Literature of the Western World

LITERATURE OF THE WESTERN WORLD

VOLUME II
Neoclassicism Through The Modern Period

BRIAN WILKIE JAMES HURT

University of Illinois

MACMILLAN PUBLISHING CO., INC.
NEW YORK

Printed in the United States of America

Macmillan Publishing Company
866 Third Avenue, New York, New York 10022

Collier Macmillan Canada, Inc.

Library of Congress Cataloging in Publication Data
Main entry under title:

Literature of the Western world.

Includes index.
Contents: —v. 2. Neoclassicism through the modern period.
1. Literature—Collections. I. Wilkie, Brian,
II. Hurt, James,
PN6014.L615 1984 808.8 82-20396
ISBN 0-02-427690-1 (v. 1)
ISBN 0-02-427700-2 (v. 2)

Printing: 3 4 5 6 7 8 Year: 6 7 8 9 0 1 2

ISBN 0-02-427690-1 (v.1)
ISBN 0-02-427700-2 (v.2)

Acknowledgments

BANTAM BOOKS, INC.: "Miss Julie": Copyright © Arvid Paulson, from *Seven Plays by August Strindberg,* translated by Arvid Paulson, copyright © 1960 by Bantam Books, Inc. Reprinted by permission of the publisher. All rights reserved.

DOUBLEDAY & COMPANY, INC.: "Sonny's Blues" from *Going to Meet the Man* by James Baldwin. Copyright © 1948, 1951, 1957, 1958, 1960, 1965 by James Baldwin. A Dial Press Book. Reprinted by permission of Doubleday & Company, Inc.

ELSEVIER-DUTTON PUBLISHING CO., INC.: "The Circular Ruins" from *The Aleph and Other Stories* by Jorge Luis Borges, edited and translated by Norman Thomas di Giovanni in collaboration with the author. English translation copyright © 1968, 1969, 1970 by Emece Editores, S. A., and Norman Thomas di Giovanni. Reprinted by permission of the publisher, E. P. Dutton. *Six Characters in Search of an Author* by Luigi Pirandello, translated by Frederick May, copyright, 1922, by E. P. Dutton & Co., Inc. Renewal, 1950, in the names of Stefano, Fausto, Lietta Pirandello. Reprinted by permission of E. P. Dutton & Co. Inc. "Candide" from *Candide and Other Tales* by Voltaire, translated by Tobias Smollett and revised by J. C. Thornton. An Everyman's Library Edition, 1937. Reprinted by permission of the publisher in the United States, E. P. Dutton.

FARRAR, STRAUS & GIROUX, INC.: *A Sorrow Beyond Dreams* by Peter Handke, translated from the German by Ralph Manheim. Copyright © 1974 by Farrar, Straus & Giroux, Inc. Reprinted by permission of Farrar, Straus & Giroux, Inc.

GROVE PRESS, INC.: "Krapp's Last Tape" from *Krapp's Last Tape and Other Dramatic Pieces* by Samuel Beckett, 1960. Copyright © 1958, 1959, 1960 by Grove Press, Inc. Reprinted by permission of Grove Press, Inc.

HARCOURT BRACE JOVANOVICH, INC.: "The Love Song of J. Alfred Prufrock," "The Waste Land," and "The Hollow Men" from *Complete Poems and Plays, 1909–1950* by T. S. Eliot, copyright © 1963, 1964, by T. S. Eliot. Reprinted by permission of the publishers. "Tradition and the Individual Talent" and excerpts from "Hamlet and His Problems" from *Selected Essays* by T. S. Eliot, copyright 1950 by Harcourt Brace Jovanovich, Inc.; renewed 1978 by Esme Valerie Eliot. Reprinted by permission of the publisher. "Tartuffe" by Moliere, translated and © 1961, 1962 by Richard Wilbur, is reprinted by permission of Harcourt Brace Jovanovich, Inc. "The River" from *A Good Man Is Hard to Find and Other Stories* by Flannery O'Connor, © 1953 by Flannery O'Connor, renewed 1981 by Mrs. Regina O'Connor. Reprinted by permission of Harcourt Brace Jovanovich, Inc. "Pale Horse, Pale Rider" from *Pale Horse, Pale Rider* by Katherine Anne Porter, © 1937, 1965 by Katherine Anne Porter. Reprinted by permission of Harcourt Brace Jovanovich, Inc. "The New Dress" from *A Haunted House and Other Stories* by Virginia Woolf, copyright 1944, 1972 by Harcourt Brace Jovanovich, Inc. Reprinted by permission of the publisher.

HARPER & ROW, PUBLISHERS, INC.: "The Man Who Lived Underground" from *Eight Men* by Richard Wright. Copyright 1944 by L. B. Fischer Publishing Corp. Copyright © 1961 by Richard Wright. Reprinted by permission of Harper & Row, Publishers, Inc.

HARVARD UNIVERSITY PRESS: "Success is counted sweetest," "I'm 'wife'—I've finished that—," "I taste a liquor never brewed," "There's a certain Slant of light," "I felt a Funeral, in my Brain," "The Soul selects her own Society," "Before I got my eye put out," "A Bird came down the Walk—," "What Soft—Cherubic Creatures," "Much Madness is divinest Sense," "I heard a Fly buzz—when I died—," "I am alive—I guess—," "I like to see it lap the Miles—," "Because I could not stop for Death—," "Presentiment—is that long Shadow—on the Lawn—," "Tell all the Truth but tell it slant," and "My life closed twice before its close—" as they appear in *The Poems of Emily Dickinson* by Emily Dickinson, Thomas H. Johnson, ed. Reprinted by permission of the publishers and the Trustees of Amherst College from *The Poems of Emily Dickinson,* edited by Thomas H. Johnson, Cambridge, Mass.: The Belknap Press of Harvard University Press, Copyright 1951, © 1955, 1979 by the President and Fellows of Harvard College.

Alfred A. Knopf, Inc.: "The Renegade" from *Exile and the Kingdom* by Albert Camus, translated by Justin O'Brien. Copyright © 1957, 1958 by Alfred A. Knopf, Inc. Reprinted by permission of the publisher. "A Simple Heart" from *Three Tales* by Gustave Flaubert, translated by Arthur McDowall. Published 1924 by Alfred A. Knopf, Inc. Reprinted by permission of the publisher. "Felix Krull" and "Disorder and Early Sorrow" by Thomas Mann. Copyright 1936 and renewed 1964 by Alfred A. Knopf, Inc. Reprinted from *Stories of Three Decades,* by Thomas Mann, translated by H. T. Lowe-Porter, by permission of the publisher.

Macmillan Publishing Company: "Gooseberries" from *The Wife and Other Stories* by Anton Chekhov, translated by Constance Garnett. Copyright 1918 by Macmillan Publishing Co., renewed 1946 by Constance Garnett. Reprinted by permission of Macmillan Publishing Company. "The Grand Inquisitor" from *The Brothers Karamazov* by Fyodor Dostoevsky, translated from the Russian by Constance Garnett. Copyright 1923 by Macmillan Publishing Co. Reprinted by permission of Macmillan Publishing Company. "Notes from Underground" from *White Nights and Other Stories* by Fyodor Dostoevsky, translated from the Russian by Constance Garnett. Copyright 1918 by Macmillan Publishing Co. Reprinted by permission of Macmillan Publishing Company. "The Lake Isle of Innisfree," "To Ireland in the Coming Times," and "He Remembers Forgotten Beauty" by W. B. Yeats, reprinted by permission of Macmillan Publishing Company from *Collected Poems* by W. B. Yeats. Copyright 1956 by Macmillan Publishing Co. Reprinted by permission of Macmillan Publishing Company. "A Coat" by W. B. Yeats, reprinted with permission of Macmillan Publishing Company from *Collected Poems* by W. B. Yeats. Copyright 1916 by Macmillan Publishing Co., Inc., renewed 1944 by Bertha Georgie Yeats. "Easter 1916" and "The Second Coming" by W. B. Yeats, reprinted with permission of Macmillan Publishing Company from *Collected Poems* by W. B. Yeats. Copyright 1924 by Macmillan Publishing Co., Inc., renewed 1952 by Bertha Georgie Yeats. "Sailing to Byzantium," "Two Songs from a Play," "Leda and the Swan," and "Among School Children" by W. B. Yeats, reprinted with permission of Macmillan Publishing Company from *Collected Poems* by W. B. Yeats. Copyright 1928 by Macmillan Publishing Co., Inc., renewed 1956 by Georgie Yeats. "Crazy Jane Talks with the Bishop" by W. B. Yeats, reprinted with permission of Macmillan Publishing Company from *Collected Poems* by W. B. Yeats. Copyright 1933 by Macmillan Publishing Co., Inc., renewed 1961 by Bertha Georgie Yeats. "Lapis Lazuli," "The Circus Animals' Desertion," and "Under Ben Bulben" by W. B. Yeats, reprinted with permission of Macmillan Publishing Company from *Collected Poems* by W. B. Yeats. Copyright 1940 by Georgie Yeats, renewed 1968 by Bertha Georgie Yeats, Michael Butler Yeats and Anne Yeats.

The New American Library, Inc.: "A Doll House" from *The Complete Major Prose Plays* by Henrik Ibsen, translated by Rolf Fjelde. Copyright © 1965, 1970, 1978 by Rolf Fjelde. Reprinted by arrangement with The New American Library, Inc., New York, New York.

New Directions Publishing Corporation: "Tlön, Uqbar, Orbis Tertius" from *Labyrinths and Other Writings* by Jorge Luis Borges, translated by James E. Irby. Copyright © 1962, 1964 by New Directions Publishing Corporation. Reprinted by permission of New Directions Publishing Corporation. "The House of Bernarda Alba" from *Three Tragedies* by Federico García Lorca, translated by James Graham-Lujan and Richard L. O'Connell. Copyright © 1962, 1964 by New Directions Publishing Corporation. Reprinted by permission of New Directions Publishing Corporation.

Penguin Books Ltd.: "Phaedra" from *Phaedra and Other Plays* by Jean Racine, translated by John Cairncross. © 1963 by Penguin Books Ltd. Reprinted by permission of Penguin Books Ltd.

Random House, Inc.: "Battle Royal" copyright 1947 by Ralph Ellison. Reprinted from *Invisible Man* by Ralph Ellison, by permission of Random House, Inc. "An Odor of Verbena" by William Faulkner. Copyright 1938 and renewed 1966 by Estelle Faulkner and Jill Faulkner Summers. Reprinted from *The Faulkner Reader* by William Faulkner, by permission of Random House, Inc. "The Wall" by Jean-Paul Sartre, translated by Maria Jolas. Copyright 1945 and renewed 1973 by Random House, Inc. Reprinted from *Bedside Book of Famous*

French Stories, edited by Belle Becker and Robert N. Linscott, by permission of New Directions Publishing Corp. and Random House, Inc.

SCHOCKEN BOOKS, INC.: "The Metamorphosis" from *Franz Kafka: The Complete Stories* by Franz Kafka, translated by Willa and Edwin Muir. Copyright © 1946, 1947, 1948, 1949, 1954, 1958, 1971 by Schocken Books, Inc. Reprinted by permission of Schocken Books, Inc.

UNIVERSITY OF MINNESOTA PRESS: "The Good Woman of Setzuan" from *Parables for the Theatre: Two Plays by Bertolt Brecht,* translated by Eric Bentley. Copyright © 1948 by Eric Bentley. Reprinted by permission of the University of Minnesota Press.

VIKING PENGUIN INC.: "Looking for Mr. Green" from *Mosby's Memoirs & Other Stories* by Saul Bellow. Copyright 1951 by Saul Bellow. Copyright renewed 1979 by Saul Bellow. Reprinted by permission of Viking Penguin Inc. "Araby" and "The Dead" from *Dubliners* by James Joyce. Copyright © 1967 by the Estate of James Joyce. Reprinted by permission of Viking Penguin Inc. "Odour of Chrysanthemums" and "The Horse Dealer's Daughter" from *The Complete Short Stories,* Vol. II, by D. H. Lawrence. Copyright 1922 by Thomas Seltzer, Inc., copyright renewed 1950 by Frieda Lawrence. Reprinted by permission of Viking Penguin Inc.

Preface

Our goals in putting together *Literature of the Western World* have been, one, to produce the most comprehensive collection of world literature currently available, and, two, to present that literature as accurately and accessibly as possible. Edgar Lee Masters' unglamorous metaphor for anthologists—"humble gleaners in the fields of literature"—describes one way in which we have seen our role. But our labors in the fields have also given us, not to mention intellectual rewards, a great deal of pleasure; after all, an anthology is literally a "gathering of flowers." We hope the book will provide corresponding rewards and pleasure for its readers.

In selecting works to include, we have started from scratch; we have consciously resisted the notion of a single, unchanging list of canonized great books elevated beyond the shifting winds of human literary tastes and needs. We have recognized, nevertheless, that certain works have an enduring centrality in literary history, and we have honored the claims of this tradition. Here are the *Odyssey,* the great tragedies of ancient Greece, the *Divine Comedy, Don Quixote, King Lear,* and *Paradise Lost.* At the same time, an anthology that included only such monumental works would be as misleading as a map that showed only mountain tops. With the monumental we have included the urgent and immediate, the perhaps unexpected by the side of the inevitable. And so we include Wollstonecraft's *Vindication of the Rights of Woman,* for example, and such acknowledged but not easily available masterpieces as Lermontov's *A Hero of Our Time.*

In every selection, the paramount consideration has been to provide a substantial and satisfying reading experience. Whenever possible, we have chosen complete works—representing prose fiction, for example, by five complete short novels, by Voltaire, Goethe, Lermontov, Chopin, and Conrad, and a dozen novellas of the nineteenth and twentieth centuries. For works too long to include in their entirety, such as the *Aeneid* and *Don Quixote,* we have selected sustained units and provided detailed summaries of omitted sections in order to preserve the overall shape of the work. Rather than offer sketchy representations of two authors of equal rank, we have occasionally chosen to represent one of them much more extensively, as with More and Machiavelli, or Tennyson and Browning. The result, we hope, is depth as well as breadth of coverage and a series of substantial works or selections.

In making our choices, we have been acutely aware of T. S. Eliot's conception of literary tradition as fluid and dynamic rather than fixed and unchanging; the new must alter our perception of the "ideal order" of the past. The course of Western literature must look slightly different now from the way it looked even, say, twenty years ago. Certain of the authors and individual works in this book are here because—for sometimes obvious, sometimes more elusive reasons—they seem to have a special appeal for contemporary readers; hence, for example, the complete *Odyssey* rather than the complete *Iliad,* and *King Lear* rather than, say, *Hamlet* or *Macbeth.* We believe the final selection honors equally the claims of old and new and contains, despite its length, nothing of merely historical interest that cannot speak with a special urgency and vitality to a contemporary reader.

In presentation, as in selection, we have tried to keep firmly in mind the needs of teachers and students. Choice of translations was crucial. We live in an age, we have come to realize, of great translations, and choices have often been difficult. We have been guided throughout by considerations of both accessibility and accuracy. We are proud to present a number of distinguished recent translations that combine these virtues: Robert Fagles' translation of the *Oresteia,* for example, which captures, perhaps better than ever before in English, both the lucidity and the wildness of that great dramatic poem of violence, Robert Fitzgerald's wonderfully readable translation of the *Odyssey,* and Mary Barnard's sensitive renderings of Sappho's difficult texts. We are happy, too, to be able to include Stephen Berg's and Diskin Clay's *Oedipus the King,* William Arrowsmith's *Alcestis,* Patricia Terry's *Song of Roland,* Richard Wilbur's *Tartuffe,* Rolf Fjelde's *A Doll House,* Arvid Paulson's *Miss Julie,* and Willa and Edwin Muir's *The Metamorphosis.* But we have never assumed that the most recent translation is necessarily the best and have correspondingly chosen Walter Starkie's earthy, vigorous translation of *Don Quixote* and Tobias Smollett's rollicking English version of *Candide* over more recent but, to our minds, less lively versions. Challenges of translation have also forced upon us the difficult decision to minimize the amount of translated lyric poetry. Poets who travel well in borrowed languages are rare, and so lyric poetry is represented primarily by poets who wrote originally in English, especially those whose forms and themes reflect the currents of Western literature in other languages.

In our introductions to the major periods and to the individual selections, our goal has been to provide the most useful information, while suppressing the professorial temptation to explain everything. Like many other readers in these post-New-Critical days, we have tried to combine a sense of the integrity and autonomy of art with a heightened awareness of the roots of art in particular, time-bound human experience. Our introductions to periods and authors give biography and history their due, especially the history of ideas and culture. For the three period introductions of Volume One we have aimed, within the limits of space, to be at least moderately comprehensive, mentioning the salient facts and tendencies of the three enormously varied periods—the Ancient World, the Middle Ages, and the Renaissance—without attempting to reduce complex historical movements to formulas. The period introductions in Volume Two, on Neoclassicism and Romanticism, Realism and Naturalism, and Modernism, are more thematically organized, but we have tried there too not to be simplistic. In the author introductions, we have done as many of the following things as are relevant to individual authors: give a fairly detailed biographical summary, describe their personal artistic development (including the titles of their most important works), identify their recurrent themes, place them in the context of their times and of the development of literature and ideas, and help readers focus on the selections that follow in this book. Sometimes we venture brief critical commentary, suggesting alternative standard interpretations or advancing our own views, chiefly as whetstones against which we hope students and teachers will hone the edges of their own interpretive tools.

Footnotes are intended to be, above all, functional. From among the dozens of facts worth knowing about Apollo or Stoicism or the French Revolution, we restrict ourselves to the facts relevant to the immediate passage glossed. As in the introductions, our policy is to leave interpretation to our readers. On a very few occasions we depart from this policy for special reasons; in Aeschylus, for example, we stop a few times to point out the richness of meaning and imagery in a passage, by way of alerting readers to the scores of other passages that deserve similar close reading. On matters of general knowledge and of vocabulary, we probably err on the side of over-annotation, hoping that none of our readers will mind being given what they may not need. Among the facts of life that we have tried to keep in mind is that few readers take side trips to the dictionary, especially if they are absorbed in their reading, as we hope our readers will be.

Each period and author introduction is followed by a list of "Further Reading." With a few exceptions, and with some slight modifications, these bibliographies are the work of three people to whom we are deeply indebted: Nancy K. Barry, Frances Stickney Newman, and Willard J. Rusch. Their initials identify the respective reading lists for which they are mainly responsible. They and we have tried to restrict the books listed to reliable and authoritative ones, but a good many works indispensable for advanced scholarly study have been consciously omitted. Each bibliography focuses on a few books we think might be useful to accompany a first reading of the author.

Finally, the obvious: this is a pair of very big books, the most comprehensive collection of world literature, we think, currently available. It is not a course, but a small library from which many courses can be constructed. But despite its size, it contains nothing that has not proved a source of delight to the editors over many years of studying and teaching literature. Our greatest pleasure in making this book has been the hope that it will introduce others to works we love and give them something of the same delight.

By "our" goals, we sometimes mean those of the two editors, but more often we mean those of several dozen teachers, from widely scattered colleges and universities, who before this book was made and while it was in the making have told us what they and their students wanted. In no case did this consensus contradict our own teaching experience, but it has made possible a perspective that no two or even ten anthologists could have achieved confidently on their own. These valued colleagues include:

Professor Jesse T. Airaudi, Baylor University; Professor Beatrice Batson, Wheaton College; Professor J. A. Bryant, University of Kentucky; Professor Leslie Chard, University of Cincinnati; Professor Keith Cohen, University of Wisconsin, Madison; Professor Charles L. Crow, Bowling Green State University; Professor Prescott Evarts, Jr., Monmouth College; Professor Robert Fagles, Princeton University; Professor Betty S. Flowers, The

University of Texas at Austin; Professor Barbara L. Gerber; Professor John F. Hennedy, Providence College; Professor Thomas G. Jones, Jr., Western Kentucky University; Professor Beuford W. Keene, University of Tennessee, Martin; Professor James King, Hillsdale College; Professor Alfred Kloeckner, Norwich University; Professor Stanley J. Kozikowski, Bryant College; Professor Lawrence F. Laban, Virginia Commonwealth University; Professor Frederick Z. Lesher, University of Wisconsin, La Crosse; Professor Irving Lord, South Oregon State College; Professor Christiaan T. Lievestro, University of Santa Clara; Professor John M. Long, Eastern Kentucky University; Professor Littleton Long, University of Vermont; Professor Joan McCarthy, Southern Connecticut State College; Professor H. Thomas McCracken; Professor Ronald E. MacFarland, University of Idaho; Professor Ronald E. McReynolds, Central Missouri State University; Professor Charles Miller, Western State College; Professor Zenobia Mistri, Purdue University, Calumet Campus; Professor Martin Mueller, Northwestern University; Professor Helen H. Naugle, Georgia Institute of Technology; Professor R. W. Parker, Wittenberg University; Professor Erling W. Peterson, Indiana Central University; Professor Willard Potts, Oregon State University; Professor Carroll Y. Rich, North Texas State University; Professor William Patrick Riley, Mississippi Valley State University; Professor J. E. Rivers, University of Colorado, Boulder; Professor Allen Robb, Florida State University; Professor Thomas G. Rosenmeyer, University of California, Berkeley; Professor Silvia Ruffo-Fiore, University of South Florida; Professor Susan Rusinko, Bloomsburg State College; Professor Richard Savage, Bloomsburg State College; Professor Gerald H. Strauss, Bloomsburg State College; Professor Woodruff C. Thomson, Brigham Young University; Professor Willa F. Valencia, Valdosta State College; Professor Robert A. Wiggins, University of California, Davis; Professor Heinz D. Woehlk, Northeast Missouri State University; Professor Edith Williams, Eastern Kentucky University.

For advice on particular authors and periods we warmly thank Lynn Altenbernd, John Bateman, Barbara Bowen, Vincent Bowen, Edward Brandabur, David Bright, Jackson Campbell, Howard Cole, John Dussinger, Chester Fontenot, Eva Frayne, John Frayne, John Friedman, Stanley Gray, Achsah Guibbory, Jan Hinely, Bernard Hirsch, Frank Hodgins, Allan Holaday, Anthony Kaufman, David Kay, Keneth Kinnamon, Joan Klein, Dale Kramer, James Marchand, Donald Masterson, Linda Mazer, Michael Mullin, John K. Newman, Michael Palencia-Roth, Vernon Robbins, Michael Shapiro, Charles Shattuck, Janet Levarie Smarr, Arnold Stein, Jack Stillinger, Zohreh Sullivan, Benjamin Uroff, Leon Waldoff, Emily Watts, and Richard Wheeler.

For their skilled secretarial help we are indebted to Marjorie Beasley, Marlyn Ehlers, Sherri George, Jenny Maden, and Irene Wahlfeldt.

For expert guidance throughout the project we thank D. Anthony English. Our production editor, Patricia Cabeza, helped us immensely with the task of getting the manuscript through the press. Berta Lewis provided excellent design assistance. And finally, we thank Joyce Rappaport, Kevin McLaughlin, and Ann Wilkie for help with the formidable and exacting labor of copyediting and proofreading.

Contents

Neoclassicism and Romanticism

Western literature from about 1650 to about 1850 was dominated by two impulses: Neoclassicism until about 1760, Romanticism thereafter. The impulses were international, although the typical masterpieces of Neoclassicism were written in French and English. The two labels (imposed, for the most part, after the fact by historians of literature) are not adequate to describe either period comprehensively; many writers and works, novels especially, resist such classification. The term *Neoclassicism* and other related terms into which it blends are applied somewhat differently to different parts of Europe. In France, for example, the purest form of Neoclassicism precedes 1700; the form of aggressive secular French rationalism that dominated the eighteenth century is more properly called the Enlightenment. The entire period from the philosopher René Descartes' *Discourse on Method* (1637) to the outbreak of the French Revolution in 1789 can also be called the Age of Reason, in France and outside it. It is this constellation of roughly allied trends that for the sake of simplicity is called Neoclassicism in the present essay. As for *Romanticism,* the problem has been almost the opposite: not rivalry between competing labels but a proliferation of meanings for the single label *Romanticism,* some of them so wildly unrelated or contradictory that certain historians of literature a few decades ago came to consider the word useless. Attempts at definition since then have produced some hard thinking on the subject. The result has been, if not a generally accepted definition, at least a better understanding of the complex phenomena the word is meant to reflect.

The terms *Neoclassic* and *Romantic,* despite their limitations, are useful in identifying the basic models various artists conformed to or reacted against, each in his or her different way. The periods described by the two terms are generally considered not only as distinct—with some blurring along their mid-eighteenth-century border—but as antithetical. For that very reason, and also because the contrast between the two manners was pressed belligerently by Romantics rebelling against their forebears, it seems useful to consider both together. Another reason for doing so is that the two terms describe not merely historical epochs in the arts and general culture but also recurrent types that have existed in every epoch. A "romantic" person is impulsive (or irresponsible), idealistic (or impractical), imaginative (or unbalanced), and so on. We do not ordinarily apply the word *classic* to persons, but it is widely applied to things, not only books and pieces of music but also automobile designs, sweaters, athletic events (the "Fall Classic"), and almost anything whose appeal is stable, perennial, immune to the whims of fashion. One of the more interesting questions about literary history is how closely the historical senses of the two words correspond to their popular usages.

One feasible way to examine Neoclassicism and Romanticism in literature is to state as baldly as possible the general formulas commonly used to distinguish them and then modify the formulas, as necessary, so as to reflect the truth more closely, if still in a general way. Three such formulas have to do with order, emotion, and nature. As one might expect, the clichés describe the third-rate talents better than the greatest ones, but that does not mean the clichés are useless. All wars are fought partly with slogans, and slogans tell us something, if not the whole truth.

Formula One: Neoclassicism values the orderly, social, and general; Romanticism values the exceptional, individual, and particular.

The Neoclassic age did value order, and it had good reason to do so. The early and middle seventeenth century witnessed an apocalyptic outpouring of hatred, in the form of religious civil wars fought not only between Catholics and Protestants but between factions within Protestantism. The prototype is the great English civil war of the 1640s and 1650s between the Calvinist Puritans, who were both political and religious radicals, and their Anglican-Royalist enemies. In the course of this war King Charles I was beheaded. Theological doctrines and the political philosophies tied up with them were literally fighting words in the hands of partisan pamphleteers such as John Milton. The unrest continued in England even after the Restoration of the monarchy in 1660, culminating in the Glorious Revolution of 1688–89. This reorientation of political power, reducing the stature of the king and elevating the parliament and merchants, cost some people, notably Catholics, civil liberties. But for most people it enlarged these liberties, and it opened the way to a more settled era. Political strife was far from over, but the relative calm was welcomed with relief. (An analogy exists with the 1950s in the United States, when, after two decades when people stood in breadlines and then slept in muddy foxholes, the normal and tranquil seemed to many people heaven itself.) The English began to think of themselves as "Augustans," living in a time like that of Caesar Augustus, Virgil, and Horace after Augustus ended decades of Roman civil war and made civilized life—and civilized art—possible.

Something similar was happening on the European continent. The German states had the terrible Thirty Years War (1618–1648) in their recent past; the French, the bitterly divided period of the Fronde (1648–1653). Political order in the English manner was not possible in Germany, still divided into separate states. In France, the new order meant the triumph of the monarchy, especially under the resplendent "Sun King" Louis XIV and his satellite aristocracy. The middle class, ascendant in England after 1688, had to wait a century to assert itself politically in France. When it did so in the revolution of 1789, which within a few years took a more radical turn toward democracy, the nation and all Europe witnessed the end of eighteenth-century versions of order. A new apocalypse had begun.

Civil disorder in the seventeenth century synchronized ironically with the achievement of a new scientific order, the product of an international synthesis of the kind that ever since has been the rule in scientific advancement. Developing from the discoveries and theories of such astronomer-physicists as Galileo (1564–1642), an Italian, and Johannes Kepler (1571–1630), a German, the Scientific Revolution culminated in the Englishman Isaac Newton's (1642–1727) formulation of the laws of motion and of universal gravitation, describable in terms of a new branch of mathematics, calculus, that Newton himself and the German mathematician Gottfried Wilhelm Leibnitz (1646–1716) invented at about the same time. Newton's astounding achievement, probably the greatest in the history of science, had a historically dramatic timing; his *Principia* was published in 1687, a year before the Glorious Revolution. It was as though the cosmos itself, as revealed in the orderly minds of men intent on natural truth rather than the chimeras of religious "enthusiasm," were giving humankind a broad hint: put your political and cultural house in order too. The ruling model, for government, art, and even human nature, became an inorganic one—sometimes a machine, sometimes an architectural edifice, but at any rate a model articulated by reason, understandable by secular good sense, and governed by widely recognizable rules.

The relationship between the art and science of any period is always a chicken-and-egg problem. The "rules" that came to govern literature and literary theory (especially in France, with its Latinate tradition of the absolute) may have been conditioned by the new science, or it may be that the great seventeenth-century scientific revolution was conditioned by the humanities, specifically the Renaissance adulation of balanced rationality as manifested in ancient literature. At any rate, the Neoclassicists tried to subsume literature under strict rules, infusing rigorous method into the Renaissance version of classicism. As one might expect, the most insistent of the rules governed the most public of the literary genres, the drama, in the form of the three "unities" of action, time, and place. (The first two of these are inferrable from Aristotle's *Poetics;* the third, apparently dictated by pure logic, is found nowhere in his works.) A tragedy had to deal with a single action, its plot had to unfold within twelve (or sometimes twenty-four) hours, and it had to be set in a single place. The most effortlessly perfect realizations of these dramatic rules were the tragedies of Racine, such as his *Phaedra.* Similar rules defined and governed many other genres. A carefully graded scale of diction was elaborated, the loftiest language being reserved for tragedy and the lowest for satire. These rules were to remain in force for a long time. When Victor Hugo's experimental Romantic drama *Hernani* was first staged in 1830, a grand commotion was stirred among Parisian partisans of the old and new by the play's daring opening lines: Hugo had displaced the caesura, or pause, in the twelve-syllable French line from its regular place after the sixth syllable and had actually put in the mouth of a high-born lady the word *escalier,* "stairs."

In doctrinaire Romantics the rules stirred anger; to most people today they seem merely absurd. To keep things in perspective, however, we should stop to consider how many rules still operate, in behavior and the arts—in the popular arts most of all. People dress differently for funerals and for cookouts. One can scan the shelves of a bookstore for a long time before finding on a dust jacket a picture of a novelist who would dare wear a suit and tie. No one would score Dixieland jazz for string quartet or country music for two grand pianos. Much of science fiction observes conventions about how freely scientific laws can be fantasized, and very rigid rules for murder mysteries were codified by the late Dorothy L. Sayers. A more fundamental modern misunderstanding, however, arises from the inherent ambiguity of the word *rules.* Like its sibling, *laws,* the word can mean either prescriptive, legislated rules, like those of baseball, or rules that purport to describe the nature of reality, like the commutative rule of multiplication (3 times 2 equals 2 times 3). To most Neoclassicists the rules were descriptive, reflecting the almost unalterable conditions necessary for literature to be effective. Thus Pope could write that rules are "Nature methodised; / Nature, like liberty, is but restrained / By the same laws which first herself ordained" (*Essay on Criticism,* I.89–91). To depart from the rules in this sense would cause literature not to work, as on a vaster scale the solar system would not work if the planet Jupiter went its own headstrong way unbeholden to the rules of gravitation. Pope's analogy with liberty is very significant; he and other Neoclassicists wanted literature to be *free* to perform its proper role in the scheme of nature, as environmentalists today want the snail darter to be free to do. (Pope believed, moreover, that there were "nameless graces" beyond the reach of precepts.) But *nature* is a tricky word; about it, more later.

The Romantic penchant for the exceptional and individual needs less explanation, since it accords with twentieth-century attitudes. The audiences for art—"high" art at least—take it for granted that a good artist or work does something not done before, and such originality usually implies novelty of subject matter or artistic method. Here again, however, we can deceive ourselves. Certain stock figures—the alienated hero, for example—can hardly be called original any more, but the alienated hero seems tolerable by modern tastes in almost limitless near-duplication, as his cousin the Byronic hero was for Romantic audiences. Goethe's Werther, that prototype of the misunderstood, eccentric Romantic man of genius and sensibility, was adopted as a blood brother by countless thousands of readers, who felt they understood him perfectly.

The fact is that the best Romantic authors, like their modern counterparts, are not drawn to the eccentric simply for its own sake. To say, in Matthew Arnold's words, "We mortal millions live *alone*" is verbally a paradox, but it is easy enough to understand. A similar paradox—that what all humans share is uniqueness—is fundamental to Romantic literature and thought. Significantly, the French Revolutionists, who in so many ways set the stage for the Romantics, were able to accommodate (along with *equality*) among their three watchwords both *liberty* and *fraternity,* two notions with considerable potential for incompatibility. Wordsworth, following up but modifying Rousseau's choice of "Myself alone" as the subject matter of his *Confessions,* can single himself out in *The Prelude* as a Romantic epic hero exactly because he believes that somehow he can discern and reveal the essence of humanity at large by looking into himself. That is why he continually moves grammatically between *I* and *we, my* and *our, me* and *us.* That is also why the American arch-Romantic, Walt Whitman, can launch *Song of Myself* with the statement "I celebrate myself" but add almost immediately, "For every atom belonging to me as good belongs to you." The exception, for many Romantics, proves the rule in the relevant sense of *prove:* "put to the test." When human nature is thus "proved" by the seeming uniqueness of the individuals who partake in it, we learn something about the norm of human nature, as the study of abnormal psychology today throws light on what normal behavior is. In a way, then, the Romantics pursued the same objective—the understanding of the universal—that the Neoclassicists pursued. But the Romantics approached this norm by the circuitous paths and side entrances of inference and surprise; the Neoclassicists made frontal assaults on the norm, through explicit generalizations such as Pope utters in almost every couplet.

Romantic individualism marks a real shift from Neoclassicism all the same, and one way to understand the shift is to ask what the alternative to individualism was in each of the two ages. When a person in the early eighteenth century felt threatened *as an individual,* the threat was something localizable, indeed mechanical. It usually operated through the oppressive machinery of the state (sometimes of the church). The threat came from bad laws or the perversion of good laws by identifiable authorities, from the king down, and their official agencies. This kind of mechanical threat to freedom is what the American revolutionists and founding fathers sensed, and against such political malfunctions their safeguard was another machine: the Constitution. It had "checks," "balances," and, one is tempted to add, gears, pulleys, and flywheels.

The Romantics, a generation or two later than the thinkers who influenced James Madison, came to fear something more insidious: the spiritually pervasive, often poisoned atmosphere we have come to call "society." Like its American equivalent, the French Revolution had begun as an attempt to repair or replace political machinery—by reconvening the long-dormant Estates General, for example, and thus renovating the legislative process. But within a few years this daring but still limited rationalist impulse became a total spiritual imperative, exacting allegiance in everything from religion to manners to language to dress. A state had become a society. And the change was permanent, as Balzac's vision of post-Revolutionary France makes clear. Ironically, it was Rousseau, himself a patron saint of the Revolution, who first clearly articulated the dangerous pressure exerted on the individual by society so understood. Almost all the Romantics shared this vision. Goethe's Werther, a Romantic in Rousseau's footsteps, is totally unconcerned with governments; the officialdom he tries briefly to become part of and learns to loathe is not a mechanism but a noxious moral atmosphere. It would be ludicrous to imagine Byron's Manfred voting for a bill or opposing a political party. What both these protagonists reject in their environment (apart from certain metaphysical aspects of the human condition in itself) is the deadening spiritual miasma that attacks not one's circumstantial freedom but the integrity of one's psyche, a miasma both omnipresent and intangible. The eighteenth-century mode of establishing freedom was to "charter" a group or corporation, guaranteeing or conceding specified legal rights and immunities. The American Bill of Rights is a charter in this sense. But by the end of the eighteenth century we can also hear voices like that of the speaker in Blake's "London," who almost vomits up the word *chartered* in disgust at the hypocritical mystification implicit in the specious order it expresses. What nauseates him is not merely commercial and other institutionalized mechanisms of oppression but a whole moral complex that, besides corporations, includes poverty, prostitution, loveless marriage, disease, war, and—at the heart of all—the enslavement of mind by mind. This is no longer political protest but recognizably Romantic—and modern—social protest.

Not incidentally, the social protest in "London" is couched in lyric poetry, uttered by the voice of an individual speaker. The lyric poem is sometimes considered the distinctive Romantic genre. Strictly speaking, this is not true; the lyric is not the form the greatest Romantics consciously chose for their most serious utterances. Goethe's most nearly definitive values are expressed in the two parts of the drama *Faust.* Wordsworth in *The Prelude,* Byron in *Don Juan,* and Blake in *The Four Zoas, Milton,* and *Jerusalem* chose the long verse epic. Victor Hugo (1802–1885) was a great lyricist but is even better known for his novels *Notre Dame de Paris* and *Les Misérables;* Hawthorne's medium was also fiction; Melville brought the novel and the epic together in *Moby-Dick.* But many of these long Romantic works are written in an intensely lyrical vein. Tennyson's *In Memoriam* and Whitman's *Leaves of Grass* are large edifices, but their components are separable lyrics. The quintessence of Romanticism, if not its extended rationale, is isolable in the lyrics, especially the odes, of Keats, despite his heroic attempts to write great long poems. In the last analysis, then, Romanticism is a lyrical impulse, in keeping with its veneration of the individual.

Conversely, Neoclassicism distrusted idiosyncrasy and ranked the lyric rather low in its elaborate hierarchy of literary genres. The loftiest of the genres were tragedy and epic. Theory outstripped achievement here; comedy thrived in Restoration England, and France produced Molière, one of the world's great comic dramatists, but the only really great tragedians were Pierre Corneille (1606–1684) and Racine. The closest approaches to important Neoclassic epic were John Dryden's translation (1697) of Virgil, Pope's of Homer (1715–26), and Voltaire's *Henriade* (1723), an epic that almost no one reads today. The literature of protest took the form of satire, for which the lyric form and voice would have been considered inappropriate and inadequate. Significantly, the great Neoclassic satires do not portray distinctive individuals. Characters have *traits*—Pope's Belinda is charming and vain, Swift's Gulliver is sturdily commonsensical and pragmatic, Voltaire's Candide is resiliently naive and his Pangloss optimistic to the point of lunacy—but they do not have *personalities.* Although they are not allegorical figures like those in the medieval *Everyman,* they are nonetheless generalizations: Candide's name means "open, ingenuous," *Pangloss* means "explainer-away of everything" (the subtitle of the book, "The Optimist," is itself a generalization), *Gulliver* puns on *gull* ("dupe"), *Belinda* puns on *belle,* and her misadventures are further generalized by being filtered through the conventions of classical and Miltonic epic. The typical result of such generalizing is a blend of serious purpose with hilarity, matched in Aristophanes but in scarcely anyone else in the earlier history of literature. Stereotyping can be cruel and unjust in life, but a great deal of humor depends on such reductionism, and satire thrives on it. Like other forms of comedy, comic satire distances us from the intimate personal understanding and empathy that render almost everything tragic or poignant or sentimental. It thus clears the way for the savage moral indignation of a Swift and the keen intellectual indignation of a Voltaire.

Formula Two: Neoclassicism values reason; Romanticism values emotion.

On the face of it, this statement seems so indisputably true as to require no further comment, and it is true. But misunderstandings are possible. No one can read Racine's *Phaedra* or Swift's account of the Yahoos without recognizing that the Neoclassicists considered human passion an immensely powerful force. Their very compulsion for order was conditioned by an awareness of its dangerous alternatives, as the seismographic vigilance of Victorian chaperones attested not their undervaluation of sex but their hyperalert awareness of its power. In general, Neoclassicists regarded passion as a threat to health, in the polity and in the individual psyche. It was also an obstacle to clear understanding, an unavoidable but undesirable contaminant of reason. Not all people of the time took that view, however. The optimist followers of the third Earl of Shaftesbury (1671–1713), for example, believed that benevolent feelings were an inherent part of humankind at its best, and this philosophy encouraged a sentimentalizing strain in literature that grew stronger as the eighteenth century progressed. (The middle to late eighteenth century is sometimes called the Age of Sensibility; its preoccupation with tender feelings and the beauties of rustic nature is usually traced to Rousseau, but Shaftesbury was an earlier herald.) Moreover, even for the rationalists reason meant different things. For some of them it meant a severe, secularist intellectuality; this was the basic view of Voltaire and other *philosophes* of the French Enlightenment. For others (Swift, for example), it meant almost the opposite: a pragmatic common sense that rejected fine-spun theorizing as contemptible, immoral, or even insane. This distrust of pure ratiocination harks back to the Renaissance humanists' disdain for cobweb-spinning medieval scholasticism.

Among the Romantics there was unquestionably a cult of feeling. Doubtless some of its initiates indulged their emotions for the simplest of reasons: because feeling strongly felt good. The more one felt, the better; emotion was fine but ecstasy finer still. This deliberate luxuriating in feeling, largely for its own sake, is a charge brought against Goethe's Werther, for example, by readers unsympathetic to him. But it will be immediately obvious that the passion Werther feels is very different from what Pope or Racine or Swift means by passion. In Werther passion has less to do with primal appetites (though there is some evidence that he sublimates these drives) than with softness on one hand and sublimity on the other. Compared with the Neoclassicists' passion, his is both more domestic and more exotic, a combination typical of Romantic sensibility. In other words, the Romantics did not only give emotion a new level of value but also redefined its special quality.

They also redefined the role of emotion in understanding reality. As the philosopher Alfred North Whitehead observed in *Science and the Modern World,* models of reality are constructed by a selective process, and what the models ignore clamors to be readmitted. This, he argued, is what happened in the eighteenth century; understandably, people were so awed by the spectacular success of rationalist science that they excluded from their adopted model something vital and human. The Romantics' task, as the more thoughtful among them saw it, was to rehumanize mankind's sense of itself (and of the cosmos too; we shall get to that later). They envisaged a more comprehensive model of reality, less exclusively ruled by reason. But they knew their new model would be unsatisfactory if it simply substituted feeling for reason; feeling had to ally itself to what is best in the mind, not oppose it. The literary result, especially among the great English Romantics, was a poetry of intense feeling that was also intellectual in an almost unprecedented degree. They were obsessed with the importance of love, for example, but except in Byron and Shelley one would be hard pressed to find many confessional English Romantic love poems, the kind of thing one could include in a letter to one's sweetheart. (Shakespeare, Donne, and other Elizabethan poets are a much more fertile field. The continental Romantics were also more personally amatory, even—in fact, especially—that thinking man's poet, Goethe.) For all his subjectivity, there is scarcely a more intellectual poet than Wordsworth, who wanted not only to reestablish the essential role of human feeling but to redeem poetry from its status as genteel adornment and make it an avenue to truth. The poetry of Blake, the most uncompromising opponent of eighteenth-century rationalism, is as intellectual as that of Dante or Milton, perhaps more so.

The centerpiece of the Romantics' endeavor was a new theory of creative understanding based on the faculty of imagination. This theory, stated by Coleridge in the *Biographia Literaria* (1817) and urged most extravagantly by Blake, was essentially a reaction against John Locke (1632–1704), the philosopher who defined the basic model for eighteenth-century theories of perceiving and knowing (and for much modern thought on these matters as well). Locke held that the human mind begins as a *tabula rasa,* or blank slate. (If he were writing today, one feels sure his metaphor would have been unexposed photographic film.) The blankness is first touched by elementary sense impressions which, subsequently modified and combined in more and more complex overlays (like multi-exposed film), result at last in what we call ideas. The process is essentially passive, positing a reality that exists most fully in material things and agencies outside the mind. What draws human beings together is that their minds respond to things they perceive in common—the same sun, the same trees, and, in well-educated readers, the same great books, poems, and plays. The term *common sense* assumes a new meaning when we interpret it literally as implying sense impressions we have in common.

It is not hard to see how this philosophical model could generate among Neoclassicists a corresponding theory of literature, namely an updated version of the ancient theory of art as imitation, especially imitation of the basic, uneccentric experiences that all human beings share. The Neoclassic term for the creative power was *wit.* The term may surprise us unless we recognize that (1) it goes back to Anglo-Saxon for "reason" or "intelligence"—hence the surviving word *half-wit;* and (2) even today witticisms impress us apparently because of their novelty but basically because behind their cleverness we recognize a familiar truth. ("Punctuality"—not procrastination, as in the proverb—"is the thief of time," says Oscar Wilde; we are startled, and then we remember how much time we have spent waiting for the habitually late.) Hence Pope's famous formula: "True wit is Nature to advantage dressed, / What oft was thought, but ne'er so well expressed" (*Essay on Criticism,* II.297–98). Implicit in this view of mind and of art is a noble ideal of human community, united by collectively endorsed realities as sensed by the best minds from antiquity to the present. The dreadful alternative was enthrallment by irresponsibly mutant values and quirks of feeling, which in turn could produce a spiritual and social malaise not entirely different from what today is called "the inability to communicate."

This notion of creativity, symbolized as a mirror, was central to Neoclassic art. The alternative Romantic metaphor, as M. H. Abrams has pointed out, was the lamp, which emits light rather than receiving and reflecting it. *Wit* was transformed into *imagination,* which Coleridge defined on two levels. The artist wields the "secondary imagination," becoming a fairly literal creator by shaping and forming the welter of raw experiences, which in themselves are a chaos. In order to do so, he must bring into play all the powers of the psyche, emotion as well as reason, for the goal is an organic integration, not the analytic dissection for which unimpassioned reason alone would suffice. Moreover, underlying the artist's secondary imagination is the primary imagination, an even more basic faculty that Coleridge identifies with all normal human perception. This kind of perception, however, is not to be understood as a receptive act; rather, it is the shaping of chaotic matter into forms such as trees and chairs, which in themselves are a welter of meaningless bits of matter. Both forms of creation are echoes of the ultimate act of creation by God, whose power is manifested less by making matter out of nothing than by giving it living form and order. Coleridge thus achieves a brilliant *tour de force,* asserting the sublime dignity of artistic creation by linking it to the divine, but also defending it on the Lockeans' own ground by linking it with familiar, ordinary sense experiences such as perfectly "unimaginative" people have hundreds of times every minute. Either way, the Coleridgean, Romantic model of creation is a far cry from the undisciplined indulgence of emotion. Wordsworth called imagination "another name for absolute power / And clearest insight, amplitude of mind, / And reason in her most exalted mood" (*The Prelude,* XIV.190–192).

This notion of imagination, and its conflict with Lockean models, is a basic theme on which the Romantics composed countless variations. Wordsworth sounds it continually, now leaning to a Lockean position that nature influences us (as in parts of *The Prelude*), now in the opposite direction of mind's independence (as in other parts of *The Prelude* and the "Intimations" ode), now toward a compromise according to which we create but half-perceive (as in "Tintern Abbey"). For Blake, his contemporary, there could be no compromise. His Oothoon, in *Visions of the Daughters of Albion,* spits out her repeated question "With what sense . . . ?" in a feminist manifesto that is simultaneously an attack on Locke. All animals have senses, she insists, but all animals are different, fulfilling themselves as unique species, not reduced to uniformity by the natural world they experience in common. Analogously, all human beings are unique, each of them being the center of his or her created world. To ignore this fact is to acquiesce in a system which defines people in terms of their sense experience (in Oothoon's case, her history of having been "defiled" by rape) and implicitly to acquiesce in a system of social classification that reduces some classes, such as women and Blacks, to slavery. All this becomes more moving when we understand that Oothoon is in some sense a version of Mary Wollstonecraft, the feminist pioneer whose message in her *Vindication of the Rights of Woman* strains uneasily, as it probably seemed to Blake, against her misplaced eighteenth-century faith in the reforming power of reason. Transformed into Oothoon, she sees rationalism as "Urizen" ("your reason"), the "mistaken Demon of Heaven." The explosive anger of the poem is more than a tone, then; it is an assertion of the need for the whole person, not just her reason but her feelings also, to engage the question of what is true and false, right and wrong. Letting off steam is not enough either; one must also *see.* This need explains the poem's form, a debate, which dramatically seems so incongruous with Oothoon's personal crisis. She is the Romantic imagination incarnate, attempting to see life whole if not steadily.

Formula Three: Neoclassicism values ____________, Romanticism values nature.

The second half of this theorem is the commonest of all generalizations on the subject, but before we go any further the reader is invited to fill in the blank for Neoclassicism by supplying the antonym for *nature.* If one says "indoor scenes," the contrast will make sense and will even be roughly valid. One will search Pope in vain for the mountaintop ecstasies recorded in Wordsworth's *Prelude* and search Wordsworth in vain for anything like Belinda's dressing table in Pope's *Rape of the Lock.* When the mock-epic card game of Pope's poem is playfully recalled in Book I of *The Prelude,* the cardplayers, significantly, are huddled in a cottage, sheltered precariously from the mountain rain and bitter cold. To most Neoclassicists city life did seem the normal human environment; Samuel Johnson, the last great literary voice before the Romantics, equated London with life and sniffed that people who chose to live in the country deserved their fate. This preference for the urban seems to many modern readers, even some confirmed city dwellers, to be a perverse aberration, but one can make a good case for the opposite. Through most of history, cities have been the definitive emblem of the good life, secular and sacred. Socrates envisaged a structured republic, not a pastoral commune. The Lord can be imaged as a shepherd (though even this emblem of nature is half-domesticated), but the basic Christian image of heaven is the City of God. "America the Beautiful" admires "purple mountain majesties," but its highest, futurist vision of America is one wherein "alabaster cities gleam / Undimmed by human tears."

The word *nature* is not so simple, though; in fact, it is one of the most complicated in the language. The range of its meanings is illustrated in Shakespeare's *King Lear,* where the word refers both to the divinely sanctioned human order typified in the loving bond that should unite parent and child and also to the Godless brute creation, so that when Edmund says, "Thou, nature, art my goddess," he is uttering the most blood-curdling blasphemy. C. S. Lewis, in his *Studies in Words,* discusses about twenty senses of *nature,* and even standard collegiate dictionaries record more than a dozen. These are best discriminated by the antonyms for *natural,* which include *artificial* (synthetic vitamins), *man-made* (the Hoover Dam as opposed to a beaver's), *pretentiously affected* (baby talk by an adult), *interfered with* ("don't stunt the child's natural development"), *acquired* ("are males breadwinners by nature or by culture?"), *legislated* (unlike natural laws), *wearing clothes* (*au naturel* now usually means "nude"), *not pertaining to matter* (social as opposed to natural sciences), *supernatural* (transcending nature, as God does), *magic* ("does demonic possession have a natural explanation?"), *trained* ("did he take lessons or is he just naturally good?"), *socially organized* ("in the state of nature there was no police force"), and many others. The most comprehensive antonym, probably, is *alien to what something, or someone, really is,* a concept especially useful to people never perplexed by the question of what is real.

All these senses are relevant to Neoclassicism and Romanticism, but to test the two impulses against each of them would take far more space than we have here. Let us say only that some of the meanings support our formula, some do not, and some are ambiguous. For example, what it means to *interfere with someone's true nature,* and whether or not it is good to do so, depends on one's premises. One might send children to a *progressive* school because one believes that their natural, good impulses should be unfettered but send them to a progressive *school* because one thinks that what nature has done for their minds must be improved on; whether a Neoclassicist or a Romantic would be the more likely to choose such a school is hard to say. If *nature* means the physical world as illuminated by science, the Neoclassicists probably valued nature even more than the Romantics did. Romantics might value the beaver's dam more than a man-made one, but that man does and should shape his world in a metaphysical sense is a distinctive Romantic idea, as we have seen.

Similar ambiguities cloud the distinctions between Neoclassical and Romantic theories of art and literature. For the Neoclassicists, art was an act of cultivating, but the thing to be cultivated ("to advantage dressed") was nature, understood as the governing reality of the world and life. The complication, as we said earlier, lies in the way one understands reality. Dazzled by the scientifically described cosmic machine, the Neoclassicists naturally (what does the word mean *here,* by the way?) thought of art as having an inorganic order and regularity. As their respect for the rules implies, they saw the literary genres—epic, tragedy, elegy, pastoral, ode, lyric, satire, and so on—as having intrinsic reality as containers, apart from the content poured into them by individual authors. But as the eighteenth century drew to a close and the nineteenth ran its course, scientific models changed. The focus of investigation shifted from astronomy and physics to chemistry to geology (a blend of physical science and history) to the life sciences, culminating in Charles Darwin's (1809–1882) evolutionary theories. An organic model replaced the mechanical one, a shift conditioned by science or conditioning it (another chicken-egg problem). The American founding fathers had invented a machine of government, but by 1863 Abraham Lincoln in the Gettysburg address was describing the origin of the nation in metaphors of conception and childbirth and diagnosing its mid-life crisis. Similarly, the human individual was imaged differently, not as having achieved a definitive human status in being born (*natus*) but as having thus embarked on the evolutionary journey called life. Every stage of life had its own reality and integrity, not excepting childhood. Indeed, childhood had its own special importance, as what Wordsworth called the "seed time" of the soul (note the organic metaphor). The Neoclassicists had internalized nature, modeling the human on an inorganic environment. Conversely, the Romantics projected the life they subjectively experienced onto the cosmos, now seen as vital instead of mechanical.

Two implications of organicism are especially relevant to literature: vital interconnectedness and growth. Both the inorganic models of machines or buildings and the organic models of plants or animals have parts, but in organisms the parts are not discrete and separable as they are in, say, modern component stereo systems. Rather, they are subordinated to a central vital principle, all the parts intimately interdependent, meaningless in isolation, and unable to survive alone. (The validity of this distinction, by the way, is being tested today by surgical organ transplants.) "The spirit of poetry," Coleridge wrote, "like all other living powers . . . must embody in order to reveal itself; but a living body is of necessity an organized one,—and what is organization, but the connection of parts to a whole, so that each part is at once end and means." This implies, first, that every work of art is unique, governed by its own internal ecology; second, that the distinction between form and subject matter is annihilated, because form grows from the essential idea or inspiration of a work as a plant does from its seed; and third, that the process of creation is inseparable from the product created. Perhaps the best example of all three of these implications is Wordsworth's *Prelude,* generating from a literary parentage (not from rules) its unique form of epic, taking the poet's own life as its subject, and incorporating in itself an account of how it was written.

The organicist emphasis on development and growth is even more important for literature. It accounts for the emergence of new forms such as the spiritual autobiography, which is less concerned with circumstances than with the evolution of the author's psyche. The fictional sibling of this form was the "apprenticeship" novel or poem, represented by *The Prelude,* Goethe's *Wilhelm Meister's Apprenticeship* (1795–96), and in our century by James Joyce's *Portrait of the Artist as a Young Man* (1916). This genre, going today as strong as ever, is still the norm for a writer's first novel, frequently combining the autobiographical and fictional impulses. The view of literature as process is reflected also in Tennyson's *In Memoriam,* which grows as naturally but unpredictably as a tree, by way of lyrics we are meant to take as spontaneous records of the passing months and years, from its autobiographical seed in the death of his friend Hallam. Growth and striving became themes also, in innumerable works including Goethe's *Faust.* The medieval romance theme of the quest was revived and adapted to modern subjects, including metaphysical quests for fulfillment. Even the texture of literature became organic for the Romantics; metaphor and symbol, used as in Keats's odes to blend idea and image inseparably, became more typical than the simile, which says only that something is *like* something else. Between Pope's "Bright as the sun, her eyes the gazers strike, / And, like the sun, they shine on all alike" (*The Rape of the Lock,* II.13–14) and Keats's "Thou still unravished bride of quietness" ("Ode on a Grecian Urn," line 1) lies an immense difference in ways of perceiving things. The breathtaking emblems of the spirit Thoreau finds in nature are climactic expressions of this metaphorical vision.

The Romantic love of nature is more than a taste for pretty scenery; it is an attempt to humanize nature, to replace man's view of himself as part of a machine, however well and benignly made, with a vision of the world as essentially an extension of soul. To call the Romantic view optimistic, as many people do, seems therefore a vast understatement. To other historians of literature and culture, though, there is a darker side to all this. On the simplest level, it is argued, the Romantic celebration of nature is defensive, a reflexive countermovement to the ominous rise of urban industrialization, analogous to modern environmentalist movements inspired not by security but by a sense of danger. On a spiritual level, the Romantics can be seen as claiming kinship to a humanized nature exactly because they feared that that strange phenomenon, human consciousness, is no more than a meaningless freak in a mindless cosmos. This sense of the utter strangeness of consciousness is the central theme of Byron's *Manfred*. The fear that, unconcerned with us or anything else, the stars "blindly run" is quite explicit in Tennyson's *In Memoriam* (III.5); compared with that frightening vision, the eighteenth-century deists' vision of a clockwork universe, however impersonal its Designer, seems almost cozy. That Wordsworth, the "worshipper" of nature, should even say "nature never did betray / The heart that loved her" suggests to some readers a fear on his part that she may indeed betray him ("Tintern Abbey," 152, 122–23). Seen in this light, the Byronic hero and his many nineteenth-century progeny are not mere picturesque period types toying with gloom from the security of their spiritual confidence but rather mythic embodiments of a sense of loneliness that dwells at the heart of Romanticism.

Furthermore, it seems inevitable that the Romantics, envisioning themselves and the world in organic terms of growth, should have seen with equal clarity the ultimate implication: that the terminus of organic process in all living things is death. The middle section of Wordsworth's "Intimations" ode traces the human movement toward spiritual as well as physical death; the final intimations—hints, not proofs—of immortality are found not in nature but in the mind's ability to transcend this mere "homely nurse." The implicitness of death in both our ordinary existence and our attempts to escape it is also the central theme of Keats's odes, especially the "Ode to a Nightingale," and it is not coincidental that the poem calls into question the validity of the Romantic imagination in general. Blake saw these negative implications from the beginning of the Romantic age; he may have loved the countryside as much as his brother Romantics, but toward nature as a thing in itself—mechanical or organic, dead or alive—he felt a profound hostility. As a metaphysical entity, it was "satanic," antithetical to the human.

Both Neoclassicists and Romantics, then, in their different ways, revered nature. The Romantics' reverence for it had both bright and dark sides, however. The same is true of their view of human possibilities. The theme of aspiration in their work coexists tensely with their awareness of the limitations imposed on the human spirit by the world, social organization, the mortality of the body, and even certain blocking agents in the psyche itself. These dualities help explain one of the paradoxes of twentieth-century literature. Modern writers rebelled against Romanticism, scorning its moonlit atmosphere, gossamer texture, and spiritual affirmations as unsustaining or irrelevant. On the other hand, they sometimes seem very similar to the Romantics, especially when they turn inward and face up to doubt as the Romantics did in their great crisis lyrics.

A sense of kinship to the Romantics, companionable or hostile, operates also in the many modern readers who find it easier to love or hate the Romantics than to respond in either way to the Neoclassicists. What we owe the latter is best appreciated if we move back from literature and take a wider view. The Neoclassical music of Wolfgang Amadeus Mozart (1756–1791) and of his eighteenth-century Baroque predecessor Johann Sebastian Bach (1685–1750), impassioned yet disciplined by formal clarity, has never since been rivaled except by Ludwig van Beethoven (1770–1827), a Romantic with one foot in the age of Neoclassicism. Many of the practical arts of graceful elegance—typified in the furniture designed by Thomas Chippendale (1718–1779)—have advanced little if at all since the eighteenth century. The roots of modern totalitarianism have been traced by some theorists of history to the Puritan regime in seventeenth-century England against which the Neoclassicists reacted and to the French Revolution, which killed Neoclassicism. These allegations have been largely discredited; for example, the nineteenth-century extension of civil and economic rights to the lowest social classes is in the line of descent from the French Revolution. It is significant, however, that such charges could not be brought against the Age of Reason with any plausibility at all. We owe to people of that age—great and ordinary—the theory and much of the machinery in accordance with which most free societies operate to the extent that they are free.

But we should not turn away too fast from literature and language. Besides its imaginative masterpieces, the Neoclassicists excelled in the "nonimaginative" genres dedicated to fact: biography, history, letters, the essay. When the Romantics revived metaphor in literature, they enriched it immeasurably, but the attempt by advocates of science in the latter seventeenth century to kill metaphor were, in the long run, a good thing too. To compare the energy, muscularity, and lucidity of Swift's prose—what in old sexist days was called its virility—with anything written two generations earlier is to recognize that the Neoclassic period created functional modern prose, the syntax and diction of, say, our better magazines. This is also the prose used or aspired to by authors of fiction when clear communication is their main concern. The human spirit needs poetry, both literal poetry and the spiritual adventure symbolized by the word, and these are what the Romantics give us. The spirit also needs Neoclassical prose and the vision of sane order implicit in it.

This distinction, including the poetry-prose metaphor, goes back more than a century, and it is valid enough to be worth preserving. Increasingly, however, students of literature have found it too facile. The Neoclassic and eighteenth-century vision of order seems, on the personal level, to have been more vision that fact; among the English authors alone, Swift, William Collins, Thomas Gray, Samuel Johnson, Christopher Smart, William Cowper, and Robert Burns all suffered from depression, serious mental illness, or the fear of such illness; Thomas Chatterton committed suicide in his teens. In their literary works too there are glimpses of mysterious and irrational psychic depths; for example, that most civilized of poems, Pope's *Rape of the Lock,* includes in its Cave of Spleen a surrealistic fantasy world where, among other things, "Men prove with child, as powerful fancy works, / And maids turned bottles, call aloud for corks" (IV.53–54). The personal lives of the Romantics were, for the most part, not really adventurous, a few such as Byron excepted. Their works, apparently so much closer to wish-fulfillment fantasy than to reality, have come to seem more and more realistic in their depiction of basic truths about the human personality, as depth psychologists have recognized. Behind most human acts and language lies their opposite, according to one maxim of popular psychology; the determined life-of-the-party is really shy, the notorious lecher really hates women, and so on. Applying that rule to the periods we are considering, we would conclude that the Neoclassic age was an age of unreason and that the Romantic age was one of sober responsibility. To go that far would surely be perverse and absurd, yet in reading particular works it sometimes helps to keep the theory of opposites and compensations in mind. If we do so, especially when reading the greatest authors, we find that the Neoclassicists and the Romantics are not totally dissimilar, since they are writing about the one world that ultimately all people in all ages inhabit.

FURTHER READING *(prepared by B. W.):* Among the words discussed at length in C. S. Lewis's *Studies in Words,* 1960, are *nature, wit,* and *sense,* all key terms in Neoclassicism or Romanticism. The distinguished philosopher-mathematician Alfred North Whitehead, in *Science and the Modern World,* 1925, speculates provocatively and with enduring relevance on the relationship between science, philosophy, and literature since the Renaissance. Martin S. Day's *History of English Literature 1660–1837,* 1963, in the Doubleday College Course Guide series, is an excellent handbook that covers a good deal of ground economically. For a general history of political and many other aspects of eighteenth-century Europe, see Isser Woloch's *Eighteenth-Century Europe, Tradition and Progress 1715–1789,* 1982. Derek Jarrett's *England in the Age of Hogarth,* 1974, is an engrossing, illustrated social history of the eighteenth century. The spirit of the century is also well captured in Peter Gay's *The Enlightenment,* 2 vols., 1966–69. Donald Greene's *The Age of Exuberance,* 1970, is an intellectual and literary history that re-evaluates the adequacy of labels such as *Enlightenment.* On the transition from Neoclassicism to Romanticism many good things have been written. One is Walter Jackson Bate's *From Classic to Romantic,* 1946, which treats the relationship of literature to other currents of thought in the two periods; Basil Willey's *The Eighteenth-Century Background,* 1940, which concentrates chiefly on the idea of nature, is also very good. Two volumes in the Viking Portable series, *The Portable Age of Reason Reader,* ed. Crane Brinton, 1956, and *The Portable Romantic Reader,* ed. Howard E. Hugo, 1957, provide good introductions to the periods and wide samplings of characteristic writings, drawn from several national literatures. On the shift in imagery, the replacement in Romanticism of a God- and nature-centered world view by a human-centered one, and a number of other important issues, see Northrop Frye's *A Study of English Romanticism,* 1968, and "The Imaginative and the Imaginary" in his *Fables of Identity,* 1963. On the transition between Neoclassical models of reality and Romantic organicism, see A. O. Lovejoy's *The Great Chain of Being,* 1936; René Wellek's "The Concept of 'Romanticism' in Literary History" in the 1949 volume of *Comparative Literature;* Morse Peckham's "Toward a Theory of Romanticism" in the 1951 volume of *PMLA;* and Peckham's sequel to that article in the 1961 volume of *Studies in Romanticism.* A variety of essays on the transition to Romanticism are collected in *From Sensibility to Romanticism,* ed. Frederick W. Hilles and Harold Bloom, 1965. On the emergence of the Romantic theory of poetic creation from earlier models, see M. H. Abrams, *The Mirror and the Lamp,* 1953, one of the most highly honored books of modern literary scholarship. For an excellent guide to and description of books and articles on the Romantics, some of which have an international focus, see "The Romantic Movement" by Ernest Bernbaum and Frank Jordan, in *The English Romantic Poets: A Review of Research and Criticism,* 3rd ed., ed. Frank Jordan, 1972. *Romanticism Reconsidered,* ed. Northrop Frye, 1963, contains appraisals of its subject by four distinguished authorities: Frye, M. H. Abrams, Lionel Trilling, and René Wellek. On the coherence of Romanticism as a movement, see Wellek's broad-ranging second volume, *The Romantic Age,* 1955, in his *History of Modern Criticism 1750–1950.* His "German and English Romanticism: A Confrontation," in the 1964 volume of *Studies in Romanticism,* is valuable on the subject it addresses. An immensely spirited, polemical defense of Romanticism against charges brought against it on political and other grounds is presented by Jacques Barzun in *Classic, Romantic, and Modern,* 1961, a book that also compares "historic" and "perennial" Romanticism. Also lively and penetrating is Harold Bloom's *The Visionary Company;* mainly a series of readings of individual English Romantic poets, the 2nd edition, 1971, includes also a stimulating general preface on the radical, Protestant political impulse in Romanticism. For a cultural history of the United States in the nineteenth century, see Daniel Boorstin, *The Americans: The National Experience,* 1965. A guide to writings about the major authors is available in *Eight American Authors: A Review of Research and Criticism,* rev. ed., ed. James Woodress, 1971. The central American theme of optimism is explored in R. W. B. Lewis's *The American Adam: Innocence, Tragedy, and Tradition in the Nineteenth Century,* 1955. F. O. Matthiessen's *American Renaissance,* 1941, though in some ways a little outdated, remains one of the classic treatments of nineteenth-century American literature.

Molière

(1622–1673)

Jean-Baptiste Poquelin, whose stage name was Molière, was born in Paris in 1622, into a respectable, well-to-do, middle-class family; his father was an upholsterer who included the king among his customers. Molière was educated at the excellent Collège de Clermont in Paris and then enrolled in a law course in Orléans. At the age of twenty-one, however, he shocked and disappointed his father (his mother had died when he was ten) by abandoning the study of law and becoming an actor. Part of the lure of the theater apparently was the beautiful and talented Madeleine Béjart, six years older than Molière and an experienced actress. Molière joined Madeleine, her brother Joseph, and her sister Genevieve in forming L'Illustre Théâtre; *upon entering the theater, he took the name of Molière, possibly to spare his father embarrassment. The dozen youthful members of the Illustrious Theater performed sporadically and unsuccessfully for two years in Paris; Molière was twice briefly imprisoned for debt during this time. Finally, Molière and the three Béjarts, with three other loyal members of the company, decided to leave Paris and perform in the provinces. Their tour lasted twelve years, during which the members of the company became seasoned performers and Molière began to write plays.*

In 1658, these performers decided to try their luck once more in Paris. They played before the king's brother Philippe (known as "Monsieur"), pleased him, and became established as the "Troupe de Monsieur." During the remaining fifteen years of his life, Molière remained in Paris, writing, directing, and acting in the more than thirty plays upon which his reputation still rests. His career was marked by almost constant intrigue and turmoil, and each major success won him not only admirers but enemies among those his satiric wit had touched. The success of The Pretentious Young Ladies *in 1659 caused a storm of protest which forced a suspension of the production for two weeks and eventually the closing of the theater in which Molière was then performing, the Petit Bourbon.* The School for Wives *in 1662 launched another series of attacks upon both his art and his character, and* Tartuffe *(1664) provoked such a scandal that public performances were forbidden for five years.*

In 1662, at the age of forty, Molière married Armande Béjart, the twenty-year-old youngest sister of his long-time mistress and close friend Madeleine Béjart. Armande was an accomplished actress, specializing in the roles of witty coquettes, many of which Molière wrote for her, such as Eliza in The School for Wives Criticized *and Célimène in* The Misanthrope. *The couple had three children, two of whom died in infancy, but the marriage was not happy, and they lived separately for several years.*

Louis XIV was an enthusiastic though erratic supporter of Molière. In 1665, he conferred upon Molière's company the title of "Troupe of the King," and Molière wrote a number of plays, opera-ballets, and other entertainments for presentation at Versailles and other locations of the court. In 1672, however, the king withdrew his favor from Molière and conferred it upon the devious and manipulative court composer Jean Baptiste Lully. Hurt by this rejection and by the recent deaths of Madeleine Béjart and of a son and suffering from a worsening of a long-time lung ailment, probably tuberculosis, Molière completed his last play, The Imaginary Invalid, *paradoxically one of the wittiest and most sparkling of his works. On February 17, 1673, he collapsed, hemorrhaging from the lungs, in the middle of a performance of*

The Imaginary Invalid *in which he was playing the role of the hypochondriac Argan. He managed to finish the performance but died later that night in his home. The local priests at first refused to bury him in holy ground, but on the intervention of the king he was finally buried in the Cemetery Saint-Joseph, although his body was taken to the grave in darkness so as to "avoid scandal."*

The physical theaters Molière wrote for differed considerably from the theaters of Shakespeare and Calderón. The earliest seventeenth-century French theaters were converted from unused indoor tennis courts, survivals of a short-lived vogue for tennis. These and later theaters were long, narrow rooms with a raised stage at one end and an ornate proscenium arch and a front curtain, much like a modern stage. The stage, unlike Shakespeare's, represented a particular place throughout, depicted in perspective scenery made of wood and canvas. This scenery remained in place throughout the play; because of both the difficulty of shifting scenery and the influence of the idea of "unity of place" (the limitation of a play to one location), no attempt was made to change the set in the course of the action.

All these theatrical conditions affected the form and structure of French neoclassical plays. Molière's casts of characters are small, by Shakespearean standards at least; his plots are comparatively simple and usually confined to domestic, family matters; and the action takes place over a short span of time and in a single place, even when such constriction results in some improbability.

Molière's revolutionary impact upon French drama was in the creation of "character comedy." When he and his company began performing his plays in Paris, the dominant forms of stage comedy were the improvised low comedy of the Italian commedia dell'arte *and high comedy that depended upon elaborate, complex plots. Molière revived the popular farcical comedy of a quarter-century before, with its preoccupation with cuckoldry and its slapstick devices, and used it to deal with contemporary fashions and customs. The result was a hilarious comedy that shifted the focus from elaborate plotting to character.*

In his comedy Molière is recurringly preoccupied with the contrast between mask *and* face. *His characters are usually drawn from the stock types of popular farce—young lovers, witty servants, tyrannical parents, absurd pedants—but he humanizes these masks by hinting at the psychological forces behind them. His major characters are usually great egotists who disguise their drives to satisfy their appetites behind conventional roles or masks. There is thus frequently a rather infantile quality about Molière's comedy; we sometimes feel that we are watching great babies playing at being fathers, mothers, husbands, wives, or courtiers. Their appetites are frequently so urgent and so all-engulfing that they can be controlled only by theatrical illusion. Tartuffe seems destined to triumph over Orgon and his family up until the very end, when a "messenger from the king" rather improbably reverses the action.*

Tartuffe, *like all of Molière's greatest plays, comes perilously close to tragedy. Tartuffe is one of dramatic literature's greatest comic creations. Molière daringly delays his entrance until the third act, after he has been discussed thoroughly. When he finally enters, calling with a delicious absurdity for his valet to hang up his hair shirt and his scourge, he fascinates us with his completely amoral and childlike pursuit of his own gratification. But, in many ways, Orgon is even more interesting. Why is he so blind to Tartuffe's true nature? What needs of his own lead him to accept Tartuffe so completely and so self-destructively, while hiding behind his own mask of piety and righteousness? Man seems woefully ill-equipped to deal with evil in this play. Cléante, Molière's familiar touchstone character of moderation and the normal, asks his brother-in-law, "Is not a face quite different from a mask? / Cannot sincerity and cunning art, / Reality and semblance, be told apart?" But his good sense cannot prevail against the masked irrational drives of either Orgon or Tartuffe; only the playwright's hand can avert a calamitous ending. The best comedy, Freud told us, has a sting in it; we laugh hardest at things that, if we did not laugh, would make us weep. We laugh all the more at* Tartuffe's *comic masks, perhaps, because we are aware of the tragic faces behind them.*

FURTHER READING *(prepared by W. J. R.):* A good biography and survey of Molière's writings can be found in John Palmer's *Molière,* 1930, rpt. 1970. Palmer provides particularly good chapters on Molière's acting career and on the theater of his day. D. B. Wyndham Lewis's witty *Molière: The Comic Mask,* 1959, combines biography and criticism of works including *Tartuffe.* Gertrud Mander's *Molière,* trans. by Diana Stone Peters, 1973, begins with a chronology and an essay on Molière's times and then proceeds to introductory discussions of fourteen Molière plays. Reviews of significant modern productions of Molière are collected in the conclusion. Five major plays are discussed in Lionel Gossman's *Men and Masks,* 1963, concluding with an examination of Molière's modern reputation. Nineteen essays on technique, theme, and tradition are collected in *Molière: Stage and Study,* ed. W. D. Howarth and Merlin Thomas, 1973. Gaston Hall's essay on comic images and W. H. Barber's essay on Voltaire and Molière may be of particular interest. W. G. Moore's *Molière: A New Criticism,* 1949, is still an important work in Molière scholarship. Moore identifies several problems in interpreting Molière's drama and analyzes multiple levels of comedy in several major works. An interesting complement to Moore's study is provided in Brian Nicholas's "Is Tartuffe a Comic Character?" *Modern Language Review,* 75 (1980), 753–65. Nicholas responds to Moore's analysis of *Tartuffe* and speculates interestingly on the relationship between comedy and satirical ideas. *Molière: A Collection of Critical Essays,* ed. Jacques Guicharnaud, 1964, contains several fine essays on the art of comedy and on *Dom Juan,* but does not offer essays on *Tartuffe.* Roger W. Herzel provides an interesting essay on a rather neglected topic in "The Decor of Molière's Stage: The Testimony of Brissart and Chauveau," *PMLA,* 93 (1978), 925–54. Using many illustrations, Herzel explains why the stage designs for Molière's comedies may have differed considerably from the barren, static designs used for Racinian tragedies. (See also the bibliography for Racine.)

TARTUFFE

Translated by Richard Wilbur

CHARACTERS

MME. PERNELLE, *Orgon's mother*
ORGON, *Elmire's husband*
ELMIRE, *Orgon's wife*
DAMIS, *Orgon's son, Elmire's stepson*
MARIANE, *Orgon's daughter, Elmire's stepdaughter, in love with Valère*
VALÈRE, *in love with Mariane*
CLÉANTE, *Orgon's brother-in-law*
TARTUFFE, *a hypocrite*
DORINE, *Mariane's lady's-maid*
M. LOYAL, *a bailiff*
A POLICE OFFICER
FLIPOTE, *Mme. Pernelle's maid*

THE SCENE THROUGHOUT: ORGON'S *house in Paris*

ACT I

SCENE 1

MADAME PERNELLE *and* FLIPOTE, *her maid*
ELMIRE DORINE CLÉANTE
MARIANE DAMIS

MADAME PERNELLE. Come, come, Flipote; it's time I left this place.
ELMIRE. I can't keep up, you walk at such a pace.
MADAME PERNELLE. Don't trouble, child; no need to show me out.
It's not your manners I'm concerned about.
ELMIRE. We merely pay you the respect we owe.
But, Mother, why this hurry? Must you go?
MADAME PERNELLE. I must. This house appalls me. No one in it
Will pay attention for a single minute.
Children, I take my leave much vexed in spirit.
I offer good advice, but you won't hear it.
You all break in and chatter on and on.
It's like a madhouse with the keeper gone.
DORINE. If . . .
MADAME PERNELLE. Girl, you talk too much, and I'm afraid
You're far too saucy for a lady's-maid.
You push in everywhere and have your say.
DAMIS. But . . .
MADAME PERNELLE. You, boy, grow more foolish every day.
To think my grandson should be such a dunce!
I've said a hundred times, if I've said it once,
That if you keep the course on which you've started,
You'll leave your worthy father broken-hearted.
MARIANE. I think . . .
MADAME PERNELLE. And you, his sister, seem so pure,
So shy, so innocent, and so demure.

But you know what they say about still waters.
I pity parents with secretive daughters.

ELMIRE. Now, Mother . . .

MADAME PERNELLE. And as for you, child, let me add
That your behavior is extremely bad,
And a poor example for these children, too.
Their dear, dead mother did far better than you.
You're much too free with money, and I'm distressed
To see you so elaborately dressed.
When it's one's husband that one aims to please,
One has no need of costly fripperies.

CLÉANTE. Oh, Madame, really . . .

MADAME PERNELLE. You are her brother, Sir,
And I respect and love you; yet if I were
My son, this lady's good and pious spouse,
I wouldn't make you welcome in my house.
You're full of worldly counsels which, I fear,
Aren't suitable for decent folk to hear.
I've spoken bluntly, Sir; but it behooves us
Not to mince words when righteous fervor moves us.

DAMIS. Your man Tartuffe is full of holy speeches . . .

MADAME PERNELLE. And practises precisely what he preaches.
He's a fine man, and should be listened to.
I will not hear him mocked by fools like you.

DAMIS. Good God! Do you expect me to submit
To the tyranny of that carping hypocrite?
Must we forgo all joys and satisfactions
Because that bigot censures all our actions?

DORINE. To hear him talk—and he talks all the time—
There's nothing one can do that's not a crime.
He rails at everything, your dear Tartuffe.

MADAME PERNELLE. Whatever he reproves deserves reproof.
He's out to save your souls, and all of you
Must love him, as my son would have you do.

DAMIS. Ah no, Grandmother, I could never take
To such a rascal, even for my father's sake.
That's how I feel, and I shall not dissemble.
His every action makes me seethe and tremble
With helpless anger, and I have no doubt
That he and I will shortly have it out.

DORINE. Surely it is a shame and a disgrace
To see this man usurp the master's place—
To see this beggar who, when first he came,
Had not a shoe or shoestring to his name
So far forget himself that he behaves
As if the house were his, and we his slaves.

MADAME PERNELLE. Well, mark my words, your souls would fare far better
If you obeyed his precepts to the letter.

DORINE. You see him as a saint. I'm far less awed;
In fact, I see right through him. He's a fraud.
MADAME PERNELLE. Nonsense.
DORINE. His man Laurent's the same, or worse;
I'd not trust either with a penny purse.
MADAME PERNELLE. I can't say what his servant's morals may be;
His own great goodness I can guarantee.
You all regard him with distaste and fear
Because he tells you what you're loath to hear,
Condemns your sins, points out your moral flaws,
And humbly strives to further Heaven's cause.
DORINE. If sin is all that bothers him, why is it
He's so upset when folk drop in to visit?
Is Heaven so outraged by a social call
That he must prophesy against us all?
I'll tell you what I think: if you ask me,
He's jealous of my mistress' company.
MADAME PERNELLE. Rubbish! [*To* ELMIRE.] He's not alone, child, in complaining
Of all your promiscuous entertaining.
Why, the whole neighborhood's upset, I know,
By all these carriages that come and go,
With crowds of guests parading in and out
And noisy servants loitering about.
In all of this, I'm sure there's nothing vicious;
But why give people cause to be suspicious?
CLÉANTE. They need no cause; they'll talk in any case.
Madam, this world would be a joyless place
If, fearing what malicious tongues might say,
We locked our doors and turned our friends away.
And even if one did so dreary a thing,
D'you think those tongues would cease their chattering?
One can't fight slander; it's a losing battle;
Let us instead ignore their tittle-tattle.
Let's strive to live by conscience' clear decrees,
And let the gossips gossip as they please.
DORINE. If there is talk against us, I know the source:
It's Daphne and her little husband, of course.
Those who have greatest cause for guilt and shame
Are quickest to besmirch a neighbor's name.
When there's a chance for libel, they never miss it;
When something can be made to seem illicit
They're off at once to spread the joyous news,
Adding to fact what fantasies they choose.
By talking up their neighbor's indiscretions
They seek to camouflage their own transgressions,
Hoping that others' innocent affairs
Will lend a hue of innocence to theirs,
Or that their own black guilt will come to seem
Part of a general shady color-scheme.

MADAME PERNELLE. All that is quite irrelevant. I doubt
That anyone's more virtuous and devout
Than dear Orante; and I'm informed that she
Condemns your mode of life most vehemently.

DORINE. Oh, yes, she's strict, devout, and has no taint
Of worldliness, in short, she seems a saint.
But it was time which taught her that disguise;
She's thus because she can't be otherwise.
So long as her attractions could enthrall,
She flounced and flirted and enjoyed it all,
But now that they're no longer what they were
She quits a world which fast is quitting her,
And wears a veil of virtue to conceal
Her bankrupt beauty and her lost appeal.
That's what becomes of old coquettes today:
Distressed when all their lovers fall away,
They see no recourse but to play the prude,
And so confer a style on solitude.
Thereafter, they're severe with everyone,
Condemning all our actions, pardoning none,
And claiming to be pure, austere, and zealous
When, if the truth were known, they're merely jealous,
And cannot bear to see another know
The pleasures time has forced them to forgo.

MADAME PERNELLE [*initially to* ELMIRE]. That sort of talk is what you like to hear,
Therefore you'd have us all keep still, my dear,
While Madam rattles on the livelong day.
Nevertheless, I mean to have my say.
I tell you that you're blest to have Tartuffe
Dwelling, as my son's guest, beneath this roof;
That Heaven has sent him to forestall its wrath
By leading you, once more, to the true path;
That all he reprehends is reprehensible,
And that you'd better heed him, and be sensible.
These visits, balls, and parties in which you revel
Are nothing but inventions of the Devil.
One never hears a word that's edifying:
Nothing but chaff and foolishness and lying,
As well as vicious gossip in which one's neighbor
Is cut to bits with epee, foil, and saber.
People of sense are driven half-insane
At such affairs, where noise and folly reign
And reputations perish thick and fast.
As a wise preacher said on Sunday last,
Parties are Towers of Babylon, because
The guests all babble on with never a pause;
And then he told a story which, I think . . .
[*To* CLÉANTE.] I heard that laugh, Sir, and I saw that wink!
Go find your silly friends and laugh some more!

Enough; I'm going; don't show me to the door.
I leave this household much dismayed and vexed;
I cannot say when I shall see you next.
[*Slapping* FLIPOTE.] Wake up, don't stand there gaping into space!
I'll slap some sense into that stupid face.
Move, move, you slut.

SCENE 2

CLÉANTE DORINE

CLÉANTE. I think I'll stay behind;
I want no further pieces of her mind.
How that old lady . . .
DORINE. Oh, what wouldn't she say
If she could hear you speak of her that way!
She'd thank you for the *lady,* but I'm sure
She'd find the *old* a little premature.
CLÉANTE. My, what a scene she made, and what a din!
And how this man Tartuffe has taken her in!
DORINE. Yes, but her son is even worse deceived;
His folly must be seen to be believed.
In the late troubles, he played an able part
And served his king with wise and loyal heart,
But he's quite lost his senses since he fell
Beneath Tartuffe's infatuating spell.
He calls him brother, and loves him as his life,
Preferring him to mother, child, or wife.
In him and him alone will he confide;
He's made him his confessor and his guide;
He pets and pampers him with love more tender
Than any pretty mistress could engender,
Gives him the place of honor when they dine,
Delights to see him gorging like a swine,
Stuffs him with dainties till his guts distend,
And when he belches, cries "God bless you, friend!"
In short, he's mad; he worships him; he dotes;
His deeds he marvels at, his words he quotes,
Thinking each act a miracle, each word
Oracular as those that Moses heard.
Tartuffe, much pleased to find so easy a victim,
Has in a hundred ways beguiled and tricked him,
Milked him of money, and with his permission
Established here a sort of Inquisition.
Even Laurent, his lackey, dares to give
Us arrogant advice on how to live;
He sermonizes us in thundering tones
And confiscates our ribbons and colognes.
Last week he tore a kerchief into pieces
Because he found it pressed in a *Life of Jesus:*

He said it was a sin to juxtapose
Unholy vanities and holy prose.

SCENE 3
ELMIRE DAMIS DORINE
MARIANE CLÉANTE

ELMIRE [*to* CLÉANTE]. You did well not to follow; she stood in the door
And said *verbatim* all she'd said before.
I saw my husband coming. I think I'd best
Go upstairs now, and take a little rest.
CLÉANTE. I'll wait and greet him here; then I must go.
I've really only time to say hello.
DAMIS. Sound him about my sister's wedding, please.
I think Tartuffe's against it, and that he's
Been urging Father to withdraw his blessing.
As you well know, I'd find that most distressing.
Unless my sister and Valère can marry,
My hopes to wed *his* sister will miscarry,
And I'm determined . . .
DORINE. He's coming.

SCENE 4
ORGON CLÉANTE DORINE

ORGON. Ah, Brother, good-day.
CLÉANTE. Well, welcome back. I'm sorry I can't stay.
How was the country? Blooming, I trust, and green?
ORGON. Excuse me, Brother; just one moment.
[*To* DORINE.] Dorine . . .
[*To* CLÉANTE.] To put my mind at rest, I always learn
The household news the moment I return.
[*To* DORINE.] Has all been well, these two days I've been gone?
How are the family? What's been going on?
DORINE. Your wife, two days ago, had a bad fever,
And a fierce headache which refused to leave her.
ORGON. Ah. And Tartuffe?
DORINE. Tartuffe? Why, he's round and red,
Bursting with health, and excellently fed.
ORGON. Poor fellow!
DORINE. That night, the mistress was unable
To take a single bite at the dinner-table.
Her headache-pains, she said, were simply hellish.
ORGON. Ah. And Tartuffe?
DORINE. He ate his meal with relish,
And zealously devoured in her presence
A leg of mutton and a brace of pheasants.

ORGON. Poor fellow!
DORINE. Well, the pains continued strong,
And so she tossed and tossed the whole night long,
Now icy-cold, now burning like a flame.
We sat beside her bed till morning came.
ORGON. Ah. And Tartuffe?
DORINE. Why, having eaten, he rose
And sought his room, already in a doze,
Got into his warm bed, and snored away
In perfect peace until the break of day.
ORGON. Poor fellow!
DORINE. After much ado, we talked her
Into dispatching someone for the doctor.
He bled her, and the fever quickly fell.
ORGON. Ah. And Tartuffe?
DORINE. He bore it very well.
To keep his cheerfulness at any cost,
And make up for the blood *Madame* had lost,
He drank, at lunch, four beakers full of port.
ORGON. Poor fellow!
DORINE. Both are doing well, in short.
I'll go and tell *Madame* that you've expressed
Keen sympathy and anxious interest.

SCENE 5

ORGON CLÉANTE

CLÉANTE. That girl was laughing in your face, and though
I've no wish to offend you, even so
I'm bound to say that she had some excuse.
How can you possibly be such a goose?
Are you so dazed by this man's hocus-pocus
That all the world, save him, is out of focus?
You've given him clothing, shelter, food, and care;
Why must you also . . .
ORGON. Brother, stop right there.
You do not know the man of whom you speak.
CLÉANTE. I grant you that. But my judgment's not so weak
That I can't tell, by his effect on others . . .
ORGON. Ah, when you meet him, you two will be like brothers!
There's been no loftier soul since time began.
He is a man who . . . a man who . . . an excellent man.
To keep his precepts is to be reborn,
And view this dunghill of a world with scorn.
Yes, thanks to him I'm a changed man indeed.
Under his tutelage my soul's been freed
From earthly loves, and every human tie:

My mother, children, brother, and wife could die,
And I'd not feel a single moment's pain.
CLÉANTE. That's a fine sentiment, Brother; most humane.
ORGON. Oh, had you seen Tartuffe as I first knew him,
Your heart, like mine, would have surrendered to him.
He used to come into our church each day
And humbly kneel nearby, and start to pray.
He'd draw the eyes of everybody there
By the deep fervor of his heartfelt prayer;
He'd sigh and weep, and sometimes with a sound
Of rapture he would bend and kiss the ground;
And when I rose to go, he'd run before
To offer me holy-water at the door.
His serving-man, no less devout than he,
Informed me of his master's poverty;
I gave him gifts, but in his humbleness
He'd beg me every time to give him less.
"Oh, that's too much," he'd cry, "too much by twice!
I don't deserve it. The half, Sir, would suffice."
And when I wouldn't take it back, he'd share
Half of it with the poor, right then and there.
At length, Heaven prompted me to take him in
To dwell with us, and free our souls from sin.
He guides our lives, and to protect my honor
Stays by my wife, and keeps an eye upon her;
He tells me whom she sees, and all she does,
And seems more jealous than I ever was!
And how austere he is! Why, he can detect
A mortal sin where you would least suspect;
In smallest trifles, he's extremely strict.
Last week, his conscience was severely pricked
Because, while praying, he had caught a flea
And killed it, so he felt, too wrathfully.
CLÉANTE. Good God, man! Have you lost your common sense—
Or is this all some joke at my expense?
How can you stand there and in all sobriety . . .
ORGON. Brother, your language savors of impiety.
Too much free-thinking's made your faith unsteady,
And as I've warned you many times already,
'Twill get you into trouble before you're through.
CLÉANTE. So I've been told before by dupes like you:
Being blind, you'd have all others blind as well;
The clear-eyed man you call an infidel,
And he who sees through humbug and pretense
Is charged, by you, with want of reverence.
Spare me your warnings, Brother; I have no fear
Of speaking out, for you and Heaven to hear,
Against affected zeal and pious knavery.
There's true and false in piety, as in bravery,

And just as those whose courage shines the most
In battle, are the least inclined to boast,
So those whose hearts are truly pure and lowly
Don't make a flashy show of being holy.
There's a vast difference, so it seems to me,
Between true piety and hypocrisy:
How do you fail to see it, may I ask?
Is not a face quite different from a mask?
Cannot sincerity and cunning art,
Reality and semblance, be told apart?
Are scarecrows just like men, and do you hold
That a false coin is just as good as gold?
Ah, Brother, man's a strangely fashioned creature
Who seldom is content to follow Nature,
But recklessly pursues his inclination
Beyond the narrow bounds of moderation,
And often, by transgressing Reason's laws,
Perverts a lofty aim or noble cause.
A passing observation, but it applies.

ORGON. I see, dear Brother, that you're profoundly wise;
You harbor all the insight of the age.
You are our one clear mind, our only sage,
The era's oracle, its Cato too,
And all mankind are fools compared to you.

CLÉANTE. Brother, I don't pretend to be a sage,
Nor have I all the wisdom of the age.
There's just one insight I would dare to claim:
I know that true and false are not the same;
And just as there is nothing I more revere
Than a soul whose faith is steadfast and sincere,
Nothing that I more cherish and admire
Than honest zeal and true religious fire,
So there is nothing that I find more base
Than specious piety's dishonest face—
Than these bold mountebanks, these histrios
Whose impious mummeries and hollow shows
Exploit our love of Heaven, and make a jest
Of all that men think holiest and best;
These calculating souls who offer prayers
Not to their Maker, but as public wares,
And seek to buy respect and reputation
With lifted eyes and sighs of exaltation;
These charlatans, I say, whose pilgrim souls
Proceed, by way of Heaven, toward earthly goals,
Who weep and pray and swindle and extort,
Who preach the monkish life, but haunt the court,
Who make their zeal the partner of their vice—
Such men are vengeful, sly, and cold as ice,
And when there is an enemy to defame

They cloak their spite in fair religion's name,
Their private spleen and malice being made
To seem a high and virtuous crusade,
Until, to mankind's reverent applause,
They crucify their foe in Heaven's cause.
Such knaves are all too common; yet, for the wise,
True piety isn't hard to recognize,
And, happily, these present times provide us
With bright examples to instruct and guide us.
Consider Ariston and Périandre;
Look at Oronte, Alcidamas, Clitandre;
Their virtue is acknowledged; who could doubt it?
But you won't hear them beat the drum about it.
They're never ostentatious, never vain,
And their religion's moderate and humane;
It's not their way to criticize and chide:
They think censoriousness a mark of pride,
And therefore, letting others preach and rave,
They show, by deeds, how Christians should behave.
They think no evil of their fellow man,
But judge of him as kindly as they can.
They don't intrigue and wangle and conspire;
To lead a good life is their one desire;
The sinner wakes no rancorous hate in them;
It is the sin alone which they condemn;
Nor do they try to show a fiercer zeal
For Heaven's cause than Heaven itself could feel.
These men I honor, these men I advocate
As models for us all to emulate.
Your man is not their sort at all, I fear:
And, while your praise of him is quite sincere,
I think that you've been dreadfully deluded.

ORGON. Now then, dear Brother, is your speech concluded?
CLÉANTE. Why, yes.
ORGON. Your servant, Sir. [*He turns to go.*]
CLÉANTE. No, Brother; wait.
There's one more matter. You agreed of late
That young Valère might have your daughter's hand.
ORGON. I did.
CLÉANTE. And set the date, I understand.
ORGON. Quite so.
CLÉANTE. You've now postponed it; is that true?
ORGON. No doubt.
CLÉANTE. The match no longer pleases you?
ORGON. Who knows?
CLÉANTE. D'you mean to go back on your word?
ORGON. I won't say that.
CLÉANTE. Has anything occurred
Which might entitle you to break your pledge?

ORGON. Perhaps.
CLÉANTE. Why must you hem, and haw, and hedge?
The boy asked me to sound you in this affair . . .
ORGON. It's been a pleasure.
CLÉANTE. But what shall I tell Valère?
ORGON. Whatever you like.
CLÉANTE. But what have you decided?
What are your plans?
ORGON. I plan, Sir, to be guided
By Heaven's will.
CLÉANTE. Come, Brother, don't talk rot.
You've given Valère your word; will you keep it, or not?
ORGON. Good day.
CLÉANTE. This looks like poor Valère's undoing;
I'll go and warn him that there's trouble brewing.

ACT II

SCENE 1

ORGON MARIANE

ORGON. Mariane.
MARIANE. Yes, Father?
ORGON. A word with you; come here.
MARIANE. What are you looking for?
ORGON [*peering into a small closet*]. Eavesdroppers, dear.
I'm making sure we shan't be overheard.
Someone in there could catch our every word.
Ah, good, we're safe. Now, Mariane, my child,
You're a sweet girl who's tractable and mild,
Whom I hold dear, and think most highly of.
MARIANE. I'm deeply grateful, Father, for your love.
ORGON. That's well said, Daughter; and you can repay me
If, in all things, you'll cheerfully obey me.
MARIANE. To please you, Sir, is what delights me best.
ORGON. Good, good. Now, what d'you think of Tartuffe, our guest?
MARIANE. I, Sir?
ORGON. Yes. Weigh your answer; think it through.
MARIANE. Oh, dear. I'll say whatever you wish me to.
ORGON. That's wisely said, my Daughter. Say of him, then,
That he's the very worthiest of men,
And that you're fond of him, and would rejoice
In being his wife, if that should be my choice.
Well?
MARIANE. What?
ORGON. What's that?
MARIANE. I . . .
ORGON. Well?

MARIANE. Forgive me, pray.
ORGON. Did you not hear me?
MARIANE. Of *whom,* Sir, must I say
That I am fond of him, and would rejoice
In being his wife, if that should be your choice?
ORGON. Why, of Tartuffe.
MARIANE. But, Father, that's false, you know.
Why would you have me say what isn't so?
ORGON. Because I am resolved it shall be true.
That it's my wish should be enough for you.
MARIANE. You can't mean, Father . . .
ORGON. Yes, Tartuffe shall be
Allied by marriage to this family,
And he's to be your husband, is that clear?
It's a father's privilege . . .

SCENE 2

DORINE ORGON MARIANE

ORGON [*to* DORINE]. What are you doing in here?
Is curiosity so fierce a passion
With you, that you must eavesdrop in this fashion?
DORINE. There's lately been a rumor going about—
Based on some hunch or chance remark, no doubt—
That you mean Mariane to wed Tartuffe.
I've laughed it off, of course, as just a spoof.
ORGON. You find it so incredible?
DORINE. Yes, I do.
I won't accept that story, even from you.
ORGON. Well, you'll believe it when the thing is done.
DORINE. Yes, yes, of course. Go on and have your fun.
ORGON. I've never been more serious in my life.
DORINE. Ha!
ORGON. Daughter, I mean it; you're to be his wife.
DORINE. No, don't believe your father; it's all a hoax.
ORGON. See here, young woman . . .
DORINE. Come, Sir, no more jokes;
You can't fool us.
ORGON. How dare you talk that way?
DORINE. All right, then: we believe you, sad to say.
But how a man like you, who looks so wise
And wears a moustache of such splendid size,
Can be so foolish as to . . .
ORGON. Silence, please!
My girl, you take too many liberties.
I'm master here, as you must not forget.
DORINE. Do let's discuss this calmly; don't be upset.
You can't be serious, Sir, about this plan.
What should that bigot want with Mariane?

Praying and fasting ought to keep him busy.
And then, in terms of wealth and rank, what is he?
Why should a man of property like you
Pick out a beggar son-in-law?

ORGON. That will do.
Speak of his poverty with reverence.
His is a pure and saintly indigence
Which far transcends all worldly pride and pelf.
He lost his fortune, as he says himself,
Because he cared for Heaven alone, and so
Was careless of his interests here below.
I mean to get him out of his present straits
And help him to recover his estates—
Which, in his part of the world, have no small fame.
Poor though he is, he's a gentleman just the same.

DORINE. Yes, so he tells us; and, Sir, it seems to me
Such pride goes very ill with piety.
A man whose spirit spurns this dungy earth
Ought not to brag of lands and noble birth;
Such worldly arrogance will hardly square
With meek devotion and the life of prayer.
. . . But this reproach, I see, has drawn a blank;
Let's speak, then, of his person, not his rank.
Doesn't it seem to you a trifle grim
To give a girl like her to a man like him?
When two are so ill-suited, can't you see
What the sad consequence is bound to be?
A young girl's virtue is imperilled, Sir,
When such a marriage is imposed on her;
For if one's bridegroom isn't to one's taste,
It's hardly an inducement to be chaste,
And many a man with horns upon his brow
Has made his wife the thing that she is now.
It's hard to be a faithful wife, in short,
To certain husbands of a certain sort,
And he who gives his daughter to a man she hates
Must answer for her sins at Heaven's gates.
Think, Sir, before you play so risky a role.

ORGON. This servant-girl presumes to save my soul!

DORINE. You would do well to ponder what I've said.

ORGON. Daughter, we'll disregard this dunderhead.
Just trust your father's judgment. Oh, I'm aware
That I once promised you to young Valère;
But now I hear he gambles, which greatly shocks me;
What's more, I've doubts about his orthodoxy.
His visits to church, I note, are very few.

DORINE. Would you have him go at the same hours as you,
And kneel nearby, to be sure of being seen?

ORGON. I can dispense with such remarks, Dorine.
[*To* MARIANE.] Tartuffe, however, is sure of Heaven's blessing,

And that's the only treasure worth possessing.
This match will bring you joys beyond all measure;
Your cup will overflow with every pleasure;
You two will interchange your faithful loves
Like two sweet cherubs, or two turtle-doves.
No harsh word shall be heard, no frown be seen,
And he shall make you happy as a queen.

DORINE. And she'll make him a cuckold, just wait and see.

ORGON. What language!

DORINE. Oh, he's a man of destiny;
He's *made* for horns, and what the stars demand
Your daughter's virtue surely can't withstand.

ORGON. Don't interrupt me further. Why can't you learn
That certain things are none of your concern?

DORINE. It's for your own sake that I interfere.

[*She repeatedly interrupts* ORGON *just as he is turning to speak to his daughter.*]

ORGON. Most kind of you. Now, hold your tongue, d'you hear?

DORINE. If I didn't love you . . .

ORGON. Spare me your affection.

DORINE. I love you, Sir, in spite of your objection.

ORGON. Blast!

DORINE. I can't bear, Sir, for your honor's sake,
To let you make this ludicrous mistake.

ORGON. You mean to go on talking?

DORINE. If I didn't protest
This sinful marriage, my conscience couldn't rest.

ORGON. If you don't hold your tongue, you little shrew . . .

DORINE. What, lost your temper? A pious man like you?

ORGON. Yes! Yes! You talk and talk. I'm maddened by it.
Once and for all, I tell you to be quiet.

DORINE. Well, I'll be quiet. But I'll be thinking hard.

ORGON. Think all you like, but you had better guard
That saucy tongue of yours, or I'll . . .
[*Turning back to* MARIANE.] Now, child,
I've weighed this matter fully.

DORINE [*aside*]. It drives me wild
That I can't speak.

[ORGON *turns his head, and she is silent.*]

ORGON. Tartuffe is no young dandy,
But, still, his person . . .

DORINE [*aside*]. Is as sweet as candy.

ORGON. Is such that, even if you shouldn't care
For his other merits . . .

[*He turns and stands facing* DORINE, *arms crossed.*]

DORINE [*aside*]. They'll make a lovely pair.
If I were she, no man would marry me

Against my inclination, and go scot-free.
He'd learn, before the wedding-day was over,
How readily a wife can find a lover.

ORGON [*to* DORINE]. It seems you treat my orders as a joke.

DORINE. Why, what's the matter? 'Twas not to you I spoke.

ORGON. What *were* you doing?

DORINE. Talking to myself, that's all.

ORGON. Ah! [*Aside.*] One more bit of impudence and gall,
And I shall give her a good slap in the face.

[*He puts himself in position to slap her;* DORINE, *whenever he glances at her, stands immobile and silent.*]

Daughter, you shall accept, and with good grace,
The husband I've selected . . . Your wedding-day . . .
[*To* DORINE.] Why don't you talk to yourself?

DORINE. I've nothing to say.

ORGON. Come, just one word.

DORINE. No thank you, Sir. I pass.

ORGON. Come, speak; I'm waiting.

DORINE. I'd not be such an ass.

ORGON [*turning to* MARIANE]. In short, dear Daughter, I mean to be obeyed,
And you must bow to the sound choice I've made.

DORINE [*moving away*]. I'd not wed such a monster, even in jest.

[ORGON *attempts to slap her, but misses.*]

ORGON. Daughter, that maid of yours is a thorough pest;
She makes me sinfully annoyed and nettled.
I can't speak further; my nerves are too unsettled.
She's so upset me by her insolent talk,
I'll calm myself by going for a walk.

SCENE 3

DORINE MARIANE

DORINE [*returning*]. Well, have you lost your tongue, girl? Must I play
Your part, and say the lines you ought to say?
Faced with a fate so hideous and absurd,
Can you not utter one dissenting word?

MARIANE. What good would it do? A father's power is great.

DORINE. Resist him now, or it will be too late.

MARIANE. But . . .

DORINE. Tell him one cannot love at a father's whim;
That you shall marry for yourself, not him;
That since it's you who are to be the bride,
It's you, not he, who must be satisfied;
And that if his Tartuffe is so sublime,
He's free to marry him at any time.

Mariane. I've bowed so long to Father's strict control,
I couldn't oppose him now, to save my soul.
Dorine. Come, come, Mariane. Do listen to reason, won't you?
Valère has asked your hand. Do you love him, or don't you?
Mariane. Oh, how unjust of you! What can you mean
By asking such a question, dear Dorine?
You know the depth of my affection for him;
I've told you a hundred times how I adore him.
Dorine. I don't believe in everything I hear;
Who knows if your professions were sincere?
Mariane. They were, Dorine, and you do me wrong to doubt it;
Heaven knows that I've been all too frank about it.
Dorine. You love him, then?
Mariane. Oh, more than I can express.
Dorine. And he, I take it, cares for you no less?
Mariane. I think so.
Dorine. And you both, with equal fire,
Burn to be married?
Mariane. That is our one desire.
Dorine. What of Tartuffe, then? What of your father's plan?
Mariane. I'll kill myself, if I'm forced to wed that man.
Dorine. I hadn't thought of that recourse. How splendid!
Just die, and all your troubles will be ended!
A fine solution. Oh, it maddens me
To hear you talk in that self-pitying key.
Mariane. Dorine, how harsh you are! It's most unfair.
You have no sympathy for my despair.
Dorine. I've none at all for people who talk drivel
And, faced with difficulties, whine and snivel.
Mariane. No doubt I'm timid, but it would be wrong . . .
Dorine. True love requires a heart that's firm and strong.
Mariane. I'm strong in my affection for Valère,
But coping with my father is his affair.
Dorine. But if your father's brain has grown so cracked
Over his dear Tartuffe that he can retract
His blessing, though your wedding-day was named,
It's surely not Valère who's to be blamed.
Mariane. If I defied my father, as you suggest,
Would it not seem unmaidenly, at best?
Shall I defend my love at the expense
Of brazenness and disobedience?
Shall I parade my heart's desires, and flaunt . . .
Dorine. No, I ask nothing of you. Clearly you want
To be Madame Tartuffe, and I feel bound
Not to oppose a wish so very sound.
What right have I to criticize the match?
Indeed, my dear, the man's a brilliant catch.
Monsieur Tartuffe! Now, there's a man of weight!
Yes, yes, Monsieur Tartuffe, I'm bound to state,

Is quite a person; that's not to be denied;
'Twill be no little thing to be his bride.
The world already rings with his renown;
He's a great noble—in his native town;
His ears are red, he has a pink complexion,
And all in all, he'll suit you to perfection.

MARIANE. Dear God!

DORINE. Oh, how triumphant you will feel
At having caught a husband so ideal!

MARIANE. Oh, do stop teasing, and use your cleverness
To get me out of this appalling mess.
Advise me, and I'll do whatever you say.

DORINE. Ah no, a dutiful daughter must obey
Her father, even if he weds her to an ape.
You've a bright future; why struggle to escape?
Tartuffe will take you back where his family lives,
To a small town aswarm with relatives—
Uncles and cousins whom you'll be charmed to meet.
You'll be received at once by the elite,
Calling upon the bailiff's wife, no less—
Even, perhaps, upon the mayoress,
Who'll sit you down in the *best* kitchen chair.
Then, once a year, you'll dance at the village fair
To the drone of bagpipes—two of them, in fact—
And see a puppet-show, or an animal act.
Your husband . . .

MARIANE. Oh, you turn my blood to ice!
Stop torturing me, and give me your advice.

DORINE [*threatening to go*]. Your servant, Madam.

MARIANE. Dorine, I beg of you . . .

DORINE. No, you deserve it; this marriage must go through.

MARIANE. Dorine!

DORINE. No.

MARIANE. Not Tartuffe! You know I think him . . .

DORINE. Tartuffe's your cup of tea, and you shall drink him.

MARIANE. I've always told you everything, and relied . . .

DORINE. No. You deserve to be tartuffified.

MARIANE. Well, since you mock me and refuse to care,
I'll henceforth seek my solace in despair:
Despair shall be my counsellor and friend,
And help me bring my sorrows to an end.
[*She starts to leave.*]

DORINE. There now, come back; my anger has subsided.
You do deserve some pity, I've decided.

MARIANE. Dorine, if Father makes me undergo
This dreadful martyrdom, I'll die, I know.

DORINE. Don't fret; it won't be difficult to discover
Some plan of action . . . But here's Valère, your lover.

SCENE 4

VALÈRE MARIANE DORINE

VALÈRE. Madame, I've just received some wondrous news
Regarding which I'd like to hear your views.
MARIANE. What news?
VALÈRE. You're marrying Tartuffe.
MARIANE. I find
That Father does have such a match in mind.
VALÈRE. Your father, Madam . . .
MARIANE. . . . has just this minute said
That it's Tartuffe he wishes me to wed.
VALÈRE. Can he be serious?
MARIANE. Oh, indeed he can;
He's clearly set his heart upon the plan.
VALÈRE. And what position do you propose to take, Madam?
MARIANE. Why—I don't know.
VALÈRE. For heaven's sake—
You don't know?
MARIANE. No.
VALÈRE. Well, well!
MARIANE. Advise me, do.
VALÈRE. Marry the man. That's my advice to you.
MARIANE. That's your advice?
VALÈRE. Yes.
MARIANE. Truly?
VALÈRE. Oh, absolutely.
You couldn't choose more wisely, more astutely.
MARIANE. Thanks for this counsel; I'll follow it, of course.
VALÈRE. Do, do; I'm sure 'twill cost you no remorse.
MARIANE. To give it didn't cause your heart to break.
VALÈRE. I gave it, Madam, only for your sake.
MARIANE. And it's for your sake that I take it, Sir.
DORINE [*withdrawing to the rear of the stage*]. Let's see which fool will prove the stubborner.
VALÈRE. So! I am nothing to you, and it was flat
Deception when you . . .
MARIANE. Please, enough of that.
You've told me plainly that I should agree
To wed the man my father's chosen for me,
And since you've designed to counsel me so wisely,
I promise, Sir, to do as you advise me.
VALÈRE. Ah, no, 'twas not by me that you were swayed.
No, your decision was already made;
Though now, to save appearances, you protest
That you're betraying me at my behest.
MARIANE. Just as you say.
VALÈRE. Quite so. And I now see
That you were never truly in love with me.

MARIANE. Alas, you're free to think so if you choose.
VALÈRE. I choose to think so, and here's a bit of news:
You've spurned my hand, but I know where to turn
For kinder treatment, as you shall quickly learn.
MARIANE. I'm sure you do. Your noble qualities
Inspire affection . . .
VALÈRE. Forget my qualities, please.
They don't inspire you overmuch, I find.
But there's another lady I have in mind
Whose sweet and generous nature will not scorn
To compensate me for the loss I've borne.
MARIANE. I'm no great loss, and I'm sure that you'll transfer
Your heart quite painlessly from me to her.
VALÈRE. I'll do my best to take it in my stride.
The pain I feel at being cast aside
Time and forgetfulness may put an end to.
Or if I can't forget, I shall pretend to.
No self-respecting person is expected
To go on loving once he's been rejected.
MARIANE. Now, that's a fine, high-minded sentiment.
VALÈRE. One to which any sane man would assent.
Would you prefer it if I pined away
In hopeless passion till my dying day?
Am I to yield you to a rival's arms
And not console myself with other charms?
MARIANE. Go then: console yourself; don't hesitate.
I wish you to; indeed, I cannot wait.
VALÈRE. You wish me to?
MARIANE. Yes.
VALÈRE. That's the final straw.
Madam, farewell. Your wish shall be my law.
[*He starts to leave, and then returns: this repeatedly.*]
MARIANE. Splendid.
VALÈRE [*coming back again*].
This breach, remember, is of your making;
It's you who've driven me to the step I'm taking.
MARIANE. Of course.
VALÈRE [*coming back again*].
Remember, too, that I am merely
Following your example.
MARIANE. I see that clearly.
VALÈRE. Enough. I'll go and do your bidding, then.
MARIANE. Good.
VALÈRE [*coming back again*].
You shall never see my face again.
MARIANE. Excellent.
VALÈRE [*walking to the door, then turning about*].
Yes?
MARIANE. What?

VALÈRE. What's that? What did you say?
MARIANE. Nothing. You're dreaming.
VALÈRE. Ah. Well, I'm on my way.
Farewell, *Madame.*
[*He moves slowly away.*]
MARIANE. Farewell.
DORINE [*to* MARIANE]. If you ask me,
Both of you are as mad as mad can be.
Do stop this nonsense, now. I've only let you
Squabble so long to see where it would get you.
Whoa there, Monsieur Valère!
[*She goes and seizes* VALÈRE *by the arm; he makes a great show of resistance.*]
VALÈRE. What's this, Dorine?
DORINE. Come here.
VALÈRE. No, no, my heart's too full of spleen.
Don't hold me back; her wish must be obeyed.
DORINE. Stop!
VALÈRE. It's too late now; my decision's made.
DORINE. Oh, pooh!
MARIANE [*aside*]. He hates the sight of me, that's plain.
I'll go, and so deliver him from pain.
DORINE [*leaving* VALÈRE, *running after* MARIANE].
And now *you* run away! Come back.
MARIANE. No, no.
Nothing you say will keep me here. Let go!
VALÈRE [*aside*]. She cannot bear my presence, I perceive.
To spare her further torment, I shall leave.
DORINE [*leaving* MARIANE, *running after* VALÈRE]. Again! You'll not escape, Sir; don't you try it.
Come here, you two. Stop fussing, and be quiet.
[*She takes* VALÈRE *by the hand, then* MARIANE, *and draws them together.*]
VALÈRE [*to* DORINE]. What do you want of me?
MARIANE [*to* DORINE]. What is the point of this?
DORINE. We're going to have a little armistice.
[*To* VALÈRE.] Now weren't you silly to get so overheated?
VALÈRE. Didn't you see how badly I was treated?
DORINE [*to* MARIANE]. Aren't you a simpleton, to have lost your head?
MARIANE. Didn't you hear the hateful things he said?
DORINE [*to* VALÈRE]. You're both great fools. Her sole desire, Valère,
Is to be yours in marriage. To that I'll swear.
[*To* MARIANE.] He loves you only, and he wants no wife
But you, Mariane. On that I'll stake my life.
MARIANE [*to* VALÈRE]. Then why you advised me so, I cannot see.
VALÈRE [*to* MARIANE]. On such a question, why ask advice of *me?*
DORINE. Oh, you're impossible. Give me your hands, you two.

[*To* VALÈRE.] Yours first.
VALÈRE [*giving* DORINE *his hand*]. But why?
DORINE [*to* MARIANE]. And now a hand from you.
MARIANE [*also giving* DORINE *her hand*].
What are you doing?
DORINE. There: a perfect fit.
You suit each other better than you'll admit.

[VALÈRE *and* MARIANE *hold hands for some time without looking at each other.*]

VALÈRE [*turning toward* MARIANE]. Ah, come, don't be so haughty. Give a man
A look of kindness, won't you, Mariane?

[MARIANE *turns toward* VALÈRE *and smiles.*]

DORINE. I tell you, lovers are completely mad!
VALÈRE [*to* MARIANE]. Now come, confess that you were very bad
To hurt my feelings as you did just now.
I have a just complaint, you must allow.
MARIANE. *You* must allow that you were most unpleasant . . .
DORINE. Let's table that discussion for the present;
Your father has a plan which must be stopped.
MARIANE. Advise us, then; what means must we adopt?
DORINE. We'll use all manner of means, and all at once.
[*To* MARIANE.] Your father's addled; he's acting like a dunce.
Therefore you'd better humor the old fossil.
Pretend to yield to him, be sweet and docile,
And then postpone, as often as necessary,
The day on which you have agreed to marry.
You'll thus gain time, and time will turn the trick.
Sometimes, for instance, you'll be taken sick,
And that will seem good reason for delay;
Or some bad omen will make you change the day—
You'll dream of muddy water, or you'll pass
A dead man's hearse, or break a looking-glass.
If all else fails, no man can marry you
Unless you take his ring and say "I do."
But now, let's separate. If they should find
Us talking here, our plot might be divined.
[*To* VALÈRE.] Go to your friends, and tell them what's occurred,
And have them urge her father to keep his word.
Meanwhile, we'll stir her brother into action,
And get Elmire, as well, to join our faction.
Good-bye.
VALÈRE [*to* MARIANE]. Though each of us will do his best,
It's your true heart on which my hopes shall rest.
MARIANE [*to* VALÈRE]. Regardless of what Father may decide,
None but Valère shall claim me as his bride.
VALÈRE. Oh, how those words content me! Come what will . . .

Dorine. Oh, lovers, lovers! Their tongues are never still.
Be off, now.
Valère [*turning to go, then turning back*].
One last word . . .
Dorine. No time to chat:
You leave by this door; and *you* leave by that.
[Dorine *pushes them, by the shoulders, toward opposing doors.*]

ACT III

SCENE 1

Damis Dorine

Damis. May lightning strike me even as I speak,
May all men call me cowardly and weak,
If any fear or scruple holds me back
From settling things, at once, with that great quack!
Dorine. Now, don't give way to violent emotion.
Your father's merely talked about this notion,
And words and deeds are far from being one.
Much that is talked about is left undone.
Damis. No, I must stop that scoundrel's machinations;
I'll go and tell him off; I'm out of patience.
Dorine. Do calm down and be practical. I had rather
My mistress dealt with him—and with your father.
She has some influence with Tartuffe, I've noted.
He hangs upon her words, seems most devoted,
And may, indeed, be smitten by her charm.
Pray Heaven it's true! 'Twould do our cause no harm.
She sent for him, just now, to sound him out
On this affair you're so incensed about;
She'll find out where he stands, and tell him, too,
What dreadful strife and trouble will ensue
If he lends countenance to your father's plan.
I couldn't get in to see him, but his man
Says that he's almost finished with his prayers.
Go, now. I'll catch him when he comes downstairs.
Damis. I want to hear this conference, and I will.
Dorine. No, they must be alone.
Damis. Oh, I'll keep still.
Dorine. Not you. I know your temper. You'd start a brawl,
And shout and stamp your foot and spoil it all.
Go on.
Damis. I won't; I have a perfect right . . .
Dorine. Lord, you're a nuisance! He's coming; get out of sight.
[Damis *conceals himself in a closet at the rear of the stage.*]

SCENE 2
TARTUFFE DORINE

TARTUFFE [*observing* DORINE, *and calling to his manservant offstage*].
Hang up my hair-shirt, put my scourge in place,
And pray, Laurent, for Heaven's perpetual grace.
I'm going to the prison now, to share
My last few coins with the poor wretches there.
DORINE [*aside*]. Dear God, what affectation! What a fake!
TARTUFFE. You wished to see me?
DORINE. Yes . . .
TARTUFFE [*taking a handkerchief from his pocket*].
For mercy's sake,
Please take this handkerchief, before you speak.
DORINE. What?
TARTUFFE. Cover that bosom, girl. The flesh is weak,
And unclean thoughts are difficult to control.
Such sights as that can undermine the soul.
DORINE. Your soul, it seems, has very poor defenses,
And flesh makes quite an impact on your senses.
It's strange that you're so easily excited;
My own desires are not so soon ignited,
And if I saw you naked as a beast,
Not all your hide would tempt me in the least.
TARTUFFE. Girl, speak more modestly; unless you do,
I shall be forced to take my leave of you.
DORINE. Oh, no, it's I who must be on my way;
I've just one little message to convey.
Madame is coming down, and begs you, Sir,
To wait and have a word or two with her.
TARTUFFE. Gladly.
DORINE [*aside*]. *That* had a softening effect!
I think my guess about him was correct.
TARTUFFE. Will she be long?
DORINE. No: that's her step I hear.
Ah, here she is, and I shall disappear.

SCENE 3
ELMIRE TARTUFFE

TARTUFFE. May Heaven, whose infinite goodness we adore,
Preserve your body and soul forevermore,
And bless your days, and answer thus the plea
Of one who is its humblest votary.
ELMIRE. I thank you for that pious wish. But please,
Do take a chair and let's be more at ease.
[*They sit down.*]

TARTUFFE. I trust that you are once more well and strong?
ELMIRE. Oh, yes: the fever didn't last for long.
TARTUFFE. My prayers are too unworthy, I am sure,
 To have gained from Heaven this most gracious cure;
 But lately, Madam, my every supplication
 Has had for object your recuperation.
ELMIRE. You shouldn't have troubled so. I don't deserve it.
TARTUFFE. Your health is priceless, Madam, and to preserve it
 I'd gladly give my own, in all sincerity.
ELMIRE. Sir, you outdo us all in Christian charity.
 You've been most kind. I count myself your debtor.
TARTUFFE. 'Twas nothing, Madam. I long to serve you better.
ELMIRE. There's a private matter I'm anxious to discuss.
 I'm glad there's no one here to hinder us.
TARTUFFE. I too am glad; it floods my heart with bliss
 To find myself alone with you like this.
 For just this chance I've prayed with all my power—
 But prayed in vain, until this happy hour.
ELMIRE. This won't take long, Sir, and I hope you'll be
 Entirely frank and unconstrained with me.
TARTUFFE. Indeed, there's nothing I had rather do
 Than bare my inmost heart and soul to you.
 First, let me say that what remarks I've made
 About the constant visits you are paid
 Were prompted not by any mean emotion,
 But rather by a pure and deep devotion,
 A fervent zeal . . .
ELMIRE. No need for explanation.
 Your sole concern, I'm sure, was my salvation.
TARTUFFE [*taking* ELMIRE*'s hand and pressing her fingertips*]. Quite so; and such great fervor do I feel . . .
ELMIRE. Ooh! Please! You're pinching!
TARTUFFE. 'Twas from excess of zeal.
 I never meant to cause you pain, I swear.
 I'd rather . . .
 [*He places his hand on* ELMIRE*'s knee.*]
ELMIRE. What can your hand be doing there?
TARTUFFE. Feeling your gown; what soft, fine-woven stuff!
ELMIRE. Please, I'm extremely ticklish. That's enough.
 [*She draws her chair away;* TARTUFFE *pulls his after her.*]
TARTUFFE. [*fondling the lace collar of her gown*]. My, my what lovely lacework on your dress!
 The workmanship's miraculous, no less.
 I've not seen anything to equal it.
ELMIRE. Yes, quite. But let's talk business for a bit.
 They say my husband means to break his word
 And give his daughter to you, Sir. Had you heard?

TARTUFFE. He did once mention it. But I confess
I dream of quite a different happiness.
It's elsewhere, Madam, that my eyes discern
The promise of that bliss for which I yearn.
ELMIRE. I see: you care for nothing here below.
TARTUFFE. Ah, well—my heart's not made of stone, you know.
ELMIRE. All your desires mount heavenward, I'm sure,
In scorn of all that's earthly and impure.
TARTUFFE. A love of heavenly beauty does not preclude
A proper love for earthly pulchritude;
Our senses are quite rightly captivated
By perfect works our Maker has created.
Some glory clings to all that Heaven has made;
In you, all Heaven's marvels are displayed.
On that fair face, such beauties have been lavished,
The eyes are dazzled and the heart is ravished;
How could I look on you, O flawless creature,
And not adore the Author of all Nature,
Feeling a love both passionate and pure
For you, his triumph of self-portraiture?
At first, I trembled lest that love should be
A subtle snare that Hell had laid for me;
I vowed to flee the sight of you, eschewing
A rapture that might prove my soul's undoing;
But soon, fair being, I became aware
That my deep passion could be made to square
With rectitude, and with my bounden duty.
I thereupon surrendered to your beauty.
It is, I know, presumptuous on my part
To bring you this poor offering of my heart,
And it is not my merit, Heaven knows,
But your compassion on which my hopes repose.
You are my peace, my solace, my salvation;
On you depends my bliss—or desolation;
I bide your judgment and, as you think best,
I shall be either miserable or blest.
ELMIRE. Your declaration is most gallant, Sir,
But don't you think it's out of character?
You'd have done better to restrain your passion
And think before you spoke in such a fashion.
It ill becomes a pious man like you . . .
TARTUFFE. I may be pious, but I'm human too:
With your celestial charms before his eyes,
A man has not the power to be wise.
I know such words sound strangely, coming from me,
But I'm no angel, nor was meant to be,
And if you blame my passion, you must needs
Reproach as well the charms on which it feeds.

Your loveliness I had no sooner seen
Than you became my soul's unrivalled queen;
Before your seraph glance, divinely sweet,
My heart's defenses crumbled in defeat,
And nothing fasting, prayer, or tears might do
Could stay my spirit from adoring you.
My eyes, my sighs have told you in the past
What now my lips make bold to say at last,
And if, in your great goodness, you will deign
To look upon your slave, and ease his pain,—
If, in compassion for my soul's distress,
You'll stoop to comfort my unworthiness,
I'll raise to you, in thanks for that sweet manna,
An endless hymn, an infinite hosanna.
With me, of course, there need be no anxiety,
No fear of scandal or of notoriety.
These young court gallants, whom all the ladies fancy,
Are vain in speech, in action rash and chancy;
When they succeed in love, the world soon knows it;
No favor's granted them but they disclose it
And by the looseness of their tongues profane
The very altar where their hearts have lain.
Men of my sort, however, love discreetly,
And one may trust our reticence completely.
My keen concern for my good name insures
The absolute security of yours;
In short, I offer you, my dear Elmire,
Love without scandal, pleasure without fear.

ELMIRE. I've heard your well-turned speeches to the end,
And what you urge I clearly apprehend.
Aren't you afraid that I may take a notion
To tell my husband of your warm devotion,
And that, supposing he were duly told,
His feelings toward you might grow rather cold?

TARTUFFE. I know, dear lady, that your exceeding charity
Will lead your heart to pardon my temerity;
That you'll excuse my violent affection
As human weakness, human imperfection;
And that—O fairest!—you will bear in mind
That I'm but flesh and blood, and am not blind.

ELMIRE. Some women might do otherwise, perhaps,
But I shall be discreet about your lapse;
I'll tell my husband nothing of what's occurred
If, in return, you'll give your solemn word
To advocate as forcefully as you can
The marriage of Valère and Mariane,
Renouncing all desire to dispossess
Another of his rightful happiness,
And . . .

SCENE 4

DAMIS ELMIRE TARTUFFE

DAMIS [*emerging from the closet where he has been hiding*].
No! We'll not hush up this vile affair;
I heard it all inside that closet there,
Where Heaven, in order to confound the pride
Of this great rascal, prompted me to hide.
Ah, now I have my long-awaited chance
To punish his deceit and arrogance,
And give my father clear and shocking proof
Of the black character of his dear Tartuffe.

ELMIRE. Ah no, Damis; I'll be content if he
Will study to deserve my leniency.
I've promised silence—don't make me break my word;
To make a scandal would be too absurd.
Good wives laugh off such trifles, and forget them;
Why should they tell their husbands, and upset them?

DAMIS. You have your reasons for taking such a course,
And I have reasons, too, of equal force.
To spare him now would be insanely wrong.
I've swallowed my just wrath for far too long
And watched this insolent bigot bringing strife
And bitterness into our family life.
Too long he's meddled in my father's affairs,
Thwarting my marriage-hopes, and poor Valère's.
It's high time that my father was undeceived,
And now I've proof that can't be disbelieved—
Proof that was furnished me by Heaven above.
It's too good not to take advantage of.
This is my chance, and I deserve to lose it
If, for one moment, I hesitate to use it.

ELMIRE. Damis . . .

DAMIS. No, I must do what I think right.
Madam, my heart is bursting with delight,
And, say whatever you will, I'll not consent
To lose the sweet revenge on which I'm bent.
I'll settle matters without more ado;
And here, most opportunely, is my cue.

SCENE 5

ORGON TARTUFFE DAMIS ELMIRE

DAMIS. Father, I'm glad you've joined us. Let us advise you
Of some fresh news which doubtless will surprise you.
You've just now been repaid with interest
For all your loving-kindness to our guest.
He's proved his warm and grateful feelings toward you;
It's with a pair of horns he would reward you.

Yes, I surprised him with your wife, and heard
His whole adulterous offer, every word.
She, with her all too gentle disposition,
Would not have told you of his proposition;
But I shall not make terms with brazen lechery,
And feel that not to tell you would be treachery.

ELMIRE. And I hold that one's husband's peace of mind
Should not be spoilt by tattle of this kind.
One's honor doesn't require it: to be proficient
In keeping men at bay is quite sufficient.
These are my sentiments, and I wish, Damis,
That you had heeded me and held your peace.

SCENE 6

ORGON DAMIS TARTUFFE

ORGON. Can it be true, this dreadful thing I hear?

TARTUFFE. Yes, Brother, I'm a wicked man, I fear:
A wretched sinner, all depraved and twisted,
The greatest villain that has ever existed.
My life's one heap of crimes, which grows each minute;
There's naught but foulness and corruption in it;
And I perceive that Heaven, outraged by me,
Has chosen this occasion to mortify me.
Charge me with any deed you wish to name;
I'll not defend myself, but take the blame.
Believe what you are told, and drive Tartuffe
Like some base criminal from beneath your roof;
Yes, drive me hence, and with a parting curse:
I shan't protest, for I deserve far worse.

ORGON [*to* DAMIS]. Ah, you deceitful boy, how dare you try
To stain his purity with so foul a lie?

DAMIS. What! Are you taken in by such a bluff?
Did you not hear . . .?

ORGON. Enough, you rogue, enough!

TARTUFFE. Ah, Brother, let him speak: you're being unjust.
Believe his story; the boy deserves your trust.
Why, after all, should you have faith in me?
How can you know what I might do, or be?
Is it on my good actions that you base
Your favor? Do you trust my pious face?
Ah, no, don't be deceived by hollow shows;
I'm far, alas, from being what men suppose;
Though the world takes me for a man of worth,
I'm truly the most worthless man on earth.
[*To* DAMIS.] Yes, my dear son, speak out now: call me the chief
Of sinners, a wretch, a murderer, a thief;
Load me with all the names men most abhor;
I'll not complain; I've earned them all, and more;

I'll kneel here while you pour them on my head
As a just punishment for the life I've led.
ORGON [*to* TARTUFFE]. This is too much, dear Brother.
[*To* DAMIS.] Have you no heart?
DAMIS. Are you so hoodwinked by this rascal's art . . . ?
ORGON. Be still, you monster.
[*To* TARTUFFE.] Brother, I pray you, rise.
[*To* DAMIS.] Villain!
DAMIS. But . . .
ORGON. Silence!
DAMIS. Can't you realize . . . ?
ORGON. Just one word more, and I'll tear you limb from limb.
TARTUFFE. In God's name, Brother, don't be harsh with him.
I'd rather far be tortured at the stake
Than see him bear one scratch for my poor sake.
ORGON [*to* DAMIS]. Ingrate!
TARTUFFE. If I must beg you, on bended knee,
To pardon him . . .
ORGON [*falling to his knees, addressing* TARTUFFE].
Such goodness cannot be!
[*To* DAMIS.] Now, *there's* true charity!
DAMIS. What, you . . . ?
ORGON. Villain, be still!
I know your motives; I know you wish him ill:
Yes, all of you—wife, children, servants, all—
Conspire against him and desire his fall,
Employing every shameful trick you can
To alienate me from this saintly man.
Ah, but the more you seek to drive him away,
The more I'll do to keep him. Without delay,
I'll spite this household and confound its pride
By giving him my daughter as his bride.
DAMIS. You're going to force her to accept his hand?
ORGON. Yes, and this very night, d'you understand?
I shall defy you all, and make it clear
That I'm the one who gives the orders here.
Come, wretch, kneel down and clasp his blessed feet,
And ask his pardon for your black deceit.
DAMIS. I ask that swindler's pardon? Why, I'd rather . . .
ORGON. So! You insult him, and defy your father!
A stick! A stick! [*To* TARTUFFE.] No, no—release me, do.
[*To* DAMIS.] Out of my house this minute! Be off with you,
And never dare set foot in it again.
DAMIS. Well, I shall go, but . . .
ORGON. Well, go quickly, then.
I disinherit you; an empty purse
Is all you'll get from me—except my curse!

SCENE 7
ORGON TARTUFFE

ORGON. How he blasphemed your goodness! What a son!
TARTUFFE. Forgive him, Lord, as I've already done.
[*To* ORGON.] You can't know how it hurts when someone tries
To blacken me in my dear Brother's eyes.
ORGON. Ahh!
TARTUFFE. The mere thought of such ingratitude
Plunges my soul into so dark a mood . . .
Such horror grips my heart . . . I gasp for breath,
And cannot speak, and feel myself near death.
ORGON. [*He runs, in tears, to the door through which he has just driven his son.*] You blackguard! Why did I spare you? Why did I not
Break you in little pieces on the spot?
Compose yourself, and don't be hurt, dear friend.
TARTUFFE. These scenes, these dreadful quarrels, have got to end.
I've much upset your household, and I perceive
That the best thing will be for me to leave.
ORGON. What are you saying!
TARTUFFE. They're all against me here;
They'd have you think me false and insincere.
ORGON. Ah, what of that? Have I ceased believing in you?
TARTUFFE. Their adverse talk will certainly continue,
And charges which you now repudiate
You may find credible at a later date.
ORGON. No, Brother, never.
TARTUFFE. Brother, a wife can sway
Her husband's mind in many a subtle way.
ORGON. No, no.
TARTUFFE. To leave at once is the solution;
Thus only can I end their persecution.
ORGON. No, no, I'll not allow it; you shall remain.
TARTUFFE. Ah, well; 'twill mean much martyrdom and pain,
But if you wish it . . .
ORGON. Ah!
TARTUFFE. Enough; so be it.
But one thing must be settled, as I see it.
For your dear honor, and for our friendship's sake,
There's one precaution I feel bound to take.
I shall avoid your wife, and keep away . . .
ORGON. No, you shall not, whatever they may say.
It pleases me to vex them, and for spite
I'd have them see you with her day and night.
What's more, I'm going to drive them to despair
By making you my only son and heir;
This very day, I'll give to you alone
Clear deed and title to everything I own.
A dear, good friend and son-in-law-to-be

Is more than wife, or child, or kin to me.
Will you accept my offer, dearest son?
TARTUFFE. In all things, let the will of Heaven be done.
ORGON. Poor fellow! Come, we'll go draw up the deed.
Then let them burst with disappointed greed!

ACT IV

SCENE 1

CLÉANTE TARTUFFE

CLÉANTE. Yes, all the town's discussing it, and truly,
Their comments do not flatter you unduly.
I'm glad we've met, Sir, and I'll give my view
Of this sad matter in a word or two.
As for who's guilty, that I shan't discuss;
Let's say it was Damis who caused the fuss;
Assuming, then, that you have been ill-used
By young Damis, and groundlessly accused,
Ought not a Christian to forgive, and ought
He not to stifle every vengeful thought?
Should you stand by and watch a father make
His only son an exile for your sake?
Again I tell you frankly, be advised:
The whole town, high and low, is scandalized;
This quarrel must be mended, and my advice is
Not to push matters to a further crisis.
No, sacrifice your wrath to God above,
And help Damis regain his father's love.
TARTUFFE. Alas, for my part I should take great joy
In doing so. I've nothing against the boy.
I pardon all, I harbor no resentment;
To serve him would afford me much contentment.
But Heaven's interest will not have it so:
If he comes back, then I shall have to go.
After his conduct—so extreme, so vicious—
Our further intercourse would look suspicious.
God knows what people would think! Why, they'd describe
My goodness to him as a sort of bribe;
They'd say that out of guilt I made pretense
Of loving-kindness and benevolence—
That, fearing my accuser's tongue, I strove
To buy his silence with a show of love.
CLÉANTE. Your reasoning is badly warped and stretched,
And these excuses, Sir, are most far-fetched.
Why put yourself in charge of Heaven's cause?
Does Heaven need our help to enforce its laws?
Leave vengeance to the Lord, Sir; while we live,

Our duty's not to punish, but forgive;
And what the Lord commands, we should obey
Without regard to what the world may say.
What! Shall the fear of being misunderstood
Prevent our doing what is right and good?
No, no; let's simply do what Heaven ordains,
And let no other thoughts perplex our brains.

TARTUFFE. Again, Sir, let me say that I've forgiven
Damis, and thus obeyed the laws of Heaven;
But I am not commanded by the Bible
To live with one who smears my name with libel.

CLÉANTE. Were you commanded, Sir, to indulge the whim
Of poor Orgon, and to encourage him
In suddenly transferring to your name
A large estate to which you have no claim?

TARTUFFE. 'Twould never occur to those who know me best
To think I acted from self-interest.
The treasures of this world I quite despise;
Their specious glitter does not charm my eyes;
And if I have resigned myself to taking
The gift which my dear Brother insists on making,
I do so only, as he well understands,
Lest so much wealth fall into wicked hands,
Lest those to whom it might descend in time
Turn it to purposes of sin and crime,
And not, as I shall do, make use of it
For Heaven's glory and mankind's benefit.

CLÉANTE. Forget these trumped-up fears. Your argument
Is one the rightful heir might well resent;
It *is* a moral burden to inherit
Such wealth, but give Damis a chance to bear it.
And would it not be worse to be accused
Of swindling, than to see that wealth misused?
I'm shocked that you allowed Orgon to broach
This matter, and that you feel no self-reproach;
Does true religion teach that lawful heirs
May freely be deprived of what is theirs?
And if the Lord has told you in your heart
That you and young Damis must dwell apart,
Would it not be the decent thing to beat
A generous and honorable retreat,
Rather than let the son of the house be sent,
For your convenience, into banishment?
Sir, if you wish to prove the honesty
Of your intentions . . .

TARTUFFE. Sir, it is half-past three.
I've certain pious duties to attend to,
And hope my prompt departure won't offend you.

CLÉANTE [*alone*]. Damn.

SCENE 2

ELMIRE CLÉANTE MARIANE DORINE

DORINE. Stay, Sir, and help Mariane, for Heaven's sake!
She's suffering so, I fear her heart will break.
Her father's plan to marry her off tonight
Has put the poor child in a desperate plight.
I hear him coming. Let's stand together, now,
And see if we can't change his mind, somehow,
About this match we all deplore and fear.

SCENE 3

ORGON MARIANE DORINE
ELMIRE CLÉANTE

ORGON. Hah! Glad to find you all assembled here.
[*To* MARIANE.] This contract, child, contains your happiness,
And what it says I think your heart can guess.
MARIANE [*falling to her knees*]. Sir, by that Heaven which sees me here distressed,
And by whatever else can move your breast,
Do not employ a father's power, I pray you,
To crush my heart and force it to obey you,
Nor by your harsh commands oppress me so
That I'll begrudge the duty which I owe—
And do not so embitter and enslave me
That I shall hate the very life you gave me.
If my sweet hopes must perish, if you refuse
To give me to the one I've dared to choose,
Spare me at least—I beg you, I implore—
The pain of wedding one whom I abhor;
And do not, by a heartless use of force,
Drive me to contemplate some desperate course.
ORGON [*feeling himself touched by her*]. Be firm, my soul. No human weakness, now.
MARIANE. I don't resent your love for him. Allow
Your heart free rein, Sir; give him your property,
And if that's not enough, take mine from me;
He's welcome to my money; take it, do,
But don't, I pray, include my person too.
Spare me, I beg you; and let me end the tale
Of my sad days behind a convent veil.
ORGON. A convent! Hah! When crossed in their amours,
All lovesick girls have the same thought as yours.
Get up! The more you loathe the man, and dread him,
The more ennobling it will be to wed him.
Marry Tartuffe, and mortify your flesh!
Enough; don't start that whimpering afresh.
DORINE. But why . . . ?

ORGON. Be still, there. Speak when you're spoken to.
Not one more bit of impudence out of you.
CLÉANTE. If I may offer a word of counsel here . . .
ORGON. Brother, in counseling you have no peer;
All your advice is forceful, sound, and clever;
I don't propose to follow it, however.
ELMIRE [*to* ORGON]. I am amazed, and don't know what to say;
Your blindness simply takes my breath away.
You are indeed bewitched, to take no warning
From our account of what occurred this morning.
ORGON. Madam, I know a few plain facts, and one
Is that you're partial to my rascal son;
Hence, when he sought to make Tartuffe the victim
Of a base lie, you dared not contradict him.
Ah, but you underplayed your part, my pet;
You should have looked more angry, more upset.
ELMIRE. When men make overtures, must we reply
With righteous anger and a battle-cry?
Must we turn back their amorous advances
With sharp reproaches and with fiery glances?
Myself, I find such offers merely amusing,
And make no scenes and fusses in refusing;
My taste is for good-natured rectitude,
And I dislike the savage sort of prude
Who guards her virtue with her teeth and claws,
And tears men's eyes out for the slightest cause:
The Lord preserve me from such honor as that,
Which bites and scratches like an alley-cat!
I've found that a polite and cool rebuff
Discourages a lover quite enough.
ORGON. I know the facts, and I shall not be shaken.
ELMIRE. I marvel at your power to be mistaken.
Would it, I wonder, carry weight with you
If I could *show* you that our tale was true?
ORGON. Show me?
ELMIRE. Yes.
ORGON. Rot.
ELMIRE. Come, what if I found a way
To make you see the facts as plain as day?
ORGON. Nonsense.
ELMIRE. Do answer me; don't be absurd.
I'm not now asking you to trust our word.
Suppose that from some hiding-place in here
You learned the whole sad truth by eye and ear—
What would you say of your good friend, after that?
ORGON. Why, I'd say . . . nothing, by Jehoshaphat!
It can't be true.
ELMIRE. You've been too long deceived,
And I'm quite tired of being disbelieved.
Come now: let's put my statements to the test,

And you shall see the truth made manifest.
ORGON. I'll take that challenge. Now do your uttermost.
We'll see how you make good your empty boast.
ELMIRE [*to* DORINE]. Send him to me.
DORINE. He's crafty; it may be hard
To catch the cunning scoundrel off his guard.
ELMIRE. No, amorous men are gullible. Their conceit
So blinds them that they're never hard to cheat.
Have him come down. [*To* CLÉANTE and MARIANE.] Please leave us, for a bit.

SCENE 4
ELMIRE ORGON

ELMIRE. Pull up this table, and get under it.
ORGON. What?
ELMIRE. It's essential that you be well-hidden.
ORGON. Why there?
ELMIRE. Oh, Heavens! Just do as you are bidden.
I have my plans; we'll soon see how they fare.
Under the table, now; and once you're there,
Take care that you are neither seen nor heard.
ORGON. Well, I'll indulge you, since I gave my word
To see you through this infantile charade.
ELMIRE. Once it is over, you'll be glad we played.
[*To her husband, who is now under the table.*] I'm going to act quite strangely, now, and you
Must not be shocked at anything I do.
Whatever I may say, you must excuse
As part of that deceit I'm forced to use.
I shall employ sweet speeches in the task
Of making that impostor drop his mask;
I'll give encouragement to his bold desires,
And furnish fuel to his amorous fires.
Since it's for your sake, and for his destruction,
That I shall seem to yield to his seduction,
I'll gladly stop whenever you decide
That all your doubts are fully satisfied.
I'll count on you, as soon as you have seen
What sort of man he is, to intervene,
And not expose me to his odious lust
One moment longer than you feel you must.
Remember: you're to save me from my plight
Whenever . . . He's coming! Hush! Keep out of sight!

SCENE 5
TARTUFFE ELMIRE ORGON

TARTUFFE. You wish to have a word with me, I'm told.
ELMIRE. Yes. I've a little secret to unfold.

Before I speak, however, it would be wise
To close that door, and look about for spies.

[TARTUFFE *goes to the door, closes it, and returns.*]

The very last thing that must happen now
Is a repetition of this morning's row.
I've never been so badly caught off guard.
Oh, how I feared for you! You saw how hard
I tried to make that troublesome Damis
Control his dreadful temper, and hold his peace.
In my confusion, I didn't have the sense
Simply to contradict his evidence;
But as it happened, that was for the best,
And all has worked out in our interest.
This storm has only bettered your position;
My husband doesn't have the least suspicion,
And now, in mockery of those who do,
He bids me be continually with you.
And that is why, quite fearless of reproof,
I now can be alone with my Tartuffe,
And why my heart—perhaps too quick to yield—
Feels free to let its passion be revealed.

TARTUFFE. Madam, your words confuse me. Not long ago,
You spoke in quite a different style, you know.

ELMIRE. Ah, Sir, if that refusal made you smart,
It's little that you know of woman's heart,
Or what that heart is trying to convey
When it resists in such a feeble way!
Always, at first, our modesty prevents
The frank avowal of tender sentiments;
However high the passion which inflames us,
Still, to confess its power somehow shames us.
Thus we reluct, at first, yet in a tone
Which tells you that our heart is overthrown,
That what our lips deny, our pulse confesses,
And that, in time, all noes will turn to yesses.
I fear my words are all too frank and free,
And a poor proof of woman's modesty;
But since I'm started, tell me, if you will—
Would I have tried to make Damis be still,
Would I have listened, calm and unoffended,
Until your lengthy offer of love was ended,
And been so very mild in my reaction,
Had your sweet words not given me satisfaction?
And when I tried to force you to undo
The marriage-plans my husband has in view,
What did my urgent pleading signify
If not that I admired you, and that I
Deplored the thought that someone else might own
Part of a heart I wished for mine alone?

TARTUFFE. Madam, no happiness is so complete
As when, from lips we love, come words so sweet;
Their nectar floods my every sense, and drains
In honeyed rivulets through all my veins.
To please you is my joy, my only goal;
Your love is the restorer of my soul;
And yet I must beg leave, now, to confess
Some lingering doubts as to my happiness.
Might this not be a trick? Might not the catch
Be that you wish me to break off the match
With Mariane, and so have feigned to love me?
I shan't quite trust your fond opinion of me
Until the feelings you've expressed so sweetly
Are demonstrated somewhat more concretely,
And you have shown, by certain kind concessions,
That I may put my faith in your professions.
ELMIRE. [*She coughs, to warn her husband.*] Why be in such a hurry? Must my heart
Exhaust its bounty at the very start?
To make that sweet admission cost me dear,
But you'll not be content, it would appear,
Unless my store of favors is disbursed
To the last farthing, and at the very first.
TARTUFFE. The less we merit, the less we dare to hope,
And with our doubts, mere words can never cope.
We trust no promised bliss till we receive it;
Not till a joy is ours can we believe it.
I, who so little merit your esteem,
Can't credit this fulfillment of my dream,
And shan't believe it, Madam, until I savor
Some palpable assurance of your favor.
ELMIRE. My, how tyrannical your love can be,
And how it flusters and perplexes me!
How furiously you take one's heart in hand,
And make your every wish a fierce command!
Come, must you hound and harry me to death?
Will you not give me time to catch my breath?
Can it be right to press me with such force,
Give me no quarter, show me no remorse,
And take advantage, by your stern insistence,
Of the fond feelings which weaken my resistance?
TARTUFFE. Well, if you look with favor upon my love,
Why, then, begrudge me some clear proof thereof?
ELMIRE. But how can I consent without offense
To Heaven, toward which you feel such reverence?
TARTUFFE. If Heaven is all that holds you back, don't worry.
I can remove that hindrance in a hurry.
Nothing of that sort need obstruct our path.
ELMIRE. Must one not be afraid of Heaven's wrath?

TARTUFFE. Madam, forget such fears, and be my pupil,
And I shall teach you how to conquer scruple.
Some joys, it's true, are wrong in Heaven's eyes;
Yet Heaven is not averse to compromise;
There is a science, lately formulated,
Whereby one's conscience may be liberated,
And any wrongful act you care to mention
May be redeemed by purity of intention.
I'll teach you, Madam, the secrets of that science;
Meanwhile, just place on me your full reliance.
Assuage my keen desires, and feel no dread:
The sin, if any, shall be on my head.
[ELMIRE *coughs, this time more loudly.*]
You've a bad cough.
ELMIRE. Yes, yes. It's bad indeed.
TARTUFFE [*producing a little paper bag*]. A bit of licorice may be what you need.
ELMIRE. No, I've a stubborn cold, it seems. I'm sure it
Will take much more than licorice to cure it.
TARTUFFE. How aggravating.
ELMIRE. Oh, more than I can say.
TARTUFFE. If you're still troubled, think of things this way:
No one shall know our joys, save us alone,
And there's no evil till the act is known;
It's scandal, Madam, which makes it an offense,
And it's no sin to sin in confidence.
ELMIRE [*having coughed once more*]. Well, clearly I must do as you require,
And yield to your importunate desire.
It is apparent, now, that nothing less
Will satisfy you, and so I acquiesce.
To go so far is much against my will;
I'm vexed that it should come to this; but still,
Since you are so determined on it, since you
Will not allow mere language to convince you,
And since you ask for concrete evidence, I
See nothing for it, now, but to comply.
If this is sinful, if I'm wrong to do it,
So much the worse for him who drove me to it.
The fault can surely not be charged to me.
TARTUFFE. Madam, the fault is mine, if fault there be,
And . . .
ELMIRE. Open the door a little, and peek out;
I wouldn't want my husband poking about.
TARTUFFE. Why worry about the man? Each day he grows
More gullible; one can lead him by the nose.
To find us here would fill him with delight,
And if he saw the worst, he'd doubt his sight.

ELMIRE. Nevertheless, do step out for a minute
Into the hall, and see that no one's in it.

SCENE 6

ORGON ELMIRE

ORGON [*coming out from under the table*]. That man's a perfect monster, I must admit!
I'm simply stunned. I can't get over it.
ELMIRE. What, coming out so soon? How premature!
Get back in hiding, and wait until you're sure.
Stay till the end, and be convinced completely;
We mustn't stop till things are proved concretely.
ORGON. Hell never harbored anything so vicious!
ELMIRE. Tut, don't be hasty. Try to be judicious.
Wait, and be certain that there's no mistake.
No jumping to conclusions, for Heaven's sake!
[*She places* ORGON *behind her, as* TARTUFFE *re-enters.*]

SCENE 7

TARTUFFE ELMIRE ORGON

TARTUFFE [*not seeing* ORGON]. Madam, all things have worked out to perfection;
I've given the neighboring rooms a full inspection;
No one's about; and now I may at last . . .
ORGON [*intercepting him*]. Hold on, my passionate fellow, not so fast!
I should advise a little more restraint.
Well, so you thought you'd fool me, my dear saint!
How soon you wearied of the saintly life—
Wedding my daughter, and coveting my wife!
I've long suspected you, and had a feeling
That soon I'd catch you at your double-dealing.
Just now, you've given me evidence galore;
It's quite enough; I have no wish for more.
ELMIRE [*to* TARTUFFE]. I'm sorry to have treated you so slyly,
But circumstances forced me to be wily.
TARTUFFE. Brother, you can't think . . .
ORGON. No more talk from you;
Just leave this household, without more ado.
TARTUFFE. What I intended . . .
ORGON. That seems fairly clear.
Spare me your falsehoods and get out of here.
TARTUFFE. No, I'm the master, and you're the one to go!
This house belongs to me, I'll have you know,
And I shall show you that you can't hurt *me*
By this contemptible conspiracy,

That those who cross me know not what they do,
And that I've means to expose and punish you,
Avenge offended Heaven, and make you grieve
That ever you dared order me to leave.

SCENE 8
ELMIRE ORGON

ELMIRE. What was the point of all that angry chatter?
ORGON. Dear God, I'm worried. This is no laughing matter.
ELMIRE. How so?
ORGON. I fear I understood his drift.
I'm much disturbed about that deed of gift.
ELMIRE. You gave him . . . ?
ORGON. Yes, it's all been drawn and signed.
But one thing more is weighing on my mind.
ELMIRE. What's that?
ORGON. I'll tell you; but first let's see if there's
A certain strong-box in his room upstairs.

ACT V

SCENE 1
ORGON CLÉANTE

CLÉANTE. Where are you going so fast?
ORGON. God knows!
CLÉANTE. Then wait;
Let's have a conference, and deliberate
On how this situation's to be met.
ORGON. That strong-box has me utterly upset;
This is the worst of many, many shocks.
CLÉANTE. Is there some fearful mystery in that box?
ORGON. My poor friend Argas brought that box to me
With his own hands, in utmost secrecy;
'Twas on the very morning of his flight.
It's full of papers which, if they came to light,
Would ruin him—or such is my impression.
CLÉANTE. Then why did you let it out of your possession?
ORGON. Those papers vexed my conscience, and it seemed best
To ask the counsel of my pious guest.
The cunning scoundrel got me to agree
To leave the strong-box in his custody,
So that, in case of an investigation,
I could employ a slight equivocation
And swear I didn't have it, and thereby,
At no expense to conscience, tell a lie.
CLÉANTE. It looks to me as if you're out on a limb.

Trusting him with that box, and offering him
That deed of gift, were actions of a kind
Which scarcely indicate a prudent mind.
With two such weapons, he has the upper hand,
And since you're vulnerable, as matters stand,
You erred once more in bringing him to bay.
You should have acted in some subtler way.

ORGON. Just think of it: behind that fervent face,
A heart so wicked, and a soul so base!
I took him in, a hungry beggar, and then . . .
Enough, by God! I'm through with pious men:
Henceforth I'll hate the whole false brotherhood,
And persecute them worse than Satan could.

CLÉANTE. Ah, there you go—extravagant as ever!
Why can you not be rational? You never
Manage to take the middle course, it seems,
But jump, instead, between absurd extremes.
You've recognized your recent grave mistake
In falling victim to a pious fake;
Now, to correct that error, must you embrace
An even greater error in its place,
And judge our worthy neighbors as a whole
By what you've learned of one corrupted soul?
Come, just because one rascal made you swallow
A show of zeal which turned out to be hollow,
Shall you conclude that all men are deceivers,
And that, today, there are no true believers?
Let atheists make that foolish inference;
Learn to distinguish virtue from pretense,
Be cautious in bestowing admiration,
And cultivate a sober moderation.
Don't humor fraud, but also don't asperse
True piety; the latter fault is worse,
And it is best to err, if err one must,
As you have done, upon the side of trust.

SCENE 2

DAMIS   ORGON   CLÉANTE

DAMIS. Father, I hear that scoundrel's uttered threats
Against you; that he pridefully forgets
How, in his need, he was befriended by you,
And means to use your gifts to crucify you.

ORGON. It's true, my boy. I'm too distressed for tears.

DAMIS. Leave it to me, Sir; let me trim his ears.
Faced with such insolence, we must not waver.
I shall rejoice in doing you the favor
Of cutting short his life, and your distress.

CLÉANTE. What a display of young hotheadedness!

Do learn to moderate your fits of rage.
In this just kingdom, this enlightened age,
One does not settle things by violence.

SCENE 3

MADAME PERNELLE DORINE ORGON
MARIANE DAMIS CLÉANTE ELMIRE

MADAME PERNELLE. I hear strange tales of very strange events.
ORGON. Yes, strange events which these two eyes beheld.
The man's ingratitude is unparalleled.
I save a wretched pauper from starvation,
House him, and treat him like a blood relation,
Shower him every day with my largesse,
Give him my daughter, and all that I possess;
And meanwhile the unconscionable knave
Tries to induce my wife to misbehave;
And not content with such extreme rascality,
Now threatens me with my own liberality,
And aims, by taking base advantage of
The gifts I gave him out of Christian love,
To drive me from my house, a ruined man,
And make me end a pauper, as he began.
DORINE. Poor fellow!
MADAME PERNELLE. No, my son, I'll never bring
Myself to think him guilty of such a thing.
ORGON. How's that?
MADAME PERNELLE. The righteous always were maligned.
ORGON. Speak clearly, Mother. Say what's on your mind.
MADAME PERNELLE. I mean that I can smell a rat, my dear.
You know how everybody hates him, here.
ORGON. That has no bearing on the case at all.
MADAME PERNELLE. I told you a hundred times, when you were small,
That virtue in this world is hated ever;
Malicious men may die, but malice never.
ORGON. No doubt that's true, but how does it apply?
MADAME PERNELLE. They've turned you against him by a clever lie.
ORGON. I've told you, I was there and saw it done.
MADAME PERNELLE. Ah, slanderers will stop at nothing, Son.
ORGON. Mother, I'll lose my temper . . . For the last time,
I tell you I was witness to the crime.
MADAME PERNELLE. The tongues of spite are busy night and noon,
And to their venom no man is immune.
ORGON. You're talking nonsense. Can't you realize
I saw it; saw it; saw it with my eyes?
Saw, do you understand me? Must I shout it
Into your ears before you'll cease to doubt it?
MADAME PERNELLE. Appearances can deceive, my son. Dear me,
We cannot always judge by what we see.

ORGON. Drat! Drat!
MADAME PERNELLE. One often interprets things awry;
Good can seem evil to a suspicious eye.
ORGON. Was I to see his pawing at Elmire
As an act of charity?
MADAME PERNELLE. Till his guilt is clear,
A man deserves the benefit of the doubt.
You should have waited, to see how things turned out.
ORGON. Great God in Heaven, what more proof did I need?
Was I to sit there, watching, until he'd . . .
You drive me to the brink of impropriety.
MADAME PERNELLE. No, no, a man of such surpassing piety
Could not do such a thing. You cannot shake me.
I don't believe it, and you shall not make me.
ORGON. You vex me so that, if you weren't my mother,
I'd say to you . . . some dreadful thing or other.
DORINE. It's your turn now, Sir, not to be listened to;
You'd not trust us, and now she won't trust you.
CLÉANTE. My friends, we're wasting time which should be spent
In facing up to our predicament.
I fear that scoundrel's threats weren't made in sport.
DAMIS. Do you think he'd have the nerve to go to court?
ELMIRE. I'm sure he won't: they'd find it all too crude
A case of swindling and ingratitude.
CLÉANTE. Don't be too sure. He won't be at a loss
To give his claims a high and righteous gloss;
And clever rogues with far less valid cause
Have trapped their victims in a web of laws.
I say again that to antagonize
A man so strongly armed was most unwise.
ORGON. I know it; but the man's appalling cheek
Outraged me so, I couldn't control my pique.
CLÉANTE. I wish to Heaven that we could devise
Some truce between you, or some compromise.
ELMIRE. If I had known what cards he held, I'd not
Have roused his anger by my little plot.
ORGON [*to* DORINE, *as* M. LOYAL *enters*]. What is that fellow looking for? Who is he?
Go talk to him—and tell him that I'm busy.

SCENE 4

MONSIEUR LOYAL DAMIS ELMIRE
MADAME PERNELLE MARIANE CLÉANTE
ORGON DORINE

MONSIEUR LOYAL. Good day, dear sister. Kindly let me see
Your master.
DORINE. He's involved with company,
And cannot be disturbed just now, I fear.

MONSIEUR LOYAL. I hate to intrude; but what has brought me here
Will not disturb your master, in any event.
Indeed, my news will make him most content.
DORINE. Your name?
MONSIEUR LOYAL. Just say that I bring greetings from
Monsieur Tartuffe, on whose behalf I've come.
DORINE [*to* ORGON]. Sir, he's a very gracious man, and bears
A message from Tartuffe, which, he declares,
Will make you most content.
CLÉANTE. Upon my word,
I think this man had best be seen, and heard.
ORGON. Perhaps he has some settlement to suggest.
How shall I treat him? What manner would be best?
CLÉANTE. Control your anger, and if he should mention
Some fair adjustment, give him your full attention.
MONSIEUR LOYAL. Good health to you, good Sir. May Heaven confound
Your enemies, and may your joys abound.
ORGON [*aside, to* CLÉANTE]. A gentle salutation: it confirms
My guess that he is here to offer terms.
MONSIEUR LOYAL. I've always held your family most dear;
I served your father, Sir, for many a year.
ORGON. Sir, I must ask your pardon; to my shame,
I cannot now recall your face or name.
MONSIEUR LOYAL. Loyal's my name; I come from Normandy,
And I'm a bailiff, in all modesty.
For forty years, praise God, it's been my boast
To serve with honor in that vital post,
And I am here, Sir, if you will permit
The liberty, to serve you with this writ . . .
ORGON. To—*what?*
MONSIEUR LOYAL. Now, please, Sir, let us have no friction:
It's nothing but an order of eviction.
You are to move your goods and family out
And make way for new occupants, without
Deferment or delay, and give the keys . . .
ORGON. I? Leave this house?
MONSIEUR LOYAL. Why yes, Sir, if you please.
This house, Sir, from the cellar to the roof,
Belongs now to the good Monsieur Tartuffe,
And he is lord and master of your estate
By virtue of a deed of present date,
Drawn in due form, with clearest legal phrasing . . .
DAMIS. Your insolence is utterly amazing!
MONSIEUR LOYAL. Young man, my business here is not with you,
But with your wise and temperate father, who,
Like every worthy citizen, stands in awe
Of justice, and would never obstruct the law.
ORGON. But . . .
MONSIEUR LOYAL. Not for a million, Sir, would you rebel

Against authority; I know that well.
You'll not make trouble, Sir, or interfere
With the execution of my duties here.

DAMIS. Someone may execute a smart tattoo
On that black jacket of yours, before you're through.

MONSIEUR LOYAL. Sir, bid your son be silent. I'd much regret
Having to mention such a nasty threat
Of violence, in writing my report.

DORINE [*aside*]. This man Loyal's a most disloyal sort!

MONSIEUR LOYAL. I love all men of upright character,
And when I agreed to serve these papers, Sir,
It was your feelings that I had in mind.
I couldn't bear to see the case assigned
To someone else, who might esteem you less
And so subject you to unpleasantness.

ORGON. What's more unpleasant than telling a man to leave
His house and home?

MONSIEUR LOYAL. You'd like a short reprieve?
If you desire it, Sir, I shall not press you,
But wait until tomorrow to dispossess you.
Splendid. I'll come and spend the night here, then,
Most quietly, with half a score of men.
For form's sake, you might bring me, just before
You go to bed, the keys to the front door.
My men, I promise, will be on their best
Behavior, and will not disturb your rest.
But bright and early, Sir, you must be quick
And move out all your furniture, every stick:
The men I've chosen are both young and strong,
And with their help it shouldn't take you long.
In short, I'll make things pleasant and convenient,
And since I'm being so extremely lenient,
Please show me, Sir, a like consideration,
And give me your entire cooperation.

ORGON [*aside*]. I may be all but bankrupt, but I vow
I'd give a hundred louis, here and now,
Just for the pleasure of landing one good clout
Right on the end of that complacent snout.

CLÉANTE. Careful; don't make things worse.

DAMIS. My bootsole itches
To give that beggar a good kick in the breeches.

DORINE. Monsieur Loyal, I'd love to hear the whack
Of a stout stick across your fine broad back.

MONSIEUR LOYAL. Take care: a woman too may go to jail if
She uses threatening language to a bailiff.

CLÉANTE. Enough, enough, Sir. This must not go on.
Give me that paper, please, and then begone.

MONSIEUR LOYAL. Well, *au revoir*. God give you all good cheer!

ORGON. May God confound you, and him who sent you here!

SCENE 5

ORGON ELMIRE DORINE MARIANE
CLÉANTE MADAME PERNELLE DAMIS

ORGON. Now, Mother, was I right or not? This writ
Should change your notion of Tartuffe a bit.
Do you perceive his villainy at last?
MADAME PERNELLE. I'm thunderstruck. I'm utterly aghast.
DORINE. Oh, come, be fair. You mustn't take offense
At this new proof of his benevolence.
He's acting out of selfless love, I know.
Material things enslave the soul, and so
He kindly has arranged your liberation
From all that might endanger your salvation.
ORGON. Will you not ever hold your tongue, you dunce?
CLÉANTE. Come, you must take some action, and at once.
ELMIRE. Go tell the world of the low trick he's tried.
The deed of gift is surely nullified
By such behavior, and public rage will not
Permit the wretch to carry out his plot.

SCENE 6

VALÈRE ELMIRE
DAMIS ORGON MARIANE
DORINE CLÉANTE MADAME PERNELLE

VALÈRE. Sir, though I hate to bring you more bad news,
Such is the danger that I cannot choose.
A friend who is extremely close to me
And knows my interest in your family
Has, for my sake, presumed to violate
The secrecy that's due to things of state,
And sends me word that you are in a plight
From which your one salvation lies in flight.
That scoundrel who's imposed upon you so
Denounced you to the King an hour ago
And, as supporting evidence, displayed
The strong-box of a certain renegade
Whose secret papers, so he testified,
You had disloyally agreed to hide.
I don't know just what charges may be pressed,
But there's a warrant out for your arrest;
Tartuffe has been instructed, furthermore,
To guide the arresting officer to your door.
CLÉANTE. He's clearly done this to facilitate
His seizure of your house and your estate.
ORGON. That man, I must say, is a vicious beast!
VALÈRE. Quick, Sir; you mustn't tarry in the least.

My carriage is outside, to take you hence;
This thousand louis should cover all expense.
Let's lose no time, or you shall be undone;
The sole defense, in this case, is to run.
I shall go with you all the way, and place you
In a safe refuge to which they'll never trace you.
ORGON. Alas, dear boy, I wish that I could show you
My gratitude for everything I owe you.
But now is not the time; I pray the Lord
That I may live to give you your reward.
Farewell, my dears; be careful . . .
CLÉANTE. Brother, hurry.
We shall take care of things; you needn't worry.

SCENE 7

THE OFFICER ELMIRE DORINE
TARTUFFE MARIANE CLÉANTE ORGON
VALÈRE MADAME PERNELLE DAMIS

TARTUFFE. Gently, Sir, gently; stay right where you are.
No need for haste; your lodging isn't far.
You're off to prison, by order of the Prince.
ORGON. This is the crowning blow, you wretch; and since
It means my total ruin and defeat,
Your villainy is now at last complete.
TARTUFFE. You needn't try to provoke me; it's no use.
Those who serve Heaven must expect abuse.
CLÉANTE. You are indeed most patient, sweet, and blameless.
DORINE. How he exploits the name of Heaven! It's shameless.
TARTUFFE. Your taunts and mockeries are all for naught;
To do my duty is my only thought.
MARIANE. Your love of duty is most meritorious,
And what you've done is little short of glorious.
TARTUFFE. All deeds are glorious, Madam, which obey
The sovereign prince who sent me here today.
ORGON. I rescued you when you were destitute;
Have you forgotten that, you thankless brute?
TARTUFFE. No, no, I well remember everything;
But my first duty is to serve my King.
That obligation is so paramount
That other claims, beside it, do not count;
And for it I would sacrifice my wife,
My family, my friend, or my own life.
ELMIRE. Hypocrite!
DORINE. All that we most revere, he uses
To cloak his plots and camouflage his ruses.
CLÉANTE. If it is true that you are animated
By pure and loyal zeal, as you have stated,
Why was this zeal not roused until you'd sought

To make Orgon a cuckold, and been caught?
Why weren't you moved to give your evidence
Until your outraged host had driven you hence?
I shan't say that the gift of all his treasure
Ought to have damped your zeal in any measure;
But if he is a traitor, as you declare,
How could you condescend to be his heir?

TARTUFFE [*to the* OFFICER]. Sir, spare me all this clamor; it's growing shrill.
Please carry out your orders, if you will.

OFFICER. Yes, I've delayed too long, Sir. Thank you kindly.
You're just the proper person to remind me.
Come, you are off to join the other boarders
In the King's prison, according to his orders.

TARTUFFE. Who? I, Sir?

OFFICER. Yes.

TARTUFFE. To prison? This can't be true!

OFFICER. I owe an explanation, but not to you.
[*To* ORGON.] Sir, all is well; rest easy, and be grateful.
We serve a Prince to whom all sham is hateful,
A Prince who sees into our inmost hearts,
And can't be fooled by any trickster's arts.
His royal soul, though generous and human,
Views all things with discernment and acumen;
His sovereign reason is not lightly swayed,
And all his judgments are discreetly weighed.
He honors righteous men of every kind,
And yet his zeal for virtue is not blind,
Nor does his love of piety numb his wits
And make him tolerant of hypocrites.
'Twas hardly likely that this man could cozen
A King who's foiled such liars by the dozen.
With one keen glance, the King perceived the whole
Perverseness and corruption of his soul,
And thus high Heaven's justice was displayed:
Betraying you, the rogue stood self-betrayed.
The King soon recognized Tartuffe as one
Notorious by another name, who'd done
So many vicious crimes that one could fill
Ten volumes with them, and be writing still.
But to be brief: our sovereign was appalled
By this man's treachery toward you, which he called
The last, worst villainy of a vile career,
And bade me follow the impostor here
To see how gross his impudence could be,
And force him to restore your property.
Your private papers, by the King's command,
I hereby seize and give into your hand.
The King, by royal order, invalidates
The deed which gave this rascal your estates,

And pardons, furthermore, your grave offense
In harboring an exile's documents.
By these decrees, our Prince rewards you for
Your loyal deeds in the late civil war,
And shows how heartfelt is his satisfaction
In recompensing any worthy action,
How much he prizes merit, and how he makes
More of men's virtues than of their mistakes.

DORINE. Heaven be praised!
MADAME PERNELLE. I breathe again, at last.
ELMIRE. We're safe.
MARIANE. I can't believe the danger's past.
ORGON [*to* TARTUFFE]. Well, traitor, now you see . . .
CLÉANTE. Ah, Brother, please,
Let's not descend to such indignities.
Leave the poor wretch to his unhappy fate,
And don't say anything to aggravate
His present woes; but rather hope that he
Will soon embrace an honest piety,
And mend his ways, and by a true repentance
Move our just King to moderate his sentence.
Meanwhile, go kneel before your sovereign's throne
And thank him for the mercies he has shown.
ORGON. Well said: let's go at once and, gladly kneeling,
Express the gratitude which all are feeling.
Then, when that first great duty has been done,
We'll turn with pleasure to a second one,
And give Valère, whose love has proven so true,
The wedded happiness which is his due.

Jean Racine
(1639–1699)

Of all the drama of Western literature, the Neoclassic drama of seventeenth-century France seems the most remote from modern tastes, which are likely to find the moral values, revolving around a rigid view of honor, and the stage practice, shackled by a strict observance of the unities, both impossibly narrow and artificial. This is a pity, because at its best the drama of seventeenth-century France turns its limitations into virtues and uses its concentration to deal with depths of the human mind rarely plumbed elsewhere. What it sacrifices in breadth it compensates for in intensity and penetration. What Molière is to French Neoclassic comedy, Racine is to Neoclassic tragedy. Both are poets of obsession, of the manias that flourish in the human mind in narrow, repressive societies. But where Molière reaps laughter from man's obsessive delusions, Racine explores their tragic implications.

Jean Racine was born in 1639, seventeen years after Molière, in La Ferté-Milon, about fifty miles northeast of Paris. Orphaned at the age of four, he was taken in by the nuns of Port-Royal, an abbey which was a center of Jansenism, a strict and austere Catholic sect that had much in common with Calvinism in its belief in predestination and emphasis upon divine grace, personal holiness, and austerity. All his life, Racine was to be torn between Jansenist ideas and contrary worldly impulses. He remained at Port-Royal until he was nineteen, when he enrolled in the Collège d'Harcourt in the University of Paris. There he fell under the influence of the literary and theatrical life of the capital and won some notice as a poet. His progress was briefly interrupted when his family removed him to the provincial town of Uzès, where his uncle, a canon of the church, was to prepare him for the priesthood. He returned to Paris after two years, however, and committed himself to a literary career.

The critic Nicolas Boileau, at the threshold of his own career, befriended him and gave him valuable direction, as did Jean de La Fontaine, then at work on the Fables *which were to make him famous. Molière, who was at the height of his career, helped the ambitious young playwright, read and criticized his work, and finally accepted Racine's fourth play,* The Theban Brothers *(1664), for production at the Théâtre du Palais-Royal. The play was a modest success, and Molière also accepted Racine's next play,* Alexander the Great *(1665). Racine, however, turned against his benefactor and, while Molière was performing the play, turned it over to the rival theater of the Hôtel de Bourgogne. The breach between the two playwrights was further widened two years later when Racine persuaded his mistress Thérèse du Parc, one of Molière's leading actresses, to quit Molière's troupe and join that of the Hôtel du Bourgogne. Racine at the age of twenty-eight began the series of seven tragedies that were to establish him as the master of French tragedy:* Andromache *(1667),* Brittanicus *(1668),* Berenice *(1670),* Bajazet *(1672),* Mithridates *(1673),* Iphigenia *(1674), and* Phaedra *(1677).*

During the years of his theatrical triumphs, Racine was a familiar figure at the court of Louis XIV, the "Sun King," and gained an apparently well-deserved reputation for unscrupulous ambition and intrigue, often using his influence at court to gain the upper hand over his theatrical rivals, especially the elderly Pierre Corneille. He had quarreled bitterly with his Jansenist friends, who disapproved strongly of the theater, in 1665. But in 1677, soon after the production of Phaedra, *he suddenly renounced the theater, married, was reconciled with the Jansenists, and was appointed royal historiographer. The last twenty-two years of his life were spent in chronicling the activities of the king, in religious studies, and in rearing his seven children. He returned to dramatic writing twice during these latter years, composing the religious plays* Esther *(1689) and* Athalie *(1691), at the request of the king's wife, Mme. de Maintenon, who wanted plays to be performed in her school at Saint-Cyr. Racine fell from the king's favor in 1698 and died the following year.*

The physical theater for which Racine wrote was the same one Molière wrote for: a long, narrow room with a raised stage at one end, a proscenium arch, a front curtain, and painted scenery representing a particular place, often "a room in the palace," a theater very different from the spacious, open, and indeterminate space of Shakespeare's stage. The unities were insisted upon even more in tragedy than in comedy: the unity of time, requiring that the plot cover no more than twelve or at most twenty-four hours; the unity of place, dictating that the action take place in one location; and the unity of action, demanding that every speech and every action bear upon the main plot. A number of subordinate rules, or proprieties, were to be observed: the characters should be noble, their language should be appropriate to their rank, they should never touch each other, either in anger or in love, and no violence should be directly depicted.

It is Racine's triumph that he turned these seeming shackles into dramatic tools, accepting their limitations, and using them to create a drama of intense inner action, as if the violent action proscribed in the outer world found its alternative outlet in the psychological conflicts of the characters.

Racine's source for Phaedra *is Euripides'* Hippolytus *(428 B.C.). The change of title is significant. Euripides' drama places the ascetic and virginal Hippolytus at center stage, and Phaedra's suffering is only incidental to the main action of Aphrodite's punishing an arrogant rebel against her power. In Euripides' play, when Hippolytus learns of Phaedra's helpless love, he lashes out in a vicious attack on all womankind. Phaedra hangs herself but leaves a letter accusing Hippolytus of raping her. Theseus condemns his son, who is attacked by the monster from the sea and dies, but not before a final deathbed scene with his father, whom he forgives.*

Racine is rather disingenuous in his "Preface to Phaedra*" when he says that he "followed a slightly different route from Euripides." It is true that he follows the main outline of the plot fairly closely, but the emphases, the motivations, and the meanings of the story are more than "slightly" changed. Phaedra, strictly a secondary character in Euripides, dominates Racine's play. Hippolytus, far from being a woman-hater, is a rather tediously normal young man, in love with the insipid Aricia. He is shocked by his stepmother's profession of love, but hardly rabid; he would prefer to forget it, to "consign this shameful secret to oblivion." Phaedra's decision to allow Oenone to tell the fatal lie to Theseus is motivated only by Hippolytus's "bold gaze"; one critic has pointed out that this is the only tragedy in history whose climax rests upon the misinterpretation of a look. Thus the focus stays firmly upon Phaedra and her thought processes. Her passion, explained in Euripides as the result of Aphrodite's curse, is here presented in wholly naturalistic terms, as a result of her heredity (her mother Pasiphae was also given to monstrous love, having copulated with a bull and given birth to the Minotaur) and her thoroughly human subjection to the arbitrary forces of uncontrollable passion. The lesson of Euripides' play seems to be that the forces of life and fertility must be acknowledged along with the complementary human impulses toward purity and isolation. The vision of passionate love in Racine's play is very nearly the opposite; it seems to be a curse which can lead only to destruction.*

If the classical gods have no place in the action of Phaedra, *the stern God of the Jansenists may. There is none of the "joy of sex" in* Phaedra; *the queen, from the moment she enters, supported in her agony by Oenone, is devoured by the most wrenching guilt and self-hate. She never wavers in her conviction that her love is wholly loathsome, not only hopeless but adulterous and incestuous as well. She does not even like the object of her obsession: Hippolytus is a "fearful monster" in her eyes. How are we to explain this strange fixation? In his Preface, Racine says that her passion is "a punishment of the gods rather than an urge flowing from her own will." In the absence of the classical gods, we may suspect that "the gods" are the wrathful God of the Jansenists and that Phaedra, as the Jansenist theologian Arnauld is said to have believed, is "one of the just to whom grace was not vouchsafed." The two gods who figure in the play—Phaedra's grandfather, the Sun, and her father, Minos, now god of the underworld—sound suspiciously like the Jansenist God, who like the*

Sun sees every human action and who like Minos prepares a punishment in the afterlife below.

Whatever its explanation, the fatal passion of Phaedra is one of the givens in the play, and the real power of the tragedy is in the human reactions to this passion. Phaedra is on the rack, and in her great scenes she reveals all the twistings and turnings of the human mind in conflict with itself. Everything else in the drama is subordinated to this inner struggle. Racine has taken the story of Phaedra as it came down to him and wrought his play so that every detail serves his central action on some level or another. The monstrous story of Phaedra's family on Crete serves as a frightful analogue of her own state of mind. (The word monster *chimes like a bell throughout the play.) Theseus's double career as monster-killer and amorous adventurer and his son's prowess with horses and his pallid love affair with Aricia stand as ironic commentaries on Phaedra's suffering. Even the setting, the claustrophobic backwater town of Troezen, echoes the theme of Phaedra's entrapment. No finer achievement exists in the narrowly circumscribed but emotionally concentrated drama of Neoclassicism.*

FURTHER READING *(prepared by W. J. R.):* A fine account of Racine's life and works is Geoffrey Brereton's *Jean Racine, A Critical Biography,* 1951, which includes good general discussions of *Phèdre, Andromaque,* and other plays. Two enduring general works on the period of Racine and Molière are C. H. C. Wright's *French Classicism,* 1920, and Martin Turnell's *The Classical Moment,* 1946. Both discuss in detail the seventeenth-century French artistic environment. Fine background information on the French theater of Racine's day is available in P. J. Yarrow's *Racine,* 1978. The concluding chapters of this work discuss tragedy and style and offer new theories on Racine's artistry. Odette de Mourgues's *Racine, or The Triumph of Relevance,* 1967, written for the general English reader, argues convincingly for the lasting effectiveness of Racinian tragedy. Bernard Weinberg's *The Art of Jean Racine,* 1963, discusses eleven of the later plays in separate chapters. Weinberg's work is of particular value for acquainting the new reader of Racine with less famous works, such as *Bajazet* and *Athalie.* A chronology of Racine's life and fourteen critical essays are offered in *Racine: Modern Judgments,* ed. R. C. Knight, 1969. The introduction surveys the development of Racine's modern reputation.

PHAEDRA

A TRAGEDY

Translated by John Cairncross

RACINE'S PREFACE TO *PHAEDRA*

Here is another tragedy of which I have borrowed the subject from Euripides. Although I have followed a slightly different route from that author as regards the plot, I have not failed to enrich my play with everything which seemed to me to be most striking in his. Even if I owed him only the idea of Phaedra's character, I should be justified in saying that I owe him what is probably the clearest and most closely-knit play I have written. I am not surprised that this character should have met with such a favourable reception in Euripides' day and that it should still be so successful in our time, since it possesses all the qualities required by Aristotle in a tragic hero, that is, the ability to arouse pity and terror. For Phaedra is neither entirely guilty nor altogether innocent. She is involved by her destiny, and by the anger of the gods, in an unlawful passion at which she is the very first to be horrified. She makes every effort to overcome it. She prefers to let herself die rather than declare it to anyone. And, when she is forced to disclose it, she speaks with such embarrassment that it is clear that her crime is a punishment of the gods rather than an urge flowing from her own will.

I have even been at pains to make her slightly less odious than in the tragedies of the ancients, where she resolves of her own accord to accuse Hippolytus. I felt that calumny was somewhat too low and foul to be put in the mouth of a princess whose sentiments were otherwise so noble and virtuous. This baseness seemed to me to be more appropriate to a nurse, who could well have more slave-like inclinations, and who nevertheless launches this false accusation only in order to save the life and honour of her mistress. Phaedra consents to it only because she is in such a state of excitement as to be out of her mind, and she appears a moment later in order to exculpate her innocent victim and declare the truth.

In Euripides and Seneca, Hippolytus is accused of having violated his stepmother: *Vim corpus tulit.* But here he is only accused of having intended to do so. I wished to spare Theseus a degree of agitation which could have detracted from the sympathy aroused by him among the spectators.

As regards the role of Hippolytus, I had noticed that the ancients reproached Euripides with having portrayed him as a sage free from any imperfection. As a result, the young prince's death caused much more indignation than pity. I felt obliged to leave him one weakness which would make him slightly guilty towards his father, without however depriving him in any way of the nobility with which he spares Phaedra's honour and allows himself to be mistreated without accusing her. I regard as a weakness the passion he feels in spite of himself for Aricia, who is the daughter and sister of his father's mortal enemies.

This character—Aricia—was not invented by me. Virgil says that Hippolytus married her, and had a son by her, after Aesculapius had brought him back to life. And I have also read in certain authors that Hippolytus married and took to Italy a young Athenian lady of high birth who was called Aricia and who gave her name to a small Italian town.

I cite these authorities, because I have been very scrupulous in trying to follow the classical account. I have even been faithful to the story of Theseus as recounted by Plutarch.

It was in this historian that I found that what gave rise to the belief that Theseus went down to the underworld to abduct Proserpine was a journey by this prince in Epirus towards the source of the Acheron to a king whose wife Pirithous wished to carry off and who kept Theseus prisoner after having put Pirithous to death.[1] In this way, I have endeavoured to retain the credibility of the story without losing anything of the ornaments of the legend which constitutes a rich source of poetry. And the rumour of Theseus' death, based on this legendary journey, gives rise to Phaedra's profession of love which becomes one of the main causes of her downfall, since she would never have dared to speak had she believed that her husband was alive.

For the rest, I do not as yet dare to affirm that this play is my best tragedy. I leave it to the readers and to time to decide as to its real value. What I can affirm is that in no other play of mine is virtue given greater prominence. The slightest transgressions are severely punished. The very thought of crime is regarded with as much horror as crime itself. Weaknesses caused by love are treated as real weak-

[1] This sentence is neither more nor less involved than in the original. (All notes to *Phaedra* are by the translator, John Cairncross.)

nesses. The passions are portrayed merely in order to show the aberrations to which they give rise; and vice is painted throughout in colours which bring out its hideousness and hatefulness. That is really the objective which everyone working for the public should have in mind. And it is what the tragedians of early times aimed at above all else. Their theatre was a school in which virtue was taught not less well than in the schools of the philosophers. Hence it was that Aristotle was prepared to lay down rules for drama; and Socrates, the wisest of philosophers, did not disdain to lend a hand to the composition of Euripides' tragedies. It would be greatly to be desired that modern writings were as sound and full of useful precepts as the works of these poets. This might perhaps provide a means of reconciling to tragedy a host of people famous for their piety and their doctrine who have recently condemned it and who would no doubt pass a more favourable judgement on it if writers were as keen to edify their spectators as to amuse them, thereby complying with the real purpose of tragedy.

PHAEDRA

CAST

THESEUS,[2] *son of Aegeus, King of Athens*
PHAEDRA, *wife of Theseus, daughter of Minos and Pasiphae*
HIPPOLYTUS, *son of Theseus and Antiope, Queen of the Amazons*
ARICIA,[3] *princess of the blood royal of Athens*
THERAMENES, *Hippolytus's governor*
OENONE, *Phaedra's nurse and confidante*
ISMENE, *Aricia's confidante*
PANOPE, *a woman of Phaedra's retinue*

THE SCENE *is in Troezen, a town in the Peloponnese*

ACT ONE

SCENE ONE

HIPPOLYTUS THERAMENES

HIPPOLYTUS. It is resolved, Theramenes. I go.
I will depart from Troezen's pleasant land.
Torn by uncertainty about the King,
I am ashamed of standing idly by.
For over half a year I have not heard
Of my dear father Theseus' destiny
Nor even by what far sky he is concealed.
THERAMENES. And, where, my lord, would you make search for him?
Already, to allay your rightful fears,

[2] Pronounced as two syllables. [3] Pronounced as four syllables.

I have scoured both the seas that Corinth joins;
I have sought news of Theseus on the shores
Of Acheron, the river of the dead;
Elis I searched, then sailed past Tenaros
On to the sea where Icarus came down.[4]
What makes you hope that you may find his trace
In some more favoured region of the world?
Who knows indeed if it is his desire
To have the secret of his absence known?
And whether, as we tremble for his life,
He is not tasting all the joys of love,
And soon the outraged victim of his wiles. . . .

HIPPOLYTUS. No more of this, Theramenes. The King
Has seen the errors of his amorous youth.
He is above unworthy dalliance,
And, stronger than his old inconstancy,
Phaedra has in his heart long reigned alone.
But, to be brief, I must make search for him
Far from this city where I dare not stay.

THERAMENES. Since when do you, my lord, fear to frequent
These peaceful haunts you cherished as a boy,
Which I have seen you many a time prefer
To the loud pomp of Athens and the court?
What peril, or what trouble, drives you hence?

HIPPOLYTUS. Those happy days are gone, and all is changed,
Since to these shores the mighty gods have sent
The child of Minos and Pasiphae.[5]

THERAMENES. I understand. The cause of your distress
Is known. The sight of Phaedra vexes you.
Theseus' new wife had scarcely seen you than
Your exile gave the measure of her power.
But now her hate that never let you be
Has vanished or is greatly on the wane.
Besides what perils threaten you from her—
A woman dying or who seeks to die?
Racked by a malady she will not name,
Tired of herself and of the light of day,
Phaedra has not the strength to do you ill.

HIPPOLYTUS. I do not fear her vain hostility.
If I go hence, I flee, let me confess,

[4] The isthmus of Corinth links the main part of Greece with the peninsula of the Peloponnese. The two seas are the Ionian and the Aegean. The River Acheron has its source in the mountains of Epirus in northwest Greece. Theramenes' wanderings took him from there southward to Elis, a province on the western shore of the Peloponnese, then to Tenaros on its southern tip, and finally to the Aegean Sea on the east side of Greece.

[5] Minos was King of Crete, and later judge in Hades. Pasiphae was the daughter of the Sun. She had two daughters by Minos—Ariadne and Phaedra (the latter being the one that Hippolytus has in mind). Aphrodite, the goddess of love, inspired Pasiphae with a monstrous passion for a bull, and from this union there was born the Minotaur, half man, half bull. Theseus brought back Phaedra from Crete after killing the monster in its labyrinth.

Another enemy . . . Aricia,
Last of a line that plotted Theseus' death.

THERAMENES. What! Would you stoop to persecute her too?
Though she is sprung of Pallas' cruel race,
She never joined in her false brothers' schemes.[6]
Why hate her then if she is innocent?

HIPPOLYTUS. I would not flee her if I hated her.

THERAMENES. My lord, may I explain your sudden flight?
Are you no more the man that once you were,
Relentless foe of all the laws of love
And of a yoke Theseus himself has borne?
Will Venus whom you haughtily disdained
Vindicate Theseus after all these years
By forcing you to worship with the throng
Of ordinary mortals at her shrine?
Are you in love?

HIPPOLYTUS.
My friend, what have you said?
You who have known me since I first drew breath,
You ask me shamefully to disavow
The feelings of a proud disdainful heart?
The Amazon, my mother,[7] with her milk
Suckled me on that pride you wonder at.
And I myself, on reaching man's estate,
Approved my nature when I knew myself.
Serving me with unfeignéd loyalty,
You would relate my father's history.
You know how, as I hung upon your words,
My heart would glow at tales of his exploits
When you portrayed Theseus, that demi-god,
Consoling mortals for Alcides'[8] loss,
Monsters suppressed and brigands brought to book—
Procrustes, Sciron, Sinis, Cercyon;
The giants' bones in Epidaurus strewn
And Crete red with the slaughtered Minotaur.
But, when you told me of less glorious deeds,
His word pledged and believed in countless lands:
Helen in Sparta ravished from her home,
Salamis, scene of Periboea's tears;
Others whose very names he has forgot,
Too trusting spirits all deceived by him;
Wronged Ariadne[9] crying to the winds;
Phaedra abducted, though for lawful ends;

[6] Pallas was descended from Erechtheus, the original King of Athens and son of the earth god. Aegeus, Theseus's father, had obtained the throne by adoption. Aricia's brothers plotted Theseus's downfall, but were discovered and put to death.

[7] Antiope (Hippolyta). [8] Hercules.

[9] Minos' daughter, Phaedra's sister, who led Theseus through the labyrinth and thus enabled him to kill the Minotaur; she eloped with Theseus, and was abandoned by him on the island of Naxos.

You know how, loath to hear this sorry tale,
I often urged you quickly to conclude,
Happy could I have kept the shameful half
Of these adventures from posterity.
And am I to be vanquished in my turn?
And can the gods have humbled me so far?
In base defeat the more despicable
Since countless exploits plead on his behalf,
Whereas no monsters overcome by me
Have given me the right to err like him.
And, even if I were fated to succumb,
Should I have chosen to love Aricia?
Should not my wayward feelings have recalled
That she is barred from me eternally?
King Theseus frowns upon her and decrees
That she shall not prolong her brothers' line:
He fears this guilty stock will blossom forth,
And, to ensure her name shall end with her,
Condemns her to be single till she dies—
No marriage torch shall ever blaze for her.
Should I espouse her cause and brave his wrath?
Set an example to foolhardiness?
And, on a foolish passion launched, my youth. . .

THERAMENES. Ah! when your hour has once but struck, my lord,
Heaven of our reasons takes but little heed.
Theseus opens your eyes despite yourself.
His hatred of Aricia has fanned
Your passion and has lent her added grace.
Besides, my lord, why fear a worthy love?
If it is sweet, will you not dare to taste?
Will you be always ruled by modesty?
Can you go wrong where Hercules has trod?
What hearts has Venus' power not subdued?
Where would you be yourself, who fight her now,
If, combating her love, Antiope
Had never been consumed for Theseus?
However, what avails this haughty tone?
Confess it, all is changed; for some days past
You are less often seen, aloof and proud,
Speeding your chariot along the shore,
Or, skilful in the seagod Neptune's art,
Bending an untamed courser to the curb.
The woods less often to your cries resound;
Your eyes grow heavier with secret fire.
There is no doubt, you are consumed with love.
You perish from a malady you hide.
Has fair Aricia enraptured you?

HIPPOLYTUS. Theramenes, I go to seek the King.

THERAMENES. And will you see Phaedra before you leave,
My lord?

HIPPOLYTUS.
I mean to. You may tell her so.
See her I must, since duty so commands.
But what new burden weighs Oenone down?

SCENE TWO

HIPPOLYTUS OENONE THERAMENES

OENONE. Alas, my lord, what cares can equal mine?
The Queen is almost at her destined end.
In vain I watch over her night and day.
She's dying from a hidden malady;
Eternal discord reigns within her mind.
Her restless anguish tears her from her bed.
She longs to see the light, and yet, distraught
With pain, she bids me banish everyone. . .
But here she comes.
HIPPOLYTUS.
Enough. I'll take my leave
And will not show her my detested face.

SCENE THREE

PHAEDRA OENONE

PHAEDRA. No further. Here, Oenone, let us stay.
I faint, I fall; my strength abandons me.
My eyes are dazzled by the daylight's glare,
And my knees, trembling, give beneath my weight.
Alas!
OENONE.
May our tears move you, mighty gods!
PHAEDRA. How these vain jewels, these veils weigh on me!
What meddling hand has sought to re-arrange
My hair, by braiding it across my brow?
All things contrive to grieve and thwart me, all.
OENONE. How all her wishes war among themselves!
Yourself, condemning your unlawful plans,
A moment past, bade us adorn your brow;
Yourself, summoning up your former strength,
Wished to come forth and see the light again.
Scarce have you seen it than you long to hide,
You hate the daylight you came forth to see.
PHAEDRA. O shining founder of an ill-starred line,
You, whom my mother dared to boast her sire,[10]
Who blush perhaps to see me thus distraught,
Sungod, for the last time, I look on you.

[10] The Sun was Pasiphae's father and hence Phaedra's grandfather.

OENONE. What? you will not give up this fell desire?
And will you, always saying no to life,
Make mournful preparation for your death?
PHAEDRA. Would I were seated in the forest's shade!
When can I follow through the swirling dust
The lordly chariot's flight along the course?
OENONE. What?
PHAEDRA.
Madness! Where am I, what have I said?
Whither have my desires, my reason strayed?
Lost, lost, the gods have carried it away.
Oenone, blushes sweep across my face;
My grievous shame stands all too clear revealed,
And tears despite me fill my aching eyes.
OENONE. If you must blush, blush for your silence, for
It but inflames the fury of your ills.
Deaf to our wild entreaties, pitiless,
Will you allow yourself to perish thus?
What madness cuts you off in mid career?
What spell, what poison, has dried up the source?
Thrice have the shades of night darkened the skies
Since sleep last made its entry in your eyes,
And thrice the day has driven forth dim night
Since last your fainting lips took nourishment.
What dark temptation lures you to your doom?
What right have you to plot to end your life?
In this you wrong the gods from whom you spring,
You are unfaithful to your wedded lord;
Unfaithful also to your hapless sons,
Whom you would thrust beneath a heavy yoke.
Remember, that same day their mother dies,
Hope for the alien woman's son revives,
For that fierce enemy of you and yours,
That youth whose mother was an Amazon,
Hippolytus. . .
PHAEDRA.
God!
OENONE.
That reproach struck home.
PHAEDRA. Ah! wretched woman, what name crossed your lips?
OENONE. Your anger now bursts forth, and rightly so.
I love to see you shudder at the name.
Live then. Let love and duty spur you on.
Live on. Do not allow a Scythian's son
To lord it with his harsh and odious rule
Over the pride of Greece and of the gods.
Do not delay! for every moment kills.
Haste to replenish your enfeebled strength
While yet the fires of life, though all but spent,
Are burning and can still flame bright again.

Phaedra. I have prolonged my guilty days too far.
Oenone. What, are you harried by some keen remorse?
What crime could ever bring you to this pass?
Your hands were never stained with guiltless blood.
Phaedra. Thanks be to heaven, my hands have done no wrong.
Would God my heart were innocent as they!
Oenone. What fearful project then have you conceived
Which strikes such terror deep into my heart?
Phaedra. I have revealed enough. Spare me the rest.
I die, and my grim secret dies with me.
Oenone. Keep silence then, inhuman one, and die;
But seek some other hand to close your eyes.
Although the candle of your life burns low,
I will go down before you to the dead.
Thither a thousand different roads converge,
My misery will choose the shortest one.
When have I ever failed you, cruel one?
Remember, you were born into my arms.
For you I have lost country, children, all.[11]
Is this how you reward fidelity?
Phaedra. What do you hope to gain by violence?
If I should speak, you would be thunderstruck.
Oenone. And what, ye gods, could be more terrible
Than seeing you expire before my eyes?
Phaedra. Even when you know my crime and cruel fate,
I yet will die, and die the guiltier.
Oenone. By all the tears that I have shed for you,
And by your faltering knees I hold entwined,
Deliver me from dire uncertainty.
Phaedra. You wish it. Rise.
Oenone.
Speak. I await your words.
Phaedra. What shall I say to her and where begin?
Oenone. Wound me no longer by such vain affrights!
Phaedra. Oh hate of Venus! Anger-laden doom!
Into what dark abyss love hurled my mother![12]
Oenone. Ah, Queen, forget; and for all time to come
Eternal silence seal this memory.
Phaedra. Oh sister Ariadne, from what love
You died deserted on a barren shore!
Oenone. What ails you, and what mortal agony
Drives you to fury against all your race?
Phaedra. Since Venus wills it, of this unblest line
I perish, I, the last and wretchedest.
Oenone. You are in love?
Phaedra.
Love's furies rage in me.

[11] The nurse had accompanied Phaedra from her native Crete to Athens.
[12] An allusion to Pasiphae's monstrous passion for the bull.

OENONE. For whom?

PHAEDRA.
Prepare to hear the crowning woe.
I love . . . I tremble, shudder at the name;
I love . . .

[OENONE *leans forward.*]

PHAEDRA.
You know that prince whom I myself
So long oppressed, son of the Amazon?

OENONE. Hippolytus?

PHAEDRA.
You have pronounced his name.

OENONE. Merciful heavens! My blood chills in my veins.
O grief! O crime! O lamentable race!
Ill-fated journey and thrice ill-starred coast!
Would we had never neared your dangerous shores!

PHAEDRA. My malady goes further back. I scarce
Was bound by marriage to Aegeus' son;[13]
My peace of mind, my happiness seemed sure—
Athens revealed to me my haughty foe.
As I beheld, I reddened, I turned pale.
A tempest raged in my distracted mind.
My eyes no longer saw. I could not speak.
I felt my body freezing, burning; knew
Venus was on me with her dreaded flames,
The fatal torments of a race she loathes.
By sleepless vows, I thought to ward her off.
I built a temple to her, rich and fair.
No hour went by but I made sacrifice,
Seeking my reason in the victims' flanks.
Weak remedies for love incurable!
In vain my hand burned incense on the shrine.
Even when my lips invoked the goddess' name,
I worshipped *him.* His image followed me.
Even on the altar's steps, my offerings
Were only to the god I dared not name.
I shunned him everywhere. O crowning woe!
I found him mirrored in his father's face!
Against myself at last I dared revolt.
I spurred my feelings on to harass him.
To banish my adoréd enemy,
I feigned a spite against this stepson, kept
Urging his exile, and my ceaseless cries
Wrested him from a father's loving arms.
I breathed more freely since I knew him gone.
The days flowed by, untroubled, innocent.
Faithful to Theseus, hiding my distress,

[13] Theseus.

I nursed the issue of our ill-starred bed.
Ah vain precautions! Cruel destiny!
Brought by my lord himself to Troezen's shores,
I saw once more the foe I had expelled.
My open wound at once poured blood again.
The fire no longer slumbers in the veins.
All Venus' might has fastened on her prey.
I have a fitting horror for my crime;
I hate this passion and I loathe my life.
Dying, I could have kept my name unstained,
And my dark passion from the light of day;
Your tears, your pleas have forced me to confess,
And I shall not regret what I have done,
If you, respecting the approach of death,
Will cease to vex me with reproaches, and
Your vain assistance will not try to fan
The last faint flicker still alight in me.

SCENE FOUR

PHAEDRA OENONE PANOPE

PANOPE. Would I could hide from you the grievous news,
My lady, but I cannot hold it back.
Death has abducted your unconquered lord
And this mischance is known to all but you.
OENONE. What, Panope?
PANOPE.
The Queen in vain, alas!
Importunes heaven for Theseus' safe return,
For, from the vessels just arrived in port,
Hippolytus, his son, has learned his death.
PHAEDRA. God!
PANOPE.
Athens is divided in its choice
Of master. Some favor the prince, your son,
Others, forgetful of the State's decrees,[14]
Dare to support the foreign woman's son.
Rumour even has it that a bold intrigue
Wishes to give Aricia the throne.
I deemed it right to warn you of this threat.
Hippolytus is ready to set sail,
And in this turmoil it is to be feared
He may win fickle Athens to his cause.
OENONE. Panope, cease! You may be sure the Queen
Will give due heed to this important news.

[14] Which ruled out the succession of anyone even partly of non-Greek blood.

SCENE FIVE

PHAEDRA OENONE

OENONE. Ah Queen, I had relinquished you to death
And thought to follow you down to the tomb.
I had no longer words to turn you back;
But this news bids you steer another course.
Now all is changed, and fortune smiles on you.
The King is dead, and you must take his place.
He leaves a son with whom your duty lies:
A slave without you; if you live, a king.
On whom in his misfortune can he lean?
If you are dead, no hand will dry his tears;
And his fond cries, borne upwards to the gods,
Will bring his forebears' anger down on you.
Live then, no longer tortured by reproach.
Your love becomes like any other love.
Theseus, in dying, has dissolved the bonds
Which made your love a crime to be abhorred.
You need no longer dread Hippolytus,
And you may see him and be guiltless still.
Perhaps, convinced of your hostility,
He is prepared to captain the revolt.
Quick, undeceive him; bend him to your will.
King of these fertile shores, Troezen is his.
But well he knows the laws assign your son
The soaring ramparts that Minerva built.[15]
Both of you have a common enemy.
Join forces then against Aricia.
PHAEDRA. Then be it so. Your counsels have prevailed.
I'll live, if I can be recalled to life,
And if the love I bear my son can still
In this grim hour revive my failing strength.

ACT TWO

SCENE ONE

ARICIA ISMENE

ARICIA. Hippolytus has asked to see me here?
Hippolytus wishes to say farewell?
Ismene, are you not mistaken?
ISMENE.
No.
This is the first result of Theseus' death.
Make ready to receive from every side
Allegiances that Theseus filched from you.

[15] Athens.

Aricia is mistress of her fate,
And soon all Greece will bow the knee to her.
ARICIA. This was no rumour then, Ismene. Now
My enemy, my tyrant is no more.
ISMENE. Indeed. The gods no longer frown on you,
And Theseus wanders with your brothers' shades.
ARICIA. By what adventure did he meet his end?
ISMENE. The tales told of his death are past belief.
They say that in some amorous escapade
The waters closed over his faithless head.
The thousand tongues of rumour even assert
That with Pirithous he went down to Hell,
Beheld Cocytus[16] and the sombre shores,
Showed himself living to the shades below,
But that he could not, from the house of death,
Recross the river whence is no return.
ARICIA. Can mortal man, before he breathes his last,
Descend into the kingdom of the dead?
What magic lured him to that dreaded shore?
ISMENE. You alone doubt it. Theseus is no more.
Athens is stricken; Troezen knows the news,
And now pays tribute to Hippolytus.
Here in this palace, trembling for her son,
Phaedra takes counsel with her anxious friends.
ARICIA. But will Hippolytus be kinder than
His father was to me, loosen my chains,
And pity my mishaps?
ISMENE.
I think he will.
ARICIA. Do you not know severe Hippolytus?
How can you hope that he will pity me,
Honouring in me alone a sex he spurns?
How constantly he has avoided us,
Haunting those places which he knows we shun!
ISMENE. I know the tales of his unfeelingness;
But I have seen him in your presence, and
The legend of Hippolytus' reserve
Doubled my curiosity in him.
His aspect did not tally with his fame;
At the first glance from you he grew confused.
His eyes, seeking in vain to shun your gaze,
Brimming with languor, took their fill of you.
Although the name of lover wounds his pride,
He has a lover's eye, if not his tongue.
ARICIA. How avidly, Ismene, does my heart
Drink in these sweet, perhaps unfounded words!
O you who know me, can it be believed
That the sad plaything of a ruthless fate,

[16] The river of the underworld.

A heart that always fed on bitterness,
Should ever know the frenzied pangs of love?
Last of the issue of Earth's royal son,[17]
I only have escaped the scourge of war.
I lost, all in their springtime's flowering,
Six brothers, pride of an illustrious line.
The sword swept all away and drenched the earth,
Which drank, unwillingly, Erechtheus' blood.
You know that, since their death, a cruel law
Forbids all Greeks to seek me as their wife,
Since it was feared my marriage might some day
Kindle my brothers' ashes into life.
But you recall with what disdain I viewed
These moves of a suspicious conqueror,
For, as a lifelong enemy of love,
I rendered thanks to Theseus' tyranny,
Which merely helped to keep me fancy free.
My eyes had not yet lighted on his son.
Not that my eyes alone yield to the charm
Of his much vaunted grace, his handsomeness,
Bestowed by nature, but which he disdains,
And seems not even to realize he owns.
I love and prize in him far nobler gifts—
His father's virtues, not his weaknesses.
I love, let me confess, that manly pride,
Which never yet has bowed beneath love's yoke.
Phaedra in vain gloried in Theseus' sighs.
I am more proud, and spurn the easy prize
Of homage to a thousand others paid
And of a heart accessible to all.
But to bring an unbending spirit down,
To cause an aching where no feeling was,
To stun a conqueror with his defeat,
In vain revolt against a yoke he loves:
That rouses my ambition, my desire.
Even Hercules was easier to disarm.
Vanquished more often than Hippolytus,
He yielded a less glorious victory.
But, dear Ismene, what rash hopes are these?
For his resistance will be all too strong.
You yet may hear me, humble in my grief,
Bewail the very pride I now admire.
Hippolytus in love? By what excess
Of fortune could I . . .

ISMENE.

You yourself will hear.
Hither he comes.

[17] Erechtheus.

SCENE TWO

HIPPOLYTUS ARICIA ISMENE

HIPPOLYTUS.
Princess, before I go,
I deemed it right to let you know your fate.
My father is no more. My fears divined
The secret of his lengthy absence. Death,
Death only, ending his illustrious deeds,
Could hide him from the universe so long.
The gods at last deliver to the Fates
Alcides' friend, companion, and his heir.
I feel that, silencing your hate, even you
Hear in good part the honours due to him.
One hope alone tempers my mortal grief.
I can release you from a stern control,
Revoking laws whose harshness I deplore.
Yourself, your heart, do with them what you will;
And in this Troezen, now assigned to me
As my sage grandsire Pittheus' heritage,
Which with a single voice proclaimed me king,
I leave you free as I am; nay, more free.
ARICIA. Limit your boundless generosity.
By honouring me, despite adversity,
My lord, you place me, more than you believe,
Beneath those laws from which you set me free.
HIPPOLYTUS. Athens, uncertain whom to choose as heir,
Talks of yourself, of me, and the Queen's son.
ARICIA. Me?
HIPPOLYTUS.
I would not wish to deceive myself.
My claim appears to be annulled by law
Because my mother was an Amazon.
But, if my only rival for the throne
Were Phaedra's son, my stepbrother, I could
Protect my rights against the law's caprice.
If I do not assert my claim, it is
To hand, or rather to return, to you
A sceptre given to your ancestors
By that great mortal whom the earth begot.
Adoption placed it in Aegeus' hands.
Theseus, his son, defended and enlarged
The bounds of Athens, which proclaimed him king
And left your brothers in oblivion.
Athens recalls you now within her walls.
Too long has she deplored this endless feud;
Too long your noble kinsmen's blood has flown,
Drenching the very fields from which it sprang.
If Troezen falls to me, the lands of Crete

Offer a rich domain to Phaedra's son.
But Attica is yours. And I go hence
To unify our votes on your behalf.

ARICIA. At all I hear, astounded and amazed,
I almost fear a dream deceives my ears.
Am I awake? Is it to be believed?
What god, my lord, inspired you with the thought?
How rightly is your glory spread abroad!
And how the truth surpasses your renown!
You in my favour will renounce your claim?
Surely it was enough to keep your heart
So long free from that hatred of my line,
That enmity . . .

HIPPOLYTUS.
I hate you, Princess? No.
However my aloofness be decried,
Do you believe a monster gave me birth?
What churlish breeding, what unbending hate
Would not have melted at the sight of you?
Could I resist the soft beguiling spell . . .

ARICIA. What! My lord . . .

HIPPOLYTUS.
No, I cannot now draw back!
Reason, I see, gives way to violence.
And, since I have begun to speak my mind,
Princess, I must go on: I must reveal
A secret that my heart can not conceal.
Before you stands a pitiable prince,
Signal example of rash arrogance.
I who, in proud rebellion against love,
Have long mocked other captives' sufferings,
Who, pitying the shipwrecks of the weak,
Had thought to watch them always from the shore,
Am now, in bondage to the common law,
Cut from my moorings by a surging swell.
A single blow has quelled my recklessness:
My haughty spirit is at last in thrall.
For six long months ashamed and in despair,
Pierced by the shaft implanted in my side,
I battle with myself, with you, in vain.
Present I flee you; absent, you are near.
Deep in the woods, your image follows me.
The light of day, the shadows of the night,
Everything conjures up the charms I flee;
Each single thing delivers up my heart.
And, sole reward for all my fruitless care,
I seek but cannot find myself again.
Bow, chariot, javelins, all importune me;

The lessons Neptune taught me are forgot.[18]
My idle steeds no longer know my voice,
And only to my cries the woods resound.
Perhaps the tale of so uncouth a love
Brings, as you listen, blushes to your face.
What words with which to offer you a heart!
How strange a conquest for so fair a maid!
But you should prize the offering the more.
Remember that I speak an unknown tongue,
And do not scorn my clumsy gallantry,
Which, but for you, I never would have known.

SCENE THREE

HIPPOLYTUS ARICIA
THERAMENES ISMENE

THERAMENES. The Queen is coming, Prince. She looks for you.
HIPPOLYTUS. For me?
THERAMENES.
I do not know what she intends.
You have been sent for by her messenger.
Before you leave, Phaedra would speak with you.
HIPPOLYTUS. What can I say? And what can she expect . . .
ARICIA. Consent at least, my lord, to hear her speak.
Although she was your bitter enemy,
You owe some shade of pity to her tears.
HIPPOLYTUS. Meanwhile you go. I leave, and am in doubt
Whether I have offended my beloved,
Or if my heart that I commit to you . . .
ARICIA. Go, Prince. Pursue your generous designs.
Make Athens' State pay homage to me. All
The gifts you offer to me I accept.
But Athens' empire, glorious though it be,
Is not your most endearing offering.

SCENE FOUR

HIPPOLYTUS THERAMENES

HIPPOLYTUS. Are you all ready? But here comes the Queen.
Let everyone prepare with all despatch
To sail. Go, give the signal; hasten back,
And free me from a tedious interview.

[18] The seagod was also the god of horses.

SCENE FIVE

PHAEDRA HIPPOLYTUS OENONE

PHAEDRA [*to* OENONE *at the back of the stage*].
He comes . . . My blood sweeps back into my heart.
Forgotten are the words I had prepared.
OENONE. Think of your son, who hopes in you alone.
PHAEDRA. They say that you are leaving us at once,
My lord. I come to join my tears to yours.
I come to tell you of a mother's fears.
My son is fatherless, and soon, too soon,
He must behold my death as well. Even now,
Numberless enemies beset his youth.
You, only you, can see to his defence.
But I am harried by remorse within.
I fear lest you refuse to hear his cries.
I tremble lest you visit on a son
Your righteous anger at a mother's crimes.
HIPPOLYTUS. How could I ever be so infamous?
PHAEDRA. If you should hate me, I would not complain,
For I appeared resolved to do you ill.
Deep in my inmost heart you could not read.
I drew upon myself your enmity,
And where I dwelt, I would not suffer you.
With unrelenting hate, I sought to be
Divided from you by a waste of seas.
I even ordained by an express decree
That in my presence none should speak your name.
But, if the punishment should fit the crime,
If hate alone could bring your hate on me,
Never did woman merit pity more
And less, my lord, deserve your enmity.
HIPPOLYTUS. A mother jealous of her children's rights
Rarely forgives another woman's son,
I realize; and from a second bed
Awkward suspicion all too often springs.
Another would have taken like offence,
And at her hands I might have suffered more.
PHAEDRA. Ah! My lord, heaven, I dare here attest,
Has quite dispensed me from the common rule.
Far other is the care that weighs on me.
HIPPOLYTUS. Lady, it is too early yet to grieve.
Who knows, your husband may be still alive.
Heaven may vouchsafe him to your tears again.
Protected by the seagod, not in vain
Will Theseus call on mighty Neptune's aid.
PHAEDRA. No mortal visits twice the house of death.
Since Theseus has beheld the sombre shores,
In vain you hope a god will send him back,
And hungry Acheron holds fast his prey.

But no, he is not dead; he lives, in you.
Always I think I see my husband's face.
I see him, speak to him, and my fond heart . . .
My frenzied love bursts forth in spite of me.

HIPPOLYTUS. In this I see the wonder of your love.
Dead as he is, Theseus still lives for you.
Still does his memory inflame your heart.

PHAEDRA. Yes, Prince, I pine, I am on fire for him.
I love King Theseus, not as once he was,
The fickle worshipper at countless shrines,
Dishonouring the couch of Hades' god;[19]
But constant, proud, and even a little shy;
Enchanting, young, the darling of all hearts,
Fair as the gods; or fair as you are now.
He had your eyes, your bearing, and your speech.
His face flushed with your noble modesty.
When towards my native Crete he cleft the waves,[20]
Well might the hearts of Minos' daughters burn!
What were you doing then? Why without you
Did he assemble all the flower of Greece?
Why could you not, too young, alas, have fared
Forth with the ship that brought him to our shores?
You would have slain the monstrous Cretan bull
Despite the windings of his endless lair.
My sister[21] would have armed you with the thread
To lead you through the dark entangled maze—
No. *I* would have forestalled her. For my love
Would instantly have fired me with the thought.
I, only I, would have revealed to you
The subtle windings of the labyrinth.
What care I would have lavished on your head!
A thread would not have reassured my fears.
Affronting danger side by side with you,
I would myself have wished to lead the way,
And Phaedra, with you in the labyrinth,
Would have returned with you or met her doom.

HIPPOLYTUS. What do I hear? Have you forgotten that
King Theseus is my father, you his wife?

PHAEDRA. What makes you think, my lord, I have forgot,
Or am no longer mindful of my name?

HIPPOLYTUS. Forgive me. Blushing, I confess your words
Were innocent, and I misunderstood.
For very shame I cannot bear your gaze.
I go . . .

PHAEDRA.
Ah, cruel, you have understood
Only too well. I have revealed enough.

[19] Pluto, King of the underworld.
[20] On the expedition to Crete against the Minotaur. [21] Ariadne.

Know Phaedra then, and all her wild desires.
I burn with love. Yet, even as I speak,
Do not imagine I feel innocent,
Nor think that my complacency has fed
The poison of the love that clouds my mind.
The hapless victim of heaven's vengeances,
I loathe myself more than you ever will.
The gods are witness, they who in my breast
Have lit the fire fatal to all my line.
Those gods whose cruel glory it has been
To lead astray a feeble mortal's heart.
Yourself recall to mind the past, and how
I shunned you, cruel one, nay, drove you forth.
I strove to seem to you inhuman, vile;
The better to resist, I sought your hate.
But what availed my needless sufferings?
You hated me the more, I loved not less.
Even your misfortunes lent you added charms.
I pined, I dropped, in torments and in tears.
Your eyes alone could see that it is so,
If for a moment they could look at me.
Nay, this confession to you, ah! the shame,
Think you I made it of my own free will?
I meant to beg you, trembling, not to hate
My helpless children, whom I dared not fail.
My foolish heart, alas, too full of you,
Could talk to you of nothing but yourself.
Take vengeance. Punish me for loving you.
Come, prove yourself your father's worthy son,
And of a vicious monster rid the world.
I, Theseus' widow, dare to love his son!
This frightful monster must not now escape.
Here is my heart. Here must your blow strike home.
Impatient to atone for its offence,
I feel it strain to meet your mighty arm.
Strike. Or if it's unworthy of your blows,
Or such a death too mild for my deserts,
Or if you deem my blood too vile to stain
Your hand, lend me, if not your arm, your sword.
Give me it!

OENONE.
Ah! What are you doing? God!
Someone is coming. You must not be seen.
Come, let's go in, quick, to avoid disgrace.

SCENE SIX

HIPPOLYTUS THERAMENES

THERAMENES. Can that be Phaedra who was dragged away?

Why, my lord, why this sudden, sharp dismay?
I find you without sword, aghast and pale.
HIPPOLYTUS. Flee, flee, Theramenes. I cannot speak,
Nor without horror look upon myself.
Phaedra. . . . No, mighty gods, let us consign
This shameful secret to oblivion.
THERAMENES. If you will leave, the sails are all unfurled.
But Athens has already made her choice.
Her chieftains have consulted all the tribes.
Your brother rules;[22] and Phaedra wins the day.
HIPPOLYTUS. Phaedra?
THERAMENES.
A herald speaking Athens' will
Into her hands conveyed the reins of state.
Her son is king, my lord.
HIPPOLYTUS.
Oh God, who knows
Her heart, is it her virtue you reward?
THERAMENES. Meanwhile, vague rumours say the King still lives,
And even that in Epirus he was seen.
But I, who sought him there, my lord, I know . . .
HIPPOLYTUS. No matter. Let us study every clue.
Have this new rumour traced back to its source.
But, if it does not then prove credible,
Let us depart and, at whatever cost,[23]
Replace the sceptre in more worthy hands.

ACT THREE

SCENE ONE
PHAEDRA OENONE

PHAEDRA. Ah, take away those royal honours. How
Can you importune me to show myself?
And why seek to beguile my grieving heart?
Rather conceal me. I have said too much.
My frantic passion has revealed itself.
I have said what should never have been heard.
God! how he listened to me. By what shifts
He long pretended not to understand.
How his whole being hankered to be gone.
And how his blushes added to my shame.
Why did you ever thwart my baneful plan?
Ah! when his sword was pointed at my breast,
Did he turn pale for me, or did he wrench
It from me? I had but to touch it once

[22] i.e., half-brother, son of Theseus and Phaedra, whereas Hippolytus' mother was Antiope (Hippolyta).
[23] That is, even at the cost of a rebellion.

To make it horrible for him, and for
The wretched sword to soil his cruel hands.
OENONE. Thus your misfortunes breed self-pity, and
Only inflame a fire you ought to quench.
Daughter of Minos, should you not aspire
To seek your peace of mind in nobler cares?
Resort to flight from an ungrateful youth,
Reign, and assume the guidance of the State?
PHAEDRA. *I* reign? *I* bring a State beneath my rule,
When reason reigns no longer over me;
When I have lost my self-dominion; when
Beneath a shameful sway I scarcely breathe;
When I am dying?
OENONE.
Flee.
PHAEDRA.
I cannot go.
OENONE. You sent him into exile. Shun him now.
PHAEDRA. Too late, too late. He knows my mad desires.
I have transgressed the bounds of modesty.
I to Hippolytus have bared my shame,
And hope, despite me, has seduced my heart.
You yourself, rallying my failing strength
When on my lips my soul was hovering,
By guileful counsels brought me back to life.
You gave me glimpses of a sinless love.
OENONE. Alas! guilty or no of your mishaps,
What would I not have done to save your life?
But, if by insults you were ever stung,
Can you forget a haughty youth's disdain?
God! with what cruel, stern, unfeeling heart
He left you well-nigh prostrate at his feet!
How hateful was his virtuous haughtiness!
Why did not Phaedra see him with my eyes?
PHAEDRA. He may discard this pride that angers you.
Bred in the forests, he is wild like them.
Hardened by rude upbringing, he perhaps
For the first time listens to words of love.
Perhaps his silence mirrors his surprise,
And our reproaches are too violent.
OENONE. An Amazon, forget not, gave him birth.
PHAEDRA. Though a barbarian, yet did she love.
OENONE. He hates all women with a deadly hate.
PHAEDRA. No rival, then, will triumph over me.
In short, the time for good advice is past.
Serve my wild heart, Oenone, not my head.
If he is inaccessible to love,
Let us attack him at some weaker point.
He seemed attracted by an empire's rule.
He could not hide it; Athens beckoned him.

Thither his vessels' prows were headed, and
The white sails fluttered, streaming in the wind.
Oenone, play on his ambition. Go,
Dazzle him with the glitter of the crown.
Let him assume the sacred diadem.
Myself to bind it on is all I ask,
Yielding to him the power I cannot hold.
He will instruct my son how to command;
Perhaps he will be father to the boy.
Mother and son I will commit to him.
In short, try every means to win him round.
Your words will find a readier ear than mine.
Urge! Weep! Paint Phaedra at death's door.
You may assume a supplicating tone.
I will endorse it, whatsoe'er you do.
Go. Upon your success depends my fate.

SCENE TWO
PHAEDRA [*alone*]

PHAEDRA. O you who see the depths of this my shame,
Relentless Venus, is my fall complete?
Your cruelty could go no further. Now
You triumph. All your arrows have struck home.
O cruel goddess! if you seek new fame,
Attack a more rebellious enemy.
Frigid Hippolytus, flouting your wrath,
Has at your altars never bowed the knee.
Your name seems to offend his haughty ear.
Goddess, avenge yourself. Our cause is one.
Make him love . . . but Oenone, you are back.
Did he not listen? Does he loathe me still?

SCENE THREE
PHAEDRA OENONE

OENONE. Your love is vain and you must stifle it,
O Queen, and summon up your former strength.
The King we thought was dead will soon be here;
Theseus is come; Theseus is on his way.
Headlong, the crowd rushes to welcome him.
I had gone out to seek Hippolytus
When, swelling to the heavens, a thousand cries . . .
PHAEDRA. My husband lives. Oenone, say no more.
I have confessed a love that soils his name.
He is alive, and more I will not know.
OENONE. What?
PHAEDRA.
I foretold it but you would not hear.

Your tears prevailed over my keen remorse.
I died this morning worthy to be mourned;
I took your counsel and dishonoured die.

OENONE. You mean to die?

PHAEDRA.
Great God, what have I done?
My husband and his son are on their way.
I will behold the witness of my guilt
Observe me as I dare approach the King,
My heart heavy with sighs he heard unmoved,
My eyes wet with tears the wretch disdained.
Mindful of Theseus' honour, as he is,
Will he conceal from him my fierce desires?
Will he be false to father and to king,
Restrain the horror that he feels for me?
His silence would be vain, Oenone, for
I know my baseness, and do not belong
To those bold wretches who with brazen front
Can revel in their crimes unblushingly.
I know my transports and recall them all.
Even now I feel these very walls, these vaults,
Will soon give tongue and, with accusing voice,
Await my husband to reveal the truth.
Then, death, come free me from so many woes.
Is it so terrible to cease to live?
Death holds no terrors for the wretched. No.
I fear only the name I leave behind,
For my poor children what a heritage.
The blood of Jove should make their spirit swell;[24]
But, whatsoever pride that blood inspires,
A mother's crime lies heavy on her sons.
I tremble lest reports, alas, too true,
One day upbraid them with a mother's guilt.
I tremble lest, crushed by this odious weight,
Neither will ever dare hold up his head.

OENONE. Ah! do not doubt it. Pity both of them.
Never was fear more justified than yours.
But why expose them to such base affronts?
And why bear witness now against yourself?
That way lies ruin. Phaedra, they will say,
Fled from the dreaded aspect of her lord.
Hippolytus is fortunate indeed.
By laying down your life, you prove him right.
How can I answer your accuser's charge?
I shall be all too easy to confound.
I shall behold his hideous triumph as
He tells your shame to all who care to hear.

[24]Jove (Zeus) was father to Minos and grandfather to Phaedra.

Ah! sooner let the flames of heaven descend.
But tell me frankly, do you love him still?
How do you view this overweening prince?

PHAEDRA. He is a fearful monster in my eyes.

OENONE. Then why concede him such a victory?
You fear him. Dare then to accuse him first
Of the offence he soon may charge you with.
Nothing is in his favour; all is yours—
His sword, left by good fortune in your hands,
Your present agitation, your past grief,
His father, turned against him by your cries,
And, last, his exile you yourself obtained.

PHAEDRA. Should I oppress and blacken innocence?

OENONE. All I need is your silence to succeed.
Like you I tremble and I feel remorse.
Sooner would I affront a thousand deaths,
But, since without this remedy you die,
For me your life must come before all else.
Therefore I'll speak. Despite his wrath, the King
Will do naught to his son but banish him.
A father when he punishes is still
A father, and his judgement will be mild.
But, even if guiltless blood must still be shed,
What does your threatened honour not demand?
It is too precious to be compromised.
Its dictates, all of them, must be obeyed.
And, to safeguard your honour, everything,
Yes, even virtue, must be sacrificed.
But who comes here? Theseus!

PHAEDRA.
Hippolytus!
In his bold gaze my ruin is writ large.
Do as you will. My fate is in your hands.
My whirling mind has left me powerless.

SCENE FOUR

THESEUS HIPPOLYTUS PHAEDRA
OENONE THERAMENES

THESEUS. Fortune at last ceases to frown on me,
O Queen, and in your arms again . . .

PHAEDRA.
No more.
Do not profane your transports of delight.
No more do I deserve this tenderness.
You have been outraged. Jealous fortune's blows
During your absence have not spared your wife.

I am unworthy to approach you, and
Henceforth my only thought must be to hide.

SCENE FIVE

THESEUS HIPPOLYTUS THERAMENES

THESEUS. Why this cold welcome to your father?
HIPPOLYTUS.
Sire,
Phaedra alone can solve this mystery.
But, if my ardent wish can move you still,
Allow me never to set eyes on her.
Suffer your trembling son to disappear
For ever from the place where Phaedra dwells.
THESEUS. You, my son, leave me?
HIPPOLYTUS.
Yes. It was not I
Who sought her. You, my lord, you brought her here.
For you, on leaving, brought Aricia
And your Queen, Phaedra, here to Troezen's shore.
You even committed them into my care.
But, since your safe return, why should I stay?
Long have I squandered in the woods of Greece
My manhood's skill on paltry enemies.
Should not I, fleeing shameful idleness,
Redden my javelins in more glorious blood?
Before you had attained my present years,
More than one tyrant, monsters more than one,
Had felt the might of your unconquered arm;
Even then, you were the scourge of insolence.
You had cleared all the shores of both the seas.
The traveller now fares freely through the land.
Hercules, resting on his laurels' fame,
Already for his labours looked to you.
And I, a glorious father's unknown son,
Lag far behind even my mother's deeds.
Let me at least show you my mettle and,
If some fell monster has escaped your sword,
Place at your feet its honourable spoils.
Or let the memory of a glorious death,
Engraving in eternity my life,
Prove to the universe I was your son.
THESEUS. What do I see? What horror spread around
Drives back from me, distraught, my family?
If I return, so feared, so undesired,
O heaven! why did you free me from my gaol?
I had one friend alone.[25] He rashly tried

[25] Pirithous.

To seize the consort of Epirus' King.
I served his amorous plan reluctantly;
But fate in anger blinded both of us.
The tyrant took me by surprise unarmed.
Pirithous I beheld, a woeful sight,
Thrown to fierce monsters by the barbarous king,
Who fed them on the blood of helpless men.
Me he confined in sombre caves profound
Nearby the shadowy kingdom of the dead.
The gods at last relented towards me and
Allowed me to outwit my guardian.
I purged the world of a perfidious knave,
And his own monsters battened on his flesh.
But when I joyfully prepare to meet
My dearest ones, all that the gods have spared,
Nay, when my soul, that is its own again,
Would feast itself upon so dear a sight,
Only with shudders am I welcomed home;
Everyone flees, rejecting my embrace.
Myself, filled with the horror I inspire,
Would I were prisoner in Epirus still.
Speak! Phaedra tells of outrage done to me.
Who played me false? Why am I unavenged?
Has Greece, so often guarded by my arm,
Afforded shelter to the criminal?
You do not answer. Is my son, my own
Dear son, in league, then, with my enemies?
Let us go in and end this grim suspense.
Let us discover criminal and crime,
And Phaedra tell us why she is distraught.

SCENE SIX

Hippolytus Theramenes

Hippolytus. What meant these words that made my blood run cold?
Will Phaedra, still in her delirium,
Denounce herself, bring ruin on her head?
O God! What will the King say then? How love
Has spread its baleful poison through the house!
Myself, full of a passion he condemns,
As once he knew me, so he finds me still.
Gloomy forebodings terrify my soul.
But innocence has surely naught to fear.
Come, let me with some new and happier
Approach revive my father's tenderness,
And tell him of a love he may oppose
But which it is not in his power to change.

ACT FOUR

SCENE ONE
THESEUS OENONE

THESEUS. What do I hear? A reckless libertine
Conceived this outrage on his father's name?
How harshly you pursue me, destiny.
I know not where I am, whither I go.
O son! O ill-rewarded tenderness!
Daring the scheme, detestable the thought.
To gain his lustful and nefarious ends,
The shameless villain had resort to force.
I recognized the sword he drew on her,
That sword I gave him for a nobler use.
Could all the ties of blood not hold him back?
Phaedra was slow in bringing him to book?
In keeping silent, Phaedra spared the knave?
OENONE. Rather did Phaedra spare a father's tears.
Ashamed of a distracted lover's suit,
And of the vicious passion she had caused,
Phaedra, my lord, was dying and her hand
Was on the point of cutting short her days.
I saw her raise her arm, I ran to her.
I, only I, preserved her for your love,
And, pitying her distress and your alarm,
Reluctantly I lent her tears a voice.
THESEUS. The criminal! He blenched despite himself.
As I drew near, I saw him start with fear.
I was astonished by his joyless mien;
His cold embraces froze my tenderness.
But had this guilty love that eats him up
Already, even in Athens, shown itself?
OENONE. My lord, recall how oft the Queen complained.
Infamous love gave rise to all her hate.
THESEUS. And here in Troezen this flamed up again?
OENONE. My lord, I have related all I know.
The grieving Queen too long remains alone;
Allow me to withdraw and go to her.

SCENE TWO
THESEUS HIPPOLYTUS

THESEUS. Ah, it is he. Great gods! what eye would not
Be duped like mine by such nobility?
Must needs the brow of an adulterer
Be bright with virtue's sacred character?
And ought we not by fixed certain signs
To see into perfidious mortals' hearts?

HIPPOLYTUS. May I inquire of you what baleful cloud
Has overcast, my lord, your regal brow?
Will you not venture to confide in me?
THESEUS. Villain! How dare you come before me now?
Monster, the thunderbolt too long has spared!
Last of the brigands whom I swept away!
After the frenzy of your wicked lust
Has driven you to assault your father's bed,
You dare to show your hateful face to me,
Here in this place full of your infamy,
And seek not out, under an unknown sky,
Countries to which your fame has never spread.
Flee, villain, flee. Brave not my hatred here
Nor tempt my anger that I scarce restrain.
I have my portion of eternal shame
To have begot so criminal a son,
Without his death, disgrace to my renown,
Soiling the glory of my labours past.
Flee, and if you desire not to be joined
To all the villains fallen by my hand,
Take care that never does the shining sun
Behold you in these palaces again.
Flee then, and never more return;
And of your hideous presence purge my realm.
And, Neptune, in time past if my strong hand
Of infamous assassins cleared your shores,
Remember that, to recompense my deeds,
You swore to grant the first of my desires.
In the long hardships of a cruel gaol
I did not call on your immortal power;
With miser's care I put aside your aid,
Holding it in reserve for greater needs.
I call upon you now. Revenge my wrong.
I give this villain over to your wrath;
Drown in his blood his shameless foul desires.
Your favours will be measured by your rage.
HIPPOLYTUS. Phaedra accuses me of sinful love?
So infinite a horror numbs my soul,
So many unforeseen and heavy blows
Rain down upon me that I cannot speak.
THESEUS. Villain, you thought that Phaedra would conceal
In craven silence your vile insolence.
You should not, as you fled, have dropped the sword
That, in her hands, establishes your guilt.
Rather should you have crowned your perfidy
And at one stroke robbed her of speech and life.
HIPPOLYTUS. Rightly indignant at so black a lie,
I ought, my lord, to let the truth speak out,
But I will not resolve this mystery
Out of the deep respect that seals my lips.

And, if you will not deepen your distress,
Look at my life; remember who I am.
Some little crimes lead up to greater crimes.
Whoever goes beyond the bounds of law
Can in the end flout the most sacred rules.
No less than virtue, crime has its degrees,
And innocence has never yet been known
To swing at once to licence's extreme.
A single day cannot change virtuous men
To craven and incestuous murderers.
Reared by a virtuous Amazon from birth,
I never have belied my mother's blood.
Pittheus, esteemed the wisest far of men,
Instructed me after I left her hands.
I do not seek to paint myself too fair;
But, if one virtue is my birthright, that
Is above all, my lord, as I have shown,
Hate of the crime that they accuse me of.
That is what I am famous for in Greece.
I carried virtue to the sternest lengths,
My obdurate austerity is known;
The daylight is not purer than my heart.
Yet I, they say, fired by unholy love. . .

THESEUS. Yes, by that very pride you stand condemned.
The reason why you were so cold is clear;
Phaedra alone entranced your lustful eyes.
And, by all other charms unmoved, your heart
Disdained to glow with innocent desire.

HIPPOLYTUS. No, father, for this may not be concealed,
I have not scorned to glow with virtuous love,
And at your feet confess my real offence.
I am in love; in love despite your ban.
Aricia is mistress of my heart
And Pallas' daughter has subdued your son.
I worship her and, flouting your command,
For her alone I pine, I am consumed.

THESEUS. You love her? God! The ruse is gross indeed!
You feign to err to justify yourself.

HIPPOLYTUS. For half a year I have been deep in love.
Trembling, I came to tell you so myself.
What! Can no word of mine unseal your eyes?
What fearful oath, to move you, must I swear?
May heaven and earth and everything that is. . .

THESEUS. Foulness goes hand in hand with perjury.
Cease! Spare me an importunate harangue,
If your false virtue has no other stay.

HIPPOLYTUS. To you I may seem false and full of guile.
Phaedra does justice to me in her heart.

THESEUS. Ah! how my wrath grows at your shamelessness.

HIPPOLYTUS. What time and what the place of banishment?

THESEUS. Were you beyond Alcides' pillars,[26] still
Would I believe your villainy too near.
HIPPOLYTUS. Crushed by the crime that you suspect me of,
If you desert me who will pity me?
THESEUS. Go seek out friends who in their viciousness
Applaud adultery and incest. These
Villains and ingrates, lawless, honourless,
Will shelter evildoers such as you.
HIPPOLYTUS. You harp on incest and adultery.
I will say nought; but Phaedra, as you know,
My lord, is of a mother, of a line,
Richer in all these horrors than my own.
THESEUS. What! are there no bounds to your frantic rage?
For the last time, begone from out my sight.
Go, libertine, before a father's wrath
Has you with ignominy torn from hence.

SCENE THREE

THESEUS [*alone*]

THESEUS. Unhappy youth! Haste to your certain doom.
By the stream dreaded even of the gods
Neptune has given and will fulfill his word.
A god of vengeance follows hard on you.
I loved you and, in spite of your offence,
My heart is stirred for you forebodingly.
But you have forced me to pronounce your doom.
Was ever wretched father outraged so?
O God who see my overwhelming grief,
How could I have begot so foul a child?

SCENE FOUR

PHAEDRA THESEUS

PHAEDRA. My Lord, I come stricken with terror, for
Your dreaded voice has reached me and I fear
Your menace may be given prompt effect.
If it is not too late, then spare your son.
Respect your flesh and blood, I beg of you,
And save me from the horror of his cries.
Do not lay up for me the endless grief
Of causing bloodshed by a father's hand.
THESEUS. No, Queen, my hand has not bathed in his blood,
But still the villain will not now escape.
Immortal hands are with his ruin charged.

[26] The Pillars of Hercules, at the western end of the Mediterranean; hence any extremely remote locality.

This Neptune owes me. You will be avenged.
PHAEDRA. This Neptune owes you. What? Your anger calls. . .
THESEUS. How! You already fear I may be heard?
Rather unite your wishes with my own.
In all their heinousness depict his crimes;
Stir up my sluggish cold resentment, for
You do not know the measure of his crimes.
His fury showers affronts upon your name.
Your mouth, he says, speaks nothing but deceit;
He swears Aricia has won his heart,
And that he loves her.
PHAEDRA.
What!
THESEUS.
Those were his words.
But I am not the dupe of vain pretence.
Let us expect swift justice from the god.
I shall myself to Neptune's altars, there
To urge fulfilment of immortal oaths.

SCENE FIVE

PHAEDRA [*alone*]

PHAEDRA. He's gone. What tidings have assailed my ears!
What smouldering fire awakens in my heart!
God! What a thunderbolt! What baleful news!
Flying with but one thought to aid his son,
I tore myself from pale Oenone's arms,
Yielding to the remorse that tortured me.
Who knows how far repentance would have gone?
Perhaps I might even have accused myself?
Perhaps, had not my voice died in my throat,
The frightful truth would have escaped my lips.
Hippolytus can love but loves not me.
Aricia has won his heart, his troth.
Ah! when, inexorable to my pleas,
Hippolytus put on a front of steel,
I thought his heart for ever closed to love,
And against women all alike was armed.
Another none the less has conquered him.
She has found favour in his cruel eyes.
Perhaps he has a heart easy to move.
Alone of women me he cannot bear.
And I was hastening to his defence!

SCENE SIX

PHAEDRA OENONE

PHAEDRA. Oenone, do you know what I have heard?

OENONE. No, but I still am trembling, to be frank.
As you rushed forth, I blenched at your intent.
I was afraid you would destroy yourself.
PHAEDRA. Who would have thought it? There was someone else.
OENONE. What!
PHAEDRA.
Yes. Hippolytus is deep in love.
This shy, invincible antagonist,
Whom my respect displeased, my tears annoyed,
Whom I could never speak to unafraid,
Submissive, tamed, proclaims his own defeat.
Aricia is mistress of his heart.
OENONE. Aricia?
PHAEDRA.
Ah! unplumbed depths of woe!
For what new torments have I spared myself?
All I have suffered, jealous torments, fears,
Raging desire, the horror of remorse,
A cruel, harsh, intolerable slight,
Were a mere foretaste of my torments now.
They love each other. By what spell did they
Deceive me? How, where did they meet, since when?
You knew. Why did you let me be misled?
Why did you keep from me their stealthy love?
Were they seen oft exchanging looks and words?
Deep in the forests were they wont to hide?
Alas! They had the utmost liberty.
Heaven smiled upon their innocent desires.
They followed where love led them, conscience free.
For them the dawn rose shining and serene.
And I, rejected by all living things,
I hid myself from day, I shunned the light;
Death was the only god I dared invoke.
I waited for the moment of my end,
Feeding on gall and drinking deep of tears.
Too closely watched, I did not even dare
Give myself up in freedom to my grief.
Trembling, this baleful pleasure I enjoyed
And, cloaking with a feignéd calm my woes,
Was often driven to forego my tears.
OENONE. What good will their love do them? Never will
They meet again.
PHAEDRA.
Their love will always live.
Even as I speak, ah cruel, deadly thought!
They flout the fury of my insane rage.
Despite this exile which will sever them
They swear a thousand oaths never to part.
No. No. Their happiness is gall to me.
Oenone, pity my wild jealousy.

Aricia must perish, and the King
Be stirred to wrath against her odious race.
No trifling retribution will suffice.
The sister has outdone her brothers' crime.
I will implore him in my jealous rage.
What am I doing? I have lost my mind!
I, jealous? and 'tis Theseus I implore!
My husband is alive and yet I pine.
For whom? Whose heart have I been coveting?
At every word my hair stands up on end.
Henceforth the measure of my crimes is full.
I reek with foulest incest and deceit.
My hands, that strain for murder and revenge,
Burn with desire to plunge in guiltless blood.
Wretch! and I live and can endure the gaze
Of the most sacred sun from which I spring.
My grandsire is the lord of all the gods;
My forebears fill the sky, the universe.
Where can I hide? In dark infernal night?
No, there my father holds the urn of doom.
Destiny placed it in his ruthless hands.
Minos judges in hell the trembling dead.
Ah! how his horror-stricken shade will start
To see before him his own daughter stand,
Forced to admit to such a host of sins
And some, perhaps, unknown even in hell!
What, father, will you say to that dread sight?
I see your hand slip from the fateful urn;
I see you searching for new punishments,
Yourself your own kin's executioner.
Forgive me. Venus' wrath has doomed your race.
Your daughter's frenzy shows that vengeance forth.
Alas, my sad heart never has enjoyed
The fruits of crimes whose dark shame follows me.
Dogged by misfortune to my dying breath,
I end upon the rack a life of pain.

OENONE. Ah, Queen! dismiss these unbecoming fears,
And of your error take a different view.
You are in love. We cannot change our fate.
By destined magic you were swept along.
Is that so strange or so miraculous?
Has love then triumphed only over you?
Frailty is human and but natural.
Mortal, you must a mortal's lot endure.
This thraldom was imposed long, long ago.
The gods themselves that in Olympus dwell,
Who smite the evildoer with their bolt,
Have sometimes felt unlawful passions' fire.

PHAEDRA. Great gods! What counsels dare you offer me?
Even to the last you seek to poison me.

Wretch! Thus it is that you have caused my doom.
You, when I fled from life, you called me back;
At your entreaties duty was forgot;
It was *you* made me see Hippolytus.
You meddling fool. Why did your impious lips,
Falsely accusing him, besmirch his life?
You may have killed him, if the gods have heard
A maddened father's sacrilegious wish.
I'll hear no more. Hence, loathsome monster, hence.
Go, leave me to my pitiable fate.
May the just heavens reward you fittingly,
And may your punishment forever fright
All who, as you have done, by base deceit,
Pander to ill-starred princes' weaknesses,
Urging them on to yield to their desires,
And dare to smooth the path of crime for them,
Vile flatterers, the most ill-fated boon
The anger of the gods can make to kings!

OENONE. Ah God! to save her what have I not done;
But this is the reward I have deserved.

ACT FIVE

SCENE ONE

HIPPOLYTUS ARICIA

ARICIA. What, in this peril you refuse to speak?
You leave a loving father undeceived?
Cruel one, can you, by my tears unmoved,
Consent without a sigh to part from me?
Go hence and leave me to my grieving heart.
But, if you go, at least preserve your life.
Defend your honour from a foul reproach
And force your father to revoke your doom.
There still is time. Wherefore, from what caprice,
Will you let Phaedra's slander hold the field?
Tell Theseus all.

HIPPOLYTUS.
Ah, what have I not said?
Should I make known the outrage to his bed
And by an all too frank relation bring
Over my father's brow a blush of shame?
This odious secret you alone have pierced.
My sole confidants are the gods and you.
Judge of my love, I have not hid from you
All I desired to hide even from myself.
But, since you have been sworn to secrecy,
Forget, if it be possible, my words.
And never may your pure unsullied lips

Recount the details of this horrid scene.
Let's trust the justice of the gods above.
Their interest lies in vindicating me.
Sooner or later Phaedra will be brought
To book and meet an ignominious doom.
That is the only boon I ask of you.
My anger takes all other liberties.
Reject the bondage under which you pine;
Dare to accompany me in my flight.
Tear yourself free from an unhallowed spot
Where virtue breathes a foul, polluted air.
Let us to cover our escape exploit
The wild confusion that my downfall spreads.
I can provide you with the means for flight.
The only guards controlling you are mine.
Mighty defenders will take up our cause.
Argos awaits us; Sparta summons us.
Let's bear our grievance to our new allies.
Phaedra must never profit from our fall[27]
And drive us both from off my father's throne,
Making her son the heir to our estates.
Now is our chance. We must lay hands on it.
What holds you back? You seem to hesitate.
Only your interest thus emboldens me.
When I am ardent, why are you so cold?
Are you afraid to share an exile's lot?

ARICIA. Alas! How pleasant to be banished thus!
With what delight, linking my fate with yours,
By all the world forgotten I would live!
But, since we are not joined by that sweet bond,
Could I in honour flee from here with you?
I know that, even by the strictest code,
I may throw off your father's tutelage.
No bond of home or parents holds me back,
And flight from tyrants is permissible.
You love me, though, my lord, and my good name. . .

HIPPOLYTUS. No. No. Your honour is too dear to me.
I come before you with a nobler plan.
Flee from my foes. Flee as my wedded wife.
Alone in exile, since heaven wills it so,
We need no man's consent to pledge our faith.
Not always torches blaze for Hymen's rites.
Not far from Troezen's gates, among these tombs,
My princely forebears' ancient burial place,
There stands a shrine dreaded of perjurers.
There mortals never swear an oath in vain.
Who breaks his word is punished instantly,

[27] i.e., profit by obtaining the kingdom which normally would have gone to Hippolytus and Aricia.

And men forsworn, afraid of certain death,
Are held in check by this most dreaded threat.
There, if you trust me, we will ratify
By solemn oath our everlasting love,
Taking to witness this old temple's god.
We'll pray him to be father to us both.
I'll call to witness the most sacred gods,
And chaste Diana, Juno the august,
And all the gods, witnesses of my love,
Will lend their blessing to my holy vows.

ARICIA. The King is coming. Flee, make haste. To cloak
My own departure, I will stay awhile.
Go now, but leave me someone I can trust
To lead my steps to the appointed place.

SCENE TWO

THESEUS ARICIA ISMENE

THESEUS. O God! lighten the darkness of my mind.
Show me the truth that I am searching for.

ARICIA. Make ready, dear Ismene, for our flight.

SCENE THREE

THESEUS ARICIA

THESEUS. Your colour changes and you seem aghast,
Lady. What was the young prince doing here?

ARICIA. My lord, he took eternal leave of me.

THESEUS. You have subdued that proud rebellious heart,
And his first raptures were inspired by you.

ARICIA. My lord, I cannot well deny the truth.
Your unjust hatred is not shared by him.
He did not treat me like a criminal.

THESEUS. I know. He swore eternal love to you.
Do not rely on that inconstant heart,
For he to others swore the self same oaths.

ARICIA. He, Sire?

THESEUS.
You ought to have restrained him. How
Could you endure to share his fickle heart?

ARICIA. And how could you allow such calumny
To tarnish the bright glory of his life?
Have you so little knowledge of his heart?
Can you not tell baseness from innocence?
Must from your eyes alone an odious cloud
Conceal his virtues which shine bright to all?
I cannot let him further be maligned.
Stop and repent of your assassin's prayer.

Fear, my lord, fear lest the unbending heavens
Hate you enough to grant you your desire.
Oft in their wrath they take our sacrifice.
Often their gifts are sent to scourge our sins.
THESEUS. In vain you seek to cover his offence.
Your passion blinds you to his faults. But I
Have faith in sure, trustworthy witnesses.
I have seen tears which surely were not feigned.
ARICIA. Take care, my lord. Invincible, your hands
Have freed the world from monsters numberless;
But all are not destroyed. You still let live
One . . . But your son forbids me to proceed.
Knowing his wishes, I respect you still.
I would but grieve him if I dared to speak.
Following his restraint, I will withdraw
Rather than let the truth escape my lips.

SCENE FOUR
THESEUS [*alone*]

THESEUS. What does she mean, and what do these words hide,
Begun and broken off, begun again?
Is it their aim to trick me by a feint?
Are they in league to put me on the rack?
But I myself, despite my stern resolve,
What plaintive voice cries in my inmost heart?
A lurking flash of pity harrows me.
I'll have Oenone questioned once again;
I must have more light thrown upon the crime.
Guards, bring Oenone out to me alone.

SCENE FIVE
THESEUS PANOPE

PANOPE. I do not know what the Queen purposes,
But her distraction is a fearful sight.
Mortal despair cries from her haggard face,
And death has laid its paleness on her cheeks.
Oenone, driven out with shame, has plunged
Already into the unsounded sea.
We do not know what led her to this death;
The waves have closed for ever over her.
THESEUS. What?
PANOPE.
This dark action did not calm the Queen.
Distraction seems to swell her wavering heart.
Sometimes, to soothe her secret sufferings,
She takes her children, bathes them in her tears;

Then, suddenly, renouncing mother's love,
Shuddering with horror, will have none of them.
This way and that, she wanders aimlessly;
Wildly she looks at us, but knows us not.
She thrice has written, then has changed her mind,
And thrice torn up the letter she began.
See her, we beg you. We implore your help.

THESEUS. Oenone's dead, and Phaedra seeks to die.
Call back my son, let him defend himself
And speak to me! I'll lend a willing ear.
[*Alone.*]
Do not be overhasty with your gifts,
Neptune! I wish my prayer may not be heard.
Perhaps I have believed false witnesses,
Lifting too soon my cruel hand to you.
Ah! if you act, what will be my despair!

SCENE SIX

THESEUS THERAMENES

THESEUS. What have you done with him, Theramenes?
I put him as a boy into your hands.
But why the tears that trickle down your cheeks?
What of my son?

THERAMENES.
O tardy vain concern!
O unavailing love! Your son's no more.

THESEUS. God!

THERAMENES.
I have seen the best of mortals die,
And the most innocent, I dare to add.

THESEUS. Dead? When I open wide my arms to him,
The gods, impatient, hasten on his death?
What blow, what thunderbolt snatched him away?

THERAMENES. Scarce were we issuing from Troezen's gates;
He drove his chariot; round about him ranged,
Copying his silence, were his cheerless guards.
Pensive, he followed the Mycenae road,
And let the reins hang loose upon his steeds.
These haughty steeds, that once upon a time,
Noble, high-spirited, obeyed his voice,
Now dull of eye and with dejected air
Seemed to conform to his despondent thoughts.
A ghastly cry from out the water's depths
That moment rent the quiet of the air.
From the earth's entrails then a fearful voice
Made answer with a groan to that dread cry.
Deep in our hearts our blood with horror froze.
The coursers' manes, on hearing, stood erect.

And now, there rose upon the liquid plain
A watery mountain seething furiously.
The surge drew near, dissolved and vomited
A raging monster from among the foam.
His forehead huge was armed with fearsome horns
And his whole body sheathed in yellow scales,
Half bull, half dragon, wild, impetuous.
His crupper curved in many a winding fold.
The shore quaked with his long-drawn bellowings.
The heavens beheld the monster, horror-struck;
It poisoned all the air; it rocked the earth.
The wave that brought it in recoiled aghast.
Everyone, throwing courage to the winds,
Took refuge in the temple near at hand.
Hippolytus alone, undaunted, stayed,
Reined in his steeds and seized his javelins,
Had at the monster and, with sure-flung dart,
Dealt him a gaping wound deep in his flank.
With rage and pain the monster, starting up,
Collapsed and, falling at the horses' feet,
Rolled over, opening wide his flaming jaws,
And covered them with smoke and blood and fire.
Carried away by terror, deaf, the steeds
No more responded to his curb or voice.
Their master spent his efforts all in vain.
They stained the bridle with their bloody foam.
In this wild tumult, it is even said,
A god appeared, goading their dusty flanks.
Over the rocks fear drove them headlong on;
The axle groaned and broke. Hippolytus
Saw his whole chariot shattered into bits.
He fell at last, entangled in the reins.
Forgive my grief. For me this picture spells
Eternal sorrow and perpetual tears.
I have beheld, my lord, your ill-starred son
Dragged by the horses that his hand had fed.
His voice that called them merely frightened them.
Onward they flew—his body one whole wound.
The plain resounded with our cries of woe.
At last they slackened their impetuous course.
They halted near the old ancestral tombs
Where all his royal forebears lie in state.
I and his guards hastened to him in tears.
The traces of his blood showed us the way.
The rocks were stained with it, the cruel thorns
Dripped with the bleeding remnants of his hair.
I saw him, called him; giving me his hand,
He opened, then that moment closed, his eyes.
"Heaven takes my life, though innocent," he cried.
"When I am dead, protect Aricia.

Friend, if my father ever learns the truth,
And pities the misfortunes of his son,
And would appease me in the life to come,
Tell him to show that princess clemency,
To give her back. . . ." And then he passed away,
And in my arms lay a disfigured corpse,
A tribute to the anger of the gods
That even his father would not recognize.

THESEUS. My son, fond hope I have myself destroyed!
Inexorable, all too helpful gods!
What keen remorse will haunt me all my life!

THERAMENES. Aricia then came upon the scene.
She came, my lord, fleeing your royal wrath,
Before the gods to pledge her faith to him.
As she drew near, she saw the reeking grass.
She saw, a grim sight for a lover's eyes,
Hippolytus, disfigured, deadly pale.
A while she tried to doubt her evil fate.
She sees the body of Hippolytus,
Yet still pursues the quest for her beloved.
But, in the end, only too sure 'tis he,
With one sad look, accusing heaven's spite,
Cold, moaning, and well nigh inanimate,
She falls, unconscious, at her sweetheart's feet.
Ismene, bending over her, in tears,
Summons her back to life, a life of pain.
And I have come, my lord, hating the world,
To tell you of Hippolytus' last wish
And to discharge the bitter embassy
Which he entrusted to me as he died.
But hither comes his deadly enemy.

SCENE SEVEN

THESEUS PHAEDRA THERAMENES
PANOPE GUARDS

THESEUS. Well, then, you triumph and my son's no more.
What grounds I have for fear! What cruel doubt
Gnaws at my heart, pleading his innocence!
But he is dead. Accept your victim. Joy
In his undoing, justified or no,
For I am willing to deceive myself.
Since you accuse him, I accept his guilt.
His death will make my tears flow fast enough
Without my seeking for enlightenment
Which could not ever bring him back to me
And might perhaps but sharpen my distress.
Let me flee, far from you and from these shores,
The bloody vision of my mangled son.

Stunned and pursued by this grim memory,
Would I were in another universe!
Everything seems to brand my wicked wrath.
My very name increases my despair.
Less known of mortals, I could hide myself.
I hate even the favours of the gods.
And now I must bewail their murderous gifts,
No longer tiring them with fruitless prayers.
Whatever they have done for me, their aid
Cannot give back what they have robbed me of.

PHAEDRA. No, Theseus. No, I must at last speak out.
I must redress the wrong I did your son,
For he was innocent,

THESEUS.
Wretch that I am!
If I condemned him, it was on your word.
Cruel one, do you hope to be forgiven. . .

PHAEDRA. Each moment's precious. Listen. It was I,
Theseus, who on your virtuous, filial son
Made bold to cast a lewd, incestuous eye.
Heaven in my heart lit an ill-omened fire.
Detestable Oenone did the rest.
She feared your son, knowing my frenzy, might
Reveal a guilty passion he abhorred.
The wretch, exploiting my enfeebled state,
Rushed to denounce Hippolytus to you.
She has exacted justice on herself
And found beneath the waves too mild a death.
By now I would have perished by the sword,
But first I wished to clear my victim's name.
I wished, revealing my remorse to you,
To choose a slower road down to the dead.
I have instilled into my burning veins
A poison that Medea brought to Greece.[28]
Already it has reached my heart and spread
A strange chill through my body. Even now
Only as through a cloud I see the bright
Heaven and the husband whom I still defile.
But death, robbing my eyes of light, will give
Back to the sun its tarnished purity.

PANOPE. Ah! she is dying.

THESEUS.
Would the memory
Of her appalling misdeeds die with her!
Let us, now that my error's all too clear,

[28] Medea, princess of Colchis, helped Jason win the Golden Fleece and fled with him. When Jason lost interest in her and wanted to marry Creusa, Medea, who had powers of sorcery, sent her a gown that burned her to death. She then killed her own children and escaped to Athens.

Go out and mourn over my ill-starred son.
Let us embrace my cherished son's remains
And expiate my mad atrocious wish,
Rendering him the honours he deserves,
And, to appease the anger of his shade,
Let his beloved, despite her brothers' crime,
Be as a daughter to me from this day.

Jonathan Swift

(1667–1745)

The most powerful English satirist in an age of great satire, Jonathan Swift was also a dedicated clergyman, a political journalist, an accomplished poet, and a master of English prose style whose interest in language reflects his attitude toward the integrity or corruption of society. He was born in 1667 in Dublin, a descendant of a family that had supported the monarchy in the English civil wars of the mid-seventeenth century. His father died before Jonathan was born. Supported by uncles, he attended Kilkenny, an excellent school, and then Trinity College, Dublin, where he had a mediocre career as a student. Because of the disturbances in Ireland following on the English revolution of 1688, Swift emigrated to England, where in 1689 he became secretary in the household of Sir William Temple, a writer and retired diplomat, with whom Swift spent the greater part of the next ten years. There Swift met a young girl named Esther Johnson (the "Stella" to whom he later wrote a series of engrossing letters). Swift's subsequent relationship with her is still mysterious. He may have married her, but if so the marriage was not consummated, possibly (to cite one of several speculations on the matter) because of a blood kinship between the two. In 1692 Swift took a master's degree from Oxford, and in 1695 he was ordained a priest of the Anglican church of Ireland. He read a good deal while he was with Temple and embarked there on his literary career. After some early experiments in the Pindaric ode, which were discouraged by the poet John Dryden, he adopted a drier and more direct poetic style closer to the mordant prose that would become characteristic of him.

During this decade he also began work on two early satiric masterpieces in prose: A Tale of a Tub *and* The Battle of the Books. *These works, published together in 1704, illustrate the conservative bent that Swift shares with many other great satirists. The former is a dazzling, difficult, kaleidoscopic work attacking religious, scientific, and scholarly corruptions, including what seemed to Swift an illusory theory of human progress and modernist forms of rationalism. (Swift believed strongly in the value of reason, but he hated abstract and metaphysical systems.)* The Battle of the Books *is a mock epic in which Swift sides with the "ancients," who favored the "old" learning and especially the classics, in a contemporary debate between them and the "moderns," who resisted intellectual authority and tended to champion the new science. A famous passage in* The Battle *compares the moderns to the spider, absorbed in itself and producing only excrement and venom, whereas the ancients are like the bee, bringing home from its wide-ranging flights honey and wax and thus producing "the two noblest of things, which are sweetness and light."*

After Temple's death, Swift went through several years of unsettledness. He lived partly in Ireland and partly in England, where he began to acquire some prestige and fame, although his hopes for a high appointment in the Church were frustrated. He associated with prominent Whigs including the essayists Addison and Steele and the playwright Congreve. But, although Swift was still a Whig and supported the Whig position that royal power must be balanced by parliament, he was uncomfortable with that party's encouragement of religious Dissenters. In 1710 he shifted his allegiance to the Tories, who were then in power. Swift soon became their foremost political journalist. He also became part of the "Scriblerus Club," a group of brilliant Tory wits that included Alexander Pope and the dramatist John Gay. Some years later, in 1728, Swift helped inspire Pope's satire The Dunciad *and Gay's* The Beggar's Opera.

This period, the height of Swift's political influence, ended in 1714 with the death of Queen Anne and the overthrow of the Tories. Although disappointed in his desire for a deanery in England, Swift was named in 1713 dean of St. Patrick's Cathedral in Dublin. He spent most of the rest of his life in Ireland. There, after a period of discouragement, he resumed his political writing, attacking the Whigs and defending the Irish against oppressive English economic policy. His Drapier's Letters *(1724–25) brought charges of sedition against him, but he was now a hero of the Irish and, although known to have written the work, was not prosecuted. The best known today of his pieces about the Irish is the brief, brilliant tract* A Modest Proposal *(1729), a parody of social scientism that turns on its head the economic theory that the wealth of a nation lies in its population. Swift's calculating, "public-spirited" persona recommends a scheme of cannibalism of Irish children that is symbolically the equivalent of what was actually happening to them and their parents.*

Despite a fallacious tradition that Swift was uncontrollably irascible and even mad, his mental powers remained firm until his very last years, and he received public honors in Ireland as late as 1739. He later suffered a stroke, and in 1742 he had to be entrusted to guardians. He died in Dublin in 1745. The epitaph he composed for himself was later rendered as follows by the great modern Anglo-Irishman William Butler Yeats:

Swift has sailed into his rest;
Savage indignation there
Cannot lacerate his breast.
Imitate him if you dare,
World-besotted traveller; he
Served human liberty.

Gulliver's Travels, *Swift's greatest work, was begun around 1720 and published in 1726. It was brought out anonymously, or rather as the work of Lemuel Gulliver himself. It was an immediate success with all manner of readers. A famous anecdote cites an Irish bishop who declared that it was "full of improbable lies, and for his part he hardly believed a word of it"—a strangely oblique acknowledgment of an ingenious circumstantial realism in the book that has made it popular as early science fiction and (in cut versions) as a children's fantasy. Its meticulous factuality owes something to the many travel books that, among other things, it satirizes. It also owes something to the genres of allegory and beast fable; "philosophical voyages" that took an admiring primitivist view of non-European peoples; utopias; and sermon literature of the day that dwelt on the fallen corruption of mankind. The rhetorical forms of irony understatement, exaggeration, sarcasm, the bland utterance of shocking statements, the assumption that the reasonable is outrageous or vice versa—succeed one another, often without transition, so that the reader's mental nimbleness is continually tested. The satiric strategy, even when it springs from essentially simple devices, is equally versatile. Size, in itself and as a metaphor, is used tellingly in Parts I and II, the visits to Lilliput and Brobdingnag, realizing in literal terms psychological associations with size that are half-latent in our vocabulary ("magnanimous," "small-minded"). Thus, the literally petite Lilliputians often (though not always) seem mentally petty too, whereas the big Brobdingnagians often (though not always) seem broad-minded. Physically, on the other hand, the Lilliputians, who can be seen only from a "distance," are more attractive than the giants, whose coarse skin and body hairs (our own, of course) can be seen "close up." The metaphor of seeing is, in fact, used repeatedly and intricately. The slipperiness of the satire can be seen also in the episode of the Grand Academy of Lagado in Part III, where we are first drawn into feeling contempt for the scientists' insane experiments and immediately afterward see their colleagues pursuing even more ludicrous schemes such as rewarding integrity and altruism in politics.*

Much of the book's satire reaches us indirectly, through the medium of Gulliver's mind and personality. An avidly curious observer and a dutiful reporter of what he encounters, Gulliver remains essentially impressionable and naive in his value judgments. But that general fact about him does not by any means solve all our problems with the satire, for he is just as protean as everything else in the book. At times he merely reports without reaction what ought to stir a strong response in him, and when he does respond he is frequently out of phase (though in unpredictable ways) with the moral judgment expected of the reader. He can accept enormities without blinking and can defend the indefensible. He is especially good at missing connections. The unbending dogmatist whom we see after his return from Houyhnhnmland is the same man who can say of the ill-fated Captain Pocock: "He was an honest man, and a good sailor, but a little too positive in his own opinions, which was the cause of his destruction, as it hath been of several others" (IV, Chapter 1). Lest we miss this irony, we have Gulliver's letter to Cousin Sympson in which Gulliver complains that even "after above six months' warning" the evils of the human race have not been totally cured by his book. Perhaps more than anything else, it is the distance between Gulliver's judgment (or his failure to make one) and our own that marks the effect and intensity of the satire.

It is ironic, then, and an index to fluctuations in senses of humor, that for the better part of two centuries readers have often identified Gulliver's judgment of the Houyhnhnms and yahoos with Swift's. Although no reader could have missed the satiric intent of at least parts of Gulliver's Travels, *it was first enjoyed largely for its wit and inventiveness. Before long, though, readers began to find in the book a repellent misanthropy (an especially serious evil by the standards of Swift's contemporaries) and later the signs of a seriously deranged mind. The most extreme formulation of this judgment on Swift was that of the Victorian novelist Thackeray: "a monster gibbering shrieks and gnashing imprecations against mankind—tearing down all shreds of modesty, past all sense of manliness and shame; filthy in word, filthy in thought, furious, raging, obscene." The occasions for charges in this vein include occasional ribaldry and misogyny, as well as Swift's so-called "excremental vision"; but the crux of the matter is his treatment of the yahoos and Houyhnhnms. The nauseating yahoos, it is assumed, are Swift's considered picture of humanity, set off by the sober, reasonable, and admirable horses. In the last fifty years or so, most authorities on Swift have repudiated this view as wrong or at best simplistic. They point to the book's comic tone and to the character Gulliver's limitations and errors—for example, his condescension toward the humane captain Don Pedro de Mendez, the obtuseness of the final, prideful attack on pride, and ludicrous details such as Gulliver's acquired habit of conversing with his horses.*

This corrective view of the book has been widely, if not universally, accepted. But no one wants to deny that Part IV is satire, like the earlier parts, and the question is "On what?" One possibility is to see the yahoos as a symbolic extreme, derived partly from the tradition of Christian sermons on fallen man, representing the bestiality and decay of reason in the fallen state, and the Houyhnhnms as equally extreme in their rationalism without Christian charity, the real human being lying somewhere between and possibly above both. The comic touches in the descriptions of the Houyhnhnms—their threading of needles, for example—may hint at a deeper critique of them: in their coldness and rigidity they may be a hostile caricature of the thoroughgoing rationalistic ideal of benevolent natural mankind espoused by deists and freethinkers. Or the Houyhnhnms may be a positive but still limited ideal, implying that if human beings were truly rational and not merely capable *of reason they might be imperfect but would at least avoid the worst excesses of their passions (the yahoos) and of their perversions of reason (European man). And many other readings are possible.*

Welcome though such corrective modern interpretations are, it can be objected that they tend to make Swift seem too blandly normal. Granted that Gulliver's Travels *is funny, it still seems impossible to regard the fourth part as primarily comedy. And the explanations of his satire as fundamentally an expression of values current in his time may seem to deny the unique energy, passion, and urgency that make* Gulliver's Travels *so powerful a work. It seems certain that the debate about it, and especially about Part IV, will continue.*

FURTHER READING *(prepared by W. J. R.):* Carl Van Doren's *Swift,* 1930, is a highly readable biographical introduction; somewhat more extensive is A. L. Rowse's generously illustrated *Jonathan Swift,* 1975. An excellent survey of Swift's major works can be found in Ricardo Quintana's *Swift: An Introduction,* 1955, especially helpful on Lemuel Gulliver and Swift's career. Another good survey appears in Robert Hunting's *Jonathan Swift,* 1967. William A. Eddy's *"Gulliver's Travels": A Critical Study,* 1923, rpt. 1963, examines each of the four voyages separately and discusses the influence of *Gulliver's Travels* on later eighteenth-century literature. John M. Bullitt's *Jonathan Swift and the Anatomy of Satire,* 1961, discusses technical accomplishments in Swift's satire, approaching the satiric devices as an organic outgrowth of Swift's perception of the human condition. Claude J. Rawson's *Gulliver and the Gentle Reader: Studies in Swift and Our Time,* 1973, is a provocative study of Swift and modern literature. Rawson devotes one section of this work to examining how Swift anticipates the techniques of Mailer, Ionesco, and other contemporary writers. Herbert Davis's *Jonathan Swift: Essays on His Satire and Other Studies,* 1964, is a particularly good collection of critical essays.

GULLIVER'S TRAVELS

SUMMARY OF PARTS I, II, AND III

PART I. Lemuel Gulliver is an English physician who, after unsuccessful attempts to practice medicine at home, sails as a ship's doctor. A storm destroys his ship, and Gulliver has to swim for his life to a nearby coast, where he falls asleep in exhaustion. When he awakes, he finds himself surrounded by the Lilliputians, people six inches tall, who have tied him down with ropes, which to Gulliver are threads. Given drugged wine, Gulliver falls asleep again, after which the little people load him onto a platform and with 1,500 tiny horses haul him to the capital. There he is lodged snugly in what for Lilliput is a vast building. Gulliver learns the language, becomes more at home, and is allowed some freedom to move about in a country that proves to have many similarities (which Swift exploits for satiric purposes) to England, especially in politics and religion. The effect is to make the supposedly momentous events of European history seem trivial. In some respects, however, the Lilliputian ways and institutions seem admirable.

Gulliver aids the Lilliputians in their war with the neighboring island of Blefuscu (representing France), wading across the intervening channel and single-handedly towing away the enemy fleet of tiny ships. Gulliver is honored by the Lilliputian emperor but later falls out with him over Gulliver's unwillingness to destroy and enslave Blefuscu. Amid much court intrigue, Gulliver is charged with treason and threatened with the loss of his eyesight. He goes to Blefuscu and is received cordially. While there, he finds a human-size small boat that has been washed ashore. Aided by a vast number of Blefuscu craftsmen, he refits the boat, sets out to sea, and is picked up by an English ship, which takes him home. Gulliver is able to vouch for and profit from his amazing adventure through displaying some tiny cattle he has brought away with him.

PART II. After two months at home, Gulliver goes to sea again. A storm takes the ship far off its course. Gulliver goes ashore with a foraging party in a land we later learn is called Brobdingnag. He strays from his comrades and is abandoned by them when they have to row for safety from a gigantic human being who pursues them. Gulliver hides like a small insect in a giant-scale wheat field but is discovered by a sixty-foot-tall farm laborer, who carries him to the landowner's house. Gulliver becomes a kind of toy there and is entrusted to the care of the farmer's nine-year-old daughter. He learns the giants' language. The farmer makes money by displaying his tiny curiosity, taking him to the metropolis for this purpose. After Gulliver's health begins to suffer, the farmer sells him to the queen, the farmer's daughter being retained as his guardian and nurse. He finds himself constantly beset with dangers from normally small creatures like wasps that in Brobdingnag are enormous. Conversing with the king, Gulliver loyally and proudly describes civilization and what we know to be its evils. The king, representing in his size a moral perspective larger than Gulliver's, concludes that Gulliver's race are "the most pernicious race of little odious vermin that nature ever suffered to crawl upon the surface of the earth."

A "little" box is constructed in which Gulliver can be carried around. During a visit to the seacoast, he and his box are carried off by a giant bird, which later drops them into the ocean. Gulliver is rescued by a ship bound for England; there he finds it hard to adjust to life among such "tiny" men as his countrymen.

PART III. Bored in England, Gulliver once more goes to sea, this time to Indo-China. From there he sets out on a trading excursion to the nearby islands. He is captured by pirates who then abandon him in a small boat, in which he reaches an uninhabited island. One day he sights overhead the flying island named Laputa; the inhabitants spot Gulliver and draw him aboard. The ruling-class men of Laputa (unlike the servants and women, who are much earthier and more normal) are an excessively intellectual people, interested only in the theoretical subtleties of mathematics, science, and music. They are so absent-minded that they must have their servants cue them when it is their turn to reply in a conversation with one another. They also terrorize the regions they control on the earth below by hurling down large stones or threatening to let the island drop on them.

When the flying island reaches the country of Balnibarbi, Gulliver gets permission to visit it. There he inspects the Grand Academy of Lagado, a parody of the Royal Society, an association of English scientists. The experimenters in the Academy are engaged in such lunatic schemes as trying to extract sunbeams from cucumbers and to construct buildings from the top down. At the same time the social scientists are engaged in equally "absurd" schemes—for example, choosing political leaders on the basis of their devotion to the public good.

Gulliver visits Glubbdubdrib, a land of magicians. The ghosts of the illustrious dead are conjured up, and Gulliver learns from them, among other things, how false and flattering history books are. Moving on to Luggnagg, he is shown the struldbruggs, who will never die. Gulliver's admiration and enthusiasm over these immortals cease when he finds that they nevertheless continue to age throughout their endless lives.

Finally, Gulliver arrives in Japan, where he finds a ship to take him back to England.

PART IV: A VOYAGE TO THE COUNTRY OF THE HOUYHNHNMS.

CHAPTER I

The author sets out as captain of a ship. His men conspire against him, confine him a long time to his cabin, set him on shore in an unknown land. He travels up in the country. The yahoos, a strange sort of animal, described. The author meets two Houyhnhnms.

I continued at home with my wife and children about five months in a very happy condition, if I could have learned the lesson of knowing when I was well. I left my poor wife big with child, and accepted an advantageous offer made me to be captain of the *Adventure,* a stout merchantman of 350 tons: for I understood navigation well, and being grown weary of a surgeon's employment at sea, which however I could exercise upon occasion, I took a skilful young man of that calling, one Robert Purefoy, into my ship. We set sail from Portsmouth[1] upon the 7th day of September, 1710;[2] on the 14th, we met with Captain Pocock of Bristol, at Tenariff, who was going to the bay of Campechy, to cut logwood.[3] On the 16th, he was parted from us by a storm; I heard since my return that his ship foundered, and none es-

[1] A port on the south coast of England. [2] Gulliver's age is now forty-nine.

[3] Tenariff is the largest of the Canary Islands, off northwest Africa. The bay of Campechy is the southern part of the Gulf of Mexico, off Yucatan. Logwood is a Central American tree from which a dye is derived.

caped, but one cabin-boy. He was an honest man, and a good sailor, but a little too positive in his own opinions, which was the cause of his destruction, as it hath been of several others. For if he had followed my advice, he might at this time have been safe at home with his family as well as myself.

I had several men died in my ship of calentures,[4] so that I was forced to get recruits out of Barbadoes, and the Leeward Islands,[5] where I touched by the direction of the merchants who employed me, which I had soon too much cause to repent; for I found afterwards that most of them had been buccaneers.[6] I had fifty hands on board, and my orders were, that I should trade with the Indians in the South Sea, and make what discoveries I could. These rogues whom I had picked up debauched my other men, and they all formed a conspiracy to seize the ship and secure me; which they did one morning, rushing into my cabin, and binding me hand and foot, threatening to throw me overboard, if I offered to stir. I told them, I was their prisoner, and would submit. This they made me swear to do, and then unbound me, only fastening one of my legs with a chain near my bed, and placed a sentry at my door with his piece[7] charged, who was commanded to shoot me dead if I attempted my liberty. They sent me down victuals and drink, and took the government of the ship to themselves. Their design was to turn pirates, and plunder the Spaniards, which they could not do till they got more men. But first they resolved to sell the goods in the ship, and then go to Madagascar[8] for recruits, several among them having died since my confinement. They sailed many weeks, and traded with the Indians, but I knew not what course they took, being kept close prisoner in my cabin, and expecting nothing less than to be murdered, as they often threatened me.

Upon the 9th day of May, 1711, one James Welch came down to my cabin; and said he had orders from the captain to set me ashore. I expostulated with him, but in vain; neither would he so much as tell me who their new captain was. They forced me into the long-boat, letting me put on my best suit of clothes, which were as good as new, and a small bundle of linen, but no arms except my hanger;[9] and they were so civil as not to search my pockets, into which I conveyed what money I had, with some other little necessaries. They rowed about a league, and then set me down on a strand.[10] I desired them to tell me what country it was. They all swore, they knew no more than myself, but said, that the captain (as they called him) was resolved, after they had sold the lading,[11] to get rid of me in the first place where they discovered land. They pushed off immediately, advising me to make haste, for fear of being overtaken by the tide, and bade me farewell.

In this desolate condition I advanced forward, and soon got upon firm ground, where I sat down on a bank to rest myself, and consider what I had

[4] Delirious tropical fever or sunstroke. [5] Islands in the West Indies.

[6] Seventeenth-century pirates frequenting the West Indies. The occasions for Gulliver's adventures are progressively more evil in the four Parts: in I he was shipwrecked; in II he was left behind when his shipmates had to flee to save themselves; in III he was captured by pirates; in IV he is the victim of treachery.

[7] Firearm. [8] A large island off southeastern Africa, now the Malagasy Republic.

[9] A small sword hanging from the belt. [10] Beach. [11] Cargo.

best to do. When I was a little refreshed I went up into the country, resolving to deliver myself to the first savages I should meet, and purchase my life from them by some bracelets, glass rings, and other toys, which sailors usually provide themselves with in those voyages, and whereof I had some about me: the land was divided by long rows of trees, not regularly planted, but naturally growing; there was great plenty of grass, and several fields of oats. I walked very circumspectly for fear of being surprised, or suddenly shot with an arrow from behind or on either side. I fell into a beaten road, where I saw many tracks of human feet, and some of cows, but most of horses. At last I beheld several animals in a field, and one or two of the same kind sitting in trees. Their shape was very singular, and deformed, which a little discomposed me, so that I lay down behind a thicket to observe them better. Some of them coming forward near the place where I lay, gave me an opportunity of distinctly marking their form. Their heads and breasts were covered with a thick hair, some frizzled and others lank; they had beards like goats, and a long ridge of hair down their backs, and the foreparts of their legs and feet, but the rest of their bodies were bare, so that I might see their skins, which were of a brown buff colour. They had no tails, nor any hair at all on their buttocks, except about the anus; which, I presume, nature had placed there to defend them as they sat on the ground; for this posture they used, as well as lying down, and often stood on their hind feet. They climbed high trees, as nimbly as a squirrel, for they had strong extended claws before and behind, terminating in sharp points, and hooked. They would often spring, and bound, and leap with prodigious agility. The females were not so large as the males; they had long lank hair on their heads, and only a sort of down on the rest of their bodies, except about the anus, and pudenda. Their dugs[12] hung between their fore-feet, and often reached almost to the ground as they walked. The hair of both sexes was of several colours, brown, red, black, and yellow. Upon the whole, I never beheld in all my travels so disagreeable an animal, or one against which I naturally conceived so strong antipathy. So that thinking I had seen enough, full of contempt and aversion, I got up and pursued the beaten road, hoping it might direct me to the cabin of some Indian. I had not gone far when I met one of these creatures full in my way, and coming up directly to me. The ugly monster, when he saw me, distorted several ways every feature of his visage, and stared as at an object he had never seen before; then approaching nearer, lifted up his forepaw, whether out of curiosity or mischief, I could not tell. But I drew my hanger, and gave him a good blow with the flat side of it, for I durst not strike him with the edge, fearing the inhabitants might be provoked against me, if they should come to know that I had killed or maimed any of their cattle. When the beast felt the smart, he drew back, and roared so loud, that a herd of at least forty came flocking about me from the next field, howling and making odious faces; but I ran to the body of a tree, and leaning my back against it, kept them off, by waving my hanger. Several of this cursed brood getting hold of the branches behind leaped up into the tree, from whence they began to discharge their excrements on my head: however, I escaped

[12] Breasts.

pretty well, by sticking close to the stem of a tree, but was almost stifled with the filth, which fell about me on every side.

In the midst of this distress, I observed them all to run away on a sudden as fast as they could, at which I ventured to leave the tree, and pursue the road, wondering what it was that could put them into this fright. But looking on my left hand, I saw a horse walking softly in the field, which my persecutors having sooner discovered, was the cause of their flight. The horse started a little when he came near me, but soon recovering himself, looked full in my face with manifest tokens of wonder: he viewed my hands and feet, walking round me several times. I would have pursued my journey, but he placed himself directly in the way, yet looking with a very mild aspect, never offering the least violence. We stood gazing at each other for some time; at last I took the boldness to reach my hand towards his neck, with a design to stroke it, using the common style and whistle of jockeys when they are going to handle a strange horse. But this animal, seeming to receive my civilities with disdain, shook his head, and bent his brows, softly raising up his left forefoot to remove my hand. Then he neighed three or four times, but in so different a cadence, that I almost began to think he was speaking to himself in some language of his own.

While he and I were thus employed, another horse came up; who applying himself to the first in a very formal manner, they gently struck each other's right hoof before, neighing several times by turns, and varying the sound, which seemed to be almost articulate. They went some paces off, as if it were to confer together, walking side by side, backward and forward, like persons deliberating upon some affair of weight, but often turning their eyes towards me, as it were to watch that I might not escape. I was amazed to see such actions and behaviour in brute beasts, and concluded with myself, that if the inhabitants of this country were endued with a proportionable degree of reason, they must needs be the wisest people upon earth. This thought gave me so much comfort, that I resolved to go forward until I could discover some house or village, or meet with any of the natives, leaving the two horses to discourse together as they pleased. But the first, who was a dapple grey, observing me to steal off, neighed after me in so expressive a tone, that I fancied myself to understand what he meant; whereupon I turned back, and came near him, to expect[13] his farther commands. But concealing my fear as much as I could, for I began to be in some pain, how this adventure might terminate; and the reader will easily believe I did not much like my present situation.

The two horses came up close to me, looking with great earnestness upon my face and hands. The grey steed rubbed my hat all round with his right fore-hoof, and discomposed it so much, that I was forced to adjust it better, by taking it off, and settling it again; whereat both he and his companion (who was a brown bay) appeared to be much surprised; the latter felt the lappet[14] of my coat, and finding it to hang loose about me, they both looked with new signs of wonder. He stroked my right hand, seeming to admire[15] the softness, and colour; but he squeezed it so hard between his

[13] Wait for. [14] Lapel. [15] Wonder at.

hoof and his pastern,[16] that I was forced to roar; after which they both touched me with all possible tenderness. They were under great perplexity about my shoes and stockings, which they felt very often, neighing to each other, and using various gestures, not unlike those of a philosopher, when he would attempt to solve some new and difficult phenomenon.

Upon the whole, the behaviour of these animals was so orderly and rational, so acute and judicious, that I at last concluded, they must needs be magicians, who had thus metamorphosed themselves upon some design,[17] and seeing a stranger in the way, were resolved to divert themselves with him; or perhaps were really amazed at the sight of a man so very different in habit, feature, and complexion from those who might probably live in so remote a climate. Upon the strength of this reasoning, I ventured to address them in the following manner: Gentlemen, if you be conjurers, as I have good cause to believe, you can understand any language; therefore I make bold to let your Worships know, that I am a poor distressed English man, driven by his misfortunes upon your coast, and I entreat one of you, to let me ride upon his back, as if he were a real horse, to some house or village, where I can be relieved. In return of which favour, I will make you a present of this knife and bracelet (taking them out of my pocket). The two creatures stood silent while I spoke, seeming to listen with great attention; and when I had ended, they neighed frequently towards each other, as if they were engaged in serious conversation. I plainly observed, that their language expressed the passions very well, and the words might with little pains be resolved into an alphabet more easily than the Chinese.

I could frequently distinguish the word *yahoo,* which was repeated by each of them several times; and although it was impossible for me to conjecture what it meant, yet while the two horses were busy in conversation, I endeavoured to practice this word upon my tongue; and as soon as they were silent, I boldly pronounced *yahoo* in a loud voice, imitating, at the same time, as near as I could, the neighing of a horse; at which they were both visibly surprised, and the grey repeated the same word twice, as if he meant to teach me the right accent, wherein I spoke after him as well as I could, and found myself perceivably to improve every time, although very far from any degree of perfection. Then the bay tried me with a second word, much harder to be pronounced; but reducing it to the English orthography, may be spelt thus, *Houyhnhnm.*[18] I did not succeed in this so well as the former, but after two or three farther trials, I had better fortune; and they both appeared amazed at my capacity.

After some farther discourse, which I then conjectured might relate to me, the two friends took their leaves, with the same compliment of striking each other's hoof; and the grey made me signs that I should walk before him, wherein I thought it prudent to comply, till I could find a better director. When I offered to slacken my pace, he would cry *hhuun, hhuun;* I guessed his meaning, and gave him to understand, as well as I could, that I was weary, and not able to walk faster; upon which he would stand a while to let me rest.

[16] The back of a horse's foot, just above the hoof. [17] For some purpose.
[18] Imitative of the whinnying of a horse; probably pronounced *hwinnum.*

CHAPTER II

The author conducted by a Houyhnhnm to his house. The house described. The author's reception. The food of the Houyhnhnms. The author in distress for want of meat, is at last relieved. His manner of feeding in that country.

Having travelled about three miles, we came to a long kind of building, made of timber stuck in the ground, and wattled[1] across; the roof was low, and covered with straw. I now began to be a little comforted, and took out some toys, which travellers usually carry for presents to the savage Indians of America and other parts, in hopes the people of the house would be thereby encouraged to receive me kindly. The horse made me a sign to go in first; it was a large room with a smooth clay floor, and a rack and manger extending the whole length on one side. There were three nags, and two mares, not eating, but some of them sitting down upon their hams,[2] which I very much wondered at; but wondered more to see the rest employed in domestic business. They seemed but ordinary cattle; however, this confirmed my first opinion, that a people who could so far civilize brute animals must needs excel in wisdom all the nations of the world. The grey came in just after, and thereby prevented any ill treatment which the others might have given me. He neighed to them several times in a style of authority, and received answers.

Beyond this room there were three others, reaching the length of the house, to which you passed through three doors, opposite to each other, in the manner of a vista;[3] we went through the second room towards the third; here the grey walked in first, beckoning me to attend:[4] I waited in the second room, and got ready my presents for the master and mistress of the house: they were two knives, three bracelets of false pearl, a small looking-glass and a bead necklace. The horse neighed three or four times, and I waited to hear some answers in a human voice, but I heard no other returns than in the same dialect, only one or two a little shriller than his. I began to think that this house must belong to some person of great note among them, because there appeared so much ceremony before I could gain admittance. But that a man of quality should be served all by horses was beyond my comprehension. I feared my brain was disturbed by my sufferings and misfortunes: I roused myself, and looked about me in the room where I was left alone; this was furnished as the first, only after a more elegant manner. I rubbed my eyes often, but the same objects still occurred. I pinched my arms and sides, to awake myself, hoping I might be in a dream. I then absolutely concluded, that all these appearances could be nothing else but necromancy and magic. But I had no time to pursue these reflections; for the grey horse came to the door, and made me a sign to follow him into the third room, where I saw a very comely mare, together with a colt and foal, sitting on their haunches, upon mats of straw, not unartfully made, and perfectly neat and clean.

[1] Made of intertwined reeds or twigs. [2] Buttocks.

[3] A long view; the doorways are so arranged that one can see through them the length of the building.

[4] Wait.

The mare, soon after my entrance, rose from her mat, and coming up close, after having nicely[5] observed my hands and face, gave me a most contemptuous look; then turning to the horse, I heard the word *yahoo* often repeated betwixt them; the meaning of which word I could not then comprehend, although it were the first I had learned to pronounce; but I was soon better informed, to my everlasting mortification: for the horse beckoning to me with his head, and repeating the word *hhuun, hhuun,* as he did upon the road, which I understood was to attend him, led me out into a kind of court, where was another building at some distance from the house. Here we entered, and I saw three of those detestable creatures, which I first met after my landing, feeding upon roots, and the flesh of some animals, which I afterwards found to be that of asses and dogs, and now and then a cow dead by accident or disease. They were all tied by the neck with strong withes,[6] fastened to a beam; they held their food between the claws of their forefeet, and tore it with their teeth.

The master horse ordered a sorrel nag, one of his servants, to untie the largest of these animals, and take him into the yard. The beast and I were brought close together, and our countenances diligently compared, both by master and servant, who thereupon repeated several times the word *yahoo.* My horror and astonishment are not to be described, when I observed, in this abominable animal, a perfect human figure; the face of it indeed was flat and broad, the nose depressed, the lips large, and the mouth wide. But these differences are common to all savage nations, where the lineaments of the countenance are distorted by the natives suffering their infants to lie grovelling on the earth, or by carrying them on their backs, nuzzling with their face against the mother's shoulders. The forefeet of the yahoo differed from my hands in nothing else but the length of the nails, the coarseness and brownness of the palms, and the hairiness on the backs. There was the same resemblance between our feet, with the same differences, which I knew very well, although the horses did not, because of my shoes and stockings; the same in every part of our bodies, except as to hairiness and colour, which I have already described.

The great difficulty that seemed to stick with the two horses, was to see the rest of my body so very different from that of a yahoo, for which I was obliged to my clothes, whereof they had no conception: the sorrel nag offered me a root, which he held (after their manner, as we shall describe in its proper place) between his hoof and pastern; I took it in my hand, and having smelt it, returned it to him as civilly as I could. He brought out of the yahoo's kennel a piece of ass's flesh, but it smelt so offensively that I turned from it with loathing: he then threw it to the yahoo, by whom it was greedily devoured. He afterwards showed me a wisp of hay, and a fetlock[7] full of oats; but I shook my head, to signify, that neither of these were food for me. And indeed, I now apprehended, that I must absolutely starve, if I did not get to some of my own species: for as to those filthy yahoos, although there were few greater lovers of mankind, at that time, than myself, yet I confess I never saw any sensitive[8] being so detestable on all accounts;

[5] Carefully and fastidiously. [6] Flexible willow twigs.
[7] A projection above and behind the hoof. [8] Sentient.

and the more I came near them, the more hateful they grew, while I stayed in that country. This the master horse observed by my behaviour, and therefore sent the yahoo back to his kennel. He then put his fore-hoof to his mouth, at which I was much surprised, although he did it with ease, and with a motion that appeared perfectly natural, and made other signs to know what I would eat; but I could not return him such an answer as he was able to apprehend; and if he had understood me, I did not see how it was possible to contrive any way for finding myself nourishment. While we were thus engaged, I observed a cow passing by, whereupon I pointed to her, and expressed a desire to let me go and milk her. This had its effect; for he led me back into the house, and ordered a mare-servant to open a room, where a good store of milk lay in earthen and wooden vessels, after a very orderly and cleanly manner. She gave me a large bowl full, of which I drank very heartily, and found myself well refreshed.

About noon I saw coming towards the house a kind of vehicle drawn like a sledge by four yahoos. There was in it an old steed, who seemed to be of quality; he alighted with his hind feet forward, having by accident got a hurt in his left forefoot. He came to dine with our horse, who received him with great civility. They dined in the best room, and had oats boiled in milk for the second course, which the old horse eat[9] warm, but the rest cold. Their mangers were placed circular in the middle of the room, and divided into several partitions, round which they sat on their haunches upon bosses[10] of straw. In the middle was a large rack with angles answering to every partition of the manger. So that each horse and mare eat their own hay, and their own mash of oats and milk, with much decency and regularity. The behaviour of the young colt and foal appeared very modest, and that of the master and mistress extremely cheerful and complaisant to their guest. The grey ordered me to stand by him, and much discourse passed between him and his friend concerning me, as I found by the stranger's often looking on me, and the frequent repetition of the word *yahoo*.

I happened to wear my gloves, which the master grey observing, seemed perplexed, discovering[11] signs of wonder what I had done to my forefeet; he put his hoof three or four times to them, as if he would signify, that I should reduce them to their former shape, which I presently did, pulling off both my gloves, and putting them into my pocket. This occasioned farther talk, and I saw the company was pleased with my behaviour, whereof I soon found the good effects. I was ordered to speak the few words I understood, and while they were at dinner, the master taught me the names for oats, milk, fire, water, and some others: which I could readily pronounce after him, having from my youth a great facility in learning languages.

When dinner was done, the master horse took me aside, and by signs and words made me understand the concern he was in, that I had nothing to eat. Oats in their tongue are called *hlunnh*. This word I pronounced two or three times; for although I had refused them at first, yet upon second thoughts, I considered that I could contrive to make of them a kind of

[9] Ate. [10] Hassocks. [11] Revealing.

bread, which might be sufficient with milk to keep me alive, till I could make my escape to some other country, and to creatures of my own species. The horse immediately ordered a white mare-servant of his family to bring me a good quantity of oats in a sort of wooden tray. These I heated before the fire as well as I could, and rubbed them till the husks came off, which I made a shift[12] to winnow from the grain; I ground and beat them between two stones, then took water, and made them into a paste or cake, which I toasted at the fire, and eat warm with milk. It was at first a very insipid[13] diet, although common enough in many parts of Europe, but grew tolerable by time; and having been often reduced to hard fare in my life, this was not the first experiment I had made how easily nature is satisfied. And I cannot but observe, that I never had one hour's sickness, while I stayed in this island. It is true, I sometimes made a shift to catch a rabbit, or bird, by springes[14] made of yahoos' hairs, and I often gathered wholesome herbs, which I boiled, or eat as salads with my bread, and now and then, for a rarity, I made a little butter, and drank the whey.[15] I was at first at a great loss for salt; but custom soon reconciled the want of it; and I am confident that the frequent use of salt among us is an effect of luxury, and was first introduced only as a provocative to drink; except where it is necessary for preserving of flesh in long voyages, or in places remote from great markets. For we observe no animal to be fond of it but man:[16] and as to myself, when I left this country, it was a great while before I could endure the taste of it in anything that I eat.

This is enough to say upon the subject of my diet, wherewith other travellers fill their books, as if the readers were personally concerned whether we fared well or ill. However, it was necessary to mention this matter, lest the world should think it impossible that I could find sustenance for three years in such a country, and among such inhabitants.

When it grew towards evening, the master horse ordered a place for me to lodge in; it was but six yards from the house, and separated from the stable of the yahoos. Here I got some straw, and covering myself with my own clothes, slept very sound. But I was in a short time better accommodated, as the reader shall know hereafter, when I come to treat more particularly about my way of living.

CHAPTER III

The author studious to learn the language, the Houyhnhnm his master assists in teaching him. The language described. Several Houyhnhnms of quality come out of curiosity to see the author. He gives his master a short account of his voyage.

My principal endeavour was to learn the language, which my master (for so I shall henceforth call him) and his children and every servant of his house were desirous to teach me. For they looked upon it as a prodigy that a brute animal should discover[1] such marks of a rational creature. I pointed to

[12] Managed. [13] Lacking flavor. [14] Snares. [15] The watery ingredient in milk.
[16] An error (by Swift or Gulliver); many animals like and need salt, especially herbivorous ones.
[1] Reveal; evince.

every thing, and enquired the name of it, which I wrote down in my journal-book when I was alone, and corrected my bad accent, by desiring those of the family to pronounce it often. In this employment, a sorrel nag, one of the under servants, was very ready to assist me.

In speaking, they pronounce through the nose and throat, and their language approaches nearest to the High Dutch or German, of any I know in Europe; but is much more graceful and significant. The Emperor Charles V made almost the same observation, when he said, that if he were to speak to his horse, it should be in High Dutch.[2]

The curiosity and impatience of my master were so great, that he spent many hours of his leisure to instruct me. He was convinced (as he afterwards told me) that I must be a yahoo, but my teachableness, civility and cleanliness astonished him; which were qualities altogether so opposite to those animals. He was most perplexed about my clothes, reasoning sometimes with himself, whether they were a part of my body; for I never pulled them off till the family were asleep, and got them on before they waked in the morning. My master was eager to learn from whence I came, how I acquired those appearances of reason which I discovered in all my actions, and to know my story from my own mouth, which he hoped he should soon do by the great proficiency I made in learning and pronouncing their words and sentences. To help my memory, I formed all I learned into the English alphabet, and writ the words down with the translations. This last, after some time, I ventured to do in my master's presence. It cost me much trouble to explain to him what I was doing; for the inhabitants have not the least idea of books or literature.

In about ten weeks time I was able to understand most of his questions, and in three months could give him some tolerable answers. He was extremely curious to know from what part of the country I came, and how I was taught to imitate a rational creature, because the yahoos (whom he saw I exactly resembled in my head, hands and face, that were only visible), with some appearance of cunning, and the strongest disposition to mischief, were observed to be the most unteachable of all brutes. I answered, that I came over the sea, from a far place, with many others of my own kind, in a great hollow vessel made of the bodies of trees. That my companions forced me to land on this coast, and then left me to shift for myself. It was with some difficulty, and by the help of many signs, that I brought him to understand me. He replied, that I must needs be mistaken, or that I "said the thing which was not." (For they have no words in their language to express lying or falsehood.) He knew it was impossible that there could be a country beyond the sea, or that a parcel of brutes could move a wooden vessel whither they pleased upon water. He was sure no Houyhnhnm alive could make such a vessel, or would trust yahoos to manage it.

The word *Houyhnhnm,* in their tongue, signifies a *horse,* and in its etymology, *the perfection of nature.* I told my master, that I was at a loss for

[2]Charles V was Holy Roman Emperor and king of Spain. He is said to have remarked that he would address his God in Spanish, his mistress in Italian, and his horse in German. The German (Hanoverian) kings who, beginning with George I in 1714, had become rulers of England were not popular with the Tories.

expression, but would improve as fast as I could; and hoped in a short time I should be able to tell him wonders: he was pleased to direct his own mare, his colt and foal, and the servants of the family to take all opportunities of instructing me, and every day for two or three hours he was at the same pains himself: several horses and mares of quality in the neighbourhood came often to our house upon the report spread of a wonderful yahoo, that could speak like a Houyhnhnm, and seemed in his words and actions to discover some glimmerings of reason. These delighted to converse with me; they put many questions, and received such answers as I was able to return. By all which advantages, I made so great a progress, that in five months from my arrival I understood whatever was spoke, and could express myself tolerably well.

The Houyhnhnms who came to visit my master, out of a design of seeing and talking with me, could hardly believe me to be a right[3] yahoo, because my body had a different covering from others of my kind. They were astonished to observe me without the usual hair or skin except on my head, face, and hands; but I discovered that secret to my master, upon an accident, which happened about a fortnight before.

I have already told the reader, that every night, when the family were gone to bed, it was my custom to strip and cover myself with my clothes: it happened one morning early, that my master sent for me, by the sorrel nag, who was his valet; when he came, I was fast asleep, my clothes fallen off on one side, and my shirt above my waist. I awaked at the noise he made, and observed him to deliver his message in some disorder; after which he went to my master, and in a great fright gave him a very confused account of what he had seen: this I presently discovered; for going, as soon as I was dresssed, to pay my attendance upon his Honour, he asked me the meaning of what his servant had reported, that I was not the same thing when I slept as I appeared to be at other times; that his valet assured him, some part of me was white, some yellow, at least not so white, and some brown.

I had hitherto concealed the secret of my dress, in order to distinguish myself as much as possible from that cursed race of yahoos; but now I found it in vain to do so any longer. Besides, I considered that my clothes and shoes would soon wear out, which already were in a declining condition, and must be supplied by some contrivance from the hides of yahoos or other brutes; whereby the whole secret would be known: I therefore told my master, that in the country from whence I came those of my kind always covered their bodies with the hairs of certain animals prepared by art, as well for decency, as to avoid inclemencies of air both hot and cold; of which, as to my own person, I would give him immediate conviction, if he pleased to command me; only desiring his excuse, if I did not expose those parts that nature taught us to conceal. He said my discourse was all very strange, but especially the last part; for he could not understand why nature should teach us to conceal what nature had given. That neither himself nor family were ashamed of any parts of their bodies; but however I might do as I pleased. Whereupon, I first unbuttoned my coat, and pulled it off. I did the same with my waistcoat; I drew off my shoes, stockings, and

[3] True; genuine.

breeches. I let my shirt down to my waist, and drew up the bottom, fastening it like a girdle about my middle to hide my nakedness.

My master observed the whole performance with great signs of curiosity and admiration.[4] He took up all my clothes in his pastern, one piece after another, and examined them diligently; he then stroked my body very gently and looked round me several times, after which he said, it was plain I must be a perfect yahoo; but that I differed very much from the rest of my species, in the whiteness and smoothness of my skin, my want of hair in several parts of my body, the shape and shortness of my claws behind and before, and my affectation of walking continually on my two hinder feet. He desired to see no more, and gave me leave to put on my clothes again, for I was shuddering with cold.

I expressed my uneasiness at his giving me so often the appellation of *yahoo,* an odious animal, for which I had so utter an hatred and contempt; I begged he would forbear applying that word to me, and take the same order in his family, and among his friends whom he suffered[5] to see me. I requested likewise, that the secret of my having a false covering to my body might be known to none but himself, at least as long as my present clothing should last; for as to what the sorrel nag his valet had observed, his Honour might command him to conceal it.

All this my master very graciously consented to, and thus the secret was kept till my clothes began to wear out, which I was forced to supply by several contrivances, that shall hereafter be mentioned. In the mean time, he desired I would go on with my utmost diligence to learn their language, because he was more astonished at my capacity for speech and reason than at the figure of my body, whether it were covered or no; adding, that he waited with some impatience to hear the wonders which I promised to tell him.

From thenceforward he doubled the pains he had been at to instruct me; he brought me into all company, and made them treat me with civility, because, as he told them privately, this would put me into good humour, and make me more diverting.

Every day when I waited on him, beside the trouble he was at in teaching, he would ask me several questions concerning myself, which I answered as well as I could; and by those means he had already received some general ideas, although very imperfect. It would be tedious to relate the several steps by which I advanced to a more regular conversation: but the first account I gave of myself in any order and length, was to this purpose:

That I came from a very far country, as I already had attempted to tell him, with about fifty more of my own species; that we travelled upon the seas, in a great hollow vessel made of wood, and larger than his Honour's house. I described the ship to him in the best terms I could, and explained by the help of my handkerchief displayed, how it was driven forward by the wind. That upon a quarrel among us, I was set on shore on this coast, where I walked forward without knowing whither, till he delivered me from the persecution of those execrable yahoos. He asked me, who made the ship, and how it was possible that the Houyhnhnms of my country would leave it to the management of brutes? My answer was, that I durst

[4] Wonder [5] Permitted.

proceed no farther in my relation, unless he would give me his word and honour that he would not be offended, and then I would tell him the wonders I had so often promised. He agreed; and I went on by assuring him, that the ship was made by creatures like myself, who in all the countries I had travelled, as well as in my own, were the only governing, rational animals; and that upon my arrival hither, I was as much astonished to see the Houyhnhnms act like rational beings, as he or his friends could be in finding some marks of reason in a creature he was pleased to call a yahoo, to which I owned[6] my resemblance in every part, but could not account for their degenerate and brutal nature. I said farther, that if good fortune ever restored me to my native country, to relate my travels hither, as I resolved to do, every body would believe that I "said the thing which was not"; that I invented the story out of my own head; and with all possible respect to himself, his family and friends, and under his promise of not being offended, our countrymen would hardly think it probable, that a Houyhnhnm should be the presiding creature of a nation, and a yahoo the brute.

CHAPTER IV

The Houyhnhnms' notion of truth and falsehood. The author's discourse disapproved by his master. The author gives a more particular account of himself, and the accidents of his voyage.

My master heard me with great appearances of uneasiness in his countenance, because *doubting* or *not believing,* are so little known in this country, that the inhabitants cannot tell how to behave themselves under such circumstances. And I remember in frequent discourses with my master concerning the nature of manhood,[1] in other parts of the world, having occasion to talk of *lying* and *false representation,* it was with much difficulty that he comprehended what I meant, although he had otherwise a most acute judgment. For he argued thus; that the use of speech was to make us understand one another, and to receive information of facts; now if any one *said the thing which was not,* these ends were defeated; because I cannot properly be said to understand him, and I am so far from receiving information, that he leaves me worse than in ignorance, for I am led to believe a thing black when it is white, and short when it is long. And these were all the notions he had concerning that faculty of lying, so perfectly well understood, and so universally practised among human creatures.

To return from this digression; when I asserted that the yahoos were the only governing animals in my country, which my master said was altogether past his conception, he desired to know, whether we had Houyhnhnms among us, and what was their employment: I told him, we had great numbers, that in summer they grazed in the fields, and in winter were kept in houses, with hay and oats, where yahoo servants were employed to rub their skins smooth, comb their manes, pick their feet, serve them with food, and make their beds. I understand you well, said my mas-

[6] Admitted; acknowledged. [1] Humanity.

ter, it is now very plain, from all you have spoken, that whatever share of reason the yahoos pretend to, the Houyhnhnms are your masters; I heartily wish our yahoos would be so tractable.[2] I begged his Honour would please to excuse me from proceeding any farther, because I was very certain that the account he expected from me would be highly displeasing. But he insisted in commanding me to let him know the best and the worst: I told him, he should be obeyed. I owned, that the Houyhnhnms among us, whom we called horses, were the most generous[3] and comely animal we had, that they excelled in strength and swiftness; and when they belonged to persons of quality, employed in travelling, racing, and drawing chariots, they were treated with much kindness and care, till they fell into diseases, or became foundered[4] in the feet; but then they were sold, and used to all kind of drudgery till they died; after which their skins were stripped and sold for what they were worth, and their bodies left to be devoured by dogs and birds of prey. But the common race of horses had not so good fortune, being kept by farmers and carriers and other mean people,[5] who put them to greater labour, and feed them worse. I described, as well as I could, our way of riding, the shape and use of a bridle, a saddle, a spur, and a whip, of harness and wheels. I added, that we fastened plates of a certain hard substance called "iron" at the bottom of their feet, to preserve their hoofs from being broken by the stony ways on which we often travelled.

My master, after some expressions of great indignation, wondered how we dared to venture upon a Houyhnhnm's back, for he was sure that the weakest servant in his house would be able to shake off the strongest yahoo, or by lying down, and rolling upon his back, squeeze the brute to death. I answered, that our horses were trained up from three or four years old to the several uses we intended them for; that if any of them proved intolerably vicious, they were employed for carriages; that they were severely beaten while they were young, for any mischievous tricks; that the males, designed for the common use of riding or draught,[6] were generally castrated about two years after their birth, to take down their spirits, and make them more tame and gentle; that they were indeed sensible[7] of rewards and punishments; but his Honour would please to consider, that they had not the least tincture of reason any more than the yahoos in this country.

It put me to the pains of many circumlocutions to give my master a right idea of what I spoke; for their language doth not abound in variety of words, because their wants and passions are fewer than among us. But it is impossible to express his noble resentment at our savage treatment of the Houyhnhnm race, particularly after I had explained the manner and use of castrating horses among us, to hinder them from propagating their kind, and to render them more servile. He said, if it were possible there could be any country where yahoos alone were endued with reason, they certainly must be the governing animal, because reason will in time always prevail against brutal strength. But, considering the frame of our bodies, and especially of mine, he thought no creature of equal bulk was so ill contrived for employing that reason in the common offices of life; where-

[2] Easily controlled. [3] Noble. [4] Lamed. [5] People of the lower classes.
[6] Hauling of heavy loads. [7] Aware.

upon he desired to know whether those among whom I lived resembled me or the yahoos of his country. I assured him, that I was as well shaped as most of my age: but the younger and the females were much more soft and tender, and the skins of the latter generally as white as milk. He said, I differed indeed from other yahoos, being much more cleanly, and not altogether so deformed, but in point of real advantage he thought I differed for the worse. That my nails were of no use either to my fore or hinder feet; as to my forefeet, he could not properly call them by that name, for he never observed me to walk upon them; that they were too soft to bear the ground; that I generally went with them uncovered, neither was the covering I sometimes wore on them of the same shape or so strong as that on my feet behind. That I could not walk with any security, for if either of my hinder feet slipped, I must inevitably fall. He than began to find fault with other parts of my body, the flatness of my face, the prominence of my nose, my eyes placed directly in front, so that I could not look on either side without turning my head: that I was not able to feed myself without lifting one of my forefeet to my mouth: and therefore nature had placed those joints to answer that necessity. He knew not what could be the use of those several clefts and divisions in my feet behind; that these were too soft to bear the hardness and sharpness of stones without a covering made from the skin of some other brute; that my whole body wanted a fence[8] against heat and cold, which I was forced to put on and off every day with tediousness and trouble. And lastly, that he observed every animal in this country naturally to abhor the yahoos, whom the weaker avoided, and the stronger drove from them. So that supposing us to have the gift of reason, he could not see how it were possible to cure that natural antipathy which every creature discovered against us; nor consequently, how we could tame and render them serviceable. However, he would (as he said) debate the matter no farther, because he was more desirous to know my own story, the country where I was born, and the several actions and events of my life before I came hither.

I assured him how extremely desirous I was that he should be satisfied in every point; but I doubted much, whether it would be possible for me to explain myself on several subjects whereof his Honour could have no conception, because I saw nothing in his country to which I could resemble them. That however, I would do my best, and strive to express myself by similitudes, humbly desiring his assistance when I wanted proper words; which he was pleased to promise me.

I said, my birth was of honest parents, in an island called England, which was remote from this country as many days' journey as the strongest of his Honour's servants could travel in the annual course of the sun. That I was bred a surgeon, whose trade is to cure wounds and hurts in the body, got by accident or violence; that my country was governed by a female man, whom we called *queen.*[9] That I left it to get riches, whereby I might maintain myself and family when I should return. That in my last voyage I was

[8] Defense.

[9] At the time of this voyage, England was ruled by Queen Anne (reigned 1702–14), daughter of James II and last of the Stuart rulers.

commander of the ship, and had about fifty yahoos under me, many of which died at sea, and I was forced to supply them by others picked out from several nations. That our ship was twice in danger of being sunk; the first time by a great storm, and the second, by striking against a rock. Here my master interposed, by asking me, how I could persuade strangers out of different countries to venture with me, after the losses I had sustained, and the hazards I had run. I said, they were fellows of desperate fortunes, forced to fly from the places of their birth, on account of their poverty or their crimes. Some were undone by lawsuits; others spent all they had in drinking, whoring, and gaming; others fled for treason; many for murder, theft, poisoning, robbery, perjury, forgery, coining false money, for committing rapes or sodomy, for flying from their colours, or deserting to the enemy, and most of them had broken prison; none of these durst return to their native countries for fear of being hanged, or of starving in a jail; and therefore were under a necessity of seeking a livelihood in other places.

During this discourse, my master was pleased often to interrupt me; I had made use of many circumlocutions in describing to him the nature of the several crimes, for which most of our crew had been forced to fly their country. This labour took up several days' conversation before he was able to comprehend me. He was wholly at a loss to know what could be the use or necessity of practising those vices. To clear up which I endeavoured to give him some ideas of the desire of power and riches, of the terrible effects of lust, intemperance, malice and envy. All this I was forced to define and describe by putting of cases, and making suppositions. After which, like one whose imagination was struck with something never seen or heard of before, he would lift up his eyes with amazement and indignation. Power, government, war, law, punishment, and a thousand other things had no terms wherein that language could express them, which made the difficulty almost insuperable to give my master any conception of what I meant. But being of an excellent understanding, much improved by contemplation and converse, he at last arrived at a competent knowledge of what human nature in our parts of the world is capable to perform, and desired I would give him some particular account of that land which we call Europe, especially of my own country.

CHAPTER V

The author, at his master's commands, informs him of the state of England. The causes of war among the princes of Europe. The author begins to explain the English constitution.

The reader may please to observe, that the following extract of many conversations I had with my master contains a summary of the most material points which were discoursed at several times for above two years; his Honour often desiring fuller satisfaction as I farther improved in the Houyhnhnm tongue. I laid before him, as well as I could, the whole state of Europe; I discoursed of trade and manufactures, of arts and sciences; and the answers I gave to all the questions he made, as they arose upon several subjects, were a fund of conversation not to be exhausted. But I shall here only set down the substance of what passed between us concerning my own country, reducing it into order as well as I can, without any regard to time or other circumstances, while I strictly adhere to truth. My only concern is, that I shall hardly be able to do justice to my master's arguments and expressions, which must needs suffer by my want of capacity, as well as by a translation into our barbarous English.

In obedience therefore to his Honour's commands, I related to him the Revolution under the Prince of Orange; the long war with France entered into by the said prince, and renewed by his successor the present queen, wherein the greatest powers of Christendom were engaged, and which still continued: I computed, at his request, that about a million of yahoos might have been killed in the whole progress of it, and perhaps a hundred or more cities taken, and five times as many ships burnt or sunk.[1]

He asked me what were the usual causes or motives that made one country go to war with another. I answered they were innumerable, but I should only mention a few of the chief. Sometimes the ambition of princes, who never think they have land or people enough to govern: sometimes the corruption of ministers, who engage their master in a war in order to stifle or divert the clamour of the subjects against their evil administration. Difference in opinions hath cost many millions of lives: for instance, whether flesh be bread, or bread be flesh; whether the juice of a certain berry be blood or wine; whether whistling be a vice or a virtue; whether it be better to kiss a post, or throw it into the fire; what is the best colour for a coat, whether black, white, red, or grey; and whether it should be long or short, narrow or wide, dirty or clean, with many more.[2] Neither are any wars so furious and bloody, or of so long continuance, as those occasioned by difference in opinion, especially if it be in things indifferent.[3]

Sometimes the quarrel between two princes is to decide which of them shall dispossess a third of his dominions, where neither of them pretend to any right. Sometimes one prince quarrelleth with another, for fear the other should quarrel with him. Sometimes a war is entered upon, because the enemy is too strong, and sometimes because he is too weak. Sometimes our neighbours want the things which we have, or have the things which we want; and we both fight, till they take ours or give us theirs. It is a very justifiable cause of war to invade a country after the people have been

[1] In the "Glorious Revolution" of 1688, King James II, a Catholic and an unpopular ruler, was dethroned in favor of his Protestant daughter, who then became Mary II and ruled jointly with her Dutch husband and cousin William of Orange, who became William III. James fled to France, and the "Declaration of Rights" of 1689 made Parliament the supreme power in England. Wars with France followed, including (after Anne came to the throne in 1702) the War of the Spanish Succession, in which many European nations were involved and which was still continuing when Gulliver arrived in the Houyhnhnms' land. Swift exaggerates the number of casualties.

[2] The references are to divisions among Protestants and between them and Catholics over the doctrine of transubstantiation (the changing of bread and wine into Christ's body and blood), the proper use of music in church, the veneration of images and particularly of the crucifix, and liturgical vestments.

[3] Unimportant.

wasted by famine, destroyed by pestilence, or embroiled by factions amongst themselves. It is justifiable to enter into a war against our nearest ally, when one of his towns lies convenient for us, or a territory of land, that would render our dominions round and compact. If a prince send forces into a nation where the people are poor and ignorant, he may lawfully put half of them to death, and make slaves of the rest, in order to civilize and reduce them from their barbarous way of living. It is a very kingly, honourable, and frequent practice, when one prince desires the assistance of another to secure him against an invasion, that the assistant, when he hath driven out the invader, should seize on the dominions himself, and kill, imprison or banish the prince he came to relieve. Alliance by blood or marriage is a sufficient cause of war between princes, and the nearer the kindred is, the greater is their disposition to quarrel: poor nations are hungry, and rich nations are proud, and pride and hunger will ever be at variance. For these reasons, the trade of a soldier is held the most honourable of all others: because a soldier is a yahoo hired to kill in cold blood as many of his own species, who have never offended him, as possibly he can.

There is likewise a kind of beggarly princes in Europe, not able to make war by themselves, who hire out their troops to richer nations, for so much a day to each man; of which they keep three fourths to themselves, and it is the best part of their maintenance; such are those in Germany[4] and many northern parts of Europe.

What you have told me (said my master) upon the subject of war, does indeed discover most admirably the effects of that reason you pretend to: however, it is happy that the shame is greater than the danger; and that nature hath left you utterly uncapable of doing much mischief. For your mouths lying flat with your faces, you can hardly bite each other to any purpose, unless by consent. Then as to the claws upon your feet before and behind, they are so short and tender, that one of our yahoos would drive a dozen of yours before him. And therefore in recounting the numbers of those who have been killed in battle, I cannot but think that you have *said the thing which is not.*

I could not forbear shaking my head and smiling a little at his ignorance. And being no stranger to the art of war, I gave him a description of cannons, culverins,[5] muskets, carabines, pistols, bullets, powder, swords, bayonets, battles, sieges, retreats, attacks, undermines, countermines, bombardments, sea-fights; ships sunk with a thousand men, twenty thousand killed on each side; dying groans, limbs flying in the air, smoke, noise, confusion, trampling to death under horses' feet; flight, pursuit, victory; fields strewed with carcases left for food to dogs, and wolves, and birds of prey; plundering, stripping, ravishing, burning and destroying. And to set forth the valour of my own dear countrymen, I assured him, that I had seen them blow up a hundred enemies at once in a siege, and as many in a ship, and beheld the dead bodies drop down in pieces from the clouds, to the great diversion of all the spectators.

[4] King George I, while he was Elector of Hanover, had been involved in this trade in mercenaries. The early editions of *Gulliver's Travels* omit the provocative reference to Germany.

[5] Thin-barreled cannons.

I was going on to more particulars, when my master commanded me silence. He said, whoever understood the nature of yahoos might easily believe it possible for so vile an animal to be capable of every action I had named, if their strength and cunning equalled their malice. But as my discourse had increased his abhorrence of the whole species, so he found it gave him a disturbance in his mind, to which he was wholly a stranger before. He thought his ears being used to such abominable words, might by degrees admit them with less detestation. That although he hated the yahoos of this country, yet he no more blamed them for their odious qualities, than he did a *gnnayh* (a bird of prey) for its cruelty, or a sharp stone for cutting his hoof. But when a creature pretending to reason could be capable of such enormities, he dreaded lest the corruption of that faculty might be worse than brutality itself. He seemed therefore confident, that instead of reason, we were only possessed of some quality fitted to increase our natural vices; as the reflection from a troubled stream returns the image of an ill-shapen body, not only larger, but more distorted.

He added, that he had heard too much upon the subject of war, both in this and some former discourses. There was another point which a little perplexed him at present. I had said, that some of our crew left their country on account of being ruined by *law;* that I had already explained the meaning of the word; but he was at a loss how it should come to pass, that the *law* which was intended for every man's preservation, should be any man's ruin. Therefore he desired to be farther satisfied what I meant by *law,* and the dispensers thereof according to the present practice in my own country; because he thought nature and reason were sufficient guides for a reasonable animal, as we pretended to be, in showing us what we ought to do, and what to avoid.

I assured his Honour, that law was a science wherein I had not much conversed, further than by employing advocates in vain, upon some injustices that had been done me. However, I would give him all the satisfaction I was able.

I said there was a society of men among us, bred up from their youth in the art of proving by words multiplied for the purpose, that white is black, and black is white, according as they are paid. To this society all the rest of the people are slaves.

For example, if my neighbour hath a mind to my cow, he hires a lawyer to prove that he ought to have my cow from me. I must then hire another to defend my right, it being against all rules of law that any man should be allowed to speak for himself. Now in this case, I who am the true owner lie under two great disadvantages. First, my lawyer, being practiced almost from his cradle in defending falsehood, is quite out of his element when he would be an advocate for justice, which as an office unnatural, he always attempts with great awkwardness, if not with ill will. The second disadvantage is, that my lawyer must proceed with great caution, or else he will be reprimanded by the judges, and abhorred by his brethren, as one who would lessen the practice of the law. And therefore I have but two methods to preserve my cow. The first is to gain over my adversary's lawyer with a double fee, who will then betray his client by insinuating that he hath justice on his side. The second way is for my lawyer to make my cause appear as unjust as he can, by allowing the cow to belong to my adversary; and this if it be skilfully done will certainly bespeak the favour of the bench.

Now, your Honour is to know that these judges are persons appointed to decide all controversies of property, as well as for the trial of criminals, and picked out from the most dextrous lawyers who are grown old or lazy, and having been biassed all their lives against truth and equity, lie under such a fatal necessity of favouring fraud, perjury, and oppression, that I have known several of them refuse a large bribe from the side where justice lay, rather than injure the faculty[6] by doing any thing unbecoming their nature or their office.

It is a maxim among these lawyers, that whatever hath been done before may legally be done again: and therefore they take special care to record all the decisions formerly made against common justice and the general reason of mankind. These, under the name of *precedents,* they produce as authorities, to justify the most iniquitous opinions; and the judges never fail of decreeing accordingly.

In pleading, they studiously avoid entering into the merits of the cause, but are loud, violent, and tedious in dwelling upon all circumstances which are not to the purpose. For instance, in the case already mentioned; they never desire to know what claim or title my adversary hath to my cow, but whether the said cow were red or black, her horns long or short; whether the field I graze her in be round or square, whether she was milked at home or abroad, what diseases she is subject to, and the like; after which they consult precedents, adjourn the cause from time to time, and in ten, twenty, or thirty years come to an issue.

It is likewise to be observed that this society hath a peculiar cant and jargon of their own, that no other mortal can understand, and wherein all their laws are written, which they take special care to multiply; whereby they have wholly confounded the very essence of truth and falsehood, of right and wrong; so that it will take thirty years to decide whether the field left me by my ancestors for six generations belongs to me or to a stranger three hundred miles off.

In the trial of persons accused for crimes against the state the method is much more short and commendable: the judge first sends to sound the disposition of those in power, after which he can easily hang or save the criminal, strictly preserving all due forms of law.

Here my master, interposing, said it was a pity, that creatures endowed with such prodigious abilities of mind as these lawyers, by the description I gave of them, must certainly be, were not rather encouraged to be instructors of others in wisdom and knowledge. In answer to which I assured his Honour, that in all points out of their own trade they were usually the most ignorant and stupid generation among us, the most despicable in common conversation, avowed enemies to all knowledge and learning, and equally disposed to pervert the general reason of mankind in every other subject of discourse, as in that of their own profession.

[6] The legal profession.

CHAPTER VI

A continuation of the state of England under Queen Anne. The character of a first minister in the courts of Europe.

My master was yet wholly at a loss to understand what motives could incite this race of lawyers to perplex, disquiet, and weary themselves by engaging in a confederacy of injustice, merely for the sake of injuring their fellow-animals; neither could he comprehend what I meant in saying they did it for hire. Whereupon I was at much pains to describe to him the use of money, the materials it was made of, and the value of the metals; that when a yahoo had got a great store of this precious substance, he was able to purchase whatever he had a mind to, the finest clothing, the noblest houses, great tracts of land, the most costly meats and drinks, and have his choice of the most beautiful females. Therefore since money alone was able to perform all these feats, our yahoos thought they could never have enough of it to spend or to save, as they found themselves inclined from their natural bent either to profusion or avarice. That the rich man enjoyed the fruit of the poor man's labour, and the latter were a thousand to one in proportion to the former. That the bulk of our people were forced to live miserably, by labouring every day for small wages to make a few live plentifully. I enlarged myself much on these and many other particulars to the same purpose: but his Honour was still to seek,[1] for he went upon a supposition that all animals had a title to their share in the productions of the earth, and especially those[2] who presided over the rest. Therefore he desired I would let him know what these costly meats were, and how any of us happened to want[3] them. Whereupon I enumerated as many sorts as came into my head, with the various methods of dressing them, which could not be done without sending vessels by sea to every part of the world, as well for liquors to drink, as for sauces, and innumerable other conveniencies. I assured him, that this whole globe of earth must be at least three times gone round, before one of our better female yahoos could get her breakfast, or a cup to put it in. He said, that must needs be a miserable country which cannot furnish food for its own inhabitants. But what he chiefly wondered at was how such vast tracts of ground as I described should be wholly without fresh water, and the people put to the necessity of sending over the sea for drink. I replied, that England (the dear place of my nativity) was computed to produce three times the quantity of food more than its inhabitants are able to consume, as well as liquors extracted from grain, or pressed out of the fruit of certain trees, which made excellent drink, and the same proportion in every other convenience of life. But in order to feed the luxury and intemperance of the males, and the vanity of the females, we sent away the greatest part of our necessary things to other countries, from whence in return we brought the materials of diseases, folly, and vice, to spend among ourselves. Hence it follows of necessity that vast numbers of our people are compelled to seek their livelihood by begging, robbing, stealing, cheating, pimping, forswearing, flattering, suborning,[4]

[1] Unable to understand. [2] That species. [3] Lack.
[4] Inducing a person to do wrong, especially commit perjury.

forging, gaming, lying, fawning, hectoring,[5] voting, scribbling, star-gazing,[6] poisoning, whoring, canting,[7] libelling, free-thinking,[8] and the like occupations: every one of which terms, I was at much pains to make him understand.

That wine was not imported among us from foreign countries to supply the want of water or other drinks, but because it was a sort of liquid which made us merry, by putting us out of our senses; diverted all melancholy thoughts, begat wild extravagant imaginations in the brain, raised our hopes, and banished our fears, suspended every office of reason for a time, and deprived us of the use of our limbs, until we fell into a profound sleep; although it must be confessed, that we always awaked sick and dispirited, and that the use of this liquor filled us with diseases, which made our lives uncomfortable and short.

But beside all this, the bulk of our people supported themselves by furnishing the necessities or conveniencies of life to the rich, and to each other. For instance, when I am at home and dressed as I ought to be, I carry on my body the workmanship of an hundred tradesmen; the building and furniture of my house employ as many more, and five times the number to adorn my wife.

I was going on to tell him of another sort of people, who get their livelihood by attending the sick, having upon some occasions informed his Honour that many of my crew had died of diseases. But here it was with the utmost difficulty that I brought him to apprehend what I meant. He could easily conceive that a Houyhnhnm grew weak and heavy[9] a few days before his death, or by some accident might hurt a limb. But that Nature, who works all things to perfection, should suffer any pains to breed in our bodies, he thought impossible, and desired to know the reason of so unaccountable an evil. I told him, we fed on a thousand things which operated contrary to each other; that we eat when we were not hungry, and drank without the provocation of thirst; that we sat whole nights drinking strong liquors without eating a bit, which disposed us to sloth, enflamed our bodies, and precipitated or prevented digestion. That prostitute female yahoos acquired a certain malady, which bred rottenness in the bones of those who fell into their embraces; that this and many other diseases were propagated from father to son, so that great numbers come into the world with complicated maladies upon them; that it would be endless to give him a catalogue of all diseases incident to human bodies; for they could not be fewer than five or six hundred, spread over every limb and joint; in short, every part, external and intestine,[10] having diseases appropriated to each. To remedy which, there was a sort of people bred up among us, in the profession or pretence of curing the sick. And because I had some skill in the faculty, I would, in gratitude to his Honour, let him know the whole mystery and method by which they proceed.

Their fundamental is, that all diseases arise from repletion,[11] from whence they conclude that a great evacuation of the body is necessary,

[5] Threatening. [6] Using astrology. [7] Using jargon, especially of piety.
[8] Rationalist rejection of religious doctrine. [9] Weary. [10] Internal.
[11] Fullness.

either through the natural passage, or upwards at the mouth. Their next business is, from herbs, minerals, gums, oils, shells, salts, juices, seaweed, excrements, barks of trees, serpents, toads, frogs, spiders, dead men's flesh and bones, birds, beasts and fishes, to form a composition for smell and taste the most abominable, nauseous and detestable that they can possibly contrive, which the stomach immediately rejects with loathing; and this they call a vomit; or else from the same storehouse, with some other poisonous additions, they command us to take in at the orifice above or below (just as the physician then happens to be disposed) a medicine equally annoying and disgustful to the bowels, which, relaxing the belly, drives down all before it, and this they call a purge or a clyster.[12] For nature (as the physicians allege) having intended the superior anterior orifice only for the intromission of solids and liquids, and the inferior posterior for ejection, these artists ingeniously considering that in all diseases Nature is forced out of her seat, therefore to replace her in it, the body must be treated in a manner directly contrary, by interchanging the use of each orifice, forcing solids and liquids in at the anus, and making evacuations at the mouth.

But besides real diseases we are subject to many that are only imaginary, for which the physicians have invented imaginary cures; these have their several names, and so have the drugs that are proper for them, and with these our female yahoos are always infested.

One great excellency in this tribe is their skill at prognostics, wherein they seldom fail; their predictions in real diseases, when they rise to any degree of malignity, generally portending death, which is always in their power, when recovery is not: and therefore, upon any unexpected signs of amendment, after they have pronounced their sentence, rather than be accused as false prophets, they know how to approve[13] their sagacity to the world by a seasonable dose.

They are likewise of special use to husbands and wives who are grown weary of their mates, to eldest sons, to great ministers of state, and often to princes.

I had formerly upon occasion discoursed with my master upon the nature of our government in general, and particularly of our own excellent constitution, deservedly the wonder and envy of the whole world. But having here accidentally mentioned a "minister of state," he commanded me some time after to inform him, what species of yahoo I particularly meant by that appellation.

I told him that a first or chief minister[14] of state, who was the person I intended to describe, was a creature wholly exempt from joy and grief, love and hatred, pity and anger; at least makes use of no other passions but a violent desire of wealth, power, and titles; that he applies his words to all uses, except to the indication of his mind; that he never tells a truth, but with an intent that you should take it for a lie; nor a lie, but with a design that you should take it for a truth; that those he speaks worst of behind their backs are in the surest way to preferment;[15] and whenever he begins to praise you to others or to yourself, you are from that day forlorn. The worst mark you can receive is a promise, especially when it is confirmed with an oath; after which every wise man retires, and gives over all hopes.

[12] Enema. [13] Prove. [14] Prime Minister. [15] Promotion.

There are three methods by which a man may rise to be chief minister: the first is, by knowing how with prudence to dispose of a wife, a daughter, or a sister: the second, by betraying or undermining his predecessor: and the third is, by a furious zeal in public assemblies against the corruptions of the court. But a wise prince would rather choose to employ those who practise the last of these methods; because such zealots prove always the most obsequious and subservient to the will and passions of their master. That these "ministers" having all employments at their disposal, preserve themselves in power by bribing the majority of a senate or great council; and at last, by an expedient called an "act of indemnity"[16] (whereof I described the nature to him) they secure themselves from after reckonings, and retire from the public, laden with the spoils of the nation.

The palace of a chief minister is a seminary to breed up others in his own trade; the pages, lackeys, and porter, by imitating their master, become ministers of state in their several districts, and learn to excel in the three principal ingredients, of insolence, lying, and bribery. Accordingly, they have a subaltern[17] court paid to them by persons of the best rank, and sometimes by the force of dexterity and impudence arrive through several gradations to be successors to their lord.

He is usually governed by a decayed wench or favourite footman, who are the tunnels through which all graces are conveyed, and may properly be called, in the last resort, the governors of the kingdom.

One day my master, having heard me mention the nobility of my country, was pleased to make me a compliment which I could not pretend to deserve: that he was sure I must have been born of some noble family, because I far exceeded in shape, colour, and cleanliness, all the yahoos of his nation, although I seemed to fail in strength and agility, which must be imputed to my different way of living from those other brutes, and besides, I was not only endowed with the faculty of speech, but likewise with some rudiments of reason, to a degree that with all his acquaintance I passed for a prodigy.

He made me observe, that among the Houyhnhnms, the white, the sorrel, and the iron-grey were not so exactly shaped as the bay, the dapple-grey, and the black; nor born with equal talents of the mind, or a capacity to improve them; and therefore continued always in the condition of servants, without ever aspiring to match out of their own race, which in that country would be reckoned monstrous and unnatural.

I made his Honour my most humble acknowledgments for the good opinion he was pleased to conceive of me; but assured him at the same time that my birth was of the lower sort, having been born of plain honest parents, who were just able to give me a tolerable education: that nobility among us was altogether a different thing from the idea he had of it; that our young noblemen are bred from their childhood in idleness and luxury; that as soon as years will permit, they consume their vigor and contract odious diseases among lewd females; and when their fortunes are almost ruined, they marry some woman of mean birth, disagreeable person, and unsound constitution, merely for the sake of money, whom they hate and despise. That the productions of such marriages are generally scrofulous,

[16] A law exempting an official from punishment for illegal acts. [17] Subordinate.

ricketty, or deformed children, by which means the family seldom continues above three generations, unless the wife takes care to provide a healthy father among her neighbours or domestics, in order to improve and continue the breed. That a weak diseased body, a meager countenance, and sallow complexion are the true marks of noble blood; and a healthy robust appearance is so disgraceful in a man of quality, that the world concludes his real father to have been a groom, or a coachman. The imperfections of his mind run parallel with those of his body, being a composition of spleen,[18] dulness, ignorance, caprice, sensuality, and pride.

Without the consent of this illustrious body[19] no law can be enacted, repealed, or altered, and these nobles have likewise the decision of all our possessions without appeal.

CHAPTER VII

The author's great love of his native country. His master's observations upon the constitution and administration of England, as described by the author, with parallel cases and comparisons. His master's observations upon human nature.

The reader may be disposed to wonder how I could prevail on myself to give so free a representation of my own species, among a race of mortals who were already too apt to conceive the vilest opinion of human kind from that entire congruity betwixt me and their yahoos. But I must freely confess, that the many virtues of those excellent quadrupeds, placed in opposite view to human corruptions, had so far opened my eyes and enlarged my understanding, that I began to view the actions and passions of man in a very different light, and to think the honour of my own kind not worth managing;[1] which, besides, it was impossible for me to do before a person of so acute a judgment as my master, who daily convinced me of a thousand faults in myself, whereof I had not the least perception before, and which with us would never be numbered even among human infirmities: I had likewise learned from his example an utter detestation of all falsehood or disguise; and truth appeared so amiable to me, that I determined upon sacrificing every thing to it.

Let me deal so candidly with the reader as to confess, that there was yet a much stronger motive for the freedom I took in my representation of things. I had not been a year in this country before I contracted such a love and veneration for the inhabitants, that I entered on a firm resolution never to return to human kind, but to pass the rest of my life among these admirable Houyhnhnms in the contemplation and practice of every virtue; where I could have no example or incitement to vice. But it was decreed by Fortune, my perpetual enemy, that so great a felicity should not fall to my share. However, it is now some comfort to reflect, that in what I said of my countrymen I extenuated their faults as much as I durst before so strict an examiner, and upon every article gave as favourable a turn as the matter

[18] A vague malady characterized by ill temper, gloom, outbursts of passion, and melancholy.

[19] The House of Lords.

[1] Carefully protecting.

would bear. For, indeed, who is there alive that will not be swayed by his bias and partiality to the place of his birth?

I have related the substance of several conversations I had with my master, during the greatest part of the time I had the honour to be in his service, but have indeed for brevity sake omitted much more than is here set down.

When I had answered all his questions, and his curiosity seemed to be fully satisfied, he sent for me one morning early, and commanding me to sit down at some distance (an honour which he had never before conferred upon me), he said he had been very seriously considering my whole story, as far as it related both to myself and my country: that he looked upon us as a sort of animals to whose share, by what accident he could not conjecture, some small pittance of reason had fallen, whereof we made no other use than by its assistance to aggravate our natural corruptions, and to acquire new ones which Nature had not given us. That we disarmed ourselves of the few abilities she had bestowed, had been very successful in multiplying our original wants, and seemed to spend our whole lives in vain endeavours to supply them by our own inventions. That as to myself, it was manifest I had neither the strength or agility of a common yahoo, that I walked infirmly on my hinder feet, had found out a contrivance to make my claws of no use or defence, and to remove the hair from my chin, which was intended as a shelter from the sun and the weather. Lastly, that I could neither run with speed, nor climb trees like my brethren (as he called them) the yahoos in this country.

That our institutions of government and law were plainly owing to our gross defects in reason, and by consequence, in virtue; because reason alone is sufficient to govern a rational creature; which was therefore a character we had no pretence to challenge,[2] even from the account I had given of my own people, although he manifestly perceived, that in order to favour them I had concealed many particulars, and often *said the thing which was not.*

He was the more confirmed in this opinion, because he observed, that as I agreed in every feature of my body with other yahoos, except where it was to my real disadvantage in point of strength, speed, and activity, the shortness of my claws, and some other particulars where nature had no part; so from the representation I had given him of our lives, our manners, and our actions, he found as near a resemblance in the disposition of our minds. He said the yahoos were known to hate one another more than they did any different species of animals; and the reason usually assigned was the odiousness of their own shapes, which all could see in the rest, but not in themselves. He had therefore begun to think it not unwise in us to cover our bodies, and, by that invention, conceal many of our deformities from each other, which would else be hardly supportable. But he now found he had been mistaken, and that the dissensions of those brutes in his country were owing to the same cause with ours, as I had described them. For if (said he) you throw among five yahoos as much food as would be sufficient for fifty, they will, instead of eating peaceably, fall together by the ears, each single one impatient to have all to itself, and therefore a servant was

[2] A title we had no right to claim.

usually employed to stand by while they were feeding abroad, and those kept at home were tied at a distance from each other; that if a cow died of age or accident, before a Houyhnhnm could secure it for his own yahoos, those in the neighbourhood would come in herds to seize it, and then would ensue such a battle as I had described, with terrible wounds made by their claws on both sides, although they seldom were able to kill one another, for want of such convenient instruments of death as we had invented. At other times the like battles have been fought between the yahoos of several neighbourhoods without any visible cause; those of one district watching all opportunities to surprise the next before they are prepared. But if they find their project hath miscarried, they return home, and, for want of enemies, engage in what I call a civil war among themselves.

That in some fields of his country there are certain shining stones of several colours, whereof the yahoos are violently fond, and when part of these stones are fixed in the earth, as it sometimes happeneth, they will dig with their claws for whole days to get them out, carry them away, and hide them by heaps in their kennels; but still looking round with great caution, for fear their comrades should find out their treasure. My master said, he could never discover the reason of this unnatural appetite, or how these stones could be of any use to a yahoo; but now he believed it might proceed from the same principle of avarice which I had ascribed to mankind; that he had once, by way of experiment, privately removed a heap of these stones from the place where one of his yahoos had buried it: whereupon the sordid animal, missing his treasure, by his loud lamenting brought the whole herd to the place, there miserably howled, then fell to biting and tearing the rest, began to pine away, would neither eat, nor sleep, nor work, till he ordered a servant privately to convey the stones into the same hole and hide them as before; which when his yahoo had found, he presently recovered his spirits and good humour, but took care to remove them to a better hiding-place, and hath ever since been a very serviceable brute.

My master farther assured me, which I also observed myself, that in the fields where these shining stones abound, the fiercest and most frequent battles are fought, occasioned by perpetual inroads of the neighbouring yahoos.

He said, it was common, when two yahoos discovered such a stone in a field, and were contending which of them should be the proprietor, a third would take the advantage, and carry it away from them both; which my master would needs contend to have some resemblance with our suits at law; wherein I thought it for our credit not to undeceive him; since the decision he mentioned was much more equitable than many decrees among us: because the plaintiff and defendant there lost nothing beside the stone they contended for, whereas our courts of equity would never have dismissed the cause while either of them had any thing left.

My master, continuing his discourse, said, there was nothing that rendered the yahoos more odious than their undistinguishing[3] appetite to devour every thing that came in their way, whether herbs, roots, berries, corrupted flesh of animals, or all mingled together: and it was peculiar in their temper, that they were fonder of what they could get by rapine or

[3] Undiscriminating.

stealth at a greater distance, than much better food provided for them at home. If their prey held out, they would eat till they were ready to burst, after which Nature had pointed out to them a certain root that gave them a general evacuation.

There was also another kind of root very juicy, but somewhat rare and difficult to be found, which the yahoos sought for with much eagerness, and would suck it with great delight; and it produced in them the same effects that wine hath upon us. It would make them sometimes hug, and sometimes tear one another; they would howl and grin, and chatter, and reel, and tumble, and then fall asleep in the mud.

I did indeed observe, that the yahoos were the only animals in this country subject to any diseases; which, however, were much fewer than horses have among us, and contracted not by any ill treatment they meet with, but by the nastiness and greediness of that sordid brute. Neither has their language any more than a general appellation for those maladies, which is borrowed from the name of the beast, and called *hnea-yahoo,* or the *yahoo's-evil,* and the cure prescribed is a mixture of their own dung and urine forcibly put down the yahoo's throat. This I have since often known to have been taken with success, and do here freely recommend it to my countrymen, for the public good, as an admirable specific[4] against all diseases produced by repletion.

As to learning, government, arts, manufactures, and the like, my master confessed he could find little or no resemblance between the yahoos of that country and those in ours. For he only meant to observe what parity[5] there was in our natures. He had heard indeed some curious[6] Houyhnhnms observe, that in most herds there was a sort of ruling yahoo (as among us there is generally some leading or principal stag in a park), who was always more deformed in body, and mischievous in disposition, than any of the rest. That this leader had usually a favourite as like himself as he could get, whose employment was to lick his master's feet and posteriors, and drive the female yahoos to his kennel; for which he was now and then rewarded with a piece of ass's flesh. This favourite is hated by the whole herd, and therefore, to protect himself, keeps always near the person of his leader. He usually continues in office till a worse can be found; but the very moment he is discarded, his successor, at the head of all the yahoos in that district, young and old, male and female, come in a body, and discharge their excrements upon him from head to foot. But how far this might be applicable to our courts and favourites, and ministers of state, my master said I could best determine.

I durst make no return to this malicious insinuation, which debased human understanding below the sagacity of a common hound, who has judgment enough to distinguish and follow the cry of the ablest dog in the pack, without being ever mistaken.

My master told me, there were some qualities remarkable in the yahoos, which he had not observed me to mention, or at least very slightly, in the accounts I had given him of human kind; he said, those animals, like other brutes, had their females in common; but in this they differed, that the she-yahoo would admit the male while she was pregnant, and that the hees

[4] Medication; remedy. [5] Resemblance. [6] Carefully observant.

would quarrel and fight with the females as fiercely as with each other. Both which practices were such degrees of infamous brutality, that no other sensitive creature ever arrived at.

Another thing he wondered at in the yahoos was their strange disposition to nastiness and dirt, whereas there appears to be a natural love of cleanliness in all other animals. As to the two former accusations, I was glad to let them pass without any reply, because I had not a word to offer upon them in defence of my species, which otherwise I certainly had done from my own inclinations. But I could have easily vindicated human kind from the imputation of singularity upon the last article, if there had been any swine in that country (as unluckily for me there were not), which, although it may be a sweeter quadruped than a yahoo, cannot, I humbly conceive, in justice pretend to more cleanliness; and so his Honour himself must have owned, if he had seen their filthy way of feeding, and their custom of wallowing and sleeping in the mud.

My master likewise mentioned another quality which his servants had discovered in several yahoos, and to him was wholly unaccountable. He said, a fancy would sometimes take a yahoo to retire into a corner, to lie down and howl, and groan, and spurn away all that came near him, although he were young and fat, and wanted neither food nor water; nor did the servants imagine what could possibly ail him. And the only remedy they found was to set him to hard work, after which he would infallibly come to himself. To this I was silent out of partiality to my own kind; yet here I could plainly discover the true seeds of spleen, which only seizeth on the lazy, the luxurious, and the rich; who, if they were forced to undergo the same regimen, I would undertake for the cure.

His Honour had farther observed, that a female yahoo would often stand behind a bank or a bush, to gaze on the young males passing by, and then appear, and hide, using many antic gestures and grimaces, at which time it was observed, that she had a most offensive smell; and when any of the males advanced, would slowly retire, looking often back, and with a counterfeit show of fear, run off into some convenient place where she knew the male would follow her.

At other times if a female stranger came among them, three or four of her own sex would get about her, and stare and chatter, and grin, and smell her all over, and then turn off with gestures that seemed to express contempt and disdain.

Perhaps my master might refine[7] a little in these speculations, which he had drawn from what he observed himself, or had been told him by others: however, I could not reflect without some amazement, and much sorrow, that the rudiments of lewdness, coquetry, censure, and scandal, should have place by instinct in womankind.

I expected every moment that my master would accuse the yahoos of those unnatural appetites[8] in both sexes, so common among us. But Nature, it seems, hath not been so expert a school-mistress; and these politer pleasures are entirely the productions of art and reason, on our side of the globe.

[7] Be excessively subtle. [8] Sodomy, presumably.

CHAPTER VIII

The author relates several particulars of the yahoos. The great virtues of the Houyhnhnms. The education and exercise of their youth. Their general assembly.

As I ought to have understood human nature much better than I supposed it possible for my master to do, so it was easy to apply the character[1] he gave of the yahoos to myself and my countrymen, and I believed I could yet make farther discoveries from my own observation. I therefore often begged his Honour to let me go among the herds of yahoos in the neighbourhood, to which he always very graciously consented, being perfectly convinced that the hatred I bore those brutes would never suffer me to be corrupted by them; and his Honour ordered one of his servants, a strong sorrel nag, very honest and good-natured, to be my guard, without whose protection I durst not undertake such adventures. For I have already told the reader how much I was pestered by those odious animals upon my first arrival. And I afterwards failed very narrowly three or four times of falling into their clutches, when I happened to stray at any distance without my hanger. And I have reason to believe they had some imagination that I was of their own species, which I often assisted myself, by stripping up my sleeves, and showing my naked arms and breast in their sight, when my protector was with me. At which times they would approach as near as they durst, and imitate my actions after the manner of monkeys, but ever with great signs of hatred, as a tame jackdaw,[2] with cap and stockings, is always persecuted by the wild ones, when he happens to be got among them.

They are prodigiously nimble from their infancy; however, I once caught a young male of three years old, and endeavoured by all marks of tenderness to make it quiet; but the little imp fell a squalling, and scratching, and biting with such violence, that I was forced to let it go, and it was high time, for a whole troop of old ones came about us at the noise, but finding the cub was safe (for away it ran), and my sorrel nag being by, they durst not venture near us. I observed the young animal's flesh to smell very rank, and the stink was somewhat between a weasel and a fox, but much more disagreeable. I forgot another circumstance (and perhaps I might have the reader's pardon if it were wholly omitted) that while I held the odious vermin in my hands, it voided its filthy excrements of a yellow liquid substance all over my clothes; but by good fortune there was a small brook hard by, where I washed myself as clean as I could, although I durst not come into my master's presence, until I were sufficiently aired.

By what I could discover, the yahoos appear to be the most unteachable of all animals, their capacities never reaching higher than to draw or carry burthens. Yet I am of opinion this defect ariseth chiefly from a perverse, restive disposition. For they are cunning, malicious, treacherous and revengeful. They are strong and hardy, but of a cowardly spirit, and by consequence insolent, abject, and cruel. It is observed, that the redhaired of both sexes are more libidinous and mischievous than the rest, whom yet they much exceed in strength and activity.

[1] Description; sketch. [2] A bird resembling a crow.

The Houyhnhnms keep the yahoos for present use in huts not far from the house; but the rest are sent abroad to certain fields, where they dig up roots, eat several kinds of herbs, and search about for carrion,[3] or sometimes catch weasels and *luhimuhs* (a sort of wild rat), which they greedily devour. Nature hath taught them to dig deep holes with their nails on the side of a rising ground, wherein they lie by themselves, only the kennels of the females are larger, sufficient to hold two or three cubs.

They swim from their infancy like frogs, and are able to continue long under water, where they often take fish, which the females carry home to their young. And upon this occasion, I hope the reader will pardon my relating an odd adventure.

Being one day abroad with my protector the sorrel nag, and the weather exceeding hot, I entreated him to let me bathe in a river that was near. He consented, and I immediately stripped myself stark naked, and went down softly into the stream. It happened that a young female yahoo, standing behind a bank, saw the whole proceeding, and inflamed by desire, as the nag and I conjectured, came running with all speed, and leaped into the water within five yards of the place where I bathed. I was never in my life so terribly frighted; the nag was grazing at some distance, not suspecting any harm. She embraced me after a most fulsome manner; I roared as loud as I could, and the nag came galloping towards me, whereupon she quitted her grasp, with the utmost reluctancy, and leaped upon the opposite bank, where she stood gazing and howling all the time I was putting on my clothes.

This was matter of diversion to my master and his family, as well as of mortification to myself. For now I could no longer deny that I was a real yahoo in every limb and feature, since the females had a natural propensity to me as one of their own species: neither was the hair of this brute of a red colour (which might have been some excuse for an appetite a little irregular) but black as a sloe,[4] and her countenance did not make an appearance altogether so hideous as the rest of the kind; for, I think, she could not be above eleven years old.

Having already lived three years in this country, the reader I suppose will expect that I should, like other travellers, give him some account of the manners and customs of its inhabitants, which it was indeed my principal study to learn.

As these noble Houyhnhnms are endowed by nature with a general disposition to all virtues, and have no conceptions or ideas of what is evil in a rational creature, so their grand maxim is, to cultivate reason, and to be wholly governed by it. Neither is reason among them a point problematical as with us, where men can argue with plausibility on both sides of a question; but strikes you with immediate conviction; as it must needs do where it is not mingled, obscured, or discoloured by passion and interest. I remember it was with extreme difficulty that I could bring my master to understand the meaning of the word *opinion,* or how a point could be disputable; because reason taught us to affirm or deny only where we are certain; and beyond our knowledge we cannot do either. So that controver-

[3] The flesh of dead animals. [4] A blue-black fruit.

sies, wranglings, disputes, and positiveness in false or dubious propositions are evils unknown among the Houyhnhnms. In the like manner, when I used to explain to him our several systems of natural philosophy,[5] he would laugh that a creature pretending to reason should value itself upon the knowledge of other people's conjectures, and in things where that knowledge, if it were certain, could be of no use. Wherein he agreed entirely with the sentiments of Socrates, as Plato delivers them;[6] which I mention as the highest honour I can do that prince of philosophers. I have often since reflected what destruction such a doctrine would make in the libraries of Europe, and how many paths to fame would be then shut up in the learned world.

Friendship and benevolence are the two principal virtues among the Houyhnhnms, and these not confined to particular objects, but universal to the whole race. For a stranger from the remotest part is equally treated with the nearest neighbour, and wherever he goes, looks upon himself as at home. They preserve decency and civility in the highest degrees, but are altogether ignorant of ceremony. They have no fondness[7] for their colts or foals, but the care they take in educating them proceeds entirely from the dictates of reason. And I observed my master to show the same affection to his neighbour's issue that he had for his own. They will have it that nature teaches them to love the whole species, and it is reason only that maketh a distinction of persons, where there is a superior degree of virtue.

When the matron Houyhnhnms have produced one of each sex, they no longer accompany with their consorts, except they lose one of their issue by some casualty, which very seldom happens: but in such a case they meet again, or when the like accident befalls a person whose wife is past bearing, some other couple bestows on him one of their own colts, and then go together a second time till the mother be pregnant. This caution is necessary to prevent the country from being overburthened with numbers. But the race of inferior Houyhnhnms bred up to be servants is not so strictly limited upon this article; these are allowed to produce three of each sex, to be domestics in the noble families.

In their marriages they are exactly careful to choose such colours as will not make any disagreeable mixture in the breed. Strength is chiefly valued in the male, and comeliness in the female, not upon the account of love, but to preserve the race from degenerating; for where a female happens to excel in strength, a consort is chosen with regard to comeliness. Courtship, love, presents, jointures, settlements,[8] have no place in their thoughts, or terms whereby to express them in their language. The young couple meet and are joined, merely because it is the determination of their parents and friends: it is what they see done every day, and they look upon it as one of the necessary actions in a reasonable being. But the violation of marriage, or any other unchastity, was never heard of: and the married pair pass

[5] Physical science.

[6] In Book V of Plato's *Republic,* Socrates distinguishes between vague opinion and true (therefore morally useful) knowledge.

[7] Doting affection.

[8] Jointures and settlements are property and money legally apportioned to a woman upon her marriage.

their lives with the same friendship and mutual benevolence that they bear to all others of the same species who come in their way; without jealousy, fondness, quarrelling, or discontent.

In educating the youth of both sexes, their method is admirable, and highly deserves our imitation. These are not suffered to taste a grain of oats, except upon certain days, till eighteen years old; nor milk, but very rarely; and in summer they graze two hours in the morning, and as many in the evening, which their parents likewise observe, but the servants are not allowed above half that time, and a great part of the grass is brought home, which they eat at the most convenient hours, when they can be best spared from work.

Temperance, industry, exercise and cleanliness, are the lessons equally enjoined to the young ones of both sexes: and my master thought it monstrous in us to give the females a different kind of education from the males, except in some articles of domestic management; whereby, as he truly observed, one half of our natives were good for nothing but bringing children into the world: and to trust the care of their children to such useless animals, he said, was yet a greater instance of brutality.

But the Houyhnhnms train up their youth to strength, speed, and hardiness, by exercising them in running races up and down steep hills, or over hard stony grounds, and when they are all in a sweat, they are ordered to leap over head and ears into a pond or a river. Four times a year the youth of certain districts meet to show their proficiency in running and leaping, and other feats of strength or agility, where the victor is rewarded with a song made in his or her praise. On this festival the servants drive a herd of yahoos into the field, laden with hay, and oats, and milk for a repast to the Houyhnhnms; after which these brutes are immediately driven back again, for fear of being noisome[9] to the assembly.

Every fourth year, at the vernal equinox, there is a representative council of the whole nation, which meets in a plain about twenty miles from our house, and continues about five or six days. Here they inquire into the state and condition of the several districts; whether they abound or be deficient in hay or oats, or cows or yahoos. And wherever there is any want (which is but seldom) it is immediately supplied by unanimous consent and contribution. Here likewise the regulation of children is settled: as for instance, if a Houyhnhnm hath two males, he changeth one of them with another who hath two females: and when a child hath been lost by any casualty, where the mother is past breeding, it is determined what family in the district shall breed another to supply the loss.

CHAPTER IX

A grand debate at the general assembly of the Houyhnhnms, and how it was determined. The learning of the Houyhnhnms. Their buildings. Their manner of burials. The defectiveness of their language.

One of these grand assemblies was held in my time, about three months

[9] Offensive, especially in odor.

before my departure, whither my master went as the representative of our district. In this council was resumed their old debate, and indeed, the only debate that ever happened in their country; whereof my master after his return gave me a very particular account.

The question to be debated was, whether the yahoos should be exterminated from the face of the earth. One of the members for the affirmative offered several arguments of great strength and weight, alleging, that as the yahoos were the most filthy, noisome, and deformed animal which nature ever produced, so they were the most restive and indocible,[1] mischievous and malicious: they would privately suck the teats of the Houyhnhnms' cows, kill and devour their cats, trample down their oats and grass, if they were not continually watched, and commit a thousand other extravagancies. He took notice of a general tradition, that yahoos had not been always in their country: but that many ages ago two of these brutes appeared together upon a mountain, whether produced by the heat of the sun upon corrupted mud and slime, or from the ooze and froth of the sea, was never known. That these yahoos engendered, and their brood in a short time grew so numerous as to overrun and infest the whole nation. That the Houyhnhnms, to get rid of this evil, made a general hunting, and at last enclosed the whole herd; and destroying the older, every Houyhnhnm kept two young ones in a kennel, and brought them to such a degree of tameness, as an animal so savage by nature can be capable of acquiring; using them for draught and carriage. That there seemed to be much truth in this tradition, and that those creatures could not be *ylnhniamshy* (or *aborigines* of the land) because of the violent hatred the Houyhnhnms, as well as all other animals, bore them; which although their evil disposition sufficiently deserved, could never have arrived at so high a degree, if they had been aborigines, or else they would have long since been rooted out. That the inhabitants taking a fancy to use the service of the yahoos, had very imprudently neglected to cultivate the breed of asses, which were a comely animal, easily kept, more tame and orderly, without any offensive smell, strong enough for labour, although they yield to the other in agility of body; and if their braying be no agreeable sound, it is far preferable to the horrible howlings of the yahoos.

Several others declared their sentiments to the same purpose, when my master proposed an expedient to the assembly, whereof he had indeed borrowed the hint from me. He approved of the tradition, mentioned by the "honourable member" who spoke before, and affirmed, that the two yahoos said to be first seen among them had been driven thither over the sea; that coming to land, and being forsaken by their companions, they retired to the mountains, and degenerating by degrees, became in process of time much more savage than those of their own species in the country from whence these two originals came. The reason of his assertion was, that he had now in his possession a certain wonderful yahoo (meaning myself) which most of them had heard of, and many of them had seen. He then related to them how he first found me; that my body was all covered with an artificial composure of the skins and hairs of other animals: that I spoke in a language of my own, and had thoroughly learned theirs: that I had

[1] Restless and unteachable.

related to him the accidents which brought me thither: that when he saw me without my covering, I was an exact yahoo in every part, only of a whiter colour, less hairy, and with shorter claws. He added, how I had endeavoured to persuade him, that in my own and other countries the yahoos acted as the governing, rational animal, and held the Houyhnhnms in servitude: that he observed in me all the qualities of a yahoo, only a little more civilized by some tincture of reason, which however was in a degree as far inferior to the Houyhnhnm race as the yahoos of their country were to me: that, among other things, I mentioned a custom we had of castrating Houyhnhnms when they were young, in order to render them tame; that the operation was easy and safe; that it was no shame to learn wisdom from brutes, as industry is taught by the ant, and building by the swallow. (For so I translate the word *lyhannh,* although it be a much larger fowl.) That this invention might be practised upon the younger yahoos here, which, besides rendering them tractable and fitter for use, would in an age put an end to the whole species without destroying life. That in the mean time the Houyhnhnms should be exhorted to cultivate the breed of asses, which, as they are in all respects more valuable brutes, so they have this advantage, to be fit for service at five years old, which the others are not till twelve.

This was all my master thought fit to tell me at that time of what passed in the grand council. But he was pleased to conceal one particular, which related personally to myself, whereof I soon felt the unhappy effect, as the reader will know in its proper place, and from whence I date all the succeeding misfortunes of my life.

The Houyhnhnms have no letters,[2] and consequently their knowledge is all traditional. But there happening few events of any moment among a people so well united, naturally disposed to every virtue, wholly governed by reason, and cut off from all commerce with other nations, the historical part is easily preserved without burthening their memories. I have already observed, that they are subject to no diseases, and therefore can have no need of physicians. However, they have excellent medicines composed of herbs, to cure accidental bruises and cuts in the pastern or frog[3] of the foot by sharp stones, as well as other maims and hurts in the several parts of the body.

They calculate the year by the revolution of the sun and the moon, but use no subdivisions into weeks. They are well enough acquainted with the motions of those two luminaries, and understand the nature of eclipses; and this is the utmost progress of their astronomy.

In poetry they must be allowed to excel all other mortals; wherein the justness of their similes, and the minuteness, as well as exactness of their descriptions, are indeed inimitable. Their verses abound very much in both of these, and usually contain either some exalted notions of friendship and benevolence, or the praises of those who were victors in races and other bodily exercises. Their buildings, although very rude and simple, are not inconvenient, but well contrived to defend them from all injuries of cold and heat. They have a kind of tree, which at forty years old loosens in the root, and falls with the first storm; it grows very straight, and being pointed like stakes with a sharp stone (for the Houyhnhnms know not the use of

[2] Writings. [3] Part of the sole of the hoof.

iron), they stick them erect in the ground about ten inches asunder, and then weave in oat-straw, or sometimes wattles betwixt them. The roof is made after the same manner, and so are the doors.

The Houyhnhnms use the hollow part between the pastern and the hoof of their forefeet as we do our hands, and this with greater dexterity than I could at first imagine. I have seen a white mare of our family thread a needle (which I lent her on purpose) with that joint. They milk their cows, reap their oats, and do all the work which requires hands, in the same manner. They have a kind of hard flints, which, by grinding against other stones, they form into instruments, that serve instead of wedges, axes, and hammers. With tools made of these flints they likewise cut their hay, and reap their oats, which there groweth naturally in several fields: the yahoos draw home the sheaves in carriages, and the servants tread them in certain covered huts, to get out the grain, which is kept in stores. They make a rude kind of earthen and wooden vessels, and bake the former in the sun.

If they can avoid casualties, they die only of old age, and are buried in the obscurest places that can be found, their friends and relations expressing neither joy nor grief at their departure; nor does the dying person discover the least regret that he is leaving the world, any more than if he were upon[4] returning home from a visit to one of his neighbours; I remember my master having once made an appointment with a friend and his family to come to his house upon some affair of importance; on the day fixed, the mistress and her two children came very late; she made two excuses, first for her husband, who, as she said, happened that very morning to *lhnuwnh*. The word is strongly expressive in their language, but not easily rendered into English; it signifies, "to retire to his first mother." Her excuse for not coming sooner was, that her husband dying late in the morning, she was a good while consulting her servants about a convenient place where his body should be laid; and I observed she behaved herself at our house as cheerfully as the rest: she died about three months after.

They live generally to seventy or seventy-five years, very seldom to fourscore: some weeks before their death they feel a gradual decay, but without pain. During this time they are much visited by their friends, because they cannot go abroad[5] with their usual ease and satisfaction. However, about ten days before their death, which they seldom fail in computing, they return the visits that have been made them by those who are nearest in the neighbourhood, being carried in a convenient sledge drawn by yahoos, which vehicle they use, not only upon this occasion, but when they grow old, upon long journeys, or when they are lamed by any accident. And therefore when the dying Houyhnhnms return those visits, they take a solemn leave of their friends, as if they were going to some remote part of the country, where they designed to pass the rest of their lives.

I know not whether it may be worth observing, that the Houyhnhnms have no word in their language to express any thing that is evil, except what they borrow from the deformities or ill qualities of the yahoos. Thus they denote the folly of a servant, an omission of a child, a stone that cuts their feet, a continuance of foul or unseasonable weather, and the like, by adding to each the epithet of *yahoo*. For instance, *hhnm yahoo, whnaholm yahoo,*

[4] On the point of. [5] Away from home.

ynlhnmawihlma yahoo, and an ill-contrived house *ynholmhnmrohlnw yahoo.*

I could with great pleasure enlarge farther upon the manners and virtues of this excellent people; but intending in a short time to publish a volume by itself expressly upon that subject, I refer the reader thither. And in the mean time, proceed to relate my own sad catastrophe.[6]

CHAPTER X

The author's economy[1] *and happy life among the Houyhnhnms. His great improvement in virtue, by conversing with them. Their conversations. The author has notice given him by his master that he must depart from the country. He falls into a swoon for grief, but submits. He contrives and finishes a canoe, by the help of a fellow-servant, and puts to sea at a venture.*[2]

I had settled my little economy to my own heart's content. My master had ordered a room to be made for me after their manner, about six yards from the house, the sides and floors of which I plastered with clay, and covered with rush mats of my own contriving; I had beaten hemp, which there grows wild, and made of it a sort of ticking: this I filled with the feathers of several birds I had taken with springes made of yahoos' hairs, and were excellent food. I had worked two chairs with my knife, the sorrel nag helping me in the grosser and more laborious part. When my clothes were worn to rags, I made myself others with the skins of rabbits, and of a certain beautiful animal about the same size, called *nnuhnoh,* the skin of which is covered with a fine down. Of these I likewise made very tolerable stockings. I soled my shoes with wood which I cut from a tree, and fitted to the upper leather, and when this was worn out, I supplied it with the skins of yahoos dried in the sun. I often got honey out of hollow trees, which I mingled with water, or eat it with my bread. No man could more verify the truth of these two maxims, *That nature is very easily satisfied;* and *That necessity is the mother of invention.* I enjoyed perfect health of body and tranquillity of mind; I did not feel the treachery or inconstancy of a friend, nor the injuries of a secret or open enemy. I had no occasion of bribing, flattering or pimping to procure the favour of any great man or of his minion.[3] I wanted no fence against fraud or oppression; here was neither physician to destroy my body, nor lawyer to ruin my fortune; no informer to watch my words and actions, or forge accusations against me for hire: here were no gibers, censurers, backbiters, pickpockets, highwaymen, housebreakers, attorneys, bawds, buffoons, gamesters, politicans, wits, splenetics,[4] tedious talkers, controvertists,[5] ravishers, murderers, robbers, virtuosos: no leaders or followers of party and faction: no encouragers to vice, by seducement or examples: no dungeon, axes, gibbets, whipping-posts, or pillories: no cheating shopkeepers or mechanics:[6] no pride, vanity, or affectation: no

[6] Conclusion (as of a play). [1] Living arrangements. [2] At random.
[3] Obsequious favorite. [4] People suffering from spleen.
[5] Disputers; controversialists. [6] Craftsmen; low fellows.

fops, bullies, drunkards, strolling whores, or poxes:[7] no ranting, lewd, expensive wives: no stupid, proud pedants: no importunate, overbearing, quarrelsome, noisy, roaring, empty, conceited, swearing companions: no scoundrels, raised from the dust upon the merit of their vices, or nobility thrown into it on account of their virtues: no lords, fiddlers, judges or dancing-masters.

I had the favour of being admitted to several Houyhnhnms, who came to visit or dine with my master; where his Honour graciously suffered me to wait in the room, and listen to their discourse. Both he and his company would often descend to ask me questions, and receive my answers. I had also sometimes the honour of attending my master in his visits to others. I never presumed to speak, except in answer to a question, and then I did it with inward regret, because it was a loss of so much time for improving myself: but I was infinitely delighted with the station of an humble auditor in such conversations, where nothing passed but what was useful, expressed in the fewest and most significant words: where (as I have already said) the greatest decency was observed, without the least degree of ceremony; where no person spoke without being pleased himself, and pleasing his companions; where there was no interruptions, tediousness, heat, or difference of sentiments. They have a notion, that when people are met together, a short silence doth much improve conversation: this I found to be true; for during those little intermissions of talk, new ideas would arise in their minds, which very much enlivened the discourse. Their subjects are generally on friendship and benevolence, or order and economy, sometimes upon the visible operations of nature, or ancient traditions, upon the bounds and limits of virtue, upon the unerring rules of reason, or upon some determinations to be taken at the next great assembly, and often upon the various excellencies of poetry. I may add without vanity, that my presence often gave them sufficient matter for discourse, because it afforded my master an occasion of letting his friends into the history of me and my country, upon which they were all pleased to descant[8] in a manner not very advantageous to human kind; and for that reason I shall not repeat what they said: only I may be allowed to observe, that his Honour, to my great admiration, appeared to understand the nature of yahoos much better than myself. He went through all our vices and follies, and discovered many which I had never mentioned to him, by only supposing what qualities a yahoo of their country, with a small proportion of reason, might be capable of exerting; and concluded, with too much probability, how vile as well as miserable such a creature must be.

I freely confess, that all the little knowledge I have of any value was acquired by the lectures I received from my master, and from hearing the discourses of him and his friends; to which I should be prouder to listen, than to dictate to the greatest and wisest assembly in Europe. I admired the strength, comeliness, and speed of the inhabitants; and such a constellation of virtues in such amiable persons produced in me the highest veneration. At first, indeed, I did not feel that natural awe which the yahoos and all other animals bear towards them; but it grew upon me by degrees, much sooner than I imagined, and was mingled with a respectful love and grati-

[7] Skin diseases, especially syphilis. [8] Discourse.

tude, that they would condescend to distinguish me from the rest of my species.

When I thought of my family, my friends, my countrymen, or human race in general, I considered them as they really were, yahoos in shape and disposition, only a little more civilized, and qualified with the gift of speech, but making no other use of reason than to improve and multiply those vices whereof their brethren in this country had only the share that nature allotted them. When I happened to behold the reflection of my own form in a lake or fountain, I turned away my face in horror and detestation of myself, and could better endure the sight of a common yahoo, than of my own person. By conversing with the Houyhnhnms, and looking upon them with delight, I fell to imitate their gait and gesture, which is now grown into a habit, and my friends often tell me in a blunt way that I "trot like a horse"; which, however, I take for a great compliment: neither shall I disown, that in speaking I am apt to fall into the voice and manner of the Houyhnhnms, and hear myself ridiculed on that account without the least mortification.

In the midst of all this happiness, when I looked upon myself to be fully settled for life, my master sent for me one morning a little earlier than his usual hour. I observed by his countenance that he was in some perplexity, and at a loss how to begin what he had to speak. After a short silence, he told me, he did not know how I would take what he was going to say; that in the last general assembly, when the affair of the yahoos was entered upon, the representatives had taken offence at his keeping a yahoo (meaning myself) in his family more like a Houyhnhnm than a brute animal. That he was known frequently to converse with me, as if he could receive some advantage or pleasure in my company: that such a practice was not agreeable to reason or nature, or a thing ever heard of before among them. The assembly did therefore exhort him, either to employ me like the rest of my species, or command me to swim back to the place from whence I came. That the first of these expedients was utterly rejected by all the Houyhnhnms who had ever seen me at his house or their own: for they alleged, that because I had some rudiments of reason, added to the natural pravity[9] of those animals, it was to be feared, I might be able to seduce them into the woody and mountainous parts of the country, and bring them in troops by night to destroy the Houyhnhnms' cattle, as being naturally of the ravenous kind, and averse from labour.

My master added, that he was daily pressed by the Houyhnhnms of the neighbourhood to have the assembly's exhortation executed, which he could not put off much longer. He doubted[10] it would be impossible for me to swim to another country, and therefore wished I would contrive some sort of vehicle resembling those I had described to him, that might carry me on the sea, in which work I should have the assistance of his own servants, as well as those of his neighbours. He concluded, that for his own part he could have been content to keep me in his service as long as I lived, because he found I had cured myself of some bad habits and dispositions, by endeavouring, as far as my inferior nature was capable, to imitate the Houyhnhnms.

I should here observe to the reader, that a decree of the general assem-

[9] Depravity. [10] Suspected.

bly in this country is expressed by the word *hnhloayn,* which signifies an *exhortation,* as near as I can render it: for they have no conception how a rational creature can be compelled, but only advised or exhorted, because no person can disobey reason, without giving up his claim to be a rational creature.

I was struck with the utmost grief and despair at my master's discourse, and being unable to support the agonies I was under, I fell into a swoon at his feet; when I came to myself he told me that he concluded I had been dead. (For these people are subject to no such imbecilities of nature.) I answered, in a faint voice, that death would have been too great an happiness; that although I could not blame the assembly's exhortation, or the urgency of his friends, yet, in my weak and corrupt judgment, I thought it might consist with reason to have been less rigorous. That I could not swim a league, and probably the nearest land to theirs might be distant above an hundred; that many materials, necessary for making a small vessel to carry me off, were wholly wanting in this country, which, however, I would attempt in obedience and gratitude to his Honour, although I concluded the thing to be impossible, and therefore looked on my self as already devoted[11] to destruction. That the certain prospect of an unnatural death was the least of my evils: for, supposing I should escape with life by some strange adventure, how could I think with temper[12] of passing my days among yahoos, and relapsing into my old corruptions, for want of examples to lead and keep me within the paths of virtue? That I knew too well upon what solid reasons all the determinations of the wise Houyhnhnms were founded, not to be shaken by arguments of mine, a miserable yahoo; and therefore, after presenting him with my humble thanks for the offer of his servants' assistance in making a vessel, and desiring a reasonable time for so difficult a work, I told him I would endeavour to preserve a wretched being; and, if ever I returned to England, was not without hopes of being useful to my own species, by celebrating the praises of the renowned Houyhnhnms, and proposing their virtues to the imitation of mankind.

My master in a few words made me a very gracious reply, allowed me the space of two months to finish my boat; and ordered the sorrel nag, my fellow-servant (for so at this distance I may presume to call him) to follow my instructions, because I told my master, that his help would be sufficient, and I knew he had a tenderness for me.

In his company my first business was to go to that part of the coast where my rebellious crew had ordered me to be set on shore. I got upon a height, and looking on every side into the sea, fancied I saw a small island, towards the northeast: I took out my pocket-glass, and could then clearly distinguish it about five leagues off, as I computed; but it appeared to the sorrel nag to be only a blue cloud: for as he had no conception of any country beside his own, so he could not be as expert in distinguishing remote objects at sea as we who so much converse in[13] that element.

After I had discovered this island, I considered no farther; but resolved it should, if possible, be the first place of my banishment, leaving the consequence to fortune.

[11] Doomed. [12] Calmness. [13] Are familiar with.

I returned home, and consulting with the sorrel nag, we went into a copse at some distance, where I with my knife, and he with a sharp flint fastened very artificially[14] after their manner, to a wooden handle, cut down several oak wattles about the thickness of a walking-staff, and some larger pieces. But I shall not trouble the reader with a particular description of my own mechanics; let it suffice to say that in six weeks' time, with the help of the sorrel nag, who performed the parts that required most labour, I finished a sort of Indian canoe, but much larger, covering it with the skins of yahoos well stitched together, with hempen threads of my own making. My sail was likewise composed of the skins of the same animal; but I made use of the youngest I could get, the older being too tough and thick, and I likewise provided myself with four paddles. I laid in a stock of boiled flesh, of rabbits and fowls, and took with me two vessels, one filled with milk, and the other with water.

I tried my canoe in a large pond near my master's house, and then corrected in it what was amiss; stopping all the chinks with yahoos' tallow, till I found it staunch, and able to bear me and my freight. And when it was as complete as I could possibly make it, I had it drawn on a carriage very gently by yahoos to the seaside, under the conduct of the sorrel nag and another servant.

When all was ready, and the day came for my departure, I took leave of my master and lady, and the whole family, my eyes flowing with tears, and my heart quite sunk with grief. But his Honour, out of curiosity, and perhaps (if I may speak it without vanity) partly out of kindness, was determined to see me in my canoe, and got several of his neighbouring friends to accompany him. I was forced to wait above an hour for the tide, and then observing the wind very fortunately bearing towards the island, to which I intended to steer my course, I took a second leave of my master: but as I was going to prostrate myself to kiss his hoof, he did me the honour to raise it gently to my mouth. I am not ignorant how much I have been censured for mentioning this last particular. Detractors are pleased to think it improbable, that so illustrious a person should descend to give so great a mark of distinction to a creature so inferior as I. Neither have I forgot how apt some travellers are to boast of extraordinary favours they have received. But if these censurers were better acquainted with the noble and courteous disposition of the Houyhnhnms, they would soon change their opinion.

I paid my respects to the rest of the Houyhnhnms in his Honour's company; then getting into my canoe, I pushed off from shore.

CHAPTER XI

The author's dangerous voyage. He arrives at New Holland,[1] hoping to settle there. Is wounded with an arrow by one of the natives. Is seized and carried by force into a Portuguese ship. The great civilities of the captain. The author arrives at England.

[14] Ingeniously. [1] The coast of Australia.

I began this desperate voyage on February 15, 1714–5,[2] at 9 o'clock in the morning. The wind was very favourable; however, I made use at first only of my paddles, but considering I should soon be weary, and that the wind might probably chop about, I ventured to set up my little sail; and thus with the help of the tide I went at the rate of a league and a half an hour, as near as I could guess. My master and his friends continued on the shore till I was almost out of sight; and I often heard the sorrel nag (who always loved me) crying out, *Hnuy illa nyha maiah yahoo,* Take care of thyself, gentle yahoo.

My design was, if possible, to discover some small island uninhabited, yet sufficient by my labour to furnish me with the necessaries of life, which I would have thought a greater happiness than to be first minister in the politest court of Europe; so horrible was the idea I conceived of returning to live in the society and under the government of yahoos. For in such a solitude as I desired, I could at least enjoy my own thoughts, and reflect with delight on the virtues of those inimitable Houyhnhnms, without any opportunity of degenerating into the vices and corruptions of my own species.

The reader may remember what I related when my crew conspired against me, and confined me to my cabin. How I continued there several weeks, without knowing what course we took, and when I was put ashore in the long-boat, how the sailors told me with oaths, whether true or false, that they knew not in what part of the world we were. However, I did then believe us to be about ten degrees southward of the Cape of Good Hope, or about 45 degrees southern latitude, as I gathered from some general words I overheard among them, being I supposed to the southeast in their intended voyage to Madagascar. And although this were but little better than conjecture, yet I resolved to steer my course eastward, hoping to reach the southwest coast of New Holland,[3] and perhaps some such island as I desired, lying westward of it. The wind was full west, and by six in the evening I computed I had gone eastward at least eighteen leagues, when I spied a very small island about half a league off, which I soon reached.[4] It was nothing but a rock, with one creek, naturally arched by the force of tempests. Here I put in my canoe, and climbing a part of the rock, I could plainly discover land to the east, extending from south to north. I lay all night in my canoe, and repeating my voyage early in the morning, I arrived in seven hours to the southeast point of New Holland. This confirmed me in the opinion I have long entertained, that the maps and charts place this country at least three degrees more to the east than it really is; which thought I communicated many years ago to my worthy friend Mr. Herman Moll,[5] and gave him my reasons for it, although he hath rather chosen to follow other authors.

I saw no inhabitants in the place where I landed, and being unarmed, I

[2] That is, 1714 in England (which, still using the old calendar, dated the new year from March 25), but 1715 elsewhere in Europe. England did not adopt the new calendar until 1752.

[3] Swift or Gulliver is in error; the western coast of Australia, or New Holland, is thousands of miles from Africa.

[4] Another lapse; in Book X the plan had been to sail to an island five leagues (15 miles) from Houyhnhnmland.

[5] A Dutch-English mapmaker.

was afraid of venturing far into the country. I found some shellfish on the shore, and eat them raw, not daring to kindle a fire, for fear of being discovered by the natives. I continued three days feeding on oysters and limpets,[6] to save my own provisions, and I fortunately found a brook of excellent water, which gave me great relief.

On the fourth day, venturing out early a little too far, I saw twenty or thirty natives upon a height, not above five hundred yards from me. They were stark naked, men, women, and children, round a fire, as I could discover by the smoke. One of them spied me, and gave notice to the rest; five of them advanced towards me, leaving the women and children at the fire. I made what haste I could to the shore, and getting into my canoe, shoved off: the savages observing me retreat, ran after me; and before I could get far enough into the sea, discharged an arrow, which wounded me deeply on the inside of my left knee (I shall carry the mark to my grave). I apprehended the arrow might be poisoned, and paddling out of the reach of their darts (being a calm day), I made a shift to suck the wound, and dress it as well as I could.

I was at a loss what to do, for I durst not return to the same landing-place, but stood to the north, and was forced to paddle; for the wind, although very gentle, was against me, blowing northwest.[7] As I was looking about for a secure landing-place, I saw a sail to the north-northeast, which appearing every minute more visible, I was in some doubt, whether I should wait for them or no; but at last my detestation of the yahoo race prevailed, and turning my canoe, I sailed and paddled together to the south, and got into the same creek from whence I set out in the morning, choosing rather to trust myself among these barbarians, than live with European yahoos. I drew up my canoe as close as I could to the shore, and hid myself behind a stone by the little brook, which, as I have already said, was excellent water.

The ship came within a half a league of this creek, and sent out her long-boat with vessels to take in fresh water (for the place it seems was very well known) but I did not observe it until the boat was almost on shore, and it was too late to seek another hiding-place. The seamen at their landing observed my canoe, and rummaging it all over, easily conjectured that the owner could not be far off. Four of them well armed searched every cranny and lurking-hole, till at last they found me flat on my face behind the stone. They gazed a while in admiration[8] at my strange uncouth dress, my coat made of skins, my wooden-soled shoes, and my furred stockings; from whence, however, they concluded I was not a native of the place, who all go naked. One of the seamen in Portuguese bid me rise, and asked who I was. I understood that language very well, and getting upon my feet, said, I was a poor yahoo, banished from the Houyhnhnms, and desired they would please to let me depart. They admired to hear me answer them in their own tongue, and saw by my complexion I must be an European; but were at loss to know what I meant by yahoos and Houyhnhnms, and at the same time fell a laughing at my strange tone in speaking, which resembled the neighing of a horse. I trembled all the while betwixt fear and hatred: I again desired leave to depart, and was gently moving to my canoe; but they laid

[6] A kind of shellfish. [7] Out of the northwest. [8] Wonder.

hold on me, desiring to know, what country I was of, whence I came, with many other questions. I told them I was born in England, from whence I came about five years ago, and then their country and ours were at peace. I therefore hoped they would not treat me as an enemy, since I meant them no harm, but was a poor yahoo, seeking some desolate place where to pass the remainder of his unfortunate life.

When they began to talk, I thought I never heard or saw any thing so unnatural; for it appeared to me as monstrous as if a dog or a cow should speak in England, or a yahoo in Houyhnhnmland. The honest[9] Portuguese were equally amazed at my strange dress, and the odd manner of delivering my words, which however they understood very well. They spoke to me with great humanity, and said they were sure their captain would carry me *gratis* to Lisbon, from whence I might return to my own country; that two of the seamen would go back to the ship, inform the captain of what they had seen, and receive his orders; in the mean time, unless I would give my solemn oath not to fly, they would secure me by force. I thought it best to comply with their proposal. They were very curious to know my story, but I gave them very little satisfaction; and they all conjectured that my misfortunes had impaired my reason. In two hours the boat, which went loaden with vessels of water, returned with the captain's commands to fetch me on board. I fell on my knees to preserve my liberty; but all was in vain, and the men having tied me with cords, heaved me into the boat, from whence I was taken into the ship, and from thence into the captain's cabin.

His name was Pedro de Mendez; he was a very courteous and generous person; he entreated me to give some account of my self, and desired to know what I would eat or drink; said, I should be used as well as himself, and spoke so many obliging things, that I wondered to find such civilities from a yahoo. However, I remained silent and sullen; I was ready to faint at the very smell of him and his men. At last I desired something to eat out of my own canoe; but he ordered me a chicken and some excellent wine, and then directed that I should be put to bed in a very clean cabin. I would not undress myself, but lay on the bed-clothes, and in half an hour stole out, when I thought the crew was at dinner, and getting to the side of the ship was going to leap into the sea, and swim for my life, rather than continue among yahoos. But one of the seamen prevented me, and having informed the captain, I was chained to my cabin.

After dinner Don Pedro came to me, and desired to know my reason for so desperate an attempt: assured me he only meant to do me all the service he was able, and spoke so very movingly, that at last I descended[10] to treat him like an animal which had some little portion of reason. I gave him a very short relation of my voyage, of the conspiracy against me by my own men, of the country where they set me on shore, and of my three years' residence there. All which he looked upon as if it were a dream or a vision; whereat I took great offence; for I had quite forgot the faculty of lying, so peculiar to yahoos in all countries where they preside, and, consequently, the disposition of suspecting truth in others of their own species. I asked him, whether it were the custom of his country to *say the thing that was not.* I assured him I had almost forgot what he meant by falsehood, and if

[9] Unpretentious; ingenuous. [10] Condescended.

I had lived a thousand years in Houyhnhnmland, I should never have heard a lie from the meanest servant; that I was altogether indifferent whether he believed me or no; but however, in return for his favours, I would give so much allowance to the corruption of his nature as to answer any objection he would please to make, and he might easily discover the truth.

The captain, a wise man, after many endeavours to catch me tripping in some part of my story, at last began to have a better opinion of my veracity. But he added, that since I professed so inviolable an attachment to truth, I must give him my word of honour to bear him company in this voyage without attempting anything against my life, or else he would continue me a prisoner till we arrived in Lisbon. I gave him the promise he required; but at the same time protested that I would suffer the greatest hardships rather than return to live among yahoos.

Our voyage passed without any considerable accident.[11] In gratitude to the captain I sometimes sat with him at his earnest request, and strove to conceal my antipathy to human kind, although it often broke out, which he suffered to pass without observation. But the greatest part of the day, I confined myself to my cabin, to avoid seeing any of the crew. The captain had often entreated me to strip myself of my savage dress, and offered to lend me the best suit of clothes he had. This I would not be prevailed on to accept, abhorring to cover myself with anything that had been on the back of a yahoo. I only desired he would lend me two clean shirts, which having been washed since he wore them, I believed would not so much defile me. These I changed every second day, and washed them myself.

We arrived at Lisbon, Nov. 5, 1715. At our landing the captain forced me to cover myself with his cloak, to prevent the rabble from crowding about me. I was conveyed to his own house, and, at my earnest request, he led me up to the highest room backwards.[12] I conjured him to conceal from all persons what I had told him of the Houyhnhnms, because the least hint of such a story would not only draw numbers of people to see me, but probably put me in danger of being imprisoned, or burnt by the Inquisition.[13] The captain persuaded me to accept a suit of clothes newly made, but I would not suffer the tailor to take my measure; however, Don Pedro being almost of my size, they fitted me well enough. He accoutred me with other necessaries all new, which I aired for twenty-four hours before I would use them.

The captain had no wife, nor above three servants, none of which were suffered to attend at meals, and his whole deportment was so obliging, added to very good *human* understanding, that I really began to tolerate his company. He gained so far upon me, that I ventured to look out of the back window. By degrees I was brought into another room, from whence I peeped into the street, but drew my head back in a fright. In a week's time he seduced me down to the door. I found my terror gradually lessened, but my hatred and contempt seemed to increase. I was at last bold enough to

[11] Incident. [12] In the rear (of the house).

[13] The Roman Catholic court designed to prosecute heresy. (To claim that horses were superior to humans in rationality would be heretical.)

walk the street in his company, but kept my nose well stopped with rue,[14] or sometimes with tobacco.

In ten days Don Pedro, to whom I had given some account of my domestic affairs, put it upon me as a point of honour and conscience, that I ought to return to my native country, and live at home with my wife and children. He told me, there was an English ship in the port just ready to sail, and he would furnish me with all things necessary. It would be tedious to repeat his arguments, and my contradictions. He said it was altogether impossible to find such a solitary island as I had desired to live in; but I might command in my own house, and pass my time in a manner as recluse as I pleased.

I complied at last, finding I could not do better. I left Lisbon the 24th day of November, in an English merchantman, but who was the master I never inquired. Don Pedro accompanied me to the ship, and lent me twenty pounds. He took kind leave of me, and embraced me at parting, which I bore as well as I could. During this last voyage I had no commerce[15] with the master or any of his men, but pretending I was sick kept close in my cabin. On the fifth of December, 1715, we cast anchor in the Downs[16] about nine in the morning, and at three in the afternoon I got safe to my house at Redriff.[17]

My wife and family received me with great surprise and joy, because they concluded me certainly dead; but I must freely confess the sight of them filled me only with hatred, disgust and contempt, and the more by reflecting on the near alliance I had to them. For although, since my unfortunate exile from the Houyhnhnm country, I had compelled myself to tolerate the sight of yahoos, and to converse with Don Pedro de Mendez, yet my memory and imaginations were perpetually filled with the virtues and ideas of those exalted Houyhnhnms. And when I began to consider, that by copulating with one of the yahoo species I had become a parent of more, it struck me with the utmost shame, confusion, and horror.

As soon as I entered the house, my wife took me in her arms, and kissed me, at which, having not been used to the touch of that odious animal[18] for so many years, I fell in a swoon for almost an hour. At the time I am writing it is five years since my last return to England: during the first year I could not endure my wife or children in my presence, the very smell of them was intolerable, much less could I suffer them to eat in the same room. To this hour they dare not presume to touch my bread, or drink out of the same cup, neither was I ever able to let one of them take me by the hand. The first money I laid out was to buy two young stone-horses,[19] which I keep in a good stable, and next to them the groom is my greatest favourite; for I feel my spirits revived by the smell he contracts in the stable. My horses understand me tolerably well; I converse with them at least four hours every day. They are strangers to bridle or saddle; they live in great amity with me, and friendship to each other.

[14] An aromatic herb. [15] Social contact.
[16] An anchorage area in the English Channel, off the coast of Kent in southeast England.
[17] A district in south London.
[18] This may refer to the yahoo species rather than to the wife personally.
[19] Ungelded horses; stallions.

CHAPTER XII

The author's veracity. His design in publishing this work. His censure of those travellers who swerve from the truth. The author clears himself from any sinister ends in writing. An objection answered. The method of planting colonies. His native country commended. The right of the crown to those countries described by the author is justified. The difficulty of conquering them. The author takes his last leave of the reader, proposeth his manner of living for the future, gives good advice, and concludes.

Thus, gentle reader, I have given thee a faithful history of my travels for sixteen years, and above seven months, wherein I have not been so studious of[1] ornament as of truth. I could perhaps like others have astonished thee with strange improbable tales; but I rather chose to relate plain matter of fact in the simplest manner and style, because my principal design was to inform, and not to amuse thee.

It is easy for us who travel into remote countries, which are seldom visited by Englishmen or other Europeans, to form descriptions of wonderful animals both at sea and land. Whereas a traveller's chief aim should be to make men wiser and better, and to improve their minds by the bad as well as good example of what they deliver concerning foreign places.

I could heartily wish a law were enacted, that every traveller, before he were permitted to publish his voyages, should be obliged to make oath before the Lord High Chancellor that all he intended to print was absolutely true to the best of his knowledge; for then the world would no longer be deceived as it usually is, while some writers, to make their works pass the better upon the public, impose the grossest falsities on the unwary reader. I have perused several books of travels with great delight in my younger days; but having since gone over most parts of the globe, and been able to contradict many fabulous accounts from my own observation, it hath given me a great disgust against this part of reading, and some indignation to see the credulity of mankind so impudently abused. Therefore since my acquaintance were pleased to think my poor endeavours might not be unacceptable to my country, I imposed on myself as a maxim, never to be swerved from, that I would *strictly adhere to truth;* neither indeed can I be ever under the least temptation to vary from it, while I retain in my mind the lectures and example of my noble master, and the other illustrious Houyhnhnms, of whom I had so long the honour to be an humble hearer.

—Nec si miserum Fortuna Sinonem
Finxit, vanum etiam mendacemque improba finget.[2]

I know very well how little reputation is to be got by writings which

[1] Zealous for.

[2] From Virgil's *Aeneid,* Book II: "Sinon is wretched, / Fortune has made him so, but she will never / Make him a liar" (Rolfe Humphries translation). This is a literary joke, because Sinon is indeed a liar who hoodwinks the Trojans into harboring the wooden horse inside which are concealed the Greek soldiers who will sack Troy. For Sinon, see also Dante, *Inferno,* XXX.98 ff.

require neither genius nor learning, nor indeed any other talent, except a good memory or an exact journal. I know likewise, that writers of travels, like dictionary-makers, are sunk into oblivion by the weight and bulk of those who come after, and therefore lie uppermost. And it is highly probable, that such travellers who shall hereafter visit the countries described in this work of mine, may, by detecting my errors (if there be any), and adding many new discoveries of their own, jostle me out of vogue, and stand in my place, making the world forget that ever I was an author. This indeed would be too great a mortification if I wrote for fame: but, as my sole intention was the PUBLIC GOOD, I cannot be altogether disappointed. For who can read of the virtues I have mentioned in the glorious Houyhnhnms, without being ashamed of his own vices, when he considers himself as the reasoning, governing animal of his country? I shall say nothing of those remote nations where yahoos preside, amongst which the least corrupted are the Brobdingnagians,[3] whose wise maxims in morality and government it would be our happiness to observe. But I forbear descanting further, and rather leave the judicious reader to his own remarks and applications.

I am not a little pleased that this work of mine can possibly meet with no censurers: for what objections can be made against a writer who relates only plain facts that happened in such distant countries, where we have not the least interest with respect either to trade or negotiations? I have carefully avoided every fault with which common writers of travels are often too justly charged. Besides, I meddle not the least with any *party*,[4] but write without passion, prejudice, or ill-will against any man or number of men whatsover. I write for the noblest end, to inform and instruct mankind, over whom I may, without breach of modesty, pretend to some superiority from the advantages I received by conversing so long among the most accomplished Houyhnhnms. I write without any view towards profit or praise. I never suffer a word to pass that may look like reflection,[5] or possibly give the least offence even to those who are most ready to take it. So that I hope I may with justice pronounce myself an author perfectly blameless, against whom the tribe of answerers, considerers, observers, reflecters, detecters, remarkers, will never be able to find matter for exercising their talents.

I confess, it was whispered to me that I was bound in duty, as a subject of England, to have given in a memorial to a secretary of state, at my first coming over; because, whatever lands are discovered by a subject belong to the crown. But I doubt whether our conquests in the countries I treat of would be as easy as those of Ferdinando Cortez over the naked Americans.[6] The Lilliputians,[7] I think, are hardly worth the charge of a fleet and army to reduce them, and I question whether it might be prudent or safe to attempt the Brobdingnagians. Or whether an English army would be much

[3] Giants whose land Gulliver visited in Part II.

[4] The earlier parts of *Gulliver's Travels* are actually full of political gibes, especially against the Whig party in England.

[5] Censure.

[6] The Spanish explorer Cortez conquered the Aztecs of Mexico in 1521 with only a small force of men.

[7] The tiny humans visited by Gulliver in Part I.

at their ease with the Flying Island[8] over their heads. The Houyhnhnms, indeed, appear not to be so well prepared for war, a science to which they are perfect strangers, and especially against missive weapons.[9] However, supposing myself to be a minister of state, I could never give my advice for invading them. Their prudence, unanimity, unacquaintedness with fear, and their love of their country would amply supply all defects in the military art. Imagine twenty thousand of them breaking into the midst of an European army, confounding the ranks, overturning the carriages,[10] battering the warriors' faces into mummy,[11] by terrible yerks[12] from their hinder hoofs. For they would well deserve the character given to Augustus; *Recalcitrat undique tutus.*[13] But instead of proposals for conquering that magnanimous nation, I rather wish they were in a capacity or disposition to send a sufficient number of their inhabitants for civilizing Europe, by teaching us the first principles of honour, justice, truth, temperance, public spirit, fortitude, chastity, friendship, benevolence, and fidelity. The names of all which virtues are still retained among us in most languages, and are to be met with in modern as well as ancient authors; which I am able to assert from my own small reading.

But I had another reason which made me less forward to enlarge his Majesty's dominions by my discoveries. To say the truth, I had conceived a few scruples with relation to the distributive justice[14] of princes upon those occasions. For instance, a crew of pirates are driven by a storm they know not whither, at length a boy discovers land from the topmast, they go on shore to rob and plunder, they see an harmless people, are entertained with kindness, they give the country a new name, they take formal possession of it for the king, they set up a rotten plank or a stone for a memorial, they murder two or three dozen of the natives, bring away a couple more by force for a sample, return home, and get their pardon. Here commences a new dominion acquired with a title by *divine right.* Ships are sent with the first opportunity, the natives driven out or destroyed, their princes tortured to discover their gold, a free license given to all acts of inhumanity and lust, the earth reeking with the blood of its inhabitants: and this execrable crew of butchers employed in so pious an expedition, is a modern colony sent to convert and civilize an idolatrous and barbarous people.

But this description, I confess, doth by no means affect the British nation, who may be an example to the whole world for their wisdom, care, and justice in planting colonies; their liberal endowments for the advancement of religion and learning; their choice of devout and able pastors to propagate Christianity; their caution in stocking their provinces with people of sober lives and conversations[15] from this the mother kingdom; their strict regard to the distribution of justice, in supplying the civil administration through all their colonies with officers of the greatest abilities, utter strangers to corruption; and to crown all, by sending the most vigilant and

[8] The flying island of Laputa, described in Part III, can crush the towns underneath it by descending on them.

[9] Weapons hurled or shot. [10] Gun carriages. [11] Pulp. [12] Kicks.

[13] From Horace's *Satires,* II: "He kicks on all sides with safety."

[14] The branch of justice concerned with giving to different people their proper shares.

[15] Way of living; behavior. Some of the British colonists were, in fact, convicted felons.

virtuous governors, who have no other views than the happiness of the people over whom they preside, and the honour of the king their master.

But as those countries which I have described do not appear to have any desire of being conquered, and enslaved, murdered or driven out by colonies, nor abound either in gold, silver, sugar or tobacco; I did humbly conceive they were by no means proper objects of our zeal, our valour, or our interest. However, if those whom it may concern think fit to be of another opinion, I am ready to depose, when I shall be lawfully called, that no European did ever visit these countries before me. I mean, if the inhabitants ought to be believed; unless a dispute may arise about the two yahoos, said to have been seen many ages ago on a mountain in Houyhnhnmland, from whence the opinion is, that the race of those brutes hath descended; and these, for any thing I know, may have been English, which indeed I was apt to suspect from the lineaments of their posterity's countenances, although very much defaced. But, how far that will go to make out a title, I leave to the learned in colony-law.

But as to the formality of taking possession in my sovereign's name, it never came once into my thoughts; and if it had, yet as my affairs then stood, I should perhaps, in point of prudence and self-preservation, have put it off to a better opportunity.

Having thus answered the *only* objection that can ever be raised against me as a traveller, I here take a final leave of my courteous readers, and return to enjoy my own speculations in my little garden at Redriff, to apply those excellent lessons of virtue which I learned among the Houyhnhnms, to instruct the yahoos of my own family as far as I shall find them docible[16] animals, to behold my figure often in a glass, and thus if possible habituate myself by time to tolerate the sight of a human creature; to lament the brutality[17] of Houyhnhnms in my own country, but always treat their persons with respect, for the sake of my noble master, his family, his friends, and the whole Houyhnhnm race, whom these of ours have the honour to resemble in all their lineaments, however their intellectuals[18] came to degenerate.

I began last week to permit my wife to sit at dinner with me, at the farthest end of a long table, and to answer (but with the utmost brevity) the few questions I ask her. Yet the smell of a yahoo continuing very offensive, I always keep my nose well stopped with rue, lavender, or tobacco leaves. And although it be hard for a man late in life to remove old habits, I am not altogether out of hopes in some time to suffer a neighbour yahoo in my company without the apprehensions I am yet under of his teeth or his claws.

My reconcilement to the yahoo-kind in general might not be so difficult if they would be content with those vices and follies only which nature hath entitled them to. I am not in the least provoked at the sight of a lawyer, a pickpocket, a colonel, a fool, a lord, a gamester, a politician, a whoremonger, a physician, an evidence,[19] a suborner, an attorney, a traitor, or the like; this is all according to the due course of things: but when I behold a lump of deformity and diseases both in body and mind, smitten with

[16]Teachable. [17]Brutalization. [18]Intellects. [19]Paid false witness.

pride, it immediately breaks all the measures of my patience; neither shall I be ever able to comprehend how such an animal and such a vice could tally together. The wise and virtuous Houyhnhnms, who abound in all excellencies that can adorn a rational creature, have no name for this vice in their language, which hath no terms to express any thing that is evil, except those whereby they describe the detestable qualities of their yahoos, among which they were not able to distinguish this of pride, for want of thoroughly understanding human nature, as it showeth itself in other countries, where that animal presides. But I, who had more experience, could plainly observe some rudiments of it among the wild yahoos.

But the Houyhnhnms, who live under the government of reason, are no more proud of the good qualities they possess, than I should be for not wanting a leg or an arm, which no man in his wits would boast of, although he must be miserable without them. I dwell the longer upon this subject from the desire I have to make the society of an English yahoo by any means not insupportable, and therefore I here entreat those who have any tincture of this absurd vice, that they will not presume to appear in my sight.

FINIS

A LETTER FROM CAPT. GULLIVER TO HIS COUSIN SYMPSON.[1]

I hope you will be ready to own publicly, whenever you shall be called to it, that by your great and frequent urgency you prevailed on me to publish a very loose and uncorrect account of my travels; with direction to hire some young gentlemen of either university to put them in order, and correct the style, as my cousin Dampier[2] did by my advice, in his book called *A Voyage round the World*. But I do not remember I gave you power to consent, that any thing should be omitted, and much less that any thing should be inserted: therefore, as to the latter, I do here renounce every thing of that kind; particularly a paragraph about her Majesty the late Queen Anne,[3] of most pious and glorious memory; although I did reverence and esteem her more than any of human species. But you, or your interpolator, ought to have considered, that as it was not my inclination, so was it not decent to praise any animal of our composition[4] before my master Houyhnhnm: and besides, the fact was altogether false; for to my knowledge, being in England during some part of her Majesty's reign, she did govern by a chief minister; nay, even by two successively; the first whereof was the Lord of Godolphin, and the second the Lord of Oxford; so that you have made me *say the thing that was not*. Likewise, in the account of the Academy of Projec-

[1] A fictitious person. The present letter first appeared in the 1735 edition, nine years after the first edition. Although the letter is largely a spoof, it expresses Swift's genuine resentment about changes in the text made by the publisher in the interests of political safety.

[2] William Dampier (1652–1715), a well known buccaneer, explorer, and adventurer. He rescued the castaway Alexander Selkirk, the model for Daniel Defoe's *Robinson Crusoe*.

[3] This passage, inserted in Part IV, chapter 6, was removed in later editions.

[4] Make-up.

tors,[5] and several passages of my discourse to my master Houyhnhnm, you have either omitted some material circumstances, or minced or changed them in such a manner, that I do hardly know mine own work. When I formerly hinted to you something of this in a letter, you were pleased to answer, that you were afraid of giving offence; that people in power were very watchful over the press, and apt not only to interpret, but to punish every thing which looked like an *innuendo* (as I think you called it). But pray, how could that which I spoke so many years ago, and at above five thousand leagues distance, in another reign, be applied to any of the yahoos who now are said to govern the herd; especially at a time when I little thought on or feared the unhappiness of living under them? Have not I the most reason to complain, when I see these very yahoos carried by Houyhnhnms in a vehicle, as if these were brutes, and those the rational creatures? And, indeed, to avoid so monstrous and detestable a sight was one principal motive of my retirement hither.[6]

Thus much I thought proper to tell you in relation to your self, and to the trust I reposed in you.

I do in the next place complain of my own great want of judgment, in being prevailed upon by the intreaties and false reasonings of you and some others, very much against mine own opinion, to suffer my travels to be published. Pray bring to your mind how often I desired you to consider, when you insisted on the motive of public good, that the yahoos were a species of animals utterly incapable of amendment by precepts or examples, and so it hath proved; for instead of seeing a full stop put to all abuses and corruptions, at least in this little island, as I had reason to expect: behold, after above six months' warning, I cannot learn that my book hath produced one single effect according to mine intentions: I desired you would let me know by a letter, when party and faction were extinguished; judges learned and upright; pleaders honest and modest, with some tincture of common sense; and Smithfield[7] blazing with pyramids of law-books; the young nobility's education entirely changed; the physicians banished; the female yahoos abounding in virtue, honour, truth and good sense; courts and levees[8] of great ministers thoroughly weeded and swept; wit, merit and learning rewarded; all disgracers of the press in prose and verse condemned to eat nothing but their own cotton,[9] and quench their thirst with their own ink. These, and a thousand other reformations, I firmly counted upon by your encouragement; as indeed they were plainly deducible from the precepts delivered in my book. And, it must be owned, that seven months were a sufficient time to correct every vice and folly to which yahoos are subject, if their natures had been capable of the least disposition to virtue or wisdom; yet so far have you been from answering mine expectation in any of your letters, that on the contrary you are loading our carrier every week with libels, and keys, and reflections, and mem-

[5] An organization of scientists, portrayed in Part III, engaged in ingenious but insane experiments.

[6] Gulliver is supposed to have retired from London to Nottinghamshire, in central England.

[7] An area of London where alleged heretics and criminals had formerly been burned.

[8] Receptions held in the morning. [9] Used to make paper and to clean type.

oirs, and second parts;[10] wherein I see myself accused of reflecting upon great states-folk; of degrading human nature (for so they have still the confidence to style it), and of abusing the female sex. I find likewise, that the writers of those bundles are not agreed among themselves; for some of them will not allow me to be author of mine own travels; and others make me author of books to which I am wholly a stranger.

I find likewise that your printer hath been so careless as to confound the times, and mistake the dates of my several voyages and returns, neither assigning the true year, or the true month, or day of the month; and I hear the original manuscript is all destroyed since the publication of my book. Neither have I any copy left; however, I have sent you some corrections, which you may insert if ever there should be a second edition: and yet I cannot stand to[11] them, but shall leave that matter to my judicious and candid readers, to adjust it as they please.

I hear some of our sea-yahoos find fault with my sea-language, as not proper in many parts, nor now in use. I cannot help it. In my first voyages, while I was young, I was instructed by the oldest mariners, and learned to speak as they did. But I have since found that the sea-yahoos are apt, like the land ones, to become new-fangled in their words; which the latter change every year, insomuch as I remember upon each return to mine own country, their old dialect was so altered that I could hardly understand the new. And I observe, when any yahoo comes from London out of curiosity to visit me at mine own house, we neither of us are able to deliver our conceptions in a manner intelligible to the other.

If the censure of yahoos could any way affect me, I should have great reason to complain that some of them are so bold as to think my book of travels a mere fiction out of mine own brain; and have gone so far as to drop hints that the Houyhnhnms and yahoos have no more existence than the inhabitants of Utopia.[12]

Indeed I must confess, that as to the people of Lilliput, Brobdingrag (for so the word should have been spelt, and not erroneously 'Brobdingnag') and Laputa, I have never yet heard of any yahoo so presumptuous as to dispute their being, or the facts I have related concerning them; because the truth immediately strikes every reader with conviction. And is there less probability in my account of the Houyhnhnms or yahoos, when it is manifest as to the latter, there are so many thousands even in this city,[13] who only differ from their brother brutes in Houyhnhnmland, because they use a sort of a jabber, and do not go naked? I wrote for their amendment, and not their approbation. The united praise of the whole race would be of less consequence to me than the neighing of those two degenerate Houyhnhnms I keep in my stable; because from these, degenerate as they are, I still improve in some virtues, without any mixture of vice.

Do these miserable animals presume to think that I am so far degener-

[10] Spurious commentaries on and continuations of *Gulliver's Travels* began to appear immediately after its first publication.

[11] Stand behind.

[12] Thomas More's great satire *Utopia* (1516) depicts an ideal state flourishing in a far-away part of the world.

[13] London, apparently, although Gulliver is supposed to have moved away.

ated as to defend my veracity? Yahoo as I am, it is well known through all Houyhnhnmland, that by the instructions and example of my illustrious master, I was able in the compass of two years (although I confess with the utmost difficulty) to remove that infernal habit of lying, shuffling,[14] deceiving, and equivocating, so deeply rooted in the very souls of all my species, especially the Europeans.

I have other complaints to make upon this vexatious occasion; but I forbear troubling myself or you any further. I must freely confess, that since my last return some corruptions of my yahoo nature have revived in me by conversing with a few of your species, and particularly those of mine own family, by an unavoidable necessity; else I should never have attempted so absurd a project as that of reforming the yahoo race in this kingdom; but I have now done with all such visionary schemes for ever.

April 2, 1727

A MODEST PROPOSAL

FOR

PREVENTING THE CHILDREN OF POOR PEOPLE IN IRELAND FROM BEING A BURDEN TO THEIR PARENTS OR COUNTRY, AND FOR MAKING THEM BENEFICIAL TO THE PUBLIC

It is a melancholy object to those who walk through this great town,[1] or travel in the country, when they see the streets, the roads and cabin-doors crowded with beggars of the female sex, followed by three, four, or six children, all in rags, and importuning every passenger for an alms. These mothers, instead of being able to work for their honest livelihood, are forced to employ all their time in strolling, to beg sustenance for their helpless infants, who, as they grow up, either turn thieves for want of work, or leave their dear native country to fight for the Pretender[2] in Spain, or sell themselves to the Barbadoes.[3]

I think it is agreed by all parties that this prodigious number of children, in the arms, or on the backs, or at the heels of their mothers, and frequently of their fathers, is in the present deplorable state of the kingdom a very great additional grievance; and therefore whoever could find out a fair, cheap, and easy method of making these children sound and useful members of the commonwealth would deserve so well of the public as to have his statue set up for a preserver of the nation.

[14] Acting deceitfully; equivocating. [1] Dublin.

[2] The Stuart claimant of the English throne; the exiled family had been deposed and succeeded by the house of Hanover (George I and his descendants). The Old Pretender was James Francis Edward Stuart (1688–1766), son of James II; his son Charles Edward ("Bonnie Prince Charlie," 1720–1788) was the Young Pretender.

[3] Barbados, in the West Indies. Emigrants agreed to work for a period in return for the cost of their transportation.

But my intention is very far from being confined to provide only for the children of professed beggars; it is of a much greater extent, and shall take in the whole number of infants at a certain age who are born of parents in effect as little able to support them as those who demand our charity in the streets.

As to my own part, having turned my thoughts for many years upon this important subject, and maturely weighed the several schemes of other projectors,[4] I have always found them grossly mistaken in their computation. It is true a child just dropped from its dam may be supported by her milk for a solar year with little other nourishment, at most not above the value of two shillings, which the mother may certainly get, or the value in scraps, by her lawful occupation of begging, and it is exactly at one year old that I propose to provide for them, in such a manner as, instead of being a charge[5] upon their parents, or the parish, or wanting food and raiment for the rest of their lives, they shall, on the contrary, contribute to the feeding and partly to the clothing of many thousands.

There is likewise another great advantage in my scheme, that it will prevent those voluntary abortions, and that horrid practice of women murdering their bastard children, alas, too frequent among us, sacrificing the poor innocent babes, I doubt,[6] more to avoid the expense than the shame, which would move tears and pity in the most savage and inhuman breast.

The number of souls in Ireland being usually reckoned one million and a half, of these I calculate there may be about two hundred thousand couples whose wives are breeders, from which number I subtract thirty thousand couples who are able to maintain their own children, although I apprehend there cannot be so many under the present distresses of the kingdom, but this being granted, there will remain an hundred and seventy thousand breeders. I again subtract fifty thousand for those women who miscarry, or whose children die by accident or disease within the year. There only remain an hundred and twenty thousand children of poor parents annually born: the question therefore is, how this number shall be reared, and provided for, which, as I have already said, under the present situation of affairs is utterly impossible by all the methods hitherto proposed, for we can neither employ them in handicraft or agriculture; we neither build houses (I mean in the country), nor cultivate land: they can very seldom pick up a livelihood by stealing until they arrive at six years old, except where they are of towardly parts,[7] although I confess they learn the rudiments much earlier, during which time they can however be properly looked upon only as probationers,[8] as I have been informed by a principal gentleman in the County of Cavan, who protested to me that he never knew above one or two instances under the age of six, even in a part of the kingdom so renowned for the quickest proficiency in that art.

I am assured by our merchants that a boy or a girl before twelve years old, is no saleable commodity, and even when they come to this age, they will not yield above three pounds, or three pounds and half-a-crown at

[4] Experimental reformers; a pejorative term for Swift. [5] Financial burden.
[6] Suspect. [7] Precocious talents.
[8] Persons undergoing a trial period; apprentices.

most on the Exchange, which cannot turn to account either to the parents or the kingdom, the charge of nutriment and rags having been at least four times that value.

I shall now therefore humbly propose my own thoughts, which I hope will not be liable to the least objection.

I have been assured by a very knowing American of my acquaintance in London, that a young healthy child well nursed is at a year old a most delicious, nourishing and wholesome food, whether stewed, roasted, baked, or boiled, and I make no doubt that it will equally serve in a fricassee, or a ragout.

I do therefore humbly offer it to public consideration, that of the hundred and twenty thousand children already computed, twenty thousand may be reserved for breed, whereof only one fourth part to be males, which is more than we allow to sheep, black-cattle, or swine, and my reason is that these children are seldom the fruits of marriage, a circumstance not much regarded by our savages, therefore one male will be sufficient to serve four females. That the remaining hundred thousand may at a year old be offered in sale to the persons of quality, and fortune, through the kingdom, always advising the mother to let them suck plentifully in the last month, so as to render them plump, and fat for a good table. A child will make two dishes at an entertainment for friends, and when the family dines alone, the fore or hind quarter will make a reasonable dish, and seasoned with a little pepper or salt will be very good boiled on the fourth day, especially in winter.

I have reckoned upon a medium,[9] that a child just born will weigh twelve pounds, and in a solar year if tolerably nursed increaseth to twenty-eight pounds.

I grant this food will be somewhat dear, and therefore very proper for landlords, who, as they have already devoured most of the parents, seem to have the best title to the children.

Infant's flesh will be in season throughout the year, but more plentiful in March, and a little before and after, for we are told by a grave author, an eminent French physician,[10] that fish being a prolific diet, there are more children born in Roman Catholic countries about nine months after Lent[11] than at any other season; therefore reckoning a year after Lent, the markets will be more glutted than usual, because the number of Popish infants is at least three to one in this kingdom, and therefore it will have one other collateral advantage by lessening the number of Papists[12] among us.

I have already computed the charge of nursing a beggar's child (in which list I reckon all cottagers, labourers, and four-fifths of the farmers) to be about two shillings *per annum,* rags included, and I believe no gentleman would repine to give ten shillings for the carcass of a good fat child, which, as I have said, will make four dishes of excellent nutritive meat, when he hath only some particular friend or his own family to dine with him. Thus the Squire will learn to be a good landlord and grow popular among his

[9] On the average. [10] François Rabelais, author of *Gargantua and Pantagruel.*
[11] Abstention from meat was practiced in Lent by Catholics.
[12] This term for Catholics, like "Popish," was a pejorative one.

tenants, the mother will have eight shillings net profit, and be fit for work until she produces another child.

Those who are more thrifty (as I must confess the times require) may flay the carcass; the skin of which artificially[13] dressed, will make admirable gloves for ladies, and summer boots for fine gentlemen.

As to our city of Dublin, shambles[14] may be appointed for this purpose, in the most convenient parts of it, and butchers we may be assured will not be wanting, although I rather recommend buying the children alive, and dressing them hot from the knife, as we do roasting pigs.

A very worthy person, a true lover of his country, and whose virtues I highly esteem, was lately pleased, in discoursing on this matter to offer a refinement upon my scheme. He said that many gentlemen of this kingdom, having of late destroyed their deer, he conceived that the want of venison might be well supplied by the bodies of young lads and maidens, not exceeding fourteen years of age, nor under twelve, so great a number of both sexes in every county being now ready to starve, for want of work and service: and these to be disposed of by their parents if alive, or otherwise by their nearest relations. But with due deference to so excellent a friend, and so deserving a patriot, I cannot be altogether in his sentiments. For as to the males, my American acquaintance assured me from frequent experience that their flesh was generally tough and lean, like that of our schoolboys, by continual exercise, and their taste disagreeable, and to fatten them would not answer the charge. Then as to the females, it would, I think with humble submission, be a loss to the public, because they soon would become breeders themselves: and besides, it is not improbable that some scrupulous people might be apt to censure such a practice (although indeed very unjustly) as a little bordering upon cruelty, which I confess, hath always been with me the strongest objection against any project, howsoever well intended.

But in order to justify my friend, he confessed that this expedient was put into his head by the famous Psalmanazar,[15] a native of the island Formosa, who came from thence to London, above twenty years ago, and in conversation told my friend that in his country when any young person happened to be put to death, the executioner sold the carcass to persons of quality, as a prime dainty, and that, in his time, the body of a plump girl of fifteen, who was crucified for an attempt to poison the emperor, was sold to his Imperial Majesty's Prime Minister of State, and other great Mandarins of the Court, in joints from the gibbet, at four hundred crowns. Neither indeed can I deny that if the same use were made of several plump young girls in this town who, without one single groat to their fortunes, cannot stir abroad without a chair,[16] and appear at the playhouse and assemblies in foreign fineries, which they never will pay for, the kingdom would not be the worse.

Some persons of a desponding spirit are in great concern about that vast number of poor people, who are aged, diseased, or maimed, and I have been desired to employ my thoughts what course may be taken to ease the

[13] Skillfully. [14] Slaughterhouses.
[15] A literary fraud who published a fictitious description of Formosa.
[16] Sedan chair.

nation of so grievous an encumbrance. But I am not in the least pain upon that matter, because it is very well known that they are every day dying, and rotting, by cold, and famine, and filth, and vermin, as fast as can be reasonably expected. And as to the younger labourers they are now in almost as hopeful a condition. They cannot get work, and consequently pine away from want of nourishment, to a degree that if at any time they are accidentally hired to common labour, they have not strength to perform it; and thus the country and themselves are in a fair way of being soon delivered from the evils to come.

I have too long digressed, and therefore shall return to my subject. I think the advantages by the proposal which I have made are obvious and many, as well as of the highest importance.

For first, as I have already observed, it would greatly lessen the number of Papists, with whom we are yearly over-run, being the principal breeders of the nation, as well as our most dangerous enemies, and who stay at home on purpose with a design to deliver the kingdom to the Pretender, hoping to take their advantage by the absence of so many good Protestants, who have chosen rather to leave their country than stay at home and pay tithes[17] against their conscience to an idolatrous Episcopal curate.

Secondly, the poorer tenants will have something valuable of their own, which by law may be made liable to distress,[18] and help to pay their landlord's rent, their corn and cattle being already seized, and money a thing unknown.

Thirdly, whereas the maintenance of an hundred thousand children, from two years old, and upwards, cannot be computed at less than ten shillings a piece *per annum,* the nation's stock will be thereby increased fifty thousand pounds *per annum,* besides the profit of a new dish, introduced to the tables of all gentlemen of fortune in the kingdom, who have any refinement in taste, and the money will circulate among ourselves, the goods being entirely of our own growth and manufacture.

Fourthly, the constant breeders, besides the gain of eight shillings sterling *per annum,* by the sale of their children, will be rid of the charge of maintaining them after the first year.

Fifthly, this food would likewise bring great custom to taverns, where the vintners will certainly be so prudent as to procure the best receipts[19] for dressing it to perfection, and consequently have their houses frequented by all the fine gentlemen, who justly value themselves upon their knowledge in good eating; and a skilful cook, who understands how to oblige his guests, will contrive to make it as expensive as they please.

Sixthly, this would be a great inducement to marriage, which all wise nations have either encouraged by rewards, or enforced by laws and penalties. It would increase the care and tenderness of mothers towards their children, when they were sure of a settlement for life, to the poor babes, provided in some sort by the public to their annual profit instead of expense. We should soon see an honest emulation[20] among the married women, which of them could bring the fattest child to the market. Men would become as fond of their wives, during the time of their pregnancy, as

[17] Contributions of a tenth of one's income for the support of the church.
[18] Seizure of goods for the payment of debt. [19] Recipes. [20] Rivalry.

they are now of their mares in foal, their cows in calf, or sows when they are ready to farrow, nor offer to beat or kick them (as it is too frequent a practice) for fear of a miscarriage.

Many other advantages might be enumerated. For instance, the addition of some thousand carcasses in our exportation of barrelled beef; the propagation of swine's flesh, and improvement in the art of making good bacon, so much wanted among us by the great destruction of pigs, too frequent at our tables, which are no way comparable in taste or magnificence to a well-grown, fat yearling child, which roasted whole will make a considerable figure at a Lord Mayor's feast, or any other public entertainment. But this and many others I omit, being studious of brevity.

Supposing that one thousand families in this city would be constant customers for infants' flesh, besides others who might have it at merry meetings, particularly weddings and christenings; I compute that Dublin would take off annually about twenty thousand carcasses, and the rest of the kingdom (where probably they will be sold somewhat cheaper) the remaining eighty thousand.

I can think of no one objection that will possibly be raised against this proposal, unless it should be urged that the number of people will be thereby much lessened in the kingdom. This I freely own,[21] and it was indeed one principal design in offering it to the world. I desire the reader will observe, that I calculate my remedy *for this one individual Kingdom of* Ireland, *and for no other that ever was, is, or, I think, ever can be upon earth.* Therefore let no man talk to me of other expedients: *Of taxing our absentees at five shillings a pound: Of using neither clothes, nor household furniture, except what is of our own growth and manufacture: Of utterly rejecting the materials and instruments that promote foreign luxury: Of curing the expensiveness of pride, vanity, idleness, and gaming in our women: Of introducing a vein of parsimony, prudence, and temperance: Of learning to love our country, wherein we differ even from* Laplanders, *and the inhabitants of* Topinamboo:[22] *Of quitting our animosities and factions, nor act any longer like the* Jews, *who were murdering one another at the very moment their city was taken: Of being a little cautious not to sell our country and consciences for nothing: Of teaching landlords to have at least one degree of mercy towards their tenants.* Lastly, *of putting a spirit of honesty, industry, and skill into our shopkeepers, who, if a resolution could now be taken to buy only our native goods, would immediately unite to cheat and exact upon us in the price, the measure and the goodness, nor could ever yet be brought to make one fair proposal of just dealing, though often and earnestly invited to it.*

Therefore I repeat, let no man talk to me of these and the like expedients, till he hath at least a glimpse of hope that there will ever be some hearty and sincere attempt to put them in practice.

But as to myself, having been wearied out for many years with offering vain, idle, visionary thoughts, and at length utterly despairing of success, I fortunately fell upon this proposal, which as it is wholly new, so it hath something solid and real, of no expense and little trouble, full in our own power, and whereby we can incur no danger in disobliging England. For this kind of commodity will not bear exportation, the flesh being of too

[21] Admit. [22] An area of Brazil.

tender a consistence to admit a long continuance in salt, *although perhaps I could name a country*[23] *which would be glad to eat up our whole nation without it.*

After all I am not so violently bent upon my own opinion as to reject any offer, proposed by wise men, which shall be found equally innocent, cheap, easy and effectual. But before some thing of that kind shall be advanced in contradiction to my scheme, and offering a better, I desire the author, or authors, will be pleased maturely to consider two points. First, as things now stand, how they will be able to find food and raiment for a hundred thousand useless mouths and backs? And secondly, there being a round million of creatures in human figure, throughout this kingdom, whose whole subsistence put into a common stock would leave them in debt two millions of pounds sterling; adding those who are beggars by profession, to the bulk of farmers, cottagers, and labourers with their wives and children, who are beggars in effect; I desire those politicians who dislike my overture, and may perhaps be so bold to attempt an answer, that they will first ask the parents of these mortals whether they would not at this day think it a great happiness to have been sold for food at a year old, in the manner I prescribe, and thereby have avoided such a perpetual scene of misfortunes as they have since gone through, by the oppression of landlords, the impossibility of paying rent without money or trade, the want of common sustenance, with neither house nor clothes to cover them from the inclemencies of weather, and the most inevitable prospect of entailing the like, or greater miseries upon their breed for ever.

I profess in the sincerity of my heart that I have not the least personal interest in endeavouring to promote this necessary work, having no other motive than the *public good of my country, by advancing our trade, providing for infants, relieving the poor, and giving some pleasure to the rich.* I have no children by which I can propose to get a single penny; the youngest being nine years old, and my wife past child-bearing.

[23] England.

Alexander Pope

(1688–1744)

Perhaps the quintessential writer of the Neoclassic period in Europe was the English poet Alexander Pope. Pope was born in 1688 into a middle-class Roman Catholic family in London. In the same year, the Glorious Revolution deposed the Catholic James II and placed the Protestant William and Mary on the English throne; Pope suffered all his life from the anti-Catholicism of the strongly Protestant age that followed. Barred as a Catholic from universities, he was educated by tutors and at small private schools and by his own reading and study. When he was twelve, his family moved to a country house in Windsor Forest, in an area more tolerant of

Catholics. He contracted tuberculosis in childhood; it left him with a curved spine, a stunted, twisted body only four feet, six inches tall, and a lifetime of recurring pain.

Publication of his PASTORALS *in 1709 and of the* ESSAY ON CRITICISM *in 1711 catapulted him at the age of twenty-one into the exciting but sometimes cut-throat life of literary London. He met the magisterial Joseph Addison and was briefly a member of the group of young Whig writers who gathered around Addison at Button's Coffeehouse. He soon gravitated, however, to the more congenial circle of the Tory satirists Jonathan Swift, John Arbuthnot, Thomas Parnell, and John Gay. Together, these five made up the "Scriblerus Club," which met regularly at the apartments of Arbuthnot, a court physician, to compose the* Memoirs of Martinus Scriblerus, *a burlesque of all the kinds of pedantry and literary folly that fell under their scrutiny. The* Memoirs *did not see the light of publication until 1741, when Pope published them, much rewritten, long after the deaths of Arbuthnot, Parnell, and Gay. But the spirit of the group inspired a number of satirical works, most notably Swift's* Gulliver's Travels, *Pope's* Dunciad, *and perhaps Gay's* Beggar's Opera.

In 1717, Pope's father died, and a few months later, Pope leased the villa of Twickenham on the Thames, near Richmond, and moved there with his mother. Here he lived the rest of his life, moving in a glittering social circle and participating vigorously in London artistic life and controversy. Among his friends were the philosopher George Berkeley, the composer Handel, and a number of painters (Pope himself was an accomplished amateur): William Kent, Charles Jervas, Sir Godfrey Kneller, and the two Jonathan Richardsons.

Pope's literary career consists of three clearly marked periods. The first, from the beginning to 1717, Pope described in the Epistle to Dr. Arbuthnot *as devoted to noncontroversial topics: "a painted mistress or a purling stream." The 1717 collected* Poems, *which brought together his early work, contained the* Pastorals *and the bucolic* Windsor Forest; *a number of imitations and translations of Virgil, Ovid, and Chaucer; the highly emotional* Verses to the Memory of an Unfortunate Lady *and* Eloisa to Abelard; *the* Essay on Criticism; *and* The Rape of the Lock.

After the appearance of the 1717 Poems, *Pope turned to ten years of editing and translating in a successful attempt to gain financial security. The first volume of his translation of Homer's* Iliad, *in a deluxe edition for advance subscribers, appeared in 1715. It involved Pope in the first of many literary wars, since Addison, no longer friendly, had arranged for a rival translation by Thomas Tickell to appear at the same time. Pope's translation was a great success, however, and he followed it by a translation of the* Odyssey; *his income from the two translations has been estimated at the considerable sum of £9,000. His fortune was further augmented by his six-volume edition of Shakespeare, which appeared in 1725.*

When Pope returned to original composition in 1727, he, as he wrote, "stooped to truth, and moralized his song": that is, he became a satirist. This third period produced the Dunciad, *the* Moral Essays, *the imitations of Horace, and other satires. The* Dunciad, *originally conceived as a project of the Scriblerus Club, was a mock epic devoted to counterattacks on all Pope's literary enemies, especially the Shakespearian scholar and editor Lewis Theobald, who had attacked Pope's Shakespeare edition, and Colley Cibber, actor, playwright, and poet laureate. Pope continued to revise the* Dunciad *for the rest of his life to accommodate new enemies, and it appeared in three distinct versions over a period of fifteen years. The* Moral Essays, *which included the* Essay on Man, *were part of a large plan for a series of poems which would comprise a complete ethical system. The first part was to consist of the four epistles of the* Essay on Man; *the second was to consist of nine further epistles. Of this second group, four were actually written:* Of the Knowledge and Characters of Men, Of the Characters of Women, *and two both called* Of the Use of Riches. *During the years in which the ethical poems were appearing, Pope continued to publish a number of satires in which he was able to attack the policies of George II and his Whig prime minister Robert Walpole under the guise of Horace's satires on the court of the Emperor Augustus. Also in this period belongs the* Epistle to Dr. Arbuthnot, *Pope's brilliant and moving defense of the moral basis of his satire, written as a tribute to his dying friend.*

Pope's pen was often dipped in acid, and during the nineteenth-century Romantic reaction to Neoclassicism, it was common to think of him only as a shallow and spiteful controversialist, the "wasp of Twickenham." More recent readers have recognized the consistent and thoughtful morality of his satire. Deeply conservative by temperament and background, Pope lived at a time when economic and political power in England was passing from the established landed aristocracy to a new commercial class. Pope, like his fellow Tory Swift, saw this shift as threatening a general deterioration of the quality of English life, in public and private morality, in intellectual life, and in art. Pope's "dunces" matched Swift's "yahoos" as images of a rising tide of vulgarity, opportunism, and "dullness," which the two writers thought they saw in the Whig ascendancy, Pope stressing the corruption of civilized man as Swift satirized the debasement of brute human nature. But Pope's vision, no more than Swift's, is wholly negative, as the Epistle to Dr. Arbuthnot *makes clear. He measured contemporary life against a generous and humane standard of honesty, charity, and selflessness, qualities that he found both in his parents and in his friend John Arbuthnot. Pope's celebration of the individual, his reverence for the classics, his keen appreciation of nature, and his vision of a humane and ordered society all identify him as a true heir of English Renaissance thought.*

An Essay on Criticism, *begun when Pope was only seventeen and published when he was twenty-three, anticipates many of his later poetic principles and practices. As a poetic "essay," it is the only one of Pope's early poems not based on a traditional genre; its didacticism and satiric tone were to reappear often in Pope's later work. Pope did not attempt in his* Essay *to break any new ground; the ideas he expressed were familiar enough. But in the position he took on some familiar issues he managed to generate considerable controversy and to irritate such traditionalists as the irascible John Dennis. These issues include the relationship between such apparent opposites as "art" and "nature," "wit" and "judgment," and "rules" and "nameless graces." Pope's emphasis is upon common sense and compromise. There need be no conflict between the rules of art and the imitation of nature ("nature" being for Pope the generalized, universal patterns of the created world). The "rules" are not inviolate laws but merely statements of natural patterns and designs: "Those RULES of old discovered, not devised, / Are Nature still, but Nature methodised." Similarly, there need not be any real conflict between "wit" (a complex word, but meaning something like "imaginative and original perception of relationships") and "judgment" (sound knowledge and reasoning), for "true wit" is "Nature to advantage dressed," that is, it follows Nature's order rather than being merely ingenious and therefore complements rather than conflicts with "judgment." The same sort of reconciliation may be effected between the objective rules of art and the individual genius; within the regularity of nature expressed by the rules, there is also room for variety and individuality, "nameless graces" which "no Precepts can declare." Pope was to be faithful to these sensible compromises between the universal and the individual throughout the rest of his poetic career.*

The Essay on Criticism *also heralds Pope's later work in the mastery it displays of the metrical form he was to make triumphantly his own, the heroic couplet: two rhymed iambic pentameter lines, closed and end-stopped; that is, with grammatical pauses coinciding with the ends of both the first and second lines. Within this seemingly rigid and mechanical form, Pope is able to effect the same compromise between the "regular" and the personal that he does with his key critical concepts. By careful substitutions for the regular iambic feet, variation of the lengths of phrases and clauses, and sensitive use of such sound effects as alliteration and assonance, he is able to give his couplets the fluid movement of a lively mind at work. Pope's success in this early poem in saying "what oft was thought, but ne'er so well expressed" has made it perhaps the most frequently quoted of his poems.*

Eloisa to Abelard *is unusual among Pope's works in that it is a highly impassioned dramatic monologue. Peter Abelard was a twelfth-century French cleric and philosopher who fell in love with and secretly married one of his pupils, Heloise, or Eloisa. Her uncle discovered the affair and had Abelard castrated by a group of ruffians. He became a monk and built a monastery, the Paraclete, which he later gave to Eloisa, who became abbess of a sisterhood there, while he retired to the abbey of Cluny. Their letters survive and were translated into English by John Hughes; Pope based his poem on this translation. The form of the piece, however, is based upon a classical model, Ovid's* Heroides, *a collection of imaginary letters from famous women to their absent lovers.*

The masterwork of the 1717 volume of Pope's poems, however, was The Rape of the Lock, *which he had written in a short first version in 1711. In Pope's home village of Binfield, a certain Lord Petre had cut off one of Miss Arabella Fermor's curls without her consent. The incident provoked a quarrel and a serious breach between the two families. Pope's friend John Caryll, who knew both families, suggested that he write a poem to reconcile them. The result was a delightful, miniature mock epic, which Pope expanded in 1714 by adding the Rosicrucian "supernatural machinery" of sylphs and gnomes. Every convention of the epic finds its diminished echo in* The Rape of the Lock. *The epic hero becomes a fashionable belle, the epic battle is a game of cards, the journey to the underworld becomes Belinda pouting in the "Cave of Spleen," the arming of the hero is a scene at a dressing table, and the gods and goddesses who oversee the epic action become Rosicrucian sylphs and gnomes. In addition, the poem is an intricate web of verbal echoes from the* Iliad, *the* Odyssey, *the* Aeneid, *and most of all* Paradise Lost. *The basis of* The Rape of the Lock *is a trick of perspective; Pope tries to bring the real-life participants in the incident of the lock back to common sense and good humor by showing how trivial the incident was in the context of greater things. But on another level,* The Rape of the Lock *is not trivial at all; it takes on some of the seriousness of its heroic models as it traces Belinda's Eve-like fall from innocence to experience, delicately articulated in the poem's recurring imagery of broken china.*

As an aside, one might add that Pope's attempt at peace-making was not an unqualified success. He sent advance copies of the poem to both Lord Petre and Miss Fermor, and both seemed pleased. But when the poem appeared and friends commented on the strong sexual undercurrent of the poem, they began to have doubts. Pope, however, restored good relations by dedicating the final version of the poem to Miss Fermor, with a warm introductory letter.

An Essay on Man *was intended as the cornerstone of the ethical system that Pope developed in a series of poems late in his life. The* Moral Epistles *were to explore particular problems of human life; the* Essay *was to present an overview of the human condition, "a* general Map *of MAN." Pope quite deliberately invites comparison with Milton when he declares that his purpose is to "vindicate the ways of God to Man," but a comparison suggests more differences than similarities. Milton's orientation is thoroughly religious; Pope is attempting to construct an ethical system independent of religion, although not necessarily incompatible with it. There is nothing particularly original in this system; here, as in the* Essay on Criticism, *Pope is merely attempting to say "what oft was thought, but ne'er so well expressed." Readers of* Candide *may be tempted, especially when they read the famous line "Whatever is, is right," to identify Pope's position with the Leibnitzian Optimism of Dr. Pangloss. But none of the ideas in the poem can be traced to a single source. Rather the poem is an attempt to weave commonplace, well-established ideas of Pope's day into an orderly and coherent whole: the hierarchical conception of the universe as organized in a Great Chain of Being, with man in the middle of the Chain; the view of evil as a good viewed from a partial perspective; a theory of human character as defined by "humors" and organized by a "ruling passion"; the conception of society as having declined from an earlier "Golden Age," and several other such familiar ideas.*

But the Essay on Man *is memorable not as philosophy but as art. Pope chose verse instead of prose for the* Essay, *he said, not only because it was more concise but also because it could capture better the "force" and "grace" of arguments. What the reader takes away from the* Essay on Man *is not so much a body of doctrine as the sense of a lively and orderly mind "expatiating free" over received ideas and communicating vividly and movingly what it feels like to hold such ideas.*

FURTHER READING *(prepared by W. J. R.):* There is no completely satisfactory biography of Pope. George Sherburn's *The Early Career of Alexander Pope,* 1934, is reliable, though it ends its account in 1726. Two recent works provide fine introductions to Pope's poetry for the general reader: Pat Rogers' *Introduction to Pope,* 1976, considers Pope's work poem by poem and surveys earlier scholarship; I. R. F. Gordon's *A Preface to Pope,* 1976, contains a lengthy biographical section and surveys the major works more briefly. Frederick M. Keener's *An Essay on Pope,* 1974, studies eight poems, including *Eloisa to Abelard* and *The Rape of the Lock.* Keener discusses Pope's life in relation to his work and concludes with a discussion of how to read Pope. Reuben Arthur Brower's important *Alexander Pope: The Poetry of Allusion,* 1959, traces Pope's development in terms of his use of allusion. Murray Cohen's "Versions of the Lock: Readers of *The Rape of the Lock,*" *ELH,* 43 (1976), 53–73, discusses the lock's fate as an implicit warning to readers against misinterpreting the meaning of the poem. Major critical trends in Pope criticism are discussed in Ralph Cohen's "Pope's Meanings and the Strategies of Interrelation," in *English Literature in the Age of Disguise,* ed. Maximillian Novak, 1977. A superlative collection of critical essays is *Pope: Recent Essays by Several Hands,* ed. Maynard Mack and James A. Winn, 1980. This extensive collection covers all of Pope's writings and represents a great variety of critical approaches.

AN ESSAY ON CRITICISM

PART I

'Tis hard to say, if greater want of skill
Appear in writing or in judging ill;
But, of the two, less dang'rous is th' offence
To tire our patience, than mislead our sense.
Some few in that, but numbers err in this,
Ten censure wrong for one who writes amiss;
A fool might once himself alone expose,
Now one in verse makes many more in prose.
'Tis with our judgments as our watches, none
Go just alike, yet each believes his own.
In Poets as true genius is but rare,
True Taste as seldom is the Critic's share;
Both must alike from Heaven derive their light,
These born to judge, as well as those to write.
Let such teach others who themselves excel,
And censure freely who have written well.
Authors are partial to their wit, 'tis true,
But are not Critics to their judgment too?
Yet if we look more closely, we shall find
Most have the seeds of judgment in their mind:
Nature affords at least a glimm'ring light;
The lines, though touched but faintly, are drawn right.
But as the slightest sketch, if justly traced,
Is by ill-colouring but the more disgraced,
So by false learning is good sense defaced:
Some are bewildered in the maze of schools,
And some made coxcombs Nature meant but fools.
In search of wit these lose their common sense,
And then turn Critics in their own defence:
Each burns alike, who can, or cannot write,
Or with a Rival's, or an Eunuch's spite.
All fools have still an itching to deride,
And fain would be upon the laughing side.
If Maevius[1] scribble in Apollo's spite,
There are who judge still worse than he can write.
Some have at first for Wits, then Poets past,
Turned Critics next, and proved plain fools at last.[2]
Some neither can for Wits nor Critics pass,
As heavy mules are neither horse nor ass.
Those half-learned witlings, num'rous in our isle,
As half-formed insects on the banks of Nile;

[1] A foolish poet referred to by both Virgil and Horace.

[2] Pope may be referring to a contemporary critic, John Dennis, an enemy of Pope's known for his dogmatism and bad temper. Pope later wrote that when Dennis read these lines, he flung down the book, crying, "By God, he means me!"

Unfinished things, one knows not what to call,
Their generation's so equivocal:[3]
To tell 'em, would a hundred tongues require,
Or one vain wit's, that might a hundred tire.
  But you who seek to give and merit fame,
And justly bear a Critic's noble name,
Be sure yourself and your own reach to know,
How far your genius, taste, and learning go;
Launch not beyond your depth, but be discreet,
And mark that point where sense and dullness meet.
  Nature to all things fixed the limits fit,
And wisely curbed proud man's pretending wit.
As on the land while here the ocean gains,
In other parts it leaves wide sandy plains;
Thus in the soul while memory prevails,
The solid power of understanding fails;
Where beams of warm imagination play,
The memory's soft figures melt away.
One science only will one genius fit;
So vast is art, so narrow human wit:
Not only bounded to peculiar arts,
But oft in those confined to single parts.
Like kings we lose the conquests gained before,
By vain ambition still to make them more;
Each might his sev'ral province well command,
Would all but stoop to what they understand.
  First follow Nature, and your judgment frame
By her just standard, which is still the same:
Unerring NATURE, still divinely bright,
One clear, unchanged, and universal light,
Life, force, and beauty, must to all impart,
At once the source, and end, and test of Art.
Art from that fund each just supply provides,
Works without show, and without pomp presides:
In some fair body thus th' informing soul
With spirits feeds, with vigour fills the whole,
Each motion guides, and every nerve sustains;
Itself unseen, but in the effects, remains.
Some, to whom heaven in wit has been profuse,
Want as much more, to turn it to its use;
For wit and judgment often are at strife,
Though meant each other's aid, like man and wife.
'Tis more to guide, than spur the Muse's steed;
Restrain his fury, than provoke his speed;
The winged courser, like a gen'rous horse,
Shows most true mettle when you check his course.
  Those RULES of old discovered, not devised,

[3] Pope is alluding to the belief that insects were spontaneously generated by the flooding of the Nile.

Are Nature still, but Nature methodised;
Nature, like liberty, is but restrained
By the same laws which first herself ordained.
  Hear how learned Greece her useful rules indites,
When to repress, and when indulge our flights:
High on Parnassus'[4] top her sons she showed,
And pointed out those arduous paths they trod;
Held from afar, aloft, th' immortal prize,
And urged the rest by equal steps to rise.
Just precepts thus from great examples given,
She drew from them what they derived from Heaven.
The generous Critic fanned the Poet's fire,
And taught the world with reason to admire.
Then Criticism the Muses' handmaid proved,
To dress her charms, and make her more beloved:
But following wits from that intention strayed,
Who could not win the mistress, wooed the maid;
Against the Poets their own arms they turned,
Sure to hate most the men from whom they learned.
So modern 'Pothecaries, taught the art
By Doctor's bills to play the Doctor's part,
Bold in the practice of mistaken rules,
Prescribe, apply, and call their masters fools.
Some on the leaves of ancient authors prey,
Nor time nor moths e'er spoiled so much as they.
Some drily plain, without invention's aid,
Write dull receipts[5] how poems may be made.
These leave the sense, their learning to display,
And those explain the meaning quite away.
  You then whose judgment the right course would steer,
Know well each ANCIENT's proper character;
His fable, subject, scope in every page;
Religion, Country, genius of his Age:
Without all these at once before your eyes,
Cavil you may, but never criticise.
Be Homer's works your study and delight,
Read them by day, and meditate by night;
Thence form your judgment, thence your maxims bring,
And trace the Muses upward to their spring.
Still with itself compared, his text peruse;
And let your comment be the Mantuan Muse.[6]
  When first young Maro in his boundless mind
A work t' outlast immortal Rome designed,
Perhaps he seemed above the critic's law,
And but from Nature's fountains scorned to draw:

[4] The Greek mountain sacred to Apollo and poetry. [5] Recipes.

[6] The "Mantuan Muse" or "Maro" is Virgil (Publius Vergilius Maro), who was born near Mantua. Because the *Aeneid* is modeled upon Homer's *Iliad* and *Odyssey*, it can be considered a "comment" or commentary upon them.

But when t' examine every part he came,
Nature and Homer were, he found, the same.
Convinced, amazed, he checks the bold design;
And rules as strict his laboured work confine,
As if the Stagirite[7] o'erlooked each line.
Learn hence for ancient rules a just esteem;
To copy nature is to copy them.
   Some beauties yet no Precepts can declare,
For there's a happiness as well as care.
Music resembles Poetry, in each
Are nameless graces which no methods teach,
And which a master-hand alone can reach.
If, where the rules not far enough extend,
(Since rules were made but to promote their end)
Some lucky Licence answer to the full
Th' intent proposed, that Licence is a rule.
Thus Pegasus,[8] a nearer way to take,
May boldly deviate from the common track;
From vulgar bounds with brave disorder part,
And snatch a grace beyond the reach of art,
Which without passing through the judgment, gains
The heart, and all its end at once attains.
In prospects[9] thus, some objects please our eyes,
Which out of nature's common order rise,
The shapeless rock, or hanging precipice.
Great wits sometimes may gloriously offend,
And rise to faults true Critics dare not mend.
But though the Ancients thus their rules invade,
(As Kings dispense with laws themselves have made)
Moderns, beware! or if you must offend
Against the precept, ne'er transgress its End;
Let it be seldom, and compelled by need;
And have, at least, their precedent to plead.
The Critic else proceeds without remorse,
Seizes your fame, and puts his laws in force.
   I know there are, to whose presumptuous thoughts
Those freer beauties, even in them, seem faults.
Some figures monstrous and mis-shaped appear,
Considered singly, or beheld too near,
Which, but proportioned to their light, or place,
Due distance reconciles to form and grace.
A prudent chief not always must display
His powers in equal ranks, and fair array,
But with th' occasion and the place comply,
Conceal his force, nay seem sometimes to fly.

[7] Aristotle, who came from Stagira.

[8] The winged horse of Greek legend, symbolic of poetic inspiration; his hoofstroke brought forth the spring of Hippocrene, which gave the gift of song to those who drank from it

[9] Scenic views.

Those oft are stratagems which error seem,
Nor is it Homer nods, but we that dream.
  Still green with bays each ancient Altar stands,
Above the reach of sacrilegious hands;
Secure from Flames, from Envy's fiercer rage,
Destructive War, and all-involving Age.
See, from each clime the learned their incense bring!
Hear, in all tongues consenting Paeans ring!
In praise so just let every voice be joined,
And fill the general chorus of mankind.
Hail, Bards triumphant! born in happier days;
Immortal heirs of universal praise!
Whose honours with increase of ages grow,
As streams roll down, enlarging as they flow;
Nations unborn your mighty names shall sound,
And worlds applaud that must not yet be found!
Oh may some spark of your celestial fire,
The last, the meanest of your sons inspire,
(That on weak wings, from far, pursues your flights;
Glows while he reads, but trembles as he writes)
To teach vain Wits a science little known,
T' admire superior sense, and doubt their own!

PART II

  Of all the Causes which conspire to blind
Man's erring judgment, and misguide the mind,
What the weak head with strongest bias rules
Is *Pride,* the never-failing vice of fools.
Whatever nature has in worth denied,
She gives in large recruits of needful pride;
For as in bodies, thus in souls, we find
What wants in blood and spirits, swelled with wind:
Pride, where wit fails, steps in to our defence,
And fills up all the mighty Void of sense.
If once right reason drives that cloud away,
Truth breaks upon us with resistless day.
Trust not yourself; but your defects to know,
Make use of every friend—and every foe.
  A *little learning* is a dang'rous thing;
Drink deep, or taste not the Pierian spring:[10]
There shallow draughts intoxicate the brain,
And drinking largely sobers us again.
Fired at first sight with what the Muse imparts,
In fearless youth we tempt the heights of Arts,
While from the bounded level of our mind
Short views we take, nor see the lengths behind;

[10] The Pierian spring on Mount Olympus bubbled with the water of learning and the arts.

But more advanced, behold with strange surprise
New distant scenes of endless science rise!
So pleased at first the tow'ring Alps we try,
Mount o'er the vales, and seem to tread the sky,
Th' eternal snows appear already past,
And the first clouds and mountains seem the last;
But, those attained, we tremble to survey
The growing labours of the lengthened way,
Th' increasing prospect tires our wand'ring eyes,
Hills peep o'er hills, and Alps on Alps arise!
  A perfect Judge will read each work of Wit
With the same spirit that its author writ:
Survey the WHOLE, nor seek slight faults to find
Where nature moves, and rapture warms the mind:
Nor lose, for that malignant dull delight,
The gen'rous pleasure to be charmed with Wit.
But in such lays as neither ebb, nor flow,
Correctly cold, and regularly low,
That shunning faults, one quiet tenour keep;
We cannot blame indeed—but we may sleep.
In wit, as nature, what affects our hearts
Is not th' exactness of peculiar parts;
'Tis not a lip, or eye, we beauty call,
But the joint force and full result of all.
Thus when we view some well-proportioned dome,[11]
(The world's just wonder, and even thine, O Rome!)
No single parts unequally surprise,
All comes united to th' admiring eyes;
No monstrous height, or breadth, or length appear;
The Whole at once is bold, and regular.
  Whoever thinks a faultless piece to see,
Thinks what ne'er was, nor is, nor e'er shall be.
In every work regard the writer's End,
Since none can compass more than they intend;
And if the means be just, the conduct true,
Applause, in spight of trivial faults, is due;
As men of breeding, sometimes men of wit,
T' avoid great errors, must the less commit:
Neglect the rules each verbal Critic lays,
For not to know some trifles, is a praise.
Most Critics, fond of some subservient art,
Still make the Whole depend upon a Part:
They talk of principles, but notions prize,
And all to one loved Folly sacrifice.
  Once on a time, La Mancha's Knight,[12] they say,

[11] The dome of Saint Peter's in Rome.

[12] Don Quixote. This episode appears, as Pope pointed out, not in Cervantes' novel but in a spurious "continuation" of it, published by a "false Cervantes" who signed himself Alonzo Fernandez de Avellaneda. It was translated into English in 1705.

A certain bard encount'ring on the way,
Discoursed in terms as just, with looks as sage,
As e'er could Dennis[13] of the Grecian stage;
Concluding all were desperate sots and fools,
Who durst depart from Aristotle's rules.
Our Author, happy in a judge so nice,
Produced his Play, and begged the Knight's advice;
Made him observe the subject, and the plot,
The manners, passions, unities; what not?
All which, exact to rule, were brought about,
Were but a Combat in the lists left out.
"What! leave the Combat out?" exclaims the Knight;
Yes, or we must renounce the Stagirite.
"Not so by Heaven" (he answers in a rage),
"Knights, squires, and steeds, must enter on the stage."
So vast a throng the stage can ne'er contain.
"Then build a new, or act it in a plain."
Thus Critics, of less judgment than caprice,
Curious not knowing, not exact but nice,
Form short Ideas; and offend in arts
(As most in manners) by a love to parts.
Some to *Conceit*[14] alone their taste confine,
And glitt'ring thoughts struck out at every line;
Pleased with a work where nothing's just or fit;
One glaring Chaos and wild heap of wit.
Poets like painters, thus, unskilled to trace
The naked nature and the living grace,
With gold and jewels cover every part,
And hide with ornaments their want of art.
True Wit is Nature to advantage dressed,
What oft was thought, but ne'er so well expressed;
Something, whose truth convinced at sight we find,
That gives us back the image of our mind.
As shades more sweetly recommend the light,
So modest plainness sets off sprightly wit.
For works may have more wit than does 'em good,
As bodies perish through excess of blood.
Others for *Language* all their cares express,
And value books, as women men, for Dress:
Their praise is still,—the Style is excellent:
The Sense, they humbly take upon content.
Words are like leaves; and where they most abound,
Much fruit of sense beneath is rarely found:
False Eloquence, like the prismatic glass,
Its gaudy colours spreads on every place;
The face of Nature we no more survey,

[13] John Dennis. Further satiric references to him in Part III incurred his enmity when the poem appeared.

[14] Strained, fanciful, and over-ingenious expressions.

All glares alike, without distinction gay:
But true expression, like th' unchanging Sun,
Clears and improves whate'er it shines upon,
It gilds all objects, but it alters none.
Expression is the dress of thought, and still
Appears more decent, as more suitable;
A vile conceit in pompous words expressed,
Is like a clown[15] in regal purple dressed:
For diff'rent styles with diff'rent subjects sort,
As several garbs with country, town, and court.
Some by old words to fame have made pretence,
Ancients in phrase, mere moderns in their sense;
Such laboured nothings, in so strange a style,
Amaze th' unlearned, and make the learnèd smile.
Unlucky, as Fungoso[16] in the play,
These sparks with awkward vanity display
What the fine gentleman wore yesterday;
And but so mimic ancient wits at best,
As apes our grandsires, in their doublets drest.
In words, as fashions, the same rule will hold;
Alike fantastic, if too new, or old:
Be not the first by whom the new are tried,
Nor yet the last to lay the old aside.
　But most by Numbers judge a Poet's song;
And smooth or rough, with them is right or wrong:
In the bright Muse though thousand charms conspire,
Her voice is all these tuneful fools admire;
Who haunt Parnassus but to please their ear,
Not mend their minds; as some to Church repair,
Not for the doctrine, but the music there.
These equal syllables alone require,
Though oft the ear the open vowels tire;
While expletives their feeble aid do join;
And ten low words oft creep in one dull line:
While they ring round the same unvaried chimes,
With sure returns of still expected rhymes;
Where'er you find "the cooling western breeze,"
In the next line, it "whispers through the trees":
If crystal streams "with pleasing murmurs creep,"
The reader's threatened (not in vain) with "sleep":
Then, at the last and only couplet fraught
With some unmeaning thing they call a thought,
A needless Alexandrine[17] ends the song
That, like a wounded snake, drags its slow length along.
Leave such to tune their own dull rhymes, and know
What's roundly smooth or languishingly slow;
And praise the easy vigour of a line,

[15] Rustic. [16] A character in Ben Jonson's *Every Man Out of His Humor* (1599).
[17] A line with six iambic feet (like the next one).

Where Denham's strength, and Waller's sweetness join.[18]
True ease in writing comes from art, not chance,
As those move easiest who have learned to dance.
'Tis not enough no harshness gives offence,
The sound must seem an Echo to the sense:
Soft is the strain when Zephyr gently blows,
And the smooth stream in smoother numbers flows;
But when loud surges lash the sounding shore,
The hoarse, rough verse should like the torrent roar:
When Ajax[19] strives some rock's vast weight to throw,
The line too labours, and the words move slow;
Not so, when swift Camilla[20] scours the plain,
Flies o'er th' unbending corn, and skims along the main.
Hear how Timotheus'[21] varied lays surprise,
And bid alternate passions fall and rise!
While, at each change, the son of Libyan Jove[22]
Now burns with glory, and then melts with love,
Now his fierce eyes with sparkling fury glow,
Now sighs steal out, and tears begin to flow:
Persians and Greeks like turns of nature[23] found,
And the world's victor stood subdued by Sound!
The power of Music all our hearts allow,
And what Timotheus was, is DRYDEN now.
  Avoid Extremes; and shun the fault of such,
Who still are pleased too little or too much.
At every trifle scorn to take offence,
That always shows great pride, or little sense;
Those heads, as stomachs, are not sure the best,
Which nauseate all, and nothing can digest.
Yet let not each gay Turn thy rapture move;
For fools admire, but men of sense approve:[24]
As things seem large which we through mists descry,
Dullness is ever apt to magnify.
  Some foreign writers, some our own despise;
The Ancients only, or the Moderns prize.
Thus Wit, like Faith, by each man is applied
To one small sect, and all are damned beside.
Meanly they seek the blessing to confine,
And force that sun but on a part to shine,
Which not alone the southern wit sublimes,
But ripens spirits in cold northern climes;

[18] Sir John Denham (1615–69) and Edmund Waller (1606–87). John Dryden had contrasted Denham's "strength" with Waller's "sweetness."

[19] Hero of the Trojan War, slow-witted but enormously strong.

[20] A princess in Virgil's *Aeneid,* so fleet-footed that her steps did not bend grain beneath her.

[21] The musician in Dryden's *Alexander's Feast.* The following lines refer to this poem.

[22] Alexander the Great, who was said to be the son of Jove.

[23] Shifts of mood or feeling.

[24] To "admire" is to wonder; to "approve" is to judge thoughtfully.

Which from the first has shone on ages past,
Enlights the present, and shall warm the last;
Though each may feel increases and decays,
And see now clearer and now darker days.
Regard not then if Wit be old or new,
But blame the false, and value still the true.
  Some ne'er advance a Judgment of their own,
But catch the spreading notion of the Town;
They reason and conclude by precedent,
And own stale nonsense which they ne'er invent.
Some judge of authors' names, not works, and then
Nor praise nor blame the writings, but the men.
Of all this servile herd the worst is he
That in proud dullness joins with Quality.
A constant Critic at the great man's board,
To fetch and carry nonsense for my Lord.
What woful stuff this madrigal would be,
In some starved hackney sonneteer, or me?
But let a Lord once own the happy lines,
How the wit brightens! how the style refines!
Before his sacred name flies every fault,
And each exalted stanza teems with thought!
  The Vulgar thus through Imitation err;
As oft the Learned by being singular;
So much they scorn the crowd, that if the throng
By chance go right, they purposely go wrong;
So Schismatics[25] the plain believers quit,
And are but damned for having too much wit.
Some praise at morning what they blame at night;
But always think the last opinion right.
A Muse by these is like a mistress used,
This hour she's idolised, the next abused;
While their weak heads like towns unfortified,
'Twixt sense and nonsense daily change their side,
Ask them the cause; they're wiser still, they say;
And still to-morrow's wiser than to-day.
We think our fathers fools, so wise we grow;
Our wiser sons, no doubt, will think us so.
Once School-divines this zealous isle o'er-spread;
Who knew most Sentences, was deepest read;[26]
Faith, Gospel, all, seemed made to be disputed,
And none had sense enough to be confuted:
Scotists and Thomists, now, in peace remain,
Amidst their kindred cobwebs in Duck-lane.[27]

[25] Those who divide the Church over doctrinal differences.

[26] "School-divines" are medieval theologians; the "sentences" are Peter Lombard's *Book of Sentences*, a compilation of extracts from various theologians.

[27] "Scotists and Thomists" are followers of Duns Scotus and St. Thomas Aquinas. "Duck-lane" was a street with many secondhand bookstores.

If Faith itself has diff'rent dresses worn,
What wonder modes in Wit should take their turn?
Oft, leaving what is natural and fit,
The current folly proves the ready wit;
And authors think their reputation safe,
Which lives as long as fools are pleased to laugh.
  Some valuing those of their own side or mind,
Still make themselves the measure of mankind:
Fondly[28] we think we honour merit then,
When we but praise ourselves in other men.
Parties in Wit attend on those of State,
And public faction doubles private hate.
Pride, Malice, Folly, against Dryden rose,
In various shapes of Parsons, Critics, Beaus;
But sense survived, when merry jests were past;
For rising merit will buoy up at last.
Might he return, and bless once more our eyes,
New Blackmores and new Milbourns[29] must arise:
Nay should great Homer lift his awful head,
Zoilus[30] again would start up from the dead.
Envy will merit, as its shade, pursue;
But like a shadow, proves the substance true;
For envied Wit, like Sol eclipsed, makes known
Th' opposing body's grossness, not its own,
When first that sun too powerful beams displays,
It draws up vapours which obscure its rays;
But even those clouds at last adorn its way,
Reflect new glories, and augment the day.
  Be thou the first true merit to befriend;
His praise is lost, who stays, till all commend.
Short is the date, alas, of modern rhymes,
And 'tis but just to let them live betimes.
No longer now that golden age appears,
When Patriarch-wits survived a thousand years:
Now length of Fame (our second life) is lost,
And bare threescore is all even that can boast;
Our sons their fathers' failing language see,
And such as Chaucer is, shall Dryden be.
So when the faithful pencil has designed
Some bright Idea of the master's mind,
Where a new world leaps out at his command,
And ready Nature waits upon his hand;
When the ripe colours soften and unite,
And sweetly melt into just shade and light;

[28] Foolishly.

[29] Sir Richard Blackmore and the Reverend Luke Milbourn had been harsh critics of Dryden.

[30] Fourth-century B.C. author of an attack on Homer.

When mellowing years their full perfection give,
And each bold figure just begins to live,
The treach'rous colours the fair art betray,
And all the bright creation fades away!
Unhappy Wit, like most mistaken things,
Atones not for that envy which it brings.
In youth alone its empty praise we boast,
But soon the short-lived vanity is lost:
Like some fair flower the early spring supplies,
That gaily blooms, but even in blooming dies.
What is this Wit, which must our cares employ?
The owner's wife, that other men enjoy;
Then most our trouble still when most admired,
And still the more we give, the more required;
Whose fame with pains we guard, but lose with ease,
Sure some to vex, but never all to please;
'Tis what the vicious fear, the virtuous shun,
By fools 'tis hated, and by knaves undone!
If Wit so much from Ign'rance undergo,
Ah let not Learning too commence its foe!
Of old, those met rewards who could excel,
And such were praised who but endeavoured well:
Though triumphs were to generals only due,
Crowns were reserved to grace the soldiers too.
Now, they who reach Parnassus' lofty crown,
Employ their pains to spurn some others down;
And while self-love each jealous writer rules,
Contending wits become the sport of fools:
But still the worst with most regret commend,
For each ill Author is as bad a Friend.
To what base ends, and by what abject ways,
Are mortals urged through sacred[31] lust of praise!
Ah ne'er so dire a thirst of glory boast,
Nor in the Critic let the Man be lost.
Good-nature and good-sense must ever join;
To err is human, to forgive, divine.
But if in noble minds some dregs remain
Not yet purged off, of spleen and sour disdain;
Discharge that rage on more provoking crimes,
Nor fear a dearth in these flagitious times.
No pardon vile Obscenity should find,
Though wit and art conspire to move your mind;
But Dullness with Obscenity must prove
As shameful sure as Impotence in love.
In the fat age of pleasure, wealth and ease,
Sprung the rank weed, and thrived with large increase:
When love was all an easy Monarch's care;

[31] Accursed.

Seldom at council, never in a war:
Jilts[32] ruled the state, and statesmen farces writ;
Nay wits had pensions, and young Lords had wit:
The Fair sat panting at a Courtier's play,
And not a Mask[33] went unimproved away:
The modest fan was lifted up no more,
And Virgins smiled at what they blushed before.
The following licence of a Foreign reign
Did all the dregs of bold Socinus[34] drain;
Then unbelieving priests reformed the nation,
And taught more pleasant methods of salvation;
Where Heaven's free subjects might their rights dispute,
Lest God himself should seem too absolute:
Pulpits their sacred satire learned to spare,
And Vice admired to find a flatt'rer there!
Encouraged thus, Wit's Titans braved the skies,
And the press groaned with licensed blasphemies.
These monsters, Critics! with your darts engage,
Here point your thunder, and exhaust your rage!
Yet shun their fault, who, scandalously nice,[35]
Will needs mistake an author into vice;
All seems infected that th' infected spy,
As all looks yellow to the jaundiced eye.

PART III

Learn then what MORALS Critics ought to show,
For 'tis but half a Judge's task, to know.
'Tis not enough, taste, judgment, learning, join;
In all you speak, let truth and candour shine:
That not alone what to your sense is due
All may allow; but seek your friendship too.
Be silent always when you doubt your sense;
And speak, though sure, with seeming diffidence:
Some positive, persisting fops we know,
Who, if once wrong, will needs be always so;
But you, with pleasure own your errors past,
And make each day a Critic on the last.
'Tis not enough, your counsel still be true;
Blunt truths more mischief than nice falsehoods do;
Men must be taught as if you taught them not,
And things unknown proposed as things forgot.
Without Good Breeding, truth is disapproved;

[32] Kept mistresses.
[33] Women wearing masks, fashionable at public events, later identified with prostitutes.
[34] Laelius Socinus (1525–62) and his nephew Faustus Socinus (1539–1604) formed an anti-Trinitarian sect which denied the divinity of Jesus. The "foreign reign" is that of William III, a Dutchman.
[35] Fastidious, over-precise.

That only makes superior sense beloved.
  Be niggards of advice on no pretence;
For the worst avarice is that of sense.
With mean complacence ne'er betray your trust,
Nor be so civil as to prove unjust.
Fear not the anger of the wise to raise;
Those best can bear reproof, who merit praise.
  'Twere well might critics still this freedom take,
But Appius[36] reddens at each word you speak,
And stares, tremendous, with a threat'ning eye,
Like some fierce Tyrant in old tapestry.
Fear most to tax an Honourable fool,
Whose right it is, uncensured, to be dull;
Such, without wit, are Poets when they please,
As without learning they can take Degrees.
Leave dangerous truths to unsuccessful Satires,
And flattery to fulsome Dedicators,
Whom, when they praise, the world believes no more,
Than when they promise to give scribbling o'er.
'Tis best sometimes your censure to restrain,
And charitably let the dull be vain:
Your silence there is better than your spite,
For who can rail so long as they can write?
Still humming on, their drowsy course they keep,
And lashed so long, like tops, are lashed asleep.
False steps but help them to renew the race,
As, after stumbling, Jades will mend their pace.
What crowds of these, impenitently bold,
In sounds and jingling syllables grown old,
Still run on Poets, in a raging vein,
Even to the dregs and squeezings of the brain,
Strain out the last dull droppings of their sense,
And rhyme with all the rage of Impotence.
  Such shameless Bards we have; and yet 'tis true,
There are as mad abandoned Critics too.
The bookful blockhead, ignorantly read,
With loads of learnèd lumber in his head,
With his own tongue still edifies his ears,
And always list'ning to himself appears.
All books he reads, and all he reads assails,
From Dryden's Fables down to Durfey's Tales.[37]
With him, most authors steal their works, or buy;
Garth did not write his own Dispensary.[38]
Name a new Play, and he's the Poet's friend,

[36] "Appius" is John Dennis, who had written an unsuccessful play named *Appius and Virginia* (1709).

[37] John Dryden's *Fables Ancient and Modern* (1700), the most popular of Dryden's works in the eighteenth century, and Thomas D'Urfey's *Tales Tragical and Comical* (1704).

[38] Sir Samuel Garth's satirical mock epic *The Dispensary* (1699).

Nay showed his faults—but when would Poets mend?
No place so sacred from such fops is barred,
Nor is Paul's church more safe than Paul's churchyard:[39]
Nay, fly to Altars; there they'll talk you dead:
For Fools rush in where Angels fear to tread.
Distrustful sense with modest caution speaks,
It still looks home, and short excursions makes;
But rattling nonsense in full volleys breaks,
And never shocked, and never turned aside,
Bursts out, resistless, with a thund'ring tide.
 But where's the man, who counsel can bestow,
Still pleased to teach, and yet not proud to know?
Unbiased, or by favour, or by spite;
Not dully prepossessed, nor blindly right;
Though learned, well-bred; and though well-bred, sincere,
Modestly bold, and humanly severe:
Who to a friend his faults can freely show,
And gladly praise the merit of a foe?
Blest with a taste exact, yet unconfined;
A knowledge both of books and human kind:
Gen'rous converse; a soul exempt from pride;
And love to praise, with reason on his side?
 Such once were Critics; such the happy few,
Athens and Rome in better ages knew.
The mighty Stagirite first left the shore,
Spread all his sails, and durst the deeps explore:
He steered securely, and discovered far,
Led by the light of the Maeonian Star.[40]
Poets, a race long unconfined, and free,
Still fond and proud of savage liberty,
Received his laws; and stood convinced 'twas fit,
Who conquered Nature, should preside o'er Wit.
 Horace[41] still charms with graceful negligence,
And without method talks us into sense,
Will, like a friend, familiarly convey
The truest notions in the easiest way.
He, who supreme in judgment, as in wit,
Might boldly censure, as he boldly writ,
Yet judged with coolness, though he sung with fire:
His Precepts teach but what his works inspire.
Our Critics take a contrary extreme,
They judge with fury, but they write with fle'me:
Nor suffers Horace more in wrong Translations

[39] Saint Paul's Cathedral, London. Paul's Churchyard was the adjoining booksellers' quarter.

[40] Homer, who was born in Lydia, or Maeonia.

[41] Horace (65 B.C.–8 B.C.), Roman Augustan poet and author of the *Ars Poetica,* which influenced the *Essay on Criticism* heavily.

By Wits, than Critics in as wrong Quotations.
  See Dionysius Homer's thoughts refine,[42]
And call new beauties forth from every line!
  Fancy and art in gay Petronius[43] please,
The scholar's learning, with the courtier's ease.
  In grave Quintilian's[44] copious work, we find
The justest rules, and clearest method joined:
Thus useful arms in magazines we place,
All ranged in order, and disposed with grace,
But less to please the eye, than arm the hand,
Still fit for use, and ready at command.
  Thee, bold Longinus![45] all the Nine inspire,
And bless their Critic with a Poet's fire.
An ardent Judge, who zealous in his trust,
With warmth gives sentence, yet is always just;
Whose own example strengthens all his laws;
And is himself that great Sublime he draws.
  Thus long succeeding Critics justly reigned,
Licence repressed, and useful laws ordained.
Learning and Rome alike in empire grew;
And Arts still followed where her Eagles flew;
From the same foes, at last, both felt their doom,
And the same age saw Learning fall, and Rome.
With Tyranny, then Superstition joined,
As that the body, this enslaved the mind;
Much was believed, but little understood,
And to be dull was construed to be good;
A second deluge Learning thus o'er-run,
And the Monks finished what the Goths begun.
  At length Erasmus,[46] that great injured name,
(The glory of the Priesthood, and the shame!)
Stemmed the wild torrent of a barb'rous age,
And drove those holy Vandals off the stage.
  But see! each Muse, in LEO's[47] golden days,
Starts from her trance, and trims her withered bays,
Rome's ancient Genius, o'er its ruins spread,
Shakes off the dust, and rears his rev'rend head.
Then Sculpture and her sister-arts revive;
Stones leaped to form, and rocks began to live;
With sweeter notes each rising Temple rung;

[42] Dionysius of Halicarnassus was a first-century B.C. Greek critic and commentator on Homer.

[43] Petronius Arbiter (d. A.D. 66), Roman satirist and author of the *Satyricon.*

[44] Quintilian (A.D. c. 35–A.D. c. 95) wrote the twelve-volume *Institutes,* a survey of rhetoric with acute comments on writers.

[45] First-century A.D. author of *On the Sublime.*

[46] Dutch humanist and satirist (1469?–1536), author of *The Praise of Folly.* He was the "glory" of the priesthood because of his learning and its "shame" because of its attacks on him.

[47] Pope Leo X (1475–1521), patron of Raphael and of a circle of writers.

A Raphael painted, and a Vida sung.[48]
Immortal Vida: on whose honoured brow
The Poet's bays and Critic's ivy grow:
Cremona now shall ever boast thy name,
As next in place to Mantua, next in fame!
  But soon by impious arms from Latium chased,
Their ancient bounds the banished Muses passed;
Thence Arts o'er all the northern world advance,
But Critic-learning flourished most in France:
The rules a nation, born to serve, obeys;
And Boileau[49] still in right of Horace sways.
But we, brave Britons, foreign laws despised,
And kept unconquered, and uncivilised;
Fierce for the liberties of wit, and bold,
We still defied the Romans, as of old.
Yet some there were, among the sounder few
Of those who less presumed, and better knew,
Who durst assert the juster ancient cause,
And here restored Wit's fundamental laws.
Such was the Muse, whose rules and practice tell,
"Nature's chief Master-piece is writing well."[50]
Such was Roscommon,[51] not more learned than good,
With manners gen'rous as his noble blood;
To him the wit of Greece and Rome was known,
And every author's merit, but his own.
Such late was Walsh[52]—the Muse's judge and friend,
Who justly knew to blame or to commend;
To failings mild, but zealous for desert;
The clearest head, and the sincerest heart.
This humble praise, lamented shade! receive,
This praise at least a grateful Muse may give:
The Muse, whose early voice you taught to sing,
Prescribed her heights, and pruned her tender wing,
(Her guide now lost) no more attempts to rise,
But in low numbers short excursions tries:
Content, if hence th' unlearned their wants may view,
The learned reflect on what before they knew:
Careless of censure, nor too fond of fame;
Still pleased to praise, yet not afraid to blame,
Averse alike to flatter, or offend;
Not free from faults, nor yet too vain to mend.

[48] The Italian painter Raphael (1483–1520) was chief architect of Saint Peter's and painter of the Sistine Madonna. Vida was M. Hieronymus Vida, a contemporary of Raphael who wrote an *Art of Poetry*.

[49] Nicolas Boileau (1636–1711), French critic and poet, was the foremost spokesman of Neoclassicism.

[50] A line from John Sheffield, Duke of Buckingham's *Essay on Poetry* (1682).

[51] Wentworth Dillon, the Earl of Roscommon, published a metrical translation of Horace's *Art of Poetry* in 1680 and an *Essay on Translated Verse* in 1684.

[52] William Walsh, poet and early friend of Pope.

ELOÏSA TO ABELARD[1]

In these deep solitudes and awful cells,
Where heavenly-pensive contemplation dwells,
And ever-musing melancholy reigns;
What means this tumult in a Vestal's[2] veins?
Why rove my thoughts beyond this last retreat?
Why feels my heart its long-forgotten heat?
Yet, yet I love!—From Abelard it came,
And Eloïsa yet must kiss the name.
Dear fatal name! rest ever unrevealed,
Nor pass these lips in holy silence sealed:
Hide it, my heart, within that close disguise,
Where mixed with God's, his loved Idea[3] lies:
O write it not my hand—the name appears
Already written—wash it out, my tears!
In vain lost Eloïsa weeps and prays,
Her heart still dictates, and her hand obeys.
Relentless walls! whose darksome round contains
Repentant sighs, and voluntary pains:
Ye rugged rocks! which holy knees have worn;
Ye grots and caverns shagged with horrid thorn!
Shrines! where their vigils pale-eyed virgins keep,
And pitying saints, whose statues learn to weep!
Though cold like you, unmoved and silent grown,
I have not yet forgot myself to stone.
All is not Heaven's while Abelard has part,
Still rebel nature holds out half my heart;
Nor prayers nor fasts its stubborn pulse restrain,
Nor tears for ages taught to flow in vain.
Soon as thy letters trembling I unclose,
That well-known name awakens all my woes.
Oh name for ever sad! for ever dear!
Still breathed in sighs, still ushered with a tear.
I tremble too, where'er my own I find,
Some dire misfortune follows close behind.
Line after line my gushing eyes o'erflow,
Led through a sad variety of woe:
Now warm in love, now with'ring in my bloom,
Lost in a convent's solitary gloom!
There stern Religion quenched th' unwilling flame,
There died the best of passions, Love and Fame.
Yet write, oh write me all, that I may join
Griefs to thy griefs, and echo sighs to thine.
Nor foes nor fortune take this power away;
And is my Abelard less kind than they?
Tears still are mine, and those I need not spare,

[1] For the historical background of "Eloïsa to Abelard," see the Introduction.
[2] A virgin. [3] Image.

Love but demands what else were shed in prayer;
No happier task these faded eyes pursue;
To read and weep is all they now can do.
  Then share thy pain, allow that sad relief;
Ah, more than share it, give me all thy grief.
Heaven first taught letters for some wretch's aid,
Some banished lover, or some captive maid;
They live, they speak, they breathe what love inspires,
Warm from the soul, and faithful to its fires,
The virgin's wish without her fears impart,
Excuse[4] the blush, and pour out all the heart,
Speed the soft intercourse from soul to soul,
And waft a sigh from Indus to the Pole.
  Thou know'st how guiltless first I met thy flame,
When Love approached me under Friendship's name;
My fancy formed thee of angelic kind,
Some emanation of th' all-beauteous Mind.
Those smiling eyes, attemp'ring every ray,
Shone sweetly lambent with celestial day.
Guiltless I gazed; heaven listened while you sung;
And truths divine came mended from that tongue.
From lips like those what precept failed to move?
Too soon they taught me 'twas no sin to love:
Back through the paths of pleasing sense I ran,
Nor wished an Angel whom I loved a Man.
Dim and remote the joys of saints I see;
Nor envy them that heaven I lose for thee.
  How oft, when pressed to marriage, have I said,
Curse on all laws but those which love has made?
Love, free as air, at sight of human ties,
Spreads his light wings, and in a moment flies.
Let wealth, let honour, wait the wedded dame,
August her deed, and sacred be her fame;
Before true passion all those views remove,
Fame, wealth, and honour! what are you to Love?
The jealous God, when we profane his fires,
Those restless passions in revenge inspires,
And bids them make mistaken mortals groan,
Who seek in love for aught but love alone.
Should at my feet the world's great master fall,
Himself, his throne, his world, I'd scorn 'em all:
Not Caesar's empress would I deign to prove;
No, make me mistress to the man I love;
If there be yet another name more free,
More fond than mistress, make me that to thee!
Oh! happy state! when souls each other draw,
When love is liberty, and nature law:

[4] Exempt from the need of.

All then is full, possessing, and possessed,
No craving void left aching in the breast:
Even thought meets thought, ere from the lips it part,
And each warm wish springs mutual from the heart.
This sure is bliss (if bliss on earth there be)
And once the lot of Abelard and me.
  Alas, how changed! what sudden horrors rise!
A naked Lover bound and bleeding lies!
Where, where was Eloïse? her voice, her hand,
Her poniard, had opposed the dire command.
Barbarian, stay! that bloody stroke restrain;
The crime was common, common be the pain.
I can no more; by shame, by rage suppressed,
Let tears, and burning blushes speak the rest.
  Canst thou forget that sad, that solemn day,
When victims at yon altar's foot we lay?
Canst thou forget what tears that moment fell,
When, warm in youth, I bade the world farewell?
As with cold lips I kissed the sacred veil,
The shrines all trembled, and the lamps grew pale:
Heaven scarce believed the Conquest it surveyed,
And Saints with wonder heard the vows I made.
Yet then, to those dread altars as I drew,
Not on the Cross my eyes were fixed, but you:
Not grace, or zeal, love only was my call,
And if I lose thy love, I lose my all.
Come! with thy looks, thy words, relieve my woe;
Those still at least are left thee to bestow.
Still on that breast enamoured let me lie,
Still drink delicious poison from thy eye,
Pant on thy lip, and to thy heart be pressed;
Give all thou canst—and let me dream the rest.
Ah no! instruct me other joys to prize,
With other beauties charm my partial eyes,
Full in my view set all the bright abode,
And make my soul quit Abelard for God.
  Ah, think at least thy flock deserves thy care,
Plants of thy hand, and children of thy prayer.
From the false world in early youth they fled,
By thee to mountains, wilds, and deserts led.
You raised these hallowed walls; the desert smiled,
And Paradise was opened in the Wild.
No weeping orphan saw his father's stores
Our shrines irradiate, or emblaze the floors;
No silver saints, by dying misers given,
Here bribed the rage of ill-requited heaven:
But such plain roofs as Piety could raise,
And only vocal with the Maker's praise.
In these lone walls (their days eternal bound)

These moss-grown domes[5] with spiry turrets crowned,
Where awful arches make a noon-day night,
And the dim windows shed a solemn light;
Thy eyes diffused a reconciling ray,
And gleams of glory brightened all the day.
But now no face divine contentment wears,
'Tis all blank sadness, or continual tears.
See how the force of others' prayers I try,
(O pious fraud of am'rous charity!)
But why should I on others' prayers depend?
Come thou, my father, brother, husband, friend!
Ah let thy handmaid, sister, daughter move,
And all those tender names in one, thy love!
The darksome pines that o'er yon rocks reclined
Wave high, and murmur to the hollow wind,
The wandering streams that shine between the hills,
The grots that echo to the tinkling rills,
The dying gales that pant upon the trees,
The lakes that quiver to the curling breeze;
No more these scenes my meditation aid,
Or lull to rest the visionary maid.
But o'er the twilight groves and dusky caves,
Long-sounding aisles, and intermingled graves,
Black Melancholy sits, and round her throws
A death-like silence, and a dead repose:
Her gloomy presence saddens all the scene,
Shades every flower, and darkens every green,
Deepens the murmur of the falling floods,
And breathes a browner horror on the woods.
Yet here for ever, ever must I stay;
Sad proof how well a lover can obey!
Death, only death, can break the lasting chain:
And here, even then, shall my cold dust remain,
Here all its frailties, all its flames resign,
And wait till 'tis no sin to mix with thine.
Ah wretch! believed the spouse of God in vain,
Confessed within the slave of love and man.
Assist me, heaven! but whence arose that prayer?
Sprung it from piety, or from despair?
Even here, where frozen chastity retires,
Love finds an altar for forbidden fires.
I ought to grieve, but cannot what I ought;
I mourn the lover, not lament the fault;
I view my crime, but kindle at the view,
Repent old pleasures, and solicit new;
Now turned to heaven, I weep my past offence,
Now think of thee, and curse my innocence.
Of all affliction taught a lover yet,

[5] Dignified buildings.

'Tis sure the hardest science to forget!
How shall I lose the sin, yet keep the sense,
And love th' offender, yet detest th' offence?
How the dear object from the crime remove,
Or how distinguish penitence from love?
Unequal task! a passion to resign,
For hearts so touched, so pierced, so lost as mine.
Ere such a soul regains its peaceful state,
How often must it love, how often hate!
How often hope, despair, resent, regret,
Conceal, disdain,—do all things but forget.
But let heaven seize it, all at once 'tis fired:
Not touched, but rapt; not wakened, but inspired!
Oh come! oh teach me nature to subdue,
Renounce my love, my life, myself—and you.
Fill my fond heart with God alone, for he
Alone can rival, can succeed to thee.
  How happy is the blameless Vestal's lot!
The world forgetting, by the world forgot:
Eternal sunshine of the spotless mind!
Each prayer accepted, and each wish resigned;
Labour and rest, that equal periods keep;
"Obedient slumbers that can wake and weep;"[6]
Desires composed, affections ever even;
Tears that delight, and sighs that waft to heaven.
Grace shines around her with serenest beams,
And whisp'ring Angels prompt her golden dreams.
For her th' unfading rose of Eden blooms,
And wings of Seraphs shed divine perfumes,
For her the Spouse prepares the bridal ring,
For her white virgins Hymeneals sing,[7]
To sounds of heavenly harps she dies away,
And melts in visions of eternal day.
  Far other dreams my erring soul employ,
Far other raptures, of unholy joy:
When at the close of each sad, sorrowing day,
Fancy restores what vengeance snatched away,
Then conscience sleeps, and leaving nature free,
All my loose soul unbounded springs to thee.
Oh curst, dear horrors of all-conscious night;
How glowing guilt exalts the keen delight!
Provoking Demons all restraint remove,
And stir within me every source of love.
I hear thee, view thee, gaze o'er all thy charms,
And round thy phantom glue my clasping arms.
I wake:—no more I hear, no more I view,

[6] A quotation from "Description of a Religious House," by Richard Crashaw (1612–49), l. 16.

[7] A reference to the ceremony by which a nun becomes the "bride of Christ."

The phantom flies me, as unkind as you.
I call aloud; it hears not what I say:
I stretch my empty arms; it glides away.
To dream once more I close my willing eyes;
Ye soft illusions, dear deceits, arise!
Alas, no more! methinks we wand'ring go
Through dreary wastes, and weep each other's woe,
Where round some mould'ring tower pale ivy creeps,
And low-browed rocks hang nodding o'er the deeps.
Sudden you mount, you beckon from the skies;
Clouds interpose, waves roar, and winds arise.
I shriek, start up, the same sad prospect find,
And wake to all the griefs I left behind.
  For thee the fates, severely kind, ordain
A cool suspense from pleasure and from pain;
Thy life a long dead calm of fixed repose;
No pulse that riots, and no blood that glows.
Still as the sea, ere winds were taught to blow,
Or moving spirit bade the waters flow;
Soft as the slumbers of a saint forgiven,
And mild as opening gleams of promised heaven.
  Come, Abelard! for what hast thou to dread?
The torch of Venus burns not for the dead.
Nature stands checked; Religion disapproves;
Even thou art cold—yet Eloïsa loves.
Ah hopeless, lasting flames! like those that burn
To light the dead, and warm th' unfruitful urn.
  What scenes appear where'er I turn my view?
The dear Ideas, where I fly, pursue,
Rise in the grove, before the altar rise,
Stain all my soul, and wanton in my eyes.
I waste the Matin lamp in sighs for thee,
Thy image steals between my God and me,
Thy voice I seem in every hymn to hear,
With every bead I drop too soft a tear.
When from the censer clouds of fragrance roll,
And swelling organs lift the rising soul,
One thought of thee puts all the pomp to flight,
Priests, tapers, temples, swim before my sight:
In seas of flame my plunging soul is drowned,
While Altars blaze, and Angels tremble round.
  While prostrate here in humble grief I lie,
Kind, virtuous drops just gath'ring in my eye,
While praying, trembling, in the dust I roll,
And dawning grace is opening on my soul:
Come, if thou dar'st, all charming as thou art!
Oppose thyself to heaven; dispute my heart;
Come, with one glance of those deluding eyes
Blot out each bright Idea of the skies;
Take back that grace, those sorrows, and those tears;

Take back my fruitless penitence and prayers;
Snatch me, just mounting, from the blest abode;
Assist the fiends, and tear me from my God!
  No, fly me, fly me, far as Pole from Pole;
Rise Alps between us! and whole oceans roll!
Ah, come not, write not, think not once of me,
Nor share one pang of all I felt for thee.
Thy oaths I quit, thy memory resign;
Forget, renounce me, hate whate'er was mine.
Fair eyes, and tempting looks (which yet I view!)
Long loved, adored ideas, all adieu!
Oh Grace serene! oh virtue heavenly fair!
Divine oblivion of low-thoughted care!
Fresh blooming Hope, gay daughter of the sky!
And Faith, our early immortality!
Enter, each mild, each amicable guest;
Receive, and wrap me in eternal rest!
  See in her cell sad Eloïsa spread,
Propt on some tomb, a neighbour of the dead.
In each low wind methinks a Spirit calls,
And more than Echoes talk along the walls.
Here, as I watched the dying lamps around,
From yonder shrine I heard a hollow sound.
"Come, sister, come!" (it said, or seemed to say)
"Thy place is here, sad sister, come away!
Once like thyself, I trembled, wept, and prayed,
Love's victim then, though now a sainted maid:
But all is calm in this eternal sleep;
Here grief forgets to groan, and love to weep,
Even superstition loses every fear:
For God, not man, absolves our frailties here."
  I come, I come! prepare your roseate bowers,
Celestial palms, and ever-blooming flowers.
Thither, where sinners may have rest, I go,
Where flames refined in breasts seraphic glow:
Thou, Abelard! the last sad office pay,
And smooth my passage to the realms of day;
See my lips tremble, and my eye-balls roll,
Suck my last breath, and catch my flying soul!
Ah no—in sacred vestments may'st thou stand,
The hallowed taper trembling in thy hand,
Present the Cross before my lifted eye,
Teach me at once, and learn of me to die.
Ah then, thy once-loved Eloïsa see!
It will be then no crime to gaze on me.
See from my cheek the transient roses fly!
See the last sparkle languish in my eye!
'Til every motion, pulse, and breath be o'er;
And even my Abelard be loved no more.
O Death all-eloquent! you only prove

What dust we dote on, when 'tis man we love.
Then too when fate shall thy fair frame destroy,
(That cause of all my guilt, and all my joy)
In trance ecstatic may thy pangs be drowned,
Bright clouds descend, and Angels watch thee round,
From opening skies may streaming glories shine,
And saints embrace thee with a love like mine.
May one kind grave unite each hapless name,
And graft my love immortal on thy fame!
Then, ages hence, when all my woes are o'er,
When this rebellious heart shall beat no more;
If ever chance two wand'ring lovers brings
To Paraclete's[8] white walls and silver springs,
O'er the pale marble shall they join their heads,
And drink the falling tears each other sheds;
Then sadly say, with mutual pity moved,
"Oh may we never love as these have loved!"
From the full choir when loud Hosannas rise,
And swell the pomp of dreadful sacrifice,[9]
Amid that scene if some relenting eye
Glance on the stone where our cold relics lie,
Devotion's self shall steal a thought from heaven,
One human tear shall drop and be forgiven.
And sure, if fate some future bard shall join
In sad similitude of griefs to mine,
Condemned whole years in absence to deplore,
And image charms he must behold no more;
Such if there be, who loves so long, so well;
Let him our sad, our tender story tell;
The well-sung woes will soothe my pensive ghost;
He best can paint 'em who shall feel 'em most.

[8] The Monastery of the Paraclete (Holy Ghost), where Eloïsa and Abelard were buried together.
[9] The celebration of the Eucharist.

THE RAPE OF THE LOCK

AN HEROI-COMICAL POEM

Nolueram, Belinda, tuos violare capillos;
Sed juvat, hoc precibus me tribuisse tuis.
Mart. *Epigr.* xii. 84.[1]

To Mrs. Arabella Fermor

CANTO I

What dire offence from am'rous causes springs,
What mighty contests rise from trivial things,
I sing—This verse to Caryll,[2] Muse! is due:
This, even Belinda may vouchsafe to view:
Slight is the subject, but not so the praise,
If She inspire, and He approve my lays.
Say what strange motive, Goddess! could compel
A well-bred Lord t' assault a gentle Belle?
O say what stranger cause, yet unexplored,
Could make a gentle Belle reject a Lord?
In tasks so bold, can little men engage,
And in soft bosoms dwells such mighty Rage?
Sol through white curtains shot a tim'rous ray,
And oped those eyes that must eclipse the day:
Now lap-dogs give themselves the rousing shake,
And sleepless lovers, just at twelve, awake:
Thrice rung the bell, the slipper knocked the ground,[3]
And the pressed watch returned a silver sound.[4]
Belinda still her downy pillow prest,
Her guardian Sylph[5] prolonged the balmy rest:
'Twas He had summoned to her silent bed
The morning-dream that hovered o'er her head;

[1] "I was unwilling, Belinda, to ravish your locks; but I rejoice to have conceded this to your prayers." (Pope changes Martial's "Polytimus" to "Belinda.")

[2] John Caryll, the friend who suggested the poem. The beginning is a mock epic invocation.

[3] Since her bell was not answered, she knocked on the floor with her slipper.

[4] A "repeater" watch that sounded the hours and the quarters when a pin was pushed.

[5] This is the first reference to the "supernatural machinery" of the poem. As Pope explained in his introductory letter to Arabella Fermor, the spirits are borrowed from Rosicrucian lore: "According to these Gentlemen [the Rosicrucians], the four Elements are inhabited by Spirits, which they call *Sylphs, Gnomes, Nymphs,* and *Salamanders.* The *Gnomes,* or Daemons of Earth, delight in Mischief; but the *Sylphs,* whose Habitation is in the Air, are the best-condition'd Creatures imaginable. For they say, any Mortals may enjoy the most intimate Familiarities with these gentle Spirits, upon a Condition very easie to all true *Adepts,* an inviolate Preservation of Chastity." In epics, the gods often communicate with the hero through apparitions during sleep.

A Youth more glitt'ring than a Birth-night Beau,[6]
(That even in slumber caused her cheek to glow)
Seemed to her ear his winning lips to lay,
And thus in whispers said, or seemed to say.
"Fairest of mortals, thou distinguished care
Of thousand bright Inhabitants of Air!
If e'er one vision touched thy infant thought,
Of all the Nurse and all the Priest have taught;
Of airy Elves by moonlight shadows seen,
The silver token, and the circled green,[7]
Or virgins visited by Angel-powers,
With golden crowns and wreaths of heav'nly flowers;
Hear and believe! thy own importance know,
Nor bound thy narrow views to things below.
Some secret truths, from learnéd pride concealed,
To Maids alone and Children are revealed:
What though no credit doubting Wits may give?
The Fair and Innocent shall still believe.
Know, then, unnumbered Spirits round thee fly,
The light Militia of the lower sky:
These, though unseen, are ever on the wing,
Hang o'er the Box, and hover round the Ring.[8]
Think what an equipage thou hast in Air,
And view with scorn two Pages and a Chair.
As now your own, our beings were of old,
And once inclosed in Woman's beauteous mould;
Thence, by a soft transition, we repair
From earthly Vehicles to these of air.
Think not, when Woman's transient breath is fled,
That all her vanities at once are dead;
Succeeding vanities she still regards,
And though she plays no more, o'erlooks the cards.
Her joy in gilded Chariots, when alive,
And love of Ombre,[9] after death survive.
For when the Fair in all their pride expire,
To their first Elements their Souls retire:
The Sprites of fiery Termagants[10] in Flame
Mount up, and take a Salamander's name.
Soft yielding minds to Water glide away,
And sip, with Nymphs, their elemental Tea.
The graver Prude sinks downward to a Gnome,
In search of mischief still on Earth to roam.
The light Coquettes in Sylphs aloft repair,
And sport and flutter in the fields of Air.

[6] Beaux dressed with particular splendor for the royal birthday celebrations.

[7] Fairies were supposed to leave coins (the "silver token") and rings of green grass, where they held fairy dances.

[8] That is, a theater box and the fashionable circular drive for coaches in Hyde Park.

[9] A popular card game. See III.27–104.

[10] Scolding, bad-tempered women.

"Know further yet; whoever fair and chaste
Rejects mankind, is by some Sylph embraced:
For Spirits, freed from mortal laws, with ease
Assume what sexes and what shapes they please.
What guards the purity of melting Maids,
In courtly balls, and midnight masquerades,
Safe from the treach'rous friend, the daring spark,[11]
The glance by day, the whisper in the dark,
When kind occasion prompts their warm desires,
When music softens, and when dancing fires?
'Tis but their Sylph, the wise Celestials know,
Though Honour is the word with Men below.
"Some nymphs there are, too conscious of their face,[12]
For life predestined to the Gnomes' embrace.
These swell their prospects and exalt their pride,
When offers are disdained, and love denied:
Then gay Ideas crowd the vacant brain,
While Peers, and Dukes, and all their sweeping train,
And Garters, Stars, and Coronets appear,
And in soft sounds, Your Grace salutes their ear.
'Tis these that early taint the female soul,
Instruct the eyes of young Coquettes to roll,
Teach Infant-cheeks a bidden blush to know,
And little hearts to flutter at a Beau.
"Oft, when the world imagine women stray,
The Sylphs through mystic mazes guide their way,
Through all the giddy circle they pursue,
And old impertinence[13] expel by new.
What tender maid but must a victim fall
To one man's treat, but for another's ball?
When Florio speaks what virgin could withstand,
If gentle Damon did not squeeze her hand?
With varying vanities, from every part,
They shift the moving Toyshop[14] of their heart;
Where wigs with wigs, with sword-knots sword-knots strive,[15]
Beaux banish beaux, and coaches coaches drive.
This erring mortals Levity may call;
Oh blind to truth! the Sylphs contrive it all.
"Of these am I, who thy protection claim,
A watchful sprite, and Ariel is my name.
Late, as I ranged the crystal wilds of air,
In the clear Mirror of thy ruling Star
I saw, alas! some dread event impend,
Ere to the main this morning sun descend,
But heaven reveals not what, or how, or where:

[11] A fashionable, foppish man. [12] Too aware of their beauty. [13] A trifling bauble.
[14] A shop for trinkets and baubles.
[15] "Sword-knots" were ribbons tied to the hilts of ornamental swords.

Warned by the Sylph, oh pious maid, beware!
This to disclose is all thy guardian can:
Beware of all, but most beware of Man!"
  He said; when Shock,[16] who thought she slept too long,
Leaped up, and waked his mistress with his tongue.
'Twas then, Belinda, if report say true,
Thy eyes first opened on a Billet-doux;[17]
Wounds, Charms, and Ardors were no sooner read,
But all the Vision vanished from thy head.
  And now, unveiled, the Toilet stands displayed,[18]
Each silver Vase in mystic order laid.
First, robed in white, the Nymph intent adores,
With head uncovered, the Cosmetic powers.
A heav'nly image in the glass appears,
To that she bends, to that her eyes she rears;
Th' inferior Priestess, at her altar's side,
Trembling begins the sacred rites of Pride.
Unnumbered treasures ope at once, and here
The various off'rings of the world appear;
From each she nicely culls with curious toil,
And decks the Goddess with the glitt'ring spoil.
This casket India's glowing gems unlocks,
And all Arabia breathes from yonder box.
The Tortoise here and Elephant unite,
Transformed to combs, the speckled, and the white.
Here files of pins extend their shining rows,
Puffs, Powders, Patches, Bibles, Billet-doux.
Now awful Beauty puts on all its arms;
The fair each moment rises in her charms,
Repairs her smiles, awakens every grace,
And calls forth all the wonders of her face;
Sees by degrees a purer blush arise,
And keener lightnings quicken in her eyes.
The busy Sylphs surround their darling care,
These set the head, and those divide the hair,
Some fold the sleeve, whilst others plait the gown;
And Betty's[19] praised for labours not her own.

CANTO II

Not with more glories, in th' etherial plain,
The Sun first rises o'er the purpled main,
Than, issuing forth, the rival of his beams

[16] Belinda's lapdog. A "shock" or "shough" was a breed of small dog. [17] Love letter.

[18] The following passage parodies an epic ceremonial worship of a goddess. Belinda is the chief priestess, and the goddess is her own image in the mirror. The passage also parodies the arming of the epic hero.

[19] "Betty" was a generic term for a lady's maid.

Launched on the bosom of the silver Thames.
Fair Nymphs, and well-drest Youths around her shone,
But every eye was fixed on her alone.
On her white breast a sparkling Cross she wore,
Which Jews might kiss, and Infidels adore.
Her lively looks a sprightly mind disclose,
Quick as her eyes, and as unfixed as those:
Favours to none, to all she smiles extends;
Oft she rejects, but never once offends.
Bright as the sun, her eyes the gazers strike,
And, like the sun, they shine on all alike.
Yet graceful ease, and sweetness void of pride,
Might hide her faults, if Belles had faults to hide:
If to her share some female errors fall,
Look on her face, and you'll forget 'em all.
  This Nymph, to the destruction of mankind,
Nourished two Locks, which graceful hung behind
In equal curls, and well conspired to deck
With shining ringlets the smooth iv'ry neck.
Love in these labyrinths his slaves detains,
And mighty hearts are held in slender chains.
With hairy springes[20] we the birds betray,
Slight lines of hair surprise the finny prey,
Fair tresses man's imperial race ensnare,
And beauty draws us with a single hair.
  Th' advent'rous Baron the bright locks admired;
He saw, he wished, and to the prize aspired.
Resolved to win, he meditates the way,
By force to ravish, or by fraud betray;
For when success a Lover's toil attends,
Few ask, if fraud or force attained his ends.
  For this, ere Phoebus rose, he had implored
Propitious heaven, and every power adored,
But chiefly Love—to Love an Altar built,
Of twelve vast French Romances, neatly gilt.
There lay three garters, half a pair of gloves;
And all the trophies of his former loves;
With tender Billet-doux he lights the pyre,
And breathes three am'rous sighs to raise the fire.
Then prostrate falls, and begs with ardent eyes
Soon to obtain, and long possess the prize:
The powers gave ear, and granted half his prayer,
The rest, the winds dispersed in empty air.
  But now secure the painted vessel glides,
The sun-beams trembling on the floating tides:
While melting music steals upon the sky,
And softened sounds along the waters die;

[20] Snares.

Smooth flow the waves, the Zephyrs gently play,
Belinda smiled, and all the world was gay.
All but the Sylph—with careful thoughts oppresst,
Th' impending woe sat heavy on his breast.
He summons strait his Denizens of air;
The lucid squadrons round the sails repair:
Soft o'er the shrouds aërial whispers breathe,
That seemed but Zephyrs to the train beneath.
Some to the sun their insect-wings unfold,
Waft on the breeze, or sink in clouds of gold;
Transparent forms, too fine for mortal sight,
Their fluid bodies half dissolved in light,
Loose to the wind their airy garments flew,
Thin glitt'ring textures of the filmy dew,
Dipt in the richest tincture of the skies,
Where light disports in ever-mingling dyes,
While every beam new transient colours flings,
Colours that change whene'er they wave their wings.
Amid the circle, on the gilded mast,
Superior by the head, was Ariel placed;
His purple pinions opening to the sun,
He raised his azure wand, and thus begun.
"Ye Sylphs and Sylphids, to your chief give ear!
Fays, Fairies, Genii, Elves, and Daemons, hear!
Ye know the spheres and various tasks assigned
By laws eternal to th' aërial kind.
Some in the fields of purest Aether play,
And bask and whiten in the blaze of day.
Some guide the course of wand'ring orbs on high,
Or roll the planets through the boundless sky.
Some less refined, beneath the moon's pale light
Pursue the stars that shoot athwart the night,
Or suck the mists in grosser air below,
Or dip their pinions in the painted bow,
Or brew fierce tempests on the wintry main,
Or o'er the glebe[21] distil the kindly rain.
Others on earth o'er human race preside,
Watch all their ways, and all their actions guide:
Of these the chief the care of Nations own,
And guard with Arms divine the British Throne.
"Our humbler province is to tend the Fair,
Not a less pleasing, though less glorious care;
To save the powder from too rude a gale,
Nor let th' imprisoned essences exhale;
To draw fresh colours from the vernal flowers;
To steal from rainbows e'er they drop in showers
A brighter wash; to curl their waving hairs,
Assist their blushes, and inspire their airs;

[21] Cultivated field.

Nay oft, in dreams, invention we bestow,
To change a Flounce, or add a Furbelow.
"This day, black Omens threat the brightest Fair,
That e'er deserved a watchful spirit's care;
Some dire disaster, or by force, or slight;
But what, or where, the fates have wrapt in night.
Whether the nymph shall break Diana's law,[22]
Or some frail China jar receive a flaw;
Or stain her honour or her new brocade;
Forget her prayers, or miss a masquerade;
Or lose her heart, or necklace, at a ball;
Or whether Heaven has doomed that Shock must fall.
Haste, then, ye spirits! to your charge repair:
The flutt'ring fan be Zephyretta's care;
The drops to thee, Brillante, we consign;
And, Momentilla, let the watch be thine;
Do thou, Crispissa,[23] tend her fav'rite Lock;
Ariel himself shall be the guard of Shock.
"To fifty chosen Sylphs, of special note,
We trust th' important charge, the Petticoat:[24]
Oft have we known that seven-fold fence to fail,
Though stiff with hoops, and armed with ribs of whale;
Form a strong line about the silver bound,
And guard the wide circumference around.
"Whatever spirit, careless of his charge,
His post neglects, or leaves the fair at large,
Shall feel sharp vengeance soon o'ertake his sins,
Be stopped in vials, or transfixed with pins;
Or plunged in lakes of bitter washes lie,
Or wedged whole ages in a bodkin's eye:[25]
Gums and Pomatums shall his flight restrain,
While clogged he beats his silken wings in vain;
Or Alum styptics with contracting power
Shrink his thin essence like a rivelled[26] flower:
Or, as Ixion[27] fixed, the wretch shall feel
The giddy motion of the whirling Mill,
In fumes of burning Chocolate shall glow,
And tremble at the sea that froths below!"
He spoke; the spirits from the sails descend;
Some, orb in orb, around the nymph extend;
Some thrid the mazy ringlets of her hair;
Some hang upon the pendants of her ear:

[22] That is, the law of chastity.
[23] "Crispissa" is derived from the Latin *crispere,* to curl.
[24] Pope is parodying epic descriptions of the hero's shield.
[25] Here "bodkin" means a blunt-pointed needle. Later (IV.98 and V.95) it means a hair ornament, and (V.55 and 88), a dagger. Pope plays on these various meanings.
[26] Wrinkled, shrunken.
[27] In Greek mythology, Ixion was punished by being tied to an everturning wheel in the underworld.

With beating hearts the dire event they wait,
Anxious, and trembling for the birth of Fate.

CANTO III

Close by those meads, forever crowned with flowers,
Where Thames with pride surveys his rising towers,
There stands a structure of majestic frame,
Which from the neighb'ring Hampton[28] takes its name.
Here Britain's statesmen oft the fall foredoom
Of foreign Tyrants and of Nymphs at home;
Here thou, great ANNA![29] whom three realms obey,
Dost sometimes counsel take—and sometimes Tea.
  Hither the heroes and the nymphs resort,
To taste awhile the pleasures of a Court;
In various talk th' instructive hours they past,
Who gave the ball, or paid the visit last;
One speaks the glory of the British Queen,
And one describes a charming Indian screen;
A third interprets motions, looks, and eyes;
At every word a reputation dies.
Snuff, or the fan, supply each pause of chat,
With singing, laughing, ogling, *and all that.*
  Meanwhile, declining from the noon of day,
The sun obliquely shoots his burning ray;
The hungry Judges soon the sentence sign,
And wretches hang that jury-men may dine;
The merchant from th' Exchange returns in peace,
And the long labours of the Toilet cease.
Belinda now, whom thirst of fame invites,
Burns to encounter two advent'rous Knights,
At Ombre[30] singly to decide their doom;
And swells her breast with conquests yet to come.
Straight the three bands prepare in arms to join,
Each band the number of the sacred nine.
Soon as she spreads her hand, th' aërial guard
Descend, and sit on each important card:
First Ariel perched upon a Matadore,
Then each, according to the rank they bore;

[28] Hampton Court is the royal palace about fifteen miles up the Thames from London.

[29] Queen Anne. The "three realms" are Great Britain, Ireland, and (inaccurately) France.

[30] The epic battle is the card game of ombre. Ombre was a Spanish game (Spanish *hombre,* man), somewhat like bridge or whist. It was played with a pack of forty cards; the 8's, 9's and 10's were not used. The "Matadores" were the Ace of Spades ("Spadillio"), the Ace of Clubs ("Basto"), and one other card ("Manillio"), in this case the two of spades. The principal player was the Ombre; if one of the other players won the game, he was said to "give Codille" to the Ombre. Pope describes a real game so precisely that it is possible to reconstruct it and replay it. Belinda is the Ombre and wins by a narrow margin. The Baron has a strong hand, but the third player (never directly mentioned) has a weak one.

For Sylphs, yet mindful of their ancient race,
Are, as when women, wondrous fond of place.
  Behold, four Kings in majesty revered,
With hoary whiskers and a forky beard;
And four fair Queens whose hands sustain a flower,
Th' expressive emblem of their softer power;
Four Knaves in garbs succinct, a trusty band,
Caps on their heads, and halberts in their hand;
And particoloured troops, a shining train,
Draw forth to combat on the velvet plain.
  The skilful Nymph reviews her force with care:
Let Spades be trumps! she said, and trumps they were.
  Now move to war her sable Matadores,
In show like leaders of the swarthy Moors.
Spadillio first, unconquerable Lord!
Led off two captive trumps, and swept the board.
As many more Manillio forced to yield,
And marched a victor from the verdant field.
Him Basto followed, but his fate more hard
Gained but one trump and one Plebeian card.
With his broad sabre next, a chief in years,
The hoary Majesty of Spades appears,
Puts forth one manly leg, to sight revealed,
The rest, his many-coloured robe concealed.
The rebel Knave, who dares his prince engage,
Proves the just victim of his royal rage.
Even mighty Pam, that Kings and Queens o'erthrew
And mowed down armies in the fights of Lu,[31]
Sad chance of war! now destitute of aid,
Falls undistinguished by the victor spade!
  Thus far both armies to Belinda yield;
Now to the Baron fate inclines the field.
His warlike Amazon her host invades,
Th' imperial consort of the crown of Spades.
The Club's black Tyrant first her victim dyed,
Spite of his haughty mien, and barb'rous pride:
What boots the regal circle on his head,
His giant limbs, in state unwieldy spread;
That long behind he trails his pompous robe,
And, of all monarchs, only grasps the globe?
  The Baron now his Diamonds pours apace;
Th' embroidered King who shows but half his face,
And his refulgent Queen, with powers combined
Of broken troops an easy conquest find.
Clubs, Diamonds, Hearts, in wild disorder seen,
With throngs promiscuous strew the level green.
Thus when dispersed a routed army runs,
Of Asia's troops, and Afric's sable sons,

[31] "Pam" is the knave of clubs, the highest trump in the game of loo.

With like confusion different nations fly,
Of various habit, and of various dye,
The pierced battalions dis-united fall,
In heaps on heaps; one fate o'erwhelms them all.
  The Knave of Diamonds tries his wily arts,
And wins (oh shameful chance!) the Queen of Hearts.
At this, the blood the virgin's cheek forsook,
A livid paleness spreads o'er all her look;
She sees, and trembles at th' approaching ill,
Just in the jaws of ruin, and Codille.
And now (as oft in some distempered State)
On one nice Trick depends the general fate.
An Ace of Hearts steps forth: The King unseen
Lurked in her hand, and mourned his captive Queen:
He springs to Vengeance with an eager pace,
And falls like thunder on the prostrate Ace.
The nymph exulting fills with shouts the sky;
The walls, the woods, and long canals reply.
  Oh thoughtless mortals! ever blind to fate,
Too soon dejected, and too soon elate.
Sudden, these honours shall be snatched away,
And cursed for ever this victorious day.
  For lo! the board with cups and spoons is crowned,
The berries crackle, and the mill turns round;
On shining Altars of Japan[32] they raise
The silver lamp; the fiery spirits blaze:
From silver spouts the grateful liquors glide,
While China's earth receives the smoking tide:
At once they gratify their scent and taste,
And frequent cups prolong the rich repast.
Straight hover round the Fair her airy band;
Some, as she sipped, the fuming liquor fanned,
Some o'er her lap their careful plumes displayed,
Trembling, and conscious of the rich brocade.
Coffee, (which makes the politician wise,
And see through all things with his half-shut eyes)
Sent up in vapours to the Baron's brain
New Stratagems, the radiant Lock to gain.
Ah cease, rash youth! desist ere 'tis too late,
Fear the just Gods, and think of Scylla's Fate!
Changed to a bird, and sent to flit in air,
She dearly pays for Nisus' injured hair![33]
  But when to mischief mortals bend their will,
How soon they find fit instruments of ill!

[32] The mill is a coffee mill and the "shining Altars of Japan" are lacquered oriental coffee tables. Pope is parodying epic feasts.

[33] Scylla, daughter of King Nisus, fell in love with King Minos and cut off for him a purple hair from her father's head, upon which the safety of his kingdom depended. She was punished by being turned into a bird. The story appears in Ovid's *Metamorphoses*.

Just then, Clarissa drew with tempting grace
A two-edged weapon[34] from her shining case:
So Ladies in Romance assist their Knight,
Present the spear, and arm him for the fight.
He takes the gift with rev'rence, and extends
The little engine on his fingers' ends;
This just behind Belinda's neck he spread,
As o'er the fragrant steams she bends her head.
Swift to the Lock a thousand Sprites repair,
A thousand wings, by turns, blow back the hair;
And thrice they twitched the diamond in her ear;
Thrice she looked back, and thrice the foe drew near.
Just in that instant, anxious Ariel sought
The close recesses of the Virgin's thought;
As on the nosegay in her breast reclined,
He watched th' Ideas rising in her mind,
Sudden he viewed, in spite of all her art,
An earthly Lover lurking at her heart.
Amazed, confused, he found his power expired,
Resigned to fate, and with a sigh retired.
  The Peer now spreads the glitt'ring Forfex wide,
T' inclose the Lock; now joins it, to divide.
Even then, before the fatal engine closed,
A wretched Sylph too fondly interposed;
Fate urged the shears, and cut the Sylph in twain,
(But airy substance soon unites again)
The meeting points the sacred hair dissever
From the fair head, forever, and forever!
  Then flashed the living lightning from her eyes,
And screams of horror rend th' affrighted skies.
Not louder shrieks to pitying heaven are cast,
When husbands, or when lap-dogs breathe their last;
Or when rich China vessels fall'n from high,
In glitt'ring dust and painted fragments lie!
  Let wreaths of triumph now my temples twine,
(The victor cried) the glorious Prize is mine!
While fish in streams, or birds delight in air,
Or in a coach and six the British Fair,
As long as Atalantis[35] shall be read,
Or the small pillow grace a Lady's bed,
While visits shall be paid on solemn days,
When num'rous wax-lights in bright order blaze,
While nymphs take treats, or assignations give,
So long my honour, name, and praise shall live!
What Time would spare, from Steel receives its date,

[34] Scissors.

[35] Mrs. Manley's *Secret Memories and Manners of several Persons of Quality, of Both Sexes. From the New Atalantis, an Island in the Mediterranean* (1709) was a fashionable book of thinly veiled allusions to current scandals.

And monuments, like men, submit to fate!
Steel could the labour of the Gods destroy,
And strike to dust th' imperial towers of Troy;
Steel could the works of mortal pride confound,
And hew triumphal arches to the ground.
What wonder then, fair nymph! thy hairs should feel,
The conq'ring force of unresisted steel?

CANTO IV

But anxious cares the pensive nymph oppressed,
And secret passions laboured in her breast.
Not youthful kings in battle seized alive,
Not scornful virgins who their charms survive,
Not ardent lovers robbed of all their bliss,
Not ancient ladies when refused a kiss,
Not tyrants fierce that unrepenting die,
Not Cynthia when her manteau's[36] pinned awry,
E'er felt such rage, resentment, and despair,
As thou, sad Virgin! for thy ravished Hair.
  For, that sad moment, when the Sylphs withdrew
And Ariel weeping from Belinda flew,
Umbriel,[37] a dusky, melancholy sprite,
As ever sullied the fair face of light,
Down to the central earth, his proper scene,
Repaired to search the gloomy Cave of Spleen.
  Swift on his sooty pinions flits the Gnome,
And in a vapour[38] reached the dismal dome.
No cheerful breeze this sullen region knows,
The dreaded East is all the wind that blows.
Here in a grotto, sheltered close from air,
And screened in shades from day's detested glare,
She sighs for ever on her pensive bed,
Pain at her side, and Megrim[39] at her head.
  Two handmaids wait the throne: alike in place,
But diff'ring far in figure and in face.
Here stood Ill-nature like an ancient maid,
Her wrinkled form in black and white arrayed;
With store of prayers, for mornings, nights, and noons.
Her hand is filled; her bosom with lampoons.
  There Affectation, with a sickly mien,
Shows in her cheek the roses of eighteen,

[36] A loose robe.

[37] The name Umbriel suggests shadows and darkness. The episode of the Cave of Spleen (ill-humor) represents Belinda's sulking and parodies the epic visit to the underworld.

[38] Here and later, Pope puns on "vapour," which is both mist and the fashionable feminine malady of the "vapours."

[39] Headache. The organ called the spleen is on the left side of the body; therefore Pain is at Spleen's side and Megrim at her head.

Practised to lisp, and hang the head aside,
Faints into airs, and languishes with pride,
On the rich quilt sinks with becoming woe,
Wrapt in a gown, for sickness, and for show.
The fair ones feel such maladies as these,
When each new night-dress gives a new disease.
  A constant Vapour o'er the palace flies;
Strange phantoms rising as the mists arise;
Dreadful, as hermit's dreams in haunted shades,
Or bright, as visions of expiring maids.
Now glaring fiends, and snakes on rolling spires,
Pale spectres, gaping tombs, and purple fires:
Now lakes of liquid gold, Elysian scenes,
And crystal domes, and angels in machines.[40]
  Unnumbered throngs on every side are seen,
Of bodies changed to various forms by Spleen.
Here living Tea-pots stand, one arm held out,
One bent; the handle this, and that the spout:
A Pipkin there, like Homer's Tripod[41] walks;
Here sighs a Jar, and there a Goose-pie talks;
Men prove with child, as powerful fancy works,
And maids turned bottles, call aloud for corks.
  Safe past the Gnome through this fantastic band,
A branch of healing Spleenwort[42] in his hand.
Then thus addressed the power: "Hail, wayward Queen!
Who rule the sex to fifty from fifteen:
Parent of vapours and of female wit,
Who give th' hysteric or poetic fit,
On various tempers act by various ways,
Make some take physic, others scribble plays;
Who cause the proud their visits to delay,
And send the godly in a pet to pray.
A nymph there is, that all thy power disdains,
And thousands more in equal mirth maintains.
But oh! if e'er thy Gnome could spoil a grace,
Or raise a pimple on a beauteous face,
Like Citron-waters[43] matrons' cheeks inflame,
Or change complexions at a losing game;
If e'er with airy horns[44] I planted heads,
Or rumpled petticoats, or tumbled beds,
Or caus'd suspicion when no soul was rude,
Or discomposed the head-dress of a Prude,
Or e'er to costive lap-dog gave disease,

[40] These are both splenetic hallucinations and, satirically, scenic effects in contemporary opera and pantomime.

[41] A pipkin is an earthenware pot. According to Homer, Vulcan made self-propelling tripods, or stools, for the gods.

[42] An herb, so called because it was supposed to cure the spleen.

[43] Brandy distilled with the rind of citrons.

[44] Suspicions of adultery, "airy" because the horns exist only in the jealous husband's mind.

Which not the tears of brightest eyes could ease:
Hear me, and touch Belinda with chagrin,
That single act gives half the world the spleen."
  The Goddess with a discontented air
Seems to reject him, though she grants his prayer.
A wondrous Bag with both her hands she binds,
Like that where once Ulysses held the winds;[45]
There she collects the force of female lungs,
Sighs, sobs, and passions, and the war of tongues.
A Vial next she fills with fainting fears,
Soft sorrows, melting griefs, and flowing tears.
The Gnome rejoicing bears her gifts away,
Spreads his black wings, and slowly mounts to day.
  Sunk in Thalestris'[46] arms the nymph he found,
Her eyes dejected and her hair unbound.
Full o'er their heads the swelling bag he rent,
And all the Furies issued at the vent.
Belinda burns with more than mortal ire,
And fierce Thalestris fans the rising fire.
"Oh wretched maid!" she spread her hands, and cried,
(While Hampton's echoes, "Wretched maid!" replied)
"Was it for this you took such constant care
The bodkin, comb, and essence to prepare?
For this your locks in paper durance bound,
For this with torturing irons wreathed around?
For this with fillets strained your tender head,
And bravely bore the double loads of lead?[47]
Gods! shall the ravisher display your hair,
While the Fops envy, and the Ladies stare!
Honour forbid! at whose unrivalled shrine
Ease, pleasure, virtue, all our sex resign.
Methinks already I your tears survey,
Already hear the horrid things they say,
Already see you a degraded toast,
And all your honour in a whisper lost!
How shall I, then, your helpless fame defend?
'Twill then be infamy to seem your friend!
And shall this prize, th' inestimable prize,
Exposed through crystal to the gazing eyes,
And heightened by the diamond's circling rays,
On that rapacious hand for ever blaze?
Sooner shall grass in Hyde-park Circus grow,
And wits take lodgings in the sound of Bow;[48]

[45] Aeolus, god of the winds, gave Ulysses a bag containing all the winds that would hamper his voyage home. See the *Odyssey*, Book X.

[46] Queen of the Amazons. Belinda is being comforted by a rather intimidating matron.

[47] The torturing irons are curling irons. Curl papers were fastened with flexible strips of lead.

[48] An unfashionable neighborhood in the City of London proper, within sound of the bells of St. Mary-le-Bow in Cheapside.

Sooner let earth, air, sea, to Chaos fall,
Men, monkeys, lap-dogs, parrots, perish all!"
She said; then raging to Sir Plume repairs,
And bids her Beau demand the precious hairs:
(Sir Plume of amber snuff box justly vain,
And the nice conduct of a clouded cane)
With earnest eyes, and round unthinking face,
He first the snuff-box opened, then the case,
And thus broke out—"My Lord, why, what the devil?
Z—ds! damn the lock! 'fore Gad, you must be civil!
Plague on't! 'tis past a jest—nay prithee, pox!
Give her the hair"—he spoke, and rapped his box.
"It grieves me much" (replied the Peer again)
"Who speaks so well should ever speak in vain.
But by this Lock, this sacred Lock I swear,
(Which never more shall join its parted hair;
Which never more its honours shall renew,
Clipped from the lovely head where late it grew)
That while my nostrils draw the vital air,
This hand, which won it, shall for ever wear."
He spoke, and speaking, in proud triumph spread
The long-contended honours of her head.
But Umbriel, hateful Gnome! forbears not so;
He breaks the Vial whence the sorrows flow.
Then see! the nymph in beauteous grief appears,
Her eyes half-languishing, half-drowned in tears;
On her heaved bosom hung her drooping head,
Which, with a sigh, she raised; and thus she said.
"For ever cursed be this detested day,
Which snatched my best, my fav'rite curl away!
Happy! ah, ten times happy had I been,
If Hampton-Court these eyes had never seen!
Yet am not I the first mistaken maid,
By love of Courts to numerous ills betrayed.
Oh had I rather un-admired remained
In some lone isle, or distant Northern land;
Where the gilt Chariot never marks the way,
Where none learn Ombre, none e'er taste Bohea![49]
There kept my charms concealed from mortal eye,
Like roses, that in deserts bloom and die.
What moved my mind with youthful Lords to roam?
Oh had I stayed, and said my prayers at home!
'Twas this, the morning omens seemed to tell,
Thrice from my trembling hand the patch-box[50] fell;
The tott'ring China shook without a wind,
Nay, Poll sat mute, and Shock was most unkind!
A Sylph too warned me of the threats of fate,

[49] An expensive and fashionable kind of tea.
[50] A box to hold "beauty-patches" of court plaster.

In mystic visions, now believed too late!
See the poor remnants of these slighted hairs!
My hands shall rend what even thy rapine spares:
These in two sable ringlets taught to break,
Once gave new beauties to the snowy neck;
The sister-lock now sits uncouth, alone,
And in its fellow's fate foresees its own;
Uncurled it hangs, the fatal shears demands,
And tempts once more, thy sacrilegious hands.
Oh hadst thou, cruel! been content to seize
Hairs less in sight, or any hairs but these!"

CANTO V

She said: the pitying audience melt in tears.
But Fate and Jove had stopped the Baron's ears.
In vain Thalestris with reproach assails,
For who can move when fair Belinda fails?
Not half so fixed the Trojan could remain,
While Anna begged and Dido raged in vain.[51]
Then grave Clarissa graceful waved her fan;
Silence ensued, and thus the nymph began.
"Say why are Beauties praised and honoured most,
The wise man's passion, and the vain man's toast?
Why decked with all that land and sea afford,
Why Angels called, and Angel-like adored?
Why round our coaches crowd the white-gloved Beaux,
Why bows the side-box[52] from its inmost rows;
How vain are all these glories, all our pains,
Unless good sense preserve what beauty gains:
That men may say, when we the front-box grace:
'Behold the first in virtue as in face!'
Oh! if to dance all night, and dress all day,
Charmed the small-pox, or chased old-age away;
Who would not scorn what housewife's cares produce,
Or who would learn one earthly thing of use?
To patch, nay ogle, might become a Saint,
Nor could it sure be such a sin to paint.
But since, alas! frail beauty must decay,
Curled or uncurled, since Locks will turn to grey;
Since painted, or not painted, all shall fade,
And she who scorns a man, must die a maid;
What then remains but well our power to use,
And keep good-humour still whate'er we lose?
And trust me, dear! good-humour can prevail,

[51] The Trojan is Aeneas, who abandoned Dido despite her anger and the pleas of her sister Anna.

[52] The "side-box" and the "front-box" are theater boxes.

When airs, and flights, and screams, and scolding fail.
Beauties in vain their pretty eyes may roll;
Charms strike the sight, but merit wins the soul."[53]
  So spoke the Dame, but no applause ensued;
Belinda frowned, Thalestris called her Prude.
"To arms, to arms!" the fierce Virago cries,
And swift as lightning to the combat flies.
All side in parties, and begin th' attack;
Fans clap, silks rustle, and tough whalebones crack;
Heroes' and Heroines' shouts confus'dly rise,
And bass and treble voices strike the skies.
No common weapons in their hands are found,
Like Gods they fight, nor dread a mortal wound.
  So when bold Homer makes the Gods engage,
And heavenly breasts with human passions rage;
'Gainst Pallas, Mars; Latona, Hermes arms;
And all Olympus rings with loud alarms:
Jove's thunder roars, heaven trembles all around,
Blue Neptune storms, the bellowing deeps resound:
Earth shakes her nodding towers, the ground gives way,
And the pale ghosts start at the flash of day!
  Triumphant Umbriel on a sconce's[54] height
Clapped his glad wings, and sat to view the fight:
Propped on their bodkin spears, the Sprites survey
The growing combat, or assist the fray.
  While through the press enraged Thalestris flies,
And scatters death around from both her eyes,
A Beau and Witling perished in the throng,
One died in metaphor, and one in song.
"O cruel nymph! a living death I bear,"
Cried Dapperwit, and sunk beside his chair.
A mournful glance Sir Fopling upwards cast,
"Those eyes are made so killing"—was his last.[55]
Thus on Meander's flowery margin lies
Th' expiring Swan, and as he sings he dies.
  When bold Sir Plume had drawn Clarissa down,
Chloe stepped in, and killed him with a frown;
She smiled to see the doughty hero slain,
But, at her smile, the Beau revived again.
  Now Jove suspends his golden scales in air,
Weighs the Men's wits against the Lady's hair;
The doubtful beam long nods from side to side;
At length the wits mount up, the hairs subside.
  See, fierce Belinda on the Baron flies,
With more than usual lightning in her eyes:

[53] Clarissa's speech is a parody of the speech of Sarpedon to Glaucus in the *Iliad*.
[54] A wall bracket for a candlestick.
[55] Pope pointed out that Sir Fopling's last words are from the fashionable opera *Camilla*, by Buononcini.

Nor feared the Chief th' unequal fight to try,
Who sought no more than on his foe to die.
But this bold Lord with manly strength endued,
She with one finger and a thumb subdued:
Just where the breath of life his nostrils drew,
A charge of Snuff the wily virgin threw;
The Gnomes direct, to every atom just,
The pungent grains of titillating dust.
Sudden, with starting tears each eye o'erflows,
And the high dome re-echoes to his nose.
"Now meet thy fate," incensed Belinda cried,
And drew a deadly bodkin from her side,
(The same, his ancient personage to deck,
Her great great grandsire wore about his neck,
In three seal-rings; which after, melted down,
Formed a vast buckle for his widow's gown:
Her infant grandame's whistle next it grew,
The bells she jingled, and the whistle blew;
Then in a bodkin graced her mother's hairs,
Which long she wore, and now Belinda wears.)
"Boast not my fall" (he cried) "insulting foe!
Thou by some other shalt be laid as low,
Nor think, to die dejects my lofty mind:
All that I dread is leaving you behind!
Rather than so, ah let me still survive,
And burn in Cupid's flames—but burn alive."
"Restore the Lock!" she cries; and all around
"Restore the Lock!" the vaulted roofs rebound.
Not fierce Othello in so loud a strain
Roared for the handkerchief that caused his pain.[56]
But see how oft ambitious aims are crossed,
And chiefs contend 'till all the prize is lost!
The Lock, obtained with guilt, and kept with pain,
In every place is sought, but sought in vain:
With such a prize no mortal must be blest,
So heaven decrees! with heaven who can contest?
Some thought it mounted to the Lunar sphere,
Since all things lost on earth are treasured there.
There Heroes' wits are kept in pond'rous vases,
And beaux's in snuff-boxes and tweezer-cases.
There broken vows and death-bed alms are found,
And lovers' hearts with ends of riband bound,
The courtier's promises, and sick man's prayers,
The smiles of harlots, and the tears of heirs,
Cages for gnats, and chains to yoke a flea,

[56] In Shakespeare's *Othello,* Iago steals a handkerchief decorated with strawberries from Desdemona, gives it to Cassio, and leads Othello to believe that Desdemona has given it to Cassio as a love gift. Othello confronts Desdemona and "roars for the handkerchief" in Act III, Scene iv.

Dried butterflies, and tomes of casuistry.
  But trust the Muse—she saw it upward rise,
Though marked by none but quick, poetic eyes:
(So Rome's great founder to the heavens withdrew,[57]
To Proculus alone confessed in view)
A sudden Star, it shot through liquid air,
And drew behind a radiant trail of hair.
Not Berenice's Locks first rose so bright,[58]
The heavens bespangling with dishevelled light.
The Sylphs behold it kindling as it flies,
And pleased pursue its progress through the skies.
  This the Beau monde shall from the Mall[59] survey,
And hail with music its propitious ray.
This the blest Lover shall for Venus take,
And send up vows from Rosamonda's lake.[60]
This Partridge[61] soon shall view in cloudless skies,
When next he looks through Galileo's eyes;[62]
And hence th' egregious wizard shall foredoom
The fate of Louis, and the fall of Rome.
Then cease, bright Nymph! to mourn thy ravished hair,
Which adds new glory to the shining sphere!
Not all the tresses that fair head can boast,
Shall draw such envy as the Lock you lost.
For, after all the murders of your eye,
When, after millions slain, yourself shall die:
When those fair suns shall set, as set they must,
And all those tresses shall be laid in dust,
This Lock, the Muse shall consecrate to fame,
And 'midst the stars inscribe Belinda's name.

from *AN ESSAY ON MAN*

To Henry St. John, Lord Bolingbroke

THE DESIGN

Having proposed to write some pieces on Human Life and Manners, such as (to use my Lord Bacon's expression) *come home to Men's Business and Bosoms,* I thought it more satisfactory to begin with considering *Man* in the abstract, his *Nature* and his *State;* since, to prove any moral duty, to enforce any moral precept, or to examine

[57] Romulus, legendary founder of Rome, was said to have been carried to heaven in a storm cloud.

[58] Berenice dedicated a lock of her hair to the gods for the safe return from war of her husband Ptolemy III. It became a constellation.

[59] An enclosed walk in St. James' Park. [60] A pond in St. James' Park.

[61] "John Partridge was a ridiculous star-gazer, who in his Almanacs every year never failed to predict the downfall of the Pope and the King of France, then at war with the English" (Pope).

[62] That is, a telescope.

the perfection or imperfection of any creature whatsoever, it is necessary first to know what *condition* and *relation* it is placed in, and what is the proper *end* and *purpose* of its *being*.

The science of Human Nature is, like all other sciences, reduced to a *few clear points:* There are not *many certain truths* in this world. It is therefore in the Anatomy of the mind as in that of the Body; more good will accrue to mankind by attending to the large, open, and perceptible parts, than by studying too much such finer nerves and vessels, the conformations and uses of which will forever escape our observation. The *disputes* are all upon these last, and, I will venture to say, they have less sharpened the *wits* than the *hearts* of men against each other, and have diminished the practice, more than advanced the theory of Morality. If I could flatter myself that this Essay has any merit, it is in steering betwixt the extremes of doctrines seemingly opposite, in passing over terms utterly unintelligible, and in forming a *temperate* yet not *inconsistent,* and a *short* yet not *imperfect* system of Ethics.

This I might have done in prose, but I chose verse, and even rhyme, for two reasons. The one will appear obvious; that principles, maxims, or precepts so written, both strike the reader more strongly at first, and are more easily retained by him afterwards: The other may seem odd, but is true, I found I could express them more *shortly* this way than in prose itself; and nothing is more certain, than that much of the *force* as well as *grace* of arguments or instructions, depends on their *conciseness.* I was unable to treat this part of my subject more in *detail,* without becoming dry and tedious; or more *poetically,* without sacrificing perspicuity to ornament, without wandering from the precision, or breaking the chain of reasoning: If any man can unite all these without diminution of any of them, I freely confess he will compass a thing above my capacity.

What is now published, is only to be considered as a *general Map of* MAN, marking out no more than the *greater parts,* their *extent,* their *limits,* and their *connection,* and leaving the particular to be more fully delineated in the charts which are to follow. Consequently, these Epistles in their progress (if I have health and leisure to make any progress) will be less dry, and more susceptible of poetical ornament. I am here only opening the *fountains,* and clearing the passage. To deduce the *rivers,* to follow them in their course, and to observe their effects, may be a task more agreeable.

EPISTLE I

Of the Nature and State of Man, with respect to the Universe

Awake, my ST. JOHN![1] leave all meaner things
To low ambition, and the pride of Kings.
Let us (since Life can little more supply
Than just to look about us and to die)
Expatiate[2] free o'er all this scene of Man;
A mighty maze! but not without a plan;
A Wild, where weeds and flowers promiscuous shoot;
Or Garden, tempting with forbidden fruit.
Together let us beat this ample field,
Try what the open, what the covert yield;
The latent tracts, the giddy heights, explore
Of all who blindly creep, or sightless soar;

[1] Pope's friend, Henry St. John, Viscount Bolingbroke. [2] Wander at will.

Eye Nature's walks, shoot Folly as it flies,
And catch the Manners living as they rise;
Laugh where we must, be candid[3] where we can;
But vindicate the ways of God to Man.[4]
  I. Say first, of God above, or Man below,
What can we reason, but from what we know?
Of Man, what see we but his station here,
From which to reason, or to which refer?
Through worlds unnumbered though the God be known,
'Tis ours to trace him only in our own.
He, who through vast immensity can pierce,
See worlds on worlds compose one universe,
Observe how system into system runs,
What other planets circle other suns,
What varied Being peoples every star,
May tell why Heaven has made us as we are.
But of this frame the bearings, and the ties,
The strong connexions, nice dependencies,
Gradations[5] just, has thy pervading soul
Looked through? or can a part contain the whole?
  Is the great chain,[6] that draws all to agree,
And drawn supports, upheld by God, or thee?
  II. Presumptuous Man! the reason wouldst thou find,
Why formed so weak, so little, and so blind?
First, if thou canst, the harder reason guess,
Why formed no weaker, blinder, and no less?
Ask of thy mother earth, why oaks are made
Taller or stronger than the weeds they shade?
Or ask of yonder argent fields above,
Why Jove's satellites are less than Jove?
  Of Systems possible, if 'tis confest
That Wisdom infinite must form the best,
Where all must full or not coherent be,
And all that rises, rise in due degree;
Then, in the scale of reas'ning life, 'tis plain,
There must be, somewhere, such a rank as Man:
And all the question (wrangle e'er so long)
Is only this, if God has placed him wrong?
  Respecting Man, whatever wrong we call,
May, must be right, as relative to all.
In human works, though labored on with pain,
A thousand movements scarce one purpose gain;
In God's, one single can its end produce;
Yet serves to second too some other use.

[3] Kindly or benign.

[4] An allusion to Milton's *Paradise Lost,* I.26: "And justify the ways of God to men."

[5] "Connexions," "dependencies," and "gradations" were technical astronomical terms relating to the hierarchies of the stellar systems.

[6] The Great Chain of Being, the traditional expression of the hierarchical arrangement of the universe.

So Man, who here seems principal alone,
Perhaps acts second to some sphere unknown,
Touches some wheel, or verges to some goal;
'Tis but a part we see, and not a whole.
When the proud steed shall know why Man restrains
His fiery course, or drives him o'er the plains:
When the dull Ox, why now he breaks the clod,
Is now a victim, and now Egypt's God:
Then shall Man's pride and dulness comprehend
His actions', passions', being's, use and end;
Why doing, suffering, checked, impelled; and why
This hour a slave, the next a deity.
Then say not Man's imperfect, Heaven in fault;
Say rather, Man's as perfect as he ought:
His knowledge measured to his state and place;
His time a moment and a point his space.
If to be perfect in a certain sphere,
What matter, soon or late, or here or there?
The blest today is as completely so,
As who began a thousand years ago.
III. Heaven from all creatures hides the book of Fate,
All but the page prescribed, their present state:
From brutes what men, from men what spirits know:
Or who could suffer Being here below?
The lamb thy riot dooms to bleed today,
Had he thy Reason, would he skip and play?
Pleased to the last, he crops the flowery food,
And licks the hand just raised to shed his blood.
Oh blindness to the future! kindly given,
That each may fill the circle marked by Heaven:
Who sees with equal eye, as God of all,
A hero perish, or a sparrow fall,
Atoms or systems[7] into ruin hurled,
And now a bubble burst, and now a world.
Hope humbly then; with trembling pinions soar;
Wait the great teacher Death; and God adore.
What future bliss, he gives not thee to know,
But gives that Hope to be thy blessing now.
Hope springs eternal in the human breast:
Man never Is, but always To be blest:
The soul, uneasy and confined from home,
Rests and expatiates in a life to come.
Lo, the poor Indian! whose untutored mind
Sees God in clouds, or hears him in the wind;
His soul, proud Science never taught to stray
Far as the solar walk, or milky way;
Yet simple Nature to his hope has given,
Behind the cloud-topt hill, an humbler heaven;

[7] Solar systems.

Some safer world in depth of woods embraced,
Some happier island in the watery waste,
Where slaves once more their native land behold,
No fiends torment, no Christians thirst for gold.
To Be, contents his natural desire,
He asks no Angel's wing, no Seraph's fire;
But thinks, admitted to that equal sky,
His faithful dog shall bear him company.
IV. Go, wiser thou! and, in thy scale of sense,
Weigh thy Opinion against Providence;
Call imperfection what thou fanciest such,
Say, here he gives too little, there too much:
Destroy all Creatures for thy sport or gust,[8]
Yet cry, If Man's unhappy, God's unjust;
If Man alone engross not Heaven's high care,
Alone made perfect here, immortal there:
Snatch from his hand the balance and the rod,
Re-judge his justice, be the God of God.
In Pride, in reas'ning Pride, our error lies;
All quit their sphere, and rush into the skies.
Pride still is aiming at the blest abodes,
Men would be Angels, Angels would be Gods.
Aspiring to be Gods, if Angels fell,
Aspiring to be Angels, Men rebel:
And who but wishes to invert the laws
Of Order, sins against th' Eternal Cause.
V. Ask for what end the heavenly bodies shine,
Earth for whose use? Pride answers, "'Tis for mine:
For me kind Nature wakes her genial[9] Power,
Suckles each herb, and spreads out every flower;
Annual for me, the grape, the rose renew
The juice nectareous, and the balmy dew;
For me, the mine a thousand treasures brings;
For me, health gushes from a thousand springs;
Seas roll to waft me, suns to light me rise;
My foot-stool earth, my canopy the skies."
But errs not Nature from this gracious end,
From burning suns when livid deaths[10] descend,
When earthquakes swallow, or when tempests sweep
Towns to one grave, whole nations to the deep?
"No, ('tis replied) the first Almighty Cause
Acts not by partial, but by gen'ral laws;
Th' exceptions few; some change since all began:
And what created perfect?"—Why then Man?
If the great end be human Happiness,
Then Nature deviates; and can Man do less?
As much that end a constant course requires
Of showers and sun-shine, as of Man's desires;

[8] Taste or appetite. [9] Generative. [10] Plague victims had a gray or bluish color.

As much eternal springs and cloudless skies,
As Men for ever temp'rate, calm, and wise.
If plagues or earthquakes break not Heaven's design,
Why then a Borgia, or a Catiline?[11]
Who knows but he, whose hand the lightning forms,
Who heaves old Ocean, and who wings the storms;
Pours fierce Ambition in a Caesar's mind,
Or turns young Ammon[12] loose to scourge mankind?
From pride, from pride, our very reasoning springs;
Account for moral, as for natural things:
Why charge we Heaven in those, in these acquit?
In both, to reason right is to submit.
  Better for Us, perhaps, it might appear,
Were there all harmony, all virtue here;
That never air or ocean felt the wind;
That never passion discomposed the mind.
But ALL subsists by elemental strife;
And Passions are the elements of Life.
The gen'ral ORDER, since the whole began,
Is kept in Nature, and is kept in Man.
  VI. What would this Man? Now upward will he soar,
And little less than Angel, would be more;
Now looking downwards, just as grieved appears
To want the strength of bulls, the fur of bears.
Made for his use all creatures if he call,
Say what their use, had he the powers of all?
Nature to these, without profusion, kind,
The proper organs, proper powers assigned;
Each seeming want compensated of course,[13]
Here with degrees of swiftness, there of force;
All in exact proportion to the state;
Nothing to add, and nothing to abate.
Each beast, each insect, happy in its own:
Is heaven unkind to Man, and Man alone?
Shall he alone, whom rational we call,
Be pleased with nothing, if not blessed with all?
  The bliss of Man (could Pride that blessing find)
Is not to act or think beyond mankind;
No powers of body or of soul to share,
But what his nature and his state can bear.
Why has not Man a microscopic eye?
For this plain reason, Man is not a Fly.[14]
Say what the use, were finer optics given,
T' inspect a mite, not comprehend the heaven?
Or touch, if tremblingly alive all o'er,

[11] The Borgia family of Renaissance Italy was famous for its cruelty. Catiline led a first-century B.C. revolt against the Roman consuls.

[12] Alexander the Great.

[13] In the normal course of events.

[14] Flies were thought to have eyes with microscopic powers.

To smart and agonize at every pore?
Or quick effluvia[15] darting through the brain,
Die of a rose in aromatic pain?
If nature thundered in his opening ears,
And stunned him with the music of the spheres,
How would he wish that Heaven had left him still
The whisp'ring Zephyr, and the purling rill?
Who finds not Providence all good and wise,
Alike in what it gives, and what denies?
VII. Far as Creation's ample range extends,
The scale of sensual, mental powers ascends:
Mark how it mounts, to Man's imperial race,
From the green myriads in the peopled grass:
What modes of sight betwixt each wide extreme,
The mole's dim curtain, and the lynx's beam:[16]
Of smell, the headlong lioness between,
And hound sagacious[17] on the tainted green:
Of hearing, from the life that fills the Flood,
To that which warbles through the vernal wood:
The spider's touch, how exquisitely fine!
Feels at each thread, and lives along the line:
In the nice[18] bee, what sense so subtly true
From pois'nous herbs extracts the healing dew?[19]
How Instinct varies in the grov'lling swine,
Compared, half-reas'ning elephant, with thine!
'Twixt that, and Reason, what a nice barrier,
For ever sep'rate, yet for ever near![20]
Remembrance and Reflection how allied;
What thin partitions Sense from Thought divide:
And Middle natures, how they long to join,
Yet never pass th' insuperable line!
Without this just gradation, could they be
Subjected, these to those, or all to thee?
The powers of all subdued by thee alone,
Is not thy Reason all these powers in one?
VIII. See, through this air, this ocean, and this earth,
All matter quick, and bursting into birth.
Above, how high, progressive life may go!
Around, how wide! how deep extend below!
Vast chain of Being! which from God began,
Natures ethereal, human, angel, man,
Beast, bird, fish, insect, what no eye can see,
No glass can reach; from Infinite to thee,

[15] Epicurus believed that odors were communicated to the brain by means of streams of invisible particles or "effluvia."

[16] Sight was thought to involve an emission of rays from the eye.

[17] Acute in the senses, especially that of smell. [18] Accurate, precise.

[19] Honey was used medicinally in Pope's day.

[20] Pope expresses the orthodox view, opposed by Montaigne and others, that man differs from animals in kind, not merely in degree.

From thee to Nothing.—On superior powers
Were we to press, inferior might on ours:
Or in the full creation leave a void,
Where, one step broken, the great scale's destroyed:
From Nature's chain whatever link you strike,
Tenth or ten thousandth, breaks the chain alike.
  And, if each system in gradation roll
Alike essential to th' amazing Whole,
The least confusion but in one, not all
That system only, but the Whole must fall.
Let Earth unbalanced from her orbit fly,
Planets and Suns run lawless through the sky;
Let ruling Angels from their spheres be hurled,
Being on Being wrecked, and world on world;
Heaven's whole foundations to their centre nod,
And Nature tremble to the throne of God.
All this dread ORDER break—for whom? for thee?
Vile worm!—Oh Madness! Pride! Impiety!
  IX. What if the foot, ordained the dust to tread,
Or hand, to toil, aspired to be the head?
What if the head, the eye, or ear repined
To serve mere engines[21] to the ruling Mind?
Just as absurd, for any part to claim
To be another, in this gen'ral frame:
Just as absurd, to mourn the tasks or pains,
The great directing MIND of ALL ordains.
  All are but parts of one stupendous whole,
Whose body Nature is, and God the soul;
That, changed through all, and yet in all the same;
Great in the earth, as in th' ethereal frame;
Warms in the sun, refreshes in the breeze,
Glows in the stars, and blossoms in the trees,
Lives through all life, extends through all extent,
Spreads undivided, operates unspent;
Breathes in our soul, informs our mortal part,
As full, as perfect, in a hair as heart:
As full, as perfect, in vile Man that mourns,
As the rapt Seraph that adores and burns:[22]
To him no high, no low, no great, no small;
He fills, he bounds, connects, and equals all.
  X. Cease then, nor ORDER Imperfection name:
Our proper bliss depends on what we blame.
Know thy own point: this kind, this due degree
Of blindness, weakness, Heaven bestows on thee.
Submit.—In this, or any other sphere,

[21] Tools or instruments.

[22] The Seraphim, the highest order of angels, were said to be pure flame. Cf. l. 110 preceding.

Secure to be as blest as thou canst bear:
Safe in the hand of one disposing Power,
Or in the natal, or the mortal hour.
All Nature is but Art, unknown to thee;
All Chance, Direction, which thou canst not see;
All Discord, Harmony not understood;
All partial Evil, universal Good:
And, spite of Pride, in erring Reason's spite,
One truth is clear, WHATEVER IS, IS RIGHT.

EPISTLE II

Of the Nature and State of Man with respect to HIMSELF,
as an Individual

I. Know then thyself, presume not God to scan;
The proper study of Mankind is Man.
Placed on this isthmus of a middle state,
A Being darkly wise, and rudely great:
With too much knowledge for the Sceptic side,
With too much weakness for the Stoic's pride,[23]
He hangs between; in doubt to act, or rest;
In doubt to deem himself a God, or Beast;
In doubt his Mind or Body to prefer;
Born but to die, and reas'ning but to err;
Alike in ignorance, his reason such,
Whether he thinks too little, or too much:
Chaos of Thought and Passion, all confused;
Still by himself abused, or disabused;
Created half to rise, and half to fall;
Great lord of all things, yet a prey to all;
Sole judge of Truth, in endless Error hurled:
The glory, jest, and riddle of the world!
Go, wondrous creature! mount where Science guides.
Go, measure earth, weigh air, and state the tides;
Instruct the planets in what orbs to run,
Correct old Time, and regulate the Sun;
Go, soar with Plato to th' empyreal sphere,[24]
To the first good, first perfect, and first fair;
Or tread the mazy round his follow'rs trod,
And quitting sense[25] call imitating God;
As Eastern priests in giddy circles run,

[23] The Skeptics maintained that real knowledge of things was impossible. The Stoics were said to be "proud" because they believed that men could escape their passions and achieve the serenity of God.

[24] The empyreal sphere was the outermost sphere of the Ptolemaic universe, the abode of God. Pope thinks of it as also the location of Plato's archetypes or Ideas.

[25] Neoplatonic trances.

And turn their heads to imitate the Sun.
Go, teach Eternal Wisdom how to rule—
Then drop into thyself, and be a fool!
  Superior beings, when of late they saw
A mortal Man unfold all Nature's law,
Admired such wisdom in an earthly shape,
And shewed a NEWTON as we shew an Ape.[26]
  Could he, whose rules the rapid Comet bind,
Describe or fix one movement of his Mind?
Who saw its fires here rise, and there descend,
Explain his own beginning, or his end?
Alas what wonder! Man's superior part
Unchecked may rise, and climb from art to art;
But when his own great work is but begun,
What Reason weaves, by Passion is undone.
  Trace Science then, with Modesty thy guide;
First strip off all her equipage of Pride;
Deduct what is but Vanity, or Dress,
Or Learning's Luxury, or Idleness;
Or tricks to shew the stretch of human brain,
Mere curious pleasure, or ingenious pain;
Expunge the whole, or lop th' excrescent parts
Of all, our Vices have created Arts;
Then see how little the remaining sum,
Which served the past, and must the times to come!
  II. Two Principles in human nature reign;
Self-love,[27] to urge, and Reason, to restrain;
Nor this a good, nor that a bad we call,
Each works its end, to move or govern all:
And to their proper operation still,
Ascribe all Good; to their improper, Ill.
  Self-love, the spring of motion, acts[28] the soul;
Reason's comparing balance rules the whole.
Man, but for that, no action could attend,
And but for this, were active to no end:
Fixed like a plant on his peculiar spot,
To draw nutrition, propagate, and rot;
Or, meteor-like, flame lawless through the void,
Destroying others, by himself destroyed.
  Most strength the moving principle requires;
Active its task, it prompts, impels, inspires.
Sedate and quiet the comparing lies,
Formed but to check, delib'rate, and advise.
Self-love still stronger, as its objects nigh;
Reason's at distance, and in prospect lie:
That sees immediate good by present sense;
Reason, the future and the consequence.

[26] The English translation of Sir Isaac Newton's *Principia* had been published in 1729.
[27] Self-preservation; maintenance of life. [28] Activates.

Thicker than arguments, temptations throng,
At best more watchful this, but that more strong.
The action of the stronger to suspend,
Reason still use, to Reason still attend.
Attention, habit and experience gains;
Each strengthens Reason, and Self-love restrains.
Let subtle schoolmen teach these friends to fight,
More studious to divide than to unite;
And Grace and Virtue, Sense and Reason split,
With all the rash dexterity of wit.
Wits, just like Fools, at war about a name,
Have full as oft no meaning, or the same.
Self-love and Reason to one end aspire,
Pain their aversion, Pleasure their desire;
But greedy That, its object would devour,
This taste the honey, and not wound the flower:
Pleasure, or wrong or rightly understood,
Our greatest evil, or our greatest good.
III. Modes of Self-love the Passions we may call:
'Tis real good, or seeming, moves them all:
But since not every good we can divide,
And Reason bids us for our own provide;
Passions, though selfish, if their means be fair,
List[29] under Reason, and deserve her care;
Those, that imparted,[30] court a nobler aim,
Exalt their kind, and take some Virtue's name.
In lazy Apathy let Stoics boast
Their Virtue fixed; 'tis fixed as in a frost;
Contracted all, retiring to the breast;
But strength of mind is Exercise, not Rest:
The rising tempest puts in act the soul,
Parts it may ravage, but preserves the whole.
On life's vast ocean diversely we sail,
Reason the card,[31] but Passion is the gale;
Nor God alone in the still calm we find,
He mounts the storm, and walks upon the wind.
Passions, like Elements, though born to fight,
Yet, mixed and softened, in his work unite:
These 'tis enough to temper and employ;
But what composes Man, can Man destroy?
Suffice that Reason keep to Nature's road,
Subject, compound them, follow her and God.
Love, Hope, and Joy, fair pleasure's smiling train,
Hate, Fear, and Grief, the family of pain,
These mixed with art, and to due bounds confined,
Make and maintain the balance of the mind:
The lights and shades, whose well accorded strife

[29] Enlist. [30] That is, the passions when reason is imparted to them.
[31] A mariner's chart or map.

Gives all the strength and colour of our life.
  Pleasures are ever in our hands or eyes;
And when in act they cease, in prospect rise:
Present to grasp, and future still to find,
The whole employ of body and of mind.
All spread their charms, but charm not all alike;
On diff'rent senses diff'rent objects strike;
Hence diff'rent Passions more or less inflame,
As strong or weak, the organs of the frame;
And hence one MASTER PASSION in the breast,
Like Aaron's serpent, swallows up the rest.[32]
  As Man, perhaps, the moment of his breath,
Receives the lurking principle of death;
The young disease, that must subdue at length,
Grows with his growth, and strengthens with his strength:
So, cast and mingled with his very frame,
The Mind's disease, its RULING PASSION came;
Each vital humour[33] which should feed the whole,
Soon flows to this, in body and in soul:
Whatever warms the heart, or fills the head,
As the mind opens, and its functions spread,
Imagination plies her dang'rous art,
And pours it all upon the peccant[34] part.
  Nature its mother, Habit is its nurse;
Wit, Spirit, Faculties, but make it worse;
Reason itself but gives it edge and power;
As Heaven's blest beam turns vinegar more sour.
  We, wretched subjects, though to lawful sway,
In this weak queen some fav'rite still obey:
Ah! if she lend not arms, as well as rules,
What can she more than tell us we are fools?
Teach us to mourn our Nature, not to mend,
A sharp accuser, but a helpless friend!
Or from a judge turn pleader, to persuade
The choice we make, or justify it made;
Proud of an easy conquest all along,
She but removes weak passions for the strong:
So, when small humours gather to a gout,[35]
The doctor fancies he has driven them out.
  Yes, Nature's road must ever be preferred;
Reason is here no guide, but still a guard:
'Tis hers to rectify, not overthrow,
And treat this passion more as friend than foe:

[32] Aaron was Moses' brother. In a miracle before the Pharaoh's court, Aaron's rod became a serpent. When the Egyptian magicians turned their own rods into serpents, Aaron's serpent swallowed them. See Exodus 7:8–13.

[33] The fluids or "spirits" that were thought to govern physical and mental functions.

[34] "Peccant" humours were either diseased or too abundant.

[35] Gout was thought to be caused by the body driving diseased humours into the extremities.

A mightier Power the strong direction sends,
And several Men impels to several ends:
Like varying winds, by other passions tossed.
This drives them constant to a certain coast.
Let power or knowledge, gold, or glory, please,
Or (oft more strong than all) the love of ease;
Through life 'tis followed, even at life's expense;
The merchant's toil, the sage's indolence,
The monk's humility, the hero's pride,
All, all alike find Reason on their side.
  Th' Eternal Art educing good from ill,
Grafts on this Passion our best principle:
'Tis thus the Mercury of Man is fixed,[36]
Strong grows the Virtue with his nature mixed;
The dross cements what else were too refined,
And in one interest body acts with mind.
  As fruits, ungrateful to the planter's care,
On savage stocks inserted, learn to bear;
The surest Virtues thus from Passions shoot,
Wild Nature's vigor working at the root.
What crops of wit and honesty appear
From spleen, from obstinacy, hate, or fear!
See anger, zeal and fortitude supply;
Even av'rice, prudence; sloth, philosophy;
Lust, through some certain strainers well refined,
Is gentle love, and charms all womankind;
Envy, to which th' ignoble mind's a slave,
Is emulation in the learned or brave;
Nor Virtue, male or female, can we name,
But what will grow on Pride, or grow on Shame.
  Thus Nature gives us (let it check our pride)
The virtue nearest to our vice allied:
Reason the bias turns to good from ill,
And Nero reigns a Titus, if he will.
The fiery soul abhorred in Catiline,
In Decius charms, in Curtius is divine:[37]
The same ambition can destroy or save,
And makes a patriot as it makes a knave.
  IV. This light and darkness in our chaos joined,
What shall divide? The God within the mind.
  Extremes in Nature equal ends produce,
In Man they join to some mysterious use;
Though each by turns the other's bound invade,
As, in some well-wrought picture, light and shade,

[36] A metallurgical metaphor. "Primal mercury" was thought to be the basis of all metals, which were "fixed" in different forms by different "sulphurs." Pope is saying that the ruling passion "sets" one's personality.

[37] Nero was a "bad" emperor of Rome, Titus a "good" one. Catiline was a famous rebel against Rome; Decius and Curtius performed acts of patriotic self-sacrifice described by the Roman historian Livy.

And oft so mix, the diff'rence is too nice
Where ends the Virtue, or begins the Vice.
  Fools! who from hence into the notion fall,
That Vice or Virtue there is none at all.
If white and black blend, soften, and unite
A thousand ways, is there no black or white?
Ask your own heart, and nothing is so plain;
'Tis to mistake them, costs the time and pain.
  V. Vice is a monster of so frightful mien,
As, to be hated, needs but to be seen;
Yet seen too oft, familiar with her face,
We first endure, then pity, then embrace.
But where th' Extreme of Vice, was ne'er agreed:
Ask where's the North? at York, 'tis on the Tweed;
In Scotland, at the Orcades; and there,
At Greenland, Zembla, or the Lord knows where.
No creature owns it in the first degree,
But thinks his neighbour further gone than he;
Even those who dwell beneath its very zone,
Or never feel the rage, or never own;
What happier natures shrink at with affright,
The hard inhabitant contends is right.
  VI. Virtuous and vicious every Man must be,
Few in th' extreme, but all in the degree;
The rogue and fool by fits is fair and wise;
And even the best, by fits, what they despise.
'Tis but by parts we follow good or ill;
For, Vice or Virtue, Self directs it still;
Each individual seeks a sev'ral goal;
But HEAVEN's great view is One, and that the Whole.
That counter-works each folly and caprice;
That disappoints th' effect of every vice;
That, happy frailties to all ranks applied,
Shame to the virgin, to the matron pride,
Fear to the statesman, rashness to the chief,
To kings presumption, and to crowds belief:
That, Virtue's ends from Vanity can raise,
Which seeks no int'rest, no reward but praise;
And build on wants, and on defects of mind,
The joy, the peace, the glory of Mankind.
  Heaven forming each on other to depend,
A master, or a servant, or a friend,
Bids each on other for assistance call,
Till one Man's weakness grows the strength of all.
Wants, frailties, passions, closer still ally
The common int'rest, or endear the tie.
To these we owe true friendship, love sincere,
Each home-felt joy that life inherits here;
Yet from the same we learn, in its decline,
Those joys, those loves, those int'rests to resign;

Taught half by Reason, half by mere decay,
To welcome death, and calmly pass away.
Whate'er the Passion, knowledge, fame, or pelf,
Not one will change his neighbour with himself.
The learned is happy nature to explore,
The fool is happy that he knows no more;
The rich is happy in the plenty given,
The poor contents him with the care of Heaven.
See the blind beggar dance, the cripple sing,
The sot a hero, lunatic a king;
The starving chemist in his golden views
Supremely blest, the poet in his Muse.
See some strange comfort every state attend,
And Pride bestowed on all, a common friend;
See some fit Passion every age supply,
Hope travels through, nor quits us when we die.
Behold the child, by Nature's kindly law,
Pleased with a rattle, tickled with a straw:
Some livelier play-thing gives his youth delight,
A little louder, but as empty quite:
Scarfs,[38] garters, gold, amuse his riper stage,
And beads and prayer-books are the toys of age:
Pleased with this bauble still, as that before;
'Til tired he sleeps, and Life's poor play is o'er.
Meanwhile Opinion gilds with varying rays
Those painted clouds that beautify our days;
Each want of happiness by hope supplied,
And each vacuity of sense by Pride:
These build as fast as knowledge can destroy;
In Folly's cup still laughs the bubble, joy;
One prospect lost, another still we gain;
And not a vanity is given in vain;
Even mean Self-love becomes, by force divine,
The scale to measure others' wants by thine.
See! and confess, one comfort still must rise,
'Tis this, Though Man's a fool, yet GOD IS WISE.

[38] The traditional badge of doctors of divinity.

Voltaire

(1694–1778)

Perhaps no single figure better embodies what is meant by the "Enlightenment," in all its many senses, than the French philosophe, *playwright, historian, novelist, and poet François-Marie Arouet, who wrote under the pen name Voltaire. During a career that spanned six decades, from 1718 to 1778, he poured out an astonishing number of plays, poems, historical works, polemical pamphlets and essays, satires, and philosophical tales; his collected works run to fifty-two volumes. The recurring rallying cry through all these works is* Écrasez l'infâme! *or "Crush infamy." By infamy, he seems to have meant all forms of intolerance and dogmatism, especially religious, but political, social, artistic, and moral as well, all forms of "darkness" that oppress mankind.*

Voltaire was born in 1694 into a prosperous middle-class family in Paris. He was educated at the Jesuit Collège Louis-le-Grand, studied law, and became a member of a circle of Paris wits and free-thinkers who jibed at the intellectual stagnation of the court of Louis XIV. When he was twenty-two, Voltaire was exiled to Sully-sur-Loire for political satires, and a year later he was imprisoned in the Bastille for a similar offense. During the eleven months he spent in prison, he wrote a tragedy, Oedipus, *which was produced upon his release and made a great success. When it was printed a year later, he took the name Voltaire, a rough anagram of "Arouet," by which he was known for the rest of his life.*

Voltaire's long career was marked by enormous energy and productivity and by continual political and religious controversy. In 1726, he was again imprisoned in the Bastille and then exiled to England, where he learned English, studied English literature, and became the friend of Pope, Swift, and other prominent English writers of the time. By the age of thirty, he had become wealthy as a result of shrewd speculations; his fortune increased rapidly for the rest of his life, making him one of the richest writers of all time. His wealth gave him a certain measure of independence and allowed him to maintain a series of lavish establishments, where he entertained distinguished visitors from all over the world. During the five years that followed his return from England in 1729, he wrote voluminously, producing a number of successful plays and satiric poems, as well as a history of Charles XII which has been called the first modern history.

In 1734, Voltaire was forced to flee Paris again as the result of the publication of the daring Philosophical Letters. *He took up residence with the brilliant Madame du Châtelet, at Cirey, in the region of Lorraine in eastern France. Although he was allowed to return to Paris in 1735, he made his home at Cirey during ten years of vigorous literary activity, during which he continued to write tragedies, as well as satires and philosophical and scientific works. After 1743, he recovered some measure of favor at court and was made official Historiographer of France and elected to the French Academy.*

In 1749, Madame du Châtelet died; she and Voltaire had continued on good terms, although she had ceased to be his mistress some time before and he had become involved with his niece, the vulgar and ugly Madame Denis. In 1750, he accepted an invitation from Frederick II to take up residence in Prussia, where he remained for three years, until he quarreled with Frederick and was forced to leave. Voltaire then resettled in Switzerland, where he purchased an estate named Les Délices *(The Delights). Controversy still followed him, especially over the publication of a sardonic article on Geneva in the French* Encyclopedia, *and he left Switzerland after three years to purchase his great estate Ferney, in France near the Swiss frontier. He spent the rest of his life there. Voltaire wrote* Candide *in 1758, the same year he bought Ferney.*

During Voltaire's last twenty years, the years at Ferney, he devoted more of his time to political, philosophical, and religious controversy than to literature. He con-

tinued to propagandize vigorously in a steady stream of essays, pamphlets, satirical dialogues, didactic tales, and a massive number of private letters. (Voltaire's published correspondence fills 107 volumes.) He was also closely involved in the operation of Ferney, carrying out a number of agricultural experiments and projects to employ the poor. He also took an active part in defenses of a number of people persecuted for their beliefs, including campaigns to rehabilitate the memories of the Huguenots Jean Calas and Sirven, both executed on false charges of murder; La Barre, a youth beheaded on a minor religious charge; and the comte de Lally, governor-general of the French posts in India, who was executed after their loss. In 1778, Voltaire, aged and ill, returned to Paris for the first time in twenty-eight years to be lionized with wild enthusiasm. He witnessed a performance of his last tragedy, Irene, *at the Comédie-Française and was crowned with a wreath of laurel. The celebration weakened him, and he died a few weeks later. He had to be buried secretly, the Church having refused him burial; thirteen years later, his body was exhumed and triumphantly reinterred in the Pantheon.*

Even after two centuries, the meaning and significance of Voltaire's work remain controversial. The French critic Faguet wittily summed up one view of his work in the famous phrase, "a chaos of clear ideas." Voltaire was often inconsistent in a body of work that was voluminous, produced over a long period of time, and often inspired by immediate circumstances. But certain ideas remain consistent throughout his work, especially his hostility toward all extremes and all forms of absolutism and fanaticism, whether religious, political, or social. In general, Voltaire moved from a rather optimistic rationalism in his early life to a period of comparative pessimism in the early 1750s, a response, perhaps, to a number of personal misfortunes as well as such external events as the Seven Years' War and the Lisbon earthquake, which inspired the despairing "Poem on the Disaster of Lisbon" (1756). In his later years, he turned to a modestly melioristic position, in which he largely abandoned abstract speculation in favor of an emphasis upon small, immediate reforms, expressed in his various crusades and by his work on the Encyclopedia, *as well as by his reforming projects in his own "garden" of Ferney.*

As a writer, Voltaire is one of those men for whom no single masterpiece or handful of major works seems to sum up their total achievement or impact. In his own day, Voltaire was regarded as a great dramatist, historian, and philosopher, as well as a controversialist and general man of letters. Our own perspective has shifted; his tragedies, his epic The Henriad, *and his massive histories are not much read, and he is valued primarily for his work in minor forms—epigrams, satiric verse, letters, and especially philosophic tales—as well as for the record of his vigorous personality.*

Candide *is the single work for which Voltaire is now most widely known, and it contains an excellent sampling of Voltaire's sardonic wit as well as many of his most fundamental ideas. Much of the humor is very broad. Candide, Dr. Pangloss, and Cunegund are two-dimensional characters; we could hardly bear the sadism of their horrifying mishaps in this ultimate hard-luck story if they were more real and if we did not know that even after each apparent death, ravishing, or mutilation, they would pop up again, marvelously and comically restored, like characters in a film cartoon.*

Voltaire's satiric point is aimed at a larger target than the ostensible one of Leibnitz's philosophy of Optimism. (The subtitle refers not just to a general attitude but to a formal philosophical concept.) His subject is the problem of how one should live one's life in the face of the pervasive evil of the world, both physical and social, and his satire is directed against all the various dogmas and fanaticisms which man uses to shield himself against reality and to veil his naked self-interest. The various episodes of the book read like a catalogue of the ills flesh is heir to: uncontrollable natural calamities such as tempests and earthquakes, great human disasters that transcend any individual human responsibility such as syphilis and the plague, and calamities in which the innocent suffer along with the guilty such as the naval battle in Chapter 20. But Voltaire saves his most sardonic anger for those evils that have their origin in human illusions: war, the Inquisition, colonialism and proselytizing by the sword, rabid nationalism, and all the other manifestations of man's cruelty, hypocrisy, and greed.

The comically naive Candide wanders through all these woes, spiritually girded up by the wonderfully absurd Dr. Pangloss, encountering as he goes a great range of possible worlds or human societies. Westphalia, the garden from which he is expelled to begin his wanderings, is a false paradise in the grip of Panglossian self-delusion and petty aristocratic tyranny. Bulgaria, Paraguay, and Holland are ruled by various sorts of military, religious, and economic despotisms, and Lisbon is the seat of religious fanaticism and sadism. The primitive society of the Oreillons represents Voltaire's sardonic commentary on the idealization of the Noble Savage, such as Montaigne's in his essay "Of Cannibals." The world of cities is no better: Paris is a viper's nest of venom and intrigue, and the palace of Pococurante is a place of purposelessness and decadent boredom. Among all these possible worlds, one impossible one stands out as a sort of utopian dream of human happiness, that of El Dorado.

The famous ending of the tale, in which Candide resolves to "take care of his garden," deserves close attention. Candide has remained unshaken in his Panglossian optimism and idealization until the episode in Surinam, when "the villainy of mankind presented itself to his mind in all its deformity, and his soul was a prey to the most gloomy ideas." His drift toward pessimism is spurred by the arrival on the scene of Martin, the "Manichaean" pessimist to balance the optimistic Pangloss. Candide never quite comes to accept Martin's "detestable principles," however, and at the end of the book, he becomes the center of a modest micro-society devoted neither to optimism nor to pessimism but to a meliorism based on honest labor, cooperation, and a realistic view of the possible. This conclusion may sum up the final wisdom of Voltaire, who wrote in his old age: "I have done a bit of good; that is my finest work."

FURTHER READING *(prepared by W. J. R.):* Theodore Besterman's *Voltaire,* 1969, rpt. 1976, is a massive and excellent biography, which utilizes a great deal of new information. An appendix offers a long excerpt from Voltaire's autobiography. A less ambitious, introductory work is Wayne Andrews's *Voltaire,* 1981. Andrews writes in an easy, anecdotal style with liberal dashes of wit. Voltaire is admirably portrayed in the context of his own times in Owen Aldridge's *Voltaire and the Century of Light,* 1975. Aldridge uses the methods of comparative literature to present Voltaire's eighteenth-century France. Gustave Lanson's *Voltaire,* 1906, trans. by Robert A. Wagoner, 1960, is an excellent introduction to Voltaire's work, carefully distinguishing between Voltaire's philosophical views and his more whimsical speculations. Haydn Mason's *Voltaire,* 1975, attempts to make the writer more accessible to the general public. Mason's work is organized according to significant aspects of Voltaire's career, such as his work as historian and as poet. Ira O. Wade's *Voltaire and "Candide,"* 1959, is an important work in *Candide* criticism, divided into sections on the philosophical background, genesis, publication, and meaning. Ten essays, mostly on topics related to Voltaire as philosopher, are collected in *Voltaire: A Collection of Critical Essays,* ed. William F. Bottiglia, 1968.

CANDIDE

OR

THE OPTIMIST

Translated from the German of Doctor Ralph
With the additions which were found in the Doctor's pocket
when he died at Minden, in the year of grace 1759.[1]

Translated by Tobias Smollett and revised by J. C. Thornton

CHAPTER I

How Candide was brought up in a magnificent castle, and how he was driven from thence.

In the country of Westphalia, in the castle of the most noble Baron of Thunder-ten-tronckh,[2] lived a youth whom nature had endowed with a most sweet disposition. His face was the true index of mind. He had a solid judgment joined to the most unaffected simplicity; and hence, I presume, he had his name of Candide. The old servants of the house suspected him to have been the son of the Baron's sister, by a mighty good sort of a gentleman of the neighborhood, whom that young lady refused to marry, because he could produce no more than threescore and eleven quarterings in his arms;[3] the rest of the genealogical tree belonging to the family having been lost through the injuries of time.

The Baron was one of the most powerful lords in Westphalia; for his castle had not only a gate, but even windows; and his great hall was hung with tapestry. He used to hunt with his mastiffs and spaniels instead of greyhounds; his groom served him for huntsman; and the parson of the parish officiated as grand almoner.[4] He was called "My Lord" by all his people, and he never told a story but every one laughed at it.

My lady Baroness weighed three hundred and fifty pounds, consequently was a person of no small consideration; and then she did the honors of the house with a dignity that commanded universal respect. Her daughter Cunegund was about seventeen years of age, fresh colored, comely, plump, and desirable.[5] The Baron's son seemed to be a youth in

[1] "Doctor Ralph" is, of course, a fiction. The battle of Minden, in Westphalia, was an episode in the Seven Years' War (1756–1763).

[2] Westphalia is a region in northwest Germany. The castle of "Thunder-ten-tronckh" is fictitious, Voltaire's idea of an absurd German name.

[3] "Quarterings" are groupings of coats of arms upon one shield, to indicate family alliances. Seventy-one quarterings is an absurdly high number.

[4] Dispenser of alms, or charity.

[5] Cunegund is apparently a namesake of Queen Kunigunda, who walked barefoot on red-hot irons to prove her faithfulness to her husband, Emperor Henry II. The name is somewhat inappropriate in the light of Cunegund's later sexual career.

every respect worthy of his father. Pangloss the preceptor was the oracle of the family, and little Candide listened to his instructions with all the simplicity natural to his age and disposition.[6]

Master Pangloss taught the metaphysico-theologo-cosmolo-nigology. He could prove to admiration that there is no effect without a cause; and that, in this best of all possible worlds, the Baron's castle was the most magnificent of all castles, and my lady the best of all possible baronesses.[7]

"It is demonstrable," said he, "that things cannot be otherwise than they are; for as all things have been created for some end, they must necessarily be created for the best end. Observe, for instance, the nose is formed for spectacles, therefore we wear spectacles. The legs are visibly designed for stockings, accordingly we wear stockings. Stones were made to be hewn, and to construct castles, therefore my lord has a magnificent castle; for the greatest baron in the province ought to be the best lodged. Swine were intended to be eaten; therefore we eat pork all the year round: and they who assert that everything is right do not express themselves correctly; they should say, that everything is best."[8]

Candide listened attentively, and believed implicitly; for he thought Miss Cunegund excessively handsome, though he never had the courage to tell her so. He concluded that next to the happiness of being Baron of Thunder-ten-tronckh, the next was that of being Miss Cunegund, the next that of seeing her every day, and the last that of hearing the doctrine of Master Pangloss, the greatest philosopher of the whole province, and consequently of the whole world.

One day, when Miss Cunegund went to take a walk in a little neighboring wood, which was called a park, she saw, through the bushes, the sage Doctor Pangloss giving a lecture in experimental physics to her mother's chambermaid, a little brown wench, very pretty, and very tractable. As Miss Cunegund had a great disposition for the sciences, she observed with the utmost attention the experiments which were repeated before her eyes; she perfectly well understood the force of the doctor's reasoning upon causes and effects. She retired greatly flurried, quite pensive, and filled with the desire of knowledge, imagining that she might be a sufficing reason for young Candide, and he for her.

On her way back she happened to meet Candide; she blushed, he blushed also: she wished him a good morning in a faltering tone; he returned the salute, without knowing what he said. The next day, as they were rising from dinner, Cunegund and Candide slipped behind the screen; she dropped her handkerchief, the young man picked it up. She innocently took hold of his hand, and he as innocently kissed hers with a warmth, a sensibility, a grace—all very extraordinary; their lips met; their eyes sparkled; their knees trembled; their hands strayed. The Baron of

[6] Pangloss means "all-tongue," or "explainer-away of everything." Candide suggests "candid" or the French *candide* (ingenuous or artless).

[7] Master Pangloss is a follower of the German philosopher and mathematician Leibnitz (1646–1716), who viewed the world as a hierarchical system of "monads," or units of spiritual force or matter, rising up to the supreme monad, God. His system emphasized strict cause-and-effect relationships and regarded God as allowing freedom of the will while still shaping the world as the best of all possible worlds.

[8] Voltaire is here reducing to absurdity the philosophical "argument from design."

Thunder-ten-tronckh chanced to come by; he beheld the cause and effect, and, without hesitation, saluted Candide with some notable kicks on the breech, and drove him out of doors. Miss Cunegund fainted away, and, as soon as she came to herself, the Baroness boxed her ears. Thus a general consternation was spread over this most magnificent and most agreeable of all possible castles.

CHAPTER II

What befell Candide among the Bulgarians.[9]

Candide, thus driven out of this terrestrial paradise, wandered a long time, without knowing where he went; sometimes he raised his eyes, all bedewed with tears, towards heaven, and sometimes he cast a melancholy look towards the magnificent castle where dwelt the fairest of young baronesses. He laid himself down to sleep in a furrow, heartbroken and supperless. The snow fell in great flakes, and, in the morning when he awoke, he was almost frozen to death; however, he made shift to crawl to the next town, which was called Waldberghoff-trarbkdikdorff, without a penny in his pocket, and half dead with hunger and fatigue. He took up his stand at the door of an inn. He had not been long there, before two men dressed in blue[10] fixed their eyes steadfastly upon him.

"Faith, comrade," said one of them to the other, "yonder is a well-made young fellow, and of the right size."

Thereupon they made up to Candide, and with the greatest civility and politeness invited him to dine with them.

"Gentlemen," replied Candide, with a most engaging modesty, "you do me much honor, but, upon my word, I have no money."

"Money, Sir!" said one of the men in blue to him, "young persons of your appearance and merit never pay anything; why, are not you five feet five inches high?"

"Yes, gentlemen, that is really my size," replied he, with a low bow.

"Come then, Sir, sit down along with us; we will not only pay your reckoning, but will never suffer such a clever young fellow as you to want money. Mankind were born to assist one another."

"You are perfectly right, gentlemen," said Candide; "that is precisely the doctrine of Master Pangloss; and I am convinced that everything is for the best."

His generous companions next entreated him to accept of a few crowns, which he readily complied with, at the same time offering them his note for payment, which they refused, and sat down to table.

"Have you not a great affection for—"

"O yes!" he replied, "I have a great affection for the lovely Miss Cunegund."

[9] The "Bulgarians" are the Prussian troops of Frederick the Great. Voltaire chose the name to suggest sodomy (compare French *bougre* and English "buggery").

[10] Frederick the Great's recruiting officers wore blue uniforms. The recruiters are tall and regard Candide as "the right size" in reference to Prussian regiments that would accept only men over six feet tall.

"Maybe so," replied one of the men, "but that is not the question! We are asking you whether you have not a great affection for the King of the Bulgarians?"

"For the King of the Bulgarians?" said Candide. "Not at all. Why, I never saw him in my life."

"Is it possible! Oh, he is a most charming king! Come, we must drink his health."

"With all my heart, gentlemen," Candide said, and he tossed off his glass.

"Bravo!" cried the blues; "you are now the support, the defender, the hero of the Bulgarians; your fortune is made; you are on the high road to glory."

So saying, they put him in irons, and carried him away to the regiment. There he was made to wheel about to the right, to the left, to draw his ramrod, to return his ramrod, to present, to fire, to march, and they gave him thirty blows with a cane; the next day he performed his exercise a little better, and they gave him but twenty; the day following he came off with ten, and was looked upon as a young fellow of surprising genius by all his comrades.

Candide was struck with amazement, and could not for the soul of him conceive how he came to be a hero. One fine spring morning, he took it into his head to take a walk, and he marched straight forward, conceiving it to be a privilege of the human species, as well as of the brute creation, to make use of their legs how and when they pleased. He had not gone above two leagues when he was overtaken by four other heroes, six feet high, who bound him neck and heels, and carried him to a dungeon. A court-martial sat upon him, and he was asked which he liked best, either to run the gauntlet six and thirty times through the whole regiment, or to have his brains blown out with a dozen musket-balls. In vain did he remonstrate to them that the human will is free, and that he chose neither; they obliged him to make a choice, and he determined, in virtue of that divine gift called free will, to run the gauntlet six and thirty times. He had gone through his discipline twice, and the regiment being composed of two thousand men, they composed for him exactly four thousand strokes, which laid bare all his muscles and nerves, from the nape of his neck to his rump. As they were preparing to make him set out the third time, our young hero, unable to support it any longer, begged as a favor they would be so obliging as to shoot him through the head. The favor being granted, a bandage was tied over his eyes, and he was made to kneel down. At that very instant, his Bulgarian Majesty, happening to pass by, inquired into the delinquent's crime, and being a prince of great penetration, he found, from what he heard of Candide, that he was a young metaphysician, entirely ignorant of the world; and therefore, out of his great clemency, he condescended to pardon him, for which his name will be celebrated in every journal, and in every age.[11] A skillful surgeon made a cure of Candide in three weeks, by

[11] The incident of Candide's desertion is based on an episode in which Voltaire intervened with Frederick the Great for the release of a French deserter. Leibnitz's doctrine of free will was said to encourage soldiers to desert.

means of emollient unguents prescribed by Dioscorides.[12] His sores were now skinned over, and he was able to march, when the King of the Bulgarians gave battle to the King of the Abares.[13]

CHAPTER III

How Candide escaped from the Bulgarians. And what befell him afterwards.

Never was anything so gallant, so well accoutred, so brilliant, and so finely disposed as the two armies. The trumpets, fifes, hautboys, drums, and cannon, made such harmony as never was heard in hell itself. The entertainment began by a discharge of cannon, which, in the twinkling of an eye, laid flat about six thousand men on each side. The musket bullets swept away, out of the best of all possible worlds, nine or ten thousand scoundrels that infested its surface. The bayonet was next the sufficient reason for the deaths of several thousands. The whole might amount to thirty thousand souls. Candide trembled like a philosopher, and concealed himself as well as he could during this heroic butchery.

At length, while the two kings were causing *Te Deum*[14] to be sung in each of their camps, Candide took a resolution to go and reason somewhere else upon causes and effects. After passing over heaps of dead or dying men, the first place he came to was a neighboring village, in the Abarian territories, which had been burned to the ground by the Bulgarians in accordance with international law. Here lay a number of old men covered with wounds, who beheld their wives dying with their throats cut, and hugging their children to their breasts all stained with blood. There several young virgins, whose bellies had been ripped open after they had satisfied the natural necessities of the Bulgarian heroes, breathed their last; while others, half burned in the flames, begged to be dispatched out of the world. The ground about them was covered with the brains, arms, and legs of dead men.

Candide made all the haste he could to another village, which belonged to the Bulgarians, and there he found that the heroic Abares had enacted the same tragedy. From thence continuing to walk over palpitating limbs, or through ruined buildings, at length he arrived beyond the theater of war, with a little provision in his pouch, and Miss Cunegund's image in his heart. When he arrived in Holland his provisions failed him; but having heard that the inhabitants of that country were all rich and Christians, he made himself sure of being treated by them in the same manner as at the Baron's castle, before he had been driven from thence through the power of Miss Cunegund's bright eyes.

He asked charity of several grave-looking people, who one and all answered him that if he continued to follow this trade, they would have him

[12] Dioscorides was a first-century A.D. Greek physician and author of a textbook on medicines.

[13] There was actually a barbaric tribe named the Abares, but here the name is used for the French, opponents of the Prussians in the Seven Years' War.

[14] An ancient Latin hymn of praise and thanksgiving for victory.

sent to the house of correction, where he should be taught to earn his bread.

He next addressed himself to a person who had just been haranguing a numerous assembly for a whole hour on the subject of charity. The orator, squinting at him under his broad-brimmed hat, asked him sternly, what brought him thither? and whether he was for the good cause?

"Sir," said Candide, in a submissive manner, "I conceive there can be no effect with a cause; everything is necessarily concatenated and arranged for the best. It was necessary that I should be banished from the presence of Miss Cunegund; that I should afterwards run the gauntlet; and it is necessary I should beg my bread, till I am able to earn it: all this could not have been otherwise."

"Hark ye, friend," said the orator, "do you hold the Pope to be Antichrist?"

"Truly, I never heard anything about it," said Candide; "but whether he is or not, I am in want of something to eat."

"Thou deservest not to eat or to drink," replied the orator, "wretch, monster that thou art! hence! avoid my sight, nor ever come near me again while thou livest."

The orator's wife happened to put her head out of the window at that instant, when, seeing a man who doubted whether the Pope was Antichrist, she discharged upon his head a chamber-pot full of ——. Good heavens, to what excess does religious zeal transport the female kind!

A man who had never been christened, an honest Anabaptist, named James, was witness to the cruel and ignominious treatment showed to one of his brethren, to a rational, two-footed, unfledged being.[15] Moved with pity, he carried him to his own house, cleaned him up, gave him meat and drink, and made him a present of two florins, at the same time proposing to instruct him in his own trade of weaving Persian silks which are fabricated in Holland. Candide threw himself at his feet, crying:

"Now I am convinced that Master Pangloss told me truth, when he said that everything was for the best in this world; for I am infinitely more affected by your extraordinary generosity than by the inhumanity of that gentleman in the black cloak and his wife."

The next day, as Candide was walking out, he met a beggar all covered with scabs, his eyes were sunk in his head, the end of his nose was eaten off, his mouth drawn on one side, his teeth as black as coal, snuffling and coughing most violently, and every time he attempted to spit, out dropped a tooth.

CHAPTER IV

How Candide found his old master in philosophy, Dr. Pangloss, again, and what happened to them.

Candide, divided between compassion and horror, but giving way to the

[15]"Anabaptist" was the scornful name applied to certain sixteenth-century sects who opposed infant baptism; Voltaire respected a number of contemporary Anabaptists. "A rational, two-footed, unfledged (or unfeathered) being" is Plato's definition of man.

former, bestowed on this shocking figure the two florins which the honest Anabaptist James had just before given to him. The spectre looked at him very earnestly, shed tears, and threw his arms about his neck. Candide started back aghast.

"Alas!" said the one wretch to the other, "don't you know your dear Pangloss?"

"What do I hear? Is it you, my dear master! you I behold in this piteous plight? What dreadful misfortune has befallen you? What has made you leave the most magnificent and delightful of all castles? What is become of Miss Cunegund, the mirror of young ladies, and nature's masterpiece?"

"Oh Lord!" cried Pangloss, "I am so weak I cannot stand."

Thereupon Candide instantly led him to the Anabaptist's stable, and procured him something to eat. As soon as Pangloss had a little refreshed himself, Candide began to repeat his inquiries concerning Miss Cunegund.

"She is dead," replied the other.

Candide immediately fainted away: his friend recovered him by the help of a little bad vinegar which he found by chance in the stable. Candide opened his eyes.

"Dead! Miss Cunegund dead!" he said. "Ah, where is the best of worlds now? But of what illness did she die? Was it for grief upon seeing her father kick me out of his magnificent castle?"

"No," replied Pangloss; "her belly was ripped open by the Bulgarian soldiers, after they had ravished her as much as it was possible for damsel to be ravished: they knocked the Baron her father on the head for attempting to defend her; my lady her mother was cut in pieces; my poor pupil was served just in the same manner as his sister;[16] and as for the castle, they have not left one stone upon another; they have destroyed all the ducks, and the sheep, the barns, and the trees: but we have had our revenge, for the Abares have done the very same thing in a neighboring barony, which belonged to a Bulgarian lord."

At hearing this, Candide fainted away a second time; but, having come to himself again, he said all that it became him to say; he inquired into the cause and effect, as well as into the sufficing reason, that had reduced Pangloss to so miserable a condition.

"Alas!" replied the other, "it was love: love, the comfort of the human species; love, the preserver of the universe, the soul of all sensible beings; love! tender love!"

"Alas," replied Candide, "I have had some knowledge of love myself, this sovereign of hearts, this soul of souls; yet it never cost me more than a kiss, and twenty kicks on the backside. But how could this beautiful cause produce in you so hideous an effect?"

Pangloss made answer in these terms: "O my dear Candide, you must remember Pacquette, that pretty wench, who waited on our noble Baroness; in her arms I tasted the pleasures of paradise, which produced these hell-torments with which you see me devoured. She was infected with the disease, and perhaps is since dead of it; she received this present of a learned cordelier,[17] who derived it from the fountain-head; he was in-

[16] Voltaire slyly associates Cunegund's brother with homosexuality throughout.
[17] A cordelier is a Franciscan friar, so called because of his girtle of knotted cord.

debted for it to an old countess, who had it of a captain of horse, who had it of a marchioness, who had it of a page; the page had it of a Jesuit, who, during his novitiate, had it in a direct line from one of the fellow-adventurers of Christopher Columbus;[18] for my part I shall give it to nobody, I am a dying man."

"O Pangloss," cried Candide, "what a strange genealogy is this! Is not the devil the root of it?"

"Not at all," replied the great man, "it was a thing unavoidable, a necessary ingredient in the best of worlds; for if Columbus had not, in an island of America, caught this disease, which contaminates the source of generation, and frequently impedes propagation itself, and is evidently opposite to the great end of nature, we should have had neither chocolate nor cochineal. It is also to be observed that, even to the present time, in this continent of ours, this malady, like our religious controversies, is peculiar to ourselves. The Turks, the Indians, the Persians, the Chinese, the Siamese, and the Japanese are entirely unacquainted with it; but there is a sufficing reason for them to know it in a few centuries. In the meantime, it is making prodigious progress among us, especially in those armies composed of well-disciplined hirelings, who determine the fate of nations; for we may safely affirm that, when an army of thirty thousand men fights another equal in number, there are about twenty thousand of them poxed on each side."

"Very surprising, indeed," said Candide, "but you must get cured."

"How can I?" said Pangloss: "my dear friend, I have not a penny in the world; and you know one cannot be bled, or have a clyster,[19] without a fee."

This last speech had its effect on Candide; he flew to the charitable Anabaptist James, he flung himself at his feet, and gave him so touching a picture of the miserable situation of his friend, that the good man, without any further hesitation, agreed to take Dr. Pangloss into his house, and to pay for his cure. The cure was effected with only the loss of one eye and an ear. As he wrote a good hand and understood accounts tolerably well, the Anabaptist made him his book-keeper. At the expiration of two months, being obliged to go to Lisbon, about some mercantile affairs, he took the two philosophers with him in the same ship; Pangloss, during the voyage, explained to him how everything was so constituted that it could not be better. James did not quite agree with him on this point.

"Mankind," said he, "must, in some things, have deviated from their original innocence; for they were not born wolves, and yet they worry one another like those beasts of prey. God never gave them twenty-four pounders nor bayonets, and yet they have made cannon and bayonets to destroy one another. To this account I might add, not only bankruptcies, but the law, which seizes on the effects of bankrupts, only to cheat the creditors."

"All this was indispensably necessary," replied the one-eyed doctor; "for private misfortunes are public benefits; so that the more private misfortunes there are, the greater is the general good."

While he was arguing in this manner, the sky was overcast, the winds

[18] Voltaire is reflecting the belief that syphilis came to Europe from America.
[19] An enema.

blew from the four quarters of the compass, and the ship was assailed by a most terrible tempest, within sight of the port of Lisbon.

CHAPTER V

A tempest, a shipwreck, an earthquake; and what else befell Dr. Pangloss, Candide, and James the Anabaptist.

One half of the passengers, weakened and half dead with the inconceivable anguish which the rolling of a vessel at sea occasions to the nerves and all the humors of the body, tossed about in opposite directions, were lost to all sense of the danger that surrounded them. The other made loud outcries, or betook themselves to their prayers; the sails were blown into shivers, and the masts were brought by the board. The vessel leaked. Every one was busily employed, but nobody could be either heard or obeyed. The Anabaptist, being upon deck, lent a helping hand as well as the rest, when a brutish sailor gave him a blow, and laid him speechless; but, with the violence of the blow, the tar himself tumbled head foremost overboard, and fell upon a piece of the broken mast, which he immediately grasped. Honest James flew to his assistance, and hauled him in again, but, in the attempt, was thrown overboard himself in sight of the sailor, who left him to perish without taking the least notice of him. Candide, who beheld all that passed, and saw his benefactor one moment rising above water, and the next swallowed up by the merciless waves, was preparing to jump after him; but was prevented by the philosopher Pangloss, who demonstrated to him that the coast of Lisbon had been made on purpose for the Anabaptist to be drowned there. While he was proving his argument *à priori*,[20] the ship foundered, and the whole crew perished, except Pangloss, Candide, and the brute of a sailor who had been the means of drowning the good Anabaptist. The villain swam ashore; but Pangloss and Candide got to land upon a plank.

As soon as they had recovered a little, they walked towards Lisbon; with what little money they had left they thought to save themselves from starving after having escaped drowning.

Scarce had they done lamenting the loss of their benefactor and set foot in the city, when they perceived the earth to tremble under their feet, and the sea, swelling and foaming in the harbor, dash in pieces the vessels that were riding at anchor. Large sheets of flames and cinders covered the streets and public places; the houses tottered, and were tumbled topsy-turvy, even to their foundations, which were themselves destroyed, and thirty thousand inhabitants of both sexes, young and old, were buried beneath the ruins.[21]

The sailor, whistling and swearing, cried, "Damn it, there's something to be got here."

[20] An *a priori* argument is independent of factual support.

[21] Lisbon was destroyed by a major earthquake and fire on November 1, 1755. Voltaire wrote a long poem on the subject, "Poem on the Disaster of Lisbon" (1756), in which he used the incident to attack the idea of a benevolent Providence.

"What can be the sufficing reason of this phenomenon?" said Pangloss.

"It is certainly the day of judgment," said Candide.

The sailor, defying death in the pursuit of plunder, rushed into the midst of the ruin, where he found some money, with which he got drunk, and after he had slept himself sober, he purchased the favors of the first good-natured wench that came his way, amidst the ruins of demolished houses, and the groans of half-buried and expiring persons. Pangloss pulled him by the sleeve.

"Friend," said he, "this is not right, you trespass against the universal reason, and have mistaken your time."

"Death and zounds!" answered the other, "I am a sailor, and born at Batavia, and have trampled four times upon the crucifix in as many voyages to Japan:[22] you are come to a good hand with your universal reason."

Candide, who had been wounded by some pieces of stone that fell from the houses, lay stretched in the street, almost covered with rubbish.

"For God's sake," said he to Pangloss, "get me a little wine and oil. I am dying."

"This concussion of the earth is no new thing," replied Pangloss, "the city of Lima, in America, experienced the same last year; the same cause, the same effects: there is certainly a train of sulphur all the way under ground from Lima to Lisbon."

"Nothing more probable," said Candide; "but, for the love of God, a little oil and wine."

"Probable!" replied the philosopher, "I maintain that the thing is demonstrable."

Candide fainted away, and Pangloss fetched him some water from a neighboring spring.

The next day, in searching among the ruins, they found some eatables with which they repaired their exhausted strength. After this, they assisted the inhabitants in relieving the distressed and wounded. Some, whom they had humanely assisted, gave them as good a dinner as could be expected under such terrible circumstances. The repast, indeed, was mournful, and the company moistened their bread with their tears; but Pangloss endeavored to comfort them under this affliction by affirming that things could not be otherwise than they were.

"For," said he, "all this is for the very best end; for if there is a volcano at Lisbon, it could be on no other spot; for it is impossible for things not to be as they are, for everything is for the best."

By his side sat a little man dressed in black, who was one of the familiars of the Inquisition.[23] This person, taking him up with great politeness, said, "Possibly, my good Sir, you do not believe in original sin; for if everything is best, there could have been no such thing as the fall or punishment of man."

"I humbly ask your Excellency's pardon," answered Pangloss, still more

[22] Batavia is the former Dutch name for Djakarta, in Java. The Dutch were the only Europeans allowed into Japan in the seventeenth century. The belief that they had to trample on the crucifix to gain entry was a widespread slander.

[23] A familiar was an undercover agent of the Inquisition.

politely; "for the fall of man, and the curse consequent thereupon necessarily entered into the system of the best of worlds."

"That is as much as to say, Sir," rejoined the familiar, "you do not believe in free will."

"Your Excellency will be so good as to excuse me," said Pangloss; "free will is consistent with absolute necessity; for it was necessary we should be free, for in that the will——"

Pangloss was in the midst of his proposition, when the familiar made a sign to the attendant who was helping him to a glass of port wine.

CHAPTER VI

How the Portuguese made a superb auto-da-fé to prevent any future earthquakes, and how Candide underwent public flagellation.

After the earthquake which had destroyed three-quarters of the city of Lisbon, the sages of that country could think of no means more effectual to preserve the kingdom from utter ruin, than to entertain the people with an *auto-da-fé*,[24] it having been decided by the University of Coimbra that burning a few people alive by a slow fire, and with great ceremony, is an infallible secret to prevent earthquakes.

In consequence thereof they had seized on a Biscayan for marrying his godmother, and on two Portuguese for taking out the bacon of a larded pullet they were eating.[25] After dinner they came and secured Dr. Pangloss, and his pupil Candide; the one for speaking his mind, and the other for seeming to approve what he had said. They were conducted to separate apartments, extremely cool, where they were never incommoded with the sun. Eight days afterwards they were each dressed in a *fanbenito*,[26] and their heads were adorned with paper mitres. The mitre and *fanbenito* worn by Candide were painted with flames reversed, and with devils that had neither tails nor claws; but Dr. Pangloss's devils had both tails and claws, and his flames were upright. In these habits they marched in procession, and heard a very pathetic sermon, which was followed by a chant, beautifully intoned. Candide was flogged in regular cadence, while the chant was being sung; the Biscayan, and the two men who would not eat bacon, were burnt, and Pangloss was hanged, although this is not a common custom at these solemnities. The same day there was another earthquake, which made most dreadful havoc.[27]

Candide, amazed, terrified, confounded, astonished, and trembling from head to foot, said to himself, "If this is the best of all possible worlds, what are the others? If I had only been whipped, I could have put up with it, as I did among the Bulgarians; but, O my dear Pangloss! thou greatest of

[24] An *auto de fé* (literally "act of faith") was the public announcement of a judgment of the Inquisition, followed by execution of the judgment.

[25] The Biscayan is accused of violating the ecclesiastical laws against spiritual incest. The Portuguese are suspected of being Jews.

[26] A *fanbenito* was a long yellow cape worn by prisoners of the Inquisition.

[27] Lisbon experienced a second earthquake on December 21, 1755.

philosophers! that ever I should live to see thee hanged, without knowing for what! O my dear Anabaptist, thou best of men, that it should be thy fate to be drowned in the very harbor! O Miss Cunegund, you mirror of young ladies! that it should be your fate to have your belly ripped open."

He was making the best of his way from the place where he had been preached to, whipped, absolved, and received benediction, when he was accosted by an old woman, who said to him, "Take courage, my son, and follow me."

CHAPTER VII

How the old woman took care of Candide, and how he found the object of his love.

Candide followed the old woman, though without taking courage, to a decayed house where she gave him a pot of pomatum to anoint his sores, showed him a very neat bed, with a suit of clothes hanging up by it; and set victuals and drink before him.

"There," said she, "eat, drink, and sleep, and may our blessed Lady of Atocha, and the great St. Anthony of Padua, and the illustrious St. James of Compostella, take you under their protection. I shall be back to-morrow."

Candide, struck with amazement at what he had seen, at what he had suffered, and still more with the charity of the old woman, would have shown his acknowledgment by kissing her hand.

"It is not my hand you ought to kiss," said the old woman, "I shall be back to-morrow. Anoint your back, eat, and take your rest."

Candide, notwithstanding so many disasters, ate and slept. The next morning, the old woman brought him his breakfast; examined his back, and rubbed it herself with another ointment. She returned at the proper time, and brought him his dinner; and at night she visited him again with his supper. The next day she observed the same ceremonies.

"Who are you?" said Candide to her. "What god has inspired you with so much goodness? What return can I ever make you?"

The good old beldame kept a profound silence. In the evening she returned, but without his supper.

"Come along with me," said she, "but do not speak a word."

She took him by the arm, and walked with him about a quarter of a mile into the country, till they came to a lonely house surrounded with moats and gardens. The old woman knocked at a little door, which was immediately opened, and she showed him up a pair of back stairs into a small, but richly furnished apartment. There she made him sit down on a brocaded sofa, shut the door upon him, and left him. Candide thought himself in a trance; he looked upon his whole life hitherto as a frightful dream, and the present moment as a very agreeable one.

The old woman soon returned, supporting with great difficulty a young lady, who appeared scarce able to stand. She was of a majestic mien and stature; her dress was rich, and glittering with diamonds, and her face was covered with a veil.

"Take off that veil," said the old woman to Candide.

The young man approached, and, with a trembling hand, took off her veil. What a happy moment! What surprise! He thought he beheld Miss Cunegund; he did behold her, it was she herself. His strength failed him, he could not utter a word, he fell at her feet. Cunegund fainted upon the sofa. The old woman bedewed them with spirits; they recovered; they began to speak. At first they could express themselves only in broken accents; their questions and answers were alternately interrupted with sighs, tears, and exclamations. The old woman desired them to make less noise; and left them together.

"Good heavens!" cried Candide, "is it you? Is it Miss Cunegund I behold, and alive? Do I find you again in Portugal? Then you have not been ravished? They did not rip open your belly, as the philosopher Pangloss informed me?"

"Indeed but they did," replied Miss Cunegund; "but these two accidents do not always prove mortal."

"But were your father and mother killed?"

"Alas!" answered she, "it is but too true!" and she wept.

"And your brother?"

"And my brother also."

"And how did you come to Portugal? And how did you know of my being here? And by what strange adventure did you contrive to have me brought into this house?"

"I will tell you all," replied the lady, "but first you must acquaint me with all that has befallen you since the innocent kiss you gave me, and the rude kicking you received."

Candide, with the greatest submission, obeyed her, and though he was still wrapped in amazement, though his voice was low and tremulous, though his back pained him, yet he gave her a most ingenuous account of everything that had befallen him since the moment of their separation. Cunegund, with her eyes uplifted to heaven, shed tears when he related the death of the good Anabaptist James, and of Pangloss; after which, she thus related her adventures to Candide, who lost not one syllable she uttered, and seemed to devour her with his eyes all the time she was speaking.

CHAPTER VIII

The history of Cunegund.

"I was in bed and fast asleep, when it pleased heaven to send the Bulgarians to our delightful castle of Thunder-ten-tronckh, where they murdered my father and brother, and cut my mother in pieces. A tall Bulgarian soldier, six feet high, perceiving that I had fainted away at this sight, attempted to ravish me; the operation brought me to my senses. I cried, I struggled, I bit, I scratched, I would have torn the tall Bulgarian's eyes out, not knowing that what had happened at my father's castle was a customary thing. The brutal soldier gave me a cut in the left groin with his hanger,[28] the mark of which I still carry."

[28] A light sabre.

"I hope I shall see it," said Candide, with all imaginable simplicity.

"You shall," said Cunegund; "but let me proceed."

"Pray do," replied Candide.

She continued. "A Bulgarian captain came in and saw me weltering in my blood, and the soldier still as busy as if no one had been present. The officer, enraged at the fellow's want of respect to him, killed him with one stroke of his sabre as he lay upon me. This captain took care of me, had me cured, and carried me prisoner of war to his quarters. I washed what little linen he was master of, and dressed his victuals: he thought me very pretty, it must be confessed; neither can I deny that he was well made, and had a white soft skin, but he was very stupid, and knew nothing of philosophy: it might plainly be perceived that he had not been educated under Doctor Pangloss. In three months' time, having gamed away all his money, and being grown tired of me, he sold me to a Jew, named Don Issachar, who traded in Holland and Portugal, and was passionately fond of women. This Jew showed me great kindness in hopes to gain my favors; but he never could prevail on me. A modest woman may be once ravished; but her virtue is greatly strengthened thereby. In order to make sure of me, he brought me to this country house you now see. I had hitherto believed that nothing could equal the beauty of the castle of Thunder-ten-tronckh; but I found I was mistaken.

"The Grand Inquisitor saw me one day at mass, ogled me all the time of service, and, when it was over, sent to let me know he wanted to speak with me about some private business. I was conducted to his palace, where I told him of my parentage: he represented to me how much it was beneath a person of my birth to belong to an Israelite. He caused a proposal to be made to Don Issachar that he should resign me to his lordship. Don Issachar, being the court banker, and a man of credit, was not easily to be prevailed upon. His lordship threatened him with an *auto-da-fé;* in short, my Jew was frightened into a compromise, and it was agreed between them that the house and myself should belong to both in common; that the Jew should have Monday, Wednesday, and the Sabbath to himself; and the Inquisitor the other days of the week. This agreement has lasted almost six months; but not without several disputes, whether the space from Saturday night to Sunday morning belonged to the old or the new law.[29] For my part, I have hitherto withstood them both, and truly I believe this is the very reason why they both still love me.

"At length, to turn aside the scourge of earthquakes, and to intimidate Don Issachar, my lord Inquisitor was pleased to celebrate an *auto-da-fé*. He did me the honor to invite me to the ceremony. I had a very good seat; and refreshments were offered the ladies between mass and the execution. I was dreadfully shocked at the burning of the two Jews, and the honest Biscayan who married his godmother; but how great was my surprise, my consternation, and concern, when I beheld a figure so like Pangloss, dressed in a *sanbenito* and mitre! I rubbed my eyes, I looked at him attentively. I saw him hanged, and I fainted away: scarce had I recovered my senses, when I beheld you stark naked; this was the height of horror, grief,

[29] The "old law" is that of the Old Testament, hence of the Jew; the "new law" that of the New Testament, or the Christian.

and despair. I must confess to you for a truth, that your skin is far whiter and more blooming than that of the Bulgarian captain. This spectacle worked me up to a pitch of distraction. I screamed out, and would have said, 'Hold, barbarians!' but my voice failed me; and indeed my cries would have been useless. After you had been severely whipped I said to myself, 'How is it possible that the lovely Candide and the sage Pangloss should be at Lisbon, the one to receive a hundred lashes, and the other to be hanged by order of my lord Inquisitor, of whom I am so great a favorite? Pangloss deceived me most cruelly, in saying that everything is fittest and best.'

"Thus agitated and perplexed, now distracted and lost, now half dead with grief, I revolved in my mind the murder of my father, mother, and brother; the insolence of the rascally Bulgarian soldier; the wound he gave me in the groin; my servitude; my being a cook wench to my Bulgarian captain; my subjection to the villainous Don Issachar, and my cruel Inquisitor; the hanging of Doctor Pangloss; the *Miserere*[30] sung while you were whipped; and particularly the kiss I gave you behind the screen the last day I ever beheld you. I returned thanks to God for having brought you to the place where I was, after so many trials. I charged the old woman who attends me to bring you hither, as soon as possible. She has carried out my orders well, and I now enjoy the inexpressible satisfaction of seeing you, hearing you, and speaking to you. But you must certainly be half dead with hunger; I myself have got a good appetite, and so let us sit down to supper."

Upon this the two lovers immediately placed themselves at table, and, after having supped they returned to seat themselves again on the magnificent sofa already mentioned; they were there when Signor Don Issachar, one of the masters of the house, entered unexpectedly; it was the Sabbath day, and he came to enjoy his privilege, and sigh forth his tender passion.

CHAPTER IX

What happened to Cunegund, Candide, the Grand Inquisitor, and the Jew.

This same Issachar was the most choleric little Hebrew that had ever been in Israel since the captivity in Babylon.

"What," said he, "you Galilean bitch, my lord Inquisitor was not enough for thee, but this rascal must come in for a share with me?"

Uttering these words, he drew out a long poniard[31] which he always carried about him, and never dreaming that his adversary had any arms, he attacked him most furiously; but our honest Westphalian had received a handsome sword from the old woman with the suit of clothes. Candide drew his rapier; and though he was the most gentle, sweet-tempered young man breathing, he whipped it into the Israelite and laid him sprawling on the floor at the fair Cunegund's feet.

"Holy Virgin!" cried she, "what will become of us? A man killed in my apartment! If the peace-officers come, we are undone."

"Had not Pangloss been hanged," replied Candide, "he would have

[30] The *Miserere* ("have pity") is the 51st Psalm, a penitential hymn. [31] Dagger.

given us most excellent advice in this emergency, for he was a profound philosopher. But, since he is not here, let us consult the old woman."

She was very intelligent, and was beginning to give her advice when another door opened suddenly. It was now one o'clock in the morning, and of course the beginning of Sunday, which, by agreement, fell to the lot of my lord Inquisitor. Entering, he discovered the flagellated Candide with his drawn sword in his hand, a dead body stretched on the floor, Cunegund frightened out of her wits, and the old woman giving advice.

At that very moment a sudden thought came into Candide's head. "If this holy man," thought he, "should call assistance, I shall most undoubtedly be consigned to the flames, and Miss Cunegund may perhaps meet with no better treatment; besides, he was the cause of my being so cruelly whipped; he is my rival; and I have now begun to dip my hands in blood; there is no time to hesitate."

This whole train of reasoning was clear and instantaneous; so that, without giving time to the Inquisitor to recover from his surprise, he ran him through the body, and laid him by the side of the Jew.

"Good God!" cried Cunegund, "here's another fine piece of work! now there can be no mercy for us, we are excommunicated; our last hour is come. But how in the name of wonder could you, who are of so mild a temper, dispatch a Jew and a prelate in two minutes' time?"

"Beautiful lady," answered Candide, "when a man is in love, is jealous, and has been flogged by the Inquisition, he becomes lost to all reflection."

The old woman then put in her word.

"There are three Andalusian horses in the stable," said she, "with as many bridles and saddles; let the brave Candide get them ready; madam has moidores[32] and jewels; let us mount immediately, though I have only one buttock to sit upon; let us set out for Cadiz; it is the finest weather in the world, and there is great pleasure in travelling in the cool of the night."

Candide, without any further hesitation, saddled the three horses; and Miss Cunegund, the old woman, and he set out, and travelled thirty miles without once stopping. While they were making the best of their way, the Holy Brotherhood[33] entered the house. My Lord the Inquisitor was interred in a magnificent manner, and Issachar's body was thrown upon a dunghill.

Candide, Cunegund, and the old woman had, by this time, reached the little town of Aracena, in the midst of the mountains of Sierra Morena, and were engaged in the following conversation in an inn.

CHAPTER X

In what distress Candide, Cunegund, and the old woman arrive at Cadiz; and of their embarkation.

"Who could it be who has robbed me of my moidores and jewels?" exclaimed Miss Cunegund, all bathed in tears. "How shall we live? What shall

[32] Portuguese and Brazilian coins.
[33] The "Holy Brotherhood" was a Spanish semi-religious order with police powers.

we do? Where shall I find Inquisitors and Jews who can give me more?"

"Alas!" said the old woman, "I have a shrewd suspicion of a reverend father cordelier, who lay last night in the same inn with us at Badajoz: God forbid I should condemn any one wrongfully, but he came into our room twice, and he set off in the morning long before us."

"Alas!" said Candide, "Pangloss has often demonstrated to me that the goods of this world are common to all men, and that every one has an equal right to the enjoyment of them; but, according to these principles, the cordelier ought to have left us enough to carry us to the end of our journey. Have you nothing at all left, my beautiful Cunegund?"

"Not a sou," replied she.

"What is to be done then?" said Candide.

"Sell one of the horses," replied the old woman, "I will get behind my young lady though I have only one buttock to ride on, and we shall reach Cadiz, never fear."

In the same inn there was a Benedictine prior who bought the horse very cheap. Candide, Cunegund, and the old woman, after passing through Lucena, Chellas, and Lebrija, arrived at length at Cadiz. A fleet was then getting ready, and troops were assembling in order to reduce the reverend fathers, the Jesuits of Paraguay, who were accused of having excited one of the Indian tribes, in the neighborhood of the town of the Holy Sacrament,[34] to revolt against the Kings of Spain and Portugal. Candide, having been in the Bulgarian service, performed the military exercise of that nation before the general of this little army with so intrepid an air, and with such agility and expedition that he gave him the command of a company of foot. Being now made a captain, he embarked with Miss Cunegund, the old woman, two valets, and the two Andalusian horses which had belonged to the Grand Inquisitor of Portugal.

During their voyage they amused themselves with many profound reasonings on poor Pangloss's philosophy.

"We are now going into another world," said Candide, "and surely it must be there that everything is best; for I must confess that we have had some little reason to complain of what passes in ours, both as to the physical and moral part."

"Though I have a sincere love for you," said Miss Cunegund, "yet I still shudder at the reflection of what I have seen and experienced."

"All will be well," replied Candide, "the sea of this new world is already better than our European seas: it is smoother, and the winds blow more regularly."

"God grant it," said Cunegund; "but I have met with such terrible treatment in this that I have almost lost all hopes of a better."

"What murmuring and complaining is here indeed!" cried the old woman. "If you had suffered half what I have done, there might be some reason for it."

Miss Cunegund could scarcely refrain from laughing at the good old woman, and thought it droll enough to pretend to a greater share of misfortunes than herself.

"Alas! my good dame," said she, "unless you have been ravished by two

[34] Colonia del Sacramento, in Paraguay

Bulgarians, have received two deep wounds in your belly, have seen two of your own castles demolished, and beheld two fathers and two mothers barbarously murdered before your eyes, and, to sum up all, have had two lovers whipped at an *auto-da-fé,* I cannot see how you could be more unfortunate than me. Add to this, though born a baroness and bearing seventy-two quarterings, I have been reduced to a cook-wench."

"Miss," replied the old woman, "you do not know my family as yet; but if I were to show you my backside, you would not talk in this manner, but suspend your judgment."

This speech raised a high curiosity in Candide and Cunegund; and the old woman continued as follows.

CHAPTER XI

The history of the old woman.

"I have not always been blear-eyed. My nose did not always touch my chin, nor was I always a servant. You must know that I am the daughter of Pope Urban X,[35] and of the Princess of Palestrina. Up to the age of fourteen I was brought up in a castle, compared with which all the castles of the German barons would not have been fit for stabling, and one of my robes would have bought half the province of Westphalia. I grew in beauty, in wit, and in every graceful accomplishment, in the midst of pleasures, homage, and the highest expectations. I already began to inspire the men with love: my breast began to take its right form; and such a breast! white, firm, and formed like that of Venus of Medici: my eyebrows were as black as jet; and as for my eyes, they darted flames, and eclipsed the lustre of the stars, as I was told by the poets of our part of the world. My maids, when they dressed and undressed me, used to fall into an ecstasy in viewing me before and behind: and all the men longed to be in their places.

"I was contracted to a sovereign prince of Massa-Carrara. Such a prince! as handsome as myself, sweet-tempered, agreeable, of brilliant wit, and in love with me over head and ears. I loved him too, as our sex generally do for the first time, with transport and idolatry. The nuptials were prepared with surprising pomp and magnificence; the ceremony was attended with a succession of feasts, carousals, and burlesques: all Italy composed sonnets in my praise, though not one of them was tolerable. I was on the point of reaching the summit of bliss, when an old marchioness who had been mistress to the Prince my husband invited him to drink chocolate. In less than two hours after he returned from the visit he died of most terrible convulsions: but this is a mere trifle. My mother, in despair, and yet less afflicted than me, determined to absent herself for some time from so fatal a place. As she had a very fine estate in the neighborhood of Gaeta, we embarked on board a galley which was gilded like the high altar of St. Peter's at Rome. In our passage we were boarded by a Sallee corsair. Our men defended themselves like true Pope's soldiers; they flung themselves

[35] As Voltaire pointed out in a note, there was never a pope named Urban X.

upon their knees, laid down their arms and begged the corsair to give them absolution *in articulo mortis.*[36]

"The Moors presently stripped us as bare as monkeys. My mother, my maids of honor, and myself, were served all in the same manner. It is amazing how quick these gentry are at undressing people. But what surprised me most was that they thrust their fingers into that part of our bodies where we women seldom permit anything but enemas to enter. I thought it a very strange kind of ceremony; for thus we are generally apt to judge of things when we have not seen the world. I afterwards learnt that it was to discover if we had any diamonds concealed. This practice has been established since time immemorial among those civilized nations that scour the seas. I was informed that the religious Knights of Malta never fail to make this search, whenever any Moors of either sex fall into their hands. It is a part of the law of nations from which they never deviate.

"I need not tell you how great a hardship it was for a young princess and her mother to be made slaves and carried to Morocco. You may easily imagine what we must have suffered on board a corsair. My mother was still extremely handsome, our maids of honor, and even our common waiting-women, had more charms than were to be found in all Africa. As to myself, I was enchanting; I was beauty itself, and then I had my virginity. But, alas! I did not retain it long; this precious flower, which was reserved for the lovely Prince of Massa-Carrara, was cropped by the captain of the Moorish vessel, who was a hideous negro, and thought he did me infinite honor. Indeed, both the Princess of Palestrina and myself must have had very strong constitutions to undergo all the hardships and violences we suffered till our arrival at Morocco. But I will not detain you any longer with such common things; they are hardly worth mentioning.

"Upon our arrival at Morocco, we found that kingdom bathed in blood. Fifty sons of the Emperor Muley Ishmael[37] were each at the head of a party. This produced fifty civil wars of blacks against blacks, of blacks against tawnies, of tawnies against tawnies, and of mulattoes against mulattoes. In short, the whole empire was one continual scene of carnage.

"No sooner were we landed than a party of blacks, of a contrary faction to that of my captain, came to rob him of his booty. Next to the money and jewels, we were the most valuable things he had. I was witness on this occasion to such a battle as you never beheld in your cold European climates. The northern nations have not that fermentation in their blood, nor that raging lust for women that is so common in Africa. The natives of Europe seem to have their veins filled with milk only; but fire and vitriol circulate in those of the inhabitants of Mount Atlas and the neighboring provinces. They fought with the fury of the lions, tigers, and serpents of their country, to know who should have us. A Moor seized my mother by the right arm, while my captain's lieutenant held her by the left; another Moor laid hold of her by one leg, and one of our corsairs held her by the other. In this manner were almost every one of our women dragged between soldiers. My captain kept me concealed behind him, and with his

[36] "At the point of death."
[37] Muley Ishmael was a real Sultan of Morocco (1646?–1727).

drawn scimitar cut down every one who opposed him; at length I saw all our Italian women and my mother mangled and torn in pieces by the monsters who contended for them. The captives, my companions, the Moors who had taken them, the soldiers, the sailors, the blacks, the tawnies, the whites, the mulattoes, and lastly my captain himself, were all slain, and I remained alone expiring upon a heap of dead bodies. The like barbarous scenes were enacted every day over the whole country, which is an extent of three hundred leagues, and yet they never missed the five stated times of prayer enjoined by their prophet Mahomet.

"I disentangled myself with great difficulty from such a heap of slaughtered bodies, and made shift to crawl to a large orange tree that stood on the bank of a neighboring rivulet, where I fell down exhausted with terror, and overwhelmed with horror, despair, and hunger. My senses being overpowered, I fell asleep, or rather seemed to be in a trance. Thus I lay in a state of weakness and insensibility between life and death, when I felt myself pressed by something that moved up and down upon my body. This brought me to myself; I opened my eyes, and saw a pretty fair-faced man, who sighed and muttered these words between his teeth, '*O che sciagura d'essere senza coglioni!*' "[38]

CHAPTER XII

The adventures of the old woman continued.

"Astonished and delighted to hear my native language, and no less surprised at the young man's words, I told him that there were far greater misfortunes in the world than what he complained of. And to convince him of it, I gave him a short history of the horrible disasters that had befallen me; and again fell into a swoon. He carried me in his arms to a neighboring cottage, where he had me put to bed, procured me something to eat, waited on me, comforted me, caressed me, told me that he had never seen anything so perfectly beautiful as myself, and that he had never so much regretted the loss of what no one could restore to him."

" 'I was born at Naples,' said he, 'where they caponize[39] two or three thousand children every year: several die of the operation; some acquire voices far beyond the most tuneful of your ladies; and others are sent to govern states and empires. I underwent this operation very happily, and was one of the singers in the Princess of Palestrina's chapel.'

" 'How,' cried I, 'in my mother's chapel!'

" 'The Princess of Palestrina, your mother!' cried he, bursting into a flood of tears, 'is it possible you should be the beautiful young princess whom I had the care of bringing up till she was six years old, and who, at that tender age, promised to be as fair as I now behold you?'

" 'I am the same,' I replied. 'My mother lies about a hundred yards from here, cut in pieces, and buried under a heap of dead bodies.'

"I then related to him all that had befallen me, and he in return ac-

[38] "Oh, what a misfortune to have no testicles!" [39] Castrate.

quainted me with all his adventures, and how he had been sent to the court of the King of Morocco by a Christian prince to conclude a treaty with that monarch; in consequence of which he was to be furnished with military stores, and ships to enable him to destroy the commerce of other Christian governments.

" 'I have executed my commission,' said the eunuch; 'I am going to take shipping at Ceuta, and I'll take you along with me to Italy. *Ma che sciagura d'essere senza coglioni!*'

"I thanked him with tears of joy; but, instead of taking me with him into Italy, he carried me to Algiers, and sold me to the dey of that province. I had not been long a slave when the plague, which had made the tour of Africa, Asia, and Europe, broke out at Algiers with redoubled fury. You have seen an earthquake; but tell me, miss, had you ever the plague?"

"Never," answered the young Baroness.

"If you ever had," continued the old woman, "you would own an earthquake was a trifle to it. It is very common in Africa; I was seized with it. Figure to yourself the situation of the daughter of a pope, only fifteen years old, and who in less than three months had felt the miseries of poverty and slavery; had been ravished almost every day; had beheld her mother cut into four quarters; had experienced the scourges of famine and war, and was now dying of the plague at Algiers. I did not, however, die of it; but my eunuch, and the dey, and almost the whole seraglio of Algiers, were swept off.

"As soon as the first fury of this dreadful pestilence was over, a sale was made of the dey's slaves. I was purchased by a merchant, who carried me to Tunis. This man sold me to another merchant, who sold me again to another at Tripoli; from Tripoli I was sold to Alexandria, from Alexandria to Smyrna, and from Smyrna to Constantinople. After many changes, I at length became the property of an aga of the janissaries, who, soon after I came into his possession, was ordered away to the defence of Azov, then besieged by the Russians.[40]

"The aga being fond of women, took his whole seraglio with him, and lodged us in a small fort on Lake Maeotis, with two black eunuchs and twenty soldiers for our guard. Our army made a great slaughter among the Russians, but they soon returned us the compliment. Azov was taken by storm, and the enemy spared neither age nor sex, but put all to the sword, and laid the city in ashes. Our little fort alone held out; they resolved to reduce us by famine. The twenty janissaries had bound themselves by an oath never to surrender the place. Being reduced to the extremity of famine, they found themselves obliged to eat two eunuchs rather than violate their oath. After a few days they determined to devour the women.

"We had a very pious and humane imam,[41] who made them a most excellent sermon on this occasion, exhorting them not to kill us all at once.

" 'Only cut off one of the buttocks of each of those ladies,' said he, 'and you will fare extremely well; if ye are still under the necessity of having

[40] The Crimean town of Azov was besieged by Russia in 1696. A janissary is an elite Turkish soldier.

[41] Moslem priest.

recourse to the same expedient again, ye will find the like supply a few days hence. Heaven will approve of so charitable an action, and work your deliverance.'

"By the force of this eloquence he easily persuaded them, and all underwent the operation. The imam applied the same balsam as they do to children after circumcision. We were all ready to give up the ghost.

"The janissaries had scarcely time to finish the repast with which we had supplied them, when the Russians attacked the place by means of flat-bottomed boats, and not a single janissary escaped. The Russians paid no regard to the condition we were in; but as there are French surgeons in all parts of the world, a skillful operator took us under his care, and made a cure of us; and I shall never forget, while I live, that as soon as my wounds were perfectly healed, he made me certain proposals. In general, he desired us all to have a good heart, assuring us that the like had happened in many sieges; and that it was the law of war.

"As soon as my companions were in a condition to walk, they were sent to Moscow. As for me, I fell to the lot of a boyard,[42] who put me to work in his garden, and gave me twenty lashes a-day. But this nobleman having, in about two years afterwards, been broken alive upon the wheel, with about thirty others, for some court intrigues,[43] I took advantage of the event, and made my escape. I travelled over a great part of Russia. I was a long time an innkeeper's servant at Riga, then at Rostock, Wismar, Leipsic, Cassel, Utrecht, Leyden, The Hague, and Rotterdam: I have grown old in misery and disgrace, living with only one buttock, and in the perpetual remembrance that I was a pope's daughter. I have been an hundred times upon the point of killing myself, but still was fond of life. This ridiculous weakness is, perhaps, one of the dangerous principles implanted in our nature. For what can be more absurd than to persist in carrying a burden of which we wish to be eased? to detest, and yet to strive to preserve our existence? In a word, to caress the serpent that devours us, and hug him close to our bosoms till he has gnawed into our hearts?

"In the different countries which it has been my fate to traverse, and the many inns where I have been a servant, I have observed a prodigious number of people who held their existence in abhorrence, and yet I never knew more than twelve who voluntarily put an end to their misery; namely, three negroes, four Englishmen, as many Genoese, and a German professor named Robek.[44] My last place was with the Jew, Don Issachar, who placed me near your person, my fair lady; to your fortunes I have attached myself, and have been more affected by your adventures than my own. I should never have even mentioned the latter to you, had you not a little piqued me on the head of sufferings; and if it were not customary to tell stories on board a ship in order to pass away the time. In short, my dear miss, I have a great deal of knowledge and experience of the world, therefore take my advice; divert yourself, and prevail upon each passenger to tell his story,

[42] Russian nobleman.

[43] Voltaire is referring to an abortive revolt against Peter the Great in 1698.

[44] Johann Robeck (1672–1739) wrote a treatise advocating suicide and actually drowned himself.

and if there is one of them all that has not cursed his existence many times, and said to himself over and over again, that he was the most wretched of mortals, I give you leave to throw me headforemost into the sea."

CHAPTER XIII

How Candide was obliged to leave the fair Cunegund and the old woman.

The fair Cunegund, being thus made acquainted with the history of the old woman's life and adventures, paid her all the respect and civility due to a person of her rank and merit. She very readily came into her proposal of engaging every one of the passengers to relate their adventures in their turns, and was at length, as well as Candide, compelled to acknowledge that the old woman was in the right.

"It is a thousand pities," said Candide, "that the sage Pangloss should have been hanged contrary to the custom of an *auto-da-fé,* for he would have read us a most admirable lecture on the moral and physical evil which overspreads the earth and sea; and I think I should have courage enough to presume to offer (with all due respect) some few objections."

While everyone was reciting his adventures, the ship continued her way, and at length arrived at Buenos Ayres, where Cunegund, Captain Candide, and the old woman landed and went to wait upon the Governor Don Fernando d'Ibaraa y Figueora y Mascarenas y Lampourdos y Souza. This nobleman carried himself with a haughtiness suitable to a person who bore so many names. He spoke with the most noble disdain to every one, carried his nose so high, strained his voice to such a pitch, assumed so imperious an air, and stalked with so much loftiness and pride, that everyone who had the honor of conversing with him was violently tempted to bastinade[45] his Excellency. He was immoderately fond of women, and Cunegund appeared in his eyes a paragon of beauty. The first thing he did was to ask her if she was the captain's wife. The air with which he made this demand alarmed Candide; he did not dare to say he was married to her, because, indeed, he was not; neither durst he say she was his sister, because she was not that either: and though a lie of this nature proved of great service to one of the ancients,[46] and might possibly be useful to some of the moderns, yet the purity of his heart would not permit him to violate the truth.

"Miss Cunegund," replied he, "is to do me the honor of marrying me, and we humbly beseech your Excellency to condescend to grace the ceremony with your presence."

Don Fernando d'Ibaraa y Figueora y Mascarenas y Lampourdos y Souza, twirling his mustachio, and putting on a sarcastic smile, ordered Captain Candide to go and review his company. Candide obeyed, and the Governor was left with Miss Cunegund. He made her a strong declaration of love, protesting that he was ready on the morrow to give her his hand in the face of the Church, or otherwise, as should appear most agreeable to a

[45] Beat with a stick. [46] See the story of Abraham and Sarah, Genesis, chapter 12.

young lady of her prodigious beauty. Cunegund desired leave to retire a quarter of an hour to consult the old woman, and determine how she should proceed.

The old woman gave her the following counsel: "Miss, you have seventy-two quarterings in your arms, it is true, but you have not a penny to bless yourself with: it is your own fault if you are not wife to one of the greatest noblemen in South America, with an exceeding fine mustachio. What business have you to pride yourself upon an unshaken constancy? You have been ravished by a Bulgarian soldier; a Jew and an Inquisitor have both tasted of your favors. People take advantage of misfortunes. I must confess, were I in your place, I should, without the least scruple, give my hand to the Governor, and thereby make the fortune of the brave Captain Candide."

While the old woman was thus haranguing, with all the prudence that old age and experience furnish, a small bark entered the harbor, in which was a magistrate and his alguazils.[47] Matters had fallen out as follows.

The old woman rightly guessed that the cordelier with the long sleeves was the person who had taken Cunegund's money and jewels while they and Candide were at Badajoz, in their hasty flight from Lisbon. This same friar attempted to sell some of the diamonds to a jeweller, who at once knew them to have belonged to the Grand Inquisitor. The cordelier, before he was hanged, confessed that he had stolen them, and described the persons, and the road they had taken. The flight of Cunegund and Candide was already the town-talk. They sent in pursuit of them to Cadiz; and the vessel which had been sent, to make the greater dispatch, had now reached the port of Buenos Ayres. A report was spread that a magistrate was going to land, and that he was in pursuit of the murderers of my lord the Grand Inquisitor. The wise old woman immediately saw what was to be done. "You cannot run away," said she to Cunegund; "but you have nothing to fear; it was not you who killed my lord Inquisitor: besides, as the Governor is in love with you, he will not suffer you to be ill-treated; therefore stand your ground."

Then hurrying away to Candide, "Be gone," said she, "from hence this instant, or you will be burned alive."

Candide found there was no time to be lost; but how could he part from Cunegund, and whither must he fly for shelter?

CHAPTER XIV

The reception Candide and Cacambo met with among the Jesuits in Paraguay.

Candide had brought with him from Cadiz such a footman as one often meets with on the coasts of Spain and in the colonies. He was the fourth part of a Spaniard, of a mongrel breed, and born in Tucuman.[48] He had successively gone through the profession of a choirboy, sexton, sailor, monk, peddler, soldier, and lackey. His name was Cacambo; he had a great

[47] Police officers. [48] A province in Argentina.

affection for his master because his master was a mighty good man. He immediately saddled the two Andalusian horses.

"Come, my good master," he said, "let us follow the old woman's advice, and make all the haste we can from this place, without staying to look behind us."

Candide burst into a flood of tears.

"O my dear Cunegund, must I then be compelled to quit you, just as the Governor was going to honor us with his presence at our wedding! Cunegund, so long lost, and found again, what will become of you?"

"Lord!" said Cacambo, "she must do as well as she can; women are never at a loss. God takes care of them, and so let us make the best of our way."

"But whither wilt thou carry me? Where can we go? What can we do without Cunegund?" cried the disconsolate Candide.

"By St. James of Compostella," said Cacambo, "you were going to fight against the Jesuits of Paraguay; now, let us go and fight for them: I know the road perfectly well; I'll conduct you to their kingdom; they will be delighted with a captain that understands the Bulgarian exercise; you will certainly make a prodigious fortune. If we cannot find our account in one world, we may in another. It is a great pleasure to see new objects, and perform new exploits."

"Then you have been in Paraguay?" said Candide.

"Ay, marry, have I," replied Cacambo: "I was a scout in the College of the Assumption, and I am as well acquainted with the new government of Los Padres[49] as I am with the streets of Cadiz. Oh, it is an admirable government, that is most certain! The kingdom is at present upwards of three hundred leagues in diameter, and divided into thirty provinces; the fathers are there masters of everything, and the people have no money at all; this is the masterpiece of justice and reason. For my part, I see nothing so divine as the good fathers, who wage war in this part of the world against the King of Spain and the King of Portugal, at the same time they hear the confessions of those very princes in Europe; who kill Spaniards in America, and send them to Heaven in Madrid. This pleases me exceedingly, but let us push forward; you are going to be most fortunate of all mortals. How charmed will those fathers be to hear that a captain who understands the Bulgarian exercise is coming among them!"

As soon as they reached the first barrier, Cacambo called to the advance guard, and told them that a captain wanted to speak to my Lord the General. Notice was given to the main guard, and immediately a Paraguayan officer ran to throw himself at the feet of the Commandant to impart this news to him. Candide and Cacambo were immediately disarmed, and their two Andalusian horses were seized. The two strangers were now conducted between two files of musketeers, the Commandant was at the farther end with a three-cornered cap on his head, his gown tucked up, a sword by his side, and a half-pike in his hand; he made a sign, and instantly four-and-twenty soldiers drew up round the newcomers. A sergeant told them that they must wait, the Commandant could not speak to them; and that

[49] "Los Padres" were the Jesuit fathers.

the Reverend Father Provincial did not suffer any Spaniard to open his mouth but in his presence, or to stay above three hours in the province.

"And where is the Reverend Father Provincial?" said Cacambo.

"He is just come from mass, and is at the parade," replied the sergeant, "and in about three hours' time, you may possibly have the honor to kiss his spurs."

"But," said Cacambo, "the captain, who, as well as myself, is perishing with hunger, is no Spaniard, but a German; therefore, pray, might we not be permitted to break our fast till we can be introduced to his Reverence?"

The sergeant immediately went, and acquainted the Commandant with what he heard.

"God be praised," said the Reverend Commandant, "since he is a German, I will hear what he has to say; let him be brought to my arbor."

Immediately they conducted Candide to a beautiful pavilion, adorned with a colonnade of green and gold marble, and with trellises of vines, which served as a kind of cage for parrots, humming-birds, fly-birds, guinea-hens, and all other curious kinds of birds. An excellent breakfast was provided in vessels of gold; and while the Paraguayans were eating coarse Indian corn out of wooden dishes in the open air, and exposed to the burning heat of the sun, the Reverend Father Commandant retired to his cool arbor.

He was a very handsome young man, round-faced, fair, and fresh-colored, his eyebrows were finely arched, he had a piercing eye, the tips of his ears were red, his lips vermilion, and he had a bold and commanding air; but such a boldness as neither resembled that of a Spaniard nor of a Jesuit. He ordered Candide and Cacambo to have their arms restored to them, together with their two Andalusian horses. Cacambo gave the poor beasts some oats to eat close by the arbor, keeping a strict eye upon them all the while for fear of surprise.

Candide having kissed the hem of the Commandant's robe, they sat down to table.

"It seems you are a German?" said the Jesuit to him in that language.

"Yes, Reverend Father," answered Candide.

As they pronounced these words, they looked at each other with great amazement, and with an emotion that neither could conceal.

"From what part of Germany do you come?" said the Jesuit.

"From the dirty province of Westphalia," answered Candide: "I was born in the castle of Thunder-ten-tronckh."

"Oh heavens! is it possible?" said the Commandant.

"What a miracle!" cried Candide.

"Can it be you?" said the Commandant.

On this they both retired a few steps backwards, then embraced, and let fall a shower of tears.

"Is it you then, Reverend Father? You are the brother of the fair Cunegund? you who were slain by the Bulgarians! you the Baron's son! you a Jesuit in Paraguay! I must confess this is a strange world we live in. O Pangloss! Pangloss! what joy would this have given you, if you had not been hanged."

The Commandant dismissed the negro slaves, and the Paraguayans who were presenting them with liquor in crystal goblets. He returned thanks to God and St. Ignatius a thousand times; he clasped Candide in his arms, and both their faces were bathed in tears.

"You will be more surprised, more affected, more transported," said Candide, "when I tell you that Miss Cunegund, your sister, whose belly was supposed to have been ripped open, is in perfect health."

"Where?"

"In your neighborhood, with the Governor of Buenos Ayres; and I myself was going to fight against you."

Every word they uttered during this long conversation was productive of some new matter of astonishment. Their souls fluttered on their tongues, listened in their ears, and sparkled in their eyes. Like true Germans, they continued a long time at table, waiting for the Reverend Father Provincial; and the Commandant spoke to his dear Candide as follows:

CHAPTER XV

How Candide killed the brother of his dear Cunegund.

"Never while I live shall I lose the remembrance of that horrible day on which I saw my father and mother barbarously butchered before my eyes, and my sister ravished. When the Bulgarians retired, we found no sign of my dear sister; but the bodies of my father, mother, and myself, with two servant maids, and three little boys with their throats cut, were thrown into a cart, to be buried in a chapel belonging to the Jesuits, within two leagues of our family seat. A Jesuit sprinkled us with some holy water, which was confoundedly salt, and a few drops of it went into my eyes; the father perceived that my eyelids stirred a little; he put his hand on my breast, and felt my heart beat; upon which he gave me proper assistance, and at the end of three weeks I was perfectly recovered. You know, my dear Candide, I was very handsome; I became still more so, and the Reverend Father Croust,[50] Superior of the House, took a great fancy to me; he gave me a novice's habit, and some years afterwards I was sent to Rome. Our general stood in need of new levies of young German Jesuits. The sovereigns of Paraguay admit as few Spanish Jesuits as possible; they prefer those of other nations, as being more obedient to command. The Reverend Father General looked upon me as a proper person to work in that vineyard. I set out in company with a Pole and a Tyrolese. Upon my arrival, I was honored with a subdeaconship and a lieutenancy. Now I am colonel and priest. We shall give a warm reception to the King of Spain's troops; I can assure you, they will be well excommunicated and beaten. Providence has sent you hither to assist us. But is it true that my dear sister Cunegund is in the neighborhood with the Governor of Buenos Ayres?"

Candide swore that nothing could be more true; and the tears began again to trickle down their cheeks.

The Baron knew no end of embracing Candide: he called him his brother, his deliverer.

[50] There really was a Father Croust, a French Jesuit with whom Voltaire had quarreled. Voltaire is, of course, implying a homosexual relationship.

"Perhaps," said he, "my dear Candide, we shall be fortunate enough to enter the town sword in hand, and rescue my sister Cunegund."

"Ah! that would crown my wishes," replied Candide, "for I intended to marry her; and I hope I shall still be able to do so."

"Insolent fellow!" replied the Baron. "You! you have the impudence to marry my sister, who bears seventy-two quarterings! I think you have an insufferable degree of assurance to dare so much as to mention such an audacious design to me."

Candide, thunder-struck at the oddness of this speech, answered, "Reverend Father, all the quarterings in the world are of no significance. I have delivered your sister from a Jew and an Inquisitor; she is under many obligations to me, and she is resolved to give me her hand. Master Pangloss always told me that mankind are by nature equal. Therefore, you may depend upon it, that I will marry your sister."

"We shall see about that, villain!" said the Jesuit Baron of Thunder-ten-tronckh, and struck him across the face with the flat side of his sword.

Candide, in an instant, drew his rapier, and plunged it up to the hilt in the Jesuit's body; but, in pulling it out reeking hot, he burst into tears.

"Good God!" cried he, "I have killed my old master, my friend, my brother-in-law; I am the mildest man in the world, and yet I have already killed three men; and of these three two were priests."

Cacambo, standing sentry near the door of the arbor, instantly ran up.

"Nothing remains," said his master, "but to sell our lives as dearly as possible; they will undoubtedly look into the arbor; we must die sword in hand."

Cacambo, who had seen many of these kind of adventures, was not discouraged! He stripped the Baron of his Jesuit's habit, and put it upon Candide, then gave him the dead man's three-cornered cap, and made him mount on horseback. All this was done as quick as thought.

"Gallop, master," cried Cacambo; "everybody will take you for a Jesuit going to give orders; and we shall have passed the frontiers before they are able to overtake us."

He flew as he spoke these words, crying out aloud in Spanish, "Make way, make way for the Reverend Father Colonel."

CHAPTER XVI

What happened to our two travellers with two girls, two monkeys, and the savages, called Oreillons.

Candide and his servant had already passed the frontiers before it was known that the German Jesuit was dead. The wary Cacambo had taken care to fill his wallet with bread, chocolate, ham, fruit, and a few bottles of wine. They penetrated with their Andalusian horses into a strange country where they could discover no beaten path. At length, a beautiful meadow, intersected with streams, opened to their view. Our two travellers allowed their steeds to graze. Cacambo urged his master to take some food, and he set him an example.

"How can you desire me to eat ham, when I have killed the son of my

Lord the Baron, and am doomed never more to see the beautiful Cunegund? What will it avail me to prolong a wretched life that might be spent far from her in remorse and despair; and then, what will the *Journal of Trevoux* say?"[51]

While he was making these reflections, he still continued eating. The sun was now on the point of setting, when the ears of our two were assailed with cries which seemed to be uttered by a female voice. They could not tell whether these were cries of grief or joy: however, they instantly started up, full of that uneasiness and apprehension which a strange place inspires. The cries proceeded from two young women who were tripping stark naked on the edge of the prairie, while two monkeys followed close at their heels biting their buttocks. Candide was touched with compassion; he had learned to shoot while he was among the Bulgarians, and he could hit a filbert in a hedge without touching a leaf. Accordingly, he took up his double-barrelled Spanish musket, pulled the trigger, and laid the two monkeys lifeless on the ground.

"God be praised, my dear Cacambo, I have rescued two poor girls from a most perilous situation: if I have committed a sin in killing an Inquisitor and a Jesuit, I made ample amends by saving the lives of these two girls. Who knows but they may be young ladies of a good family, and that this assistance I have been so happy to give them may procure great advantage in this country."

He was about to continue, when he felt himself struck speechless at seeing the two girls embracing the dead bodies of the monkeys in the tenderest manner, bathing their wounds with their tears, and rending the air with the most doleful lamentations.

"Really," said he to Cacambo, "I should not have expected to see such a prodigious share of good nature."

"Master," replied Cacambo, "you have made a precious piece of work of it; do you know that you have killed the lovers of these two ladies!"

"Their lovers! Cacambo, you are jesting! it cannot be! I can never believe it?"

"Dear Sir," replied Cacambo, "you are surprised at everything; why should you think it so strange that there should be a country where monkeys insinuate themselves into the good graces of the ladies? They are the fourth part of a man as I am the fourth part of a Spaniard."

"Alas!" replied Candide, "I remember to have heard Master Pangloss say that such accidents as these frequently came to pass in former times, and that these commixtures are productive of centaurs, fauns, and satyrs; and that many of the ancients had seen such monsters: but I looked upon the whole as fabulous."

"Now you are convinced," said Cacambo, "that it is very true, and you see what use is made of those creatures by persons who have not had a proper education: all I am afraid of is that these same ladies will play us some ugly trick."

These judicious reflections operated so far on Candide, as to make him quit the meadow and strike into a thicket. There he and Cacambo supped, and after heartily cursing the Grand Inquisitor, the Governor of Buenos

[51] The *Journal of Trevoux* was a Jesuit journal which regularly attacked Voltaire.

Ayres, and the Baron, they fell asleep on the ground. When they awoke, they were surprised to find that they could not move; the reason was that the Oreillons[52] who inhabit that country, and to whom the two girls had denounced them, had bound them with cords made of the bark of trees. They were surrounded by fifty naked Oreillons armed with bows and arrows, clubs, and hatchets of flint; some were making a fire under a large cauldron; and others were preparing spits, crying out one and all, "A Jesuit! a Jesuit! We shall be revenged; we shall have excellent cheer; let us eat this Jesuit; let us eat him up."

"I told you, master," cried Cacambo mournfully, "that those two wenches would play us some scurvy trick."

Candide seeing the cauldron and the spits, cried out, "I suppose they are going either to boil or roast us. Ah! what would Master Pangloss say if he were to see how pure nature is formed! Everything is right: it may be so: but I must confess it is something hard to be bereft of Miss Cunegund, and to be spitted by these Oreillons."

Cacambo, who never lost his presence of mind in distress, said to the disconsolate Candide, "Do not despair; I understand a little of the jargon of these people; I will speak to them."

"Ay, pray do," said Candide, "and be sure you make them sensible of the horrid barbarity of boiling and roasting human creatures, and how little of Christianity there is in such practices."

"Gentlemen," said Cacambo, "you think perhaps you are going to feast upon a Jesuit; if so, it is mighty well; nothing can be more agreeable to justice than thus to treat your enemies. Indeed, the law of nature teaches us to kill our neighbor, and accordingly we find this practiced all over the world; and if we do not indulge ourselves in eating human flesh, it is because we have much better fare; but you have not such resources as we have; it is certainly much better judged to feast upon your enemies than to abandon to the fowls of the air the fruits of your victory. But surely, gentlemen, you would not choose to eat your friends. You imagine you are going to roast a Jesuit, whereas my master is your friend, your defender, and you are going to spit the very man who has been destroying your enemies: as to myself, I am your countryman; this gentleman is my master, and so far from being a Jesuit, he has very lately killed one of that order, whose spoils he now wears, and which have probably occasioned your mistake. To convince you of the truth of what I say, take the habit he now has on, and carry it to the first barrier of the Jesuits' kingdom, and inquire whether my master did not kill one of their officers. There will be little or no time lost by this, and you may still reserve our bodies in your power to feast on, if you should find what we have told you to be false. But, on the contrary, if you find it to be true, I am persuaded you are too well acquainted with the principles of the laws of society, humanity, and justice, not to use us courteously."

This speech appeared very reasonable to the Oreillons; they deputed two of their people with all expedition to inquire into the truth of this

[52] The name "Oreillons" is an attempt to render the American-Spanish *Orejones* ("long-eared," "unbranded," or "wild"). Voltaire got the name and a number of other details from a 1609 book on Peru by Garcilaso de Vega.

affair. The two delegates acquitted themselves of their commission like men of sense, and soon returned with good tidings. Upon this the Oreillons released their two prisoners, showed them all sorts of civilities, offered them girls, gave them refreshments, and reconducted them to the confines of their country, crying before them all the way, in token of joy, "He is no Jesuit, he is no Jesuit."

Candide could not help admiring the cause of his deliverance.

"What men! what manners!" cried he: "if I had not fortunately run my sword up to the hilt in the body of Miss Cunegund's brother, I should have infallibly been eaten alive. But, after all, pure nature is an excellent thing; since these people, instead of eating me, showed me a thousand civilities, as soon as they knew I was not a Jesuit."

CHAPTER XVII

Candide and his servant arrive in the country of El Dorado. What they saw there.

When they got to the frontiers of the Oreillons, Cacambo said to Candide, "You see, this hemisphere is no better than the other: take my advice, and let us return to Europe by the shortest way possible."

"But how can we get back?" said Candide; "and whither shall we go? To my own country? the Bulgarians and the Abares are laying that waste with fire and sword. Or shall we go to Portugal? there I shall be burned; and if we abide here, we are every moment in danger of being spitted. But how can I bring myself to quit that part of the world where Miss Cunegund has her residence?"

"Let us turn towards Cayenne," said Cacambo; "there we shall meet with some Frenchmen; for you know those gentry ramble all over the world; perhaps they will assist us, and God will look with pity on our distress."

It was not so easy to get to Cayenne. They knew pretty nearly whereabouts it lay; but the mountains, rivers, precipices, robbers, savages, were dreadful obstacles in the way. Their horses died with fatigue, and their provisions were at an end. They subsisted a whole month upon wild fruit, till at length they came to a little river bordered with cocoa-nut palms, the sight of which at once sustained life and hope.

Cacambo, who was always giving as good advice as the old woman herself, said to Candide, "You see there is no holding out any longer; we travelled enough on foot. I see an empty canoe near the river-side; let us fill it with cocoa-nuts, get into it, and go down with the stream; a river always leads to some inhabited place. If we do not meet with agreeable things, we shall at least meet with something new."

"Agreed," replied Candide; "let us recommend ourselves to Providence."

They rowed a few leagues down the river, the banks of which were in some places covered with flowers; in others barren; in some parts smooth and level, and in others steep and rugged. The stream widened as they went further on, till at length it passed under one of the frightful rocks whose summits seemed to reach the clouds. Here our two travellers had the courage to commit themselves to the stream beneath this vault, which, contracting in this part, hurried them along with a dreadful noise and rapidity. At the end of four-and-twenty hours, they saw daylight again; but their canoe was dashed to pieces against the rocks. They were obliged to creep along, from rock to rock, for the space of a league, till at last a spacious plain presented itself to their sight, bound by inaccessible mountains. The country appeared cultivated equally for pleasure, and to produce the necessaries of life. The useful and agreeable were here equally blended. The roads were covered, or rather adorned, with carriages formed of glittering materials, in which were men and women of a surprising beauty, drawn with great rapidity by red sheep of a very large size, which far surpassed in speed the finest coursers of Andalusia, Tetuan, or Mequinez.

"Here is a country, however," said Candide, "preferable to Westphalia."

He and Cacambo landed near the first village they saw, at the entrance of which they perceived some children covered with tattered garments of the richest brocade, playing at quoits. Our two inhabitants of the other hemisphere amused themselves greatly with what they saw. The quoits were large round pieces, yellow, red, and green, which cast a most glorious lustre. Our travellers picked some of them up, and they proved to be gold, emeralds, rubies, and diamonds, the least of which would have been the greatest ornament to the superb throne of the great Mogul.

"Without doubt," said Cacambo, "those children must be the king's sons, that are playing at quoits."

As he was uttering those words, the schoolmaster of the village appeared, who came to call them to school.

"There," said Candide, "is the preceptor of the royal family."

The little ragamuffins immediately quitted their game, leaving the quoits on the ground with all their other playthings. Candide gathered them up, ran to the schoolmaster, and, with a most respectful bow, presented them to him, giving him to understand by signs that their Royal Highnesses had forgotten their gold and precious stones. The schoolmaster, with a smile, flung them upon the ground, then having examined Candide from head to foot with an air of great surprise, went on his way.

Our travellers took care, however, to gather up the gold, the rubies, and the emeralds.

"Where are we?" cried Candide. "The king's children in this country must have an excellent education, since they are taught to show such a contempt for gold and precious stones."

Cacambo was as much surprised as his master.

They at length drew near the first house in the village, which was built after the manner of a European palace. There was a crowd of people round the door, and a still greater number in the house. The sound of the most delightful musical instruments was heard, and the most agreeable smell came from the kitchen. Cacambo went up to the door, and heard those within talking in the Peruvian language, which was his mother tongue; for every one knows that Cacambo was born in a village of Tucuman where no other language is spoken.

"I will be your interpreter here," said he to Candide, "let us go in; this is an eating-house."

Immediately two waiters, and two servant-girls, dressed in cloth of gold, and their hair braided with ribbons of tissue, accosted the strangers, and invited them to sit down to the ordinary. Their dinner consisted of four dishes of different soups, each garnished with two young paroquets, a large dish of bouille[53] that weighed two hundredweight, two roasted monkeys of a delicious flavor, three hundred humming-birds in one dish, and six hundred fly-birds in another; some excellent ragouts, delicate tarts, and the whole served up in dishes of rock-crystal. Several sorts of liquors, extracted from the sugar-cane, were handed about by the servants who attended.

Most of the company were chapmen and wagoners,[54] all extremely polite: they asked Cacambo a few questions, with the utmost discretion and circumspection; and replied to his in a most obliging and satisfactory manner.

As soon as dinner was over, both Candide and Cacambo thought they would pay very handsomely for their entertainment by laying down two of those large gold pieces which they had picked off the ground; but the landlord and landlady burst into a fit of laughing and held their sides for some time before they were able to speak.

"Gentlemen," said the landlord, "I plainly perceive you are strangers, and such we are not accustomed to see; pardon us, therefore, for laughing when you offered us the common pebbles of our highways for payment of your reckoning. To be sure, you have none of the coin of this kingdom; but there is no necessity to have any money at all to dine in this house. All the inns, which are established for the convenience of those who carry on the trade of this nation, are maintained by the government. You have found but very indifferent entertainment here, because this is only a poor village; but in almost every other of these public houses you will meet with a reception worthy of persons of your merit."

Cacambo explained the whole of this speech of the landlord to Candide, who listened to it with the same astonishment with which his friend communicated it.

"What sort of a country is this," said the one to the other, "that is unknown to all the world, and in which Nature has everywhere so different an appearance from what she has in ours? Possibly this is that part of the globe where everything is right, for there must certainly be some such place; and, for all the Master Pangloss could say, I often perceived that things went very ill in Westphalia."

CHAPTER XVIII

What they saw in the country of El Dorado.

Cacambo vented all his curiosity upon the landlord by a thousand different questions.

The honest man answered him thus: "I am very ignorant, Sir, but I am contented with my ignorance; however, we have in this neighborhood an old man retired from court, who is the most learned and communicative person in the whole kingdom."

[53] Stew. [54] Merchants and wagondrivers.

He then directed Cacambo to the old man; Candide acted now only a second character, and attended his servant. They entered a quite plain house, for the door was nothing but silver, and the ceiling was only of beaten gold, but wrought in so elegant a taste as to vie with the richest. The antechamber, indeed, was only encrusted with rubies and emeralds; but the order in which everything was disposed made amends for this great simplicity.

The old man received the strangers on a sofa, which was stuffed with humming-birds' feathers; and ordered his servants to present them with liquors in golden goblets, after which he satisfied their curiosity in the following terms:

"I am now one hundred and seventy-two years old; and I learned of my late father who was equerry to the king the amazing revolutions of Peru, to which he had been an eye-witness. This kingdom is the ancient patrimony of the Incas, who very imprudently quitted it to conquer another part of the world, and were at length conquered and destroyed themselves by the Spaniards.

"Those princes of their family who remained in their native country acted more wisely. They ordained, with the consent of their whole nation, that none of the inhabitants of our little kingdom should ever quit it; and to this wise ordinance we owe the preservation of our innocence and happiness. The Spaniards had some confused notion of this country, to which they gave the name of El Dorado; and Sir Walter Raleigh, an Englishman, actually came very near it, about a hundred years ago:[55] but the inaccessible rocks and precipices with which our country is surrounded on all sides have hitherto secured us from the rapacious fury of the people of Europe, who have an unaccountable fondness for the pebbles and dirt of our land, for the sake of which they would murder us all to the very last man."

The conversation lasted some time and turned chiefly on the form of government, the customs, the women, the public diversions, and the arts. At length, Candide, who had always had a taste for metaphysics, asked whether the people of that country had any religion.

The old man reddened a little at this question.

"Can you doubt it?" said he. "Do you take us for wretches lost to all sense of gratitude?"

Cacambo asked in a respectful manner what was the established religion of El Dorado. The old man blushed again.

"Can there be two religions then?" he said. "Ours, I apprehend, is the religion of the whole world; we worship God from morning till night."

"Do you worship but one God?" said Cacambo, who still acted as the interpreter of Candide's doubts.

"Certainly," said the old man; "there are not two, nor three, nor four Gods. I must confess the people of your world ask very extraordinary questions."

However, Candide could not refrain from making many more inquiries

[55] The myth of El Dorado, the land of gold, was very widespread. Sir Walter Raleigh explored the Orinoco River in 1595 and again in 1616, in search of this mythical land.

of the old man; he wanted to know in what manner they prayed to God in El Dorado.

"We do not pray to him at all," said the reverend sage; "we have nothing to ask of him, he has given us all we want, and we give him thanks incessantly."

Candide had a curiosity to see some of their priests, and desired Cacambo to ask the old man where they were.

At this he, smiling, said, "My friends, we are all of us priests; the King and all the heads of families sing solemn hymns of thanksgiving every morning, accompanied by five or six thousand musicians."

"What!" said Cacambo, "have you no monks among you, to dispute, to govern, to intrigue, and to burn people who are not of the same opinion with themselves?"

"Do you take us for fools?" said the old man. "Here we are all of one opinion, and know not what you mean by your monks."

During the whole of this discourse Candide was in raptures, and he said to himself:

"What a prodigious difference is there between this place and Westphalia, and this house and the Baron's castle! If our friend Pangloss had seen El Dorado, he would no longer have said that the castle of Thunder-ten-Tronckh was the finest of all possible edifices: there is nothing like seeing the world, that's certain."

This long conversation being ended, the old man ordered six sheep to be harnessed, and put to the coach, and sent twelve of his servants to escort the travellers to Court.

"Excuse me," said he, "for not waiting on you in person; my age deprives me of that honor. The King will receive you in such a manner that you will have no reason to complain; and doubtless you will make a proper allowance for the customs of the country, if they should not happen altogether to please you."

Candide and Cacambo got into the coach, the six sheep flew, and in less than a quarter of an hour they arrived at the King's palace, which was situated at the further end of the capital. At the entrance was a portal two hundred and twenty feet high, and one hundred wide; but it is impossible for words to express the materials of which it was built. The reader, however, will readily conceive they must have a prodigious superiority over the pebbles and sand which we call gold and precious stones.

Twenty beautiful young virgins-in-waiting received Candide and Cacambo at their alighting from the coach, conducted them to the bath, and clad them in robes woven of the down of humming-birds; after this they were introduced by the great officers of the crown of both sexes to the King's apartment, between two files of musicians, each file consisting of a thousand, according to the custom of the country. When they drew near to the presence chamber, Cacambo asked one of the officers in what manner they were to pay their obeisance to his Majesty: whether it was the custom to fall upon their knees, or to prostrate themselves upon the ground? whether they were to put their hands upon their heads, or behind their backs? whether they were to lick the dust off the floor? in short, what was the ceremony usual on such occasions?

"The custom," said the great officer, "is to embrace the King, and kiss him on each cheek."

Candide and Cacambo accordingly threw their arms round his Majesty's neck; and he received them in the most gracious manner imaginable, and very politely asked them to sup with him.

While supper was preparing, orders were given to show them the city, where they saw public structures that reared their lofty heads to the clouds; the market-places decorated with a thousand columns; fountains of spring water, besides others of rose water, and of liquors drawn from the sugar-cane, incessantly flowing in the great squares; these were paved with a kind of precious stone that emitted an odor like that of cloves and cinnamon. Candide asked to see the high court of justice, the parliament; but was answered that they have none in that country, being utter strangers to lawsuits. He then inquired if they had any prisons; they replied, "None." But what gave him at once the greatest surprise and pleasure was the Palace of Sciences, where he saw a gallery two thousand feet long, filled with the various apparatus of mathematics and natural philosophy.

After having spent the whole afternoon in seeing only about the thousandth part of the city, they were brought back to the King's palace. Candide sat down at the table with his Majesty, his servant Cacambo, and several ladies of the Court. Never was entertainment more elegant, nor could any one possibly show more wit than his Majesty displayed while they were at supper. Cacambo explained all the King's *bons mots*[56] to Candide, and although they were translated they still appeared to be *bons mots*. Of all the things that surprised Candide, this was not the least. They spent a whole month in this hospitable place, during which time Candide was continually saying to Cacambo:

"I own, my friend, once more, that the castle where I was born is a mere nothing in comparison with the place where we now are; but still Miss Cunegund is not here, and you yourself have doubtless some mistress in Europe. If we remain here, we shall only be as others are: whereas, if we return to our own world with only a dozen of El Dorado sheep, loaded with the pebbles of this country, we shall be richer than all the kings in Europe; we shall no longer need to stand in awe of the Inquisitors; and we may easily recover Miss Cunegund."

This speech pleased Cacambo. A fondness for roving, for making a figure in their own country, and for boasting of what they had seen in their travels, was so strong in our two wanderers that they resolved to be no longer happy; and demanded permission of his Majesty to quit the country.

"You are about to do a rash and silly action," said the King; "I am sensible my kingdom is an inconsiderable spot; but when people are tolerably at their ease in any place, I should think it would be their interest to remain there. Most assuredly, I have no right to detain you or any strangers against your wills; this is an act of tyranny to which our manners and our laws are equally repugnant: all men are free; you have an undoubted liberty to depart whenever you please, but you will have many difficulties in

[56] Witticisms.

passing the frontiers. It is impossible to ascend that rapid river which runs under high and vaulted rocks, and by which you were conveyed hither by a miracle. The mountains by which my kingdom is hemmed in on all sides are ten thousand feet high, and perfectly perpendicular; they are above ten leagues over each, and the descent from them is one continued precipice. However, since you are determined to leave us, I will immediately give orders to the superintendent of machines to cause one to be made that will convey you safely. When they have conducted you to the back of the mountains, nobody can attend you further; for my subjects have made a vow never to quit the kingdom, and they are too prudent to break it. Ask me whatever else you please."

"All we shall ask of your Majesty," said Cacambo, "is a few sheep laden with provisions, pebbles, and the clay of your country."

The King smiled at the request, and said, "I cannot imagine what pleasure you Europeans find in our yellow clay; but take away as much of it as you will, and much good may it do you."

He immediately gave orders to his engineers to make a machine to hoist these two extraordinary men out of the kingdom. Three thousand good mathematicians went to work and finished it in about fifteen days; and it did not cost more than twenty millions sterling of that country's money. Candide and Cacambo were placed on this machine, and they took with them two large red sheep, bridled and saddled, to ride upon when they got on the other side of the mountains; twenty others to serve as pack-horses for carrying provisions; thirty laden with presents of whatever was most curious in the country; and fifty with gold, diamonds, and other precious stones. The King embraced the two wanderers with the greatest cordiality.

It was a curious sight to behold the manner of their setting off, and the ingenious method by which they and their sheep were hoisted to the top of the mountains. The mathematicians and engineers took leave of them as soon as they had conveyed them to a place of safety, and Candide was wholly occupied with the thoughts of presenting his sheep to Miss Cunegund.

"Now," said he, "thanks to heaven, we have more than sufficient to pay the Governor of Buenos Ayres for Miss Cunegund, if she is redeemable. Let us make the best of our way to Cayenne, where we will take ship, and then we may at leisure think of what kingdom we shall purchase."

CHAPTER XIX

What happened to them at Surinam, and how Candide became acquainted with Martin.

Our travellers' first day's journey was very pleasant; they were elated with the prospect of possessing more riches than were to be found in Europe, Asia, and Africa together. Candide, in amorous transports, cut the name of Miss Cunegund on the trees. The second day, two of their sheep sank into a morass, and were swallowed up with their loads; two more died of fatigue some few days afterwards; seven or eight perished with hunger in a desert, and others, at different times, tumbled down precipices; so that, after travelling about a hundred days, they had only two sheep left.

Said Candide to Cacambo, "You see, my dear friend, how perishable the riches of this world are; there is nothing solid but virtue and the joy of seeing Miss Cunegund again."

"Very true," said Cacambo; "but we have still two sheep remaining, with more treasure than ever the King of Spain will be possessed of; and I espy a town at a distance, which I take to be Surinam, a town belonging to the Dutch. We are now at the end of our troubles, and at the beginning of happiness."

As they drew near the town, they saw a negro stretched on the ground with only one half of his habit, which was a pair of blue cotton drawers; for the poor man had lost his left leg, and his right hand.

"Good God," said Candide in Dutch, "what dost thou here, friend, in this deplorable condition?"

"I am waiting for my master Mynheer Vanderdendur, the famous trader," answered the negro.

"Was it Mynheer Vanderdendur that used you in this cruel manner?"

"Yes, Sir," said the negro; "it is the custom here. They give a pair of cotton drawers twice a year, and that is all our covering. When we labor in the sugar-works, and the mill happens to snatch hold of a finger, they instantly chop off our hand; and when we attempt to run away, they cut off a leg. Both these cases have happened to me, and it is at this expense that you eat sugar in Europe; and yet when my mother sold me for ten pattacoons on the coast of Guinea, she said to me, "My dear child, bless our fetishes;[57] adore them for ever; they will make thee live happy; thou hast the honor to be a slave to our lords the whites, by which thou wilt make the fortune of us thy parents." Alas! I know not whether I have made their fortunes; but they have not made mine: dogs, monkeys, and parrots, are a thousand times less wretched than me. The Dutch fetishes who converted me tell me every Sunday that, blacks and whites, we are all children of Adam. As for me, I do not understand anything of genealogies; but if what these preachers say is true, we are all second cousins; and you must allow, that it is impossible to be worse treated by our relations than we are."

"O Pangloss!" cried out Candide, "such horrid doings never entered thy imagination. Here is an end of the matter; I find myself, after all, obliged to renounce thy Optimism."

"Optimism!" said Cacambo, "what is that?"

"Alas!" replied Candide, "it is the obstinacy of maintaining that everything is best when it is worst": and so saying, he turned his eyes towards the poor negro, and shed a flood of tears; and in this weeping mood he entered the town of Surinam.

Immediately upon their arrival, our travellers inquired if there was any vessel in the harbor which they might send to Buenos Ayres. The person they addressed themselves to happened to be the master of a Spanish bark, who offered to agree with them on moderate terms, and appointed them a

[57] Priests.

meeting at a public-house. Thither Candide and his faithful Cacambo went to wait for him, taking with them their two sheep.

Candide, who was all frankness and sincerity, made an ingenuous recital of his adventures to the Spaniard, declaring to him at the same time his resolution of carrying off Miss Cunegund.

"In that case," said the shipmaster, "I'll take good care not to take you to Bueno Ayres. It would prove a hanging matter to us all. The fair Cunegund is the Governor's favorite mistress."

These words were like a clap of thunder to Candide; he wept bitterly for a long time, and, taking Cacambo aside, he said to him:

"I'll tell you, my dear friend, what you must do. We have each of us in our pockets to the value of five or six millions in diamonds; you are cleverer at these matters than I; you must go to Buenos Ayres and bring off Miss Cunegund. If the Governor makes any difficulty, give him a million; if he holds out, give him two; as you have not killed an Inquisitor, they will have no suspicion of you: I'll fit out another ship and go to Venice, where I will wait for you. Venice is a free country, where we shall have nothing to fear from Bulgarians, Abares, Jews, or Inquisitors."

Cacambo greatly applauded this wise resolution. He was inconsolable at the thought of parting with so good a master, who treated him more like an intimate friend than a servant; but the pleasure of being able to do him a service soon got the better of his sorrow. They embraced each other with a flood of tears. Candide charged him not to forget the old woman. Cacambo set out the same day. This Cacambo was a very honest fellow.

Candide continued some days longer at Surinam, waiting for any captain to carry him and his two remaining sheep to Italy. He hired domestics and purchased many things necessary for a long voyage; at length, Mynheer Vanderdendur, skipper of a large Dutch vessel, came and offered his service.

"What will you take," said Candide, "to carry me, my servants, my baggage, and these two sheep you see here, direct to Venice?"

The skipper asked ten thousand piastres; and Candide agreed to his demand without hesitation.

"Oh, ho!" said the cunning Vanderdendur to himself, "this stranger must be very rich; he agrees to give me ten thousand piastres without hesitation."

Returning a little while after, he told Candide that upon second consideration he could not undertake the voyage for less than twenty thousand.

"Very well, you shall have them," said Candide.

"Zounds!" said the skipper to himself, "this man agrees to pay twenty thousand piastres with as much ease as ten."

Accordingly he went back again, and told him roundly that he would not carry him to Venice for less than thirty thousand piastres.

"Then you shall have thirty thousand," said Candide.

"Odso!" said the Dutchman once more to himself, "thirty thousand piastres seem a trifle to this man. Those sheep must certainly be laden with an immense treasure. I'll stop here and ask no more; but make him pay down the thirty thousand piastres, and then we shall see."

Candide sold two small diamonds, the least of which was worth more than all the skipper asked. He paid him before-hand, and the two sheep were put on board, and Candide followed in a small boat to join the vessel in the road. The skipper took his opportunity, hoisted his sails, and put out to sea with a favorable wind. Candide, confounded and amazed, soon lost sight of the ship.

"Alas!" said he, "this is a trick like those in our old world!"

He returned back to the shore overwhelmed with grief; and, indeed, he had lost what would have been the fortune of twenty monarchs.

Immediately upon his landing, he applied to the Dutch magistrate: being transported with passion, he thundered at the door; which being opened, he went in, told his case, and talked a little louder than necessary. The magistrate began with fining him ten thousand piastres for his petulance, and then listened very patiently to what he had to say, promised to examine into the affair at the skipper's return, and ordered him to pay ten thousand piastres more for the fees of the court.

This treatment put Candide out of all patience: it is true, he had suffered misfortunes a thousand times more grievous; but the cool insolence of the judge and of the skipper who robbed him raised his choler and threw him into a deep melancholy. The villainy of mankind presented itself to his mind in all its deformity, and his soul was a prey to the most gloomy ideas. After some time, hearing that the captain of a French ship was ready to set sail for Bordeaux, as he had no more sheep loaded with diamonds to put on board, he hired the cabin at the usual price; and made it known in the town that he would pay the passage and board of any honest man who would give him his company during the voyage; besides making him a present of ten thousand piastres, on condition that such person was the most dissatisfied with his condition and the most unfortunate in the whole province.

Upon this there appeared such a crowd of candidates that a large fleet could not have contained them. Candide, willing to choose from among those who appeared most likely to answer his intention, selected twenty, who seemed to him the most sociable, and who all pretended to merit the preference. He invited them to his inn, and promised to treat them with a supper, on condition that every man should bind himself by an oath to relate his own history. He declared at the same time that he would make choice of that person who should appear to him the most deserving of compassion, and the most justly dissatisfied with his condition of life; and that he would make a present to the rest.

This extraordinary assembly continued sitting till four in the morning. Candide, while he was listening to their adventures, called to mind what the old woman had said to him on their voyage to Buenos Ayres, and the wager she had laid that there was not a person on board the ship but had met with some great misfortune. Every story he heard put him in mind of Pangloss.

"My old master," said he, "would be confoundedly put to it to demonstrate his favorite system. Would he were here! Certainly if everything is for the best, it is in El Dorado, and not in the other parts of the world."

At length he determined in favor of a poor scholar who had labored ten years for the booksellers at Amsterdam, being of opinion that no employment could be more detestable.

This scholar, who was in fact a very honest man, had been robbed by his wife, beaten by his son, and forsaken by his daughter, who had run away with a Portuguese. He had been likewise deprived of a small employment on which he subsisted, and he was persecuted by the clergy of Surinam, who took him for a Socinian.[58] It must be acknowledged that the other competitors were, at least, as wretched as he; but Candide was in hopes that the company of a man of letters would relieve the tediousness of the voyage. All the other candidates complained that Candide had done them great injustice; but he stopped their mouths by a present of a hundred piastres to each.

CHAPTER XX

What befell Candide and Martin on their voyage.

The old scholar, whose name was Martin, took shipping with Candide for Bordeaux. They both had seen and suffered a great deal; and if the ship had been destined to sail from Surinam to Japan round the Cape of Good Hope, they could have found sufficient entertainment for each other during the whole voyage in discoursing upon moral and natural evil.

Candide, however, had one advantage over Martin: he lived in the pleasing hopes of seeing Miss Cunegund once more; whereas the poor philosopher had nothing to hope for. Besides, Candide had money and jewels, and, notwithstanding he had lost a hundred red sheep, laden with the greatest treasure on the earth, and though he still smarted from the reflection of the Dutch skipper's knavery, yet when he considered what he had still left, and repeated the name of Cunegund, especially after mealtimes, he inclined to Pangloss's doctrine.

"And pray," said he to Martin, "what is your opinion of the whole of this system? What notion have you of moral and natural evil?"

"Sir," replied Martin, "our priests accused me of being a Socinian; but the real truth is, I am a Manichaean."[59]

"Nay, now you are jesting," said Candide; "there are no Manichaeans existing at present in the world."

"And yet I am one," said Martin; "but I cannot help it; I cannot for the soul of me think otherwise."

"Surely the devil must be in you," said Candide.

"He concerns himself so much," replied Martin, "in the affairs of this world that it is very probable he may be in me as well as everywhere else; but I must confess, when I cast my eye on this globe, or rather globule, I cannot help thinking that God has abandoned it to some malignant being. I always except El Dorado. I scarce ever knew a city that did not wish the destruction of its neighboring city; nor a family that did not desire to exterminate some other family. The poor, in all parts of the world, bear an

[58] Follower of a rationalist, anti-Trinitarian religious system, founded by the sixteenth-century Polish reformers Laelius and Faustus Socinus.

[59] Manichaeanism was a religion founded by a third-century Persian named Mani, who taught that the world was ruled by two powers, one good and one evil.

inveterate hatred to the rich, even while they creep and cringe to them; and the rich treat the poor like sheep, whose wool and flesh they barter for money: a million of regimented assassins traverse Europe from one end to the other to get their bread by regular depredation and murder, because it is the most gentleman-like profession. Even in those cities which seem to enjoy the blessings of peace, and where the arts flourish, the inhabitants are devoured with envy, care, and anxiety, which are greater plagues than any experienced in a town besieged. Private chagrins are still more dreadful than public calamities. In a word, I have seen and suffered so much, that I am a Manichaean."

"And yet there is some good in the world," replied Candide.

"May be," said Martin, "but it has escaped my knowledge."

While they were deeply engaged in this dispute they heard the report of cannon, which redoubled every moment. Each took out his glass, and they espied two ships warmly engaged at the distance of about three miles. The wind brought them both so near the French ship that those on board her had the pleasure of seeing the fight with great ease. At last one of the two vessels gave the other a shot between wind and water, which sank her outright. Then could Candide and Martin plainly perceive a hundred men on the deck of the vessel which was sinking, who, with hands uplifted to heaven, sent forth piercing cries, and were in a moment swallowed up by the waves.

"Well," said Martin, "you now see in what manner mankind treat each other."

"It is certain," said Candide, "that there is something diabolical in this affair."

As he was speaking thus, he saw something of a shining red hue, which swam close to the vessel. The boat was hoisted out to see what it might be, when it proved to be one of his sheep. Candide felt more joy at the recovery of this one animal than he did grief when he lost the other hundred, though laden with the large diamonds of El Dorado.

The French captain quickly perceived that the victorious ship belonged to the crown of Spain; that the other which sank was a Dutch pirate, and the very same captain who had robbed Candide. The immense riches which this villain had amassed were buried with him in the deep, and only this one sheep saved out of the whole.

"You see," said Candide to Martin, "that vice is sometimes punished: this villain, the Dutch skipper, has met with the fate he deserved."

"Very true," said Martin; "but why should the passengers be doomed also to destruction? God has punished the knave, and the devil has drowned the rest."

The French and Spanish ships continued their cruise, and Candide and Martin their conversation. They disputed fourteen days successively, at the end of which they were just as far advanced as the first moment they began. However, they had the satisfaction of disputing, of communicating their ideas, and of mutually comforting each other. Candide embraced his sheep.

"Since I have found thee again," said he, "I may possibly find my Cunegund once more."

CHAPTER XXI

Candide and Martin, while thus reasoning with each other, draw near to the coast of France.

At length they sighted the coast of France.

"Pray, Mr. Martin," said Candide, "have you ever been in France?"

"Yes, Sir," said Martin, "I have been in several provinces of that kingdom. In some, one half of the people are madmen; in some, they are too artful; in others, again, they are in general either very good-natured or very brutal; while in others, they affect to be witty, and in all, their ruling passion is love, the next is slander, and the last is to talk nonsense."

"But pray, Mr. Martin, were you ever in Paris?"

"Yes, Sir, I have been in that city, and it is a place that contains the several species just described; it is a chaos, a confused multitude, where everyone seeks for pleasure without being able to find it; at least, as far as I have observed during my short stay in that city. At my arrival, I was robbed of all I had in the world by pickpockets and sharpers, at the fair of St. Germain. I was taken up myself for a robber, and confined in prison a whole week; after that I hired myself as corrector to a press in order to get a little money towards defraying my expenses back to Holland on foot. I knew the whole tribe of scribblers, malcontents, and religious convulsionaries.[60] It is said the people of that city are very polite; I believe that may be so."

"For my part, I have no curiosity to see France," said Candide, "you may easily conceive, my friend, that, after spending a month at El Dorado, I can desire to behold nothing upon earth but Miss Cunegund; I am going to wait for her at Venice; I intend to pass through France on my way to Italy; will you not bear me company?"

"With all my heart," said Martin: "they say Venice is agreeable to none but noble Venetians; but that, nevertheless, strangers are well received there when they have plenty of money; now I have none, but you have, therefore I will attend you wherever you please."

"Now we are upon this subject," said Candide, "do you think that the earth was originally sea, as we read in that great book[61] which belongs to the captain of the ship?"

"I believe nothing of it," replied Martin, "any more than I do of the many other chimeras which have been related to us for some time past."

"But then, to what end," said Candide, "was the world formed?"

"To make us mad," said Martin.

"Are you not surprised," continued Candide, "at the love which the two girls in the country of the Oreillons had for those two monkeys?—You know I have told you the story."

"Surprised!" replied Martin, "not in the least; I see nothing strange in

[60] The "religious convulsionaries" were Jansenists, a conservative Catholic sect whose members made public display of their spiritual ecstasies.

[61] The "great book" is the Bible, which in Genesis describes the earth as originally covered with water.

this passion. I have seen so many extraordinary things, that there is nothing extraordinary to me now."

"Do you think," said Candide, "that mankind always massacred each other as they do now? Were they always guilty of lies, fraud, treachery, ingratitude, inconstancy, envy, ambition, and cruelty? Were they always thieves, fools, cowards, gluttons, drunkards, misers, calumniators, debauchees, fanatics, and hypocrites?"

"Do you believe," said Martin, "that hawks have always been accustomed to eat pigeons when they came in their way?"

"Doubtless," said Candide.

"Well, then," replied Martin, "if hawks have always had the same nature, why should you pretend that mankind change theirs?"

"Oh!" said Candide, "there is a great deal of difference, for free will . . ."

Reasoning thus, they arrived at Bordeaux.

CHAPTER XXII

What happened to Candide and Martin in France.

Candide stayed no longer at Bordeaux than was necessary to dispose of a few of the pebbles he had brought from El Dorado, and to provide himself with a post-chaise for two persons, for he could no longer stir a step without his philosopher Martin. The only thing that gave him concern was the being obliged to leave his sheep behind him, which he entrusted to the care of the Academy of Sciences at Bordeaux. The academicians proposed, as a prize-subject for the year, to prove why the wool of this sheep was red; and the prize was adjudged to a northern sage,[62] who demonstrated by A plus B, minus C, divided by Z, that the sheep must necessarily be red, and die of the rot.

In the meantime, all the travellers whom Candide met with in the inns, or on the road, told him to a man that they were going to Paris. This general eagerness gave him likewise a great desire to see this capital, and it was not much out of his way to Venice.

He entered the city by the suburbs of St. Marceau, and thought himself in one of the vilest hamlets in all Westphalia.

Candide had not been long at his inn before he was seized with a slight disorder owing to the fatigue he had undergone. As he wore a diamond of an enormous size on his finger, and had, among the rest of his equipage, a strong box that seemed very weighty, he soon found himself between two physicians whom he had not sent for, a number of intimate friends whom he had never seen, and who would not quit his bedside, and two female devotees who warmed his soup for him.

"I remember," said Martin to him, "that the first time I came to Paris I was likewise taken ill; I was very poor, and, accordingly, I had neither friends, nurses, nor physicians, and yet I did very well."

[62] The "northern sage" is Maupertius Le Lapon, who was said to prove the existence of God by mathematics.

However, by dint of purging and bleeding Candide's disorder became very serious. The priest of the parish came with all imaginable politeness to desire a note of him, payable to the bearer in the other world.[63] Candide refused to comply with his request; but the two devotees assured him that it was a new fashion. Candide replied that he was not one that followed the fashion. Martin was for throwing the priest out of the window. The clerk swore Candide should not have Christian burial. Martin swore in turn that he would bury the clerk alive, if he continued to plague them any longer. The dispute grew warm; Martin took him by the shoulders, and turned him out of the room, which gave great scandal, and occasioned a lawsuit.

Candide recovered; and, till he was in a condition to go abroad, had a great deal of very good company to pass the evenings with him in his chamber. They played deep.[64] Candide was surprised to find he could never turn a trick; and Martin was not at all surprised at the matter.

Among those who did him the honors of the place was a little spruce Abbé from Périgord, one of those insinuating, busy, fawning, impudent, accommodating fellows that lie in wait for strangers at their arrival, tell them all the scandal of the town, and offer to minister to their pleasures at various prices. This man conducted Candide and Martin to the playhouse: they were acting a new tragedy. Candide found himself placed near a cluster of wits: this, however, did not prevent him from shedding tears at some scenes which were perfectly acted. One of these talkers said to him between the acts:

"You are greatly to blame in shedding tears; that actress plays horribly, and the man that plays with her still worse, and the piece itself is still more execrable than the representation. The author does not understand a word of Arabic, and yet he has laid his scene in Arabia; and what is more, he is a fellow who does not believe in innate ideas.[65] To-morrow I will bring you a score of pamphlets that have been written against him."

"Pray, Sir," said Candide to the Abbé, "how many theatrical pieces have you in France?"

"Five or six thousand," replied the other.

"Indeed! that is a great number," said Candide: "but how many good ones may there be?"

"About fifteen or sixteen."

"Oh! that is a great number," said Martin.

Candide was greatly taken with an actress who performed the part of Queen Elizabeth in a dull kind of tragedy that is played sometimes.[66]

"That actress," said he to Martin, "pleases me greatly; she has some sort of resemblance to Miss Cunegund. I should be very glad to pay my respects to her."

The Abbé of Périgord offered his services to introduce him to her at her own house. Candide, who was brought up in Germany, desired to

[63] *Billets de confession* were required of seriously ill persons in eighteenth-century France. These authorized a priest to give such persons the last rites and bury them in consecrated ground.

[64] A card game.

[65] Descartes believed that certain ideas were innate rather than acquired; Locke denied that any ideas were innate. Neither theory, of course, has anything to do with tragedy.

[66] Thomas Corneille's *The Earl of Essex* (1678).

know what might be the ceremonial used on those occasions, and how a Queen of England was treated in France.

"There is a necessary distinction to be observed in these matters," said the Abbé. "In a country town we take them to a tavern; here in Paris, they are treated with great respect during their lifetime, provided they are handsome, and when they die, we throw their bodies upon a dunghill."[67]

"How," said Candide, "throw a queen's body upon a dunghill!"

"The gentleman is quite right," said Martin; "he tells you nothing but the truth. I happened to be in Paris when Mlle. Monime made her exit, as one may say, out of this world into another.[68] She was refused what they call here the rights of sepulture; that is to say, she was denied the privilege of rotting in a churchyard by the side of all the beggars in the parish. She was buried alone by her troupe at the corner of Burgundy Street, which must certainly have shocked her extremely, as she had very exalted notions of things."

"This is acting very impolitely," said Candide.

"Lord!" said Martin, "what can be said to it? It is the way of these people. Figure to yourself all the contradictions, all the inconsistencies possible, and you may meet with them in the government, the courts of justice, the churches, and the public spectacles of this odd nation."

"Is it true," said Candide, "that the people of Paris are always laughing?"

"Yes," replied the Abbé, "but it is with anger in their hearts; they express all their complaints by loud bursts of laughter, and commit the most detestable crimes with a smile on their faces."

"Who was that great overgrown beast," said Candide, "who spoke so ill to me of the piece with which I was so much affected, and of the players who gave me so much pleasure?"

"A good-for-nothing sort of a man," answered the Abbé, "one who gets his livelihood by abusing every new book and play; he abominates to see anyone meet with success, like eunuchs, who detest every one that possesses those powers they are deprived of; he is one of those vipers in literature who nourish themselves with their own venom; a pamphlet-monger."

"A pamphlet-monger!" said Candide, "what is that?"

"Why, a pamphlet-monger," replied the Abbé, "is a writer of pamphlets, a Fréron."[69]

Candide, Martin, and the Abbé of Périgord argued thus on the staircase, while they stood to see people go out of the playhouse.

"Though I am very earnest to see Miss Cunegund again," said Candide, "yet I have a great inclination to sup with Mlle. Clairon,[70] for I am really much taken with her."

[67] Voltaire campaigned vigorously against the ban on burying actors and actresses in consecrated ground.

[68] "Mlle. Monime" was Adrienne Lecouvreur (1690–1730), who made her debut as Monime in Racine's *Mithridate* and became the greatest tragic actress of her age. Voltaire's "Ode on the death of Mlle. Lecouvreur" protests the Church's refusal to allow her to be buried in holy ground; he was present at her secret, midnight funeral.

[69] Fréron was a journalist who had attacked Voltaire's plays.

[70] Mlle. Clairon was Claire Leris, an actress who had performed in Voltaire's plays.

The Abbé was not a person to show his face at this lady's house, which was frequented by none but the best company.

"She is engaged this evening," said he; "but I will do myself the honor of introducing you to a lady of quality of my acquaintance, at whose house you will see as much of the manners of Paris as if you had lived here for four years."

Candide, who was naturally curious, suffered himself to be conducted to this lady's house, which was in the suburb of St. Honoré. The company were engaged at faro;[71] twelve melancholy punters held each in his hand a small pack of cards, the corners of which doubled down were so many registers of their ill-fortune. A profound silence reigned throughout the assembly, a pallid dread was in the countenances of the punters, and restless anxiety in the face of him who kept the bank; and the lady of the house, who was seated next to him, observed pitilessly with lynx's eyes every parole, and sept-et-la-va as they were going, as likewise those who tallied, and made them undouble their cards with a severe exactness, though mixed with a politeness which she thought necessary not to frighten away her customers. This lady assumed the title of Marchioness of Parolignac. Her daughter, a girl of about fifteen years of age, was one of the punters, and took care to give her mamma an item, by signs, when any one of them attempted to repair the rigor of their ill fortune by a little innocent deception. The company were thus occupied, when Candide, Martin, and the Abbé made their entrance: not a creature rose to salute them, or indeed took the least notice of them, being wholly intent upon the business in hand.

"Ah!" said Candide, "my lady Baroness of Thunder-ten-tronckh would have behaved more civilly."

However, the Abbé whispered in the ear of the marchioness, who half rose, and honored Candide with a gracious smile and Martin with a dignified inclination of her head. She then ordered a seat for Candide and a hand of cards. He lost fifty thousand francs in two rounds. After that, they supped very elegantly, and every one was astounded that Candide was not disturbed at his loss. The servants said to each other in their servants' language:

"This must be some English lord!"

Supper was like most others of this kind in Paris; at first there was silence, then there was an indistinguishable babel of words, then jokes, most of them insipid, false reports, bad reasonings, a little political talk, and much scandal. They spoke also of new books.

"Have you seen," said the Abbé of Périgord, "the romance written by Monsieur Gauchat, the doctor of theology?"[72]

"Yes," replied one of the guests, "but I had not the patience to go through it. We have a throng of impertinent writers, but all of them together do not approach Gauchat, the doctor of theology, in impertinence. I

[71] A card game. The players are called "punters" and they bet against the banker. A "parole" is an illegal doubling of one's bet. (Hence the lady's title of "Marchioness of Parolignac.") A "sept-et-la-va" is a bet at high odds, and "tallying" is folding down a card as a signal.

[72] Another literary enemy of Voltaire's.

am so sated with reading these piles of vile stuff that flood upon us that I even resolved to come here and make a party at faro."

"But what say you to Archdeacon Trublet's miscellanies?"[73] said the Abbé.

"Oh," cried the Marchioness of Parolignac, "tedious creature. What pains he is at to tell one things that all the world knows. How he labors an argument that is hardly the slightest consideration! How absurdly he makes use of other people's wit! How he mangles what he pilfers from them! How he disgusts me! But he will disgust me no more. It is enough to have read a few pages of the Archdeacon."

There was at the table a person of learning and taste, who supported what the Marchioness had advanced. They next began to talk of tragedies. The lady desired to know how it came about that there were several tragedies which still continued to be played, but which were unreadable. The man of taste explained very clearly how a piece may be in some manner interesting, without having a grain of merit. He showed, in a few words, that it is not sufficient to throw together a few incidents that are to be met with in every romance, and that dazzle the spectator; the thoughts should be new without being far-fetched; frequently sublime, but always natural; the author should have a thorough knowledge of the human heart and make it speak properly. He should be a complete poet, without showing an affectation of it in any of the characters of his piece; he should be a perfect master of his language, speak it with all its purity, and with the utmost harmony, and yet not so as to make the sense a slave to the rhyme.

"Whoever," added he, "neglects any of these rules, though he may write two or three tragedies with tolerable success, will never be reckoned in the number of good authors. There are a few good tragedies, some are idylls, in well-written and harmonious dialogue, and others a chain of political reasonings that send one to sleep, or else pompous and high-flown amplifications that disgust rather than please. Others again are the ravings of a madman, in an uncouth style, with unmeaning flights, or long apostrophes, to the deities, for want of knowing how to address mankind; in a word, a collection of false maxims and dull commonplaces."

Candide listened to this discourse with great attention, and conceived a high opinion for the person who delivered it; and as the Marchioness had taken care to place him at her side, he took the liberty to whisper softly in her ear and ask who this person was who spoke so well.

"It is a man of letters," replied her ladyship, "who never plays and whom the Abbé brings with him to my house sometimes to spend an evening. He is a great judge of writing, especially in tragedy; he has composed one himself which was damned, and has written a book which was never seen out of his bookseller's shop, excepting only one copy, which he sent me with a dedication."

"What a great man," cried Candide, "he is a second Pangloss."

Then, turning towards him, "Sir," said he, "you are doubtless of the opinion that everything is for the best in the physical and moral world and that nothing could be otherwise than it is?"

"I, Sir," replied the man of letters, "I think no such thing, I assure you. I

[73] Trublet had also attacked Voltaire's writing.

find that all in this world is set the wrong end uppermost. No one knows what is his rank, his office, nor what he does, nor what he should do; and that except for our evenings which we generally pass tolerably merrily, the rest of our time is spent in idle disputes and quarrels, Jansenists against Molinists,[74] the Parliament against the Church, men of letters against men of letters, countries against countries, financiers against the people, wives against husbands, relations against relations. In short, there is eternal warfare."

"Yes," said Candide, "and I have seen worse than all that; and yet a learned man, who had the misfortune to be hanged, taught me that everything was marvellously well, and that these evils you are speaking of were only so many shadows in a beautiful picture."

"Your hempen sage," said Martin, "laughed at you. These shadows as you call them are most horrible blemishes."

"It is men who make these blemishes," rejoined Candide, "and they cannot do otherwise."

"Then it is not their fault," added Martin.

The great part of the gamesters, who did not understand a syllable of this discourse, continued to drink, while Martin reasoned with the learned gentleman, and Candide recounted some of his adventures to the lady of the house.

After supper, the Marchioness conducted Candide into her dressing-room, and made him sit down on a sofa.

"Well," said she, "are you still so violently fond of Miss Cunegund of Thunder-ten-tronckh?"

"Yes, Madam," replied Candide.

The Marchioness said to him with a tender smile, "You answer like a young man from Westphalia. A Frenchman would have said 'It is true, Madam, I had a great passion for Miss Cunegund, but since I have seen you, I fear I can no longer love her as I did.' "

"Alas! Madam," replied Candide, "I'll make you what answer you please."

"You fell in love with her, I find, in picking up her handkerchief. You shall pick up my garter."

"With all my heart," said Candide.

"But you must tie it on," said the lady; and Candide tied it on.

"Look you," said the lady, "you are a stranger. I make some of my lovers here in Paris languish for me a fortnight, but I surrender to you the first night, because I am willing to do the honors of my country to a young Westphalian."

The fair one having cast her eye on two large diamonds on the young stranger's finger, praised them in so earnest a manner that they passed from Candide's fingers to those of the Marchioness.

As Candide was going home with the Abbé, he felt some qualms of conscience for having been guilty of infidelity to Miss Cunegund. The Abbé shared with him in his uneasiness; he had but an inconsiderable share in the fifty thousand francs that Candide had lost at play, and in the value

[74] For the Jansenists, see footnote 60. The Molinists were the Jesuit party. They differed on the issue of grace and good works in attaining salvation.

of the two jewels, half given, half extorted from him. His plan was to profit as much as he could from the advantages which his acquaintance with Candide could procure for him. He spoke to him much of Miss Cunegund, and Candide assured him that he would heartily ask pardon of that fair one for his infidelity to her, when he saw her at Venice.

The Abbé redoubled his civilities and seemed to interest himself warmly in everything that Candide said, did, or seemed inclined to do.

"And so, Sir, you have a *rendez-vous* at Venice?"

"Yes, Monsieur l'Abbé," answered Candide. "I must indeed go and find Miss Cunegund."

Then the pleasure he took in talking about the object he loved led him insensibly to relate, according to custom, part of his adventures with the illustrious Westphalian beauty.

"I fancy," said the Abbé "Miss Cunegund has a great deal of wit, and that her letters must be very entertaining."

"I never received any from her," said Candide, "for you are to consider that being kicked out of the castle on her account, I could not write to her; especially as, soon after my departure, I heard she was dead; that though I found her again, I lost her, and that I have sent a messenger to her two thousand five hundred leagues from here, and I wait here for his return with an answer from her."

The Abbé listened attentively—and seemed a little thoughtful. He soon took leave of the two strangers, after having embraced them tenderly. The next day, immediately on waking, Candide received a letter couched in these terms:

"My dearest lover, I have been ill in this city these eight days. I have heard of your arrival and should fly to your arms, were I able to move a limb of me. I was informed of your procedure at Bordeaux. I left there the faithful Cacambo and the old woman who will soon follow me. The Governor of Buenos Ayres has taken everything from me; but I still have your heart. Come. Your presence will restore me to life or will make me die with pleasure."

At the receipt of this charming, this unexpected letter, Candide felt the utmost joy, though the malady of his beloved Cunegund overwhelmed him with grief. Distracted between these two passions, he took his gold and his diamonds and procured a person to direct him with Martin to the house where Miss Cunegund lodged. He entered, trembling with emotion, his heart fluttered, his tongue faltered. He attempted to draw the curtain apart, and called for a light to the bedside.

"Take care," said the servant, "the light is unbearable to her"; and immediately she closed the curtains again.

"My beloved," said Candide, weeping, "how are you? If you cannot see me, at least speak to me."

"She cannot speak," said the servant. The lady then put from the bed a plump hand which Candide bathed with his tears; then filled with diamonds, leaving a purse full of gold on the arm-chair.

In the midst of his transports there arrived an officer, followed by the Abbé of Périgord and a file of musketeers.

"There," said he, "are the two suspected foreigners."

He had them seized forthwith and bade the soldiers carry them off to prison.

"Travellers are not treated in this manner in El Dorado," said Candide.

"I am more of a Manichaean now than ever," said Martin.

"But pray, good Sir, where are you taking us?" asked Candide.

"To a dungeon," said the officer.

Martin having recovered his calm judged that the lady who pretended to be Cunegund was a cheat, that the Abbé of Périgord was a sharper, who had imposed upon Candide's simplicity so quickly as he could, and the officer another knave whom they might easily get rid of.

Candide, following the advice of his friend Martin, and burning with impatience to see the real Cunegund, rather than be obliged to appear at a court of justice, proposed to the officer to make him a present of three small diamonds, each of them worth three thousand pistoles.

"Ah, Sir," said this understrapper of justice, "had you committed ever so much villainy, this would render you the honestest man living in my eyes. Three diamonds, worth three thousand pistoles. Why, my dear Sir, so far from leading you to jail, I would lose my life to serve you. There are orders to arrest all strangers, but leave it to me. I have a brother at Dieppe in Normandy. I myself will conduct you thither, and if you have a diamond left to give him, he will take as much care of you as I myself should."

"But why," said Candide, "do they arrest all strangers?"

The Abbé of Périgord answered that it was because a poor devil of the province of Atrébatie heard somebody tell foolish stories, and this induced him to commit a parricide; not such a one as that in the month of May, 1610, but such as that in the month of December in the year 1594, and such as many that have been perpetrated in other months and years by other poor devils who had heard foolish stories.[75]

The officer then explained to them what the Abbé meant.

"Monsters," exclaimed Candide. "Is it possible that such horrors should pass among a people who are continually singing and dancing? Is there no immediate means of flying this abominable country, where monkeys provoke tigers? I have seen bears in my country, but men I have beheld nowhere but in El Dorado. In the name of God, Sir," said he to the officer, "do me the kindness to conduct me to Venice, where I am to wait upon Miss Cunegund."

"I cannot conduct you further than Lower Normandy," said the officer.

So saying, he ordered Candide's irons to be struck off and sent his followers about their business, after which he conducted Candide and Martin to Dieppe, and left them to the care of his brother. There happened just then to be a small Dutch ship in the roads. The Norman, whom the other three diamonds had converted into the most obliging, serviceable being that ever breathed, took care to see Candide and his attendants safe on board the vessel, that was just ready to sail for Portsmouth in England. This was not the nearest way to Venice indeed; but Candide thought himself

[75] Atrébatie is the Latin name for the district of Artois, the home of a man who attempted to assassinate Louis XV in 1757. The years 1594 and 1610 were the dates of attempted assassinations of Henry IV (Henry of Navarre), the second one successful.

escaped out of hell, and did not in the least doubt but he should quickly find an opportunity of resuming his voyage to Venice.

CHAPTER XXIII

Candide and Martin touch upon the English coast; what they saw there.

"Ah Pangloss! Pangloss! Ah, Martin! Martin! Ah, my dear Miss Cunegund! What sort of a world is this?" Thus exclaimed Candide, as soon as he had got on board the Dutch ship.

"Why, something very foolish, and very abominable," said Martin.

"You are acquainted with England," said Candide; "are they as great fools in that country, as in France?"

"Yes, but in a different manner," answered Martin. "You know that these two nations are at war about a few acres of snow in the neighborhood of Canada, and that they have expended much greater sums in the contest than all Canada is worth.[76] To say exactly whether there are a greater number fit to be inhabitants of a mad-house in the one country than the other, exceeds the limits of my imperfect capacity; I know, in general, that the people we are going to visit are of a very dark and gloomy disposition."

As they were chatting thus together, they arrived at Portsmouth. The shore, on each side of the harbor, was lined with a multitude of people, whose eyes were steadfastly fixed on a lusty man, who was kneeling down on the deck of one of the men of war, with his eyes bound. Opposite to this personage stood four soldiers, each of whom shot three bullets into his skull, with all the composure imaginable; and when it was done, the whole company went away perfectly well satisfied.[77]

"What the devil is all this for?" said Candide; "and what demon lords it thus over all the world?"

He then asked who was that lusty man who had been sent out of the world with so much ceremony, and he received for answer, that it was an admiral.

"And, pray," he said, "why do you put your admiral to death?"

"Because he did not put a sufficient number of his fellow creatures to death. You must know, he had an engagement with a French admiral, and it has been proved against him that he was not near enough to his antagonist."

"But," replied Candide, "the French admiral must have been as far from him."

"There is no doubt of that; but in this country it is found requisite, now and then, to put one admiral to death, in order to spirit up the others."

Candide was so shocked at what he saw and heard that he would not set foot on shore, but made a bargain with the Dutch skipper (were he even to rob him like the captain of Surinam) to carry him directly to Venice.

The skipper was ready in two days. They sailed along the coast of France, and passed within sight of Lisbon, at which Candide trembled.

[76] The wars of the French and English over Canada lasted until 1763.

[77] Voltaire based this incident on the execution of the English admiral John Byng, in 1757.

From thence they proceeded to the straits, entered the Mediterranean, and at length arrived at Venice.

"God be praised," said Candide, embracing Martin, "this is the place where I am to behold my beloved Cunegund once again. I can rely on Cacambo, like another self. All is well, all very well, all as well as possible."

CHAPTER XXIV

Of Pacquette and Friar Giroflée.

Upon their arrival at Venice, he went in search of Cacambo at every inn and coffee-house, and among all the ladies of pleasure; but could hear nothing of him. He sent every day to inquire of every ship and every vessel that came in: still no news of Cacambo.

"It is strange!" said he to Martin, "very strange! that I should have had time to sail from Surinam to Bordeaux; to travel from thence to Paris, to Dieppe, to Portsmouth; to sail along the coast of Portugal and Spain, and up the Mediterranean, to spend some months in Venice; and that my lovely Cunegund should not have arrived. Instead of her, I only met with a Parisian impostor, and a rascally Abbé of Périgord. Cunegund is actually dead, and I have nothing to do but to follow her. Alas! how much better would it have been for me to have remained in the paradise of El Dorado than to have returned to this cursed Europe! You are in the right, my dear Martin; you are certainly in the right; all is misery and deceit."

He fell into a deep melancholy, and neither went to the opera in vogue, nor partook of any of the diversions of the Carnival; not a woman caused him even a moment's temptation.

Martin said to him, "Upon my word, I think you are very simple to imagine that a rascally valet, with five or six millions in his pocket, would go in search of your mistress to the further end of the world, and bring her to Venice to meet you. If he finds her, he will take her for himself; if he does not, he will take another. Let me advise you to forget your valet Cacambo, and your mistress Cunegund."

Martin's speech was not consoling. Candide's melancholy increased, and Martin never left proving to him that there is very little virtue or happiness in this world; except, perhaps, in El Dorado where hardly anybody can gain admittance.

While they were disputing on this important subject, and still expecting Miss Cunegund, Candide perceived a young Theatine friar[78] in St. Mark's Place, with a girl under his arm. The Theatine looked fresh-colored, plump, and vigorous; his eyes sparkled; his air and gait were bold and lofty. The girl was very pretty, and was singing a song; and every now and then gave her Theatine an amorous ogle and wantonly pinched his ruddy cheeks.

"You will at least allow," said Candide to Martin, "that these two are happy. Hitherto I have met with none but unfortunate people in the whole habitable globe, except in El Dorado; but, as to this couple, I would venture to lay a wager they are happy."

[78] Member of a Catholic order founded in 1524.

"Done," said Martin; "they are not, for what you will."

"Well, we have only to ask them to dine with us," said Candide, "and you will see whether I am mistaken or not."

Thereupon he accosted them, and with great politeness invited them to his inn to eat some macaroni, with Lombard partridges and caviare, and to drink a bottle of Montepulciano, Lacrima Christi, Cyprus and Samos wine. The girl blushed; the Theatine accepted the invitation, and she followed him, eyeing Candide every now and then with a mixture of surprise and confusion, while the tears stole down her cheeks. No sooner did she enter his apartment than she cried out:

"How, Mr. Candide, have you quite forgotten poor Pacquette? Do you not know her again?"

Candide, who had not regarded her with any degree of attention before, being wholly occupied with the thoughts of his dear Cunegund, exclaimed:

"Ah! is it you, child? Was it you that reduced Dr. Pangloss to that fine condition I saw him in?"

"Alas! Sir," answered Pacquette, "it was I, indeed. I find you are acquainted with everything; and I have been informed of all the misfortunes that happened to the whole family of my lady Baroness and the fair Cunegund. But I can safely swear to you that my lot was no less deplorable; I was innocence itself when you saw me last. A cordelier, who was my confessor, easily seduced me; the consequences proved terrible. I was obliged to leave the castle some time after the Baron kicked you out by the backside from there; and if a famous surgeon had not taken compassion on me, I had been a dead woman. Gratitude obliged me to live with him some time as a mistress: his wife, who was a very devil for jealousy, beat me unmercifully every day. Oh! she was a perfect fury. The doctor himself was the most ugly of all mortals, and I the most wretched creature existing, to be continually beaten for a man whom I did not love. You are sensible, Sir, how dangerous it was for an ill-natured woman to be married to a physician. Incensed at the behavior of his wife, he one day gave her so affectionate a remedy for a slight cold she had caught, that she died in less than two hours in most dreadful convulsions. Her relations prosecuted the husband, who was obliged to fly, and I was sent to prison. My innocence would not have saved me, if I had not been tolerably handsome. The judge gave me my liberty on condition he should succeed the doctor. However, I was soon supplanted by a rival, turned off without a farthing, and obliged to continue the abominable trade which you men think so pleasing, but which to us unhappy creatures is the most dreadful of all sufferings. At length I came to follow the business at Venice. Ah! Sir, did you but know what it is to be obliged to lie indifferently with old tradesmen, with counsellors, with monks, gondoliers, and abbés; to be exposed to all their insolence and abuse; to find it often necessary to borrow a petticoat, only that it may be taken up by some disagreeable wretch; to be robbed by one gallant of what we get from another; to be subject to the extortions of civil magistrates; and to have for ever before one's eyes the prospect of old age, a hospital, or a dunghill, you would conclude that I am one of the most unhappy wretches breathing."

Thus did Pacquette unbosom herself to honest Candide in his closet, in the presence of Martin, who took occasion to say to him:

"You see I have half won the wager already."

Friar Giroflée[79] was all this time in the parlor refreshing himself with a glass or two of wine till dinner was ready.

"But," said Candide to Pacquette, "you looked so gay and content, when I met you, you were singing, and caressing the Theatine with so much fondness that I absolutely thought you as happy as you say you are now miserable."

"Ah! dear Sir," said Pacquette, "this is one of the miseries of the trade; yesterday I was stripped and beaten by an officer; yet to-day I must appear good-humored and gay to please a friar."

Candide was convinced, and acknowledged that Martin was in the right. They sat down to table with Pacquette and the Theatine; the entertainment was very agreeable, and towards the end they began to converse together with some freedom.

"Father," said Candide, to the friar, "you seem to me to enjoy a state of happiness that even kings might envy; joy and health are painted in your countenance. You have a tight pretty wench to divert you; and you seem to be perfectly well contented with your condition as a Theatine."

"Faith, Sir," said Friar Giroflée, "I wish with all my soul the Theatines were every one of them at the bottom of the sea. I have been tempted a thousand times to set fire to the convent and go and turn Turk. My parents obliged me, at the age of fifteen, to put on this detestable habit only to increase the fortune of an elder brother of mine, whom God confound! Jealousy, discord, and fury reside in our convent. It is true, I have preached some paltry sermons, by which I have got a little money, half of which the prior robs me of, and the remainder helps to pay my girls; but, at night, when I go hence to my convent, I am ready to dash my brains against the walls of the dormitory; and this is the case with all the rest of our fraternity."

Martin, turning towards Candide, with his usual indifference, said, "Well, what think you now? Have I won the wager entirely?"

Candide gave two thousand piastres to Pacquette, and a thousand to Friar Giroflée, saying, "I will answer that this will make them happy."

"I am not of your opinion," said Martin; "perhaps this money will only make them much more wretched."

"Be that as it may," said Candide, "one thing comforts me; I see that one often meets with those whom we expected never to see again; so that, perhaps, as I have found my red sheep and Pacquette, I may be lucky enough to find Miss Cunegund also."

"I wish," said Martin, "she one day may make you happy, but I doubt it much."

"You are very hard of belief," said Candide.

"It is because," said Martin, "I have seen the world."

"Observe those gondoliers," said Candide; "are they not perpetually singing?"

[79] Giroflée means "gillyflower," and Paquette means "daisy."

"You do not see them," answered Martin, "at home with their wives and brats. The doge[80] has his chagrin, gondoliers theirs. Nevertheless, in the main, I look upon the gondolier's life as preferable to that of the doge; but the difference is so trifling that it is not worth the trouble of examining into."

"I have heard great talk," said Candide, "of the senator Pococurante,[81] who lives in that fine house at the Brenta, where, they say, he entertains foreigners in the most polite manner. They claim that this man is a perfect stranger to uneasiness."

"I should be glad to see so extraordinary a being," said Martin.

Candide thereupon sent a messenger to Signor Pococurante, desiring permission to wait on him the next day.

CHAPTER XXV

Candide and Martin pay a visit to Signor Pococurante, a noble Venetian.

Candide and his friend Martin went in a gondola on the Brenta, and arrived at the palace of the noble Pococurante: the gardens were laid out in an elegant taste, and adorned with beautiful marble statues; his palace was architecturally magnificent. The master of the house, who was a man of sixty, and very rich, received our two travellers with great politeness, but without much ceremony, which somewhat disconcerted Candide, but was not at all displeasing to Martin.

First, two very pretty girls, neatly dressed, brought in chocolate, which was extremely well frothed. Candide could not help praising their beauty and graceful carriage.

"The creatures are well enough," said the senator; "I make them lie with me sometimes, for I am heartily tired of the women of the town, their coquetry, their jealousy, their quarrels, their humors, their meannesses, their pride, and their folly; I am weary of making sonnets, or of paying for sonnets to be made on them; but, after all, these two girls begin to grow very indifferent to me."

After having refreshed himself, Candide walked into a large gallery, where he was struck with the sight of a fine collection of paintings. He asked what master had painted the two first.

"They are Raphael's," answered the senator. "I gave a great deal of money for them some years ago, purely out of conceit, as they were said to be the finest pieces in Italy; but I cannot say they please me: the coloring is dark and heavy; the figures do not swell nor come out enough, and the drapery has no resemblance to the actual material. In short, notwithstanding the encomiums lavished upon them, they are not, in my opinion, a true representation of nature. I approve of no paintings but where I think I behold nature herself; and there are none of that kind to be met with. I have what is called a fine collection, but I take no manner of delight in them."

While dinner was getting ready, Pococurante ordered a concert. Candide praised the music to the skies.

[80] Chief magistrate of Venice. [81] Pococurante means "small care."

"This noise," said the noble Venetian, "may amuse one for a little time, but if it was to last above half an hour, it would grow tiresome to everybody, though perhaps no one would care to own it. Music is become the art of executing what is difficult; now, whatever is difficult cannot be long pleasing. I believe I might take more pleasure in an opera, if they had not made such a monster of it as perfectly shocks me; and I am amazed how people can bear to see wretched tragedies set to music; where the scenes are contrived for no other purpose than to lug in, as it were by the ears, three or four ridiculous songs, to give a favorite actress an opportunity of exhibiting her pipe. Let who will, or can, die away in raptures at the trills of an eunuch quavering the majestic part of Caesar or Cato, and strutting in a foolish manner upon the stage; for my part, I have long ago renounced these paltry entertainments which constitute the glory of modern Italy, and are so dearly purchased by crowned heads."

Candide opposed these sentiments; but he did it in a discreet manner; as for Martin, he was entirely of the old senator's opinion.

Dinner being served they sat down to table, and after a very hearty repast returned to the library. Candide, observing Homer richly bound, commended the noble Venetian's taste.

"This," said he, "is a book that was once the delight of the great Pangloss, the best philosopher in Germany."

"Homer is no favorite of mine," answered Pococurante, very coolly: "I was made to believe once that I took a pleasure in reading him; but his continual repetitions of battles have all such a resemblance with each other; his gods that are for ever in a hurry and bustle, without ever doing anything; his Helen, that is the cause of the war, and yet hardly acts in the whole performance; his Troy, that holds out so long, without being taken: in short, all these things together make the poem very insipid to me. I have asked some learned men, whether they are not in reality as much tired as myself with reading this poet: those who were sincere assured me that he had made them fall asleep; and yet, that they could not well avoid giving him a place in their libraries as a monument of antiquity or like those rusty medals which are of no use in commerce."

"But your Excellency does not surely form the same opinion of Virgil?" said Candide.

"Why, I grant," replied Pococurante, "that the second, third, fourth, and sixth book of his *Aeneid* are excellent; but as for his pious Aeneas, his strong Cloanthus, his friendly Achates, his boy Ascanius, his silly king Latinus, his ill-bred Amata, his insipid Lavinia, I think there cannot in nature be anything more flat and disagreeable. I must confess, I prefer Tasso far beyond him; nay, even that sleepy tale-teller Ariosto."

"May I take the liberty to ask if you do not receive great pleasure from reading Horace?" said Candide.

"There are maxims in this writer," replied Pococurante, "from whence a man of the world may reap some benefit; and the short and forceful measure of the verse makes them more easily to be retained in the memory. But I see nothing extraordinary in his journey to Brundisium, and his account of his bad dinner; nor in his dirty low quarrel between one Rupilius, whose words, as he expresses it, were full of poisonous filth, and another, whose language was dipped in vinegar. His indelicate verses against old women and witches have frequently given me great offense; nor can I discover the great merit of his telling his friend Maecenas that if he will but rank him in the class of lyric poets, his lofty head shall touch the stars. Ignorant readers are apt to praise everything by the lump in a writer of reputation. For my part, I read only to please myself. I like nothing but what makes for my purpose."

Candide, who had been brought up with a notion of never making use of his own judgment, was astonished at what he had heard; but Martin found there was a good deal of reason in the senator's remarks.

"Oh! here is a Cicero," said Candide: "this great man, I fancy, you are never tired of reading?"

"Indeed, I never read him at all," replied Pococurante. "What a deuce is it to me whether he pleads for Rabirius or Cluentius? I try causes enough myself. I had once some liking for his philosophical works; but when I found he doubted of everything, I thought I knew as much as he, and had no need of a guide to learn ignorance."

"Ha!" cried Martin, "here are fourscore volumes of the memoirs of the Academy of Science; perhaps there may be something valuable in them."

"Yes," answered Pococurante; "so there might if any one of the compilers of this rubbish had only invented the art of pin-making: but all these volumes are filled with mere chimerical systems without one single article conducive to real utility."

"I see a prodigious number of plays," said Candide, "in Italian, Spanish, and French."

"Yes," replied the Venetian; "there are I think three thousand, and not three dozen of them good for anything. As to these huge volumes of divinity, and those enormous collections of sermons, they are altogether not worth one single page in Seneca; and I fancy you will readily believe that neither myself, nor any one else, ever looks into them."

Martin noticed some shelves filled with English books.

"I fancy," he said, "that a republican must be highly delighted with those books, which are most of them written with a noble spirit of freedom."

"It is noble to write as we think," said Pococurante; "it is the privilege of humanity. Throughout Italy we write only what we do not think; and the present inhabitants of the country of the Caesars and Antoninuses dare not acquire a single idea without the permission of a Dominican friar. I should be enamored of the spirit of the English nation, did it not utterly frustrate the good effects it would produce, by passion and the spirit of party."

Candide, seeing a Milton, asked the senator if he did not think that author a great man.

"Who?" said Pococurante sharply; "that barbarian who writes a tedious commentary in ten books of rumbling verse, on the first chapter of Genesis? that slovenly imitator of the Greeks, who disfigures the creation, by making the Messiah take a pair of compasses from heaven's armory to plan the world; whereas Moses represented the Deity as producing the whole universe by his fiat? Can I, think you, have any esteem for a writer who has spoiled Tasso's hell and the devil? who transforms Lucifer sometimes into a toad, and, at others, into a pigmy? who makes him say the same thing over again a hundred times? who metamorphoses him into a school-divine? and who, by an absurdly serious imitation of Ariosto's comic invention of firearms, represents the devils and angels cannonading each other in heaven? Neither I nor any other Italian can possibly take pleasure in such melancholy reveries; but the marriage of Sin and Death, and snakes issuing from the womb of the former, are enough to make any person sick that is not lost to all sense of delicacy, while his long description of a lazar-house is fit only for a gravedigger. This obscene, whimsical and disagreeable poem met with neglect at its first publication; and I only treat the author now as he was treated in his own country by his contemporaries."

Candide was sensibly grieved at this speech, as he had a great respect for Homer and was very fond of Milton.

"Alas!" said he softly to Martin, "I am afraid this man holds our German poets in great contempt."

"There would be no such great harm in that," said Martin.

"O what a surprising man!" said Candide, still to himself; "what a prodigious genius is this Pococurante! nothing can please him."

After finishing their survey of the library, they went down into the garden, when Candide commended the several beauties that offered themselves to his view.

"I know nothing upon earth laid out in such bad taste," said Pococurante; "everything about it is childish and trifling; but I shall have another laid out to-morrow upon a nobler plan."

As soon as our two travellers had taken leave of his Excellency, Candide said to Martin:

"I hope you will own that this man is the happiest of all mortals, for he is above everything he possesses."

"But do not you see," answered Martin, "that he likewise dislikes everything he possesses? It was an observation of Plato, long since, that those are not the best stomachs that reject, without distinction, all sorts of aliments."

"True," said Candide, "but still there must certainly be a pleasure in criticizing everything, and in perceiving faults where others think they see beauties."

"That is," replied Martin, "there is a pleasure in having no pleasure."

"Well, well," said Candide, "I find that I shall be the only happy man at last, when I am blessed with the sight of my dear Cunegund."

"It is good to hope," said Martin.

In the meanwhile, days and weeks passed away, and no news of Cacambo. Candide was so overwhelmed with grief, that he did not reflect on the behavior of Pacquette and Friar Giroflée, who never stayed to return him thanks for the presents he had so generously made them.

CHAPTER XXVI

Candide and Martin sup with six strangers; and who they were.

One evening when Candide, with his attendant Martin, were going to sit down to supper with some foreigners who lodged in the same inn, a man, with a face the color of soot, came behind him, and taking him by the arm, said:

"Hold yourself in readiness to go along with us, be sure you do not fail."

He turned and beheld Cacambo. Nothing but the sight of Cunegund could have given greater joy and surprise. He was almost beside himself with joy. After embracing this dear friend, he said:

"Cunegund must be here? Where, where is she? Carry me to her this instant, that I may die with joy in her presence."

"Cunegund is not here," answered Cacambo; "she is at Constantinople."

"Good heavens, at Constantinople! but no matter if she was in China, I would fly thither. Let us be gone."

"We depart after supper," said Cacambo. "I cannot at present stay to say anything more to you; I am a slave, and my master waits for me; I must go and attend him at table: but say not a word, only get your supper, and hold yourself in readiness."

Candide, divided between joy and grief, charmed to have thus met with his faithful agent again, and surprised to hear he was a slave, his heart palpitating, his senses confused, but full of the hopes of recovering his mistress, sat down to table with Martin, who beheld all these scenes with great unconcern, and with six strangers who had come to spend the carnival at Venice.

Cacambo waited at table upon one of these strangers. When supper was nearly over, he drew near to his master, and whispered him in the ear:

"Sire, your Majesty may go when you please, the ship is ready."

Having said these words, he left the room. The guests, surprised at what they had heard, looked at each other without speaking a word; when another servant drawing near to his master, in like manner said:

"Sire, your Majesty's post-chaise is at Padua, and the bark is ready."

His master made him a sign, and he instantly withdrew. The company all stared at each other again, and the general astonishment was increased. A third servant then approached another of the strangers, and said:

"Sire, if your Majesty will be advised by me, you will not stay any longer in this place; I will go and get everything ready"—and he instantly disappeared.

Candide and Martin then took it for granted that this was some of the diversions of the carnival, and that these were characters in masquerade. Then a fourth domestic said to the fourth stranger:

"Your Majesty may set out when you please." Saying this, he went away like the rest.

A fifth valet said the same to a fifth master. But the sixth domestic spoke in a different style to the person on whom he waited, and who sat next to Candide.

"Troth, Sir," said he, "they will trust your Majesty no longer, nor myself neither; and we may both of us chance to be sent to jail this very night; and therefore I shall take care of myself, and so adieu."

The servants being all gone, the six strangers, with Candide and Martin, remained in a profound silence. At length Candide broke it by saying:

"Gentlemen, this is a very singular joke, upon my word; why, how came you all to be kings? For my part, I own frankly, that neither my friend Martin here nor myself have any claim to royalty."

Cacambo's master then began, with great gravity, to deliver himself thus in Italian:

"I am not joking in the least, my name is Achmet III. I was Grand Sultan for many years; I dethroned my brother, my nephew dethroned me, my viziers lost their heads, and I am condemned to end my days in the old seraglio. My nephew, the Grand Sultan Mahmud, gives me permission to travel sometimes for my health, and I am come to spend the carnival at Venice."

A young man who sat by Achmet spoke next, and said:

"My name is Ivan. I was once Emperor of all the Russias, but was dethroned in my cradle. My parents were confined, and I was brought up in a prison; yet I am sometimes allowed to travel, though always with persons to keep a guard over me, and I am come to spend the carnival at Venice."

The third said:

"I am Charles Edward, King of England; my father has renounced his right to the throne in my favor. I have fought in defense of my rights, and eight hundred of my followers have had their hearts taken out of their bodies alive and thrown in their faces. I have myself been confined in a prison. I am going to Rome to visit the King my father, who was dethroned as well as myself and my grandfather; and I am come to spend the carnival at Venice."

The fourth spoke thus:

"I am the King of Poland; the fortune of war has stripped me of my hereditary dominions. My father experienced the same vicissitudes of fate. I resign myself to the will of Providence, in the same manner as Sultan Achmet, the Emperor Ivan, and King Charles Edward, whom God long preserve; and I am come to spend the carnival at Venice."

The fifth said:

"I am King of Poland also. I have twice lost my kingdom; but Providence has given me other dominions, where I have done more good than all the Sarmatian kings put together were ever able to do on the banks of the Vistula: I resign myself likewise to Providence; and am come to spend the carnival at Venice."

It now came to the sixth monarch's turn to speak.

"Gentlemen," said he, "I am not so great a prince as the rest of you, it is true; but I am, however, a crowned head. I am Theodore, elected King of Corsica. I have had the title of Majesty, and am now hardly treated with common civility. I have coined money, and am not now worth a single ducat. I have had two secretaries of state, and am now without a valet. I was once seated on a throne, and since that have lain upon a truss of straw in a common jail in London, and I very much fear I shall meet with the same fate here in Venice, where I come, like your Majesties, to divert myself at the carnival."[82]

The other five kings listened to this speech with great attention; it excited their compassion; each of them made the unhappy Theodore a present of twenty sequins to get clothes and shirts, and Candide gave him a diamond worth just an hundred times that sum.

[82] The six kings are real historical figures: Achmet III of Turkey (1673–1736); Ivan VI of Russia (1740–1764); Charles Edward of England, "Bonnie Prince Charlie" (1720–1788); Augustus III of Poland (1696–1763); Stanislas Leczinski of Poland (1677–1766); and Theodore von Neuhof (1690–1756), who served as elected king of Corsica for about eight months.

"Who can this private person be," said the five kings, "who is able to give, and has actually given, a hundred times as much as any of us? Are you, Sir, also a king?"

"No, gentlemen, and I have no wish to be one."

Just as they rose from table, in came four Serene Highnesses who had also been stripped of their territories by the fortune of war, and were come to spend the remainder of the carnival at Venice. Candide took no manner of notice of them; for his thoughts were wholly employed on his voyage to Constantinople, whither he intended to go in search of his beloved Cunegund.

CHAPTER XXVII

Candide's voyage to Constantinople.

The trusty Cacambo had already engaged the captain of the Turkish ship that was to carry Sultan Achmet back to Constantinople, to take Candide and Martin on board. Accordingly, they both embarked, after paying their obeisance to his miserable Highness. As they were going on board, Candide said to Martin:

"You see we supped in company with six dethroned kings, and to one of them I gave charity. Perhaps there may be a great many other princes still more unfortunate. For my part, I have lost only a hundred sheep, and am now going to fly to the arms of Cunegund. My dear Martin, I must insist on it, that Pangloss was in the right. All is for the best."

"I wish it may be," said Martin.

"But this was an odd adventure we met with at Venice. I do not think there ever was an instance before, of six dethroned monarchs supping together at a public inn."

"This is no more extraordinary," said Martin, "than most of what has happened to us. It is a very common thing for kings to be dethroned; and as for our having the honor to sup with six of them, it is a mere accident, not deserving our attention. What does it matter with whom one sups, provided one has good fare?"

As soon as Candide set his foot on board the vessel, he flew to his old friend and servant Cacambo; and throwing his arms about his neck, embraced him with transports of joy.

"Well," said he, "what news of Cunegund? Does she still continue the paragon of beauty? Does she love me still? How is she? You have, doubtless, purchased a palace for her at Constantinople?"

"My dear master," replied Cacambo, "Cunegund washes dishes on the banks of the Propontis, in the house of a prince who has very few to wash. She is at present a slave in the family of an ancient sovereign, named Ragotsky,[83] whom the Grand Turk allows three crowns a day to maintain him in his exile; but the most melancholy circumstance of all is, that she has lost her beauty and turned horribly ugly."

[83] Or Rakoczy, briefly king of Transylvania, later interned in Turkey from 1720 to 1735.

"Ugly or handsome," said Candide, "I am a man of honor; and, as such, am obliged to love her still. But how could she possibly have been reduced to so abject a condition, when I sent five or six millions to her by you?"

"Lord bless me," said Cacambo, "was not I obliged to give two millions to Senor Don Fernando d'Ibaraa y Figueora y Mascarenas y Lampourdos y Souza, Governor of Buenos Ayres, for liberty to take Miss Cunegund away with me? and then did not a brave fellow of a pirate very gallantly strip us of all the rest? and then did not this same pirate carry us with him to Cape Matapan, to Milo, to Nicaria, to Samos, to Petra, to the Dardanelles, to Marmora, to Scutari? Cunegund and the old woman are now servants to the prince I have told you of; and I myself am slave to the dethroned Sultan."

"What a chain of terrible calamities!" exclaimed Candide. "But, after all, I have still some diamonds left, with which I can easily procure Cunegund's liberty. It is a pity she is grown so very ugly."

Then turning to Martin, "What think you, friend," said he, "whose condition is most to be pitied, the Emperor Achmet's, the Emperor Ivan's, King Charles Edward's, or mine?"

"Faith, I cannot resolve your question," said Martin, "unless I had been in the breasts of you all."

"Ah!" cried Candide, "was Pangloss here now, he would have known, and satisfied me at once."

"I know not," said Martin, "in what balance your Pangloss could have weighed the misfortunes of mankind, and have set a just estimation on their sufferings. All that I pretend to know of the matter is that there are millions of men on the earth whose conditions are an hundred times more pitiable than those of King Charles Edward, the Emperor Ivan, or Sultan Achmet."

"Why, that may be," answered Candide.

In a few days they reached the Bosphorus; and the first thing Candide did was to pay a high ransom for Cacambo: then, without losing time, he and his companions went on board a galley, in order to search for his Cunegund, on the banks of the Propontis, notwithstanding she was grown so ugly.

There were two slaves among the crew of the galley, who rowed very ill, and to whose bare backs the master of the vessel frequently applied a lash of oxhide. Candide, from natural sympathy, looked at these two slaves more attentively than at any of the rest, and drew near them with a look of pity. Their features, though greatly disfigured, appeared to him to bear a strong resemblance with those of Pangloss and the unhappy Baron Jesuit, Miss Cunegund's brother. This idea affected him with grief and compassion: he examined them more attentively than before.

"In troth," said he, turning to Martin, "if I had not seen my master Pangloss fairly hanged, and had not myself been unlucky enough to run the Baron through the body, I could believe these are they rowing in the galley."

No sooner had Candide uttered the names of the Baron and Pangloss than the two slaves gave a great cry, ceased rowing, and let fall their oars out of their hands. The master of the vessel, seeing this, ran up to them, and redoubled the discipline of the lash.

"Hold, hold," cried Candide, "I will give you what money you ask for these two persons."

"Good heavens! it is Candide," said one of the men.

"Candide!" cried the other.

"Do I dream," said Candide, "or am I awake? Am I actually on board this galley? Is this my lord Baron, whom I killed? and that my master Pangloss, whom I saw hanged?"

"It is I! it is I!" cried they both together.

"What! is this your great philosopher?" said Martin.

"My dear Sir," said Candide to the master of the galley, "how much do you ask for the ransom of the Baron of Thunder-ten-tronckh, who is one of the first barons of the empire, and of Mr. Pangloss, the most profound metaphysician in Germany?"

"Why then, Christian cur," replied the Turkish captain, "since these two dogs of Christian slaves are barons and metaphysicians, who no doubt are of high rank in their own country, thou shalt give me fifty thousand sequins."

"You shall have them, Sir: carry me back as quick as thought to Constantinople, and you shall receive the money immediately. No! carry me first to Miss Cunegund."

The captain, upon Candide's first proposal, had already tacked about, and he made the crew apply their oars so effectively that the vessel flew through the water quicker than a bird cleaves the air.

Candide bestowed a thousand embraces on the Baron and Pangloss.

"And so then, my dear Baron, I did not kill you? and you, my dear Pangloss, are come to life again after your hanging? But how came you slaves on board a Turkish galley?"

"And is it true that my dear sister is in this country?" said the Baron.

"Yes," said Cacambo.

"And do I once again behold my dear Candide?" said Pangloss.

Candide presented Martin and Cacambo to them; they embraced each other, and all spoke together. The galley flew like lightning, and now they were got back to the port. Candide instantly sent for a Jew, to whom he sold for fifty thousand sequins a diamond richly worth one hundred thousand, though the fellow swore to him all the time, by Abraham, that he gave him the most he could possibly afford. He no sooner got the money into his hands than he paid it down for the ransom of the Baron and Pangloss. The latter flung himself at the feet of his deliverer, and bathed him with his tears: the former thanked him with a gracious nod, and promised to return him the money at the first opportunity.

"But is it possible," said he, "that my sister should be in Turkey?"

"Nothing is more possible," answered Cacambo; "for she scours the dishes in the house of a Transylvanian prince."

Candide sent directly for two Jews, and sold more diamonds to them; and then he set out with his companions in another galley, to deliver Cunegund from slavery.

CHAPTER XXVIII

What befell Candide, Cunegund, Pangloss, Martin, &c.

"Pardon," said Candide to the Baron; "once more let me entreat your pardon, Reverend Father, for running you through the body."

"Say no more about it," replied the Baron; "I was a little too hasty I must own: but as you seem to be anxious to know by what accident I came to be a slave on board the galley where you saw me, I will inform you. After I had been cured of the wound you gave me, by the apothecary of the College, I was attacked and carried off by a party of Spanish troops, who clapped me up in prison in Buenos Ayres, at the very time my sister was setting out from there. I asked leave to return to Rome, to the general of my Order, who appointed me chaplain to the French Ambassador at Constantinople. I had not been a week in my new office, when I happened to meet one evening with a young icoglan;[84] extremely handsome and well made. The weather was very hot; the young man had an inclination to bathe. I took the opportunity to bathe likewise. I did not know it was a crime for a Christian to be found naked in company with a young Turk. A cadi ordered me to receive a hundred blows on the soles of my feet, and sent me to the galleys. I do not believe that there was ever an act of more flagrant injustice. But I would fain know how my sister came to be a scullion to a Transylvanian prince who has taken refuge among the Turks?"

"But how happens it that I behold you again, my dear Pangloss?" said Candide.

"It is true," answered Pangloss, "you saw me hanged, though I ought properly to have been burned; but you may remember that it rained extremely hard when they were going to roast me. The storm was so violent that they found it impossible to light the fire; so they hanged me because they could do no better. A surgeon purchased my body, carried it home, and prepared to dissect me. He began by making a crucial incision from my navel to the clavicle. It is impossible for any one to have been more lamely hanged than I had been. The executioner of the Holy Inquisition was a subdeacon, and knew how to burn people very well, but as for hanging, he was a novice at it, being quite out of the way of his practice; the cord being wet, and not slipping properly, the noose did not join. In short, I still continued to breathe; the crucial incision made me scream to such a degree that my surgeon fell flat upon his back; and imagining it was the devil he was dissecting, ran away, and in his fright tumbled downstairs. His wife hearing the noise flew from the next room, and, seeing me stretched upon the table with my crucial incision, was still more terrified than her husband. She took to her heels and fell over him. When they had a little recovered themselves, I heard her say to her husband, 'My dear, how could you think of dissecting an heretic? Don't you know that the devil is always in them? I'll run directly to a priest to come and drive the evil spirit out.' I trembled from head to foot at hearing her talk in this manner, and exerted what little strength I had left to cry out, 'Have mercy on me!' At length the Portuguese barber took courage, sewed up my wound, and his wife nursed me;

[84] Page to the sultan. The Baron is again presented, by implication, as homosexual.

and I was upon my legs in a fortnight's time. The barber got me a place as lackey to a Knight of Malta who was going to Venice; but finding my master had no money to pay me my wages, I entered into the service of a Venetian merchant, and went with him to Constantinople.

"One day I happened to enter a mosque, where I saw no one but an old imam and a very pretty young female devotee, who was saying her prayers; her neck was quite bare, and in her bosom she had a beautiful nosegay of tulips, roses, anemones, ranunculuses, hyacinths, and auriculas. She let fall her nosegay. I ran immediately to take it up, and presented it to her with a most respectful bow. I was so long in delivering it, that the imam began to be angry; and, perceiving I was a Christian, he cried out for help; they carried me before the cadi, who ordered me to receive one hundred bastinadoes, and sent me to the galleys. I was chained in the very galley, and to the very same bench with my lord the Baron. On board this galley there were four young men belonging to Marseilles, five Neapolitan priests, and two monks of Corfu, who told us that the like adventures happened every day. The Baron pretended that he had been worse used than myself; and I insisted that there was far less harm in taking up a nosegay, and putting it into a woman's bosom, than to be found stark naked with a young icoglan. We were continually in dispute, and received twenty lashes a-day with a thong, when the concatenation of sublunary events brought you on board our galley to ransom us from slavery."

"Well, my dear Pangloss," said Candide to him, "when you were hanged, dissected, whipped, and tugging at the oar, did you continue to think that every thing in this world happens for the best?"

"I have always abided by my first opinion," answered Pangloss; "for, after all, I am a philosopher; and it would not become me to retract my sentiments; especially, as Leibnitz could not be in the wrong; and that pre-established harmony is the finest thing in the world, as well as the *plenum* and the *materia subtilis*."[85]

CHAPTER XXIX

In what manner Candide found Cunegund and the old woman again.

While Candide, the Baron, Pangloss, Martin, and Cacambo were relating their several adventures, and reasoning on the contingent or non-contingent events of this world; while they were disputing on causes and effects, on moral and physical evil, on free will and necessity, and on the consolation that may be felt by a person when a slave and chained to an oar in a Turkish galley, they arrived at the house of the Transylvanian prince on the coasts of the Propontis. The first objects they beheld there were Miss Cunegund and the old woman, who were hanging some table-cloths on a line to dry.

The Baron turned pale at the sight. Even the tender Candide, that affectionate lover, upon seeing his fair Cunegund all sun-burned, with

[85] "Pre-established harmony," the *plenum* (matter presumed to fill all space), and the *materia subtilis* (all spiritual agencies) are terms and concepts in Leibnitz's system.

blear eyes, a withered neck, wrinkled face and arms, all covered with a red scurf,[86] started back with horror; but, recovering himself, he advanced towards her out of good manners. She embraced Candide and her brother; they embraced the old woman, and Candide ransomed them both.

There was a small farm in the neighborhood, which the old woman proposed to Candide to make a shift with till the company should meet with a more favorable destiny. Cunegund, not knowing that she was grown ugly, as no one had informed her of it, reminded Candide of his promise in so peremptory a manner that the simple lad did not dare to refuse her; he then acquainted the Baron that he was going to marry his sister.

"I will never suffer," said the Baron, "my sister to be guilty of an action so derogatory to her birth and family; nor will I bear this insolence on your part: no, I never will be reproached that my nephews are not qualified for the first ecclesiastical dignities in Germany; nor shall a sister of mine ever be the wife of any person below the rank of a baron of the Empire."

Cunegund flung herself at her brother's feet, and bedewed them with her tears, but he still continued inflexible.

"Thou foolish fellow," said Candide, "have I not delivered thee from the galleys, paid thy ransom, and thy sister's too who was a scullion, and is very ugly, and yet I condescend to marry her? and shalt thou make claim to oppose the match? If I were to listen only to the dictates of my anger, I should kill thee again."

"Thou mayest kill me again," said the Baron, "but thou shalt not marry my sister while I am living."

CHAPTER XXX

Conclusion.

Candide had, in truth, no great inclination to marry Cunegund; but the extreme impertinence of the baron determined him to conclude the match; and Cunegund pressed him so warmly that he could not recant. He consulted Pangloss, Martin, and the faithful Cacambo. Pangloss composed a fine memorial, by which he proved that the Baron had no right over his sister; and that she might, according to all the laws of the Empire, marry Candide with the left hand.[87] Martin concluded that they should throw the Baron into the sea: Cacambo decided that he must be delivered to the Turkish captain and sent to the galleys; after which he should be conveyed by the first ship to the Father General at Rome. This advice was found to be very good; the old woman approved of it, and not a syllable was said to his sister; the business was executed for a little money: and they had the pleasure of tricking a Jesuit and punishing the pride of a German baron.

It was altogether natural to imagine that after undergoing so many disasters, Candide married to his mistress, and living with the philosopher Pangloss, the philosopher Martin, the prudent Cacambo, and the old

[86] Scales.

[87] A marriage "with the left hand" is a morganatic marriage, one in which the partner of lower rank relinquishes any claim to rank or property.

woman, having besides brought home so many diamonds from the country of the ancient Incas, would lead the most agreeable life in the world. But he had been so much cheated by the Jews that he had nothing else left but his little farm; his wife, every day growing more and more ugly, became ill-natured and insupportable; the old woman was infirm, and more bad-tempered yet than Cunegund. Cacambo, who worked in the garden, and carried the produce of it to sell at Constantinople, was past his labor, and cursed his fate. Pangloss despaired of making a figure in any of the German universities. And as to Martin, he was firmly persuaded that a person is equally ill-situated everywhere. He took things with patience. Candide, Martin, and Pangloss disputed sometimes about metaphysics and morality. Boats were often seen passing under the windows of the farm fraught with effendis, pashas, and cadis, that were going into banishment to Lemnos, Mytilene, and Erzeroum. And other cadis, pashas, and effendis were seen coming back to succeed the place of the exiles, and were driven out in their turns. They saw several heads very curiously stuffed with straw, being carried as presents to the Sublime Porte. Such sights gave occasion to frequent dissertations; and when no disputes were carried on, the irksomeness was so excessive that the old woman ventured one day to say to them:

"I would be glad to know which is worst, to be ravished a hundred times by negro pirates, to have one buttock cut off, to run the gauntlet among the Bulgarians, to be whipped and hanged at an *auto-da-fé,* to be dissected, to be chained to an oar in a galley, and in short to experience all the miseries through which every one of us hath passed,—or to remain here doing nothing?"

"This," said Candide, "is a big question."

This discourse gave birth to new reflections, and Martin especially concluded that man was born to live in the convulsions of disquiet, or in the lethargy of idleness. Though Candide did not absolutely agree to this; yet he was sure of nothing. Pangloss avowed that he had undergone dreadful sufferings; but having once maintained that everything went on as well as possible, he still maintained it, and at the same time believed nothing of it.

There was one thing which, more than ever, confirmed Martin in his detestable principles, made Candide hesitate, and embarrassed Pangloss. This was the arrival of Pacquette and Friar Giroflée one day at their farm. This couple had been in the utmost distress; they had very speedily made away with their three thousand piastres; they had parted, been reconciled; quarrelled again, been thrown into prison; had made their escape, and at last Brother Giroflée turned Turk. Pacquette still continued to follow her trade wherever she came; but she got little or nothing by it.

"I foresaw very well," said Martin to Candide, "that your presents would soon be squandered, and only make them more miserable. You and Cacambo have spent millions of piastres, and yet you are not more happy than Brother Giroflée and Pacquette."

"Ah!" said Pangloss to Pacquette. "It is heaven who has brought you here among us, my poor child! Do you know that you have cost me the tip of my nose, one eye, and one ear? What a handsome shape is here! and what is this world!"

This new adventure engaged them more deeply than ever in philosophical disputations.

In the neighborhood lived a very famous dervish,[88] who passed for the best philosopher in Turkey; him they went to consult: Pangloss, who was their spokesman, addressed him thus:

"Master, we come to entreat you to tell us why so strange an animal as man has been formed?"

"Why do you trouble your head about it?" said the dervish. "Is it any business of yours?"

"But, my Reverend Father," said Candide, "there is a horrible deal of evil on the earth."

"What signifies it," said the dervish, "whether there is evil or good? When his Highness sends a ship to Egypt, does he trouble his head whether the rats in the vessel are at their ease or not?"

"What must then be done?" said Pangloss.

"Be silent," answered the dervish.

"I flattered myself," replied Pangloss, "that we should have the pleasure of arguing with you on causes and effects, on the best of possible worlds, the origin of evil, the nature of the soul, and the pre-established harmony."

At these words the dervish shut the door in their faces.

During this conversation, news was spread abroad that two viziers of the bench and the mufti[89] had just been strangled at Constantinople, and several of their friends impaled. This catastrophe made a great noise for some hours. Pangloss, Candide, and Martin, as they were returning to the little farm, met with a good-looking old man, who was taking the air at his door, under an alcove formed of orange-trees. Pangloss, who was as inquisitive as he was argumentative, asked him what was the name of the mufti who was lately strangled.

"I cannot tell," answered the good old man; "I never knew the name of any mufti or vizier breathing. I am entirely ignorant of the event you speak of; I presume that, in general, such as are concerned in public affairs sometimes come to a miserable end; and that they deserve it: but I never inquire what is happening at Constantinople; I am content with sending thither the produce of the garden which I cultivate."

After saying these words, he invited the strangers to come into his house. His two daughters and two sons presented them with diverse sorts of iced sherbet of their own making; besides *caymac*,[90] heightened with the peel of candied citrons, oranges, lemons, pine-apples, pistachio-nuts, and Mocha coffee unadulterated with the bad coffee of Batavia or the West Indies. After which the two daughters of this good mussulman perfumed the beards of Candide, Pangloss, and Martin.

"You must certainly have a vast estate," said Candide to the Turk.

"I have no more than twenty acres of ground," he replied, "the whole of which I cultivate myself with the help of my children; and our labor keeps off from us three great evils, idleness, vice, and want."

Candide, as he was returning home, made profound reflections on the Turk's discourse.

"This good old man," he said to Pangloss and Martin, "appears to me to

[88] Member of a Moslem ascetic order. [89] A Moslem advisor on religious law.
[90] A Turkish dessert.

have chosen for himself a lot much preferable to that of the six kings with whom we had the honor to sup."

"Human grandeur," said Pangloss, "is very dangerous, if we believe the testimonies of almost all philosophers; for we find Eglon, King of the Moabites, was assassinated by Ehud; Absalom was hanged by the hair of his head, and run through with three darts; King Nadab, son of Jeroboam, was slain by Baasha; King Elah by Zimri; Ahaziah by Jehu; Athaliah by Jehoiada; the Kings Jehoiakim, Jechoniah, and Zedekiah were led into captivity: I need not tell you what was the fate of Croesus, Astyages, Darius, Dionysius of Syracuse, Pyrrhus, Perseus, Hannibal, Jugurtha, Ariovistus, Caesar, Pompey, Nero, Otho, Vitellius, Domitian, Richard III of England, Edward II, Henry VI, Richard II, Mary Stuart, Charles I, the three Henrys of France, and the Emperor Henry IV."

"Neither need you tell me," said Candide, "that we must take care of our garden."

"You are in the right," said Pangloss; "for when man was put into the Garden of Eden, it was with an intent to dress it: and this proves that man was not born to be idle."

"Work then without disputing," said Martin; "it is the only way to render life supportable."

The little society, one and all, entered into this laudable design; and set themselves to exert their different talents. The little piece of ground yielded them a plentiful crop. Cunegund indeed was very ugly, but she became an excellent hand at pastry-work; Pacquette embroidered; the old woman had the care of the linen. There was none, down to Brother Giroflée, but did some service; he was a very good carpenter, and became an honest man. Pangloss used now and then to say to Candide:

"There is a concatenation of all events in the best of possible worlds; for, in short, had you not been kicked out of a fine castle by the backside for the love of Miss Cunegund, had you not been put into the Inquisition, had you not travelled over America on foot, had you not run the Baron through the body, and had you not lost all your sheep which you brought from the good country of El Dorado, you would not have been here to eat preserved citrons and pistachio-nuts."

"Excellently observed," answered Candide; "but let us take care of our garden."

Jean-Jacques Rousseau
(1712–1778)

It might be argued that, compared with the eighteenth century, the nineteenth and twentieth centuries produced more striking and widespread changes in the outward conditions of life, especially in technology and social organization. But it is at least tenable that the eighteenth century witnessed a greater intellectual ferment, especially in new ethical norms, in new images of human nature, and in new views of the relationship between human beings and their natural and social surroundings. To single out any one person, therefore, as the central figure of the century is to put a heavy weight of responsibility on him, for better or worse. But many people would so identify Jean-Jacques Rousseau. His most immediate, verifiable impact was on the democratic political theory that strongly influenced the direction of the American and especially the French Revolution. His ideas on education have come into their own in the twentieth century, in now orthodox theories of learning and even more clearly in the movements loosely summarized as "progressive education"; even earlier, though, these ideas produced a new view of the nature of childhood. In literature, he propagated the vogues of sentiment and reverence for natural scenery, and he pioneered a new kind of spiritual autobiography centered on the psychological development and personal uniqueness of the author, a confessional mode that influenced poetry and fiction as well; in these respects, and others, he is clearly a founding father of Romanticism. Perhaps the most comprehensive of his achievements was to familiarize the intellectual world with a new model of innate human goodness and dignity.

Rousseau was born in 1712 in Geneva, the son of a Swiss watchmaker. He grew up in an atmosphere in which democratic workers' associations helped instill in him the egalitarian principles he was to preach later in his life, the more persuasively for the working class origins that distinguished him from the typically aristocratic radicals of his time. In his childhood and boyhood, described in Book I of his Confessions, *he had a passion for reading but got little formal education; Rousseau is one of the prototypes of the self-taught genius. The youthful personality he recalls was a curious mixture of mental sordidness and dreaming idealism. Not surprisingly, his revelations—about the effects upon him and his father of his mother's death in giving birth to him, and about the lasting effect of spankings upon his personality, especially his sexual urges—have intrigued psychoanalytic interpreters and biographers, especially because Rousseau explicitly articulates ideas resembling Freud's on the lasting effect of childhood experiences.*

After being unhappily apprenticed to an engraver, he ran away in 1728, fearful of punishment for having been stranded outside the city walls one night. He found refuge with a Madame de Warens, who for several years thereafter was a mother figure to him. Under her influence he was converted from his Genevan Calvinism to Catholicism, and at twenty-one he became her lover. During the next two decades he was a vagabond, geographically and vocationally; in Paris and many other parts of Europe, he was at different times a lackey, an engraver, a seminarian for the Catholic priesthood, a census clerk, a tutor (unsuccessful), and a secretary to the French ambassador in Venice. For a time he read intensively, becoming an admirer of Voltaire (later his bitter enemy). More than anything else, he defined his vocation as music; he tried to win Parisian recognition for a new system of musical notation and later was to write an opera performed before the king. In 1745 he entered into a liaison with a servant named Thérèse Le Vasseur, by whom he had five children, all consigned to a home for foundlings. (More than twenty years later, in 1768, he married her.) He met several of the French "Encyclopedists," the rationalist radicals of the time, including D'Alembert and Diderot. The latter became a close friend of Rousseau's.

In 1749, while walking to Vincennes to visit Diderot, who had been imprisoned there for violating the press laws, Rousseau came upon an announcement in a French journal of an essay contest, sponsored by the Academy of Dijon, on the question of whether the arts and sciences had improved human morals. Rousseau, feverishly excited and feeling that he had struck upon the ideas that would define his role in life, began immediately a prize-winning essay, published the following year, arguing that the arts and sciences had corrupted the primitive virtues of mankind and were tools by which the wealthy and powerful enslaved others. In this rather extreme form appeared Rousseau's first important statement of his lifelong theme: the conflict between corrupting civilization and natural virtue. In the following years he wrote articles on music and other subjects for the Encyclopedia. *Although courted by the fashionable world, Rousseau chose to live a life of sturdy independence and poverty, eking out a small income as a music copyist. By 1753 he was notorious enough to have come under police scrutiny.*

In an essay written that year for another Dijon contest, on the question of inequality, Rousseau posited and praised a former golden age of human existence when man, having moved from his first natural condition into a healthy communal one, lived still uncorrupted by private property and oppressive laws. In 1754 he revisited Geneva, reconverting to Protestantism. His theistic convictions, although unorthodox in some important respects, were emerging as one source of increasing friction between him and the anti-religious Encyclopedists, and he made a sharp break with them when, in 1758, he opposed a scheme favored by Voltaire to introduce a theater in Geneva. Rousseau argued, in a long Letter to D'Alembert on Plays, *that the introduction in Geneva of aristocratic dramas such as those of Molière and Voltaire himself would corrupt a still healthy community. Rousseau had now forfeited his standing in both the conservative and radical camps; increasingly thereafter his life was to be a series of persecutions, some real and many imaginary, culminating in the mental derangement of his very last years.*

Rousseau never felt comfortable in the refined and structured social life of Paris, and he left the city in 1756, settling near the wood of Montmorency. In 1761 and 1762, after a few years of intense productivity, he published the three works that, along with the Confessions, *are his greatest: the novel* Julie, or The New Heloise; The Social Contract; *and* Emile, or Education. The New Heloise *was one of the most spectacularly popular novels of the century, going through fifty editions; for a time it was rented out by lending libraries for ten sous per hour. Influenced by Rousseau's platonic but intense love for the Countess d'Houdetot, the book is a triangular love story, a sentimental novel of passion set in simple rustic surroundings and saturated by a deep feeling for nature. One of its incidental but not insignificant effects was to make Swiss scenery a poetic symbol for such poets as Byron and Shelley and a tourist mecca for them and for thousands of lesser devotees through the eighteenth and nineteenth centuries.*

The same concern with nature, in a somewhat different sense, pervades Emile, *a combination of tract and narrative outlining Rousseau's ideas on education. One of the book's basic themes is Rousseau's familiar premise that human nature is originally good; the child will be corrupted only if outside, alien forces of social evil are allowed to infect his world. For this reason, much of the pupil Emile's early education is "negative," a guarding against pernicious outside influences; that is why he is reared in the country. Moreover, childhood is defined as a period with its own autonomy; it is not merely potential adulthood: "Nature wants children to be children before being men." Because the faculty of reason develops late, children in their early years should learn not through precepts or books but by doing and experiencing* things, *things they recognize as useful and interesting. Memorization has no place in this regime. Each child must be led to discover his real self and to express it. An atmosphere of trust should exist between the adolescent pupil and the teacher, the two linked by an unforced mutual contract. Parental affection is important; therefore, for instance, mothers should breast-feed their children instead of relegating them to wet-nurses,* but, far from being coddled, the children should be inured to natural physical rigors. The last goal should be the introduction of the child into the responsibilities of mature adult social relations.

This goal of humane socialization is one of the links between Rousseau's ideas of education and his political theory as expressed in The Social Contract. There may seem to be a conflict between such socialization and Rousseau's view of society as an evil force, but he was realist enough to recognize that civilization could not just return to its primitive forms of organization. The challenge for him was to envision a principle (not necessarily concrete institutions) of social order that would enhance human freedom to the greatest possible extent. Building on but transforming ideas of earlier political theorists, including Hobbes and Locke, Rousseau posited an implicit agreement, or contract, made freely among free citizens, to yield their absolute individualism to a state in which the "general will" would represent their own best interests. The state exists, then, as the creation of its subjects, all its subjects, who in renouncing the right to indulge their own individual impulses fulfill their higher needs. Similarly, because the citizens are sovereign, they may undo the contract (a notion also stated in the opening sentences of the American Declaration of Independence). It is not surprising that the leaders of the French Revolution hailed Rousseau as its sacred prophet.

The publication of these definitive works so nearly at the same time marked another epoch in Rousseau's life. Alienated from the intellectual left, he also suffered now a rapid series of blows from the political and religious right: the Catholic hierarchy, the French royal court, the Parlement of Paris, the city council of Geneva, and Protestant ministers. (Emile contained a section arguing that the child's education in Christianity could be accomplished through nature rather than revelation.) Emile and The Social Contract were condemned and burned in Paris and Geneva, and an order was issued in Paris for Rousseau's arrest. As if these real persecutions were not enough, Rousseau developed strong delusions of persecution that remained with him to the end of his life. The man who had felt ready to retire, his great work accomplished, now found that he had to move repeatedly from one refuge to another, all over western Europe.

In 1766, at the invitation of the philosopher David Hume, he went to England, where he worked on his Confessions, but he came to believe that Hume too was involved in a conspiracy against him and fled the country in 1767. In 1770, the Confessions completed (though not published until two years after his death), Rousseau returned to Paris, where in 1775 there occurred an incident characteristic of his last years: convinced that all human beings were against him, he tried to deposit one of his autobiographical works on the altar of Notre Dame Cathedral but found the altar barred by an iron grille, so that even God seemed to have disowned him. In the last two years of his life, he wrote his Reveries of a Solitary Walker, a work of tranquil charm that shows once more Rousseau's intense feeling for nature. He died in 1778, of an apoplectic stroke, in Ermenonville, a town near Paris. (Voltaire had died a month earlier.) Soon after Rousseau's death came the universal acclaim and affection he had despaired of before he died. Among his worshipers were Robespierre and the other men who, a few years later, directed the French Revolution—not to mention many of the great Romantic poets of the next generation.

The Confessions has been vastly influential. The first paragraph reveals Rousseau's purported intention, which he claims was unprecedented: total self-revelation for its own sake. (This goal will seem somewhat less egoistic if we recall Rousseau's premise in works such as Emile that every individual is unique.) The book is more concerned with Rousseau's private self than with public events. "Myself alone!"—that is its theme. Perhaps only in Montaigne had anyone attempted the like before, since the one earlier great Confessions, that of St. Augustine, was written not so much to reveal its author as to praise and help reveal God.

Rousseau's Confessions is a spiritual autobiography, but that label is misleading if it obscures Rousseau's emphasis that in him spirit was indissociably attached to an animal nature. The combination of high idealism with sleaziness in Rousseau's character can be unedifying to some readers; others, however, recognizing in themselves traits and impulses that are less than noble, will be comforted to recognize that such faults do not necessarily exclude one from sympathy and understanding. For Rousseau in Book I, embarrassing self-revelation is the voucher for his honesty, since, as he asserts in connection with his "spankings" fetish, it is easier to acknowledge criminal faults than ridiculous ones. Even granting Rousseau's honesty, though, there remain questions about the quality of that honesty; for example, is the revelation of one's petty vices a sign of humility or of a perverse pride? However we answer such questions, we can see in the stated aim of the Confessions an early milestone in the evolution of "sincerity," one of the great, almost mythic watchwords of the modern personality, a characteristically modern measure of value in personal relationships and literature alike.

In many other respects too Rousseau was one of the great mythmakers of modern times, if we take "myth" to mean a deep-seated image or belief that governs a culture's ideas, ideals, values, premises, and behavior. Rousseau held some views that make modernists uneasy: his view of female education in Emile is very conservative, and some people detect a disturbingly statist mystique in his political theory of the "general will" (something different from the sum of individual wills) and in his insistence that religious tolerance coexist with certain articles of civic religion. But in many more respects Rousseau was the spokesman, supremely eloquent, for ideas accepted by many people today so unselfconsciously that they are hardly aware of them as distinct beliefs open to challenge: that man is naturally good; that crime and vice are extrinsic evils curable by education and by adjustments in the political and economic environment; that the innocence and integrity of childhood are not merely negative conditions of inexperience but an idyll that later life in the world tragically shatters; that education ought not to be the bending and beating of resistant iron in a smithy but the nurturing of a plant; that the tendency of complex civilization is to corrupt the hardy virtues of earlier times; that city life is not the normal milieu for human beings; that what is artificial is inferior, and that intellect is more artificial than instinctual feeling; that each of us must labor to discern and realize the elusive, unique, inner being whose enemy is conformity and convention, in short, to "be ourselves"; that autobiography (like first novels) should tell, in effect, "how I got to be me." The most fundamental myth of all (in the sense defined earlier) is the existence of something called "society," understood not merely as a convenient term for statistical tendencies in the human world around us but as an organized, almost conscious force against which our aspirations and needs bruise themselves. Stated so, these are simplifications of what Rousseau wrote, as most myths are simplifications. And some of these notions go back to earlier writers and ages. But that they are often attributed to Rousseau is itself revelatory of the impact of his dynamic literary personality; he is a good person to pin things on, from Romanticism to the totalitarian state to modern radicalism. If he did not in fact create all the myths associated with him, for many of them he is at least the accredited mythographer.

FURTHER READING *(prepared by W. J. R.):* Frances Winwar's *Jean-Jacques Rousseau: Conscience of an Era,* 1961, is a thorough biography written with sympathy for Rousseau's theories; also reliable is Matthew Josephson's *Jean-Jacques Rousseau,* 1931, rpt. 1959. C. H. Dobinson's *Jean-Jacques Rousseau: His Thought and Its Relevance Today,* 1969, examines Rousseau's views of education and discusses his life and intellectual development. The coherence of Rousseau's thought, a disputed subject, is defended in Ernst Cassirer's *The Question of Jean-Jacques Rousseau,* 1932, trans. and ed. Peter Gay, 1954, which attempts a comprehensive interpretation. The unity of Rousseau's political thinking is the subject of Stephen Ellenburg's *Rousseau's Political Philosophy,* 1976. The central idea of sovereign citizenry is examined in particular detail, and Ellenburg argues lucidly for Rousseau's consistency. Judith N. Shklar's *Men and Citizens: A Study of Rousseau's Social Theory,* 1969, contains interesting chapters on Rousseau and utopias and on his theories of authority. Several excellent essays on Rousseau's politics, relationships with other writers, and other topics are collected in *Reappraisals of Rousseau,* ed. Simon Harvey, Marian Hobson, David Kelley, and others, 1980 (French articles are not translated into English).

*CONFESSIONS**

BOOK I

[1712–1719.]—I am commencing an undertaking, hitherto without precedent, and which will never find an imitator. I desire to set before my fellows the likeness of a man in all the truth of nature, and that man myself.

Myself alone! I know the feelings of my heart, and I know men. I am not made like any of those I have seen; I venture to believe that I am not made like any of those who are in existence. If I am not better, at least I am different. Whether Nature has acted rightly or wrongly in destroying the mold in which she cast me, can only be decided after I have been read.

Let the trumpet of the Day of Judgment sound when it will, I will present myself before the Sovereign Judge with this book in my hand. I will say boldly: "This is what I have done, what I have thought, what I was. I have told the good and the bad with equal frankness. I have neither omitted anything bad, nor interpolated anything good. If I have occasionally made use of some immaterial embellishments, this has only been in order to fill a gap caused by lack of memory. I may have assumed the truth of that which I knew might have been true, never of that which I knew to be false. I have shown myself as I was: mean and contemptible, good, high-minded and sublime, according as I was one or the other. I have unveiled my inmost self even as Thou hast seen it, O Eternal Being. Gather round me the countless host of my fellow-men; let them hear my confessions, lament for my unworthiness, and blush for my imperfections. Then let each of them in turn reveal, with the same frankness, the secrets of his heart at the foot of the Throne, and say, if he dare, *'I was better than that man!'*"

I was born at Geneva, in the year 1712, and was the son of Isaac Rousseau and Susanne Bernard, citizens. The distribution of a very moderate

*Translator anonymous. Reprinted from *The Confessions of Jean-Jacques Rousseau,* Modern Library, Random House, Inc., New York, 1945.

inheritance amongst fifteen children had reduced my father's portion almost to nothing; and his only means of livelihood was his trade of watchmaker, in which he was really very clever. My mother, a daughter of the Protestant minister[1] Bernard, was better off. She was clever and beautiful, and my father had found difficulty in obtaining her hand. Their affection for each other had commenced almost as soon as they were born. When only eight years old, they walked every evening upon the Treille;[2] at ten, they were inseparable. Sympathy and union of soul strengthened in them the feeling produced by intimacy. Both, naturally full of tender sensibility, only waited for the moment when they should find the same disposition in another—or, rather, this moment waited for them, and each abandoned his heart to the first which opened to receive it. Destiny, which appeared to oppose their passion, only encouraged it. The young lover, unable to obtain possession of his mistress, was consumed by grief. She advised him to travel, and endeavor to forget her. He travelled, but without result, and returned more in love than ever. He found her whom he loved still faithful and true. After this trial of affection, nothing was left for them but to love each other all their lives. This they swore to do, and Heaven blessed their oath.

Gabriel Bernard, my mother's brother, fell in love with one of my father's sisters, who only consented to accept the hand of the brother, on condition that her own brother married the sister. Love arranged everything, and the two marriages took place on the same day.[3] Thus my uncle became the husband of my aunt, and their children were doubly my first cousins. At the end of a year, a child was born to both, after which they were again obliged to separate.

My uncle Bernard was an engineer. He took service in the Empire[4] and in Hungary, under Prince Eugène. He distinguished himself at the siege and battle of Belgrade. My father, after the birth of my only brother, set out for Constantinople, whither he was summoned to undertake the post of watchmaker to the Sultan. During his absence, my mother's beauty, intellect and talents gained for her the devotion of numerous admirers.[5] M. de la Closure, the French Resident, was one of the most eager to offer his. His passion must have been great, for, thirty years later, I saw him greatly affected when speaking to me of her. To enable her to resist such advances, my mother had more than her virtue: she loved her husband tenderly. She pressed him to return; he left all, and returned. I was the unhappy fruit of this return. Ten months later I was born, a weak and ailing child; I cost my mother her life, and my birth was the first of my misfortunes.

[1] Susanne was actually the daughter of a clockmaker, although she was reared by a minister uncle after her father died when she was nine. Rousseau is not always exact in his facts and dates.

[2] A public walk on the Geneva city walls.

[3] The two marriages were really five years apart. This statement, like some other errors early in the book, may either be deliberate poeticizing or represent family traditions Rousseau believed were true.

[4] The Austrian empire; Prince Eugène was an Austrian general.

[5] "Her talents were too brilliant for her position, since her father, the minister, who worshipped her, had educated her with great care. She drew, sang, accompanied herself on the téorbe [a stringed instrument, resembling a lute]; she read much, and wrote tolerable verses. . . ." [Rousseau's note.]

I have never heard how my father bore this loss, but I know that he was inconsolable. He believed that he saw his wife again in me, without being able to forget that it was I who had robbed him of her; he never embraced me without my perceiving, by his sighs and the convulsive manner in which he clasped me to his breast, that a bitter regret was mingled with his caresses, which were on that account only the more tender. When he said to me, "Jean-Jacques, let us talk of your mother," I used to answer, "Well, then, my father, we will weep!"—and this word alone was sufficient to move him to tears. "Ah!" said he, with a sigh, "give her back to me, console me for her loss, fill the void which she has left in my soul. Should I love you as I do, if you were only my son?" Forty years after he had lost her, he died in the arms of a second wife, but the name of the first was on his lips and her image at the bottom of his heart.

Such were the authors of my existence. Of all the gifts which Heaven had bestowed upon them, a sensitive heart is the only one they bequeathed to me; it had been the source of their happiness, but for me it proved the source of all the misfortunes of my life.

I was brought into the world in an almost dying condition; little hope was entertained of saving my life. I carried within me the germs of a complaint[6] which the course of time has strengthened, and which at times allows me a respite only to make me suffer more cruelly in another manner. One of my father's sisters, an amiable and virtuous young woman, took such care of me that she saved my life. At this moment, while I am writing, she is still alive, at the age of eighty, nursing a husband younger than herself, but exhausted by excessive drinking. Dear aunt, I forgive you for having preserved my life; and I deeply regret that, at the end of your days, I am unable to repay the tender care which you lavished upon me at the beginning of my own.[7] My dear old nurse Jacqueline is also still alive, healthy and robust. The hands which opened my eyes at my birth will be able to close them for me at my death.

I felt before I thought: this is the common lot of humanity. I experienced it more than others. I do not know what I did until I was five or six years old. I do not know how I learned to read; I only remember my earliest reading, and the effect it had upon me; from that time I date my uninterrupted self-consciousness. My mother had left some romances behind her, which my father and I began to read after supper. At first it was only a question of practicing me in reading by the aid of amusing books; but soon the interest became so lively, that we used to read in turns without stopping, and spent whole nights in this occupation. We were unable to leave off until the volume was finished. Sometimes, my father, hearing the swallows begin to twitter in the early morning, would say, quite ashamed, "Let us go to bed; I am more of a child than yourself."

In a short time I acquired, by this dangerous method, not only extreme facility in reading and understanding what I read, but a knowledge of the passions that was unique in a child of my age. I had no idea of things in

[6] Probably uremia, a symptom of kidney disease accompanied by nausea, headache, and coma.

[7] "The name of this aunt was Madame Gonceru. In March, 1767, Rousseau settled upon her an income of one hundred livres, and, even in the time of his greatest distress, always paid it with scrupulous exactitude." [Translator's note.]

themselves, although all the feelings of actual life were already known to me. I had conceived nothing, but felt everything. These confused emotions which I felt one after the other, certainly did not warp the reasoning powers which I did not as yet possess; but they shaped them in me of a peculiar stamp, and gave me odd and romantic notions of human life, of which experience and reflection have never been able wholly to cure me.

[1719–1723.]—The romances came to an end in the summer of 1719. The following winter brought us something different. My mother's library being exhausted, we had recourse to the share of her father's which had fallen to us. Luckily, there were some good books in it; in fact, it could hardly have been otherwise, for the library had been collected by a minister, who was even a learned man according to the fashion of the day, and was at the same time a man of taste and intellect. The "History of the Empire and the Church," by Le Sueur; Bossuet's "Treatise upon Universal History"; Plutarch's "Lives of Famous Men"; Nani's "History of Venice"; Ovid's "Metamorphoses"; La Bruyère; Fontenelle's "Worlds"; his "Dialogues of the Dead"; and some volumes of Molière—all these were brought over into my father's room, and I read to him out of them while he worked. I conceived a taste for them that was rare and perhaps unique at my age. Plutarch, especially, became my favorite author. The pleasure I took in reading him over and over again cured me a little of my taste for romance, and I soon preferred Agesilaus, Brutus, and Aristides to Orondates, Artamenes, and Juba.[8] This interesting reading, and the conversations between my father and myself to which it gave rise, formed in me the free and republican spirit, the proud and indomitable character unable to endure slavery or servitude, which has tormented me throughout my life in situations the least fitted to afford it scope. Unceasingly occupied with thoughts of Rome and Athens, living as it were amongst their great men, myself by birth the citizen of a republic and the son of a father whose patriotism was his strongest passion, I was fired by his example; I believed myself a Greek or a Roman; I lost my identity in that of the individual whose life I was reading; the recitals of the qualities of endurance and intrepidity which arrested my attention made my eyes glisten and strengthened my voice. One day, while I was relating the history of Scaevola at table, those present were alarmed to see me come forward and hold my hand over a chafing-dish, to illustrate his action.[9]

I had a brother seven years older than myself, who was learning my father's trade. The excessive affection which was lavished upon myself caused him to be somewhat neglected, which treatment I cannot approve of. His education felt the consequences of this neglect. He took to evil courses before he was old enough to be a regular profligate. He was put with another master, from whom he was continually running away, as he had done from home. I hardly ever saw him; I can scarcely say that I knew him; but I never ceased to love him tenderly, and he loved me as much as a vagabond can love anything. I remember that, on one occasion, when my

[8] The first three are among the heroes in the *Parallel Lives* of the ancient Greeks and Romans by Plutarch (c. A.D. 46–120), a lifelong favorite author of Rousseau's; the last three are heroes of romances.

[9] Scaevola was an ancient Roman who put his hand on a brazier to dramatize an oath to kill the king of the Etruscan enemies.

father was chastising him harshly and in anger, I threw myself impetuously between them and embraced him closely. In this manner I covered his body with mine, and received the blows which were aimed at him; I so obstinately maintained my position that at last my father was obliged to leave off, being either disarmed by my cries and tears, or afraid of hurting me more than him. At last, my brother turned out so badly that he ran away and disappeared altogether. Sometime afterwards we heard that he was in Germany. He never once wrote to us. From that time nothing more has been heard of him, and thus I have remained an only son.

If this poor boy was carelessly brought up, this was not the case with his brother; the children of kings could not be more carefully looked after than I was during my early years—worshipped by all around me, and, which is far less common, treated as a beloved, never as a spoiled child. Till I left my father's house, I was never once allowed to run about the streets by myself with the other children; in my case no one ever had to satisfy or check any of those fantastic whims which are attributed to Nature, but are all in reality the result of education. I had the faults of my age: I was a chatterbox, a glutton, and, sometimes, a liar. I would have stolen fruits, bonbons, or eatables; but I have never found pleasure in doing harm or damage, in accusing others, or in tormenting poor dumb animals. I remember, however, that I once made water[10] in a saucepan belonging to one of our neighbors, Madame Clot, while she was at church. I declare that, even now, the recollection of this makes me laugh, because Madame Clot, a good woman in other respects, was the most confirmed old grumbler I have ever known. Such is the brief and true story of all my childish offenses.

How could I become wicked, when I had nothing but examples of gentleness before my eyes, and none around me but the best people in the world? My father, my aunt, my nurse, my relations, our friends, our neighbors, all who surrounded me, did not, it is true, obey me, but they loved me; and I loved them in return. My wishes were so little excited and so little opposed, that it did not occur to me to have any. I can swear that, until I served under a master, I never knew what a fancy was. Except during the time I spent in reading or writing in my father's company, or when my nurse took me for a walk, I was always with my aunt, sitting or standing by her side, watching her at her embroidery or listening to her singing; and I was content. Her cheerfulness, her gentleness and her pleasant face have stamped so deep and lively an impression on my mind that I can still see her manner, look, and attitude; I remember her affectionate language: I could describe what clothes she wore and how her head was dressed, not forgetting the two little curls of black hair on her temples, which she wore in accordance with the fashion of the time.

I am convinced that it is to her I owe the taste, or rather passion, for music, which only became fully developed in me a long time afterwards. She knew a prodigious number of tunes and songs which she used to sing in a very thin, gentle voice. This excellent woman's cheerfulness of soul banished dreaminess and melancholy from herself and all around her. The attraction which her singing possessed for me was so great that not only

[10] Urinated.

have several of her songs always remained in my memory, but even now, when I have lost her, and as I grew older, many of them, totally forgotten since the days of my childhood, return to my mind with inexpressible charm. Would anyone believe that I, an old dotard, eaten up by cares and troubles, sometimes find myself weeping like a child, when I mumble one of those little airs in a voice already broken and trembling? One of them, especially, has come back to me completely, as far as the tune is concerned; the second half of the words, however, has obstinately resisted all my efforts to recall it, although I have an indistinct recollection of the rhymes. Here is the beginning, and all that I can remember of the rest:

Tircis, je n'ose
Écouter ton chalumeau
Sous l'ormeau:
Car on en cause
Déjà dans notre hameau.
. . . .
. . . . *un berger*
. . . . *s'engager*
. . . . . *sans danger*
Et toujours l'épine est sous la rose.[11]

I ask, where is the affecting charm which my heart finds in this song? it is a whim, which I am quite unable to understand; but, be that as it may, it is absolutely impossible for me to sing it through without being interrupted by my tears. I have intended, times without number, to write to Paris to make inquiries concerning the remainder of the words, in case anyone should happen to know them; but I am almost certain that the pleasure which I feel in recalling the air would partly disappear, if it should be proved that others besides my poor aunt Suson have sung it.

Such were my earliest emotions on my entry into life; thus began to form or display itself in me that heart at once so proud and tender, that character so effeminate but yet indomitable, which, ever wavering between timidity and courage, weakness and self-control, has throughout my life made me inconsistent, and has caused abstinence and enjoyment, pleasure and prudence equally to elude my grasp.

This course of education was interrupted by an accident, the consequences of which have exercised an influence upon the remainder of my life. My father had a quarrel with a captain in the French army, named Gautier, who was connected with some of the members of the Common Council. This Gautier, a cowardly and insolent fellow (whose nose happened to bleed during the affray), in order to avenge himself, accused my father of having drawn his sword within the city walls. My father, whom they wanted to send to prison, persisted that, in accordance with the law, the accuser ought to be imprisoned as well as himself. Being unable to have his way in this, he preferred to quit Geneva and expatriate himself for the

[11] Including the words Rousseau could not remember, the song goes: "Tircis, I dare not listen to your pipe under the elm; people are beginning to talk about it in the village. It is dangerous for a heart to have too much to do with a shepherd; there is no rose without its thorn."

rest of his life, than to give way on a point in which honor and liberty appeared to him to be compromised.

I remained under the care of my uncle Bernard, who was at the time employed upon the fortifications of Geneva. His eldest daughter was dead, but he had a son of the same age as myself. We were sent together to Bossey,[12] to board with the Protestant minister Lambercier, in order to learn, together with Latin, all the sorry trash which is included under the name of education.

Two years spent in the village in some degree softened my Roman roughness and made me a child again. At Geneva, where no tasks were imposed upon me, I loved reading and study, which were almost my only amusements; at Bossey, my tasks made me love the games which formed a break in them. The country was so new to me, that my enjoyment of it never palled. I conceived so lively an affection for it, that it has never since died out. The remembrance of the happy days I have spent there filled me with regretful longing for its pleasures, at all periods of my life, until the day which has brought me back to it. M. Lambercier was a very intelligent person, who, without neglecting our education, never imposed excessive tasks upon us. The fact that, in spite of my dislike of restraint, I have never recalled my hours of study with any feeling of disgust—and also that, even if I did not learn much from him, I learnt without difficulty what I did learn and never forgot it—is sufficient proof that his system of instruction was a good one.

The simplicity of this country life was of inestimable value to me, in that it opened my heart to friendship. Up to that time I had only known lofty but imaginary sentiments. The habit of living peacefully together with my cousin Bernard drew us together in tender bonds of union. In a short time, my feelings towards him became more affectionate than those with which I had regarded my brother, and they have never been effaced. He was a tall, lanky, weakly boy, as gentle in disposition as he was feeble in body, who never abused the preference which was shown to him in the house as the son of my guardian. Our tasks, our amusements, our tastes were the same: we were alone, we were of the same age, each of us needed a companion: separation was to us, in a manner, annihilation. Although we had few opportunities of proving our mutual attachment, it was very great; not only were we unable to live an instant apart, but we did not imagine it possible that we could ever be separated. Being, both of us, ready to yield to tenderness, and docile, provided compulsion was not used, we always agreed in everything. If, in the presence of those who looked after us, he had some advantage over me in consequence of the favor with which they regarded him, when we were alone I had an advantage over him which restored the equilibrium. When we were saying our lessons, I prompted him if he hesitated; when I had finished my exercise, I helped him with his; and in our amusements, my more active mind always led the way. In short, our two characters harmonized so well, and the friendship which united us was so sincere, that, in the five years and more, during which, whether at Bossey or Geneva, we were almost inseparable, although I confess that we often fought, it was never necessary to separate us, none of our quarrels ever

[12] A village about three miles from Geneva.

lasted longer than a quarter of an hour, and neither of us ever made any accusation against the other. These observations are, if you will, childish, but they furnish an example which, since the time that there have been children, is perhaps unique.

The life which I led at Bossey suited me so well that, had it only lasted longer, it would have completely decided my character. Tender, affectionate and gentle feelings formed its foundation. I believe that no individual of our species was naturally more free from vanity than myself. I raised myself by fits and starts to lofty flights, but immediately fell down again into my natural languor. My liveliest desire was to be loved by all who came near me. I was of a gentle disposition; my cousin and our guardians were the same. During two whole years I was neither the witness nor the victim of any violent feeling. Everything nourished in my heart those tendencies which it received from Nature. I knew no higher happiness than to see all the world satisfied with me and with everything. I shall never forget how, if I happened to hesitate when saying my catechism in church, nothing troubled me more than to observe signs of restlessness and dissatisfaction on Mademoiselle Lambercier's face. That alone troubled me more than the disgrace of failing in public, which, nevertheless, affected me greatly: for, although little susceptible to praise, I felt shame keenly; and I may say here that the thought of Mademoiselle's reproaches caused me less uneasiness than the fear of offending her.

When it was necessary, however, neither she nor her brother were wanting in severity; but, since this severity was nearly always just, and never passionate, it pained me without making me insubordinate. Failure to please grieved me more than punishment, and signs of dissatisfaction hurt me more than corporal chastisement. It is somewhat embarrassing to explain myself more clearly, but, nevertheless, I must do so. How differently would one deal with youth, if one could more clearly see the remote effects of the usual method of treatment, which is employed always without discrimination, frequently without discretion! The important lesson which may be drawn from an example as common as it is fatal makes me decide to mention it.

As Mademoiselle Lambercier had the affection of a mother for us, she also exercised the authority of one, and sometimes carried it so far as to inflict upon us the punishment of children when we had deserved it. For some time she was content with threats, and this threat of a punishment that was quite new to me appeared very terrible; but, after it had been carried out, I found the reality less terrible than the expectation; and, what was still more strange, this chastisement made me still more devoted to her who had inflicted it. It needed all the strength of this devotion and all my natural docility to keep myself from doing something which would have deservedly brought upon me a repetition of it; for I had found in the pain, even in the disgrace, a mixture of sensuality which had left me less afraid than desirous of experiencing it again from the same hand. No doubt some precocious sexual instinct was mingled with this feeling, for the same chastisement inflicted by her brother would not have seemed to me at all pleasant. But, considering his disposition, there was little cause to fear the substitution; and if I kept myself from deserving punishment, it was solely for fear of displeasing Mademoiselle Lambercier; for, so great is the power exercised over me by kindness, even by that which is due to the senses, that it has always controlled the latter in my heart.

The repetition of the offense, which I avoided without being afraid of it, occurred without any fault of mine, that is to say, of my will, and I may say that I profited by it without any qualm of conscience. But this second time was also the last; for Mademoiselle Lambercier, who had no doubt noticed something which convinced her that the punishment did not have the desired effect, declared that it tired her too much, and that she would abandon it. Until then we had slept in her room, sometimes even in her bed during the winter. Two days afterwards we were put to sleep in another room, and from that time I had the honor, which I would gladly have dispensed with, of being treated by her as a big boy.

Who would believe that this childish punishment, inflicted upon me when only eight years old by a young woman of thirty,[13] disposed of my tastes, my desires, my passions, and my own self for the remainder of my life, and that in a manner exactly contrary to that which should have been the natural result? When my feelings were once inflamed, my desires so went astray that, limited to what I had already felt, they did not trouble themselves to look for anything else. In spite of my hot blood, which has been inflamed with sensuality almost from my birth, I kept myself free from every taint until the age when the coldest and most sluggish temperaments begin to develop. In torments for a long time, without knowing why, I devoured with burning glances all the pretty women I met; my imagination unceasingly recalled them to me, only to make use of them in my own fashion, and to make of them so many Mlles. Lambercier.

Even after I had reached years of maturity, this curious taste, always abiding with me and carried to depravity and even frenzy, preserved my morality, which it might naturally have been expected to destroy. If ever a bringing-up was chaste and modest, assuredly mine was. My three aunts were not only models of propriety, but reserved to a degree which has long since been unknown amongst women. My father, a man of pleasure, but a gallant of the old school, never said a word, even in the presence of women whom he loved more than others, which would have brought a blush to a maiden's cheek; and the respect due to children has never been so much insisted upon as in my family and in my presence. In this respect I found M. Lambercier equally careful; and an excellent servant was dismissed for having used a somewhat too free expression in our presence. Until I was a young man, I not only had no distinct idea of the union of the sexes, but the confused notion which I had regarding it never presented itself to me except in a hateful and disgusting form. For common prostitutes I felt a loathing which has never been effaced: the sight of a profligate always filled me with contempt, even with affright. My horror of debauchery became thus pronounced ever since the day when, walking to Little Sacconex[14] by a hollow way, I saw on both sides holes in the ground, where I was told that these creatures carried on their intercourse. The thought of the one always brought back to my mind the copulation of dogs, and the bare recollection was sufficient to disgust me.

[13] Actually, at the time described, Mlle. Lambercier was about 38 and Rousseau about 11.
[14] A village on the outskirts of Geneva.

This tendency of my bringing-up, in itself adapted to delay the first outbreaks of an inflammable temperament, was assisted, as I have already said, by the direction which the first indications of sensuality took in my case. Only busying my imagination with what I had actually felt, in spite of most uncomfortable effervescence of blood, I only knew how to turn my desires in the direction of that kind of pleasure with which I was acquainted, without ever going as far as that which had been made hateful to me, and which, without my having the least suspicion of it, was so closely related to the other. In my foolish fancies, in my erotic frenzies, in the extravagant acts to which they sometimes led me, I had recourse in my imagination to the assistance of the other sex, without ever thinking that it was serviceable for any purpose than that for which I was burning to make use of it.

In this manner, then, in spite of an ardent, lascivious and precocious temperament, I passed the age of puberty without desiring, even without knowing of any other sensual pleasures than those of which Mademoiselle Lambercier had most innocently given me the idea; and when, in course of time, I became a man, that which should have destroyed me again preserved me. My old childish taste, instead of disappearing, became so associated with the other, that I could never banish it from the desires kindled by my senses; and this madness, joined to my natural shyness, has always made me very unenterprising with women, for want of courage to say all or power to do all. The kind of enjoyment, of which the other was only for me the final consummation, could neither be appropriated by him who longed for it, nor guessed by her who was able to bestow it. Thus I have spent my life in idle longing, without saying a word, in the presence of those whom I loved most. Too bashful to declare my taste, I at least satisfied it in situations which had reference to it and kept up the idea of it. To lie at the feet of an imperious mistress, to obey her commands, to ask her forgiveness—this was for me a sweet enjoyment; and, the more my lively imagination heated my blood, the more I presented the appearance of a bashful lover. It may be easily imagined that this manner of making love does not lead to very speedy results, and is not very dangerous to the virtue of those who are its object. For this reason I have rarely possessed, but have none the less enjoyed myself in my own way—that is to say, in imagination. Thus it has happened that my senses, in harmony with my timid disposition and my romantic spirit, have kept my sentiments pure and my morals blameless, owing to the very tastes which, combined with a little more impudence, might have plunged me into the most brutal sensuality.

I have taken the first and most difficult step in the dark and dirty labyrinth of my confessions. It is easier to admit that which is criminal than that which is ridiculous and makes a man feel ashamed. Henceforth I am sure of myself; after having ventured to say so much, I can shrink from nothing. One may judge what such confessions have cost me, from the fact that, during the whole course of my life, I have never dared to declare my folly to those whom I loved with the frenzy of a passion which deprived me of sight and hearing, which robbed me of my senses and caused me to tremble all over with a convulsive movement. I have never brought myself, even when on most intimate terms, to ask women to grant me the only favor of all which was wanting. This never happened to me but once—in my childhood, with a girl of my own age;[15] even then, it was she who first proposed it.

While thus going back to the first traces of my inner life, I find elements which sometimes appear incompatible, and yet have united in order to produce with vigor a simple and uniform effect; and I find others which, although apparently the same, have formed combinations so different, owing to the co-operation of certain circumstances, that one would never imagine that these elements were in any way connected. Who, for instance, would believe that one of the most powerful movements of my soul was tempered in the same spring from which a stream of sensuality and effeminacy has entered my blood? Without leaving the subject of which I have just spoken, I shall produce by means of it a very different impression.

One day I was learning my lesson by myself in the room next to the kitchen. The servant had put Mademoiselle Lambercier's combs in front of the fire-place to dry. When she came back to fetch them, she found one with a whole row of teeth broken. Who was to blame for the damage? No one except myself had entered the room. On being questioned, I denied that I had touched the comb. M. and Mademoiselle Lambercier both began to admonish, to press, and to threaten me; I obstinately persisted in my denial; but the evidence was too strong, and outweighed all my protestations, although it was the first time that I had been found to lie so boldly. The matter was regarded as serious, as in fact it deserved to be. The mischievousness, the falsehood, the obstinacy appeared equally deserving of punishment; but this time it was not by Mademoiselle Lambercier that chastisement was inflicted. My uncle Bernard was written to, and he came. My poor cousin was accused of another equally grave offense; we were involved in the same punishment. It was terrible. Had they wished to look for the remedy in the evil itself and to deaden for ever my depraved senses, they could not have set to work better, and for a long time my senses left me undisturbed.

They could not draw from me the desired confession. Although I was several times brought up before them and reduced to a pitiable condition, I remained unshaken. I would have endured death, and made up my mind to do so. Force was obliged to yield to the diabolical obstinacy of a child—as they called my firmness. At last I emerged from this cruel trial, utterly broken, but triumphant.

It is now nearly fifty years since this incident took place, and I have no fear of being punished again for the same thing. Well, then, I declare in the sight of heaven that I was innocent of the offense, that I neither broke nor touched the comb, that I never went near the fire-place, and had never even thought of doing so. It would be useless to ask me how the damage was done: I do not know, and I cannot understand; all that I know for certain is that I had nothing to do with it.

Imagine a child, shy and obedient in ordinary life, but fiery, proud, and unruly in his passions: a child who had always been led by the voice of reason and always treated with gentleness, justice, and consideration, who had not even a notion of injustice, and who for the first time becomes

[15] A Mlle. Goton, described later in Book I.

acquainted with so terrible an example of it on the part of the very people whom he most loves and respects! What an upset of ideas! what a disturbance of feelings! what revolution in his heart, in his brain, in the whole of his little intellectual and moral being! Imagine all this, I say, if possible. As for myself, I feel incapable of disentangling and following up the least trace of what then took place within me.

I had not yet sense enough to feel how much appearances were against me, and to put myself in the place of the others. I kept to my own place, and all that I felt was the harshness of a frightful punishment for an offense which I had not committed. The bodily pain, although severe, I felt but little: all I felt was indignation, rage, despair. My cousin, whose case was almost the same, and who had been punished for an involuntary mistake as if it had been a premeditated act, following my example, flew into a rage, and worked himself up to the same pitch of excitement as myself. Both in the same bed, we embraced each other with convulsive transports: we felt suffocated; and when at length our young hearts, somewhat relieved, were able to vent their wrath, we sat upright in bed and began to shout, times without number, with all our might: *Carnifex! carnifex! carnifex!*[16]

While I write these words, I feel that my pulse beats faster; those moments will always be present to me though I should live a hundred thousand years. That first feeling of violence and injustice has remained so deeply graven on my soul, that all the ideas connected with it bring back to me my first emotion; and this feeling, which, in its origin, had reference only to myself, has become so strong in itself and so completely detached from all personal interest, that, when I see or hear of any act of injustice—whoever is the victim of it, and wherever it is committed—my heart kindles with rage, as if the effect of it recoiled upon myself. When I read of the cruelties of a ferocious tyrant, the crafty atrocities of a rascally priest, I would gladly set out to plunge a dagger into the heart of such wretches, although I had to die for it a hundred times. I have often put myself in a perspiration, pursuing or stoning a cock, a cow, a dog, or any animal which I saw tormenting another merely because it felt itself the stronger. This impulse may be natural to me, and I believe that it is; but the profound impression left upon me by the first injustice I suffered was too long and too strongly connected with it, not to have greatly strengthened it.

With the above incident the tranquillity of my childish life was over. From that moment I ceased to enjoy a pure happiness, and even at the present day I feel that the recollection of the charms of my childhood ceases there. We remained a few months longer at Bossey. We were there, as the first man is represented to us—still in the earthly paradise, but we no longer enjoyed it; in appearance our condition was the same, in reality it was quite a different manner of existence. Attachment, respect, intimacy, and confidence no longer united pupils and guides: we no longer regarded them as gods, who were able to read in our hearts; we became less ashamed of doing wrong and more afraid of being accused; we began to dissemble, to be insubordinate, to lie. All the vices of our age corrupted our innocence and threw a veil of ugliness over our amusements. Even the country lost in our eyes that charm of gentleness and simplicity which goes to the heart. It

[16] Executioner; tormentor (Latin).

appeared to us lonely and somber: it seemed as it were covered with a veil which concealed its beauties from our eyes. We ceased to cultivate our little gardens, our plants, our flowers. We no longer scratched up the ground gently, or cried with joy when we saw the seed which we had sown beginning to sprout. We were disgusted with the life, and others were disgusted with us; my uncle took us away, and we separated from M. and Mademoiselle Lambercier, having had enough of each other, and feeling but little regret at the separation.

Nearly thirty years have passed since I left Bossey, without my recalling to mind my stay there with any connected and pleasurable recollections; but, now that I have passed the prime of life and am approaching old age, I feel these same recollections springing up again while others disappear; they stamp themselves upon my memory with features, the charm and strength of which increase daily, as if, feeling life already slipping away, I were endeavoring to grasp it again by its commencement. The most trifling incidents of that time please me, simply because they belong to that period. I remember all the details of place, persons, and time. I see the maid or the manservant busy in the room, a swallow darting through the window, a fly settling on my hand while I was saying my lesson: I see the whole arrangement of the room in which we used to live; M. Lambercier's study on the right, a copperplate engraving of all the Popes, a barometer, a large almanac hanging on the wall, the raspberry bushes which, growing in a garden situated on very high ground facing the back of the house, shaded the window and sometimes forced their way through it. I am quite aware that the reader does not want to know all this; but I am bound to tell him. Why have I not the courage to relate to him in like manner all the trifling anecdotes of that happy time, which still make me tremble with joy when I recall them? Five or six in particular—but let us make a bargain. I will let you off five, but I wish to tell you one, only one, provided that you will permit me to tell it in as much detail as possible, in order to prolong my enjoyment.

If I only had your pleasure in view, I might choose the story of Mademoiselle Lambercier's backside, which, owing to an unfortunate somersault at the bottom of the meadow, was exhibited in full view to the King of Sardinia, who happened to be passing by;[17] but that of the walnut-tree on the terrace is more amusing for me who took an active part in it, whereas I was merely a spectator of the somersault; besides, I declare that I found absolutely nothing to laugh at in an accident which, although comic in itself, alarmed me for the safety of a person whom I loved as a mother and, perhaps, even more.

Now, O curious readers of the important history of the walnut-tree on the terrace, listen to the horrible tragedy, and keep from shuddering if you can!

Outside the gate of the court, on the left of the entrance, there was a terrace, where we often went to sit in the afternoon. As it was entirely unprotected from the sun, M. Lambercier had a walnut-tree planted there. The process of planting was carried out with the greatest solemnity. The two boarders were its godfathers; and, while the hole was being filled up, we each of us held the tree with one hand and sang songs of triumph. In

[17] This royal procession passed through in August 1724.

order to water it, a kind of basin was made round the foot. Every day, eager spectators of this watering, my cousin and I became more strongly convinced, as was natural, that it was a finer thing to plant a tree on a terrace than a flag upon a breach, and we resolved to win this glory for ourselves without sharing it with anyone.

With this object, we proceeded to cut a slip from a young willow, and planted it on the terrace, at a distance of about eight or ten feet from the august walnut-tree. We did not forget to dig a similar trench round our tree; the difficulty was how to fill it, for the water came from some distance, and we were not allowed to run and fetch it. However, it was absolutely necessary to have some for our willow. For a few days, we had recourse to all kinds of devices to get some, and we succeeded so well that we saw it bud and put forth little leaves, the growth of which we measured every hour, convinced that, although not yet a foot high, it would soon afford us a shade.

As our tree so completely claimed our attention that we were quite incapable of attending to or learning anything else, and were in a sort of delirium: as our guardians, not knowing what was the matter with us, kept a tighter hand upon us, we saw the fatal moment approaching when we should be without water, and were inconsolable at the thought of seeing our tree perish from drought. At length necessity, the mother of invention, suggested to us how to save ourselves from grief and the tree from certain death; this was, to make a channel underground, which should secretly conduct part of the water intended for the walnut-tree to our willow. This undertaking was at first unsuccessful, in spite of the eagerness with which it was carried out. We had made the incline so clumsily that the water did not run at all. The earth fell in and stopped up the channel; the entrance was filled with mud; everything went wrong. But nothing disheartened us: *Labor omnia vincit improbus.*[18] We dug our basin deeper, in order to allow the water to run; we cut some bottoms of boxes into small narrow planks, some of which were laid flat, one after the other, and others set up on both sides of these at an angle, thus forming a triangular canal for our conduit. At the entrance we stuck small pieces of wood, some little distance apart, which, forming a kind of grating or lattice-work, kept back the mud and stones, without stopping the passage of the water. We carefully covered our work with well-trodden earth; and when all was ready, we awaited, in the greatest excitement of hope and fear, the time of watering. After centuries of waiting, the hour at length arrived; M. Lambercier came as usual to assist at the operation, during which we both kept behind him, in order to conceal our tree, to which very luckily he turned his back.

No sooner had the first pail of water been poured out, than we saw some of it running into our basin. At this sight, our prudence deserted us: we began to utter cries of joy which made M. Lambercier turn round; this was a pity, for he took great delight in seeing how good the soil of the walnut-tree was, and how greedily it absorbed the water. Astonished at seeing it distribute itself into two basins, he cried out in his turn, looked, perceived the trick, ordered a pickaxe to be brought, and, with one blow, broke off two or three pieces from our planks; then, crying loudly, "An

[18] "Tenacious work overcomes all obstacles" (from Virgil's *Georgics*, I. 145–146).

aqueduct, an aqueduct!" he dealt merciless blows in every direction, each of which went straight to our hearts. In a moment planks, conduit, basin, willow, everything was destroyed and uprooted, without his having uttered a single word, during this terrible work of destruction, except the exclamation which he incessantly repeated. "An aqueduct!" he cried, while demolishing everything, "an aqueduct, an aqueduct!"

It will naturally be imagined that the adventure turned out badly for the little architects: that would be a mistake: it was all over. M. Lambercier never uttered a single word of reproach, or looked upon us with displeasure, and said nothing more about it; shortly afterwards, we even heard him laughing loudly with his sister, for his laughter could be heard a long way off; and what was still more astonishing, when the first fright was over, we ourselves were not much troubled about the matter. We planted another tree somewhere else, and often reminded ourselves of the disaster that overtook the first, by repeating with emphasis, "An aqueduct, an aqueduct!" Hitherto I had had intermittent attacks of pride, when I was Aristides or Brutus;[19] then it was that I felt the first well-defined promptings of vanity. To have been able to construct an aqueduct with our own hands, to have put a cutting in competition with a large tree, appeared to me the height of glory. At ten years of age I was a better judge on this point than Caesar at thirty.

The thought of this walnut-tree and the little history connected with it has remained so vivid in my memory, or returned to it, that one of the plans which gave me the greatest pleasure, on my journey to Geneva, in 1754, was to go to Bossey and revisit the memorials of my boyish amusements, above all, the dear walnut-tree, which by that time must have been a third of a century old; but I was so continually occupied, so little my own master, that I could never find the moment to afford myself this satisfaction. There is little prospect of the opportunity ever occurring again; yet the wish has not disappeared with the hope; and I am almost certain that, if ever I should return to those beloved spots and find my dear walnut-tree still alive, I should water it with my tears.

After my return to Geneva, I lived for two or three years[20] with my uncle, waiting until my friends had decided what was to be done with me. As he intended his own son to be an engineer, he made him learn a little drawing and taught him the elements of Euclid.[21] I learned these subjects together with him, and acquired a taste for them, especially for drawing. In the meantime, it was debated whether I should be a watchmaker, an attorney, or a minister. My own preference was for the last, for preaching seemed to me to be a very fine thing; but the small income from my mother's property, which had to be divided between my brother and myself, was not sufficient to allow me to prosecute my studies. As, considering my age at that time, there was no immediate need to decide, I remained for the present with my uncle, making little use of my time and, in addition, as was only fair, paying a tolerably large sum for my board. My uncle, a man of pleasure like my father, was unable, like him, to tie himself down to his

[19] Ancient heroes, mentioned earlier, whom Rousseau had read about in Plutarch.
[20] Actually, this period lasted only about eight months.
[21] Greek author, third century B.C., of the ancient classic on geometry.

duties, and troubled himself little enough about us. My aunt was somewhat of a pietist, and preferred to sing psalms rather than attend to our education. We were allowed almost absolute freedom, which we never abused. Always inseparable, we were quite contented with our own society; and, having no temptation to make companions of the street boys of our own age, we learned none of the dissolute habits into which idleness might have led us. I am even wrong in saying that we were idle, for we were never less so in our lives; and the most fortunate thing was that all the ways of amusing ourselves, with which we successively became infatuated, kept us together busy in the house, without our being even tempted to go out into the street. We made cages, flutes, shuttlecocks, drums, houses, squirts,[22] and cross-bows. We spoilt my good old grandfather's tools in trying to make watches as he did. We had a special taste for wasting paper, drawing, painting in water-colors, illuminating, and spoiling colors. An Italian showman, named Gamba-Corta, came to Geneva; we went to see him once and never wanted to go again. But he had a marionette-show, and we proceeded to make marionettes; his marionettes played comedies and we composed comedies for ours. For want of a squeaker, we imitated Punch's[23] voice in our throat, in order to play the charming comedies, which our poor and kind relations had the patience to sit and listen to. But, my uncle Bernard having one day read aloud in the family circle a very fine sermon which he had composed himself, we abandoned comedy and began to write sermons. These details are not very interesting, I confess, but they show how exceedingly well-conducted our early education must have been, seeing that we, almost masters of our time and ourselves at so tender an age, were so little tempted to abuse our opportunities. We had so little need of making companions, that we even neglected the chances of doing so. When we went for a walk, we looked at their amusements as we passed by without the slightest desire, or even the idea of taking part in them. Our friendship so completely filled our hearts, that it was enough for us to be together to make the simplest amusements a delight.

Being thus inseparable, we began to attract attention: the more so as, my cousin being very tall while I was very short, we made an oddly-assorted couple. His long, slim figure, his little face like a boiled apple, his gentle manner, and his slovenly walk excited the children's ridicule. In the *patois*[24] of the district he was nicknamed Barna Bredanna,[25] and, directly we went out, we heard nothing but "Barna Bredanna!" all round us. He endured it more quietly than I did: I lost my temper and wanted to fight. This was just what the little rascals desired. I fought and was beaten. My poor cousin helped me as well as he could; but he was weak, and a single blow of the fist knocked him down. Then I became furious. However, although I received blows in abundance, I was not the real object of attack, but Barna Bredanna; but my obstinate anger made matters so much worse, that, in future, we only ventured to go out during school-hours, for fear of being hooted and followed.

[22] Toy pistols.

[23] Punch and Judy are characters in an old tradition of slapstick puppet shows; they make raucous sounds but don't utter words.

[24] Dialect; slang (French).

[25] A regional term equivalent to "bridled or saddled donkey," or "ignorant lout."

Behold me already a redresser of wrongs! In order to be a regular Paladin[26] I only wanted a lady; I had two. From time to time I went to see my father at Nyon, a little town in the Vaud[27] country, where he had settled. He was very much liked, and his son felt the effects of his popularity. During the short time I stayed with him, friends vied with each other in making me welcome. A certain Madame de Vulson, especially, bestowed a thousand caresses upon me, and, to crown all, her daughter took me for her lover. It is easy to understand the meaning of a lover eleven years old[28] for a girl of twenty-two. But all these roguish young women are so ready to put little puppets in front in order to hide larger ones, or to tempt them with the idea of an amusement which they know how to render attractive! As for myself, I saw no incongruity between us and took the matter seriously; I abandoned myself with all my heart, or rather with all my head—for it was only in that part of me that I was in love, although madly—and my transports, excitement and frenzy produced scenes enough to make anyone split his sides with laughing.

I am acquainted with two very distinct and very real kinds of love, which have scarcely anything in common, although both are very fervent, and which both differ from tender friendship. The whole course of my life has been divided between these two kinds of love, essentially so different, and I have even felt them both at the same time; for instance, at the time of which I am speaking, while I took possession of Mademoiselle de Vulson so openly and so tyrannically that I could not endure that any man should approach her, I had several meetings, brief but lively, with a certain little Mademoiselle Goton, in which she deigned to play the schoolmistress,[29] and that was all; but this all, which was really all for me, seemed to me the height of happiness; and, already feeling the value of the mystery, although I only knew how to make use of it as a child, I paid Mademoiselle de Vulson, who had scarcely any suspicion of it, in the same coin for the assiduity with which she made use of me to conceal other amours. But, to my great regret, my secret was discovered, or not so well kept on the part of my little schoolmistress as on my own; we were soon separated; and, some time afterwards, on my return to Geneva, while passing through Coutance, I heard some little girls cry, in an undertone, "Goton tic-tac[30] Rousseau!"

This little Mademoiselle Goton was really a singular person. Without being pretty, she had a face which was not easy to forget, and which I still recall to mind, often too tenderly for an old fool. Neither her form, nor her manner, nor, above all, her eyes were in keeping with her age. She had a proud and commanding air, which suited her part admirably, and which in fact had suggested the first idea of it to us. But the oddest thing about her was a mixture of impudence and reserve which it was difficult to comprehend. She took the greatest liberties with me, but never allowed me to take

[26] A hero of chivalry (originally, one of Charlemagne's twelve nobles, as in *The Song of Roland*).

[27] A region of western Switzerland northeast of Geneva.

[28] To be exact, Rousseau was 12 at the time.

[29] That is, spank him. This is the "girl of my own age" mentioned earlier as having performed this service for Rousseau.

[30] Either "has come to blows with" or "is in love with." Coutance is a neighborhood in Geneva where Rousseau's family lived after 1718.

any with her. She treated me just like a child, which makes me believe, either that she was no longer one herself, or that, on the contrary, she was still childish enough to see nothing but an amusement in the danger to which she exposed herself.

I belonged entirely, so to say, to each of these two persons, and so completely, that, when I was with one, I never thought of the other. In other respects, there was not the slightest similarity between the feelings with which they inspired me. I could have spent all my life with Mademoiselle de Vulson, without ever thinking of leaving her; but, when I approached her, my joy was tranquil and free from emotion. I loved her above all in fashionable society; the witty sallies, railleries, and even the petty jealousies attracted and interested me; I felt a pride and glory in the marks of preference she bestowed upon me in the presence of grown-up rivals whom she appeared to treat with disdain. I was tormented, but I loved the torment. The applause, encouragement, and laughter warmed and inspirited me. I had fits of passion and broke out into audacious sallies. In society, I was transported with love; in a *tête-à-tête*[31] I should have been constrained, cold, perhaps wearied. However, I felt a real tenderness for her; I suffered when she was ill; I would have given my own health to restore her own, and, observe! I knew very well from experience the meaning of illness and health. When absent from her, I thought of her and missed her; when I was by her side, her caresses reached my heart—not my senses. I was intimate with her with impunity; my imagination demanded no more than she granted; yet I could not have endured to see her do even as much for others. I loved her as a brother, but I was as jealous of her as a lover.

I should have been as jealous of Mademoiselle Goton as a Turk, a madman, or a tiger, if I had once imagined that she could accord the same treatment to another as to myself; for even that was a favor which I had to ask on my knees. I approached Mademoiselle de Vulson with lively pleasure, but without emotion; whereas, if I only saw Mademoiselle Goton, I saw nothing else, all my senses were bewildered. With the former I was familiar without familiarity; while on the contrary, in the presence of the latter, I was as bashful as I was excited, even in the midst of our greatest familiarities. I believe that, if I had remained with her long, I should have died; the throbbings of my heart would have suffocated me. I was equally afraid of displeasing either; but I was more attentive to the one and more obedient to the other. Nothing in the world would have made me annoy Mademoiselle de Vulson; but if Mademoiselle Goton had ordered me to throw myself into the flames, I believe I should have obeyed her immediately.

My amour, or rather my meetings, with the latter, continued only for a short time—happily for both of us. Although my relations with Mademoiselle de Vulson had not the same danger, they were not without their catastrophe, after they had lasted a little longer. The end of all such connections should always be somewhat romantic, and furnish occasion for exclamations of sorrow. Although my connection with Mademoiselle de Vulson was less lively, it was perhaps closer. We never separated without tears, and it is

[31] Private conversation.

remarkable into what an overwhelming void I felt myself plunged as soon as I had left her. I could speak and think of nothing but her; my regret was genuine and lively; but I believe that, at bottom, this heroic regret was not felt altogether for her, and that, without my perceiving it, the amusements, of which she was the center, played their part in it. To moderate the pangs of absence, we wrote letters to each other, pathetic enough to melt the heart of a stone. At last I triumphed; she could endure it no longer, and came to Geneva to see me. This time my head was completely turned; I was drunk and mad during the two days she remained. When she left I wanted to throw myself in the water after her, and the air resounded with my screams. Eight days afterwards she sent me some bonbons and gloves, which I should have considered a great compliment, if I had not learnt at the same time that she was married, and that the visit with which she had been pleased to honor me was really made in order to buy her weddingdress. I will not attempt to describe my fury; it may be imagined. In my noble rage I swore that I would never see the faithless one again, being unable to imagine a more terrible punishment for her. She did not, however, die of it; for, twenty years afterwards, when on a visit to my father, while rowing with him on the lake, I asked who the ladies were whom I saw in a boat not far from ours. "What!" said my father with a smile, "does not your heart tell you? it is your old love, Mademoiselle de Vulson that was, now Madame Cristin." I started at the almost forgotten name, but I told the boatmen to change their course. Although I had a fine opportunity of avenging myself at that moment, I did not think it worth while to perjure myself and to renew a quarrel, twenty years old, with a woman of forty.

[1723–1728.]—Thus the most valuable time of my boyhood was wasted in follies, before my future career had been decided upon. After long deliberation as to the bent of my natural inclination, a profession was determined upon for which I had the least taste; I was put with M. Masseron, the town clerk, in order to learn, under his tuition, the useful trade of a *fee-grabber*.[32] This nickname was extremely distasteful to me; the hope of gaining a number of crowns in a somewhat sordid business by no means flattered my pride; the occupation itself appeared to me wearisome and unendurable; the constant application, the feeling of servitude completed my dislike, and I never entered the office without a feeling of horror, which daily increased in intensity. M. Masseron, on his part, was ill-satisfied with me, and treated me with contempt; he continually reproached me with my dullness and stupidity, dinning into my ears every day that my uncle had told him that I knew something, whereas, in reality, I knew nothing; that he had promised him a sharp lad, and had given him a jackass. At last I was dismissed from the office in disgrace as being utterly incapable, and M. Masseron's clerks declared that I was good for nothing except to handle a file.

My calling being thus settled, I was apprenticed, not, however, to a watchmaker, but to an engraver. The contempt with which I had been treated by M. Masseron had made me very humble, and I obeyed without a murmur. My new master, M. Ducommun, was a rough and violent young

[32] Disparaging term for "lawyer."

man, who in a short time succeeded in tarnishing all the brightness of my childhood, stupefying my loving and lively nature, and reducing me, in mind as well as in position, to a real state of apprenticeship. My Latin, my antiquities, my history, were all for a long time forgotten; I did not even remember that there had ever been any Romans in the world. My father, when I went to see him, no longer found in me his idol; for the ladies I was no longer the gallant Jean Jacques; and I felt so certain myself that the Lamberciers would not have recognised their pupil in me, that I was ashamed to pay them a visit, and have never seen them since. The vilest tastes, the lowest street-blackguardism took the place of my simple amusements and effaced even the remembrance of them. I must, in spite of a most upright training, have had a great propensity to degenerate; for the change took place with great rapidity, without the least trouble, and never did so precocious a Caesar so rapidly become a Laridon.[33]

The trade in itself was not disagreeable to me; I had a decided taste for drawing; the handling of a graving-tool amused me; and as the claims upon the skill of a watchmaker's engraver were limited, I hoped to attain perfection. I should, perhaps, have done so, had not my master's brutality and excessive restraint disgusted me with my work. I stole some of my working hours to devote to similar occupations, but which had for me the charm of freedom. I engraved medals for an order of knighthood for myself and my companions. My master surprised me at this contraband occupation, and gave me a sound thrashing, declaring that I was training for a coiner, because our medals bore the arms of the Republic. I can swear that I had no idea at all of bad, and only a very faint one of good, money. I knew better how the Roman *As*[34] was made than our three-sou pieces.

My master's tyranny at length made the work, of which I should have been very fond, altogether unbearable, and filled me with vices which I should otherwise have hated, such as lying, idleness and thieving. The recollection of the alteration produced in me by that period of my life has taught me, better than anything else, the difference between filial dependence and abject servitude. Naturally shy and timid, no fault was more foreign to my disposition than impudence; but I had enjoyed an honorable liberty, which hitherto had only been gradually restrained, and at length disappeared altogether. I was bold with my father, unrestrained with M. Lambercier, and modest with my uncle; I became timid with my master, and from that moment I was a lost child. Accustomed to perfect equality in my intercourse with my superiors, knowing no pleasure which was not within my reach, seeing no dish of which I could not have a share, having no desire which I could not have openly expressed, and carrying my heart upon my lips—it is easy to judge what I was bound to become, in a house in which I did not venture to open my mouth, where I was obliged to leave the table before the meal was half over, and the room as soon as I had nothing more to do there; where, incessantly fettered to my work, I saw only objects of enjoyment for others and of privation for myself; where the sight of the liberty enjoyed by my master and companions increased the weight of my

[33] In one of La Fontaine's fables, a name for degenerate dogs.
[34] A Roman unit of weight and money.

servitude; where, in disputes about matters as to which I was best informed, I did not venture to open my mouth; where, in short, everything that I saw became for my heart an object of longing, simply because I was deprived of all. From that time my ease of manner, my gaiety, the happy expressions which, in former times, when I had done something wrong, had gained me immunity from punishment—all were gone. I cannot help laughing when I remember how, one evening, at my father's house, having been sent to bed without any supper for some piece of roguery, I passed through the kitchen with my melancholy piece of bread, and, seeing the joint turning on the spit, sniffed at it. All the household was standing round the hearth, and, in passing, I was obliged to say good-night to everybody. When I had gone the round, I winked at the joint, which looked so nice and smelt so good, and could not help bowing to it as well, and saying in a mournful voice, "Good-night, roast beef!" This naïve sally amused them so much that they made me stop to supper. Perhaps it might have had the same effect with my master, but I am sure that it would never have occurred to me, and that I should not have had the courage to say it in his presence.

In this manner I learnt to covet in silence, to dissemble, to lie, and, lastly, to steal—an idea which, up to that time, had never even entered my mind, and of which since then I have never been able to cure myself completely. Covetousness and weakness always lead in that direction. This explains why all servants are rogues, and why all apprentices ought to be; but the latter, in a peaceful state of equality, where all that they see is within their reach, lose, as they grow up, this disgraceful propensity. Not having had the same advantages, I have not been able to reap the same benefits.

It is nearly always good, but badly-directed principles, that make a child take the first step towards evil. In spite of continual privations and temptations, I had been more than a year with my master without being able to make up my mind to take anything, even eatables. My first theft was a matter of obliging some one else, but it opened the door to others, the motive of which was not so praiseworthy.

My master had a journeyman,[35] named M. Verrat, whose house was in the neighborhood, and had a garden some way off which produced very fine asparagus. M. Verrat, who was not too well supplied with money, conceived the idea of stealing some of his mother's young asparagus and selling it in order to provide himself with two or three good breakfasts. As he was unwilling to run the risk himself, and was not very active, he selected me for the expedition. After some preliminary cajoleries, which the more easily succeeded with me as I did not see their aim, he proposed it to me as an idea that had struck him on the spur of the moment. I strongly opposed it; he persisted. I have never been able to resist flattery: I gave in. I went every morning to gather a crop of the finest asparagus, and carried it to the Molard, where some good woman, who saw that I had just stolen it, told me so to my face in order to get it cheaper. In my fright I took whatever she chose to offer me, and took it to Verrat. The amount was immediately

[35] A person who has completed his apprenticeship but is not yet an independent master craftsman.

converted into a breakfast, of which I was the purveyor, and which he shared with another companion; I myself was quite satisfied with a few scraps, and never even touched their wine.

This little arrangement continued several days, without its even occurring to me to rob the robber, and to levy my tithe[36] of the proceeds of M. Verrat's asparagus. I performed my part in the transaction with the greatest loyalty; my only motive was to please him who prompted me to carry it out. And yet, if I had been caught, what blows, abuse, and cruel treatment should I have had to endure, while the wretch, who would have been sure to give me the lie, would have been believed on his word, and I should have suffered double punishment for having had the impudence to accuse him, seeing that he was a journeyman, while I was only an apprentice! So true it is that, in every condition of life, the strong man who is guilty saves himself at the expense of the innocent who is weak.

In this manner I learned that stealing was not so terrible a thing as I had imagined, and I soon knew how to make such good use of my discovery, that nothing I desired, if it was within my reach, was safe from me. I was not absolutely ill-fed, and abstinence was only rendered difficult to me from seeing that my master observed it so ill himself. The custom of sending young people from the table when the most appetizing dishes are brought on appears to me admirably adapted to make them gluttons as well as thieves. In a short time I became both the one and the other; and, as a rule, I came off very well; occasionally, when I was caught, very badly.

I shudder, and at the same time laugh, when I remember an apple hunt which cost me dear. These apples were at the bottom of a store-room, which was lighted from the kitchen by means of a high grating. One day, when I was alone in the house, I climbed upon the kneading-trough, in order to look at the precious fruit in the garden of the Hesperides,[37] which was out of my reach. I went to fetch the spit[38] to see if I could touch the apples; it was too short. To make it longer, I tied on to it another little spit which was used for small game, for my master was very fond of sport. I thrust several times without success; at last, to my great delight, I felt that I had secured an apple. I pulled very gently; the apple was close to the grating; I was ready to catch hold of it. But who can describe my grief, when I found that it was too large to pass through the bars? How many expedients I tried, to get it through! I had to find supports to keep the spit in its place, a knife long enough to divide the apple, a lath to hold it up. At last I managed to divide it, and hoped to be able to pull the pieces towards me one after the other; but no sooner were they separated than they both fell into the store-room. Compassionate reader, share my affliction!

I by no means lost courage; but I had lost considerable time. I was afraid of being surprised. I put off a more lucky attempt till the following day, and returned to my work as quietly as if I had done nothing, without thinking of the two tell-tale witnesses in the store-room.

The next day, finding the opportunity favorable, I made a fresh at-

[36] Small share (literally, one-tenth of one's goods contributed to the church).

[37] In Greek myth, nymphs who, along with a dragon, guarded a tree with golden apples in the western Isles of the Blest.

[38] A sharpened rod or stick used to support meat cooked over a fire.

tempt. I climbed upon my stool, lengthened the spit, adjusted it, and was ready to make a lunge. . . . but, unfortunately, the dragon was not asleep; all at once the door of the store-room opened, my master came out, folded his arms, looked at me, and said, "Courage!". . . . the pen falls from my hand.

In consequence of continuous ill-treatment I soon became less sensitive to it, and regarded it as a kind of compensation for theft, which gave me the right to continue the latter. Instead of looking back and considering the punishment, I looked forward and thought of revenge. I considered that, if I were beaten as a rogue, I was entitled to behave like one. I found that stealing and a flogging went together, and constituted a sort of bargain, and that, if I performed my part, I could safely leave my master to carry out his own. With this idea, I began to steal more quietly than before. I said to myself: "What will be the result? I shall be flogged. Never mind; I am made to be flogged."

I am fond of eating, but am not greedy; I am sensual, but not a gourmand;[39] too many other tastes prevent that. I have never troubled myself about my food except when my heart has been unoccupied: and that has so seldom been the case during my life that I have scarcely had time to think about dainties. For this reason I did not long confine my thievish propensities to eatables, but soon extended them to everything which tempted me; and, if I did not become a regular thief, it was because I have never been much tempted by money. Leading out of the common workshop was a private room belonging to my master, the door of which I found means to open and shut without being noticed. There I laid under contribution his best tools, drawings, proofs—in fact, everything which attracted me and which he purposely kept out of my reach. At bottom, these thefts were quite innocent, being only committed to serve him; but I was transported with joy at having these trifles in my power; I thought that I was robbing him of his talent together with its productions. Besides, I found boxes containing gold and silver filings, little trinkets, valuables and coins. When I had four or five sous[40] in my pocket, I thought I was rich; and yet, far from touching anything of what I found there, I do not even remember that I ever cast longing eyes upon it. I looked upon it with more affright than pleasure. I believe that this horror of stealing money and valuables was in great part the result of my bringing-up. With it were combined secret thoughts of disgrace, prison, punishment and the gallows, which would have made me shudder if I had been tempted; whereas my tricks only appeared to me in the light of pieces of mischief, and in fact were nothing else. They could lead to nothing but a sound flogging from my master, and I prepared myself for that beforehand.

But, I repeat, I never felt sufficient longing to need to control myself; I had nothing to contend with. A single sheet of fine drawing-paper tempted me more than money enough to buy a ream of it. This singularity is connected with one of the peculiarities of my character; it has exercised such great influence upon my conduct that it is worthwhile to explain it.

I am a man of very strong passions, and, while I am stirred by them,

[39] A person passionately fond of eating. [40] Coins of very small value.

nothing can equal my impetuosity; I forget all discretion, all feelings of respect, fear and decency; I am cynical, impudent, violent and fearless; no feeling of shame keeps me back, no danger frightens me; with the exception of the single object which occupies my thoughts, the universe is nothing to me. But all this lasts only for a moment, and the following moment plunges me into complete annihilation. In my calmer moments I am indolence and timidity itself; everything frightens and discourages me; a fly, buzzing past, alarms me; a word which I have to say, a gesture which I have to make, terrifies my idleness; fear and shame overpower me to such an extent that I would gladly hide myself from the sight of my fellow-creatures. If I have to act, I do not know what to do; if I have to speak, I do not know what to say; if anyone looks at me, I am put out of countenance. When I am strongly moved I sometimes know how to find the right words, but in ordinary conversation I can find absolutely nothing, and my condition is unbearable for the simple reason that I am obliged to speak.

Add to this, that none of my prevailing tastes center in things that can be bought. I want nothing but unadulterated pleasures, and money poisons all. For instance, I am fond of the pleasures of the table; but, as I cannot endure either the constraint of good society or the drunkenness of the tavern, I can only enjoy them with a friend; alone, I cannot do so, for my imagination then occupies itself with other things, and eating affords me no pleasure. If my heated blood longs for women, my excited heart longs still more for affection. Women who could be bought for money would lose for me all their charms; I even doubt whether it would be in me to make use of them. I find it the same with all pleasures within my reach; unless they cost me nothing, I find them insipid. I only love those enjoyments which belong to no one but the first man who knows how to enjoy them.

Money has never appeared to me as valuable as it is generally considered. More than that, it has never even appeared to me particularly convenient. It is good for nothing in itself; it has to be changed before it can be enjoyed; one is obliged to buy, to bargain, to be often cheated, to pay dearly, to be badly served. I should like something which is good in quality; with my money I am sure to get it bad. If I pay a high price for a fresh egg, it is stale; for a nice piece of fruit, it is unripe; for a girl, she is spoilt. I am fond of good wine, but where am I to get it? At a wine merchant's? Whatever I do, he is sure to poison me. If I really wish to be well served, what trouble and embarrassment it entails! I must have friends, correspondents, give commissions, write, go backwards and forwards, wait, and in the end be often deceived! What trouble with my money! my fear of it is greater than my fondness for good wine.

Times without number, during my apprenticeship and afterwards, I have gone out with the intention of buying some delicacy. Coming to a pastrycook's shop, I notice some women at the counter; I think I can already see them laughing amongst themselves at the little glutton. I go on to a fruiterer's; I eye the fine pears; their smell tempts me. Two or three young people close by me look at me; a man who knows me is standing in front of his shop; I see a girl approaching in the distance: is it the housemaid? My short-sightedness causes all kinds of illusions. I take all the passers-by for acquaintances; everywhere I am intimidated, restrained by some obstacle; my desire increases with my shame, and at last I return home like a fool, consumed with longing, having in my pocket the means of satisfying it, and yet not having had the courage to buy anything.

I should enter into the most insipid details if, in relating how my money was spent by myself or others, I were to describe the embarrassment, the shame, the repugnance, the inconvenience, the annoyances of all kinds which I have always experienced. In proportion as the reader, following the course of my life, becomes acquainted with my real temperament, he will understand all this, without my taking the trouble to tell him.

This being understood, it will be easy to comprehend one of my apparent inconsistencies—the union of an almost sordid avarice with the greatest contempt for money. It is a piece of furniture in which I find so little convenience, that it never enters my mind to long for it when I have not got it, and that, when I have got it, I keep it for a long time without spending it, for want of knowing how to make use of it in a way to please myself; but if a convenient and agreeable opportunity presents itself, I make such good use of it that my purse is empty before I know it. Besides this, one need not expect to find in me that curious characteristic of misers—that of spending for the sake of ostentation; on the contrary, I spend in secret for the sake of enjoyment; far from glorying in my expenditure, I conceal it. I feel so strongly that money is of no use to me, that I am almost ashamed to have any, still more to make use of it. If I had ever had an income sufficient to live comfortably upon, I am certain that I should never have been tempted to be a miser. I should have spent it all, without attempting to increase it; but my precarious circumstances make me careful. I worship freedom; I abhor restraint, trouble, dependence. As long as the money in my purse lasts, it assures my independence; it relieves me of the trouble of finding expedients to replenish it, a necessity which always inspired me with dread; but the fear of seeing it exhausted makes me hoard it carefully. The money which a man possesses is the instrument of freedom; that which we eagerly pursue is the instrument of slavery. Therefore I hold fast to that which I have, and desire nothing.

My disinterestedness is, therefore, nothing but idleness; the pleasure of possession is not worth the trouble of acquisition. In like manner, my extravagance is nothing but idleness; when the opportunity of spending agreeably presents itself, it cannot be too profitably employed. Money tempts me less than things, because between money and the possession of the desired object there is always an intermediary, whereas between the thing itself and the enjoyment of it there is none. If I see the thing, it tempts me; if I only see the means of gaining possession of it, it does not. For this reason I have committed thefts, and even now I sometimes pilfer trifles which tempt me, and which I prefer to take rather than to ask for; but neither when a child nor a grown-up man do I ever remember to have robbed anyone of a farthing,[41] except on one occasion, fifteen years ago, when I stole seven *livres* ten *sous*. The incident is worth recording, for it contains a most extraordinary mixture of folly and impudence, which I should have found difficulty in believing if it concerned anyone but myself.

It took place at Paris, I was walking with M. de Franceuil in the Palais-Royal about five o'clock. He pulled out his watch, looked at it, and said:

[41] One-fourth of a British penny.

"Let us go to the Opera." I agreed; we went. He took two tickets for the amphitheater,[42] gave me one, and went on in front with the other. I followed him; he went in. Entering after him, I found the door blocked. I looked, and seeing everybody standing up, thought it would be easy to lose myself in the crowd, or at any rate to make M. de Franceuil believe that I had lost myself. I went out, took back my check,[43] then my money, and went off, without thinking that as soon as I had reached the door everybody had taken their seats, and that M. de Franceuil clearly saw that I was no longer there.

As nothing was ever more foreign to my disposition than such behavior, I mention it in order to show that there are moments of semi-delirium during which men must not be judged by their actions. I did not exactly want to steal the money, I wanted to steal the employment of it; the less of a theft it was, the greater its disgracefulness.

I should never finish these details if I were to follow all the paths along which, during my apprenticeship, I descended from the sublimity of heroism to the depths of worthlessness. And yet, although I adopted the vices of my position, I could not altogether acquire a taste for them. I wearied of the amusements of my companions; and when excessive restraint had rendered work unendurable to me, I grew tired of everything. This renewed my taste for reading, which I had for some time lost. This reading, for which I stole time from my work, became a new offense which brought new punishment upon me. The taste for it, provoked by constraint, became a passion, and soon a regular madness. La Tribu, a well-known lender of books, provided me with all kinds of literature. Good or bad, all were alike to me; I had no choice, and read everything with equal avidity. I read at the work-table, I read on my errands, I read in the wardrobe, and forgot myself for hours together; my head became giddy with reading; I could do nothing else. My master watched me, surprised me, beat me, took away my books. How many volumes were torn, burnt, and thrown out of the window! how many works were left in odd volumes in La Tribu's stock! When I had no more money to pay her, I gave her my shirts, neckties and clothes; my three sous of pocket-money were regularly taken to her every Sunday.

Well, then, I shall be told, money had become necessary to me. That is true; but it was not until my passion for reading had deprived me of all activity. Completely devoted to my new hobby, I did nothing but read, and no longer stole. Here again is one of my characteristic peculiarities. In the midst of a certain attachment to any manner of life, a mere trifle distracts me, alters me, rivets my attention, and finally becomes a passion. Then everything is forgotten; I no longer think of anything except the new object which engrosses my attention. My heart beat with impatience to turn over the leaves of the new book which I had in my pocket; I pulled it out as soon as I was alone, and thought no more of rummaging my master's work-room. I can hardly believe that I should have stolen even if I had had more expensive tastes. Limited to the present, it was not in my way to make preparations in this manner for the future. La Tribu gave me credit, the

[42] Gallery; balcony.

[43] A ticket given to theatergoers allowing them to leave and then re-enter. In the present instance, Rousseau uses it to get a refund, which he keeps, of money his friend has paid.

payments on account were small, and, as soon as I had my book in my pocket, I forgot everything else. The money which came to me honestly passed in the same manner into the hands of this woman; and, when she pressed me, nothing was easier to dispose of than my own property. It required too much foresight to steal in advance, and I was not even tempted to steal in order to pay.

In consequence of quarrels, blows, and secret and ill-chosen reading, my disposition became savage and taciturn; my mind became altogether perverted, and I lived like a misanthrope. However, if my good taste did not keep me from silly and insipid books, my good fortune preserved me from such as were filthy and licentious; not that La Tribu, a woman in all respects most accommodating, would have made any scruple about lending them to me; but, in order to increase their importance, she always mentioned them to me with an air of mystery which had just the effect of making me refuse them, as much from disgust as from shame; and chance aided my modest disposition so well that I was more than thirty years old before I set eyes upon any of those dangerous books which a fine lady finds inconvenient because they can only be read with one hand.

In less than a year I exhausted La Tribu's little stock, and want of occupation, during my spare time, became painful to me. I had been cured of my childish and knavish propensities by my passion for reading, and even by the books I read, which, although ill-chosen and frequently bad, filled my heart with nobler sentiments than those with which my sphere of life had inspired me. Disgusted with everything that was within my reach, and feeling that everything which might have tempted me was too far removed from me, I saw nothing possible which might have flattered my heart. My excited senses had long clamored for an enjoyment, the object of which I could not even imagine. I was as far removed from actual enjoyment as if I had been sexless; and, already fully developed and sensitive, I sometimes thought of my crazes, but saw nothing beyond them. In this strange situation, my restless imagination entered upon an occupation which saved me from myself and calmed my growing sensuality. This consisted in feeding myself upon the situations which had interested me in the course of my reading, in recalling them, in varying them, in combining them, in making them so truly my own that I became one of the persons who filled my imagination, and always saw myself in the situations most agreeable to my taste; and that, finally, the fictitious state in which I succeeded in putting myself made me forget my actual state with which I was so dissatisfied. This love of imaginary objects, and the readiness with which I occupied myself with them, ended by disgusting me with everything around me, and decided that liking for solitude which has never left me. In the sequel we shall see more than once the curious effects of this disposition, apparently so gloomy and misanthropic, but which is really due to a too affectionate, too loving and too tender heart, which, being unable to find any in existence resembling it, is obliged to nourish itself with fancies. For the present, it is sufficient for me to have defined the origin and first cause of a propensity which has modified all my passions, and which, restraining them by means of themselves, has always made me slow to act, owing to my excessive impetuosity in desire.

In this manner I reached my sixteenth year, restless, dissatisfied with myself and everything, without any of the tastes of my condition of life, without any of the pleasures of my age, consumed by desires of the object of which I was ignorant, weeping without any cause for tears, sighing without knowing why—in short, tenderly caressing my chimeras,[44] since I saw nothing around me which counterbalanced them. On Sundays, my fellow-apprentices came to fetch me after service to go and amuse myself with them. I would gladly have escaped from them if I had been able; but, once engaged in their amusements, I became more excited and went further than any of them; it was as difficult to set me going as to stop me. Such was always my disposition. During our walks outside the city I always went further than any of them without thinking about my return, unless others thought of it for me. Twice I was caught: the gates[45] were shut before I could get back. The next day I was treated as may be imagined; the second time I was promised such a reception if it ever happened again that I resolved not to run the risk of it; yet this third time, so dreaded, came to pass. My watchfulness was rendered useless by a confounded Captain Minutoli, who always shut the gate at which he was on guard half-an-hour before the others. I was returning with two companions. About half a league from the city I heard the retreat sounded: I doubled my pace: I heard the tattoo[46] beat, and ran with all my might. I arrived out of breath and bathed in perspiration; my heart beat; from a distance I saw the soldiers at their posts; I rushed up and cried out with a voice half-choked. It was too late! Twenty paces from the outposts, I saw the first bridge raised. I shuddered when I saw those terrible horns rising in the air—a sinister and fatal omen of the destiny which that moment was opening for me.

In the first violence of my grief I threw myself on the *glacis*[47] and bit the ground. My companions, laughing at their misfortune, immediately made up their minds what to do. I did the same, but my resolution was different from theirs. On the spot I swore never to return to my master; and the next morning, when they entered the city after the gates were opened, I said good-bye to them for ever, only begging them secretly to inform my cousin Bernard of the resolution *I* had taken, and of the place where he might be able to see me once more.

After I had entered upon my apprenticeship I saw less of him. For some time we used to meet on Sunday, but gradually each of us adopted other habits, and we saw one another less frequently. I am convinced that his mother had much to do with this change. He was a child of the upper city; I, a poor apprentice, was only a child of Saint-Gervais.[48] In spite of our relationship, there was no longer any equality between us; it was derogatory to him to associate with me. However, relations were not entirely broken off between us, and, as he was a good-natured lad, he sometimes followed the dictates of his heart instead of his mother's instructions. When he was informed of my resolution, he hastened to me, not to try and dissuade me from it or to share it, but to lessen the inconveniences of my flight by some small presents, since my own resources could not take me very far.

[44] Unreal products of the imagination. [45] The gates of the city.

[46] Military signals sounded at the end of the day. This decisive event in Rousseau's life took place on March 14, 1728, a few months before his sixteenth birthday.

[47] A slope in front of a military fortification.

[48] Part of the lower-class section of Geneva.

Amongst other things he gave me a small sword, which had taken my fancy exceedingly, and which I carried as far as Turin, where necessity obliged me to dispose of it, and where, as the saying is, I passed it through my body.[49] The more I have since reflected upon the manner in which he behaved towards me at this critical moment, the more I have felt convinced that he followed the instructions of his mother, and perhaps of his father; for it is inconceivable that, left to himself, he would not have made some effort to keep me back, or would not have been tempted to follow; but, no! he rather encouraged me in my plan than tried to dissuade me; and, when he saw me quite determined, he left me without shedding many tears. We have never corresponded or seen each other since. It is a pity; his character was essentially good; we were made to love each other.

Before I abandon myself to the fatality of my lot, allow me to turn my eyes for a moment upon the destiny which, in the nature of things, would have awaited me if I had fallen into the hands of a better master. Nothing was more suitable to my disposition or better adapted to make me happy than the quiet and obscure lot of a respectable artisan,[50] especially of a certain class such as that of the engravers of Geneva. Such a position, sufficiently lucrative to afford a comfortable livelihood, but not sufficiently so to lead to fortune, would have limited my ambition for the rest of my days, and, leaving me an honorable leisure to cultivate modest tastes, would have confined me within my own sphere, without offering me the means of getting out of it. My imaginative powers were rich enough to beautify all callings with their chimeras, and strong enough to transport me, so to speak, at will from one to another; so it would have been immaterial to me in what position I actually found myself. It could not have been so far from the place where I was to my first castle in the air, that I could not have taken up my abode there without any difficulty. From this alone it followed that the simplest vocation, that which involved the least trouble and anxiety, that which allowed the greatest mental freedom, was the one which suited me best: and that was exactly my own. I should have passed a peaceful and quiet life, such as my disposition required, in the bosom of my religion, my country, my family and my friends, in the monotony of a profession that suited my taste, and in a society after my own heart. I should have been a good Christian, a good citizen, a good father of a family, a good friend, a good workman, a good man in every relation of life. I should have loved my position in life, perhaps honored it; and, having spent a life—simple, indeed, and obscure, but calm and serene—I should have died peacefully in the bosom of my family. Though, doubtless, soon forgotten, I should at least have been regretted as long as anyone remembered me.

Instead of that—what picture am I going to draw? Let us not anticipate the sorrows of my life; I shall occupy my readers more than enough with this melancholy subject.

[49] Said of a poor soldier who sells his arms for food.
[50] A person skilled in a manual craft.

Johann Wolfgang von Goethe
(1749–1832)

Johann Wolfgang von Goethe, supreme in German literature, is also one of the titans of world literature, not only because of the international fame of his works but also because he was interested in many national literatures and was one of the first men to conceive of them as an organic global entity. Beginning in childhood, he wrote almost continuously throughout his long life, so that—even discounting work he was dissatisfied with and destroyed—we have an enormous body of writing, in virtually every literary genre: short poems including ballads and some of the world's most beautiful lyrics, in many modes and meters; prose fiction of several different types; dramas in both prose and verse treating historical, classical, and mythical subjects; and a considerable amount of autobiographical writing. Nor did he limit himself to imaginative literature; he studied and wrote extensively on science, especially botany, zoology, geology, anatomy, optics, the history of science, and the psychology of scientific research. He was a painter of significant if limited gifts and a practical man of the theater. He was trained as a lawyer, and his official profession was that of a public statesman, concerned with matters ranging from diplomacy to technology. He had many love affairs, as one might expect of a man who made the "eternal feminine," as he called it, a symbol and vehicle of spiritual salvation. Although he was one of the great romanticists, his work is also profoundly classical. In short, he transcends and redefines the categories we usually use to classify human beings and their achievements.

Goethe was born in 1749 (on August 28, the birthday he assigns to Werther), in Frankfurt-am-Main in western Germany, the son of a lawyer. His early years were happy ones, and he mixed easily with people. His cultured parents provided him with a good education that fostered both his intellectual and esthetic gifts. From 1765 to 1768 he was a law student at the University of Leipzig, a sophisticated city he later dubbed the Paris of Germany. There he continued to write, especially in established eighteenth-century modes of drama and light poetry, besides occupying himself with music, medicine, and the visual arts. His first published book was the anonymous New Songs, *which appeared in 1769.*

Illness forced Goethe to leave Leipzig and ushered in a darker and more intense period of his life. When he resumed his law studies in Strasbourg (where he took his degree in 1771), he was ready to indulge a new kind of sensibility, expressed in the Sturm und Drang *(Storm and Stress) movement of which J. G. Herder was the principal apologist. This intensely emotional literary vogue, a herald of Romanticism, rebelled against Enlightenment rationalism and the art associated with it, calling instead for a more organically natural literature freed from formal rules, a more direct link between experience and expression, a new mystique of external nature as a model for art and human conduct, the use of national subjects and folk forms, and the celebration of the unaffectedly spontaneous, represented in life by children and the lower classes and in literature by "primitive" or "natural" poets like Homer and Shakespeare. (Some of these goals were clearly influenced by Rousseau.) Goethe's first great contribution to the Storm and Stress movement was the rousing historical drama* Götz von Berlichingen *(1773), which made him a name in Germany. He became an international name the following year, with* The Sorrows of Young Werther, *one of the most popular and influential books ever written. Like much of Goethe's work, it drew largely on his life, specifically an intense, hopeless love he felt,* while living in the town of Wetzlar in 1772, for Charlotte Buff, a young woman engaged to Goethe's friend Johann Kestner. With this autobiographical experience Goethe united another source from life, the suicide of his acquaintance Karl Jerusalem, an embassy secretary snubbed by the aristocracy and hopelessly in love with another man's wife. From these events Goethe fashioned not merely a roguish period piece from the Age of Sensibility (Werther's dress, ideas, and even his unhappy exit from the world were aped) but a work of enduring eloquence and artistry, one of literature's best specimens of the psychological novel and a milestone in the development of Romanticism.

In 1775 Goethe entered into an engagement, soon broken off, with Lili Schönemann, the fashionable daughter of a banker. The same year he entered the service of his admirer Duke Karl August of Saxe-Weimar, and the east-central German city of Weimar was to be his home during most of the remainder of his life. He soon was a member of the cabinet, and he became a noble in 1782. His social and civic duties were to occupy a good deal of his time at Weimar; he supervised activities ranging from theatricals to finance to mining to military recruiting. Goethe was a good administrator, but he did not sell his independence. Although his duties slowed him, he continued to write (his Storm-and-Stress mood having calmed considerably) and to immerse himself in scientific subjects; among other achievements he discovered the intermaxillary bone. A close attachment to Charlotte von Stein, a woman of great intelligence and gifts but, once more, another man's wife, evoked some of his finest lyrics. The counter-Romantic strain in him was reinforced by a trip to Italy in 1786–1788. There, while experimenting with a career as painter and sculptor and (as always) writing, he immeasurably deepened his commitment to classical art and its values of order, harmony, and proportion. Thereafter one finds in his work a fruitful tension between romantic individualism and classical discipline and universality. In 1787 two of his dramatic masterpieces were published: Egmont is a treatment of the theme of freedom based on the struggle for Dutch independence from Spain, building to a musical ending for which Beethoven later wrote incidental music; Iphigenia in Tauris is a reshaping of the Orestes myth that supremely illustrates Goethe's vision of woman as redeemer. Three years later, another great play appeared: Torquato Tasso, at once a penetrating psychological study of the Italian Renaissance poet and an examination of the nature of poetry.

After returning from Italy in 1788, Goethe took as his mistress Christiane Vulpius, a woman of modest social station by whom he had several children and whom he married eighteen years later. She helped inspire the sensuous Roman Elegies, one of Goethe's lyrical triumphs. The next years, until 1794, were a time of relative retirement and spiritual unsettledness. Although still supported by the Duke, Goethe had few state duties. The French Revolution erupted, and Goethe accompanied the Duke's army on an ill-fated campaign against France. One literary offshoot of the Revolutionary experience was to be Hermann and Dorothea (1797), an experiment in the adaptation of the ancient epic manner and meter to a modern love story in a setting of war.

In 1794 Goethe began a new phase of productivity enhanced by his friendship and collaboration with the poet Friedrich Schiller, a cross-fertilization of minds comparable to what was happening at the same time in England between Wordsworth and Coleridge. In 1796 Goethe published Wilhelm Meister's Apprenticeship, which he had started some years earlier; this work is one of the central models for the Bildungsroman, or "apprenticeship novel," which relates fictionally the process through which a young person is educated for living. One of Goethe's most popular *works, it was extended three decades later by a sequel,* Wilhelm Meister's Travels, *which tried to bring the earlier work into line with the much changed world of the Industrial Revolution.*

The greatest result of this productive decade, however, was Faust, *the First Part of which (following on earlier fragmentary versions) was published in 1808. This was Goethe's supreme work, ranking with the world's greatest dramas. The despair of translators because of its many intricate verse forms and the mixture of tones including the sublime, lyrically melodious, grotesque, and farcical, it nevertheless enjoys a worldwide eminence. It expresses one of the most deep-seated myths of modern consciousness: the highly gifted man who contracts with the Devil in return for fuller existence and self-realization. Goethe gives the issue an even more cosmic setting by placing the story in the framework of a bet, like that in the Book of Job, between God and the Devil over the redemption of Faust, whose identity is the arena for a struggle between good and evil. Part One leaves the outcome unresolved, and not until more than twenty years later did Goethe complete the drama in Part Two, which he reserved for publication after his death. Part Two is far-ranging symbolism that takes Faust from the smaller world he had encountered in Margarete, the heroine of Part One, into the larger public world where he meets his ultimate test and—in some sense about which interpreters differ—triumphs.*

Schiller died in 1805, a loss Goethe felt keenly. He found some compensation, however, in the society of the young Romantics of the day, whose values he shared in many ways although he felt they were insufficiently respectful of the ideal of form. In 1809 he published Elective Affinities, *a complex psychological novel on the issue of marriage and divorce, and in 1808–1810 one of his major scientific works,* On the Theory of Colors, *a study he ranked high among his achievements. He embarked on serious study of non-Western literatures, stirred by an ideal of world literature as an agency for international understanding and universal culture. The culmination of these studies in his own creative work was the Persian-inspired* West-Easterly Divan *(1819), a collection that includes some of his most beautiful poems. Much of his very last writing was autobiographical.*

Goethe's international stature, well established by the turn of the century, grew ever greater in his last decades; great public figures, including Napoleon, paid him homage. Thomas Mann created an interesting imaginative picture of Goethe's late years of fame in Lotte in Weimar, *a novel about a visit to Goethe some forty years after* Werther *by the real-life prototype of Lotte. A celebrity's celebrity, his status late in life was that of a godlike sage. He remained concerned to the end with new currents of events and social tendencies, especially the problems and promise of technology. And, one hardly needs to add, he wrote until the end, completing the aforementioned sequel to* Wilhelm Meister *and Second Part of* Faust, *which was published a year after his death in 1832.*

The Sorrows of Young Werther, *the selection from Goethe that follows in this book, has been in some ways the victim of its own notoriety. Safely pigeonholed as part of Storm-and-Stress (and therefore "low") Romanticism, as a representation in caricature of a passing mood in the history of taste, it invites new readers to be tolerantly amused at best by things that people once, inexplicably, took seriously. This misjudgment seldom survives an actual reading of the novel. To be sure, some things in it are dated—most obviously, the vogue of "Ossian's" poetry, which Werther reads to Lotte near the end with such cyclonic effect. Even things like this, however, are often redeemed by the narrative context; certainly that final scene gives the murky gloom of Ossianic poetry a power it does not possess in itself.* Werther *is, in fact, by no means low Romanticism; in its treatment of nature as half the creation of the human mind, in its exploration of the conflict between the quest for absolutes and the confinements of the actual, in its examination of the role of work and social convention in the life of the idealist, in its treatment of love as both spiritual and fleshly desire, and above all in the acuity of its psychological analysis of the relationship between neurosis (if that is the right word) and genius,* Werther *is very near in sophistication to high Romanticism at its best.*

These great themes are half-concealed by the realistic, seemingly effortless flow of the epistolary novel form. But it would be a mistake, the protagonist's penchant for artlessness notwithstanding, to underestimate Goethe's artistry in Werther. *Enough eloquence survives translation to make the book linguistically impressive. Its general movement, modulating skillfully between calm and storm (both literally in nature and psychologically), shows firm control of form. The themes are introduced early and deftly; this is most obviously true in the lengthy discussion of suicide, but there are subtler touches too, including the irony of Werther's tirade against the poisoning effect of ill-humor (1 July 1771) and the still more subtle irony—a mere sugges-tion—in Werther's very first letter, in which he shows concern over having broken a woman's heart. Expressive threads of imagery weave their patterns throughout. For example, Werther's outrage at the chopping down of the walnut trees is more than tenderness toward flora; significantly, it blends in his mind with the perpetrator's rationalist modern theology and the sleaziness of commerce. The large patterns are hard to miss, like those sustained in the Biblical references, but even the smallest details can pull their weight, as in the two acts of gathering flowers described on 10 August 1771 and 30 November 1772.*

The abiding challenge in reading Werther *is to understand the psychology of its hero (to some extent, Lotte and Albert too) and to evaluate him. A distinguishing quality of certain great books is that they evoke widely different responses, all of which can be plausibly defended. This is certainly true of* Werther. *To some readers its hero is the man described in the opening paragraph as certain to win our "admiration and love," a noble victim either of hopeless passion for a woman or of the more metaphysi-cal doom that sent him with an unquenchable thirst for being into a world that ultimately reveals itself as a parched wasteland. To some readers he is exasperating, perversely ignoring not only the sensible advice of other people but his own best wisdom, including his conviction, already mentioned, that we need to control our ill-humor in the interests of our friends' happiness. Some readers find in him a case study of morbid, pathological neurosis and then go on (somewhat inconsistently, since they are talking about a man they define as sick) to condemn him roundly not just as contemptible but even as cruel. These wildly varying interpretations of him suggest that, however Goethe wanted us to respond to it,* Werther *is a touchstone by which readers reveal certain of their fundamental values—the degree of their idealism and realism (and how they understand those problematical terms), the importance they attribute to love as an emotional experience, and—in the psychologist's phrase—their "threshold of pain interpretation" (a matter Werther and Albert explicitly address; see the letter of 12 August 1771). That a book which engages our interest so intensely as sheer story can do all this is surely a sign that its author, even at twenty-five, was a man of extraordinary vision and intelligence.*

FURTHER READING *(prepared by W. J. R.):* A fine introduction to *The Sorrows of Young Werther* can be found in the Bantam bilingual edition of the work, with intro-duction by Harry Steinhauer, 1962. Steinhauer sketches Goethe's life, discusses

Werther as a drama, and considers controversial interpretations of Werther himself. Stuart Pratt Atkins's *The Testament of Werther in Poetry and Drama,* 1949, is a fascinating examination of *Werther's* tremendous impact on Romanticism. The first chapter, "The Cult of Werther," will be the most interesting for those concerned only with *Werther* itself rather than its successors. Critical surveys of Goethe's total output are legion; Barker Fairley's *A Study of Goethe,* 1947, is probably still the best one available in English. Fairley provides fine biographical information and discusses the writing of *Faust* at particular length. Liselotte Dieckmann's *Johann Wolfgang Goethe,* 1974, is also a good introductory piece, taking a traditional approach. Ronald Gray's *Goethe: A Critical Introduction,* 1967, can also be highly recommended; Gray's biographical account is particularly useful for the influences on Goethe's development. On a more advanced critical level, Ilse Graham's *Goethe: Portrait of the Artist,* 1977, takes a thematic approach to the problem of defining what constitutes a "Goethean" work. Using a great variety of Goethe's writings, Graham makes a rewarding attempt to elucidate a complex artistic sensibility. For those approaching *Faust* for the first time, the following works can provide assistance: F. Melian Stawell and G. Lewis Dickinson's *Goethe and "Faust": An Interpretation,* 1929, is primarily a commentary on the work; Alexander Gillies's *Goethe's "Faust": An Interpretation,* 1957, stresses allegorical interpretations and also uses a commentary format; H. G. Haile's *Invitation to Goethe's "Faust,"* 1978, is probably the best of the group, examining difficult textual matters and several thematic concerns.

THE SORROWS OF YOUNG WERTHER

(1774 Version)[1]

Translated by William Rose

Whatever I have been able to discover of the story of poor Werther I have industriously collected, and put it now before you, and I know that you will thank me for it. You will not be able to withhold your admiration and love for his mind and character or your tears for his fate.

And you, good soul, who are laboring under the same distress as he, draw consolation from his sufferings and, if you should be prevented by fate or your own fault from finding one more intimate, let this little book be your friend.

PART ONE

4 May, 1771.

How glad I am to have got away! My dear friend, what a thing is the heart of man! To leave you whom I love so much, from whom I was inseparable—and yet be cheerful! I know you will forgive me. Were not all my other

[1] Goethe revised *Werther* in 1786. In the later version, the fictional editor, after he steps in to tell the story near the end, portrays Albert more sympathetically than in the present version. The other most significant difference is the insertion of a brief episode of tragic love, summarized in the footnote to Werther's letter of 6 December 1772. Stylistically, the second version is smoother, the first more colloquial and closer to the mood of the Storm-and-Stress period.

friendships veritably chosen by Fate to oppress a heart like mine? Poor Leonore! And yet the blame was not mine! Could I help it if her poor heart conceived a passion for me while the capricious charms of her sister afforded me agreeable entertainment! And yet—am I altogether blameless? Did I not feed her emotions? Did I not myself find pleasure in the sincere manifestations of Nature which so often made us laugh, however little conducive they were to laughter? Did I not—Oh! what is man, that he may bewail his lot?—I will, dear friend, I promise you, I will mend my ways; I will no longer chew the cud of misfortune that Fate ekes out to us, as I have always done. I will enjoy the present, and the past shall be done with. You are surely right, my best of friends. The sufferings of men would be less if they did not so busily engage their imagination—God knows why they are so constituted—in recalling the memory of bygone ills, rather than bear an indifferent present.

Will you be so good as to tell my mother that I shall look after her business as well as I can and that I shall write to her about it in a day or two? I called on my aunt and did not by any means find the ill-tempered woman that they make her out to be at home. She is lively, impetuous and very warm-hearted. I explained to her my mother's grievances about the legacy that had been held back. She told me the reasons that had impelled her to do it and the terms under which she would be ready to hand everything over—more, in fact, than we asked.—In short, I don't want to write about it now, but tell my mother everything will be all right. And in dealing with this little matter I have again found that misunderstandings and indolence are perhaps the cause of more disturbance in the world than cunning or malice. At any rate the last two are certainly more rare.

For the rest, I am quite happy here. Solitude is delicious balm to my heart in this heavenly spot, and this youthful season pours the fulness of its warmth into my oft-shivering heart. Every tree, every hedge is a nosegay, and one would like to turn into a cockchafer[2] to float in a sea of fragrance and find in it all the nourishment one needs.

The town itself is not very agreeable, but it lies amidst the most inexpressible natural beauty, which led the late Count von M. to lay out a garden on one of the intersecting hills which form the most charming valleys in the loveliest diversity of Nature. The garden is simple, and one feels as soon as one enters that it was planned not by a scientific gardener but by an impressionable soul that wanted here to take its pleasure. I have shed many a tear for the departed owner in the crumbling arbor which was his favorite sojourn, and is also mine. Soon I shall be the master of the garden. The gardener has become devoted to me during the few days I have been here, and he will not do at all badly by it.

10 MAY.

My whole soul is imbued with a wondrous serenity, like the pleasant spring mornings which I enjoy with all my heart. I am completely alone and find life so enjoyable in this spot which was created for souls like mine. I am so happy, so absorbed in the sensation of a tranquil existence, that my art is

[2] A beetle.

suffering. I could not draw a line at this moment, and yet I have never been more of a painter than I am now. When the mist is rising from the lovely valley and the sun is high above the impenetrable shade of my wood, so that only now and then a ray steals into the inner sanctuary, and I lie in the tall grass by the falling brook, and discover a thousand different grasses on the surface of the earth; when I feel nearer to my heart the teeming little world among the blades, the innumerable, unfathomable creatures in the shape of worms and insects, and when I feel the presence of the Almighty Spirit Who created us all in His image, the breath of the All-loving One who sustains us as we float in illimitable bliss—Oh! friend, when the world then grows dim before my eyes and earth and sky are absorbed into my soul like the form of a beloved, I am often consumed with longing and think, ah! would that I could express it, would that I could breathe on to paper that which lives so warm and full within me, so that it might become the mirror of my soul as my soul is the mirror of the eternal God! My friend—but it is beyond my power, and I succumb to the splendor of what lies before me.

12 MAY.

I know not whether deluding spirits are hovering round this spot, or whether it is the divine and ardent fancy of my heart which turns everything around me into a Paradise. Right in front of the gate is a spring, a spring by which I am enchanted like Melusine[3] and her sisters. On descending a small hill you come to an arch, with about twenty steps going down to where the clearest of water gushes from the marble rock. The little wall above which encloses it, the tall trees all round, the coolness of the place—there is something so attractive, so awesome about it all. Hardly a day passes without my sitting there for an hour. Then the girls come from the town to fetch water, the most innocent and necessary of services which once even the daughters of kings performed. As I sit there I am reminded vividly of the days of the patriarchs,[4] all striking up acquaintance or plighting their troth at the well, and kindly spirits hovering round the springs and fountains. Oh! he can never have refreshed himself at the coolness of a spring, after a hard walk on a summer's day, who is unable to sympathize with my emotion.

13 MAY.

You ask whether you are to send my books along? I entreat you, for the Lord's sake, do not bother me with books. I no longer want to be guided, enlivened or excited. This heart is in sufficient of a ferment without their help. I need lullabies and I have found them in abundance in my Homer. How often do I lull my stormy spirit, for never have you seen anything so restless, so changeable as this heart. Dear friend! do I need to tell *you* who have so often borne the burden of my transition from grief to excessive joy,

[3] A mermaid.

[4] Abraham, Isaac, and Jacob. Episodes at wells led to the betrothals of Isaac to Rebekah and of Jacob to Rachel (Genesis, chs. 24, 29).

from gentle melancholy to devastating passion? I treat my heart like a sick child and gratify its every whim. Don't repeat this, there are people who would take it amiss.

15 MAY.

The poor folk here know me already and have an affection for me, especially the children. I have noticed something which saddens me. When I first mixed with them and asked in a friendly manner about one thing or another, some of them thought I wanted to scoff, and they put me off very rudely. I did not take offense, but I felt very keenly, what I have often noticed, that people in a better position always keep coldly aloof from the common folk as though they feared to lose something by proximity, and there are even heedless, mischievous wags who appear to act condescendingly in order to make poor people all the more sensitive to their arrogance. I know quite well that we are not all equal, and that we never can be so. But I maintain that anyone who thinks it necessary to hold himself aloof from the so-called rabble, in order to keep its respect, is quite as blameworthy as a coward who hides from the enemy because he is afraid of defeat.

A little while ago I came to the spring and found a young maidservant who had put her pitcher on the lowest step and was looking round for one of her friends to help her lift it on to her head. I went down and looked at her. "Shall I help you, young woman?" I asked. She blushed to the roots of her hair. "Oh no sir!" she said. "Come, don't stand on ceremony."—She adjusted her headpiece and I helped her. She thanked me and went up the steps.

17 MAY.

I have made all sorts of acquaintances but have not yet got into any circle. I do not know what there is about me that attracts people, so many like me and become attached to me, and it always grieves me when our paths are the same for only such a very short distance. When you ask what the people here are like, I must reply, like everywhere else. The human race does not vary much. Most people pass the greater part of their lives in work, in order to live, and the modicum of free time they have to themselves makes them so uneasy that they seek every means they can to kill it. Alas, the destiny of man!

But they are a very worthy type of folk! When I on occasion forget myself, and am able to enjoy with them the pleasures that still remain to man, to exchange jests in all candor and sincerity at a well-set board, to arrange a walk or a dance at the proper time and so on, it has a good effect on me, so long as I do not remember all the other forces lying dormant in me, all untried and becoming atrophied, which I must carefully conceal. Oh! all this clutches at my heart—and yet! It is the fate of a man like me to be misunderstood.

Alas! that the friend of my youth is gone, alas! that I ever knew her! I would say to myself "You are a fool! You are seeking what does not exist down here." But she was mine, I felt the heart, the great soul in whose presence I seemed to myself to be more than I really was, since I was everything that I could be. God! was there a single force in my soul that remained untried, was I not able to develop in her presence all the wondrous perception with which my heart embraces Nature, was not our intercourse an endless weaving of the most delicate feeling, the keenest wit, whose variations were all stamped, even to the extent of extravagance, with the impress of genius? And now—Alas! she descended before me to the grave, for she had the advantage in years. Never shall I forget her, never shall I cease to recall her steadfast mind and divine fortitude.

A few days ago I met a young man named V., a straightforward youth with very pleasing features. He has just come down from the University, does not exactly consider himself a sage but yet thinks he knows more than other people. He was very diligent, as I can tell from various signs, in short, he is pretty well informed. As he had heard that I draw a great deal and know Greek (two unusual phenomena in these parts) he came to me and dug out his store of learning, from Batteux to Wood, from de Piles to Winckelmann, assuring me that he had read right through the first part of Sulzer's *Theory* and possessed a manuscript of Heyne's about the study of antiquity.[5] I did not pursue the subject.

I have made the acquaintance of another very worthy fellow, the prince's bailiff.[6] A straightforward, simple man. They say it does one's heart good to see him among his children, of whom he has nine. In particular they talk a great deal about his eldest daughter. He has invited me to come and see him, and I am going to call on him very soon. He lives in one of the prince's hunting lodges, an hour and a half from here, to which he received permission to move after the death of his wife, since he found staying here in the town, in the bailiff's lodge, too painful.

In addition I have come across a few eccentric oddities whom I find quite insufferable, most insupportable of all being their attestations of friendship.

Farewell! you will like this letter, it is all about things that have happened.

22 MAY.

That the life of man is only a dream has already occurred to many, and I also am always haunted by this feeling. When I see the restrictions by which the active, speculative powers of man are hemmed in, when I see how all activity is directed toward the satisfaction of needs which themselves have no other purpose than to prolong our wretched existence, and that the only way to meet certain speculations is by a dreamy resignation, in which we paint the walls of our prison with colored figures and bright prospects—all this, Wilhelm, makes me dumb. I turn in upon myself and find a world! But again more with presentiment and obscure craving than plastic[7] power and vital force. Everything swims before my senses and I continue on my way through the world with a dreamy smile.

All learned teachers and instructors are agreed that children do not

[5] The six men named were authorities on esthetics, archeology, and language.
[6] Manager of an estate. [7] Shaping.

know the reason for their desires. But nobody likes to believe that grown-ups are also walking unsteadily upon this earth, that, like children, they do not know whence they come nor whither they are going, that their actions are equally devoid of true purpose, that they are ruled in the same way by the promise of biscuits, cake or the birch,[8] and yet it seems to me the thing is evident.

I willingly admit, for I know what your reply will be, that the happiest mortals are those who, like children, live for the day, drag about their dolls, don and doff their clothes, creep respectfully round the cupboard where mother keeps the tarts and, when they at last snatch what they are after, stuff their cheeks and cry for more.—Such beings are happy. And they also are well-off who give high-sounding names to their miserable pursuits, or even their passions, and attribute to them a colossal influence on the welfare and prosperity of the human race. He is lucky who can do so! But whoever in his humbleness recognizes what all this leads to, who sees how neatly every contented citizen trims his little garden into an Eden, and how even unhappy mortals pant along patiently under their heavy load and everybody alike is eager to see the light of the sun for another minute—such a man is tranquil and likewise creates his world out of his own soul, happy because he is a human being. And then, circumscribed as he is, he yet always preserves in his heart the sweet feeling of freedom and the thought that he can leave this prison when he will.

26 MAY.

You know of old the way I settle down, build myself a cabin in some intimate spot and take up my modest quarters there. I have again found a corner that attracts me.

About an hour's journey from the town lies a hamlet called Wahlheim.[9] It is very interestingly situated on a hill and, when you walk out of the village by the footpath above, you see the whole valley spread out at your feet. A kindly landlady, obliging and cheerful in her old age, dispenses wine, beer and coffee and, what is most delightful of all, there are two limes whose spreading branches cast their shade over the little open space in front of the church, which is closed in on all sides by the cottages of the peasants, their barns and farmyards. I have rarely found a spot more intimate or cozy, and I have my little table and chair brought out from the inn, drink my coffee and read my Homer. The first time I came by accident upon the limes one fine afternoon, the place was a solitude. Everybody was in the fields. Only one little boy about four years of age was sitting on the ground, holding a child of about six months between his feet, clasping him with both arms to his breast so that he formed a kind of armchair for him and, in spite of the vivacity which sparkled in his black eyes, he was quite still. The sight pleased me and, sitting down on a plow opposite them, I amused myself by drawing their brotherly attitude, including the neighbor-

[8] Rod for punishing children.

[9] "The reader need not exert himself to find out which are the places referred to here, as it has been necessary to change the names mentioned in the original letters."—Note in original German text.

ing hedge, the doorway of a threshing-floor and some broken cartwheels, just as they all stood, so that in an hour I had made a well-grouped and very interesting sketch without adding anything at all that was not in my model. This strengthened my resolution to keep to Nature in the future. Nature alone is infinitely rich, and Nature alone forms the great artist. Much can be adduced in favor of rules that can be applied with more or less equal justice in praise of middle-class society. The man who models himself on them will never produce anything inferior or in bad taste, just as one who allows his life to be fashioned by precepts and the laws of propriety will never become a disagreeable neighbor or a remarkable villain; on the other hand, whatever people may say, rules destroy the true feeling for Nature and its true expression. You will say, "That is too severe! they only act as a check, prune the rank[10] tendrils, and so on." My good friend, shall I submit a parable to you? It is like love. A youth cleaves wholly to a maid, passes all his hours in her company, expends all his forces, all his fortune, to express to her at every moment that he is completely devoted to her. And then there comes a Philistine,[11] a man engaged in a public office, who says to him, "Young Man, to love is human, only you must love in a human way! Divide up your hours, giving some to work, and your hours of recreation you may dedicate to your maid; calculate your fortune, and from whatever you have beyond your needs you may offer her a gift, say on her birth or name day,[12] only not too often, and so on." If he obeys, he will become an efficient young man and I would advise any prince to give him a post in the government service; but there will be an end to his love and, if he is an artist, to his art. Oh my friends! Why does the stream of genius break forth so rarely, so rarely roar down in a raging torrent, mountain high, to convulse your wondering souls? My friends, there are tranquil fellows dwelling on both banks whose arbors, tulip-beds and cabbage-plots would be devastated, and so they are able to ward off the threatening danger by timely damming and draining.

27 MAY.

I see that I have lapsed into parable and ecstatic declamation, and have quite forgotten to tell you the sequel to my adventure with the children. I had been sitting on my plow for about two hours entirely absorbed in perceptions of the picturesque which my letter of yesterday will have transmitted to you in a very fragmentary manner. Towards evening a young woman comes up to the children, who during all this time had not moved, with a little basket on her arm, and calls out when she is still some distance away, "Philip, you are a very good boy." She greeted me, I thanked her, stood up, went up to her and inquired whether she was the mother of the children. She said she was and, giving the older one half a roll, she picked up the baby and kissed it with every sign of maternal affection. "I gave my Philip the baby to hold," she said, "and went into the town with my eldest boy to buy white bread and sugar and an earthenware saucepan for porridge." I saw all this in the basket from which the lid had fallen off. "I want

[10] Growing wild; overfertile. [11] An insensitive middle-class opponent of culture.
[12] Feast day of the saint whose name one bears.

to cook Hans (that was the name of the baby) some broth before he goes to bed; my scamp of an eldest broke my saucepan yesterday as he was quarrelling with Philip over what was left of the porridge." I inquired about the eldest boy, and she had hardly told me that he was chasing a couple of geese on the common when he came running up with a hazel switch for Philip. In further conversation with the mother I learned that she was the daughter of the schoolmaster, and that her husband was on his way to Switzerland to fetch a legacy that had been left him by a cousin. "They tried to cheat him out of it," she said, "and did not answer his letters, so he has gone there himself. I hope nothing has happened to him, as I have not heard from him since." I found it difficult to tear myself away. I gave each of the children a *Kreuzer,*[13] including one for the baby which I gave to the mother to buy him a roll for his broth when she went into the town, and so I left them.

I tell you, my dear fellow, when my mind is all a riot, it is soothed by the sight of such a mortal pursuing in tranquil contentment the narrow round of her existence, making both ends meet from day to day, and with no other thought, when she sees the leaves falling, but that winter is near.

I have often gone out since, and the children have become quite used to me. When I drink my coffee they have their share of the sugar, and they share my bread and butter and sour milk in the evening. On Sundays they never fail to receive their *Kreuzer,* and if I am not there after the hour of prayer the landlady has orders to pay it to them.

I have won their confidence and they tell me all sorts of things. I find it particularly delightful to watch them vent their passions and express their desires so naively when a number of children from the village are collected together.

I had a lot of trouble to relieve the mother of her apprehension lest they might "incommode the gentleman."

16 JUNE.

Why don't I write to you? You ask me that though you are also numbered among the scholars! You should be able to divine that I am well, and indeed—in short, I have met someone in whom my heart is interested. I have—I do not know.

To tell you in proper order how it happened that I made the acquaintance of one of the most charming of beings will be no easy matter; I am content and happy, so am not likely to be a satisfactory narrator.

An angel! By Heaven, everybody says that of his mistress! Doesn't he? And yet I am incapable of telling you how perfect she is, or why she is perfect, enough, she has taken complete possession of my mind.

So much naïvete combined with such intelligence, such kindness and such resolve, such tranquillity of soul in such an active life.

This is all hopeless twaddle that I am saying about her, mere abstractions which fail to express a single feature of her real self. Another time—No, not another time, I will tell you now, immediately. If I don't do it now, I never shall. For, between ourselves, since I began this letter I have been

[13] Small coin.

three times on the verge of laying down my pen, saddling my horse and riding off though I vowed early this morning that I would not—and yet every minute I go to the window to see how high the sun stands. . . .

I could not help it, I had to go out to her. I am back once more, Wilhelm, and will eat my supper and finish this letter. How it enraptures my soul to see her among the dear happy children, her eight brothers and sisters.

If I continue like this, you will be no wiser at the end than you were at the beginning, so listen, I will force myself to give you details.

I wrote to you recently that I had made the acquaintance of the bailiff S., and that he had invited me to come and visit him soon at his hermitage, or rather his little kingdom. I neglected to do so and would perhaps never have gone, if there had not been revealed to me by accident the treasure concealed in that tranquil spot.

The young people here had arranged a ball in the country, and I gladly agreed to go. I offered my escort to a nice, good-looking, but not otherwise interesting girl in this town, and it was settled that I was to hire a coach to drive out to the scene of the festivities with my partner and her cousin, and that we were to pick up Charlotte S. on the way. "You will make the acquaintance of a beautiful girl," my partner said, as we drove through a broad avenue in the wood towards the hunting lodge. "Take care," her cousin added, "that you don't fall in love." "What do you mean?" I asked. "She is already betrothed," the former replied, "to a very worthy man who has gone to put his affairs in order after his father's death and to apply for an important post." The information did not interest me particularly.

The sun was still a quarter of an hour from the hilltop when we reached the lodge gate; it was very sultry and the ladies expressed their anxiety lest we should be overtaken by a storm which we could see gathering in heavy, whitish-gray little clouds round the horizon. I relieved their fears by pretending to a knowledge of the weather, though I began myself to have a foreboding that our festivities would be interrupted.

I had alighted, and a maid who came to the gate begged us to wait a moment, Mamselle Lottchen[14] would be with us straightway. I went across the courtyard to the well-built house and, when I had ascended the steps in front and entered at the door, I caught sight of the most charming scene that I have ever witnessed. In the entrance hall there swarmed six children, from two to eleven years of age, round a handsome girl of middle height, who wore a simple white frock with pink bows on the breast and arms. She was holding a loaf of black bread and cutting a slice for each of the children round her in proportion to its age and appetite, offering it with such an amiable air and each one crying "Thank you!" so artlessly, after he had stretched his little hands up as high as he could before his slice was cut, and then springing away contentedly with his supper or, if he was of a quieter nature, walking tranquilly towards the gate to see the strangers and the coach in which their Lotte was to drive away.—"I beg your pardon," she said, "for giving you the trouble of coming in and making the ladies wait. While I was dressing and making all sorts of arrangements for the house in my absence, I forgot to give my children their supper, and they

[14] Diminutive form of *Charlotte*.

won't have their bread cut by anyone but me." I paid her some harmless compliment while my whole soul was absorbed in the contemplation of her figure, her voice, her bearing, and I had just time to recover from my surprise when she ran into the room to fetch her gloves and fan. The children kept at a little distance, casting sidelong glances at me, and I went up to the youngest who was a most pleasant looking child. He had just drawn back when Lotte appeared in the doorway and said, "Louis, shake hands with your cousin." The boy did so with a very frank air, and I could not refrain from kissing him heartily in spite of his dirty little nose. "Cousin?" I said, as I offered her my hand. "Do you consider that I deserve the happiness of being related to you?" "Oh!" she said, with a roguish smile, "our circle of cousins is very extensive, and I should be very sorry if you were the least worthy among them." As we went she ordered Sophie, the next oldest sister to herself, a girl of about eleven, to keep an eye on the little ones, and greet their father when he came back from his ride. The little ones she admonished to obey their sister Sophie as they would herself, and some of them expressly promised to do so. A pert little blonde, however, of about six years, said, "But it isn't you, after all, Lottchen! we like you better." The two eldest boys had climbed up behind the coach, and at my request she allowed them to travel with us until we reached the edge of the wood, so long as they promised not to tease each other and to hold on firmly.

Hardly had we fitted ourselves in and the ladies greeted one another, each in turn expressing her views about the others' costumes, particularly bonnets, and duly passing in review the company that they expected to meet, when Lotte stopped the coach for her brothers to descend; they asked to kiss her hand once more, and the older one did so with all the delicacy that could be expected of a boy of fifteen, the other with impetuousness and levity. She bade them give her love once more to the little ones, and the coach rolled on.

The cousin inquired whether she had finished the book she had recently sent her. "No," said Lotte. "I do not like it; you can have it back. The one you sent me before was no better." When I asked what the books were, I was amazed at her reply.[15] There was so much character in all she said, and with every word I discovered fresh charms, saw new flashes of intelligence lighting up her features, which appeared gradually to brighten with pleasure because she felt that I understood her.

"When I was younger," she said, "I liked nothing so much as novels. Heaven knows I felt happy when I could sit in some corner on Sundays and share with my whole heart the fortune or distress of some Miss Jenny. Nor do I deny that this kind of romance still has some charm for me. But since I now so seldom have time for a book, it must be suited to my taste. And the author I most prefer is the one in whom I find my own world again, who describes happenings such as I see around me and yet whose story I find as interesting, as sympathetic as my own domestic existence, which is, to be

[15] "It has been thought necessary to suppress this passage in the manuscript so as not to afford anyone grounds for complaint. Although, as a matter of fact, no author can be much concerned at the judgment of a single girl and an unbalanced young man."—Note in original German text.

sure, not a Paradise, but nevertheless on the whole a source of inexpressible bliss."

I did my best to conceal my emotions at these words. I was not, it is true, very successful, for when I heard her speak incidentally, but with such truth, about the Vicar of Wakefield and about[16]—, I lost my control and told her everything that forced itself to my lips, and only noticed after some time, when Lotte directed her remarks to the others, that these had been sitting there the whole time with wide-open eyes, as though they were not there at all. The cousin looked at me more than once with a mocking air, which however was of little consequence to me.

The conversation turned upon the pleasure of dancing. "If this passion is a fault," said Lotte, "I willingly confess I know nothing that excels dancing. And when I have something on my mind and drum out a quadrille on my squeaky old harpsichord, then everything is all right again."

How I gazed into her black eyes as she spoke, how her vivacious lips and her fresh, lively mien drew my whole soul on, how totally absorbed I became in the glorious feeling of listening to her, so that I often did not even hear the words by which she expressed herself!—Of this you can have some idea, since you know me. In short, I descended from the coach as though in a dream when we came to a halt in front of the summer house, and I was still so immersed in dreams amid the darkling world around me that I hardly noticed the music which was wafted down to us from the brightly lit hall.

Two gentlemen named Audran and a certain N.N.—who can remember everybody's name!—who were the partners of Lotte and the cousin, met us at the coach door, took charge of their ladies, and I escorted mine upstairs.

We glided round one another in minuets, I engaged one lady after another, and it was just the least attractive ones who could not manage to change hands and end the figure. Lotte and her partner began an English quadrille,[17] and you can imagine how happy I was when the turn came for her to begin the figure with us. You should see her dance! She is so absorbed in it, heart and soul, her whole body *one* harmony, as care-free, as unaffected, as though nothing else mattered, as though she thought or felt nothing else, and it is certain that at such moments everything else has ceased to exist for her.

I asked her for the second quadrille, but she promised me the third, and with the most charming ingenuousness in the world she assured me that she was very fond of dancing in the German way. "It is the fashion here," she continued, "that each couple who are together remain together in the German dance, but my partner is an indifferent waltzer and he will be grateful if I relieve him of the labor. Your lady can't waltz either and doesn't like it, and I saw during the quadrille that you waltz well; if you care to be my partner for the German dance, go and ask leave of my partner

[16]"The names of some of our native authors have been omitted here also. Whoever shares Lotte's appreciation will certainly feel in his own heart who they are, if he should read these lines. And there is no necessity for anybody else to know."—Note in original German text. Oliver Goldsmith's sentimental novel *The Vicar of Wakefield* (1766) enjoyed a considerable popularity.

[17]A square dance involving four couples and five "figures," or patterns of steps.

while I go and ask your lady." I agreed, and it was soon arranged that her partner should sit out the waltz with mine.

We then began, and took delight in interlacing our arms in diverse ways. What charm, what fleetness of movement! And when we came to the waltz, and the dancers revolved round each other like planets, there was at first a certain amount of confusion since very few are expert at it. We were prudent and let them wear themselves out, and when the clumsiest couples had left the floor we joined in and held out valiantly to the end together with another pair, Audran and his partner. Never have I danced so easily. I was no longer a mortal. To have the most charming creature in the world in my arms and to fly around with her like lightning, so that everything round about ceased to exist and—Wilhelm, to be candid, I *did* vow that the girl I loved, on whom I had claims, should never waltz with another, even if it meant the end of me. You understand!

We took a turn or two round the room after the dance in order to recover our breath. Then she sat down, and the lemons I had stolen when the punch was being brewed, which were now the only ones left and which I brought her cut into slices with sugar, had an excellent refreshing effect, except that with every slice the lady sitting next to her took out of the cup a stab went through my heart, though for the sake of decency I had to offer it to her also.

In the third quadrille we were the second couple. As we danced through the ranks and I, God knows with what rapture, kept my eyes, as she hung upon my arm, fixed upon hers, in which shone the sincerest expression of frank and pure enjoyment, we reached a lady who had attracted my attention on account of her sympathetic mien, though her face was no longer exactly young. She looked at Lotte with a smile, lifted a minatory[18] finger, and mentioned the name Albert twice with considerable emphasis as she whirled past.

"Who is Albert," I asked Lotte, "if it is not presumption on my part?" She was about to reply when we had to separate to make the figure of eight, and it seemed to me that I saw a certain pensiveness shade her brow as we crossed in front of each other. "Why should I keep it from you?" she said, as she gave me her hand for the promenade. "Albert is a worthy man to whom I am as good as betrothed." This was not news to me, for the girls had told me in the carriage, and yet it *was* entirely new to me, since I had not thought of it in connection with her who had come to mean so much to me in such a short time. Enough—I became confused, forgot the steps, and danced in between the wrong couple so that everything became mixed up and Lotte's whole presence of mind and pulling and tugging were necessary to restore order.

The dance had not yet come to an end when the flashes of lightning, which we had for some time seen gleaming on the horizon and which I had pretended were sheet lightning, began to grow more pronounced and the thunder drowned the music. Three ladies ran out of the ranks, followed by their partners, confusion became general, and the music ceased. It is natural, when our pleasure is interrupted by an accident or something terrifying, that the impression made upon us should be stronger than usual,

[18] Of warning disapproval.

partly because of the contrast which is felt so vividly, partly and even more because our senses are susceptible and receive an impression all the more quickly. To these causes must be attributed the wondrous grimaces which I saw appear on the faces of several ladies. The wisest of them sat down in a corner with her back to the window and held her hands over her ears, another knelt down and buried her face in the lap of the first one, a third pushed her way in between them both and clasped her little sisters to her with a thousand tears. Some wanted to drive home, others, who were even less aware what they were doing, had not sufficient presence of mind to avoid the impertinences of some of the young gentlemen who had had a little to drink, and who appeared to be busily engaged in capturing from the lips of the beauties in distress the timorous prayers which were meant for Heaven. Some of the gentlemen had gone downstairs to smoke a quiet pipe, and the rest of the company did not refuse when the hostess hit upon the clever idea of showing us into a room which had curtains and shutters. Hardly had we entered when Lotte began to arrange chairs in a circle, to seat the guests and suggest a game.

I saw more than one gentleman purse his lips and stretch his limbs in expectation of a luscious forfeit.[19] "We are going to play at Counting," she said, "so pay attention. I am going round in a circle from right to left, and each of you must also count round the number that comes to him, but it must go like wildfire, and whoever hesitates or makes a mistake receives a box on the ears, and so on to a thousand."—It was a merry sight. She went round the circle with her arm stretched out. "One," cried the first, his neighbor "two," "three" the next and so on. Then she began to go more quickly, more and more quickly. One man missed his number, *smack!* a box on the ears; the next man laughed so much that he also missed, *smack!* And more and more quickly. I received two slaps on the face myself, and with secret pleasure I thought I felt that they were harder than those she gave the others. A general uproar and outburst of laughter brought the game to an end before the thousand was counted. Those who were most intimate with each other drew aside, the storm was over, and I followed Lotte into the ballroom. On the way she said, "During the ear-boxing they forgot the weather and everything!" I did not know what to reply. "I was one of the most timorous," she said, "and by pretending to be brave in order to give the others courage I became courageous myself." We stepped to the window, the thunder could be heard away to the side, and the glorious rain was pattering down on to the earth, while the most refreshing fragrance rose up to us in a full, warm vapor. She stood leaning on her elbow, her gaze searching the landscape; she looked up to the heavens and then at me, I saw her eyes fill with tears, she put her hand on mine and murmured—*Klopstock!*[20] I became submerged in the flood of emotions which this name let loose upon me. I could not bear it, I bent over her hand and kissed it amidst the most ecstatic tears. And looked up again into her eyes—Noble Poet! would that thou hadst seen thy apotheosis[21] in that gaze, and would that I might never hear again thy so oft desecrated name!

[19] Penalty, in a parlor game.

[20] German poet (1724–1803); Charlotte is thinking of an emotional description of a thunderstorm in his ode "The Rite of Spring."

[21] Transformation into a god.

19 JUNE.
I no longer know where I broke off my story. All I know is that it was two o'clock in the morning when I went to bed, and that if, instead of writing, I had been able to babble to you, I should probably have kept you up till daybreak.

I have not yet told you what happened on our way home from the ball and I haven't time to tell you to-day either.

There was a lovely sunrise. The dripping wood and the freshened fields round about! Our companions in the coach were nodding off. She asked if I did not want to join them, as far as she was concerned I need not be embarrassed. "As long as I see your eyes open," I said, looking at her firmly, "there is no danger of that." And we both held out until we reached the gates of her home, when the maid opened gently and assured her, in answer to her inquiries, that her father and the little ones were all right and were still asleep. Then I took leave with the protestation that I would see her that same day, and I kept my promise; and since that time sun, moon and stars can journey calmly on their round, I know not whether it is night or day and the whole world about me has ceased to have any existence.

21 JUNE.
My days are as happy as those God allots to His saints; and whatever the future may have in store for me, I shall not be able to say that I have not experienced the joys, the purest joys of life. You know my Wahlheim. I am quite settled there. It is only half an hour away from Lotte, and there I feel I am myself and possess all the happiness that is granted to mankind.

Had I but thought, when I selected Wahlheim as the goal of my walks, that it lies so near to Heaven! How often in the course of my long wanderings did I see the hunting lodge, which now encompasses all my desires, either from the hill or in the plain across the river.

Dear Wilhelm, I have pondered over so many things, man's craving to extend, to make new discoveries, to rove about; and then again his inward urge to submit willingly to his limitations, to travel along the path of custom and have no thought for the right hand or the left.

It is wonderful how I came here and gazed down from the hilltop into the lovely valley, how I was enchanted by everything round about. There the little wood! Oh could you but mingle in its shade! There the summit of the mount! Oh could you but survey from there the broad landscape! The chain of hills and intimate valleys! Oh could I but lose myself in them! I hurried thither and returned, and had not found that which I sought. Oh! distant vistas are like the distant future! A vast darkling whole lies before our soul, our emotions merge into it, like our gaze, and we yearn to surrender our entire being, to be filled with all the rapture of a single great glorious feeling.—And oh! when we rush up to it, when the distant *there* becomes *here,* everything is as it was before, and we stand hemmed in by our poverty, while our soul pants for the draft that is beyond its reach.

And so even the most restless wanderer longs at last for his native land, and finds in his poor cabin, at the breast of his wife, amidst his children and the occupations necessary for their sustenance, all the rapture which he sought in vain in the wide and dreary world.

When I set out at daybreak to walk to my Wahlheim and pick peas for myself in the garden of the inn, and sit down and shell them while I read my Homer; when I then go into the little kitchen to find a pot, cut off a piece of butter, put my peas on the fire, cover the pot and sit down to keep turning them—then I feel so vividly how the glorious haughty suitors of Penelope[22] slaughtered oxen and swine, cut them up and roasted them. Nothing so fills me with a sincere, calm emotion as the features of patriarchal life which I, thanks be to God, am able without affectation to weave into my mode of living.

How happy I am that my heart can feel the simple, innocent joy of the man who brings to his table a cabbage that he has grown himself, and enjoys at the same moment not only the cabbage but also all the fine days, the beautiful morning when he planted it, the pleasant evenings when he watered it and when he rejoiced in its increasing size.

29 JUNE.

The physician came here from the town the day before yesterday to visit the bailiff and found me on the floor among Lotte's children, some crawling over me and the others teasing me while I was tickling them, and we all made a great uproar. The doctor, who is a very dogmatic puppet and arranges the folds of his cuffs while he is discoursing and pulls out his frill as far as his navel, thought this beneath the dignity of an intelligent person, as I could see by the way he turned up his nose. I did not let myself be put out, however, but let him pursue his wise disquisition, and continued to rebuild a house of cards that the children had knocked down. He afterwards went about the town complaining that the bailiff's children were sufficiently badly brought up without that fellow Werther spoiling them completely.

Yes, Wilhelm, children are nearer to my heart than anything else on earth. When I watch them and see in the little creatures the germs of all the virtues and all the powers that they will one day find so indispensable, when I see in their obstinacy all the future constancy and firmness of character, in their wantonness all the future good humor and facility in gliding over the hazards of life, all so unspoilt, so undiminished—I always, always repeat the golden words of the Teacher of men, "Unless ye become even as one of these!"[23] And yet we treat them, who are such as we, whom we should look upon as our models, after the manner of inferior beings. They are said to be lacking in will!—Have we then none? And in what lies our superiority? In our age and maturer wisdom? God in Heaven, Thou seest old children and young children, and that is all, and Thy Son has long since proclaimed in which Thou findest greater joy. But they do not believe in Him and do not hear Him—that is also out of fashion!—and they model their children upon themselves, and —Adieu, Wilhelm, I have no wish to continue this idle talk.

[22] The wife of Odysseus in Homer's *Odyssey;* during the ten years it took him to return from the Trojan war, Penelope was courted by princes who fed off Odysseus' stock.

[23] "Except ye be converted, and become as little children, ye shall not enter into the kingdom of heaven."—Matthew 18:3.

1 JULY.
What Lotte must be to a sick man I feel in my own poor heart, which is worse off than many a one which is languishing on a bed of sickness. She is to pass some days in the town at the bedside of an honest woman who, so the doctors say, is nearing her end, and who wishes to have Lotte near her in her last moments. I went with her last week to visit the pastor of St., a hamlet an hour's journey away in the mountains. We arrived about four. Lotte had brought her second sister with her. When we entered the courtyard of the parsonage, which is shaded by two tall walnut trees, we found the good old man sitting on a bench before the house door, and when he saw Lotte it was as though he were imbued with new life. He forgot his knotted stick and made an effort to rise and come towards her. She ran towards him and made him sit down, while she took a seat at his side, gave him her father's best greetings, and embraced his youngest child, an unclean, ugly lad but the darling of his father's old age. You ought to have seen her occupying the old man's attention, raising her voice to reach his half-deaf ears, telling him about robust young people who had unexpectedly died, how excellent Karlsbad[24] was and praising his resolve to go there next summer, and how she thought that he looked much better and more cheerful than the last time she had seen him. I had meantime paid my respects to the pastor's wife. The old man became quite cheerful, and since I could not help praising the handsome walnut trees that shaded us so pleasantly, he began, though with a little difficulty, to tell us their history. "The old one," he said, "we don't know who planted that, some say one pastor, some say another. But the young one over there is the same age as my wife, fifty years next October. Her father planted it the morning of the day she was born. He was my predecessor in the living,[25] and I cannot tell you how much he loved that tree; it is in truth no less dear to me. My wife was seated beneath it on a log with her knitting when I first entered this courtyard as a poor student seven and twenty years ago." Lotte inquired after his daughter, and he told her that she had gone out to the workmen in the meadow with Mr. Schmidt; then, continuing his narrative, he explained how his predecessor had grown fond of him, and the daughter as well, and how he had first become his curate and then his successor. He had hardly finished his story when his daughter came through the garden with the said Mr. Schmidt. She welcomed Lotte with considerable warmth, and I must admit that I found her by no means unattractive. A lively brunette with a good figure, who would have been quite entertaining company during a short stay in the country. Her suitor, for as such Mr. Schmidt soon presented himself, was a cultivated but reserved individual, who did not show any desire to join in our conversation, although Lotte kept turning to him, and what most depressed me was that I thought I could gather from his expression that it was caprice and ill-humor rather than limited intelligence which prevented him from being more communicative. In the sequel this unfortunately grew only too evident, for when Friederike, as we walked along, kept to the side of Lotte or occasionally came over to me, the gentleman's face, which was in any case of a brownish hue, darkened so

[24] City in what is now Czechoslovakia; site of medicinal baths.
[25] Appointment as pastor to a church.

visibly that it was time for Lotte to tug me by the sleeve and advise me to refrain from making myself agreeable to Friederike. Now nothing aggravates me more than when people torment each other, especially when young couples, who might be most receptive to all the joys that come in the prime of life, spoil the few days that might be so pleasant with crotchets,[26] and only realize when it is too late that they have wasted what cannot be recovered. It vexed me mightily, and when we returned to the parsonage towards evening and were supping at a table in the courtyard on bread dipped in milk, I could not help taking up the subject when the conversation turned on the joys and sorrows of this world, and attacking most heartily the vice of ill-humor. "We mortals frequently complain," I began, "that the days of our happiness are too few and those of our sorrow too many, and I think we are generally wrong. If our hearts were always open to enjoy the good which God gives us each day, then we should also have sufficient strength to bear misfortune when it comes." "But we have not control over our natures," replied the pastor's wife. "How much depends on our bodies! When we feel unwell, everything seems wrong." I admitted that. "Then let us regard it as a disease and inquire whether there is no remedy for it." "That is worth considering," said Lotte. "I believe at least that much depends on ourselves. I know it from my own nature. When anything worries me and is inclined to make me depressed, I jump up and sing a couple of quadrille airs up and down the garden, and it goes immediately." "That is just what I wanted to say," I rejoined. "Ill-humor is like laziness, for it is a kind of laziness; our natures are strongly inclined that way, and yet, when we only have the strength to assume control of ourselves, our tasks are done with no difficulty and we find a real pleasure in activity." Friederike was very attentive, and her young suitor objected that man is not his own master, having control least of all over his emotions. "We are referring here to a disagreeable emotion," I replied. "Everyone is anxious to get rid of it, and nobody knows the extent of his strength until he has tried. A sick man will certainly consult all the physicians and will not reject the greatest trials, the bitterest medicines, in order to win back the health he desires." I noticed that the worthy old man was straining his hearing to take part in the conversation, and I raised my voice as I directed my remarks to him. "People preach against so many vices," I said, "but I have never heard anyone denouncing ill-humor from the pulpit."[27] "The pastors in the towns ought to do that," he answered, "the peasants are never ill-tempered. Though it would not hurt occasionally and would at least be a lesson to our wives—to say nothing of the bailiff." Everybody burst out laughing, and he joined in heartily until he fell into a fit of coughing, which interrupted the conversation for a time, before the young man again took up the thread. "You called ill-humor a vice. I think that is an exaggeration." "Not at all," I declared, "if that which harms oneself and one's dear ones deserves the name. Is it not enough that we cannot make each other happy; must we in addition deprive each other of the pleasure that each heart is able at times to afford

[26] Ill-natured whims.

[27] "We now possess an excellent sermon by Lavater on this text, among those on the Book of Jonah."—Note in original German text. Johann Kaspar Lavater (1741–1801) was a Swiss thinker whom Goethe highly admired.

itself? And I should like to know the name of the man who is in an ill-humor and yet has the virtue to conceal it, to bear it alone without destroying the happiness of those around him. Is it not rather an inward displeasure at our own unworthiness, a dissatisfaction with ourselves which is always combined with an envy that a foolish conceit has incited? We see happy people whose happiness has not been caused by *us*, and we cannot bear it." Lotte smiled at me when she saw the vehemence with which I spoke, and a tear in the eye of Friederike spurred me on to continue. "Woe be to those," I said, "who abuse their power over the heart of another to deprive it of the simplest joys that spring up in it. All the gifts, all the good-will in the world, cannot replace a moment of pure pleasure which the envious constraint of a tyrant has embittered."

My whole heart was full at this moment, the memory of so much that had happened in the past rushed into my soul, and my eyes filled with tears.

"If people would only think to themselves every day," I cried, "that you can do nothing for your friends save leave them their pleasure and augment their happiness by enjoying it with them. Have you the power, when their inmost soul is tortured by an agony of passion, torn with grief, to offer them a drop of comfort? And when the last fatal sickness overtakes the being whom you helped to wear away in the days of her youth, and she lies there in pitiable exhaustion, her eyes raised unseeingly to Heaven, the death-sweat coming and going on her brow, and you stand at the bedside like one of the damned, with the feeling in your inmost soul that with all your power you can do nothing, you are inwardly convulsed with the agonizing thought that you would give your all to be able to instill into the dying being a particle of vigor, a spark of courage."

The memory of such a scene, at which I had been present, took possession of me with undiminished force as I uttered these words. I put my handkerchief to my eyes and left the company. Only the voice of Lotte, who called to me that it was time to go, brought me to myself. And how she scolded me on the way home for taking too warm an interest in everything, declaring that it would be my ruin, that I should spare myself!—Oh angel! For thy sake I must live!

6 JULY.

She is still looking after her dying friend and is always the same, always the devoted, lovely creature who soothes pain and spreads happiness wherever she goes. She went for a walk yesterday evening with Marianne and little Amalie. I knew of this and went to meet them. After an hour and a half we had come back to the town and the spring which is so precious to me, and which became a thousand times more precious when Lotte sat down on the wall beside it. I gazed around, and alas! the time when my heart was so solitary again came vividly into my mind. "Beloved spring," I said, "I have not rested since then in thy cool shade, and often have I hastened past thee without a glance." I looked down and saw that Amalie was ascending the steps with a glass of water. I looked at Lotte and felt all that she means to me. Amalie meanwhile approached with the glass and Marianne wanted to take it from her, but "No!" cried the child with the sweetest expression, "no, you shall drink first, Lotte!" I was so enraptured with the sincerity, the goodness with which she said this, that I found no other way to express my emotion but to take the child up in my arms and kiss her so violently that she straightway began to scream and weep. "That was wrong of you," said Lotte. I was disconcerted. "Come, Amy," she continued, taking the child by the hand and leading her down the steps, "quick, wash your face in the running water and it won't hurt you." As I stood there and watched the child busily rubbing her cheeks with her wet hands; when I saw the faith she had that the miraculous spring would wash away all defilement and prevent the disgrace of growing an ugly beard; how she even continued to wash away after Lotte had said, "It's enough!", as though too much was better than too little—I tell you, Wilhelm, I have never felt more reverent at a baptism. And when Lotte came up, I would have liked to cast myself at her feet as before a prophet who has washed away in consecrated water the sins of a nation.

That evening I could not help, in the happiness of my heart, relating the incident to a man from whom I expected human understanding, since he is a man of common sense. But what did I find! He said it was very wrong of Lotte, that children should not be told such stories, since they gave rise to all sorts of misconceptions and superstitions, against which children should be guarded at an early age. It occurred to me, however, that he had had a child of his own baptized a week previously, so I said nothing and silently kept to my conviction that we ought to treat children as God treats us.—He makes us happiest when He lets us wander on under the intoxication of agreeable illusions.

8 JULY.

What children we are! How we crave a glance! What children we are! We had gone to Wahlheim. The ladies were driving out, and during our walks I thought I could see in Lotte's black eyes—I am foolish, forgive me, but you should see these eyes. In short, for I can hardly keep my eyes open, the ladies were getting into the coach round which young W., Selstadt, Audran and I were standing. They were talking through the window to the fellows who were, to be sure, pretty thoughtless and frivolous. I sought Lotte's eyes! Alas! they were glancing from one to the other! But on me! me! me! who stood there absorbed in her alone, they did not fall! My heart bade her a thousand adieux! And she did not see me! The coach drove past and a tear stood in my eye. I gazed after her! And I saw Lotte's coiffure leaning out of the window as she turned to look back. Oh! at me?—It is in this uncertainty that I hover! It is this which is my consolation. Perhaps it was I at whom she turned to look. Perhaps—good night! Oh! how childish I am!

10 JULY.

You should see what a foolish figure I make when she is spoken of in company. And when I am asked how I like her—like! I hate the word. What sort of a fellow must he be who likes Lotte and whose whole mind, whose whole heart is not entirely absorbed by her. Like! The other day someone asked me how I liked Ossian![28]

11 JULY.

Mrs. M. is very ill. I pray for her, for I suffer with Lotte. I see her rarely at a friend's, and to-day she told me of a marvelous happening. Old M. is a miserly curmudgeon who has curbed and harassed his wife pretty well during her life, though she has always been able to manage tolerably. A few days ago, when the doctor said there was no hope for her, she sent for her husband while Lotte was in the room and spoke to him thus: "I must confess something that might cause you confusion and vexation after my death. Hitherto I have kept house in as orderly and economical a manner as possible, but you will forgive me for having deceived you these thirty years. When we first married, you allowed me a trifling sum for food and other domestic expenses. When our household became larger and our business grew, I could not move you to increase my weekly allowance to meet the altered circumstances. In short, you know that when our expenses were greatest I had to manage with seven florins a week. I accepted this amount without protest and abstracted the remainder from the receipts every week, since no one had any suspicion that your wife would steal from the till. I have never been extravagant and would have gone tranquilly to my eternal rest without confessing this, if it were not that the one who follows me in keeping house for you will not know how to make both ends meet, and yet you might still insist that your first wife had been able to manage."

I talked with Lotte concerning the incredible delusion of the human mind, which can prevent a man from suspecting that there is something wrong when seven florins suffice to cover an obvious outlay of possibly twice as much. I have, however, myself known people who would not have been surprised at the presence in their house of the widow's inexhaustible cruse.[29]

13 JULY.

No, I am not deceiving myself! I can read in her black eyes a real interest in me and my destiny. Yes, I feel (and in this matter I can trust my heart) that she—Oh! may I, can I express the Paradise that lies in these words?—that she loves me.

Loves me! How the thought exalts me in my own eyes! How I—I may tell you, perhaps, for you can sympathize with such an emotion—how I worship myself since she loves me.

And be it presumption or perception of the true state of affairs—I do

[28] In one of the great literary frauds of the century, James Macpherson published in the 1760s supposed translations of a legendary third-century Gaelic poet named Ossian. Goethe shared the widespread craze over these works. A passage from Macpherson-Ossian appears later in *Werther.*

[29] Jar. God sustained the prophet Elijah during a drought and famine by having him lodge with a widow whose store of food was miraculously replenished. 1 Kings 17:1–16.

not know the man whose rivalry I would have to fear in Lotte's heart. And yet—when she speaks of her betrothed with such warmth, with such affection, I feel like one who has been deprived of all his honors and dignities and has had to yield up his sword.

16 JULY.

Oh! how the blood rushes through my veins when my finger accidentally touches hers, when our feet meet under the table. I draw back as from a flame, and a secret force thrusts me forward again. All my senses swim. And oh! her innocence, her pure soul, does not feel the torment which these little intimacies occasion me. When she lays her hand on mine as we converse, and moves nearer to me as she grows more interested, so that her divine breath is wafted to my lips—I feel that I am about to sink to the ground as though struck by lightning. And, Wilhelm, if I should ever dare to—but no, my heart is not so depraved! Weak! weak enough! Is that not depravity?

She is sacred to me. All lust ceases in her presence. I am never aware what I feel when I am with her; it is as though my soul were revolving in all my nerves. There is a melody which she plays on the harpsichord with the touch of an angel, so simple and spiritual. It is her favorite song, and I am cured of all my harassing bewilderment and melancholy so soon as she strikes the first note.

I do not find it difficult to believe the stories of the magic power of music in ancient times. How this simple song fascinates me! And how well she knows when to play it, often at a time when I feel like putting a bullet in my brain! All the confusion and gloom in my soul are dispersed, and I breathe more freely again.

18 JULY.

What meaning has the world for our souls without love, Wilhelm? It is a magic lantern[30] without its lamp. Hardly have you inserted the lamp when the most colorful pictures appear on the white screen. And even if that were all there is, nothing but passing phantoms, yet it makes us happy when we stand in front like simple children and are enraptured by the wonderful pictures. I was unable to visit Lotte to-day, being detained by an unavoidable engagement. What could I do? I sent my lad out, just to have somebody about me who had been in her presence to-day. How impatiently I awaited his return, how glad I was to see him again! I would have liked to take him in my arms and embrace him, had I not been ashamed to do so.

It is said of the Bologna stone that when it is placed in the sun it attracts the rays, and is luminous for a time by night. So it was with the lad. The feeling that her eyes had rested on his face, his cheeks, his coat buttons, the collar of his surtout,[31] made them all so sacred and precious to me that I would not at that moment have exchanged the lad for a thousand *Talers*.[32] I felt so happy in his presence.—May God preserve you from laughing at this. Can these be phantoms, Wilhelm, that make us so happy?

[30] An early form of the slide projector. [31] Long, close-fitting coat.
[32] German silver coins.

19 JULY.
"I am going to see her!" I cry aloud every morning, when I am aroused and gaze happily at the glorious sun. "I am going to see her!" And I have no further wish for the rest of the day. Everything, everything is absorbed in this prospect.

20 JULY.
I cannot yet accept your suggestion that I should accompany the ambassador to * * *. I am not fond of discipline, and we all know that he is, in any case, a disagreeable fellow. You write that my mother would like to see me occupied? It makes me laugh. Am I not now occupied? And is it not, at bottom, a matter of indifference whether I count peas or lentils? Everything in this world ends in nothingness, after all, and a fellow who wears himself out for somebody else's sake, without its being his own ambition, in order to achieve wealth or dignity or anything else, is simply a fool.

24 JULY.
Since you are so anxious that I should not neglect my drawing, I would rather say nothing about it than confess that hitherto I have done little.

I was never happier, never has my sympathy with Nature down to the stones and blades of grass been fuller and more ardent, and yet—I know not how to express myself, but my powers of perception are so weak, everything swims and trembles before my soul so that I cannot seize the outline; but I think, if I had clay or wax, I could probably fashion it out. If this lasts much longer I shall procure some clay and mold it, even if all I can make is cakes.

I have begun Lotte's portrait three times, and each time I have made a mess of it, which vexes me all the more since I got it quite successfully some time ago. Then I cut out her silhouette, and that will have to suffice.

26 JULY.
I have often made up my mind not to see her so frequently. If I could only keep to my resolution! Every day I succumb to temptation and promise myself sacredly that I will stay away next day, and when the morning comes I again discover some irresistible reason and find myself there before I am aware of it. Either she has said the evening before, "You will come tomorrow, won't you?" (who could remain away under such circumstances?)—or the day is so very lovely, I walk to Wahlheim, and when I am there it is only half an hour to her. I am too near to her presence—in a trice I am there. My grandmother used to tell me a story of a magnetic mountain. The ships which approached too closely to it were suddenly deprived of all their ironwork, the nails shot towards the mountain, and the poor wretches sank amidst the collapsing planks.

30 JULY.
Albert has arrived, and I shall go. Even if he were the best, the most noble

of men, to whom I were prepared in every respect to give way, it would be intolerable to see him before my eyes in possession of so many perfections. Possession!—Enough, Wilhelm, her betrothed has arrived. A worthy, agreeable fellow, whom one cannot help liking. Luckily, I was not present when she welcomed him. It would have torn my heartstrings. He is so honorable and has never even kissed Lotte when I was there. May God reward him for it! I must love him for the respect with which he treats the girl. He is well-intentioned towards me, but I suspect that is due to Lotte more than to his own disposition, for in this matter women are delicate, and rightly so. If they can keep two admirers on good terms with each other, the advantage is always theirs, though it is seldom practicable.

Meanwhile I cannot deny Albert my esteem. His outward calm is in very vivid contrast to the restlessness of my character, which I am unable to conceal. He is a man of feeling and knows what he possesses in Lotte. He appears rarely to be in an ill-humor and, as you know, that is the sin I hate more than any other.

He considers me a man of intellect, and my attachment to Lotte, with the ardent pleasure I take in all her actions, increases his triumph, and he loves me all the more. Whether he does not sometimes plague her privately with petty jealousy is a matter about which I will offer no opinion. At any rate, I should not in his place be altogether free from the demon.

Be that as it may, my pleasure in Lotte's company is gone. Am I to call it foolishness or infatuation? What do names matter? The thing itself is evident. I knew everything that I know now before Albert came. I knew that I could have no claim on her, nor did I make any, that is to say, as far as it is possible to be without desire in the case of so many charms. And the ridiculous fellow opens his eyes wide now that the other man has arrived and takes the girl away.

I grit my teeth and mock at my wretchedness, and mock doubly and trebly at those who might say I should be resigned, since it cannot be helped.—Rid me of these fellows!—I wander about in the woods, and when I come to Lotte's and Albert is sitting with her in the summer house in the garden, and I can get no further, I behave in an extravagant manner, practice all sorts of crazy buffoonery. "For Heaven's sake," Lotte said to me to-day, "I beg of you! no more scenes like that of yesterday evening! You are dreadful when you act so wildly." Between ourselves, I wait till he is occupied elsewhere; *presto!* I am there in a trice, and I am always happy when I find her alone.

8 AUGUST.

Please, Wilhelm, I did not mean you when I wrote, "Rid me of the fellows who say I ought to be resigned." I really did not think that you could be of that opinion. And at bottom you are right. Only one thing, my dear friend! In this world it is rarely possible to settle matters with an "either, or," since there are as many gradations of emotion and conduct as there are stages between a hooked nose and one that turns up.

So you will not take it amiss if I grant you your whole argument and nevertheless try to steal my way between your "either, or."

Either I have hopes of Lotte, you say, or I have not. Good! In the former case I must seek to realize them, seek to achieve the fulfilment of my desires; in the latter case I must pull myself together and try to rid myself of a wretched emotion which is bound to consume all my energies. That is well said, my friend, and—soon said.

Can you demand of the unhappy man whose life is gradually and irremediably ebbing under the influence of an insidious malady, can you demand of him that he should put an end to his torture with a dagger? Does not the disease which is consuming his energies at the same time rob him of the courage to procure his own deliverance?

You can of course answer me with a similar allegory—who would not rather submit to the amputation of an arm than risk his life by doubts and hesitations? I do not know. And we will not attack each other with allegories. Enough . . . Yes, Wilhelm, I often have such moments of bounding, vehement courage, and then, if I only knew whither, I would probably go.

10 AUGUST.

I could lead the happiest and best of lives were I not a fool. Such a combination of favorable circumstances is rarely found for the delight of a man's heart as that in which I am now placed. Alas! how true it is that our heart is alone responsible for its own happiness. To be a member of this charming family, loved by the old man like a son, by the little ones like a father, and by Lotte . . . and now this worthy Albert, who never disturbs my happiness by any display of ill-humor, who regards me with sincere friendship, who, next to Lotte, loves me more than anything in the world. Wilhelm, it is a joy to hear us on our walks, when we talk about Lotte. There has never been anything more ridiculous than this relationship, and yet it often brings the tears to my eyes.

When he tells me about her righteous mother, how she entrusted her house and children to Lotte on her deathbed and confided Lotte to his care, how since then Lotte has been imbued with a new spirit, how in her concern for the household she has really become a mother, how not a moment of her time but has been occupied or absorbed in some task of affection, and yet she has not lost her cheerful lightheartedness. I walk along beside him and pluck flowers by the wayside, bind them very carefully into a nosegay and—cast them into the brook that flows past to watch them gently float along. I do not know whether I have written to you that Albert is to remain here and receive a post at a handsome salary from the Court,[33] where he is in very good favor. I have rarely seen his equal for regularity and diligence at his occupation.

12 AUGUST.

Albert is certainly the most excellent of men. There was an extraordinary scene between us yesterday. I went to his house to take leave of him, for I had conceived a desire to ride into the hills, whence I am now writing to you, and as I was walking up and down the room I caught sight of a pair of

[33] The sovereign or the people around him.

pistols. "Lend me your pistols," I said, "for my journey." "Certainly," he replied, "if you will take the trouble to load them; I only keep them here *pro forma*."[34] I took one of them down, and he continued, "Since my prudence played me such a scurvy trick, I don't like having anything more to do with the things." I was curious to hear the story. "When I was staying with a friend in the country for about three months," he told me, "I had a brace of unloaded pocket-pistols with me and slept unperturbed. One rainy afternoon, as I was sitting idly thinking, it occurred to me for some reason or other that we might be attacked, that we might have need of the pistols and—you know the sort of thing I mean. I gave them to the servant to clean and load. He dallies with the maidservants, tries to frighten them, and, the Lord knows how, the pistol goes off with the ramrod still in it, and shoots the latter through the ball of the thumb of the right hand of one of the girls, smashing it. I had to bear the lamentation and pay the surgeon into the bargain, and since that time I leave my pistols unloaded. My dear fellow, what's the use of precautions? One cannot guard against every peril. To be sure. . . ." Now, you know, I am very fond of the man until he says "to be sure . . ."; for is it not a matter of course that every general proposition is subject to exceptions? But he is so anxious to justify his opinion, that when he thinks he has said anything rash, made a general statement, or uttered a half-truth, he never ceases to qualify, modify, add to, or subtract from what he has said, until finally there is nothing left of his original assertion. On this occasion he dilated at great length on the subject, till I at last ceased to listen to him, subsided into a state of melancholy, and pressed the mouth of the pistol with a flourish to my forehead above the right eye. "Come!" said Albert, snatching at the pistol. "What is the meaning of this?" "It is not loaded," I said. "And even so, what is the meaning of it?" he asked impatiently. "I cannot imagine how a man can be so foolish as to shoot himself. The very thought is repellent."

"Why do you people," I cried, "when you speak of anything, declare immediately 'this is foolish, this is wise, this is good, this is bad!' What is the meaning of it all? Have you discovered the inward circumstances of an action? Can you determine exactly why it happened, why it was bound to happen? Had you done that, you would be less hasty in your judgments."

"You will admit," said Albert, "that certain actions are vicious from whatever motive they may occur."

I shrugged my shoulders and granted him that. "But, my dear fellow," I continued, "even in that case there are exceptions. It is true that thieving is a vice, but does a man who sets out to steal in order to preserve himself and his family from a miserable death by starvation, deserve punishment or sympathy? Who will be the first to cast a stone at the man who sacrifices an unfaithful wife and her worthless seducer to his righteous wrath? Against the girl who in a moment of rapture loses herself amid the impetuous joys of love? Even our laws, those cold-blooded pedants, are not insensible, and refrain from punishment."

"That is a very different matter," Albert replied, "because a man who is swept away by passion is deprived of all power of reflection and is in the same category as a drunkard or a madman."—"Oh you men of reason!" I

[34] As a matter of form (Latin).

cried with a smile. "Passion! Drunkenness! Madness! You stand there so calmly, you moral creatures, so unsympathetic, scolding the drunkard, abhorring the lack of reason, passing by like the priest and thanking your God like the Pharisee that he has not made you like one of these.[35] I have been drunk more than once, my passions were never far from madness, and for neither do I feel remorse, for I have learned in my own measure to understand that all men above the ordinary who have done anything great or seemingly impossible have invariably been decried as drunkards or madmen.

"But even in our daily life it is intolerable to hear it said of a man who has done anything at all generous, noble or unexpected, 'The fellow is crazy,' or 'The fellow is drunk.' Shame upon you sober beings! Shame upon you sages!"

"This is another of your crotchets," said Albert. "You exaggerate everything, and here at least you are certainly wrong in comparing suicide, which we are now discussing, with exalted actions, since it is not possible to regard it as anything but a weakness, for it is surely easier to die than to bear a life of agony without flinching."

I was about to break off, for no argument in the world so disconcerts me as when a fellow comes out with some insignificant platitude when I am speaking with my whole heart. But I contained myself, for it had often occurred to me and I had often been vexed at it, and rejoined with some heat, "You call that weakness? I beg of you not to be deceived by appearances. When a nation is groaning under the intolerable yoke of a tyrant, can you term it weak if it finally rises up and bursts its fetters? When a man, under the influence of horror at seeing his house break out in flames, is able to put forth all his strength and bear with ease burdens which in a calmer mood he can scarcely move—when a man, in a rage at some injury, attacks half a dozen foes single-handed and conquers them—are these to be called weak? And, my friend, if exertion is strength, why should over-tension be the reverse?"

Albert looked at me and said, "Do not take it amiss, but the instances you quote appear to me to be quite inapplicable." "It may be so," I replied, "I have often been informed that my method of argument verges on the absurd. Let us see then whether we can in any other way depict the state of mind of a man who has resolved to cast off the burden of life, which is generally so agreeable, for only in so far as we experience his emotions can we have the right to discuss the matter."

"Human nature," I continued, "has its limits; it can bear joy, sorrow and pain to a certain degree, but it succumbs when this is exceeded.

"The question, therefore, is not whether a man is strong or weak, but whether he can endure the measure of his suffering, moral or physical, and I find it just as extraordinary to say that a man is a coward who takes his own life, as it would be improper to call a man a coward who dies of a virulent fever."

"Paradoxical, very paradoxical," cried Albert. "Not so much as you

[35] In the parable of the Good Samaritan, the priest passes by the man in distress without helping him; Luke 10:31. For the Pharisee's self-righteous boast of superiority to sinners, see Luke 18:11.

imagine," I replied. "You will admit we call it a mortal disease when nature is so seriously affected that its forces are partly consumed, partly so put out of action that it cannot be set right, that the ordinary course of life can not by any happy transformation be restored.

"Well, let us apply this to the mind. Let us see how man is circumscribed, how he is affected by impressions, obsessed by ideas, until finally a growing passion robs him of the power of calm reflection and brings him to grief.

"It is in vain that a cool, reasoning individual perceives the unhappy man's condition and talks to him in a persuasive manner, just as a healthy man is unable to inspire an invalid with even a modicum of his own vigor."

This was speaking in terms too general for Albert. I reminded him of a girl who had been found dead in the water some time previously, and recapitulated her story. "A respectable young creature, who had grown up within the restricted sphere of her domestic occupations, with no other prospect of amusement than being able to walk out on a Sunday in the best clothes which she had gradually accumulated, her companions being girls in a similar situation to herself, with an occasional dance on the chief holidays, or the opportunity of whiling away an hour or two by a lively chat with a neighbor about the cause of a quarrel or some scandalous rumor; whose ardent nature eventually felt more inward cravings, which were intensified by the flatteries of men. All her former pleasures gradually grew insipid, till she finally met a man to whom she was irresistibly attracted by some hitherto unknown emotion, on whom she cast all her hopes, forgetting the world about her, hearing nothing, seeing nothing, sensing nothing but him alone, longing for nothing but him alone. Unspoilt by the empty pleasures of an inconstant vanity, her desire marches straight to its fulfilment; she wants to be his, to find in an indissoluble union all the happiness which she has missed, to experience all the combined joys for which she has longed. Reiterated promises, which seal the certainty of all her hopes, bold caresses, which intensify her cravings, encompass her whole being; she hovers in a semi-conscious state of bliss, with the premonitory feeling of supreme rapture, worked up to the highest pitch, until at last she stretches forth her arms to embrace her desires—and is abandoned by her lover. Stupefied, out of her mind, she stands on the verge of an abyss, everything is dark around her, with no hope for the future, no solace, since he has left her with whom alone her existence was bound up. She is blind to the world which lies before her, to those who could replace what she has lost, she feels herself alone, abandoned by all the world. And unseeingly, oppressed by the dreadful agony in her soul, she hurls herself down to still her torment in an encircling death.—That, Albert, is the story of so many mortals, and tell me, is it not analogous to the condition of an invalid? Nature can find no way out of the entangled labyrinth of confused and contradictory instincts, and the mortal must die.

"Woe to him who would say, 'Foolish woman! Had she but waited till time had exerted its healing effect, her despair would have abated and another would have come to give her solace.' That is as though one would say, 'The fool! to die of a fever! Had he but waited till his strength was restored, his humors were adjusted, the tumult of his blood had subsided, all would have been well and he would still be alive to-day!' "

Albert, who was still unwilling to accept my analogy, continued to put forward objections, among others, that I had only adduced the case of a simple girl; and he wanted to know what excuse could be found for a reasoning being who was not so circumscribed and understood better the connections of things.

"My friend," I cried, "a man is a man, and the little reasoning power he may possess is of small advantage, or of none at all, when passion rages and he is oppressed by the limits of humanity. Much rather—but another time," I said, and seized my hat. Oh! my heart was so full. And we parted, without having understood each other. How difficult it is for one to understand the other in this world!

15 AUGUST.

It is, after all, certain that nothing in the world renders a man indispensable save love. I feel that Lotte would not willingly lose me, and the children have no other notion but that I shall return every morning. I went out to-day to tune Lotte's harpsichord, but I was unable to set to work at it, for the children besought me to tell them a fairy tale, and then Lotte herself asked me to comply with their wish. I cut the bread for their supper, which they now accept almost as eagerly from me as from Lotte, and told them their favorite tale of the princess who was served by hands. It teaches me a great deal, I assure you, and I am amazed at the impression it makes on them. Since I often have to invent an episode, which on the next occasion I forget, they tell me at once that it was different at the previous telling, so that I now practice reciting it mechanically in a sort of chant. This has taught me that an author must necessarily spoil his book when he alters the story for a second edition, however much it may be improved from the artistic point of view. The first impression finds us receptive, and man is so constituted that he can be convinced of the most extravagant incidents; these, however, are immediately embedded in his mind, and woe to him who attempts to erase and obliterate them.

18 AUGUST.

Was it ordained by Fate that that which renders a man happy becomes later the source of his misery?

My heart's full and ardent sympathy with Nature, which flooded me with such bliss and made the world round about into a Paradise, has now become an unbearable torment, a torturing spirit which pursues me everywhere. When I used to stand upon the rock and survey the fertile valley across the river as far as the distant hills, when I saw everything about me surge forth and germinate, the mountains clad thickly from foot to summit with tall trees, all the vales in their manifold windings shaded by the most delightful forests, with the river gently flowing among the whispering reeds, mirroring the clouds which were wafted along by the gentle evening breeze; when I heard the birds awakening the forest and the myriad swarms of midges danced merrily in the red rays of the setting sun, whose last quivering glance roused the humming chafer from his grassy bed, while the whirring life about me drew my attention to the ground, where the moss, which wrests its nourishment from the hard rock, and the broom, which grows down the arid sandhill, revealed to me the inward, fervent, sacred life of Nature—how I took all this into my ardent heart, lost myself in its unending abundance, while the glorious forms of the unending world stirred within my animated soul. Vast mountains surrounded me, precipices lay at my feet, torrents poured down, rivers streamed below me, and forest and hills resounded. I saw all the unfathomable forces at their interweaving work of creation in the depths of the earth. Above the earth and below the sky there swarm the innumerable species of creatures. Everything, everything populated with a thousand kinds of shapes, and mankind secures itself in little houses and settles down and rules in its own way over the wide world. Poor fool! you who deem everything of little significance because you are yourself so small. From the inaccessible mountain, across the wilderness which no foot has ever trod, to the end of the unknown ocean there breathes the spirit of the Eternal Creator Who rejoices at every speck of dust that receives it and lives. How often have I longed to be borne on the wings of the crane which flew above my head to the shores of the immeasurable ocean, to quaff the swelling rapture of life from the foaming goblet of the infinite, and to feel for but a moment the curbed forces of my soul extended by one drop of the bliss of that Being Who brings forth all things in and through Himself.

Brother, it is only the memory of those hours that gives me ease. Even the exertion of recalling and again clothing in words those inexpressible emotions, exalts my soul above itself, only to let me feel in double measure the anguish of my condition.

It is as though a curtain has been drawn from before my soul, and the scene of eternal life is being transformed before my eyes into the abyss of the ever open grave. Can you say *This is,* when everything is transitory, everything rolls past with the speed of lightning, only rarely endures till its life force is spent, but is carried away by the current, submerged and smashed against the rocks? Not a moment but consumes you and yours, not a moment when you do not yourself destroy something, and inevitably so. The most innocent stroll costs a myriad tiny creatures their lives, one step annihilates the laborious construction of a nation of ants and crushes a world in little to ignominious ruin. It is not the great occasional catastrophes of the world, the floods that sweep away your villages, the earthquakes that devour your cities, by which I am moved. It is the consuming force latent in universal Nature, that has formed nothing that has not destroyed its neighbor and itself, which saps my soul. And so I reel along in anguish, surrounded by earth and sky and all the weaving forces of Nature. I see nothing but a monster, eternally devouring, eternally chewing the cud.

21 AUGUST.

In vain I stretch out my arms towards her in the morning when I wake from troubled dreams. In vain I seek her at night in my bed when an innocent dream has made me happy with the illusion that I am sitting beside her in the meadow, holding her hand and covering it with a thousand kisses. Oh! when I put out my hand to touch her, still drunk with sleep, and rouse myself by doing so, a stream of tears wells up from my oppressed heart, and I weep for the hopelessness of the gloomy future.

22 AUGUST.

My condition is wretched, Wilhelm! All my energies are reduced to a restless inactivity. I cannot be idle, and yet I am unable to take up any task. I have no power of imagination, no interest in Nature, and my books all repel me. When we lose ourselves, we have lost everything. I vow I could sometimes wish to be a laborer, so as to have every morning, when I awake, some prospect for the ensuing day, some urge, some hope. I often envy Albert, whom I see buried to the ears in his documents, and pretend to myself that I should like to be in his place. More than once it has suddenly occurred to me to write to you and the minister in order to apply for the post at the legation which you assure me I should not fail to obtain. I believe so too. The minister has long been fond of me, and used frequently to urge me to take up some profession. For an hour or so I occupy myself with the notion, but later, when I think about it again, I remember the fable of the horse that was tired of its freedom, allowed itself to be saddled and bridled, and was ridden to death. I do not know what to do, and is not perhaps my longing for a change in my situation a deep-seated, uneasy impatience which will pursue me wherever I may go?

28 AUGUST.

Truly, if my malady could be cured, these people would do it. It is my birthday to-day, and very early this morning I received a packet from Albert. As soon as I opened it I caught sight of one of the pink bows that Lotte was wearing on her bosom when I first met her, and which I had since then more than once asked her for. There were also two little books in duodecimo[36] in the packet, the Wetstein edition of Homer, which I had so often wanted to possess so as not to have to drag about the edition of Ernesti on my walks. You see! that is how they anticipate my desires, how they think of all the small friendly services which are a thousand times more appreciated than the brilliant presents that humiliate us and are due to the vanity of the giver. I kiss the bow a thousand times, and with every breath I drink in the memory of the rapture which more than filled those few happy days that can return no more. The blossoms of life are only a mirage. It is so, Wilhelm, and I do not complain. How many fade and do not leave a trace behind; how few bear fruit, and how little of the fruit reaches maturity! And yet sufficient remain, but—Oh my brother! can we neglect, despise the ripened fruit, let it wither and rot without having been enjoyed?

Farewell! The summer is glorious and I often sit in the fruit trees in Lotte's orchard, picking pears from the highest branches with a long rod. She stands below and receives them when I reach them down.

[36] Pocket-size book format.

30 AUGUST.

Foolish wretch that I am! Do I not deceive myself? What is the purpose of all this endless raging passion? I offer no prayers now save to her; no form appears before my mind save hers; and everything in the world about me I see only in relation to her. And this affords me so many happy hours—till I must again tear myself away from her. Oh! Wilhelm, whither does my heart so often urge me! When I have sat with her thus for two hours or three, feasting my eyes on her form, her bearing, listening to the divine words that come from her lips, and then gradually all my senses become taut, my eyes grow dim, I hardly hear what is said, and I feel as though some assassin were gripping me by the throat, while my heart beats wildly in the endeavor to free my oppressed senses but only increases their confusion—Wilhelm, I am scarcely aware at such times whether I am in this world! And often, if melancholy does not gain the ascendancy and Lotte offer me the wretched solace of pouring forth my anguish in tears upon her hand, I am compelled to rush away, out into the fields where I rove about, or to find pleasure in climbing a steep hill, thrusting my way through a trackless wood, being wounded by hedges and torn by thorns. Then I feel somewhat relieved. Somewhat! And when I sometimes sink down on the way, overcome with weariness and thirst, in the dead of night when the full moon is floating above my head, or sit on a crooked tree in the lonely forest to rest the aching soles of my feet, and fall asleep in the lulling stillness of the half light. . . . Oh! Wilhelm, a solitary cell, a hair-shirt[37] and a belt of thorns were the relief for which my soul is languishing. Adieu! I see no end to all this misery but the grave.

3 SEPTEMBER.

I must away. I thank you, Wilhelm, that you have confirmed my wavering resolve. For a fortnight I have been trying to make up my mind to leave her. I must. She is again in the town on a visit to a friend. And Albert—and—I must away.

10 SEPTEMBER.

What a night that was! Now, Wilhelm, I can surmount anything. I shall not see her again. Oh! that I cannot fly to your breast, tell you amid a thousand tears and transports all the emotions which are assailing my heart. Here I sit and gasp for air, try to calm myself, and await the morning. The horses are to be ready at dawn.

She sleeps peacefully and does not think that she will never see me again. I have torn myself away, was strong enough, during a conversation lasting two hours, not to reveal my purpose. And God! what a conversation!

Albert had promised me that he would be in the garden with Lotte immediately after supper. I stood on the terrace beneath the tall chestnuts and gazed at the sun, which I saw for the last time sinking over the lovely valley and the gentle stream. How often I had stood with her at this spot watching the same glorious scene, and now. . . . I walked to and fro along

[37] A painfully rough undergarment worn by religious ascetics.

the avenue which was so dear to me; I had so often been bound here by some mysterious, sympathetic attraction before ever I knew Lotte—and how we rejoiced when we discovered, at the beginning of our friendship, our mutual inclination for the place, which is really one of the most romantic productions of art that I have ever seen.

First, you have the broad prospect between the chestnut trees—Oh! I remember I have, I think, already written you a lot about how one is finally closed in by a high rampart of beeches and the avenue grows darker and darker on account of a plantation[38] that adjoins it, until one at last emerges into a confined clearing over which there hovers the awe of solitude. I can still feel the queer emotion by which I was stirred when I first entered it one high noon; I had a faint presentiment of all the pain and bliss of which it was to be the scene.

I had been revelling for about half an hour in the sweet languishing thoughts of parting and seeing her again, when I heard them coming up the terrace, ran towards them, seized her hand with an inward shudder and kissed it. We had just reached the top when the moon rose behind the tree-clad hill; we spoke of a diversity of things and approached imperceptibly the gloomy recess. Lotte entered and sat down, Albert at her side, and I also seated myself, but my restlessness soon made me start up again; I stood in front of her, walked to and fro, sat down again and was most distressed. She drew our attention to the beautiful effect of the moonlight which illuminated the whole terrace at the end of the rampart of beeches, a glorious sight which was rendered all the more striking by the deep twilight which closed us in all round. We were silent, and after a time she said, "I never go for a walk in the moonlight without being accompanied by the thought of my dead ones, without being oppressed by the feeling of death, of what is to come. We shall exist, Werther," she continued with the most exalted emotion in her voice, "but shall we meet again? and recognize one another? What do you surmise, what do you say?"

"Lotte," I replied, giving her my hand, my eyes filling with tears, "we shall meet again! Here and beyond!"—I could say no more. . . . Wilhelm, why did she have to ask me that, at the moment when I bore the anguish of this parting in my heart?

"And do our dear departed ones know anything about us?" she continued. "Do they feel, when it fares well with us, that we remember them with warm affection? Oh! my mother's form is always hovering about me, in the quiet evenings when I am sitting among her children, my children, and they are gathered round me as they were once gathered round her. When I gaze yearningly up to Heaven with tears in my eyes and wish that she might for a moment be able to look down and see how I am keeping the promise I gave on her deathbed to be a mother to her children. A hundred times I cry out, 'Forgive me, dearest one, if I am not to them what you were. Oh! I do whate'er I can, they are clad, fed, and oh! what is more than all, cared for and loved. Could you but see the harmony in which we live, dear saint! You would glorify with the most fervent gratitude the God Whom you entreated with your last bitter tears to protect your children!'"

That is what she said. Oh! Wilhelm! who can repeat her words, how can

[38] Grove of cultivated trees.

the dead cold letter depict the divine efflorescence of her spirit? Albert broke in gently, "It affects you too deeply, dear Lotte; I know your soul clings strongly to these notions, but I beg of you . . ." "Oh! Albert!" she said, "I know you do not forget the evenings when we sat together at the small round table, when father was away on a journey and we had sent the little ones to bed. You often had a good book with you, but you seldom succeeded in reading anything. Was not intercourse with this splendid soul more than all else? The beautiful, gentle, cheerful, ever busy woman! God knows with what tears I often cast myself before Him as I lay in bed, and entreated Him to make me as she was."

"Lotte!" I cried, throwing myself at her feet and seizing her hands, which I moistened with a thousand tears. "Lotte! the blessing of God and the spirit of your mother rest upon you." "If you had known her," she said, pressing my hand, "she was worthy to be known by you." I thought I should swoon. Never had anything so exalted, so proud been said in my praise. She continued, "And this woman was taken away in the prime of her life, when her youngest son was not yet six months old. Her illness did not last long, she was tranquil, resigned, regretting only her children, especially the babe. As the end drew near she said to me, 'Let them come up to me,' and I brought them in, the little ones who did not understand, and the older ones who were beside themselves; they stood round the bed and she raised her hands and prayed over them, and kissed them one after the other and sent them away, and said to me, 'Be a mother to them!' I gave her my hand as I made the vow. 'It is no little thing which you are promising, my daughter,' she said, 'the heart of a mother and the eye of a mother. I have often seen by your grateful tears that you know what that means. Let your brothers and sisters find them in you, and show to your father the faithfulness and obedience of a wife. You will afford him consolation.' She asked after him, but he had gone out to conceal from us the unbearable grief he felt. His heart was lacerated.

"You were in the room, Albert! She heard someone walking, inquired who it was, and asked you to approach. And as she gazed at you and at me, with a tranquil look, confident that we should be happy, happy together. . . ." Albert fell on her neck and kissed her, and cried, "We are! we shall be!" The usually serene Albert had entirely lost his self-possession, and I myself was on the verge of losing consciousness.

"Werther," she began, "this is the woman that we have lost! God! when I think, as I so often do, how we thus let the dearest thing in our life be taken away, and no one feels it so keenly as the children; who long continued to complain that the black men had carried away their mama."

She rose, but I was agitated and shaken and remained seated, holding her hand. "We must go," she said, "it is growing late." She wished to withdraw her hand, but I held it more firmly. "We shall meet again," I cried. "We shall come together, under whatever form we shall recognize one another. I go, I go willingly, and yet, if I had to say 'for ever,' I could not bear it. Farewell, Lotte! Farewell, Albert! We shall meet again." "To-morrow, I think," she replied jestingly. I was affected by this "to-morrow." Oh! she did not know as she withdrew her hand from mine . . . They went out along the avenue, I stood, looked after them in the moonlight, then threw myself on the earth and wept my fill, sprang up, ran out on to the terrace and could still perceive below, in the shadow of the tall limes, her white frock gleaming on the way to the garden door, I stretched out my arms, and it disappeared.

PART TWO

20 OCTOBER.

We arrived at this place yesterday. The ambassador is unwell, & will therefore keep to the house for some days. If only he were not so ungracious, all would be well. I perceive, I perceive that Fate has hard trials in store for me. But I must be of good courage! A light heart can bear everything. A light heart! I cannot help laughing as the word falls from my pen. A little more lightness of heart would make me the happiest being under the sun. What! where other men, with their modicum of energy and talent, are strutting around me in complacent self-assurance, do I despair of my energy, of my talents? God in Heaven, Who didst endow me with all this, why didst Thou not withhold the half and give me instead self-confidence and contentment!

Patience! Patience! Things will mend. For I tell you my friend, you are right. Since I have been compelled to move about among the people like this every day, and see what they do and how they go about things, I am on much better terms with myself. To be sure, since we are, after all, so constituted that we compare everything with ourselves and ourselves with everything, happiness or misery lies in the things with which we establish the analogy, and so nothing is more dangerous than solitude. Our power of imagination, forced by its nature to assert itself, nourished by the fantastic visions of poetry, raises for itself a series of beings of which we are the lowest, and where everything that is external to ourselves appears more splendid, everyone else more perfect. And the process is quite natural. We feel so often that there is something lacking in us, and it is just what we lack that often appears to us to be possessed by someone else, to whom we then impute, in addition, everything that we have ourselves and a certain ideal ease to boot. And so the happy being is perfect, the creature of our own imagination.

When, on the other hand, weak as we are, we only continue laboriously with our work, we very often find that with all our dawdling and tacking[39] we get further than others with their sails and oars—and—it does impart a feeling of self-confidence when one keeps up with or even outstrips others.

10 NOVEMBER.

I am beginning to settle down tolerably well here so far. The best of it is that there is enough to do, and then the various kinds of people, the diversity of new faces, present a motley scene to my soul. I have made the acquaintance of Count C., a man whom I learn to esteem more every day. A broad and lofty mind, making allowances for much and therefore by no means unsympathetic. One's connection with him is illumined by such feel-

[39] Laborious zigzag sailing into the wind.

ing for friendship and affection. He took an interest in me when I had some business to arrange with him, and he perceived at the opening of our conversation that we understood one another, that he could talk to me as he could not talk to everybody. And I cannot sufficiently praise his frank bearing towards me. There is no real ardent pleasure to equal that of being given access to a great soul.

24 DECEMBER.

The ambassador causes me much chagrin, as I anticipated. He is the most meticulous fool that can be imagined. He proceeds step by step and is as fussy as an old woman. A man who is never satisfied with himself and whom therefore nobody can please. I like to work quickly, and as a thing turns out so I leave it, but he is capable of giving me back a memorandum and saying, "It is good, but look through it again, there is always a better word, a more precise particle." It is enough to drive me crazy. No "and" or other conjunction may be omitted, and he is a mortal enemy of all the inversions which occasionally escape me. If one's periods[40] are not ground out in accordance with the time-honored rhythm, he is unable to understand them. It is a penance to have to deal with such a man.

The confidence of Count von C. is the only thing which compensates me. He confessed to me quite openly the other day how dissatisfied he is with the dull-witted scrupulousness of my ambassador. Such people make things more difficult for themselves and for others. "But," he said, "we must be resigned, like a traveller who has a mountain to cross. Of course, if the mountain weren't there, the way would be easier and shorter, but it *is* there and it has to be got over."

My chief probably feels, also, the preference the Count gives me over him, and that vexes him, so that he seizes every opportunity to speak ill of the Count to me. I oppose him, of course, and thereby only render matters worse. Yesterday he even made me fly into a passion, for he included me in his remarks—that the Count was quite good for affairs of the world, being a very quick worker and having a facile pen, but he was lacking in solid erudition, like all literary folk. I would have liked to thrash him for this, for there is no other way of reasoning with such fellows, but since this was not possible, I disputed with some heat and told him that the Count was a man who inspires esteem not only on account of his character but also of his knowledge. "I have never known anyone," I said, "who has so succeeded in enlarging his mind, to embrace matters innumerable, without surrendering his activity in ordinary life." This was all Greek to his brain, and I took my leave to avoid having to choke down more choler at further nonsensical talk.

You are all responsible for this, who talked me into assuming the yoke and prated so much of "activity." Activity! If the man who plants potatoes and rides to town to sell his corn, is not doing more than I, then I will wear myself out for another ten years in the galley to which I am now fettered.

And the gilded misery, the boredom among the loathsome people who

[40] Sentence constructions.

are assembled here! Their love of rank, the way they keep watch and guard to steal the smallest march[41] upon each other, their most wretched and pitiable passions which they make no attempt to conceal. There is a woman, for instance, who tells everybody about her noble birth and her country, so that every stranger must think, "What a fool she is with her conceited notions of her trivial patent of nobility and the fame of her country." That isn't the worst of it, however, for this very woman is the daughter of a district clerk in these parts. I cannot understand the human race that has so little sense as to make such a downright fool of itself.

To be sure, I perceive more clearly every day how foolish it is to judge others by oneself . . . And since I have so much to occupy me in myself, and my heart and mind are so tempestuous—oh! I would gladly let the others go their way, if they could only let me go my way too.

What irritates me most of all is the odious social conditions. To be sure, I am as well aware as anybody of the necessity for class distinctions and of the advantages that I myself receive from them; but they ought not to stand in my way just when I could enjoy a little pleasure, a gleam of happiness on this earth. During one of my walks recently I made the acquaintance of a Fräulein von B., a charming creature, who has preserved considerable naturalness in spite of the stiff conventional life here. We found one another's conversation agreeable and, when we parted, I asked permission to call upon her. This she granted with such frankness, that I could hardly await the appropriate hour to go to her. She does not come from this part, and is staying with an aunt, an old maid whose physiognomy was displeasing to me. I paid the latter much attention, applied my conversation mostly to her, and in less than half an hour I had pretty well conjectured what the young lady herself afterwards admitted to me—that the aunt, lacking everything, with neither a respectable fortune nor qualities of mind, has no support in her old age other than her ancestral tree, no protection other than the rank behind which she barricades herself, and no pleasure except to look down from her height and ignore the middle classes. She is said to have been beautiful in her youth and to have trifled away her life, first tormenting many a poor young man with her capriciousness, and in later years bowing to the domination of an elderly officer, who, in return for this and a passable income, passed the brass age[42] with her and then died. And now she has reached the iron age, she is alone, and would not receive any consideration, if her niece were not so charming.

8 JANUARY, 1772.

What creatures they are whose whole soul is bound up with ceremonial, whose thoughts and aims are for years directed towards the means of worming their way on to a chair which is one move higher up the table! And it is not as though the fellows had no other opportunities. No! there is work in abundance, for the very reason that the petty vexations hinder the

[41] Stealthily gain the slightest advantage.

[42] According to myth, the human race degenerated from golden to silver to bronze (or brass) to iron ages.

progress of the important matters. Last week there was a quarrel during a sledge drive and all the fun was spoilt.

Fools, not to see that the place does not really matter at all, and that he who occupies the first very rarely plays the chief part! How many kings are ruled by their ministers, and how many ministers by their secretaries! And who is then the first? The one, it seems to me, who can take in the others at a glance, and has sufficient power or cunning to harness their energies and passions to the execution of his plans.

20 JANUARY.
I must write to you, dear Lotte, here in the taproom of a poor rustic inn where I have taken refuge from a heavy storm. Since I have been moving about in that wretched hole of a town, among strangers, complete strangers to my heart, there has not been a moment, not a single one, when my heart bade me write to you. And now in this hut, in this solitude, where I am so hemmed in, and snow and hail are beating furiously against the window panes, here my first thought was of you. As I entered, your form appeared before my mind. Oh, Lotte! with such sacred fervor! God! the first happy moment recaptured!

If you could see me now, in this deluge of distraction! How dried up my senses are becoming, not one moment when I can allow my heart full play, not one single hour of tearful bliss! Nothing! Nothing! It is as though I am standing in front of a raree-show,[43] watching the mannikins and the little horses moving about, and I often ask myself whether it is not an optical illusion. I join in the general movement, or rather I am moved like a marionette, and often seize the wooden hand of my neighbor and start back with a shudder.

I have only discovered a single feminine being here. A Fräulein von B. She resembles you, Lotte, if it is possible for anyone to resemble you. "Ah!" you will say, "the fellow is paying compliments!" There is some truth in that. For some time I have been very well-mannered, since, after all, I cannot help myself. I have a ready wit, and the ladies say nobody utters such delicate compliments as I do (and lies, you will add, for otherwise they cannot be successful, do you follow me?). I was speaking about Fräulein B. She has much soul which shines from her blue eyes, and is oppressed by her rank which does not satisfy any of her heart's desires. She longs to escape from the turmoil, and we pass many an hour in fanciful conversation about rural scenes of unalloyed happiness—and about you. How often does she have to pay you homage! There is no "must," she does it with all her heart, likes so much to hear about you, loves you.

Oh! would that I were sitting at your feet in the dear familiar room, and our little ones were tumbling about around me, and when they grew too noisy for you I would collect them round me and quieten them with a weird fairy tale. The sun is setting gloriously over a gleaming, snow-white earth, and the storm has passed on. And I—must again shut myself up in my cage. Adieu! Is Albert with you! And how—? God forgive me the question!

[43] Exhibition viewed through a small peephole.

17 FEBRUARY.

I fear that my ambassador and I will not stay together much longer. The fellow is perfectly unbearable. His way of working and doing business is so ridiculous, that I cannot refrain from contradicting him and frequently doing a thing in my own way and to my own mind, which, of course, then never suits him. He recently complained of me at Court on this account, and the minister reproved me, mildly to be sure, but nevertheless it was a reproof, and I was about to send in my resignation when I received a private letter[44] from him, a letter before which I sank on my knees and worshipped the lofty, wise and noble mind that knows so well how to correct my too great sensitiveness, respecting, indeed, my exaggerated notions of activity, of influence over others, of getting the mastery in affairs, as a praiseworthy, youthful spirit, trying not to eradicate them, but only to temper them and guide them to where they can have full scope and achieve their most useful purpose. I am now fortified for a week, and in harmony with myself. Tranquillity of soul is a glorious thing, and joy in oneself. Dear friend, if only the thing were not just as fragile as it is beautiful and precious.

20 FEBRUARY.

God bless you, my dear ones, and grant you all the happy days that He takes from me.

I thank you, Albert, for deceiving me; I was awaiting news when your wedding day was to be, and had intended on that day solemnly to take down Lotte's silhouette from the wall and bury it under other papers. Now you are married, and her portrait is still here! Well, it shall stay! Why not? I know that I am also with you, that I am in Lotte's heart, without prejudice to you. I have, yes, I have the second place in it, and will and must retain it. Oh! I would go mad, if she were able to forget. . . . Albert, hell lies in the thought. Albert, farewell! Farewell, angel from heaven, farewell, Lotte!

15 MARCH.

I have been subjected to a mortification that will drive me away from here, and makes me gnash my teeth. The Devil! It cannot be made good, and the whole fault is yours, all of you who spurred me on, and drove me and worried me to accept a post that was not to my mind. Well, here I am! You have got your way! And in order that you may not tell me again that my exaggerated notions spoil everything—here, my dear Sir, is a story, clear and simple, as a chronicler would record it.

Count von C. is fond of me, pays me special attention, that is well known and I have already told you so a hundred times. I was dining with him yesterday, on the particular day when the aristocratic company of ladies and gentlemen assembles at his house in the evening. I had forgotten this,

[44] "This letter, together with another which is referred to later on, has been withdrawn from this collection out of respect for this excellent man, as it was not thought that such boldness could be excused by the gratitude, however warm, of the public."—Note in original German text.

and it never occurred to me that we of inferior rank are not acceptable on such occasions. Good. I dine with the Count, and after table we walk up and down the great hall, I converse with him and with Colonel B. who puts in an appearance, and thus the hour for the party approaches. God knows, I suspect nothing. Then there enters the more-than-gracious Madame von S. with her consort and her nobly hatched little goose of a flat-chested, tight-laced daughter. They widen their eyes and nostrils in the traditional, highly-aristocratic manner *en passant,*[45] and, as I loathe the herd with all my heart, I was about to take my leave, waiting only until the Count should be free from the exchange of dreadful twaddle, when suddenly my Fräulein von B. entered. Since it always raises my spirits a little when I see her, I remained, took my place behind her chair, and only noticed after some time that she was talking to me with less frankness than usual, indeed with some embarrassment. I was struck by this. If she is like all these people, I thought to myself, may the Devil take her! I was irritated and wanted to depart, and yet remained, for I was intrigued and wished for more light on the matter. Meanwhile the room was filling up. Baron F., wearing his whole wardrobe dating from the coronation of the Emperor Francis the First,[46] Hofrat[47] R., here called *in qualitate* Herr *von* R.,[48] with his deaf wife etc., to say nothing of J., who is badly off, his antiquated garments contrasting strangely with the fashionable oddments he wore with them—all these were arriving, and I was conversing with some of the people I knew, who were all very laconic.[49] I was occupied with my thoughts, and only concerned with my Fräulein B. I did not notice that the women were whispering to each other at the end of the room, that this infected the men, that Frau von S. was talking to the Count (Fräulein B. told me all this afterwards), until finally the Count came up to me and led me to a window. "You are aware," he said, "of our odd conventions. The company, I observe, is displeased to see you here. I would not for anything in the world. . . ." "Your Excellency," I interrupted, "I beg a thousand pardons. I should have thought of it before, but I know you will forgive my *faux pas.*[50] I was about to take my leave some time ago, but" I added with a smile as I bowed, "an evil genius held me back." The Count pressed my hand with a sympathy which said more than words. I made my bow to the distinguished company, and took a coach as far as M. to see the sun setting from the top of the hill, and read in my Homer the glorious canto where Ulysses is entertained by the worthy swineherd.[51] This was all delightful.

In the evening I returned home to sup. There were only a few people left in the coffee-room, and they had turned back the table cloth and were throwing dice in a corner. Then Adelin came in, put down his hat, as he glanced at me, came up and said softly, "You were rebuffed?" "*I* was?" I said. "The Count asked you to leave the company." "The Devil take them,"

[45] In passing (French).

[46] Holy Roman Emperor from 1745 to 1765. The present date is 1772.

[47] Court Councillor.

[48] Given the aristocratic preposition *von* ("of"), since he has been accepted in aristocratic company.

[49] Abrupt in speech. [50] Social blunder.

[51] In Homer's *Odyssey,* the disguised Odysseus, after returning to Ithaca, enjoys the hospitality of his faithful old swineherd Eumaeus.

I said. "I was glad to get out into the fresh air." "Good," he said, "that you treat it lightly. But I am annoyed. Everybody is talking about it." Now for the first time the matter began to vex me. I thought everyone who looked at me at table did so because he knew about it. This began to rouse my choler.[52]

And now, when I am pitied wherever I go, when I hear those who are jealous of me exclaiming triumphantly that one could see what happened to arrogant fellows who boasted of their modicum of intellect and thought it gave them a right to set themselves above all conventions, and that sort of twaddle—it is enough to make a man stick a knife in his heart. For whatever people may say about independence, I would like to see who can bear scoundrels talking about him when they have him at a disadvantage. If it is only empty talk, oh! then one can easily ignore them.

16 MARCH.

Everything is combining to provoke me! Today I met Fräulein B. in the avenue. I could not refrain from addressing her, and showing her, as soon as we were some distance from the rest of the company, that I was hurt at her recent behavior. "Oh! Werther!" she said, in a tone of deep sincerity, "could you thus interpret my confusion, knowing my heart as you do? How I suffered for your sake, from the moment when I entered the room! I foresaw everything, a hundred times it was on the tip of my tongue to warn you, I knew that Madame von S. and Madame von T., together with their husbands, would rather take their departure than stay in your company, I knew that the Count would not venture to fall out with them—and now all this fuss . . ." "What do you mean?" I asked, and concealed my dismay, for everything that Adelin had told me the day before yesterday coursed through my veins like boiling water at this moment. "How much it has already cost me!" said the sweet creature, with tears in her eyes. I could no longer control myself, was about to throw myself at her feet. "Tell me what you mean," I cried. The tears ran down her cheeks. I was beside myself. She dried them without any attempt at concealment. "You know my aunt," she began. "She was there, and oh! how she opened her eyes! Werther, I endured last night and this morning a sermon about my intercourse with you, and had to listen to you being disparaged, degraded, and was only half able to defend you."

Every word she uttered pierced my heart like a sword. She did not see what a mercy it would have been to hide all this from me, and she now told me all the further gossip there would be, how all the malicious fellows would be triumphant. How from now on they would proclaim that my arrogance and disdain of others, which they had long blamed in me, was now punished and humbled. To hear all this from her lips, Wilhelm, in a tone of sincerest sympathy—I was overcome, and am still raging inwardly. I wish someone would dare to cast it in my teeth,[53] that I might thrust my sword through his body! If I were to see blood I should feel better. Oh! I have taken up a knife a hundred times to let air into my suffocating heart. It is related of a noble species of horses that, when they are frightfully

[52] Anger. [53] Reproach me (and thus provoke a duel).

heated and at their last gasp, they instinctively bite open a vein to help them to breathe. I often feel like that. I would like to open a vein and achieve eternal freedom.

24 MARCH.
I have handed in my resignation at Court and hope it will be accepted. You will forgive me for not asking your permission first. I *had* to go away, and I already know everything you would say to persuade me to stay, so—sugar the pill for my mother. I cannot help myself so she must put up with it, though I cannot help her either. It will certainly grieve her. To see the brilliant career which was leading her son to a privy councillorship or an embassy suddenly interrupted and the horse put back in its stable! Make of it what you will and add up the possible eventualities which might have made it possible for me to stay, or obliged me to do so. Enough, I am going. And that you may know whither I am going, Prince ***, who relishes my society, is here, and asked me, when he heard of my intention, to accompany him to his estates and spend the beautiful spring there. He has promised that I shall be left entirely to myself and, since we understand each other up to a certain point, I will try my luck and go with him.

19 APRIL.
For your Information.
I thank you for your two letters. I did not reply, since I was leaving this letter until my resignation had been accepted at Court, for I feared my mother might apply to the minister and render my purpose difficult. Now, however, it is all over, and I have my discharge. I hardly like to tell you how unwillingly they gave it me, and what the minister has written; you would break out into fresh lamentations. The hereditary prince has sent me a parting gift of twenty-five ducats, with a letter that moved me to tears. So my mother need not send me the money I wrote for recently.

5 MAY.
I leave here to-morrow, and since the place where I was born is only a few miles away, I would like to see it again, and recall the happy days I used to dream away. I will enter by the very gate from which I drove out with my mother when she left the dear, familiar spot after my father's death, to shut herself up in her unbearable town. Adieu, Wilhelm, you shall have news of my progress.

9 MAY.
I have fulfilled the pilgrimage to my home with a pilgrim's reverence and have been affected by many an unexpected emotion. I stopped at the great lime tree, a quarter of an hour's journey outside the town on the way to S. I alighted and bade the postillion[54] take the coach on, that I might go on

[54] Coachman.

foot to savor each memory anew, vividly, and in my own way. There I stood beneath the lime which used to be the goal and boundary of my walks as a boy. How different the circumstances! Then, in my blissful ignorance, I had yearned to go out into the unknown world, where my heart hoped to find all the nourishment, all the enjoyment of which I so often felt the lack in my bosom. Now I was coming back from the wide world—with oh! how many hopes miscarried, how many plans shattered!—I saw the range of mountains in front of me, that had times without number been the object of my desires. I had sat here for hours at a time, yearning to be there, fervently absorbed in the woods and valleys which appeared before me in an intimate halflight—and then, when the time came to return home, how unwillingly I left the beloved spot! I approached the town, greeted all the old familiar summer-houses, and disliked the new ones as well as all the other changes which had taken place. I went in through the gate and there I found myself again completely. I will not give you all the details, for, charming as they were to me, the record would only be monotonous. I had made up my mind to take a lodging in the market-place, next door to our old house. As I walked along I noticed that the little school, where our childhood had been penned up by an honest old dame, was turned into a shop. I recalled the restlessness, the tears, the mental apathy and heart-aches I had endured in that den.—Every step I took was fraught with interest. No pilgrim in the Holy Land comes across so many shrines of pious memory, and the souls of few are so filled with sacred emotion. One more detail that must suffice for a thousand. I went down the river to a certain farm, which used also to be one of my walks, and looked at the places where we boys tried who could make the flat stones rebound most often as we skimmed them along the surface of the water. I remember most vividly how I often stood there and gazed at the stream, the wondrous presentiments with which I followed it, how romantic the country appeared to me to which it was flowing, how I soon found that there were limits to my imagination and yet I had to penetrate further, ever further, until I had completely lost myself in the illimitable distance. Is that not just what the glorious patriarchs felt! When Ulysses[55] speaks of the immeasurable ocean and the unbounded earth, is not that more true, more human, more fervent, than nowadays when every schoolboy thinks himself a miracle of wisdom because he can repeat that the world is round?

Here I am in the Prince's hunting-box.[56] He is quite agreeable to live with, being simple and sincere. I am often pained, however, when he talks about things that he only knows from hearsay or reading, and always from a second-hand point of view.

And he has more understanding for my intellect and talents than for my heart, which is, after all, my only pride, the sole source of everything, all vigor, all bliss and all misery. Oh! anyone can know what I know.—My heart is my own.

25 MAY.

I had something in my mind about which I was unwilling to tell you any-

[55] Homer's Odysseus. [56] Hunting lodge.

thing until it had been put into execution but, now that it has come to nothing, I may just as well do so. I wanted to go to the wars! My heart was long intent on it. It was the chief reason why I came here with the Prince, who is a general in the *** service. I revealed my intention to him during one of our walks, he dissuaded me, and it would have had to be a passion rather than a whim to prevent me listening to his arguments.

11 JUNE.
Say what you will, I cannot stay any longer. What is the use? I am finding it tedious. The Prince treats me as an equal and yet I do not feel at home. And we have not really anything in common. He is a man of intellect, but of a low order, and I find his conversation no more entertaining than a well-written book. I shall stay another week and then resume my wanderings. The best thing I have done here is my sketching. The Prince has a feeling for art, though this would be deeper if he were not limited by the abominations of science and the usual terminology. It often makes me gnash my teeth when, upon my introducing with warmth and imagination topics of nature and art, he thinks he is doing quite well as he suddenly blunders in with some conventional technical term.

18 JUNE.
Where am I going? I will tell you in confidence. I have to remain here another fortnight after all, and then I pretend to myself that I am going to visit the mines in ***. Nothing of the sort, however. I only want to see Lotte again. That is all. And I ridicule my own heart—but shall do what it demands.

29 JULY.
No, it is all right! Everything is all right! I—her husband! Oh! God, Who made me, if Thou hadst granted me that bliss, my whole life would be one continual prayer. I will not complain, and crave pardon for these tears, pardon for my vain desires.—She—my wife! If I had the dearest being under the sun enfolded in my arms—a shudder goes through my whole body, Wilhelm, when Albert embraces her slender waist.

And—ought I to say it? Why not, Wilhelm? She would have been happier with me than with him! Oh! he is not the man to fulfill all the longings of that heart. A certain lack of delicacy, a lack—take it as you will, that his heart does not beat in sympathy at—oh!—at a passage in a beloved book where my heart and Lotte's meet as one. In a hundred other cases, when it happens that we express our feelings at the action of someone else. Dear Wilhelm!—He *does* love her with his whole soul, and what is such a love not worth. . . .

I have been interrupted by an insupportable fellow. My tears are dried. I am distracted. Adieu, dear friend!

4 AUGUST.
I am not the only one to suffer thus. All men find their hopes deceived,

their expectations betrayed. I visited the good woman who lives by the lime tree. Her eldest boy ran towards me, and his shouts of joy attracted his mother, who looked very downcast. Her first words were, "Good Sir! Alas, my Hans is dead."—He was the youngest of her sons. I was silent.—"And my husband," she continued, "has returned from Switzerland with empty hands, and were it not for some kind people he would have had to go a-begging. He fell ill of a fever on the way." I knew not what to say to her, and gave something to the little one. She asked me to accept some apples, which I did and left the place of melancholy memory.

21 AUGUST.

I change in a flash. Sometimes I find a gleam of joy in life once more, but alas! only for a moment. When I thus lose myself in my dreams, I cannot avoid the thought—"What if Albert were to die! You would, she would—," and then I pursue the will o' the wisp till it leads me to the verge of abysses before which I shudder back.

When I go out at the town gate, the way I first went when I fetched Lotte to the ball—how different it all was! All, all is over. Not a vestige of the former world, not a throb of the emotion I then felt. I feel like a ghost that has returned to the burnt-out castle which it once built in its princely glory and bequeathed on its death-bed, splendidly furnished, to a beloved son.

3 SEPTEMBER.

I am sometimes unable to comprehend how another can, or may love her, when I love her so singleheartedly, so fervently, so completely, and know nothing, am aware of nothing, have nothing but her.

6 SEPTEMBER.

I had a difficult struggle before I was able to make up my mind to put aside the simple blue coat in which I first danced with Lotte, but it grew at last too shabby. I have had a new one made, just like the last, with collar and facings, and another yellow waistcoat and pair of breeches.

But it has not quite the same effect. I do not know—perhaps, with time, I shall grow to like it more.

15 SEPTEMBER.

It is enough to make one resign oneself to the Devil to see all the hounds that God tolerates on this earth, without sense or feeling for what little there is of value on it. You know the walnut trees beneath which I sat with Lotte at the honest old clergyman's in St., the glorious walnut trees which, God knows, always filled my soul with the greatest content. How intimate and cool they made the courtyard, how glorious their branches were. And the memories they held, back to the good clergymen who had planted them so many years ago. The schoolmaster often mentioned the name of one of them, which he had learned from his grandfather. He is said to have been such a worthy man and his memory was always sacred to me under the trees. I tell you there were tears in the schoolmaster's eyes yesterday when we discussed their having been cut down.—Cut down! The thought makes me frenzied, I could murder the hound who struck the first blow. I, who could pine away with grief if a few trees stood in my courtyard and one of them withered with age—I have to look on at this. But there is one point worth mentioning. What a thing is human feeling! The whole village is muttering, and I hope the minister's wife will feel the difference in the way of butter, eggs and other presents, to show how she has wounded the villagers. For it is she who is to blame, the wife of the new minister (the old one is dead), a scraggy, sickly brute with very good cause to take no interest in the world, since no one takes any in her. An ugly creature who puts forth pretensions to learning, takes a hand in the examination of the canon,[57] works a great deal at the new-fangled, critico-moral reformation of Christianity and shrugs her shoulders at the enthusiasms of Lavater, is quite shattered in health and therefore without joy on God's earth. Only such a creature could find it possible to cut down my walnut trees. I cannot keep cool! Just imagine, the falling leaves make the courtyard dank and dirty, the trees take away the light and, when the nuts are ripe, the boys throw stones at them and that jars her nerves, disturbs the profundity of her meditations when she is pondering the differing views of Kennicott, Semler and Michaelis.[58] When I saw how discontented the villagers were, especially the old ones, I asked why they had suffered it. "When the mayor wants a thing hereabouts," they replied, "what can we do?" But one justice was done at least. The mayor and the parson, who at any rate wanted to make something out of his wife's whims, which don't bring him in much profit, thought of sharing the proceeds, but the revenue-office heard of it and said, "This way please!", and sold the trees to the highest bidder. There they lie! Oh if I were but a Prince! The parson's wife, the mayor and the revenue-office would be—Prince!—Well, if I were a Prince, would I worry about the trees in my country!

10 OCTOBER.
If I only look into her black eyes, I am already cured! And what mortifies me is that Albert does not appear to be as happy as he—expected—as I—thought I would be—if—I am not fond of dashes, but it is the only way I can express myself here—and I think it is clear enough.

12 OCTOBER.
Ossian has crowded Homer out of my heart. To what a world this glorious poet has introduced me! To wander over the heath, with the storm wind howling round me, carrying along in the steaming mists the ghosts of ancestors under the light of the moon. To hear from the mountains, amid the roaring of the forest river, the fading groans of spirits in their caves and the laments of the maiden pining with grief by the four moss-covered, grass-grown stones that mark the grave of her noble lover. Then when I find him, the wandering gray bard, who seeks on the broad heath the

[57] Of the authenticity of books of the Bible. [58] Biblical scholars.

foot-steps of his fathers, and finds alas! their tombstones, and then gazes lamenting at the evening star which is hiding in the rolling ocean, and ages long gone by re-awaken in the soul of the hero, when the friendly beam shed its light upon the perils of the brave ones and the moon illumined their ship returning wreathed in victory; when I read the deep sorrow on his brow, see the last forlorn hero tottering exhausted to the grave, drinking in ever fresh, grievously glowing joys in the impotent presence of the shades of his departed ones, and looking down on the cold earth and the high waving grass, crying out: "The traveller will come, will come, who knew me in my beauty and will ask, 'Where is the minstrel, Fingal's worthy son?'[59] His foot-step will pass over my grave and he will ask for me upon the earth in vain."—Oh Friend! I would like to draw my sword like a noble armor-bearer[60] and free my lord with one blow from the quivering torment of this slowly receding life, and send my soul to follow the freed demi-god.

19 OCTOBER.

Oh! this void, this dreadful void within my breast. I often think—if you could but press her once, only once, to your heart, the void would all be filled.

26 OCTOBER.

Yes, I am growing certain, friend, certain and ever more certain, that the existence of any creature matters little, very little. One of Lotte's friends came to see her, and I went into the next room to find a book, but could not read, so took up a pen to write. I heard them speaking softly, exchanging trifling gossip, news of the town, how one girl had married, another was very sick. "She has a dry cough, the bones are sticking out of her face, she gets fainting fits, I wouldn't give a penny for her life," said the friend. "So and so is also in a bad way," said Lotte. "He has swollen up already," said the other. My vivid imagination set me at the bedsides of these poor people, I saw how reluctantly they turned their backs on this life, how they—and Wilhelm, these ladies were discussing the matter in the way we usually discuss a stranger's death. And when I look round, and see the room, with Lotte's clothes lying about, her ear-rings here on the table, and Albert's papers and the furniture with which I am so familiar, even this ink-pot, and think to myself, "See what you are to this house! All in all. Your friends esteem you. You often make them happy and your heart feels that it could not exist without them; and yet—if you were to go? if you were to leave this circle? would they, and for how long, feel the void which your loss would make in their lot? for how long?"—Oh! man is so transitory that even where he finds the actual certainty of his existence, where he leaves the only true impress of his presence, in the memory, in the soul of those he loves—even there he must be extinguished, must disappear, and oh! how soon!

[59] Fingal was the legendary Ossian's father.
[60] Warrior who carried his ruler's weapons.

27 OCTOBER.
I would often like to tear my breast and dash out my brains at the thought that two mortals can be so little to one another. The love, the joy, the ardor, the rapture that do not come from myself will not be given me by another, and though my whole heart be full of bliss I cannot make another happy if he stands before me cold and limp.

30 OCTOBER.
If I have not a hundred times been on the verge of embracing her! The great God knows what it feels like to see so much charm about one and not be able to grasp it. And that is yet the most natural of human instincts. Do not children grasp at everything they see?—And I?

3 NOVEMBER.
God knows, I lie down to sleep so often with the wish, sometimes with the hope, that I shall not wake again; and in the morning I open my eyes, see the sun again and am wretched. Oh! that I could be peevish, could shift the blame to the weather, to a third party, to an unsuccessful venture; the intolerable burden of ill-humor would then only half rest upon myself. Woe is me, I feel only too truly that the whole fault is mine alone—not fault! Enough that the source of all my misery lies concealed within myself, as formerly was the source of all my happiness. Am I not still the same who formerly hovered amidst all the abundance of emotion, with a Paradise following on every step, with a heart able to embrace a whole world with love? And this heart is now dead, no more delights flow from it, my eyes are dry, and my faculties, no longer revived by refreshing tears, draw uneasy furrows across my brow. I am suffering much, because I have lost what was the sole delight of my life, the holy vivifying power with which I created worlds around me. It has gone!—When I look out of my window at the distant hill, as the morning sun pierces the mist above it and illumines the tranquil meadows in the valley, and the gentle stream winds towards me between its leafless willows—oh! when this glorious scene appears before me as fixed as a varnished picture and all this rapture is incapable of pumping a single drop of happiness from my heart up into my brain, and my whole churlish self stands before the face of God like a dried-up spring, like a cracked pitcher! I have so often cast myself upon the ground and implored God to send me tears as a husbandman[61] prays for rain, when the sky is brazen[62] overhead and the earth about him is parched.

But oh! I feel that God does not send rain and sunshine at our impetuous bidding, and those times, the memory of which torments me, why were they so happy if not because I patiently awaited His spirit and received with a grateful fervent heart the rapture which He caused to descend upon me!

8 NOVEMBER.
She has reproached me with my lack of control, and oh! so gently! That I

[61] Farmer. [62] Like brass.

sometimes allow myself to be seduced by a glass of wine into drinking the whole bottle. "Don't do it," she said, "think of Lotte!" "Think!" I said. "Do you need to bid me do that? I think!—or do not think! You are always present to my soul. I sat to-day at the spot where you alighted lately from the coach. . . ." She changed the topic, to stop me pursuing the subject further. Friend, I am lost! She can do with me what she will.

15 NOVEMBER.

I am grateful to you, Wilhelm, for your sincere sympathy, for your well-meant advice, and would beg you to be tranquil. Let me endure it to the end; with all my lassitude I have strength enough to see it out. I have respect for religion, as you know, I feel that it is a staff for many a weary soul, refreshment for many who are faint. But—can it, must it then be for everyone? When you look at the great world, you see thousands for whom it has not been, thousands for whom it will not be—preached or not preached—must it then be for me? Does not even the Son of God say that those would be about Him whom His Father has given to Him?[63] Suppos-ing our Father wishes to keep me for Himself, as my heart tells me? I beg you, do not interpret this falsely, do not look for mockery in these innocent words; it is my whole soul that I am baring to you. Otherwise I would rather have remained silent, for I do not willingly waste words about things of which no one knows any more than I do. What is it but the fate of man to endure his lot, to drain his cup?—And if the cup was too bitter for the human lips of the God Who came from Heaven,[64] why should I brag and pretend it tastes sweet to me? And why should I be ashamed, in the dread moment when my whole existence is trembling between being and not being, when the past is gleaming like lightning over the dark abyss of the future, when everything around me is falling away and the world crashing to ruin over my head?—Is it not the voice of the mortal who is thrust wholly in upon himself, insufficient unto himself, plunging headlong into the chasm, which grates from the secret recesses of his vainly upward-striving soul: "My God, My God, why hast Thou forsaken me?"[65] And should I be ashamed to say this, should I stand in dread of the moment when even He did not escape it Who rolls the Heavens together like a cloth?

21 NOVEMBER.

She does not see, she does not feel that she is preparing a poison which will bring us both to grief. And I am voluptuously draining the cup that she is handing me for my destruction. What is the meaning of the kindly glance with which she often—often?—no, not often, but nevertheless sometimes looks at me, the favor with which she receives an involuntary expression of my feeling, the sympathy with my suffering that I see on her brow?

[63] John 6:37, 17:24.

[64] The reference is to Jesus' prayer in Gethsemane on the night before the Crucifixion: "O my Father, if it be possible, let this cup pass from me: nevertheless, not as I will, but as thou wilt" (Matthew 26:39; compare also Mark 14:36 and Luke 22:42).

[65] Jesus' words on the cross (Matthew 27:46; Mark 15:34), quoted from Psalms 22:1.

Yesterday, as I was leaving, she gave me her hand and said, "Adieu, dear Werther!" Dear Werther! It was the first time that she called me "dear," and it penetrated to my very marrow. I repeated it to myself a hundred times, and last night, as I was going to bed, as I was chattering to myself about nothing in particular, I suddenly said, "Good night, dear Werther!" and had to laugh at myself afterwards.

24 NOVEMBER.
She feels what I am suffering. Her gaze went deep into my heart to-day. I found her alone. I said nothing, and she looked at me. And I no longer saw in her the charming beauty, no longer saw the shining of her fine spirit; all that disappeared from before my eyes. The gaze which affected me was far more glorious, full of an expression of the most ardent interest, the sweetest sympathy. Why could I not cast myself at her feet? Why could I not embrace her in reply with a thousand kisses?—She took refuge at the harpsichord, and in a sweet, soft voice breathed harmonious sounds to accompany her playing. Never have I seen her lips so alluring; it was as though they opened thirstily to drink in the sweet tones that welled forth from the instrument, and only the secret echo was returning from her sweet mouth—if I could only tell you what it was like! I no longer resisted; I bowed my head and vowed that I would never venture to imprint a kiss on those lips on which the spirits of Heaven are hovering. And yet—I will—Ha! you see, it stands like a barrier before my soul—this bliss—and then to go down to do penance for my sin—sin?

30 NOVEMBER.
I cannot, I cannot regain command of myself. Wherever I go I encounter an apparition which totally deranges me. To-day! Oh fate! Oh humanity!

At noon I went down to the river, I had no desire for food. Everything was so dreary. A damp, cold west wind was blowing from the mountains and the gray storm clouds were being wafted along the valley. From a distance I saw a man in a shabby green coat crawling about among the rocks and appearing to search for herbs. When I came close to him, and the noise I made caused him to turn round, I saw a very interesting physiognomy of which the chief feature was a quiet melancholy, but which otherwise expressed only a good and frank disposition; his black hair was held in two coils by pins, and the rest woven into a thick plait which hung down his back. Since his dress seemed to me to denote a man of inferior rank, I thought he would not take it amiss if I betrayed an interest in his occupation, so I asked him what he was looking for. "I am looking for flowers," he replied with a deep sigh, "and can find none." "This is not the season for them," I said with a smile. "There are so many flowers," he said, coming down towards me. "In my garden there are roses and two kinds of honeysuckle, one of which my father gave me; they grow like weeds; I have been searching for two days and cannot find any. Out there also there are always flowers, yellow and blue and red, and the centaury has a beautiful flower. I cannot find any at all." There seemed to be something queer about this, so I asked him in a roundabout way, "What do you want the flowers for then?" His mouth twitched with an odd wry smile. "If you will not give me away," he said, pressing his finger to his lips, "I have promised to take a nosegay to my sweetheart." "That is fine," I said. "Oh!" he replied, "She has a lot of other things, she is rich." "And yet she would like your nosegay," I said. "Oh!" he continued, "she has jewels and a crown." "What is her name?" "If the States General[66] were to pay me," he replied, "I should be another man. Yes, there was once a time when I was so well off. Now it is all over with me, now I am. . . ."—a tearful gaze at the heavens expressed everything. "So you were happy?" I asked. "Oh! I wish I were so again!" he said, "then I was so well off, so gay, as happy as a fish in water." "Heinrich!" cried an old woman who came along the path, "Heinrich, where have you been? We have looked for you everywhere. Come and eat." "Is he your son?" I asked, going up to her. "Yes, my poor son," she replied. "God has given me a heavy cross to bear." "How long has he been like this?" I asked. "He has been as quiet as this for half a year now. Thank God he has got so far! Before that he was in a frenzy for a whole year, and he lay in chains in the madhouse. Now he would not harm anybody, and is only occupied with kings and emperors. He was such a good quiet boy, who helped to keep me and wrote a good hand; but suddenly he grew melancholy, fell into a violent fever, then into a frenzy, and now he is as you see him. If I were to tell you, Sir . . ." I broke in upon her stream of reminiscences by asking what he meant by the time when he was so happy and well off. "The crazy fellow," she cried with a smile of compassion. "He means the time when he was out of his mind; he always praises it. That was when he was in the madhouse, when he was unaware of his condition."—I was thunderstruck. I pressed a piece of money in her hand and rushed away.

"When you were happy!" I cried aloud, as I hastened towards the town. "Happy as a fish in water.—God in Heaven! hast Thou made it the fate of man that he is only to be happy when he has come to his senses and when he loses them again! Poor fellow! yet how I envy your melancholy, the confusion of mind in which you are languishing! You set out hopefully to pluck flowers for your queen—in Winter—and are sad that you can find none, and cannot comprehend why you can find none. And I—and I set out without hope or purpose, and return home as I came. You indulge your fancy of what you would do if the States General were to pay you. Blissful being, who can impute his lack of happiness to an earthly obstacle. You do not feel! you do not feel that your misery springs from your ravaged heart, from your unhinged brain, and that all the kings on earth cannot help you."

He should perish without hope who mocks a sick man for traveling to the furthermost spring that will only intensify his malady and render his death more painful, who assumes himself superior to an oppressed being when the latter, to rid himself of remorse and the sufferings of the spirit, makes a pilgrimage to the Holy Tomb. Every footprint on an untrodden path is a drop of balsam for the anguished soul, and with every day's toilsome journey he lies down relieved of so much affliction. And can you call that madness—you armchair windbags?—Madness!—Oh God! Thou seest my tears! Why didst Thou, Who createdst man in wretchedness enough,

[66] The Dutch government, a symbol of great wealth.

put brothers at his side to rob him of his morsel of wretchedness, the morsel of trust he has in Thee, in Thee, Thou All-loving One? For what is trust in a healing root, in the tears of the vine,[67] but trust in Thee, that Thou hast laid in all the things about us the power to heal and soothe which we need at every step? Father, Whom I do not know! Father, Who didst formerly fill my whole soul and now hast turned away Thy face from me! Call me to Thee! Break Thy silence! Thy silence cannot sustain this thirsting soul—and could a man, a father, be angry whose son returned before his time and fell upon his neck and cried, "I am returned, my father. Be not angry that I have broken off my journey which, according to thy will, I should have prolonged. The world is everywhere the same, for work and toil, reward and joy, but what is that to me? I am only well where thou art, and in thy presence I will suffer and rejoice."—And Thou, dear Heavenly Father, wouldst *Thou* turn him from Thee?

1 DECEMBER.
Wilhelm! the man I wrote to you about, the happy unhappy one, was a clerk in the employ of Lotte's father, and an unhappy passion for her which he nourished, concealed, and then revealed, so that he was dismissed from his office, sent him mad. Feel, fellow, at these dry words, the distraction with which I listened to this story when Albert related it as calmly as you, perhaps, will read it.

4 DECEMBER.
I beg of you—you see, it is all over with me—I can bear it all no longer. I sat by her to-day—sat, she played on the harpsichord, various melodies, with such expression! such expression!—what will you?—her little sister sat on my knee and dressed her doll. Tears came into my eyes. I bent my head and caught sight of her wedding ring.—My tears flowed.—And suddenly she played the divine old melody, suddenly, and through my soul there coursed a feeling of solace and memory of all the past, all the occasions when I had heard the song, all the dismal intervals of chagrin and hopes miscarried, and then—I walked up and down the room, my heart suffocating under it all. "For God's sake," I said, going up to her in a violent outburst. "For God's sake, stop!" She ceased playing and gazed at me fixedly. "Werther," she said, with a smile that went to my soul, "Werther, you are very ill, you have taken a dislike to your favorite dishes. Go, I beg you! Calm yourself!" I tore myself away, and—God! Thou seest my misery and wilt put an end to it.

6 DECEMBER.
How her form pursues me! Waking and dreaming she absorbs my soul. Here, when I close my eyes, here in my forehead, at the focus of inward vision, are her black eyes. Here! I cannot explain it to you. When I close my

[67] Wine.

eyes, they are there, like an ocean, like an abyss they lie before me, in me, absorb my mental faculties.

What is man? The lauded demi-god! Are not his powers deficient just when he has most need of them? And when he soars up in bliss or sinks down in suffering, is he not held back, is he not again restored to cold dull consciousness, just at the moment when he longed to lose himself in the fullness of the infinite?[68]

8 DECEMBER.

Dear Wilhelm, my condition is that in which those unhappy beings must have been who were believed to be driven about by evil spirits. I am often possessed by something which is not fear, not craving. It is an unknown inward raging that threatens to tear my breast, that clutches my throat. I am wretched! wretched! And then I wander about the dread nocturnal countryside of this inhuman season.

Last night I was impelled to go out. I had heard in the evening that the stream had overflowed, and all the brooks, and that the whole of my dear valley, from Wahlheim downwards, was inundated. At night, some time after eleven, I hastened out. A dreadful scene. To see the turbulent flood whirling down from the rock in the moonlight over fields, meadows and hedges, and up and down the broad valley a raging sea lashed by the howling wind. When the moon came out again and illumined the black clouds and the booming flood rolled out in front of me in the dreadful glorious reflection, I was overcome by awe and longing. Oh! I faced the abyss with widespread arms and breathed, "Down! down!", and was immersed in the rapture of hurling down there all my torment and all my suffering, to rage along like the torrent. And oh! I was incapable of raising my foot from the ground to put an end to all my affliction!—My clock has not yet run down—I feel it! Oh Wilhelm! how willingly would I have surrendered all my humanity to tear the clouds apart with the storm wind, to embrace the flood. Ha! Will not perhaps the prisoner one day share this rapture?—

And as I gazed down pensively at a spot where I had rested with Lotte beneath a willow when we were heated with our walk, it was also submerged, and I could hardly make out where the willow was. And I thought of her

[68] The fictional editor begins his narrative at this point in the later, 1786 version. Besides commenting on Werther's situation and state of mind, he relates an episode for which that version has prepared us through two earlier letters by Werther. In May of 1771 he had described meeting a peasant servant who loved his mistress, a widow, purely but passionately, and Werther had entered sympathetically into the man's feelings. Later, about three months before the present date in December 1772, he learned that the servant, who had previously received some encouragement from the widow, had lost control of himself, tried to force himself on her, and been dismissed from her service, partly at the insistence of her brother, who feared that her money would be lost to his children if she remarried. Now Werther learns that the desperately jealous peasant, determined that no one else shall have the widow, has murdered the man who has replaced him both as servant and in her affections. Although Werther knows the man committed the murder, he believes in his essential guiltlessness and pleads fervently for him before the bailiff, who insists that the law must take its course. Albert sides with the bailiff. After this last fruitless burst of quixotic energy, Werther's depression sets in once more.

meadows, and the whole region round her hunting-lodge! how our summer-house was now scattered by the raging stream! And a sunbeam from the past gleamed out as when a captive dreams of herds, meadows and cornfields. I stayed.—I do not blame myself, for I have the courage to die.—I should have. . . . Now I am sitting here like an old woman gleaning wood from hedges and begging bread at doors to prolong and alleviate her wasting, joyless life for yet another moment.

17 DECEMBER.
What is this, my friend? I start back in terror from myself! Is not my love for her the holiest, purest, most brotherly love? Have I ever borne in my soul a culpable desire?—I will not maintain. . . . and now—dreams! Oh! how true a perception they had when they ascribed such contradictory effects to strange forces! Last night, I shudder to say it, I held her in my arms, clasped her tightly to my bosom and covered her love-lisping lips with unending kisses. My eyes swam in the intoxication of hers. God! am I to blame that I even yet feel an ecstasy in recalling with all their fervor these glowing joys? Lotte! Lotte!—And it is all over with me! My senses are confused. For a week I have lost my powers of deliberation, my eyes have been filled with tears. I am at ease nowhere and everywhere. I desire nothing, require nothing. It is better that I should go.

THE EDITOR

To The Reader

In order to supply the detailed story of our friend's last remarkable days, I am compelled to interrupt his letters by a narration, the material for which I gathered from the mouth of Lotte, Albert, his servant and other witnesses.

Werther's passion had gradually undermined the peace of Albert and his wife. The latter loved her with the tranquil faithfulness of an honorable man, and his amiable intercourse with her was in time subordinated more and more to his profession. To be sure, he did not want to admit to himself the difference which distinguished the present situation from the days when they were betrothed, but he felt a certain inward resentment at Werther's attentions to Lotte, which must have seemed both an interference with his privileges and a silent reproach. This increased the ill-humor which was often generated by overwork in his hampered and badly-paid profession, and, since Werther's situation made him also a depressing companion, the anguish of his heart having consumed his remaining spiritual faculties, his vivacity and his acumen, it was unavoidable that at last Lotte should also be infected and that she fell into a kind of melancholy in which Albert thought he could perceive a growing passion for the lover, and Werther a deep chagrin at the changed demeanor of her husband. The distrust with which the two friends regarded one another rendered their mutual presence very embarrassing to them. Albert avoided his wife's room when Werther was with her, and the latter, noticing it, after some fruitless attempts to keep away from her altogether, seized the opportunity of visiting her when her husband was detained at his office. This gave cause for fresh discontent, their tempers grew more and more exasperated, until at last Albert said rather curtly to his wife that she should at least for people's sake give a different turn to her relations to Werther, and put an end to his too-frequent visits.

It was about this time that the resolve to quit the world had taken shape in the poor youth's soul. It had always been a favorite idea of his, which had occupied him particularly since his return to Lotte.

It was, however, to be no precipitate, rash act; he wanted to take the step with the firmest conviction, with the most tranquil resolution.

His doubts, his struggle with himself, can be seen in a note that is probably the beginning of a letter to Wilhelm, and was found undated among his papers.

> Her presence, her fate, her sympathy with mine, press the last tears from my parched brain.
>
> To raise the curtain and step behind, that is all! So why this fear and hesitation?—Because we do not know what it is like behind?—And because there is no return?—And because it is the quality of our mind to forebode confusion and darkness where we know nothing definite.

He could not forget the rebuff at the embassy. He rarely mentioned it, but one could feel imperceptibly that he considered his honor irretrievably outraged, and that the episode had inspired him with a dislike for a profession or political activity. He therefore resigned himself totally to the odd emotional and mental idiosyncrasies with which we are acquainted from his letters, and to a bottomless passion which was bound to cause the eventual extinction of all his vital energies. The eternal monotony of a melancholy attachment to the charming and beloved being whose peace of mind he was upsetting, the tempestuous wearing down of his vitality, without hope or purpose, drove him at last to the dreadful act.

20 DECEMBER.

I am grateful, Wilhelm, for the affection that has prompted you to accept my remark as you have. Yes, you are right, it is better that I should go. Your suggestion that I should return to you does not please me altogether; at least, I would like to come by a roundabout way, especially as it is to be expected that the frost will last and the roads be good. I am glad that you will come to fetch me, but postpone it for a fortnight until you have received a letter from me with further news. Nothing should be plucked until it is ripe. And a fortnight more or less can do much. Ask my mother to pray for her son, and to forgive all the trouble I have caused her. It was my fate to sadden those to whom I owed happiness. Farewell, my dearest friend. All the blessing of Heaven be upon you! Farewell!

On that very day—it was the Sunday before Christmas—he came to Lotte in the evening, and found her alone. She was occupied in arranging some toys that she had prepared as Christmas presents for her little brothers and sisters. He talked about the pleasure the little ones would experience, and about the times when the unexpected opening of the door and the appearance of a decorated Christmas tree with wax candles, sweetmeats

& apples inspired a heavenly ecstasy. "You also," said Lotte, concealing her embarrassment with a sweet smile, "you also are to receive Christmas presents, if you behave properly, a little roll of wax tapers and something else." "And what do you call behaving properly?" he cried. "What am I to do, what can I do, dearest Lotte?" "Thursday evening," she said, "is Christmas Eve, when the children are coming, and my father also, then everyone will receive his present, and you are to come as well—but not before." Werther was taken aback. "I beg of you," she continued, "that is how things are, and I beg you for the sake of my peace of mind, we cannot, we cannot continue like this!"—He turned his eyes away from her, went up and down the room, and muttered, "we cannot continue like this!" between his teeth. Lotte, who perceived the terrible state these words had put him in, tried to divert his thoughts by asking him all manner of questions, but without avail. "No, Lotte," he cried, "I shall not see you again!"—"Why?" she rejoined, "you can, you must see us again, only control yourself. Oh! why were you born with this impetuosity, this persistent passion for everything that you once touch! I beg of you," she continued, taking his hand, "control yourself. Your intellect, your knowledge, your talents—what diverse enjoyments do these not offer you! Be a man. Rid yourself of this melancholy attachment to a person who can do nought but pity you." He grated his teeth and looked at her gloomily. She held his hand. "Only one moment of calm thinking, Werther," she said. "Do you not perceive that you are deceiving yourself, that you are the voluntary cause of your own undoing? Why me, Werther? Just me, who belong to another? Just this? I fear, I fear it is only the impossibility of possessing me that makes this desire so alluring." He withdrew his hand from hers, gazing at her with a fixed and angry look. "Clever!" he cried. "Very clever! Did Albert say that, I wonder? Subtle! Very subtle!"—"Anyone might say it," she replied. "Is there then no maiden in the wide world who could fulfil the desires of your heart? Bring yourself to look for her, and I swear to you that you will find her. For a long time I have feared for you and for us the restriction you have imposed upon yourself. Bring yourself to it! A journey will and must distract you! Seek and find a worthy object for all your love, then return and let us enjoy together the happiness of a true friendship."

"That ought to be printed," he said with a cold laugh, "and recommended to all tutors. Dear Lotte, let me have just a little repose, and everything will be all right."—"Only this, Werther! that you do not come back till Christmas Eve."—He was about to reply, when Albert entered the room. They bade one another a frigid good evening, and walked up and down the room together with some embarrassment. Werther began some trifling conversation, which soon petered out. Albert did the same and then asked his wife about some commissions and, when he heard that they had not yet been carried out, returned a sharp answer that cut Werther to the heart. He wanted to go, could not, and delayed till eight o'clock. Their irritation and ill-humor with one another increased more and more until the table was laid and he took his hat and stick, when Albert, with conventional politeness, invited him to take pot-luck with them.

He arrived at his lodging, took the candle from his servant who wanted to light him on his way, and went alone to his room, where he wept aloud, spoke in an excited manner to himself, strode violently up and down, and finally threw himself, fully clad, on his bed, where he was found by his man who ventured about eleven o'clock to go in and ask whether he should take off his master's boots. This he let him do, and then ordered him not to come into the room the next morning until he was called.

On Monday morning, the twenty-first of December, he wrote the fol lowing letter to Lotte, which was found sealed on his writing-desk after his death and brought to her. I will insert it here at intervals, just as—and this is evident from what happened—he wrote it.

My mind is made up, Lotte. I intend to die, and I am writing you this calmly, without romantic exaltation, on the morning of the day when I shall see you for the last time. When you read this, my dearest, the cool grave will already cover the stiffened remains of the restless, unhappy man who knows no sweeter bliss in the last moments of his life than to converse with you. I have had a terrible night, which has strengthened, has fixed my wavering resolve. I intend to die. When I tore myself away from you yesterday, with my senses in a state of fearful excitement, when it all rushed in upon my heart, and the thought of my hopeless, joyless existence at your side seized hold of me with chill horror—I was hardly able to reach my room, beside myself I fell upon my knees, and oh! God! Thou didst grant me the final boon of bitter tears! A thousand plans, a thousand possibilities coursed through my brain, and at last it was there, firmly, wholly, the one ultimate thought—I intend to die!—I lay down, and this morning, in all the tranquillity of my awakening, it is still firm, still strong in my heart—I intend to die!—It is not despair, but the certainty that I have reached the end, and that I am sacrificing myself for you. Yes, Lotte! Why should I not say it? One of us three must go, and I will be the one. Oh! my dearest, the frenzy has often crept through my torn heart, often—to murder your husband!—You!—Myself! So let it be then!—When you climb up the hill, on a beautiful summer evening, remember me, how I often came thus up the valley, and then gaze across at the churchyard to my grave, as the wind gently waves the grass to and fro in the rays of the setting sun.—I was calm when I began, and now I am weeping like a child when I see it all so vividly.

Towards ten o'clock Werther called his servant, and said to him as he dressed that he was going away in a few days, and his clothes should therefore be turned out and made ready for packing. He also ordered him to ask everywhere for bills to be sent in, to collect some books that had been lent, and to pay two months advance to some poor people to whom he was accustomed to give something every week.

He had his meal brought to his room, and rode out afterwards to the bailiff, whom he did not find at home. He walked pensively up and down the garden, and appeared to want to bury himself at the last moment under all his melancholy memories.

The little ones did not long leave him in peace, but pursued him, sprang up at him, told him that when tomorrow had come, and then another day, and another day after that, they were going to Lotte's to fetch their Christmas presents, and spoke of the wonders that their little imaginations promised them. "Tomorrow!" he cried, "and then another day, and another day after that!" And he kissed them all affectionately, and was about to go when the smallest one tried to whisper something in his ear. He confided to him that his big brothers had written beautiful New Year greetings, so big! one for papa, one for Albert and Lotte, and also one for Herr Werther. They were going to hand them over early on New Year's Day.

This overcame him. He gave each one something, mounted his horse, asked them to give his regards to the old man, and rode away with tears in his eyes.

He reached home towards five, ordered the maid to see to the fire and to keep it going till night time. He told his servant to pack his books and linen in his trunk downstairs and to sew his clothes up in a bale. Then he probably wrote the following passage in his last letter to Lotte.

> You do not expect me. You think I shall obey you and not see you again till Christmas Eve. Oh, Lotte! To-day or never again. On Christmas Eve you will hold this letter in your hand and tremble as you moisten it with your sweet tears. I will, I must! Oh! how glad I am that I have made up my mind!

At half past six he went to Albert's house, and found Lotte alone, very alarmed at his visit. She had told her husband in the course of conversation that Werther would not return until Christmas Eve. Soon after he had had his horse saddled, saying he was riding to an official in the neighborhood with whom he had some business to settle, and had gone out in spite of the inclement weather. Lotte, who knew quite well that he had long postponed this matter and that it would keep him from home all night, understood the pantomime only too well, and was very depressed. She sat alone, her heart was touched, she thought of the past, feeling how precious it had been, and her love for her husband, who now, instead of the promised happiness, was beginning to make her life wretched. Her thoughts came back to Werther. She blamed him, but could not hate him. A mysterious trait had attracted her to him from the beginning of their friendship and now, after so long, after having lived through so many experiences, the impression on her heart was bound to be inextinguishable. Her oppressed heart at last found relief in tears, and she fell into a quiet melancholy in which she became more and more deeply immersed. But how her heart hammered when she heard Werther ascending the steps and asking for her outside! It was too late to say she was not at home, and she had only half recovered from her confusion when he entered the room. "You have not kept your word!" she cried. "I made no promise," was his answer. "Then you should at least have acceded to my request," she said, "it was for both our sakes." As she spoke, she made up her mind to send for some girl friends. These should be witnesses to her conversation with Werther and, since he would have to see them home, she would be able to get rid of him early. He had brought her back some books, and she inquired about some others, trying to keep the conversation on a general level until her friends arrived, when the maid returned and informed her that they both begged to be excused, one of them having some relations visiting her whom she could not send away, and the other not wanting to dress and go out in such wretched weather.

This made her ponder for a few minutes, until the feeling of her innocence roused her pride. She decided to defy Albert's crotchets, and the purity of her heart fortified her, so that she did not, as she at first intended, call her maid into the room but, after she had played a number of minuets on the harpsichord to recover herself and allay the confusion of her heart, sat down calmly on the sofa at Werther's side. "Have you nothing to read?" she said. He had nothing. "In my drawer there," she began, "is your translation of some of the songs of Ossian. I have not read them yet, for I hoped to hear you recite them, but ever since you haven't been fit for anything." He smiled, fetched the songs, a tremor ran through him as he took them in his hand, and his eyes filled with tears as he looked at them. He sat down and read:[69]

"Star of descending night! fair is thy light in the west! thou liftest thy unshorn head from thy cloud: thy steps are stately on thy hill. What dost thou behold in the plain? The stormy winds are laid. The murmur of the torrent comes from afar. Roaring waves climb the distant rock. The flies of evening are on their feeble wings; the hum of their course is on the field. What dost thou behold, fair light? But thou dost smile and depart. The waves come with joy around thee: they bathe thy lovely hair. Farewell, thou silent beam! Let the light of Ossian's soul arise!

"And it does arise in its strength! I behold my departed friends. Their gathering is on Lora, as in the days of other years. Fingal comes like a watry column of mist! his heroes are around: and see the bards of song, grey-haired Ullin! stately Ryno! Alpin, with the tuneful voice! the soft complaint of Minona! How are ye changed, my friends, since the days of Selma's feast? when we contended, like gales of spring, as they fly along the hill, and bend by turns the feebly-whistling grass.

"Minona[70] came forth in her beauty; with down-cast look and tearful eye. Her hair flew slowly on the blast, that rushed unfrequent from the hill. The souls of the heroes were sad when she raised the tuneful voice. Often had they seen the grave of Salgar, the dark dwelling of white-bosomed Colma. Colma left alone on the hill, with all her voice of song! Salgar promised to come:[71] but the night descended around. Hear the voice of Colma, when she sat alone on the hill!

COLMA

"It is night; I am alone, forlorn on the hill of storms. The wind is heard on the mountain. The torrent pours down the rock. No hut receives me from the rain; forlorn on the hill of winds!

"Rise, moon! from behind thy clouds. Stars of the night, arise! Lead me, some light, to the place, where my love rests from the chase alone! his bow near him, unstrung: his dogs panting around him. But here I must sit alone, by the rock of the mossy stream. The stream and the wind roar aloud. I hear not the voice of my love! Why delays my Salgar, why the chief of the hill, his promise? Here is the rock, and here the tree! here is the roaring stream! Thou didst promise with night to be here. Ah! whither is my Salgar gone? With thee I would fly, from my father; with thee, from my brother of pride. Our races have long been foes; we are not foes, O Salgar!

"Cease a little while, O wind! stream, be thou silent a while! let my voice be heard

[69] "This extract from Ossian's *The Songs of Selma* is here reproduced in the original." —Translator's note. On Ossian, see the note to Werther's letter of 10 July 1771. The excerpt that follows begins with a passage about the evening star by the bard Ossian. He then relates three stories he heard in the past at the feast of Selma, in Lora, the palace of his father Fingal, a Scottish king.

[70] Minona was the first of the bards to sing at the feast. She told of the death at each other's hands of Colma's lover Salgar and her brother.

[71] To keep a lovers' tryst with Colma.

around. Let my wanderer hear me! Salgar! it is Colma who calls. Here is the tree, and the rock. Salgar, my love! I am here. Why delayest thou thy coming? Lo! the calm moon comes forth. The flood is bright in the vale. The rocks are grey on the steep. I see him not on the brow. His dogs come not before him, with tidings of his near approach. Here I must sit alone!

"Who lie on the heath beside me? Are they my love and my brother? Speak to me, O my friends! To Colma they give no reply. Speak to me: I am alone! My soul is tormented with fears! Ah! they are dead! Their swords are red from the fight. O my brother! my brother! why hast thou slain my Salgar? why, O Salgar! hast thou slain my brother? Dear were ye both to me! what shall I say in your praise? Thou wert fair on the hill among thousands! he was terrible in fight. Speak to me; hear my voice; hear me, sons of my love! They are silent; silent for ever! Cold, cold are their breasts of clay! Oh! from the rock on the hill; from the top of the windy steep, speak, ye ghosts of the dead! speak, I will not be afraid! Whither are ye gone to rest? In what cave of the hill shall I find the departed? No feeble voice is on the gale: no answer half-drowned in the storm!

"I sit in my grief; I wait for morning in my tears! Rear the tomb, ye friends of the dead. Close it not till Colma come. My life flies away like a dream: why should I stay behind? Here shall I rest with my friends, by the stream of the sounding rock. When night comes on the hill; when the loud winds arise; my ghost shall stand in the blast, and mourn the death of my friends. The hunter shall hear from his booth. He shall fear but love my voice! For sweet shall my voice be for my friends: pleasant were her friends to Colma!

"Such was thy song, Minona, softly-blushing daughter of Torman. Our tears descended for Colma, and our souls were sad! Ullin[72] came with his harp! he gave the song of Alpin. The voice of Alpin was pleasant: the soul of Ryno was a beam of fire! But they had rested in the narrow house: their voice had ceased in Selma. Ullin had returned, one day, from the chase, before the heroes fell. He heard their strife[73] on the hill; their song was soft but sad! They mourned the fall of Morar, first of mortal men! His soul was like the soul of Fingal; his sword like the sword of Oscar.[74] But he fell, and his father mourned: his sister's eyes were full of tears, Minona's eyes were full of tears, the sister of car-borne Morar. She retired from the song of Ullin, like the moon in the west, when she foresees the shower, and hides her fair head in a cloud. I touched the harp with Ullin; the song of mourning rose!

Ryno

"The wind and the rain are past: calm is the noon of day. The clouds are divided in heaven. Over the green hills flies the inconstant sun. Red through the stony vale comes down the stream of the hill. Sweet are thy murmurs, O stream! but more sweet is the voice I hear. It is the voice of Alpin, the son of song, mourning for the dead! Bent is his head of age; red his tearful eye. Alpin, thou son of song, why alone on the silent hill? why complainest thou, as a blast in the wood; as a wave on the lonely shore?

[72] Another bard who sang at the remembered feast. He mourned Morar, brother to the Minona who had just sung, by way of repeating a dialogue between Ryno and Alpin, who were both dead at the time of the feast. Ullin sang the part of Alpin and Ossian himself the part of Ryno.

[73] The strife of the dead heroes Ryno and Alpin, contending with each other in song.

[74] Ossian's son.

ALPIN

"My tears, O Ryno! are for the dead; my voice for those that have passed away. Tall thou art on the hill; fair among the sons of the vale. But thou shalt fall like Morar; the mourner shall sit on thy tomb. The hills shall know thee no more; thy bow shall lie in thy hall unstrung!

"Thou wert swift, O Morar! as a roe on the desert; terrible as a meteor of fire. Thy wrath was as the storm. Thy sword in battle, as lightning in the field. Thy voice was a stream after rain; like thunder on distant hills. Many fell by thy arm; they were consumed in the flames of thy wrath. But when thou didst return from war, how peaceful was thy brow! Thy face was like the sun after rain; like the moon in the silence of night; calm as the breast of the lake when the loud wind is laid.

"Narrow is thy dwelling now! dark the place of thine abode! With three steps I compass thy grave, O thou who wast so great before! Four stones, with their heads of moss, are the only memorial of thee. A tree with scarce a leaf, long grass, which whistles in the wind, mark to the hunter's eye the grave of the mighty Morar. Morar! thou art low indeed. Thou hast no mother to mourn thee; no maid with her tears of love. Dead is she that brought thee forth. Fallen is the daughter of Morglan.

"Who on his staff is this? who is this, whose head is white with age? whose eyes are red with tears? who quakes at every step? It is thy father, O Morar! the father of no son but thee. He heard of thy fame in war; he heard of foes dispersed. He heard of Morar's renown; why did he not hear of his wound? Weep, thou father of Morar! weep; but thy son heareth thee not. Deep is the sleep of the dead; low their pillow of dust. No more shall he hear thy voice; no more awake at thy call. When shall it be morn in the grave, to bid the slumberer awake? Farewell, thou bravest of men! thou conqueror in the field! but the field shall see thee no more; nor the dark wood be lightened with the splendour of thy steel. Thou hast left no son. The song shall preserve thy name. Future times shall hear of thee; they shall hear of the fallen Morar!

"The grief of all arose, but most the bursting sigh of Armin.[75] He remembers the death of his son, who fell in the days of his youth. Carmor was near the hero, the chief of the echoing Galmal. Why bursts the sigh of Armin? he said. Is there a cause to mourn? The song comes, with its music, to melt and please the soul. It is like soft mist, that, rising from a lake, pours on the silent vale; the green flowers are filled with dew, but the sun returns in his strength, and the mist is gone. Why art thou sad, O Armin, chief of sea-surrounded Gorma?

"Sad! I am! nor small is my cause of woe! Carmor, thou hast lost no son; thou hast lost no daughter of beauty. Colgar the valiant lives; and Annira fairest maid. The boughs of thy house ascend, O Carmor! but Armin is the last of his race. Dark is thy bed, O Daura! deep thy sleep in the tomb! When shalt thou awake with thy songs? with all thy voice of music?

"Arise, winds of autumn, arise; blow along the heath! streams of the mountains, roar! roar, tempests, in the groves of my oaks! walk through broken clouds, O moon! show thy pale face, at intervals! bring to my mind the night, when all my children fell; when Arindal the mighty fell; when Daura the lovely failed! Daura, my daughter! thou wert fair; fair as the moon on Fura; white as the driven snow; sweet as the breathing gale. Arindal, thy bow was strong. Thy spear was swift in the

[75] One of the guests at the feast. The mourning song he had just heard reminded him of the deaths of his son Arindal, his daughter Daura, and Daura's betrothed Armar, because of the treachery of Erath, Armar's enemy.

field. Thy look was like mist on the wave: thy shield, a red cloud in a storm. Armar, renowned in war, came, and sought Daura's love. He was not long refused: fair was the hope of their friends!

"Erath, son of Odgal, repined: his brother had been slain by Armar. He came disguised like a son of the sea: fair was his skiff on the wave; white his locks of age; calm his serious brow. Fairest of women, he said, lovely daughter of Armin! a rock not distant in the sea, bears a tree on its side; red shines the fruit afar! There Armar waits for Daura. I come to carry his love! She went; she called on Armar. Nought answered, but the son of the rock, Armar, my love! my love! why tormentest thou me with fear? hear, son of Arnart, hear: it is Daura who calleth thee! Erath the traitor fled laughing to the land. She lifted up her voice; she called for her brother and her father. Arindal! Armin! none to relieve your Daura!

"Her voice came over the sea. Arindal my son descended from the hill; rough in the spoils of the chase. His arrows rattled by his side; his bow was in his hand: five dark grey dogs attend his steps. He saw fierce Erath on the shore: he seized and bound him to an oak. Thick wind the thongs of the hide around his limbs; he loads the wind with his groans. Arindal ascends the deep in his boat, to bring Daura to land. Armar came in his wrath, and let fly the grey-feathered shaft.[76] It sung; it sunk in thy heart, O Arindal my son! for Erath the traitor thou diedst. The oar is stopped at once; he panted on the rock and expired. What is thy grief, O Daura, when round thy feet is poured thy brother's blood! The boat is broken in twain. Armar plunges into the sea, to rescue his Daura, or die. Sudden a blast from the hill came over the waves. He sunk, and he rose no more.

"Alone, on the sea-beat rock, my daughter was heard to complain. Frequent and loud were her cries. What could her father do? All night I stood on the shore. I saw her by the faint beam of the moon. All night I heard her cries. Loud was the wind; the rain beat hard on the hill. Before morning appeared, her voice was weak. It died away, like the evening-breeze among the grass of the rocks. Spent with grief she expired; and left thee, Armin, alone. Gone is my strength in war! fallen my pride among women![77] When the storms aloft arise; when the north lifts the wave on high; I sit by the sounding shore, and look on the fatal rock. Often by the setting moon, I see the ghost of my children. Half-viewless,[78] they walk in mournful conference together."

A stream of tears, which gushed from Lotte's eyes and afforded relief to her oppressed heart, interrupted Werther's reading. He threw down the sheets, seized her hand and wept bitterly. Lotte supported herself on her other arm and hid her eyes in her handkerchief. The agitation of both of them was terrible. They felt their own misery in the fate of those noble ones, felt it together, and their tears mingled. Werther's lips and eyes burned on Lotte's arms, a tremor ran through her, she tried to withdraw, and all her grief, all her pity lay heavy as lead upon her. She took a deep breath to recover herself and begged him with a sob to continue, begged him with the whole voice of Heaven. Werther trembled, his heart felt as though it would burst, he picked up the sheet and read in a broken voice:[79]

[76] He thinks Arindal is Erath.
[77] His "strength" and "pride" are his son and daughter.
[78] Half invisible. [79] "From Ossian's *Berrathon.*"—Translator's note.

"Why dost thou awake me, O breath of Spring, thou dost woo me and say: 'I cover thee with the drops of heaven.' But the time of my fading is near, the blast that shall scatter my leaves. To-morrow shall the traveller come; he that saw me in my beauty shall come. His eyes will search the field, but they will not find me."

The whole force of these words deprived the unhappy man of his self-possession. He threw himself at Lotte's feet in utter despair, seized her hands, pressed them against his eyes, against his forehead, and a foreboding of his dreadful intention appeared to flash through her soul. Her mind grew confused, she clasped his hands, pressed them against her breast, bent over him with a sorrowful air, and their burning cheeks touched. They were lost to the world, he twined his arms round her, pressed her to his breast, and covered her trembling, stammering lips with frenzied kisses. "Werther!" she cried in a suffocating voice, turning away her face, "Werther!", and she thrust him away from her breast with a nerveless hand. "Werther!" she cried in a calm tone with noble dignity. He did not resist, released her from his embrace, and threw himself madly at her feet. She got up hastily and, in nervous confusion, trembling between love and anger, she said, "This is the last time, Werther! You shall not see me again." With a look, fraught with love, at the unhappy man, she rushed into the next room and locked the door behind her. Werther stretched his arms out towards her, not daring to hold her back. He lay on the ground, his head on the sofa, and in this attitude he remained for half an hour, until a sound recalled him to himself. It was the maid who wanted to lay the table. He walked up and down the room and, when he saw that he was alone again, went to the door of the cabinet and called gently, "Lotte! Lotte! only one word more, in farewell!"—She was silent, he waited—and begged—and waited, then tore himself away and cried, "Farewell, Lotte! Farewell for ever!"

He came to the town gate. The watchmen, who were used to him, let him out without a word. There was a drizzle, half rain half snow, and it was getting on for eleven when he knocked at the gate again. His servant noticed, when Werther returned home, that he was without his hat. He did not venture to say anything and undressed him. Everything was wet. The hat was found afterwards on a rock, on the slope of the hill towards the valley, and it is inconceivable how he managed to climb up there on a wet dark night without falling headlong.

He lay down in bed and slept for many hours. His servant found him writing, when, at his call, he brought in his coffee next morning. He added the following to the letter to Lotte:

For the last time then, for the last time I open these eyes. They are alas! to see the sun no more; it is hidden by a dark and misty day. Mourn then, Nature! thy son, thy friend, thy lover nears his end. Lotte, it is a feeling without compare, and yet it is most akin to a twilight dream, to say to oneself, 'This is the last morning.' The last! Lotte, I have no conception of the word—the last! Do I not stand here in all my strength, and to-morrow I shall lie stretched out and inert on the ground! Die! What does that mean? We are dreaming when we speak of death. I have seen many people die, yet humanity is so limited that it has no conception of the beginning and end of its existence. Still mine, thine! thine! beloved, and the next moment—separated, parted—perhaps for ever.—No, Lotte, no.—How can I pass away, how can you pass away, do we not exist!—Pass away!—What does that mean? It is again a word! an empty sound, that awakes no echo in my heart.—Dead, Lotte! Interred in the cold earth, so narrow, so dark!—There was a girl who was everything to me in my helpless youth; she died, and I followed her corpse and stood beside her grave. As they let down the coffin and pulled up the whirring ropes again from under it, as the first shovelful of earth thudded down and the fearful shell gave back a muffled sound, becoming more and more muffled till it was at last entirely covered—I sank down beside the grave—moved, shaken, in anguish, my soul torn, but I knew not what had happened to me—what will happen to me—Death! The grave! I do not understand the words!

Oh, forgive me! Yesterday! It should have been the last hour of my life. Oh, you angel! for the first time, for the first time there glowed through the depths of my soul, without room for doubt, the feeling of rapture: She loves me! She loves me! The sacred fire that streamed from your lips still burns on mine, a fresh rapturous warmth is in my heart. Forgive me, forgive me.

Oh, I knew that you loved me, knew from the first soulful glances, the first hand pressure, and yet when I went away again, when I saw Albert at your side, I again despaired with feverish doubtings.

Do you remember the flowers you sent me, when you were unable to say a word to me, or give me your hand, at that odious party? Oh! I have knelt in front of them half the night and they put the seal on your love for me. But alas! these impressions faded, as the believer gradually loses the sense of his God's loving kindness which was accorded him with all Heaven's abundance in sacred and visible symbols.

All this is transitory, but no eternity can extinguish the glowing essence that I imbibed yesterday from your lips, that I feel within me. She loves me! This arm has embraced her, these lips have trembled on her lips, this mouth has stammered against hers. She is mine! You are mine! Yes, Lotte, for ever!

And what does it mean, that Albert is your husband? Husband!—That is to say in this world—and in this world it is a sin that I love you, that I would like to snatch you from his arms into mine? A sin? Good! I am punishing myself for it. I have tasted this sin in all its divine rapture, have drunk restoring balsam and strength into my heart. From that moment you were mine! mine, Lotte! I go ahead! to my Father and to yours. To Him I will bring my plaint, and He will solace me till you come and I can fly to you, clasp you, stay with you before the face of the Infinite in an eternal embrace.

This is no dream, no delusion! On the verge of the grave I saw more clearly. We *shall* exist! We shall see one another again! See your mother! I shall see her, find her, and oh! pour out all my heart before her. Your mother, bearing the semblance of yourself.

Towards eleven o'clock Werther inquired of his servant whether Albert had yet returned. The servant said that he had, for he had seen his horse being led. His master then gave him an unsealed note with the following contents:

Would you lend me your pistols for a journey I am about to undertake? Farewell.

Lotte had slept little that night; she was in a state of feverish agitation, and her heart was ravaged with a thousand emotions. In spite of herself, she felt deep within her breast the passion of Werther's embraces, and at the same time she saw with double beauty the days of her artless innocence, of her care-free confidence in herself. She already feared beforehand her husband's gaze and his half-vexed, half-mocking questions, when he should hear of Werther's visit. She had never dissembled, she had never lied, and now she was faced, for the first time, with the unavoidable necessity of doing so. The reluctance, the embarrassment she felt, made the fault all the greater in her eyes, and yet she could neither hate him who was the cause of it nor promise herself never to see him again. She wept till morning, when she sank into a sleep of exhaustion, from which she had hardly risen and dressed when her husband returned, whose presence for the first time she found quite unbearable. For she trembled lest he should discover in her the traces of a sleepless night spent in tears, and this increased her confusion, so that she greeted him with an impetuous embrace which was more expressive of consternation and remorse than passionate delight, thereby attracting the attention of Albert, who asked her curtly, after he had opened some letters and packets, whether anything had happened, whether any one had called. She answered hesitatingly that Werther had been there for an hour on the previous day.—"He chooses his time well," he replied, and went to his study. Lotte remained alone for a quarter of an hour. The presence of her husband, whom she loved and honored, had made a fresh impression on her heart. She remembered all his kindness, generosity and affection, and reproached herself for having so ill requited them. An obscure impulse made her follow him; she took her work, as she was sometimes wont to do, and went to his room. She asked him whether he needed anything, but he said that he did not and sat down at his desk to write, while she sat down to do her knitting. They had been together for an hour in this way, when Albert began to walk up and down the room. Lotte spoke to him, but he made little or no reply, only sitting down at his desk again, and she fell into a train of melancholy thoughts which were all the more distressing since she tried to hide them and to stay her tears.

The appearance of Werther's boy plunged her in the greatest embarrassment. He handed the note to Albert, who turned coldly to his wife and said, "Give him the pistols."—"I wish him a good journey," he said to the youth. This was like a thunderclap to her. She faltered in an attempt to rise. She could not understand her feelings. Slowly she went to the wall, took them down trembling, wiped off the dust and hesitated, and would have delayed still more if Albert's inquiring glance had not impelled her. She gave the fatal weapons to the boy, without being able to utter a word, and when he had gone she gathered her work together and went to her room in a state of the most inexpressible anguish. Her heart prophesied all sorts of catastrophes. At first she was on the verge of throwing herself at her husband's feet and revealing everything—what had happened on the previous evening, her own fault and forebodings. Then she could not see what would be the advantage of such a step. Least of all could she hope to persuade her husband to go to Werther. The table was laid, and a friend of Lotte's, who only came to make some inquiry but was not allowed by Lotte to leave, made conversation bearable during the meal. They constrained themselves, discussed sundry matters, and were able to forget.

The boy brought the pistols to Werther, who took them from him in a transport of delight when he heard that they had been handed to him by Lotte. He had bread and wine brought in, told the boy to go and have his dinner, and sat down to write.

They have passed through your hands, you have wiped the dust from them, I kiss them a thousand times for you have touched them. Thou, Spirit of Heaven, dost favor my resolve! And you, Lotte, offer me the weapon, you, at whose hands I wished to encounter death and alas! now encounter it! Oh! I made my servant tell me everything—you trembled when you handed them to him, you bade me no farewell!—Alas! Alas!—no farewell! Is it possible that you have closed your heart to me on account of the moment which sealed me to you for ever? Lotte, a thousand years cannot wipe out the impress! And I feel that you cannot hate him who burns for you thus.

After the meal he ordered his boy to finish packing everything, destroyed a number of papers, and went out to settle some small debts. He returned home, went out again beyond the gate, in spite of the rain, as far as the Count's garden, roved about the neighborhood, came back as night fell, and wrote:

I have seen field, wood and sky for the last time, Wilhelm. I bid you farewell, also! Forgive me, mother! Console her, Wilhelm. God bless you both! My affairs are all in order. Farewell! We shall meet again in happier circumstances.

I have ill rewarded you, Albert, but you will forgive me. I have ruined the peace of your house and sowed distrust between you. Farewell, I am about to make an end. Oh! that my death might restore your happiness! Albert! Albert! Make the angel happy. And may God's blessing rest upon you!

He spent much time turning out his papers during the evening, tore many of them up and threw them in the stove, and sealed a number of packages which he addressed to Wilhelm. They contained small essays and disconnected ideas, several of which I have seen. After having the fire made up and a flask of wine brought in, he sent his servant, who slept some distance away, as did the other domestics, to bed. The boy lay down in his clothes in order to be at hand at an early hour, for his master had told him that the coach horses would be at the door before six.

AFTER ELEVEN.

All is so still around me and my soul so calm. I thank thee, Lord, for these last moments of strength and ardor.

I step to the window, my dearest, and still see some stars shining through the fleeting storm-clouds. No, you will not fall! The Eternal One bears you at his heart, and me. I saw the wheeler stars of Charles's Wain,[80] the loveliest of all the constella-

[80]The Big Dipper; located in the north, it wheels around the North Star as the night passes.

tions. When I left you at night, as I went out at the gate, it was in front of me. With what intoxication have I so often gazed at it, raised aloft my hands and made it a symbol, a sacred token of the bliss I felt, and still—Oh! Lotte, what is there that does not remind me of you! Are you not about me always! And have I not always, like a child, insatiably, seized every trifle that your saintly hands had touched!

Beloved silhouette! I now return it to you at my death, Lotte, and beg you to hold it in honor. I have pressed a thousand, thousand kisses on it, waved a thousand greetings to it when I went out or returned.

I have left a note for your father entreating him to protect my body. In the churchyard there are two lime trees, at the back in a corner, towards the field, and there I wish to lie. He can and will do this for his friend. Add your entreaties to mine. I will not ask pious Christians to allow their bodies to rest beside that of a poor wretch. Oh! I could wish to be buried by the wayside, or in the lonely valley, that priest and Levite might cross themselves as they passed by the stone which marked the spot, and the Samaritan shed a tear.[81]

Here, Lotte! I do not shudder to take the dread cold cup from which I am to drink the ecstasy of death! It is you who have handed it to me, and I do not fear. All! All! thus are the desires and hopes of my life fulfilled! To knock so cold, so stiff, at the brazen gate of death.

That I might have been granted the happiness to die for you! To sacrifice myself for you, Lotte! I would die with a stout heart, I would die gladly, if I could restore the tranquillity, the rapture of your life. But alas! it was granted to but few noble souls to shed their blood for those they loved, and by their deaths to kindle for them a new life enhanced a hundredfold.

I wish to be buried in these clothes, Lotte. You have touched and sanctified them. I have asked your father to grant me this favor. My soul will hover over my coffin. Let them not search my pockets. This pink bow which you wore on your bosom, when I met you first among your children—Oh! kiss them a thousand times and tell them the fate of their unhappy friend. The darlings, how they swarm about me. Oh! how I attached myself to you, could not keep away from you from the first moment! Let this bow be buried with me. You gave it me on my birthday! How eagerly I accepted it all!—Alas, I did not think that the way would lead to this!—Be calm! I beg you, be calm!—

They are loaded—it is striking twelve!—So be it then—Lotte! Lotte, farewell! Farewell!

A neighbor saw the flash of the powder and heard the shot, but as everything remained still he paid no more attention.

At six next morning the servant entered with a candle and found his master stretched on the floor, with blood about and the pistol by him. He called to him, seized hold of him, but there was no answer, only a rattling in the throat. He ran for a doctor, for Albert. Lotte heard the bell, all her limbs began to tremble. She woke her husband, they got up, the servant stammered the news amid sobs, Lotte sank to the ground in a swoon in front of Albert.

When the physician arrived, he found the unhappy youth on the floor beyond all hope; his pulse was still beating but all his limbs were paralyzed.

[81] A despised Samaritan helped the man in distress, while the conventionally pious priest and Levite passed him by. Luke 10:31–33.

He had shot himself through the head above the right eye, and his brains were protruding. He was bled[82] in the arm, the blood flowed and he still breathed.

From the blood on the arm of his chair it was concluded that he had committed the deed sitting at his desk. He had then sunk down and twisted convulsively round the chair. He lay on his back in the direction of the window, deprived of strength, fully dressed in boots, blue coat and yellow waistcoat.

The house, the neighbors, the whole town were in a turmoil. Albert entered. Werther had been laid on the bed, his forehead tied up, his face already like that of a dead man, without moving a limb. A dreadful rattling noise still came from his lungs, now faintly, now more loudly; the end was near.

He had only drunk one glass of the wine. *Emilia Galotti*[83] lay open on his desk.

I cannot describe Albert's dismay, Lotte's grief.

The old bailiff came galloping up at the news, and he kissed the dying youth as the hot tears coursed down his cheeks. His eldest sons arrived soon afterwards on foot and sank beside the bed with expressions of the most unrestrained sorrow, kissed his hands and mouth, and the eldest, of whom he had been the most fond, clung to his lips and had to be torn away by force. He died at noon. The presence of the bailiff and the arrangements he made prevented a crowd from assembling. He had him buried towards eleven o'clock at night at the spot that he had chosen. The old man and his sons followed the body. Albert could not. Lotte's life was in danger. He was carried by workmen. There was no pastor present.

[82] To draw blood from the sick was a standard medical treatment.
[83] A tragedy by Gotthold Ephraim Lessing (1729–1781).

Mary Wollstonecraft
(1759–1797)

Mary Wollstonecraft's Vindication of the Rights of Woman *(1792) holds a high place in the "literature of fact" as an impassioned expression of Enlightenment libertarianism, a celebration of Natural Woman to match Rousseau's glorification of Natural Man.*

Born in London in 1759, Wollstonecraft had a restless, unhappy childhood, full of family conflict and frequent moves as her father tried to use a family inheritance to establish himself as a farmer on one piece of land after another in Essex, Yorkshire, Wales, and other places. When she was sixteen, an intense friendship sprang up with Fanny Blood, a neighbor two years older than herself who helped Wollstonecraft in a course of self-education. After her mother died in 1780, Wollstonecraft moved in with the Bloods and helped to support the family through needlework. In 1783,

Wollstonecraft, her sister Eliza, whom Mary had helped rescue from a brutal, unhappy marriage, another sister named Everina, and Fanny Blood opened a school in London. The school failed four years later, after the marriage and death in childbirth of Fanny Blood.

Wollstonecraft's literary career began in 1786 with Thoughts on the Education of Daughters, *which she wrote to raise money for her school. After a brief, unhappy experience as governess to the elder daughters of Viscount Kingsborough of Mitchelstown, County Cork, Ireland, she returned to London, determined to earn her living as a writer. Here she became part of a distinguished group of radical artists and writers who gathered around the establishment of Joseph Johnson, her first publisher. This circle included the visionary poet and engraver William Blake, the liberal Dissenting minister Richard Price, the Anglo-Swiss artist Henry Fuseli, the American radical Thomas Paine, and the anarchist philosopher William Godwin. Within the next five years she published a thinly disguised autobiographical novel called* Mary, a Fiction, *a children's book named* Original Stories from Real Life, *an anthology named* The Female Reader, *a number of miscellaneous translations, and a great many articles for Johnson's* Analytical Review. *Fame came in 1791 with the publication under her own name of* A Vindication of the Rights of Man, *written and published anonymously the year before as a response to Edmund Burke's conservative* Reflections on the Revolution in France. A Vindication of the Rights of Woman *followed in 1792.*

The five years of life that remained to Wollstonecraft were turbulent ones. Always impetuous and passionate, as well as subject to fits of deep depression, she fell in love with Henry Fuseli and proposed to move in with him—and his wife. Her proposal rejected, she moved to Paris to write a history of the Revolution. There she met and fell in love with a young American businessman, Gilbert Imlay, by whom in 1794 she had a child, named Fanny in memory of Fanny Blood. Even before the birth of the child, Imlay's passion had cooled and he eventually moved to London and a new mistress, an actress. Wollstonecraft, in despair, made two suicide attempts, the first prevented by Imlay, the second frustrated by two English boatmen on the Thames after she had flung herself off Putney Bridge.

Imlay and his new mistress returned to Paris, while Wollstonecraft remained in London, continuing to write and reestablishing contact with the Johnson circle. Falling in love with William Godwin, she set up housekeeping with him, although they continued to maintain separate working quarters. When she became pregnant a few months after she and Godwin became lovers, they were married, out of consideration for the child's legal status, despite the objection of both to the institution of marriage. She spent the months of her pregnancy working on several books, including a didactic novel to be entitled The Wrongs of Woman; or, Maria. *A daughter, named Mary, was born on August 30, 1797; Wollstonecraft died a little over a week later.*

The grieving Godwin almost immediately wrote a tender tribute to his wife: Memoirs of the Author of "A Vindication of the Rights of Woman." *Left alone to rear the children Fanny and Mary, he eventually married a widow with two children, Charles and Claire, and with her had a fifth child, William. When she was seventeen, Mary Godwin eloped with the already married Percy Bysshe Shelley; they were married in 1816, after the death of his first wife. Claire, at the age of seventeen, pursued an affair with Lord Byron and bore him a daughter, Allegra.*

As A Vindication of the Rights of Man *had been written as an immediate, impassioned reply to Burke's offensive* Reflections, *so* A Vindication of the Rights of Woman *was written in response to another book,* Report on Public

Instruction (1791), in which the French legislator and diplomat Talleyrand presented his proposals for national education under the new French constitution. Wollstonecraft generally approved of Talleyrand's proposals but took strong exception to his recommendation that girls be educated along with boys only to the age of eight, after which they should return home to learn domestic skills. In a strongly-worded introductory letter, she called for the French to extend their championship of the rights of man to the rights of woman as well.

In the main body of the Vindication, however, Wollstonecraft focuses not upon Talleyrand but upon targets nearer home, the numerous English books on female education which advanced the orthodox view that women should be educated only for marriage and domesticity. She regarded as especially objectionable two then current popular manuals: James Fordyce's Sermons to Young Women (1787), and John Gregory's A Father's Legacy to His Daughters (1789). She also attacked interpretations of the book of Genesis, especially Milton's, as giving divine sanction to the theory of women's secondary and subordinate role.

Wollstonecraft's chief opponent in the Vindication, however, was Rousseau, and especially his didactic novel Emile, or Education. Rousseau was an especially infuriating foe, perhaps, because there was so much in Emile that she could accept. Although she ridicules his glorification of Natural Man as a "ferocious flight back to the night of sensual ignorance," her own instincts are strongly on the side of natural simplicity in matters of child-rearing. She advocates simple clothing, an emphasis upon outdoor exercise, and a free expression of sexuality when it naturally develops. Where she parts company with Rousseau is over Book V of Emile, entitled "Sophy, or Woman," in which, in Wollstonecraft's paraphrase, Rousseau argues that "a woman should never, for a moment, feel herself independent, that she should be governed by fear to exercise her natural cunning, and made a coquettish slave in order to render her a more alluring object of desire, a sweeter companion to man, whenever he chooses to relax himself." (Oothoon, heroine of Blake's Visions of the Daughters of Albion and probably modeled in part on Wollstonecraft, scathingly attacks this ideal of woman as artful coquette.)

To Rousseau's view, and to those of Talleyrand, Fordyce, Gregory, and Milton, Wollstonecraft opposes the weapon of reason. "In what does man's pre-eminence over the brute creation consist?" she cries at the opening of her first chapter, and the answer is "as clear as that a half is less than the whole; in Reason." For Wollstonecraft the rationalist, "free enquiry" is all that is needed to correct the injustices women suffer. Once men and women are educated to perceive the irrationality of these injustices, they will cease. If, to a modern reader, such a view seems to omit too many complexities of political and economic conditions and to assume too optimistic a view of man's love of reason, Wollstonecraft's statement of it is so personal and so eloquently expressed that we must agree with Virginia Woolf's appraisal of her:

> Many millions have died and been forgotten in the hundred and thirty years that have passed since she was buried; and yet as we read her letters and listen to her arguments and consider her experiments, above all that most fruitful experiment, her relation with Godwin, and realise the high-handed and hot-blooded manner in which she cut her way to the quick of life, one form of immortality is hers undoubtedly: she is alive and active, she argues and experiments, we hear her voice and trace her influence even now among the living.

FURTHER READING *(prepared by N. K. B.)*: A recent collection of Mary Wollstonecraft's writings, *A Wollstonecraft Anthology*, ed. Janet M. Todd, 1977, contains an extensive sample of her writings, and illustrates both her creative and intellectual energies. Ralph Wardle's critical biography, *Mary Wollstonecraft*, 1951, is an invaluable aid in understanding the political and literary context surrounding her career. It contains a detailed examination of her intellectual and political growth as evidenced in her letters, fiction and essays. More recently, Eleanor Flexner's *Mary Wollstonecraft*, 1972, supplements and corrects several details in Wardle's study, with an emphasis on Wollstonecraft's childhood and psychological development. Emily Sunstein's *A Different Face: The Life of Mary Wollstonecraft*, 1975, is useful for its analysis of and sympathy toward those incidents in her life that many biographers and commentators have condemned. "Mary Wollstonecraft," a short essay by Virginia Woolf in *The Second Common Reader*, 1932, is a highly appreciative and poetically succinct summary of Wollstonecraft's life and character, emphasizing her passionate attempts "to make human conventions conform more closely to human needs." Woolf's article provides a useful companion to George Eliot's essay "Margaret Fuller and Mary Wollstonecraft," 1855 (rpt. in *Essays of George Eliot*, 1963), in which she stresses the moral purpose and rationality behind Wollstonecraft's plea for women's rights. For a discussion of Wollstonecraft in relation to the French Revolution and the European tradition, see Jacob Bouten's 1922 study, *Mary Wollstonecraft and the Beginning of Female Emancipation in France and England*.

from *A VINDICATION OF THE RIGHTS OF WOMAN*

INTRODUCTION

After considering the historic page, and viewing the living world with anxious solicitude, the most melancholy emotions of sorrowful indignation have depressed my spirits, and I have sighed when obliged to confess, that either nature has made a great difference between man and man, or that the civilization which has hitherto taken place in the world has been very partial. I have turned over various books written on the subject of education, and patiently observed the conduct of parents and the management of schools; but what has been the result?—a profound conviction that the neglected education of my fellow-creatures is the grand source of the misery I deplore; and that women, in particular, are rendered weak and wretched by a variety of concurring causes, originating from one hasty conclusion. The conduct and manners of women, in fact, evidently prove that their minds are not in a healthy state; for, like the flowers which are planted in too rich a soil, strength and usefulness are sacrificed to beauty; and the flaunting leaves, after having pleased a fastidious eye, fade, disregarded on the stalk, long before the season when they ought to have arrived at maturity. One cause of this barren blooming I attribute to a false system of education, gathered from the books written on this subject by men who, considering females rather as women than human creatures, have been more anxious to make them alluring mistresses than affectionate wives and rational mothers; and the understanding of the sex has been so bubbled by this specious homage, that the civilized women of the present century, with a few exceptions, are only anxious to inspire love, when they ought to cherish a nobler ambition, and by their abilities and virtues exact respect. . . .

My own sex, I hope, will excuse me, if I treat them like rational creatures, instead of flattering their *fascinating* graces, and viewing them as if they were in a state of perpetual childhood, unable to stand alone. I earnestly wish to point out in what true dignity and human happiness consists—I wish to persuade women to endeavour to acquire strength, both of mind and body, and to convince them that the soft phrases, susceptibility of heart, delicacy of sentiment, and refinement of taste, are almost synonymous with epithets of weakness, and that those beings who are only the objects of pity and that kind of love, which has been termed its sister, will soon become objects of contempt.

Dismissing, then, those pretty feminine phrases, which the men condescendingly use to soften our slavish dependence, and despising that weak elegancy of mind, exquisite sensibility, and sweet docility of manners, supposed to be the sexual characteristics of the weaker vessel, I wish to shew that elegance is inferior to virtue, that the first object of laudable ambition is to obtain a character as a human being, regardless of the distinction of sex; and that secondary views should be brought to this simple touchstone. . . .

The education of women has, of late, been more attended to than formerly; yet they are still reckoned a frivolous sex, and ridiculed or pitied by the writers who endeavour by satire or instruction to improve them. It is acknowledged that they spend many of the first years of their lives in acquiring a smattering of accomplishments; meanwhile strength of body and mind are sacrificed to libertine notions of beauty, to the desire of establishing themselves,—the only way women can rise in the world,—by marriage. And this desire making mere animals of them, when they marry they act as such children may be expected to act:—they dress; they paint, and nickname God's creatures.[1] Surely these weak beings are only fit for a seraglio!—Can they be expected to govern a family with judgment, or take care of the poor babes whom they bring into the world?

If then it can be fairly deduced from the present conduct of the sex, from the prevalent fondness for pleasure which takes the place of ambition and those nobler passions that open and enlarge the soul; that the instruction which women have hitherto received has only tended, with the constitution of civil society, to render them insignificant objects of desire—mere propagators of fools!—if it can be proved that in aiming to accomplish them, without cultivating their understandings, they are taken out of their sphere of duties, and made ridiculous and useless when the short-lived bloom of beauty is over, I presume that *rational* men will excuse me for endeavouring to persuade them to become more masculine and respectable.

Indeed the word masculine is only a bugbear: there is little reason to fear that women will acquire too much courage or fortitude; for their apparent inferiority with respect to bodily strength, must render them, in

[1]One of the accusations Hamlet flings at Ophelia is that women paint their faces and "nickname God's creatures." See *Hamlet* III.i.142–46.

some degree, dependent on men in the various relations of life; but why should it be increased by prejudices that give a sex to virtue, and confound simple truths with sensual reveries?

Women are, in fact, so much degraded by mistaken notions of female excellence, that I do not mean to add a paradox when I assert, that this artificial weakness produces a propensity to tyrannize, and gives birth to cunning, the natural opponent of strength, which leads them to play off those contemptible infantine airs that undermine esteem even whilst they excite desire. Let men become more chaste and modest, and if women do not grow wiser in the same ratio, it will be clear that they have weaker understandings. It seems scarcely necessary to say, that I now speak of the sex in general. Many individuals have more sense than their male relatives; and, as nothing preponderates where there is a constant struggle for an equilibrium, without it has naturally more gravity, some women govern their husbands without degrading themselves, because intellect will always govern.

CHAPTER I

THE RIGHTS AND INVOLVED DUTIES OF MANKIND CONSIDERED

In the present state of society it appears necessary to go back to first principles in search of the most simple truths, and to dispute with some prevailing prejudice every inch of ground. To clear my way, I must be allowed to ask some plain questions, and the answers will probably appear as unequivocal as the axioms on which reasoning is built; though, when entangled with various motives of action, they are formally contradicted, either by the words or conduct of men.

In what does man's pre-eminence over the brute creation consist? The answer is as clear as that a half is less than the whole; in Reason.

What acquirement exalts one being above another? Virtue, we spontaneously reply.

For what purpose were the passions implanted? That man by struggling with them might attain a degree of knowledge denied to the brutes; whispers Experience.

Consequently the perfection of our nature and capability of happiness, must be estimated by the degree of reason, virtue, and knowledge, that distinguish the individual, and direct the laws which bind society: and that from the exercise of reason, knowledge and virtue naturally flow is equally undeniable, if mankind be viewed collectively. . . .

That the society is formed in the wisest manner, whose constitution is founded on the nature of man, strikes, in the abstract, every thinking being so forcibly, that it looks like presumption to endeavour to bring forward proofs; though proof must be brought, or the strong hold of prescription will never be forced by reason; yet to urge prescription as an argument to justify the depriving men (or women) of their natural rights, is one of the absurd sophisms which daily insult common sense.

The civilization of the bulk of the people of Europe is very partial; nay, it may be made a question, whether they have acquired any virtues in exchange for innocence, equivalent to the misery produced by the vices that have been plastered over unsightly ignorance, and the freedom which has been bartered for splendid slavery. The desire of dazzling by riches, the most certain pre-eminence that man can obtain, the pleasure of commanding flattering sycophants, and many other complicated low calculations of doting self-love, have all contributed to overwhelm the mass of mankind, and make liberty a convenient handle for mock patriotism. For whilst rank and titles are held of the utmost importance, before which Genius "must hide its diminished head," it is, with a few exceptions, very unfortunate for a nation when a man of abilities, without rank or property, pushes himself forward to notice. Alas! what unheard-of misery have thousands suffered to purchase a cardinal's hat for an intriguing obscure adventurer, who longed to be ranked with princes, or lord it over them by seizing the triple crown!

Such, indeed, has been the wretchedness that has flowed from hereditary honours, riches, and monarchy, that men of lively sensibility have almost uttered blasphemy in order to justify the dispensations of providence. Man has been held out as independent of his power who made him, or as a lawless planet darting from its orbit to steal the celestial fire of reason; and the vengeance of heaven, lurking in the subtile flame, like Pandora's pent-up mischiefs,[2] sufficiently punished his temerity, by introducing evil into the world.

Impressed by this view of the misery and disorder which pervaded society, and fatigued with jostling against artificial fools, Rousseau became enamoured of solitude, and, being at the same time an optimist, he labours with uncommon eloquence to prove that man was naturally a solitary animal.[3] Misled by his respect for the goodness of God, who certainly—for what man of sense and feeling can doubt it!—gave life only to communicate happiness, he considers evil as positive, and the work of man; not aware that he was exalting one attribute at the expense of another, equally necessary to divine perfection.

Reared on a false hypothesis his arguments in favour of a state of nature are plausible, but unsound. I say unsound; for to assert that a state of nature is preferable to civilization, in all its possible perfection, is, in other words, to arraign supreme wisdom; and the paradoxical exclamation, that God has made all things right, and that error has been introduced by the creature, whom he formed, knowing what he formed, is as unphilosophical as impious.

When that wise Being who created us and placed us here, saw the fair idea, he willed, by allowing it to be so, that the passions should unfold our reason, because he could see that present evil would produce future good. Could the helpless creature whom he called from nothing break loose from his providence, and boldly learn to know good by practising evil, without his permission? No. How could that energetic advocate for immortality argue so inconsistently? Had mankind remained for ever in the brutal state of nature, which even his magic pen cannot paint as a state in which a single

[2] Pandora, in the Greek myth, against Zeus's orders, opened a box which contained all human ills.

[3] Rousseau's idealization of "natural man" appears primarily in "Concerning the Origin of Inequality among Men" (1754) and *The Social Contract* (1762). His comments on women are mainly found in *Emile*, Book V: "Sophy, or Woman."

virtue took root, it would have been clear, though not to the sensitive unreflecting wanderer, that man was born to run the circle of life and death, and adorn God's garden for some purpose which could not easily be reconciled with his attributes.

But if, to crown the whole, there were to be rational creatures produced, allowed to rise in excellence by the exercise of powers implanted for that purpose; if benignity itself thought fit to call into existence a creature above the brutes, who could think and improve himself, why should that inestimable gift, for a gift it was, if man was so created as to have a capacity to rise above the state in which sensation produced brutal ease, be called, in direct terms, a curse? A curse it might be reckoned, if the whole of our existence were bounded by our continuance in this world; for why should the gracious fountain of life give us passions, and the power of reflecting, only to imbitter our days and inspire us with mistaken notions of dignity? Why should he lead us from love of ourselves to the sublime emotions which the discovery of his wisdom and goodness excites, if these feelings were not set in motion to improve our nature, of which they make a part, and render us capable of enjoying a more godlike portion of happiness? Firmly persuaded that no evil exists in the world that God did not design to take place, I build my belief on the perfection of God.

Rousseau exerts himself to prove that all *was* right originally: a crowd of authors that all *is* now right: and I, that all will *be* right.

But, true to his first position, next to the state of nature, Rousseau celebrates barbarism, and apostrophizing the shade of Fabricius,[4] he forgets that, in conquering the world, the Romans never dreamed of establishing their own liberty on a firm basis, or of extending the reign of virtue. Eager to support his system, he stigmatizes, as vicious, every effort of genius; and, uttering the apotheosis of savage virtues, he exalts those to demi-gods, who were scarcely human—the brutal Spartans, who, in defiance of justice and gratitude, sacrificed, in cold blood, the slaves who had shewn themselves heroes to rescue their oppressors.

Disgusted with artificial manners and virtues, the citizen of Geneva,[5] instead of properly sifting the subject, threw away the wheat with the chaff, without waiting to inquire whether the evils which his ardent soul turned from indignantly, were the consequence of civilization or the vestiges of barbarism. He saw vice trampling on virtue, and the semblance of goodness taking place of the reality; he saw talents bent by power to sinister purposes, and never thought of tracing the gigantic mischief up to arbitrary power, up to the hereditary distinctions that clash with the mental superiority that naturally raises a man above his fellows. He did not perceive that regal power, in a few generations, introduces idiotism into the noble stem, and holds out baits to render thousands idle and vicious.

Nothing can set the regal character in a more contemptible point of view, than the various crimes that have elevated men to the supreme dignity. Vile intrigues, unnatural crimes, and every vice that degrades our nature, have been the steps to this distinguished eminence; yet millions of

[4] Gaius Fabricius (third century B.C.) called for Rome to return to its ancient virtues. Rousseau praises him in "A Discourse on the Sciences and the Arts" (1750).

[5] Rousseau, who was born and spent much of his life in Geneva.

men have supinely allowed the nerveless limbs of the posterity of such rapacious prowlers to rest quietly on their ensanguined thrones.

What but a pestilential vapour can hover over society when its chief director is only instructed in the invention of crimes, or the stupid routine of childish ceremonies? Will men never be wise?—will they never cease to expect corn from tares, and figs from thistles?

It is impossible for any man, when the most favourable circumstances concur, to acquire sufficient knowledge and strength of mind to discharge the duties of a king, entrusted with uncontrolled power; how then must they be violated when his very elevation is an insuperable bar to the attainment of either wisdom or virtue; when all the feelings of a man are stifled by flattery, and reflection shut out by pleasure! Surely it is madness to make the fate of thousands depend on the caprice of a weak fellow creature, whose very station sinks him *necessarily* below the meanest of his subjects! But one power should not be thrown down to exalt another—for all power inebriates weak man; and its abuse proves that the more equality there is established among men, the more virtue and happiness will reign in society. But this and any similar maxim deduced from simple reason, raises an outcry—the church or the state is in danger, if faith in the wisdom of antiquity is not implicit; and they who, roused by the sight of human calamity, dare to attack human authority, are reviled as despisers of God, and enemies of man. . . .

After attacking the sacred majesty of Kings, I shall scarcely excite surprise by adding my firm persuasion that every profession, in which great subordination of rank constitutes its power, is highly injurious to morality.

A standing army, for instance, is incompatible with freedom; because subordination and rigour are the very sinews of military discipline; and despotism is necessary to give vigour to enterprizes that one will directs. A spirit inspired by romantic notions of honour, a kind of morality founded on the fashion of the age, can only be felt by a few officers, whilst the main body must be moved by command, like the waves of the sea; for the strong wind of authority pushes the crowd of subalterns forward, they scarcely know or care why, with headlong fury.

Besides, nothing can be so prejudicial to the morals of the inhabitants of country towns as the occasional residence of a set of idle superficial young men, whose only occupation is gallantry, and whose polished manners render vice more dangerous, by concealing its deformity under gay ornamental drapery. An air of fashion, which is but a badge of slavery, and proves that the soul has not a strong individual character, awes simple country people into an imitation of the vices, when they cannot catch the slippery graces of politeness. Every corps is a chain of despots, who, submitting and tyrannizing without exercising their reason, become dead weights of vice and folly on the community. A man of rank or fortune, sure of rising by interest, has nothing to do but to pursue some extravagant freak; whilst the needy *gentleman,* who is to rise, as the phrase turns, by his merit, becomes a servile parasite or vile pander.

Sailors, the naval gentlemen, come under the same description, only their vices assume a different and a grosser cast. They are more positively indolent, when not discharging the ceremonials of their station; whilst the insignificant fluttering of soldiers may be termed active idleness. More confined to the society of men, the former acquire a fondness for humour and mischievous tricks; whilst the latter, mixing frequently with well-bred women, catch a sentimental cant. But mind is equally out of the question, whether they indulge the horse-laugh, or polite simper.

May I be allowed to extend the comparison to a profession where more mind is certainly to be found; for the clergy have superior opportunities of improvement, though subordination almost equally cramps their faculties? The blind submission imposed at college to forms of belief serves as a novitiate to the curate, who must obsequiously respect the opinion of his rector or patron, if he mean to rise in his profession. Perhaps there cannot be a more forcible contrast than between the servile dependant gait of a poor curate and the courtly mien of a bishop. And the respect and contempt they inspire render the discharge of their separate functions equally useless.

It is of great importance to observe that the character of every man is, in some degree, formed by his profession. A man of sense may only have a cast of countenance that wears off as you trace his individuality, whilst the weak, common man has scarcely ever any character, but what belongs to the body; at least, all his opinions have been so steeped in the vat consecrated by authority, that the faint spirit which the grape of his own vine yields cannot be distinguished.

Society, therefore, as it becomes more enlightened, should be very careful not to establish bodies of men who must necessarily be made foolish or vicious by the very constitution of their profession.

In the infancy of society, when men were just emerging out of barbarism, chiefs and priests, touching the most powerful springs of savage conduct, hope and fear, must have had unbounded sway. An aristocracy, of course, is naturally the first form of government. But, clashing interests soon losing their equipoise, a monarchy and hierarchy break out of the confusion of ambitious struggles, and the foundation of both is secured by feudal tenures. This appears to be the origin of monarchical and priestly power, and the dawn of civilization. But such combustible materials cannot long be pent up; and, getting vent in foreign wars and intestine insurrections, the people acquire some power in the tumult, which obliges their rulers to gloss over their oppression with a shew of right. Thus, as wars, agriculture, commerce, and literature, expand the mind, despots are compelled to make covert corruption hold fast the power which was formerly snatched by open force. And this baneful lurking gangrene is most quickly spread by luxury and superstition, the sure dregs of ambition. The indolent puppet of a court first becomes a luxurious monster, or fastidious sensualist, and then makes the contagion which his unnatural state spread, the instrument of tyranny.

It is the pestiferous purple which renders the progress of civilization a curse, and warps the understanding, till men of sensibility doubt whether the expansion of intellect produces a greater portion of happiness or misery. But the nature of the poison points out the antidote; and had Rousseau mounted one step higher in his investigation, or could his eye have pierced through the foggy atmosphere, which he almost disdained to breathe, his active mind would have darted forward to contemplate the perfection of man in the establishment of true civilization, instead of taking his ferocious flight back to the night of sensual ignorance.

CHAPTER II

The Prevailing Opinion of a Sexual Character Discussed

To account for, and excuse the tyranny of man, many ingenious arguments have been brought forward to prove, that the two sexes, in the acquirement of virtue, ought to aim at attaining a very different character; or, to speak explicitly, women are not allowed to have sufficient strength of mind to acquire what really deserves the name of virtue. Yet it should seem, allowing them to have souls, that there is but one way appointed by Providence to lead *mankind* to either virtue or happiness.

If then women are not a swarm of ephemeron triflers, why should they be kept in ignorance under the specious name of innocence? Men complain, and with reason, of the follies and caprices of our sex, when they do not keenly satirize our headstrong passions and grovelling vices. Behold, I should answer, the natural effect of ignorance! The mind will ever be unstable that has only prejudices to rest on, and the current will run with destructive fury when there are no barriers to break its force. Women are told from their infancy, and taught by the example of their mothers, that a little knowledge of human weakness, justly termed cunning, softness of temper, *outward* obedience, and a scrupulous attention to a puerile kind of propriety, will obtain for them the protection of man; and should they be beautiful, everything else is needless, for, at least, twenty years of their lives.

Thus Milton describes our first frail mother;[6] though when he tells us that women are formed for softness and sweet attractive grace, I cannot comprehend his meaning, unless, in the true Mahometan strain, he meant to deprive us of souls,[7] and insinuate that we were beings only designed by sweet attractive grace, and docile blind obedience, to gratify the senses of man when he can no longer soar on the wing of contemplation.

How grossly do they insult us who thus advise us only to render ourselves gentle, domestic brutes! For instance, the winning softness so warmly, and frequently, recommended, that governs by obeying. What childish expressions, and how insignificant is the being—can it be an immortal one? who will condescend to govern by such sinister methods! "Certainly," says Lord Bacon, "man is of kin to the beasts by his body; and if he be not of kin to God by his spirit, he is a base and ignoble creature!"[8] Men, indeed, appear to me to act in a very unphilosophical manner when they try to secure the good conduct of women by attempting to keep them always in a state of childhood. Rousseau was more consistent when he wished to stop the progress of reason in both sexes, for if men eat of the

[6] See *Paradise Lost* IV.295ff: "For contemplation he and valor form'd, / For softness she and sweet attractive grace."

[7] Wollstonecraft follows the common Western misconception that the Koran denies that women have souls.

[8] See Francis Bacon, "Of Atheism" (1597).

tree of knowledge, women will come in for a taste; but, from the imperfect cultivation which their understandings now receive, they only attain a knowledge of evil

Children, I grant, should be innocent; but when the epithet is applied to men, or women, it is but a civil term for weakness. For if it be allowed that women were destined by Providence to acquire human virtues, and by the exercise of their understandings, that stability of character which is the firmest ground to rest our future hopes upon, they must be permitted to turn to the fountain of light, and not forced to shape their course by the twinkling of a mere satellite. Milton, I grant, was of a very different opinion; for he only bends to the indefeasible right of beauty, though it would be difficult to render two passages which I now mean to contrast, consistent. But into similar inconsistencies are great men often led by their senses.

> To whom thus Eve with *perfect beauty* adorn'd.
> "My Author and Disposer, what thou bidst
> *Unargued* I obey; so God ordains;
> God is *thy law, thou mine:* to know no more
> Is Woman's *happiest* knowledge and her *praise*."[9]

These are exactly the arguments that I have used to children; but I have added, your reason is now gaining strength, and, till it arrives at some degree of maturity, you must look up to me for advice—then you ought to *think,* and only rely on God.

Yet in the following lines Milton seems to coincide with me; when he makes Adam thus expostulate with his Maker.

> "Hast thou not made me here thy substitute,
> And these inferior far beneath me set?
> Among *unequals* what society
> Can sort, what harmony or true delight?
> Which must be mutual, in proportion due
> Giv'n and receiv'd; but in *disparity*
> The one intense, the other still remiss
> Cannot well suit with either, but soon prove
> Tedious alike: of *fellowship* I speak
> Such as I seek, fit to participate
> All rational delight—"[10]

In treating, therefore, of the manners of women, let us, disregarding sensual arguments, trace what we should endeavour to make them in order to co-operate, if the expression be not too bold, with the supreme Being.

By individual education, I mean, for the sense of the word is not precisely defined, such an attention to a child as will slowly sharpen the senses, form the temper, regulate the passions as they begin to ferment, and set the understanding to work before the body arrives at maturity; so that the man may only have to proceed, not to begin, the important task of learning to think and reason.

[9] *Paradise Lost* IV.634–38. [10] *Paradise Lost* VIII.381–92.

To prevent any misconstruction, I must add, that I do not believe that a private education can work the wonders which some sanguine writers have attributed to it. Men and women must be educated, in a great degree, by the opinions and manners of the society they live in. In every age there has been a stream of popular opinion that has carried all before it, and given a family character, as it were, to the century. It may then fairly be inferred, that, till society be differently constituted, much cannot be expected from education. It is, however, sufficient for my present purpose to assert, that, whatever effect circumstances have on the abilities, every being may become virtuous by the exercise of its own reason; for if but one being was created with vicious inclinations, that is positively bad, what can save us from atheism? or if we worship a God, is not that God a devil?

Consequently, the most perfect education, in my opinion, is such an exercise of the understanding as is best calculated to strengthen the body and form the heart. Or, in other words, to enable the individual to attain such habits of virtue as will render it independent. In fact, it is a farce to call any being virtuous whose virtues do not result from the exercise of its own reason. This was Rousseau's opinion respecting men: I extend it to women, and confidently assert that they have been drawn out of their sphere by false refinement, and not by an endeavour to acquire masculine qualities. Still the regal homage which they receive is so intoxicating, that till the manners of the times are changed, and formed on more reasonable principles, it may be impossible to convince them that the illegitimate power, which they obtain, by degrading themselves, is a curse, and that they must return to nature and equality, if they wish to secure the placid satisfaction that unsophisticated affections impart. But for this epoch we must wait—wait, perhaps, till kings and nobles, enlightened by reason, and, preferring the real dignity of man to childish state, throw off their gaudy hereditary trappings: and if then women do not resign the arbitrary power of beauty—they will prove that they have *less* mind than man.

I may be accused of arrogance; still I must declare what I firmly believe, that all the writers who have written on the subject of female education and manners, from Rousseau to Dr. Gregory,[11] have contributed to render women more artificial, weak characters, than they would otherwise have been; and consequently, more useless members of society. I might have expressed this conviction in a lower key; but I am afraid it would have been the whine of affectation, and not the faithful expression of my feelings, of the clear result which experience and reflection have led me to draw. When I come to that division of the subject, I shall advert to the passages that I more particularly disapprove of, in the works of the authors I have just alluded to; but it is first necessary to observe, that my objection extends to the whole purport of those books, which tend, in my opinion, to degrade one half of the human species, and render women pleasing at the expense of every solid virtue.

Though, to reason on Rousseau's ground, if man did attain a degree of perfection of mind when his body arrived at maturity, it might be proper, in order to make a man and his wife *one*, that she should rely entirely on his understanding; and the graceful ivy, clasping the oak that supported it,

[11] John Gregory, author of *A Father's Legacy to His Daughters* (1789).

would form a whole in which strength and beauty would be equally conspicuous. But, alas! husbands, as well as their helpmates, are often only overgrown children; nay, thanks to early debauchery, scarcely men in their outward form—and if the blind lead the blind, one need not come from heaven to tell us the consequence.

Many are the causes that, in the present corrupt state of society, contribute to enslave women by cramping their understandings and sharpening their senses. One, perhaps, that silently does more mischief than all the rest, is their disregard of order.

To do everything in an orderly manner, is a most important precept, which women, who, generally speaking, receive only a disorderly kind of education, seldom attend to with that degree of exactness that men, who from their infancy are broken into method, observe. This negligent kind of guess-work, for what other epithet can be used to point out the random exertions of a sort of instinctive common sense, never brought to the test of reason? prevents their generalizing matters of fact—so they do to-day, what they did yesterday, merely because they did it yesterday.

This contempt of the understanding in early life has more baneful consequences than is commonly supposed; for the little knowledge which women of strong minds attain, is, from various circumstances, of a more desultory kind than the knowledge of men, and it is acquired more by sheer observations on real life, than from comparing what has been individually observed with the results of experience generalized by speculation. Led by their dependent situation and domestic employments more into society, what they learn is rather by snatches; and as learning is with them, in general, only a secondary thing, they do not pursue any one branch with that persevering ardour necessary to give vigour to the faculties, and clearness to the judgment. In the present state of society, a little learning is required to support the character of a gentleman; and boys are obliged to submit to a few years of discipline. But in the education of women, the cultivation of the understanding is always subordinate to the acquirement of some corporeal accomplishment; even while enervated by confinement and false notions of modesty, the body is prevented from attaining that grace and beauty which relaxed half formed limbs never exhibit. Besides, in youth their faculties are not brought forward by emulation; and having no serious scientific study, if they have natural sagacity it is turned too soon on life and manners. They dwell on effects, and modifications, without tracing them back to causes; and complicated rules to adjust behaviour are a weak substitute for simple principles.

As a proof that education gives this appearance of weakness to females, we may instance the example of military men, who are, like them, sent into the world before their minds have been stored with knowledge or fortified by principles. The consequences are similar; soldiers acquire a little superficial knowledge, snatched from the muddy current of conversation, and, from continually mixing with society, they gain, what is termed a knowledge of the world; and this acquaintance with manners and customs has frequently been confounded with a knowledge of the human heart. But can the crude fruit of casual observation, never brought to the test of judgment, formed by comparing speculation and experience, deserve such a distinction? Soldiers, as well as women, practice the minor virtues with punctilious politeness. Where is then the sexual difference, when the education has been the same? All the difference that I can discern, arises from the superior advantage of liberty, which enables the former to see more of life. . . .

Standing armies can never consist of resolute robust men; they may be well disciplined machines, but they will seldom contain men under the influence of strong passions, or with very vigorous faculties. And as for any depth of understanding, I will venture to affirm, that it is as rarely to be found in the army as amongst women; and the cause, I maintain, is the same. It may be further observed, that officers are also particularly attentive to their persons, fond of dancing, crowded rooms, adventures, and ridicule. Like the *fair* sex, the business of their lives is gallantry. They were taught to please, and they only live to please. Yet they do not lose their rank in the distinction of sexes, for they are still reckoned superior to women, though in what their superiority consists, beyond what I have just mentioned, it is difficult to discover.

The great misfortune is this, that they both acquire manners before morals, and a knowledge of life before they have, from reflection, any acquaintance with the grand ideal outline of human nature. The consequence is natural; satisfied with common nature, they become a prey to prejudices, and taking all their opinions on credit, they blindly submit to authority. So that, if they have any sense, it is a kind of instinctive glance, that catches proportions, and decides with respect to manners; but fails when arguments are to be pursued below the surface, or opinions analyzed.

May not the same remark be applied to women? Nay, the argument may be carried still further, for they are both thrown out of a useful station by the unnatural distinctions established in civilized life. Riches and hereditary honours have made cyphers of women to give consequence to the numerical figure; and idleness has produced a mixture of gallantry and despotism into society, which leads the very men who are the slaves of their mistresses to tyrannize over their sisters, wives, and daughters. This is only keeping them in rank and file, it is true. Strengthen the female mind by enlarging it, and there will be an end to blind obedience; but, as blind obedience is ever sought for by power, tyrants and sensualists are in the right when they endeavour to keep women in the dark, because the former only want slaves, and the latter a plaything. The sensualist, indeed, has been the most dangerous of tyrants, and women have been duped by their lovers, as princes by their ministers, whilst dreaming that they reigned over them.

I now principally allude to Rousseau, for his character of Sophia[12] is, undoubtedly, a captivating one, though it appears to me grossly unnatural; however it is not the superstructure, but the foundation of her character, the principles on which her education was built, that I mean to attack; nay, warmly as I admire the genius of that able writer, whose opinions I shall often have occasion to cite, indignation always takes place of admiration, and the rigid frown of insulted virtue effaces the smile of complacency,

[12] In Book V of *Emile.*

which his eloquent periods are wont to raise, when I read his voluptuous reveries. Is this the man, who, in his ardour for virtue, would banish all the soft arts of peace, and almost carry us back to Spartan discipline? Is this the man who delights to paint the useful struggles of passion, the triumphs of good dispositions, and the heroic flights which carry the glowing soul out of itself?—How are these mighty sentiments lowered when he describes the pretty foot and enticing airs of his little favourite! But, for the present, I waive the subject, and, instead of severely reprehending the transient effusions of overweening sensibility, I shall only observe, that whoever has cast a benevolent eye on society, must often have been gratified by the sight of humble mutual love, not dignified by sentiment, or strengthened by a union in intellectual pursuits. The domestic trifles of the day have afforded matters for cheerful converse, and innocent caresses have softened toils which did not require great exercise of mind or stretch of thought: yet, has not the sight of this moderate felicity excited more tenderness than respect? An emotion similar to what we feel when children are playing, or animals sporting, whilst the contemplation of the noble struggles of suffering merit has raised admiration, and carried out thoughts to that world where sensation will give place to reason.

Women are, therefore, to be considered either as moral beings, or so weak that they must be entirely subjected to the superior faculties of men.

Let us examine this question. Rousseau declares that a woman should never, for a moment, feel herself independent, that she should be governed by fear to exercise her *natural* cunning, and made a coquettish slave in order to render her a more alluring object of desire, a *sweeter* companion to man, whenever he chooses to relax himself. He carries the arguments, which he pretends to draw from the indications of nature, still further, and insinuates that truth and fortitude, the cornerstones of all human virtue, should be cultivated with certain restrictions, because, with respect to the female character, obedience is the grand lesson which ought to be impressed with unrelenting rigour.

What nonsense! when will a great man arise with sufficient strength of mind to puff away the fumes which pride and sensuality have thus spread over the subject! If women are by nature inferior to men, their virtues must be the same in quality, if not in degree, or virtue is a relative idea; consequently, their conduct should be founded on the same principles, and have the same aim.

Connected with man as daughters, wives, and mothers, their moral character may be estimated by their manner of fulfilling those simple duties; but the end, the grand end of their exertions should be to unfold their own faculties and acquire the dignity of conscious virtue. They may try to render their road pleasant; but ought never to forget, in common with man, that life yields not the felicity which can satisfy an immortal soul. I do not mean to insinuate that either sex should be so lost in abstract reflections or distant views, as to forget the affections and duties that lie before them, and are, in truth, the means appointed to produce the fruit of life; on the contrary, I would warmly recommend them, even while I assert, that they afford most satisfaction when they are considered in their true, sober light.

Probably the prevailing opinion, that woman was created for man, may have taken its rise from Moses's poetical story;[13] yet, as very few, it is presumed, who have bestowed any serious thought on the subject, ever supposed that Eve was, literally speaking, one of Adam's ribs, the deduction must be allowed to fall to the ground; or, only be so far admitted as it proves that man, from the remotest antiquity, found it convenient to exert his strength to subjugate his companion, and his invention to show that she ought to have her neck bent under the yoke, because the whole creation was only created for his convenience or pleasure.

Let it not be concluded that I wish to invert the order of things; I have already granted, that, from the constitution of their bodies, men seem to be designed by Providence to attain a greater degree of virtue. I speak collectively of the whole sex; but I see not the shadow of a reason to conclude that their virtues should differ in respect to their nature. In fact, how can they, if virtue has only one eternal standard? I must therefore, if I reason consequentially, as strenuously maintain that they have the same simple direction, as that there is a God.

It follows then that cunning should not be opposed to wisdom, little cares to great exertions, or insipid softness, varnished over with the name of gentleness, to that fortitude which grand views alone can inspire.

I shall be told that woman would then lose many of her peculiar graces, and the opinion of a well known poet might be quoted to refute my unqualified assertion. For Pope has said, in the name of the whole male sex,

> Yet ne'er so sure our passion to create,
> As when she touch'd the brink of all we hate.[14]

In what light this sally places men and women, I shall leave to the judicious to determine; meanwhile I shall content myself with observing, that I cannot discover why, unless they are mortal, females should always be degraded by being made subservient to love or lust.

To speak disrespectfully of love is, I know, high treason against sentiment and fine feelings; but I wish to speak the simple language of truth, and rather to address the head than the heart. To endeavour to reason love out of the world, would be to out Quixote Cervantes,[15] and equally offend against common sense; but an endeavour to restrain this tumultuous passion, and to prove that it should not be allowed to dethrone superior powers, or to usurp the sceptre which the understanding should ever coolly wield, appears less wild.

Youth is the season for love in both sexes; but in those days of thoughtless enjoyment provision should be made for the more important years of life, when reflection takes place of sensation. But Rousseau, and most of the male writers who have followed his steps, have warmly inculcated that the whole tendency of female education ought to be directed to one point:—to render them pleasing.

[13] See Genesis 2:21–23, in which Eve is created from Adam's rib.
[14] Alexander Pope, *Moral Essays,* II.51–52.
[15] To "out Quixote Cervantes" is to attempt the impossible.

Let me reason with the supporters of this opinion who have any knowledge of human nature, do they imagine that marriage can eradicate the habitude of life? The woman who has only been taught to please will soon find that her charms are oblique sunbeams, and that they cannot have much effect on her husband's heart when they are seen every day, when the summer is passed and gone. Will she then have sufficient native energy to look into herself for comfort, and cultivate her dormant faculties? or, is it not more rational to expect that she will try to please other men; and, in the emotions raised by the expectation of new conquests, endeavour to forget the mortification her love or pride has received? When the husband ceases to be a lover—and the time will inevitably come, her desire of pleasing will then grow languid, or become a spring of bitterness; and love, perhaps, the most evanescent of all passions, gives place to jealousy or vanity.

I now speak of women who are restrained by principle or prejudice; such women, though they would shrink from an intrigue with real abhorrence, yet, nevertheless, wish to be convinced by the homage of gallantry that they are cruelly neglected by their husbands; or, days and weeks are spent in dreaming of the happiness enjoyed by congenial souls till their health is undermined and their spirits broken by discontent. How then can the great art of pleasing be such a necessary study? it is only useful to a mistress; the chaste wife, and serious mother, should only consider her power to please as the polish of her virtues, and the affection of her husband as one of the comforts that render her task less difficult and her life happier. But, whether she be loved or neglected, her first wish should be to make herself respectable, and not to rely for all her happiness on a being subject to like infirmities with herself. . . .

Women ought to endeavour to purify their heart; but can they do so when their uncultivated understandings make them entirely dependent on their senses for employment and amusement, when no noble pursuit sets them above the little vanities of the day, or enables them to curb the wild emotions that agitate a reed over which every passing breeze has power? To gain the affections of a virtuous man, is affectation necessary? Nature has given woman a weaker frame than man; but, to ensure her husband's affections, must a wife, who by the exercise of her mind and body whilst she was discharging the duties of a daughter, wife, and mother, has allowed her constitution to retain its natural strength, and her nerves a healthy tone, is she, I say, to condescend to use art and feign a sickly delicacy in order to secure her husband's affection? Weakness may excite tenderness, and gratify the arrogant pride of man; but the lordly caresses of a protector will not gratify a noble mind that pants for, and deserves to be respected. Fondness is a poor substitute for friendship!

In a seraglio, I grant, that all these arts are necessary; the epicure must have his palate tickled, or he will sink into apathy; but have women so little ambition as to be satisfied with such a condition? Can they supinely dream life away in the lap of pleasure, or the languor of weariness, rather than assert their claim to pursue reasonable pleasures and render themselves conspicuous by practising the virtues which dignify mankind? Surely she has not an immortal soul who can loiter life away merely employed to adorn her person, that she may amuse the languid hours, and soften the cares of a fellow-creature who is willing to be enlivened by her smiles and tricks, when the serious business of life is over.

Besides, the woman who strengthens her body and exercises her mind will, by managing her family and practising various virtues, become the friend, and not the humble dependent of her husband; and if she, by possessing such substantial qualities, merit his regard, she will not find it necessary to conceal her affection, nor to pretend to an unnatural coldness of constitution to excite her husband's passions. In fact, if we revert to history, we shall find that the women who have distinguished themselves have neither been the most beautiful nor the most gentle of their sex. . . .

Gentleness of manners, forbearance and long-suffering, are such amiable God-like qualities, that in sublime poetic strains the Deity has been invested with them; and, perhaps, no representation of his goodness so strongly fastens on the human affections as those that represent him abundant in mercy and willing to pardon. Gentleness, considered in this point of view, bears on its front all the characteristics of grandeur, combined with the winning graces of condescension; but what a different aspect it assumes when it is the submissive demeanour of dependence, the support of weakness that loves, because it wants protection; and is forbearing, because it must silently endure injuries; smiling under the lash at which it dare not snarl. Abject as this picture appears, it is the portrait of an accomplished woman, according to the received opinion of female excellence, separated by specious reasoners from human excellence. Or, they kindly restore the rib, and make one moral being of a man and woman; not forgetting to give her all the "submissive charms."[16]

How women are to exist in that state where there is to be neither marrying or giving in marriage,[17] we are not told. For though moralists have agreed that the tenor of life seems to prove that *man* is prepared by various circumstances for a future state, they constantly concur in advising *woman* only to provide for the present. Gentleness, docility, and a spaniel-like affection are, on this ground, consistently recommended as the cardinal virtues of the sex; and, disregarding the arbitrary economy of nature, one writer has declared that it is masculine for a woman to be melancholy. She was created to be the toy of man, his rattle, and it must jingle in his ears whenever, dismissing reason, he chooses to be amused.

To recommend gentleness, indeed, on a broad basis is strictly philosophical. A frail being should labour to be gentle. But when forbearance confounds right and wrong, it ceases to be a virtue; and, however convenient it may be found in a companion—that companion will ever be considered as an inferior, and only inspire a vapid tenderness, which easily degenerates into contempt. Still, if advice could really make a being gentle, whose natural disposition admitted not of such a fine polish, something towards the advancement of order would be attained; but if, as might quickly be demonstrated, only affectation be produced by this indiscriminate counsel, which throws a stumbling-block in the way of gradual improvement, and true melioration of temper, the sex is not much benefited

[16] Adam (*Paradise Lost* IV.498) delights in Eve's beauty and "submissive charms."
[17] That is, in Heaven.

by sacrificing solid virtues to the attainment of superficial graces, though for a few years they may procure the individuals regal sway. . . .

But to view the subject in another point of view. Do passive indolent women make the best wives? Confining our discussion to the present moment of existence, let us see how such weak creatures perform their part. Do the women who, by the attainment of a few superficial accomplishments, have strengthened the prevailing prejudice, merely contribute to the happiness of their husbands? Do they display their charms merely to amuse them? And have women, who have early imbibed notions of passive obedience, sufficient character to manage a family or educate children? So far from it, that, after surveying the history of woman, I cannot help, agreeing with the severest satirist, considering the sex as the weakest as well as the most oppressed half of the species. What does history disclose but marks of inferiority, and how few women have emancipated themselves from the galling yoke of sovereign man?—So few, that the exceptions remind me of an ingenious conjecture respecting Newton:[18] that he was probably a being of superior order, accidentally caged in a human body. Following the same train of thinking, I have been led to imagine that the few extraordinary women who have rushed in eccentrical directions out of the orbit prescribed to their sex, were *male* spirits, confined by mistake in female frames. But if it be not philosophical to think of sex when the soul is mentioned, the inferiority must depend on the organs; or the heavenly fire, which is to ferment the clay, is not given in equal portions.

But avoiding, as I have hitherto done, any direct comparison of the two sexes collectively, or frankly acknowledging the inferiority of woman, according to the present appearance of things, I shall only insist that men have increased that inferiority till women are almost sunk below the standard of rational creatures. Let their faculties have room to unfold, and their virtues to gain strength, and then determine where the whole sex must stand in the intellectual scale. Yet let it be remembered, that for a small number of distinguished women I do not ask a place. . . .

I love man as my fellow; but his sceptre, real, or usurped, extends not to me, unless the reason of an individual demands my homage; and even then the submission is to reason, and not to man. In fact, the conduct of an accountable being must be regulated by the operations of its own reason; or on what foundation rests the throne of God?

It appears to me necessary to dwell on these obvious truths, because females have been insulated, as it were; and, while they have been stripped of the virtues that should clothe humanity, they have been decked with artificial graces that enable them to exercise a short-lived tyranny. Love, in their bosoms, taking place of every nobler passion, their sole ambition is to be fair, to raise emotion instead of inspiring respect; and this ignoble desire, like the servility in absolute monarchies, destroys all strength of character. Liberty is the mother of virtue, and if women be, by their very constitution, slaves, and not allowed to breathe the sharp invigorating air of freedom, they must ever languish like exotics, and be reckoned beautiful flaws in nature. . . .

I will allow that bodily strength seems to give man a natural superiority

[18]Sir Isaac Newton (1642–1727), physicist and mathematician.

over woman; and this is the only solid basis on which the superiority of the sex can be built. But I still insist, that not only the virtue, but the *knowledge* of the two sexes should be the same in nature, if not in degree, and that women, considered not only as moral, but rational creatures, ought to endeavour to acquire human virtues (or perfections) by the *same* means as men, instead of being educated like a fanciful kind of *half* being—one of Rousseau's wild chimeras.

But, if strength of body be, with some show of reason, the boast of men, why are women so infatuated as to be proud of a defect? Rousseau has furnished them with a plausible excuse, which could only have occurred to a man, whose imagination had been allowed to run wild, and refine on the impressions made by exquisite senses;—that they might, forsooth, have a pretext for yielding to a natural appetite without violating a romantic species of modesty, which gratifies the pride and libertinism of man.

Women, deluded by these sentiments, sometimes boast of their weakness, cunningly obtaining power by playing on the *weakness* of men; and they may well glory in their illicit sway, for, like Turkish bashaws,[19] they have more real power than their masters: but virtue is sacrificed to temporary gratifications, and the respectability of life to the triumph of an hour.

Women, as well as despots, have now, perhaps, more power than they would have if the world, divided and subdivided into kingdoms and families, were governed by laws deduced from the exercise of reason; but in obtaining it, to carry on the comparison, their character is degraded, and licentiousness spread through the whole aggregate of society. The many become pedestal to the few. I, therefore, will venture to assert, that till women are more rationally educated, the progress of human virtue and improvement in knowledge must receive continual checks. And if it be granted that woman was not created merely to gratify the appetite of man, or to be the upper servant, who provides his meals and takes care of his linen, it must follow, that the first care of those mothers or fathers, who really attend to the education of females, should be, if not to strengthen the body, at least, not to destroy the constitution by mistaken notions of beauty and female excellence; nor should girls ever be allowed to imbibe the pernicious notion that a defect can, by any chemical process of reasoning, become an excellence. . . .

But should it be proved that woman is naturally weaker than man, whence does it follow that it is natural for her to labour to become still weaker than nature intended her to be? Arguments of this cast are an insult to common sense, and savour of passion. The *divine right* of husbands, like the divine right of kings, may, it is to be hoped, in this enlightened age, be contested without danger, and, though conviction may not silence many boisterous disputants, yet, when any prevailing prejudice is attacked, the wife will consider, and leave the narrow-minded to rail with thoughtless vehemence at innovation.

The mother, who wishes to give true dignity of character to her daughter, must, regardless of the sneers of ignorance, proceed on a plan diametrically opposite to that which Rousseau has recommended with all the deluding charms of eloquence and philosophical sophistry: for his elo-

[19] Officers or governors.

quence renders absurdities plausible, and his dogmatic conclusions puzzle, without convincing, those who have not ability to refute them.

Throughout the whole animal kingdom every young creature requires almost continual exercise, and the infancy of children, conformable to this intimation, should be passed in harmless gambols, that exercise the feet and hands, without requiring very minute direction from the head, or the constant attention of a nurse. In fact, the care necessary for self-preservation is the first natural exercise of the understanding, as little inventions to amuse the present moment unfold the imagination. But these wise designs of nature are counteracted by mistaken fondness or blind zeal. The child is not left a moment to its own direction, particularly a girl, and thus rendered dependent—dependence is called natural.

To preserve personal beauty, woman's glory! the limbs and faculties are cramped with worse than Chinese bands,[20] and the sedentary life which they are condemned to live, whilst boys frolic in the open air, weakens the muscles and relaxes the nerves. As for Rousseau's remarks, which have since been echoed by several writers, that they have naturally, that is from their birth, independent of education, a fondness for dolls, dressing, and talking—they are so puerile as not to merit a serious refutation. That a girl, condemned to sit for hours together listening to the idle chat of weak nurses, or to attend at her mother's toilet, will endeavour to join the conversation, is, indeed, very natural; and that she will imitate her mother or aunts, and amuse herself by adorning her lifeless doll, as they do in dressing her, poor innocent babe! is undoubtedly a most natural consequence. For men of the greatest abilities have seldom had sufficient strength to rise above the surrounding atmosphere; and, if the page of genius have always been blurred by the prejudices of the age, some allowance should be made for a sex, who, like kings, always see things through a false medium.

Pursuing these reflections, the fondness for dress, conspicuous in women, may be easily accounted for, without supposing it the result of a desire to please the sex on which they are dependent. The absurdity, in short, of supposing that a girl is naturally a coquette, and that a desire connected with the impulse of nature to propagate the species, should appear even before an improper education has, by heating the imagination, called it forth prematurely, is so unphilosophical, that such a sagacious observer as Rousseau would not have adopted it, if he had not been accustomed to make reason give way to his desire of singularity, and truth to a favourite paradox. . . .

I have, probably, had an opportunity of observing more girls in their infancy than J. J. Rousseau—I can recollect my own feelings, and I have looked steadily around me; yet, so far from coinciding with him in opinion respecting the first dawn of the female character, I will venture to affirm, that a girl, whose spirits have not been damped by inactivity, or innocence tainted by false shame, will always be a romp, and the doll will never excite attention unless confinement allows her no alternative. Girls and boys, in short, would play harmlessly together, if the distinction of sex was not inculcated long before nature makes any difference. I will go further, and affirm, as an indisputable fact, that most of the women, in the circle of my

[20] The Chinese bound girls' feet to make them unnaturally small.

observation, who have acted like rational creatures, or shown any vigour of intellect, have accidentally been allowed to run wild—as some of the elegant formers of the fair sex would insinuate.

The baneful consequences which flow from inattention to health during infancy, and youth, extend further than is supposed—dependence of body naturally produces dependence of mind; and how can she be a good wife or mother, the greater part of whose time is employed to guard against or endure sickness? Nor can it be expected that a woman will resolutely endeavour to strengthen her constitution and abstain from enervating indulgences, if artificial notions of beauty, and false descriptions of sensibility, have been early entangled with her motives of action. Most men are sometimes obliged to bear with bodily inconveniences, and to endure, occasionally, the inclemency of the elements; but genteel women are, literally speaking, slaves to their bodies, and glory in their subjection.

I once knew a weak woman of fashion, who was more than commonly proud of her delicacy and sensibility. She thought a distinguishing taste and puny appetite the height of all human perfection, and acted accordingly. I have seen this weak sophisticated being neglect all the duties of life, yet recline with self-complacency on a sofa, and boast of her want of appetite as a proof of delicacy that extended to, or, perhaps, arose from, her exquisite sensibility: for it is difficult to render intelligible such ridiculous jargon.—Yet, at the moment, I have seen her insult a worthy old gentlewoman, whom unexpected misfortunes had made dependent on her ostentatious bounty, and who, in better days, had claims on her gratitude. Is it possible that a human creature could have become such a weak and depraved being if, like the Sybarites,[21] dissolved in luxury, everything like virtue had not been worn away, or never impressed by precept, a poor substitute, it is true, for cultivation of mind, though it serves as a fence against vice?. . . .

Women are everywhere in this deplorable state; for, in order to preserve their innocence, as ignorance is courteously termed, truth is hidden from them, and they are made to assume an artificial character before their faculties have acquired any strength. Taught from their infancy that beauty is woman's sceptre, the mind shapes itself to the body, and, roaming round its gilt cage, only seeks to adore its prison. Men have various employments and pursuits which engage their attention, and give a character to the opening mind; but women, confined to one, and having their thoughts constantly directed to the most insignificant part of themselves, seldom extend their views beyond the triumph of the hour. But were their understanding once emancipated from the slavery to which the pride and sensuality of man and their short-sighted desire, like that of dominion in tyrants, of present sway, has subjected them, we should probably read of their weaknesses with surprise. . . .

Let not men then in the pride of power, use the same arguments that tyrannic kings and venal ministers have used, and fallaciously assert that women ought to be subjected because she has always been so. But, when man, governed by reasonable laws, enjoys his natural freedom, let him

[21] Inhabitants of the ancient Greek city of Sybaris, noted for its wealth and luxury.

despise woman, if she do not share it with him; and, till that glorious period arrives, in descanting on the folly of the sex, let him not overlook his own.

Women, it is true, obtaining power by unjust means, by practising or fostering vice, evidently lose the rank which reason would assign them, and they become either abject slaves or capricious tyrants. They lose all simplicity, all dignity of mind, in acquiring power, and act as men are observed to act when they have been exalted by the same means.

It is time to effect a revolution in female manners—time to restore to them their lost dignity—and make them, as a part of the human species, labour by reforming themselves to reform the world. It is time to separate unchangeable morals from local manners. If men be demi-gods—why let us serve them! And if the dignity of the female soul be as disputable as that of animals—if their reason does not afford sufficient light to direct their conduct whilst unerring instinct is denied—they are surely of all creatures the most miserable! and, bent beneath the iron hand of destiny, must submit to be a *fair defect* in creation. But to justify the ways of Providence respecting them, by pointing out some irrefragable reason for thus making such a large portion of mankind accountable and not accountable, would puzzle the subtilest casuist. . . .

It were to be wished that women would cherish an affection for their husbands, founded on the same principle that devotion ought to rest upon. No other firm base is there under heaven—for let them beware of the fallacious light of sentiment; too often used as a softer phrase for sensuality. It follows then, I think, that from their infancy women should either be shut up like eastern princes, or educated in such a manner as to be able to think and act for themselves.

Why do men halt between two opinions, and expect impossibilities? Why do they expect virtue from a slave, from a being whom the constitution of civil society has rendered weak, if not vicious?

Still I know that it will require a considerable length of time to eradicate the firmly rooted prejudices which sensualists have planted; it will also require some time to convince women that they act contrary to their real interest on an enlarged scale, when they cherish or affect weakness under the name of delicacy, and to convince the world that the poisoned source of female vices and follies, if it be necessary, in compliance with custom, to use synonymous terms in a lax sense, has been the sensual homage paid to beauty:—to beauty of features; for it has been shrewdly observed by a German writer, that a pretty woman, as an object of desire, is generally allowed to be so by men of all descriptions; whilst a fine woman, who inspires more sublime emotions by displaying intellectual beauty, may be overlooked or observed with indifference by those men who find their happiness in the gratification of their appetites. I foresee an obvious retort—whilst man remains such an imperfect being as he appears hitherto to have been, he will, more or less, be the slave of his appetites; and those women obtaining most power who gratify a predominant one, the sex is degraded by a physical, if not by a moral necessity.

This objection has, I grant, some force; but while such a sublime precept exists, as, "Be pure as your heavenly Father is pure;" it would seem that the virtues of man are not limited by the Being who alone could limit them; and that he may press forward without considering whether he steps out of his sphere by indulging such a noble ambition. To the wild billows it has been said, "Thus far shalt thou go, and no further; and here shall thy proud waves be stayed."[22] Vainly then do they beat and foam, restrained by the power that confines the struggling planets in their orbits, matter yields to the great governing Spirit. But an immortal soul, not restrained by mechanical laws and struggling to free itself from the shackles of matter, contributes to, instead of disturbing, the order of creation, when, co-operating with the Father of spirits, it tries to govern itself by the invariable rule that, in a degree, before which our imagination faints, regulates the universe.

Besides, if women be educated for dependence; that is, to act according to the will of another fallible being, and submit, right or wrong, to power, where are we to stop? Are they to be considered as vicegerents allowed to reign over a small domain, and answerable for their conduct to a higher tribunal, liable to error?

It will not be difficult to prove that such delegates will act like men subjected by fear, and make their children and servants endure their tyrannical oppression. As they submit without reason, they will, having no fixed rules to square their conduct by, be kind, or cruel, just as the whim of the moment directs; and we ought not to wonder if sometimes, galled by their heavy yoke, they take a malignant pleasure in resting it on weaker shoulders.

But, supposing a woman, trained up to obedience, be married to a sensible man, who directs her judgment without making her feel the servility of her subjection, to act with as much propriety by this reflected light as can be expected when reason is taken at second hand, yet she cannot ensure the life of her protector; he may die and leave her with a large family.

A double duty devolves on her: to educate them in the character of both father and mother; to form their principles and secure their property. But alas! she has never thought, much less acted for herself. She has only learned to please men, to depend gracefully on them; yet, encumbered with children, how is she to obtain another protector—a husband to supply the place of reason? A rational man, for we are not treading on romantic ground, though he may think her a pleasing docile creature, will not choose to marry a *family* for love, when the world contains many more pretty creatures. What is then to become of her? She either falls an easy prey to some mean fortune-hunter, who defrauds her children of their paternal inheritance, and renders her miserable; or becomes the victim of discontent and blind indulgence. Unable to educate her sons, or impress them with respect; for it is not a play on words to assert, that people are never respected, though filling an important station, who are not respectable; she pines under the anguish of unavailing impotent regret. The serpent's tooth enters into her very soul, and the vices of licentious youth bring her with sorrow, if not with poverty also, to the grave.

This is not an overcharged picture; on the contrary, it is a very possible case, and something similar must have fallen under every attentive eye.

I have, however, taken it for granted, that she was well-disposed, though experience shows, that the blind may as easily be led into a ditch as

[22]Job 38:11.

along the beaten road. But supposing no very improbable conjecture, that a being only taught to please must still find her happiness in pleasing;—what an example of folly, not to say vice, will she be to her innocent daughters! The mother will be lost in the coquette, and, instead of making friends of her daughters, view them with eyes askance, for they are rivals—rivals more cruel than any other, because they invite a comparison, and drive her from the throne of beauty, who has never thought of a seat on the bench of reason.

It does not require a lively pencil, or the discriminating outline of a caricature, to sketch the domestic miseries and petty vices which such a mistress of a family diffuses. Still she only acts as a woman ought to act, brought up according to Rousseau's system. She can never be reproached for being masculine, or turning out of her sphere; nay, she may observe another of his grand rules, and, cautiously preserving her reputation free from spot, be reckoned a good kind of woman. Yet in what respect can she be termed good? She abstains, it is true, without any great struggle, from committing gross crimes; but how does she fulfil her duties? Duties!—in truth she has enough to think of to adorn her body and nurse a weak constitution.

With respect to religion, she never presumed to judge for herself; but conformed, as a dependent creature should, to the ceremonies of the church which she was brought up in, piously believing that wiser heads than her own have settled that business:—and not to doubt is her point of perfection. She therefore pays her tithe of mint and cummin[23]—and thanks her God that she is not as other women are. These are the blessed effects of a good education! These the virtues of man's help-mate!

I must relieve myself by drawing a different picture.

Let fancy now present a woman with a tolerable understanding, for I do not wish to leave the line of mediocrity, whose constitution, strengthened by exercise, has allowed her body to acquire its full vigour; her mind, at the same time, gradually expanding itself to comprehend the moral duties of life, and in what human virtue and dignity consist.

Formed thus by the discharge of the relative duties of her station, she marries from affection, without losing sight of prudence, and looking beyond matrimonial felicity, she secures her husband's respect before it is necessary to exert mean arts to please him and feed a dying flame, which nature doomed to expire when the object became familiar, when friendship and forbearance take place of a more ardent affection. This is the natural death of love, and domestic peace is not destroyed by struggles to prevent its extinction. I also suppose the husband to be virtuous; or she is still more in want of independent principles.

Fate, however, breaks this tie. She is left a widow, perhaps, without a sufficient provision; but she is not desolate! The pang of nature is felt; but after time has softened sorrow into melancholy resignation, her heart turns to her children with redoubled fondness, and anxious to provide for them, affection gives a sacred heroic cast to her maternal duties. She thinks that not only the eye sees her virtuous efforts from whom all her comfort now must flow, and whose approbation is life; but her imagination, a little ab-

[23] A Hebrew ceremonial offering. See Matthew 23:23.

stracted and exalted by grief, dwells on the fond hope that the eyes which her trembling hand closed, may still see how she subdues every wayward passion to fulfil the double duty of being the father as well as the mother of her children. Raised to heroism by misfortunes, she represses the first faint dawning of a natural inclination, before it ripens into love, and in the bloom of life forgets her sex—forgets the pleasure of an awakening passion, which might again have been inspired and returned. She no longer thinks of pleasing, and conscious dignity prevents her from priding herself on account of the praise which her conduct demands. Her children have her love, and her brightest hopes are beyond the grave, where her imagination often strays.

I think I see her surrounded by her children, reaping the reward of her care. The intelligent eye meets hers, whilst health and innocence smile on their chubby cheeks, and as they grow up the cares of life are lessened by their grateful attention. She lives to see the virtues which she endeavoured to plant on principles, fixed into habits, to see her children attain a strength of character sufficient to enable them to endure adversity without forgetting their mother's example.

The task of life thus fulfilled, she calmly waits for the sleep of death, and rising from the grave, may say—Behold, thou gavest me a talent—and here are five talents.[24]

I wish to sum up what I have said in a few words, for I here throw down my gauntlet, and deny the existence of sexual virtues, not excepting modesty. For man and woman, truth, if I understand the meaning of the word, must be the same; yet the fanciful female character, so prettily drawn by poets and novelists, demanding the sacrifice of truth and sincerity, virtue becomes a relative idea, having no other foundation than utility, and of that utility men pretend arbitrarily to judge, shaping it to their own convenience.

Women, I allow, may have different duties to fulfil; but they are *human* duties, and the principles that should regulate the discharge of them, I sturdily maintain, must be the same.

To become respectable, the exercise of their understanding is necessary, there is no other foundation for independence of character; I mean explicitly to say that they must only bow to the authority of reason, instead of being the *modest* slaves of opinion.

In the superior ranks of life how seldom do we meet with a man of superior abilities, or even common acquirements? The reason appears to me clear, the state they are born in was an unnatural one. The human character has ever been formed by the employments the individual, or class, pursues; and if the faculties are not sharpened by necessity, they must remain obtuse. The argument may fairly be extended to women; for, seldom occupied by serious business, the pursuit of pleasure gives that insignificancy to their character which renders the society of the *great* so insipid. The same want of firmness, produced by a similiar cause, forces

[24] In Christ's parable of the talents (Matthew 25:15–28), the servant entrusted with a talent (a sum of money) who merely kept it and returned it to his master was punished; the one who invested it and returned five talents was rewarded.

them both to fly from themselves to noisy pleasures, and artificial passions, till vanity takes place of every social affection, and the characteristics of humanity can scarcely be discerned. Such are the blessings of civil governments, as they are at present organized, that wealth and female softness equally tend to debase mankind, and are produced by the same cause; but allowing women to be rational creatures, they should be incited to acquire virtues which they may call their own, for how can a rational being be ennobled by anything that is not obtained by its *own* exertions?

CHAPTER IX

OF THE PERNICIOUS EFFECTS WHICH ARISE FROM THE UNNATURAL DISTINCTIONS ESTABLISHED IN SOCIETY

From the respect paid to property flow, as from a poisoned fountain, most of the evils and vices which render this world such a dreary scene to the contemplative mind. For it is in the most polished society that noisome reptiles and venomous serpents lurk under the rank herbage; and there is voluptuousness pampered by the still sultry air, which relaxes every good disposition before it ripens into virtue.

One class presses on another; for all are aiming to procure respect on account of their property: and property, once gained, will procure the respect due only to talents and virtue. Men neglect the duties incumbent on man, yet are treated like demi-gods; religion is also separated from morality by a ceremonial veil, yet men wonder that the world is, almost literally speaking, a den of sharpers or oppressors. . . .

It is vain to expect virtue from women till they are in some degree independent of men; nay, it is vain to expect that strength of natural affection which would make them good wives and mothers. Whilst they are absolutely dependent on their husbands they will be cunning, mean, and selfish, and the men who can be gratified by the fawning fondness of spaniel-like affection have not much delicacy, for love is not to be bought, in any sense of the words; its silken wings are instantly shrivelled up when anything beside a return in kind is sought. Yet whilst wealth enervates men, and women live, as it were, by their personal charms, how can we expect them to discharge those ennobling duties which equally require exertion and self-denial? Hereditary property sophisticates[25] the mind, and the unfortunate victims to it, if I may so express myself, swathed from their birth, seldom exert the locomotive faculty of body or mind; and, thus viewing everything through one medium, and that a false one, they are unable to discern in what true merit and happiness consist. False, indeed, must be the light when the drapery of situation hides the man, and makes him stalk in masquerade, dragging from one scene of dissipation to another the nerveless limbs that hang with stupid listlessness, and rolling round the vacant eye which plainly tells us that there is no mind at home.

I mean, therefore, to infer that the society is not properly organized which does not compel men and women to discharge their respective duties, by making it the only way to acquire that countenance from their

[25] Corrupts.

fellow-creatures which every human being wishes some way to attain. The respect, consequently, which is paid to wealth and mere personal charms, is a true north-east blast that blights the tender blossoms of affection and virtue. Nature has wisely attached affections to duties to sweeten toil, and to give that vigour to the exertions of reason which only the heart can give. But the affection which is put on merely because it is the appropriated insignia of a certain character, when its duties are not fulfilled, is one of the empty compliments which vice and folly are obliged to pay to virtue and the real nature of things.

To illustrate my opinion, I need only observe that when a woman is admired for her beauty, and suffers herself to be so far intoxicated by the admiration she receives as to neglect to discharge the indispensable duty of a mother, she sins against herself by neglecting to cultivate an affection that would equally tend to make her useful and happy. True happiness, I mean all the contentment and virtuous satisfaction that can be snatched in this imperfect state, must arise from well regulated affections; and an affection includes a duty. Men are not aware of the misery they cause and the vicious weakness they cherish by only inciting women to render themselves pleasing; they do not consider that they thus make natural and artificial duties clash by sacrificing the comfort and respectability of woman's life to voluptuous notions of beauty when in nature they all harmonize.

Cold would be the heart of a husband, were he not rendered unnatural by early debauchery, who did not feel more delight at seeing his child suckled by its mother, than the most artful wanton tricks could ever raise; yet this natural way of cementing the matrimonial tie and twisting esteem with fonder recollections, wealth leads women to spurn. To preserve their beauty and wear the flowery crown of the day, which gives them a kind of right to reign for a short time over the sex, they neglect to stamp impressions on their husbands' hearts that would be remembered with more tenderness when the snow on the head began to chill the bosom than even their virgin charms. The maternal solicitude of a reasonable affectionate woman is very interesting, and the chastened dignity with which a mother returns the caresses that she and her child receive from a father who has been fulfilling the serious duties of his station, is not only a respectable but a beautiful sight. So singular indeed are my feelings, and I have endeavoured not to catch factitious ones, that after having been fatigued with the sight of insipid grandeur and the slavish ceremonies that with cumbrous pomp supplied the place of domestic affections, I have turned to some other scene to relieve my eye by resting it on the refreshing green everywhere scattered by nature. I have then viewed with pleasure a woman nursing her children, and discharging the duties of her station with, perhaps, merely a servant maid to take off her hands the servile part of the household business. I have seen her prepare herself and children, with only the luxury of cleanliness, to receive her husband, who returning weary home in the evening found smiling babes and a clean hearth. My heart has loitered in the midst of the group, and has even throbbed with sympathetic emotion, when the scraping of the well known foot has raised a pleasing tumult. . . .

The preposterous distinctions of rank, which render civilization a curse by dividing the world between voluptuous tyrants and cunning envious dependents, corrupt, almost equally, every class of people, because respectability is not attached to the discharge of the relative duties of life, but to the station, and when the duties are not fulfilled the affections cannot gain sufficient strength to fortify the virtue of which they are the natural reward. Still there are some loopholes out of which a man may creep, and dare to think and act for himself; but for a woman it is a herculean task, because she has difficulties peculiar to her sex to overcome which require almost superhuman powers.

A truly benevolent legislator always endeavours to make it the interest of each individual to be virtuous; and this private virtue becoming the cement of public happiness, an orderly whole is consolidated by the tendency of all the parts towards a common centre. But, the private or public virtue of woman is very problematical; for Rousseau, and a numerous list of male writers, insist that she should all her life be subjected to a severe restraint, that of propriety. Why subject her to propriety—blind propriety, if she be capable of acting from a nobler spring, if she be an heir of immortality? Is sugar always to be produced by vital blood? Is one half of the human species, like the poor African slaves, to be subject to prejudices that brutalize them, when principles would be a surer guard, only to sweeten the cup of man? Is not this indirectly to deny woman reason? for a gift is a mockery, if it be unfit for use.

Women are, in common with men, rendered weak and luxurious by the relaxing pleasures which wealth procures; but added to this they are made slaves to their persons, and must render them alluring that man may lend them his reason to guide their tottering steps aright. Or should they be ambitious, they must govern their tyrants by sinister tricks, for without rights there cannot be any incumbent duties. The laws respecting woman, which I mean to discuss in a future part, make an absurd unit of a man and his wife; and then, by the easy transition of only considering him as responsible, she is reduced to a mere cypher.[26]

The being who discharges the duties of its station is independent; and, speaking of women at large, their first duty is to themselves as rational creatures, and the next in point of importance, as citizens, is that which includes so many, of a mother. The rank in life which dispenses with their fulfilling this duty necessarily degrades them by making them mere dolls. Or, should they turn to something more important than merely fitting drapery upon a smooth block, their minds are only occupied by some soft platonic attachment; or, the actual management of an intrigue may keep their thoughts in motion; for when they neglect domestic duties, they have it not in their own power to take the field and march and counter-march like soldiers, or wrangle in the senate to keep their faculties from rusting. . . .

But, to render her really virtuous and useful, she must not, if she discharges her civil duties, want, individually, the protection of civil laws; she must not be dependent on her husband's bounty for her subsistence during his life or support after his death—for how can a being be generous who has nothing of its own? or virtuous, who is not free? The wife, in the pres-

[26] English common law regarded a married couple as a legal unit, with the legally responsible person the husband.

ent state of things, who is faithful to her husband, and neither suckles nor educates her children, scarcely deserves the name of a wife, and has no right to that of a citizen. But take away natural rights, and duties become null.

Women then must be considered as only the wanton solace of men when they become so weak in mind and body that they cannot exert themselves, unless to pursue some frothy pleasure or to invent some frivolous fashion. What can be a more melancholy sight to a thinking mind than to look into the numerous carriages that drive helter-skelter about this metropolis in a morning full of pale-faced creatures who are flying from themselves. I have often wished, with Dr. Johnson, to place some of them in a little shop with half a dozen children looking up to their languid countenances for support.[27] I am much mistaken if some latent vigour would not soon give health and spirit to their eyes, and some lines drawn by the exercise of reason on the blank cheeks, which before were only undulated by dimples, might restore lost dignity to the character, or rather enable it to attain the true dignity of its nature. Virtue is not to be acquired even by speculation, much less by the negative supineness that wealth naturally generates.

Besides, when poverty is more disgraceful than even vice, is not morality cut to the quick? Still to avoid misconstruction, though I consider that women in the common walks of life are called to fulfil the duties of wives and mothers, by religion and reason, I cannot help lamenting that women of a superior cast have not a road open by which they can pursue more extensive plans of usefulness and independence. I may excite laughter by dropping a hint which I mean to pursue some future time, for I really think that women ought to have representatives, instead of being arbitrarily governed without having any direct share allowed them in the deliberations of government.

But, as the whole system of representation is now in this country only a convenient handle for despotism, they need not complain, for they are as well represented as a numerous class of hard-working mechanics, who pay for the support of royalty when they can scarcely stop their children's mouths with bread. How are they represented whose very sweat supports the splendid stud of an heir apparent, or varnishes the chariot of some female favourite who looks down on shame? Taxes on the very necessaries of life enable an endless tribe of idle princes and princesses to pass with stupid pomp before a gaping crowd, who almost worship the very parade which costs them so dear. This is mere gothic grandeur, something like the barbarous useless parade of having sentinels on horseback at Whitehall,[28] which I could never view without a mixture of contempt and indignation. . . .

But what have women to do in society? I may be asked, but to loiter with easy grace; surely you would not condemn them all to suckle fools and chronicle small beer![29] No. Women might certainly study the art of healing, and be physicians as well as nurses. And midwifery, decency seems to allot

[27] Samuel Johnson says something of this kind in "The Mischiefs of Total Idleness" (*Rambler* essay, no. 85, Jan. 8, 1751).

[28] Palace in central London, seat of the British government.

[29] This is Iago's description of the function of women: *Othello* II.i.159.

to them, though I am afraid the word midwife in our dictionaries will soon give place to *accoucheur*,[30] and one proof of the former delicacy of the sex be effaced from the language.

They might also study politics, and settle their benevolence on the broadest basis; for the reading of history will scarcely be more useful than the perusal of romances, if read as mere biography; if the character of the times, the political improvements, arts, &c., be not observed. In short, if it be not considered as the history of man; and not of particular men, who filled a niche in the temple of fame, and dropped into the black rolling stream of time, that silently sweeps all before it, into the shapeless void called—eternity. For shape, can it be called, "that shape hath none"?

Business of various kinds they might likewise pursue, if they were educated in a more orderly manner, which might save many from common and legal prostitution. Women would not then marry for a support, as men accept of places under government, and neglect the implied duties; nor would an attempt to earn their own subsistence—a most laudable one!—sink them almost to the level of those poor abandoned creatures who live by prostitution. For are not milliners and mantua-makers[31] reckoned the next class? The few employments open to women, so far from being liberal, are menial; and when a superior education enables them to take charge of the education of children as governesses, they are not treated like the tutors of sons, though even clerical tutors are not always treated in a manner calculated to render them respectable in the eyes of their pupils, to say nothing of the private comfort of the individual. But as women educated like gentlewomen are never designed for the humiliating situation which necessity sometimes forces them to fill, these situations are considered in the light of a degradation; and they know little of the human heart, who need to be told that nothing so painfully sharpens sensibility as such a fall in life.

Some of these women might be restrained from marrying by a proper spirit or delicacy, and others may not have had it in their power to escape in this pitiful way from servitude; is not that government then very defective, and very unmindful of the happiness of one half of its members, that does not provide for honest, independent women, by encouraging them to fill respectable stations? But in order to render their private virtue a public benefit, they must have a civil existence in the state, married or single; else we shall continually see some worthy woman, whose sensibility has been rendered painfully acute by undeserved contempt, droop like "the lily broken down by a plow-share."

It is a melancholy truth—yet such is the blessed effect of civilization!—the most respectable women are the most oppressed; and, unless they have understandings far superior to the common run of understandings, taking in both sexes, they must, from being treated like contemptible beings, become contemptible. How many women thus waste life away the prey of discontent, who might have practised as physicians, regulated a farm, managed a shop, and stood erect, supported by their own industry, instead of hanging their heads surcharged with the dew of sensibility, that consumes the beauty to which it at first gave lustre; nay, I doubt whether pity and love

[30] A male attendant at childbirth. [31] Dressmakers.

are so near akin as poets feign, for I have seldom seen much compassion excited by the helplessness of females, unless they were fair; then, perhaps, pity was the soft handmaid of love, or the harbinger of lust.

How much more respectable is the woman who earns her own bread by fulfilling any duty, than the most accomplished beauty!—beauty did I say?—so sensible am I of the beauty of moral loveliness, or the harmonious propriety that attunes the passions of a well-regulated mind, that I blush at making the comparison; yet I sigh to think how few women aim at attaining this respectability by withdrawing from the giddy whirl of pleasure, or the indolent calm that stupefies the good sort of women it sucks in.

Proud of their weakness, however, they must always be protected, guarded from care, and all the rough toils that dignify the mind. If this be the fiat of fate, if they will make themselves insignificant and contemptible, sweetly to waste "life away," let them not expect to be valued when their beauty fades, for it is the fate of the fairest flowers to be admired and pulled to pieces by the careless hand that plucked them. In how many ways do I wish, from the purest benevolence, to impress this truth on my sex; yet I fear that they will not listen to a truth that dear-bought experience has brought home to many an agitated bosom, nor willingly resign the privileges of rank and sex for the privileges of humanity, to which those have no claim who do not discharge its duties.

Those writers are particularly useful, in my opinion, who make man feel for man, independent of the station he fills, or the drapery of factitious sentiments. I then would fain convince reasonable men of the importance of some of my remarks; and prevail on them to weigh dispassionately the whole tenor of my observations. I appeal to their understandings; and, as a fellow-creature, claim, in the name of my sex, some interest in their hearts. I entreat them to assist to emancipate their companion, to make her a *help meet* for them!

Would men but generously snap our chains, and be content with rational fellowship instead of slavish obedience, they would find us more observant daughters, more affectionate sisters, more faithful wives, more reasonable mothers—in a word, better citizens. We should then love them with true affection, because we should learn to respect ourselves; and the peace of mind of a worthy man would not be interrupted by the idle vanity of his wife, nor the babes sent to nestle in a strange bosom, having never found a home in their mother's.

CHAPTER X

Parental Affection

Parental affection is, perhaps, the blindest modification of perverse self-love. . . . Parents often love their children in the most brutal manner, and sacrifice every relative duty to promote their advancement in the world.—To promote, such is the perversity of unprincipled prejudices, the future welfare of the very beings whose present existence they embitter by the most despotic stretch of power. Power, in fact, is ever true to its vital principle, for in every shape it would reign without control or inquiry. Its throne is built across a dark abyss, which no eye must dare to explore, lest the baseless fabric should totter under investigation. Obedience, unconditional obedience, is the catch-word of tyrants of every description, and to render "assurance doubly sure,"[32] one kind of despotism supports another. Tyrants would have cause to tremble if reason were to become the rule of duty in any of the relations of life, for the light might spread till perfect day appeared. And when it did appear, how would men smile at the sight of the bugbears at which they started during the night of ignorance, or the twilight of timid inquiry.

Parental affection, indeed, in many minds, is but a pretext to tyrannize where it can be done with impunity, for only good and wise men are content with the respect that will bear discussion. Convinced that they have a right to what they insist on, they do not fear reason, or dread the sifting of subjects that recur to natural justice: because they firmly believe that the more enlightened the human mind becomes the deeper root will just and simple principles take. . . .

Woman, however, a slave in every situation to prejudice, seldom exerts enlightened maternal affection; for she either neglects her children, or spoils them by improper indulgence. Besides, the affection of some women for their children is, as I have before termed it, frequently very brutish: for it eradicates every spark of humanity. Justice, truth, everything is sacrificed by these Rebekahs,[33] and for the sake of their *own* children they violate the most sacred duties, forgetting the common relationship that binds the whole family on earth together. Yet, reason seems to say, that they who suffer one duty, or affection, to swallow up the rest, have not sufficient heart or mind to fulfil that one conscientiously. It then loses the venerable aspect of a duty, and assumes the fantastic form of a whim.

As the care of children in their infancy is one of the grand duties annexed to the female character by nature, this duty would afford many forcible arguments for strengthening the female understanding, if it were properly considered.

The formation of the mind must be begun very early, and the temper, in particular, requires the most judicious attention—an attention which women cannot pay who only love their children because they are their children, and seek no further for the foundation of their duty, than in the feelings of the moment. It is this want of reason in their affections which makes women so often run into extremes, and either be the most fond or most careless and unnatural mothers.

To be a good mother—a woman must have sense, and that independence of mind which few women possess who are taught to depend entirely on their husbands. Meek wives are, in general, foolish mothers; wanting their children to love them best, and take their part, in secret, against the father, who is held up as a scarecrow. When chastisement is necessary, though they have offended the mother, the father must inflict the punishment; he must be the judge in all disputes: but I shall more fully discuss this subject when I treat of private education; I now only mean to insist, that unless the understanding of woman be enlarged, and her character ren-

[32] *Macbeth* IV.i.83

[33] Scheming mothers, from Rebekah, who tried to get Isaac's blessing for her favorite son Jacob over his brother Esau (Genesis 27).

dered more firm, by being allowed to govern her own conduct, she will never have sufficient sense or command of temper to manage her children properly. Her parental affection, indeed, scarcely deserves the name, when it does not lead her to suckle her children, because the discharge of this duty is equally calculated to inspire maternal and filial affection: and it is the indispensable duty of men and women to fulfil the duties which give birth to affections that are the surest preservatives against vice. Natural affection, as it is termed, I believe to be a very faint tie; affections must grow out of the habitual exercise of a mutual sympathy: and what sympathy does a mother exercise who sends her babe to a nurse, and only takes it from a nurse to send it to a school?

In the exercise of their maternal feelings providence has furnished women with a natural substitute for love, when the lover becomes only a friend, and mutual confidence takes place of overstrained admiration—a child then gently twists the relaxing cord, and a mutual care produces a new mutual sympathy. But a child, though a pledge of affection, will not enliven it, if both father and mother be content to transfer the charge to hirelings; for they who do their duty by proxy should not murmur if they miss the reward of duty—parental affection produces filial duty.

CHAPTER XII

On National Education

I have already animadverted on the bad habits which females acquire when they are shut up together; and I think that the observation may fairly be extended to the other sex, till the natural inference is drawn which I have had in view throughout—that to improve both sexes they ought, not only in private families, but in public schools, to be educated together. If marriage be the cement of society, mankind should all be educated after the same model, or the intercourse of the sexes will never deserve the name of fellowship, nor will women ever fulfil the peculiar duties of their sex, till they become enlightened citizens, till they become free by being enabled to earn their own subsistence, independent of men; in the same manner, I mean, to prevent misconstruction, as one man is independent of another. Nay, marriage will never be held sacred till women, by being brought up with men, are prepared to be their companions rather than their mistresses; for the mean doublings of cunning will ever render them contemptible, whilst oppression renders them timid. So convinced am I of this truth, that I will venture to predict that virtue will never prevail in society till the virtues of both sexes are founded on reason; and, till the affections common to both are allowed to gain their due strength by the discharge of mutual duties.

Were boys and girls permitted to pursue the same studies together, those graceful decencies might early be inculcated which produce modesty without those sexual distinctions that taint the mind. Lessons of politeness, and that formulary of decorum which treads on the heels of falsehood, would be rendered useless by habitual propriety of behaviour. Not, indeed, put on for visitors like the courtly robe of politeness, but the sober effect of cleanliness of mind. Would not this simple elegance of sincerity be a chaste homage paid to domestic affections, far surpassing the meretricious compliments that shine with false lustre in the heartless intercourse of fashionable life? But, till more understanding preponderates in society, there will ever be a want of heart and taste, and the harlot's *rouge* will supply the place of that celestial suffusion which only virtuous affections can give to the face. Gallantry, and what is called love, may subsist without simplicity of character; but the main pillars of friendship are respect and confidence—esteem is never founded on it cannot tell what! . . .

True taste is ever the work of the understanding employed in observing natural effects; and till women have more understanding, it is vain to expect them to possess domestic taste. Their lively senses will ever be at work to harden their hearts, and the emotions struck out of them will continue to be vivid and transitory, unless a proper education store their mind with knowledge.

It is the want of domestic taste, and not the acquirement of knowledge, that takes women out of their families, and tears the smiling babe from the breast that ought to afford it nourishment. Women have been allowed to remain in ignorance, and slavish dependence, many, very many years, and still we hear of nothing but their fondness of pleasure and sway, their preference of rakes and soldiers, their childish attachment to toys, and the vanity that makes them value accomplishments more than virtues. . . .

Let an enlightened nation then try what effect reason would have to bring them back to nature, and their duty; and allowing them to share the advantages of education and government with man, see whether they will become better as they grow wiser and become free. They cannot be injured by the experiment; for it is not in the power of man to render them more insignificant than they are at present.

To render this practicable, day schools, for particular ages, should be established by government, in which boys and girls might be educated together. The school for the younger children, from five to nine years of age, ought to be absolutely free and open to all classes. A sufficient number of masters should also be chosen by a select committee, in each parish, to whom any complaint of negligence, &c., might be made, if signed by six of the children's parents. . . .

To prevent any of the distinctions of vanity, they should be dressed alike, and all obliged to submit to the same discipline, or leave the school. The school-room ought to be surrounded by a large piece of ground, in which the children might be usefully exercised, for at this age they should not be confined to any sedentary employment for more than an hour at a time. But these relaxations might all be rendered a part of elementary education, for many things improve and amuse the senses, when introduced as a kind of show, to the principles of which, dryly laid down, children would turn a deaf ear. For instance, botany, mechanics, and astronomy. Reading, writing, arithmetic, natural history, and some simple experiments in natural philosophy, might fill up the day; but these pursuits should never encroach on gymnastic plays in the open air. The elements of religion, history, the history of man, and politics, might also be taught by conversations, in the socratic form.

After the age of nine, girls and boys, intended for domestic employments, or mechanical trades, ought to be removed to other schools, and receive instruction in some measure appropriated to the destination of each individual, the two sexes being still together in the morning; but in the afternoon the girls should attend a school where plain-work, mantua-making, millinery, &c., would be their employment.

The young people of superior abilities, or fortune, might now be taught, in another school, the dead and living languages, the elements of science, and continue the study of history and politics, on a more extensive scale, which would not exclude polite literature.

Girls and boys still together? I hear some readers ask: yes. And I should not fear any other consequence than that some early attachment might take place; which, whilst it had the best effect on the moral character of the young people, might not perfectly agree with the views of the parents, for it will be a long time, I fear, before the world will be so far enlightened that parents, only anxious to render their children virtuous, shall allow them to choose companions for life themselves.

Besides, this would be a sure way to promote early marriages, and from early marriages the most salutary physical and moral effects naturally flow. What a different character does a married citizen assume from the selfish coxcomb, who lives but for himself, and who is often afraid to marry lest he should not be able to live in a certain style. Great emergencies excepted, which would rarely occur in a society of which equality was the basis, a man can only be prepared to discharge the duties of public life by the habitual practice of those inferior ones which form the man.

In this plan of education the constitution of boys would not be ruined by the early debaucheries which now make men so selfish, or girls rendered weak and vain by indolence and frivolous pursuits. But, I presuppose that such a degree of equality should be established between the sexes as would shut out gallantry and coquetry, yet allow friendship and love to temper the heart for the discharge of higher duties.

These would be schools of morality—and the happiness of man, allowed to flow from the pure springs of duty and affection, what advances might not the human mind make? Society can only be happy and free in proportion as it is virtuous; but the present distinctions, established in society, corrode all private and blast all public virtue.

I have already inveighed against the custom of confining girls to their needle, and shutting them out from all political and civil employments; for by thus narrowing their minds they are rendered unfit to fulfill the peculiar duties which nature has assigned them.

Only employed about the little incidents of the day, they necessarily grow up cunning. My very soul has often sickened at observing the sly tricks practised by women to gain some foolish thing on which their silly hearts were set. Not allowed to dispose of money, or call anything their own, they learn to turn the market penny; or, should a husband offend, by staying from home, or give rise to some emotions of jealousy—a new gown, or any pretty bawble, smooths Juno's angry brow.[34]

But these *littlenesses* would not degrade their character, if women were led to respect themselves, if political and moral subjects were opened to them; and I will venture to affirm that this is the only way to make them

[34]Juno (Hera) is the wife of Jupiter (Zeus) in classical mythology.

properly attentive to their domestic duties. An active mind embraces the whole circle of its duties, and finds time enough for all. It is not, I assert, a bold attempt to emulate masculine virtues; it is not the enchantment of literary pursuits, or the steady investigation of scientific subjects, that leads women astray from duty. No, it is indolence and vanity—the love of pleasure and the love of sway, that will reign paramount in an empty mind. I say empty emphatically, because the education which women now receive scarcely deserves the name. For the little knowledge that they are led to acquire, during the important years of youth, is merely relative to accomplishments; and accomplishments without a bottom, for unless the understanding be cultivated, superficial and monotonous is every grace. Like the charms of a made up face, they only strike the senses in a crowd; but at home, wanting mind, they want variety. The consequence is obvious; in gay scenes of dissipation we meet the artificial mind and face, for those who fly from solitude dread, next to solitude, the domestic circle; not having it in their power to amuse or interest, they feel their own insignificance, or find nothing to amuse or interest themselves.

Besides, what can be more indelicate than a girl's *coming out* in the fashionable world? Which, in other words, is to bring to market a marriageable miss, whose person is taken from one public place to another, richly caparisoned. Yet, mixing in the giddy circle under restraint, these butterflies long to flutter at large, for the first affection of their souls is their own persons, to which their attention has been called with the most sedulous care whilst they were preparing for the period that decides their fate for life. Instead of pursuing this idle routine, sighing for tasteless show and heartless state, with what dignity would the youths of both sexes form attachments in the schools that I have cursorily pointed out; in which, as life advanced, dancing, music, and drawing might be admitted as relaxations, for at these schools young people of fortune ought to remain, more or less, till they were of age. Those who were designed for particular professions might attend, three or four mornings in the week, the schools appropriated for their immediate instruction. . . .

I know that libertines will also exclaim, that woman would be unsexed by acquiring strength of body and mind, and that beauty, soft bewitching beauty! would no longer adorn the daughters of men. I am of a very different opinion, for I think that, on the contrary, we should then see dignified beauty, and true grace; to produce which, many powerful physical and moral causes would concur. Not relaxed beauty, it is true, or the graces of helplessness; but such as appears to make us respect the human body as a majestic pile fit to receive a noble inhabitant, in the relics of antiquity. . . .

My observations on national education are obviously hints; but I principally wish to enforce the necessity of educating the sexes together to perfect both, and of making children sleep at home that they may learn to love home; yet to make private support, instead of smothering, public affections, they should be sent to school to mix with a number of equals, for only by the jostlings of equality can we form a just opinion of ourselves.

To render mankind more virtuous, and happier of course, both sexes must act from the same principle; but how can that be expected when only one is allowed to see the reasonableness of it? To render also the social compact truly equitable, and in order to spread those enlightening principles which alone can meliorate the fate of man, women must be allowed to found their virtue on knowledge, which is scarcely possible unless they be educated by the same pursuits as men. For they are made so inferior by ignorance and low desires, as not to deserve to be ranked with them; or, by the serpentine wrigglings of cunning they mount the tree of knowledge, and only acquire sufficient to lead men astray.

It is plain from the history of all nations, that women cannot be confined to merely domestic pursuits, for they will not fulfil family duties, unless their minds take a wider range, and whilst they are kept in ignorance they become in the same proportion the slaves of pleasure as they are the slaves of man. Nor can they be shut out of great enterprises, though the narrowness of their minds often make them mar, what they are unable to comprehend.

The libertinism, and even the virtues of superior men, will always give women, of some description, great power over them; and these weak women, under the influence of childish passions and selfish vanity, will throw a false light over the objects which the very men view with their eyes, who ought to enlighten their judgment. Men of fancy, and those sanguine characters who mostly hold the helm of human affairs, in general, relax in the society of women; and surely I need not cite to the most superficial reader of history the numerous examples of vice and oppression which the private intrigues of female favourites have produced; not to dwell on the mischief that naturally arises from the blundering interposition of well-meaning folly. For in the transactions of business it is much better to have to deal with a knave than a fool, because a knave adheres to some plan; and any plan of reason may be seen through much sooner than a sudden flight of folly. The power which vile and foolish women have had over wise men, who possessed sensibility, is notorious; I shall only mention one instance.

Who ever drew a more exalted female character than Rousseau? though in the lump he constantly endeavoured to degrade the sex. And why was he thus anxious? Truly to justify to himself the affection which weakness and virtue had made him cherish for that fool Theresa.[35] He could not raise her to the common level of her sex; and therefore he laboured to bring woman down to hers. He found her a convenient humble companion, and pride made him determine to find some superior virtues in the being whom he chose to live with; but did not her conduct during his life, and after his death, clearly show how grossly he was mistaken who called her a celestial innocent? Nay, in the bitterness of his heart he himself laments, that when his bodily infirmities made him no longer treat her like a woman, she ceased to have an affection for him. And it was very natural that she should, for having so few sentiments in common, when the sexual tie was broken, what was to hold her? To hold her affection whose sensibility was confined to one sex, nay, to one man, it requires sense to turn sensibility into the broad channel of humanity; many women have not mind enough to have an affection for a woman, or a friendship for a man. But the sexual weakness that makes woman depend upon a man for subsistence, produces a kind of cattish affection which leads a wife to purr about her husband as she would about any man who fed and caressed her.

[35] Thérèse Le Vasseur was Rousseau's common-law wife.

Men are, however, often gratified by this kind of fondness, which is confined in a beastly manner to themselves; but should they ever become more virtuous, they will wish to converse at their fireside with a friend, after they cease to play with a mistress.

Besides, understanding is necessary to give variety and interest to sensual enjoyments, for low, indeed, in the intellectual scale is the mind that can continue to love when neither virtue nor sense give a human appearance to an animal appetite. But sense will always preponderate; and if women be not, in general, brought more on a level with men, some superior women, like the Greek courtezans, will assemble the men of abilities around them, and draw from their families many citizens who would have stayed at home had their wives had more sense, or the graces which result from the exercise of understanding and fancy, the legitimate parents of taste. A woman of talents, if she be not absolutely ugly, will always obtain great power, raised by the weakness of her sex; and in proportion as men acquire virtue and delicacy, by the exertion of reason, they will look for both in women, but they can only acquire them in the same way that men do.

In France or Italy, have the women confined themselves to domestic life? though they have not hitherto had a political existence, yet, have they not illicitly had great sway? corrupting themselves and the men with whose passions they played. In short, in whatever light I view the subject, reason and experience convince me that the only method of leading women to fulfil their peculiar duties, is to free them from all restraint by allowing them to participate in the inherent rights of mankind.

Make them free, and they will quickly become wise and virtuous, as men become more so; for the improvement must be mutual, or the injustice which one half of the human race are obliged to submit to, retorting on their oppressors, the virtue of man will be worm-eaten by the insect whom he keeps under his feet.

Let men take their choice, man and woman were made for each other, though not to become one being; and if they will not improve women, they will deprave them!

I speak of the improvement and emancipation of the whole sex, for I know that the behaviour of a few women, who, by accident, or by following a strong bent of nature, have acquired a portion of knowledge superior to that of the rest of their sex, has often been overbearing; but there have been instances of women who, attaining knowledge, have not discarded modesty, nor have they always pedantically appeared to despise the ignorance which they laboured to disperse in their own minds. The exclamations then which any advice respecting female learning commonly produces, especially from pretty women, often arise from envy. When they chance to see that even the lustre of their eyes and the flippant sportiveness of refined coquetry will not always secure them attention, during a whole evening, should a woman of a more cultivated understanding endeavour to give a rational turn to the conversation, the common source of consolation is, that such women seldom get husbands. What arts have I not seen silly women use to interrupt by *flirtation*—a very significant word to describe such a maneuver—a rational conversation which made the men forget that they were pretty women.

But, allowing what is very natural to man, that the possession of rare abilities is calculated to excite overweening pride, disgusting in both men and women—in what a state of inferiority must the female faculties have rusted when such a small portion of knowledge as those women attained, who have sneeringly been termed learned women, could be singular?—Sufficiently so to puff up the possessor, and excite envy in her contemporaries, and some of the other sex. Nay, has not a little rationality exposed many women to the severest censure? I advert to well known facts, for I have frequently heard women ridiculed, and every little weakness exposed, only because they adopted the advice of some medical men, and deviated from the beaten track in their mode of treating their infants. I have actually heard this barbarous aversion to innovation carried still further, and a sensible woman stigmatized as an unnatural mother, who has thus been wisely solicitous to preserve the health of her children, when in the midst of her care she has lost one by some of the casualties of infancy, which no prudence can ward off. Her acquaintance has observed, that this was the consequence of new-fangled notions—the new-fangled notions of ease and cleanliness. And those who pretending to experience, though they have long adhered to prejudices that have, according to the opinions of the most sagacious physicians, thinned the human race, almost rejoiced at the disaster that gave a kind of sanction to prescription.

Indeed, if it were only on this account, the national education of women is of the utmost consequence, for what a number of human sacrifices are made to that moloch[36] prejudice! And in how many ways are children destroyed by the lasciviousness of man? The want of natural affection in many women, who are drawn from their duty by the admiration of men, and the ignorance of others, render the infancy of man a much more perilous state than that of brutes; yet men are unwilling to place women in situations proper to enable them to acquire sufficient understanding to know how even to nurse their babes.

So forcibly does this truth strike me, that I would rest the whole tendency of my reasoning upon it, for whatever tends to incapacitate the maternal character, takes woman out of her sphere. . . .

In public schools women, to guard against the errors of ignorance, should be taught the elements of anatomy and medicine, not only to enable them to take proper care of their own health, but to make them rational nurses of their infants, parents, and husbands; for the bills of mortality are swelled by the blunders of self-willed old women, who give nostrums of their own without knowing anything of the human frame. It is likewise proper only in a domestic view, to make women acquainted with the anatomy of the mind, by allowing the sexes to associate together in every pursuit; and by leading them to observe the progress of the human understanding in the improvement of the sciences and arts; never forgetting the science of morality, or the study of the political history of mankind.

A man has been termed a microcosm; and every family might also be called a state. States, it is true, have mostly been governed by arts that disgrace the character of man; and the want of a just constitution, and equal laws, have so perplexed the notions of the worldly wise, that they

[36] A "moloch" is an idol, from the Canaanite god of fire, to whom children were sacrificed.

more than question the reasonableness of contending for the rights of humanity. Thus morality, polluted in the national reservoir, sends off streams of vice to corrupt the constituent part of the body politic; but should more noble, or rather more just principles regulate the laws, which ought to be the government of society, and not those who execute them, duty might become the rule of private conduct.

Besides, by the exercise of their bodies and minds women would acquire that mental activity so necessary in the maternal character, united with the fortitude that distinguishes steadiness of conduct from the obstinate perverseness of weakness. For it is dangerous to advise the indolent to be steady, because they instantly become rigorous, and to save themselves trouble, punish with severity faults that the patient fortitude of reason might have prevented.

But fortitude presupposes strength of mind; and is strength of mind to be acquired by indolent acquiescence? by asking advice instead of exerting the judgment? by obeying through fear, instead of practising the forbearance, which we all stand in need of ourselves?—The conclusion which I wish to draw is obvious; make women rational creatures, and free citizens, and they will quickly become good wives and mothers; that is—if men do not neglect the duties of husbands and fathers.

Discussing the advantages which a public and private education combined, as I have sketched, might rationally be expected to produce, I have dwelt most on such as are particularly relative to the female world, because I think the female world oppressed; yet the gangrene, which the vices engendered by oppression have produced, is not confined to the morbid part, but pervades society at large: so that when I wish to see my sex become more like moral agents, my heart bounds with the anticipation of the general diffusion of that sublime contentment which only morality can diffuse.

William Blake

(1757–1827)

The number of spiritually lonely artists neglected in their time and canonized by posterity only after their deaths is not as great as popular imagination conceives, but there have been some, and William Blake was among them. His writings (he was also a great painter) reached only a tiny audience during his life. For forty years after he died almost none of his work was known, and then for another sixty it was very imperfectly understood. The fault did not lie entirely with a blind and unfeeling world. Most of Blake's literary work was issued in a format that—contrary to his hopes and intentions—precluded wide readership, and his last, longest poems are forbiddingly complex to the point of seeming incoherent. Those who have committed their minds and imaginative energies to Blake's kaleidoscopic, mythic epics have been rewarded with an awed exhilaration comparable to what James Joyce's devotees get from Finnegans Wake, *but there are still people who doubt that the effort (for either* writer) is worth it. Whoever is right, there is a strong irony here, for in lyrics like *Songs of Innocence and of Experience*, most of *The Marriage of Heaven and Hell*, the wonderful marginalia he recorded in books he owned, and notebook epigrams, Blake proves that he can say things with an almost unique gnomic economy and bluntness. He hated "mystery"—religious or scientifically rationalist—with his whole soul and mind. The crowning irony is that there is far greater agreement, among those who have studied them, about the meaning of his "incomprehensible" poems than about the more accessible ones such as *Thel* and the *Songs*, which have been read in wildly different ways.

The intensity of Blake's work contrasts with the tenor of his life, in which there were few dramatic peaks. The son of a hosier and haberdasher, he was born in 1757, in London, where except for three years he spent his whole life. He was endowed with hyperacute visual powers, from boyhood onward seeing and imagining things with a preternatural clarity that must be distinguished from the mystic's sensory blackout where, in Wordsworth's phrase, "we are laid asleep in body and become a living soul." At ten Blake began formal study of drawing (of conventional education he had none), and by twenty-one he had completed a seven-year apprenticeship as an engraver, which thereafter was his bread-and-butter occupation. He also studied for a time at the Royal Academy of Art, developing an antipathy to its eminent president, Sir Joshua Reynolds, and his approved style of painting. Blake believed that the line was everything in artistic technique and despised painters like Rembrandt who produced murky "blurs." This principle remained with him, his passion for clarity of outline in art, and for watercolors instead of oils, coalescing with his philosophical detestation of "mystery." In 1782 he married the illiterate Catherine Boucher, who seems to have fallen in love with him at first sight; Blake taught her to write, and she became a valuable collaborator in his artistic work. In 1787 he lost a beloved younger brother, Robert, who according to Blake remained a source of visionary inspiration to him thereafter.

In 1783 Blake's only conventionally printed book appeared, a collection of youthful poems and other pieces called *Poetical Sketches*. In 1789 he produced *Songs of Innocence*, his first important volume in the unique format of illuminated etching he continued to use, with some variation, in his literary work from then on. The method was to compose a design, usually a combination of text and picture, transfer it to a copper plate in an acid-resistant medium, etch away the remaining surface, make inked impressions on good paper, and then hand-color each page of each work. This process was not only an effort by a man uniquely gifted as both great poet and painter to exercise both his talents; it was also symptomatic of a synthesizing impulse in Blake's mind as a whole, a physical emblem of the unification of the powers of the human psyche whose division from one another, he believed, is reflected in the personal and political distresses of the world. The relationship of picture to text is sometimes straightforward, but more often it is indirect, and frequently it is ironical. The text of the last plate of *The Book of Thel*, for example, dramatizes a world of tortured sexuality, but the picture shows three naked children of both sexes—true innocents—riding a phallic serpent-monster with blithe nonchalance.

Between 1789 and 1795 Blake created a number of relatively short volumes by this method. (Their dates overlap somewhat.) Two of them—*Thel* and *Visions of the Daughters of Albion*—explore the theme of human growth in connection with sexual repression and freedom, *Visions* extending the theme to include the status of women and black slavery. This poem was written under the influence of Mary Wollstonecraft, author of A Vindication of the Rights of Woman (1792), who along with Blake and other radicals gathered around the leftist publisher Joseph Johnson in the revolutionary 1790s. The Marriage of Heaven and Hell, written in reaction against the Swedish mystic Emanuel Swedenborg whom Blake had once admired, is a titanically impudent satire calling for the release of creative "infernal" energies from the control imposed by an "angelic" Establishment in state, church, and personal morality. Three works—America, Europe, and The Song of Los—make up a political trilogy, in the vein of the "Song of Liberty" which concludes The Marriage, placing the American and French Revolutions in the context of a long-range myth going back beyond the time of Christ but also presenting historical protagonists. George III, Washington, Paine, Franklin, Hancock, and the others are cast in colossal molds, like Greek titans or Norse gods; these for Blake were truer portraits than "realistic" depictions of bewigged, bespectacled Enlightenment colonists. Another trilogy—the Books of Urizen, Ahania, and Los—is psychological, tracing the causes of the fallen—that is, crippled—human psyche in terms of a secession by Urizen ("your reason") from the primal unity of the human faculties. In 1794 Blake issued Songs of Experience, combining it pointedly with the earlier Innocence to produce one of the world's greatest volumes of lyric poetry.

In several of these works, especially the political and psychological trilogies, Blake was working toward a grander mythic vision that after 1795 absorbed his energies as poet. The first epic was The Four Zoas (about 1795 to 1803; left in manuscript), in which Blake personified in Zoas—"living creatures"—the four basic faculties in man—reason, passion, imagination, and instinct—whose strife with one another and alienation from what is best in themselves (personified in female "Emanations") are the root of both individual neurosis and social evil. As in Visions of the Daughters of Albion, the vehicle for these themes is "the torments of love and jealousy." His next epic, Milton (about 1800 to 1810), arose in part from personal frictions. William Hayley, a prominent if undistinguished poet and man of letters, invited Blake to join him in the country at Felpham on the coast south of London, where Blake lived from 1800 to 1803. Despite Hayley's sincere wish to help him, Blake came to see Hayley as a spiritual enemy, threatening to lead Blake from his true vocation as poet-prophet into the byways of genteel art. Milton allegorizes this test of artistic integrity as part of its larger story, in which the great poet, admired by Blake above all others except the biblical authors, renounces his place in Heaven and goes back to earth so that, reincarnated in Blake, he may fulfill his revolutionary, visionary potential and redeem his Puritan errors. This concept, outrageous on its face, was typical of Blake's attitude toward writers of the past; in his book illustrations he treated them not as having had their final say but rather as still-living presences continually striving to correct and perfect their prophetic visions with the collaboration of their fellow-prophet Blake. While he was at Felpham, the most dramatic incident in Blake's life occurred when he expelled a soldier from his garden and in turn was charged with, then tried for, treason. He was acquitted, but the episode helped shape the symbolism of Blake's final epic, Jerusalem: The Emanation of the Giant Albion (about 1804 to 1820). It was the culmination of his many attempts to fuse the themes of personal and social redemption. The title epitomizes Blake's view of his place in the tradition of biblical prophecy: Albion is England and also mankind; Jerusalem—a city and a woman—is the holy city of the biblical Jews and also man's exiled spiritual freedom, enslaved as the Jews were by Babylon. The symbolic juxtapositions reflect Blake's conviction that he must be to his own nation what prophets like Ezekiel were to theirs. It is these three epics especially that have earned Blake his reputation for obscurity. They are unquestionably difficult, but also sublime; in their combination of intensity of feeling, extravagance of thematic elaboration, boldness of formal innovation, and sheer mental power, they have a close analogue in the late music of Beethoven (which, in fact, was written at the same time).

In 1809 Blake gave a public exhibition of his paintings, partly to promote his idea for the use of portable frescos in public buildings, but he won no converts. The next decade of his life was an unhappy one about which we do not know a great deal. But in his last years Blake was discovered admiringly by a band of gifted young artists, and he responded with some of his best pictorial work, including illustrations to the Book of Job and Dante, where his reinterpretations of his sources merged their visions with his own in the way typical of him. He died—while singing, it is said—in August, 1827 (four months after Beethoven).

Those who regret Blake's turn from lyric to epic prophecy may have a case, but to see it as simply a move from clarity to obscurity is misleading. The *Songs* are plain in their language and rather conventional in symbolism, but the impression of forthright directness one gets from a first reading does not survive re-readings. Actually, they are enormously complex. "My Pretty Rose Tree," for example, obviously portrays a man whose marital fidelity goes unappreciated by his wife, but a half dozen other possible scenarios gradually emerge, some of them very different in their implications. And if this richness is discernible within individual poems, it is further enhanced when one reads the *Songs* complete, as one should, and listens for the powerful resonances between them. They are most patent in the explicitly contrasting poems with identical or parallel titles, but in fact they pulsate throughout. The relation of the black "little black boy" in the poem so named and the white little black boy of the "Chimney Sweeper" poems is synergistic.

The *Songs* make one of the most powerful statements ever of social protest; yet, in Blake's characteristic way, they simultaneously explore the intimate recesses of individual minds. "London" is a howl of anger over the tyranny of institutions, but, like all the *Songs*, it also reveals the speaker's attitudes; one notes the intention stated in the volume's subtitle to show "the two contrary states of the human soul." He is a sensitive and acute social critic, but his repeated "every" may suggest his own victimization by "mind-forged manacles" that blind him to everything except horror. If that is true, it by no means lets the world's tyrants off the hook; damaged psyches are as tragic as damaged bodies. The problem that challenges him and the other speakers is how to integrate the innocent's trust with experience, love with knowledge, in a vision that transcends half-truths.

Innocence and Experience are "contraries" between which there should exist, Blake believed, a healthily creative rather than a mutually destructive relationship. This theme of "contraries" is explicit in *The Marriage of Heaven and Hell*, but the desired war between energy and its containment preached there is problematical. Blake suggests that the "prolific" devils need the "devouring" angels; yet he is clearly of the devil's party. One can hardly imagine a reader at all attuned to Blake opting to be an "angel" on the grounds that it takes all types, stodgy as well as vibrant, to make a world. *The Marriage* is satire, and even-handed fairness is not the satirist's business. *Thel* and *Visions of the Daughters of Albion* present an even more complex problem. Superficially, that may seem untrue, since it is hard to imagine Blake's endorsing Thel's apparent retreat from the world or his not endorsing the views of his noble, rhetorically irresistible Oothoon. But there is a question, for some readers at least, whether Thel should be dismissed as simply a coward avoiding the challenge to grow. As for Oothoon, we may wonder whether the price of her spiritual liberation (her external condition is still slavery) includes not only rape and the contemptible Theotormon's neurotic jealousy but also psychic damage. For example, are we to accept her sordid vision of marriage as necessarily more realistic than what the Clod of Clay in Thel says about it? It is such questions as these, not the meaning of the seemingly incoherent long epics, that divide Blakeans most passionately.

Probably the most vexing problems for new readers of Blake (and some more seasoned ones) arise from his views of religion and of the relationship between nature, mind, and the senses. The key to both problems is Blake's belief in the literal divinity of humankind. The fundamental reality for Blake is the human imagination, which is almost identical with one's identity and consciousness. He therefore believed in the divine inspiration of the Old Testament, with its fundamental premise that man is God's image (Genesis 1:26–27; and see Blake's "The Divine Image") and its history of intimacy between man and God. (He rejected the complementary Jewish idea that God is unapproachably Other.) Even more emphatically, Blake was a Christian, believing that the New Testament shows the literal union, in time and eternity, of the divine and human in the person of Jesus. (Blake's Christianity is most evident in his later works, but it is implicit from the beginning.) He believed that most of the evils in the world are actually parodies of the true and good; war between nations, for example, is an appallingly twisted version of the life-giving war of contraries that energizes the healthy human mind and ought to operate in society. Christianity as the churches teach it is for Blake one of these demonic parodies, turning the doctrine of the Incarnation into a one-way avenue by which a suprahuman and infinitely superior God descends to a lesser human condition, patiently tolerating in his human disguise the misconception that he is one of us. Blake believed in the Incarnation too, literally, but he reversed the direction of its thrust, seeing Jesus as achieving the Godhood latent but paralyzed in other human beings. This view is not to be confused with that of certain nineteenth-century religious liberals who saw in Jesus an incomparable ethical model on the plane of mere nature. Blake's view of the divine humanity in Jesus is just as supernatural as that of the theologians: Jesus transcended nature, among other things through his miracles (if the subject believed), and so can we all. In fact, Blake believed we all do so in the imaginative act of perception, which creates nature in as real a sense as that ascribed to the God of Genesis.

To Blake nature has no true existence in itself if by existence we understand meaningful form. For all Blake cares, there may well exist "out there" a cloud of atoms or other particles bumping one another around into blobs, some of which are denser than others. But to mistake that for reality would be false, and in extreme cases it would be mental derangement. Fortunately, most people escape this insanity; for example, to save them from their "rational" conviction that immaterial mind cannot possibly affect the behavior of matter in the form of human bodies and speedily approaching automobiles, imagination intervenes with the happy "illusion" that people have the freedom to jump back and avoid getting run over. Even the most casual acts of perception are acts of imaginative sculpture; when we see a desk or refrigerator or tree we mentally carve it out of space, giving it significant reality in the only way possible. If, rising to a higher level, we bring the entire force of our imaginations to these acts, giving vital intensity to what we see, as an inspired painter observes his *subject or a lover his beloved, we create an even fuller reality, because we have made it more fully human. And in these acts our sense organs are not causes but apertures allowing creative energy to move freely. The "doors of perception" are to be cleansed, as* The Marriage *stipulates, not to let objects penetrate to our passive minds but to let our mental and spiritual powers move out and create. It is this creative power that Oothoon is talking about in her frustrating debate with Bromion and Theotormon, both of whom remain locked up in the self-imposed delusion that the world is physically and mentally intractable. For Blake this freedom of and from the senses, so that we use them rather than the other way around, has ethical and political implications, as it does for Oothoon. We can be as free from the tyrannical forms of God, neurotic conscience, and institutions as we can from the mere machinery of our sense organs. For Blake this truth applies to all kinds of sense experience, but he dwells most emphatically on vision and the sexual sense of touch, the two coming together in Oothoon's daring metaphor of seeing as copulation (*Visions, *6:23–7:2). And so, although Blake could and did love the world of outdoors, he would have no part of Wordsworthian "guidance" by nature, or of its indirect deification by scientists implicitly worshipping its "laws," and least of all of deism, a religion whose remote, clockwork God combines the worst of both religious orthodoxy and of fallen science.*

What makes Blake exciting, though at times difficult, is his organic vision of things: the cross-fertilization of words and images in different works, the fusion of the personal and public, the ultimate unity of his religious, psychological, and political mythology, his marriage of the arts, his annihilation of the barrier between feeling and intelligence. As one might expect, then, his influence today is very great not only in literature but in other fields including psychology, theology, and politics. His vision is also organic in endowing everything, from stars to grains of sand, with an intense life both vast and intimately human. In his essay on his painting The Vision of the Last Judgment, *he exhorts his public to "enter into these images in . . . imagination, approaching them on the fiery chariot of . . . contemplative thought," making "a friend and companion of . . . these images of wonder." He calls for the same vivifying effort by his readers.*

The text in the selections that follow is as edited by David V. Erdman, except for a few slight changes.

FURTHER READING *(prepared by B. W.):* Good introductory books on Blake include Max Plowman's *An Introduction to the Study of Blake,* 1927; H. M. Margoliouth's *William Blake,* 1950; and J. Middleton Murry's *William Blake,* 1933. Murry's is the most detailed and takes a somewhat personal approach. Very possibly the best study of Blake is Northrop Frye's *Fearful Symmetry,* 1947; most of it is for advanced students, but the first two chapters, on Blake's ideas of imagination, mind, perception, and religion, make an exciting introduction for any reader. Good biographies that also give some attention to Blake's individual works include Mona Wilson's *The Life of William Blake,* 1927, 1971 ed. by Geoffrey Keynes; and Michael Davis's *William Blake: A New Kind of Man,* 1977. Stimulating explications of a variety of works by Blake appear in Harold Bloom's *Blake's Apocalypse,* 1963, and the Blake section of Bloom's *The Visionary Company,* 1961. For the *Songs,* including their designs, Joseph H. Wicksteed's *Blake's Innocence and Experience,* 1928, can still be recommended; more modern, and more controversial, readings appear in D. G. Gillham's *Blake's Contrary States,* 1966, in which the *Songs* are treated as "dramatic poems." Zachary Leader, in *Reading Blake's "Songs,"* 1981, explicates the *Songs* and their pictorial designs in detail, while arguing that in them Blake confronted central problems in his art and thought. On sexual and feminist themes in Blake, see Diana Hume George's eloquent, even-handed study, *Blake and Freud,* 1980. David V. Erdman's *The Illuminated Blake,* 1974, contains black-and-white reproductions of all the plates in Blake's illuminated poetry, along with commentary on each plate. Inexpensive color reproductions of various Blake works appear from time to time, from various publishers. Those who wish to read further in Blake, with good help, are directed to *Blake's Poetry and Designs,* ed. Mary Lynn Johnson and John E. Grant, 1979, which includes good annotations, selected color illustrations, and a sampling of critical essays.

SONGS OF INNOCENCE AND OF EXPERIENCE

Shewing the Two Contrary States of the Human Soul

Songs of Innocence

INTRODUCTION

Piping down the valleys wild
Piping songs of pleasant glee
On a cloud I saw a child.
And he laughing said to me.[1]

Pipe a song about a Lamb;
So I piped with merry chear,
Piper pipe that song again—
So I piped, he wept to hear.

Drop thy pipe thy happy pipe
Sing thy songs of happy chear,
So I sung the same again
While he wept with joy to hear

Piper sit thee down and write
In a book that all may read—
So he vanish'd from my sight.
And I pluck'd a hollow reed.

And I made a rural pen,
And I stain'd the water clear,
And I wrote my happy songs
Every child may joy to hear

[1] Blake's eccentric punctuation and capitalization have been left as in the text he engraved, because he probably intended them to affect the rhetorical rhythms and meaning, as with the dashes in Emily Dickinson's poems. Quotation marks sometimes supplied by editors have been avoided because (as in "Infant Joy" of *Innocence* and "The Chimney Sweeper" of *Experience*) they can do away with ambiguities Blake almost certainly intended.

THE SHEPHERD

How sweet is the Shepherds sweet lot,
From the morn to the evening he strays:
He shall follow his sheep all the day
And his tongue shall be filled with praise.

For he hears the lambs innocent call,
And he hears the ewes tender reply,
He is watchful while they are in peace,
For they know when their Shepherd is nigh.

THE ECCHOING GREEN

The Sun does arise,
And make happy the skies.
The merry bells ring
To welcome the Spring.
The sky-lark and thrush,
The birds of the bush,
Sing louder around,
To the bells chearful sound.
While our sports shall be seen
On the Ecchoing Green.

Old John with white hair
Does laugh away care,
Sitting under the oak,
Among the old folk,
They laugh at our play,
And soon they all say.
Such such were the joys.
When we all girls & boys,
In our youth-time were seen,
On the Ecchoing Green.

Till the little ones weary
No more can be merry
The sun does descend,
And our sports have an end:
Round the laps of their mothers,
Many sisters and brothers,
Like birds in their nest,
Are ready for rest;
And sport no more seen,
On the darkening Green.

THE LAMB

Little Lamb who made thee
Dost thou know who made thee
Gave thee life & bid thee feed.
By the stream & o'er the mead;[1]
Gave thee clothing of delight,
Softest clothing wooly bright;
Gave thee such a tender voice,
Making all the vales rejoice!
Little Lamb who made thee
Dost thou know who made thee

Little Lamb I'll tell thee,
Little Lamb I'll tell thee!
He is called by thy name,
For he calls himself a Lamb:
He is meek & he is mild,
He became a little child:
I a child & thou a lamb,
We are called by his name.
Little Lamb God bless thee.
Little Lamb God bless thee.

THE LITTLE BLACK BOY

My mother bore me in the southern wild,
And I am black, but O! my soul is white;
White as an angel is the English child:
But I am black as if bereav'd[1] of light.

My mother taught me underneath a tree
And sitting down before the heat of day,
She took me on her lap and kissed me,
And pointing to the east began to say.

Look on the rising sun: there God does live
And gives his light, and gives his heat away.
And flowers and trees and beasts and men recieve
Comfort in morning joy in the noon day.

And we are put on earth a little space,[2]
That we may learn to bear the beams of love,
And these black bodies and this sun-burnt face
Is but a cloud, and like a shady grove.

[1] Meadow. [1] Deprived. [2] Period of time.

For when our souls have learn'd the heat to bear
The cloud will vanish we shall hear his voice.
Saying: come out from the grove my love & care,
And round my golden tent like lambs rejoice.

Thus did my mother say and kissed me,
And thus I say to little English boy.
When I from black and he from white cloud free,
And round the tent of God like lambs we joy:

Ill shade him from the heat till he can bear,
To lean in joy upon our fathers knee.
And then I'll stand and stroke his silver hair,
And be like him and he will then love me.

THE BLOSSOM

Merry Merry Sparrow
Under leaves so green
A happy Blossom
Sees you swift as arrow
Seek your cradle narrow
Near my Bosom.

Pretty Pretty Robin
Under leaves so green
A happy Blossom
Hears you sobbing sobbing
Pretty Pretty Robin
Near my Bosom.

THE CHIMNEY SWEEPER

When my mother died I was very young,
And my father sold me[1] while yet my tongue,
Could scarcely cry weep weep weep weep.[2]
So your chimneys I sweep & in soot I sleep.

Theres little Tom Dacre, who cried when his head
That curl'd like a lambs back, was shav'd,[3] so I said.

[1] "Sold" is a more accurate word than "apprenticed" would be. A 1788 law prohibited the use of children under eight years old as sweeps, but it was not enforced. The sweeps' plight was even worse than Blake paints it in the poem.

[2] The boys' slurred street-cry, for "Sweep."

[3] The shaving was for streamlining in crawling into chimneys. The sweeps worked naked in them.

Hush Tom never mind it, for when your head's bare,
You know that the soot cannot spoil your white hair.

And so he was quiet, & that very night,
As Tom was a sleeping he had such a sight,
That thousands of sweepers Dick, Joe Ned & Jack
Were all of them lock'd up in coffins of black

And by came an Angel who had a bright key,
And he open'd the coffins & set them all free.
Then down a green plain leaping laughing they run
And wash in a river and shine in the Sun.

Then naked & white, all their bags[4] left behind,
They rise upon clouds, and sport in the wind.
And the Angel told Tom if he'd be a good boy,
He'd have God for his father & never want joy.

And so Tom awoke and we rose in the dark
And got with our bags & our brushes to work.
Tho' the morning was cold, Tom was happy & warm,
So if all do their duty, they need not fear harm.

THE LITTLE BOY LOST

Father, father, where are you going
O do not walk so fast.
Speak father, speak to your little boy
Or else I shall be lost,

The night was dark no father was there
The child was wet with dew.
The mire was deep, & the child did weep
And away the vapour flew.

THE LITTLE BOY FOUND

The little boy lost in the lonely fen,[1]
Led by the wand'ring light,
Began to cry, but God ever nigh,
Appeard like his father in white.

He kissed the child & by the hand led
And to his mother brought,
Who in sorrow pale, thro' the lonely dale
Her little boy weeping sought.

[4] Bags for hauling soot. [1] Marsh.

LAUGHING SONG

When the green woods laugh, with the voice of joy
And the dimpling stream runs laughing by,
When the air does laugh with our merry wit,
And the green hill laughs with the noise of it.

When the meadows laugh with lively green
And the grasshopper laughs in the merry scene,
When Mary and Susan and Emily,
With their sweet round mouths sing Ha, Ha, He.

When the painted[1] birds laugh in the shade
Where our table with cherries and nuts is spread
Come live & be merry and join with me,
To sing the sweet chorus of Ha, Ha, He.

A CRADLE SONG

Sweet dreams form a shade,
O'er my lovely infants head.
Sweet dreams of pleasant streams,
By happy silent moony beams.

Sweet sleep with soft down,
Weave thy brows an infant crown.
Sweet sleep Angel mild,
Hover o'er my happy child.

Sweet smiles in the night,
Hover over my delight.
Sweet smiles Mothers smiles
All the livelong night beguiles.

Sweet moans, dovelike sighs,
Chase not slumber from thy eyes.
Sweet moans, sweeter smiles,
All the dovelike moans beguiles.

Sleep sleep happy child.
All creation slept and smil'd.
Sleep sleep, happy sleep,
While o'er thee thy mother weep.

Sweet babe in thy face,
Holy image I can trace.

[1] Variously colored.

Sweet babe once like thee,
Thy maker lay and wept for me

Wept for me for thee for all,
When he was an infant small.
Thou his image ever see,
Heavenly face that smiles on thee.

Smiles on thee on me on all,
Who became an infant small,
Infant smiles are his own smiles.
Heaven & earth to peace beguiles.

THE DIVINE IMAGE

To Mercy Pity Peace and Love,
All pray in their distress:
And to these virtues of delight
Return their thankfulness.

For Mercy Pity Peace and Love,
Is God our father dear:
And Mercy Pity Peace and Love,
Is Man his child and care.

For Mercy has a human heart
Pity, a human face:
And Love, the human form divine,
And Peace, the human dress.

Then every man of every clime,
That prays in his distress,
Prays to the human form divine
Love Mercy Pity Peace.

And all must love the human form,
In heathen, turk or jew.
Where Mercy, Love & Pity dwell
There God is dwelling too.

HOLY THURSDAY[1]

Twas on a Holy Thursday their innocent faces clean
The children walking two & two in red & blue & green

[1] The poor children of London's charity schools attended a service at St. Paul's Cathedral on the first Thursday in May.

Grey headed beadles[2] walkd before with wands as white as snow
Till into the high dome of Pauls they like Thames waters flow

O what a multitude they seemd these flowers of London town
Seated in companies they sit with radiance all their own
The hum of multitudes was there but multitudes of lambs
Thousands of little boys & girls raising their innocent hands

Now like a mighty wind they raise to heaven the voice of song
Or like harmonious thunderings the seats of heaven among
Beneath them[3] sit the aged men wise guardians of the poor
Then cherish pity, lest you drive an angel from your door

NIGHT

The sun descending in the west
The evening star does shine.
The birds are silent in their nest,
And I must seek for mine,
The moon like a flower,
In heavens high bower;
With silent delight,
Sits and smiles on the night.

Farewell green fields and happy groves,
Where flocks have took delight;
Where lambs have nibbled, silent moves
The feet of angels bright;
Unseen they pour blessing,
And joy without ceasing,
On each bud and blossom,
And each sleeping bosom.

They look in every thoughtless nest,
Where birds are coverd warm;
They visit caves of every beast,
To keep them all from harm;
If they see any weeping,
That should have been sleeping
They pour sleep on their head
And sit down by their bed.

When wolves and tygers howl for prey
They pitying stand and weep;
Seeking to drive their thirst away,
And keep them from the sheep.

[2] Minor church officers. [3] The children sat in temporary grandstands.

But if they rush dreadful;
The angels most heedful,
Recieve each mild spirit,
New worlds to inherit.

And there the lions ruddy eyes,
Shall flow with tears of gold:
And pitying the tender cries,
And walking round the fold:
Saying: wrath by his meekness
And by his health, sickness,
Is driven away,
From our immortal day.

And now beside thee bleating lamb,
I can lie down and sleep;
Or think on him who bore thy name,
Grase after thee and weep.
For wash'd in lifes river,
My bright mane for ever,
Shall shine like the gold,
As I guard o'er the fold.

SPRING

Sound the Flute!
Now it's mute.
Birds delight
Day and Night.
Nightingale
In the dale
Lark in Sky
Merrily
Merrily Merrily to welcome in the Year

Little Boy
Full of joy.
Little Girl
Sweet and small,
Cock does crow
So do you.
Merry voice
Infant noise
Merrily Merrily to welcome in the Year.

Little Lamb
Here I am,
Come and lick

My white neck.
Let me pull
Your soft Wool.
Let me kiss
Your soft face.
Merrily Merrily we welcome in the Year

NURSE'S SONG

When the voices of children are heard on the green
And laughing is heard on the hill,
My heart is at rest within my breast
And every thing else is still

Then come home my children, the sun is gone down
And the dews of night arise
Come come leave off play, and let us away
Till the morning appears in the skies

No no let us play, for it is yet day
And we cannot go to sleep
Besides in the sky, the little birds fly
And the hills are all coverd with sheep

Well well go & play till the light fades away
And then go home to bed
The little ones leaped & shouted & laugh'd
And all the hills ecchoed

INFANT JOY

I have no name
I am but two days old.—
What shall I call thee?
I happy am
Joy is my name,—
Sweet joy befall thee!

Pretty joy!
Sweet joy but two days old.
Sweet joy I call thee:
Thou dost smile.
I sing the while
Sweet joy befall thee.

A DREAM

Once a dream did weave a shade,
O'er my Angel-guarded bed,
That an Emmet[1] lost it's way
Where on grass methought I lay.

Troubled wilderd[2] and folorn
Dark benighted travel-worn,
Over many a tangled spray
All heart-broke I heard her say.

O my children! do they cry
Do they hear their father sigh.
Now they look abroad to see,
Now return and weep for me.

Pitying I drop'd a tear:
But I saw a glow-worm near:
Who replied. What wailing wight[3]
Calls the watchman of the night.

I am set to light the ground,
While the beetle goes his round:
Follow now the beetles hum,
Little wanderer hie[4] thee home.

ON ANOTHERS SORROW

Can I see anothers woe,
And not be in sorrow too.
Can I see anothers grief,
And not seek for kind relief.

Can I see a falling tear,
And not feel my sorrows share,
Can a father see his child,
Weep, nor be with sorrow fill'd.

Can a mother sit and hear,
An infant groan an infant fear—
No no never can it be.
Never never can it be.

[1] Ant. [2] Lost. [3] Creature. [4] Hurry.

And can he who smiles on all
Hear the wren with sorrows small,
Hear the small birds grief & care
Hear the woes that infants bear—

And not sit beside the nest
Pouring pity in their breast,
And not sit the cradle near
Weeping tear on infants tear.

And not sit both night & day,
Wiping all our tears away.
O! no never can it be.
Never never can it be.

He doth give his joy to all.
He becomes an infant small.
He becomes a man of woe
He doth feel the sorrow too.

Think not, thou canst sigh a sigh,
And thy maker is not by.
Think not, thou canst weep a tear,
And thy maker is not near.

O! he gives to us his joy,
That our grief he may destroy
Till our grief is fled & gone
He doth sit by us and moan

Songs of Experience

INTRODUCTION

Hear the voice of the Bard![1]
Who Present, Past, & Future sees
Whose ears have heard,
The Holy Word,
That walk'd among the ancient trees.

Calling the lapsed Soul
And weeping in the evening dew;[2]
That might controll,

[1] Inspired poet.

[2] In Genesis 3:8–19 God appears to the fallen ("lapsed") Adam and Eve in the evening, condemning them to death. Blake substitutes "Holy Word"—the Son of God—for God. Antecedents and pronoun references in lines 1–8 are ambiguous, and several readings are possible.

The starry pole;
And fallen fallen light renew!

O Earth O Earth return!
Arise from out the dewy grass;
Night is worn,
And the morn
Rises from the slumberous mass.

Turn away no more:
Why wilt thou turn away
The starry floor
The watry shore[3]
Is giv'n thee till the break of day.

EARTH'S ANSWER

Earth rais'd up her head,
From the darkness dread & drear.
Her light fled:
Stony dread!
And her locks cover'd with grey despair.

Prison'd on watry shore
Starry Jealousy does keep my den
Cold and hoar
Weeping o'er
I hear the Father of the ancient men[1]

Selfish father of men
Cruel jealous selfish fear
Can delight
Chain'd in night
The virgins of youth and morning bear.[2]

Does spring hide its joy
When buds and blossoms grow?
Does the sower?
Sow by night?
Or the plowman in darkness plow?

Break this heavy chain,
That does freeze my bones around

[3] *Starry floor* and *watry shore* are paradoxical symbols in Blake, both for humanity's fallen condition and for a saving limit that preserves it from a final, irreversible fallenness.

[1] The Father is in pointed parallel-contrast with "Holy Word" in the "Introduction."

[2] Probably "If they are chained in night, can the virgins of youth and morning bear delight?", but the word order is ambiguous.

Selfish! vain,
Eternal bane![3]
That free Love with bondage bound.

THE CLOD & THE PEBBLE

Love seeketh not Itself to please,
Nor for itself hath any care;
But for another gives its ease,
And builds a Heaven in Hells despair.

So sang a little Clod of Clay,
Trodden with the cattles feet:
But a Pebble of the brook,
Warbled out these metres meet.[1]

Love seeketh only Self to please,
To bind another to its delight;
Joys in anothers loss of ease,
And builds a Hell in Heavens despite.[2]

HOLY THURSDAY[1]

Is this a holy thing to see,
In a rich and fruitful land,
Babes reducd to misery,
Fed with cold and usurous hand?

Is that trembling cry a song?
Can it be a song of joy?
And so many children poor?
It is a land of poverty!

And their sun does never shine.
And their fields are bleak & bare.
And their ways are fill'd with thorns.
It is eternal winter there.

For where-e'er the sun does shine,
And where-e'er the rain does fall:
Babe can never hunger there,
Nor poverty the mind appall.

[3] Ruin. [1] Appropriate. [2] Spiteful defiance.
[1] For the situation described, see note to title of "Holy Thursday" in *Innocence.*

THE LITTLE GIRL LOST[1]

In futurity
I prophetic see,
That the earth from sleep,
(Grave the sentence[2] deep)

Shall arise and seek
For her maker meek:
And the desart wild
Become a garden mild.

In the southern clime,
Where the summers prime,
Never fades away;
Lovely Lyca lay.

Seven summers old
Lovely Lyca told,[3]
She had wanderd long,
Hearing wild birds song.

Sweet sleep come to me
Underneath this tree;
Do father, mother weep.—
"Where can Lyca sleep".

Lost in desart wild
Is your little child.
How can Lyca sleep,
If her mother weep.

If her heart does ake,
Then let Lyca wake;
If my mother sleep,
Lyca shall not weep.

Frowning frowning night,
O'er this desart bright,
Let thy moon arise,
While I close my eyes.

Sleeping Lyca lay;
While the beasts of prey,
Come from caverns deep,
View'd the maid asleep

[1] This poem and its "Found" sequel were originally in *Songs of Innocence*.
[2] A complex pun; "grave" includes the meaning "engrave." [3] Numbered.

The kingly lion stood
And the virgin view'd,
Then he gambold[4] round
O'er the hallowd ground:

Leopards, tygers play,
Round her as she lay;
While the lion old,
Bow'd his mane of gold.

And her bosom lick,
And upon her neck,
From his eyes of flame,
Ruby tears there came;

While the lioness,
Loos'd her slender dress,
And naked they convey'd
To caves the sleeping maid.

THE LITTLE GIRL FOUND

All the night in woe
Lyca's parents go:
Over vallies deep,
While the desarts weep.

Tired and woe-begone,
Hoarse with making moan:
Arm in arm seven days,
They trac'd the desart ways.

Seven nights they sleep,
Among shadows deep:
And dream they see their child
Starv'd in desart wild.

Pale thro pathless ways
The fancied image strays,
Famish'd, weeping, weak
With hollow piteous shriek

Rising from unrest,
The trembling woman prest,
With feet of weary woe;
She could no further go.

[4] Skipped playfully.

In his arms he bore,
Her arm'd with sorrow sore;
Till before their way,
A couching lion lay.

Turning back was vain,
Soon his heavy mane,
Bore them to the ground;
Then he stalk'd around,

Smelling to his prey.
But their fears allay,
When he licks their hands;
And silent by them stands.

They look upon his eyes
Fill'd with deep surprise:
And wondering behold,
A spirit arm'd in gold.

On his head a crown
On his shoulders down,
Flow'd his golden hair.
Gone was all their care.

Follow me he said,
Weep not for the maid;
In my palace deep,
Lyca lies asleep.

Then they followed,
Where the vision led:
And saw their sleeping child,
Among tygers wild.

To this day they dwell
In a lonely dell
Nor fear the wolvish howl,
Nor the lions growl.

THE CHIMNEY SWEEPER[1]

A little black thing among the snow:
Crying weep, weep, in notes of woe!
Where are thy father & mother? say?
They are both gone up to the church to pray.

[1] See notes to "The Chimney Sweeper" in *Innocence*.

Because I was happy upon the heath,
And smil'd among the winters snow:
They clothed me in the clothes of death,
And taught me to sing the notes of woe.

And because I am happy, & dance & sing,
They think they have done me no injury:
And are gone to praise God & his Priest & King
Who make up a heaven of our misery.

NURSES SONG

When the voices of children, are heard on the green
And whisprings are in the dale:
The days of my youth rise fresh in my mind,
My face turns green and pale.

Then come home my children, the sun is gone down
And the dews of night arise
Your spring & your day, are wasted in play
And your winter and night in disguise.

THE SICK ROSE

O Rose thou art sick.
The invisible worm,
That flies in the night
In the howling storm:

Has found out thy bed
Of crimson joy:
And his dark secret love
Does thy life destroy.

THE FLY

Little Fly
Thy summers play,
My thoughtless hand
Has brush'd away.

Am not I
A fly like thee?
Or art not thou
A man like me?

For I dance
And drink & sing;
Till some blind hand
Shall brush my wing.

If thought is life
And strength & breath;
And the want
Of thought is death;

Then am I
A happy fly,
If I live,
Or if I die.

THE ANGEL

I Dreamt a Dream! what can it mean?
And that I was a maiden Queen:
Guarded by an Angel mild;
Witless[1] woe, was ne'er beguil'd![2]

And I wept both night and day
And he wip'd my tears away
And I wept both day and night
And hid from him my hearts delight

So he took his wings and fled:
Then the morn blush'd rosy red:
I dried my tears & armd my fears,
With ten thousand shields and spears.

Soon my Angel came again:
I was arm'd, he came in vain:
For the time of youth was fled
And grey hairs were on my head.

THE TYGER

Tyger Tyger, burning bright,
In the forests of the night;
What immortal hand or eye,
Could frame[1] thy fearful symmetry?

[1] Possibly "unwitting"—unaware, naive. The word also means "stupid."

[2] Taken in by guile.

[1] If there is also a pun on picture-framing here, line 20 refers not only to the creation of the world but also to the artist's creative process. Blake's works contain many symbols based on his graphic methods.

In what distant deeps or skies
Burnt the fire of thine eyes!
On what wings dare he aspire?
What the hand, dare sieze the fire?

And what shoulder, & what art,
Could twist the sinews of thy heart?
And when thy heart began to beat,
What dread hand? & what dread feet?

What the hammer? what the chain,
In what furnace was thy brain?
What the anvil? what dread grasp,
Dare its deadly terrors clasp?

When the stars threw down their spears
And water'd heaven with their tears:[2]
Did he smile his work to see?
Did he who made the Lamb make thee?

Tyger, Tyger burning bright,
In the forests of the night:
What immortal hand or eye,
Dare frame thy fearful symmetry?

MY PRETTY ROSE TREE[1]

A flower was offerd to me;
Such a flower as May never bore.
But I said I've a Pretty Rose-tree,
And I passed the sweet flower o'er.

Then I went to my Pretty Rose-tree;
To tend her by day and by night.
But my Rose turnd away with jealousy:
And her thorns were my only delight.

AH! SUN-FLOWER

Ah Sun-flower! weary of time,
Who countest the steps of the Sun:

[2] These words recur in a passage in Blake's *Four Zoas,* V, in which Urizen, fallen reason, marshals forces (called "stars") to rebel against his creator, as Satan did against God. The present line therefore probably refers to a primordial time just before the creation of the world and man.

[1] This and the following two poems, all of them about passivity versus activity in love, form a single plate.

Seeking after that sweet golden clime
Where the travellers journey is done.

Where the Youth pined away with desire,
And the pale Virgin shrouded in snow:
Arise from their graves and aspire,
Where my Sun-flower wishes to go.

THE LILLY

The modest Rose puts forth a thorn:
The humble Sheep, a threatning horn:
While the Lilly white, shall in Love delight,
Nor a thorn nor a threat stain her beauty bright

THE GARDEN OF LOVE

I went to the Garden of Love,
And saw what I never had seen:
A Chapel was built in the midst,
Where I used to play on the green.

And the gates of this Chapel were shut,
And Thou shalt not. writ over the door;
So I turn'd to the Garden of Love,
That so many sweet flowers bore,

And I saw it was filled with graves,
And tomb-stones where flowers should be:
And Priests in black gowns, were walking their rounds,
And binding with briars, my joys & desires.

THE LITTLE VAGABOND

Dear Mother, dear Mother, the Church is cold.
But the Ale-house is healthy & pleasant & warm;
Besides I can tell where I am use'd well,
Such usage in heaven will never do well.

But if at the Church they would give us some Ale.
And a pleasant fire, our souls to regale;
We'd sing and we'd pray, all the live-long day;
Nor ever once wish from the Church to stray,

Then the Parson might preach & drink & sing.
And we'd be as happy as birds in the spring:
And modest dame Lurch, who is always at Church,
Wou'ld not have bandy[1] children nor fasting nor birch.[2]

And God like a father rejoicing to see,
His children as pleasant and happy as he:
Would have no more quarrel with the Devil or the Barrel
But kiss him & give him both drink and apparel.

LONDON

I wander thro' each charter'd[1] street,
Near where the charter'd Thames does flow.
And mark in every face I meet
Marks of weakness, marks of woe.

In every cry of every Man,
In every Infants cry of fear,
In every voice: in every ban,[2]
The mind-forg'd manacles I hear

How the Chimney-sweepers cry
Every blackning Church appalls,
And the hapless Soldiers sigh,
Runs in blood down Palace walls

But most thro' midnight streets I hear
How the youthful Harlots curse
Blasts the new-born Infants tear[3]
And blights with plagues the Marriage hearse

THE HUMAN ABSTRACT

Pity would be no more,
If we did not make somebody Poor:
And Mercy no more could be,
If all were as happy as we;

And mutual fear brings peace;
Till the selfish loves increase.

[1] Bent like a bow. [2] Stick for punishing children.

[1] Rented out; also, given prerogatives by charter. In the latter sense the word was part of the jargon of patriotism, as in "the chartered rights of Englishmen."

[2] Decree of prohibition; also curse; possibly also a pun on "banns (announcement) of marriage."

[3] Produces congenital blindness through venereal disease.

Then Cruelty knits a snare,
And spreads his baits with care.

He sits down with holy fears,
And waters the ground with tears:
Then Humility takes its root
Underneath his foot.

Soon spreads the dismal shade
Of Mystery[1] over his head;
And the Catterpiller and Fly,
Feed on the Mystery.

And it bears the fruit of Deceit,
Ruddy and sweet to eat;
And the Raven his nest has made
In its thickest shade.

The Gods of the earth and sea,
Sought thro' Nature to find this Tree
But their search was all in vain:
There grows one in the Human Brain

INFANT SORROW

My mother groand! my father wept.
Into the dangerous world I leapt:
Helpless, naked, piping loud;
Like a fiend hid in a cloud.

Struggling in my fathers hands:
Striving against my swadling bands:[1]
Bound and weary I thought best
To sulk upon my mothers breast.

A POISON TREE[1]

I was angry with my friend;
I told my wrath, my wrath did end.

[1] In Blake's myth, Mystery (often in the form of a tree) represents the counter-human tendencies of both religious worship of a remote God and of scientific rationalism implicitly worshipping the hidden god Nature. Blake regarded the churches and the rationalists, apparent enemies of each other, as merely different forms of the same thing, although the attack on religious hypocrisy is the more explicit in this poem.

[1] Cloths wound restrictively around infants.

[1] In Blake's notebook draft entitled "Christian Forbearance."

I was angry with my foe:
I told it not, my wrath did grow.

And I waterd it in fears,
Night & morning with my tears:
And I sunned it with smiles,
And with soft deceitful wiles.

And it grew both day and night.
Till it bore an apple bright.
And my foe beheld it shine.
And he knew that it was mine.

And into my garden stole,
When the night had veild the pole;
In the morning glad I see;
My foe outstretchd beneath the tree.

A LITTLE BOY LOST

Nought loves another as itself
Nor venerates another so.
Nor is it possible to Thought
A greater than itself to know:

And Father, how can I love you,
Or any of my brothers more?
I love you like the little bird
That picks up crumbs around the door.

The Priest sat by and heard the child.
In trembling zeal he siez'd his hair:
He led him by his little coat:
And all admir'd the Priestly care.

And standing on the altar high,
Lo what a fiend is here! said he:
One who sets reason up for judge
Of our most holy Mystery.[1]

The weeping child could not be heard.
The weeping parents wept in vain:
They strip'd him to his little shirt.
And bound him in an iron chain.

[1] See note to "The Human Abstract," line 14.

And burn'd him in a holy place,
Where many had been burn'd before:
The weeping parents wept in vain.
Are such things done on Albions[2] shore.

A LITTLE GIRL LOST

Children of the future Age,
Reading this indignant page:
Know that in a former time,
Love! sweet Love! was thought a crime.

In the Age of Gold,
Free from winters cold:
Youth and maiden bright,
To the holy light,
Naked in the sunny beams delight.

Once a youthful pair
Fill'd with softest care:
Met in garden bright,
Where the holy light,
Had just removd the curtains of the night.

There in rising day,
On the grass they play:
Parents were afar:
Strangers came not near:
And the maiden soon forgot her fear.

Tired with kisses sweet
They agree to meet,
When the silent sleep
Waves o'er heavens deep;
And the weary tired wanderers weep.

To her father white
Came the maiden bright:
But his loving look,
Like the holy book,
All her tender limbs with terror shook.

Ona! pale and weak!
To thy father speak:
O the trembling fear!
O the dismal care!
That shakes the blossoms of my hoary[1] hair

[2] England's. The literal answer to the question is no. [1] White with age.

TO TIRZAH[1]

Whate'er is Born of Mortal Birth,
Must be consumed with the Earth
To rise from Generation[2] free;
Then what have I to do with thee?[3]

The Sexes sprung from Shame & Pride
Blow'd[4] in the morn: in evening died
But Mercy changd Death into Sleep;
The Sexes rose to work & weep.[5]

Thou Mother of my Mortal part
With cruelty didst mould my Heart,
And with false self-decieving tears,
Didst bind my Nostrils Eyes & Ears.

Didst close my Tongue in senseless clay
And me to Mortal Life betray:
The Death of Jesus set me free,
Then what have I to do with thee?

THE SCHOOL BOY[1]

I love to rise in a summer morn,
When the birds sing on every tree;
The distant huntsman winds his horn,
And the sky-lark sings with me.
O! what sweet company.

But to go to school in a summer morn
O! it drives all joy away;
Under a cruel eye outworn,
The little ones spend the day,
In sighing and dismay.

[1] This poem was written some years after the other *Songs* and appears only in late copies of the volume. It reflects Blake's later myth, where Tirzah appears as a demonic female who tortures men sexually. Here she is Nature seen as the mother of what is perishable rather than immortal in us, a connection Blake made clear in a text from I Corinthians 15:44, "it is raised a spiritual body," engraved on the pictorial plate.

[2] The life of material and temporal flux; also, the world of Experience, where our souls can succumb or win their freedom.

[3] Jesus' words to his mother, in John 2:4, in apparent resistance to her plea for his help when the wine runs out at the wedding at Cana; he nevertheless goes on to change water into wine, his first miracle.

[4] Blossomed. Tradition held that Adam and Eve sinned on the same day they were created.

[5] After the fall, Eve was cursed with pain in childbirth, Adam with painfully hard labor, and both with death (Genesis 3:16–19), but Christianity changed death into sleep through the doctrine of the resurrection of the body.

[1] Blake sometimes placed this poem in *Innocence*.

Ah! then at times I drooping sit,
And spend many an anxious hour.
Nor in my book can I take delight,
Nor sit in learnings bower,
Worn thro' with the dreary shower

How can the bird that is born for joy,
Sit in a cage and sing.
How can a child when fears annoy,[2]
But droop his tender wing,
And forget his youthful spring.

O! father & mother, if buds are nip'd,
And blossoms blown away,
And if the tender plants are strip'd
Of their joy in the springing day,
By sorrow and cares dismay,

How shall the summer arise in joy
Or the summer fruits appear
Or how shall we gather what griefs destroy
Or bless the mellowing year,
When the blasts of winter appear.

THE VOICE OF THE ANCIENT BARD[1]

Youth of delight come hither:
And see the opening morn,
Image of truth new born
Doubt is fled & clouds of reason
Dark disputes & artful teazing.
Folly is an endless maze,
Tangled roots perplex her ways,
How many have fallen there!
They stumble all night over bones of the dead;
And feel they know not what but care;
And wish to lead others when they should be led.

A DIVINE IMAGE[1]

[A rejected Song of Experience]

Cruelty has a Human Heart
And Jealousy a Human Face

[2] Harm (a stronger word than it is today).
[1] Another poem sometimes placed in *Innocence*.
[1] Blake substituted "The Human Abstract" for this poem.

Terror, the Human Form Divine
And Secrecy, the Human Dress

The Human Dress, is forged Iron
The Human Form, a fiery Forge.
The Human Face, a Furnace seal'd
The Human Heart, its hungry Gorge.[2]

THE BOOK OF THEL[1]

PLATE i

THEL'S MOTTO

Does the Eagle know what is in the pit?
Or wilt thou go ask the Mole:
Can Wisdom be put in a silver rod?
Or Love in a golden bowl?[2]

PLATE 1

THEL

I

The daughters of Mne Seraphim[3] led round their sunny flocks,
All but the youngest. she in paleness sought the secret air.
To fade away like morning beauty from her mortal day:
Down by the river of Adona[4] her soft voice is heard:
And thus her gentle lamentation falls like morning dew.

O life of this our spring! why fades the lotus of the water?
Why fade these children of the spring? born but to smile & fall.
Ah! Thel is like a watry bow, and like a parting cloud,
Like a reflection in a glass. like shadows in the water.
Like dreams of infants. like a smile upon an infants face,

[2] Gullet.

[1] The name Thel comes from the Greek for "wish" or "will." The poem is an illuminated engraving and thus is divided into "plates"; see the Introduction to Blake.

[2] The silver rod and golden bowl are male and female sexual symbols and also recall a description in Ecclesiastes 12:5–6 of a time when "desire shall fail because man goeth to his long home . . . or ever the . . . golden bowl be broken."

[3] "Mne" is the root of the Greek word for "memory," which in Blake has sinister associations with living in the past; yoked here with "Seraphim," the order of angels associated with love, it suggests the division within Thel.

[4] Derived from Adonis, the personification in myth of fertility arising from death.

Like the doves voice, like transient day, like music in the air;
Ah! gentle may I lay me down, and gentle rest my head.
And gentle sleep the sleep of death. and gentle hear the voice
Of him that walketh in the garden in the evening time.[5]

The Lilly of the valley breathing in the humble grass
Answer'd the lovely maid and said; I am a watry weed,
And I am very small, and love to dwell in lowly vales;
So weak, the gilded butterfly scarce perches on my head
Yet I am visited from heaven and he that smiles on all.
Walks in the valley. and each morn over me spreads his hand
Saying, rejoice thou humble grass, thou new-born lilly flower,
Thou gentle maid of silent valleys. and of modest brooks;
For thou shalt be clothed in light, and fed with morning manna:[6]
Till summers heat melts thee beside the fountains and the springs
To flourish in eternal vales: then why should Thel complain,

PLATE 2

Why should the mistress of the vales of Har,[7] utter a sigh.

She ceasd & smild in tears, then sat down in her silver shrine.

Thel answerd. O thou little virgin of the peaceful valley.
Giving to those that cannot crave, the voiceless, the o'ertired.
Thy breath doth nourish the innocent lamb, he smells thy milky garments,
He crops thy flowers. while thou sittest smiling in his face,
Wiping his mild and meekin[8] mouth from all contagious taints.
Thy wine doth purify the golden honey, thy perfume,
Which thou dost scatter on every little blade of grass that springs
Revives the milked cow, & tames the fire-breathing steed.
But Thel is like a faint cloud kindled at the rising sun:
I vanish from my pearly throne, and who shall find my place.

Queen of the vales the Lilly answerd, ask the tender cloud,
And it shall tell thee why it glitters in the morning sky,
And why it scatters its bright beauty thro' the humid air.
Descend O little cloud & hover before the eyes of Thel.

The Cloud descended, and the Lilly bowd her modest head:
And went to mind her numerous charge[9] among the verdant grass.

[5] God, declaring the sentence of death to Adam and Eve after their fall (Genesis 3:8–19).

[6] In Exodus 16:14–21, the miraculous but highly perishable food (the sun melted it) provided by God to the Israelites in the wilderness.

[7] In Blake's *Tiriel*, an Adam-figure who lives with his mate Heva ("Eve") in childish senility in an artificially preserved paradise.

[8] Meek. [9] Those in her custody.

PLATE 3

II

O little Cloud the virgin said, I charge thee tell to me,
Why thou complainest not when in one hour thou fade away:
Then we shall seek thee but not find; ah Thel is like to Thee.
I pass away. yet I complain, and no one hears my voice.

The Cloud then shew'd his golden head & his bright form emerg'd,
Hovering and glittering on the air before the face of Thel.

O virgin know'st thou not. our steeds drink of the golden springs
Where Luvah[10] doth renew his horses: look'st thou on my youth,
And fearest thou because I vanish and am seen no more.
Nothing remains; O maid I tell thee, when I pass away,
It is to tenfold life, to love, to peace, and raptures holy:
Unseen descending, weigh my light wings upon balmy flowers;
And court the fair eyed dew. to take me to her shining tent;[11]
The weeping virgin, trembling kneels before the risen sun,
Till we arise link'd in a golden band, and never part;
But walk united, bearing food to all our tender flowers

Dost thou O little Cloud? I fear that I am not like thee;
For I walk through the vales of Har. and smell the sweetest flowers;
But I feed not the little flowers: I hear the warbling birds,
But I feed not the warbling birds. they fly and seek their food;
But Thel delights in these no more because I fade away,
And all shall say, without a use this shining woman liv'd,
Or did she only live. to be at death the food of worms.

The Cloud reclind upon his airy throne and answer'd thus.

Then if thou art the food of worms. O virgin of the skies,
How great thy use. how great thy blessing; every thing that lives,
Lives not alone, nor for itself: fear not and I will call
The weak worm from its lowly bed, and thou shalt hear its voice.
Come forth worm of the silent valley, to thy pensive queen.

The helpless worm arose, and sat upon the Lillys leaf,
And the bright Cloud saild on, to find his partner in the vale.

PLATE 4

III

Then Thel astonish'd view'd the Worm upon its dewy bed.

Art thou a Worm? image of weakness. art thou but a Worm?
I see thee like an infant wrapped in the Lillys leaf:

[10] A pun on "love"; in Blake's later myth, the representative of passion.
[11] Biblical image for consummation of marriage.

Ah weep not little voice, thou can'st not speak. but thou can'st weep;
Is this a Worm? I see thee lay helpless & naked: weeping,
And none to answer, none to cherish thee with mothers smiles.

The Clod of Clay[12] heard the Worms voice, & raisd her pitying head;
She bow'd over the weeping infant, and her life exhal'd
In milky fondness, then on Thel she fix'd her humble eyes.

O beauty of the vales of Har. we live not for ourselves,
Thou seest me the meanest thing, and so I am indeed;
My bosom of itself is cold. and of itself is dark,

PLATE 5

But he that loves the lowly, pours his oil upon my head.
And kisses me, and binds his nuptial bands around my breast,
And says; Thou mother of my children, I have loved thee.
And I have given thee a crown that none can take away
But how this is sweet maid, I know not, and I cannot know,
I ponder, and I cannot ponder; yet I live and love.

The daughter of beauty wip'd her pitying tears with her white veil,
And said. Alas! I knew not this, and therefore did I weep:
That God would love a Worm I knew, and punish the evil foot
That wilful, bruis'd its helpless form: but that he cherish'd it
With milk and oil. I never knew; and therefore did I weep,
And I complaind in the mild air, because I fade away,
And lay me down in thy cold bed, and leave my shining lot.

Queen of the vales, the matron Clay answerd; I heard thy sighs.
And all thy moans flew o'er my roof. but I have call'd them down:
Wilt thou O Queen enter my house. 'tis given thee to enter,
And to return; fear nothing. enter with thy virgin feet.

PLATE 6

IV

The eternal gates terrific porter lifted the northern bar:[13]
Thel enter'd in & saw the secrets of the land unknown;
She saw the couches of the dead, & where the fibrous roots
Of every heart on earth infixes deep its restless twists:
A land of sorrows & of tears where never smile was seen.

She wanderd in the land of clouds thro' valleys dark, listning
Dolours & lamentations: waiting oft beside a dewy grave

[12] Compare Blake's "The Clod and the Pebble," in *Songs of Experience*. Here the Clod is a version of Mother Earth.

[13] In Homer's *Odyssey*, Book XIII, mortals enter the cave of the Naiads (sea nymphs) by the northern gate, deities by the southern gate. This sixth plate, with its account of a subterranean descent, was composed later than the rest of the poem.

She stood in silence. listning to the voices of the ground,
Till to her own grave plot she came, & there she sat down.
And heard this voice of sorrow breathed from the hollow pit.

Why cannot the Ear be closed to its own destruction?
Or the glistning Eye to the poison of a smile!
Why are Eyelids stord with arrows ready drawn,
Where a thousand fighting men in ambush lie?
Or an Eye of gifts & graces, show'ring fruits & coined gold!
Why a Tongue impress'd with honey from every wind?
Why an Ear, a whirlpool fierce to draw creations in?
Why a Nostril wide inhaling terror trembling & affright
Why a tender curb upon the youthful burning boy!
Why a little curtain of flesh on the bed of our desire?[14]

The Virgin started from her seat, & with a shriek.
Fled back unhinderd till she came into the vales of Har

The End

VISIONS OF THE DAUGHTERS OF ALBION

The Eye sees more than the Heart knows.

This poem is an antithetical twin to *The Book of Thel.* There are many parallels and contrasts in structure and imagery (for example, the opening dialogues with flowers, one a retiring lily, the other a bold marigold). The most obvious parallel-contrast is in the situations and actions of the two heroines. Both begin in a state of virginity and longing, but Oothoon passes almost at the outset from a Thel-like hesitancy to decisive action. She loves Theotormon (whose name, from Greek, suggests that he is "tormented by God"). Her plucking of the marigold is symbolic of a conversion in her psyche, through which she accepts sexuality and growth. Then tragedy strikes: while winging her way to join Theotormon, she is raped by Bromion (a thunder-titan whose name suggests the Greek for "roarer"). After a period of shame, penitence, and attempted atonement, she suddenly has a breakthrough, in a way the poem does not explicitly describe, recognizing that shame in her situation is absurd and is born of false values that the two men still share (despite the superficial difference between the introvert Theotormon and the brute Bromion).

The poem is also sociology. "Albion" means England, and in that context his "Daughters" are Englishwomen, the potential recipients of a message of liberation sent from the New World of America, of which Oothoon is the "soft soul." In Blake's later myth Albion is also humanity; his daughters, then, would be all womankind, the audience for the message on a more universal level. Bromion is identified as a slave trader, so that America, the land of freedom darkened by slavery,

[14] The boy is probably Cupid, god of love; the curtain is the hymen, or "maidenhead." These two lines protest against the restraint of the sexual sense (touch); the preceding lines protest against the hyperactivity of the other four senses.

suffers from a moral cancer. This concern with racial slavery blends with the more obvious feminist theme, derived in part from Blake's acquaintance with Mary Wollstonecraft, author of *A Vindication of the Rights of Woman* (1792), who probably provided one model for Oothoon. With all these themes Blake interweaves his ideas about the proper use of the senses (tyrannously hyperactive in Bromion, repressed in Theotormon) and about jealousy, the psychological analogue in Blake for all forms of tyranny. [*Editors' headnote.*]

PLATE iii[1]

THE ARGUMENT[2]

I loved Theotormon
And I was not ashamed
I trembled in my virgin fears
And I hid in Leutha's[3] vale!

I plucked Leutha's flower,
And I rose up from the vale;
But the terrible thunders[4] tore
My virgin mantle in twain.

PLATE 1

VISIONS

Enslav'd, the Daughters of Albion weep: a trembling lamentation
Upon their mountains; in their valleys.[5] sighs toward America.

For the soft soul of America, Oothoon[6] wanderd in woe,
Along the vales of Leutha seeking flowers to comfort her;
And thus she spoke to the bright Marygold of Leutha's vale

Art thou a flower! art thou a nymph! I see thee now a flower;
Now a nymph! I dare not pluck thee from thy dewy bed?

The Golden nymph replied; pluck thou my flower Oothoon the mild
Another flower shall spring, because the soul of sweet delight
Can never pass away. she ceas'd & closd her golden shrine.

Then Oothoon pluck'd the flower saying, I pluck thee from thy bed
Sweet flower. and put thee here to glow between my breasts
And thus I turn my face to where my whole soul seeks.

[1] For Blake's method of engraved illuminations, see the Introduction to Blake. Plates i and ii are a pictorial frontispiece and the title page.
[2] Subject matter.
[3] In Blake's larger myth, a female embodiment of sexual repression and guilt.
[4] Bromion. (See Headnote.)
[5] On Blake's punctuation, see note to "Introduction" to *Songs of Innocence*.
[6] Oothoon's name derives ironically from a character in Ossian (see Goethe's *Werther*, note to letter of 10 July 1771) who is suicidally gloomy over a sexual abduction.

Over the waves she went in wing'd exulting swift delight;
And over Theotormons reign,[7] took her impetuous course.

Bromion rent her with his thunders. on his stormy bed
Lay the faint maid, and soon her woes appalld his thunders hoarse

Bromion spoke. behold this harlot here on Bromions bed,
And let the jealous dolphins sport around the lovely maid;
Thy soft American plains are mine, and mine thy north & south:
Stampt with my signet are the swarthy children of the sun:[8]
They are obedient, they resist not, they obey the scourge:
Their daughters worship terrors and obey the violent:

PLATE 2

Now thou maist marry Bromions harlot, and protect the child
Of Bromions rage, that Oothoon shall put forth in nine moons time

Then storms rent Theotormons limbs; he rolld his waves around.
And folded his black jealous waters round the adulterate pair
Bound back to back in Bromions caves terror & meekness dwell

At entrance Theotormon sits wearing the threshold hard
With secret tears; beneath him sound like waves on a desart shore
The voice of slaves beneath the sun, and children bought with money.[9]
That shiver in religious caves beneath the burning fires
Of lust, that belch incessant from the summits of the earth

Oothoon weeps not: she cannot weep! her tears are locked up;
But she can howl incessant writhing her soft snowy limbs.
And calling Theotormons Eagles to prey upon her flesh.

I call with holy voice! kings of the sounding air,
Rend away this defiled bosom that I may reflect.
The image of Theotormon on my pure transparent breast.

The Eagles at her call descend & rend their bleeding prey;
Theotormon severely smiles. her soul reflects the smile;
As the clear spring mudded with feet of beasts grows pure & smiles.

The Daughters of Albion hear her woes. & eccho back her sighs.

Why does my Theotormon sit weeping upon the threshold;[10]
And Oothoon hovers by his side, perswading him in vain:
I cry arise O Theotormon for the village dog
Barks at the breaking day. the nightingale has done lamenting.

[7] Over the Atlantic ocean. [8] A reference to the branding of slaves.
[9] Exploited child labor blends with the other forms of oppression.
[10] We get no explanation of the transition to the new Oothoon we hear from this point on.

The lark does rustle in the ripe corn, and the Eagle returns
From nightly prey, and lifts his golden beak to the pure east;
Shaking the dust from his immortal pinions[11] to awake
The sun that sleeps too long. Arise my Theotormon I am pure.
Because the night is gone that clos'd me in its deadly black.
They told me that the night & day were all that I could see;
They told me that I had five senses[12] to inclose me up.
And they inclos'd my infinite brain into a narrow circle.
And sunk my heart into the Abyss, a red round globe hot burning
Till all from life I was obliterated and erased.
Instead of morn arises a bright shadow, like an eye
In the eastern cloud: instead of night a sickly charnel house;[13]
That Theotormon hears me not! to him the night and morn
Are both alike: a night of sighs, a morning of fresh tears;

PLATE 3

And none but Bromion can hear my lamentations.

With what sense[14] is it that the chicken shuns the ravenous hawk?
With what sense does the tame pigeon measure out the expanse?
With what sense does the bee form cells? have not the mouse & frog
Eyes and ears and sense of touch? yet are their habitations.
And their pursuits, as different as their forms and as their joys:
Ask the wild ass why he refuses burdens: and the meek camel
Why he loves man: is it because of eye ear mouth or skin
Or breathing nostrils? No. for these the wolf and tyger have.
Ask the blind worm the secrets of the grave, and why her spires
Love to curl round the bones of death; and ask the rav'nous snake
Where she gets poison: & the wing'd eagle why he loves the sun
And then tell me the thoughts of man, that have been hid of old.

Silent I hover all the night, and all day could be silent.
If Theotormon once would turn his loved eyes upon me;
How can I be defild when I reflect thy image pure?
Sweetest the fruit that the worm feeds on. & the soul prey'd on
by woe
The new wash'd lamb ting'd with the village smoke & the bright
swan
By the red earth of our immortal river: I bathe my wings.
And I am white and pure to hover round Theotormons breast.

Then Theotormon broke his silence. and he answered.

[11] Wings.

[12] For Blake, the senses can be either avenues to spiritual freedom or a form of imprisonment; see the Introduction to Blake.

[13] Tomb.

[14] Oothoon's speech, like the following ones by Theotormon and Bromion, explores the relationship between inner mental or spiritual realities and their physical embodiments in sense experience. Implicit in the debate are the questions whether virginity is a condition of the soul or a matter of physical intactness and whether universal laws rather than the uniqueness of each individual should govern values and one's sense of reality.

Tell me what is the night or day to one o'erflowd with woe?
Tell me what is a thought? & of what substance is it made?
Tell me what is a joy? & in what gardens do joys grow?
And in what rivers swim the sorrows? and upon what mountains

PLATE 4
Wave shadows of discontent? and in what houses dwell the wretched
Drunken with woe forgotten. and shut up from cold despair.

Tell me where dwell the thoughts forgotten till thou call them forth
Tell me where dwell the joys of old! & where the ancient loves?
And when will they renew again & the night of oblivion past?
That I might traverse times & spaces far remote and bring
Comforts into a present sorrow and a night of pain
Where goest thou O thought? to what remote land is thy flight?
If thou returnest to the present moment of affliction
Wilt thou bring comforts on thy wings. and dews and honey and
balm;
Or poison from the desart wilds, from the eyes of the envier.

Then Bromion said: and shook the cavern with his lamentation

Thou knowest that the ancient trees seen by thine eyes have fruit;
But knowest thou that trees and fruits flourish upon the earth
To gratify senses unknown? trees beasts and birds unknown:
Unknown, not unpercievd, spread in the infinite microscope,
In places yet unvisited by the voyager. and in worlds
Over another kind of seas, and in atmospheres unknown:
Ah! are there other wars, beside the wars of sword and fire!
And are there other sorrows, beside the sorrows of poverty!
And are there other joys, beside the joys of riches and ease?
And is there not one law for both the lion and the ox?
And is there not eternal fire, and eternal chains?
To bind the phantoms of existence from eternal life?

Then Oothoon waited silent all the day. and all the night,

PLATE 5
But when the morn arose, her lamentation renewd,
The Daughters of Albion hear her woes, & eccho back her sighs.

O Urizen![15] Creator of men! mistaken Demon of heaven:
Thy joys are tears! thy labour vain, to form men to thine image.

[15] The name ("your reason," with a further pun on "horizon," a circular limit) refers to a figure in Blake's later myth who embodies reason (usually in its familiar "fallen" or corrupted form), God seen as a remote but vindictive tyrant, political tyranny, and compulsively rigid conscience.

How can one joy absorb another? are not different joys
Holy, eternal, infinite! and each joy is a Love.

Does not the great mouth laugh at a gift? & the narrow eyelids
mock
At the labour that is above payment, and wilt thou take the ape
For thy councellor? or the dog, for a schoolmaster to thy children?
Does he who contemns poverty,[16] and he who turns with abhorrence
From usury: feel the same passion or are they moved alike?
How can the giver of gifts experience the delights of the merchant?
How the industrious citizen the pains of the husbandman.[17]
How different far the fat fed hireling with hollow drum;
Who buys whole corn fields into wastes, and sings upon the heath:[18]
How different their eye and ear! how different the world to them!
With what sense does the parson claim the labour of the farmer?[19]
What are his nets & gins & traps. & how does he surround him
With cold floods of abstraction, and with forests of solitude,
To build him castles and high spires. where kings & priests may
dwell.
Till she who burns with youth. and knows no fixed lot; is bound
In spells of law to one she loaths: and must she drag the chain
Of life, in weary lust! must chilling murderous thoughts. obscure
The clear heaven of her eternal spring? to bear the wintry rage
Of a harsh terror driv'n to madness, bound to hold a rod
Over her shrinking shoulders all the day; & all the night
To turn the wheel of false desire: and longings that wake her womb
To the abhorred birth of cherubs in the human form
That live a pestilence & die a meteor & are no more.
Till the child dwell with one he hates. and do the deed he loaths
And the impure scourge force his seed into its unripe birth
E'er yet his eyelids can behold the arrows of the day.[20]

Does the whale worship at thy footsteps as the hungry dog?
Or does he scent the mountain prey, because his nostrils wide
Draw in the ocean? does his eye discern the flying cloud
As the ravens eye? or does he measure the expanse like the vulture?
Does the still spider view the cliffs where eagles hide their young?
Or does the fly rejoice. because the harvest is brought in?
Does not the eagle scorn the earth & despise the treasures beneath?
But the mole[21] knoweth what is there, & the worm shall tell it thee.
Does not the worm erect a pillar in the mouldering church yard?

[16] Feels contempt for the poor. [17] Farmer. (The "citizen" is the city-dweller.)

[18] The servant of the rich landowner and the military recruiter, who turn farmland into hunting land and conscript farm workers.

[19] The parson forces the payment of tithes, taxes to support the church.

[20] As often in Blake, the transitions are breathless, here moving rapidly from marriage to parenthood to children in a catalogue of the ills resulting from marriage understood as slavery to law.

[21] Compare the eagle and mole in "Thel's Motto" in *The Book of Thel*—one of hundreds of such interconnections between Blake's works.

PLATE 6

And a palace of eternity in the jaws of the hungry grave
Over his porch these words are written. Take thy bliss O Man!
And sweet shall be thy taste & sweet thy infant joys renew!

Infancy, fearless, lustful, happy! nestling for delight
In laps of pleasure; Innocence! honest, open, seeking
The vigorous joys of morning light; open to virgin bliss,
Who taught thee modesty, subtil modesty! child of night & sleep
When thou awakest. wilt thou dissemble[22] all thy secret joys
Or wert thou not, awake when all this mystery was disclos'd!
Then com'st thou forth a modest virgin knowing to dissemble
With nets found under thy night pillow, to catch virgin joy,
And brand it with the name of whore; & sell it in the night,
In silence. ev'n without a whisper, and in seeming sleep:
Religious dreams and holy vespers,[23] light thy smoky fires:
Once were thy fires lighted by the eyes of honest morn
And does my Theotormon seek this hypocrite modesty!
This knowing, artful, secret, fearful, cautious, trembling hypocrite.
Then is Oothoon a whore indeed! and all the virgin joys
Of life are harlots: and Theotormon is a sick mans dream
And Oothoon is the crafty slave of selfish holiness.

But Oothoon is not so, a virgin fill'd with virgin fancies
Open to joy and to delight where ever beauty appears
If in the morning sun I find it: there my eyes are fix'd

PLATE 7

In happy copulation;[24] if in evening mild. wearied with work;
Sit on a bank and draw the pleasures of this free born joy.

The moment of desire! the moment of desire! The virgin
That pines for man; shall awaken her womb to enormous joys
In the secret shadows of her chamber; the youth shut up from
The lustful joy. shall forget to generate. & create an amorous image
In the shadows of his curtains and in the folds of his silent pillow.
Are not these the places of religion? the rewards of continence?
The self enjoyings of self denial? Why dost thou seek religion?
Is it because acts are not lovely, that thou seekest solitude,
Where the horrible darkness is impressed with reflections of desire.

Father of Jealousy.[25] be thou accursed from the earth!
Why hast thou taught my Theotormon this accursed thing?
Till beauty fades from off my shoulders darken'd and cast out,
A solitary shadow wailing on the margin of non-entity.[26]

[22] Conceal one's true nature. [23] Evening prayers.
[24] The act of seeing is described as a sexual union. [25] Urizen.
[26] A state described elsewhere in Blake as psychic disintegration.

I cry, Love! Love! Love! happy happy Love! free as the mountain wind!
Can that be Love, that drinks another as a sponge drinks water?
That clouds with jealousy his nights, with weepings all the day:
To spin a web of age around him. grey and hoary! dark!
Till his eyes sicken at the fruit that hangs before his sight.
Such is self-love that envies all! a creeping skeleton
With lamplike eyes watching around the frozen marriage bed.

But silken nets and traps of adamant[27] will Oothoon spread,
And catch for thee girls of mild silver, or of furious gold;
I'll lie beside thee on a bank & view their wanton play
In lovely copulation bliss on bliss with Theotormon:
Red as the rosy morning, lustful as the first born beam,
Oothoon shall view his dear delight, nor e'er with jealous cloud
Come in the heaven of generous love; nor selfish blightings bring.

Does the sun walk in glorious raiment. on the secret floor

PLATE 8

Where the cold miser spreads his gold? or does the bright cloud drop
On his stone threshold? does his eye behold the beam that brings
Expansion to the eye of pity? or will he bind himself
Beside the ox to thy hard furrow? does not that mild beam blot
The bat, the owl, the glowing tyger, and the king of night.
The sea fowl takes the wintry blast. for a cov'ring to her limbs:
And the wild snake, the pestilence to adorn him with gems & gold.
And trees. & birds. & beasts. & men. behold their eternal joy.
Arise you little glancing wings, and sing your infant joy!
Arise and drink your bliss, for every thing that lives is holy!

Thus every morning wails Oothoon. but Theotormon sits
Upon the margind ocean conversing with shadows dire.

The Daughters of Albion hear her woes, & eccho back her sighs.

The End

[27] A very hard stone or other substance. The nets and traps are Oothoon's ironic reversal of the nets used by hypocritical modesty in 6:10–11.

THE MARRIAGE OF HEAVEN AND HELL

PLATE 2[1]

THE ARGUMENT[2]

Rintrah[3] roars & shakes his fires in the burdend air;
Hungry clouds swag on the deep[4]

Once meek, and in a perilous path,
The just man kept his course along
The vale of death.
Roses are planted where thorns grow.
And on the barren heath
Sing the honey bees.

Then the perilous path was planted:
And a river, and a spring
On every cliff and tomb;
And on the bleached bones
Red clay[5] brought forth.

Till the villain left the paths of ease,
To walk in perilous paths, and drive
The just man into barren climes.

Now the sneaking serpent walks
In mild humility.
And the just man rages in the wilds
Where lions roam.

Rintrah roars & shakes his fires in the burdend air;
Hungry clouds swag on the deep.

PLATE 3

As a new heaven is begun, and it is now thirty-three years since its advent: the Eternal Hell revives. And lo! Swedenborg[6] is the Angel sitting

[1] Plate 1 is the title page. For Blake's use of illuminated engravings, see the Introduction to Blake.

[2] Theme; subject. The "Argument" is an account of how good and evil, the "just man" and the "villain," have come to be confused with each other. The just man's perilous position and role are usurped by the villain as soon as they cease to be perilous.

[3] A stern prophet-figure in Blake, he heralds a new age of revolutionary cataclysm, in France, England, and the human psyche.

[4] Hang over the ocean. On Blake's punctuation, see note to "Introduction" to *Songs of Innocence*.

[5] "Red clay" is the literal meaning of "Adam" in Hebrew; this phrase and the "serpent" of line 17 indicate that Blake is giving us a revised version of the story of creation and fall in Genesis 1–3.

[6] Blake first admired the Swedish visionary Emanuel Swedenborg (1688–1772) but later saw in him one more exponent of such false orthodoxies as predestination and punishment in eternity. *The Marriage* is an elaborate parody of some of his writings. According to Swedenborg, a Last Judgment had begun in 1757, which happens also to be the year Blake was born. He is now, in 1790 (the presumed present), 33 years old, as was Jesus when he died.

at the tomb; his writings are the linen clothes folded up.[7] Now is the dominion of Edom,[8] & the return of Adam into Paradise; see Isaiah xxxiv and XXXV Chap:[9]

Without Contraries is no progression. Attraction and Repulsion, Reason and Energy, Love and Hate, are necessary to Human existence.

From these contraries spring what the religious call Good & Evil. Good is the passive that obeys Reason [.] Evil is the active springing from Energy.

Good is Heaven. Evil is Hell.

PLATE 4

THE VOICE OF THE DEVIL

All Bibles or sacred codes. have been the causes of the following Errors.

1. That Man has two real existing principles Viz: a Body & a Soul.
2. That Energy. calld Evil. is alone from the Body. & that Reason. calld Good. is alone from the Soul.
3. That God will torment Man in Eternity for following his Energies.

But the following Contraries to these are True

1 Man has no Body distinct from his Soul for that calld Body is a portion of Soul discernd by the five Senses, the chief inlets of Soul in this age

2 Energy is the only life and is from the Body and Reason is the bound or outward circumference of Energy.

3 Energy is Eternal Delight

PLATE 5

Those who restrain desire, do so because theirs is weak enough to be restrained; and the restrainer or reason usurps its place & governs the unwilling.

And being restraind it by degrees becomes passive till it is only the shadow of desire.

The history of this is written in Paradise Lost. & the Governor or Reason is call'd Messiah.

And the original Archangel or possessor of the command of the heavenly host, is calld the Devil or Satan and his children are call'd Sin & Death[10]

[7] The garments left in the tomb by the resurrected Jesus; John 20:6–7.

[8] Esau (tricked out of his birthright by the crafty Jacob but promised revenge; Genesis 27); also, revolutionary France.

[9] Isaiah 34 prophesies war and divine retribution in Edom (the land of Esau's descendants, which will produce an avenger mentioned in Isaiah 63). Isaiah 35 describes restored peace and redemption. Blake is expressing the paradoxical condition of his time (and of this crisis in the human psyche), one of fear and promise, destruction and restoration.

[10] In *Paradise Lost,* II.746–787, Milton describes the birth of Sin from the rebellious Satan's head, his copulation with her, and the birth of their son Death.

But in the Book of Job Miltons Messiah is call'd Satan.[11]

For this history has been adopted by both parties

It indeed appear'd to Reason as if Desire was cast out, but the Devils account is, that the Messi[PL 6]ah fell. & formed a heaven of what he stole from the Abyss

This is shewn in the Gospel, where he prays to the Father to send the comforter[12] or Desire that Reason may have Ideas to build on, the Jehovah of the Bible being no other than he, who dwells in flaming fire. Know that after Christs death, he became Jehovah.

But in Milton; the Father is Destiny, the Son, a Ratio of the five senses. & the Holy-ghost, Vacuum![13]

Note. The reason Milton wrote in fetters when he wrote of Angels & God, and at liberty when of Devils & Hell,[14] is because he was a true Poet and of the Devils party without knowing it

A Memorable Fancy

As I was walking among the fires of hell, delighted with the enjoyments of Genius; which to Angels look like torment and insanity. I collected some of their Proverbs: thinking that as the sayings used in a nation, mark its character, so the Proverbs of Hell, shew the nature of Infernal wisdom better than any description of buildings or garments.

When I came home; on the abyss of the five senses, where a flat sided steep frowns over the present world. I saw a mighty Devil folded in black clouds, hovering on the sides of the rock, with cor[PL 7]roding[15] fires he wrote the following sentence now percieved by the minds of men, & read by them on earth.

How do you know but ev'ry Bird that cuts the airy way,
Is an immense world of delight, clos'd by your senses five?

Proverbs of Hell

In seed time learn, in harvest teach, in winter enjoy.
Drive your cart and your plow over the bones of the dead.
The road of excess leads to the palace of wisdom.
Prudence is a rich ugly old maid courted by Incapacity.
He who desires but acts not, breeds pestilence.
The cut worm forgives the plow.

[11] In Job 1–2 Satan is a cynical accuser and tormentor of Job. In *Paradise Lost,* Book VI, the Messiah, or Son of God, drives the defeated rebel angels into a tormenting hell. For Blake, Satan is generally utterly evil and should not necessarily be identified with the "devils" in the *Marriage.*

[12] In John 14:16–17. The Comforter is the Holy Ghost, whom Blake reinterprets as Desire, an "infernal" virtue.

[13] Milton assigned no role to the third person of the Trinity. A "ratio" (the root of the word *rationalism*) is a view of reality as a least common denominator founded on sense impressions available to even the least imaginative mind. Thus the "ratio" perception of a tree would be merely a bunch of mixed-up sticks and leaves. Blake thinks Milton's Messiah is unimaginatively conceived.

[14] To many readers Milton's God in Book III sounds like a querulous, hair-splitting theologian, whereas Satan and Hell in Books I and II are full of titanic energy.

[15] Blake's etching process used acid to create raised lines on the plates.

Dip him in the river who loves water.
A fool sees not the same tree that a wise man sees.
He whose face gives no light, shall never become a star.
Eternity is in love with the productions of time.
The busy bee has no time for sorrow.
The hours of folly are measur'd by the clock, but of wisdom: no clock can measure.
All wholsom food is caught without a net or a trap.
Bring out number weight & measure in a year of dearth.[16]
No bird soars too high. if he soars with his own wings.
A dead body. revenges not injuries.
The most sublime act is to set another before you.
If the fool would persist in his folly he would become wise
Folly is the cloke of knavery.
Shame is Prides cloke.

PLATE 8

Prisons are built with stones of Law, Brothels with bricks of Religion.
The pride of the peacock is the glory of God.
The lust of the goat is the bounty of God.
The wrath of the lion is the wisdom of God.
The nakedness of woman is the work of God.
Excess of sorrow laughs. Excess of joy weeps.
The roaring of lions, the howling of wolves, the raging of the stormy sea, and the destructive sword. are portions of eternity too great for the eye of man.
The fox condemns the trap, not himself.
Joys impregnate. Sorrows bring forth.
Let man wear the fell[17] of the lion. woman the fleece of the sheep.
The bird a nest, the spider a web, man friendship.
The selfish smiling fool. & the sullen frowning fool. shall be both thought wise. that they may be a rod.[18]
What is now proved was once, only imagin'd.
The rat, the mouse, the fox, the rabbet; watch the roots, the lion, the tyger, the horse, the elephant, watch the fruits.
The cistern contains: the fountain overflows
One thought. fills immensity.
Always be ready to speak your mind, and a base man will avoid you.
Every thing possible to be believ'd is an image of truth.
The eagle never lost so much time. as when he submitted to learn of the crow.

PLATE 9

The fox provides for himself. but God provides for the lion.
Think in the morning, Act in the noon, Eat in the evening, Sleep in the night.

[16] Scarcity. [17] Hide. [18] Chastisement; punishment.

He who has sufferd[19] you to impose on him knows you.
As the plow follows words, so God rewards prayers.
The tygers of wrath are wiser than the horses of instruction
Expect poison from the standing water.
You never know what is enough unless you know what is more than enough.
Listen to the fools reproach! it is a kingly title!
The eyes of fire, the nostrils of air, the mouth of water, the beard of earth.
The weak in courage is strong in cunning.
The apple tree never asks the beech how he shall grow, nor the lion. the horse, how he shall take his prey.
The thankful reciever bears a plentiful harvest.
If others had not been foolish, we should be so.
The soul of sweet delight, can never be defil'd,
When thou seest an Eagle, thou seest a portion of Genius. lift up thy head!
As the catterpiller chooses the fairest leaves to lay her eggs on, so the priest lays his curse on the fairest joys.
To create a little flower is the labour of ages.
Damn. braces: Bless relaxes.
The best wine is the oldest. the best water the newest.
Prayers plow not! Praises reap not!
Joys laugh not! Sorrows weep not!

PLATE 10

The head Sublime, the heart Pathos, the genitals Beauty, the hands & feet Proportion.
As the air to a bird or the sea to a fish, so is contempt to the contemptible.
The crow wish'd every thing was black, the owl, that every thing was white.
Exuberance is Beauty.
If the lion was advise'd by the fox. he would be cunning.
Improve[me]nt makes strait roads, but the crooked roads without Improvement, are roads of Genius.
Sooner murder an infant in its cradle than nurse unacted desires
Where man is not nature is barren.
Truth can never be told so as to be understood, and not be believ'd.
Enough! or Too much

PLATE 11

The ancient Poets animated all sensible objects with Gods or Geniuses, calling them by the names and adorning them with the properties of woods, rivers, mountains, lakes, cities, nations, and whatever their enlarged & numerous senses could percieve.

[19] Allowed.

And particularly they studied the genius[20] of each city & country. placing it under its mental deity.

Till a system was formed, which some took advantage of & enslav'd the vulgar by attempting to realize or abstract the mental deities from their objects; thus began Priesthood.

Choosing forms of worship from poetic tales.

And at length they pronouncd that the Gods had orderd such things.

Thus men forgot that All deities reside in the human breast.

PLATE 12

A MEMORABLE FANCY

The Prophets Isaiah and Ezekiel dined with me, and I asked them how they dared so roundly to assert. that God spake to them; and whether they did not think at the time, that they would be misunderstood, & so be the cause of imposition.[21]

Isaiah answer'd. I saw no God, nor heard any, in a finite organical perception; but my senses discover'd the infinite in every thing, and as I was then perswaded, & remain confirm'd; that the voice of honest indignation is the voice of God, I cared not for consequences but wrote.

Then I asked: does a firm perswasion that a thing is so, make it so?

He replied. All poets believe that it does, & in ages of imagination this firm perswasion removed mountains; but many are not capable of a firm perswasion of any thing.

Then Ezekiel said. The philosophy of the east taught the first principles of human perception some nations held one principle for the origin & some another, we of Israel taught that the Poetic Genius (as you now call it) was the first principle and all the others merely derivative, which was the cause of our despising the Priests & Philosophers of other countries, and prophecying that all Gods [PL 13] would at last be proved to originate in ours & to be the tributaries of the Poetic Genius. it was this. that our great poet King David desired so fervently & invokes so patheticly, saying by this he conquers enemies & governs kingdoms; and we so loved our God. that we cursed in his name all the deities of surrounding nations, and asserted that they had rebelled; from these opinions the vulgar came to think that all nations would at last be subject to the jews.

This said he, like all firm perswasions, is come to pass, for all nations believe the jews code and worship the jews god, and what greater subjection can be

I heard this with some wonder, & must confess my own conviction. After dinner I ask'd Isaiah to favour the world with his lost works, he said none of equal value was lost. Ezekiel said the same of his.

I also asked Isaiah what made him go naked and barefoot three years? he answerd, the same that made our friend Diogenes[22] the Grecian.

I then asked Ezekiel. why he eat dung, & lay so long on his right & left

[20] Distinctive character. [21] Fraud.

[22] A Greek philosopher (412?–323 B.C.) who chose to live in poverty. Isaiah's nakedness was to be a sign of the stripping of Egyptian prisoners by the Assyrians. Isaiah 20:2–5.

side?[23] he answerd. the desire of raising other men into a perception of the infinite this the North American tribes practise. & is he honest who resists his genius or conscience. only for the sake of present ease or gratification?

PLATE 14

The ancient tradition that the world will be consumed in fire at the end of six thousand years[24] is true. as I have heard from Hell.

For the cherub with his flaming sword is hereby commanded to leave his guard at tree of life,[25] and when he does, the whole creation will be consumed, and appear infinite. and holy whereas it now appears finite & corrupt.

This will come to pass by an improvement of sensual enjoyment.

But first the notion that man has a body distinct from his soul, is to be expunged; this I shall do, by printing in the infernal method, by corrosives, which in Hell are salutary and medicinal, melting apparent surfaces away, and displaying the infinite which was hid.

If the doors of perception were cleansed every thing would appear to man as it is, infinite.

For man has closed himself up, till he sees all things thro' narrow chinks of his cavern.

PLATE 15

A MEMORABLE FANCY

I was in a Printing house[26] in Hell & saw the method in which knowledge is transmitted from generation to generation.

In the first chamber was a Dragon-Man, clearing away the rubbish from a caves mouth; within, a number of Dragons were hollowing the cave,

In the second chamber was a Viper folding round the rock & the cave, and others adorning it with gold silver and precious stones.

In the third chamber was an Eagle with wings and feathers of air, he caused the inside of the cave to be infinite, around were numbers of Eagle like men, who built palaces in the immense cliffs.

In the fourth chamber were Lions of flaming fire raging around & melting the metals into living fluids.

In the fifth chamber were Unnam'd forms, which cast the metals into the expanse.

There they were reciev'd by Men who occupied the sixth chamber, and took the forms of books & were arranged in libraries.

[23] In Ezekiel 4 the prophet enacts symbolically the captivity and iniquity of Israel and Judah, lying on his side for 430 days to represent 430 years and eating cakes baked "with dung" (that is, as a fuel, not, as Blake read the passage, mixed with the meal).

[24] In other words, soon, because tradition held that the world had been created a little more than 4,000 years B.C.

[25] The angel stationed to prevent Adam from re-entering Eden; Genesis 3:24.

[26] This passage, clearly some kind of allegory of the creative process, has had many interpretations, no one of which seems more worthy of mention than the others. Its contrast with the straightforwardness of most of *The Marriage* suggests the possiblity that Blake is being deliberately and playfully esoteric.

PLATE 16

The Giants who formed this world into its sensual existence and now seem to live in it in chains, are in truth. the causes of its life & the sources of all activity, but the chains are, the cunning of weak and tame minds. which have power to resist energy, according to the proverb, the weak in courage is strong in cunning.

Thus one portion of being, is the Prolific. the other, the Devouring: to the devourer it seems as if the producer was in his chains, but it is not so, he only takes portions of existence and fancies that the whole.

But the Prolific would cease to be Prolific unless the Devourer as a sea recieved the excess of his delights.

Some will say, Is not God alone the Prolific? I answer, God only Acts & Is, in existing beings or Men.

These two classes of men are always upon earth, & they should be enemies;[27] whoever tries [PL 17] to reconcile them seeks to destroy existence.

Religion is an endeavour to reconcile the two.

Note. Jesus Christ did not wish to unite but to seperate them, as in the Parable of sheep and goats! & he says I came not to send Peace but a Sword.[28]

Messiah or Satan or Tempter was formerly thought to be one of the Antediluvians[29] who are our Energies.

A Memorable Fancy

An Angel came to me and said O pitiable foolish young man! O horrible! O dreadful state! consider the hot burning dungeon thou art preparing for thyself to all eternity, to which thou art going in such career.[30]

I said, perhaps you will be willing to shew me my eternal lot & we will contemplate together upon it and see whether your lot or mine is most desirable

So he took me thro' a stable & thro' a church & down into the church vault at the end of which was a mill:[31] thro' the mill we went, and came to a cave. down the winding cavern we groped our tedious way till a void boundless as a nether sky appeard beneath us. & we held by the roots of trees and hung over this immensity, but I said, if you please we will commit ourselves to this void, and see whether providence is here also, if you will not I will? but he answerd, do not presume O young man but as we here remain behold thy lot which will soon appear when the darkness passes away

So I remaind with him sitting in the twisted [PL 18] root of an oak. he was suspended in a fungus which hung with the head downward into the deep;

[27] The need to keep the two classes (corresponding to Hell and Heaven) separate raises the question how their apparently desired "marriage" is to be understood.

[28] The sheep and goats (saved and damned) are to be separated at the Last Judgment (Matthew 25:31–46); in Matthew 10:34–39, Jesus says he brings not peace but a sword, forcing his followers to choose between him and even their closest kindred.

[29] Those who lived before the Flood of Genesis 7–8.

[30] Haste.

[31] The mill is a complex symbol in Blake for the destruction of what is human and individual: as a flour mill reduces grain to indistinguishable particles, industrial mills (as Blake may have foreseen) reduce people to things, and the stars revolving around the poles suggest imprisonment in an indifferent universe.

By degrees we beheld the infinite Abyss, fiery as the smoke of a burning city; beneath us at an immense distance was the sun, black but shining[;] round it were fiery tracks on which revolv'd[32] vast spiders, crawling after their prey; which flew or rather swum in the infinite deep, in the most terrific shapes of animals sprung from corruption. & the air was full of them, & seemd composed of them; these are Devils. and are called Powers of the air, I now asked my companion which was my eternal lot? he said, between the black & white spiders

But now, from between the black & white spiders a cloud and fire burst and rolled thro the deep blackning all beneath, so that the nether deep grew black as a sea & rolled with a terrible noise: beneath us was nothing now to be seen but a black tempest, till looking east between the clouds & the waves, we saw a cataract of blood mixed with fire and not many stones throw from us appeard and sunk again the scaly fold of a monstrous serpent[.] at last to the east, distant about three degrees appeard a fiery crest above the waves[.] slowly it reared like a ridge of golden rocks till we discoverd two globes of crimson fire, from which the sea fled away in clouds of smoke, and now we saw, it was the head of Leviathan,[33] his forehead was divided into streaks of green & purple like those on a tygers forehead: soon we saw his mouth & red gills hang just above the raging foam tinging the black deep with beams of blood, advancing toward [PL 19] us with all the fury of a spiritual existence.

My friend the Angel climb'd up from his station into the mill; I remain'd alone, & then this appearance was no more, but I found myself sitting on a pleasant bank beside a river by moon light hearing a harper who sung to the harp, & his theme was, The man who never alters his opinion is like standing water, & breeds reptiles of the mind.

But I arose, and sought for the mill, & there I found my Angel, who surprised asked me, how I escaped?

I answerd. All that we saw was owing to your metaphysics: for when you ran away, I found myself on a bank by moonlight hearing a harper, But now we have seen my eternal lot, shall I shew you yours? he laughd at my proposal; but I by force suddenly caught him in my arms, & flew westerly thro' the night, till we were elevated above the earths shadow: then I flung myself with him directly into the body of the sun, here I clothed myself in white, & taking in my hand Swedenborgs volumes sunk from the glorious clime, and passed all the planets till we came to saturn, here I staid to rest & then leap'd into the void, between saturn & the fixed stars.[34]

Here said I! is your lot, in this space, if space it may be calld, Soon we saw the stable and the church, & I took him to the altar and open'd the Bible, and lo! it was a deep pit, into which I descended driving the Angel before me, soon we saw seven houses of brick, one we enterd; in it were a [PL 20] number of monkeys, baboons, & all of that species[35] chaind by the middle, grinning and snatching at one another, but witheld by the shortness of their chains: however I saw that they sometimes grew numerous,

[32] A parody of the solar system seen rationalistically.

[33] The giant sea-beast of Job 41:1–10.

[34] Saturn was traditionally the outermost planet (although in 1781 Uranus had been discovered).

[35] The animals are quarreling theologians; the seven houses, different Churches.

and then the weak were caught by the strong and with a grinning aspect, first coupled with & then devourd, by plucking off first one limb and then another till the body was left a helpless trunk. this after grinning & kissing it with seeming fondness they devourd too; and here & there I saw one savourily picking the flesh off of his own tail; as the stench terribly annoyd us both we went into the mill, & I in my hand brought the skeleton of a body, which in the mill was Aristotles Analytics.[36]

So the Angel said: thy phantasy has imposed upon me & thou oughtest to be ashamed.

I answerd: we impose on one another, & it is but lost time to converse with you whose works are only Analytics

Opposition is true Friendship.

PLATE 21

I have always found that Angels have the vanity to speak of themselves as the only wise; this they do with a confident insolence sprouting from systematic reasoning;

Thus Swedenborg boasts that what he writes is new; tho' it is only the Contents or Index of already publish'd books

A man carried a monkey about for a shew, & because he was a little wiser than the monkey, grew vain, and conciev'd himself as much wiser than seven men. It is so with Swedenborg; he shews the folly of churches & exposes hypocrites, till he imagines that all are religious. & himself the single [PL 22] one on earth that ever broke a net.

Now hear a plain fact: Swedenborg has not written one new truth: Now hear another: he has written all the old falshoods.

And now hear the reason. He conversed with Angels who are all religious, & conversed not with Devils who all hate religion, for he was incapable thro' his conceited notions.

Thus Swedenborgs writings are a recapitulation of all superficial opinions, and an analysis of the more sublime, but no further.

Have now another plain fact: Any man of mechanical talents may from the writings of Paracelsus or Jacob Behmen,[37] produce ten thousand volumes of equal value with Swedenborg's. and from those of Dante or Shakespear, an infinite number.

But when he has done this, let him not say that he knows better than his master, for he only holds a candle in sunshine.

A Memorable Fancy

Once I saw a Devil in a flame of fire. who arose before an Angel that sat on a cloud. and the Devil utterd these words.

The worship of God is. Honouring his gifts in other men each according to his genius. and loving the [PL 23] greatest men best, those who envy or calumniate great men hate God, for there is no other God.

The Angel hearing this became almost blue but mastering himself he grew yellow, & at last white pink & smiling, and then replied,

[36] Treatises on formal reasoning.
[37] Paracelsus (1493–1541) and Boehme (1575–1624) wrote on the occult and mysticism.

Thou Idolater, is not God One? & is not he visible in Jesus Christ? and has not Jesus Christ given his sanction to the law of ten commandments and are not all other men fools, sinners, & nothings?

The Devil answer'd; bray a fool in a morter[38] with wheat. yet shall not his folly be beaten out of him: if Jesus Christ is the greatest man, you ought to love him in the greatest degree; now hear how he has given his sanction to the law of ten commandments: did he not mock at the sabbath, and so mock the sabbaths God? murder those who were murderd because of him? turn away the law from the woman taken in adultery? steal the labor of others to support him? bear false witness when he omitted making a defence before Pilate? covet when he pray'd for his disciples, and when he bid them shake off the dust of their feet against such as refused to lodge them?[39] I tell you, no virtue can exist without breaking these ten commandments. Jesus was all virtue, and acted from im[PL 24]pulse. not from rules.

When he had so spoken: I beheld the Angel who stretched out his arms embracing the flame of fire & he was consumed and arose as Elijah.[40]

Note. This Angel, who is now become a Devil, is my particular friend: we often read the Bible together in its infernal or diabolical sense which the world shall have if they behave well

I have also: The Bible of Hell:[41] which the world shall have whether they will or no.

One Law for the Lion & Ox is Oppression

PLATE 25

A Song of Liberty[42]

1. The Eternal Female[43] groand! it was heard over all the Earth:
2. Albions[44] coast is sick silent; the American meadows faint!
3. Shadows of Prophecy shiver along by the lakes and the rivers and mutter across the ocean? France rend down thy dungeon;[45]
4. Golden Spain burst the barriers of old Rome;
5. Cast thy keys[46] O Rome into the deep down falling, even to eternity down falling,
6. And weep

[38] Pound with a mortar and pestle.

[39] The Devil is interpreting passages including Mark 2:23–28 (on the sabbath); Matthew 2:16 (Herod's slaughter of the innocents; Blake may also mean all the Christian martyrs); John 8:3–11 (the adulterous woman); Matthew 10:9–15 (support and lodging for the disciples); and Matthew 27:13–14 (silence before Pilate).

[40] Carried up to heaven in a whirlwind (II Kings 2:11).

[41] Probably Blake's subsequent "prophetic works" such as the *Book of Urizen,* which describes the hell of fallen human consciousness and uses a biblical double-column format of chapters and verses.

[42] This tailpiece to *The Marriage* is in the style of Blake's later prophetic myths *America* and *Europe,* where the characters here are named and fully developed.

[43] This mother, in labor with the "new born terror" (verse 7) who personifies revolution, is in later versions of Blake's myth the mate of Urthona (verse 16). There the parents represent imagination; here they may be mere earth-figures, but if they have their later meaning they underline the origin of revolution in imagination, not nature.

[44] England's. [45] The Bastille, stormed in 1789. [46] The papal keys of St. Peter.

7. In her trembling hands she took the new born terror howling:
8 On those infinite mountains of light[47] now barr'd out by the atlantic sea, the new born fire stood before the starry king![48]
9. Flag'd[49] with grey brow'd snows and thunderous visages the jealous wings wav'd over the deep.
10. The speary hand burned aloft, unbuckled was the shield, forth went the hand of jealousy among the flaming hair, and [PL 26] hurl'd the new born wonder thro' the starry night.
11. The fire, the fire, is falling!
12. Look up! look up! O citizen of London. enlarge thy countenance; O Jew, leave counting gold! return to thy oil and wine; O African! black African! (go. winged thought widen his forehead.)
13. The fiery limbs, the flaming hair, shot like the sinking sun into the western sea.
14. Wak'd from his eternal sleep, the hoary element roaring fled away:
15. Down rushd beating his wings in vain the jealous king; his grey brow'd councellors, thunderous warriors, curl'd veterans, among helms, and shields, and chariots[,] horses, elephants: banners, castles, slings and rocks,
16. Falling, rushing, ruining! buried in the ruins, on Urthona's[50] dens.
17. All night beneath the ruins, then their sullen flames faded emerge round the gloomy king,
18. With thunder and fire: leading his starry hosts thro' the waste wilderness [PL 27] he promulgates his ten commands, glancing his beamy eyelids over the deep in dark dismay,
19. Where the son of fire[51] in his eastern cloud, while the morning plumes her golden breast,
20. Spurning the clouds written with curses, stamps the stony law[52] to dust, loosing the eternal horses from the dens of night, crying

Empire is no more! and now the lion & wolf shall cease.

CHORUS

Let the Priests of the Raven[53] of dawn, no longer in deadly black. with hoarse note curse the sons of joy. Nor his accepted brethren whom, tyrant, he calls free: lay the bound or build the roof. Nor pale religious letchery call that virginity, that wishes but acts not!

For every thing that lives is Holy

[47] The lost continent of Atlantis.
[48] Urizen, the principle of tyranny by state, religion, and rigid morality.
[49] Weighed down. [50] See note to verse 1.
[51] The spirit of revolution, risen again like the sun. [52] The Ten Commandments.
[53] The priests substitute the gloomy raven for the joyful birds of day.

William Wordsworth
(1770–1850)

Like several other Romantic poets, William Wordsworth is a paradox. In much of his best poetry his aim was to celebrate the changeless things in nature and man. Yet his contemporaries sensed in his work a strangeness and bold originality that were bracing or unsettling depending on how willing they were to accept a new kind of poetry. In retrospect, we can see still more clearly how original he was, and if he no longer startles us that is partly because so many later poets—Matthew Arnold and Robert Frost, to name just two—have made his strategies familiar, especially his habit of philosophizing from natural emblems. Wordsworth embarked on his most creative period by trying to chasten and chastise eighteenth-century poetry, using a language of limpid, plate-glass purity freed from mannered artifice. Yet his own manner was so distinctive that he is among the most parodied of poets. His plainness of diction, along with the unpretentious, aggressively banal subjects he sometimes wrote on, earned him the dubious epithet "the simple Wordsworth." Yet much of his work was and still is difficult, groping as it does toward the expression of elusive states of the mind and soul. (In Don Juan, *I.xc, a clowning Byron calls him "unintelligible," which would hardly be funny if no one else agreed.) In his lifetime, Wordsworth was rightly considered, along with Byron, one of the two pivotal figures of English Romanticism, and this despite the fact that his greatest, most characteristic, and in some respects most revolutionary work remained unpublished until after his death.*

Wordsworth once defined the imagination, which he considered the highest faculty of the creative mind, as something which "produces impressive effects out of simple elements." We could apply this phrase to his life, which was outwardly rather uneventful except for a few years in his early twenties that we don't know much about. He was born in 1770 in Cockermouth, in northwest England, the scenic "Lake District" he was to make famous. His father was business agent to Sir James Lowther, a tightfisted man whose failure to repay a debt to his agent created money problems for the five Wordsworth children until his heir finally made amends in 1802. Wordsworth's mother, the daughter of a linen draper, died when the poet was eight, his father five years later. (As they also do with the nature-loving, motherless Rousseau, critics with a psychoanalytic bent make much of the maternal and nurse images the orphaned Wordsworth applies to nature; see, for example, "Ode: Intimations of Immortality," lines 77–84.) When he was nine Wordsworth was sent to a very good school at Hawkshead, about thirty miles from home, where for eight years he boarded during school terms with a townswoman. Hawkshead was the center of the intense boyhood experiences in nature he describes in the early books of The Prelude*—a discipline in both "beauty" and "fear" to which he later ascribed the formation of his character. When he was seventeen he enrolled in St. John's College, Cambridge. The uncles who had become his guardians expected him to win a fellowship and become a clergyman, but that career had no appeal for Wordsworth, and for several years his worldly prospects were to be perilous and indeterminate.*

In his third year at Cambridge he took the walking tour to the Alps described in Book VI of The Prelude. *After returning to Cambridge and taking an undistinguished degree in 1791, he spent some time in London; according to* The Prelude, *he found the metropolis a phantasmagoria, the antithesis of the stable grandeur and dignity of his native hills. In late 1791 he went to France again, this time for a year. The French Revolution was moving toward its critical phase, and Wordsworth* learned to understand what it was about from a French officer named Michael Beaupuy. In France Wordsworth also fell in love with a surgeon's daughter named Annette Vallon, by whom he had an illegitimate child—a well-kept secret until the twentieth century. Forced by lack of money to come back to England, Wordsworth was prevented by the outbreak of war from seeing mother or child for ten years, and he never married Annette as they had once intended. (In 1802, during a brief peace just before his marriage to Mary Hutchinson, Wordsworth did revisit Annette and their daughter Caroline, to whose support he later contributed.) And another, mental crisis emerged from the war. As an Englishman, Wordsworth felt guilty about his French sympathies, which in themselves became a source of anguish when the Revolution turned more violently bloody and France turned from self-defense to military aggression. Taking psychological refuge in the uncompromising rationalism of the London radicals only made things worse, and he reached a state he called "despair." At this dark moment a modest but sufficient bequest from Raisley Calvert, whom Wordsworth had helped care for before his death in 1795, allowed Wordsworth and his adoring and loved sister Dorothy to establish a home in Dorsetshire, in southern England. She helped restore his mental health and remained with him through old age, her journals providing Wordsworth with material for his poems and us with valuable insights into his creative methods.

In 1797 they cemented a recent friendship with Samuel Taylor Coleridge and moved again in order to be near his home in Somerset, in the southwest. The friendship between the two men, like that between Goethe and Schiller at the same time, was one of the most fruitful relationships in literary history. In 1793 Wordsworth had published two long poems (An Evening Walk and Descriptive Sketches) more or less in the prevailing eighteenth-century style, and Coleridge's poetry too had been derivative. Now they conceived together both a new poetic style and a whole new rationale of what poetry should do. It was to be an agency not of mere diversion but of the profoundest truth, truth uniting the best insights of mind and heart in an imaginative union that would enlighten and help heal a spiritually ailing world. According to Coleridge's account some years later, their division of labor called for him to treat supernatural or exotic subjects with psychological realism and for Wordsworth to treat everyday subjects in such a way as to give them the novelty and excitement we normally expect only from the supernatural. The medium would be an honest language really spoken by men, cleansed of unfunctional conventionality. This program produced their epoch-making volume Lyrical Ballads, first published in 1798. Its rationale was expressed in the famous Preface of 1800 (revised in 1802), written by Wordsworth and traditionally considered the manifesto of English Romanticism. Of the poems themselves, Coleridge contributed only four, but they included his masterpiece "The Rime of the Ancient Mariner." Wordsworth contributed nineteen, adding many more in the new editions that followed in the next few years. A few (including "Tintern Abbey") are not ballads at all but elevated blank-verse meditations. Wordsworth's ballads in the volume fell, roughly speaking, into two groups: 1) treatments of almost absurdly "unpoetic" subjects like that of "The Idiot Boy," expressed in aggressively commonplace language; and 2) certain quintessentially Wordsworthian poems about simple situations, written in a chaste basic English—neither lofty nor low. (The first four poems that follow in this anthology belong to this second set.) However simple-minded or disarming they may seem, all the poems have, in Wordsworth's portentous phrase, "a worthy purpose" (the emphasis is his). These "purposes" are easy to miss or mistake, but almost always they have to do with the way our minds work. For example, it may well be valid and in keeping with the Words-

worthian spirit to read "We Are Seven" as a poem illustrating the child's higher religious insight (though this presents problems, for the child apparently does not have any notion of an afterlife, while the adult does speak of heaven); what emerges from a closer reading is the pattern of differences between the mental mechanics of adult and child. Oddly, one of the things that obscure the "purposes" in many of Wordsworth's poems is the very simplicity of the language; one of the hardest things in reading his works is to concentrate on the behavior of words that seem not to be doing anything special at all. For example: "Come forth into the light of things" ("The Tables Turned," line 15), where things *is emphatic, in contrast with the light of* books. *Or, from the same poem: "She [nature] has a world of ready wealth" (line 17), where "ready wealth" is a financial metaphor equivalent to "liquid assets"; in other words, nature gives us something we can use immediately, like money in our pockets, while books represent an investment tied up and transferable into profit only at some time in the future.*

In 1799, after a winter in Germany, Wordsworth and his sister moved back permanently to the northern Lake District where they had been children. The friendship with Coleridge continued, interrupted by an estrangement in 1810–1812 that was later healed but not completely. Under Coleridge's influence, Wordsworth had early projected a monumental "philosophical poem" on no less a subject than man, nature, and society. Understandably, he found this a heavy task. More congenial was the poem on his own life which for a long time he considered as an appendage to the projected philosophical work. The poetic autobiography grew from a two-book version completed in the late 1790's to a five-book version in 1804 to the full-scale epic Prelude *he completed in 1804–1805. This work tells the story of his life from infancy to the era of* Lyrical Ballads. *The philosophical poem, to be called* The Recluse, *remained unwritten except for an opening passage and the entire second part (of three parts planned), which appeared in 1814 as* The Excursion. *That poem was, and is, a disappointment, at least when compared with Wordsworth's earlier poetry. Wordsworth was uneasy about publishing so apparently self-centered a work as* The Prelude, *but it meant much to him and he carefully revised it several times over the next decades. It was published after his death, his wife providing the now familiar title (Wordsworth had never given it one). As for the unrealized philosophical poem, there is probably no cause to grieve, since it is hard to believe that Wordsworth had much more to say than he said in* The Prelude.

With the magnificent Poems in Two Volumes *of 1807—which included the "Intimations" ode, some sonnets unsurpassed in English, and other fine lyrics—Wordsworth's "great decade" ended. Thereafter, although his discriminating critical sense helped him to clarify the form and (some believe) to improve the style of* The Prelude, *his new poems suddenly and mysteriously declined in quality. There have been innumerable guesses about why this happened, the most common ones having to do with his growing conservatism in politics and especially in religion. But that is only a guess, and it begs many questions about the relationship between creativity and belief. At any rate, the most salient fact about Wordsworth's last four decades is the growth in his reputation. At first the object of enthusiasm by a cult, he became better known when Coleridge wrote a brilliant assessment of his friend in the* Biographia Literaria *(1817), and by 1843 he was well enough known and accepted to be named Poet Laureate. He died in 1850. In that year Matthew Arnold wrote the poem "Memorial Verses," in which he mourns Goethe, Byron, and Wordsworth. The first two, long dead, had taught us "how to dare, / And against fear our breast to steel; / Others will strengthen us to bear." But, now that Wordsworth is dead, "who, ah! who, will make us feel?"*

The typical movement of Wordsworth's major works is oscillation—between observation of the external scene and introspective analysis of feelings, between experiences and the ideas they generate, between the remembered past and present circumstances, between personal confession (I) *and universal truths* (We). *He himself called attention to this movement in connection with "Tintern Abbey," but it is discernible also in the "Intimations" ode and it governs the narrative ebb and flow in* The Prelude. *(If the poem were an automobile, we could say that it has a lot of play in the steering.) Sometimes the juxtapositions are sharply dramatic, as in the "Intimations" ode, but more often they are leisurely, producing the characteristic Wordsworthian hovering effect, by which ideas seem to grow unforcedly and organically from the scene or incident described.*

We need to keep this back-and-forth movement in mind when we call Wordsworth a "nature poet." Though it is everywhere in his work, nature rarely appears simply for its own sake, and there are not many sharp-focused close-ups. Rather, nature is a mythic emblem—of a mysterious, perhaps divine "presence" (to use one of Wordsworth's typical soft-focus nouns), of a dynamic of steady order in the universe, and especially of the meaningful development and spiritual experience of individual persons. Moreover, nature can cut two ways. It is beauty, but it is also fear—the salutary fear that comes as a vivid aftermath to transgressions like stealing boats, the soul-ennobling fear inherent in the sublime (as in the "apocalypse" passage of Book VI), the chilling fear that, while nature remains the same, we human beings perish, bodily and emotionally. This last fear is at the heart of "Tintern Abbey" and the "Intimations" ode, which present almost the same problem of the loss of inner vitality but offer very different answers, one naturalistic and the other metaphysical. (Some readers, satisfied with the answers given, regard Wordsworth as a poet of joy; others, more skeptical, find in him the deepest anxiety.) In these poems, as in many others, Wordsworth's subject is not ultimately nature but the psyche.

That does not mean that the psyche can ever be sufficient unto itself; it needs a "nurse" or "anchor" in the "mighty world / Of eye and ear" ("Tintern Abbey," lines 105–109). This last phrase is justly famous, since it leads us toward the center of Wordsworth's poetry. On the simplest level, it helps us focus on what he is saying; in the "Intimations" ode, for example, patterns of sight- and sound-imagery parallel the movements between hope and fear, reality and self-delusion. More important, by pointing at once to the world "out there" and the organic human instruments necessary for communication with that world, the phrase hints at an "ennobling interchange / Of action from without and from within"—still another form of oscillation—that ensures "spiritual dignity" (Prelude, *XIII.373–376). If we need nature, it is equally true that nature needs us. (For Blake, it is the second half of this statement that counts, as perhaps also for Wordsworth in the "Intimations" ode, a poem Blake loved.)*

This give-and-take with nature is at the heart of The Prelude. *The subject of Rousseau's* Confessions *had been "Myself alone!", but Wordsworth's plan is broader. He intends the poem to be a true epic, though—in keeping with the Romantic premise that art is an organic process—he discovers only in the act of writing that the growth of the mind is "heroic argument" (III. 184), after having (as he thought) settled for mere autobiography at the end of Book I. Virgil had transformed Homeric heroism, substituting for sheer action an ideal of civic morality; Milton had further internalized heroism by identifying it with Christian freedom-in-obedience. Wordsworth goes one step further, substituting imagination for biblical religion. In taking this bold and daunting step (daunting because it at least seems so egoistic), Wordsworth dignifies the doctrine and metaphor of guidance by nature that may seem facile in lyrics like "Expostulation and Reply" or "The Tables Turned" and perhaps even "Tintern Abbey." For nature is Wordsworth's epic "machinery," the providential force leading him by dark ways to heroism, which in* The Prelude *is the development of imaginative—that is, truly human—power. The ultimate function of his "divine" but natural guide is to make the hero independent of it. Nature teaches, but it is man who must act. Virgil's Aeneas is a passive recipient of education by the gods early in the* Aeneid; *matured, he can achieve things without their direct help. Similarly, Wordsworth is taught to go beyond nature to man: "the mind of man becomes / A thousand times more beautiful than the earth / On which he dwells" (XIV.448–450). Not just Wordsworth's mind but* man's; *as Milton's Adam is all humankind, so Wordsworth has moved from the first-person pronoun of his poem's opening passage to a universal application.*

FURTHER READING *(prepared by B. W.):* Since Wordsworth's poetry is uneven, a selection is advisable for new readers; a good choice is the Riverside edition *Selected Poems and Prefaces,* ed. by Jack Stillinger, 1965, which is well annotated and includes the entire 1850 *Prelude.* The three main versions of *The Prelude*—1799, 1805, and 1850—with good notes and a selection of critical essays are accessible in a format that facilitates comparison in the Norton Critical Edition of *The Prelude,* ed. Jonathan Wordsworth, M. H. Abrams, and Stephen Gill, 1979. The most reliable biography is Mary Moorman's *William Wordsworth: A Biography,* 2 vols., 1957–65. An excellent general work on Wordsworth, usable as an introduction but intelligently meaty, is Carl Woodring's *Wordsworth,* 1965; Helen Darbishire's *The Poet Wordsworth,* 1949, can also be recommended. Lionel Trilling has an exciting essay (first published in 1942) on the "Intimations" ode in *The Liberal Imagination,* 1950; Cleanth Brooks gives the poem a close reading in *The Well Wrought Urn,* 1947, especially good on imagery. Geoffrey H. Hartman, in *The Unmediated Vision,* 1954, has an excellent section on Wordsworth, especially on "Tintern Abbey" and the conflicts in it. This essay, along with Basil Willey's "On Wordsworth and the Locke Tradition" in *The Seventeenth-Century Background,* 1934, depicts a Wordsworth struggling to find value in a world vacated of older forms of supernatural certainty. Raymond Dexter Havens's *The Mind of A Poet,* 1941, is a detailed commentary on *The Prelude.* Herbert Lindenberger's *On Wordsworth's "Prelude,"* 1963, is good on several aspects of the poem, including the style. R. J. Onorato's *The Character of the Poet: Wordsworth in "The Prelude,"* 1971, is a psychoanalytic study of the poem. Frank D. McConnell's *The Confessional Imagination: A Reading of Wordsworth's "Prelude,"* 1974, incorporates a brilliant and unhackneyed reading of the poem with good comments on its narrative voice and its theme of continuity. John T. Ogden's "The Structure of Imaginative Experience in Wordsworth's *Prelude,*" in *The Wordsworth Circle,* 6 (1975), 290–98, analyzes the dynamics and phases in the mind's response to the external world. The tensions between Wordsworth's faith in nature and his faith in human mind-imagination-spirit are explored in John Jones's *The Egotistical Sublime,* 1954; David Perkins's *The Quest for Permanence,* 1959; David Ferry's *The Limits of Mortality,* 1959; and Geoffrey H. Hartman's *Wordsworth's Poetry 1787–1814,* 1964. Robert Rehder's *Wordsworth and the Beginnings of Modern Poetry,* 1981, discusses the poet in the context of European literature, focusing particularly on the theme of consciousness. *Discussions of William Wordsworth,* ed. by Jack Davis, 1964, begins with classic evaluations of the poet by Coleridge and Matthew Arnold and moves to important modern critics.

ANECDOTE FOR FATHERS[1]

I have a boy of five years old,
His face is fair and fresh to see;
His limbs are cast in beauty's mould,
And dearly he loves me.

One morn we strolled on our dry walk,
Our quiet home all full in view,
And held such intermitted talk
As we are wont to do.

My thoughts on former pleasures ran;
I thought of Kilve's delightful shore,
Our pleasant home when spring began,
A long, long year before.

A day it was when I could bear
Some fond regrets to entertain;
With so much happiness to spare,
I could not feel a pain.

The green earth echoed to the feet
Of lambs that bounded through the glade,
From shade to sunshine, and as fleet
From sunshine back to shade.

Birds warbled round me—and each trace
Of inward sadness had its charm;
Kilve, thought I, was a favoured place,
And so is Liswyn farm.

My boy beside me tripped, so slim
And graceful in his rustic dress!
And, as we talked, I questioned him,
In very idleness.

"Now tell me, had you rather be,"
I said, and took him by the arm,
"On Kilve's smooth shore, by the green sea,
Or here at Liswyn farm?"

In careless mood he looked at me,
While still I held him by the arm,
And said, "At Kilve I'd rather be
Than here at Liswyn farm."

[1] In the first edition of 1798, this poem had the subtitle "Showing How the Art of Lying May be Taught." In 1845 Wordsworth gave the poem a Latin epigraph which may be translated "Restrain your force or else you will make me tell lies."

"Now, little Edward, say why so:
My little Edward, tell me why."—
"I cannot tell, I do not know."—
"Why, this is strange," said I;

"For here are woods, hills smooth and warm:
There surely must some reason be
Why you would change sweet Liswyn farm
For Kilve by the green sea."

At this my boy hung down his head,
He blushed with shame, nor made reply;
And three times to the child I said,
"Why, Edward, tell me why?"

His head he raised—there was in sight,
It caught his eye, he saw it plain—
Upon the house-top, glittering bright,
A broad and gilded vane.

Then did the boy his tongue unlock,
And eased his mind with this reply:
"At Kilve there was no weather-cock;[2]
And that's the reason why."

O dearest, dearest boy! my heart
For better lore would seldom yearn,
Could I but teach the hundredth part
Of what from thee I learn.

WE ARE SEVEN

—A simple child,
That lightly draws its breath,
And feels its life in every limb,
What should it know of death?[1]

I met a little cottage girl:
She was eight years old, she said;
Her hair was thick with many a curl
That clustered round her head.

She had a rustic, woodland air,
And she was wildly clad:
Her eyes were fair, and very fair;
—Her beauty made me glad.

[2] Weather vane in the shape of a rooster. [1] Lines 1–4 were supplied by Coleridge.

"Sisters and brothers, little maid,
How many may you be?"
"How many? Seven in all," she said,
And wondering looked at me.

"And where are they? I pray you tell."
She answered, "Seven are we;
And two of us at Conway dwell,
And two are gone to sea.

"Two of us in the church-yard lie,
My sister and my brother;
And, in the church-yard cottage, I
Dwell near them with my mother."

"You say that two at Conway dwell,
And two are gone to sea,
Yet ye are seven! I pray you tell,
Sweet maid, how this may be."

Then did the little maid reply,
"Seven boys and girls are we;
Two of us in the church-yard lie,
Beneath the church-yard tree."

"You run about, my little maid,
Your limbs they are alive;
If two are in the church-yard laid,
Then ye are only five."

"Their graves are green, they may be seen,"
The little maid replied,
"Twelve steps or more from my mother's door,
And they are side by side.

"My stockings there I often knit,
My kerchief there I hem;
And there upon the ground I sit,
And sing a song to them.

"And often after sun-set, sir,
When it is light and fair,
I take my little porringer,[2]
And eat my supper there.

"The first that died was sister Jane;
In bed she moaning lay,
Till God released her of her pain;
And then she went away.

[2] Bowl with a handle.

"So in the church-yard she was laid;
And, when the grass was dry,
Together round her grave we played,
My brother John and I.

"And when the ground was white with snow,
And I could run and slide,
My brother John was forced to go,
And he lies by her side."

"How many are you, then," said I,
"If they two are in heaven?"
Quick was the little maid's reply,
"O master! we are seven."

"But they are dead; those two are dead!
Their spirits are in heaven!"
'Twas throwing words away; for still
The little maid would have her will,
And said, "Nay, we are seven!"

EXPOSTULATION AND REPLY

"Why, William, on that old grey stone,
Thus for the length of half a day,
Why, William, sit you thus alone,
And dream your time away?

"Where are your books?—that light bequeathed
To beings else forlorn and blind!
Up! up! and drink the spirit breathed
From dead men to their kind.[1]

"You look round on your Mother Earth,
As if she for no purpose bore you;
As if you were her first-born birth,
And none had lived before you!"

One morning thus, by Esthwaite lake,
When life was sweet, I knew not why,
To me my good friend Matthew spake,
And thus I made reply:

"The eye—it cannot choose but see;
We cannot bid the ear be still;
Our bodies feel, where'er they be,
Against or with our will.

[1] Their species, with a pun on "those like them."

"Nor less I deem that there are powers
Which of themselves our minds impress;
That we can feed this mind of ours
In a wise passiveness.

"Think you, 'mid all this mighty sum
Of things for ever speaking,
That nothing of itself will come,
But we must still be seeking?

"—Then ask not wherefore, here, alone,
Conversing[2] as I may,
I sit upon this old grey stone,
And dream my time away."

THE TABLES TURNED

AN EVENING SCENE
ON THE SAME SUBJECT

Up! up! my friend, and quit your books;
Or surely you'll grow double:
Up! up! my friend, and clear your looks;
Why all this toil and trouble?

The sun, above the mountain's head,
A freshening lustre mellow
Through all the long green fields has spread,
His first sweet evening yellow.

Books! 'tis a dull and endless strife:
Come, hear the woodland linnet,
How sweet his music! on my life,
There's more of wisdom in it.

And hark! how blithe the throstle[1] sings!
He, too, is no mean preacher:
Come forth into the light of things,
Let nature be your teacher.

She has a world of ready wealth,
Our minds and hearts to bless—
Spontaneous wisdom breathed by health,
Truth breathed by cheerfulness.

One impulse from a vernal wood
May teach you more of man,

[2] Associating with others. [1] Thrush.

Of moral evil and of good,
Than all the sages can.

Sweet is the lore which nature brings;
Our meddling intellect
Mis-shapes the beauteous forms of things:—
We murder to dissect.

Enough of science and of art;
Close up those barren leaves;
Come forth, and bring with you a heart
That watches and receives.

LINES

COMPOSED A FEW MILES ABOVE TINTERN ABBEY ON REVISITING THE BANKS OF THE WYE[1] DURING A TOUR, JULY 13, 1798

Five years have past; five summers, with[2] the length
Of five long winters! and again I hear
These waters, rolling from their mountain-springs
With a soft inland murmur.—Once again
Do I behold these steep and lofty cliffs,
That on a wild secluded scene impress
Thoughts of more deep seclusion; and connect
The landscape with the quiet of the sky.
The day is come when I again repose
Here, under this dark sycamore, and view
These plots of cottage-ground, these orchard-tufts,
Which at this season, with their unripe fruits,
Are clad in one green hue, and lose themselves
'Mid groves and copses. Once again I see
These hedge-rows, hardly hedge-rows, little lines
Of sportive wood run wild: these pastoral farms,
Green to the very door; and wreaths of smoke
Sent up, in silence, from among the trees!
With some uncertain notice, as might seem
Of vagrant dwellers in the houseless woods,
Or of some hermit's cave, where by his fire
The hermit sits alone.

These beauteous forms,
Through a long absence, have not been to me
As is a landscape to a blind man's eye:

[1] A river in Wales and western England flowing into the Severn. Tintern Abbey is an old ruined monastery.
[2] And also.

But oft, in lonely rooms, and 'mid the din
Of towns and cities, I have owed to them
In hours of weariness, sensations sweet,
Felt in the blood, and felt along the heart;
And passing even into my purer mind,
With tranquil restoration:—feelings too
Of unremembered pleasure: such, perhaps,
As have no slight or trivial influence
On that best portion of a good man's life,
His little, nameless, unremembered, acts
Of kindness and of love. Nor less, I trust,
To them I may have owed another gift,
Of aspect more sublime; that blessed mood,
In which the burthen[3] of the mystery,
In which the heavy and the weary weight
Of all this unintelligible world,
Is lightened:—that serene and blessed mood,
In which the affections gently lead us on,—
Until, the breath of this corporeal frame
And even the motion of our human blood
Almost suspended, we are laid asleep
In body, and become a living soul:
While with an eye made quiet by the power
Of harmony, and the deep power of joy,
We see into the life of things.
If this
Be but a vain belief, yet, oh! how oft—
In darkness and amid the many shapes
Of joyless daylight; when the fretful stir
Unprofitable, and the fever of the world,
Having hung upon the beatings of my heart—
How oft, in spirit, have I turned to thee,
O sylvan Wye! thou wanderer thro' the woods,
How often has my spirit turned to thee!

And now, with gleams of half-extinguished thought,
With many recognitions dim and faint,
And somewhat of a sad perplexity,
The picture of the mind revives again:
While here I stand, not only with the sense
Of present pleasure, but with pleasing thoughts
That in this moment there is life and food
For future years. And so I dare to hope,
Though changed, no doubt, from what I was when first
I came among these hills; when like a roe
I bounded o'er the mountains, by the sides
Of the deep rivers, and the lonely streams,
Wherever nature led: more like a man

[3] Burden.

Flying from something that he dreads, than one
Who sought the thing he loved. For nature then
(The coarser pleasures of my boyish days,
And their glad animal movements all gone by)
To me was all in all.—I cannot paint
What then I was. The sounding cataract
Haunted me like a passion: the tall rock,
The mountain, and the deep and gloomy wood,
Their colours and their forms, were then to me
An appetite; a feeling and a love,
That had no need of a remoter charm,
By thought supplied, nor any interest
Unborrowed from the eye.—That time is past,
And all its aching joys are now no more,
And all its dizzy raptures. Not for this
Faint[4] I, nor mourn nor murmur;[5] other gifts
Have followed; for such loss, I would believe,
Abundant recompense. For I have learned
To look on nature, not as in the hour
Of thoughtless youth; but hearing oftentimes
The still, sad music of humanity,
Nor harsh nor grating, though of ample power
To chasten and subdue. And I have felt
A presence that disturbs me with the joy
Of elevated thoughts; a sense sublime
Of something far more deeply interfused,
Whose dwelling is the light of setting suns,
And the round ocean and the living air,
And the blue sky, and in the mind of man:
A motion and a spirit, that impels
All thinking things, all objects of all thought,
And rolls through all things. Therefore am I still
A lover of the meadows and the woods,
And mountains; and of all that we behold
From this green earth; of all the mighty world
Of eye, and ear,—both what they half create,
And what perceive; well pleased to recognise
In nature and the language of the sense
The anchor of my purest thoughts, the nurse,
The guide, the guardian of my heart, and soul
Of all my moral being.
Nor perchance,
If I were not thus taught, should I the more
Suffer my genial[6] spirits to decay:
For thou art with me here upon the banks

[4] Grow weak in spirit. [5] Complain.

[6] A key word in Romantic poetry, *genial* can mean "innate," "sociable," "creative," "life-giving," or "pertaining to genius"; the meanings often overlap in any specific usage and have to be determined by the context. Compare Coleridge's "Dejection: An Ode," line 39.

Of this fair river; thou my dearest friend,
My dear, dear friend; and in thy voice I catch
The language of my former heart,[7] and read
My former pleasures in the shooting lights
Of thy wild eyes. Oh! yet a little while
May I behold in thee what I was once,
My dear, dear sister! and this prayer I make,
Knowing that nature never did betray
The heart that loved her; 'tis her privilege,
Through all the years of this our life, to lead
From joy to joy: for she can so inform[8]
The mind that is within us, so impress
With quietness and beauty, and so feed
With lofty thoughts, that neither evil tongues,
Rash judgments, nor the sneers of selfish men,
Nor greetings where no kindness is, nor all
The dreary intercourse of daily life,
Shall e'er prevail against us, or disturb
Our cheerful faith, that all which we behold
Is full of blessings. Therefore let the moon
Shine on thee in thy solitary walk;
And let the misty mountain-winds be free
To blow against thee: and, in after years,
When these wild ecstasies shall be matured
Into a sober pleasure; when thy mind
Shall be a mansion for all lovely forms,
Thy memory be as a dwelling-place
For all sweet sounds and harmonies; oh! then,
If solitude, or fear, or pain, or grief,
Should be thy portion, with what healing thoughts
Of tender joy wilt thou remember me,
And these my exhortations! Nor, perchance—
If I should be where I no more can hear
Thy voice, nor catch from thy wild eyes these gleams
Of past existence—wilt thou then forget
That on the banks of this delightful stream
We stood together; and that I, so long
A worshipper of nature, hither came
Unwearied in that service: rather say
With warmer love—oh! with far deeper zeal
Of holier love. Nor wilt thou then forget
That after many wanderings, many years
Of absence, these steep woods and lofty cliffs,
And this green pastoral landscape, were to me
More dear, both for themselves and for thy sake!

[7] Wordsworth's sister Dorothy, to whom he was very close, was only a year and a half younger than he, but in this poem he suggests that she is in the stage he went through five years earlier.

[8] Mold.

A Summary of Wordsworth's *Prelude*

BOOK I. Wordsworth describes his impulse to write a great poem, presumably an epic, and the difficulties he has in finding the right theme and the sufficient firmness in himself. He begins reviewing his life from infancy and decides that for the time being he will renounce his grand plans and settle for a limited, autobiographical subject.

BOOK II. He continues the account of his growth through adolescence, describing how nature, at first a backdrop, gradually came to be loved for its own sake.

BOOK III. He describes his first year at Cambridge University, which he entered at seventeen. On the whole, his description of the place is ambivalent; he attacks it for its artificiality and triviality, but he also confesses his own failure to pursue learning with greater dedication and acknowledges the beauty of the ideal of learning. He also confesses to a kind of inner falling-off of imaginative dedication which he experienced while there. He felt that he had a great task in life that he was not fulfilling and that had little to do with the university.

BOOK IV. He describes his first summer vacation from the university, when he returned to his rural home and felt himself more than ever enamored of nature. Yet even during this summer there was too much triviality, he feels, in view of what he was cut out to be. The moment of his half-unconscious "poetic dedication" occurs, at the end of a night-long dancing party.

BOOK V. He confesses his deep obligation to books, especially those (like romances, the Arabian Nights, *and fairy tales) that nurture imagination. He attacks an artificial kind of modern education that purports to rear children with careful solicitude but in fact is a kind of fussy interference with their natural development and freedom. He believes children ought to be free from their mentors' scrupulous overwatchfulness.*

BOOK VI. After his third year at Cambridge, Wordsworth and a companion take a walking tour through France and the Alps. It is now about a year after the storming of the Bastille, and the French Revolution is in its early, innocent, relatively bloodless stage. Wordsworth responds sympathetically to the euphoria sweeping France, though he also feels some pangs at the usurpation of the ancient Chartreuse monastery, a symbol of religious faith in the past. He describes the great hopes he had of finding the Alps an overwhelming experience, and also how these hopes were dashed when he found out that he had crossed the Alps without recognizing the fact. From the very disappointment, however, he learns a lesson about the greatness of the imagination and the human soul.

BOOK VII. Wordsworth moves to London. He describes the city as, despite its awesomeness and power, an artificial phantasmagoria, the antithesis of the solidity, peace, and meaningfulness of nature amid his native hills.

BOOK VIII. It is common in epic poems that, just before the crisis of the action, there be a retrospective flashback. Book VIII serves this purpose in The Prelude. *Words-*

worth describes a dynamic that, working even when he lived in nature, away from society, would ultimately teach him the supremacy of human life and values to those of mere nature.

BOOKS IX, X, AND XI. Wordsworth describes a second sojourn in France, this one longer, lasting about a year. He is no longer a naive and uninformed foreigner looking on in relative detachment, but (as the result of tutoring by a noble friend, Captain Beaupuy) an ardent zealot of the French Revolution. But near the end of his stay in France he travels to Paris and finds the city suffering from fears brought on by the first wave of what later was to be called the Reign of Terror. He feels that the Revolution has lost its initial generous impulses and that France is in danger of being usurped by mindless and bloody vengefulness. While in Paris he even considers the possibility of becoming an active leader so that he can stem the bloody tide—this despite the fact that Wordsworth is a nobody in France. But he is prevented from taking such a step, for circumstantial reasons, and he returns to London. He acknowledges gratefully that by having to return to England he was saved from a fate which would have meant betraying his true poetic mission in life. But back in England he feels alienated from both France and his own country. England, he feels, is pursuing a reactionary course in leaguing itself with old imperial regimes against Revolutionary France, while France has betrayed its own revolution by invading other countries. Thoroughly bewildered and disillusioned, Wordsworth retreats into a protective shell of uncompromising rationalism. This was the crisis of his soul's disease, from which he was rescued by friends like Coleridge and his sister Dorothy and by the dynamic of his relationship to nature, which had implanted emotional and imaginative resources that in the end could not fail him.

BOOKS XII, XIII, AND XIV. These are, for the most part, discursive rather than narrative books, and they state Wordsworth's definitive ideas on a multitude of subjects, especially on the importance of imagination. (The "spots of time" passage in Book XII is an example.) He recovers, and confirms in himself for the first time since his age of innocence, the imaginative powers that had grown in childhood; they are confirmed because they have withstood the test of despair and disillusionment. He now hopes that he, in collaboration with his colleague and friend Coleridge, can help heal the sickness of England and of the age, and he projects a career for them as prophets and healers and poets, teaching people in an age of despair how to feel and how to summon confidence from the existence of perennial truths of human nature. In Book XIV he describes an ascent of Mount Snowdon, in Wales, and a vision of the moon shining on top of clouds, which he feels is an emblem of the way in which the imaginative mind works on the material of the world. The poem ends with a joyful acknowledgment of the nobility of the human mind, which is even more beautiful than the nature he had celebrated early in the poem. In its unpredictable and mysterious way, nature has led him to love man and to understand what is permanently valuable in human nature.

from THE PRELUDE[1]

OR, GROWTH OF A POET'S MIND

An Autobiographical Poem
(1850 Version)

BOOK FIRST

INTRODUCTION—CHILDHOOD
AND SCHOOL-TIME

O there is blessing in this gentle breeze,
A visitant that while it fans my cheek
Doth seem half-conscious of the joy it brings
From the green fields, and from yon azure sky.
Whate'er its mission, the soft breeze can come
To none more grateful than to me; escaped
From the vast city,[2] where I long had pined
A discontented sojourner: now free,
Free as a bird to settle where I will.
What dwelling shall receive me? in what vale
Shall be my harbour? underneath what grove
Shall I take up my home? and what clear stream
Shall with its murmur lull me into rest?
The earth is all before me.[3] With a heart
Joyous, nor scared at its own liberty,
I look about; and should the chosen guide
Be nothing better than a wandering cloud,
I cannot miss my way. I breathe again!
Trances of thought and mountings of the mind
Come fast upon me: it is shaken off,
That burthen[4] of my own unnatural self,
The heavy weight of many a weary day
Not mine, and such as were not made for me.

[1] This title and the subtitle were supplied by Mrs. Wordsworth when the poem was first published in 1850 shortly after her husband's death. At one time he had intended it as an appendage to a long philosophical poem on man, nature, and society, only part of which was ever written. Some readers prefer the earliest (1805) full-length version of the poem, partly on the grounds that it is closer to Wordsworth's early views on politics and especially on religion. It is unquestionably true that in revising *The Prelude* over the last half of his life Wordsworth made the poem more conservative, but the differences between the two versions have been exaggerated; Wordsworth in 1805 had already moved away from political or religious radicalism. The text of 1850 has seemed to us preferable because of its general superiority in poetic style (for example, it adds the great lines about Newton in III.62–63) and because the epic pattern in it is even clearer than in the version of 1805.

[2] London.

[3] An allusion to the departure of Adam and Eve from Eden in Milton's *Paradise Lost,* XII.646–647: "The world was all before them, where to choose / Their place of rest, and Providence their guide."

[4] Burden.

Long months of peace (if such bold word accord
With any promises of human life),
Long months of ease and undisturbed delight
Are mine in prospect; whither shall I turn,
By road or pathway, or through trackless field,
Up hill or down, or shall some floating thing
Upon the river point me out my course?

Dear liberty! Yet what would it avail
But for a gift that consecrates the joy?
For I, methought, while the sweet breath of heaven
Was blowing on my body, felt within
A correspondent breeze, that gently moved
With quickening[5] virtue, but is now become
A tempest, a redundant[6] energy,
Vexing its own creation. Thanks to both,
And their congenial[7] powers, that, while they join
In breaking up a long-continued frost,
Bring with them vernal promises, the hope
Of active days urged on by flying hours,—
Days of sweet leisure, taxed with patient thought
Abstruse, nor wanting punctual service high,
Matins and vespers[8] of harmonious verse!

Thus far, O friend![9] did I, not used to make
A present joy the matter of a song,[10]
Pour forth that day my soul in measured[11] strains
That would not be forgotten, and are here
Recorded: to the open fields I told
A prophecy: poetic numbers[12] came
Spontaneously to clothe in priestly robe
A renovated spirit singled out,
Such hope was mine, for holy services.
My own voice cheered me, and, far more, the mind's
Internal echo of the imperfect sound;
To both I listened, drawing from them both
A cheerful confidence in things to come.

Content and not unwilling now to give
A respite to this passion, I paced on
With brisk and eager steps; and came, at length,
To a green shady place, where down I sate

[5] Life-giving. [6] A Latinism: "overflowing."
[7] *Con* means "together"; for *genial,* see "Lines Composed a Few Miles Above Tintern Abbey," note to line 113.
[8] *Matins and vespers.* In monasteries, morning and evening services.
[9] Samuel Taylor Coleridge, to whom the poem is addressed.
[10] *not used . . . song.* In the Preface to *Lyrical Ballads,* Wordsworth wrote that poetry originates in "emotion recollected in tranquillity."
[11] In poetic meter. [12] Versification.

Beneath a tree, slackening my thoughts by choice,
And settling into gentler happiness.
T'was autumn, and a clear and placid day,
With warmth, as much as needed, from a sun
Two hours declined towards the west; a day
With silver clouds, and sunshine on the grass,
And in the sheltered and the sheltering grove
A perfect stillness. Many were the thoughts
Encouraged and dismissed, till choice was made
Of a known vale, whither my feet should turn,
Nor rest till they had reached the very door
Of the one cottage which methought I saw.
No picture of mere memory ever looked
So fair; and while upon the fancied scene
I gazed with growing love, a higher power
Than fancy[13] gave assurance of some work
Of glory there forthwith to be begun,
Perhaps too there performed. Thus long I mused,
Nor e'er lost sight of what I mused upon,
Save when, amid the stately grove of oaks,
Now here, now there, an acorn, from its cup
Dislodged, through sere leaves rustled, or at once
To the bare earth dropped with a startling sound.
From that soft couch I rose not, till the sun
Had almost touched the horizon; casting then
A backward glance upon the curling cloud
Of city smoke, by distance ruralised;
Keen as a truant or a fugitive,
But as a pilgrim resolute, I took,
Even with the chance equipment of that hour,
The road that pointed toward the chosen vale.
It was a spendid evening, and my soul
Once more made trial of her strength, nor lacked
Aeolian[14] visitations; but the harp
Was soon defrauded, and the banded host
Of harmony dispersed in straggling sounds,
And lastly utter silence! "Be it so;
Why think of anything but present good?"
So, like a home-bound labourer I pursued
My way beneath the mellowing sun, that shed
Mild influence; nor left in me one wish
Again to bend the Sabbath of that time
To a servile yoke. What need of many words?
A pleasant loitering journey, through three days
Continued, brought me to my hermitage.
I spare to tell of what ensued, the life

[13] Wordsworth generally thought of fancy as a creative power inferior to imagination.

[14] Wind-like; Aeolus was god of the winds. For the Aeolian harp and its symbolism, see Coleridge's "Dejection: An Ode" and the note to line 7.

In common things—the endless store of things,
Rare, or at least so seeming, every day
Found all about me in one neighbourhood—
The self-congratulation, and, from morn
To night, unbroken cheerfulness serene.
But speedily an earnest longing rose
To brace myself to some determined aim,
Reading or thinking; either to lay up
New stores, or rescue from decay the old
By timely interference: and therewith
Came hopes still higher, that with outward life[15]
I might endue some airy phantasies
That had been floating loose about for years,
And to such beings temperately deal forth
The many feelings that oppressed my heart.
That hope hath been discouraged; welcome light
Dawns from the east, but dawns to disappear
And mock me with a sky that ripens not
Into a steady morning: if my mind,
Remembering the bold promise of the past,
Would gladly grapple with some noble theme,
Vain is her wish; where'er she turns she finds
Impediments from day to day renewed.

And now it would content me to yield up
Those lofty hopes awhile, for present gifts
Of humbler industry. But, oh, dear friend!
The poet, gentle creature as he is,
Hath, like the lover, his unruly times;
His fits when he is neither sick nor well,
Though no distress be near him but his own
Unmanageable thoughts: his mind, best pleased
While she as duteous as the mother dove
Sits brooding, lives not always to that end,
But like the innocent bird, hath goadings on
That drive her as in trouble through the groves;
With me is now such passion, to be blamed
No otherwise than as it lasts too long.

When, as becomes a man who would prepare
For such an arduous work, I through myself
Make rigorous inquisition, the report
Is often cheering; for I neither seem
To lack that first great gift, the vital soul,
Nor general truths, which are themselves a sort
Of elements and agents, under-powers,
Subordinate helpers of the living mind:
Nor am I naked of external things,

[15] With poetic form.

Forms, images, nor numerous other aids
Of less regard, though won perhaps with toil
And needful to build up a poet's praise.
Time, place, and manners do I seek, and these
Are found in plenteous store, but nowhere such
As may be singled out with steady choice;
No little band of yet remembered names[16]
Whom I, in perfect confidence, might hope
To summon back from lonesome banishment,
And make them dwellers in the hearts of men
Now living, or to live in future years.
Sometimes the ambitious power of choice, mistaking
Proud spring-tide swellings for a regular sea,
Will settle on some British theme, some old
Romantic tale by Milton left unsung;[17]
More often turning to some gentle place
Within the groves of chivalry,[18] I pipe
To shepherd swains, or seated harp in hand,
Amid reposing knights by a river side
Or fountain, listen to the grave reports
Of dire enchantments faced and overcome
By the strong mind, and tales of warlike feats,
Where spear encountered spear, and sword with sword
Fought, as if conscious of the blazonry[19]
That the shield bore, so glorious was the strife;
Whence inspiration for a song that winds
Through ever-changing scenes of votive[20] quest
Wrongs to redress, harmonious tribute paid
To patient courage and unblemished truth,
To firm devotion, zeal unquenchable,
And Christian meekness hallowing faithful loves.
Sometimes, more sternly moved, I would relate
How vanquished Mithridates[21] northward passed,
And, hidden in the cloud of years, became
Odin, the father of a race by whom
Perished the Roman Empire: how the friends
And followers of Sertorius,[22] out of Spain

[16] Wordsworth is groping for an epic theme, and the standard epic approach was to write on legendary or historical rather than fictional heroes.

[17] Milton had considered an early medieval theme for his epic before deciding to write *Paradise Lost,* on the fall of man. Throughout *The Prelude* Wordsworth has Milton in mind as his model.

[18] Wordsworth is thinking of the medieval and Renaissance romance.

[19] Coat of arms.

[20] Related to a vow, like that of a knight to save a maiden in distress.

[21] A king in Asia Minor, defeated by the Roman general Pompey in 66 B.C. Wordsworth blends him with the legendary Odin, who out of hatred of the Romans developed the Goths living in Sweden to the point where they could overthrow Rome.

[22] A Roman general, defeated by the party in power in Rome. Legend held that, after he died in 72 B.C., his followers settled the Canary Islands (identified with the Fortunate Isles, the mythical abode of dead heroes), where fifteen hundred years later the Spaniards had great difficulty overcoming them.

Flying, found shelter in the Fortunate Isles,
And left their usages, their arts and laws,
To disappear by a slow gradual death,
To dwindle and to perish one by one,
Starved in those narrow bounds: but not the soul
Of liberty, which fifteen hundred years
Survived, and, when the European came
With skill and power that might not be withstood,
Did, like a pestilence, maintain its hold
And wasted down by glorious death that race
Of natural heroes: or I would record
How, in tyrannic times, some high-souled man,
Unnamed among the chronicles of kings,
Suffered in silence for truth's sake: or tell,
How that one Frenchman,[23] through continued force
Of meditation on the inhuman deeds
Of those who conquered first the Indian Isles,
Went single in his ministry across
The ocean; not to comfort the oppressed,
But, like a thirsty wind, to roam about
Withering the oppressor: how Gustavus[24] sought
Help at his need in Dalecarlia's mines:
How Wallace[25] fought for Scotland; left the name
Of Wallace to be found, like a wild flower,
All over his dear country; left the deeds
Of Wallace, like a family of ghosts,
To people the steep rocks and river banks,
Her natural sanctuaries, with a local soul
Of independence and stern liberty.
Sometimes it suits me better to invent
A tale from my own heart, more near akin
To my own passions and habitual thoughts;
Some variegated story, in the main
Lofty, but the unsubstantial structure melts
Before the very sun that brightens it,
Mist into air dissolving! Then a wish,
My last and favourite aspiration, mounts
With yearning toward some philosophic song
Of truth that cherishes our daily life;
With meditations passionate from deep
Recesses in man's heart, immortal verse
Thoughtfully fitted to the Orphean[26] lyre;
But from this awful burthen I full soon
Take refuge and beguile myself with trust

[23] Dominique de Gourges, who in 1567 sailed from France to Florida to avenge the slaughter of French Protestants by Spain.
[24] A sixteenth-century king of Sweden who liberated his people from the Danes; for a time he hid out in Dalecarlia, a mining district.
[25] Sir William Wallace (1272–1305), Scots hero who led his people's resistance to England.
[26] Related to Orpheus, legendary poet-musician.

That mellower years will bring a riper mind
And clearer insight. Thus my days are past
In contradiction; with no skill to part
Vague longing, haply bred by want of power,
From paramount impulse not to be withstood,
A timorous capacity from prudence,
From circumspection,[27] infinite delay.
Humility and modest awe themselves
Betray me, serving often for a cloak
To a more subtle selfishness; that now
Locks every function up in blank reserve,[28]
Now dupes me, trusting to an anxious eye[29]
That with intrusive restlessness beats off
Simplicity and self-presented truth.
Ah! better far than this, to stray about
Voluptuously through fields and rural walks,
And ask no record of the hours, resigned
To vacant musing, unreproved neglect
Of all things, and deliberate holiday.
Far better never to have heard the name
Of zeal and just ambition, than to live
Baffled and plagued by a mind that every hour
Turns recreant[30] to her task; takes heart again,
Then feels immediately some hollow thought
Hang like an interdict[31] upon her hopes.
This is my lot; for either still I find
Some imperfection in the chosen theme,
Or see of absolute accomplishment
Much wanting, so much wanting, in myself,
That I recoil and droop, and seek repose
In listlessness from vain perplexity,
Unprofitably travelling toward the grave,
Like a false steward who hath much received
And renders nothing back.[32]
                                        Was it for this
That one, the fairest of all rivers,[33] loved
To blend his murmurs with my nurse's song,
And, from his alder shades and rocky falls,
And from his fords and shallows, sent a voice
That flowed along my dreams? For this, didst thou,
O Derwent! winding among grassy holms
Where I was looking on, a babe in arms,
Make ceaseless music that composed my thoughts

[27] Prudent concern about the result. [28] Hoarding of energies.
[29] Crippling self-consciousness. [30] Like an unfaithful coward. [31] Prohibition.
[32] *steward . . . back.* Wordsworth is thinking of the parable of the "talents" (sums of money); the servant who did not take investment risks with what his master had entrusted to him was severely punished. See Matthew 25:14–30.
[33] *fairest . . . rivers.* The Derwent flowed past the house in Cockermouth where Wordsworth was born.

To more than infant softness, giving me
Amid the fretful dwellings of mankind
A foretaste, a dim earnest,[34] of the calm
That nature breathes among the hills and groves.
When he had left the mountains and received
On his smooth breast the shadow of those towers[35]
That yet survive, a shattered monument
Of feudal sway, the bright blue river passed
Along the margin of our terrace walk;
A tempting playmate whom we dearly loved.
Oh, many a time have I, a five years' child,
In a small mill-race severed from his stream,
Made one long bathing of a summer's day;
Basked in the sun, and plunged and basked again
Alternate, all a summer's day, or scoured
The sandy fields, leaping through flowery groves
Of yellow ragwort; or, when rock and hill,
The woods, and distant Skiddaw's lofty height,
Were bronzed with deepest radiance, stood alone
Beneath the sky, as if I had been born
On Indian[36] plains, and from my mother's hut
Had run abroad in wantonness, to sport
A naked savage, in the thunder shower.

Fair seed-time had my soul, and I grew up
Fostered alike by beauty and by fear:
Much favoured in my birth-place, and no less
In that beloved vale to which erelong
We were transplanted[37]—there were we let loose
For sports of wider range. Ere I had told[38]
Ten birth-days, when among the mountain slopes
Frost, and the breath of frosty wind, had snapped
The last autumnal crocus, 'twas my joy
With store of springes[39] o'er my shoulder hung
To range the open heights where woodcocks run
Along the smooth green turf. Through half the night,
Scudding away from snare to snare, I plied
That anxious visitation;—moon and stars
Were shining o'er my head. I was alone,
And seemed to be a trouble to the peace
That dwelt among them. Sometimes it befell
In these night wanderings, that a strong desire
O'erpowered my better reason, and the bird
Which was the captive of another's toil
Became my prey; and when the deed was done

[34] Assurance (literally, a down payment). [35] Of Cockermouth Castle.
[36] American Indian.
[37] When he was nine, Wordsworth was sent to school at Hawkshead, in the Vale of Esthwaite, about thirty miles from Cockermouth.
[38] Numbered. [39] Snares.

I heard among the solitary hills
Low breathings coming after me, and sounds
Of undistinguishable motion, steps
Almost as silent as the turf they trod.

Nor less, when spring had warmed the cultured[40] vale,
Roved we as plunderers where the mother-bird
Had in high places built her lodge; though mean
Our object and inglorious, yet the end[41]
Was not ignoble. Oh! when I have hung
Above the raven's nest, by knots of grass
And half-inch fissures in the slippery rock
But ill sustained, and almost (so it seemed)
Suspended by the blast that blew amain,
Shouldering the naked crag, oh, at that time
While on the perilous ridge I hung alone,
With what strange utterance did the loud dry wind
Blow through my ear! the sky seemed not a sky
Of earth—and with what motion moved the clouds!

Dust as we are, the immortal spirit grows
Like harmony in music; there is a dark
Inscrutable workmanship that reconciles
Discordant elements, makes them cling together
In one society. How strange that all
The terrors, pains, and early miseries,
Regrets, vexations, lassitudes interfused
Within my mind, should e'er have borne a part,
And that a needful part, in making up
The calm existence that is mine when I
Am worthy of myself! Praise to the end!
Thanks to the means which nature deigned to employ;
Whether her fearless visiting, or those
That came with soft alarm, like hurtless light
Opening the peaceful clouds; or she may use
Severer interventions, ministry
More palpable, as best might suit her aim.

One summer evening (led by her) I found
A little boat tied to a willow tree
Within a rocky cave, its usual home.
Straight I unloosed her chain, and stepping in
Pushed from the shore. It was an act of stealth
And troubled pleasure, nor without the voice
Of mountain-echoes did my boat move on;
Leaving behind her still, on either side,
Small circles glittering idly in the moon,
Until they melted all into one track

[40] Cultivated (farmland). [41] Result (not "purpose").

Of sparkling light. But now, like one who rows,
Proud of his skill, to reach a chosen point
With an unswerving line, I fixed my view
Upon the summit of a craggy ridge,
The horizon's utmost boundary; for above
Was nothing but the stars and the grey sky.
She was an elfin pinnace;[42] lustily
I dipped my oars into the silent lake,
And, as I rose upon the stroke, my boat
Went heaving through the water like a swan;
When, from behind the craggy steep till then
The horizon's bound, a huge peak, black and huge,
As if with voluntary power instinct[43]
Upreared its head. I struck and struck again,
And growing still in stature the grim shape
Towered up between me and the stars, and still,
For so it seemed, with purpose of its own
And measured motion like a living thing,
Strode after me. With trembling oars I turned,
And through the silent water stole my way
Back to the covert of the willow tree;
There in her mooring-place I left my bark[44]—
And through the meadows homeward went, in grave
And serious mood; but after I had seen
That spectacle, for many days, my brain
Worked with a dim and undetermined sense
Of unknown modes of being; o'er my thoughts
There hung a darkness, call it solitude
Or blank desertion. No familiar shapes
Remained, no pleasant images of trees,
Of sea or sky, no colours of green fields;
But huge and mighty forms, that do not live
Like living men, moved slowly through the mind
By day, and were a trouble to my dreams.

Wisdom and Spirit of the universe!
Thou Soul that art the eternity of thought,
That givest to forms and images a breath
And everlasting motion, not in vain
By day or star-light thus from my first dawn
Of childhood didst thou intertwine for me
The passions that build up our human soul;
Not with the mean and vulgar[45] works of man,
But with high objects, with enduring things—
With life and nature—purifying thus

[42] Elfish small boat.
[43] *with . . . instinct.* Endowed with a will of its own. The natural explanation for the apparition is that the line of sight from farther out on the lake made visible a tall peak that had been hidden by a smaller one when the boy was looking almost straight up from the shore.
[44] Boat. [45] Ordinary.

The elements of feeling and of thought,
And sanctifying, by such discipline,
Both pain and fear, until we recognise
A grandeur in the beatings of the heart.
Nor was this fellowship vouchsafed to me
With stinted[46] kindness. In November days,
When vapours rolling down the valley made
A lonely scene more lonesome, among woods
At noon, and 'mid the calm of summer nights
When, by the margin of the trembling lake,
Beneath the gloomy hills homeward I went
In solitude, such intercourse was mine;
Mine was it in the fields both day and night,
And by the waters, all the summer long.

And in the frosty season, when the sun
Was set, and visible for many a mile
The cottage windows blazed through twilight gloom,
I heeded not their summons: happy time
It was indeed for all of us—for me
It was a time of rapture! Clear and loud
The village clock tolled six,—I wheeled about,
Proud and exulting like an untired horse
That cares not for his home. All shod with steel,[47]
We hissed along the polished ice in games
Confederate,[48] imitative of the chase
And woodland pleasures—the resounding horn,
The pack loud chiming, and the hunted hare.
So through the darkness and the cold we flew,
And not a voice was idle; with the din
Smitten, the precipices rang aloud;
The leafless trees and every icy crag
Tinkled like iron; while far distant hills
Into the tumult sent an alien sound
Of melancholy not unnoticed, while the stars
Eastward were sparkling clear, and in the west
The orange sky of evening died away.
Not seldom from the uproar I retired
Into a silent bay, or sportively
Glanced sideway, leaving the tumultuous throng,
To cut across the reflex[49] of a star
That fled, and, flying still before me, gleamed
Upon the glassy plain; and oftentimes,
When we had given our bodies to the wind,
And all the shadowy banks on either side

[46] Restricted; stingy. [47] Wearing ice skates.

[48] Joined together (a Latinism). The children are playing a game in which the pack chases one of the skaters, in imitation of hunting dogs.

[49] Reflection. The impossible attempt to skate around it is a good example of childhood whimsy.

Came sweeping through the darkness, spinning still
The rapid line of motion, then at once
Have I, reclining back upon my heels,
Stopped short; yet still the solitary cliffs
Wheeled by me—even as if the earth had rolled
With visible motion her diurnal round![50]
Behind me did they stretch in solemn train,[51]
Feebler and feebler, and I stood and watched
Till all was tranquil as a dreamless sleep.

Ye presences of nature in the sky
And on the earth! Ye visions of the hills!
And souls of lonely places! can I think
A vulgar hope was yours when ye employed
Such ministry, when ye, through many a year
Haunting me thus among my boyish sports,
On caves and trees, upon the woods and hills,
Impressed upon all forms the characters[52]
Of danger or desire; and thus did make
The surface of the universal earth
With triumph and delight, with hope and fear,
Work like a sea?

Not uselessly employed,
Might I pursue this theme through every change
Of exercise and play, to which the year
Did summon us in his delightful round.

We were a noisy crew; the sun in heaven
Beheld not vales more beautiful than ours;
Nor saw a band in happiness and joy
Richer, or worthier of the ground they trod.
I could record with no reluctant voice
The woods of autumn, and their hazel bowers
With milk-white clusters hung; the rod and line,
True symbol of hope's foolishness, whose strong
And unreproved enchantment led us on
By rocks and pools shut out from every star,
All the green summer, to forlorn cascades
Among the windings hid of mountain brooks.
—Unfading recollections! at this hour
The heart is almost mine with which I felt,
From some hill-top on sunny afternoons,
The paper kite high among fleecy clouds
Pull at her rein like an impetuous courser;[53]
Or, from the meadows sent on gusty days,
Beheld her breast the wind, then suddenly
Dashed headlong, and rejected by the storm.

[50] Daily rotation on her axis. [51] Line; succession. [52] Marks. [53] Swift horse.

Ye lowly cottages wherein we dwelt,[54]
A ministration of your own was yours;
Can I forget you, being as you were
So beautiful among the pleasant fields
In which ye stood? or can I here forget
The plain and seemly countenance with which
Ye dealt out your plain comforts? Yet had ye
Delights and exultations of your own.
Eager and never weary we pursued
Our home-amusements by the warm peat-fire
At evening, when with pencil, and smooth slate
In square divisions parcelled out and all
With crosses and with cyphers scribbled o'er,[55]
We schemed and puzzled, head opposed to head
In strife too humble to be named in verse:
Or round the naked table, snow-white deal,[56]
Cherry or maple, sate in close array,
And to the combat, loo or whist,[57] led on
A thick-ribbed army; not, as in the world,
Neglected and ungratefully thrown by
Even for the very service they had wrought,
But husbanded[58] through many a long campaign.
Uncouth assemblage was it, where no few
Had changed their functions: some, plebeian cards
Which fate, beyond the promise of their birth,
Had dignified, and called to represent
The persons of departed potentates.[59]
Oh, with what echoes on the board they fell!
Ironic diamonds,—clubs, hearts, diamonds, spades,
A congregation piteously akin!
Cheap matter offered they to boyish wit,
Those sooty knaves,[60] precipitated down
With scoffs and taunts, like Vulcan out of heaven:[61]
The paramount ace, a moon in her eclipse,
Queens gleaming through their splendour's last decay,
And monarchs surly at the wrongs sustained
By royal visages. Meanwhile abroad
Incessant rain was falling, or the frost
Raged bitterly, with keen and silent tooth;
And, interrupting oft that eager game,
From under Esthwaite's splitting fields of ice
The pent-up air, struggling to free itself,

[54] During his schooldays at Hawkshead, Wordsworth boarded with Ann Tyson, a woman of the village.

[55] Wordsworth is describing tick-tack-toe. [56] Fir or pine.

[57] Loo and whist were popular card games in the eighteenth century. In the following mock-epic description of card-playing Wordsworth echoes Pope's *Rape of the Lock*, III.25–98.

[58] Carefully conserved. [59] Rulers (that is, face cards). [60] Jacks.

[61] Vulcan (also called Mulciber), blacksmith god of fire, was thrown out of heaven by Zeus; compare Milton's *Paradise Lost*, I.739–746.

Gave out to meadow grounds and hills a loud
Protracted yelling, like the noise of wolves
Howling in troops along the Bothnic Main.[62]

Nor, sedulous as I have been to trace
How nature by extrinsic passion[63] first
Peopled the mind with forms sublime or fair,
And made me love them, may I here omit
How other pleasures have been mine, and joys
Of subtler origin; how I have felt,
Not seldom even in that tempestuous time,
Those hallowed and pure motions of the sense
Which seem, in their simplicity, to own
An intellectual charm; that calm delight
Which, if I err not, surely must belong
To those first-born affinities that fit
Our new existence to existing things,
And, in our dawn of being, constitute
The bond of union between life and joy.[64]

Yes, I remember when the changeful earth,
And twice five summers on my mind had stamped
The faces of the moving year, even then
I held unconscious intercourse with beauty
Old as creation, drinking in a pure
Organic pleasure from the silver wreaths
Of curling mist, or from the level plain
Of waters coloured by impending clouds.

The sands of Westmoreland, the creeks and bays
Of Cumbria's[65] rocky limits, they can tell
How, when the sea threw off his evening shade,
And to the shepherd's hut on distant hills
Sent welcome notice of the rising moon,
How I have stood, to fancies such as these[66]
A stranger, linking with the spectacle
No conscious memory of a kindred sight,
And bringing with me no peculiar sense
Of quietness or peace; yet have I stood,
Even while mine eye hath moved o'er many a league
Of shining water, gathering as it seemed,

[62] Northern part of the Baltic Sea.

[63] Emotion felt not for nature intrinsically but for childhood activities performed in the setting of nature.

[64] *lines 554–558.* Possibly an allusion to the myth of pre-existence, or possibly a suggestion that something (nature, presumably) establishes connections ("affinities") in our infancy between our newborn souls and the world.

[65] Westmoreland and Cumberland (Cumbria) are the counties in northwest England that include the Wordsworthian "Lake District."

[66] *fancies such as these.* Perhaps the speculations expressed in lines 554–558.

Through every hair-breadth in that field of light,
New pleasure like a bee among the flowers.

Thus oft amid those fits of vulgar joy
Which, through all seasons, on a child's pursuits
Are prompt attendants, 'mid that giddy bliss
Which, like a tempest, works along the blood
And is forgotten; even then I felt
Gleams like the flashing of a shield;—the earth
And common face of nature spake to me
Rememberable things; sometimes, 'tis true,
By chance collisions and quaint accidents
(Like those ill-sorted unions, work supposed
Of evil-minded fairies), yet not vain
Nor profitless, if haply they impressed
Collateral objects[67] and appearances,
Albeit lifeless then, and doomed to sleep
Until maturer seasons called them forth
To impregnate and to elevate the mind.
—And if the vulgar joy by its own weight
Wearied itself out of the memory,
The scenes which were a witness of that joy
Remained in their substantial lineaments
Depicted on the brain, and to the eye
Were visible, a daily sight; and thus
By the impressive[68] discipline of fear,
By pleasure and repeated happiness,
So frequently repeated, and by force
Of obscure feelings representative
Of things forgotten, these same scenes so bright,
So beautiful, so majestic in themselves,
Though yet the day was distant, did become
Habitually dear, and all their forms
And changeful colours by invisible links
Were fastened to the affections.
I began
My story early—not misled, I trust,
By an infirmity of love for days
Disowned by memory—fancying flowers where none
Not even the sweetest do or can survive
For him at least whose dawning day they cheered.
Nor will it seem to thee, O friend! so prompt
In sympathy, that I have lengthened out
With fond and feeble tongue a tedious tale.
Meanwhile, my hope has been, that I might fetch
Invigorating thoughts from former years;
Might fix the wavering balance of my mind,

[67] Objects associated with them.

[68] To be taken literally: "making an impression."

And haply meet reproaches too, whose power
May spur me on, in manhood now mature,
To honourable toil. Yet should these hopes
Prove vain and thus should neither I be taught
To understand myself, nor thou to know
With better knowledge how the heart was framed
Of him thou lovest; need I dread from thee
Harsh judgments, if the song be loth to quit
Those recollected hours that have the charm
Of visionary things, those lovely forms
And sweet sensations that throw back our life,
And almost make remotest infancy
A visible scene, on which the sun is shining?

One end at least hath been attained; my mind
Hath been revived, and if this genial mood
Desert me not, forthwith shall be brought down
Through later years the story of my life.
The road lies plain before me[69]—'tis a theme
Single and of determined bounds; and hence
I choose it rather at this time, than work
Of ampler or more varied argument,[70]
Where I might be discomfited[71] and lost:
And certain hopes are with me, that to thee
This labour will be welcome, honoured friend!

from BOOK THIRD

RESIDENCE AT CAMBRIDGE

It was a dreary morning when the wheels
Rolled over a wide plain o'erhung with clouds,
And nothing cheered our way till first we saw
The long-roofed chapel of King's College[1] lift
Turrets and pinnacles in answering files,
Extended high above a dusky grove.

Advancing, we espied upon the road
A student clothed in gown and tasselled cap,
Striding along as if o'ertasked by time,
Or covetous of exercise and air;
He passed—nor was I master of my eyes
Till he was left an arrow's flight behind.
As near and nearer to the spot we drew,
It seemed to suck us in with an eddy's force.

[69] See I.14 and note. [70] Subject matter; theme. [71] Thwarted; defeated.
[1] One of the colleges that make up Cambridge University. Wordsworth is now seventeen.

Onward we drove beneath the Castle; caught,
While crossing Magdalene Bridge, a glimpse of Cam;[2]
And at the *Hoop* alighted, famous inn.

My spirit was up, my thoughts were full of hope;
Some friends I had, acquaintances who there
Seemed friends, poor simple schoolboys, now hung round
With honour and importance; in a world
Of welcome faces up and down I roved;
Questions, directions, warnings and advice,
Flowed in upon me from all sides; fresh day
Of pride and pleasure! to myself I seemed
A man of business and expense, and went
From shop to shop about my own affairs,
To tutor or to tailor, as befell,
From street to street with loose and careless mind.

I was the dreamer, they the dream; I roamed
Delighted through the motley spectacle;
Gowns grave, or gaudy, doctors,[3] students, streets,
Courts, cloisters, flocks of churches, gateways, towers:
Migration strange for a stripling of the hills,
A northern villager.
As if the change
Had waited on some fairy's wand, at once
Behold me rich in monies, and attired
In splendid garb, with hose of silk, and hair
Powdered like rimy[4] trees, when frost is keen.
My lordly dressing-gown, I pass it by,
With other signs of manhood that supplied[5]
The lack of beard.—The weeks went roundly on,
With invitations, suppers, wine and fruit,
Smooth housekeeping within, and all without
Liberal,[6] and suiting gentleman's array,

The Evangelist St. John[7] my patron was:
Three Gothic courts are his, and in the first
Was my abiding-place, a nook obscure;
Right underneath, the College kitchens made
A humming sound, less tuneable than bees,
But hardly less industrious; with shrill notes
Of sharp command and scolding intermixed.
Near me hung Trinity's loquacious clock,
Who never let the quarters, night or day,
Slip by him unproclaimed, and told the hours

[2] The river of Cambridge. [3] Faculty. [4] Frost-covered.
[5] Compensated for. [6] Relaxedly free-spending.
[7] Wordsworth attended St. John's College from 1787 to 1791. It adjoins Trinity College (see line 53).

Twice over with a male and female voice.
Her pealing organ was my neighbour too;
And from my pillow, looking forth by light
Of moon or favouring stars, I could behold
The antechapel where the statue stood
Of Newton[8] with his prism and silent face,
The marble index of a mind for ever
Voyaging through strange seas of thought, alone.

Of college labours, of the lecturer's room
All studded round, as thick as chairs could stand,
With loyal students, faithful to their books,
Half-and-half idlers, hardy recusants,[9]
And honest dunces—of important days,
Examinations, when the man was weighed
As in a balance! of excessive hopes,
Tremblings withal and commendable fears,
Small jealousies, and triumphs good or bad,
Let others that know more speak as they know.
Such glory was but little sought by me,
And little won. Yet from the first crude days
Of settling time in this untried abode,
I was disturbed at times by prudent thoughts,
Wishing to hope without a hope, some fears
About my future worldly maintenance,
And, more than all, a strangeness in the mind,
A feeling that I was not for that hour,
Nor for that place. But wherefore be cast down?
For (not to speak of reason and her pure
Reflective acts to fix the moral law
Deep in the conscience, nor of Christian Hope,
Bowing her head before her sister Faith
As one far mightier), hither I had come,
Bear witness truth, endowed with holy powers
And faculties, whether to work or feel.
Oft when the dazzling show no longer new
Had ceased to dazzle, ofttimes did I quit
My comrades, leave the crowd, buildings and groves,
And as I paced alone the level fields
Far from those lovely sights and sounds sublime
With which I had been conversant,[10] the mind
Drooped not; but there into herself returning,
With prompt rebound seemed fresh as heretofore.
At least I more distinctly recognised
Her native instincts: let me dare to speak

[8] Sir Isaac Newton (1642–1727), the great mathematician and physicist. The word *prism* suggests Newton's discoveries about the refraction of light.
[9] Literally, religious independents; here, "loafers." [10] Familiar.

A higher language, say that now I felt
What independent solaces were mine,
To mitigate the injurious sway[11] of place
Or circumstance, how far soever changed
In youth, or *to* be changed in manhood's prime;
Or for the few who shall be called to look
On the long shadows in our evening years,
Ordained precursors to the night of death.
As if awakened, summoned, roused, constrained,
I looked for universal things; perused
The common countenance of earth and sky:
Earth, nowhere unembellished by some trace
Of that first Paradise whence man was driven;
And sky, whose beauty and bounty are expressed
By the proud name she bears—the name of Heaven.
I called on both to teach me what they might;
Or, turning the mind in upon herself,
Pored, watched, expected, listened, spread my thoughts
And spread them with a wider creeping; felt
Incumbencies more awful,[12] visitings
Of the Upholder of the tranquil soul,
That tolerates the indignities of time,
And, from the centre of Eternity
All finite motions overruling, lives
In glory immutable. But peace! enough
Here to record I had ascended now
To such community with highest truth—
A track pursuing, not untrod before,
From strict analogies by thought supplied
Or consciousnesses not to be subdued.
To every natural form, rock, fruit or flower,
Even the loose stones that cover the highway,
I gave a moral life: I saw them feel,
Or linked them to some feeling: the great mass
Lay bedded in a quickening[13] soul, and all
That I beheld respired with inward meaning.
Add that whate'er of terror or of love
Or beauty, nature's daily face put on
From transitory passion, unto this
I was as sensitive as waters are
To the sky's influence; in a kindred mood
Of passion was obedient as a lute
That waits upon the touches of the wind.[14]
Unknown, unthought of, yet I was most rich—
I had a world about me—'twas my own;

[11] Influence. [12] More awe-inspiring spiritual weights or responsibilities.

[13] Life-giving.

[14] *lute . . . wind.* Another reference to the Aeolian harp; see note to Coleridge's "Dejection: An Ode," line 7.

I made it, for it only lived to me,
And to the God who sees into the heart.
Such sympathies, though rarely, were betrayed
By outward gestures and by visible looks:
Some called it madness—so indeed it was,
If child-like fruitfulness in passing joy,
If steady moods of thoughtfulness matured
To inspiration, sort[15] with such a name;
If prophecy be madness; if things viewed
By poets in old time, and higher up
By the first men, earth's first inhabitants,
May in these tutored days no more be seen
With undisordered sight. But leaving this,
It was no madness, for the bodily eye
Amid my strongest workings[16] evermore
Was searching out the lines of difference
As they lie hid in all external forms,
Near or remote, minute or vast; an eye
Which, from a tree, a stone, a withered leaf,
To the broad ocean and the azure heavens
Spangled with kindred multitudes of stars,
Could find no surface where its power might sleep;
Which spake perpetual logic to my soul,
And by an unrelenting agency
Did bind my feelings even as in a chain.

And here, O friend! have I retraced my life
Up to an eminence,[17] and told a tale
Of matters which not falsely may be called
The glory of my youth. Of genius, power,
Creation and divinity itself
I have been speaking, for my theme has been
What passed[18] within me. Not of outward things
Done visibly for other minds, words, signs,
Symbols or actions, but of my own heart
Have I been speaking, and my youthful mind.
O Heavens! how awful is the might of souls,
And what they do within themselves while yet
The yoke of earth is new to them, the world
Nothing but a wild field where they were sown.
This is, in truth, heroic argument,[19]
This genuine prowess, which I wished to touch
With hand however weak, but in the main
It lies far hidden from the reach of words.
Points have we all of us within our souls

[15] Are consistent; agree.
[16] Times of mental turmoil (what "some called . . . madness," line 149).
[17] High point. [18] Happened. [19] Epic subject matter.

Where all stand single; this I feel, and make
Breathings for incommunicable powers;[20]
But is not each a memory to himself,
And, therefore, now that we must quit this theme,
I am not heartless,[21] for there's not a man
That lives who hath not known his god-like hours,
And feels not what an empire we inherit
As natural beings in the strength of nature.

from BOOK SIXTH

Cambridge and the Alps

'Tis not my present purpose to retrace
That variegated journey[1] step by step.
A march it was of military speed,
And Earth did change her images and forms
Before us, fast as clouds are changed in heaven.
Day after day, up early and down late,
From hill to vale we dropped, from vale to hill
Mounted—from province on to province swept,
Keen hunters in a chase of fourteen weeks,
Eager as birds of prey, or as a ship
Upon the stretch, when winds are blowing fair:
Sweet coverts did we cross of pastoral life,
Enticing valleys, greeted them and left
Too soon, while yet the very flash and gleam
Of salutation were not passed away.
Oh! sorrow for the youth who could have seen,
Unchastened, unsubdued, unawed, unraised
To patriarchial[2] dignity of mind,
And pure simplicity of wish and will,
Those sanctified abodes of peaceful man,
Pleased (though to hardship born, and compassed round
With danger, varying as the seasons change),
Pleased with his daily task, or, if not pleased,
Contented, from the moment that the dawn
(Ah! surely not without attendant gleams
Of soul-illumination) calls him forth
To industry, by glistenings flung on rocks,
Whose evening shadows lead him to repose.

[20] *make . . . powers.* A notoriously obscure phrase; it may mean "utter (make breathings for) what is incommunicable" or possibly "pray for poetic powers that cannot be given (communicated) to human beings." The next lines seem to take consolation in the fact that, since all other human beings have their own unique memories and have had analogous experiences of the divinity in themselves, they will know what Wordsworth means.

[21] Disheartened.

[1] A walking-tour through France and the Alps that Wordsworth took with his friend Robert Jones in 1790.

[2] Associated with the early, simple ages of mankind.

Well might a stranger look with bounding heart
Down on a green recess, the first I saw
Of those deep haunts, an aboriginal vale,
Quiet and lorded over and possessed
By naked huts, wood-built, and sown like tents
Or Indian cabins over the fresh lawns
And by the river side.

That very day,
From a bare ridge we also first beheld
Unveiled the summit of Mont Blanc,[3] and grieved
To have a soulless image on the eye
That had usurped upon a living thought
That never more could be. The wondrous Vale
Of Chamouny stretched far below, and soon
With its dumb cataracts and streams of ice,
A motionless array of mighty waves,[4]
Five rivers broad and vast, made rich amends,
And reconciled us to realities;
There small birds warble from the leafy trees,
The eagle soars high in the element,
There doth the reaper bind the yellow sheaf,
The maiden spread the haycock in the sun,
While winter like a well-tamed lion walks,
Descending from the mountain to make sport
Among the cottages by beds of flowers.

Whate'er in this wide circuit we beheld,
Or heard, was fitted to our unripe state
Of intellect and heart. With such a book
Before our eyes, we could not choose but read
Lessons of genuine brotherhood, the plain
And universal reason of mankind,
The truths of young and old. Nor, side by side
Pacing, two social pilgrims, or alone
Each with his humour, could we fail to abound
In dreams and fictions, pensively composed:
Dejection taken up for pleasure's sake,
And gilded sympathies, the willow wreath,[5]
And sober posies of funereal flowers,
Gathered among those solitudes sublime
From formal gardens of the lady Sorrow,
Did sweeten many a meditative hour.

Yet still in me with those soft luxuries
Mixed something of stern mood, an under-thirst

[3] The most famous of the Alps; the travelers' disappointment with it anticipates lines 557–591.
[4] *dumb . . . waves.* Glaciers. [5] Conventional emblem of sorrow.

Of vigour seldom utterly allayed.
And from that source how different a sadness
Would issue, let one incident make known.
When from the Vallais we had turned, and clomb
Along the Simplon's[6] steep and rugged road,
Following a band of muleteers, we reached
A halting-place, where all together took
Their noon-tide meal. Hastily rose our guide,
Leaving us at the board; awhile we lingered,
Then paced the beaten downward way that led
Right to a rough stream's edge, and there broke off;
The only track now visible was one
That from the torrent's further brink held forth
Conspicuous invitation to ascend
A lofty mountain. After brief delay
Crossing the unbridged stream, that road we took,
And clomb with eagerness, till anxious fears
Intruded, for we failed to overtake
Our comrades gone before. By fortunate chance,
While every moment added doubt to doubt,
A peasant met us, from whose mouth we learned
That to the spot which had perplexed us first
We must descend, and there should find the road,
Which in the stony channel of the stream
Lay a few steps, and then along its banks;
And, that our future course, all plain to sight,
Was downwards, with the current of that stream.[7]
Loth[8] to believe what we so grieved to hear,
For still we had hopes that pointed to the clouds,
We questioned him again, and yet again;
But every word that from the peasant's lips
Came in reply, translated by our feelings,
Ended in this,—*that we had crossed the Alps.*

Imagination—here[9] the power so called
Through sad incompetence of human speech,
That awful power rose from the mind's abyss
Like an unfathered vapour that enwraps,
At once, some lonely traveller. I was lost;[10]

[6] A pass through the Alps.

[7] *with . . . stream.* The implication of walking with the current is that they have passed the continental divide.

[8] Unwilling.

[9] Not "at this point in our journey" but "at this point in my writing of the poem"—fourteen years after the incident related. Wordsworth suddenly realizes, in retrospect, the implication of the disappointment felt years earlier: the soul is glorious precisely because it can make demands on life that mere factual reality cannot satisfy.

[10] *I was lost.* This phrase does not refer to the literal getting-lost just described but to the bafflement Wordsworth felt, while writing the poem, just before the insight heralded in lines 598 ff.

Halted without an effort to break through;
But to my conscious soul I now can say—
"I recognise thy glory:" in such strength
Of usurpation, when the light of sense
Goes out, but with a flash that has revealed
The invisible world, doth greatness make abode,
There harbours whether we be young or old.
Our destiny, our being's heart and home,
Is with infinitude, and only there;
With hope it is, hope that can never die,
Effort, and expectation, and desire,
And something evermore about to be.
Under such banners militant,[11] the soul
Seeks for no trophies, struggles for no spoils
That may attest her prowess, blest in thoughts
That are their own perfection and reward,
Strong in herself and in beatitude
That hides her, like the mighty flood of Nile[12]
Poured from his fount of Abyssinian clouds
To fertilise the whole Egyptian plain.

The melancholy slackening that ensued
Upon those tidings by the peasant given
Was soon dislodged. Downwards we hurried fast,
And, with the half-shaped road which we had missed,
Entered a narrow chasm. The brook and road
Were fellow-travellers in this gloomy strait,
And with them did we journey several hours
At a slow pace. The immeasurable height
Of woods decaying, never to be decayed,
The stationary blasts of waterfalls,
And in the narrow rent at every turn
Winds thwarting winds, bewildered and forlorn,
The torrents shooting from the clear blue sky,
The rocks that muttered close upon our ears,
Black drizzling crags that spake by the way-side
As if a voice were in them, the sick sight
And giddy prospect of the raving stream,
The unfettered clouds and region of the heavens,
Tumult and peace, the darkness and the light—
Were all like workings of one mind, the features
Of the same face, blossoms upon one tree;
Characters of the great apocalypse,[13]
The types and symbols of eternity,
Of first, and last, and midst, and without end.

[11] This word probably modifies "soul," not "banner."
[12] The sources of the Nile were also mysteriously remote and hidden.
[13] Ultimate revelation, as in the last book of the New Testament.

from BOOK ELEVENTH

France

From that time forth, authority in France
Put on a milder face; terror had ceased,[1]
Yet every thing was wanting that might give
Courage to them who looked for good by light
Of rational experience, for the shoots
And hopeful blossoms of a second spring:
Yet, in me, confidence was unimpaired;
The Senate's language, and the public acts
And measures of the government, though both
Weak, and of heartless[2] omen, had not power
To daunt me; in the people was my trust,[3]
And in the virtues which mine eyes had seen;
I knew that wound external could not take
Life from the young republic;[4] that new foes
Would only follow, in the path of shame,
Their brethren, and her triumphs be in the end
Great, universal, irresistible.
This intuition led me to confound[5]
One victory with another, higher far,—
Triumphs of unambitious peace at home,
And noiseless fortitude. Beholding still
Resistance strong as heretofore, I thought
That what was in degree the same was likewise
The same in quality,—that, as the worse
Of the two spirits then at strife remained
Untired, the better, surely, would preserve
The heart that first had roused him.[6] Youth maintains,
In all conditions of society,
Communion more direct and intimate
With nature,—hence, ofttimes, with reason too—
Than age or manhood, even. To nature, then,
Power had reverted: habit, custom, law,

[1] Wordsworth is referring to the fall and execution in July 1794 of Maximilien Robespierre, who during the preceding twelve months had presided over the Reign of Terror in France, when multitudes of accused enemies of the revolutionary regime were sent to the guillotine. At this point in the poem, Wordsworth is back in England, having returned from revolutionary France after living there from November 1791 until near the end of 1792. His sympathies remained with the French for some time, as Book XI makes clear.

[2] Disheartening.

[3] In the people of France, as opposed to its legislature and government, mentioned in the preceding lines.

[4] *that wound . . . republic.* That France could not be defeated by the foreign countries at war with it and with the principles of the Revolution.

[5] Associate. Wordsworth hopes that the principles of reform will spread, bloodlessly, to England.

[6] *lines 21–27.* Wordsworth trusted that, since the opposition to France by the "worse" spirit remained strong, the better cause of revolutionary France itself must have remained equally strong.

Had left an interregnum's[7] open space
For *her* to move about in, uncontrolled.
Hence could I see how Babel-like[8] their task,
Who, by the recent deluge stupified,
With their whole souls went culling from the day
Its petty promises, to build a tower
For their own safety; laughed with my compeers[9]
At gravest heads, by enmity to France
Distempered,[10] till they found, in every blast
Forced from the street-disturbing newsman's horn,
For her great cause record or prophecy
Of utter ruin. How might we believe
That wisdom could, in any shape, come near
Men clinging to delusions so insane?
And thus, experience proving that no few
Of our opinions had been just, we took
Like credit to ourselves where less was due,
And thought that other notions were as sound,
Yea, could not but be right, because we saw
That foolish men opposed them.
To a strain
More animated I might here give way,
And tell, since juvenile errors are my theme,
What in those days, through Britain, was performed
To turn *all* judgments out of their right course;
But this is passion over-near ourselves,
Reality too close and too intense,
And intermixed with something, in my mind,
Of scorn and condemnation personal,
That would profane the sanctity of verse.
Our shepherds,[11] this say merely, at that time
Acted, or seemed at least to act, like men
Thirsting to make the guardian crook[12] of law
A tool of murder; they who ruled the state,
Though with such awful proof before their eyes
That he, who would sow death, reaps death, or worse,
And can reap nothing better, child-like longed
To imitate,[13] not wise enough to avoid;
Or left (by mere timidity betrayed)
The plain straight road, for one no better chosen
Than if their wish had been to undermine
Justice, and make an end of liberty.

[7] An interregnum is an interval between two reigns. Old laws and customs have been overthrown, and new ones have not been perfected; nature reigns alone in the interim.

[8] Hopeless, like the attempt by the builders of the Tower of Babel to reach heaven; see Genesis 11:1–9.

[9] Companions. [10] Disordered.

[11] Governmental rulers of England. Wordsworth is describing the anti-Revolutionary political witch-hunting in England in the 1790s; he and Coleridge had been among the suspects (hence his allusion to "personal" feelings in lines 57–60).

[12] Shepherd's staff. [13] To imitate the political repression in France.

But from these bitter truths I must return
To my own history. It hath been told
That I was led to take an eager part
In arguments of civil polity,
Abruptly, and indeed before my time:[14]
I had approached, like other youths, the shield
Of human nature from the golden side,
And would have fought, even to the death, to attest
The quality of the metal which I saw.[15]
What there is best in individual man,
Of wise in passion, and sublime in power,
Benevolent in small societies,
And great in large ones, I had oft revolved,
Felt deeply, but not thoroughly understood
By reason: nay, far from it; they were yet,
As cause was given me afterwards to learn,
Not proof against[16] the injuries of the day;
Lodged only at the sanctuary's door,
Not safe within its bosom. Thus prepared,
And with such general insight into evil,
And of the bounds which sever it from good,
As books and common intercourse with life
Must needs have given—to the inexperienced mind,
When the world travels in a beaten road,
Guide faithful as is needed—I began
To meditate with ardour on the rule
And management of nations; what it is
And ought to be; and strove to learn how far
Their power or weakness, wealth or poverty,
Their happiness or misery, depends
Upon their laws, and fashion of the state.

O pleasant exercise of hope and joy!
For mighty were the auxiliars[17] which then stood
Upon our side, we who were strong in love!
Bliss was it in that dawn to be alive,
But to be young was very heaven! O times,
In which the meagre, stale, forbidding ways
Of custom, law, and statute, took at once
The attraction of a country in romance!
When reason seemed the most to assert her rights
When most intent on making of herself
A prime enchantress—to assist the work,
Which then was going forward in her name!
Not favoured spots alone, but the whole earth,
The beauty wore of promise—that which sets

[14] Wordsworth had had his initiation in political theory in France, from conversations with the French captain Michael Beaupuy.

[15] *attest . . . saw.* Defend my belief that human nature was "golden," that is, basically good.

[16] *proof against.* Immune to. [17] Aids.

(As at some moments might not be unfelt
Among the bowers of Paradise itself)
The budding rose above the rose full blown.
What temper[18] at the prospect did not wake
To happiness unthought of? The inert
Were roused, and lively natures rapt[19] away!
They who had fed their childhood upon dreams,
The play-fellows of fancy, who had made
All powers of swiftness, subtilty, and strength
Their ministers,—who in lordly wise had stirred
Among the grandest objects of the sense,
And dealt with whatsoever they found there
As if they had within some lurking right
To wield it;—they, too, who of gentle mood
Had watched all gentle motions, and to these
Had fitted their own thoughts, schemers more mild,
And in the region of their peaceful selves;—
Now was it that *both* found, the meek and lofty
Did both find, helpers to their hearts' desire,
And stuff at hand, plastic[20] as they could wish,—
Were called upon to exercise their skill,
Not in Utopia,[21]—subterranean fields,—
Or some secreted island, heaven knows where!
But in the very world, which is the world
Of all of us,—the place where, in the end,
We find our happiness, or not at all!

Why should I not confess that earth was then
To me, what an inheritance, new-fallen,
Seems, when the first time visited, to one
Who thither comes to find in it his home?
He walks about and looks upon the spot
With cordial transport, moulds it and remoulds,
And is half-pleased with things that are amiss,[22]
'Twill be such joy to see them disappear.

An active partisan, I thus convoked[23]
From every object pleasant circumstance
To suit my ends; I moved among mankind
With genial feelings still predominant;
When erring, erring on the better part,
And in the kinder spirit; placable,[24]
Indulgent, as not uninformed that men
See as they have been taught, and that antiquity
Gives rights to error; and aware, no less,
That throwing off oppression must be work

[18] What kind of person. [19] Swept. [20] Capable of being shaped.
[21] Thomas More's *Utopia* (1516) had described the supposedly perfect society as existing on an island far away.
[22] Faulty. [23] Called up. [24] Easygoing; tolerant.

As well of license[25] as of liberty;
And above all— for this was more than all—
Not caring if the wind did now and then
Blow keen upon an eminence that gave
Prospect so large[26] into futurity;
In brief, a child of nature, as at first,
Diffusing only those affections wider
That from the cradle had grown up with me,
And losing, in no other way than light
Is lost in light, the weak in the more strong.

In the main outline, such it might be said
Was my condition, till with open war
Britain opposed the liberties of France.[27]
This threw me first out of the pale[28] of love;
Soured and corrupted, upwards to the source,
My sentiments; was not, as hitherto,
A swallowing up of lesser things in great,
But change of them into their contraries;
And thus a way was opened for mistakes
And false conclusions, in degree as gross,
In kind more dangerous. What had been a pride,
Was now a shame; my likings and my loves
Ran in new channels, leaving old ones dry;
And hence a blow that, in maturer age,
Would but have touched the judgment, struck more deep
Into sensations near the heart: meantime,
As from the first, wild theories were afloat,
To whose pretensions, sedulously urged,[29]
I had but lent a careless ear, assured
That time was ready to set all things right,
And that the multitude, so long oppressed,
Would be oppressed no more.
But when events
Brought less encouragement, and unto these
The immediate proof of principles no more
Could be entrusted, while the events themselves,
Worn out in greatness, stripped of novelty,
Less occupied the mind, and sentiments
Could through my understanding's natural growth
No longer keep their ground, by faith maintained
Of inward consciousness, and hope that laid
Her hand upon her object—evidence
Safer, of universal application, such
As could not be impeached, was sought elsewhere.

[25] Going too far; excess. [26] So far-ranging a view.
[27] Britain declared war in February 1793. [28] Outside the region.
[29] Eagerly argued.

But now, become oppressors in their turn,
Frenchmen had changed a war of self-defence
For one of conquest,[30] losing sight of all
Which they had struggled for: and mounted up,
Openly in the eye of earth and heaven,
The scale of liberty.[31] I read her doom,
With anger vexed, with disappointment sore,
But not dismayed, nor taking to the shame
Of a false prophet. While resentment rose
Striving to hide, what nought could heal, the wounds
Of mortified presumption, I adhered
More firmly to old tenets, and, to prove
Their temper,[32] strained them more; and thus, in heat
Of contest, did opinions every day
Grow into consequence, till round my mind
They clung, as if they were its life, nay more,
The very being of the immortal soul.

This was the time, when, all things tending fast
To depravation, speculative schemes—
That promised to abstract the hopes of man
Out of his feelings, to be fixed thenceforth
For ever in a purer element[33]—
Found ready welcome. Tempting region *that*
For Zeal to enter and refresh herself,
Where passions had the privilege to work,
And never hear the sound of their own names.
But, speaking more in charity, the dream
Flattered the young, pleased with extremes, nor least
With that which makes our reason's naked self
The object of its fervour. What delight!
How glorious! in self-knowledge and self-rule,
To look through all the frailties of the world,
And, with a resolute mastery shaking off
Infirmities of nature, time, and place,
Build social upon personal liberty,
Which, to the blind restraints of general laws
Superior, magisterially adopts
One guide, the light of circumstances, flashed
Upon an independent intellect.
Thus expectation rose again; thus hope,

[30] In the latter part of 1794, France had turned into an aggressor against Germany, the Netherlands, Spain, and Italy.

[31] What is opposed to liberty proves to have more weight. The scale image is often used in epics to indicate crucial decisions by the gods.

[32] Strength and durability, as of tempered metal.

[33] The element of pure, emotionless reason, as typified in the influential book *An Enquiry Concerning Political Justice* (1793) by William Godwin, husband of Mary Wollstonecraft and father of Mary Shelley.

From her first ground expelled, grew proud once more.
Oft, as my thoughts were turned to human kind,
I scorned indifference; but, inflamed with thirst
Of a secure intelligence, and sick
Of other longing, I pursued what seemed
A more exalted nature; wished that man
Should start out of his earthly, worm-like state,
And spread abroad the wings of liberty,
Lord of himself, in undisturbed delight—
A noble aspiration! *yet*[34] I feel
(Sustained by worthier as by wiser thoughts)
The aspiration, nor shall ever cease
To feel it;—but return we to our course.

Enough, 'tis true—could such a plea excuse
Those aberrations—had the clamorous friends
Of ancient institutions said and done
To bring disgrace upon their very names;
Disgrace, of which custom and written law,
And sundry moral sentiments as props
Or emanations of those institutes,
Too justly bore a part. A veil had been
Uplifted;[35] why deceive ourselves? in sooth,
'Twas even so; and sorrow for the man
Who either had not eyes wherewith to see,
Or, seeing, had forgotten! A strong shock
Was given to old opinions; all men's minds
Had felt its power, and mine was both let loose,
Let loose and goaded. After what hath been
Already said of patriotic love,
Suffice it here to add, that, somewhat stern
In temperament, withal[36] a happy man,
And therefore bold to look on painful things,
Free likewise of the world, and thence more bold,
I summoned my best skill, and toiled, intent
To anatomise[37] the frame of social life;
Yea, the whole body of society
Searched to its heart. Share with me, friend![38] the wish
That some dramatic tale, endued with shapes
Livelier, and flinging out less guarded words
Than suit the work we fashion, might set forth
What then I learned, or think I learned, of truth,
And the errors into which I fell, betrayed
By present objects, and by reasonings false
From their beginnings, inasmuch as drawn
Out of a heart that had been turned aside

[34] Even now.
[35] *veil . . . Uplifted.* Old concealments of the truth had been removed (by the Revolution).
[36] And in addition. [37] Intellectually dissect.
[38] Coleridge, the addressee of the whole poem.

From nature's way by outward accidents,
And which was thus confounded, more and more
Misguided, and misguiding. So I fared,
Dragging all precepts, judgments, maxims, creeds,
Like culprits to the bar;[39] calling the mind,
Suspiciously, to establish in plain day
Her titles and her honours; now believing,
Now disbelieving; endlessly perplexed
With impulse, motive, right and wrong, the ground
Of obligation, what the rule and whence
The sanction; till, demanding formal *proof*,
And seeking it in every thing, I lost
All feeling of conviction, and, in fine,[40]
Sick, wearied out with contrarieties,
Yielded up moral questions in despair.

This was the crisis of that strong disease,
This the soul's last and lowest ebb; I drooped,
Deeming our blessed reason of least use
Where wanted most: "The lordly attributes
Of will and choice," I bitterly exclaimed,
"What are they but a mockery of a being
Who hath in no concerns of his a test
Of good and evil; knows not what to fear
Or hope for, what to covet or to shun;
And who, if those could be discerned, would yet
Be little profited, would see, and ask
Where is the obligation to enforce?
And, to acknowledged law rebellious, still,
As selfish passion urged, would act amiss;
The dupe of folly, or the slave of crime."

Depressed, bewildered thus, I did not walk
With scoffers, seeking light and gay revenge
From indiscriminate laughter, nor sate down
In reconcilement with an utter waste
Of intellect; such sloth I could not brook,
(Too well I loved, in that my spring of life,
Pains-taking thoughts, and truth, their dear reward)
But turned to abstract science, and there sought
Work for the reasoning faculty enthroned
Where the disturbances of space and time—
Whether in matter's various properties
Inherent, or from human will and power
Derived—find no admission.[41] Then it was—
Thanks to the bounteous Giver of all good!—
That the beloved sister[42] in whose sight

[39] Into the courtroom. [40] At last. [41] Wordsworth apparently means mathematics.
[42] Wordsworth was reunited with his beloved sister Dorothy, after a long separation, in September 1795.

Those days were passed, now speaking in a voice
Of sudden admonition—like a brook
That did but *cross* a lonely road, and now
Is seen, heard, felt, and caught at every turn,
Companion never lost through many a league—
Maintained for me a saving intercourse
With my true self; for, though bedimmed and changed
Much, as it seemed, I was no further changed
Than as a clouded and a waning moon:
She whispered still that brightness would return,
She, in the midst of all, preserved me still
A poet, made me seek beneath that name,
And that alone, my office upon earth;
And, lastly, as hereafter will be shown,
If willing audience fail not, nature's self,
By all varieties of human love
Assisted, led me back through opening day
To those sweet counsels between head and heart
Whence grew that genuine knowledge, fraught with peace,
Which, through the later sinkings of this cause,[43]
Hath still upheld me, and upholds me now
In the catastrophe[44] (for so they dream,
And nothing less), when, finally to close
And rivet down all the gains of France, a Pope
Is summoned in, to crown an Emperor—
This last opprobrium, when we see a people
That once looked up in faith, as if to heaven
For manna, take a lesson from the dog
Returning to his vomit; when the sun
That rose in splendour, was alive, and moved
In exultation with a living pomp
Of clouds—his glory's natural retinue—
Hath dropped all functions by the gods bestowed,
And, turned into a gewgaw,[45] a machine,
Sets like an opera phantom. . . .[46]

from BOOK TWELFTH

Imagination and taste, How Impaired and Restored

There are in our existence spots of time,
That with distinct pre-eminence retain
A renovating virtue, whence, depressed
By false opinion and contentious thought,

[43] The cause of the Revolution.

[44] In drama, the *catastrophe* is the outcome of the play. Monarchy in a new form was revived in France in 1804 when Napoleon Bonaparte was crowned Emperor of the French, Pope Pius VII assisting at the ceremony.

[45] Cheap decoration. [46] Like an absurdly artificial piece of stage machinery.

Or aught of heavier or more deadly weight,
In trivial occupations, and the round
Of ordinary intercourse, our minds
Are nourished and invisibly repaired;
A virtue, by which pleasure is enhanced,
That penetrates, enables us to mount,
When high, more high, and lifts us up when fallen.
This efficacious spirit chiefly lurks
Among those passages of life that give
Profoundest knowledge to what point, and how,
The mind is lord and master—outward sense
The obedient servant of her will. Such moments
Are scattered everywhere, taking their date
From our first childhood. I remember well,
That once, while yet my inexperienced hand
Could scarcely hold a bridle, with proud hopes
I mounted, and we journeyed towards the hills:
An ancient servant of my father's house
Was with me, my encourager and guide:
We had not travelled long, ere some mischance
Disjoined me from my comrade; and, through fear
Dismounting, down the rough and stony moor
I led my horse, and, stumbling on, at length
Came to a bottom, where in former times
A murderer had been hung in iron chains.
The gibbet-mast[1] had mouldered down, the bones
And iron case were gone: but on the turf,
Hard by,[2] soon after that fell deed was wrought,
Some unknown hand had carved the murderer's name.
The monumental letters were inscribed
In times long past; but still, from year to year
By superstition of the neighbourhood,
The grass is cleared away, and to this hour
The characters are fresh and visible:
A casual glance had shown them, and I fled,
Faltering and faint, and ignorant of the road:
Then, reascending the bare common, saw
A naked pool that lay beneath the hills,
The beacon[3] on the summit, and, more near,
A girl, who bore a pitcher on her head,
And seemed with difficult steps to force her way
Against the blowing wind. It was, in truth,
An ordinary sight; but I should need
Colours and words that are unknown to man,
To paint the visionary dreariness
Which, while I looked all round for my lost guide,
Invested moorland waste, and naked pool,
The beacon crowning the lone eminence,

[1] Gallows. [2] Nearby. [3] A stone signal-tower.

The female and her garments vexed and tossed
By the stong wind. When, in the blessed hours
Of early love,[4] the loved one at my side,
I roamed, in daily presence of this scene,
Upon the naked pool and dreary crags,
And on the melancholy beacon, fell
A spirit of pleasure and youth's golden gleam;
And think ye not with radiance more sublime
For these remembrances, and for the power
They had left behind? So feeling comes in aid
Of feeling, and diversity of strength
Attends us, if but once we have been strong.
Oh! mystery of man, from what a depth
Proceed thy honours. I am lost, but see
In simple childhood something of the base
On which thy greatness stands; but this I feel,
That from thyself it comes, that thou must give,
Else never canst receive. The days gone by
Return upon me almost from the dawn
Of life: the hiding-places of man's power
Open; I would approach them, but they close.
I see by glimpses now; when age comes on,
May scarcely see at all; and I would give,
While yet we may, as far as words can give,
Substance and life to what I feel, enshrining,
Such is my hope, the spirit of the past
For future restoration.—Yet another
Of these memorials:—
                                        One Christmas-time,[5]
On the glad eve of its dear holidays,
Feverish, and tired, and restless, I went forth
Into the fields, impatient for the sight
Of those led palfreys[6] that should bear us home;[7]
My brothers and myself. There rose a crag,
That, from the meeting-point of two highways
Ascending, overlooked them both, far stretched;
Thither, uncertain on which road to fix
My expectation, thither I repaired,
Scout-like, and gained the summit; 'twas a day
Tempestuous, dark, and wild, and on the grass
I sate half-sheltered by a naked wall;
Upon my right hand couched a single sheep,
Upon my left a blasted hawthorn stood;
With those companions at my side, I watched,
Straining my eyes intensely, as the mist
Gave intermitting prospect of the copse

[4] *hours . . . love.* In 1787; the "loved one" was Mary Hutchinson, whom Wordsworth married fifteen years later.

[5] In 1783, when Wordsworth was thirteen. [6] Saddle horses. [7] From school.

And plain beneath. Ere we to school returned,—
That dreary time,—ere we had been ten days
Sojourners in my father's house, he died,
And I and my three brothers, orphans then,[8]
Followed his body to the grave. The event,
With all the sorrow that it brought, appeared
A chastisement; and when I called to mind
That day so lately past, when from the crag
I looked in such anxiety of hope;
With trite reflections of morality,
Yet in the deepest passion, I bowed low
To God, Who thus corrected my desires;
And, afterwards, the wind and sleety rain,
And all the business of the elements,
The single sheep, and the one blasted tree,
And the bleak music from that old stone wall,
The noise of wood and water, and the mist
That on the line of each of those two roads
Advanced in such indisputable shapes;
All these were kindred spectacles and sounds
To which I oft repaired, and thence would drink,
As at a fountain; and on winter nights,
Down to this very time, when storm and rain
Beat on my roof, or, haply, at noon-day,
While in a grove I walk, whose lofty trees,
Laden with summer's thickest foliage, rock
In a strong wind, some working of the spirit,
Some inward agitations thence are brought,
Whate'er their office,[9] whether to beguile
Thoughts over busy in the course they took,
Or animate an hour of vacant ease.

from BOOK FOURTEENTH

CONCLUSION

In one of those excursions (may they ne'er
Fade from remembrance!) through the northern tracts
Of Cambria ranging with a youthful friend,[1]
I left Bethgelert's[2] huts at couching-time,
And westward took my way, to see the sun
Rise, from the top of Snowdon. To the door
Of a rude cottage at the mountain's base
We came, and roused the shepherd who attends

[8] Wordsworth's mother had died five years earlier. [9] Function.

[1] The Robert Jones of Book VI. The poet's ascent of Mount Snowdon, highest mountain in England or Wales ("Cambria"), took place in 1791, earlier than the events described in the immediately preceding books.

[2] A village near the mountain.

The adventurous stranger's steps, a trusty guide;
Then, cheered by short refreshment, sallied forth.

It was a close, warm, breezeless summer night,
Wan, dull, and glaring, with a dripping fog
Low-hung and thick that covered all the sky;
But, undiscouraged, we began to climb
The mountain-side. The mist soon girt us round,
And, after ordinary travellers' talk
With our conductor, pensively we sank
Each into commerce with his private thoughts:
Thus did we breast the ascent, and by myself
Was nothing either seen or heard that checked
Those musings or diverted, save that once
The shepherd's lurcher,[3] who, among the crags,
Had to his joy unearthed a hedgehog, teased
His coiled-up prey with barkings turbulent.
This small adventure, for even such it seemed
In that wild place and at the dead of night,
Being over and forgotten, on we wound
In silence as before. With forehead bent
Earthward, as if in opposition set
Against an enemy, I panted up
With eager pace, and no less eager thoughts.
Thus might we wear a midnight hour away,
Ascending at loose distance each from each,
And I, as chanced, the foremost of the band;
When at my feet the ground appeared to brighten,
And with a step or two seemed brighter still;
Nor was time given to ask or learn the cause,
For instantly a light upon the turf
Fell like a flash, and lo! as I looked up
The moon hung naked in a firmament
Of azure without cloud, and at my feet
Rested a silent sea of hoary mist.
A hundred hills their dusky backs upheaved
All over this still ocean; and beyond,
Far, far beyond, the solid vapours stretched,
In headlands, tongues, and promontory shapes,
Into the main Atlantic, that appeared
To dwindle, and give up his majesty,
Usurped upon far as the sight could reach.
Not so the ethereal vault; encroachment none
Was there, nor loss; only the inferior stars
Had disappeared, or shed a fainter light
In the clear presence of the full-orbed moon,
Who, from her sovereign elevation, gazed
Upon the billowy ocean, as it lay

[3] Hunting dog.

All meek and silent, save that through a rift—
Not distant from the shore whereon we stood,
A fixed, abysmal, gloomy, breathing-place—
Mounted the roar of waters, torrents, streams
Innumerable, roaring with one voice!
Heard over earth and sea, and, in that hour,
For so it seemed, felt by the starry heavens.

When into air had partially dissolved
That vision, given to spirits of the night
And three chance human wanderers, in calm thought
Reflected, it appeared to me the type
Of a majestic intellect, its acts
And its possessions, what it has and craves,
What in itself it is, and would become.
There I beheld the emblem of a mind
That feeds upon infinity, that broods
Over the dark abyss, intent to hear
Its voices issuing forth to silent light
In one continuous stream; a mind sustained
By recognitions of transcendent power,
In sense conducting to ideal form,
In soul of more than mortal privilege.
One function, above all, of such a mind
Had nature shadowed there, by putting forth,
'Mid circumstances awful and sublime,
That mutual domination which she loves
To exert upon the face of outward things,
So moulded, joined, abstracted, so endowed
With interchangeable supremacy,
That men, least sensitive, see, hear, perceive,
And cannot choose but feel. The power, which all
Acknowledge when thus moved, which nature thus
To bodily sense exhibits, is the express
Resemblance of that glorious faculty
That higher minds bear with them as their own.
This is the very spirit in which they deal
With the whole compass of the universe:
They from their native selves can send abroad
Kindred mutations; for themselves create
A like existence; and, whene'er it dawns
Created for them, catch it, or are caught
By its inevitable mastery,
Like angels stopped upon the wing by sound
Of harmony from Heaven's remotest spheres.
Them the enduring and the transient both
Serve to exalt; they build up greatest things
From least suggestions; ever on the watch,
Willing to work and to be wrought upon,
They need not extraordinary calls

To rouse them; in a world of life they live,
By sensible impressions not enthralled,
But by their quickening impulse made more prompt
To hold fit converse with the spiritual world,
And with the generations of mankind
Spread over time, past, present, and to come,
Age after age, till time shall be no more.
Such minds are truly from the Deity,
For they are powers; and hence the highest bliss
That flesh can know is theirs—the consciousness
Of Whom[4] they are, habitually infused
Through every image and through every thought,
And all affections by communion raised
From earth to heaven, from human to divine;
Hence endless occupation for the soul,
Whether discursive[5] or intuitive;
Hence cheerfulness for acts of daily life,
Emotions which best foresight need not fear,
Most worthy then of trust when most intense.
Hence, amid ills that vex and wrongs that crush
Our hearts—if here the words of Holy Writ
May with fit reverence be applied—that peace
Which passeth understanding,[6] that repose
In moral judgments which from this pure source
Must come, or will by man be sought in vain.

* * *

This spiritual love acts not nor can exist
Without imagination, which, in truth,
Is but another name for absolute power
And clearest insight, amplitude of mind,
And reason in her most exalted mood.
This faculty hath been the feeding source
Of our long labour: we have traced the stream
From the blind cavern whence is faintly heard
Its natal murmur; followed it to light
And open day; accompanied its course
Among the ways of nature, for a time
Lost sight of it bewildered and engulphed:[7]
Then given it greeting as it rose once more

[4] The posthumous text of 1850 is sprinkled with capital letters (for example, "Truant," "Fugitive," and "Pilgrim" in I.90–91, "Terror," "Love," and "Beauty" in III.136–37), and most of these have been removed from the present text. Here the capital in "Whom" has been retained, on the assumption that Wordsworth means "God." This interpretation is, however, not certain. The text of 1805 capitalizes the "Deity" of line 112 but has "whom" instead of the "Whom" of line 115.

[5] Using formal methods of reasoning. [6] *peace . . . understanding.* Philippians 4:7.

[7] *bewildered and engulphed.* During the mental crisis brought on by the French Revolution; see XI.173–333.

In strength, reflecting from its placid breast
The works of man and face of human life;
And lastly, from its progress have we drawn
Faith in life endless, the sustaining thought
Of human being, eternity, and God.

Imagination having been our theme,
So also hath that intellectual love,
For they are each in each, and cannot stand
Dividually.—Here must thou be, O man!
Power to thyself; no helper hast thou here;
Here keepest thou in singleness thy state:
No other can divide with thee this work:
No secondary hand can intervene
To fashion this ability; 'tis thine,
The prime and vital principle is thine
In the recesses of thy nature, far
From any reach of outward fellowship,
Else is not thine at all. . . .

* * *

And now, O friend! this history is brought
To its appointed close: the discipline
And consummation of a poet's mind,
In everything that stood most prominent,
Have faithfully been pictured; we have reached
The time (our guiding object from the first)
When we may, not presumptuously, I hope,
Suppose my powers so far confirmed, and such
My knowledge, as to make me capable
Of building up a work that shall endure.

* * *

Oh! yet a few short years of useful life,
And all will be complete, thy race[8] be run,
Thy monument of glory will be raised;
Then, though (too weak to tread the ways of truth)
This age fall back to old idolatry,
Though men return to servitude as fast
As the tide ebbs, to ignominy and shame
By nations sink together, we shall still
Find solace—knowing what we have learnt to know,
Rich in true happiness if allowed to be
Faithful alike in forwarding a day
Of firmer trust, joint labourers in the work
(Should Providence such grace to us vouchsafe)

[8] Thy (Coleridge's) career.

Of their deliverance, surely yet to come.
Prophets of nature, we to them will speak
A lasting inspiration, sanctified
By reason, blest by faith: what we have loved,
Others will love, and we will teach them how;
Instruct them how the mind of man becomes
A thousand times more beautiful than the earth
On which he dwells, above this frame of things
(Which, 'mid all revolution in the hopes
And fears of men, doth still remain unchanged)
In beauty exalted, as it is itself
Of quality and fabric more divine.

MY HEART LEAPS UP WHEN I BEHOLD

My heart leaps up when I behold
    A rainbow in the sky:
So was it when my life began;
So is it now I am a man;
So be it when I shall grow old,
    Or let me die!
The child is father of the man;
And I could wish my days to be
Bound each to each by natural piety.

ODE

INTIMATIONS OF IMMORTALITY FROM RECOLLECTIONS OF EARLY CHILDHOOD

The child is father of the man;
And I could wish my days to be
Bound each to each by natural piety.[1]

I

There was a time when meadow, grove, and stream,
The earth, and every common sight,
        To me did seem
    Apparelled in celestial light,
The glory[2] and the freshness of a dream.

[1] These three lines are from "My Heart Leaps Up When I Behold." The theme of human continuity in that poem makes it an appropriate epigraph for the ode.

[2] Here and later in the poem, the concrete meaning of the word is "halo" or "nimbus of light," as also in "glorious " and "glories."

It is not now as it hath been of yore;—
Turn wheresoe'er I may,
By night or day,
The things which I have seen I now can see no more.

II

The Rainbow comes and goes,
And lovely is the rose,
The moon doth with delight
Look round her when the heavens are bare,
Waters on a starry night
Are beautiful and fair;
The sunshine is a glorious birth;
But yet I know, where'er I go,
That there hath past away a glory from the earth.

III

Now, while the birds thus sing a joyous song,
And while the young lambs bound
As to the tabor's[3] sound,
To me alone there came a thought of grief:
A timely utterance gave that thought relief,
And I again am strong:
The cataracts blow their trumpets from the steep;
No more shall grief of mine the season wrong;
I hear the echoes through the mountains throng,
The winds come to me from the fields of sleep,[4]
And all the earth is gay;
Land and sea
Give themselves up to jollity,
And with the heart of May
Doth every beast keep holiday;—
Thou child of joy,
Shout round me, let me hear thy shouts, thou happy
shepherd-boy!

IV

Ye blessèd creatures, I have heard the call
Ye to each other make; I see
The heavens laugh with you in your jubilee;
My heart is at your festival,
My head hath its coronal,
The fulness of your bliss, I feel—I feel it all.
Oh evil day! if I were sullen
While earth herself is adorning,
This sweet May-morning,

[3] Small drum. Strophes III and IV combine realism with the conventional imagery of classical pastoral—e.g., the "coronal" (wreath of flowers) of line 40.

[4] *fields of sleep.* An obscure phrase; the meaning may be that the winds of morning seem to be blowing out of the night (fields of sleep) that has just ended.

And the children are culling
On every side,
In a thousand valleys far and wide,
Fresh flowers; while the sun shines warm,
And the babe leaps up on his mother's arm:—
I hear, I hear, with joy I hear!
—But there's a tree, of many, one,[5]
A single field which I have looked upon,
Both of them speak of something that is gone:
The pansy at my feet
Doth the same tale repeat:
Whither is fled the visionary gleam?
Where is it now, the glory and the dream?

V

Our birth is but a sleep and a forgetting:
The soul that rises with us, our life's star,
Hath had elsewhere its setting,
And cometh from afar:
Not in entire forgetfulness,
And not in utter nakedness,
But trailing clouds of glory do we come
From God, who is our home:
Heaven lies about us in our infancy!
Shades of the prison-house begin to close
Upon the growing boy,
But he beholds the light, and whence it flows,
He sees it in his joy;
The youth, who daily farther from the east
Must travel, still is nature's priest,
And by the vision splendid
Is on his way attended;
At length the man perceives it die away,
And fade into the light of common day.

VI

Earth fills her lap with pleasures of her own;
Yearnings she hath in her own natural kind,[6]
And, even with something of a mother's mind,
And no unworthy aim,
The homely nurse doth all she can
To make her foster-child, her inmate man,
Forget the glories he hath known,
And that imperial palace whence he came.

[5] *of many, one.* An individual tree singled out from many around it because it is associated with something that happened in the past. What the memory is we are not told.

[6] Mode; way.

VII

Behold the child among his new-born blisses,
A six years' darling of a pigmy size!
See, where 'mid work of his own hand he lies,
Fretted by sallies[7] of his mother's kisses,
With light upon him from his father's eyes!
See, at his feet, some little plan or chart,
Some fragment from his dream of human life,
Shaped by himself with newly-learned art;
A wedding or a festival,
A mourning or a funeral;
And this hath now his heart,
And unto this he frames his song:
Then will he fit his tongue
To dialogues of business, love, or strife;
But it will not be long
Ere this be thrown aside,
And with new joy and pride
The little actor cons[8] another part;
Filling from time to time his "humorous stage"[9]
With all the persons, down to palsied age,
That life brings with her in her equipage;[10]
As if his whole vocation
Were endless imitation.

VIII

Thou, whose exterior semblance doth belie
Thy soul's immensity;
Thou best philosopher, who yet dost keep
Thy heritage, thou eye among the blind,
That, deaf and silent, read'st the eternal deep,[11]
Haunted for ever by the eternal mind,—
Mighty prophet! Seer blest!
On whom those truths do rest,
Which we are toiling all our lives to find,
In darkness lost, the darkness of the grave;
Thou, over whom thy immortality
Broods like the day, a master o'er a slave,
A presence which is not to be put by;[12]
Thou little child, yet glorious in the might
Of heaven-born freedom on thy being's height,
Why with such earnest pains dost thou provoke
The years to bring the inevitable yoke,

[7] Attacked by (almost military) raids. [8] Memorizes.

[9] Quoted from the dedicatory sonnet of Samuel Daniel's *Musophilus* (1599). There is probably also an allusion to Jaques' speech describing the "seven ages" of human life ("All the world's a stage . . ."), in Shakespeare's *As You Like It*, II.vii.139–166.

[10] Ceremonial procession. [11] Ocean. [12] Got rid of.

Thus blindly with thy blessedness at strife?
Full soon thy soul shall have her earthly freight,
And custom lie upon thee with a weight,
Heavy as frost, and deep almost as life!

IX

O joy! that in our embers
Is something that doth live,
That nature yet remembers
What was so fugitive!
The thought of our past years in me doth breed
Perpetual benediction: not indeed
For that which is most[13] worthy to be blest;
Delight and liberty, the simple creed
Of childhood, whether busy or at rest,
With new-fledged hope still fluttering in his breast:—
Not for these I raise
The song of thanks and praise;
But for those obstinate questionings
Of sense and outward things,
Fallings from us, vanishings;
Blank misgivings of a creature
Moving about in worlds not realised,[14]
High instincts before which our mortal nature
Did tremble like a guilty thing surprised:[15]
But for those first affections,
Those shadowy recollections,
Which, be they what they may,[16]
Are yet the fountain-light of all our day,
Are yet a master-light of all our seeing;
Uphold us, cherish, and have power to make
Our noisy years seem moments in the being
Of the eternal silence: truths that wake,
To perish never:
Which neither listlessness, nor mad endeavour,
Nor man nor boy,
Nor all that is at enmity with joy,
Can utterly abolish or destroy.
Hence in a season of calm weather
Though inland far we be,
Our souls have sight of that immortal sea
Which brought us hither,
Can in a moment travel thither,

[13] Very. [14] Made real.

[15] Like a supernatural spirit taken by surprise. (The words "guilty thing" are a quotation from Shakespeare's *Hamlet,* I.i.148, where they refer to the ghost of Hamlet's father.)

[16] *lines 141–150.* This groping passage, according to statements Wordsworth made later in life, is based on his memory from childhood of feeling an immunity to death and an "abyss of idealism" in which physical objects seemed merely the emanations of his inner self.

And see the children sport upon the shore,
And hear the mighty waters rolling evermore.

X

Then sing, ye birds, sing, sing a joyous song!
And let the young lambs bound
As to the tabor's sound!
We in thought will join your throng,
Ye that pipe and ye that play,
Ye that through your hearts to-day
Feel the gladness of the May!
What though the radiance which was once so bright
Be now for ever taken from my sight,
Though nothing can bring back the hour
Of splendour in the grass, of glory in the flower;
We will grieve not, rather find
Strength in what remains behind;
In the primal sympathy
Which having been must ever be;
In the soothing thoughts that spring
Out of human suffering;
In the faith that looks through death,
In years that bring the philosophic mind.

XI

And O, ye fountains, meadows, hills, and groves,
Forebode not any severing of our loves!
Yet in my heart of hearts I feel your might;
I only have relinquished one delight
To live beneath your more habitual sway.
I love the brooks which down their channels fret,
Even more than when I tripped lightly as they;
The innocent brightness of a new-born day
Is lovely yet;
The clouds that gather round the setting sun
Do take a sober colouring from an eye
That hath kept watch o'er man's mortality;
Another race hath been, and other palms[17] are won.
Thanks to the human heart by which we live,
Thanks to its tenderness, its joys, and fears,
To me the meanest flower that blows[18] can give
Thoughts that do often lie too deep for tears.

[17] Emblems of victories. [18] *meanest . . . blows.* Most lowly flower that blooms.

Samuel Taylor Coleridge
(1772–1834)

"Dejection: An Ode" is inserted here for comparison with Wordsworth's "Ode: Intimations of Immortality," which it sometimes echoes. In 1802 Coleridge heard recited the opening four strophes of his friend Wordsworth's poem (all that Wordsworth had then written), and in reply Coleridge wrote "Dejection." The unhappiness the poem expresses arose from Coleridge's ill health, his unhappy marriage to Sara Fricker, and his hopeless love for Sara Hutchinson, sister of the Mary Hutchinson whom Wordsworth married later in 1802. The first version of "Dejection," addressed to "Sara" (Hutchinson), ran 340 lines; in later versions Coleridge changed the addressee to "William," then to "Edmund," and finally to "Lady." He published an early version in a newspaper on Wordsworth's wedding day, which was also Coleridge's wedding anniversary. The version printed here is the final one, published in 1817.

DEJECTION: AN ODE

Late, late yestreen I saw the new moon,
With the old moon in her arms;[1]
And I fear, I fear, my master dear!
We shall have a deadly storm.
—*Ballad of* SIR PATRICK SPENCE

I

Well! If the bard was weather-wise, who made
The grand old ballad of Sir Patrick Spence,
This night, so tranquil now, will not go hence
Unroused by winds, that ply a busier trade
Than those which mould yon cloud in lazy flakes,
Or the dull sobbing draft, that moans and rakes
Upon the strings of this Aeolian lute,[2]
Which better far were mute.
For lo! the new-moon winter-bright!
And overspread with phantom light,
(With swimming phantom light o'erspread
But rimmed and circled by a silver thread)
I see the old moon in her lap, foretelling
The coming-on of rain and squally blast.
And oh! that even now the gust were swelling,

[1] *new moon . . . arms.* Coleridge gives a visual description of this phenomenon in lines 9–13 below. Astronomers call it the "ashen light"—a grayish light covering the whole disc of the very new moon and caused by sunlight reflected off the earth. (When it is new moon on Earth, it is "full Earth" on the moon.) Almost wholly back-lighted, the moon has a fine bright line around the entire disc. The phenomenon is especially noticeable in April, the setting for "Dejection." According to the old ballad Coleridge quotes, the ashen light is a sign of a coming storm.

[2] An Aeolian lute is an instrument that produces music when the wind blows over it. Several of the Romantics used it as a symbol of inspiration.

And the slant night-shower driving loud and fast!
Those sounds which oft have raised me, whilst they awed,
And sent my soul abroad,
Might now perhaps their wonted[3] impulse give,
Might startle this dull pain, and make it move and live!

II

A grief without a pang, void, dark, and drear,
A stifled, drowsy, unimpassioned grief,
Which finds no natural outlet, no relief,
In word, or sigh, or tear—
O lady! in this wan and heartless mood,
To other thoughts by yonder throstle[4] woo'd,
All this long eve, so balmy and serene,
Have I been gazing on the western sky,
And its peculiar tint of yellow green:
And still I gaze—and with how blank an eye!
And those thin clouds above, in flakes and bars,
That give away their motion to the stars;
Those stars, that glide behind them or between,
Now sparkling, now bedimmed, but always seen:
Yon crescent moon, as fixed as if it grew
In its own cloudless, starless lake of blue;
I see them all so excellently fair,
I see, not feel, how beautiful they are!

III

My genial[5] spirits fail;
And what can these[6] avail
To lift the smothering weight from off my breast?
It were a vain endeavour,
Though I should gaze for ever
On that green light that lingers in the west:
I may not hope from outward forms to win
The passion and the life, whose fountains are within.

IV

O lady! we receive but what we give,
And in our life alone does nature live:
Ours is her wedding garment, ours her shroud!
And would we aught behold, of higher worth,
Than that inanimate cold world allowed
To the poor loveless ever-anxious crowd,
Ah! from the soul itself must issue forth
A light, a glory, a fair luminous cloud
Enveloping the Earth—

[3] Usual. [4] Thrush.

[5] A key word for the Romantics; see note to Wordsworth's "Lines Composed a Few Miles Above Tintern Abbey," line 113.

[6] The natural objects described above.

And from the soul itself must there be sent
  A sweet and potent voice, of its own birth,
Of all sweet sounds the life and element!

V

O pure of heart! thou need'st not ask of me
What this strong music in the soul may be!
What, and wherein it doth exist,
This light, this glory, this fair luminous mist,
This beautiful and beauty-making power.
  Joy, virtuous lady! Joy that ne'er was given,
Save to the pure, and in their purest hour,
Life, and life's effluence,[7] cloud at once and shower,
Joy, lady! is the spirit and the power,
Which wedding nature to us gives in dower
  A new Earth and new Heaven,[8]
Undreamt of by the sensual and the proud—
Joy is the sweet voice, joy the luminous cloud—
    We in ourselves rejoice!
And thence flows all that charms or ear or[9] sight,
  All melodies the echoes of that voice,
All colours a suffusion[10] from that light.

VI

There was a time when, though my path was rough,
  This joy within me dallied with distress,
And all misfortunes were but as the stuff[11]
  Whence fancy made me dreams of happiness:
For hope grew round me, like the twining vine,
And fruits, and foliage, not my own, seemed mine.
But now afflictions bow me down to earth:
Nor care I that they rob me of my mirth;
    But oh! each visitation
Suspends what nature gave me at my birth,
  My shaping spirit of imagination.
For not to think of what I needs must feel,
  But to be still and patient, all I can;
And haply[12] by abstruse research to steal
  From my own nature all the natural man—
  This was my sole resource, my only plan:
Till that which suits a part infects the whole,
And now is almost grown the habit of my soul.

VII

Hence, viper thoughts, that coil around my mind,
    Reality's dark dream!

[7] Something that flows out.
[8] Joy achieves a wedding between the bride nature and us, giving as the bride's dowry a new earth and new heaven. (The reader should mentally supply commas after "Which" and "us" in line 68.)
[9] *or ear or.* Either ear or. [10] Something that spreads. [11] Material. [12] Perhaps.

I turn from you, and listen to the wind,
Which long has raved unnoticed. What a scream
Of agony by torture lengthened out
That lute sent forth! Thou wind, that rav'st without,[13]
Bare crag, or mountain-tairn,[14] or blasted tree,
Or pine-grove whither woodman never clomb,
Or lonely house, long held the witches' home,
Methinks were fitter instruments for thee,
Mad lutanist! who in this month of showers,
Of dark-brown gardens, and of peeping flowers,
Mak'st devils' yule, with worse than wintry song,
The blossoms, buds, and timorous leaves among.
Thou actor, perfect in all tragic sounds!
Thou mighty poet, e'en to frenzy bold!
What tell'st thou now about?
'Tis of the rushing of an host in rout,
With groans, of trampled men, with smarting wounds—
At once they groan with pain, and shudder with the cold!
But hush! there is a pause of deepest silence!
And all that noise, as of a rushing crowd,
With groans, and tremulous shudderings—all is over—
It tells another tale, with sounds less deep and loud!
A tale of less affright,
And tempered with delight,
As Otway's[15] self had framed the tender lay,—
'Tis of a little child
Upon a lonesome wild,
Not far from home, but she hath lost her way:
And now moans low in bitter grief and fear,
And now screams loud, and hopes to make her mother hear.

VIII

'Tis midnight, but small thoughts have I of sleep:
Full seldom may my friend such vigils keep!
Visit her, gentle sleep! with wings of healing,
And may this storm be but a mountain-birth,
May all the stars hang bright above her dwelling,
Silent as though they watched the sleeping Earth!
With light heart may she rise,
Gay fancy, cheerful eyes,
Joy lift her spirit, joy attune her voice;
To her may all things live, from pole to pole,
Their life the eddying of her living soul!
O simple spirit, guided from above,
Dear lady! friend devoutest of my choice,
Thus mayest thou ever, evermore rejoice.

[13] Outdoors. [14] Small lake.
[15] Thomas Otway (1652–1685), dramatist known for pathetic effects. Coleridge's original version read "William's."

George Gordon, Lord Byron

(1788–1824)

George Gordon, sixth Baron Byron, created in the "Byronic hero" one of the most pervasive literary myths of the last two centuries, and he was himself part of that myth. With a few exceptions, attempts in the last few decades to escape the tyranny of Byron biography and concentrate on his poems in themselves have been only indifferently successful, relapsing despite the critics' resolve into much the same old gossip and speculation about his politics, personality, and amours. This may be just as well. Byron, along with Sir Walter Scott, influenced literature throughout Europe—not to mention painting, orchestral music, and opera—more than any other English writers of their century. But while Scott did this through his novels as such (many of which in fact appeared anonymously), Byron's impact came through the compound of his work and public personality, a blend of author with hero that Byron teased the public into accepting at the same time that he stoutly disclaimed any resemblance to his protagonists. We may, if we wish, talk about the "persona" speaking in poems like Don Juan, *or rather personas (the innocent embarrassed by the story he tells, the leering lecher, the bouncy clown, the sensitive spirit bruised by life), but for his readers all such real or assumed guises belonged to the notorious Lord Byron, and the poet's awareness of his public image is what gives point to many of the poem's jokes and laments. This is not to say that Byron's life is more important than his works, since it was poetry that launched his fame in the first place, but rather that the two are for most purposes inseparable.*

The thirty-six years of Byron's life were crowded and often lurid. There was bad, if aristocratic, blood on the paternal side of the family, and his father, "Mad Jack" Byron, was a profligate rake who married Byron's mother (the descendant of a distinguished old Scottish family) for her money and rapidly squandered it. (He had a daughter Augusta by an earlier marriage who would turn up again in Byron's life.) After leaving her husband, Byron's impoverished mother gave birth to the future poet in London in 1788. He was born lame—with a club foot, apparently, that seems to have embittered him but also gave him a touch of infernal glamor in his later years of social success. Mother and son lived in straitened circumstances in Aberdeen, Scotland, until the boy was ten, when after the death of the old baron's immediate heirs (Byron's father and cousin) and then of the baron himself, Byron inherited the title. His religious upbringing had a strong flavor of Scottish Calvinism, one of the most uncheerful of religions, and some critics find in that background a source of the darker side of Byron's later work. The scope Byron's life affords armchair psychologists (and some more serious ones) is also illustrated in the fact that the servant girl entrusted with teaching Byron his Bible played another role too: as one of Byron's friends later put it, she used to go to bed with the nine-year-old boy and "play tricks with his person." So began his flagrant sexual career.

Byron's succession to the title and to Newstead Abbey, a half-ruined, romantic old family home that Henry VIII had taken from the monks, revolutionized his life, and as if to make up for poverty and lost time he became in his later youth and young manhood almost a caricature of the eighteenth-century roué in the last years before middle-class morality began to set the stage for Victorianism. He acquired a snobbish class-consciousness that throughout his life mingled uneasily with militant political liberalism. He got a gentleman's education at its best, at Harrow and Trinity College, Cambridge, and after a few disappointed, idealized adolescent loves plunged into a life of debauchery and debt in London during his college years. He also wrote lyric poetry in his teens—some of it cynically rakish, some sentimental—a foreshadowing of the seemingly inexplicable division of his later work between worldly rambunctiousness and melodramatic romanticism. His first published volume (after the naughty Fugitive Pieces, *which Byron suppressed) was called* Hours of Idleness *(1807)—a title invented by the publisher but prophetically apt, since all his life Byron would cultivate the image of a gentleman who condescendingly dabbled in poetry as a sideline to more authentically aristocratic—generally dissipated—activities. Many critics and biographers, conscious that Byron wrote prolifically and continuously during almost all his adult life, see this stance as one of Byron's many "poses," but it was more than that. Despite his addiction to versifying and his love for neoclassical authors like Pope (at a time when his contemporary Romantics were in strident rebellion against the patrician eighteenth-century models), one side of Byron really did despise poetry, which he sometimes saw as an intellectually fashionable form of lying. Still, when* Hours of Idleness *got a bad reception from the* Edinburgh Review, *Byron retaliated with* English Bards and Scotch Reviewers *(1809), a rhymed-couplet poem more or less in the tradition of Popean satire, in which Byron attacked virtually all the prominent poets and critics of the day. (Later, when some of his targets, including Scott, had become his friends, he regretted the persistently popular poem.)*

In the same year, the twenty-one-year-old Byron took his seat in the House of Lords and then embarked on the Grand Tour customary for young gentlemen. But instead of the usual sojourn in the central cities of Europe, Byron set out with his best friend John Cam Hobhouse on a two-year trip to Portugal, Spain (at the time the focal center of the Napoleonic wars), Gibraltar, Malta, Albania, Greece, and Constantinople (en route, Byron swam the Hellespont, or Dardanelles). This trip represented a real adventure in Byron's day and permanently impressed his imagination. During the voyage he began Childe Harold, *a colorful travelogue anomalously overlaid with the portrait of Harold, the first "Byronic hero," a brooding, cynical, jaded expatriate alienated from mankind and from life itself. After his return to England in 1811, Byron made a few speeches in the House of Lords, taking daringly liberal positions in 1812 on the issue of capital punishment for the technologically unemployed who were breaking the new textile machinery in England and on the rights of Roman Catholics. As he reminisced years later, Byron might have had a political career; he had always had a penchant for oratory, and in fact the style of his parliamentary speeches has much in common with the expansive style of his poems, especially the melodramatic ones.*

Instead, the die was cast otherwise for him when, in March 1812, Cantos I and II of Childe Harold *were published and Byron became overnight the most feverishly sought-after poet-celebrity in London, his allure heightened by the popular identification of him with his Harold. Over the next four years he wrote, sometimes hundreds of* lines at a time in the early morning after a night on the town, a series of oriental verse tales that were incredibly popular best-sellers, including The Giaour, The Bride of Abydos, and The Corsair. All of them, and some later works including Manfred, feature amoral, personally magnetic egoists, alienated from society or the human condition or both, tied to humanity only by their love (often a guilty one) for a woman. Actual or potential leaders, they really serve their own egos rather than any cause pursued for its own sake. It was works like these that made Byron a household word in the nineteenth century and a powerful influence on great writers including Stendhal, Lermontov, Emily and Charlotte Brontë, Melville, the elder Dumas, Jules Verne, and a host of others. (The decorous heroine of Jane Austen's Persuasion chats about The Giaour, and on the Missouri frontier we find Byron's "Destruction of Sennacherib" on the declamation program in Tom Sawyer's schoolroom.) The vogue of the Byronic hero persists, indeed, into the twentieth century, in the loners of Hemingway and Raymond Chandler and the swashbucklers who provided movie roles for the likes of both senior and junior Douglas Fairbanks. No one has quite satisfactorily explained why the Byronic hero made such a sensation; Rousseau, spine-tingling gothic novels, and Goethe's Werther and Faust had anticipated him. Byron's vogue may have had something to do with the spiritual weariness of Europe after a quarter-century of revolution and war, but that does not explain his influence since then, on levels ranging from masterpieces to trash.

Byron's love affairs during the four years of his fame in England were notorious, conducted in veins ranging from farce (as with the madcap Lady Caroline Lamb) to desperation. It now seems certain that he and his half-sister Augusta were lovers. On the other hand, partly in reaction to the affair with Augusta, he was drawn in a curiously ambivalent way to Annabella Milbanke, a primly serious young woman whom he married in January 1815. This must rank with the most incompatible marriages ever contracted, and it lasted just a year, during which Byron acted so outrageously—not to mention his hints to his wife about Augusta and him—that Annabella had some reason to question Byron's sanity. After bearing him a daughter, Augusta Ada, Lady Byron left him in January 1816. In the succeeding months a separation was arranged, in an atmosphere of juicy public scandal that permanently left Byron with a contempt for what he considered English moral hypocrisy. He left England, never to return there alive, in April.

On the continent, the psychologically maimed Byron visited the field of Waterloo (the great battle there only a year old but already fading from memory), the Rhineland, and Switzerland. He recorded his impressions in a third canto of Childe Harold, one of the episodes in the "pageant of his bleeding heart" that, in Matthew Arnold's phrase, Byron bore through Europe to his final end in Greece. Life had, after all, ironically cast him as the Byronic hero he had devised but resisted comparison to. During a memorable summer on Lake Geneva in Switzerland, Byron met the idealistic young poet Percy Bysshe Shelley and Mary Godwin (whom Shelley later married) and renewed an affair with Claire Clairmont, Mary's stepsister, one of the many women who had thrown themselves at Byron while he was still in England. Claire was already pregnant with Byron's daughter Allegra. (Born early in 1817, she later died at the age of five in a convent to which Byron, following one of his fitful quasi-orthodox religious impulses, had entrusted her over the mother's protests.) The friendship between the two poets, utterly unlike each other, remained close until Shelley died in Italy six years later by drowning. In the meantime, the foursome of 1816 spawned scandalous if inaccurate charges of a "league of incest" in Switzer-

land, a situation not improved when Shelley's wife Harriet drowned herself in London a few months later.

In terms of literary production, the year was fruitful. Mary began her novel Frankenstein *as part of a horror story competition among the friends. Byron, besides writing Canto III of* Childe Harold, *began* Manfred *(completed a year later), which is haunted by the memory of Augusta as Astarte, and wrote* The Prisoner of Chillon. *These last two works, the first showing the spirit as invincible, the second revealing it as inevitably destroyed by the brute facts of imprisonment, make a notable contrast. That Byron should have conceived such wholly contradictory visions at almost the same time is striking evidence of the romantic and realist sides which did not so much alternate as coexist in him.*

Late in 1816 Byron moved to Italy, where he lived for the next seven years, first at Venice (where he indulged a frenzy of sensuality), then at Ravenna, Pisa, Leghorn, and Genoa, besides visiting other parts of Italy, including Rome. Some of these settings are reflected in the fourth (and final) canto of Childe Harold *(1818) and in the last act of* Manfred. *A turning point in Byron's sexual life was his liaison with the Countess Teresa Gamba Guiccioli, a nineteen-year-old married woman with whom, by his standards, Byron settled down almost cozily in 1819. In Italy, Byron continued to work the vein of the Byronic hero, mainly in a series of closet dramas of which the greatest is* Cain *(published 1821), a daring piece of cosmological speculation and religious unorthodoxy very similar, given the difference of the Biblical subject, to* Manfred. *But he also turned to a wholly different kind of poetry that for most modern readers represents Byron at his greatest. He used as his vehicle the ottava-rima stanza (eight pentameter lines rhyming abababcc) he discovered in a satirist named Frere and in the Italian Renaissance epic poets. His first poem in this form was* Beppo *(published 1818), a rollicking, playful satire on Venetian manners in which Byron strings out on an almost nonexistent plot thread a series of comments on anything he feels like mentioning, in a bracingly colloquial style further enlivened by outrageous rhymes. In the same genre he wrote* The Vision of Judgment *(1822), in which he remorselessly pilloried Robert Southey, the poet laureate he loathed, and a truly despicable poem Southey had written on the reception of George III into heaven after his death. Byron's poem ranks with Pope's* Rape of the Lock *as one of the two greatest verse satires of their length in English. The* magnum opus *among the ottava-rima poems was* Don Juan, *which Byron began in 1818 and wrote away at until his death, piling up a total of sixteen-plus cantos. The poem, which is unlike anything else in English, allowed Byron to indulge all the sides of himself—his worldly cynicism and sociability as well as his "Byronic" sadness, his poetic exuberance and his contempt for poetic pretensions, his love of life and his profound dissatisfaction with it, his thoughts and his jaundiced opinion of Thinkers. The narrative and geographical sweep is comprehensive: Juan moves from his native Spain of Canto I to the Greek islands (where he escapes a shipwreck and has a love affair with a "child of nature" that ends tragically) to slavery in Constantinople to shenanigans in a harem to service under the Russians in a battle against the Turks to the court of Catherine the Great of Russia (where he is the queen's lover) to England, though the narrative plot thins out to such an extent that the late cantos are almost all digression, like* Beppo. *Despite several mock-solemn outlines of his "plan" for the poem, it seems doubtful that Byron meant it ever to end.*

The final chapter in Byron's life is political. Along with Shelley and Teresa's family, the Gambas, Byron was distressed by the subjugation of Italy to Austria in the wake of the Napoleonic wars, and he got into trouble with the reactionary ruling forces. The same political liberalism, combined with personal restlessness and his inveterate pain over modern Greece, once the glory of the world but now reduced to mean subservience under the Turks, led him to leave Italy in 1823 for Greece, where he planned to vindicate himself to the world by providing both military leadership and financial help to the liberationists. He did in fact help substantially with money, but his hopes for an honored military role were aborted when he incurred a fever after horseback-riding in the rain and, after a week of suffering, died in April 1824 at Missolonghi. (The ironic tawdriness of his exit from the world is exactly the kind of thing he would have exploited bemusedly in Don Juan.*) Mourned by the world, and especially by the Greeks, who have since worshiped him, his body was returned to England, where he was buried near his old country estate, having been denied burial in the hallowed Westminster Abbey. The* Memoirs *he had written and transmitted to his friend Thomas Moore a few years earlier were burned by his publisher, who apparently considered them too hot for even posterity to handle.*

Manfred *and* Don Juan *clearly represent two visions so different that it seems hard to imagine them as the products of the same creative mind.* Manfred *is all claustrophobic gloom (despite its Alpine scenery). Its hero is the "Byronic hero"* par excellence. Don Juan *is the most open of poems, in form and theme impudently free to go anywhere and say anything. Its hero, far from being the sulfurously masterful figure of legend who in defiance of heaven and earth undermines marriage, the family, and consequently the social order, is a well-balanced, genial young man at home in society with men and women, and of the latter the prey rather than the predator. The solemn* Manfred *has two incongruous lines (III.iv.71–72) that might be considered funny, when the startled Manfred turns from dire warnings directed at the Abbot to wonder how the devil got into the house. (It would not be unlike Byron to have played this joke on purpose, out of pure mischievousness; he does this kind of thing in a few other works.)* Don Juan *is one laugh (belly or cerebral) after another, though people have also been known to cry over parts like Julia's letter (I.cxcii–cxcvii).* Manfred *is a kind of apotheosis of death, though ironically its protagonist seems tragically exempt from it;* Don Juan *is vitality itself ("is it not* life, *is it not* the thing?" *Byron wrote to a friend, with an epistolary dig in the ribs).*

Yet Manfred *and* Don Juan *were written by the same man, and if one examines them more closely the fact does not seem so incredible after all. For one thing, the styles have something in common: both are based on swelling rhetorical expansiveness, the parliamentary orator's trick of saying almost the same thing several times (see Manfred's hymn to the sun in III.ii and the "sweet" stanzas in* Don Juan, *I.cxxii–cxxvii). Both poems scorn conventional society. Above all, both poems explore, though in utterly different moods, a serious matter that Byron returns to often in his work: the undeniable but unthinkable combination in man of "dust" and "deity," the utter strangeness of the thing we call consciousness in a being made of matter. Seen in this light,* Manfred, *a play about a man who seems unique, immune to material or spiritual influence from outside himself, singled out for exemption from death, is really an exploration of a more universal intuition: that the "I" within us could not possibly be subject to mere circumstance—for example, the accident that the trajectory of a lump of lead projected from a machine we call a gun passes through the muscle in us that pumps blood. The same unspeakable irony underlies much of* Don Juan—*for example, in the strange relationship between an adolescent's airiest reveries and his hormones (I.xc–xciii) or between Julia's platonic rationalizations and biological destiny (I.lxxvii–lxxix, cxvi). Following on her letter, the quiet little stanza (I.cxcviii) describing Julia's stationery is a heartrending reminder that at this supreme spiritual crisis in her life she is bound to* things, *having to use (and possibly choose consciously) a certain kind of bordered writing paper and a new pen and red sealing wax, having to perform the absurd, mechanical acts required to write and mail a letter. It is as if we were watching a man on the morning of his execution as he chooses which shirt to wear and whether to put on the good socks or the ones with the hole in them.*

Don Juan *contains plenty of satire, but to call it a satire seems inadequate. Rather—and this becomes even more apparent in the later cantos—it is a philosophical poem, though it scoffs at Philosophy as it does at everything else that tries to systematically tidy up the incongruous welter of momentous, trivial, blithe, heartbreaking episodes that are life. It is a profoundly skeptical work, though its darker vision throws into relief its vivacity and sparkle. Similarly, though there is mock-epic in* Don Juan *it is also meant as a genuine epic—not an absurd use of literary heavy machinery to lift fluff but a seriocomic examination of the role of poetry, especially epic poetry, in the present and the past. Byron says that most poets lie—whether they are double talking minor ones like Campbell (I.lxxxviii–lxxxix) or major ones like Homer, Virgil, and Milton, who tell us that glory is more real than love (a cliché of epic convention since Virgil's Dido) or that heaven is more real than earth. It is no accident that, just as Byron chooses a Byronic-hero figure, Don Juan, and makes him wholly un-"Byronic," he takes the archetypal erotic hero and measures him against an epic tradition in which sexual love is a desecration of duty. This poem, for once, will tell it as it is, with nothing of the "poetic" in it, nothing of the thematic or stylistic dignity that poets use to evade reality. It most certainly will not have the kind of intricacy and self-important intensity Byron despised in most of his Romantic contemporaries and sometimes in himself when he was like them. Instead, it will be "the thing."*

FURTHER READING *(prepared by B. W.)*: A general reader's edition of the (nearly complete) poetry is the Oxford Standard Authors *Poetical Works of Lord Byron,* first published in 1904. Well-annotated student editions of the complete *Don Juan* include one edited by T. G. Steffan, E. Steffan, and W. W. Pratt, 1982, and Leslie A. Marchand's Riverside edition, 1958. Byron's incomparably readable letters, with other fascinating material, appear in *Byron's Letters and Journals,* 12 vols., ed. by Marchand, 1973–82; a selection from this work is available as *Lord Byron: Selected Letters and Journals,* 1982. The poet's extraordinary life is recounted in full detail in Marchand's marvelous *Byron: A Biography,* 3 vols., 1957, skillfully condensed in the one-volume *Byron: A Portrait,* 1970. Northrop Frye's essay on Byron in *Fables of Identity,* 1963, is a brief, witty, incisive introduction to the poet and his distinctive achievement. Bernard Blackstone's *Byron: A Survey,* 1975, provides a useful overview of the poetry, with biographical information where it is relevant. Jerome J. McGann's excellent *Fiery Dust: Byron's Poetic Development,* 1968, is recommended especially for students who go on to read widely in Byron. Robert F. Gleckner's *Byron and the Ruins of Paradise,* 1967, concentrates on the dark, existential side of Byron, providing some good readings of often-neglected nonsatiric works. Peter L. Thorslev's *The Byronic Hero: Types and Prototypes,* 1962, is valuable for tracing the literary antecedents of Manfred and other "Byronic" heroes. On their psychology, see Peter J. Manning's psychoanalytic study *Byron and His Fictions,* 1978, which also discusses *Don Juan.* On that poem, a number of essays are gathered in *Twentieth Century Interpretations of "Don Juan,"* ed. by Edward E. Bostetter, 1969. George M. Ridenour's *The Style of "Don Juan,"* 1960, finds the poem coherent, discussing it in terms of its speaking persona, governing images of the fall of man, and stylistic levels. The poem's epic status is treated by Brian Wilkie in the Byron chapter of *Romantic Poets and Epic Tradition,* 1965. Jerome J. McGann's *"Don Juan" in Context,* 1976, treats the poem's language, theme, and structure in social, biographical, and artistic contexts.

MANFRED

A DRAMATIC POEM

"There are more things in heaven and earth, Horatio,
Than are dreamt of in your philosophy."[1]

DRAMATIS PERSONAE

MANFRED
CHAMOIS HUNTER
ABBOT OF ST. MAURICE
MANUEL
HERMAN
WITCH OF THE ALPS
ARIMANES
NEMESIS
THE DESTINIES
SPIRITS, &C.

THE SCENE *of the drama is amongst the higher Alps —partly in the castle of Manfred, and partly in the mountains.*

ACT I

SCENE I

MANFRED *alone.—Scene, a Gothic gallery. Time, midnight.*

MANFRED. The lamp must be replenished, but even then
It will not burn so long as I must watch:[2]
My slumbers—if I slumber—are not sleep,
But a continuance of enduring thought,
Which then I can resist not: in my heart
There is a vigil, and these eyes but close
To look within; and yet I live, and bear

[1] Quoted from Shakespeare's *Hamlet,* I.v.166–167. [2] Remain awake.

The aspect and the form of breathing men.
But grief should be the instructor of the wise;
Sorrow is knowledge: they who know the most
Must mourn the deepest o'er the fatal truth,
The tree of knowledge is not that of life.
Philosophy and science, and the springs
Of wonder, and the wisdom of the world,
I have essayed, and in my mind there is
A power to make these subject to itself—
But they avail not: I have done men good,
And I have met with good even among men—
But this availed not: I have had my foes,
And none have baffled, many fallen before me—
But this availed not:—Good, or evil, life,
Powers, passions, all I see in other beings,
Have been to me as rain unto the sands,
Since that all-nameless hour.[3] I have no dread,
And feel the curse to have no natural fear,
Nor fluttering throb, that beats with hopes or wishes,
Or lurking love of something on the earth.
Now to my task.—
Mysterious agency!
Ye spirits of the unbounded universe!
Whom I have sought in darkness and in light—
Ye, who do compass earth about, and dwell
In subtler essence—ye, to whom the tops
Of mountains inaccessible are haunts,
And earth's and ocean's caves familiar things—
I call upon ye by the written charm[4]
Which gives me power upon you—Rise! Appear!
[*A pause.*]
They come not yet.—Now by the voice of him
Who is the first[5] among you—by this sign,
Which makes you tremble—by the claims of him
Who is undying,—Rise! Appear——Appear!
[*A pause.*]
If it be so—Spirits of earth and air,
Ye shall not thus elude me! By a power,
Deeper than all yet urged, a tyrant-spell,
Which had its birthplace in a star condemned,
The burning wreck of a demolished world,
A wandering hell in the eternal space;
By the strong curse which is upon my soul,
The thought which is within me and around me,
I do compel ye to my will—Appear!

[3] The first of several references to Manfred's fatal, guilt-ridden relationship with his beloved Astarte, often identified with Byron's half-sister and lover Augusta.

[4] Formula of magic.

[5] Possibly Arimanes, chief of the evil spirits, whom Manfred will confront later in the play, but possibly a broader religious reference is intended.

[A star is seen at the darker end of the gallery: it is stationary; and a voice is heard singing.]

FIRST SPIRIT[6]

Mortal! to thy bidding bowed,
From my mansion in the cloud,
Which the breath of twilight builds
And the summer's sunset gilds
With the azure and vermilion,
Which is mixed for my pavilion;
Though thy quest may be forbidden,
On a star-beam I have ridden,
To thine adjuration bowed:
Mortal—be thy wish avowed![7]

VOICE OF THE SECOND SPIRIT

Mont Blanc[8] is the monarch of mountains;
  They crowned him long ago
On a throne of rocks, in a robe of clouds,
  With a diadem[9] of snow.
Around his waist are forests braced,
  The avalanche in his hand;
But ere it fall, that thundering ball
  Must pause for my command.
The glacier's cold and restless mass
  Moves onward day by day;
But I am he who bids it pass,
  Or with its ice delay.
I am the spirit of the place,
  Could make the mountain bow
And quiver to his caverned base—
  And what with me wouldst *thou?*

VOICE OF THE THIRD SPIRIT

In the blue depth of the waters,
  Where the wave hath no strife,
Where the wind is a stranger,
  And the sea-snake hath life,
Where the mermaid is decking
  Her green hair with shells,
Like the storm on the surface
  Came the sound of thy spells;
O'er my calm hall of coral
  The deep echo rolled—
To the Spirit of Ocean
  Thy wishes unfold!

[6] The seven spirits are identified below, in line 132. [7] Confessed.
[8] Highest of the Alps. [9] Crown.

FOURTH SPIRIT

Where the slumbering earthquake
Lies pillowed on fire,
And the lakes of bitumen[10]
Rise boilingly higher;
Where the roots of the Andes[11]
Strike deep in the earth,
As their summits to heaven
Shoot soaringly forth;
I have quitted my birthplace
Thy bidding to bide—
Thy spell hath subdued me,
Thy will be my guide!

FIFTH SPIRIT

I am the rider of the wind,
The stirrer of the storm;
The hurricane I left behind
Is yet with lightning warm;
To speed to thee, o'er shore and sea
I swept upon the blast:
The fleet I met sailed well, and yet
'Twill sink ere night be past.

SIXTH SPIRIT

My dwelling is the shadow of the night,
Why doth thy magic torture me with light?

SEVENTH SPIRIT

The star which rules thy destiny
Was ruled, ere earth began, by me:
It was a world as fresh and fair
As e'er revolved round sun in air;
Its course was free and regular,
Space bosomed not a lovelier star.
The hour arrived—and it became
A wandering mass of shapeless flame,
A pathless comet, and a curse,
The menace of the universe;
Still rolling on with innate force,
Without a sphere, without a course,
A bright deformity on high,
The monster of the upper sky!
And thou! beneath its influence born—
Thou worm! whom I obey and scorn—
Forced by a power (which is not thine,
And lent thee but to make thee mine)

[10] Molten volcanic asphalt.
[11] Great mountain chain along the west coast of South America.

For this brief moment to descend,
Where these weak spirits round thee bend
And parley with a thing like thee—
What wouldst thou, child of clay! with me?

THE SEVEN SPIRITS

Earth, ocean, air, night, mountains, winds, thy star,
Are at thy beck and bidding, child of clay!
Before thee at thy quest their spirits are—
What wouldst thou with us, son of mortals—say!

MAN. Forgetfulness—
FIRST SPIRIT. Of what—of whom—and why?
MAN. Of that which is within me; read it there—
Ye know it, and I cannot utter it.
SPIRIT. We can but give thee that which we possess:
Ask of us subjects, sovereignty, the power
O'er earth—the whole, or portion—or a sign
Which shall control the elements, whereof
We are the dominators,—each and all,
These shall be thine.
MAN. Oblivion, self-oblivion!
Can ye not wring from out the hidden realms
Ye offer so profusely what I ask?
SPIRIT. It is not in our essence, in our skill;
But—thou may'st die.
MAN. Will death bestow it on me?
SPIRIT. We are immortal, and do not forget;
We are eternal; and to us the past
Is, as the future, present. Art thou answered?
MAN. Ye mock me—but the power which brought ye here
Hath made you mine. Slaves, scoff not at my will!
The mind, the spirit, the Promethean spark,[12]
The lightning of my being, is as bright,
Pervading, and far darting as your own,
And shall not yield to yours, though cooped in clay![13]
Answer, or I will teach you what I am.
SPIRIT. We answer as we answered; our reply
Is even in thine own words.
MAN. Why say ye so?
SPIRIT. If, as thou say'st, thine essence be as ours,
We have replied in telling thee, the thing
Mortals call death hath naught to do with us.
MAN. I then have called ye from your realms in vain;
Ye cannot, or ye will not, aid me.
SPIRIT. Say;

[12] The divine element in humanity. (In myth, Prometheus stole the fire of the gods and bestowed it on man.)

[13] Mortal flesh; the word *clay* recurs in Byron, often in opposition to spirit. He uses "dust" in the same sense.

What we possess we offer; it is thine:
Bethink ere thou dismiss us; ask again—
Kingdom, and sway,[14] and strength, and length of days—

MAN. Accursed! what have I to do with days?
They are too long already.—Hence—begone!

SPIRIT. Yet pause: being here, our will would do thee service;
Bethink thee, is there then no other gift
Which we can make not worthless in thine eyes?

MAN. No, none: yet stay—one moment, ere we part,
I would behold ye face to face. I hear
Your voices, sweet and melancholy sounds,
As music on the waters; and I see
The steady aspect of a clear large star;
But nothing more. Approach me as ye are,
Or one, or all, in your accustomed forms.

SPIRIT. We have no forms, beyond the elements
Of which we are the mind and principle:
But choose a form—in that we will appear.

MAN. I have no choice; there is no form on earth
Hideous or beautiful to me. Let him,
Who is most powerful of ye, take such aspect
As unto him may seem most fitting—Come!

SEVENTH SPIRIT [*appearing in the shape of a beautiful female figure*]. Behold!

MAN. Oh God! if it be thus, and *thou*
Art not a madness and a mockery,
I yet might be most happy. I will clasp thee,
And we again will be—

[*The figure vanishes.*]

My heart is crushed!

[MANFRED *falls senseless.*]

[*A voice is heard in the Incantation which follows.*]

When the moon is on the wave,
  And the glow-worm in the grass,
And the meteor on the grave,
  And the wisp on the morass;
When the falling stars are shooting,
And the answered owls are hooting,
And the silent leaves are still
In the shadow of the hill,
Shall my soul be upon thine,
With a power and with a sign.

Though thy slumber may be deep,
Yet thy spirit shall not sleep;
There are shades which will not vanish,
There are thoughts thou canst not banish;
By a power to thee unknown,

[14] Power; rulership.

Thou canst never be alone;
Thou art wrapt as with a shroud,
Thou art gathered in a cloud;
And forever shalt thou dwell
In the spirit of this spell.

Though thou seest me not pass by,
Thou shalt feel me with thine eye
As a thing that, though unseen,
Must be near thee, and hath been;
And when in that secret dread
Thou hast turned around thy head,
Thou shalt marvel I am not
As thy shadow on the spot,
And the power which thou dost feel
Shall be what thou must conceal.

And a magic voice and verse
Hath baptized thee with a curse;
And a spirit of the air
Hath begirt[15] thee with a snare;
In the wind there is a voice
Shall forbid thee to rejoice;
And to thee shall night deny
All the quiet of her sky;
And the day shall have a sun,
Which shall make thee wish it done.

From thy false tears I did distil
An essence which hath strength to kill;
From thy own heart I then did wring
The black blood in its blackest spring;
From thy own smile I snatched the snake,
For there it coiled as in a brake;[16]
From thy own lip I drew the charm
Which gave all these their chiefest harm;
In proving[17] every poison known,
I found the strongest was thine own.

By thy cold breast and serpent smile,
By thy unfathomed gulfs of guile,
By that most seeming virtuous eye,
By thy shut soul's hypocrisy;
By the perfection of thine art
Which passed for human thine own heart;
By thy delight in others' pain,
And by thy brotherhood of Cain,[18]

[15] Encircled. [16] Brushwood thicket. [17] Trying out.

[18] The first murderer; an outcast from human society, he was protected by a special mark from human retribution; see Genesis 4:1–15.

I call upon thee! and compel
Thyself to be thy proper hell!

And on thy head I pour the vial
Which doth devote[19] thee to this trial;
Nor to slumber, nor to die,
Shall be in thy destiny,
Though thy death shall still seem near
To thy wish, but as a fear;
Lo! the spell now works around thee,
And the clankless chain hath bound thee;
O'er thy heart and brain together
Hath the word been passed—now wither!

SCENE II

The mountain of the Jungfrau.[20]*—Time, morning.—*
MANFRED *alone upon the cliffs.*

MAN. The spirits I have raised abandon me,
The spells which I have studied baffle me,
The remedy I recked of tortured me;
I lean no more on superhuman aid;
It hath no power upon the past, and for
The future, till the past be gulfed in darkness,
It is not of my search.—My mother earth!
And thou fresh breaking day, and you, ye mountains,
Why are ye beautiful? I cannot love ye.
And thou, the bright eye of the universe,
That openest over all, and unto all
Art a delight—thou shin'st not on my heart.
And you, ye crags, upon whose extreme edge
I stand, and on the torrent's brink beneath
Behold the tall pines dwindled as to shrubs
In dizziness of distance; when a leap,
A stir, a motion, even a breath, would bring
My breast upon its rocky bosom's bed
To rest forever—wherefore do I pause?
I feel the impulse—yet I do not plunge;
I see the peril—yet do not recede;
And my brain reels—and yet my foot is firm:
There is a power upon me which withholds,
And makes it my fatality to live;
If it be life to wear within myself
This barrenness of spirit, and to be
My own soul's sepulchre, for I have ceased
To justify my deeds unto myself—
The last infirmity of evil. Aye,

[19] Set apart; doom by a curse. [20] "The Virgin," a peak in the Alps.

Thou winged and cloud-cleaving minister,
[*An eagle passes.*]
Whose happy flight is highest into heaven,
Well may'st thou swoop so near me—I should be
Thy prey, and gorge thine eaglets; thou art gone
Where the eye cannot follow thee; but thine
Yet pierces downward, onward, or above,
With a pervading vision.—Beautiful!
How beautiful is all this visible world!
How glorious in its action and itself!
But we, who name ourselves its sovereigns, we,
Half dust, half deity, alike unfit
To sink or soar, with our mixed essence make
A conflict of its elements, and breathe
The breath of degradation and of pride,
Contending with low wants and lofty will,
Till our mortality predominates,
And men are—what they name not to themselves,
And trust not to each other. Hark! the note,
[*The shepherd's pipe in the distance is heard.*]
The natural music of the mountain reed—
For here the patriarchal[21] days are not
A pastoral fable—pipes in the liberal air,
Mixed with the sweet bells of the sauntering herd;
My soul would drink those echoes. Oh, that I were
The viewless[22] spirit of a lovely sound,
A living voice, a breathing harmony,
A bodiless enjoyment—born and dying
With the blest tone which made me!
[*Enter from below a* CHAMOIS[23] HUNTER.]

CHAMOIS HUNTER. Even so
This way the chamois leapt: her nimble feet
Have baffled me; my gains today will scarce
Repay my break-neck travail.[24]—What is here?
Who seems not of my trade, and yet hath reached
A height which none even of our mountaineers,
Save our best hunters, may attain: his garb
Is goodly, his mien manly, and his air
Proud as a free-born peasant's, at this distance:
I will approach him nearer.

MAN. [*not perceiving the other*]. To be thus—
Gray-haired with anguish, like these blasted pines,
Wrecks of a single winter, barkless, branchless,
A blighted trunk upon a cursed root,
Which but supplies a feeling to decay—
And to be thus, eternally but thus,

[21] Primitively simple. [22] Invisible. [23] Goatlike mountain antelope. [24] Labor.

Having been otherwise! Now furrowed o'er
With wrinkles, ploughed by moments,—not by years,—
And hours, all tortured into ages—hours
Which I outlive!—Ye toppling crags of ice!
Ye avalanches, whom a breath draws down
In mountainous o'erwhelming, come and crush me!
I hear ye momently[25] above, beneath,
Crash with a frequent conflict; but ye pass,
And only fall on things that still would live;
On the young flourishing forest, or the hut
And hamlet of the harmless villager.

C. HUN. The mists begin to rise from up the valley;
I'll warn him to descend, or he may chance
To lose at once his way and life together.

MAN. The mists boil up around the glaciers; clouds
Rise curling fast beneath me, white and sulphury,
Like foam from the roused ocean of deep hell,
Whose every wave breaks on a living shore,
Heaped with the damned like pebbles.—I am giddy.

C. HUN. I must approach him cautiously; if near,
A sudden step will startle him, and he
Seems tottering already.

MAN. Mountains have fallen,
Leaving a gap in the clouds, and with the shock
Rocking their Alpine brethren; filling up
The ripe green valleys with destruction's splinters;
Damming the rivers with a sudden dash,
Which crushed the waters into mist and made
Their fountains find another channel—thus,
Thus, in its old age, did Mount Rosenberg[26]—
Why stood I not beneath it?

C. HUN. Friend! have a care,
Your next step may be fatal!—for the love
Of him who made you, stand not on that brink!

MAN. [*not hearing him*]. Such would have been for me a fitting tomb;
My bones had then been quiet in their depth;
They had not then been strewn upon the rocks
For the wind's pastime—as thus—thus they shall be—
In this one plunge.—Farewell, ye opening heavens!
Look not upon me thus reproachfully—
You were not meant for me—Earth! take these atoms!

[*As* MANFRED *is in act to spring from the cliff, the* CHAMOIS HUNTER *seizes and retains him with a sudden grasp.*]

C. HUN. Hold, madman!—though aweary of thy life,

[25] From moment to moment.

[26] A 1,000-by-100-foot facade of this mountain collapsed in 1806, falling on four villages and killing about 450 people.

Stain not our pure vales with thy guilty blood:
Away with me—I will not quit my hold.
MAN. I am most sick at heart—nay, grasp me not—
I am all feebleness—the mountains whirl
Spinning around me—I grow blind—What art thou?
C. HUN. I'll answer that anon. Away with me!
The clouds grow thicker—there—now lean on me—
Place your foot here—here, take this staff, and cling
A moment to that shrub—now give me your hand,
And hold fast by my girdle—softly—well—
The chalet[27] will be gained within an hour:
Come on, we'll quickly find a surer footing,
And something like a pathway, which the torrent
Hath washed since winter.—Come, 'tis bravely done—
You should have been a hunter.—Follow me.
[*As they descend the rocks with difficulty, the scene closes.*]

ACT II

SCENE I

A cottage among the Bernese Alps.
MANFRED *and the* CHAMOIS HUNTER.

C. HUN. No, no—yet pause—thou must not yet go forth:
Thy mind and body are alike unfit
To trust each other, for some hours, at least;
When thou art better, I will be thy guide—
But whither?
MAN. It imports not: I do know
My route full well, and need no further guidance.
C. HUN. Thy garb and gait bespeak thee of high lineage—
One of the many chiefs, whose castled crags
Look o'er the lower valleys—which of these
May call thee lord? I only know their portals;
My way of life leads me but rarely down
To bask by the huge hearths of those old halls,
Carousing with the vassals;[1] but the paths,
Which step from out our mountains to their doors,
I know from childhood—which of these is thine?
MAN. No matter.
C. HUN. Well, sir, pardon me the question,
And be of better cheer. Come, taste my wine;
'Tis of an ancient vintage; many a day
'T has thawed my veins among our glaciers, now
Let it do thus for thine. Come, pledge[2] me fairly.
MAN. Away, away! there's blood upon the brim!

[27] An Alpine hut. [1] The chiefs' followers. [2] Drink a toast.

Will it then never—never sink in the earth?
C. HUN. What dost thou mean? thy senses wander from thee.
MAN. I say 'tis blood—my blood! the pure warm stream
Which ran in the veins of my fathers, and in ours
When we were in our youth, and had one heart,
And loved each other as we should not love,
And this was shed: but still it rises up,
Colouring the clouds, that shut me out from heaven,
Where thou art not—and I shall never be.
C. HUN. Man of strange words, and some half-maddening sin,
Which makes thee people vacancy,[3] whate'er
Thy dread and sufferance be, there's comfort yet—
The aid of holy men, and heavenly patience—
MAN. Patience and patience! Hence—that word was made
For brutes of burthen,[4] not for birds of prey;
Preach it to mortals of a dust like thine,—
I am not of thine order.
C. HUN. Thanks to heaven!
I would not be of thine for the free fame
Of William Tell;[5] but whatsoe'er thine ill,
It must be borne, and these wild starts are useless.
MAN. Do I not bear it?—Look on me—I live.
C. HUN. This is convulsion, and no healthful life.
MAN. I tell thee, man! I have lived many years,
Many long years, but they are nothing now
To those which I must number: ages—ages—
Space and eternity—and consciousness,
With the fierce thirst of death—and still unslaked!
C. HUN. Why, on thy brow the seal of middle age
Hath scarce been set; I am thine elder far.
MAN. Think'st thou existence doth depend on time?
It doth; but actions are our epochs: mine
Have made my days and nights imperishable,
Endless, and all alike, as sands on the shore,
Innumerable atoms; and one desert,
Barren and cold, on which the wild waves break,
But nothing rests, save carcasses and wrecks,
Rocks, and the salt-surf weeds of bitterness.
C. HUN. Alas! he's mad—but yet I must not leave him.
MAN. I would I were—for then the things I see
Would be but a distempered[6] dream.
C. HUN. What is it
That thou dost see, or think thou look'st upon?
MAN. Myself, and thee—a peasant of the Alps—
Thy humble virtues, hospitable home,
And spirit patient, pious, proud, and free;
Thy self-respect, grafted on innocent thoughts;

[3] Makes you see people in the empty air. [4] Burden.
[5] Legendary champion of Swiss freedom. [6] Caused by illness.

Thy days of health, and nights of sleep; thy toils,
By danger dignified, yet guiltless; hopes
Of cheerful old age and a quiet grave,
With cross and garland over its green turf,
And thy grandchildren's love for epitaph;
This do I see—and then I look within—
It matters not—my soul was scorched already!

C. HUN. And wouldst thou then exchange thy lot for mine?

MAN. No, friend! I would not wrong thee, nor exchange
My lot with living being: I can bear—
However wretchedly, 'tis still to bear—
In life what others could not brook[7] to dream,
But perish in their slumber.

C. HUN. And with this—
This cautious feeling for another's pain,
Canst thou be black with evil?—say not so.
Can one of gentle thoughts have wreaked revenge
Upon his enemies?

MAN. Oh! no, no, no!
My injuries came down on those who loved me—
On those whom I best loved: I never quelled
An enemy, save in my just defence—
But my embrace was fatal.

C. HUN. Heaven give thee rest!
And penitence restore thee to thyself;
My prayers shall be for thee.

MAN. I need them not—
But can endure thy pity. I depart—
'Tis time—farewell!—Here's gold, and thanks for thee;
No words—it is thy due. Follow me not—
I know my path—the mountain peril's past:
And once again I charge thee, follow not!
[*Exit* MANFRED.]

SCENE II

A lower valley in the Alps.—A cataract.
Enter MANFRED.

MAN. It is not noon—the sunbow's[8] rays still arch
The torrent with the many hues of heaven,
And roll the sheeted silver's waving column
O'er the crag's headlong perpendicular,
And fling its lines of foaming light along
And to and fro, like the pale courser's tail,
The giant steed, to be bestrode by death,
As told in the Apocalypse.[9] No eyes

[7] Bear. [8] Rainbow-effect seen in the waterfall; visible in the morning.
[9] The Book of Revelation 6:8, in which Death rides a pale horse.

But mine now drink this sight of loveliness;
I should be sole in this sweet solitude,
And with the Spirit of the place divide
The homage of these waters.—I will call her.

[MANFRED *takes some of the water into the palm of his hand and flings it into the air, muttering the adjuration.*[10] *After a pause, the* WITCH OF THE ALPS *rises beneath the arch of the sunbow of the torrent.*]

Beautiful spirit! with thy hair of light,
And dazzling eyes of glory, in whose form
The charms of earth's least mortal daughters grow
To an unearthly stature, in an essence
Of purer elements; while the hues of youth,—
Carnationed like a sleeping infant's cheek,
Rocked by the beating of her mother's heart,
Or the rose tints, which summer's twilight leaves
Upon the lofty glacier's virgin snow,
The blush of earth embracing with her heaven,—
Tinge thy celestial aspect, and make tame
The beauties of the sunbow which bends o'er thee.
Beautiful Spirit! in thy calm clear brow,
Wherein is glassed serenity of soul,
Which of itself shows immortality,
I read that thou wilt pardon to a son
Of Earth, whom the abstruser powers permit
At times to commune with them—if that he
Avail him of his spells—to call thee thus,
And gaze on thee a moment.

WITCH OF THE ALPS. Son of Earth!
I know thee, and the powers which give thee power;
I know thee for a man of many thoughts,
And deeds of good and ill, extreme in both,
Fatal and fated in thy sufferings.
I have expected this—what wouldst thou with me?

MAN. To look upon thy beauty—nothing further.
The face of the earth hath maddened me, and I
Take refuge in her mysteries, and pierce
To the abodes of those who govern her—
But they can nothing aid me. I have sought
From them what they could not bestow, and now
I search no further.

WITCH. What could be the quest
Which is not in the power of the most powerful,
The rulers of the invisible?

MAN. A boon;[11]
But why should I repeat it? 'twere in vain.

[10] Magical appeal. [11] Favor.

WITCH. I know not that; let thy lips utter it.
MAN. Well, though it torture me, 'tis but the same;
My pang shall find a voice. From my youth upwards
My spirit walked not with the souls of men,
Nor looked upon the earth with human eyes;
The thirst of their ambition was not mine,
The aim of their existence was not mine;
My joys, my griefs, my passions, and my powers,
Made me a stranger; though I wore the form,
I had no sympathy with breathing flesh,
Nor midst the creatures of clay that girded me
Was there but one who—but of her anon.[12]
I said with men, and with the thoughts of men,
I held but slight communion; but instead,
My joy was in the wilderness,—to breathe
The difficult air of the iced mountain's top,
Where the birds dare not build, nor insect's wing
Flit o'er the herbless granite; or to plunge
Into the torrent, and to roll along
On the swift whirl of the new breaking wave
Of river-stream, or ocean, in their flow.
In these my early strength exulted; or
To follow through the night the moving moon,
The stars and their development; or catch
The dazzling lightnings till my eyes grew dim;
Or to look, list'ning, on the scattered leaves,
While autumn winds were at their evening song.
These were my pastimes, and to be alone;
For if the beings, of whom I was one,—
Hating to be so,—crossed me in my path,
I felt myself degraded back to them,
And was all clay again. And then I dived,
In my lone wanderings, to the caves of death,
Searching its cause in its effect; and drew
From withered bones, and skulls, and heaped up dust,
Conclusions most forbidden. Then I passed
The nights of years in sciences untaught,
Save in the old time; and with time and toil,
And terrible ordeal, and such penance
As in itself hath power upon the air,
And spirits that do compass air and earth,
Space, and the peopled infinite, I made
Mine eyes familiar with Eternity,
Such as, before me, did the Magi,[13] and
He who from out their fountain dwellings raised
Eros and Anteros, at Gadara,[14]

[12] A little later. [13] Persian priests of the Zoroastrian religion.

[14] At the baths of Gadara, in Syria, the philosopher Iamblichus (fourth century A.D.) called up the spirits of two springs, Eros (love) and Anteros (avenger of unhappy love).

As I do thee;—and with my knowledge grew
The thirst of knowledge, and the power and joy
Of this most bright intelligence, until—
WITCH. Proceed.
MAN. Oh! I but thus prolonged my words,
Boasting these idle attributes, because
As I approach the core of my heart's grief—
But to my task. I have not named to thee
Father, or mother, mistress, friend, or being,
With whom I wore the chain of human ties;
If I had such, they seemed not such to me;
Yet there was one—
WITCH. Spare not thyself—proceed.
MAN. She was like me in lineaments; her eyes,
Her hair, her features, all, to the very tone
Even of her voice, they said were like to mine;
But softened all, and tempered into beauty:
She had the same lone thoughts and wanderings,
The quest of hidden knowledge, and a mind
To comprehend the universe: nor these
Alone, but with them gentler powers than mine,
Pity, and smiles, and tears—which I had not;
And tenderness—but that I had for her;
Humility—and that I never had.
Her faults were mine—her virtues were her own—
I loved her, and destroyed her!
WITCH. With thy hand?
MAN. Not with my hand, but heart—which broke her heart;
It gazed on mine, and withered. I have shed
Blood, but not hers—and yet her blood was shed;
I saw—and could not stanch[15] it.
WITCH. And for this—
A being of the race thou dost despise,
The order, which thine own would rise above,
Mingling with us and ours,—thou dost forego
The gifts of our great knowledge, and shrink'st back
In recreant[16] mortality—Away!
MAN. Daughter of air! I tell thee, since that hour—
But words are breath—look on me in my sleep,
Or watch my watchings—Come and sit by me!
My solitude is solitude no more,
But peopled with the furies;[17]—I have gnashed
My teeth in darkness till returning morn,
Then cursed myself till sunset;—I have prayed
For madness as a blessing—'tis denied me.
I have affronted[18] death—but in the war

[15] Stop the flow of. [16] Cowardly; unfaithful.
[17] In Greek myth, the primitive female beings who avenged crimes, especially against blood kindred. See Aeschylus, *The Eumenides.*
[18] Confronted defiantly.

Of elements the waters shrunk from me,
And fatal things passed harmless; the cold hand
Of an all-pitiless demon held me back,
Back by a single hair, which would not break.
In fantasy, imagination, all
The affluence of my soul—which one day was
A Croesus[19] in creation—I plunged deep,
But, like an ebbing wave, it dashed me back
Into the gulf of my unfathomed thought.
I plunged amidst mankind—Forgetfulness
I sought in all, save where 'tis to be found,
And that I have to learn; my sciences,
My long-pursued and superhuman art,
Is mortal here: I dwell in my despair—
And live—and live forever.

WITCH. It may be
That I can aid thee.

MAN. To do this thy power
Must wake the dead, or lay me low with them.
Do so—in any shape—in any hour—
With any torture—so it be the last.

WITCH. That is not in my province; but if thou
Wilt swear obedience to my will, and do
My bidding, it may help thee to thy wishes.

MAN. I will not swear—Obey! and whom? the spirits
Whose presence I command, and be the slave
Of those who served me—Never!

WITCH. Is this all?
Hast thou no gentler answer?—Yet bethink thee,
And pause ere thou rejectest.

MAN. I have said it.

WITCH. Enough! I may retire then—say!

MAN. Retire!

[*The* WITCH *disappears.*]

MAN. [*alone*]. We are the fools of time and terror. Days
Steal on us, and steal from us; yet we live,
Loathing our life, and dreading still to die.
In all the days of this detested yoke—
This vital weight upon the struggling heart,
Which sinks with sorrow, or beats quick with pain,
Or joy that ends in agony or faintness—
In all the days of past and future, for
In life there is no present, we can number
How few—how less than few—wherein the soul
Forbears to pant for death, and yet draws back
As from a stream in winter, though the chill
Be but a moment's. I have one resource
Still in my science—I can call the dead,

[19] Sixth-century B.C. king of Lydia in Asia Minor, enormously wealthy.

And ask them what it is we dread to be:
The sternest answer can but be the grave,
And that is nothing. If they answer not—
The buried prophet answered to the Hag
Of Endor;[20] and the Spartan Monarch drew
From the Byzantine maid's unsleeping spirit
An answer and his destiny—he slew
That which he loved, unknowing what he slew,
And died unpardoned—though he called in aid
The Phyxian Jove, and in Phigalia roused
The Arcadian Evocators to compel
The indignant shadow to depose her wrath,
Or fix her term of vengeance—she replied
In words of dubious import, but fulfilled.[21]
If I had never lived, that which I love
Had still been living; had I never loved,
That which I love would still be beautiful,
Happy and giving happiness. What is she?
What is she now?—a sufferer for my sins—
A thing I dare not think upon—or nothing.
Within few hours I shall not call in vain—
Yet in this hour I dread the thing I dare:
Until this hour I never shrunk to gaze
On spirit, good or evil—now I tremble,
And feel a strange cold thaw upon my heart.
But I can act even what I most abhor,
And champion human fears.—The night approaches.
[*Exit.*]

SCENE III

The summit of the Jungfrau Mountain.
Enter FIRST DESTINY.

FIRST DESTINY. The moon is rising broad, and round, and bright;
And here on snows, where never human foot
Of common mortal trod,[22] we nightly tread,
And leave no traces: o'er the savage sea,
The glassy ocean of the mountain ice,
We skim its rugged breakers, which put on
The aspect of a tumbling tempest's foam,

[20] The ghost of Samuel (the "buried prophet"), called up by the witch of Endor at the request of the king Saul, prophesied Saul's death. See I Samuel 28.

[21] *Lines 183–192.* Pausanias, an arrogant king of Sparta in the fifth century B.C., forced the parents of Cleonice (a "Byzantine maid") to yield her up to be his mistress. Approaching his bed in the dark, out of modesty, she was mistaken for an enemy by the king, who killed her. Haunted thereafter by her and his guilt, he had the mediums of Arcadia summon her spirit so that she might pardon him, but her reply was an equivocal prediction of his death.

[22] Actually, the Jungfrau had been climbed for the first time in 1811, six years before *Manfred* was published.

Frozen in a moment—a dead whirlpool's image:
And this most steep fantastic pinnacle,
The fretwork[23] of some earthquake—where the clouds
Pause to repose themselves in passing by—
Is sacred to our revels, or our vigils;
Here do I wait my sisters, on our way
To the Hall of Arimanes,[24] for tonight
Is our great festival—'tis strange they come not.

A VOICE [*without, singing*]

The captive usurper,[25]
  Hurled down from the throne,
Lay buried in torpor,
  Forgotten and lone;
I broke through his slumbers,
  I shivered his chain,
I leagued him with numbers—
  He's tyrant again!
With the blood of a million he'll answer my care,
With a nation's destruction—his flight and despair.

SECOND VOICE [*without*]

The ship sailed on, the ship sailed fast,
But I left not a sail, and I left not a mast;
There is not a plank of the hull or the deck,
And there is not a wretch to lament o'er his wreck;
Save one, whom I held, as he swam, by the hair,
And he was a subject well worthy my care;
A traitor on land, and a pirate at sea—
But I saved him to wreak further havoc for me!

FIRST DESTINY [*answering*]

The city lies sleeping;
  The morn, to deplore[26] it,
May dawn on it weeping:
  Sullenly, slowly,
The black plague flew o'er it—
  Thousands lie lowly;
Tens of thousands shall perish;
  The living shall fly from
The sick they should cherish;
  But nothing can vanquish
The touch that they die from.

[23] Ornamentation in geometrical shapes.

[24] Ahriman—in the Zoroastrian religion of the ancient Persians, the spirit of evil who wars against the spirit of good (Ormazd).

[25] Napoleon Bonaparte, at the time of the poem imprisoned on the island of St. Helena after his defeat in 1815 at Waterloo. The prediction here is that he will return to power, as he had done from the island of Elba in 1815. (The voice is heard "without," that is, offstage.)

[26] Mourn for.

Sorrow and anguish,
And evil and dread,
Envelop a nation;
The blest are the dead,
Who see not the sight
Of their own desolation;
This work of a night—
This wreck of a realm—this deed of my doing—
For ages I've done, and shall still be renewing!

[*Enter the* Second *and* Third Destinies.]

The Three

Our hands contain the hearts of men,
Our footsteps are their graves;
We only give to take again
The spirits of our slaves!

First Destiny. Welcome!—Where's Nemesis?[27]
Second Destiny. At some great work;
But what I know not, for my hands were full.
Third Destiny. Behold she cometh.

[*Enter* Nemesis.]

First Des. Say, where hast thou been?
My sisters and thyself are slow tonight.
Nemesis. I was detained repairing shattered thrones,[28]
Marrying fools, restoring dynasties,
Avenging men upon their enemies,
And making them repent their own revenge;
Goading the wise to madness; from the dull
Shaping out oracles[29] to rule the world
Afresh, for they were waxing out of date,
And mortals dared to ponder for themselves,
To weigh kings in the balance, and to speak
Of freedom, the forbidden fruit.—Away!
We have outstayed the hour—mount we our clouds.

[*Exeunt.*]

SCENE IV

The Hall of Arimanes. Arimanes *on his throne, a globe of fire, surrounded by the* Spirits.

Hymn of the Spirits

Hail to our Master!—Prince of earth and air!

[27] The Greek goddess of vengeance.
[28] Restoring the old monarchies of Europe, eclipsed during the French Revolution and Napoleonic period (1789–1815).
[29] Infallible authorities or their statements.

Who walks the clouds and waters—in his hand
The sceptre of the elements, which tear
Themselves to chaos at his high command!
He breatheth—and a tempest shakes the sea;
He speaketh—and the clouds reply in thunder;
He gazeth—from his glance the sunbeams flee;
He moveth—earthquakes rend the world asunder.
Beneath his footsteps the volcanoes rise;
His shadow is the pestilence; his path
The comets herald through the crackling skies;
And planets turn to ashes at his wrath.
To him war offers daily sacrifice;
To him death pays his tribute; life is his,
With all its infinite of agonies—
And his the spirit of whatever is!

[*Enter the* DESTINIES *and* NEMESIS.]

FIRST DES. Glory to Arimanes! on the earth
His power increaseth—both my sisters did
His bidding, nor did I neglect my duty!
SECOND DES. Glory to Arimanes! we who bow
The necks of men, bow down before his throne!
THIRD DES. Glory to Arimanes! we await His nod!
NEM. Sovereign of sovereigns! we are thine,
And all that liveth, more or less, is ours,
And most things wholly so; still to increase
Our power, increasing thine, demands our care,
And we are vigilant. Thy late commands
Have been fulfilled to the utmost.

[*Enter* MANFRED.]

A SPIRIT. What is here?
A mortal!—Thou most rash and fatal wretch,
Bow down and worship!
SECOND SPIRIT. I do know the man—
A magian[30] of great power, and fearful skill!
THIRD SPIRIT. Bow down and worship, slave!—What, know'st thou not
Thine and our sovereign?—Tremble, and obey!
ALL THE SPIRITS. Prostrate thyself, and thy condemned clay,
Child of the earth! or dread the worst.
MAN. I know it;
And yet ye see I kneel not.
FOURTH SPIRIT. 'Twill be taught thee.
MAN. 'Tis taught already;—many a night on the earth,
On the bare ground, have I bowed down my face,
And strewed my head with ashes; I have known
The fullness of humiliation, for
I sunk before my vain despair, and knelt
To my own desolation.

[30] Magician.

FIFTH SPIRIT. Dost thou dare
Refuse to Arimanes on his throne
What the whole earth accords, beholding not
The terror of his glory?—Crouch, I say.
MAN. Bid *him* bow down to that which is above him,
The overruling Infinite—the Maker
Who made him not for worship—let him kneel,
And we will kneel together.
THE SPIRITS. Crush the worm!
Tear him in pieces!—
FIRST DES. Hence! avaunt![31]—he's mine.
Prince of the powers invisible! This man
Is of no common order, as his port[32]
And presence here denote; his sufferings
Have been of an immortal nature, like
Our own; his knowledge, and his powers and will,
As far as is compatible with clay,
Which clogs the ethereal essence, have been such
As clay hath seldom borne; his aspirations
Have been beyond the dwellers of the earth,
And they have only taught him what we know—
That knowledge is not happiness, and science
But an exchange of ignorance for that
Which is another kind of ignorance.
This is not all—the passions, attributes
Of earth and heaven, from which no power, nor being,
Nor breath from the worm upwards is exempt,
Have pierced his heart, and in their consequence
Made him a thing which I, who pity not,
Yet pardon those who pity. He is mine,
And thine, it may be; be it so, or not,
No other spirit in this region hath
A soul like his—or power upon his soul.
NEM. What doth he here then?
FIRST DES. Let him answer that.
MAN. Ye know what I have known; and without power
I could not be amongst ye: but there are
Powers deeper still beyond—I come in quest
Of such, to answer unto what I seek.
NEM. What wouldst thou?
MAN. *Thou* canst not reply to me.
Call up the dead—my question is for them.
NEM. Great Arimanes, doth thy will avouch[33]
The wishes of this mortal?
ARIMANES. Yea.
NEM. Whom wouldst thou
Uncharnel?[34]

[31] Be gone. [32] Posture; bearing. [33] Sanction.
[34] Call from the charnel house (tomb).

MAN. One without a tomb—call up
Astarte.[35]

NEMESIS

Shadow! or spirit!
Whatever thou art,
Which still doth inherit[36]
The whole or a part
Of the form of thy birth,
Of the mould of thy clay,
Which returned to the earth,—
Reappear to the day!
Bear what thou borest,
The heart and the form,
And the aspect thou worest
Redeem from the worm.
Appear!—Appear!—Appear!
Who sent thee there requires thee here!

[*The* PHANTOM OF ASTARTE *rises and stands in the midst.*]

MAN. Can this be death? there's bloom upon her cheek;
But now I see it is no living hue,
But a strange hectic[37]—like the unnatural red
Which autumn plants upon the perished leaf.
It is the same! Oh, God! that I should dread
To look upon the same—Astarte!—No,
I cannot speak to her—but bid her speak—
Forgive me or condemn me.

NEMESIS

By the power which hath broken
The grave which enthralled thee,
Speak to him who hath spoken,
Or those who have called thee!

MAN. She is silent,
And in that silence I am more than answered.
NEM. My power extends no further. Prince of Air!
It rests with thee alone—command her voice.
ARI. Spirit—obey this sceptre!
NEM. Silent still!
She is not of our order, but belongs
To the other powers. Mortal! thy quest is vain,
And we are baffled also.
MAN. Hear me, hear me—
Astarte! my beloved! speak to me:
I have so much endured—so much endure—

[35] The name is that of the Phoenician goddess of fertility and love. [36] Possess.
[37] Fever symptom.

Look on me! the grave hath not changed thee more
Than I am changed for thee. Thou lovedst me
Too much, as I loved thee; we were not made
To torture thus each other, though it were
The deadliest sin to love as we have loved.
Say that thou loath'st me not—that I do bear
This punishment for both—that thou wilt be
One of the blessed—and that I shall die;
For hitherto all hateful things conspire
To bind me in existence—in a life
Which makes me shrink from immortality—
A future like the past. I cannot rest.
I know not what I ask, nor what I seek:
I feel but what thou art, and what I am;
And I would hear yet once before I perish
The voice which was my music—Speak to me!
For I have called on thee in the still night,
Startled the slumbering birds from the hushed boughs,
And woke the mountain wolves, and made the caves
Acquainted with thy vainly echoed name,
Which answered me—many things answered me—
Spirits and men—but thou wert silent all.
Yet speak to me! I have outwatched the stars,
And gazed o'er heaven in vain in search of thee.
Speak to me! I have wandered o'er the earth,
And never found thy likeness—Speak to me!
Look on the fiends around—they feel for me:
I fear them not, and feel for thee alone—
Speak to me! though it be in wrath;—but say—
I reck not what—but let me hear thee once—
This once—once more!

PHANTOM OF ASTARTE. Manfred!

MAN. Say on, say on—
I live but in the sound—it is thy voice!

PHAN. Manfred! Tomorrow ends thine earthly ills.
Farewell!

MAN. Yet one word more—am I forgiven?

PHAN. Farewell!

MAN. Say, shall we meet again?

PHAN. Farewell!

MAN. One word for mercy! Say thou lovest me.

PHAN. Manfred!

[*The* SPIRIT OF ASTARTE *disappears.*]

NEM. She's gone, and will not be recalled;
Her words will be fulfilled. Return to the earth.

A SPIRIT. He is convulsed.—This is to be a mortal
And seek the things beyond mortality.

ANOTHER SPIRIT. Yet, see, he mastereth himself, and makes
His torture tributary to his will.

Had he been one of us, he would have made
An awful[38] spirit.

NEM. Hast thou further question
Of our great sovereign, or his worshippers?

MAN. None.

NEM. Then for a time farewell.

MAN. We meet then! Where? On the earth?—
Even as thou wilt: and for the grace accorded
I now depart a debtor. Fare ye well!

[*Exit* MANFRED.]

[*Scene closes.*]

ACT III

SCENE I

A hall in the castle of MANFRED.

MANFRED *and* HERMAN.

MAN. What is the hour?

HERMAN. It wants but one till sunset,
And promises a lovely twilight.

MAN. Say,
Are all things so disposed of in the tower
As I directed?

HER. All, my lord, are ready:
Here is the key and casket.[1]

MAN. It is well:
Thou may'st retire.

[*Exit* HERMAN.]

MAN. [*alone*]. There is a calm upon me—
Inexplicable stillness! which till now,
Did not belong to what I knew of life.
If that I did not know philosophy
To be of all our vanities the motliest,[2]
The merest word that ever fooled the ear
From out the schoolman's jargon, I should deem
The golden secret, the sought "Kalon,"[3] found,
And seated in my soul. It will not last,
But it is well to have known it, though but once:
It hath enlarged my thoughts with a new sense,
And I within my tablets would note down
That there is such a feeling. Who is there?

[*Re-enter* HERMAN.]

HER. My lord, the abbot of St. Maurice craves

[38] Awesome. [1] A small box for precious objects.
[2] Most foolish (from *motley,* the many-colored dress of court jesters).
[3] Greek for highest good—that is, beauty.

To greet your presence.

[*Enter the* ABBOT OF ST. MAURICE.]

ABBOT. Peace be with Count Manfred!
MAN. Thanks, holy father! welcome to these walls;
Thy presence honours them, and blesseth those
Who dwell within them.
ABBOT. Would it were so, Count!—
But I would fain[4] confer with thee alone.
MAN. Herman, retire—What would my reverend guest?
ABBOT. Thus, without prelude:—Age and zeal, my office,
And good intent, must plead my privilege;
Our near, though not acquainted neighbourhood,[5]
May also be my herald. Rumours strange,
And of unholy nature, are abroad,
And busy with thy name; a noble name
For centuries: may he who bears it now
Transmit it unimpaired!
MAN. Proceed,—I listen.
ABBOT. 'Tis said thou holdest converse with the things
Which are forbidden to the search of man;
That with the dwellers of the dark abodes,
The many evil and unheavenly spirits
Which walk the valley of the shade of death,
Thou communest. I know that with mankind,
Thy fellows in creation, thou dost rarely
Exchange thy thoughts, and that thy solitude
Is as an anchorite's,[6] were it but holy.
MAN. And what are they who do avouch these things?
ABBOT. My pious brethren—the scared peasantry—
Even thy own vassals—who do look on thee
With most unquiet eyes. Thy life's in peril.
MAN. Take it.
ABBOT. I come to save, and not destroy:
I would not pry into thy secret soul;
But if these things be sooth,[7] there still is time
For penitence and pity: reconcile thee
With the true church, and through the church to heaven.
MAN. I hear thee. This is my reply: whate'er
I may have been, or am, doth rest between
Heaven and myself. I shall not choose a mortal
To be my mediator. Have I sinned
Against your ordinances? prove and punish!
ABBOT. My son! I did not speak of punishment,
But penitence and pardon;—with thyself
The choice of such remains—and for the last,
Our institutions and our strong belief
Have given me power to smooth the path from sin
To higher hope and better thoughts; the first

[4] Preferably. [5] Situation as neighbors. [6] Religious hermit. [7] Truth.

I leave to heaven,—"Vengeance is mine alone!"[8]
So saith the Lord, and with all humbleness
His servant echoes back the awful word.
MAN. Old man! there is no power in holy men,
Nor charm in prayer, nor purifying form
Of penitence, nor outward look, nor fast,
Nor agony—nor, greater than all these,
The innate tortures of that deep despair,
Which is remorse without the fear of hell,
But all in all sufficient to itself
Would make a hell of heaven[9]—can exorcise
From out the unbounded spirit the quick sense
Of its own sins, wrongs, sufferance, and revenge
Upon itself; there is no future pang
Can deal that justice on the self-condemned
He deals on his own soul.
ABBOT. All this is well;
For this will pass away, and be succeeded
By an auspicious hope, which shall look up
With calm assurance to that blessed place,
Which all who seek may win, whatever be
Their earthly errors, so they be atoned:
And the commencement of atonement is
The sense of its necessity. Say on—
And all our church can teach thee shall be taught;
And all we can absolve thee shall be pardoned.
MAN. When Rome's sixth emperor[10] was near his last,
The victim of a self-inflicted wound,
To shun the torments of a public death
From senates once his slaves, a certain soldier,
With show of loyal pity, would have stanched
The gushing throat with his officious robe;
The dying Roman thrust him back, and said—
Some empire still in his expiring glance—
"It is too late—is this fidelity?"
ABBOT. And what of this?
MAN. I answer with the Roman—
"It is too late!"
ABBOT. It never can be so,
To reconcile thyself with thy own soul,
And thy own soul with heaven. Hast thou no hope?
'Tis strange—even those who do despair above,
Yet shape themselves some fantasy on earth,
To which frail twig they cling, like drowning men.
MAN. Aye—father! I have had those earthly visions,

[8] "Vengeance is mine; I will repay, saith the Lord."—Romans 12:19.
[9] An echo of Satan's words in Milton's *Paradise Lost*, I. 254–255: "The mind is its own place, and in itself / Can make a heaven of hell, a hell of heaven."
[10] Nero (A.D. 37–68).

And noble aspirations in my youth,
To make my own the mind of other men,
The enlightener of nations; and to rise
I knew not whither—it might be to fall;
But fall, even as the mountain-cataract,
Which, having leapt from its more dazzling height,
Even in the foaming strength of its abyss
(Which casts up misty columns that become
Clouds raining from the re-ascended skies),
Lies low but mighty still.—But this is past,
My thoughts mistook themselves.
ABBOT. And wherefore so?
MAN. I could not tame my nature down; for he
Must serve who fain would sway; and soothe, and sue,
And watch all time, and pry into all place,
And be a living lie, who would become
A mighty thing amongst the mean, and such
The mass are; I disdained to mingle with
A herd, though to be leader—and of wolves.
The lion is alone, and so am I.
ABBOT. And why not live and act with other men?
MAN. Because my nature was averse from life;
And yet not cruel; for I would not make,
But find a desolation. Like the wind,
The red-hot breath of the most lone simoom,[11]
Which dwells but in the desert, and sweeps o'er
The barren sands which bear no shrubs to blast,
And revels o'er their wild and arid waves,
And seeketh not, so that it is not sought,
But being met is deadly,—such hath been
The course of my existence; but there came
Things in my path which are no more.
ABBOT. Alas!
I 'gin to fear that thou art past all aid
From me and from my calling; yet so young,
I still would—
MAN. Look on me! there is an order
Of mortals on the earth, who do become
Old in their youth, and die ere middle age,
Without the violence of warlike death;
Some perishing of pleasure, some of study,
Some worn with toil, some of mere weariness,
Some of disease, and some insanity,
And some of withered or of broken hearts;
For this last is a malady which slays
More than are numbered in the lists of fate,
Taking all shapes, and bearing many names.
Look upon me! for even of all these things

[11] Hot wind of the African and Arabian deserts.

Have I partaken; and of all these things,
One were enough; then wonder not that I
Am what I am, but that I ever was,
Or having been, that I am still on earth.

ABBOT. Yet, hear me still—

MAN. Old man! I do respect
Thine order, and revere thine years; I deem
Thy purpose pious, but it is in vain:
Think me not churlish; I would spare thyself,
Far more than me, in shunning at this time
All further colloquy; and so—farewell.

[*Exit* MANFRED.]

ABBOT. This should have been a noble creature: he
Hath all the energy which would have made
A goodly frame of glorious elements,
Had they been wisely mingled; as it is,
It is an awful chaos—light and darkness,
And mind and dust, and passions and pure thoughts
Mixed, and contending without end or order,—
All dormant or destructive; he will perish,
And yet he must not; I will try once more.
For such are worth redemption; and my duty
Is to dare all things for a righteous end.
I'll follow him—but cautiously, though surely.

[*Exit* ABBOT.]

SCENE II

Another chamber.

MANFRED *and* HERMAN.

HER. My lord, you bade me wait on you at sunset:
He sinks behind the mountain.

MAN. Doth he so?
I will look on him.

[MANFRED *advances to the window of the hall.*]

Glorious orb! the idol
Of early nature, and the vigorous race
Of undiseased mankind, the giant sons
Of the embrace of angels, with a sex
More beautiful than they, which did draw down
The erring spirits who can ne'er return.[12]—
Most glorious orb! that wert a worship, ere
The mystery of thy making was revealed!
Thou earliest minister of the Almighty,
Which gladdened, on their mountain tops, the hearts

[12] Genesis 6:4 tells of a time when there were "giants in the earth," when beautiful "daughters of men" bore to "sons of God" a breed of "mighty men."

Of the Chaldean[13] shepherds, till they poured
Themselves in orisons![14] Thou material God!
And representative of the unknown—
Who chose thee for his shadow! Thou chief star!
Centre of many stars! which mak'st our earth
Endurable, and temperest the hues
And hearts of all who walk within thy rays!
Sire of the seasons! Monarch of the climes,
And those who dwell in them! for near or far,
Our inborn spirits have a tint of thee
Even as our outward aspects;—thou dost rise,
And shine, and set in glory. Fare thee well!
I ne'er shall see thee more. As my first glance
Of love and wonder was for thee, then take
My latest look; thou wilt not beam on one
To whom the gifts of life and warmth have been
Of a more fatal nature. He is gone:
I follow.

[*Exit* MANFRED.]

SCENE III

The mountains—The castle of MANFRED *at some distance—A terrace before a tower.—Time, twilight.*
HERMAN, MANUEL, *and other dependants of* MANFRED.

HER. 'Tis strange enough; night after night, for years,
He hath pursued long vigils in this tower,
Without a witness. I have been within it,—
So have we all been ofttimes; but from it,
Or its contents, it were impossible
To draw conclusions absolute, of aught
His studies tend to. To be sure, there is
One chamber where none enter: I would give
The fee[15] of what I have to come these three years,
To pore upon its mysteries.
MANUEL. 'Twere dangerous:
Content thyself with what thou know'st already.
HER. Ah! Manuel! thou art elderly and wise,
And couldst say much; thou hast dwelt within the castle—
How many years is 't?
MANUEL. Ere Count Manfred's birth,
I served his father, whom he nought resembles.
HER. There be more sons in like predicament.
But wherein do they differ?
MANUEL. I speak not
Of features or of form, but mind and habits;

[13] Babylonian (a people much interested in astronomy). [14] Prayers. [15] Ownership.

Count Sigismund was proud, but gay and free,—
A warrior and a reveller; he dwelt not
With books and solitude, nor made the night
A gloomy vigil, but a festal time,
Merrier than day; he did not walk the rocks
And forests like a wolf, nor turn aside
From men and their delights.

HER. Beshrew[16] the hour,
But those were jocund times! I would that such
Would visit the old walls again; they look
As if they had forgotten them.

MANUEL. These walls
Must change their chieftain first. Oh! I have seen
Some strange things in them, Herman.

HER. Come, be friendly,
Relate me some to while away our watch:
I've heard thee darkly speak of an event
Which happened hereabouts, by this same tower.

MANUEL. That was a night indeed! I do remember
'Twas twilight, as it may be now, and such
Another evening;—yon red cloud, which rests
On Eigher's[17] pinnacle, so rested then,—
So like that it might be the same; the wind
Was faint and gusty, and the mountain snows
Began to glitter with the climbing moon;
Count Manfred was, as now, within his tower,—
How occupied, we knew not, but with him
The sole companion of his wanderings
And watchings—her, whom of all earthly things
That lived, the only thing he seemed to love,—
As he, indeed, by blood was bound to do,
The lady Astarte, his—
Hush! who comes here?

[*Enter the* ABBOT.]

ABBOT. Where is your master?

HER. Yonder in the tower.

ABBOT. I must speak with him.

MANUEL. 'T is impossible;
He is most private, and must not be thus
Intruded on.

ABBOT. Upon myself I take
The forfeit of my fault, if fault there be—
But I must see him.

HER. Thou hast seen him once
This eve already.

ABBOT. Herman! I command thee,
Knock, and apprize[18] the Count of my approach.

HER. We dare not.

[16] Curse. [17] A famous Alpine mountain peak, today spelled *Eiger*. [18] Inform.

ABBOT. Then it seems I must be herald
Of my own purpose.
MANUEL. Reverend father, stop—
I pray you pause.
ABBOT. Why so?
MANUEL. But step this way,
And I will tell you further.
[*Exeunt.*]

SCENE IV

Interior of the tower.
MANFRED *alone.*

MAN. The stars are forth, the moon above the tops
Of the snow-shining mountains.—Beautiful!
I linger yet with nature, for the night
Hath been to me a more familiar face
Than that of man; and in her starry shade
Of dim and solitary loveliness,
I learned the language of another world.
I do remember me, that in my youth,
When I was wandering,—upon such a night
I stood within the Coliseum's[19] wall,
'Midst the chief relics of almighty Rome;
The trees which grew along the broken arches
Waved dark in the blue midnight, and the stars
Shone through the rents of ruin; from afar
The watch-dog bayed beyond the Tiber;[20] and
More near from out the Caesar's palace came
The owl's long cry, and, interruptedly,
Of distant sentinels the fitful song
Begun and died upon the gentle wind.
Some cypresses beyond the time-worn breach[21]
Appeared to skirt the horizon, yet they stood
Within a bowshot. Where the Caesars dwelt,
And dwell the tuneless birds of night, amidst
A grove which springs through levelled battlements,
And twines its roots with the imperial hearths,
Ivy usurps the laurel's[22] place of growth;
But the gladiators' bloody Circus[23] stands,
A noble wreck in ruinous perfection,
While Caesar's chambers, and the Augustan[24] halls,

[19] A vast stadium built in Rome in the first century A.D.
[20] River that flows through Rome.
[21] Part of the outside wall of the Coliseum no longer stands.
[22] Used to make wreaths for heroes.
[23] Circular stadium; gladiators were men who fought to the death as public entertainment in the Coliseum.
[24] Pertaining to Caesar Augustus (63 B.C.–14 A.D.) or to the Roman emperors in general.

Grovel on earth in indistinct decay.
And thou didst shine, thou rolling moon, upon
All this, and cast a wide and tender light,
Which softened down the hoar austerity
Of rugged desolation, and filled up,
As 't were anew, the gaps of centuries;
Leaving that beautiful which still was so,
And making that which was not, till the place
Became religion, and the heart ran o'er
With silent worship of the great of old,—
The dead but sceptred sovereigns, who still rule
Our spirits from their urns.
'Twas such a night!
'Tis strange that I recall it at this time;
But I have found our thoughts take wildest flight
Even at the moment when they should array
Themselves in pensive order.
[*Enter the* ABBOT.]

ABBOT. My good lord!
I crave a second grace for this approach;
But yet let not my humble zeal offend
By its abruptness—all it hath of ill
Recoils on me; its good in the effect
May light upon your head—could I say *heart*—
Could I touch *that,* with words or prayers, I should
Recall a noble spirit which hath wandered
But is not yet all lost.

MAN. Thou know'st me not;
My days are numbered, and my deeds recorded;
Retire, or 't will be dangerous—Away!

ABBOT. Thou dost not mean to menace me?

MAN. Not I;
I simply tell thee peril is at hand,
And would preserve thee.

ABBOT. What dost thou mean?

MAN. Look there!
What dost thou see?

ABBOT. Nothing.

MAN. Look there, I say,
And steadfastly;—now tell me what thou seest.

ABBOT. That which should shake me, but I fear it not;
I see a dusk and awful figure rise,
Like an infernal god, from out the earth;
His face wrapt in a mantle, and his form
Robed as with angry clouds: he stands between
Thyself and me—but I do fear him not.

MAN. Thou hast no cause; he shall not harm thee, but
His sight may shock thine old limbs into palsy.
I say to thee—Retire!

ABBOT. And I reply—

Never—till I have battled with this fiend:—
What doth he here?
MAN. Why—aye—what doth he here?
I did not send for him,—he is unbidden.
ABBOT. Alas! lost mortal! what with guests like these
Hast thou to do? I tremble for thy sake:
Why doth he gaze on thee, and thou on him?
Ah! he unveils his aspect: on his brow
The thunder-scars are graven: from his eye
Glares forth the immortality of hell—
Avaunt!—
MAN. Pronounce—what is thy mission?
SPIRIT. Come!
ABBOT. What art thou, unknown being? answer!—speak!
SPIRIT. The genius[25] of this mortal.—Come! 'tis time.
MAN. I am prepared for all things, but deny
The power which summons me. Who sent thee here?
SPIRIT. Thou 'lt know anon—Come! come!
MAN. I have commanded
Things of an essence greater far than thine,
And striven with thy masters. Get thee hence!
SPIRIT. Mortal! thine hour is come—Away! I say.
MAN. I knew, and know my hour is come, but not
To render up my soul to such as thee:
Away! I'll die as I have lived—alone.
SPIRIT. Then I must summon up my brethren.—Rise!
[*Other* SPIRITS *rise up.*]
ABBOT. Avaunt! ye evil ones!—Avaunt! I say;
Ye have no power where piety hath power,
And I do charge ye in the name—
SPIRIT. Old man!
We know ourselves, our mission, and thine order;
Waste not thy holy words on idle uses,
It were in vain: this man is forfeited.
Once more I summon him—Away! Away!
MAN. I do defy ye,—though I feel my soul
Is ebbing from me, yet I do defy ye;
Nor will I hence, while I have earthly breath
To breathe my scorn upon ye—earthly strength
To wrestle, though with spirits; what ye take
Shall be ta'en limb by limb.
SPIRIT. Reluctant mortal!
Is this the Magian who would so pervade
The world invisible, and make himself
Almost our equal? Can it be that thou
Art thus in love with life? the very life
Which made thee wretched!
MAN. Thou false fiend, thou liest!

[25] Presiding spirit.

My life is in its last hour,—*that* I know,
Nor would redeem a moment of that hour;
I do not combat against death, but thee
And thy surrounding angels; my past power
Was purchased by no compact with thy crew,
But by superior science—penance, daring,
And length of watching, strength of mind, and skill
In knowledge of our fathers—when the earth
Saw men and spirits walking side by side,
And gave ye no supremacy: I stand
Upon my strength—I do defy—deny—
Spurn back, and scorn ye!—

SPIRIT. But thy many crimes
Have made thee—

MAN. What are they to such as thee?
Must crimes be punished but by other crimes,
And greater criminals?—Back to thy hell!
Thou hast no power upon me, *that* I feel;
Thou never shalt possess me, *that* I know:
What I have done is done; I bear within
A torture which could nothing gain from thine:
The mind which is immortal makes itself
Requital[26] for its good or evil thoughts,—
Is its own origin of ill and end
And its own place and time; its innate sense,
When stripped of this mortality, derives
No colour from the fleeting things without,
But is absorbed in sufferance or in joy,
Born from the knowledge of its own desert.[27]
Thou didst not tempt me, and thou couldst not tempt me;
I have not been thy dupe, nor am thy prey—
But was my own destroyer, and will be
My own hereafter.—Back, ye baffled fiends!—
The hand of death is on me—but not yours!

[*The* DEMONS *disappear.*]

ABBOT. Alas! how pale thou art—thy lips are white—
And thy breast heaves—and in thy gasping throat
The accents rattle: Give thy prayers to heaven—
Pray—albeit but in thought,—but die not thus.

MAN. 'Tis over—my dull eyes can fix thee not;
But all things swim around me, and the earth
Heaves as it were beneath me. Fare thee well!
Give me thy hand.

ABBOT. Cold—cold—even to the heart—
But yet one prayer—Alas! how fares it with thee?

MAN. Old man! 'tis not so difficult to die.

[MANFRED *expires.*]

[26] Repayment. [27] What it deserves; deserts.

ABBOT. He's gone—his soul hath ta'en its earthless flight;
Whither? I dread to think—but he is gone.

DON JUAN

CANTO THE FIRST

I

I want a hero: an uncommon want,
When every year and month sends forth a new one,
Till, after cloying the gazettes[1] with cant,
The age discovers he is not the true one;
Of such as these I should not care to vaunt,
I'll therefore take our ancient friend Don Juan[2]—
We all have seen him, in the pantomime,
Sent to the Devil somewhat ere his time.

II

Vernon, the butcher Cumberland, Wolfe, Hawke,
Prince Ferdinand, Granby, Burgoyne, Keppel, Howe,
Evil and good, have had their tithe[3] of talk,
And filled their sign-posts then, like Wellesley[4] now;
Each in their turn like Banquo's monarchs stalk,
Followers of fame, "nine farrow" of that sow:[5]
France, too, had Buonaparté and Dumourier
Recorded in the Moniteur and Courier.[6]

III

Barnave, Brissot, Condorcet, Mirabeau,
Pétion, Clootz, Danton, Marat, La Fayette
Were French, and famous people, as we know;
And there were others, scarce forgotten yet,
Joubert, Hoche, Marceau, Lannes, Desaix, Moreau,[7]

[1] Military newspapers.

[2] The legendary seducer, familiar in theatrical versions including "pantomime" (line 7); he is usually condemned to hell at the end. (Compare Molière's *Don Juan* and Mozart's opera *Don Giovanni.*) Byron pronounces "Juan" throughout as having two syllables and rhyming with "new one" and "true one" (as in lines 2, 4).

[3] Share.

[4] The Duke of Wellington, victor over Napoleon Bonaparte at Waterloo in 1815. "Sign-posts" alludes to streets named after the heroes. The men named in lines 9–10 were eighteenth-century British generals and admirals.

[5] In Shakespeare's *Macbeth,* IV.i.110–124, witches reveal to Macbeth a vision of a whole series of kings descending from his murdered rival Banquo. The "nine farrow" (offspring) eaten by the sow, quoted from *Macbeth,* IV.i.65, are here an emblem of fame's devouring of her short-lived favorites.

[6] French newspapers. Dumourier was a French general of the Revolutionary period.

[7] French leaders and heroes of the Revolutionary (lines 17–18) and Napoleonic (line 21) periods.

With many of the military set,
Exceedingly remarkable at times,
But not at all adapted to my rhymes.

IV

Nelson was once Britannia's god of war,
And still should be so, but the tide is turned;
There's no more to be said of Trafalgar,[8]
'T is with our hero quietly inurned;
Because the army's grown more popular,
At which the naval people are concerned;
Besides, the prince[9] is all for the land-service,
Forgetting Duncan, Nelson, Howe, and Jervis.[10]

V

Brave men were living before Agamemnon[11]
And since, exceeding valorous and sage,
A good deal like him too, though quite the same none;
But then they shone not on the poet's page,
And so have been forgotten:—I condemn none,
But can't find any in the present age
Fit for my poem (that is, for my new one);
So, as I said, I'll take my friend Don Juan.

VI

Most epic poets plunge "in medias res"[12]
(Horace makes this the heroic turnpike road),
And then your hero tells, whene'er you please,
What went before—by way of episode,
While seated after dinner at his ease,
Beside his mistress in some soft abode,
Palace, or garden, paradise, or cavern,
Which serves the happy couple for a tavern.

VII

That is the usual method, but not mine—
My way is to begin with the beginning;
The regularity of my design
Forbids all wandering as the worst of sinning,
And therefore I shall open with a line

[8] Famous victory in 1805 over the French fleet by the British under the great admiral Horatio Nelson, who was killed in the battle.

[9] The Prince Regent (later George IV), who ruled England from 1811 to 1820 during the mental incapacity of George III.

[10] *Duncan . . . Jervis.* British naval leaders.

[11] Commander of the Greek army against Troy in Homer's *Iliad;* in the *Agamemnon,* Aeschylus tells of his murder by his wife and her lover after Agamemnon's return from the war.

[12] The Roman poet Horace (65–8 B.C.), in his *Art of Poetry,* sanctions the Homeric and Virgilian epic method, where the poet plunges "into the middle of things" and then relates the earlier action through a flashback.

(Although it cost me half an hour in spinning)
Narrating somewhat of Don Juan's father,
And also of his mother, if you'd rather.

VIII

In Seville was he born, a pleasant city,
Famous for oranges and women—he
Who has not seen it will be much to pity,
So says the proverb—and I quite agree;
Of all the Spanish towns is none more pretty,
Cadiz, perhaps—but that you soon may see;—
Don Juan's parents lived beside the river,
A noble stream, and called the Guadalquivir.

IX

His father's name was Jóse—*Don,* of course,—
A true Hidalgo,[13] free from every stain
Of Moor[14] or Hebrew blood, he traced his source
Through the most Gothic gentlemen of Spain;
A better cavalier ne'er mounted horse,
Or, being mounted, e'er got down again,
Than Jóse, who begot our hero, who
Begot—but that's to come—Well, to renew:

X

His mother[15] was a learned lady, famed
For every branch of every science known—
In every Christian language ever named,
With virtues equalled by her wit alone:
She made the cleverest people quite ashamed,
And even the good with inward envy groan,
Finding themselves so very much exceeded
In their own way by all the things that she did.

XI

Her memory was a mine: she knew by heart
All Calderon and greater part of Lopé,[16]
So that if any actor missed his part
She could have served him for the prompter's copy;
For her Feinagle's[17] were an useless art,
And he himself obliged to shut up shop—he
Could never make a memory so fine as
That which adorned the brain of Donna Inez.

[13] *Don* and *Hidalgo* are titles of nobility.
[14] Moslems controlled much of Spain during the Middle Ages.
[15] Juan's mother is in part a satire on Byron's wife, from whom he had separated in 1816 in a spirit of bitterness.
[16] *Calderon, Lopé (de Vega).* Great Spanish Renaissance dramatists.
[17] An expert on memory systems.

XII

Her favorite science was the mathematical,
Her noblest virtue was her magnanimity,
Her wit (she sometimes tried at wit) was Attic[18] all,
Her serious sayings darkened to sublimity;
In short, in all things she was fairly what I call
A prodigy—her morning dress was dimity,
Her evening silk, or, in the summer, muslin,
And other stuffs, with which I won't stay puzzling.

XIII

She knew the Latin—that is, "the Lord's prayer,"
And Greek—the alphabet—I'm nearly sure;
She read some French romances here and there,
Although her mode of speaking was not pure;
For native Spanish she had no great care,
At least her conversation was obscure;
Her thoughts were theorems, her words a problem,
As if she deemed that mystery would ennoble 'em.

XIV

She liked the English and the Hebrew tongue,
And said there was analogy between 'em;
She proved it somehow out of sacred song,
But I must leave the proofs to those who've seen 'em;
But this I heard her say, and can't be wrong,
And all may think which way their judgments lean 'em,
"'T is strange—the Hebrew noun which means 'I am,'[19]
The English always use to govern d—n."

XV

Some women use their tongues—she *looked* a lecture,
Each eye a sermon, and her brow a homily,
An all-in-all sufficient self-director,
Like the lamented late Sir Samuel Romilly,[20]
The law's expounder, and the State's corrector,
Whose suicide was almost an anomaly—
One sad example more, that "All is vanity,"[21]—
(The jury brought their verdict in "Insanity.")

XVI

In short, she was a walking calculation,
Miss Edgeworth's novels stepping from their covers,

[18] Greek—that is, intellectual.

[19] At the burning bush, God revealed to Moses His mysterious name, traditionally translated "I am" (Exodus 3:14).

[20] A reformer and lawyer, Romilly shifted from Byron's side to Lady Byron's during the separation proceedings. He committed suicide in 1818 a few days after the loss of his wife—a circumstance in which Byron found bitter irony.

[21] Quoted from Ecclesiastes 1:2.

Or Mrs. Trimmer's books on education,
Or "Coelebs' Wife"[22] set out in quest of lovers,
Morality's prim personification,
In which not Envy's self a flaw discovers;
To others' share let "female errors fall,"[23]
For she had not even one—the worst of all.

XVII

Oh! she was perfect past all parallel—
Of any modern female saint's comparison;
So far above the cunning powers of hell,
Her guardian angel had given up his garrison;
Even her minutest motions went as well
As those of the best time-piece made by Harrison:[24]
In virtues nothing earthly could surpass her,
Save thine "incomparable oil," Macassar![25]

XVIII

Perfect she was, but as perfection is
Insipid in this naughty world of ours,
Where our first parents never learned to kiss
Till they were exiled from their earlier bowers,
Where all was peace, and innocence, and bliss
(I wonder how they got through the twelve hours),
Don Jòse, like a lineal son of Eve,
Went plucking various fruit without her leave.

XIX

He was a mortal of the careless kind,
With no great love for learning, or the learned,
Who chose to go where'er he had a mind,
And never dreamed his lady was concerned;
The world, as usual, wickedly inclined
To see a kingdom or a house o'erturned,
Whispered he had a mistress, some said *two*,
But for domestic quarrels *one* will do.

XX

Now Donna Inez had, with all her merit,
A great opinion of her own good qualities;
Neglect, indeed, requires a saint to bear it,
And such, indeed, she was in her moralities;
But then she had a devil of a spirit,
And sometimes mixed up fancies with realities,
And let few opportunities escape
Of getting her liege lord into a scrape.

[22] A novel by Hannah More, who, like Maria Edgeworth and Sara Trimmer, wrote sentimental or moralizing books.
[23] Words spoken indulgently of Belinda in Pope's *Rape of the Lock,* II.17.
[24] John Harrison, famous for his marine chronometers. [25] Popular hair oil.

XXI

This was an easy matter with a man
Oft in the wrong, and never on his guard;
And even the wisest, do the best they can,
Have moments, hours, and days, so unprepared,
That you might "brain them with their lady's fan";[26]
And sometimes ladies hit exceeding hard,
And fans turn into falchions[27] in fair hands,
And why and wherefore no one understands.

XXII

'T is pity learned virgins ever wed
With persons of no sort of education,
Or gentlemen, who, though well born and bred,
Grow tired of scientific conversation;
I don't choose to say much upon this head,
I'm a plain man, and in a single station,
But—Oh! ye lords of ladies intellectual,
Inform us truly, have they not hen-pecked you all?

XXIII

Don Jóse and his lady quarrelled—*why*,
Not any of the many could divine,
Though several thousand people chose to try,
'T was surely no concern of theirs nor mine;
I loathe that low vice—curiosity;
But if there's anything in which I shine,
'T is in arranging all my friends' affairs,
Not having, of my own, domestic cares.

XXIV

And so I interfered, and with the best
Intentions, but their treatment was not kind;
I think the foolish people were possessed,
For neither of them could I ever find,
Although their porter afterwards confessed—
But that's no matter, and the worst's behind,
For little Juan o'er me threw, down stairs,
A pail of housemaid's water unawares.

XXV

A little curly-headed, good-for-nothing,
And mischief-making monkey from his birth;
His parents ne'er agreed except in doting
Upon the most unquiet imp on earth;
Instead of quarrelling, had they been but both in
Their senses, they'd have sent young master forth

[26] From Shakespeare's *1 Henry IV*, II.iii.20–21. [27] Medieval swords.

To school, or had him soundly whipped at home,
To teach him manners for the time to come.

XXVI

Don Jóse and the Donna Inez led
For some time an unhappy sort of life,
Wishing each other, not divorced, but dead;
They lived respectably as man and wife,
Their conduct was exceedingly well-bred,
And gave no outward signs of inward strife,
Until at length the smothered fire broke out,
And put the business past all kind of doubt.

XXVII

For Inez called some druggists and physicians,
And tried to prove her loving lord was *mad,*[28]
But as he had some lucid intermissions,
She next decided he was only *bad;*
Yet when they asked her for her depositions,
No sort of explanation could be had,
Save that her duty both to man and God
Required this conduct—which seemed very odd.

XXVIII

She kept a journal, where his faults were noted,
And opened certain trunks of books and letters,
All which might, if occasion served, be quoted;
And then she had all Seville for abettors,
Besides her good old grandmother (who doted);
The hearers of her case became repeaters,
Then advocates, inquisitors, and judges,
Some for amusement, others for old grudges.

XXIX

And then this best and meekest woman bore
With such serenity her husband's woes,
Just as the Spartan ladies[29] did of yore,
Who saw their spouses killed, and nobly chose
Never to say a word about them more—
Calmly she heard each calumny that rose,
And saw *his* agonies with such sublimity,
That all the world exclaimed, "What magnanimity!"

XXX

No doubt this patience, when the world is damning us,
Is philosophic in our former friends;

[28] At the time of the marital separation, Lady Byron had questioned Byron's sanity.
[29] Proverbial for their stern militarism.

'T is also pleasant to be deemed magnanimous,
The more so in obtaining our own ends;
And what the lawyers call a *"malus animus"*[30]
Conduct like this by no means comprehends:
Revenge in person's certainly no virtue,
But then 't is not *my* fault, if *others* hurt you.

XXXI

And if our quarrels should rip up old stories,
And help them with a lie or two additional,
I'm not to blame, as you well know—no more is
Any one else—they were become traditional;
Besides, their resurrection aids our glories
By contrast, which is what we just were wishing all:
And science profits by this resurrection—
Dead scandals form good subjects for dissection.

XXXII

Their friends had tried at reconciliation,
Then their relations, who made matters worse.
('T were hard to tell upon a like occasion
To whom it may be best to have recourse—
I can't say much for friend or yet relation):
The lawyers did their utmost for divorce,
But scarce a fee was paid on either side
Before, unluckily, Don Jóse died.

XXXIII

He died: and most unluckily, because,
According to all hints I could collect
From counsel learned in those kinds of laws
(Although their talk's obscure and circumspect),
His death contrived to spoil a charming cause;[31]
A thousand pities also with respect
To public feeling, which on this occasion
Was manifested in a great sensation.

XXXIV

But ah! he died; and buried with him lay
The public feeling and the lawyers' fees:
His house was sold, his servants sent away,
A Jew took one of his two mistresses,
A priest the other—at least so they say:
I asked the doctors after his disease—
He died of the slow fever called the tertian,[32]
And left his widow to her own aversion.

[30] Malice aforethought. [31] Case. [32] A form of malaria.

XXXV

Yet Jóse was an honourable man,
  That I must say, who knew him very well;
Therefore his frailties I'll no further scan,
  Indeed there were not many more to tell:
And if his passions now and then outran
  Discretion, and were not so peaceable
As Numa's[33] (who was also named Pompilius),
He had been ill brought up, and was born bilious.

XXXVI

Whate'er might be his worthlessness or worth,
  Poor fellow! he had many things to wound him.
Let's own—since it can do no good on earth—
  It was a trying moment that which found him
Standing alone beside his desolate hearth,
  Where all his household gods lay shivered round him:
No choice was left his feelings or his pride,
Save death or Doctors' Commons[34]—so he died.

XXXVII

Dying intestate, Juan was sole heir
  To a chancery[35] suit, and messuages[36] and lands,
Which, with a long minority and care,
  Promised to turn out well in proper hands:
Inez became sole guardian, which was fair,
  And answered but to nature's just demands;
An only son left with an only mother
Is brought up much more wisely than another.

XXXVIII

Sagest of women, even of widows, she
  Resolved that Juan should be quite a paragon,
And worthy of the noblest pedigree:
  (His sire was of Castile, his dam from Aragon[37]).
Then, for accomplishments of chivalry,
  In case our lord the king should go to war again,
He learned the arts of riding, fencing, gunnery,
And how to scale a fortress—or a nunnery.

XXXIX

But that which Donna Inez most desired,
  And saw into herself each day before all
The learned tutors whom for him she hired,
  Was, that his breeding should be strictly moral:
Much into all his studies she inquired,

[33] Legendary early king of Rome whose reign was peaceful. [34] The divorce court.
[35] The court that dealt with inheritances. [36] Dwellings. [37] Noble Spanish families.

And so they were submitted first to her, all,
Arts, sciences—no branch was made a mystery
To Juan's eyes, excepting natural history.

XL

The languages, especially the dead,
The sciences, and most of all the abstruse,
The arts, at least all such as could be said
To be the most remote from common use,
In all these he was much and deeply read:
But not a page of anything that's loose,
Or hints continuation of the species,
Was ever suffered, lest he should grow vicious.

XLI

His classic studies made a little puzzle,
Because of filthy loves of gods and goddesses,
Who in the earlier ages raised a bustle,
But never put on pantaloons or bodices;
His reverend tutors had at times a tussle,
And for their Aeneids, Iliads, and Odysseys,
Were forced to make an odd sort of apology,
For Donna Inez dreaded the Mythology.

XLII

Ovid's a rake, as half his verses show him,
Anacreon's morals are a still worse sample,
Catullus scarcely has a decent poem,
I don't think Sappho's[38] Ode a good example,
Although Longinus[39] tells us there is no hymn
Where the sublime soars forth on wings more ample;
But Virgil's songs are pure, except that horrid one
Beginning with "Formosum Pastor Corydon."[40]

XLIII

Lucretius'[41] irreligion is too strong
For early stomachs, to prove wholesome food;
I can't help thinking Juvenal was wrong,
Although no doubt his real intent was good,
For speaking out so plainly in his song,
So much indeed as to be downright rude;
And then what proper person can be partial
To all those nauseous epigrams of Martial?[42]

[38] *Ovid . . . Sappho.* Great Greek and Roman poets of love or drinking.
[39] Name given to the author of a Greek work entitled *On the Sublime.* Sappho's passionate ode is the one translated by Catullus in his poem 51.
[40] *horrid . . . Corydon.* Virgil's second *Eclogue,* a poem about homosexual love.
[41] Latin author of *On the Nature of Things,* which expresses a materialist philosophy.
[42] *Juvenal, Martial.* Roman satirists.

XLIV

Juan was taught from out the best edition,
Expurgated by learned men, who place,
Judiciously, from out the schoolboy's vision,
The grosser parts; but, fearful to deface
Too much their modest bard by this omission,
And pitying sore this mutilated case,
They only add them all in an appendix,
Which saves, in fact, the trouble of an index;

XLV

For there we have them all "at one fell swoop,"
Instead of being scattered through the pages;
They stand forth marshalled in a handsome troop,
To meet the ingenuous youth of future ages,
Till some less rigid editor shall stoop
To call them back into their separate cages,
Instead of standing staring all together,
Like garden gods[43]—and not so decent either.

XLVI

The Missal too (it was the family Missal)
Was ornamented in a sort of way
Which ancient mass-books often are, and this all
Kinds of grotesques illumined; and how they,
Who saw those figures on the margin kiss all,
Could turn their optics to the text and pray,
Is more than I know—But Don Juan's mother
Kept this herself, and gave her son another.

XLVII

Sermons he read, and lectures he endured,
And homilies, and lives of all the saints;
To Jerome and to Chrysostom[44] inured,
He did not take such studies for restraints;
But how faith is acquired, and then insured,
So well not one of the aforesaid paints
As Saint Augustine in his fine Confessions,[45]
Which make the reader envy his transgressions.

XLVIII

This, too, was a sealed book to little Juan—
I can't but say that his mamma was right,
If such an education was the true one.
She scarcely trusted him from out her sight;

[43] Phallic fertility statues. [44] Fourth-century saints and church fathers.

[45] In this work Augustine (354–430 A.D.) tells of his conversion from a dissolute life to Christianity.

Her maids were old, and if she took a new one,
    You might be sure she was a perfect fright;
She did this during even her husband's life—
I recommend as much to every wife.

XLIX

Young Juan waxed in godliness and grace;
    At six a charming child and at eleven
With all the promise of as fine a face
    As e'er to man's maturer growth was given.
He studied steadily and grew apace,
    And seemed, at least, in the right road to heaven,
For half his days were passed at church, the other
Between his tutors, confessor, and mother.

L

At six, I said, he was a charming child,
    At twelve he was a fine, but quiet boy;
Although in infancy a little wild,
    They tamed him down amongst them: to destroy
His natural spirit not in vain they toiled,
    At least it seemed so; and his mother's joy
Was to declare how sage, and still, and steady,
Her young philosopher was grown already.

LI

I had my doubts, perhaps I have them still,
    But what I say is neither here nor there:
I knew his father well, and have some skill
    In character—but it would not be fair
From sire to son to augur good or ill:
    He and his wife were an ill sorted pair—
But scandal's my aversion—I protest
Against all evil speaking, even in jest.

LII

For my part I say nothing—nothing—but
    This I will say—my reasons are my own—
That if I had an only son to put
    To school (as God be praised that I have none),
'T is not with Donna Inez I would shut
    Him up to learn his catechism alone,
No—no—I'd send him out betimes[46] to college,
For there it was I picked up my own knowledge.

LIII

For there one learns—'t is not for me to boast,
    Though I acquired—but I pass over *that*,

[46] Early.

As well as all the Greek I since have lost:
    I say that there's the place—but *"Verbum sat,"*[47]
I think I picked up too, as well as most,
    Knowledge of matters—but no matter *what*—
I never married—but, I think, I know
That sons should not be educated so.

LIV

Young Juan now was sixteen years of age,
    Tall, handsome, slender, but well knit: he seemed
Active, though not so sprightly, as a page;
    And everybody but his mother deemed
Him almost man; but she flew in a rage
    And bit her lips (for else she might have screamed)
If any said so, for to be precocious
Was in her eyes a thing the most atrocious.

LV

Amongst her numerous acquaintance, all
    Selected for discretion and devotion,
There was the Donna Julia, whom to call
    Pretty were but to give a feeble notion
Of many charms in her as natural
    As sweetness to the flower, or salt to ocean,
Her zone[48] to Venus, or his bow to Cupid,
(But this last simile is trite and stupid).

LVI

The darkness of her Oriental eye
    Accorded with her Moorish origin;
(Her blood was not all Spanish, by the by;
    In Spain, you know, this is a sort of sin).
When proud Granada fell, and, forced to fly,
    Boabdil[49] wept, of Donna Julia's kin
Some went to Africa, some stayed in Spain,
Her great great grandmamma chose to remain.

LVII

She married (I forget the pedigree)
    With an Hidalgo, who transmitted down
His blood less noble than such blood should be;
    At such alliances his sires would frown,
In that point so precise in each degree
    That they bred *in and in,* as might be shown,
Marrying their cousins—nay, their aunts, and nieces,
Which always spoils the breed, if it increases.

[47] Abbreviated form of the Latin proverb "A word to the wise is sufficient." [48] Belt.
[49] Last Moorish king of Grenada, driven out by King Ferdinand in 1492.

LVIII

This heathenish cross restored the breed again,
Ruined its blood, but much improved its flesh;
For from a root the ugliest in old Spain
Sprung up a branch as beautiful as fresh;
The sons no more were short, the daughters plain:
But there's a rumour which I fain would hush,
'T is said that Donna Julia's grandmamma
Produced her Don more heirs at love than law.

LIX

However this might be, the race went on
Improving still through every generation,
Until it centred in an only son,
Who left an only daughter: my narration
May have suggested that this single one
Could be but Julia (whom on this occasion
I shall have much to speak about), and she
Was married, charming, chaste, and twenty-three.

LX

Her eye (I'm very fond of handsome eyes)
Was large and dark, suppressing half its fire
Until she spoke, then through its soft disguise
Flashed an expression more of pride than ire,
And love than either; and there would arise
A something in them which was not desire,
But would have been, perhaps, but for the soul
Which struggled through and chastened down the whole.

LXI

Her glossy hair was clustered o'er a brow
Bright with intelligence, and fair, and smooth;
Her eyebrow's shape was like the aërial bow,
Her cheek all purple with the beam of youth,
Mounting, at times, to a transparent glow,
As if her veins ran lightning; she, in sooth,
Possessed an air and grace by no means common:
Her stature tall—I hate a dumpy woman.

LXII

Wedded she was some years, and to a man
Of fifty, and such husbands are in plenty;
And yet, I think, instead of such a ONE
'T were better to have TWO of five-and-twenty,
Especially in countries near the sun:
And now I think on 't, "mi vien in mente,"[50]

[50] "It comes to my mind."

Ladies even of the most uneasy virtue
Prefer a spouse whose age is short of thirty.

LXIII

'T is a sad thing, I cannot choose but say,
And all the fault of that indecent sun,
Who cannot leave alone our helpless clay,
But will keep baking, broiling, burning on,
That howsoever people fast and pray,
The flesh is frail, and so the soul undone:
What men call gallantry, and gods adultery,
Is much more common where the climate's sultry.

LXIV

Happy the nations of the moral North!
Where all is virtue, and the winter season
Sends sin, without a rag on, shivering forth
('T was snow that brought St. Anthony to reason[51]);
Where juries cast up what a wife is worth,
By laying whate'er sum, in mulct,[52] they please on
The lover, who must pay a handsome price,
Because it is a marketable vice.

LXV

Alfonso was the name of Julia's lord,
A man well looking for his years, and who
Was neither much beloved nor yet abhorred:
They lived together as most people do,
Suffering each others' foibles by accord,
And not exactly either *one* or *two;*
Yet he was jealous, though he did not show it,
For jealousy dislikes the world to know it.

LXVI

Julia was—yet I never could see why—
With Donna Inez quite a favourite friend;
Between their tastes there was small sympathy,
For not a line had Julia ever penned:
Some people whisper (but, no doubt, they lie,
For malice still imputes some private end)
That Inez had, ere Don Alfonso's marriage,
Forgot with him her very prudent carriage;[53]

LXVII

And that still keeping up the old connection,
Which time had lately rendered much more chaste,

[51] *snow . . . reason.* A slip (as Byron himself first pointed out) for St. Francis of Assisi, who considered snow an antidote to lust.
[52] A fine—in this context, for adultery. [53] Conduct.

She took his lady also in affection,
And certainly this course was much the best:
She flattered Julia with her sage protection,
And complimented Don Alfonso's taste;
And if she could not (who can?) silence scandal,
At least she left it a more slender handle.

LXVIII

I can't tell whether Julia saw the affair
With other people's eyes, or if her own
Discoveries made, but none could be aware
Of this, at least no symptom e'er was shown;
Perhaps she did not know, or did not care,
Indifferent from the first, or callous grown:
I'm really puzzled what to think or say,
She kept her counsel in so close a way.

LXIX

Juan she saw, and, as a pretty child,
Caressed him often—such a thing might be
Quite innocently done, and harmless styled,
When she had twenty years, and thirteen he;
But I am not so sure I should have smiled
When he was sixteen, Julia twenty-three;
These few short years make wondrous alterations,
Particularly amongst sun-burnt nations.

LXX

Whate'er the cause might be, they had become
Changed; for the dame grew distant, the youth shy,
Their looks cast down, their greetings almost dumb,
And much embarrassment in either eye;
There surely will be little doubt with some
That Donna Julia knew the reason why,
But as for Juan, he had no more notion
Than he who never saw the sea, of ocean.

LXXI

Yet Julia's very coldness still was kind,
And tremulously gentle her small hand
Withdrew itself from his, but left behind
A little pressure, thrilling, and so bland
And slight, so very slight, that to the mind
'T was but a doubt; but ne'er magician's wand
Wrought change with all Armida's[54] fairy art
Like what this light touch left on Juan's heart.

[54] A sorceress in Torquato Tasso's epic *Jerusalem Delivered* (1575).

LXXII

And if she met him, though she smiled no more,
She looked a sadness sweeter than her smile,
As if her heart had deeper thoughts in store
She must not own,[55] but cherished more the while
For that compression in its burning core;
Even innocence itself has many a wile,
And will not dare to trust itself with truth,
And love is taught hypocrisy from youth.

LXXIII

But passion most dissembles, yet betrays
Even by its darkness; as the blackest sky
Foretells the heaviest tempest, it displays
Its workings through the vainly guarded eye,
And in whatever aspect it arrays
Itself, 't is still the same hypocrisy:
Coldness or anger, even disdain or hate,
Are masks it often wears, and still[56] too late.

LXXIV

Then there were sighs, the deeper for suppression,
And stolen glances, sweeter for the theft,
And burning blushes, though for no transgression,
Tremblings when met, and restlessness when left;
All these are little preludes to possession,
Of which young passion cannot be bereft,[57]
And merely tend to show how greatly love is
Embarrassed at first starting with a novice.

LXXV

Poor Julia's heart was in an awkward state;
She felt it going, and resolved to make
The noblest efforts for herself and mate,
For honour's, pride's, religion's, virtue's sake.
Her resolutions were most truly great,
And almost might have made a Tarquin[58] quake:
She prayed the Virgin Mary for her grace,
As being the best judge of a lady's case.

LXXVI

She vowed she never would see Juan more,
And next day paid a visit to his mother,
And looked extremely at the opening door,
Which, by the Virgin's grace, let in another;
Grateful she was, and yet a little sore—
Again it opens, it can be no other,

[55] Admit to. [56] Always. [57] Deprived.
[58] Rapist in Shakespeare's *Rape of Lucrece.*

'T is surely Juan now—No! I'm afraid
That night the Virgin was no further prayed.

LXXVII

She now determined that a virtuous woman
Should rather face and overcome temptation,
That flight was base and dastardly, and no man
Should ever give her heart the least sensation;
That is to say, a thought beyond the common
Preference, that we must feel upon occasion,
For people who are pleasanter than others,
But then they only seem so many brothers.

LXXVIII

And even if by chance—and who can tell?
The devil's so very sly—she should discover
That all within was not so very well,
And, if still free, that such or such a lover
Might please perhaps, a virtuous wife can quell
Such thoughts, and be the better when they're over;
And if the man should ask, 't is but denial:
I recommend young ladies to make trial.

LXXIX

And then there are such things as love divine,
Bright and immaculate, unmixed and pure,
Such as the angels think so very fine,
And matrons, who would be no less secure,[59]
Platonic, perfect, "just such love as mine":
Thus Julia said—and thought so, to be sure;
And so I'd have her think, were *I* the man
On whom her reveries celestial ran.

LXXX

Such love is innocent, and may exist
Between young persons without any danger:
A hand may first, and then a lip be kist;
For my part, to such doings I'm a stranger,
But *hear* these freedoms form the utmost list[60]
Of all o'er which such love may be a ranger:
If people go beyond, 't is quite a crime,
But not my fault—I tell them all in time.

LXXXI

Love, then, but love within its proper limits
Was Julia's innocent determination
In young Don Juan's favour, and to him its
Exertion might be useful on occasion;

[59] Heedless of danger. [60] Boundary.

And, lighted at too pure a shrine to dim its
Ethereal lustre, with what sweet persuasion
He might be taught, by love and her together—
I really don't know what, nor Julia either.

LXXXII

Fraught with[61] this fine intention, and well fenced
In mail of proof[62]—her purity of soul,
She, for the future of her strength convinced,
And that her honour was a rock, or mole,[63]
Exceeding sagely from that hour dispensed
With any kind of troublesome control;
But whether Julia to the task was equal
Is that which must be mentioned in the sequel.

LXXXIII

Her plan she deemed both innocent and feasible,
And, surely, with a stripling of sixteen
Not scandal's fangs could fix on much that's seizable,
Or if they did so, satisfied to mean
Nothing but what was good, her breast was peaceable:
A quiet conscience makes one so serene!
Christians have burnt each other, quite persuaded
That all the Apostles would have done as they did.

LXXXIV

And if in the mean time her husband died,
But Heaven forbid that such a thought should cross
Her brain, though in a dream! (and then she sighed)
Never could she survive that common loss;
But just suppose that moment should betide,
I only say suppose it—*inter nos.*[64]
(This should be *entre nous,* for Julia thought
In French, but then the rhyme would go for nought.)

LXXXV

I only say, suppose this supposition:
Juan being then grown up to man's estate
Would fully suit a widow of condition,
Even seven years hence it would not be too late;
And in the interim (to pursue this vision)
The mischief, after all, could not be great,
For he would learn the rudiments of love,
I mean the *seraph*[65] way of those above.

LXXXVI

So much for Julia. Now we'll turn to Juan.
Poor little fellow! he had no idea

[61] Carrying. [62] Armor proved to be impenetrable.
[63] Heavy stone wall as in a harbor. [64] Between you and me (Latin). [65] Angel.

Of his own case, and never hit the true one;
In feelings quick as Ovid's Miss Medea,[66]
He puzzled over what he found a new one,
But not as yet imagined it could be a
Thing quite in course, and not at all alarming,
Which, with a little patience, might grow charming.

LXXXVII

Silent and pensive, idle, restless, slow,
His home deserted for the lonely wood,
Tormented with a wound he could not know,
His, like all deep grief, plunged in solitude:
I'm fond myself of solitude or so,
But then, I beg it may be understood,
By solitude I mean a Sultan's, not
A hermit's, with a harem for a grot.[67]

LXXXVIII

"Oh Love! in such a wilderness as this,
Where transport and security entwine,
Here is the empire of thy perfect bliss,
And here thou art a god indeed divine."[68]
The bard I quote from does not sing amiss,
With the exception of the second line,
For that same twining "transport and security"
Are twisted to a phrase of some obscurity.

LXXXIX

The poet meant, no doubt, and thus appeals
To the good sense and senses of mankind,
The very thing which everybody feels,
As all have found on trial, or may find,
That no one likes to be disturbed at meals
Or love.—I won't say more about "entwined"
Or "transport," as we knew all that before,
But beg "security" will bolt the door.

XC

Young Juan wandered by the glassy brooks,
Thinking unutterable things; he threw
Himself at length within the leafy nooks
Where the wild branch of the cork forest grew;
There poets find materials for their books,
And every now and then we read them through,

[66] In *Metamorphoses,* Book VII, Ovid portrays Medea's sudden awakening to love for Jason.
[67] Grotto; cave.
[68] *lines 697–700.* From Thomas Campbell's poem *Gertrude of Wyoming* (1809), III.i.1–4.

So that their plan and prosody[69] are eligible,
Unless, like Wordsworth,[70] they prove unintelligible.

XCI

He, Juan (and not Wordsworth), so pursued
His self-communion with his own high soul,
Until his mighty heart, in its great mood,
Had mitigated part, though not the whole
Of its disease; he did the best he could
With things not very subject to control,
And turned, without perceiving his condition,
Like Coleridge, into a metaphysician.[71]

XCII

He thought about himself, and the whole earth,
Of man the wonderful, and of the stars,
And how the deuce they ever could have birth;
And then he thought of earthquakes, and of wars,
How many miles the moon might have in girth,
Of air-balloons,[72] and of the many bars
To perfect knowledge of the boundless skies;—
And then he thought of Donna Julia's eyes.

XCIII

In thoughts like these true wisdom may discern
Longings sublime, and aspirations high,
Which some are born with, but the most part learn
To plague themselves withal, they know not why:
'T was strange that one so young should thus concern
His brain about the action of the sky;
If *you* think 't was philosophy that this did,
I can't help thinking puberty assisted.

XCIV

He pored upon the leaves, and on the flowers,
And heard a voice in all the winds; and then
He thought of wood-nymphs and immortal bowers,
And how the goddesses came down to men:
He missed the pathway, he forgot the hours,
And when he looked upon his watch again,
He found how much old Time had been a winner—
He also found that he had lost his dinner.

[69] Metrics; versification.

[70] On poetic, personal, and political grounds, Byron took a dim view of the "Lake poets," including Wordsworth, Coleridge, and above all Southey.

[71] *turned . . . metaphysician.* The same charge Coleridge brings against himself in "Dejection: An Ode," lines 87–93.

[72] Ballooning had a vogue in England in Byron's day.

XCV

Sometimes he turned to gaze upon his book,
Boscan, or Garcilasso;[73]—by the wind
Even as the page is rustled while we look,
So by the poesy of his own mind
Over the mystic leaf his soul was shook,
As if 't were one whereon magicians bind
Their spells, and give them to the passing gale,
According to some good old woman's tale.

XCVI

Thus would he while his lonely hours away
Dissatisfied, not knowing what he wanted;
Nor glowing reverie, nor poet's lay,[74]
Could yield his spirit that for which it panted,
A bosom whereon he his head might lay,
And hear the heart beat with the love it granted,
With—several other things which I forget,
Or which, at least, I need not mention yet.

XCVII

Those lonely walks, and lengthening reveries,
Could not escape the gentle Julia's eyes;
She saw that Juan was not at his ease;
But that which chiefly may, and must surprise,
Is, that the Donna Inez did not tease
Her only son with question or surmise;
Whether it was she did not see, or would not,
Or, like all very clever people, could not.

XCVIII

This may seem strange, but yet 't is very common;
For instance—gentlemen, whose ladies take
Leave to o'erstep the written rights of woman,
And break the—Which commandment is 't they break?
(I have forgot the number, and think no man
Should rashly quote, for fear of a mistake.)
I say, when these same gentlemen are jealous,
They make some blunder, which their ladies tell us.

XCIX

A real husband always is suspicious,
But still no less suspects in the wrong place,
Jealous of some one who had no such wishes,
Or pandering blindly to his own disgrace,
By harbouring some dear friend extremely vicious;
The last indeed's infallibly the case:
And when the spouse and friend are gone off wholly,
He wonders at their vice, and not his folly.

[73] Juan Boscan and Garcilaso de la Vega, 16th-century Spanish poets. [74] Poem.

C

Thus parents also are at times short-sighted;
Though watchful as the lynx, they ne'er discover,
The while the wicked world beholds delighted,
Young Hopeful's mistress, or Miss Fanny's lover,
Till some confounded escapade has blighted
The plan of twenty years, and all is over;
And then the mother cries, the father swears,
And wonders why the devil he got heirs.

CI

But Inez was so anxious, and so clear
Of sight, that I must think, on this occasion,
She had some other motive much more near
For leaving Juan to this new temptation,
But what that motive was, I shan't say here;
Perhaps to finish Juan's education,
Perhaps to open Don Alfonso's eyes,
In case he thought his wife too great a prize.

CII

It was upon a day, a summer's day;—
Summer's indeed a very dangerous season,
And so is spring about the end of May;
The sun, no doubt, is the prevailing reason;
But whatsoe'er the cause is, one may say,
And stand convicted of more truth than treason,
That there are months which nature grows more merry in,—
March has its hares, and May must have its heroine.

CIII

'T was on a summer's day— the sixth of June:—
I like to be particular in dates,
Not only of the age, and year, but moon;
They are a sort of post-house, where the Fates
Change horses, making history change its tune,
Then spur away o'er empires and o'er states,
Leaving at last not much besides chronology,
Excepting the post-obits[75] of theology.

CIV

'T was on the sixth of June, about the hour
Of half-past six—perhaps still nearer seven—
When Julia sate within as pretty a bower
As e'er held houri[76] in that heathenish heaven

[75] Loans (often contracted by young noblemen, including Byron, at very high interest) to be repaid when a relative dies and the debtor inherits his estate.
[76] One of the women promised to faithful Mohammedans in their paradise.

Described by Mahomet, and Anacreon Moore,[77]
To whom the lyre and laurels have been given,
With all the trophies of triumphant song—
He won them well, and may he wear them long!

CV

She sate, but not alone; I know not well
How this same interview had taken place,
And even if I knew, I should not tell—
People should hold their tongues in any case;
No matter how or why the thing befell,
But there were she and Juan, face to face—
When two such faces are so, 't would be wise,
But very difficult, to shut their eyes.

CVI

How beautiful she looked! her conscious[78] heart
Glowed in her cheek, and yet she felt no wrong.
Oh Love! how perfect is thy mystic art,
Strengthening the weak, and trampling on the strong!
How self-deceitful is the sagest part
Of mortals whom thy lure hath led along!—
The precipice she stood on was immense,
So was her creed in her own innocence.

CVII

She thought of her own strength, and Juan's youth,
And of the folly of all prudish fears,
Victorious virtue, and domestic truth,
And then of Don Alfonso's fifty years:
I wish these last had not occurred, in sooth,
Because that number rarely much endears,
And through all climes, the snowy and the sunny,
Sounds ill in love, whate'er it may in money.

CVIII

When people say, "I've told you *fifty* times,"
They mean to scold, and very often do;
When poets say, "I've written *fifty* rhymes,"
They make you dread that they'll recite them too;
In gangs of *fifty*, thieves commit their crimes;
At *fifty* love for love is rare, 't is true,
But then, no doubt, it equally as true is,
A good deal may be bought for *fifty* louis.[79]

[77] Byron's good friend Thomas Moore (1779–1852), an Irish poet who had written the oriental poem *Lalla Rookh* and translated Anacreon, a sixth-century B.C. Greek poet of love and wine.

[78] Sexually self-conscious. [79] French gold coins.

CIX

Julia had honour, virtue, truth, and love
For Don Alfonso; and she inly swore,
By all the vows below to powers above,
She never would disgrace the ring she wore,
Nor leave a wish which wisdom might reprove;
And while she pondered this, besides much more,
One hand on Juan's carelessly was thrown,
Quite by mistake—she thought it was her own;

CX

Unconsciously she leaned upon the other,
Which played within the tangles of her hair;
And to contend with thoughts she could not smother
She seemed, by the distraction of her air.
'T was surely very wrong in Juan's mother
To leave together this imprudent pair,
She who for many years had watched her son so—
I'm very certain *mine* would not have done so.

CXI

The hand which still held Juan's, by degrees
Gently, but palpably confirmed its grasp,
As if it said, "Detain me, if you please";
Yet there's no doubt she only meant to clasp
His fingers with a pure Platonic squeeze;
She would have shrunk as from a toad or asp,
Had she imagined such a thing could rouse
A feeling dangerous to a prudent spouse.

CXII

I cannot know what Juan thought of this,
But what he did, is much what you would do;
His young lip thanked it with a grateful kiss,
And then, abashed at its own joy, withdrew
In deep despair, lest he had done amiss,—
Love is so very timid when 't is new:
She blushed, and frowned not, but she strove to speak,
And held her tongue, her voice was grown so weak.

CXIII

The sun set, and up rose the yellow moon;
The devil's in the moon for mischief; they
Who called her CHASTE, methinks, began too soon
Their nomenclature; there is not a day,
The longest, not the twenty-first of June,
Sees half the business in a wicked way,
On which three single hours of moonshine smile—
And then she looks so modest all the while.

CXIV

There is a dangerous silence in that hour,
A stillness, which leaves room for the full soul
To open all itself, without the power
Of calling wholly back its self-control;
The silver light which, hallowing tree and tower,
Sheds beauty and deep softness o'er the whole,
Breathes also to the heart, and o'er it throws
A loving languor, which is not repose.

CXV

And Julia sate with Juan, half embraced
And half retiring from the glowing arm,
Which trembled like the bosom where 't was placed;
Yet still she must have thought there was no harm,
Or else 't were easy to withdraw her waist;
But then the situation had its charm,
And then—God knows what next—I can't go on;
I'm almost sorry that I e'er begun.

CXVI

Oh Plato! Plato! you have paved the way,
With your confounded phantasies, to more
Immoral conduct by the fancied sway
Your system feigns o'er the controlless core
Of human hearts, than all the long array
Of poets and romancers:—You're a bore,
A charlatan, a coxcomb[80]—and have been,
At best, no better than a go-between.

CXVII

And Julia's voice was lost, except in sighs,
Until too late for useful conversation;
The tears were gushing from her gentle eyes;
I wish, indeed, they had not had occasion;
But who, alas! can love, and then be wise?
Not that remorse did not oppose temptation;
A little still she strove, and much repented,
And whispering "I will ne'er consent"—consented.

CXVIII

'T is said that Xerxes[81] offered a reward
To those who could invent him a new pleasure:
Methinks the requisition's rather hard,
And must have cost his majesty a treasure;
For my part, I'm a moderate-minded bard,
Fond of a little love (which I call leisure);

[80] A conceited, showy person. [81] Persian king, fifth century B.C.

I care not for new pleasures, as the old
Are quite enough for me, so they but hold.

CXIX

Oh Pleasure! you're indeed a pleasant thing,
Although one must be damned for you, no doubt:
I make a resolution every spring
Of reformation, ere the year run out,
But somehow, this my vestal[82] vow takes wing,
Yet still, I trust, it may be kept throughout;
I'm very sorry, very much ashamed,
And mean, next winter, to be quite reclaimed.

CXX

Here my chaste Muse a liberty must take—
Start not! still chaster reader—she'll be nice[83] hence-
Forward, and there is no great cause to quake;
This liberty is a poetic licence,
Which some irregularity may make
In the design, and as I have a high sense
Of Aristotle and the rules,[84] 't is fit
To beg his pardon when I err a bit.

CXXI

This licence is to hope the reader will
Suppose from June the sixth (the fatal day
Without whose epoch my poetic skill
For want of facts would all be thrown away),
But keeping Julia and Don Juan still
In sight, that several months have passed; we'll say
'T was in November, but I'm not so sure
About the day—the era's more obscure.

CXXII

We'll talk of that anon.—'T is sweet to hear
At midnight on the blue and moonlit deep
The song and oar of Adria's[85] gondolier,
By distance mellowed, o'er the waters sweep;
'T is sweet to see the evening star appear;
'T is sweet to listen as the night-winds creep
From leaf to leaf; 't is sweet to view on high
The rainbow, based on ocean, span the sky.

CXXIII

'T is sweet to hear the watch-dog's honest bark
Bay deep-mouthed welcome as we draw near home;

[82] Chaste (like the virginal priestesses of Vesta in ancient Rome).
[83] Behaving with propriety.
[84] Neoclassical rules based on Aristotle—here, the rule of the unity of time.
[85] City on the Adriatic Sea—that is, Venice.

'T is sweet to know there is an eye will mark
Our coming, and look brighter when we come;
'T is sweet to be awakened by the lark,
Or lulled by falling waters; sweet the hum
Of bees, the voice of girls, the song of birds,
The lisp of children, and their earliest words.

CXXIV

Sweet is the vintage, when the showering grapes
In Bacchanal[86] profusion reel to earth,
Purple and gushing; sweet are our escapes
From civic revelry to rural mirth;
Sweet to the miser are his glittering heaps,
Sweet to the father is his first-born's birth,
Sweet is revenge—especially to women,
Pillage to soldiers, prize-money[87] to seamen.

CXXV

Sweet is a legacy, and passing sweet
The unexpected death of some old lady
Or gentleman of seventy years complete,
Who've made "us youth"[88] wait too—too long already
For an estate, or cash, or country seat,
Still breaking, but with stamina so steady
That all the Israelites[89] are fit to mob its
Next owner for their double-damned post-obits.

CXXVI

'T is sweet to win, no matter how, one's laurels,
By blood or ink; 't is sweet to put an end
To strife; 't is sometimes sweet to have our quarrels,
Particularly with a tiresome friend:
Sweet is old wine in bottles, ale in barrels;
Dear is the helpless creature we defend
Against the world; and dear the schoolboy spot
We ne'er forget, though there we are forgot.

CXXVII

But sweeter still than this, than these, than all,
Is first and passionate love—it stands alone,
Like Adam's recollection of his fall;
The tree of knowledge has been plucked—all's known—
And life yields nothing further to recall
Worthy of this ambrosial[90] sin, so shown,

[86] Related to Bacchus, god of wine.
[87] A navy man's share in the wealth of a captured ship.
[88] A phrase used absurdly by the aging Falstaff in Shakespeare's *1 Henry IV,* II.ii.93.
[89] Moneylenders (whether Jews or not). For "post-obits" see the note to stanza ciii.
[90] Ambrosia was the food of the gods.

No doubt in fable, as the unforgiven
Fire which Prometheus filched for us from heaven.[91]

CXXVIII

Man's a strange animal, and makes strange use
Of his own nature, and the various arts,
And likes particularly to produce
Some new experiment to show his parts;[92]
This is the age of oddities let loose,
Where different talents find their different marts;
You'd best begin with truth, and when you've lost your
Labour, there's a sure market for imposture.

CXXIX

What opposite discoveries we have seen!
(Signs of true genius, and of empty pockets.)
One makes new noses, one a guillotine,
One breaks your bones, one sets them in their sockets;
But vaccination certainly has been
A kind antithesis to Congreve's[93] rockets,
With which the Doctor paid off an old pox,
By borrowing a new one from an ox.[94]

CXXX

Bread has been made (indifferent) from potatoes;
And galvanism[95] has set some corpses grinning,
But has not answered like the apparatus
Of the Humane Society's[96] beginning,
By which men are unsuffocated gratis:
What wondrous new machines have late been spinning!
I said the small pox has gone out of late;
Perhaps it may be followed by the great.[97]

CXXXI

'T is said the great came from America;[98]
Perhaps it may set out on its return,—
The population there so spreads, they say
'T is grown high time to thin it in its turn,[99]
With war, or plague, or famine, any way,
So that civilisation they may learn;

[91] *Prometheus . . . heaven.* See note to Byron's *Manfred,* I.i.154. [92] Talents.
[93] Sir William Congreve, inventor of an artillery shell in 1808.
[94] *vaccination . . . ox.* Smallpox vaccine, invented by Edward Jenner (1749–1823), was made from parts of animals infected with cowpox.
[95] Electricity—used to experiment on muscle movement in corpses.
[96] An organization designed to rescue drowning persons.
[97] Syphilis was known as the "great pox."
[98] Brought back by Columbus's sailors, it was believed.
[99] *population . . . turn.* A reference to Thomas Malthus' (1766–1834) concern about over-population.

And which in ravage the more loathsome evil is—
Their real lues,[1] or our pseudo-syphilis?

CXXXII

This is the patent age of new inventions
For killing bodies, and for saving souls,
All propagated with the best intentions;
Sir Humphry Davy's[2] lantern, by which coals
Are safely mined for in the mode he mentions,
Tombuctoo[3] travels, voyages to the poles,
Are ways to benefit mankind, as true
Perhaps, as shooting them at Waterloo.

CXXXIII

Man's a phenomenon, one knows not what,
And wonderful beyond all wondrous measure;
'T is pity though, in this sublime world, that
Pleasure's a sin, and sometimes sin's a pleasure;
Few mortals know what end they would be at,
But whether glory, power, or love, or treasure,
The path is through perplexing ways, and when
The goal is gained, we die, you know—and then—

CXXXIV

What then?—I do not know, no more do you—
And so good night.—Return we to our story:
'T was in November, when fine days are few,
And the far mountains wax a little hoary,
And clap a white cape on their mantles blue;
And the sea dashes round the promontory,
And the loud breaker boils against the rock,
And sober suns must set at five o'clock.

CXXXV

'T was, as the watchmen say, a cloudy night;
No moon, no stars, the wind was low or loud
By gusts, and many a sparkling hearth was bright
With the piled wood, round which the family crowd;
There's something cheerful in that sort of light,
Even as a summer sky's without a cloud;
I'm fond of fire, and crickets, and all that,
A lobster salad, and champagne, and chat.

CXXXVI

'T was midnight—Donna Julia was in bed,
Sleeping, most probably,—when at her door

[1] Syphilis.
[2] Famous chemist (1778–1829), who also invented a safety lamp for miners.
[3] Timbuktu, city in western Africa.

Arose a clatter might awake the dead,
  If they had never been awoke before,
And that they have been so we all have read,
  And are to be so, at the least, once more;—
The door was fastened, but with voice and fist
First knocks were heard, then "Madam—Madam—hist!

CXXXVII

"For God's sake, Madam—Madam—here's my master,
  With more than half the city at his back—
Was ever heard of such a curst disaster!
  'T is not my fault—I kept good watch—Alack!
Do pray undo the bolt a little faster—
  They're on the stair just now, and in a crack
Will all be here; perhaps he yet may fly—
Surely the window's not so *very* high!"

CXXXVIII

By this time Don Alfonso was arrived,
  With torches, friends, and servants in great number;
The major part of them had long been wived,
  And therefore paused not to disturb the slumber
Of any wicked woman, who contrived
  By stealth her husband's temples[4] to encumber:
Examples of this kind are so contagious,
Were *one* not punished, *all* would be outrageous.

CXXXIX

I can't tell how, or why, or what suspicion
  Could enter into Don Alfonso's head;
But for a cavalier of his condition
  It surely was exceedingly ill-bred,
Without a word of previous admonition,
  To hold a levee[5] round his lady's bed,
And summon lackeys, armed with fire and sword,
To prove himself the thing he most abhorred.

CXL

Poor Donna Julia! starting as from sleep
  (Mind that I do not say she had not slept),
Began at once to scream, and yawn, and weep;
  Her maid, Antonia, who was an adept,
Contrived to fling the bed-clothes in a heap,
  As if she had just now from out them crept:
I can't tell why she should take all this trouble
To prove her mistress had been sleeping double.

[4] Cuckolded husbands, according to the tradition, grew horns.
[5] Ceremony at a king's getting out of bed in the morning.

CXLI

But Julia mistress, and Antonia maid,
Appeared like two poor harmless women, who
Of goblins, but still more of men afraid,
Had thought one man might be deterred by two,
And therefore side by side were gently laid,
Until the hours of absence should run through,
And truant husband should return, and say,
"My dear, I was the first who came away."

CXLII

Now Julia found at length a voice, and cried,
"In heaven's name, Don Alfonso, what d' ye mean?
Has madness seized you? would that I had died
Ere such a monster's victim I had been!
What may this midnight violence betide,[6]
A sudden fit of drunkenness or spleen?[7]
Dare you suspect me, whom the thought would kill?
Search, then, the room!"—Alfonso said, "I will."

CXLIII

He searched, *they* searched, and rummaged everywhere,
Closet and clothes-press, chest and window-seat.
And found much linen, lace, and several pair
Of stockings, slippers, brushes, combs, complete,
With other articles of ladies fair,
To keep them beautiful, or leave them neat:
Arras[8] they pricked and curtains with their swords,
And wounded several shutters, and some boards.

CXLIV

Under the bed they searched, and there they found—
No matter what—it was not that they sought;
They opened windows, gazing if the ground
Had signs of footmarks, but the earth said nought;
And then they stared each other's faces round:
'T is odd, not one of all these seekers thought,
And seems to me almost a sort of blunder,
Of looking *in* the bed as well as under.

CXLV

During this inquisition Julia's tongue
Was not asleep—"Yes, search and search," she cried,
"Insult on insult heap, and wrong on wrong!
It was for this that I became a bride!
For this in silence I have suffered long
A husband like Alfonso at my side;

[6] Signify. [7] Caprice; bad temper. [8] Tapestry.

But now I'll bear no more, nor here remain,
If there be law or lawyers in all Spain.

CXLVI

"Yes, Don Alfonso! husband now no more.
If ever you indeed deserved the name,
Is 't worthy of your years?—you have three-score—
Fifty, or sixty, it is all the same—
Is 't wise or fitting, causeless to explore
For facts against a virtuous woman's fame?
Ungrateful, perjured, barbarous Don Alfonso,
How dare you think your lady would go on so?

CXLVII

"Is it for this I have disdained to hold
The common privileges of my sex?
That I have chosen a confessor so old
And deaf, that any other it would vex,[9]
And never once he has had cause to scold,
But found my very innocence perplex
So much, he always doubted I was married—
How sorry you will be when I've miscarried!

CXLVIII

"Was it for this that no Cortejo[10] e'er
I yet have chosen from out the youth of Seville?
Is it for this I scarce went anywhere,
Except to bull-fights, mass, play, rout,[11] and revel?
Is it for this, whate'er my suitors were,
I favoured none—nay, was almost uncivil?
Is it for this that General Count O'Reilly,
Who took Algiers, declares I used him vilely?

CXLIX

"Did not the Italian Musico Cazzani[12]
Sing at my heart six months at least in vain?
Did not his countryman, Count Corniani,[13]
Call me the only virtuous wife in Spain?
Were there not also Russians, English, many?
The Count Strongstroganoff I put in pain,
And Lord Mount Coffeehouse, the Irish peer,
Who killed himself for love (with wine) last year.

CL

"Have I not had two bishops at my feet?
The Duke of Ichar, and Don Fernan Nunez?

[9] *any . . . vex.* Julia implies that *she* does not mind shouting to the deaf priest in the confessional, since her sins are so trivial.
[10] Publicly acknowledged lover. [11] Lively party.
[12] Pun on the Italian for "penis." [13] Pun on the Italian for "horned" (cuckold).

And is it thus a faithful wife you treat?
I wonder in what quarter now the moon is:[14]
I praise your vast forbearance not to beat
Me also, since the time so opportune is—
Oh, valiant man! with sword drawn and cocked trigger,
Now, tell me, don't you cut a pretty figure?

CLI

"Was it for this you took your sudden journey,
Under pretence of business indispensable,
With that sublime of rascals your attorney,
Whom I see standing there, and looking sensible
Of having played the fool? though both I spurn, he
Deserves the worst, his conduct's less defensible,
Because, no doubt, 't was for his dirty fee,
And not from any love to you nor me.

CLII

"If he comes here to take a deposition,
By all means let the gentleman proceed;
You've made the apartment in a fit condition:—
There's pen and ink for you, sir, when you need—
Let everything be noted with precision,
I would not you for nothing should be fee'd—
But as my maid's undressed, pray turn your spies out."
"Oh!" sobbed Antonia, "I could tear their eyes out."

CLIII

"There is the closet, there the toilet,[15] there
The antechamber—search them under, over;
There is the sofa, there the great arm-chair,
The chimney—which would really hold a lover.
I wish to sleep, and beg you will take care
And make no further noise, till you discover
The secret cavern of this lurking treasure—
And when 't is found, let me, too, have that pleasure.

CLIV

"And now, Hidalgo! now that you have thrown
Doubt upon me, confusion over all,
Pray have the courtesy to make it known
Who is the man you search for? how d' ye call
Him? what's his lineage? let him but be shown—
I hope he's young and handsome—is he tall?
Tell me—and be assured, that since you stain
Mine honour thus, it shall not be in vain.

[14] Lunatics were at their worst at full moon. [15] Dressing table.

CLV

"At least, perhaps, he has not sixty years,
    At that age he would be too old for slaughter,
Or for so young a husband's jealous fears
    (Antonia! let me have a glass of water.)
I am ashamed of having shed these tears,
    They are unworthy of my father's daughter;
My mother dreamed not in my natal hour,
That I should fall into a monster's power.

CLVI

"Perhaps 't is of Antonia you are jealous,
    You saw that she was sleeping by my side,
When you broke in upon us with your fellows;
    Look where you please—we've nothing, sir, to hide;
Only another time, I trust, you'll tell us,
    Or for the sake of decency abide
A moment at the door, that we may be
Dressed to receive so much good company.

CLVII

"And now, sir, I have done, and say no more;
    The little I have said may serve to show
The guileless heart in silence may grieve o'er
    The wrongs to whose exposure it is slow:—
I leave you to your conscience as before,
    'T will one day ask you, *why* you used me so?
God grant you feel not then the bitterest grief!
Antonia! where's my pocket-handkerchief?"

CLVIII

She ceased, and turned upon her pillow; pale
    She lay, her dark eyes flashing through their tears,
Like skies that rain and lighten; as a veil
    Waved and o'ershading her wan cheek, appears
Her streaming hair; the black curls strive, but fail,
    To hide the glossy shoulder, which uprears
Its snow through all;—her soft lips lie apart,
And louder than her breathing beats her heart.

CLIX

The Senhor Don Alfonso stood confused;
    Antonia bustled round the ransacked room,
And, turning up her nose, with looks abused
    Her master, and his myrmidons,[16] of whom
Not one, except the attorney, was amused;
    He, like Achates,[17] faithful to the tomb,

[16] Followers (from Achilles' men in Homer's *Iliad*).
[17] Faithful friend of Aeneas in Virgil's *Aeneid*.

So there were quarrels, cared not for the cause,
Knowing they must be settled by the laws.

CLX

With prying snub-nose, and small eyes, he stood,
    Following Antonia's motions here and there,
With much suspicion in his attitude;
    For reputations he had little care;
So that a suit or action[18] were made good,
    Small pity had he for the young and fair,
And ne'er believed in negatives, till these
Were proved by competent false witnesses.

CLXI

But Don Alfonso stood with downcast looks,
    And, truth to say, he made a foolish figure;
When, after searching in five hundred nooks,
    And treating a young wife with so much rigour,
He gained no point, except some self-rebukes,
    Added to those his lady with such vigour
Had poured upon him for the last half hour,
Quick, thick, and heavy—as a thunder-shower.

CLXII

At first he tried to hammer an excuse,
    To which the sole reply was tears and sobs,
And indications of hysterics, whose
    Prologue is always certain throes, and throbs,
Gasps, and whatever else the owners choose:
    Alfonso saw his wife, and thought of Job's;[19]
He saw too, in perspective, her relations,
And then he tried to muster all his patience.

CLXIII

He stood in act to speak, or rather stammer,
    But sage Antonia cut him short before
The anvil of his speech received the hammer,
    With "Pray, sir, leave the room and say no more,
Or madam dies."—Alfonso muttered, "D—n her."
    But nothing else, the time of words was o'er;
He cast a rueful look or two, and did,
He knew not wherefore, that which he was bid.

CLXIV

With him retired his "*posse comitatus*,"[20]
    The attorney last, who lingered near the door
Reluctantly, still tarrying there as late as

[18] Right to go to court. [19] Traditionally considered a nagging wife.
[20] Body of men gathered to enforce the law; nowadays called simply *posse*.

Antonia let him—not a little sore
At this most strange and unexplained *"hiatus"*[21]
In Don Alfonso's facts, which just now wore
An awkward look; as he revolved the case,
The door was fastened in his legal face.

CLXV

No sooner was it bolted, than—Oh shame!
Oh sin! Oh sorrow! and Oh womankind!
How can you do such things and keep your fame,
Unless this world, and t' other too, be blind?
Nothing so dear as an unfilched good name!
But to proceed—for there is more behind:
With much heartfelt reluctance be it said,
Young Juan slipped, half-smothered, from the bed.

CLXVI

He had been hid—I don't pretend to say
How, nor can I indeed describe the where—
Young, slender, and packed easily, he lay,
No doubt, in little compass,[22] round or square;
But pity him I neither must nor may
His suffocation by that pretty pair;
'T were better, sure, to die so, than be shut
With maudlin Clarence in his Malmsey butt.[23]

CLXVII

And, secondly, I pity not, because
He had no business to commit a sin,
Forbid by heavenly, fined by human laws,
At least 't was rather early to begin;
But at sixteen the conscience rarely gnaws
So much as when we call our old debts in
At sixty years, and draw the accompts of evil,
And find a deuced balance with the devil.

CLXVIII

Of his position I can give no notion:
'T is written in the Hebrew Chronicle,
How the physicians, leaving pill and potion,
Prescribed, by way of blister,[24] a young belle,
When old King David's blood grew dull in motion,
And that the medicine answered very well;
Perhaps 't was in a different way applied,
For David lived, but Juan nearly died.

[21] Gap. [22] Space.
[23] *Clarence . . . butt.* In Shakespeare's *Richard III,* I.iv, Richard's brother Clarence is drowned in a cask ("butt") of Malmsey wine.
[24] Remedy. This therapy by the beauty Abishag is described in I Kings 1–4.

CLXIX

What's to be done? Alfonso will be back
The moment he has sent his fools away.
Antonia's skill was put upon the rack,
But no device could be brought into play—
And how to parry the renewed attack?
Besides, it wanted but few hours of day:
Antonia puzzled; Julia did not speak,
But pressed her bloodless lip to Juan's cheek.

CLXX

He turned his lip to hers, and with his hand
Called back the tangles of her wandering hair;
Even then their love they could not all command,
And half forgot their danger and despair:
Antonia's patience now was at a stand—
"Come, come, 't is no time now for fooling there,"
She whispered in great wrath—"I must deposit
This pretty gentleman within the closet:

CLXXI

"Pray, keep your nonsense for some luckier night—
Who can have put my master in this mood?
What will become on 't—I'm in such a fright,
The devil's in the urchin, and no good—
Is this a time for giggling? this a plight?
Why, don't you know that it may end in blood?
You'll lose your life, and I shall lose my place,
My mistress all, for that half-girlish face.

CLXXII

"Had it but been for a stout cavalier
Of twenty-five or thirty—(come, make haste)
But for a child, what piece of work is here!
I really, madam, wonder at your taste—
(Come, sir, get in)—my master must be near:
There, for the present, at the least, he's fast,[25]
And if we can but till the morning keep
Our counsel—(Juan, mind, you must not sleep)."

CLXXIII

Now, Don Alfonso entering, but alone,
Closed the oration of the trusty maid:
She loitered, and he told her to be gone,
An order somewhat sullenly obeyed;
However, present remedy was none,
And no great good seemed answered if she staid;

[25] Secure.

Regarding both with slow and sidelong view,
She snuffed the candle, curtsied, and withdrew.

CLXXIV

Alfonso paused a minute—then begun
Some strange excuses for his late proceeding:
He would not justify what he had done,
To say the best, it was extreme ill-breeding;
But there were ample reasons for it, none
Of which he specified in this his pleading:
His speech was a fine sample, on the whole,
Of rhetoric, which the learned call *"rigmarole."*

CLXXV

Julia said nought; though all the while there rose
A ready answer, which at once enables
A matron, who her husband's foible knows,
By a few timely words to turn the tables,
Which, if it does not silence, still must pose,[26]—
Even if it should comprise a pack of fables;
'T is to retort with firmness, and when he
Suspects with *one,* do you reproach with *three.*

CLXXVI

Julia, in fact, had tolerable grounds,—
Alfonso's loves with Inez were well known;
But whether 't was that one's own guilt confounds—
But that can't be, as has been often shown,
A lady with apologies abounds;—
It might be that her silence sprang alone
From delicacy to Don Juan's ear,
To whom she knew his mother's fame was dear.

CLXXVII

There might be one more motive, which makes two;
Alfonso ne'er to Juan had alluded,—
Mentioned his jealousy, but never who
Had been the happy lover, he concluded,
Concealed amongst his premises; 't is true,
His mind the more o'er this its mystery brooded;
To speak of Inez now were, one may say,
Like throwing Juan in Alfonso's way.

CLXXVIII

A hint, in tender cases, is enough;
Silence is best: besides there is a *tact*—
(That modern phrase appears to me sad stuff,

[26] Confuse; make him stop to think.

But it will serve to keep my verse compact)—
Which keeps, when pushed by questions rather rough,
A lady always distant from the fact:
The charming creatures lie with such a grace,
There's nothing so becoming to the face.

CLXXIX

They blush, and we believe them, at least I
Have always done so; 't is of no great use,
In any case, attempting a reply,
For then their eloquence grows quite profuse;
And when at length they're out of breath, they sigh,
And cast their languid eyes down, and let loose
A tear or two, and then we make it up;
And then—and then—and then—sit down and sup.

CLXXX

Alfonso closed his speech, and begged her pardon,
Which Julia half withheld, and then half granted,
And laid conditions he thought very hard on,
Denying several little things he wanted:
He stood like Adam lingering near his garden,
With useless penitence perplexed and haunted,
Beseeching she no further would refuse,
When, lo! he stumbled o'er a pair of shoes.

CLXXXI

A pair of shoes!—what then? not much, if they
Are such as fit with ladies' feet, but these
(No one can tell how much I grieve to say)
Were masculine; to see them, and to seize,
Was but a moment's act.—Ah! well-a-day!
My teeth begin to chatter, my veins freeze—
Alfonso first examined well their fashion,
And then flew out into another passion.

CLXXXII

He left the room for his relinquished sword,
And Julia instant to the closet flew.
"Fly, Juan, fly; for heaven's sake—not a word—
The door is open—you may yet slip through
The passage you so often have explored—
Here is the garden-key—Fly—fly—Adieu!
Haste—haste! I hear Alfonso's hurrying feet—
Day has not broke—there's no one in the street."

CLXXXIII

None can say that this was not good advice,
The only mischief was, it came too late;
Of all experience 't is the usual price,

A sort of income-tax laid on by fate:
Juan had reached the room-door in a trice,
And might have done so by the garden-gate,
But met Alfonso in his dressing-gown,
Who threatened death—so Juan knocked him down.

CLXXXIV

Dire was the scuffle, and out went the light;
Antonia cried out "Rape!" and Julia "Fire!"
But not a servant stirred to aid the fight.
Alfonso, pommelled to his heart's desire,
Swore lustily he'd be revenged this night;
And Juan, too, blasphemed an octave higher;
His blood was up: though young, he was a Tartar,[27]
And not at all disposed to prove a martyr.

CLXXXV

Alfonso's sword had dropped ere he could draw it,
And they continued battling hand to hand,
For Juan very luckily ne'er saw it;
His temper not being under great command,
If at that moment he had chanced to claw it,
Alfonso's days had not been in the land
Much longer.—Think of husbands', lovers' lives!
And how ye may be doubly widows—wives!

CLXXXVI

Alfonso grappled to detain the foe,
And Juan throttled him to get away,
And blood ('t was from the nose) began to flow;
At last, as they more faintly wrestling lay,
Juan contrived to give an awkward blow,
And then his only garment quite gave way;
He fled, like Joseph, leaving it; but there,
I doubt, all likeness ends between the pair.[28]

CLXXXVII

Lights came at length, and men, and maids, who found
An awkward spectacle their eyes before;
Antonia in hysterics, Julia swooned,
Alfonso leaning, breathless, by the door;
Some half-torn drapery scattered on the ground,
Some blood, and several footsteps, but no more:
Juan the gate gained, turned the key about,
And liking not the inside, locked the out.

[27] A violent person (from the fierce warriors of Genghis Khan in the thirteenth century).
[28] *fled . . . pair.* Fleeing from the sexual advances of Potiphar's wife, Joseph left his garment in her hand; she then accused him of making the advances, and he was thrown into prison. Genesis 39:6–20.

CLXXXVIII

Here ends this canto.—Need I sing, or say,
How Juan, naked, favoured by the night,
Who favours what she should not, found his way,
And reached his home in an unseemly plight?
The pleasant scandal which arose next day,
The nine days' wonder which was brought to light,
And how Alfonso sued for a divorce,
Were in the English newspapers, of course.

CLXXXIX

If you would like to see the whole proceedings,
The depositions and the cause at full,
The names of all the witnesses, the pleadings
Of counsel to nonsuit,[29] or to annul,
There's more than one edition, and the readings
Are various, but they none of them are dull;
The best is that in short-hand ta'en by Gurney,[30]
Who to Madrid on purpose made a journey.

CXC

But Donna Inez, to divert the train
Of one of the most circulating scandals
That had for centuries been known in Spain,
At least since the retirement of the Vandals,[31]
First vowed (and never had she vowed in vain)
To Virgin Mary several pounds of candles;
And then, by the advice of some old ladies,
She sent her son to be shipped off from Cadiz.

CXCI

She had resolved that he should travel through
All European climes, by land or sea,
To mend his former morals, and get new,
Especially in France and Italy
(At least this is the thing most people do).
Julia was sent into a convent: she
Grieved, but, perhaps, her feelings may be better
Shown in the following copy of her letter:—

CXCII

"They tell me 't is decided you depart:
'T is wise—'t is well, but not the less a pain;
I have no further claim on your young heart,
Mine is the victim, and would be again:

[29] Dismiss the case.
[30] William Gurney, shorthand reporter for the British Parliament and for several trials involving British nobility and royalty.
[31] A destructive people who committed rape and pillage in Spain in the fifth century A.D.

To love too much has been the only art
I used;—I write in haste, and if a stain
Be on this sheet, 't is not what it appears;
My eyeballs burn and throb, but have no tears.

CXCIII

"I loved, I love you, for this love have lost
State, station, heaven, mankind's, my own esteem,
And yet cannot regret what it hath cost,
So dear is still the memory of that dream;
Yet, if I name my guilt, 't is not to boast,
None can deem harshlier of me than I deem:[32]
I trace this scrawl because I cannot rest—
I've nothing to reproach or to request.

CXCIV

"Man's love is of man's life a thing apart,
'T is woman's whole existence; man may range
The court, camp, church, the vessel, and the mart;
Sword, gown, gain, glory, offer in exchange
Pride, fame, ambition, to fill up his heart,
And few there are whom these cannot estrange;
Men have all these resources, we but one,
To love again, and be again undone.

CXCV

"You will proceed in pleasure, and in pride,
Beloved and loving many; all is o'er
For me on earth, except some years to hide
My shame and sorrow deep in my heart's core:
These I could bear, but cannot cast aside
The passion which still rages as before,—
And so farewell—forgive me, love me—No,
That word is idle now—but let it go.

CXCVI

"My breast has been all weakness, is so yet;
But still I think I can collect my mind;
My blood still rushes where my spirit's set,
As roll the waves before the settled wind;
My heart is feminine, nor can forget—
To all, except one image, madly blind;
So shakes the needle,[33] and so stands the pole,
As vibrates my fond heart to my fixed soul.

CXCVII

"I have no more to say, but linger still,
And dare not set my seal upon this sheet,

[32] Judge. [33] Compass needle.

And yet I may as well the task fulfil,
My misery can scarce be more complete:
I had not lived till now, could sorrow kill;
Death shuns the wretch who fain the blow would meet,
And I must even survive this last adieu,
And bear with life to love and pray for you!"

CXCVIII

This note was written upon gilt-edged paper
With a neat little crow-quill, slight and new;
Her small white hand could hardly reach the taper,[34]
It trembled as magnetic needles do,
And yet she did not let one tear escape her:
The seal a sun-flower; *"Elle vous suit partout,"*[35]
The motto, cut upon a white cornelian;[36]
The wax was superfine, its hue vermilion.

CXCIX

This was Don Juan's earliest scrape; but whether
I shall proceed with his adventures is
Dependent on the public altogether;
We'll see, however, what they say to this;
Their favour in an author's cap's a feather,
And no great mischief's done by their caprice;
And if their approbation we experience,
Perhaps they'll have some more about a year hence.

CC

My poem's epic,[37] and is meant to be
Divided in twelve books; each book containing,
With love, and war, a heavy gale at sea,
A list of ships, and captains, and kings reigning,
New characters; the episodes are three:
A panoramic view of hell's in training
After the style of Virgil and of Homer,
So that my name of Epic's no misnomer.

CCI

All these things will be specified in time,
With strict regard to Aristotle's rules,
The *Vade Mecum*[38] of the true sublime,

[34] Candle for melting the sealing-wax.

[35] French for "It (the sunflower) follows you (the sun) everywhere," with a pun on "*She* follows."

[36] A jewel-stone.

[37] Stanzas CC-CCII are an elaborate serious parody of the standard elements in classical epic, critical theories of it (including the debate over rhyme vs. blank verse that Milton airs in his headnote to *Paradise Lost*), and the standard epic poet's boast to have achieved a higher level of truth than his predecessors in the genre.

[38] Latin for "handbook."

Which makes so many poets, and some fools:
Prose poets like blank-verse, I'm fond of rhyme,
Good workmen never quarrel with their tools;
I've got new mythological machinery,[39]
And very handsome supernatural scenery.

CCII

There's only one slight difference between
Me and my epic brethren gone before,
And here the advantage is my own, I ween[40]
(Not that I have not several merits more,
But this will more peculiarly be seen);
They so embellish, that 't is quite a bore
Their labyrinth of fables to thread through,
Whereas this story's actually true.

CCIII

If any person doubt it, I appeal
To history, tradition, and to facts,
To newspapers, whose truth all know and feel,
To plays in five, and operas in three acts:
All these confirm my statement a good deal,
But that which more completely faith exacts
Is, that myself, and several now in Seville,
Saw Juan's last elopement with the devil.[41]

CCIV

If ever I should condescend to prose,
I'll write poetical commandments, which
Shall supersede beyond all doubt all those
That went before; in these I shall enrich
My text with many things that no one knows,
And carry precept to the highest pitch:
I'll call the work "Longinus o'er a Bottle,
Or, Every Poet his *own* Aristotle."

CCV

Thou shalt believe[42] in Milton, Dryden, Pope;
Thou shalt not set up Wordsworth, Coleridge, Southey;
Because the first is crazed beyond all hope,
The second drunk, the third so quaint and mouthy:
With Crabbe it may be difficult to cope,

[39] The term in critical theory for the divinities who intervene in the human action.
[40] Think. [41] *Saw . . . devil.* Byron probably means a theatrical performance.
[42] *Thou shalt believe, etc.* As Byron foresaw, this parody of the Ten Commandments seemed outrageously blasphemous to some readers. His praise of Milton and the neoclassical poets Pope and Dryden at the expense of his Romantic contemporaries, which is typical of his poetic conservatism, is intensified by his linking of the Lake poets, whom he detested, even with modern poets whom he admired, including George Crabbe, Thomas Campbell, Samuel Rogers, and Thomas Moore.

And Campbell's Hippocrene is somewhat drouthy:[43]
Thou shalt not steal from Samuel Rogers, nor
Commit—flirtation with the muse of Moore.

CCVI

Thou shalt not covet Mr. Sotheby's Muse,
His Pegasus,[44] nor anything that's his;
Thou shalt not bear false witness like "the Blues"[45]—
(There's *one,* at least, is very fond of this);
Thou shalt not write, in short, but what I choose;
This is true criticism, and you may kiss—
Exactly as you please, or not,—the rod;
And if you don't, I'll lay it on, by G—d!

CCVII

If any person should presume to assert
This story is not moral, first, I pray,
That they will not cry out before they're hurt,
Then that they'll read it o'er again, and say
(But, doubtless, nobody will be so pert),
That this is not a moral tale, though gay;
Besides, in Canto Twelfth,[46] I mean to show
The very place where wicked people go.

CCVIII

If, after all, there should be some so blind
To their own good this warning to despise,
Led by some tortuosity of mind,
Not to believe my verse and their own eyes,
And cry that they "the moral cannot find,"
I tell him, if a clergyman, he lies;
Should captains the remark, or critics, make,
They also lie too—under a mistake.[47]

CCIX

The public approbation I expect,
And beg they'll take my word about the moral,
Which I with their amusement will connect
(So children cutting teeth receive a coral);
Meantime they'll doubtless please to recollect
My epical pretensions to the laurel:

[43] *Hippocrene . . . drouthy.* The fountain of poetic inspiration (in mythology) is dry.

[44] Winged horse that opened the fountain of Hippocrene with a blow of its hoof. William Sotheby was a poet and translator whom Byron disliked.

[45] "Bluestockings," or intellectual women; the "one" in the next line is Byron's wife.

[46] One of many conflicting statements Byron made about the planned length of *Don Juan,* which in fact he spun out indefinitely, completing more than sixteen cantos before his death arbitrarily ended the poem.

[47] Byron jestingly adds this saving phrase because such men, unlike clergymen, would fight duels if called liars literally.

For fear some prudish readers should grow skittish,
I've bribed my grandmother's review—the British.[48]

CCX

I sent it in a letter to the Editor,
Who thanked me duly by return of post—
I'm for a handsome article[49] his creditor;
Yet, if my gentle Muse he please to roast,
And break a promise after having made it her,
Denying the receipt of what it cost,
And smear his page with gall instead of honey,
All I can say is—that he had the money.

CCXI

I think that with this holy *new*[50] alliance
I may ensure the public, and defy
All other magazines of art or science,
Daily, or monthly, or three monthly; I
Have not essayed to multiply their clients,
Because they tell me 't were in vain to try,
And that the Edinburgh Review and Quarterly[51]
Treat a dissenting author very martyrly.

CCXII

"Non ego hoc ferrem calida juventâ
Consule Planco,"[52] Horace said, and so
Say I; by which quotation there is meant a
Hint that some six or seven good years ago
(Long ere I dreamt of dating from the Brenta[53])
I was most ready to return a blow,
And would not brook at all this sort of thing
In my hot youth—when George the Third was King.

CCXIII

But now at thirty years my hair is gray—
(I wonder what it will be like at forty?
I thought of a peruke[54] the other day—)
My heart is not much greener; and, in short, I
Have squandered my whole summer while 't was May,

[48] A journal hostile to Byron on moral grounds. The editor later played into Byron's hands by taking seriously the present joke about bribing him.

[49] Review of the poem.

[50] As opposed to the so-called Holy Alliance formed in 1815 between Russia, Austria, and Prussia to suppress democracy after the Revolutionary and Napoleonic periods. The moralistic *British Review* was also "holy."

[51] Two of the most powerful journals of Byron's time.

[52] *"Non . . . Planco."* "I would not have put up with this in my hot youth, when Plancus was consul"—Horace, *Odes,* III.14.

[53] *Long . . . Brenta.* When I was in England and not, as now, dating my letters from Venice (near the Brenta river).

[54] Wig.

And feel no more the spirit to retort; I
Have spent my life, both interest and principal,
And deem not, what I deemed, my soul invincible.

CCXIV

No more—no more—Oh! never more on me
The freshness of the heart can fall like dew,
Which out of all the lovely things we see
Extracts emotions beautiful and new,
Hived in our bosoms like the bag o' the bee.
Think'st thou the honey with those objects grew?
Alas! 't was not in them, but in thy power
To double even the sweetness of a flower.

CCXV

No more—no more—Oh! never more, my heart,
Canst thou be my sole world, my universe!
Once all in all, but now a thing apart,
Thou canst not be my blessing or my curse:
The illusion's gone for ever, and thou art
Insensible, I trust, but none the worse,
And in thy stead I've got a deal of judgment,
Though heaven knows how it ever found a lodgment.

CCXVI

My days of love are over; me no more
The charms of maid, wife, and still less of widow,
Can make the fool of which they made before,—
In short, I must not lead the life I did do;
The credulous hope of mutual minds is o'er,
The copious use of claret is forbid too,[55]
So for a good old-gentlemanly vice,
I think I must take up with avarice.

CCXVII

Ambition was my idol, which was broken
Before the shrines of Sorrow, and of Pleasure;
And the two last have left me many a token
O'er which reflection may be made at leisure;
Now, like Friar Bacon's brazen head, I've spoken
"Time is, Time was, Time's past":[56]—a chymic[57] treasure
Is glittering youth, which I have spent betimes—
My heart in passion, and my head on rhymes.

CCXVIII

What is the end of fame? 't is but to fill
A certain portion of uncertain paper:

[55] *Lines 1721–1726.* Loosely paraphrased from Horace, *Odes,* IV.i.
[56] *"Time . . . past."* Spoken by a magic brass head in Robert Greene (1558–1592), *Friar Bacon and Friar Bungay,* scene xi.
[57] Transforming, as with alchemy.

Some liken it to climbing up a hill,
Whose summit, like all hills, is lost in vapour;
For this men write, speak, preach, and heroes kill,
And bards burn what they call their "midnight taper,"
To have, when the original is dust,
A name, a wretched picture, and worse bust.

CCXIX

What are the hopes of man? Old Egypt's King
Cheops erected the first pyramid
And largest, thinking it was just the thing
To keep his memory whole, and mummy hid:
But somebody or other rummaging,
Burglariously broke his coffin's lid:
Let not a monument give you or me hopes,
Since not a pinch of dust remains of Cheops.[58]

CCXX

But I, being fond of true philosophy,
Say very often to myself, "Alas!
All things that have been born were born to die,
And flesh (which Death mows down to hay) is grass;
You've passed your youth not so unpleasantly,
And if you had it o'er again—'t would pass—
So thank your stars that matters are no worse,
And read your Bible, sir, and mind your purse."

CCXXI

But for the present, gentle reader! and
Still gentler purchaser! the bard—that's I—
Must, with permission, shake you by the hand,
And so your humble servant, and good-bye!
We meet again, if we should understand
Each other; and if not, I shall not try
Your patience further than by this short sample—
'T were well if others followed my example.

CCXXII

"Go, little book, from this my solitude!
I cast thee on the waters—go thy ways!
And if, as I believe, thy vein be good,
The world will find thee after many days."
When Southey's read, and Wordsworth understood,
I can't help putting in my claim to praise—
The four first rhymes are Southey's,[59] every line:
For God's sake, reader! take them not for mine!

[58] It had recently been discovered that the body of Cheops (c. 2900–2877 B.C.) was missing from the burial chamber in the Great Pyramid.

[59] From his Epilogue to *The Lay of the Laureate*.

from CANTO THE SECOND

XVIII

"Farewell,[1] my Spain! a long farewell!" he cried,
"Perhaps I may revisit thee no more,
But die, as many an exiled heart hath died,
Of its own thirst to see again thy shore:
Farewell, where Guadalquivir's waters glide!
Farewell, my mother! and, since all is o'er
Farewell, too, dearest Julia!—(here he drew
Her letter out again, and read it through.)

XIX

"And oh! if e'er I should forget, I swear—
But that's impossible, and cannot be—
Sooner shall this blue ocean melt to air,
Sooner shall earth resolve itself to sea,
Than I resign thine image, oh, my fair!
Or think of anything, excepting thee;
A mind diseased no remedy can physic—
(Here the ship gave a lurch, and he grew sea-sick.)

XX

"Sooner shall heaven kiss earth—(here he fell sicker)
Oh Julia! what is every other woe?—
(For God's sake let me have a glass of liquor;
Pedro, Battista,[2] help me down below.)
Julia, my love!—(you rascal, Pedro, quicker)—
Oh, Julia!—(this curst vessel pitches so)—
Belovéd Julia, hear me still beseeching!"
(Here he grew inarticulate with retching.)

XXI

He felt that chilling heaviness of heart,
Or rather stomach, which, alas! attends,
Beyond the best apothecary's[3] art,
The loss of love, the treachery of friends,
Or death of those we dote on, when a part
Of us dies with them as each fond hope ends:
No doubt he would have been much more pathetic,
But the sea acted as a strong emetic.

XXII

Love's a capricious power: I've known it hold
Out through a fever caused by its own heat,

[1] *"Farewell," etc.* Because of the scandal arising from his affair with Julia, Juan is sent abroad. The Julia story ends and her tender letter is presented from a very different perspective in this brief passage from Canto II. Juan's ship is sailing from the harbor of Cadiz, a port near Gibraltar.

[2] Juan's servants. [3] Pharmacist.

But be much puzzled by a cough and cold,
And find a quinsy[4] very hard to treat;
Against all noble maladies he's bold,
But vulgar illnesses don't like to meet,
Nor that a sneeze should interrupt his sigh,
Nor inflammation redden his blind eye.

[4] Inflammation of the tonsils.

John Keats

(1795–1821)

The world could ill spare Adonais, *Percy Bysshe Shelley's great funeral elegy for John Keats, but it could easily spare the myth that sprang from the poem and long persisted among its readers: that Keats was a hypersensitively vulnerable flower nipped in its early bud by a cold world personified in a hostile literary critic. That picturesque image is a sad one, but the truth about Keats is different and infinitely sadder. The blows life dealt him were less airily abstract and until near the end of his short life were borne bravely, almost uncomplainingly, by a young man with guts and a tough mind, not to mention a thoroughly engaging, vital personality. Posterity's loss is almost equally painful to contemplate. Had disease and then death not cut short his career at the height of his powers, he almost certainly would have reached even greater heights, for, like certain other great artists who died young—including Mozart, Schubert, and Shelley himself—he was driven by a dynamic of experiment and growth. It is hard to imagine him outliving his genius as, say, Wordsworth did.*

Keats was born in London in 1795. His mother's father owned a livery stable that Keats's father eventually took over. The latter was killed in an accident when John was not quite nine, the first of a series of deaths in the family that would shadow the poet's life. His mother remarried some two months later and then separated from her second husband. Keats and his three younger siblings lived with their grandmother for much of this unsettled time, and Keats had to learn early the role of surrogate parent, especially after his mother died of tuberculosis, which ran in the family, when he was fourteen. One finds in Keats's mature personality a combination of dependence on others and self-reliance shaped by these early years.

Keats went to a good school and was a good student, but he showed no precocious talent for, or even deep interest in, literature. He was more conspicuous for getting into fights; one of his schoolmates recalled years later that Keats seemed cut out more for a military career than for poetry. At sixteen he began a four-year apprenticeship as a "surgeon," a term that in Keats's day described a kind of skilled paramedic, after which he spent a year in training at Guy's Hospital. This medical background—in the days before anesthesia—is significant, showing that the unparalleled concrete sensuousness of his later poetry was grounded in an intimate knowledge of the brute facts of pain.

In the meantime, Keats had been converted (in the strongest sense of the word) to poetry, largely through the influence of Charles Cowden Clarke, his schoolmaster's son. Keats soon abandoned his medical prospects. His first enthusiasm was Spenser, whose Faerie Queene *made a striking impact on him. Spenser (whose stanza Keats later used in* The Eve of St. Agnes*) pointed the young poet toward romance, a genre that, whether indulged for its own sake or as a vehicle of serious themes, took Keats's imagination into exotic settings far removed in time and place from familiar scenes. This side of Keats persisted through his last poetry, but increasingly it came into conflict with a sterner ambition to face and explore poetically the harsher side of life, the side most people (however simplistically) call "reality." He half-foresaw, half-willed this progression in himself in his early "Sleep and Poetry." The thirst for sternness he came to associate with epic rather than romance. The polarity was to take many other forms for Keats in his never-ceasing attempt to see life in its wholeness: the value of thought versus feeling; philosophy versus art (including poetry); active striving versus passive, open receptivity; waking versus sleep; humanity versus deity; earth versus the sky.*

Spenser was also the first of a line of poets Keats learned from over the next five years, quickly bleeding them white, one after another, of everything he felt he could assimilate to himself from their minds and styles. One early, and unfortunate, model was Leigh Hunt, a prominent man of letters who in 1816 made a protégé of Keats, introduced him to a public circle of writers and artists (including Shelley), and instilled in the impressionable young poet the stylistic principles of an undiscriminating reaction against Pope and the other neoclassicists. The result in Keats's early poems was the substitution for eighteenth-century aphoristic tightness of a limp, simpering softness that helped conceal his real promise and did his reputation no good at the time. The worst excesses of this style emerge in Keats's first published volume, the Poems *of 1817. They reappear in his next published work, the long romance* Endymion *(1818) about the love of a mortal for the goddess of the moon, where they mar an ambitious and interesting work that, in its tension between the demands of earthly life and aspiration to the heavens, foreshadows the greater poetry to come. One dwells on these shortcomings in a novice poet only because they illustrate tendencies he later turned to good account. The "luxuries" he loved to dwell on in his early poems would be transformed into the powerful symbols of rich imaginative experience in the great odes, and his early fumblings with new-coined words and the romance mode were the matrix from which emerged the magical language and atmosphere of* The Eve of St. Agnes.

The bad reception his work got from influential literary journals (inspired partly by opposition to Hunt's leftist politics and social snobbery that contemptuously relegated Keats to a "Cockney" school of poetry) did not devastate Keats as legend was to assert but rather confirmed in part his own dissatisfaction with his poetry and turned him toward models he could profit from. Shakespeare (especially as interpreted in the lectures of William Hazlitt) had already begun to teach Keats the value of the poet's selfless impersonality and empathy with his creations; from the other direction, Wordsworth had made him see the possibilities of making high poetry from inner, subjective experience. This dialectic, over the next year or two, would coalesce with influences from Milton, for his Latinate grandeur of tone and the serious universality of his public themes; Dryden, for his lithe, energetic versification; and Dante, for his directness of diction and image and his allegorical sure-footedness.

The growth in Keats's poetic powers was also shaped by two key events in his private life. One was the death, in December 1818, of his younger brother Tom (again, from tuberculosis). In nursing him over the last months of his life, Keats sharpened his awareness of pain and death in the most vivid way possible while also learning to appreciate by contrast the beauty of life, its claims all the more urgent for its perishability. A similar clash of feelings arose from his love for Fanny Brawne, a young woman Keats met some time in 1818 and became engaged to late in 1819. His consuming love for her was dashed with intense anxieties and insecurities about their relationship. The paradoxical feelings generated by these experiences of death and love, blending with other paradoxes that had always obsessed Keats and with his rapidly developed craftsmanship, gave birth to a miraculous year. Between September 1818 and September 1819 Keats produced the Miltonic epic fragment Hyperion; The Eve of St. Agnes; *the five great odes on Psyche, the nightingale, the Grecian urn, melancholy, and autumn;* Lamia; The Fall of Hyperion *(a more personal reworking of his epic); and such great lyrics as "La Belle Dame Sans Merci" and the sonnet "To Sleep." No poet ever produced a richer variety of great poems in twelve months. Most of these poems appeared in Keats's third volume,* Lamia, Isabella, The Eve of St. Agnes, and Other Poems, *published in 1820.*

But that marked the end. Early in 1820 the symptoms of tuberculosis had become unmistakable, and the last year of Keats's life makes an almost unbearable story. Suffering agonies not only over his approaching death in itself but also over the loss of Fanny and the failure, as he thought, of his poetic ambitions, Keats left England in September 1820, on money his friends had raised, and sailed for Italy, where it was hoped the climate would help him. It did not. Nursed by a friend, the young painter Joseph Severn, Keats lingered on for a few months in pain, then died in Rome in February 1821, at the age of twenty-five, and was buried there. The mood of his last days is captured in the epitaph he devised for himself: "Here lies one whose name was writ in water."

Keats's development can be seen in cameo form by comparing the sonnets "On First Looking into Chapman's Homer" (1816), his first really fine poem, and "To Sleep" (1819). Apart from their themes, which illustrate respectively the exuberance of Keats's love of poetry and his heavily freighted recurring symbol of sleep, the two poems reflect opposite strategies. "Chapman's Homer" is the work of a young poet at play, a tour de force that cleverly separates the sustained image of geographical exploration from the exploration of literature it allegorizes. The geographical metaphor can stand on its own, and our pleasure in the poem comes partly from solving a puzzle by matching its details, one by one, with what they stand for. "To Sleep" typifies the way in which Keats, three years later, had learned to interfuse *meaning and metaphor, the hymn to sleep and its image of death blending inseparably and mysteriously to produce an effect both morbid and, somehow, sensuously vital.*

The Eve of St. Agnes *illustrates most of Keats's characteristic themes and techniques. Its movement is like that of many poems by Keats, which in time, space, or intensity of emotion penetrate and then withdraw, or rise and then descend, or move from* now *to* then *back to* now. *Its imagery is typically Keatsian in exploiting not only the Wordsworthian "mighty world of eye and ear" but also the earthier senses—smell, taste, touch—that depend on physical contact. Thematically, the gorgeousness of the love story and of the cozy but fragile shelteredness of the lovers from a world of danger and death reflects Keats's recurrent concern with "luxury" versus pain. It also examines, not discursively but in the symbolic and dramatic manner of Keats at his best, the validity of imaginative experience, asking in effect whether or not dreams come true, and if so how and with what result.*

This testing of imagination is also the theme of the great odes, which have been called the "essence"—idea, distillation, and perfume—of Romanticism. They cap the Romantic tradition of "crisis" lyric that includes Wordsworth's "Tintern Abbey" and "Intimations" ode and Coleridge's "Dejection." Keats's odes, like the others, are compressed dramas in which the self confronts the threats to it, from the world and from within. They image a state of ecstatic bliss and at the same time the perils of achieving or even aspiring to it. If bliss is by definition free from the threat of change, under what conditions, if at all, can it exist in a world where change seems to be the only certainty? On the other hand, can anything really be called happiness that does not *change, grow, even die? One way to appreciate Keats is to compare the abstractions in those last two sentences with the concreteness of the odes. Keats creates symbols—the nightingale, the urn, and the others—of almost inexhaustible implications, rendered in words whose meanings seem to open like doors, revealing an endless series of other doors. We approach the core of the poems as we approach a limit in calculus, always getting closer but never quite reaching it. At the same time, Keats wholly engages our senses as always, often in a peculiarly kinesthetic way typical of him, balancing motion against frozen stillness so that we feel an almost literal muscular tension, as if we were the figures on the Grecian urn.*

Like some other poets (and unlike some), Keats had both intelligence and imagination. Perhaps what makes him unique is his almost unparalleled honesty. This was part of his personal character, as we learn from his matchless letters, many of which rival the poems by combining opalescent brilliance with rich suggestiveness, but always with an eye to what is really true, about the world and the author himself. Both the letters and the poems are full of tensions and contradictions, showing a man willing to entertain almost all possibilities but finally endorsing no axiom until, in his own words, it has "been proved on the pulses" of both mind and heart. In the odes especially, he shows the need both to explore and to verify, so that many readers feel they can profitably retrace his steps in exploring for their own forms of truth. Victorian poets like Tennyson learned a great deal from Keats. His kinship with poets—and many other people—of our century is even stronger, if less obvious, providing a model for their own efforts to affirm life in the teeth of doubt.

FURTHER READING *(prepared by B. W.):* The moving story of Keats's brief life is told in Walter Jackson Bate's superb biography *John Keats,* 1963, which also includes sensitive criticism of the poetry. Sophisticated knowledge about Keats is combined with detailed close readings of key poems in Earl Wasserman's *The Finer Tone,* 1953. David Perkins's *The Quest for Permanence,* 1959, approaches Keats's meaning by way of his symbolism, stressing the tension between flux and permanence. The close readings in Stuart Sperry's *Keats the Poet,* 1973, are both searching and cogently argued. *Keats: A Collection of Critical Essays,* ed. Walter Jackson Bate, 1964, includes several important essays, including a highly original and somewhat controversial one by Jack Stillinger on *The Eve of St. Agnes* ("The Hoodwinking of Madeline," included also in his book so named, 1971). Stillinger also is the editor of the collection *Twentieth Century Interpretations of Keats's Odes,* 1968. Harold Bloom, in *The Visionary Company,* rev. ed. 1971, is at his brilliant best in his brief readings of key poems by Keats.

ON FIRST LOOKING INTO CHAPMAN'S HOMER[1]

Much have I travell'd in the realms of gold,
And many goodly states and kingdoms seen;
Round many western islands have I been
Which bards in fealty to Apollo[2] hold.
Oft of one wide expanse had I been told
That deep-brow'd Homer ruled as his demesne;[3]
Yet did I never breathe its pure serene[4]
Till I heard Chapman speak out loud and bold:
Then felt I like some watcher of the skies
When a new planet swims into his ken;[5]
Or like stout Cortez when with eagle eyes
He star'd at the Pacific—and all his men
Look'd at each other with a wild surmise—
Silent, upon a peak in Darien.[6]

THE EVE OF ST. AGNES[1]

I

St. Agnes' Eve—Ah, bitter chill it was!
The owl, for all his feathers, was a-cold;
The hare limped trembling through the frozen grass,
And silent was the flock in woolly fold:
Numb were the beadsman's[2] fingers, while he told[3]
His rosary, and while his frosted breath,
Like pious incense from a censer old,
Seemed taking flight for Heaven, without a death,
Past the sweet Virgin's picture, while his prayer he saith.

II

His prayer he saith, this patient, holy man;
Then takes his lamp, and riseth from his knees,
And back returneth, meagre, barefoot, wan,
Along the chapel aisle by slow degrees:
The sculptured dead on each side seem to freeze,

[1] George Chapman (1559?–1634) published his translations of Homer's *Iliad* and *Odyssey* between 1598 and 1616.

[2] *Bards* are poets. *Fealty* is the allegiance of a feudal underlord to his lord. *Apollo* is the god of poetry.

[3] Domain. [4] Clear sky or air.

[5] View. Uranus was discovered by F. W. (later Sir William) Herschel in 1781; the planets out through Saturn had been known to antiquity.

[6] Panama. The Pacific was actually discovered by Balboa (1475–1517), not by Cortez.

[1] Third-century patron saint of virgins. Her feast day is January 21.

[2] A religious man supported by a family in return for his prayers for them.

[3] Counted.

Imprisoned in black, purgatorial rails:
Knights, ladies, praying in dumb orat'ries,[4]
He passeth by; and his weak spirit fails
To think how they may ache in icy hoods and mails.[5]

III

Northward he turneth through a little door,
And scarce three steps, ere music's golden tongue
Flattered to tears this agéd man and poor;
But no—already had his deathbell rung:
The joys of all his life were said and sung;
His was harsh penance on St. Agnes' Eve:
Another way he went, and soon among
Rough ashes sat he for his soul's reprieve,
And all night kept awake, for sinners' sake to grieve.

IV

That ancient beadsman heard the prelude soft;
And so it chanced, for many a door was wide,
From hurry to and fro. Soon, up aloft,
The silver, snarling trumpets 'gan to chide:[6]
The level chambers, ready with their pride,[7]
Were glowing to receive a thousand guests:
The carvéd angels, ever eager-eyed,
Stared, where upon their heads the cornice[8] rests,
With hair blown back, and wings put crosswise on their breasts.

V

At length burst in the argent revelry,[9]
With plume, tiara, and all rich array,
Numerous as shadows haunting faerily
The brain, new stuffed in youth, with triumphs gay
Of old romance. These let us wish away,
And turn, sole-thoughted, to one lady there,
Whose heart had brooded, all that wintry day,
On love, and winged St. Agnes' saintly care,
As she had heard old dames full many times declare.

VI

They told her how, upon St. Agnes' Eve,
Young virgins might have visions of delight,
And soft adorings from their loves receive
Upon the honeyed middle of the night,
If ceremonies due they did aright;
As, supperless to bed they must retire,
And couch supine their beauties, lily white;

[4] Oratories; side-chapels. [5] Coats of armor. [6] Scold. [7] Gorgeousness.
[8] Horizontal top supported by columns.
[9] Revelers. "Argent" is the term for "silver" in heraldry (the study of coats of arms).

Nor look behind, nor sideways, but require[10]
Of Heaven with upward eyes for all that they desire.

VII

Full of this whim was thoughtful Madeline:
The music, yearning like a god in pain,
She scarcely heard: her maiden eyes divine,
Fixed on the floor, saw many a sweeping train[11]
Pass by—she heeded not at all: in vain
Came many a tiptoe, amorous cavalier,
And back retired; not cooled by high disdain,
But she saw not: her heart was otherwhere:
She sighed for Agnes' dreams, the sweetest of the year.

VIII

She danced along with vague, regardless eyes,
Anxious her lips, her breathing quick and short:
The hallowed hour was near at hand: she sighs
Amid the timbrels,[12] and the thronged resort
Of whisperers in anger, or in sport;
'Mid looks of love, defiance, hate, and scorn,
Hoodwinked with faery fancy; all amort,[13]
Save to St. Agnes and her lambs unshorn,[14]
And all the bliss to be before tomorrow morn.

IX

So, purposing each moment to retire,
She lingered still. Meantime, across the moors,
Had come young Porphyro, with heart on fire
For Madeline. Beside the portal doors,
Buttressed[15] from moonlight, stands he, and implores
All saints to give him sight of Madeline
But for one moment in the tedious hours,
That he might gaze and worship all unseen;
Perchance speak, kneel, touch, kiss—in sooth[16] such things have been.

X

He ventures in: let no buzzed whisper tell:
All eyes be muffled, or a hundred swords
Will storm his heart, love's fev'rous citadel:
For him, those chambers held barbarian hordes,
Hyena foemen, and hot-blooded lords,
Whose very dogs would execrations[17] howl
Against his lineage: not one breast affords

[10] Ask. [11] Of skirts (Keats's explanation). [12] Tambourines.
[13] Equivalent of "dead to the world."
[14] At the "Agnus Dei" ("Lamb of God") prayer in the Mass on St. Agnes' feast day, lambs with virgin wool were presented at the altar. ("Agnes" also derives from "lamb.")
[15] In the shadow of a buttress, a massive stone support for a wall. [16] Truly.
[17] Curses.

Him any mercy, in that mansion foul,
Save one old beldame,[18] weak in body and in soul.

XI

Ah, happy chance! the agéd creature came,
Shuffling along with ivory-headed wand,
To where he stood, hid from the torch's flame,
Behind a broad hall-pillar, far beyond
The sound of merriment and chorus bland:
He startled her; but soon she knew his face,
And grasped his fingers in her palsied hand,
Saying, "Mercy, Porphyro! hie thee from this place:
They are all here to-night, the whole blood-thirsty race!

XII

"Get hence! get hence! there's dwarfish Hildebrand;
He had a fever late, and in the fit
He curséd thee and thine, both house and land:
Then there's that old Lord Maurice, not a whit
More tame for his gray hairs—Alas me! flit!
Flit like a ghost away."—"Ah, gossip[19] dear,
We're safe enough; here in this arm chair sit,
And tell me how"—"Good saints! not here, not here;
Follow me, child, or else these stones will be thy bier."

XIII

He followed through a lowly archéd way,
Brushing the cobwebs with his lofty plume,
And as she muttered "Well-a—well-a-day!"
He found him in a little moonlight room,
Pale, latticed, chill, and silent as a tomb.
"Now tell me where is Madeline," said he,
"Oh tell me, Angela, by the holy loom
Which none but secret sisterhood[20] may see,
When they St. Agnes' wool are weaving piously."

XIV

"St. Agnes! Ah! it is St. Agnes' Eve—
Yet men will murder upon holy days:
Thou must hold water in a witch's sieve,
And be liege-lord of all the elves and fays,[21]
To venture so: it fills me with amaze
To see thee, Porphyro!—St. Agnes' Eve!
God's help! my lady fair the conjuror[22] plays
This very night: good angels her deceive!
But let me laugh awhile, I've mickle[23] time to grieve."

[18] Old woman. [19] Archaic term for a female crony.
[20] See note to line 71. After the ceremony, nuns spun the wool. [21] Fairies.
[22] Summoner of spirits. [23] Much.

XV

Feebly she laugheth in the languid moon
While Porphyro upon her face doth look,
Like puzzled urchin on an agéd crone
Who keepeth closed a wond'rous riddle-book,
As spectacled she sits in chimney nook.
But soon his eyes grew brilliant, when she told
His lady's purpose; and he scarce could brook[24]
Tears, at the thought of those enchantments cold,
And Madeline asleep in lap of legends old.

XVI

Sudden a thought came like a full-blown[25] rose,
Flushing his brow, and in his painéd heart
Made purple riot: then doth he propose
A stratagem, that makes the beldame start:
"A cruel man and impious thou art:
Sweet lady, let her pray, and sleep, and dream
Alone with her good angels, far apart
From wicked men like thee. Go, go!—I deem
Thou canst not surely be the same that thou didst seem."

XVII

"I will not harm her, by all saints I swear,"
Quoth Porphyro: "O may I ne'er find grace
When my weak voice shall whisper its last prayer,
If one of her soft ringlets I displace,
Or look with ruffian passion in her face:
Good Angela, believe me by these tears;
Or I will, even in a moment's space,
Awake, with horrid shout, my foemen's ears,
And beard them, though they be more fanged than wolves and bears."

XVIII

"Ah! why wilt thou affright a feeble soul?
A poor, weak, palsy-stricken, churchyard thing,
Whose passing-bell[26] may ere the midnight toll;
Whose prayers for thee, each morn and evening,
Were never missed."—Thus plaining,[27] doth she bring
A gentler speech from burning Porphyro;
So woful, and of such deep sorrowing,
That Angela gives promise she will do
Whatever he shall wish, betide her weal or woe.[28]

XIX

Which was, to lead him, in close secrecy,
Even to Madeline's chamber, and there hide

[24] Hold back. [25] Full-blossomed. [26] Bell tolled for the dead. [27] Complaining.
[28] *betide . . . woe.* Whatever happens to her, good or bad.

Him in a closet,[29] of such privacy
That he might see her beauty unespied,
And win perhaps that night a peerless bride,
While legioned faeries paced the coverlet,
And pale enchantment held her sleepy-eyed.
Never on such a night have lovers met,
Since Merlin paid his demon all the monstrous debt.[30]

XX

"It shall be as thou wishest," said the Dame:
"All cates[31] and dainties shall be storéd there
Quickly on this feast-night: by the tambour frame[32]
Her own lute thou wilt see: no time to spare,
For I am slow and feeble, and scarce dare
On such a catering trust my dizzy head.
Wait here, my child, with patience; kneel in prayer
The while: Ah! thou must needs the lady wed,
Or may I never leave my grave among the dead."

XXI

So saying, she hobbled off with busy fear.
The lover's endless minutes slowly passed;
The dame returned, and whispered in his ear
To follow her, with agéd eyes aghast
From fright of dim espial. Safe at last,
Through many a dusky gallery, they gain
The maiden's chamber, silken, hushed, and chaste;
Where Porphyro took covert, pleased amain.[33]
His poor guide hurried back with agues[34] in her brain.

XXII

Her faltering hand upon the balustrade,
Old Angela was feeling for the stair,
When Madeline, St. Agnes' charméd maid,
Rose, like a missioned spirit, unaware:
With silver taper's[35] light, and pious care,
She turned, and down the agéd gossip led
To a safe level matting. Now prepare,
Young Porphyro, for gazing on that bed;
She comes, she comes again, like ring-dove frayed[36] and fled.

XXIII

Out went the taper as she hurried in;
Its little smoke, in pallid moonshine, died:
She closed the door, she panted, all akin

[29] Small room.
[30] *Merlin . . . debt.* Merlin was a magician in the King Arthur legends. The obscure reference to paying a debt may refer to his dying, on a stormy and magic-filled night.
[31] Delicate foods. [32] Embroidery frame. [33] Greatly. [34] Fevers; chills.
[35] Candle's. [36] Frightened.

To spirits of the air, and visions wide:
No uttered syllable, or, woe betide!
But to her heart, her heart was voluble,[37]
Paining with eloquence her balmy side;
As though a tongueless nightingale should swell
Her throat in vain, and die, heart-stifled, in her dell.

XXIV

A casement high and triple-arched there was,
All garlanded with carven imag'ries
Of fruits, and flowers, and bunches of knot-grass,
And diamonded with panes of quaint device,
Innumerable of stains and splendid dyes,
As are the tiger-moth's deep-damasked wings;
And in the midst, 'mong thousand heraldries,
And twilight saints, and dim emblazonings,[38]
A shielded scutcheon blushed with blood of queens and kings.[39]

XXV

Full on this casement shone the wintry moon,
And threw warm gules[40] on Madeline's fair breast,
As down she knelt for heaven's grace and boon;[41]
Rose-bloom fell on her hands, together prest,
And on her silver cross soft amethyst,
And on her hair a glory,[42] like a saint:
She seemed a splendid angel, newly drest,
Save wings, for heaven:—Porphyro grew faint:
She knelt, so pure a thing, so free from mortal taint.

XXVI

Anon his heart revives: her vespers[43] done,
Of all its wreathéd pearls her hair she frees;
Unclasps her warméd jewels one by one;
Loosens her fragrant bodice; by degrees
Her rich attire creeps rustling to her knees:
Half-hidden like a mermaid in sea-weed,
Pensive awhile she dreams awake, and sees,
In fancy, fair St. Agnes in her bed,
But dares not look behind, or all the charm is fled.

XXVII

Soon trembling in her soft and chilly nest,
In sort of wakeful swoon, perplexed she lay,
Until the poppied warmth of sleep oppressed
Her soothéd limbs, and soul fatigued away;
Flown, like a thought, until the morrow day;

[37] Speaking fluently. [38] Ornamentations from heraldry.
[39] *shielded . . . kings.* The description is of a red coat of arms, in the shape of a shield, showing the family's royal connections.
[40] Red (in heraldry). [41] Blessing; favor. [42] Halo. [43] Evening prayers.

Blissfully havened both from joy and pain;
Clasped like a missal where swart Paynims pray;[44]
Blinded alike from sunshine and from rain,
As though a rose should shut, and be a bud again.

XXVIII

Stolen to this paradise, and so entranced,
Porphyro gazed upon her empty dress,
And listened to her breathing, if it chanced
To wake into a slumberous tenderness;
Which when he heard, that minute did he bless,
And breathed himself: then from the closet crept,
Noiseless as fear in a wide wilderness,
And over the hushed carpet, silent stept,
And 'tween the curtains peeped, where lo!—how fast she slept.

XXIX

Then by the bedside, where the faded moon
Made a dim, silver twilight, soft he set
A table, and, half anguished, threw thereon
A cloth of woven crimson, gold, and jet:—
O for some drowsy Morphean amulet![45]
The boisterous, midnight, festive clarion,[46]
The kettle-drum, and far-heard clarinet,
Affray[47] his ears, though but in dying tone:—
The hall door shuts again, and all the noise is gone.

XXX

And still she slept an azure-lidded sleep,
In blanchéd[48] linen, smooth, and lavendered,
While he from forth the closet brought a heap
Of candied apple, quince, and plum, and gourd;
With jellies soother[49] than the creamy curd,
And lucent syrups, tinct[50] with cinnamon;
Manna and dates, in argosy[51] transferred
From Fez; and spicéd dainties, every one,
From silken Samarcand[52] to cedared Lebanon.

XXXI

These delicates he heaped with glowing hand
On golden dishes and in baskets bright
Of wreathéd silver: sumptuous they stand
In the retiréd quiet of the night,

[44] *Clasped . . . pray.* Either locked with a clasp or grasped protectively, like a Catholic Mass-book in a land of dark-skinned ("swart") pagans.
[45] Charm inducing sleep (from Morpheus, god of sleep).
[46] Trumpet with a piercing sound. [47] Frighten. [48] Bleached.
[49] Smoother. [50] *lucent.* Translucent. *tinct.* Tinctured; containing a touch of.
[51] *Manna.* Delicious fruit. *argosy.* Trading ship.
[52] *Fez, Samarcand.* Cities in, respectively, Morocco and Persia, the latter noted for its silk.

Filling the chilly room with perfume light.—
"And now, my love, my seraph fair, awake!
Thou art my heaven, and I thine eremite:[53]
Open thine eyes for meek St. Agnes' sake,
Or I shall drowse beside thee, so my soul doth ache."

XXXII

Thus whispering, his warm, unnervéd[54] arm
Sank in her pillow. Shaded was her dream
By the dusk curtains:—'twas a midnight charm
Impossible to melt as icéd stream:
The lustrous salvers in the moonlight gleam;
Broad golden fringe upon the carpet lies:
It seemed he never, never could redeem
From such a steadfast spell his lady's eyes;
So mused awhile, entoiled in wooféd phantasies.[55]

XXXIII

Awakening up, he took her hollow lute,—
Tumultuous,—and, in chords that tenderest be,
He played an ancient ditty, long since mute,
In Provence called, "La belle dame sans mercy":[56]
Close to her ear touching the melody;—
Wherewith disturbed, she uttered a soft moan:
He ceased—she panted quick—and suddenly
Her blue affrayéd eyes wide open shone:
Upon his knees he sank, pale as smooth-sculptured stone.

XXXIV

Her eyes were open, but she still beheld,
Now wide awake, the vision of her sleep:
There was a painful change, that nigh expelled
The blisses of her dream so pure and deep;
At which fair Madeline began to weep,
And moan forth witless[57] words with many a sigh;
While still her gaze on Porphyro would keep;
Who knelt, with joinéd hands and piteous eye,
Fearing to move or speak, she looked so dreamingly.

XXXV

"Ah, Porphyro!" said she, "but even now
Thy voice was at sweet tremble in mine ear,
Made tuneable with every sweetest vow;
And those sad eyes were spiritual and clear:
How changed thou art! how pallid, chill, and drear!

[53] Religious hermit. [54] Nerveless; inert.
[55] *entoiled . . . phantasies.* Ensnared in woven fantasies.
[56] *"La belle . . . mercy."* "The beautiful lady without pity." Provence was the land of the troubadour poets, in southern France.
[57] Unwitting; unaware or unintentional.

Give me that voice again, my Porphyro,
Those looks immortal, those complainings dear!
Oh leave me not in this eternal woe,
For if thou diest, my love, I know not where to go."

XXXVI

Beyond a mortal man impassioned far
At these voluptuous accents, he arose,
Ethereal, flushed, and like a throbbing star
Seen mid the sapphire heaven's deep repose;
Into her dream he melted, as the rose
Blendeth its odour with the violet,—
Solution sweet: meantime the frost-wind blows
Like love's alarum[58] pattering the sharp sleet
Against the window-panes; St. Agnes' moon hath set.

XXXVII

'Tis dark: quick pattereth the flaw-blown[59] sleet:
"This is no dream, my bride, my Madeline!"
'Tis dark: the icéd gusts still rave and beat:
"No dream, alas! alas! and woe is mine!
Porphyro will leave me here to fade and pine,—
Cruel! what traitor could thee hither bring?
I curse not, for my heart is lost in thine,
Though thou forsakest a deceivéd thing;—
A dove forlorn and lost with sick unpruned[60] wing."

XXXVIII

"My Madeline! sweet dreamer! lovely bride!
Say, may I be for ay thy vassal[61] blest?
Thy beauty's shield, heart-shaped and vermeil[62] dyed?
Ah, silver shrine, here will I take my rest
After so many hours of toil and quest,
A famished pilgrim,—saved by miracle.
Though I have found, I will not rob thy nest
Saving of thy sweet self; if thou think'st well
To trust, fair Madeline, to no rude infidel.

XXXIX

"Hark! 'tis an elfin-storm from faery land,
Of haggard[63] seeming, but a boon indeed:
Arise—arise! the morning is at hand;—
The bloated wassailers[64] will never heed:—
Let us away, my love, with happy speed;
There are no ears to hear, or eyes to see,—
Drowned all in Rhenish and the sleepy mead:[65]

[58] Warning. [59] Squall-blown. [60] Unpreened; disheveled. [61] Bondman.
[62] Vermilion. [63] Wild. [64] Drunken carousers.
[65] *Rhenish.* Rhine wine. *mead.* Fermented beverage made from honey.

Awake! arise! my love, and fearless be,
For o'er the southern moors I have a home for thee."

XL

She hurried at his words, beset with fears,
For there were sleeping dragons all around,
At glaring watch, perhaps, with ready spears—
Down the wide stairs a darkling way they found.—
In all the house was heard no human sound.
A chain-drooped lamp was flickering by each door;
The arras,[66] rich with horseman, hawk, and hound,
Fluttered in the besieging wind's uproar;
And the long carpets rose along the gusty floor.

XLI

They glide, like phantoms, into the wide hall;
Like phantoms, to the iron porch they glide;
Where lay the porter, in uneasy sprawl,
With a huge empty flagon by his side:
The wakeful bloodhound rose, and shook his hide,
But his sagacious eye an inmate owns:[67]
By one, and one, the bolts full easy slide:—
The chains lie silent on the footworn stones;—
The key turns, and the door upon its hinges groans.

XLII

And they are gone: aye, ages long ago
These lovers fled away into the storm.
That night the Baron dreamt of many a woe,
And all his warrior-guests, with shade and form
Of witch, and demon, and large coffin-worm
Were long be-nightmared. Angela the old
Died palsy-twitched, with meagre face deform;
The beadsman, after thousand aves[68] told,
For ay unsought for slept among his ashes cold.

LA BELLE DAME SANS MERCI[1]

I

O what can ail thee, knight-at-arms,
Alone and palely loitering?
The sedge[2] has withered from the lake,
And no birds sing.

[66] Tapestry. [67] Acknowledges.
[68] Prayers beginning "Hail, Mary," part of the rosary (line 6).
[1] *La Belle . . . Merci.* Keats got the title, which means "The beautiful lady without pity," from a medieval poem by Alain Chartier.
[2] Grasslike plant.

II

O what can ail thee, knight-at-arms,
So haggard and so woe-begone?
The squirrel's granary is full,
And the harvest's done.

III

I see a lily on thy brow,
With anguish moist and fever dew,
And on thy cheek a fading rose
Fast withereth too.

IV

"I met a lady in the meads,[3]
Full beautiful—a faery's child,
Her hair was long, her foot was light,
And her eyes were wild.

V

"I made a garland for her head,
And bracelets too, and fragrant zone;[4]
She looked at me as she did love,
And made sweet moan.

VI

"I set her on my pacing steed,
And nothing else saw all day long,
For sidelong would she bend and sing
A faery's song.

VII

"She found me roots of relish sweet,
And honey wild, and manna dew,[5]
And sure in language strange she said
'I love thee true.'

VIII

"She took me to her elfin grot,[6]
And there she wept and sighed full sore,
And there I shut her wild wild eyes
With kisses four.

IX

"And there she lulléd me asleep,
And there I dreamed—Ah! woe betide!
The latest dream I ever dreamt
On the cold hill side.

[3] Meadows. [4] Belt of flowers. [5] The juice of an exotic fruit. [6] Grotto; cave.

X

"I saw pale kings and princes too,
    Pale warriors, death-pale were they all;
They cried, 'La Belle Dame sans Merci
    Hath thee in thrall!'[7]

XI

"I saw their starved lips in the gloam[8]
    With horrid warning gapéd wide,
And I awoke, and found me here,
    On the cold hill's side.

XII

"And this is why I sojourn here,
    Alone and palely loitering,
Though the sedge is withered from the lake,
    And no birds sing."

TO SLEEP

O soft embalmer of the still midnight,
    Shutting, with careful fingers and benign,
Our gloom-pleas'd eyes, embower'd from the light,
    Enshaded in forgetfulness divine:
O soothest[1] Sleep! if so it please thee, close
    In midst of this thine hymn my willing eyes,
Or wait the "Amen," ere thy poppy throws
    Around my bed its lulling charities.
Then save me, or the passéd day will shine
Upon my pillow, breeding many woes,—
    Save me from curious[2] conscience, that still lords[3]
Its strength for darkness, burrowing like a mole;
    Turn the key deftly in the oiléd wards,[4]
And seal the hushéd casket[5] of my soul.

[7] Bondage. [8] Twilight. [1] Most soothing.

[2] Besides its ordinary meaning, this may have the Latinate sense of scrupulously careful, painstaking. "Conscience" may include its older meaning of consciousness.

[3] Proudly assembles. Some editions have "hoards" instead of "lords."

[4] Ridges inside a lock.

[5] Small box for precious objects. (The meaning "coffin" is an Americanism.)

ODE TO PSYCHE[1]

O Goddess! hear these tuneless numbers, wrung
By sweet enforcement and remembrance dear,
And pardon that thy secrets should be sung
Even into thine own soft-conchéd[2] ear:
Surely I dreamt to-day, or did I see
The wingéd Psyche with awaken'd eyes?
I wander'd in a forest thoughtlessly,
And, on the sudden, fainting with surprise,
Saw two fair creatures, couchéd side by side
In deepest grass, beneath the whisp'ring roof
Of leaves and trembled blossoms, where there ran
A brooklet, scarce espied:
'Mid hush'd, cool-rooted flowers, fragrant-eyed,
Blue, silver-white, and budded Tyrian,[3]
They lay calm-breathing on the bedded grass;
Their arms embracéd, and their pinions[4] too;
Their lips touch'd not, but had not bade adieu,
As if disjoinéd by soft-handed slumber,
And ready still past kisses to outnumber
At tender eye-dawn of aurorean[5] love:
The wingéd boy[6] I knew;
But who wast thou, O happy, happy dove?
His Psyche true!

O latest born and loveliest vision far
Of all Olympus'[7] faded hierarchy!
Fairer than Phoebe's sapphire-region'd star,[8]
Or Vesper,[9] amorous glow-worm of the sky;
Fairer than these, though temple thou hast none,
Nor altar heap'd with flowers;
Nor virgin-choir to make delicious moan
Upon the midnight hours;
No voice, no lute, no pipe, no incense sweet
From chain-swung censer teeming;
No shrine, no grove, no oracle,[10] no heat
Of pale-mouth'd prophet dreaming.

O brightest! though too late for antique vows,
Too, too late for the fond believing lyre,[11]

[1] Goddess of the mind, or soul, described by Keats as a latecomer among the classical deities and therefore never properly worshiped by the ancients. Cupid, or Eros, god of love, fell in love with her.

[2] Like a conch shell, which is spiral-shaped.

[3] Purple (from the dye made in ancient Tyre). [4] Wings.

[5] Awakening (from Aurora, goddess of the dawn). [6] Cupid.

[7] Mountain-home of the classical gods.

[8] *Phoebe's . . . star.* The moon, of which Phoebe (Artemis, Diana) was the virgin goddess.

[9] The evening star; Venus (Aphrodite).

[10] Priest who is the earthly spokesman of the goddess. [11] Harp (of worshipers and of poets).

When holy were the haunted forest boughs,
  Holy the air, the water, and the fire;
Yet even in these days so far retir'd
  From happy pieties, thy lucent fans,[12]
  Fluttering among the faint Olympians,
I see, and sing, by my own eyes inspir'd.
So let me be thy choir, and make a moan
    Upon the midnight hours;
Thy voice, thy lute, thy pipe, thy incense sweet
  From swingéd censer teeming;
Thy shrine, thy grove, thy oracle, thy heat
  Of pale-mouth'd prophet dreaming.

Yes, I will be thy priest, and build a fane[13]
  In some untrodden region of my mind,
Where branchéd thoughts, new grown with pleasant pain,
  Instead of pines shall murmur in the wind:
Far, far around shall those dark-cluster'd trees
  Fledge[14] the wild-ridgéd mountains steep by steep;
And there by zephyrs,[15] streams, and birds, and bees,
  The moss-lain Dryads[16] shall be lull'd to sleep;
And in the midst of this wide quietness
A rosy sanctuary will I dress
With the wreath'd trellis of a working brain,
  With buds, and bells, and stars without a name,
With all the gardener Fancy e'er could feign,
  Who breeding flowers, will never breed the same:
And there shall be for thee all soft delight
  That shadowy thought can win,
A bright torch, and a casement ope at night,
  To let the warm Love[17] in!

ODE TO A NIGHTINGALE

I

My heart aches, and a drowsy numbness pains
  My sense, as though of hemlock[1] I had drunk,
Or emptied some dull opiate to the drains
  One minute past, and Lethe-wards[2] had sunk:
'Tis not through envy of thy happy lot,
  But being too happy in thine happiness,—
    That thou, light-wingéd Dryad[3] of the trees,
      In some melodious plot

[12] Luminous wings. [13] Temple. [14] Fringe.
[15] Soft breezes. [16] Tree-nymphs. [17] Cupid. [1] A poison; usable also as a sedative.
[2] Toward Lethe, in ancient myth the river of forgetfulness in the underworld.
[3] Tree-nymph.

Of beechen green, and shadows numberless,
Singest of summer in full-throated ease.

II

O, for a draught of vintage! that hath been
Cool'd a long age in the deep-delvéd earth,
Tasting of Flora[4] and the country green,
Dance, and Provençal[5] song, and sunburnt mirth!
O for a beaker full of the warm South,
Full of the true, the blushful Hippocrene,[6]
With beaded bubbles winking at the brim,
And purple-stainéd mouth;
That I might drink, and leave the world unseen,
And with thee fade away into the forest dim:

III

Fade far away, dissolve, and quite forget
What thou among the leaves hast never known,
The weariness, the fever, and the fret
Here, where men sit and hear each other groan;
Where palsy shakes a few, sad, last gray hairs,
Where youth grows pale, and spectre-thin, and dies;[7]
Where but to think is to be full of sorrow
And leaden-eyed despairs,
Where Beauty cannot keep her lustrous eyes,
Or new Love pine at them beyond to-morrow.

IV

Away! away! for I will fly to thee,
Not charioted by Bacchus and his pards,[8]
But on the viewless[9] wings of Poesy,
Though the dull brain perplexes and retards:
Already with thee! tender is the night,
And haply[10] the Queen-Moon is on her throne,
Cluster'd around by all her starry Fays;[11]
But here there is no light,
Save what from heaven is with the breezes blown
Through verdurous glooms and winding mossy ways.

V

I cannot see what flowers are at my feet,
Nor what soft incense hangs upon the boughs,
But, in embalméd darkness, guess each sweet

[4] Roman goddess of flowers. [5] Of Provence, in southern France.
[6] In Greek myth, the fountain of poetic inspiration.
[7] *youth . . . dies.* Keats's brother Tom had died in December, 1818, about five months before this poem was written.
[8] *Bacchus . . . pards.* The god of wine and the leopards who drew his chariot.
[9] Invisible; also, unseeing. [10] Perhaps. [11] Fairies.

Wherewith the seasonable month endows
The grass, the thicket, and the fruit-tree wild;
White hawthorn, and the pastoral eglantine;
Fast fading violets cover'd up in leaves;
And mid-May's eldest child,
The coming musk-rose, full of dewy wine,
The murmurous haunt of flies on summer eves.

VI

Darkling[12] I listen; and, for many a time
I have been half in love with easeful Death,
Call'd him soft names in many a muséd rhyme,
To take into the air my quiet breath;
Now more than ever seems it rich to die,
To cease upon the midnight with no pain,
While thou art pouring forth thy soul abroad
In such an ecstasy!
Still wouldst thou sing, and I have ears in vain—
To thy high requiem[13] become a sod.

VII

Thou wast not born for death, immortal Bird!
No hungry generations tread thee down;
The voice I hear this passing night was heard
In ancient days by emperor and clown:[14]
Perhaps the self-same song that found a path
Through the sad heart of Ruth,[15] when, sick for home,
She stood in tears amid the alien corn;
The same that oft-times hath
Charm'd magic casements, opening on the foam
Of perilous seas, in faery lands forlorn.

VIII

Forlorn! the very word is like a bell
To toll me back from thee to my sole self!
Adieu! the fancy cannot cheat so well
As she is fam'd to do, deceiving elf.
Adieu! adieu! thy plaintive anthem fades
Past the near meadows, over the still stream,
Up the hill-side; and now 'tis buried deep
In the next valley-glades:
Was it a vision, or a waking dream?
Fled is that music:—Do I wake or sleep?

[12] In the dark. [13] A high requiem (Mass for the dead) is one with music.
[14] Peasant.
[15] In the Old Testament book of Ruth, chapter 2, Ruth works in the fields while exiled from her homeland. "Corn" means "barley," not what Americans call corn.

ODE ON A GRECIAN URN

I

Thou still unravish'd[1] bride of quietness,
Thou foster-child of silence and slow time,
Sylvan[2] historian, who canst thus express
A flowery tale more sweetly than our rhyme:
What leaf-fring'd legend haunts about thy shape
Of deities or mortals, or of both,
In Tempe or the dales of Arcady?[3]
What men or gods are these? What maidens loth?[4]
What mad pursuit? What struggle to escape?
What pipes and timbrels?[5] What wild ecstasy?

II

Heard melodies are sweet, but those unheard
Are sweeter; therefore, ye soft pipes, play on;
Not to the sensual[6] ear, but, more endear'd,
Pipe to the spirit ditties of no tone:
Fair youth, beneath the trees, thou canst not leave
Thy song, nor ever can those trees be bare;
Bold lover, never, never canst thou kiss,
Though winning near the goal—yet, do not grieve;
She cannot fade, though thou hast not thy bliss,
For ever wilt thou love, and she be fair!

III

Ah, happy, happy boughs! that cannot shed
Your leaves, nor ever bid the spring adieu;
And, happy melodist, unweariéd,
For ever piping songs for ever new:
More happy love! more happy, happy love!
For ever warm and still to be enjoy'd,
For ever panting, and for ever young;
All breathing human passion far above,[7]
That leaves a heart high-sorrowful and cloy'd,
A burning forehead, and a parching tongue.

IV

Who are these coming to the sacrifice?
To what green altar, O mysterious priest,
Lead'st thou that heifer lowing at the skies,
And all her silken flanks with garlands drest?
What little town by river or sea shore,

[1] Virginal. [2] Of forests.
[3] *Tempe, Arcady.* Sites associated with ancient Greek pastoral. Tempe (a valley) was also sacred to Apollo, god of poetry.
[4] Reluctant. [5] Tambourines. [6] Sensory.
[7] *All . . . above.* Normal word order would be "Far above all breathing human passion."

Or mountain-built with peaceful citadel,
Is emptied of this folk, this pious morn?
And, little town, thy streets for evermore
Will silent be; and not a soul to tell
Why thou art desolate, can e'er return.

V

O Attic shape! Fair attitude! with brede[8]
Of marble men and maidens overwrought,[9]
With forest branches and the trodden weed;
Thou, silent form, dost tease us out of thought
As doth eternity: Cold pastoral!
When old age shall this generation waste,
Thou shalt remain, in midst of other woe
Than ours, a friend to man, to whom thou say'st,
"Beauty is truth, truth beauty,"—that is all
Ye know on earth, and all ye need to know.[10]

ODE ON MELANCHOLY

I

No, no, go not to Lethe, neither twist
Wolf's bane, tight-rooted, for its poisonous wine;
Nor suffer thy pale forehead to be kiss'd
By nightshade, ruby grape of Proserpine;
Make not your rosary of yew-berries,
Nor let the beetle, nor the death-moth be
Your mournful Psyche, nor the downy owl[1]
A partner in your sorrow's mysteries;[2]
For shade to shade will come too drowsily,
And drown the wakeful anguish of the soul.

II

But when the melancholy fit shall fall
Sudden from heaven like a weeping cloud,

[8] *Attic.* Greek. *attitude.* Pose (as of an artist's model). *brede.* Embroidery.

[9] Covered with (artistic) work.

[10] *Beauty . . . know.* Possibly the two lines in English poetry most discussed and debated, on the scores of meaning, appropriateness to the poem, and punctuation. Punctuated as here, there is more than one possible answer to the question who is addressing whom, and the possibilities are multiplied if, like many critics and editors, one puts the entire last two lines in quotation marks.

[1] *lines 1-7.* Keats piles up images of gloom and oblivion. Lethe is the river of forgetfulness in the mythological underworld; wolfsbane is a poisonous plant; nightshade is another, with red berries here associated with Proserpine, the queen of the dead; yew-berries are also poisonous; the "beetle" is the Egyptian scarab, buried with the dead; the death moth has markings resembling a skull (and contrasts with the butterfly that often symbolizes Psyche, the living soul); the owl is a nocturnal bird.

[2] Secret rituals of a pagan religious cult.

That fosters the droop-headed flowers all,
  And hides the green hill in an April shroud;
Then glut thy sorrow on a morning rose,
  Or on the rainbow of the salt sand-wave,[3]
    Or on the wealth of globéd peonies;
Or if thy mistress some rich anger shows,
  Emprison her soft hand, and let her rave,
    And feed deep, deep upon her peerless eyes.

III

She dwells with Beauty—Beauty that must die;
  And Joy, whose hand is ever at his lips
Bidding adieu; and aching Pleasure nigh,
  Turning to poison while the bee-mouth sips:
Ay, in the very temple of delight
  Veil'd Melancholy has her sovran[4] shrine,
    Though seen of none save him whose strenuous tongue
  Can burst Joy's grape against his palate fine;
His soul shall taste the sadness of her might,
    And be among her cloudy trophies hung.[5]

TO AUTUMN

I

Season of mists and mellow fruitfulness,
  Close bosom-friend of the maturing sun;
Conspiring with him how to load and bless
  With fruit the vines that round the thatch-eves[1] run;
To bend with apples the moss'd cottage-trees,
  And fill all fruit with ripeness to the core;
    To swell the gourd, and plump the hazel shells
  With a sweet kernel; to set budding more,
And still more, later flowers for the bees,
Until they think warm days will never cease,
    For Summer has o'er-brimm'd their clammy cells.

II

Who hath not seen thee oft amid thy store?[2]
  Sometimes whoever seeks abroad[3] may find
Thee sitting careless on a granary floor,
  Thy hair soft-lifted by the winnowing[4] wind;

[3] *rainbow . . . wave.* Rainbow effects seen in the moisture on beaches.
[4] *sovran.* Supreme. (Apollo, for example, had many lesser temples, but his "sovran" one was at Delphi.)
[5] *among . . . hung.* Trophies, or spoils, of victory were often hung on the walls of ancient temples and thus dedicated to their deities.
[1] Eaves of thatched roofs. [2] Abundance. [3] Outdoors.
[4] Separating grain from chaff by air currents.

Or on a half-reap'd furrow sound asleep,
Drows'd with the fume of poppies, while thy hook
Spares the next swath[5] and all its twinéd flowers:
And sometimes like a gleaner[6] thou dost keep
Steady thy laden head across a brook;
Or by a cyder-press, with patient look,
Thou watchest the last oozings hours by hours.

III

Where are the songs of Spring? Ay, where are they?
Think not of them, thou hast thy music too,—
While barréd clouds bloom the soft-dying day,
And touch the stubble-plains with rosy hue;
Then in a wailful choir the small gnats mourn
Among the river sallows,[7] borne aloft
Or sinking as the light wind lives or dies;
And full-grown lambs loud bleat from hilly bourn;[8]
Hedge-crickets sing; and now with treble soft
The red-breast whistles from a garden-croft;[9]
And gathering swallows twitter in the skies.

[5] Amount of crop cut by one stroke. [6] One who gathers grain the reapers missed. [7] Willow trees. [8] Boundary between fields. [9] Small plot.

Mary Shelley

(1797–1851)

One of the most durable myths of the modern world was born on the evening of June 16, 1816, in a villa on the shore of Lake Léman in Switzerland, when the English poet Lord Byron proposed to his companions that they compete in writing ghost stories. The companions were Percy Bysshe Shelley, his future wife Mary Godwin, Mary's stepsister Claire Clairmont, and an Italian physician named Dr. John William Polidori. Byron began and abandoned a vampire story, Polidori completed a story called "The Vampyre: A Tale" which, later published and then adapted into a play, became the ultimate source of innumerable horror stories and films, and Mary Godwin Shelley wrote Frankenstein, or The Modern Prometheus.

Mary Godwin was born in 1797, the daughter of the anarchist William Godwin and the feminist Mary Wollstonecraft. (See the introduction to Mary Wollstonecraft.) The mother died eleven days after Mary was born; Godwin was remarried four years later to Mary Jane Clairmont, a widow with two children. Mary disliked her stepmother and spent much of her childhood, as she later wrote, in "scribbling" and in "waking dreams." In 1814, when she was seventeen, she met Shelley, then twenty-one, married, the father of one child, and with a pregnant wife. Three months later, they eloped to the Continent, in the company of Mary's stepsister Claire Clairmont. After two months they returned to England, where over a period of fourteen months, Mary gave birth to two children, the first of which died after less than two weeks. In May of 1816, Shelley, Mary, their second baby, named William, and Claire went to Switzerland, the trip on which Frankenstein was begun.

When Shelley and Mary returned to England in September, they faced a series of disasters. In October, Fanny Imlay, Mary's halfsister, committed suicide; Shelley's wife followed her in suicide in December, drowning herself in the Serpentine in Hyde Park, London. Shelley and Mary were married later in December; in March, a court denied them custody of his and Harriet's two children on the grounds of his "atheism" and "immorality." Frankenstein was published a year later; on the same day, the Shelleys sailed for Italy, where they were to remain until Shelley's death by drowning in 1822. Clara, born in 1817, died a few months after they reached Italy; William, born in 1816, died in 1819. Percy Florence Shelley, the only child to survive infancy, was born in November, 1819. Added to these bereavements was Mary's misery over rapidly worsening relations with her husband, based upon his attentions to other women, his indifference to her, and his mercurial moods.

Mary Shelley returned to England with her two-year-old son a year after Shelley's death. She had already written, in addition to Frankenstein, some verse plays, a long story called Mathilda (not published until 1959), and a second novel, Valperga. Now she turned, for financial reasons, to professional writing. In the next few years, she turned out journal articles, short stories, encyclopedia articles, and four more novels: The Last Man (1826), Perkin Warbeck (1830), Lodore (1835), and Falkner (1837). In addition, she devoted herself to the perpetuation of her late husband's memory, preparing an annotated Poetical Works. She also issued a revised edition of the enormously popular Frankenstein in 1831.

Mary Shelley died in London in 1851 and was buried in Bournemouth between the bodies of her father and mother. When her only surviving son, Percy Florence Shelley, died in 1889, he, too, was buried there. His father's heart was placed in his coffin; it had been taken from the funeral flames in Italy, and Mary Shelley had preserved it, pressed, according to family legend, in a volume of his poetry.

Frankenstein is an elaborate structure of narratives within narratives. Most of the story is told by Victor Frankenstein himself to Robert Walton, an English explorer who finds him on an ice floe in the Arctic. As a young man in Geneva, Frankenstein has become enthralled with the natural sciences; at the University of Ingolstadt, he has stumbled upon the secret of creating life and has built and animated an eight-foot monster, who has fled soon after his creation. Frankenstein falls ill with a brain fever. He returns to Geneva when he learns that his young brother William has been strangled to death and that a faithful family servant, Justine, has been accused of the crime. The evidence against her is a miniature portrait from William's neck which was found in her pocket. Despite Frankenstein's efforts to save her, Justine is condemned and executed. Hiking over the mountainous landscape, Frankenstein meets the monster, who tells him his story (the narrative reprinted here). The monster tells Frankenstein that he will kill at random if Frankenstein will not make him a mate. If he will, the monster will retire with the mate to the wilds of South America. Frankenstein goes to the Orkney Islands with his best friend Clerval and builds the female monster but destroys it at the last moment. Enraged, the monster, who has followed him, vows that he will take terrible vengeance upon Frankenstein *on his wedding night. He then kills Clerval. Back in Geneva, Frankenstein marries his childhood foster sister and lifelong love Elizabeth, but the monster breaks in and strangles her on the wedding night. Frankenstein, in quest of vengeance, has pursued the monster to the Arctic wastes. Having told his story, the weakened Frankenstein dies in Walton's ship's cabin. The novel ends with a scene between Walton and the monster, who breaks into the cabin. The monster expresses his self-loathing for the evil he has done and vows to kill himself on a funeral pyre. He then vanishes over the icefield.*

It is difficult to arrive at an interpretation of Frankenstein *that can account for its remarkable, nightmarelike suggestiveness. In outline, it sounds like a tragedy of the* hubris *of a scientist who tries to rival God by creating life and is punished by having his creation turn out to be monstrous. And this theme does appear in the book. But the situation is complicated by the fact that the monster is not merely monstrous. As Harold Bloom puts it, "The greatest paradox and most astonishing achievement of Mary Shelley's novel is that the monster is* more human *than his creator." The monster, in his suffering, his longing to be human, even in his lacerating guilt over his own murderous acts, arrests our attention and holds our sympathies in a way that the comparatively pallid and narcissistic Victor Frankenstein never does.*

But the key to Frankenstein *is not in either Frankenstein or the monster individually but in their complex relationship. They form two halves of a single self; in creating the monster Frankenstein has created—or freed—part of himself. Self-absorbed, megalomaniacal, irresponsible, Frankenstein discovers in the monster his own repressed, primitive self, the "Natural Man" within himself, capable of becoming a new Adam or a horrid demon. "I ought to be thy Adam," the monster tells Frankenstein, "but I am rather the fallen angel, whom thou drivest from joy for no misdeed."*

Much of the richness of the novel comes from the monster's account to his creator of his own history. The monster has passed through a foreshortened childhood and adolescence, but he has also retraced the history of the race, discovering the patterns of nature, fire, and eventually language and even writing. With civilization, though, comes self-consciousness and such questions as "Who was I? What was I? Whence did I come? What was my destination?" The gap between the dreams of the unfettered imagination and earthy reality widens each time the monster glimpses his reflection in the water or his shadow in the moonlight. With the disastrous collapse of his secret relationship with his beloved cottagers, he falls prey to powerful contrary impulses toward kindness and human fellowship and toward murderous revenge.

The monster's story can be read as a philosophical exploration of Rousseau's doctrines of the Natural Man, as an allegory of Romantic conceptions of education, and as a reply to Milton's Paradise Lost. *But the image that haunts the memory, beneath the thematic content of the story, is of the profoundly and paradoxically human monster peering longingly through the chinks in his pigsty at the ordinary, loving life of the cottagers, a life from which he is forever exiled.*

FURTHER READING *(prepared by N. K. B.):* For a complete text of *Frankenstein,* see the New American Library edition, 1965, which includes a provocative essay by Harold Bloom. James Rieger's scholarly edition of *Frankenstein,* 1974, compares the 1818 and 1831 texts and includes an introduction and notes. For other fiction by Mary Shelley, see *Mary Shelley: Collected Tales and Stories, With Original Engravings,* ed. by Charles E. Robinson, 1976, which contains twenty-five stories (eight previously unpublished). *The Letters of Mary Shelley,* 2 vols., 1944, and *Mary Shelley's Journal,* 1947, both ed. by Frederick L. Jones, are reliable, nearly complete editions.

R. Glynn Grylls, *Mary Shelley: A Biography,* 1938, is the standard biography and contains commentary on *Frankenstein.* Muriel Spark's *Child of Light: A Reassessment of Mary Shelley,* 1951, is a sympathetic treatment valuable for its thorough discussion of critical approaches to *Frankenstein.* For a briefer synopsis of Mary Shelley's life and work, see Sylva Norman, "Mary Wollstonecraft Shelley," in Kenneth Neill Cameron, ed., *Romantic Rebels: Essays on Shelley and His Circle,* 1973. A short, valuable introduction to the novel is M. A. Goldberg's "Moral and Myth in Mrs. Shelley's *Frankenstein,*" *Keats-Shelley Journal,* 8 (1959), 27–38. Elizabeth Nitchie's *Mary Shelley, Author of Frankenstein,* 1953, is an essential reference work providing intelligent and provocative criticism of Shelley's writings. William Walling, *Mary Shelley,* 1972, includes a biographical sketch, a thorough analysis of *Frankenstein* from a Freudian perspective, and a balanced treatment of the political writings. Martin Tropp, *Mary Shelley's Monster: The Story of Frankenstein,* 1976, analyzes the novel's themes and imagery.

from *FRANKENSTEIN*

THE MONSTER'S STORY

CHAPTER 11

"It is with considerable difficulty that I remember the original era of my being; all the events of that period appear confused and indistinct. A strange multiplicity of sensations seized me, and I saw, felt, heard, and smelt at the same time; and it was, indeed, a long time before I learned to distinguish between the operations of my various senses. By degrees, I remember, a stronger light pressed upon my nerves, so that I was obliged to shut my eyes. Darkness then came over me and troubled me, but hardly had I felt this when, by opening my eyes, as I now suppose, the light poured in upon me again. I walked and, I believe, descended, but I presently found a great alteration in my sensations. Before, dark and opaque bodies had surrounded me, impervious to my touch or sight; but I now found that I could wander on at liberty, with no obstacles which I could not either surmount or avoid. The light became more and more oppressive to me, and the heat wearying me as I walked, I sought a place where I could receive shade. This was the forest near Ingolstadt; and here I lay by the side of a brook resting from my fatigue, until I felt tormented by hunger and thirst. This roused me from my nearly dormant state, and I ate some berries which I found hanging on the trees or lying on the ground. I slaked my thirst at the brook, and then lying down, was overcome by sleep.

"It was dark when I awoke; I felt cold also, and half frightened, as it were, instinctively, finding myself so desolate. Before I had quitted your apartment, on a sensation of cold, I had covered myself with some clothes, but these were insufficient to secure me from the dews of night. I was a poor, helpless, miserable wretch; I knew, and could distinguish, nothing; but feeling pain invade me on all sides, I sat down and wept.

"Soon a gentle light stole over the heavens and gave me a sensation of pleasure. I started up and beheld a radiant form rise from among the trees.[1] I gazed with a kind of wonder. It moved slowly, but it enlightened my path, and I again went out in search of berries. I was still cold when under one of the trees I found a huge cloak, with which I covered myself, and sat down upon the ground. No distinct ideas occupied my mind; all was confused. I felt light, and hunger, and thirst, and darkness; innumerable sounds rang in my ears, and on all sides various scents saluted me; the only object that I could distinguish was the bright moon, and I fixed my eyes on that with pleasure.

"Several changes of day and night passed, and the orb of night had greatly lessened, when I began to distinguish my sensations from each other. I gradually saw plainly the clear stream that supplied me with drink and the trees that shaded me with their foliage. I was delighted when I first discovered that a pleasant sound, which often saluted my ears, proceeded from the throats of the little winged animals who had often intercepted the light from my eyes. I began also to observe, with greater accuracy, the forms that surrounded me and to perceive the boundaries of the radiant roof of light which canopied me. Sometimes I tried to imitate the pleasant songs of the birds but was unable. Sometimes I wished to express my sensations in my own mode, but the uncouth and inarticulate sounds which broke from me frightened me into silence again.

"The moon had disappeared from the night, and again, with a lessened form, showed itself, while I still remained in the forest. My sensations had by this time become distinct, and my mind received every day additional ideas. My eyes became accustomed to the light and to perceive objects in their right forms; I distinguished the insect from the herb, and by degrees, one herb from another. I found that the sparrow uttered none but harsh notes, whilst those of the blackbird and thrush were sweet and enticing.

"One day, when I was oppressed by cold, I found a fire which had been left by some wandering beggars, and was overcome with delight at the warmth I experienced from it. In my joy I thrust my hand into the live embers, but quickly drew it out again with a cry of pain. How strange, I thought, that the same cause should produce such opposite effects! I examined the materials of the fire, and to my joy found it to be composed of wood. I quickly collected some branches, but they were wet and would not burn. I was pained at this and sat still watching the operation of the fire. The wet wood which I had placed near the heat dried and itself became inflamed. I reflected on this, and by touching the various branches, I discovered the cause and busied myself in collecting a great quantity of wood, that I might dry it and have a plentiful supply of fire. When night came on and brought sleep with it, I was in the greatest fear lest my fire should be extinguished. I covered it carefully with dry wood and leaves and placed wet branches upon it; and then, spreading my cloak, I lay on the ground and sank into sleep.

"It was morning when I awoke, and my first care was to visit the fire. I uncovered it, and a gentle breeze quickly fanned it into a flame. I observed this also and contrived a fan of branches, which roused the embers when they were nearly extinguished. When night came again I found, with plea-

[1] The moon (Mary Shelley's note).

sure, that the fire gave light as well as heat and that the discovery of this element was useful to me in my food, for I found some of the offals that the travellers had left had been roasted, and tasted much more savoury than the berries I gathered from the trees. I tried, therefore, to dress my food in the same manner, placing it on the live embers. I found that the berries were spoiled by this operation, and the nuts and roots much improved.

"Food, however, became scarce, and I often spent the whole day searching in vain for a few acorns to assuage the pangs of hunger. When I found this, I resolved to quit the place that I had hitherto inhabited, to seek for one where the few wants I experienced would be more easily satisfied. In this emigration I exceedingly lamented the loss of the fire which I had obtained through accident, and knew not how to reproduce it. I gave several hours to the serious consideration of this difficulty, but I was obliged to relinquish all attempt to supply it, and wrapping myself up in my cloak, I struck across the wood towards the setting sun. I passed three days in these rambles and at length discovered the open country. A great fall of snow had taken place the night before, and the fields were of one uniform white; the appearance was disconsolate, and I found my feet chilled by the cold damp substance that covered the ground.

"It was about seven in the morning, and I longed to obtain food and shelter; at length I perceived a small hut, on a rising ground, which had doubtless been built for the convenience of some shepherd. This was a new sight to me, and I examined the structure with great curiosity. Finding the door open, I entered. An old man sat in it, near a fire, over which he was preparing his breakfast. He turned on hearing a noise, and perceiving me, shrieked loudly, and quitting the hut, ran across the fields with a speed of which his debilitated form hardly appeared capable. His appearance, different from any I had ever before seen, and his flight somewhat surprised me. But I was enchanted by the appearance of the hut; here the snow and rain could not penetrate; the ground was dry; and it presented to me then as exquisite and divine a retreat as Pandemonium appeared to the demons of hell after their sufferings in the lake of fire.[2] I greedily devoured the remnants of the shepherd's breakfast, which consisted of bread, cheese, milk, and wine; the latter, however, I did not like. Then, overcome by fatigue, I lay down among some straw and fell asleep.

"It was noon when I awoke, and allured by the warmth of the sun, which shone brightly on the white ground, I determined to recommence my travels; and, depositing the remains of the peasant's breakfast in a wallet I found, I proceeded across the fields for several hours, until at sunset I arrived at a village. How miraculous did this appear! The huts, the neater cottages, and stately houses engaged my admiration by turns. The vegetables in the gardens, the milk and cheese that I saw placed at the windows of some of the cottages, allured my appetite. One of the best of these I entered, but I had hardly placed my foot within the door before the children shrieked, and one of the women fainted. The whole village was roused; some fled, some attacked me, until, grievously bruised by stones and many other kinds of missile weapons, I escaped to the open country and fearfully

[2] Pandemonium is the palace the demons in *Paradise Lost* build in hell. See *Paradise Lost* I.670–751. The name literally means "All-Demons."

took refuge in a low hovel, quite bare, and making a wretched appearance after the palaces I had beheld in the village. This hovel, however, joined a cottage of a neat and pleasant appearance, but after my late dearly bought experience, I dared not enter it. My place of refuge was constructed of wood, but so low that I could with difficulty sit upright in it. No wood, however, was placed on the earth, which formed the floor, but it was dry; and although the wind entered it by innumerable chinks, I found it an agreeable asylum from the snow and rain.

"Here, then, I retreated and lay down happy to have found a shelter, however miserable, from the inclemency of the season, and still more from the barbarity of man.

"As soon as morning dawned I crept from my kennel, that I might view the adjacent cottage and discover if I could remain in the habitation I had found. It was situated against the back of the cottage and surrounded on the sides which were exposed by a pig sty and a clear pool of water. One part was open, and by that I had crept in; but now I covered every crevice by which I might be perceived with stones and wood, yet in such a manner that I might move them on occasion to pass out; all the light I enjoyed came through the sty, and that was sufficient for me.

"Having thus arranged my dwelling and carpeted it with clean straw, I retired, for I saw the figure of a man at a distance, and I remembered too well my treatment the night before to trust myself in his power. I had first, however, provided for my sustenance for that day by a loaf of coarse bread, which I purloined, and a cup with which I could drink more conveniently than from my hand of the pure water which flowed by my retreat. The floor was a little raised, so that it was kept perfectly dry, and by its vicinity to the chimney of the cottage it was tolerably warm.

"Being thus provided, I resolved to reside in this hovel until something should occur which might alter my determination. It was indeed a paradise compared to the bleak forest, my former residence, the rain-dropping branches, and dank earth. I ate my breakfast with pleasure and was about to remove a plank to procure myself a little water when I heard a step, and looking through a small chink, I beheld a young creature, with a pail on her head, passing before my hovel. The girl was young and of gentle demeanour, unlike what I have since found cottagers and farmhouse servants to be. Yet she was meanly dressed, a coarse blue petticoat and a linen jacket being her only garb; her fair hair was plaited but not adorned: she looked patient yet sad. I lost sight of her, and in about a quarter of an hour she returned bearing the pail, which was now partly filled with milk. As she walked along, seemingly incommoded by the burden, a young man met her, whose countenance expressed a deeper despondence. Uttering a few sounds with an air of melancholy, he took the pail from her head and bore it to the cottage himself. She followed, and they disappeared. Presently I saw the young man again, with some tools in his hand, cross the field behind the cottage; and the girl was also busied, sometimes in the house and sometimes in the yard.

"On examining my dwelling, I found that one of the windows of the cottage had formerly occupied a part of it, but the panes had been filled up with wood. In one of these was a small and almost imperceptible chink through which the eye could just penetrate. Through this crevice a small room was visible, whitewashed and clean but very bare of furniture. In one corner, near a small fire, sat an old man, leaning his head on his hands in a disconsolate attitude. The young girl was occupied in arranging the cottage; but presently she took something out of a drawer, which employed her hands, and she sat down beside the old man, who, taking up an instrument, began to play and to produce sounds sweeter than the voice of the thrush or the nightingale. It was a lovely sight, even to me, poor wretch who had never beheld aught beautiful before. The silver hair and benevolent countenance of the aged cottager won my reverence, while the gentle manners of the girl enticed my love. He played a sweet mournful air which I perceived drew tears from the eyes of his amiable companion, of which the old man took no notice, until she sobbed audibly; he then pronounced a few sounds, and the fair creature, leaving her work, knelt at his feet. He raised her and smiled with such kindness and affection that I felt sensations of a peculiar and overpowering nature; they were a mixture of pain and pleasure, such as I had never before experienced, either from hunger or cold, warmth or food; and I withdrew from the window, unable to bear these emotions.

"Soon after this the young man returned, bearing on his shoulders a load of wood. The girl met him at the door, helped to relieve him of his burden, and taking some of the fuel into the cottage, placed it on the fire; then she and the youth went apart into a nook of the cottage, and he showed her a large loaf and a piece of cheese. She seemed pleased and went into the garden for some roots and plants, which she placed in water, and then upon the fire. She afterwards continued her work, whilst the young man went into the garden and appeared busily employed in digging and pulling up roots. After he had been employed thus about an hour, the young woman joined him and they entered the cottage together.

"The old man had, in the meantime, been pensive, but on the appearance of his companions he assumed a more cheerful air, and they sat down to eat. The meal was quickly dispatched. The young woman was again occupied in arranging the cottage, the old man walked before the cottage in the sun for a few minutes, leaning on the arm of the youth. Nothing could exceed in beauty the contrast between these two excellent creatures. One was old, with silver hairs and a countenance beaming with benevolence and love; the younger was slight and graceful in his figure, and his features were moulded with the finest symmetry, yet his eyes and attitude expressed the utmost sadness and despondency. The old man returned to the cottage, and the youth, with tools different from those he had used in the morning, directed his steps across the fields.

"Night quickly shut in, but to my extreme wonder, I found that the cottagers had a means of prolonging light by the use of tapers, and was delighted to find that the setting of the sun did not put an end to the pleasure I experienced in watching my human neighbours. In the evening the young girl and her companion were employed in various occupations which I did not understand; and the old man again took up the instrument which produced the divine sounds that had enchanted me in the morning. So soon as he had finished, the youth began, not to play, but to utter sounds that were monotonous, and neither resembling the harmony of the old man's instrument nor the songs of the birds: I since found that he read aloud, but at that time I knew nothing of the science of words or letters.

"The family, after having been thus occupied for a short time, extinguished their lights and retired, as I conjectured, to rest."

CHAPTER 12

"I lay on my straw, but I could not sleep. I thought of the occurrences of the day. What chiefly struck me was the gentle manners of these people, and I longed to join them, but dared not. I remembered too well the treatment I had suffered the night before from the barbarous villagers, and resolved, whatever course of conduct I might hereafter think it right to pursue, that for the present I would remain quietly in my hovel, watching and endeavouring to discover the motives which influenced their actions.

"The cottagers arose the next morning before the sun. The young woman arranged the cottage and prepared the food, and the youth departed after the first meal.

"This day was passed in the same routine as that which preceded it. The young man was constantly employed out of doors, and the girl in various laborious occupations within. The old man, whom I soon perceived to be blind, employed his leisure hours on his instrument or in contemplation. Nothing could exceed the love and respect which the younger cottagers exhibited towards their venerable companion. They performed towards him every little office of affection and duty with gentleness, and he rewarded them by his benevolent smiles.

"They were not entirely happy. The young man and his companion often went apart and appeared to weep. I saw no cause for their unhappiness, but I was deeply affected by it. If such lovely creatures were miserable, it was less strange that I, an imperfect and solitary being, should be wretched. Yet why were these gentle beings unhappy? They possessed a delightful house (for such it was in my eyes) and every luxury; they had a fire to warm them when chill and delicious viands when hungry; they were dressed in excellent clothes; and, still more, they enjoyed one another's company and speech, interchanging each day looks of affection and kindness. What did their tears imply? Did they really express pain? I was at first unable to solve these questions, but perpetual attention and time explained to me many appearances which were at first enigmatic.

"A considerable period elapsed before I discovered one of the causes of the uneasiness of this amiable family: it was poverty, and they suffered that evil in a very distressing degree. Their nourishment consisted entirely of the vegetables of their garden and the milk of one cow, which gave very little during the winter, when its masters could scarcely procure food to support it. They often, I believe, suffered the pangs of hunger very poignantly, especially the two younger cottagers, for several times they placed food before the old man when they reserved none for themselves.

"This trait of kindness moved me sensibly. I had been accustomed, during the night, to steal a part of their store for my own consumption, but when I found that in doing this I inflicted pain on the cottagers, I abstained and satisfied myself with berries, nuts, and roots which I gathered from a neighbouring wood.

"I discovered also another means through which I was enabled to assist their labours. I found that the youth spent a great part of each day in collecting wood for the family fire, and during the night I often took his tools, the use of which I quickly discovered, and brought home firing sufficient for the consumption of several days.

"I remember, the first time that I did this, the young woman, when she opened the door in the morning, appeared greatly astonished on seeing a great pile of wood on the outside. She uttered some words in a loud voice, and the youth joined her, who also expressed surprise. I observed, with pleasure, that he did not go to the forest that day, but spent it in repairing the cottage and cultivating the garden.

"By degrees I made a discovery of still greater moment. I found that these people possessed a method of communicating their experience and feelings to one another by articulate sounds. I perceived that the words they spoke sometimes produced pleasure or pain, smiles or sadness, in the minds and countenances of the hearers. This was indeed a godlike science, and I ardently desired to become acquainted with it. But I was baffled in every attempt I made for this purpose. Their pronunciation was quick, and the words they uttered, not having any apparent connection with visible objects, I was unable to discover any clue by which I could unravel the mystery of their reference. By great application, however, and after having remained during the space of several revolutions of the moon in my hovel, I discovered the names that were given to some of the most familiar objects of discourse; I learned and applied the words 'fire,' 'milk,' 'bread,' and 'wood.' I learned also the names of the cottagers themselves. The youth and his companion had each of them several names, but the old man had only one, which was 'father.' The girl was called 'sister' or 'Agatha,' and the youth 'Felix,' 'brother,' or 'son.' I cannot describe the delight I felt when I learned the ideas appropriated to each of these sounds and was able to pronounce them. I distinguished several other words without being able as yet to understand or apply them, such as 'good,' 'dearest,' 'unhappy.'

"I spent the winter in this manner. The gentle manners and beauty of the cottagers greatly endeared them to me; when they were unhappy, I felt depressed; when they rejoiced, I sympathized in their joys. I saw few human beings besides them, and if any other happened to enter the cottage, their harsh manners and rude gait only enhanced to me the superior accomplishments of my friends. The old man, I could perceive, often endeavoured to encourage his children, as sometimes I found that he called them, to cast off their melancholy. He would talk in a cheerful accent, with an expression of goodness that bestowed pleasure even upon me. Agatha listened with respect, her eyes sometimes filled with tears, which she endeavoured to wipe away unperceived; but I generally found that her countenance and tone were more cheerful after having listened to the exhortations of her father. It was not thus with Felix. He was always the saddest of the group, and even to my unpractised senses, he appeared to have suffered more deeply than his friends. But if his countenance was more sorrowful, his voice was more cheerful than that of his sister, especially when he addressed the old man.

"I could mention innumerable instances which, although slight, marked the dispositions of these amiable cottagers. In the midst of poverty and want, Felix carried with pleasure to his sister the first little white flower that peeped out from beneath the snowy ground. Early in the morning, before she had risen, he cleared away the snow that obstructed her path to the milk-house, drew water from the well, and brought the wood from the out-house, where, to his perpetual astonishment, he found his store always replenished by an invisible hand. In the day, I believe, he worked sometimes for a neighbouring farmer, because he often went forth and did not return until dinner, yet brought no wood with him. At other times he worked in the garden, but as there was little to do in the frosty season, he read to the old man and Agatha.

"This reading had puzzled me extremely at first, but by degrees I discovered that he uttered many of the same sounds when he read as when he talked. I conjectured, therefore, that he found in the paper signs for speech which he understood, and I ardently longed to comprehend these also; but how was that possible when I did not even understand the sounds for which they stood as signs? I improved, however, sensibly in this science, but not sufficiently to follow up any kind of conversation, although I applied my whole mind to the endeavour, for I easily perceived that, although I eagerly longed to discover myself to the cottagers, I ought not to make the attempt until I had first become master of their language, which knowledge might enable me to make them overlook the deformity of my figure, for with this also the contrast perpetually presented to my eyes had made me acquainted.

"I had admired the perfect forms of my cottagers—their grace, beauty, and delicate complexions; but how was I terrified when I viewed myself in a transparent pool! At first I started back, unable to believe that it was indeed I who was reflected in the mirror; and when I became fully convinced that I was in reality the monster that I am, I was filled with the bitterest sensations of despondence and mortification. Alas! I did not yet entirely know the fatal effects of this miserable deformity.

"As the sun became warmer and the light of day longer, the snow vanished, and I beheld the bare trees and the black earth. From this time Felix was more employed, and the heart-moving indications of impending famine disappeared. Their food, as I afterwards found, was coarse, but it was wholesome; and they procured a sufficiency of it. Several new kinds of plants sprang up in the garden, which they dressed; and these signs of comfort increased daily as the season advanced.

"The old man, leaning on his son, walked each day at noon, when it did not rain, as I found it was called when the heavens poured forth its waters. This frequently took place, but a high wind quickly dried the earth, and the season became far more pleasant than it had been.

"My mode of life in my hovel was uniform. During the morning I attended the motions of the cottagers, and when they were dispersed in various occupations, I slept; the remainder of the day was spent in observing my friends. When they had retired to rest, if there was any moon or the night was star-light, I went into the woods and collected my own food and fuel for the cottage. When I returned, as often as it was necessary, I cleared their path from the snow and performed those offices that I had seen done by Felix. I afterwards found that these labours, performed by an invisible hand, greatly astonished them; and once or twice I heard them, on these occasions, utter the words 'good spirit,' 'wonderful'; but I did not then understand the signification of these terms.

"My thoughts now became more active, and I longed to discover the motives and feelings of these lovely creatures; I was inquisitive to know why Felix appeared so miserable and Agatha so sad. I thought (foolish wretch!) that it might be in my power to restore happiness to these deserving people. When I slept or was absent, the forms of the venerable blind father, the gentle Agatha, and the excellent Felix flitted before me. I looked upon them as superior beings who would be the arbiters of my future destiny. I formed in my imagination a thousand pictures of presenting myself to them, and their reception of me. I imagined that they would be disgusted, until, by my gentle demeanour and conciliating words, I should first win their favour and afterwards their love.

"These thoughts exhilarated me and led me to apply with fresh ardour to the acquiring the art of language. My organs were indeed harsh, but supple; and although my voice was very unlike the soft music of their tones, yet I pronounced such words as I understood with tolerable ease. It was as the ass and the lap-dog; yet surely the gentle ass whose intentions were affectionate, although his manners were rude, deserved better treatment than blows and execration.[3]

"The pleasant showers and genial warmth of spring greatly altered the aspect of the earth. Men who before this change seemed to have been hid in caves dispersed themselves and were employed in various arts of cultivation. The birds sang in more cheerful notes, and the leaves began to bud forth on the trees. Happy, happy earth! Fit habitation for gods, which, so short a time before, was bleak, damp, and unwholesome. My spirits were elevated by the enchanting appearance of nature; the past was blotted from my memory, the present was tranquil, and the future gilded by bright rays of hope and anticipations of joy."

CHAPTER 13

"I now hasten to the more moving part of my story. I shall relate events that impressed me with feelings which, from what I had been, have made me what I am.

"Spring advanced rapidly; the weather became fine and the skies cloudless. It surprised me that what before was desert and gloomy should now bloom with the most beautiful flowers and verdure. My senses were gratified and refreshed by a thousand scents of delight and a thousand sights of beauty.

"It was on one of these days, when my cottagers periodically rested from labour—the old man played on his guitar, and the children listened to him—that I observed the countenance of Felix was melancholy beyond expression; he sighed frequently, and once his father paused in his music, and I conjectured by his manner that he inquired the cause of his son's sorrow. Felix replied in a cheerful accent, and the old man was recommencing his music when someone tapped at the door.

[3] The story of the ass who tried to behave like a lap-dog is told by La Fontaine (*Fables* IV.5).

"It was a lady on horseback, accompanied by a countryman as a guide. The lady was dressed in a dark suit and covered with a thick black veil. Agatha asked a question, to which the stranger only replied by pronouncing, in a sweet accent, the name of Felix. Her voice was musical but unlike that of either of my friends. On hearing this word, Felix came up hastily to the lady, who, when she saw him, threw up her veil, and I beheld a countenance of angelic beauty and expression. Her hair of a shining raven black, and curiously braided; her eyes were dark, but gentle, although animated; her features of a regular proportion, and her complexion wondrously fair, each cheek tinged with a lovely pink.

"Felix seemed ravished with delight when he saw her, every trait of sorrow vanished from his face, and it instantly expressed a degree of ecstatic joy, of which I could hardly have believed it capable; his eyes sparkled, as his cheek flushed with pleasure; and at that moment I thought him as beautiful as the stranger. She appeared affected by different feelings; wiping a few tears from her lovely eyes, she held out her hand to Felix, who kissed it rapturously and called her, as well as I could distinguish, his sweet Arabian. She did not appear to understand him, but smiled. He assisted her to dismount, and dismissing her guide, conducted her into the cottage. Some conversation took place between him and his father, and the young stranger knelt at the old man's feet and would have kissed his hand, but he raised her and embraced her affectionately.

"I soon perceived that although the stranger uttered articulate sounds and appeared to have a language of her own, she was neither understood by nor herself understood the cottagers. They made many signs which I did not comprehend, but I saw that her presence diffused gladness through the cottage, dispelling their sorrow as the sun dissipates the morning mists. Felix seemed peculiarly happy and with smiles of delight welcomed his Arabian. Agatha, the ever-gentle Agatha, kissed the hands of the lovely stranger, and pointing to her brother, made signs which appeared to me to mean that he had been sorrowful until she came. Some hours passed thus, while they, by their countenances, expressed joy, the cause of which I did not comprehend. Presently I found, by the frequent recurrence of some sound which the stranger repeated after them, that she was endeavouring to learn their language; and the idea instantly occurred to me that I should make use of the same instructions to the same end. The stranger learned about twenty words at the first lesson; most of them, indeed, were those which I had before understood, but I profited by the others.

"As night came on Agatha and the Arabian retired early. When they separated Felix kissed the hand of the stranger and said, 'Good night, sweet Safie.' He sat up much longer, conversing with his father, and by the frequent repetition of her name I conjectured that their lovely guest was the subject of their conversation. I ardently desired to understand them, and bent every faculty towards that purpose, but found it utterly impossible.

"The next morning Felix went out to his work, and after the usual occupations of Agatha were finished, the Arabian sat at the feet of the old man, and taking his guitar, played some airs so entrancingly beautiful that they at once drew tears of sorrow and delight from my eyes. She sang, and her voice flowed in a rich cadence, swelling or dying away like a nightingale of the woods.

"When she had finished, she gave the guitar to Agatha, who at first declined it. She played a simple air, and her voice accompanied it in sweet accents, but unlike the wondrous strain of the stranger. The old man appeared enraptured and said some words which Agatha endeavoured to explain to Safie, and by which he appeared to wish to express that she bestowed on him the greatest delight by her music.

"The days now passed as peaceably as before, with the sole alteration that joy had taken place of sadness in the countenances of my friends. Safie was always gay and happy; she and I improved rapidly in the knowledge of language, so that in two months I began to comprehend most of the words uttered by my protectors.

"In the meanwhile also the black ground was covered with herbage, and the green banks interspersed with innumerable flowers, sweet to the scent and the eyes, stars of pale radiance among the moonlight woods; the sun became warmer, the nights clear and balmy; and my nocturnal rambles were an extreme pleasure to me, although they were considerably shortened by the late setting and early rising of the sun, for I never ventured abroad during daylight, fearful of meeting with the same treatment I had formerly endured in the first village which I entered.

"My days were spent in close attention, that I might more speedily master the language; and I may boast that I improved more rapidly than the Arabian, who understood very little and conversed in broken accents, whilst I comprehended and could imitate almost every word that was spoken.

"While I improved in speech, I also learned the science of letters as it was taught to the stranger, and this opened before me a wide field for wonder and delight.

"The book from which Felix instructed Safie was Volney's *Ruins of Empires*.[4] I should not have understood the purport of this book had not Felix, in reading it, given very minute explanations. He had chosen this work, he said, because the declamatory style was framed in imitation of the Eastern authors. Through this work I obtained a cursory knowledge of history and a view of the several empires at present existing in the world; it gave me an insight into the manners, governments, and religions of the different nations of the earth. I heard of the slothful Asiatics, of the stupendous genius and mental activity of the Grecians, of the wars and wonderful virtue of the early Romans—of their subsequent degenerating—of the decline of that mighty empire, of chivalry, Christianity, and kings. I heard of the discovery of the American hemisphere and wept with Safie over the hapless fate of its original inhabitants.

"These wonderful narrations inspired me with strange feelings. Was man, indeed, at once so powerful, so virtuous, and magnificent, yet so vicious and base? He appeared at one time a mere scion of the evil principle and at another as all that can be conceived of noble and godlike. To be a great and virtuous man appeared the highest honour that can befall a sensitive being; to be base and vicious, as many on record have been, appeared the lowest degradation, a condition more abject than that of the

[4] *The Ruins, or Meditations upon the Revolutions of Empires* (1791), by Constantine François Chasseboeuf, Count of Volney, was a popular historical work of the day.

blind mole or harmless worm. For a long time I could not conceive how one man could go forth to murder his fellow, or even why there were laws and governments; but when I heard details of vice and bloodshed, my wonder ceased and I turned away with disgust and loathing.

"Every conversation of the cottagers now opened new wonders to me. While I listened to the instructions which Felix bestowed upon the Arabian, the strange system of human society was explained to me. I heard of the division of property, of immense wealth and squalid poverty, of rank, descent, and noble blood.

"The words induced me to turn towards myself. I learned that the possessions most esteemed by your fellow creatures were high and unsullied descent united with riches. A man might be respected with only one of these advantages, but without either he was considered, except in very rare instances, as a vagabond and a slave, doomed to waste his powers for the profits of the chosen few! And what was I? Of my creation and creator I was absolutely ignorant, but I knew that I possessed no money, no friends, no kind of property. I was, besides, endued with a figure hideously deformed and loathsome; I was not even of the same nature as man. I was more agile than they and could subsist upon coarser diet; I bore the extremes of heat and cold with less injury to my frame; my stature far exceeded theirs. When I looked around I saw and heard of none like me. Was I, then, a monster, a blot upon the earth, from which all men fled and whom all men disowned?

"I cannot describe to you the agony that these reflections inflicted upon me; I tried to dispel them, but sorrow only increased with knowledge. Oh, that I had forever remained in my native wood, nor known nor felt beyond the sensations of hunger, thirst, and heat!

"Of what a strange nature is knowledge! It clings to the mind when it has once seized on it like a lichen on the rock. I wished sometimes to shake off all thought and feeling, but I learned that there was but one means to overcome the sensation of pain, and that was death—a state which I feared yet did not understand. I admired virtue and good feelings and loved the gentle manners and amiable qualities of my cottagers, but I was shut out from intercourse with them, except through means which I obtained by stealth, when I was unseen and unknown, and which rather increased than satisfied the desire I had of becoming one among my fellows. The gentle words of Agatha and the animated smiles of the charming Arabian were not for me. The mild exhortations of the old man and the lively conversation of the loved Felix were not for me. Miserable, unhappy wretch!

"Other lessons were impressed upon me even more deeply. I heard of the difference of sexes, and the birth and growth of children, how the father doted on the smiles of the infant, and the lively sallies of the older child, how all the life and cares of the mother were wrapped up in the precious charge, how the mind of youth expanded and gained knowledge, of brother, sister, and all the various relationships which bind one human being to another in mutual bonds.

"But where were my friends and relations? No father had watched my infant days, no mother had blessed me with smiles and caresses; or if they had, all my past life was now a blot, a blind vacancy in which I distinguished nothing. From my earliest remembrance I had been as I then was in height and proportion. I had never yet seen a being resembling me or who claimed any intercourse with me. What was I? The question again recurred, to be answered only with groans.

"I will soon explain to what these feelings tended, but allow me now to return to the cottagers, whose story excited in me such various feelings of indignation, delight, and wonder, but which all terminated in additional love and reverence for my protectors (for so I loved, in an innocent, half-painful self-deceit, to call them)."

CHAPTER 14

"Some time elapsed before I learned the history of my friends. It was one which could not fail to impress itself deeply on my mind, unfolding as it did a number of circumstances, each interesting and wonderful to one so utterly inexperienced as I was.

"The name of the old man was De Lacey. He was descended from a good family in France, where he had lived for many years in affluence, respected by his superiors and beloved by his equals. His son was bred in the service of his country, and Agatha had ranked with ladies of the highest distinction. A few months before my arrival they had lived in a large and luxurious city called Paris, surrounded by friends and possessed of every enjoyment which virtue, refinement of intellect, or taste, accompanied by a moderate fortune, could afford.

"The father of Safie had been the cause of their ruin. He was a Turkish merchant and had inhabited Paris for many years, when, for some reason which I could not learn, he became obnoxious to the government. He was seized and cast into prison the very day that Safie arrived from Constantinople to join him. He was tried and condemned to death. The injustice of his sentence was very flagrant; all Paris was indignant; and it was judged that his religion and wealth rather than the crime alleged against him had been the cause of his condemnation.

"Felix had accidentally been present at the trial; his horror and indignation were uncontrollable when he heard the decision of the court. He made, at that moment, a solemn vow to deliver him and then looked around for the means. After many fruitless attempts to gain admittance to the prison, he found a strongly grated window in an unguarded part of the building, which lighted the dungeon of the unfortunate Muhammadan, who, loaded with chains, waited in despair the execution of the barbarous sentence. Felix visited the grate at night and made known to the prisoner his intentions in his favour. The Turk, amazed and delighted, endeavoured to kindle the zeal of his deliverer by promises of reward and wealth. Felix rejected his offers with contempt, yet when he saw the lovely Safie, who was allowed to visit her father and who by her gestures expressed her lively gratitude, the youth could not help owning to his own mind that the captive possessed a treasure which would fully reward his toil and hazard.

"The Turk quickly perceived the impression that his daughter had made on the heart of Felix and endeavoured to secure him more entirely in his interests by the promise of her hand in marriage so soon as he should be conveyed to a place of safety. Felix was too delicate to accept this offer, yet he looked forward to the probability of the event as to the consummation of his happiness.

"During the ensuing days, while the preparations were going forward for the escape of the merchant, the zeal of Felix was warmed by several letters that he received from this lovely girl, who found means to express her thoughts in the language of her lover by the aid of an old man, a servant of her father who understood French. She thanked him in the most ardent terms for his intended services towards her parent, and at the same time she gently deplored her own fate.

"I have copies of these letters, for I found means, during my residence in the hovel, to procure the implements of writing; and the letters were often in the hands of Felix or Agatha. Before I depart I will give them to you; they will prove the truth of my tale; but at present, as the sun is already far declined, I shall only have time to repeat the substance of them to you.

"Safie related that her mother was a Christian Arab, seized and made a slave by the Turks; recommended by her beauty, she had won the heart of the father of Safie, who married her. The young girl spoke in high and enthusiastic terms of her mother, who, born in freedom, spurned the bondage to which she was now reduced. She instructed her daughter in the tenets of her religion and taught her to aspire to higher powers of intellect and an independence of spirit forbidden to the female followers of Muhammad. This lady died, but her lessons were indelibly impressed on the mind of Safie, who sickened at the prospect of again returning to Asia and being immured within the walls of a harem, allowed only to occupy herself with infantile amusements, ill-suited to the temper of her soul, now accustomed to grand ideas and a noble emulation for virtue. The prospect of marrying a Christian and remaining in a country where women were allowed to take a rank in society was enchanting to her.

"The day for the execution of the Turk was fixed, but on the night previous to it he quitted his prison and before morning was distant many leagues from Paris. Felix had procured passports in the name of his father, sister, and himself. He had previously communicated his plan to the former, who aided the deceit by quitting his house, under the pretence of a journey, and concealed himself, with his daughter, in an obscure part of Paris.

"Felix conducted the fugitives through France to Lyons and across Mont Cenis to Leghorn, where the merchant had decided to wait a favourable opportunity of passing into some part of the Turkish dominions.

"Safie resolved to remain with her father until the moment of his departure, before which time the Turk renewed his promise that she should be united to his deliverer; and Felix remained with them in expectation of that event; and in the meantime he enjoyed the society of the Arabian, who exhibited towards him the simplest and tenderest affection. They conversed with one another through the means of an interpreter, and sometimes with the interpretation of looks; and Safie sang to him the divine airs of her native country.

"The Turk allowed this intimacy to take place and encouraged the hopes of the youthful lovers, while in his heart he had formed far other plans. He loathed the idea that his daughter should be united to a Christian, but he feared the resentment of Felix if he should appear lukewarm, for he knew that he was still in the power of his deliverer if he should choose to betray him to the Italian state which they inhabited. He revolved a thousand plans by which he should be enabled to prolong the deceit until it might be no longer necessary, and secretly to take his daughter with him when he departed. His plans were facilitated by the news which arrived from Paris.

"The government of France were greatly enraged at the escape of their victim and spared no pains to detect and punish his deliverer. The plot of Felix was quickly discovered, and De Lacey and Agatha were thrown into prison. The news reached Felix and roused him from his dream of pleasure. His blind and aged father and his gentle sister lay in a noisome dungeon while he enjoyed the free air and the society of her whom he loved. This idea was torture to him. He quickly arranged with the Turk that if the latter should find a favourable opportunity for escape before Felix could return to Italy, Safie should remain as a boarder at a convent at Leghorn; and then, quitting the lovely Arabian, he hastened to Paris and delivered himself up to the vengeance of the law, hoping to free De Lacey and Agatha by this proceeding.

"He did not succeed. They remained confined for five months before the trial took place, the result of which deprived them of their fortune and condemned them to a perpetual exile from their native country.

"They found a miserable asylum in the cottage in Germany, where I discovered them. Felix soon learned that the treacherous Turk, for whom he and his family endured such unheard-of oppression, on discovering that his deliverer was thus reduced to poverty and ruin, became a traitor to good feeling and honour and had quitted Italy with his daughter, insultingly sending Felix a pittance of money to aid him, as he said, in some plan of future maintenance.

"Such were the events that preyed on the heart of Felix and rendered him, when I first saw him, the most miserable of his family. He could have endured poverty, and while this distress had been the meed of his virtue, he gloried in it; but the ingratitude of the Turk and the loss of his beloved Safie were misfortunes more bitter and irreparable. The arrival of the Arabian now infused new life into his soul.

"When the news reached Leghorn that Felix was deprived of his wealth and rank, the merchant commanded his daughter to think no more of her lover, but to prepare to return to her native country. The generous nature of Safie was outraged by this command; she attempted to expostulate with her father, but he left her angrily, reiterating his tyrannical mandate.

"A few days after, the Turk entered his daughter's apartment and told her hastily that he had reason to believe that his residence at Leghorn had been divulged and that he should speedily be delivered up to the French government; he had consequently hired a vessel to convey him to Constantinople, for which city he should sail in a few hours. He intended to leave his daughter under the care of a confidential servant, to follow at her leisure with the greater part of his property, which had not yet arrived at Leghorn.

"When alone, Safie resolved in her own mind the plan of conduct that it would become her to pursue in this emergency. A residence in Turkey was abhorrent to her; her religion and her feelings were alike averse to it. By some papers of her father which fell into her hands she heard of the exile of her lover and learnt the name of the spot where he then resided. She hesitated some time, but at length she formed her determination. Taking with her some jewels that belonged to her and a sum of money, she quitted Italy with an attendant, a native of Leghorn, but who understood the common language of Turkey, and departed for Germany.

"She arrived in safety at a town about twenty leagues from the cottage of De Lacey, when her attendant fell dangerously ill. Safie nursed her with the most devoted affection, but the poor girl died, and the Arabian was left alone, unacquainted with the language of the country and utterly ignorant of the customs of the world. She fell, however, into good hands. The Italian had mentioned the name of the spot for which they were bound, and after her death the woman of the house in which they had lived took care that Safie should arrive in safety at the cottage of her lover."

CHAPTER 15

"Such was the history of my beloved cottagers. It impressed me deeply. I learned, from the views of social life which it developed, to admire their virtues and to deprecate the vices of mankind.

"As yet I looked upon crime as a distant evil, benevolence and generosity were ever present before me, inciting within me a desire to become an actor in the busy scene where so many admirable qualities were called forth and displayed. But in giving an account of the progress of my intellect, I must not omit a circumstance which occurred in the beginning of the month of August of the same year.

"One night during my accustomed visit to the neighbouring wood where I collected my own food and brought home firing for my protectors, I found on the ground a leathern portmanteau containing several articles of dress and some books. I eagerly seized the prize and returned with it to my hovel. Fortunately the books were written in the language, the elements of which I had acquired at the cottage; they consisted of *Paradise Lost,* a volume of Plutarch's *Lives,* and the *Sorrows of Werter.*[5] The possession of these treasures gave me extreme delight; I now continually studied and exercised my mind upon these histories, whilst my friends were employed in their ordinary occupations.

"I can hardly describe to you the effect of these books. They produced in me an infinity of new images and feelings, that sometimes raised me to ecstasy, but more frequently sunk me into the lowest dejection. In the *Sorrows of Werter,* besides the interest of its simple and affecting story, so many opinions are canvassed and so many lights thrown upon what had hitherto been to me obscure subjects that I found in it a never-ending source of speculation and astonishment. The gentle and domestic manners it described, combined with lofty sentiments and feelings, which had for their

[5] Plutarch's *Parallel Lives* (first century A.D.) consists of forty-six paired Greek and Roman biographies and four single biographies. Goethe's *Sorrows of Young Werther* (1774; revised 1786) was an enormously popular novel of the period; Werther, lonely and alienated like the monster, broods over his frustrated love for Charlotte and finally shoots himself.

object something out of self, accorded well with my experience among my protectors and with the wants which were forever alive in my own bosom. But I thought Werter himself a more divine being than I had ever beheld or imagined; his character contained no pretension, but it sank deep. The disquisitions upon death and suicide were calculated to fill me with wonder. I did not pretend to enter into the merits of the case, yet I inclined towards the opinions of the hero, whose extinction I wept, without precisely understanding it.

"As I read, however, I applied much personally to my own feelings and condition. I found myself similar yet at the same time strangely unlike to the beings concerning whom I read and to whose conversation I was a listener. I sympathized with and partly understood them, but I was unformed in mind; I was dependent on none and related to none. 'The path of my departure was free,'[6] and there was none to lament my annihilation. My person was hideous and my stature gigantic. What did this mean? Who was I? What was I? Whence did I come? What was my destination? These questions continually recurred, but I was unable to solve them.

"The volume of Plutarch's *Lives* which I possessed contained the histories of the first founders of the ancient republics. This book had a far different effect upon me from the *Sorrows of Werter*. I learned from Werter's imaginations despondency and gloom, but Plutarch taught me high thoughts; he elevated me above the wretched sphere of my own reflections, to admire and love the heroes of past ages. Many things I read surpassed my understanding and experience. I had a very confused knowledge of kingdoms, wide extents of country, mighty rivers, and boundless seas. But I was perfectly unacquainted with towns and large assemblages of men. The cottage of my protectors had been the only school in which I had studied human nature, but this book developed new and mightier scenes of action. I read of men concerned in public affairs, governing or massacring their species. I felt the greatest ardour for virtue rise within me, and abhorrence for vice, as far as I understood the significance of those terms, relative as they were, as I applied them, to pleasure and pain alone. Induced by these feelings, I was of course led to admire peaceable lawgivers, Numa, Solon, and Lycurgus, in preference to Romulus and Theseus.[7] The patriarchal lives of my protectors caused these impressions to take a firm hold on my mind; perhaps, if my first introduction to humanity had been made by a young soldier, burning for glory and slaughter, I should have been imbued with different sensations.

"But *Paradise Lost* excited different and far deeper emotions. I read it, as I had read the other volumes which had fallen into my hands, as a true history. It moved every feeling of wonder and awe that the picture of an omnipotent God warring with his creatures was capable of exciting. I often referred the several situations, as their similarity struck me, to my own. Like Adam, I was apparently united by no link to any other being in existence; but his state was far different from mine in every other respect. He

[6] A line, slightly altered, from Percy Bysshe Shelley's poem "On Mutability."

[7] Numa, Solon, and Lycurgus, traditionally the founders of Rome, Athens, and Sparta, were renowned as peaceful lawgivers. Romulus, with his twin brother Remus another legendary founder of Rome, and the Greek mythological hero Theseus were violent, warlike heroes.

had come forth from the hands of God a perfect creature, happy and prosperous, guarded by the especial care of his Creator; he was allowed to converse with and acquire knowledge from beings of a superior nature, but I was wretched, helpless, and alone. Many times I considered Satan as the fitter emblem of my condition, for often, like him, when I viewed the bliss of my protectors, the bitter gall of envy rose within me.

"Another circumstance strengthened and confirmed these feelings. Soon after my arrival in the hovel I discovered some papers in the pocket of the dress which I had taken from your laboratory. At first I had neglected them, but now that I was able to decipher the characters in which they were written, I began to study them with diligence. It was your journal of the four months that preceded my creation. You minutely described in these papers every step you took in the progress of your work; this history was mingled with accounts of domestic occurrences. You doubtless recollect these papers. Here they are. Everything is related in them which bears reference to my accursed origin; the whole detail of that series of disgusting circumstances which produced it is set in view; the minutest description of my odious and loathsome person is given, in language which painted your own horrors and rendered mine indelible. I sickened as I read. 'Hateful day when I received life!' I exclaimed in agony. 'Accursed creator! Why did you form a monster so hideous that even *you* turned from me in disgust? God, in pity, made man beautiful and alluring, after his own image; but my form is a filthy type of yours, more horrid even from the very resemblance. Satan had his companions, fellow devils, to admire and encourage him, but I am solitary and abhorred.'

"These were the reflections of my hours of despondency and solitude; but when I contemplated the virtues of the cottagers, their amiable and benevolent dispositions, I persuaded myself that when they should become acquainted with my admiration of their virtues they would compassionate me and overlook my personal deformity. Could they turn from their door one, however monstrous, who solicited their compassion and friendship? I resolved, at least, not to despair, but in every way to fit myself for an interview with them which would decide my fate. I postponed this attempt for some months longer, for the importance attached to its success inspired me with a dread lest I should fail. Besides, I found that my understanding improved so much with every day's experience that I was unwilling to commence this undertaking until a few more months should have added to my sagacity.

"Several changes, in the meantime, took place in the cottage. The presence of Safie diffused happiness among its inhabitants, and I also found that a greater degree of plenty reigned there. Felix and Agatha spent more time in amusement and conversation, and were assisted in their labours by servants. They did not appear rich, but they were contented and happy; their feelings were serene and peaceful, while mine became every day more tumultuous. Increase of knowledge only discovered to me more clearly what a wretched outcast I was. I cherished hope, it is true, but it vanished when I beheld my person reflected in water or my shadow in the moonshine, even as that frail image and that inconstant shade.

"I endeavoured to crush these fears and to fortify myself for the trial which in a few months I resolved to undergo; and sometimes I allowed my thoughts, unchecked by reason, to ramble in the fields of Paradise, and dared to fancy amiable and lovely creatures sympathizing with my feelings and cheering my gloom; their angelic countenances breathed smiles of consolation. But it was all a dream; no Eve soothed my sorrows nor shared my thoughts; I was alone. I remembered Adam's supplication to his Creator. But where was mine? He had abandoned me, and in the bitterness of my heart I cursed him.

"Autumn passed thus. I saw, with surprise and grief, the leaves decay and fall, and nature again assume the barren and bleak appearance it had worn when I first beheld the woods and the lovely moon. Yet I did not heed the bleakness of the weather; I was better fitted by my conformation for the endurance of cold than heat. But my chief delights were the sight of the flowers, the birds, and all the gay apparel of summer; when those deserted me, I turned with more attention towards the cottagers. Their happiness was not decreased by the absence of summer. They loved and sympathized with one another; and their joys, depending on each other, were not interrupted by the casualties that took place around them. The more I saw of them, the greater became my desire to claim their protection and kindness; my heart yearned to be known and loved by these amiable creatures; to see their sweet looks directed towards me with affection was the utmost limit of my ambition. I dared not think that they would turn them from me with disdain and horror. The poor that stopped at their door were never driven away. I asked, it is true, for greater treasures than a little food or rest: I required kindness and sympathy; but I did not believe myself utterly unworthy of it.

"The winter advanced, and an entire revolution of the seasons had taken place since I awoke into life. My attention at this time was solely directed towards my plan of introducing myself into the cottage of my protectors. I revolved many projects, but that on which I finally fixed was to enter the dwelling when the blind old man should be alone. I had sagacity enough to discover that the unnatural hideousness of my person was the chief object of horror with those who had formerly beheld me. My voice, although harsh, had nothing terrible in it; I thought, therefore, that if in the absence of his children I could gain the good will and mediation of the old De Lacey, I might by his means be tolerated by my younger protectors.

"One day, when the sun shone on the red leaves that strewed the ground and diffused cheerfulness, although it denied warmth, Safie, Agatha, and Felix departed on a long country walk, and the old man, at his own desire, was left alone in the cottage. When his children had departed, he took up his guitar and played several mournful but sweet airs, more sweet and mournful than I had ever heard him play before. At first his countenance was illuminated with pleasure, but as he continued, thoughtfulness and sadness succeeded; at length, laying aside the instrument, he sat absorbed in reflection.

"My heart beat quick; this was the hour and moment of trial, which would decide my hopes or realize my fears. The servants were gone to a neighbouring fair. All was silent in and around the cottage; it was an excellent opportunity; yet, when I proceeded to execute my plan, my limbs failed me and I sank to the ground. Again I rose, and exerting all the firmness of which I was master, removed the planks which I had placed before my hovel to conceal my retreat. The fresh air revived me, and with renewed determination I approached the door of their cottage.

"I knocked. 'Who is there?' said the old man. 'Come in.'

"I entered. 'Pardon this intrusion,' said I; 'I am a traveller in want of a little rest; you would greatly oblige me if you would allow me to remain a few minutes before the fire.'

"'Enter,' said De Lacey, 'and I will try in what manner I can to relieve your wants; but, unfortunately, my children are from home, and as I am blind, I am afraid I shall find it difficult to procure food for you.'

"'Do not trouble yourself, my kind host; I have food; it is warmth and rest only that I need.'

"I sat down, and a silence ensued. I knew that every minute was precious to me, yet I remained irresolute in what manner to commence the interview, when the old man addressed me. 'By your language, stranger, I suppose you are my countryman; are you French?'

"'No; but I was educated by a French family and understand that language only. I am now going to claim the protection of some friends, whom I sincerely love, and of whose favour I have some hopes.'

"'Are they Germans?'

"'No, they are French. But let us change the subject. I am an unfortunate and deserted creature; I look around and I have no relation or friend upon earth. These amiable people to whom I go have never seen me and know little of me. I am full of fears, for if I fail there, I am an outcast in the world forever.'

"'Do not despair. To be friendless is indeed to be unfortunate, but the hearts of men, when unprejudiced by any obvious self-interest, are full of brotherly love and charity. Rely, therefore, on your hopes; and if these friends are good and amiable, do not despair.'

"'They are kind—they are the most excellent creatures in the world; but, unfortunately, they are prejudiced against me. I have good dispositions; my life has been hitherto harmless and in some degree beneficial; but a fatal prejudice clouds their eyes, and where they ought to see a feeling and kind friend, they behold only a detestable monster.'

"'That is indeed unfortunate; but if you are really blameless, cannot you undeceive them?'

"'I am about to undertake that task; and it is on that account that I feel so many overwhelming terrors. I tenderly love these friends; I have, unknown to them, been for many months in the habits of daily kindness towards them; but they believe that I wish to injure them, and it is that prejudice which I wish to overcome.'

"'Where do these friends reside?'

"'Near this spot.'

"The old man paused and then continued, 'If you will unreservedly confide to me the particulars of your tale, I perhaps may be of use in undeceiving them. I am blind and cannot judge of your countenance, but there is something in your words which persuades me that you are sincere. I am poor and an exile, but it will afford me true pleasure to be in any way serviceable to a human creature.'

"'Excellent man! I thank you and accept your generous offer. You raise me from the dust by this kindness; and I trust that, by your aid, I shall not be driven from the society and sympathy of your fellow creatures.'

"'Heaven forbid! Even if you were really criminal, for that can only drive you to desperation, and not instigate you to virtue. I also am unfortunate; I and my family have been condemned, although innocent; judge, therefore, if I do not feel for your misfortunes.'

"'How can I thank you, my best and only benefactor? From your lips first have I heard the voice of kindness directed towards me; I shall be forever grateful; and your present humanity assures me of success with those friends whom I am on the point of meeting.'

"'May I know the names and residence of those friends?'

"I paused. This, I thought, was the moment of decision, which was to rob me of or bestow happiness on me forever. I struggled vainly for firmness sufficient to answer him, but the effort destroyed all my remaining strength; I sank on the chair and sobbed aloud. At that moment I heard the steps of my younger protectors. I had not a moment to lose, but seizing the hand of the old man, I cried, 'Now is the time! Save and protect me! You and your family are the friends whom I seek. Do not you desert me in the hour of trial!'

"'Great God!' exclaimed the old man. 'Who are you?'

"At that instant the cottage door was opened, and Felix, Safie, and Agatha entered. Who can describe their horror and consternation on beholding me? Agatha fainted, and Safie, unable to attend to her friend, rushed out of the cottage. Felix darted forward, and with supernatural force tore me from his father, to whose knees I clung; in a transport of fury, he dashed me to the ground and struck me violently with a stick. I could have torn him limb from limb, as the lion rends the antelope. But my heart sank within me as with bitter sickness, and I refrained. I saw him on the point of repeating his blow, when, overcome by pain and anguish, I quitted the cottage, and in the general tumult escaped unperceived to my hovel."

CHAPTER 16

"Cursed, cursed creator! Why did I live? Why, in that instant, did I not extinguish the spark of existence which you had so wantonly bestowed? I know not; despair had not yet taken possession of me; my feelings were those of rage and revenge. I could with pleasure have destroyed the cottage and its inhabitants and have glutted myself with their shrieks and misery.

"When night came I quitted my retreat and wandered in the wood; and now, no longer restrained by the fear of discovery, I gave vent to my anguish in fearful howlings. I was like a wild beast that had broken the toils, destroying the objects that obstructed me and ranging through the wood with a staglike swiftness. Oh! What a miserable night I passed! The cold stars shone in mockery, and the bare trees waved their branches above me; now and then the sweet voice of a bird burst forth amidst the universal stillness. All, save I, were at rest or in enjoyment; I, like the arch-fiend, bore a hell within me,[8] and finding myself unsympathized with, wished to tear up the trees, spread havoc and destruction around me, and then to have sat down and enjoyed the ruin.

"But this was a luxury of sensation that could not endure; I became fatigued with excess of bodily exertion and sank on the damp grass in the sick impotence of despair. There was none among the myriads of men that existed who would pity or assist me; and should I feel kindness towards my enemies? No; from that moment I declared everlasting war against the species, and more than all, against him who had formed me and sent me forth to this insupportable misery.

"The sun rose; I heard the voices of men and knew that it was impossible to return to my retreat during that day. Accordingly I hid myself in some thick underwood, determining to devote the ensuing hours to reflection on my situation.

"The pleasant sunshine and the pure air of day restored me to some degree of tranquillity; and when I considered what had passed at the cottage, I could not help believing that I had been too hasty in my conclusions. I had certainly acted imprudently. It was apparent that my conversation had interested the father in my behalf, and I was a fool in having exposed my person to the horror of his children. I ought to have familiarized the old De Lacey to me, and by degrees to have discovered myself to the rest of his family, when they should have been prepared for my approach. But I did not believe my errors to be irretrievable, and after much consideration I resolved to return to the cottage, seek the old man, and by my representations win him to my party.

"These thoughts calmed me, and in the afternoon I sank into a profound sleep; but the fever of my blood did not allow me to be visited by peaceful dreams. The horrible scene of the preceding day was forever acting before my eyes; the females were flying and the enraged Felix tearing me from his father's feet. I awoke exhausted, and finding that it was already night, I crept forth from my hiding-place, and went in search of food.

"When my hunger was appeased, I directed my steps towards the well-known path that conducted to the cottage. All there was at peace. I crept into my hovel and remained in silent expectation of the accustomed hour when the family arose. That hour passed, the sun mounted high in the heavens, but the cottagers did not appear. I trembled violently, apprehending some dreadful misfortune. The inside of the cottage was dark, and I heard no motion; I cannot describe the agony of this suspense.

"Presently two countrymen passed by, but pausing near the cottage, they entered into conversation, using violent gesticulations; but I did not understand what they said, as they spoke the language of the country, which differed from that of my protectors. Soon after, however, Felix approached with another man; I was surprised, as I knew that he had not quitted the cottage that morning, and waited anxiously to discover from his discourse the meaning of these unusual appearances.

"'Do you consider,' said his companion to him, 'that you will be obliged

[8] In *Paradise Lost* (IV.75), Satan says, "Which way I fly is Hell; myself am Hell . . . ."

to pay three months' rent and to lose the produce of your garden? I do not wish to take any unfair advantage, and I beg therefore that you will take some days to consider of your determination.'

"'It is utterly useless,' replied Felix; 'we can never again inhabit your cottage. The life of my father is in the greatest danger, owing to the dreadful circumstance that I have related. My wife and my sister will never recover from their horror. I entreat you not to reason with me any more. Take possession of your tenement and let me fly from this place.'

"Felix trembled violently as he said this. He and his companion entered the cottage, in which they remained for a few minutes, and then departed. I never saw any of the family of De Lacey more.

"I continued for the remainder of the day in my hovel in a state of utter and stupid despair. My protectors had departed and had broken the only link that held me to the world. For the first time the feelings of revenge and hatred filled my bosom, and I did not strive to control them, but allowing myself to be borne away by the stream, I bent my mind towards injury and death. When I thought of my friends, of the mild voice of De Lacey, the gentle eyes of Agatha, and the exquisite beauty of the Arabian, these thoughts vanished and a gush of tears somewhat soothed me. But again when I reflected that they had spurned and deserted me, anger returned, a rage of anger, and unable to injure anything human, I turned my fury towards inanimate objects. As night advanced I placed a variety of combustibles around the cottage, and after having destroyed every vestige of cultivation in the garden, I waited with forced impatience until the moon had sunk to commence my operations.

"As the night advanced, a fierce wind arose from the woods and quickly dispersed the clouds that had loitered in the heavens; the blast tore along like a mighty avalanche and produced a kind of insanity in my spirits that burst all bounds of reason and reflection. I lighted the dry branch of a tree and danced with fury around the devoted cottage, my eyes still fixed on the western horizon, the edge of which the moon nearly touched. A part of its orb was at length hid, and I waved my brand; it sank, and with a loud scream I fired the straw, and heath, and bushes, which I had collected. The wind fanned the fire, and the cottage was quickly enveloped by the flames, which clung to it and licked it with their forked and destroying tongues.

"As soon as I was convinced that no assistance could save any part of the habitation, I quitted the scene and sought for refuge in the woods.

"And now, with the world before me, whither should I bend my steps?[9] I resolved to fly far from the scene of my misfortunes; but to me, hated and despised, every country must be equally horrible. At length the thought of you crossed my mind. I learned from your papers that you were my father, my creator; and to whom could I apply with more fitness than to him who had given me life? Among the lessons that Felix had bestowed upon Safie, geography had not been omitted; I had learned from these the relative situations of the different countries of the earth. You had mentioned Geneva as the name of your native town, and towards this place I resolved to proceed.

[9] See *Paradise Lost* XII.646–7. Adam and Eve are leaving Eden: "The World was all before them, where to choose / Their place of rest, and Providence their guide."

"But how was I to direct myself? I knew that I must travel in a southwesterly direction to reach my destination, but the sun was my only guide. I did not know the names of the towns that I was to pass through, nor could I ask information from a single human being; but I did not despair. From you only could I hope for succour, although towards you I felt no sentiment but that of hatred. Unfeeling, heartless creator! You had endowed me with perceptions and passions and then cast me abroad an object for the scorn and horror of mankind. But on you only had I any claim for pity and redress, and from you I determined to seek that justice which I vainly attempted to gain from any other being that wore the human form.

"My travels were long and the sufferings I endured intense. It was late in autumn when I quitted the district where I had so long resided. I travelled only at night, fearful of encountering the visage of a human being. Nature decayed around me, and the sun became heatless; rain and snow poured around me; mighty rivers were frozen; the surface of the earth was hard and chill, and bare, and I found no shelter. Oh, earth! How often did I imprecate curses on the cause of my being! The mildness of my nature had fled, and all within me was turned to gall and bitterness. The nearer I approached to your habitation, the more deeply did I feel the spirit of revenge enkindled in my heart. Snow fell, and the waters were hardened, but I rested not. A few incidents now and then directed me, and I possessed a map of the country; but I often wandered wide from my path. The agony of my feelings allowed me no respite; no incident occurred from which my rage and misery could not extract its food; but a circumstance that happened when I arrived on the confines of Switzerland, when the sun had recovered its warmth and the earth again began to look green, confirmed in an especial manner the bitterness and horror of my feelings.

"I generally rested during the day and travelled only when I was secured by night from the view of man. One morning, however, finding that my path lay through a deep wood, I ventured to continue my journey after the sun had risen; the day, which was one of the first of spring, cheered even me by the loveliness of its sunshine and the balminess of the air. I felt emotions of gentleness and pleasure, that had long appeared dead, revive within me. Half surprised by the novelty of these sensations, I allowed myself to be borne away by them, and forgetting my solitude and deformity, dared to be happy. Soft tears again bedewed my cheeks, and I even raised my humid eyes with thankfulness towards the blessed sun, which bestowed such joy upon me.

"I continued to wind among the paths of the wood, until I came to its boundary, which was skirted by a deep and rapid river, into which many of the trees bent their branches, now budding with the fresh spring. Here I paused, not exactly knowing what path to pursue, when I heard the sound of voices, that induced me to conceal myself under the shade of a cypress. I was scarcely hid when a young girl came running towards the spot where I was concealed, laughing, as if she ran from someone in sport. She continued her course along the precipitous sides of the river, when suddenly her foot slipped, and she fell into the rapid stream. I rushed from my hiding-place and, with extreme labour from the force of the current, saved her and dragged her to shore. She was senseless, and I endeavoured by every means in my power to restore animation, when I was suddenly interrupted by the approach of a rustic, who was probably the person from whom she had playfully fled. On seeing me, he darted towards me, and tearing the girl from my arms, hastened towards the deeper parts of the wood. I followed speedily, I hardly knew why; but when the man saw me draw near, he aimed a gun, which he carried, at my body and fired. I sank to the ground, and my injurer, with increased swiftness, escaped into the wood.

"This was then the reward of my benevolence! I had saved a human being from destruction, and as a recompense I now writhed under the miserable pain of a wound which shattered the flesh and bone. The feelings of kindness and gentleness which I had entertained but a few moments before gave place to hellish rage and gnashing of teeth. Inflamed by pain, I vowed eternal hatred and vengeance to all mankind. But the agony of my wound overcame me; my pulses paused, and I fainted.

"For some weeks I led a miserable life in the woods, endeavouring to cure the wound which I had received. The ball had entered my shoulder, and I knew not whether it had remained there or passed through; at any rate I had no means of extracting it. My sufferings were augmented also by the oppressive sense of the injustice and ingratitude of their infliction. My daily vows rose for revenge—a deep and deadly revenge, such as would alone compensate for the outrages and anguish I had endured.

"After some weeks my wound healed, and I continued my journey. The labours I endured were no longer to be alleviated by the bright sun or gentle breezes of spring; all joy was but a mockery which insulted my desolate state and made me feel more painfully that I was not made for the enjoyment of pleasure.

"But my toils now drew near a close, and in two months from this time I reached the environs of Geneva.

"It was evening when I arrived, and I retired to a hiding-place among the fields that surround it to meditate in what manner I should apply to you. I was oppressed by fatigue and hunger and far too unhappy to enjoy the gentle breezes of evening or the prospect of the sun setting behind the stupendous mountains of Jura.

"At this time a slight sleep relieved me from the pain of reflection, which was disturbed by the approach of a beautiful child, who came running into the recess I had chosen, with all the sportiveness of infancy. Suddenly, as I gazed on him, an idea seized me that this little creature was unprejudiced and had lived too short a time to have inbibed a horror of deformity. If, therefore, I could seize him and educate him as my companion and friend, I should not be so desolate in this peopled earth.

"Urged by this impulse, I seized on the boy as he passed and drew him towards me. As soon as he beheld my form, he placed his hands before his eyes and uttered a shrill scream; I drew his hand forcibly from his face and said, 'Child, what is the meaning of this? I do not intend to hurt you; listen to me.'

"He struggled violently. 'Let me go,' he cried; 'monster! Ugly wretch! You wish to eat me and tear me to pieces. You are an ogre. Let me go, or I will tell my papa.'

"'Boy, you will never see your father again; you must come with me.'

"'Hideous monster! Let me go. My papa is a syndic[10]—he is M. Frankenstein—he will punish you. You dare not keep me.'

"'Frankenstein! You belong then to my enemy—to him towards whom I have sworn eternal revenge; you shall be my first victim.'

"The child still struggled and loaded me with epithets which carried despair to my heart; I grasped his throat to silence him, and in a moment he lay dead at my feet.

"I gazed on my victim, and my heart swelled with exultation and hellish triumph; clapping my hands, I exclaimed, 'I too can create desolation; my enemy is not invulnerable; this death will carry despair to him, and a thousand other miseries shall torment and destroy him.'

"As I fixed my eyes on the child, I saw something glittering on his breast. I took it; it was a portrait of a most lovely woman. In spite of my malignity, it softened and attracted me. For a few moments I gazed with delight on her dark eyes, fringed by deep lashes, and her lovely lips; but presently my rage returned; I remembered that I was forever deprived of the delights that such beautiful creatures could bestow and that she whose resemblance I contemplated would, in regarding me, have changed that air of divine benignity to one expressive of disgust and affright.

"Can you wonder that such thoughts transported me with rage? I only wonder that at that moment, instead of venting my sensations in exclamations and agony, I did not rush among mankind and perish in the attempt to destroy them.

"While I was overcome by these feelings, I left the spot where I had committed the murder, and seeking a more secluded hiding-place, I entered a barn which had appeared to me to be empty. A woman was sleeping on some straw; she was young, not indeed so beautiful as her whose portrait I held, but of an agreeable aspect and blooming in the loveliness of youth and health. Here, I thought, is one of those whose joy-imparting smiles are bestowed on all but me. And then I bent over her and whispered, 'Awake, fairest, thy lover is near—he who would give his life but to obtain one look of affection from thine eyes; my beloved, awake!'

"The sleeper stirred; a thrill of terror ran through me. Should she indeed awake, and see me, and curse me, and denounce the murderer? Thus would she assuredly act if her darkened eyes opened and she beheld me. The thought was madness; it stirred the fiend within me—not I, but she, shall suffer; the murder I have committed because I am forever robbed of all that she could give me, she shall atone. The crime had its source in her; be hers the punishment! Thanks to the lessons of Felix and the sanguinary laws of man, I had learned now to work mischief. I bent over her and placed the portrait securely in one of the folds of her dress. She moved again, and I fled.

"For some days I haunted the spot where these scenes had taken place, sometimes wishing to see you, sometimes resolved to quit the world and its miseries forever. At length I wandered towards these mountains, and have ranged through their immense recesses, consumed by a burning passion which you alone can gratify. We may not part until you have promised to comply with my requisition. I am alone and miserable; man will not associ-

[10] A Swiss civil magistrate.

ate with me; but one as deformed and horrible as myself would not deny herself to me. My companion must be of the same species and have the same defects. This being you must create."

Honoré de Balzac
(1799–1850)

Honoré de Balzac, sometimes called the "father of the modern novel," was born in 1799 in Tours, a city about 125 miles southwest of Paris. His father was of peasant origin but rose to the status of a civil servant, changing his name from Balssa and adding the aristocratic preposition "de"; later, the son would emulate his father's tendency to social-climb, notwithstanding his ruthless portraits of parvenus in his fiction. The boy was educated at Vendôme, near Tours, where he proved to be a problematical pupil but a voracious reader (even of the dictionary), with a phenomenal memory for detail. This period in his life was later reflected in his novella Louis Lambert. *In 1814, a year before the final defeat of Napoleon, Balzac's family moved to Paris, the city he came to love but portrayed in many of his works as a demonic hell. There he continued his studies, concentrating in law, and also worked for three years in a law office, acquiring the inside knowledge of the profession that later helped him picture it convincingly in several works, including* Colonel Chabert. *He forsook the law, however, for a career as a writer. In his twenties he produced, under pseudonyms, a good deal of factory-made trash. It is noteworthy that Balzac was not precocious—contrary to what one would expect of a writer whose later serious work runs to nearly a hundred novels and tales, filling some forty volumes, written with incredible speed, and of an impressively consistent level of high quality.*

Balzac also tried his hand at the publishing and printing businesses, which failed and left him badly debt-ridden, a financial problem that oppressed him throughout his life. But, again, he salvaged literary capital from these enterprises (and some wild, unsuccessful ones later), learning the ins and outs of money and finance that he examines repeatedly in his fiction. Many nineteenth-century novelists were concerned with this theme, fascinated as they were with middle-class values, but few if any of them can equal Balzac's ability to describe money as a relentless driving force on the same elemental level as hunger and sex. In 1829 he published under his own name his first successful piece of fiction, later revised as The Chouans, *a historical novel in the line of Walter Scott, whom Balzac enthusiastically admired.*

Balzac's life over the next twenty years was a crowded one. He wrote for and edited journals. He had a number of love affairs, including one with the Polish countess Eveline Hanska that ran, concurrently with others, for seventeen years and culminated in a marriage a few months before Balzac's death. He led a flamboyant social life. But, above all, he wrote—feverishly, obsessively. Getting by on five or six hours of sleep, he often wrote for sixteen or eighteen hours at a stretch, beginning at midnight and continuing almost without a break until the following afternoon. Nor did he merely dash off stories, send them to the printer, and forget them; rather, he composed at lightning speed and then revised repeatedly, often from printers' proofs. He reworked the proofs of one of his stories, Pierrette, *seventeen times. The result was that, although his works are not perfectly polished and opinions differ on his prose style, his fiction is artistically crafted—well-constructed and powerful in symbolic imagery. But no one, even with Balzac's strong constitution, could keep up such a pace indefinitely, and after several years of failing health he died in 1850, in Paris, at the age of fifty-one. In working himself to death in this way, Balzac resembles, as his work frequently does too, his British contemporary Charles Dickens. Among the many pseudo-scientific notions that Balzac entertained seriously was a belief that human beings were endowed with a definite quantity of vital energy, which they could conserve or spend. Balzac, clearly, was a spender. He had projected works he did not live to write; among the many he did complete are dozens still widely read, including such masterpieces as* Father Goriot, Eugenie Grandet, Cousin Pons, Cousin Bette, The Wild Ass's Skin, *and* Lost Illusions. *He also wrote masterful novellas and short stories, including the Rabelaisian collection entitled* Droll Stories.

The chief sources of Balzac's literary power are an astonishingly prolific imagination, an intensity of vision that lends preternatural vividness to his people and scenes, and the keenest powers of psychological and material observation. He can render human emotions with great subtlety and conviction, but they are linked almost always to material surroundings, on a large scale (social position, professional milieu, residential neighborhood) and a small scale (furniture, dress, personal belongings). It is this ability to describe the external as both the conditioning cause and the reflection of inner personality that allows him to combine two literary modes often considered mutually exclusive: realism and melodrama. Balzac's studies of villainy are among the most effective ever written; he has a peculiar power to command his reader's feelings, creating hope, antipathy, and dread that can be felt as physical tension. Typical of Balzac are the stories in which evil people are pitted against naive or noble innocent victims who, no match for the wicked, are victimized by the very unguardedness that the villains know so well how to take advantage of. Colonel Chabert is one such victim. In confrontations like these and in the narrator's tone of urgency lies melodrama, though raised as in Dickens to a high level of art. The realism appears in the scrupulously exact accounts of the characters' lives, environments, and motives; the villains' nefarious and the victims' altruistic behavior is rooted in very specific traits and situations that, good or evil, are realistically credible—like Chabert's sense of military pride and his alienated wife's need to use her fortune to keep her second husband dependent on her. Balzac is like a detective, tracing the movements of his characters step by deliberate step. He can also alternate with the melodramatist's impassioned rhetoric a drier tone of analysis, of individuals and society, that suggests the method of the realists.

These combinations—detachment with passion, broad moral vision with circumstantial accuracy—are related to Balzac's larger goals as an author. Not content to record and create, he came to see himself as a systematic historian, cataloguer, diagnostician, and finally judge of his society. As his published works accumulated during the 1830s, he began to devise classifications for them and for the aspects of life they described. In 1842 he wrote an important preface outlining the comprehensive scheme he invented for his works, written or projected, naming the total corpus The Human Comedy *in implicit parallel with Dante's* Divine Comedy. *It was to record French life from about 1800 on and was to be divided into three basic groups. The first, and much the largest, was to include "studies" of manners, or behavior, subdivided into "scenes" from private or familiar, provincial, Parisian, political, military, and country life; the second group was to include philosophical studies and the third analytical studies. (The word "scenes" had overtones of theatrical drama, and the elaborate descriptive passages in his fiction are very much like the specifications of a set designer.) In one of his letters Balzac explained that the studies of manners would show social* effects: *the history of the human heart and of society, "the play of emotions, the movement of life." The philosophical studies would penetrate a further layer by showing* causes, *or "rules of the game" of life. The analytical studies would uncover ultimate* principles. *According to a list Balzac drew up in 1845, there would be 144 "studies" in all.*

The three great divisions Balzac outlined not only serve to distinguish works from one another but also reflect his mingling of approaches within individual works—his habit, for example, of pausing to generalize, editorialize, theorize. Moreover, in giving a comprehensive title to the body of his works Balzac was certifying what his novels had in fact been doing: creating a vast panorama of interlocking lives and people. Characters encountered in one work reappear in others, in major or minor roles or mere passing mention, showing us different sides of themselves, growing, changing, in short revealing themselves much as people do whom we know in our lives. One of the volumes in the Pléiade French edition of Balzac lists his fictional characters, many of whom appear in more than one work, summarizing in severely condensed form their actions in the various stories. The list runs to over four hundred pages of tiny print (not to mention another 260 pages indexing references to historical and literary figures). In creating this kind of saga, with its vast network of interconnections, Balzac anticipated a number of later novelists including Anthony Trollope and William Faulkner.

Oddly enough, in the preface of 1842 mentioned above Balzac takes the conservative position that society—or at least society organized by the monarchial and Catholic institutions he had come to support—was the desired norm, self-interest being a source of evil. He explicitly rejects Rousseau's vision of society as oppressor of the individual. What we actually find in much of Balzac's work, though, is a scorching exposé of society. This is certainly true in Colonel Chabert, *a "scene from private life" first written and published in 1832 and later much revised. The plot, in which a supposedly dead spouse returns, has a perennial appeal, but Balzac integrates the personal tale with a social theme, so that Chabert's crusade to reestablish his identity is set against the social-climbing element in post-Napoleonic France represented by his wife and the cold indifference and impersonality of society represented by official institutions. The governing metaphor for all this is law, which represents both the obstacles Chabert must face and the weaponry that he (and his bigamous wife too, for her purposes) must use. In fighting this labyrinthine battle, he is handicapped by the fact that he is* literally *a soldier, accustomed to the simple moral outlines and speedy execution of basic justice he has known in the army.*

As everywhere in Balzac, intangibles are reflected in external things: the physical properties of Derville's law office, and of the court anteroom where sentenced vagabonds gather like Dante's damned at the Acheron, are explicitly symbolic for Balzac. The characters themselves can also be symbolists. Chabert once cries out, "I have been buried beneath the dead, but now I am buried beneath the living—beneath facts, beneath records, beneath society itself, which seeks to thrust me back underground!" Derville recognizes in Madame Ferraud's elegant dining room, where she offers coffee to her pet monkey, the external correlative of her heartless injustice to the colonel, who also lives "with the beasts" but in Vergniaud's squalid cowhouse. But not all the symbolism is made explicit; for example, we might find in the boisterous hairsplitting of the law clerks trying to define what constitutes a play mere extraneous "atmosphere," but in fact it is atmosphere of the revelatory, Balzacian kind, in this case a grotesquely diminished specimen of the legalism that runs through the larger issues of the story.

Colonel Chabert *is typical of Balzac in several other ways too. We find the cross-fertilization with other works: Derville, Madame Ferraud (who will become Louis XVIII's mistress), Vergniaud (who will wind up in jail), Godeschal, Crottat, and other characters more casually mentioned appear elsewhere in Balzac. The last paragraph contains a very brief plot summary of* Father Goriot; *if we have read it, we know that Derville is not just emoting but knows exactly what he is talking about. We find also the melodrama of the tense confrontation between calculating greed and ingenuous honesty, the terrible indictment of Paris, the description of the tortuous ways of status-seeking, the concern with inheritances and money, the intricacies of sociopolitical currents in the days of the restored monarchy. In short, we find Balzac playing his typical twin roles: chronicler of the human heart and anatomist of society.*

FURTHER READING *(prepared by W. J. R.):* V. S. Pritchett's *Balzac,* 1973, combines a close biographical account with a lavish pictorial portrait of nineteenth-century Paris. Stefan Zweig's *Balzac,* trans. William and Dorothy Rose, 1946, is another thorough biography. The fictional world of *The Human Comedy* is viewed comprehensively in Felicien Marceau's *Balzac and His World,* 1955, trans. Derek Coltman, 1966, a good introduction to the author. George B. Raser's *The Heart of Balzac's Paris,* 1970, studies Balzac's Paris—boulevards, theaters, the Palais Royal—in order to explore Balzac's attitudes toward his city and social climate. Samuel Rogers, in *Balzac and the Novel,* 1953, provides a fine overview of *The Human Comedy,* establishing a broad context for Balzac's art. A somewhat more specialized treatment of *The Human Comedy,* but still valuable for the new student of Balzac, is Anthony R. Pugh's *Balzac's Recurring Characters,* 1974. Pugh's study is a reference work, but it also elucidates various methods of Balzac's art. *Balzac and the Nineteenth Century,* ed. by D. G. Charlton, J. Gaudon, and Anthony R. Pugh, 1972, is a collection of critical essays divided between Balzac and other nineteenth-century writers.

*COLONEL CHABERT**

"There's our old topcoat again!"

This exclamation came from the lips of a clerk of the species called in Parisian law-offices "gutter-jumpers," who was at the moment munching with a very good appetite a slice of bread. He took a little of the crumb and made a pellet, which he flung, with a laugh, through the blinds of the window against which he was leaning. Well-aimed, the pellet rebounded nearly to the height of the window after hitting the hat of a stranger who was crossing the courtyard of a house in the rue Vivienne, where Maître Derville, the lawyer, resided.

"Come, come, Simonnin, don't play tricks, or I'll turn you off. No matter how poor a client may be, he is a man, the devil take you!" said the head-clerk, pausing as he added up a bill of costs.

*Translator anonymous. Reprinted from *The Short Novels of Balzac,* The Dial Press, New York, 1948.

The gutter-jumper is usually, like Simonnin, a lad of thirteen or fourteen years of age, who in all law-offices is under the particular supervision of the head-clerk, whose errands he does, and whose love-letters he carries, together with the writs of the courts and the petitions entered. He belongs to the *gamin*[1] *de Paris* through his ethics, and to the pettifogging[2] side of law through fate. The lad is usually pitiless, undisciplined, totally without reverence, a scoffer, a writer of epigrams, lazy, and also greedy. Nevertheless, all such little fellows have an old mother living on some fifth story, with whom they share the thirty or forty francs they earn monthly.

"If it is a man, why do you call him an 'old topcoat?' " said Simonnin, in the tone of a scholar[3] who detects his master in a mistake.

Thereupon he returned to the munching of his bread with a bit of cheese, leaning his shoulder against the window-frame; for he took his rest standing, like the horses of the hackney-coaches, with one leg raised and supported against the other.

"Couldn't we play that old guy some trick?" said the third clerk, Godeschal, in a low voice, stopping in the middle of a legal document he was dictating to be engrossed[4] by the fourth clerk and copied by two neophytes from the provinces. Having made the above suggestion, he went on with his dictation: *"But in his gracious and benevolent wisdom His Majesty Louis the Eighteenth*[5]— Write all the letters, hi, there! Desroches the learned!— *so soon as he recovered the reins of power, understood*— What did that fat joker understand, I'd like to know?— *the high mission to which Divine Providence had called him!* . . . . . . Put an exclamation mark and six dots; they are pious enough at the Palais[6] to let 'em pass— *and his first thought was, as is proved by the date of the ordinance herein named, to repair evils caused by the frightful and lamentable disasters of the revolutionary period by restoring to his faithful and numerous adherents*— 'Numerous' is a bit of flattery which ought to please the court— *all their unsold property wheresoever situate, whether in the public domain or the ordinary and extraordinary crown domains, or in the endowments of public institutions; for we contend and hold ourselves able to maintain that such is the spirit and the meaning of the gracious ordinance, rendered in*—"

"Stop, stop," said Godeschal to the three clerks. "That rascally sentence has come to the end of my paper and isn't done yet. Well," he added, stopping to wet the back of the cahier[7] with his tongue to turn the thick page of his stamped paper, "if you want to play the old topcoat a trick tell him that the master is so busy he can talk to clients only between two and three o'clock in the morning; we'll see if he comes then, the old villain!" and Godeschal returned to his dictation. "*—gracious ordinance rendered in*— Have you got that down?"

"Yes," cried the three copyists.

[1]Street urchin. [2]Pettily unscrupulous. [3]Pupil. [4]Written for official use.

[5]The present date in the story is 1819. The French Revolution broke out in 1789; in 1793 King Louis XVI was executed. Following the Revolution, Napoleon Bonaparte rose to power in France and conquered much of Europe. After suffering several military defeats, he abdicated in 1814, and the monarchy was restored in Louis XVIII, brother of the executed king. Napoleon was permitted to retire to the island of Elba in the Mediterranean, but he made a dramatic return to power in March 1815. The ensuing "Hundred Days" ended with Napoleon's final overthrow at Waterloo in Belgium on June 18, 1815.

[6]*Palais de Justice;* the law-courts. [7]Notebook.

"Rendered in— Hi, papa Boucard, what's the date of that ordinance? Dot your i's, *unam et omnes*[8]—it fills up."

"Omnes," repeated one of the clerks before Boucard, the head-clerk, could answer.

"Good heavens! you haven't written that, have you?" cried Godeschal, looking at the provincial newcomer with a truculent air.

"Yes, he has," said Desroches, the fourth clerk, leaning over to look at his neighbor's copy, "he has written, Dot your i's, and he spells it e-y-e-s."

All the clerks burst into a roar of laughter.

"Do you call that a law-term, Monsieur Huré?" cried Simonnin. "And you say you come from Mortagne!"

"Scratch it out carefully," said the head-clerk. "If one of the judges were to get hold of the petition and see that, the master would never hear the last of it. Come, no more such blunders, Monsieur Huré; a Norman[9] ought to know better than to write a petition carelessly; it's the 'Shoulder-arms!' of the legal guild."

"Rendered in—in—" went on Godeschal. "Do tell me when, Boucard?"

"June, 1814," replied the head-clerk, without raising his head from his work.

A knock at the door interrupted the next sentence of the prolix petition. Five grinning clerks, with lively, satirical eyes and curly heads, turned their noses towards the door, having all shouted with one voice, "Come in!" Boucard remained with his head buried in a mound of deeds, and went on making out the bill of costs on which he was employed.

The office was a large room, furnished with the classic stove that adorns all other pettifogging precincts. The pipes went diagonally across the room and entered the chimney, on the marble mantel-shelf of which were diverse bits of bread, triangles of Brie cheese, fresh pork chops, glasses, bottles, and a cup of chocolate for the head-clerk. The smell of these comestibles amalgamated so well with the offensive odor of the overheated stove and the peculiar exhalations of desks and papers that the stench of a fox would hardly have been perceived. The floor was covered with mud and snow brought in by the clerks. Near the window stood the rolling-top desk of the head-clerk, and next to it the little table of the second clerk. The latter was now on duty in the courts, where he usually went between eight and nine o'clock in the morning. The sole decorations of the office were the well-known large yellow posters which announce attachments on property, mortgagee-sales, litigations between guardians and minors, and auctions, final or postponed, the glory of legal offices.

Behind the head-clerk, and covering the wall from top to bottom, was a case with an enormous number of pigeon-holes, each stuffed with bundles of papers, from which hung innumerable tags and those bits of red tape which give special character to legal documents. The lower shelves of the case were filled with pasteboard boxes, yellowed by time and edged with blue paper, on which could be read the names of the more distinguished clients whose affairs were cooking at the present time. The dirty window-panes let in but a small amount of light; besides, in the month of February

[8]"One and all" (Latin). [9]Native of Normandy, in northwestern France.

there are very few law-offices in Paris where the clerks can write without a lamp before ten o'clock in the day. Such offices are invariably neglected, and for the reason that while everyone goes there nobody stays; no personal interest attaches to so mean a spot; neither the lawyers, nor the clients, nor the clerks, care for the appearance of the place which is to the latter a school, to the clients a means, to the master a laboratory. The greasy furniture is transmitted from lawyer to lawyer with such scrupulous exactness that certain offices still possess boxes of "residues," parchments engrossed in black-letter,[10] and bags, which have descended from the solicitors of the "Chlet," an abbreviation of the word "Châtelet," an institution which represented under the old order of things what a court of common pleas is in our day.

This dark office, choked with dust and dirt, was therefore, like all such offices, repulsive to clients, and one of the ugly monstrosities of Paris. Certainly, if the damp sacristies[11] where prayers are weighted and paid for like spices, if the second-hand shops, where flutter rags which blight the illusions of life by revealing to us the end of our festive arrays, if these two sewers of poesy did not exist, a lawyer's office would be the most horrible of all social dens. But the same characteristic may be seen in gambling-houses, in court-rooms, in the lottery bureaus, and in evil resorts. Why? Perhaps because the drama played in such places within the soul renders men indifferent to externals—a thought which likewise explains the simplicity of great thinkers and men of great ambitions.

"Where's my penknife?"

"I shall eat my breakfast."

"Look out! there's a blot on the petition."

"Hush, gentlemen!"

These various exclamations went off all at once just as the old client entered and closed the door, with the sort of humility which gives an unnatural air to the movements of a poverty-stricken man. The stranger tried to smile, but the muscles of his face relaxed when he had vainly looked for symptoms of civility on the inexorably indifferent faces of the six clerks. Accustomed, no doubt, to judge men, he addressed himself politely to the gutter-jumper, hoping that the office drudge might answer him civilly:

"Monsieur, can I see your master?"

The mischievous youngster replied by tapping his ear with the fingers of his left hand, as much as to say, "I am deaf."

"What is it you want, monsieur?" asked Godeschal, swallowing an enormous mouthful as he asked the question—brandishing his knife and crossing his legs till the foot of the upper one came on a line with his nose.

"I have called five times, monsieur," replied the visitor. "I wish to speak to Monsieur Derville."

"On business?"

"Yes; but I can explain my business only to him."

"He's asleep; if you wish to consult him you'll have to come at night; he never gets to work before midnight. But if you will explain the matter to us we can perhaps do as well—"

[10] Old-fashioned, "gothic" letters. [11] Rooms behind the altars of churches; vestries.

The stranger was impassive. He looked humbly about him like a dog slipping into a strange kitchen and afraid of kicks. Thanks to their general condition, law-clerks are not afraid of thieves; so they felt no suspicion of the topcoat, but allowed him to look round in search of a seat, for he was evidently fatigued. It is a matter of calculation with lawyers to have few chairs in their offices. The common client, weary of standing, goes away grumbling.

"Monsieur," replied the stranger, "I have already had the honor of telling you that I can explain my business to no one but Monsieur Derville. I will wait until he is up."

Boucard had now finished his accounts. He smelt the fumes of his chocolate, left his cane chair, came up to the chimney, looked the old man over from head to foot, gazed at the topcoat and made an indescribable grimace. He probably thought that no matter how long they kept this client on the rack not a penny could be got out of him; and he now interposed, meaning with a few curt words to rid the office of an unprofitable client.

"They tell you the truth, monsieur," he said. "Monsieur Derville works only at night. If your business is important I advise you to come back here at one or two in the morning."

The client looked at the head-clerk with a stupid air, and remained for an instant motionless. Accustomed to see many changes of countenance, and many singular expressions produced by the hesitation and the dreaminess which characterize persons who go to law, the clerks took no notice of the old man, but continued to eat their breakfasts with as much noise of their jaws as if they were horses at a manger.

"Monsieur, I shall return to-night," said the visitor, who, with the tenacity of an unhappy man, was determined to put his tormentors in the wrong.

The only retaliation granted to poverty is that of forcing justice and benevolence to unjust refusals. When unhappy souls have convicted society of falsehood then they fling themselves the more ardently upon the bosom of God.

"Did you ever see such a skull?" cried Simonnin, without waiting till the door had closed on the old man.

"He looks as if he had been buried and dug up again," said one.

"He's some colonel who wants his back-pay," said the head-clerk.

"No, he's an old porter."

"Who'll bet he's a nobleman?" cried Boucard.

"I'll bet he has been a porter," said Godeschal. "None but porters are gifted by nature with topcoats as greasy and ragged round the bottom as that old fellow's. Didn't you notice his cracked boots which let in water, and that cravat in place of a shirt? That man slept last night under a bridge."

"He may be a nobleman and have burnt his candle at both ends—that's nothing new!" cried Desroches.

"No," replied Boucard, in the midst of much laughter, "I maintain he was a brewer in 1789 and a colonel under the Republic."

"Ha! I'll bet tickets for a play all round that he never was a soldier," said Godeschal.

"Done," said Boucard.

"Monsieur, monsieur!" called the gutter-jumper, opening the window.

"What are you doing, Simonnin?" asked Boucard.

"I'm calling him back to know if he is a colonel or a porter—he ought to know, himself."

"What shall we say to him?" exclaimed Godeschal.

"Leave it to me," said Boucard.

The poor man re-entered timidly, with his eyes lowered, perhaps not to show his hunger by looking too eagerly at the food.

"Monsieur," said Boucard, "will you have the kindness to give us your name, so that Monsieur Derville may—"

"Chabert."

"The colonel who was killed at Eylau?"[12] asked Huré, who had not yet spoken, but was anxious to get in his joke like the rest.

"The same, monsieur," answered the old man, with classic simplicity. Then he left the room.

"Thunder!"

"Sold!"

"Puff!"

"Oh!"

"Ah!"

"Boum!"

"The old oddity!"

"Done for!"

"Monsieur Desroches, you and I will go to the theater for nothing!" cried Huré to the fourth clerk, with a rap on the shoulders fit to have killed a rhinoceros.

Then followed a chorus of shouts, laughs, and exclamations, to describe which we should have to use all the onomatopoeias[13] of the language.

"Which theater shall we choose?"

"The Opera," said the head-clerk.

"In the first place," said Godeschal, "I never said theater at all. I can take you, if I choose, to Madame Saqui."[14]

"Madame Saqui is not a play," said Desroches.

"What's a play?" retorted Godeschal. "Let's first establish the fact. What did I bet, gentlemen? tickets for a play. What's a play? a thing we go to see—"

"If that's so, you can take us to see the water running under the Pont Neuf,"[15] interrupted Simonnin.

"—see for money," went on Godeschal.

"But you can see a great many things for money that are not plays. The definition is not exact," said Desroches.

"But just listen to me—"

"You are talking nonsense, my dear fellow," said Boucard.

"Do you call Curtius a play?" asked Godeschal.

"No," said the head-clerk, "I call it a gallery of wax figures."

"I'll bet a hundred francs to a sou," retorted Godeschal, "that Curtius'

[12] A bloody battle fought in 1807 by the French against the Russians and Prussians, near what is now the Polish-Soviet border.

[13] Words that sound like what they mean, such as "boom."

[14] A famous dancer-acrobat. [15] The "New Bridge."

gallery constitutes a collection of things which may legally be called a play. They combine into one thing which can be seen at different prices according to the seats you occupy—"

"You can't get out of it!" said Simonnin.

"Take care I don't box your ears!" said Godeschal.

The clerks all shrugged their shoulders.

"Besides, we don't know that that old baboon wasn't making fun of us," he continued, changing his argument amid roars of laughter. "The fact is, Colonel Chabert is as dead as a door nail; his widow married Comte Ferraud, councillor of state. Madame Ferraud is one of our clients."

"The cause stands over for to-morrow," said Boucard. "Come, get to work, gentlemen. Heavens and earth! nothing ever gets done here. Finish with that petition—it has to be sent in before the session of the fourth court which meets to-day. Come, to work!"

"If it was really Colonel Chabert, wouldn't he have kicked that little Simonnin when he pretended to be deaf?" said the provincial Huré, considering that observation quite as conclusive as those of Godeschal.

"Nothing is decided," said Boucard. "Let us agree to accept the second tier of boxes at the Français and see Talma in Nero. Simonnin can sit in the pit."[16]

Thereupon the head-clerk sat down at his desk, and the others followed his example.

"Rendered June one thousand eight hundred and fourteen— Write it in letters, mind," said Godeschal. "Have you written it?"

"Yes," replied the copyists and the engrosser, whose pens began to squeak along the stamped paper with a noise, well known in all law-offices, like that of scores of cockchafers[17] tied by schoolboys in a paper bag.

"And we pray that the gentlemen of this tribunal— Hold on! let me read that sentence over to myself; I don't know what I'm about."

"Forty-six—should think that often happened—and three, forty-nine," said Boucard.

"We pray," resumed Godeschal, having re-read his clause, *"that the gentlemen of this tribunal will not show less magnanimity than the august author of the ordinance, and that they will deny the miserable pretensions of the administration of the grand chancellor of the Legion of honor*[18] *by determining the jurisprudence of this matter in the broad sense in which we have established it here—"*

"Monsieur Godeschal, don't you want a glass of water?" said the gutter-jumper.

"That imp of a Simonnin!" said Boucard. "Come here, saddle your double-soled horses, and take this package and skip over to the Invalides."[19]

"Which we have established it here—" went on Godeschal. "Did you get to that? Well, then add *in the interests of Madame* (full length) *la Vicomtesse de Grandlieu—"*

"What's that?" cried the head-clerk, "the idea of petitioning in that affair! Vicomtesse de Grandlieu against the Legion of honor! Ah! you must

[16] The rear part of the orchestra. [17] Beetles.

[18] *Legion of honor.* Recipients of a high French honor, military or civilian, inaugurated in 1802.

[19] A veterans' hospital.

be a fool! Have the goodness to put away your copies and your minute—they'll answer for the Navarreins affair against the monasteries. It's late, and I must be off with the other petitions; I'll attend to that myself at the Palais."

Towards one o'clock in the morning the individual calling himself Colonel Chabert knocked at the door of Maître Derville, solicitor in the court of common pleas for the department of the Seine. The porter told him that Monsieur Derville had not yet come in. The old man declared he had an appointment and passed up to the rooms of the celebrated lawyer, who, young as he was, was even then considered one of the best legal heads in France. Having rung and been admitted, the persistent client was not a little astonished to find the head-clerk laying out on a table in the dining-room a number of documents relating to affairs which were to come up on the morrow. The clerk, not less astonished at the apparition of the old man, bowed to the colonel and asked him to sit down, which he did.

"Upon my word, monsieur, I thought you were joking when you named such a singular hour for a consultation," said the old man, with the factitious liveliness of a ruined man who tries to smile.

"The clerks were joking and telling the truth also," said the head-clerk, going on with his work. "Monsieur Derville selects this hour to examine his causes, give directions for the suits, and plan his defenses. His extraordinary intellect works freer at this hour, the only one in which he can get the silence and tranquillity he requires to evolve his ideas. You are the third person only who has been admitted here for a consultation at this time of night. After Monsieur Derville comes in he will talk over each affair, read everything connected with it, and spend perhaps five or six hours at his work; then he rings for me, and explains his intentions. In the morning, from ten to two, he listens to his clients; the rest of the day he passes in visiting. In the evening he goes about in society to keep up his relations with the great world. He has no other time than at night to delve into his cases, rummage the arsenals of the Code, make his plans of campaign. He is determined, out of love for his profession, not to lose a single case. And for that reason he won't take all that are brought to him, as other lawyers do. That's his life; it's extraordinarily active. He makes a lot of money."

The old man was silent as he listened to this explanation, and his singular face assumed a look so devoid of all intelligence that the clerk after glancing at him once or twice took no further notice of him. A few moments later Derville arrived, in evening dress; his head-clerk opened the door to him and then went back to the papers. The young lawyer looked amazed when he saw in the dim light the strange client who awaited him. Colonel Chabert was as motionless as the wax figures of Curtius' gallery where Godeschal proposed to take his comrades. This immovability might have been less noticeable than it was, if it had not, as it were, completed the supernatural impression conveyed by the whole appearance of the man. The old soldier was lean and shrunken. The concealment of his forehead, which was carefully hidden beneath a wig brushed smoothly over it, gave a mysterious expression to his person. The eyes seemed covered with a film; you might have thought them bits of dirty mother-of-pearl, their bluish reflections quivering in the candlelight. The pale, livid, hatchet face, if I may borrow that term, seemed dead. An old black-silk stock was fastened round the neck. The shadow of the room hid the body so effectually below the dark line of the ragged article that a man of vivid imagination might have taken that old head for a sketch drawn at random on the wall or for a portrait by Rembrandt[20] without its frame. The brim of the hat worn by the strange old man cast a black line across the upper part of his face. This odd effect, though perfectly natural, brought out in abrupt contrast the white wrinkles, the stiffened lines, the unnatural hue of that cadaverous countenance. The absence of all motion in the body, all warmth in the glance, combined with a certain expression of mental alienation, and with the degrading symptoms which characterize idiocy, to give that face a nameless horror which no words can describe.

But an observer, and especially a lawyer, would have seen in that blasted man the signs of some deep anguish, indications of a misery that degraded that face as the drops of rain falling from the heavens on pure marble gradually disfigure it. A doctor, an author, a magistrate would have felt intuitively a whole drama as they looked at this sublime wreck, whose least merit was a resemblance to those fantastic sketches drawn by artists on the margins of their lithographic stones as they sit conversing with their friends.

When the stranger saw the lawyer he shuddered with the convulsive movement which seizes a poet when a sudden noise recalls him from some fecund revery amid the silence of the night. The old man rose quickly and took off his hat to the young lawyer. The leather that lined it was no doubt damp with grease, for his wig stuck to it without his knowledge and exposed his skull, horribly mutilated and disfigured by a scar running from the crown of his head to the angle of his right eye and forming a raised welt. The sudden removal of that dirty wig, worn by the poor soul to conceal his wound, caused no desire to laugh in the minds of the two young men, so awful was the sight of that skull. "The mind fled through it!" was the first thought suggested to them as they saw that wound.

"If he is not Colonel Chabert he is some bold trooper," thought Boucard.

"Monsieur," said Derville, "to whom have I the honor of speaking?"

"To Colonel Chabert."

"Which one?"

"The one who was killed at Eylau," replied the old man.

Hearing those extraordinary words the clerk and the lawyer looked at each other as if to say, "He is mad."

"Monsieur," said the colonel, "I desire to confide my secrets to you in private."

The intrepidity which characterizes lawyers is worthy of remark. Whether from their habit of receiving great numbers of persons, whether from an abiding sense of the protection of the law, or from perfect confidence in their ministry, certain it is they go everywhere and take all risks, like priests and doctors. Derville made a sign to Boucard, who left the room.

[20] Rembrandt's portraits often show a bright face surrounded by semidarkness.

"Monsieur," said the lawyer, "during the day I am not very chary of my time; but in the middle of the night every moment is precious to me. Therefore, be brief and concise. Tell your facts without digression; I will ask you any explanations I may find necessary. Go on."

Bidding his strange client be seated, the young man sat down before the table, and while listening to the tale of the late colonel he turned over the pages of a brief.

"Monsieur," said the deceased, "perhaps you know that I commanded a regiment of cavalry at Eylau. I was the chief cause of the success of Murat's[21] famous charge which won the day. Unhappily for me, my death is given as an historic fact in 'Victories and Conquests'[22] where all the particulars are related. We cut the three Russian lines in two; then they closed behind us and we were obliged to cut our way back again. Just before we reached the Emperor,[23] having dispersed the Russians, a troop of the enemy's cavalry met us. I flung myself upon them. Two Russian officers, actual giants, attacked me together. One of them cut me over the head with his sabre, which went through everything, even to the silk cap which I wore, and laid my skull open. I fell from my horse. Murat came up to support us, and he and his whole party, fifteen hundred men, rode over me. They reported my death to the Emperor, who sent (for he loved me a little, the master!) to see if there were no hope of saving a man to whom he owed the vigor of our attack. He despatched two surgeons to find me and bring me in to the ambulances, saying—perhaps too hurriedly, for he had work to attend to—'Go and see if my poor Chabert is still living.' Those cursed saw-bones had just seen me trampled under the hoofs of two regiments; no doubt they never took the trouble to feel my pulse, but reported me as dead. The certificate of my death was doubtless drawn up in due form of military law."

Gradually, as he listened to his client, who expressed himself with perfect clearness, and related facts that were quite possible, though somewhat strange, the young lawyer pushed away his papers, rested his left elbow on the table, put his head on his hand, and looked fixedly at the colonel.

"Are you aware, monsieur," he said, "that I am the solicitor[24] of the Countess Ferraud, widow of Colonel Chabert?"

"Of my wife? Yes, monsieur. And therefore, after many fruitless efforts to obtain a hearing from lawyers, who all thought me mad, I determined to come to you. I shall speak of my sorrows later. Allow me now to state the facts, and explain to you how they probably happened, rather than how they actually did happen. Certain circumstances, which can never be known except to God Almighty, oblige me to relate much in the form of hypotheses. I must tell you, for instance, that the wounds I received probably produced something like lockjaw, or threw me into a state analogous to a disease called, I believe, catalepsy.[25] Otherwise, how can I suppose that I was stripped of my clothing and flung into a common grave, according to the customs of war, by the men whose business it was to bury the dead?

[21] Joachim Murat was a French general and brother-in-law of Napoleon.

[22] A multivolume military history of France, especially of the Revolutionary and Napoleonic periods, published after the wars and based largely on official bulletins.

[23] Napoleon (crowned as Emperor of the French in 1804).

[24] Legal counselor. [25] A condition accompanied by unawareness of external things.

Here let me state a circumstance which I only knew much later than the event which I am forced to call my death. In 1814 I met in Stuttgart[26] an old cavalry sergeant of my regiment. That dear man—the only human being willing to recognize me, of whom I will presently speak to you—explained to me the extraordinary circumstances of my preservation. He said that my horse received a bullet in the body at the same moment when I myself was wounded. Horse and rider were therefore knocked over together like a stand of muskets. In turning, either to the right or to the left, I had doubtless been protected by the body of my horse which saved me from being crushed by the riders or hit by bullets."

The old man paused for a moment as if to collect himself and then resumed:

"When I came to myself, monsieur, I was in a place and in an atmosphere of which I could give you no idea, even if I talked for days. The air I breathed was mephitic.[27] I tried to move but I found no space. My eyes were open but I saw nothing. The want of air was the worst sign, and it showed me the dangers of my position. I felt I was in some place where the atmosphere was stagnant, and that I should die of it. This thought overcame the sense of extreme pain which had brought me to my senses. My ears hummed violently. I heard, or thought I heard (for I can affirm nothing), groans from the heap of dead bodies among whom I lay. Though the recollection of those moments is dark, though my memory is confused, and in spite of still greater sufferings which I experienced later and which have bewildered my ideas, there are nights, even now, when I think I hear those smothered moans. But there was something more horrible than even those cries—a silence that I have never known elsewhere, the silence of the grave. At last, raising my hands and feeling for the dead, I found a void between my head and the human carrion about me. I could even measure the space thus left to me by some mere chance, the cause of which I did not know. It seemed as if, thanks to the carelessness or to the haste with which we had been flung pell-mell into the trench, that two dead bodies had fallen across each other above me, so as to form an angle like that of two cards which children lay together to make houses. Quickly feeling in all directions—for I had no time to idle—I happily came across an arm, the arm of a Hercules, detached from its body; and those good bones saved me! Without that unlooked-for succor I must have perished. But now, with a fury you will readily understand, I began to work my way upward through the bodies which separated me from the layer of earth hastily flung over us—I say 'us,' as though there were others living. I worked with a will, monsieur, for here I am! Still, I don't know to-day how it was that I managed to tear through the covering of flesh that lay between me and life. I had, as it were, three arms. The Herculean crow-bar, which I used carefully, brought me a little air confined among the bodies which it helped me to displace, and I economized my breathing. At last I saw daylight, but through the snow, monsieur! Just then I noticed for the first time that my head was cut open. Happily, my blood—that of my comrades, possibly, how should I know? of the bleeding flesh of my horse—had coagulated on my wound and formed a natural plaster. But in spite of that scab I fainted

[26] City in southwest Germany. [27] Having a poisonously foul odor.

when my head came in contact with the snow. The little heat still left in my body melted the snow about me, and when I came to myself my head was in the middle of a little opening, through which I shouted as long as I was able. But the sun had risen and I was little likely to be heard. People seemed already in the fields. I raised myself to my feet, making stepping-stones of the dead whose thighs were solid—for it wasn't the moment to stop and say, 'Honor to heroes!'

"In short, monsieur," continued the old man, who had stopped speaking for a moment, "after going through the anguish—if that word describes the rage—of seeing those cursed Germans, ay, many of them, run away when they heard the voice of a man they could not see, I was at last taken from my living grave by a woman, daring enough or inquisitive enough to come close to my head, which seemed to grow from the ground like a mushroom. The woman fetched her husband, and together they took me to their poor hovel. It seems that there I had a return of catalepsy—allow me that term with which to describe a state of which I have no idea, but which I judge, from what my hosts told me, must have been an effect of that disease. I lay for six months between life and death, not speaking, or wandering in mind when I did speak. At last my benefactors placed me in the hospital at Heilsberg.[28] Of course you understand, monsieur, that I issued from my grave as naked as I came from my mother's womb; so that when, many months later, I remembered that I was Colonel Chabert, and endeavored to make my nurses treat me with more respect than if I were a poor devil of a private, all the men in the ward laughed. Happily for me, the surgeon made it a point of honor or vanity to cure me; and he naturally became interested in his patient. When I spoke to him in a connected manner of my former life, the good man (his name was Sparchmann) had my statements recorded in the legal forms of his country, also a statement of the miraculous manner in which I had escaped from the trench, and the day and hour my benefactress and her husband had rescued me, together with the nature and exact position of my wounds and a careful description of my person. Well, monsieur, I do not possess a single one of those important papers, nor the declaration I made before a notary at Heilsberg to establish my identity. The events of the war drove us from the town, and from that day I have wandered like a vagabond, begging my bread, treated as a lunatic when I told my story, unable to earn a single sou[29] that would enable me to send for those papers, which alone can prove the truth of what I say and restore me to my social status. Often my physical sufferings have kept me for weeks and months in some obscure country town, where the greatest kindness has been shown to the sick Frenchman, but where they laughed in his face when he asserted he was Colonel Chabert. For a long while such doubts and laughter made me furious, and that injured my cause, and once I was shut up as a madman at Stuttgart. You can imagine, from what I have told you, that there were reasons to lock me up. After two years in a madhouse, where I was forced to hear my keepers say: 'This poor man fancies he was once Colonel Chabert,' to visitors, who replied compassionately, 'Ah, poor man!' I myself was convinced of the impossibility of my story being true; I grew sad, resigned, tranquil, and I ceased to call myself

[28] Town about eighteen miles from Eylau. [29] Penny.

Colonel Chabert, so as to get my release and return to France. Oh, monsieur! to see Paris once more! it was a joy I—"

With those unfinished words Colonel Chabert sank into a revery, which the lawyer did not disturb.

"Monsieur," resumed the client presently, "one fine day, a spring day, they gave me my freedom and ten thalers,[30] on the ground that I talked sensibly on all subjects and had given up calling myself Colonel Chabert; and, God knows, at that time my name was disagreeable to me, and has been at intervals ever since. I would like not to be myself; the sense of my rights kills me. If my illness had only taken from me forever the remembrance of my past existence, I might be happy. I might have reentered the service under some other name; and, who knows? perhaps I should have ended as a Russian or an Austrian field-marshal."

"Monsieur," said the lawyer, "you have upset all my ideas; I fancy I dream as I listen to you. Let us pause here for a moment, I beg of you."

"You are the only person," said the colonel sadly, "who have ever listened to me patiently. No lawyer has been willing to lend me ten napoleons,[31] that I might send to Germany for the papers necessary for my suit."

"What suit?" asked the lawyer, who had forgotten the unfortunate present position of his client, as he listened to the recital of his past misery.

"Why, monsieur, you are well aware that the Comtesse Ferraud is my wife. She possesses an income of thirty thousand francs which belongs to me, and she refuses to give me one penny of it. When I tell this to lawyers and to men of common-sense, when I, a beggar, propose to sue a count and countess, when I, risen from the dead, deny the proofs of my death, they put me off—they refuse to listen to me, either with that coldly polite air with which you lawyers know so well how to rid yourselves of hapless creatures, or brutally, as men do when they think they are dealing with a swindler or a madman. I have been buried beneath the dead, but now I am buried beneath the living—beneath facts, beneath records, beneath society itself, which seeks to thrust me back underground!"

"Monsieur, have the goodness to sue, to prosecute now," said the lawyer.

"Have the goodness! Ah!" exclaimed the unfortunate old man, taking the hand of the young lawyer, "that is the first polite word I have heard since—"

He wept. Gratitude stifled his voice. The all-penetrative, indescribable eloquence of look, gesture—even silence—clinched Derville's conviction, and touched him keenly.

"Listen to me, monsieur," he said. "I won three hundred francs at cards to-night; I can surely afford to give half that sum to procure the happiness of a man. I will make all the investigations and orders necessary to obtain the papers you mention; and, until their arrival, I will allow you five francs a day. If you are Colonel Chabert, you will know how to pardon the smallness of the loan offered by a young man who has his fortune to make. Continue."

The self-styled colonel remained for an instant motionless, and as if stupefied; his great misfortunes had, perhaps, destroyed his powers of be-

[30] German silver coins. [31] French gold coins worth twenty francs.

lief. If he were seeking to recover his illustrious military fame, his home, his fortune—himself, in short—it may have been only in obedience to that inexplicable feeling, that germ in the hearts of all men, to which we owe the researches of the alchemists, the passion for glory, the discoveries of astronomy and of physics—all that urges a man to magnify himself by the magnitude of the facts or the ideas that are a part of him. The *ego* was now but a secondary consideration to his mind, just as the vanity of triumph or the satisfaction of gain are dearer to a man who bets than the object of his wager. The words of the young lawyer came, therefore, like a miracle to this man, repudiated for the last ten years by wife, by justice, by the whole social creation. To receive from a lawyer those ten gold pieces so long denied him, by so many persons, in so many ways! The colonel was like the lady who had been ill so long, that when she was cured she thought she was suffering from a new malady. There are joys in which we no longer believe; they come, and we find them thunderbolts—they blast us. So now the poor man's gratitude was so deep that he could not utter it. He might have seemed cold to a superficial mind, but Derville saw integrity in that very stupor. A swindler would have spoken.

"Where was I?" said the colonel, with the guilelessness of a child or a soldier; for there is much of the child in the true soldier, and nearly always something of a soldier in a child, especially in France.

"At Stuttgart; they had set you at liberty."

"You know my wife?" asked the colonel.

"Yes," replied Derville, with a nod of his head.

"How is she?"

"Always fascinating."

The old man made a gesture with his hand, and seemed to conquer some secret pang with the grave and solemn resignation that characterizes men who have been tried in the fire and blood of battle-fields.

"Monsieur," he said, with a sort of gayety; for he breathed anew, poor soul; he had issued a second time from the grave; he had broken through a crust of ice and snow harder to melt than that which once had frozen his wounded head; he inhaled the air as though he were just issuing from a dungeon. "Monsieur," he said, "if I were a handsome fellow I shouldn't be where I am now. Women believe men when they lard their sentences with words of love. Then they'll fetch and carry, and come and go, and do anything to serve you. They'll intrigue; they'll swear to facts; they'll play the devil for the man they love. But how could I make a woman listen to one like me? With a face like a death's head, and clothed like a sans-culotte,[32] I was more of an Eskimo than a Frenchman—I, who in 1799 was the finest coxcomb[33] in the service!—I, Chabert, count of the Empire! At last the day came when I knew I was an outcast on the streets, like a pariah[34] dog. That day I met the sergeant I told you of; his name was Boutin. That poor devil and I made the finest pair of broken-down old brutes I have ever seen. I met him, and recognized him; but he couldn't even guess who I was. We went into a tavern. When I told him my name his mouth split open with a

[32] Literally, "without breeches"; the term for the radicals of the French Revolution who wore long trousers instead of the aristocratic knee-breeches.

[33] A conceited, finely dressed person. [34] Outcast.

roar of laughter like a burst mortar. Monsieur, that laugh is among the bitterest of my sorrows. It revealed, without disguise, the changes there were in me. I saw myself unrecognizable, even to the humblest and most grateful of my friends; for I had once saved Boutin's life, though that was a return for something I owed him. I needn't tell you the whole story; the thing happened in Italy, at Ravenna. The house where Boutin saved me from being stabbed was none too decent. At that time I was not colonel, only a trooper, like Boutin. Happily, there were circumstances in the affair known only to him and me; when I reminded him of them, his incredulity lessened. Then I told him the story of my extraordinary fate. Though my eyes and my voice were, he told me, strangely altered; though I had neither hair, nor teeth, nor eyebrows, and was as white as an albino, he did finally recognize his old colonel in the beggar before him, after putting a vast number of questions to which I answered triumphantly.

"Ah!" went on the old soldier, after a moment's pause, "he told me his adventures too, and they were hardly less extraordinary than mine. He was just back from the borders of China, to which he had escaped from Siberia. He told me of the disasters of the Russian campaign[35] and Napoleon's first abdication; that news was another of my worst pangs. We were two strange wrecks drifting over the globe, as the storms of ocean drift the pebbles from shore to shore. We had each seen Egypt, Syria, Spain, Russia, Holland, Germany, Italy, Dalmatia, England, China, Tartary, Siberia; nothing was left for us to know but the Indies and America. Boutin, who was more active on his legs than I, agreed to go to Paris as quickly as he could, and tell my wife the state in which I was. I wrote a long and detailed letter to Madame Chabert; it was the fourth I had written her. Monsieur, if I had had relatives of my own, the thing could not have happened; but, I must tell you plainly, I was a foundling, a soldier whose patrimony was his courage, the world his family, France his country, God his sole protector—no! I am wrong; I had a father—the Emperor! Ah! if he, dear man, were still among us; if he saw 'his Chabert,' as he called me, in such a plight, he would be furious. But what's to be done? our sun has set; we are all left out in the cold! After all, political events might be the reason of my wife's silence; at least I thought so. Boutin departed. He was lucky, *he* was, poor fellow! he had two white bears who danced and kept him in food. I could not accompany him; my pains were so great I could not go long distances. I wept when we parted, having walked as far as I had strength with the bears and him. At Karlsruhe[36] I was taken with neuralgia in my head, and lay six weeks in the straw of an inn barn.

"Ah! monsieur," continued the unhappy man, "there is no end to what I might tell you of my miserable life. Moral anguish, before which all physical sufferings are as nought, excites less pity because it is not seen. I remember weeping before a mansion in Strasbourg[37] where I once gave a ball, and where they now refused me a crust of bread. Having agreed with Boutin as to the road I should follow, I went to every post-office on my way

[35] The French forces, probably the largest army in history up to that time, were routed disastrously after Napoleon led them into Russia in 1812.
[36] A German city on the Rhine river.
[37] A French city on the Rhine near the German border.

expecting to find a letter and some money. I reached Paris at last without a line. Despair was in my heart! Boutin must be dead, I thought; and I was right; the poor fellow died at Waterloo, as I heard later and accidentally. His errand to my wife was no doubt fruitless. Well, I reached Paris just as the Cossacks entered it. To me, that was grief upon grief. When I saw those Russians in France I no longer remembered that I had neither shoes on my feet nor money in my pocket. Yes, monsieur, my clothes were literally in shreds. The evening of my arrival I was forced to bivouac in the woods of Claye. The chilliness of the night gave me a sort of illness, I hardly know what it was, which seized me as I was crossing the faubourg Saint-Martin. I fell, half-unconscious, close by the door of an ironmonger. When I came to my senses I was in a bed at the Hôtel-Dieu.[38] There I stayed a month in some comfort; then I was discharged. I had no money, but I was cured and I had my feet on the blessed pavements of Paris. With what joy and speed I made my way to the rue du Mont-Blanc, where I supposed my wife was living in my house. Bah! the rue du Mont-Blanc had become the rue de la Chaussée-d'Antin. My house was no longer standing; it was pulled down. Speculators had built houses in my gardens. Not knowing that my wife had married Monsieur Ferraud, I could hear nothing of her. At last I went to an old lawyer who formerly took charge of my affairs. The good man was dead, and his office had passed into the hands of a young man. The latter informed me, to my great astonishment, of the settlement of my estate, the marriage of my wife, and the birth of her two children. When I told him that I was Colonel Chabert, he laughed so loudly in my face that I turned and left him without a word. My detention at Stuttgart made me mindful of Charenton,[39] and I resolved to act prudently. Then, monsieur, knowing where my wife lived, I made my way to the house—Ah!" cried the colonel, with a gesture of intense anger, "I was not received when I gave a borrowed name, but when I sent in my own I was turned out of the house! I have stood night after night leaning against the buttress of her porte-cochère[40] to see her returning from a ball or from the theater. I have plunged my eyes into that carriage where I could see the woman who is mine and who is not mine! Oh! from that day I have lived for vengeance," cried the old man, in a hollow voice, standing suddenly erect in front of Derville. "She knows I am living; she has received three letters which I have written to her since my return. She loves me no longer! I—I don't know if I love her or if I hate her; I long for her and I curse her by turns! She owes her prosperity and all her happiness to me, and she denies me even the meanest succor! Sometimes I don't know where to turn!"

The old man fell back into a chair, motionless and silent. Derville too was silent, contemplating his client.

"The matter is serious," he said at last in a mechanical way. "Even admitting the authenticity of the papers which ought to be found at Heilsberg, it is not clear that we can establish our case—certainly not at once. The suit will have to go before three courts. I must reflect at my leisure over such a case. It is exceptional."

[38] An ancient hospital in Paris.

[39] An eastern suburb of Paris, site of an insane asylum.

[40] Entrance for carriages.

"Oh!" replied the colonel, coldly, lifting his head with a proud gesture, "if I am compelled to succumb, I can die—but not alone."

With the words the old man seemed to vanish; the eyes of the man of energy shone with the fires of desire and vengeance.

"Perhaps we shall have to compromise," said the lawyer.

"Compromise!" repeated Colonel Chabert. "Am I dead, or am I living?"

"Monsieur," said the lawyer, "you will, I hope, follow my advice. Your cause shall be my cause. You will soon, I trust, see the true interest I take in your situation, which is almost without precedent in legal annals. Meantime let me give you an order on my notary, who will remit you fifty francs every ten days on your receipt. It is not desirable that you should come here for this money. If you are Colonel Chabert you ought not to be beholden to anyone. I shall make these advances in the form of a loan. You have property to recover; you are a rich man."

This last delicate consideration for his feelings brought tears from the old man's eyes. Derville rose abruptly, for assuredly it is not the thing for a lawyer to show feeling; he went into his private study and returned presently with an unsealed letter, which he gave to Colonel Chabert. When the old man took it he felt two gold pieces within the paper.

"Tell me precisely what the papers are; give me the exact name of the town and kingdom," said the lawyer.

The colonel dictated the necessary information and corrected the spelling of the names. Then he took his hat in one hand, looked at Derville, offered him the other hand, a horny hand, and said in a simple way—

"After the Emperor you are the man to whom I owe most. You are a noble man."

The lawyer clasped the colonel's hand, and went with him to the stairway to light him down.

"Boucard," said the lawyer to his head-clerk, whom he summoned, "I have just heard a tale which may cost me some money. If I am deceived I shall never regret what I pay, for I shall have seen the greatest comedian[41] of our time."

When the colonel reached the street, he stopped under a lamp, drew the two pieces of twenty francs each from the letter which the lawyer had given him, and looked at them for a moment in the dim light. He saw gold for the first time in nine years.

"I can smoke cigars," he said to himself.

About three months after the nocturnal consultation of Colonel Chabert with Derville, the notary whom the latter had directed to pay the stipend he allowed to his singular client went to the lawyer's office one day to confer on some important matter, and opened the conversation by asking for the six hundred francs he had already paid to the old soldier.

"Do you find it amusing to support the old army?" said the notary, laughing. His name was Crottat—a young man who had just bought a practice in which he was head-clerk, the master of which, a certain Roguin, had lately absconded after a frightful failure.

[41] Actor.

"Thank you, my dear fellow, for reminding me of that affair," replied Derville. "My philanthropy does not go beyond twenty-five louis;[42] I fear I have been the dupe of my patriotism."

As Derville uttered the words his eyes lighted on a packet of papers the head-clerk had laid upon his desk. His attention was drawn to one of the letters by the postmarks, oblong, square, and triangular, and red and blue stamped upon it in the Prussian, Austrian, Bavarian, and French post-offices.

"Ah!" said he, laughing, "here's the conclusion of the comedy; now we shall see if I have been taken in."

He took up the letter and opened it, but was unable to read a word, for it was in German.

"Boucard!" he called, opening the door and holding out the letter to his head-clerk, "go yourself and get that letter translated, and come back with it as fast as you can."

The Berlin notary to whom Derville had written now replied by informing the latter that the papers he had asked for would reach him a few days after this letter of advice. They were all, he said, perfectly regular, and were fully certified with the necessary legal forms. He added, moreover, that nearly all the witnesses to the facts were still living, and that the woman to whom Monsieur le Comte Chabert owed his life could be found in a certain suburb of Heilsberg.

"It is getting serious," said Derville, when Boucard had told him the substance of the letter. "But see here, my dear fellow, I want some information which I am sure you must have in your office. When that old swindler of a Roguin—"

"We say 'the unfortunate Roguin,' " said Crottat, laughing, as he interrupted Derville.

"Well—when that unfortunate Roguin ran off with eight hundred thousand francs of his clients' money and reduced many families to pauperism, what was done about the Chabert property? It seems to me I have seen something about it among our Ferraud papers."

"Yes," replied Crottat, "I was third clerk at the time, and I remember copying and studying the documents. Rose Chapotel, wife and widow of Hyacinthe, called Chabert, count of the Empire, grand officer of the Legion of honor. They had married without a contract and therefore they held their property in common. As far as I can recollect, the assets amounted to about six hundred thousand francs. Before his marriage Comte Chabert had made a will leaving one fourth of the property of which he might die possessed to the Parisian hospitals; the State inherited another fourth. There was an auction sale and a distribution of the property, for the lawyers made good speed with the affair. Upon the settlement of the estate the monster[43] who then ruled France made a decree restoring the amount which had gone to the Treasury to the colonel's widow."

"So that Comte Chabert's individual property," said Derville, "does not amount to more than three hundred thousand francs?"

"Just that, old man," said Crottat. "You solicitors do occasionally get

[42] Coins each worth twenty gold francs. [43] Napoleon.

things right—though some people accuse you of arguing just as well against as for the truth."

Comte Chabert, whose address was written at the foot of the first receipt he had given to the notary, lived in the faubourg Saint Marceau, rue du Petit-Banquier, with an old sergeant of the Imperial Guard named Vergniaud, now a cow-keeper. When Derville reached the place he was obliged to go on foot to find his client, for his groom positively refused to drive through an unpaved street the ruts of which were deep enough to break the wheels of a cabriolet. Looking about him on all sides, the lawyer at length discovered at the end of the street nearest to the boulevard and between two walls built of bones and mud, two shabby rough stone pillars, much defaced by wheels in spite of wooden posts placed in front of them. These pillars supported a beam covered with a tiled hood, on which, painted red, were the words, "VERGNIAUD, COW-KEEPER." To the right of the name was a cow, and to the left eggs, all painted white. The gate was open.

At the farther end of a good-sized yard and opposite to the gate stood the house, if indeed that name rightfully belongs to one of those hovels built in the suburbs of Paris, the squalor of which cannot be matched elsewhere, not even in the most wretched of country huts; for they have all the poverty of the latter without their poetry. In fact, a cabin in the open country has the charm that pure air, verdure, the meadow vistas, a hill, a winding road, creepers, evergreen hedges, a mossy roof and rural implements can give to it; but in Paris poverty is heightened only by horrors. Though recently built, the house seemed tumbling to ruins. None of its materials were originally destined for it; they came from the "demolitions" which are daily events in Paris. On a shutter made of an old sign Derville read the words "Fancy-articles." No two of the windows were alike, and all were placed haphazard. The ground-floor, which seemed to be the habitable part of the hovel, was raised from the earth on one side, while on the other the rooms were sunk below a bank. Between the gate and the house was a slough of manure, into which flowed the rain-water and the drainage from the house. The wall upon which this rickety building rested was surrounded by hutches in which rabbits brought forth their numerous young. To the right of the gate was the cow-shed, which communicated with the house through a dairy, and over it the hay-loft. To the left was a poultry-yard, a stable, and a pig-sty, all of which were finished off, like the house, with shabby planks of white-wood nailed one above the other and filled in with rushes. Like most of the purlieus[44] whence the elements of the grand dinners daily eaten in Paris are derived, the yard in which Derville now stood showed signs of the haste required for the prompt filling of orders. The great tin cans in which the milk was carried, the smaller cans with their linen stoppers which contained the cream, were tossed higgledy-piggledy in front of the dairy. The rags used to wipe them out were hanging in the sun to dry, on lines fastened to hooks. The steady horse, of a race extinct except among milk-dealers, had walked a few steps away from the cart and stood in front of the stable, the door of which was locked. A goat browsed

[44] Neighborhoods.

upon the spindling, powdery vine-shoots which crept along the cracked and yellow walls of the house. A cat was creeping among the cream-cans and licking the outside of them. The hens, scared at Derville's advent, scuttled away cackling, and the watch-dog barked.

"The man who decided the victory of Eylau lives here!" thought Derville, taking in at a glance the whole of this squalid scene.

The house seemed to be under the guardianship of three little ragamuffins. One, who had clambered to the top of a cart laden with green fodder, was throwing stones down the chimney of the next house, probably hoping that they would fall into the saucepans below; another was trying to lead a pig up the floor of a tip-cart, one end of which touched the ground, while the third, hanging on to the other end, was waiting till the pig was fairly in to tip the cart up again. When Derville asked if that was where Monsieur Chabert lived none of them answered; and all three gazed at him with lively stupidity—if it is allowable to unite those words. Derville repeated his question without result. Provoked at the saucy air of the little scamps, he spoke sharply, in a tone which young men think they can use to children, and the boys broke silence with a roar of laughter. Derville was angry. The colonel, who heard the noise, came out of a little room near the dairy and stood on the sill of his door with the imperturbable phlegm of a military training. In his mouth was a pipe in process of being "colored"[45]—one of those humble pipes of white clay with short stems called "muzzle-scorchers." He raised the peak of a cap which was horribly greasy, saw Derville, and came across the manure heap in haste to meet his benefactor, calling out in a friendly tone to the boys, "Silence in the ranks!" The children became instantly and respectfully silent, showing the power the old soldier had over them.

"Why haven't you written to me?" he said to Derville. "Go along by the cow-house; see, the yard is paved on that side," he cried, noticing the hesitation of the young lawyer, who did not care to set his feet in the wet manure.

Jumping from stone to stone, Derville at last reached the door through which the colonel had issued. Chabert seemed annoyed at the necessity of receiving him in the room he was occupying. In fact, there was only one chair. The colonel's bed was merely a few bundles of straw on which his landlady had spread some ragged bits of old carpet, such as milk-women lay upon the seats of their wagons, and pick up, heaven knows where. The floor was neither more nor less than the earth beaten hard. Such dampness exuded from the nitrified walls, greenish in color and full of cracks, that the side where the colonel slept had been covered with a mat made of reeds. The topcoat was hanging on a nail. Two pairs of broken boots lay in a corner. Not a vestige of under-clothing was seen. The "Bulletins of the Grand Army,"[46] reprinted by Plancher, was lying open on a mouldy table, as if constantly read by the colonel, whose face was calm and serene in the midst of this direful poverty. His visit to Derville seemed to have changed the very character of his features, on which the lawyer now saw traces of happy thought, the special gleam which hope had cast.

[45] Seasoned. [46] Military chronicle of the Napoleonic wars.

"Does the smoke of a pipe annoy you?" he asked, offering the one chair, and that half-denuded of straw.

"But colonel, you are shockingly ill-lodged here!"

The words were wrung from Derville by the natural distrust of lawyers, caused by the deplorable experience that comes to them so soon from the dreadful, mysterious dramas in which they are called professionally to take part.

"That man," thought Derville to himself, "has no doubt spent my money in gratifying the three cardinal virtues of a trooper—wine, women, and cards."

"True enough, monsieur; we don't abound in luxury. It is a bivouac, tempered, as you may say, by friendship; but" (here the soldier cast a searching look at the lawyer) "I have done wrong to no man, I have repulsed no man, and I sleep in peace."

Derville felt there would be a want of delicacy in asking his client to account for his use of the money he had lent him, so he merely said: "Why don't you come into Paris, where you could live just as cheaply as you do here, and be much better off?"

"Because," replied the colonel, "the good, kind people I am with took me in and fed me gratis for a year, and how could I desert them the moment I got a little money? Besides, the father of these young scamps is an Egyptian."

"An Egyptian?"

"That's what we call the troopers who returned from the expedition to Egypt,[47] in which I took part. Not only are we all brothers in heart, but Vergniaud was in my regiment; he and I shared the water of the desert. Besides, I want to finish teaching those little monkeys to read."

"He might give you a better room for your money," said the lawyer.

"Bah!" said the colonel, "the children sleep as I do on straw. He and his wife have no better bed themselves. They are very poor, you see; they have more of an establishment here than they can manage. But if I get back my fortune—Well, enough!"

"Colonel, I expect to receive your papers from Heilsberg to-morrow; your benefactress is still living."

"Oh! cursed money! to think I haven't any!" cried the colonel, flinging down his pipe.

A "colored" pipe is a precious pipe to a smoker; but the action was so natural and so generous that all smokers would have forgiven him that act of leze-tobacco;[48] the angels might have picked up the pieces.

"Colonel, your affair is very complicated," said Derville, leaving the room to walk up and down in the sun before the house.

"It seems to me," said the soldier, "perfectly simple. They thought me dead, and here I am! Give me back my wife and my property; give me the rank of general—to which I have a right, for I had passed colonel in the Imperial Guard the night before the battle of Eylau."

"Matters are not managed that way in law," said Derville. "Listen to me. You are Comte Chabert—I'll admit that; but the thing is to prove it legally

[47] Napoleon's army campaigned in Egypt in 1798–1799. [48] "Treason" against tobacco.

against those persons whose interest it is to deny your existence. All your papers and documents will be disputed; and the very first discussions will open a dozen or more preliminary questions. Every step will be fought over up to the supreme court. All that will involve expensive suits, which will drag along, no matter how much energy I put into them. Your adversaries will demand an inquiry, which we cannot refuse, and which will perhaps necessitate sending a commission to Prussia. But suppose all went well, and you were promptly and legally recognized as Colonel Chabert, what then? Do we know how the question of Madame Ferraud's innocent bigamy would be decided? Here's a case where the question of rights is outside of the Code, and can be decided by the judges only under the laws of conscience, as a jury does in many delicate cases which social perversities bring up in criminal courts. Now, here's a point: you had no children by your marriage, and Monsieur Ferraud has two; the judges may annul the marriage where the ties are weakest, in favor of a marriage which involves the well-being of children, admitting that the parents married in good faith. Would it be a fine or moral position for you, at your age, and under these circumstances, to insist on having—will ye, nill ye[49]—a wife who no longer loves you? You would have against you a husband and wife who are powerful and able to bring influence upon the judges. The case has many elements of duration in it. You may spend years and grow an old man still struggling with the sharpest grief and anxiety."

"But my property?"

"You think you have a large fortune?"

"I had an income of thirty thousand francs."

"My dear colonel, in 1799, before your marriage, you made a will leaving a quarter of your whole property to the hospitals."

"That is true."

"Well, you were supposed to be dead; then of course an inventory of your property was made and the whole wound up in order to give that fourth part to the said hospitals. Your wife had no scruples about cheating the poor. The inventory, in which she took care not to mention the cash on hand or her jewelry, or the full amount of the silver, and in which the furniture was appraised at two-thirds below its real value (either to please her or to lessen the treasury tax, for appraisers are liable for the amount of their valuations)—this inventory, I say, gave your property as amounting to six hundred thousand francs. Your widow had a legal right to half. Everything was sold and bought in by her; she gained on the whole transaction, and the hospitals got their seventy-five thousand francs. Then, as the Treasury inherited the rest of your property (for you had not mentioned your wife in your will), the Emperor made a decree returning the portion which reverted to the Treasury to your widow. Now, then, the question is, to what have you any legal right?—to three hundred thousand francs only, less costs."

"You call that justice?" said the colonel, thunder-struck.

"Of course."

"Fine justice!"

"It is always so, my poor colonel. You see now that what you thought so

[49] No matter what anyone else wants.

easy is not easy at all. Madame Ferraud may also try to keep the portion the Emperor returned to her."

"But she was not a widow, and therefore the decree was null."

"I admit that. But everything can be argued. Listen to me. Under these circumstances, I think a compromise is the best thing both for you and for her. You could get a larger sum that way than by asserting your rights."

"It would be selling my wife!"

"With an income of twenty-four thousand francs you would be in a position to find another who would suit you better and make you happier. I intend to go and see the Comtesse Ferraud to-day, and find out how the land lies; but I did not wish to take that step without letting you know."

"We will go together."

"Dressed as you are?" said the lawyer. "No, no, colonel, no! You might lose your case."

"Can I win it?"

"Yes, under all aspects," answered Derville. "But my dear Colonel Chabert, there is one thing you pay no heed to. I am not rich, and my practice is not yet wholly paid for. If the courts should be willing to grant you a provisional maintenance they will only do so after recognizing your claims as Colonel Chabert, grand officer of the Legion of honor."

"So I am!" said the old man, naïvely, "grand officer of the Legion of honor—I had forgotten that."

"Well, as I was saying," resumed Derville, "till then you will have to bring suits, pay lawyers, serve writs, employ sheriffs, and live. The cost of those preliminary steps will amount to more than twelve or even fifteen thousand francs. I can't lend you the money for I am crushed by the enormous interest I am forced to pay to those who lent me money to buy my practice. Where, then, can you get it?"

Big tears fell from the faded eyes of the old soldier and rolled down his cheeks. The sight of these difficulties discouraged him. The social and judicial world lay upon his breast like a nightmare.

"I will go to the column of the place Vêndome," he said, "and cry aloud, 'I am Colonel Chabert, who broke the Russian square at Eylau!' The man of iron[50] up there—ah! he'll recognize me!"

"They would put you in Charenton."

At that dreaded name the soldier's courage fell.

"Perhaps I should have a better chance at the ministry of war," he said.

"In a government office? Well, try it," said Derville. "But you must take with you a legal judgment declaring your death disproved. The government would prefer to get rid of the Empire people."

The colonel remained for a moment speechless, motionless, gazing before him and seeing nothing, plunged in a bottomless despair. Military justice is prompt and straight-forward; it decides peremptorily, and is generally fair; this was the only justice Chabert knew. Seeing the labyrinth of difficulty which lay before him, and knowing that he had no money with which to enter it, the poor soldier was mortally wounded in that particular power of human nature which we call *will*. He felt it was impossible for him to live in a legal struggle; far easier to his nature was it to stay poor and a

[50] Statue of Napoleon.

beggar, or to enlist in some cavalry regiment if they would still take him. Physical and mental suffering had vitiated his body in some of its important organs. He was approaching one of those diseases for which the science of medicine has no name, the seat of which is, in a way, movable (like the nervous system which is the part of our machinery most frequently attacked), an affection which we must fain call "the spleen of sorrow." However serious this invisible but most real disease might be, it was still curable by a happy termination of his griefs. To completely unhinge and destroy that vigorous organization some final blow was needed, some unexpected shock which might break the weakened springs and produce those strange hesitations, those vague, incomplete, and inconsequent actions which physiologists notice in all persons wrecked by grief.

Observing symptoms of deep depression in his client, Derville hastened to say: "Take courage; the issue[51] of the affair must be favorable to you in some way or other. Only, examine your own mind and see if you can place implicit trust in me, and accept blindly the course that I shall think best for you."

"Do what you will," said Chabert.

"Yes, but will you surrender yourself to me completely, like a man marching to his death?"

"Am I to live without a status and without a name? Is that bearable?"

"I don't mean that," said the lawyer. "We will bring an amicable suit to annul the record of your decease, and also your marriage; then you will resume your rights. You could even be, through Comte Ferraud's influence, restored to the army with the rank of general, and you would certainly obtain a pension."

"Well, go on, then," replied Chabert. "I trust implicitly in you."

"I will send you a power-of-attorney[52] to sign," said Derville. "Adieu, keep up your courage; if you want money let me know."

Chabert wrung the lawyer's hand, and stood with his back against the wall, unable to follow him except with his eyes. During this conference the face of a man had every now and then looked round one of the gate pillars, behind which its owner was posted waiting for Derville's departure. The man now accosted the young lawyer. He was old, and he wore a blue jacket, a pleated white smock like those worn by brewers, and on his head a cap of otter fur. His face was brown, hollow, and wrinkled, but red at the cheekbones from hard work and exposure to the weather.

"Excuse me, monsieur, if I take the liberty of speaking to you," he said, touching Derville on the arm. "But I supposed when I saw you that you were the general's friend."

"Well," said Derville, "what interest have you in him? Who are you?" added the distrustful lawyer.

"I am Louis Vergniaud," answered the man, "and I want to have a word with you."

"Then it is you who lodge the Comte Chabert in this way, is it?"

"Pardon it, monsieur. He has the best room in the house. I would have given him mine if I had had one, and slept myself in the stable. A man who has suffered as he has and who is teaching my kids to read, a general, an

[51] Outcome. [52] A legal authorization of another person to act in one's place.

Egyptian, the first lieutenant under whom I served—why, all I have is his! I've shared all with him. Unluckily it is so little—bread and milk and eggs! However, when you're on a campaign you must live with the mess;[53] and little as it is, it is given with a full heart, monsieur. But he has vexed us."

"He!"

"Yes, monsieur, vexed us; there's no going behind that. I took this establishment, which is more than I can manage, and he saw that. It troubled him, and he would do my work and take care of the horse! I kept saying to him, 'No, no, my general!' But there! he only answered, 'Am I a lazybones? don't I know how to put my shoulder to the wheel?' So I gave notes for the value of my cow-house to a man named Grados. Do you know him, monsieur?"

"But, my good friend, I haven't the time to listen to all this. Tell me only how Colonel Chabert vexed you."

"He did vex us, monsieur, just as true as my name is Louis Vergniaud, and my wife cried about it. He heard from the neighbors that I couldn't meet that note; and the old fellow, without a word to us, took all you gave him, and, little by little, paid the note! Wasn't it a trick! My wife and I knew he went without tobacco all that time, poor old man! But now, yes, he has the cigars—I'd sell my own self sooner! But it does vex us. Now, I propose to you to lend me on this establishment three hundred francs, so that we may get him some clothes and furnish his room. He thinks he had paid us, doesn't he? Well, the truth is, he has made us his debtors. Yes, he has vexed us; he shouldn't have played us such a trick—wasn't it almost an insult? Such friends as we are! As true as my name is Louis Vergniaud, I will mortgage myself rather than not return you that money."

Derville looked at the cow-keeper, then he made a step backward and looked at the house, the yard, the manure, the stable, the rabbits, and the children.

"Faith!" thought he to himself, "I do believe one of the characteristics of virtue is to own nothing. Yes," he said aloud, "you shall have your three hundred francs, and more too. But it is not I who give them to you, it is the colonel; he will be rich enough to help you, and I shall not deprive him of that pleasure."

"Will it be soon?"

"Yes, soon."

"Good God! how happy my wife will be." The tanned face of the cow-keeper brightened into joy.

"Now," thought Derville as he jumped into his cabriolet, "to face the enemy. She must not see our game, but we must know hers, and win it at one trick. She is a woman. What are women most afraid of? Why, of—"

He began to study the countess' position, and fell into one of those deep reveries to which great politicians are prone when they prepare their plans and try to guess the secrets of foreign powers. Lawyers are, in a way, statesmen, to whom the management of individual interests is entrusted. A glance at the situation of Monsieur le Comte Ferraud and his wife is necessary for a full comprehension of the lawyer's genius.

Monsieur le Comte Ferraud was the son of a former councillor of the

[53] Military meals.

parliament of Paris, who had emigrated during the Terror,[54] and who, though he saved his head, lost his property. He returned to France under the Consulate,[55] and remained faithful to the interests of Louis XVIII, in whose suite his father had been before the Revolution. His son, therefore, belonged to that section of the faubourg Saint-Germain[56] which nobly resisted the Napoleonic seductions. The young count's reputation for good sense and sagacity when he was called simply "Monsieur Ferraud" made him the object of a few imperial blandishments; for the Emperor took as much satisfaction in his conquests over the aristocracy as he did in winning a battle. The count was promised the restitution of his title, also that of all his property which was not sold, and hopes were held out of a ministry in the future, and a senatorship. The Emperor failed. At the time of Comte Chabert's death Monsieur Ferraud was a young man twenty-six years of age, without fortune, agreeable in appearance and manner, and a social success, whom the faubourg Saint-Germain adopted as one of its distinguished figures.

Madame la Comtesse Chabert had managed the property derived from her late husband so well that after a widowhood of eighteen months she possessed an income of nearly forty thousand francs a year. Her marriage with the young count was not regarded as news[57] by the coteries of the faubourg. Napoleon, who was pleased with an alliance which met his ideas of fusion, returned to Madame Chabert the money derived by the Treasury from her late husband's estate; but here again Napoleon's hopes were foiled. Madame Ferraud not only adored a lover in the young man, but she was attracted by the idea of entering that haughty society which, in spite of its political abasement, was still far above that of the imperial court. Her various vanities as well as her passions were gratified by this marriage. She felt she was about to become "an elegant woman."

When the faubourg Saint-Germain ascertained that the young count's marriage was not a defection from their ranks, all salons were opened to his wife. The Restoration took place. The political fortunes of the Comte Ferraud made no rapid strides. He understood very well the exigencies of Louis XVIII's position; he was one of the initiated who waited until "the revolutionary gulf was closed"—a royal phrase which the liberals laughed at, but which, nevertheless, hid a deep political meaning. However, the ordinance with its long-winded clerical phrases quoted by Godeschal in the first pages of this story restored to the Comte Ferraud two forests and an estate which had risen in value during its sequestration.[58] At the period of which we write Comte Ferraud was Councillor of State, also a director-general, and he considered his position as no more than the opening of his political career. Absorbed in the pursuit of an eager ambition, he depended much on his secretary, a ruined lawyer named Delbecq—a man

[54] During the "Reign of Terror" in 1793–1794, thousands of people, including aristocrats and others considered hostile to the regime, were sent to the guillotine by the French Revolutionists.

[55] The early years of Napoleon's political supremacy, from the end of the Revolutionary period in 1799 to his crowning as Emperor in 1804.

[56] The old aristocratic district ("faubourg") of Paris.

[57] The meaning, probably, is that she had been known to be his mistress.

[58] Seizure of the property.

who was more than able, one who knew every possible resource of pettifogging sophistry, to whom the count left the management of all his private affairs. This clever practitioner understood his position in the count's household far too well not to be honest out of policy. He hoped for some place under government through the influence of his patron, whose property he took care of to the best of his ability. His conduct so completely refuted the dark story of his earlier life that he was now thought to be a calumniated man.

The countess, however, with the shrewd tact of a woman, fathomed the secretary, watched him carefully, and knew so well how to manage him, that she had already largely increased her fortune by his help. She contrived to convince Delbecq that she ruled Monsieur Ferraud, and promised that she would get him made judge of a municipal court in one of the most important cities in France if he devoted himself wholly to her interests. The promise of an irremovable office, which would enable him to marry advantageously and improve his political career until he became in the end a deputy, made Delbecq Madame Ferraud's abject tool. His watchfulness enabled her to profit by all those lucky chances which the fluctuations of the Bourse[59] and the rise of property in Paris during the first three years of the Restoration offered to clever manipulators of money. Delbecq had tripled her capital with all the more ease because his plans commended themselves to the countess as a rapid method of making her fortune enormous. She spent the emoluments[60] of the count's various offices on the household expenses, so as to invest every penny of her own income, and Delbecq aided and abetted this avarice without inquiring into its motives. Men of his kind care nothing for the discovery of any secrets that do not affect their own interests. Besides, he accounted for it naturally by that thirst for gold which possesses nearly all Parisian women; and as he knew how large a fortune Comte Ferraud's ambitions needed to support them, he sometimes fancied that he saw in the countess' greed a sign of her devotion to a man with whom she was still in love.

Madame Ferraud buried the motives of her conduct in the depths of her own heart. There lay the secrets of life and death to her; there is the kernel of our present history.

At the beginning of the year 1818 the Restoration was established on an apparently firm and immovable basis; its governmental doctrines, as understood by superior minds, seemed likely to lead France into an era of renewed prosperity. Then it was that society changed front. Madame la Comtesse Ferraud found that she had made a marriage of love and wealth and ambition. Still young and beautiful, she played the part of a woman of fashion and lived in the court atmosphere. Rich herself, and rich through her husband, who had the credit of being one of the ablest men of the royalist party, a friend of the king and likely to become a minister, she belonged to the aristocracy and shared its glamour.

In the midst of this triumphant prosperity a moral cancer fastened upon her. Men have feelings which women guess in spite of every effort made by such men to bury them. At the time of the king's first return Comte Ferraud was conscious of some regrets for his marriage. The widow

[59] Stock Exchange. [60] Income; salary.

of Colonel Chabert had brought him no useful connections; he was alone and without influence, to make his way in a career full of obstacles and full of enemies. Then, perhaps, after he had coolly judged his wife, he saw certain defects of education which made her unsuitable, and unable, to further his projects. A word he once said about Talleyrand's[61] marriage enlightened the countess and showed her that if the past had to be done over again he would never make her his wife. What woman would forgive that regret, containing as it did, the germs of all insults, nay, of all crimes and all repudiations!

Let us conceive the wound that this discovery made in the heart of a woman who feared the return of her first husband. She knew that he lived; she had repulsed him. Then, for a short time, she heard no more of him, and took comfort in the hope that he was killed at Waterloo together with the imperial eagles and Boutin. She then conceived the idea of binding her second husband to her by the strongest of ties, by a chain of gold; and she determined to be so rich that her great fortune should make that second marriage indissoluble if by chance Comte Chabert reappeared. He had reappeared; and she was unable to understand why the struggle she so much dreaded was not begun. Perhaps the man's sufferings, perhaps an illness had delivered her from him. Perhaps he was half-crazy and Charenton might restore his reason. She was not willing to set Delbecq or the police on his traces, for fear of putting herself in their power, or bringing on a catastrophe. There are many women in Paris who, like the Comtesse Ferraud, are living secretly with moral monsters, or skirting the edges of some abyss; they make for themselves a callus over the region of their wound and still continue to laugh and be amused.

"There is something very singular in Comte Ferraud's situation," said Derville to himself, after long meditation, as the cabriolet stopped before the gate of the hôtel[62] Ferraud in the rue de Varennes. "How is it that he, so wealthy and a favorite of the king, is not already a peer of France? Perhaps Madame de Grandlieu[63] is right in saying that the king's policy is to give higher importance to the peerage by not lavishing it. Besides, the son of a councillor of the old parliament is neither a Crillon nor a Rohan.[64] Comte Ferraud can enter the upper Chamber[65] only, as it were, on sufferance.[66] But if his marriage were ruptured wouldn't it be a satisfaction to the king if the peerage of some of those old senators who have daughters only could descend to him? Certainly that's a pretty good fear to dangle before the countess," thought Derville, as he went up the steps of the hôtel Ferraud.

Without knowing it the lawyer had laid his finger on the secret wound, he had plunged his hand into the cancer that was destroying Madame Ferraud's life. She received him in a pretty winter dining-room, where she was breakfasting and playing with a monkey, which was fastened by a chain to a sort of little post with iron bars. The countess was wrapped in an elegant morning-gown; the curls of her pretty hair, carelessly caught up, escaped from a little cap which gave her a piquant air. She was fresh and

[61] French diplomat (1754–1838); his wife is said to have been stupid. [62] Mansion.
[63] A member of a fictional old aristocratic family, several of whom figure in Balzac's works.
[64] *Crillon, Rohan.* Distinguished old families.
[65] French equivalent of the House of Lords. [66] Tolerance.

smiling. The table glittered with the silver-gilt service, the plate, the mother-of-pearl articles; rare plants were about her, growing in splendid porcelain vases.

As the lawyer looked at Comte Chabert's wife, rich with his property, surrounded by luxury, and she herself at the apex of society, while the unhappy husband lived with the beasts in a cow-house, he said to himself: "The moral of this is that a pretty woman will never acknowledge a husband, nor even a lover, in a man with an old topcoat, a shabby wig, and broken boots." A bitter and satirical smile expressed the half-philosophic, half-sarcastic ideas that necessarily come to a man who is so placed that he sees to the bottom of things in spite of the lies under which so many Parisian families hide their existence.

"Good morning, Monsieur Derville," said the countess, continuing to make the monkey drink coffee.

"Madame," he said, abruptly, for he was offended at the careless tone in which the countess greeted him. "I have come to talk to you on a serious matter."

"Oh! I am so very sorry, but the count is absent—"

"I am glad, madame; for he would be out of place at this conference. Besides, I know from Delbecq that you prefer to do business yourself, without troubling Monsieur le comte."

"Very good; then I will send for Delbecq," she said.

"He could do you no good, clever as he is," returned Derville. "Listen to me, madame; one word will suffice to make you serious. Comte Chabert is living."

"Do you expect me to be serious when you talk such nonsense as that?" she said, bursting into a fit of laughter.

But the countess was suddenly subdued by the strange lucidity of the fixed look with which Derville questioned her, seeming to read into the depths of her soul.

"Madame," he replied, with cold and incisive gravity, "you are not aware of the dangers of your position. I do not speak of the undeniable authenticity of the papers in the case, nor of the positive proof that can be brought of Comte Chabert's existence. I am not a man, as you know, to take charge of a hopeless case. If you oppose our steps to prove the falsity of the death-record, you will certainly lose that first suit, and that question once settled in our favor determines all the others."

"Then, what do you wish to speak of?"

"Not of the colonel, nor of you; neither shall I remind you of the costs a clever lawyer in possession of all the facts of the case might charge upon you, nor of the game such a man could play with those letters which you received from your first husband before you married your second—"

"It is false!" she cried, with the violence of a spoilt beauty. "I have never received a letter from Comte Chabert. If any one calls himself the colonel he is a swindler, a galley-slave perhaps, like Cogniard;[67] it makes me shud-

[67] Balzac's misspelling of Coignard, the name of a notorious adventurer. An escaped convict, he rose to eminence under a false identity while continuing to work with a band of robbers. After being recognized by a former fellow-convict, he was tried and sentenced to hard labor for life.

der to think of it. How can the colonel come to life again? Bonaparte himself sent me condolences on his death by an aid-de-camp; and I now draw a pension of three thousand francs granted to his widow by the Chambers. I have every right to reject all Chaberts past, present, and to come."

"Happily we are alone, madame, and we can lie at our ease," he said, coldly, inwardly amused by inciting the anger which shook the countess, for the purpose of forcing her into some betrayal—a trick familiar to all lawyers, who remain calm and impassible themselves when their clients or their adversaries get angry.

"Now then, to measure swords!" he said to himself, thinking of a trap he could lay to force her to show her weakness. "The proof that Colonel Chabert's first letter reached you exists, madame," he said aloud. "It contained a draft."

"No, it did not; there was no draft," she said.

"Then the letter did reach you," continued Derville, smiling. "You are caught in the first trap a lawyer lays for you, and yet you think you can fight the law!"

The countess blushed, turned pale, and hid her face in her hands. Then she shook off her shame, and said, with the coolness which belongs to women of her class, "As you are the lawyer of the impostor Chabert, have the goodness to—"

"Madame," said Derville, interrupting her, "I am at this moment your lawyer as well as the colonel's. Do you think I wish to lose a client as valuable to me as you are? But you are not listening to me."

"Go on, monsieur," she said, graciously.

"Your fortune came from Monsieur le Comte Chabert, and you have repudiated him. Your property is colossal, and you let him starve. Madame, lawyers can be very eloquent when their cases are eloquent; here are circumstances which can raise the hue-and-cry of public opinion against you."

"But, Monsieur," said the countess, irritated by the manner in which Derville turned and returned her on his gridiron, "admitting that your Monsieur Chabert exists, the courts will sustain my second marriage on account of my children, and I shall get off by repaying two hundred and fifty thousand francs to Monsieur Chabert."

"Madame, there is no telling how a court of law may view a matter of feeling. If, on the one hand, we have a mother and two children, on the other there is a man overwhelmed by undeserved misfortune, aged by you, left to starve by your rejection. Besides, the judges cannot go against the law. Your marriage with the colonel puts the law on his side; he has the prior right. But if you appear in such an odious light you may find an adversary you little expect. That, madame, is the danger I came to warn you of."

"Another adversary!" she said, "who?"

"Monsieur le Comte Ferraud, madame."

"Monsieur Ferraud is too deeply attached to me, and respects the mother of his children too—"

"Ah, madame," said Derville, interrupting her, "why talk such nonsense to a lawyer who can read hearts. At the present moment Monsieur Ferraud has not the slightest desire to annul his marriage, and I have no doubt he adores you. But if someone went to him and told him that his marriage could be annulled, that his wife would be arraigned before the bar of public opinion—"

"He would defend me, monsieur."

"No, madame."

"What reason would he have for deserting me?"

"That of marrying the only daughter of some peer of France, whose title would descend to him by the king's decree."

The countess turned pale.

"I have her!" thought Derville. "Good, the poor colonel's cause is won. Moreover, madame," he said aloud, "Monsieur Ferraud will feel the less regret because a man covered with glory, a general, a count, a grand officer of the Legion of honor, is certainly not a derogation to you—if such a man asks for his wife—"

"Enough, enough, monsieur," she cried. "I can have no lawyer but you. What must I do?"

"Compromise."

"Does he still love me?"

"How could it be otherwise?"

At these words the countess threw up her head. A gleam of hope shone in her eyes; perhaps she thought of speculating on her husband's tenderness and winning her way by some female wile.

"I shall await your orders, madame; you will let me know whether we are to serve notices of Comte Chabert's suit upon you, or whether you will come to my office and arrange the basis of a compromise," said Derville, bowing as he left the room.

Eight days after these visits paid by Derville, on a fine June morning, the husband and wife, parted by an almost supernatural circumstance, were making their way from the opposite extremes of Paris, to meet again in the office of their mutual lawyer. Certain liberal advances made by Derville to the colonel enabled the latter to clothe himself in accordance with his rank. He came in a clean cab. His head was covered with a suitable wig; he was dressed in dark-blue cloth and spotlessly white linen, and he wore beneath his waist-coat the broad red ribbon of the grand officers of the Legion of honor. In resuming the dress and the habits of affluence he had also recovered his former martial elegance. He walked erect. His face, grave and mysterious, and bearing the signs of happiness and renewed hope, seemed younger and fuller; he was no more like the old Chabert in the topcoat than a two-sous piece is like a forty-franc coin just issued. All who passed him knew him at once for a noble relic of our old army, one of those heroic men on whom the light of our national glory shines, who reflect it, as shattered glass illuminated by the sun returns a thousand rays. Such old soldiers are books and pictures too.

The count sprang from the carriage to enter Derville's office with the agility of a young man. The cab had hardly turned away before a pretty coupé with armorial bearings drove up. Madame la Comtesse Ferraud got out of it in a simple dress, but one well suited to display her youthful figure. She wore a pretty drawn bonnet lined with pink, which framed her face delightfully, concealed its exact outline, and restored its freshness.

Though the clients were thus rejuvenated, the office remained its old self, such as we saw it when this history began. Simonnin was eating his breakfast, one shoulder leaning against the window, which was now open; he was gazing at the blue sky above the courtyard formed by four blocks of black buildings.

"Ha!" cried the gutter-jumper, "who wants to bet a play now that Colonel Chabert is a general and a red-ribbon?"

"Derville is a downright magician," said Godeschal.

"There's no trick to play him this time," said Desroches.

"His wife will do that, the Comtesse Ferraud," said Boucard.

"Then she'll have to belong to two—"

"Here she is!" cried Simonnin.

Just then the colonel came in and asked for Derville.

"He is in, Monsieur le Comte," said Simonnin.

"So you are not deaf, you young scamp," said Chabert, catching the gutter-jumper by the ear and twisting it, to the great satisfaction of the other clerks, who laughed and looked at the colonel with the inquisitive interest due to so singular a personage.

Colonel Chabert was in Derville's room when his wife entered the office.

"Say, Boucard, what a queer scene there's going to be in the master's room! She can live the even days with Comte Ferraud, and the uneven days with Comte Chabert—"

"Leap-year the colonel will gain," said Godeschal.

"Hold your tongues, gentlemen," said Boucard, severely. "You'll be overheard. I never knew an office in which the clerks made such fun of the clients as you do here."

Derville had put the colonel into an adjoining room by the time the countess was ushered in.

"Madame," he said to her, "not knowing if it would be agreeable to you to meet Monsieur le Comte Chabert, I have separated you. If, however, you wish—"

"I thank you for that consideration, monsieur."

"I have prepared the draft of an agreement, the conditions of which can be discussed here and now, between you and Monsieur Chabert. I will go from one to the other and convey the remarks of each."

"Begin, monsieur," said the countess, showing signs of impatience.

Derville read: "Between the undersigned—Monsieur Hyacinthe, called Chabert, count, brigadier-general, and grand officer of the Legion of honor, living in Paris, in the rue du Petit-Banquier, of the first part, and Madame Rose Chapotel, wife of the above-named Monsieur le Comte Chabert, born—"

"That will do," she said. "Skip the preamble and come to the conditions."

"Madame," said the lawyer, "the preamble explains succinctly the position which you hold to each other. Then, in article one, you recognize in presence of three witnesses, namely, two notaries, and the cow-keeper with whom your husband lives, to all of whom I have confided your secret and who will keep it faithfully—you recognize, I say, that the individual mentioned in the accompanying deeds and whose identity is elsewhere established by affidavits prepared by Alexander Crottat, your notary, is the

Comte Chabert, your first husband. In article two Comte Chabert, for the sake of your welfare, agrees to make no use of his rights except under circumstances provided for in the agreement—and those circumstances," remarked Derville in a parenthesis, "are the non-fulfilment of the clauses of this private agreement. Monsieur Chabert, on his part," he continued, "consents to sue with you for a judgment which shall set aside the record of his death, and also dissolve his marriage."

"But that will not suit me at all," said the countess, astonished. "I don't wish a lawsuit, you know why."

"In article three," continued the lawyer, with imperturbable coolness, "you agree to secure to the said Hyacinthe, Comte Chabert, an annuity of twenty-four thousand francs now invested in the public Funds, the capital of which will devolve on you at his death."

"But that is far too dear!" cried the countess.

"Can you compromise for less?"

"Perhaps so."

"What is it you want, madame?"

"I want—I don't want a suit. I want—"

"To keep him dead," said Derville, quickly.

"Monsieur," said the countess, "if he asks twenty-four thousand francs a year, I'll demand justice."

"Yes, justice!" cried a hollow voice, as the colonel opened the door and appeared suddenly before his wife, with one hand in his waistcoat and the other pointing to the floor, a gesture to which the memory of his great disaster gave a horrible meaning.

"It is he!" said the countess in her own mind.

"Too dear?" continued the old soldier. "I gave you a million and now you trade on my poverty. Well, then, I will have you and my property both; our marriage is not void."

"But monsieur is not Colonel Chabert!" cried the countess, feigning surprise.

"Ah!" said the old man, in a tone of irony, "do you want proofs? Well, did I not take you from the pavements of the Palais-Royal?"[68]

The countess turned pale. Seeing her color fade beneath her rouge, the old soldier, sorry for the suffering he was inflicting on a woman he had once loved ardently, stopped short; but she gave him such a venomous look that he suddenly added, "You were with—"

"For heaven's sake, monsieur," said the countess, appealing to the lawyer, "allow me to leave this place. I did not come here to listen to such insults."

She left the room. Derville sprang into the office after her; but she seemed to have taken wings and was already gone. When he returned to his own room he found the colonel walking up and down in a paroxysm of rage.

"In those days men took their wives where they liked," he said. "But I chose ill; I ought never to have trusted her; she has no heart!"

"Colonel, you will admit I was right in begging you not to come here! I

[68] At the time notorious for gambling, prostitution, and other forms of low life; much frequented by tourists.

am now certain of your identity. When you came in the countess made a little movement the meaning of which was not to be doubted. But you have lost your cause. Your wife now knows that you are unrecognizable."

"I will kill her."

"Nonsense! then you would be arrested and guillotined as a criminal. Besides, you might miss your stroke; it is unpardonable not to kill a wife when you attempt it. Leave me to undo your folly, you big child! Go away; but take care of yourself, for she is capable of laying some trap and getting you locked up at Charenton. I will see about serving the notices of the suit on her at once; that will be some protection to you."

The poor colonel obeyed his young benefactor, and went away, stammering a few excuses. He was going slowly down the dark staircase lost in gloomy thought, overcome perhaps by the blow he had just received, to him the worst, the one that went deepest to his heart, when, as he reached the lower landing, he heard the rustle of a gown, and his wife appeared.

"Come, monsieur," she said, taking his arm with a movement like others he once knew so well.

The action, the tones of her voice, now soft and gentle, calmed the colonel's anger, and he allowed her to lead him to her carriage.

"Get in," she said, when the footman had let down the steps.

And he suddenly found himself, as if by magic, seated beside his wife in the coupé.

"Where to, madame?" asked the footman.

"To Groslay," she replied.

The horses started, and the carriage crossed the whole city.

"Monsieur!" said the countess, in a tone of voice that seemed to betray one of those rare emotions, few in life, which shake our whole being. At such moments heart, fibers, nerves, soul, body, countenance, all, even the pores of the skin, quiver. Life seems no longer in us; it gushes out, it conveys itself like a contagion, it transmits itself in a look, in a tone of the voice, in a gesture, in the imposition of our will on others. The old soldier trembled, hearing that word, that first, that expressive "Monsieur!" It was at once a reproach, a prayer, a pardon, a hope, a despair, a question, an answer. That one word included all. A woman must needs be a great comedian[69] to throw such eloquence and so many feelings into one word. Truth is never so complete in its expression; it cannot utter itself wholly—it leaves something to be seen within. The colonel was filled with remorse for his suspicions, his exactions, his anger, and he lowered his eyes to conceal his feelings.

"Monsieur," continued the countess, after an almost imperceptible pause, "I knew you at once."

"Rosine," said the old soldier, "that word contains the only balm that can make me forget my troubles."

Two great tears fell hotly on his wife's hands, which he pressed as if to show her a paternal affection.

"Monsieur," she continued, "how is it you did not see what it cost me to appear before a stranger in a position so false as mine. If I am forced to blush for what I am, at least let it be in my own home. Ought not such a

[69] Actress.

secret to remain buried in our own hearts? You will, I hope, forgive my apparent indifference to the misfortunes of a Chabert in whom I had no reason to believe. I did receive your letters," she said, hastily, seeing a sudden objection on her husband's face, "but they reached me thirteen months after the battle of Eylau; they were open, torn, dirty; the writing was unknown to me; and I, who had just obtained Napoleon's signature to my new marriage contract, supposed that some clever swindler was trying to impose upon me. Not wishing to trouble Monsieur Ferraud's peace of mind, or to bring future trouble into the family, I was right, was I not, to take every precaution against a false Chabert?"

"Yes, you were right; and I have been a fool, a dolt, a beast, not to have foreseen the consequences of such a situation. But where are we going?" asked the colonel, suddenly noticing that they had reached the Barrière de la Chapelle.

"To my country-place near Groslay, in the valley of Montmorency," she replied. "There, monsieur, we can think over, together, the course we ought to take. I know my duty. Though I am yours legally, I am no longer yours in fact. Surely, you cannot wish that we should be the common talk of Paris. Let us hide from the public a situation which, for me, has a mortifying side, and strive to maintain our dignity. You love me still," she continued, casting a sad and gentle look upon the colonel, "but I, was I not authorized to form other ties? In this strange position a secret voice tells me to hope in your goodness, which I know so well. Am I wrong in taking you, you only, for the sole arbiter of my fate? Be judge and pleader both; I confide in your noble nature. You will forgive the consequences of my innocent fault. I dare avow to you, therefore, that I love Monsieur Ferraud; I thought I had the right to love him. I do not blush for this confession; it may offend you, but it dishonors neither of us. I cannot hide the truth from you. When accident made me a widow, I was not a mother—"

The colonel made a sign with his hand as if to ask silence of his wife; and they remained silent, not saying a word for over a mile. Chabert fancied he saw her little children before him.

"Rosine!"

"Monsieur?"

"The dead do wrong to reappear."

"Oh, monsieur, no, no! Do not think me ungrateful. But you find a mother, a woman who loves another man, where you left a wife. If it is no longer in my power to love you, I know what I owe to you, and I offer you still the devotion of a daughter."

"Rosine," said the old man, gently, "I feel no resentment towards you. We will forget all that once was," he said, with one of those smiles whose charm is the reflection of a noble soul. "I am not so lost to delicacy as to ask a show of love from a woman who no longer loves me."

The countess gave him such a grateful glance that poor Chabert wished in his heart he could return to that grave at Eylau. Certain men have souls capable of vast sacrifices, whose recompense to them is the certainty of the happiness of one they love.

"My friend, we will talk of all this later, with a quiet mind," said the countess.

The conversation took another turn, for it was impossible to continue it long in this strain. Though husband and wife constantly touched upon their strange position, either by vague allusions, or grave remarks, they nevertheless made a charming journey, recalling many of the events of their union, and of the Empire. The countess knew how to impart a tender charm to these memories, and to cast a tinge of melancholy upon the conversation, enough at least to keep it serious. She revived love without exciting desire, and showed her first husband the mental graces and knowledge she had acquired—trying to let him taste the happiness of a father beside a cherished daughter. The colonel had known the countess of the Empire, he now saw a countess of the Restoration.

They at last arrived, through a cross-road, at a fine park in the little valley which separates the heights of Margency from the pretty village of Groslay. The house was a delightful one, and the colonel saw on arriving that all was prepared for their stay. Misfortune is a sort of talisman,[70] the power of which lies in strengthening and fulfilling our natural man; it increases the distrust and evil tendencies of certain natures just as it increases the goodness of those whose heart is sound. Misfortune had made the colonel more helpful and better than he had ever been; he was therefore able to enter into those secrets of woman's suffering which are usually unknown to men. And yet, in spite of his great lack of distrust, he could not help saying to his wife:

"You seem to have been sure of bringing me here?"

"Yes," she answered, "if I found Colonel Chabert in the petitioner."

The tone of truth which she gave to that answer dispersed the few doubts which the colonel already felt ashamed of admitting.

For three days the countess was truly admirable in her conduct to her first husband. By tender care and constant gentleness she seemed to try to efface even the memory of the sufferings he had endured, and to win pardon for the misfortunes she had, as she admitted, innocently caused. She took pleasure in displaying for his benefit, though always with a sort of melancholy, the particular charms under the influence of which she knew him to be feeble—for men are more particularly susceptible to certain ways, to certain graces of heart and mind; and those they are unable to resist. She wanted to interest him in her situation, to move his feelings enough to control his mind and so bend him absolutely to her will. Resolved to take any means to reach her ends, she was still uncertain what to do with the man, though she meant, undoubtedly, to destroy him socially.

On the evening of the third day she began to feel that in spite of all her efforts she could no longer conceal the anxiety she felt as to the result of her maneuvers. To obtain a moment's relief she went up to her own room, sat down at her writing-table, and took off the mask of tranquillity she had worn before the colonel, like an actress returning weary to her room after a trying fifth act and falling half-dead upon a couch, while the audience retains an image of her to which she bears not the slightest resemblance. She began to finish a letter already begun to Delbecq, telling him to go to Derville and ask in her name for a sight of the papers which concerned Colonel Chabert, to copy them, and come immediately to Groslay. She had

[70] Instrument of magic.

hardly finished before she heard the colonel's step in the corridor; for he was coming, full of anxiety, to find her.

"Oh!" she said aloud, "I wish I were dead! my position is intolerable—"

"What is it? is anything the matter?" said the worthy man.

"Nothing, nothing," she said.

She rose, left the colonel where he was, and went to speak to her maid without witnesses, telling her to go at once to Paris and deliver the letter, which she gave her, into Delbecq's own hands, and to bring it back to her as soon as he read it. Then she went out and seated herself on a bench in the garden, where she was in full view of the colonel if he wished to find her. He was already searching for her and he soon came.

"Rosine," he said, "tell me what is the matter."

She did not answer. It was one of those glorious calm evenings of the month of June, when all secret harmonies diffuse such peace, such sweetness in the sunsets. The air was pure, the silence deep, and a distant murmur of children's voices added a sort of melody to the consecrated scene.

"You do not answer me," said the colonel.

"My husband—" began the countess, then she stopped, made a movement, and said, appealingly, with a blush, "What ought I to say in speaking of Monsieur le Comte Ferraud?"

"Call him your husband, my poor child," answered the colonel, in a kind tone. "He is the father of your children."

"Well, then," she continued, "if he asks me what I am doing here, if he learns that I have shut myself up with an unknown man, what am I to say? Hear me, monsieur," she went on, taking an attitude that was full of dignity, "decide my fate; I feel I am resigned to everything—"

"Dear," said the colonel, grasping his wife's hands, "I have resolved to sacrifice myself wholly to your happiness—"

"That is impossible," she cried, with a convulsive movement. "Remember that in that case you must renounce your own identity—and do so legally."

"What!" exclaimed the colonel, "does not my word satisfy you?"

The term "legally" fell like lead upon the old man's heart and roused an involuntary distrust. He cast a look upon his wife which made her blush; she lowered her eyes, and for a moment he feared he should be forced to despise her. The countess was alarmed lest she had startled the honest shame, the stern uprightness of a man whose generous nature and whose primitive virtues were well-known to her. Though these ideas brought a cloud to each brow they were suddenly dispelled, harmony was restored—and thus: A child's cry resounded in the distance.

"Jules, let your sister alone!" cried the countess.

"What! are your children here?" exclaimed the colonel.

"Yes, but I forbade them to come in your way."

The old soldier understood the delicacy and the womanly tact shown in that graceful consideration, and he took her hand to kiss it.

"Let them come!" he said.

The little girl ran up to complain of her brother.

"Mamma! he plagued me—"

"Mamma!"

"It was his fault—"

"It was hers—"

The hands were stretched out to the mother, and the two voices mingled. It was a sudden, delightful picture.

"My poor children!" exclaimed the countess, not restraining her tears, "must I lose them? To whom will the court give them? A mother's heart cannot be shared. I will have them! yes, I—"

"You are making mamma cry," said Jules, the elder, with an angry look at the colonel.

"Hush, Jules!" cried his mother, peremptorily.

The two children examined their mother and the stranger with an indescribable curiosity.

"Yes," continued the countess, "if I am parted from Monsieur Ferraud, they must leave me my children; if I have them, I can bear all."

Those words brought the success she expected.

"Yes," cried the colonel, as if completing a sentence he had begun mentally. "I must return to the grave; I have thought so already."

"How can I accept such a sacrifice?" replied the countess. "If men have died to save the honor of their mistresses, they gave their lives but once. But this would be giving your daily life, your lifetime! No, no, it is impossible; if it were only your existence perhaps it might be nothing, but to sign a record that you are not Colonel Chabert, to admit yourself an impostor, to sacrifice your honor, to live a lie for all the days of your life—no; human devotion cannot go to such a length! No, no! if it were not for my poor children I would fly with you to the ends of the earth."

"But," said Chabert, "why can I not live here, in that little cottage, as a friend and relative. I am as useless as an old cannon; all I need is a little tobacco and the *Constitutionnel*."[71]

The countess burst into tears. Then followed a struggle of generosity between them, from which Colonel Chabert came forth a conqueror. One evening, watching the mother in the midst of her children, deeply moved by that picture of a home, influenced, too, by the silence and the quiet of the country, he came to the resolution of remaining dead; no longer resisting the thought of a legal instrument, he asked his wife what steps he should take to secure, irrevocably, the happiness of that home.

"Do what you will," replied the countess. "I declare positively that I will have nothing to do with it—I ought not."

Delbecq had then been in the house a few days, and, in accordance with the countess' verbal instructions, he had wormed himself into the confidence of the old soldier. The morning after this little scene Colonel Chabert accompanied the former lawyer to Saint-Leu-Taverny, where Delbecq had already had an agreement drawn up by a notary, in terms so crude and brutal that on hearing them the colonel abruptly left the office.

"Good God! would you make me infamous! why, I should be called a forger!"

"Monsieur," said Delbecq, "I advise you not to sign too quickly. You could get at least thirty thousand francs a year out of this affair; Madame would give them."

[71] A liberal, Bonapartist journal.

Blasting that scoundrel emeritus[72] with the luminous glance of an indignant honest man, the colonel rushed from the place driven by a thousand conflicting feelings. He was again distrustful, indignant, and merciful by turns. After a time he re-entered the park of Groslay by a breach in the wall, and went, with slow steps, to rest and think at his ease, in a little study built beneath a raised kiosk[73] which commanded a view of the road from Saint-Leu.

The path was made of that yellow earth which now takes the place of river-gravel, and the countess, who was sitting in the kiosk above, did not hear the slight noise of the colonel's footstep, being preoccupied with anxious thoughts as to the success of her plot. Neither did the old soldier become aware of the presence of his wife in the kiosk above him.

"Well, Monsieur Delbecq, did he sign?" asked the countess, when she saw the secretary, over the sunk-fence, alone upon the road.

"No, Madame; and I don't even know what has become of him. The old horse reared."

"We shall have to put him in Charenton," she said. "We can do it."

The colonel, recovering the elasticity of his youth, jumped the ha-ha,[74] and in the twinkling of an eye applied the hardest pair of slaps that ever two cheeks received. "Old horses kick!" he said.

His anger once over, the colonel had no strength left to jump the ditch again. The truth lay before him in its nakedness. His wife's words and Delbecq's answer had shown him the plot to which he had so nearly been a victim. The tender attentions he had received were the bait of the trap. That thought was like a sudden poison, and it brought back to the old hero his past sufferings, physical and mental. He returned to the kiosk through a gate of the park, walking slowly like a broken man. So, then, there was no peace, no truce for him! Must he enter upon that odious struggle with a woman which Derville had explained to him? must he live a life of legal suits? must he feed on gall, and drink each morning the cup of bitterness? Then, dreadful thought! where was the money for such suits to come from? So deep a disgust of life came over him, that had a pistol been at hand he would have blown out his brains. Then he fell back into the confusion of ideas which, ever since his interview with Derville in the cow-yard, had changed his moral being. At last, reaching the kiosk, he went up the stairs to the upper chamber, whose oriel windows looked out on all the enchanting perspectives of that well-known valley, and where he found his wife sitting on a chair. The countess was looking at the landscape, with a calm and quiet demeanor, and that impenetrable countenance which certain determined women know so well how to assume. She dried her eyes, as though she had shed tears, and played, as if abstractedly, with the ribbons of her sash. Nevertheless, in spite of this apparent composure, she could not prevent herself from trembling when she saw her noble benefactor before her—standing, his arms crossed, his face pale, his brow stern.

"Madame," he said, looking at her so fixedly for a moment that he forced her to blush. "Madame, I do not curse you, but I despise you. I now thank the fate which has parted us. I have no desire for vengeance; I have ceased to love you. I want nothing from you. Live in peace upon the faith

[72] Master scoundrel. [73] A pavilion or summerhouse. [74] A ditch or sunken fence.

of my word; it is worth more than the legal papers of all the notaries in Paris. I shall never take the name I made, perhaps, illustrious. Henceforth, I am but a poor devil named Hyacinthe, who asks no more than a place in God's sunlight. Farewell—"

The countess flung herself at his feet and tried to hold him by catching his hands, but he repulsed her with disgust, saying, "Do not touch me!"

The countess made a gesture which no description can portray when she heard the sound of her husband's departing steps. Then, with that profound sagacity which comes of great wickedness, or of the savage, material selfishness of this world, she felt she might live in peace, relying on the promise and the contempt of that loyal soldier.

Chabert disappeared. The cow-keeper failed and became a cab-driver. Perhaps the colonel at first found some such occupation. Perhaps, like a stone flung into the rapids, he went from fall to fall until he sank engulfed in that great pool of filth and penury which welters in the streets of Paris.

Six months after these events Derville, who had heard nothing of Colonel Chabert or of the Comtesse Ferraud, thought that they had probably settled on a compromise, and that the countess, out of spite, had employed some other lawyer to draw the papers. Accordingly, one morning, he summed up the amounts advanced to the said Chabert, added the costs, and requested the Comtesse Ferraud to obtain from Monsieur le Comte Chabert the full amount, presuming that she knew the whereabouts of her first husband.

The next day Comte Ferraud's secretary sent the following answer:

MONSIEUR—I am directed by Madame la Comtesse Ferraud to inform you that your client totally deceived you, and that the individual calling himself the Comte Chabert admitted having falsely taken that name.

Receive the assurance, etc., etc.

DELBECQ.

"Well, some people are, upon my honor, as devoid of sense as the beasts of the field—they've stolen their baptism!" cried Derville. "Be human, be generous, be philanthropic, and you'll find yourself in the lurch! Here's a business that has cost me over two thousand francs."

Not long after the reception of this letter Derville was at the Palais, looking for a lawyer with whom he wished to speak, and who was in the habit of practicing in the criminal courts. It so chanced that Derville entered the sixth court-room as the judge was sentencing a vagrant named Hyacinthe to two months' imprisonment, the said vagrant to be conveyed at the expiration of the sentence to the mendicity[75] office of the Saint-Denis quarter—a sentence which was equivalent to perpetual imprisonment. The name, Hyacinthe, caught Derville's ear, and he looked at the delinquent sitting between two gendarmes on the prisoner's bench, and recognized at once his false Colonel Chabert. The old soldier was calm, motionless, almost absent-minded. In spite of his rags, in spite of the poverty marked on every feature of the face, his countenance was instinct with noble pride. His

[75] Begging.

glance had an expression of stoicism which a magistrate ought not to have overlooked; but when a man falls into the hands of justice, he is no longer anything but an entity, a question of law and facts; in the eyes of statisticians, he is a numeral.

When the soldier was taken from the court-room to wait until the whole batch of vagabonds who were then being sentenced were ready for removal, Derville used his privilege as a lawyer to follow him into the room adjoining the sheriff's office, where he watched him for a few moments, together with the curious collection of beggars who surrounded him. The ante-chamber of a sheriff's office presents at such times a sight which, unfortunately, neither legislators, nor philanthropists, nor painters, nor writers, ever study. Like all the laboratories of the law this ante-chamber is dark and ill-smelling; the walls are protected by a bench, blackened by the incessant presence of the poor wretches who come to this central rendezvous from all quarters of social wretchedness—not one of which is unrepresented there. A poet would say that the daylight was ashamed to lighten that terrible sink-hole of all miseries. There is not one spot within it where crime, planned or committed, has not stood; not a spot where some man, rendered desperate by the stigma which justice lays upon him for his first fault, has not begun a career leading to the scaffold or to suicide. All those who fall in Paris rebound against these yellow walls, on which a philanthropist could decipher the meaning of many a suicide about which hypocritical writers, incapable of taking one step to prevent them, rail; written on those walls he will find a preface to the dramas of the Morgue and those of the Place de Grève.[76] Colonel Chabert was now sitting in the midst of this crowd of men with nervous faces, clothed in the horrible liveries of poverty, silent at times or talking in a low voice, for three gendarmes paced the room as sentries, their sabres clanging against the floor.

"Do you recognize me?" said Derville to the old soldier.

"Yes, Monsieur," said Chabert, rising.

"If you are an honest man," continued Derville, in a low voice, "how is it that you have remained my debtor?"

The old soldier colored like a young girl accused by her mother of a clandestine love.

"Is it possible," he cried in a loud voice, "that Madame Ferraud has not paid you?"

"Paid me!" said Derville, "she wrote me you were an impostor."

The colonel raised his eyes with a majestic look of horror and invocation as if to appeal to heaven against this new treachery. "Monsieur," he said, in a voice that was calm though it faltered, "ask the gendarmes to be so kind as to let me go into the sheriff's office; I will there write you an order which will certainly be paid."

Derville spoke to the corporal, and was allowed to take his client into the office, where the colonel wrote a few lines and addressed them to the Comtesse Ferraud.

"Send that to her," he said, "and you will be paid for your loans and all costs. Believe me, Monsieur, if I have not shown the gratitude I owe you for your kind acts it is none the less *there*," he said, laying his hand upon his

[76] *Morgue, Place de Grève.* Respectively, the Paris mortuary and a place of public executions.

heart. "Yes, it is there, full, complete. But the unfortunate ones can do nothing—they love, that is all."

"Can it be," said Derville, "that you did not stipulate for an income?"

"Don't speak of that," said the old man. "You can never know how utterly I despise this external life to which the majority of men cling so tenaciously. I was taken suddenly with an illness—a disgust for humanity. When I think that Napoleon is at Saint-Helena[77] all things here below are nothing to me. I can no longer be a soldier, that is my only sorrow. Ah, well," he added, with a gesture that was full of childlike playfulness, "it is better to have luxury in our feelings than in our clothes. I fear no man's contempt."

He went back to the bench and sat down. Derville went away. When he reached his office, he sent Godeschal, then advanced to be second clerk, to the Comtesse Ferraud, who had no sooner read the missive he carried than she paid the money owing to Comte Chabert's lawyer.

In 1840, towards the close of the month of June, Godeschal, then a lawyer on his own account, was on his way to Ris, in company with Derville. When they reached the avenue which leads into the mail road to Bicêtre, they saw beneath an elm by the roadside one of those hoary, broken-down old paupers who rule the beggars about them, and live at Bicêtre just as pauper women live at La Salpêtrière. This man, one of the two thousand inmates of the "Almshouse for Old Age," was sitting on a stone and seemed to be giving all his mind to an operation well-known to the dwellers in charitable institutions; that of drying the tobacco in their handkerchiefs in the sun—possibly to escape washing them. The old man had an interesting face. He was dressed in that gown of dark, reddish cloth which the Almshouse provides for its inmates, a dreadful sort of livery.

"Derville," said Godeschal to his companion, "do look at that old fellow. Isn't he like those grotesque figures that are made in Germany. But I suppose he lives, and perhaps he is happy!"

Derville raised his glass, looked at the pauper, and gave vent to an exclamation of surprise; then he said: "That old man, my dear fellow, is a poem, or, as the romanticists say, a drama.[78] Did you ever meet the Comtesse Ferraud?"

"Yes, a clever woman and very agreeable, but too pious."

"That old man is her legitimate husband, Comte Chabert, formerly colonel. No doubt she has had him placed here. If he lives in an almshouse instead of a mansion, it is because he reminded the pretty countess that he took her, like a cab, from the streets. I can still see the tigerish look she gave him when he said it."

These words so excited Godeschal's curiosity that Derville told him the whole story. Two days later, on the following Monday morning, as they were returning to Paris, the two friends glanced at Bicêtre, and Derville proposed that they should go and see Colonel Chabert. Half-way up the

[77] *Saint-Helena.* After his defeat at Waterloo in 1815, Napoleon was exiled on this Atlantic island, a British possession, until his death in 1821.

[78] The French word *drame* referred to a certain kind of relatively realistic play, neither strict classical tragedy nor comedy, designed to have a strong emotional appeal.

avenue they found the old man sitting on the trunk of a fallen tree, and amusing himself by drawing lines on the gravel with a stick which he held in his hand. When they looked at him attentively they saw that he had been breakfasting elsewhere than at the almshouse.

"Good-morning, Colonel Chabert," said Derville.

"Not Chabert! not Chabert! my name is Hyacinthe," answered the old man. "I'm no longer a man; I'm number 164, seventh room," he added, looking at Derville with timid anxiety—the fear of old age or of childhood. "You can see the condemned prisoner," he said, after a moment's silence; "he's not married, no! he's happy—"

"Poor man!" said Godeschal, "don't you want some money for tobacco?"

The colonel extended his hand with all the naïveté of a street boy to the two strangers, who each gave him a twenty-franc gold piece. He thanked them both, with a stupid look, and said, "Brave troopers!" Then he pretended to shoulder arms and take aim at them, calling out with a laugh, "Fire the two pieces, and long live Napoleon!" after which he described an imaginary arabesque[79] in the air, with a flourish of his cane.

"The nature of his wound must have made him childish," said Derville.

"He childish!" cried another old pauper who was watching them. "Ha! there are days when it won't do to step on his toes. He's a knowing one, full of philosophy and imagination. But to-day, don't you see, he's been keeping Monday. Why, Monsieur, he was here in 1820. Just about that time a Prussian officer, whose carriage was going over the Villejuif hill, walked by on foot. Hyacinthe and I were sitting by the roadside. The officer was talking with another, I think it was a Russian or some animal of that kind, and when they saw the old fellow, the Prussian, just to tease him, says he: 'Here's an old acrobat who must have been at Rosbach—' 'I was too young to be at Rosbach,' says Hyacinthe, 'but I'm old enough to have been at Jena!'[80] Ha, ha! that Prussian cleared off—and no more questions—"

"What a fate!" cried Derville. "Born in the Foundling, he returns to die in the asylum of old age, having in the interval helped Napoleon to conquer Egypt and Europe!— Do you know, my dear fellow," continued Derville, after a long pause, "that there are three men in our social system who cannot respect or value the world—the priest, the physician, and the lawyer. They wear black gowns, perhaps because they mourn for all virtues, all illusions. The most unhappy among them is the lawyer. When a man seeks a priest he is forced to it by repentance, by remorse, by beliefs which make him interesting, which ennoble him and comfort the soul of his mediator, whose duty is not without a certain sort of joy; the priest purifies, heals, reconciles. But we lawyers! we see forever the same evil feelings, never corrected; our offices are sink-holes which nothing can cleanse.

"How many things have I not seen and known and learned in my practice! I have seen a father die in a garret, penniless, abandoned by daughters, to each of whom he had given an income of forty thousand francs.[81] I have seen wills burned. I have seen mothers robbing their children, hus-

[79] An elaborate design.
[80] Battle fought in Germany in 1806 where Napoleon's forces routed the Prussians.
[81] *I have seen . . . francs.* This story is told in Balzac's novel *Father Goriot.*

bands stealing from their wives, wives killing their husbands by the very love they inspired, so as to live in peace with their lovers. I have seen women giving to their children of a first marriage tastes which led them to their death, so that the child of love might be enriched. I could not tell you what I have seen, for I have seen crimes against which justice is powerless. All the horrors that romance-writers think they invent are forever below the truth. You are about to make acquaintance with such things; as for me, I shall live in the country with my wife; I have a horror of Paris."

Nathaniel Hawthorne
(1804–1864)

In the most famous lines ever written about Nathaniel Hawthorne, Herman Melville, his neighbor in Lenox, Massachusetts, said, "For spite of all the Indian-summer sunlight on the hither side of Hawthorne's soul, the other side—like the dark half of the physical sphere—is shrouded in a blackness, ten times black. . . . This great power of blackness in him derives its force from its appeals to that Calvinistic sense of Innate Depravity and Original Sin, from whose visitations, in some shape or other, no deeply thinking mind is always and wholly free." The old conception of Hawthorne as a melancholy recluse, a brooding, black-clad Hamlet among the cheerful Transcendentalists, has been abandoned—he was in some ways a vigorous man of the world—but the doubleness Melville saw in his work, the "Indian-summer sunlight" and the "blackness, ten times black," is a continual presence in his haunting studies of the human heart.

Hawthorne was born in 1804 in Salem, Massachusetts, a setting which was to play a large part in shaping his imagination. Settled in 1626, the town was the scene of the shocking Witch Trials of 1692, in which nineteen men and women and two dogs were hanged for "witchcraft"; one of Hawthorne's ancestors had been a judge at the trials. Salem and its history were to suggest to Hawthorne many of his major themes—the burden of fathers and the past, the sins of intellectual and moral pride, the persistence of "blackness" even in a society dedicated to infinite progress.

Hawthorne's father, a sea captain, died when Hawthorne was four; his mother gradually withdrew from life and became a recluse. The writer's childhood was spent in Salem and, after he was twelve, in a remote Maine village. When he was seventeen, he went to Bowdoin College in Maine, where his classmates included Henry Wadsworth Longfellow and Franklin Pierce, who was later President of the United States. Hawthorne seems to have enjoyed the ordinary rowdiness of college life but had already begun to develop what he called later his "accursed habits" of solitude. Upon graduation, he returned to Salem to live; "I felt it," he said, "almost my destiny to make Salem my home." Here, for twelve years, he led a quiet, secluded life, reading and developing, fitfully and circuitously, the highly personal mode of fiction that was to make him famous. A false start was Fanshawe, *a Gothic novel set in Bowdoin College, which he published privately in 1828; he later tried to destroy all surviving copies. He was not to return to the novel form for twenty years; instead he concentrated on short sketches and tales, often little more than brief essays or historical anecdotes which subtly modulated into symbolic dreams or parables. He began to publish these in the early 1830's, often anonymously, in a number of popular magazines and annual "gift-books."*

Fame came in 1837 with the publication of a collection of these stories, Twice-Told Tales. *A second, expanded version appeared in 1842; Edgar Allan Poe, in one of the most generous reviews, wrote, "The style is purity itself. Force abounds. High imagination gleams from every page. Mr. Hawthorne is a man of the truest genius." Poe used the review as the occasion for developing his own theory of the "brief tale" which can be read in one sitting and thus can achieve an effect of "totality" or perfect unity, an effect which Hawthorne achieves magnificently. With public recognition, Hawthorne began to emerge from his isolation in Salem. He continued to write voluminously, mostly magazine stories and children's books, and, to supplement his small income from writing, worked from 1839 to 1841 as salt and coal measurer in the Boston Custom House. He also became involved in the utopian community Brook Farm in 1840 but soon withdrew, apparently finding the highminded optimism of the utopians incompatible with his own darker vision. He married Sophia Peabody in 1842, when he was thirty-eight, after a prolonged engagement, and moved with his new wife to Concord, where they lived in the Old Manse, where Emerson had lived. Another collection of tales,* Mosses from an Old Manse, *appeared in 1846, the year in which he also obtained a political appointment as Surveyor of the United States Customhouse at Salem. A change in the administration ended this job in 1849; out of work, he wrote, in four intense months, his masterpiece,* The Scarlet Letter, *published in 1850. All Hawthorne's experiences and concerns were focused in this story of the consequences of the adultery of the Puritan minister Arthur Dimmesdale with one of his parishioners, Hester Prynne: the psychology of Puritanism, the consequences of guilt and isolation, the relationship between private, inner experience and public, social institutions. The book also established the major form in which Hawthorne was to work for the rest of his life: the "romance," as he preferred to call it—not a detailed, realistic depiction of social life, but a psychological and symbolic narrative of the inner, moral life.*

The success of The Scarlet Letter *eased the Hawthornes' financial situation, and they moved to Lenox, Massachusetts. Herman Melville was writing* Moby-Dick *in the neighboring village of Pittsfield, and he and Hawthorne became close friends. Hawthorne was at the height of his powers and wrote prolifically in the early 1850's.* The House of the Seven Gables *and* The Snow Image *appeared in 1851. Three more books followed in 1852:* The Blithedale Romance, *a satirical novel based on the Brook Farm experiment;* A Wonder Book for Girls and Boys, *retellings of Greek myths for children; and* The Life of Franklin Pierce, *a campaign biography of his old friend from college. Another children's book,* Tanglewood Tales, *appeared in 1853.*

When Pierce was elected President on the Democratic ticket in 1852, he appointed Hawthorne United States Consul in Liverpool, England. Hawthorne and his family lived in Liverpool for four years (1853–57) and then spent three more years in Italy, where he wrote The Marble Faun *(1860), a novel that anticipates Henry James' studies of Americans in Europe. It was to be his last completed novel. He returned to Concord in 1860 as the Civil War was beginning; depressed by the War and by family illness and uncertain of what direction to take in his writing, he worked sporadically at three novels, all left unfinished at his death. He died in 1864 while on a walking tour of New Hampshire with his old friend Franklin Pierce.*

Hawthorne's career was uneven and problematical. There is no steady movement from apprentice-work to confident, fully achieved work, but instead a series of probings and experiments, many of them failures. The great works—a handful of early tales and The Scarlet Letter*—are surrounded by inferior work. In retrospect, we can see, perhaps, artistic reasons for this unevenness. Hawthorne's challenge as an artist was to discover a new form appropriate to his vision of the inner life—to invent, in effect, modern psychological fiction in America. The form that he discovered is, like the man himself, complex and ambivalent. The content of a Hawthorne story often seems unpromising—a slight, quasi-historical anecdote or a rather mechanical allegorical incident. But the story is told in a voice that deepens and enriches it, continually generating insights into human problems of the self and its relations with others. The anonymous narrator himself often seems to be the most important character in a Hawthorne story, almost hovering over the narrative, probing, questioning, wondering, frequently retreating into quaintness, protestations of bewilderment, or such protective devices as symbol, allegory, or rumor, sometimes seeming reluctant to probe too deeply into his characters, lest he violate their delicate mysteries, as one of his own heartless Rappaccinis might do. The Hawthorne voice, despite its occasional quaintness and its echoes of eighteenth-century rhetoric, is essentially a modern voice, forerunner of a long line of uncertain, questioning, haunted narrators in modern fiction. It is one of the many paradoxes of Hawthorne that this idiosyncratic, seemingly eccentric and inimitable writer has cast such a long shadow over later American literature.*

FURTHER READING *(prepared by W. J. R.):* Arlin Turner's *Nathaniel Hawthorne,* 1980, narrates Hawthorne's life while also exploring his efforts to comprehend and represent the American experience. Hubert Hoeltje's *Inward Sky: The Mind and Heart of Nathaniel Hawthorne,* 1962, was written in reaction to much of the previous criticism and emphasizes the literary relationship between Emerson and Hawthorne. A critical study of Hawthorne's career and times is provided by James R. Mellow's *Nathaniel Hawthorne in His Times,* 1980. Two companion studies by Richard Harter Fogle, *Hawthorne's Fiction: The Light and the Dark,* 1952, rev. 1964, and *Hawthorne's Imagery,* 1969, are valuable. The former uses the methods of New Criticism in its analyses of "Rappaccini's Daughter," five other short stories, and the four major novels; the latter restricts its attention to the novels. A helpful guide to Hawthorne's fifty-four short stories can be found in Lea Bertani Vozar Newman's *A Reader's Guide to the Short Stories of Nathaniel Hawthorne,* 1979. Newman gives information on publication history, composition, criticism, and other topics for each entry. *Hawthorne Centenary Essays,* ed. Roy Harvey Pearce, 1964, is a superior collection of essays on "Tales and Romances," "Art and Substance," and "Discovery and Rediscovery." *Critics on Hawthorne,* ed. Thomas J. Rountree, 1972, offers early reviews of Hawthorne's work and a selection of modern critical essays. *Nathaniel Hawthorne: New Critical Essays,* ed. A. Robert Lee, 1982, is a reassessment of Hawthorne; the essays illuminate Hawthorne's relation to the past, nature, American culture, and European literature.

YOUNG GOODMAN BROWN

Young Goodman[1] Brown came forth at sunset into the street at Salem village;[2] but put his head back, after crossing the threshold, to exchange a parting kiss with his young wife. And Faith, as the wife was aptly named, thrust her own pretty head into the street, letting the wind play with the pink ribbons of her cap while she called to Goodman Brown.

"Dearest heart," whispered she, softly and rather sadly, when her lips were close to his ear, "prithee put off your journey until sunrise and sleep in your own bed to-night. A lone woman is troubled with such dreams and such thoughts that she's afeard of herself sometimes. Pray tarry with me this night, dear husband, of all nights in the year."

"My love and my Faith," replied young Goodman Brown, "of all nights in the year, this one night must I tarry away from thee. My journey, as thou callest it, forth and back again, must needs be done 'twixt now and sunrise. What, my sweet wife, dost thou doubt me already, and we but three months married?"

"Then God bless you!" said Faith, with the pink ribbons; "and may you find all well when you come back."

"Amen!" cried Goodman Brown. "Say thy prayers, dear Faith, and go to bed at dusk, and no harm will come to thee."

So they parted; and the young man pursued his way until, being about to turn the corner by the meeting-house, he looked back and saw the head of Faith still peeping after him with a melancholy air, in spite of her pink ribbons.

"Poor little Faith!" thought he, for his heart smote him, "What a wretch am I to leave her on such an errand! She talks of dreams, too. Methought as she spoke there was trouble in her face, as if a dream had warned her what work is to be done to-night. But no, no; 'twould kill her to think it. Well, she's a blessed angel on earth; and after this one night I'll cling to her skirts and follow her to heaven."

With this excellent resolve for the future, Goodman Brown felt himself justified in making more haste on his present evil purpose. He had taken a dreary road, darkened by all the gloomiest trees of the forest, which barely stood aside to let the narrow path creep through, and closed immediately behind. It was all as lonely as could be; and there is this peculiarity in such a solitude, that the traveller knows not who may be concealed by the innumerable trunks and the thick boughs overhead; so that with lonely footsteps he may yet be passing through an unseen multitude.

"There may be a devilish Indian behind every tree," said Goodman Brown to himself; and he glanced fearfully behind him as he added, "What if the devil himself should be at my very elbow!"

His head being turned back, he passed a crook of the road, and, looking forward again, beheld the figure of a man, in grave and decent attire, seated at the foot of an old tree. He arose at Goodman Brown's approach and walked onward side by side with him.

[1] A seventeenth-century title of respect for those below the rank of gentleman, especially for a farmer or yeoman.

[2] A village in Massachusetts, location of the Salem witch trials and executions in 1692.

"You are late, Goodman Brown," said he. "The clock of the Old South[3] was striking as I came through Boston, and that is full fifteen minutes agone."

"Faith kept me back a while," replied the young man, with a tremor in his voice, caused by the sudden appearance of his companion, though not wholly unexpected.

It was now deep dusk in the forest, and deepest in that part of it where these two were journeying. As nearly as could be discerned, the second traveller was about fifty years old, apparently in the same rank of life as Goodman Brown, and bearing a considerable resemblance to him, though perhaps more in expression than features. Still they might have been taken for father and son. And yet, though the elder person was as simply clad as the younger, and as simple in manner too, he had an indescribable air of one who knew the world, and who would not have felt abashed at the governor's dinner table or in King William's[4] court, were it possible that his affairs should call him thither. But the only thing about him that could be fixed upon as remarkable was his staff, which bore the likeness of a great black snake, so curiously wrought that it might almost be seen to twist and wriggle itself like a living serpent. This, of course, must have been an ocular deception, assisted by the uncertain light.

"Come, Goodman Brown," cried his fellow-traveller, "this is a dull pace for the beginning of a journey. Take my staff, if you are so soon weary."

"Friend," said the other, exchanging his slow pace for a full stop, "having kept convenant by meeting thee here, it is my purpose now to return whence I came. I have scruples touching the matter thou wot'st[5] of."

"Sayest thou so?" replied he of the serpent, smiling apart. "Let us walk on, nevertheless, reasoning as we go; and if I convince thee not thou shalt turn back. We are but a little way in the forest yet."

"Too far! too far!" exclaimed the goodman, unconsciously resuming his walk. "My father never went into the woods on such an errand, nor his father before him. We have been a race of honest men and good Christians since the days of the martyrs;[6] and shall I be the first of the name of Brown that ever took this path and kept"—

"Such company, thou wouldst say," observed the elder person, interpreting his pause. "Well said, Goodman Brown! I have been as well acquainted with your family as with ever a one among the Puritans; and that's no trifle to say. I helped your grandfather, the constable, when he lashed the Quaker woman so smartly through the streets of Salem;[7] and it was I that brought your father a pitch-pine knot, kindled at my own hearth, to set fire to an Indian village, in King Philip's war.[8] They were my good friends, both; and many a pleasant walk have we had along this path, and returned merrily after midnight. I would fain be friends with you for their sake."

"If it be as thou sayest," replied Goodman Brown, "I marvel they never

[3] The Old South Church in Boston. [4] William III was the reigning king of England.
[5] Knowest.
[6] That is, since the sixteenth-century persecutions of English Protestants by Queen Mary.
[7] Quakers were persecuted by the Puritans.
[8] An uprising of New England Indians in 1675 and 1676.

spoke of these matters; or, verily, I marvel not, seeing that the least rumor of the sort would have driven them from New England. We are a people of prayer, and good works to boot, and abide no such wickedness."

"Wickedness or not," said the traveller with the twisted staff, "I have a very general acquaintance here in New England. The deacons of many a church have drunk the communion wine with me; the selectmen of divers towns make me their chairman; and a majority of the Great and General Court[9] are firm supporters of my interest. The governor and I, too— But these are state secrets."

"Can this be so?" cried Goodman Brown, with a stare of amazement at his undisturbed companion. "Howbeit, I have nothing to do with the governor and council; they have their own ways, and are no rule for a simple husbandman[10] like me. But, were I to go on with thee, how should I meet the eye of that good old man, our minister, at Salem village? Oh, his voice would make me tremble both Sabbath day and lecture day."[11]

Thus far the elder traveller had listened with due gravity; but now burst into a fit of irrepressible mirth, shaking himself so violently that his snake-like staff actually seemed to wriggle in sympathy.

"Ha! ha! ha!" shouted he again and again; then composing himself, "Well, go on, Goodman Brown, go on; but, prithee, don't kill me with laughing."

"Well, then, to end the matter at once," said Goodman Brown, considerably nettled, "there is my wife, Faith. It would break her dear little heart; and I'd rather break my own."

"Nay, if that be the case," answered the other, "e'en go thy ways, Goodman Brown. I would not for twenty old women like the one hobbling before us that Faith should come to any harm."

As he spoke he pointed his staff at a female figure on the path, in whom Goodman Brown recognized a very pious and exemplary dame, who had taught him his catechism in youth, and was still his moral and spiritual adviser, jointly with the minister and Deacon Gookin.[12]

"A marvel, truly, that Goody[13] Cloyse should be so far in the wilderness at nightfall," said he. "But with your leave, friend, I shall take a cut through the woods until we have left this Christian woman behind. Being a stranger to you, she might ask whom I was consorting with and whither I was going."

"Be it so," said his fellow-traveller. "Betake you to the woods, and let me keep the path."

Accordingly the young man turned aside, but took care to watch his companion, who advanced softly along the road until he had come within a staff's length of the old dame. She, meanwhile, was making the best of her way, with singular speed for so aged a woman, and mumbling some indistinct words—a prayer, doubtless—as she went. The traveller put forth his staff and touched her withered neck with what seemed the serpent's tail.

[9] The main Puritan legislative body. [10] Farmer, humble man.

[11] A day set aside during the week for lectures on the Scriptures.

[12] Hawthorne uses actual Puritan names; there was a Puritan magistrate named Daniel Gookin, though he was never a Deacon at Salem. Goody Cloyse and Goody Cory, mentioned below, were executed in the 1692 witch trials.

[13] Contraction of "Goodwife," the feminine equivalent of "Goodman."

"The devil!" screamed the pious old lady.

"Then Goody Cloyse knows her old friend?" observed the traveller, confronting her and leaning on his writhing stick.

"Ah, forsooth, and is it your worship indeed?" cried the good dame. "Yea, truly is it, and in the very image of my old gossip, Goodman Brown, the grandfather of the silly fellow that now is. But—would your worship believe it?—my broomstick hath strangely disappeared, stolen, as I suspect, by that unhanged witch, Goody Cory, and that, too, when I was all anointed with the juice of smallage, and cinquefoil, and wolf's bane[14] —"

"Mingled with fine wheat and the fat of a new-born babe," said the shape of old Goodman Brown.

"Ah, your worship knows the recipe," cried the old lady, cackling aloud. "So, as I was saying, being all ready for the meeting, and no horse to ride on, I made up my mind to foot it; for they tell me there is a nice young man to be taken into communion to-night. But now your good worship will lend me your arm, and we shall be there in a twinkling."

"That can hardly be," answered her friend. "I may not spare you my arm, Goody Cloyse; but here is my staff, if you will."

So saying, he threw it down at her feet, where, perhaps, it assumed life, being one of the rods which its owner had formerly lent to the Egyptian magi.[15] Of this fact, however, Goodman Brown could not take cognizance. He had cast up his eyes in astonishment, and, looking down again, beheld neither Goody Cloyse nor the serpentine staff, but his fellow-traveller alone, who waited for him as calmly as if nothing had happened.

"That old woman taught me my catechism," said the young man; and there was a world of meaning in this simple comment.

They continued to walk onward, while the elder traveller exhorted his companion to make good speed and persevere in the path, discoursing so aptly that his arguments seemed rather to spring up in the bosom of his auditor than to be suggested by himself. As they went, he plucked a branch of maple to serve for a walking stick, and began to strip it of the twigs and little boughs, which were wet with evening dew. The moment his fingers touched them they became strangely withered and dried up as with a week's sunshine. Thus the pair proceeded, at a good free pace, until suddenly, in a gloomy hollow of the road, Goodman Brown sat himself down on the stump of a tree and refused to go any farther.

"Friend," said he, stubbornly, "my mind is made up. Not another step will I budge on this errand. What if a wretched old woman do choose to go to the devil when I thought she was going to heaven: is that any reason why I should quit my dear Faith and go after her?"

"You will think better of this by and by," said his acquaintance, composedly. "Sit here and rest yourself a while; and when you feel like moving again, there is my staff to help you along."

Without more words, he threw his companion the maple stick, and was as speedily out of sight as if he had vanished into the gloom. The young man sat a few moments by the roadside, applauding himself greatly, and

[14] Wild plants thought to be used by witches for magical purposes.

[15] Pharaoh's magicians, in their confrontation with Moses, cast down rods which become serpents. See Exodus 7.

thinking with how clear a conscience he should meet the minister in his morning walk, nor shrink from the eye of good old Deacon Gookin. And what calm sleep would be his that very night, which was to have been spent so wickedly, but so purely and sweetly now, in the arms of Faith! Amidst these pleasant and praiseworthy meditations, Goodman Brown heard the tramp of horses along the road, and deemed it advisable to conceal himself within the verge of the forest, conscious of the guilty purpose that had brought him thither, though now so happily turned from it.

On came the hoof tramps and the voices of the riders, two grave old voices, conversing soberly as they drew near. These mingled sounds appeared to pass along the road, within a few yards of the young man's hiding-place; but, owing doubtless to the depth of the gloom at that particular spot, neither the travellers nor their steeds were visible. Though their figures brushed the small boughs by the wayside, it could not be seen that they intercepted, even for a moment, the faint gleam from the strip of bright sky athwart which they must have passed. Goodman Brown alternately crouched and stood on tiptoe, pulling aside the branches and thrusting forth his head as far as he durst without discerning so much as a shadow. It vexed him the more, because he could have sworn, were such a thing possible, that he recognized the voices of the minister and Deacon Gookin, jogging along quietly, as they were wont to do, when bound to some ordination or ecclesiastical council. While yet within hearing, one of the riders stopped to pluck a switch.

"Of the two, reverend sir," said the voice like the deacon's, "I had rather miss an ordination dinner than to-night's meeting. They tell me that some of our community are to be here from Falmouth and beyond, and others from Connecticut and Rhode Island, besides several of the Indian powwows, who, after their fashion know almost as much deviltry as the best of us. Moreover, there is a goodly young woman to be taken into communion."

"Mighty well, Deacon Gookin!" replied the solemn old tones of the minister. "Spur up, or we shall be late. Nothing can be done, you know, until I get on the ground."

The hoofs clattered again; and the voices, talking so strangely in the empty air, passed on through the forest, where no church had ever been gathered or solitary Christian prayed. Whither, then, could these holy men be journeying so deep into the heathen wilderness? Young Goodman Brown caught hold of a tree for support, being ready to sink down on the ground, faint and overburdened with the heavy sickness of his heart. He looked up to the sky, doubting whether there really was a heaven above him. Yet there was the blue arch, and the stars brightening in it.

"With heaven above and Faith below, I will yet stand firm against the devil!" cried Goodman Brown.

While he still gazed upward into the deep arch of the firmament and had lifted his hands to pray, a cloud, though no wind was stirring, hurried across the zenith and hid the brightening stars. The blue sky was still visible, except directly overhead, where this black mass of cloud was sweeping swiftly northward. Aloft in the air, as if from the depths of the cloud, came a confused and doubtful sound of voices. Once the listener fancied that he could distinguish the accents of townspeople of his own, men and women, both pious and ungodly, many of whom he had met at the communion table, and had seen others rioting at the tavern. The next moment, so indistinct were the sounds, he doubted whether he had heard aught but the murmur of the old forest, whispering without a wind. Then came a stronger swell of those familiar tones, heard daily in the sunshine at Salem village, but never until now from a cloud of night. There was one voice, of a young woman, uttering lamentations, yet with an uncertain sorrow, and entreating for some favor, which, perhaps, it would grieve her to obtain; and all the unseen multitude, both saints and sinners, seemed to encourage her onward.

"Faith!" shouted Goodman Brown, in a voice of agony and desperation; and the echoes of the forest mocked him, crying, "Faith! Faith!" as if bewildered wretches were seeking her all through the wilderness.

The cry of grief, rage, and terror was yet piercing the night, when the unhappy husband held his breath for a response. There was a scream, drowned immediately in a louder murmur of voices, fading into far-off laughter, as the dark cloud swept away, leaving the clear and silent sky above Goodman Brown. But something fluttered lightly down through the air and caught on the branch of a tree. The young man seized it, and beheld a pink ribbon.

"My Faith is gone!" cried he, after one stupefied moment. "There is no good on earth; and sin is but a name. Come, devil; for to thee is this world given."

And, maddened with despair, so that he laughed loud and long, did Goodman Brown grasp his staff and set forth again, at such a rate that he seemed to fly along the forest path rather than to walk or run. The road grew wilder and drearier and more faintly traced, and vanished at length, leaving him in the heart of the dark wilderness, still rushing onward with the instinct that guides mortal man to evil. The whole forest was peopled with frightful sounds—the creaking of the trees, the howling of wild beasts, and the yell of Indians; while sometimes the wind tolled like a distant church bell, and sometimes gave a broad roar around the traveller, as if all Nature were laughing him to scorn. But he was himself the chief horror of the scene, and shrank not from its other horrors.

"Ha! ha! ha!" roared Goodman Brown when the wind laughed at him. "Let us hear which will laugh loudest. Think not to frighten me with your deviltry. Come witch, come wizard, come Indian powwow, come devil himself, and here comes Goodman Brown. You may as well fear him as he fear you."

In truth, all through the haunted forest there could be nothing more frightful than the figure of Goodman Brown. On he flew among the black pines, brandishing his staff with frenzied gestures, now giving vent to an inspiration of horrid blasphemy, and now shouting forth such laughter as set all the echoes of the forest laughing like demons around him. The fiend in his own shape is less hideous than when he rages in the breast of man. Thus sped the demoniac on his course, until, quivering among the trees, he saw a red light before him, as when the felled trunks and branches of a clearing have been set on fire, and throw up their lurid blaze against the sky, at the hour of midnight. He paused, in a lull of the tempest that had driven him onward, and heard the swell of what seemed a hymn, rolling solemnly from a distance with the weight of many voices. He knew the tune; it was a familiar one in the choir of the village meeting-house. The verse died heavily away, and was lengthened by a chorus, not of human voices, but of all the sounds of the benighted wilderness pealing in awful harmony together. Goodman Brown cried out, and his cry was lost to his own ear by its unison with the cry of the desert.

In the interval of silence he stole forward until the light glared full upon his eyes. At one extremity of an open space, hemmed in by the dark wall of the forest, arose a rock, bearing some rude, natural resemblance either to an altar or a pulpit, and surrounded by four blazing pines, their tops aflame, their stems untouched, like candles at an evening meeting. The mass of foliage that had over-grown the summit of the rock was all on fire, blazing high into the night and fitfully illuminating the whole field. Each pendent twig and leafy festoon was in a blaze. As the red light arose and fell, a numerous congregation alternately shone forth, then disappeared in shadow, and again grew, as it were, out of the darkness, peopling the heart of the solitary woods at once.

"A grave and dark-clad company," quoth Goodman Brown.

In truth they were such. Among them, quivering to and fro between gloom and splendor, appeared faces that would be seen next day at the council board of the province, and others which, Sabbath after Sabbath, looked devoutly heavenward, and benignantly over the crowded pews, from the holiest pulpits in the land. Some affirm that the lady of the governor was there.[16] At least there were high dames well known to her, and wives of honored husbands, and widows, a great multitude, and ancient maidens, all of excellent repute, and fair young girls, who trembled lest their mothers should espy them. Either the sudden gleams of light flashing over the obscure field bedazzled Goodman Brown, or he recognized a score of the church members of Salem village famous for their especial sanctity. Good old Deacon Gookin had arrived, and waited at the skirts of that venerable saint, his revered pastor. But, irreverently consorting with these grave, reputable, and pious people, these elders of the church, these chaste dames and dewy virgins, there were men of dissolute lives and women of spotted fame, wretches given over to all mean and filthy vice, and suspected even of horrid crimes. It was strange to see that the good shrank not from the wicked, nor were the sinners abashed by the saints. Scattered also among their palefaced enemies were the Indian priests, or powwows, who had often scared their native forest with more hideous incantations than any known to English witchcraft.

"But where is Faith?" thought Goodman Brown; and, as hope came into his heart, he trembled.

Another verse of the hymn arose, a slow and mournful strain, such as the pious love, but joined to words which expressed all that our nature can conceive of sin, and darkly hinted at far more. Unfathomable to mere mortals is the lore of fiends. Verse after verse was sung; and still the chorus of the desert swelled between like the deepest tone of a mighty organ; and with the final peal of that dreadful anthem there came a sound, as if the

[16] The wife of Sir William Phips, royal Governor of Massachusetts in 1692, is said to have been accused of witchcraft, though she was not tried.

roaring wind, the rushing streams, the howling beasts, and every other voice of the unconcerted wilderness were mingling and according with the voice of guilty man in homage to the prince of all. The four blazing pines threw up a loftier flame, and obscurely discovered shapes and visages of horror on the smoke wreaths above the impious assembly. At the same moment the fire on the rock shot redly forth and formed a glowing arch above its base, where now appeared a figure. With reverence be it spoken, the figure bore no slight similitude, both in garb and manner, to some grave divine of the New England churches.

"Bring forth the converts!" cried a voice that echoed through the field and rolled into the forest.

At the word, Goodman Brown stepped forth from the shadow of the trees and approached the congregation, with whom he felt a loathful brotherhood by the sympathy of all that was wicked in his heart. He could have well-nigh sworn that the shape of his own dead father beckoned him to advance, looking downward from a smoke wreath, while a woman, with dim features of despair, threw out her hand to warn him back. Was it his mother? But he had no power to retreat one step, nor to resist, even in thought, when the minister and good old Deacon Gookin seized his arms and led him to the blazing rock. Thither came also the slender form of a veiled female, led between Goody Cloyse, that pious teacher of the catechism, and Martha Carrier,[17] who had received the devil's promise to be queen of hell. A rampant hag was she. And there stood the proselytes beneath the canopy of fire.

"Welcome, my children," said the dark figure, "to the communion of your race. Ye have found thus young your nature and your destiny. My children, look behind you!"

They turned; and flashing forth, as it were, in a sheet of flame, the fiend worshippers were seen; the smile of welcome gleamed darkly on every visage.

"There," resumed the sable form, "are all whom ye have reverenced from youth. Ye deemed them holier than yourselves, and shrank from your own sin, contrasting it with their lives of righteousness and prayerful aspirations heavenward. Yet here are they all in my worshipping assembly. This night it shall be granted you to know their secret deeds: how hoary-bearded elders of the church have whispered wanton words to the young maids of their households; how many a woman, eager for widow's weeds, has given her husband a drink at bedtime and let him sleep his last sleep in her bosom; how beardless youths have made haste to inherit their fathers' wealth: and how fair damsels—blush not, sweet ones—have dug little graves in the garden, and bidden me, the sole guest, to an infant's funeral. By the sympathy of your human hearts for sin ye shall scent out all the places—whether in church, bed-chamber, street, field, or forest—where crime has been committed, and shall exult to behold the whole earth one stain of guilt, one mighty bloody spot. Far more than this. It shall be yours to penetrate, in every bosom, the deep mystery of sin, the fountain of all wicked arts, and which inexhaustibly supplies more evil impulses than

[17] Another actual historical figure. Charged with witchcraft in 1692, she testified that the devil had promised that she would be "queen of hell." She was among those executed.

human power—than my power at its utmost—can make manifest in deeds. And now, my children, look upon each other."

They did so; and, by the blaze of the hell-kindled torches, the wretched man beheld his Faith, and the wife her husband, trembling before that unhallowed altar.

"Lo, there ye stand, my children," said the figure, in a deep and solemn tone, almost sad with its despairing awfulness, as if his once angelic nature could yet mourn for our miserable race. "Depending upon one another's hearts, ye had still hoped that virtue were not all a dream. Now are ye undeceived. Evil is the nature of mankind. Evil must be your only happiness. Welcome again, my children, to the communion of your race."

"Welcome," repeated the fiend worshippers, in one cry of despair and triumph.

And there they stood, the only pair, as it seemed, who were yet hesitating on the verge of wickedness in this dark world. A basin was hollowed, naturally, in the rock. Did it contain water, reddened by the lurid light? or was it blood? or, perchance, a liquid flame? Herein did the shape of evil dip his hand and prepare to lay the mark of baptism upon their foreheads, that they might be partakers of the mystery of sin, more conscious of the secret guilt of others, both in deed and thought, than they could now be of their own. The husband cast one look at his pale wife, and Faith at him. What polluted wretches would the next glance show them to each other, shuddering alike at what they disclosed and what they saw!

"Faith! Faith!" cried the husband, "look up to heaven, and resist the wicked one."

Whether Faith obeyed he knew not. Hardly had he spoken when he found himself amid calm night and solitude, listening to a roar of the wind which died heavily away through the forest. He staggered against the rock, and felt it chill and damp; while a hanging twig, that had been all on fire, besprinkled his cheek with the coldest dew.

The next morning young Goodman Brown came slowly into the street of Salem village, staring around him like a bewildered man. The good old minister was taking a walk along the graveyard to get an appetite for breakfast and meditate his sermon, and bestowed a blessing, as he passed, on Goodman Brown. He shrank from the venerable saint as if to avoid an anathema.[18] Old Deacon Gookin was at domestic worship, and the holy words of his prayer were heard through the open window. "What God doth the wizard pray to?" quoth Goodman Brown. Goody Cloyse, that excellent old Christian, stood in the early sunshine at her own lattice, catechizing a little girl who had brought her a pint of morning's milk. Goodman Brown snatched away the child as from the grasp of the fiend himself. Turning the corner by the meeting-house, he spied the head of Faith, with the pink ribbons, gazing anxiously forth, and bursting into such joy at sight of him that she skipped along the street and almost kissed her husband before the whole village. But Goodman Brown looked sternly and sadly into her face, and passed on without a greeting.

Had Goodman Brown fallen asleep in the forest and only dreamed a wild dream of a witch-meeting?

[18] Curse.

Be it so if you will; but, alas! it was a dream of evil omen for young Goodman Brown. A stern, a sad, a darkly meditative, a distrustful, if not a desperate man did he become from the night of that fearful dream. On the Sabbath day, when the congregation were singing a holy psalm, he could not listen because an anthem of sin rushed loudly upon his ear and drowned all the blessed strain. When the minister spoke from the pulpit with power and fervid eloquence, and, with his hand on the open Bible, of the sacred truths of our religion, and of saint-like lives and triumphant deaths, and of future bliss or misery unutterable, then did Goodman Brown turn pale, dreading lest the roof should thunder down upon the gray blasphemer and his hearers. Often, waking suddenly at midnight, he shrank from the bosom of Faith; and at morning or eventide, when the family knelt down at prayer, he scowled and muttered to himself, and gazed sternly at his wife, and turned away. And when he had lived long, and was borne to his grave a hoary corpse, followed by Faith, an aged woman, and children and grandchildren, a goodly procession, besides neighbors not a few, they carved no hopeful verse upon his tombstone, for his dying hour was gloom.

RAPPACCINI'S DAUGHTER

A young man, named Giovanni Guasconti, came, very long ago, from the more southern region of Italy, to pursue his studies at the University of Padua. Giovanni, who had but a scanty supply of gold ducats in his pocket, took lodgings in a high and gloomy chamber of an old edifice which looked not unworthy to have been the palace of a Paduan noble, and which, in fact, exhibited over its entrance the armorial bearings of a family long since extinct. The young stranger, who was not unstudied in the great poem of his country, recollected that one of the ancestors of this family, and perhaps an occupant of this very mansion, had been pictured by Dante as a partaker of the immortal agonies of his Inferno. These reminiscences and associations, together with the tendency to heartbreak natural to a young man for the first time out of his native sphere, caused Giovanni to sigh heavily as he looked around the desolate and ill-furnished apartment.

"Holy Virgin, signor!" cried old Dame Lisabetta, who, won by the youth's remarkable beauty of person, was kindly endeavoring to give the chamber a habitable air, "what a sigh was that to come out of a young man's heart! Do you find this old mansion gloomy? For the love of Heaven, then, put your head out of the window, and you will see as bright sunshine as you have left in Naples."

Guasconti mechanically did as the old woman advised, but could not quite agree with her that the Paduan sunshine was as cheerful as that of southern Italy. Such as it was, however, it fell upon a garden beneath the window and expended its fostering influences on a variety of plants, which seemed to have been cultivated with exceeding care.

"Does this garden belong to the house?" asked Giovanni.

"Heaven forbid, signor, unless it were fruitful of better pot herbs than any that grow there now," answered old Lisabetta. "No; that garden is cultivated by the own hands of Signor Giacomo Rappaccini, the famous doctor, who, I warrant him, has been heard of as far as Naples. It is said that he distils these plants into medicines that are as potent as a charm. Oftentimes you may see the signor doctor at work, and perchance the signora, his daughter, too, gathering the strange flowers that grow in the garden."

The old woman had now done what she could for the aspect of the chamber; and, commending the young man to the protection of the saints, took her departure.

Giovanni still found no better occupation than to look down into the garden beneath his window. From its appearance, he judged it to be one of those botanic gardens which were of earlier date in Padua than elsewhere in Italy or in the world. Or, not improbably, it might once have been the pleasure-place of an opulent family; for there was the ruin of a marble fountain in the centre, sculptured with rare art but so wofully shattered that it was impossible to trace the original design from the chaos of remaining fragments. The water, however, continued to gush and sparkle into the sunbeams as cheerfully as ever. A little gurgling sound ascended to the young man's window, and made him feel as if the fountain were an immortal spirit that sung its song unceasingly and without heeding the vicissitudes around it, while one century imbodied it in marble and another scattered the perishable garniture[1] on the soil. All about the pool into which the water subsided grew various plants, that seemed to require a plentiful supply of moisture for the nourishment of gigantic leaves, and, in some instances, flowers gorgeously magnificent. There was one shrub in particular, set in a marble vase in the midst of the pool, that bore a profusion of purple blossoms, each of which had the lustre and richness of a gem; and the whole together made a show so resplendent that it seemed enough to illuminate the garden, even had there been no sunshine. Every portion of the soil was peopled with plants and herbs, which, if less beautiful, still bore tokens of assiduous care, as if all had their individual virtues,[2] known to the scientific mind that fostered them. Some were placed in urns, rich with old carving, and others in common garden pots; some crept serpent-like along the ground or climbed on high, using whatever means of ascent was offered them. One plant had wreathed itself round a statue of Vertumnus,[3] which was thus quite veiled and shrouded in a drapery of hanging foliage, so happily arranged that it might have served a sculptor for a study.

While Giovanni stood at the window he heard a rustling behind a screen of leaves, and became aware that a person was at work in the garden. His figure soon emerged into view, and showed itself to be that of no common laborer, but a tall, emaciated, sallow, and sickly-looking man, dressed in a scholar's garb of black. He was beyond the middle term of life, with grey hair, a thin, grey beard, and a face singularly marked with intellect and cultivation, but which could never, even in his more youthful days, have expressed much warmth of heart.

Nothing could exceed the intentness with which this scientific gardener

[1] Decoration; adornment. [2] Powers; potencies.
[3] Roman god of gardens, orchards, and the changing seasons.

examined every shrub which grew in his path: it seemed as if he was looking into their inmost nature, making observations in regard to their creative essence, and discovering why one leaf grew in this shape and another in that, and wherefore such and such flowers differed among themselves in hue and perfume. Nevertheless, in spite of this deep intelligence on his part, there was no approach to intimacy between himself and these vegetable existences. On the contrary, he avoided their actual touch or the direct inhaling of their odors with a caution that impressed Giovanni most disagreeably; for the man's demeanor was that of one walking among malignant influences, such as savage beasts, or deadly snakes, or evil spirits, which, should he allow them one moment of license, would wreak upon him some terrible fatality. It was strangely frightful to the young man's imagination to see this air of insecurity in a person cultivating a garden, that most simple and innocent of human toils, and which had been alike the joy and labor of the unfallen parents of the race. Was this garden, then, the Eden of the present world? And this man, with such a perception of harm in what his own hands caused to grow,—was he the Adam?

The distrustful gardener, while plucking away the dead leaves or pruning the too luxuriant growth of the shrubs, defended his hands with a pair of thick gloves. Nor were these his only armor. When, in his walk through the garden, he came to the magnificent plant that hung its purple gems beside the marble fountain, he placed a kind of mask over his mouth and nostrils, as if all this beauty did but conceal a deadlier malice; but, finding his task still too dangerous, he drew back, removed the mask, and called loudly, but in the infirm voice of a person affected with inward disease,—

"Beatrice! Beatrice!"

"Here am I, my father. What would you?" cried a rich and youthful voice from the window of the opposite house—a voice as rich as a tropical sunset, and which made Giovanni, though he knew not why, think of deep hues of purple or crimson and of perfumes heavily delectable. "Are you in the garden?"

"Yes, Beatrice," answered the gardener, "and I need your help."

Soon there emerged from under a sculptured portal the figure of a young girl, arrayed with as much richness of taste as the most splendid of the flowers, beautiful as the day, and with a bloom so deep and vivid that one shade more would have been too much. She looked redundant with life, health, and energy; all of which attributes were bound down and compressed, as it were, and girdled tensely, in their luxuriance, by her virgin zone.[4] Yet Giovanni's fancy must have grown morbid while he looked down into the garden; for the impression which the fair stranger made upon him was as if here were another flower, the human sister of those vegetable ones, as beautiful as they, more beautiful than the richest of them, but still to be touched only with a glove, nor to be approached without a mask. As Beatrice came down the garden path, it was observable that she handled and inhaled the odor of several of the plants which her father had most sedulously avoided.

"Here, Beatrice," said the latter, "see how many needful offices require to be done to our chief treasure. Yet, shattered as I am, my life might pay

[4] A belt or girdle.

the penalty of approaching it so closely as circumstances demand. Henceforth, I fear, this plant must be consigned to your sole charge."

"And gladly will I undertake it," cried again the rich tones of the young lady, as she bent towards the magnificent plant and opened her arms as if to embrace it. "Yes, my sister, my splendor, it shall be Beatrice's task to nurse and serve thee; and thou shalt reward her with thy kisses and perfumed breath, which to her is as the breath of life."

Then, with all the tenderness in her manner that was so strikingly expressed in her words, she busied herself with such attentions as the plant seemed to require; and Giovanni, at his lofty window, rubbed his eyes and almost doubted whether it were a girl tending her favorite flower, or one sister performing the duties of affection to another. The scene soon terminated. Whether Dr. Rappaccini had finished his labors in the garden, or that his watchful eye had caught the stranger's face, he now took his daughter's arm and retired. Night was already closing in; oppressive exhalations seemed to proceed from the plants and steal upward past the open window; and Giovanni, closing the lattice, went to his couch and dreamed of a rich flower and beautiful girl. Flower and maiden were different, and yet the same, and fraught with some strange peril in either shape.

But there is an influence in the light of morning that tends to rectify whatever errors of fancy, or even of judgment, we may have incurred during the sun's decline, or among the shadows of the night, or in the less wholesome glow of moonshine. Giovanni's first movement, on starting from sleep, was to throw open the window and gaze down into the garden which his dreams had made so fertile of mysteries. He was surprised and a little ashamed to find how real and matter-of-fact an affair it proved to be, in the first rays of the sun which gilded the dew-drops that hung upon leaf and blossom, and, while giving a brighter beauty to each rare flower, brought everything within the limits of ordinary experience. The young man rejoiced that, in the heart of the barren city, he had the privilege of overlooking this spot of lovely and luxuriant vegetation. It would serve, he said to himself, as a symbolic language to keep him in communion with Nature. Neither the sickly and thought-worn Dr. Giacomo Rappaccini, it is true, nor his brilliant daughter, were now visible; so that Giovanni could not determine how much of the singularity which he attributed to both was due to their own qualities and how much to his wonder-working fancy; but he was inclined to take a most rational view of the whole matter.

In the course of the day he paid his respects to Signor Pietro Baglioni, professor of medicine in the university, a physician of eminent repute, to whom Giovanni had brought a letter of introduction. The professor was an elderly personage, apparently of genial nature, and habits that might almost be called jovial. He kept the young man to dinner, and made himself very agreeable by the freedom and liveliness of his conversation, especially when warmed by a flask or two of Tuscan wine. Giovanni, conceiving that men of science, inhabitants of the same city, must needs be on familiar terms with one another, took an opportunity to mention the name of Dr. Rappaccini. But the professor did not respond with so much cordiality as he had anticipated.

"Ill would it become a teacher of the divine art of medicine," said Professor Pietro Baglioni, in answer to a question of Giovanni, "to withhold due and well-considered praise of a physician so eminently skilled as Rappaccini; but, on the other hand, I should answer it but scantily to my conscience were I to permit a worthy youth like yourself, Signor Giovanni, the son of an ancient friend, to imbibe erroneous ideas respecting a man who might hereafter chance to hold your life and death in his hands. The truth is, our worshipful Dr. Rappaccini has as much science as any member of the faculty—with perhaps one single exception—in Padua, or all Italy; but there are certain grave objections to his professional character."

"And what are they?" asked the young man.

"Has my friend Giovanni any disease of body or heart, that he is so inquisitive about physicians?" said the professor, with a smile. "But as for Rappaccini, it is said of him—and I, who know the man well, can answer for its truth—that he cares infinitely more for science than for mankind. His patients are interesting to him only as subjects for some new experiment. He would sacrifice human life, his own among the rest, or whatever else was dearest to him, for the sake of adding so much as a grain of mustard seed to the great heap of his accumulated knowledge."

"Methinks he is an awful man indeed," remarked Guasconti, mentally recalling the cold and purely intellectual aspect of Rappaccini. "And yet, worshipful professor, is it not a noble spirit? Are there many men capable of so spiritual a love of science?"

"God forbid," answered the professor, somewhat testily; "at least, unless they take sounder views of the healing art than those adopted by Rappaccini. It is his theory that all medicinal virtues are comprised within those substances which we term vegetable poisons. These he cultivates with his own hands, and is said even to have produced new varieties of poison, more horribly deleterious than Nature, without the assistance of this learned person, would ever have plagued the world withal. That the signor doctor does less mischief than might be expected with such dangerous substances is undeniable. Now and then, it must be owned, he has effected, or seemed to effect, a marvellous cure; but, to tell you my private mind, Signor Giovanni, he should receive little credit for such instances of success,—they being probably the work of chance,—but should be held strictly accountable for his failures, which may justly be considered his own work."

The youth might have taken Baglioni's opinions with many grains of allowance had he known that there was a professional warfare of long continuance between him and Dr. Rappaccini, in which the latter was generally thought to have gained the advantage. If the reader be inclined to judge for himself, we refer him to certain black-letter tracts on both sides, preserved in the medical department of the University of Padua.

"I know not, most learned professor," returned Giovanni, after musing on what had been said of Rappaccini's exclusive zeal for science,—"I know not how dearly this physician may love his art; but surely there is one object more dear to him. He has a daughter."

"Aha!" cried the professor, with a laugh. "So now our friend Giovanni's secret is out. You have heard of this daughter, whom all the young men in Padua are wild about, though not half a dozen have ever had the good hap to see her face. I know little of the Signora Beatrice save that Rappaccini is said to have instructed her deeply in his science, and that, young and beautiful as fame reports her, she is already qualified to fill a professor's chair. Perchance her father destines her for mine! Other absurd rumors there be, not worth talking about or listening to. So now, Signor Giovanni, drink off your glass of lachryma."[5]

Guasconti returned to his lodgings somewhat heated with the wine he had quaffed, and which caused his brain to swim with strange fantasies in reference to Dr. Rappaccini and the beautiful Beatrice. On his way, happening to pass by a florist's, he bought a fresh bouquet of flowers.

Ascending to his chamber, he seated himself near the window, but within the shadow thrown by the depth of the wall, so that he could look down into the garden with little risk of being discovered. All beneath his eye was a solitude. The strange plants were basking in the sunshine, and now and then nodding gently to one another, as if in acknowledgment of sympathy and kindred. In the midst, by the shattered fountain, grew the magnificent shrub, with its purple gems clustering all over it; they glowed in the air, and gleamed back again out of the depths of the pool, which thus seemed to overflow with colored radiance from the rich reflection that was steeped in it. At first, as we have said, the garden was a solitude. Soon, however,—as Giovanni had half hoped, half feared, would be the case,—a figure appeared beneath the antique sculptured portal, and came down between the rows of plants, inhaling their various perfumes as if she were one of those beings of old classic fable that lived upon sweet odors. On again beholding Beatrice, the young man was even startled to perceive how much her beauty exceeded his recollection of it; so brilliant, so vivid, was its character, that she glowed amid the sunlight, and, as Giovanni whispered to himself, positively illuminated the more shadowy intervals of the garden path. Her face being now more revealed than on the former occasion, he was struck by its expression of simplicity and sweetness,—qualities that had not entered into his idea of her character, and which made him ask anew what manner of mortal she might be. Nor did he fail again to observe, or imagine, an analogy between the beautiful girl and the gorgeous shrub that hung its gem-like flowers over the fountain,—a resemblance which Beatrice seemed to have indulged a fantastic humor in heightening, both by the arrangement of her dress and the selection of its hues.

Approaching the shrub, she threw open her arms, as with a passionate ardor, and drew its branches into an intimate embrace—so intimate that her features were hidden in its leafy bosom and her glistening ringlets all intermingled with the flowers.

"Give me thy breath, my sister," exclaimed Beatrice; "for I am faint with common air. And give me this flower of thine, which I separate with gentlest fingers from the stem and place it close beside my heart."

With these words the beautiful daughter of Rappaccini plucked one of the richest blossoms of the shrub, and was about to fasten it in her bosom. But now, unless Giovanni's draughts of wine had bewildered his senses, a singular incident occurred. A small orange-colored reptile, of the lizard or chameleon species, chanced to be creeping along the path, just at the feet of Beatrice. It appeared to Giovanni,—but, at the distance from which he gazed, he could scarcely have seen anything so minute,—it appeared to

[5] A sweet Italian wine.

him, however, that a drop or two of moisture from the broken stem of the flower descended upon the lizard's head. For an instant the reptile contorted itself violently, and then lay motionless in the sunshine. Beatrice observed this remarkable phenomenon, and crossed herself, sadly, but without surprise; nor did she therefore hesitate to arrange the fatal flower in her bosom. There it blushed, and almost glimmered with the dazzling effect of a precious stone, adding to her dress and aspect the one appropriate charm which nothing else in the world could have supplied. But Giovanni, out of the shadow of his window, bent forward and shrank back, and murmured and trembled.

"Am I awake? Have I my senses?" said he to himself. "What is this being? Beautiful shall I call her, or inexpressibly terrible?"

Beatrice now strayed carelessly through the garden, approaching closer beneath Giovanni's window, so that he was compelled to thrust his head quite out of its concealment in order to gratify the intense and painful curiosity which she excited. At this moment there came a beautiful insect over the garden wall; it had, perhaps, wandered through the city, and found no flowers or verdure among those antique haunts of men until the heavy perfumes of Dr. Rappaccini's shrubs had lured it from afar. Without alighting on the flowers, this winged brightness seemed to be attracted by Beatrice, and lingered in the air and fluttered about her head. Now, here it could not be but that Giovanni Guasconti's eyes deceived him. Be that as it might, he fancied that, while Beatrice was gazing at the insect with childish delight, it grew faint and fell at her feet; its bright wings shivered; it was dead—from no cause that he could discern, unless it were the atmosphere of her breath. Again Beatrice crossed herself and sighed heavily as she bent over the dead insect.

An impulsive movement of Giovanni drew her eyes to the window. There she beheld the beautiful head of the young man—rather a Grecian than an Italian head, with fair, regular features, and a glistening of gold among his ringlets—gazing down upon her like a being that hovered in mid air. Scarcely knowing what he did, Giovanni threw down the bouquet which he had hitherto held in his hand.

"Signora," said he, "there are pure and healthful flowers. Wear them for the sake of Giovanni Guasconti."

"Thanks, signor," replied Beatrice, with her rich voice, that came forth as it were like a gush of music, and with a mirthful expression half childish and half woman-like. "I accept your gift, and would fain recompense it with this precious purple flower; but if I toss it into the air it will not reach you. So Signor Guasconti must even content himself with my thanks."

She lifted the bouquet from the ground, and then, as if inwardly ashamed at having stepped aside from her maidenly reserve to respond to a stranger's greeting, passed swiftly homeward through the garden. But few as the moments were, it seemed to Giovanni, when she was on the point of vanishing beneath the sculptured portal, that his beautiful bouquet was already beginning to wither in her grasp. It was an idle thought; there could be no possibility of distinguishing a faded flower from a fresh one at so great a distance.

For many days after this incident the young man avoided the window that looked into Dr. Rappaccini's garden, as if something ugly and monstrous would have blasted his eyesight had he been betrayed into a glance. He felt conscious of having put himself, to a certain extent, within the influence of an unintelligible power by the communication which he had opened with Beatrice. The wisest course would have been, if his heart were in any real danger, to quit his lodgings and Padua itself at once; the next wiser, to have accustomed himself, as far as possible, to the familiar and daylight view of Beatrice—thus bringing her rigidly and systematically within the limits of ordinary experience. Least of all, while avoiding her sight, ought Giovanni to have remained so near this extraordinary being that the proximity and possibility even of intercourse should give a kind of substance and reality to the wild vagaries which his imagination ran riot continually in producing. Guasconti had not a deep heart—or, at all events, its depths were not sounded now; but he had a quick fancy and an ardent southern temperament, which rose every instant to a higher fever pitch. Whether or no Beatrice possessed those terrible attributes, that fatal breath, the affinity with those so beautiful and deadly flowers which were indicated by what Giovanni had witnessed, she had at least instilled a fierce and subtle poison in his system. It was not love, although her rich beauty was a madness to him; nor horror, even while he fancied her spirit to be imbued with the same baneful essence that seemed to pervade her physical frame; but a wild offspring of both love and horror that had each parent in it, and burned like one and shivered like the other. Giovanni knew not what to dread; still less did he know what to hope; yet hope and dread kept a continual warfare in his breast, alternately vanquishing one another and starting up afresh to renew the contest. Blessed are all simple emotions, be they dark or bright! It is the lurid intermixture of the two that produces the illuminating blaze of the infernal regions.

Sometimes he endeavored to assuage the fever of his spirit by a rapid walk through the streets of Padua or beyond its gates: his footsteps kept time with the throbbings of his brain, so that the walk was apt to accelerate itself to a race. One day he found himself arrested; his arm was seized by a portly personage, who had turned back on recognizing the young man and expended much breath in overtaking him.

"Signor Giovanni! Stay, my young friend!" cried he. "Have you forgotten me? That might well be the case if I were as much altered as yourself."

It was Baglioni, whom Giovanni had avoided ever since their first meeting, from a doubt[6] that the professor's sagacity would look too deeply into his secrets. Endeavoring to recover himself, he started forth wildly from his inner world into the outer one and spoke like a man in a dream.

"Yes; I am Giovanni Guasconti. You are Professor Pietro Baglioni. Now let me pass!"

"Not yet, not yet, Signor Giovanni Guasconti," said the professor, smiling, but at the same time scrutinizing the youth with an earnest glance. "What! did I grow up side by side with your father? and shall his son pass me like a stranger in these old streets of Padua? Stand still, Signor Giovanni; for we must have a word or two before we part."

"Speedily, then, most worshipful professor, speedily," said Giovanni, with feverish impatience. "Does not your worship see that I am in haste?"

[6] Suspicion.

Now, while he was speaking there came a man in black along the street, stooping and moving feebly like a person in inferior health. His face was all overspread with a most sickly and sallow hue, but yet so pervaded with an expression of piercing and active intellect that an observer might easily have overlooked the merely physical attributes and have seen only this wonderful energy. As he passed, this person exchanged a cold and distant salutation with Baglioni, but fixed his eyes upon Giovanni with an intentness that seemed to bring out whatever was within him worthy of notice. Nevertheless, there was a peculiar quietness in the look, as if taking merely a speculative, not a human, interest in the young man.

"It is Dr. Rappaccini!" whispered the professor when the stranger had passed. "Has he ever seen your face before?"

"Not that I know," answered Giovanni, starting at the name.

"He *has* seen you! he must have seen you!" said Baglioni, hastily. "For some purpose or other, this man of science is making a study of you. I know that look of his! It is the same that coldly illuminates his face as he bends over a bird, a mouse, or a butterfly, which, in pursuance of some experiment, he has killed by the perfume of a flower; a look as deep as Nature itself, but without Nature's warmth of love. Signor Giovanni, I will stake my life upon it, you are the subject of one of Rappaccini's experiments!"

"Will you make a fool of me?" cried Giovanni, passionately. "*That,* signor professor, were an untoward experiment."

"Patience! patience!" replied the imperturbable professor. "I tell thee, my poor Giovanni, that Rappaccini has a scientific interest in thee. Thou hast fallen into fearful hands! and the Signora Beatrice,—what part does she act in this mystery?"

But Guasconti, finding Baglioni's pertinacity intolerable, here broke away, and was gone before the professor could again seize his arm. He looked after the young man intently and shook his head.

"This must not be," said Baglioni to himself. "The youth is the son of my old friend, and shall not come to any harm from which the arcana[7] of medical science can preserve him. Besides, it is too insufferable an impertinence in Rappaccini, thus to snatch the lad out of my own hands, as I may say, and make use of him for his infernal experiments. This daughter of his! It shall be looked to. Perchance, most learned Rappaccini, I may foil you where you little dream of it!"

Meanwhile Giovanni had pursued a circuitous route, and at length found himself at the door of his lodgings. As he crossed the threshold he was met by old Lisabetta, who smirked and smiled, and was evidently desirous to attract his attention; vainly, however, as the ebullition of his feelings had momentarily subsided into a cold and dull vacuity. He turned his eyes full upon the withered face that was puckering itself into a smile, but seemed to behold it not. The old dame, therefore, laid her grasp upon his cloak.

"Signor! signor!" whispered she, still with a smile over the whole breadth of her visage, so that it looked not unlike a grotesque carving in

[7]Secret lore.

wood, darkened by centuries. "Listen, signor! There is a private entrance into the garden!"

"What do you say?" exclaimed Giovanni, turning quickly about, as if an inanimate thing should start into feverish life. "A private entrance into Dr. Rappaccini's garden?"

"Hush! hush! not so loud!" whispered Lisabetta, putting her hand over his mouth. "Yes; into the worshipful doctor's garden, where you may see all his fine shrubbery. Many a young man in Padua would give gold to be admitted among those flowers."

Giovanni put a piece of gold into her hand.

"Show me the way," said he.

A surmise, probably excited by his conversation with Baglioni, crossed his mind, that this interposition of old Lisabetta might perchance be connected with the intrigue, whatever were its nature, in which the professor seemed to suppose that Dr. Rappaccini was involving him. But such a suspicion, though it disturbed Giovanni, was inadequate to restrain him. The instant that he was aware of the possibility of approaching Beatrice, it seemed an absolute necessity of his existence to do so. It mattered not whether she were angel or demon; he was irrevocably within her sphere, and must obey the law that whirled him onward, in ever-lessening circles, towards a result which he did not attempt to foreshadow; and yet, strange to say, there came across him a sudden doubt whether this intense interest on his part were not delusory; whether it were really of so deep and positive a nature as to justify him in now thrusting himself into an incalculable position; whether it were not merely the fantasy of a young man's brain, only slightly or not at all connected with his heart.

He paused, hesitated, turned half about, but again went on. His withered guide led him along several obscure passages, and finally undid a door, through which, as it was opened, there came the sight and sound of rustling leaves, with the broken sunshine glimmering among them. Giovanni stepped forth, and, forcing himself through the entanglement of a shrub that wreathed its tendrils over the hidden entrance, stood beneath his own window in the open area of Dr. Rappaccini's garden.

How often is it the case that, when impossibilities have come to pass and dreams have condensed their misty substance into tangible realities, we find ourselves calm, and even coldly self-possessed, amid circumstances which it would have been a delirium of joy or agony to anticipate! Fate delights to thwart us thus. Passion will choose his own time to rush upon the scene, and lingers sluggishly behind when an appropriate adjustment of events would seem to summon his appearance. So was it now with Giovanni. Day after day his pulses had throbbed with feverish blood at the improbable idea of an interview with Beatrice, and of standing with her, face to face, in this very garden, basking in the Oriental sunshine of her beauty, and snatching from her full gaze the mystery which he deemed the riddle of his own existence. But now there was a singular and untimely equanimity within his breast. He threw a glance around the garden to discover if Beatrice or her father were present, and, perceiving that he was alone, began a critical observation of the plants.

The aspect of one and all of them dissatisfied him; their gorgeousness seemed fierce, passionate, and even unnatural. There was hardly an individual shrub which a wanderer, straying by himself through a forest, would not have been startled to find growing wild, as if an unearthly face had glared at him out of the thicket. Several also would have shocked a delicate instinct by an appearance of artificialness indicating that there had been such commixture, and, as it were, adultery, of various vegetable species, that the production was no longer of God's making, but the monstrous offspring of man's depraved fancy, glowing with only an evil mockery of beauty. They were probably the result of experiment, which in one or two cases had succeeded in mingling plants individually lovely into a compound possessing the questionable and ominous character that distinguished the whole growth of the garden. In fine, Giovanni recognized but two or three plants in the collection, and those of a kind that he well knew to be poisonous. While busy with these contemplations he heard the rustling of a silken garment, and, turning, beheld Beatrice emerging from beneath the sculptured portal.

Giovanni had not considered with himself what should be his deportment; whether he should apologize for his intrusion into the garden, or assume that he was there with the privity[8] at least, if not by the desire, of Dr. Rappaccini or his daughter; but Beatrice's manner placed him at his ease, though leaving him still in doubt by what agency he had gained admittance. She came lightly along the path and met him near the broken fountain. There was surprise in her face, but brightened by a simple and kind expression of pleasure.

"You are a connoisseur in flowers, signor," said Beatrice, with a smile, alluding to the bouquet which he had flung her from the window. "It is no marvel, therefore, if the sight of my father's rare collection has tempted you to take a nearer view. If he were here, he could tell you many strange and interesting facts as to the nature and habits of these shrubs; for he has spent a lifetime in such studies, and this garden is his world."

"And yourself, lady," observed Giovanni; "if fame says true,—you likewise are deeply skilled in the virtues indicated by these rich blossoms and these spicy perfumes. Would you deign to be my instructress, I should prove an apter scholar than if taught by Signor Rappaccini himself."

"Are there such idle rumors?" asked Beatrice, with the music of a pleasant laugh. "Do people say that I am skilled in my father's science of plants? What a jest is there! No; though I have grown up among these flowers, I know no more of them than their hues and perfume; and sometimes methinks I would fain rid myself of even that small knowledge. There are many flowers here, and those not the least brilliant, that shock and offend me when they meet my eye. But pray, signor, do not believe these stories about my science. Believe nothing of me save what you see with your own eyes."

"And must I believe all that I have seen with my own eyes?" asked Giovanni, pointedly, while the recollection of former scenes made him shrink. "No, signora; you demand too little of me. Bid me believe nothing save what comes from your own lips."

It would appear that Beatrice understood him. There came a deep flush

[8] Concurrence or consent.

to her cheek; but she looked full into Giovanni's eyes, and responded to his gaze of uneasy suspicion with a queenlike haughtiness.

"I do so bid you, signor," she replied. "Forget whatever you may have fancied in regard to me. If true to the outward senses, still it may be false in its essence; but the words of Beatrice Rappaccini's lips are true from the depths of the heart outward. Those you may believe."

A fervor glowed in her whole aspect and beamed upon Giovanni's consciousness like the light of truth itself; but while she spoke there was a fragrance in the atmosphere around her, rich and delightful, though evanescent, yet which the young man, from an indefinable reluctance, scarcely dared to draw into his lungs. It might be the odor of the flowers. Could it be Beatrice's breath which thus embalmed her words with a strange richness, as if by steeping them in her heart? A faintness passed like a shadow over Giovanni and flitted away; he seemed to gaze through the beautiful girl's eyes into her transparent soul, and felt no more doubt or fear.

The tinge of passion that had colored Beatrice's manner vanished; she became gay, and appeared to derive a pure delight from her communion with the youth not unlike what the maiden of a lonely island might have felt conversing with a voyager from the civilized world. Evidently her experience of life had been confined within the limits of that garden. She talked now about matters as simple as the daylight or summer clouds, and now asked questions in reference to the city, or Giovanni's distant home, his friends, his mother, and his sisters—questions indicating such seclusion, and such lack of familiarity with modes and forms, that Giovanni responded as if to an infant. Her spirit gushed out before him like a fresh rill that was just catching its first glimpse of the sunlight and wondering at the reflections of earth and sky which were flung into its bosom. There came thoughts, too, from a deep source, and fantasies of a gemlike brilliancy, as if diamonds and rubies sparkled upward among the bubbles of the fountain. Ever and anon there gleamed across the young man's mind a sense of wonder that he should be walking side by side with the being who had so wrought upon his imagination, whom he had idealized in such hues of terror, in whom he had positively witnessed such manifestations of dreadful attributes,—that he should be conversing with Beatrice like a brother, and should find her so human and so maidenlike. But such reflections were only momentary; the effect of her character was too real not to make itself familiar at once.

In this free intercourse they had strayed through the garden, and now, after many turns among its avenues, were come to the shattered fountain, beside which grew the magnificent shrub, with its treasury of glowing blossoms. A fragrance was diffused from it which Giovanni recognized as identical with that which he had attributed to Beatrice's breath, but incomparably more powerful. As her eyes fell upon it, Giovanni beheld her press her hand to her bosom as if her heart were throbbing suddenly and painfully.

"For the first time in my life," murmured she, addressing the shrub, "I had forgotten thee."

"I remember, signora," said Giovanni, "that you once promised to reward me with one of these living gems for the bouquet which I had the happy boldness to fling to your feet. Permit me now to pluck it as a memorial of this interview."

He made a step towards the shrub with extended hand; but Beatrice darted forward, uttering a shriek that went through his heart like a dagger. She caught his hand and drew it back with the whole force of her slender figure. Giovanni felt her touch thrilling through his fibres.

"Touch it not!" exclaimed she, in a voice of agony. "Not for thy life! It is fatal!"

Then, hiding her face, she fled from him and vanished beneath the sculptured portal. As Giovanni followed her with his eyes, he beheld the emaciated figure and pale intelligence of Dr. Rappaccini, who had been watching the scene, he knew not how long, within the shadow of the entrance.

No sooner was Guasconti alone in his chamber than the image of Beatrice came back to his passionate musings, invested with all the witchery that had been gathering around it ever since his first glimpse of her, and now likewise imbued with a tender warmth of girlish womanhood. She was human; her nature was endowed with all gentle and feminine qualities; she was worthiest to be worshipped; she was capable, surely, on her part, of the height and heroism of love. Those tokens which he had hitherto considered as proofs of a frightful peculiarity in her physical and moral system were now either forgotten, or, by the subtle sophistry of passion, transmitted into a golden crown of enchantment, rendering Beatrice the more admirable by so much as she was the more unique. Whatever had looked ugly was now beautiful; or, if incapable of such a change, it stole away and hid itself among those shapeless half ideas which throng the dim region beyond the daylight of our perfect consciousness. Thus did he spend the night, nor fell asleep until the dawn had begun to awake the slumbering flowers in Dr. Rappaccini's garden, whither Giovanni's dreams doubtless led him. Up rose the sun in his due season, and, flinging his beams upon the young man's eyelids, awoke him to a sense of pain. When thoroughly aroused, he became sensible of a burning and tingling agony in his hand—in his right hand—the very hand which Beatrice had grasped in her own when he was on the point of plucking one of the gemlike flowers. On the back of that hand there was now a purple print like that of four small fingers, and the likeness of a slender thumb upon his wrist.

Oh, how stubbornly does love,—or even that cunning semblance of love which flourishes in the imagination, but strikes no depth of root into the heart,—how stubbornly does it hold its faith until the moment comes when it is doomed to vanish into thin mist! Giovanni wrapped a handkerchief about his hand and wondered what evil thing had stung him, and soon forgot his pain in a reverie of Beatrice.

After the first interview, a second was in the inevitable course of what we call fate. A third; a fourth; and a meeting with Beatrice in the garden was no longer an incident in Giovanni's daily life, but the whole space in which he might be said to live; for the anticipation and memory of that ecstatic hour made up the remainder. Nor was it otherwise with the daughter of Rappaccini. She watched for the youth's appearance, and flew to his side with confidence as unreserved as if they had been playmates from early infancy—as if they were such playmates still. If, by any unwonted chance, he failed to come at the appointed moment, she stood beneath the window and sent up the rich sweetness of her tones to float around him in his chamber and echo and reverberate throughout his heart: "Giovanni! Giovanni! Why tarriest thou? Come down!" And down he hastened into that Eden of poisonous flowers.

But, with all this intimate familiarity, there was still a reserve in Beatrice's demeanor, so rigidly and invariably sustained that the idea of infringing it scarcely occurred to his imagination. By all appreciable signs, they loved; they had looked love with eyes that conveyed the holy secret from the depths of one soul into the depths of the other, as if it were too sacred to be whispered by the way; they had even spoken love in those gushes of passion when their spirits darted forth in articulated breath like tongues of long-hidden flame; and yet there had been no seal of lips, no clasp of hands, nor any slightest caress such as love claims and hallows. He had never touched one of the gleaming ringlets of her hair; her garment—so marked was the physical barrier between them—had never been waved against him by a breeze. On the few occasions when Giovanni had seemed tempted to overstep the limit, Beatrice grew so sad, so stern, and withal wore such a look of desolate separation, shuddering at itself, that not a spoken word was requisite to repel him. At such times he was startled at the horrible suspicions that rose, monster-like, out of the caverns of his heart and stared him in the face; his love grew thin and faint as the morning mist, his doubts alone had substance. But, when Beatrice's face brightened again after the momentary shadow, she was transformed at once from the mysterious, questionable being whom he had watched with so much awe and horror; she was now the beautiful and unsophisticated girl whom he felt that his spirit knew with a certainty beyond all other knowledge.

A considerable time had now passed since Giovanni's last meeting with Baglioni. One morning, however, he was disagreeably surprised by a visit from the professor, whom he had scarcely thought of for whole weeks, and would willingly have forgotten still longer. Given up as he had long been to a pervading excitement, he could tolerate no companions except upon condition of their perfect sympathy with his present state of feeling. Such sympathy was not to be expected from Professor Baglioni.

The visitor chatted carelessly for a few minutes about the gossip of the city and the university, and then took up another topic.

"I have been reading an old classic author lately," said he, "and met with a story that strangely interested me.[9] Possibly you may remember it. It is of an Indian prince, who sent a beautiful woman as a present to Alexander the Great. She was as lovely as the dawn and gorgeous as the sunset; but what especially distinguished her was a certain rich perfume in her breath—richer than a garden of Persian roses. Alexander, as was natural to a youthful conqueror, fell in love at first sight with this magnificent stranger; but a certain sage physician, happening to be present, discovered a terrible secret in regard to her."

"And what was that?" asked Giovanni, turning his eyes downward to avoid those of the professor.

"That this lovely woman," continued Baglioni, with emphasis, "had

[9]The author is Sir Thomas Browne; the story appears in his *Pseudodoxia Epidemica,* Book VII, chapter 17.

been nourished with poisons from her birth upward, until her whole nature was so imbued with them that she herself had become the deadliest poison in existence. Poison was her element of life. With that rich perfume of her breath she blasted the very air. Her love would have been poison—her embrace death. Is not this a marvellous tale?"

"A childish fable," answered Giovanni, nervously starting from his chair. "I marvel how your worship finds time to read such nonsense among your graver studies."

"By the by," said the professor, looking uneasily about him, "what singular fragrance is this in your apartment? Is it the perfume of your gloves? It is faint, but delicious; and yet, after all, by no means agreeable. Were I to breathe it long, methinks it would make me ill. It is like the breath of a flower; but I see no flowers in the chamber."

"Nor are there any," replied Giovanni, who had turned pale as the professor spoke; "nor, I think, is there any fragrance except in your worship's imagination. Odors, being a sort of element combined of the sensual and the spiritual, are apt to deceive us in this manner. The recollection of a perfume, the bare idea of it, may easily be mistaken for a present reality."

"Ay; but my sober imagination does not often play such tricks," said Baglioni; "and, were I to fancy any kind of odor, it would be that of some vile apothecary drug, wherewith my fingers are likely enough to be imbued. Our worshipful friend Rappaccini, as I have heard, tinctures his medicaments with odors richer than those of Araby. Doubtless, likewise, the fair and learned Signora Beatrice would minister to her patients with draughts as sweet as a maiden's breath; but woe to him that sips them!"

Giovanni's face evinced many contending emotions. The tone in which the professor alluded to the pure and lovely daughter of Rappaccini was a torture to his soul; and yet the intimation of a view of her character, opposite to his own, gave instantaneous distinctness to a thousand dim suspicions, which now grinned at him like so many demons. But he strove hard to quell them and to respond to Baglioni with a true lover's perfect faith.

"Signor professor," said he, "you were my father's friend; perchance, too, it is your purpose to act a friendly part towards his son. I would fain feel nothing towards you save respect and deference; but I pray you to observe, signor, that there is one subject on which we must not speak. You know not the Signora Beatrice. You cannot, therefore, estimate the wrong—the blasphemy, I may even say—that is offered to her character by a light or injurious word."

"Giovanni! my poor Giovanni!" answered the professor, with a calm expression of pity, "I know this wretched girl far better than yourself. You shall hear the truth in respect to the poisoner Rappaccini and his poisonous daughter; yes, poisonous as she is beautiful. Listen; for, even should you do violence to my gray hairs, it shall not silence me. That old fable of the Indian woman has become a truth by the deep and deadly science of Rappaccini and in the person of the lovely Beatrice."

Giovanni groaned and hid his face.

"Her father," continued Baglioni, "was not restrained by natural affection from offering up his child in this horrible manner as the victim of his insane zeal for science; for, let us do him justice, he is as true a man of science as ever distilled his own heart in an alembic.[10] What, then, will be your fate? Beyond a doubt you are selected as the material of some new experiment. Perhaps the result is to be death; perhaps a fate more awful still. Rappaccini, with what he calls the interest of science before his eyes, will hesitate at nothing."

"It is a dream," muttered Giovanni to himself; "surely it is a dream."

"But," resumed the professor, "be of good cheer, son of my friend. It is not yet too late for the rescue. Possibly we may even succeed in bringing back this miserable child within the limits of ordinary nature, from which her father's madness has estranged her. Behold this little silver vase! It was wrought by the hands of the renowned Benvenuto Cellini,[11] and is well worthy to be a love gift to the fairest dame in Italy. But its contents are invaluable. One little sip of this antidote would have rendered the most virulent poisons of the Borgias[12] innocuous. Doubt not that it will be as efficacious against those of Rappaccini. Bestow the vase, and the precious liquid within it, on your Beatrice, and hopefully await the result."

Baglioni laid a small, exquisitely wrought silver vial on the table and withdrew, leaving what he had said to produce its effect upon the young man's mind.

"We will thwart Rappaccini yet," thought he, chuckling to himself, as he descended the stairs; "but, let us confess the truth of him, he is a wonderful man—a wonderful man indeed; a vile empiric,[13] however, in his practice, and therefore not to be tolerated by those who respect the good old rules of the medical profession."

Throughout Giovanni's whole acquaintance with Beatrice, he had occasionally, as we have said, been haunted by dark surmises as to her character; yet so thoroughly had she made herself felt by him as a simple, natural, most affectionate, and guileless creature, that the image now held up by Professor Baglioni looked as strange and incredible as if it were not in accordance with his own original conception. True, there were ugly recollections connected with his first glimpses of the beautiful girl; he could not quite forget the bouquet that withered in her grasp, and the insect that perished amid the sunny air, by no ostensible agency save the fragrance of her breath. These incidents, however, dissolving in the pure light of her character, had no longer the efficacy of facts, but were acknowledged as mistaken fantasies, by whatever testimony of the senses they might appear to be substantiated. There is something truer and more real than what we can see with the eyes and touch with the finger. On such better evidence had Giovanni founded his confidence in Beatrice, though rather by the necessary force of her high attributes than by any deep and generous faith on his part. But now his spirit was incapable of sustaining itself at the height to which the early enthusiasm of passion had exalted it; he fell down, grovelling among earthly doubts, and defiled therewith the pure whiteness of Beatrice's image. Not that he gave her up; he did but distrust.

[10] A retort; a vessel used for distilling.

[11] Famous sixteenth-century Italian artist who worked in metal.

[12] Cesare Borgia (c. 1475–1507) and his sister Lucrezia Borgia (1480–1519), members of a powerful Italian Renaissance family, were famous for their skill in poisons.

[13] Experimenter; one who follows the empirical method.

He resolved to institute some decisive test that should satisfy him, once for all, whether there were those dreadful peculiarities in her physical nature which could not be supposed to exist without some corresponding monstrosity of soul. His eyes, gazing down afar, might have deceived him as to the lizard, the insect, and the flowers; but if he could witness, at the distance of a few paces, the sudden blight of one fresh and healthful flower in Beatrice's hand, there would be room for no further question. With this idea he hastened to the florist's and purchased a bouquet that was still gemmed with the morning dew-drops.

It was now the customary hour of his daily interview with Beatrice. Before descending into the garden, Giovanni failed not to look at his figure in the mirror,—a vanity to be expected in a beautiful young man, yet, as displaying itself at that troubled and feverish moment, the token of a certain shallowness of feeling and insincerity of character. He did gaze, however, and said to himself that his features had never before possessed so rich a grace, nor his eyes such vivacity, nor his cheeks so warm a hue of superabundant life.

"As least," thought he, "her poison has not yet insinuated itself into my system. I am no flower to perish in her grasp."

With that thought he turned his eyes on the bouquet, which he had never once laid aside from his hand. A thrill of indefinable horror shot through his frame on perceiving that those dewy flowers were already beginning to droop; they wore the aspect of things that had been fresh and lovely yesterday. Giovanni grew white as marble, and stood motionless before the mirror, staring at his own reflection there as at the likeness of something frightful. He remembered Baglioni's remark about the fragrance that seemed to pervade the chamber. It must have been the poison in his breath! Then he shuddered—shuddered at himself. Recovering from his stupor, he began to watch with curious eye a spider that was busily at work hanging its web from the antique cornice of the apartment, crossing and recrossing the artful system of interwoven lines—as vigorous and active a spider as ever dangled from an old ceiling. Giovanni bent towards the insect, and emitted a deep, long breath. The spider suddenly ceased its toil; the web vibrated with a tremor originating in the body of the small artisan. Again Giovanni sent forth a breath, deeper, longer, and imbued with a venomous feeling out of his heart: he knew not whether he were wicked, or only desperate. The spider made a convulsive gripe with his limbs and hung dead across the window.

"Accursed! accursed!" muttered Giovanni, addressing himself. "Hast thou grown so poisonous that this deadly insect perished by thy breath?"

At that moment a rich, sweet voice came floating up from the garden.

"Giovanni! Giovanni! It is past the hour! Why tarriest thou? Come down!"

"Yes," muttered Giovanni again. "She is the only being whom my breath may not slay! Would that it might!"

He rushed down, and in an instant was standing before the bright and loving eyes of Beatrice. A moment ago his wrath and despair had been so fierce that he could have desired nothing so much as to wither her by a glance; but with her actual presence there came influences which had too real an existence to be at once shaken off: recollections of the delicate and benign power of her feminine nature, which had so often enveloped him in a religious calm; recollections of many a holy and passionate outgush of her heart, when the pure fountain had been unsealed from its depths and made visible in its transparency to his mental eye; recollections which, had Giovanni known how to estimate them, would have assured him that all this ugly mystery was but an earthly illusion, and that, whatever mist of evil might seem to have gathered over her, the real Beatrice was a heavenly angel. Incapable as he was of such high faith, still her presence had not utterly lost its magic. Giovanni's rage was quelled into an aspect of sullen insensibility. Beatrice, with a quick spiritual sense, immediately felt that there was a gulf of blackness between them which neither he nor she could pass. They walked on together, sad and silent, and came thus to the marble fountain and to its pool of water on the ground, in the midst of which grew the shrub that bore gem-like blossoms. Giovanni was affrighted at the eager enjoyment—the appetite, as it were—with which he found himself inhaling the fragrance of the flowers.

"Beatrice," asked he, abruptly, "whence came this shrub?"

"My father created it," answered she, with simplicity.

"Created it! created it!" repeated Giovanni. "What mean you, Beatrice?"

"He is a man fearfully acquainted with the secrets of Nature," replied Beatrice; "and, at the hour when I first drew breath, this plant sprang from the soil, the offspring of his science, of his intellect, while I was but his earthly child. Approach it not!" continued she, observing with terror that Giovanni was drawing nearer to the shrub. "It has qualities that you little dream of. But I, dearest Giovanni,—I grew up and blossomed with the plant and was nourished with its breath. It was my sister, and I loved it with a human affection; for, alas!—hast thou not suspected it?—there was an awful doom."

Here Giovanni frowned so darkly upon her that Beatrice paused and trembled. But her faith in his tenderness reassured her, and made her blush that she had doubted for an instant.

"There was an awful doom," she continued, "the effect of my father's fatal love of science, which estranged me from all society of my kind. Until Heaven sent thee, dearest Giovanni, oh, how lonely was thy poor Beatrice!"

"Was it a hard doom?" asked Giovanni, fixing his eyes upon her.

"Only of late have I known how hard it was," answered she, tenderly. "Oh, yes; but my heart was torpid, and therefore quiet."

Giovanni's rage broke forth from his sullen gloom like a lightning flash out of a dark cloud.

"Accursed one!" cried he, with venomous scorn and anger. "And, finding thy solitude wearisome, thou hast severed me likewise from all the warmth of life and enticed me into thy region of unspeakable horror!"

"Giovanni!" exclaimed Beatrice, turning her large bright eyes upon his face. The force of his words had not found its way into her mind; she was merely thunderstruck.

"Yes, poisonous thing!" repeated Giovanni, beside himself with passion. "Thou hast done it! Thou hast blasted me! Thou hast filled my veins with poison! Thou hast made me as hateful, as ugly, as loathsome and deadly a creature as thyself—a world's wonder of hideous monstrosity! Now, if our breath be happily as fatal to ourselves as to all others, let us join our lips in one kiss of unutterable hatred, and so die!"

"What has befallen me?" murmured Beatrice, with a low moan out of her heart. "Holy Virgin, pity me, a poor heart-broken child!"

"Thou,—dost thou pray?" cried Giovanni, still with the same fiendish scorn. "Thy very prayers, as they come from thy lips, taint the atmosphere with death. Yes, yes; let us pray! Let us to church and dip our fingers in the holy water at the portal! They that come after us will perish as by a pestilence! Let us sign crosses in the air! It will be scattering curses abroad in the likeness of holy symbols!"

"Giovanni," said Beatrice, calmly, for her grief was beyond passion, "why dost thou join thyself with me thus in those terrible words? I, it is true, am the horrible thing thou namest me. But thou,—what hast thou to do, save with one other shudder at my hideous misery to go forth out of the garden and mingle with thy race, and forget that there ever crawled on earth such a monster as poor Beatrice?"

"Dost thou pretend ignorance?" asked Giovanni, scowling upon her. "Behold! this power have I gained from the pure daughter of Rappaccini."

There was a swarm of summer insects flitting through the air in search of the food promised by the flower odors of the fatal garden. They circled round Giovanni's head, and were evidently attracted towards him by the same influence which had drawn them for an instant within the sphere of several of the shrubs. He sent forth a breath among them, and smiled bitterly at Beatrice as at least a score of the insects fell dead upon the ground.

"I see it! I see it!" shrieked Beatrice. "It is my father's fatal science! No, no, Giovanni; it was not I! Never! never! I dreamed only to love thee and be with thee a little time, and so to let thee pass away, leaving but thine image in mine heart; for, Giovanni, believe it, though my body be nourished with poison, my spirit is God's creature, and craves love as its daily food. But my father,—he has united us in this fearful sympathy. Yes; spurn me, tread upon me, kill me! Oh, what is death after such words as thine? But it was not I. Not for a world of bliss would I have done it."

Giovanni's passion had exhausted itself in its outburst from his lips. There now came across him a sense, mournful, and not without tenderness, of the intimate and peculiar relationship between Beatrice and himself. They stood, as it were, in an utter solitude, which would be made none the less solitary by the densest throng of human life. Ought not, then, the desert of humanity around them to press this insulated pair closer together? If they should be cruel to one another, who was there to be kind to them? Besides, thought Giovanni, might there not still be a hope of his returning within the limits of ordinary nature, and leading Beatrice, the redeemed Beatrice, by the hand? O, weak, and selfish, and unworthy spirit, that could dream of an earthly union and earthly happiness as possible, after such deep love had been so bitterly wronged as was Beatrice's love by Giovanni's blighting words! No, no; there could be no such hope. She must pass heavily, with that broken heart, across the borders of Time—she must bathe her hurts in some fount of paradise, and forget her grief in the light of immortality, and *there* be well.

But Giovanni did not know it.

"Dear Beatrice," said he, approaching her, while she shrank away as always at his approach, but now with a different impulse, "dearest Beatrice, our fate is not yet so desperate. Behold! there is a medicine, potent, as a wise physician has assured me, and almost divine in its efficacy. It is composed of ingredients the most opposite to those by which thy awful father has brought this calamity upon thee and me. It is distilled of blessed herbs. Shall we not quaff it together, and thus be purified from evil?"

"Give it me!" said Beatrice, extending her hand to receive the little silver vial which Giovanni took from his bosom. She added, with a peculiar emphasis, "I will drink; but do thou await the result."

She put Baglioni's antidote to her lips; and, at the same moment, the figure of Rappaccini emerged from the portal and came slowly towards the marble fountain. As he drew near, the pale man of science seemed to gaze with a triumphant expression at the beautiful youth and maiden, as might an artist who should spend his life in achieving a picture or a group of statuary and finally be satisfied with his success. He paused; his bent form grew erect with conscious power; he spread out his hands over them in the attitude of a father imploring a blessing upon his children; but those were the same hands that had thrown poison into the stream of their lives. Giovanni trembled. Beatrice shuddered nervously, and pressed her hand upon her heart.

"My daughter," said Rappaccini, "thou art no longer lonely in the world. Pluck one of those precious gems from thy sister shrub and bid thy bridegroom wear it in his bosom. It will not harm him now. My science and the sympathy between thee and him have so wrought within his system, that he now stands apart from common men, as thou dost, daughter of my pride and triumph, from ordinary women. Pass on, then, through the world, most dear to one another and dreadful to all besides!"

"My father," said Beatrice, feebly,—and still as she spoke she kept her hand upon her heart,—"wherefore didst thou inflict this miserable doom upon thy child?"

"Miserable!" exclaimed Rappaccini. "What mean you, foolish girl? Dost thou deem it misery to be endowed with marvellous gifts against which no power nor strength could avail an enemy—misery, to be able to quell the mightiest with a breath—misery, to be as terrible as thou art beautiful? Wouldst thou, then, have preferred the condition of a weak woman, exposed to all evil and capable of none?"

"I would fain have been loved, not feared," murmured Beatrice, sinking down upon the ground. "But now it matters not. I am going, father, where the evil which thou hast striven to mingle with my being will pass away like a dream—like the fragrance of these poisonous flowers, which will no longer taint my breath among the flowers of Eden. Farewell, Giovanni! Thy words of hatred are like lead within my heart; but they, too, will fall away as I ascend. Oh, was there not, from the first, more poison in thy nature than in mine?"

To Beatrice,—so radically had her earthly part been wrought upon by Rappaccini's skill,—as poison had been life, so the powerful antidote was death; and thus the poor victim of man's ingenuity and of thwarted nature, and of the fatality that attends all such efforts of perverted wisdom, perished there, at the feet of her father and Giovanni. Just at that moment

Professor Pietro Baglioni looked forth from the window, and called loudly, in a tone of triumph mixed with horror, to the thunderstricken man of science,—

"Rappaccini! Rappaccini! and is *this* the upshot of your experiment!"

Alfred, Lord Tennyson
(1809–1892)

The long and prolific career of Alfred Tennyson (Lord Tennyson after 1883) marks the road from Romantic to modern poetry. It winds gently forth from Wordsworth, Byron, Shelley, and Keats at the earlier end but meets roadblocks and S-curves at the later one. In many ways, Tennyson represented—or at least seemed to—everything turn-of-the-century modernism wanted to free itself from: a high-ceremonial style at odds with the idiom of familiar life; a tendency to subordinate literary art to statement, and complacent statement at that; an ideal of beauty too nearly synonymous with exoticism and mere prettiness; the imposition of a false vision of order on a fragmented world; cozy domestic sentimentalism; an obsessive Victorian need to resolve the darkness of life into light. These identifications with Tennyson—some of them anticipated by his own younger contemporaries—range between quarter- and half-truths. No reader of In Memoriam *can deny that Tennyson gives darkness its due. The tension between the public and private roles of poetry was something he felt keenly, and he was as much a harsh critic of Victorian society as its spokesman. Indeed, much of the early twentieth-century reaction to him amounts to a tribute to his stature; rebels rebel against what is there, and what was there at the turn of the century was, to a great extent, Tennyson. Even they could not convincingly deny Tennyson's mastery of language and technique, in a broad range of styles and forms. It is true that he did not always find matter adequate to his gifts, but one can say the same thing of most other great artists who were unstintingly prolific, like Mozart or Bach. In his best work, though, of which there is a considerable quantity, Tennyson did find apt matter, and then the result was great poetry.*

Tennyson's life is mainly the story of his poetry; he never had another profession. He was born in 1809, the third of eleven children, in Lincolnshire, a county in east-central England where some of the early lyrics in In Memoriam *are set. His father, a clergyman, was a devoted parent in most ways but was subject to drunken outbursts that provoked severe melancholy in the young Tennyson, foreshadowing a note of poignant Virgilian sadness that would later mix with optimism in his work—not to mention mental health problems in his real life. Enormously precocious, he wrote poems from the time he was five and by his mid-teens was producing ambitious, skillfully crafted poems. In 1828, at Cambridge, he met Arthur Henry Hallam, the central figure in his life. The two were members of the "Apostles," a society at Cambridge that met regularly to discuss directions in various branches of thought as well as politics and literature. The keen-minded and personally appealing Hallam was at the center of this brilliant group of young men, and Tennyson came to depend on him not only as a friend (they traveled together to Spain and to the Rhine) but also as his inspiration and guide in poetry. Hallam and the Apostles had discovered Keats and Shelley, and when in 1831 Hallam reviewed Tennyson's* Poems, Chiefly Lyrical *(1830) he saw and encouraged the sensuousness that in much of Tennyson's work, as in Keats's, is posed against a sterner acceptance of duty, social responsibility, and pain. Hallam's review (a remarkable literary essay, incidentally, for a twenty-year-old) also asserted the sufficiency and integrity of the poetic calling, the need for the artist to fix his attention on his feelings and art rather than on what distracts from them, however lofty these distractions might be. In some of Tennyson's early work we find him exploring this question of the poet's role and balancing, like Keats, the imagery of static quietude ("The Lotos-Eaters," for example), escape, and death against the need to act, suffer, immerse oneself in the life of the world. Tennyson's delicately beautiful "The Lady of Shalott" is among the poems that explore this conflict.*

Reviews of Tennyson's next volume, the Poems *of 1832, were mixed, but they included a devastating one by John Wilson Croker—appropriately, since Croker is best known today for a similar savaging of Keats. Poetically speaking, the sensitive Tennyson withdrew into himself, writing and revising but publishing almost nothing for ten years. But the review was a trifling blow compared with another one, the crucial event in Tennyson's life: Hallam died suddenly in 1833 in Vienna, at the age of twenty-two. Tennyson's grief over his lost friend and counsellor was profound, his individual loss aggravated by a further personal bond in Hallam's engagement to Tennyson's sister Emily and the public loss of a man whom his friends had believed destined to become a national leader. The poem "Tithonus," with its death-wish theme and despair over irrecoverable youth, was one response to Hallam's death, as in a different way was "Ulysses," with its contrasting heroic resolve to act and endure even though youth is gone. (We note in passing that "Ulysses" is sometimes read very differently: as a condemnation of the protagonist's escapist irresponsibility.) But the main record of Tennyson's grief, and of the troubling ideas it gave rise to, was a series of tender, pensive, anguished, speculative brief lyrics ("short swallow-flights of song"—XLVIII.15) that, written randomly at first like a diary, were later gathered, ordered, and published (anonymously) in 1850 as* In Memoriam.

The compelling private and public themes of In Memoriam *challenged the highest reaches of Tennyson's imagination and artistry, and the result is one of the centerpieces of Victorian culture. Growing from an expression of personal bereavement, it becomes also a way of exploring religious, philosophical, and social issues including the compatibility of science with faith and of spiritual with intellectual progress. Considered in its broadest aspect, the poem is a wrestling with the problem of evil and suffering, in the line of the Book of Job. What distinguishes* In Memoriam *from many other treatments of this formidable question is its nakedness and personal immediacy; written originally without any large formal or public purpose in mind, each poem is free to record honestly a passing mood or address a concrete philosophical issue, in the context not of fiction but of real life, and without subordination to an artificial consistency of plan or attitude. The result, thematically, is a work both universal (as Tennyson put it, "the voice of the human race" speaking through the poet) and personal—personal not only from the poet's viewpoint but also from that of many modern readers for whom the problem of belief takes the same form, science versus religion, that it takes in* In Memoriam. *For such readers, therefore, the poem requires little or no conversion by analogy into their own dilemmas. As art, the result is a prime example of nineteenth-century organicism: a poem that, like Wordsworth's* Prelude, *has to evolve its own themes, purpose, and organization through the process of being written and records that artistic evolution in parallel with the evolution from chaotic grief to ordered affirmation. And, again like* The Prelude, In Memoriam *emerges as a work with its own unique kind of developmental unity organically inseparable from the experiences recorded. Both art and life, at first apparently random, ultimately have pattern.*

In the year when In Memoriam *was published, a long-lapsed engagement between Tennyson, now forty-one, and Emily Sellwood was revived, and the two were married. (The obstacles had included differences in religious belief and Tennyson's unsettled financial prospects; it has been suggested that Tennyson's hauntedness with Hallam also played a part.) Still another milestone in 1850 was the death of Wordsworth and the naming of Tennyson as the new poet laureate of England. The great success of* In Memoriam *had paved the way, following on the impressive 1842 volume of poems and* The Princess *(1847), a curiously ambivalent but lyrically glorious examination of the role and education of women. Thereafter Tennyson was an institution, like Dickens. His volumes were immensely popular best sellers. Some were comfortably sentimental, like* Enoch Arden *(1864), a work about the return of a supposedly dead spouse that is remembered today mainly because its title is used to describe laws governing the subject of presumed but unproved death. Tennyson did not, however, simply become the voice of complacency. In the Byronic "Locksley Hall" (1842) Tennyson's protagonist had greeted the new age in the bracing words "Forward, forward let us range, / Let the great world spin for ever down the ringing grooves of change," but the poem had also indicted the materialism of the age, and this critique was sustained in the experimental* Maud; A Monodrama *(1855) and in the series* Idylls of the King, *Tennyson's equivalent of epic. Published over three decades beginning in 1859, this retelling of the King Arthur story emerges as a societal* memento mori *reminding the reader of how a noble civilization can undergo moral decay. In the 1870s and 1880s Tennyson wrote several plays, most of which were staged. He was made a baron in 1883. In 1892 he died, aged eighty-three, and was buried with much ceremony in Westminster Abbey.*

Tennyson's recognized poetic craftsmanship has many sides. To begin with, he is a master of what in modern filmmaking are called "special effects," though in his best poems these cannot be isolated from creative imaginative vision. A good example is lines 34–39 of "Tithonus," which simultaneously describe the goddess's body and the coming of dawn on earth; this is certainly virtuoso work, but it is also authentic mythmaking. The sustaining of a single sentence through all sixteen lines of In Memoriam *LXXXVI is a technical feat, but the technique is functional, reinforcing the theme of wind and breath that runs through the whole. Tennyson's skill in using the distant mythical past to explore contemporary, immediately personal, or universal themes (as in "The Lotos-Eaters," "Ulysses," and "Tithonus") can rightly be praised as a technique, but it represents also a remarkable act of imaginative fusion. (Hallam's review recognized this power of Tennyson's, of "embodying himself in ideal characters, or rather moods of character, with such extreme accuracy of adjustment, that the circumstances of the narration seem to have a natural correspondence with the predominant feeling, and, as it were, to be evolved from it by assimilative force.") Tennyson excels in meticulous description, though this too is often much more than mannerism. The description of the high waterfall in lines 8–9 of "The Lotos-Eaters" that "like a downward smoke . . . Along the cliff to fall and pause and fall did seem" is not mere backdrop, nor is it simply acute sensory psychology, registering the common optical illusion that the water alternately falls and is arrested; the lines also evoke the poem's theme of rest versus action. Tennyson can also create mood* *masterfully through sound, meter, and imagery. Like Keats, he is a master of vowel and consonant interplay—a "miser of sound and syllable," to borrow a phrase from Keats himself. ("The shallop flitteth silken-sail'd / Skimming down to Camelot"—"The Lady of Shallot.") He prided himself on knowing the quantity—that is, the temporal duration of the syllables—of every English word except "scissors." The range of his voice is almost unparalleled; we remember best his high sonorities, but he can also achieve a studied plainness ("He is not here; but far away / The noise of life begins again"—*In Memoriam, *VII.9–10) and even write dialect. His public rhetorical voice can be exhilarating, as in the famous New-Year's poem (*In Memoriam, *CVI), but the voice of private intimacy is equally moving, as in the lyrics about Hallam's house (VII, CXIX). Perhaps the best way to summarize Tennyson's style is to draw a negative comparison. Someone once defined poetry whimsically as language that, when printed, leaves an uneven right margin, and there are indeed poems so unassumingly prosaic as to be unrecognizable as poems without this typographic help. Tennyson's poetry is the antithesis of that. He is sometimes criticized for overpoeticizing, as in the notorious example from the epilogue to *In Memoriam *where he calls champagne "the foaming grape of eastern France" (line 80). But such excesses, if they can be called that, are a small price to pay for the verbal magic of passages like this one:*

And suck'd from out the distant gloom
A breeze began to tremble o'er
The large leaves of the sycamore,
And fluctuate all the still perfume,

And gathering freshlier overhead
Rock'd the full-foliaged elms, and swung
The heavy-folded rose, and flung
The lilies to and fro, and said,

"The dawn, the dawn," and died away;
And East and West, without a breath,
Mixt their dim lights, like life and death,
To broaden into boundless day.

[In Memoriam, *XCV.53–64*]

FURTHER READING *(prepared by W. J. R.):* The most complete life is Sir Charles Tennyson's *Alfred Tennyson,* 1949, which provides a good deal of new information and draws heavily on the correspondence. James D. Kissane's *Alfred Tennyson,* 1970, is a particularly good survey of the poet's life, works, and modern reputation. Paul Turner's *Tennyson,* 1976, is another critical survey, especially good on *Idylls of the King* and *In Memoriam.* Andrew Cecil Bradley's *A Commentary on Tennyson's "In Memoriam,"* 1901, rev. 1910, is still a valuable work, with an interpretation of the poem which has become fairly standard. *Tennyson: A Collection of Critical Essays,* ed. Elizabeth A. Francis, 1980, contains twelve essays by T. S. Eliot, Douglas Bush, and others, and is intended for the general reader. More specialized essays appear in the stimulating *Critical Essays on the Poetry of Tennyson,* ed. John Kilham, 1960, divided into seven categories. *Studies in Tennyson,* ed. Hallam Tennyson, 1981, contains essays on Tennyson's present value, his relation to ancient classical literature, and other central topics. J. M. Gray's *Thro' the Vision of the Night,* 1980, is a sympathetic estimate of *Idylls of the King,* examining Tennyson's use of sources and the poetic processes by which narrative poems recast literary traditions. W. David Shaw's *Tennyson's Style,* 1976, analyzes carefully stylistic developments in Tennyson's artistry and discusses *In Memoriam, Maud,* and *Idylls* in detail.

THE LOTOS-EATERS[1]

"Courage!" he[2] said, and pointed toward the land,
"This mounting wave will roll us shoreward soon."
In the afternoon they came unto a land
In which it seemed always afternoon.
All round the coast the languid air did swoon,
Breathing like one that hath a weary dream.
Full-faced above the valley stood the moon;
And, like a downward smoke, the slender stream
Along the cliff to fall and pause and fall did seem.

A land of streams! some, like a downward smoke,
Slow-dropping veils of thinnest lawn,[3] did go;
And some thro' wavering lights and shadows broke,
Rolling a slumbrous sheet of foam below.
They saw the gleaming river seaward flow
From the inner land; far off, three mountain-tops,
Three silent pinnacles of aged snow,
Stood sunset-flush'd; and, dew'd with showery drops,
Up-clomb the shadowy pine above the woven copse.[4]

The charmed[5] sunset linger'd low adown
In the red West; thro' mountain clefts the dale
Was seen far inland, and the yellow down[6]
Border'd with palm, and many a winding vale
And meadow, set with slender galingale;[7]
A land where all things always seem'd the same!
And round about the keel[8] with faces pale,
Dark faces pale against that rosy flame,
The mild-eyed melancholy Lotos-eaters came.

Branches they bore of that enchanted stem,
Laden with flower and fruit, whereof they gave
To each, but whoso did receive of them
And taste, to him the gushing of the wave
Far far away did seem to mourn and rave
On alien shores; and if his fellow spake,

[1] This poem was suggested by an episode in Homer's *Odyssey,* Book IX. After the ten-years' war against Troy, Odysseus (in Latin, "Ulysses") and his men underwent many perils while trying to return to Ithaca, their island home. At one point they reached the island of the lotos. When tasted, the fruit of this plant sapped the crew's willpower to continue their journey.
[2] Odysseus. [3] A thin fabric. [4] Dense shrubbery. [5] Under a magic spell.
[6] Rolling upland. [7] An herb. [8] The center beam of the ship.

His voice was thin, as voices from the grave;
And deep-asleep he seem'd, yet all awake,
And music in his ears his beating heart did make.

They sat them down upon the yellow sand,
Between the sun and moon upon the shore;
And sweet it was to dream of Fatherland,
Of child, and wife, and slave; but evermore
Most weary seem'd the sea, weary the oar,
Weary the wandering fields of barren foam.
Then some one said, "We will return no more;"
And all at once they sang, "Our island home
Is far beyond the wave; we will no longer roam."

CHORIC SONG

I

There is sweet music here that softer falls
Than petals from blown[9] roses on the grass,
Or night-dews on still waters between walls
Of shadowy granite, in a gleaming pass;
Music that gentlier on the spirit lies,
Than tired eyelids upon tired eyes;
Music that brings sweet sleep down from the blissful skies.
Here are cool mosses deep,
And thro' the moss the ivies creep,
And in the stream the long-leaved flowers weep,
And from the craggy ledge the poppy hangs in sleep.

II

Why are we weigh'd upon with heaviness,
And utterly consumed with sharp distress,
While all things else have rest from weariness?
All things have rest: why should we toil alone,
We only toil, who are the first of things,
And make perpetual moan,
Still from one sorrow to another thrown;
Nor ever fold our wings,
And cease from wanderings,
Nor steep our brows in slumber's holy balm;
Nor harken what the inner spirit sings,
"There is no joy but calm!"—
Why should we only toil, the roof and crown of things?

III

Lo! in the middle of the wood,
The folded leaf is woo'd from out the bud

[9] Past their bloom.

With winds upon the branch, and there
Grows green and broad, and takes no care,
Sun-steep'd at noon, and in the moon
Nightly dew-fed; and turning yellow
Falls, and floats adown the air.
Lo! sweeten'd with the summer light,
The full-juiced apple, waxing over-mellow,
Drops in a silent autumn night.
All its allotted length of days
The flower ripens in its place,
Ripens and fades, and falls, and hath no toil,
Fast-rooted in the fruitful soil.

IV

Hateful is the dark-blue sky,
Vaulted o'er the dark-blue sea.
Death is the end of life; ah, why
Should life all labor be?
Let us alone. Time driveth onward fast,
And in a little while our lips are dumb.
Let us alone. What is it that will last?
All things are taken from us, and become
Portions and parcels of the dreadful past.
Let us alone. What pleasure can we have
To war with evil? Is there any peace
In ever climbing up the climbing wave?
All things have rest, and ripen toward the grave
In silence—ripen, fall, and cease:
Give us long rest or death, dark death, or dreamful ease.

V

How sweet it were, hearing the downward stream,
With half-shut eyes ever to seem
Falling asleep in a half-dream!
To dream and dream, like yonder amber light,
Which will not leave the myrrh-bush on the height;
To hear each other's whisper'd speech;
Eating the Lotos day by day,
To watch the crisping[10] ripples on the beach,
And tender curving lines of creamy spray;
To lend our hearts and spirits wholly
To the influence of mild-minded melancholy;
To muse and brood and live again in memory,
With those old faces of our infancy
Heap'd over with a mound of grass,
Two handfuls of white dust, shut in an urn of brass!

[10] Curling.

VI

Dear is the memory of our wedded lives,
And dear the last embraces of our wives
And their warm tears; but all hath suffer'd change;
For surely now our household hearths are cold,
Our sons inherit us, our looks are strange,
And we should come like ghosts to trouble joy.
Or else the island princes[11] over-bold
Have eat our substance, and the minstrel sings
Before them of the ten years' war in Troy,
And our great deeds, as half-forgotten things.
Is there confusion in the little isle?
Let what is broken so remain.
The Gods are hard to reconcile;
'T is hard to settle order once again.
There *is* confusion worse than death,
Trouble on trouble, pain on pain,
Long labor unto aged breath,
Sore task to hearts worn out by many wars
And eyes grown dim with gazing on the pilot-stars.[12]

VII

But, propt on beds of amaranth and moly,[13]
How sweet—while warm airs lull us, blowing lowly—
With half-dropt eyelid still,
Beneath a heaven dark and holy,
To watch the long bright river drawing slowly
His waters from the purple hill—
To hear the dewy echoes calling
From cave to cave thro' the thick-twined vine—
To watch the emerald-color'd water falling
Thro' many a woven acanthus-wreath[14] divine!
Only to hear and see the far-off sparkling brine,
Only to hear were sweet, stretch'd out beneath the pine.

VIII

The Lotos blooms below the barren peak,
The Lotos blows by every winding creek;
All day the wind breathes low with mellower tone;
Thro' every hollow cave and alley lone
Round and round the spicy downs the yellow Lotos-dust is blown.
We have had enough of action, and of motion we,

[11] In the *Odyssey,* men from neighboring islands woo Odysseus' wife, the presumed widow Penelope, while living off his land and goods.
[12] Stars that are used in navigation.
[13] Respectively, a flower that does not fade and a magical herb.
[14] A plant sacred to the ancient gods.

Roll'd to starboard, roll'd to larboard, when the surge was seething free,
Where the wallowing monster[15] spouted his foam-fountains in the sea.
Let us swear an oath, and keep it with an equal mind,
In the hollow Lotos-land to live and lie reclined
On the hills like Gods together, careless of mankind.
For they lie beside their nectar,[16] and the bolts are hurl'd
Far below them in the valleys, and the clouds are lightly curl'd
Round their golden houses, girdled with the gleaming world;
Where they smile in secret, looking over wasted[17] lands,
Blight and famine, plague and earthquake, roaring deeps and fiery sands,
Clanging fights, and flaming towns, and sinking ships, and praying hands.
But they smile, they find a music centred in a doleful song
Steaming up, a lamentation and an ancient tale of wrong,
Like a tale of little meaning tho' the words are strong;
Chanted from an ill-used race of men that cleave the soil,
Sow the seed, and reap the harvest with enduring toil,
Storing yearly little dues of wheat, and wine and oil;
Till they perish and they suffer—some, 't is whisper'd—down in hell
Suffer endless anguish, others in Elysian valleys dwell,
Resting weary limbs at last on beds of asphodel.[18]
Surely, surely, slumber is more sweet than toil, the shore
Than labor in the deep mid-ocean, wind and wave and oar;
O, rest ye, brother mariners, we will not wander more.

ULYSSES[1]

It little profits that an idle king,
By this still hearth, among these barren crags,
Match'd with an aged wife, I mete and dole[2]
Unequal laws unto a savage race,
That hoard, and sleep, and feed, and know not me.
I cannot rest from travel; I will drink
Life to the lees.[3] All times I have enjoy'd
Greatly, have suffer'd greatly, both with those
That loved me, and alone; on shore, and when

[15] Whale. [16] The drink of the gods. [17] Laid waste.

[18] A yellow flower supposed to grow in the Elysian Fields, the Greek equivalent of Paradise.

[1] See notes 1 and 11 to "The Lotos-Eaters." Ulysses-Odysseus has come home to Ithaca and defeated the suitors but is now restless with his life there. Developing a hint from Homer's *Odyssey,* Book XI, Tennyson in "Ulysses" builds mainly on Dante's account of the hero's last voyage (*Inferno,* XXVI.90–142), in which he sails boldly westward past Gibraltar to his death.

[2] Give out in small measured quantities. [3] Dregs.

Thro' scudding drifts the rainy Hyades[4]
Vext the dim sea. I am become a name;
For always roaming with a hungry heart
Much have I seen and known,—cities of men
And manners, climates, councils, governments,
Myself not least, but honor'd of them all,—
And drunk delight of battle with my peers,
Far on the ringing plains of windy Troy.
I am a part of all that I have met;
Yet all experience is an arch wherethro'
Gleams that untravell'd world whose margin fades
For ever and for ever when I move.
How dull it is to pause, to make an end,
To rust unburnish'd,[5] not to shine in use!
As tho' to breathe were life! Life piled on life
Were all too little, and of one to me
Little remains; but every hour is saved
From that eternal silence, something more,
A bringer of new things; and vile it were
For some three suns[6] to store and hoard myself,
And this gray spirit yearning in desire
To follow knowledge like a sinking star,
Beyond the utmost bound of human thought.
  This is my son, mine own Telemachus,
To whom I leave the sceptre and the isle,—
Well-loved of me, discerning to fulfil
This labor, by slow prudence to make mild
A rugged people, and thro' soft degrees[7]
Subdue them to the useful and the good.
Most blameless is he, centred in the sphere
Of common duties, decent not to fail
In offices of tenderness, and pay
Meet adoration to my household gods,
When I am gone. He works his work, I mine.
  There lies the port; the vessel puffs her sail;
There gloom the dark, broad seas. My mariners,
Souls that have toil'd, and wrought, and thought with me,—
That ever with a frolic welcome took
The thunder and the sunshine, and opposed
Free hearts, free foreheads,—you and I are old;
Old age hath yet his honor and his toil.
Death closes all; but something ere the end,
Some work of noble note, may yet be done,
Not unbecoming men that strove with Gods.[8]
The lights begin to twinkle from the rocks;

[4] Stars associated with rain and storm. [5] Unpolished. [6] Three years.
[7] Gradual steps.
[8] In Homer's *Iliad*, gods fight on both sides in the Trojan war.

The long day wanes; the slow moon climbs; the deep
Moans round with many voices. Come, my friends.
'T is not too late to seek a newer world.
Push off, and sitting well in order smite
The sounding furrows; for my purpose holds
To sail beyond the sunset, and the baths
Of all the western stars, until I die.
It may be that the gulfs will wash us down;
It may be we shall touch the Happy Isles,
And see the great Achilles,[9] whom we knew.
Tho' much is taken, much abides; and tho'
We are not now that strength which in old days
Moved earth and heaven, that which we are, we are,—
One equal temper[10] of heroic hearts,
Made weak by time and fate, but strong in will
To strive, to seek, to find, and not to yield.

TITHONUS[1]

The woods decay, the woods decay and fall,
The vapors weep their burthen[2] to the ground,
Man comes and tills the field and lies beneath,
And after many a summer dies the swan.
Me only cruel immortality
Consumes; I wither slowly in thine arms,
Here at the quiet limit[3] of the world,
A white-hair'd shadow roaming like a dream
The ever-silent spaces of the East,
Far-folded mists, and gleaming halls of morn.
  Alas! for this gray shadow, once a man—
So glorious in his beauty and thy choice,
Who madest him thy chosen, that he seem'd
To his great heart none other than a God!
I ask'd thee, "Give me immortality."
Then didst thou grant mine asking with a smile,
Like wealthy men who care not how they give.
But thy strong Hours indignant work'd their wills,
And beat me down and marr'd and wasted me,
And tho' they could not end me, left me maim'd
To dwell in presence of immortal youth,
Immortal age beside immortal youth,

[9] The hero of the *Iliad,* foremost of the Greek warriors against Troy. After their death, heroes dwelt in the Happy Isles, located in the Atlantic.

[10] Possibly "consistent strength" (like that of a well-tempered sword), possibly "well-matched personal characters."

[1] A Trojan prince; Eos, the goddess of the dawn, loved him and persuaded Zeus to grant him immortality. She forgot, however, to ask that he be given eternal youth.

[2] Burden. [3] Eastern edge.

And all I was in ashes. Can thy love,
Thy beauty, make amends, tho' even now,
Close over us, the silver star,[4] thy guide,
Shines in those tremulous eyes that fill with tears
To hear me? Let me go; take back thy gift.
Why should a man desire in any way
To vary from the kindly[5] race of men,
Or pass beyond the goal of ordinance[6]
Where all should pause, as is most meet[7] for all?
  A soft air fans the cloud apart; there comes
A glimpse of that dark world where I was born.
Once more the old mysterious glimmer steals
From thy pure brows, and from thy shoulders pure,
And bosom beating with a heart renew'd.
Thy cheek begins to redden thro' the gloom,
Thy sweet eyes brighten slowly close to mine,
Ere yet they blind the stars, and the wild team[8]
Which love thee, yearning for thy yoke, arise,
And shake the darkness from their loosen'd manes,
And beat the twilight into flakes of fire.
  Lo! ever thus thou growest beautiful
In silence, then before thine answer given
Departest, and thy tears are on my cheek.
  Why wilt thou ever scare me with thy tears,
And make me tremble lest a saying learnt,
In days far-off, on that dark earth, be true?
"The Gods themselves cannot recall their gifts."
  Ay me! ay me! with what another heart
In days far-off, and with what other eyes
I used to watch—if I be he that watch'd—
The lucid outline forming round thee; saw
The dim curls kindle into sunny rings;
Changed with thy mystic change, and felt my blood
Glow with the glow that slowly crimson'd all
Thy presence and thy portals, while I lay,
Mouth, forehead, eyelids, growing dewy-warm
With kisses balmier than half-opening buds
Of April, and could hear the lips that kiss'd
Whispering I knew not what of wild and sweet,
Like that strange song I heard Apollo sing,
While Ilion like a mist rose into towers.[9]
  Yet hold me not for ever in thine East;
How can my nature longer mix with thine?
Coldly thy rosy shadows bathe me, cold
Are all thy lights, and cold my wrinkled feet

[4] The morning star. [5] In accordance with one's kind (species).
[6] Limit set by established custom or law. [7] Fitting.
[8] Horses that draw the dawn's chariot.
[9] Troy (Ilion) was built by the song of Apollo, god of music, poetry, and the sun.

Upon thy glimmering thresholds, when the steam
Floats up from those dim fields about the homes
Of happy men that have the power to die,
And grassy barrows[10] of the happier dead.
Release me, and restore me to the ground.
Thou seest all things, thou wilt see my grave;
Thou wilt renew thy beauty morn by morn,
I earth in earth forget these empty courts,
And thee returning on thy silver wheels.

IN MEMORIAM A. H. H.

OBIIT[1] MDCCCXXXIII

Arthur Henry Hallam, Tennyson's best friend and his sister Emily's fiancé, died unexpectedly in Vienna in 1833 when he was twenty-two and Tennyson twenty-four years old. The two men had known each other well at Cambridge University, where Hallam had been highly regarded as a thinker and a potential public figure. Over the next sixteen years Tennyson expressed his grief, its phases, and related speculations in brief lyrics, not originally intended for publication or collection together. He gave them their present sequence in 1849, a year before they were published, anonymously, as *In Memoriam.* Tennyson remarked that he intended the work as "a kind of Divine Commedia" in which grief yields ultimately to joy. He also explained that the "I" in the poems is not always Tennyson personally but "the voice of the human race speaking through him."

Strong Son of God, immortal Love,
  Whom we, that have not seen thy face,
  By faith, and faith alone, embrace,
Believing where we cannot prove;

Thine are these orbs of light and shade;[2]
  Thou madest Life in man and brute;
  Thou madest Death; and lo, thy foot
Is on the skull which thou hast made.

Thou wilt not leave us in the dust:
  Thou madest man, he knows not why,
  He thinks he was not made to die;
And thou hast made him: thou art just.

Thou seemest human and divine,
  The highest, holiest manhood, thou.
  Our wills are ours, we know not how;
Our wills are ours, to make them thine.

[10] Grave mounds.
[1] Died (Latin). The prefatory poem, written shortly before the publication of *In Memoriam,* is a retrospect on the work as a whole.
[2] *orbs . . . shade.* The moon and planets.

Our little systems[3] have their day;
They have their day and cease to be;
They are but broken[4] lights of thee,
And thou, O Lord, art more than they.

We have but faith: we cannot know,
For knowledge is of things we see;
And yet we trust it comes from thee,
A beam in darkness: let it grow.

Let knowledge grow from more to more,
But more of reverence in us dwell;
That mind and soul, according well,
May make one music as before,[5]

But vaster. We are fools and slight;
We mock thee when we do not fear:
But help thy foolish ones to bear;
Help thy vain worlds to bear thy light.

Forgive what seem'd my sin in me,
What seem'd my worth since I began;
For merit lives from man to man,
And not from man, O Lord, to thee.

Forgive my grief for one removed,
Thy creature, whom I ſound so fair.
I trust he lives in thee, and there
I find him worthier to be loved.

Forgive these wild and wandering cries,
Confusions of a wasted[6] youth;
Forgive them where they fail in truth,
And in thy wisdom make me wise.
1849

I

I held it truth, with him[7] who sings
To one clear harp in divers tones,[8]
That men may rise on stepping-stones
Of their dead selves to higher things.

But who shall so forecast the years
And find in loss a gain to match?
Or reach a hand thro' time to catch
The far-off interest[9] of tears?

[3] Philosophical systems. [4] Refracted. [5] As in past ages of faith.
[6] Laid waste; desolated. [7] Goethe, according to Tennyson's explanation.
[8] Various literary styles. [9] A commercial metaphor: like profit on an investment.

Let Love clasp Grief[10] lest both be drown'd,
Let darkness keep her raven gloss.
Ah, sweeter to be drunk with loss,
To dance with Death, to beat the ground,

Than that the victor Hours should scorn
The long result of love, and boast,
"Behold the man that loved and lost,
But all he was is overworn."[11]

II

Old yew,[12] which graspest at the stones
That name the underlying dead,
Thy fibres net the dreamless head,
Thy roots are wrapt about the bones.

The seasons bring the flower again,
And bring the firstling[13] to the flock;
And in the dusk of thee the clock
Beats out the little lives of men.

O, not for thee the glow, the bloom,
Who changest not in any gale,
Nor branding[14] summer suns avail
To touch thy thousand years of gloom;

And gazing on thee, sullen tree,
Sick for thy stubborn hardihood,
I seem to fail from out my blood
And grow incorporate into thee.

III

O Sorrow, cruel fellowship,
O Priestess in the vaults of Death,
O sweet and bitter in a breath,
What whispers from thy lying lip?

"The stars," she whispers, "blindly run;
A web is woven across the sky;
From out waste places comes a cry,
And murmurs from the dying sun;[15]

[10] Let love cling to grief so that recovery from grief will not show that the love was weak.
[11] Worn away.
[12] A yew tree in a church graveyard. The yew's leaves are less sensitive to seasonal changes than those of other trees, and it can reach a very old age.
[13] First-born. [14] "Burning," probably.
[15] *Lines 5–8.* Sorrow, personified, says that nature is blind, mechanical, and dying. The implication is that in such a world man has no special importance.

"And all the phantom, Nature, stands—
With all the music in her tone,
A hollow echo[16] of my own,—
A hollow form with empty hands."

And shall I take a thing[17] so blind,
Embrace her as my natural good;
Or crush her, like a vice of blood,
Upon the threshold of the mind?

V

I sometimes hold it half a sin
To put in words the grief I feel:
For words, like Nature, half reveal
And half conceal the Soul within.

But, for the unquiet heart and brain,
A use in measured language[18] lies;
The sad mechanic exercise,
Like dull narcotics, numbing pain.

In words, like weeds,[19] I'll wrap me o'er,
Like coarsest clothes against the cold;
But that large grief which these enfold
Is given in outline and no more.

VII

Dark house,[20] by which once more I stand
Here in the long unlovely street,
Doors, where my heart was used to beat
So quickly, waiting for a hand,

A hand that can be clasp'd no more—
Behold me, for I cannot sleep,
And like a guilty thing[21] I creep
At earliest morning to the door.

He is not here; but far away
The noise of life begins again,
And ghastly thro' the drizzling rain
On the bald street breaks the blank day.

IX

Fair ship, that from the Italian shore[22]
Sailest the placid ocean-plains

[16] Nature's voice echoes the mournful tone of Sorrow. [17] Sorrow.
[18] Language in poetic meter. [19] Garments.
[20] Hallam's house in London. With this poem compare CXIX.
[21] "Guilty thing" is quoted from Shakespeare's *Hamlet,* where the phrase refers to the ghost of Hamlet's father.
[22] The ship bearing Hallam's body home sailed from Trieste.

With my lost Arthur's loved remains,
Spread thy full wings, and waft[23] him o'er.

So draw him home to those that mourn
In vain; a favorable speed
Ruffle thy mirror'd mast, and lead
Thro' prosperous floods[24] his holy urn.

All night no ruder air perplex
Thy sliding keel, till Phosphor,[25] bright
As our pure love, thro' early light
Shall glimmer on the dewy decks.

Sphere all your lights around, above;[26]
Sleep, gentle heavens, before the prow;
Sleep, gentle winds, as he sleeps now,
My friend, the brother of my love;

My Arthur, whom I shall not see
Till all my widow'd race be run;
Dear as the mother to the son,
More than my brothers are to me.

X

I hear the noise about thy keel;
I hear the bell struck in the night;
I see the cabin-window bright;
I see the sailor at the wheel.

Thou bring'st the sailor to his wife,
And travell'd men from foreign lands;
And letters unto trembling hands;
And, thy dark freight, a vanish'd life.

So bring him; we have idle dreams;
This look of quiet flatters thus
Our home-bred fancies.[27] O, to us,
The fools of habit, sweeter seems

To rest beneath the clover sod,
That takes the sunshine and the rains,
Or where the kneeling hamlet drains
The chalice of the grapes of God;[28]

Than if with thee the roaring wells
Should gulf him fathom-deep in brine,

[23] Carry gently. [24] Favorable seas. [25] The morning star.
[26] This is addressed to the heavens.
[27] Our simple tastes (which prefer that loved ones be buried on land rather than at sea).
[28] *chalice . . . God.* The Communion chalice.

And hands so often clasp'd in mine,
Should toss with tangle[29] and with shells.

XI

Calm is the morn without a sound,
Calm as to suit a calmer grief,
And only thro' the faded leaf
The chestnut pattering to the ground;

Calm and deep peace on this high wold,[30]
And on these dews that drench the furze,[31]
And all the silvery gossamers[32]
That twinkle into green and gold;

Calm and still light on yon great plain
That sweeps with all its autumn bowers,
And crowded farms and lessening[33] towers,
To mingle with the bounding main;[34]

Calm and deep peace in this wide air,
These leaves that redden to the fall,
And in my heart, if calm at all,
If any calm, a calm despair;

Calm on the seas, and silver sleep,
And waves that sway themselves in rest,
And dead calm in that noble breast
Which heaves but with the heaving deep.

XV

To-night the winds begin to rise
And roar from yonder dropping day;
The last red leaf is whirl'd away,
The rooks[35] are blown about the skies;

The forest crack'd, the waters curl'd,
The cattle huddled on the lea;
And wildly dash'd on tower and tree
The sunbeam strikes along the world:

And but for fancies, which aver
That all thy motions[36] gently pass
Athwart a plane of molten glass,
I scarce could brook the strain and stir

[29] Seaweed. [30] Undulating plain. [31] Shrubs.
[32] Cobwebs with in the distance.dew reflecting the sunlight.
[33] Seeming to diminish in the distance. [34] Bordering ocean.
[35] Crowlike birds. [36] The motions of the ship carrying Hallam's body.

That makes the barren branches loud;
And but for fear it is not so,[37]
The wild unrest that lives in woe
Would dote and pore on yonder cloud

That rises upward always higher,
And onward drags a laboring breast,
And topples round the dreary west,
A looming bastion fringed with fire.

XVI

What words are these have fallen from me?
Can calm despair and wild unrest
Be tenants of a single breast,
Or Sorrow such a changeling[38] be?

Or doth she only seem to take
The touch of change in calm or storm,
But knows no more of transient form
In her deep self, than some dead lake

That holds the shadow of a lark
Hung in the shadow of a heaven?
Or has the shock, so harshly given,
Confused me like the unhappy bark[39]

That strikes by night a craggy shelf,
And staggers blindly ere she sink?
And stunn'd me from my power to think
And all my knowledge of myself;

And made me that delirious man
Whose fancy fuses old and new,
And flashes into false and true,
And mingles all without a plan?

XVIII

'T is well; 't is something; we may stand
Where he in English earth[40] is laid,
And from his ashes may be made
The violet of his native land.

'T is little; but it looks in truth
As if the quiet bones were blest

[37] *fear it is not so.* Fear that in fact the ship is storm-tossed. If it were not for this fear, the speaker could identify sympathetically with the storm cloud he is looking at.

[38] Fickle person. [39] Ship.

[40] Tennyson was not actually present at Hallam's funeral, nor did he visit the burial place until many years later.

Among familiar names to rest
And in the places of his youth.

Come then, pure hands, and bear the head
That sleeps or wears the mask of sleep,
And come, whatever loves to weep,
And hear the ritual of the dead.

Ah yet, even yet, if this might be,
I, falling on his faithful heart,
Would breathing thro' his lips impart
The life that almost dies in me;[41]

That dies not, but endures with pain,
And slowly forms the firmer mind,
Treasuring the look it cannot find,
The words that are not heard again.

XIX

The Danube to the Severn[42] gave
The darken'd heart that beat no more;
They laid him by the pleasant shore,
And in the hearing of the wave.

There twice a day the Severn fills;
The salt sea-water passes by,
And hushes half the babbling Wye,[43]
And makes a silence in the hills.

The Wye is hush'd nor moved along,
And hush'd my deepest grief of all,
When fill'd with tears that cannot fall,
I brim with sorrow drowning song.

The tide flows down, the wave again
Is vocal in its wooded walls;
My deeper anguish also falls,
And I can speak a little then.

XXI

I sing to him that rests below,
And, since the grasses round me wave,

[41] *breathing . . . me.* The identification of life and spirit with the physical breath is an ancient and widespread metaphor. Compare LVI.7.

[42] *Danube, Severn.* Vienna, where Hallam died, is on the Danube River; he was buried near the Severn, a river in western England that, like the Thames in the east, widens into a very broad tidal estuary.

[43] The Wye river flows into the Severn; when the tide backs it up, the sound of its flow ceases.

I take the grasses of the grave,
And make them pipes whereon to blow.[44]

The traveller hears me now and then,
And sometimes harshly will he speak:
"This fellow would make weakness weak,
And melt the waxen hearts of men."

Another answers: "Let him be,
He loves to make parade of pain,
That with his piping he may gain
The praise that comes to constancy."

A third is wroth:[45] "Is this an hour
For private sorrow's barren song,
When more and more the people throng
The chairs and thrones of civil power?[46]

"A time to sicken and to swoon,
When Science reaches forth her arms
To feel from world to world, and charms
Her secret from the latest moon?"[47]

Behold, ye speak an idle thing;
Ye never knew the sacred dust.
I do but sing because I must,
And pipe but as the linnets[48] sing;

And one is glad; her note is gay,
For now her little ones have ranged;
And one is sad; her note is changed,
Because her brood is stolen away.

XXII

The path by which we twain did go,
Which led by tracts that pleased us well,
Thro' four sweet years[49] arose and fell,
From flower to flower, from snow to snow;

And we with singing cheer'd the way,
And, crown'd with all the season lent,
From April on to April went,
And glad at heart from May to May.

[44] *pipes . . . blow.* The poet compares his verses to the pipings of the conventional shepherd of ancient pastoral poetry.
[45] Angry.
[46] *people . . . power.* A reference to social unrest in England and perhaps the revolutions in France since 1789.
[47] The planet Neptune and its satellite were discovered in 1846. [48] Songbirds.
[49] Tennyson met Hallam in 1828.

But where the path we walk'd began
To slant the fifth autumnal slope,
As we descended following Hope,
There sat the Shadow fear'd of man;

Who broke our fair companionship,
And spread his mantle dark and cold,
And wrapt thee formless in the fold,
And dull'd the murmur on thy lip,

And bore thee where I could not see
Nor follow, tho' I walk in haste,
And think that somewhere in the waste[50]
The Shadow sits and waits for me.

XXIII

Now, sometimes in my sorrow shut,
Or breaking into song by fits,
Alone, alone, to where he sits,[51]
The Shadow cloak'd from head to foot,

Who keeps the keys of all the creeds,[52]
I wander, often falling lame,
And looking back to whence I came,
Or on to where the pathway leads;

And crying, How changed from where it ran
Thro' lands where not a leaf was dumb,
But all the lavish hills would hum
The murmur of a happy Pan;[53]

When each by turns was guide to each,
And Fancy light from Fancy caught,
And Thought leapt out to wed with Thought
Ere Thought could wed itself with Speech;[54]

And all we met was fair and good,
And all was good that Time could bring,
And all the secret of the Spring
Moved in the chambers of the blood;

And many an old philosophy
On Argive[55] heights divinely sang,
And round us all the thicket rang
To many a flute of Arcady.[56]

[50] Wasteland.
[51] The main verb is "wander" in line 6: "I wander . . . to where he (the Shadow, death) sits."
[52] *keeps . . . creeds.* Reveals what is true about religious beliefs. [53] God of nature.
[54] *Lines 15–16.* Where communication preceded words. [55] Ancient Greek.
[56] In Greece, the setting for pastoral poetry.

XXIV

And was the day of my delight
As pure and perfect as I say?
The very source and fount of day
Is dash'd with wandering isles of night.[57]

If all was good and fair we met,
This earth had been[58] the Paradise
It never look'd to human eyes
Since our first sun arose and set.

And is it that the haze of grief
Makes former gladness loom so great?
The lowness of the present state,
That sets the past in this relief?

Or that the past will always win
A glory from its being far,
And orb into the perfect star
We saw not when we moved therein?[59]

XXVI

Still onward winds the dreary way;
I with it, for I long to prove
No lapse of moons[60] can canker Love,
Whatever fickle tongues may say.

And if that eye which watches guilt
And goodness, and hath power[61] to see
Within the green the moulder'd tree,
And towers fallen as soon as built—

O, if indeed that eye foresee
Or see—in Him is no before—
In more of life true life no more
And Love the indifference to be,[62]

Then might I find, ere yet the morn
Breaks hither over Indian seas,
That Shadow waiting with the keys,
To shroud me from my proper scorn.[63]

[57] *Lines 3–4.* There are spots even in the sun. [58] Would have been.
[59] *Lines 15–16.* Become a perfect circle only when seen from a distance (like the earth to an outbound astronaut). "Orb" is a verb.
[60] Passage of months, that is, of time.
[61] The power of the deity to see the future hidden within the present.
[62] *And Love . . . be.* And can see love turning to indifference in the future.
[63] My scorn of myself.

XXVII

I envy not in any moods
The captive void of noble rage,
The linnet born within the cage,
That never knew the summer woods;

I envy not the beast that takes
His license in the field of time,[64]
Unfetter'd by the sense of crime,
To whom a conscience never wakes;

Nor, what may count itself as blest,
The heart that never plighted troth[65]
But stagnates in the weeds of sloth:
Nor any want-begotten rest.[66]

I hold it true, whate'er befall;
I feel it, when I sorrow most;
'T is better to have loved and lost
Than never to have loved at all.

XXVIII

The time draws near the birth of Christ.
The moon is hid, the night is still;
The Christmas bells from hill to hill
Answer each other in the mist.

Four voices of four hamlets round,
From far and near, on mead[67] and moor,
Swell out and fail, as if a door
Were shut between me and the sound;

Each voice four changes[68] on the wind,
That now dilate, and now decrease,
Peace and goodwill, goodwill and peace,
Peace and goodwill, to all mankind.

This year[69] I slept and woke with pain,
I almost wish'd no more to wake,
And that my hold on life would break
Before I heard those bells again;

[64] *takes . . . time.* Follows its amoral natural impulses in life.
[65] Never became engaged, that is, never made an emotional commitment to someone or something.
[66] Quiet life resulting from the lack of qualities like imagination or initiative.
[67] Meadow.
[68] Combinations of tones in different orders, as in the familiar "Westminster chime." The sound is imitated in lines 11–12.
[69] 1833, the year of Hallam's death.

But they my troubled spirit rule,
For they controll'd me when a boy;
They bring me sorrow touch'd with joy,
The merry, merry bells of Yule.

XXIX

With such compelling cause to grieve
As daily vexes household peace,
And chains regret to his decease,
How dare we keep our Christmas-eve,

Which brings no more a welcome guest
To enrich the threshold of the night
With shower'd largess[70] of delight
In dance and song and game and jest?

Yet go, and while the holly boughs
Entwine the cold baptismal font,[71]
Make one wreath more for Use and Wont,[72]
That guard the portals of the house;

Old sisters of a day gone by,
Gray nurses, loving nothing new—
Why should they miss their yearly due
Before their time? They too will die.

XXX

With trembling fingers[73] did we weave
The holly round the Christmas hearth;
A rainy cloud possess'd the earth,
And sadly fell our Christmas-eve.

At our old pastimes in the hall
We gamboll'd,[74] making vain pretence
Of gladness, with an awful sense
Of one mute Shadow watching all.

We paused: the winds were in the beech;
We heard them sweep the winter land;
And in a circle hand-in-hand
Sat silent, looking each at each.

Then echo-like our voices rang;
We sung, tho' every eye was dim,

[70] Generosity in giving. [71] Sculptured basin (in the church).
[72] *Use and Wont.* Traditional custom.
[73] *With trembling fingers, etc.* This is the first of three Christmas poems that, according to many interpreters, divide *In Memoriam* into four parts. Compare the ideas and tones in LXXVIII and CV.
[74] Behaved merrily.

A merry song we sang with him
Last year; impetuously we sang.

We ceased; a gentler feeling crept
Upon us: surely rest is meet.[75]
"They rest," we said, "their sleep is sweet,"
And silence follow'd, and we wept.

Our voices took a higher range;
Once more we sang: "They do not die
Nor lose their mortal sympathy,
Nor change to us, although they change;

"Rapt[76] from the fickle and the frail
With gather'd power, yet the same,
Pierces the keen seraphic flame[77]
From orb to orb, from veil to veil."[78]

Rise, happy morn, rise, holy morn,
Draw forth the cheerful day from night:
O Father, touch the east, and light
The light that shone when Hope was born.

XXXIV

My own dim life should teach me this,
That life shall live for evermore,
Else earth is darkness at the core,
And dust and ashes all that is;

This round of green, this orb of flame,[79]
Fantastic beauty; such as lurks
In some wild poet, when he works
Without a conscience or an aim.

What then were God to such as I?
'T were hardly worth my while to choose
Of things all mortal, or to use
A little patience ere I die;

'T were best at once to sink to peace,
Like birds the charming[80] serpent draws,
To drop head-foremost in the jaws
Of vacant darkness and to cease.

[75] Appropriate. [76] Carried away.
[77] "Seraphic flame"—i.e., the soul—is the subject of "pierces."
[78] *From . . . veil.* Through different states of existence.
[79] *round . . . flame.* The earth and sun. [80] Casting a hypnotizing spell.

XXXV

Yet if some voice that man could trust
Should murmur from the narrow house,[81]
"The cheeks drop in, the body bows;
Man dies, nor is there hope in dust;"

Might I not say? "Yet even here,
But for one hour, O Love, I strive
To keep so sweet a thing alive."
But I should turn mine ears and hear

The moanings of the homeless sea,
The sound of streams that swift or slow
Draw down Aeonian[82] hills, and sow
The dust of continents to be;

And Love would answer with a sigh,
"The sound of that forgetful shore[83]
Will change my sweetness more and more,
Half-dead to know that I shall die."

O me, what profits it to put
An idle case?[84] If Death were seen
At first as Death, Love had not been,
Or been in narrowest working shut,

Mere fellowship of sluggish moods,
Or in his coarsest Satyr-shape
Had bruised the herb and crush'd the grape,
And bask'd and batten'd[85] in the woods.[86]

XLVII

That each, who seems a separate whole,
Should move his rounds, and fusing all
The skirts of self again, should fall
Remerging in the general Soul,

Is faith as vague as all unsweet.[87]
Eternal form shall still divide

[81] The grave.

[82] Lasting through vast geological ages; Charles Lyell's geological theories, which Tennyson knew, held that the earth evolved gradually.

[83] *sound . . . shore.* The voice from the grave denying life after death; "forgetful shore" refers to Lethe, the river of forgetfulness in the land of the dead.

[84] *put . . . case.* Imagine a merely hypothetical case. [85] Gorged oneself like an animal.

[86] *Lines 18–24.* If we knew from the beginning that death would be final, we would never have loved or else love would have been merely sensual (like that of Satyrs, lecherous mythological creatures).

[87] *Lines 1–5.* It is comfortless to imagine human individuality lost by absorption into an impersonal cosmic soul.

The eternal soul from all beside;
And I shall know him when we meet;

And we shall sit at endless feast,
Enjoying each the other's good.
What vaster dream can hit the mood
Of Love on earth? He seeks at least

Upon the last and sharpest height,
Before the spirits fade away,
Some landing-place, to clasp and say,
"Farewell! We lose ourselves in light."[88]

XLVIII

If these brief lays,[89] of Sorrow born,
Were taken to be such as closed[90]
Grave doubts and answers here proposed,
Then these were such as men might scorn.

Her care is not to part[91] and prove;
She takes, when harsher moods remit,
What slender shade of doubt may flit,
And makes it vassal unto love;

And hence, indeed, she sports with words,
But better serves a wholesome law,
And holds it sin and shame to draw
The deepest measure from the chords;

Nor dare she trust a larger lay,
But rather loosens from the lip
Short swallow-flights of song, that dip
Their wings in tears, and skim away.

L

Be near me[92] when my light is low,
When the blood creeps, and the nerves prick
And tingle; and the heart is sick,
And all the wheels of being slow.

Be near me when the sensuous frame
Is rack'd with pangs that conquer trust;
And Time, a maniac scattering dust,
And Life, a Fury[93] slinging flame.

[88] *Lines 12–16.* "If we are to be finally merged into the Universal Soul, Love asks to have at least one more parting before we lose ourselves."—Tennyson's note.

[89] Poems. [90] Resolved finally. [91] Intellectually classify and analyze.

[92] The speaker addresses Hallam.

[93] The terrifying Furies of Greek mythology were sometimes imagined as carrying torches.

Be near me when my faith is dry,
And men[94] the flies of latter spring,
That lay their eggs, and sting and sing
And weave their petty cells and die.

Be near me when I fade away,
To point the term of human strife,[95]
And on the low dark verge of life
The twilight of eternal day.

LIV

O, yet we trust that somehow good
Will be the final goal of ill,
To pangs of nature, sins of will,
Defects of doubt, and taints of blood;

That nothing walks with aimless feet;
That not one life shall be destroy'd,
Or cast as rubbish to the void,
When God hath made the pile[96] complete;

That not a worm is cloven in vain;
That not a moth with vain desire
Is shrivell'd in a fruitless fire,
Or but subserves another's gain.[97]

Behold, we know not anything;
I can but trust that good shall fall
At last—far off—at last, to all,
And every winter change to spring.

So runs my dream; but what am I?
An infant crying in the night;
An infant crying for the light,
And with no language but a cry.

LV

The wish, that of the living whole
No life may fail beyond the grave,
Derives it not from what we have
The likest God within the soul?[98]

[94] Men seem.
[95] *point . . . strife.* Show the final goal of human life—that is, the "twilight of eternal day" mentioned two lines later.
[96] Building; edifice.
[97] *but . . . gain.* The speaker finds no comfort in the idea of ecological cycles in which some creatures exist to be the prey of others.
[98] *Lines 3–4.* Does it not spring from what is most Godlike in us? Tennyson defined this as the "inner consciousness."

Are God and Nature then at strife,
That Nature lends such evil dreams?
So careful of the type[99] she seems,
So careless of the single life,

That I, considering everywhere
Her secret meaning in her deeds,
And finding that of fifty seeds
She often brings but one to bear,

I falter where I firmly trod,
And falling with my weight of cares
Upon the great world's altar-stairs
That slope thro' darkness up to God,

I stretch lame hands of faith, and grope,
And gather dust and chaff, and call
To what I feel is Lord of all,
And faintly trust the larger hope.[1]

LVI

"So careful of the type?" but no.
From scarped cliff and quarried stone
She cries, "A thousand types are gone;
I care for nothing, all shall go.[2]

"Thou makest thine appeal to me;
I bring to life, I bring to death;
The spirit does but mean the breath:[3]
I know no more." And he, shall he,

Man, her last work, who seem'd so fair,
Such splendid purpose in his eyes,
Who roll'd the psalm to wintry skies,
Who built him fanes of fruitless prayer,[4]

Who trusted God was love indeed
And love Creation's final law—

[99] Species, as opposed to any individual member of the species.

[1] According to Tennyson's son, this hope was "that the whole human race would through, perhaps, ages of suffering, be at length purified and saved." Or perhaps the hope is the wish stated in lines 1–2.

[2] *Lines 1–4.* Nature (the "She" of line 3) is not concerned for species either, as shown by fossil evidence of extinct species found in quarries and the rock layers in vertically cut ("scarped") cliffs. Tennyson was influenced by Lyell's writings on geology; Darwin's account of evolution in *The Origin of Species* was not published until 1859, nine years after *In Memoriam* was completed.

[3] *spirit . . . breath.* See note on XVIII.15–16. Here Nature says that breath is not a metaphor for something higher that we call spirit (as in Latin, where *spiritus* means "breath"); rather, physical acts like breathing are all there is to life.

[4] *fanes . . . prayer.* Temples where deluded man prayed to the nonexistent God of a meaningless universe.

Tho' Nature, red in tooth and claw
With ravine,[5] shriek'd against his creed—

Who loved, who suffer'd countless ills,
Who battled for the True, the Just,
Be blown about the desert dust,
Or seal'd within the iron hills?[6]

No more? A monster then, a dream,
A discord. Dragons of the prime,
That tare each other[7] in their slime,
Were mellow music match'd with him.[8]

O life as futile, then, as frail!
O for thy[9] voice to soothe and bless!
What hope of answer, or redress?
Behind the veil, behind the veil.

LVII

Peace; come away: the song of woe
Is after all an earthly song.
Peace; come away: we do him wrong
To sing so wildly: let us go.

Come; let us go: your cheeks[10] are pale;
But half my life I leave behind.
Methinks my friend is richly shrined;[11]
But I shall pass, my work will fail.

Yet in these ears, till hearing dies,
One set slow bell will seem to toll
The passing of the sweetest soul
That ever look'd with human eyes.

I hear it now, and o'er and o'er,
Eternal greetings to the dead;
And "Ave, Ave, Ave," said,
"Adieu, adieu," for evermore.[12]

[5] Ravin; predatory fierceness.

[6] *seal'd . . . hills.* Become a buried fossil, like other species.

[7] *Dragons . . . other.* Primeval monsters that tore each other.

[8] *Lines 22–24.* Because at least the monsters did not suffer from a "discord" in their natures whereby, like man, they aspired to an illusory immortality.

[9] Hallam's.

[10] Perhaps the cheeks of Tennyson's sister Emily (Hallam's fiancée), perhaps those of all mourners for Hallam.

[11] That is, shrined in these poems.

[12] *Ave, Adieu.* Hail and farewell. Tennyson alludes to the last words of Catullus's poem 101, the elegy for his dead brother.

LXX

I cannot see the features right,
When on the gloom[13] I strive to paint
The face I know; the hues are faint
And mix with hollow masks of night;

Cloud-towers by ghostly masons wrought,
A gulf that ever shuts and gapes,
A hand that points, and palled shapes[14]
In shadowy thoroughfares of thought;

And crowds that stream from yawning doors,
And shoals of pucker'd faces drive;
Dark bulks that tumble half alive,
And lazy lengths on boundless shores;

Till all at once beyond the will[15]
I hear a wizard music roll,
And thro' a lattice on the soul
Looks thy fair face and makes it still.

LXXVIII

Again at Christmas[16] did we weave
The holly round the Christmas hearth;
The silent snow possess'd the earth,
And calmly fell our Christmas-eve.

The yule-clog[17] sparkled keen with frost,
No wing of wind the region swept,
But over all things brooding slept
The quiet sense of something lost.

As in the winters left behind,
Again our ancient games had place,
The mimic picture's[18] breathing grace,
And dance and song and hoodman-blind.[19]

Who show'd a token of distress?
No single tear, no mark of pain—
O sorrow, then can sorrow wane?
O grief, can grief be changed to less?

O last regret, regret can die!
No—mixt with all this mystic frame,

[13] The darkness, as he is falling asleep. [14] Veiled figures.
[15] As he falls asleep and the will becomes powerless.
[16] The second of the Christmas poems; compare XXX and CV. [17] Log.
[18] A game, resembling charades, in which famous paintings were acted out.
[19] Blind man's buff.

Her deep relations are the same,
But with long use her tears are dry.

LXXXVI

Sweet after showers, ambrosial[20] air,
That rollest from the gorgeous gloom
Of evening over brake[21] and bloom
And meadow, slowly breathing bare

The round of space, and rapt below
Thro' all the dewy tassell'd wood,
And shadowing down the horned flood[22]
In ripples, fan my brows and blow

The fever from my cheek, and sigh
The full new life that feeds thy breath
Throughout my frame, till Doubt and Death,
Ill brethren, let the fancy fly

From belt to belt of crimson seas[23]
On leagues of odor streaming far,
To where in yonder orient[24] star
A hundred spirits whisper "Peace."

LXXXVII

I past beside the reverend walls
In which of old I wore the gown;[25]
I roved at random thro' the town,
And saw the tumult of the halls;

And heard once more in college fanes[26]
The storm their high-built organs make,
And thunder-music, rolling, shake
The prophet blazon'd on the panes;

And caught once more the distant shout,
The measured pulse of racing oars
Among the willows; paced the shores
And many a bridge, and all about

The same gray flats again, and felt
The same, but not the same; and last
Up that long walk of limes I past
To see the rooms in which he dwelt.

[20] Like ambrosia, the food of the gods; fragrant. This poem, a single sentence, describes a west wind at sundown, according to Tennyson.
[21] Fern. [22] An inlet of the ocean winding between two promontories.
[23] *belt . . . seas.* The streaks of red in the sunset. [24] Rising.
[25] The gown of a student—at Trinity College, Cambridge. [26] Chapels.

Another name was on the door.
I linger'd; all within was noise
Of songs, and clapping hands, and boys
That crash'd the glass and beat the floor;

Where once we held debate, a band[27]
Of youthful friends, on mind and art,
And labor, and the changing mart,
And all the framework of the land;

When one would aim an arrow fair,
But send it slackly from the string;[28]
And one would pierce an outer ring,
And one an inner, here and there;

And last the master-bowman, he,[29]
Would cleave the mark. A willing ear
We lent him. Who but hung to hear
The rapt oration flowing free

From point to point, with power and grace
And music in the bounds of law,
To those conclusions when we saw
The God within him light his face,

And seem to lift the form, and glow
In azure orbits heavenly-wise;
And over those ethereal eyes
The bar of Michael Angelo?[30]

XCV

By night[31] we linger'd on the lawn,
For underfoot the herb was dry;
And genial warmth; and o'er the sky
The silvery haze of summer drawn;

And calm that let the tapers[32] burn
Unwavering: not a cricket chirr'd;
The brook alone far-off was heard,
And on the board the fluttering urn.[33]

And bats went round in fragrant skies,
And wheel'd or lit the filmy shapes[34]

[27] "The Apostles," a discussion group that Hallam and Tennyson belonged to.
[28] *aim . . . string.* Try to make a good point but express it poorly.
[29] Hallam.
[30] *bar . . . Angelo.* Hallam himself once remarked that both he and Michelangelo had a ridge over the eyebrows.
[31] *By night, etc.* This poem is often considered the heart of the whole work.
[32] Candles. [33] Tea-urn, over a flame. [34] Moths.

That haunt the dusk, with ermine capes
And woolly breasts and beaded eyes;

While now we sang old songs that peal'd
From knoll to knoll, where, couch'd at ease,
The white kine[35] glimmer'd, and the trees
Laid their dark arms about the field.

But when those others, one by one,
Withdrew themselves from me and night,
And in the house light after light
Went out, and I was all alone,

A hunger seized my heart; I read
Of that glad year which once had been,
In those fallen leaves which kept their green,
The noble letters of the dead.

And strangely on the silence broke
The silent-speaking words, and strange
Was love's dumb cry defying change
To test his worth; and strangely spoke

The faith, the vigor, bold to dwell
On doubts that drive the coward back,
And keen thro' wordy snares to track
Suggestion to her inmost cell.

So word by word, and line by line,
The dead man touch'd me from the past,
And all at once it seem'd at last
The living soul was flash'd on mine,

And mine in this was wound, and whirl'd[36]
About empyreal[37] heights of thought,
And came on that which is, and caught
The deep pulsations of the world,

Aeonian[38] music measuring out
The steps of Time—the shocks of Chance—
The blows of Death. At length my trance
Was cancell'd, stricken thro' with doubt.

Vague words! but ah, how hard to frame
In matter-moulded forms of speech,

[35] Cows.

[36] *Lines 36, 37.* Tennyson's original published text read "His living soul" and "mine in his." His intention in the revision was apparently to suggest the cosmic or divine soul as including Hallam's.

[37] Heavenly. [38] Enduring for ages.

Or even for intellect to reach
Thro' memory that which I became;[39]

Till now the doubtful dusk reveal'd
The knolls once more where, couch'd at ease,
The white kine glimmer'd, and the trees
Laid their dark arms about the field;

And suck'd from out the distant gloom
A breeze began to tremble o'er
The large leaves of the sycamore,
And fluctuate all the still perfume,

And gathering freshlier overhead,
Rock'd the full-foliaged elms, and swung
The heavy-folded rose, and flung
The lilies to and fro, and said,

"The dawn, the dawn," and died away;
And East and West, without a breath,
Mixt their dim lights, like life and death,
To broaden into boundless day.

XCVI

You say, but with no touch of scorn,
Sweet-hearted, you,[40] whose light-blue eyes
Are tender over drowning flies,
You tell me, doubt is Devil-born.

I know not: one indeed I knew
In many a subtle question versed,
Who touch'd a jarring lyre at first,
But ever strove to make it true;

Perplext in faith, but pure in deeds,
At last he beat his music out.
There lives more faith in honest doubt,
Believe me, than in half the creeds.

He fought his doubts and gather'd strength,
He would not make his judgment blind,
He faced the spectres of the mind
And laid[41] them; thus he came at length

To find a stronger faith his own,
And Power was with him in the night,

[39]*Lines 45–48.* Probably an echo of the end of Dante's *Paradise,* especially XXXIII. 121–123.

[40]A woman of simple piety. [41]To lay a ghost is to exorcise or overcome it.

Which makes the darkness and the light,
And dwells not in the light alone,

But in the darkness and the cloud,
As over Sinaï's peaks of old,
While Israel made their gods of gold,
Altho' the trumpet blew so loud.[42]

CIV

The time draws near the birth of Christ;
The moon is hid, the night is still;
A single church below the hill
Is pealing, folded in the mist.

A single peal of bells below,
That wakens at this hour of rest
A single murmur in the breast,
That these are not the bells I know.[43]

Like strangers' voices here they sound,
In lands where not a memory strays,
Nor landmark breathes of other days,
But all is new unhallow'd ground.

CV

To-night[44] ungather'd let us leave
This laurel, let this holly stand:
We live within the stranger's land,
And strangely falls our Christmas-eve.

Our father's dust[45] is left alone
And silent under other snows:
There in due time the woodbine blows,[46]
The violet comes, but we are gone.

No more shall wayward grief abuse[47]
The genial hour with mask and mime;
For change of place, like growth of time,
Has broke the bond of dying use.[48]

Let cares that petty shadows cast,
By which our lives are chiefly proved,[49]

[42] *Lines 21–24.* God appeared to Moses on Mount Sinai in a dark cloud while the Israelites below were worshiping their golden calf; Exodus, chapters 19, 32. Hallam, like Moses, found truth by exploring the darkness, unlike facile but materialistic "believers."
[43] *not . . . know.* The Tennyson family had moved from their old home at Somersby in east central England to a new one in Epping Forest, north of London.
[44] *Tonight, etc.* The third of the Christmas poems; compare XXX and LXXVIII.
[45] Body in his grave. [46] Blossoms. [47] Do wrong to. [48] Custom; tradition.
[49] Tested.

A little spare the night I loved,
And hold it solemn to the past.

But let no footstep beat the floor,
Nor bowl of wassail mantle[50] warm;
For who would keep an ancient form
Thro' which the spirit breathes no more?

Be neither song, nor game, nor feast;
Nor harp be touch'd, nor flute be blown;
No dance, no motion, save alone
What lightens in the lucid East

Of rising worlds by yonder wood.
Long sleeps the summer in the seed;
Run out your measured arcs, and lead
The closing cycle[51] rich in good.

CVI

Ring out, wild bells, to the wild sky,
The flying cloud, the frosty light:
The year is dying in the night;[52]
Ring out, wild bells, and let him die.

Ring out the old, ring in the new,
Ring, happy bells, across the snow:
The year is going, let him go;
Ring out the false, ring in the true.

Ring out the grief that saps the mind,
For those that here we see no more;
Ring out the feud of rich and poor,
Ring in redress[53] to all mankind.

Ring out a slowly dying cause,
And ancient forms of party strife;
Ring in the nobler modes of life,
With sweeter manners, purer laws.

Ring out the want, the care, the sin,
The faithless coldness of the times;
Ring out, ring out my mournful rhymes,
But ring the fuller minstrel[54] in.

Ring out false pride in place and blood,[55]
The civic slander and the spite;

[50] Become frothy. [51] Final era.
[52] *year . . . night.* A week has passed; it is New Year's Eve. [53] Remedy for wrongs.
[54] Singer; poet. [55] High office and aristocratic lineage.

Ring in the love of truth and right,
Ring in the common love of good.

Ring out old shapes of foul disease;
Ring out the narrowing lust of gold;
Ring out the thousand wars of old,
Ring in the thousand years of peace.

Ring in the valiant man and free,
The larger heart, the kindlier hand;
Ring out the darkness of the land,
Ring in the Christ that is to be.[56]

CXIV

Who loves not Knowledge? Who shall rail
Against her beauty? May she mix
With men and prosper! Who shall fix
Her pillars?[57] Let her work prevail.

But on her forehead sits a fire;
She sets her forward countenance
And leaps into the future chance,
Submitting all things to desire.

Half-grown as yet, a child, and vain—
She cannot fight the fear of death.
What is she, cut from love and faith,
But some wild Pallas[58] from the brain

Of demons? fiery-hot to burst
All barriers in her onward race
For power. Let her know her place;
She is the second, not the first.

A higher hand must make her mild,
If all be not in vain, and guide
Her footsteps, moving side by side
With Wisdom, like the younger child;

For she is earthly of the mind,
But Wisdom heavenly of the soul.
O friend, who camest to thy goal
So early, leaving me behind,

[56] *Christ . . . be.* According to Tennyson, a nobler Christianity of the future, free from bigotry and sectarian controversy.

[57] Possibly an analogy to the seven pillars of Wisdom's house (Proverbs 9:1); possibly limits (from the Pillars of Hercules, or strait of Gibraltar, considered by the ancients as the limit of the world).

[58] Athene, the Greek goddess of knowledge, wisdom, and manual crafts, born from the head of Zeus, the king of the gods.

I would the great world grew like thee,
Who grewest not alone in power
And knowledge, but by year and hour
In reverence and in charity.

CXV

Now fades the last long streak of snow,
Now burgeons every maze of quick[59]
About the flowering squares,[60] and thick
By ashen roots[61] the violets blow.

Now rings the woodland loud and long,
The distance takes a lovelier hue,
And drown'd in yonder living blue
The lark becomes a sightless[62] song.

Now dance the lights on lawn and lea,
The flocks are whiter down the vale,
And milkier every milky sail
On winding stream or distant sea;

Where now the seamew pipes, or dives
In yonder greening gleam,[63] and fly
The happy birds, that change their sky
To build and brood, that live their lives

From land to land; and in my breast
Spring wakens too, and my regret
Becomes an April violet,
And buds and blossoms like the rest.

CXVIII

Contemplate all this work of Time,
The giant laboring in his youth;
Nor dream of human love and truth,
As dying Nature's earth and lime;[64]

But trust that those we call the dead
Are breathers of an ampler day
For ever nobler ends. They say,
The solid earth whereon we tread

In tracts of fluent[65] heat began,
And grew to seeming-random forms,

[59] *burgeons . . . quick.* Every hedge brings forth buds. [60] Fields.
[61] Roots of ash trees. [62] Invisible. [63] The ocean.
[64] *Lines 3–4.* Do not imagine that love and truth disappear as rotted physical bodies do; the "lime" is the calcium compounds in decayed bones.
[65] Flowing; that is, gaseous.

The seeming prey of cyclic storms,
Till at the last arose the man;

Who throve and branch'd from clime to clime,
The herald of a higher race,
And of himself in higher place,[66]
If so he type this work of time

Within himself,[67] from more to more;
Or, crown'd with attributes of woe
Like glories,[68] move his course, and show
That life is not as idle ore,

But iron dug from central gloom,
And heated hot with burning fears,
And dipt in baths of hissing tears,
And batter'd[69] with the shocks of doom

To shape and use. Arise and fly
The reeling Faun,[70] the sensual feast;
Move upward, working out the beast,
And let the ape and tiger die.

CXIX

Doors,[71] where my heart was used to beat
So quickly, not as one that weeps
I come once more; the city sleeps;
I smell the meadow in the street;

I hear a chirp of birds; I see
Betwixt the black fronts long-withdrawn
A light-blue lane of early dawn,
And think of early days and thee,

And bless thee, for thy lips are bland,
And bright the friendship of thine eye;
And in my thoughts with scarce a sigh
I take the pressure of thine hand.

CXXI

Sad Hesper[72] o'er the buried sun
And ready, thou, to die with him,

[66] The afterlife, probably.
[67] *If . . . himself.* If he follows the pattern of development in his moral nature that time followed in physical evolution.
[68] Halos.
[69] Hammered; the whole figure of speech is from the shaping of metal by a blacksmith.
[70] In mythology, a creature half man and half goat.
[71] The doors of Hallam's house in London; compare poem VII.
[72] The evening star.

Thou watchest all things ever dim
And dimmer, and a glory done.

The team is loosen'd from the wain,[73]
The boat is drawn upon the shore;
Thou listenest to the closing door,
And life is darken'd in the brain.

Bright Phosphor,[74] fresher for the night,
By thee the world's great work is heard
Beginning, and the wakeful bird;
Behind thee comes the greater light.

The market boat is on the stream,
And voices hail it from the brink;
Thou hear'st the village hammer clink,
And see'st the moving of the team.

Sweet Hesper-Phosphor, double name
For what is one,[75] the first, the last,
Thou, like my present and my past,
Thy place is changed; thou art the same.

CXXIII

There rolls the deep where grew the tree.
O earth, what changes hast thou seen!
There where the long street roars hath been
The stillness of the central sea.

The hills are shadows, and they flow
From form to form, and nothing stands;
They melt like mist, the solid lands,
Like clouds they shape themselves and go.

But in my spirit will I dwell,
And dream my dream, and hold it true;
For tho' my lips may breathe adieu,
I cannot think the thing farewell.

CXXIV

That which we dare invoke to bless;
Our dearest faith; our ghastliest doubt;[76]
He, They, One, All; within, without;
The Power in darkness whom we guess,—

[73] Farm wagon. [74] The morning star.
[75] The same planet (usually Venus) serves at different times as either morning or evening star.
[76] *Our . . . doubt.* That is, our thoughts about God inspire extremes of both faith and doubt.

I found Him not in world or sun,
Or eagle's wing, or insect's eye,[77]
Nor thro' the questions men may try,
The petty cobwebs we have spun.

If e'er when faith had fallen asleep,
I heard a voice, "believe no more,"
And heard an ever-breaking shore
That tumbled in the Godless deep,

A warmth within the breast would melt
The freezing reason's colder part,
And like a man in wrath the heart
Stood up and answer'd, "I have felt."

No, like a child[78] in doubt and fear:
But that blind clamor made me wise;
Then was I as a child that cries,
But, crying, knows his father near;

And what I am beheld again
What is, and no man understands;[79]
And out of darkness came the hands
That reach thro' nature, moulding men.

CXXVI

Love is and was my lord and king,
And in his presence I attend
To hear the tidings of my friend,
Which every hour his couriers bring.

Love is and was my king and lord,
And will be, tho' as yet I keep
Within the court[80] on earth, and sleep
Encompass'd by his faithful guard,

And hear at times a sentinel
Who moves about from place to place,
And whispers to the worlds of space,
In the deep night, that all is well.

[77] *Lines 5–6.* I did not find faith through the argument from design, namely that intricately functioning creatures must have had a conscious designer.
[78] See poem LIV.17–20.
[79] *What is . . . understands.* God, whom no man can understand.
[80] The court of Love the king.

EPILOGUE

O true and tried, so well and long,
Demand not thou a marriage lay;[81]
In that it is thy marriage day
Is music more than any song.

Nor have I felt so much of bliss
Since first he told me that he loved
A daughter of our house,[82] nor proved
Since that dark day[83] a day like this;

Tho' I since then have number'd o'er
Some thrice three years; they went and came,
Remade the blood and changed the frame,
And yet is love not less, but more;

No longer caring to embalm
In dying songs a dead regret,
But like a statue solid-set,
And moulded in colossal calm.

Regret is dead, but love is more
Than in the summers that are flown,
For I myself with these have grown
To something greater than before;

Which makes appear the songs I made
As echoes out of weaker times,
As half but idle brawling rhymes,
The sport of random sun and shade.

But where is she, the bridal flower,
That must be made a wife ere noon?
She enters, glowing like the moon
Of Eden on its bridal bower.

On me she bends her blissful eyes
And then on thee; they meet thy look
And brighten like the star that shook
Betwixt the palms of Paradise.

O, when her life was yet in bud,
He too foretold the perfect rose.[84]

[81] *Demand . . . lay.* Do not ask for an epithalamium, or formal wedding poem. This epilogue describes the wedding of Tennyson's sister Cecilia with Edmund Lushington in 1842, nine years after Hallam's death.

[82] *he told . . . house.* The "he" is Hallam, the "daughter" is Emily, another of Tennyson's sisters, who had been engaged to Hallam.

[83] The day of Hallam's death.

[84] *Lines 33–34.* Hallam had predicted Cecilia's beauty when she was still a child.

For thee she grew, for thee she grows
For ever, and as fair as good.

And thou art worthy, full of power;
As gentle; liberal-minded, great,
Consistent; wearing all that weight
Of learning[85] lightly like a flower.

But now set out: the noon is near,
And I must give away the bride;
She fears not, or with thee beside
And me behind her, will not fear.

For I that danced her on my knee,[86]
That watch'd her on her nurse's arm,
That shielded all her life from harm,
At last must part with her to thee;

Now waiting to be made a wife,
Her feet, my darling, on the dead;
Their pensive tablets round her head,[87]
And the most living words of life

Breathed in her ear. The ring is on,
The "Wilt thou?" answer'd, and again
The "Wilt thou?" ask'd, till out of twain
Her sweet "I will" has made you one.

Now sign your names, which shall be read,
Mute symbols of a joyful morn,
By village eyes as yet unborn.
The names are sign'd, and overhead

Begins the clash and clang that tells
The joy to every wandering breeze;
The blind wall rocks, and on the trees
The dead leaf trembles to the bells.

O happy hour, and happier hours
Await them. Many a merry face
Salutes them—maidens of the place,
That pelt us in the porch with flowers.

O happy hour, behold the bride
With him to whom her hand I gave.
They leave the porch, they pass the grave
That has to-day its sunny side.

[85] Lushington was a professor of Greek.
[86] Cecilia was eight years younger than Tennyson.
[87] *Lines 50–51.* There are graves under the church and commemorative tablets on the wall.

To-day the grave is bright for me,
For them the light of life increased,
Who stay to share the morning feast,
Who rest to-night beside the sea.

Let all my genial spirits advance
To meet and greet a whiter sun;
My drooping memory will not shun
The foaming grape of eastern France.[88]

It circles round, and fancy plays.
And hearts are warm'd and faces bloom,
As drinking health to bride and groom
We wish them store of happy days.

Nor count me all to blame if I
Conjecture of a stiller guest,[89]
Perchance, perchance, among the rest,
And, tho' in silence, wishing joy.

But they must go, the time draws on,
And those white-favor'd[90] horses wait:
They rise, but linger; it is late;
Farewell, we kiss, and they are gone.

A shade falls on us like the dark
From little cloudlets on the grass,
But sweeps away as out we pass
To range the woods, to roam the park,

Discussing how their courtship grew,
And talk of others that are wed,
And how she look'd, and what he said,
And back we come at fall of dew.

Again the feast, the speech, the glee,[91]
The shade of passing thought, the wealth
Of words and wit, the double health,
The crowning cup, the three-times-three,[92]

And last the dance;—till I retire.
Dumb is that tower which spake so loud,
And high in heaven the streaming cloud,
And on the downs[93] a rising fire:

And rise, O moon, from yonder down,
Till over down and over dale

[88]*foaming . . . France.* Champagne. [89]Hallam. [90]Decorated with white.
[91]Song sung in harmony (as in "glee club"). [92]Cheer. [93]Rolling pastures.

All night the shining vapor sail
And pass the silent-lighted town,

The white-faced halls, the glancing rills,
And catch at every mountain head.
And o'er the friths[94] that branch and spread
Their sleeping silver thro' the hills;

And touch with shade the bridal doors,
With tender gloom the roof, the wall;
And breaking let the splendor fall
To spangle all the happy shores

By which they rest, and ocean sounds,
And, star and system rolling past,
A soul shall draw from out the vast
And strike his being into bounds,

And, moved thro' life of lower phase,[95]
Result in man, be born and think,
And act and love, a closer link
Betwixt us and the crowning race

Of those that, eye to eye, shall look
On knowledge; under whose command
Is Earth and Earth's, and in their hand
Is Nature like an open book;

No longer half-akin to brute,
For all we thought and loved and did,
And hoped, and suffer'd, is but seed
Of what in them is flower and fruit;

Whereof the man that with me trod
This planet was a noble type[96]
Appearing ere the times were ripe,
That friend of mine who lives in God,

That God, which ever lives and loves,
One God, one law, one element,
And one far-off divine event,[97]
To which the whole creation moves.
1833–1849 (1850)

[94] Elongated bays at the mouths of rivers; fjords. (Variant of "firths.")
[95] *Lines 123–125.* The newlyweds will conceive a child that, in the womb, will pass through stages corresponding to lower animal forms.
[96] Symbolic model. [97] Final result.

Robert Browning

(1812 1889)

Robert Browning ranks with Tennyson as one of the two greatest English Victorian poets. Like Tennyson, he had an idealistic creed to express, and both his wife and his reading public encouraged him to express it. But there was also another side of Browning that made him struggle to detach himself from the men and women of his poems, presenting them as what they are in themselves, tantalizing quirky fragments of a total truth comprehensible only by God. This dialogue between the preacher and dramatic painter in Browning informs his work from beginning to end. Browning the sage did not outlast the Victorian period, but the verse dramatist in him had a strong influence on a number of modern poets.

Browning was born in 1812, near London, the son of a clerk who worked for the Bank of England. He got a spotty formal education, but he read exhaustively in the six thousand books his father had collected, and from them he derived much of the widely varied factual information he later drew on in his poems. Headstrong in his youth, he early discovered Shelley and decided to be a poet—against all financial practicalities but with the support of his family. Response to his anonymous, Shelleyan poem Pauline *(1833) brought home to him that, contrary to his intentions, he had revealed a good deal of himself in the poem, in a not very attractive light. Thereafter he made a stronger effort to efface his own personality in his work. One of the two options he explored was writing stage plays, but the convoluted self-examinations of his characters were not good theater, and those of his plays that were produced failed. The other, much more fruitful, option was the dramatic monologue; this was to be the vehicle of his most characteristic poems, long and short (though he wrote fine lyrics too).* Dramatic Lyrics *(1842) included his first triumph in the dramatic monologue, "My Last Duchess," along with other notable works like "Porphyria's Lover," "Soliloquy of the Spanish Cloister," and "The Pied Piper of Hamelin," a children's classic.* Dramatic Romances and Lyrics, *in which "The Bishop Orders His Tomb at St. Praxed's Church" appeared, was published in 1845. Neither volume sold well.*

Browning did not invent the dramatic monologue, but he perfected a distinctive form of it. The requirements of the genre (not all of them observed in every Browning monologue) call for a single speaker, addressing a silent listener or one whose words must be imagined, in a concrete situation that either represents a crisis in the speaker's life or brings out through the circumstantial setting his or her personality and values. The persons portrayed often reveal more about themselves than they are aware of doing, and they sometimes touch on ideas Browning himself felt strongly about. Much of the fascination of the dramatic monologues arises from our sense of tension between different sides of the protagonist, between his or her values and Browning's, and between the characters' limited visions and implicit fuller visions of reality. The monologues make stringent demands on the reader, who is expected to know a good deal about history and special subjects (about statuary stone, for example, in "The Bishop Orders His Tomb") and to have the mental acuity to piece out what is happening—not to mention sensing the psychological implications and appreciating the artistry. Browning developed in his own time, and has still not entirely shed, a reputation for composing difficult puzzles. But to many readers the experience of discovery in reading his poems and the need to complete the poems' meaning in their minds are part of the excitement.

In 1845 Browning met Elizabeth Barrett; the result was one of the famous love stories of the century. She was then (and remained throughout her life) much the more popular poet of the two, but she was an invalid recluse dominated by a possessive father. She and Browning, against the father's wishes, married secretly in 1846 and eloped to Italy, where they spent most of the next fifteen years, her health substantially restored. There Browning absorbed the Italian lore that he used in many of his best poems. In 1855 he published Men and Women, *one of the most marvelous poetic volumes of the century, including such masterpieces as "Andrea del Sarto," "Love Among the Ruins," "Fra Lippo Lippi," "A Toccata of Galuppi's," and the eerie "Childe Roland to the Dark Tower Came."*

After Elizabeth died in 1861, Browning, now near fifty, left Italy and returned with their son to England where Browning prepared an edition of his wife's poems. His own fame was now to arrive. In 1864 he published Dramatis Personae, *a less impressive volume than* Men and Women *but Browning's first popular success. This was crowned by* The Ring and the Book *(1868–1869), a 21,000-line poem in four volumes about a seventeenth-century murder trial in Rome. Divided into sections told from the particular, limited perspectives of the people involved, the poem uses the dramatic monologue on an epic scale. In its exploration of point-of-view storytelling it anticipates an important later novelistic technique. During the rest of his life, Browning continued to write prolifically, especially on modern themes. His public image as a genial dinner guest of his friends made a strange contrast to the imaginatively rich, often bizarre work that is typical of him. Much honored in his last years, he died in 1889, in Venice, and was buried in Westminster Abbey.*

Browning has perhaps a wider range of voices than even Tennyson; for example, the sinister haughtiness of the Duke of Ferrara, the fevered incoherencies of the dying Bishop, and the limp musings and entreaties of Andrea del Sarto could hardly be more dissimilar. The three monologues are typical of Browning in their creation of distinctive speakers in concrete situations, in their Italian settings, and in their concern with sensuousness, idealism, and other aspects of art. "My Last Duchess" and "The Bishop Orders His Tomb" are typical in their focus on climactic moments (a marriage negotiation, the approach of death), "Andrea del Sarto" in its focus on a characteristic scene and episode (Andrea's deference to but resentment of his wife, who has her own reasons for enduring his long speech). "Andrea" further explores a theme central in Browning: the relationship between a noble if impossible quest for achievement and an ignoble if understandable refusal of the challenge.

Some Victorians found in Browning's earthier form of idealism a bracing alternative to the magisterial Tennysonian manner. Early twentieth-century English and American poets, in the act of rejecting him along with the other Victorians, also found some of their paths cleared by Browning's use of "undignified" and racy language, his zest for gnarled cacaphonies ("Shrewd was that snatch from out the corner south / He graced his carrion with, God curse the same!"—"The Bishop Orders His Tomb," lines 18–19), his admiration of Donne, his concern with modern subjects, his tolerance of unedifying or grotesque characters, his interest in the vagaries of human psychology, and of course his development of the dramatic monologue, with its transitionless stream of consciousness. Poets like Ezra Pound and the T. S. Eliot who wrote "Prufrock" owe him a considerable debt.

FURTHER READING *(prepared by W. J. R.):* W. Hall Griffin's *The Life of Robert Browning,* completed and ed. by H. C. Minchin, 1938, is still the most valuable single biography; to this volume may be added John Maynard's *Browning's Youth,* 1977, an excellent study of the poet's education and the artistic climate of his day. Robert Brainard Pearsall's *Robert Browning,* 1976, surveys Browning's entire poetic career and contains extensive discussions of major themes and works. Twenty-three of the lyric poems are given individual attention in Norton B. Crowell's *A Reader's Guide to Robert Browning,* 1972, which also provides a biographical sketch. Leonard Burrows's *Browning the Poet: An Introductory Study,* 1969, contains analyses of some thirty poems. A detailed treatment of Browning's development as a poet is included in William Clyde DeVane's *A Browning Handbook,* 1935, 2nd ed. 1955, which combines factual information with excellent analyses of Browning's poetic methods and styles. A good discussion of the technique of Browning's dramatic monologues, including "Andrea del Sarto," "Fra Lippo Lippi," and "The Bishop Orders His Tomb," is Roma A. King, Jr.'s *The Bow and the Lyre,* 1957. E. Warwick Slinn's *Browning and the Fictions of Identity,* 1982, discusses Browning as a psychological dramatist in the monologues, emphasizing the tension between concerns with the self and with other people. William O. Raymond's *The Infinite Moment and Other Essays in Robert Browning,* 1950, explains the genesis and composition of *The Ring and the Book.* Eleven essays on Browning by prominent scholars are collected in *Browning's Mind and Art,* ed. by Clarence Tracy, 1968.

MY LAST DUCHESS

FERRARA[1]

That's my last Duchess painted on the wall,
Looking as if she were alive; I call
That piece a wonder, now: Frà Pandolf's[2] hands
Worked busily a day, and there she stands.
Will't please you sit and look at her? I said
'Frà Pandolf' by design, for never read
Strangers like you that pictured countenance,
The depth and passion of its earnest glance,
But to myself they turned (since none puts by
The curtain I have drawn for you, but I)
And seemed as they would ask me, if they durst,[3]
How such a glance came there; so, not the first
Are you to turn and ask thus. Sir, 'twas not
Her husband's presence only, called that spot
Of joy into the Duchess' cheek: perhaps
Frà Pandolf chanced to say 'Her mantle laps
Over my Lady's wrist too much,' or 'Paint
Must never hope to reproduce the faint
Half-flush that dies along her throat;' such stuff
Was courtesy, she thought, and cause enough
For calling up that spot of joy. She had
A heart . . . how shall I say? . . . too soon made glad,
Too easily impressed; she liked whate'er

[1] City in northern Italy. [2] Brother Pandolf, a fictitious monk and painter.
[3] Dared.

She looked on, and her looks went everywhere.
Sir, 'twas all one! My favour[4] at her breast,
The dropping of the daylight in the West,
The bough of cherries some officious fool
Broke in the orchard for her, the white mule
She rode with round the terrace—all and each
Would draw from her alike the approving speech,
Or blush, at least. She thanked men,—good; but thanked
Somehow . . . I know not how . . . as if she ranked
My gift of a nine-hundred-years-old name
With anybody's gift. Who'd stoop to blame
This sort of trifling? Even had you skill
In speech—(which I have not)—to make your will
Quite clear to such an one, and say 'Just this
Or that in you disgusts me; here you miss,
Or there exceed the mark'[5]—and if she let
Herself be lessoned so, nor plainly set
Her wits to yours, forsooth, and made excuse,
—E'en then would be some stooping, and I choose
Never to stoop. Oh, Sir, she smiled, no doubt,
Whene'er I passed her; but who passed without
Much the same smile? This grew; I gave commands;
Then all smiles stopped together. There she stands
As if alive. Will't please you rise? We'll meet
The company below, then. I repeat,
The Count your Master's known munificence
Is ample warrant that no just pretence
Of mine for dowry will be disallowed;
Though his fair daughter's self, as I avowed
At starting, is my object. Nay, we'll go
Together down, Sir! Notice Neptune, though,
Taming a sea-horse, thought a rarity,
Which Claus of Innsbruck[6] cast in bronze for me.

THE BISHOP ORDERS HIS TOMB AT SAINT PRAXED'S CHURCH[1]

ROME, 15—

Vanity, saith the preacher, vanity![2]
Draw round my bed: is Anselm keeping back?

[4] Gift. [5] Standard; criterion.
[6] Another fictitious artist. Neptune, god of the ocean, was a standard subject of Renaissance art.
[1] A church in Rome, named for a second-century Roman virgin-martyr converted to Christianity and noted for giving her goods to the poor. The characters in the poem are fictional.
[2] "Vanity of vanities, says the Preacher, . . . All is vanity." Ecclesiastes 1:2.

Nephews[3]—sons mine . . . ah God, I know not! Well—
She, men would have to be your mother once,
Old Gandolf[4] envied me, so fair she was!
What's done is done, and she is dead beside,
Dead long ago, and I am Bishop since,
And as she died so must we die ourselves,
And thence ye may perceive the world's a dream.
Life, how and what is it? As here I lie
In this state-chamber, dying by degrees,
Hours and long hours in the dead night, I ask
"Do I live, am I dead?" Peace, peace seems all.
Saint Praxed's ever was the church for peace;
And so, about this tomb of mine. I fought
With tooth and nail to save my niche, ye know:
—Old Gandolf cozened[5] me, despite my care;
Shrewd was that snatch from out the corner south
He graced his carrion[6] with, God curse the same!
Yet still my niche is not so cramped but thence
One sees the pulpit o' the epistle-side,[7]
And somewhat of the choir, those silent seats,
And up into the aëry dome where live
The angels, and a sunbeam's sure to lurk.
And I shall fill my slab of basalt[8] there,
And 'neath my tabernacle[9] take my rest,
With those nine columns round me, two and two,
The odd one at my feet where Anselm stands,
Peach-blossom marble all, the rare, the ripe,
As fresh-poured red wine of a mighty pulse.[10]
—Old Gandolf with his paltry onion-stone,[11]
Put me where I may look at him! True peach,
Rosy and flawless; how I earned the prize!
Draw close. That conflagration of my church
—What then? So much was saved if aught were missed!
My sons, ye would not be my death? Go dig
The white-grape vineyard where the oil-press stood,
Drop water gently till the surface sinks,
And if ye find . . . ah God, I know not, I! . . .
Bedded in store of rotten fig-leaves soft,
And corded up in a tight olive-frail,[12]
Some lump, ah God, of *lapis lazuli*,[13]
Big as a Jew's head cut off at the nape,
Blue as a vein o'er the Madonna's breast—
Sons, all have I bequeathed you, villas, all,

[3] In reality, illegitimate sons. He is now ready to call them that.
[4] His predecessor as bishop. [5] Cheated. [6] Rotten flesh.
[7] In the Mass, excerpts from the biblical Epistles were read at the right-hand side of the altar, from the Gospels at the left.
[8] Hard, dark-colored rock. [9] Canopy. [10] Strength.
[11] Cheap marble that peeled like an onion. [12] Basket.
[13] High-quality blue stone.

That brave Frascati[14] villa with its bath—
So, let the blue lump poise between my knees,
Like God the Father's globe on both his hands
Ye worship in the Jesu Church so gay,
For Gandolf shall not choose but see and burst!
Swift as a weaver's shuttle fleet our years;[15]
Man goeth to the grave, and where is he?
Did I say basalt for my slab, sons? Black—
'Twas ever antique-black[16] I meant! How else
Shall ye contrast my frieze[17] to come beneath?
The bas-relief in bronze ye promised me,
Those Pans and Nymphs ye wot of, and perchance
Some tripod, thyrsus,[18] with a vase or so,
The Saviour at his sermon on the mount,
St. Praxed in a glory,[19] and one Pan
Ready to twitch the Nymph's last garment off,
And Moses with the tables . . . but I know
Ye mark me not! What do they whisper thee,
Child of my bowels, Anselm? Ah, ye hope
To revel down my villas while I gasp
Bricked o'er with beggar's moldy travertine[20]
Which Gandolf from his tomb-top chuckles at!
Nay, boys, ye love me—all of jasper,[21] then!
'Tis jasper ye stand pledged to, lest I grieve
My bath must needs be left behind, alas!
One block, pure green as a pistachio-nut,
There's plenty jasper somewhere in the world—
And have I not St. Praxed's ear to pray
Horses for ye, and brown Greek manuscripts,
And mistresses with great smooth marbly limbs?
—That's if ye carve my epitaph aright,
Choice Latin, picked phrase, Tully's every word,
No gaudy ware like Gandolf's second line—
Tully, my masters? Ulpian[22] serves his need!
And then how I shall lie through centuries,
And hear the blessed mutter of the Mass,
And see God made and eaten all day long,
And feel the steady candle-flame, and taste
Good strong, thick, stupefying incense-smoke!
For as I lie here, hours of the dead night,
Dying in state and by such slow degrees,
I fold my arms as if they clasped a crook,[23]
And stretch my feet forth straight as stone can point,

[14] Fashionable area near Rome. [15] *Swift . . . years.* Loosely quoted from Job 7:6.
[16] A finer marble. [17] Decorated horizontal surface.
[18] Wand carried by Bacchus, god of wine. [19] Halo. [20] Inferior stone.
[21] A variety of quartz.
[22] *Tully, Ulpian.* Tully (Cicero) was a model for excellent and Ulpian for poor Latin style.
[23] The crozier, a bishop's symbolic staff shaped like a shepherd's crook.

And let the bedclothes for a mort-cloth[24] drop
Into great laps and folds of sculptor's-work.
And as yon tapers[25] dwindle, and strange thoughts
Grow, with a certain humming in my ears,
About the life before I lived this life,
And this life too, popes, cardinals, and priests,
St. Praxed at his sermon on the mount,
Your tall pale mother with her talking eyes,
And new-found agate urns as fresh as day,
And marble's language, Latin pure, discreet,
—Aha, ELUCESCEBAT[26] quoth our friend?
No Tully, said I, Ulpian at the best!
Evil and brief hath been my pilgrimage.
All *lapis,* all, sons! Else I give the Pope
My villas. Will ye ever eat my heart?
Ever your eyes were as a lizard's quick;
They glitter like your mother's for my soul,
Or ye would heighten my impoverished frieze,
Piece out its starved design, and fill my vase
With grapes, and add a vizor and a term,[27]
And to the tripod ye would tie a lynx
That in his struggle throws the thyrsus down,
To comfort me on my entablature[28]
Whereon I am to lie till I must ask
"Do I live, am I dead?" There, leave me, there!
For ye have stabbed me with ingratitude
To death—ye wish it—God, ye wish it! Stone—
Gritstone,[29] a-crumble! Clammy squares which sweat
As if the corpse they keep were oozing through—
And no more *lapis* to delight the world!
Well, go! I bless ye. Fewer tapers there,
But in a row. And, going, turn your backs
—Aye, like departing altar-ministrants,
And leave me in my church, the church for peace,
That I may watch at leisure if he leers—
Old Gandolf—at me, from his onion-stone,
As still he envied me, so fair she was.

[24] Funeral drapery. [25] Candles.
[26] "He was glorious." This verb form is inferior Latin; "elucebat" is purer.
[27] A vizor is a mask, a term is a bust on a pedestal.
[28] Horizontal part of a classical structure. [29] Cheap sandstone.

ANDREA DEL SARTO[1]

CALLED "THE FAULTLESS PAINTER"

But do not let us quarrel any more,
No, my Lucrezia! bear with me for once:
Sit down and all shall happen as you wish.
You turn your face, but does it bring your heart?
I'll work then for your friend's friend,[2] never fear,
Treat his own subject after his own way,
Fix his own time, accept too his own price,
And shut the money into this small hand
When next it takes mine. Will it? tenderly?
Oh, I'll content him,—but to-morrow, Love!
I often am much wearier than you think,
This evening more than usual: and it seems
As if—forgive now—should you let me sit
Here by the window, with your hand in mine,
And look a half hour forth on Fiesolè,[3]
Both of one mind, as married people use,
Quietly, quietly the evening through,
I might get up to-morrow to my work
Cheerful and fresh as ever. Let us try.
To-morrow, how you shall be glad for this!
Your soft hand is a woman of itself,
And mine, the man's bared breast she curls inside.
Don't count the time lost, neither; you must serve
For each of the five pictures we require:
It saves a model. So! keep looking so—
My serpentining beauty, rounds on rounds!
—How could you ever prick those perfect ears,
Even to put the pearl there! oh, so sweet—
My face, my moon, my everybody's moon,
Which everybody looks on and calls his,
And, I suppose, is looked on by in turn,
While she looks—no one's: very dear, no less.
You smile? why, there's my picture ready made,
There's what we painters call our harmony!
A common grayness silvers everything,—
All in a twilight, you and I alike
—You, at the point of your first pride in me
(That's gone you know),—but I, at every point;
My youth, my hope, my art, being all toned down
To yonder sober pleasant Fiesolè.

[1] Florentine painter; he was born in 1486 and died of the plague in 1531. Browning's account of him here is based largely on the *Lives of the Painters* by Giorgio Vasari, the famous art historian, who was a pupil of Andrea's.

[2] Some friend of Lucrezia's so-called "cousin" mentioned later in the poem.

[3] A town near Florence.

There's the bell clinking from the chapel-top;
That length of convent-wall across the way
Holds the trees safer, huddled more inside;
The last monk leaves the garden; days decrease,
And autumn grows, autumn in everything.
Eh? the whole seems to fall into a shape
As if I saw alike my work and self
And all that I was born to be and do,
A twilight-piece. Love, we are in God's hand.
How strange now looks the life he makes us lead;
So free we seem, so fettered fast we are!
I feel he laid the fetter: let it lie!
This chamber for example—turn your head—
All that's behind us! You don't understand,
Nor care to understand, about my art,
But you can hear at least when people speak:
And that cartoon,[4] the second from the door
—It is the thing, Love! so such things should be—
Behold Madonna!—I am bold to say.
I can do with my pencil what I know,
What I see, what at bottom of my heart
I wish for, if I ever wish so deep—
Do easily, too—when I say, perfectly,
I do not boast, perhaps: yourself are judge,
Who listened to the Legate's[5] talk last week,
And just as much they used to say in France.
At any rate, 'tis easy, all of it!
No sketches first, no studies, that's long past:
I do what many dream of all their lives,
—Dream? strive to do, and agonize to do,
And fail in doing. I could count twenty such
On twice your fingers, and not leave this town,
Who strive—you don't know how the others strive
To paint a little thing like that you smeared
Carelessly passing with your robes afloat,—
Yet do much less, so much less, Someone[6] says,
(I know his name, no matter)—so much less!
Well, less is more, Lucrezia: I am judged.
There burns a truer light of God in them,
In their vexed, beating, stuffed, and stopped-up brain,
Heart, or whate'er else, than goes on to prompt
This low-pulsed forthright craftsman's hand of mine.
Their works drop groundward, but themselves, I know,
Reach many a time a heaven that's shut to me,
Enter and take their place there sure enough,
Though they come back and cannot tell the world.
My works are nearer heaven, but I sit here.

[4] Sketch drawn as preliminary to a painting. [5] Diplomatic envoy of the Pope.
[6] Michelangelo (1475–1564); he is referred to later in the poem.

The sudden blood of these men! at a word—
Praise them, it boils, or blame them, it boils too.
I, painting from myself and to myself,
Know what I do, am unmoved by men's blame
Or their praise either. Somebody remarks
Morello's[7] outline there is wrongly traced,
His hue mistaken; what of that? or else,
Rightly traced and well ordered; what of that?
Speak as they please, what does the mountain care?
Ah, but a man's reach should exceed his grasp,
Or what's a heaven for? All is silver-gray,
Placid and perfect with my art: the worse!
I know both what I want and what might gain;
And yet how profitless to know, to sigh
"Had I been two, another and myself,
Our head would have o'erlooked the world!" No doubt.
Yonder's a work now, of that famous youth
The Urbinate[8] who died five years ago.
('Tis copied, George Vasari sent it me.)
Well, I can fancy how he did it all,
Pouring his soul, with kings and popes to see,
Reaching, that heaven might so replenish him,
Above and through his art—for it gives way;
That arm is wrongly put—and there again—
A fault to pardon in the drawing's lines,
Its body, so to speak: its soul is right,
He means right—that, a child may understand.
Still, what an arm! and I could alter it;
But all the play, the insight and the stretch—
Out of me, out of me! And wherefore out?
Had you enjoined them on me, given me soul,
We might have risen to Rafael, I and you.
Nay, Love, you did give all I asked, I think—
More than I merit, yes, by many times.
But had you—oh, with the same perfect brow,
And perfect eyes, and more than perfect mouth,
And the low voice my soul hears, as a bird
The fowler's[9] pipe, and follows to the snare—
Had you, with these the same, but brought a mind!
Some women do so. Had the mouth there urged
"God and the glory! never care for gain.
The present by the future, what is that?
Live for fame, side by side with Agnolo![10]
Rafael is waiting: up to God, all three!"
I might have done it for you. So it seems:
Perhaps not. All is as God overrules.

[7] A mountain.
[8] Native of Urbino—that is, Raphael (1483–1520), who executed work for Pope Julius II.
[9] Hunter of birds. [10] Michelangelo.

Beside, incentives come from the soul's self;
The rest avail not. Why do I need you?
What wife had Rafael, or has Agnolo?
In this world, who can do a thing, will not;
And who would[11] do it, cannot, I perceive:
Yet the will's somewhat—somewhat, too, the power—
And thus we half-men struggle. At the end,
God, I conclude, compensates, punishes.
'Tis safer for me, if the award be strict,
That I am something underrated here,
Poor this long while, despised, to speak the truth.
I dared not, do you know, leave home all day,
For fear of chancing on the Paris lords.[12]
The best is when they pass and look aside;
But they speak sometimes; I must bear it all.
Well may they speak! That Francis, that first time,
And that long festal year at Fontainebleau!
I surely then could sometimes leave the ground,
Put on the glory, Rafael's daily wear,
In that humane great monarch's golden look,—
One finger in his beard or twisted curl
Over his mouth's good mark that made the smile,
One arm about my shoulder, round my neck,
The jingle of his gold chain in my ear,
I painting proudly with his breath on me,
All his court round him, seeing with his eyes,
Such frank French eyes, and such a fire of souls
Profuse, my hand kept plying by those hearts,—
And, best of all, this, this, this face beyond,
This in the background, waiting on my work,
To crown the issue with a last reward!
A good time, was it not, my kingly days?
And had you not grown restless . . . but I know—
'Tis done and past; 'twas right, my instinct said;
Too live the life grew, golden and not gray,
And I'm the weak-eyed bat no sun should tempt
Out of his grange[13] whose four walls make his world.
How could it end in any other way?
You called me, and I came home to your heart.
The triumph was—to reach and stay there; since
I reached it ere the triumph, what is lost?
Let my hands frame your face in your hair's gold,
You beautiful Lucrezia that are mine!
"Rafael did this, Andrea painted that;

[11] Desires to.

[12] Andrea had worked in 1518 for King Francis I of France at his palace in Fontainebleau, near Paris. According to the story, now questioned, Lucrezia got Andrea to return to Florence, where she induced him to spend on a new house money entrusted to him so that he might buy paintings for the king.

[13] Barn.

The Roman's[14] is the better when you pray,
But still the other's Virgin was his wife—"
Men will excuse me. I am glad to judge
Both pictures in your presence; clearer grows
My better fortune, I resolve to think.
For, do you know, Lucrezia, as God lives,
Said one day Agnolo, his very self,
To Rafael . . . I have known it all these years . . .
(When the young man was flaming out his thoughts
Upon a palace-wall for Rome to see,
Too lifted up in heart because of it)
"Friend, there's a certain sorry little scrub
Goes up and down our Florence, none cares how,
Who, were he set to plan and execute
As you are, pricked on by your popes and kings,
Would bring the sweat into that brow of yours!"
To Rafael's!—And indeed the arm is wrong.
I hardly dare . . . yet, only you to see,
Give the chalk here—quick, thus the line should go!
Ay, but the soul! he's Rafael! rub it out!
Still, all I care for, if he spoke the truth,
(What he? why, who but Michel Agnolo?
Do you forget already words like those?)
If really there was such a chance so lost,—
Is, whether you're—not grateful—but more pleased.
Well, let me think so. And you smile indeed!
This hour has been an hour! Another smile?
If you would sit thus by me every night
I should work better, do you comprehend?
I mean that I should earn more, give you more.
See, it is settled dusk now; there's a star;
Morello's gone, the watch-lights show the wall,
The cue-owls speak the name we call them by.
Come from the window, love,—come in, at last,
Inside the melancholy little house
We built to be so gay with. God is just.
King Francis may forgive me: oft at nights
When I look up from painting, eyes tired out,
The walls become illumined, brick from brick
Distinct, instead of mortar, fierce bright gold,
That gold of his I did cement them with!
Let us but love each other. Must you go?
That cousin here again? he waits outside?
Must see you—you, and not with me? Those loans?
More gaming[15] debts to pay? you smiled for that?
Well, let smiles buy me! have you more to spend?
While hand and eye and something of a heart
Are left me, work's my ware, and what's it worth?

[14] Raphael, who painted in St. Peter's. [15] Gambling.

I'll pay my fancy. Only let me sit
The gray remainder of the evening out,
Idle, you call it, and muse perfectly
How I could paint, were I but back in France,
One picture, just one more—the Virgin's face,
Not yours this time! I want you at my side
To hear them—that is, Michel Agnolo—
Judge all I do and tell you of its worth.
Will you? To-morrow, satisfy your friend.
I take the subjects for his corridor,
Finish the portrait out of hand—there, there,
And throw him in another thing or two
If he demurs;[16] the whole should prove enough
To pay for this same cousin's freak. Beside,
What's better and what's all I care about,
Get you the thirteen scudi[17] for the ruff!
Love, does that please you? Ah, but what does he,
The cousin! what does he to please you more?
  I am grown peaceful as old age to-night.
I regret little, I would change still less.
Since there my past life lies, why alter it?
The very wrong to Francis!—it is true
I took his coin, was tempted and complied,
And built this house and sinned, and all is said.
My father and my mother died of want.
Well, had I riches of my own? you see
How one gets rich! Let each one bear his lot.
They were born poor, lived poor, and poor they died:
And I have labored somewhat in my time
And not been paid profusely. Some good son
Paint my two hundred pictures—let him try!
No doubt, there's something strikes a balance. Yes,
You loved me quite enough, it seems to-night.
This must suffice me here. What would one have?
In heaven, perhaps, new chances, one more chance—
Four great walls in the New Jerusalem[18]
Meted on each side by the angel's reed,[19]
For Leonard,[20] Rafael, Agnolo and me
To cover—the three first without a wife,
While I have mine! So—still they overcome
Because there's still Lucrezia,—as I choose.
Again the cousin's whistle! Go, my Love.

[16] Is not satisfied. [17] Italian coins. [18] Heaven.
[19] *Meted . . . reed.* Measured by the angel's yardstick.
[20] Leonardo da Vinci (1452–1519).

Mikhail Lermontov

(1814–1841)

"I have never had anything against you, Baron," Captain Solyony tells his fellow officer, the Baron Tusenbach, in Chekhov's play The Three Sisters *(1900). "But I have the temperament of Lermontov. In fact I am rather like Lermontov to look at . . . so I am told." Solyony is a foolish poseur, languidly cultivating a Byronic air of secret sorrow and compulsively sprinkling scent on his hands, as if trying to conceal the smell of death. But he is a dangerous fool, and at the end of the play, he guns Tusenbach down on the eve of his wedding, in a meaningless and arbitrary duel. Everyone in this play of uncertain self-conceptions cultivates some tentative pose, and it is significant that almost sixty years after the poet's death, Chekhov could depend upon his Russian audience instantly to recognize Solyony's pose as Lermontovian.*

Mikhail Lermontov was born in Moscow in 1814. His mother died when he was three, and his strong-willed, combative maternal grandmother wrested custody of him from his irresponsible, high-living father; she reared him on her luxurious estate in Penzenskaya province. Childhood illnesses stunted his growth and left him permanently stoop-shouldered and bowlegged. His grandmother took him three times for recuperation to the wild, scenic Caucasus area in southern Russia, to which he became passionately and permanently attached. When Lermontov was thirteen, his grandmother moved with him to Moscow so that he could attend the Moscow University Gentry Pension, the preparatory school for Moscow University. Here he studied for two years, developing a great enthusiasm for the poetry of Lord Byron, who along with the great Russian poet Alexander Pushkin, was to be the major influence upon his future writing. When he was sixteen, he enrolled at the University of Moscow but was bored and contemptuous of the lectures and withdrew after two years to transfer to the University of St. Petersburg. During his Moscow years, Lermontov had a series of youthful love affairs, of which the most important was with Varvara Lopukhina; his attachment to her survived through the rest of his life, even after her marriage to another man, and he based the character of Vera in A Hero of Our Time *upon her.*

When the University of St. Petersburg refused to honor his work at the University of Moscow, Lermontov made the fateful decision to seek an army career and entered the Guards' School in Petersburg; he spent two years there and was commissioned an officer in the Life Guard Hussars in 1834. He spent the first three years of his military service stationed with his regiment at Tsarskoye Selo, the Czar's summer palace just outside St. Petersburg, and moving in the glittering society of St. Petersburg. He had been writing lyric poetry, longer narrative poems, and plays since the age of fourteen, and now he began to write in earnest. A play, The Two Brothers *(1835), dealt with his meeting with Varvara Lopukhina's elderly husband, and another,* Masquerade *(1835), dealt satirically with Petersburg society, so pointedly that it was rejected by the censor and was published only seven years later, after heavy revision. To this period, also, belongs an unfinished short novel,* Princess Ligovskaya, *in which Lermontov introduced the character of Pechorin; this work was to provide the basis of "Princess Mary" in* A Hero of Our Time.

In 1837, there began a series of struggles between Lermontov and the tyrannical Czar Nicholas I which were to bring about, indirectly, Lermontov's death seven years later. Pushkin was killed in a sordid duel over the reputation of his wife in January,

1837, and Lermontov immediately wrote a long elegy for the poet, which included lines laying the blame for his death upon the court, "hangmen of Freedom, Genius, and Fame." The Czar, upon reading this poem, had Lermontov arrested and exiled to a regiment on active duty in the Caucasus. This first exile, which lasted a year, was not onerous; Lermontov spent much of the time convalescing from rheumatism at the famous resort in Pyatigorsk (setting of "Princess Mary"), meeting Georgian artists and intellectuals, and studying Caucasian languages and cultures. He was allowed to return to Petersburg and his old regiment in 1838. In the following two years, he wrote voluminously, completing a number of major poems and his masterpiece, A Hero of Our Time.

In 1840, however, the Czar struck again. Lermontov had fought a duel with the son of the French ambassador, for reasons not now known. The duelists were to fire simultaneously; his opponent missed, Lermontov fired to one side, and the two were reconciled. When Nicholas heard of the duel, he ordered Lermontov transferred immediately to a combat regiment in the Caucasus which, attempting to defend an isolated fortress, was suffering a casualty rate of over fifty percent. As it happened, the commander in the Caucasus assigned him to a different regiment which embarked on a six-month foray into enemy territory. On this expedition, Lermontov distinguished himself repeatedly in combat and was recommended for high decorations, which were, however, summarily refused by Nicholas.

Lermontov was granted a two-month leave at the beginning of 1841, on the appeal of his grandmother. On the expiration of the leave, Lermontov was again assigned, on specific orders of the Czar, to the dangerous Black Sea front. He never reached his regiment; on the way, he stopped at Pyatigorsk, where he quarrelled with a retired army officer named N. S. Martynov. Martynov challenged him to a duel; Lermontov is said to have fired into the air, but Martynov's first shot killed Lermontov instantly. He was twenty-seven years old.

Lermontov is usually acknowledged to be among the greatest of the Russian Romantics. He produced an astonishingly large body of poetry, despite the brevity of his busy life; even on the journey from Petersburg to the Caucasus which ended in his death, he wrote a number of poems, several of them among his finest. His poems deal with the impulse toward freedom, heroism, and mission, in what the Russians call "iron verse," heroic, energetic language, and with such other Romantic themes as nature and the lives of simple people. Many of his poems continue to hold their place among the masterworks of Russian lyric poetry.

A Hero of Our Time *holds a similarly high place among the masterpieces of Russian fiction. Some Russian critics have maintained that it is the greatest Russian novel, though it would be hard to rank this comparatively small-scale work above Tolstoy's* War and Peace *or Dostoevsky's* The Brothers Karamazov. *(Tolstoy himself called "Taman," one of the five stories in* A Hero of Our Time, *"the most artistically perfect work in Russian literature.") But it is perhaps best to consider* A Hero of Our Time *not as the rival of the great later Russian novels but as their progenitor; it established the tradition of psychological realism to which the achievements not only of Tolstoy and Dostoevsky but also of Turgenev, Gorky, and Chekhov belong.*

A Hero of Our Time *is a psychological inquiry into "Byronism," a Romantic stance so widespread in early nineteenth-century Russia as to make Pechorin an ironic "hero of our time." The Byronic hero had its origins in Byron's own self-perception and his projection of it into his own Childe Harolds and Manfreds: both passionate and cynical, oscillating between acts of heroic benevolence and cold cruelty, world-weary and bored, and above all, haunted by his own acute perception of his inner division between feeling and intellect, actor and observer. Pechorin speaks for all Byronic heroes when he confides to his friend Werner, "There are two men in me; one lives in the full sense of the word, the other reasons and passes judgment on the first." Byronism escaped the pages of books and became what amounted to a social stance in the 1820's and '30's, a way of translating the content of Romanticism into a personal style, much as perhaps the widespread affectation of a languid decadence in the England of the 1890's or the role of alienated Flower Child in the American 1960's expressed certain cultural pressures.*

It would seem that the remote Caucasus would be an inappropriate setting for a study of what is essentially a fashionable society personality. But for both personal and artistic reasons, the Caucasus is perfect. Romantic memories of childhood happiness as well as adult experience charged the area for Lermontov with associations of freedom and release, in contrast to the patterned paranoia of Czarist St. Petersburg. The wild landscape and the romantic Tatar characters are suitably Byronic, providing opportunities both for contemplation of nature and for feats of derring-do. The novel opens in 1837, and the initial narrator is traveling back to Russia from Georgia along the old "Military Georgian Road" from Tiflis, the capital of Georgia, to Vladikavkaz. The Circassian (Cherkess), Kabardian, and Ossetian characters in the novel are all members of Tatar tribes, Islamic heirs of the Mongolian invasions of the thirteenth century, now engaged in ongoing guerrilla warfare against the Russians who are attempting to incorporate them into their empire.

Lermontov's exploration of "all our generation's vices in full bloom" is richly ambivalent. Pechorin is obviously partially a self-portrait; Lermontov's physical description of Pechorin is a description of himself, even down to his bad back, and the incidents of the book are based upon his own experiences. But the novel's structure distances us from Pechorin and makes it not a confession but a dissection, and to some extent, a condemnation of his personality. The five stories that make up the novel are, except for "Maxim Maximych," complete in themselves, and "Bela," "The Fatalist," and "Taman" were published separately before they were incorporated into the novel. But it is clear that Lermontov conceived the five stories as parts of the larger structure and arranged them so as to provide a progressive series of perspectives upon his protagonist's character. The anonymous narrator of "Bela" and "Maxim Maximych" (also a version of Lermontov himself) at first hears about Pechorin as filtered through the perceptions of someone diametrically opposite, the bluff, hearty old soldier Maximych. He then observes Pechorin first hand, and we finally get, in the three sections from Pechorin's journal, Pechorin's own perceptions of himself. But even here, there is a kaleidoscope of impressions; only "Princess Mary" is presented in journal form, and the other sections impose various kinds of interpretation and myth-making. All in all, it is a complex and elegant hall of mirrors for the contemplation of this ambiguous "hero."

FURTHER READING *(prepared by J. H.):* The best account of Lermontov's life in English is Laurence Kelly's *Lermontov: Tragedy in the Caucasus,* 1978, which is scholarly, vividly written, and illustrated with a number of rare pictures of Lermontov and his world. Most of the major criticism is in Russian, of course, but John Mersereau, Jr.'s *Mikhail Lermontov,* 1962, is a good critical introduction in English and is based upon a comprehensive knowledge of the Russian sources. Janko Lavrin's *Lermontov,* 1959, is another excellent, more economical introduction. On *A*

Hero of Our Time, C. J. G. Turner's *Pechorin: An Essay on Lermontov's "A Hero of Our Time,"* 1978, is a thoughtful, extended study. Vladimir Nabokov's introduction to his translation, with Dimitri Nabokov, of the novel is a characteristically high-spirited and dogmatic, but provocative, interpretation. Otherwise, the best criticism of the novel is probably to be found in chapters of books: Henry Gifford, *The Novel in Russia from Pushkin to Pasternak,* 1964, pp. 30–41; F. D. Reeve, *The Russian Novel,* 1966, pp. 45–63; Alexander F. Boyd, "Lonely White Sail: Mikhail Lermontov and *A Hero of Our Time,*" in *Aspects of the Russian Novel,* 1972, pp. 24–45; and Richard Freeborn, *The Rise of the Russian Novel,* 1973, pp. 38–73.

A HERO OF OUR TIME

Translated by Martin Parker

FOREWORD

The foreword is at once the first and the last thing in any book; it serves either to explain the purpose of the work or to justify the author before his critics. Ordinarily, however, readers are concerned with neither the moral nor the journalistic attacks on the author; hence they do not read forewords. Yet it is a pity it should be so, especially in our country. Our public is still so immature and simple-hearted that it does not understand a fable unless it finds the moral at the end. It fails to grasp a joke or sense an irony; it is simply brought up badly. It is as yet unaware that obvious invective has no place in respectable society and respectable books, that contemporary enlightenment has devised a sharper, almost invisible but nevertheless deadly weapon, which under the guise of flattery deals a true, unparriable blow. Our public is like the provincial who overhearing a conversation between two diplomats belonging to hostile courts carries off the conviction that each is deceiving his government for the sake of a tender mutual friendship.

The present book recently had the misfortune of being taken literally by some readers and even some magazines. Some were frightfully offended in all seriousness at being given a man as amoral as the Hero of Our Time for a model; others delicately hinted that the author had drawn portraits of himself and his acquaintances. . . . A threadbare witticism! But apparently Russia is so constituted that however she may progress in every other respect, she is unable to get rid of absurdities like this. With us the most fantastic of fairy tales has hardly a chance of escaping criticism as an attempt at libel!

A Hero of Our Time, *my dear sirs, is indeed a portrait, but not of one man; it is a portrait built up of all our generation's vices in full bloom. You will again tell me that a human being cannot be so wicked, and I shall reply that if you can believe in the existence of all the villains of tragedy and romance, why should you not believe that there was a Pechorin? If you could admire far more terrifying and repulsive types, why are you not more merciful to this character, even if it is fictitious? Is it not because there is more truth in it than you might wish?*

You say that morality will gain nothing by it. I beg to differ. People have been fed enough sweetmeats to upset their stomachs; now bitter remedies, acid truths, are needed. Yet you should not think that the author of this book was ever ambitious enough to aspire to reform human vices. May God preserve him from such boorishness! It simply pleased him to portray the modern man as he sees him and as he so often, to his own and your misfortune, has found him to be. Suffice it that the disease has been diagnosed, how to cure it the Lord alone knows!

PART ONE

I. BELA

I was traveling along the post road from Tiflis. The only luggage in the carriage was one small portmanteau half-full of travel notes about Georgia. Fortunately for you the greater part of them has been lost since then, though luckily for me the case and the rest of the things in it have survived.

The sun was already slipping behind a snow-capped ridge when I drove into Koishaur Valley. The Ossetian coachman, singing at the top of his voice, urged his horses on relentlessly to reach the summit of Koishaur Mountain before nightfall. What a glorious spot this valley is! All around it tower formidable mountains, reddish crags draped with hanging ivy and crowned with clusters of plane-trees, yellow cliffs grooved by torrents, with a gilded fringe of snow high above, while down below the Aragva embraces a nameless stream that noisily bursts forth from a black, gloom-filled gorge, and then stretches in a silvery ribbon into the distance, its surface shimmering like the scaly back of a snake.

On reaching the foot of Koishaur Mountain we stopped outside a *dukhan*[1] where some twenty Georgians and mountaineers made up a noisy assemblage; nearby a camel caravan had halted for the night. I had to hire oxen to haul my carriage to the top of the confounded mountain for it was already autumn and a thin layer of ice covered the ground, and the climb was about two versts[2] in length.

There was nothing for it but to hire six oxen and several Ossetians. One of them hoisted my portmanteau on his shoulder and the others set to helping the oxen along, doing little more than shout, however.

Behind my carriage came another, pulled by four oxen with no visible exertion although the vehicle was piled high with baggage. This rather surprised me. In the wake of the carriage walked its owner, puffing at a small silver-inlaid Kabardian pipe. He was wearing an officer's coat without epaulettes and a shaggy Cherkess cap. He looked about fifty, his swarthy face betrayed a long acquaintanceship with the Caucasian sun, and his prematurely gray moustache belied his firm step and vigorous appearance. I went up to him and bowed; he silently returned my greeting, blowing out an enormous cloud of smoke.

"I take it we are fellow-travellers?"

He bowed again, but did not say a word.

"I suppose you are going to Stavropol?"

"Yes, sir, I am . . . with some government baggage."

[1] Caucasian tavern.
[2] Russian units of distance, equal to about two-thirds of a mile.

"Will you please explain to me how it is that four oxen easily manage to pull your heavy carriage while six beasts can barely haul my empty one with the help of all these Ossetians?"

He smiled shrewdly, casting an appraising glance at me.

"I daresay you haven't been long in the Caucasus?"

"About a year," I replied.

He smiled again.

"Why do you ask?"

"No particular reason, sir. They're terrific rogues, these Asiatics! You don't think their yelling helps much, do you? You can't tell what the devil they're saying. But the oxen understand them all right; hitch up twenty of the beasts if you wish and they won't budge once those fellows begin yelling in their tongue. . . . Terrific cheats, they are. And what can you do to them? They do like to skin the traveller. Spoiled, they are, the scoundrels . . . you'll see they'll make you tip them too. I know them by now, they won't fool me!"

"Have you served long in these parts?"

"Yes, ever since Alexei Petrovich[3] was here," he replied, drawing himself up. "When he arrived at the line I was a sublieutenant, and under him was promoted twice for service against the mountaineers."

"And now?"

"Now I am in the third line battalion. And you, may I ask?"

I told him.

This brought the conversation to an end and we walked along side by side in silence. On top of the mountain we ran into snow. The sun set and night followed day without any interval in between as is usual in the South; thanks to the glistening snow, however, we could easily pick out the road which still continued to climb, though less steeply than before. I gave orders to put my portmanteau in the carriage and replace the oxen with horses, and turned to look back at the valley down below for the last time, but a thick mist that rolled in waves from the gorges blanketed it completely and not a single sound reached us from its depths. The Ossetians vociferously besieged me, demanding money for vodka; but the captain shouted at them so fiercely that they dispersed in a moment.

"You see what they are like!" he grumbled. "They don't know enough Russian to ask for a piece of bread, but they've learned to beg for tips: 'Officer, give me money for vodka!' To me the Tatars are better—they're teetotalers at least. . . ."

Another verst remained to the post station. It was quiet all around, so quiet that you could trace the flight of a mosquito by its buzz. A deep gorge yawned black to the left; beyond it and ahead of us the dark-blue mountain peaks wrinkled with gorges and gullies and topped by layers of snow loomed against the pale horizon that still retained the last glimmer of twilight. Stars began to twinkle in the dark sky, and strangely enough it seemed that they were far higher here than in our northern sky. On both sides of the road naked black boulders jutted up from the ground, and here and there some shrubs peeped from under the snow; not a single

[3] General Alexei Petrovich Yermolov was governor-general of Georgia from 1817 to 1827.

dead leaf rustled, and it was pleasant to hear in the midst of this lifeless somnolence of nature the snorting of the tired post horses and the uneven tinkling of the Russian carriage bells.

"Tomorrow will be a fine day," I observed, but the captain did not reply. Instead he pointed to a tall mountain rising directly ahead of us.

"What's that?" I asked.

"Mount Goud."

"Yes?"

"See how it smokes?"

Indeed, Mount Goud was smoking; light wisps of mist crept along its sides while a black cloud rested on the summit, so black that it stood out as a blotch even against the dark sky.

We could already make out the post station and the roofs of the huts around it, and welcoming lights were dancing ahead when the gusts of cold raw wind came whistling down the gorge and it began to drizzle. Barely had I thrown a felt cape over my shoulders than the snow came. I looked at the captain with respect now. . . .

"We'll have to stay here overnight," he said, annoyed. "You can't journey through the hills in a blizzard like this. See any avalanches on Krestovaya?"he asked a coachman.

"No, sir," the Ossetian replied. "But there's a lot just waiting to come down."

As there was no room for travellers at the post house, we were given lodgings in a smoky hut. I invited my fellow-traveller to join me at tea for I had with me a cast-iron tea-kettle—my sole comfort on my Caucasian travels.

The hut was built against a cliff. Three wet, slippery steps led up to the door. I groped my way in and stumbled upon a cow, for these people have a cowshed for an anteroom. I could not make out where to go; on one side sheep were bleating and on the other a dog growled. Fortunately a glimmer of light showed through the gloom and guided me to another opening that looked like a door. Here a rather interesting scene confronted me: the spacious hut with a roof supported by two smoke-blackened posts was full of people. A fire built on the bare earth crackled in the middle and the smoke, forced back by the wind through the opening in the roof, hung so thick that it took some time before I could distinguish anything around me. By the fire sat two old women, a swarm of children and a lean Georgian man, all of them dressed in tatters. There was nothing to do but to make ourselves comfortable by the fire and light up our pipes, and soon the teakettle was singing merrily.

"Pitiable creatures!" I observed to the captain, nodding toward our grimy hosts who stared at us silently with something like stupefaction.

"A dull-witted people," he replied. "Believe me, they can't do a thing, nor can they learn anything either. Our Kabardians or Chechens, rogues and vagabonds though they be, are at least good fighters, whereas these take no interest even in arms: you won't find a decent dagger on a single one of them. But what can you expect from Ossetians!"

"Were you long in Chechna?"

"Quite a while—ten years garrisoning a fort with a company, out Kamenny Brod way. Do you know the place?"

"Heard of it."

"Yes, sir, we had enough of the ruffians; now, thank God, things are quieter, but there was a time when you couldn't venture a hundred paces beyond the rampart without some hairy devil stalking you, ready to put a halter around your neck or a bullet through the back of your head the moment he caught you napping. But they were stout fellows anyway."

"You must have had a good many adventures?" I asked, spurred by curiosity.

"Aye, many indeed. . . ."

Thereupon he began to pluck at the left tip of his moustache, his head drooped and he sank into deep thought. I very badly wanted to get some sort of story out of him—a desire that is natural to anyone who travels about, recording things. In the meantime the tea came to a boil; I dug out two traveller's tumblers from my portmanteau, poured out tea and placed one before the captain. He took a sip and muttered as if to himself: "Yes, many indeed!" The exclamation raised my hopes, for I knew that Caucasian old-timers like to talk; they seldom have a chance to do so, for a man may be stationed a full five years with a company somewhere in the backwoods without anyone to greet him with a "Good day" (that mode of address does not belong to the sergeant's vocabulary). And there is so much to talk about: the wild, strange people all around, the constant dangers, and the remarkable adventures; one cannot help thinking it is a pity that we record so little of it.

"Would you care to add a little rum?" I asked. "I have some white rum from Tiflis, it will warm you up in this cold."

"No, thanks, I don't drink."

"How is that?"

"Well . . . swore off the stuff. Once when I was still a sublieutenant we went on a bit of a spree, you know how it happens, and that very night there was an alarm. So we showed up before the ranks on the gay side, and there was the devil to pay when Alexei Petrovich found out. Lord preserve me from seeing a man as furious as he was; we escaped being court-martialled by a hair's breadth. That's the way it is: sometimes you get to spend a whole year without seeing anyone, and if you take to drink you're done for."

On hearing this I nearly lost hope.

"Take even the Cherkess," he went on. "As soon as they drink their fill of *boza*[4] at a wedding or a funeral the fight begins. Once I barely managed to escape alive although I was the guest of a peaceable prince."

"How did it happen?"

"Well," he filled and lit his pipe, took a long draw on it, and began the story, "you see, I was stationed at the time at a fort beyond the Terek with a company—that was nearly five years back. Once in the autumn a convoy came with foodstuffs, and with it an officer, a young man of about twenty-five. He reported to me in full dress uniform and announced that he had been ordered to join me at the fort. He was so slim and pale and his uniform so immaculate that I could tell at once that he was a newcomer to the Caucasus. 'You must have been transferred here from Russia?' I asked him. 'Yes, sir,' he replied. I took his hand and said: 'Glad to have you here, very

[4] A native drink made from hemp seed and darnel meal.

glad. It'll be a bit dull for you . . . but we'll get along very well, I'm sure. Call me simply Maxim Maximych, if you like, and, another thing, you need not bother wearing full dress uniform. Just come around in your forage cap.' He was shown his quarters and he settled down in the fort."

"What was his name?" I asked Maxim Maximych.

"Grigori Alexandrovich Pechorin. A fine chap he was, I assure you, though a bit queer. For instance, he would spend days on end hunting in rain or cold; everybody else would be chilled and exhausted, but not he. Yet sometimes a mere draught in his room would be enough for him to claim he had caught cold; a banging shutter might make him start and turn pale, yet I myself saw him go at a wild boar single-handed; sometimes you couldn't get a word out of him for hours on end, but when he occasionally did start telling stories you'd split your sides laughing. . . . Yes, sir, a most curious sort of fellow he was, and, apparently, rich too, judging by the quantity of expensive trinkets he had."

"How long was he with you?" I asked.

"A good year. That was a memorable year for me; he caused me plenty of trouble, God forgive him! But after all, there are people who are predestined to have all sorts of odd things happen to them!"

"Odd things?" I exclaimed eagerly as I poured him some more tea.

"I'll tell you the story. Some six versts from the fort there lived a peaceable prince. His son, a lad of about fifteen, got into the habit of riding over to see us; not a day passed that he didn't come for one reason or another. Grigori Alexandrovich and I really spoiled him. What a scapegrace he was, ready for anything, whether it was to lean down from his saddle to pick up a cap from the ground while galloping by or to try his hand at marksmanship. But there was one bad thing about him: he had a terrible weakness for money. Once for a joke Grigori Alexandrovich promised him a gold piece if he stole the best goat from his father's herd, and what do you think? The very next night he dragged the animal in by the horns. Sometimes, if we just tried teasing him, he would flare up and reach for his dagger. 'Your head's too hot for your own good, Azamat,' I would tell him. 'That's *yaman*[5] for your topknot!'

"Once the old prince himself came over to invite us to a wedding; he was giving away his elder daughter and since we were *kunaks*[6] there was no way of declining, you know, Tatar or not. So we set out. A pack of barking dogs met us in the village. On seeing us the women hid themselves; the faces we did catch a glimpse of were far from pretty. 'I had a much better opinion of Cherkess women,' Grigori Alexandrovich said to me. 'You wait a while,' I replied, smiling. I had something up my sleeve.

"There was quite a crowd assembled in the prince's house. It's the custom among Asiatics, you know, to invite to their weddings everyone they chance to meet. We were welcomed with all due honors and shown to the best room. Before going in, though, I took care to note where they put our horses, just in case something unforeseen happened, you know."

"How do they celebrate weddings?" I asked the captain.

"Oh, in the usual way. First the mullah reads them something from the Koran, then presents are given to the newly-weds and all their relatives.

[5] Tatar for "bad." [6] "Friends."

They eat and drink *boza,* until finally the horsemanship display begins, and there is always some kind of filthy, tattered creature riding a mangy lame nag playing the buffoon to amuse the company. Later, when it grows dark, what we would call a ball begins in the best room. Some miserable old man strums away on a three-stringed . . . can't remember what they call it . . . something like our balalaika. The girls and young men line up in two rows facing each other, clap their hands and sing. Then one of the girls and a man step into the center and begin to chant verses to each other improvising as they go while the rest pick up the refrain. Pechorin and I occupied the place of honor, and as we sat there the host's younger daughter, a girl of sixteen or so, came up to him and sang to him . . . what should I call it . . . a sort of compliment."

"You don't remember what she sang by any chance?"

"Yes, I think it went something like this: 'Our young horsemen are stalwart and their coats are encrusted with silver, but the young Russian officer is more stalwart still and his epaulettes are of gold. He is like a poplar among the others, yet he shall neither grow nor bloom in our orchard.' Pechorin rose, bowed to her, pressing his hand to his forehead and heart, and asked me to reply to her. Knowing their language well I translated his reply.

"When she walked away I whispered to Grigori Alexandrovich: 'Well, what do you think of her?'

"'Exquisite,' replied he. 'What is her name?' 'Her name is Bela,'[7] I replied.

"And indeed, she was beautiful: tall, slim, and her eyes as black as a chamois looked right into your soul. Pechorin grew pensive and did not take his eyes off her, and she frequently stole a glance at him. But Pechorin was not the only one who admired the pretty princess: from a corner of the room another pair of eyes, fixed and flaming, stared at her. I looked closer and recognized my old acquaintance Kazbich. He was a man you couldn't say was friendly, though there was nothing to show he was hostile towards us. There were a good many suspicions but he was never caught at any trickery. Occasionally he brought rams to us at the fort and sold them cheap, but he never bargained: you had to pay him what he asked; he would never cut a price even if his life depended on it. It was said about him that he would ride out beyond the Kuban with the *abreks,*[8] and to tell the truth, he did look like a brigand: he was short, wiry and broad-shouldered. And clever he was, as clever as the devil! The *beshmet*[9] he wore was always torn and patched, but his weapons were set in silver. As for his horse, it was famous in all Kabarda, and indeed, you couldn't think of a better horse. The horsemen all around had very good reason to envy him, and time and again they tried to steal the animal, but in vain. I can still see that horse as if it were before me now: as black as pitch, with legs like taut violin strings and eyes no worse than Bela's. He was a strong animal too, could gallop fifty versts at a stretch, and as for training, he would follow his master like a dog and even recognized his voice. Kazbich never bothered to tether the animal. A regular brigand horse!

[7] The name means "grief" in Turkish. [8] Caucasian guerrillas.
[9] Short, quilted caftan or loose coat.

"That evening Kazbich was more morose than I had ever seen him, and I noticed that he had a coat of mail under his *beshmet.* 'There must be a reason for the armor,' thought I. 'He is evidently scheming something.'

"It was stuffy indoors, so I stepped out into the fresh air. The night was settling on the hills and the mist was beginning to weave in and out among the gorges.

"It occurred to me to look into the shelter where our horses stood and see whether they were being fed, besides which caution is never amiss. After all, I had a fine horse and a good many Kabardians had cast fond glances at him and said: *'Yakshi tkhe, chok yakshi!'*[10]

"I was picking my way along the fence when suddenly I heard voices; one of the speakers I recognized right away: it was that scapegrace Azamat, our host's son. The other spoke more slowly and quietly. 'I wonder what they're up to,' thought I. 'I hope it's not about my horse.' I dropped down behind the fence and cocked my ears, trying not to miss a word. It was impossible to catch everything, for now and then the singing and the hum of voices from the hut drowned out the conversation I was so interested to hear.

"'That's a fine horse you have,' Azamat was saying. 'Were I the master of my house and the owner of a drove of three hundred mares, I'd give half of them for your horse, Kazbich!'

"'So it's Kazbich,' thought I and remembered the coat of mail.

"'You're right,' Kazbich replied after a momentary silence, 'you won't find another like him in all Kabarda. Once, beyond the Terek it was, I rode with the *abreks* to pick up some Russian horses. We were unlucky though, and had to scatter. Four Cossacks came after me; I could already hear the *gyaurs*[11] shouting behind me, and ahead of me was a thicket. I bent low in the saddle, trusted myself to Allah and for the first time in my life insulted the horse by striking him. Like a bird he flew between the branches; the thorns tore my clothes and the dry karagach twigs lashed my face. The horse leaped over stumps and crashed through the brush chest on. It would have been better for me to slip off him in some glade and take cover in the woods on foot, but I could not bear to part with him so I held on, and the Prophet rewarded me. Some bullets whistled past overhead; I could hear the Cossacks, now dismounted, running along my trail. . . . Suddenly a deep gully opened up in front; my horse hesitated for a moment, and then jumped. But on the other side his hind legs slipped off the sheer edge and he was left holding on by the forelegs. I dropped the reins and slipped into the gully. This saved the horse, who managed to pull himself up. The Cossacks saw all this, but none of them came down into the ravine to look for me; they probably gave me up for dead. Then I heard them going after my horse. My heart bled as I crawled through the thick grass of the gully until I was out of the woods. Now I saw some Cossacks riding out from the thicket into the open and my Karagöz galloping straight at them. With a shout they made a dash for him. They chased him for a long time. One of them almost got a halter around his neck once or twice; I trembled, turned away and began praying. Looking up a few moments later I saw my

[10] "Good horse, very good" (Tatar).

[11] "Infidel dogs," contemptuous Moslem term for unbelievers.

Karagöz flying free as the wind, his tail streaming while the *gyaurs* trailed far behind in the plain on their exhausted horses. I swear by Allah this is the truth! I sat in my gully until far into the night. And what do you think happened, Azamat? Suddenly through the darkness I heard a horse running along the brink of the gully, snorting, neighing and stamping his hoofs; I recognized the voice of my Karagöz, for it was he, my comrade! Since then we have never parted.'

"You could hear the man patting the smooth neck of the horse and addressing him with all kinds of endearments.

"'Had I a drove of a thousand mares,' said Azamat, 'I would give it to you for your Karagöz.'

"'*Yok*,[12] I wouldn't take it,' replied Kazbich indifferently.

"'Listen, Kazbich,' Azamat coaxed him. 'You are a good man and a brave *jigit*;[13] my father fears the Russians and does not let me go into the mountains. Give me your horse and I will do anything you want, I'll steal for you my father's best musket or saber, whatever you wish—and his saber is a real *gurda*,[14] lay the blade against your hand and it will cut deep into the flesh; mail like yours won't stop it.'

"Kazbich was silent.

"'When I first saw your horse,' Azamat went on, 'prancing under you, his nostrils dilated and sparks flying under his hoofs, something strange happened in my soul, and I lost interest in everything. I have disdained my father's best horses, ashamed to be seen riding them, and I have been sick at heart. In my misery I have spent days on end sitting on a crag, thinking of nothing but your fleet-footed Karagöz with his proud stride and sleek back as straight as an arrow, his blazing eyes looking straight into mine as if he wanted to speak to me. I shall die, Kazbich, if you will not sell him to me,' said Azamat in a trembling voice.

"I thought I heard him sob; and I must tell you that Azamat was a most stubborn lad and even when he was younger nothing could ever make him cry.

"In reply to his tears I heard something like a laugh.

"'Listen!' said Azamat his voice firm now. 'You see I am ready to do anything. I could steal my sister for you if you want. How she can dance and sing! And her gold embroidery is something wonderful! The Turkish Padishah himself never had a wife like her. If you want her, wait for me tomorrow night in the gorge where the stream flows; I shall go by with her on the way to the next village—and she'll be yours. Isn't Bela worth your steed?'

"For a long, long time Kazbich was silent. At last instead of replying, he began softly singing an old song:[15]

> Ours are the fairest of maidens that be:
> Eyes like the stars, by their light do I see.
> Sweet flits the time when we cosset a maid,
> Sweeter's the freedom of any young blade.

[12] "No." [13] "Warrior." [14] A type of fine saber.

[15] "I apologize to my readers for having put Kazbich's song, which of course was told me in prose, into verse; but habit is second nature." (Lermontov's note.)

Wives by the dozen are purchased with gold,
A mettlesome steed is worth riches untold;
Swift o'er the plains like a whirlwind he flies,
Never betrays you, and never tells lies.

"In vain Azamat pleaded with him; he tried tears, flattery, and cajolery, until finally Kazbich lost patience with him:

"'Get away with you, boy! Are you mad? You could never ride my horse! He'd throw you after the first three paces and you'd smash your head against a rock.'

"'Me?' Azamat screamed in a fury, and his child's dagger rang against the coat of mail. A strong arm flung him back and he fell against the wattle fence[16] so violently that it shook. 'Now the fun will begin,' thought I and dashed into the stable, bridled our horses and led them to the yard at the back. Two minutes later a terrific uproar broke out in the hut. This is what happened: Azamat ran into the hut in a torn *beshmet* shouting that Kazbich had tried to kill him. Everybody rushed out and went for their rifles—and the fun was on! There was screaming and shouting and shots were fired, but Kazbich was already on his horse spinning around like a demon in the midst of the crowd and warding off assailants with his saber. 'Bad business to get mixed up in this,' said I to Grigori Alexandrovich as I caught him by the arm. 'Hadn't we better clear out as fast as we can?'

"'Let's wait a bit and see how it ends.'

"'It's sure to end badly; that's what always happens with these Asiatics, as soon as they have their fill of drink they go slashing each other.' We mounted and rode home."

"What happened to Kazbich?" I asked impatiently.

"What can happen to these people?" replied the captain, finishing his glass of tea. "He got away, of course."

"Not even wounded, was he?" I asked.

"The Lord only knows. They're tough, the rogues! I have seen some of them in engagements; a man may be cut up into ribbons with bayonets and still he continues brandishing his saber." After a brief silence the captain went on, stamping his foot:

"There is one thing I'll never forgive myself for. When we got back to the fort, some devil prompted me to tell Grigori Alexandrovich what I had overheard behind the fence. He laughed—the fox—though he was already cooking up a scheme."

"What was it? I should like to hear it."

"I suppose I'll have to tell you. Since I began telling the story, I might as well finish.

"Some four days later Azamat rode up to the fort. As usual, he went in to see Grigori Alexandrovich, who always had some delicacies for him. I was there too. The talk turned to horses, and Pechorin began to praise Kazbich's horse; as spirited and beautiful as a chamois the steed was, and as Pechorin put it, there simply was no other horse like it in all the world.

"The Tatar boy's eyes lit up, but Pechorin pretended not to notice it; I

[16] A fence made of poles and interwoven branches.

tried to change the subject, but at once he brought it back to Kazbich's horse. This happened each time Azamat came. About three weeks later I noticed that Azamat was growing pale and wasting away as they do from love in novels. What was it all about?

"You see, I got the whole story later. Grigori Alexandrovich egged him on to a point when the lad was simply desperate. Finally he put it point-blank: 'I can see, Azamat, that you want that horse very badly. Yet you have as little chance of getting it as of seeing the back of your own head. Now tell me what would you give if someone gave it to you?'

"'Anything he asks,' replied Azamat.

"'In that case I'll get the horse for you, but on one condition. . . . Swear you will carry it out?'

"'I swear. . . . And you must swear too!'

"'Good! I swear you'll get the horse, only you have to give me your sister Bela in exchange. Karagöz shall be her *kalym*[17]! I hope the bargain suits you.'

"Azamat was silent.

"'You don't want to? As you wish. I thought you were a man, but I see you're still a child: you're too young to ride in the saddle.'

"Azamat flared up. 'What about my father?' he asked.

"'Doesn't he ever go anywhere?'

"'That's true, he does. . . .'

"'So you agree?'

"'I agree,' whispered Azamat, pale as death itself. 'When?'

"'The next time Kazbich comes here; he has promised to bring a dozen sheep. The rest is my business. And you take care of your end of the bargain, Azamat!'"

"So they arranged the whole business, and I must say it was a bad business indeed. Later I said so to Pechorin, but he only replied that the primitive Cherkess girl ought to be happy to have such a fine husband as himself, for, after all, he would be her husband according to the local custom, and that Kazbich was a brigand who should be punished anyway. Judge for yourself, what could I say against this? But at the time I knew nothing about the conspiracy. So one day Kazbich came asking whether we wanted sheep and honey, and I told him to bring some the day after. 'Azamat,' Grigori Alexandrovich said to the lad, 'tomorrow Karagöz will be in my hands. If Bela is not here tonight you will not see the horse. . . .'

"'Good!' said Azamat and galloped back to his village. In the evening Grigori Alexandrovich armed himself and rode out of the fort. How they managed everything, I don't know—but at night they both returned and the sentry saw a woman lying across Azamat's saddle with hands and feet tied and head wrapped in a veil."

"And the horse?" I asked the captain.

"Just a moment, just a moment. Early the next morning Kazbich came, driving along the dozen sheep he wanted to sell. Tying his horse to a fence, he came to see me and I regaled him with tea, for, scoundrel though he was, he nevertheless was a *kunak* of mine.

[17] Property given by a man for his bride, according to tribal custom.

"We began to chat about this and that. Suddenly I saw Kazbich start; his face twisted and he dashed for the window, but it unfortunately opened to the backyard. 'What happened?' I asked.

"'My horse . . . horse!' he said, shaking all over.

"And true enough, I heard the beat of hoofs. 'Some Cossack must have arrived.'

"'No! *Urus yaman, yaman,*'[18] he cried and dashed out like a wild panther. In two strides he was in the courtyard; at the gates of the fort a sentry barred his way with a musket, but he leaped over the weapon and began running down the road. In the distance a cloud of dust whirled—it was Azamat urging on the spirited Karagöz. Kazbich drew his gun from its holster and fired as he ran. For a minute he stood motionless until he was certain he had missed; then he screamed, dashed the gun to pieces against the stones, and rolled on the ground crying like a baby. . . . People from the fort gathered around him—but he did not see anyone, and after standing about for a while they all went back. I had the money for the sheep placed next to him, but he did not touch it; he only lay there face down like a corpse. Would you believe it, he lay like that all through the night? Only the next morning he returned to the fort to ask whether anyone could tell him who the thief was. A sentry who had seen Azamat untie the horse and gallop off did not think it necessary to conceal the fact. When Kazbich heard the name his eyes flashed and he set out for the village where Azamat's father lived."

"What did the father do?"

"The whole trouble was that Kazbich did not find him; he had gone off somewhere for six days or so. Had he not done so could Azamat have carried off his sister?

"The father returned to find both daughter and son gone. The lad was a wily one; he knew very well that his head wouldn't be worth anything if he got caught. So he has been missing ever since; most likely he joined some *abrek* band and perhaps ended his mad career beyond the Terek, or maybe the Kuban. And that's no more than he deserved!

"I must admit that it wasn't easy for me either. As soon as I learned that the Cherkess girl was at Grigori Alexandrovich's, I put on my epaulettes and strapped on my sword and went to see him.

"He was lying on the bed in the first room, one hand under his head and the other holding a pipe that had gone out. The door leading to the next room was locked, and there was no key in the lock; all this I noticed at once. I coughed and stamped my heels on the threshold, but he pretended not to hear.

"'Ensign! Sir!' I said as severely as I could. 'Don't you realize that I've come to see you?'

"'Ah, how do you do, Maxim Maximych. Have a pipe,' he replied without getting up.

"'I beg your pardon! I am no Maxim Maximych: I am a captain to you!'

"'Oh, it's all the same. Would you care to have some tea? If you only knew what a load I've got on my mind!'

[18] "Russian bad, bad!"

"'I know everything,' I replied, walking up to the bed.

"'That's all the better, then. I am in no mood to go over it again.'

"'Ensign, you have committed an offense for which I too may have to answer. . . .'

"'Well, why not? Have we not always shared everything equally?'

"'This is no time to joke. Will you surrender your sword?'

"Mitka brought the sword. Having thus done my duty, I sat down on the bed and said: 'Listen here, Grigori Alexandrovich, you'd best admit that it's wrong.'

"'What's wrong?'

"'To have kidnapped Bela. What a scoundrel that Azamat is! Come, now, admit it,' I said to him.

"'Why should I? She happens to please me.'

"What would you have me reply to that? I did not know what to do. Nevertheless after a moment's silence I told him he would have to give the girl back if her father insisted.

"'I don't see why I should!'

"'But what if he finds out that she is here?"

"'How will he?'

"Again I was in a blind alley.

"'Listen, Maxim Maximych,' said Pechorin, rising, 'you're a good soul—if we give the girl to that barbarian he'll either kill her or sell her. What has been done cannot be undone, and it won't do to spoil things by being overzealous. You keep my sword, but leave her with me. . . .'

"'Supposing you let me see her,' said I.

"'She's behind that door; I myself have been trying in vain to see her. She sits there in a corner all huddled up in her shawl and will neither speak nor look at you; she's as timid as a gazelle. I hired the *dukhan* keeper's wife who speaks Tatar to look after her and get her accustomed to the idea that she is mine—for she will never belong to anyone but myself,' he added, striking the table with his fist.

"I reconciled myself to this too. . . . What would you have had me do? There are people who always get their own way."

"What happened in the end?" I asked Maxim Maximych. "Did he actually win her over or did she pine away in captivity longing for her native village?"

"Now why should she have longed for her native village? She could see the very same mountains from the fort as she had seen from the village, and that's all these barbarians want. Moreover, Grigori Alexandrovich gave her some present every day. At first she proudly tossed the gifts aside without a word, whereupon they became the property of the *dukhan* keeper's wife and stimulated her eloquence. Ah, gifts! What wouldn't a woman do for a bit of colored rag! But I digress. . . . Grigori Alexandrovich strove long and hard to win her; in the meantime he learned to speak Tatar and she began to understand our language. Little by little she learned to look at him, at first askance, but she was always melancholy and I too could not help feeling sad when I heard her from the next room singing her native songs in a low voice. I shall never forget a scene I once witnessed while passing the window: Bela was seated on a bench, her head bowed, and

Grigori Alexandrovich stood before her. 'Listen, my peri,'[19] he was saying, 'don't you realize that sooner or later you must be mine—why then do you torment me so? Or perhaps you love some Chechen? If you do, I will let you go home at once.' She shuddered barely perceptibly and shook her head. 'Or,' he went on, 'am I altogether hateful to you?' She sighed. 'Perhaps your faith forbids your loving me?' She grew pale but did not say a word. 'Believe me, there is only one Allah for all people, and if he permits me to love you, why should he forbid you to return my love?' She looked him straight in the face as if struck by his new thought; her eyes betrayed suspicion and sought reassurance. And what eyes she had! They shone like two coals.

"'Listen to me, sweet, kind Bela!' Pechorin continued. 'You can see how I love you. I am ready to do anything to cheer you; I want you to be happy, and if you keep on grieving I shall die. Tell me, you will be more cheerful?' She thought for a moment, her black eyes searching his face, then smiled tenderly and nodded in agreement. He took her hand and began to persuade her to kiss him; but she resisted weakly and repeated over and over again: 'Please, please, no, no.' He became persistent; she trembled and began to sob. 'I am your captive, your slave,' she said, 'and of course you can force me.' And again there were tears.

"Grigori Alexandrovich struck his forehead with his fist and ran into the next room. I went in to him; he was gloomily pacing up and down with arms folded. 'What now, old chap?' I asked him. 'She's not a woman, but a she-devil!' he replied. 'But I give you my word that she will be mine!' I shook my head. 'Do you want to wager?' he said. 'I'll give her a week.' 'Done!' We shook on it and parted.

"The next day he sent a messenger to Kizlyar to make diverse purchases and there was no end to the array of various kinds of Persian cloth that was brought back.

"'What do you think, Maxim Maximych,' he said as he showed me the gifts, 'will an Asiatic beauty be able to resist a battery like this?' 'You don't know Cherkess women,' I replied. 'They're nothing like Georgian or Transcaucasian Tatar women—nothing like them. They have their own rules of conduct; different upbringing, you know.' Grigori Alexandrovich smiled and began whistling a march air.

"It turned out that I was right: the gifts did only half the trick; she became more amiable and confiding—but nothing more. So he decided to play his last card. One morning he ordered his horse saddled, dressed in Cherkess fashion, armed himself, and went in to her. 'Bela,' he said, 'you know how I love you. I decided to carry you off, believing that when you came to know me you would love me too. But I made a mistake; so, farewell, I leave you the mistress of everything I have, and if you wish, you can return to your father—you are free, I have wronged you and must be punished. Farewell, I shall ride away, where, I don't know. Perhaps it will not be long before I am cut down by a bullet or a saber blow; when that happens, remember me and try to forgive me.' He turned away and extended his hand to her in parting. She did not take the hand, nor did she say a word. Standing behind the door I saw her through the crack, and I

[19] Fairy or nymph (Persian folklore).

was sorry for her—such a deathly pallor had spread over her pretty little face. Hearing no reply, Pechorin took several steps towards the door. He was trembling, and do you know, I quite believe he was capable of actually doing what he threatened. The Lord knows that's the kind of man he was. But barely had he touched the door when she sprang up, sobbing and threw her arms around his neck. Believe me, I also wept standing there behind the door, that is, I didn't exactly weep, but—well, anyway it was silly."

The captain fell silent.

"I might as well confess," he said after a while, tugging at his moustache, "I was annoyed because no woman had ever loved me like that."

"How long did their happiness last?" I asked.

"Well, she admitted that Pechorin had often appeared in her dreams since the day she first saw him and that no other man had ever made such an impression on her. Yes, they were happy!"

"How boring!" I exclaimed involuntarily. Indeed, I was expecting a tragic end and it was a shock to see my hopes collapse so suddenly. "Don't tell me the father did not guess she was with you in the fort."

"I believe he did suspect. A few days later, however, we heard that the old man had been killed. This is how it happened. . . ."

My interest was again aroused.

"I must tell you that Kazbich got the idea that Azamat had stolen the horse with his father's consent, at least I think so. So he lay in ambush one day some three versts beyond the village when the old man was returning from his futile search for his daughter. The old man had left his liegemen lagging behind and was plunged deep in thought as he rode slowly down the road through the deepening twilight, when Kazbich suddenly sprang catlike from behind a bush, leaped behind him on the horse, cut him down with a blow of his dagger and seized the reins. Some of the liegemen saw it all from a hill, but though they set out in pursuit they could not overtake Kazbich."

"So he compensated himself for the loss of his horse and took revenge as well," I said in order to draw an opinion out of my companion.

"Of course, he was absolutely right according to their lights," said the captain.

I was struck by the ability of the Russian to reconcile himself to the customs of the people among whom he happens to live. I do not know whether this mental quality is a virtue or a vice, but it does reveal a remarkable flexibility and that sober common sense which forgives evil wherever it feels it to be necessary, or impossible to eradicate.

Meanwhile we had finished our tea. Outside the horses had been harnessed long since and were now standing shivering in the snow; the paling moon in the western sky was about to immerse itself in the black clouds that trailed like tattered bits of a rent curtain from the mountain peaks in the distance. We stepped out into the open. Contrary to the prediction of my companion, the weather had cleared and promised a calm morning. The stars, intertwined in garlands of a fantastic pattern in the far heavens, went out one after another as the pale glimmer of the east spread out over the dark lilac sky, gradually casting its glow on the steep mountainsides blanketed by virginal snow. To right and left yawned gloomy, mysterious abysses, and the mist, coiling and twisting like a snake, crawled into them along the cracks and crevices of the cliffs as if in apprehension of coming day.

There was a great peace in the heavens and on earth as there is in the hearts of men at morning prayers. Only now and then the cold east wind came in gusts ruffling the hoary manes of the horses. We set out, the five lean nags hauling our carriages with difficulty along the tortuous road up Mount Goud. We walked behind, setting stones under the wheels when the horses could pull no longer; it seemed as if the road must lead straight to heaven, for it rose higher and higher as far as the eye could see and finally was lost in the cloud that had been reposing on the mountain summit since the day before like a vulture awaiting its prey. The snow crunched underfoot; the air grew so rare that it was painful to breathe; I continually felt the blood rushing to my head, yet a feeling of elation coursed through my being and somehow it felt good to be so much above the world—a childish feeling, I admit, but as we drift farther away from the conventions of society and draw closer to nature we willy-nilly become children again: the soul is unburdened of whatever it has acquired and it becomes what it once was and what it will surely be again. Anyone who has had occasion as I have to roam in the deserted mountains, feasting his eyes upon their fantastic shapes and eagerly inhaling the invigorating air of the gorges, will understand my urge to describe, to portray, to paint these magic canvases. At last we reached the summit of Mount Goud, and paused to look around us: a gray cloud rested on the mountain top and its cold breath held the threat of an imminent blizzard; but the east was so clear and golden that we, that is, the captain and I, promptly forgot about it. . . . Yes, the captain too: for simple hearts feel the beauty and majesty of nature a hundred times more keenly than do we, rapturous tellers of stories spoken or written.

"You are no doubt accustomed to these magnificent scenes," I said to him.

"Yes, sir, you can get accustomed even to the whining of bullets, I mean, accustomed to concealing the involuntary quickening of your pulse."

"On the contrary, I have been told that to some old soldiers it is sweet music."

"Yes, it is sweet too, if you please; but only because it makes the heart beat faster. Look," he added, pointing to the east, "what heavenly country!"

Indeed, it was a panorama I can hardly hope to see again: below us lay Koishaur Valley, the Aragva and another river, tracing their course across it like two silver threads; a bluish mist crept over it, seeking refuge in the nearest nooks from the warm rays of the morning; to the right and to the left the mountain ridges, one higher than the other, criss-crossed and stretched out into the distance, covered with snow and brush. Mountains as far as the eye could see, but no two crags alike—and all this snow burned with a rosy glitter so gay and so vivid that one would fain have stayed there for ever. The sun barely showed from behind a dark-blue mountain which only the experienced eye could distinguish from a storm-cloud, but above it stretched a crimson belt to which my comrade now drew my attention. "I told you," he exclaimed, "there's bad weather ahead; we'll have to hurry or it may catch us on Krestovaya. Look lively, there!" he shouted to the coachmen.

Chains were passed through the wheels for brakes to prevent them from getting out of control. Leading the horses by their bridles we began the descent. To the right of us was a cliff, and to the left an abyss so deep that an Ossetian village at the bottom looked like a swallow's nest; I shuddered at the thought that a dozen times a year some courier rides through the dark night along this road too narrow for two carts to pass, without alighting from his jolting carriage. One of our drivers was a Russian peasant from Yaroslavl, the other an Ossetian. The Ossetian took the leading horse by the bridle after unhitching the first pair in good time and taking every other possible precaution, but our heedless Russian did not even bother to get down from the box. When I suggested that he might have shown some concern if only for my portmanteau, which I had no desire to go down into the abyss to recover, he replied: "Don't worry, sir! With God's help we'll get there just as well as they. This is not the first time we've done it." And he was right; true, we might not have got through safely, yet we did. And if all men gave the matter more thought they would realize that life is not worth worrying over too much. . . .

Perhaps you wish to hear the story of Bela to the end? Firstly, however, I am not writing a novel but simply travel notes, and hence I cannot make the captain resume his story sooner than he actually did. So you will have to wait, or, if you wish to do so, skip a few pages; only I do not advise you to, for the crossing of Mount Krestovaya (or le Mont St. Christophe as the learned Gamba calls it[20]) is worthy of your interest. And so we descended from Mount Goud to Chertova Valley. This is a romantic name for you. Perhaps you already visualize the den of the Evil Spirit among the inaccessible crags—but if you do, you are mistaken: Chertova Valley derives its name from the word *"cherta"* and not *"chort,"* for the boundary of Georgia once passed here.[21] The valley was buried under snow-drifts which gave the scene a rather strong resemblance to Saratov, Tambov and other spots *dear to us*[22] in our mother country.

"There's Krestovaya," said the captain as we came down to Chertova Valley, pointing to a hill shrouded by snow. On the summit the black outline of a stone cross was visible, and past it ran a barely discernible road which was used only when the road along the mountainside was snow-bound. Our drivers said that there were no snow-slips yet and in order to spare the horses they took us the roundabout way. Around a turn in the road we came upon five Ossetians who offered us their services, and seizing hold of the wheels and shouting, they began to help our carriage along. The road was dangerous indeed. To our right, masses of snow hung overhead ready, it seemed, to crash down into the gorge with the first blast of wind. Some sections of the narrow road were covered with snow, which here and there

[20] One of the earliest Europeans to describe the Caucasus was the French diplomat Jacques François Gamba, who, in his *Journey in Russia . . . and the Caucasus* (1826), mistranslated Mount Krestovaya as "Mount St. Christopher" instead of "Mount of the Cross."

[21] *"cherta" and not "chort." Cherta* means "line" and *chort* means "devil."

[22] Ironic; Saratov and Tambov were notoriously dull and provincial towns in Central Russia.

gave way underfoot; others had been turned to ice under the action of the sun's rays and night frosts, so that we made headway with difficulty. The horses kept on slipping, and to the left of us yawned a deep fissure with a turbulent stream at the bottom that now slipped out of sight under a crust of ice, now plunged in frothy fury amidst black boulders. It took us all of two hours to skirt Mount Krestovaya—two hours to negotiate two versts. In the meantime the clouds came lower and it began to hail and snow. The wind bursting into the gorges howled and whistled like Solovey the Brigand,[23] and soon the stone cross was blotted out by the mist which was coming in waves from the east, each wave thicker than the other. Incidentally, there is a queer but generally accepted legend about this cross which claims it was raised by Emperor Peter I when he travelled through the Caucasus.[24] Yet, in the first place, Peter was only in Daghestan, and, secondly, an inscription in big letters on the cross announced it had been put up on the orders of General Yermolov, in 1824, to be exact. Despite the inscription, the legend had taken such firm root that one is at a loss to know what to believe, all the more so since we are not accustomed to put our faith in inscriptions.

We had another five versts to descend along the ice-coated rocky ledges and through soft snow before reaching the station at Kobi. The horses were exhausted and we thoroughly chilled, while the blizzard blew harder and harder, much like our native, northern snow-storms, except that its wild refrain was sadder and more mournful. "You too, my exile," thought I, "are mourning your wide, boundless steppes where there was space to spread out your icy wings, whilst here you are choked and hemmed in like the eagle who beats against the bars of his iron cage."

"Looks bad!" the captain was saying. "Nothing but mist and snow. Watch out or we'll find ourselves dropping into a crevice or getting stuck in some wretched hole, and the Baidara down there will probably be running too high to cross. That's Asia for you! The rivers are as unreliable as the people."

The drivers shouted and cursed as they whipped the snorting, balking horses which refused to take another step in spite of the persuasion of the whip. "Your Honor," one of the drivers finally said, "we can't reach Kobi today. Had we not better turn to the left while there is still time? Over on that slope there are some huts, I believe. Travellers always halt there in bad weather." Then he added, pointing to an Ossetian: "They say they will guide us there if you give them some money for vodka."

"I know it, brother, I know without you telling me!" said the captain. "These rogues! They'll do anything for a tip."

"All the same you have to admit that we'd be worse off without them," said I.

"Maybe, maybe," he muttered, "but I know these guides! They can tell by instinct when to take advantage of you; as if you couldn't find your way without them."

So we turned to the left and somehow after a good deal of trouble made

[23] In Russian folklore, Solovey was a highwayman who could whistle powerfully enough to knock a man down.

[24] Czar Peter I toured the Caucasus in 1722.

our way to the scanty refuge consisting of two huts built of slabs and stones and surrounded by a wall of the same material. The tattered inhabitants gave us a cordial welcome. Later I found out that the government pays and feeds them on condition that they take in wayfarers who are caught by the storm.

"It's all for the best," said I, taking a seat by the fire. "Now you will be able to tell me the rest of the story about Bela; I am sure that wasn't the end of it."

"What makes you so sure?" replied the captain, with a sly smile and a twinkle in his eye.

"Because things don't happen like that. Anything that begins so strangely must end in the same way."

"Well, you guessed right. . . ."

"Glad to hear it."

"It's all very well for you to be glad, but for me it is really sad to recall. She was a fine girl, Bela was! I grew as fond of her in the end as if she were my own daughter, and she loved me too. I ought to tell you that I have no family; I haven't heard about my father or mother for some twelve years now, and it didn't occur to me to get myself a wife earlier—and now, you must admit, it would no longer be seemly. So I was happy to have found someone to pet. She would sing to us or dance the Lezghinka. . . . And how she danced! I've seen our provincial fine ladies and once some twenty years ago I was at the Nobles' Club in Moscow,[25] but none of them could hold a candle to her. Grigori Alexandrovich dressed her up like a doll, petted and fondled her, and she grew so lovely that it was amazing. The tan disappeared from her face and arms and her cheeks grew rosy. . . . How gay she was and how she used to tease me, the little vixen. . . . May God forgive her!"

"What happened when you told her about her father's death?"

"We kept it from her for a long time, until she became accustomed to her new position. And when she was told, she cried for a couple of days and then forgot about it.

"For about four months everything went splendidly. Grigori Alexandrovich, I must have already told you, had a passion for hunting. Some irresistible force used to draw him to the forest to stalk wild boar or goats, and now he had scarcely ventured beyond the ramparts. Then I noticed he was growing pensive again; he would pace up and down the room with his arms folded behind his back. One day without saying a word to anyone he took his gun and went out, and was lost for the whole morning; that happened once, twice, and then more and more frequently. Things are going badly, I thought, something must have come between them!

"One morning when I dropped in to see them I found Bela sitting on the bed wearing a black silk *beshmet,* so pale and sad that I was really alarmed.

"'Where's Pechorin?' I asked.

"'Hunting.'

"'When did he leave? Today?'

[25] Lermontov refers frequently to this luxurious Moscow club, founded in 1810.

"She did not reply, it seemed difficult for her to speak.

"'No, yesterday,' she finally said with a deep sigh.

"'I hope nothing has happened to him.'

"'All day yesterday I thought and thought,' she said, her eyes full of tears, 'and imagined all kinds of terrible things. First I thought a wild boar had injured him, then that the Chechen had carried him off to the mountains. . . . And now it already seems to me that he doesn't love me.'

"'Truly, my dear, you couldn't have imagined anything worse!'

"She burst into tears, and then proudly raised her head, dried her eyes, and continued:

"'If he doesn't love me, what prevents him from sending me home? I am not forcing myself on him. And if this goes on I shall leave myself; I am not his slave, I am a prince's daughter!'

"I began reasoning with her. 'Listen, Bela, he can't sit here all the time as if tied to your apron strings. He's a young man and likes to hunt. He'll go and he'll come back, and if you are going to mope he'll only get tired of you the sooner.'

"'You are right,' she replied. 'I shall be gay.' Laughing, she seized her tambourine and began to sing and dance for me. But very soon she threw herself on the bed again and hid her face in her hands.

"What was I to do with her? You see, I had never had dealings with women. I racked my brains for some way to comfort her but could not think of anything. For a time we both were silent. A most unpleasant situation, I assure you!

"At length I said: 'Would you like to go for a walk with me on the rampart? The weather's fine.' It was September, and the day was really wonderful, sunny but not too hot, the mountains as clearly visible as if laid out on a platter. We went out, and in silence walked up and down the breastwork. After a while she sat down on the turf, and I sat next to her. It's really funny to recall how I fussed over her like a nursemaid.

"Our fort was situated on an elevation, and the view from the parapet was excellent: on one side was a wide open space intersected by gullies and ending in a forest that stretched all the way to the top of the mountain ridge, and here and there on this expanse you could see the smoke of villages and droves of grazing horses; on the other side flowed a small rivulet bordered by dense brush that covered the flinty hills merging with the main chain of the Caucasus. We were sitting in a corner of a bastion whence we had a perfect view of either side. As I scanned the landscape, a man riding a gray horse emerged from the woods and came closer and closer, until he finally stopped on the far side of the rivulet some hundred sagenes[26] or so from where we were and began spinning around on his horse like mad. What the devil was that?

"'You've younger eyes than I, Bela, see if you can make out that horseman,' said I. 'I wonder whom he is honoring with a visit.'

"She looked and cried out: 'It's Kazbich!'

"'Ah, the brigand! Has he come to mock at us?' Now I could see it was Kazbich: the same swarthy features, and as tattered and dirty as ever. 'That's my father's horse,' Bela said, seizing my arm; she trembled like a

[26] A "sagene" was about two and a half yards.

leaf and her eyes flashed. 'Aha, my little one,' thought I, 'brigand blood tells in you too.'

"'Come here,' I called to a sentry, 'take aim and knock that fellow off for me and you'll get a ruble in silver.' 'Yes, Your Honor, only he doesn't stay still. . . .' 'Tell him to,' said I laughing. 'Hey, there!' shouted the sentry waving his arm, 'wait a minute, will you, stop spinning like a top!' Kazbich actually paused to listen, probably thinking we wanted to parley, the insolent beggar! My grenadier took aim . . . bang! . . and missed, for as soon as the powder flashed in the pan, Kazbich gave a jab to the horse making it leap aside. He stood up in his stirrups, shouted something in his own language, shook his whip menacingly in the air—and in a flash was gone.

"'You ought to be ashamed of yourself!' I said to the sentry.

"'Your Honor! He's gone off to die,' he replied. 'Such a cussed lot they are you can't kill them with one shot.'

"A quarter of an hour later Pechorin returned from the chase. Bela ran to meet him and threw her arms around his neck, and not a single complaint, not a single reproach for his long absence did I hear. . . . Even I had lost patience with him. 'Sir,' said I, 'Kazbich was on the other side of the river just now and we fired at him; you could easily have run into him too. These mountaineers are vengeful people, and do you think he does not suspect you helped Azamat? I'll wager he saw Bela here. And I happen to know that a year ago he was very much attracted by her—told me so himself in fact. Had he had any hope of raising a substantial *kalym* he surely would have asked for her in marriage. . . .' Pechorin was grave now. 'Yes,' he said, 'we have to be more careful. . . . Bela, after today you must not go out on the rampart any more.'

"That evening I had a long talk with him; it grieved me that he had changed toward the poor girl, for besides being out hunting half the time, he began to treat her coldly, rarely showing her any affection. She began to waste away visibly, her face grew drawn, and her big eyes lost their luster. Whenever I asked her, 'Why are you sighing, Bela? Are you sad?' she would reply, 'No.' 'Do you want anything?' 'No!' 'Are you grieving for your kinsfolk?' 'I have no kinsfolk.' For days on end you couldn't get more than 'yes' or 'no' out of her.

"I resolved to have a talk with him about this. 'Listen, Maxim Maximych,' he replied, 'I have an unfortunate character; whether it is my upbringing that made me like that or God who created me so, I do not know. I know only that if I cause unhappiness to others I myself am no less unhappy. I realize this is poor consolation for them—but the fact remains that it is so. In my early youth after leaving the guardianship of my parents, I plunged into all the pleasures money could buy, and naturally these pleasures grew distasteful to me. Then I went into society, but soon enough grew tired of it; I fell in love with beautiful society women and was loved by them, but their love only spurred on my ambition and vanity while my heart remained desolate. . . . I began to read and to study, but wearied of learning too; I saw that neither fame nor happiness depended on it in the slightest, for the happiest people were the ignorant and fame was a matter of luck, to achieve which you only had to be shrewd. And I grew bored. . . . Soon I was transferred to the Caucasus; this was the happiest time of my life. I hoped that boredom would not survive under Chechen bullets—but in vain; in a month I had become so accustomed to their whine and the proximity of death that, to tell the truth, the mosquitoes bothered me more, and life became more boring than ever because I had now lost practically my last hope. When I saw Bela at my home, when I held her on my lap and first kissed her raven locks, I foolishly thought she was an angel sent down to me by a compassionate Providence. . . . Again I erred: the love of a barbarian girl is little better than that of a well-born lady; the ignorance and simplicity of the one are as boring as the coquetry of the other. I still love her, if you wish, I am grateful to her for a few rather blissful moments, I am ready to give my life for her, but I am bored with her. I don't know whether I am a fool or a scoundrel; but the fact is that I am to be pitied as much, if not more than she. My soul has been warped by the world, my mind is restless, my heart insatiable; nothing suffices me: I grow accustomed to sorrow as readily as to joy, and my life becomes emptier from day to day. Only one expedient is left for me, and that is to travel. As soon as possible I shall set out—not for Europe, God forbid—but for America, Arabia, India—and perhaps I shall die somewhere on the road! At least I am sure that with the help of storms and bad roads this last resort will not soon cease to be a consolation.' He talked long in this vein and his words seared themselves in my memory for it was the first time I had heard such talk from a man of twenty-five, and, I hope to God, the last. Amazing! You probably were in the capital recently; perhaps you can tell me," the captain went on, addressing me, "whether the young people there are all like that?"

I replied that there are many who say the same, and that most likely some of them are speaking the truth; that, on the whole, disillusionment, having begun like all vogues in the upper strata of society, had descended to the lower which wear it threadbare, and that now those who are really bored the most endeavor to conceal that misfortune as if it were a vice. The captain did not understand these subtleties, and he shook his head and smiled slyly:

"It was the French, I suppose, who made boredom fashionable?"

"No, the English."

"Ah, so that's it!" he replied. "Of course, they've always been inveterate drunkards!"

Involuntarily I recalled one Moscow lady who claimed Byron was nothing more than a drunkard. The captain's remark, however, was more excusable, for in order to abstain from drink he naturally tried to reassure himself that all misfortunes in the world are caused by intemperance.

"Kazbich did not come again," he went on with his story. "Still, for some unknown reason, I could not get rid of the idea that his visit had not been purposeless and that he was scheming something evil.

"Once Pechorin persuaded me to go hunting wild boar with him. I tried to resist, for what was a wild boar to me, but finally he did make me go with him. We set out early in the morning, taking five soldiers with us. Until ten o'clock we poked about the reeds and the woods without seeing a single animal. 'What do you say to turning back?' said I. 'What's the use of being stubborn? You can see for yourself the day has turned out to be unlucky.' But Grigori Alexandrovich did not want to return empty-handed in spite of the heat and fatigue. . . . That's how he was; if he set his mind on something he had to get it; his mother must have spoiled him as a child. . . . At last around noon we came upon a cussed boar! . . bang! . . bang! . . but no: the beast slipped into the reeds . . . yes, it was indeed our unlucky day. After a bit of a rest we turned for home.

"We rode side by side, in silence, reins hanging loose, and had almost reached the fort, though we could not yet see it for the brush, when a shot rang out. We looked at each other, and the same suspicion flashed through our minds. Galloping in the direction of the sound, we saw a group of soldiers huddled together on the rampart, pointing to the field where a horseman was careering into the distance at breakneck speed with something white across his saddle, Grigori Alexandrovich yelled not a whit worse than any Chechen, drew his gun from its holster and dashed in pursuit, and I after him.

"Luckily, because of our poor hunting luck, our horses were quite fresh; they strained under the saddle, and with every moment we gained on our quarry. Finally I recognized Kazbich, though I could not make out what he was holding in front of him. I drew abreast of Pechorin and shouted to him: 'It's Kazbich!' He looked at me, nodded and struck his horse with the crop.

"At last we were within gunshot of Kazbich. Whether his horse was exhausted or whether it was worse than ours I do not know, but he was unable to get much speed out of the animal in spite of his efforts to urge it on. I am sure he was thinking of his Karagöz then. . . .

"I looked up and saw Pechorin aiming. 'Don't shoot!' I yelled. 'Save the charge, we'll catch up with him soon enough.' That's youth for you: always foolhardy at the wrong time. . . . But the shot rang out and the bullet wounded the horse in a hind leg; the animal made another dozen leaps before it stumbled and fell on its knees. Kazbich sprang from the saddle, and now we saw he was holding a woman bound in a veil in his arms. It was Bela . . . poor Bela! He shouted something to us in his own language and raised his dagger over her. . . . There was no time to waste and I fired at random. I must have hit him in the shoulder, for his arm suddenly dropped. When the smoke dispersed there was the wounded horse lying on the ground and Bela next to it, while Kazbich, who had thrown away his gun, was scrambling up a cliff through the underbrush like a cat. I wanted to pick him off but my gun was unloaded now. We slipped out of the saddle and ran toward Bela. The poor girl lay motionless, blood streaming from her wound. The villain! Had he struck her in the heart, it all would have been over in a moment, but to stab her in the back in the foulest way! She was unconscious. We tore the veil into strips and bandaged the wound as tightly as we could. In vain Pechorin kissed her cold lips; nothing could bring her back to consciousness.

"Pechorin mounted his horse and I raised her up from the ground, somehow managing to place her in front of him in the saddle. He put his arm around her and we started back. After several minutes of silence, Grigori Alexandrovich spoke: 'Listen, Maxim Maximych, we'll never get her home alive at this pace.' 'You're right,' I said, and we spurred the horses to full gallop. At the fort gates a crowd was awaiting us. We carried the wounded girl gently into Pechorin's quarters and sent for the surgeon. Although he was drunk, he came at our summons, and after examining the wound said the girl could not live more than a day. But he was wrong. . . ."

"She recovered then?" I asked the captain seizing his arm, glad in spite of myself.

"No," he replied, "the surgeon was wrong only in that she lived another two days."

"But tell me how did Kazbich manage to kidnap her?"

"It was like this: disobeying Pechorin's instructions, she had left the fort and gone to the river. It was very hot, and she had sat down on a rock and dipped her feet into the water. Kazbich crept up, seized and gagged her, dragged her into the bushes, jumped on his horse and galloped off. She managed to scream, however, and the sentries gave the alarm, fired after him but missed, and that's when we arrived on the scene."

"Why did Kazbich want to carry her off?"

"My dear sir! These Cherkess are a nation of thieves. Their fingers itch for anything that lies unguarded; whether they need it or not, they steal—they just can't help themselves! Besides he had long had his eye on Bela."

"And she died?"

"Yes, but she suffered a great deal, and we too were worn out watching her. About ten o'clock at night she regained consciousness; we were sitting at her bedside. As soon as she opened her eyes she asked for Pechorin. 'I am here, beside you, my *janechka,*' (that is, 'darling' in our language) he replied taking her hand. 'I shall die,' she said. We began to reassure her, saying that the surgeon had promised to cure her without fail, but she shook her head and turned to the wall. She did not want to die!

"During the night she grew delirious. Her head was on fire and every now and then she shook with fever. She was now talking incoherently about her father and brother; she wanted to go back to her mountains and home. . . . Then she also talked about Pechorin, calling him all kinds of tender names or reproaching him for not loving his *janechka* any more. . . .

"He listened in silence, his head resting on his hands. But throughout it all I did not notice a single tear on his lashes; whether he was actually incapable of weeping or whether he held himself in check, I do not know. As for myself, I had never witnessed anything more heart-rending.

"By morning the delirium passed. For about an hour she lay motionless, pale and so weak that her breathing was barely perceptible. Presently she felt better and began to speak again, but can you guess of what? Such thoughts can occur only to the dying. She regretted that she was not a Christian and that in the world beyond her soul would never meet Grigori Alexandrovich's, that some other woman would be his soulmate in paradise. It occurred to me that she might be baptized before death, but when I suggested this she gazed at me in indecision for a long time, unable to say a word. At last she replied that she would die in the faith she had been born. So the whole day passed. How she changed in that day! Her pallid cheeks grew sunken, her eyes seemed to become larger and larger, and her lips were burning. The fever within her was like red-hot iron.

"The second night came, and we sat at her bedside without closing an eyelid. She was in terrible agony, she moaned, but as soon as the pain subsided a little she tried to assure Grigori Alexandrovich that she was feeling better, urged him to get some sleep, and kissed his hand and clung to it with her own. Just before daybreak the agony of death set in, and she tossed on the bed, tearing off the bandage so that the blood flowed again. When the wound was dressed she calmed down for a moment and asked Pechorin to kiss her. He knelt by the bed, raised her head from the pillow and pressed his lips against hers, which were now growing chill; she entwined her trembling arms tightly around his neck as if by this kiss she wished to give her soul to him. Yes, it was well that she died! What would have happened to her had Grigori Alexandrovich left her? And that was bound to happen sooner or later. . . .

"The first half of the next day she was quiet, silent and submissive in spite of the way our surgeon tortured her with poultices and medicine. 'My good man!' I protested. 'You yourself said she would not live, why then all these medicines of yours?' 'Got to do it, just the same, Maxim Maximych,' he replied, 'so that my conscience should be at peace.' Conscience indeed!

"In the afternoon she was tortured by thirst. We opened the windows, but it was hotter outside than in the room. We placed ice next to her bed, but nothing helped. I knew that this unbearable thirst was a sign that the end was approaching, and I said so to Pechorin. 'Water, water,' she repeated hoarsely, raising herself from the bed.

"He went white as a sheet, seized a glass, filled it with water, and gave it to her. I covered my face with my hands and began to recite a prayer. I can't remember which. Yes, sir, I had been through a great deal in my time, had seen men die in hospitals and on the battlefield, but it had been nothing like this! I must confess that there was something else that made me sad; not once before her death did she remember me, and I think I loved her like a father. Well. . . . May God forgive her! But then who am I that anyone should remember me on his deathbed?

"As soon as she had drunk the water she felt better, and some three minutes later she passed away. We pressed a mirror to her lips, but nothing showed on it. I led Pechorin out of the room, and then we walked on the fort wall, pacing back and forth side by side for a long while without uttering a word, arms crossed behind our backs. It angered me to detect no sign of emotion on his face, for in his place I should have died of grief. Finally, he sat down on the ground in the shade and began to trace some design in the sand with a stick. I began to speak, wishing to console him, more for the sake of good form than anything else, you know, whereupon he looked up and laughed. . . . That laugh sent cold shivers running up and down my spine. . . . I went to order the coffin.

"I confess that it was partly for diversion that I occupied myself with this business. I covered the coffin with a piece of tarlatan[27] I had and ornamented it with some Cherkess silver lace Grigori Alexandrovich had bought for her.

"Early next morning we buried her beyond the fort, next to the spot on the riverbank where she had sat that last time; the small grave is now surrounded by white acacia and elder bushes. I wanted to put up a cross, but that was a bit awkward, you know, for after all she was not a Christian. . . ."

"What did Pechorin do?" I asked.

[27] Fine ornamental fabric of either sheer cotton or silk.

"He was ailing for a long time and lost weight, the poor chap. But we never spoke about Bela after that. I saw it would be painful for him, so why should I have mentioned her? Some three months later he was ordered to join the . . . regiment, and he went to Georgia. Since then we have not met. Oh yes, I remember someone telling me recently that he had returned to Russia, though it had not been mentioned in the corps orders. In general it takes a long time before news reaches us here."

Here, probably to dispel his sad memories, he launched upon a long dissertation concerning the disadvantages of hearing year-old tidings.

I neither interrupted him nor listened.

An hour later it was already possible to continue our journey. The blizzard had died down and the sky cleared up, and we set out. On the road, however, I could not help directing the conversation back to Bela and Pechorin.

"Did you ever happen to hear what became of Kazbich?" I asked.

"Kazbich? Really, I don't know. I have heard that the Shapsugi on the right flank of the line have a Kazbich, a bold fellow who wears a red *beshmet,* rides at a trot under our fire and bows with exaggerated politeness whenever a bullet whistles near him, but I doubt whether it's the same man."

Maxim Maximych and I parted at Kobi, for I took the post chaise and he could not keep pace with me because of his heavy baggage. At the time we did not think we would ever meet again, yet we did, and if you wish, I will tell you about it, but that is a story in itself. . . . You must admit, however, that Maxim Maximych is a man you can respect. If you do admit it, I shall be amply rewarded for my story, long though it may be.

II. MAXIM MAXIMYCH

After parting with Maxim Maximych, I made good time through the Terek and Daryal gorges and had breakfast at Kazbek and tea at Lars, driving into Vladikavkaz by suppertime. I shall not bore you with descriptions of mountains, exclamations that mean nothing and landscapes that convey nothing, especially to those who have never been in these parts, or with statistical observations which I am certain no one will bother to read.

I stopped at a hotel where all travellers stay and where, incidentally, there is no one to serve you a roast pheasant or a plate of cabbage soup, for the three invalids[28] in charge are either so stupid or so drunk that there is no sense to be had from them.

I was told that I should have to stop there for another three days, for the *okazia* from Yekaterinograd had not come in yet, and hence could not set out on the return trip. What an *okazia*! But a bad pun is no consolation to a Russian and in order to while away the time I decided to write down Maxim Maximych's story about Bela quite unaware that it would turn out to be the first link in a long chain of tales. So you see how an occurrence insignificant in itself may have grave consequences. . . . But perhaps you

[28] Veterans.

do not know what an *okazia*[29] is? It is an escort of half a company of infantry and a gun under whose protection the caravans cross Kabarda from Vladikavkaz to Yekaterinograd.

The first day was very dull, but early next morning a carriage drove into the yard. It was Maxim Maximych. We greeted each other like old friends. I offered him the use of my room. He did not stand on ceremony, he even clapped me on the shoulder, and his mouth twisted in what passed for a smile. A queer chap!

Maxim Maximych was well versed in the culinary art and turned out a wonderful roast pheasant with a highly successful pickled cucumber sauce. I must admit that without him I would have had to content myself with a cold snack. A bottle of Kakhetian helped us to overlook the modesty of the meal which consisted of only one course. Afterwards we lit our pipes and settled down for a smoke, I near the window and he next to the stove where a fire was going, for the day was chilly and raw. We sat in silence; what was there to say? . . . He had already told me all that was interesting about himself, and I had nothing to tell him. I looked out of the window. A multitude of low houses, sprawling along the shore of the Terek, which here spreads wider and wider, were visible through the trees, while in the distance was the blue serrated wall of the mountains with Kazbek in its white cardinal's hat peering over it. Mentally I bid them good-bye; I felt sorry to leave them.

We sat thus for a long time. The sun was setting behind the frigid peaks and a milky mist was spreading through the valleys when we heard the tinkling of bells and the shouting of drivers outside. Several carts with filthy Armenians on top drove into the courtyard followed by an empty carriage whose lightness, comfort and elegance gave it a distinctly foreign air. Behind walked a man with a huge moustache wearing a dolman;[30] he was rather well dressed for a manservant; but the way he knocked the ashes from his pipe and shouted at the coachman left no doubt as to his station. He was obviously the pampered servant of an indolent gentleman—something of a Russian Figaro.[31] "Tell me, my good man," I called to him from the window, "is it the *okazia*?" He looked at me rather insolently, straightened his neckerchief and turned away. An Armenian who had been walking beside him smiled and replied for him that it was the *okazia* and that it would set out on the return trip the next morning. "Thank God!" said Maxim Maximych who had just walked to the window. "A fine carriage!" he added. "Probably some official on his way to conduct a hearing in Tiflis. You can see he doesn't know our hills. No, my dear fellow, they're not for the likes of you; even an English carriage wouldn't stand the jolting! I wonder who it is—let's find out. . . ." We went into the corridor, at the far end of which a door was open into a side room. The valet and the driver were carrying in portmanteaus.

[29] The "bad pun" turns around the two meanings of *okazia:* "a military escort" and "an occasion or adventure." "What an *okazia!*" means "How unfortunate!"

[30] A Turkish robe.

[31] Figaro is the witty servant in Beaumarchais' *Marriage of Figaro* (1784) and in Mozart's opera based on the play (1786).

"Listen, friend," the captain asked the valet, "whose is that fine carriage, eh? A splendid carriage indeed!" The valet muttered something inaudible without turning and went on unstrapping a case. This was too much for Maxim Maximych, who tapped the insolent fellow on the shoulder and said: "I am talking to you, my good man. . . ."

"Whose carriage? My master's."

"And who is your master?"

"Pechorin."

"What did you say? Pechorin? Good God! Did he ever serve in the Caucasus?" Maxim Maximych exclaimed, pulling at my sleeve. His eyes lit up with joy.

"I believe so . . . but I haven't been with him long."

"Well, well, there you are! Grigori Alexandrovich is his name, isn't it? Your master and I used to know each other well," he added, with a friendly slap on the valet's shoulder that nearly made him lose his balance.

"Excuse me, sir, you are in my way," said the latter, frowning.

"Don't be absurd, man! Don't you know I am an old friend of your master's, we lived together, too. Now where can I find him?"

The servant announced that Pechorin had stayed behind to dine and spend the night with Colonel N.

"Will he not be here tonight?" said Maxim Maximych. "Or perhaps you, my good man, will have some reason to see him? If you do, tell him Maxim Maximych is here; you just tell him that and he'll know. . . . I'll give you a *vosmigrivenny*[32] for vodka. . . ."

The valet put on a superior air on hearing this modest offer, but nevertheless promised Maxim Maximych to do as he asked.

"He'll come at once, I warrant!" Maxim Maximych told me triumphantly. "I'll go out to the gates to meet him. Pity I don't know N."

Maxim Maximych sat down on a bench outside the gate and I went into my room. I must admit that I too awaited the appearance of this Pechorin with some eagerness, for though the captain's story had not given me too favorable a portrait of the man, some of his traits nevertheless struck me as quite remarkable. In an hour one of the invalids brought in a steaming samovar and a teapot. "Maxim Maximych, will you have some tea?" I called to him from the window.

"Thank you, I really don't care for any."

"You'd better have some. It's late already and getting chilly."

"No, thank you. . . ."

"Well, as you wish!" I said and sat down to tea alone. In ten minutes or so the old man came in. "I suppose you are right," he said. "Better have some tea. . . . You see, I was waiting. His man has been gone a long time; looks as if something has detained him."

He hastily gulped down a cup of tea, refused a second, and went back to the gate, obviously upset. It was clear that the old man was hurt by Pechorin's unconcern, all the more so since he had spoken to me so recently about their friendship and only an hour before had

[32] A small tip.

been certain that Pechorin would come running as soon as he heard his name.

It was dark when I again opened the window and called to remind Maxim Maximych that it was time to retire. He muttered something in reply and I urged him again to come in, but he did not answer.

Leaving a candle on the bench, I lay down on the couch, wrapped myself in my greatcoat and was soon asleep. I would have slept peacefully all night had not Maxim Maximych awakened me when he came in very late. He threw his pipe on the table, began pacing up and down the room, then tinkered with the stove. Finally he lay down, coughing, spitting and tossing about for a long time.

"Bedbugs bothering you?" I asked.

"Yes, bedbugs," he replied with a heavy sigh.

I woke up early next morning but Maxim Maximych had already risen. I found him sitting on the bench at the gate. "I've got to see the commandant," he said, "so if Pechorin comes will you please send for me?"

I promised to do so. He ran off as if his limbs had regained the strength and agility of youth.

It was a fresh, fine morning. Golden clouds piled up on the mountains like a new range of aerial summits. In front of the gates was a broad square, and beyond it the market-place was seething with people, for it was Sunday. Barefooted Ossetian boys, birchbark baskets laden with honeycombs strapped to their backs, crowded around me, but I drove them away for I was too preoccupied to give them much thought; the good captain's disquietude was beginning to claim me too.

Ten minutes had not passed when the man for whom we had been waiting appeared at the far end of the square. With him was Colonel N., who left him at the hotel and turned toward the fort. I immediately sent one of the invalids for Maxim Maximych.

Pechorin was met by his valet who reported that the horses would be ready in a moment, handed him a box of cigars and having received a few instructions, retired to carry them out. His master lit a cigar, yawned once or twice and sat down on a bench on the other side of the gate. Now I should like to draw you his portrait.

He was of medium stature; his erect, lithe figure and broad shoulders suggested a strong physique equal to all the hardships of the road and variations of climate, unweakened by either the dissolute life of the capital or emotional conflicts. His dusty velvet coat was open except for the last two buttons, revealing an expanse of dazzlingly white linen that betrayed the habits of a gentleman. His soiled gloves seemed to have been made for his small, aristocratic hands, and when he pulled off a glove, I was amazed at the slenderness of his white fingers. His walk was careless and indolent, but I noticed he did not swing his arms—a sure sign of a certain reticence of character. But these are my personal opinions based on my own observations, and I cannot compel you to accept them blindly. When he sank down on the bench his erect frame sagged as if his back was spineless; his whole posture now betrayed some nervous debility; he sat as a thirty-year-old Balzacian coquette might sit in a cushioned easy chair after an exhausting ball.[33] At first glance I should not have given him more than twenty-three years, though later I was ready to grant him thirty. There was something childlike in his smile. His skin was as delicate as a woman's, and his naturally curly fair hair made a pleasing frame for his pale, noble brow on which only careful scrutiny could disclose a fine network of wrinkles that probably were a good deal more in evidence at times of anger or spiritual disquietude. In spite of his light hair, his moustache and eyebrows were black—as much a sign of pedigree in a man as a black mane and tail are in a white horse. To complete the portrait, I shall say that he had a slightly turned-up nose and that his teeth were dazzlingly white and his eyes hazel—but about his eyes I must say a few more words.

Firstly, they did not laugh when he did. Have you ever had occasion to observe this peculiarity in people? It is a sign either of evil nature or deep constant sadness. They shone with a phosphorescent glow, if one may so put it, under half-closed eyelids. It was no reflection of spiritual warmth or fertile imagination; it was the flash of smooth steel, blinding but cold. His glance was brief but piercing and oppressive, it had the disturbing effect of an indiscreet question, and might have seemed challenging had it not been so calmly casual. Perhaps all these observations came to my mind only because I happened to know some details about his life, and another person might have obtained an entirely different impression, but since you will not learn about him from anyone else, you will have to be satisfied with this portrayal. I must say in conclusion that, on the whole, he was handsome indeed, and had one of those unusual faces that are particularly pleasing to ladies.

The horses were harnessed, the bell attached to the shaft bow tinkled, and the valet had already reported twice to Pechorin that the carriage was waiting, but still there was no sign of Maxim Maximych. Luckily Pechorin was deep in thought; he gazed at the blue jagged ridge of the Caucasus apparently in no hurry to be on his way. I crossed over to him. "If you would care to wait a while," said I, "you will have the pleasure of meeting an old friend. . ."

"Ah, that's right!" he replied quickly. "I was told about him yesterday. But where is he?" I looked out over the square and saw Maxim Maximych running towards us for all he was worth. . . . In a few minutes he had reached us. He could barely catch his breath, beads of perspiration rolled down his face, damp strands of gray hair that had escaped from under his cap were plastered to his face, and his knees shook. He was about to throw his arms around Pechorin's neck, but the latter extended his hand coldly, though his smile was pleasant enough. For a moment the captain was dumbfounded, then eagerly gripped the hand with both of his. He was still unable to speak.

"This is a pleasure, dear Maxim Maximych. How are you?" said Pechorin.

"And you . . ." faltered the old man, tears welling up in his eyes. "It's a long time . . . a very long time. . . . But where are you off to?"

[33] Lermontov is referring to Honoré de Balzac's "The Thirty-Year-Old Woman," a story in his *Scenes from Private Life* (1828–44).

"On my way to Persia . . . and farther. . . ."

"Not immediately, I hope? Won't you stay a while? We haven't seen each other for so long."

"I must go, Maxim Maximych," was the reply.

"My God, what is the hurry? I have so much to tell you and so many questions to ask. . . . How are things, anyway? Retired, eh? What have you been doing?"

"Bored to death," replied Pechorin, smiling.

"Remember how we used to live in the fort? Wonderful hunting country, wasn't it? How you loved to hunt! Remember Bela?"

Pechorin paled a little and turned away.

"Yes, I remember," he said, deliberately yawning almost in the same breath.

Maxim Maximych urged him to stay on for another hour or two. "We'll have a fine dinner," he said. "I have two pheasants, and the Kakhetian here is excellent . . . not the same as in Georgia, of course, but the best to be had here. And we could talk . . . you will tell me about your stay in St. Petersburg, won't you?"

"I really have nothing to tell, dear Maxim Maximych. And I have to say good-bye now, for I must be off. . . . In rather a hurry. . . . It was kind of you not to have forgotten me," he added, taking the old man's hand.

The old man frowned. He was both grieved and hurt, though he did his best to conceal his feeling. "Forgotten!" he muttered. "No, I've forgotten nothing. Oh well, never mind. . . . Only I did not expect our meeting would be like this."

"Come, now, that will do," said Pechorin, embracing him in a friendly way. "I don't think I have changed. At any rate, it can't be helped. We all are destined to go our several ways. God knows whether we'll meet again." This he said as he climbed into the carriage and the coachman was already gathering in the reins.

"Wait a minute, wait a minute!" Maxim Maximych suddenly shouted, seizing hold of the carriage door. "It completely slipped my mind. . . . I still have your papers, Grigori Alexandrovich. . . . Been carrying them around with me. . . . Thought I'd find you in Georgia, never dreaming the Lord would have us meet here. . . . What shall I do with them?"

"Whatever you wish," replied Pechorin. "Farewell!"

"So you are off to Persia. . . . When do you expect to be back?" Maxim Maximych shouted after him.

The carriage was already some distance off, but Pechorin waved in a way that could well be interpreted to mean: "I doubt whether I shall return, nor is there any reason why I should!"

Long after the tinkling of the bell and the clatter of wheels against the flinty surface of the road had faded into the distance, the poor old man stood glued to the spot, lost in his thoughts.

"Yes," he said at last, trying his best to preserve a nonchalant air though tears of disappointment still showed in his eyes, "we were friends, of course, but what is friendship nowadays? What am I to him? I am neither rich nor titled, and, besides, I am far too old. What a fop his visit to St. Petersburg has made him! Look at that carriage, and the pile of luggage and the haughty valet!" This he said with an ironic smile. "Tell me," he went on, turning to me, "what do you think of it all? What sort of a demon is driving him to Persia now? Queer, isn't it? I knew all along, of course, that he was the flighty sort of fellow you can't count on. It's a pity though that he should come to a bad end . . . but there's nothing for it, as you can see. I've always said that nothing good will come of those who forget old friends." At that he turned away to conceal his agitation and began pacing up and down the courtyard beside his carriage, pretending to examine the wheels, while the tears kept welling in his eyes.

"Maxim Maximych," said I, walking up to him. "What were the papers Pechorin left you?"

"The Lord knows! Some notes or other. . . ."

"What do you intend to do with them?"

"Eh? I'll have them made into cartridges."

"You'd better give them to me."

He looked at me in amazement, muttered something under his breath and began to rummage through his portmanteau. He took out one notebook and threw it contemptuously on the ground. The second, the third and the tenth all shared the fate of the first. There was something childish about the old man's resentment, and I was both amused and sorry for him.

"That's the lot," he said. "I congratulate you on your find."

"And I may do whatever I want with them?"

"Print them in the papers if you like, what do I care? Yes, indeed, am I a friend of his or a relative? True, we shared the same roof for a long time, but then I have lived with all sorts of people."

I seized the papers and carried them off before the captain could change his mind. Soon we were told that the *okazia* would set out in an hour, and I gave orders to harness the horses. The captain came into my room as I was putting on my hat. He showed no sign of preparing for the journey; there was a strained coldness about him.

"Aren't you coming, Maxim Maximych?"

"No."

"Why?"

"I haven't seen the commandant, and I have to deliver some government property to him."

"But didn't you go to see him?"

"Yes, of course," he stammered, "but he wasn't in and I didn't wait for him."

I understood what he meant. For the first time in his life, perhaps, the poor old man had neglected his duties for *his own convenience,* to put it in official language, and this had been his reward!

"I am very sorry, Maxim Maximych," I said, "very sorry indeed, that we have to part so soon."

"How can we ignorant old fogies keep up with you haughty young men of the world; here, with Cherkess bullets flying about, you put up with us somehow . . . but if we chanced to meet later on you would be ashamed to shake hands with the likes of us."

"I have not deserved this reproof, Maxim Maximych."

"I'm speaking in general, you know, at any rate I wish you luck and a pleasant journey."

We parted rather frigidly. Good Maxim Maximych was now an obstinate, cantankerous captain. And why? Because Pechorin through absent-mindedness or for some other reason had merely extended his hand when his old friend wanted to fall on his neck. It is sad to see a young man's finest hopes and dreams shattered, to see him lose the rosy illusions with which he viewed man's deeds and emotions, although there is still hope that he may exchange the old delusions for new ones no less transitory but also no less sweet. But what is there to exchange them for at Maxim Maximych's age? Without wishing it, the heart would harden and the soul wither. . . .

I set out alone.

PECHORIN'S DIARY

FOREWORD

Recently I learned that Pechorin had died on his way back from Persia. This news pleased me very much, for it gave me the right to publish these notes, and I took advantage of the opportunity to sign my name to another man's work. God forbid that the reader should penalize me for such an innocent deception!

Now I must explain briefly what it was that spurred me to make public the innermost secrets of a man I never knew. It might have been understandable had I been his friend; for the perfidious indiscretion of the true friend is something everyone can appreciate. But I saw him only once for a fleeting moment, and hence cannot regard him with that inexplicable hatred which, concealed under the mask of friendship, only waits for death or misfortune to overtake the object of affection in order to bring down upon his head a hailstorm of remonstrances, advice, mockery and commiseration.

Reading over these notes, I became convinced that the man must have been sincere in so mercilessly laying bare his own weaknesses and vices. The story of a human soul, even the pettiest of souls, is no less interesting and instructive than the story of a nation, especially if it is the result of the observation of a mature mind and written without the vain desire to evoke compassion or wonder. One of the defects of Rousseau's Confessions[34] *is that he read it to his friends.*

Thus it was purely the desire to do some good that impelled me to publish excerpts from the diary I happened to acquire. Though I have changed all proper names, those mentioned in it will no doubt recognize themselves and perhaps find justification for deeds they have held against a man who is no longer of this world. For we nearly always forgive that which we understand.

I have included in this book only excerpts bearing on Pechorin's stay in the Caucasus. This still leaves me with a thick notebook in which he tells the story of his whole life. Some day it too will be submitted to public judgment; now, however, I dare not take the responsibility upon myself for many important reasons.

[34] Jean-Jacques Rousseau's *Confessions* (1781–88) established the standard of self-revelation for the nineteenth century.

Some readers will probably want to know what I think of Pechorin's character. My reply may be found in the title of this book. "But that is bitter irony!" they will say. I do not know.

I. TAMAN

Taman is the most wretched of all seaboard towns in Russia. I very nearly died of hunger there, and was almost drowned into the bargain. I arrived by post chaise late at night. The coachman stopped his tired troika at the gate of the only brick building, which stood at the entrance to the town. Roused from a doze by the tinkling of the carriage bell, the Black Sea Cossack on sentry duty shouted wildly: "Who goes there?" A Cossack sergeant and a local policeman emerged from the building. I explained that I was an officer on my way to a line unit on official business and demanded lodgings for the night. The policeman took us around town. All the cottages we stopped at were occupied. It was chilly, and, not having slept for three nights running, I was exhausted and began to lose my temper. "Take me anywhere you want, you scoundrel! To the devil, if you please, as long as there's a place to stay!" I shouted. "There is still one place left," the policeman replied, scratching the back of his head. "Only you will not like it, sir; there are queer goings on there!" Failing to grasp the precise meaning of the last remark, I told him to go ahead, and after wandering about for a long time in muddy alleys lined with rickety fences, we drove up to a small hut on the seashore.

A full moon lit up the reed roof and white walls of my prospective dwelling. In the courtyard, which was fenced in by a crude stone wall, stood another miserable, crooked hut, smaller and older than the first. A cliff dropped abruptly to the sea from the very walls of the hut, and down below the dark blue waves broke against the shore with an incessant roar. The moon looked down serenely upon the restless but obedient sea, and by its light I could discern two ships at anchor far from the shore, their black rigging a motionless cobweb against the paler background of the skyline. "There are ships in the anchorage," thought I. "Tomorrow I shall leave for Gelenjik."

A Cossack from a line unit served as my batman.[35] Telling him to take down my portmanteau and dismiss the driver, I called for the master of the house. There was no answer. I knocked, and still there was no reply. What could it mean? Finally a boy of about fourteen appeared on the porch.

"Where is the master?" "No master." "What? You mean there is no master at all?" "None at all." "And the mistress?" "Gone to town." "Who's going to open the door for me?" said I, kicking at it. The door opened by itself, and a dank smell came from the hut. I struck a sulphur match and brought it close to the youngster's nose, and in its light I saw two white eyes. He was blind, totally blind from birth. As he stood motionless before me I looked closely into his face.

I admit that I am greatly prejudiced against all the blind, squint-eyed, deaf, dumb, legless, armless, hunchbacked and so on. I have observed that

[35] Orderly.

there is always some strange relationship between the external appearance of a man and his soul, as if with the loss of a limb the soul too lost some faculty of feeling.

So I examined the blind lad's face, but what would you have me read on a face without eyes? I looked at him long with involuntary pity when a faint smile flitted across his thin lips, making, I know not why, the most unpleasant impression on me. A suspicion that he was not as blind as he seemed flashed through my mind, and in vain I tried to assure myself that it is impossible to simulate a cataract. And why should anyone do that? But I couldn't help suspecting, for I am often inclined to form preconceived notions.

"Are you the master's son?" I asked him at last. "Nay." "Then who are you?" "Orphan, a poor orphan." "Has the mistress any children?" "Nay. There was a daughter but she ran away across the sea with a Tatar." "What kind of a Tatar?" "The devil knows! A Crimean Tatar, a boatman from Kerch."

I walked into the hut. Two benches, a table and a huge trunk next to the stove were the sole furnishings. Not a single icon was there on the wall—a bad sign that! The sea wind blew in through a broken window. I extracted the stub of a wax candle from my portmanteau and lighting it began to lay out my things. I put my sword and gun in a corner, laid my pistols on the table, and spread out my cloak on a bench while the Cossack laid out his on the other. In ten minutes he was snoring, but I could not sleep; the lad with the white eyes kept swimming before me in the gloom.

About an hour passed in this way. The moon shone into the window and a beam of light played on the earthen floor of the hut. Suddenly a shadow darted across the bright strip on the floor. I got up and looked out of the window. Someone again ran past and disappeared, God knows where. It did not seem possible that the creature could have run down the cliff to the shore, yet he could not have gone anywhere else. I got up, put on my *beshmet,* girded on a dagger and stole out of the hut. The blind boy was coming toward me. I drew close to the fence, and he went past with sure though cautious tread. He carried a bundle under his arm. Turning toward the boat landing, he began the descent along a narrow, steep path. "The blind receive their sight, and the deaf hear,"[36] I thought, following close enough not to lose sight of him.

In the meantime clouds began to envelop the moon and a fog rose at sea. The stern light of the ship nearest the shore was barely visible through it. On the shore gleamed the foam of the breakers, which threatened to submerge it any moment. Picking my way with difficulty down the steep incline, I saw the blind boy stop, then turn to the right and proceed so close to the water that it seemed the waves must surely seize him and carry him out to sea. It was obvious, however, that this was not the first time he was making the journey, judging by the confidence with which he stepped from stone to stone and avoided the holes. At last he stopped as if listening for something, then sat down on the ground with his bundle beside him. Hidden behind a projecting cliff I watched his movements. A few minutes later

[36]"The blind . . . the deaf hear." An allusion to Matthew 11:5, "The blind receive their sight and the lame walk, lepers are cleansed and the deaf hear."

a figure in white appeared from the other side, walked up to the blind boy and sat down beside him. The wind carried fragments of their conversation to me.

"What do you say, blind one?" a woman's voice said. "The gale is too heavy; Yanko won't come." "Yanko is not afraid of gales," the other replied. "The fog is thickening," came the woman's voice again with a note of sadness.

"It will be easier to slip by the patrol ships in the fog," was the reply. "What if he is drowned?" "Well, what of it? You'll go to church on Sunday without a new ribbon."

A silence followed. I was struck, however, by one thing: the blind boy had spoken to me in the Ukrainian dialect, and now he was speaking pure Russian.

"You see, I am right," said the blind boy again, clapping his hands. "Yanko does not fear the sea, or the winds, or the fog, or yet the coast patrols. Listen, that's not the waves splashing, you can't fool me; those are his long oars."

The woman jumped up and peered anxiously into the distance.

"You're raving, blind one," she said. "I don't see anything."

I must admit that, strain as I did, I failed to discern anything like a boat in the distance. Some ten minutes had passed thus when a black speck now growing larger, now diminishing, appeared among the mountainous billows. Slowly climbing to the crests of the waves and sharply dropping into the troughs, the boat approached the shore. It was an intrepid oarsman who ventured on a night like this to cross the twenty versts of the strait, and the reason that spurred him on must have been pressing indeed. Thus thinking, my heart involuntarily quickening its beat, I watched the frail craft dive with the dexterity of a duck and then leap up from the watery chasm through the flying foam with a swift movement of the oars that recalled the thrust of wings. I thought it must surely crash full force against the shore and be dashed to pieces, but it neatly swung around and slipped safely into a tiny bay. A man of medium stature wearing a Tatar sheepskin cap stepped from the boat. He motioned with his hand and all three commenced to haul something from the craft; the cargo was so great that to this day I cannot understand why the boat had not sunk. Each shouldering a bundle, they set out along the shore and I soon lost sight of them. I had to return to my lodgings. I must admit, however, that all these strange doings alarmed me, and I could hardly wait for the morning.

My Cossack was very much surprised when upon waking up he found me fully dressed, but I gave him no explanation. After admiring for some time the blue sky mottled with ragged little clouds and the Crimean coast which spread out in a line of mauve in the distance and ended in a crag topped by the white tower of a lighthouse, I set out for the Fanagoria fort[37] to inquire at the commandant's when I could leave for Gelenjik.

But, alas, the commandant was unable to tell me anything definite. The vessels in the harbor were either coastguard ships or merchant boats which had not even begun loading. "Perhaps there will be a packet-boat in three or four days," the commandant said, "and then we shall see." I returned to

[37] Military installation built on the ruins of an ancient Greek colony northeast of Taman.

my lodgings morose and angry. My Cossack met me at the door with a scared look on his face.

"Looks bad, sir!" he said.

"Yes, my friend. Who knows when we shall get away!" Now he looked still more worried. Bending toward me, he whispered:

"It's uncanny here! Today I met the sergeant of the Black Sea Cossacks; I happen to know him, we were in the same detachment last year. When I told him where we'd stopped he said to me: 'Brother, it's unclean there; the people are no good!' And come to think of it, what sort of fellow is this blind chap? Goes everywhere alone, to the market for bread, and to fetch water. You can see they're used to that sort of thing here."

"What of it? Has the mistress of the house appeared at least?"

"While you were out an old woman came with her daughter."

"What daughter? She has no daughter."

"God knows who she is then. The old woman is in the hut now."

I went inside. The stove had been heated well and a dinner rather sumptuous for poor folk was cooking. To all my questions the old woman replied that she was deaf and could not hear me. What could I do? I addressed the blind boy, who was sitting in front of the stove feeding brushwood into the fire. "Now tell me, you blind imp," said I, taking hold of his ear, "where did you go last night with that bundle, eh?" He burst into tears and began howling and wailing: "Where'd I go? Nowhere. And I don't know of any bundle." This time the old woman heard what was going on and began to grumble: "Of all the things to imagine, and about the poor wretch, too! Why can't you leave him alone? What has he done to you?" This disgusted me and I walked out firmly resolved to find the key to the riddle.

I wrapped my cloak around me and sat down on a boulder beside the wall, gazing into the distance. Before me spread the sea agitated by last night's gale, and its monotonous roar like the murmuring of a city falling into slumber reminded me of bygone years, carrying my thoughts to the North, to our frigid capital. Stirred by memories I forgot all else. An hour and perhaps more passed thus. Suddenly something like a song caught my ear. It was a song, and the voice was pleasant, feminine, but where did it come from? I listened to it; it was a strange melody, now slow and plaintive, now fast and lively. I looked around, but saw no one; I listened again, and the sound seemed to drop from the heavens. I looked up, and on the roof of the hut I saw a girl in a striped dress, a real mermaid with loosened tresses. Shading her eyes from the sun with her hand, she was peering into the distance, now smiling and talking to herself, now picking up the song again.

I memorized the song word for word:

Over boundless billows green,
    Over billows surging.
Fly the ships with sails a-spread,
    Onward urging.
There among those ships at sea,
    Sails my shallop sprightly,
Curtsying to wind and wave,

Kissed by combers lightly.
Stormy winds begin to blow,
Stately ships a-rocking,
Widely do they spread their wings—
To leeward flocking.
The angry ocean then I pray,
Bending low before him:
"Spare my barque, O fearsome one!"—
Thus do I implore him.—
"Precious goods are stowed on board!—
Fierce the sea is foaming!—
Keep her safe—a madcap steers
Through the gloaming!"

It occurred to me that I had heard the same voice the night before. For a moment I was lost in thought, and when I looked up at the roof again, the girl was no longer there. Suddenly she tripped past me, singing a different tune; snapping her fingers, she ran in to the old woman, and I heard their voices rise in argument. The old woman grew very angry but the girl merely laughed aloud. A short while later my mermaid came skipping along again. As she approached me she paused and looked me straight in the eyes, as if surprised at finding me there. Then she turned away carelessly and went quietly down to the boat landing. This, however, was not the end of it: all day long she hovered around my quarters, singing and skipping about without a moment's respite. She was a strange creature indeed. There was nothing insane about her expression; on the contrary, her eyes inspected me with keen penetration, they seemed to be endowed with some magnetic power, and each glance appeared to invite a question, but as soon as I opened my mouth to speak she ran away, smiling artfully.

Never had I seen a woman like her. She was far from beautiful, though I have my preconceived notions as regards beauty as well. There was much of the thoroughbred in her, and in women as in horses that is a great thing; this discovery belongs to young France.[38] It (I mean pedigree, not young France) is betrayed mainly by the walk and by the hands and feet, and particularly indicative is the nose. In Russia a classic nose is rarer than small feet. My songstress looked no more than eighteen. Her extraordinarily graceful figure, the peculiar way she had of tilting her head, her long auburn hair, the golden sheen of her slightly sun-tanned neck and shoulders, and especially her finely chiselled nose enchanted me. Though I could read something wild and suspicious in her sidelong glances and though there was something indefinable in her smile, the preconceived notions got the better of me. The chiselled nose carried me off my feet, and I fancied I had found Goethe's Mignon,[39] that queer figment of his German imagination. And indeed, there was much in common between the two, the same swift transitions from supreme agitation to utter immobility,

[38] "Young France" was a cult of antibourgeois dandyism in Paris in the 1830's.
[39] The mysterious Italian girl in Johann Wolfgang von Goethe's *Wilhelm Meister's Apprenticeship* (1796).

the same puzzling conversation, the same gambolling and the same strange songs. . . .

Toward evening I stopped her in the doorway and engaged her in the following conversation:

"Tell me, my pretty one," I asked, "what were you doing on the roof today?" "Looking where the wind blows from." "Why?" "Whence the wind blows, thence happiness." "Indeed, were you invoking happiness by song?" "Where there is song there is also good fortune." "Supposing you sing grief for yourself?" "What of it? If things will not be better, they'll be worse, and then it's not so far from bad to good." "Who taught you that song?" "No one taught it to me. I sing whatever comes to my mind; he to whom I sing will hear; others will not understand." "What is your name, my nightingale?" "Whoever named me knows." "And who named you?" "How should I know?" "You are sly! But I've learned something about you." There was no change in her expression, not even a trembling of her lips, as if it all were no concern of hers. "I know that you went down to the shore last night." Assuming an air of importance I told her everything I had seen, hoping to disconcert her, but in vain! She only burst out laughing. "You saw a lot but know little; and what you do know you'd best keep under lock and key." "Supposing I took it into my head to report to the commandant?" I adopted a very serious, even severe mien. Suddenly she bounded off and began singing, disappearing like a bird frightened into flight. My last remark was entirely out of place, though at the time I did not suspect its full purport and only later had occasion to regret ever having made it.

It was beginning to grow dark and I told the Cossack to put on the kettle, lighted a candle and sat at the table smoking my travelling pipe. I was already finishing my second glass of tea when the door suddenly creaked and I heard the soft rustle of a dress and light footsteps behind me. I started and turned around: it was she, my undine![40] She sat down opposite me without a word and looked at me with eyes that for some unfathomable reason seemed full of sweet tenderness; they reminded me of eyes that years before had so despotically ruled my life. She seemed to wait for me to speak, but I was too confused to say a word. The deathly pallor of her face betrayed the tumult within her; her hand aimlessly wandered over the table and I noticed that it trembled; now her bosom rose high, now she seemed to be holding her breath. The comedy began to pall and I was ready to cut it short in the most prosaic fashion by offering her a glass of tea when she jumped up, entwined her arms around my neck and planted a moist, fiery kiss on my lips. Everything went dark before my eyes, my head swam, and I embraced her with all my youthful passion, but she slipped like a serpent from my arms, whispering in my ear: "Meet me on the shore tonight after everyone is asleep," and ran out of the room as swift as an arrow. In the passageway she upset the tea-kettle and the candle standing on the floor. "She-devil!" shouted the Cossack, who had made himself comfortable on some straw and was intending to warm himself with the tea I had left. I came to myself with a start.

Some two hours later when all was quiet I roused my Cossack. "If you

[40] Water nymph.

hear a pistol shot," I told him, "run down to the waterfront." He opened his eyes wide but replied mechanically: "Yes, sir." I stuck a pistol under my belt and went out. She was waiting for me at the top of the slope, more than flimsily clad, a small shawl tied around her slender form.

"Follow me," she said, taking me by the hand, and we started down the embankment. I do not know how I managed not to break my neck. At the bottom we turned to the right and took the path along which I had followed the blind boy the night before. The moon had not risen yet, and only two stars like two distant lighthouses shone in the dark blue sky. The swell came in at even, regular intervals, barely lifting the lone boat moored to the shore. "Let's get into the boat," said my companion. I hesitated, for I have no predilection for sentimental sea jaunts, but this was not the time to retreat. She jumped into the boat and I followed, and before I knew it we had cast off. "What does this mean?" I asked, angrily now. "It means," she said as she pushed me on to a seat and wrapped her arms around me, "that I love you." She pressed her cheek against mine and I felt her breath hot on my face. Suddenly something splashed into the water; I reached for my belt, but the pistol was gone. Now a terrible suspicion crept into my heart and the blood rushed to my head. Looking around I saw we were already some fifty sagenes from the shore, and I unable to swim! I wanted to push her away, but she clung to my clothes like a cat, then gave me a sharp push that nearly threw me overboard. The boat rocked dangerously, but I regained my balance, and a desperate struggle began between us. Fury gave me strength, but I soon noticed that my adversary was more agile than I. "What do you want!" I shouted, gripping her small hands. I could hear her fingers crack, but she did not cry out; her snakelike nature was superior to the pain.

"You saw what happened," she replied, "and you will report on us." With a superhuman effort she forced me against the gunwale until we both hung perilously over the water and her hair dipped into it. The moment was decisive. I braced my knee against the side of the boat and seized her by the hair with one hand and the throat with the other. She let go of my clothes and in a flash I had hurled her into the sea.

It was already quite dark and after seeing her head bob up a couple of times in the foam I lost sight of her completely.

I found a piece of an old oar at the bottom of the boat, and after a great deal of effort managed to get to the landing. As I was making my way along the shore back to the hut, my eyes turned towards the spot where the blind boy had waited for the nocturnal boatman the night before. The moon was coming up and in its light I thought I saw a white-garbed figure sitting on the shore. Spurred on by curiosity I crept toward it and lay down in the grass on top of a bluff rising from the shore; by raising my head slightly I could observe everything that happened below, and I was neither too surprised nor sorry to find my mermaid there. She was wringing the sea water from her hair, and I noticed how her wet clothes outlined her lithe form and high bosom. Soon a boat appeared in the distance and quickly approached the shore. Like the night before, a man stepped out of it wearing a Tatar cap, though his hair was cropped in Cossack fashion, and he had a large knife stuck under his belt. "Yanko," she said, "everything is lost!" They continued talking, but in so low a voice that I could not hear a word.

"And where is the blind one?" Yanko finally asked in a louder tone. "I sent him off," was the reply. A few minutes later the blind boy appeared carrying a bag on his back. This was put into the boat.

"Listen, blind one," said Yanko, "take care of that spot, you know what I mean? There's a wealth of goods there. . . . And tell (the name I could not make out) that I am no longer his servant. Things have turned out badly and he'll see me no more. It's dangerous to go on. I'm going to look for work elsewhere; he won't find another daredevil like me. And tell him that had he paid more generously Yanko wouldn't have left him. I can always make my way wherever the wind blows and the sea roars!" After a brief pause, Yanko continued: "I'll take her with me, for she can't stay behind, and tell the old woman it's time she died; she's lived long enough and ought to know when her time's up. She'll never see us again."

"What about me?" the blind boy whimpered.

"What do I need you for?" was the answer.

In the meantime my undine had jumped into the boat and was waving to her comrade. Yanko put something into the blind boy's hand and muttered: "Here, buy yourself some ginger cakes." "Is that all?" asked the blind one. "All right, take this too." The coin rang as it fell on the stones. The blind boy did not pick it up. Yanko got into the boat, and as the wind was blowing out to sea, they raised a small sail and quickly slipped into the distance. For a long time the white sail was visible among the dark waves in the moonlight. The blind boy remained sitting on the shore, and I heard something that sounded like sobbing: it was the blind boy weeping, and he wept for a long, long time. . . . A sadness came over me. Why did fate have to throw me into the peaceful lives of *honest smugglers?* Like a stone hurled into the placid surface of a well I had disturbed their tranquillity, and like a stone had nearly gone to the bottom myself!

I returned to my quarters. In the passage a candle spluttered its last on a wooden platter, while my Cossack, orders notwithstanding, was fast asleep gripping a gun with both hands. I did not disturb him, and picking up the candle went into the room. But alas, my box, silver-inlaid saber and a Daghestan dagger which I had received as a present from a friend had vanished. Now I guessed what the confounded blind boy had carried. Rousing the Cossack with scant ceremony, I swore at him and raged, but there was nothing that could be done about it any more. And would it not have been ludicrous for me to complain to my superiors that I had been robbed by a blind boy and that an eighteen-year-old girl had all but drowned me? Thank God an opportunity offered itself the following morning to travel farther, and I left Taman. What happened later to the old woman and the poor blind boy, I do not know. And, after all, what have human joys and sorrows to do with me, an itinerant officer, and one travelling on official business to boot!

END OF PART ONE

PART TWO
CONCLUSION OF PECHORIN'S DIARY

II. PRINCESS MARY

MAY 11

Yesterday I arrived in Pyatigorsk[41] and rented quarters in the outskirts at the foot of Mashuk;[42] this is the highest part of the town, so high that the clouds will reach down to my roof during thunderstorms. When I opened the window at five o'clock this morning the fragrance of the flowers growing in the modest little front garden flooded my room. The flower-laden branches of the cherry-trees peep into my windows, and now and then the wind strews my writing-desk with the white petals. I have a marvellous view on three sides. Five-peaked Beshtau looms blue in the west like "the last cloud of a dispersed storm";[43] in the north rises Mashuk like a shaggy Persian cap concealing this part of the horizon. To the east the view is gayer: down below the clean new town spreads colorfully before me, the medicinal fountains babble and so do the multilingual crowds, farther in the distance the massive amphitheater of mountains grows ever bluer and mistier, while on the fringe of the horizon stretches the silvery chain of snow-capped peaks beginning with Kazbek and ending with twin-peaked Elbrus. . . . It is a joy to live in a country like this! A feeling of elation flows in all my veins. The air is pure and fresh like the kiss of a child, the sun is bright and the sky blue—what more could one desire? What place is there left for passions, yearnings and regrets? But it's time to go. I shall walk down to Elizabeth Springs where they say the spa society congregates in the mornings.[44]

. . . .

Upon reaching the center of the town I took the boulevard where I encountered several melancholy groups slowly climbing the hill. That most of them were landed families from the plains was obvious from the threadbare, old-fashioned coats of the men and the dainty dresses of the wives and daughters. They evidently had all the eligible young men at the watering place marked out, for they looked at me with fond curiosity. The Petersburg cut of my coat deceived them at first, but discovering my army epaulettes they soon turned away in disgust.

The wives of the local officials, the hostesses of the springs, so to say, were more graciously inclined. They carry lorgnettes and pay less attention to the uniform, for in the Caucasus they have learned to find ardent hearts under brass buttons and enlightened minds under white forage caps.

[41] A famous resort, noted for its medicinal springs, in the northern Caucasus.

[42] One of the mountains around Pyatigorsk alluded to frequently in the story. The others are Iron Mountain, Snake Mountain, Beshtau, and Bald Mountain.

[43] First line of Alexander Pushkin's poem "The Cloud" (1835).

[44] Here, as throughout *A Hero of Our Time,* rows of dots do not signify omissions but are Lermontov's own punctuation, a fashionable Romantic convention suggesting the indeterminate and the ineffable.

These ladies are very charming, and remain charming for a long time! Their admirers are renewed every year, which perhaps explains the secret of their indefatigable amiability. As I climbed up the narrow path leading to Elizabeth Springs I passed a crowd of men, both civilians and military, who, as I discovered later, form a class in itself among those who keep vigil at the fount. They drink, but not water, go out but little, philander in a desultory way; they gamble and complain of boredom. They are fops; they assume academic poses as they dip their wickered tumblers into the sulphur water; the civilians flaunt pale-blue cravats, and the armymen, ruffs showing above their collars. They affect deep disdain for provincial society and sigh at the thought of aristocratic drawing-rooms of the capital which are closed to them.

Here at last is the well. . . . On a site nearby, a little red-roofed building has been raised over the baths, and farther on, a gallery to shelter the promenaders when it rains. Several wounded officers—pale, sad-looking men—sat on a bench holding their crutches in front of them. Several ladies were briskly pacing back and forth, waiting for the water to take effect. Among them were two or three pretty faces. Through the avenues of vines that cover the slope of Mashuk I caught an occasional glimpse of a gay bonnet evidently belonging to a votaress of privacy for two as it was invariably accompanied by an army cap or an ugly round hat. On a steep cliff where there is a pavilion named the Aeolian Harp, sightseers were aiming a telescope at Elbrus; among them were two tutors with their charges who had come here in search of a cure for king's evil.

Panting, I had stopped at the brink of the precipice and was leaning against a corner of the building surveying the picturesque locality when I suddenly heard a familiar voice behind me:

"Pechorin! Been here long?"

I turned around and saw Grushnitsky. We embraced. I had met him in a line unit. He had a bullet wound in the leg and had left for the watering place a week earlier than I.

Grushnitsky is a cadet. He has served only a year and wears a heavy soldier's greatcoat which he flaunts as his particular brand of foppery. He has a soldier's Cross of St. George.[45] He is well-built, swarthy and dark-haired, and looks twenty-five though he can scarcely be more than twenty-one. He has a way of throwing his head back when talking, and he constantly twirls his moustache with his left hand for his right is engaged leaning on his crutch. His speech is glib and florid; he is one of those who have a pompous phrase ready for every occasion, who are unmoved by simple beauty and who grandly assume a garb of extraordinary emotions, exalted passions and exquisite anguish. They delight in creating an impression, and romantic provincial ladies are infatuated with them to the point of distraction. In their old age they become either peaceable landlords or drunkards, sometimes both. Often their souls have many kindly qualities but not a particle of poetry. Grushnitsky used to have a passion for declaiming; he would shower you under with words as soon as the conver-

[45] A highly prized medal for bravery. (Lermontov does not describe what Grushnitsky did to receive the medal, but the fact that he has won it casts a significant light on his character later in the story.)

sation transcended the bounds of everyday concepts, and I could never argue with him. He neither answers your rebuttal nor listens to what you have to say. As soon as you stop, he launches upon a long tirade which on the face of it seems to have some bearing on what you have said, but actually amounts only to a continuation of his own argument.

He is rather witty and his epigrams are frequently amusing but never pointed or malicious; he does not annihilate a person with one word. He knows neither people nor their foibles, for all his life he has been preoccupied with himself alone. His object in life is to become the hero of a romance. So often has he tried to make others believe he is a creature never intended for this world and hence doomed to some kind of occult suffering that he has practically convinced himself of it. That is why he vaunts of his heavy soldier's greatcoat. I see through him and he dislikes me for it, though on the face of it we are on the friendliest of terms. Grushnitsky has a reputation for superb courage; I have seen him in action: he brandishes his saber, and dashes forward shouting with his eyes shut. There is something very un-Russian in that brand of gallantry!

I do not like him either, and I feel we are bound to fall foul of each other one day with rueful consequences for one of us.

His coming to the Caucasus too was the result of his romantic fanaticism. I am certain that on the eve of his departure from his father's village he tragically announced to some comely neighbor that he was not going merely to serve in the army, but to seek death, because . . . at this point he probably covered his eyes with his hand and went on like this: "No, you must not know the reason! Your pure soul would shudder at the thought! And why should you? What am I to you? Can you understand me?" and so on and so forth.

He told me himself that the reason why he enlisted in the K. regiment will forever remain a secret between him and his Maker.

And yet when he discards his tragic guise Grushnitsky can be quite pleasant and amusing. I would like to see him in the company of women, for I imagine that is when he would try to be at his best.

We greeted each other as old friends. I began to ply him with questions concerning life at the spa and the interesting people there were to be met.

"We lead a rather prosaic life," he sighed. "Those who drink the waters in the mornings are listless like all sick people, and those who drink wine in the evenings are unbearable like all people who enjoy good health. There is feminine company, but it offers little consolation; they play whist, dress badly and speak terrible French. This year Princess Ligovskaya with her daughter are the only visitors from Moscow, but I have not met them. My greatcoat is like a brand of ostracism. The sympathy it evokes is as unwelcome as charity."

Just then two ladies walked past us toward the spring, one elderly, the other young and slender. I could not see their faces for the bonnets, but they were dressed in strict conformity with the very best taste: everything was as it should be. The young woman wore a high-necked pearl-gray dress; a dainty silk kerchief encircled her supple neck. A pair of dark-brown shoes encased her slender little feet up to the ankles so daintily that even one uninitiated into the mysteries of beauty would have caught his breath, if only in amazement. Her light but dignified gait had something virginal about it that eluded definition yet was perceptible to the eye. As she walked past us, that subtle fragrance was wafted from her which sometimes is exhaled by a note from a woman we love.

"That is Princess Ligovskaya," said Grushnitsky, "and her daughter, whom she calls Mary in the English manner. They've been here only three days."

"You seem to know her name already."

"Heard it quite by accident," he replied, coloring. "I must confess I have no desire to meet them. These haughty aristocrats think we armymen are savages. What is it to them if there is an intellect under a numbered cap and a heart beneath a thick greatcoat?"

"Poor greatcoat," said I, smiling. "And who is the gentleman going up to them and so obligingly offering them a tumbler?"

"Oh, that's the Moscow dandy Rayevich! He's a gambler, as you can see by the heavy gold chain across his blue waistcoat. And look at that thick cane—just like Robinson Crusoe's! Or the beard he sports, and the haircut *à la moujik*."[46]

"You seem to bear a grudge against the whole human race."

"And with good reason. . . ."

"Really?"

By this time the ladies had left the well and were again passing us. Grushnitsky hastened to strike a dramatic pose with the help of his crutch and replied loudly in French:

"Mon cher, je hais les hommes pour ne pas les mépriser, car autrement la vie serait une farce trop dégoûtante."[47]

The attractive Princess turned and bestowed on the speaker a long and searching glance. It was an obscure kind of look, but without a trace of mockery, on which I mentally congratulated him from the bottom of my heart.

"This Princess Mary is most charming," I said to him. "Her eyes are like velvet, yes, velvet. I would advise you to adopt this expression when you talk about her eyes; the eyelashes, both upper and lower, are so long that the sunbeams find no reflection in her pupils. I love eyes like that—without a shine in them, and so soft that they seem to be caressing you. By the way, I think they are the only good point in her face. . . . Are her teeth white? That is very important! It's a pity she did not smile at your grandiloquence."

"You talk about a charming woman as if she were an English thoroughbred," said Grushnitsky indignantly.

"Mon cher," I replied, trying to fall into tone, *"je méprise es femmes pour ne pas les aimer, car autrement la vie serait un mélodrame trop ridicule."*[48]

I turned and walked off. For half an hour I strolled along the vineclad walks, along the limestone cliffs and among the low bushes between them, until it grew hot and I hurried home. As I passed by the sulphur spring I stopped to rest in the shade of the covered gallery and thus became a witness of a rather curious spectacle. This is how the actors were

[46] A fashionable short haircut, affecting the style of a peasant (*moujik*).

[47] "My dear fellow, I hate men in order not to despise them, for otherwise life would be too disgusting a farce" (French).

[48] "My dear fellow, I despise women in order not to love them, for otherwise life would be too ridiculous a melodrama."

placed. The old Princess was sitting with the Moscow fop on a bench in the gallery and seemed to be engaged in a serious conversation. The young Princess, having apparently drunk her last glassful of water, was pacing thoughtfully up and down by the well. Grushnitsky was standing at the well. There was no one else around.

I went up closer and hid behind a corner of the gallery. Just then Grushnitsky dropped his tumbler on the sand and tried to stoop to pick it up, but his wounded leg made it hard for him. Poor chap! How he tried, leaning against the crutch, but in vain. His expressive face actually registered pain.

Princess Mary saw this better than I did.

Quicker than a bird she was at his side, bent down, picked up the tumbler and handed it to him with an inexpressibly sweet gesture; then she blushed furiously, cast a glance in the direction of the gallery, but seeing that her mother had not noticed anything, immediately regained her composure. When Grushnitsky opened his mouth to thank her she was already far away. A minute later she left the gallery in the company of her mother and the dandy, but as she passed Grushnitsky she assumed a most prim and proper air, not even turning her head in his direction or noticing the fervent gaze with which he escorted her until she disappeared behind the lime-trees of the boulevard at the foot of the hill. . . . He caught a last glimpse of her bonnet on the other side of the street as she ran into the gateway of one of the finest houses in Pyatigorsk. Behind her walked the old Princess, who bid farewell to Rayevich at the gate.

Only now did the poor smitten cadet become aware of my presence.

"Did you see it?" he asked, gripping my hand firmly. "She's simply an angel!"

"Why?" asked I, feigning utter innocence.

"Didn't you see?"

"Of course, I saw how she picked up your tumbler. If there had been a park-keeper around he would have done the same, only quicker in hopes of getting a tip. Though there is nothing surprising that she took pity on you; you made such an awful face when you stepped on your wounded leg. . . ."

"Weren't you moved when you saw her soul shining in her eyes?"

"No."

I was lying, but I wanted to rouse him. I have an inborn urge to contradict; my whole life has been a mere chain of sad and futile opposition to the dictates of either heart or reason. The presence of an enthusiast makes me as cold as a midwinter's day, and I believe frequent association with a listless phlegmatic would make me an impassioned dreamer. I must also admit that momentarily an unpleasant but familiar sensation lightly crept over my heart; that sensation was envy. I say "envy" frankly, because I am accustomed to being honest with myself. And it is unlikely that any young man (a man of the world accustomed to indulging his vanities, of course), who, having met a woman who attracted his idle fancy, would not be unpleasantly impressed upon seeing her favor another man no less a stranger than he.

Grushnitsky and I descended the hill in silence and walked down the boulevard past the windows of the house which our beauty had entered.

She was sitting at the window. Tugging at my sleeve, Grushnitsky gave her one of those mistily tender looks that evoke so little response in women. I directed my lorgnette at her and saw that Grushnitsky's glance brought a smile to her face while my impertinent lorgnette made her very angry. Indeed, how dare a Caucasian armyman level an eye-glass at a princess from Moscow?

MAY 13

The doctor dropped in to see me this morning. His name is Werner, but he is a Russian. There is nothing surprising in that. I once knew an Ivanov who was a German.

Werner is in many respects a remarkable man. He is a skeptic and a materialist like most medical men, but he is also a poet, and that quite in earnest—a poet in all his deeds and frequently in words, though he never wrote two verses in his life. He has studied the vital chords of the human heart the way men study the sinews of a corpse, but he has never been able to make use of his knowledge just as a splendid anatomist may not be able to cure a fever. As a rule, Werner secretly laughed at his patients, yet once I saw him weep over a dying soldier. He was poor and dreamed of possessing millions, but he would not have gone a step out of his way for the sake of money. Once he told me that he would rather do an enemy a good turn than a friend, because in the latter case it would amount to profiting by one's charity, whereas hatred grows in proportion to the generosity of the adversary. He had a malicious tongue, and, branded by his epigrams, more than one good soul came to be regarded as a vulgar fool. His competitors, envious practitioners at the spa, spread a rumor that he drew caricatures of his patients; the latter were furious and he lost practically all his clientele. His friends, that is, all the really decent people serving in the Caucasus, tried in vain to repair his fallen prestige.

His appearance was of the kind that strikes one disagreeably at first sight but subsequently becomes likeable when the eye has learned to discern behind the irregular features the impress of a soul that is tried and lofty. There have been cases when women have fallen madly in love with men like him and would not have exchanged their ugliness for the beauty of the freshest and pinkest of Endymions.[49] Women must be given credit for possessing an instinct for spiritual beauty; perhaps that is why men like Werner love women so passionately.

Werner was short of stature, thin and as frail as a child. Like Byron he had one leg shorter than the other; his head was disproportionately large; he wore his hair cropped close, and the irregularities of his skull thus exposed would have astounded a phrenologist by their queer combination of contradictory inclinations. His small, black, ever restless eyes probed your thoughts. He dressed immaculately and with good taste, and his lean, small, sinewy hands were neatly gloved in pale yellow. His coat, cravat and waistcoat were invariably black. The young set called him Mephistopheles, and though he pretended to be displeased by the appellation, in reality it

[49] In Greek mythology, Endymion was the beautiful shepherd loved by the moon goddess Selene.

flattered his vanity. We soon understood each other and became companions—for I am incapable of friendship. Between two friends one is always the slave of the other, though frequently neither will admit it; the slave I cannot be, and to dominate is an arduous task since one must employ deception as well; besides, I have the servants and the money! This is how we became acquainted: I met Werner in S., in a large and boisterous gathering of the younger set. Toward the end of the evening the conversation took a philosophical and metaphysical trend. We spoke about convictions, of which each had his own.

"As for me, I am convinced of only one thing . . ." said the doctor.

"And what is that?" I asked, wishing to hear the opinion of a man who had been silent till then.

"That some fine morning sooner or later I shall die," he replied.

"I am better off than you," said I. "I have another conviction besides, which is that one exceedingly foul night I had the misfortune to be born."

Everyone else was of the opinion that we were talking nonsense, but really nobody had anything more clever to say. From that moment we singled each other out from among the crowd. We used to meet frequently and discuss abstract matters in all seriousness until we both noticed that we were pulling each other's leg. Then, after looking each other in the eye significantly—the way Cicero tells us the Roman augurs[50] did—we would burst out laughing and separate satisfied with an evening well spent.

I was lying on a divan, my eyes fixed upon the ceiling and my hands behind my head, when Werner walked into my room. He seated himself in a chair, stood his cane in a corner, yawned and observed that it was getting hot outdoors. I replied that the flies were bothering me, and we both fell silent.

"You will have noticed, my dear doctor," said I, "that without fools the world would be very boring. . . . Now here we are, two intelligent people; we know in advance that everything can be argued about endlessly, and hence do not argue; we know nearly all of each other's innermost thoughts; a single word tells us a whole story, and we see the kernel of each of our sentiments through a triple husk.[51] Sad things strike us as funny, funny things as sad, and generally speaking if you want to know, we are rather indifferent to everything except ourselves. Hence there can be no exchange of emotions and ideas between us; we know all we want to know about each other and do not wish to know more. That leaves only one thing to talk about: the latest news. Haven't you any news to tell me?"

Fatigued by the long speech, I closed my eyes and yawned.

"There is one idea in the balderdash you are talking," he replied after a pause for thought.

"Two!" I replied.

"Tell me one of them and I will say what the other is."

"Good. You begin," said I, continuing to inspect the ceiling and smiling inwardly.

[50] Augurs foretold the future by examining the entrails of animals. The first-century B.C. philosopher Cicero, in *On Divination,* wondered how one augur could see another without laughing.

[51] The "triple husk," explained immediately, is (1) the comedy of sadness, (2) the sadness of comedy, and (3) indifference to both.

"You would like to know some details about someone who has arrived at the spa, and I can guess who it is you have in mind because that person has already been inquiring about you."

"Doctor! We definitely need not converse; we can read each other's minds."

"Now the other one. . . ."

"The second idea is this: I would like to induce you to tell me something; firstly, because listening is less tiring than talking, secondly, because in listening one does not give anything away, thirdly, because you may learn another man's secret, and, fourthly, because clever people like you prefer a listener to a talker. Now let's come to the point: what did Princess Ligovskaya have to say to you about me?"

"Are you sure it was not Princess Mary?"

"Quite certain."

"Why?"

"Because Princess Mary asked about Grushnitsky."

"You have rare sagacity. The young Princess said she was certain the young man in the ordinary soldier's greatcoat had been degraded to the ranks on account of a duel. . . ."

"I hope you did not disabuse her mind of that pleasant illusion. . . ."

"Naturally not."

"The plot thickens," I cried in elation, "and we shall see to the denouement of the comedy. Fate apparently does not wish me to be bored."

"I have a notion that poor Grushnitsky will end up as your victim," said the doctor.

"And then what happened, doctor?"

"Princess Ligovskaya said your face was familiar. I observed she must have met you somewhere in St. Petersburg society, and mentioned your name. She knew about you. It seems that your story made a sensation there. Then the Princess went on to recount your adventures, probably spicing the society gossip with her own opinions. Her daughter listened with interest, visualizing you as the hero of a novel written in the modern style. I did not contradict the Princess though I knew she was talking nonsense."

"Worthy friend!" said I, extending my hand to him. The doctor gripped it with feeling and continued.

"If you wish me to, I'll introduce you. . . ."

"My dear fellow!" said I, spreading my hands. "Have you ever heard of heroes being formally presented? They make the acquaintance of their beloved by rescuing her from certain death. . . ."

"Do you really intend to court the Princess?"

"Not at all, quite the contrary! Doctor, I score at last, for you do not understand me! Yet it is rather annoying just the same," I continued after a moment's silence. "I make it a rule never to disclose my own thoughts, and am very glad when others divine them because that leaves me a loophole for denying them when necessary. But you must describe mama and daughter to me. What sort of people are they?"

"In the first place, the old Princess is a woman of forty-five," replied Werner. "Her digestion is splendid, though her blood is not quite in order; you can tell by the red spots on her cheeks. The latter half of her life she has spent in Moscow where inactivity has caused her to put on weight. She is fond of spicy anecdotes and says improper things when her daughter is out of the room. She told me that her daughter was as innocent as a dove. Though what it had to do with me, I don't know. I wanted to tell her that she might rest assured I would tell no one about it! The Princess is taking the cure for rheumatism, and the daughter the Lord knows what for; I told them both to drink two glasses of sulphur water daily and bathe twice weekly in it. The Princess apparently is unaccustomed to ordering people about, and she respects the brains and knowledge of her daughter, who has read Byron in English and knows algebra, for it seems that the young ladies of Moscow have taken up learning—good for them, I should say. In general our men are so ill-mannered that intelligent women probably find it unbearable to flirt with them. The old Princess is very fond of young men, but Princess Mary regards them with a certain contempt—an old Moscow habit. In Moscow they go in for forty-year-old wits only."

"Were you ever in Moscow, doctor?"

"Yes, I was. Had a sort of practice there."

"Please go on."

"I believe I have said everything there is to say. . . . Oh yes, one more thing: Princess Mary appears to be fond of discussing sentiments, emotions and the like. She spent a winter in Petersburg, but the city, and particularly its society, did not please her. Evidently she was given a cool reception."

"You didn't meet anybody else at their place today, did you?"

"Yes, I did. There was an adjutant, a starched guardsman, and a lady, one of the new arrivals, some relative of the Princess' husband, a very pretty woman but a very sick one, I believe. You didn't happen to see her at the spring? She is of medium height, blond, with regular features, a consumptive complexion, and a little dark mole on her right cheek. I was struck by the expressiveness of her face."

"A mole?" I muttered. "Is it possible?"

The doctor looked at me and laying his hand on my heart said solemnly: "You know her." My heart indeed was beating faster than usual.

"It's your turn to exult now," said I. "Only I trust that you will not give me away. I have not seen her yet, but I believe I recognize in the portrait you have painted a woman I loved in the old days. . . . Don't tell her a word about me, and if she asks you, speak ill of me."

"As you wish," said Werner, shrugging his shoulders.

When he left, a terrible sadness flooded my soul. Was it fate that brought us together in the Caucasus, or had she come on purpose, knowing she would find me here? What would the meeting be like? And was it she, after all? My presentiments had never deceived me. There is not another person on earth over whom the past holds such sway as over me. Every remembrance of a past sorrow or joy sends a pang through my heart and invariably strikes the very same chords. I am stupidly constituted, for I forget nothing—nothing!

After dinner I went down to the boulevard at about six and found a crowd there. The Princess and her daughter were seated on a bench surrounded by a flock of young men who were paying them constant attention. I found myself another bench some distance away, stopped two officers I knew and began telling them a story. Apparently it amused them, because they roared with laughter like madmen. Curiosity drew to my bench some of the gallants who had clustered around the Princess; then little by little the rest too deserted her and joined my group. I talked incessantly, telling anecdotes that were witty to the point of stupidity and ridiculing the queer characters that passed by with a malice bordering on viciousness. Thus I continued to amuse my audience until sunset. Several times the young Princess strolled arm-in-arm with her mother past me, accompanied by a limping old man, and several times her gaze rested on me, expressing vexation while trying to convey indifference.

"What was he telling you?" she asked one of the young men who returned to her out of sheer politeness. "It must have been a very thrilling story—about his battle exploits no doubt." She spoke rather loudly, obviously with the intention of slighting me. "Aha," thought I, "you are thoroughly annoyed, my dear Princess! Wait, there is more to come!"

Grushnitsky has been stalking her like a wild beast, never letting her out of his sight. I daresay that tomorrow he will ask someone to present him to Princess Ligovskaya. She will be very glad to meet him, for she is bored.

MAY 16

During the past two days things have been moving fast. Princess Mary decidedly hates me. I have already been told two or three rather biting but nevertheless very flattering epigrams pointed at me. It strikes her as very odd that I who am so accustomed to good society and on such intimate terms with her Petersburg cousins and aunts should make no effort to make her acquaintance. We see each other every day at the spring and on the boulevard, and I do my best to decoy her admirers, the glittering adjutants, pallid Moscovites and others—with almost invariable success. I have always loathed entertaining guests, but now I have a full house every day, for dinner, supper and a game of cards, and lo, my champagne triumphs over the magnetism of her eyes!

Yesterday I met her at Chelakhov's shop where she was bargaining for a splendid Persian rug. The Princess pleaded with her mother not to begrudge the money, for the rug would look so well in her room. . . . I overbid forty rubles and walked away with the rug, and was rewarded with a look of the most bewitching fury. At dinner-time I deliberately had my Cherkess horse led past her windows with the rug thrown over its back. Werner, who was visiting them at the time, told me that the effect of the spectacle was most dramatic. The Princess wants to raise a levy against me; I have already noticed that in her presence two of the adjutants give me very curt nods, though they dine with me every day.

Grushnitsky has assumed a mysterious air; he walks with his hands behind his back oblivious of everybody. His leg has suddenly healed so that he scarcely limps. He found an occasion to engage the old Princess in conversation and to pay a compliment to Princess Mary; the latter apparently is not too discriminating, for ever since she has been responding to his bows with the most charming smile.

"You are sure you do not wish to meet the Ligovskys?" he asked me yesterday.

"Positive."

"Really! It's the pleasantest house at the spa. All the best local society. . . ."

"My dear friend, I'm frightfully fed up with non-local society, let alone the local. Have you been calling on them?"

"Not yet. I have no more than talked with the Princess once or twice. You know how unpleasant it is to fish for an invitation, though it is done here. . . . It would be another matter if I had epaulettes. . . ."

"My dear fellow! You are far more interesting as you are. You simply do not know how to take advantage of your favorable position. Don't you know that a soldier's greatcoat makes you a hero and a martyr in the eyes of any sensitive young lady?"

Grushnitsky smiled complacently.

"What nonsense!" he said.

"I am sure," I went on, "that the Princess has fallen in love with you."

He blushed to the roots of his hair and pouted.

O vanity! Thou art the lever with which Archimedes hoped to raise the globe.[52]

"You're always joking," he said, pretending to be angry. "In the first place she barely knows me. . . ."

"Women love only the men they don't know."

"But I have no particular desire to please her. I merely wish to make the acquaintance of a pleasant household, and it would indeed be absurd to entertain any hopes whatsoever. . . . Now you Petersburg lady-killers are another matter: you only have to look once for a woman to melt. . . . By the way, Pechorin, do you know the young Princess spoke of you?"

"What? Has she already spoken to you about me?"

"You have no reason to rejoice, though. Once quite by chance I entered into conversation with her at the spring; her third remark was, 'Who is that gentleman with the unpleasant, heavy-eyed expression? He was with you when. . . .' She blushed and was reluctant to mention the day, recalling her charming little exploit. 'You need not mention the day,' I replied, 'for I shall always remember it. . . .' Pechorin, my friend, I cannot congratulate you, for she thinks ill of you. . . . It is a pity, really, because my Mary is very charming!"

It must be noted that Grushnitsky is one of those who in speaking of a woman they hardly know call her *my Mary* or *my Sophie* if only she has the good fortune to attract them.

Assuming a serious mien I replied:

"Yes, she is rather good-looking. . . . Only take care, Grushnitsky! Russian young ladies for the most part go in only for Platonic love with no intentions of matrimony, and Platonic love is most disturbing. It seems to me that the Princess is one of those women who wish to be amused; if she is bored for two minutes in your company you are irrevocably doomed. Your silence must arouse her curiosity, your conversation must never completely satisfy her; you must keep her in a state of suspense all the time; ten times she will defy public opinion for your sake and call it a sacrifice, and as a

[52] The third-century B.C. Greek mathematician and physicist Archimedes, discoverer of the principle of the lever, is said to have boasted that if he had a lever long enough and a place to put it, he could raise the earth.

recompense she will begin to torment you and end up by saying simply that she cannot tolerate you. If you do not gain the ascendancy over her, even her first kiss will not give you the right to a second. She will flirt with you to her heart's content and a year or two later marry an ugly beast in obedience to her mother's will; then she will begin to assure you that she is unhappy, that she had loved only one man—that is, you—but that fate had not ordained that she be joined to him because he wore a soldier's greatcoat, though beneath that thick gray garment there beat an ardent and noble heart. . . ."

Grushnitsky smote the table with his fist and began to pace up and down the room.

I shook with laughter inwardly and even smiled a couple of times, but luckily he did not notice it. He is clearly in love, for he has become more credulous than ever: he even wears a new niello-silver[53] ring of local workmanship, which struck me as suspicious. On closer inspection what do you think I saw? The name *Mary* engraved in small letters on the inside and next to it the date when she picked up that famous tumbler. I said nothing of my discovery; I do not want to extract any confessions from him; I want him to make me his confidant by his own choice—and that's when I am going to enjoy myself. . . .

. . . .

Today I got up late, and by the time I reached the spring no one was there. It was getting hot, white fluffy clouds raced across the sky away from the snow-capped mountains promising a thunderstorm. Mashuk's summit was smoking like an extinguished torch, and around it gray tatters of clouds arrested in their flight and seemingly caught in the mountain brambles, writhed and crawled like serpents. The atmosphere was charged with electricity. I took the vine-flanked avenue leading to the grotto; I felt depressed. I was thinking of the young woman with the mole on her cheek whom the doctor had mentioned. What was she doing here? And was it she? And why did I think it was she? Why was I so certain about it? Are there so few women with moles on their cheeks? Ruminating thus I reached the grotto. A woman was seated on a stone bench in the cool shade of its roof; she was wearing a straw hat, a black shawl was wrapped round her shoulders, and her head was lowered so that the hat concealed her face. I was about to turn back so as not to disturb her meditations when she looked up at me.

"Vera!" I cried out involuntarily.

She started and turned pale. "I knew you were here," she said. I sat down next to her and took her hand. A long-forgotten tremor shot through my veins at the sound of that sweet voice. Her deep, tranquil eyes looked straight into mine; in them I could read distress and something akin to a reproach.

"We have not seen each other for so long," said I.

"Yes, and we both have changed a great deal."

"You mean, you do not love me any more!"

[53] Silver decorated with incised designs filled with niello, a black alloy.

"I am married!" she said.

"Again? Some years ago there was the same reason, but in spite of that. . . ."

She snatched her hand away and her cheeks flamed.

"Perhaps you are in love with your second husband?"

She made no reply and turned away.

"Or maybe he is very jealous?"

Silence.

"Well, he must be a fine, handsome fellow, very rich, I suppose, and you are afraid that. . . ." I looked at her and was startled; her face expressed dire distress, and tears glistened in her eyes.

"Tell me," she whispered at last, "does it give you so much pleasure to torment me? I ought to hate you. Ever since we have known each other you have brought me nothing but pain. . . ." Her voice shook, and she leaned towards me resting her head on my breast.

"Perhaps," I thought, "that is why you loved me, for joy is forgotten, but sorrow never. . . ."

I pressed her close to me and we remained thus for a long time. Then our lips met and merged in a burning, rapturous kiss; her hands were ice-cold, her head feverishly hot. There began one of those conversations that make no sense on paper, that cannot be repeated or even remembered, for the import of words is substituted and enriched by that of sounds, just as in Italian opera.

She is resolved that I should not meet her husband, who is the lame old man I caught a glimpse of on the boulevard. She married him for the sake of her son. He is rich and suffers from rheumatism. I did not allow myself a single disparaging remark about him, for she respects him like a father—and will deceive him as a husband. . . . A queer thing, the human heart, and a woman's heart in particular!

Vera's husband, Semyon Vasilyevich G...v, is a distant relative of Princess Ligovskaya. They are next door neighbors, and Vera is often at the Princess'. I promised her that I would meet the Ligovskys and dangle after Princess Mary so as to divert attention from her. This does not interfere with my plans at all and I will have a good time. . . .

A good time! Yes, I have already passed that period of spiritual life when people seek happiness alone and when the heart must needs love someone passionately; now I only want to be loved, and then only by very few. As a matter of fact, I believe one constant attachment would suffice for me—a wretched sentimental habit!

It has always struck me as queer that I have never become the slave of the woman I loved; on the contrary, I have always acquired an invincible sway over her mind and heart without any effort on my part. Why is that? Was it because I have never particularly prized anything and they have been afraid to let me slip out of their hands for a moment? Or was it the magnetic appeal of physical strength? Or simply because I have never met a woman with strength of character?

I must admit that I do not care for women with a mind of their own—it does not suit them!

Though I recall now that once, but only once, I loved a woman with a strong mind I never could conquer. . . . We parted enemies, yet had I met her five years later the parting might have been quite different. . . .

Vera is ill, very ill, although she will not admit it; I am afraid she has consumption or the disease they call *fiévre lente*[54]—not a Russian ailment at all and hence it has no name in our language.

The thunderstorm overtook us in the grotto and kept us there another half an hour. She did not make me vow to be faithful to her, nor did she ask me whether I had loved others since we parted. . . . She trusted me again as wholeheartedly as before—and I shall not deceive her; she is the only woman in the world I would not have the heart to deceive. I know that we shall part again soon, perhaps forever. We shall both go our different ways to the grave, but I shall always cherish her memory. I have always told her so and she believes me, though she says she does not.

At length we parted, and I stood there following her with my eyes until her bonnet disappeared behind the bushes and rocks. My heart contracted painfully, just as when we parted the first time. Oh, how I revelled in this feeling! Was it youth with its beneficent tempests reasserting itself, or merely its farewell glance, a parting gift—a souvenir? And to think that I still look like a boy; though my face is pale, it is still fresh, my limbs are supple and graceful, my locks thick and curly, eyes flashing, and my blood courses swiftly through the veins. . . .

On coming home, I mounted my horse and galloped into the steppe, for I love riding a mettlesome horse through the tall grass, with the desert wind in my face, greedily drinking in the fragrant air and gazing into the blue distance to discern hazy outlines or objects that grow more distinct every moment. Whatever sorrow weighs down the heart or anxiety plagues the mind, it all is immediately dispersed, and a peace settles over the soul as physical fatigue prevails over mental unrest. There are no feminine eyes I would not forget when gazing on the wooded mountains bathed in the southern sunshine, contemplating the blue sky, or listening to the roar of the torrent falling from crag to crag.

I should imagine the Cossack sentinels, standing drowsily in their watchtowers, must have been sorely puzzled on seeing me galloping along without aim or drift, for they most likely took me for a Cherkess on account of my costume. As a matter of fact I had been told that mounted and wearing Cherkess costume I look more like a Kabardian than many Kabardians. And indeed, as far as this noble battle garb is concerned I am a perfect dandy: not an extra bit of braiding, costly weapons in the simplest setting, the fur on my cap neither too long nor too short, leggings and soft-leather boots fitting perfectly, white *beshmet* and dark-brown Cherkess coat. I practiced long the mountaineers' way of sitting a horse; and nothing so flatters my vanity as praise for my ability to ride a horse as the Caucasians do. I keep four horses, one for myself and three for my friends, so as to avoid the boredom of riding out alone through the fields, but though they are pleased to have my horses to ride they never ride with me. It was already six o'clock in the afternoon when I remembered that it was time for dinner; moreover, my horse was exhausted. I rode out onto the road lead-

[54] A "slow" or chronic fever, as opposed to *fiévre hectique,* a sudden, acute fever.

ing from Pyatigorsk to the German colony where the spa society frequently goes *en piquenique.*[55] The road winds its way through the shrubbery, dipping into shallow gullies where noisy rivulets flow in the shadow of the tall grasses; all around are the towering blue terraces of Beshtau, Zmeinaya, Zheleznaya and Lysaya mountains. I had stopped in one of these gullies to water my horse when a noisy and brilliant cavalcade appeared down the road; there were ladies in black and sky-blue riding habits and gentlemen in garb that was a mixture of Cherkess and Nizhni-Novgorod.[56] Grushnitsky and Princess Mary rode in front.

Ladies who come to take the waters still believe the stories of Cherkess raids in broad daylight, and that probably explains why Grushnitsky had belted a saber and a pair of pistols over his soldier's greatcoat; he looked rather ridiculous in these heroic vestments. A tall bush concealed me from them, but I had a perfect view through the foliage and could tell by the expression of their faces that the conversation was in a sentimental vein. Finally they neared the dip in the road. Grushnitsky gripped the reins of the Princess' horse, and now I could hear the end of their conversation:

"And you wish to remain in the Caucasus all your life?" said the Princess.

"What is Russia to me?" replied her escort. "A country where thousands of people will despise me because they are wealthier than I, whereas here—why, here this thick greatcoat was no obstacle to my making your acquaintance. . . ."

"On the contrary . . ." said the Princess, blushing.

Grushnitsky looked pleased. He continued:

"Here my days will flow thick and fast and unnoticed under the bullets of barbarians, and if only God should send me each year one bright feminine glance, one like. . . ."

By this time they drew level with me; I struck my horse with the whip and rode out from behind the bushes.

"Mon dieu, un Circassien!"[57] cried the Princess in terror.

To reassure her I replied in French, with a slight bow:

"Ne craignez rien, madame, je ne suis pas plus dangereux que votre cavalier."[58]

She was thrown into confusion—I wonder why? Because of her mistake, or because she thought my reply insolent? I wish indeed that the latter were the case. Grushnitsky glanced at me with displeasure.

Late that night, that is, about eleven o'clock, I went for a walk along the lime avenue of the boulevard. The town was fast asleep, and only here and there a light shone in a window. On three sides loomed the black ridges of the spurs of Mashuk, on whose summit lay an ominous cloud; the moon was rising in the east; in the distance the snow-capped summits glistened in a silvery fringe. The cries of sentries intermingled with the noise of the hot

[55] Picnicking (French).

[56] *Cherkess and Nizhni-Novgorod.* Nizhni-Novgorod was a provincial Russian city, now named Gorky. To say that something was "*X* and Nizhni-Novgorod" meant that it was an impossible jumble, from a line in Alexander Griboyedov's comedy *Wit from Woe* (1833): "a confusion of tongues, French and Nizhni-Novgorodan."

[57] "Oh dear! A Circassian!" (French).

[58] "Fear nothing, madame, I am no more dangerous than your cavalier" (French).

springs now released for the night. At times the ringing hoofbeats echoed down the street accompanied by the creaking of a covered ox-wagon and the plaintive chant of a Tatar refrain. I sat down on a bench and sank into thought. I felt a need to unburden my thoughts in a friendly talk . . . but with whom? What was Vera doing now, I wondered. I would have given much to press her hand just then.

Suddenly I heard quick, uneven steps. . . . Probably Grushnitsky . . . and so it was.

"Where have you been?"

"At Princess Ligovskaya's," he said gravely. "How beautifully Mary sings!"

"You know what," said I, "I'll wager she does not know you are a cadet, but thinks you are a degraded officer."

"Maybe. What do I care!" he said absently.

"Well, I just mentioned it. . . ."

"Do you know that you made her terribly angry? She thought it was downright insolence on your part. I had a stiff job trying to assure her that you are so well bred and so much at home in society that you could not have had any intention of insulting her. She says you have an impudent look and must be very conceited."

"She is right. . . . You seem to be taking her part, don't you?"

"I'm sorry I haven't won that right yet."

"Oho!" thought I. "Evidently he already has hopes. . . ."

"It'll only be worse for you," Grushnitsky went on. "Now it will be hard for you to meet them—what a pity! It is one of the pleasantest houses I know. . . ."

I smiled inwardly.

"The pleasantest house for me just now is my own," said I yawning, and rose to go.

"Still you must admit that you regret it?"

"What nonsense! I could be at the Princess' tomorrow night if I wish. . . ."

"We'll see about that. . . ."

"To please you I can even pay court to the Princess. . . ."

"That is, if she is willing to talk to you. . . ."

"I shall wait till she gets bored with your conversation. . . . Good night!"

"And I'll go for a prowl—couldn't fall asleep for anything now. . . . Look here, let's go to the restaurant, one can gamble there. . . . Violent sensations are what I need tonight."

"I hope you lose. . . ."

I went home.

MAY 21

Nearly a week has passed and I have not met the Ligovskys yet. Am waiting for an opportunity. Grushnitsky follows Princess Mary about like a shadow, and they talk incessantly. I wonder when she'll get tired of him. Her mother takes no notice of what is going on because he is *not eligible.* There is the logic of mothers for you! I have caught two or three tender looks—this must be put a stop to.

Yesterday Vera made her first appearance at the spring. Since our meeting in the grotto she has not left the house. We dipped our tumblers into the water at the same time and as she bent down she whispered to me:

"You don't want to go to the Ligovskys'! It is the only place where we can meet."

A reproach—how boring! But I deserved it.

By the way, there is a subscription ball at the restaurant hall, and I intend to dance the mazurka with Princess Mary.

MAY 29

The restaurant hall was transformed into a Nobles' Club hall. By nine o'clock everybody was there. Princess Ligovskaya and her daughter were among the last to arrive. Many of the ladies eyed Princess Mary with envy and ill will, for she dresses with very good taste. Those who consider themselves the local aristocrats concealed their envy and attached themselves to her. What else could be expected? Wherever there is feminine society, there is an immediate division into the upper and lower circles. Grushnitsky stood among the crowd outside the window, pressing his face to the glass and devouring his goddess with his eyes; in passing she gave him a barely perceptible nod. He beamed like the sun. . . . The first dance was a polonaise; then the orchestra struck up a waltz. Spurs jingled and coat-tails whirled.

I stood behind a stout lady under a rose-colored plumage. The splendor of her gown was reminiscent of the farthingale age[59] and the blotchiness of her coarse skin of the happy epoch of the black-taffeta beauty spots. The biggest wart on her neck was concealed beneath a clasp. She was saying to her partner, a captain of dragoons:

"This Princess Ligovskaya is a minx. Think of it, she bumped into me and did not bother to apologize, and actually turned round to look at me through her lorgnette. . . . *C'est impayable!*[60] And what has she got to give herself airs for? It would do her good to be taught a lesson. . . ."

"Leave it to me!" replied the obliging captain and repaired to another room.

I went over at once to the Princess and asked for the waltz, taking advantage of the freedom of the local customs which allow one to dance with strangers.

She was scarcely able to suppress a smile and thus conceal her triumph, but quickly enough she managed to assume a totally indifferent and even severe mien. She carelessly laid her hand on my shoulder, tilted her head a bit to one side, and off we started. I know no other waist so voluptuous and supple. Her sweet breath caressed my face; now and then a ringlet broke loose from its companions in the whirl of the dance and brushed my burning cheek. . . . I made three turns round the room. (She waltzes delightfully.) She was panting, her eyes looked blurred and her parted lips could hardly whisper the necessary "*Merci, monsieur.*"

[59] The "farthingale age" was the eighteenth century, when women wore farthingales (hoopskirts) and black-taffeta beauty spots.

[60] "That's priceless!" (French).

After a few minutes of silence I said, assuming the humblest of expressions:

"I have heard, Princess, that while still an utter stranger to you, I had the misfortune to evoke your displeasure, that you found me impertinent. . . . Is that really true?"

"And you would like to strengthen that opinion now?" she replied, with an ironical little grimace that, incidentally, matched well the quick mobility of her features.

"If I had the audacity to offend you in any way, will you allow me the greater audacity of asking your forgiveness? Really, I should like very much to prove that you were mistaken in your opinion of me. . . ."

"That will be a rather difficult task for you. . . ."

"Why?"

"Because you don't come to our house and these balls probably will not be repeated frequently."

That means, thought I, their doors are closed to me for all time.

"Do you know, Princess," said I with a shade of annoyance, "that one should never spurn a repentant sinner, for out of sheer desperation he may become doubly sinful . . . and then. . . ."

Laughter and whispering around us made me break off and look round. A few paces away stood a group of men, among them the captain of dragoons who had expressed his hostile intentions toward the charming Princess. He seemed to be highly pleased with something, rubbing his hands, laughing loudly and exchanging winks with his comrades. Suddenly a gentleman in a tailcoat and with a long moustache and a red face stepped out of their midst and walked unsteadily toward the Princess. He was obviously drunk. Stopping in front of the bewildered Princess, with his hands behind his back, he directed his bleary gray eyes at her and said in a wheezy treble:

"*Permettez* . . . oh, dash it . . . I just want to have the mazurka. . . ."

"What do you want, sir?" she said with a tremor in her voice, casting about a beseeching glance. But, alas, her mother was far away, nor were there any of the gallants she knew nearby, excepting one adjutant who, I believe, saw what was going on, but hid behind the crowd to avoid being involved in an unpleasant scene.

"Well, well!" said the drunken gentleman, winking at the captain of dragoons who was spurring him on with encouraging signs. "You would rather not? I once more have the honor of inviting you *pour mazure*[61]. . . . Maybe you think I'm drunk? That's all right! Dance all the better, I assure you. . . ."

I saw she was on the verge of fainting from terror and mortification.

I stepped up to the intoxicated gentleman, gripped him firmly by the arm and looking him straight in the eyes asked him to go away, because, I added, the Princess had already promised me the mazurka.

"Oh, I see! Another time, then!" he said, with a laugh, and rejoined his cronies who, looking rather crestfallen, guided him out of the room.

I was rewarded with a charming glance.

The Princess went over to her mother and told her what had happened,

[61] "For the mazurka" (French).

and the latter sought me out in the crowd to thank me. She told me that she knew my mother and was a friend of half a dozen of my aunts.

"I simply cannot understand how it is we haven't met before," she added, "though you must admit that it's your own fault. You hold yourself so aloof you know, really. I hope the atmosphere of my drawing-room will dispel your spleen. What do you say?"

I replied with one of those polite phrases everyone must have in store for occasions like this.

The quadrilles dragged out interminably.

Finally the mazurka started and I sat down beside the young Princess.

I made no reference to the drunken gentleman, nor to my previous conduct, nor yet to Grushnitsky. The impression the unpleasant incident had made on her gradually dispersed, her face glowed, and she chatted charmingly. Her conversation was pointed without pretensions to wit, it was vivacious and free of restraint, and some of her observations were profound indeed. . . . I let her understand in a confused, rambling sort of way that I had long been attracted by her. She bent her head and blushed faintly.

"You are a strange man!" she said presently with a constrained smile, raising her velvety eyes to me.

"I did not wish to meet you," I continued, "because you are surrounded by too great a crowd of admirers and I was afraid it might engulf me completely."

"You had nothing to fear. They are all exceedingly tiresome. . . ."

"All of them? Certainly not all?"

She looked at me closely as if trying to recall something, then blushed faintly again and finally said in a decided tone: "All of them!"

"Even my friend Grushnitsky?"

"Is he your friend?" she asked dubiously.

"He is."

"He, certainly, cannot be classed as a bore."

"But an unfortunate, perhaps?" said I, laughingly.

"Of course! Why are you amused? I would like to see you in his place."

"Why? I was a cadet once myself, and believe me, that was the finest period of my life!"

"Is he a cadet?" she asked quickly, adding a moment later: "And I thought. . . ."

"What did you think?"

"Nothing, nothing at all. . . . Who is that lady?"

The conversation took a different turn and this subject was not resumed.

The mazurka ended and we parted—until we should meet again. The ladies went home. Going in for supper, I met Werner.

"Aha," he said, "so that's that! And you said you would only make the Princess' acquaintance by rescuing her from certain death?"

"I did better," I replied, "I saved her from fainting at the ball!"

"What happened? Tell me!"

"No, you will have to guess, O you who divine everything under the sun!"

MAY 30

I was walking on the boulevard about seven o'clock in the evening. Grushnitsky, seeing me from afar, came over, a ridiculously rapturous light gleaming in his eyes. He clasped my hand tightly and said in a tragic tone:

"I thank you, Pechorin. . . . You understand me, don't you?"

"No, I don't. In any case there is nothing to thank me for," I replied, for I really had no good deed on my conscience.

"Why, what about yesterday? Have you forgotten? Mary told me everything. . . ."

"You don't say you already share everything in common? And gratitude too?"

"Listen," said Grushnitsky with an impressive air. "Please don't make fun of my love if you wish to remain my friend. . . . You see, I love her madly . . . and I believe, I hope, that she loves me too. . . . I have a favor to ask of you: you will be visiting them this evening, promise me to observe everything. I know you are experienced in these matters and you know women better than I do. O women, women! Who really does understand them? Their smiles disavow their glances, their words promise and beguile, but the tone of their voice repulses. They either divine in a flash your innermost thought or they do not grasp the most obvious hint. . . . Take the Princess, for instance: yesterday her eyes glowed with passion when they dwelt on me but now they are lusterless and cold. . . ."

"That perhaps is the effect of the waters," replied I.

"You always look at the seamy side of things . . . you materialist!" he added scornfully. "But let us get down to other matters." Pleased with this bad pun, his spirits rose.

At nine o'clock we went together to the Princess'.

In passing Vera's windows I saw her looking out, and we exchanged a cursory glance. She entered the Ligovskys' drawing-room soon after us. The old Princess introduced her to me as a kinswoman. Tea was served, there were many guests, and the conversation was general. I did my best to charm the old Princess, told jokes and made her laugh heartily several times; her daughter too wanted to laugh more than once, but she suppressed the desire so as not to abandon the role she assumed, for she believes that languor is becoming to her—and perhaps she is right. I believe Grushnitsky was very glad that my gaiety did not infect her.

After tea we all repaired to the sitting-room.

"Are you pleased with my obedience, Vera?" I asked as I passed her.

She gave me a look full of love and gratitude. I am used to these glances; but there was a time when they were my heart's delight. Princess Ligovskaya made her daughter sit down to the piano and everybody begged her to sing. I said nothing, and taking advantage of the hubbub withdrew to a window with Vera who intimated that she had something to say of great importance to both of us. It turned out to be nonsense.

My indifference did not please the young Princess, however, as I could guess by the one angry flashing glance she gave me. . . . How well do I understand this dumb but eloquent conversational means, so brief yet so forceful!

She sang: her voice is pleasant but she sings badly . . . as a matter of fact, I did not listen. But Grushnitsky, with his elbows on the piano facing the Princess, devoured her with his eyes, mumbling *"Charmant! Délicieux!"* over and over again.

"Listen," Vera was saying, "I do not want you to make the acquaintance of my husband, but you must get into the old Princess' good graces; you can do it easily, you can do anything you wish. We shall meet only here. . . ."

"Nowhere else?"

She colored and went on:

"You know I am your slave, I never could resist you. And I will be punished for it. Because you will cease to love me! At least I want to save my reputation . . . not because of myself, you know that very well. But please don't torment me as before with idle doubts and feigned indifference; I may die soon, for I feel I am growing weaker day by day . . . but in spite of that I cannot think of the life beyond, I think only of you. You men do not understand the rapture one can find in a glance or a handclasp, but, I swear to you, the sound of your voice fills me with a deep, strange feeling of joy as no passionate kisses ever could do."

In the meantime Princess Mary had stopped singing. A chorus of praise broke out around her. I walked up to her last and said something very casual about her voice.

She pouted and made a mock curtsy.

"It is all the more flattering to me," she said, "because you weren't listening at all. But perhaps you do not care for music?"

"On the contrary, I do, particularly after dinner."

"Grushnitsky is right when he says that your tastes are most prosaic. Even I can see that you appreciate music from the point of view of the gourmand. . . ."

"You are wrong again. I am no gourmand and I have a poor digestion. Nevertheless, music after dinner lulls you to sleep and a nap after dinner is good for you; hence I like music in the medical sense. In the evening, on the contrary, it excites my nerves too much, and I find myself either too depressed or too gay. Both are tedious when there is no good reason either to mope or to rejoice; besides to be downcast in company is ridiculous and excessive gaiety is in bad taste. . ."

She walked off without waiting for me to finish and sat down beside Grushnitsky. The two engaged in a sentimental conversation: the Princess seemed to respond to his sapient sayings in an absent-minded, rather inept, way, though she simulated interest, and he glanced at her every now and then with a look of surprise as if trying to fathom the cause of the inner turmoil reflected in her troubled eyes.

But I have unravelled your secret, my charming Princess, so beware! You wish to repay me in the same currency by wounding my vanity—but you will not succeed in doing so! And if you declare war on me, I shall be ruthless.

Several times in the course of the evening I deliberately tried to join in their conversation, but she countered my remarks rather drily, and I finally withdrew feigning resentment. The Princess was triumphant, and so was Grushnitsky. Triumph, my friends, while you may . . . you have not long to triumph! What will happen? I have a presentiment. . . . Upon meeting a woman I have always been able to tell without error whether she will fall in love with me or not. . . .

The remainder of the evening I spent with Vera, and we talked our fill about the past. I really do not know why she loves me so. Especially since she is the only woman who has ever completely understood me with all my petty frailties and evil passions. . . . Can evil indeed be so attractive?

I left together with Grushnitsky. Outside he took my arm and after a long silence said:

"Well, what do you say?"

I wanted to tell him, "You are a fool," but restrained myself and merely shrugged my shoulders.

JUNE 6

All these days I have not once departed from my system. The Princess is beginning to enjoy my conversation. I told her some of the curious incidents of my life, and she is beginning to regard me as an unusual person. I mock at everything under the sun, emotions in particular, and this is beginning to frighten her. She does not dare to launch upon sentimental debates with Grushnitsky when I am present, and already on several occasions she has replied to him with an ironical smile. Yet each time Grushnitsky approaches her I assume a humble air and leave the two alone. The first time I did so she was glad, or tried to look pleased; the second time she lost patience with me, and the third time with Grushnitsky.

"You have very little pride!" she told me yesterday. "Why do you think I prefer Grushnitsky's society?"

I replied that I was sacrificing my own pleasure for a friend's happiness.

"And my pleasure as well," she added.

I looked at her intently and assumed an air of gravity. Then for the rest of the day I did not address her. . . . She was pensive last night, and even more wistful this morning at the spring. As I walked up to her, she was listening absently to Grushnitsky who, I believe, was harping on the beauties of nature, but as soon as she saw me she began to laugh heartily (rather irrelevantly), pretending not to notice me. I withdrew some distance away and watched her out of the corner of my eye; she turned away from her companion and yawned twice. There is no doubt about it: she is bored with Grushnitsky. But I shall not speak to her for another two days.

JUNE 11

I often ask myself why it is that I so persistently seek to win the love of a young girl whom I do not wish to seduce and whom I shall never marry. Why this feminine coquetry? Vera loves me better than Princess Mary ever will. Were she an unconquerable beauty, the difficulty of the undertaking might serve as an inducement. . . .

But far from it! Hence this is not the restless craving for love that torments us in the early years of our youth and casts us from one woman to another until we meet one who cannot endure us; this is the beginning of our constancy—the true unending passion that may mathematically be represented by a line extending from a point into space, the secret of whose endlessness consists merely in the impossibility of attaining the goal, that is, the end.

What is it that spurs me on? Envy of Grushnitsky? Poor chap! He does not deserve it. Or is it the result of that malicious but indomitable impulse to annihilate the blissful illusions of a fellow man in order to have the petty satisfaction of telling him when in desperation he appeals to us:

"My friend, the same thing happened to me! Yet as you see, I dine, sup and sleep well, and, I hope, will be able to die without any fuss or tears!"

And yet to possess a young soul that has barely burgeoned out is a source of unfathomable delight. It is like a flower whose richest perfume goes out to meet the first ray of the sun; one must pluck it at that very moment and after inhaling its perfume to one's heart's content cast it away on the chance that someone will pick it up. I sense in myself that insatiable avidity that devours everything in its path; and I regard the sufferings and joys of others merely in relation to myself, as food to sustain my spiritual strength. Passions no longer are capable of robbing me of my sanity, my ambition has been crushed by circumstances, but it has manifested itself in new form, for ambition is nothing but greed for power, and my greatest pleasure I derive from subordinating everything around me to my will. Is it not both the first token of power and its supreme triumph to inspire in others the emotions of love, devotion and fear? Is it not the sweetest fare for our vanity to be the cause of pain or joy for someone without the least claim thereto? And what is happiness? Pride gratified. Could I consider myself better and more powerful than anyone else in the world, I should be happy; were everybody to love me, I should find in myself unending well-springs of love. Evil begets evil; the first pain leads to a realization of how great is the pleasure of tormenting another; the conception of evil cannot take root in the mind of man without his desiring to apply it in practice. Someone has said that ideas are organic entities: their very birth imparts them form, and this form is action. He in whose brain most ideas are born is more active than others, and because of this a genius shackled to an office desk must either die or lose his mind, just as a man of powerful physique who leads a sedentary and chaste life dies of apoplectic stroke.

Passions are nothing more than ideas at the first stage of their development; they belong to the heart's youth, and he is foolish who thinks they will stir him all his life. Many a placid river begins in roaring waterfalls, but not a single stream leaps and froths all the way to the sea. Frequently this placidity is a symptom of great though latent force. The fullness and depth of emotions and thought precludes furious impulses, for the soul in its sufferings or rejoicings is fully alive to what is taking place and conscious that so it must be; it knows that were there no tempests the constant heat of the sun would shrivel it; it is imbued with its own life, fostering and chastising itself as a mother her favorite child. Only in this state of supreme self-cognition can a man appreciate the divine judgment.

Reading over this page I notice that I have digressed far from my subject. But what of it? For I am writing this journal for myself and hence anything I jot down will in time become a precious memory to me.

. . . .

Grushnitsky came and flung himself on my neck—he had received his commission. We had some champagne. Doctor Werner came in immediately after.

"I don't offer you my felicitations," he said to Grushnitsky.

"Why?"

"Because the soldier's greatcoat suits you very well and you will have to admit that an infantry officer's uniform tailored here at the spa will not add anything of interest to you. . . . You see, so far you have been an exception, whereas now you will be quite commonplace."

"Say what you will, doctor, you cannot prevent me from rejoicing. He does not know," Grushnitsky whispered in my ear, "what hopes I attach to these epaulettes. O epaulettes, epaulettes! Your stars are little guiding stars. . . . No! I am perfectly happy now."

"Are you coming with us for a walk to the chasm?" I asked him.

"Oh no! I wouldn't show myself to the Princess for anything until my new uniform is ready."

"Shall I tell her about your good fortune?"

"Please don't, I want it to be a surprise."

"Tell me though, how are you getting along with her?"

He was embarrassed and pondered a while. He would have liked to brag about it and lie, but his conscience forbade him, and at the same time he was ashamed to confess the truth.

"Do you think she loves you?"

"Does she love me? For goodness sake, Pechorin, what ideas you have! How can you expect it so soon? And even if she did, a respectable woman would not say so. . . ."

"Good! You probably believe that a respectable man too must conceal his passion."

"Ah, my good fellow, there is a proper way to do everything. Many things are not said but guessed. . . ."

"True enough. . . . Only the love we read in a woman's eyes is noncommittal whereas words. . . . Take care, Grushnitsky, she is deceiving you. . . ."

"She?" he replied, raising his eyes to the sky and smiling complacently. "I pity you, Pechorin!"

He left.

In the evening a large company set out on foot for the chasm.

The local savants are of the opinion that this chasm is nothing but an extinct crater. It is located in the slope of Mashuk within a verst of the town. It is approached by a narrow path winding through the brush and crags. As we climbed the mountainside I offered my arm to the Princess, who did not relinquish it throughout the entire walk.

Our conversation started with scandal; I began to go through our acquaintances both present and absent, first describing their ridiculous aspects, then their bad traits. My gall was up and after starting off in jest I finished in deadly earnest. At first she was amused, then alarmed.

"You are a dangerous man!" she told me. "I would rather risk a murderer's knife in the forest than be flayed by your tongue. I beg of you quite earnestly—if you should ever take it into your mind to speak ill of me, take a knife instead and kill me. I believe you would not find it too difficult to do."

"Do I look like a murderer?"

"You are worse. . . ."

I thought for a moment and then said, assuming a deeply touched mien:

"Yes, such has been my lot since childhood. Everyone read signs of nonexistent evil traits in my features. But since they were expected to be there, they did make their appearance. Because I was reserved, they said I was sly, so I grew reticent. I was keenly aware of good and evil, but instead of being fondled I was insulted and so I became spiteful. I was sulky while other children were merry and talkative, but though I felt superior to them I was considered inferior. So I grew envious. I was ready to love the whole world, but no one understood me, and I learned to hate. My cheerless youth passed in conflict with myself and society, and fearing ridicule I buried my finest feelings deep in my heart, and there they died. I spoke the truth, but nobody believed me, so I began to practice duplicity. Having come to know society and its mainsprings, I became versed in the art of living and saw how others were happy without that proficiency, enjoying gratuitously the boons I had so painfully striven for. It was then that despair was born in my breast—not the despair that is cured with a pistol, but a cold, impotent desperation concealed under a polite exterior and a good-natured smile. I became a moral cripple; I had lost one half of my soul, for it had shrivelled, dried up and died and I had cut it off and cast it away, while the other half stirred and lived, adapted to serve every comer. No one noticed this because no one suspected there had been another half; now, however, you awakened memories of it in me, and what I have just done is to read its epitaph to you. Many regard all epitaphs as ridiculous, but I do not, particularly when I remember what rests beneath them. Of course, I am not asking you to share my opinion; if what I have said seems funny to you, please laugh, though I warn you that it will not annoy me in the slightest."

At that moment our eyes met, and I saw that hers swam with tears. Her arm resting on mine trembled, her cheeks were flaming. She was sorry for me! Compassion—that emotion which all women so easily yield to—had sunk its talons into her inexperienced heart. Throughout the walk she was absent-minded and flirted with no one—and that is a great omen indeed!

We reached the chasm. The other ladies left their escorts, but she did not release my arm. The witticisms of the local dandies did not amuse her; the abruptness of the bluff on the brink of which she stood did not alarm her, though the other young ladies squealed and closed their eyes.

On the way back I did not resume the sad conversation, but to my idle questions and jests she gave only brief and distracted answers.

"Have you ever been in love?" I finally asked her.

She looked at me intently, shook her head and again was lost in thought. It was evident that she wanted to say something but did not know where to begin. Her breast heaved. . . . Indeed, a muslin sleeve affords but slight protection, and an electric tremor ran from my arm to hers; most passions begin thus, and we frequently deceive ourselves when we think that a woman loves us for our physical or moral qualities; true, they prepare the ground, dispose her heart to receive the sacred flame, but nevertheless it is the first contact that decides the issue.

"I have been very amiable today, have I not?" the Princess said with a forced smile when we returned from our walk.

We parted.

She is displeased with herself; she accuses herself of being cool. Ah, this is the first and most important triumph! Tomorrow she will want to reward me. I know it all by rote—and that is what makes it all so boring.

JUNE 12

I have just seen Vera. She nagged me to death with jealousy. I believe the Princess has chosen to confide her secrets of the heart to Vera. An appropriate choice, indeed!

"I can guess what it all will lead to," Vera said to me. "It would be better if you told me frankly now that you love her."

"But supposing I do not love her?"

"Then why pursue her, disturb her and stir her imagination? Oh, I know you too well! If you want me to believe you, go to Kislovodsk a week from now. We shall move there the day after tomorrow. Princess Ligovskaya is remaining here a little longer. Rent the apartment next door to ours; we shall stay in the large house near the fountain, on the mezzanine floor. Princess Ligovskaya will occupy the floor below, and next door there is another house belonging to the same owner which has not been taken yet. . . . Will you come?"

I promised, and the very same day sent a man to rent the apartments.

Grushnitsky dropped in at six in the evening and announced that his uniform would be ready the next day, just in time for the ball.

"At last I shall dance with her all evening. . . . And talk to my heart's content," he added.

"When is the ball?"

"Tomorrow. Didn't you know? It's quite a gala event, and the local authorities are sponsoring it."

"Let's go out on the boulevard."

"Goodness no, not in this hideous greatcoat. . . ."

"What? Do you mean to say you don't like it any more?"

I went out alone, and, encountering Princess Mary asked her for the mazurka. She looked surprised and pleased.

"I thought you danced only when necessary, like the last time," she said, smiling very prettily.

She seemed to be totally unaware of Grushnitsky's absence.

"You will have a pleasant surprise tomorrow," I said to her.

"What is it?"

"It's a secret. . . . You will see for yourself at the ball."

I wound up the evening at Princess Ligovskaya's. There were no guests besides Vera and a very amusing old man. I was in good form and improvised all kinds of fantastic stories. Princess Mary sat opposite me listening to my chatter with an attention so great, intense and even tender that I felt a pang of remorse. What had become of her vivacity, her coquetry, her caprices, her haughty air, her contemptuous smile and absent gaze?

Vera noticed it all and a deep sadness was reflected on her wan face; she sat in the shadows at the window sunk in a broad arm-chair. I was sorry for her. . . .

Then I related the whole dramatic story of our friendship and love, naturally using fictitious names.

So vividly did I describe my tender feelings, anxieties and raptures, and portrayed her actions and character in so favorable a light that she could not but forgive me my flirtation with the Princess.

She got up, moved to a seat closer to us and recovered her spirits . . . and only at two o'clock in the morning did we recollect that physician's orders were to retire at eleven.

JUNE 13

Half an hour before the ball Grushnitsky came to my apartment in the full splendor of an infantry officer's uniform. A bronze chain on which a double lorgnette dangled was attached to his third button; he wore epaulettes of incredible size which curled up like Cupid's wings; his boots squeaked; in his left hand he carried a pair of brown kid gloves and his cap, while with his right he kept twirling his frizzled forelock into tiny curls. Complacency tinged with a certain hesitancy was written on his face. His festive appearance and his proud carriage would have made me roar with laughter had that been in keeping with my intentions.

He threw his cap and gloves on the table and began to pull at his coattails and preen himself in front of the mirror. An enormous black kerchief twisted into a high stiffener for his cravat, with bristles that supported his chin, showed half an inch above the collar; he thought that too little and pulled it up to his ears. The exertion made his face grow purple, for the collar of the uniform coat was very tight and uncomfortable.

"They say you have been hard after my Princess these days," he said rather nonchalantly, without looking at me.

"It's not for the likes of us to drink tea!" replied I, repeating a favorite saying by one of the cleverest rakes of the past once sung by Pushkin.[62]

"Say, does this thing fit me well? Confound the Jew![63] It's tight under the armpits. Have you any perfume?"

"For goodness sake, what more do you want? You already reek of rose pomade."

"Never mind. Let's have some. . . ."

He poured half a phial on his cravat, handkerchief and sleeves.

"Going to dance?" he asked.

"I don't think so."

"I am afraid the Princess and I will have to start the mazurka, and I scarcely know a single figure. . . ."

[62] Vladimir Nabokov identifies this figure as Pavel Kaverin (1794–1855), a soldier and man-about-town, for whose portrait Alexander Pushkin wrote an inscription in 1817.

[63] This casual piece of anti-semitism is based on the fact that a large number of Russian tailors were Jews, since tailoring was one of the few trades open to them.

"Did you ask her for the mazurka?"

"No, not yet. . . ."

"Take care no one anticipates you. . . ."

"You're right, by gad!" he said, slapping his forehead. "Good-bye, I'll go and wait for her at the entrance." He seized his cap and ran off.

Half an hour later I too set out. The streets were dark and deserted. Around the club rooms or inn—whichever you want to call it—the crowds were gathering. The windows were lighted up, and the evening wind wafted to me the strains of the regimental band. I walked slowly, steeped in melancholy. Can it be, thought I, that my sole mission on earth is to destroy the hopes of others? Ever since I began to live and act, fate has somehow associated me with the denouement of other people's tragedies, as if without me no one could either die or give way to despair! I have been the inevitable fifth-act character, involuntarily playing the detestable role of the hangman or the traitor. What has been fate's object in all this? Has it destined me to be the author of middle-class tragedies and family romances—or a purveyor of tales for, say, the Reader's Library.[64] Who knows? Are there not many who begin life by aspiring to end it like Alexander the Great, or Lord Byron, and yet remain petty civil servants all their lives?

On entering the hall I mingled with the crowd of men and began making observations. Grushnitsky was standing beside the Princess and talking with great ardor; she was listening to him absent-mindedly, looking around and pressing her fan to her lips; her countenance expressed impatience and her eyes searched for someone. I quietly slipped behind them so as to overhear the conversation.

"You are tormenting me, Princess," Grushnitsky said. "You have changed terribly since I saw you last."

"You too have changed," she replied, throwing him a swift look whose veiled scorn was lost on him.

"I? Changed? Never! You know that is impossible! Whoever has seen you once will carry your divine image with him to the grave. . . ."

"Stop. . . ."

"Why will you not listen now to what you so recently and so often lent a favorable ear?"

"Because I do not like repetition," she replied, laughing.

"O, I have been bitterly mistaken! I thought, fool that I am, that at least these epaulettes would give me the right to hope. . . . Yes, it would have been better to spend the rest of my life in that despicable greatcoat of a soldier to which I perhaps owe your attention."

"Really, the greatcoat becomes you far better. . . ."

At that moment I came up and bowed to the Princess; she blushed slightly, saying hurriedly:

"Don't you think, M'sieu Pechorin, that the gray greatcoat suits M'sieu Grushnitsky much better?"

"I do not agree with you," replied I. "He looks even younger in this uniform."

Grushnitsky could not stand the thrust, for like all boys he lays claim to being a man of years. He thinks that the deep traces of passions on his face

[64] A popular St. Petersburg magazine.

can pass for the stamp of years. He threw a furious look at me, stamped his foot and strode away.

"You must admit," said I to the Princess, "that although he has always been very ridiculous he still struck you as interesting a short while ago . . . in his gray greatcoat."

She dropped her eyes and said nothing.

Grushnitsky pursued the Princess the whole evening, dancing either with her or vis-à-vis;[65] he devoured her with his eyes, sighed and wearied her with his supplications and reproaches. By the end of the third quadrille she already hated him.

"I did not expect this of you," he said, coming up to me and taking me by the arm.

"What are you talking about?"

"Are you going to dance the mazurka with her?" he asked me in a solemn tone. "She admitted as much to me. . . ."

"Well, what of it? Is it a secret?"

"Of course. . . . I should have expected it from that hussy, that flirt. . . . Never mind, I'll take my revenge!"

"Blame your greatcoat or your epaulettes, but why accuse her? Is it her fault that she no longer likes you?"

"Why did she give me reason to hope?"

"Why did you hope? To want something and to strive for it is something I can understand, but whoever hopes?"

"You have won the bet, but not entirely," he said, with a sneer.

The mazurka began. Grushnitsky invited none but the Princess, other cavaliers chose her every minute; it was obviously a conspiracy against me—but that was all for the better. She wanted to talk with me; she was prevented from doing so—good! She would want to all the more.

I pressed her hand once or twice; the second time she pulled her hand away without a word.

"I shall sleep badly tonight," she said to me when the mazurka was over.

"Grushnitsky is to blame for that."

"Oh no!" And her face grew so pensive, so sad, that I promised myself I would kiss her hand that night.

Everybody began to disperse. Having helped the Princess into her carriage, I quickly pressed her little hand to my lips. It was dark and no one could see.

I returned to the hall highly pleased with myself.

The young gallants were having supper around a large table, Grushnitsky among them. When I entered they all fell silent; they must have been talking about me. Ever since the previous ball many of them, the captain of dragoons in particular, have had a bone to pick with me, and now it seems that a hostile band is being organized against me under Grushnitsky's command. He wears such a cocky, bravura air.

I am very glad of it, for I love enemies, though not in the Christian way. They amuse me and quicken my pulse. To be always on one's guard, to catch every look and the significance of every word, to guess intentions, foil

[65] "Face to face," that is, in one of the other three couples in a quadrille set (French).

conspiracies, pretend to be deceived and then to overthrow with one blow the whole vast edifice of artifices and designs raised with so much effort—that is what I call life.

Throughout the meal Grushnitsky spoke in whspers and exchanged winks with the captain of dragoons.

JUNE 14

This morning Vera left for Kislovodsk with her husband. Their carriage passed me as I was on my way to Princess Ligovskaya's. She nodded to me; there was a reproach in her eyes.

Who is to blame, after all? Why does she not want to give me an opportunity to see her alone? Love, like fire, dies out without fuel. Perhaps jealousy will succeed where my pleadings have failed.

I stayed a whole hour at the Princess'. Mary did not come down—she was indisposed. In the evening she did not appear on the boulevard. The newly-formed gang had armed itself with lorgnettes and looked formidable indeed. I am glad that the Princess was ill, for they would have affronted her in some way. Grushnitsky's hair was dishevelled and he looked desperate; he actually seems to be embittered, his vanity especially has been wounded. But some people are really amusing even when desperate!

On returning home I felt a vague longing. *I had not seen her! She was ill!* Have I actually fallen in love? What nonsense!

JUNE 15

At eleven o'clock in the morning, at which hour Princess Ligovskaya usually sweats it out at the Yermolov baths, I walked past her house. Princess Mary was sitting at the window lost in thought; on seeing me, she jumped to her feet.

I walked into the anteroom; there was no one around and taking advantage of the freedom of the local custom, I went straight to the drawing-room without being announced.

A dull pallor had spread over the Princess' charming features. She stood by the piano, leaning with one arm on the back of a chair; the arm trembled slightly. Quietly I walked up to her and said:

"Are you angry with me?"

She raised her eyes to me with a deep, languorous look and shook her head; her lips wanted to say something, but could not; her eyes filled with tears; she sank into a chair and covered her face with her hands.

"What is the matter?" I said, taking her hand.

"You do not respect me! Oh, leave me alone!"

I stepped back a few paces. She stiffened in the chair and her eyes flashed. . . .

I paused, my hand on the door knob, and said:

"I beg your pardon, Princess! I acted rashly . . . it will not happen again, I shall see to it. Why should you know what has been going on in my heart? You shall never know it, which is all the better for you. Farewell."

As I went out I thought I heard her sobbing.

Until evening I wandered about the environs of Mashuk, tired myself out thoroughly and on returning home flung myself on the bed in utter exhaustion.

Werner dropped in to see me.

"Is it true," he asked, "that you intend to marry Princess Ligovskaya?"

"Why do you ask?"

"The whole town is talking about it. All my patients can think of nothing else but this important news, and these watering place crowds know everything!"

"This is Grushnitsky's little joke!" thought I.

"To prove to you, doctor, how unfounded these rumors are, I shall tell you in confidence that I am going to Kislovodsk tomorrow."

"And Princess Mary as well?"

"No, she will remain here another week."

"So you do not intend to marry?"

"Doctor, doctor! Look at me: do I look like a bridegroom or anything of the kind?"

"I am not saying you do. . . . But, you know, it sometimes happens," he added, smiling slyly, "that a man of honor is obliged to get married, and that there are fond mamas who at least do not prevent such eventualities from arising. . . . So as a friend, I advise you to be more cautious. The air is highly dangerous here at the waters. How many splendid young men worthy of a better fate have I seen leave here bound straight for the altar. Believe it or not, they wanted to marry me off, too. It was the doing of one provincial mama with a very pale daughter. I had the misfortune to tell her that the girl would regain her color after the nuptials; whereupon with tears of gratitude in her eyes she offered me her daughter's hand and all her property—fifty souls,[66] I believe it was. I told her, however, that I was quite unfit for matrimony."

Werner left fully confident that he had given me a timely warning.

I could tell by what he had said that diverse malicious rumors had been spread all over town about the Princess and myself: Grushnitsky will have to pay for this!

JUNE 18

It is three days since I arrived in Kislovodsk. I see Vera every day at the spring or on the promenade. When I wake up in the morning I sit at the window and direct a lorgnette at her balcony. Having dressed long before, she waits for the signal agreed upon, and we meet as if by accident in the garden which slopes down to the spring from our houses. The invigorating mountain air has returned color to her face and given her strength. It is not for nothing that Narzan is called the spring of giants. The local inhabitants claim that the air in Kislovodsk is conducive to love and that all the love affairs that ever began at the foot of Mashuk have invariably reached their denouement here. And indeed, everything here breathes of solitude; everything is mysterious—the dense shadows of the avenues of lime-trees

[66] Fifty serfs. An estate with only fifty serfs was a very small one.

hanging over the torrent, which, falling noisily and frothily from flag[67] to flag, cleaves its way through the green mountains, and the gorges, full of gloom and silence, that branch out from here in all directions, and the freshness of the fragrant air laden with the aroma of the tall southern grasses and the white acacia, and the incessant deliciously drowsy babble of the cool brooks which, mingling at the end of the valley, rush onward to hurl their waters into the Podkumok. On this side the gorge is wider and spreads out into a green depression, and through it meanders a dusty road. Each time I look at it, I seem to see a carriage approaching and a pretty rosy-cheeked face looking out of its window. Many a carriage has already rolled along that road—but there still is no sign of that particular one. The settlement beyond the fort is now densely populated; from the restaurant built on a hill a few paces from my apartment lights have begun to glimmer in the evenings through the double row of poplars, and the noise and the clinking of glasses can be heard until late at night.

Nowhere is there so much Kakhetian wine and mineral water quaffed as here.

> To jumble up such various kinds of fun
> There's many take delight: for me, I am not one.[68]

Grushnitsky and his gang carouse daily in the saloon. He hardly ever greets me now.

He arrived only yesterday, but he has already managed to pick a quarrel with three old men who wanted to take their baths before him. Bad luck is decidedly developing a bellicose spirit in him.

JUNE 22

At last they arrived. I was sitting at the window when I heard their carriage drive up, and my heart bounded. What does it mean? Could I be in love? So senselessly am I constituted that it might indeed be expected of me.

I had dinner with them. Princess Ligovskaya eyed me very tenderly and did not leave her daughter's side—a bad sign that! But Vera is jealous of Princess Mary; I have managed to achieve that felicitous state after all! What would not a woman do to hurt a rival! I recall a woman who loved me simply because I was in love with another. Nothing is more paradoxical than the feminine mind: it is hard to convince women of anything, they must be brought to a point where they will convince themselves. The method of adducing the evidence with which they annihilate their prejudices is highly original, and to come to know their dialectics one must overthrow in one's mind all the academic rules of logic. For example, the ordinary method is this:

This man loves me; but I am married; hence, I must not love him.

The feminine method is this:

I must not love him, because I am married; but he loves me, and hence. . . .

[67] Flat rock or ledge. [68] From Alexander Griboyedov's comedy *Wit from Woe* (1833).

Here follows a pregnant pause, for reason is now dumb, and all the talking is mainly done by the tongue, eyes, and eventually the heart, if there is one.

What if these notes fall into a woman's hands some day? "Libel!" she will cry indignantly.

Ever since poets began to write and women to read them (for which they must be heartily thanked), the latter have been called angels so often that in the simplicity of their hearts they have actually come to believe in this compliment, forgetting that for money the very same poets exalted Nero as a demigod.

It might appear unseemly that I should speak of them with such malice—I, who have never loved anything else under the sun, I, who have always been ready to sacrifice my peace of mind, ambition and life for their sake. . . . Yet it is not in a fit of annoyance or injured vanity that I endeavor to draw aside that magic veil which only the accustomed eye can penetrate. No, all that I say about them is only the result of

> The mind's reflections coldly noted,
> The bitter insights of the heart.[69]

Women should wish all men to know them as well as I do, for I have loved them a hundred times more since I overcame my fear of them and discovered their petty frailties.

Incidentally, Werner the other day compared women with the enchanted forest described by Tasso in his "Jerusalem Delivered."[70]

"You have but to approach it," he said, "to be assaulted from all sides by ungodly terrors: duty, pride, respectability, public opinion, ridicule, contempt. . . . You must not heed them, but go straight on; little by little the monsters vanish and before you opens a quiet, sunny glade with green myrtle blooming in its midst. But woe to you if your heart quails when you take those first steps and you turn back!"

JUNE 24

This evening was replete with events. Some three versts out of Kislovodsk, in the gorge where the Podkumok flows, there is a crag called *The Ring*, forming a natural gateway that towers above a high hill; through it the setting sun casts its last fiery glance at the world. A large cavalcade set out to watch the sunset through the rocky window. To tell the truth, though, none of the people who came along thought of the sunset. I rode next to Princess Mary. On the way back we had to ford the Podkumok. Even the smallest mountain streams are dangerous chiefly because their bottoms are a perfect kaleidoscope, changing day after day under the action of the current; where there was a rock yesterday there may be a pit today. I took the Princess' horse by the bridle and led it to the water, which did not rise above the knees; we started crossing slowly at an angle against the current.

[69] From Alexander Pushkin's *Eugene Onegin* (1831).

[70] A religious epic (1575) about the First Crusade by the Italian poet Torquato Tasso.

It is a well-known fact that in crossing rapids one should not look at the water because it makes you dizzy. I forgot to warn Princess Mary of this.

We were already in midstream, where the current is the swiftest, when she suddenly began to sway in the saddle. "I feel faint!" she gasped. Quickly I bent over toward her and put my arm around her supple waist.

"Look up!" I whispered to her. "Don't be afraid, it's quite all right; I am with you."

She felt better and wanted to free herself from my arm, but I tightened my embrace about her soft slender waist; my cheek almost touched hers; I could feel its fiery glow.

"What are you doing? My God!"

I paid no heed to her quivering confusion, and my lips touched her soft cheek; she started, but said nothing. We were riding behind the others; no one saw us. When we clambered ashore, everyone set off at a trot. The Princess, however, reined in her horse, and I remained with her; it was obvious that she was worried by my silence, but I swore to myself not to say a word—out of sheer curiosity. I wanted to see how she would extricate herself from the embarrassing situation.

"Either you despise me or you love me very much," she said at last in a voice that shook with tears. "Perhaps you wish to mock at me, play on my feelings, and then leave me. . . . That would be so vile, so low, that the very thought. . . . Oh no! Surely," she added with an air of tender trustfulness, "there is nothing in me that would preclude respect, is there? Your presumptuous conduct. . . . I must, I must forgive you because I suffered it. . . . Answer me, speak to me, I want to hear your voice!" There was so much womanly impetuosity in her last words that I could not suppress a smile; luckily, it was growing dark. I did not reply.

"You have nothing to say?" she continued. "Perhaps you wish me to be the first to say that I love you?"

I was silent.

"Do you want me to do that?" she went on, swiftly turning toward me. There was something awe-inspiring in the earnestness of her eyes and voice.

"Why should I?" I replied, shrugging my shoulders.

She struck her horse with her riding crop and set off at full gallop along the narrow, dangerous road; it all happened so quickly that I was hardly able to overtake her, and did so only when she had already joined the rest of the company. All the way home she talked and laughed incessantly. There was a feverishness in her movements; and not once did she look at me. Everybody noticed this unusual gaiety. Princess Ligovskaya rejoiced inwardly as she watched her daughter; but her daughter was merely suffering a fit of nerves and would spend a sleepless night weeping. The very thought gives me infinite pleasure; there are moments when I understand the Vampire[71]. . . . And yet I have the reputation of being a good fellow and try to live up to it!

Having dismounted, the ladies went in to Princess Ligovskaya's. I was

[71] The character in John William Polidori's "The Vampyre, A Tale" (1819), written for the same horror-story competition which produced Mary Shelley's *Frankenstein*.

agitated and galloped into the hills to dispel the thoughts that crowded into my mind. The dewy evening breathed a delicious coolness. The moon was rising from behind the darkly looming mountain pinnacles. Every step my unshod horse took echoed dully in the silence of the gorges. I watered my horse at a waterfall, eagerly drank in the invigorating air of the southern night, and retraced my steps. I rode through the village. Lights were going out in the windows; sentries on the ramparts of the fort and Cossack pickets on the outposts hallooed to each other on a sustained note.

I noticed that one of the houses in the village which had been built on the brink of a gully was unusually brightly lit, and every now and then I could hear a babble of voices and shouting which betokened an armymen's carousal. I dismounted and crept up to the window; a loose shutter made it possible for me to see the revellers and overhear what they were saying. They were talking about me.

The captain of dragoons, flushed with wine, pounded the table with his fist to command attention.

"Gentlemen!" he said. "This won't do at all. Pechorin must be taught a lesson. These Petersburg whippersnappers get uppish until they're rapped on the knuckles! Just because he always wears clean gloves and shiny boots he thinks he's the only society man around."

"And that supercilious smile of his! Yet I'm certain he's a coward—yes, a coward!"

"I believe so too," said Grushnitsky. "He turns everything into a joke. Once I told him off in such terms that another man would have cut me down on the spot, but Pechorin just laughed it off. I, of course, didn't challenge him, because it was up to him to do so; besides I did not want to bother. . . ."

"Grushnitsky is wild because he stole a march on him with the Princess," said someone.

"What nonsense! True, I did run after the Princess a bit, but I gave it up soon enough because I have no desire to marry and I do not believe in compromising a girl."

"Yes, I assure you he is a coward of the first water, Pechorin I mean, not Grushnitsky. Grushnitsky is a fine chap and a good friend of mine to boot!" said the captain of dragoons. "Gentlemen! Does anyone here want to stand up for him? No one? All the better! Do you wish to test his courage? It will be amusing. . . ."

"We do. But how?"

"Now listen to me: since Grushnitsky's grievance is the biggest, his shall be the leading role. He will take exception to some trifle and challenge Pechorin to a duel. . . . Wait, this is the point. . . . He will challenge Pechorin—so far so good! Everything, the challenge, the preparations and the conditions will be made in as solemn and awe-inspiring a fashion as possible—I shall take care of that, for I'll be your second, my poor friend! Very well! Now this is the trick: we will not load the pistols. I give you my word Pechorin will show the white feather—six paces from one another I'll place them, damn it! Are you agreeable, gentlemen?"

"Grand idea, splendid! What a lark!" came from all sides.

"And you, Grushnitsky?"

I awaited Grushnitsky's reply with trepidation; a cold fury gripped me at the thought that mere chance had saved me from being made the butt of these fools' jest. Had Grushnitsky not agreed to it, I would have flung myself on his neck. After a brief silence, however, he rose from his seat, extended his hand to the captain and said very pompously: "Very well, I agree."

The elation of the whole honorable company defies description.

I returned home a prey to two conflicting emotions. One was sadness. Why do they all hate me? I thought. Why? Had I offended anybody? No. Can it be that I am one of those whose mere appearance excites ill will? And I felt a venomous wrath gradually take possession of me. Take care, Mr. Grushnitsky, I said to myself as I paced up and down the room, you cannot trifle thus with me. You might have to pay dearly for the approbation of your stupid comrades. I am not a toy for you to play with! . . .

I lay awake all night. In the morning I looked as yellow as an orange.

Early in the day I met Princess Mary at the spring.

"Are you ill?" she asked, looking at me intently.

"I did not sleep all night."

"Neither did I. . . . I blamed you . . . unjustly perhaps? But if you would only explain I could forgive you everything."

"Everything?"

"Yes, everything. . . . Only you must tell the truth . . . be quick. . . . You see, I have gone over it again and again, trying to find some explanation that would justify your conduct. Perhaps you fear opposition on the part of my relatives? There is nothing to worry about that; when they hear of it . . ." (her voice trembled) "I shall persuade them. Or, perhaps, it is your own position . . . but I want you to know that I am capable of sacrificing everything for the sake of the man I love. . . . Oh, answer me quickly—have pity on me. . . . Tell me, you don't despise me, do you?"

She seized my hand.

Princess Ligovskaya was walking ahead of us with Vera's husband and saw nothing; but we could have been observed by the patients who were strolling about, and they are the most inquisitive of all inquisitive gossips, so I quickly disengaged my hand from her passionate clasp.

"I shall tell you the whole truth," I said, "without trying to justify myself or to explain my actions. I do not love you."

Her lips paled slightly.

"Leave me," she said in a barely audible voice.

I shrugged my shoulders, turned, and walked away.

JUNE 25

Sometimes I despise myself; is that why I despise others too? I am no longer capable of noble impulses; I am afraid of appearing ridiculous to myself. Anyone else would have offered the Princess *son coeur et sa fortune*[72] but for me the word *marriage* has an odd spell: no matter how passionately I might love a woman it is farewell to love if she as much as hints at my marrying her. My heart turns to stone, and nothing can warm it again. I would make any sacrifice but this; twenty times I can stake my life, even my

[72] "His heart and his fortune" (French).

honor, but my freedom I shall never sell. Why do I prize it so much? What do I find in it? What am I aiming at? What have I to expect from the future? Nothing, absolutely nothing. It is some innate fear, an inexplicable foreboding. . . . After all, some people have an unreasoning fear of spiders, cockroaches, mice. . . . Shall I confess? When I was still a child, some old woman told my fortune for my mother, predicting that I would *die through a wicked wife*. It made a deep impression on me at the time, and an insuperable abhorrence for marriage grew within me. And yet something tells me that her prophecy will come true; but at least I shall do my best to put off its fulfillment as long as possible.

JUNE 26

Apfelbaum, the conjurer, arrived here yesterday. A long poster appeared on the restaurant doors informing the worthy public that the above-named amazing magician, acrobat, chemist and optician would have the honor to present a magnificent spectacle this day at eight o'clock in the evening in the hall of the Nobles' Club (otherwise the restaurant); admission two rubles and a half.

Everybody intends to go and see the amazing conjurer; even Princess Ligovskaya has taken a ticket for herself, although her daughter is ill.

As I was walking past Vera's windows today after dinner—she was sitting on the balcony alone—a note fell at my feet:

"Come tonight at ten o'clock in the evening by the main staircase; my husband has gone to Pyatigorsk and will not be back until tomorrow morning. My menservants and chambermaids will not be in: I gave them all, as well as the Princess' servants, tickets to the show. I shall wait for you; come without fail."

"Aha!" thought I. "At last I am having my way."

At eight o'clock I went to see the conjurer. It was nearly nine when the audience had assembled and the performance began. In the back rows I recognized the lackeys and chambermaids of both Vera and the Princess. They were all there. Grushnitsky was sitting in the first row with his lorgnette. The conjurer turned to him each time he needed a handkerchief, watch, ring, or the like.

Grushnitsky has not bowed to me for some time, and now he eyed me rather insolently once or twice. He shall rue it when the time comes to settle scores.

It was nearly ten when I rose and went out.

It was pitch black outside. Heavy, chill clouds lay on the summits of the surrounding mountains, and only now and then did the dying breeze rustle the tops of the poplars around the restaurant. People were crowding at the windows. I went down the hill and, after turning into the gate, quickened my pace. Suddenly I felt that someone was following me. I stopped and looked around. It was too dark to see anything, but for the sake of caution I walked around the house as if merely out for a stroll. As I passed Princess Mary's windows I again heard footsteps behind me, and a man wrapped in a greatcoat ran past me. This worried me; nevertheless I crept up to the porch and hurried up the dark staircase. The door opened; a little hand seized mine. . . .

"No one saw you?" Vera whispered, clinging to me.

"No!"

"Now do you believe that I love you! Oh, I have hesitated so long, tormented myself so long . . . but I am as clay in your hands."

Her heart pounded, and her hands were cold as ice. Then followed reproaches and jealous recriminations—she demanding a full confession, vowing she would meekly endure my faithlessness, for her only desire was to see me happy. I did not quite believe that but, nevertheless, reassured her with vows, promises, and so on.

"So you are not going to marry Mary? You don't love her? And she thinks . . . do you know she is madly in love with you, the poor thing! . . ."

. . . .

. . . .

At about two o'clock in the morning I opened the window and, knotting two shawls together, let myself down from the upper balcony to the lower, holding on to a column as I did so. A light was still burning in Princess Mary's room. Something impelled me toward that window. The curtains were not drawn tight and I was able to cast a curious glance into the interior of the room. Mary was sitting on her bed, her hands crossed on her knees; her abundant tresses had been gathered under a lace night cap; a large scarlet shawl covered her white shoulders, and her tiny feet were concealed in a pair of brightly colored Persian slippers. She sat motionless, her head sunk on her breast; on a table before her lay an open book, but her fixed gaze, full of inexpressible sadness, seemed to be skimming one and the same page for the hundredth time while her thoughts were far away. . . .

Just then someone moved behind a bush. I jumped down to the lawn from the balcony. An invisible hand seized me by the shoulder. "Aha!" said a gruff voice. "Got you! I'll teach you to go prowling in princesses' rooms at night!"

"Hold him fast!" yelled another, leaping from behind the corner.

They were Grushnitsky and the captain of dragoons.

I struck the latter on the head with my fist, knocking him down, and ran for the bushes. I knew all the paths in the garden covering the slope opposite our houses.

"Thieves! Help!" they shouted; a shot was fired; the glowing wad fell almost at my feet.

A minute later I was in my own room, undressed and in bed. My manservant had scarcely locked the door when Grushnitsky and the captain began pounding on it.

"Pechorin! Are you asleep? Are you there?" the captain shouted.

"I'm in bed," I replied testily.

"Get up! Thieves! The Cherkess!"

"I have a cold," I replied, "I'm afraid of aggravating it."

They went away. I should not have answered them; they would have spent another hour searching for me in the garden. In the meantime a fearful hue and cry was raised. A Cossack galloped down from the fort. Everything was agog; Cherkess were being hunted for in every bush, but of course, none were found. Many probably carried off the firm conviction, however, that had the garrison displayed greater courage and speed at least a dozen or two marauders would have been left on the spot.

JUNE 27

The Cherkess night raid was the sole subject of conversation at the spring this morning. Having imbibed the prescribed number of glasses of Narzan and walked some ten times up and down the long linden avenue, I met Vera's husband, who had just returned from Pyatigorsk. He took my arm and we went into the restaurant for breakfast. He was exceedingly worried about his wife. "She had a terrible fright last night!" he said. "A thing like this would have to happen just when I was away!" We sat down for breakfast near the door leading to the corner room, which was occupied by a dozen gallants, Grushnitsky among them. And for the second time Providence offered me an opportunity to overhear a conversation that was to decide his fate. He did not see me, and hence I could not conclude that he was talking deliberately for my benefit; but that only enhanced his guilt in my eyes.

"Could it really have been the Cherkess?" said someone. "Did anyone see them?"

"I'll tell you the whole truth," replied Grushnitsky, "only I ask you not to give me away. This is what happened: last night a man, whose name I shall not mention, came to me with the story that he had seen someone sneaking into the Ligovsky house at about ten at night. Let me remind you that Princess Ligovskaya was here at the time, and Princess Mary at home. So I set out with him to lie in wait for the lucky fellow under her window."

I admit I was alarmed lest my companion, engrossed though he was with his breakfast, should hear some rather unpleasant things if Grushnitsky had guessed the truth. Blinded by jealousy, however, the latter did not even suspect what had happened.

"So you see," Grushnitsky continued, "we set off taking along a gun loaded with a blank charge in order to give the fellow a fright. Until two o'clock we waited in the garden. Finally he appeared, the Lord knows from where, only it wasn't through the window because it did not open—he probably came through the glass door hidden behind a column—finally, I say, we saw somebody climbing off the balcony. . . . What do you think of the Princess, eh? I must admit these Moscow ladies are beyond me! What can you believe in after this? We tried to seize him, but he broke loose and scurried for the bushes like a hare; that's when I shot at him."

A murmur of incredulity broke out around Grushnitsky.

"You do not believe me?" he continued. "I give you my word of honor that this is the downright truth, and to prove it, perhaps, I shall mention the name of the gentleman in question."

"Who was it, who was it?" came from all sides.

"Pechorin," replied Grushnitsky.

At that moment he raised his eyes—to see me standing in the doorway facing him; he flushed scarlet. I stepped up to him and said very slowly and distinctly:

"I am very sorry that I entered after you had already given your word of honor in confirmation of the most abominable piece of slander. My presence might have saved you from that added villainy."

Grushnitsky leaped to his feet, all ready to flare up.

"I beg of you," I continued in the same tone of voice, "I beg of you to retract at once what you have said; you are very well aware that it is a lie. I do not believe that the indifference of a woman to your brilliant qualities deserves such severe retaliation. Think it over well: if you persist in your opinion, you forfeit your right to a reputation of a man of honor and risk your life."

Grushnitsky stood before me, eyes downcast, in violent agitation. But the struggle between conscience and vanity was brief. The captain of dragoons, who was sitting next to him, nudged him with his elbow; he started and quickly replied to me without raising his eyes:

"My dear sir, when I say something I mean it, and am ready to repeat it. . . . Your threats do not intimidate me and I will stick at nothing."

"The last you have already proved," I replied coldly, and taking the arm of the captain of dragoons, led him out of the room.

"What do you wish with me?" asked the captain.

"You are a friend of Grushnitsky's and will probably be his second?"

The captain bowed with much hauteur.

"You have guessed right," he replied. "Moreover, I am obliged to be his second, for the insult you have offered him concerns me too . . . I was with him last night," he added, squaring his stooping shoulders.

"Ah, so it was you I hit so clumsily on the head?"

He went yellow, then blue; suppressed anger showed on his face.

"I shall have the honor to send my second to you shortly," I added, bowing very politely and pretending to ignore his fury.

On the steps of the restaurant I met Vera's husband. He had evidently been waiting for me.

He seized hold of my hand with something akin to rapture.

"Noble-minded young man!" he said with tears in his eyes. "I heard everything. What a scoundrel! The ingrate! Just think of admitting them into a respectable home after this! Thank God I have no daughters! But she for whom you are risking your life will reward you. You may be assured of my discretion for the time being," he continued. "I was young once myself and served in the army; I know one must not interfere in affairs like this. Good-bye!"

Poor fellow! He is glad that he has no daughters. . . .

I went straight to Werner, whom I found at home, and told him everything—my relations with Vera and the Princess and the conversation I had overheard which apprised me of these gentlemen's intentions to make a fool of me by having us shoot it out with blank charges. Now, however, the affair had overstepped the bounds of a joke; they probably had not expected it to end like this.

The doctor agreed to act as my second. I gave him a few instructions concerning the conditions of the duel; he was to insist on the greatest secrecy, for though I am always ready to risk my life, I am not disposed in the slightest to spoil my future in this world for all time to come.

Afterwards I went home. An hour later the doctor returned from his expedition.

"There indeed is a conspiracy against you," he said. "I found the captain of dragoons and another gentlemen whose name I do not remember at Grushnitsky's. I stopped for a moment in the hallway to take off my galoshes; inside there was a terrific noise and argument going on. 'I will not agree on any account!' Grushnitsky was saying. 'He insulted me publicly; at that time it was an entirely different matter. . . .' 'Why should it concern you?' replied the captain. 'I am taking everything upon myself. I have been a second in five duels and know how these things are arranged. I have thought it out in every detail. Only be so good as not to interfere with me. It will do good to give him a fright. And why should you run a risk if you can avoid it?' At that point I walked in. They immediately fell silent. Our parleys lasted for quite a while, and finally we came to the following arrangement: about five versts from here there is a lonely gorge; they will go there tomorrow morning at four o'clock, and we are to leave half an hour later. You will fire at six paces—Grushnitsky insisted on the distance himself. The dead man is to be credited to the Cherkess. Now I will tell you what I suspect: they, the seconds, I mean, have apparently amended the earlier scheme somewhat and want to put a bullet only into Grushnitsky's pistol. It looks rather like murder, but cunning is permitted in wartime, particularly in an Asiatic war. I daresay though that Grushnitsky is slightly better than his comrades. What do you think? Should we let them know that we have guessed their strategem?"

"Not for anything in the world, doctor! You can rest assured I shall not give in to them."

"What do you intend to do?"

"That is my secret."

"Take care you do not fall into the trap. . . . Remember the distance is only six paces!"

"Doctor, I shall expect you tomorrow at four. The horses will be saddled. Good-bye!"

I sat at home until evening, locked up in my room. A footman came with an invitation from Princess Ligovskaya, but I said I was ill.

. . . .

It is two o'clock in the morning, but I cannot fall asleep. I know I should rest, so that my hand should be steady tomorrow. It will be hard to miss at six paces though. Ah, Mr. Grushnitsky, your hoax will not succeed! We shall exchange roles, and now it will be for me to look for signs of secret terror on your pallid face. Why did you insist on these fatal six paces? You think that I shall submissively offer you my brow as a target . . . but we shall draw lots! And then . . . then . . . but what if fortune smiles on him? What if my star fails me at last? And little wonder if it did; it has served me faithfully so long.

Ah, well! If I must die, I must! The world will lose little, and I am weary enough of it all. I am like a man who yawns at a ball and does not go home to sleep only because his carriage has not come. But the carriage is here—good-bye!

I run through my past life in my mind and involuntarily ask myself:

Why have I lived? For what purpose was I born? I daresay there was a purpose, and I daresay, fate had something noble in store for me, for I am conscious of untapped powers within me. . . . But I did not divine my predestination, I allowed myself to be carried away by the temptation of vain and ignoble passions; I emerged from their crucible hard and cold like iron, but gone forever was the ardor of noble aspirations—life's finest flower. How often since then have I played the role of an axe in the hands of fate! Like that instrument of punishment I have fallen upon the heads of the condemned, often without malice, always without regret. . . . My love has never made anyone happy, for I have never sacrificed anything for those I loved; I have loved only for myself, for my own pleasure; I have striven only to satisfy a strange craving of the heart, greedily absorbing their emotions, their tenderness, their joys and sufferings—and have never been sated. I have been like the starving man who falls into a stupor from sheer exhaustion and dreams of luxurious viands and sparkling wines; exultingly he gorges himself on these ephemeral gifts of the imagination, and seems to feel better; but when he awakes the vision is gone . . . and redoubled hunger and despair remain!

Perhaps I shall die tomorrow, and there will not be a creature on earth who understands me fully. Some think of me worse, others better, than I really am. Some will say: he was a good fellow; others: he was a scoundrel. And both will be wrong. Is it worth the trouble to live after this? And yet you go on living—out of curiosity, in expectation of something new. . . . How ludicrous and how vexatious!

A month and a half has passed since I arrived at the fort of N. Maxim Maximych has gone out hunting. . . . I am all alone. I am sitting at the window; outside the gray clouds have concealed the mountains to their very base; the sun looks like a yellow blotch through the mist. It is cold; the wind is soughing and rattling the shutters. . . . How wearisome it all is! I shall resume writing my journal which has been interrupted by so many queer events.

Reading over the last page, it strikes me as humorous. I thought I would die, but that was out of the question, for I had not drained my cup of misery to the dregs, and now I feel that I still have long to live.

How clearly and sharply everything that has happened is imprinted in my memory! Time has not obliterated a single line or shade.

I recall that on the night preceding the duel I did not sleep a wink. A mysterious disquietude seized me and I could not write for long. For about an hour I paced the room; then I sat down and opened a novel by Walter Scott that had lain on my table: it was *Old Mortality.* At first I read with an effort, then, carried away by the enchanting fiction, I was soon oblivious to everything.

At last day broke. My nerves had grown calm. I examined my face in the mirror: a dull pallor had spread over my features which still showed traces of a racking sleepless night, but my eyes, though encircled by dark shadows, shone proudly and remorselessly. I was satisfied with myself.

Ordering the horses to be saddled, I dressed and hurried to the baths. As I immersed myself in the cold Narzan water, I felt my physical and spiritual strength returning. I left the baths as refreshed and vigorous as if about to attend a ball. After this no one can tell me that the soul is not dependent on the body!

On returning home I found the doctor there. He was wearing gray riding breeches, a light caftan gathered in at the waist and a Cherkess cap. I burst out laughing at the sight of his slight frame beneath the enormous shaggy cap. His countenance is anything but warlike, and this time he looked more dejected than usual.

"Why so sad, doctor?" I said to him. "Haven't you seen people off to the next world a hundred times with the greatest indifference? Imagine that I have a bilious fever, and that I have equal chances of recovering or succumbing; both eventualities are in the order of things; try to regard me as a patient stricken with a disease you have not yet diagnosed—that will stimulate your curiosity to the utmost. You may now make some important physiological observations on me. . . . Is not expectation of death by violence a real illness in itself?"

This thought impressed the doctor and his spirits rose.

We mounted. Werner clung to the reins with both hands and we set off. In a flash we had galloped through the settlement and past the fort and entered the gorge through which a road wound its way. It was half overgrown with tall grass and intersected at short intervals by noisy brooks which we had to ford to the great despair of the doctor whose horse would halt each time in the water.

I cannot remember a morning bluer or fresher. The sun had barely peeped over the green summits and the merging of the first warmth of its rays with the dying coolness of the night brought a sweet languor to the senses. The exultant ray of the young day had not yet penetrated into the gorge; now it gilded only the tips of the crags that towered above us on both sides. The dense foliage of the bushes growing in the deep crevices of the cliffs showered a silvery rain upon us at the slightest breath of wind. I remember that at that moment I loved nature as never before. With what curiosity did I gaze at each dew-drop that trembled on the broad vine leaves, reflecting millions of rainbow rays! How eagerly my eyes sought to pierce the hazy distance! There the path grew narrower and narrower, the crags bluer and more awesome, seeming to merge at last into an impregnable wall. We rode along in silence.

"Have you made your will?" Werner asked all of a sudden.

"No."

"What if you are killed?"

"The heirs will turn up themselves."

"Have you no friends you would wish to send your last farewell?"

I shook my head.

"Is there no woman in the world to whom you would want to leave a remembrance?"

"Do you want me to lay bare my soul to you, doctor?" I replied. "You see, I am past the years when people die with the names of their beloved on their lips and bequeath a lock of pomaded, or unpomaded, hair to a friend. When I think of imminent and possible death, I think only of myself; some do not even do that. Friends, who will forget me tomorrow, or, worse still, who will weave God knows what fantastic yarns about me, and women, who in the embrace of another will laugh at me in order that he might not be jealous of the departed—what do I care for them? From life's turmoil I have drawn a few ideas, but no feeling. For a long time now I have been living by my reason, not my heart. I weigh and analyze my own emotions and actions with stern curiosity, but without sympathy. There are two men in me; one lives in the full sense of the word, the other reasons and passes judgment on the first. The first will, perhaps, take leave of you and the world forever an hour from now, and the second . . . the second. . . . Look, doctor, do you see the three dark figures on the cliff to the right? I believe they are our adversaries."

We spurred our horses on.

Three horses were tethered in the bushes at the foot of the cliff. We tethered ours there too and continued on foot up a narrow path to a ledge where Grushnitsky was waiting for us with the captain of dragoons and another second by the name of Ivan Ignatych; his surname I had never heard.

"We have been waiting a long time for you," said the captain of the dragoons, with an ironical smile.

I pulled out my watch and showed it to him.

He apologized, saying that his watch was fast.

For several minutes there was an awkward silence. At last the doctor broke it, turning to Grushnitsky:

"I believe," he said, "that having both shown your readiness to fight and thereby duly discharged your debt of honor, you might, gentlemen, come to an understanding and end this affair amicably."

"I am ready to do so," said I.

The captain winked at Grushnitsky, who thinking that I was showing the white feather assumed a haughty air, although his face had been sickly gray until that moment. Now for the first time since our arrival he looked at me; the glance was uneasy and betrayed his inner conflict.

"Tell me your conditions," he said, "and you may rest assured that I shall do all I can for you. . . ."

"These are my conditions: you will today publicly retract your calumny and apologize to me. . . ."

"My dear sir, I am amazed that you dare suggest anything of the kind. . . ."

"What else could I suggest?"

"We shall shoot it out."

I shrugged my shoulders.

"So be it; only remember that one of us is bound to be killed."

"I hope it will be you."

"And I am quite certain of the contrary."

He started and flushed red, and then he forced a laugh.

The captain took him by the arm and led him aside; they spoke in whispers at some length. I had arrived quite peaceably disposed, but now these proceedings were getting on my nerves.

The doctor came up to me.

"Look here," he said, obviously worried, "have you forgotten about their conspiracy? I do not know how to load a pistol, but if that is the case. . . . You are a queer man! Tell them you are aware of their intentions, and they will not dare. . . . Where's the sense of it? They will shoot you down like a fowl. . . ."

"Please, doctor, do not alarm yourself, and wait a little. . . . I shall handle it so that they will not have any advantage. Let them whisper. . . ."

"Gentlemen, this is becoming tiresome!" I said to them in a loud voice. "If we are to fight, let us do so; you had time yesterday to talk it over. . . ."

"We are ready," replied the captain. "Take your places, gentlemen! Doctor, will you measure off six paces?"

"Take your places!" repeated Ivan Ignatych in a squeaky voice.

"I beg your pardon!" I said. "There is one more condition. Inasmuch as we intend to fight to the death, we are obliged to take every precaution that this encounter should remain a secret and that our seconds should bear no responsibility. Do you agree?"

"We agree fully."

"This is what has occurred to me. Do you see the narrow ledge on top of that sheer cliff to the right? The drop from there to the bottom is a good thirty sagenes, if not more; down below there are jagged rocks. Each of us will take his position on the very edge of the shelf, which will make even a slight wound mortal; that should coincide with your wishes since you yourselves set the distance at six paces. If one of us is wounded he will inevitably go over and be dashed to pieces; the doctor will remove the bullet, and the sudden death can easily be explained as an accident. We shall draw lots to see who is to shoot first. In conclusion I wish to make it clear that I shall fight on no other terms."

"Let it be so!" said the captain after a meaning look at Grushnitsky, who nodded his concurrence. His facial expression changed every moment. I had placed him in a difficult position. Under ordinary conditions, he could have aimed at my leg and wounded me lightly, thus getting his revenge without laying too heavy a burden on his conscience. Now, however, he either had to fire into the air or become a murderer, or, finally, abandon his dastardly scheme and run the same risk as I. I would not have wished to be in his boots at that moment. He led the captain aside and began to talk to him very heatedly; I noticed how his lips, now turned bluish, quivered. The captain, however, turned away from him with a contemptuous smile. "You are a fool!" he said to Grushnitsky rather loudly. "You don't understand anything. Let us go, gentlemen!"

A narrow path winding between the bushes led up to the steep incline; broken fragments of rock formed the precarious steps of this natural staircase; clutching at the bushes, we began climbing. Grushnitsky went ahead, followed by his seconds, and the doctor and I came last.

"You amaze me," said the doctor, clasping my hand warmly. "Let me feel your pulse. Oho, it's pounding feverishly! But your face betrays nothing; only your eyes shine brighter than usual."

Suddenly small stones rolled noisily down to our feet. What had happened? Grushnitsky had stumbled; the branch he had been holding on to snapped and he would have fallen backwards had his seconds not supported him.

"Take care!" I called out to him. "Don't fall too soon; it's an ill omen. Remember Julius Caesar!"[73]

Finally we reached the top of the projecting cliff. The ledge was covered with fine sand as if specially spread there for the duel. All around, wrapped in the golden mist of morning, the mountain peaks clustered like a numberless herd, while in the south Elbrus loomed white, bringing up the rear of a chain of icy summits among which roamed the feathery clouds blown in from the east. I walked to the brink of the ledge and looked down; my head nearly swam. Down below it was dark and cold as in a grave, and the moss-grown jagged rocks hurled down by storm and time awaited their prey.

The ledge on which we were to fight formed an almost regular triangle. Six paces were measured off from the projecting angle, and it was decided that he who would first have to face his opponent's fire should stand at the very edge with his back to the abyss; if he was not killed, the adversaries were to change places.

I decided to give Grushnitsky every advantage, for I wanted to try him; a spark of generosity might have been awakened in his soul, in which case everything would have turned out for the best; but vanity and weakness of character were bound to triumph. . . . I wanted to give myself full justification for allowing him no quarter if fate spared me. Who has not thus struck a bargain with his conscience?

"Cast the lots, doctor!" said the captain.

The doctor produced a silver coin from his pocket and held it aloft.

"Tail!" cried Grushnitsky suddenly, like a man just awakened by a friendly nudge.

"Head!" said I.

The coin rose into the air and came down with a clink; we all rushed over to look at it.

"You're lucky," I said to Grushnitsky, "you are to shoot first. But remember, if you do not kill me, I shall not miss—I give you my word of honor."

He flushed; the thought of killing an unarmed man filled him with shame. I looked at him intently, and for a moment I thought he would throw himself at my feet and beg my forgiveness; but how could he confess to a scheme so vile? One way out remained for him: to fire into the air; I was certain he would fire into the air! Only one thing might prevent him from doing so: the thought that I might demand a second duel.

"It's time now!" the doctor whispered to me, tugging at my sleeve. "If you will not tell them now that we know their intention all will be lost. See, he is loading already. If you will not, I shall tell them. . . ."

"Certainly not, doctor!" I replied, holding him by the arm. "You will spoil everything; you gave me your word you would not interfere. . . . And why should it concern you? Perhaps I want to be killed."

He looked at me in amazement.

[73] The assassination of Julius Caesar was preceded by omens, according to Plutarch's *Parallel Lives* (c. 100 A.D.) and Shakespeare's play, which is based on Plutarch.

"Oh, that's another matter! Only don't blame me in the other world. . . ."

Meanwhile the captain had loaded his pistols. One he gave Grushnitsky, smilingly whispering something to him, the other to me.

I took my place at the far corner of the ledge, firmly bracing my left foot against the rock and leaning slightly forward so as not to fall backwards in case I was lightly wounded.

Grushnitsky took his place opposite me, and when the signal was given, started to raise the pistol. He aimed straight at my forehead. . . .

Savage anger welled up in my heart.

Suddenly he lowered the muzzle of his pistol and going as white as a sheet turned to his second.

"I cannot do it," he said hoarsely.

"Coward!" replied the captain.

The shot rang out. The bullet scratched my knee. Involuntarily I took a few steps forward to get away from the brink as quickly as possible.

"Well, brother Grushnitsky, it is a pity you missed!" said the captain. "Now it's your turn, take your place! Embrace me before you go, for we shall meet no more!" They embraced, the captain scarcely able to restrain himself from laughter. "Don't be afraid," he added, with a sly look at Grushnitsky, "everything in the world's a pack of nonsense! Nature, fate, life itself, all are but worthless pelf!"

This tragic utterance made with due solemnity, the captain withdrew to his place. With tears in his eyes, Ivan Ignatych also embraced Grushnitsky, and now the latter remained alone facing me. To this day I have tried to explain to myself the emotion that then surged in my breast: it was the vexation of injured vanity, and contempt, and wrath born of the realization that this man who was now eyeing me so coolly, with such calm insolence, two minutes before had sought to kill me like a dog without endangering himself in the slightest, for had I been wounded a little more severely in the leg I would certainly have toppled over the cliff.

I looked him squarely in the face for a few minutes, trying to detect the slightest sign of repentance. Instead I thought I saw him suppressing a smile.

"I advise you to say your prayers before you die," I told him then.

"You need not be more concerned about my soul than your own. I only beg of you to fire with the least delay."

"And you will not retract your slander? Or apologize to me? Think well, has your conscience nothing to say to you?"

"Mr. Pechorin!" shouted the captain of dragoons. "You are not here to preach, allow me to observe. . . . Let us get it over and done with as quickly as possible. Someone might ride through the gorge and see us."

"Very well. Doctor, will you come to me?"

The doctor came over. Poor doctor! He was paler than Grushnitsky had been ten minutes before.

I spoke the following words with deliberation, loudly and distinctly, as sentences of death are pronounced:

"Doctor, these gentlemen, no doubt in their haste, forgot to put a bullet into my pistol; I beg you to reload it—and well!"

"It can't be!" cried the captain. "It can't be! I loaded both pistols; the bullet may have rolled out of yours. . . . That's not my fault! And you have no right to reload . . . no right whatsoever . . . it is most decidedly against the rules. I shall not allow it. . . ."

"Good!" I said to the captain. "If so, you and I shall shoot it out on the same terms. . . ."

He did not know what to say.

Grushnitsky stood there, head sunk on his breast, embarrassed and gloomy.

"Let them do as they wish!" he finally told the captain, who was trying to wrench my pistol from the doctor's hand. "You know yourself that they are right."

In vain the captain made signs to him; Grushnitsky did not even look up.

Meanwhile the doctor loaded the pistol and handed it to me.

Seeing this, the captain spat and stamped his foot. "You are a fool, my friend," he said, "a damned fool. Once you trusted me, you should have listened to me in everything. . . . You are getting what you deserve, so go ahead and die like a fly!" He turned away, muttering, "but it is altogether against the rules."

"Grushnitsky!" said I. "There is still time; retract your calumny and I shall forgive you everything. You have failed to make a fool of me, and my vanity is satisfied. Remember that once we were friends. . . ."

His face twisted with passion, his eyes flashed.

"Fire!" he replied. "I despise myself and hate you. If you do not kill me, I shall stab you in the back some night. The world is too small to hold us both. . . ."

I fired.

When the smoke cleared, there was no Grushnitsky on the ledge. Only a thin pillar of dust curled over the brink of the precipice.

Everybody cried out at once.

"Finita la commedia!"[74] I said to the doctor.

He did not reply, but turned away in horror.

I shrugged my shoulders and bowed to Grushnitsky's seconds.

As I came down the path I saw Grushnitsky's bloodstained corpse between the clefts in the rocks. Involuntarily I closed my eyes.

Untying my horse, I set out for home at a walking pace. My heart was heavy within me. The sun seemed to have lost its brilliance and its rays did not warm me. Before reaching the settlement I turned into a gorge on my right. I could not have endured to see anyone just then; I wanted to be alone. With the reins hanging loose and my head sunk on my breast, I rode on for some time until I found myself in an entirely unfamiliar spot. I turned back and sought the roadway. The sun was setting when I reached Kislovodsk, a spent man on a spent horse.

My manservant told me that Werner had called and gave me two notes, one from him, and the other from Vera.

I opened the first; it contained the following:

[74] "The comedy is over!" (Italian).

Everything has been arranged as well as possible; the mutilated body has been brought in, and the bullet removed from the breast. Everybody believes that his death was accidental; only the commandant, who probably knows of your quarrel, shook his head, but said nothing. There is no evidence against you and you may rest in peace . . . if you can. Good-bye. . . .

I hesitated long before opening the second note. What could she have to write to me? An ominous presentiment racked my soul.

Here it is, that letter whose every word ineffaceably seared itself into my memory:

I am writing to you quite certain that we shall never meet again. When we parted several years ago, I thought the same; but it pleased heaven to try me a second time; I did not withstand the test, my weak heart was again conquered by that familiar voice . . . but you will not despise me for it, will you? This letter is at once a farewell and a confession: I must tell you everything that has been stored in my heart ever since it first learned to love you. I shall not accuse you—you behaved to me as any other man might have done; you loved me as your property, as a source of the reciprocal joys, fears and sorrows without which life would be wearisome and monotonous. I realized that from the very beginning. . . . But you were unhappy, and I sacrificed myself in the hope that some day you would appreciate my sacrifice, that some day you would understand my infinite tenderness which nothing could affect. Much time has passed since then; I have fathomed all the secrets of your soul . . . and I see that mine was a vain hope. How it hurt me! But my love and my soul have melted into one: the flame is dimmer, but it has not died.

We are parting forever; yet you may be certain that I shall never love another; my soul has spent all its treasures, its tears and hopes on you. She who has once loved you cannot but regard other men with some measure of contempt, not because you are better than they—oh no!—but because there is something unique in your nature, something peculiar to you alone, something so proud and unfathomable; whatever you may be saying, your voice holds an invincible power; in no one is the desire to be loved so constant as in you; in no one is evil so attractive; in no one's glance is there such a promise of bliss; nobody knows better than you how to use his advantages, and no one else can be so genuinely unhappy as you, because nobody tries as hard as you to convince himself of the contrary.

Now I must explain the reason for my hasty departure; it will strike you as of little consequence because it concerns me alone.

This morning my husband came to me and told me about your quarrel with Grushnitsky. My face must have given me away, for he looked me straight in the eyes, long and searchingly; I nearly fainted at the thought that you would have to fight a duel and that I was the cause; I thought I would lose my mind. . . . Now, however, when I can reason clearly, I am certain that you will live; it is impossible that you should die without me, impossible! My husband paced the room for a long time; I do not know what he said to me, nor do I remember what I replied. . . . I probably told him that I loved you. . . . I only remember that at the end of our conversation he insulted me with a terrible word and left the room. I heard him order the carriage. . . . For three hours now I have been sitting at the window and awaiting your return. . . . But you are alive, you cannot die! The carriage is almost ready. . . . Farewell, farewell! I am lost—but what of it? If I could be certain that you will always remember me—I say nothing of loving me, no—only remember. . . . Good-bye! They are coming. . . . I have to hide this letter. . . .

You do not love Mary, do you? You will not marry her? Oh, but you must make this sacrifice for me; I have given up everything in the world for your sake. . . .

Like a madman I dashed outside, leaped into the saddle of my horse who was being led across the courtyard, and set off at full gallop along the road to Pyatigorsk. I mercilessly spurred on the exhausted beast which, panting and covered with froth, sped me along the rocky road.

The sun had vanished into a black cloud resting on the mountain range in the west, and it turned dark and damp in the gorge. The Podkumok picked its way through the rocks with a dull and monotonous roar. Breathless with impatience I galloped on. The thought that I might not find her in Pyatigorsk pounded like a sledge-hammer at my heart. Oh, but to see her for a minute, only one more minute, to say good-bye, to clasp her hand. . . . I prayed, I cursed, I cried, I laughed . . . no, no words can express my anxiety, my despair. Now that I realized I might lose her forever, Vera became for me the most precious thing on earth, more precious than life, honor or happiness! God only knows what odd, wild ideas swarmed in my head. . . . And all the while I rode on, spurring my horse mercilessly. Finally I noticed that the animal was breathing more laboriously, and once or twice he stumbled on a level stretch. There still remained five versts to Essentuki, a Cossack hamlet where I could get another mount.

Everything would have been redeemed had my horse had the strength to carry on for another ten minutes. But suddenly, at a sharp bend in the road coming up from a shallow ravine as we were emerging from the hills, he crashed to the ground. I leaped nimbly out of the saddle; but try as I might to help him up, pull as I might at the reins, my efforts were in vain. A scarcely audible groan escaped from between his clenched teeth and a few minutes later he was dead. I was left alone in the steppe, my last hope gone; I tried to continue on foot, but my knees gave way and exhausted by the day's anxieties and the sleepless night, I fell onto the wet grass and wept like a child.

I lay there for a long time motionless and wept bitterly without trying to check the tears and sobs; I thought my breast would be rent asunder. All my resolution, all my composure vanished like smoke; my spirit was impotent, my reason paralyzed, and had someone seen me at that moment he would have turned away in contempt.

When the nocturnal dew and mountain breeze had cooled my fevered brow and my thoughts became collected once more, I realized it was useless and senseless to pursue a happiness that was lost. What more did I want? To see her? Why? Was not everything over between us? One bitter farewell kiss would not make my memories sweeter, and it only would be the harder to part.

It is pleasant for me to know, however, that I can weep! Although, the real reason was perhaps frayed nerves, the sleepless night, the two minutes I had stood looking at the muzzle of a pistol, and an empty stomach.

Everything works out for the best. As for this new sensation of pain, it served as a happy diversion, to employ a military term. It does one good to weep, and had I not ridden my horse to death and then been compelled to walk the fifteen versts back, I perhaps should not have closed my eyes that night either.

I returned to Kislovodsk at five o'clock in the morning, threw myself on the bed and slept like Napoleon after Waterloo.

When I woke up, it was dark outside. Unfastening my jacket, I sat at an open window—and the breeze from the mountains cooled my breast not yet becalmed even by the heavy sleep of fatigue. Way out beyond the river the lights of the fort and the village twinkled through the thick crowns of the overshadowing lindens. The courtyard was deadly still, and the Princess' house plunged into darkness.

The doctor entered. His brow was furrowed, and contrary to his wont he did not offer me his hand.

"Where have you come from, doctor?"

"From Princess Ligovskaya's. Her daughter is ill—nervous breakdown. . . . But that's not why I am here; the trouble is that the authorities are beginning to suspect, and though nothing definite can be proved I would advise you to be more cautious. The Princess just told me that she was aware you fought a duel because of her daughter. That old man—what's his name?—told her. He witnessed your altercation with Grushnitsky in the restaurant. I came to warn you. So good-bye—perhaps we shall not see each other again—very likely you'll be sent away."

He paused on the threshold; he wanted to shake my hand. And had I given him the slightest encouragement he would have flung himself on my neck; but I remained as cold as a stone, and he went away.

That is just like human beings! They are all alike; though fully aware in advance of all the evil aspects of a deed, they aid and abet and even give their approbation to it when they see there is no other way out—and then they wash their hands of it and turn away with disapproval from him who dared assume the full burden of responsibility. They are all alike, even the kindest and wisest of them!

The following morning, when I had received orders from my superiors to report at the fort of N., I dropped in at the Princess' to say good-bye.

Princess Ligovskaya was taken aback when in reply to her question whether I had anything important to tell her I merely said that I had come to say good-bye.

"I must have a very serious talk with you, however."

I sat down without saying a word.

It was obvious she was at a loss how to begin; her face went red and she drummed her stubby fingers on the table. Finally she began haltingly: "Monsieur Pechorin, I believe you are an honorable man."

I bowed.

"I am even certain of it," she continued, "though your conduct has been somewhat questionable. You may have your reasons, however, of which I am not aware, and if so, you must share them with me now. You protected my daughter from calumny, engaged in a duel on her behalf, and risked your life in doing so. . . . Pray do not reply, for I know you will not admit it because Grushnitsky is dead." (She crossed herself.) "God forgive him, and you too, I hope! That is none of my concern. . . . I have no right to condemn you, for it was my daughter, blameless though she is, who was the cause. She has told me everything . . . everything, I am sure. You have declared you love her, and she has confessed her love for you." (Here the Princess drew a deep sigh.) "But she is ill and I am certain that it is not an ordinary malady. Some secret grief is killing her; she does not admit it, but I am certain that you are the cause. . . . Listen to me: you perhaps think that I am after rank and immense riches—if so, you are mistaken; I seek only my daughter's happiness. Your present position is unenviable, but it may mend. You are wealthy; my daughter loves you, and her upbringing is such that she can make her husband happy. I am rich, and she is my only child. . . . Tell me, what is it that deters you? I should not have told you all this, but I rely upon your heart and honor—remember that I have only one daughter . . . only one. . . ."

She began to sob.

"Princess," I said, "I cannot answer you; allow me to speak to your daughter alone."

"Never!" she cried, rising from her chair in great agitation.

"As you wish," replied I, preparing to leave.

She thought it over, motioned me to wait, and left the room.

Some five minutes passed; my heart pounded, but my thoughts were orderly and my head cool. Search as I might in my breast for even the tiniest spark of love for the charming Mary, all my efforts were in vain.

The door opened and she entered. Heavens! How she had changed, since I saw her last—and that but a short while ago!

When she reached the middle of the room she swayed; I leaped to her side, offered her my arm and led her to an arm-chair.

I stood facing her. For a long time neither of us said a word; her big eyes full of ineffable sorrow seemed to search mine with something akin to hope; in vain her pale lips tried to smile; her delicate hands folded on her knees were so fragile and transparent that I began to feel sorry for her.

"Princess," said I, "you know I have mocked at you, do you not? You must despise me."

A feverish flush mantled her cheeks.

"Hence, you cannot love me. . . ." I continued.

She turned away, leaned her elbows on the table and covered her eyes with her hand, and I thought I saw tears glistening in them.

"My God!" she said scarcely audibly.

The situation grew unbearable; in another minute I should have thrown myself at her feet.

"So you see for yourself," I said in as steady a voice as I could, forcing a smile, "you see for yourself that I cannot marry you. Even if you wished me to do so now, you would regret the decision very soon. The talk I had with your mother compels me to speak with you now so frankly and brutally; I hope she is mistaken but you can easily undeceive her. As you can see I am playing a most contemptible and disgusting role in your eyes, and I admit it; that is the most I can do for you. However bad your opinion may be of me, I shall accept it. You see I am abasing myself before you. . . . Even if you had loved me, you would despise me from this moment—now, wouldn't you?"

She turned to me a face as pale as marble but with eyes flashing wondrously.

"I hate you . . ." she said.

I thanked her, bowed respectfully and walked out.

An hour later a post troika was carrying me rapidly from Kislovodsk. A few versts from Essentuki I descried the carcass of my steed by the roadside; the saddle had been removed—probably by some passing Cossack—and in its place two ravens now sat on the horse's back. I sighed and turned away. . . .

And now, here in this dreary fort, as my mind dwells on the past, I frequently ask myself: why did I not wish to tread the path fate held open to me with a promise of tranquil joys and peace of mind? No, I could never have reconciled myself to such a lot. I am like a mariner born and bred on board a buccaneer brig whose soul has become so inured to storm and strife that if cast ashore he would weary and languish no matter how alluring the shady groves and how bright the gentle sun. All day long he paces the sandy beach, hearkening to the monotonous roar of the breakers and gazing into the hazy distance to catch in the pale strip dividing the blue deep from the gray clouds the flash of the long-awaited sail that at first is like the wing of a sea-gull and then gradually stands out from the white of the spray as it steadily makes for its lonely anchorage. . . .

III. THE FATALIST

I happened once to spend two weeks in a Cossack village on the left flank. A battalion of infantry was stationed there, and the officers used to meet at each other's quarters in turn, playing cards in the evenings.

On one occasion at Major C.'s, having tired of Boston[75] we threw the cards under the table and sat on talking until late, for this time the conversation was interesting. We were discussing the Moslem belief that the fate of man is preordained in heaven, which was said to find many adherents among us. Each of us had some unusual occurrences to relate pro or contra.

"All you have been saying, gentlemen, proves nothing," said the old major. "After all, none of you witnessed any of the strange happenings you adduce to support your views, did you?"

"Of course not," several said. "But we have it on reliable authority!"

"Nonsense!" someone said. "Where is the reliable authority who has seen the scroll on which our mortal hour is written? And if there is such a thing as predestination, why have we been given will and reason? Why are we held accountable for our actions?"

Meanwhile an officer who had been sitting in a corner of the room rose, walked slowly over to the table and surveyed us all with a calm, solemn glance. He was a Serbian by birth, as you could tell by his name.

[75] A card game for four players with two decks of cards.

Lieutenant Vulic's appearance was in keeping with his character. His tall stature and swarthy complexion, black hair, black piercing eyes, and the large but regular nose typical of his nation, the cold, melancholy smile that eternally played on his lips—all this was as if designed to endow him with the appearance of an unusual person incapable of sharing his thoughts and emotions with those whom fate had made his comrades.

He was brave, he spoke little but bluntly; he confided his intimate and family secrets to no one; he scarcely ever drank any wine, and he never paid court to the young Cossack women, whose charms must be seen to be appreciated. It was said, nevertheless, that the colonel's wife was smitten by his expressive eyes; but he was always angered by hints to that effect.

There was only one passion he did not conceal—his passion for gambling. At a green-topped table he was oblivious to the world. He usually lost, but persistent bad luck only fed his obstinacy. It was said that one night during an expedition when he was keeping the bank on a pillow and having a terrific run of luck, shots suddenly rang out, the alarm was given, and everyone sprang up and rushed for their arms. "Stake the pool!" cried Vulic, who had not moved, to one of the most ardent punters. "Seven!" replied the latter as he dashed off. In spite of general confusion, Vulic dealt to the end; he turned up punter.[76]

When he reached the skirmish line the firing was already heavy. Vulic paid no attention either to the bullets or the Chechen sabers; he was searching for his lucky punter.

"It was a seven!" Vulic shouted catching sight of him at last in a line of skirmishers who were beginning to dislodge the enemy from a wood, and going up to him pulled out his purse and wallet and gave them to the winner in spite of the latter's objections to this ill-timed settlement. Having performed this unpleasant duty, Vulic dashed forward at the head of the soldiers and to the very end of the engagement fought the Chechens with the utmost coolness.

When Lieutenant Vulic walked up to the table everybody fell silent, expecting as usual something original.

"Gentlemen!" he said (his voice was calm though it was pitched lower than usual). "Gentlemen, why this idle argument? You wish for proof: I propose we test it on ourselves whether a man can dispose of his own life or whether the fateful moment has been preordained for each of us. . . . Who wants to try?"

"Not I, not I!" was the response from all sides. "What a queer fellow! Of all the things to think of!"

"I suggest a wager," I said in jest.

"What sort of a wager?"

"I claim there is no such thing as predestination," I said, emptying some twenty gold pieces on the table from my pockets—all that I happened to have on me.

"Done!" replied Vulic in a low voice. "Major, will you be the umpire;

[76] The game is a variation of faro called *shtoss*. The dealer, or "banker," goes through a deck of cards, turning up cards alternately on his right and left. He wins the stake if the card designated as the winner comes up on his right; the player, or "punter," wins if the card "turns up punter," that is, on the left.

here are fifteen gold pieces; you owe me five, so will you do me the favor of making up the difference?"

"Very well," said the major. "Though I haven't the slightest idea what it's all about, or how you propose to settle the matter."

Without a word Vulic went into the major's bedroom, we following him. Going over to a wall hung with weapons, he took down at random one of the pistols, of which there were several of different calibers. We did not realize what he was up to at first; but when he cocked the weapon and primed it, several of us involuntarily cried out and seized him by the arms.

"What are you going to do? Are you mad?" they shouted at him.

"Gentlemen!" he said with deliberation, disengaging his arms. "Which of you would care to pay twenty gold pieces for me?"

Everyone fell silent and drew back.

Vulic went into the next room and sat down at the table; the rest of us followed him. He motioned us to take our seats around the table. We obeyed him in silence, for at this moment he acquired some mysterious power over us. I looked intently into his eyes, but they met my searching gaze calmly and unwaveringly, and his pale lips smiled; but in spite of his composure I thought I could read the seal of death on his pallid face. I have observed, and many old soldiers have confirmed the observation, that frequently the face of a person who is to die in a few hours' time bears some strange mark of his inevitable fate which a practiced eye can scarcely fail to detect.

"You will die today," I said to him. He turned sharply to me, but replied with calm deliberation:

"I may, and then again I may not. . . ."

Then, turning to the major, he asked whether the pistol was loaded. In his confusion, the major could not remember exactly.

"That's enough, Vulic!" someone cried. "It must be loaded once it hung at the head of the bed. What sort of a joke is this!"

"A stupid joke!" threw in another.

"I'll wager fifty to five that the pistol is not loaded!" a third shouted. Fresh bets were made.

This endless ceremony began to pall on me. "Look here," I said, "either fire or hang the pistol back in its place and let's go to bed."

"That's right," many exclaimed. "Let's go to bed."

"Gentlemen, I beg of you not to move!" said Vulic, pressing the muzzle of the pistol to his forehead. We were all petrified.

"Mr. Pechorin," he went on, "will you take a card and throw it up in the air."

As I recall now, I picked up an ace of hearts from the table and threw it up; with bated breath and eyes expressive of terror and a vague curiosity we glanced from the pistol to the fateful ace which was now slowly fluttering downwards. The moment it touched the table, Vulic pulled the trigger—but the pistol missed fire.

"Thank God!" several voices cried. "It was not loaded. . . ."

"We shall see about that," said Vulic. Again he cocked the weapon and aimed at a forage cap hanging over the window; a shot rang out and smoke filled the room; and when it dispersed the forage cap was taken down—

there was the hole in the very center of it and the bullet had embedded itself deep in the wall.

For a good three minutes no one could utter a word; Vulic calmly poured my money into his purse.

Speculation began as to why the pistol did not go off the first time; some claimed that the pan must have been clogged, others whispered that the powder was damp at first, and that Vulic had afterwards sprinkled some fresh powder on it; I, however, assured them that the latter supposition was not just, for I had not taken my eyes off the pistol for a moment.

"You have gambler's luck!" I said to Vulic.

"For the first time in my life," he replied, smiling complacently. "This is better than faro or shtoss."

"But slightly more dangerous."

"Well? Have you begun to believe in predestination?"

"I do believe in it. Only I do not understand why it seemed to me that you were doomed to die today. . . ."

The very same man who so short a time before had with supreme indifference aimed a pistol at his own forehead now suddenly flared up and looked disconcerted.

"That will do!" he said, rising. "Our wager is finished and now your remarks seem out of place to me. . . ." He picked up his cap and walked out. His behavior struck me as queer—and rightly so.

Soon everyone left, each giving his own interpretation of Vulic's eccentric behavior on the way home, and, probably, unanimously branding me an egoist for having wagered with a man who wanted to shoot himself; as if he could not have found a convenient opportunity without my help!

I returned home through the deserted sidestreets of the settlement; the full moon, red as the glow of a conflagration, was just coming up over the jagged skyline of the housetops; the stars shone placidly in the dark-blue firmament, and I was amused at the thought that there once were sages who believed the heavenly bodies have a share in our wretched squabbles over a bit of territory or some other imaginary rights. Yet these lamps, which they thought had been lighted only to illuminate their battles and triumphs, still burn with undiminished brilliance, while their passions and hopes have long since died out together with them like a campfire left burning on the fringe of a forest by a careless wayfarer. But what strength of will they drew from the certainty that all the heavens with their numberless inhabitants looked down on them with constant, though mute, sympathy! Whereas we, their wretched descendants, who roam the earth without convictions or pride, without joys or fear other than the nameless dread that constricts the heart at the thought of the inevitable end, we are no longer capable of great sacrifices either for the good of mankind or even for our personal happiness since we know that happiness is impossible; and we pass indifferently from one doubt to another just as our forebears floundered from one delusion to another, without the hopes they had and without even that vague but potent sense of joy the soul derives from any struggle with men or destiny. . . .

Many similar thoughts passed through my mind; I did not retard their passage, because I do not care to dwell upon abstract ideas—for what can they lead to? In my early youth I was a dreamer; I liked to woo the images, now gloomy, now radiant, which my restless, eager imagination drew for me. But what have I derived from it all? Only weariness, like the aftermath of a nocturnal battle with a phantom, and dim memories filled with regrets. In this futile struggle I exhausted the warmth of soul and the constancy of will which are essential to an active life; when I embarked on that life, I had already lived it through in my thoughts, and hence it has become as boring and repulsive to me as a travesty of a long-familiar book.

The evening's events had made a rather deep impression on me and worked on my nerves. I am not certain whether I now believe in predestination or not, but that night I firmly believed in it. The proof had been striking, and regardless of the fact that I had ridiculed our forebears and their complaisant astrology, I found myself thinking as they did; but I caught myself in good time on this dangerous road, and having made it a rule never to reject anything categorically and never to believe in anything blindly, I cast metaphysics aside and began to watch the ground under my feet. The caution was timely, for I nearly stumbled over something thick and soft but apparently inanimate. I bent down—the moon now lit up the road—and what did I see lying in front of me but a pig sliced into two with a saber. . . . I had hardly had time to look at it when I heard footsteps: two Cossacks came running from a sidestreet. One of them came up to me and asked whether I had seen a drunken Cossack pursuing a pig. I told them that I had not met the Cossack, but showed them the unlucky victim of his violent prowess.

"The bandit!" said the second Cossack. "As soon as he drinks his fill of *chikhir*[77] he's out to cut up everything that comes his way. Let's go after him, Yeremeich; we've got to tie him up, or else. . . ."

They went off and I continued on my way more warily than before, at last reaching my quarters safe and sound.

I was staying with an old Cossack non-commissioned officer whom I liked because of his kindly nature and particularly because of his pretty daughter, Nastya.

She was waiting for me as usual at the gate, wrapped in a fur coat; the moon shone on her sweet lips, now blue from the cold of the night. Seeing me, she smiled, but I had other things on my mind. "Good night, Nastya," I said, passing by. She was about to say something in reply, but sighed instead.

I locked the door of my room, lighted a candle and flung myself on the bed; tonight, however, sleep eluded me longer than usual. The east was already beginning to grow pale when I fell asleep, but evidently the heavens had ordained that I was not to sleep this night. At four o'clock in the morning two fists banged at my window. I sprang up; what was the matter? "Wake up and get dressed!" several voices shouted. I dressed hastily and went out. "Do you know what's happened?" the three officers who had come for me said to me in chorus; they were as pale as death.

"What?"

"Vulic has been killed."

I was stupefied.

[77] New red wine.

"Yes, killed!" they went on. "Let us go quickly."

"Where to?"

"We'll tell you on the way."

We set off. They told me everything that had happened, adding to the story various observations concerning the strange fatality that had saved Vulic from certain death half an hour before he died. The Serbian had been walking alone along a dark street when the drunken Cossack who had slashed up the pig bumped into him, and might perhaps have gone on without paying any attention to him had Vulic not stopped suddenly and said:

"Whom are you looking for, brother?"

"You!" the Cossack answered, striking him with his saber and cleaving him from the shoulder nearly to the heart. . . . The two Cossacks whom I had seen and who were pursuing the murderer reached the spot, and picked up the wounded man, but he was already breathing his last and uttered only the words: "He was right!" I alone understood the ominous portent of these words; they referred to me. I had involuntarily predicted the poor man's fate; my instinct had not failed me; I had indeed read on his altered features the stamp of imminent death.

The murderer had locked himself in a vacant cottage at the far end of the settlement, and thither we went. A large number of women were running in the same direction, crying as they went. Every now and then a Cossack sprang belatedly out of a cottage hurriedly buckling on a dagger and ran past us. There was a fearful commotion.

At last we arrived on the scene to find a crowd gathered around the cottage whose doors and shutters had been fastened from the inside. Officers and Cossacks were holding a heated argument; the women were wailing and lamenting. Among them I noticed an old woman whose face expressed frantic despair. She was seated on a thick log, her elbows on her knees and her hands supporting her head; she was the murderer's mother. At times her lips moved . . . was it with a prayer or a curse?

In the meantime some decision had to be made and the malefactor apprehended. But no one had the pluck to go in first.

I went up to the window and looked in through a crack in a shutter. The man lay on the floor, holding a pistol in his right hand; a blood-stained saber lay beside him. His face was pale, and his expressive eyes rolled fearfully; at times he shuddered and clutched at his head as if hazily recollecting the happenings of the previous day. There did not seem to be much resolution in his uneasy glance and I told the major that there was no reason why he should not order the Cossacks to break the door in and rush the cottage, for it would be better to do so now rather than later when the man would have fully recovered his senses.

Just then an old captain of the Cossacks went up to the door and called to the man inside by name; the latter responded.

"You've sinned, brother Yefimych," said the Cossack captain. "So there's nothing for it but to give yourself up!"

"I won't!" replied the Cossack.

"Fear God's wrath! You are not a heathen Chechen, you're an honest Christian. You've gone astray and it can't be helped. You can't escape your fate!"

"I won't give up!" the Cossack shouted menacingly, and we could hear the click of the pistol as he cocked it.

"Hey, mother!" the Cossack captain said to the old woman. "You speak to your son, maybe he will listen to you. . . . After all, this sort of thing is only defying God. Look, the gentlemen have been waiting for two hours now."

The old woman looked at him intently and shook her head.

"Vasili Petrovich," said the Cossack captain, walking up to the major, "he will not give himself up—I know him. And if we break in the door, he will kill many of our men. Wouldn't it be better if you ordered him to be shot? There is a wide crack in the shutter."

At that moment a queer thought flashed in my mind; like Vulic, I thought of putting fate to a test.

"Wait," I said to the major, "I'll take him alive." Telling the Cossack captain to engage him in conversation and stationing three Cossacks at the entrance with instructions to break in the door and to rush to my assistance as soon as the signal was given, I walked around the cottage and approached the fateful window, my heart pounding.

"Hey there, you wretch!" shouted the Cossack captain. "Are you mocking at us or what? Or maybe you think we won't be able to take you." He began hammering at the door with all his strength, while I, pressing my eye to the chink, followed the movements of the Cossack inside who did not expect attack from this side, then suddenly wrenched off the shutter and threw myself into the window head first. The pistol went off next to my ear and the bullet tore off an epaulette. The smoke that filled the room, however, prevented my adversary from finding his saber, which lay beside him. I seized him by the arms; the Cossacks broke in, and in less than three minutes the criminal was tied up and led off under guard. The people dispersed and the officers congratulated me—and indeed they had reason to do so.

After all this how could one possibly avoid becoming a fatalist? But who knows for certain whether he is convinced of anything or not? And how often we mistake a deception of the senses or an error of reason for conviction!

I prefer to doubt everything; such a disposition does not preclude a resolute character; on the contrary, as far as I am concerned, I always advance more boldly when I do not know what is awaiting me. After all, nothing worse than death can happen—and death you cannot escape!

On returning to the fort I told Maxim Maximych everything I had seen and experienced, and wanted to hear his opinion about predestination. At first he did not understand the word, but I explained it to him as best I could, whereupon he said, significantly shaking his head:

"Yes, sir! It's a queer business that! By the way, these Asiatic pistol cocks often miss fire if they are poorly oiled or if you don't press hard enough with your finger. I must admit I don't like the Cherkess rifles either; they are a bit inconvenient for the likes of us; the butt is so small that unless you watch out you may get your nose scorched. . . . Their sabers now are a different matter—I take off my hat to them!"

Then he added after brief reflection:

"Yes, I'm sorry for the poor chap. . . . Why the devil did he stop to talk with a drunk at night! But, I suppose, that was his destiny!"

I got nothing more out of him; in general he does not care for metaphysical discourses.

THE END

Henry David Thoreau

(1817–1862)

One of the greatest American writers wrote no fiction or drama and only a handful of eccentric, rather unsuccessful poems. His fame rests not upon any achievement in the major literary forms but upon one short essay and a peculiar autobiographical narrative about his experience of living by himself for two years in the woods. Yet no American book is more widely read, not only for its ideas but for its artistry as well, than Walden. *This paradox, this violation of received norms, is quite appropriate to the general contrariness and determination to go his own way of Henry David Thoreau.*

Thoreau was born in 1817 in Concord, Massachusetts (thus becoming the only native of Concord among the group of 1840's "Concord transcendentalists"). His father, who had failed at storekeeping, was a manufacturer of pencils; his mother was a strong, high-minded woman who insisted upon good educations for her children. Thoreau went to Concord Academy and Harvard. He thought little of Harvard, but he did acquire the classical education there which was to flavor all his writings. (The critic Marcus Cunliffe has, not unkindly, called Thoreau "a Huckleberry Finn who has been to Harvard.") When he was graduated in 1837, he returned to Concord, where he joined his father for a time in the pencil business and then opened a private school with his brother John. With John, too, he made the trip which became the subject of his first book, A Week on the Concord and Merrimack Rivers *(1849). He also made the acquaintance of Ralph Waldo Emerson, the ex-Unitarian minister, now transcendentalist seer, who had settled in Concord, and when the Thoreaus' school closed in 1841, he moved in with the Emersons, earning his room and board by working as the Emersons' handyman.*

The cluster of ideas, hardly a systematic philosophy, called "transcendentalism" is crucial in understanding what has been called "the flowering of New England" in mid-nineteenth-century American literature, not only for those writers who expressed varieties of transcendentalist thought (Emerson, Thoreau, Whitman) but also for those who in some ways reacted against it (Hawthorne and Melville). Emerson had begun his career as a Unitarian minister in Boston but had left the ministry after three years when he found he could no longer accept the Christian dogma surviving even in Unitarianism. He spent the rest of his life as a writer and lecturer. His creed, transcendentalism, can be seen as an attempt to develop a religious philosophy suited to conditions in an optimistic, expanding, and forward-looking American society. Compounded of elements of New England Puritanism, Unitarianism, and the teachings of the European Romantics, transcendentalism was based upon a faith in indi-

vidual intuition as a guide to "transcendental" truth (that beyond the grasp of the senses). "Deity" (Emerson omitted the definite article) was all-loving and present in every person; man was thus in a sense himself divine and assured of salvation. The world, both matter and spirit, was one, and man could arrive at transcendental understanding through contemplation of the self and of nature. Intuition, individualism, and nature were thus key elements in transcendentalism.

Emerson, both as man and writer, had a profound influence upon Thoreau. Emerson suggested to him that he keep a journal, and like Emerson's own journal, Thoreau's became a mine from which he cut chunks for polishing and publication; both men expressed themselves primarily in meditative, lecture-like essays studded with verse and growing out of journal entries. Thoreau contributed to the transcendentalists' magazine The Dial *and met with "the Symposium," the transcendentalist discussion group, which included Emerson, Bronson Alcott, Orestes Brownson, Nathaniel Hawthorne, and William Ellery Channing.*

In 1843, Thoreau left Concord briefly and went to New York, where he tutored the children of Emerson's brother and made some attempts to break into the New York literary world. But he soon returned to Concord. In 1845, he moved into a cabin he had built on some land Emerson owned on Walden Pond, near Concord, and began the experiment that was to form the subject of Walden. *He remained there for two years and two months, spending his time, apart from that devoted to taking care of the necessities of life, in writing the book based on his boating trip of 1839 on the Concord and Merrimack Rivers with his brother. It was during the Walden stay, too, that he spent a night in jail in July, 1846, for refusing for six years to pay his poll tax, in protest against the support the state of Massachusetts gave slavery. This incident formed the subject of his essay on "Civil Disobedience."*

Thoreau left Walden Pond in September, 1847, and moved back into Concord with the Emersons. He had already begun Walden *while in the cabin and submitted a version of it for publication in 1849, but* A Week on the Concord and Merrimack Rivers, *published earlier that year, had failed and* Walden *was rejected. He spent five years revising and polishing it, and it was published in 1854. There were few reviews, and most of those few were uncomprehending; critics viewed the book mainly as a prescription for how to live cheaply.*

After the passage of the Fugitive Slave law of 1850, requiring Northern states to return escaped slaves, Thoreau became even more involved in the Abolitionist controversy, writing for the Abolitionist paper, The Liberator, *and writing and speaking in behalf of John Brown, condemned to hang for his raid on Harpers Ferry, Virginia, in 1859.*

Thoreau spent his last years operating his father's business, which he switched from the manufacture of pencils to the grinding of graphite, making a systematic study of botany with the great American naturalist Louis Agassiz, and writing and publishing occasional essays. He had suffered from tuberculosis for some years, and his condition began to worsen rapidly in 1860. He died in 1862 at the age of forty-five. His lung condition had probably been aggravated by prolonged breathing of graphite dust in his shop. Thus, oddly, this apostle of the open air was at least partially a victim of industrial pollution. He had published only two books during his lifetime, but after his death, his sister Sophia and his friends put together, from his magazine articles, lectures, and unpublished essays half a dozen other volumes which appeared over the next twenty years. His complete works, published in 1906, fill twenty volumes.

Thoreau's most directly influential work has been "Civil Disobedience." In this essay, he raises the question, suggested by Massachusetts' collaboration in the slave system, including its support of the Mexican War, but applicable to all similar situations, of the relation of the individual to a government regarded as unjust. "That government is best which governs least," Thoreau argues, and goes on to assert that the individual is responsible for the actions of his government and that if he cannot agree with those actions, he is entitled to disobey any civil order. The essay has been translated into many languages and in many countries has been a basic text for reformers. It was a favorite of revolutionaries in Russia against czarist tyranny, and it was an important source of the ideas that went into the formation of the British Labor Party. Gandhi, in India, drew his strategy of "passive resistance" to British colonialism from Thoreau, and in America, "Civil Disobedience" inspired Martin Luther King's campaign for Black civil rights in the 1960's, as well as the resistance to the Vietnam war.

The impact of Walden *has been as great, if less directly translated into action. After the indifference and misunderstanding which greeted its first appearance, it has steadily gained readers and is now recognized as not only the supreme expression of New England transcendentalism but a work that goes beyond transcendentalism to levels of experience unrecognized by Thoreau's fellow seekers.*

Walden *is a quest narrative in which the object of the quest is not a material prize but an understanding of the self and of reality. "Let us settle ourselves," Thoreau wrote, "and work and wedge our feet downward through the mud and slush of opinion, and prejudice, and tradition, and delusion, and appearance, that alluvion which covers the globe, through Paris and London, through New York and Boston and Concord, through church and state, through poetry and philosophy and religion, till we come to a hard bottom and rocks in place, which we can call* reality, *and say, This is, and no mistake. . . ." Like a good transcendentalist, Thoreau seeks reality not through logical inquiry but by situating himself in the midst of nature and opening himself up to its influence. What nature whispers to him will be knowledge of himself as well, since for Thoreau there is no barrier between nature and himself or between his own "higher nature" and his "lower nature." The fundamental structure of the book is, appropriately, a circle. It is shaped as a whole by the single seasonal cycle to which Thoreau reduces the two years he spent at the pond, and the fundamental movement of Thoreau's mind is also circular, spiraling around each of the elements in his little world until he has drilled his way down to the "hard bottom" of its meaning.*

Walden *is also among American literature's most entertaining books. Thoreau's quest may be exalted but it is not grim or pompous. The book is full of humor that ranges from terse, twinkle-eyed Yankee aphorisms ("Some circumstantial evidence is very strong, as when you find a trout in the milk") to shrewd, ironic anecdotes (about, for example, the farmer who lectures Thoreau that a vegetarian diet provides no material to build bones while plowing behind oxen with "vegetable-made bones"). And the tone can modulate easily to other keys: passionate conviction, quiet reflection, a gnarled, eloquent poetry. To listen to the voice of* Walden *is to be in the company of perhaps the finest example of what Emerson called the American Scholar—not just a "thinker" but "man thinking."*

FURTHER READING *(prepared by W. J. R.):* For background on the transcendentalist movement see the following works: F. O. Matthiessen's *American Renaissance: Art and Expression in the Age of Emerson and Whitman,* 1941 (contains sections on Emerson and Thoreau, Hawthorne, Melville, and Whitman); Lawrence Buell's *Literary Transcendentalism,* 1973; and *American Transcendentalism: An Anthology of Criticism,* ed. Brian M. Barbour, 1973. Norman Foerster's *Nature in America,* 1923, rpt. 1953, has lengthy discussions of both Thoreau and Whitman; Alexander Kern's "The Rise of Transcendentalism," in *Transitions in American Literary History,* ed. Harry Hayden Clark, 1954, offers a compact overview of the movement which should serve the new student well. The following works are limited to Thoreau: Sherman Paul's *The Shores of America: Thoreau's Inward Journey,* 1958, chronicles Thoreau's intellectual and spiritual development. Walter Harding and Michael Meyer's *The New Thoreau Handbook,* 1980, a revised version of Harding's 1954 *Handbook,* surveys Thoreau's life, works, and ideas. An overview of Thoreau criticism may be found in *Henry David Thoreau: Studies and Commentaries,* ed. Walter Harding, George Brown, and Paul A. Doyle, 1972.

from *WALDEN*

I. ECONOMY

When I wrote the following pages, or rather the bulk of them, I lived alone, in the woods, a mile from any neighbor, in a house which I had built myself, on the shore of Walden Pond, in Concord, Massachusetts, and earned my living by the labor of my hands only. I lived there two years and two months. At present I am a sojourner in civilized life again.

I should not obtrude my affairs so much on the notice of my readers if very particular inquiries had not been made by my townsmen concerning my mode of life, which some would call impertinent, though they do not appear to me at all impertinent, but, considering the circumstances, very natural and pertinent. Some have asked what I got to eat: if I did not feel lonesome; if I was not afraid; and the like. Others have been curious to learn what portion of my income I devoted to charitable purposes; and some, who have large families, how many poor children I maintained. I will therefore ask those of my readers who feel no particular interest in me to pardon me if I undertake to answer some of these questions in this book. In most books, the *I,* or first person, is omitted; in this it will be retained; that, in respect to egotism, is the main difference. We commonly do not remember that it is, after all, always the first person that is speaking. I should not talk so much about myself if there were anybody else whom I knew as well. Unfortunately, I am confined to this theme by the narrowness of my experience. Moreover, I, on my side, require of every writer, first or last, a simple and sincere account of his own life, and not merely what he has heard of other men's lives; some such account as he would send to his kindred from a distant land; for if he has lived sincerely it must have been in a distant land to me. Perhaps these pages are more particularly addressed to poor students. As for the rest of my readers, they will accept such portions as apply to them. I trust that none will stretch the seams in putting on the coat, for it may do good service to him whom it fits.

I would fain say something, not so much concerning the Chinese and

Sandwich Islanders[1] as you who read these pages, who are said to live in New England; something about your condition, especially your outward condition or circumstances in this world, in this town, what it is, whether it is necessary that it be as bad as it is, whether it cannot be improved as well as not. I have traveled a good deal in Concord; and everywhere, in shops, and offices, and fields, the inhabitants have appeared to me to be doing penance in a thousand remarkable ways. What I have heard of Bramins[2] sitting exposed to four fires and looking in the face of the sun; or hanging suspended, with their heads downwards, over flames; or looking at the heavens over their shoulders "until it becomes impossible for them to resume their natural position, while from the twist of the neck nothing but liquids can pass into the stomach"; or dwelling, chained for life, at the foot of a tree; or measuring with their bodies, like caterpillars, the breadth of vast empires; or standing on one leg on the tops of pillars,—even these forms of conscious penance are hardly more incredible and astonishing than the scenes which I daily witness. The twelve labors of Hercules[3] were trifling in comparison with those which my neighbors have undertaken; for they were only twelve, and had an end; but I could never see that these men slew or captured any monster or finished any labor. They have no friend Iolaus[4] to burn with a hot iron the root of the hydra's head, but as soon as one head is crushed, two spring up.

I see young men, my townsmen, whose misfortune it is to have inherited farms, houses, barns, cattle, and farming tools; for these are more easily acquired than got rid of. Better if they had been born in the open pasture and suckled by a wolf, that they might have seen with clearer eyes what field they were called to labor in. Who made them serfs of the soil? Why should they eat their sixty acres, when man is condemned to eat only his peck of dirt?[5] Why should they begin digging their graves as soon as they are born? They have got to live a man's life, pushing all these things before them, and get on as well as they can. How many a poor immortal soul have I met well-nigh crushed and smothered under its load, creeping down the road of life, pushing before it a barn seventy-five feet by forty, its Augean stables[6] never cleansed, and one hundred acres of land, tillage, mowing, pasture, and wood-lot. The portionless, who struggle with no such unnecessary inherited encumbrances, find it labor enough to subdue and cultivate a few cubic feet of flesh.

But men labor under a mistake. The better part of the man is soon plowed into the soil for compost. By a seeming fate, commonly called necessity, they are employed, as it says in an old book, laying up treasures

[1] Hawaiians. James Cook, who discovered the islands in 1778, originally called them the "Sandwich Islands" after his patron, the Earl of Sandwich.

[2] Members of the highest Hindu caste; usually spelled Brahmins. They tortured themselves as a religious act.

[3] In Greek mythology, Hercules had to perform twelve seemingly impossible tasks in order to win purification after killing his wife and children in a fit of madness.

[4] Hercules' servant, who helped him kill the nine-headed Hydra.

[5] A traditional proverb says that everyone eats a peck of dirt before he dies.

[6] One of the twelve labors of Hercules was to clean the stables where King Augeas had kept a large herd of oxen for thirty years.

which moth and rust will corrupt and thieves break through and steal.[7] It is a fool's life, as they will find when they get to the end of it, if not before. It is said that Deucalion and Pyrrha[8] created men by throwing stones over their heads behind them:—

> Inde genus durum sumus, experiensque laborum,
> Et documenta damus quâ sumus origine nati.[9]

Or, as Raleigh rhymes it in his sonorous way,—

> "From thence our kind hard-hearted is, enduring pain and care,
> Approving that our bodies of a stony nature are."

So much for a blind obedience to a blundering oracle, throwing the stones over their heads behind them, and not seeing where they fell.

Most men, even in this comparatively free country, through mere ignorance and mistake, are so occupied with the factitious cares and superfluously coarse labors of life that its finer fruits cannot be plucked by them. Their fingers, from excessive toil, are too clumsy and tremble too much for that. Actually, the laboring man has not leisure for true integrity day by day; he cannot afford to sustain the manliest relations to men; his labor would be depreciated in the market. He has no time to be anything but a machine. How can he remember well his ignorance—which his growth requires—who has so often to use his knowledge? We should feed and clothe him gratuitously sometimes, and recruit him with our cordials,[10] before we judge of him. The finest qualities of our nature, like the bloom on fruits, can be preserved only by the most delicate handling. Yet we do not treat ourselves nor one another thus tenderly.

Some of you, we all know, are poor, find it hard to live, are sometimes, as it were, gasping for breath. I have no doubt that some of you who read this book are unable to pay for all the dinners which you have actually eaten, or for the coats and shoes which are fast wearing or are already worn out, and have come to this page to spend borrowed or stolen time, robbing your creditors of an hour. It is very evident what mean and sneaking lives many of you live, for my sight has been whetted by experience; always on the limits,[11] trying to get into business and trying to get out of debt, a very ancient slough, called by the Latins *aes alienum,* another's brass, for some of their coins were made of brass; still living, and dying, and buried by this other's brass; always promising to pay, promising to pay, tomorrow, and dying today, insolvent; seeking to curry favor, to get custom, by how many modes, only not state-prison offenses; lying, flattering, voting, contracting yourselves into a nutshell of civility, or dilating into an atmosphere of thin and vaporous generosity, that you may persuade your neighbor to let you make his shoes, or his hat, or his coat, or his carriage, or import his groceries for him; making yourselves sick, that you may lay up something against

[7] The "old book" is the Bible; see Matthew 6:19.
[8] In Greek mythology, Deucalion and Pyrrha were the only survivors of a worldwide flood.
[9] Ovid, *Metamorphoses,* Book I. The translation is from Sir Walter Raleigh's *History of the World* (1614).
[10] Stimulating drinks or medicines. [11] That is, the limits of indebtedness.

a sick day, something to be tucked away in an old chest, or in a stocking behind the plastering, or, more safely, in the brick bank; no matter where, no matter how much or how little.

I sometimes wonder that we can be so frivolous, I may almost say, as to attend to the gross but somewhat foreign form of servitude called Negro Slavery, there are so many keen and subtle masters that enslave both North and South. It is hard to have a Southern overseer; it is worse to have a Northern one; but worst of all when you are the slave-driver of yourself. Talk of a divinity in man! Look at the teamster on the highway, wending to market by day or night; does any divinity stir within him? His highest duty to fodder and water his horses! What is his destiny to him compared with the shipping interests? Does not he drive for Squire Make-a-stir? How god-like, how immortal, is he? See how he cowers and sneaks, how vaguely all the day he fears, not being immortal nor divine, but the slave and prisoner of his own opinion of himself, a fame won by his own deeds. Public opinion is a weak tyrant compared with our own private opinion. What a man thinks of himself, that it is which determines, or rather indicates, his fate. Self-emancipation even in the West Indian provinces of the fancy and imagination,—what Wilberforce[12] is there to bring that about? Think, also, of the ladies of the land weaving toilet[13] cushions against the last day, not to betray too green an interest in their fates! As if you could kill time without injuring eternity.

The mass of men lead lives of quiet desperation. What is called resignation is confirmed desperation. From the desperate city you go into the desperate country, and have to console yourself with the bravery of minks and muskrats. A stereotyped but unconscious despair is concealed even under what are called the games and amusements of mankind. There is no play in them, for this comes after work. But it is a characteristic of wisdom not to do desperate things.

When we consider what, to use the words of the catechism, is the chief end of man,[14] and what are the true necessaries and means of life, it appears as if men had deliberately chosen the common mode of living because they preferred it to any other. Yet they honestly think there is no choice left. But alert and healthy natures remember that the sun rose clear. It is never too late to give up our prejudices. No way of thinking or doing, however ancient, can be trusted without proof. What everybody echoes or in silence passes by as true today may turn out to be falsehood tomorrow, mere smoke of opinion, which some had trusted for a cloud that would sprinkle fertilizing rain on their fields. What old people say you cannot do, you try and find that you can. Old deeds for old people, and new deeds for new. Old people did not know enough once, perchance, to fetch fresh fuel to keep the fire a-going; new people put a little dry wood under a pot,[15] and are whirled round the globe with the speed of birds, in a way to kill old people, as the phrase is. Age is no better, hardly so well, qualified for an

[12] William Wilberforce (1759–1833) was the leading English abolitionist.

[13] Dressing room.

[14] "The chief end of man," according to the catechism in the *New England Primer,* first published before 1690 and the most popular schoolbook in eighteenth-century America, was "to glorify God and to enjoy him forever."

[15] The boiler in a steam locomotive.

instructor as youth, for it has not profited so much as it has lost. One may almost doubt if the wisest man has learned anything of absolute value by living. Practically, the old have no very important advice to give the young, their own experience has been so partial, and their lives have been such miserable failures, for private reasons, as they must believe; and it may be that they have some faith left which belies that experience, and they are only less young than they were. I have lived some thirty years on this planet, and I have yet to hear the first syllable of valuable or even earnest advice from my seniors. They have told me nothing, and probably cannot tell me anything to the purpose. Here is life, an experiment to a great extent untried by me; but it does not avail me that they have tried it. If I have any experience which I think valuable, I am sure to reflect that this my Mentors[16] said nothing about.

One farmer says to me, "You cannot live on vegetable food solely, for it furnishes nothing to make bones with;" and so he religiously devotes a part of his day to supplying his system with the raw material of bones; walking all the while he talks behind his oxen, which, with vegetable-made bones, jerk him and his lumbering plow along in spite of every obstacle. Some things are really necessaries of life in some circles, the most helpless and diseased, which in others are luxuries merely, and in others still are entirely unknown.

The whole ground of human life seems to some to have been gone over by their predecessors, both the heights and the valleys, and all things to have been cared for. According to Evelyn,[17] "the wise Solomon prescribed ordinances for the very distance of trees; and the Roman praetors[18] have decided how often you may go into your neighbor's land to gather the acorns which fall on it without trespass, and what share belongs to that neighbor." Hippocrates[19] has even left directions how we should cut our nails; that is, even with the ends of the fingers, neither shorter nor longer. Undoubtedly the very tedium and ennui which presume to have exhausted the variety and the joys of life are as old as Adam. But man's capacities have never been measured; nor are we to judge of what he can do by any precedents, so little has been tried. Whatever have been thy failures hitherto, "be not afflicted, my child, for who shall assign to thee what thou hast left undone?"[20]

We might try our lives by a thousand simple tests; as, for instance, that the same sun that ripens my beans illumines at once a system of earths like ours. If I had remembered this it would have prevented some mistakes. This was not the light in which I hoed them. The stars are the apexes of what wonderful triangles! What distant and different beings in the various mansions of the universe are contemplating the same one at the same moment! Nature and human life are as various as our several constitutions. Who shall say what prospect life offers to another? Could a greater miracle take place than for us to look through each other's eyes for an instant? We

[16] Telemachus's teacher in Homer's *Odyssey;* hence, any wise teacher.

[17] John Evelyn, seventeenth-century English diarist, also wrote a book on trees: *Sylva; or, A Discourse on Forest-Trees* (1644).

[18] Magistrates.

[19] Greek physician (c. 460–c. 370 B.C.), called "the father of medicine."

[20] From the Hindu religious text, the *Vishnu Purana.*

should live in all the ages of the world in an hour; ay, in all the worlds of the ages. History, Poetry, Mythology!—I know of no reading of another's experience so startling and informing as this would be.

The greater part of what my neighbors call good I believe in my soul to be bad, and if I repent of anything, it is very likely to be my good behavior. What demon possessed me that I behaved so well? You may say the wisest thing you can, old man,—you who have lived seventy years, not without honor of a kind,—I hear an irresistible voice which invites me away from all that. One generation abandons the enterprises of another like stranded vessels.

I think that we may safely trust a good deal more than we do. We may waive just so much care of ourselves as we honestly bestow elsewhere. Nature is as well adapted to our weakness as to our strength. The incessant anxiety and strain of some is a well-nigh incurable form of disease. We are made to exaggerate the importance of what work we do; and yet how much is not done by us! or, what if we had been taken sick? How vigilant we are! determined not to live by faith if we can avoid it; all the day long on the alert, at night we unwillingly say our prayers and commit ourselves to uncertainties. So thoroughly and sincerely are we compelled to live, reverencing our life, and denying the possibility of change. This is the only way, we say; but there are as many ways as there can be drawn radii from one center. All change is a miracle to contemplate; but it is a miracle which is taking place every instant. Confucius[21] said, "To know that we know what we know, and that we do not know what we do not know, that is true knowledge." When one man has reduced a fact of the imagination to be a fact of his understanding, I foresee that all men will at length establish their lives on that basis.

Let us consider for a moment what most of the trouble and anxiety which I have referred to is about, and how much it is necessary that we be troubled, or at least careful. It would be some advantage to live a primitive and frontier life, though in the midst of an outward civilization, if only to learn what are the gross necessaries of life and what methods have been taken to obtain them; or even to look over the old day-books of the merchants, to see what it was that men most commonly bought at the stores, what they stored, that is, what are the grossest groceries. For the improvements of ages have had but little influence on the essential laws of man's existence; as our skeletons, probably, are not to be distinguished from those of our ancestors.

By the words, *necessary of life,* I mean whatever, of all that man obtains by his own exertions, has been from the first, or from long use has become, so important to human life that few, if any, whether from savageness, or poverty, or philosophy, ever attempt to do without it. To many creatures there is in this sense but one necessary of life, Food. To the bison of the prairie it is a few inches of palatable grass, with water to drink; unless he seeks the Shelter of the forest or the mountain's shadow. None of the brute creation requires more than Food and Shelter. The necessaries of life for man in this climate may, accurately enough, be distributed under the several heads of Food, Shelter, Clothing, and Fuel; for not till we have secured

[21] Chinese ethical teacher (c. 551–479? B.C.); the quotation is from the *Analects,* II, 17.

these are we prepared to entertain the true problems of life with freedom and a prospect of success. Man has invented, not only houses, but clothes and cooked food; and possibly from the accidental discovery of the warmth of fire, and the consequent use of it, at first a luxury, arose the present necessity to sit by it. We observe cats and dogs acquiring the same second nature. By proper Shelter and Clothing we legitimately retain our own internal heat; but with an excess of these, or of Fuel, that is, with an external heat greater than our own internal, may not cookery properly be said to begin? Darwin,[22] the naturalist, says of the inhabitants of Tierra del Fuego, that while his own party, who were well clothed and sitting close to a fire, were far from too warm, these naked savages, who were farther off, were observed, to his great surprise, "to be streaming with perspiration at undergoing such a roasting." So, we are told, the New Hollander[23] goes naked with impunity, while the European shivers in his clothes. Is it impossible to combine the hardiness of these savages with the intellectualness of the civilized man? According to Liebig,[24] man's body is a stove, and food the fuel which keeps up the internal combustion in the lungs. In cold weather we eat more, in warm less. The animal heat is the result of a slow combustion, and disease and death take place when this is too rapid; or for want of fuel, or from some defect in the draught, the fire goes out. Of course the vital heat is not to be confounded with fire; but so much for analogy. It appears, therefore, from the above list, that the expression, *animal life,* is nearly synonymous with the expression, *animal heat;* for while Food may be regarded as the Fuel which keeps up the fire within us,—and Fuel serves only to prepare that Food or to increase the warmth of our bodies by addition from without,—Shelter and Clothing also serve only to retain the *heat* thus generated and absorbed.

The grand necessity, then, for our bodies, is to keep warm, to keep the vital heat in us. What pains we accordingly take, not only with our Food, and Clothing, and Shelter, but with our beds, which are our night-clothes, robbing the nests and breasts of birds to prepare this shelter within a shelter, as the mole has its bed of grass and leaves at the end of its burrow! The poor man is wont to complain that this is a cold world; and to cold, no less physical than social, we refer directly a great part of our ails. The summer, in some climates, makes possible to man a sort of Elysian life.[25] Fuel, except to cook his Food, is then unnecessary; the sun is his fire, and many of the fruits are sufficiently cooked by its rays; while Food generally is more various, and more easily obtained, and Clothing and Shelter are wholly or half unnecessary. At the present day, and in this country, as I find by my own experience, a few implements, a knife, an axe, a spade, a wheelbarrow, etc., and for the studious, lamplight, stationery, and access to a few books, rank next to necessaries, and can all be obtained at a trifling cost. Yet some, not wise, go to the other side of the globe, to barbarous and unhealthy regions, and devote themselves to trade for ten or twenty years, in order that they

[22] The English naturalist Charles Darwin (1809–1882) described the inhabitants of Tierra del Fuego, an island off the southern tip of South America, in his *Voyage of the "Beagle"* (1839).
[23] Australian aborigine.
[24] Justus von Liebig (1803–1873) was a German chemist.
[25] An idyllic or Edenic life. In Greek mythology, Elysium was the home of the blessed dead.

may live,—that is, keep comfortably warm,—and die in New England at last. The luxuriously rich are not simply kept comfortably warm, but unnaturally hot; as I implied before, they are cooked, of course, *à la mode*.[26]

Most of the luxuries, and many of the so-called comforts of life, are not only not indispensable, but positive hindrances to the elevation of mankind. With respect to luxuries and comforts, the wisest have ever lived a more simple and meager life than the poor. The ancient philosophers, Chinese, Hindoo, Persian, and Greek, were a class than which none has been poorer in outward riches, none so rich in inward. We know not much about them. It is remarkable that *we* know so much of them as we do. The same is true of the more modern reformers and benefactors of their race. None can be an impartial or wise observer of human life but from the vantage ground of what *we* should call voluntary poverty. Of a life of luxury the fruit is luxury, whether in agriculture, or commerce, or literature, or art. There are nowadays professors of philosophy, but not philosophers. Yet it is admirable to profess because it was once admirable to live. To be a philosopher is not merely to have subtle thoughts, nor even to found a school, but so to love wisdom as to live according to its dictates, a life of simplicity, independence, magnanimity, and trust. It is to solve some of the problems of life, not only theoretically, but practically. The success of great scholars and thinkers is commonly a courtier-like success, not kingly, not manly. They make shift to live merely by conformity, practically as their fathers did, and are in no sense the progenitors of a nobler race of men. But why do men degenerate ever? What makes families run out? What is the nature of the luxury which enervates and destroys nations? Are we sure that there is none of it in our own lives? The philosopher is in advance of his age even in the outward form of his life. He is not fed, sheltered, clothed, warmed, like his contemporaries. How can a man be a philosopher and not maintain his vital heat by better methods than other men?

When a man is warmed by the several modes which I have described, what does he want next? Surely not more warmth of the same kind, as more and richer food, larger and more splendid houses, finer and more abundant clothing, more numerous, incessant, and hotter fires, and the like. When he has obtained those things which are necessary to life, there is another alternative than to obtain the superfluities; and that is, to adventure on life now, his vacation from humbler toil having commenced. The soil, it appears, is suited to the seed, for it has sent its radicle[27] downward, and it may now send its shoot upward also with confidence. Why has man rooted himself thus firmly in the earth, but that he may rise in the same proportion into the heavens above?—for the nobler plants are valued for the fruit they bear at last in the air and light, far from the ground, and are not treated like the humbler esculents,[28] which, though they may be biennials, are cultivated only till they have perfected their root, and often cut down at top for this purpose, so that most would not know them in their flowering season.

[26] In the fashionable style. Thoreau is referring to central heating, then becoming popular among the prosperous.
[27] Root.
[28] Any edible vegetable, here restricted to roots and tubers, such as turnips and potatoes.

I do not mean to prescribe rules to strong and valiant natures, who will mind their own affairs whether in heaven or hell, and perchance build more magnificently and spend more lavishly than the richest, without ever impoverishing themselves, not knowing how they live,—if, indeed, there are any such, as has been dreamed; nor to those who find their encouragement and inspiration in precisely the present condition of things, and cherish it with the fondness and enthusiasm of lovers,—and, to some extent, I reckon myself in this number; I do not speak to those who are well employed, in whatever circumstances, and they know whether they are well employed or not;—but mainly to the mass of men who are discontented, and idly complaining of the hardness of their lot or of the times, when they might improve them. There are some who complain most energetically and inconsolably of any, because they are, as they say, doing their duty. I also have in my mind that seemingly wealthy, but most terribly impoverished class of all, who have accumulated dross, but know not how to use it, or get rid of it, and thus have forged their own golden or silver fetters.

If I should attempt to tell how I have desired to spend my life in years past, it would probably surprise those of my readers who are somewhat acquainted with its actual history; it would certainly astonish those who know nothing about it. I will only hint at some of the enterprises which I have cherished.

In any weather, at any hour of the day or night, I have been anxious to improve the nick of time, and notch it on my stick too; to stand on the meeting of two eternities, the past and future, which is precisely the present moment; to toe that line. You will pardon some obscurities, for there are more secrets in my trade than in most men's, and yet not voluntarily kept, but inseparable from its very nature. I would gladly tell all that I know about it, and never paint "No Admittance" on my gate.

I long ago lost a hound, a bay horse, and a turtle dove,[29] and am still on their trail. Many are the travelers I have spoken concerning them, describing their tracks and what calls they answered to. I have met one or two who had heard the hound, and the tramp of the horse, and even seen the dove disappear behind a cloud, and they seemed as anxious to recover them as if they had lost them themselves.

To anticipate, not the sunrise and the dawn merely, but, if possible, Nature herself! How many mornings, summer and winter, before yet any neighbor was stirring about his business, have I been about mine! No doubt, many of my townsmen have met me returning from this enterprise, farmers starting for Boston in the twilight, or woodchoppers going to their work. It is true, I never assisted the sun materially in his rising, but, doubt not, it was of the last importance only to be present at it.

So many autumn, ay, and winter days, spent outside the town, trying to hear what was in the wind, to hear and carry it express! I well-nigh sunk all my capital in it, and lost my own breath into the bargain, running in the face of it. If it had concerned either of the political parties, depend upon it,

[29] The symbolism of the hound, bay horse, and turtle dove, despite much debate, remains obscure. In general, they seem to be objects of a spiritual quest but they may have more specific meanings as well.

it would have appeared in the Gazette[30] with the earliest intelligence.[31] At other times watching from the observatory of some cliff or tree, to telegraph any new arrival; or waiting at evening on the hill-tops for the sky to fall, that I might catch something, though I never caught much, and that, manna-wise,[32] would dissolve again in the sun.

For a long time I was reporter to a journal,[33] of no very wide circulation, whose editor has never yet seen fit to print the bulk of my contributions, and, as is too common with writers, I got only my labor for my pains. However, in this case my pains were their own reward.

For many years I was self-appointed inspector of snow-storms and rain-storms, and did my duty faithfully; surveyor, if not of highways, then of forest paths and all across-lot routes, keeping them open, and ravines bridged and passable at all seasons, where the public heel had testified to their utility.

I have looked after the wild stock of the town, which give a faithful herdsman a good deal of trouble by leaping fences; and I have had an eye to the unfrequented nooks and corners of the farm; though I did not always know whether Jonas or Solomon worked in a particular field today; that was none of my business. I have watered the red huckleberry, the sand cherry and the nettle-tree, the red pine and the black ash, the white grape and the yellow violet, which might have withered else in dry seasons.

In short, I went on thus for a long time (I may say it without boasting), faithfully minding my business, till it became more and more evident that my townsmen would not after all admit me into the list of town officers, nor make my place a sinecure with a moderate allowance. My accounts, which I can swear to have kept faithfully, I have, indeed, never got audited, still less accepted, still less paid and settled. However, I have not set my heart on that.

Not long since, a strolling Indian went to sell baskets at the house of a well-known lawyer in my neighborhood. "Do you wish to buy any baskets?" he asked. "No, we do not want any," was the reply. "What!" exclaimed the Indian as he went out the gate, "do you mean to starve us?" Having seen his industrious white neighbors so well off,—that the lawyer had only to weave arguments, and, by some magic, wealth and standing followed,—he had said to himself: I will go into business; I will weave baskets; it is a thing which I can do. Thinking that when he had made the baskets he would have done his part, and then it would be the white man's to buy them. He had not discovered that it was necessary for him to make it worth the other's while to buy them, or at least make him think that it was so, or to make something else which it would be worth his while to buy. I too had woven a kind of basket of a delicate texture, but I had not made it worth any one's while to buy them. Yet not the less, in my case, did I think it worth my while to weave them, and instead of studying how to make it worth men's while to buy my baskets, I studied rather how to avoid the necessity

[30] The Concord *Yeoman's Gazette;* by extension, any newspaper. [31] News.

[32] Manna was the food the Lord gave the Israelites on their exodus out of Egypt (Exodus 16). What was left over dissolved in the sun.

[33] Thoreau may be referring to the transcendentalist magazine *The Dial,* which rejected some of his contributions, or he may be referring, whimsically, to his own private journal.

of selling them. The life which men praise and regard as successful is but one kind. Why should we exaggerate any one kind at the expense of the others?

Finding that my fellow-citizens were not likely to offer me any room in the court house, or any curacy or living anywhere else, but I must shift for myself, I turned my face more exclusively than ever to the woods, where I was better known. I determined to go into business at once, and not wait to acquire the usual capital, using such slender means as I had already got. My purpose in going to Walden Pond was not to live cheaply nor to live dearly there, but to transact some private business with the fewest obstacles; to be hindered from accomplishing which for want of a little common sense, a little enterprise and business talent, appeared not so sad as foolish.

I have always endeavored to acquire strict business habits; they are indispensable to every man. If your trade is with the Celestial Empire,[34] then some small counting house on the coast, in some Salem harbor, will be fixture enough. You will export such articles as the country affords, purely native products, much ice and pine timber and a little granite, always in native bottoms. These will be good ventures. To oversee all the details yourself in person; to be at once pilot and captain, and owner and underwriter; to buy and sell and keep the accounts; to read every letter received, and write or read every letter sent; to superintend the discharge of imports night and day; to be upon many parts of the coast almost at the same time,—often the richest freight will be discharged upon a Jersey shore;[35]—to be your own telegraph, unweariedly sweeping the horizon, speaking all passing vessels bound coastwise; to keep up a steady despatch of commodities, for the supply of such a distant and exorbitant market; to keep yourself informed of the state of the markets, prospects of war and peace everywhere, and anticipate the tendencies of trade and civilization,—taking advantage of the results of all exploring expeditions, using new passages and all improvements in navigation;—charts to be studied, the position of reefs and new lights and buoys to be ascertained, and ever, and ever, the logarithmic tables to be corrected, for by the error of some calculator the vessel often splits upon a rock that should have reached a friendly pier,—there is the untold fate of La Pérouse;[36]—universal science to be kept pace with, studying the lives of all great discoverers and navigators, great adventurers and merchants, from Hanno and the Phoenicians[37] down to our day; in fine, account of stock to be taken from time to time, to know how you stand. It is a labor to task the faculties of a man,—such problems of profit and loss, of interest, of tare and tret,[38] and gauging of all kinds in it, as demand a universal knowledge.

I have thought that Walden Pond would be a good place for business,

[34] China.

[35] The coast of New Jersey was notorious for the number of ships wrecked there.

[36] The eighteenth-century French explorer the Count de la Pérouse was shipwrecked and killed in 1788 in the South Pacific.

[37] Hanno was a fifth-century B.C. Carthaginian navigator who explored the northeastern coast of Africa. The Phoenicians were generally known as skillful ancient navigators and explorers.

[38] Shipping terms. "Tare" is a deduction for the weight of the container; "tret" is a deduction for waste.

not solely on account of the railroad and the ice trade; it offers advantages which it may not be good policy to divulge; it is a good port and a good foundation. No Neva[39] marshes to be filled; though you must everywhere build on piles of your own driving. It is said that a flood-tide, with a westerly wind, and ice in the Neva, would sweep St. Petersburg from the face of the earth.

As this business was to be entered into without the usual capital, it may not be easy to conjecture where those means, that will still be indispensable to every such undertaking, were to be obtained. As for Clothing, to come at once to the practical part of the question, perhaps we are led oftener by the love of novelty and a regard for the opinions of men, in procuring it, than by a true utility. Let him who has work to do recollect that the object of clothing is, first, to retain the vital heat, and secondly, in this state of society, to cover nakedness, and he may judge how much of any necessary or important work may be accomplished without adding to his wardrobe. Kings and queens who wear a suit but once, though made by some tailor or dressmaker to their majesties, cannot know the comfort of wearing a suit that fits. They are no better than wooden horses to hang the clean clothes on. Every day our garments become more assimilated to ourselves, receiving the impress of the wearer's character, until we hesitate to lay them aside without such delay and medical appliances and some such solemnity even as our bodies. No man ever stood the lower in my estimation for having a patch in his clothes; yet I am sure that there is greater anxiety, commonly, to have fashionable, or at least clean and unpatched clothes, than to have a sound conscience. But even if the rent is not mended, perhaps the worst vice betrayed is improvidence. I sometimes try my acquaintances by such tests as this,—Who could wear a patch, or two extra seams only, over the knee? Most behave as if they believed that their prospects for life would be ruined if they should do it. It would be easier for them to hobble to town with a broken leg than with a broken pantaloon. Often if an accident happens to a gentleman's legs, they can be mended; but if a similar accident happens to the legs of his pantaloons, there is no help for it; for he considers, not what is truly respectable, but what is respected. We know but few men, a great many coats and breeches. Dress a scarecrow in your last shift, you standing shiftless by, who would not soonest salute the scarecrow? Passing a cornfield the other day, close by a hat and coat on a stake, I recognized the owner of the farm. He was only a little more weather-beaten than when I saw him last. I have heard of a dog that barked at every stranger who approached his master's premises with clothes on, but was easily quieted by a naked thief. It is an interesting question how far men would retain their relative rank if they were divested of their clothes. Could you,' in such a case, tell surely of any company of civilized men which belonged to the most respected class? When Madam Pfeiffer,[40] in her adventurous travels round the world, from east to west, had got so near home as Asiatic Russia, she says that she felt the necessity of wearing other than a traveling dress, when she went to meet the authorities, for she "was now in

[39] The river upon whose delta St. Petersburg (Leningrad) is built.

[40] Ida Pfeiffer (1797–1858) was an Austrian woman who traveled around the world in the 1840's and reported her experiences in *A Woman's Journey Round the World* (1852).

a civilized country, where . . . people are judged of by their clothes." Even in our democratic New England towns the accidental possession of wealth, and its manifestation in dress and equipage alone, obtain for the possessor almost universal respect. But they who yield such respect, numerous as they are, are so far heathen, and need to have a missionary sent to them. Beside, clothes introduced sewing, a kind of work which you may call endless; a woman's dress, at least, is never done.

A man who has at length found something to do will not need to get a new suit to do it in; for him the old will do, that has lain dusty in the garret for an indeterminate period. Old shoes will serve a hero longer than they have served his valet,—if a hero ever has a valet,—bare feet are older than shoes, and he can make them do. Only they who go to soirées and legislative halls must have new coats, coats to change as often as the man changes in them. But if my jacket and trousers, my hat and shoes, are fit to worship God in, they will do; will they not? Who ever saw his old clothes,—his old coat, actually worn out, resolved into its primitive elements, so that it was not a deed of charity to bestow it on some poor boy, by him perchance to be bestowed on some poorer still, or shall we say richer, who could do with less? I say, beware of all enterprises that require new clothes, and not rather a new wearer of clothes. If there is not a new man, how can the new clothes be made to fit? If you have any enterprise before you, try it in your old clothes. All men want, not something to *do with,* but something to *do,* or rather something to *be.* Perhaps we should never procure a new suit, however ragged or dirty the old, until we have so conducted, so enterprised or sailed in some way, that we feel like new men in the old, and that to retain it would be like keeping new wine in old bottles.[41] Our moulting season, like that of the fowls, must be a crisis in our lives. The loon retires to solitary ponds to spend it. Thus also the snake casts its slough, and the caterpillar its wormy coat, by an internal industry and expansion; for clothes are but our outmost cuticle and mortal coil. Otherwise we shall be found sailing under false colors, and be inevitably cashiered at last by our own opinion, as well as that of mankind.

We don garment after garment, as if we grew like exogenous plants by addition without. Our outside and often thin and fanciful clothes are our epidermis, or false skin, which partakes not of our life, and may be stripped off here and there without fatal injury; our thicker garments, constantly worn, are our cellular integument, or cortex; but our shirts are our liber, or true bark, which cannot be removed without girdling and so destroying the man. I believe that all races at some seasons wear something equivalent to the shirt. It is desirable that a man be clad so simply that he can lay his hands on himself in the dark, and that he live in all respects so compactly and preparedly that, if an enemy take the town, he can, like the old philosopher, walk out the gate empty-handed without anxiety. While one thick garment is, for most purposes, as good as three thin ones, and cheap clothing can be obtained at prices really to suit customers; while a thick coat can be bought for five dollars, which will last as many years, thick pantaloons for two dollars, cowhide boots for a dollar and a half a pair, a summer hat for a quarter of a dollar, and a winter cap for sixty-two and a half cents, or

[41] Matthew 9:17. "Neither do men put new wine into old bottles: else the bottles break."

a better be made at home at a nominal cost, where is he so poor that, clad in such a suit, *of his own earning,* there will not be found wise men to do him reverence?

When I ask for a garment of a particular form, my tailoress tells me gravely, "They do not make them so now," not emphasizing the "They" at all, as if she quoted an authority as impersonal as the Fates,[42] and I find it difficult to get made what I want, simply because she cannot believe that I mean what I say, that I am so rash. When I hear this oracular sentence, I am for a moment absorbed in thought, emphasizing to myself each word separately that I may come at the meaning of it, that I may find out by what degree of consanguinity *They* are related to *me,* and what authority they may have in an affair which affects me so nearly; and, finally, I am inclined to answer her with equal mystery, and without any more emphasis of the "they,"—"It is true, they did not make them so recently, but they do now." Of what use this measuring of me if she does not measure my character, but only the breadth of my shoulders, as it were a peg to hang the coat on? We worship not the Graces,[43] nor the Parcae,[44] but Fashion. She spins and weaves and cuts with full authority. The head monkey at Paris puts on a traveler's cap, and all the monkeys in America do the same. I sometimes despair of getting anything quite simple and honest done in this world by the help of men. They would have to be passed through a powerful press first, to squeeze their old notions out of them, so that they would not soon get upon their legs again; and then there would be some one in the company with a maggot in his head, hatched from an egg deposited there nobody knows when, for not even fire kills these things, and you would have lost your labor. Nevertheless, we will not forget that some Egyptian wheat was handed down to us by a mummy.[45]

On the whole, I think that it cannot be maintained that dressing has in this or any country risen to the dignity of an art. At present men make shift to wear what they can get. Like shipwrecked sailors, they put on what they can find on the beach, and at a little distance, whether of space or time, laugh at each other's masquerade. Every generation laughs at the old fashions, but follows religiously the new. We are amused at beholding the costume of Henry VIII, or Queen Elizabeth, as much as if it was that of the King and Queen of the Cannibal Islands. All costume off a man is pitiful or grotesque. It is only the serious eye peering from and the sincere life passed within it which restrain laughter and consecrate the costume of any people. Let Harlequin[46] be taken with a fit of the colic and his trappings will have to serve that mood too. When the soldier is hit by a cannon-ball, rags are as becoming as purple.

The childish and savage taste of men and women for new patterns keeps how many shaking and squinting through kaleidoscopes that they may discover the particular figure which this generation requires today. The manufacturers have learned that this taste is merely whimsical. Of two

[42] In Greek mythology, the three goddesses who control human destiny.
[43] In Greek mythology, the three goddesses of beauty and charm.
[44] Roman name for the three Fates.
[45] Wheat had supposedly been sprouted from seeds found in Egyptian tombs.
[46] A stock character in old Italian comedy, dressed in multicolored clothes.

patterns which differ only by a few threads more or less of a particular color, the one will be sold readily, the other lie on the shelf, though it frequently happens that after the lapse of a season the latter becomes the most fashionable. Comparatively, tattooing is not the hideous custom which it is called. It is not barbarous merely because the printing is skin-deep and unalterable.

I cannot believe that our factory system is the best mode by which men may get clothing. The condition of the operatives is becoming every day more like that of the English;[47] and it cannot be wondered at, since, as far as I have heard or observed, the principal object is, not that mankind may be well and honestly clad, but, unquestionably, that the corporations may be enriched. In the long run men hit only what they aim at. Therefore, though they should fail immediately, they had better aim at something high.

As for a Shelter, I will not deny that this is now a necessary of life, though there are instances of men having done without it for long periods in colder countries than this. Samuel Laing[48] says that "the Laplander in his skin dress, and in a skin bag which he puts over his head and shoulders, will sleep night after night on the snow . . . in a degree of cold which would extinguish the life of one exposed to it in any woollen clothing." He had seen them asleep thus. Yet he adds, "They are not hardier than other people." But, probably, man did not live long on the earth without discovering the convenience which there is in a house, the domestic comforts, which phrase may have originally signified the satisfactions of the house more than of the family; though these must be extremely partial and occasional in those climates where the house is associated in our thoughts with winter or the rainy season chiefly, and two thirds of the year, except for a parasol, is unnecessary. In our climate, in the summer, it was formerly almost solely a covering at night. In the Indian gazettes a wigwam was the symbol of a day's march, and a row of them cut or painted on the bark of a tree signified that so many times they had camped. Man was not made so large limbed and robust but that he must seek to narrow his world, and wall in a space such as fitted him. He was at first bare and out of doors; but though this was pleasant enough in serene and warm weather, by daylight, the rainy season and the winter, to say nothing of the torrid sun, would perhaps have nipped his race in the bud if he had not made haste to clothe himself with the shelter of a house. Adam and Eve, according to the fable, wore the bower before other clothes. Man wanted a home, a place of warmth, of comfort, first of physical warmth, then the warmth of the affections.

We may imagine a time when, in the infancy of the human race, some enterprising mortal crept into a hollow in a rock for shelter. Every child begins the world again, to some extent, and loves to stay outdoors, even in wet and cold. It plays house, as well as horse, having an instinct for it. Who does not remember the interest with which when young he looked at shelv-

[47] Working conditions in English clothing mills were notoriously bad.

[48] British author of a number of travel books on Scandinavia, including *Journal of a Residence in Norway* (1837), from which the following quotation is taken.

ing rocks, or any approach to a cave? It was the natural yearning of that portion of our most primitive ancestor which still survived in us. From the cave we have advanced to roofs of palm leaves, of bark and boughs, of linen woven and stretched, of grass and straw, of boards and shingles, of stone and tiles. At last, we know not what it is to live in the open air, and our lives are domestic in more senses than we think. From the hearth the field is a great distance. It would be well, perhaps, if we were to spend more of our days and nights without any obstruction between us and the celestial bodies, if the poet did not speak so much from under a roof, or the saint dwell there so long. Birds do not sing in caves, nor do doves cherish their innocence in dovecots.

However, if one designs to construct a dwelling-house, it behooves him to exercise a little Yankee shrewdness, lest after all he find himself in a workhouse, a labyrinth without a clue, a museum, an almshouse, a prison, or a splendid mausoleum instead. Consider first how slight a shelter is absolutely necessary. I have seen Penobscot Indians,[49] in this town, living in tents of thin cotton cloth, while the snow was nearly a foot deep around them, and I thought that they would be glad to have it deeper to keep out the wind. Formerly, when how to get my living honestly, with freedom left for my proper pursuits, was a question which vexed me even more than it does now, for unfortunately I am become somewhat callous, I used to see a large box by the railroad, six feet long by three wide, in which the laborers locked up their tools at night; and it suggested to me that every man who was hard pushed might get such a one for a dollar, and, having bored a few auger holes in it, to admit the air at least, get into it when it rained and at night, and hook down the lid, and so have freedom in his love, and in his soul be free. This did not appear the worst, nor by any means a despicable alternative. You could sit up as late as you pleased, and, whenever you got up, go abroad without any landlord or house-lord dogging you for rent. Many a man is harassed to death to pay the rent of a larger and more luxurious box who would not have frozen to death in such a box as this. I am far from jesting. Economy is a subject which admits of being treated with levity, but it cannot so be disposed of. A comfortable house for a rude and hardy race, that lived mostly out of doors, was once made here almost entirely of such materials as Nature furnished ready to their hands. Gookin,[50] who was superintendent of the Indians subject to the Massachusetts Colony, writing in 1674, says, "The best of their houses are covered very neatly, tight and warm, with barks of trees, slipped from their bodies at those seasons when the sap is up, and made into great flakes, with pressure of weighty timber, when they are green. . . . The meaner sort are covered with mats which they make of a kind of bulrush, and are also indifferently tight and warm, but not so good as the former. . . . Some I have seen, sixty or a hundred feet long and thirty feet broad. . . . I have often lodged in their wigwams, and found them as warm as the best English houses." He adds that they were commonly carpeted and lined within with

[49] A tribe from northern Maine.
[50] Daniel Gookin (1612–1687) wrote *Historical Collections of the Indians in New England* (1792).

well-wrought embroidered mats, and were furnished with various utensils. The Indians had advanced so far as to regulate the effect of the wind by a mat suspended over the hole in the roof and moved by a string. Such a lodge was in the first instance constructed in a day or two at most, and taken down and put up in a few hours; and every family owned one, or its apartment in one.

In the savage state every family owns a shelter as good as the best, and sufficient for its coarser and simpler wants; but I think that I speak within bounds when I say that, though the birds of the air have their nests, and the foxes their holes,[51] and the savages their wigwams, in modern civilized society not more than one half the families own a shelter. In the large towns and cities, where civilization especially prevails, the number of those who own a shelter is a very small fraction of the whole. The rest pay an annual tax for this outside garment of all, become indispensable summer and winter, which would buy a village of Indian wigwams, but now helps to keep them poor as long as they live. I do not mean to insist here on the disadvantage of hiring compared with owning, but it is evident that the savage owns his shelter because it costs so little, while the civilized man hires his commonly because he cannot afford to own it; nor can he, in the long run, any better afford to hire. But, answers one, by merely paying this tax the poor civilized man secures an abode which is a palace compared with the savage's. An annual rent of from twenty-five to a hundred dollars (these are the country rates) entitles him to the benefit of the improvements of centuries, spacious apartments, clean paint and paper, Rumford fireplace,[52] back plastering,[53] Venetian blinds, copper pump, spring lock, a commodious cellar, and many other things. But how happens it that he who is said to enjoy these things is so commonly a *poor* civilized man, while the savage, who has them not, is rich as a savage? If it is asserted that civilization is a real advance in the condition of man,—and I think that it is, though only the wise improve their advantages,—it must be shown that it has produced better dwellings without making them more costly; and the cost of a thing is the amount of what I will call life which is required to be exchanged for it, immediately or in the long run. An average house in this neighborhood costs perhaps eight hundred dollars, and to lay up this sum will take from ten to fifteen years of the laborer's life, even if he is not encumbered with a family,—estimating the pecuniary value of every man's labor at one dollar a day, for if some receive more, others receive less;—so that he must have spent more than half his life commonly before *his* wigwam will be earned. If we suppose him to pay a rent instead, this is but a doubtful choice of evils. Would the savage have been wise to exchange his wigwam for a palace on these terms?

It may be guessed that I reduce almost the whole advantage of holding this superfluous property as a fund in store against the future, so far as the individual is concerned, mainly to the defraying of funeral expenses. But perhaps a man is not required to bury himself. Nevertheless this points to an important distinction between the civilized man and the savage; and, no

[51] See Matthew 8:20: "The foxes have holes, and the birds of the air have nests; but the Son of man hath not where to lay his head."

[52] A Rumford fireplace was a kind of smokeless stove. [53] Insulation.

doubt, they have designs on us for our benefit, in making the life of a civilized people an *institution,* in which the life of the individual is to a great extent absorbed, in order to preserve and perfect that of the race. But I wish to show at what a sacrifice this advantage is at present obtained, and to suggest that we may possibly so live as to secure all the advantage without suffering any of the disadvantage. What mean ye by saying that the poor ye have always with you, or that the fathers have eaten sour grapes, and the children's teeth are set on edge?[54]

"As I live, saith the Lord God, ye shall not have occasion any more to use this proverb in Israel.

"Behold all souls are mine; as the soul of the father, so also the soul of the son is mine: the soul that sinneth, it shall die."[55]

When I consider my neighbors, the farmers of Concord, who are at least as well off as the other classes, I find that for the most part they have been toiling twenty, thirty, or forty years, that they may become the real owners of their farms, which commonly they have inherited with encumbrances, or else bought with hired money,—and we may regard one third of that toil as the cost of their houses,—but commonly they have not paid for them yet. It is true, the encumbrances sometimes outweigh the value of the farm, so that the farm itself becomes one great encumbrance, and still a man is found to inherit it, being well acquainted with it, as he says. On applying to the assessors, I am surprised to learn that they cannot at once name a dozen in the town who own their farms free and clear. If you would know the history of these homesteads, inquire at the bank where they are mortgaged. The man who has actually paid for his farm with labor on it is so rare that every neighbor can point to him. I doubt if there are three such men in Concord. What has been said of the merchants, that a very large majority, even ninety-seven in a hundred, are sure to fail, is equally true of the farmers. With regard to the merchants, however, one of them says pertinently that a great part of their failures are not genuine pecuniary failures, but merely failures to fulfill their engagements, because it is inconvenient; that is, it is the moral character that breaks down. But this puts an infinitely worse face on the matter, and suggests, beside, that probably not even the other three succeed in saving their souls, but are perchance bankrupt in a worse sense than they who fail honestly. Bankruptcy and repudiation are the springboards from which much of our civilization vaults and turns its somersets, but the savage stands on the unelastic plank of famine. Yet the Middlesex Cattle Show[56] goes off here with *éclat*[57] annually, as if all the joints of the agricultural machine were suent.[58]

The farmer is endeavoring to solve the problem of a livelihood by a formula more complicated than the problem itself. To get his shoestrings he speculates in herds of cattle. With consummate skill he has set his trap with a hair spring[59] to catch comfort and independence, and then, as he turned away, got his own leg into it. This is the reason he is poor; and for a similar reason we are all poor in respect to a thousand savage comforts, though surrounded by luxuries. As Chapman sings,—

[54] Thoreau is quoting Matthew 26:11 and Ezekiel 18:2. [55] Ezekiel 18:3–4.
[56] This show was held in Concord every year in September. [57] Brilliance of success.
[58] A New England expression meaning "broken in." [59] That is, with a "hair trigger."

"The false society of men—
—for earthly greatness
All heavenly comforts rarefies to air."[60]

And when the farmer has got his house, he may not be the richer but the poorer for it, and it be the house that has got him. As I understand it, that was a valid objection urged by Momus against the house which Minerva made,[61] that she "had not made it movable, by which means a bad neighborhood might be avoided," and it may still be urged, for our houses are such unwieldy property that we are often imprisoned rather than housed in them; and the bad neighborhood to be avoided is our own scurvy selves. I know one or two families, at least, in this town, who, for nearly a generation, have been wishing to sell their houses in the outskirts and move into the village, but have not been able to accomplish it, and only death will set them free.

Granted that the *majority* are able at last either to own or hire the modern house with all its improvements. While civilization has been improving our houses, it has not equally improved the men who are to inhabit them. It has created palaces, but it was not so easy to create noblemen and kings. And *if the civilized man's pursuits are no worthier than the savage's, if he is employed the greater part of his life in obtaining gross necessaries and comforts merely, why should he have a better dwelling than the former?*

But how do the poor *minority* fare? Perhaps it will be found that just in proportion as some have been placed in outward circumstances above the savage, others have been degraded below him. The luxury of one class is counterbalanced by the indigence of another. On the one side is the palace, on the other are the almshouse and "silent poor."[62] The myriads who built the pyramids to be the tombs of the Pharaohs were fed on garlic, and it may be were not decently buried themselves. The mason who finishes the cornice of the palace returns at night perchance to a hut not so good as a wigwam. It is a mistake to suppose that, in a country where the usual evidences of civilization exist, the condition of a very large body of the inhabitants may not be as degraded as that of savages. I refer to the degraded poor, not now to the degraded rich. To know this I should not need to look farther than to the shanties which everywhere border our railroads, that last improvement in civilization; where I see in my daily walks human beings living in sties, and all winter with an open door, for the sake of light, without any visible, often imaginable, wood-pile, and the forms of both old and young are permanently contracted by the long habit of shrinking from cold and misery, and the development of all their limbs and faculties is checked. It certainly is fair to look at that class by whose labor the works which distinguish this generation are accomplished. Such too, to a greater or less extent, is the condition of the operatives of every denomination in England, which is the great workhouse of the world. Or I could refer you

[60] George Chapman, *Caesar and Pompey* (1631), V.ii.210 and 212–13.
[61] In Greek literary convention, Momus personified fault-finding and mockery. Minerva was, among other things, the goddess of craftsmanship.
[62] Poor people too proud to ask for assistance.

to Ireland,[63] which is marked as one of the white or enlightened spots on the map. Contrast the physical condition of the Irish with that of the North American Indian, or the South Sea Islander, or any other savage race before it was degraded by contact with the civilized man. Yet I have no doubt that that people's rulers are as wise as the average of civilized rulers. Their condition only proves what squalidness may consist with civilization. I hardly need refer now to the laborers in our Southern States who produce the staple exports of this country, and are themselves a staple production of the South.[64] But to confine myself to those who are said to be in *moderate* circumstances.

Most men appear never to have considered what a house is, and are actually though needlessly poor all their lives because they think that they must have such a one as their neighbors have. As if one were to wear any sort of coat which the tailor might cut out for him, or, gradually leaving off palm-leaf hat or cap of woodchuck skin, complain of hard times because he could not afford to buy him a crown! It is possible to invent a house still more convenient and luxurious than we have, which yet all would admit that man could not afford to pay for. Shall we always study to obtain more of these things, and not sometimes to be content with less? Shall the respectable citizen thus gravely teach, by precept and example, the necessity of the young man's providing a certain number of superflous glow-shoes,[65] and umbrellas, and empty guest chambers for empty guests, before he dies? Why should not our furniture be as simple as the Arab's or the Indian's? When I think of the benefactors of the race, whom we have apotheosized as messengers from heaven, bearers of divine gifts to man, I do not see in my mind any retinue at their heels, any car-load of fashionable furniture. Or what if I were to allow—would it not be a singular allowance?—that our furniture should be more complex than the Arab's, in proportion as we are morally and intellectually his superiors! At present our houses are cluttered and defiled with it, and a good housewife would sweep out the greater part into the dust hole, and not leave her morning's work undone. Morning work! By the blushes of Aurora and the music of Memnon,[66] what should be man's *morning work* in this world? I had three pieces of limestone on my desk, but I was terrified to find that they required to be dusted daily, when the furniture of my mind was all undusted still, and I threw them out the window in disgust. How, then, could I have a furnished house? I would rather sit in the open air, for no dust gathers on the grass, unless where man has broken ground.

It is the luxurious and dissipated who set the fashions which the herd so diligently follow. The traveler who stops at the best houses, so called, soon discovers this, for the publicans presume him to be a Sardanapalus,[67] and if he resigned himself to their tender mercies he would soon be completely emasculated. I think that in the railroad car we are inclined to spend more on luxury than on safety and convenience, and it threatens without attain-

[63] Ireland was an especially topical example of human misery, because of the Potato Famine of the 1840's.

[64] Slaves were bred and raised for sale in the South. [65] Overshoes.

[66] Aurora was the Roman goddess of the dawn; the statue of Memnon, in Egypt, was said to sing when the rays of the morning sun struck it.

[67] Ninth-century B.C. Assyrian king, noted for his effeminacy and love of luxury.

ing these to become no better than a modern drawing room, with its divans, and ottomans, and sun-shades, and a hundred other oriental things, which we are taking west with us, invented for the ladies of the harem and the effeminate natives of the Celestial Empire, which Jonathan[68] should be ashamed to know the names of. I would rather sit on a pumpkin and have it all to myself than be crowded on a velvet cushion. I would rather ride on earth in an ox cart, with a free circulation, than go to heaven in the fancy car of an excursion train and breathe a *malaria* all the way.

The very simplicity and nakedness of man's life in the primitive ages imply this advantage, at least, that they left him still but a sojourner in nature. When he was refreshed with food and sleep, he contemplated his journey again. He dwelt, as it were, in a tent in this world, and was either threading the valleys, or crossing the plains, or climbing the mountaintops. But lo! men have become the tools of their tools. The man who independently plucked the fruits when he was hungry is become a farmer; and he who stood under a tree for shelter, a housekeeper. We now no longer camp as for a night, but have settled down on earth and forgotten heaven. We have adopted Christianity merely as an improved method of *agri*-culture. We have built for this world a family mansion, and for the next a family tomb. The best works of art are the expression of man's struggle to free himself from this condition, but the effect of our art is merely to make this low state comfortable and that higher state to be forgotten. There is actually no place in this village for a work of *fine* art, if any had come down to us, to stand, for our lives, our houses and streets, furnish no proper pedestal for it. There is not a nail to hang a picture on, nor a shelf to receive the bust of a hero or a saint. When I consider how our houses are built and paid for, or not paid for, and their internal economy managed and sustained, I wonder that the floor does not give way under the visitor while he is admiring the gewgaws upon the mantelpiece, and let him through into the cellar to some solid and honest though earthy foundation. I cannot but perceive that this so-called rich and refined life is a thing jumped at, and I do not get on in the enjoyment of the *fine* arts which adorn it, my attention being wholly occupied with the jump; for I remember that the greatest genuine leap, due to human muscles alone, on record, is that of certain wandering Arabs, who are said to have cleared twenty-five feet on level ground. Without factitious support, man is sure to come to earth again beyond that distance. The first question which I am tempted to put to the proprietor of such great impropriety is, Who bolsters you? Are you one of the ninety-seven who fail, or the three who succeed? Answer me these questions, and then perhaps I may look at your baubles and find them ornamental. The cart before the horse is neither beautiful nor useful. Before we can adorn our houses with beautiful objects the walls must be stripped, and our lives must be stripped, and beautiful housekeeping and beautiful living be laid for a foundation: now, a taste for the beautiful is most cultivated out of doors, where there is no house and no housekeeper.

Old Johnson, in his "Wonder-Working Providence,"[69] speaking of the

[68] Nickname for Americans.

[69] Edward Johnson (1598–1672) wrote *Wonder-Working Providence of Sion's Saviour in New England* (1654).

first settlers of this town, with whom he was contemporary, tells us that "they burrow themselves in the earth for their first shelter under some hillside, and, casting the soil aloft upon timber, they make a smoky fire against the earth, at the highest side." They did not "provide them houses," says he, "till the earth, by the Lord's blessing, brought forth bread to feed them," and the first year's crop was so light that "they were forced to cut their bread very thin for a long season." The secretary of the Province of New Netherland, writing in Dutch, in 1650,[70] for the information of those who wished to take up land there, states more particularly that "those in New Netherland, and especially in New England, who have no means to build farm-houses at first according to their wishes, dig a square pit in the ground, cellar fashion, six or seven feet deep, as long and as broad as they think proper, case the earth inside with wood all round the wall, and line the wood with the bark of trees or something else to prevent the caving in of the earth; floor this cellar with plank, and wainscot it overhead for a ceiling, raise a roof of spars clear up, and cover the spars with bark or green sods, so that they can live dry and warm in these houses with their entire families for two, three, and four years, it being understood that partitions are run through those cellars which are adapted to the size of the family. The wealthy and principal men in New England, in the beginning of the colonies, commenced their first dwelling-houses in this fashion for two reasons: firstly, in order not to waste time in building, and not to want food the next season; secondly, in order not to discourage poor laboring people whom they brought over in numbers from Fatherland. In the course of three or four years, when the country became adapted to agriculture, they built themselves handsome houses, spending on them several thousands."

In this course which our ancestors took there was a show of prudence at least, as if their principle were to satisfy the more pressing wants first. But are the more pressing wants satisfied now? When I think of acquiring for myself one of our luxurious dwellings, I am deterred, for, so to speak, the country is not yet adapted to *human* culture, and we are still forced to cut our *spiritual* bread far thinner than our forefathers did their wheaten. Not that all architectural ornament is to be neglected even in the rudest periods; but let our houses first be lined with beauty, where they come in contact with our lives, like the tenement of the shell-fish, and not overlaid with it. But, alas! I have been inside one or two of them, and know what they are lined with.

Though we are not so degenerate but that we might possibly live in a cave or a wigwam or wear skins today, it certainly is better to accept the advantages, though so dearly bought, which the invention and industry of mankind offer. In such a neighborhood as this, boards and shingles, lime and bricks, are cheaper and more easily obtained than suitable caves, or whole logs, or bark in sufficient quantities, or even well-tempered clay or flat stones. I speak understandingly on this subject, for I have made myself acquainted with it both theoretically and practically. With a little more wit we might use these materials so as to become richer than the richest now

[70] New Netherland was the old name for New York. Thoreau quotes from a translation published in E. B. O'Callaghan, *The Documentary History of the State of New York* (1851).

are, and make our civilization a blessing. The civilized man is a more experienced and wiser savage. But to make haste to my own experiment.

Near the end of March, 1845, I borrowed an axe and went down to the woods by Walden Pond, nearest to where I intended to build my house, and began to cut down some tall, arrowy white pines, still in their youth, for timber. It is difficult to begin without borrowing, but perhaps it is the most generous course thus to permit your fellow-men to have an interest in your enterprise. The owner of the axe, as he released his hold on it, said that it was the apple of his eye; but I returned it sharper than I received it. It was a pleasant hillside where I worked, covered with pine woods, through which I looked out on the pond, and a small open field in the woods where pines and hickories were springing up. The ice in the pond was not yet dissolved, though there were some open spaces, and it was all dark-colored and saturated with water. There were some slight flurries of snow during the days that I worked there; but for the most part when I came out on to the railroad, on my way home, its yellow sand-heap stretched away gleaming in the hazy atmosphere, and the rails shone in the spring sun, and I heard the lark and pewee and other birds already come to commence another year with us. They were pleasant spring days, in which the winter of man's discontent[71] was thawing as well as the earth, and the life that had lain torpid began to stretch itself. One day, when my axe had come off and I had cut a green hickory for a wedge, driving it with a stone, and had placed the whole to soak in a pond-hole in order to swell the wood, I saw a striped snake run into the water, and he lay on the bottom, apparently without inconvenience, as long as I stayed there, or more than a quarter of an hour; perhaps because he had not yet fairly come out of the torpid state. It appeared to me that for a like reason men remain in their present low and primitive condition; but if they should feel the influence of the spring of springs arousing them, they would of necessity rise to a higher and more ethereal life. I had previously seen the snakes in frosty mornings in my path with portions of their bodies still numb and inflexible, waiting for the sun to thaw them. On the 1st of April it rained and melted the ice, and in the early part of the day, which was very foggy, I heard a stray goose groping about over the pond and cackling as if lost, or like the spirit of the fog.

So I went on for some days cutting and hewing timber, and also studs and rafters, all with my narrow axe, not having many communicable or scholar-like thoughts, singing to myself,—

> Men say they know many things;
> But lo! they have taken wings,—
> The arts and sciences,
> And a thousand appliances;
> The wind that blows
> Is all that any body knows.[72]

[71] Cf. Richard III's line, "Now is the winter of our discontent . . ." in Shakespeare's *Richard III,* I.i.l.

[72] Thoreau's own poetry, identified here, as elsewhere in *Walden,* by the absence of quotation marks.

I hewed the main timbers six inches square, most of the studs on two sides only, and the rafters and floor timbers on one side, leaving the rest of the bark on, so that they were just as straight and much stronger than sawed ones. Each stick was carefully mortised or tenoned by its stump, for I had borrowed other tools by this time. My days in the woods were not very long ones; yet I usually carried my dinner of bread and butter, and read the newspaper in which it was wrapped, at noon, sitting amid the green pine boughs which I had cut off, and to my bread was imparted some of their fragrance, for my hands were covered with a thick coat of pitch. Before I had done I was more the friend than the foe of the pine tree, though I had cut down some of them, having become better acquainted with it. Sometimes a rambler in the wood was attracted by the sound of my axe, and we chatted pleasantly over the chips which I had made.

By the middle of April, for I made no haste in my work, but rather made the most of it, my house was framed and ready for the raising. I had already bought the shanty of James Collins, an Irishman who worked on the Fitchburg Railroad, for boards. James Collins' shanty was considered an uncommonly fine one. When I called to see it he was not at home. I walked about the outside, at first unobserved from within, the window was so deep and high. It was of small dimensions, with a peaked cottage roof, and not much else to be seen, the dirt being raised five feet all around as if it were a compost heap. The roof was the soundest part, though a good deal warped and made brittle by the sun. Doorsill there was none, but a perennial passage for the hens under the door-board. Mrs. C. came to the door and asked me to view it from the inside. The hens were driven in by my approach. It was dark, and had a dirt floor for the most part, dank, clammy, and aguish, only here a board and there a board which would not bear removal. She lighted a lamp to show me the inside of the roof and the walls, and also that the board floor extended under the bed, warning me not to step into the cellar, a sort of dust hole two feet deep. In her own words, they were "good boards overhead, good boards all around, and a good window,"—of two whole squares originally, only the cat had passed out that way lately. There was a stove, a bed, and a place to sit, an infant in the house where it was born, a silk parasol, gilt-framed looking-glass, and a patent new coffee-mill nailed to an oak sapling, all told. The bargain was soon concluded, for James had in the meanwhile returned. I to pay four dollars and twenty-five cents tonight, he to vacate at five tomorrow morning, selling to nobody else meanwhile: I to take possession at six. It were well, he said, to be there early, and anticipate certain indistinct but wholly unjust claims on the score of ground rent and fuel. This he assured me was the only encumbrance. At six I passed him and his family on the road. One large bundle held their all,—bed, coffee-mill, looking-glass, hens,—all but the cat; she took to the woods and became a wild cat, and, as I learned afterward, trod in a trap set for woodchucks, and so became a dead cat at last.

I took down this dwelling the same morning, drawing the nails, and removed it to the pond-side by small cartloads, spreading the boards on the grass there to bleach and warp back again in the sun. One early thrush gave me a note or two as I drove along the woodland path. I was informed treacherously by a young Patrick[73] that neighbor Seeley, an Irishman, in the intervals of the carting, transferred the still tolerable, straight, and drivable nails, staples, and spikes to his pocket, and then stood when I came back to pass the time of day, and look freshly up, unconcerned, with spring thoughts, at the devastation; there being a dearth of work, as he said. He was there to represent spectatordom, and help make this seemingly insignificant event one with the removal of the gods of Troy.[74]

I dug my cellar in the side of a hill sloping to the south, where a woodchuck had formerly dug his burrow, down through sumach and blackberry roots, and the lowest stain of vegetation, six feet square by seven deep, to a fine sand where potatoes would not freeze in any winter. The sides were left shelving, and not stoned; but the sun having never shone on them, the sand still keeps its place. It was but two hours' work. I took particular pleasure in this breaking of ground, for in almost all latitudes men dig into the earth for an equable temperature. Under the most splendid house in the city is still to be found the cellar where they store their roots as of old, and long after the superstructure has disappeared posterity remark its dent in the earth. The house is still but a sort of porch at the entrance of a burrow.

At length, in the beginning of May, with the help of some of my acquaintances, rather to improve so good an occasion for neighborliness than from any necessity, I set up the frame of my house. No man was ever more honored in the character of his raisers than I.[75] They are destined, I trust, to assist at the raising of loftier structures one day. I began to occupy my house on the 4th of July, as soon as it was boarded and roofed, for the boards were carefully feather-edged and lapped, so that it was perfectly impervious to rain, but before boarding I laid the foundation of a chimney at one end, bringing two cartloads of stones up the hill from the pond in my arms. I built the chimney after my hoeing in the fall, before a fire became necessary for warmth, doing my cooking in the meanwhile out of doors on the ground, early in the morning: which mode I still think is in some respects more convenient and agreeable than the usual one. When it stormed before my bread was baked, I fixed a few boards over the fire, and sat under them to watch my loaf, and passed some pleasant hours in that way. In those days, when my hands were much employed, I read but little, but the least scraps of paper which lay on the ground, my holder, or tablecloth, afforded me as much entertainment, in fact answered the same purpose as the *Iliad*.[76]

It would be worth the while to build still more deliberately than I did, considering, for instance, what foundation a door, a window, a cellar, a garret, have in the nature of man, and perchance never raising any superstructure until we found a better reason for it than our temporal necessities even. There is some of the same fitness in a man's building his own house

[73] Nickname for any Irishman.

[74] In the legends of the Trojan War, Troy could not be conquered as long as the statue of Athena remained in her temple at Troy. The Greeks removed the statue and then conquered the city.

[75] Thoreau's assistants at the house-raising included Bronson Alcott, Ralph Waldo Emerson, Ellery Channing, and six other friends.

[76] Homer's epic of the Trojan War.

that there is in a bird's building its own nest. Who knows but if men constructed their dwellings with their own hands, and provided food for themselves and families simply and honestly enough, the poetic faculty would be universally developed, as birds universally sing when they are so engaged? But alas! we do like cowbirds and cuckoos, which lay their eggs in nests which other birds have built, and cheer no traveler with their chattering and unmusical notes. Shall we forever resign the pleasure of construction to the carpenter? What does architecture amount to in the experience of the mass of men? I never in all my walks came across a man engaged in so simple and natural an occupation as building his house. We belong to the community. It is not the tailor alone who is the ninth part of a man;[77] it is as much the preacher, and the merchant, and the farmer. Where is this division of labor to end? and what object does it finally serve? No doubt another *may* also think for me; but it is not therefore desirable that he should do so to the exclusion of my thinking for myself.

True, there are architects so called in this country, and I have heard of one at least possessed with the idea of making architectural ornaments have a core of truth, a necessity, and hence a beauty, as if it were a revelation to him. All very well perhaps from his point of view, but only a little better than the common dilettantism. A sentimental reformer in architecture, he began at the cornice, not at the foundation. It was only how to put a core of truth within the ornaments, that every sugar-plum, in fact, might have an almond or caraway seed in it,—though I hold that almonds are most wholesome without the sugar,—and not how the inhabitant, the indweller, might build truly within and without, and let the ornaments take care of themselves. What reasonable man ever supposed that ornaments were something outward and in the skin merely,—that the tortoise got his spotted shell, or the shell-fish its mother-o'-pearl tints, by such a contract as the inhabitants of Broadway their Trinity Church?[78] But a man has no more to do with the style of architecture of his house than a tortoise with that of its shell: nor need the soldier be so idle as to try to paint the precise *color* of his virtue on his standard. The enemy will find it out. He may turn pale when the trial comes. This man seemed to me to lean over the cornice, and timidly whisper his half truth to the rude occupants who really knew it better than he. What of architectural beauty I now see, I know has gradually grown from within outward, out of the necessities and character of the indweller, who is the only builder,—out of some unconscious truthfulness, and nobleness, without ever a thought for the appearance; and whatever additional beauty of this kind is destined to be produced will be preceded by a like unconscious beauty of life. The most interesting dwellings in this country, as the painter knows, are the most unpretending, humble log huts and cottages of the poor commonly; it is the life of the inhabitants whose shells they are, and not any peculiarity in their surfaces merely, which makes them *picturesque;* and equally interesting will be the citizen's suburban box, when his life shall be as simple and as agreeable to the imagination, and there is as little straining after effect in the style of his dwelling. A

[77] A scurrilous proverb ran, "It takes nine tailors to make a man."
[78] New York's Trinity Church had been built in the 1840's in an ornate nineteenth-century Gothic style.

great proportion of architectural ornaments are literally hollow, and a September gale would strip them off, like borrowed plumes, without injury to the substantials. They can do without *architecture* who have no olives nor wines in the cellar. What if an equal ado were made about the ornaments of style in literature, and the architects of our bibles spent as much time about their cornices as the architects of our churches do? So are made the *belles-lettres* and the *beaux-arts*[79] and their professors. Much it concerns a man, forsooth, how a few sticks are slanted over him or under him, and what colors are daubed upon his box. It would signify somewhat, if, in any earnest sense, *he* slanted them and daubed it; but the spirit having departed out of the tenant, it is of a piece with constructing his own coffin,—the architecture of the grave,—and "carpenter" is but another name for "coffinmaker." One man says, in his despair or indifference to life, take up a handful of the earth at your feet, and paint your house that color. Is he thinking of his last and narrow house?[80] Toss up a copper[81] for it as well. What an abundance of leisure he must have! Why do you take up a handful of dirt? Better paint your house your own complexion; let it turn pale or blush for you. An enterprise to improve the style of cottage architecture! When you have got my ornaments ready, I will wear them.

Before winter I built a chimney, and shingled the sides of my house, which were already impervious to rain, with imperfect and sappy shingles made of the first slice of the log, whose edges I was obliged to straighten with a plane.

I have thus a tight shingled and plastered house, ten feet wide by fifteen long, and eight-feet posts, with a garret and a closet, a large window on each side, two trap-doors, one door at the end, and a brick fireplace opposite. The exact cost of my house, paying the usual price for such materials as I used, but not counting the work, all of which was done by myself, was as follows; and I give the details because very few are able to tell exactly what their houses cost, and fewer still, if any, the separate cost of the various materials which compose them:—

Boards	$8 03½,	mostly shanty boards.
Refuse shingles for roof and sides	4 00	
Laths	1 25	
Two second-hand windows with glass	2 43	
One thousand old brick	4 00	
Two casks of lime	2 40	That was high.
Hair	0 31	More than I needed.
Mantle-tree iron	0 15	
Nails	3 90	
Hinges and screws	0 14	
Latch	0 10	

[79] High literature and the fine arts. [80] That is, the grave.
[81] A coin. The Greeks buried their dead with coins to pay Charon to ferry them over the river Styx into Hades.

Chalk	0 01	I carried a good part on my back.
Transportation	1 40	
In all	$28 12½	

These are all the materials, excepting the timber, stones, and sand, which I claimed by squatter's right. I have also a small woodshed adjoining, made chiefly of the stuff which was left after building the house.

I intend to build me a house which will surpass any on the main street in Concord in grandeur and luxury, as soon as it pleases me as much and will cost me no more than my present one.

I thus found that the student who wishes for a shelter can obtain one for a lifetime at an expense not greater than the rent which he now pays annually. If I seem to boast more than is becoming, my excuse is that I brag for humanity rather than for myself; and my shortcomings and inconsistencies do not affect the truth of my statement. Notwithstanding much cant and hypocrisy,—chaff which I find it difficult to separate from my wheat, but for which I am as sorry as any man,—I will breathe freely and stretch myself in this respect, it is such a relief to both the moral and physical system; and I am resolved that I will not through humility become the devil's attorney.[82] I will endeavor to speak a good word for the truth. At Cambridge College[83] the mere rent of a student's room, which is only a little larger than my own, is thirty dollars each year, though the corporation had the advantage of building thirty-two side by side and under one roof, and the occupant suffers the inconvenience of many and noisy neighbors, and perhaps a residence in the fourth story. I cannot but think that if we had more true wisdom in these respects, not only less education would be needed, because, forsooth, more would already have been acquired, but the pecuniary expense of getting an education would in a great measure vanish. Those conveniences which the student requires at Cambridge or elsewhere cost him or somebody else ten times as great a sacrifice of life as they would with proper management on both sides. Those things for which the most money is demanded are never the things which the student most wants. Tuition, for instance, is an important item in the term bill, while for the far more valuable education which he gets by associating with the most cultivated of his contemporaries no charge is made. The mode of founding a college is, commonly, to get up a subscription of dollars and cents, and then, following blindly the principles of a division of labor to its extreme,—a principle which should never be followed but with circumspection,—to call in a contractor who makes this a subject of speculation, and he employs Irishmen or other operatives actually to lay the foundations, while the students that are to be are said to be fitting themselves for it; and for these oversights successive generations have to pay. I think that it would be *better than this,* for the students, or those who desire to be benefited by it, even to lay the foundation themselves. The student who secures his coveted

[82] A "devil's attorney" or "devil's advocate" is one who argues for an opposing or bad cause, from the person the Roman Catholic Church appoints to present the arguments against the proposed canonization of a saint.

[83] Harvard College, Cambridge, Massachusetts.

leisure and retirement by systematically shirking any labor necessary to man obtains but an ignoble and unprofitable leisure, defrauding himself of the experience which alone can make leisure fruitful. "But," says one, "you do not mean that the students should go to work with their hands instead of their heads?" I do not mean that exactly, but I mean something which he might think a good deal like that; I mean that they should not *play* life, or *study* it merely, while the community supports them at this expensive game, but earnestly *live* it from beginning to end. How could youths better learn to live than by at once trying the experiment of living? Methinks this would exercise their minds as much as mathematics. If I wished a boy to know something about the arts and sciences, for instance, I would not pursue the common course, which is merely to send him into the neighborhood of some professor, where anything is professed and practiced but the art of life;—to survey the world through a telescope or a microscope, and never with his natural eye; to study chemistry, and not learn how his bread is made, or mechanics, and not learn how it is earned; to discover new satellites to Neptune,[84] and not detect the motes in his eyes, or to what vagabond he is a satellite himself; or to be devoured by the monsters that swarm all around him, while contemplating the monsters in a drop of vinegar. Which would have advanced the most at the end of a month,—the boy who had made his own jackknife from the ore which he had dug and smelted, reading as much as would be necessary for this—or the boy who had attended the lectures on metallurgy at the Institute in the meanwhile, and had received a Rodgers penknife[85] from his father? Which would be most likely to cut his fingers? . . . To my astonishment I was informed on leaving college that I had studied navigation!—why, if I had taken one turn down the harbor I should have known more about it. Even the *poor* student studies and is taught only *political* economy, while that economy of living which is synonymous with philosophy is not even sincerely professed in our college. The consequence is, that while he is reading Adam Smith, Ricardo, and Say,[86] he runs his father in debt irretrievably.

As with our colleges, so with a hundred "modern improvements"; there is an illusion about them; there is not always a positive advance. The devil goes on exacting compound interest to the last for his early share and numerous succeeding investments in them. Our inventions are wont to be pretty toys, which distract our attention from serious things. They are but improved means to an unimproved end, an end which it was already but too easy to arrive at; as railroads lead to Boston or New York. We are in great haste to construct a magnetic telegraph from Maine to Texas; but Maine and Texas, it may be, have nothing important to communicate. Either is in such a predicament as the man who was earnest to be introduced to a distinguished deaf woman, but when he was presented, and one end of her ear trumpet was put into his hand, had nothing to say. As if the main object were to talk fast and not to talk sensibly. We are eager to tunnel under the Atlantic and bring the Old World some weeks nearer to the New;

[84] The planet Neptune and its satellite were discovered in 1846.
[85] An expensive pocket knife manufactured in Sheffield, England.
[86] Adam Smith, David Ricardo, and Jean-Baptiste Say were all eighteenth-century and early nineteenth-century economists.

but perchance the first news that will leak through into the broad, flapping American ear will be that the Princess Adelaide[87] has the whooping cough. After all, the man whose horse trots a mile in a minute does not carry the most important messages; he is not an evangelist, nor does he come round eating locusts and wild honey.[88] I doubt if Flying Childers[89] ever carried a peck of corn to mill.

One says to me, "I wonder that you do not lay up money; you love to travel; you might take the cars and go to Fitchburg today and see the country." But I am wiser than that. I have learned that the swiftest traveler is he that goes afoot. I say to my friend, Suppose we try who will get there first. The distance is thirty miles; the fare ninety cents. That is almost a day's wages. I remember when wages were sixty cents a day for laborers on this very road. Well, I start now on foot, and get there before night; I have traveled at that rate by the week together. You will in the meanwhile have earned your fare, and arrive there some time tomorrow, or possibly this evening, if you are lucky enough to get a job in season. Instead of going to Fitchburg, you will be working here the greater part of the day. And so, if the railroad reached round the world, I think that I should keep ahead of you; and as for seeing the country and getting experience of that kind, I should have to cut your acquaintance altogether.

Such is the universal law, which no man can ever outwit, and with regard to the railroad even we may say it is as broad as it is long. To make a railroad round the world available to all mankind is equivalent to grading the whole surface of the planet. Men have an indistinct notion that if they keep up this activity of joint stocks and spades long enough all will at length ride somewhere, in next to no time, and for nothing; but though a crowd rushes to the depot, and the conductor shouts "All aboard!" when the smoke is blown away and the vapor condensed, it will be perceived that a few are riding, but the rest are run over,—and it will be called, and will be, "A melancholy accident." No doubt they can ride at last who shall have earned their fare, that is, if they survive so long, but they will probably have lost their elasticity and desire to travel by that time. This spending of the best part of one's life earning money in order to enjoy a questionable liberty during the least valuable part of it reminds me of the Englishman who went to India to make a fortune first, in order that he might return to England and live the life of a poet. He should have gone up garret at once. "What!" exclaim a million Irishmen starting up from all the shanties in the land, "is not this railroad which we have built a good thing?" Yes, I answer, *comparatively* good, that is, you might have done worse; but I wish, as you are brothers of mine, that you could have spent your time better than digging in this dirt. . . .

[87] Princess Adelaide of Orleans (1771–1847), sister of the French King Louis-Philippe; an insignificant "celebrity."

[88] The evangelist John the Baptist lived on locusts and wild honey while preaching in the wilderness. See Matthew 3:4.

[89] A famous English racehorse.

II. WHERE I LIVED, AND WHAT I LIVED FOR

At a certain season of our life we are accustomed to consider every spot as the possible site of a house. I have thus surveyed the country on every side within a dozen miles of where I live. In imagination I have bought all the farms in succession, for all were to be bought, and I knew their price. I walked over each farmer's premises, tasted his wild apples, discoursed on husbandry with him, took his farm at his price, at any price, mortgaging it to him in my mind; even put a higher price on it,—took everything but a deed of it,—took his word for his deed, for I dearly love to talk,—cultivated it, and him too to some extent, I trust, and withdrew when I had enjoyed it long enough, leaving him to carry it on. This experience entitled me to be regarded as a sort of real-estate broker by my friends. Wherever I sat, there I might live, and the landscape radiated from me accordingly. What is a house but a *sedes*, a seat?—better if a country seat. I discovered many a site for a house not likely to be soon improved, which some might have thought too far from the village, but to my eyes the village was too far from it. Well, there I might live, I said; and there I did live, for an hour, a summer and a winter life; saw how I could let the years run off, buffet the winter through, and see the spring come in. The future inhabitants of this region, wherever they may place their houses, may be sure that they have been anticipated. An afternoon sufficed to lay out the land into orchard, wood-lot, and pasture, and to decide what fine oaks or pines should be left to stand before the door, and whence each blasted tree could be seen to the best advantage; and then I let it lie, fallow perchance, for a man is rich in proportion to the number of things which he can afford to let alone.

My imagination carried me so far that I even had the refusal of several farms,—the refusal was all I wanted,—but I never got my fingers burned by actual possession. The nearest that I came to actual possession was when I bought the Hollowell place, and had begun to sort my seeds, and collected materials with which to make a wheelbarrow to carry it on or off with; but before the owner gave me a deed of it, his wife—every man has such a wife—changed her mind and wished to keep it, and he offered me ten dollars to release him. Now, to speak the truth, I had but ten cents in the world, and it surpassed my arithmetic to tell, if I was that man who had ten cents, or who had a farm, or ten dollars, or all together. However, I let him keep the ten dollars and the farm too, for I had carried it far enough; or rather, to be generous, I sold him the farm for just what I gave for it, and, as he was not a rich man, made him a present of ten dollars, and still had my ten cents, and seeds, and materials for a wheelbarrow left. I found thus that I had been a rich man without any damage to my poverty. But I retained the landscape, and I have since annually carried off what it yielded without a wheelbarrow. With respect to landscapes,—

"I am monarch of all I *survey*,
My right there is none to dispute."[1]

[1] From "Verses Supposed to be Written by Alexander Selkirk," by William Cowper (1731–1800). Selkirk, who was marooned on an island off the coast of Chile for four years, was the model for Defoe's Robinson Crusoe. Thoreau italicizes the word "survey" to point up the pun on his own profession of surveying.

I have frequently seen a poet withdraw, having enjoyed the most valuable part of a farm, while the crusty farmer supposed that he had got a few wild apples only. Why, the owner does not know it for many years when a poet has put his farm in rhyme, the most admirable kind of invisible fence, has fairly impounded it, milked it, skimmed it, and got all the cream, and left the farmer only the skimmed milk.

The real attractions of the Hollowell farm, to me, were: its complete retirement, being about two miles from the village, half a mile from the nearest neighbor, and separated from the highway by a broad field; its bounding on the river, which the owner said protected it by its fogs from frosts in the spring, though that was nothing to me; the gray color and ruinous state of the house and barn, and the dilapidated fences, which put such an interval between me and the last occupant: the hollow and lichen-covered apple trees, gnawed by rabbits, showing what kind of neighbors I should have; but above all, the recollection I had of it from my earliest voyages up the river, when the house was concealed behind a dense grove of red maples, through which I heard the house-dog bark. I was in haste to buy it before the proprietor finished getting out some rocks, cutting down the hollow apple trees, and grubbing up some young birches which had sprung up in the pasture, or, in short had made any more of his improvements. To enjoy these advantages I was ready to carry it on; like Atlas, to take the world on my shoulders,[2]—I never heard what compensation he received for that,—and do all those things which had no other motive or excuse but that I might pay for it and be unmolested in my possession of it; for I knew all the while that it would yield the most abundant crop of the kind I wanted, if I could only afford to let it alone. But it turned out as I have said.

All that I could say, then, with respect to farming on a large scale—I have always cultivated a garden—was that I had had my seeds ready. Many think that seeds improve with age. I have no doubt that time discriminates between the good and the bad; and when at last I shall plant, I shall be less likely to be disappointed. But I would say to my fellows once for all, As long as possible live free and uncommitted. It makes but little difference whether you are committed to a farm or the county jail.

Old Cato, whose "De Re Rusticâ" is my "Cultivator,"[3] says,—and the only translation I have seen makes sheer nonsense of the passage,—"When you think of getting a farm turn it thus in your mind, not to buy greedily; nor spare your pains to look at it, and do not think it enough to go round it once. The oftener you go there the more it will please you, if it is good." I think I shall not buy greedily, but go round and round it as long as I live, and be buried in it first, that it may please me the more at last.

The present was my next experiment of this kind, which I purpose to describe more at length, for convenience putting the experience of two years into one. As I have said, I do not propose to write an ode to dejection,

[2] Atlas, in Greek mythology, was a Titan whose task was to hold up the earth on his shoulders.

[3] Marcus Porcius Cato, second century B.C., wrote "Of Agriculture," sometimes known as "Of Rustic Things." A "Cultivator" is a farmer's handbook.

but to brag as lustily as chanticleer in the morning, standing on his roost, if only to wake my neighbors up.

When first I took up my abode in the woods, that is, began to spend my nights as well as days there, which, by accident, was on Independence Day, or the Fourth of July, 1845, my house was not finished for winter, but was merely a defense against the rain, without plastering or chimney, the walls being of rough, weather-stained boards, with wide chinks, which made it cool at night. The upright white hewn studs and freshly planed door and window casings gave it a clean and airy look, especially in the morning, when its timbers were saturated with dew, so that I fancied that by noon some sweet gum would exude from them. To my imagination it retained throughout the day more or less of this auroral character, reminding me of a certain house on a mountain which I had visited a year before. This was an airy and unplastered cabin, fit to entertain a traveling god, and where a goddess might trail her garments. The winds which passed over my dwelling were such as sweep over the ridges of mountains, bearing the broken strains, or celestial parts only, of terrestrial music. The morning wind forever blows, the poem of creation is uninterrupted; but few are the ears that hear it. Olympus[4] is but the outside of the earth everywhere.

The only house I had been the owner of before, if I except a boat, was a tent, which I used occasionally when making excursions in the summer, and this is still rolled up in my garret; but the boat, after passing from hand to hand, has gone down the stream of time. With this more substantial shelter about me, I had made some progress toward settling in the world. This frame, so slightly clad, was a sort of crystallization around me, and reacted on the builder. It was suggestive somewhat as a picture in outlines. I did not need to go outdoors to take the air, for the atmosphere within had lost none of its freshness. It was not so much within-doors as behind a door where I sat, even in the rainiest weather. The Harivansa[5] says, "An abode without birds is like a meat without seasoning." Such was not my abode, for I found myself suddenly neighbor to the birds; not by having imprisoned one, but having caged myself near them. I was not only nearer to some of those which commonly frequent the garden and the orchard, but to those wilder and more thrilling songsters of the forest which never, or rarely, serenade a villager,—the wood thrush, the veery, the scarlet tanager, the field sparrow, the whip-poor-will, and many others.

I was seated by the shore of a small pond, about a mile and a half south of the village of Concord and somewhat higher than it, in the midst of an extensive wood between that town and Lincoln, and about two miles south of that our only field known to fame, Concord Battle Ground;[6] but I was so low in the woods that the opposite shore, half a mile off, like the rest, covered with wood, was my most distant horizon. For the first week, whenever I looked out on the pond it impressed me like a tarn high up on the side of a mountain, its bottom far above the surface of other lakes, and, as the sun arose, I saw it throwing off its nightly clothing of mist, and here and there, by degrees, its soft ripples or its smooth reflecting surface was

[4] The mountain where the Greek gods lived.
[5] A Hindu epic (fifth century A.D.) about the god Krishna.
[6] Site of the battle, April 19, 1775, that began the American Revolution.

revealed, while the mists, like ghosts, were stealthily withdrawing in every direction into the woods, as at the breaking up of some nocturnal conventicle. The very dew seemed to hang upon the trees later into the day than usual, as on the sides of mountains.

This small lake was of most value as a neighbor in the intervals of a gentle rain-storm in August, when, both air and water being perfectly still, but the sky overcast, mid-afternoon had all the serenity of evening, and the wood thrush sang around, and was heard from shore to shore. A lake like this is never smoother than at such a time; and the clear portion of the air above it being shallow and darkened by clouds, the water, full of light and reflections, becomes a lower heaven itself so much the more important. From a hill-top near by where the wood had been recently cut off, there was a pleasing vista southward across the pond, through a wide indentation in the hills which form the shore there, where their opposite sides sloping toward each other suggested a stream flowing out in that direction through a wooded valley, but stream there was none. That way I looked between and over the near green hills to some distant and higher ones in the horizon, tinged with blue. Indeed, by standing on tiptoe I could catch a glimpse of some of the peaks of the still bluer and more distant mountain ranges in the northwest, those true-blue coins from heaven's own mint, and also of some portion of the village. But in other directions, even from this point, I could not see over or beyond the woods which surrounded me. It is well to have some water in your neighborhood, to give buoyancy to and float the earth. One value even of the smallest well is, that when you look into it you see that earth is not continent but insular. This is as important as that it keeps butter cool. When I looked across the pond from this peak toward the Sudbury meadows, which in time of flood I distinguished elevated perhaps by a mirage in their seething valley, like a coin in a basin, all the earth beyond the pond appeared like a thin crust insulated and floated even by this small sheet of intervening water, and I was reminded that this on which I dwelt was but *dry land*.

Though the view from my door was still more contracted, I did not feel crowded or confined in the least. There was pasture enough for my imagination. The low shrub oak plateau to which the opposite shore arose stretched away toward the prairies of the West and the steppes of Tartary, affording ample room for all the roving families of men. "There are none happy in the world but beings who enjoy freely a vast horizon,"—said Damodara,[7] when his herds required new and larger pastures.

Both place and time were changed, and I dwelt nearer to those parts of the universe and to those eras in history which had most attracted me. Where I lived was as far off as many a region viewed nightly by astronomers. We are wont to imagine rare and delectable places in some remote and more celestial corner of the system, behind the constellation of Cassiopeia's Chair,[8] far from noise and disturbance. I discovered that my house actually had its site in such a withdrawn, but forever new and

[7] Another quotation from the *Harivansa,* mentioned above. "Damodara" is another name for Krishna.

[8] Cassiopeia's Chair, the Pleiades, the Hyades, Aldebaran, and Altair are all constellations or stars.

unprofaned, part of the universe. If it were worth the while to settle in those parts near to the Pleiades or the Hyades, to Aldebaran or Altair, then I was really there, or at an equal remoteness from the life which I had left behind, dwindled and twinkling with as fine a ray to my nearest neighbor, and to be seen only in moonless nights by him. Such was that part of creation where I had squatted;—

"There was a shepherd that did live,
And held his thoughts as high
As were the mounts whereon his flocks
Did hourly feed him by."[9]

What should we think of the shepherd's life if his flocks always wandered to higher pastures than his thoughts?

Every morning was a cheerful invitation to make my life of equal simplicity, and I may say innocence, with Nature herself. I have been as sincere a worshipper of Aurora[10] as the Greeks. I got up early and bathed in the pond; that was a religious exercise, and one of the best things which I did. They say that characters were engraven on the bathing tub of King Tching-thang[11] to this effect: "Renew thyself completely each day; do it again, and again, and forever again." I can understand that. Morning brings back the heroic ages. I was as much affected by the faint hum of a mosquito making its invisible and unimaginable tour through my apartment at earliest dawn, when I was sitting with door and windows open, as I could be by any trumpet that ever sang of fame.[12] It was Homer's requiem; itself an Iliad and Odyssey in the air, singing its own wrath and wanderings. There was something cosmical about it; a standing advertisement, till forbidden,[13] of the everlasting vigor and fertility of the world. The morning, which is the most memorable season of the day, is the awakening hour. Then there is least somnolence in us; and for an hour, at least, some part of us awakes which slumbers all the rest of the day and night. Little is to be expected of that day, if it can be called a day, to which we are not awakened by our Genius, but by the mechanical nudgings of some servitor, are not awakened by our own newly acquired force and aspirations from within, accompanied by the undulations of celestial music, instead of factory bells, and a fragrance filling the air—to a higher life than we fell asleep from; and thus the darkness bear its fruit, and prove itself to be good, no less than the light. That man who does not believe that each day contains an earlier, more sacred, and auroral hour than he has yet profaned, has despaired of life, and is pursuing a descending and darkening way. After a partial cessa-

[9] From an anonymous poem named "The Shepherd's Love for Philliday," printed in Thomas Evans' *Old Ballads* (1810).

[10] Goddess of the dawn.

[11] Chinese king, founder of the Shang dynasty about 1500 B.C. The story is from a commentary on *The Great Learning* of Confucius.

[12] Thoreau is paraphrasing a line from "The Landing of the Pilgrim Fathers in New England," by Felicia Hemans (1793–1835): "Not as the conqueror comes, / They, the true-hearted, came; / Not with the roll of the stirring drums, / And the trumpet that sings of fame."

[13] A "standing advertisement" was one that ran continuously until it was canceled, or "till forbidden."

tion of his sensuous life, the soul of man, or its organs rather, are reinvigorated each day, and his Genius tries again what noble life it can make. All memorable events, I should say, transpire in morning time and in a morning atmosphere. The Vedas[14] say, "All intelligences awake with the morning." Poetry and art, and the fairest and most memorable of the actions of men, date from such an hour. All poets and heroes, like Memnon,[15] are the children of Aurora, and emit their music at sunrise. To him whose elastic and vigorous thought keeps pace with the sun, the day is a perpetual morning. It matters not what the clocks say or the attitudes and labors of men. Morning is when I am awake and there is a dawn in me. Moral reform is the effort to throw off sleep. Why is it that men give so poor an account of their day if they have not been slumbering? They are not such poor calculators. If they had not been overcome with drowsiness, they would have performed something. The millions are awake enough for physical labor; but only one in a million is awake enough for effective intellectual exertion, only one in a hundred millions to a poetic or divine life. To be awake is to be alive. I have never yet met a man who was quite awake. How could I have looked him in the face?

We must learn to reawaken and keep ourselves awake, not by mechanical aids, but by an infinite expectation of the dawn, which does not forsake us in our soundest sleep. I know of no more encouraging fact than the unquestionable ability of man to elevate his life by a conscious endeavor. It is something to be able to paint a particular picture, or to carve a statue, and so to make a few objects beautiful; but it is far more glorious to carve and paint the very atmosphere and medium through which we look, which morally we can do. To affect the quality of the day, that is the highest of arts. Every man is tasked to make his life, even in its details, worthy of the contemplation of his most elevated and critical hour. If we refused, or rather used up, such paltry information as we get, the oracles would distinctly inform us how this might be done.

I went to the woods because I wished to live deliberately, to front only the essential facts of life, and see if I could not learn what it had to teach, and not, when I came to die, discover that I had not lived. I did not wish to live what was not life, living is so dear; nor did I wish to practice resignation, unless it was quite necessary. I wanted to live deep and suck out all the marrow of life, to live so sturdily and Spartan-like as to put to rout all that was not life, to cut a broad swath and shave close, to drive life into a corner, and reduce it to its lowest terms, and, if it proved to be mean, why then to get the whole and genuine meanness of it, and publish its meanness to the world; or if it were sublime, to know it by experience, and be able to give a true account of it in my next excursion. For most men, it appears to me, are in a strange uncertainty about it, whether it is of the devil or of God, and have *somewhat hastily* concluded that it is the chief end of man here to "glorify God and enjoy him forever."

[14] Four Hindu religious books.

[15] Memnon, in Greek mythology, was a king of Ethiopia and son of the dawn goddess Aurora. He fought with Troy against the Greeks and was killed by Achilles. In Egypt, his name was associated with Amenhotep III. A huge statue of him which stood near Thebes was said to emit musical sounds when the first rays of the sun warmed its stones.

Still we live meanly, like ants; though the fable tells us that we were long ago changed into men;[16] like pygmies we fight with cranes;[17] it is error upon error, and clout upon clout, and our best virtue has for its occasion a superfluous and evitable wretchedness. Our life is frittered away by detail. An honest man has hardly need to count more than his ten fingers, or in extreme cases he may add his ten toes, and lump the rest. Simplicity, simplicity, simplicity! I say, let your affairs be as two or three, and not a hundred or a thousand; instead of a million count half a dozen, and keep your accounts on your thumb-nail. In the midst of this chopping sea of civilized life, such are the clouds and storms and quicksands and thousand-and-one items to be allowed for, that a man has to live, if he would not founder and go to the bottom and not make his port at all, by dead reckoning, and he must be a great calculator indeed who succeeds. Simplify, simplify. Instead of three meals a day, if it be necessary eat but one; instead of a hundred dishes, five; and reduce other things in proportion. Our life is like a German Confederacy, made up of petty states, with its boundary forever fluctuating, so that even a German cannot tell you how it is bounded at any moment.[18] The nation itself, with all its so-called internal improvements, which, by the way, are all external and superficial, is just such an unwieldy and overgrown establishment, cluttered with furniture and tripped up by its own traps, ruined by luxury and heedless expense, by want of calculation and a worthy aim, as the million households in the land; and the only cure for it, as for them, is in a rigid economy, a stern and more than Spartan simplicity of life and elevation of purpose. It lives too fast. Men think that it is essential that the *Nation* have commerce, and export ice, and talk through a telegraph, and ride thirty miles an hour, without a doubt, whether *they* do or not; but whether we should live like baboons or like men, is a little uncertain. If we do not get out sleepers,[19] and forge rails, and devote days and nights to the work, but go to tinkering upon our *lives* to improve *them,* who will build railroads? And if railroads are not built, how shall we get to heaven in season?[20] But if we stay at home and mind our business, who will want railroads? We do not ride on the railroad; it rides upon us. Did you ever think what those sleepers are that underlie the railroad? Each one is a man, an Irishman, or a Yankee man. The rails are laid on them, and they are covered with sand, and the cars run smoothly over them. They are sound sleepers, I assure you. And every few years a new lot is laid down and run over; so that, if some have the pleasure of riding on a rail,[21] others have the misfortune to be ridden upon. And when they run over a man that is walking in his sleep, a supernumerary sleeper in the wrong position, and wake him up, they suddenly stop the cars, and

[16] In Greek mythology, Zeus responded to the plea of Aeacus and turned ants into men to repopulate his plague-decimated kingdom.

[17] In Book III of Homer's *Iliad,* the Trojans and Greeks are compared to cranes and pygmies.

[18] In 1854, Germany was still divided into a number of small principalities and kingdoms. It was united, under the leadership of Bismarck, in 1871.

[19] Railroad ties.

[20] An allusion to Nathaniel Hawthorne's story "The Celestial Railroad."

[21] This passage contains a complex set of puns on "sleepers," "sound," and "rail." "Riding on a rail" is being run out of town; unwanted people were ridden out of town on a wooden fence rail.

make a hue and cry about it, as if this were an exception. I am glad to know that it takes a gang of men for every five miles to keep the sleepers down and level in their beds as it is, for this is a sign that they may sometime get up again.

Why should we live with such hurry and waste of life? We are determined to be starved before we are hungry. Men say that a stitch in time saves nine, and so they take a thousand stitches today to save nine tomorrow. As for *work,* we haven't any of any consequence. We have the Saint Vitus' dance,[22] and cannot possibly keep our heads still. If I should only give a few pulls at the parish bell-rope, as for a fire, that is, without setting the bell, there is hardly a man on his farm in the outskirts of Concord, notwithstanding that press of engagements which was his excuse so many times this morning, nor a boy, nor a woman, I might almost say, but would forsake all and follow that sound, not mainly to save property from the flames, but, if we will confess the truth, much more to see it burn, since burn it must, and we, be it known, did not set it on fire,—or to see it put out, and have a hand in it, if that is done as handsomely; yes, even if it were the parish church itself. Hardly a man takes a half-hour's nap after dinner, but when he wakes he holds up his head and asks, "What's the news?" as if the rest of mankind had stood his sentinels. Some give directions to be waked every half-hour, doubtless for no other purpose; and then, to pay for it, they tell what they have dreamed. After a night's sleep the news is as indispensable as the breakfast. "Pray tell me anything new that has happened to a man anywhere on this globe,"—and he reads it over his coffee and rolls, that a man has had his eyes gouged out this morning on the Wachito River;[23] never dreaming the while that he lives in the dark unfathomed mammoth cave of this world, and has but the rudiment of an eye himself.[24]

For my part, I could easily do without the post office. I think that there are very few important communications made through it. To speak critically, I never received more than one or two letters in my life—I wrote this some years ago—that were worth the postage. The penny-post[25] is, commonly, an institution through which you seriously offer a man that penny for his thoughts which is so often safely offered in jest. And I am sure that I never read any memorable news in a newspaper. If we read of one man robbed, or murdered, or killed by accident, or one house burned, or one vessel wrecked, or one steamboat blown up, or one cow run over on the Western Railroad, or one mad dog killed, or one lot of grasshoppers in the winter,—we never need read of another. One is enough. If you are acquainted with the principle, what do you care for a myriad instances and applications? To a philosopher all *news,* as it is called, is gossip, and they who edit and read it are old women over their tea. Yet not a few are greedy after this gossip. There was such a rush, as I hear, the other day at one of the offices to learn the foreign news by the last arrival, that several large

[22] A disease characterized by jerky, spasmodic movements.

[23] The Ouachita River in Arkansas.

[24] In the underground streams of Mammoth Cave, Kentucky, a breed of small fish have lost their eyesight through disuse.

[25] Letters could be sent up to three thousand miles for three cents in 1854; Thoreau is alluding to the British "penny post."

squares of plate glass belonging to the establishment were broken by the pressure,—news which I seriously think a ready wit might write a twelvemonth, or twelve years, beforehand with sufficient accuracy. As for Spain, for instance, if you know how to throw in Don Carlos and the Infanta, and Don Pedro and Seville and Granada,[26] from time to time in the right proportions,—they may have changed the names a little since I saw the papers,—and serve up a bullfight when other entertainments fail, it will be true to the letter, and give us as good an idea of the exact state or ruin of things in Spain as the most succinct and lucid reports under this head in the newspapers: and as for England, almost the last significant scrap of news from that quarter was the revolution of 1649; and if you have learned the history of her crops for an average year, you never need attend to that thing again, unless your speculations are of a merely pecuniary character. If one may judge who rarely looks into the newspapers, nothing new does ever happen in foreign parts, a French revolution not excepted.

What news! how much more important to know what that is which was never old! "Kieou-he-yu (great dignitary of the state of Wei) sent a man to Khoung-tseu to know his news. Khoung-tseu caused the messenger to be seated near him, and questioned him in these terms: What is your master doing? The messenger answered with respect: My master desires to diminish the number of his faults, but he cannot come to the end of them. The messenger being gone, the philosopher remarked: What a worthy messenger! What a worthy messenger!"[27] The preacher, instead of vexing the ears of drowsy farmers on their day of rest at the end of the week,—for Sunday is the fit conclusion of an ill-spent week, and not the fresh and brave beginning of a new one,—with this one other draggle-tail of a sermon, should shout with thundering voice, "Pause! Avast! Why so seeming fast, but deadly slow?"

Shams and delusions are esteemed for soundest truths, while reality is fabulous. If men would steadily observe realities only, and not allow themselves to be deluded, life, to compare it with such things as we know, would be like a fairy tale and the Arabian Nights' Entertainments. If we respected only what is inevitable and has a right to be, music and poetry would resound along the streets. When we are unhurried and wise, we perceive that only great and worthy things have any permanent and absolute existence, that petty fears and petty pleasures are but the shadow of the reality. This is always exhilarating and sublime. By closing the eyes and slumbering, and consenting to be deceived by shows, men establish and confirm their daily life of routine and habit everywhere, which still is built on purely illusory foundations. Children, who play life, discern its true law and relations more clearly than men, who fail to live it worthily, but who think that they are wiser by experience, that is, by failure. I have read in a Hindoo book,[28] that "there was a king's son, who, being expelled in infancy from

[26] These names had figured prominently in Spanish politics in the 1830's and 1840's but were out of the news by the time *Walden* was written.

[27] Khoung-tseu is Confucius. The story is from Confucius' *Analects,* XIV, 26.

[28] This Hindu book, if it exists, has not been identified. The story is a version of a widely distributed folk tale which was used as the basis for Calderón's play *Life is a Dream* (1635).

his native city, was brought up by a forester, and, growing up to maturity in that state, imagined himself to belong to the barbarous race with which he lived. One of his father's ministers having discovered him, revealed to him what he was, and the misconception of his character was removed, and he knew himself to be a prince. So soul," continues the Hindoo philosopher, "from the circumstances in which it is placed, mistakes its own character, until the truth is revealed to it by some holy teacher, and then it knows itself to be *Brahme*."[29] I perceive that we inhabitants of New England live this mean life that we do because our vision does not penetrate the surface of things. We think that that *is* which *appears* to be. If a man should walk through this town and see only the reality, where, think you, would the "Mill-dam"[30] go to? If he should give us an account of the realities he beheld there, we should not recognize the place in his description. Look at a meeting-house, or a court-house, or a jail, or a shop, or a dwelling-house, and say what that thing really is before a true gaze, and they would all go to pieces in your account of them. Men esteem truth remote, in the outskirts of the system, behind the farthest star, before Adam and after the last man. In eternity there is indeed something true and sublime. But all these times and places and occasions are now and here. God himself culminates in the present moment, and will never be more divine in the lapse of all the ages. And we are enabled to apprehend at all what is sublime and noble only by the perpetual instilling and drenching of the reality that surrounds us. The universe constantly and obediently answers to our conceptions; whether we travel fast or slow, the track is laid for us. Let us spend our lives in conceiving then. The poet or the artist never yet had so fair and noble a design but some of his posterity at least could accomplish it.

Let us spend one day as deliberately as Nature, and not be thrown off the track by every nutshell and mosquito's wing that falls on the rails. Let us rise early and fast, or break fast, gently and without perturbation; let company come and let company go, let the bells ring and the children cry,—determined to make a day of it. Why should we knock under and go with the stream? Let us not be upset and overwhelmed in that terrible rapid and whirlpool[31] called a dinner, situated in the meridian shallows. Weather this danger and you are safe, for the rest of the way is down hill. With unrelaxed nerves, with morning vigor, sail by it, looking another way, tied to the mast like Ulysses. If the engine whistles, let it whistle till it is hoarse for its pains. If the bell rings, why should we run? We will consider what kind of music they are like. Let us settle ourselves, and work and wedge our feet downward through the mud and slush of opinion, and prejudice, and tradition, and delusion, and appearance, that alluvion which covers the globe, through Paris and London, through New York and Boston and Concord, through Church and State, through poetry and philosophy and religion, till we come to a hard bottom and rocks in place, which we can call

[29] Brahma, the supreme soul and the essence of all being in Hindu thought.
[30] The "Mill-dam" was a heavily traveled section of street in Concord.
[31] An allusion to Scylla and Charybdis, the rock and the whirlpool in Homer's *Odyssey*, Book XII. The following allusion to Ulysses "tied to the mast" refers to the episode in the *Odyssey*, Book XII, in which Odysseus (Ulysses) has his sailors stuff their ears with wax and tie him to the mast so he can hear the fatal song of the Sirens without endangering the ship.

reality, and say, This is, and no mistake; and then begin, having a point d'appui,[32] below freshet and frost and fire, a place where you might found a wall or a state, or set a lamp-post safely, or perhaps a gauge, not a Nilometer,[33] but a Realometer, that future ages might know how deep a freshet of shams and appearances had gathered from time to time. If you stand right fronting and face to face to a fact, you will see the sun glimmer on both its surfaces, as if it were a cimeter,[34] and feel its sweet edge dividing you through the heart and marrow, and so you will happily conclude your mortal career. Be it life or death, we crave only reality. If we are really dying, let us hear the rattle in our throats and feel cold in the extremities; if we are alive, let us go about our business.

Time is but the stream I go a-fishing in. I drink at it; but while I drink I see the sandy bottom and detect how shallow it is. Its thin current slides away, but eternity remains. I would drink deeper; fish in the sky, whose bottom is pebbly with stars. I cannot count one. I know not the first letter of the alphabet. I have always been regretting that I was not as wise as the day I was born. The intellect is a cleaver; it discerns and rifts its way into the secret of things. I do not wish to be any more busy with my hands than is necessary. My head is hands and feet. I feel all my best faculties concentrated in it. My instinct tells me that my head is an organ for burrowing, as some creatures use their snout and fore paws, and with it I would mine and burrow my way through these hills. I think that the richest vein is somewhere hereabouts; so by the divining-rod and thin rising vapors I judge; and here I will begin to mine.

XI. HIGHER LAWS

As I came home through the woods with my string of fish, trailing my pole, it being now quite dark, I caught a glimpse of a woodchuck stealing across my path, and felt a strange thrill of savage delight, and was strongly tempted to seize and devour him raw; not that I was hungry then, except for that wildness which he represented. Once or twice, however, while I lived at the pond, I found myself ranging the woods, like a half-starved hound, with a strange abandonment, seeking some kind of venison which I might devour, and no morsel could have been too savage for me. The wildest scenes had become unaccountably familiar. I found in myself, and still find, an instinct toward a higher, or, as it is named, spiritual life, as do most men, and another toward a primitive rank and savage one, and I reverence them both. I love the wild not less than the good. The wildness and adventure that are in fishing still recommended it to me. I like sometimes to take rank hold on life and spend my day more as the animals do. Perhaps I have owed to this employment and to hunting, when quite young, my closest acquaintance with Nature. They early introduce us to and

[32] Base of operations (French).
[33] A gauge placed in the Nile River at Memphis to measure the rising water at flood times.
[34] Scimitar, an oriental sword with a curved blade.

detain us in scenery with which otherwise, at that age, we should have little acquaintance. Fishermen, hunters, wood-choppers, and others, spending their lives in the fields and woods, in a peculiar sense a part of Nature themselves, are often in a more favorable mood for observing her, in the intervals of their pursuits, than philosophers or poets even, who approach her with expectation. She is not afraid to exhibit herself to them. The traveler on the prairie is naturally a hunter, on the head waters of the Missouri and Columbia a trapper, and at the Falls of St. Mary[1] a fisherman. He who is only a traveler learns things at second-hand and by the halves, and is poor authority. We are most interested when science reports what those men already know practically or instinctively, for that alone is a true *humanity,* or account of human experience.

They mistake who assert that the Yankee has few amusements, because he has not so many public holidays, and men and boys do not play so many games as they do in England, for here the more primitive but solitary amusements of hunting, fishing, and the like have not yet given place to the former. Almost every New England boy among my contemporaries shouldered a fowling-piece between the ages of ten and fourteen; and his hunting and fishing grounds were not limited, like the preserves of an English nobleman, but were more boundless even than those of a savage. No wonder, then, that he did not oftener stay to play on the common. But already a change is taking place, owing, not to an increased humanity, but to an increased scarcity of game, for perhaps the hunter is the greatest friend of the animals hunted, not excepting the Humane Society.

Moreover, when at the pond, I wished sometimes to add fish to my fare for variety. I have actually fished from the same kind of necessity that the first fishers did. Whatever humanity I might conjure up against it was all factitious, and concerned my philosophy more than my feelings. I speak of fishing only now, for I had long felt differently about fowling, and sold my gun before I went to the woods. Not that I am less humane than others, but I did not perceive that my feelings were much affected. I did not pity the fishes nor the worms. This was habit. As for fowling, during the last years that I carried a gun my excuse was that I was studying ornithology, and sought only new or rare birds. But I confess that I am now inclined to think that there is a finer way of studying ornithology than this. It requires so much closer attention to the habits of the birds, that, if for that reason only, I have been willing to omit the gun. Yet notwithstanding the objection on the score of humanity, I am compelled to doubt if equally valuable sports are ever substituted for these; and when some of my friends have asked me anxiously about their boys, whether they should let them hunt, I have answered, yes,—remembering that it was one of the best parts of my education,—*make* them hunters, though sportsmen only at first, if possible, mighty hunters at last, so that they shall not find game large enough for them in this or any vegetable wilderness,—hunters as well as fishers of men.[2] Thus far I am of the opinion of Chaucer's nun, who

[1]The rapids of the St. Marys River between Lake Superior and Lake Huron. The Sault Sainte Marie Canals now provide a way around these rapids and falls.

[2]Christ told Simon and Andrew, "Follow me and I will make you become fishers of men" (Mark 1:17).

"yave not of the text a pulled hen
That saith that hunters ben not holy men."[3]

There is a period in the history of the individual, as of the race, when the hunters are the "best men," as the Algonquins called them. We cannot but pity the boy who has never fired a gun; he is no more humane, while his education has been sadly neglected. This was my answer with respect to those youths who were bent on this pursuit, trusting that they would soon outgrow it. No humane being, past the thoughtless age of boyhood, will wantonly murder any creature which holds its life by the same tenure that he does. The hare in its extremity cries like a child. I warn you, mothers, that my sympathies do not always make the usual phil-*anthropic* distinctions.

Such is oftenest the young man's introduction to the forest, and the most original part of himself. He goes thither at first as a hunter and fisher, until at last, if he has the seeds of a better life in him, he distinguishes his proper objects, as a poet or naturalist it may be, and leaves the gun and fish-pole behind. The mass of men are still and always young in this respect. In some countries a hunting parson is no uncommon sight. Such a one might make a good shepherd's dog, but is far from being the Good Shepherd. I have been surprised to consider that the only obvious employment, except wood-chopping, ice-cutting, or the like business, which ever to my knowledge detained at Walden Pond for a whole half-day any of my fellow-citizens, whether fathers or children of the town, with just one exception, was fishing. Commonly they did not think that they were lucky, or well paid for their time, unless they got a long string of fish, though they had the opportunity of seeing the pond all the while. They might go there a thousand times before the sediment of fishing would sink to the bottom and leave their purpose pure; but no doubt such a clarifying process would be going on all the while. The Governor and his Council faintly remember the pond, for they went a-fishing there when they were boys; but now they are too old and dignified to go a-fishing, and so they know it no more forever. Yet even they expect to go to heaven at last. If the legislature regards it, it is chiefly to regulate the number of hooks to be used there; but they know nothing about the hook of hooks with which to angle for the pond itself, impaling the legislature for a bait. Thus, even in civilized communities, the embryo man passes through the hunter stage of development.

I have found repeatedly, of late years, that I cannot fish without falling a little in self-respect. I have tried it again and again. I have skill at it, and, like many of my fellows, a certain instinct for it, which revives from time to time, but always when I have done I feel that it would have been better if I had not fished. I think that I do not mistake. It is a faint intimation, yet so are the first streaks of morning. There is unquestionably this instinct in me which belongs to the lower orders of creation; yet with every year I am less a fisherman, though without more humanity or even wisdom; at present I am no fisherman at all. But I see that if I were to live in a wilderness I

[3] From the Prologue to Chaucer's *Canterbury Tales,* where it refers to the Monk rather than the Nun. It means that he "didn't give a plucked hen for the text that says that hunters are not holy men."

should again be tempted to become a fisher and hunter in earnest. Beside, there is something essentially unclean about this diet and all flesh, and I began to see where housework commences, and whence the endeavor, which costs so much, to wear a tidy and respectable appearance each day, to keep the house sweet and free from all ill odors and sights. Having been my own butcher and scullion and cook, as well as the gentleman for whom the dishes were served up, I can speak from an unusually complete experience. The practical objection to animal food in my case was its uncleanness; and besides, when I had caught and cleaned and cooked and eaten my fish, they seemed not to have fed me essentially. It was insignificant and unnecessary, and cost more than it came to. A little bread or a few potatoes would have done as well, with less trouble and filth. Like many of my contemporaries, I had rarely for many years used animal food, or tea, or coffee, etc.; not so much because of any ill effects which I had traced to them, as because they were not agreeable to my imagination. The repugnance to animal food is not the effect of experience, but is an instinct. It appeared more beautiful to live low and fare hard in many respects; and though I never did so, I went far enough to please my imagination. I believe that every man who has ever been earnest to preserve his higher or poetic faculties in the best condition has been particularly inclined to abstain from animal food, and from much food of any kind. It is a significant fact, stated by entomologists,—I find it in Kirby and Spence,[4]—that "some insects in their perfect state, though furnished with organs of feeding, make no use of them"; and they lay it down as "a general rule, that almost all insects in this state eat much less than in that of larvae. The voracious caterpillar when transformed into a butterfly . . . and the gluttonous maggot when become a fly" content themselves with a drop or two of honey or some other sweet liquid. The abdomen under the wings of the butterfly still represents the larva. This is the tidbit which tempts his insectivorous fate. The gross feeder is a man in the larva state; and there are whole nations in that condition, nations without fancy or imagination, whose vast abdomens betray them.

It is hard to provide and cook so simple and clean a diet as will not offend the imagination; but this, I think, is to be fed when we feed the body; they should both sit down at the same table. Yet perhaps this may be done. The fruits eaten temperately need not make us ashamed of our appetites, nor interrupt the worthiest pursuits. But put an extra condiment into your dish, and it will poison you. It is not worth the while to live by rich cookery. Most men would feel shame if caught preparing with their own hands precisely such a dinner, whether of animal or vegetable food, as is every day prepared for them by others. Yet till this is otherwise we are not civilized, and, if gentlemen and ladies, are not true men and women. This certainly suggests what change is to be made. It may be vain to ask why the imagination will not be reconciled to flesh and fat. I am satisfied that it is not. Is it not a reproach that man is a carnivorous animal? True, he can and does live, in a great measure, by preying on other animals; but this is a miserable way,—as any one who will go to snaring rabbits, or slaughtering

[4] William Kirby and William Spence, *An Introduction to Entomology* (1815–1826, American edition 1846).

lambs, may learn,—and he will be regarded as a benefactor of his race who shall teach man to confine himself to a more innocent and wholesome diet. Whatever my own practice may be, I have no doubt that it is a part of the destiny of the human race, in its gradual improvement, to leave off eating animals, as surely as the savage tribes have left off eating each other when they came in contact with the more civilized.

If one listens to the faintest but constant suggestions of his genius, which are certainly true, he sees not to what extremes, or even insanity, it may lead him; and yet that way, as he grows more resolute and faithful, his road lies. The faintest assured objection which one healthy man feels will at length prevail over the arguments and customs of mankind. No man ever followed his genius till it misled him. Though the result were bodily weakness, yet perhaps no one can say that the consequences were to be regretted, for these were a life in conformity to higher principles. If the day and the night are such that you greet them with joy, and life emits a fragrance like flowers and sweet-scented herbs, is more elastic, more starry, more immortal,—that is your success. All nature is your congratulation, and you have cause momentarily to bless yourself. The greatest gains and values are farthest from being appreciated. We easily come to doubt if they exist. We soon forget them. They are the highest reality. Perhaps the facts most astounding and most real are never communicated by man to man. The true harvest of my daily life is somewhat as intangible and indescribable as the tints of morning or evening. It is a little star-dust caught, a segment of the rainbow which I have clutched.

Yet, for my part, I was never unusually squeamish; I could sometimes eat a fried rat with a good relish, if it were necessary. I am glad to have drunk water so long, for the same reason that I prefer the natural sky to an opium-eater's heaven. I would fain keep sober always; and there are infinite degrees of drunkenness. I believe that water is the only drink for a wise man; wine is not so noble a liquor; and think of dashing the hopes of a morning with a cup of warm coffee, or of an evening with a dish of tea! Ah, how low I fall when I am tempted by them! Even music may be intoxicating. Such apparently slight causes destroyed Greece and Rome, and will destroy England and America. Of all ebriosity, who does not prefer to be intoxicated by the air he breathes? I have found it to be the most serious objection to coarse labors long continued, that they compelled me to eat and drink coarsely also. But to tell the truth, I find myself at present somewhat less particular in these respects. I carry less religion to the table, ask no blessing; not because I am wiser than I was, but, I am obliged to confess, because, however much it is to be regretted, with years I have grown more coarse and indifferent. Perhaps these questions are entertained only in youth, as most believe of poetry. My practice is "nowhere," my opinion is here. Nevertheless I am far from regarding myself as one of those privileged ones to whom the Ved[5] refers when it says, that "he who has true faith in the Omnipresent Supreme Being may eat all that exists," that is, is not bound to inquire what is his food, or who prepares it; and even in their

[5] One of the Vedas, Hindu sacred writings. Thoreau took this quotation from Rajah Rammohun Roy, *Translation of Several . . . of the Vedas* (1832).

case it is to be observed, as a Hindoo commentator has remarked, that the Vedant limits this privilege to "the time of distress."

Who has not sometimes derived an inexpressible satisfaction from his food in which appetite had no share? I have been thrilled to think that I owed a mental perception to the commonly gross sense of taste, that I have been inspired through the palate, that some berries which I had eaten on a hillside had fed my genius. "The soul not being mistress of herself," says Thseng-tseu,[6] "one looks, and one does not see; one listens, and one does not hear; one eats, and one does not know the savor of food." He who distinguishes the true savor of his food can never be a glutton; he who does not cannot be otherwise. A puritan may go to his brown-bread crust with as gross an appetite as ever an alderman to his turtle. Not that food which entereth into the mouth defileth a man, but the appetite with which it is eaten. It is neither the quality nor the quantity, but the devotion to sensual savors; when that which is eaten is not a viand to sustain our animal, or inspire our spiritual life, but food for the worms that possess us. If the hunter has a taste for mud-turtles, muskrats, and other such savage tidbits, the fine lady indulges a taste for jelly made of a calf's foot, or for sardines from over the sea, and they are even. He goes to the mill-pond, she to her preserve-pot. The wonder is how they, how you and I, can live this slimy, beastly life, eating and drinking.

Our whole life is startlingly moral. There is never an instant's truce between virtue and vice. Goodness is the only investment that never fails. In the music of the harp which trembles round the world it is the insisting on this which thrills us. The harp is the traveling patterer for the Universe's Insurance Company, recommending its laws, and our little goodness is all the assessment that we pay. Though the youth at last grows indifferent, the laws of the universe are not indifferent, but are forever on the side of the most sensitive. Listen to every zephyr for some reproof, for it is surely there, and he is unfortunate who does not hear it. We cannot touch a string or move a stop but the charming moral transfixes us. Many an irksome noise, go a long way off, is heard as music, a proud, sweet satire on the meanness of our lives.

We are conscious of an animal in us, which awakens in proportion as our higher nature slumbers. It is reptile and sensual, and perhaps cannot be wholly expelled; like the worms which, even in life and health, occupy our bodies. Possibly we may withdraw from it, but never change its nature. I fear that it may enjoy a certain health of its own; that we may be well, yet not pure. The other day I picked up the lower jaw of a hog, with white and sound teeth and tusks, which suggested that there was an animal health and vigor distinct from the spiritual. This creature succeeded by other means than temperance and purity. "That in which men differ from brute beasts," says Mencius,[7] "is a thing very inconsiderable; the common herd lose it very soon; superior men preserve it carefully." Who knows what sort of life would result if we had attained to purity? If I knew so wise a man as

[6] Confucius. The quotation is from *The Great Learning*.

[7] Chinese philosopher (372?–289? B.C.). The quotation is from the *Book of Mencius*, Book IV, chapter 19, page 1.

could teach me purity I would go to seek him forthwith. "A command over our passions, and over the external senses of the body, and good acts, are declared by the Ved to be indispensable in the mind's approximation to God." Yet the spirit can for the time pervade and control every member and function of the body, and transmute what in form is the grossest sensuality into purity and devotion. The generative energy, which, when we are loose, dissipates and makes us unclean, when we are continent invigorates and inspires us. Chastity is the flowering of man; and what are called Genius, Heroism, Holiness, and the like, are but various fruits which succeed it. Man flows at once to God when the channel of purity is open. By turns our purity inspires and our impurity casts us down. He is blessed who is assured that the animal is dying out in him day by day, and the divine being established. Perhaps there is none but has cause for shame on account of the inferior and brutish nature to which he is allied. I fear that we are such gods or demigods only as fauns and satyrs, the divine allied to beasts, the creatures of appetite, and that, to some extent, our very life is our disgrace.—

> "How happy's he who hath due place assigned
> To his beasts and disafforested his mind!
>
> . . . .
>
> Can use his horse, goat, wolf, and ev'ry beast,
> And is not ass himself to all the rest!
> Else man not only is the herd of swine,
> But he's those devils too which did incline
> Them to a headlong rage, and made them worse."[8]

All sensuality is one, though it takes many forms; all purity is one. It is the same whether a man eat, or drink, or cohabit, or sleep sensually. They are but one appetite, and we only need to see a person do any one of these things to know how great a sensualist he is. The impure can neither stand nor sit with purity. When the reptile is attacked at one mouth of his burrow, he shows himself at another. If you would be chaste, you must be temperate. What is chastity? How shall a man know if he is chaste? He shall not know it. We have heard of this virtue, but we know not what it is. We speak conformably to the rumor which we have heard. From exertion come wisdom and purity; from sloth ignorance and sensuality. In the student sensuality is a sluggish habit of mind. An unclean person is universally a slothful one, one who sits by a stove, whom the sun shines on prostrate, who reposes without being fatigued. If you would avoid uncleanness, and all the sins, work earnestly, though it be at cleaning a stable. Nature is hard to be overcome, but she must be overcome. What avails it that you are Christian, if you are not purer than the heathen, if you deny yourself no more, if you are not more religious? I know of many systems of religion esteemed heathenish whose precepts fill the reader with shame, and provoke him to new endeavors, though it be to the performance of rites merely.

[8] "To Sir Edward Herbert . . . Being at the Siege of Julyers" by John Donne (1573–1631), lines 9–17.

I hesitate to say these things, but it is not because of the subject,—I care not how obscene my *words* are,—but because I cannot speak of them without betraying my impurity. We discourse freely without shame of one form of sensuality, and are silent about another. We are so degraded that we cannot speak simply of the necessary functions of human nature. In earlier ages, in some countries, every function was reverently spoken of and regulated by law. Nothing was too trivial for the Hindoo lawgiver, however offensive it may be to modern taste. He teaches how to eat, drink, cohabit, void excrement and urine and the like, elevating what is mean, and does not falsely excuse himself by calling these things trifles.

Every man is the builder of a temple, called his body, to the god he worships, after a style purely his own, nor can he get off by hammering marble instead. We are all sculptors and painters, and our material is our own flesh and blood and bones. Any nobleness begins at once to refine a man's features, any meanness or sensuality to imbrute them.

John Farmer sat at his door one September evening, after a hard day's work, his mind still running on his labor more or less. Having bathed, he sat down to re-create his intellectual man. It was a rather cool evening, and some of his neighbors were apprehending a frost. He had not attended to the train of his thoughts long when he heard some one playing on a flute,[9] and that sound harmonized with his mood. Still he thought of his work; but the burden of his thought was, that though this kept running in his head, and he found himself planning and contriving it against his will, yet it concerned him very little. It was no more than the scurf of his skin, which was constantly shuffled off. But the notes of the flute came home to his ears out of a different sphere from that he worked in, and suggested work for certain faculties which slumbered in him. They gently did away with the street, and the village, and the state in which he lived. A voice said to him,—Why do you stay here and live this mean moiling life, when a glorious existence is possible for you? Those same stars twinkle over other fields than these.—But how to come out of this condition and actually migrate thither? All that he could think of was to practice some new austerity, to let his mind descend into his body and redeem it, and treat himself with ever increasing respect.

XVII. SPRING

The opening of large tracts by the ice-cutters commonly causes a pond to break up earlier; for the water, agitated by the wind, even in cold weather, wears away the surrounding ice. But such was not the effect on Walden that year, for she had soon got a thick new garment to take the place of the old. This pond never breaks up so soon as the others in this neighborhood, on account both of its greater depth and its having no stream passing through it to melt or wear away the ice. I never knew it to open in the course of a winter, not excepting that of '52-3, which gave the ponds so severe a trial. It commonly opens about the first of April, a week or ten days later than

[9] Thoreau himself, who played the flute.

Flint's Pond and Fair Haven, beginning to melt on the north side in the shallower parts where it began to freeze. It indicates better than any water hereabouts the absolute progress of the season, being least affected by transient changes of temperature. A severe cold of a few days' duration in March may very much retard the opening of the former ponds, while the temperature of Walden increases almost uninterruptedly. A thermometer thrust into the middle of Walden on the 6th of March, 1847, stood at 32°, or freezing point; near the shore at 33°; in the middle of Flint's Pond, the same day, at 32½; at a dozen rods from the shore, in shallow water, under ice a foot thick at 36°. This difference of three and a half degrees between the temperature of the deep water and the shallow in the latter pond, and the fact that a great proportion of it is comparatively shallow, show why it should break up so much sooner than Walden. The ice in the shallowest part was at this time several inches thinner than in the middle. In midwinter the middle had been the warmest and the ice thinnest there. So, also, every one who has waded about the shores of a pond in summer must have perceived how much warmer the water is close to the shore, where only three or four inches deep, than a little distance out, and on the surface where it is deep, than near the bottom. In spring the sun not only exerts an influence through the increased temperature of the air and earth, but its heat passes through ice a foot or more thick, and is reflected from the bottom in shallow water, and so also warms the water and melts the under side of the ice, at the same time that it is melting it more directly above, making it uneven, and causing the air bubbles which it contains to extend themselves upward and downward until it is completely honeycombed, and at last disappears suddenly in a single spring rain. Ice has its grain as well as wood, and when a cake begins to rot or "comb," that is, assume the appearance of honeycomb, whatever may be its position, the air cells are at right angles with what was the water surface. Where there is a rock or a log rising near to the surface the ice over it is much thinner, and is frequently quite dissolved by this reflected heat; and I have been told that in the experiment at Cambridge to freeze water in a shallow wooden pond, though the cold air circulated underneath, and so had access to both sides, the reflection of the sun from the bottom more than counterbalanced this advantage. When a warm rain in the middle of the winter melts off the snow ice from Walden, and leaves a hard dark or transparent ice on the middle, there will be a strip of rotten though thicker white ice, a rod or more wide, about the shores, created by this reflected heat. Also, as I have said, the bubbles themselves within the ice operate as burning-glasses to melt the ice beneath.

The phenomena of the year take place every day in a pond on a small scale. Every morning, generally speaking, the shallow water is being warmed more rapidly than the deep, though it may not be made so warm after all, and every evening it is being cooled more rapidly until the morning. The day is an epitome of the year. The night is the winter, the morning and evening are the spring and fall, and the noon is the summer. The cracking and booming of the ice indicate a change of temperature. One pleasant morning after a cold night, February 24th, 1850, having gone to Flint's Pond to spend the day, I noticed with surprise, that when I struck the ice with the head of my axe, it resounded like a gong for many rods around, or as if I had struck on a tight drum-head. The pond began to boom about an hour after sunrise, when it felt the influence of the sun's rays slanted upon it from over the hills; it stretched itself and yawned like a waking man with a gradually increasing tumult, which was kept up three or four hours. It took a short siesta at noon, and boomed once more toward night, as the sun was withdrawing his influence. In the right stage of the weather a pond fires its evening gun with great regularity. But in the middle of the day, being full of cracks, and the air also being less elastic, it had completely lost its resonance, and probably fishes and muskrats could not then have been stunned by a blow on it. The fishermen say that the "thundering of the pond" scares the fishes and prevents their biting. The pond does not thunder every evening, and I cannot tell surely when to expect its thundering; but though I may perceive no difference in the weather, it does. Who would have suspected so large and cold and thick-skinned a thing to be so sensitive? Yet it has its law to which it thunders obedience when it should as surely as the buds expand in the spring. The earth is all alive and covered with papillae.[1] The largest pond is as sensitive to atmospheric changes as the globule of mercury in its tube.

One attraction in coming to the woods to live was that I should have leisure and opportunity to see the Spring come in. The ice in the pond at length begins to be honeycombed, and I can set my heel in it as I walk. Fogs and rains and warmer suns are gradually melting the snow; the days have grown sensibly longer; and I see how I shall get through the winter without adding to my wood-pile, for large fires are no longer necessary. I am on the alert for the first signs of spring, to hear the chance note of some arriving bird, or the striped squirrel's chirp, for his stores must be now nearly exhausted, or see the woodchuck venture out of his winter quarters. On the 13th of March, after I had heard the bluebird, song sparrow, and red-wing, the ice was still nearly a foot thick. As the weather grew warmer it was not sensibly worn away by the water, nor broken up and floated off as in rivers, but, though it was completely melted for half a rod in width about the shore, the middle was merely honeycombed and saturated with water, so that you could put your foot through it when six inches thick; but by the next day, evening, perhaps, after a warm rain followed by fog, it would have wholly disappeared, all gone with the fog, spirited away. One year I went across the middle only five days before it disappeared entirely. In 1845 Walden was first completely open on the 1st of April; in '46, the 25th of March; in '47, the 8th of April; in '51, the 28th of March; in '52, the 18th of April; in '53, the 23d of March; in '54, about the 7th of April.

Every incident connected with the breaking up of the rivers and ponds and the settling of the weather is particularly interesting to us who live in a climate of so great extremes. When the warmer days come, they who dwell near the river hear the ice crack at night with a startling whoop as loud as artillery, as if its icy fetters were rent from end to end, and within a few days see it rapidly going out. So the alligator comes out of the mud with quakings of the earth. One old man, who has been a close observer of Nature, and seems as thoroughly wise in regard to all her operations as if

[1] Small protuberances concerned with the senses of touch, taste, and smell, such as the papillae of the tongue.

she had been put upon the stocks when he was a boy, and he had helped to lay her keel,[2]—who has come to his growth, and can hardly acquire more of natural lore if he should live to the age of Methuselah,[3]—told me—and I was surprised to hear him express wonder at any of Nature's operations, for I thought that there were no secrets between them—that one spring day he took his gun and boat, and thought that he would have a little sport with the ducks. There was ice still on the meadows, but it was all gone out of the river, and he dropped down without obstruction from Sudbury, where he lived, to Fair Haven Pond, which he found, unexpectedly, covered for the most part with a firm field of ice. It was a warm day, and he was surprised to see so great a body of ice remaining. Not seeing any ducks, he hid his boat on the north or back side of an island in the pond, and then concealed himself in the bushes on the south side, to await them. The ice was melted for three or four rods from the shore, and there was a smooth and warm sheet of water, with a muddy bottom, such as the ducks love, within, and he thought it likely that some would be along pretty soon. After he had lain still there about an hour he heard a low and seemingly very distant sound, but singularly grand and impressive, unlike anything he had ever heard, gradually swelling and increasing as if it would have a universal and memorable ending, a sullen rush and roar, which seemed to him all at once like the sound of a vast body of fowl coming in to settle there, and, seizing his gun, he started up in haste and excited; but he found, to his surprise, that the whole body of the ice had started while he lay there, and drifted in to the shore, and the sound he had heard was made by its edge grating on the shore,—at first gently nibbled and crumbled off, but at length heaving up and scattering its wrecks along the island to a considerable height before it came to a standstill.

At length the sun's rays have attained the right angle, and warm winds blow up mist and rain and melt the snowbanks, and the sun, dispersing the mist, smiles on a checkered landscape of russet and white smoking with incense, through which the traveler picks his way from islet to islet, cheered by the music of a thousand tinkling rills and rivulets whose veins are filled with the blood of winter which they are bearing off.

Few phenomena gave me more delight than to observe the forms which thawing sand and clay assume in flowing down the sides of a deep cut on the railroad through which I passed on my way to the village, a phenomenon not very common on so large a scale, though the number of freshly exposed banks of the right material must have been greatly multiplied since railroads were invented. The material was sand of every degree of fineness and of various rich colors, commonly mixed with a little clay. When the frost comes out in the spring, and even in a thawing day in the winter, the sand begins to flow down the slopes like lava, sometimes bursting out through the snow and overflowing it where no sand was to be seen before. Innumerable little streams overlap and interlace one with another, exhibiting a sort of hybrid product, which obeys half way the law of currents, and half way that of vegetation. As it flows it takes the forms of sappy

[2] Stocks are the bracing framework of a boat under construction or repair. The keel is the main timber of a ship's hull.

[3] Methuselah, according to Genesis 5:27, lived to be 969 years old.

leaves or vines, making heaps of pulpy sprays a foot or more in depth, and resembling, as you look down on them, the laciniated, lobed, and imbricated thalluses of some lichens;[4] or you are reminded of coral, of leopards' paws or birds' feet, of brains or lungs or bowels, and excrements of all kinds. It is a truly *grotesque* vegetation, whose forms and color we see imitated in bronze, a sort of architectural foliage more ancient and typical than acanthus, chicory, ivy, vine, or any vegetable leaves; destined perhaps, under some circumstances, to become a puzzle to future geologists. The whole cut impressed me as if it were a cave with its stalactites laid open to the light. The various shades of the sand are singularly rich and agreeable, embracing the different iron colors, brown, gray, yellowish, and reddish. When the flowing mass reaches the drain at the foot of the bank it spreads out flatter into *strands,* the separate streams losing their semi-cylindrical form and gradually becoming more flat and broad, running together as they are more moist, till they form an almost flat *sand,* still variously and beautifully shaded, but in which you can trace the original forms of vegetation; till at length, in the water itself, they are converted into *banks,* like those formed off the mouths of rivers, and the forms of vegetation are lost in the ripple-marks on the bottom.

The whole bank, which is from twenty to forty feet high, is sometimes overlaid with a mass of this kind of foliage, or sandy rupture, for a quarter of a mile on one or both sides, the produce of one spring day. What makes this sand foliage remarkable is its springing into existence thus suddenly. When I see on the one side the inert bank,—for the sun acts on one side first,—and on the other this luxuriant foliage, the creation of an hour, I am affected as if in a peculiar sense I stood in the laboratory of the Artist who made the world and me,—had come to where he was still at work, sporting on this bank, and with excess of energy strewing his fresh designs about. I feel as if I were nearer to the vitals of the globe, for this sandy overflow is something such a foliaceous mass as the vitals of the animal body. You find thus in the very sands an anticipation of the vegetable leaf. No wonder that the earth expresses itself outwardly in leaves, it so labors with the idea inwardly. The atoms have already learned this law, and are pregnant by it. The overhanging leaf sees here its prototype. *Internally,* whether in the globe or animal body, it is a moist thick *lobe,* a word especially applicable to the liver and lungs and the *leaves* of fat (λείβω, *labor, lapsus,* to flow or slip downward, a lapsing; λοβός, *globus,* lobe, globe; also lap, flap, and many other words); *externally,* a dry thin *leaf,* even as the *f* and *v* are a pressed and dried *b.* The radicals of *lobe* are *lb,* the soft mass of the *b* (single-lobed, or B, double-lobed), with the liquid *l* behind it pressing it forward. In globe, *glb,* the guttural *g* adds to the meaning the capacity of the throat. The feathers and wings of birds are still drier and thinner leaves. Thus, also, you pass from the lumpish grub in the earth to the airy and fluttering butterfly. The very globe continually transcends and translates itself, and becomes winged in its orbit. Even ice begins with delicate crystal leaves, as if it had flowed into moulds which the fronds of water-plants have impressed on the watery

[4]These are botanical terms. A lichen is a mosslike plant of irregular shape. "Laciniated" means having edges cut into irregular lobes; "imbricated" means overlapping like tiles on a roof; and "thalluses" are plants so simple that they have no stems, roots, or leaves.

mirror. The whole tree itself is but one leaf, and rivers are still vaster leaves whose pulp is intervening earth, and towns and cities are the ova of insects in their axils.[5]

When the sun withdraws the sand ceases to flow, but in the morning the streams will start once more and branch and branch again into a myriad of others. You here see perchance how blood vessels are formed. If you look closely you observe that first there pushes forward from the thawing mass a stream of softened sand with a drop-like point, like the ball of the finger, feeling its way slowly and blindly downward, until at last with more heat and moisture, as the sun gets higher, the moist fluid portion, in its effort to obey the law to which the most inert also yields, separates from the latter and forms for itself a meandering channel or artery within that, in which is seen a little silvery stream glancing like lightning from one stage of pulpy leaves or branches to another, and ever and anon swallowed up in the sand. It is wonderful how rapidly yet perfectly the sand organizes itself as it flows, using the best material its mass affords to form the sharp edges of its channel. Such are the sources of rivers. In the silicious matter which the water deposits is perhaps the bony system, and in the still finer soil and organic matter the fleshy fiber or cellular tissue. What is man but a mass of thawing clay? The ball of the human finger is but a drop congealed. The fingers and toes flow to their extent from the thawing mass of the body. Who knows what the human body would expand and flow out to under a more genial heaven? Is not the hand a spreading *palm* leaf with its lobes and veins? The ear may be regarded, fancifully, as a lichen, *Umbilicaria,* on the side of the head, with its lobe or drop. The lip—*labium,* from *labor* (?)—laps or lapses from the sides of the cavernous mouth. The nose is a manifest congealed drop or stalactite. The chin is a still larger drop, the confluent dripping of the face. The cheeks are a slide from the brows into the valley of the face, opposed and diffused by the cheek bones. Each rounded lobe of the vegetable leaf, too, is a thick and now loitering drop, larger or smaller; the lobes are the fingers of the leaf; and as many lobes as it has, in so many directions it tends to flow, and more heat or other genial influences would have caused it to flow yet farther.

Thus it seemed that this one hillside illustrated the principle of all the operations of Nature. The Maker of this earth but patented a leaf. What Champollion[6] will decipher this hieroglyphic for us, that we may turn over a new leaf at last? This phenomenon is more exhilarating to me than the luxuriance and fertility of vineyards. True, it is somewhat excrementitious in its character, and there is no end to the heaps of liver, lights, and bowels, as if the globe were turned wrong side outward; but this suggests at least that Nature has some bowels, and there again is mother of humanity. This is the frost coming out of the ground; this is Spring. It precedes the green and flowery spring, as mythology precedes regular poetry. I know of nothing more purgative of winter fumes and indigestions. It convinces me that Earth is still in her swaddling-clothes, and stretches forth baby fingers on every side. Fresh curls spring from the baldest brow. There is nothing

[5] Points between the upper sides of leaves or stems and the supporting stems or branches.

[6] Jean-François Champollion (1790–1832) was a French Egyptologist who deciphered the Rosetta Stone and thus made it possible to read hieroglyphics.

inorganic. These foliaceous heaps lie along the bank like the slag of a furnace, showing that Nature is "in full blast" within. The earth is not a mere fragment of dead history, stratum upon stratum like the leaves of a book, to be studied by geologists and antiquaries chiefly, but living poetry like the leaves of a tree, which precede flowers and fruit,—not a fossil earth, but a living earth; compared with whose great central life all animal and vegetable life is merely parasitic. Its throes will heave our exuviae from their graves. You may melt your metals and cast them into the most beautiful moulds you can; they will never excite me like the forms which this molten earth flows out into. And not only it, but the institutions upon it are plastic like clay in the hands of the potter.

Ere long, not only on these banks, but on every hill and plain and in every hollow, the frost comes out of the ground like a dormant quadruped from its burrow, and seeks the sea with music, or migrates to other climes in clouds. Thaw with his gentle persuasion is more powerful than Thor[7] with his hammer. The one melts, the other but breaks in pieces.

When the ground was partially bare of snow, and a few warm days had dried its surface somewhat, it was pleasant to compare the first tender signs of the infant year just peeping forth with the stately beauty of the withered vegetation which had withstood the winter,—life-everlasting, goldenrods, pinweeds, and graceful wild grasses, more obvious and interesting frequently than in summer even, as if their beauty was not ripe till then; even cotton-grass, cat-tails, mulleins, johnswort, hardhack, meadow-sweet, and other strong-stemmed plants, those unexhausted granaries which entertain the earliest birds,—decent weeds, at least, which widowed Nature wears. I am particularly attracted by the arching and sheaf-like top of the wool-grass; it brings back the summer to our winter memories, and is among the forms which art loves to copy, and which, in the vegetable kingdom, have the same relation to types already in the mind of man that astronomy has. It is an antique style, older than Greek or Egyptian. Many of the phenomena of winter are suggestive of an inexpressible tenderness and fragile delicacy. We are accustomed to hear this king described as a rude and boisterous tyrant; but with the gentleness of a lover he adorns the tresses of Summer.

At the approach of spring the red squirrels got under my house, two at a time, directly under my feet as I sat reading or writing, and kept up the queerest chuckling and chirruping and vocal pirouetting and gurgling sounds that ever were heard; and when I stamped they only chirruped the louder, as if past all fear and respect in their mad pranks, defying humanity to stop them. No, you don't—chickaree—chickaree. They were wholly deaf to my arguments, or failed to perceive their force, and fell into a strain of invective that was irresistible.

The first sparrow of spring! The year beginning with younger hope than ever! The faint silvery warblings heard over the partially bare and moist fields from the bluebird, the song sparrow, and the red-wing, as if the last flakes of winter tinkled as they fell! What at such a time are histories, chronologies, traditions, and all written revelations? The brooks sing carols and glees to the spring. The marsh hawk, sailing low over the

[7] Norse god of thunder.

meadow, is already seeking the first slimy life that awakes. The sinking sound of melting snow is heard in all dells, and the ice dissolves apace in the ponds. The grass flames up on the hillsides like a spring fire,—*"et primitus oritur herba imbribus primoribus evocata,"*[8]—as if the earth sent form an inward heat to greet the returning sun; not yellow but green is the color of its flame;—the symbol of perpetual youth, the grass-blade, like a long green ribbon, streams from the sod into the summer, checked indeed by the frost, but anon pushing on again, lifting its spear of last year's hay with the fresh life below. It grows as steadily as the rill oozes out of the ground. It is almost identical with that, for in the growing days of June, when the rills are dry, the grass-blades are their channels, and from year to year the herds drink at this perennial green stream, and the mower draws from it betimes their winter supply. So our human life but dies down to its root, and still puts forth its green blade to eternity.

Walden is melting apace. There is a canal two rods wide along the northerly and westerly sides, and wider still at the east end. A great field of ice has cracked off from the main body. I hear a song sparrow singing from the bushes on the shore,—*olit, olit, olit,—chip, chip, chip, che char,—che wiss, wiss, wiss.* He too is helping to crack it. How handsome the great sweeping curves in the edge of the ice, answering somewhat to those of the shore, but more regular! It is unusually hard, owing to the recent severe but transient cold, and all watered or waved like a palace floor. But the wind slides eastward over its opaque surface in vain, till it reaches the living surface beyond. It is glorious to behold this ribbon of water sparkling in the sun, the bare face of the pond full of glee and youth, as if it spoke the joy of the fishes within it, and of the sands on its shore,—a silvery sheen as from the scales of a leuciscus,[9] as it were all one active fish. Such is the contrast between winter and spring. Walden was dead and is alive again.[10] But this spring it broke up more steadily, as I have said.

The change from storm and winter to serene and mild weather, from dark and sluggish hours to bright and elastic ones, is a memorable crisis which all things proclaim. It is seemingly instantaneous at last. Suddenly an influx of light filled my house, though the evening was at hand, and the clouds of winter still overhung it, and the eaves were dripping with sleety rain. I looked out the window, and lo! where yesterday was cold gray ice there lay the transparent pond already calm and full of hope as in a summer evening, reflecting a summer evening sky in its bosom, though none was visible overhead, as if it had intelligence with some remote horizon. I heard a robin in the distance, the first I had heard for many a thousand years, methought, whose note I shall not forget for many a thousand more,—the same sweet and powerful song as of yore. O the evening robin, at the end of a New England summer day! If I could ever find the twig he sits upon! I mean *he;* I mean *the twig.* This at least is not the *Turdis migratorius.*[11] The pitch pines and shrub oaks about my house, which had so long

[8]"And for the first time the grass begins to grow, called forth by the first rains." From "Of Rural Things," by the Roman Marcus Terentius Varro (116–27? B.C.).

[9]A small freshwater fish.

[10]The father in the parable of the Prodigal Son says, "This my son was dead, and is alive again" (Luke 15:24).

[11]The American robin.

drooped, suddenly resumed their several characters, looked brighter, greener, and more erect and alive, as if effectually cleansed and restored by the rain. I knew that it would not rain any more. You may tell by looking at any twig of the forest, ay, at your very wood-pile, whether its winter is past or not. As it grew darker, I was startled by the honking of geese flying low over the woods, like weary travelers getting in late from Southern lakes, and indulging at last in unrestrained complaint and mutual consolation. Standing at my door, I could hear the rush of their wings; when, driving toward my house, they suddenly spied my light, and with hushed clamor wheeled and settled in the pond. So I came in, and shut the door, and passed my first spring night in the woods.

In the morning I watched the geese from the door through the mist, sailing in the middle of the pond, fifty rods off, so large and tumultuous that Walden appeared like an artificial pond for their amusement. But when I stood on the shore they at once rose up with a great flapping of wings at the signal of their commander, and when they had got into rank circled about over my head, twenty-nine of them, and then steered straight to Canada, with a regular *honk* from the leader at intervals, trusting to break their fast in muddier pools. A "plump"[12] of ducks rose at the same time and took the route to the north in the wake of their noisier cousins.

For a week I heard the circling, groping clangor of some solitary goose in the foggy mornings, seeking its companion, and still peopling the woods with the sound of a larger life than they could sustain. In April the pigeons were seen again flying express in small flocks, and in due time I heard the martins twittering over my clearing, though it had not seemed that the township contained so many that it could afford me any, and I fancied that they were peculiarly of the ancient race that dwelt in hollow trees ere white men came. In almost all climes the tortoise and the frog are among the precursors and heralds of this season, and birds fly with song and glancing plumage, and plants spring and bloom, and winds blow, to correct this slight oscillation of the poles and preserve the equilibrium of nature.

As every season seems best to us in its turn, so the coming in of spring is like the creation of Cosmos out of Chaos and the realization of the Golden Age.—

> "Eurus ad Auroram Nabathaeaque regna recessit,
> Persidaque, et radiis juga subdita matutinis."

> "The East-Wind withdrew to Aurora and the Nabathaean kingdom,[13]
> And the Persian, and the ridges placed under the morning rays.
> . . . .
> Man was born. Whether that Artificer of things,
> The origin of a better world, made him from the divine seed;
> Or the earth, being recent and lately sundered from the high
> Ether, retained some seeds of cognate heaven."[14]

[12] Flock.

[13] The Nabathaean (or Nabataean) kingdom was the land between Syria and Arabia from the Euphrates to the Red Sea, thus "the east."

[14] Ovid, *Metamorphoses,* Book I.

A single gentle rain makes the grass many shades greener. So our prospects brighten on the influx of better thoughts. We should be blessed if we lived in the present always, and took advantage of every accident that befell us, like the grass which confesses the influence of the slightest dew that falls on it; and did not spend our time in atoning for the neglect of past opportunities, which we call doing our duty. We loiter in winter while it is already spring. In a pleasant spring morning all men's sins are forgiven. Such a day is a truce to vice. While such a sun holds out to burn, the vilest sinner may return.[15] Through our own recovered innocence we discern the innocence of our neighbors. You may have known your neighbor yesterday for a thief, a drunkard, or a sensualist, and merely pitied or despised him, and despaired of the world; but the sun shines bright and warm this first spring morning, re-creating the world, and you meet him at some serene work, and see how his exhausted and debauched veins expand with still joy and bless the new day, feel the spring influence with the innocence of infancy, and all his faults are forgotten. There is not only an atmosphere of good will about him, but even a savor of holiness groping for expression, blindly and ineffectually perhaps, like a new-born instinct, and for a short hour the south hillside echoes to no vulgar jest. You see some innocent fair shoots preparing to burst from his gnarled rind and try another year's life, tender and fresh as the youngest plant. Even he has entered into the joy of his Lord. Why the jailer does not leave open his prison doors,—why the judge does not dismiss his case,—why the preacher does not dismiss his congregation! It is because they do not obey the hint which God gives them, nor accept the pardon which he freely offers to all.

"A return to goodness produced each day in the tranquil and beneficient breath of the morning, causes that in respect to the love of virtue and the hatred of vice, one approaches a little the primitive nature of man, as the sprouts of the forest which has been felled. In like manner the evil which one does in the interval of a day prevents the germs of virtues which began to spring up again from developing themselves and destroys them.

"After the germs of virtue have thus been prevented many times from developing themselves, then the beneficent breath of evening does not suffice to preserve them. As soon as the breath of evening does not suffice longer to preserve them, then the nature of man does not differ much from that of the brute. Men seeing the nature of this man like that of the brute, think that he has never possessed the innate faculty of reason. Are those the true and natural sentiments of man?"[16]

> "The Golden Age was first created which without any avenger
> Spontaneously without law cherished fidelity and rectitude.
> Punishment and fear were not; nor were threatening words read
> On suspended brass; nor did the suppliant crowd fear
> The words of their judge; but were safe without an avenger.
> Not yet the pine felled on its mountains had descended

[15] Paraphrase of a line in a hymn by Isaac Watts (1674–1748).
[16] These paragraphs are quoted from the *Book of Mencius,* IV, part 1, chapter VIII.

To the liquid waves that it might see a foreign world,
And mortals knew no shores but their own.

. . . .

There was eternal spring, and placid zephyrs with warm
Blasts soothed the flowers born without seed."[17]

On the 29th of April, as I was fishing from the bank of the river near the Nine-Acre-Corner bridge, standing on the quaking grass and willow roots, where the muskrats lurk, I heard a singular rattling sound, somewhat like that of the sticks which boys play with their fingers, when, looking up, I observed a very slight and graceful hawk, like a nighthawk, alternately soaring like a ripple and tumbling a rod or two over and over, showing the under side of its wings, which gleamed like a satin ribbon in the sun, or like the pearly inside of a shell. This sight reminded me of falconry and what nobleness and poetry are associated with that sport. The merlin it seemed to me it might be called; but I care not for its name. It was the most ethereal flight I had ever witnessed. It did not simply flutter like a butterfly, nor soar like the larger hawks, but it sported with proud reliance in the fields of air; mounting again and again with its strange chuckle, it repeated its free and beautiful fall, turning over and over like a kite, and then recovering from its lofty tumbling, as if it had never set its foot on *terra firma.* It appeared to have no companion in the universe,—sporting there alone,—and to need none but the morning and the ether with which it played. It was not lonely, but made all the earth lonely beneath it. Where was the parent which hatched it, its kindred, and its father in the heavens? The tenant of the air, it seemed related to the earth but by an egg hatched some time in the crevice of a crag;—or was its native nest made in the angle of a cloud, woven of the rainbow's trimmings and the sunset sky, and lined with some soft midsummer haze caught up from earth? Its eyry[18] now some cliffy cloud.

Beside this I got a rare mess of golden and silver and bright cupreous[19] fishes, which looked like a string of jewels. Ah! I have penetrated to those meadows on the morning of many a first spring day, jumping from hummock to hummock, from willow root to willow root, when the wild river valley and the woods were bathed in so pure and bright a light as would have waked the dead, if they had been slumbering in their graves, as some suppose. There needs no stronger proof of immortality. All things must live in such a light. O Death, where was thy sting? O Grave, where was thy victory, then?[20]

Our village life would stagnate if it were not for the unexplored forests and meadows which surround it. We need the tonic of wildness,—to wade sometimes in marshes where the bittern and the meadow-hen lurk, and hear the booming of the snipe; to smell the whispering sedge where only some wilder and more solitary fowl builds her nest, and the mink crawls with its belly close to the ground. At the same time that we are earnest to explore and learn all things, we require that all things be mysterious and

[17] Ovid, *Metamorphoses,* Book I.
[18] A lofty nest. (Also spelled "aerie" or "eyrie.")
[19] Copper-colored.
[20] "O death, where is thy sting? O grave, where is thy victory?" (I Corinthians 15:55).

unexplorable, that land and sea be infinitely wild, unsurveyed and unfathomed by us because unfathomable. We can never have enough of nature. We must be refreshed by the sight of inexhaustible vigor, vast and titanic features, the sea-coast with its wrecks, the wilderness with its living and its decaying trees, the thunder-cloud, and the rain which lasts three weeks and produces freshets. We need to witness our own limits transgressed, and some life pasturing freely where we never wander. We are cheered when we observe the vulture feeding on the carrion which disgusts and disheartens us, and deriving health and strength from the repast. There was a dead horse in the hollow by the path to my house, which compelled me sometimes to go out of my way, especially in the night when the air was heavy, but the assurance it gave me of the strong appetite and inviolable health of Nature was my compensation for this. I love to see that Nature is so rife with life that myriads can be afforded to be sacrificed and suffered to prey on one another; that tender organizations can be so serenely squashed out of existence like pulp,—tadpoles which herons gobble up, and tortoises and toads run over in the road; and that sometimes it has rained flesh and blood! With the liability to accident, we must see how little account is to be made of it. The impression made on a wise man is that of universal innocence. Poison is not poisonous after all, nor are any wounds fatal. Compassion is a very untenable ground. It must be expeditious. Its pleadings will not bear to be stereotyped.

Early in May, the oaks, hickories, maples, and other trees, just putting out amidst the pine woods around the pond, imparted a brightness like sunshine to the landscape, especially in cloudy days, as if the sun were breaking through mists and shining faintly on the hillsides here and there. On the third or fourth of May I saw a loon in the pond, and during the first week of the month I heard the whip-poor-will, the brown thrasher, the veery, the wood pewee, the chewink, and other birds. I had heard the wood thrush long before. The phoebe had already come once more and looked in at my door and window, to see if my house was cavern-like enough for her, sustaining herself on humming wings with clinched talons, as if she held by the air, while she surveyed the premises. The sulphur-like pollen of the pitch pine soon covered the pond and the stones and rotten wood along the shore, so that you could have collected a barrelful. This is the "sulphur showers" we hear of. Even in Calidas' drama of Sacontala,[21] we read of "rills dyed yellow with the golden dust of the lotus." And so the seasons went rolling on into summer, as one rambles into higher and higher grass.

Thus was my first year's life in the woods completed; and the second year was similar to it. I finally left Walden September 6th, 1847.

XVIII. CONCLUSION

To the sick the doctors wisely recommend a change of air and scenery. Thank Heaven, here is not all the world. The buckeye does not grow in

[21] Calidas (usually spelled "Kalidasa") was a fifth-century Hindu poet and dramatist. His *Sacontala* (usually spelled *Sakuntala*) was translated into English by Sir William Jones in 1789. The work became a favorite of the German and English Romantics and has been produced in modern times.

New England, and the mockingbird is rarely heard here. The wild goose is more of a cosmopolite than we; he breaks his fast in Canada, takes a luncheon in the Ohio, and plumes himself for the night in a southern bayou. Even the bison, to some extent, keeps pace with the seasons, cropping the pastures of the Colorado only till a greener and sweeter grass awaits him by the Yellowstone. Yet we think that if rail fences are pulled down, and stone walls piled up on our farms, bounds are henceforth set to our lives and our fates decided. If you are chosen town clerk, forsooth, you cannot go to Tierra del Fuego this summer: but you may go to the land of infernal fire nevertheless. The universe is wider than our views of it.

Yet we should oftener look over the tafferel[1] of our craft, like curious passengers, and not make the voyage like stupid sailors picking oakum. The other side of the globe is but the home of our correspondent. Our voyaging is only great-circle sailing,[2] and the doctors prescribe for diseases of the skin merely. One hastens to southern Africa to chase the giraffe; but surely that is not the game he would be after. How long, pray, would a man hunt giraffes if he could? Snipes and woodcocks also may afford rare sport; but I trust it would be nobler game to shoot one's self.—

> "Direct your eye right inward, and you'll find
> A thousand regions in your mind
> Yet undiscovered. Travel them, and be
> Expert in home-cosmography."[3]

What does Africa,—what does the West stand for? Is not our own interior white on the chart? black though it may prove, like the coast, when discovered. Is it the source of the Nile, or the Niger, or the Mississippi, or a Northwest Passage around this continent, that we would find? Are these the problems which most concern mankind? Is Franklin[4] the only man who is lost, that his wife should be so earnest to find him? Does Mr. Grinnell know where he himself is? Be rather the Mungo Park, the Lewis and Clark and Frobisher,[5] of your own streams and oceans; explore your own higher latitudes,—with shiploads of preserved meats to support you, if they be necessary; and pile the empty cans sky-high for a sign.[6] Were preserved meats invented to preserve meat merely? Nay, be a Columbus to whole new

[1] Taffrail, the rail around a ship's stern. "Oakum" is tarry fiber used to calk the seams in a ship's hull. "Picking oakum," or picking apart old rope for this purpose, was a tedious shipboard job.

[2] A "great circle" is the circle formed on the surface of a sphere by a plane which passes through the center of the sphere. In navigation, "great circle sailing" is following a course along an arc of a great circle and thus taking the most direct route. Thoreau's emphasis in this metaphor, however, is upon the correspondence between one point on a great circle and the opposite point.

[3] From "To My Honoured Friend, Sir. Ed. P. Knight," by William Habington (1605–1654). "Eye right" is changed from "eye-sight" in the original.

[4] "Franklin" is Sir John Franklin, the Arctic explorer whose men and two ships were lost in 1847–1848; "Grinnell" is Henry Grinnell, an American who financed an expedition to search for Franklin.

[5] Mungo Park was an eighteenth-century Scottish explorer of Africa; Meriwether Lewis and William Clark explored the American West in 1803–1806; Sir Martin Frobisher was a sixteenth-century English explorer of Canada.

[6] A pile of tin cans was one of the few traces ever found of the lost Franklin party.

continents and worlds within you, opening new channels, not of trade, but of thought. Every man is the lord of a realm beside which the earthly empire of the Czar is but a petty state, a hummock left by the ice. Yet some can be patriotic who have no *self-respect,* and sacrifice the greater to the less. They love the soil which makes their graves, but have no sympathy with the spirit which may still animate their clay. Patriotism is a maggot in their heads. What was the meaning of that South-Sea Exploring Expedition,[7] with all its parade and expense, but an indirect recognition of the fact that there are continents and seas in the moral world to which every man is an isthmus or an inlet, yet unexplored by him, but that it is easier to sail many thousand miles through cold and storm and cannibals, in a government ship, with five hundred men and boys to assist one, than it is to explore the private sea, the Atlantic and Pacific Ocean of one's being alone.—

> "Erret, et extremos alter scrutetur Iberos.
> Plus habet hic vitae, plus habet ille viae."

> Let them wander and scrutinize the outlandish Australians.
> I have more of God, they more of the road.[8]

It is not worth the while to go round the world to count the cats in Zanzibar.[9] Yet do this even till you can do better, and you may perhaps find some "Symmes' Hole"[10] by which to get at the inside at last. England and France, Spain and Portugal, Gold Coast and Slave Coast, all front on this private sea; but no bark from them has ventured out of sight of land, though it is without doubt the direct way to India. If you would learn to speak all tongues and conform to the customs of all nations, if you would travel farther than all travelers, be naturalized in all climes, and cause the Sphinx to dash her head against a stone,[11] even obey the precept of the old philosopher, and Explore thyself.[12] Herein are demanded the eye and the nerve. Only the defeated and deserters go to the wars, cowards that run away and enlist. Start now on that farthest western way, which does not pause at the Mississippi or the Pacific, nor conduct toward a worn-out China or Japan, but leads on direct, a tangent to this sphere, summer and winter, day and night, sun down, moon down, and at last earth down too.

It is said that Mirabeau[13] took to highway robbery "to ascertain what

[7] An expedition to explore Antarctica, led by Charles Wilkes in 1839–1842.

[8] From "The Old Man of Verona," by the Roman poet Claudian (d. 404?). Thoreau changes "Spaniards" *(Iberos)* to "Australians" and "of life" *(vitae)* to "of God."

[9] Zanzibar is an island off the east coast of Africa. Thoreau had read about "the cats in Zanzibar" in Charles Pickering's *The Races of Man* (1851), according to his journal.

[10] John Symmes wrote a pamphlet named "The Symmes Theory of Concentric Spheres, demonstrating that the earth is hollow, habitable, and widely open about the poles" (1818). Both Edgar Allan Poe and Jules Verne based fantasy stories on Symmes' peculiar theory.

[11] In Greek mythology, when Oedipus answered the Sphinx's riddle, she killed herself by dashing out her brains on a rock.

[12] An allusion to "Know thyself," the inscription above the Delphic Oracle in ancient Greece.

[13] The Count de Mirabeau (1749–1791) was a French revolutionist and statesman. Thoreau is quoting from an article about Mirabeau that appeared in *Harper's New Monthly.*

degree of resolution was necessary in order to place one's self in formal opposition to the most sacred laws of society." He declared that "a soldier who fights in the ranks does not require half so much courage as a foot-pad,"—"that honor and religion have never stood in the way of a well-considered and a firm resolve." This was manly, as the world goes; and yet it was idle, if not desperate. A saner man would have found himself often enough "in formal opposition" to what are deemed "the most sacred laws of society," through obedience to yet more sacred laws, and so have tested his resolution without going out of his way. It is not for a man to put himself in such an attitude to society, but to maintain himself in whatever attitude he find himself through obedience to the laws of his being, which will never be one of opposition to a just government, if he should chance to meet with such.

I left the woods for as good a reason as I went there. Perhaps it seemed to me that I had several more lives to live, and could not spare any more time for that one. It is remarkable how easily and insensibly we fall into a particular route, and make a beaten track for ourselves. I had not lived there a week before my feet wore a path from my door to the pond-side; and though it is five or six years since I trod it, it is still quite distinct. It is true, I fear, that others may have fallen into it, and so helped to keep it open. The surface of the earth is soft and impressible by the feet of men; and so with the paths which the mind travels. How worn and dusty, then, must be the highways of the world, how deep the ruts of tradition and conformity! I did not wish to take a cabin passage, but rather to go before the mast and on the deck of the world,[14] for there I could best see the moonlight amid the mountains. I do not wish to go below now.

I learned this, at least, by my experiment: that if one advances confidently in the direction of his dreams, and endeavors to live the life which he has imagined, he will meet with a success unexpected in common hours. He will put some things behind, will pass an invisible boundary; new, universal, and more liberal laws will begin to establish themselves around and within him; or the old laws be expanded, and interpreted in his favor in a more liberal sense, and he will live with the license of a higher order of beings. In proportion as he simplifies his life, the laws of the universe will appear less complex, and solitude will not be solitude, nor poverty poverty, nor weakness weakness. If you have built castles in the air, your work need not be lost; that is where they should be. Now put the foundations under them.

It is a ridiculous demand which England and America make, that you shall speak so that they can understand you. Neither men nor toadstools grow so. As if that were important, and there were not enough to understand you without them. As if Nature could support but one order of understandings, could not sustain birds as well as quadrupeds, flying as well as creeping things, and *hush* and *who,* which Bright can understand,[15] were

[14] To "go before the mast" is to sail as a common seaman; to "take a cabin passage" is to travel as a paying passenger (with, of course, a pun on "cabin").

[15] "Bright" was a common name for an ox; in driving oxen, "hush" means "go," and "who" means "stop."

the best English. As if there were safety in stupidity alone. I fear chiefly lest my expression may not be *extra-vagant*[16] enough, may not wander far enough beyond the narrow limits of my daily experience, so as to be adequate to the truth of which I have been convinced. *Extra vagance!* it depends on how you are yarded. The migrating buffalo, which seeks new pastures in another latitude, is not extravagant like the cow which kicks over the pail, leaps the cowyard fence, and runs after her calf, in milking time. I desire to speak somewhere *without* bounds; like a man in a waking moment, to men in their waking moments; for I am convinced that I cannot exaggerate enough even to lay the foundation of a true expression. Who that has heard a strain of music feared then lest he should speak extravagantly any more forever? In view of the future or possible, we should live quite laxly and undefined in front, our outlines dim and misty on that side; as our shadows reveal an insensible perspiration toward the sun. The volatile truth of our words should continually betray the inadequacy of the residual statement. Their truth is instantly *translated;* its literal monument alone remains. The words which express our faith and piety are not definite; yet they are significant and fragrant like frankincense to superior natures.

Why level downward to our dullest perception always, and praise that as common sense? The commonest sense is the sense of men asleep, which they express by snoring. Sometimes we are inclined to class those who are once-and-a-half-witted with the half-witted, because we appreciate only a third part of their wit. Some would find fault with the morning red, if they ever got up early enough. "They pretend," as I hear, "that the verses of Kabir have four different senses; illusion, spirit, intellect, and the exoteric doctrine of the Vedas";[17] but in this part of the world it is considered a ground for complaint if a man's writings admit of more than one interpretation. While England endeavors to cure the potato-rot, will not any endeavor to cure the brain-rot, which prevails so much more widely and fatally?

I do not suppose that I have attained to obscurity, but I should be proud if no more fatal fault were found with my pages on this score than was found with the Walden ice. Southern customers objected to its blue color, which is the evidence of its purity, as if it were muddy, and preferred the Cambridge ice, which is white, but tastes of weeds. The purity men love is like the mists which envelop the earth, and not like the azure ether beyond.

Some are dinning in our ears that we Americans, and moderns generally, are intellectual dwarfs compared with the ancients, or even the Elizabethan men. But what is that to the purpose? A living dog is better than a dead lion.[18] Shall a man go and hang himself because he belongs to the race of pygmies, and not be the biggest pygmy that he can? Let every one mind his own business, and endeavor to be what he was made.

[16] Thoreau divides the word to emphasize its root meaning: *extra* means "outside" and *vagari* means "to wander."

[17] Kabar was a fifteenth-century Indian mystic who attempted to reconcile the teachings of Hinduism and Islam. Thoreau is quoting from Garcin de Tassy, *History of Hindu Literature* (1839).

[18] Ecclesiastes 9:4.

Why should we be in such desperate haste to succeed and in such desperate enterprises? If a man does not keep pace with his companions, perhaps it is because he hears a different drummer. Let him step to the music which he hears, however measured or far away. It is not important that he should mature as soon as an apple tree or an oak. Shall he turn his spring into summer? If the condition of things which we were made for is not yet, what were any reality which we can substitute? We will not be shipwrecked on a vain reality. Shall we with pains erect a heaven of blue glass over ourselves, though when it is done we shall be sure to gaze still at the true ethereal heaven far above, as if the former were not?

There was an artist in the city of Kouroo who was disposed to strive after perfection.[19] One day it came into his mind to make a staff. Having considered that in an imperfect work time is an ingredient, but into a perfect work time does not enter, he said to himself, It shall be perfect in all respects, though I should do nothing else in my life. He proceeded instantly to the forest for wood, being resolved that it should not be made of unsuitable material; and as he searched for and rejected stick after stick, his friends gradually deserted him, for they grew old in their works and died, but he grew not older by a moment. His singleness of purpose and resolution, and his elevated piety, endowed him, without his knowledge, with perennial youth. As he made no compromise with Time, Time kept out of his way, and only sighed at a distance because he could not overcome him. Before he had found a stock in all respects suitable the city of Kouroo was a hoary ruin, and he sat on one of its mounds to peel the stick. Before he had given it the proper shape the dynasty of the Candahars was at an end, and with the point of the stick he wrote the name of the last of that race in the sand, and then resumed his work. By the time he had smoothed and polished the staff Kalpa was no longer the pole-star; and ere he had put on the ferule and the head adorned with precious stones, Brahma had awoke and slumbered many times. But why do I stay to mention these things? When the finishing stroke was put to his work, it suddenly expanded before the eyes of the astonished artist into the fairest of all the creations of Brahma. He had made a new system in making a staff, a world with full and fair proportions; in which, though the old cities and dynasties had passed away, fairer and more glorious ones had taken their places. And now he saw by the heap of shavings still fresh at his feet, that, for him and his work, the former lapse of time had been an illusion, and that no more time had elapsed than is required for a single scintillation from the brain of Brahma to fall on and inflame the tinder of a mortal brain. The material was pure, and his art was pure; how could the result be other than wonderful?

No face which we can give to a matter will stead us so well at last as the truth. This alone wears well. For the most part, we are not where we are, but in a false position. Through an infirmity of our natures, we suppose a case, and put ourselves into it, and hence are in two cases at the same time, and it is doubly difficult to get out. In sane moments we regard only the facts, the case that is. Say what you have to say, not what you ought. Any truth is better than make-believe. Tom Hyde, the tinker, standing on the

[19] No source has been discovered for this "legend," and Thoreau probably invented it.

gallows, was asked if he had anything to say. "Tell the tailors," said he, "to remember to make a knot in their thread before they take the first stitch." His companion's prayer is forgotten.

However mean your life is, meet it and live it; do not shun it and call it hard names. It is not so bad as you are. It looks poorest when you are richest. The fault-finder will find faults even in paradise. Love your life, poor as it is. You may perhaps have some pleasant, thrilling, glorious hours, even in a poor-house. The setting sun is reflected from the windows of the alms-house as brightly as from the rich man's abode; the snow melts before its door as early in the spring. I do not see but a quiet mind may live as contentedly there, and have as cheering thoughts, as in a palace. The town's poor seem to me often to live the most independent lives of any. Maybe they are simply great enough to receive without misgiving. Most think that they are above being supported by the town; but it oftener happens that they are not above supporting themselves by dishonest means, which should be more disreputable. Cultivate poverty like a garden herb, like sage. Do not trouble yourself much to get new things, whether clothes or friends. Turn the old; return to them. Things do not change; we change. Sell your clothes and keep your thoughts. God will see that you do not want society. If I were confined to a corner of a garret all my days, like a spider, the world would be just as large to me while I had my thoughts about me. The philosopher said: "From an army of three divisions one can take away its general, and put it in disorder; from the man the most abject and vulgar one cannot take away his thought."[20] Do not seek so anxiously to be developed, to subject yourself to many influences to be played on; it is all dissipation. Humility like darkness reveals the heavenly lights. The shadows of poverty and meanness gather around us, "and lo! creation widens to our view."[21] We are often reminded that if there were bestowed on us the wealth of Croesus,[22] our aims must still be the same, and our means essentially the same. Moreover, if you are restricted in your range by poverty, if you cannot buy books and newspapers, for instance, you are but confined to the most significant and vital experiences; you are compelled to deal with the material which yields the most sugar and the most starch. It is life near the bone where it is sweetest.[23] You are defended from being a trifler. No man loses ever on a lower level by magnanimity on a higher. Superfluous wealth can buy superfluities only. Money is not required to buy one necessary of the soul.

I live in the angle of a leaden wall, into whose composition was poured a little alloy of bell-metal. Often, in the repose of my mid-day, there reaches my ears a confused *tintinnabulum* from without. It is the noise of my contemporaries. My neighbors tell me of their adventures with famous gentlemen and ladies, what notabilities they met at the dinner-table; but I am no more interested in such things than in the contents of the Daily Times. The interest and the conversation are about costume and manners chiefly; but a

[20] The philosopher is Confucius.

[21] Paraphrase of a line from a sonnet named "To Night," by Joseph Blanco White (1775–1841).

[22] Croesus was a king of ancient Lydia who became legendary for his great wealth.

[23] Thoreau is varying the old proverb, "The nearer the bone, the sweeter the meat."

goose is a goose still, dress it as you will. They tell me of California and Texas, of England and the Indies, of the Hon. Mr.—— of Georgia[24] or Massachusetts, all transient and fleeting phenomena, till I am ready to leap from their court-yard like the Mameluke bey.[25] I delight to come to my bearings,—not walk in procession with pomp and parade, in a conspicuous place, but to walk even with the Builder of the universe, if I may,—not to live in this restless, nervous, bustling, trivial Nineteenth Century, but stand or sit thoughtfully while it goes by. What are men celebrating? They are all on a committee of arrangements, and hourly expect a speech from somebody. God is only the president of the day, and Webster[26] is his orator. I love to weigh, to settle, to gravitate toward that which most strongly and rightfully attracts me,—not hang by the beam of the scale and try to weigh less,—not suppose a case, but take the case that is; to travel the only path I can, and that on which no power can resist me. It affords me no satisfaction to commence to spring an arch before I have got a solid foundation. Let us not play at kittly-benders.[27] There is a solid bottom everywhere. We read that the traveler asked the boy if the swamp before him had a hard bottom. The boy replied that it had. But presently the traveler's horse sank in up to the girths, and he observed to the boy, "I thought you said that this bog had a hard bottom." "So it has," answered the latter, "but you have not got half way to it yet." So it is with the bogs and quicksands of society; but he is an old boy that knows it. Only what is thought, said, or done at a certain rare coincidence is good. I would not be one of those who will foolishly drive a nail into mere lath and plastering; such a deed would keep me awake nights. Give me a hammer, and let me feel for the furring.[28] Do not depend on the putty. Drive a nail home and clinch it so faithfully that you can wake up in the night and think of your work with satisfaction,—a work at which you would not be ashamed to invoke the Muse. So will help you God, and so only. Every nail driven should be as another rivet in the machine of the universe, you carrying on the work.

Rather than love, than money, than fame, give me truth. I sat at a table where were rich food and wine in abundance, an obsequious attendance, but sincerity and truth were not; and I went away hungry from the inhospitable board. The hospitality was as cold as the ices. I thought that there was no need of ice to freeze them. They talked to me of the age of the wine and the fame of the vintage; but I thought of an older, a newer, and purer wine, of a more glorious vintage, which they had not got, and could not buy. The style, the house and grounds and "entertainment" pass for nothing with me. I called on the king, but he made me wait in his hall, and conducted like a man incapacitated for hospitality. There was a man in my

[24] Thoreau probably had in mind Robert A. Toombs, prominent Congressman, later Senator, from Georgia.

[25] The Mamelukes were an Egyptian military caste. One bey escaped a massacre in 1811 by leaping from the walls of the citadel at Cairo onto his horse.

[26] Daniel Webster (1782–1852). Thoreau is ironic in referring to him as "God's orator," since Webster had alienated the antislavery forces by sponsoring the Compromise of 1850, which among other provisions required Northern states to return escaped slaves to the South.

[27] "Kittly-benders" was a game which involved running or sliding over dangerously thin ice.

[28] Wall studs.

neighborhood who lived in a hollow tree. His manners were truly regal. I should have done better had I called on him.

How long shall we sit in our porticoes practicing idle and musty virtues, which any work would make impertinent? As if one were to begin the day with long-suffering, and hire a man to hoe his potatoes; and in the afternoon go forth to practice Christian meekness and charity with goodness aforethought! Consider the China pride and stagnant self-complacency of mankind. This generation inclines a little to congratulate itself on being the last of an illustrious line; and in Boston and London and Paris and Rome, thinking of its long descent, it speaks of its progress in art and science and literature with satisfaction. There are the Records of the Philosophical Societies, and the public Eulogies of *Great Men!* It is the good Adam contemplating his own virtue. "Yes, we have done great deeds, and sung divine songs, which shall never die,"—that is, as long as *we* can remember them. The learned societies and great men of Assyria,—where are they? What youthful philosophers and experimentalists we are! There is not one of my readers who has yet lived a whole human life. These may be but the spring months in the life of the race. If we have had the seven-years' itch, we have not seen the seventeen-year locust yet in Concord. We are acquainted with a mere pellicle[29] of the globe on which we live. Most have not delved six feet beneath the surface, nor leaped as many above it. We know not where we are. Beside, we are sound asleep nearly half our time. Yet we esteem ourselves wise, and have an established order on the surface. Truly, we are deep thinkers, we are ambitious spirits! As I stand over the insect crawling amid the pine needles on the forest floor, and endeavoring to conceal itself from my sight, and ask myself why it will cherish those humble thoughts, and hide its head from me who might, perhaps, be its benefactor, and impart to its race some cheering information, I am reminded of the greater Benefactor and Intelligence that stands over me the human insect.

There is an incessant influx of novelty into the world, and yet we tolerate incredible dullness. I need only suggest what kind of sermons are still listened to in the most enlightened countries. There are such words as joy and sorrow, but they are only the burden of a psalm, sung with a nasal twang, while we believe in the ordinary and mean. We think that we can change our clothes only. It is said that the British Empire is very large and respectable, and that the United States are a first-rate power. We do not believe that a tide rises and falls behind every man which can float the British Empire like a chip, if he should ever harbor it in his mind. Who knows what sort of seventeen-year locust will next come out of the ground? The government of the world I live in was not framed, like that of Britain, in after-dinner conversations over the wine.

The life in us is like the water in the river. It may rise this year higher than man has ever known it, and flood the parched uplands; even this may be the eventful year, which will drown out all our muskrats. It was not always dry land where we dwell. I see far inland the banks which the stream anciently washed, before science began to record its freshets. Everyone has heard the story which has gone the rounds of New England, of a strong and beautiful bug which came out of the dry leaf of an old table of apple-

[29] Skin.

tree wood, which had stood in a farmer's kitchen for sixty years, first in Connecticut, and afterward in Massachusetts,—from an egg deposited in the living tree many years earlier still, as appeared by counting the annual layers beyond it; which was heard gnawing out for several weeks, hatched perchance by the heat of an urn. Who does not feel his faith in a resurrection and immortality strengthened by hearing of this? Who knows what beautiful and winged life, whose egg has been buried for ages under many concentric layers of woodenness in the dead dry life of society, deposited at first in the alburnum of the green and living tree, which has been gradually converted into the semblance of its well-seasoned tomb,—heard perchance gnawing out now for years by the astonished family of man, as they sat round the festive board,—may unexpectedly come forth from amidst society's most trivial and handselled[30] furniture, to enjoy its perfect summer life at last!

I do not say that John or Jonathan[31] will realize all this; but such is the character of that morrow which mere lapse of time can never make to dawn. The light which puts out our eyes is darkness to us. Only that day dawns to which we are awake. There is more day to dawn. The sun is but a morning star.

[30] Cheap, shoddy.
[31] John Bull and the Yankee Jonathan, common names for Englishmen and Americans.

Walt Whitman

(1819–1892)

Among the great archetypal heroes of nineteenth-century Romanticism—Blake's Albion, Goethe's Faust, Byron's haunted protagonists—surely one of the most appealing and suggestive embodies both the exuberant individualism of Romanticism in general and the optimistic expansionism of America's Westward Movement in particular. His name was "Walt," and he was the self-conscious and deliberate creation of a New York printer and journalist named Walt Whitman. Whitman's literary persona—"an American, one of the roughs, a kosmos"—first appeared in 1855 with the initial publication of Leaves of Grass *and continued to develop over the next four decades, through eight more editions, as Whitman amplified and refined the book that was "an attempt . . . of a naïve, masculine, affectionate, contemplative, sensual, imperious person to cast into literature not only his own grit and arrogance, but his own flesh and form, undraped, regardless of all models, regardless of modesty or law; and ignorant, as at first it appears, of . . . all outside of the fiercely loved land of his birth."*

The Brooklyn of the 1830's and 1840's is preserved in Whitman's poetry as the Dublin of 1904 is preserved in Joyce's work or rural Mississippi is in Faulkner's. "Remember," Whitman told a friend late in life, "the book arose out of my life in

Brooklyn and New York from 1838 to 1853, absorbing a million people, for fifteen years, with an intimacy, an eagerness, an abandon, probably never equalled."

Whitman was born on Long Island in 1819; when he was not quite five, the family moved to what was then the small town of Brooklyn, where the father set up a carpentry shop. The peaceful woods and beaches of Long Island and the hustle and bustle of Brooklyn and of New York, just up the bay, were to figure equally in Whitman's memories of his youth and in his poetry. He left school when he was eleven and became an office boy for a lawyer and a doctor and then an apprentice to a printer. By the time he was seventeen, he was a fully qualified compositor, also working from time to time as a country schoolteacher. Printing led into journalism, and for about twelve years, from the time he was nineteen until he was thirty-one, he was caught up in the daily pressures of newspaper work, churning out news stories, editorials, some rather conventional poetry and fictional sketches, and even a hack-work temperance novel named Franklin Evans *(1842). Whitman's journalism culminated in his two-year editorship (1846–48) of the prosperous Brooklyn* Daily Eagle, *a job he lost because of his liberal politics. When the job on the* Eagle *ended, he made a three-month trip to New Orleans as an editor of the* Daily Crescent; *on the way, he also visited Chicago and the Midwest.*

The trip to New Orleans coincided with, if it did not trigger, a remarkable change in Whitman's personality and public identity. Until then, he had been something of a dandy in his dress; he had led the life of a city newspaperman on the fringes of the bohemian artistic circles of New York; and his style had been slick, conventional, and journalistic. Now, at the age of thirty-one, he began to wear workman's clothes, he grew a full beard, and, as his notebooks show, he began to conceive of himself as a potential bard and prophet of an ideal America and to forge a new poetic style to express this role. Over the next few years, he accepted some journalistic assignments, but his main energies went into the preparation of the first edition of Leaves of Grass, *which he published himself in 1855.*

The first, 1855 version of Leaves of Grass *contained a long preface in which Whitman proclaimed that "The United States themselves are essentially the greatest poem," and called for a new race of poets and a new kind of poetry adequate to express the inherent poetic content of America. It also contained "Song of Myself" and eleven shorter poems. The initial impact of the book did not appear in sales, which were very small, but in a series of reviews, which Whitman carefully arranged. A few reviewers were shocked and repelled by the unconventionality of the poetry and the book's frank egotism and explicit sexuality. But there were also some reviews, in both America and England, which recognized the book's importance. The Concord transcendentalists, especially, praised the book, and Emerson, to whom Whitman sent a copy, responded quickly with a remarkable letter to Whitman in which he said, "I give you joy of your free & brave thought. I have great joy in it. I find incomparable things said incomparably well, as they must be. . . . I greet you at the beginning of a great career, which yet must have had a long foreground somewhere, for such a start." Henry David Thoreau and Bronson Alcott, too, liked the book and made pilgrimages to Brooklyn to visit Whitman later that year; Emerson followed in 1856.*

The rest of Whitman's life was devoted primarily to producing further editions of Leaves of Grass, *each with added poems and revisions and rearrangements of earlier ones. The book thus took on a living, organic quality, as its title suggested, growing and evolving along with its creator. A second edition appeared quickly, in 1856, and eight further editions were printed at regular intervals until Whitman's death in 1892. The general direction of the revisions of* Leaves of Grass *was away from the immediate, personal, erotic emphasis of the first edition and toward the development of the "Walt" figure as a more generalized, sage-like, public embodiment of democratic man. The Civil War poems called "Drum Taps" were added in the 1867 edition, and the long "Passage to India," which used the opening of the Suez Canal as the occasion to celebrate both scientific progress and a spiritual progress to "more than India," first appeared in the edition of 1876.*

The Civil War affected Whitman deeply. His initial response was exhilaration, as in the poem "Beat! Beat! Drums!" But as the war wore on, he became more and more touched by the personal suffering of the soldiers. In 1862, he went to the front in Virginia to seek his brother George, who had been reported wounded. He remained in Washington for the rest of the war, working as a volunteer among the wounded in military hospitals, raising money for his efforts by writing war correspondence for New York and Brooklyn papers. Both his experiences with the casualties of the war and the assassination of Lincoln perhaps are responsible for a richer, more tragic tone which enters his later poetry.

After the war, Whitman worked as a clerk in government offices in Washington, first in the Department of the Interior, from which he was dismissed when it was discovered that he had written an "indecent book," and later in the office of the Attorney General. He suffered a serious paralytic stroke in 1873 and left Washington for Camden, New Jersey, where he remained, with some intervals away, for the rest of his life, frail and in ill health but revered by what amounted to a cult of worldwide admirers and followers. He died in 1892.

As Emerson shrewdly surmised in 1855, what at first seemed like a startling new voice in American poetry had "a long foreground." Part of that foreground was Emerson himself. Whitman's intensive self-education during his newspaper years had included a close reading of Emerson's essays, and the 1855 Leaves of Grass *was a "transcendental" work, in the broadest sense of that term. For Whitman, as for Emerson, the individual stood at the center of his own universe and he arrived at understanding not through received doctrines but through ecstatic and intuitive communion with a universe harmonious with his own soul. Whitman's Walt, like Emerson's American scholar, celebrates the continuous re-creation of the world in the imagination of each individual, the intuition of "a world primal again." There were other roots, too, for Whitman's joyous and genial individualism, including the Jacksonian political ideas of his carpenter father and the Quakerism of his mother's family.*

But Whitman was not just putting new American wine into old Romantic bottles. His vision of America grew less out of tradition than out of "loafing" and "inviting his soul," as he contemplated himself and his relation to the restless, hustling, Westward-moving America in which he grew up. For all his kinship with the New England transcendentalists, he is as different from them as New York is from Concord. For all their love of the natural world, Emerson and Thoreau were both nervous about the flesh; the carnal was always a steppingstone to the spiritual. Whitman had no such nervousness: "I find no sweeter fat than sticks to my own bones," he declared. And while the transcendentalists were at best ambivalent about the crude energies of a rapidly expanding America, Whitman embraced them without reserve, loving "the blab of the pave" and America at work as much as the ponds and woods and America in contemplation.

The early, energetic "Song of Myself" is at once a series of fifty-two independent lyrics and a sustained, gradually unfolding narrative, "epic" in its own eccentric way. The speaker is an infinitely protean character, becoming everybody everywhere, in a pose that is at once a triumph of imaginative identification and a quick-change vaudeville act. But if Walt "leaks out into the universe," as D. H. Lawrence put it, it is not at the expense of his own memorable identity. He is comically egotistical (saying, tongue firmly in cheek, "I dote on myself, there is that lot of me and all so luscious"), hungry to incorporate all experience, humble or exalted, male or female, minute or cosmic, spiritual or carnal. He is at once the act and the observer of the act: "My hurts turn livid upon me as I lean on a cane and observe." He can observe the particular and at the same time maintain the distance to see the "form, union, plan" of life.

The verse form of this remarkable poem strikes a similar balance between fluidity and form. Whitman abandons the traditional meters of English verse in favor of a rhythmical "free verse," in which the rhetorical phrase, rather than the foot, becomes the basic unit, and the verse is given shape by such rhetorical devices as parallelism and repetition. The result is a highly oral style, reminiscent not only of the King James version of the Bible, but also of the high rhetoric of the nineteenth-century stage and the operatic arias Whitman admired so much.

"When Lilacs Last in the Dooryard Bloom'd" reveals a different Whitman voice, equally comprehensive in its imaginative range, but with a deeper, richer music. This meditation on the death of Lincoln, for all its apparently free-associational spontaneity, is a carefully structured development of the triple images of lilac, star, and bird. Like such great predecessors in the poetic elegy as Milton's "Lycidas" and Shelley's "Adonais," the poem focuses not so much upon the person mourned as upon the sensibility of the mourner as he struggles to find meaning in the painful death and to come to terms with his grief.

Whitman is one of the great risk-takers of poetry. By daring such flamboyance and extravagance, he risks becoming merely absurd (a risk that sometimes becomes a reality). But at his exuberant best, he has been a continuing delight to readers (especially those with a sense of humor) and a continuing model for much of what is most daring and exciting in modern poetry.

FURTHER READING *(prepared by W. J. R.):* Gay Wilson Allen has written two different accounts of Whitman's life: *Solitary Singer: A Critical Biography of Walt Whitman,* 1955, rev. 1967, is a full-length work which takes an integrative approach to Whitman's life and work; *Walt Whitman,* 1969, is intended for the nonspecialist. This short biographical sketch is heavily illustrated and has a section of selected criticism. Richard Chase's *Walt Whitman Reconsidered,* 1955, examines the major works and compares Whitman with other writers. Another book by Gay Wilson Allen, the *Walt Whitman Handbook,* 1962, is a valuable guide for the new reader of Whitman. Allen discusses Whitman's prose and the techniques of *Leaves of Grass,* and evaluates a good deal of Whitman criticism. An introductory work focusing on *Leaves of Grass* is James E. Miller, Jr.'s, *A Critical Guide to "Leaves of Grass,"* 1957. Miller emphasizes the structure of Whitman's poetry, discussing several major works other than *Leaves of Grass* before attempting to define a comprehensive structure for Whitman's masterpiece. *Whitman: A Collection of Critical Essays,* ed. Roy Harvey Pearce, 1962, contains fourteen essays by leading critics, with a section devoted to *Leaves of Grass.*

SONG OF MYSELF

1

I celebrate myself, and sing myself,
And what I assume you shall assume,
For every atom belonging to me as good belongs to you.

I loafe and invite my soul,
I lean and loafe at my ease observing a spear of summer grass.

My tongue, every atom of my blood, form'd from this soil, this air,
Born here of parents born here from parents the same, and their parents the same,
I, now thirty-seven years old in perfect health begin,
Hoping to cease not till death.

Creeds and schools in abeyance,
Retiring back a while sufficed at what they are, but never forgotten,
I harbor for good or bad, I permit to speak at every hazard,
Nature without check with original energy.

2

Houses and rooms are full of perfumes, the shelves are crowded with perfumes,
I breathe the fragrance myself and know it and like it,
The distillation would intoxicate me also, but I shall not let it.

The atmosphere is not a perfume, it has no taste of the distillation, it is odorless,
It is for my mouth forever, I am in love with it,
I will go to the bank by the wood and become undisguised and naked,
I am mad for it to be in contact with me.

The smoke of my own breath,
Echoes, ripples, buzz'd whispers, love-root, silk-thread, crotch and vine,
My respiration and inspiration, the beating of my heart, the passing of blood and air through my lungs,
The sniff of green leaves and dry leaves, and of the shore and dark-color'd sea-rocks, and of hay in the barn,
The sound of the belch'd words of my voice loos'd to the eddies of the wind,
A few light kisses, a few embraces, a reaching around of arms,
The play of shine and shade on the trees as the supple boughs wag,
The delight alone or in the rush of the streets, or along the fields and hill-sides,
The feeling of health, the full-noon trill, the song of me rising from bed and meeting the sun.

Have you reckon'd a thousand acres much? have you reckon'd the
earth much?
Have you practis'd so long to learn to read?
Have you felt so proud to get at the meaning of poems?

Stop this day and night with me and you shall possess the origin of all
poems,
You shall possess the good of the earth and sun, (there are millions of
suns left,)
You shall no longer take things at second or third hand, nor look
through the eyes of the dead, nor feed on the spectres in books,
You shall not look through my eyes either, nor take things from me,
You shall listen to all sides and filter them from your self.

3

I have heard what the talkers were talking, the talk of the beginning
and the end,
But I do not talk of the beginning or the end.

There was never any more inception than there is now,
Nor any more youth or age than there is now,
And will never be any more perfection than there is now,
Nor any more heaven or hell than there is now.

Urge and urge and urge,
Always the procreant urge of the world.

Out of the dimness opposite equals advance, always substance and
increase, always sex,
Always a knit of identity, always distinction, always a breed of life.

To elaborate is no avail, learn'd and unlearn'd feel that it is so.

Sure as the most certain sure, plumb in the uprights, well entretied,[1]
braced in the beams,
Stout as a horse, affectionate, haughty, electrical,
I and this mystery here we stand.

Clear and sweet is my soul, and clear and sweet is all that is not my
soul.

Lack one lacks both, and the unseen is proved by the seen,
Till that becomes unseen and receives proof in its turn.

Showing the best and dividing it from the worst age vexes age,
Knowing the perfect fitness and equanimity of things, while they discuss I am silent, and go bathe and admire myself.

[1]Supported (a term in carpentry).

Welcome is every organ and attribute of me, and of any man hearty and clean,
Not an inch nor a particle of an inch is vile, and none shall be less familiar than the rest.

I am satisfied—I see, dance, laugh, sing;
As the hugging and loving bed-fellow sleeps at my side through the night, and withdraws at the peep of the day with stealthy tread,
Leaving me baskets cover'd with white towels swelling the house with their plenty,
Shall I postpone my acceptation and realization and scream at my eyes,
That they turn from gazing after and down the road,
And forthwith cipher and show me to a cent,
Exactly the value of one and exactly the value of two, and which is ahead?

4

Trippers and askers[2] surround me.
People I meet, the effect upon me of my early life or the ward and city I live in, or the nation,
The latest dates, discoveries, inventions, societies, authors old and new,
My dinner, dress, associates, looks, compliments, dues,
The real or fancied indifference of some man or woman I love,
The sickness of one of my folks or of myself, or ill-doing or loss or lack of money, or depressions or exaltations,
Battles, the horrors of fratricidal war, the fever of doubtful news, the fitful events;
These come to me days and nights and go from me again,
But they are not the Me myself.

Apart from the pulling and hauling stands what I am,
Stands amused, complacent, compassionating, idle, unitary,
Looks down, is erect, or bends an arm on an impalpable certain rest,
Looking with side-curved head curious what will come next,
Both in and out of the game and watching and wondering at it.

Backward I see in my own days where I sweated through fog with linguists and contenders,
I have no mockings or arguments, I witness and wait.

5

I believe in you my soul, the other I am must not abase itself to you,
And you must not be abased to the other.

Loafe with me on the grass, loose the stop from your throat,

[2] Travelers and beggars.

Not words, not music or rhyme I want, not custom or lecture, not
even the best,
Only the lull I like, the hum of your valvèd voice.

I mind how once we lay such a transparent summer morning,
How you settled your head athwart my hips and gently turn'd over
upon me,
And parted the shirt from my bosom-bone, and plunged your tongue
to my bare-stript heart,
And reach'd till you felt my beard, and reach'd till you held my feet.

Swiftly arose and spread around me the peace and knowledge that
pass all the argument of the earth,
And I know that the hand of God is the promise of my own,
And I know that the spirit of God is the brother of my own,
And that all the men ever born are also my brothers, and the women
my sisters and lovers,
And that a kelson[3] of the creation is love,
And limitless are leaves stiff or drooping in the fields,
And brown ants in the little wells beneath them,
And mossy scabs of the worm fence,[4] heap'd stones, elder, mullein
and poke-weed.

6

A child said *What is the grass?* fetching it to me with full hands;
How could I answer the child? I do not know what it is any more
than he.

I guess it must be the flag of my disposition, out of hopeful green
stuff woven.

Or I guess it is the handkerchief of the Lord,
A scented gift and remembrancer designedly dropt,
Bearing the owner's name someway in the corners, that we may see
and remark, and say *Whose?*

Or I guess the grass is itself a child, the produced babe of the
vegetation.

Or I guess it is a uniform hieroglyphic,
And it means, Sprouting alike in broad zones and narrow zones,
Growing among black folks as among white,
Kanuck, Tuckahoe, Congressman, Cuff,[5] I give them the same, I
receive them the same.

[3] Keelson, the line of timbers or iron plates that brace the keel of a ship.
[4] A zigzag, rail fence.
[5] A "Kanuck" (Canuck) is a French-Canadian. A "Tuckahoe" is a poor Southern white, presumed to live on "tuckahoe," a common fungus. "Cuff" is short for "Cuffy," a local nickname for a Negro.

And now it seems to me the beautiful uncut hair of graves.

Tenderly will I use you curling grass,
It may be you transpire from the breasts of young men,
It may be if I had known them I would have loved them,
It may be you are from old people, or from offspring taken soon out of their mothers' laps,
And here you are the mothers' laps.

This grass is very dark to be from the white heads of old mothers,
Darker than the colorless beards of old men,
Dark to come from under the faint red roofs of mouths.

O I perceive after all so many uttering tongues,
And I perceive they do not come from the roofs of mouths for nothing.

I wish I could translate the hints about the dead young men and women,
And the hints about old men and mothers, and the offspring taken soon out of their laps.

What do you think has become of the young and old men?
And what do you think has become of the women and children?

They are alive and well somewhere,
The smallest sprout shows there is really no death,
And if ever there was it led forward life, and does not wait at the end to arrest it,
And ceas'd the moment life appear'd.

All goes onward and outward, nothing collapses,
And to die is different from what any one supposed, and luckier.

7

Has any one supposed it lucky to be born?
I hasten to inform him or her it is just as lucky to die, and I know it.

I pass death with the dying and birth with the new-wash'd babe, and am not contain'd between my hat and boots,
And peruse manifold objects, no two alike and every one good,
The earth good and the stars good, and their adjuncts all good.

I am not an earth nor an adjunct of an earth,
I am the mate and companion of people, all just as immortal and fathomless as myself,
(They do not know how immortal, but I know.)

Every kind for itself and its own, for me mine male and female,
For me those that have been boys and that love women,

For me the man that is proud and feels how it stings to be slighted,
For me the sweet-heart and the old maid, for me mothers and the mothers of mothers,
For me lips that have smiled, eyes that have shed tears,
For me children and the begetters of children.

Undrape! you are not guilty to me, nor stale nor discarded,
I see through the broadcloth and gingham whether or no,
And am around, tenacious, acquisitive, tireless, and cannot be shaken away.

8

The little one sleeps in its cradle,
I lift the gauze and look a long time, and silently brush away flies with my hand.

The youngster and the red-faced girl turn aside up the bushy hill,
I peeringly view them from the top.

The suicide sprawls on the bloody floor of the bedroom,
I witness the corpse with its dabbled hair, I note where the pistol has fallen.

The blab of the pave,[6] tires of carts, sluff of boot-soles, talk of the promenaders,
The heavy omnibus, the driver with his interrogating thumb, the clank of the shod horses on the granite floor,
The snow-sleighs, clinking, shouted jokes, pelts of snow-balls,
The hurrahs for popular favorites, the fury of rous'd mobs,
The flap of the curtain'd litter, a sick man inside borne to the hospital,
The meeting of enemies, the sudden oath, the blows and fall,
The excited crowd, the policeman with his star quickly working his passage to the centre of the crowd,
The impassive stones that receive and return so many echoes,
What groans of over-fed or half-starv'd who fall sunstruck or in fits,
What exclamations of women taken suddenly who hurry home and give birth to babes,
What living and buried speech is always vibrating here, what howls restrain'd by decorum,
Arrests of criminals, slights, adulterous offers made, acceptances, rejections with convex lips,
I mind them or the show or resonance of them—I come and I depart.

9

The big doors of the country barn stand open and ready,
The dried grass of the harvest-time loads the slow-drawn wagon,
The clear light plays on the brown gray and green intertinged,

[6] Talk of the streets.

The armfuls are pack'd to the sagging mow.

I am there, I help, I came stretch'd atop of the load,
I felt its soft jolts, one leg reclined on the other,
I jump from the cross-beams and seize the clover and timothy,
And roll head over heels and tangle my hair full of wisps.

10

Alone far in the wilds and mountains I hunt,
Wandering amazed at my own lightness and glee,
In the late afternoon choosing a safe spot to pass the night,
Kindling a fire and broiling the fresh-kill'd game,
Falling asleep on the gather'd leaves with my dog and gun by my side.

The Yankee clipper is under her sky-sails, she cuts the sparkle and scud,[7]
My eyes settle the land, I bend at her prow or shout joyously from the deck.

The boatmen and clam-diggers arose early and stopt for me,
I tuck'd my trowser-ends in my boots and went and had a good time;
You should have been with us that day round the chowder-kettle.

I saw the marriage of the trapper in the open air in the far west, the bride was a red girl,
Her father and his friends sat near cross-legged and dumbly smoking, they had moccasins to their feet and large thick blankets hanging from their shoulders,
On a bank lounged the trapper, he was drest mostly in skins, his luxuriant beard and curls protected his neck, he held his bride by the hand,
She had long eyelashes, her head was bare, her coarse straight locks descended upon her voluptuous limbs and reach'd to her feet.

The runaway slave came to my house and stopt outside,
I heard his motions crackling the twigs of the woodpile,
Through the swung half-door of the kitchen I saw him, limpsy[8] and weak,
And went where he sat on a log and led him in and assured him,
And brought water and fill'd a tub for his sweated body and bruis'd feet,
And gave him a room that enter'd from my own, and gave him some coarse clean clothes,
And remember perfectly well his revolving eyes and his awkwardness,
And remember putting plasters on the galls of his neck and ankles;
He staid with me a week before he was recuperated and pass'd north,
I had him sit next me at table, my fire-lock[9] lean'd in the corner.

[7] Wind-driven spray. [8] Limp. [9] Flintlock musket.

11

Twenty-eight young men bathe by the shore,
Twenty-eight young men and all so friendly;
Twenty-eight years of womanly life and all so lonesome.

She owns the fine house by the rise of the bank,
She hides handsome and richly drest aft the blinds of the window.

Which of the young men does she like the best?
Ah the homeliest of them is beautiful to her.

Where are you off to, lady? for I see you,
You splash in the water there, yet stay stock still in your room.

Dancing and laughing along the beach came the twenty-ninth bather,
The rest did not see her, but she saw them and loved them.

The beards of the young men glisten'd with wet, it ran from their long
 hair,
Little streams pass'd all over their bodies.

An unseen hand also pass'd over their bodies,
It descended tremblingly from their temples and ribs.

The young men float on their backs, their white bellies bulge to the
 sun, they do not ask who seizes fast to them,
They do not know who puffs and declines with pendant and bending
 arch,
They do not think whom they souse with spray.

12

The butcher-boy puts off his killing-clothes, or sharpens his knife at
 the stall in the market,
I loiter enjoying his repartee and his shuffle and break-down.[10]

Blacksmiths with grimed and hairy chests environ the anvil,
Each has his main-sledge, they are all out, there is a great heat in
 the fire.

From the cinder-strew'd threshold I follow their movements,
The lithe sheer[11] of their waists plays even with their massive arms,
Overhand the hammers swing, overhand so slow, overhand so sure,
They do not hasten, each man hits in his place.

13

The negro holds firmly the reins of his four horses, the block swags[12]
 underneath on its tied-over chain,

[10] Folk dances. [11] Curve (a nautical term). [12] Hangs heavily.

The negro that drives the long dray[13] of the stone-yard, steady and tall he stands pois'd on one leg on the string-piece,[14]
His blue shirt exposes his ample neck and breast and loosens over his hip-band,
His glance is calm and commanding, he tosses the slouch of his hat away from his forehead,
The sun falls on his crispy hair and mustache, falls on the black of his polish'd and perfect limbs.

I behold the picturesque giant and love him, and I do not stop there,
I go with the team also.

In me the caresser of life wherever moving, backward as well as forward sluing,[15]
To niches aside and junior bending, not a person or object missing,
Absorbing all to myself and for this song.

Oxen that rattle the yoke and chain or halt in the leafy shade, what is that you express in your eyes?
It seems to me more than all the print I have read in my life.

My tread scares the wood-drake and wood-duck on my distant and day-long ramble,
They rise together, they slowly circle around.

I believe in those wing'd purposes,
And acknowledge red, yellow, white, playing within me,
And consider green and violet and the tufted crown intentional,
And do not call the tortoise unworthy because she is not something else,
And the jay in the woods never studied the gamut,[16] yet trills pretty well to me,
And the look of the bay mare shames silliness out of me.

14

The wild gander leads his flock through the cool night,
Ya-honk he says, and sounds it down to me like an invitation,
The pert may suppose it meaningless, but I listening close,
Find its purpose and place up there toward the wintry sky.

The sharp-hoof'd moose of the north, the cat on the house-sill, the chickadee, the prairie-dog,
The litter of the grunting sow as they tug at her teats,
The brood of the turkey-hen and she with her half-spread wings,
I see in them and myself the same old law.

[13] A cart or sledge used for heavy loads. [14] A beam that runs the length of a wagon.
[15] Swinging around. [16] Musical scale.

The press of my foot to the earth springs a hundred affections,
They scorn the best I can do to relate them.

I am enamour'd of growing out-doors,
Of men that live among cattle or taste of the ocean or woods,
Of the builders and steerers of ships and the wielders of axes and mauls, and the drivers of horses,
I can eat and sleep with them week in and week out.

What is commonest, cheapest, nearest, easiest, is Me,
Me going in for my chances, spending for vast returns,
Adorning myself to bestow myself on the first that will take me,
Not asking the sky to come down to my good will,
Scattering it freely forever.

15

The pure contralto sings in the organ loft,
The carpenter dresses his plank, the tongue of his foreplane whistles its wild ascending lisp,
The married and unmarried children ride home to their Thanksgiving dinner,
The pilot seizes the king-pin,[17] he heaves down with a strong arm,
The mate stands braced in the whale-boat, lance and harpoon are ready,
The duck-shooter walks by silent and cautious stretches,
The deacons are ordain'd with cross'd hands at the altar,
The spinning girl retreats and advances to the hum of the big wheel,
The farmer stops by the bars[18] as he walks on a First-day loafe[19] and looks at the oats and rye,
The lunatic is carried at last to the asylum a confirm'd case,
(He will never sleep any more as he did in the cot in his mother's bed-room;)
The jour[20] printer with gray head and gaunt jaws works at his case,[21]
He turns his quid of tobacco while his eyes blurr with the manuscript;
The malform'd limbs are tied to the surgeon's table,
What is removed drops horribly in a pail;
The quadroon girl is sold at the auction-stand, the drunkard nods by the bar-room stove,
The machinist rolls up his sleeves, the policeman travels his beat, the gate-keeper marks who pass,
The young fellow drives the express-wagon, (I love him, though I do not know him;)
The half-breed straps on his light boots to compete in the race,

[17] Extended spoke on a ship's pilot wheel. [18] Rails of a fence or gate.

[19] "First day" is Sunday. Whitman often uses such terminology from his Quaker childhood in his poetry.

[20] Journeyman. The description of the printer seems to have been based upon a real person, William Hartshorne, the printer who taught Whitman to set type.

[21] The case of type.

The western turkey-shooting[22] draws old and young, some lean on their rifles, some sit on logs,
Out from the crowd steps the marksman, takes his position, levels his piece;
The groups of newly-come immigrants cover the wharf or levee,
As the woolly-pates hoe in the sugar-field, the overseer views them from his saddle,
The bugle calls in the ball-room, the gentlemen run for their partners, the dancers bow to each other,
The youth lies awake in the cedar-roof'd garret and harks to the musical rain,
The Wolverine[23] sets traps on the creek that helps fill the Huron,
The squaw wrapt in her yellow-hemm'd cloth is offering moccasins and bead-bags for sale,
The connoisseur peers along the exhibition-gallery with half-shut eyes bent sideways,
As the deck-hands make fast the steamboat the plank is thrown for the shore-going passengers,
The young sister holds out the skein while the elder sister winds it off in a ball, and stops now and then for the knots,
The one-year wife is recovering and happy having a week ago borne her first child,
The clean-hair'd Yankee girl works with her sewing-machine or in the factory or mill,
The paving-man leans on his two-handed rammer, the reporter's lead flies swiftly over the note-book, the sign painter is lettering with blue and gold,
The canal boy trots on the tow-path,[24] the book-keeper counts at his desk, the shoemaker waxes his thread,
The conductor beats time for the band and all the performers follow him,
The child is baptized, the convert is making his first professions,
The regatta is spread on the bay, the race is begun, (how the white sails sparkle!)
The drover watching his drove sings out to them that would stray,
The pedler sweats with his pack on his back, (the purchaser higgling[25] about the odd cent;)
The bride unrumples her white dress, the minute-hand of the clock moves slowly,
The opium-eater reclines with rigid head and just-open'd lips,
The prostitute draggles her shawl, her bonnet bobs on her tipsy and pimpled neck,
The crowd laugh at her blackguard oaths, the men jeer and wink to each other,
(Miserable! I do not laugh at your oaths nor jeer you;)

[22] A shooting contest with a turkey for the prize. [23] Resident of Michigan.
[24] The path along a canal, where horses or oxen towed the canal boats.
[25] Bargaining.

The President holding a cabinet council is surrounded by the great Secretaries,
On the piazza walk three matrons stately and friendly with twined arms,
The crew of the fish-smack pack repeated layers of halibut in the hold,
The Missourian crosses the plains toting his wares and his cattle,
As the fare-collector goes through the train he gives notice by the jingling of loose change,
The floor-men are laying the floor, the tinners are tinning the roof, the masons are calling for mortar,
In single file each shouldering his hod pass onward the laborers;
Seasons pursuing each other the indescribable crowd is gather'd; it is the fourth of Seventh-month,[26] (what salutes of cannon and small arms!)
Seasons pursuing each other the plougher ploughs, the mower mows, and the winter-grain falls in the ground;
Off on the lakes the pike-fisher watches and waits by the hole in the frozen surface,
The stumps stand thick round the clearing, the squatter strikes deep with his axe,
Flatboatmen make fast towards dusk near the cotton-wood or pecan-trees,
Coon-seekers go through the regions of the Red river[27] or through those drain'd by the Tennessee, or through those of the Arkansas,
Torches shine in the dark that hangs on the Chattahooche or Altamahaw,[28]
Patriarchs sit at supper with sons and grandsons and great-grandsons around them,
In walls of adobie, in canvas tents, rest hunters and trappers after their day's sport,
The city sleeps and the country sleeps,
The living sleep for their time, the dead sleep for their time,
The old husband sleeps by his wife and the young husband sleeps by his wife;
And these tend inward to me, and I tend outward to them,
And such as it is to be of these more or less I am,
And of these one and all I weave the song of myself.

16

I am of old and young, of the foolish as much as the wise,
Regardless of others, ever regardful of others,
Maternal as well as paternal, a child as well as a man,
Stuff'd with the stuff that is coarse and stuff'd with the stuff that is fine,

[26] July (Quaker terminology).

[27] Southwestern river, flowing between Texas and Oklahoma, between Texas and Arkansas, and across Louisiana into the Mississippi.

[28] Rivers in Georgia.

One of the Nation of many nations, the smallest the same and the largest the same,
A Southerner soon as a Northerner, a planter nonchalant and hospitable down by the Oconee[29] I live,
A Yankee bound my own way ready for trade, my joints the limberest joints on earth and the sternest joints on earth,
A Kentuckian walking the vale of the Elkhorn[30] in my deer-skin leggings, a Louisianian or Georgian,
A boatman over lakes or bays or along coasts, a Hoosier, Badger, Buckeye;[31]
At home on Kanadian snow-shoes or up in the bush, or with fishermen off Newfoundland,
At home in the fleet of ice-boats, sailing with the rest and tacking,
At home on the hills of Vermont or in the woods of Maine, or the Texan ranch,
Comrade of Californians, comrade of free North-Westerners, (loving their big proportions,)
Comrade of raftsmen and coalmen, comrade of all who shake hands and welcome to drink and meat,
A learner with the simplest, a teacher of the thoughtfullest,
A novice beginning yet experient of myriads of seasons,
Of every hue and caste am I, of every rank and religion,
A farmer, mechanic, artist, gentleman, sailor, quaker,
Prisoner, fancy-man,[32] rowdy, lawyer, physician, priest.

I resist any thing better than my own diversity,
Breathe the air but leave plenty after me,
And am not stuck up, and am in my place.

(The moth and the fish-eggs are in their place,
The bright suns I see and the dark suns I cannot see are in their place,
The palpable is in its place and the impalpable is in its place.)

17

These are really the thoughts of all men in all ages and lands, they are not original with me,
If they are not yours as much as mine they are nothing, or next to nothing,
If they are not the riddle and the untying of the riddle they are nothing,
If they are not just as close as they are distant they are nothing.

This is the grass that grows wherever the land is and the water is,
This the common air that bathes the globe.

18

With music strong I come, with my cornets and my drums,

[29] River in Georgia. [30] Elkhorn Creek in central Kentucky.
[31] Residents, respectively, of Indiana, Wisconsin, and Ohio. [32] A prostitute's pimp.

I play not marches for accepted victors only, I play marches for conquer'd and slain persons.

Have you heard that it was good to gain the day?
I also say it is good to fall, battles are lost in the same spirit in which they are won.

I beat and pound for the dead,
I blow through my embouchures[33] my loudest and gayest for them.

Vivas[34] to those who have fail'd!
And to those whose war-vessels sank in the sea!
And to those themselves who sank in the sea!
And to all generals that lost engagements, and all overcome heroes!
And the numberless unknown heroes equal to the greatest heroes known!

19

This is the meal equally set, this the meat for natural hunger,
It is for the wicked just the same as the righteous, I make appointments with all,
I will not have a single person slighted or left away,
The kept-woman, sponger, thief, are hereby invited,
The heavy-lipp'd slave is invited, the venerealee is invited;
There shall be no difference between them and the rest.

This is the press of a bashful hand, this the float and odor of hair,
This is the touch of my lips to yours, this the murmur of yearning,
This the far-off depth and height reflecting my own face,
This the thoughtful merge of myself, and the outlet again.

Do you guess I have some intricate purpose?
Well I have, for the Fourth-month[35] showers have, and the mica on the side of a rock has.

Do you take it I would astonish?
Does the daylight astonish? does the early redstart twittering through the woods?
Do I astonish more than they?

This hour I tell things in confidence,
I might not tell everybody, but I will tell you.

20

Who goes there? hankering, gross, mystical, nude;

[33] Metal mouthpieces of musical instruments, or the mouths of players adjusted to such mouthpieces.
[34] Cheers. [35] April (Quaker terminology).

How is it I extract strength from the beef I eat?
What is a man anyhow? what am I? what are you?

All I mark as my own you shall offset it with your own,
Else it were time lost listening to me.

I do not snivel that snivel the world over,
That months are vacuums and the ground but wallow and filth.

Whimpering and truckling fold with powders for invalids,[36] conformity goes to the fourth-remov'd,
I wear my hat as I please indoors or out.

Why should I pray? why should I venerate and be ceremonious?

Having pried through the strata, analyzed to a hair, counsel'd with doctors and calculated close,
I find no sweeter fat than sticks to my own bones.

In all people I see myself; none more and not one a barley-corn less,
And the good or bad I say of myself I say of them.

I know I am solid and sound,
To me the converging objects of the universe perpetually flow,
All are written to me, and I must get what the writing means.

I know I am deathless,
I know this orbit of mine cannot be swept by a carpenter's compass,
I know I shall not pass like a child's carlacue cut with a burnt stick at night.[37]

I know I am august,
I do not trouble my spirit to vindicate itself or be understood,
I see that the elementary laws never apologize,
(I reckon I behave no prouder than the level I plant my house by, after all.)

I exist as I am, that is enough,
If no other in the world be aware I sit content,
And if each and all be aware I sit content.

One world is aware and by far the largest to me, and that is myself,
And whether I come to my own to-day or in ten thousand or ten million years,
I can cheerfully take it now, or with equal cheerfulness I can wait.

[36] That is, whimpering and submitting tamely belong with medicines for invalids.
[37] That is, like the curlicue a child makes at night by waving a glowing stick in the air.

My foothold is tenon'd and mortis'd[38] in granite,
I laugh at what you call dissolution,
And I know the amplitude of time.

21

I am the poet of the Body and I am the poet of the Soul,
The pleasures of heaven are with me and the pains of hell are with me,
The first I graft and increase upon myself, the latter I translate into a new tongue.

I am the poet of the woman the same as the man,
And I say it is as great to be a woman as to be a man,
And I say there is nothing greater than the mother of men.

I chant the chant of dilation or pride,
We have had ducking and deprecating about enough,
I show that size is only development.

Have you outstript the rest? are you the President?
It is a trifle, they will more than arrive there every one, and still pass on.

I am he that walks with the tender and growing night,
I call to the earth and sea half-held by the night.

Press close bare-bosom'd night—press close magnetic nourishing night!
Night of south winds—night of the large few stars!
Still nodding night—mad naked summer night.

Smile O voluptuous cool-breath'd earth!
Earth of the slumbering and liquid trees!
Earth of departed sunset—earth of the mountains misty-topt!
Earth of the vitreous[39] pour of the full moon just tinged with blue!
Earth of shine and dark mottling the tide of the river!
Earth of the limpid gray of clouds brighter and clearer for my sake!
Far-swooping elbow'd[40] earth—rich apple-blossom'd earth!
Smile, for your lover comes.

Prodigal, you have given me love—therefore I to you give love!
O unspeakable passionate love.

[38] Joined securely. A "mortise and tenon joint," in carpentry, is one in which a projection (tenon) on one piece of wood is fitted into a cavity (mortise) in another.

[39] Glassy.

[40] "Elbow'd" may refer to the sharp turn in the earth's elliptical orbit around the sun or to deep valleys shaped like crooked elbows.

22

You sea! I resign myself to you also—I guess what you mean,
I behold from the beach your crooked inviting fingers,
I believe you refuse to go back without feeling of me,
We must have a turn together, I undress, hurry me out of sight of the land,
Cushion me soft, rock me in billowy drowse,
Dash me with amorous wet, I can repay you.

Sea of stretch'd ground-swells,
Sea breathing broad and convulsive breaths,
Sea of the brine of life and of unshovell'd yet always-ready graves,
Howler and scooper of storms, capricious and dainty sea,
I am integral with you, I too am of one phase and of all phases.

Partaker of influx and efflux, I, extoller of hate and conciliation,
Extoller of amies[41] and those that sleep in each other's arms.

I am he attesting sympathy,
(Shall I make my list of things in the house and skip the house that supports them?)

I am not the poet of goodness only, I do not decline to be the poet of wickedness also.

What blurt is this about virtue and about vice?
Evil propels me and reform of evil propels me, I stand indifferent,
My gait is no fault-finder's or rejecter's gait,
I moisten the roots of all that has grown.

Did you fear some scrofula[42] out of the unflagging pregnancy?
Did you guess the celestial laws are yet to be work'd over and rectified?

I find one side a balance and the antipodal side a balance,
Soft doctrine as steady help as stable doctrine,
Thoughts and deeds of the present our rouse and early start.

This minute that comes to me over the past decillions,
There is no better than it and now.

What behaved well in the past or behaves well to-day is not such a wonder,
The wonder is always and always how there can be a mean man or an infidel.

[41] Friends or lovers (French).
[42] A tubercular disease affecting primarily the lymph glands and the joints.

23

Endless unfolding of words of ages!
And mine a word of the modern, the word En-Masse.

A word of the faith that never balks,
Here or henceforward it is all the same to me, I accept Time absolutely.

It alone is without flaw, it alone rounds and completes all,
That mystic baffling wonder alone completes all.

I accept Reality and dare not question it,
Materialism first and last imbuing.

Hurrah for positive science! long live exact demonstration!
Fetch stonecrop[43] mixt with cedar and branches of lilac,
This is the lexicographer, this the chemist, this made a grammar of the old cartouches,[44]
These mariners put the ship through dangerous unknown seas,
This is the geologist, this works with the scalpel, and this is a mathematician.

Gentlemen, to you the first honors always!
Your facts are useful, and yet they are not my dwelling,
I but enter by them to an area of my dwelling.

Less the reminders of properties told my words,
And more the reminders they of life untold, and of freedom and extrication,
And make short account of neuters and geldings, and favor men and women fully equipt,
And beat the gong of revolt, and stop with fugitives and them that plot and conspire.

24

Walt Whitman, a kosmos, of Manhattan the son,
Turbulent, fleshy, sensual, eating, drinking and breeding,
No sentimentalist, no stander above men and women or apart from them,
No more modest than immodest.

Unscrew the locks from the doors!
Unscrew the doors themselves from their jambs!

Whoever degrades another degrades me,
And whatever is done or said returns at last to me.

[43] A medicinal herb.
[44] That is, interpreted Egyptian hieroglyphics. (Cartouches are oval borders around hieroglyphics expressing royal names on Egyptian monuments.)

Through me the afflatus[45] surging and surging, through me the current and index.

I speak the pass-word primeval, I give the sign of democracy,
By God! I will accept nothing which all cannot have their counterpart of on the same terms.

Through me many long dumb voices,
Voices of the interminable generations of prisoners and slaves,
Voices of the diseas'd and despairing and of thieves and dwarfs,
Voices of cycles of preparation and accretion,
And of the threads that connect the stars, and of wombs and of the father-stuff.[46]
And of the rights of them the others are down upon,
Of the deform'd, trivial, flat, foolish, despised,
Fog in the air, beetles rolling balls of dung.

Through me forbidden voices,
Voices of sexes and lusts, voices veil'd and I remove the veil,
Voices indecent by me clarified and transfigur'd.

I do not press my fingers across my mouth,
I keep as delicate around the bowels as around the head and heart,
Copulation is no more rank to me than death is.

I believe in the flesh and the appetites,
Seeing, hearing, feeling, are miracles, and each part and tag of me is a miracle.

Divine am I inside and out, and I make holy whatever I touch or am touch'd from,
The scent of these arm-pits aroma finer than prayer,
This head more than churches, bibles, and all the creeds.

If I worship one thing more than another it shall be the spread of my own body, or any part of it,
Translucent mould of me it shall be you!
Shaded ledges and rests it shall be you!
Firm masculine colter[47] it shall be you!
Whatever goes to the tilth[48] of me it shall be you!
You my rich blood! your milky stream pale strippings of my life!
Breast that presses against other breasts it shall be you!
My brain it shall be your occult convolutions!
Root of wash'd sweetflag![49] timorous pond-snipe![50] nest of guarded duplicate eggs! it shall be you!

[45] Poetic inspiration. [46] Seminal fluid.
[47] Sharp blade on the beam of a plow, used to cut the ground ahead of the plowshare.
[48] Cultivation. [49] Plant with long, sword-shaped leaves and aromatic roots.
[50] A water bird.

Mix'd tussled hay of head, beard, brawn, it shall be you!
Trickling sap of maple, fibre of manly wheat, it shall be you!
Sun so generous it shall be you!
Vapors lighting and shading my face it shall be you!
You sweaty brooks and dews it shall be you!
Winds whose soft-tickling genitals rub against me it shall be you!
Broad muscular fields, branches of live oak, loving lounger in my winding paths, it shall be you!
Hands I have taken, face I have kiss'd, mortal I have ever touch'd, it shall be you.

I dote on myself, there is that lot of me and all so luscious,
Each moment and whatever happens thrills me with joy,
I cannot tell how my ankles bend, or whence the cause of my faintest wish,
Nor the cause of the friendship I emit, nor the cause of the friendship I take again.

That I walk up my stoop, I pause to consider if it really be,
A morning-glory at my window satisfies me more than the metaphysics of books.

To behold the day-break!
The little light fades the immense and diaphanous shadows,
The air tastes good to my palate.

Hefts[51] of the moving world at innocent gambols silently rising, freshly exuding,
Scooting obliquely high and low.

Something I cannot see puts upward libidinous prongs,
Seas of bright juice suffuse heaven.

The earth by the sky staid with, the daily close of their junction,
The heav'd challenge from the east that moment over my head,
The mocking taunt, See then whether you shall be master!

25

Dazzling and tremendous how quick the sun-rise would kill me,
If I could not now and always send sun-rise out of me.

We also ascend dazzling and tremendous as the sun.
We found our own O my soul in the calm and cool of the daybreak.

My voice goes after what my eyes cannot reach,
With the twirl of my tongue I encompass worlds and volumes of worlds.

[51] Bulk or main parts.

Speech is the twin of my vision, it is unequal to measure itself,
It provokes me forever, it says sarcastically,
Walt you contain enough, why don't you let it out then?

Come now I will not be tantalized, you conceive too much of articulation,
Do you not know O speech how the buds beneath you are folded?
Waiting in gloom, protected by frost,
The dirt receding before my prophetical screams,
I underlying causes to balance them at last,
My knowledge my live parts, it keeping tally with the meaning of all things,
Happiness, (which whoever hears me let him or her set out in search of this day.)

My final merit I refuse you. I refuse putting from me what I really am,
Encompass worlds, but never try to encompass me,
I crowd your sleekest and best by simply looking toward you.

Writing and talk do not prove me,
I carry the plenum[52] of proof and every thing else in my face,
With the hush of my lips I wholly confound the skeptic.

26

Now I will do nothing but listen,
To accrue[53] what I hear into this song, to let sounds contribute toward it.

I hear bravuras of birds, bustle of growing wheat, gossip of flames, clack of sticks cooking my meals,
I hear the sound I love, the sound of the human voice,
I hear all sounds running together, combined, fused or following,
Sounds of the city and sounds out of the city, sounds of the day and night,
Talkative young ones to those that like them, the loud laugh of work-people at their meals,
The angry base[54] of disjointed friendship, the faint tones of the sick,
The judge with hands tight to the desk, his pallid lips pronouncing a death-sentence,
The heave'e'yo of the stevedores unlading ships by the wharves, the refrain of the anchor-lifters,
The ring of alarm-bells, the cry of fire, the whirr of swift-streaking engines and hose-carts with premonitory tinkles and color'd lights,
The steam-whistle, the solid roll of the train of approaching cars,
The slow march play'd at the head of the association marching two and two,

[52] Fullness. [53] Add or incorporate. [54] Bass.

(They go to guard some corpse, the flag-tops are draped with black
muslin.)

I hear the violoncello, ('tis the young man's heart's complaint,)
I hear the key'd cornet, it glides quickly in through my ears,
It shakes mad-sweet pangs through my belly and breast.

I hear the chorus, it is a grand opera,
Ah this indeed is music—this suits me.

A tenor large and fresh as the creation fills me,
The orbic flex of his mouth is pouring and filling me full.

I hear the train'd soprano (what work with hers is this?)
The orchestra whirls me wider than Uranus[55] flies,
It wrenches such ardors from me I did not know I possess'd them,
It sails me, I dab with bare feet, they are lick'd by the indolent waves,
I am cut by bitter and angry hail, I lose my breath,
Steep'd amid honey'd morphine, my windpipe throttled in fakes[56] of
death,
At length let up again to feel the puzzle of puzzles,
And that we call Being.

27

To be in any form, what is that?
(Round and round we go, all of us, and ever come back thither,)
If nothing lay more develop'd the quahaug[57] in its callous shell were
enough.

Mine is no callous shell,
I have instant conductors all over me whether I pass or stop,
They seize every object and lead it harmlessly through me.

I merely stir, press, feel with my fingers, and am happy,
To touch my person to some one else's is about as much as I can stand.

28

Is this then a touch? quivering me to a new identity,
Flames and ether making a rush for my veins,
Treacherous tip of me reaching and crowding to help them,
My flesh and blood playing out lightning to strike what is hardly different from myself,
On all sides prurient provokers stiffening my limbs,
Straining the udder of my heart for its withheld drip,
Behaving licentious toward me, taking no denial,
Depriving me of my best as for a purpose,
Unbuttoning my clothes, holding me by the bare waist,

[55] The planet Uranus has a large orbit. [56] Coils of rope. [57] A kind of clam.

Deluding my confusion with the calm of the sunlight and pasture-fields,
Immodestly sliding the fellow-senses away,
They bribed to swap off with touch and go and graze at the edges of me,
No consideration, no regard for my draining strength or my anger,
Fetching the rest of the herd around to enjoy them a while,
Then all uniting to stand on a headland and worry me.

The sentries desert every other part of me,
They have left me helpless to a red marauder,
They all come to the headland to witness and assist against me.

I am given up by traitors,
I talk wildly, I have lost my wits, I and nobody else am the greatest traitor,
I went myself first to the headland, my own hands carried me there.

You villain touch! what are you doing? my breath is tight in its throat,
Unclench your floodgates, you are too much for me.

29

Blind loving wrestling touch, sheath'd hooded sharp-tooth'd touch!
Did it make you ache so, leaving me?

Parting track'd by arriving, perpetual payment of perpetual loan,
Rich showering rain, and recompense richer afterward.

Sprouts take and accumulate, stand by the curb prolific and vital,
Landscapes projected masculine, full-sized and golden.

30

All truths wait in all things,
They neither hasten their own delivery nor resist it,
They do not need the obstetric forceps of the surgeon,
The insignificant is as big to me as any,
(What is less or more than a touch?)

Logic and sermons never convince,
The damp of the night drives deeper into my soul.

(Only what proves itself to every man and woman is so,
Only what nobody denies is so.)

A minute and a drop of me settle my brain,
I believe the soggy clods shall become lovers and lamps,
And a compend[58] of compends is the meat of a man or woman,

[58] Compendium, epitome. A "compend of compends" would be a distillation of distillations.

And a summit and flower there is the feeling they have for each other,
And they are to branch boundlessly out of that lesson until it becomes omnific,[59]
And until one and all shall delight us, and we them.

31

I believe a leaf of grass is no less than the journey-work of the stars,
And the pismire[60] is equally perfect, and a grain of sand, and the egg of the wren,
And the tree-toad is a chef-d'oeuvre[61] for the highest,
And the running blackberry would adorn the parlors of heaven,
And the narrowest hinge in my hand puts to scorn all machinery,
And the cow crunching with depress'd head surpasses any statue,
And a mouse is miracle enough to stagger sextillions of infidels.

I find I incorporate gneiss,[62] coal, long-threaded moss, fruits, grains, esculent[63] roots,
And am stucco'd with quadrupeds and birds all over,
And have distanced what is behind me for good reasons,
But call any thing back again when I desire it.

In vain the speeding or shyness,
In vain the plutonic rocks[64] send their old heat against my approach,
In vain the mastodon retreats beneath its own powder'd bones,
In vain objects stand leagues off and assume manifold shapes,
In vain the ocean settling in hollows and the great monsters lying low,
In vain the buzzard houses herself with the sky,
In vain the snake slides through the creepers and logs,
In vain the elk takes to the inner passes of the woods,
In vain the razor-bill'd auk sails far north to Labrador,
I follow quickly, I ascend to the nest in the fissure of the cliff.

32

I think I could turn and live with animals, they're so placid and self-contain'd,
I stand and look at them long and long.

They do not sweat and whine about their condition,
They do not lie awake in the dark and weep for their sins,
They do not make me sick discussing their duty to God,
Not one is dissatisfied, not one is demented with the mania of owning things,
Not one kneels to another, nor to his kind that lived thousands of years ago,
Not one is respectable or unhappy over the whole earth.
So they show their relations to me and I accept them,

[59] All-creating. [60] Ant. [61] Masterpiece (French).
[62] A kind of metamorphic rock, formed by pressure and heat beneath the earth's surface.
[63] Edible. [64] Rocks that solidified far below the earth's surface.

They bring me tokens of myself, they evince them plainly in their
possession.

I wonder where they get those tokens,
Did I pass that way huge times ago and negligently drop them?

Myself moving forward then and now and forever,
Gathering and showing more always and with velocity,
Infinite and omnigenous,[65] and the like of these among them,
Not too exclusive toward the reachers of my remembrancers,
Picking out here one that I love, and now go with him on brotherly
terms.

A gigantic beauty of a stallion, fresh and responsive to my caresses,
Head high in the forehead, wide between the ears,
Limbs glossy and supple, tail dusting the ground,
Eyes full of sparkling wickedness, ears finely cut, flexibly moving.

His nostrils dilate as my heels embrace him,
His well-built limbs tremble with pleasure as we race around and return.

I but use you a minute, then I resign you, stallion,
Why do I need your paces when I myself out-gallop them?
Even as I stand or sit passing faster than you.

33

Space and Time! now I see it is true, what I guess'd at,
What I guess'd when I loaf'd on the grass,
What I guess'd while I lay alone in my bed,
And again as I walk'd the beach under the paling stars of the
morning.

My ties and ballasts leave me, my elbows rest in sea-gaps,
I skirt sierras, my palms cover continents,
I am afoot with my vision.

By the city's quadrangular houses—in log huts, camping with
lumbermen,
Along the ruts of the turnpike, along the dry gulch and rivulet bed,
Weeding my onion-patch or hoeing rows of carrots and parsnips,
crossing savannas,[66] trailing in forests,
Prospecting, gold-digging, girdling the trees of a new purchase,[67]
Scorch'd ankle-deep by the hot sand, hauling my boat down the shal-
low river,
Where the panther walks to and fro on a limb overhead, where the
buck turns furiously at the hunter,

[65] Of all kinds. [66] Grassy plains.
[67] "Girdling" trees is killing them by cutting rings around their trunks, a common practice in clearing forested land.

Where the rattlesnake suns his flabby length on a rock, where the otter is feeding on fish,
Where the alligator in his tough pimples sleeps by the bayou,
Where the black bear is searching for roots or honey, where the beaver pats the mud with his paddle-shaped tail;
Over the growing sugar, over the yellow-flower'd cotton plant, over the rice in its low moist field,
Over the sharp-peak'd farm house, with its scallop'd scum and slender shoots from the gutters,[68]
Over the western persimmon, over the long-leav'd corn, over the delicate blue-flower flax,
Over the white and brown buckwheat, a hummer and buzzer[69] there with the rest,
Over the dusky green of the rye as it ripples and shades in the breeze;
Scaling mountains, pulling myself cautiously up, holding on by low scragged[70] limbs,
Walking the path worn in the grass and beat through the leaves of the brush,
Where the quail is whistling betwixt the woods and the wheat-lot,
Where the bat flies in the Seventh-month[71] eve, where the great goldbug drops through the dark,
Where the brook puts out of the roots of the old tree and flows to the meadow,
Where cattle stand and shake away flies with the tremulous shuddering of their hides,
Where the cheese-cloth hangs in the kitchen, where andirons straddle the hearth-slab, where cobwebs fall in festoons from the rafters;
Where trip-hammers crash, where the press is whirling its cylinders,
Where the human heart beats with terrible throes under its ribs,
Where the pear-shaped balloon is floating aloft, (floating in it myself and looking composedly down,)
Where the life-car is drawn on the slip-noose,[72] where the heat hatches pale-green eggs in the dented sand,
Where the she-whale swims with her calf and never forsakes it,
Where the steam-ship trails hind-ways its long pennant of smoke,
Where the fin of the shark cuts like a black chip out of the water,
Where the half-burn'd brig is riding on unknown currents,
Where shells grow to her slimy deck, where the dead are corrupting below;
Where the dense-starr'd flag is borne at the head of the regiments,
Approaching Manhattan up by the long-stretching island,
Under Niagara, the cataract falling like a veil over my countenance,
Upon a door-step, upon the horse-block[73] of hard wood outside,
Upon the race-course, or enjoying picnics or jigs or a good game of base-ball,

[68] The "scum" and shoots are apparently fungus and vines growing on the wooden shingles and in the eaves.
[69] A hummingbird and a bee. [70] Stunted. [71] July (Quaker terminology).
[72] Lifeboat drawn by a rope from ship to shore. [73] Block used to mount a horse.

At he-festivals, with blackguard jibes, ironical license, bull-dances,[74] drinking, laughter,
At the cider-mill tasting the sweets of the brown mash, sucking the juice through a straw,
At apple-peelings wanting kisses for all the red fruit I find,
At musters,[75] beach-parties, friendly bees, huskings, house-raisings;
Where the mocking-bird sounds his delicious gurgles, cackles, screams, weeps,
Where the hay-rick stands in the barn-yard, where the dry-stalks are scatter'd, where the brood-cow waits in the hovel,
Where the bull advances to do his masculine work, where the stud to the mare, where the cock is treading the hen,
Where the heifers browse, where geese nip their food with short jerks,
Where sun-down shadows lengthen over the limitless and lonesome prairie,
Where herds of buffalo make a crawling spread of the square miles far and near,
Where the humming-bird shimmers, where the neck of the long-lived swan is curving and winding,
Where the laughing-gull scoots by the shore, where she laughs her near-human laugh,
Where bee-hives range on a gray bench in the garden half hid by the high weeds,
Where band-neck'd partridges roost in a ring on the ground with their heads out,
Where burial coaches enter the arch'd gates of a cemetery,
Where winter wolves bark amid wastes of snow and icicled trees,
Where the yellow-crown'd heron comes to the edge of the marsh at night and feeds upon small crabs,
Where the splash of swimmers and divers cools the warm noon,
Where the katy-did works her chromatic reed on the walnut-tree over the well,
Through patches of citrons[76] and cucumbers with silver-wired leaves,
Through the salt-lick or orange glade, or under conical firs,
Through the gymnasium, through the curtain'd saloon, through the office or public hall;
Pleas'd with the native and pleas'd with the foreign, pleas'd with the new and old,
Pleas'd with the homely woman as well as the handsome,
Pleas'd with the quakeress as she puts off her bonnet and talks melodiously,
Pleas'd with the tune of the choir of the whitewash'd church,
Pleas'd with the earnest words of the sweating Methodist preacher, impress'd seriously at the camp-meeting;
Looking in at the shop-windows of Broadway the whole forenoon, flatting the flesh of my nose on the thick plate glass,

[74] Indian buffalo dances. [75] Gatherings [76] Watermelons.

Wandering the same afternoon with my face turn'd up to the clouds, or down a lane or along the beach,
My right and left arms round the sides of two friends, and I in the middle;
Coming home with the silent and dark-cheek'd bush-boy,[77] (behind me he rides at the drape[78] of the day,)
Far from the settlements studying the print of animals' feet, or the moccasin print,
By the cot in the hospital reaching lemonade to a feverish patient,
Nigh the coffin'd corpse when all is still, examining with a candle;
Voyaging to every port to dicker and adventure,
Hurrying with the modern crowd as eager and fickle as any,
Hot toward one I hate, ready in my madness to knife him,
Solitary at midnight in my back yard, my thoughts gone from me a long while,
Walking the old hills of Judaea with the beautiful gentle God by my side,
Speeding through space, speeding through heaven and the stars,
Speeding amid the seven satellites and the broad ring, and the diameter of eighty thousand miles,
Speeding with tail'd meteors, throwing fire-balls like the rest,
Carrying the crescent child[79] that carries its own full mother in its belly,
Storming, enjoying, planning, loving, cautioning,
Backing and filling, appearing and disappearing,
I tread day and night such roads.

I visit the orchards of spheres and look at the product,
And look at quintillions ripen'd and look at quintillions green.

I fly those flights of a fluid and swallowing soul,
My course runs below the sounding of plummets.

I help myself to material and immaterial,
No guard can shut me off, no law prevent me.

I anchor my ship for a little while only,
My messengers continually cruise away or bring their returns to me.

I go hunting polar furs and the seal, leaping chasms with a pike-pointed staff, clinging to topples[80] of brittle and blue.

I ascend to the foretruck,[81]
I take my place late at night in the crow's-nest,[82]
We sail the arctic sea, it is plenty light enough,
Through the clear atmosphere I stretch around on the wonderful beauty,

[77] Back-woods boy. [78] Close, end. [79] The crescent moon.
[80] Fallen chunks of ice. [81] Foretop; platform at the head of a foremast.
[82] Box or platform for a lookout at the top of a mast.

The enormous masses of ice pass me and I pass them, the scenery is plain in all directions,
The white-topt mountains show in the distance, I fling out my fancies toward them,
We are approaching some great battle-field in which we are soon to be engaged,
We pass the colossal outposts of the encampment, we pass with still feet and caution,
Or we are entering by the suburbs some vast and ruin'd city,
The blocks and fallen architecture more than all the living cities of the globe.

I am a free companion, I bivouac by invading watchfires,
I turn the bridegroom out of bed and stay with the bride myself,
I tighten her all night to my thighs and lips.

My voice is the wife's voice, the screech by the rail of the stairs,
They fetch my man's body up dripping and drown'd.

I understand the large hearts of heroes,
The courage of present times and all times,
How the skipper saw the crowded and rudderless wreck of the steam-ship, and Death chasing it up and down the storm,
How he knuckled tight and gave not back an inch, and was faithful of days and faithful of nights,
And chalk'd in large letters on a board, *Be of good cheer, we will not desert you;*
How he follow'd with them and tack'd[83] with them three days and would not give it up,
How he saved the drifting company at last,
How the lank loose-gown'd women look'd when boated from the side of their prepared graves,
How the silent old-faced infants and the lifted sick, and the sharp-lipp'd unshaved men;
All this I swallow, it tastes good, I like it well, it becomes mine,
I am the man, I suffer'd, I was there.[84]

The disdain and calmness of martyrs,
The mother of old, condemn'd for a witch, burnt with dry wood, her children gazing on,
The hounded slave that flags in the race, leans by the fence, blowing, cover'd with sweat,
The twinges that sting like needles his legs and neck, the murderous buckshot and the bullets,
All these I feel or am.

I am the hounded slave, I wince at the bite of the dogs,

[83] Sailed into the wind.
[84] This shipwreck episode is based upon newspaper accounts of an actual shipwreck in January, 1854.

Hell and despair are upon me, crack and again crack the marksmen,
I clutch the rails of the fence, my gore dribs,[85] thinn'd with the ooze of my skin,
I fall on the weeds and stones,
The riders spur their unwilling horses, haul close,
Taunt my dizzy ears and beat me violently over the head with whip-stocks.

Agonies are one of my changes of garments,
I do not ask the wounded person how he feels, I myself become the wounded person,
My hurts turn livid upon me as I lean on a cane and observe.

I am the mash'd fireman with breast-bone broken,
Tumbling walls buried me in their debris,
Heat and smoke I inspired,[86] I heard the yelling shouts of my comrades,
I heard the distant click of their picks and shovels,
They have clear'd the beams away, they tenderly lift me forth.

I lie in the night air in my red shirt, the pervading hush is for my sake,
Painless after all I lie exhausted but not so unhappy,
White and beautiful are the faces around me, the heads are bared of their fire-caps,
The kneeling crowd fades with the light of the torches.

Distant and dead resuscitate,
They show as the dial or move as the hands of me, I am the clock myself.

I am an old artillerist, I tell of my fort's bombardment,
I am there again.

Again the long roll of the drummers,
Again the attacking cannon, mortars,
Again to my listening ears the cannon responsive.

I take part, I see and hear the whole,
The cries, curses, roar, the plaudits for well-aim'd shots,
The ambulanza[87] slowly passing trailing its red drip,
Workmen searching after damages, making indispensable repairs,
The fall of grenades through the rent roof, the fan-shaped explosion,
The whizz of limbs, heads, stone, wood, iron, high in the air.

Again gurgles the mouth of my dying general, he furiously waves with his hand,
He gasps through the clot *Mind not me—mind—the entrenchments.*

[85] That is, my blood drips. [86] Breathed in. [87] Military ambulance.

34

Now I tell what I knew in Texas in my early youth,[88]
(I tell not the fall of Alamo,[89]
Not one escaped to tell the fall of Alamo,
The hundred and fifty are dumb yet at Alamo,)
'Tis the tale of the murder in cold blood of four hundred and twelve young men.

Retreating they had form'd in a hollow square with their baggage for breastworks,
Nine hundred lives out of the surrounding enemy's, nine times their number, was the price they took in advance,
Their colonel was wounded and their ammunition gone,
They treated for an honorable capitulation, receiv'd writing and seal, gave up their arms and march'd back prisoners of war.

They were the glory of the race of rangers,
Matchless with horse, rifle, song, supper, courtship,
Large, turbulent, generous, handsome, proud, and affectionate,
Bearded, sunburnt, drest in the free costume of hunters,
Not a single one over thirty years of age.

The second First-day[90] morning they were brought out in squads and massacred, it was beautiful early summer,
The work commenced about five o'clock and was over by eight.

None obey'd the command to kneel,
Some made a mad and helpless rush, some stood stark and straight,
A few fell at once, shot in the temple or heart, the living and dead lay together,
The maim'd and mangled dug in the dirt, the new-comers saw them there,
Some half-kill'd attempted to crawl away,
These were despatch'd with bayonets or batter'd with the blunts of muskets,
A youth not seventeen years old seiz'd his assassin till two more came to release him,
The three were all torn and cover'd with the boy's blood.

At eleven o'clock began the burning of the bodies;
That is the tale of the murder of the four hundred and twelve young men.

[88] Whitman is maintaining his all-inclusive persona; he was never in Texas. The following story of the Texas massacre is based upon an article entitled "Fanning's Men, or The Massacre at Goliad," which, as editor, Whitman had published in the Brooklyn *Eagle* in 1846.

[89] The Texas garrison at the Alamo, in San Antonio, Texas, was annihilated by the forces of the Mexican general Santa Ana in February, 1836, after they refused to surrender.

[90] Sunday (Quaker terminology).

35

Would you hear of an old-time sea-fight?[91]
Would you learn who won by the light of the moon and stars?
List to the yarn, as my grandmother's father the sailor told it to me.

Our foe was no skulk in his ship I tell you, (said he,)
His was the surly English pluck, and there is no tougher or truer, and never was, and never will be;
Along the lower'd eve he came horribly raking us.

We closed with him, the yards entangled, the cannon touch'd,
My captain lash'd fast with his own hands.

We had receiv'd some eighteen pound shots under the water,
On our lower-gun-deck two large pieces had burst at the first fire, killing all around and blowing up overhead.

Fighting at sun-down, fighting at dark,
Ten o'clock at night, the full moon well up, our leaks on the gain, and five feet of water reported,
The master-at-arms loosing the prisoners confined in the after-hold to give them a chance for themselves.

The transit to and from the magazine[92] is now stopt by the sentinels,
They see so many strange faces they do not know whom to trust.

Our frigate takes fire,
The other asks if we demand quarter?
If our colors are struck and the fighting done?

Now I laugh content, for I hear the voice of my little captain,
We have not struck, he composedly cries, *we have just begun our part of the fighting.*[93]

Only three guns are in use,
One is directed by the captain himself against the enemy's mainmast,
Two well serv'd with grape and canister[94] silence his musketry and clear his decks.

[91] The following description of a sea-battle is based upon the engagement between the U.S. *Bon Homme Richard,* commanded by John Paul Jones, and the British *Serapis,* commanded by Richard Pearson, in the North Sea, September 23, 1779.

[92] Storeroom for gunpowder.

[93] John Paul Jones is supposed to have responded to a demand for surrender with the words, "We have just begun to fight."

[94] Two kinds of shot for a cannon. Grapeshot is a number of small cannon balls discharged simultaneously; canister shot is the same kind of small balls enclosed in an exploding canister.

The tops alone second the fire of this little battery, especially the
maintop,
They hold out bravely during the whole of the action.

Not a moment's cease,
The leaks gain fast on the pumps, the fire eats toward the powder-
magazine.

One of the pumps has been shot away, it is generally thought we are
sinking.

Serene stands the little captain,
He is not hurried, his voice is neither high nor low,
His eyes give more light to us than our battle-lanterns.

Toward twelve there in the beams of the moon they surrender to us.

36

Stretch'd and still lies the midnight,
Two great hulls motionless on the breast of the darkness,
Our vessel riddled and slowly sinking, preparations to pass to the one
we have conquer'd,
The captain on the quarter-deck coldly giving his orders through a
countenance white as a sheet,
Near by the corpse of the child that serv'd in the cabin,
The dead face of an old salt with long white hair and carefully curl'd
whiskers,
The flames spite of all that can be done flickering aloft and below,
The husky voices of the two or three officers yet fit for duty,
Formless stacks of bodies and bodies by themselves, dabs of flesh
upon the masts and spars,
Cut of cordage, dangle of rigging, slight shock of the soothe of waves,
Black and impassive guns, litter of powder-parcels,[95] strong scent,
A few large stars overhead, silent and mournful shining,
Delicate sniffs of sea-breeze, smells of sedgy grass and fields by the
shore, death-messages given in charge to survivors,
The hiss of the surgeon's knife, the gnawing teeth of his saw,
Wheeze, cluck, swash of falling blood, short wild scream, and long,
dull, tapering groan,
These so, these irretrievable.

37

You laggards there on guard! look to your arms!
In at the conquer'd doors they crowd! I am possess'd!
Embody all presences outlaw'd or suffering,
See myself in prison shaped like another man,

[95] The papers in which portions of gunpowder for the cannons were wrapped.

And feel the dull unintermitted pain.

For me the keepers of convicts shoulder their carbines and keep watch,
It is I let out in the morning and barr'd at night.

Not a mutineer walks handcuff'd to jail but I am handcuff'd to him and walk by his side,
(I am less the jolly one there, and more the silent one with sweat on my twitching lips.)

Not a youngster is taken for larceny but I go up too, and am tried and sentenced.

Not a cholera patient lies at the last gasp but I also lie at the last gasp,
My face is ash-color'd, my sinews gnarl, away from me people retreat.

Askers embody themselves in me and I am embodied in them,
I project[96] my hat, sit shame-faced, and beg.

38

Enough! enough! enough!
Somehow I have been stunn'd. Stand back!
Give me a little time beyond my cuff'd head, slumbers, dreams, gaping,
I discover myself on the verge of a usual mistake.

That I could forget the mockers and insults!
That I could forget the trickling tears and the blows of the bludgeons and hammers!
That I could look with a separate look on my own crucifixion and bloody crowning.

I remember now,
I resume the overstaid fraction,[97]
The grave of rock multiplies what has been confided to it, or to any graves,
Corpses rise, gashes heal, fastenings roll from me.

I troop forth replenish'd with supreme power, one of an average unending procession.
Inland and sea-coast we go, and pass all boundary lines,
Our swift ordinances on their way over the whole earth,
The blossoms we wear in our hats the growth of thousands of years.

Eleves,[98] I salute you! come forward!

[96] Hold out. [97] The part withheld too long.
[98] Students (French); here, seekers after divine truth.

Continue your annotations, continue your questionings.

39

The friendly and flowing savage, who is he?
Is he waiting for civilization, or past it and mastering it?

Is he some Southwesterner rais'd out-doors? is he Kanadian?
Is he from the Mississippi country? Iowa, Oregon, California?
The mountains? prairie-life, bush-life? or sailor from the sea?

Wherever he goes men and women accept and desire him,
They desire he should like them, touch them, speak to them, stay with them.

Behavior lawless as snow-flakes, words simple as grass, uncomb'd head, laughter, and naiveté,
Slow-stepping feet, common features, common modes and emanations,
They descend in new forms from the tips of his fingers,
They are wafted with the odor of his body or breath, they fly out of the glance of his eyes.

40

Flaunt of the sunshine I need not your bask—lie over!
You light surfaces only, I force surfaces and depths also.

Earth! you seem to look for something at my hands,
Say, old top-knot,[99] what do you want?

Man or woman, I might tell how I like you, but cannot,
And might tell what it is in me and what it is in you, but cannot,
And might tell that pining I have, that pulse of my nights and days.

Behold, I do not give lectures or a little charity,
When I give I give myself.

You there, impotent, loose in the knees,
Open your scarf'd chops[1] till I blow grit within you,
Spread your palms and lift the flaps of your pockets,
I am not to be denied, I compel, I have stores plenty and to spare,
And any thing I have I bestow.

I do not ask who you are, that is not important to me,
You can do nothing and be nothing but what I will infold you.

To cotton-field drudge or cleaner of privies I lean,

[99] An affectionate term of address.
[1] Grooved or creased cheeks, or, perhaps, jaws wrapped in a scarf.

On his right cheek I put the family kiss,
And in my soul I swear I never will deny him.

On women fit for conception I start bigger and nimbler babes,
(This day I am jetting[2] the stuff of far more arrogant republics.)

To any one dying, thither I speed and twist the knob of the door,
Turn the bed-clothes toward the foot of the bed,
Let the physician and the priest go home.

I seize the descending man and raise him with resistless will,
O despairer, here is my neck,
By God, you shall not go down! hang your whole weight upon me.

I dilate you with tremendous breath, I buoy you up,
Every room of the house do I fill with an arm'd force,
Lovers of me, bafflers of graves.

Sleep—I and they keep guard all night,
Not doubt, not decease shall dare to lay finger upon you,
I have embraced you, and henceforth possess you to myself,
And when you rise in the morning you will find what I tell you is so.

41

I am he bringing help for the sick as they pant on their backs,
And for strong upright men I bring yet more needed help.

I heard what was said of the universe,
Heard it and heard it of several thousand years;
It is middling well as far as it goes—but is that all?

Magnifying and applying come I,
Outbidding at the start the old cautious hucksters,[3]
Taking myself the exact dimensions of Jehovah,
Lithographing Kronos, Zeus his son, and Hercules his grandson,
Buying drafts of Osiris, Isis, Belus, Brahma, Buddha,
In my portfolio placing Manito loose, Allah on a leaf, the crucifix
engraved,
With Odin and the hideous-faced Mexitli and every idol and image,[4]
Taking them all for what they are worth and not a cent more,
Admitting they were alive and did the work of their days,
(They bore mites as for unfledg'd birds who have now to rise and fly
and sing for themselves,)

[2] Spouting or shooting forth. [3] Peddlers.

[4] Whitman is listing a wide range of gods of various cultures. Kronos, in Greek mythology, was the Titan dethroned by his son Zeus. Osiris and his sister-wife Isis were the chief Egyptian gods. Belus (usually "Baal" or "Bel") was the principal Babylonian god; Brahma is the supreme deity of Hinduism, Buddha the founder of Buddhism. A manito, or manitou, was one of the spirits in the Algonquian Indian religion; Allah is the Supreme Being of the Muslims; and "the crucifix," of course, suggests Christianity. Odin was the chief god in Norse religion, and Mexitli was an Aztec war god.

Accepting the rough deific[5] sketches to fill out better in myself, bestowing them freely on each man and woman I see,
Discovering as much or more in a framer framing a house,
Putting higher claims for him there with his roll'd-up sleeves driving the mallet and chisel,
Not objecting to special revelations, considering a curl of smoke or a hair on the back of my hand just as curious as any revelation,
Lads ahold of fire-engines and hook-and-ladder ropes no less to me than the gods of the antique wars,
Minding their voices peal through the crash of destruction,
Their brawny limbs passing safe over charr'd laths, their white foreheads whole and unhurt out of the flames;
By the mechanic's wife with her babe at her nipple interceding for every person born,
Three scythes at harvest whizzing in a row from three lusty angels with shirts bagg'd out at their waists,
The snag-tooth'd hostler[6] with red hair redeeming sins past and to come,
Selling all he possesses, traveling on foot to fee lawyers for his brother and sit by him while he is tried for forgery;
What was strewn in the amplest strewing the square rod about me, and not filling the square rod then,
The bull and the bug never worshipp'd half enough,
Dung and dirt more admirable than was dream'd,
The supernatural of no account, myself waiting my time to be one of the supremes,
The day getting ready for me when I shall do as much good as the best, and be as prodigious;
By my life-lumps![7] becoming already a creator,
Putting myself here and now to the ambush'd womb of the shadows.

42

A call in the midst of the crowd,
My own voice, orotund sweeping and final.

Come my children,
Come my boys and girls, my women, household and intimates,
Now the performer launches his nerve, he has pass'd his prelude on the reeds within.

Easily written loose-finger'd chords—I feel the thrum of your climax and close.

My head slues round on my neck,
Music rolls, but not from the organ,
Folks are around me, but they are no household of mine.

Ever the hard unsunk ground,

[5] Divine. [6] Someone who takes care of horses. [7] Testicles.

Ever the eaters and drinkers, ever the upward and downward sun, ever the air and the ceaseless tides,
Ever myself and my neighbors, refreshing, wicked, real,
Ever the old inexplicable query, ever that thorn'd thumb, that breath of itches and thirsts,
Ever the vexer's *hoot! hoot!* till we find where the sly one hides and bring him forth,
Ever love, ever the sobbing liquid of life,
Ever the bandage under the chin, ever the trestles[8] of death.

Here and there with dimes on the eyes[9] walking,
To feed the greed of the belly the brains liberally spooning,
Tickets buying, taking, selling, but in to the feast never once going,
Many sweating, ploughing, thrashing, and then the chaff for payment receiving,
A few idly owning, and they the wheat continually claiming.

This is the city and I am one of the citizens,
Whatever interests the rest interests me, politics, wars, markets, newspapers, schools,
The mayor and councils, banks, tariffs, steamships, factories, stocks, stores, real estate and personal estate.

The little plentiful manikins skipping around in collars and tail'd coats,
I am aware who they are, (they are positively not worms or fleas,)
I acknowledge the duplicates of myself, the weakest and shallowest is deathless with me,
What I do and say the same waits for them,
Every thought that flounders in me the same flounders in them.

I know perfectly well my own egotism,
Know my omnivorous lines and must not write any less,
And would fetch you whoever you are flush[10] with myself.

Not words of routine this song of mine,
But abruptly to question, to leap beyond yet nearer bring;
This printed and bound book—but the printer and the printing-office boy?
The well-taken photographs—but your wife or friend close and solid in your arms?
The black ship mail'd with iron, her mighty guns in her turrets—but the pluck of the captain and engineers?
In the houses the dishes and fare and furniture—but the host and hostess, and the look out of their eyes?

[8] Supports for coffins.
[9] Both the dead (with coins on their eyes to hold them shut) and the greedy (with a money-look in their eyes).
[10] Even or equal.

The sky up there—yet here or next door, or across the way?
The saints and sages in history—but you yourself?
Sermons, creeds, theology—but the fathomless human brain,
And what is reason? and what is love? and what is life?

13

I do not despise you priests, all time, the world over,
My faith is the greatest of faiths and the least of faiths,
Enclosing worship ancient and modern and all between ancient and modern,
Believing I shall come again upon the earth after five thousand years,
Waiting responses from oracles, honoring the gods, saluting the sun,
Making a fetich[11] of the first rock or stump, powowing with sticks in the circle of obis,[12]
Helping the llama[13] or brahmin[14] as he trims the lamps of the idols,
Dancing yet through the streets in a phallic procession, rapt and austere in the woods a gymnosophist,[15]
Drinking mead from the skull-cup, to Shastas and Vedas[16] admirant,[17] minding the Koran,
Walking the teokallis,[18] spotted with gore from the stone and knife, beating the serpent-skin drum,
Accepting the Gospels, accepting him that was crucified, knowing assuredly that he is divine,
To the mass kneeling or the puritan's prayer rising, or sitting patiently in a pew,
Ranting and frothing in my insane crisis, or waiting dead-like till my spirit arouses me,
Looking forth on pavement and land, or outside of pavement and land,
Belonging to the winders of the circuit of circuits.

One of that centripetal and centrifugal gang I turn and talk like a man leaving charges before a journey.

Down-hearted doubters, dull and excluded,
Frivolous, sullen, moping, angry, affected, dishearten'd, atheistical,
I know every one of you, I know the sea of torment, doubt, despair and unbelief.

How the flukes[19] splash!
How they contort rapid as lightning, with spasms and spouts of blood!

Be at peace bloody flukes of doubters and sullen mopers,
I take my place among you as much as among any,
The past is the push of you, me, all, precisely the same,

[11] Fetish, an object of worship. [12] Charms used in West African religion.
[13] Lama, a Tibetan high priest. [14] A member of the Hindu priestly caste.
[15] A Hindu ascetic. [16] Sacred Hindu texts. [17] Admiring (French)
[18] Aztec temple. [19] Tail of a whale.

And what is yet untried and afterward is for you, me, all precisely the same.

I do not know what is untried and afterward,
But I know it will in its turn prove sufficient, and cannot fail.

Each who passes is consider'd, each who stops is consider'd, not a single one can it fail.

It cannot fail the young man who died and was buried,
Nor the young woman who died, and was put by his side,
Nor the little child that peep'd in at the door, and then drew back and was never seen again,
Nor the old man who has lived without purpose, and feels it with bitterness worse than gall,
Nor him in the poor house tubercled by rum and the bad disorder,
Nor the numberless slaughter'd and wreck'd, nor the brutish koboo[20] call'd the ordure[21] of humanity,
Nor the sacs merely floating with open mouths for food to slip in,
Nor any thing in the earth, or down in the oldest graves of the earth,
Nor any thing in the myriads of spheres, nor the myriads of myriads that inhabit them,
Nor the present, nor the least wisp that is known.

44

It is time to explain myself—let us stand up.

What is known I strip away,
I launch all men and women forward with me into the Unknown.

The clock indicates the moment—but what does eternity indicate?

We have thus far exhausted trillions of winters and summers,
There are trillions ahead, and trillions ahead of them.

Births have brought us richness and variety,
And other births will bring us richness and variety.

I do not call one greater and one smaller,
That which fills its period and place is equal to any.

Were mankind murderous or jealous upon you, my brother, my sister?
I am sorry for you, they are not murderous or jealous upon me,
All has been gentle with me, I keep no account with lamentation,
(What have I to do with lamentation?)

I am an acme of things accomplish'd, and I an encloser of things to be.

[20] Primitive natives of Sumatra. [21] Filth, excrement.

My feet strike an apex of the apices[22] of the stairs,
On every step bunches of ages, and larger bunches between the steps,
All below duly travel'd, and still I mount and mount.

Rise after rise bow the phantoms behind me,
Afar down I see the huge first Nothing, I know I was even there,
I waited unseen and always, and slept through the lethargic mist,
And took my time, and took no hurt from the fetid carbon.

Long I was hugg'd close—long and long.

Immense have been the preparations for me,
Faithful and friendly the arms that have help'd me.

Cycles ferried my cradle, rowing and rowing like cheerful boatmen,
For room to me stars kept aside in their own rings,
They sent influences to look after what was to hold me.

Before I was born out of my mother generations guided me,
My embryo has never been torpid, nothing could overlay it.

For it the nebula cohered to an orb,[23]
The long slow strata piled to rest it on,
Vast vegetables gave it sustenance,
Monstrous sauroids[24] transported it in their mouths and deposited it
with care.

All forces have been steadily employ'd to complete and delight me,
Now on this spot I stand with my robust soul!

45

O span of youth! ever-push'd elasticity!
O manhood, balanced, florid and full.

My lovers suffocate me,
Crowding my lips, thick in the pores of my skin,
Jostling me through streets and public halls, coming naked to me at
night,
Crying by day *Ahoy!* from the rocks of the river, swinging and chirp-
ing over my head,
Calling my name from flower-beds, vines, tangled underbrush,
Lighting on every moment of my life,
Bussing[25] my body with soft balsamic[26] busses,
Noiselessly passing handfuls out of their hearts and giving them to be
mine.

Old age superbly rising! O welcome, ineffable grace of dying days!

[22] Plural of apex.
[23] A cloudlike mass of gas attached itself to a globe. (Whitman is describing the formation of the earth.)
[24] Prehistoric reptiles. [25] Kissing. [26] With the sweet odor of balsam.

Every condition promulges[27] not only itself, it promulges what grows
after and out of itself,
And the dark hush promulges as much as any.

I open my scuttle[28] at night and see the far-sprinkled systems,
And all I see multiplied as high as I can cipher edge but the rim of the
farther systems.

Wider and wider they spread, expanding, always expanding,
Outward and outward and forever outward.

My sun has his sun and round him obediently wheels,
He joins with his partners a group of superior circuit,
And greater sets follow, making specks of the greatest inside them.

There is no stoppage and never can be stoppage,
If I, you, and the worlds, and all beneath or upon their surfaces, were
this moment reduced back to a pallid float, it would not avail in the
long run,
We should surely bring up again where we now stand,
And surely go as much farther, and then farther and farther.

A few quadrillions of eras, a few octillions of cubic leagues, do not
hazard the span or make it impatient,
They are but parts, any thing is but a part.

See ever so far, there is limitless space outside of that,
Count ever so much, there is limitless time around that.

My rendezvous is appointed, it is certain,
The Lord will be there and wait till I come on perfect terms,
The great Camerado,[29] the lover true for whom I pine will be there.

46

I know I have the best of time and space, and was never measured
and never will be measured.

I tramp a perpetual journey, (come listen all!)
My signs are a rain-proof coat, good shoes, and a staff cut from the
woods,
No friend of mine takes his ease in my chair,
I have no chair, no church, no philosophy,
I lead no man to a dinner-table, library, exchange,
But each man and each woman of you I lead upon a knoll,
My left hand hooking you round the waist,
My right hand pointing to landscapes of continents and the public
road.

[27] Promulgates; generates. [28] An opening in a roof (nautical term).
[29] Comrade (Spanish).

Not I, not any one else can travel that road for you,
You must travel it for yourself.

It is not far, it is within reach,
Perhaps you have been on it since you were born and did not know,
Perhaps it is everywhere on water and on land.

Shoulder your duds[30] dear son, and I will mine, and let us hasten forth,
Wonderful cities and free nations we shall fetch[31] as we go.

If you tire, give me both burdens, and rest the chuff[32] of your hand on my hip,
And in due time you shall repay the same service to me,
For after we start we never lie by again.

This day before dawn I ascended a hill and look'd at the crowded heaven,
And I said to my spirit *When we become the enfolders of those orbs, and the pleasure and knowledge of every thing in them, shall we be fill'd and satisfied then?*
And my spirit said *No, we but level that lift*[33] *to pass and continue beyond.*

You are also asking me questions and I hear you,
I answer that I cannot answer, you must find out for yourself.

Sit a while dear son,
Here are biscuits to eat and here is milk to drink,
But as soon as you sleep and renew yourself in sweet clothes, I kiss you with a good-by kiss and open the gate for your egress[34] hence.

Long enough have you dream'd contemptible dreams,
Now I wash the gum from your eyes,
You must habit yourself to the dazzle of the light and of every moment of your life.

Long have you timidly waded holding a plank by the shore,
Now I will you to be a bold swimmer,
To jump off in the midst of the sea, rise again, nod to me, shout, and laughingly dash with your hair.

47

I am the teacher of athletes.
He that by me spreads a wider breast than my own proves the width of my own.
He most honors my style who learns under it to destroy the teacher.

The boy I love, the same becomes a man not through derived power but in his own right,

[30] Clothes (in a pack). [31] Reach. [32] Heel. [33] Rising ground. [34] Exit.

Wicked rather than virtuous out of conformity or fear,
Fond of his sweetheart, relishing well his steak,
Unrequited love or a slight cutting him worse than sharp steel cuts,
First-rate to ride, to fight, to hit the bull's eye, to sail a skiff, to sing a song or play on the banjo,
Preferring scars and the beard and faces pitted with small-pox over all latherers,
And those well-tann'd to those that keep out of the sun.

I teach straying from me, yet who can stray from me?
I follow you whoever you are from the present hour,
My words itch at your ears till you understand them.

I do not say these things for a dollar or to fill up the time while I wait for a boat,
(It is you talking just as much as myself, I act as the tongue of you,
Tied in your mouth, in mine it begins to be loosen'd.)

I swear I will never again mention love or death inside a house,
And I swear I will never translate myself at all, only to him or her who privately stays with me in the open air.

If you would understand me go to the heights or water-shore,
The nearest gnat is an explanation, and a drop or motion of waves a key,
The maul, the oar, the hand-saw, second my words.

No shutter'd room or school can commune with me,
But roughs and little children better than they.

The young mechanic is closest to me, he knows me well,
The woodman that takes his axe and jug with him shall take me with him all day,
The farm-boy ploughing in the field feels good at the sound of my voice,
In vessels that sail my words sail, I go with fishermen and seamen and love them.

The soldier camp'd or upon the march is mine,
On the night ere the pending battle many seek me, and I do not fail them,
On that solemn night (it may be their last) those that know me seek me.

My face rubs to the hunter's face when he lies down alone in his blanket,
The driver thinking of me does not mind the jolt of his wagon,
The young mother and old mother comprehend me,

The girl and the wife rest the needle a moment and forget where they are,
They and all would resume[35] what I have told them.

48

I have said that the soul is not more than the body,
And I have said that the body is not more than the soul,
And nothing, not God, is greater to one than one's self is,
And whoever walks a furlong without sympathy walks to his own funeral drest in his shroud,
And I or you pocketless of a dime may purchase the pick of the earth,
And to glance with an eye or show a bean in its pod confounds the learning of all times,
And there is no trade or employment but the young man following it may become a hero,
And there is no object so soft but it makes a hub for the wheel'd universe,
And I say to any man or woman, Let your soul stand cool and composed before a million universes.

And I say to mankind, Be not curious about God,
For I who am curious about each am not curious about God,
(No array of terms can say how much I am at peace about God and about death.)

I hear and behold God in every object, yet understand God not in the least,
Nor do I understand who there can be more wonderful than myself.

Why should I wish to see God better than this day?
I see something of God each hour of the twenty-four, and each moment then,
In the faces of men and women I see God, and in my own face in the glass,
I find letters from God dropt in the street, and every one is sign'd by God's name,
And I leave them where they are, for I know that whereso'er I go
Others will punctually come for ever and ever.

49

And as to you Death, and you bitter hug of mortality, it is idle to try to alarm me.

To his work without flinching the accoucheur[36] comes,
I see the elder-hand[37] pressing receiving supporting,
I recline by the sills of the exquisite flexible doors,
And mark the outlet, and mark the relief and escape.

[35] Sum up. [36] Male assistant at childbirth. [37] Left hand.

And as to you Corpse I think you are good manure, but that does not offend me,
I smell the white roses sweet-scented and growing,
I reach to the leafy lips, I reach to the polish'd breasts of melons.

And as to you Life I reckon you are the leavings of many deaths,
(No doubt I have died myself ten thousand times before.)

I hear you whispering there O stars of heaven,
O suns—O grass of graves—O perpetual transfers and promotions,
If you do not say any thing how can I say any thing?

Of the turbid[38] pool that lies in the autumn forest,
Of the moon that descends the steeps of the soughing[39] twilight,
Toss, sparkles of day and dusk—toss on the black stems that decay in the muck,
Toss to the moaning gibberish of the dry limbs.

I ascend from the moon, I ascend from the night,
I perceive that the ghastly glimmer is noonday sunbeams reflected,
And debouch[40] to the steady and central from the offspring great or small.

50

There is that in me—I do not know what it is—but I know it is in me.

Wrench'd and sweaty—calm and cool then my body becomes,
I sleep—I sleep long.

I do not know it—it is without name—it is a word unsaid,
It is not in any dictionary, utterance, symbol.

Something it swings on more than the earth I swing on,
To it the creation is the friend whose embracing awakes me.

Perhaps I might tell more. Outlines! I plead for my brothers and sisters.

Do you see O my brothers and sisters?
It is not chaos or death—it is form, union, plan—it is eternal life—it is Happiness.

51

The past and present wilt—I have fill'd them, emptied them,
And proceed to fill my next fold of the future.

Listener up there! what have you to confide to me?

[38] Cloudy, muddy. [39] Rustling, murmuring. [40] Emerge.

Look in my face while I snuff the sidle[41] of evening,
(Talk honestly, no one else hears you, and I stay only a minute longer.)

Do I contradict myself?
Very well then I contradict myself,
(I am large, I contain multitudes.)

I concentrate toward them that are nigh, I wait on the door-slab.

Who has done his day's work? who will soonest be through with his supper?
Who wishes to walk with me?

Will you speak before I am gone? will you prove already too late?

52

The spotted hawk swoops by and accuses me, he complains of my gab and my loitering.

I too am not a bit tamed, I too am untranslatable,
I sound my barbaric yawp[42] over the roofs of the world.

The last scud[43] of day holds back for me,
It flings my likeness after the rest and true as any on the shadow'd wilds,
It coaxes me to the vapor and the dusk.

I depart as air, I shake my white locks at the runaway sun,
I effuse[44] my flesh in eddies, and drift it in lacy jags.

I bequeath myself to the dirt to grow from the grass I love,
If you want me again look for me under your boot-soles.

You will hardly know who I am or what I mean,
But I shall be good health to you nevertheless,
And filter and fibre your blood.

Failing to fetch me at first keep encouraged,
Missing me one place search another,
I stop somewhere waiting for you.

[41] Fading light. [42] Shout, cry. [43] Clouds or mist driven by the wind.
[44] Pour out.

WHEN LILACS LAST IN THE DOORYARD BLOOM'D

1

When lilacs last in the dooryard bloom'd,
And the great star[1] early droop'd in the western sky in the night,
I mourn'd, and yet shall mourn with ever-returning spring.

Ever-returning spring, trinity sure to me you bring,
Lilac blooming perennial and drooping star in the west,
And thought of him I love.

2

O powerful western fallen star!
O shades of night—O moody, tearful night!
O great star disappear'd—O the black murk that hides the star!
O cruel hands that hold me powerless—O helpless soul of me!
O harsh surrounding cloud that will not free my soul.

3

In the dooryard fronting an old farm-house near the white-wash'd palings,
Stands the lilac-bush tall-growing with heart-shaped leaves of rich green,
With many a pointed blossom rising delicate, with the perfume strong I love,
With every leaf a miracle—and from this bush in the dooryard,
With delicate-color'd blossoms and heart-shaped leaves of rich green,
A sprig with its flower I break.

4

In the swamp in secluded recesses,
A shy and hidden bird is warbling a song.

Solitary the thrush,
The hermit withdrawn to himself, avoiding the settlements,
Sings by himself a song.

Song of the bleeding throat,
Death's outlet song of life, (for well dear brother I know,
If thou wast not granted to sing thou would'st surely die.)

5

Over the breast of the spring, the land, amid cities,
Amid lanes and through old woods, where lately the violets peep'd from the ground, spotting the gray debris,

[1] Venus, the evening star.

Amid the grass in the fields each side of the lanes, passing the endless grass,
Passing the yellow-spear'd wheat, every grain from its shroud in the dark-brown fields uprisen,
Passing the apple-tree blows of white and pink in the orchards,
Carrying a corpse to where it shall rest in the grave,
Night and day journeys a coffin.[2]

6

Coffin that passes through lanes and streets,
Through day and night with the great cloud darkening the land,
With the pomp of the inloop'd flags with the cities draped in black,
With the show of the States themselves as of crape-veil'd women standing,
With processions long and winding and the flambeaus[3] of the night,
With the countless torches lit, with the silent sea of faces and the unbared heads,
With the waiting depot, the arriving coffin, and the sombre faces,
With dirges through the night, with the thousand voices rising strong and solemn,
With all the mournful voices of the dirges pour'd around the coffin,
The dim-lit churches and the shuddering organs—where amid these you journey,
With the tolling tolling bells' perpetual clang,
Here, coffin that slowly passes,
I give you my sprig of lilac.

7

(Nor for you, for one alone,
Blossoms and branches green to coffins all I bring,
For fresh as the morning, thus would I chant a song for you O sane and sacred death.

All over bouquets of roses,
O death, I cover you over with roses and early lilies,
But mostly and now the lilac that blooms the first,
Copious I break, I break the sprigs from the bushes,
With loaded arms I come, pouring for you,
For you and the coffins all of you O death.)

8

O western orb sailing the heaven,
Now I know what you must have meant as a month since I walk'd,

[2] Lincoln was assassinated on Good Friday, April 14, 1865. After a funeral service in Washington, his body was taken by train to Springfield, Illinois for burial. The journey, at twenty miles an hour, took two weeks, through scenes of grief like those Whitman describes.
[3] Torches.

As I walk'd in silence the transparent shadowy night,
As I saw you had something to tell as you bent to me night after night,
As you droop'd from the sky low down as if to my side, (while the other stars all look'd on,)
As we wander'd together the solemn night, (for something I know not what kept me from sleep,)
As the night advanced, and I saw on the rim of the west how full you were of woe,
As I stood on the rising ground in the breeze in the cool transparent night,
As I watch'd where you pass'd and was lost in the netherward black of the night,
As my soul in its trouble dissatisfied sank, as where you sad orb,
Concluded, dropt in the night, and was gone.

9

Sing on there in the swamp,
O singer bashful and tender, I hear your notes, I hear your call,
I hear, I come presently, I understand you,
But a moment I linger, for the lustrous star has detain'd me,
The star my departing comrade holds and detains me.

10

O how shall I warble myself for the dead one there I loved?
And how shall I deck my song for the large sweet soul that has gone?
And what shall my perfume be for the grave of him I love?

Sea-winds blown from east and west,
Blown from the Eastern sea and blown from the Western sea, till there on the prairies meeting,
These and with these and the breath of my chant,
I'll perfume the grave of him I love.

11

O what shall I hang on the chamber walls?
And what shall the pictures be that I hang on the walls,
To adorn the burial-house of him I love?

Pictures of growing spring and farms and homes,
With the Fourth-month[4] eve at sundown, and the gray smoke lucid and bright,
With floods of the yellow gold of the gorgeous, indolent, sinking sun, burning, expanding the air,
With the fresh sweet herbage under foot, and the pale green leaves of the trees prolific,
In the distance the flowing glaze, the breast of the river, with a wind-dapple here and there,

[4] The Quaker term for April.

With ranging hills on the banks, with many a line against the sky, and shadows,
And the city at hand with dwellings so dense, and stacks of chimneys,
And all the scenes of life and the workshops, and the workmen homeward returning.

12

Lo, body and soul—this land,
My own Manhattan with spires, and the sparkling and hurrying tides, and the ships,
The varied and ample land, the South and the North in the light, Ohio's shores and flashing Missouri,
And ever the far-spreading prairies cover'd with grass and corn.

Lo, the most excellent sun so calm and haughty,
The violet and purple morn with just-felt breezes,
The gentle soft-born measureless light,
The miracle spreading bathing all, the fulfill'd noon,
The coming eve delicious, the welcome night and the stars,
Over my cities shining all, enveloping man and land.

13

Sing on, sing on you gray-brown bird,
Sing from the swamps, the recesses, pour your chant from the bushes,
Limitless out of the dusk, out of the cedars and pines.

Sing on dearest brother, warble your reedy song,
Loud human song, with voice of uttermost woe.

O liquid and free and tender!
O wild and loose to my soul—O wondrous singer,
You only I hear—yet the star holds me, (but will soon depart,)
Yet the lilac with mastering odor holds me.

14

Now while I sat in the day and look'd forth,
In the close of the day with its light and the fields of spring, and the farmers preparing their crops,
In the large unconscious scenery of my land with its lakes and forests,
In the heavenly aerial beauty, (after the perturb'd winds and the storms,)
Under the arching heavens of the afternoon swift passing, and the voices of children and women,
The many-moving sea-tides, and I saw the ships how they sail'd,
And the summer approaching with richness, and the fields all busy with labor,
And the infinite separate houses, how they all went on, each with its meals and minutia of daily usages,

And the streets how their throbbings throbb'd, and the cities pent—lo, then and there,
Falling upon them all and among them all, enveloping me with the rest,
Appear'd the cloud, appear'd the long black trail,
And I knew death, its thought, and the sacred knowledge of death.

Then with the knowledge of death as walking one side of me,
And the thought of death close-walking the other side of me,
And I in the middle as with companions, and as holding the hands of companions,
I fled forth to the hiding receiving night that talks not,
Down to the shores of the water, the path by the swamp in the dimness,
To the solemn shadowy cedars and ghostly pines so still.

And the singer so shy to the rest receiv'd me,
The gray-brown bird I know receiv'd us comrades three,
And he sang the carol of death, and a verse for him I love.

From deep secluded recesses,
From the fragrant cedars and the ghostly pines so still,
Came the carol of the bird.

And the charm of the carol rapt me,
As I held as if by their hands my comrades in the night,
And the voice of my spirit tallied the song of the bird.

Come lovely and soothing death,
Undulate round the world, serenely arriving, arriving,
In the day, in the night, to all, to each,
Sooner or later delicate death.

Prais'd be the fathomless universe,
For life and joy, and for objects and knowledge curious,
And for love, sweet love—but praise! praise! praise!
For the sure-enwinding arms of cool-enfolding death.

Dark mother always gliding near with soft feet,
Have none chanted for thee a chant of fullest welcome?
Then I chant it for thee, I glorify thee above all,
I bring thee a song that when thou must indeed come, come unfalteringly.

Approach strong deliveress,
When it is so, when thou hast taken them I joyously sing the dead,
Lost in the loving floating ocean of thee,
Laved[5] *in the flood of thy bliss O death.*

[5] Bathed.

From me to thee glad serenades,
Dances for thee I propose saluting thee, adornments and feastings for thee,
And the sights of the open landscape and the high-spread sky are fitting,
And life and the fields, and the huge and thoughtful night.

The night in silence under many a star,
The ocean shore and the husky whispering wave whose voice I know,
And the soul turning to thee O vast and well-veil'd death,
And the body gratefully nestling close to thee.

Over the tree-tops I float thee a song,
Over the rising and singing waves, over the myriad fields and the prairies wide,
Over the dense-pack'd cities all and the teeming wharves and ways,
I float this carol with joy, with joy to thee O death.

15

To the tally of my soul,
Loud and strong kept up the gray-brown bird,
With pure deliberate notes spreading filling the night.

Loud in the pines and cedars dim,
Clear in the freshness moist and the swamp-perfume,
And I with my comrades there in the night.

While my sight that was bound in my eyes unclosed,
As to long panoramas of visions.

And I saw askant[6] the armies,
I saw as in noiseless dreams hundreds of battle-flags,
Borne through the smoke of the battles and pierc'd with missiles I saw them,
And carried hither and yon through the smoke, and torn and bloody,
And at last but a few shreds left on the staffs, (and all in silence,)
And the staffs all splinter'd and broken.

I saw battle-corpses, myriads of them,
And the white skeletons of young men, I saw them,
I saw the debris and debris of all the slain soldiers of the war,
But I saw they were not as was thought,
They themselves were fully at rest, they suffer'd not,
The living remain'd and suffer'd, the mother suffer'd,
And the wife and the child and the musing comrade suffer'd,
And the armies that remain'd suffer'd.

16

Passing the visions, passing the night,
Passing, unloosing the hold of my comrades' hands,

[6] With suspicion or mistrust.

Passing the song of the hermit bird and the tallying song of my soul,
Victorious song, death's outlet song, yet varying ever-altering song,
As low and wailing, yet clear the notes, rising and falling, flooding the night,
Sadly sinking and fainting, as warning and warning, and yet again bursting with joy,
Covering the earth and filling the spread of the heaven,
As that powerful psalm in the night I heard from recesses,
Passing, I leave thee lilac with heart-shaped leaves,
I leave thee there in the door-yard, blooming, returning with spring.

I cease from my song for thee,
From my gaze on thee in the west, fronting the west, communing with thee,
O comrade lustrous with silver face in the night.

Yet each to keep and all, retrievements out of the night,
The song, the wondrous chant of the gray-brown bird,
And the tallying chant, the echo arous'd in my soul,
With the lustrous and drooping star with the countenance full of woe,
With the holders holding my hand nearing the call of the bird,
Comrades mine and I in the midst, and their memory ever to keep, for the dead I loved so well,
For the sweetest, wisest soul of all my days and lands—and this for his dear sake,
Lilac and star and bird twined with the chant of my soul,
There in the fragrant pines and the cedars dusk and dim.

Herman Melville
(1819–1891)

Masterpieces came close upon one another's heels in America in the 1850's. Ralph Waldo Emerson's Representative Men *and Nathaniel Hawthorne's* The Scarlet Letter *were both published in 1850; Herman Melville's* Moby-Dick *followed in 1851; Henry David Thoreau's* Walden *in 1854; and Walt Whitman's* Leaves of Grass *in 1855. All these books have had a major impact upon modern world literature, but they are also intensely American; all touch universal concerns through the local and the topical. Together, they constitute a sort of five-voiced discussion of the question of the prospects of the American Adam in an Edenic continent rapidly being filled up through Yankee hustle. The five voices, it is generally held, are on two sides:*

on one, Emerson, Thoreau, and Whitman, from their own particular points of view, argue optimistically for the almost unlimited development of democratic man; on the other, Hawthorne and Melville point to the serpent in the shrubbery, the blackness in the human situation that persists despite changes in social organization.

Herman Melville, born in New York City in 1819, learned the lessons of blackness early. When he was eleven, his father, a well-to-do merchant, went bankrupt; two years later he died, driven insane through worry and overwork. The widow moved with her children to Albany. By the time Melville was twenty, he had worked as a bank clerk, a salesman, a farmhand, and a schoolteacher. In 1839, he signed on as a cabinboy for a voyage to Liverpool and back, a shocking experience of brutality and vice. In 1841, he sailed, this time as a seaman, on the whaler Acushnet, *bound for the South Seas. After eighteen months, he jumped ship in the Marquesas Islands, encountered a tribe of cannibals, and left the islands on an Australian whaler, whose crew mutinied. Melville was briefly imprisoned in Tahiti for his share in the mutiny. After a period of beachcombing in Tahiti and clerking in Hawaii, he signed on as part of the crew of the American frigate* United States; *during the fourteen-month voyage home, Melville witnessed firsthand the injustice and brutality of navy life. The ship arrived in Boston in October, 1844, and Melville was discharged along with the rest of the crew. The experiences of this three-year adventure were to furnish him with the materials of his books and to shape his attitudes for the rest of his life.*

Typee, *a barely fictionalized account of his experiences in the Marquesas, appeared in 1846, and* Omoo, *which continues the story of the voyage through the mutiny and Tahiti, followed in 1847. Both books were successful, but Melville's next book,* Mardi, *was greeted with bafflement. Again the book dealt with a young American deserter in the South Seas, but the narrative burst the bonds of the romantic adventure genre to become a dense political and religious allegory. The protagonist Taji, in quest of the beautiful Yillah, sails through the allegorical islands of the Mardi archipelago, discussing metaphysical questions with the philosopher Babbalanja. Stung by the failure of this strange, experimental book, Melville returned to more conventional sea stories with* Redburn *(1849), the story of his first voyage to Liverpool, and* White Jacket *(1850), based on his voyage home from Hawaii aboard the* United States.

Melville had married in 1847, and in 1850, he moved with his wife to the village of Pittsfield, Massachusetts, where he began a new sea novel, Moby-Dick. *Nathaniel Hawthorne lived only seven miles away, in the village of Lenox, and the two writers developed a close friendship that was to leave a lasting mark on Melville's work. Melville, as* Mardi *demonstrates, had already begun to experiment with ways to enrich literal narrative, making it suggest deeper levels of experience, and the personal influence of Hawthorne, as well as that of his cryptic, suggestive tales, led him to develop the allusive and symbolic dimensions of his story. The first draft of* Moby-Dick *seems to have been a fairly literal, documentary whaling narrative; the second draft, completed under Hawthorne's influence, became a richly symbolic quest story, "broiled in hell fire." It is narrated by a young man named Ishmael, superficially at least much like the narrator of* Typee, *but it deals with the obsessed, demonic Captain Ahab, perhaps Ishmael's double, who, like many of Hawthorne's protagonists, has arrogantly isolated himself from life in a quest not only for the white whale but for more than human knowledge.*

The commercial failure of Moby-Dick, *which he knew was his masterpiece, embittered Melville, who became increasingly alienated from his family and friends. He continued to write.* Pierre *(1852), a bitter, dreamlike allegory, mystified readers even more than* Moby-Dick. Israel Potter, *a historical novel, appeared in 1855, and* Piazza Tales, *a collection of short stories which included "Bartleby the Scrivener," appeared in 1856.* The Confidence Man *(1857) explores, aboard a Mississippi riverboat, the theme of truth and illusion.*

In 1866, Melville obtained the post of deputy customs inspector in New York, a job that provided the financial security his books had never provided but which left him little time for writing. Clarel, *a book-length symbolic poem about a trip to Palestine, was published in 1876; three collections of shorter poems also appeared during Melville's lifetime. He resigned the customs job in 1885 and died six years later, virtually forgotten as a writer but leaving one of his finest stories, the novella* Billy Budd, *in manuscript among his effects. It was not until the 1930's that Melville's works were rediscovered and republished and he began the rapid rise to fame that has now placed him with Hawthorne, Thoreau, and Whitman among the giants of American literature.*

Melville's contemporaries (or those who had heard of him at all) thought of him as a writer of adventure stories who had lapsed into writing jumbled, possibly crazed, allegories. From our perspective, we can see his work as perhaps complex and sometimes tortured but remarkably unified around a handful of rich and profoundly explored themes. The most important of these is evil and the individual's recognition and response to it, both in the outside world and in himself. Even the comparatively simple sea stories explore sardonically the intrusion of Western, "Christian" culture, with its burden of vice, disease, and guilt, into the Edenic societies of the South Seas. Captain Ahab, the Promethean Romantic individualist, thinks he is pursuing Evil itself in the form of the white whale. But is Moby-Dick "Evil" (or even "evil"?) As whiteness contains all colors, so the whiteness of the whale contains all possibilities; it is infinite in its possibilities and in its mysteriousness. And as Ahab pursues the monster upon which he has projected aspects of his own nature that he has denied, he ironically comes more and more to resemble his hated antagonist; at the end, he goes to his death bound by the harpoon lines to the whale. Captain Vere, in Billy Budd, *for all his apparent humaneness and moral sensitivity, is Captain Ahab's brother in one respect; like him, he is blind to his own evil. He rationalizes his own actions by conservative appeals to law and institutions, but Billy hangs just the same.*

Melville was at his best within the roominess of the novel, but he wrote a number of short stories and novellas as well, and in at least two, "Benito Cereno" and "Bartleby the Scrivener," he was able to achieve effective expressions of his sardonic vision. Bartleby is one of those isolates, dropouts from ordinary life, whom both Melville and his friend Hawthorne liked to dissect. But Bartleby is no Ahab, or even a Young Goodman Brown; he is just a crank, and his story is told as black comedy. Why does Bartleby decide that he "would prefer not to," and what does his polite but firm disengagement from life and drift toward death mean? Critics have varied widely in their answers. For one, the story is an economic allegory and Bartleby is a working-class hero who refuses to compete within the capitalist system. Another finds in the story a fable of Melville's attempts to write commercial magazine fiction in the 1850's (he would have preferred not to). But is Bartleby even the main character? A case could equally well be made that the real center of interest is the genial, liberal narrator, who prides himself on his connection with John Jacob Astor and who is "filled with a profound conviction that the easiest way of life is the best." The rest of his staff—the grotesque Turkey, Nippers, and Ginger Nut—seem to suggest some aspects of himself that he has repressed, and perhaps the sepulchral Bartleby, to whom he feels bound in so intimate and sympathetic a relationship, may represent the emergence of a hidden blackness in himself.

FURTHER READING *(prepared by W. J. R.):* A superior introduction to Melville is Newton Arvin's *Herman Melville,* 1950, rpt. 1957, which received a National Book Award. Tyrus Hillway's *Herman Melville,* 1963, rev. 1979, contains a fine critical survey of Melville, with chapters on his life and individual treatments of the major works. Milton R. Stern's *The Fine Hammered Steel of Herman Melville,* 1957, deals extensively with Melville's anti-idealism. Further direction for the new reader can be found in James E. Miller, Jr.'s *A Reader's Guide to Herman Melville,* 1973. Miller offers a good overview, with detailed discussions of the major works. M. O. Percival's *A Reading of "Moby Dick,"* 1950, is an excellent introduction to Melville's masterpiece. Percival discusses the primary themes and provides a good background for more specialized Melville criticism. Leading critical perspectives on *Moby-Dick* are represented in *Discussions of "Moby-Dick,"* ed. Milton R. Stern, 1960. The sections on "Ahab and Evil" and "Ritual, Myth, and Psychology" are of particular interest. Critical reactions to a number of Melville works are offered in *Melville: A Collection of Critical Essays,* ed. Richard Chase, 1962.

BARTLEBY THE SCRIVENER

A STORY OF WALL STREET

I am a rather elderly man. The nature of my avocations, for the last thirty years, has brought me into more than ordinary contact with what would seem an interesting and somewhat singular set of men, of whom, as yet, nothing, that I know of, has ever been written—I mean, the law-copyists, or scriveners. I have known very many of them, professionally and privately, and, if I pleased, could relate divers histories, at which good-natured gentlemen might smile, and sentimental souls might weep. But I waive the biographies of all other scriveners, for a few passages in the life of Bartleby, who was a scrivener, the strangest I ever saw, or heard of. While, of other law-copyists, I might write the complete life, of Bartleby nothing of that sort can be done. I believe that no materials exist, for a full and satisfactory biography of this man. It is an irreparable loss to literature. Bartleby was one of those beings of whom nothing is ascertainable, except from the original sources, and, in his case, those are very small. What my own astonished eyes saw of Bartleby, *that* is all I know of him, except, indeed, one vague report, which will appear in the sequel.

Ere introducing the scrivener, as he first appeared to me, it is fit I make some mention of myself, my *employés,* my business, my chambers, and general surroundings; because some such description is indispensable to an adequate understanding of the chief character about to be presented. Imprimis:[1] I am a man who, from his youth upwards, has been filled with a profound conviction that the easiest way of life is the best. Hence, though I belong to a profession proverbially energetic and nervous, even to turbu-

[1] In the first place.

lence, at times, yet nothing of that sort have I ever suffered to invade my peace. I am one of those unambitious lawyers who never address a jury, or in any way draw down public applause; but, in the cool tranquillity of a snug retreat, do a snug business among rich men's bonds, and mortgages, and title-deeds. All who know me, consider me an eminently *safe* man. The late John Jacob Astor,[2] a personage little given to poetic enthusiasm, had no hesitation in pronouncing my first grand point to be prudence; my next, method. I do not speak it in vanity, but simply record the fact, that I was not unemployed in my profession by the late John Jacob Astor; a name which, I admit, I love to repeat; for it hath a rounded and orbicular sound to it, and rings like unto bullion. I will freely add, that I was not insensible to the late John Jacob Astor's good opinion.

Some time prior to the period at which this little history begins, my avocations had been largely increased. The good old office, now extinct in the State of New York, of a Master of Chancery,[3] had been conferred upon me. It was not a very arduous office, but very pleasantly remunerative. I seldom lose my temper; much more seldom indulge in dangerous indignation at wrongs and outrages; but I must be permitted to be rash here and declare, that I consider the sudden and violent abrogation of the office of Master in Chancery, by the new Constitution, as a —— premature act; inasmuch as I had counted upon a life-lease of the profits, whereas I only received those of a few short years. But this is by the way.

My chambers were up stairs, at No. — Wall Street. At one end, they looked upon the white wall of the interior of a spacious skylight shaft, penetrating the building from top to bottom.

This view might have been considered rather tame than otherwise, deficient in what landscape painters call "life." But, if so, the view from the other end of my chambers offered, at least, a contrast, if nothing more. In that direction, my windows commanded an unobstructed view of a lofty brick wall, black by age and everlasting shade; which wall required no spy-glass to bring out its lurking beauties, but, for the benefit of all near-sighted spectators, was pushed up to within ten feet of my window-panes. Owing to the great height of the surrounding buildings, and my chambers being on the second floor, the interval between this wall and mine not a little resembled a huge square cistern.

At the period just preceding the advent of Bartleby, I had two persons as copyists in my employment, and a promising lad as an office-boy. First, Turkey; second, Nippers; third, Ginger Nut. These may seem names, the like of which are not usually found in the Directory. In truth, they were nicknames, mutually conferred upon each other by my three clerks, and were deemed expressive of their respective persons or characters. Turkey was a short, pursy Englishman, of about my own age—that is, somewhere not far from sixty. In the morning, one might say, his face was of a fine florid hue, but after twelve o'clock, meridian—his dinner hour—it blazed like a grate full of Christmas coals; and continued blazing—but, as it were, with a gradual wane—till six o'clock, P.M., or thereabouts; after which, I saw no more of the proprietor of the face, which, gaining its meridian with

[2] American merchant (1763–1848); at his death, the richest man in the United States.
[3] A Master of Chancery presided over equity cases, without a jury.

the sun, seemed to set with it, to rise, culminate, and decline the following day, with the like regularity and undiminished glory. There are many singular coincidences I have known in the course of my life, not the least among which was the fact, that, exactly when Turkey displayed his fullest beams from his red and radiant countenance, just then, too, at that critical moment, began the daily period when I considered his business capacities as seriously disturbed for the remainder of the twenty-four hours. Not that he was absolutely idle, or averse to business then; far from it. The difficulty was, he was apt to be altogether too energetic. There was a strange, inflamed, flurried, flighty recklessness of activity about him. He would be incautious in dipping his pen into his inkstand. All his blots upon my documents were dropped there after twelve o'clock, meridian. Indeed, not only would he be reckless, and sadly given to making blots in the afternoon, but, some days, he went further, and was rather noisy. At such times, too, his face flamed with augmented blazonry, as if cannel coal had been heaped on anthracite. He made an unpleasant racket with his chair; spilled his sandbox; in mending his pens, impatiently split them all to pieces, and threw them on the floor in a sudden passion; stood up, and leaned over his table, boxing his papers about in a most indecorous manner, very sad to behold in an elderly man like him. Nevertheless, as he was in many ways a most valuable person to me, and all the time before twelve o'clock, meridian, was the quickest, steadiest creature, too, accomplishing a great deal of work in a style not easily to be matched—for these reasons, I was willing to overlook his eccentricities, though, indeed, occasionally, I remonstrated with him. I did this very gently, however, because, though the civilest, nay, the blandest and most reverential of men in the morning, yet, in the afternoon, he was disposed, upon provocation, to be slightly rash with his tongue—in fact, insolent. Now, valuing his morning services as I did, and resolved not to lose them—yet, at the same time, made uncomfortable by his inflamed ways after twelve o'clock—and being a man of peace, unwilling by my admonitions to call forth unseemly retorts from him, I took upon me, one Saturday noon (he was always worse on Saturdays) to hint to him, very kindly, that, perhaps, now that he was growing old, it might be well to abridge his labors; in short, he need not come to my chambers after twelve o'clock, but, dinner over, had best go home to his lodgings, and rest himself till tea-time. But no; he insisted upon his afternoon devotions. His countenance became intolerably fervid, as he oratorically assured me—gesticulating with a long ruler at the other end of the room—that if his services in the morning were useful, how indispensable, then, in the afternoon?

"With submission, sir" said Turkey, on this occasion, "I consider myself your right-hand man. In the morning I but marshall and deploy my columns; but in the afternoon I put myself at their head, and gallantly charge the foe, thus"—and he made a violent thrust with the ruler.

"But the blots, Turkey," intimated I.

"True; but, with submission, sir, behold these hairs! I am getting old. Surely, sir, a blot or two of a warm afternoon is not to be severely urged against gray hairs. Old age—even if it blot the page—is honorable. With submission, sir, we *both* are getting old."

This appeal to my fellow-feeling was hardly to be resisted. At all events, I saw that go he would not. So, I made up my mind to let him stay, resolving, nevertheless, to see to it that, during the afternoon, he had to do with my less important papers.

Nippers, the second on my list, was a whiskered, sallow, and, upon the whole, rather piratical-looking young man, of about five-and-twenty. I alway deemed him the victim of two evil powers—ambition and indigestion. The ambition was evinced by a certain impatience of the duties of a mere copyist, an unwarrantable usurpation of strictly professional affairs such as the original drawing up of legal documents. The indigestion seemed betokened in an occasional nervous testiness and grinning irritability, causing the teeth to audibly grind together over mistakes committed in copying; unnecessary maledictions, hissed, rather than spoken, in the heat of business; and especially by a continual discontent with the height of the table where he worked. Though of a very ingenious mechanical turn, Nippers could never get this table to suit him. He put chips under it, blocks of various sorts, bits of pasteboard, and at last went so far as to attempt an exquisite adjustment, by final pieces of folded blotting-paper. But no invention would answer. If, for the sake of easing his back, he brought the table-lid at a sharp angle well up towards his chin, and wrote there like a man using the steep roof of a Dutch house for his desk, then he declared that it stopped the circulation in his arms. If now he lowered the table to his waistbands, and stooped over it in writing, then there was a sore aching in his back. In short, the truth of the matter was, Nippers knew not what he wanted. Or, if he wanted anything, it was to be rid of a scrivener's table altogether. Among the manifestations of his diseased ambition was a fondness he had for receiving visits from certain ambiguous-looking fellows in seedy coats, whom he called his clients. Indeed, I was aware that not only was he, at times, considerable of a ward-politician, but he occasionally did a little business at the justices' courts, and was not unknown on the steps of the Tombs.[4] I have good reason to believe, however, that one individual who called upon him at my chambers, and who, with a grand air, he insisted was his client, was no other than a dun, and the alleged title-deed, a bill. But, with all his failings, and the annoyances he caused me, Nippers, like his compatriot Turkey, was a very useful man to me; wrote a neat, swift hand; and, when he chose, was not deficient in a gentlemanly sort of deportment. Added to this, he always dressed in a gentlemanly sort of way; and so, incidentally, reflected credit upon my chambers. Whereas, with respect to Turkey, I had much ado to keep him from being a reproach to me. His clothes were apt to look oily, and smell of eating-houses. He wore his pantaloons very loose and baggy in summer. His coats were execrable; his hat not to be handled. But while the hat was a thing of indifference to me, inasmuch as his natural civility and deference, as a dependent Englishman, always led him to doff it the moment he entered the room, yet his coat was another matter. Concerning his coats, I reasoned with him; but with no effect. The truth was, I suppose, that a man with so small an income could not afford to sport such a lustrous face and a lustrous coat at one and the same time. As Nippers once observed, Turkey's money went chiefly for red

[4]The New York Halls of Justice and House of Detention, familiarly called the "Tombs" because its architecture is reminiscent of Egyptian temples and tombs.

ink. One winter day, I presented Turkey with a highly respectable-looking coat of my own—a padded gray coat, of a most comfortable warmth, and which buttoned straight up from the knee to the neck. I thought Turkey would appreciate the favor, and abate his rashness and obstreperousness of afternoons. But no; I verily believe that buttoning himself up in so downy and blanket-like a coat had a pernicious effect upon him—upon the same principle that too much oats are bad for horses. In fact, precisely as a rash, restive horse is said to feel his oats, so Turkey felt his coat. It made him insolent. He was a man whom prosperity harmed.

Though, concerning the self-indulgent habits of Turkey, I had my own private surmises, yet, touching Nippers, I was well persuaded that, whatever might be his faults in other respects, he was, at least, a temperate young man. But, indeed, nature herself seemed to have been his vintner, and, at his birth, charged him so thoroughly with an irritable, brandy-like disposition, that all subsequent potations were needless. When I consider how, amid the stillness of my chambers, Nippers would sometimes impatiently rise from his seat, and stooping over his table, spread his arms wide apart, seize the whole desk, and move it, and jerk it, with a grim, grinding motion on the floor, as if the table were a perverse voluntary agent, intent on thwarting and vexing him, I plainly perceive that, for Nippers, brandy-and-water were altogether superfluous.

It was fortunate for me that, owing to its peculiar cause—indigestion—the irritability and consequent nervousness of Nippers were mainly observable in the morning, while in the afternoon he was comparatively mild. So that, Turkey's paroxysms only coming on about twelve o'clock, I never had to do with their eccentricities at one time. Their fits relieved each other, like guards. When Nippers' was on, Turkey's was off; and *vice versa.* This was a good natural arrangement, under the circumstances.

Ginger Nut, the third on my list, was a lad, some twelve years old. His father was a carman, ambitious of seeing his son on the bench instead of a cart, before he died. So he sent him to my office, as student at law, errand-boy, cleaner and sweeper, at the rate of one dollar a week. He had a little desk to himself, but he did not use it much. Upon inspection, the drawer exhibited a great array of the shells of various sorts of nuts. Indeed, to this quick-witted youth, the whole noble science of the law was contained in a nutshell. Not the least among the employments of Ginger Nut, as well as one which he discharged with the most alacrity, was his duty as cake and apple purveyor for Turkey and Nippers. Copying law-papers being proverbially a dry, husky sort of business, my two scriveners were fain to moisten their mouths very often with Spitzenbergs,[5] to be had at the numerous stalls nigh the Custom House and Post office. Also, they sent Ginger Nut very frequently for that peculiar cake—small, flat, round, and very spicy—after which he had been named by them. Of a cold morning, when business was but dull, Turkey would gobble up scores of these cakes, as if they were mere wafers—indeed, they sell them at the rate of six or eight for a penny—the scrape of his pen blending with the crunching of the crisp particles in his mouth. Of all the fiery afternoon blunders and flurried

[5]A kind of apple.

rashness of Turkey, was his once moistening a ginger-cake between his lips, and clapping it on to a mortgage, for a seal. I came within an ace of dismissing him then. But he mollified me by making an oriental bow, and saying—

"With submission, sir, it was generous of me to find you in stationery on my own account."

Now my original business—that of a conveyancer and title hunter, and drawer-up of recondite documents of all sorts—was considerably increased by receiving the Master's office. There was now great work for scriveners. Not only must I push the clerks already with me, but I must have additional help.

In answer to my advertisement, a motionless young man one morning stood upon my office threshold, the door being open, for it was summer. I can see that figure now—pallidly neat, pitiably respectable, incurably forlorn! It was Bartleby.

After a few words touching his qualifications, I engaged him, glad to have among my corps of copyists a man of so singularly sedate an aspect, which I thought might operate beneficially upon the flighty temper of Turkey, and the fiery one of Nippers.

I should have stated before that ground-glass folding-doors divided my premises into two parts, one of which was occupied by my scriveners, the other by myself. According to my humor, I threw open these doors, or closed them. I resolved to assign Bartleby a corner by the folding-doors, but on my side of them, so as to have this quiet man within easy call, in case any trifling thing was to be done. I placed his desk close up to a small side-window in that part of the room, a window which originally had afforded a lateral view of certain grimy brickyards and bricks, but which, owing to subsequent erections, commanded at present no view at all, though it gave some light. Within three feet of the panes was a wall, and the light came down from far above, between two lofty buildings, as from a very small opening in a dome. Still further to a satisfactory arrangement, I procured a high green folding screen, which might entirely isolate Bartleby from my sight, though not remove him from my voice. And thus, in a manner, privacy and society were conjoined.

At first, Bartleby did an extraordinary quantity of writing. As if long famishing for something to copy, he seemed to gorge himself on my documents. There was no pause for digestion. He ran a day and night line, copying by sunlight and by candle-light. I should have been quite delighted with his application, had he been cheerfully industrious. But he wrote on silently, palely, mechanically.

It is, of course, an indispensable part of a scrivener's business to verify the accuracy of his copy, word by word. Where there are two or more scriveners in an office, they assist each other in this examination, one reading from the copy, the other holding the original. It is a very dull, wearisome, and lethargic affair. I can readily imagine that, to some sanguine temperaments, it would be altogether intolerable. For example, I cannot credit that the mettlesome poet, Byron, would have contentedly sat down with Bartleby to examine a law document of, say five hundred pages, closely written in a crimpy hand.

Now and then, in the haste of business, it had been my habit to assist in comparing some brief document myself, calling Turkey or Nippers for this purpose. One object I had, in placing Bartleby so handy to me behind the screen, was, to avail myself of his services on such trivial occasions. It was on the third day, I think, of his being with me, and before any necessity had arisen for having his own writing examined, that, being much hurried to complete a small affair I had in hand, I abruptly called to Bartleby. In my haste and natural expectancy of instant compliance, I sat with my head bent over the original on my desk, and my right hand sideways, and somewhat nervously extended with the copy, so that, immediately upon emerging from his retreat, Bartleby might snatch it and proceed to business without the least delay.

In this very attitude did I sit when I called to him, rapidly stating what it was I wanted him to do—namely, to examine a small paper with me. Imagine my surprise, nay, my consternation, when, without moving from his privacy, Bartleby, in a singularly mild, firm voice, replied, "I would prefer not to."

I sat awhile in perfect silence, rallying my stunned faculties. Immediately it occurred to me that my ears had deceived me, or Bartleby had entirely misunderstood my meaning. I repeated my request in the clearest tone I could assume; but in quite as clear a one came the previous reply, "I would prefer not to."

"Prefer not to," echoed I, rising in high excitement, and crossing the room with a stride. "What do you mean? Are you moonstruck? I want you to help me compare this sheet here—take it," and I thrust it towards him.

"I would prefer not to," said he.

I looked at him steadfastly. His face was leanly composed; his gray eye dimly calm. Not a wrinkle of agitation rippled him. Had there been the least uneasiness, anger, impatience or impertinence in his manner; in other words, had there been anything ordinarily human about him, doubtless I should have violently dismissed him from the premises. But as it was, I should have as soon thought of turning my pale plaster-of-paris bust of Cicero out of doors. I stood gazing at him awhile, as he went on with his own writing, and then reseated myself at my desk. This is very strange, thought I. What had one best do? But my business hurried me. I concluded to forget the matter for the present, reserving it for my future leisure. So, calling Nippers from the other room, the paper was speedily examined.

A few days after this, Bartleby concluded four lengthy documents, being quadruplicates of a week's testimony taken before me in my High Court of Chancery. It became necessary to examine them. It was an important suit, and great accuracy was imperative. Having all things arranged, I called Turkey, Nippers, and Ginger Nut, from the next room, meaning to place the four copies in the hands of my four clerks, while I should read from the original. Accordingly, Turkey, Nippers, and Ginger Nut had taken their seats in a row, each with his document in his hand, when I called to Bartleby to join this interesting group.

"Bartleby! quick, I am waiting."

I heard a slow scrape of his chair legs on the uncarpeted floor, and soon he appeared standing at the entrance of his hermitage.

"What is wanted?" said he, mildly.

"The copies, the copies," said I, hurriedly. "We are going to examine them. There"—and I held towards him the fourth quadruplicate.

"I would prefer not to," he said, and gently disappeared behind the screen.

For a few moments I was turned into a pillar of salt,[6] standing at the head of my seated column of clerks. Recovering myself, I advanced towards the screen, and demanded the reason for such extraordinary conduct.

"*Why* do you refuse?"

"I would prefer not to."

With any other man I should have flown outright into a dreadful passion, scorned all further words, and thrust him ignominiously from my presence. But there was something about Bartleby that not only strangely disarmed me, but, in a wonderful manner, touched and disconcerted me. I began to reason with him.

"These are your own copies we are about to examine. It is labor saving to you, because one examination will answer for your four papers. It is common usage. Every copyist is bound to help examine his copy. Is it not so? Will you not speak? Answer!"

"I prefer not to," he replied in a flute-like tone. It seemed to me that, while I had been addressing him, he carefully revolved every statement that I made; fully comprehended the meaning; could not gainsay the irresistible conclusion; but, at the same time, some paramount consideration prevailed with him to reply as he did.

"You are decided, then, not to comply with my request—a request made according to common usage and common sense?"

He briefly gave me to understand, that on that point my judgment was sound. Yes: his decision was irreversible.

It is not seldom the case that, when a man is browbeaten in some unprecedented and violently unreasonable way, he begins to stagger in his own plainest faith. He begins, as it were, vaguely to surmise that, wonderful as it may be, all the justice and all the reason is on the other side. Accordingly, if any disinterested persons are present, he turns to them for some reinforcement for his own faltering mind.

"Turkey," said I, "what do you think of this? Am I not right?"

"With submission, sir," said Turkey, in his blandest tone, "I think that you are."

"Nippers," said I, "what do *you* think of it?"

"I think I should kick him out of the office."

(The reader of nice perceptions will here perceive that, it being morning, Turkey's answer is couched in polite and tranquil terms, but Nippers replies in ill-tempered ones. Or, to repeat a previous sentence, Nippers' ugly mood was on duty, and Turkey's off.)

"Ginger Nut," said I, willing to enlist the smallest suffrage in my behalf, "what do *you* think of it?"

"I think, sir, he's a little *luny,*" replied Ginger Nut, with a grin.

[6] Lot's wife was turned into a pillar of salt when she disobeyed the Lord's command and looked back on Sodom. See Genesis 19:26.

"You hear what they say," said I, turning towards the screen, "come forth and do your duty."

But he vouchsafed no reply. I pondered a moment in sore perplexity. But once more business hurried me. I determined again to postpone the consideration of this dilemma to my future leisure. With a little trouble we made out to examine the papers without Bartleby, though at every page or two Turkey deferentially dropped his opinion, that this proceeding was quite out of the common; while Nippers, twitching in his chair with a dyspeptic nervousness, ground out, between his set teeth, occasional hissing maledictions against the stubborn oaf behind the screen. And for his (Nippers') part, this was the first and the last time he would do another man's business without pay.

Meanwhile Bartleby sat in his hermitage, oblivious to everything but his own peculiar business there.

Some days passed, the scrivener being employed upon another lengthy work. His late remarkable conduct led me to regard his ways narrowly. I observed that he never went to dinner; indeed, that he never went anywhere. As yet I had never, of my personal knowledge, known him to be outside of my office. He was a perpetual sentry in the corner. At about eleven o'clock though, in the morning, I noticed that Ginger Nut would advance toward the opening in Bartleby's screen, as if silently beckoned thither by a gesture invisible to me where I sat. The boy would then leave the office, jingling a few pence, and reappear with a handful of ginger-nuts, which he delivered in the hermitage, receiving two of the cakes for his trouble.

He lives, then, on ginger-nuts, thought I; never eats a dinner, properly speaking; he must be a vegetarian, then, but no; he never eats even vegetables, he eats nothing but ginger-nuts. My mind then ran on in reveries concerning the probable effects upon the human constitution of living entirely on ginger-nuts. Ginger-nuts are so called, because they contain ginger as one of their peculiar constituents, and the final flavoring one. Now, what was ginger? A hot, spicy thing. Was Bartleby hot and spicy? Not at all. Ginger, then, had no effect upon Bartleby. Probably he preferred it should have none.

Nothing so aggravates an earnest person as a passive resistance. If the individual so resisted be of a not inhumane temper, and the resisting one perfectly harmless in his passivity, then, in the better moods of the former, he will endeavor charitably to construe to his imagination what proves impossible to be solved by his judgment. Even so, for the most part, I regarded Bartleby and his ways. Poor fellow! thought I, he means no mischief; it is plain he intends no insolence; his aspect sufficiently evinces that his eccentricities are involuntary. He is useful to me. I can get along with him. If I turn him away, the chances are he will fall in with some less indulgent employer, and then he will be rudely treated, and perhaps driven forth miserably to starve. Yes. Here I can cheaply purchase a delicious self-approval. To befriend Bartleby; to humor him in his strange wilfulness, will cost me little or nothing, while I lay up in my soul what will eventually prove a sweet morsel for my conscience. But this mood was not invariable with me. The passiveness of Bartleby sometimes irritated me. I felt strangely goaded on to encounter him in new opposition—to elicit some angry spark from him answerable to my own. But, indeed, I might as well have essayed to strike fire with my knuckles against a bit of Windsor soap. But one afternoon the evil impulse in me mastered me, and the following little scene ensued:

"Bartleby," said I, "when those papers are all copied, I will compare them with you."

"I would prefer not to."

"How? Surely you do not mean to persist in that mulish vagary?"

No answer.

I threw open the folding-doors nearby, and turning upon Turkey and Nippers, exclaimed:

"Bartleby a second time says, he won't examine his papers. What do you think of it, Turkey?"

It was afternoon, be it remembered. Turkey sat glowing like a brass boiler; his bald head steaming; his hands reeling among his blotted papers.

"Think of it?" roared Turkey. "I think I'll just step behind his screen, and black his eyes for him!"

So saying, Turkey rose to his feet and threw his arms into a pugilistic position. He was hurrying away to make good his promise, when I detained him, alarmed at the effect of incautiously rousing Turkey's combativeness after dinner.

"Sit down, Turkey," said I, "and hear what Nippers has to say. What do you think of it, Nippers? Would I not be justified in immediately dismissing Bartleby?"

"Excuse me, that is for you to decide, sir. I think his conduct quite unusual, and, indeed, unjust, as regards Turkey and myself. But it may only be a passing whim."

"Ah," exclaimed I, "you have strangely changed your mind, then—you speak very gently of him now."

"All beer," cried Turkey; "gentleness is effects of beer—Nippers and I dined together today. You see how gentle *I* am, sir. Shall I go and black his eyes?"

"You refer to Bartleby, I suppose. No, not today, Turkey," I replied; "pray, put up your fists."

I closed the doors, and again advanced towards Bartleby. I felt additional incentives tempting me to my fate. I burned to be rebelled against again. I remembered that Bartleby never left the office.

"Bartleby," said I, "Ginger Nut is away; just step around to the Post Office, won't you?" (it was but a three minutes' walk) "and see if there is anything for me."

"I would prefer not to."

"You *will* not?"

"I *prefer* not."

I staggered to my desk, and sat there in a deep study. My blind inveteracy returned. Was there any other thing in which I could procure myself to be ignominiously repulsed by this lean, penniless wight?—my hired clerk? What added thing is there, perfectly reasonable, that he will be sure to refuse to do?

"Bartleby!"

No answer.

"Bartleby," in a louder tone.

No answer.

"Bartleby," I roared.

Like a very ghost, agreeably to the laws of magical invocation, at the third summons, he appeared at the entrance of his hermitage.

"Go to the next room, and tell Nippers to come to me."

"I prefer not to," he respectfully and slowly said, and mildly disappeared.

"Very good, Bartleby," said I, in a quiet sort of serenely-severe self-possessed tone, intimating the unalterable purpose of some terrible retribution very close at hand. At the moment I half intended something of the kind. But upon the whole, as it was drawing towards my dinner-hour, I thought it best to put on my hat and walk home for the day, suffering much from perplexity and distress of mind.

Shall I acknowledge it? The conclusion of this whole business was, that it soon became a fixed fact of my chambers, that a pale young scrivener, by the name of Bartleby, had a desk there; that he copied for me at the usual rate of four cents a folio (one hundred words); but he was permanently exempt from examining the work done by him, that duty being transferred to Turkey and Nippers, out of compliment, doubtless, to their superior acuteness; moreover, said Bartleby was never, on any account, to be dispatched on the most trivial errand of any sort; and that even if entreated to take upon him such a matter, it was generally understood that he would "prefer not to"—in other words, that he would refuse point-blank.

As days passed on, I became considerably reconciled to Bartleby. His steadiness, his freedom from all dissipation, his incessant industry (except when he chose to throw himself into a standing revery behind his screen), his great stillness, his unalterableness of demeanor under all circumstances, made him a valuable acquisition. One prime thing was this—*he was always there*—first in the morning, continually through the day, and the last at night. I had a singular confidence in his honesty. I felt my most precious papers perfectly safe in his hands. Sometimes, to be sure, I could not, for the very soul of me, avoid falling into sudden spasmodic passions with him. For it was exceeding difficult to bear in mind all the time those strange peculiarities, privileges, and unheard of exemptions, forming the tacit stipulations on Bartleby's part under which he remained in my office. Now and then, in the eagerness of dispatching pressing business, I would inadvertently summon Bartleby, in a short, rapid tone, to put his finger, say, on the incipient tie of a bit of red tape with which I was about compressing some papers. Of course, from behind the screen the usual answer, "I prefer not to," was sure to come; and then, how could a human creature, with the common infirmities of our nature, refrain from bitterly exclaiming upon such perverseness—such unreasonableness? However, every added repulse of this sort which I received only tended to lessen the probability of my repeating the inadvertence.

Here it must be said, that, according to the custom of most legal gentlemen occupying chambers in densely-populated law buildings, there were several keys to my door. One was kept by a woman residing in the attic, which person weekly scrubbed and daily swept and dusted my apartments. Another was kept by Turkey for convenience sake. The third I sometimes carried in my own pocket. The fourth I knew not who had.

Now, one Sunday morning I happened to go to Trinity Church,[7] to hear a celebrated preacher, and finding myself rather early on the ground I thought I would walk round to my chambers for a while. Luckily I had my key with me; but upon applying it to the lock, I found it resisted by something inserted from the inside. Quite surprised, I called out; when to my consternation a key was turned from within; and thrusting his lean visage at me, and holding the door ajar, the apparition of Bartleby appeared, in his shirt-sleeves, and otherwise in a strangely tattered deshabille, saying quietly that he was sorry, but he was deeply engaged just then, and—preferred not admitting me at present. In a brief word or two, he moreover added, that perhaps I had better walk round the block two or three times, and by that time he would probably have concluded his affairs.

Now, the utterly unsurmised appearance of Bartleby, tenanting my law-chambers of a Sunday morning, with his cadaverously gentlemanly *nonchalance,* yet withal firm and self-possessed, had such a strange effect upon me, that incontinently I slunk away from my own door, and did as desired. But not without sundry twinges of impotent rebellion against the mild effrontery of this unaccountable scrivener. Indeed, it was his wonderful mildness chiefly, which not only disarmed me, but unmanned me, as it were. For I consider that one, for the time, is sort of unmanned when he tranquilly permits his hired clerk to dictate to him, and order him away from his own premises. Furthermore, I was full of uneasiness as to what Bartleby could possibly be doing in my office in his shirt-sleeves, and in an otherwise dismantled condition of a Sunday morning. Was anything amiss going on? Nay, that was out of the question. It was not to be thought of for a moment that Bartleby was an immoral person. But what could he be doing there?—copying? Nay again, whatever might be his eccentricities, Bartleby was an eminently decorous person. He would be the last man to sit down to his desk in any state approaching to nudity. Besides, it was Sunday; and there was something about Bartleby that forbade the supposition that he would by any secular occupation violate the properties of the day.

Nevertheless, my mind was not pacified; and full of a restless curiosity, at last I returned to the door. Without hindrance I inserted my key, opened it, and entered. Bartleby was not to be seen. I looked round anxiously, peeped behind his screen; but it was very plain that he was gone. Upon more closely examining the place, I surmised that for an indefinite period Bartleby must have ate, dressed, and slept in my office, and that too without plate, mirror, or bed. The cushioned seat of a rickety old sofa in one corner bore the faint impress of a lean, reclining form. Rolled away under his desk, I found a blanket; under the empty grate, a blacking box and brush; on the chair, a tin basin, with soap and a ragged towel; in a newspaper a few crumbs of ginger-nuts and a morsel of cheese. Yes, thought I, it is evident enough that Bartleby has been making his home here, keeping bachelor's hall all by himself. Immediately then the thought came sweeping across me, what miserable friendlessness and loneliness are here revealed!

[7] A large and elaborate Episcopal church in the Wall Street area of New York.

His poverty is great; but his solitude, how horrible! Think of it. Of a Sunday, Wall Street is deserted as Petra;[8] and every night of every day it is an emptiness. This building, too, which of week-days hums with industry and life, at nightfall echoes with sheer vacancy, and all through Sunday is forlorn. And here Bartleby makes his home; sole spectator of a solitude which he has seen all populous—a sort of innocent and transformed Marius brooding among the ruins of Carthage![9]

For the first time in my life a feeling of overpowering stinging melancholy seized me. Before, I had never experienced aught but a not unpleasing sadness. The bond of a common humanity now drew me irresistibly to gloom. A fraternal melancholy! For both I and Bartleby were sons of Adam. I remembered the bright silks and sparkling faces I had seen that day, in gala trim, swan-like sailing down the Mississippi of Broadway; and I contrasted them with the pallid copyist, and thought to myself, Ah, happiness courts the light, so we deem the world is gay; but misery hides aloof, so we deem that misery there is none. These sad fancyings—chimeras, doubtless, of a sick and silly brain—led on to other and more special thoughts, concerning the eccentricities of Bartleby. Presentiments of strange discoveries hovered round me. The scrivener's pale form appeared to me laid out, among uncaring strangers, in its shivering winding-sheet.

Suddenly I was attracted by Bartleby's closed desk, the key in open sight left in the lock.

I mean no mischief, seek the gratification of no heartless curiosity, thought I; besides, the desk is mine, and its contents, too, so I will make bold to look within. Everything was methodically arranged, the papers smoothly placed. The pigeon-holes were deep, and removing the files of documents, I groped into their recesses. Presently I felt something there, and dragged it out. It was an old bandanna handkerchief, heavy and knotted. I opened it, and saw it was a saving's bank.

I now recalled all the quiet mysteries which I had noted in the man. I remembered that he never spoke but to answer; that, though at intervals he had considerable time to himself, yet I had never seen him reading—no, not even a newspaper; that for long periods he would stand looking out, at his pale window behind the screen, upon the dead brick wall; I was quite sure he never visited any refectory or eating-house; while his pale face clearly indicated that he never drank beer like Turkey, or tea and coffee even, like other men; that he never went anywhere in particular that I could learn; never went out for a walk, unless, indeed, that was the case at present; that he had declined telling who he was, or whence he came, or whether he had any relatives in the world; that though so thin and pale, he never complained of ill-health. And more than all, I remembered a certain unconscious air of pallid—how shall I call it?—of pallid haughtiness, say, or rather an austere reserve about him, which had positively awed me into my tame compliance with his eccentricities, when I had feared to ask him to do the slightest incidental thing for me, even though I might know, from

[8]An ancient city of Jordan, it was forgotten until J. L. Burckhardt discovered its ruins in 1812.

[9]Caius Marius (c. 155–86 B.C.) was a Roman general who won a number of victories in Africa but was exiled by his enemy Sulla. He was a favorite subject of nineteenth-century painting.

his long-continued motionlessness, that behind his screen he must be standing in one of those dead-wall reveries of his.

Revolving all these things, and coupling them with the recently discovered fact, that he made my office his constant abiding place and home, and not forgetful of his morbid moodiness; revolving all these things, a prudential feeling began to steal over me. My first emotions had been those of pure melancholy and sincerest pity; but just in proportion as the forlornness of Bartleby grew and grew to my imagination, did that same melancholy merge into fear, that pity into repulsion. So true it is, and so terrible, too, that up to a certain point the thought or sight of misery enlists our best affections; but, in certain special cases, beyond that point it does not. They err who would assert that invariably this is owing to the inherent selfishness of the human heart. It rather proceeds from a certain hopelessness of remedying excessive and organic ill. To a sensitive being, pity is not seldom pain. And when at last it is perceived that such pity cannot lead to effectual succor, common sense bids the soul be rid of it. What I saw that morning persuaded me that the scrivener was the victim of innate and incurable disorder. I might give alms to his body; but his body did not pain him; it was his soul that suffered, and his soul I could not reach.

I did not accomplish the purpose of going to Trinity Church that morning. Somehow, the things I had seen disqualified me for the time from church-going. I walked homeward, thinking what I would do with Bartleby. Finally, I resolved upon this—I would put certain calm questions to him the next morning, touching his history, etc., and if he declined to answer them openly and unreservedly (and I supposed he would prefer not), then to give him a twenty dollar bill over and above whatever I might owe him, and tell him his services were no longer required; but that if in any other way I could assist him, I would be happy to do so, especially if he desired to return to his native place, wherever that might be, I would willingly help to defray the expenses. Moreover, if, after reaching home, he found himself at any time in want of aid, a letter from him would be sure of a reply.

The next morning came.

"Bartleby," said I, gently calling to him behind his screen.

No reply.

"Bartleby," said I, in a still gentler tone, "come here; I am not going to ask you to do anything you would prefer not to do—I simply wish to speak to you."

Upon this he noiselessly slid into view.

"Will you tell me, Bartleby, where you were born?"

"I would prefer not to."

"Will you tell me *anything* about yourself?"

"I would prefer not to."

"But what reasonable objection can you have to speak to me? I feel friendly towards you."

He did not look at me while I spoke, but kept his glance fixed upon my bust of Cicero, which, as I then sat, was directly behind me, some six inches above my head.

"What is your answer, Bartleby?" said I, after waiting a considerable time for a reply, during which his countenance remained immovable, only there was the faintest conceivable tremor of the white attenuated mouth.

"At present I prefer to give no answer," he said, and retired into his hermitage.

It was rather weak in me I confess, but his manner, on this occasion, nettled me. Not only did there seem to lurk in it a certain calm disdain, but his perverseness seemed ungrateful, considering the undeniable good usage and indulgence he had received from me.

Again I sat ruminating what I should do. Mortified as I was at his behavior, and resolved as I had been to dismiss him when I entered my office, nevertheless I strangely felt something superstitious knocking at my heart, and forbidding me to carry out my purpose, and denouncing me for a villain if I dared to breathe one bitter word against this forlornest of mankind. At last, familiarly drawing my chair behind his screen, I sat down and said: "Bartleby, never mind, then, about revealing your history; but let me entreat you, as a friend, to comply as far as may be with the usages of this office. Say now, you will help to examine papers tomorrow or next day: in short, say now, that in a day or two you will begin to be a little reasonable:—say so, Bartleby."

"At present I would prefer not to be a little reasonable," was his mildly cadaverous reply.

Just then the folding-doors opened, and Nippers approached. He seemed suffering from an unusually bad night's rest, induced by severer indigestion than common. He overheard those final words of Bartleby.

"*Prefer not,* eh?" gritted Nippers—"I'd *prefer* him, if I were you, sir," addressing me—"I'd *prefer* him; I'd give him preferences, the stubborn mule! What is it, sir, pray, that he *prefers* not to do now?"

Bartleby moved not a limb.

"Mr. Nippers," said I, "I'd prefer that you would withdraw for the present."

Somehow, of late, I had got into the way of involuntarily using this word "prefer" upon all sorts of not exactly suitable occasions. And I trembled to think that my contact with the scrivener had already and seriously affected me in a mental way. And what further and deeper aberration might it not yet produce? This apprehension had not been without efficacy in determining me to summary measures.

As Nippers, looking very sour and sulky, was departing, Turkey blandly and deferentially approached.

"With submission, sir," said he, "yesterday I was thinking about Bartleby here, and I think that if he would but prefer to take a quart of good ale every day, it would do much towards mending him, and enabling him to assist in examining his papers."

"So you have got the word, too," said I, slightly excited.

"With submission, what word, sir?" asked Turkey, respectfully crowding himself into the contracted space behind the screen, and by so doing, making me jostle the scrivener. "What word, sir?"

"I would prefer to be left alone here," said Bartleby, as if offended at being mobbed in his privacy.

"*That's* the word, Turkey," said I—"*that's* it."

"Oh, *prefer*? Oh yes—queer word. I never use it myself. But, sir, as I was saying, if he would but prefer—"

"Turkey," interrupted I, "you will please withdraw."

"Oh certainly, sir, if you prefer that I should."

As he opened the folding-door to retire, Nippers at his desk caught a glimpse of me, and asked whether I would prefer to have a certain paper copied on blue paper or white. He did not in the least roguishly accent the word "prefer." It was plain that it involuntarily rolled from his tongue. I thought to myself, surely I must get rid of a demented man, who already has in some degree turned the tongues, if not the heads of myself and clerks. But I thought it prudent not to break the dismission at once.

The next day I noticed that Bartleby did nothing but stand at his window in his dead-wall revery. Upon asking him why he did not write, he said that he had decided upon doing no more writing.

"Why, how now? what next?" exclaimed I, "do no more writing?"

"No more."

"And what is the reason?"

"Do you not see the reason for yourself?" he indifferently replied.

I looked steadfastly at him, and perceived that his eyes looked dull and glazed. Instantly it occurred to me, that his unexampled diligence in copying by his dim window for the first few weeks of his stay with me might have temporarily impaired his vision.

I was touched. I said something in condolence with him. I hinted that of course he did wisely in abstaining from writing for a while; and urged him to embrace that opportunity of taking wholesome exercise in the open air. This, however, he did not do. A few days after this, my other clerks being absent, and being in a great hurry to dispatch certain letters by the mail, I thought that, having nothing else earthly to do, Bartleby would surely be less inflexible than usual, and carry these letters to the post-office. But he blankly declined. So, much to my inconvenience, I went myself.

Still added days went by. Whether Bartleby's eyes improved or not, I could not say. To all appearance, I thought they did. But when I asked him if they did, he vouchsafed no answer. At all events, he would do no copying. At last, in reply to my urgings, he informed me that he had permanently given up copying.

"What!" exclaimed I; "suppose your eyes should get entirely well—better than ever before—would you not copy then?"

"I have given up copying," he answered, and slid aside.

He remained as ever, a fixture in my chamber. Nay—if that were possible—he became still more of a fixture than before. What was to be done? He would do nothing in the office; why should he stay there? In plain fact, he had now become a millstone to me, not only useless as a necklace, but afflictive to bear. Yet I was sorry for him. I speak less than truth when I say that, on his own account, he occasioned me uneasiness. If he would but have named a single relative or friend, I would instantly have written, and urged their taking the poor fellow away to some convenient retreat. But he seemed alone, absolutely alone in the universe. A bit of wreck in the mid-Atlantic. At length, necessities connected with my business tyrannized over all other considerations. Decently as I could, I told Bartleby that in six days' time he must unconditionally leave the office. I warned him to take measures, in the interval, for procuring some other abode. I offered to assist him in this endeavor, if he himself would but take the first step towards a removal. "And when you finally quit me, Bartleby," added I, "I shall see that you go not away entirely unprovided. Six days from this hour, remember."

At the expiration of that period, I peeped behind the screen, and lo! Bartleby was there.

I buttoned up my coat, balanced myself; advanced slowly towards him, touched his shoulder, and said, "The time has come; you must quit this place; I am sorry for you; here is money; but you must go."

"I would prefer not," he replied, with his back still towards me.

"You *must.*"

He remained silent.

Now I had an unbounded confidence in this man's common honesty. He had frequently restored to me sixpences and shillings carelessly dropped upon the floor, for I am apt to be very reckless in such shirt-button affairs. The proceeding, then, which followed will not be deemed extraordinary.

"Bartleby," said I, "I owe you twelve dollars on account; here are thirty-two; the odd twenty are yours—Will you take it?" and I handed the bills towards him.

But he made no motion.

"I will leave them here, then," putting them under a weight on the table. Then taking my hat and cane and going to the door, I tranquilly turned and added—"After you have removed your things from these offices, Bartleby, you will of course lock the door—since every one is now gone for the day but you—and if you please, slip your key underneath the mat, so that I may have it in the morning. I shall not see you again; so good-bye to you. If, hereafter, in your new place of abode, I can be of any service to you, do not fail to advise me by letter. Good-bye, Bartleby, and fare you well."

But he answered not a word; like the last column of some ruined temple, he remained standing mute and solitary in the middle of the otherwise deserted room.

As I walked home in a pensive mood, my vanity got the better of my pity. I could not but highly plume myself on my masterly management in getting rid of Bartleby. Masterly I call it, and such it must appear to any dispassionate thinker. The beauty of my procedure seemed to consist in its perfect quietness. There was no vulgar bullying, no bravado of any sort, no choleric hectoring, and striding to and fro across the apartment, jerking out vehement commands for Bartleby to bundle himself off with his beggarly traps. Nothing of the kind. Without loudly bidding Bartleby depart—as an inferior genius might have done—I *assumed* the ground that depart he must; and upon that assumption built all I had to say. The more I thought over my procedure, the more I was charmed with it. Nevertheless, next morning, upon awakening, I had my doubts—I had somehow slept off the fumes of vanity. One of the coolest and wisest hours a man has, is just after he awakes in the morning. My procedure seemed as sagacious as ever—but only in theory. How it would prove in practice—there was the rub. It was truly a beautiful thought to have assumed Bartleby's departure;

but, after all, that assumption was simply my own, and none of Bartleby's. The great point was, not whether I had assumed that he would quit me, but whether he would prefer to do so. He was more a man of preferences than assumptions.

After breakfast, I walked down town, arguing the probabilities *pro* and *con*. One moment I thought it would prove a miserable failure, and Bartleby would be found all alive at my office as usual; the next moment it seemed certain that I should find his chair empty. And so I kept veering about. At the corner of Broadway and Canal Street, I saw quite an excited group of people standing in earnest conversation.

"I'll take odds he doesn't," said a voice as I passed.

"Doesn't go?—done!" said I, "put up your money."

I was instinctively putting my hand in my pocket to produce my own, when I remember that this was an election day. The words I had overheard bore no reference to Bartleby, but to the success or non-success of some candidate for the mayoralty. In my intent frame of mind, I had, as it were, imagined that all Broadway shared in my excitement, and were debating the same question with me. I passed on, very thankful that the uproar of the street screened my momentary absent-mindedness.

As I had intended, I was earlier than usual at my office door. I stood listening for a moment. All was still. He must be gone. I tried the knob. The door was locked. Yes, my procedure had worked to a charm; he indeed must be vanished. Yet a certain melancholy mixed with this: I was almost sorry for my brilliant success. I was fumbling under the door mat for the key which Bartleby was to have left there for me, when accidentally my knee knocked against a panel, producing a summoning sound, and in response a voice came to me from within—"Not yet; I am occupied."

It was Bartleby.

I was thunderstruck. For an instant I stood like the man who, pipe in mouth, was killed one cloudless afternoon long ago in Virginia, by summer lightning; at his own warm open window he was killed, and remained leaning out there upon the dreamy afternoon, till some one touched him, when he fell.

"Not gone!" I murmured at last. But again obeying that wondrous ascendancy which the inscrutable scrivener had over me, and from which ascendancy, for all my chafing, I could not completely escape, I slowly went down stairs and out into the street, and while walking round the block, considered what I should next do in this unheard-of perplexity. Turn the man out by an actual thrusting I could not; to drive him away by calling him hard names would not do; calling in the police was an unpleasant idea; and yet, permit him to enjoy his cadaverous triumph over me—this, too, I could not think of. What was to be done? or, if nothing could be done, was there anything further that I could *assume* in the matter? Yes, as before I had prospectively assumed that Bartleby would depart, so now I might retrospectively assume that departed he was. In the legitimate carrying out of this assumption, I might enter my office in a great hurry, and pretending not to see Bartleby at all, walk straight against him as if he were air. Such a proceeding would in a singular degree have the appearance of a home-thrust. It was hardly possible that Bartleby could withstand such an application of the doctrine of assumption. But upon second thoughts the success of the plan seemed rather dubious. I resolved to argue the matter over with him again.

"Bartleby," said I, entering the office, with a quietly severe expression, "I am seriously displeased. I am pained, Bartleby. I had thought better of you. I had imagined you of such a gentlemanly organization, that in any delicate dilemma a slight hint would suffice—in short, an assumption. But it appears I am deceived. Why," I added, unaffectedly starting, "you have not even touched that money yet," pointing to it, just where I had left it the evening previous.

He answered nothing.

"Will you, or will you not, quit me?" I now demanded in a sudden passion, advancing close to him.

"I would prefer *not* to quit you," he replied, gently emphasizing the *not*.

"What earthly right have you to stay here? Do you pay any rent? Do you pay any taxes? Or is this property yours?"

He answered nothing.

"Are you ready to go on and write now? Are your eyes recovered? Could you copy a small paper for me this morning? or help examine a few lines? or step round to the post-office? In a word, will you do anything at all, to give a coloring to your refusal to depart the premises?"

He silently retired into his hermitage.

I was now in such a state of nervous resentment that I thought it but prudent to check myself at present from further demonstrations. Bartleby and I were alone. I remembered the tragedy of the unfortunate Adams[10] and the still more unfortunate Colt in the solitary office of the latter; and how poor Colt, being dreadfully incensed by Adams, and imprudently permitting himself to get wildly excited, was at unawares hurried into his fatal act—an act which certainly no man could possibly deplore more than the actor himself. Often it had occurred to me in my ponderings upon the subject that had that altercation taken place in the public street, or at a private residence, it would not have terminated as it did. It was the circumstance of being alone in a solitary office, up stairs, of a building entirely unhallowed by humanizing domestic associations—an uncarpeted office, doubtless, of a dusty, haggard sort of appearance—this it must have been, which greatly helped to enhance the irritable desperation of the hapless Colt.

But when this old Adam of resentment rose in me and tempted me concerning Bartleby, I grappled him and threw him. How? Why, simply by recalling the divine injunction: "A new commandment give I unto you, that ye love one another."[11] Yes, this it was that saved me. Aside from higher considerations, charity often operates as a vastly wise and prudent principle—a great safeguard to its possessor. Men have committed murder for jealousy's sake, and anger's sake, and hatred's sake, and selfishness' sake, and spiritual pride's sake; but no man, that ever I heard of, ever committed a diabolical murder for sweet charity's sake. Mere self-interest, then, if no better motive can be enlisted, should, especially with high-tempered men,

[10]Melville is alluding to a sensational murder case of 1842. John C. Colt killed Samuel Adams and was sentenced to be hanged but committed suicide just before the execution.

[11]These are Christ's words to his disciples, John 13:34.

prompt all beings to charity and philanthropy. At any rate, upon the occasion in question, I strove to drown my exasperated feelings towards the scrivener by benevolently construing his conduct. Poor fellow, poor fellow! thought I, he don't mean anything; and besides, he has seen hard times, and ought to be indulged.

I endeavored, also, immediately to occupy myself, and at the same time to comfort my despondency. I tried to fancy, that in the course of the morning, at such time as might prove agreeable to him, Bartleby, of his own free accord, would emerge from his hermitage and take up some decided line of march in the direction of the door. But no. Half-past twelve o'clock came; Turkey began to glow in the face, overturn his inkstand, and become generally obstreperous; Nippers abated down into quietude and courtesy; Ginger Nut munched his noon apple; and Bartleby remained standing at his window in one of his profoundest dead-wall reveries. Will it be credited? Ought I to acknowledge it? That afternoon I left the office without saying one further word to him.

Some days now passed, during which, at leisure intervals I looked a little into "Edwards on the Will," and "Priestley on Necessity."[12] Under the circumstances, those books induced a salutary feeling. Gradually I slid into the persuasion that these troubles of mine, touching the scrivener, had been all predestinated from eternity, and Bartleby was billeted upon me for some mysterious purpose of an all-wise Providence, which it was not for a mere mortal like me to fathom. Yes, Bartleby, stay there behind your screen, thought I; I shall persecute you no more; you are harmless and noiseless as any of these old chairs; in short, I never feel so private as when I know you are here. At last I see it, I feel it; I penetrate to the predestinated purpose of my life. I am content. Others may have loftier parts to enact; but my mission in this world, Bartleby, is to furnish you with office-room for such period as you may see fit to remain.

I believe that this wise and blessed frame of mind would have continued with me, had it not been for the unsolicited and uncharitable remarks obtruded upon me by my professional friends who visited the rooms. But thus it often is, that the constant friction of illiberal minds wears out at last the best resolves of the more generous. Though to be sure, when I reflected upon it, it was not strange that people entering my office should be struck by the peculiar aspect of the unaccountable Bartleby, and so be tempted to throw out some sinister observations concerning him. Sometimes an attorney, having business with me, and calling at my office, and finding no one but the scrivener there, would undertake to obtain some sort of precise information from him touching my whereabouts; but without heeding his idle talk, Bartleby would remain standing immovable in the middle of the room. So after contemplating him in that position for a time, the attorney would depart, no wiser than he came.

Also, when a reference[13] was going on, and the room full of lawyers and witnesses, and business driving fast, some deeply-occupied legal gentleman

[12] Jonathan Edwards (1703–1758), the American theologian, presented the Calvinist argument for predestination, especially in *The Freedom of the Will* (1754). Joseph Priestley (1773–1804), English scientist and Unitarian, also argued for determinism, though on scientific grounds.

[13] A conference with a legal referee.

present, seeing Bartleby wholly unemployed, would request him to run round to his (the legal gentleman's) office and fetch some papers for him. Thereupon, Bartleby would tranquilly decline, and yet remain idle as before. Then the lawyer would give a great stare, and turn to me. And what could I say? At last I was made aware that all through the circle of my professional acquaintance, a whisper of wonder was running round, having reference to the strange creature I kept at my office. This worried me very much. And as the idea came upon me of his possibly turning out a long-lived man, and keeping occupying my chambers, and denying my authority; and perplexing my visitors; and scandalizing my professional reputation; and casting a general gloom over the premises; keeping soul and body together to the last upon his savings (for doubtless he spent but half a dime a day), and in the end perhaps outlive me, and claim possession of my office by right of his perpetual occupancy: as all these dark anticipations crowded upon me more and more, and my friends continually intruded their relentless remarks upon the apparition in my room; a great change was wrought in me. I resolved to gather all my faculties together, and forever rid me of this intolerable incubus.[14]

Ere revolving any complicated project, however, adapted to this end, I first simply suggested to Bartleby the propriety of his permanent departure. In a calm and serious tone, I commended the idea to his careful and mature consideration. But, having taken three days to meditate upon it, he apprised me, that his original determination remained the same; in short, that he still preferred to abide with me.

What shall I do? I now said to myself, buttoning up my coat to the last button. What shall I do? what ought I to do? what does conscience say I *should* do with this man, or, rather, ghost. Rid myself of him, I must; go, he shall. But how? You will not thrust him, the poor, pale, passive mortal—you will not thrust such a helpless creature out of your door? you will not dishonor yourself by such cruelty? No, I will not, I cannot do that. Rather would I let him live and die here, and then mason up his remains in the wall. What, then, will you do? For all your coaxing, he will not budge. Bribes he leaves under your own paper-weight on your table; in short, it is quite plain that he prefers to cling to you.

Then something severe, something unusual must be done. What! surely you will not have him collared by a constable, and commit his innocent pallor to the common jail? And upon what ground could you procure such a thing to be done?—a vagrant, is he? What! he a vagrant, a wanderer, who refuses to budge? It is because he will *not* be a vagrant, then, that you seek to count him *as* a vagrant. That is too absurd. No visible means of support: there I have him. Wrong again: for indubitably he *does* support himself, and that is the only unanswerable proof that any man can show of his possessing the means so to do. No more, then. Since he will not quit me, I must quit him. I will change my offices; I will move elsewhere, and give him fair notice, that if I find him on my new premises I will then proceed against him as a common trespasser.

Acting accordingly, next day I thus addressed him: "I find these chambers too far from the City Hall; the air is unwholesome. In a word, I pro-

[14] Something that weighs upon one like a nightmare.

pose to remove my offices next week, and shall no longer require your services. I tell you this now, in order that you may seek another place."

He made no reply, and nothing more was said.

On the appointed day I engaged carts and men, proceeded to my chambers, and, having but little furniture, everything was removed in a few hours. Throughout, the scrivener remained standing behind the screen, which I directed to be removed the last thing. It was withdrawn; and, being folded up like a huge folio, left him the motionless occupant of a naked room. I stood in the entry watching him a moment, while something from within me upbraided me.

I re-entered, with my hand in my pocket—and—and my heart in my mouth.

"Good-bye, Bartleby; I am going—good-bye, and God some way bless you; and take that," slipping something in his hand. But it dropped upon the floor, and then—strange to say—I tore myself from him whom I had so longed to be rid of.

Established in my new quarters, for a day or two I kept the door locked, and started at every footfall in the passages. When I returned to my rooms, after any little absence, I would pause at the threshold for an instant, and attentively listen, ere applying my key. But these fears were needless. Bartleby never came nigh me.

I thought all was going well, when a perturbed-looking stranger visited me, inquiring whether I was the person who had recently occupied rooms at No.—Wall Street.

Full of forebodings, I replied that I was.

"Then, sir," said the stranger, who proved a lawyer, "you are responsible for the man you left there. He refuses to do any copying; he refuses to do anything; he says he prefers not to; and he refuses to quit the premises."

"I am very sorry, sir," said I, with assumed tranquillity, but an inward tremor, "but, really, the man you allude to is nothing to me—he is no relation or apprentice of mine, that you should hold me responsible for him."

"In mercy's name, who is he?"

"I certainly cannot inform you. I know nothing about him. Formerly I employed him as a copyist; but he has done nothing for me now for some time past."

"I shall settle him, then—good morning, sir."

Several days passed, and I heard nothing more; and, though I often felt a charitable prompting to call at the place and see poor Bartleby, yet a certain squeamishness, of I know not what, withheld me.

All is over with him, by this time, thought I, as last, when, through another week, no further intelligence reached me. But, coming to my room the day after, I found several persons waiting at my door in a high state of nervous excitement.

"That's the man—here he comes," cried the foremost one, whom I recognized as the lawyer who had previously called upon me alone.

"You must take him away, sir, at once," cried a portly person among them, advancing upon me, and whom I knew to be the landlord of No.—Wall Street. "These gentlemen, my tenants, cannot stand it any longer; Mr. B——," pointing to the lawyer, "has turned him out of his room, and he now persists in haunting the building generally, sitting upon the banisters of the stairs by day, and sleeping in the entry by night. Everybody is concerned; clients are leaving the offices; some fears are entertained of a mob; something you must do, and that without delay."

Aghast at this torrent, I fell back before it, and would fain have locked myself in my new quarters. In vain I persisted that Bartleby was nothing to me—no more than to any one else. In vain—I was the last person known to have anything to do with him, and they held me to the terrible account. Fearful, then, of being exposed in the papers (as one person present obscurely threatened), I considered the matter, and, at length, said, that if the lawyer would give me a confidential interview with the scrivener, in his (the lawyer's) own room, I would, that afternoon, strive my best to rid them of the nuisance they complained of.

Going up stairs to my old haunt, there was Bartleby silently sitting upon the banister at the landing.

"What are you doing here, Bartleby?" said I.

"Sitting upon the banister," he mildly replied.

I motioned him into the lawyer's room, who then left us.

"Bartleby," said I, "are you aware that you are the cause of great tribulation to me, by persisting in occupying the entry after being dismissed from the office?"

No answer.

"Now one of two things must take place. Either you must do something, or something must be done to you. Now what sort of business would you like to engage in? Would you like to re-engage in copying for some one?"

"No; I would prefer not to make any change."

"Would you like a clerkship in a dry-goods store?"

"There is too much confinement about that. No, I would not like a clerkship; but I am not particular."

"Too much confinement," I cried, "why, you keep yourself confined all the time!"

"I would prefer not to take a clerkship," he rejoined, as if to settle that little item at once.

"How would a bar-tender's business suit you? There is no trying of the eye-sight in that."

"I would not like it at all; though, as I said before, I am not particular."

His unwonted wordiness inspirited me. I returned to the charge.

"Well, then, would you like to travel through the country collecting bills for the merchants? That would improve your health."

"No, I would prefer to be doing something else."

"How, then, would going as a companion to Europe, to entertain some young gentleman with your conversation—how would that suit you?"

"Not at all. It does not strike me that there is anything definite about that. I like to be stationary. But I am not particular."

"Stationary you shall be, then," I cried, now losing all patience, and, for the first time in all my exasperating connection with him, fairly flying into a passion. "If you do not go away from these premises before night, I shall feel bound—indeed, I *am* bound—to—to—to quit the premises myself!" I rather absurdly concluded, knowing not with what possible threat to try to frighten his immobility into compliance. Despairing of all further efforts, I was precipitately leaving him, when a final thought occurred to me—one which had not been wholly unindulged before.

"Bartleby," said I, in the kindest tone I could assume under such exciting circumstances, "will you go home with me now—not to my office, but my dwelling—and remain there till we can conclude upon some convenient arrangement for you at our leisure? Come, let us start now, right away."

"No: at present I would prefer not to make any change at all."

I answered nothing; but, effectually dodging every one by the suddenness and rapidity of my flight, rushed from the building, ran up Wall Street towards Broadway, and, jumping into the first omnibus, was soon removed from pursuit. As soon as tranquillity returned, I distinctly perceived that I had now done all that I possibly could, both in respect to the demands of the landlord and his tenants, and with regard to my own desire and sense of duty, to benefit Bartleby, and shield him from rude persecution. I now strove to be entirely care-free and quiescent; and my conscience justified me in the attempt; though, indeed, it was not so successful as I could have wished. So fearful was I of being again hunted out by the incensed landlord and his exasperated tenants, that, surrendering my business to Nippers, for a few days, I drove about the upper part of the town and through the suburbs, in my rockaway;[15] crossed over to Jersey City and Hoboken, and paid fugitive visits to Manhattanville and Astoria. In fact, I almost lived in my rockaway for the time.

When again I entered my office, lo, a note from the landlord lay upon the desk. I opened it with trembling hands. It informed me that the writer had sent to the police, and had Bartleby removed to the Tombs as a vagrant. Moreover, since I knew more about him than any one else, he wished me to appear at that place, and make a suitable statement of the facts. These tidings had a conflicting effect upon me. At first I was indignant; but, at last, almost approved. The landlord's energetic, summary disposition, had led him to adopt a procedure which I do not think I would have decided upon myself; and yet, as a last resort, under such peculiar circumstances, it seemed the only plan.

As I afterwards learned, the poor scrivener, when told that he must be conducted to the Tombs, offered not the slightest obstacle, but, in his pale, unmoving way, silently acquiesced.

Some of the compassionate and curious by-standers joined the party; and headed by one of the constables arm-in-arm with Bartleby, the silent procession filed its way through all the noise, and heat, and joy of the roaring thoroughfares at noon.

The same day I received the note, I went to the Tombs, or, to speak more properly, the Halls of Justice. Seeking the right officer, I stated the purpose of my call, and was informed that the individual I described was, indeed, within. I then assured the functionary that Bartleby was a perfectly honest man, and greatly to be compassionated, however unaccountably eccentric. I narrated all I knew, and closed by suggesting the idea of letting him remain in as indulgent confinement as possible, till something less harsh might be done—though, indeed, I hardly knew what. At all events, if

[15] A light, four-wheeled carriage.

nothing else could be decided upon, the alms-house must receive him. I then begged to have an interview.

Being under no disgraceful charge, and quite serene and harmless in all his ways, they had permitted him freely to wander about the prison, and, especially, in the inclosed grass-platted yards thereof. And so I found him there, standing all alone in the quietest of the yards, his face towards a high wall, while all around, from the narrow slits of the jail windows, I thought I saw peering out upon him the eyes of murderers and thieves.

"Bartleby!"

"I know you," he said, without looking round—"and I want nothing to say to you."

"It was not I that brought you here, Bartleby," said I, keenly pained at his implied suspicion. "And to you, this should not be so vile a place. Nothing reproachful attaches to you by being here. And see, it is not so sad a place as one might think. Look, there is the sky, and here is the grass."

"I know where I am," he replied, but would say nothing more, and so I left him.

As I entered the corridor again, a broad meat-like man, in an apron, accosted me, and, jerking his thumb over his shoulder, said—"Is that your friend?"

"Yes."

"Does he want to starve? If he does, let him live on the prison fare, that's all."

"Who are you?" asked I, not knowing what to make of such an unofficially speaking person in such a place.

"I am the grub-man. Such gentlemen as have friends here, hire me to provide them with something good to eat."

"Is this so?" said I, turning to the turnkey.

He said it was.

"Well, then," said I, slipping some silver into the grub-man's hands (for so they called him), "I want you to give particular attention to my friend there; let him have the best dinner you can get. And you must be as polite to him as possible."

"Introduce me, will you?" said the grub-man, looking at me with an expression which seemed to say he was all impatience for an opportunity to give a specimen of his breeding.

Thinking it would prove of benefit to the scrivener, I acquiesced; and, asking the grub-man his name, went up with him to Bartleby.

"Bartleby, this is a friend; you will find him very useful to you."

"Your sarvant, sir, your sarvant," said the grub-man, making a low salutation behind his apron. "Hope you find it pleasant here, sir; nice grounds—cool apartments—hope you'll stay with us some time—try to make it agreeable. What will you have for dinner today?"

"I prefer not to dine today," said Bartleby, turning away. "It would disagree with me; I am unused to dinners." So saying, he slowly moved to the other side of the inclosure, and took up a position fronting the dead-wall.

"How's this?" said the grub-man, addressing me with a stare of astonishment. "He's odd, ain't he?"

"I think he is a little deranged," said I, sadly.

"Deranged? deranged is it? Well, now, upon my word, I thought that friend of yourn was a gentleman forger; they are always pale and genteel-like, them forgers. I can't help pity 'em—can't help it, sir. Did you know Monroe Edwards?" he added, touchingly, and paused. Then, laying his hand piteously on my shoulder, sighed, "he died of consumption at Sing-Sing.[16] So you weren't acquainted with Monroe?"

"No, I was never socially acquainted with any forgers. But I cannot stop longer. Look to my friend yonder. You will not lose by it. I will see you again."

Some few days after this, I again obtained admission to the Tombs, and went through the corridors in quest of Bartleby; but without finding him.

"I saw him coming from his cell not long ago," said a turnkey, "may be he's gone to loiter in the yards."

So I went in that direction.

"Are you looking for the silent man?" said another turnkey, passing me. "Yonder he lies—sleeping in the yard there. 'Tis not twenty minutes since I saw him lie down."

The yard was entirely quiet. It was not accessible to the common prisoners. The surrounding walls, of amazing thickness, kept off all sounds behind them. The Egyptian character of the masonry weighed upon me with its gloom. But a soft imprisoned turf grew under foot. The heart of the eternal pyramids, it seemed, wherein, by some strange magic, through the clefts, grass-seed, dropped by birds, had sprung.

Strangely huddled at the base of the wall, his knees drawn up, and lying on his side, his head touching the cold stones, I saw the wasted Bartleby. But nothing stirred. I paused; then went close up to him; stooped over, and saw that his dim eyes were open; otherwise he seemed profoundly sleeping. Something prompted me to touch him. I felt his hand, when a tingling shiver ran up my arm and down my spine to my feet.

The round face of the grub-man peered upon me now. "His dinner is ready. Won't he dine today, either? Or does he live without dining?"

"Lives without dining," said I, and closed the eyes.

"Eh!—He's asleep, ain't he?"

"With kings and counselors,"[17] murmured I.

There would seem little need for proceeding further in this history. Imagination will readily supply the meager recital of poor Bartleby's interment. But, ere parting with the reader, let me say, that if this little narrative has sufficiently interested him, to awaken curiosity as to who Bartleby was, and what manner of life he led prior to the present narrator's making his acquaintance, I can only reply, that in such curiosity I fully share, but am wholly unable to gratify it. Yet here I hardly know whether I should divulge one little item of rumor, which came to my ear a few months after the scrivener's decease. Upon what basis it rested, I could never ascertain; and hence, how true it is I cannot now tell. But, inasmuch as this vague report has not been without a certain suggestive interest to me, however sad, it

[16] New York state prison at Ossining.

[17] Job wishes he were dead and "at rest, with kings and counselors of the earth." Job 3:13–14.

may prove the same with some others; and so I will briefly mention it. The report was this: that Bartleby had been a subordinate clerk in the Dead Letter Office at Washington, from which he had been suddenly removed by a change in the administration. When I think over this rumor, hardly can I express the emotions which seize me. Dead letters! does it not sound like dead men? Conceive a man by nature and misfortune prone to a pallid hopelessness, can any business seem more fitted to heighten it than that of continually handling these dead letters, and assorting them for the flames? For by the cart-load they are annually burned. Sometimes from out the folded paper the pale clerk takes a ring—the finger it was meant for, perhaps, moulders in the grave; a bank-note sent in swiftest charity—he whom it would relieve, nor eats nor hungers any more; pardon for those who died despairing; hope for those who died unhoping; good tidings for those who died stifled by unrelieved calamities. On errands of life, these letters speed to death.

Ah, Bartleby! Ah, humanity!

Emily Dickinson
(1830–1886)

The two greatest poets of nineteenth-century America are, arguably, Walt Whitman and Emily Dickinson. Their contemporaries would have been stupefied by this judgment. Henry Wadsworth Longfellow, James Russell Lowell, Oliver Wendell Holmes, and a handful of lesser names seemed the best bets for time's palm. Whitman, until late in his life, was known as a faintly obscene bohemian with a barbaric yawp, and nobody had heard of Emily Dickinson at all. Two poets could not, at least superficially, be less similar. Whitman is a poet of expansiveness, Dickinson of compression; Whitman's poetic persona is that of a boisterous outdoorsman, Dickinson's that of a painfully self-conscious recluse; Whitman is an aggressively male rooster, Dickinson a little white hen. But they were parallel in one respect, which perhaps put the steel in their poetry: they were both outside the paralyzing genteelism of the public culture, Whitman through his defiance of dominant codes of taste and restraint, Dickinson through her withdrawal into an intensely private world.

Dickinson was born in 1830 in Amherst, Massachusetts. The family constellation is crucial, since family and home constituted almost her entire poetic world. There was her strong, upright father, a prominent lawyer and the treasurer of Amherst College; Dickinson adored and feared him, and his image lies just beneath the surface of many of her poems, including ones about God. Her fragile mother was a chronic invalid who required long periods of nursing by her daughters. Dickinson was very close both to her sister Lavinia, a competent, loving friend, and to her brother Austin, a lawyer like his father. Dickinson seems to have been normally lively and outgoing as a young girl, but during her teens, despite a brief period away from home at Mount Holyoke Female Seminary, she began a gradual withdrawal from the outside world back into the family home. By the time she was twenty-three, she could write, "I do not go from home," and she did not, except for brief, rare trips to Boston or Philadelphia in the early years of her seclusion, for the rest of her life. Her fellow villagers in Amherst came to think of her as a village eccentric, who always dressed in white and was seldom seen, even when they came to call, when she sometimes listened to music or conversation from behind a door left ajar. They called her "the myth."

Within the house, Dickinson carried on a regular domestic routine, supervising the gardening, tending the greenhouse, and, especially, baking bread, which her father regarded as her special talent. She also carried on an extensive correspondence with a small circle of friends, read voluminously, and wrote her poetry. Although she showed her poems occasionally to others throughout her life, apparently not even her family suspected the extent and the quality of her writing.

A personal crisis of some sort occurred between the ages of twenty-nine and thirty-four, peaking in 1862, when Dickinson was thirty-two. Early romantic biographers attributed this crisis, quite evident in her poems, to a love affair, and it is true that her emotional turbulence of 1862 was apparently triggered by the departure, for California, of Charles Wadsworth, a Philadelphia minister with whom she seems to have been in love, although probably concealing the fact from him and everyone else. She had similarly ambiguous relationships with Benjamin Newton, a student in her father's law office, and with the distinguished critic Thomas Wentworth Higginson, both of whom she regarded, overtly at least, as mentors or "preceptors." But the 1862 breakdown, if it was that, now seems to have had much more complex causes than a disappointment in love, and certainly the poems which probably allude to this crisis, such as "I felt a Funeral, in my Brain," suggest a very serious and deep-seated mental disturbance.

The crisis passed, however, and Dickinson resumed the even tenor of her quiet life. Her father died suddenly in 1873, and her mother was paralyzed by a stroke a year later; Emily and Lavinia nursed her for seven years, until her death. Dickinson survived her for only four years, dying in 1886.

After her death, a box was found containing about nine hundred poems. Higginson assisted the family in editing a selection of them, published as Poems by Emily Dickinson *in 1890; two more collections appeared in 1891 and 1896. Her reputation spread and more editions of her work appeared beginning in 1914 and culminating in Thomas Johnson's definitive edition of her complete poems—totaling 1775—in 1955. Dickinson did not title her poems or, of course, prepare them for publication by providing conventional capitalization and punctuation. The numbers given in this selection are those assigned by Johnson, and the capitalization and punctuation follow the manuscripts. The dates on the left are the approximate dates of composition, as determined by Johnson; those on the right are the original publication dates. (Only seven poems of her total production were published during her lifetime.)*

Dickinson's poetry, as her life seems to have done, sets up a passionate tension between constraint and freedom. She works within the narrow limits of the rhymed quatrains of Protestant hymn-books, but she stretches the form as far as it will go with rhythmic variations and "slant rhymes" (hand/end, star/door, *etc.). For the most part, she assumes a persona of almost childlike naiveté, who "tells all the truth but tells it slant," but on occasion, she adopts a dramatic character (as she does in "I'm 'wife'—I've finished that," for example) or adopts a grave, mature tone very far from childlike whimsy (as in "I felt a Funeral, in my Brain," and "My life closed twice before its close—"). Her themes burst the limits of her characteristically small, domes-*

tic subjects to range out into cosmic speculations, especially on God, death, love, and nature. A description of a bird on her walk can become an unpretentious but powerful meditation upon both the cruelty and the grandeur of nature, and a complex and ambivalent attitude toward death can be expressed as an afternoon carriage-ride with a gentleman caller.

Some critics have insisted upon Dickinson's close, though eccentric, relation to her own time and have denied that she is, in any sense, a "modern" poet. It is true that, as her poetic form is an extension of traditional psalmody, so her themes show a post-Calvinist preoccupation with the relationships among man, God, and nature. It is nevertheless hard not to see, in her sense of the centrality and complexity of her own inner life and the frankness with which she deals with it and in her characteristic delight in ambiguity, paradox, and "slantness," qualities which speak very directly to modern readers.

FURTHER READING *(prepared by W. J .R.):* George Frisbie Whicher's *This Was A Poet: A Critical Biography of Emily Dickinson,* 1938, the first reliable biography of the poet, is still significant and contains excellent information on the New England background. Richard B. Sewall's *The Life of Emily Dickinson,* 1974, rpt. in one volume 1980, is a more extensive biography with sections on Dickinson's forebears and her family life. A critical survey of life and work can be found in Douglas Duncan's *Emily Dickinson,* 1965. Duncan analyzes several of Dickinson's most important poems. The new student of Dickinson should also consult John B. Pickard's *Emily Dickinson: An Introduction and Interpretation,* 1967, which focuses both on biography and on typical themes. Also organized for the college student, with critical analyses and lists of study questions, is *14 by Emily Dickinson,* ed. Thomas M. Davis, 1964. Close readings of a great many poems are available in Charles R. Anderson's *Emily Dickinson's Poetry: Stairway of Surprise,* 1960. This important work in Dickinson scholarship organizes the poems according to theme; it places particular emphasis on Dickinson's language. John Cody's *After Great Pain: The Inner Life of Emily Dickinson,* 1971, is a sensitive and thorough account by a professional psychoanalyst of Dickinson's personality and its expression in her poetry. Essays on Dickinson's poetry by three later poets are collected in Archibald MacLeish, Louise Bogan, and Richard Wilbur's *Emily Dickinson: Three Views,* 1960.

67

Success is counted sweetest
By those who ne'er succeed.
To comprehend a nectar
Requires sorest need.

Not one of all the purple Host
Who took the Flag today
Can tell the definition
So clear of Victory

As he defeated—dying—
On whose forbidden ear

The distant strains of triumph
Burst agonized and clear!

c. 1859 *1878*

199

I'm "wife"—I've finished that—
That other state—
I'm Czar—I'm "Woman" now—
It's safer so—

How odd the Girl's life looks
Behind this soft Eclipse—
I think that Earth feels so
To folks in Heaven—now—

This being comfort—then
That other kind—was pain—
But why compare?
I'm "Wife"! Stop there!

c. 1860 *1890*

214

I taste a liquor never brewed—
From Tankards scooped in Pearl—
Not all the Vats upon the Rhine
Yield such an Alcohol!

Inebriate of Air—am I—
And Debauchee of Dew—
Reeling—thro endless summer days—
From inns of Molten Blue—

When "Landlords" turn the drunken Bee
Out of the Foxglove's[1] door—
When Butterflies—renounce their "drams"[2]—
I shall but drink the more!

Till Seraphs swing their snowy Hats—
And Saints—to windows run—

[1] *Foxglove* is a flower with dotted white or purple tubular blossoms.
[2] Shots of liquor.

To see the little Tippler
Leaning against the—Sun—

c. 1860 *1861*

258

There's a certain Slant of light,
Winter Afternoons—
That oppresses, like the Heft[1]
Of Cathedral Tunes—

Heavenly Hurt, it gives us—
We can find no scar,
But internal difference,
Where the Meanings, are—

None may teach it—Any—
'Tis the Seal Despair—
An imperial affliction
Sent us of the Air—

When it comes, the Landscape listens—
Shadows—hold their breath—
When it goes, 'tis like the Distance
On the look of Death—

c. 1861 *1890*

280

I felt a Funeral, in my Brain,
And Mourners to and fro
Kept treading—treading—till it seemed
That Sense was breaking through—

And when they all were seated,
A Service, like a Drum—
Kept beating—beating—till I thought
My Mind was going numb—

And then I heard them lift a Box
And creak across my Soul
With those same Boots of Lead, again,
Then Space—began to toll,

[1] A colloquial term for "weight," as in the "heft" of an ax.

As all the Heavens were a Bell,
And Being, but an Ear,
And I, and Silence, some strange Race
Wrecked, solitary, here—

And then a Plank in Reason, broke,
And I dropped down, and down—
And hit a World, at every plunge,
And Finished knowing—then—

c. 1861 *1896*

303

The Soul selects her own Society—
Then—shuts the Door—
To her divine Majority—
Present no more—

Unmoved—she notes the Chariots—pausing—
At her low Gate—
Unmoved—an Emperor be kneeling
Upon her Mat—

I've known her—from an ample nation—
Choose One—
Then—close the Valves of her attention—
Like Stone—

c. 1862 *1890*

327

Before I got my eye put out
I liked as well to see—
As other Creatures, that have Eyes
And know no other way—

But were it told to me—Today—
That I might have the sky
For mine—I tell you that my Heart
Would split, for size of me—

The Meadows—mine—
The Mountains—mine—
All Forests—Stintless Stars—

As much of Noon as I could take
Between my finite eyes—

The Motions of the Dipping Birds—
The Morning's Amber Road—
For mine—to look at when I liked—
The News would strike me dead—

So safer—guess—with just my soul
Upon the Window pane—
Where other Creatures put their eyes—
Incautious—of the Sun—

c. 1862 *1891*

328

A Bird came down the Walk—
He did not know I saw—
He bit an Angleworm in halves
And ate the fellow, raw,

And then he drank a Dew
From a convenient Grass—
And then hopped sidewise to the Wall
To let a Beetle pass—

He glanced with rapid eyes
That hurried all around—
They looked like frightened Beads, I thought—
He stirred his Velvet Head

Like one in danger, Cautious,
I offered him a Crumb
And he unrolled his feathers
And rowed him softer home—

Than Oars divide the Ocean,
Too silver for a seam—
Or Butterflies, off Banks of Noon
Leap, plashless[1] as they swim.

c. 1862 *1891*

[1] Splashless.

401

What Soft—Cherubic Creatures—
These Gentlewomen are—
One would as soon assault a Plush[1]—
Or violate a Star—

Such Dimity[2] Convictions—
A Horror so refined
Of freckled Human Nature—
Of Deity—ashamed—

It's such a common—Glory—
A Fisherman's—Degree—
Redemption—Brittle Lady—
Be so—ashamed of Thee—

c. 1862 *1896*

435

Much Madness is divinest Sense—
To a discerning Eye—
Much Sense—the starkest Madness—
'Tis the Majority
In this, as All, prevail—
Assent—and you are sane—
Demur—you're straightway dangerous—
And handled with a Chain—

c. 1862 *1890*

465

I heard a Fly buzz—when I died—
The Stillness in the Room
Was like the Stillness in the Air—
Between the Heaves of Storm—

The Eyes around—had wrung them dry—
And Breaths were gathering firm

[1] A soft, piled fabric; perhaps, by extension, a cushion made of such a fabric.

[2] A sheer cotton fabric in checks or stripes often used in nineteenth-century ladies' clothing.

For that last Onset—when the King
Be witnessed—in the Room—

I willed my Keepsakes—Signed away
What portion of me be
Assignable—and then it was
There interposed a Fly—

With Blue—uncertain stumbling Buzz—
Between the light—and me—
And then the Windows failed—and then
I could not see to see—

c. 1862 *1896*

470

I am alive—I guess—
The Branches on my Hand
Are full of Morning Glory—
And at my finger's end—

The Carmine[1]—tingles warm—
And if I hold a Glass
Across my Mouth—it blurs it—
Physician's—proof of Breath—

I am alive—because
I am not in a Room—
The Parlor—Commonly—it is—
So Visitors may come—

And lean—and view it sidewise—
And add "How cold—it grew"—
And "Was it conscious—when it stepped
In Immortality?"

I am alive—because
I do not own a House—
Entitled to myself—precise—
And fitting no one else—

And marked my Girlhood's name—
So Visitors may know
Which Door is mine—and not mistake—
And try another Key—

[1] Crimson (blood).

How good—to be alive!
How infinite—to be
Alive—two-fold—The Birth I had—
And this—besides, in—Thee!

c. 1862 *1945*

585

I like to see it lap the Miles—
And lick the Valleys up—
And stop to feed itself at Tanks—
And then—prodigious step

Around a Pile of Mountains—
And supercilious peer
In Shanties—by the sides of Roads—
And then a Quarry pare

To fit its Ribs
And crawl between
Complaining all the while
In horrid—hooting stanza—
Then chase itself down Hill—

And neigh like Boanerges[1]—
Then—punctual as a Star
Stop—docile and omnipotent
At its own stable door—

c. 1862 *1891*

712

Because I could not stop for Death—
He kindly stopped for me—
The Carriage held but just Ourselves—
And Immortality.

We slowly drove—He knew no haste
And I had put away
My labor and my leisure too,
For His Civility—

[1] Name given by Christ to James and John, meaning "sons of thunder." See Mark 3:17. In Dickinson's day, it was a humorous term for any loud, ranting preacher or orator.

We passed the School, where Children strove
At Recess—in the Ring—
We passed the Fields of Gazing Grain—
We passed the Setting Sun—

Or rather—He passed Us—
The Dews drew quivering and chill—
For only Gossamer, my Gown—
My Tippet[1]—only Tulle[2]—

We paused before a House that seemed
A Swelling of the Ground—
The Roof was scarcely visible—
The Cornice—in the Ground—

Since then—'tis Centuries—and yet
Feels shorter than the Day
I first surmised the Horses' Heads
Were toward Eternity—

c. 1863 *1890*

764

Presentiment—is that long Shadow—on the Lawn—
Indicative that Suns go down—

The Notice to the startled Grass
That Darkness—is about to pass—

c. 1863 *1890*

1129

Tell all the Truth but tell it slant—
Success in Circuit lies
Too bright for our infirm Delight
The Truth's superb surprise

As Lightning to the Children eased
With explanation kind
The Truth must dazzle gradually
Or every man be blind—

c. 1868 *1945*

[1] Scarf. [2] A thin, fine, silk netting.

1732

My life closed twice before its close—
It yet remains to see
If Immortality unveil
A third event to me

So huge, so hopeless to conceive
As these that twice befell.
Parting is all we know of heaven,
And all we need of hell.

(*date uncertain*) *1896*

Realism and Naturalism

THERE is now only one consuming interest left in our life, the passion for the study of living reality," the Goncourt brothers, Jules and Edmond, wrote in 1865 in their great joint diary of the French literary life. "We are like a man accustomed to drawing from a wax dummy who has suddenly been presented with a living model, or rather life itself with its entrails warm and active, its guts palpitating." The Goncourts rather slyly and disingenuously reflect the baiting of the middle class inherent in the realist movement; a large portion of the reading public preferred its literature without the palpitating guts. But the Goncourts also express the heady exhilaration the realists felt when they took off (as they thought) the rosy glasses of romanticism and gazed unspectacled at "life itself." From a later, more disillusioned perspective, it may appear that they merely exchanged one pair of spectacles for another, darker pair. But if nineteenth-century realism sometimes seems somber and humorless, we would do well to remember how brave the new world of reality seemed to the realists, how deeply their assumptions about art have become embedded in the modern mind, and how vital the impulse toward "the study of living reality" has been in literature since their time.

The most straightforward definition of realism is probably the one given by the American realist William Dean Howells: it is "the truthful treatment of material." But what material? And what is truthful treatment? The realists tended to be highly selective in their choice of material, focusing upon what seemed real to their largely middle-class readers. The subjects of realistic fiction thus tended to be contemporary, ordinary, and middle-class. "Truthful" treatment of such subjects usually consisted of a faithful imitation of surface details with the goal of creating the illusion of reality. Henrik Ibsen spoke for most of his fellow realists when he said that the effect of his plays depended upon "making the spectator feel as if he were actually sitting, listening, and looking on events happening in real life."

Creating such an illusion required certain artistic choices. Characters had to be ordinary, average, contemporary people rather than the exceptional extremists—the Agamemnons, the King Lears, and the Manfreds—who had formed the central subjects of much earlier literature. Plots had to be unobtrusive, made up of the trivial incidents of everyday life, as "natural" as possible in their development, capturing the wandering, indeterminate nature of ordinary experience rather than contriving the tensions and climaxes of traditional plots. And the language had to be equally natural or at least give the impression of being so; not only were characters made to speak in the intonations of everyday life but the author himself strove to make his language as invisible as possible, a neutral reflector of impersonal reality.

Why this sudden interest, in the middle of the nineteenth century, in the direct imitation of ordinary life? Realism was to some extent an extension of romanticism, which included ordinary, "natural" life among its concerns. It was Wordsworth, after all, who proposed in *Lyrical Ballads* to "choose incidents and situations from common life, and to relate or describe them, throughout, as far as was possible in a selection of language really used by men." But the realists' concern with ordinary life represented a considerable shift in basic assumptions. Wordsworth proposed to throw over ordinary life " a certain colouring of imagination" and to trace through simple incidents "the primary laws of our nature," especially the ways "the passions of men are incorporated with the beautiful and permanent forms of nature." The realists' vision of ordinary life was a darker one. The " ordinary man" of the realists was not a rural laborer, in harmony with the cycles of nature, but an urban bourgeois, alienated from both nature and himself by the pressures of a scrambling, competitive, materialistic society.

Discontent with the optimistic premises of romanticism became evident in European literature as early as the 1840's, especially in France. Balzac's flood of novels during the 1830's and 1840's were basically antiromantic in their subordination of the individual will to external circumstance. His famous Preface to *The Human Comedy* (1842) sets forth some of the basic tenets of realism, including a materialistic determinism ("Tell me what you possess and I will tell you what you think"), and outlines a quasi-scientific project of producing a comprehensive classification of human types. His divisions resemble zoological categories: "By drawing up an inventory of vices and virtues, by collecting the chief facts of the passions, by depicting characters, by choosing the principal incidents of social life, by composing types out of a combination of homogeneous characteristics, I might perhaps succeed in writing the history which so many historians have neglected: that of Manners."

To see the reasons for the shift in emphasis between romanticism and realism, we must look outside literature to society and politics and especially to the triumph of the commercial middle class after the mid-century. The collapse of the 1848 revolutions that swept France, Germany, Austria, and Italy marked a major turning point in European life. Artists and intellectuals had taken an active part in these revolutions; the idealistic poet and novelist Alphonse de Lamartine had actually headed the French provisional government after the 1848 February Revolution, and the poet-patriot Giuseppe Mazzini was a leading figure in the 1848 Milan Revolution and in the 1849 Roman republic. The backlash of conservative reaction after 1848 drove artists all over Europe from the political arena and back into a kind of art that provided a refuge from a society they more and more perceived as crude, brutal, and unredeemable. In France, the decisive defeat of liberalism came with the 1851 *coup d'état* by which Napoleon III transformed the short-lived Second Republic into the Second Empire. Jules Goncourt spoke for many French intellectuals when he called the Second Empire "decadence in its vilest form, a new invasion of the barbarians." English intellectuals reacted similarly to the Crystal Palace exhibition of the same year, a celebration which, from one point of view, magnified England's material progress and industrial dominance and, from another, more jaundiced one, her crassness, vulgarity, and social injustice.

The bourgeois triumph of the 1850's was far from the unqualified disaster that aesthetes considered it. The French Bonapartist government built broad boulevards and laid water lines and sewer pipes in Paris; the diplomacy of Cavour in Italy and Bismarck in Germany unified those countries at last; and all over Europe the wealth created by industrialization brought about a new prosperity, at least some of which trickled down to the working class. Growth was so rapid that the ordinary man came to believe in inevitable, limitless progress. But it was a kind of growth to which most artists felt irreconcilably hostile. The gap between the artist and society, already wide during the age of romanticism, became a yawning gulf even now not wholly bridged.

Middle-class expansionism found its ideology in Positivism and an exaggerated faith in science or "scientism." Positivism was the creation of the French philosopher Auguste Comte, who set forth the system in his *Course of Positive Philosophy* (1830–42). For Comte, the greatest of the sciences was sociology (a term he coined), and the goal of science was to reform society so that all people could live together in comfort and harmony. Metaphysics he rejected as superstition; trustworthy knowledge was derivable from sense experience and the "positive" sciences only. Comte's brisk, commonsense optimism and his faith in progress perfectly suited the temper of his age, and by the 1850's, Positivism was the ruling ideology of many European intellectuals. In England, the Utilitarianism preached by John Stuart Mill and others was thoroughly Positivistic in its insistence upon empiricism as the basis of all knowledge and its demystification of morality as "the greatest good for the greatest number." Karl Marx, whose *Communist Manifesto* (written with Friedrich Engels) appeared in 1848, was also Positivistic in his "scientific" theory of social change, a theory developed in full in *Capital*, the influential first volume of which appeared in 1867. Mill's Utilitarianism was paralleled in Germany by the philosophy of Ludwig Feuerbach, who defined religion as nothing more than a symbolic dream and philosophy as the study of man as defined by experience. Marx's attempt at scientific history was similarly pursued by the English historian Henry Thomas Buckle, whose *History of Civilization in England* (1857–61), with its broad sweep and its supposedly scientific method, created a sensation. Even Charles Darwin's evolutionary bombshell *The Origin of Species* (1859) was essentially Positivistic in its application of the methods of science to areas that had traditionally been the province of religion: man's origins, his nature, and his relation to the rest of the natural world.

The realist writers felt an uneasy ambivalence toward this world of explosive prosperity, dizzying progress, and scientific Positivism. On the one hand, they maintained their stance of disapproval and estrangement; on the other, they shaped an art based upon the methods if not the values of the larger society. None of the great realist writers was in any sense an apologist for his society; all were more or less in open revolt against it. And yet all to some degree brought to art the habits of mind pervasive in that society: a sceptical secularism, a concern for the here and now, and a loosely scientific objectivity. It is almost as if the realists were saying to their contemporaries: "We will use your own methods to reveal to you the meanness, the cruelty, and the vulgarity of the society you take such pride in." The result was a paradoxically avant-garde art in which the bourgeoisie was taunted in its own common-sense terms. This ambivalence is especially powerful in the work of the great French realist Gustave Flaubert, who had to drive himself to write about a contemporary reality he found nauseating and who periodically escaped into lush, neoromantic fantasies. "Do you really believe that this mean reality, whose reproduction disgusts you, does not make my gorge rise as much as yours?" he wrote to a friend who had taken exception to *Madame Bovary* (1857). "If you knew me better, you would know that I hold the everyday life in detestation. Personally I have always kept myself as far away from it as I could. But aesthetically I wanted this time, and only this time, to exhaust it thoroughly. So I took the thing in an heroic fashion, I mean a minute one, accepting everything, saying everything, depicting everything—an ambitious statement!"

The desire to shock the middle class became even more pointed when realism darkened still further into naturalism, the movement that dominated the 1870's and 1880's as realism had dominated the 1850's and 1860's. Naturalism is not merely an extreme form of realism; it is informed by a very different philosophical view, a post-Darwinian form of scientific determinism in which man is the prisoner of his biological inheritance and his social environment. The naturalists abandoned the middle-class drawing rooms of the realists for the "lower depths," working-class settings where the impact of environment was especially clear, and for violent, animalistic characters whose inherited drives, especially hunger and sex, are particularly vivid. Naturalism, for all its claims to a scientific objectivity, was an even better stick with which to beat the middle class than realism had been. The Goncourt brothers, at the same time fastidious aesthetes and the first architects of the naturalistic novel, wrote in their preface to what has been called the first naturalistic novel, *Germinie Lacerteux* (1864), "The public loves to read pleasant, soothing stories, adventures that end happily, imaginative works that disturb neither its digestion nor its peace of mind: this book furnishes entertainment of a melancholy, violent sort calculated to disarrange the habits and injure the health of the public."

The Goncourts denied that their work, for all its disturbing qualities, was pessimistic or despairing; their aim, they said, was to make the novel a "serious, impassioned, living form of literary study and social investigation" and to bring about social reform. Their friend, Émile Zola, theoretician and practitioner of the "experimental novel"—the novel designed like a medical experiment—similarly denied that he was a fatalist: "We are not fatalists, we are determinists, which is not at all the same thing. . . . The moment that we can act, and that we do act, on the determining cause of phenomena—by modifying their surroundings, for example—we cease to be fatalists." Such explanations cut little ice with middle-class readers, however; Zola's works were frequently banned and Tennyson, speaking for the bourgeoisie, rejected modern literature as "wallowing in the troughs of Zolaism."

Realism and naturalism transcended national boundaries. France took the lead, but the realist impulse quickly spread throughout Europe. Scandinavia, long a backwater of European culture, became the center of a new drama, vitalized by realism, when Henrik Ibsen, an obscure, failed Norwegian playwright living in exile in Germany, read the Danish critic Georg Brandes' lecture on "Main Currents in Nineteenth-Century Literature." Brandes had applied for the chair of aesthetics at the University of Copenhagen and, to demonstrate his qualifications for the post, had been asked to deliver a series of lectures. His opening lecture, delivered on November 3, 1871, was a scathing attack on Danish literature, which he said was forty years behind the times and lost in a haze of dreamy, abstract idealism. The only living literature, he said, pointing to the French writers as examples, was realistic literature, literature that "submitted contemporary social problems to debate." When Ibsen read the lecture in Dresden in 1872, he wrote to his friend Brandes: "No more dangerous book could fall into the hands of a pregnant writer. It is one of those works that place a yawning gulf between yesterday and today." Ibsen's *Pillars of Society* followed in 1877, the first in the series of twelve realistic dramas that debated contemporary social problems. The progression in the French novel from realism to naturalism was echoed in the Scandinavian drama when Ibsen's realistic plays were followed by August Strindberg's naturalistic ones, such as *The Father* (1887) and *Miss Julie* (1888). These display the quasi-Darwinian spectacle of brutal, primitive characters triumphing in the struggle for survival over more sensitive and highly developed types.

In England, George Eliot cultivated, in *Adam Bede* (1859), *Middlemarch* (1871–72), and other works, a gentle realism which she compared to Dutch genre paintings. "Let us always have men," she wrote, "ready to give the loving pains of a life to the faithful representation of commonplace things—men who see beauty in these commonplace things, and delight in showing how kindly the light of heaven falls on them." The realistic impulse touched Charles Dickens, too, as he turned from the romantic optimism of his early novels to the more somber studies of society that began to appear in the 1850's, especially *Bleak House* (1853), *Hard Times* (1854), and *Great Expectations* (1860–61). George Meredith, Thomas Hardy, George Moore, and Joseph Conrad carried the realist-naturalist tradition down to the early years of the twentieth century.

In Russia, a realistic movement flourished that surpassed even its French inspiration. Nikolay Gogol, though a conservative upholder of autocracy and serfdom, established, especially in his comedy *The Inspector General* (1836) and his story "The Overcoat" (1842), a "natural" school of writing that was to foster the greatest achievements of Russian fiction. Ivan Turgenev added to Gogol's influence that of his friends Flaubert in France and George Eliot in England. His *A Sportsman's Sketches* (1852), a series of realistic stories of Russian peasant life, played a role in the emancipation of the serfs in 1861, and his *Fathers and Sons* (1862) is one of the great works of nineteenth-century realism. The most brilliant member of the "natural" school, however, was Fyodor Dostoevsky, whose four greatest novels, *Crime and Punishment* (1866), *The Idiot* (1868–69), *The Possessed* (1871–72), and *The Brothers Karamazov* (1879–80), all probe in their different ways the classic realist theme: the fate of the individual living in a problematical modern world stripped of faith. Leo Tolstoy's *War and Peace* (1865–69) and *Anna Karenina* (1875–76), a book often compared to *Madame Bovary*, are also in the main realistic tradition, as are his "post-conversion" masterpieces "The Death of Ivan Ilyitch" (1886) and "The Kreutzer Sonata" (1891). Anton Chekhov, besides writing magnificent realistic short stories, carried realistic drama beyond even Ibsen, to a point where photographic and phonographic literalism takes on a shimmering intensity on the borders of symbolism.

Realism crossed the Atlantic, too, to generate a vigorous movement in America. The chief theoretician of American realism was William Dean Howells, who in his column "The Editor's Study" in *Harper's Magazine* vigorously advocated an American realism somewhat milder than that of Flaubert, Zola, and Dostoevsky. America, he thought, was dominated, as France and Russia were not, by "the large, cheerful average of health and success and happy life." Therefore, American realists should concern themselves with "the more smiling aspects of life, which are the more American." Timid as this program sounds, Howells' proselytizing and his example, in such novels as *The Rise of Silas Lapham* (1885), opened the way for the great American realists, Mark Twain and Henry James, and for the later American naturalists: Frank Norris, Hamlin Garland, Theodore Dreiser, Upton Sinclair, and Jack London.

America was somewhat late in following the realist-naturalist flag; in Europe the movement had run its course by the late 1880's, when the artists' withdrawal from society that had been latent in realism was extended in the symbolist movement, which like realism originated in France and spread thoughout Europe to dominate the closing years of the century.

Realism, of course, did not disappear when it ceased to be the dominant style of serious art. It has survived as the style of most popular literature, drama, film, and television, where frequently a realistic manner is used to present the most unrealistic views of life. But it has also survived in serious art as one of the styles available to modern writers and has found special favor with socially committed writers, such as the proletarian authors of the 1930's and the "Angry Young Men" novelists of post-World War II Britain. It seems likely that as long as writers are drawn to "the study of living reality," they will continue to draw upon the models of the great nineteenth-century realists.

FURTHER READING *(prepared by J. H.):* A number of basic documents in which the nineteenth-century realists and naturalists directly declared their goals are available in the "Realism" section of *The Modern Tradition: Backgrounds of Modern Literature,* ed. by Richard Ellmann and Charles Feidelson, Jr., 1965. Two other useful collections are *Documents of Modern Literary Realism,* ed. by George L. Becker, 1963, and *Realism, Naturalism, and Symbolism: Modes of Thought and Expression in Europe, 1848–1914,* ed. by Roland N. Stromberg, 1968. The critical issues implied by the terms *realism* and *naturalism* are well treated in René Wellek's "The Concept of Realism in Literary Scholarship," in *Concepts of Criticism,* 1963, and in Harry Levin's "What is Realism?" in *Contexts of Criticism,* 1957. Levin's *The Gates of Horn,* 1963, is a standard study of the French nineteenth-century realist novelists. On the development of the realistic novel elsewhere, see Ian Watt, *The Rise of the Novel,* 1957, and R. Stang, *The Theory of the Novel in England, 1850–1870,* 1961. Erich Auerbach's masterful *Mimesis: The Representation of Reality in Western Literature,* trans. by Willard R. Trask, 1953, furnishes for the nineteenth-century realists the context of the treatment of reality throughout literary history.

Gustave Flaubert
(1821–1880)

"The author, in his work," the great French novelist Gustave Flaubert wrote, "must be like God in the Universe, present everywhere and visible nowhere." The metaphor is significant. Flaubert conceived of the artist as a sort of God, bringing his own world into being in an act of creation analogous to God's, exercising so scrupulous a fidelity to the reality of that world that his own personality is totally subsumed in it. This rigorous conception of the novelist's work and Flaubert's realization of it in his fiction played a crucial role in the making of the modern novel, no longer a slightly tawdry medium of bourgeois diversion but as lofty a form as tragedy or the epic. With Flaubert, however, the ideal of perfect objectivity was a reaction to powerful contrary impulses in his own character. He possessed a lush romantic strain and a continual temptation to retreat into his own imagination which he subdued only by herculean effort and which constantly threatened to reassert itself. Flaubert's realism was born of a heroic struggle not to be romantic.

Flaubert was born in Rouen in 1821 into the sort of prosperous middle-class background he was to treat with profound ambivalence in his greatest fiction. His father was chief surgeon at the Hôtel-Dieu hospital in Rouen, while his mother, daughter of a doctor in the small town of Pont-l'Évêque, came from a family of distinguished magistrates. His father's profession and his contact with operating rooms and anatomy classes had a permanent influence upon Flaubert, who was later to hold that he observed his subjects with "a doctor's eye." While still at school, he formed a close friendship with a young philosopher named Alfred Le Poittevin. The two young men adopted pessimistic views and cultivated an anti-bourgeois stance, compiling lists of banal idées reçues *("received ideas") to be ridiculed. By the age of sixteen, Flaubert was writing stories, mostly in a fervent romantic style, which remained unpublished. He also wrote, when he was sixteen, a long manuscript he called* Memoirs of a Fool, *an impassioned account of his secret love for a much older married woman, Elisa Schlesinger.*

Flaubert's family determined upon a law career for him, and he was enrolled at the age of twenty in the Faculty of Law at the University of Paris. Two years later, after failing his examinations, he suffered a severe nervous collapse, diagnosed at the time as epilepsy, and was forced to withdraw from his studies and return home. After the death of his father in 1846, he moved, with his mother and his orphaned infant niece, to the family estate of Croisset, near Rouen, and remained there for most of the rest of his life, devoting his full energies to literature.

The history of the composition of Flaubert's books is complex, because of his meticulous working habits and his protracted revisions. His first major book was Madame Bovary, *published in 1856 but composed during an extended interlude of five years between work on other, very different books. One of the stories Flaubert had written when he was sixteen was "Passion and Virtue," which dealt with a woman much like Emma Bovary. Twelve years later, when he read the manuscript of his* Temptation of St. Anthony *to his friends Louis Bouilhet and Maxime du Camp, they condemned its romantic excesses, advised him to burn it, and recommended that he discipline his imagination by writing a "down-to-earth" novel of ordinary life; they suggested as a topic the true story of Delphine Delamare, wife of a country doctor in Normandy who had died of grief after she deceived and ruined him. Flaubert accepted the challenge and, drawing upon the story of Delphine Delamare as well as the similar one of an acquaintance named Louise Pradier, began the five-year composition of* Madame Bovary. *Flaubert's own letters and journals record the psychological as well as artistic struggle the novel required. Contemptuous of his commonplace characters and his sordid story of provincial adultery, he nevertheless forced himself to identify sympathetically with them and to re-create meticulously their constricted world. At the same time, he strove to find beauty even in the ordinary. Through an exacting search for* le seul mot juste *("the only right word") he aimed to achieve a style that was "as rhythmical as verse and as precise as the language of science." Emma Bovary's conflict between romantic escapism and hard reality was Flaubert's own, so that he could justly say, when questioned about the model for Emma, "Madame Bovary is myself."* Madame Bovary *was published in magazine installments in 1856, and Flaubert was almost immediately brought to trial on charges of "outraging public morals and religion"; he was acquitted only narrowly. The novel made Flaubert famous and has since come to be regarded as the cornerstone of the modern art novel.*

After the long submission to reality that Madame Bovary *required, Flaubert's next novel swung to the other extreme of his divided artistic personality.* Salammbô *(1862) is a lush historical novel set in ancient Carthage; to write it, Flaubert made a trip to Tunisia to inspect the ruins of the city and to gather material on the third-century* B.C. *revolt of mercenaries against Carthage which forms the background of the novel.*

Publication of The Sentimental Education *(1869) brought to an end a process of composition even more protracted than that of* Madame Bovary. *The story of the passion of the young Frederic Moreau for the older wife of a businessman, the novel had its roots in Flaubert's youthful* Memoirs of a Fool. *Flaubert had completely rewritten this manuscript twice before the final version, once in 1842 and again between 1843 and 1845. In the process, the novel became a large-scale social panorama in which the love story is set against the background of French society under the "July Monarchy" of King Louis Philippe.*

The writing of The Temptation of St. Anthony *(1874) was spread out over a period of thirty-five years. Again, it had its start in a youthful manuscript,* Smarh, *which Flaubert wrote when he was eighteen. He radically revised the plot in 1846–49, 1856, and 1870. The successive versions of the book reflect Flaubert's developing view of religion, from the anti-religious nihilism of the early versions to a final view that religion and science are complementary, a position influenced by his reading of the English evolutionary philosopher Herbert Spencer.*

"A Simple Heart" appeared in 1877 as part of Three Tales, *which also included the stories "The Legend of St. Julian the Hospitaller" and "Herodias." These three stories, sharply contrasted in content and style, are linked by the fact that all three deal with various kinds of saints.* Three Tales *challenges* Madame Bovary *as Flaubert's masterpiece, exhibiting the same consummate craftsmanship as the earlier novel but exercised upon a wider range of material.*

When Flaubert died suddenly of an apoplectic stroke in 1880, at the age of fifty-eight, he left an unfinished novel named Bouvard and Pecuchet, *a wry satirical work about two clerks who take advantage of an unexpected legacy to retire to the country and dabble with various utopian schemes. A satire on the naive bourgeois faith in half-understood science, the novel can also be seen as Flaubert's whimsical account of his own journey to understanding.*

Flaubert's books tend to oscillate between the poles of romanticism and realism which he himself was quick to describe as the basic dichotomy in his art as in his life. But the opposition appears in individual works as well. "A Simple Heart" belongs with Madame Bovary *among the works in which Flaubert develops with painstaking realism a story of ordinary, contemporary life. Flaubert seems, like the God of creation, to be "visible nowhere" in this simple tale of a humble life. Félicité's life is built up, detail by detail, from concrete reality, with the barest minimum of authorial commentary or explicit interpretation. The servant's painful, lonely life is a deeply moving account of "the wretched of the earth," all the more touching because of the restraint and objectivity with which it is told.*

And yet Flaubert's realism is very far from a merely photographic record of life in which reality is left to determine form and facts are presumed to "speak for themselves." Again like God, if Flaubert is "nowhere visible," he is "present everywhere," shaping Félicité's story artistically and providing a subtle, ironic commentary upon it by the most indirect of means. Félicité (even her name—"happiness"—is delicately ironic) is a secular saint; her story is a series of trials—including the losses of her lover, her nephew, her parrot—from which she emerges ambiguously triumphant. She defeats monsters (the bull in the field), is scourged like Christ by the angry coachman, and is finally vouchsafed a vision of God (and her parrot). And what are we to think of that parrot? When Félicité's simple heart stops beating as the vulgar but sumptuous festival procession pauses outside her window and the beatific vision of Loulou appears, are we to laugh or cry? Is Flaubert ironically satirizing the absurdity of a constrained life or asserting the holiness of the most ordinary details of a simple life? He is doing both, and the achievement exemplifies the richness and resonance of Flaubert's complex art.

FURTHER READING *(prepared by W. J. R.):* Good biographies include Stratton Buck's *Gustave Flaubert,* 1966, and Philip Spencer's *Flaubert: A Biography,* 1952. Victor Brombert's *The Novels of Flaubert,* 1966, devotes a chapter to "A Simple Heart," discussing the tenderness and irony of the piece. *Madame Bovary, Salammbô,* and several other major works are also discussed at length. Introductory discussions of *Madame Bovary, Three Tales,* and *The Sentimental Education,* as well as a survey of Flaubert criticism, are offered in Peter Cortland's *A Reader's Guide to Flaubert,* 1968. *Flaubert: A Collection of Critical Essays,* ed. Raymond Giraud, 1964, includes essays by Jean-Paul Sartre, Erich Auerbach, and others. A general appreciation of Flaubert's artistry is provided in Margaret G. Tillett's *On Reading Flaubert,* 1961. Tillett discusses six major works, among them "A Simple Heart." *Madame Bovary, Salammbô,* and *The Sentimental Education* are the subjects of R. L. Sherrington's *Three Novels by Flaubert,* 1970. Sherrington explores in particular detail Flaubert's use of restricted point of view in these novels. Flaubert's significance for American readers is discussed in the opening chapter of Ernest Jackson's *The Critical Reception of Gustave Flaubert in the United States, 1860–1960,* 1966. Later chapters offer a good survey of critical reactions to *Madame Bovary, Three Tales,* and other works.

A SIMPLE HEART

Translated by Arthur McDowall

I

Madame Aubain's servant Félicité was the envy of the ladies of Pont-l'Évêque[1] for half a century.

She received a hundred francs a year. For that she was cook and general servant, and did the sewing, washing, and ironing; she could bridle a horse, fatten poultry, and churn butter—and she remained faithful to her mistress, unamiable as the latter was.

Mme. Aubain had married a gay bachelor without money who died at the beginning of 1809, leaving her with two small children and a quantity of debts. She then sold all her property except the farms of Toucques and Geffosses, which brought in five thousand francs a year at most, and left her house in Saint-Melaine for a less expensive one that had belonged to her family and was situated behind the market.

This house had a slate roof and stood between an alley and a lane that went down to the river. There was an unevenness in the levels of the rooms which made you stumble. A narrow hall divided the kitchen from the "parlor" where Mme. Aubain spent her day, sitting in a wicker easy chair by the window. Against the panels, which were painted white, was a row of eight mahogany chairs. On an old piano under the barometer a heap of wooden and cardboard boxes rose like a pyramid. A stuffed armchair stood on either side of the Louis-Quinze chimney-piece, which was in yellow marble with a clock in the middle of it modelled like a temple of Vesta.[2] The whole room was a little musty, as the floor was lower than the garden.

The first floor began with "Madame's" room: very large, with a pale-flowered wallpaper and a portrait of "Monsieur" as a dandy of the period. It led to a smaller room, where there were two children's cots without mattresses. Next came the drawing-room, which was always shut up and full of furniture covered with sheets. Then there was a corridor leading to a study. The shelves of a large bookcase were respectably lined with books and papers, and its three wings surrounded a broad writing-table in darkwood. The two panels at the end of the room were covered with pen-drawings, water-color landscapes, and engravings by Audran,[3] all relics of better days and vanished splendor. Félicité's room on the top floor got its light from a dormer-window, which looked over the meadows.

She rose at daybreak to be in time for Mass, and worked till evening without stopping. Then, when dinner was over, the plates and dishes in order, and the door shut fast, she thrust the log under the ashes and went to sleep in front of the hearth with her rosary in her hand. Félicité was the

[1] A village in Normandy, home of Flaubert's mother.

[2] Vesta was the Roman goddess of the hearth. *Louis-Quinze* is the fussy, rococo decorative style which prevailed in France in the first half of the eighteenth century.

[3] Gérard Audran was a seventeenth-century French engraver whose copies of famous paintings were popular household decorations.

stubbornest of all bargainers; and as for cleanness, the polish on her saucepans was the despair of other servants. Thrifty in all things, she ate slowly, gathering off the table in her fingers the crumbs of her loaf—a twelve-pound loaf expressly baked for her, which lasted for three weeks.

At all times of year she wore a print handkerchief fastened with a pin behind, a bonnet that covered her hair, gray stockings, a red skirt, and a bibbed apron—such as hospital nurses wear—over her jacket.

Her face was thin and her voice sharp. At twenty-five she looked like forty. From fifty onwards she seemed of no particular age; and with her silence, straight figure, and precise movements she was like a woman made of wood, and going by clockwork.

II

She had had her love-story like another.

Her father, a mason, had been killed by falling off some scaffolding. Then her mother died, her sisters scattered, and a farmer took her in and employed her, while she was still quite little, to herd the cows at pasture. She shivered in rags and would lie flat on the ground to drink water from the ponds; she was beaten for nothing, and finally turned out for the theft of thirty sous[4] which she did not steal. She went to another farm, where she became dairy-maid; and as she was liked by her employers her companions were jealous of her.

One evening in August (she was then eighteen) they took her to the assembly at Colleville. She was dazed and stupefied in an instant by the noise of the fiddlers, the lights in the trees, the gay medley of dresses, the lace, the gold crosses, and the throng of people jigging all together. While she kept shyly apart a young man with a well-to-do air, who was leaning on the shaft of a cart and smoking his pipe, came up to ask her to dance. He treated her to cider, coffee, and cake, and bought her a silk handkerchief; and then, imagining she had guessed his meaning, offered to see her home. At the edge of a field of oats he pushed her roughly down. She was frightened and began to cry out; and he went off.

One evening later she was on the Beaumont road. A big hay-wagon was moving slowly along; she wanted to get in front of it, and as she brushed past the wheels she recognized Theodore. He greeted her quite calmly, saying she must excuse it all because it was "the fault of the drink." She could not think of any answer and wanted to run away.

He began at once to talk about the harvest and the worthies of the commune, for his father had left Colleville for the farm at Les Écots, so that now he and she were neighbors. "Ah!" she said. He added that they thought of settling him in life. Well, he was in no hurry; he was waiting for a wife to his fancy. She dropped her head; and then he asked her if she thought of marrying. She answered with a smile that it was mean to make fun of her.

"But I am not, I swear!"—and he passed his left hand round her waist. She walked in the support of his embrace; their steps grew slower. The

[4] A very small sum of money. (A *sou* is worth five *centimes* or one twentieth of a *franc*.)

wind was soft, the stars glittered, the huge wagon-load of hay swayed in front of them, and dust rose from the dragging steps of the four horses. Then, without a word of command, they turned to the right. He clasped her once more in his arms, and she disappeared into the shadow.

The week after Theodore secured some assignations with her.

They met at the end of farmyards, behind a wall, or under a solitary tree. She was not innocent as young ladies are—she had learned knowledge from the animals—but her reason and the instinct of her honor would not let her fall. Her resistance exasperated Theodore's passion; so much so that to satisfy it—or perhaps quite artlessly—he made her an offer of marriage. She was in doubt whether to trust him, but he swore great oaths of fidelity.

Soon he confessed to something troublesome; the year before his parents had bought him a substitute for the army, but any day he might be taken again, and the idea of serving was a terror to him. Félicité took this cowardice of his as a sign of affection, and it redoubled hers. She stole away at night to see him, and when she reached their meeting-place Theodore racked her with his anxieties and urgings.

At last he declared that he would go himself to the prefecture[5] for information, and would tell her the result on the following Sunday, between eleven and midnight.

When the moment came she sped towards her lover. Instead of him she found one of his friends.

He told her that she would not see Theodore any more. To ensure himself against conscription he had married an old woman, Madame Lehoussais, of Toucques, who was very rich.

There was an uncontrollable burst of grief. She threw herself on the ground, screamed, called to the God of mercy, and moaned by herself in the fields till daylight came. Then she came back to the farm and announced that she was going to leave; and at the end of the month she received her wages, tied all her small belongings with a handkerchief, and went to Pont-l'Évêque.

In front of the inn there she made inquiries of a woman in a widow's cap, who, as it happened, was just looking for a cook. The girl did not know much, but her willingness seemed so great and her demands so small that Mme. Aubain ended by saying:

"Very well, then, I will take you."

A quarter of an hour afterwards Félicité was installed in her house.

She lived there at first in a tremble, as it were, at "the style of the house" and the memory of "Monsieur" floating over it all. Paul and Virginie, the first aged seven and the other hardly four, seemed to her beings of a precious substance; she carried them on her back like a horse; it was a sorrow to her that Mme. Aubain would not let her kiss them every minute. And yet she was happy there. Her grief had melted in the pleasantness of things all round.

Every Thursday regular visitors came in for a game of boston,[6] and Félicité got the cards and foot-warmers ready beforehand. They arrived punctually at eight and left before the stroke of eleven.

[5] Office of the prefect, or magistrate.
[6] Card game, played by four people with two decks of cards.

On Monday mornings the dealer who lodged in the covered passage spread out all his old iron on the ground. Then a hum of voices began to fill the town, mingled with the neighing of horses, bleating of lambs, grunting of pigs, and the sharp rattle of carts along the street. About noon, when the market was at its height, you might see a tall, hook-nosed old countryman with his cap pushed back making his appearance at the door. It was Robelin, the farmer of Geffosses. A little later came Liébard, the farmer from Toucques—short, red, and corpulent—in a gray jacket and gaiters[7] shod with spurs.

Both had poultry or cheese to offer their landlord. Félicité was invariably a match for their cunning, and they went away filled with respect for her.

At vague intervals Mme. Aubain had a visit from the Marquis de Gremanville, one of her uncles, who had ruined himself by debauchery and now lived at Falaise on his last remaining morsel of land. He invariably came at the luncheon hour, with a dreadful poodle whose paws left all the furniture in a mess. In spite of efforts to show his breeding, which he carried to the point of raising his hat every time he mentioned "my late father," habit was too strong for him; he poured himself out glass after glass and fired off improper remarks. Félicité edged him politely out of the house—"You have had enough, Monsieur de Gremanville! Another time!"—and she shut the door on him.

She opened it with pleasure to M. Bourais, who had been a lawyer. His baldness, his white stock, frilled shirt, and roomy brown coat, his way of rounding the arm as he took snuff—his whole person, in fact, created that disturbance of mind which overtakes us at the sight of extraordinary men.

As he looked after the property of "Madame" he remained shut up with her for hours in "Monsieur's" study, though all the time he was afraid of compromising himself. He respected the magistracy immensely, and had some pretensions to Latin.

To combine instruction and amusement he gave the children a geography book made up of a series of prints. They represented scenes in different parts of the world: cannibals with feathers on their heads, a monkey carrying off a young lady, Bedouins in the desert, the harpooning of a whale, and so on. Paul explained these engravings to Félicité; and that, in fact, was the whole of her literary education. The children's education was undertaken by Guyot, a poor creature employed at the town hall, who was famous for his beautiful hand and sharpened his penknife on his boots.

When the weather was bright the household set off early for a day at Geffosses Farm.

Its courtyard is on a slope, with the farmhouse in the middle, and the sea looks like a gray streak in the distance.

Félicité brought slices of cold meat out of her basket, and they breakfasted in a room adjoining the dairy. It was the only surviving fragment of a country house which was now no more. The wallpaper hung in tatters, and quivered in the draughts. Mme. Aubain sat with bowed head, overcome by her memories; the children became afraid to speak. "Why don't you play, then?" she would say, and off they went.

[7] Boots with fabric uppers.

Paul climbed into the barn, caught birds, played at ducks and drakes over the pond, or hammered with his stick on the big casks which boomed like drums. Virginie fed the rabbits or dashed off to pick cornflowers, her quick legs showing their embroidered little drawers.

One autumn evening they went home by the fields. The moon was in its first quarter, lighting part of the sky; and mist floated like a scarf over the windings of the Toucques. Cattle, lying out in the middle of the grass, looked quietly at the four people as they passed. In the third meadow some of them got up and made a half-circle in front of the walkers. "There's nothing to be afraid of," said Félicité, as she stroked the nearest on the back with a kind of crooning song; he wheeled round and the others did the same. But when they crossed the next pasture there was a formidable bellow. It was a bull, hidden by the mist. Mme. Aubain was about to run. "No! no! don't go so fast!" They mended their pace, however, and heard a loud breathing behind them which came nearer. His hoofs thudded on the meadow grass like hammers; why, he was galloping now! Félicité turned round, and tore up clods of earth with both hands and threw them in his eyes. He lowered his muzzle, waved his horns, and quivered with fury, bellowing terribly. Mme. Aubain, now at the end of the pasture with her two little ones, was looking wildly for a place to get over the high bank. Félicité was retreating, still with her face to the bull, keeping up a shower of clods which blinded him, and crying all the time, "Be quick! be quick!"

Mme. Aubain went down into the ditch, pushed Virginie first and then Paul, fell several times as she tried to climb the bank, and managed it at last by dint of courage.

The bull had driven Félicité to bay against a rail-fence; his slaver[8] was streaming into her face; another second, and he would have gored her. She had just time to slip between two of the rails, and the big animal stopped short in amazement.

This adventure was talked of at Pont-l'Évêque for many a year. Félicité did not pride herself on it in the least, not having the barest suspicion that she had done anything heroic.

Virginie was the sole object of her thoughts, for the child developed a nervous complaint as a result of her fright, and M. Poupart, the doctor, advised sea-bathing at Trouville. It was not a frequented place then. Mme. Aubain collected information, consulted Bourais, and made preparations as though for a long journey.

Her luggage started a day in advance, in Liébard's cart. The next day he brought round two horses, one of which had a lady's saddle with a velvet back to it, while a cloak was rolled up to make a kind of seat on the crupper of the other. Mme. Aubain rode on that, behind the farmer. Félicité took charge of Virginie, and Paul mounted M. Lechaptois' donkey, lent on condition that great care was taken of it.

The road was so bad that its five miles took two hours. The horses sank in the mud up to their pasterns, and their haunches jerked abruptly in the effort to get out; or else they stumbled in the ruts, and at other moments had to jump. In some places Liébard's mare came suddenly to a halt. He

[8] Saliva.

waited patiently until she went on again, talking about the people who had properties along the road, and adding moral reflections to their history. So it was that as they were in the middle of Toucques, and passed under some windows bowered with nasturtiums, he shrugged his shoulders and said: "There's a Mme. Lehoussais lives there; instead of taking a young man she. . ." Félicité did not hear the rest; the horses were trotting and the donkey galloping. They all turned down a bypath; a gate swung open and two boys appeared; and the party dismounted in front of a manure-heap at the very threshold of the farmhouse door.

When Mme. Liébard saw her mistress she gave lavish signs of joy. She served her a luncheon with a sirloin of beef, tripe, black-pudding, a fricassee of chicken, sparkling cider, a fruit tart, and brandied plums; seasoning it all with compliments to Madame, who seemed in better health; Mademoiselle, who was "splendid" now; and Monsieur Paul, who had "filled out" wonderfully. Nor did she forget their deceased grandparents, whom the Liébards had known, as they had been in the service of the family for several generations. The farm, like them, had the stamp of antiquity. The beams on the ceiling were worm-eaten, the walls blackened with smoke, and the window-panes gray with dust. There was an oak dresser laden with every sort of useful article—jugs, plates, pewter bowls, wolf-traps, and sheep-shears; and a huge syringe made the children laugh. There was not a tree in the three courtyards without mushrooms growing at the bottom of it or a tuft of mistletoe on its boughs. Several of them had been thrown down by the wind. They had taken root again at the middle; and all were bending under their wealth of apples. The thatched roofs, like brown velvet and of varying thickness, withstood the heaviest squalls. The cart-shed, however, was falling into ruin. Mme. Aubain said she would see about it, and ordered the animals to be saddled again.

It was another half-hour before they reached Trouville. The little caravan dismounted to pass Écores—it was an overhanging cliff with boats below it—and three minutes later they were at the end of the quay and entered the courtyard of the Golden Lamb, kept by good Mme. David.

From the first days of their stay Virginie began to feel less weak, thanks to the change of air and the effect of the sea-baths. These, for want of a bathing-dress, she took in her chemise; and her nurse dressed her afterwards in a coastguard's cabin which was used by the bathers.

In the afternoons they took the donkey and went off beyond the Black Rocks, in the direction of Hennequeville. The path climbed at first through ground with dells in it like the green sward of a park, and then reached a plateau where grass fields and arable lay side by side. Hollies rose stiffly out of the briary tangle at the edge of the road; and here and there a great withered tree made zigzags in the blue air with its branches.

They nearly always rested in a meadow, with Deauville on their left, Havre on their right, and the open sea in front. It glittered in the sunshine, smooth as a mirror and so quiet that its murmur was scarcely to be heard; sparrows chirped in hiding and the immense sky arched over it all. Mme. Aubain sat doing her needlework; Virginie plaited rushes by her side; Félicité pulled up lavender, and Paul was bored and anxious to start home.

Other days they crossed the Toucques in a boat and looked for shells.

When the tide went out sea-urchins, starfish, and jelly-fish were left exposed; and the children ran in pursuit of the foam-flakes which scudded in the wind. The sleepy waves broke on the sand and unrolled all along the beach; it stretched away out of sight, bounded on the land-side by the dunes which parted it from the Marsh, a wide meadow shaped like an arena. As they came home that way, Trouville, on the hill-slope in the background, grew bigger at every step, and its miscellaneous throng of houses seemed to break into a gay disorder.

On days when it was too hot they did not leave their room. From the dazzling brilliance outside light fell in streaks between the laths of the blinds. There were no sounds in the village; and on the pavement below not a soul. This silence round them deepened the quietness of things. In the distance, where men were caulking,[9] there was a tap of hammers as they plugged the hulls, and a sluggish breeze wafted up the smell of tar.

The chief amusement was the return of the fishing-boats. They began to tack[10] as soon as they had passed the buoys. The sails came down on two of the three masts; and they drew on with the foresail swelling like a balloon, glided through the splash of the waves, and when they had reached the middle of the harbor suddenly dropped anchor. Then the boats drew up against the quay. The sailors threw quivering fish over the side; a row of carts was waiting, and women in cotton bonnets darted out to take the baskets and give their men a kiss.

One of them came up to Félicité one day, and she entered the lodgings a little later in a state of delight. She had found a sister again—and then Nastasie Barette, "wife of Leroux," appeared, holding an infant at her breast and another child with her right hand, while on her left was a little cabin boy with his hands on his hips and a cap over his ear.

After a quarter of an hour Mme. Aubain sent them off; but they were always to be found hanging about the kitchen, or encountered in the course of a walk. The husband never appeared.

Félicité was seized with affection for them. She bought them a blanket, some shirts, and a stove; it was clear that they were making a good thing out of her. Mme. Aubain was annoyed by this weakness of hers, and she did not like the liberties taken by the nephew, who said "thee" and "thou" to Paul.[11] So as Virginie was coughing and the fine weather gone, she returned to Pont-l'Évêque.

There M. Bourais enlightened her on the choice of a boys' school. The one at Caen was reputed to be the best, and Paul was sent to it. He said his good-byes bravely, content enough at going to live in a house where he would have companions.

Mme. Aubain resigned herself to her son's absence as a thing that had to be. Virginie thought about it less and less. Félicité missed the noise he made. But she found an occupation to distract her; from Christmas onward she took the little girl to catechism every day.

[9] Filling the seams of ships with oakum or other material.
[10] Sail in a zigzag pattern against the wind.
[11] That is, the nephew used the familiar forms of the French second-person pronoun.

III

After making a genuflexion at the door she walked up between the double rows of chairs under the lofty nave, opened Mme. Aubain's pew, sat down, and began to look about her. The choir stalls were filled with the boys on the right and the girls on the left, and the curé[12] stood by the lectern. On a painted window in the apse the Holy Ghost looked down upon the Virgin. Another window showed her on her knees before the child Jesus, and a group carved in wood behind the altar-shrine represented St. Michael overthrowing the dragon.

The priest began with a sketch of sacred history. The Garden, the Flood, the Tower of Babel, cities in flames, dying nations, and overturned idols passed like a dream before her eyes; and the dizzying vision left her with reverence for the Most High and fear of His wrath. Then she wept at the story of the Passion. Why had they crucified Him, when He loved the children, fed the multitudes, healed the blind, and had willed, in His meekness, to be born among the poor, on the dung-heap of a stable? The sowings, harvests, wine-presses, all the familiar things that the Gospel speaks of, were a part of her life. They had been made holy by God's passing; and she loved the lambs more tenderly for her love of the Lamb, and the doves because of the Holy Ghost.

She found it hard to imagine Him in person, for He was not merely a bird, but a flame as well, and a breath at other times. It may be His light, she thought, which flits at night about the edge of the marshes, His breathing which drives on the clouds, His voice which gives harmony to the bells; and she would sit rapt in adoration, enjoying the cool walls and the quiet of the church.

Of doctrines she understood nothing—did not even try to understand. The curé discoursed, the children repeated their lesson, and finally she went to sleep, waking up with a start when their wooden shoes clattered on the flagstones as they went away.

It was thus that Félicité, whose religious education had been neglected in her youth, learned the catechism by dint of hearing it; and from that time she copied all Virginie's observances, fasting as she did and confessing with her. On Corpus Christi Day they made a festal altar together.

The first communion loomed distractingly ahead. She fussed over the shoes, the rosary, the book and gloves; and how she trembled as she helped Virginie's mother to dress her!

All through the mass she was racked with anxiety. She could not see one side of the choir because of M. Bourais but straight in front of her was the flock of maidens, with white crowns above their hanging veils, making the impression of a field of snow; and she knew her dear child at a distance by her dainty neck and thoughtful air. The bell tinkled. The heads bowed, and there was silence. As the organ pealed, singers and congregation took up the "Agnus Dei";[13] then the procession of the boys began, and after

[12] Parish priest.

[13] A liturgical prayer to Christ (from its opening words: "Lamb of God").

them the girls rose. Step by step, with their hands joined in prayer, they went towards the lighted altar, knelt on the first step, received the sacrament in turn, and came back in the same order to their places. When Virginie's turn came Félicité leaned forward to see her; and with the imaginativeness of deep and tender feeling it seemed to her that she actually was the child; Virginie's face became hers, she was dressed in her clothes, it was her heart beating in her breast. As the moment came to open her mouth she closed her eyes and nearly fainted.

She appeared early in the sacristy[14] next morning for Monsieur the curé to give her the communion. She took it with devotion, but it did not give her the same exquisite delight.

Mme. Aubain wanted to make her daughter into an accomplished person; and as Guyot could not teach her music or English she decided to place her in the Ursuline Convent at Honfleur as a boarder. The child made no objection. Félicité sighed and thought that Madame lacked feeling. Then she reflected that her mistress might be right; matters of this kind were beyond her.

So one day an old spring-van drew up at the door, and out of it stepped a nun to fetch the young lady. Félicité hoisted the luggage on to the top, admonished the driver, and put six pots of preserves, a dozen pears, and a bunch of violets under the seat.

At the last moment Virginie broke into a fit of sobbing; she threw her arms round her mother, who kissed her on the forehead, saying over and over "Come, be brave! be brave!" The step was raised, and the carriage drove off.

Then Mme. Aubain's strength gave way; and in the evening all her friends—the Lormeau family, Mme. Lechaptois, the Rochefeuille ladies, M. de Houppeville, and Bourais—came in to console her.

To be without her daughter was very painful for her at first. But she heard from Virginie three times a week, wrote to her on the other days, walked in the garden, and so filled up the empty hours.

From sheer habit Félicité went into Virginie's room in the mornings and gazed at the walls. It was boredom to her not to have to comb the child's hair now, lace up her boots, tuck her into bed—and not to see her charming face perpetually and hold her hand when they went out together. In this idle condition she tried making lace. But her fingers were too heavy and broke the threads; she could not attend to anything, she had lost her sleep, and was, in her own words, "destroyed."

To "divert herself" she asked leave to have visits from her nephew Victor.

He arrived on Sundays after mass, rosy-cheeked, bare-chested, with the scent of the country he had walked through still about him. She laid her table promptly and they had lunch, sitting opposite each other. She ate as little as possible herself to save expense, but stuffed him with food so generous that at last he went to sleep. At the first stroke of vespers she woke him up, brushed his trousers, fastened his tie, and went to church, leaning on his arm with maternal pride.

Victor was always instructed by his parents to get something out of

[14] Vestry, the room in a church where the sacred vestments and utensils are kept.

her—a packet of moist sugar, it might be, a cake of soap, spirits, or even money at times. He brought his things for her to mend and she took over the task, only too glad to have a reason for making him come back.

In August his father took him off on a coasting voyage. It was holiday time, and she was consoled by the arrival of the children. Paul, however, was getting selfish, and Virginie was too old to be called "thou" any longer; this put a constraint and barrier between them.

Victor went to Morlaix, Dunkirk, and Brighton in succession and made Félicité a present on his return from each voyage. It was a box made of shells the first time, a coffee cup the next, and on the third occasion a large gingerbread man. Victor was growing handsome. He was well made, had a hint of a moustache, good honest eyes, and a small leather hat pushed backwards like a pilot's. He entertained her by telling stories embroidered with nautical terms.

On a Monday, July 14, 1819 (she never forgot the date), he told her that he had signed on for the big voyage and next night but one he would take the Honfleur boat and join his schooner, which was to weigh anchor from Havre before long. Perhaps he would be gone two years.

The prospect of this long absence threw Félicité into deep distress; one more good-bye she must have, and on the Wednesday evening, when Madame's dinner was finished, she put on her clogs and made short work of the twelve miles between Pont-l'Évêque and Honfleur.

When she arrived in front of the Calvary she took the turn to the right instead of the left, got lost in the timber-yards, and retraced her steps; some people to whom she spoke advised her to be quick. She went all round the harbor basin, full of ships, and knocked against hawsers;[15] then the ground fell away, lights flashed across each other, and she thought her wits had left her, for she saw horses up in the sky.

Others were neighing by the quay-side, frightened at the sea. They were lifted by a tackle and deposited in a boat, where passengers jostled each other among cider casks, cheese baskets, and sacks of grain; fowls could be heard clucking, the captain swore; and a cabin-boy stood leaning over the bows, indifferent to it all. Félicité, who had not recognized him, called "Victor!" and he raised his head; all at once, as she was darting forwards, the gangway was drawn back.

The Honfleur packet, women singing as they hauled it, passed out of harbor. Its framework creaked and the heavy waves whipped its bows. The canvas had swung round, no one could be seen on board now; and on the moon-silvered sea the boat made a black speck which paled gradually, dipped, and vanished.

As Félicité passed by the Calvary she had a wish to commend to God what she cherished most, and she stood there praying a long time with her face bathed in tears and her eyes towards the clouds. The town was asleep, coastguards were walking to and fro; and water poured without cessation through the holes in the sluice, with the noise of a torrent. The clocks struck two.

The convent parlor would not be open before day. If Félicité were late Madame would most certainly be annoyed; and in spite of her desire to kiss

[15] Heavy ropes for mooring ships.

the other child she turned home. The maids at the inn were waking up as she came in to Pont-l'Évêque.

So the poor slip of a boy was going to toss for months and months at sea! She had not been frightened by his previous voyages. From England or Brittany you came back safe enough; but America, the colonies, the islands—these were lost in a dim region at the other end of the world.

Félicité's thoughts from that moment ran entirely on her nephew. On sunny days she was harassed by the idea of thirst; when there was a storm she was afraid of the lightning on his account. As she listened to the wind growling in the chimney or carrying off the slates she pictured him lashed by that same tempest, at the top of a shattered mast, with his body thrown backwards under a sheet of foam; or else (with a reminiscence of the illustrated geography) he was being eaten by savages, captured in a wood by monkeys, or dying on a desert shore. And never did she mention her anxieties.

Mme. Aubain had anxieties of her own, about her daughter. The good sisters found her an affectionate but delicate child. The slightest emotion unnerved her. She had to give up the piano.

Her mother stipulated for regular letters from the convent. She lost patience one morning when the postman did not come, and walked to and fro in the parlor from her armchair to the window. It was really amazing; not a word for four days!

To console Mme. Aubain by her own example Félicité remarked:

"As for me, Madame, it's six months since I heard. . ."

"From whom, pray?"

"Why . . . from my nephew," the servant answered gently.

"Oh! your nephew!" And Mme. Aubain resumed her walk with a shrug of the shoulders, as much as to say: "I was not thinking of him! And what is more, it's absurd! A scamp of a cabin-boy—what does he matter? . . . whereas my daughter . . . why, just think!"

Félicité, though she had been brought up on harshness, felt indignant with Madame—and then forgot. It seemed the simplest thing in the world to her to lose one's head over the little girl. For her the two children were equally important; a bond in her heart made them one, and their destinies must be the same.

She heard from the chemist that Victor's ship had arrived at Havana. He had read this piece of news in a gazette.

Cigars—they made her imagine Havana as a place where no one does anything but smoke, and there was Victor moving among the negroes in a cloud of tobacco. Could you, she wondered, "in case you needed," return by land? What was the distance from Pont-l'Évêque? She questioned M. Bourais to find out.

He reached for his atlas and began explaining the longitudes; Félicité's consternation provoked a fine pedantic smile. Finally he marked with his pencil a black, imperceptible point in the indentations of an oval spot, and said as he did so, "Here it is." She bent over the map; the maze of colored lines wearied her eyes without conveying anything; and on an invitation from Bourais to tell him her difficulty she begged him to show her the house where Victor was living. Bourais threw up his arms, sneezed, and laughed immensely: a simplicity like hers was a positive joy. And Félicité did not understand the reason; how could she when she expected, very likely, to see the actual image of her nephew—so stunted was her mind!

A fortnight afterwards Liébard came into the kitchen at market-time as usual and handed her a letter from her brother-in-law. As neither of them could read she took it to her mistress.

Mme. Aubain, who was counting the stitches in her knitting, put the work down by her side, broke the seal of the letter, started, and said in a low voice, with a look of meaning:

"It is bad news . . . that they have to tell you. Your nephew. . ."

He was dead. The letter said no more.

Félicité fell on to a chair, leaning her head against the wainscot; and she closed her eyelids, which suddenly flushed pink. Then with bent forehead, hands hanging, and fixed eyes, she said at intervals:

"Poor little lad! poor little lad!"

Liébard watched her and heaved sighs. Mme. Aubain trembled a little.

She suggested that Félicité should go to see her sister at Trouville. Félicité answered by a gesture that she had no need.

There was a silence. The worthy Liébard thought it was time for them to withdraw.

Then Félicité said:

"They don't care, not they!"

Her head dropped again; and she took up mechanically, from time to time, the long needles on her work-table.

Women passed in the yard with a barrow of dripping linen.

As she saw them through the window-panes she remembered her washing; she had put it to soak the day before, to-day she must wring it out; and she left the room.

Her plank and tub were at the edge of the Toucques. She threw a pile of linen on the bank, rolled up her sleeves, and taking her wooden beater dealt lusty blows whose sound carried to the neighboring gardens. The meadows were empty, the river stirred in the wind; and down below long grasses wavered, like the hair of corpses floating in the water. She kept her grief down and was very brave until the evening; but once in her room she surrendered to it utterly, lying stretched on the mattress with her face in the pillow and her hands clenched against her temples.

Much later she heard, from the captain himself, the circumstances of Victor's end. They had bled him too much at the hospital for yellow fever. Four doctors held him at once. He had died instantly, and the chief had said:

"Bah! there goes another!"

His parents had always been brutal to him. She preferred not to see them again; and they made no advances, either because they forgot her or from the callousness of the wretchedly poor.

Virginie began to grow weaker.

Tightness in her chest, coughing, continual fever, and veinings on her cheek-bones betrayed some deep-seated complaint. M. Poupart had advised a stay in Provence. Mme. Aubain determined on it, would have brought her daughter home at once but for the climate of Pont-l'Évêque.

She made an arrangement with a job-master, and he drove her to the convent every Tuesday. There is a terrace in the garden, with a view over the Seine. Virginie took walks there over the fallen vine-leaves, on her mother's arm. A shaft of sunlight through the clouds made her blink sometimes, as she gazed at the sails in the distance and the whole horizon from the castle of Tancarville to the lighthouses at Havre. Afterwards they rested in the arbor. Her mother had secured a little cask of excellent Malaga; and Virginie, laughing at the idea of getting tipsy, drank a thimble-full of it, no more.

Her strength came back visibly. The autumn glided gently away. Félicité reassured Mme. Aubain. But one evening, when she had been out on a commission in the neighborhood, she found M. Poupart's gig[16] at the door. He was in the hall, and Mme. Aubain was tying her bonnet.

"Give me my foot-warmer, purse, gloves! Quicker, come!"

Virginie had inflammation of the lungs; perhaps it was hopeless.

"Not yet!" said the doctor, and they both got into the carriage under whirling flakes of snow. Night was coming on and it was very cold.

Félicité rushed into the church to light a taper. Then she ran after the gig, came up with it in an hour, and jumped lightly in behind. As she hung on by the fringes a thought came into her mind: "The courtyard has not been shut up; supposing burglars got in!" And she jumped down.

At dawn next day she presented herself at the doctor's. He had come in and started for the country again. Then she waited in the inn, thinking that a letter would come by some hand or other. Finally, when it was twilight, she took the Lisieux coach.

The convent was at the end of a steep lane. When she was about halfway up it she heard strange sounds—a death-bell tolling. "It is for someone else," thought Félicité, and she pulled the knocker violently.

After some minutes there was a sound of trailing slippers, the door opened ajar, and a nun appeared.

The good sister, with an air of compunction, said that "she had just passed away." On the instant the bell of St. Leonard's tolled twice as fast.

Félicité went up to the second floor.

From the doorway she saw Virginie stretched on her back, with her hands joined, her mouth open, and head thrown back under a black crucifix that leaned towards her, between curtains that hung stiffly, less pale than was her face. Mme. Aubain, at the foot of the bed which she clasped with her arms, was choking with sobs of agony. The mother superior stood on the right. Three candlesticks on the chest of drawers made spots of red, and the mist came whitely through the windows. Nuns came and took Mme. Aubain away.

For two nights Félicité never left the dead child. She repeated the same prayers, sprinkled holy water over the sheets, came and sat down again, and watched her. At the end of the first vigil she noticed that the face had grown yellow, the lips turned blue, the nose was sharper, and the eyes sunk in. She kissed them several times, and would not have been immensely surprised if Virginie had opened them again; to minds like hers the supernatural is quite simple. She made the girl's toilette, wrapped her in her shroud, lifted her down into her bier, put a garland on her head, and spread out her hair. It was fair, and extraordinarily long for her age.

[16] A light two-wheeled carriage.

Félicité cut off a big lock and slipped half of it into her bosom, determined that she should never part with it.

The body was brought back to Pont-l'Évêque, as Mme. Aubain intended; she followed the hearse in a closed carriage.

It took another three-quarters of an hour after the mass to reach the cemetery. Paul walked in front, sobbing. M. Bourais was behind, and then came the chief residents, the women shrouded in black mantles, and Félicité. She thought of her nephew; and because she had not been able to pay these honors to him her grief was doubled, as though the one were being buried with the other.

Mme. Aubain's despair was boundless. It was against God that she first rebelled, thinking it unjust of Him to have taken her daughter from her—she had never done evil and her conscience was so clear! Ah, no!—she ought to have taken Virginie off to the south. Other doctors would have saved her. She accused herself now, wanted to join her child, and broke into cries of distress in the middle of her dreams. One dream haunted her above all. Her husband, dressed as a sailor, was returning from a long voyage, and shedding tears he told her that he had been ordered to take Virginie away. Then they consulted how to hide her somewhere.

She came in once from the garden quite upset. A moment ago—and she pointed out the place—the father and daughter had appeared to her, standing side by side, and they did nothing, but they looked at her.

For several months after this she stayed inertly in her room. Félicité lectured her gently; she must live for her son's sake, and for the other, in remembrance of "her."

"Her?" answered Mme. Aubain, as though she were just waking up. "Ah, yes! . . . yes! . . . You do not forget her!" This was an allusion to the cemetery, where she was strictly forbidden to go.

Félicité went there every day.

Precisely at four she skirted the houses, climbed the hill, opened the gate, and came to Virginie's grave. It was a little column of pink marble with a stone underneath and a garden plot enclosed by chains. The beds were hidden under a coverlet of flowers. She watered their leaves, freshened the gravel, and knelt down to break up the earth better. When Mme. Aubain was able to come there she felt a relief and a sort of consolation.

Then years slipped away, one like another, and their only episodes were the great festivals as they recurred—Easter, the Assumption, All Saints' Day. Household occurrences marked dates that were referred to afterwards. In 1825, for instance, two glaziers white-washed the hall; in 1827 a piece of the roof fell into the courtyard and nearly killed a man. In the summer of 1828 it was Madame's turn to offer the consecrated bread; Bourais, about this time, mysteriously absented himself; and one by one the old acquaintances passed away: Guyot, Liébard, Mme. Lechaptois, Robelin, and Uncle Gremanville, who had been paralyzed for a long time.

One night the driver of the mail-coach announced the Revolution of July[17] in Pont-l'Évêque. A new sub-prefect was appointed a few days later—Baron de Larsonnière, who had been consul in America, and

[17] In 1830, when the Bourbons were expelled and Louis-Philippe was placed on the throne.

brought with him, besides his wife, a sister-in-law and three young ladies, already growing up. They were to be seen about on their lawn, in loose blouses, and they had a negro and a parrot. They paid a call on Mme. Aubain which she did not fail to return. The moment they were seen in the distance Félicité ran to let her mistress know. But only one thing could really move her feelings—the letters from her son.

He was swallowed up in a tavern life and could follow no career. She paid his debts, he made new ones; and the sighs that Mme. Aubain uttered as she sat knitting by the window reached Félicité at her spinning-wheel in the kitchen.

They took walks together along the espaliered[18] wall, always talking of Virginie and wondering if such and such a thing would have pleased her and what, on some occasion, she would have been likely to say.

All her small belongings filled a cupboard in the two-bedded room. Mme. Aubain inspected them as seldom as she could. One summer day she made up her mind to it—and some moths flew out of the wardrobe.

Virginie's dresses were in a row underneath a shelf, on which there were three dolls, some hoops, a set of toy pots and pans, and the basin that she used. They took out her petticoats as well, and the stockings and handkerchiefs, and laid them out on the two beds before folding them up again. The sunshine lit up these poor things, bringing out their stains and the creases made by the body's movements. The air was warm and blue, a blackbird warbled, life seemed bathed in a deep sweetness. They found a little plush hat with thick, chestnut-colored pile; but it was eaten all over by moths. Félicité begged it for her own. Their eyes met fixedly and filled with tears; at last the mistress opened her arms, the servant threw herself into them, and they embraced each other, satisfying their grief in a kiss that made them equal.

It was the first time in their lives, Mme. Aubain's nature not being expansive. Félicité was as grateful as though she had received a favor, and cherished her mistress from that moment with the devotion of an animal and a religious worship.

The kindness of her heart unfolded.

When she heard the drums of a marching regiment in the street she posted herself at the door with a pitcher of cider and asked the soldiers to drink. She nursed cholera patients and protected the Polish refugees;[19] one of these even declared that he wished to marry her. They quarrelled, however; for when she came back from the Angelus[20] one morning she found that he had got into her kitchen and made himself a vinegar salad which he was quietly eating.

After the Poles came father Colmiche, an old man who was supposed to have committed atrocities in '93.[21] He lived by the side of the river in the ruins of a pigsty. The little boys watched him through the cracks in the wall, and threw pebbles at him which fell on the pallet where he lay constantly shaken by a catarrh; his hair was very long, his eyes inflamed, and there was a tumor on his arm bigger than his head. She got him some linen and

[18] Covered with fruit trees or shrubs trained to grow flat against the wall.
[19] From the Polish uprisings against Russia in 1831. [20] Morning devotion.
[21] The Reign of Terror began in France in 1793.

tried to clean up his miserable hole; her dream was to establish him in the bake-house, without letting him annoy Madame. When the tumor burst she dressed it every day; sometimes she brought him cake, and would put him in the sunshine on a truss of straw. The poor old man, slobbering and trembling, thanked her in his worn-out voice, was terrified that he might lose her, and stretched out his hands when he saw her go away. He died; and she had a mass said for the repose of his soul.

That very day a great happiness befell her; just at dinner-time appeared Mme. de Larsonnière's negro, carrying the parrot in its cage, with perch, chain, and padlock. A note from the baroness informed Mme. Aubain that her husband had been raised to a prefecture and they were starting that evening; she begged her to accept the bird as a memento and mark of her regard.

For a long time he had absorbed Félicité's imagination, because he came from America; and that name reminded her of Victor, so much so that she made inquiries of the negro. She had once gone so far as to say "How Madame would enjoy having him!"

The negro repeated the remark to his mistress; and as she could not take the bird away with her she chose this way of getting rid of him.

IV

His name was Loulou. His body was green and the tips of his wings rose-pink; his forehead was blue and his throat golden.

But he had the tiresome habits of biting his perch, tearing out his feathers, sprinkling his dirt about, and spattering the water of his tub. He annoyed Mme. Aubain, and she gave him to Félicité for good.

She endeavored to train him; soon he could repeat "Nice boy! Your servant, sir! Good morning, Marie!" He was placed by the side of the door, and astonished several people by not answering to the name Jacquot, for all parrots are called Jacquot. People compared him to a turkey and a log of wood, and stabbed Félicité to the heart each time. Strange obstinacy on Loulou's part!—directly you looked at him he refused to speak.

None the less he was eager for society; for on Sundays, while the Rochefeuille ladies, M. de Houppeville, and new familiars—Onfroy the apothecary, Monsieur Varin, and Captain Mathieu—were playing their game of cards, he beat the windows with his wings and threw himself about so frantically that they could not hear each other speak.

Bourais' face, undoubtedly, struck him as extremely droll. Directly he saw it he began to laugh—and laugh with all his might. His peals rang through the courtyard and were repeated by the echo; the neighbors came to their windows and laughed too; while M. Bourais, gliding along under the wall to escape the parrot's eye, and hiding his profile with his hat, got to the river and then entered by the garden gate. There was a lack of tenderness in the looks which he darted at the bird.

Loulou had been slapped by the butcher-boy for making so free as to plunge his head into his basket; and since then he was always trying to nip him through his shirt. Fabu threatened to wring his neck, although he was not cruel, for all his tattooed arms and large whiskers. Far from it; he really rather liked the parrot, and in a jovial humor even wanted to teach him to swear. Félicité, who was alarmed by such proceedings, put the bird in the kitchen. His little chain was taken off and he roamed about the house.

His way of going downstairs was to lean on each step with the curve of his beak, raise the right foot, and then the left; and Félicité was afraid that these gymnastics brought on fits of giddiness. He fell ill and could not talk or eat any longer. There was a growth under his tongue, such as fowls have sometimes. She cured him by tearing the pellicle off with her finger-nails. Mr. Paul was thoughtless enough one day to blow some cigar smoke into his nostrils, and another time when Mme. Lormeau was teasing him with the end of her umbrella he snapped at the ferrule. Finally he got lost.

Félicité had put him on the grass to refresh him, and gone away for a minute, and when she came back—no sign of the parrot! She began by looking for him in the shrubs, by the waterside, and over the roofs, without listening to her mistress's cries of "Take care, do! You are out of your wits!" Then she investigated all the gardens in Pont-l'Évêque, and stopped the passers-by. "You don't ever happen to have seen my parrot, by any chance, do you?" And she gave a description of the parrot to those who did not know him. Suddenly, behind the mills at the foot of the hill she thought she could make out something green that fluttered. But on the top of the hill there was nothing. A hawker assured her that he had come across the parrot just before, at Saint-Melaine, in Mère Simon's shop. She rushed there; they had no idea of what she meant. At last she came home exhausted, with her slippers in shreds and despair in her soul; and as she was sitting in the middle of the garden-seat at Madame's side, telling the whole story of her efforts, a light weight dropped on to her shoulder—it was Loulou! What on earth had he been doing? Taking a walk in the neighborhood, perhaps!

She had some trouble in recovering from this, or rather never did recover. As the result of a chill she had an attack of quinsy,[22] and soon afterwards an earache. Three years later she was deaf; and she spoke very loud, even in church. Though Félicité's sins might have been published in every corner of the diocese without dishonor to her or scandal to anybody, his Reverence the priest thought it right now to hear her confession in the sacristy only.

Imaginary noises in the head completed her upset. Her mistress often said to her, "Heavens! how stupid you are!" "Yes, Madame," she replied, and looked about for something.

Her little circle of ideas grew still narrower; the peal of church bells and the lowing of cattle ceased to exist for her. All living beings moved as silently as ghosts. One sound only reached her ears now—the parrot's voice.

Loulou, as though to amuse her, reproduced the click-clack of the turn-spit,[23] the shrill call of a man selling fish, and the noise of the saw in the joiner's house opposite; when the bell rang he imitated Mme. Aubain's "Félicité! the door! the door!"

They carried on conversations, he endlessly reciting the three phrases

[22] Tonsillitis. [23] Device to turn meat over a fire.

in his repertory, to which she replied with words that were just as disconnected but uttered what was in her heart. Loulou was almost a son and a lover to her in her isolated state. He climbed up her fingers, nibbled at her lips, and clung to her kerchief; and when she bent her forehead and shook her head gently to and fro, as nurses do, the great wings of her bonnet and the bird's wings quivered together.

When the clouds massed and the thunder rumbled Loulou broke into cries, perhaps remembering the downpours in his native forests. The streaming rain made him absolutely mad; he fluttered wildly about, dashed up to the ceiling, upset everything, and went out through the window to dabble in the garden; but he was back quickly to perch on one of the fire-dogs and hopped about to dry himself, exhibiting his tail and his beak in turn.

One morning in the terrible winter of 1837 she had put him in front of the fireplace because of the cold. She found him dead, in the middle of his cage: head downwards, with his claws in the wires. He had died from congestion, no doubt. But Félicité thought he had been poisoned with parsley, and though there was no proof of any kind her suspicions inclined to Fabu.

She wept so piteously that her mistress said to her, "Well, then, have him stuffed!"

She asked advice from the chemist, who had always been kind to the parrot. He wrote to Havre, and a person called Fellacher undertook the business. But as parcels sometimes got lost in the coach she decided to take the parrot as far as Honfleur herself.

Along the sides of the road were leafless apple-trees, one after the other. Ice covered the ditches. Dogs barked about the farms; and Félicité, with her hands under her cloak, her little black sabots[24] and her basket, walked briskly in the middle of the road.

She crossed the forest, passed High Oak, and reached St. Gatien.

A cloud of dust rose behind her, and in it a mail-coach, carried away by the steep hill, rushed down at full gallop like a hurricane. Seeing this woman who would not get out of the way, the driver stood up in front and the postilion shouted too. He could not hold in his four horses, which increased their pace, and the two leaders were grazing her when he threw them to one side with a jerk of the reins. But he was wild with rage, and lifting his arm as he passed at full speed, gave her such a lash from waist to neck with his big whip that she fell on her back.

Her first act, when she recovered consciousness, was to open her basket. Loulou was happily none the worse. She felt a burn in her right cheek, and when she put her hands against it they were red; the blood was flowing.

She sat down on a heap of stones and bound up her face with her handkerchief. Then she ate a crust of bread which she had put in the basket as a precaution, and found a consolation for her wound in gazing at the bird.

When she reached the crest of Ecquemauville she saw the Honfleur lights sparkling in the night sky like a company of stars; beyond, the sea stretched dimly. Then a faintness overtook her and she stopped; her

[24] Wooden shoes.

wretched childhood, the disillusion of her first love, her nephew's going away, and Virginie's death all came back to her at once like the waves of an oncoming tide, rose to her throat, and choked her.

Afterwards, at the boat, she made a point of speaking to the captain, begging him to take care of the parcel, though she did not tell him what was in it.

Fellacher kept the parrot a long time. He was always promising it for the following week. After six months he announced that a packing-case had started, and then nothing more was heard of it. It really seemed as though Loulou was never coming back. "Ah, they have stolen him!" she thought.

He arrived at last, and looked superb. There he was, erect upon a branch which screwed into a mahogany socket, with a foot in the air and his head on one side, biting a nut which the bird-stuffer—with a taste for impressiveness—had gilded.

Félicité shut him up in her room. It was a place to which few people were admitted, and held so many religious objects and miscellaneous things that it looked like a chapel and bazaar in one.

A big cupboard impeded you as you opened the door. Opposite the window commanding the garden a little round one looked into the court; there was a table by the folding-bed with a water-jug, two combs, and a cube of blue soap in a chipped plate. On the walls hung rosaries, medals, several benign Virgins, and a holy water vessel made out of coconut; on the chest of drawers, which was covered with a cloth like an altar, was the shell box that Victor had given her, and after that a watering-can, a toy-balloon, exercise-books, the illustrated geography, and a pair of young lady's boots; and, fastened by its ribbons to the nail of the looking-glass, hung the little plush hat! Félicité carried observances of this kind so far as to keep one of Monsieur's frock-coats. All the old rubbish which Mme. Aubain did not want any longer she laid hands on for her room. That was why there were artificial flowers along the edge of the chest of drawers and a portrait of the Comte d'Artois[25] in the little window recess.

With the aid of a bracket Loulou was established over the chimney, which jutted into the room. Every morning when she woke up she saw him there in the dawning light, and recalled old days and the smallest details of insignificant acts in a deep quietness which knew no pain.

Holding, as she did, no communication with anyone, Félicité lived as insensibly as if she were walking in her sleep. The Corpus Christi processions roused her to life again. Then she went round begging mats and candlesticks from the neighbors to decorate the altar they put up in the street.

In church she was always gazing at the Holy Ghost in the window, and observed that there was something of the parrot in him. The likeness was still clearer, she thought, on a crude color-print representing the baptism of Our Lord. With his purple wings and emerald body he was the very image of Loulou.

She bought him, and hung him up instead of the Comte d'Artois, so that she could see them both together in one glance. They were linked in

[25] Title of Charles X, last of the Bourbon kings, who ruled between 1824 and 1830.

her thoughts; and the parrot was consecrated by his association with the Holy Ghost, which became more vivid to her eye and more intelligible. The Father could not have chosen to express Himself through a dove, for such creatures cannot speak; it must have been one of Loulou's ancestors, surely. And though Félicité looked at the picture while she said her prayers she swerved a little from time to time towards the parrot.

She wanted to join the Ladies of the Virgin,[26] but Mme. Aubain dissuaded her.

And then a great event loomed up before them—Paul's marriage.

He had been a solicitor's clerk to begin with, and then tried business, the Customs, the Inland Revenue, and made efforts, even, to get into the Rivers and Forests. By an inspiration from heaven he had suddenly, at thirty-six, discovered his real line—the Registrar's Office. And there he showed such marked capacity that an inspector had offered him his daughter's hand and promised him his influence.

So Paul, grown serious, brought the lady to see his mother.

She sniffed at the ways of Pont-l'Évêque, gave herself great airs, and wounded Félicité's feelings. Mme. Aubain was relieved at her departure.

The week after came news of M. Bourais' death in an inn in Lower Brittany. The rumor of suicide was confirmed, and doubts arose as to his honesty. Mme. Aubain studied his accounts, and soon found out the whole tale of his misdoings—embezzled arrears, secret sales of wood, forged receipts, etc. Besides that he had an illegitimate child, and "relations with a person at Dozulé."

These shameful facts distressed her greatly. In March 1853 she was seized with a pain in the chest; her tongue seemed to be covered with film, and leeches did not ease the difficult breathing. On the ninth evening of her illness she died, just at seventy-two.

She passed as being younger, owing to the bands of brown hair which framed her pale, pock-marked face. There were few friends to regret her, for she had a stiffness of manner which kept people at a distance.

But Félicité mourned for her as one seldom mourns for a master. It upset her ideas and seemed contrary to the order of things, impossible and monstrous, that Madame should die before her.

Ten days afterwards, which was the time it took to hurry there from Besançon, the heirs arrived. The daughter-in-law ransacked the drawers, chose some furniture, and sold the rest; and then they went back to their registering.

Madame's armchair, her small round table, her foot-warmer, and the eight chairs were gone! Yellow patches in the middle of the panels showed where the engravings had hung. They had carried off the two little beds and the mattresses, and all Virginie's belongings had disappeared from the cupboard. Félicité went from floor to floor dazed with sorrow.

The next day there was a notice on the door, and the apothecary shouted in her ear that the house was for sale.

She tottered, and was obliged to sit down. What distressed her most of all was to give up her room, so suitable as it was for poor Loulou. She enveloped him with a look of anguish when she was imploring the Holy

[26] A lay religious organization.

Ghost, and formed the idolatrous habit of kneeling in front of the parrot to say her prayers. Sometimes the sun shone in at the attic window and caught his glass eye, and a great luminous ray shot out of it and put her in an ecstasy.

She had a pension of three hundred and eighty francs a year which her mistress had left her. The garden gave her a supply of vegetables. As for clothes, she had enough to last her to the end of her days, and she economized in candles by going to bed at dusk.

She hardly ever went out, as she did not like passing the dealer's shop, where some of the old furniture was exposed for sale. Since her fit of giddiness she dragged one leg; and as her strength was failing Mère Simon, whose grocery business had collapsed, came every morning to split the wood and pump water for her.

Her eyes grew feeble. The shutters ceased to be thrown open. Years and years passed, and the house was neither let nor sold.

Félicité never asked for repairs because she was afraid of being sent away. The boards on the roof rotted; her bolster was wet for a whole winter. After Easter she spat blood.

Then Mère Simon called in a doctor. Félicité wanted to know what was the matter with her. But she was too deaf to hear, and the only word which reached her was "pneumonia." It was a word she knew, and she answered softly "Ah! like Madame," thinking it natural that she should follow her mistress.

The time for the festal shrines was coming near. The first one was always at the bottom of the hill, the second in front of the post office, and the third towards the middle of the street. There was some rivalry in the matter of this one, and the women of the parish ended by choosing Mme. Aubain's courtyard.

The hard breathing and fever increased. Félicité was vexed at doing nothing for the altar. If only she could at least have put something there! Then she thought of the parrot. The neighbors objected that it would not be decent. But the priest gave her permission, which so intensely delighted her that she begged him to accept Loulou, her sole possession, when she died.

From Tuesday to Saturday, the eve of the festival, she coughed more often. By the evening her face had shrivelled, her lips stuck to her gums, and she had vomitings; and at twilight next morning, feeling herself very low, she sent for a priest.

Three kindly women were round her during the extreme unction. Then she announced that she must speak to Fabu. He arrived in his Sunday clothes, by no means at his ease in the funereal atmosphere.

"Forgive me," she said, with an effort to stretch out her arm; "I thought it was you who had killed him."

What did she mean by such stories? She suspected him of murder—a man like him! He waxed indignant, and was on the point of making a row.

"There," said the women, "she is no longer in her senses, you can see it well enough!"

Félicité spoke to shadows of her own from time to time. The women went away, and Mère Simon had breakfast. A little later she took Loulou and brought him close to Félicité with the words:

"Come, now, say good-bye to him!"

Loulou was not a corpse, but the worms devoured him; one of his wings was broken, and the tow was coming out of his stomach. But she was blind now; she kissed him on the forehead and kept him close against her cheek. Mère Simon took him back from her to put him on the altar.

V

Summer scents came up from the meadows; flies buzzed; the sun made the river glitter and heated the slates. Mère Simon came back into the room and fell softly asleep.

She woke at the noise of bells; the people were coming out from vespers. Félicité's delirium subsided. She thought of the procession and saw it as if she had been there.

All the school children, the church-singers, and the firemen walked on the pavement, while in the middle of the road the verger armed with his hallebard and the beadle with a large cross[27] advanced in front. Then came the schoolmaster, with an eye on the boys, and the sister, anxious about her little girls; three of the daintiest, with angelic curls, scattered rose-petals in the air; the deacon controlled the band with outstretched arms; and two censer-bearers turned back at every step towards the Holy Sacrament, which was borne by Monsieur the curé, wearing his beautiful chasuble,[28] under a canopy of dark-red velvet held up by four churchwardens. A crowd of people pressed behind, between the white cloths covering the house walls, and they reached the bottom of the hill.

A cold sweat moistened Félicité's temples. Mère Simon sponged her with a piece of linen, saying to herself that one day she would have to go that way.

The hum of the crowd increased, was very loud for an instant, and then went further away.

A fusillade shook the window-panes. It was the postilions saluting the monstrance.[29] Félicité rolled her eyes and said as audibly as she could: "Does he look well?" The parrot was weighing on her mind.

Her agony began. A death-rattle that grew more and more convulsed made her sides heave. Bubbles of froth came at the corners of her mouth and her whole body trembled.

Soon the booming of the ophicleides,[30] the high voices of the children, and the deep voices of the men were distinguishable. At intervals all was silent, and the tread of feet, deadened by the flowers they walked on, sounded like a flock pattering on grass.

The clergy appeared in the courtyard. Mère Simon clambered on to a chair to reach the attic window, and so looked down straight upon the shrine. Green garlands hung over the altar, which was decked with a flounce of English lace. In the middle was a small frame with relics in it;

[27] A verger is the official who carries the symbol of office (the hallebard) before a church dignitary. A beadle is a minor parish officer with such duties as keeping order during services.

[28] Outer vestment.

[29] Container in which the consecrated host is exposed for adoration.

[30] Old-fashioned bass horns.

there were two orange-trees at the corners, and all along stood silver candlesticks and china vases, with sunflowers, lilies, peonies, foxgloves, and tufts of hortensia. This heap of blazing color slanted from the level of the altar to the carpet which went on over the pavement; and some rare objects caught the eye. There was a silver-gilt sugar-basin with a crown of violets; pendants of Alençon stone[31] glittered on the moss, and two Chinese screens displayed their landscapes. Loulou was hidden under roses, and showed nothing but his blue forehead, like a plaque of lapis lazuli.

The churchwardens, singers, and children took their places round the three sides of the court. The priest went slowly up the steps, and placed his great, radiant golden sun[32] upon the lace. Everyone knelt down. There was a deep silence; and the censers glided to and fro on the full swing of their chains.

An azure vapor rose up into Félicité's room. Her nostrils met it; she inhaled it sensuously, mystically; and then closed her eyes. Her lips smiled. The beats of her heart lessened one by one, vaguer each time and softer, as a fountain sinks, an echo disappears; and when she sighed her last breath she thought she saw an opening in the heavens, and a gigantic parrot hovering above her head.

[31] A semi-precious stone from the region around the town of Alençon in northern France.
[32] The monstrance.

Fyodor Dostoevsky

(1821–1881)

"It would be possible," the Russian philosopher Nikolai Berdyaev wrote, "to determine two patterns, two types among men's souls, the one inclined toward the spirit of Tolstoy, the other toward that of Dostoevsky." Even their contemporaries noted the contrasting, if complementary, qualities of the two men's works, and in our own time, the critic George Steiner has elaborated at book length the contrast between Tolstoy's "epic" vision and Dostoevsky's "tragic" one. The differences can be overstated—the two men had much in common—but it is true that it is as if a shadow had passed over the sun when we move from the outward-looking, rationalistic, social world of Tolstoy to the inward-looking, visionary, existential world of Dostoevsky.

Tolstoy's fervent, questing life is like the plot of a Tolstoy novel; Dostoevsky's painful life is like the outline of one by Dostoevsky. Born in Moscow in 1821, Dostoevsky had early experiences very different from those of the wealthy, privileged Tolstoy. One biographer comments that his family "could have provided a case-study of morbid pathology." His father, a former army surgeon and at the time of Dostoevsky's birth resident physician in a hospital for the poor, was a violent, domineering alcoholic, his mother a weak, defeated woman who died when Dostoevsky was sixteen. He entered the military engineering school in St. Petersburg; while he was in school, his father was murdered by serfs on his small estate, whom he had viciously mistreated. Dostoevsky brooded over this tragedy for forty years, finally exorcizing its horror in his last novel, The Brothers Karamazov. *Dostoevsky was graduated from the engineering school in 1843 and was commissioned a lieutenant, almost immediately resigning his commission, however, to try to make his way as a writer. Two novels appeared in 1846:* Poor People *and* The Double. Poor People, *as the title suggests, is a realistic, proletarian novel; its originality lay, however, in Dostoevsky's sensitive psychological analysis of its clerk-protagonist's love for an orphan girl. The novel's public success was not matched by* The Double, *the story of a paranoid civil servant who meets a man who looks just like himself and who is conspiring against him. The novel inaugurated a long line of Dostoevskian studies of divided personalities. Over the next three years, Dostoevsky published a number of short stories and portions of a new novel.*

In 1849, however, the most shattering event of Dostoevsky's life occurred. For some time he had been a member of the "Petrashevsky Circle," a socialist discussion group, and now the Czar's government arrested the group and sentenced twenty-one of them, including Dostoevsky, to be shot. The police staged a grisly mock-execution, actually leading the prisoners to the execution wall, before announcing that the sentences had been commuted. Dostoevsky's sentence was changed to four years in a Siberian labor camp, to be followed by four years as a soldier in the ranks. He later described his experiences in prison in The House of the Dead *(1862): "A period of burial alive. I was put in a coffin. The torture was unutterable and unbearable." After four years, he was released from the camp and sent to the Siberian frontier post of Semipalatinsk as a soldier. In 1859, he was permitted to resign from the army and return to St. Petersburg.*

The impact of these ten years upon Dostoevsky's life and work was incalculable. His sufferings aggravated a mild epilepsy he had had for several years; this condition was to plague him the rest of his life. Prolonged association with criminals was to influence his writings; each of his major novels turns around a serious crime. In prison, he also gained a deep respect for the Russian peasantry that was to shape his thinking, and repeated readings of the Bible, the only book permitted in the prison, deepened and confirmed his previous faith. But perhaps most crucially, and certainly most paradoxically, Dostoevsky, who had gone into prison a mild socialist, emerged a profound political conservative, believing that his punishment had been deserved and that the Czar was kind and merciful. His life is perhaps a classic case of "identifying with the oppressor."

Back in Petersburg, Dostoevsky struggled to reestablish his long-interrupted literary career. With his brother Mikhail he founded a journal, Time, *in which he published* The House of the Dead *and* The Insulted and Injured *(both in 1861) and a travel book,* Winter Notes on Summer Impressions *(1863). He had taken the journey described in the latter book, through Germany, France, Italy, Switzerland, and England, in 1862 in the company of Appolinaria Suslova, a woman with whom he had a passionate and tempestuous love affair which ended in 1865. He had married in 1857, while still at Semipalatinsk, a high-tempered widow named Maria Isaeva, who suffered from tuberculosis. The marriage was a desperately unhappy one, and the two were frequently separated before her death from tuberculosis in 1864.*

In 1865, plagued by debts in St. Petersburg, Dostoevsky fled to Germany to work on a new novel, Crime and Punishment, *which he hoped would pay off his debts. He further exacerbated his financial difficulties, however, by obsessive and self-destructive gambling, for which he retained a passion all his life. Returning to*

Russia with the unfinished manuscript of Crime and Punishment, *he interrupted work on it to write, in twenty-six days,* The Gambler, *in order to satisfy a publisher who threatened to seize the rights to all his works to satisfy claims against him. Dostoevsky fell in love with Anna Grigorevna Snitkina, the stenographer he hired to take his dictation of* The Gambler. *They were married in 1867, and for the rest of his life, she was to provide a quiet, stabilizing influence upon him.*

Again pursued by creditors, Dostoevsky left St. Petersburg with his new wife in 1867, not to return until 1871. Crime and Punishment, *a great critical success but not a financial one, was published just before they left;* The Idiot *appeared serially in 1868.*

The last decade of Dostoevsky's life was his most peaceful and fruitful period. He continued to be at the center of political and ideological quarrels—for a time he edited a reactionary magazine named The Citizen—*but his wife's quiet efficiency brought a stable domestic routine and some relief from debt.* The Possessed *appeared in 1873,* A Raw Youth *in 1876, and his masterpiece,* The Brothers Karamazov, *in 1880. The climax of his public career came the same year, when he delivered a stirring speech in commemoration of the great poet Aleksandr Pushkin in Moscow, praising such "Russian" qualities in Pushkin as spirituality and faith and calling for contemporaries to draw upon those same qualities to lead the world toward peace and brotherhood. The crowd responded with chants of "Prophet! Prophet!" and he was lionized as a national hero. He died of complications of emphysema, from which he had suffered for years, only a few months after this triumph, in January, 1881.*

Much of Dostoevsky's massive and complex achievement can be understood in terms of his central figure of "the underground man." The convicts in The House of the Dead, *despised, thrust out of society, veering between self-hate and self-justification, anticipate this figure, but he takes center stage with the first words of* Notes from Underground *(1864): "I am a sick man. . . . I am a spiteful man. I am an unattractive man. I believe my liver is diseased." The speaker, like Raskolnikov, the main character in* Crime and Punishment, *lurks in his scruffy room, peering out at society, but spending most of his time spinning out great verbal webs rationalizing his own inner division. All Dostoevsky's subsequent protagonists are variations of the type, in their psychological positions if not in their living conditions: Natasha in* The Insulted and Injured, *Prince Myshkin in* The Idiot, *and all three of the Karamazov brothers—Dmitri, Ivan, and Alyosha. For Dostoevsky, to be Russian is, almost by definition, to be "underground"; Russians have been enslaved, impoverished, and degraded for centuries and have developed characteristic responses to their subjection: a permanent stance of resentment, wild swings between brutality and self-sacrificing altruism, a bewildering blend of sadism and masochism.*

The "underground" position, however, is not confined to Russia; the Russian underground man is representative of the response of modern men everywhere to the conditions of society. Three centuries of scientific rationalism, capitalism, and industrialism have produced mass man, faceless, hopeless, deprived of his freedom by being regarded only as a cog in the economic machine. The person who would preserve his freedom in such a world must drop out of it, go "underground" in a refusal to be dehumanized and stripped of the right to choose. The underground man, for all his perverse absurdity, thus is man at his most real and most human; being "underground," in its broadest sense, becomes Dostoevsky's metaphor for the human condition itself. Man, even when he is not oppressed by political despotism or by a soulless social philosophy, is thwarted in his fundamental drive toward freedom by his own reason and by his physical needs. The Dostoevskian underground man is not only divided from society but divided within himself, his drive toward freedom inevitably generating, in its act of revolt, cruel and aggressive impulses. The psychological results of this division appear in the studies of extreme mental states—sadomasochism, schizophrenia, paranoia—that fill Dostoevsky's novels.

The underground man as modern man is almost inevitably a city man, and Dostoevsky's St. Petersburg is, along with Balzac's Paris and Dickens's London, one of the most powerful urban nightmares. The agrarian Tolstoy generally stayed out of Petersburg, artistically as well as personally, but Dostoevsky found in the city the perfect symbol for his view of the modern world. The impression we get of the city from his novels is of a labyrinth of winding passageways and narrow streets and of tiny, rathole-like rooms from which lonely strangers scurry out from time to time. The sun may shine on the fashionable crowd passing along Nevsky Prospect, but we see it, from the perspective of the underground, as a procession of vaguely threatening automatons, a polite battlefield of egotism and self-interest.

Dostoevsky is a wonderfully dramatic writer; George Steiner argues that he possessed "the most comprehensive and natural dramatic temper since Shakespeare's." Notes from Underground *is, first of all, a great one-character play, a sustained dramatic monologue by a vivid, monstrous, tragicomic character. It began as a satirical attack on the popular utopian novel* What Is To Be Done? *(1863) by the Russian socialist Nikolai Chernyshevsky, and whole sections of the* Notes*—the attempt to bump into the officer on the Nevsky Prospect and the climactic encounter with the prostitute Liza—parody specific incidents in* What Is To Be Done? *Chernyshevsky's novel, an optimistic picture of a perfectly rational society, infuriated Dostoevsky, and he has his underground man reply at length, predicting that perverse, unregenerate, irrational man will do anything, even against his self-interest, to maintain the freedom that makes him human, to keep from being a mere "organ-stop" or "piano-key" in Chernyshevsky's Crystal Palace. The complexity and the comic irony of the story, and what raises it above the level of a satire on a long-forgotten novel, is that the underground man is not just a mouthpiece for Dostoevsky's ideas but an unforgettable character, crankily haranguing his imagined Chernyshevskian listeners on behalf of human freedom while at the same time demonstrating his own bondage, paralysis, and cruelty.*

The dirty, spiteful, human "louse" of Notes from Underground *seems very far from the Ivan Karamazov of "The Grand Inquisitor," but they are spiritual brothers. The Karamazov brothers—long separated but brought together by circumstances leading up to and including the murder of their drunken, profligate father—are all underground men, acutely self-conscious, deeply divided within themselves, torn between violent extremes. Each has made an existential, "underground" choice of self-definition, Dmitri of evil and Alyosha of saintliness, while the haunted Ivan has chosen rationalistic nihilism. (Criminal, saint, and rationalist are recurring figures throughout Dostoevsky's fiction.)*

In "The Grand Inquisitor," Ivan Karamazov unfolds for his shocked brother Alyosha a sardonic view of human nature and of human history. The Grand Inquisitor speaks for Catholicism, but he might as well speak for socialism or "nihilism," any system which would deprive man of his moral freedom in return for the comforting security of "miracle, mystery, and authority." The Inquisitor thinks of himself as the benefactor of mankind; he and his Church know that the mass of men cannot bear the terrible burden of freedom which Christ laid upon man by refusing Satan's comforting escapes of bread, miracles, and authority, and so they have supplied these means of escape. The Inquisitor is satanically persuasive, but his counsel of moral slavery is refuted by Christ's silent kiss at the end, an act implying what the saintly Father Zossima makes explicit in the following section, that harmony is not attained through the reason but through freedom and love.

FURTHER READING *(prepared by W. J. R.):* Konstantin Mochulsky's *Dostoevsky,* trans. by Michael A. Minihan, 1967, probably the most important critical biography available in English, discusses the major works and has a good section on *Notes from Underground.* On the social and political climates of St. Petersburg and Moscow, see Joseph Frank's *Dostoevsky, The Seeds of Revolt, 1821–49,* 1976, the first part of a four-volume biography. Ronald Hingley's well illustrated *Dostoevsky, His Life and Work,* 1978, discusses the major works and some of the minor ones. Anna Dostoevsky's *Dostoevsky: Reminiscences,* trans. and ed. by Beatrice Stillman, 1975, is an intimate view of the fourteen years she was married to the writer, the time of his greatest productivity. William J. Leatherbarrow's *Fedor Dostoevsky,* 1981, contains good introductory discussions of *Crime and Punishment, The Idiot,* and several other works. Richard Peace's *Dostoyevsky, An Examination of the Major Novels,* 1971, contains good close readings and gives special attention to the theme of religion. The major novels and most of the shorter fictional works are treated in Erik Krag's *Dostoevsky: The Literary Artist,* trans. by Sven Larr, 1976. Malcolm V. Jones's *Dostoevsky: The Novel of Discord,* 1976, examines the novels (and *Notes*) as illustrations of political and philosophical disorders in Dostoevsky's times. *Dostoevsky: A Collection of Critical Essays,* ed. René Wellek, 1962, is a good survey of criticism.

NOTES FROM UNDERGROUND[1]

Translated by Constance Garnett

PART I

UNDERGROUND

I

I am a sick man. . . . I am a spiteful man. I am an unattractive man. I believe my liver is diseased. However, I know nothing at all about my disease, and do not know for certain what ails me. I don't consult a doctor for it, and never have, though I have a respect for medicine and doctors. Besides, I am extremely superstitious, sufficiently so to respect medicine, anyway (I am well-educated enough not to be superstitious, but I am superstitious). No, I refuse to consult a doctor from spite. That you probably will

[1] The author of the diary and the diary itself are, of course, imaginary. Nevertheless, it is clear that such persons as the writer of these notes not only may, but positively must, exist in our society, when we consider the circumstances in the midst of which our society is formed. I have tried to expose to the view of the public, more distinctly than is commonly done, one of the characters of the recent past. He is one of the representatives of a generation still living. In this fragment, entitled "Underground," this person introduces himself and his views, and, as it were, tries to explain the causes owing to which he has made his appearance and was bound to make his appearance in our midst. In the second fragment there are added the actual notes of this person concerning certain events in his life. (Dostoevsky's note.)

not understand. Well, I understand it, though. Of course I can't explain who it is precisely that I am mortifying in this case by my spite: I am perfectly well aware that I cannot "pay out" the doctors by not consulting them; I know better than any one that by all this I am only injuring myself and no one else. But still, if I don't consult a doctor it is from spite. My liver is bad, well—let it get worse!

I have been going on like that for a long time—twenty years. Now I am forty. I used to be in the government service, but am no longer. I was a spiteful official. I was rude and took pleasure in being so. I did not take bribes, you see, so I was bound to find a recompense in that, at least. (A poor jest, but I will not scratch it out. I wrote it thinking it would sound very witty; but now that I have seen myself that I only wanted to show off in a despicable way, I will not scratch it out on purpose!)

When petitioners used to come for information to the table at which I sat, I used to grind my teeth at them, and felt intense enjoyment when I succeeded in making anybody unhappy. I almost always did succeed. For the most part they were all timid people—of course, they were petitioners. But of the uppish ones there was one officer in particular I could not endure. He simply would not be humble, and clanked his sword in a disgusting way. I carried on a feud with him for eighteen months over that sword. At last I got the better of him. He left off clanking it. That happened in my youth, though.

But do you know, gentlemen, what was the chief point about my spite? Why, the whole point, the real sting of it lay in the fact that continually, even in the moment of the acutest spleen, I was inwardly conscious with shame that I was not only not a spiteful but not even an embittered man, that I was simply scaring sparrows at random and amusing myself by it. I might foam at the mouth, but bring me a doll to play with, give me a cup of tea with sugar in it, and maybe I should be appeased. I might even be genuinely touched, though probably I should grind my teeth at myself afterwards and lie awake at night with shame for months after. That was my way.

I was lying when I said just now that I was a spiteful official. I was lying from spite. I was simply amusing myself with the petitioners and with the officer, and in reality I never could become spiteful. I was conscious every moment in myself of many, very many elements absolutely opposite to that. I felt them positively swarming in me, these opposite elements. I knew that they had been swarming in me all my life and craving some outlet from me, but I would not let them, would not let them, purposely would not let them come out. They tormented me till I was ashamed: they drove me to convulsions and—sickened me, at last, how they sickened me! Now, are not you fancying, gentlemen, that I am expressing remorse for something now, that I am asking your forgiveness for something? I am sure you are fancying that . . . However, I assure you I do not care if you are. . .[2]

It was not only that I could not become spiteful, I did not know how to become anything: neither spiteful nor kind, neither a rascal nor an honest man, neither a hero nor an insect. Now, I am living out my life in my

[2] Here, as elsewhere in the text, repeated periods do not indicate an omission but are punctuation marks.

corner, taunting myself with the spiteful and useless consolation that an intelligent man cannot become anything seriously, and it is only the fool who becomes anything. Yes, a man in the nineteenth century must and morally ought to be pre-eminently a characterless creature; a man of character, an active man is preeminently a limited creature. That is my conviction of forty years. I am forty years old now, and you know forty years is a whole lifetime; you know it is extreme old age. To live longer than forty years is bad manners, is vulgar, immoral. Who lives beyond forty? Answer that, sincerely and honestly. I will tell you who do: fools and worthless fellows. I tell all old men that to their face, all these venerable old men, all these silver-haired and reverend seniors! I tell the whole world that to its face! I have a right to say so, for I shall go on living to sixty myself. To seventy! To eighty! . . . Stay, let me take breath. . . .

You imagine no doubt, gentlemen, that I want to amuse you. You are mistaken in that, too. I am by no means such a mirthful person as you imagine, or as you may imagine; however, irritated by all this babble (and I feel that you are irritated) you think fit to ask me who am I—then my answer is, I am a collegiate assessor.[3] I was in the service that I might have something to eat (and solely for that reason), and when last year a distant relation left me six thousand roubles in his will I immediately retired from the service and settled down in my corner. I used to live in this corner before, but now I have settled down in it. My room is a wretched, horrid one in the outskirts of the town. My servant is an old country-woman, ill-natured from stupidity, and, moreover, there is always a nasty smell about her. I am told that the Petersburg climate is bad for me, and that with my small means it is very expensive to live in Petersburg. I know all that better than all these sage and experienced counsellors and monitors. . . . But I am remaining in Petersburg; . . . I am not going away from Petersburg! I am not going away because . . . ech! Why, it is absolutely no matter whether I am going away or not going away.

But what can a decent man speak of with most pleasure?

Answer: Of himself.

Well, so I will talk about myself.

II

I want now to tell you, gentlemen, whether you care to hear it or not, why I could not even become an insect. I tell you solemnly, that I have many times tried to become an insect. But I was not equal even to that. I swear, gentlemen, that to be too conscious is an illness—a real thoroughgoing illness. For man's everyday needs, it would have been quite enough to have the ordinary human consciousness, that is, half or a quarter of the amount which falls to the lot of a cultivated man of our unhappy nineteenth century, especially one who has the fatal ill-luck to inhabit Petersburg, the most theoretical and intentional town on the whole terrestrial globe. (There are intentional and unintentional towns.) It would have been quite enough, for instance, to have the consciousness by which all so-called direct persons and men of action live. I bet you think I am writing all this from affectation, to be witty at the expense of men of action; and what is more, that from

[3] A minor civil servant.

ill-bred affectation, I am clanking a sword like my officer. But, gentlemen, whoever can pride himself on his diseases and even swagger over them?

Though, after all, every one does do that; people do pride themselves on their diseases, and I do, may be, more than any one else. We will not dispute it; my contention was absurd. But yet I am firmly persuaded that a great deal of consciousness, every sort of consciousness, in fact, is a disease. I stick to that. Let us leave that, too, for a minute. Tell me this: why does it happen that at the very, yes, at the very moments when I am most capable of feeling every refinement of all that is "good and beautiful," as they used to say at one time, it would, as though of design, happen to me not only to feel but to do such ugly things, such that . . . Well, in short, actions that all, perhaps, commit; but which, as though purposely, occurred to me at the very time when I was most conscious that they ought not to be committed. The more conscious I was of goodness and of all that was "good and beautiful," the more deeply I sank into my mire and the more ready I was to sink in it altogether. But the chief point was that all this was, as it were, not accidental in me, but as though it were bound to be so. It was as though it were my most normal condition, and not in the least disease or depravity, so that at last all desire in me to struggle against this depravity passed. It ended by my almost believing (perhaps actually believing) that this was perhaps my normal condition. But at first, in the beginning, what agonies I endured in that struggle! I did not believe it was the same with other people, and all my life I hid this fact about myself as a secret. I was ashamed (even now, perhaps, I am ashamed): I got to the point of feeling a sort of secret abnormal, despicable enjoyment in returning home to my corner on some disgusting Petersburg night, acutely conscious that that day I had committed a loathsome action again, that what was done could never be undone, and secretly, inwardly gnawing, gnawing at myself for it, tearing and consuming myself till at last the bitterness turned into a sort of shameful accursed sweetness, and at last—into positive real enjoyment! Yes into enjoyment, into enjoyment! I insist upon that. I have spoken of this because I keep wanting to know for a fact whether other people feel such enjoyment? I will explain; the enjoyment was just from the too intense consciousness of one's own degradation; it was from feeling oneself that one had reached the last barrier, that it was horrible, but that it could not be otherwise; that there was no escape for you; that you never could become a different man; that even if time and faith were still left you to change into something different you would most likely not wish to change; or if you did wish to, even then you would do nothing; because perhaps in reality there was nothing for you to change into.

And the worst of it was, and the root of it all, that it was all in accord with the normal fundamental laws of over-acute consciousness, and with the inertia that was the direct result of those laws, and that consequently one was not only unable to change but could do absolutely nothing. Thus it would follow, as the result of acute consciousness, that one is not to blame in being a scoundrel; as though that were any consolation to the scoundrel once he has come to realize that he actually is a scoundrel. But enough. . . . Ech, I have talked a lot of nonsense, but what have I explained? How is enjoyment in this to be explained? But I will explain it. I will get to the bottom of it! That is why I have taken up my pen. . . .

I, for instance, have a great deal of *amour propre.*[4] I am as suspicious and prone to take offense as a hunchback or a dwarf. But upon my word I sometimes have had moments when if I had happened to be slapped in the face I should, perhaps, have been positively glad of it. I say, in earnest, that I should probably have been able to discover even in that a peculiar sort of enjoyment—the enjoyment, of course, of despair; but in despair there are the most intense enjoyments, especially when one is very acutely conscious of the hopelessness of one's position. And when one is slapped in the face—why then the consciousness of being rubbed into a pulp would positively overwhelm one. The worst of it is, look at it which way one will, it still turns out that I was always the most to blame in everything. And what is most humiliating of all, to blame for no fault of my own but, so to say, through the laws of nature. In the first place, to blame because I am cleverer than any of the people surrounding me. (I have always considered myself cleverer than any of the people surrounding me, and sometimes, would you believe it, have been positively ashamed of it. At any rate, I have all my life, as it were, turned my eyes away and never could look people straight in the face.) To blame, finally, because even if I had had magnanimity, I should only have had more suffering from the sense of its uselessness. I should certainly have never been able to do anything from being magnanimous—neither to forgive, for my assailant would perhaps have slapped me from the laws of nature, and one cannot forgive the laws of nature; nor to forget, for even if it were owing to the laws of nature, it is insulting all the same. Finally, even if I had wanted to be anything but magnanimous, had desired on the contrary to revenge myself on my assailant, I could not have revenged myself on any one for anything because I should certainly never have made up my mind to do anything, even if I had been able to. Why should I not have made up my mind? About that in particular I want to say a few words.

III

With people who know how to revenge themselves and to stand up for themselves in general, how is it done? Why, when they are possessed, let us suppose, by the feeling of revenge, then for the time there is nothing else but that feeling left in their whole being. Such a gentleman simply dashes straight for his object like an infuriated bull with its horns down, and nothing but a wall will stop him. (By the way: facing the wall, such gentlemen—that is, the "direct" persons and men of action—are genuinely nonplussed. For them a wall is not an evasion, as for us people who think and consequently do nothing; it is not an excuse for turning aside, an excuse for which we are always very glad, though we scarcely believe in it ourselves, as a rule. No, they are nonplussed in all sincerity. The wall has for them something tranquillizing, morally soothing, final—maybe even something mysterious . . . but of the wall later.)

Well, such a direct person I regard as the real normal man, as his tender mother nature wished to see him when she graciously brought him into

[4] Self-esteem.

being on the earth. I envy such a man till I am green in the face. He is stupid. I am not disputing that, but perhaps the normal man should be stupid, how do you know? Perhaps it is very beautiful, in fact. And I am the more persuaded of that suspicion, if one can call it so, by the fact that if you take, for instance, the antithesis of the normal man, that is, the man of acute consciousness, who has come, of course, not out of the lap of nature but out of a retort (this is almost mysticism, gentlemen, but I suspect this, too), this retort-made man is sometimes so nonplussed in the presence of his antithesis that with all his exaggerated consciousness he genuinely thinks of himself as a mouse and not a man. It may be an acutely conscious mouse, yet it is a mouse, while the other is a man, and therefore, et cetera, et cetera. And the worst of it is, he himself, his very own self, looks on himself as a mouse; no one asks him to do so; and that is an important point. Now let us look at this mouse in action. Let us suppose, for instance, that it feels insulted, too (and it almost always does feel insulted), and wants to revenge itself, too. There may even be a greater accumulation of spite in it than in *l'homme de la nature et de la vérité*.[5] The base and nasty desire to vent that spite on its assailant rankles perhaps even more nastily in it than in *l'homme de la nature et de la vérité*. For through his innate stupidity the latter looks upon his revenge as justice pure and simple; while in consequence of his acute consciousness the mouse does not believe in the justice of it. To come at last to the deed itself, to the very act of revenge. Apart from the one fundamental nastiness the luckless mouse succeeds in creating around it so many other nastinesses in the form of doubts and questions, adds to the one question so many unsettled questions that there inevitably works up around it a sort of fatal brew, a stinking mess, made up of its doubts, emotions, and of the contempt spat upon it by the direct men of action who stand solemnly about it as judges and arbitrators, laughing at it till their healthy sides ache. Of course the only thing left for it is to dismiss all that with a wave of its paw, and, with a smile of assumed contempt in which it does not even itself believe, creep ignominiously into its mousehole. There in its nasty, stinking, underground home our insulted, crushed and ridiculed mouse promptly becomes absorbed in cold, malignant and, above all, everlasting spite. For forty years together it will remember its injury down to the smallest, most ignominious details, and every time will add, of itself, details still more ignominious, spitefully teasing and tormenting itself with its own imagination. It will itself be ashamed of its imaginings, but yet it will recall it all, it will go over and over every detail, it will invent unheard of things against itself, pretending that those things might happen, and will forgive nothing. Maybe it will begin to revenge itself, too, but, as it were, piecemeal, in trivial ways, from behind the stove, incognito, without believing either in its own right to vengeance, or in the success of its revenge, knowing that from all its efforts at revenge it will suffer a hundred times more than he on whom it revenges itself, while he, I daresay, will not even scratch himself. On its deathbed it will recall it all over again, with interest accumulated over all the years and. . . .

[5] "The man of nature and of truth." This is the phrase Rousseau uses to describe himself in his *Confessions* (1781–88), somewhat disingenuously, the speaker suggests.

But it is just in that cold, abominable half despair, half belief, in that conscious burying oneself alive for grief in the underworld for forty years, in that acutely recognized and yet partly doubtful hopelessness of one's position, in that hell of unsatisified desires turned inward, in that fever of oscillations, or resolutions determined for ever and repented of again a minute later—that the savor of that strange enjoyment of which I have spoken lies. It is so subtle, so difficult of analysis, that persons who are a little limited, or even simply persons of strong nerves, will not understand a single atom of it. "Possibly," you will add on your own account with a grin, "people will not understand it either who have never received a slap in the face," and in that way you will politely hint to me that I, too, perhaps, have had the experience of a slap in the face in my life, and so I speak as one who knows. I bet that you are thinking that. But set your minds at rest, gentlemen, I have not received a slap in the face, though it is absolutely a matter of indifference to me what you may think about it. Possibly, I even regret, myself, that I have given so few slaps in the face during my life. But enough . . . not another word on that subject of such extreme interest to you.

I will continue calmly concerning persons with strong nerves who do not understand a certain refinement of enjoyment. Though in certain circumstances these gentlemen bellow their loudest like bulls, though this, let us suppose, does them the greatest credit, yet, as I have said already, confronted with the impossible they subside at once. The impossible means the stone wall! What stone wall? Why, of course, the laws of nature, the deductions of natural science, mathematics. As soon as they prove to you, for instance, that you are descended from a monkey, then it is no use scowling, accept it for a fact. When they prove to you that in reality one drop of your own fat must be dearer to you than a hundred thousand of your fellow-creatures, and that this conclusion is the final solution of all so-called virtues and duties and all such prejudices and fancies, then you have just to accept it, there is no help for it, for twice two is a law of mathematics. Just try refuting it.

"Upon my word," they will shout at you, "it is no use protesting: it is a case of twice two makes four! Nature does not ask your permission, she has nothing to do with your wishes, and whether you like her laws or dislike them, you are bound to accept her as she is, and consequently all her conclusions. A wall, you see, is a wall . . ." and so on, and so on.

Merciful Heavens! but what do I care for the laws of nature and arithmetic, when, for some reason I dislike those laws and the fact that twice two makes four? Of course I cannot break through the wall by battering my head against it if I really have not the strength to knock it down, but I am not going to be reconciled to it simply because it is a stone wall and I have not the strength.

As though such a stone wall really were a consolation, and really did contain some word of conciliation, simply because it is as true as twice two makes four. Oh, absurdity of absurdities! How much better it is to understand it all, to recognize it all, all the impossibilities and the stone wall; not to be reconciled to one of those impossibilities and stone walls if it disgusts you to be reconciled to it; by the way of the most inevitable, logical combinations to reach the most revolting conclusions on the everlasting theme, than even for the stone wall you are yourself somehow to blame, though again it is as clear as day you are not to blame in the least, and therefore grinding your teeth in silent impotence to sink into luxurious inertia, brooding on the fact that there is no one even for you to feel vindictive against, that you have not, and perhaps never will have, an object for your spite, that it is a sleight of hand, a bit of juggling, a card-sharper's trick, that it is simply a mess, no knowing what and no knowing who, but in spite of all these uncertainties and jugglings, still there is an ache in you, and the more you do not know, the worse the ache.

IV

"Ha, ha, ha! You will be finding enjoyment in toothache next," you cry, with a laugh.

"Well? Even in toothache there is enjoyment," I answer. I had toothache for a whole month and I know there is. In that case, of course, people are not spiteful in silence, but moan; but they are not candid moans, they are malignant moans, and the malignancy is the whole point. The enjoyment of the sufferer finds expression in those moans; if he did not feel enjoyment in them he would not moan. It is a good example, gentlemen, and I will develop it. Those moans express in the first place all the aimlessness of your pain, which is so humiliating to your consciousness; the whole legal system of nature on which you spit disdainfully, of course, but from which you suffer all the same while she does not. They express the consciousness that you have no enemy to punish, but that you have pain; the consciousness that in spite of all possible Wagenheims[6] you are in complete slavery to your teeth; that if some one wishes it, your teeth will leave off aching, and if he does not, they will go on aching another three months; and that finally if you are still contumacious and still protest, all that is left you for your own gratification is to thrash yourself or beat your wall with your fist as hard as you can, and absolutely nothing more. Well, these mortal insults, these jeers on the part of some one unknown, end at last in an enjoyment which sometimes reaches the highest degree of voluptuousness. I ask you, gentlemen, listen sometimes to the moans of an educated man of the nineteenth century suffering from toothache, on the second or third day of the attack, when he is beginning to moan, not as he moaned on the first day, that is, not simply because he has toothache, not just as any coarse peasant, but as a man affected by progress and European civilization, a man who is "divorced from the soil and the national elements," as they express it nowadays. His moans become nasty, disgustingly malignant, and go on for whole days and nights. And of course he knows himself that he is doing himself no sort of good with his moans; he knows better than any one that he is only lacerating and harassing himself and others for nothing; he knows that even the audience before whom he is making his efforts, and his whole family, listen to him with loathing, do not put the least faith in him, and inwardly understand that he might moan differently, more simply, without trills and flourishes, and that he is only amusing himself like that from ill-humor, from malignancy. Well, in all these recognitions and

[6] Two dentists, both named Wagenheim, advertised "painless dentistry" in the Petersburg newspaper in 1864.

disgraces it is that there lies a voluptuous pleasure. As though he would say: "I am worrying you, I am lacerating your hearts, I am keeping every one in the house awake. Well, stay awake then, you, too, feel every minute that I have toothache. I am not a hero to you now, as I tried to seem before, but simply a nasty person, an impostor. Well, so be it, then! I am very glad that you see through me. It is nasty for you to hear my despicable moans: well, let it be nasty; here I will let you have a nastier flourish in a minute . . . ." You do not understand even now, gentlemen? No, it seems our development and our consciousness must go further to understand all the intricacies of this pleasure. You laugh? Delighted. My jests, gentlemen, are of course in bad taste, jerky, involved, lacking self-confidence. But of course that is because I do not respect myself. Can a man of perception respect himself at all?

V

Come, can a man who attempts to find enjoyment in the very feeling of his own degradation possibly have a spark of respect for himself? I am not saying this now from any mawkish kind of remorse. And, indeed, I could never endure saying, "Forgive me, Papa, I won't do it again," not because I am incapable of saying that—on the contrary, perhaps just because I have been too capable of it, and in what a way, too! As though of design I used to get into trouble in cases when I was not to blame in any way. That was the nastiest part of it. At the same time I was genuinely touched and penitent, I used to shed tears and, of course, deceived myself, though I was not acting in the least and there was a sick feeling in my heart at the time. . . . For that one could not blame even the laws of nature, though the laws of nature have continually all my life offended me more than anything. It is loathsome to remember it all, but it was loathsome even then. Of course, a minute or so later I would realize wrathfully that it was all a lie, a revolting lie, an affected lie, that is, all this penitence, this emotion, these vows of reform. You will ask why did I worry myself with such antics: answer, because it was very dull to sit with one's hands folded, and so one began cutting capers. That is really it. Observe yourselves more carefully, gentlemen, then you will understand that it is so. I invented adventures for myself and made up a life, so as at least to live in some way. How many times it has happened to me—well, for instance, to take offense simply on purpose, for nothing; and one knows oneself, of course, that one is offended at nothing, that one is putting it on, but yet one brings oneself, at last, to the point of being really offended. All my life I have had an impulse to play such pranks, so that in the end I could not control it in myself. Another time, twice, in fact, I tried hard to be in love. I suffered, too, gentlemen, I assure you. In the depth of my heart there was no faith in my suffering, only a faint stir of mockery, but yet I did suffer, and in the real, orthodox way; I was jealous, beside myself . . . and it was all from *ennui,*[7] gentlemen, all from *ennui;* inertia overcame me. You know the direct, legitimate fruit of consciousness is inertia, that is, conscious sitting-with-the-hands-folded. I have referred to this already. I repeat, I repeat with emphasis: all "direct" persons and men of action are active just because they are stupid and lim-

[7] A feeling of weariness or dissatisfaction.

ited. How explain that? I will tell you: in consequence of their limitation they take immediate and secondary causes for primary ones, and in that way persuade themselves more quickly and easily than other people do that they have found an infallible foundation for their activity, and their minds are at ease and you know that is the chief thing. To begin to act, you know, you must first have your mind completely at ease and no trace of doubt left in it. Why, how am I, for example, to set my mind at rest? Where are the primary causes on which I am to build? Where are my foundations?. Where am I to get them from? I exercise myself in reflection, and consequently with me every primary cause at once draws after itself another still more primary, and so on to infinity. That is just the essence of every sort of consciousness and reflection. It must be a case of the laws of nature again. What is the result of it in the end? Why, just the same. Remember I spoke just now of vengeance. (I am sure you did not take it in.) I said that a man revenges himself because he sees justice in it. Therefore he has found a primary cause, that is, justice. And so he is at rest on all sides, and consequently he carries out his revenge calmly and successfully, being persuaded that he is doing a just and honest thing. But I see no justice in it, I find no sort of virtue in it either, and consequently if I attempt to revenge myself, it is only out of spite. Spite, of course, might overcome everything, all my doubts, and so might serve quite successfully in place of a primary cause, precisely because it is not a cause. But what is to be done if I have not even spite (I began with that just now, you know)? In consequence again of those accursed laws of consciousness, anger in me is subject to chemical disintegration. You look into it, the object flies off into air, your reasons evaporate, the criminal is not to be found, the wrong becomes not a wrong but a phantom, something like the toothache, for which no one is to blame, and consequently there is only the same outlet left again—that is, to beat the wall as hard as you can. So you give it up with a wave of the hand because you have not found a fundamental cause. And try letting yourself be carried away by your feelings, blindly, without reflection, without a primary cause, repelling consciousness at least for a time; hate or love, if only not to sit with your hands folded. The day after tomorrow, at the latest, you will begin despising yourself for having knowingly deceived yourself. Result: a soap-bubble and inertia. Oh, gentlemen, do you know, perhaps I consider myself an intelligent man, only because all my life I have been able neither to begin nor to finish anything. Granted I am a babbler,[8] a harmless vexatious babbler, like all of us. But what is to be done if the direct and sole vocation of every intelligent man is babble, that is, the intentional pouring of water through a sieve?

VI

Oh, if I had done nothing simply from laziness! Heavens, how I should have respected myself, then. I should have respected myself because I should at least have been capable of being lazy; there would at least have been one quality, as it were, positive in me, in which I could have believed myself. Question: What is he? Answer: A sluggard; how very pleasant it would have been to hear that of oneself! It would mean that I was positively

[8] One who chatters or talks excessively.

defined, it would mean that there was something to say about me. "Sluggard"—why, it is a calling and vocation, it is a career. Do not jest, it is so. I should then be a member of the best club by right, and should find my occupation in continually respecting myself. I knew a gentlemen who prided himself all his life on being a connoisseur of Lafitte.[9] He considered this as his positive virtue, and never doubted himself. He died, not simply with a tranquil, but with a triumphant, conscience, and he was quite right, too. Then I should have chosen a career for myself, I should have been a sluggard and a glutton, not a simple one, but, for instance, one with sympathies for everything good and beautiful. How do you like that?. I have long had visions of it. That "good and beautiful" weighs heavily on my mind at forty. But that is at forty; then—oh, then it would have been different! I should have found for myself a form of activity in keeping with it, to be precise, drinking to the health of everything "good and beautiful." I should have snatched at every opportunity to drop a tear into my glass and then to drain it to all that is "good and beautiful." I should then have turned everything into the good and the beautiful; in the nastiest, unquestionable trash, I should have sought out the good and the beautiful. I should have exuded tears like a wet sponge. An artist, for instance, paints a picture worthy of Gay.[10] At once I drink to the health of the artist who painted the picture worthy of Gay, because I love all that is "good and beautiful." An author has written *What you will:*[11] at once I drink to the health of "what you will" because I love all that is "good and beautiful."

I should claim respect for doing so. I should persecute any one who would not show me respect. I should live at ease, I should die with dignity, why, it is charming, perfectly charming! And what a good round belly I should have grown, what a triple chin I should have established, what a ruby nose I should have colored for myself, so that every one would have said, looking at me: "Here is an asset! Here is something real and solid!" And, say what you like, it is very agreeable to hear such remarks about oneself in this negative age.

VII

But these are all golden dreams. Oh, tell me, who was it first announced, who was it first proclaimed, that man only does nasty things because he does not know his own interests; and that if he were enlightened, if his eyes were opened to his real normal interests, man would at once cease to do nasty things, would at once become good and noble because, being enlightened and understanding his real advantage, he would see his own advantage in the good and nothing else, and we all know that not one man can, consciously, act against his own interests, consequently, so to say, through necessity, he would begin doing good? Oh, the babe! Oh, the pure, innocent child! Why, in the first place, when in all these thousands of years has there been a time when man has acted only from his own interest? What is to be done with the millions of facts that bear witness that men, *consciously*, that is fully understanding their real interests, have left them in the back-

[9] A kind of wine. [10] Nikolay Nikolaevich Gay, a popular painter of historical subjects.
[11] The subtitle of Shakespeare's *Twelfth Night.*

ground and have rushed headlong on another path, to meet peril and danger, compelled to this course by nobody and by nothing, but, as it were, simply disliking the beaten track, and have obstinately, willfully, struck out another difficult, absurd way, seeking it almost in the darkness. So, I suppose, this obstinacy and perversity were pleasanter to them than any advantage. . . . Advantage! What is advantage? And will you take it upon yourself to define with perfect accuracy in what the advantage of man consists? And what if it so happens that a man's advantage, *sometimes,* not only may, but even must, consist in his desiring in certain cases what is harmful to himself and not advantageous. And if so, if there can be such a case, the whole principle falls into dust. What do you think—are there such cases? You laugh; laugh away, gentlemen, but only answer me: have man's advantages been reckoned up with perfect certainty? Are there not some which not only have not been included but cannot possibly be included under any classification? You see, you gentlemen have, to the best of my knowledge, taken your whole register of human advantages from the averages of statistical figures and politico-economical formulas. Your advantages are prosperity, wealth, freedom, peace—and so on, and so on. So that the man who should, for instance, go openly and knowingly in opposition to all that list would, to your thinking, and indeed mine, too, of course, be an obscurantist[12] or an absolute madman: would not he? But, you know, this is what is surprising: why does it so happen that all these statisticians, sages and lovers of humanity, when they reckon up human advantages invariably leave out one? They don't even take it into their reckoning in the form in which it should be taken, and the whole reckoning depends upon that. It would be no great matter, they would simply have to take it, this advantage, and add it to the list. But the trouble is, that this strange advantage does not fall under any classification and is not in place in any list. I have a friend for instance . . . Ech! gentlemen, but of course he is your friend, too; and indeed there is no one, no one, to whom he is not a friend! When he prepares for any undertaking this gentleman immediately explains to you, elegantly and clearly, exactly how he must act in accordance with the laws of reason and truth. What is more, he will talk to you with excitement and passion of the true normal interests of man; with irony he will upbraid the shortsighted fools who do not understand their own interests, nor the true significance of virtue; and, within a quarter of an hour, without any sudden outside provocation, but simply through something inside him which is stronger than all his interests, he will go off on quite a different tack—that is, act in direct opposition to what he has just been saying about himself, in opposition to the laws of reason, in opposition to his own advantage, in fact in opposition to everything . . . I warn you that my friend is a compound personality, and therefore it is difficult to blame him as an individual. The fact is, gentlemen, it seems there must really exist something that is dearer to almost every man than his greatest advantages, or (not to be illogical) there is a most advantageous advantage (the very one omitted of which we spoke just now) which is more important and more advantageous than all other advantages, for the sake of which a man if necessary is ready to act in

[12] One who deliberately tries to make things obscure or vague.

opposition to all laws; that is, in opposition to reason, honor, peace, prosperity—in fact, in opposition to all those excellent and useful things if only he can attain that fundamental, most advantageous advantage which is dearer to him than all. "Yes, but it's advantage all the same," you will retort. But excuse me, I'll make the point clear, and it is not a case of playing upon words. What matters is, that this advantage is remarkable from the very fact that it breaks down all our classifications, and continually shatters every system constructed by lovers of mankind for the benefit of mankind. In fact, it upsets everything. But before I mention this advantage to you, I want to compromise myself personally, and therefore I boldly declare that all these fine systems, all these theories for explaining to mankind their real normal interests, in order that inevitably striving to pursue these interests they may at once become good and noble—are, in my opinion, so far, mere logical exercises! Yes, logical exercises. Why, to maintain this theory of the regeneration of mankind by means of the pursuit of his own advantage is to my mind almost the same thing as . . . as to affirm, for instance, following Buckle,[13] that through civilization mankind becomes softer, and consequently less bloodthirsty and less fitted for warfare. Logically it does seem to follow from his arguments. But man has such a predilection for systems and abstract deductions that he is ready to distort the truth intentionally, he is ready to deny the evidence of his senses only to justify his logic. I take this example because it is the most glaring instance of it. Only look about you: blood is being spilt in streams, and in the merriest way, as though it were champagne. Take the whole of the nineteenth century in which Buckle lived. Take Napoleon—the Great and also the present one. Take North America—the eternal union. Take the farce of Schleswig-Holstein.[14] . . . And what is it that civilization softens in us? The only gain of civilization for mankind is the greater capacity for variety of sensations—and absolutely nothing more. And through the development of this many-sidedness man may come to finding enjoyment in bloodshed. In fact, this has already happened to him. Have you noticed that it is the most civilized gentlemen who have been the subtlest slaughterers, to whom the Attilas[15] and Stenka Razins[16] could not hold a candle, and if they are not so conspicuous as the Attilas and Stenka Razins it is simply because they are so often met with, are so ordinary and have become so familiar to us. In any case civilization has made mankind if not more bloodthirsty, at least more vilely, more loathsomely bloodthirsty. In old days he saw justice in bloodshed and with his conscience at peace exterminated those he thought proper. Now we do think bloodshed abominable and yet we engage in this abomination, and with more energy than ever. Which is worse? Decide that for yourselves. They say that Cleopatra (excuse an instance from Roman history) was fond of sticking gold pins into her slave-girls' breasts and derived gratification

[13] Henry Thomas Buckle, in his popular *History of Civilization in England* (1857–61), maintained the thesis the speaker summarizes.

[14] An area disputed by Germany and Denmark and the subject of the Dano-Prussian War (1864). The English Lord Palmerston once said that of the three men who had ever understood the Schleswig-Holstein dispute, one was dead (Prince Albert), one was insane (a professor), and the third (Palmerston himself) had forgotten it.

[15] Attila was a notorious fifth-century A.D. King of the Huns.

[16] Stenka Razin was a seventeenth-century Cossack leader, noted for his fierce conquests.

from their screams and writhings. You will say that that was in the comparatively barbarous times; that these are barbarous times too, because also, comparatively speaking, pins are stuck in even now; that though man has now learned to see more clearly than in barbarous ages, he is still far from having learned to act as reason and science would dictate. But yet you are fully convinced that he will be sure to learn when he gets rid of certain old bad habits, and when common sense and science have completely re-educated human nature and turned it in a normal direction. You are confident that then man will cease from *intentional* error and will, so to say, be compelled not to want to set his will against his normal interests. That is not all; then, you say, science itself will teach man (though to my mind it's a superfluous luxury) that he never has really had any caprice or will of his own, and that he himself is something of the nature of a piano-key or the stop of an organ, and that there are, besides, things called the laws of nature; so that everything he does is not done by his willing it, but is done of itself, by the laws of nature. Consequently we have only to discover these laws of nature, and man will no longer have to answer for his actions and life will become exceedingly easy for him. All human actions will then, of course, be tabulated according to these laws, mathematically, like tables of logarithms up to 108,000, and entered in an index; or, better still, there would be published certain edifying works of the nature of encyclopedic lexicons, in which everything will be so clearly calculated and explained that there will be no more incidents or adventures in the world.

Then—this is all what you say—new economic relations will be established, all ready-made and worked out with mathematical exactitude, so that every possible question will vanish in the twinkling of an eye, simply because every possible answer to it will be provided. Then the "Crystal Palace"[17] will be built. Then . . . . In fact, those will be halcyon days. Of course there is no guaranteeing (this is my comment) that it will not be, for instance, frightfully dull then (for what will one have to do when everything will be calculated and tabulated), but on the other hand everything will be extraordinarily rational. Of course boredom may lead you to anything. It is boredom sets one sticking golden pins into people, but all that would not matter. What is bad (this is my comment again) is that I dare say people will be thankful for the gold pins then. Man is stupid, you know, phenomenally stupid; or rather he is not at all stupid, but he is so ungrateful that you could not find another like him in all creation. I, for instance, would not be in the least surprised if all of a sudden, *à propos* of nothing, in the midst of general prosperity a gentleman with an ignoble, or rather with a reactionary and ironical, countenance were to arise and, putting his arms akimbo, say to us all: "I say, gentlemen, hadn't we better kick over the whole show and scatter rationalism to the winds, simply to send these loga-

[17] The speaker is alluding to the utopian society, organized on wholly rational principles, in Nikolai Chernyshevsky's didactic novel *What Is To Be Done?* (1863). Chernyshevsky's "Crystal Palace" is closely based on the utopian "phalansteries" projected by the French social philosopher Charles Fourier (1772–1837), hypothetical communities so meticulously planned that one critic remarked that they were "the Arcadias of a bureaucrat." Chernyshevsky, for the name and architecture of his utopia (a great dome of iron and glass), drew upon London's Crystal Palace, built for the Great Exhibition of 1851 and widely regarded as a marvel of progressive architecture.

rithms to the devil, and to enable us to live once more at our own sweet foolish will!" That again would not matter, but what is annoying is that he would be sure to find followers—such is the nature of man. And all that for the most foolish reason, which, one would think, was hardly worth mentioning: that is, that man everywhere and at all times, whoever he may be, has preferred to act as he chose and not in the least as his reason and advantage dictated. And one may choose what is contrary to one's own interests, and sometimes one *positively ought* (that is my idea). One's own free unfettered choice, one's own caprice, however wild it may be, one's own fancy worked up at times to frenzy—is that very "most advantageous advantage" which we have overlooked, which comes under no classification and against which all systems and theories are continually being shattered to atoms. And how do these wiseacres know that man wants a normal, a virtuous choice? What has made them conceive that man must want a rationally advantageous choice? What man wants is simply *independent* choice, whatever that independence may cost and wherever it may lead. And choice, of course, the devil only knows what choice. . . .

VIII

"Ha! ha! ha! But you know there is no such thing as choice in reality, say what you like," you will interpose with a chuckle. "Science has succeeded in so far analyzing man that we know already that choice and what is called freedom of will is nothing else than——"

Stay, gentlemen, I meant to begin with that myself. I confess, I was rather frightened. I was just going to say that the devil only knows what choice depends on, and that perhaps that was a very good thing, but I remembered the teaching of science . . . and pulled myself up. And here you have begun upon it. Indeed, if there really is some day discovered a formula for all our desires and caprices—that is, an explanation of what they depend upon, by what laws they arise, how they develop, what they are aiming at in one case and in another and so on, that is, a real mathematical formula—then, most likely, man will at once cease to feel desire, indeed, he will be certain to. For who would want to choose by rule? Besides, he will at once be transformed from a human being into an organ-stop or something of the sort; for what is a man without desires, without freewill and without choice, if not a stop in an organ? What do you think? Let us reckon the chances—can such a thing happen or not?

"H'm!" you decide. "Our choice is usually mistaken from a false view of our advantage. We sometimes choose absolute nonsense because in our foolishness we see in that nonsense the easiest means for attaining a supposed advantage. But when all that is explained and worked out on paper (which is perfectly possible, for it is contemptible and senseless to suppose that some laws of nature man will never understand), then certainly so-called desires will no longer exist. For if a desire should come into conflict with reason we shall then reason and not desire, because it will be impossible retaining our reason to be *senseless* in our desires, and in that way knowingly act against reason and desire to injure ourselves. And as all choice and reasoning can be really calculated—because there will some day be discovered the laws of our so-called freewill—so, joking apart, there may one day be something like a table constructed of them, so that we really shall choose in accordance with it. If, for instance, some day they calculate and prove to me that I make a long nose at some one because I could not help making a long nose at him and that I had to do it in that particular way, what *freedom* is left me, especially if I am a learned man and have taken my degree somewhere? Then I should be able to calculate my whole life for thirty years beforehand. In short, if this could be arranged there would be nothing left for us to do; anyway, we should have to understand that. And, in fact, we ought unwearyingly to repeat to ourselves that at such and such a time and in such and such circumstances nature does not ask our leave; that we have got to take her as she is and not fashion her to suit our fancy, and if we really aspire to formulas and tables of rules, and well, even . . . to the chemical retort, there's no help for it, we must accept the retort too, or else it will be accepted without our consent. . . ."

Yes, but here I come to a stop! Gentlemen, you must excuse me for being over-philosophical; it's the result of forty years underground! Allow me to indulge my fancy. You see, gentlemen, reason is an excellent thing, there's no disputing that, but reason is nothing but reason and satisfies only the rational side of man's nature, while will is a manifestation of the whole life, that is, of the whole human life including reason and all the impulses. And although our life, in this manifestation of it, is often worthless, yet it is life and not simply extracting square roots. Here I, for instance, quite naturally want to live, in order to satisfy all my capacities for life, and not simply my capacity for reasoning, that is, not simply one twentieth of my capacity for life. What does reason know? Reason only knows what it has succeeded in learning (some things, perhaps, it will never learn; this is a poor comfort, but why not say so frankly?) and human nature acts as a whole, with everything that is in it, consciously or unconsciously, and, even if it goes wrong, it lives. I suspect, gentlemen, that you are looking at me with compassion; you tell me again that an enlightened and developed man, such, in short, as the future man will be, cannot consciously desire anything disadvantageous to himself, that that can be proved mathematically. I thoroughly agree, it can—by mathematics. But I repeat for the hundredth time, there is one case, one only, when man may consciously, purposely, desire what is injurious to himself, what is stupid, very stupid—simply in order to have the right to desire for himself even what is very stupid and not to be bound by an obligation to desire only what is sensible. Of course, this very stupid thing, this caprice of ours, may be in reality, gentlemen, more advantageous for us than anything else on earth, especially in certain cases. And in particular it may be more advantageous than any advantage even when it does us obvious harm, and contradicts the soundest conclusions of our reason concerning our advantage—for in any circumstances it preserves for us what is most precious and most important—that is, our personality, our individuality. Some, you see, maintain that this really is the most precious thing for mankind; choice can, of course, if it chooses, be in agreement with reason; and especially if this be not abused but kept within bounds. It is profitable and sometimes even praiseworthy. But very often, and even most often, choice is utterly and stubbornly opposed to reason . . . and . . . and . . . do you know that that, too, is profitable, sometimes even praiseworthy? Gentlemen, let us suppose that man is not stupid. (Indeed one cannot refuse to suppose that, if only from the one consideration, that, if man is stupid, then who is wise?) But if he is not stupid, he is monstrously ungrateful! Phenomenally ungrateful. In fact, I believe that the best definition of man is the ungrateful biped. But that is not all, that is not his worst defect; his worst defect is his perpetual moral obliquity, perpetual—from the days of the Flood to the Schleswig-Holstein period. Moral obliquity and consequently lack of good sense; for it has long been accepted that lack of good sense is due to no other cause than moral obliquity. Put it to the test and cast your eyes upon the history of mankind. What will you see? Is it a grand spectacle? Grand, if you like. Take the Colossus of Rhodes,[18] for instance, that's worth something. With good reason Mr. Anaevsky[19] testifies of it that some say that it is the work of man's hands, while others maintain that it has been created by nature herself. Is it many-colored? May be it is many-colored, too: if one takes the dress uniforms, military and civilian, of all peoples in all ages—that alone is worth something, and if you take the undress uniforms you will never get to the end of it; no historian would be equal to the job. Is it monotonous? May be it's monotonous too: it's fighting and fighting; they are fighting now, they fought first and they fought last—you will admit, that it is almost too monotonous. In short, one may say anything about the history of the world—anything that might enter the most disordered imagination. The only thing one can't say is that it's rational. The very word sticks in one's throat. And, indeed, this is the odd thing that is continually happening: there are continually turning up in life moral and rational persons, sages and lovers of humanity who make it their object to live all their lives as morally and rationally as possible, to be, so to speak, a light to their neighbors simply in order to show them that it is possible to live morally and rationally in this world. And yet we all know that those very people sooner or later have been false to themselves, playing some queer trick, often a most unseemly one. Now I ask you: what can be expected of man since he is a being endowed with such strange qualities? Shower upon him every earthly blessing, drown him in a sea of happiness, so that nothing but bubbles of bliss can be seen on the surface; give him economic prosperity, such that he should have nothing else to do but sleep, eat cakes and busy himself with the continuation of his species, and even then out of sheer ingratitude, sheer spite, man would play you some nasty trick. He would even risk his cakes and would deliberately desire the most fatal rubbish, the most uneconomical absurdity, simply to introduce into all this positive good sense his fatal fantastic element. It is just his fantastic dreams, his vulgar folly that he will desire to retain, simply in order to prove to himself—as though that were so necessary—that men still are men and not the keys of a piano, which the laws of nature threaten to control so completely that soon one will be able to desire nothing but by the calendar. And that is not all: even if man were nothing but a piano-key, even if this were proved to him by natural science and mathematics, even then he would not become reasonable, but would purposely do something perverse out of simple ingratitude,

[18] Large bronze statue of the sun god Helios in Rhodes harbor. One of the ancient Seven Wonders of the World.

[19] A. E. Anaevsky (1788–1886) wrote a number of potboiler "reference" books in the 1850's and 1860's.

simply to gain his point. And if he does not find means he will contrive destruction and chaos, will contrive sufferings of all sorts, only to gain his point! He will launch a curse upon the world, and as only man can curse (it is his privilege, the primary distinction between him and other animals), may be by his curse alone he will attain his object—that is, convince himself that he is a man and not a piano-key! If you say that all this, too, can be calculated and tabulated—chaos and darkness and curses, so that the mere possibility of calculating it all beforehand would stop it all, and reason would reassert itself, then man would purposely go mad in order to be rid of reason and gain his point! I believe in it, I answer for it, for the whole work of man really seems to consist in nothing but proving to himself every minute that he is a man and not a piano-key! It may be at the cost of his skin, it may be by cannibalism! And this being so, can one help being tempted to rejoice that it has not yet come off, and that desire still depends on something we don't know?

You will scream at me (that is, if you condescend to do so) that no one is touching my free will, that all they are concerned with is that my will should of itself, of its own free will, coincide with my own normal interests, with the laws of nature and arithmetic.

Good Heavens, gentlemen, what sort of free will is left when we come to tabulation and arithmetic, when it will all be a case of twice two makes four? Twice two makes four without my will. As if free will meant that!

IX

Gentlemen, I am joking, and I know myself that my jokes are not brilliant, but you know one can't take everything as a joke. I am, perhaps, jesting against the grain. Gentlemen, I am tormented by questions; answer them for me. You, for instance, want to cure men of their old habits and reform their will in accordance with science and good sense. But how do you know, not only that it is possible, but also that it is *desirable*, to reform man in that way? And what leads you to the conclusion that man's inclinations *need* reforming? In short, how do you know that such a reformation will be a benefit to man? And to go to the root of the matter, why are you so positively convinced that not to act against his real normal interests guaranteed by the conclusions of reason and arithmetic is certainly always advantageous for man and must always be a law for mankind? So far, you know, this is only your supposition. It may be the law of logic, but not the law of humanity. You think, gentlemen, perhaps that I am mad? Allow me to defend myself. I agree that man is pre-eminently a creative animal, predestined to strive consciously for an object and to engage in engineering—that is, incessantly and eternally to make new roads, *wherever they may lead*. But the reason why he wants sometimes to go off at a tangent may just be that he is *predestined* to make the road, and perhaps, too, that however stupid the "direct" practical man may be, the thought sometimes will occur to him that the road almost always does lead *somewhere*, and that the destination it leads to is less important than the process of making it, and that the chief thing is to save the well-conducted child from despising engineering, and so giving way to the fatal idleness, which, as we all know, is the mother of all the vices. Man likes to make roads and to create, that is a fact beyond dispute. But why has he such a passionate love for destruction and chaos also? Tell me that! But on that point I want to say a couple of words myself. May it not be that he loves chaos and destruction (there can be no disputing that he does sometimes love it) because he is instinctively afraid of attaining his object and completing the edifice he is constructing? Who knows, perhaps he only loves that edifice from a distance, and is by no means in love with it at close quarters; perhaps he only loves building it and does not want to live in it, but will leave it, when completed, for the use of *les animaux domestiques*[20]—such as the ants, the sheep, and so on. Now the ants have quite a different taste. They have a marvelous edifice of that pattern which endures for ever—the ant heap.

With the ant-heap the respectable race of ants began and with the ant-heap they will probably end, which does the greatest credit to their perseverance and good sense. But man is a frivolous and incongruous creature, and perhaps, like a chess player, loves the process of the game, not the end of it. And who knows (there is no saying with certainty), perhaps the only goal on earth to which mankind is striving lies in this incessant process of attaining, in other words, in life itself, and not in the thing to be attained, which must always be expressed as a formula, as positive as twice two makes four, and such positiveness is not life, gentlemen, but is the beginning of death. Anyway, man has always been afraid of this mathematical certainty, and I am afraid of it now. Granted that man does nothing but seek that mathematical certainty, he traverses oceans, sacrifices his life in the quest, but to succeed, really to find it, he dreads, I assure you. He feels that when he has found it there will be nothing for him to look for. When workmen have finished their work they do at least receive their pay, they go to the tavern, then they are taken to the police-station—and there is occupation for a week. But where can man go? Anyway, one can observe a certain awkwardness about him when he has attained such objects. He loves the process of attaining, but does not quite like to have attained, and that, of course, is very absurd. In fact, man is a comical creature; there seems to be a kind of jest in it all. But yet mathematical certainty is, after all, something insufferable. Twice two makes four seems to me simply a piece of insolence. Twice two makes four is a pert coxcomb[21] who stands with arms akimbo barring your path and spitting. I admit that twice two makes four is an excellent thing, but if we are to give everything its due, twice two makes five is sometimes a very charming thing too.

And why are you so firmly, so triumphantly, convinced that only the normal and the positive—in other words, only what is conducive to welfare—is for the advantage of man? Is not reason in error as regards advantage? Does not man, perhaps, love something besides well-being? Perhaps he is just as fond of suffering? Perhaps suffering is just as great a benefit to him as well-being? Man is sometimes extraordinarily, passionately, in love with suffering, and that is a fact. There is no need to appeal to universal history to prove that; only ask yourself, if you are a man and have lived at all. As far as my personal opinion is concerned, to care only for well-being seems to me positively ill-bred. Whether it's good or bad, it is sometimes very pleasant, too, to smash things. I hold no brief for suffering nor for well-being either. I am standing for . . . my caprice, and for its being guar-

[20] The domestic animals (French) [21] A conceited, foolish person.

anteed to me when necessary. Suffering would be out of place in vaudevilles, for instance; I know that. In the "Crystal Palace" it is unthinkable; suffering means doubt, negation, and what would be the good of a crystal palace if there could be any doubt about it? And yet I think man will never renounce real suffering, that is, destruction and chaos. Why, suffering is the sole origin of consciousness. Though I did lay it down at the beginning that consciousness is the greatest misfortune for man, yet I know man prizes it and would not give it up for any satisfaction. Consciousness, for instance, is infinitely superior to twice two makes four. Once you have mathematical certainty there is nothing left to do or to understand. There will be nothing left but to bottle up your five senses and plunge into contemplation. While if you stick to consciousness, even though the same result is attained, you can at least flog yourself at times, and that will, at any rate, liven you up. Reactionary as it is, corporal punishment is better than nothing.

X

You believe in a crystal palace that can never be destroyed—a palace at which one will not be able to put out one's tongue or make a long nose on the sly. And perhaps that is just why I am afraid of this edifice, that it is of crystal and can never be destroyed and that one cannot put one's tongue out at it even on the sly.

You see, if it were not a palace, but a hen-house, I might creep into it to avoid getting wet, and yet I would not call the hen-house a palace out of gratitude to it for keeping me dry. You laugh and say that in such circumstances a hen-house is as good as a mansion. Yes, I answer, if one had to live simply to keep out of the rain.

But what is to be done if I have taken it into my head that that is not the only object in life, and that if one must live one had better live in a mansion. That is my choice, my desire. You will only eradicate it when you have changed my preference. Well, do change it, allure me with something else, give me another ideal. But meanwhile I will not take a hen-house for a mansion. The crystal palace may be an idle dream, it may be that it is inconsistent with the laws of nature and that I have invented it only through my own stupidity, through the old-fashioned irrational habits of my generation. But what does it matter to me that it is inconsistent? That makes no difference since it exists in my desires, or rather exists as long as my desires exist. Perhaps you are laughing again? Laugh away; I will put up with any mockery rather than pretend that I am satisfied when I am hungry. I know, anyway, that I will not be put off with a compromise, with a recurring zero, simply because it is consistent with the laws of nature and actually exists. I will not accept as the crown of my desires a block of slum tenements on a lease of a thousand years, and perhaps with a sign-board of Wagenheim the dentist hanging out. Destroy my desires, eradicate my ideals, show me something better, and I will follow you. You will say, perhaps, that it is not worth your trouble; but in that case I can give you the same answer. We are discussing things seriously; but if you won't deign to give me your attention, I will drop your acquaintance. I can retreat into my underground hole.

But while I am alive and have desires I would rather my hand were withered off than bring one brick to such a building! Don't remind me that I have just rejected the crystal palace for the sole reason that one cannot put out one's tongue at it. I did not say that because I am so fond of putting my tongue out. Perhaps the thing I resented was, that of all your edifices there has not been one at which one could not put out one's tongue. On the contrary, I would let my tongue be cut off out of gratitude if things could be so arranged that I should lose all desire to put it out. It is not my fault that things cannot be so arranged, and that one must be satisfied with model flats. Then why am I made with such desires? Can I have been constructed simply in order to come to the conclusion that all my construction is a cheat? Can this be my whole purpose? I do not believe it.

But do you know what: I am convinced that we underground folk ought to be kept on a curb. Though we may sit forty years underground without speaking, when we do come out into the light of day and break out we talk and talk and talk. . . .

XI

The long and the short of it is, gentlemen, that it is better to do nothing! Better conscious inertia! And so hurrah for underground! Though I have said that I envy the normal man to the last drop of my bile, yet I should not care to be in his place such as he is now (though I shall not cease envying him). No, no; anyway the underground life is more advantageous. There, at any rate, one can. . . . Oh, but even now I am lying! I am lying because I know myself that it is not underground that is better, but something different, quite different, for which I am thirsting, but which I cannot find! Damn underground!

I will tell you another thing that would be better, and that is, if I myself believed in anything of what I have just written. I swear to you, gentlemen, there is not one thing, not one word of what I have written that I really believe. That is, I believe it, perhaps, but at the same time I feel and suspect that I am lying like a cobbler.

"Then why have you written all this?" you will say to me. "I ought to put you underground for forty years without anything to do and then come to you in your cellar, to find out what stage you have reached! How can a man be left with nothing to do for forty years?"

"Isn't that shameful, isn't that humiliating?" you will say, perhaps, wagging your heads contemptuously. "You thirst for life and try to settle the problems of life by a logical tangle. And how persistent, how insolent are your sallies, and at the same time what a scare you are in! You talk nonsense and are pleased with it; you say impudent things and are in continual alarm and apologizing for them. You declare that you are afraid of nothing and at the same time try to ingratiate yourself in our good opinion. You declare that you are gnashing your teeth and at the same time you try to be witty so as to amuse us. You know that your witticisms are not witty, but you are evidently well satisfied with their literary value. You may, perhaps, have really suffered, but you have no respect for your own suffering. You may have sincerity, but you have no modesty; out of the pettiest vanity you expose your sincerity to publicity and ignominy. You doubtlessly mean to say something, but hide your last word through fear, because you have not the resolution to utter it, and only have a cowardly impudence. You boast of consciousness, but you are not sure of your ground, for though your mind works, yet your heart is darkened and corrupt, and you cannot have a full, genuine consciousness without a pure heart. And how intrusive you are, how you insist and grimace! Lies, lies, lies!"

Of course I have myself made up all the things you say. That, too, is from underground. I have been for forty years listening to you through a crack under the floor. I have invented them myself, there was nothing else I could invent. It is no wonder that I have learned it by heart and it has taken a literary form. . .

But can you really be so credulous as to think that I will print all this and give it to you to read too? And another problem: why do I call you "gentlemen," why do I address you as though you really were my readers? Such confessions as I intend to make are never printed nor given to other people to read. Anyway, I am not strong-minded enough for that, and I don't see why I should be. But you see a fancy has occurred to me and I want to realize it at all costs. Let me explain.

Every man has reminiscences which he would not tell to every one, but only to his friends. He has other matters in his mind which he would not reveal even to his friends, but only to himself, and that in secret. But there are other things which a man is afraid to tell even to himself, and every decent man has a number of such things stored away in his mind. The more decent he is, the greater the number of such things in his mind. Anyway, I have only lately determined to remember some of my early adventures. Till now I have always avoided them, even with a certain uneasiness. Now, when I am not only recalling them, but have actually decided to write an account of them, I want to try the experiment whether one can, even with oneself, be perfectly open and not take fright at the whole truth. I will observe, in parenthesis, that Heine[22] says that a true autobiography is almost an impossibility, and that man is bound to lie about himself. He considers that Rousseau certainly told lies about himself in his *Confessions,* and even intentionally lied, out of vanity. I am convinced that Heine is right; I quite understand how sometimes one may, out of sheer vanity, attribute regular crimes to oneself, and indeed I can very well conceive that kind of vanity. But Heine judged of people who made their confessions to the public. I write only for myself, and I wish to declare once and for all that if I write as though I were addressing readers, that is simply because it is easier for me to write in that form. It is a form, an empty form—I shall never have readers. I have made this plain already. . .

I don't wish to be hampered by any restrictions in the compilation of my notes. I shall not attempt any system or method. I will jot things down as I remember them.

But here, perhaps, some one will catch at the word and ask me: if you really don't reckon on readers, why do you make such compacts with yourself—and on paper too—that is, that you won't attempt any system or method, that you jot things down as you remember them, and so on, and so on? Why are you explaining? Why do you apologize?

Well, there it is, I answer.

[22] Heinrich Heine, German poet, who, in his *Confessions* (1854), made these comments about autobiography and about Rousseau.

There is a whole psychology in all this, though. Perhaps it is simply that I am a coward. And perhaps that I purposely imagine an audience before me in order that I may be more dignified while I write. There are perhaps thousands of reasons. Again, what is my object precisely in writing? If it is not for the benefit of the public why should I not simply recall these incidents in my own mind without putting them on paper?

Quite so; but yet it is more imposing on paper. There is something more impressive in it; I shall be better able to criticize myself and improve my style. Besides, I shall perhaps obtain actual relief from writing. Today, for instance, I am particularly oppressed by one memory of a distant past. It came back vividly to my mind a few days ago, and has remained haunting me like an annoying tune that one cannot get rid of. And yet I must get rid of it somehow. I have hundreds of such reminiscences; but at times some one stands out from the hundreds and oppresses me. For some reason I believe that if I write it down I should get rid of it. Why not try?

Besides, I am bored, and I never have anything to do. Writing will be a sort of work. They say work makes man kind-hearted and honest. Well, here is a chance for me, anyway.

Snow is falling today, yellow and dingy. It fell yesterday, too, and a few days ago. I fancy it is the wet snow that has reminded me of that incident which I cannot shake off now. And so let it be a story *à propos* of the falling snow.

PART II

A PROPOS OF THE WET SNOW

When from dark error's subjugation
My words of passionate exhortation
  Had wrenched thy fainting spirit free;
And writhing prone in thine affliction
Thou didst recall with malediction
  The vice that had encompassed thee:
And when thy slumbering conscience, fretting
  By recollection's torturing flame,
Thou didst reveal the hideous setting
  Of thy life's current ere I came:
When suddenly I saw thee sicken,
  And weeping, hide thine anguished face,
Revolted, maddened, horror-stricken,
  At memories of foul disgrace, etc., etc., etc. . . .

—NEKRASOV[23] (*translated by Juliet Soskice*)

[23] Nikolay A. Nekrasov, Russian poet and radical. The poem deals with the favorite romantic theme of the redemption of a prostitute by love, the theme Dostoevsky in Part II is to present from a devastating, "underground" point of view. The speaker breaks off the poem with an impatient "etc., etc., etc." The omitted last lines—"Into my house come bold and free, / Its rightful mistress there to be"—appear ironically later in Part II.

I

At that time I was only twenty-four. My life was even then gloomy, ill-regulated, and as solitary as that of a savage. I made friends with no one and positively avoided talking, and buried myself more and more in my hole. At work in the office I never looked at any one, and I was perfectly well aware that my companions looked upon me, not only as a queer fellow, but even looked upon me—I always fancied this—with a sort of loathing. I sometimes wondered why it was that nobody except me fancied that he was looked upon with aversion? One of the clerks had a most repulsive, pock-marked face, which looked positively villainous. I believe I should not have dared to look at any one with such an unsightly countenance. Another had such a very dirty old uniform that there was an unpleasant odor in his proximity. Yet not one of these gentlemen showed the slightest self-consciousness—either about their clothes or their countenance or their character in any way. Neither of them ever imagined that they were looked at with repulsion; if they had imagined it they would not have minded—so long as their superiors did not look at them in that way. It is clear to me now that, owing to my unbounded vanity and to the high standard I set for myself, I often looked at myself with furious discontent, which verged on loathing, and so I inwardly attributed the same feeling to every one. I hated my face, for instance: I thought it disgusting, and even suspected that there was something base in my expression, and so every day when I turned up at the office I tried to behave as independently as possible, and to assume a lofty expression, so that I might not be suspected of being abject. "My face may be ugly," I thought, "but let it be lofty, expressive, and, above all, *extremely* intelligent." But I was positively and painfully certain that it was impossible for my countenance ever to express those qualities. And what was worst of all, I thought it actually stupid looking, and I would have been quite satisfied if I could have looked intelligent. In fact, I would even have put up with looking base if, at the same time, my face could have been thought strikingly intelligent.

Of course, I hated my fellow clerks one and all, and I despised them all, yet at the same time I was, as it were, afraid of them. In fact, it happened at times that I thought more highly of them than of myself. It somehow happened quite suddenly that I alternated between despising them and thinking them superior to myself. A cultivated and decent man cannot be vain without setting a fearfully high standard for himself, and without despising and almost hating himself at certain moments. But whether I despised them or thought them superior I dropped my eyes almost every time I met any one. I even made experiments whether I could face so and so's looking at me, and I was always the first to drop my eyes. This worried me to distraction. I had a sickly dread, too, of being ridiculous, and so had a slavish passion for the conventional in everything external. I loved to fall into the common rut, and had a whole-hearted terror of any kind of eccentricity in myself. But how could I live up to it? I was morbidly sensitive, as a man of our age should be. They were all stupid, and as like one another as so many sheep. Perhaps I was the only one in the office who fancied that I was a coward and a slave, and I fancied it just because I was more highly developed. But it was not only that I fancied it, it really was so. I was a coward and a slave. I say this without the slightest embarrassment. Every decent man of our age must be a coward and a slave. That is his normal condition. Of that I am firmly persuaded. He is made and constructed to that very end. And not only at the present time owing to some casual circumstances, but always, at all times, a decent man is bound to be a coward and a slave. It is the law of nature for all decent people all over the earth. If any one of them happens to be valiant about something, he need not be comforted nor carried away by that; he would show the white feather just the same before something else. That is how it invariably and inevitably ends. Only donkeys and mules are valiant, and they only till they are pushed up to the wall. It is not worth while to pay attention to them for they really are of no consequence.

Another circumstance, too, worried me in those days: that there was no one like me and I was unlike any one else. "I am unique and they are all alike," I thought—and pondered.

From that it is evident that I was still a youngster.

The very opposite sometimes happened. It was loathsome sometimes to go to the office; things reached such a point that I often came home ill. But all at once *à propos* of nothing, there would come a phase of skepticism and indifference (everything happened in phases to me), and I would laugh myself at my intolerance and fastidiousness, I would reproach myself with being *romantic*. At one time I was unwilling to speak to any one, while at other times I would not only talk, but go to the length of contemplating making friends with them. All my fastidiousness would suddenly, for no rhyme or reason, vanish. Who knows, perhaps I never had really had it, and it had simply been affected, and got out of books. I have not decided that question even now. Once I quite made friends with them, visited their homes, played preference, drank vodka, talked of promotions. . . . But here let me make a digression.

We Russians, speaking generally, have never had those foolish transcendental "romantics"—German, and still more French—on whom nothing produces any effect; if there were an earthquake, if all France perished at the barricades, they would still be the same, they would not even have the decency to affect a change, but would still go on singing their transcendental songs to the hour of their death, because they are fools. We, in Russia, have no fools; that is well known. That is what distinguishes us from foreign lands. Consequently these transcendental natures are not found amongst us in their pure form. The idea that they are is due to our "realistic" journalists and critics of that day, always on the look out for Kostanzhoglos[24] and Uncle Pyotr Ivanichs[25] and foolishly accepting them as our ideal; they have slandered our romantics, taking them for the same transcendental sort as in Germany or France. On the contrary, the characteristics of our "romantics" are absolutely and directly opposed to the transcendental European type, and no European standard can be applied to them. (Allow me to make use of this word "romantic"—an old-fashioned and much respected word which has done good service and is familiar to

[24] An idealized landowner in Nikolai Gogol's *Dead Souls,* Part II (1851).
[25] A sympathetic character in Ivan Goncharov's *A Common Story* (1847).

all.) The characteristics of our romantic are to understand everything, *to see everything and to see it often incomparably more clearly than our most realistic minds see it;* to refuse to accept anyone or anything, but at the same time not to despise anything; to give way, to yield, from policy; never to lose sight of a useful practical object (such as rent-free quarters at the government expense, pensions, decorations), to keep their eye on that object through all the enthusiasms and volumes of lyrical poems, and at the same time to preserve "the good and the beautiful" inviolate within them to the hour of their death, and to preserve themselves also, incidentally, like some precious jewel wrapped in cotton wool if only for the benefit of "the good and the beautiful." Our "romantic" is a man of great breadth and the greatest rogue of all our rogues, I assure you. . . . I can assure you from experience, indeed. Of course, that is, if he is intelligent. But what am I saying! The romantic is always intelligent, and I only meant to observe that although we have had foolish romantics they don't count, and they were only so because in the flower of their youth they degenerated into Germans, and to preserve their precious jewel more comfortably, settled somewhere out there—by preference in Weimar or the Black Forest.[26]

I, for instance, genuinely despised my official work and did not openly abuse it simply because I was in it myself and got a salary for it. Anyway, take note, I did not openly abuse it. Our romantic would rather go out of his mind—a thing, however, which very rarely happens—than take to open abuse, unless he had some other career in view; and he is never kicked out. At most, they would take him to the lunatic asylum as "the King of Spain"[27] if he should go very mad. But it is only the thin, fair people who go out of their minds in Russia. Innumerable "romantics" attain later in life to considerable rank in the service. Their many-sidedness is remarkable! And what a faculty they have for the most contradictory sensations! I was comforted by this thought even in those days, and I am of the same opinion now. That is why there are so many "broad natures" among us who never lose their ideal even in the depths of degradation; and though they never stir a finger for their ideal, though they are arrant thieves and knaves, yet they tearfully cherish their first ideal and are extraordinarily honest at heart. Yes, it is only among us that the most incorrigible rogue can be absolutely and loftily honest at heart without in the least ceasing to be a rogue. I repeat, our romantics, frequently, become such accomplished rascals (I use the term "rascals" affectionately), suddenly display such a sense of reality and practical knowledge that their bewildered superiors and the public generally can only ejaculate in amazement.

Their many-sidedness is really amazing, and goodness knows what it may develop into later on, and what the future has in store for us. It is not a poor material! I do not say this from any foolish or boastful patriotism. But I feel sure that you are again imagining that I am joking. Or perhaps

[26]The town of Weimar, in east Germany, was the home of Johann Wolfgang von Goethe and of such other Romantics as Johann Gottfried von Herder, Friedrich von Schiller, and Franz Liszt. The Black Forest, a mountainous area in southwest Germany, was also a favorite Romantic locale because of its natural beauty.

[27]The main character in Nikolai Gogol's story "Memoirs of a Madman" (1835) believes that he is the King of Spain and ends up in a lunatic asylum.

it's just the contrary and you are convinced that I really think so. Anyway, gentlemen, I shall welcome both views as an honor and a special favor. And do forgive my digression.

I did not, of course, maintain friendly relations with my comrades and soon was at loggerheads with them, and in my youth and inexperience I even gave up bowing to them, as though I had cut off all relations. That, however, only happened to me once. As a rule, I was always alone.

In the first place I spent most of my time at home, reading. I tried to stifle all that was continually seething within me by means of external impressions. And the only external means I had was reading. Reading, of course, was a great help—exciting me, giving me pleasure and pain. But at times it bored me fearfully. One longed for movement in spite of everything, and I plunged all at once into dark, underground, loathsome vice of the pettiest kind. My wretched passions were acute, smarting, from my continual, sickly irritability, I had hysterical impulses, with tears and convulsions. I had no resource except reading, that is, there was nothing in my surroundings which I could respect and which attracted me. I was overwhelmed with depression, too; I had a hysterical craving for incongruity and for contrast, and so I took to vice. I have not said all this to justify myself. . . . But, no! I am lying. I did want to justify myself. I make that little observation for my own benefit, gentlemen. I don't want to lie. I vowed to myself I would not.

And so, furtively, timidly, in solitude, at night, I indulged in filthy vice, with a feeling of shame which never deserted me, even at the most loathsome moments, and which at such moments nearly made me curse. Already even then I had my underground world in my soul. I was fearfully afraid of being seen, of being met, of being recognized. I visited various obscure haunts.

One night as I was passing a tavern I saw through a lighted window some gentlemen fighting with billiard cues, and saw one of them thrown out of a window. At other times I should have felt very much disgusted, but I was in such a mood at the time, that I actually envied the gentleman thrown out of a window—and I envied him so much that I even went into the tavern and into the billiard-room. "Perhaps," I thought, "I'll have a fight, too, and they'll throw me out of the window."

I was not drunk—but what is one to do—depression will drive a man to such a pitch of hysteria? But nothing happened. It seemed that I was not even equal to being thrown out of the window and I went away without having my fight.

An officer put me in my place from the first moment.

I was standing by the billiard-table and in my ignorance blocking up the way, and he wanted to pass; he took me by the shoulders and without a word—without a warning or explanation—moved me from where I was standing to another spot and passed by as though he had not noticed me. I could have forgiven blows, but I could not forgive his having moved me without noticing me.

Devil knows what I would have given for a real regular quarrel—a more decent, a more *literary* one, so to speak. I had been treated like a fly. This officer was over six foot, while I was a spindly little fellow. But the quarrel was in my hands. I had only to protest and I certainly would have been thrown out of the window. But I changed my mind and preferred to beat a resentful retreat.

I went out of the tavern straight home, confused and troubled, and the next night I went out again with the same lewd intentions, still more furtively, abjectly and miserably than before, as it were, with tears in my eyes—but still I did go out again. Don't imagine, though, it was cowardice made me slink away from the officer: I never have been a coward at heart, though I have always been a coward in action. Don't be in a hurry to laugh—I assure you I can explain it all.

Oh, if only that officer had been one of the sort who would consent to fight a duel! But no, he was one of those gentlemen (alas, long extinct!) who preferred fighting with cues or, like Gogol's Lieutenant Pirogov,[28] appealing to the police. They did not fight duels and would have thought a duel with a civilian like me an utterly unseemly procedure in any case—and they looked upon the duel altogether as something impossible, something free-thinking and French. But they were quite ready to bully, especially when they were over six foot.

I did not slink away through cowardice, but through an unbounded vanity. I was afraid not of his six foot, not of getting a sound thrashing and being thrown out of the window; I should have had physical courage enough, I assure you; but I had not the moral courage. What I was afraid of was that every one present, from the insolent marker down to the lowest little stinking, pimply clerk in a greasy collar, would jeer at me and fail to understand when I began to protest and to address them in literary language. For of the point of honor—not of honor, but of the point of honor (*point d'honneur*)—one cannot speak among us except in literary language. You can't allude to the "point of honor" in ordinary language. I was fully convinced (the sense of reality, in spite of all my romanticism!) that they would all simply split their sides with laughter, and that the officer would not simply beat me, that is, without insulting me, but would certainly prod me in the back with his knee, kick me round the billiard-table, and only then perhaps have pity and drop me out of the window.

Of course, this trivial incident could not with me end in that. I often met that officer afterwards in the street and noticed him very carefully. I am not quite sure whether he recognized me, I imagine not; I judge from certain signs. But I—I stared at him with spite and hatred and so it went on . . . for several years! My resentment grew even deeper with years. At first I began making stealthy inquiries about this officer. It was difficult for me to do so, for I knew no one. But one day I heard some one shout his surname in the street as I was following him at a distance, as though I were tied to him—and so I learnt his surname. Another time I followed him to his flat, and for ten kopecks learned from the porter where he lived, on which story, whether he lived alone or with others, and so on—in fact, everything one could learn from a porter. One morning, though I had never tried my hand with the pen, it suddenly occurred to me to write a satire on this officer in the form of a novel which would unmask his villainy. I wrote the novel with relish. I did unmask his villainy, I even exaggerated it; at first I so altered his surname that it could easily be recognized,

[28] This incident occurs in Nikolai Gogol's story "The Nevsky Prospect" (1835).

but on second thoughts I changed it, and sent the story to the *Otechestvenniye Zapiski.*[29] But at that time such attacks were not the fashion and my story was not printed. That was a great vexation to me.

Sometimes I was positively choked with resentment. At last I determined to challenge my enemy to a duel. I composed a splendid, charming letter to him, imploring him to apologize to me, and hinting rather plainly at a duel in case of refusal. The letter was so composed that if the officer had had the least understanding of the good and the beautiful he would certainly have flung himself on my neck and have offered me his friendship. And how fine that would have been! How we should have got on together! "He could have shielded me with his higher rank, while I could have improved his mind with my culture, and, well . . . my ideas, and all sorts of things might have happened." Only fancy, this was two years after his insult to me, and my challenge would have been a ridiculous anachronism, in spite of all the ingenuity of my letter in disguising and explaining away the anachronism. But, thank God (to this day I thank the Almighty with tears in my eyes) I did not send the letter to him. Cold shivers run down my back when I think of what might have happened if I had sent it.

And all at once I revenged myself in the simplest way, by a stroke of genius! A brilliant thought suddenly dawned upon me. Sometimes on holidays I used to stroll along the sunny side of the Nevsky[30] about four o'clock in the afternoon. Though it was hardly a stroll so much as a series of innumerable miseries, humiliations and resentments; but no doubt that was just what I wanted. I used to wriggle along in a most unseemly fashion, like an eel, continually moving aside to make way for generals, for officers of the guards and the hussars, or for ladies. At such minutes there used to be a convulsive twinge at my heart, and I used to feel hot all down my back at the mere thought of the wretchedness of my attire, of the wretchedness and abjectness of my little scurrying figure. This was a regular martyrdom, a continual, intolerable humiliation at the thought, which passed into an incessant and direct sensation, that I was a mere fly in the eyes of all this world, a nasty, disgusting fly—more intelligent, more highly developed, more refined in feeling than any of them, of course—but a fly that was continually making way for every one, insulted and injured by every one. Why I inflicted this torture upon myself, why I went to the Nevsky, I don't know. I felt simply drawn there at every possible opportunity.

Already then I began to experience a rush of the enjoyment of which I spoke in the first chapter. After my affair with the officer I felt even more drawn there than before: it was on the Nevsky that I met him most frequently, there I could admire him. He, too, went there chiefly on holidays. He, too, turned out of his path for generals and persons of high rank, and he, too, wriggled between them like an eel; but people, like me, or even better dressed than me, he simply walked over; he made straight for them as though there was nothing but empty space before him, and never, under any circumstances, turned aside. I gloated over my resentment watching him and . . . always resentfully made way for him. It exasperated me that even in the street I could not be on an even footing with him.

[29] A well-known radical Russian journal. The title means *Notes of the Fatherland.*
[30] Nevsky Prospect, the fashionable main street of St. Petersburg.

"Why must you invariably be the first to move aside?" I kept asking myself in hysterical rage, waking up sometimes at three o'clock in the morning. "Why is it you and not he? There's no regulation about it; there's no written law. Let the making way be equal as it usually is when refined people meet: he moves half-way and you move half-way; you pass with mutual respect."

But that never happened, and I always moved aside, while he did not even notice my making way for him. And lo and behold a bright idea dawned upon me! "What," I thought, "if I meet him and don't move on one side? What if I don't move aside on purpose, even if I knock up against him? How would that be?" This audacious idea took such a hold on me that it gave me no peace. I was dreaming of it continually, horribly, and I purposely went more frequently to the Nevsky in order to picture more vividly how I should do it when I did do it. I was delighted. This intention seemed to me more and more practical and possible.

"Of course I shall not really push him," I thought, already more good-natured in my joy. "I will simply not turn aside, will run up against him, not very violently, but just shouldering each other—just as much as decency permits. I will push against him just as much as he pushes against me." At last I made up my mind completely. But my preparations took a great deal of time. To begin with, when I carried out my plan I should need to be looking rather more decent, and so I had to think of my get-up. "In case of emergency, if, for instance, there were any sort of public scandal (and the public there is of the most *recherché:*[31] the Countess walks there; Prince D. walks there; all the literary world is there), I must be well dressed; that inspires respect and of itself puts us on an equal footing in the eyes of society."

With this object I asked for some of my salary in advance, and bought at Churkin's a pair of black gloves and a decent hat. Black gloves seemed to me both more dignified and *bon ton*[32] than the lemon-colored ones which I had contemplated at first. "The color is too gaudy, it looks as though one were trying to be conspicuous," and I did not take the lemon-colored ones. I had got ready long beforehand a good shirt, with white bone studs; my overcoat was the only thing that held me back. The coat in itself was a very good one, it kept me warm; but it was wadded and it had a raccoon collar which was the height of vulgarity. I had to change the collar at any sacrifice, and to have a beaver one like an officer's. For this purpose I began visiting the Gostiny Dvor[33] and after several attempts I pitched upon a piece of cheap German beaver. Though these German beavers soon grow shabby and look wretched, yet at first they look exceedingly well, and I only needed it for one occasion. I asked the price; even so, it was too expensive. After thinking it over thoroughly I decided to sell my raccoon collar. The rest of the money—a considerable sum for me, I decided to borrow from Anton Antonich Syetochkin, my immediate superior, an unassuming person, though grave and judicious. He never lent money to any one, but I had, on entering the service, been specially recommended to him by an important personage who had got me my berth. I was horribly worried. To

[31] Exquisite, exceedingly refined (French)
[32] Literally, "good tone" (French); tasteful, fashionable. [33] Market for foreign goods.

borrow from Anton Antonich seemed to me monstrous and shameful. I did not sleep for two or three nights. Indeed, I did not sleep well at that time, I was in a fever; I had a vague sinking at my heart or else a sudden throbbing, throbbing, throbbing! Anton Antonich was surprised at first, then he frowned, then he reflected, and did after all lend me the money, receiving from me a written authorization to take from my salary a fortnight later the sum that he had lent me.

In this way everything was at last ready. The handsome beaver replaced the mean-looking raccoon, and I began by degrees to get to work. It would never have done to act off-hand, at random; the plan had to be carried out skillfully, by degrees. But I must confess that after many efforts I began to despair: we simply could not run into each other. I made every preparation, I was quite determined—it seemed as though we should run into one another directly—and before I knew what I was doing I had stepped aside for him again and he had passed without noticing me. I even prayed as I approached him that God would grant me determination. One time I had made up my mind thoroughly, but it ended in my stumbling and falling at his feet because at the very last instant when I was six inches from him my courage failed me. He very calmly stepped over me, while I flew on one side like a ball. That night I was ill again, feverish and delirious.

And suddenly it ended most happily. The night before I had made up my mind not to carry out my fatal plan and to abandon it all, and with that object I went to the Nevsky for the last time, just to see how I would abandon it all. Suddenly, three paces from my enemy, I unexpectedly made up my mind—I closed my eyes, and we ran full tilt, shoulder to shoulder, against one another! I did not budge an inch and passed him on a perfectly equal footing! He did not even look round and pretended not to notice it; but he was only pretending, I am convinced of that. I am convinced of that to this day! Of course, I got the worst of it—he was stronger, but that was not the point. The point was that I had attained my object, I had kept up my dignity, I had not yielded a step, and had put myself publicly on an equal social footing with him. I returned home feeling that I was fully avenged for everything. I was delighted. I was triumphant and sang Italian arias. Of course, I will not describe to you what happened to me three days later; if you have read my first chapter you can guess that for yourself. The officer was afterwards transferred; I have not seen him now for fourteen years. What is the dear fellow doing now? Whom is he walking over?

II

But the period of my dissipation would end and I always felt very sick afterwards. It was followed by remorse—I tried to drive it away: I felt too sick. By degrees, however, I grew used to that too. I grew used to everything, or rather I voluntarily resigned myself to enduring it. But I had a means of escape that reconciled everything—that was to find refuge in "the good and the beautiful," in dreams, of course. I was a terrible dreamer, I would dream for three months on end, tucked away in my corner, and you may believe me that at those moments I had no resemblance to the gentleman who, in the perturbation of his chicken heart, put a collar of German beaver on his great coat. I suddenly became a hero. I would not have admitted my six-foot lieutenant even if he had called on me. I could not even picture him before me then. What were my dreams and how I could satisfy myself with them—it is hard to say now, but at the time I was satisfied with them. Though, indeed, even now, I am to some extent satisfied with them. Dreams were particularly sweet and vivid after a spell of dissipation; they came with remorse and with tears, with curses and transports. There were moments of such positive intoxication, of such happiness, that there was not the faintest trace of irony within me, on my honor. I had faith, hope, love. I believed blindly at such times that by some miracle, by some external circumstance, all this would suddenly open out, expand; that suddenly a vista of suitable activity—beneficent, good, and, above all, *ready made* (what sort of activity I had no idea, but the great thing was that it should be all ready for me)—would rise up before me—and I should come out into the light of day, almost riding a white horse and crowned with laurel. Anything but the foremost place I could not conceive for myself, and for that very reason I quite contentedly occupied the lowest in reality. Either to be a hero or to grovel in the mud—there was nothing between. That was my ruin, for when I was in the mud I comforted myself with the thought that at other times I was a hero, and the hero was a cloak for the mud: for an ordinary man it was shameful to defile himself, but a hero was too lofty to be utterly defiled, and so he might defile himself. It is worth noting that these attacks of the "good and the beautiful" visited me even during the period of dissipation and just at the times when I was touching bottom. They came in separate spurts, as though reminding me of themselves, but did not banish the dissipation by their appearance. On the contrary, they seemed to add a zest to it by contrast, and were only sufficiently present to serve as an appetizing sauce. That sauce was made up of contradictions and sufferings, of agonizing inward analysis, and all these pangs and pinpricks gave a certain piquancy, even a significance to my dissipation—in fact, completely answered the purpose of an appetizing sauce. There was a certain depth of meaning in it. And I could hardly have resigned myself to the simple, vulgar, direct debauchery of a clerk and have endured all the filthiness of it. What could have allured me about it then and have drawn me at night into the street? No, I had a lofty way of getting out of it all.

And what loving-kindness, oh Lord, what loving-kindness I felt at times in those dreams of mine! in those "flights into the good and the beautiful"; though it was fantastic love, though it was never applied to anything human in reality, yet there was so much of this love that one did not feel afterwards even the impulse to apply it in reality; that would have been superfluous. Everything, however, passed satisfactorily by a lazy and fascinating transition into the sphere of art, that is, into the beautiful forms of life, lying ready, largely stolen from the poets and novelists and adapted to all sorts of needs and uses. I, for instance, was triumphant over every one; every one, of course, was in dust and ashes, and was forced spontaneously to recognize my superiority, and I forgave them all. I was a poet and a grand gentleman, I fell in love; I came in for countless millions and immediately devoted them to humanity, and at the same time I confessed before all the people my shameful deeds, which, of course, were not merely shameful, but had in them much that was "good and beautiful" something in the Manfred style.[34] Every one would kiss me and weep (what idiots they would be if they did not), while I should go barefoot and hungry preaching new ideas and fighting a victorious Austerlitz[35] against the obscurantists. Then the band would play a march, an amnesty would be declared, the Pope would agree to retire from Rome to Brazil; then there would be a ball for the whole of Italy at the Villa Borghese[36] on the shores of the Lake of Como,[37] the Lake of Como being for that purpose transferred to the neighborhood of Rome; then would come a scene in the bushes, and so on, and so on—as though you did not know all about it? You will say that it is vulgar and contemptible to drag all this into public after all the tears and transports which I have myself confessed. But why is it contemptible? Can you imagine that I am ashamed of it all, and that it was stupider than anything in your life, gentlemen? And I can assure you that some of these fancies were by no means badly composed. . . . It did not all happen on the shores of Lake Como. And yet you are right—it really is vulgar and contemptible. And most contemptible of all it is that now I am attempting to justify myself to you. And even more contemptible than that is my making this remark now. But that's enough, or there will be no end to it: each step will be more contemptible than the last. . . .

I could never stand more than three months of dreaming at a time without feeling an irresistible desire to plunge into society. To plunge into society meant to visit my superior at the office, Anton Antonich Syetochkin. He was the only permanent acquaintance I have had in my life, and wonder at the fact myself now. But I only went to see him when that phase came over me, and when my dreams had reached such a point of bliss that it became essential at once to embrace my fellows and all mankind; and for that purpose I needed, at least, one human being, actually existing. I had to call on Anton Antonich, however, on Tuesday—his at-home day; so I had always to time my passionate desire to embrace humanity so that it might fall on a Tuesday.

This Anton Antonich lived on the fourth story in a house in Five Corners, in four low-pitched rooms, one smaller than the other, of a particularly frugal and sallow appearance. He had two daughters and their aunt, who used to pour out the tea. Of the daughters one was thirteen and another fourteen, they both had snub noses, and I was awfully shy of them because they were always whispering and giggling together. The master of the house usually sat in his study on a leather couch in front of the table with some gray-headed gentleman, usually a colleague from our office or some other department. I never saw more than two or three visitors there, always the same. They talked about the excise duty; about business in the Senate,[38] about salaries, about promotions, about His Excellency, and the best means of pleasing him, and so on. I had the patience to sit like a fool beside these people for four hours at a stretch, listening to them without knowing what to say to them or venturing to say a word. I became stupe-

[34] Manfred, the title hero of Byron's play (1817), has committed unspecified sins which serve to make him even more romantic and attractive.

[35] Battle in which Napoleon defeated the combined Austrian and Russian armies in 1805.

[36] In Rome. [37] Between Italy and Switzerland. [38] A high court.

fied, several times I felt myself perspiring, I was overcome by a sort of paralysis; but this was pleasant and good for me. On returning home I deferred for a time my desire to embrace all mankind.

I had however one other acquaintance of a sort, Simonov, who was an old schoolfellow. I had a number of schoolfellows, indeed, in Petersburg, but I did not associate with them and had even given up nodding to them in the street. I believe I had transferred into the department I was in simply to avoid their company and to cut off all connection with my hateful childhood. Curses on that school and all those terrible years of penal servitude! In short, I parted from my schoolfellows as soon as I got out into the world. There were two or three left to whom I nodded in the street. One of them was Simonov, who had been in no way distinguished at school, was of a quiet and equable disposition; but I discovered in him a certain independence of character and even honesty. I don't even suppose that he was particularly stupid. I had at one time spent some rather soulful moments with him, but these had not lasted long and had somehow been suddenly clouded over. He was evidently uncomfortable at these reminiscences, and was, I fancy, always afraid that I might take up the same tone again. I suspected that he had an aversion for me, but still I went on going to see him, not being quite certain of it.

And so on one occasion, unable to endure my solitude and knowing that as it was Thursday Anton Antonich's door would be closed, I thought of Simonov. Climbing up to his fourth story I was thinking that the man disliked me and that it was a mistake to go and see him. But as it always happened that such reflections impelled me, as though purposely, to put myself into a false position, I went in. It was almost a year since I had last seen Simonov.

III

I found two of my old schoolfellows with him. They seemed to be discussing an important matter. All of them took scarcely any notice of my entrance, which was strange, for I had not met them for years. Evidently they looked upon me as something on the level of a common fly. I had not been treated like that even at school, though they all hated me. I knew, of course, that they must despise me now for my lack of success in the service, and for my having let myself sink so low, going about badly dressed and so on—which seemed to them a sign of my incapacity and insignificance. But I had not expected such contempt. Simonov was positively surprised at my turning up. Even in old days he had always seemed surprised at my coming. All this disconcerted me: I sat down, feeling rather miserable, and began listening to what they were saying.

They were engaged in warm and earnest conversation about a farewell dinner which they wanted to arrange for the next day to a comrade of theirs called Zverkov, an officer in the army, who was going away to a distant province. This Zverkov had been all the time at school with me too. I had begun to hate him particularly in the upper grades. In the lower grades he had simply been a pretty, playful boy whom everybody liked. I had hated him, however, even in the lower grades, just because he was a pretty and playful boy. He was always bad at his lessons and got worse and worse as he went on; however, he left with a good certificate, as he had powerful interest. During his last year at school he came in for an estate of two hundred serfs, and as almost all of us were poor he took up a swaggering tone among us. He was vulgar in the extreme, but at the same time he was a good-natured fellow, even in his swaggering. In spite of superficial, fantastic and sham notions of honor and dignity, all but very few of us positively grovelled before Zverkov, and the more so the more he swaggered. And it was not from any interested motive that they grovelled, but simply because he had been favored by the gifts of nature. Moreover, it was, as it were, an accepted idea among us that Zverkov was a specialist in regard to tact and the social graces. This last fact particularly infuriated me. I hated the abrupt self-confident tone of his voice, his admiration of his own witticisms, which were often frightfully stupid, though he was bold in his language; I hated his handsome, but stupid face (for which I would, however, have gladly exchanged my intelligent one), and the free-and-easy military manners in fashion in the 'forties. I hated the way in which he used to talk of his future conquests of women (he did not venture to begin his attack upon women until he had the epaulettes of an officer, and was looking forward to them with impatience), and boasted of the duels he would constantly be fighting. I remember how I, invariably so taciturn, suddenly fastened upon Zverkov, when one day talking at a leisure moment with his schoolfellows of his future relations with the fair sex, and growing as sportive as a puppy in the sun, he all at once declared that he would not leave a single village girl on his estate unnoticed, that that was his *droit de seigneur,*[39] and that if the peasants dared to protest he would have them all flogged and double the tax on them, the bearded rascals. Our servile rabble applauded, but I attacked him, not from compassion for the girls and their fathers, but simply because they were applauding such an insect. I got the better of him on that occasion, but though Zverkov was stupid he was lively and impudent, and so laughed it off, and in such a way that my victory was not really complete: the laugh was on his side. He got the better of me on several occasions afterwards, but without malice, jestingly, casually. I remained angrily and contemptuously silent and would not answer him. When we left school he made advances to me; I did not rebuff them, for I was flattered, but we soon parted and quite naturally. Afterwards I heard of his barrack-room success as a lieutenant, and of the fast life he was leading. Then there came other rumors—of his successes in the service. By then he had taken to cutting me in the street, and I suspected that he was afraid of compromising himself by greeting a personage as insignificant as me. I saw him once in the theater, in the third tier of boxes. By then he was wearing shoulder-straps. He was twisting and twirling about, ingratiating himself with the daughters of an ancient General. In three years he had gone off considerably, though he was still rather handsome and adroit. One could see that by the time he was thirty he would be corpulent. So it was to this Zverkov that my school-fellows were going to give a dinner on his departure. They had kept up with him for those three years, though privately they did not consider themselves on an equal footing with him, I am convinced of that.

Of Simonov's two visitors, one was Ferfichkin, a Russianized German—

[39] "The right of the master," that is, to all the peasant women (French).

a little fellow with the face of a monkey, a blockhead who was always deriding every one, a very bitter enemy of mine from our days in the lower grades—a vulgar, impudent, swaggering fellow, who affected a most sensitive feeling of personal honor, though, of course, he was a wretched little coward at heart. He was one of those worshippers of Zverkov who made up to the latter from interested motives, and often borrowed money from him. Simonov's other visitor, Trudolyubov, was a person in no way remarkable—a tall young fellow, in the army, with a cold face, fairly honest, though he worshipped success of every sort, and was only capable of thinking of promotion. He was some sort of distant relation of Zverkov's, and this, foolish as it seems, gave him a certain importance among us. He always thought me of no consequence whatever; his behavior to me, though not quite courteous, was tolerable.

"Well, with seven roubles each," said Trudolyubov, "twenty-one roubles between the three of us, we ought to be able to get a good dinner. Zverkov, of course, won't pay."

"Of course not, since we are inviting him," Simonov decided.

"Can you imagine," Ferfichkin interrupted hotly and conceitedly, like some insolent flunky boasting of his master the General's decorations, "can you imagine that Zverkov will let us pay alone? He will accept from delicacy, but he will order half a dozen bottles of champagne."

"Do we want half a dozen for the four of us?" observed Trudolyubov, taking notice only of the half dozen.

"So the three of us, with Zverkov for the fourth, twenty-one roubles, at the Hôtel de Paris at five o'clock tomorrow," Simonov, who had been asked to make the arrangements, concluded finally.

"How twenty-one roubles?" I asked in some agitation, with a show of being offended; "if you count me it will not be twenty-one, but twenty-eight roubles."

It seemed to me that to invite myself so suddenly and unexpectedly would be positively graceful, and that they would all be conquered at once and would look at me with respect.

"Do you want to join, too?" Simonov observed, with no appearance of pleasure, seeming to avoid looking at me. He knew me through and through.

It infuriated me that he knew me so thoroughly.

"Why not? I am an old schoolfellow of his, too, I believe, and I must own I feel hurt that you have left me out," I said, boiling over again.

"And where were we to find you?" Ferfichkin put in roughly.

"You never were on good terms with Zverkov," Trudolyubov added, frowning.

But I had already clutched at the idea and would not give it up.

"It seems to me that no one has a right to form an opinion upon that," I retorted in a shaking voice, as though something tremendous had happened. "Perhaps that is just my reason for wishing it now, that I have not always been on good terms with him."

"Oh, there's no making you out . . . with these refinements," Trudolyubov jeered.

"We'll put your name down," Simonov decided, addressing me. "Tomorrow at five o'clock at the Hôtel de Paris."

"What about the money?" Ferfichkin began in an undertone, indicating me to Simonov, but he broke off, for even Simonov was embarrassed.

"That will do," said Trudolyubov, getting up. "If he wants to come so much, let him."

"But it's a private thing, between us friends," Ferfichkin said crossly, as he, too, picked up his hat. "It's not an official gathering."

"We do not want at all, perhaps . . ."

They went away. Ferfichkin did not greet me in any way as he went out, Trudolyubov barely nodded. Simonov, with whom I was left *tête-à-tête*, was in a state of vexation and perplexity, and looked at me queerly. He did not sit down and did not ask me to.

"H'm . . . yes . . . tomorrow, then. Will you pay your subscription now? I just ask so as to know," he muttered in embarrassment.

I flushed crimson, and as I did so I remembered that I had owed Simonov fifteen roubles for ages which I had, indeed, never forgotten, though I had not paid it.

"You will understand, Simonov, that I could have no idea when I came here. . . . I am very much vexed that I have forgotten. . . ."

"All right, all right, that doesn't matter. You can pay tomorrow after the dinner. I simply wanted to know. . . . Please don't . . ."

He broke off and began pacing the room still more vexed. As he walked he began to stamp with his heels.

"Am I keeping you?" I asked, after two minutes of silence.

"Oh!" he said, starting, "that is—to be truthful—yes. I have to go and see some one . . . not far from here," he added in an apologetic voice, somewhat abashed.

"My goodness, why didn't you say so?" I cried, seizing my cap, with an astonishingly free-and-easy air, which was the last thing I should have expected of myself.

"It's close by . . . not two paces away," Simonov repeated, accompanying me to the front door with a fussy air which did not suit him at all. "So five o'clock, punctually, tomorrow," he called down the stairs after me. He was very glad to get rid of me. I was in a fury.

"What possessed me, what possessed me to force myself upon them?" I wondered, grinding my teeth as I strode along the street, "for a scoundrel, a pig like that Zverkov! Of course, I had better not go; of course, I must just snap my fingers at them. I am not bound in any way. I'll send Simonov a note by tomorrow's post. . . ."

But what made me furious was that I knew for certain that I should go, that I should make a point of going; and the more tactless, the more unseemly my going would be, the more certainly I would go.

And there was a positive obstacle to my going: I had no money. All I had was nine roubles, I had to give seven of that to my servant, Apollon, for his monthly wages. That was all I paid him—he had to keep himself.

Not to pay him was impossible, considering his character. But I will talk about that fellow, about that plague of mine, another time.

However, I knew I should go and should not pay him his wages.

That night I had the most hideous dreams. No wonder; all the evening I had been oppressed by memories of my miserable days at school, and I could not shake them off. I was sent to the school by distant relations, upon whom I was dependent and of whom I have heard nothing since—they sent me there a forlorn, silent boy, already crushed by their reproaches, already troubled by doubt, and looking with savage distrust at every one. My schoolfellows met me with spiteful and merciless jibes because I was not like any of them. But I could not endure their taunts; I could not give in to them with the ignoble readiness with which they gave in to one another. I hated them from the first, and shut myself away from every one in timid, wounded and disproportionate pride. Their coarseness revolted me. They laughed cynically at my face, at my clumsy figure; and yet what stupid faces they had themselves. In our school the boys' faces seemed in a special way to degenerate and grow stupider. How many fine-looking boys came to us! In a few years they became repulsive. Even at sixteen I wondered at them morosely; even then I was struck by the pettiness of their thoughts, the stupidity of their pursuits, their games, their conversations. They had no understanding of such essential things, they took no interest in such striking, impressive subjects, that I could not help considering them inferior to myself. It was not wounded vanity that drove me to it, and for God's sake do not thrust upon me your hackneyed remarks, repeated to nausea, that "I was only a dreamer," while they even then had an understanding of life. They understood nothing, they had no idea of real life, and I swear that that was what made me most indignant with them. On the contrary, the most obvious, striking reality they accepted with fantastic stupidity and even at that time were accustomed to respect success. Everything that was just, but oppressed and looked down upon, they laughed at heartlessly and shamefully. They took rank for intelligence; even at sixteen they were already talking about a snug berth. Of course, a great deal of it was due to their stupidity, to the bad examples with which they had always been surrounded in their childhood and boyhood. They were monstrously depraved. Of course a great deal of that, too, was superficial and an assumption of cynicism; of course there were glimpses of youth and freshness even in their depravity; but even that freshness was not attractive, and showed itself in a certain rakishness. I hated them horribly, though perhaps I was worse than any of them. They repaid me in the same way, and did not conceal their aversion for me. But by then I did not desire their affection: on the contrary I continually longed for their humiliation. To escape from their derision I purposely began to make all the progress I could with my studies and forced my way to the very top. This impressed them. Moreover, they all began by degrees to grasp that I had already read books none of them could read, and understood things (not forming part of our school curriculum) of which they had not even heard. They took a savage and sarcastic view of it, but were morally impressed, especially as the teachers began to notice me on those grounds. The mockery ceased, but the hostility remained, and cold and strained relations became permanent between us. In the end I could not put up with it: with years a craving for society, for friends, developed in me. I attempted to get on friendly terms with some of my schoolfellows; but somehow or other my intimacy with them was always strained and soon ended of itself. Once, indeed, I did have a friend. But I was already a tyrant at heart; I wanted to exercise unbounded sway over him; I tried to instill into him a contempt for his surroundings; I required of him a disdainful and complete break with those surroundings. I frightened him with my passionate affection; I reduced him to tears, to hysterics. He was a simple and devoted soul; but when he devoted himself to me entirely I began to hate him immediately and repulsed him—as though all I needed him for was to win a victory over him, to subjugate him and nothing else. But I could not subjugate all of them; my friend was not at all like them either, he was, in fact, a rare exception. The first thing I did on leaving school was to give up the special job for which I had been destined so as to break all ties, to curse my past and shake the dust from off my feet. . . . And goodness knows why, after all that, I should go trudging off to Simonov's!

Early next morning I roused myself and jumped out of bed with excitement, as though it were all about to happen at once. But I believed that some radical change in my life was coming, and would inevitably come that day. Owing to its rarity, perhaps, any external event, however trivial, always made me feel as though some radical change in my life were at hand. I went to the office, however, as usual, but sneaked away home two hours earlier to get ready. The great thing, I thought, is not to be the first to arrive, or they will think I am overjoyed at coming. But there were thousands of such great points to consider, and they all agitated and overwhelmed me. I polished my boots a second time with my own hands; nothing in the world would have induced Apollon to clean them twice a day, as he considered that it was more than his duties required of him. I stole the brushes to clean them from the passage, being careful he should not detect it, for fear of his contempt. Then I minutely examined my clothes and thought that everything looked old, worn and threadbare. I had let myself get too slovenly. My uniform, perhaps, was tidy, but I could not go out to dinner in my uniform. The worst of it was that on the knee of my trousers was a big yellow stain. I had a foreboding that that stain would deprive me of nine-tenths of my personal dignity. I knew, too, that it was very bad to think so. "But this is no time for thinking: now I am in for the real thing," I thought, and my heart sank. I knew, too, perfectly well even then, that I was monstrously exaggerating the facts. But how could I help it? I could not control myself and was already shaking with fever. With despair I pictured to myself how coldly and disdainfully that "scoundrel" Zverkov would meet me; with what dull-witted, invincible contempt the blockhead Trudolyubov would look at me; with what impudent rudeness the insect Ferfichkin would snigger at me in order to curry favor with Zverkov; how completely Simonov would take it all in, and how he would despise me for the abjectness of my vanity and lack of spirit—and, worst of all, how paltry, *unliterary,* commonplace it would all be. Of course, the best thing would be not to go at all. But that was most impossible of all: if I feel impelled to do anything, I seem to be pitchforked into it. I should have jeered at myself ever afterwards: "So you funked it, you funked it, you funked the *real thing!*" On the contrary, I passionately longed to show all that "rabble" that I was by no means such a spiritless creature as I seemed to myself. What is more, even in the acutest paroxysm of this cowardly fever, I dreamed of getting the upper hand, of dominating them, carrying them away, making them like me—if only for my "elevation of thought and unmistakable wit." They would abandon Zverkov, he would sit on one side, silent and ashamed, while I should crush him. Then, perhaps, we would be reconciled and drink to our everlasting friendship; but what was most bitter and most humiliating for me was that I knew even then, knew fully and for certain, that I needed nothing of all this really, that I did not really want to crush, to subdue, to attract them, and that I did not care a straw really for the result, even if I did achieve it. Oh, how I prayed for the day to pass quickly! In unutterable anguish I went to the window, opened the movable pane and looked out into the troubled darkness of the thickly falling wet snow. At last my wretched little clock hissed out five. I seized my hat and trying not to look at Apollon, who had been all day expecting his month's wages, but in his foolishness was unwilling to be the first to speak about it, I slipped between him and the door and jumping into a high-class sledge, on which I spent my last half rouble, I drove up in grand style to the Hôtel de Paris.

IV

I had been certain the day before that I should be the first to arrive. But it was not a question of being the first to arrive. Not only were they not there, but I had difficulty in finding our room. The table was not laid even. What did it mean? After a good many questions I elicited from the waiters that the dinner had been ordered not for five, but for six o'clock. This was confirmed at the buffet too. I felt really ashamed to go on questioning them. It was only twenty-five minutes past five. If they changed the dinner hour they ought at least to have let me know—that is what the post is for, and not to have put me in an absurd position in my own eyes and . . . and even before the waiters. I sat down; the servant began laying the table; I felt even more humiliated when he was present. Towards six o'clock they brought in candles, though there were lamps burning in the room. It had not occurred to the waiter, however, to bring them in at once when I arrived. In the next room two gloomy, angry-looking persons were eating their dinners in silence at two different tables. There was a great deal of noise, even shouting, in a room further away; one could hear the laughter of a crowd of people, and nasty little shrieks in French: there were ladies at the dinner. It was sickening, in fact. I rarely passed more unpleasant moments, so much so that when they did arrive all together punctually at six I was overjoyed to see them, as though they were my deliverers, and even forgot that it was incumbent upon me to show resentment.

Zverkov walked in at the head of them; evidently he was the leading spirit. He and all of them were laughing; but, seeing me, Zverkov drew himself up a little, walked up to me deliberately with a slight, rather jauntly bend from the waist. He shook hands with me in a friendly, but not overfriendly, fashion, with a sort of circumspect courtesy like that of a General, as though in giving me his hand he were warding off something. I had imagined, on the contrary, that on coming in he would at once break into his habitual thin, shrill laugh and fall to making his insipid jokes and witticisms. I had been preparing for them ever since the previous day, but I had not expected such condescension, such high-official courtesy. So, then, he felt himself ineffably superior to me in every respect! If he only meant to insult me by that high-official tone, it would not matter, I thought—I could pay him back for it one way or another. But what if, in reality, without the least desire to be offensive, that sheepshead had a notion in earnest that he was superior to me and could only look at me in a patronizing way? The very supposition made me gasp.

"I was surprised to hear of your desire to join us," he began, lisping and drawling, which was something new. "You and I seem to have seen nothing of one another. You fight shy of us. You shouldn't. We are not such terrible people as you think, Well, anyway, I am glad to renew our acquaintance."

And he turned carelessly to put down his hat on the window.

"Have you been waiting long?" Trudolyubov inquired.

"I arrived at five o'clock as you told me yesterday," I answered aloud, with an irritability that threatened an explosion.

"Didn't you let him know that we had changed the hour?" said Trudolyubov to Simonov.

"No, I didn't. I forgot," the latter replied, with no sign of regret, and without even apologizing to me he went off to order the *hors d'oeuvres*.

"So you've been here a whole hour? Oh, poor fellow!" Zverkov cried ironically, for to his notions this was bound to be extremely funny. That rascal Ferfichkin followed with his nasty little snigger like a puppy yapping. My position struck him, too, as exquisitely ludicrous and embarrassing.

"It isn't funny at all!" I cried to Ferfichkin, more and more irritated. "It wasn't my fault, but other people's. They neglected to let me know. It was . . . it was . . . it was simply absurd."

"It's not only absurd, but something else as well," muttered Trudolyubov, naïvely taking my part. "You are not hard enough upon it. It was simply rudeness—unintentional, of course. And how could Simonov . . . h'm!"

"If a trick like that had been played on me," observed Ferfichkin, "I should . . ."

"But you should have ordered something for yourself," Zverkov interrupted, "or simply asked for dinner without waiting for us."

"You will allow that I might have done that without your permission," I rapped out. "If I waited, it was. . ."

"Let us sit down, gentlemen," cried Simonov, coming in. "Everything is ready; I can answer for the champagne; it is capitally frozen. . . . You see, I did not know your address, where was I to look for you?" he suddenly turned to me, but again he seemed to avoid looking at me. Evidently he had something against me. It must have been what happened yesterday.

All sat down; I did the same. It was a round table. Trudolyubov was on my left, Simonov on my right. Zverkov was sitting opposite, Ferfichkin next to him, between him and Trudolyubov.

"Tell me, are you . . . in a government office?" Zverkov went on attending to me. Seeing that I was embarrassed, he seriously thought that he ought to be friendly to me, and, so to speak, cheer me up.

"Does he want me to throw a bottle at his head?" I thought, in a fury. In my novel surroundings I was unnaturally ready to be irritated.

"In the N——office," I answered jerkily, with my eyes on my plate.

"And ha-ave you a go-od berth? I say, what ma-a-de you leave your original job?"

"What ma-a-de me was that I wanted to leave my original job," I drawled more than he, hardly able to control myself. Ferfichkin went off into a guffaw. Simonov looked at me ironically. Trudolyubov left off eating and began looking at me with curiosity.

Zverkov winced, but he tried not to notice it.

"And the remuneration?"

"What remuneration?"

"I mean, your sa-a-lary?"

"Why are you cross-examining me?" However, I told him at once what my salary was. I turned horribly red.

"It is not very handsome," Zverkov observed majestically.

"Yes, you can't afford to dine at cafés on that," Ferfichkin added insolently.

"To my thinking it's very poor," Trudolyubov observed gravely.

"And how thin you have grown! How you have changed!" added Zverkov, with a shade of venom in his voice, scanning me and my attire with a sort of insolent compassion.

"Oh, spare his blushes," cried Ferfichkin, sniggering.

"My dear sir, allow me to tell you I am not blushing," I broke out at last; "do you hear? I am dining here, at this café, at my own expense, not at other people's—note that, Mr. Ferfichkin."

"Wha-at? Isn't every one here dining at his own expense? You would seem to be . . ." Ferfichkin flew out at me, turning as red as a lobster, and looking me in the face with fury.

"Tha-at," I answered, feeling I had gone too far, "and I imagine it would be better to talk of something more intelligent."

"You intend to show off your intelligence, I suppose?"

"Don't disturb yourself, that would be quite out of place here."

"Why are you clacking away like that, my good sir, eh? Have you gone out of your wits in your office?"

"Enough, gentlemen, enough!" Zverkov cried, authoritatively.

"How stupid it is!" muttered Simonov.

"It really is stupid. We have met here, a company of friends, for a farewell dinner to a comrade and you carry on an altercation," said Trudolyubov, rudely addressing himself to me alone. "You invited yourself to join us, so don't disturb the general harmony."

"Enough, enough!" cried Zverkov. "Give over, gentlemen, it's out of place. Better let me tell you how I nearly got married the day before yesterday. . . ."

And then followed a burlesque narrative of how this gentleman had almost been married two days before. There was not a word about the marriage, however, but the story was adorned with generals, colonels and gentlemen-in-waiting, while Zverkov almost took the lead among them. It was greeted with approving laughter; Ferfichkin positively squealed.

No one paid any attention to me, and I sat crushed and humiliated.

"Good Heavens, these are not the people for me!" I thought. "And what a fool I have made of myself before them! I let Ferfichkin go too far, though. The brutes imagine they are doing me an honor in letting me sit down with them. They don't understand that it's an honor to them and not to me! I've grown thinner! My clothes! Oh, damn my trousers! Zverkov noticed the yellow stain on the knee as soon as he came in. . . . But what's the use! I must get up at once, this very minute, take my hat and simply go without a word . . . with contempt! And tomorrow I can send a challenge. The scoundrels! As though I cared about the seven roubles.

They may think. . . . Damn it! I don't care about the seven roubles. I'll go this minute!"

Of course I remained. I drank sherry and Lafitte[40] by the glassful in my discomfiture. Being unaccustomed to it, I was quickly affected. My annoyance increased as the wine went to my head. I longed all at once to insult them all in a most flagrant manner and then go away. To seize the moment and show what I could do, so that they would say, "He's clever, though he is absurd," and . . . and . . . in fact, damn them all!

I scanned them all insolently with my drowsy eyes. But they seemed to have forgotten me altogether. They were noisy, vociferous, cheerful. Zverkov was talking all the time. I began listening. Zverkov was talking of some exuberant lady whom he had at last led on to declaring her love (of course, he was lying like a horse), and how he had been helped in this affair by an intimate friend of his, a Prince Kolya, an officer in the hussars, who had three thousand serfs.

"And yet this Kolya, who has three thousand serfs, has not put in an appearance here tonight to see you off," I cut in suddenly.

For a minute every one was silent. "You are drunk already." Trudolyubov deigned to notice me at last, glancing contemptuously in my direction. Zverkov, without a word, examined me as though I were an insect. I dropped my eyes. Simonov made haste to fill up the glasses with champagne.

Trudolyubov raised his glass, as did every one else but me.

"Your health and good luck on the journey!" he cried to Zverkov. "To old times, to our future, hurrah!"

They all tossed off their glasses, and crowded round Zverkov to kiss him. I did not move; my full glass stood untouched before me.

"Why, aren't you going to drink it?" roared Trudolyubov, losing patience and turning menacingly to me.

"I want to make a speech separately, on my own account . . . and then I'll drink it, Mr. Trudolyubov."

"Spiteful brute!" muttered Simonov. I drew myself up in my chair and feverishly seized my glass, prepared for something extraordinary, though I did not know myself precisely what I was going to say.

"Silence!" cried Ferfichkin. "Now for a display of wit!"

Zverkov waited very gravely, knowing what was coming.

"Mr. Lieutenant Zverkov," I began, "let me tell you that I hate phrases, phrasemongers and men in corsets . . . that's the first point, and there is a second one to follow it."

There was a general stir.

"The second point is: I hate ribaldry and ribald talkers. Especially ribald talkers! The third point: I love justice, truth and honesty." I went on almost mechanically, for I was beginning to shiver with horror myself and had no idea how I came to be talking like this. "I love thought, Monsieur Zverkov; I love true comradeship, on an equal footing and not . . . H'm . . . I love. . . . But, however, why not? I will drink your health, too, Mr.

[40] A kind of wine.

Zverkov. Seduce the Circassian[41] girls, shoot the enemies of the fatherland and . . . and . . . to your health, Monsieur Zverkov!"

Zverkov got up from his seat, bowed to me and said:

"I am very much obliged to you." He was frightfully offended and turned pale.

"Damn the fellow!" roared Trudolyubov, bringing his fist down on the table.

"Well, he wants a punch in the face for that," squealed Ferfichkin.

"We ought to turn him out," muttered Simonov.

"Not a word, gentlemen, not a movement!" cried Zverkov solemnly, checking the general indignation. "I thank you all, but I can show him for myself how much value I attach to his words."

"Mr. Ferfichkin, you will give me satisfaction tomorrow for your words just now!" I said aloud, turning with dignity to Ferfichkin.

"A duel, you mean? Certainly," he answered. But probably I was so ridiculous as I challenged him and it was so out of keeping with my appearance that everyone, including Ferfichkin, was prostrate with laughter.

"Yes, let him alone, of course! He is quite drunk," Trudolyubov said with disgust.

"I shall never forgive myself for letting him join us," Simonov muttered again.

"Now is the time to throw a bottle at their heads," I thought to myself. I picked up the bottle . . . and filled my glass. . . . "No, I'd better sit on to the end," I went on thinking; "you would be pleased, my friends, if I went away. Nothing will induce me to go. I'll go on sitting here and drinking to the end, on purpose, as a sign that I don't think you of the slightest consequence. I will go on sitting and drinking, because this is a public-house and I paid my entrance money. I'll sit here and drink, for I look upon you as so many pawns, as inanimate pawns. I'll sit here and drink . . . and sing if I want to, yes, sing, for I have the right to . . . to sing . . . H'm!"

But I did not sing. I simply tried not to look at any of them. I assumed most unconcerned attitudes and waited with impatience for them to speak *first.* But alas, they did not address me! And oh, how I wished, how I wished at that moment to be reconciled to them! It struck eight, at last nine. They moved from the table to the sofa. Zverkov stretched himself on a lounge and put one foot on a round table. Wine was brought there. He did, as a fact, order three bottles on his own account. I, of course, was not invited to join them. They all sat round him on the sofa. They listened to him, almost with reverence. It was evident that they were fond of him. "What for? What for?" I wondered. From time to time they were moved to drunken enthusiasm and kissed each other. They talked of the Caucasus, of the nature of true passion, of snug berths in the service, of the income of an hussar[42] called Podkharzhevsky, whom none of them knew personally, and rejoiced in the largeness of it, of the extraordinary grace and beauty of a Princess

[41] The Circassians were an Islamic people in the rebellious Caucasus area near the Black Sea, where Zverkov is to be stationed. See Lermontov's *A Hero of Our Time.*

[42] Cavalryman.

D., whom none of them had ever seen; then it came to Shakespeare's being immortal.

I smiled contemptuously and walked up and down the other side of the room, opposite the sofa, from the table to the stove and back again. I tried my very utmost to show them that I could do without them, and yet I purposely made a noise with my boots, thumping with my heels. But it was all in vain. They paid no attention. I had the patience to walk up and down in front of them from eight o'clock till eleven, in the same place, from the table to the stove and back again. "I walk up and down to please myself and no one can prevent me." The waiter who came into the room stopped, from time to time, to look at me. I was somewhat giddy from turning round so often; at moments it seemed to me that I was in delirium. During those three hours I was three times soaked with sweat and dry again. At times, with an intense, acute pang I was stabbed to the heart by the thought that ten years, twenty years, forty years would pass, and that even in forty years I would remember with loathing and humiliation those filthiest, most ludicrous, and most awful moments of my life. No one could have gone out of his way to degrade himself more shamelessly, and I fully realized it, fully, and yet I went on pacing up and down from the table to the stove. "Oh, if you only knew what thought and feelings I am capable of, how cultured I am!" I thought at moments, mentally addressing the sofa on which my enemies were sitting. But my enemies behaved as though I were not in the room. Once—only once—they turned towards me, just when Zverkov was talking about Shakespeare, and I suddenly gave a contemptuous laugh. I laughed in such an affected and disgusting way that they all at once broke off their conversation, and silently and gravely for two minutes watched me walking up and down from the table to the stove, *taking no notice of them.* But nothing came of it: they said nothing, and two minutes later they ceased to notice me again. It struck eleven.

"Friends," cried Zverkov getting up from the sofa, "let us all be off now, *there!*"

"Of course, of course," the others assented. I turned sharply to Zverkov. I was so harassed, so exhausted, that I would have cut my throat to put an end to it. I was in a fever; my hair, soaked with perspiration, stuck to my forehead and temples.

"Zverkov, I beg your pardon," I said abruptly and resolutely. "Ferfichkin, yours too, and every one's, every one's: I have insulted you all!"

"Aha! A duel is not in your line, old man," Ferfichkin hissed venomously.

It sent a sharp pang to my heart.

"No, it's not the duel I am afraid of, Ferfichkin! I am ready to fight you tomorrow, after we are reconciled. I insist upon it, in fact, and you cannot refuse. I want to show you that I am not afraid of a duel. You shall fire first and I shall fire into the air."

"He is comforting himself," said Simonov.

"He's simply raving," said Trudolyubov.

"But let us pass. Why are you barring our way? What do you want?" Zverkov answered disdainfully.

They were all flushed, their eyes were bright: they had been drinking heavily.

"I ask for your friendship, Zverkov; I insulted you, but . . ."

"Insulted? *You* insulted *me?* Understand, sir, that you never, under any circumstances, could possibly insult *me*."

"And that's enough for you. Out of the way!" concluded Trudolyubov.

"Olympia is mine, friends, that's agreed!" cried Zverkov.

"We won't dispute your right, we won't dispute your right," the others answered, laughing.

I stood as though spat upon. The party went noisily out of the room. Trudolyubov struck up some stupid song. Simonov remained behind for a moment to tip the waiters. I suddenly went up to him.

"Simonov! give me six roubles!" I said, with desperate resolution.

He looked at me in extreme amazement, with vacant eyes. He, too, was drunk.

"You don't mean you are coming with us?"

"Yes."

"I've no money," he snapped out, and with a scornful laugh he went out of the room.

I clutched at his overcoat. It was a nightmare.

"Simonov, I saw you had money. Why do you refuse me? Am I a scoundrel? Beware of refusing me: if you knew, if you knew why I am asking! My whole future, my whole plans depend upon it!"

Simonov pulled out the money and almost flung it at me.

"Take it, if you have no sense of shame!" he pronounced pitilessly, and ran to overtake them.

I was left for a moment alone. Disorder, the remains of dinner, a broken wine-glass on the floor, spilt wine, cigarette ends, fumes of drink and delirium in my brain, an agonizing misery in my heart and finally the waiter, who had seen and heard all and was looking inquisitively into my face.

"I am going there!" I cried. "Either they shall all go down on their knees to beg for my friendship, or I will give Zverkov a slap in the face!"

V

"So this is it, this is it at last—contact with real life," I muttered as I ran headlong downstairs. "This is very different from the Pope's leaving Rome and going to Brazil, very different from the ball on Lake Como!"

"You are a scoundrel," a thought flashed through my mind, "if you laugh at this now."

"No matter!" I cried, answering myself. "Now everything is lost!"

There was no trace to be seen of them, but that made no difference—I knew where they had gone.

At the steps was standing a solitary night sledge-driver in a rough peasant coat, powdered over with the still falling, wet, and as it were warm, snow. It was hot and steamy. The little shaggy piebald horse was also covered with snow and coughing, I remember that very well. I made a rush for the roughly made sledge; but as soon as I raised my foot to get into it, the recollection of how Simonov had just given me six roubles seemed to double me up and I tumbled into the sledge like a sack.

"No, I must do a great deal to make up for all that," I cried. "But I will make up for it or perish on the spot this very night. Start!"

We set off. There was a perfect whirl in my head.

"They won't go down on their knees to beg for my friendship. That is a mirage, cheap mirage, revolting, romantic and fantastical—that's another ball on Lake Como. And so I am bound to slap Zverkov's face! It is my duty to. And so it is settled; I am flying to give him a slap in the face. Hurry up!"

The driver tugged at the reins.

"As soon as I go in I'll give it him. Ought I before giving him the slap to say a few words by way of preface? No. I'll simply go in and give it him. They will all be sitting in the drawing-room, and he with Olympia on the sofa. That damned Olympia! She laughed at my looks on one occasion and refused me. I'll pull Olympia's hair, pull Zverkov's ears! No, better one ear, and pull him by it round the room. Maybe they will all begin beating me and will kick me out. That's most likely, indeed. No matter! Anyway, I shall first slap him; the initiative will be mine; and by the laws of honor that is everything: he will be branded and cannot wipe off the slap by any blows, by nothing but a duel. He will be forced to fight. And let them beat me now. Let them, the ungrateful wretches! Trudolyubov will beat me hardest, he is so strong; Ferfichkin will be sure to catch hold sideways and tug at my hair. But no matter, no matter! That's what I am going for. The blockheads will be forced at last to see the tragedy of it all! When they drag me to the door I shall call out to them that in reality they are not worth my little finger. Get on, driver, get on!" I cried to the driver. He started and flicked his whip, I shouted so savagely.

"We shall fight at daybreak, that's a settled thing. I've done with the office. Ferfichkin made a joke about it just now. But where can I get pistols? Nonsense! I'll get my salary in advance and buy them. And powder, and bullets? That the second's business. And how can it all be done by daybreak? And where am I to get a second? I have no friends. Nonsense!" I cried, lashing myself up more and more. "It's of no consequence! the first person I meet in the street is bound to be my second, just as he would be bound to pull a drowning man out of water. The most eccentric things may happen. Even if I were to ask the director himself to be my second tomorrow, he would be bound to consent, if only from a feeling of chivalry, and to keep the secret! Anton Antonich. . . ."

The fact is, that at that very minute the disgusting absurdity of my plan and the other side of the question was clearer and more vivid to my imagination than it could be to any one on earth. But. . . .

"Get on, driver, get on, you rascal, get on!"

"Ugh, sir!" said the son of toil.

Cold shivers suddenly ran down me.

Wouldn't it be better . . . to go straight home? My God, my God! Why did I invite myself to this dinner yesterday? But no, it's impossible. And my walking up and down for three hours from the table to the stove? No, they, they and no one else must pay for my walking up and down! They must wipe out this dishonor! Drive on!

And what if they give me into custody? They won't dare! They'll be afraid of the scandal. And what if Zverkov is so contemptuous that he refuses to fight a duel? He is sure to; but in that case I'll show them . . . I will turn up at the posting station when he is setting off tomorrow, I'll catch him by the leg, I'll pull off his coat when he gets into the carriage. I'll get my teeth into his hand, I'll bite him. "See what lengths you can drive a desperate man to!" He may hit me on the head and they may belabor me from behind. I will shout to the assembled multitude: "Look at this young puppy who is driving off to captivate the Circassian girls after letting me spit in his face!"

Of course, after that everything will be over! The office will have vanished off the face of the earth. I shall be arrested, I shall be tried, I shall be dismissed from the service, thrown in prison, sent to Siberia. Never mind! In fifteen years when they let me out of prison I will trudge off to him, a beggar, in rags. I shall find him in some provincial town. He will be married and happy. He will have a grown-up daughter. . . . I shall say to him: "Look, monster, at my hollow cheeks and my rags! I've lost everything—my career, my happiness, art, science, *the woman I loved,* and all through you. Here are pistols. I have come to discharge my pistol and . . . and I . . . forgive you. Then I shall fire into the air and he will hear nothing more of me. . . ."

I was actually on the point of tears, though I knew perfectly well at that moment that all this was out of Pushkin's *Silvio*[43] and Lermontov's *Masquerade.*[44] And all at once I felt horribly ashamed, so ashamed that I stopped the horse, got out of the sledge, and stood still in the snow in the middle of the street. The driver gazed at me, sighing and astonished.

What was I to do? I could not go on there—it was evidently stupid, and I could not leave things as they were, because that would seem as though . . . Heavens, how could I leave things! And after such insults! "No!" I cried, throwing myself into the sledge again. "It is ordained! It is fate! Drive on, drive on!"

And in my impatience I punched the sledge-driver on the back of the neck.

"What are you up to? What are you hitting me for?" the peasant shouted, but he whipped up his nag so that it began kicking.

The wet snow was falling in big flakes; I unbuttoned myself, regardless of it. I forgot everything else, for I had finally decided on the slap, and felt with horror that it was going to happen *now, at once,* and that *no force could stop it.* The deserted street lamps gleamed sullenly in the snowy darkness like torches at a funeral. The snow drifted under my great-coat, under my coat, under my cravat, and melted there. I did not wrap myself up—all was lost, anyway.

At last we arrived. I jumped out, almost unconscious, ran up the steps and began knocking and kicking at the door. I felt fearfully weak, particularly in my legs and my knees. The door was opened quickly as though they knew I was coming. As a fact, Simonov had warned them that perhaps another gentleman would arrive, and this was a place in which one had to give notice and to observe certain precautions. It was one of those "millinery establishments" which were abolished by the police a good time ago. By day it really was a shop; but at night, if one had an introduction, one might visit it for other purposes.

[43] The speaker is thinking of Alexander Pushkin's story "The Shot" (1830), in which the main character is named Silvio and which turns around attempted revenge.

[44] A romantic verse play (1835) by Mikhail Lermontov.

I walked rapidly through the dark shop into the familiar drawing-room, where there was only one candle burning, and stood still in amazement: there was no one there. "Where are they?" I asked somebody. But by now, of course, they had separated. Before me was standing a person with a stupid smile, the "madam" herself, who had seen me before. A minute later a door opened and another person came in.

Taking no notice of anything I strode about the room, and, I believe, I talked to myself. I felt as though I had been saved from death and was conscious of this, joyfully, all over: I should have given that slap, I should certainly, certainly have given it! But now they were not here and . . . everything had vanished and changed! I looked round. I could not realize my condition yet. I looked mechanically at the girl who had come in: and had a glimpse of a fresh, young, rather pale face, with straight, dark eyebrows, and with grave, as it were wondering, eyes that attracted me at once; I should have hated her if she had been smiling. I began looking at her more intently and, as it were, with effort. I had not fully collected my thoughts. There was something simple and good-natured in her face, but something strangely grave. I am sure that this stood in her way here, and no one of those fools had noticed her. She could not, however, have been called a beauty, though she was tall, strong-looking, and well built. She was very simply dressed. Something loathsome stirred within me. I went straight up to her.

I chanced to look into the glass. My harassed face struck me as revolting in the extreme, pale, angry, abject, with dishevelled hair. "No matter, I am glad of it," I thought; "I am glad that I shall seem repulsive to her; I like that."

VI

. . . Somewhere behind a screen a clock began wheezing, as though oppressed by something, as though some one were strangling it. After an unnaturally prolonged wheezing there followed a shrill, nasty, and as it were unexpectedly rapid, chime—as though some one were suddenly jumping forward. It struck two. I woke up, though I had indeed not been asleep but lying half conscious.

It was almost completely dark in the narrow, cramped, low-pitched room, cumbered up with an enormous wardrobe and piles of cardboard boxes and all sorts of frippery and litter. The candle end that had been burning on the table was going out and gave a faint flicker from time to time. In a few minutes there would be complete darkness.

I was not long in coming to myself; everything came back to my mind at once, without an effort, as though it had been in ambush to pounce upon me again. And, indeed, even while I was unconscious a point seemed continually to remain in my memory unforgotten, and round it my dreams moved drearily. But strange to say, everything that had happened to me in that day seemed to me now, on waking, to be in the far, far away past, as though I had long, long ago lived all that down.

My head was full of fumes. Something seemed to be hovering over me, rousing me, exciting me, and making me restless. Misery and spite seemed surging up in me again and seeking an outlet. Suddenly I saw beside me two wide open eyes scrutinizing me curiously and persistently. The look in those eyes was coldly detached, sullen, as it were utterly remote; it weighed upon me.

A grim idea came into my brain and passed all over my body, as a horrible sensation, such as one feels when one goes into a damp and moldy cellar. There was something unnatural in those two eyes, beginning to look at me only now. I recalled, too, that during those two hours I had not said a single word to this creature, and had, in fact, considered it utterly superfluous; in fact, the silence had for some reason gratified me. Now I suddenly realized vividly the hideous idea—revolting as a spider—of vice, which, without love, grossly and shamelessly begins with that in which true love finds its consummation. For a long time we gazed at each other like that, but she did not drop her eyes before mine and her expression did not change, so that at last I felt uncomfortable.

"What is your name?" I asked abruptly, to put an end to it.

"Liza," she answered almost in a whisper, but somehow far from graciously, and she turned her eyes away.

I was silent.

"What weather! The snow . . . it's disgusting!" I said, almost to myself, putting my arm under my head despondently, and gazing at the ceiling.

She made no answer. This was horrible.

"Have you always lived in Petersburg?" I asked a minute later, almost angrily, turning my head slightly towards her.

"No."

"Where do you come from?"

"From Riga," she answered reluctantly.

"Are you a German?"

"No, Russian."

"Have you been here long?"

"Where?"

"In this house?"

"A fortnight."

She spoke more and more jerkily. The candle went out; I could no longer distinguish her face.

"Have you a father and mother?"

"Yes . . . no . . . I have."

"Where are they?"

"There . . . in Riga."

"What are they?"

"Oh, nothing."

"Nothing? Why, what class are they?"

"Tradespeople."

"Have you always lived with them?"

"Yes."

"How old are you?"

"Twenty."

"Why did you leave them?"

"Oh, for no reason."

That answer meant "Let me alone; I feel sick, sad."

We were silent.

God knows why I did not go away. I felt myself more and more sick and dreary. The images of the previous day began of themselves, apart from my will, flitting through my memory in confusion. I suddenly recalled something I had seen that morning when, full of anxious thoughts, I was hurrying to the office.

"I saw them carrying a coffin out yesterday and they nearly dropped it," I suddenly said aloud, not that I desired to open the conversation, but as it were by accident.

"A coffin?"

"Yes, in the Haymarket; they were bringing it up out of a cellar."

"From a cellar?"

"Not from a cellar, but from a basement. Oh, you know . . . down below . . . from a house of ill-fame. It was filthy all round . . . Egg-shells, litter . . . stench. It was loathsome."

Silence.

"A nasty day to be buried," I began, simply to avoid being silent.

"Nasty, in what way?"

"The snow, the wet." (I yawned.)

"It makes no difference," she said suddenly, after a brief silence.

"No, it's horrid." (I yawned again.) "The gravediggers must have sworn at getting drenched by the snow. And there must have been water in the grave."

"Why water in the grave?" she asked, with a sort of curiosity, but speaking even more harshly and abruptly than before.

I suddenly began to feel provoked.

"Why, there must have been water at the bottom a foot deep. You can't dig a dry grave in Volkovo Cemetery."

"Why?"

"Why? Why, the place is waterlogged. It's a regular marsh. So they bury them in water. I've seen it myself . . . many times."

(I had never seen it once, indeed I had never been in Volkovo, and had only heard stories of it.)

"Do you mean to say, you don't mind how you die?"

"But why should I die?" she answered, as though defending herself.

"Why, some day you will die, and you will die just the same as that dead woman. She was . . . a girl like you. She died of consumption."

"A wench would have died in a hospital . . ." (She knows all about it already: she said "wench," not "girl.")

"She was in debt to her madam," I retorted, more and more provoked by the discussion; "and went on earning money for her up to the end, though she was in consumption. Some sledge-drivers standing by were talking about her to some soldiers and telling them so. No doubt they knew her. They were laughing. They were going to meet in a pot-house to drink to her memory."

A great deal of this was my invention. Silence followed, profound silence. She did not stir.

"And is it better to die in a hospital?"

"Isn't it just the same? Besides, why should I die?" she added irritably.

"If not now, a little later."

"Why a little later?"

"Why, indeed? Now you are young, pretty, fresh, you fetch a high price.

But after another year of this life you will be very different—you will go off."

"In a year?"

"Anyway, in a year you will be worth less," I continued malignantly. "You will go from here to something lower, another house; a year later—to a third, lower and lower, and in seven years you will come to a basement in the Haymarket. That will be if you were lucky. But it would be much worse if you got some disease, consumption, say . . . and caught a chill, or something or other. It's not easy to get over an illness in your way of life. If you catch anything you may not get rid of it. And so you would die."

"Oh, well, then I shall die," she answered, quite vindictively, and she made a quick movement.

"But one is sorry."

"Sorry for whom?"

"Sorry for life."

Silence.

"Have you been engaged to be married? Eh?"

"What's that to you?"

"Oh, I am not cross-examining you. It's nothing to me. Why are you so cross? Of course you may have had your own troubles. What is it to me? It's simply that I felt sorry."

"Sorry for whom?"

"Sorry for you."

"No need," she whispered hardly audibly, and again made a faint movement.

That incensed me at once. What! I was so gentle with her, and she. . . .

"Why, do you think that you are on the right path?"

"I don't think anything."

"That's what's wrong, that you don't think. Realize it while there is still time. There still is time. You are still young, good-looking; you might love, be married, be happy. . . ."

"Not all married women are happy," she snapped out in the rude abrupt tone she used at first.

"Not all, of course, but anyway it is much better than the life here. Infinitely better. Besides, with love one can live even without happiness. Even in sorrow life is sweet; life is sweet, however one lives. But here what is there but . . . filth? Phew!"

I turned away with disgust; I was no longer reasoning coldly. I began to feel myself what I was saying and warmed to the subject. I was already longing to expound the cherished ideas I had brooded over in my corner. Something suddenly flared up in me. An object had appeared before me.

"Never mind my being here, I am not an example for you. I am, perhaps, worse than you are. I was drunk when I came here, though," I hastened, however, to say in self-defense. "Besides, a man is no example for a woman. It's a different thing. I may degrade and defile myself, but I am not any one's slave. I come and go, and that's an end of it. I shake it off, and I am a different man. But you are a slave from the start. Yes, a slave! You give up everything, your whole freedom. If you want to break your chains afterwards, you won't be able to: you will be more and more fast in the snares. It is an accursed bondage. I know it. I won't speak of anything else, maybe you won't understand, but tell me: no doubt you are in debt to your madam? There, you see," I added, though she made no answer, but only listened in silence, entirely absorbed, "that's a bondage for you! You will never buy your freedom. They will see to that. It's like selling your soul to the devil. . . . And besides . . . perhaps I, too, am just as unlucky—how do you know—and wallow in the mud on purpose, out of misery? You know, men take to drink from grief; well, maybe I am here from grief. Come, tell me, what is there good here? Here you and I . . . came together . . . just now and did not say one word to one another all the time, and it was only afterwards you began staring at me like a wild creature, and I at you. Is that loving? Is that how one human being should meet another? It's hideous, that's what it is!"

"Yes!" she assented sharply and hurriedly.

I was positively astounded by the promptitude of this "Yes." So the same thought may have been straying through her mind when she was staring at me just before. So she, too, was capable of certain thoughts? "Damn it all, this was interesting, this was a point of likeness!" I thought, almost rubbing my hands. And indeed it's easy to turn a young soul like that!

It was the exercise of my power that attracted me most.

She turned her head nearer to me, and it seemed to me in the darkness that she propped herself on her arm. Perhaps she was scrutinizing me. How I regretted that I could not see her eyes. I heard her deep breathing.

"Why have you come here?" I asked her, with a note of authority already in my voice.

"Oh, I don't know."

"But how nice it would be to be living in your father's house! It's warm and free; and you have a home of your own."

"But what if it's worse than this?"

"I must take the right tone," flashed through my mind. "I may not get far with sentimentality." But it was only a momentary thought. I swear she really did interest me. Besides, I was exhausted and moody. And cunning so easily goes hand-in-hand with feeling.

"Who denies it!" I hastened to answer. "Anything may happen. I am convinced that some one has wronged you, and that you are more sinned against than sinning. Of course, I know nothing of your story, but it's not likely a girl like you has come here of her own inclination. . . ."

"A girl like me?" she whispered, hardly audibly; but I heard it.

Damn it all, I was flattering her. That was horrid. But perhaps it was a good thing. . . . She was silent.

"See, Liza, I will tell you about myself. If I had had a home from childhood, I shouldn't be what I am now. I often think that. However bad it may be at home, anyway they are your father and mother, and not enemies, strangers. Once a year at least, they'll show their love of you. Anyway, you know you are at home. I grew up without a home; and perhaps that's why I've turned so . . . unfeeling."

I waited again. "Perhaps she doesn't understand," I thought, "and, indeed, it is absurd—it's moralizing."

"If I were a father and had a daughter, I believe I should love my daughter more than my sons, really," I began indirectly, as though talking of something else, to distract her attention. I must confess I blushed.

"Why so?" she asked.

Ah! so she was listening!

"I don't know, Liza. I knew a father who was a stern, austere man, but used to go down on his knees to his daughter, used to kiss her hands, her feet, he couldn't make enough of her, really. When she danced at parties he used to stand for five hours at a stretch, gazing at her. He was mad over her: I understand that! She would fall asleep tired at night, and he would wake to kiss her in her sleep and make the sign of the cross over her. He would go about in a dirty old coat, he was stingy to every one else, but would spend his last penny for her, giving her expensive presents, and it was his greatest delight when she was pleased with what he gave her. Fathers always love their daughters more than the mothers do. Some girls live happily at home! And I believe I should never let my daughters marry."

"What next?" she said, with a faint smile.

"I should be jealous, I really should. To think that she should kiss any one else! That she should love a stranger more than her father! It's painful to imagine it. Of course, that's all nonsense, of course every father would be reasonable at last. But I believe before I should let her marry, I should worry myself to death; I should find fault with all her suitors. But I should end by letting her marry whom she herself loved. The one whom the daughter loves always seems the worst to the father, you know. That is always so. So many family troubles come from that."

"Some are glad to sell their daughters, rather than marrying them honorably."

Ah, so that was it!

"Such a thing, Liza, happens in those accursed families in which there is neither love nor God," I retorted warmly, "and where there is no love, there is no sense either. There are such families, it's true, but I am not speaking of them. You must have seen wickedness in your own family, if you talk like that. Truly, you must have been unlucky. H'm! . . . that sort of thing mostly comes about through poverty."

"And is it any better with the gentry? Even among the poor, honest people live happily."

"H'm . . . yes. Perhaps. Another thing, Liza, man is fond of reckoning up his troubles, but does not count his joys. If he counted them up as he ought, he would see that every lot has enough happiness provided for it. And what if all goes well with the family, if the blessing of God is upon it, if the husband is a good one, loves you, cherishes you, never leaves you! There is happiness in such a family! Even sometimes there is happiness in the midst of sorrow; and indeed sorrow is everywhere. If you marry *you will find out for yourself*. But think of the first years of married life with one you love: what happiness, what happiness there sometimes is in it! And indeed it's the ordinary thing. In those early days even quarrels with one's husband end happily. Some women get up quarrels with their husbands just because they love them. Indeed, I knew a woman like that: she seemed to say that because she loved him, she would torment him and make him feel it. You know that you may torment a man on purpose through love. Women are particularly given to that, thinking to themselves 'I will love him so, I will make so much of him afterwards, that it's no sin to torment him a little now.' And all in the house rejoice in the sight of you, and you are happy and gay and peaceful and honorable. . . . Then there are some women who are jealous. If he went off anywhere—I knew one such woman, she couldn't restrain herself, but would jump up at night and run off on the sly to find out where he was, whether he was with some other woman. That's a pity. And the woman knows herself it's wrong, and her heart fails her and she suffers, but she loves—it's all through love. And how sweet it is to make it up after quarrels, to own herself in the wrong or to forgive him! And they are both so happy all at once—as though they had met anew, been married over again; as though their love had begun afresh. And no one, no one should know what passes between husband and wife if they love one another. And whatever quarrels there may be between them they ought not to call in their own mother to judge between them and tell tales of one another. They are their own judges. Love is a holy mystery and ought to be hidden from all other eyes, whatever happens. That makes it holier and better. They respect one another more, and much is built on respect. And if once there has been love, if they have been married for love, why should love pass away? Surely one can keep it! It is rare that one cannot keep it. And if the husband is kind and straightforward, why should not love last? The first phase of married love will pass, it is true, but then there will come a love that is better still. Then there will be the union of souls, they will have everything in common, there will be no secrets between them. And once they have children, the most difficult times will seem to them happy, so long as there is love and courage. Even toil will be a joy, you may deny yourself bread for your children and even that will be a joy. They will love you for it afterwards; so you are laying by for your future. As the children grow up you feel that you are an example, a support for them; that even after you die your children will always keep your thoughts and feelings, because they have received them from you, they will take on your semblance and likeness. So you see this is a great duty. How can it fail to draw the father and mother nearer? People say it's a trial to have children. Who says that? It is heavenly happiness! Are you fond of little children, Liza? I am awfully fond of them. You know—a little rosy baby boy at your bosom, and what husband's heart is not touched, seeing his wife nursing his child! A plump little rosy baby, sprawling and snuggling, chubby little hands and feet, clean tiny little nails, so tiny that it makes one laugh to look at them; eyes that look as if they understand everything. And while it sucks it clutches at your bosom with its little hand, plays. When its father comes up, the child tears itself away from the bosom, flings itself back, looks at its father, laughs, as though it were fearfully funny and falls to sucking again. Or it will bite its mother's breast when its little teeth are coming, while it looks sideways at her with its little eyes as though to say, 'Look, I am biting!' Is not all that happiness when they are the three together, husband, wife and child? One can forgive a great deal for the sake of such moments. Yes, Liza, one must first learn to live oneself before one blames others!"

"It's by pictures, pictures like that one must get at you," I thought to myself, though I did speak with real feeling, and all at once I flushed crimson. "What if she were suddenly to burst out laughing, what should I do then?" That idea drove me to fury. Towards the end of my speech I really was excited, and now my vanity was somehow wounded. The silence continued. I almost nudged her.

"Why are you——" she began and stopped. But I understood: there was a quiver of something different in her voice, not abrupt, harsh and unyielding as before, but something soft and shamefaced, so shamefaced that I suddenly felt ashamed and guilty.

"What?" I asked, with tender curiosity.

"Why, you . . ."

"What?"

"Why, you . . . speak somehow like a book," she said, and again there was a note of irony in her voice.

That remark sent a pang to my heart. It was not what I was expecting.

I did not understand that she was hiding her feelings under irony, that this is usually the last refuge of modest and chaste-souled people when the privacy of their soul is coarsely and intrusively invaded, and that their pride makes them refuse to surrender till the last moment and shrink from giving expression to their feelings before you. I ought to have guessed the truth from the timidity with which she had repeatedly approached her sarcasm, only bringing herself to utter it at last with an effort. But I did not guess, and an evil feeling took possession of me.

"Wait a bit!" I thought.

VII

"Oh, hush, Liza! How can you talk about being like a book, when it makes even me, an outsider, feel sick? Though I don't look at it as an outsider, for, indeed, it touches me to the heart. . . . Is it possible, is it possible that you do not feel sick at being here yourself? Evidently habit does wonders! God knows what habit can do with any one. Can you seriously think that you will never grow old, that you will always be good-looking, and that they will keep you here for ever and ever? I say nothing of the loathsomeness of the life here. . . . Though let me tell you this about it—about your present life, I mean; here though you are young now, attractive, nice, with soul and feeling, yet you know as soon as I came to myself just now I felt at once sick at being here with you! One can only come here when one is drunk. But if you were anywhere else, living as good people live, I should perhaps be more than attracted by you, should fall in love with you, should be glad of a look from you, let alone a word; I should hang about your door, should go down on my knees to you, should look upon you as my betrothed and think it an honor to be allowed to. I should not dare to have an impure thought about you. But here, you see, I know that I have only to whistle and you have to come with me whether you like it or not. I don't consult your wishes, but you mine. The lowest laborer hires himself as a workman, but he doesn't make a slave of himself altogether; besides, he knows that he will be free again presently. But when are you free? Only think what you are giving up here? What is it you are making a slave of? It is your soul, together with your body; you are selling your soul which you have no right to dispose of! You give your love to be outraged by every drunkard! Love! But that's everything, you know, it's a priceless diamond, it's a maiden's treasure, love—why, a man would be ready to give his soul, to face death to gain that love. But how much is your love worth now? You are sold, all of you, body and soul, and there is no need to strive for love when you can have everything without love. And you know there is no greater insult to a girl than that, do you understand? To be sure, I have heard that they comfort you, poor fools, they let you have lovers of your own here. But you know that's simply a farce, that's simply a sham, it's just laughing at you, and you are taken in by it! Why, do you suppose he really loves you, that lover of yours? I don't believe it. How can he love you when he knows you may be called away from him any minute? He would be a low fellow if he did! Will he have a grain of respect for you? What have you in common with him? He laughs at you and robs you—that is all his love amounts to! You are lucky if he does not beat you. Very likely he does beat you, too. Ask him, if you have got one, whether he will marry you. He will laugh in your face, if he doesn't spit in it or give you a blow—though maybe he is not worth a bad halfpenny himself. And for what have you ruined your life, if you come to think of it? For the coffee they give you to drink and the plentiful meals? But with what object are they feeding you up? An honest girl couldn't swallow the food, for she would know what she was being fed for. You are in debt here, and, of course, you will always be in debt, and you will go on in debt to the end, till the visitors here begin to scorn you. And that will soon happen, don't rely upon your youth—all that flies by express train here, you know. You will be kicked out. And not simply kicked out; long before that she'll begin nagging at you, scolding you, abusing you, as though you had not sacrificed your health for her, had not thrown away your youth and your soul for her benefit, but as though you had ruined her, beggared her, robbed her. And don't expect any one to take your part: the others, your companions, will attack you, too, to win her favor, for all are in slavery here, and have lost all conscience and pity here long ago. They have become utterly vile, and nothing on earth is viler, more loathsome, and more insulting than their abuse. And you are laying down everything here, unconditionally, youth and health and beauty and hope, and at twenty-two you will look like a woman of five-and-thirty, and you will be lucky if you are not diseased, pray to God for that! No doubt you are thinking now that you have a gay time and no work to do! Yet there is no work harder or more dreadful in the world or ever has been. One would think that the heart alone would be worn out with tears. And you won't dare to say a word, not half a word when they drive you away from here; you will go away as though you were to blame. You will change to another house, then to a third, then somewhere else, till you come down at last to the Haymarket. There you will be beaten at every turn; that is good manners there, the visitors don't know how to be friendly without beating you. You don't believe that it is so hateful there? Go and look for yourself some time, you can see with your own eyes. Once, one New Year's Day, I saw a woman at a door. They had turned her out as a joke, to give her a taste of the frost because she had been crying so much, and they shut the door behind her. At nine o'clock in the morning she was already quite drunk, dishevelled, half-naked, covered with bruises, her face was powdered, but she had a black-eye, blood was trickling from her nose and her teeth; some cabman had just given her a drubbing. She was sitting on the stone steps, a salt fish of some sort was in her hand; she was crying, wailing something about her luck and beating with the fish on the steps, and cabmen and drunken soldiers were crowding in the doorway taunting her. You don't believe that you will ever be like that? I should be sorry to believe it, too, but how do you know; maybe ten years, eight years ago that very woman with the salt fish came here fresh as a cherub, innocent, pure, knowing no evil, blushing at every word. Perhaps she was like you, proud, ready to take offense, not like the others; perhaps she looked like a queen, and knew what happiness was in store for the man who should love her and whom she should love. Do you see how it ended? And what if at that very minute when she was beating on the filthy steps with that fish, drunken and dishevelled—what if at that very minute she recalled the pure early days in her father's house, when she used to go to school and the neighbor's son watched for her on the way, declaring that he would love her as long as he lived, that he would devote his life to her, and when they vowed to love one another for ever and be married as soon as they were grown up! No, Liza, it would be happy for you if you were to die soon of consumption in some corner, in some cellar like that woman just now. In the hospital, do you say? You will be lucky if they take you, but what if you are still of use to the madam here? Consumption is a queer disease, it is not like fever. The patient goes on hoping till the last minute and says he is all right. He deludes himself. And that just suits your madam. Don't doubt it, that's how it is; you have sold your soul, and what is more you owe money, so you daren't say a word. But when you are dying, all will abandon you, all will turn away from you, for then there will be nothing to get from you. What's more, they will reproach you for cumbering the place, for being so long over dying. However you beg you won't get a drink of water without abuse: 'Whenever are you going off, you nasty hussy, you won't let us sleep with your moaning, you make the gentlemen sick.' That's true, I have heard such things said myself. They will thrust you dying into the filthiest corner in the cellar—in the damp and darkness; what will your thoughts be, lying there alone? When you die, strange hands will lay you out, with grumbling and impatience; no one will bless you, no one will sigh for you, they only want to get rid of you as soon as may be; they will buy a coffin, take you to the grave as they did that poor woman today, and celebrate your memory at the tavern. In the gravest sleet, filth, wet snow—no need to put themselves out for you—'Let her down, Vanyukha; it's just like her luck—even here, she is head-foremost,[45] the hussy. Shorten the cord, you rascal.' 'It's all right as it is.' 'All right, is it? Why, she's on her side! She was a fellow-creature, after all! But, never mind, throw the earth on her.' And they won't care to waste much time quarrelling over you. They will scatter the wet blue clay as quick as they can and go off to the tavern . . . and there your memory on earth will end; other women have children to go to their graves, fathers, husbands. While for you neither tear, nor sigh, nor remembrance; no one in the whole world will ever come to you, your name will vanish from the face of the earth—as though you had never existed, never been born at all! Nothing but filth and mud, however you knock at your coffin lid at night, when the dead arise, however you cry: 'Let me out, kind people, to live in the light of day! My life was no life at all; my life has been thrown away like a dish-clout;[46] it was drunk away in the tavern at the Haymarket; let me out, kind people, to live in the world again.'"

And I worked myself up to such a pitch that I began to have a lump in

[45] Both "head first" and "buffeted by fate." [46] Dishcloth.

my throat myself, and . . . and all at once I stopped, sat up in dismay, and bending over apprehensively, began to listen with a beating heart. I had reason to be troubled.

I had felt for some time that I was turning her soul upside down and rending her heart, and—and the more I was convinced of it, the more eagerly I desired to gain my object as quickly and as effectually as possible. It was the exercise of my skill that carried me away; yet it was not merely sport. . . .

I knew I was speaking stiffly, artificially, even bookishly, in fact, I could not speak except "like a book." But that did not trouble me: I knew, I felt that I should be understood and that this very bookishness might be an assistance. But now, having attained my effect, I was suddenly panic-stricken. Never before had I witnessed such despair! She was lying on her face, thrusting her face into the pillow and clutching it in both hands. Her heart was being torn. Her youthful body was shuddering all over as though in convulsions. Suppressed sobs rent her bosom and suddenly burst out in weeping and wailing, then she pressed closer into the pillow: she did not want any one here, not a living soul, to know of her anguish and her tears. She bit the pillow, bit her hand till it bled (I saw that afterwards), or, thrusting her fingers into her dishevelled hair, seemed rigid with the effort of restraint, holding her breath and clenching her teeth. I began saying something, begging her to calm herself, but felt that I did not dare; and all at once, in a sort of cold shiver, almost in terror, began fumbling in the dark, trying hurriedly to get dressed to go. It was dark: though I tried my best I could not finish dressing quickly. Suddenly I felt a box of matches and a candlestick with a whole candle in it. As soon as the room was lighted up, Liza sprang up, sat up in bed, and with a contorted face, with a half insane smile, looked at me almost senselessly. I sat down beside her and took her hands; she came to herself, made an impulsive movement towards me, would have caught hold of me, but did not dare, and slowly bowed her head before me.

"Liza, my dear, I was wrong . . . forgive me, my dear," I began, but she squeezed my hand in her fingers so tightly that I felt I was saying the wrong thing and stopped.

"This is my address, Liza, come to me."

"I will come," she answered resolutely, her head still bowed.

"But now I am going, good-bye . . . till we meet again."

I got up; she, too, stood up and suddenly flushed all over, gave a shudder, snatched up a shawl that was lying on a chair and muffled herself in it to her chin. As she did this she gave another sickly smile, blushed and looked at me strangely. I felt wretched; I was in haste to get away—to disappear.

"Wait a minute," she said suddenly, in the passage just at the doorway, stopping me with her hand on my overcoat. She put down the candle in hot haste and ran off; evidently she had thought of something or wanted to show me something. As she ran away she flushed, her eyes shone, and there was a smile on her lips—what was the meaning of it? Against my will I waited: she came back a minute later with an expression that seemed to ask forgiveness for something. In fact, it was not the same face, not the same look as the evening before: sullen, mistrustful and obstinate. Her eyes now were imploring, soft, and at the same time trustful, caressing, timid. The expression with which children look at people they are very fond of, of whom they are asking a favor. Her eyes were a light hazel, they were lovely eyes, full of life, and capable of expressing love as well as sullen hatred.

Making no explanation, as though I, as a sort of higher being, must understand everything without explanations, she held out a piece of paper to me. Her whole face was positively beaming at that instant with naïve, almost childish, triumph. I unfolded it. It was a letter to her from a medical student or some one of that sort—a very high-flown and flowery, but extremely respectful, love-letter. I don't recall the words now, but I remember well that through the high-flown phrases there was apparent a genuine feeling, which cannot be feigned. When I had finished reading it I met her glowing, questioning, and childishly impatient eyes fixed upon me. She fastened her eyes upon my face and waited impatiently for what I should say. In a few words, hurriedly, but with a sort of joy and pride, she explained to me that she had been to a dance somewhere in a private house, a family of "very nice people *who knew nothing*, absolutely nothing, for she had only come here so lately and it had all happened . . . and she hadn't made up her mind to stay and was certainly going away as soon as she had paid her debt . . ." and at that party there had been the student who had danced with her all the evening. He had talked to her, and it turned out that he had known her in old days at Riga when he was a child, they had played together, but a very long time ago—and he knew her parents, but *about this* he knew nothing, nothing whatever, and had no suspicion! And the day after the dance (three days ago) he had sent her that letter through the friend with whom she had gone to the party . . . and . . . well, that was all."

She dropped her shining eyes with a sort of bashfulness as she finished.

The poor girl was keeping that student's letter as a precious treasure, and had run to fetch it, her only treasure, because she did not want me to go away without knowing that she, too, was honestly and genuinely loved; that she, too, was addressed respectfully. No doubt that letter was destined to lie in her box and lead to nothing. But none the less, I am certain that she would keep it all her life as a precious treasure, as her pride and justification, and now at such a minute she had thought of that letter and brought it with naïve pride to raise herself in my eyes that I might see, that I, too, might think well of her. I said nothing, pressed her hand and went out. I so longed to get away. . . . I walked all the way home, in spite of the fact that the melting snow was still falling in heavy flakes. I was exhausted, shattered, in bewilderment. But behind the bewilderment the truth was already gleaming. The loathsome truth.

VIII

It was some time, however, before I consented to recognize that truth. Waking up in the morning after some hours of heavy, leaden sleep, and immediately realizing all that had happened on the previous day, I was positively amazed at my last night's *sentimentality* with Liza, at all those "outcries of horror and pity." "To think of having such an attack of womanish hysteria, pah!" I concluded. And what did I thrust my address upon her for? What if she comes? Let her come, though; it doesn't matter. . . . But *obviously,* that was not now the chief and the most important matter: I had to make haste and at all costs save my reputation in the eyes of Zverkov and Simonov as quickly as possible; that was the chief business. And I was so taken up that morning that I actually forgot all about Liza.

First of all I had at once to repay what I had borrowed the day before from Simonov. I resolved on a desperate measure: to borrow fifteen roubles straight off from Anton Antonich. As luck would have it he was in the best of humors that morning, and gave it to me at once, on the first asking. I was so delighted at this that, as I signed the I O U with a swaggering air, I told him casually that the night before "I had been keeping it up with some friends at the Hôtel de Paris; we were giving a farewell party to a comrade, in fact, I might say a friend of my childhood, and you know—a desperate rake, fearfully spoiled—of course, he belongs to a good family, and has considerable means, a brilliant career; he is witty, charming, a regular Lovelace,[47] you understand; we drank an extra 'half-dozen' and . . ."

And it went off all right; all this was uttered very easily, unconstrainedly and complacently.

On reaching home I promptly wrote to Simonov.

To this hour I am lost in admiration when I recall the truly gentlemanly, good-humored, candid tone of my letter. With tact and good-breeding, and, above all, entirely without superfluous words, I blamed myself for all that had happened. I defended myself, "if I really may be allowed to defend myself," by alleging that, being utterly unaccustomed to wine, I had been intoxicated with the first glass, which I said I had drunk before they arrived, while I was waiting for them at the Hôtel de Paris between five and six o'clock. I begged Simonov's pardon especially; I asked him to convey my explanations to all the others, especially to Zverkov, whom "I seemed to remember as though in a dream" I had insulted. I added that I would have called upon all of them myself, but my head ached, and besides I had not the face to. I was particularly pleased with a certain lightness, almost carelessness (strictly within the bounds of politeness, however), which was apparent in my style, and better than any possible arguments, gave them at once to understand that I took rather an independent view of "all that unpleasantness last night"; that I was by no means so utterly crushed as you, my friends, probably imagine; but on the contrary, looked upon it as a gentleman serenely respecting himself should look upon it. "On a young hero's past no censure is cast!"

"There is actually an aristocratic playfulness about it!" I thought admiringly, as I read over the letter. And it's all because I am an intellectual and cultivated man! Another man in my place would not have known how to extricate himself, but here I have got out of it and am as jolly as ever again, and all because I am "a cultivated and educated man of our day." And, indeed, perhaps, everything was due to the wine yesterday. H'm! . . . no, it was not the wine. I did not drink anything at all between five and six when I was waiting for them. I had lied to Simonov; I had lied shamelessly; and indeed I wasn't ashamed now. . . . Hang it all though, the great thing was that I was rid of it.

[47] A seducer, from a major character in Samuel Richardson's *Clarissa Harlowe* (1747–48).

I put six roubles in the letter, sealed it up, and asked Apollon to take it to Simonov. When he learned that there was money in the letter, Apollon became more respectful and agreed to take it. Towards evening I went out for a walk. My head was still aching and giddy after yesterday. But as evening came on and the twilight grew denser, my impressions and, following them, my thoughts, grew more and more different and confused. Something was not dead within me, in the depths of my heart and conscience it would not die, and it showed itself in acute depression. For the most part I jostled my way through the most crowded business streets, along Myeshchansky Street, along Sadovy Street and in Yusupov Garden. I always liked particularly sauntering along these streets in the dusk, just when there were crowds of working people of all sorts going home from their daily work, with faces looking cross with anxiety. What I liked was just that cheap bustle, that bare prose. On this occasion the jostling of the streets irritated me more than ever. I could not make out what was wrong with me, I could not find the clue, something seemed rising up continually in my soul, painfully, and refusing to be appeased. I returned home completely upset, it was just as though some crime were lying on my conscience.

The thought that Liza was coming worried me continually. It seemed queer to me that of all my recollections of yesterday this tormented me, as it were, especially, as it were, quite separately. Everything else I had quite succeeded in forgetting by the evening; I dismissed it all and was still perfectly satisfied with my letter to Simonov. But on this point I was not satisfied at all. It was as though I were worried only by Liza. "What if she comes," I thought incessantly, "well, it doesn't matter, let her come! H'm! it's horrid that she should see, for instance, how I live. Yesterday I seemed such a hero to her, while now, h'm! It's horrid, though, that I have let myself go so, the room looks like a beggar's. And I brought myself to go out to dinner in such a suit! And my American leather[48] sofa with the stuffing sticking out. And my dressing-gown, which will not cover me, such tatters, and she will see all this and she will see Apollon. That beast is certain to insult her. He will fasten upon her in order to be rude to me. And I, of course, shall be panic-stricken as usual, I shall begin bowing and scraping before her and pulling my dressing-gown round me, I shall begin smiling, telling lies. Oh, the beastliness! And it isn't the beastliness of it that matters most! There is something more important, more loathsome, viler! Yes, viler! And to put on that dishonest lying mask again!" . . .

When I reached that thought I fired up all at once.

"Why dishonest? How dishonest? I was speaking sincerely last night. I remember there was real feeling in me, too. What I wanted was to excite an honorable feeling in her. . . . Her crying was a good thing, it will have a good effect."

Yet I could not feel at ease. All that evening, even when I had come back home, even after nine o'clock, when I calculated that Liza could not possibly come, she still haunted me, and what was worse, she came back to my mind always in the same position. One moment out of all that had happened last night stood vividly before my imagination; the moment when I struck a match and saw her pale, distorted face, with its look of torture.

[48] A cheap kind of artificial leather.

And what a pitiful, what an unnatural, what a distorted smile she had at that moment! But I did not know then, that fifteen years later I should still in my imagination see Liza, always with the pitiful, distorted, inappropriate smile which was on her face at that minute.

Next day I was ready again to look upon it all as nonsense, due to over-excited nerves, and, above all, as *exaggerated.* I was always conscious of that weak point of mine, and sometimes very much afraid of it. "I exaggerate everything, that is where I go wrong," I repeated to myself every hour. But, however, "Liza will very likely come all the same," was the refrain with which all my reflections ended. I was so uneasy that I sometimes flew into a fury: "She'll come, she is certain to come!" I cried, running about the room, "if not today, she will come tomorrow; she'll find me out! The damnable romanticism of these pure hearts! Oh, the vileness—oh, the silliness—oh, the stupidity of these 'wretched sentimental souls!' Why, how fail to understand? How could one fail to understand? . . ."

But at this point I stopped short, and in great confusion, indeed.

And how few, how few words, I thought, in passing, were needed; how little of the idyllic (and affectedly, bookishly, artificially idyllic too) had sufficed to turn a whole human life at once according to my will. That's virginity, to be sure! Freshness of soil!

At times a thought occurred to me, to go to her, "to tell her all," and beg her not to come to me. But this thought stirred such wrath in me that I believed I should have crushed that "damned" Liza if she had chanced to be near me at the time. I should have insulted her, have spat at her, have turned her out, have struck her!

One day passed, however, another and another; she did not come and I began to grow calmer. I felt particularly bold and cheerful after nine o'clock, I even sometimes began dreaming, and rather sweetly: I, for instance, became the salvation of Liza, simply through her coming to me and my talking to her. . . . I develop her, educate her. Finally, I notice that she loves me, loves me passionately. I pretend not to understand (I don't know, however, why I pretend, just for effect, perhaps). At last all confusion, transfigured, trembling and sobbing, she flings herself at my feet and says that I am her savior, and that she loves me better than anything in the world. I am amazed, but. . . . "Liza," I say, "can you imagine that I have not noticed your love, I saw it all, I divined it, but I did not dare to approach you first, because I had an influence over you and was afraid that you would force yourself, from gratitude, to respond to my love, would try to rouse in your heart a feeling which was perhaps absent, and I did not wish that . . . because it would be tyranny . . . it would be indelicate (in short, I launch off at that point into European, inexplicably lofty subtleties à la George Sand[49]), but now, now you are mine, you are my creation, you are pure, you are good, you are my noble wife.

'Into my house come bold and free,
Its rightful mistress there to be.'"[50]

[49] Pseudonym of the French novelist and feminist Aurore Dupin (1804–76). Her novels are marked by a high moral idealism.

[50] These are the last lines of the poem by Nekrasov quoted at the beginning of Part II.

Then we begin living together, go abroad and so on, and so on. In fact, in the end it seemed vulgar to me myself, and I began putting out my tongue at myself.

Besides, they won't let her out, "the hussy!" I thought. They don't let them go out very readily, especially in the evening (for some reason I fancied she would come in the evening, and at seven o'clock precisely). Though she did say she was not altogether a slave there yet, and had certain rights; so, h'm! Damn it all, she will come, she is sure to come!

It was a good thing, in fact, that Apollon distracted my attention at that time by his rudeness. He drove me beyond all patience! He was the bane of my life, the curse laid upon me by Providence. We had been squabbling continually for years, and I hated him. My God, how I hated him! I believe I had never hated any one in my life as I hated him, especially at some moments. He was an elderly, dignified man, who worked part of his time as a tailor. But for some unknown reason he despised me beyond all measure, and looked down upon me insufferably. Though, indeed, he looked down upon every one. Simply to glance at that flaxen, smoothly brushed head, at the tuft of hair he combed up on his forehead and oiled with sunflower oil, at that dignified mouth, compressed into the shape of the letter V, made one feel one was confronting a man who never doubted of himself. He was a pedant, to the most extreme point, the greatest pedant I had met on earth, and with that had a vanity only befitting Alexander of Macedon.[51] He was in love with every button on his coat, every nail on his fingers—absolutely in love with them, and he looked it! In his behavior to me he was a perfect tyrant, he spoke very little to me, and if he chanced to glance at me he gave me a firm, majestically self-confident and invariably ironical look that drove me sometimes to fury. He did his work with the air of doing me the greatest favor. Though he did scarcely anything for me, and did not, indeed, consider himself bound to do anything. There could be no doubt that he looked upon me as the greatest fool on earth, and that "he did not get rid of me" was simply that he could get wages from me every month. He consented to do nothing for me for seven roubles a month. Many sins should be forgiven me for what I suffered from him. My hatred reached such a point that sometimes his very step almost threw me into convulsions. What I loathed particularly was his lisp. His tongue must have been a little too long or something of that sort, for he continually lisped, and seemed to be very proud of it, imagining that it greatly added to his dignity. He spoke in a slow, measured tone, with his hands behind his back and his eyes fixed on the ground. He maddened me particularly when he read aloud the psalms to himself behind his partition. Many a battle I waged over that reading! But he was awfully fond of reading aloud in the evenings, in a slow, even, sing-song voice, as though over the dead. It is interesting that that is how he has ended: he hires himself out to read the psalms over the dead, and at the same time he kills rats and makes blacking.[52] But at that time I could not get rid of him, it was as though he were chemically combined with my existence. Besides, nothing would have induced him to consent to leave me. I could not live in furnished lodgings:

[51] Alexander the Great (356–323 B.C.).
[52] Compound to make things black, either shoes or stoves.

my lodging was my private solitude, my shell, my cave, in which I concealed myself from all mankind, and Apollon seemed to me, for some reason, an integral part of that flat, and for seven years I could not turn him away.

To be two or three days behind with his wages, for instance, was impossible. He would have made such a fuss, I should not have known where to hide my head. But I was so exasperated with every one during those days, that I made up my mind for some reason and with some object to *punish* Apollon and not to pay him for a fortnight the wages that were owing him. I had for a long time—for the last two years—been intending to do this, simply in order to teach him not to give himself airs with me, and to show him that if I liked I could withhold his wages. I purposed to say nothing to him about it, and was purposely silent indeed, in order to score off his pride and force him to be the first to speak of his wages. Then I would take the seven roubles out of a drawer, show him I have the money put aside on purpose, but that I won't, I won't, I simply won't pay him his wages, I won't just because that is "what I wish," because "I am master, and it is for me to decide," because he has been disrespectful, because he has been rude; but if he were to ask respectfully I might be softened and give it to him, otherwise he might wait another fortnight, another three weeks, a whole month. . . .

But angry as I was, yet he got the better of me. I could not hold out for four days. He began as he always did begin in such cases, for there had been such cases already, there had been attempts (and it may be observed I knew all this beforehand, I knew his nasty tactics by heart). He would begin by fixing upon me an exceedingly severe stare, keeping it up for several minutes at a time, particularly on meeting me or seeing me out of the house. If I held out and pretended not to notice these stares, he would, still in silence, proceed to further tortures. All at once, *à propos* of nothing, he would walk softly and smoothly into my room, when I was pacing up and down or reading, stand at the door, one hand behind his back and one foot behind the other, and fix upon me a stare more than severe, utterly contemptuous. If I suddenly asked him what he wanted, he would make me no answer, but continue staring at me persistently for some seconds, then, with a peculiar compression of his lips and a most significant air, deliberately turn round and deliberately go back to his room. Two hours later he would come out again and again present himself before me in the same way. It had happened that in my fury I did not even ask him what he wanted, but simply raised my head sharply and imperiously and began staring back at him. So we stared at one another for two minutes; at last he turned with deliberation and dignity and went back again for two hours.

If I were still not brought to reason by all this, but persisted in my revolt, he would suddenly begin sighing while he looked at me, long, deep sighs as though measuring by them the depths of my moral degradation, and, of course, it ended at last by his triumphing completely: I raged and shouted, but still was forced to do what he wanted.

This time the usual staring maneuvers had scarcely begun when I lost my temper and flew at him in a fury. I was irritated beyond endurance apart from him.

"Stay," I cried, in a frenzy, as he was slowly and silently turning, with one hand behind his back, to go to his room, "stay! Come back, come back,

I tell you!" and I must have bawled so unnaturally, that he turned round and even looked at me with some wonder. However, he persisted in saying nothing, and that infuriated me.

"How dare you come and look at me like that without being sent for? Answer!"

After looking at me calmly for half a minute, he began turning round again.

"Stay!" I roared, running up to him, "don't stir! There. Answer, now: what did you come in to look at?"

"If you have any order to give me it's my duty to carry it out," he answered, after another silent pause, with a slow, measured lisp, raising his eyebrows and calmly twisting his head from one side to another, all this with exasperating composure.

"That's not what I am asking you about, you torturer!" I shouted, turning crimson with anger. "I'll tell you why you came here myself: you see, I don't give you your wages, you are so proud you don't want to bow down and ask for it, and so you come to punish me with your stupid stares, to worry me and you have no sus . . . pic . . . ion how stupid it is—stupid, stupid, stupid, stupid!" . . .

He would have turned round again without a word, but I seized him.

"Listen," I shouted to him. "Here's the money, do you see, here it is" (I took it out of the table drawer); "here's the seven roubles complete, but you are not going to have it, you . . . are . . . not . . . going . . . to . . . have it until you come respectfully with bowed head to beg my pardon. Do you hear?"

"That cannot be," he answered, with the most unnatural self-confidence.

"It shall be so," I said, "I give you my word of honor, it shall be!"

"And there's nothing for me to beg your pardon for," he went on, as though he had not noticed my exclamations at all. "Why, besides, you called me a 'torturer,' for which I can summon you at the police-station at any time for insulting behavior."

"Go, summon me," I roared, "go at once, this very minute, this very second! You are a torturer all the same! a torturer!"

But he merely looked at me, then turned, and regardless of my loud calls to him, he walked to his room with an even step and without looking round.

"If it had not been for Liza nothing of this would have happened," I decided inwardly. Then, after waiting a minute, I went myself behind his screen with a dignified and solemn air, though my heart was beating slowly and violently.

"Apollon," I said quietly and emphatically, though I was breathless, "go at once without a minute's delay and fetch the police-officer."

He had meanwhile settled himself at his table, put on his spectacles and taken up some sewing. But, hearing my order, he burst into a guffaw.

"At once, go this minute! Go on, or else you can't imagine what will happen."

"You are certainly out of your mind," he observed, without even raising his head, lisping as deliberately as ever and threading his needle. "Whoever heard of a man sending for the police against himself? And as for being frightened—you are upsetting yourself about nothing, for nothing will come of it."

"Go!" I shrieked, clutching him by the shoulder. I felt I should strike him in a minute.

But I did not notice the door from the passage softly and slowly open at that instant and a figure come in, stop short, and begin staring at us in perplexity. I glanced, nearly swooned with shame, and rushed back to my room. There, clutching at my hair with both hands, I leaned my head against the wall and stood motionless in that position.

Two minutes later I heard Apollon's deliberate footsteps. "There is some woman asking for you," he said, looking at me with peculiar severity. Then he stood aside and let in Liza. He would not go away, but stared at us sarcastically.

"Go away, go away," I commanded in desperation. At that moment my clock began whirring and wheezing and struck seven.

IX

"Into my house come bold and free,
Its rightful mistress there to be."
(From the same poem)

I stood before her crushed, crestfallen, revoltingly confused, and I believe I smiled as I did my utmost to wrap myself in the skirts of my ragged wadded dressing-gown—exactly as I had imagined the scene not long before in a fit of depression. After standing over us for a couple of minutes Apollon went away, but that did not make me more at ease. What made it worse was that she, too, was overwhelmed with confusion, more so, in fact, than I should have expected. At the sight of me, of course.

"Sit down," I said mechanically, moving a chair up to the table, and I sat down on the sofa. She obediently sat down at once and gazed at me open-eyed, evidently expecting something from me at once. This naïveté of expectation drove me to fury, but I restrained myself.

She ought to have tried not to notice, as though everything had been as usual, while instead of that, she . . . and I dimly felt that I should make her pay dearly for *all this*.

"You have found me in a strange position, Liza," I began, stammering and knowing that this was the wrong way to begin. "No, no, don't imagine anything," I cried, seeing that she had suddenly flushed. "I am not ashamed of my poverty. . . . On the contrary I look with pride on my poverty. I am poor but honorable. . . . One can be poor and honorable," I muttered. "However . . . would you like tea?". . .

"No," she was beginning.

"Wait a minute."

I leaped up and ran to Apollon. I had to get out of the room somehow.

"Apollon," I whispered in feverish haste, flinging down before him the seven roubles which had remained all the time in my clenched fist, "here are your wages, you see I give them to you; but for that you must come to my rescue: bring me tea and a dozen rusks from the restaurant. If you won't go, you'll make me a miserable man! You don't know what this woman is. . . . This is—everything! You may be imagining something. . . . But you don't know what that woman is!" . . .

Apollon, who had already sat down to his work and put on his spectacles again, at first glanced askance at the money without speaking or putting down his needle; then, without paying the slightest attention to me or making any answer he went on busying himself with his needle, which he had not yet threaded. I waited before him for three minutes with my arms crossed *à la Napoléon.* My temples were moist with sweat. I was pale, I felt it. But, thank God, he must have been moved to pity, looking at me. Having threaded his needle he deliberately got up from his seat, deliberately moved back his chair, deliberately took off his spectacles, deliberately counted the money, and finally asking me over his shoulder: "Shall I get a whole portion?" deliberately walked out of the room. As I was going back to Liza, the thought occurred to me on the way: shouldn't I run away just as I was in my dressing-gown, no matter where, and then let happen what would.

I sat down again. She looked at me uneasily. For some minutes we were silent.

"I will kill him," I shouted suddenly, striking the table with my fist so that the ink spurted out of the inkstand.

"What are you saying!" she cried, starting.

"I will kill him! kill him!" I shrieked, suddenly striking the table in absolute frenzy, and at the same time fully understanding how stupid it was to be in such a frenzy. "You don't know, Liza, what that torturer is to me. He is my torturer. . . . He has gone now to fetch some rusks; he . . ."

And suddenly I burst into tears. It was an hysterical attack. How ashamed I felt in the midst of my sobs; but still I could not restrain them.

She was frightened.

"What is the matter? What is wrong?" she cried, fussing about me.

"Water, give me water, over there!" I muttered in a faint voice, though I was inwardly conscious that I could have got on very well without water and without muttering in a faint voice. But I was, what is called, *putting it on,* to save appearances, though the attack was a genuine one.

She gave me water, looking at me in bewilderment. At that moment Apollon brought in the tea. It suddenly seemed to me that this commonplace, prosaic tea was horribly undignified and paltry after all that had happened, and I blushed crimson. Liza looked at Apollon with positive alarm. He went out without a glance at either of us.

"Liza, do you despise me?" I asked, looking at her fixedly, trembling with impatience to know what she was thinking.

She was confused, and did not know what to answer.

"Drink your tea," I said to her angrily. I was angry with myself, but, of course, it was she who would have to pay for it. A horrible spite against her suddenly surged up in my heart; I believe I could have killed her. To revenge myself on her I swore inwardly not to say a word to her all the time. "She is the cause of it all," I thought.

Our silence lasted for five minutes. The tea stood on the table; we did not touch it. I had got to the point of purposely refraining from beginning in order to embarrass her further; it was awkward for her to begin alone. Several times she glanced at me with mournful perplexity. I was obstinately silent. I was, of course, myself the chief sufferer, because I was fully conscious of the disgusting meanness of my spiteful stupidity, and yet at the same time I could not restrain myself.

"I want to . . . get away . . . from there altogether," she began, to break the silence in some way, but, poor girl, that was just what she ought not to have spoken about at such a stupid moment to a man so stupid as I was. My heart positively ached with pity for her tactless and unnecessary straightforwardness. But something hideous at once stifled all compassion in me; it even provoked me to greater venom. I did not care what happened. Another five minutes passed.

"Perhaps I am in your way," she began timidly, hardly audibly, and was getting up.

But as soon as I saw this first impulse of wounded dignity I positively trembled with spite, and at once burst out.

"Why have you come to me, tell me that, please?" I began, gasping for breath and regardless of logical connection in my words. I longed to have it all out at once, at one burst; I did not even trouble how to begin. "Why have you come? Answer, answer," I cried, hardly knowing what I was doing. "I'll tell you, my good girl, why you have come. You've come because I talked sentimental stuff to you then. So now you are soft as butter and longing for fine sentiments again. So you may as well know that I was laughing at you then. And I am laughing at you now. Why are you shuddering? Yes, I was laughing at you! I had been insulted just before, at dinner, by the fellows who came that evening before me. I came to you, meaning to thrash one of them, an officer; but I didn't succeed, I didn't find him; I had to avenge the insult on some one to get back my own again; you turned up, I vented my spleen on you and laughed at you. I had been humiliated, so I wanted to humiliate; I had been treated like a rag, so I wanted to show my power. . . . That's what it was, and you imagined I had come there on purpose to save you. Yes? You imagined that? You imagined that?"

I knew that she would perhaps be muddled and not take it all in exactly, but I knew, too, that she would grasp the gist of it, very well indeed. And so, indeed, she did. She turned white as a handkerchief, tried to say something, and her lips worked painfully; but she sank on a chair as though she had been felled by an axe. And all the time afterwards she listened to me with her lips parted and her eyes wide open, shuddering with awful terror. The cynicism, the cynicism of my words overwhelmed her. . . .

"Save you!" I went on, jumping up from my chair and running up and down the room before her. "Save you from what? But perhaps I am worse than you myself. Why didn't you throw it in my teeth when I was giving you that sermon: 'But what did you come here yourself for? was it to read us a sermon?' Power, power was what I wanted then, sport was what I wanted, I wanted to wring out your tears, your humiliation, your hysteria—that was what I wanted then! Of course, I couldn't keep it up then, because I am a wretched creature, I was frightened, and, the devil knows why, gave you my address in my folly. Afterwards, before I got home, I was cursing and swearing at you because of that address, I hated you already because of the lies I had told you. Because I only like playing with words, only dreaming, but, do you know, what I really want is that you should all go to hell. That is what I want. I want peace; yes, I'd sell the whole world for a farthing, straight off, so long as I was left in peace. Is the world to go to pot, or am I to go without my tea? I say that the world may go to pot for me so long as I always get my tea. Did you know that, or not? Well, anyway, I know that I am a blackguard, a scoundrel, an egoist, a sluggard. Here I have been shuddering for the last three days at the thought of your coming. And do you know what has worried me particularly for these three days? That I posed as such a hero to you, and now you would see me in a wretched torn dressing-gown, beggarly, loathsome. I told you just now that I was not ashamed of my poverty; so you may as well know that I am ashamed of it; I am more ashamed of it than of anything, more afraid of it than of being found out if I were a thief, because I am as vain as though I had been skinned and the very air blowing on me hurts. Surely by now you must realize that I shall never forgive you for having found me in this wretched dressing-gown, just as I was flying at Apollon like a spiteful cur. The savior, the former hero, was flying like a mangy, unkempt sheep-dog at his lackey, and the lackey was jeering at him! And I shall never forgive you for the tears I could not help shedding before you just now, like some silly woman put to shame! And for what I am confessing to you now, I shall never forgive *you* either! Yes—you must answer for it all because you turned up like this, because I am a blackguard, because I am the nastiest, stupidest, absurdest and most envious of all the worms on earth, who are not a bit better than I am, but, the devil knows why, are never put to confusion; while I shall always be insulted by every louse, that is my doom! And what is it to me that you don't understand a word of this! And what do I care, what do I care about you, and whether you go to ruin there or not? Do you understand? How I shall hate you now after saying this, for having been here and listening. Why, it's not once in a lifetime a man speaks out like this, and then it is in hysterics! . . . What more do you want? Why do you still stand confronting me, after all this? Why are you worrying me? Why don't you go?"

But at this point a strange thing happened. I was so accustomed to think and imagine everything from books, and to picture everything in the world to myself just as I had made it up in my dreams beforehand, that I could not all at once take in this strange circumstance. What happened was this: Liza, insulted and crushed by me, understood a great deal more than I imagined. She understood from all this what a woman understands first of all, if she feels genuine love, that is, that I was myself unhappy.

The frightened and wounded expression on her face was followed first by a look of sorrowful perplexity. When I began calling myself a scoundrel and a blackguard and my tears flowed (the tirade was accompanied throughout by tears) her whole face worked convulsively. She was on the point of getting up and stopping me; when I finished she took no notice of my shouting: "Why are you here, why don't you go away?" but realized only that it must have been very bitter to me to say all this. Besides, she was so crushed, poor girl; she considered herself infinitely beneath me; how could she feel anger or resentment? She suddenly leaped up from her chair with an irresistible impulse and held out her hands, yearning towards me, though still timid and not daring to stir. . . . At this point there was a revulsion in my heart, too. Then she suddenly rushed to me, threw her arms round me and burst into tears. I, too, could not restrain myself, and sobbed as I never had before.

"They won't let me . . . I can't be good!" I managed to articulate; then I went to the sofa, fell on it face downwards, and sobbed on it for a quarter of an hour in genuine hysterics. She came close to me, put her arms round me and stayed motionless in that position. But the trouble was that the hysterics could not go on for ever, and (I am writing the loathsome truth) lying face downwards on the sofa with my face thrust into my nasty leather pillow, I began by degrees to be aware of a far-away, involuntary but irresistible feeling that it would be awkward now for me to raise my head and look Liza straight in the face. Why was I ashamed? I don't know, but I was ashamed. The thought, too, came into my overwrought brain that our parts now were completely changed, that she was now the heroine, while I was just such a crushed and humiliated creature as she had been before me that night—four days before. . . . And all this came into my mind during the minutes I was lying on my face on the sofa.

My God! surely I was not envious of her then.

I don't know, to this day I cannot decide, and at the time, of course, I was still less able to understand what I was feeling than now. I cannot get on without domineering and tyrannizing over some one, but . . . there is no explaining anything by reasoning and so it is useless to reason.

I conquered myself, however, and raised my head; I had to do so sooner or later . . . and I am convinced to this day that it was just because I was ashamed to look at her that another feeling was suddenly kindled and flamed up in my heart . . . a feeling of mastery and possession. My eyes gleamed with passion, and I gripped her hands tightly. How I hated her and how I was drawn to her at that minute! The one feeling intensified the other. It was almost like an act of vengeance. At first there was a look of amazement, even of terror on her face, but only for one instant. She warmly and rapturously embraced me.

X

A quarter of an hour later I was rushing up and down the room in frenzied impatience, from minute to minute I went up to the screen and peeped through the crack at Liza. She was sitting on the ground with her head leaning against the bed, and must have been crying. But she did not go away, and that irritated me. This time she understood it all. I had insulted her finally, but . . . there's no need to describe it. She realized that my outburst of passion had been simply revenge, a fresh humiliation, and that to my earlier, almost causeless hatred was added a *personal hatred,* born of envy. . . . Though I do not maintain positively that she understood all this distinctly; but she certainly did fully understand that I was a despicable man, and what was worse, incapable of loving her.

I know I shall be told that this is incredible—but it is incredible to be as spiteful and stupid as I was; it may be added that it was strange I should not love her, or at any rate, appreciate her love. Why is it strange? In the first place, by then I was incapable of love, for I repeat, with me loving meant tyrannizing and showing my moral superiority. I have never in my life been able to imagine any other sort of love, and have nowadays come to the point of sometimes thinking that love really consists in the right—freely given by the beloved object—to tyrannize over her.

Even in my underground dreams I did not imagine love except as a struggle. I began it always with hatred and ended it with moral subjugation, and afterwards I never knew what to do with the subjugated object. And what is there to wonder at in that, since I had succeeded in so corrupting myself, since I was so out of touch with "real life," as to have actually thought of reproaching her, and putting her to shame for having come to me to hear "fine sentiments"; and did not even guess that she had come not to hear fine sentiments, but to love me, because to a woman all reformation, all salvation from any sort of ruin, and all moral renewal is included in love and can only show itself in that form.

I did not hate her so much, however, when I was running about the room and peeping through the crack in the screen. I was only insufferably oppressed by her being here. I wanted her to disappear. I wanted "peace," to be left alone in my underground world. Real life oppressed me with its novelty so much that I could hardly breathe.

But several minutes passed and she still remained, without stirring, as though she were unconscious. I had the shamelessness to tap softly at the screen as though to remind her. . . . She started, sprang up, and flew to seek her kerchief, her hat, her coat, as though making her escape from me. . . . Two minutes later she came from behind the screen and looked with heavy eyes at me. I gave a spiteful grin, which was forced, however, to *keep up appearances,* and I turned away from her eyes.

"Good-bye," she said, going towards the door.

I ran up to her, seized her hand, opened it, thrust something in it and closed it again. Then I turned at once and dashed away in haste to the other corner of the room to avoid seeing her, anyway. . . .

I did not mean a moment since to tell a lie—to write that I did this accidentally, not knowing what I was doing through foolishness, through losing my head. But I don't want to lie, and so I will say straight out that I opened her hand and put the money in it . . . from spite. It came into my head to do this while I was running up and down the room and she was sitting behind the screen. But this I can say for certain: though I did that cruel thing purposely, it was not an impulse from the heart, but came from my evil brain. This cruelty was so affected, so purposely made up, so completely a product of the brain, of books, that I could not even keep it up a minute—first I dashed away to avoid seeing her, and then in shame and despair rushed after Liza. I opened the door in the passage and began listening.

"Liza! Liza!" I cried on the stairs, but in a low voice, not boldly.

There was no answer, but I fancied I heard her footsteps, lower down on the stairs.

"Liza!" I cried, more loudly.

No answer. But at that minute I heard the stiff outer glass door open heavily with a creak and slam violently, the sound echoed up the stairs.

She had gone. I went back to my room in hesitation. I felt horribly oppressed.

I stood still at the table, beside the chair on which she had sat and looked aimlessly before me. A minute passed, suddenly I started; straight before me on the table I saw. . . . In short, I saw a crumpled blue five-rouble note, the one I had thrust into her hand a minute before. It was the same note; it could be no other, there was no other in the flat. So she had managed to fling it from her hand on the table at the moment when I had dashed into the further corner.

Well! I might have expected that she would do that. Might I have expected it? No, I was such an egoist, I was so lacking in respect for my fellow-creatures that I could not even imagine she would do so. I could not endure it. A minute later I flew like a madman to dress, flinging on what I could at random and ran headlong after her. She could not have got two hundred paces away when I ran out into the street.

It was a still night and the snow was coming down in masses and falling almost perpendicularly, covering the pavement and the empty street as though with a pillow. There was no one in the street, no sound was to be heard. The street lamps gave a disconsolate and useless glimmer. I ran two hundred paces to the cross-roads and stopped short.

Where had she gone? And why was I running after her?

Why? To fall down before her, to sob with remorse, to kiss her feet, to entreat her forgiveness! I longed for that, my whole breast was being rent to pieces, and never, never shall I recall that minute with indifference. But—what for? I thought. Should I not begin to hate her, perhaps, even tomorrow, just because I had kissed her feet today? Should I give her happiness? Had I not recognized that day, for the hundredth time, what I was worth? Should I not torture her?

I stood in the snow, gazing into the troubled darkness, and pondered this.

"And will it not be better?" I mused fantastically, afterwards at home, stifling the living pang of my heart with fantastic dreams. "Will it not be better that she should keep the resentment of the insult for ever? Resentment—why, it is purification; it is a most stinging and painful consciousness! Tomorrow I should have defiled her soul and have exhausted her heart, while now the feeling of insult will never die in her heart, and however loathsome the filth awaiting her—the feeling of insult will elevate and purify her . . . by hatred . . . h'm! . . . perhaps, too, by forgiveness. . . . Will all that make things easier for her though? . . ."

And, indeed, I will ask on my own account here, an idle question: which is better—cheap happiness or exalted sufferings? Well, which is better?

So I dreamed as I sat at home that evening, almost dead with the pain in my soul. Never had I endured such suffering and remorse, yet could there have been the faintest doubt when I ran out from my lodging that I should turn back half-way? I never met Liza again and I have heard nothing of her. I will add, too, that I remained for a long time afterwards pleased with the phrase about the benefit from resentment and hatred in spite of the fact that I almost fell ill from misery.

Even now, so many years later, all this is somehow a very evil memory. I have many evil memories now, but . . . hadn't I better end my "Notes" here? I believe I made a mistake in beginning to write them, anyway I have felt ashamed all the time I've been writing this story; so it's hardly literature so much as a corrective punishment. Why, to tell long stories, showing how

I have spoiled my life through morally rotting in my corner, through lack of fitting environment, through divorce from real life, and rankling spite in my underground world, would certainly not be interesting; a novel needs a hero, and all the traits for an anti-hero are *expressly* gathered together here, and what matters most, it all produces an unpleasant impression, for we are all divorced from life, we are all cripples, every one of us, more or less. We are so divorced from it that we feel at once a sort of loathing for real life, and so cannot bear to be reminded of it. Why, we have come almost to looking upon real life as an effort, almost as hard labor, and we are all privately agreed that it is better in books. And why do we fuss and fume sometimes? Why are we perverse and ask for something else? We don't know what ourselves. It would be the worse for us if our petulant prayers were answered. Come, try, give any one of us, for instance, a little more independence, untie our hands, widen the spheres of our activity, relax the control and we . . . yes, I assure you . . . we should be begging to be under control again at once. I know that you will very likely be angry with me for that, and will begin shouting and stamping. Speak for yourself, you will say, and for your miseries in your underground holes, and don't dare to say "all of us"—excuse me, gentlemen, I am not justifying myself with that "all of us." As for what concerns me in particular I have only in my life carried to an extreme what you have not dared to carry half-way, and what's more, you have taken your cowardice for good sense, and have found comfort in deceiving yourselves. So that perhaps, after all, there is more life in me than in you. Look into it more carefully! Why, we don't even know what living means now, what it is, and what it is called? Leave us alone without books and we shall be lost and in confusion at once. We shall not know what to join on to, what to cling to, what to love and what to hate, what to respect and what to despise. We are oppressed at being men—men with a real individual flesh and blood, we are ashamed of it, we think it a disgrace and try to contrive to be some sort of impossible generalized man. We are stillborn, and for generations past have been begotten, not by living fathers, and that suits us better and better. We are developing a taste for it. Soon we shall contrive to be born somehow from an idea. But enough; I don't want to write more from "Underground."

(The notes of this paradoxalist do not end here, however. He could not refrain from going on with them, but it seems to us that we may stop here.)

from *THE BROTHERS KARAMAZOV*

Translated by Constance Garnett

THE GRAND INQUISITOR

"You wrote a poem?"

"Oh, no, I didn't write it," laughed Ivan, "and I've never written two lines of poetry in my life. But I made up this poem in prose and I remembered it. I was carried away when I made it up. You will be my first reader—that is, listener. Why should an author forego even one listener?" smiled Ivan. "Shall I tell it to you?"

"I am all attention," said Alyosha.

"My poem is called 'The Grand Inquisitor'; it's a ridiculous thing, but I want to tell it to you. . . ."

"Fifteen centuries have passed since He promised to come in His glory, fifteen centuries since His prophet wrote, 'Behold, I come quickly';[1] 'Of that day and that hour knoweth no man, neither the Son, but the Father,'[2] as He Himself predicted on earth. But humanity awaits Him with the same faith and with the same love. Oh, with greater faith, for it is fifteen centuries since man has ceased to see signs from heaven.

> No signs from heaven come today
> To add to what the heart doth say.

There was nothing left but faith in what the heart doth say. It is true there were many miracles in those days. There were saints who performed miraculous cures; some holy people, according to their biographies, were visited by the Queen of Heaven herself. But the devil did not slumber, and doubts were already arising among men of the truth of these miracles. And just then there appeared in the north of Germany a terrible new heresy. 'A huge star like to a torch' (that is, to a church) 'fell on the sources of the waters and they became bitter.' These heretics began blasphemously denying miracles. But those who remained faithful were all the more ardent in their faith. The tears of humanity rose up to Him as before, awaited His coming, loved Him, hoped for Him, yearned to suffer and die for Him as before. And so many ages mankind had prayed with faith and fervor, 'O Lord our God, hasten Thy coming,' so many ages called upon Him, that in His infinite mercy He deigned to come down to His servants. Before that day He had come down, He had visited some holy men, martyrs and hermits, as is written in their lives. Among us, Tyutchev,[3] with absolute faith in the truth of his words, bore witness that

> Bearing the Cross, in slavish dress,
> Weary and worn, the Heavenly King
> Our mother, Russia, came to bless,
> And through our land went wandering.

And that certainly was so, I assure you.

"And behold, He deigned to appear for a moment to the people, to the tortured, suffering people, sunk in iniquity, but loving Him like children. My story is laid in Spain, in Seville, in the most terrible time of the Inquisition, when fires were lighted every day to the glory of God, and 'in the splendid *auto da fé*[4] the wicked heretics were burnt.' Oh, of course, this was not the coming in which He will appear according to His promise at the

[1] Revelation 22:7. [2] Mark 13:32. [3] Fëdor Tyutchev, Russian poet (1803–73).
[4] Literally, "act of the faith" (Portuguese); the burning of a heretic.

end of time in all His heavenly glory, and which will be sudden 'as lightning flashing from east to west.'[5] No, He visited His children only for a moment, and there where the flames were crackling around the heretics. In His infinite mercy He came once more among men in that human shape in which He walked among men for three years fifteen centuries ago. He came down to the 'hot pavements' of the southern town in which on the day before almost a hundred heretics had, *ad majorem gloriam Dei,*[6] been burnt by the cardinal, the Grand Inquisitor, in a magnificent *auto da fé,* in the presence of the king, the court, the knights, the cardinals, the most charming ladies of the court, and the whole population of Seville.

"He came softly, unobserved, and yet, strange to say, every one recognized Him. That might be one of the best passages in the poem. I mean, why they recognized Him. The people are irresistibly drawn to Him, they surround Him, they flock about Him, follow Him. He moves silently in their midst with a gentle smile of infinite compassion. The sun of love burns in His heart, light and power shine from His eyes, and their radiance, shed on the people, stirs their hearts with responsive love. He holds out His hands to them, blesses them, and a healing virtue comes from contact with Him, even with His garments. An old man in the crowd, blind from childhood, cries out, 'O Lord, heal me and I shall see Thee!' and, as it were, scales fall from his eyes and the blind man sees Him. The crowd weeps and kisses the earth under His feet. Children throw flowers before Him, sing, and cry hosannah. 'It is He—it is He!' all repeat. 'It must be He, it can be no one but Him!' He stops at the steps of the Seville cathedral at the moment when the weeping mourners are bringing in a little open white coffin. In it lies a child of seven, the only daughter of a prominent citizen. The dead child lies hidden in flowers. 'He will raise your child,' the crowd shouts to the weeping mother. The priest, coming to meet the coffin, looks perplexed, and frowns, but the mother of the dead child throws herself at His feet with a wail. 'If it is Thou, raise my child!' she cries, holding out her hands to Him. The procession halts, the coffin is laid on the steps at His feet. He looks with compassion, and His lips once more softly pronounce, 'Maiden, arise!'[7] and the maiden arises. The little girl sits up in the coffin and looks round, smiling with wide-open wondering eyes, holding a bunch of white roses they had put in her hand.

"There are cries, sobs, confusion among the people, and at that moment the cardinal himself, the Grand Inquisitor, passes by the cathedral. He is an old man, almost ninety, tall and erect, with a withered face and sunken eyes, in which there is still a gleam of light. He is not dressed in his gorgeous cardinal's robes, as he was the day before, when he was burning the enemies of the Roman Church—at this moment he is wearing his coarse, old, monk's cassock. At a distance behind him come his gloomy assistants and slaves and the 'holy guard.' He stops at the sight of the crowd and watches it from a distance. He sees everything; he sees them set the coffin down at His feet, sees the child rise up, and his face darkens. He knits his thick gray brows and his eyes gleam with a sinister fire. He holds

[5] Matthew 24:27. [6] "For the greater glory of God," the motto of the Jesuits.
[7] Mark 5:41.

out his finger and bids the guards take Him. And such is his power, so completely are the people cowed into submission and trembling obedience to him, that the crowd immediately makes way for the guards, and in the midst of deathlike silence they lay hands on Him and lead Him away. The crowd instantly bows down to the earth, like one man, before the old Inquisitor. He blesses the people in silence and passes on. The guards lead their prisoner to the close, gloomy vaulted prison in the ancient palace of the Holy Inquisition and shut Him in it. The day passes and is followed by the dark, burning, 'breathless' night of Seville. The air is 'fragrant with laurel and lemon.' In the pitch darkness the iron door of the prison is suddenly opened and the Grand Inquisitor himself comes in with a light in his hand. He is alone; the door is closed at once behind him. He stands in the doorway and for a minute or two gazes into His face. At last he goes up slowly, sets the light on the table and speaks.

"'Is it Thou? Thou?' but receiving no answer, he adds at once, 'Don't answer, be silent. What canst Thou say, indeed? I know too well what Thou wouldst say. And Thou hast no right to add anything to what Thou hadst said of old. Why, then, art Thou come to hinder us? For Thou hast come to hinder us, and Thou knowest that. But dost Thou know what will be tomorrow? I know not who Thou art and care not to know whether it is Thou or only a semblance of Him, but tomorrow I shall condemn Thee and burn Thee at the stake as the worst of heretics. And the very people who have today kissed Thy feet, tomorrow at the faintest sign from me will rush to heap up the embers of Thy fire. Knowest Thou that? Yes, maybe Thou knowest it,' he added with thoughtful penetration, never for a moment taking his eyes off the Prisoner."

"I don't quite understand, Ivan. What does it mean?" Alyosha, who had been listening in silence, said with a smile. "Is it simply a wild fantasy, or a mistake on the part of the old man—some impossible *quiproquo*?"[8]

"Take it as the last," said Ivan, laughing, "if you are so corrupted by modern realism and can't stand anything fantastic. If you like it to be a case of mistaken identity, let it be so. It is true," he went on, laughing, "the old man was ninety, and he might well be crazy over his set idea. He might have been struck by the appearance of the Prisoner. It might, in fact, be simply his ravings, the delusion of an old man of ninety, over-excited by the *auto da fé* of a hundred heretics the day before. But does it matter to us after all whether it was a mistake of identity or a wild fantasy? All that matters is that the old man should speak out, should speak openly of what he has thought in silence for ninety years."

"And the Prisoner too is silent? Does He look at him and not say a word?"

"That's inevitable in any case," Ivan laughed again. "The old man has told Him He hasn't the right to add anything to what He has said of old. One may say it is the most fundamental feature of Roman Catholicism, in my opinion at least. 'All has been given by Thee to the Pope,' they say, 'and all, therefore, is still in the Pope's hands, and there is no need for Thee to come now at all. Thou must not meddle for the time, at least.' That's how they speak and write too—the Jesuits, at any rate. I have read it myself in

[8] Misunderstanding.

the works of their theologians. 'Hast Thou the right to reveal to us one of the mysteries of that world from which Thou hast come?' my old man asks Him, and answers the question for Him. 'No, Thou hast not; that Thou mayest not add to what has been said of old, and mayest not take from men the freedom which Thou didst exalt when Thou wast on earth. Whatsoever Thou revealest anew will encroach on men's freedom of faith; for it will be manifest as a miracle, and the freedom of their faith was dearer to Thee than anything in those days fifteen hundred years ago. Didst Thou not often say then, "I will make you free"?[9] But now Thou hast seen these "free" men,' the old man adds suddenly, with a pensive smile. 'Yes, we've paid dearly for it,' he goes on, looking sternly at Him, 'but at last we have completed that work in Thy name. For fifteen centuries we have been wrestling with Thy freedom, but now it is ended and over for good. Dost Thou not believe that it's over for good? Thou lookest meekly at me and deignest not even to be wroth with me. But let me tell Thee that now, today, people are more persuaded than ever that they have perfect freedom, yet they have brought their freedom to us and laid it humbly at our feet. But that has been our doing. Was this what Thou didst? Was this Thy freedom?'"

"I don't understand again," Alyosha broke in. "Is he ironical, is he jesting?"

"Not a bit of it! He claims it as a merit for himself and his Church that at last they have vanquished freedom and have done so to make men happy. 'For now' (he is speaking of the Inquisition, of course) 'for the first time it has become possible to think of the happiness of men. Man was created a rebel; and how can rebels be happy? Thou wast warned,' he says to Him. 'Thou hast had no lack of admonitions and warnings, but Thou didst not listen to those warnings; Thou didst reject the only way by which men might be made happy. But, fortunately, departing Thou didst hand on the work to us. Thou hast promised, Thou hast established by Thy word, Thou hast given to us the right to bind and to unbind, and now, of course, Thou canst not think of taking it away. Why, then, hast Thou come to hinder us?'"

"And what's the meaning of 'no lack of admonitions and warnings'?" asked Alyosha.

"Why, that's the chief part of what the old man must say.

"'The wise and dread spirit, the spirit of self-destruction and non-existence,' the old man goes on, 'the great spirit talked with Thee in the wilderness, and we are told in the books that he "tempted" Thee.[10] Is that so? And could anything truer be said than what he revealed to Thee in three questions and what Thou didst reject, and what in the books is called "the temptation"? And yet if there has ever been on earth a real stupendous miracle, it took place on that day, on the day of the three temptations. The statement of those three questions was itself the miracle. If it were possible to imagine simply for the sake of argument that those three ques-

[9] See John 8:36.

[10] The story of Satan's temptation of Christ in the Wilderness appears in Matthew 4:1–11, Mark 1:12–13, and Luke 4:1–13. Satan first tempts him to turn stones into bread, then tempts him to test God by flinging himself off a pinnacle, and finally offers him all the kingdoms of the world.

tions of the dread spirit had perished utterly from the books, and that we had to restore them to invent them anew, and to do so had gathered together all the wise men of the earth—rulers, chief priests, learned men, philosophers, poets—and had set them the task to invent three questions, such as would not only fit the occasion, but express in three words, three human phrases, the whole future history of the world and of humanity—dost Thou believe that all the wisdom of the earth united could have invented anything in depth and force equal to the three questions which were actually put to Thee then by the wise and mighty spirit in the wilderness? From those questions alone, from the miracle of their statement, we can see that we have here to do not with the fleeting human intelligence, but with the absolute and eternal. For in those three questions the whole subsequent history of mankind is, as it were, brought together into one whole, and foretold, and in them are united all the unsolved historical contradictions of human nature. At the time it could not be so clear, since the future was unknown; but now that fifteen hundred years have passed, we see that everything in those three questions was so justly divined and foretold, and has been so truly fulfilled, that nothing can be added to them or taken from them.

"'Judge Thyself who was right—Thou or he who questioned Thee then? Remember the first question; its meaning, in other words, was this: "Thou wouldst go into the world, and art going with empty hands, with some promise of freedom which men in their simplicity and their natural unruliness cannot even understand, which they fear and dread—for nothing has ever been more insupportable for a man and a human society than freedom. But seest Thou these stones in this parched and barren wilderness? Turn them into bread, and mankind will run after Thee like a flock of sheep, grateful and obedient, though for ever trembling, lest Thou withdraw Thy hand and deny them Thy bread." But Thou wouldst not deprive man of freedom and didst reject the offer, thinking, what is that freedom worth, if obedience is bought with bread? Thou didst reply that man lives not by bread alone. But dost Thou know that for the sake of that earthly bread the spirit of the earth will rise up against Thee and will strive with Thee and overcome Thee, and all will follow him, crying, "Who can compare with this beast? He has given us fire from heaven!"[11] Dost Thou know that the ages will pass, and humanity will proclaim by the lips of their sages that there is no crime, and therefore no sin; there is only hunger?' "Feed men, and then ask of them virtue!" that's what they'll write on the banner, which they will raise against Thee, and with which they will destroy Thy temple. Where Thy temple stood will rise a new building; the terrible tower of Babel[12] will be built again, and though, like the one of old, it will not be finished, yet Thou mightest have prevented that new tower and have cut short the sufferings of men for a thousand years; for they will come back to us after a thousand years of agony with their tower. They will seek us again, hidden underground in the catacombs,[13] for we shall be again persecuted

[11] Revelation 13:4,13.

[12] The building of the Tower of Babel, an act of pride against God, is described in Genesis 11.

[13] Underground tombs, where early Christians met to avoid Roman persecution.

and tortured. They will find us and cry to us, "Feed us, for those who have promised us fire from heaven haven't given it!" And then we shall finish building their tower, for he finishes the building who feeds them. And we alone shall feed them in Thy name, declaring falsely that it is in Thy name. Oh, never, never can they feed themselves without us! No science will give them bread so long as they remain free. In the end they will lay their freedom at our feet, and say to us, "Make us your slaves, but feed us." They will understand themselves, at last, that freedom and bread enough for all are inconceivable together, for never, never will they be able to share between them! They will be convinced, too, that they can never be free, for they are weak, vicious, worthless and rebellious. Thou didst promise them the bread of Heaven, but, I repeat again, can it compare with earthly bread in the eyes of the weak, ever sinful and ignoble race of man? And if for the sake of the bread of Heaven thousands shall follow Thee, what is to become of the millions and tens of thousands of millions of creatures who will not have the strength to forego the earthly bread for the sake of the heavenly? Or dost Thou care only for the tens of thousands of the great and strong, while the millions, numerous as the sands of the sea, who are weak but love Thee, must exist only for the sake of the great and strong? No, we care for the weak too. They are sinful and rebellious, but in the end they too will become obedient. They will marvel at us and look on us as gods, because we are ready to endure the freedom which they have found so dreadful and to rule over them—so awful it will seem to them to be free. But we shall tell them that we are Thy servants and rule them in Thy name. We shall deceive them again, for we will not let Thee come to us again. That deception will be our suffering, for we shall be forced to lie.

"'This is the significance of the first question in the wilderness, and this is what Thou hast rejected for the sake of that freedom which Thou hast exalted above everything. Yet in this question lies hid the great secret of this world. Choosing "bread," Thou wouldst have satisfied the universal and everlasting craving of humanity—to find some one to worship. So long as man remains free he strives for nothing so incessantly and so painfully as to find some one to worship. But man seeks to worship what is established beyond dispute, so that all men would agree at once to worship it. For these pitiful creatures are concerned not only to find what one or the other can worship, but to find something that all would believe in and worship; what is essential is that all may be *together* in it. This craving for *community* of worship is the chief misery of every man individually and of all humanity from the beginning of time. For the sake of common worship they've slain each other with the sword. They have set up gods and challenged one another, "Put away your gods and come and worship ours, or we will kill you and your gods!" And so it will be to the end of the world, even when gods disappear from the earth; they will fall down before idols just the same. Thou didst know, Thou couldst not but have known, this fundamental secret of human nature, but Thou didst reject the one infallible banner which was offered Thee to make all men bow down to Thee alone—the banner of earthly bread; and Thou hast rejected it for the sake of freedom and the bread of Heaven. Behold what Thou didst further. And all again in the name of freedom! I tell Thee that man is tormented by no greater anxiety than to find some one quickly to whom he can hand over that gift of freedom with which the ill-fated creature is born. But only one who can appease their conscience can take over their freedom. In bread there was offered Thee an invincible banner; give bread, and man will worship thee, for nothing is more certain than bread. But if some one else gains possession of his conscience—oh! then he will cast away Thy bread and follow after him who has ensnared his conscience. In that Thou wast right. For the secret of man's being is not only to live but to have something to live for. Without a stable conception of the object of life, man would not consent to go on living, and would rather destroy himself than remain on earth, though he had bread in abundance. That is true. But what happened? Instead of taking men's freedom from them, Thou didst make it greater than ever! Didst Thou forget that man prefers peace, and even death, to freedom of choice in the knowledge of good and evil? Nothing is more seductive for man than his freedom of conscience, but nothing is a greater cause of suffering. And behold, instead of giving a firm foundation for setting the conscience of man at rest for ever, Thou didst choose all that is exceptional, vague and enigmatic; Thou didst choose what was utterly beyond the strength of men, acting as though Thou didst not love them at all—Thou who didst come to give Thy life for them! Instead of taking possession of men's freedom, Thou didst increase it, and burdened the spiritual kingdom of mankind with its sufferings for ever. Thou didst desire man's free love, that he should follow Thee freely, enticed and taken captive by Thee. In place of the rigid ancient law, man must hereafter with free heart decide for himself what is good and what is evil, having only Thy image before him as his guide. But didst Thou not know that he would at last reject even Thy image and Thy truth, if he is weighed down with the fearful burden of free choice? They will cry aloud at last that the truth is not in Thee, for they could not have been left in greater confusion and suffering than Thou hast caused, laying upon them so many cares and unanswerable problems.

"'So that, in truth, Thou didst Thyself lay the foundation for the destruction of Thy kingdom, and no one is more to blame for it. Yet what was offered Thee? There are three powers, three powers alone, able to conquer and to hold captive for ever the conscience of these impotent rebels for their happiness—those forces are miracle, mystery and authority. Thou hast rejected all three and hast set the example for doing so. When the wise and dread spirit set Thee on the pinnacle of the temple and said to Thee, "If Thou wouldst know whether Thou art the Son of God then cast Thyself down, for it is written: the angels shall hold him up lest he fall and bruise himself, and Thou shalt know then whether Thou art the Son of God and shalt prove then how great is Thy faith in Thy Father." But Thou didst refuse and wouldst not cast Thyself down. Oh, of course, Thou didst proudly and well, like God; but the weak, unruly race of men, are they gods? Oh, Thou didst know then that in taking one step, in making one movement to cast Thyself down, Thou wouldst be tempting God and have lost all Thy faith in Him, and wouldst have been dashed to pieces against that earth which Thou didst come to save. And the wise spirit that tempted Thee would have rejoiced. But I ask again, are there many like Thee? And couldst Thou believe for one moment that men, too, could face such a temptation? Is the nature of men such, that they can reject miracle, and at the great moments of their life, the moments of their deepest, most agonizing spiritual difficulties, cling only to the free verdict of the heart? Oh, Thou didst know that Thy deed would be recorded in books, would be handed down to remote times and the utmost ends of the earth, and Thou didst hope that man, following Thee, would cling to God and not ask for a miracle. But Thou didst not know that when man rejects miracle he rejects God too; for man seeks not so much God as the miraculous. And as man cannot bear to be without the miraculous, he will create new miracles of his own for himself, and will worship deeds of sorcery and witchcraft, though he might be a hundred times over a rebel, heretic and infidel. Thou didst not come down from the Cross when they shouted to Thee, mocking and reviling Thee, "Come down from the cross and we will believe that Thou art He."[14] Thou didst not come down, for again Thou wouldst not enslave man by a miracle, and didst crave faith given freely, not based on miracle. Thou didst crave for free love and not the base raptures of the slave before the might that has overawed him for ever. But Thou didst think too highly of men therein, for they are slaves, of course, though rebellious by nature. Look round and judge; fifteen centuries have passed, look upon them. Whom hast Thou raised up to Thyself? I swear, man is weaker and baser by nature than Thou hast believed him! Can he, can he do what Thou didst? By showing him so much respect, Thou didst, as it were, cease to feel for him, for Thou didst ask far too much from him—Thou who hast loved him more than Thyself! Respecting him less, Thou wouldst have asked less of him. That would have been more like love, for his burden would have been lighter. He is weak and vile. What though he is everywhere now rebelling against our power, and proud of his rebellion? It is the pride of a child and a schoolboy. They are little children rioting and barring out the teacher at school. But their childish delight will end; it will cost them dear. They will cast down temples and drench the earth with blood. But they will see at last, the foolish children, that, though they are rebels, they are impotent rebels, unable to keep up their own rebellion. Bathed in their foolish tears, they will recognize at last that He who created them rebels must have meant to mock at them. They will say this in despair, and their utterance will be a blasphemy which will make them more unhappy still, for man's nature cannot bear blasphemy, and in the end always avenges it on itself. And so unrest, confusion and unhappiness—that is the present lot of man after Thou didst bear so much for their freedom! The great prophet tells in vision and in image, that he saw all those who took part in the first resurrection and that there were of each tribe twelve thousand. But if there were so many of them, they must have been not men but gods. They had borne Thy cross, they had endured scores of years in the barren, hungry wilderness, living upon locusts and roots—and Thou mayest indeed point with pride at those children of freedom, of free love, of free and splendid sacrifice for Thy name. But remember that they were only some thousands; and what of the rest? And how are the other weak ones to blame, because they could not endure what the strong have endured? How is the weak soul to blame that it is unable to receive such terrible gifts? Canst Thou have simply come to the elect and for the elect? But if so, it is a

[14] Mark 15:32.

mystery and we cannot understand it. And if it is a mystery, we too have a right to preach a mystery, and to teach them that it's not the free judgment of their hearts, not love that matters, but a mystery which they must follow blindly, even against their conscience. So we have done. We have corrected Thy work and have founded it upon *miracle, mystery* and *authority*. And men rejoiced that they were again led like sheep, and that the terrible gift that had brought them such suffering was, at last, lifted from their hearts. Were we right teaching them this? Speak! Did we not love mankind, so meekly acknowledging their feebleness, lovingly lightening their burden, and permitting their weak nature even sin with our sanction? Why hast Thou come now to hinder us? And why dost Thou look silently and searchingly at me with Thy mild eyes? Be angry. I don't want Thy love, for I love Thee not. And what use is it for me to hide anything from Thee? Don't I know to Whom I am speaking? All that I can say is known to Thee already. And is it for me to conceal from Thee our mystery? Perhaps it is Thy will to hear it from my lips. Listen, then. We are not working with Thee, but with *him*—that is our mystery. It's long—eight centuries—since we have been on *his* side and not on Thine. Just eight centuries ago, we took from him what Thou didst reject with scorn, that last gift he offered Thee, showing Thee all the kingdoms of the earth.[15] We took from him Rome and the sword of Caesar, and proclaimed ourselves sole rulers of the earth, though hitherto we have not been able to complete our work. But whose fault is that? Oh, the work is only beginning, but it has begun. It has long to await completion and the earth has yet much to suffer, but we shall triumph and shall be Caesars, and then we shall plan the universal happiness of man. But Thou mightest have taken even then the sword of Caesar. Why didst Thou reject that last gift? Hadst Thou accepted that last counsel of the mighty spirit, Thou wouldst have accomplished all that man seeks on earth—that is, some one to worship, some one to keep his conscience, and some means of uniting all in one unanimous and harmonious ant-heap, for the craving for universal unity is the third and last anguish of men. Mankind as a whole has always striven to organize a universal state. There have been many great nations with great histories, but the more highly they were developed the more unhappy they were, for they felt more acutely than other people the craving for world-wide union. The great conquerors, Timours and Ghenghis-Khans,[16] whirled like hurricanes over the face of the earth striving to subdue its people, and they too were but the unconscious expression of the same craving for universal unity. Hadst Thou taken the world and Caesar's purple, Thou wouldst have founded the universal state and have given universal peace. For who can rule men if not he who holds their conscience and their bread in his hands? We have taken the sword of Caesar, and in taking it, of course, have rejected Thee and followed *him*. Oh, ages are yet to come of the confusion of free thought, of their science and cannibalism. For having begun to build their tower of Babel without us, they will end, of course, with cannibalism. But then the beast will crawl

[15] In 401, Pope Innocent I claimed jurisdiction over the entire Roman Church, thus replacing the Roman Empire as the only "universal" authority.

[16] Timour, or Tamerlane (c. 1336–1405), was the famous Mongol conqueror; Ghenghis-Khan (1167?–1227), also a Mongol, conquered most of China and penetrated into southeast Europe.

to us and lick our feet and spatter them with tears of blood. And we shall sit upon the beast and raise the cup, and on it will be written, "Mystery." But then, and only then, the reign of peace and happiness will come for men. Thou art proud of Thine elect, but Thou hast only the elect, while we give rest to all. And besides, how many of those elect, those mighty ones who could become elect, have grown weary waiting for Thee, and have transferred and will transfer the powers of their spirit and the warmth of their heart to the other camp, and end by raising their *free* banner against Thee. Thou didst Thyself lift up that banner. But with us all will be happy and will no more rebel nor destroy one another as under Thy freedom. Oh, we shall persuade them that they will only become free when they renounce their freedom to us and submit to us. And shall we be right or shall we be lying? They will be convinced that we are right, for they will remember the horrors of slavery and confusion to which Thy freedom brought them. Freedom, free thought and science, will lead them into such straits and will bring them face to face with such marvels and insoluble mysteries, that some of them, the fierce and rebellious, will destroy themselves, others, rebellious but weak, will destroy one another, while the rest, weak and unhappy, will crawl fawning to our feet and whine to us: "Yes, you were right, you alone possess His mystery, and we come back to you, save us from ourselves!"

"'Receiving bread from us, they will see clearly that we take the bread made by their hands from them, to give it to them, without any miracle. They will see that we do not change the stones to bread, but in truth they will be more thankful for taking it from our hands than for the bread itself! For they will remember only too well that in old days, without help, even the bread they made turned to stones in their hands, while since they have come back to us, the very stones have turned to bread in their hands. Too, too well will they know the value of complete submission! And until men know that, they will be unhappy. Who is most to blame for their not knowing it?—speak! Who scattered the flock and sent it astray on unknown paths? But the flock will come together again and will submit once more, and then it will be once for all. Then we shall give them the quiet humble happiness of weak creatures such as they are by nature. Oh, we shall persuade them at last not to be proud, for Thou didst lift them up and thereby taught them to be proud. We shall show them that they are weak, that they are only pitiful children, but that childlike happiness is the sweetest of all. They will become timid and will look to us and huddle close to us in fear, as chicks to the hen. They will marvel at us and will be awe-stricken before us,[17] and will be proud at our being so powerful and clever, that we have been able to subdue such a turbulent flock of thousands of millions. They will tremble impotently before our wrath, their minds will grow fearful, they will be quick to shed tears like women and children, but they will be just as ready at a sign from us to pass to laughter and rejoicing, to happy mirth and childish song. Yes, we shall set them to work, but in their leisure hours we shall make their life like a child's game, with children's songs and innocent dance. Oh, we shall allow them even sin, they are weak and helpless, and they will love us like children because we allow them to sin. We

[17] See Revelation 17:6.

shall tell them that every sin will be expiated, if it is done with our permission, that we allow them to sin because we love them, and the punishment for these sins we take upon ourselves. And we shall take it upon ourselves, and they will adore us as their saviors who have taken on themselves their sins before God. And they will have no secrets from us. We shall allow or forbid them to live with their wives and mistresses, to have or not to have children—according to whether they have been obedient or disobedient—and they will submit to us gladly and cheerfully. The most painful secrets of their conscience, all, all they will bring to us, and we shall have an answer for all. And they will be glad to believe our answer, for it will save them from the great anxiety and terrible agony they endure at present in making a free decision for themselves. And all will be happy, all the millions of creatures except the hundred thousand who rule over them. For only we, we who guard the mystery, shall be unhappy. There will be thousands of millions of happy babes, and a hundred thousand sufferers who have taken upon themselves the curse of the knowledge of good and evil. Peacefully they will die, peacefully they will expire in Thy name, and beyond the grave they will find nothing but death. But we shall keep the secret, and for their happiness we shall allure them with the reward of heaven and eternity. Though if there were anything in the other world, it certainly would not be for such as they. It is prophesied that Thou wilt come again in victory, Thou wilt come with Thy chosen, the proud and strong, but we will say that they have only saved themselves, but we have saved all. We are told that the harlot who sits upon the beast, and holds in her hands the *mystery,* shall be put to shame, that the weak will rise up again, and will rend her royal purple and will strip naked her loathsome body.[18] But then I will stand up and point out to Thee the thousand millions of happy children who have known no sin. And we who have taken their sins upon us for their happiness will stand up before Thee and say: "Judge us if Thou canst and darest." Know that I fear Thee not. Know that I too have been in the wilderness, I too have lived on roots and locusts, I too prized the freedom with which Thou hast blessed men, and I too was striving to stand among Thy elect, among the strong and powerful, thirsting "to make up the number." But I awakened and would not serve madness. I turned back and joined the ranks of those *who have corrected Thy work.* I left the proud and went back to the humble, for the happiness of the humble. What I say to Thee will come to pass, and our dominion will be built up. I repeat, tomorrow Thou shalt see that obedient flock who at a sign from me will hasten to heap up the hot cinders about the pile on which I shall burn Thee for coming to hinder us. For if any one has ever deserved our fires, it is Thou. Tomorrow I shall burn Thee. *Dixi.*'"[19]

Ivan stopped. He was carried away as he talked, and spoke with excitement; when he had finished, he suddenly smiled.

Alyosha had listened in silence; towards the end he was greatly moved and seemed several times on the point of interrupting, but restrained himself. Now his words came with a rush.

"But . . . that's absurd!" he cried, flushing. "Your poem is in praise of

[18] The vision of the Whore of Babylon is described in Revelation 17.
[19] Literally, "I have spoken" (Latin), closing formula for an ecclesiastical pronouncement.

Jesus, not in blame of Him—as you meant it to be. And who will believe you about freedom? Is that the way to understand it? That's not the idea of it in the Orthodox Church. . . . That's Rome, and not even the whole of Rome, it's false—those are the worst of the Catholics, the Inquisitors, the Jesuits! . . . And there could not be such a fantastic creature as your Inquisitor. What are these sins of mankind they take on themselves? Who are these keepers of the mystery who have taken some curse upon themselves for the happiness of mankind? When have they been seen? We know the Jesuits, they are spoken ill of, but surely they are not what you describe? They are not that at all, not at all. . . . They are simply the Romish army for the earthly sovereignty of the world in the future, with the Pontiff of Rome for Emperor . . . that's their ideal, but there's no sort of mystery or lofty melancholy about it. . . . It's simple lust of power, of filthy earthly gain, of domination—something like a universal serfdom with them as masters—that's all they stand for. They don't even believe in God perhaps. Your suffering Inquisitor is a mere fantasy."

"Stay, stay," laughed Ivan, "how hot you are! A fantasy you say, let it be so! Of course it's a fantasy. But allow me to say: do you really think that the Roman Catholic movement of the last centuries is actually nothing but the lust of power, of filthy earthly gain? Is that Father Païssy's teaching?"

"No, no, on the contrary, Father Païssy did once say something rather the same as you . . . but of course it's not the same, not a bit the same," Alyosha hastily corrected himself.

"A precious admission, in spite of your 'not a bit the same.' I ask you why your Jesuits and Inquisitors have united simply for vile material gain? Why can there not be among them one martyr oppressed by great sorrow and loving humanity? You see, only suppose that there was one such man among all those who desire nothing but filthy material gain—if there's only one like my old Inquisitor, who had himself eaten roots in the desert and made frenzied efforts to subdue his flesh to make himself free and perfect. But yet all his life he loved humanity, and suddenly his eyes were opened, and he saw that it is no great moral blessedness to attain perfection and freedom, if at the same time one gains the conviction that millions of God's creatures have been created as a mockery, that they will never be capable of using their freedom, that these poor rebels can never turn into giants to complete the tower, that it was not for such geese that the great idealist dreamt his dream of harmony. Seeing all that he turned back and joined—the clever people. Surely that could have happened?"

"Joined whom, what clever people?" cried Alyosha, completely carried away. "They have no such great cleverness and no mysteries and secrets. . . . Perhaps nothing but Atheism, that's all their secret. Your Inquisitor does not believe in God, that's his secret!"

"What if it is so! At last you have guessed it. It's perfectly true, it's true that that's the whole secret, but isn't that suffering, at least for a man like that, who has wasted his whole life in the desert and yet could not shake off his incurable love of humanity? In his old age he reached the clear conviction that nothing but the advice of the great dread spirit could build up any tolerable sort of life for the feeble, unruly, 'incomplete, empirical creatures created in jest.' And so, convinced of this, he sees that he must follow the counsel of the wise spirit, the dread spirit of death and destruction, and therefore accept lying and deception, and lead men consciously to death and destruction, and yet deceive them all the way so that they may not notice where they are being led, that the poor blind creatures may at least on the way think themselves happy. And note, the deception is in the name of Him in Whose ideal the old man had so fervently believed all his life long. Is not that tragic? And if only one such stood at the head of the whole army 'filled with the lust of power only for the sake of filthy gain'—would not one such be enough to make a tragedy? More than that, one such standing at the head is enough to create the actual leading idea of the Roman Church with all its armies and Jesuits, its highest idea. I tell you frankly that I firmly believe that there has always been such a man among those who stood at the head of the movement. Who knows, there may have been some such even among the Roman Popes. Who knows, perhaps the spirit of that accursed old man who loves mankind so obstinately in his own way, is to be found even now in a whole multitude of such old men, existing not by chance but by agreement, as a secret league formed long ago for the guarding of the mystery, to guard it from the weak and the unhappy, so as to make them happy. No doubt it is so, and so it must be indeed. I fancy that even among the Masons there's something of the same mystery at the bottom, and that that's why the Catholics so detest the Masons as their rivals breaking up the unity of the idea, while it is so essential that there should be one flock and one shepherd. . . .[20] But from the way I defend my idea I might be an author impatient of your criticism. Enough of it."

"You are perhaps a Mason yourself!" broke suddenly from Alyosha. "You don't believe in God," he added, speaking this time very sorrowfully. He fancied besides that his brother was looking at him ironically. "How does your poem end?" he asked, suddenly looking down. "Or was it the end?"

"I meant to end it like this. When the Inquisitor ceased speaking he waited some time for his Prisoner to answer him. His silence weighed down upon him. He saw that the Prisoner had listened intently all the time, looking gently in his face and evidently not wishing to reply. The old man longed for Him to say something, however bitter and terrible. But He suddenly approached the old man in silence and softly kissed him on his bloodless aged lips. That was all His answer. The old man shuddered. His lips moved. He went to the door, opened it, and said to Him: 'Go, and come no more . . . come not at all, never, never!' And he let Him out into the dark alleys of the town. The Prisoner went away."

"And the old man?"

"The kiss glows in his heart, but the old man adheres to his idea."

"And you with him, you too?" cried Alyosha, mournfully.

Ivan laughed.

"Why, it's all nonsense, Alyosha. It's only a senseless poem of a senseless student, who could never write two lines of verse. Why do you take it so seriously? Surely you don't suppose I am going straight off to the Jesuits, to join the men who are correcting His work? Good Lord, it's no business of

[20] John 10:16. The Masons, or the order of Free and Accepted Masons, is a secret fraternal order originating in the medieval stoneworkers' guild. Its secrecy has inspired strong opposition from many sources, including the Roman Catholic Church.

mine. I told you, all I want is to live on to thirty, and then . . . dash the cup to the ground!" . . .

Alyosha looked at him in silence.

"I thought that going away from here I have you at least," Ivan said suddenly, with unexpected feeling; "but now I see that there is no place for me even in your heart, my dear hermit. The formula, 'all is lawful,' I won't renounce—will you renounce me for that, yes?"

Alyosha got up, went to him and softly kissed him on the lips.

"That's plagiarism," cried Ivan, highly delighted. "You stole that from my poem. Thank you though. Get up, Alyosha, it's time we were going, both of us." . . .

Leo Tolstoy

(1828–1910)

The figure of Count Leo Tolstoy, both as writer and as man, towers over the remarkable flowering of Russian fiction in the nineteenth century. The titanic War and Peace *and* Anna Karenina *are the greatest products of that flowering, and the conflicts and tensions in human life, which Tolstoy examined with such unflinching honesty in those works, were acted out in his own extraordinary life. They were the tensions and conflicts arising from Romantic liberalism—between the individual and society, between self-realization and self-abnegation in the service of others, between an inability to accept orthodox religion and a deep need to believe—but Tolstoy's agonized probings of them reach depths beyond those of his own intellectual milieu to reach a sort of bedrock of existential concerns.*

Tolstoy was born in 1828 into a wealthy, aristocratic Russian family at Yasnaya Polyana, about a hundred miles south of Moscow, and he grew up on the family estate. His parents died when he was still a child, and he was reared by relatives and educated by private tutors. He studied at Kazan University, but returned home after three years to manage the family estate and lead a rather shallow, dissolute life in the upper social circles of Moscow and St. Petersburg. When he was twenty-three, he rejected this idle life and joined his soldier brother Nikolay in the Caucasus; he was a soldier for five years, distinguishing himself in engagements against the Caucasian hill tribes and taking part in the defense of Sevastopol in the Crimean War. While in the army, he began to write sketches and stories of his childhood and of military life; these tales were published in various Russian magazines. When he left the army, Tolstoy lived briefly in St. Petersburg, where he had already developed a literary reputation, but soon left to return to his estate and then to travel in Europe, continuing to write short stories and to pursue a growing interest in the education of the Russian peasantry.

In 1862, Tolstoy married Sonya Bers, a lively, intelligent young woman from a middle-class family, and returned to manage his estate and rear a family which came to number thirteen children. He also wrote, between 1863 and 1877, his two great masterpieces, War and Peace *(1869) and* Anna Karenina *(1877).* War and Peace, *an immense panorama of Russian life in the early nineteenth century, including Napoleon's 1812 invasion of Russia, centers upon the lives of five aristocratic Russian families and especially upon two major characters, Andrey and Pierre. These two men exemplify the major moral conflict of the book: between Romantic self-realization and service to others. Tolstoy also develops in the novel, sometimes directly and didactically, a theory of history which minimizes the influence of "great men" on historical events in favor of historical processes and natural laws which transcend individuals.* Anna Karenina, *set in the upper-class Russian society of the 1860's, while still large in scale, does not attempt the epic sweep of* War and Peace *but focuses more narrowly upon a private action, the adulterous love of Anna and Count Vronsky. The tone is darker and more pessimistic; the epigraph of the novel is "Vengeance is mine, I will repay," but the vengeance exacted from Anna is not the Lord's, but society's, not for her moral transgression but for her refusal to comply with society's hypocritical proprieties.*

The inner tensions Tolstoy dramatized so powerfully in War and Peace *and* Anna Karenina *began to overwhelm him personally. He underwent a shattering spiritual and perhaps psychological crisis which culminated in 1879 and was recorded in* A Confession *(written at the time, but not published until 1882). Tolstoy emerged from his agonized quest for the purpose of life with the simple answer that it was "to do good," an insight that he elaborated into a system of Christian anarchy. He renounced organized religion, government, and private property in favor of a faith in the individual's divinely given power to discern the good, a conviction derived from his perception of the simple faith of the peasants and from his study of Christ's words.*

Most of Tolstoy's writing during the last thirty years of his life was devoted to advancing these ideas, most fully stated in What Then Must We Do? *(1886). Didactic books, pamphlets, and articles poured from his pen; he transferred control of his estate to his family; and he attempted to bring his own daily life into conformity with his philosophical views. He gave up smoking and drinking, became a vegetarian, dressed in peasant clothes, and engaged in manual labor, attempting to avoid in every way dependence upon the labor of others. He also renounced sexual relations with his wife, in conformity with the commandment "Do not lust," one of five basic commandments he had derived from the words of Christ. Both Tolstoy's writings and the reports of his exemplary life began to attract disciples all over the world, many of whom made the pilgrimage to Yasnaya Polyana to talk with him.*

Tolstoy developed the artistic implications of his new philosophy in What is Art? *(1897). In this work, he rejected all art that does not achieve the moral purpose of communicating to the reader, through sympathetic identification, the state of the writer's soul. On these grounds, he developed his notorious rejection of Shakespeare's plays as "bad art," along with a number of other established masterpieces, including his own earlier works. Tolstoy tried to exemplify his new theory of art in a number of fictional and dramatic works, many of them marred by explicit moralizing but many among his finest achievements, including "The Death of Ivan Ilyitch" (1886), "The Kreutzer Sonata" (1891),* Resurrection *(1899), the drama* The Power of Darkness *(1888), and the unfinished drama* The Light Shines in Darkness *(1910).*

Tolstoy's commitment to his prophetic role increasingly alienated his wife and his older sons, who refused to join him in his ascetic life and who eventually obtained control of copyrights to all his works printed before 1880, in order to maintain an income satisfactory to them. The tensions of his domestic situation finally led Tolstoy, in 1910, at the age of eighty-two, to leave the estate secretly one night, in the company of his doctor and his youngest daughter Aleksandra, in order to seek a place where he could lead the kind of simple, hermit's life he sought. He caught a severe cold on the journey, however, and died a few days later of pneumonia in the house of a station-master on the railway.

Tolstoy's acute, conscience-stricken perception of the injustice of the Russian class system, his glorification of the people, and his vision of a stateless, classless society superficially seem to anticipate the revolutionary upheaval that was to transform Russia within a decade after his death. But in reality, Tolstoy's philosophy came out of a tradition of Romantic individualism and mysticism that was anathema to the makers of the Revolution; it derived not from Marx but from Rousseau, in its glorification of "natural man," its attempt to reconstruct a primitive Christianity, and its rejection of all received political or religious doctrine. For Tolstoy, the earthly paradise would not come through the inexorable unfolding of impersonal historical process or through violent class struggle; it would begin in the heart of each individual and would be achieved through the rule of love and nonviolence.

The post-conversion "Death of Ivan Ilyitch" is one of Tolstoy's finest works, profoundly moral in the sense that he defined in What is Art? *and yet never (or seldom) marred by explicit, inorganic moralizing. Inevitably, it suggests comparison with the medieval* Everyman, *in which a journey to death similarly becomes a journey toward illumination. (The persistence of the theme is demonstrated by such recent works as Ingmar Bergman's* Wild Strawberries *and Iris Murdoch's* Bruno's Dream.*) The point of Ivan Ilyitch's life is its ordinariness; it is "the simplest, the most ordinary, and the most awful." Ivan Ilyitch's very name is ordinary, a Russian equivalent of "John Smith." The protagonist has not been a great sinner, any more than Everyman has; he has led a perfectly respectable life, always doing what was expected of him as best he could. But in the face of death, a terrible question pushes itself forward: "What if in reality all my life, my conscious life, has been not the right thing?" In his crisis, as in Everyman's, "Fellowship," "Kindred and Cousin," and "Goods" fall away from him. But—and here Tolstoy parts company with the conventionally Christian vision of* Everyman*—it is not the priesthood, the "sacraments seven," and "Good Deeds" that accompany Ivan Ilyitch to the grave; he receives the last rites but they are a speciously comforting deception, like the other conventions whose hollowness he now sees. The qualities that do bring about Ivan's final illumination are those that form the core of Tolstoy's deeply moving faith.*

FURTHER READING *(prepared by W. J. R.):* The standard English biography is Ernest J. Simmons's *Leo Tolstoy,* 1947, which includes extensive chapters on the writing of *War and Peace* and *Anna Karenina.* Edward Crankshaw's *Tolstoy: The Making of a Novelist,* 1974, less detailed, is generously illustrated. Students of Tolstoy may also find Anne Edwards's biography of Tolstoy's remarkable wife, *Sonya: The Life of Countess Tolstoy,* 1981, of considerable interest. Ernest J. Simmons's *Tolstoy,* 1973, an introduction for the nonspecialist, surveys the works and discusses such topics as religion and politics. R. F. Christian's *Tolstoy: A Critical Introduction,* 1969, described by its title, is especially penetrating, concentrating on the major novels but discussing also a good deal of the short fiction. Janko Lavrin's *Tolstoy: An Approach,* 1946, rpt. 1968, interprets Tolstoy's artistry and philosophy. John Bayley's *Tolstoy and the Novel,* 1966, is good on *War and Peace,* historical background, and Tolstoy's influence on later Russian literature. Isaiah Berlin's *The Hedgehog and the Fox,* 1967 (first published 1951), is an important brief study of Tolstoy's use of philosophy and history. Essays on the cultural background of Tolstoy's fiction, the critical reception of his work, and the fiction itself are gathered in *New Essays on Tolstoy*, ed. Malcolm Jones, 1978. Thirteen very good essays are collected in *Tolstoy: A Collection of Critical Essays*, ed. Ralph E. Matlaw, 1967.

THE DEATH OF IVAN ILYITCH

Translated by Constance Garnett

I

Inside the great building of the Law Courts, during the interval in the hearing of the Melvinsky case, the members of the judicial council and the public prosecutor were gathered together in the private room of Ivan Yegorovitch Shebek, and the conversation turned upon the celebrated Krasovsky case. Fyodor Vassilievitch hotly maintained that the case was not in the jurisdiction of the court. Yegor Ivanovitch stood up for his own view; but from the first Pyotr Ivanovitch, who had not entered into the discussion, took no interest in it, but was looking through the newspapers which had just been brought in.

"Gentlemen!" he said, "Ivan Ilyitch is dead!"

"You don't say so!"

"Here, read it," he said to Fyodor Vassilievitch, handing him the fresh still damp-smelling paper.

Within a black margin was printed: "Praskovya Fyodorovna Golovin with heartfelt affliction informs friends and relatives of the decease of her beloved husband, member of the Court of Justice, Ivan Ilyitch Golovin, who passed away on the 4th of February. The funeral will take place on Thursday at one o'clock."

Ivan Ilyitch was a colleague of the gentlemen present, and all liked him. It was some weeks now since he had been taken ill; his illness had been said to be incurable. His post had been kept open for him, but it had been thought that in case of his death Alexyeev might receive his appointment, and either Vinnikov or Shtabel would succeed to Alexyeev's. So that on hearing of Ivan Ilyitch's death, the first thought of each of the gentlemen in the room was of the effect this death might have on the transfer or promotion of themselves or their friends.

"Now I am sure of getting Shtabel's place or Vinnikov's," thought Fyodor Vassilievitch. "It was promised me long ago, and the promotion means eight hundred rubles additional income, besides the grants for office expenses."

"Now I shall have to petition for my brother-in-law to be transferred from Kaluga," thought Pyotr Ivanovitch. "My wife will be very glad. She won't be able to say now that I've never done anything for her family."

"I thought somehow that he'd never get up from his bed again," Pyotr Ivanovitch said aloud. "I'm sorry!"

"But what was it exactly was wrong with him?"

"The doctors could not decide. That's to say, they did decide, but differently. When I saw him last, I thought he would get over it."

"Well, I positively haven't called there ever since the holidays. I've kept meaning to go."

"Had he any property?"

"I think there's something, very small, of his wife's. But something quite trifling."

"Yes, one will have to go and call. They live such a terribly long way off."

"A long way from you, you mean. Everything's a long way from your place."

"There, he can never forgive me for living the other side of the river," said Pyotr Ivanovitch, smiling at Shebek. And they began to talk of the great distances between different parts of the town, and went back into the court.

Besides the reflections upon the changes and promotions in the service likely to ensue from this death, the very fact of the death of an intimate acquaintance excited in every one who heard of it, as such a fact always does, a feeling of relief that "it is he that is dead, and not I."

"Only think! he is dead, but here am I all right," each one thought or felt. The more intimate acquaintances, the so-called friends of Ivan Ilyitch, could not help thinking too that now they had the exceedingly tiresome social duties to perform of going to the funeral service and paying the widow a visit of condolence.

The most intimately acquainted with their late colleague were Fyodor Vassilievitch and Pyotr Ivanovitch.

Pyotr Ivanovitch had been a comrade of his at the school of jurisprudence, and considered himself under obligations to Ivan Ilyitch.

Telling his wife at dinner of the news of Ivan Ilyitch's death and his reflections as to the possibility of getting her brother transferred into their circuit, Pyotr Ivanovitch, without lying down for his usual nap, put on his frockcoat and drove to Ivan Ilyitch's.

At the entrance before Ivan Ilyitch's flat stood a carriage and two hired flies.[1] Downstairs in the entry near the hat-stand there was leaning against the wall a coffin-lid with tassels and braiding freshly rubbed up with pipeclay. Two ladies were taking off their cloaks. One of them he knew, the sister of Ivan Ilyitch; the other was a lady he did not know. Pyotr Ivanovitch's colleague, Shvarts, was coming down; and from the top stair, seeing who it was coming in, he stopped and winked at him, as though to say: "Ivan Ilyitch has made a mess of it; it's a very different matter with you and me."

Shvarts's face, with his English whiskers[2] and all his thin figure in his frockcoat, had, as it always had, an air of elegant solemnity; and this solemnity, always such a contrast to Shvarts's playful character, had a special piquancy here. So thought Pyotr Ivanovitch.

Pyotr Ivanovitch let the ladies pass on in front of him, and walked slowly up the stairs after them. Shvarts had not come down, but was waiting at the top. Pyotr Ivanovitch knew what for; he wanted obviously to settle with him where their game of *vint*[3] was to be that evening. The ladies went up to the widow's room; while Shvarts, with his lips tightly and gravely shut

[1] Light, covered, horse-drawn cabs. [2] Long, flowing side whiskers.
[3] A game similar to auction bridge.

and amusement in his eyes, with a twitch of his eyebrows motioned Pyotr Ivanovitch to the right, to the room where the dead man was.

Pyotr Ivanovitch went in, as people always do on such occasions, in uncertainty as to what he would have to do there. One thing he felt sure of—that crossing oneself never comes amiss on such occasions. As to whether it was necessary to bow down while doing so, he did not feel quite sure, and so chose a middle course. On entering the room he began crossing himself, and made a slight sort of bow. So far as the movements of his hands and head permitted him, he glanced while doing so about the room. Two young men, one a high school boy, nephews probably, were going out of the room, crossing themselves. An old lady was standing motionless; and a lady, with her eyebrows queerly lifted, was saying something to her in a whisper. A deacon in a frockcoat, resolute and hearty, was reading something aloud with an expression that precluded all possibility of contradiction. A young peasant who used to wait at table, Gerasim, walking with light footsteps in front of Pyotr Ivanovitch, was sprinkling something on the floor. Seeing this, Pyotr Ivanovitch was at once aware of the faint odor of the decomposing corpse. On his last visit to Ivan Ilyitch Pyotr Ivanovitch had seen this peasant in his room; he was performing the duties of a sicknurse, and Ivan Ilyitch liked him particularly. Pyotr Ivanovitch continued crossing himself and bowing in a direction intermediate between the coffin, the deacon, and the holy pictures on the table in the corner. Then when this action of making the sign of the cross with his hand seemed to him to have been unduly prolonged, he stood still and began to scrutinize the dead man.

The dead man lay, as dead men always do lie, in a peculiarly heavy dead way, his stiffened limbs sunk in the cushions of the coffin, and his head bent back forever on the pillow, and thrust up, as dead men always do, his yellow waxen forehead with bald spots on the sunken temples, and his nose that stood out sharply and, as it were, squeezed on the upper lip. He was much changed, even thinner since Pyotr Ivanovitch had seen him, but his face—as always with the dead—was more handsome, and, above all, more impressive than it had been when he was alive. On the face was an expression of what had to be done having been done, and rightly done. Besides this, there was too in that expression a reproach or a reminder for the living. This reminder seemed to Pyotr Ivanovitch uncalled for, or, at least, to have nothing to do with him. He felt something unpleasant; and so Pyotr Ivanovitch once more crossed himself hurriedly, and, as it struck him, too hurriedly, not quite in accordance with the proprieties, turned and went to the door. Shvarts was waiting for him in the adjoining room, standing with his legs apart and both hands behind his back playing with his top hat. A single glance at the playful, sleek, and elegant figure of Shvarts revived Pyotr Ivanovitch. He felt that he, Shvarts, was above it, and would not give way to depressing impressions. The mere sight of him said plainly: the incident of the service over the body of Ivan Ilyitch cannot possibly constitute a sufficient ground for recognizing the business of the session suspended,—in other words, in no way can it hinder us from shuffling and cutting a pack of cards this evening, while the footman sets four unsanctified candles on the table for us; in fact, there is no ground for supposing that this incident could prevent us from spending the evening agreeably. He said as much indeed to Pyotr Ivanovitch as he came out, proposing that the party should meet at Fyodor Vassilievitch's. But apparently it was Pyotr Ivanovitch's destiny not to play *vint* that evening. Praskovya Fyodorovna, a short, fat woman who, in spite of all efforts in a contrary direction, was steadily broader from her shoulders downwards, all in black, with lace on her head and her eyebrows as queerly arched as those of the lady standing beside the coffin, came out of her own apartments with some other ladies, and conducting them to the dead man's room, said: "The service will take place immediately; come in."

Shvarts, making an indefinite bow, stood still, obviously neither accepting nor declining this invitation. Praskovya Fyodorovna, recognizing Pyotr Ivanovitch, sighed, went right up to him, took his hand, and said, "I know that you were a true friend of Ivan Ilyitch's . . ." and looked at him, expecting from him the suitable action in response to these words. Pyotr Ivanovitch knew that, just as before he had to cross himself, now what he had to do was to press her hand, to sigh and to say, "Ah, I was indeed!" And he did so. And as he did so, he felt that the desired result had been attained; that he was touched, and she was touched.

"Come, since it's not begun yet, I have something I want to say to you," said the widow. "Give me your arm."

Pyotr Ivanovitch gave her his arm, and they moved towards the inner rooms, passing Shvarts, who winked gloomily at Pyotr Ivanovitch.

"So much for our *vint!* Don't complain if we find another partner. You can make a fifth when you do get away," said his humorous glance.

Pyotr Ivanovitch sighed still more deeply and despondently, and Praskovya Fyodorovna pressed his hand gratefully. Going into her drawing-room, which was upholstered with pink cretonne and lighted by a dismal-looking lamp, they sat down at the table, she on a sofa and Pyotr Ivanovitch on a low ottoman with deranged springs which yielded spasmodically under his weight. Praskovya Fyodorovna was about to warn him to sit on another seat, but felt such a recommendation out of keeping with her position, and changed her mind. Sitting down on the ottoman, Pyotr Ivanovitch remembered how Ivan Ilyitch had arranged this drawing-room, and had consulted him about this very pink cretonne with green leaves. Seating herself on the sofa, and pushing by the table (the whole drawing-room was crowded with furniture and things), the widow caught the lace of her black fichu[4] in the carving of the table. Pyotr Ivanovitch got up to disentangle it for her; and the ottoman, freed from his weight, began bobbing up spasmodically under him. The widow began unhooking her lace herself, and Pyotr Ivanovitch again sat down, suppressing the mutinous ottoman springs under him. But the widow could not quite free herself, and Pyotr Ivanovitch rose again, and again the ottoman became mutinous and popped up with a positive snap. When this was all over, she took out a clean cambric handkerchief and began weeping. Pyotr Ivanovitch had been chilled off by the incident with the lace and the struggle with the ottoman springs, and he sat looking sullen. This awkward position was cut short by the entrance of Sokolov, Ivan Ilyitch's butler, who came in to announce that the place in the cemetery fixed on by Praskovya Fyodorovna would

[4]Shawl or scarf draped over the shoulders and fastened in front to hide a low neckline.

cost two hundred rubles. She left off weeping, and with the air of a victim glancing at Pyotr Ivanovitch, said in French that it was very terrible for her. Pyotr Ivanovitch made a silent gesture signifying his unhesitating conviction that it must indeed be so.

"Please, smoke," she said in a magnanimous, and at the same time, crushed voice, and she began discussing with Sokolov the question of the price of the site for the grave.

Pyotr Ivanovitch, lighting a cigarette, listened to her very circumstantial inquiries as to the various prices of sites and her decision as to the one to be selected. Having settled on the site for the grave, she made arrangements also about the choristers. Sokolov went away.

"I see to everything myself," she said to Pyotr Ivanovitch, moving on one side the albums that lay on the table; and noticing that the table was in danger from the cigarette-ash, she promptly passed an ash-tray to Pyotr Ivanovitch, and said: "I consider it affectation to pretend that my grief prevents me from looking after practical matters. On the contrary, if anything could—not console me . . . but distract me, it is seeing after everything for him." She took out her handkerchief again, as though preparing to weep again; and suddenly, as though struggling with herself, she shook herself, and began speaking calmly: "But I've business to talk about with you."

Pyotr Ivanovitch bowed, carefully keeping in check the springs of the ottoman, which had at once begun quivering under him.

"The last few days his sufferings were awful."

"Did he suffer very much?" asked Pyotr Ivanovitch.

"Oh, awfully! For the last moments, hours indeed, he never left off screaming. For three days and nights in succession he screamed incessantly. It was insufferable. I can't understand how I bore it; one could hear it through three closed doors. Ah, what I suffered!"

"And was he really conscious?" asked Pyotr Ivanovitch.

"Yes," she whispered, "up to the last minute. He said good-bye to us a quarter of an hour before his death, and asked Volodya to be taken away too."

The thought of the sufferings of a man he had known so intimately, at first as a light-hearted boy, a schoolboy, then grown up as a partner at whist, in spite of the unpleasant consciousness of his own and this woman's hypocrisy, suddenly horrified Pyotr Ivanovitch. He saw again that forehead, the nose that seemed squeezing the lip, and he felt frightened for himself. "Three days and nights of awful suffering and death. Why, that may at once, any minute, come upon me too," he thought, and he felt for an instant terrified. But immediately, he could not himself have said how, there came to his support the customary reflection that this had happened to Ivan Ilyitch and not to him, and that to him this must not and could not happen; that in thinking thus he was giving way to depression, which was not the right thing to do, as was evident from Shvarts's expression of face. And making these reflections, Pyotr Ivanovitch felt reassured, and began with interest inquiring details about Ivan Ilyitch's end, as though death were a mischance peculiar to Ivan Ilyitch, but not at all incidental to himself.

After various observations about the details of the truly awful physical sufferings endured by Ivan Ilyitch (these details Pyotr Ivanovitch learned only through the effect Ivan Ilyitch's agonies had had on the nerves of Praskovya Fyodorovna), the widow apparently thought it time to get to business.

"Ah, Pyotr Ivanovitch, how hard it is, how awfully, awfully hard!" and she began to cry again.

Pyotr Ivanovitch sighed, and waited for her to blow her nose. When she had done so, he said, "Indeed it is," and again she began to talk, and brought out what was evidently the business she wished to discuss with him; that business consisted in the inquiry as to how on the occasion of her husband's death she was to obtain a grant from the government. She made a show of asking Pyotr Ivanovitch's advice about a pension. But he perceived that she knew already to the minutest details, what he did not know himself indeed, everything that could be got out of the government on the ground of this death; but that what she wanted to find out was, whether there were not any means of obtaining a little more? Pyotr Ivanovitch tried to imagine such means; but after pondering a little, and out of politeness abusing the government for its stinginess, he said that he believed that it was impossible to obtain more. Then she sighed and began unmistakably looking about for an excuse for getting rid of her visitor. He perceived this, put out his cigarette, got up, pressed her hand, and went out into the passage.

In the dining-room, where was the bric-à-brac clock that Ivan Ilyitch had been so delighted at buying, Pyotr Ivanovitch met the priest and several people he knew who had come to the service for the dead, and saw too Ivan Ilyitch's daughter, a handsome young lady. She was all in black. Her very slender figure looked even slenderer than usual. She had a gloomy, determined, almost wrathful expression. She bowed to Pyotr Ivanovitch as though he were to blame in some way. Behind the daughter, with the same offended air on his face, stood a rich young man, whom Pyotr Ivanovitch knew, too, an examining magistrate, the young lady's *fiancé,* as he had heard. He bowed dejectedly to him, and would have gone on into the dead man's room, when from the staircase there appeared the figure of the son, the high school boy, extraordinarily like Ivan Ilyitch. He was the little Ivan Ilyitch over again as Pyotr Ivanovitch remembered him at school. His eyes were red with crying, and had that look often seen in unclean boys of thirteen or fourteen.[5] The boy, seeing Pyotr Ivanovitch, scowled morosely and bashfully. Pyotr Ivanovitch nodded to him and went into the dead man's room. The service for the dead began—candles, groans, incense, tears, sobs. Pyotr Ivanovitch stood frowning, staring at his feet in front of him. He did not once glance at the dead man, and right through to the end did not once give way to depressing influences, and was one of the first to walk out. In the hall there was no one. Gerasim, the young peasant, darted out of the dead man's room, tossed over with his strong hand all the fur cloaks to find Pyotr Ivanovitch's, and gave it him.

"Well, Gerasim, my boy?" said Pyotr Ivanovitch, so as to say something. "A sad business, isn't it?"

"It's God's will. We shall come to the same," said Gerasim, showing his white, even, peasant teeth in a smile, and, like a man in a rush of extra

[5] Tolstoy apparently means the boy engages in masturbation.

work, he briskly opened the door, called up the coachman, saw Pyotr Ivanovitch into the carriage, and darted back to the steps as though bethinking himself of what he had to do next.

Pyotr Ivanovitch had a special pleasure in the fresh air after the smell of incense, of the corpse, and of carbolic acid.

"Where to?" asked the coachman.

"It's not too late, I'll still go round to Fyodor Vassilievitch's."

And Pyotr Ivanovitch drove there. And he did, in fact, find them just finishing the first rubber, so that he came just at the right time to take a hand.

II

The previous history of Ivan Ilyitch was the simplest, the most ordinary, and the most awful.

Ivan Ilyitch died at the age of forty-five, a member of the Judicial Council. He was the son of an official, whose career in Petersburg through various ministries and departments had been such as leads people into that position in which, though it is distinctly obvious that they are unfit to perform any kind of real duty, they yet cannot, owing to their long past service and their official rank, be dismissed; and they therefore receive a specially created fictitious post, and by no means fictitious thousands—from six to ten—on which they go on living till extreme old age. Such was the privy councilor, the superfluous member of various superfluous institutions, Ilya Efimovitch Golovin.

He had three sons. Ivan Ilyitch was the second son. The eldest son's career was exactly like his father's, only in a different department, and he was by now close upon that stage in the service in which the same sinecure would be reached. The third son was the unsuccessful one. He had in various positions always made a mess of things, and was now employed in the railway department. And his father and his brothers, and still more their wives, did not merely dislike meeting him, but avoided, except in extreme necessity, recollecting his existence. His sister had married Baron Greff, a Petersburg official of the same stamp as his father-in-law. Ivan Ilyitch was *le phénix de la famille,*[6] as people said. He was not so frigid and precise as the eldest son, nor so wild as the youngest. He was the happy mean between them—a shrewd, lively, pleasant, and well-bred man. He had been educated with his younger brother at the school of jurisprudence. The younger brother had not finished the school course, but was expelled when in the fifth class. Ivan Ilyitch completed the course successfully. At school he was just the same as he was later on all his life—an intelligent fellow, highly good-humored and sociable, but strict in doing what he considered to be his duty. His duty he considered whatever was so considered by those persons who were set in authority over him. He was not a toady as a boy, nor later on as a grown-up person; but from his earliest years he was attracted, as a fly to the light, to persons of good standing in the world,

[6] *Le phénix de la famille.* "The phoenix of the family," a paragon (French).

assimilated their manners and their views of life, and established friendly relations with them. All the enthusiasms of childhood and youth passed, leaving no great traces in him; he gave way to sensuality and to vanity, and latterly when in the higher classes at school to liberalism, but always keeping within certain limits which were unfailingly marked out for him by his instincts.

At school he had committed actions which had struck him beforehand as great vileness, and gave him a feeling of loathing for himself at the very time he was committing them. But later on, perceiving that such actions were committed also by men of good position, and were not regarded by them as base, he was able, not to regard them as good, but to forget about them completely, and was never mortified by recollections of them.

Leaving the school of jurisprudence in the tenth class, and receiving from his father a sum of money for his outfit, Ivan Ilyitch ordered his clothes at Sharmer's, hung on his watchchain a medallion inscribed *respice finem,*[7] said good-bye to the prince who was the principal of his school, had a farewell dinner with his comrades at Donon's, and with all his new fashionable belongings—traveling trunk, linen, suits of clothes, shaving and toilet appurtenances, and traveling rug, all ordered and purchased at the very best shops—set off to take the post of secretary on special commissions for the governor of a province, a post which had been obtained for him by his father.

In the province Ivan Ilyitch without loss of time made himself a position as easy and agreeable as his position had been in the school of jurisprudence. He did his work, made his career, and at the same time led a life of well-bred social gaiety. Occasionally he visited various districts on official duty, behaved with dignity both with his superiors and his inferiors; and with exactitude and an incorruptible honesty of which he could not help feeling proud, performed the duties with which he was entrusted, principally having to do with the dissenters.[8] When engaged in official work he was, in spite of his youth and taste for frivolous amusement, exceedingly reserved, official, and even severe. But in social life he was often amusing and witty, and always good-natured, well-bred, and *bon enfant,*[9] as was said of him by his chief and his chief's wife, with whom he was like one of the family.

In the province there was, too, a connection with one of the ladies who obtruded their charms on the stylish young lawyer. There was a dressmaker, too, and there were drinking bouts with smart officers visiting the neighborhood, and visits to a certain outlying street after supper; there was a rather cringing obsequiousness in his behavior, too, with his chief, and even his chief's wife. But all this was accompanied with such a tone of the highest breeding, that it could not be called by harsh names; it all came under the rubric of the French saying, *Il faut que la jeunesse se passe.*[10] Everything was done with clean hands, in clean shirts, with French phrases, and,

[7] "Look to the end" (Latin).

[8] The Old Believers, members of a sect broken off from the Russian Orthodox Church in the seventeenth century and subjects of a number of legal restrictions.

[9] Literally, "good child"; congenial (French).

[10] French for "Youth must pass" (That's the way young people are).

what was of most importance, in the highest society, and consequently with the approval of people of rank.

Such was Ivan Ilyitch's career for five years, and then came a change in his official life. New methods of judicial procedure were established; new men were wanted to carry them out. And Ivan Ilyitch became such a new man. Ivan Ilyitch was offered the post of examining magistrate, and he accepted it in spite of the fact that this post was in another province, and he would have to break off all the ties he had formed and form new ones. Ivan Ilyitch's friends met together to see him off, had their photographs taken in a group, presented him with a silver cigarette-case, and he set off to his new post.

As an examining magistrate, Ivan Ilyitch was as *comme il faut,*[11] as well-bred, as adroit in keeping official duties apart from private life, and as successful in gaining universal respect, as he had been as secretary of private commissions. The duties of his new office were in themselves of far greater interest and attractiveness for Ivan Ilyitch. In his former post it had been pleasant to pass in his smart uniform from Sharmer's through the crowd of petitioners and officials waiting timorously and envying him, and to march with his easy swagger straight into the governor's private room, there to sit down with him to tea and cigarettes. But the persons directly subject to his authority were few. The only such persons were the district police superintendents and the dissenters, when he was serving on special commissions. And he liked treating such persons affably, almost like comrades; liked to make them feel that he, able to annihilate them, was behaving in this simple, friendly way with them. But such people were then few in number. Now as an examining magistrate Ivan Ilyitch felt that every one—every one without exception—the most dignified, the most self-satisfied people, all were in his hands, and that he had but to write certain words on a sheet of paper with a printed heading, and this dignified self-satisfied person would be brought before him in the capacity of a defendant or a witness; and if he did not care to make him sit down, he would have to stand up before him and answer his questions. Ivan Ilyitch never abused this authority of his; on the contrary, he tried to soften the expression of it. But the consciousness of this power and the possibility of softening its effect constituted for him the chief interest and attractiveness of his new position. In the work itself, in the preliminary inquiries, that is, Ivan Ilyitch very rapidly acquired the art of setting aside every consideration irrelevant to the official aspect of the case, and of reducing every case, however complex, to that form in which it could in a purely external fashion be put on paper, completely excluding his personal view of the matter, and what was of paramount importance, observing all the necessary formalities. All this work was new. And he was one of the first men who put into practical working the reforms in judicial procedure enacted in 1864.[12]

On settling in a new town in his position as examining magistrate, Ivan Ilyitch made new acquaintances, formed new ties, took up a new line, and adopted a rather different attitude. He took up an attitude of somewhat dignified aloofness towards the provincial authorities, while he picked out

[11]"As it should be"; proper (French).
[12]Russian law was reformed in 1864, following the emancipation of the serfs in 1861.

the best circle among the legal gentlemen and wealthy gentry living in the town, and adopted a tone of slight dissatisfaction with the government, moderate liberalism, and lofty civic virtue. With this, while making no change in the elegance of his get-up, Ivan Ilyitch in his new office gave up shaving, and left his beard free to grow as it liked. Ivan Ilyitch's existence in the new town proved to be very agreeable; the society which took the line of opposition to the governor was friendly and good; his income was larger, and he found a source of increased enjoyment in whist, at which he began to play at this time; and having a faculty for playing cards good-humoredly, and being rapid and exact in his calculations, he was as a rule on the winning side.

After living two years in the new town, Ivan Ilyitch met his future wife. Praskovya Fyodorovna Mihel was the most attractive, clever, and brilliant girl in the set in which Ivan Ilyitch moved. Among other amusements and recreations after his labors as a magistrate, Ivan Ilyitch started a light, playful flirtation with Praskovya Fyodorovna.

Ivan Ilyitch when he was an assistant secretary had danced as a rule; as an examining magistrate he danced only as an exception. He danced now as it were under protest, as though to show "that though I am serving on the new reformed legal code, and am of the fifth class in official rank, still if it comes to a question of dancing, in that line, too, I can do better than others." In this spirit he danced now and then towards the end of the evening with Praskovya Fyodorovna, and it was principally during these dances that he won the heart of Praskovya Fyodorovna. She fell in love with him. Ivan Ilyitch had no clearly defined intention of marrying; but when the girl fell in love with him, he put the question to himself: "After all, why not get married?"

The young lady, Praskovya Fyodorovna, was of good family, nice-looking. There was a little bit of property. Ivan Ilyitch might have reckoned on a more brilliant match, but this was a good match. Ivan Ilyitch had his salary; she, he hoped, would have as much of her own. It was a good family; she was a sweet, pretty, and perfectly *comme il faut* young woman. To say that Ivan Ilyitch got married because he fell in love with his wife and found in her sympathy with his views of life, would be as untrue as to say that he got married because the people of his world approved of the match. Ivan Ilyitch was influenced by both considerations; he was doing what was agreeable to himself in securing such a wife, and at the same time doing what persons of higher standing looked upon as the correct thing.

And Ivan Ilyitch got married.

The process itself of getting married and the early period of married life, with the conjugal caresses, the new furniture, the new crockery, the new house linen, all up to the time of his wife's pregnancy, went off very well; so that Ivan Ilyitch had already begun to think that so far from marriage breaking up that kind of frivolous, agreeable, lighthearted life, always decorous and always approved by society, which he regarded as the normal life, it would even increase its agreeableness. But at that point, in the early months of his wife's pregnancy, there came in a new element, unexpected, unpleasant, tiresome and unseemly, which could never have been anticipated, and from which there was no escape.

His wife, without any kind of reason, it seemed to Ivan Ilyitch, *de gaieté de coeur,*[13] as he expressed it, began to disturb the agreeableness and decorum of their life. She began without any sort of justification to be jealous, exacting in her demands on his attention, squabbled over everything, and treated him to the coarsest and most unpleasant scenes.

At first Ivan Ilyitch hoped to escape from the unpleasantness of this position by taking up the same frivolous and well-bred line that had served him well on other occasions of difficulty. He endeavored to ignore his wife's ill-humor, went on living lightheartedly and agreeably as before, invited friends to play cards, tried to get away himself to the club or to his friends. But his wife began on one occasion with such energy, abusing him in such coarse language, and so obstinately persisted in her abuse of him every time he failed in carrying out her demands, obviously having made up her mind firmly to persist till he gave way, that is, stayed at home and was as dull as she was, that Ivan Ilyitch took alarm. He perceived that matrimony, at least with his wife, was not invariably conducive to the pleasures and proprieties of life; but, on the contrary, often destructive of them, and that it was therefore essential to erect some barrier to protect himself from these disturbances. And Ivan Ilyitch began to look about for such means of protecting himself. His official duties were the only thing that impressed Praskovya Fyodorovna, and Ivan Ilyitch began to use his official position and the duties arising from it in his struggle with his wife to fence off his own independent world apart.

With the birth of the baby, the attempts at nursing it, and the various unsuccessful experiments with foods, with the illnesses, real and imaginary, of the infant and its mother, in which Ivan Ilyitch was expected to sympathize, though he never had the slightest idea about them, the need for him to fence off a world apart for himself outside his family life became still more imperative. As his wife grew more irritable and exacting, so did Ivan Ilyitch more and more transfer the center of gravity of his life to his official work. He became fonder and fonder of official life, and more ambitious than he had been.

Very quickly, not more than a year after his wedding, Ivan Ilyitch had become aware that conjugal life, though providing certain comforts, was in reality a very intricate and difficult business towards which one must, if one is to do one's duty, that is, lead the decorous life approved by society, work out for oneself a definite line, just as in the government service.

And such a line Ivan Ilyitch did work out for himself in his married life. He expected from his home life only those comforts—of dinner at home, of housekeeper and bed—which it could give him, and, above all, that perfect propriety in external observances required by public opinion. For the rest, he looked for good-humored pleasantness, and if he found it he was very thankful. If he met with antagonism and querulousness, he promptly retreated into the separate world he had shut off for himself in his official life, and there he found solace.

Ivan Ilyitch was prized as a good official, and three years later he was made assistant public prosecutor. The new duties of this position, their dignity, the possibility of bringing any one to trial and putting any one in

[13] "Out of gaiety of heart"; willfully or arbitrarily (French).

prison, the publicity of the speeches and the success Ivan Ilyitch had in that part of his work,—all this made his official work still more attractive to him.

Children were born to him. His wife became steadily more querulous and ill-tempered, but the line Ivan Ilyitch had taken up for himself in home life put him almost out of reach of her grumbling.

After seven years of service in the same town, Ivan Ilyitch was transferred to another province with the post of public prosecutor. They moved, money was short, and his wife did not like the place they had moved to. The salary was indeed a little higher than before, but their expenses were larger. Besides, a couple of children died, and home life consequently became even less agreeable for Ivan Ilyitch.

For every mischance that occurred in their new place of residence, Praskovya Fyodorovna blamed her husband. The greater number of subjects of conversation between husband and wife, especially the education of the children, led to questions which were associated with previous quarrels, and quarrels were ready to break out at every instant. There remained only those rare periods of being in love which did indeed come upon them, but never lasted long. These were the islands at which they put in for a time, but they soon set off again upon the ocean of concealed hostility, that was made manifest in their aloofness from one another. This aloofness might have distressed Ivan Ilyitch if he had believed that this ought not to be so, but by now he regarded this position as perfectly normal, and it was indeed the goal towards which he worked in his home life. His aim was to make himself more and more free from the unpleasant aspects of domestic life and to render them harmless and decorous. And he attained this aim by spending less and less time with his family; and when he was forced to be at home, he endeavored to secure his tranquillity by the presence of outsiders. The great thing for Ivan Ilyitch was having his office. In the official world all the interest of life was concentrated for him. And this interest absorbed him. The sense of his own power, the consciousness of being able to ruin any one he wanted to ruin, even the external dignity of his office, when he made his entry into the court or met subordinate officials, his success in the eyes of his superiors and his subordinates, and, above all, his masterly handling of cases, of which he was conscious,—all this delighted him and, together with chats with his colleagues, dining out, and whist, filled his life. So that, on the whole, Ivan's life still went on in the way he thought it should go—agreeably, decorously.

So he lived for another seven years. His eldest daughter was already sixteen, another child had died, and there was left only one other, a boy at the high school, a subject of dissension. Ivan Ilyitch wanted to send him to the school of jurisprudence, while Praskovya Fyodorovna to spite him sent him to the high school. The daughter had been educated at home, and had turned out well; the boy too did fairly well at his lessons.

III

Such was Ivan Ilyitch's life for seventeen years after his marriage. He had been prosecutor a long while by now, and had refused several appointments offered him, looking out for a more desirable post, when there occurred an unexpected incident which utterly destroyed his peace of mind. Ivan Ilyitch had been expecting to be appointed presiding judge in a university town, but a certain Goppe somehow stole a march on him and secured the appointment. Ivan Ilyitch took offense, began upbraiding him, and quarrelled with him and with his own superiors. A coolness was felt towards him, and on the next appointment that was made he was again passed over.

This was in the year 1880. That year was the most painful one in Ivan Ilyitch's life. During that year it became evident on the one hand that his pay was insufficient for his expenses; on the other hand, that he had been forgotten by every one, and that what seemed to him the most monstrous, the cruelest injustice, appeared to other people as a quite commonplace fact. Even his father felt no obligation to assist him. He felt that every one had deserted him, and that every one regarded his position with an income of three thousand five hundred rubles as a quite normal and even fortunate one. He alone, with a sense of the injustice done him, and the everlasting nagging of his wife and the debts he had begun to accumulate, living beyond his means, knew that his position was far from being normal.

The summer of that year, to cut down his expenses, he took a holiday and went with his wife to spend the summer in the country at her brother's.

In the country, with no official duties to occupy him, Ivan Ilyitch was for the first time a prey not to simple boredom, but to intolerable depression; and he made up his mind that things could not go on like that, and that it was absolutely necessary to take some decisive steps.

After a sleepless night spent by Ivan Ilyitch walking up and down the terrace, he determined to go to Petersburg to take active steps and to get transferred to some other department, so as to revenge himself on *them,* the people, that is, who had not known how to appreciate him.

Next day, in spite of all the efforts of his wife and his mother-in-law to dissuade him, he set off to Petersburg.

He went with a single object before him—to obtain a post with an income of five thousand. He was ready now to be satisfied with a post in any department, of any tendency, with any kind of work. He must only have a post—a post with five thousand, in the executive department, the banks, the railways, the Empress Marya's institutions,[14] even in the customs duties—what was essential was five thousand, and essential it was, too, to get out of the department in which they had failed to appreciate his value.

And, behold, this quest of Ivan Ilyitch's was crowned with wonderful, unexpected success. At Kursk there got into the same first-class carriage F. S. Ilyin, an acquaintance, who told him of a telegram just received by the governor of Kursk, announcing a change about to take place in the ministry—Pyotr Ivanovitch was to be superseded by Ivan Semyonovitch.

The proposed change, apart from its significance for Russia, had special significance for Ivan Ilyitch from the fact that by bringing to the front a new person, Pyotr Petrovitch, and obviously, therefore, his friend Zahar Ivanovitch, it was in the highest degree propitious to Ivan Ilyitch's own plans. Zahar Ivanovitch was a friend and school-fellow of Ivan Ilyitch's.

[14]The Empress Marya, wife of Paul I, founded a number of charitable institutions.

At Moscow the news was confirmed. On arriving at Petersburg, Ivan Ilyitch looked up Zahar Ivanovitch, and received a positive promise of an appointment in his former department—that of justice.

A week later he telegraphed to his wife: *"Zahar Miller's place. At first report I receive appointment."*

Thanks to these changes, Ivan Ilyitch unexpectedly obtained, in the same department as before, an appointment which placed him two stages higher than his former colleagues, and gave him an income of five thousand, together with the official allowance of three thousand five hundred for traveling expenses. All his ill-humor with his former enemies and the whole department was forgotten, and Ivan Ilyitch was completely happy.

Ivan Ilyitch went back to the country more lighthearted and good-tempered than he had been for a very long while. Praskovya Fyodorovna was in better spirits, too, and peace was patched up between them. Ivan Ilyitch described what respect every one had shown him in Petersburg; how all those who had been his enemies had been put to shame, and were cringing now before him; how envious they were of his appointment, and still more of the high favor in which he stood at Petersburg.

Praskovya Fyodorovna listened to this, and pretended to believe it, and did not contradict him in anything, but confined herself to making plans for her new arrangements in the town to which they would be moving. And Ivan Ilyitch saw with delight that these plans were his plans; that they were agreed; and that his life after this disturbing hitch in its progress was about to regain its true, normal character of lighthearted agreeableness and propriety.

Ivan Ilyitch had come back to the country for a short stay only. He had to enter upon the duties of his new office on the 10th of September; and besides, he needed some time to settle in a new place, to move all his belongings from the other province, to purchase and order many things in addition; in short, to arrange things as settled in his own mind, and almost exactly as settled in the heart too of Praskovya Fyodorovna.

And now when everything was so successfully arranged, and when he and his wife were agreed in their aim, and were, besides, so little together, they got on with one another as they had not got on together since the early years of their married life. Ivan Ilyitch had thought of taking his family away with him at once; but his sister and his brother-in-law, who had suddenly become extremely cordial and intimate with him and his family, were so pressing in urging them to stay that he set off alone.

Ivan Ilyitch started off; and the lighthearted temper produced by his success, and his good understanding with his wife, one thing backing up another, did not desert him all the time. He found a charming set of apartments, the very thing both husband and wife had dreamed of. Spacious, lofty reception-rooms in the old style, a comfortable, dignified-looking study for him, rooms for his wife and daughter, a schoolroom for his son, everything as though planned on purpose for them. Ivan Ilyitch himself looked after the furnishing of them, chose the wallpapers, bought furniture, by preference antique furniture, which had a peculiar *comme-il-faut* style to his mind, and it all grew up and grew up, and really attained the ideal he had set before himself. When he had half finished arranging the house, his arrangement surpassed his own expectations. He saw the *comme-il-faut* character, elegant and free from vulgarity, that the whole would have when it was all ready. As he fell asleep he pictured to himself the reception-room as it would be. Looking at the drawing-room, not yet finished, he could see the hearth, the screen, the *étagère*,[15] and the little chairs dotted here and there, the plates and dishes on the wall, and the bronzes as they would be when they were all put in their places. He was delighted with the thought of how he would impress Praskovya and Lizanka, who had taste too in this line. They would never expect anything like it. He was particularly successful in coming across and buying cheap old pieces of furniture, which gave a peculiarly aristocratic air to the whole. In his letters he purposely disparaged everything so as to surprise them. All this so absorbed him that the duties of his new office, though he was so fond of his official work, interested him less than he had expected. During sittings of the court he had moments of inattention; he pondered the question which sort of cornices to have on the window-blinds, straight or fluted. He was so interested in this business that he often set to work with his own hands, moved a piece of furniture, or hung up curtains himself. One day he went up a ladder to show a workman, who did not understand, how he wanted some hangings draped, made a false step and slipped; but, like a strong and nimble person, he clung on, and only knocked his side against the corner of a frame. The bruised place ached, but it soon passed off. Ivan Ilyich felt all this time particularly good-humored and well. He wrote: "I feel fifteen years younger." He thought his house-furnishing would be finished in September, but it dragged on to the middle of October. But then the effect was charming; not he only said so, but every one who saw it told him so too.

In reality, it was all just what is commonly seen in the houses of people who are not exactly wealthy but want to look like wealthy people, and so succeed only in being like one another—hangings, dark wood, flowers, rugs and bronzes, everything dark and highly polished, everything that all people of a certain class have so as to be like all people of a certain class. And in his case it was all so like that it made no impression at all; but it all seemed to him somehow special. When he met his family at the railway station and brought them to his newly furnished rooms, all lighted up in readiness, and a footman in a white tie opened the door into an entry decorated with flowers, and then they walked into the drawing-room and the study, uttering cries of delight, he was very happy, conducted them everywhere, eagerly drinking in their praises, and beaming with satisfaction. The same evening, while they talked about various things at tea, Praskovya Fyodorovna inquired about his fall, and he laughed and showed them how he had gone flying, and how he had frightened the upholsterer.

"It's as well I'm something of an athlete. Another man might have been killed, and I got nothing worse than a blow here; when it's touched it hurts, but it's going off already; just a bruise."

And they began to live in their new abode, which, as is always the case, when they had got thoroughly settled in they found to be short of just one room, and with their new income, which, as always, was only a little—some five hundred rubles—too little, and everything went very well. Things

[15] Cabinet with a tier of open shelves; bookcase (French).

went particularly well at first, before everything was quite finally arranged, and there was still something to do to the place—something to buy, something to order, something to move, something to make to fit. Though there were indeed several disputes between husband and wife, both were so well satisfied, and there was so much to do, that it all went off without serious quarrels. When there was nothing left to arrange, it became a little dull, and something seemed to be lacking, but by then they were making acquaintances and forming habits, and life was filled up again.

Ivan Ilyitch, after spending the morning in the court, returned home to dinner, and at first he was generally in a good humor, although this was apt to be upset a little, and precisely on account of the new abode. Every spot on the table-cloth, on the hangings, the string of a window blind broken, irritated him. He had devoted so much trouble to the arrangement of the rooms that any disturbance of their order distressed him. But, on the whole, the life of Ivan Ilyitch ran its course as, according to his conviction, life ought to do—easily, agreeably, and decorously. He got up at nine, drank his coffee, read the newspaper, then put on his official uniform, and went to the court. There the routine of the daily work was ready mapped out for him, and he stepped into it at once. People with petitions, inquiries in the office, the office itself, the sittings—public and preliminary. In all this the great thing necessary was to exclude everything with the sap of life in it, which always disturbs the regular course of official business, not to admit any sort of relations with people except the official relations; the motive of all intercourse had to be simply the official motive, and the intercourse itself to be only official. A man would come, for instance, anxious for certain information. Ivan Ilyitch, not being the functionary on duty, would have nothing whatever to do with such a man. But if this man's relation to him as a member of the court is such as can be formulated on official stamped paper—within the limits of such a relation Ivan Ilyitch would do everything, positively everything he could, and in doing so would observe the semblance of human friendly relations, that is, the courtesies of social life. But where the official relation ended, there everything else stopped too. This art of keeping the official aspect of things apart from his real life, Ivan Ilyitch possessed in the highest degree; and through long practice and natural aptitude, he had brought it to such a pitch of perfection that he even permitted himself at times, like a skilled specialist as it were in jest, to let the human and official relations mingle. He allowed himself this liberty just because he felt he had the power at any moment if he wished it to take up the purely official line again and to drop the human relation. This thing was not simply easy, agreeable, and decorous; in Ivan Ilyitch's hands it attained a positively artistic character. In the intervals of business he smoked, drank tea, chatted a little about politics, a little about public affairs, a little about cards, but most of all about appointments in the service. And tired, but feeling like some artist who has skillfully played his part in the performance, one of the first violins in the orchestra, he returned home. At home his daughter and her mother had been paying calls somewhere, or else some one had been calling on them; the son had been at school, had been preparing his lessons with his teachers, and duly learning correctly what was taught at the high school. Everything was as it should be. After dinner, if there were no visitors, Ivan Ilyitch sometimes read some book of which people were talking, and in the evening sat down to work, that is, read official papers, compared them with the laws, sorted depositions, and put them under the laws. This he found neither tiresome nor entertaining. It was tiresome when he might have been playing *vint;* but if there were no *vint* going on, it was better anyway than sitting alone or with his wife. Ivan Ilyitch's pleasures were little dinners, to which he invited ladies and gentlemen of good social position, and such methods of passing the time with them as were usual with such persons, so that his drawing-room might be like all other drawing-rooms.

Once they even gave a party—a dance. And Ivan Ilyitch enjoyed it, and everything was very successful, except that it led to a violent quarrel with his wife over the tarts and sweetmeats. Praskovya Fyodorovna had her own plan; while Ivan Ilyitch insisted on getting everything from an expensive pastry-cook, and ordered a great many tarts, and the quarrel was because these tarts were left over and the pastry-cook's bill came to forty-five rubles. The quarrel was a violent and unpleasant one, so much so that Praskovya Fyodorovna called him "Fool, imbecile." And he clutched at his head, and in his anger made some allusion to a divorce. But the party itself was enjoyable. There were all the best people, and Ivan Ilyitch danced with Princess Trufanov, the sister of the one so well known in connection with the charitable association called "Bear my Burden." His official pleasures lay in the gratification of his pride; his social pleasures lay in the gratification of his vanity. But Ivan Ilyitch's most real pleasure was the pleasure of playing *vint.* He admitted to himself that, after all, after whatever unpleasant incidents there had been in his life, the pleasure which burned like a candle before all others was sitting with good players, and not noisy partners, at *vint;* and, of course, a four-hand game (playing with five was never a success, though one pretends to like it particularly), and with good cards, to play a shrewd, serious game, then supper and a glass of wine. And after *vint,* especially after winning some small stakes (winning large sums was unpleasant), Ivan Ilyitch went to bed in a particularly happy frame of mind.

So they lived. They moved in the very best circle, and were visited by people of consequence and young people.

In their views of their circle of acquaintances, the husband, the wife, and the daughter were in complete accord; and without any expressed agreement on the subject, they all acted alike in dropping and shaking off various friends and relations, shabby persons who swooped down upon them in their drawing-room with Japanese plates on the walls, and pressed their civilities on them. Soon these shabby persons ceased fluttering about them, and none but the very best society was seen at the Golovins. Young men began to pay attention to Lizanka; and Petrishtchev, the son of Dmitry Ivanovitch Petrishtchev, and the sole heir of his fortune, an examining magistrate, began to be so attentive to Lizanka, that Ivan Ilyitch had raised the question with his wife whether it would not be as well to arrange a sledge drive for them, or to get up some theatricals. So they lived. And everything went on in this way without change, and everything was very nice.

IV

All were in good health. One could not use the word ill-health in connection with the symptoms Ivan Ilyitch sometimes complained of, namely, a queer taste in his mouth and a sort of uncomfortable feeling on the left side of the stomach.

But it came to pass that this uncomfortable feeling kept increasing, and became not exactly a pain, but a continual sense of weight in his side and the cause of an irritable temper. This irritable temper, continually growing, began at last to mar the agreeable easiness and decorum that had reigned in the Golovin household. Quarrels between the husband and wife became more and more frequent, and soon all the easiness and amenity of life had fallen away, and mere propriety was maintained with difficulty. Scenes became again more frequent. Again there were only islands in the sea of contention—and but few of these—at which the husband and wife could meet without an outbreak. And Praskovya Fyodorovna said now, not without grounds, that her husband had a trying temper. With her characteristic exaggeration, she said he had always had this awful temper, and she had needed all her sweetness to put up with it for twenty years. It was true that it was he now who began the quarrels. His gusts of temper always broke out just before dinner, and often just as he was beginning to eat, at the soup. He would notice that some piece of the crockery had been chipped, or that the food was not nice, or that his son put his elbow on the table, or his daughter's hair was not arranged as he liked it. And whatever it was, he laid the blame of it on Praskovya Fyodorovna. Praskovya Fyodorovna had at first retorted in the same strain, and said all sorts of horrid things to him; but on two occasions, just at the beginning of dinner, he had flown into such a frenzy that she perceived that it was due to physical derangement, and was brought on by taking food, and she controlled herself; she did not reply, but simply made haste to get dinner over. Praskovya Fyodorovna took great credit to herself for this exercise of self-control. Making up her mind that her husband had a fearful temper, and made her life miserable, she began to feel sorry for herself. And the more she felt for herself, the more she hated her husband. She began to wish he were dead; yet could not wish it, because then there would be no income. And this exasperated her against him even more. She considered herself dreadfully unfortunate, precisely because even his death could not save her, and she felt irritated and concealed it, and this hidden irritation on her side increased his irritability.

After one violent scene, in which Ivan Ilyitch had been particularly unjust, and after which he had said in explanation that he certainly was irritable, but that it was due to illness, she said that if he were ill he ought to take steps, and insisted on his going to see a celebrated doctor.

He went. Everything was as he had expected; everything was as it always is. The waiting and the assumption of dignity, that professional dignity he knew so well, exactly as he assumed it himself in court, and the sounding and listening and questions that called for answers that were foregone conclusions and obviously superfluous, and the significant air that seemed to insinuate—you only leave it all to us, and we will arrange everything, for us it is certain and incontestable how to arrange everything, everything in one way for every man of every sort. It was all exactly as in his court of justice. Exactly the same air as he put on in dealing with a man brought up for judgment, the doctor put on for him.

The doctor said: This and that proves that you have such-and-such a thing wrong inside you; but if that is not confirmed by analysis of this and that, then we must assume this and that. If we assume this and that, then—and so on. To Ivan Ilyitch there was only one question of consequence, Was his condition dangerous or not? But the doctor ignored that irrelevant inquiry. From the doctor's point of view this was a side issue, not the subject under consideration; the only real question was the balance of probabilities between a loose kidney, chronic catarrh, and appendicitis. It was not a question of the life of Ivan Ilyitch, but the question between the loose kidney and the intestinal appendix. And this question, as it seemed to Ivan Ilyitch, the doctor solved in a brilliant manner in favor of the appendix, with the reservation that analysis of the water[16] might give a fresh clue, and that then the aspect of the case would be altered. All this was point for point identical with what Ivan Ilyitch had himself done in brilliant fashion a thousand times over in dealing with some man on his trial. Just as brilliantly the doctor made his summing-up, and triumphantly, gaily even, glanced over his spectacles at the prisoner in the dock. From the doctor's summing-up Ivan Ilyitch deduced the conclusion—that things looked bad, and that he, the doctor, and most likely every one else, did not care, but that things looked bad for him. And this conclusion impressed Ivan Ilyitch morbidly, arousing in him a great feeling of pity for himself, of great anger against this doctor who could be unconcerned about a matter of such importance.

But he said nothing of that. He got up, and, laying the fee on the table, he said, with a sigh, "We sick people probably often ask inconvenient questions. Tell me, is this generally a dangerous illness or not?"

The doctor glanced severely at him with one eye through his spectacles, as though to say: "Prisoner at the bar, if you will not keep within the limits of the questions allowed you, I shall be compelled to take measures for your removal from the precincts of the court." "I have told you what I thought necessary and suitable already," said the doctor; "the analysis will show anything further." And the doctor bowed him out.

Ivan Ilyitch went out slowly and dejectedly, got into his sledge, and drove home. All the way home he was incessantly going over all the doctor had said, trying to translate all these complicated, obscure, scientific phrases into simple language, and to read in them an answer to the question, Is it bad—is it very bad, or nothing much as yet? And it seemed to him that the upshot of all the doctor had said was that it was very bad. Everything seemed dismal to Ivan Ilyitch in the streets. The sledge-drivers were dismal, the houses were dismal, the people passing, and the shops were dismal. This ache, this dull gnawing ache, that never ceased for a second, seemed, when connected with the doctor's obscure utterances, to have

[16] Urine.

gained a new, more serious significance. With a new sense of misery Ivan Ilyitch kept watch on it now.

He reached home and began to tell his wife about it. His wife listened; but in the middle of his account his daughter came in with her hat on, ready to go out with her mother. Reluctantly she half sat down to listen to these tedious details, but she could not stand it for long, and her mother did not hear his story to the end.

"Well, I'm very glad," said his wife; "now you must be sure and take the medicine regularly. Give me the prescription; I'll send Gerasim to the chemist's!" And she went to get ready to go out.

He had not taken breath while she was in the room, and he heaved a deep sigh when she was gone.

"Well," he said, "may be it really is nothing as yet."

He began to take the medicine, to carry out the doctor's directions, which were changed after the analysis of the water. But it was just at this point that some confusion arose, either in the analysis or in what ought to have followed from it. The doctor himself, of course, could not be blamed for it, but it turned out that things had not gone as the doctor had told him. Either he had forgotten or told a lie, or was hiding something from him.

But Ivan Ilyitch still went on just as exactly carrying out the doctor's direction, and in doing so he found comfort at first.

From the time of his visit to the doctor Ivan Ilyitch's principal occupation became the exact observance of the doctor's prescriptions as regards hygiene and medicine and the careful observation of his ailment in all the functions of his organism. Ivan Ilyitch's principal interest came to be people's ailments and people's health. When anything was said in his presence about sick people, about deaths and recoveries, especially in the case of an illness resembling his own, he listened, trying to conceal his excitement, asked questions, and applied what he heard to his own trouble.

The ache did not grow less; but Ivan Ilyitch made great efforts to force himself to believe that he was better. And he succeeded in deceiving himself so long as nothing happened to disturb him. But as soon as he had a mischance, some unpleasant words with his wife, a failure in his official work, an unlucky hand at *vint,* he was at once acutely sensible of his illness. In former days he had borne with such mishaps, hoping soon to retrieve the mistake, to make a struggle, to reach success later, to have a lucky hand. But now he was cast down by every mischance and reduced to despair. He would say to himself: "Here I'm only just beginning to get better, and the medicine has begun to take effect, and now this mischance or disappointment." And he was furious against the mischance or the people who were causing him the disappointment and killing him, and he felt that this fury was killing him, but could not check it. One would have thought that it should have been clear to him that this exasperation against circumstances and people was aggravating his disease, and that therefore he ought not to pay attention to the unpleasant incidents. But his reasoning took quite the opposite direction. He said that he needed peace, and was on the watch for everything that disturbed his peace, and at the slightest disturbance of it he flew into a rage. What made his position worse was that he read medical books and consulted doctors. He got worse so gradually that he might have deceived himself, comparing one day with another, the difference was so slight. But when he consulted the doctors, then it seemed to him that he was getting worse, and very rapidly so indeed. And in spite of this, he was continually consulting the doctors.

That month he called on another celebrated doctor. The second celebrity said almost the same as the first, but put his questions differently; and the interview with this celebrity only redoubled the doubts and terrors of Ivan Ilyitch. A friend of a friend of his, a very good doctor, diagnosed the disease quite differently; and in spite of the fact that he guaranteed recovery, by his questions and his suppositions he confused Ivan Ilyitch even more and strengthened his suspicions. A homeopath[17] gave yet another diagnosis of the complaint, and prescribed medicine, which Ivan Ilyitch took secretly for a week; but after a week of the homeopathic medicine he felt no relief, and losing faith both in the other doctor's treatment and in this, he fell into even deeper depression. One day a lady of his acquaintance talked to him of the healing wrought by the holy pictures. Ivan Ilyitch caught himself listening attentively and believing in the reality of the facts alleged. This incident alarmed him. "Can I have degenerated to such a point of intellectual feebleness?" he said to himself. "Nonsense! it's all rubbish. I must not give way to nervous fears, but fixing on one doctor, adhere strictly to his treatment. That's what I will do. Now it's settled. I won't think about it, but till next summer I will stick to the treatment, and then I shall see. Now I'll put a stop to this wavering!" It was easy to say this, but impossible to carry it out. The pain in his side was always dragging at him, seeming to grow more acute and ever more incessant; it seemed to him that the taste in his mouth was queerer, and there was a loathsome smell even from his breath, and his appetite and strength kept dwindling. There was no deceiving himself; something terrible, new, and so important that nothing more important had ever been in Ivan Ilyitch's life, was taking place in him, and he alone knew of it. All about him did not or would not understand, and believed that everything in the world was going on as before. This was what tortured Ivan Ilyitch more than anything. Those of his own household, most of all his wife and daughter, who were absorbed in a perfect whirl of visits, did not, he saw, comprehend it at all, and were annoyed that he was so depressed and exacting, as though he were to blame for it. Though they tried indeed to disguise it, he saw he was a nuisance to them; but that his wife had taken up a definite line of her own in regard to his illness, and stuck to it regardless of what he might say and do. This line was expressed thus: "You know," she would say to acquaintances, "Ivan Ilyitch cannot, like all other simple-hearted folks, keep to the treatment prescribed him. One day he'll take his drops and eat what he's ordered, and go to bed in good time; the next day, if I don't see to it, he'll suddenly forget to take his medicine, eat sturgeon (which is forbidden by the doctors), yes, and sit up at *vint* till past midnight."

[17] Practitioner of homeopathy, a system of medicine that treats illnesses by administering minute doses of substances that, in healthy persons, would produce symptoms of the disease treated.

"Why, when did I do that?" Ivan Ilyitch asked in vexation one day at Pyotr Ivanovitch's.

"Why, yesterday, with Shebek."

"It makes no difference. I couldn't sleep for pain."

"Well, it doesn't matter what you do it for, only you'll never get well like that, and you make us wretched."

Praskovya Fyodorovna's external attitude to her husband's illness, openly expressed to others and to himself, was that Ivan Ilyitch was to blame in the matter of his illness, and that the whole illness was another injury he was doing to his wife. Ivan Ilyitch felt that the expression of this dropped from her unconsciously, but that made it no easier for him.

In his official life, too, Ivan Ilyitch noticed, or fancied he noticed, a strange attitude to him. At one time it seemed to him that people were looking inquisitively at him, as a man who would shortly have to vacate his position; at another time his friends would suddenly begin chaffing him in a friendly way over his nervous fears, as though that awful and horrible, unheard-of thing that was going on within him, incessantly gnawing at him, and irresistibly dragging him away somewhere, were the most agreeable subject for joking. Shvarts especially, with his jocoseness, his liveliness, and his *comme-il-faut* tone, exasperated Ivan Ilyitch by reminding him of himself ten years ago.

Friends came sometimes to play cards. They sat down to the card-table; they shuffled and dealt the new cards. Diamonds were led and followed by diamonds, the seven. His partner said, "Can't trump," and played the two of diamonds. What then? Why, delightful, capital, it should have been—he had a trump hand. And suddenly Ivan Ilyitch feels that gnawing ache, that taste in his mouth, and it strikes him as something grotesque that with that he could be glad of a trump hand.

He looks at Mihail Mihailovitch, his partner, how he taps on the table with his red hand, and affably and indulgently abstains from snatching up the trick, and pushes the cards towards Ivan Ilyitch so as to give him the pleasure of taking them up, without any trouble, without even stretching out his hand. "What, does he suppose that I'm so weak that I can't stretch out my hand?" thinks Ivan Ilyitch, and he forgets the trumps, and trumps his partner's cards, and plays his trump hand without making three tricks; and what's the most awful thing of all is that he sees how upset Mihail Mihailovitch is about it, while he doesn't care a bit, and it's awful for him to think why he doesn't care.

They all see that he's in pain, and say to him, "We can stop if you're tired. You go and lie down." Lie down? No, he's not in the least tired; they will play the rubber. All are gloomy and silent. Ivan Ilyitch feels that it is he who has brought this gloom upon them, and he cannot disperse it. They have supper, and the party breaks up, and Ivan Ilyitch is left alone with the consciousness that his life is poisoned for him and poisons the life of others, and that this poison is not losing its force, but is continually penetrating more and more deeply into his whole existence.

And with the consciousness of this, and with the physical pain in addition, and the terror in addition to that, he must lie in his bed, often not able to sleep for pain the greater part of the night; and in the morning he must get up again, dress, go to the law-court, speak, write, or, if he does not go out, stay at home for all the four-and-twenty hours of the day and night, of which each one is a torture. And he had to live thus on the edge of the precipice alone, without one man who would understand and feel for him.

V

In this way one month, then a second, passed by. Just before the New Year his brother-in-law arrived in the town on a visit to them. Ivan Ilyitch was at the court when he arrived. Praskovya Fyodorovna had gone out shopping. Coming home and going into his study, he found there his brother-in-law, a healthy, florid man, engaged in unpacking his trunk. He raised his head, hearing Ivan Ilyitch's step, and for a second stared at him without a word. That stare told Ivan Ilyitch everything. His brother-in-law opened his mouth to utter an "Oh!" of surprise, but checked himself. That confirmed it all.

"What! have I changed?"

"Yes, there is a change."

And all Ivan Ilyitch's efforts to draw him into talking of his appearance his brother-in-law met with obstinate silence. Praskovya Fyodorovna came in; the brother-in-law went to see her. Ivan Ilyitch locked his door and began gazing at himself in the looking-glass, first full face, then in profile. He took up his photograph, taken with his wife, and compared the portrait with what he saw in the looking-glass. The change was immense. Then he bared his arm to the elbow, looked at it, pulled the sleeve down again, sat down on an ottoman and felt blacker than night.

"I mustn't, I mustn't," he said to himself, jumped up, went to the table, opened some official paper, tried to read it, but could not. He opened the door, went into the drawing-room. The door into the drawing-room was closed. He went up to it on tiptoe and listened.

"No, you're exaggerating," Praskovya Fyodorovna was saying.

"Exaggerating? You can't see it. Why, he's a dead man. Look at his eyes—there's no light in them. But what's wrong with him?"

"No one can tell. Nikolaev" (that was another doctor) "said something, but I don't know, Leshtchetitsky" (this was the celebrated doctor) "said the opposite."

Ivan Ilyitch walked away, went to his own room, lay down, and fell to musing. "A kidney—a loose kidney." He remembered all the doctors had told him, how it had been detached, and how it was loose; and by an effort of imagination he tried to catch that kidney and to stop it, to strengthen it. So little was needed, he fancied. "No, I'll go again to Pyotr Ivanovitch" (this was the friend who had a friend a doctor). He rang, ordered the horse to be put in, and got ready to go out.

"Where are you off too, Jean?"[18] asked his wife with a peculiarly melancholy and exceptionally kind expression.

This exceptionally kind expression exasperated him. He looked darkly at her.

[18] French form of "Ivan."

"I want to see Pyotr Ivanovitch."

He went to the friend who had a friend a doctor. And with him to the doctor's. He found him in, and had a long conversation with him.

Reviewing the anatomical and physiological details of what, according to the doctor's view, was taking place within him, he understood it all. It was just one thing—a little thing wrong with the intestinal appendix. It might all come right. Only strengthen one sluggish organ, and decrease the undue activity of another, and absorption would take place, and all would be set right. He was a little late for dinner. He ate his dinner, talked cheerfully, but it was a long while before he could go to his own room to work. At last he went to his study, and at once sat down to work. He read his legal documents and did his work, but the consciousness never left him of having a matter of importance very near to his heart which he had put off, but would look into later. When he had finished his work, he remembered that the matter near his heart was thinking about the intestinal appendix. But he did not give himself up to it; he went into the drawing-room to tea. There were visitors; and there was talking, playing on the piano, and singing; there was the young examining magistrate, the desirable match for the daughter. Ivan Ilyitch spent the evening, as Praskovya Fyodorovna observed, in better spirits than any of them; but he never forgot for an instant that he had the important matter of the intestinal appendix put off for consideration later. At eleven o'clock he said good night and went to his own room. He had slept alone since his illness in a little room adjoining his study. He went in, undressed, and took up a novel of Zola,[19] but did not read it; he fell to thinking. And in his imagination the desired recovery of the intestinal appendix had taken place. There had been absorption, rejection, re-establishment of the regular action.

"Why, it's all simply that," he said to himself. "One only wants to assist nature." He remembered the medicine, got up, took it, lay down on his back, watching for the medicine to act beneficially and overcome the pain. "It's only to take it regularly and avoid injurious influences; why, already I feel rather better, much better." He began to feel his side; it was not painful to the touch. "Yes, I don't feel it—really, much better already." He put out the candle and lay on his side. "The appendix is getting better, absorption." Suddenly he felt the familiar, old, dull, gnawing ache, persistent, quiet, in earnest. In his mouth the same familiar loathsome taste. His heart sank, and his brain felt dim, misty. "My God, my God!" he said, "again, again, and it will never cease." And suddenly the whole thing rose before him in quite a different aspect. "Intestinal appendix! kidney!" he said to himself. "It's not a question of the appendix, not a question of the kidney, but of life and . . . death. Yes, life has been and now it's going, going away, and I cannot stop it. Yes. Why deceive myself? Isn't it obvious to every one, except me, that I'm dying, and it's only a question of weeks, of days—at once perhaps. There was light, and now there is darkness. I was here, and now I am going! Where?" A cold chill ran over him, his breath stopped. He heard nothing but the throbbing of his heart.

"I shall be no more, then what will there be? There'll be nothing. Where

[19] Émile Zola, contemporary French naturalist writer. Tolstoy disliked Zola's work and regarded it as indecent and demoralizing.

then shall I be when I'm no more? Can this be dying? No; I don't want to!" He jumped up, tried to light the candle; and fumbling with trembling hands, he dropped the candle and the candlestick on the floor and fell back again on the pillow. "Why trouble? it doesn't matter," he said to himself, staring with open eyes into the darkness. "Death. Yes, death. And they—all of them—don't understand, and don't want to understand, and feel no pity. They are playing." (He caught through the closed doors the far-away cadence of a voice and the accompaniment.) "They don't care, but they will die too. Fools! Me sooner and them later; but it will be the same for them. And they are merry. The beasts!" Anger stifled him. And he was agonizingly, insufferably miserable. "It cannot be that all men always have been doomed to this awful horror!" He raised himself.

"There is something wrong in it; I must be calm. I must think it all over from the beginning." And then he began to consider. "Yes, the beginning of my illness. I knocked my side, and I was just the same, that day and the days after; it ached a little, then more, then doctors, then depression, misery, and again doctors; and I've gone on getting closer and closer to the abyss. Strength growing less. Nearer and nearer. And here I am, wasting away, no light in my eyes. I think of how to cure the appendix, but this is death. Can it be death?" Again a horror came over him; gasping for breath, he bent over, began feeling for the matches, and knocked his elbow against the bedside table. It was in his way and hurt him; he felt furious with it, in his anger knocked against it more violently, and upset it. And in despair, breathless, he fell back on his spine waiting for death to come that instant.

The visitors were leaving at that time. Praskovya Fyodorovna was seeing them out. She heard something fall, and came in.

"What is it?"

"Nothing. I dropped something by accident."

She went out, brought a candle. He was lying, breathing hard and fast, like a man who has run a mile, and staring with fixed eyes at her.

"What is it, Jean?"

"No—othing, I say. I dropped something."—"Why speak? She won't understand," he thought.

She certainly did not understand. She picked up the candle, lighted it for him, and went out hastily. She had to say good-bye to a departing guest. When she came back, he was lying in the same position on his back, looking upwards.

"How are you—worse?"

"Yes."

She shook her head, sat down.

"Do you know what, Jean? I wonder if we hadn't better send for Leshtchetitsky to see you here?"

This meant calling in the celebrated doctor, regardless of expense. He smiled malignantly, and said no. She sat a moment longer, went up to him, and kissed him on the forehead.

He hated her with all the force of his soul when she was kissing him, and had to make an effort not to push her away.

"Good night. Please God, you'll sleep."

"Yes."

VI

Ivan Ilyitch saw that he was dying, and was in continual despair.

At the bottom of his heart Ivan Ilyitch knew that he was dying; but so far from growing used to this idea, he simply did not grasp it—he was utterly unable to grasp it.

The example of the syllogism that he had learned in Kiseveter's logic[20]—Caius is a man, men are mortal, therefore Caius is mortal—had seemed to him all his life correct only as regards Caius, but not at all as regards himself. In that case it was a question of Caius, a man, an abstract man, and it was perfectly true, but he was not Caius, and was not an abstract man; he had always been a creature quite, quite different from all others; he had been little Vanya with a mamma and papa, and Mitya and Volodya, with playthings and a coachman and a nurse; afterwards with Katenka, with all the joys and griefs and ecstasies of childhood, boyhood, and youth. What did Caius know of the smell of the leathern ball Vanya had been so fond of? Had Caius kissed his mother's hand like that? Caius had not heard the silk rustle of his mother's skirts. He had not made a riot at school over the pudding. Had Caius been in love like that? Could Caius preside over the sittings of the court?

And Caius certainly was mortal, and it was right for him to die; but for me, little Vanya, Ivan Ilyitch, with all my feelings and ideas—for me it's a different matter. And it cannot be that I ought to die. That would be too awful.

That was his feeling.

"If I had to die like Caius, I should have known it was so, some inner voice would have told me so. But there was nothing of the sort in me. And I and all my friends, we felt that it was not at all the same as with Caius. And now here it is!" he said to himself. "It can't be! It can't be, but it is! How is it? How's one to understand it?" And he could not conceive it, and tried to drive away this idea as false, incorrect, and morbid, and to supplant it by other, correct, healthy ideas. But this idea, not as an idea merely, but as it were an actual fact, came back again and stood confronting him.

And to replace this thought he called up other thoughts, one after another, in the hope of finding support in them. He tried to get back into former trains of thought, which in old days had screened off the thought of death. But, strange to say, all that had in old days covered up, obliterated the sense of death, could not now produce the same effect. Latterly, Ivan Ilyitch spent the greater part of his time in these efforts to restore his old trains of thought which had shut off death. At one time he would say to himself, "I'll put myself into my official work; why, I used to live in it." And he would go to the law-courts, banishing every doubt. He would enter into conversation with his colleagues, and would sit carelessly, as his old habit was, scanning the crowd below dreamily, and with both his wasted hands he would lean on the arms of the oak arm-chair just as he always did; and bending over to a colleague, pass the papers to him and whisper to him,

[20] Ivan is remembering a school textbook, *Outline of Logic* (1796), by the German Karl Kiesewetter.

then suddenly dropping his eyes and sitting up straight, he would pronounce the familiar words that opened the proceedings. But suddenly in the middle, the pain in his side, utterly regardless of the stage he had reached in his conduct of the case, began its work. It riveted Ivan Ilyitch's attention. He drove away the thought of it, but it still did its work, and then *It* came and stood confronting him and looked at him, and he felt turned to stone, and the light died away in his eyes, and he began to ask himself again, "Can it be that It is the only truth?" And his colleagues and his subordinates saw with surprise and distress that he, the brilliant, subtle judge, was losing the thread of his speech, was making blunders. He shook himself, tried to regain his self-control, and got somehow to the end of the sitting, and went home with the painful sense that his judicial labors could not as of old hide from him what he wanted to hide; that he could not by means of his official work escape from *It.* And the worst of it was that It drew him to itself not for him to do anything in particular, but simply for him to look at It straight in the face, to look at It and, doing nothing, suffer unspeakably.

And to save himself from this, Ivan Ilyitch sought amusements, other screens, and these screens he found, and for a little while they did seem to save him; but soon again they were not so much broken down as let the light through, as though It pierced through everything, and there was nothing that could shut It off.

Sometimes during those days he would go into the drawing-room he had furnished, that drawing-room where he had fallen, for which—how bitterly ludicrous it was for him to think of it!—for the decoration of which he had sacrificed his life, for he knew that it was that bruise that had started his illness. He went in and saw that the polished table had been scratched by something. He looked for the cause, and found it in the bronze clasps of the album, which had been twisted on one side. He took up the album, a costly one, which he had himself arranged with loving care, and was vexed at the carelessness of his daughter and her friends. Here a page was torn, here the photographs had been shifted out of their places. He carefully put it to rights again and bent the clasp back.

Then the idea occurred to him to move all this setting up of the albums to another corner where the flowers stood. He called the footman; or his daughter or his wife came to help him. They did not agree with him, contradicted him; he argued, got angry. But all that was very well, since he did not think of It; It was not in sight.

But then his wife would say, as he moved something himself, "Do let the servants do it, you'll hurt yourself again," and all at once It peeped through the screen; he caught a glimpse of It. He caught a glimpse of It, but still he hoped It would hide itself. Involuntarily, though, he kept watch on his side; there it is just the same still, aching still, and now he cannot forget it, and *It* is staring openly at him from behind the flowers. What's the use of it all?

"And it's the fact that here, at that curtain, as if it had been storming a fort, I lost my life. Is it possible? How awful and how silly! It cannot be! It cannot be, and it is."

He went into his own room, lay down, and was again alone with It. Face to face with It, and nothing to be done with It. Nothing but to look at It and shiver.

VII

How it came to pass during the third month of Ivan Ilyitch's illness, it would be impossible to say, for it happened little by little, imperceptibly, but it had come to pass that his wife and his daughter and his son and their servants and their acquaintances, and the doctors, and, most of all, he himself—all were aware that all interest in him for other people consisted now in the question how soon he would leave his place empty, free the living from the constraint of his presence, and be set free himself from his sufferings.

He slept less and less; they gave him opium, and began to inject morphine. But this did not relieve him. The dull pain he experienced in the half-asleep condition at first only relieved him as a change, but then it became as bad, or even more agonizing, than the open pain. He had special things to eat prepared for him according to the doctors' prescriptions; but these dishes became more and more distasteful, more and more revolting to him.

Special arrangements, too, had to be made for his other physical needs, and this was a continual misery to him. Misery from the uncleanliness, the unseemliness, and the stench, from the feeling of another person having to assist in it.

But just from this most unpleasant side of his illness there came comfort to Ivan Ilyitch. There always came into his room on these occasions to clear up for him the peasant who waited on table, Gerasim.

Gerasim was a clean, fresh, young peasant, who had grown stout and hearty on the good fare in town. Always cheerful and bright. At first the sight of this lad, always cleanly dressed in the Russian style, engaged in this revolting task, embarrassed Ivan Ilyitch.

One day, getting up from the night-stool,[21] too weak to replace his clothes, he dropped on to a soft low chair and looked with horror at his bare, powerless thighs, with the muscles so sharply standing out on them.

Then there came in with light, strong steps Gerasim, in his thick boots, diffusing a pleasant smell of tar from his boots, and bringing in the freshness of the winter air. Wearing a clean hempen apron, and a clean cotton shirt, with his sleeves tucked up on his strong, bare young arms, without looking at Ivan Ilyitch, obviously trying to check the radiant happiness in his face so as not to hurt the sick man, he went up to the night-stool.

"Gerasim," said Ivan Ilyitch faintly.

Gerasim started, clearly afraid that he had done something amiss, and with a rapid movement turned towards the sick man his fresh, good-natured, simple young face, just beginning to be downy with the first growth of beard.

[21] Commode; seat over a chamber pot.

"Yes, your honor."

"I'm afraid this is very disagreeable for you. You must excuse me. I can't help it."

"Why, upon my word, sir!" And Gerasim's eyes beamed, and he showed his white young teeth in a smile. "What's a little trouble? It's a case of illness with you, sir."

And with his deft, strong arms he performed his habitual task, and went out, stepping lightly. And five minutes later, treading just as lightly, he came back.

Ivan Ilyitch was still sitting in the same way in the arm-chair.

"Gerasim," he said, when the latter had replaced the night-stool all sweet and clean, "please help me; come here." Gerasim went up to him. "Lift me up. It's difficult for me alone, and I've sent Dmitry away."

Gerasim went up to him; as lightly as he stepped he put his strong arms round him, deftly and gently lifted and supported him, with the other hand pulled up his trousers, and would have set him down again. But Ivan Ilyitch asked him to carry him to the sofa. Gerasim, without effort, carefully not squeezing him, led him, almost carrying him, to the sofa, and settled him there.

"Thank you; how neatly and well . . . you do everything."

Gerasim smiled again, and would have gone away. But Ivan Ilyitch felt his presence such a comfort that he was reluctant to let him go.

"Oh, move that chair near me, please. No, that one, under my legs. I feel easier when my legs are higher."

Gerasim picked up the chair, and without letting it knock, set it gently down on the ground just at the right place, and lifted Ivan Ilyitch's legs on to it. It seemed to Ivan Ilyitch that he was easier just at the moment when Gerasim lifted his legs higher.

"I'm better when my legs are higher," said Ivan Ilyitch. "Put that cushion under me."

Gerasim did so. Again he lifted his legs to put the cushion under them. Again it seemed to Ivan Ilyitch that he was easier at that moment when Gerasim held his legs raised. When he laid them down again, he felt worse.

"Gerasim," he said to him, "are you busy just now?"

"Not at all, sir," said Gerasim, who had learned among the town-bred servants how to speak to gentlefolks.

"What have you left to do?"

"Why, what have I to do? I've done everything, there's only the wood to chop for to-morrow."

"Then hold my legs up like that—can you?"

"To be sure, I can." Gerasim lifted the legs up. And it seemed to Ivan Ilyitch that in that position he did not feel the pain at all.

"But how about the wood?"

"Don't you trouble about that, sir. We shall have time enough."

Ivan Ilyitch made Gerasim sit and hold his legs, and began to talk to him. And, strange to say, he fancied he felt better while Gerasim had hold of his legs.

From that time forward Ivan Ilyitch would sometimes call Gerasim, and get him to hold his legs on his shoulders, and he liked talking with him. Gerasim did this easily, readily, simply, and with a good-nature that touched Ivan Ilyitch. Health, strength, and heartiness in all other people were offensive to Ivan Ilyitch; but the strength and heartiness of Gerasim did not mortify him, but soothed him.

Ivan Ilyitch's great misery was due to the deception that for some reason or other every one kept up with him—that he was simply ill, and not dying, and that he need only keep quiet and follow the doctor's orders, and then some great change for the better would be the result. He knew that whatever they might do, there would be no result except more agonizing sufferings and death. And he was made miserable by this lie, made miserable at their refusing to acknowledge what they all knew and he knew, by their persisting in lying to him about his awful position, and in forcing him too to take part in this lie. Lying, lying, this lying carried on over him on the eve of his death, and destined to bring that terrible, solemn act of his death down to the level of all their visits, curtains, sturgeons for dinner . . . was a horrible agony for Ivan Ilyitch. And, strange to say, many times when they had been going through the regular performance over him, he had been within a hair's-breadth of screaming at them: "Cease your lying! You know, and I know, that I'm dying; so do, at least, give over lying!" But he had never had the spirit to do this. The terrible, awful act of his dying was, he saw, by all those about him, brought down to the level of a casual, unpleasant, and to some extent indecorous, incident (somewhat as they would behave with a person who should enter a drawing-room smelling unpleasant). It was brought down to this level by that very decorum to which he had been enslaved all his life. He saw that no one felt for him, because no one would even grasp his position. Gerasim was the only person who recognized the position, and felt sorry for him. And that was why Ivan Ilyitch was only at ease with Gerasim. He felt comforted when Gerasim sometimes supported his legs for whole nights at a stretch, and would not go away to bed, saying, "Don't you worry yourself, Ivan Ilyitch, I'll get sleep enough yet," or when suddenly dropping into the familiar peasant forms of speech, he added: "If thou weren't sick, but as 'tis, 'twould be strange if I didn't wait on thee." Gerasim alone did not lie; everything showed clearly that he alone understood what it meant, and saw no necessity to disguise it, and simply felt sorry for his sick, wasting master. He even said this once straight out, when Ivan Ilyitch was sending him away.

"We shall all die. So what's a little trouble?" he said, meaning by this to express that he did not complain of the trouble just because he was taking this trouble for a dying man, and he hoped that for him too some one would be willing to take the same trouble when his time came.

Apart from this deception, or in consequence of it, what made the greatest misery for Ivan Ilyitch was that no one felt for him as he would have liked them to feel for him. At certain moments, after prolonged suffering, Ivan Ilyitch, ashamed as he would have been to own it, longed more than anything for some one to feel sorry for him, as for a sick child. He longed to be petted, kissed, and wept over, as children are petted and comforted. He knew that he was an important member of the law-courts, that he had a beard turning grey, and that therefore it was impossible. But still he longed for it. And in his relations with Gerasim there was something approaching to that. And that was why being with Gerasim was a comfort to him. Ivan Ilyitch longs to weep, longs to be petted and wept over, and then there comes in a colleague, Shebek; and instead of weeping and being petted, Ivan Ilyitch puts on his serious, severe, earnest face, and from mere inertia gives his views on the effect of the last decision in the Court of Appeal, and obstinately insists upon them. This falsity around him and within him did more than anything to poison Ivan Ilyitch's last days.

VIII

It was morning. All that made it morning for Ivan Ilyitch was that Gerasim had gone away, and Pyotr the footman had come in; he had put out the candles, opened one of the curtains, and begun surreptitiously setting the room to rights. Whether it were morning or evening, Friday or Sunday, it all made no difference; it was always just the same thing. Gnawing, agonizing pain never ceasing for an instant; the hopeless sense of life always ebbing away, but still not yet gone; always swooping down on him that fearful, hated death, which was the only reality, and always the same falsity. What were days, or weeks, or hours of the day to him?

"Will you have tea, sir?"

"He wants things done in their regular order. In the morning the family should have tea," he thought, and only said—

"No."

"Would you care to move on to the sofa?"

"He wants to make the room tidy, and I'm in his way. I'm uncleanness, disorder," he thought, and only said—

"No, leave me alone."

The servant still moved busily about his work. Ivan Ilyitch stretched out his hand. Pyotr went up to offer his services.

"What can I get you?"

"My watch."

Pyotr got out the watch, which lay just under his hand, and gave it to him.

"Half-past eight. Are they up?"

"Not yet, sir. Vladimir Ivanovitch" (that was his son) "has gone to the high school, and Praskovya Fyodorovna gave orders that she was to be waked if you asked for her. Shall I send word?"

"No, no need." Should I try some tea? he thought.

"Yes, tea . . . bring it."

Pyotr was on his way out. Ivan Ilyitch felt frightened of being left alone. "How keep him? Oh, the medicine. Pyotr, give me my medicine. Oh well, may be, medicine may still be some good." He took the spoon, drank it. "No, it does no good. It's all rubbish, deception," he decided, as soon as he tasted the familiar, mawkish, hopeless taste. "No, I can't believe it now. But the pain, why this pain? If it would only cease for a minute." And he groaned. Pyotr turned round. "No, go on. Bring the tea."

Pyotr went away. Ivan Ilyitch, left alone, moaned, not so much from the pain, awful as it was, as from misery. Always the same thing again and again, all these endless days and nights. If it would only be quicker. Quicker to what? Death, darkness. No, no. Anything better than death!

When Pyotr came in with the tea on a tray, Ivan Ilyitch stared for some time absent-mindedly at him, not grasping who he was and what he wanted. Pyotr was disconcerted by this stare. And when he showed he was disconcerted, Ivan Ilyitch came to himself.

"Oh yes," he said, "tea, good, set it down. Only help me to wash and put on a clean shirt."

And Ivan Ilyitch began his washing. He washed his hands slowly, and then his face, cleaned his teeth, combed his hair, and looked in the looking-glass. He felt frightened at what he saw, especially at the way his hair clung limply to his pale forehead. When his shirt was being changed, he knew he would be still more terrified if he glanced at his body, and he avoided looking at himself. But at last it was all over. He put on his dressing-gown, covered himself with a rug, and sat in the armchair to drink his tea. For one moment he felt refreshed; but as soon as he began to drink the tea, again there was the same taste, the same pain. He forced himself to finish it, and lay down, stretched out his legs. He lay down and dismissed Pyotr.

Always the same. A gleam of hope flashes for a moment, then again the sea of despair roars about him again, and always pain, always pain, always heartache, and always the same thing. Alone it is awfully dreary; he longs to call some one, but he knows beforehand that with others present it will be worse. "Morphine again—only to forget again. I'll tell him, the doctor, that he must think of something else. It can't go on; it can't go on like this."

One hour, two hours pass like this. Then there is a ring at the front door. The doctor, perhaps. Yes, it is the doctor, fresh, hearty, fat, and cheerful, wearing that expression that seems to say, "You there are in a panic about something, but we'll soon set things right for you." The doctor is aware that this expression is hardly fitting here, but he has put it on once and for all, and can't take it off, like a man who has put on a frockcoat to pay a round of calls.

In a hearty, reassuring manner the doctor rubs his hands.

"I'm cold. It's a sharp frost. Just let me warm myself," he says with an expression, as though it's only a matter of waiting a little till he's warm, and as soon as he's warm he'll set everything to rights.

"Well, now, how are you?"

Ivan Ilyitch feels that the doctor would like to say, "How's the little trouble?" but that he feels that he can't talk like that, and says, "How did you pass the night?"

Ivan Ilyitch looks at the doctor with an expression that asks—

"Is it possible you're never ashamed of lying?"

But the doctor does not care to understand this look.

And Ivan Ilyitch says—

"It's always just as awful. The pain never leaves me, never ceases. If only there were something!"

"Ah, you're all like that, all sick people say that. Come, now, I do believe I'm thawed; even Praskovya Fyodorovna, who's so particular, could find no fault with my temperature. Well, now I can say good morning." And the doctor shakes hands.

And dropping his former levity, the doctor, with a serious face, proceeds to examine the patient, feeling his pulse, to take his temperature, and then the tappings and soundings begin.

Ivan Ilyitch knows positively and indubitably that it's all nonsense and empty deception; but when the doctor, kneeling down, stretches over him, putting his ear first higher, then lower, and goes through various gymnastic evolutions over him with a serious face, Ivan Ilyitch is affected by this, as he used sometimes to be affected by the speeches of the lawyers in court, though he was perfectly well aware that they were telling lies all the while and why they were telling lies.

The doctor, kneeling on the sofa, was still sounding him, when there was the rustle of Praskovya Fyodorovna's silk dress in the doorway, and she was heard scolding Pyotr for not having let her know that the doctor had come.

She comes in, kisses her husband, and at once begins to explain that she has been up a long while, and that it was only through a misunderstanding that she was not there when the doctor came.

Ivan Ilyitch looks at her, scans her all over, and sets down against her her whiteness and plumpness, and the cleanness of her hands and neck, and the glossiness of her hair, and the gleam full of life in her eyes. With all the force of his soul he hates her. And when she touches him it makes him suffer from the thrill of hatred he feels for her.

Her attitude to him and his illness is still the same. Just as the doctor had taken up a certain line with the patient which he was not now able to drop, so she too had taken up a line with him—that he was not doing something he ought to do, and was himself to blame, and she was lovingly reproaching him for his neglect, and she could not now get out of this attitude.

"Why, you know, he won't listen to me; he doesn't take his medicine at the right times. And what's worse still, he insists on lying in a position that surely must be bad for him—with his legs in the air."

She described how he made Gerasim hold his legs up.

The doctor smiled with kindly condescension that said, "Oh well, it can't be helped, these sick people do take up such foolish fancies; but we must forgive them."

When the examination was over, the doctor looked at his watch, and then Praskovya Fyodorovna informed Ivan Ilyitch that it must, of course, be as he liked, but she had sent to-day for a celebrated doctor, and that he would examine him, and have a consultation with Mihail Danilovitch (that was the name of their regular doctor).

"Don't oppose it now, please. This I'm doing entirely for my own sake," she said ironically, meaning it to be understood that she was doing it all for his sake, and was only saying this to give him no right to refuse her request. He lay silent, knitting his brows. He felt that he was hemmed in by such a tangle of falsity that it was hard to disentangle anything from it.

Everything she did for him was entirely for her own sake, and she told him she was doing for her own sake what she actually was doing for her own sake as something so incredible that he would take it as meaning the opposite.

At half-past eleven the celebrated doctor came. Again came the sounding, and then grave conversation in his presence and in the other room about the kidney and the appendix, and questions and answers, with such an air of significance, that again, instead of the real question of life and death, which was now the only one that confronted him, the question that came uppermost was of the kidney and the appendix, which were doing something not as they ought to do, and were for that reason being attacked by Mihail Danilovitch and the celebrated doctor, and forced to mend their ways.

The celebrated doctor took leave of him with a serious, but not a hopeless face. And to the timid question that Ivan Ilyitch addressed to him while he lifted his eyes, shining with terror and hope, up towards him, Was there a chance of recovery? he answered that he could not answer for it, but that there was a chance. The look of hope with which Ivan Ilyitch watched the doctor out was so piteous that, seeing it, Praskovya Fyodorovna positively burst into tears, as she went out of the door to hand the celebrated doctor his fee in the next room.

The gleam of hope kindled by the doctor's assurance did not last long. Again the same room, the same pictures, the curtains, the wallpaper, the medicine-bottles, and ever the same, his aching suffering body. And Ivan Ilyitch began to moan; they gave him injections, and he sank into oblivion. When he waked up it was getting dark; they brought him his dinner. He forced himself to eat some broth; and again everything the same, and again the coming night.

After dinner at seven o'clock, Praskovya Fyodorovna came into his room, dressed as though to go to a *soirée*,[22] with her full bosom laced in tight, and traces of powder on her face. She had in the morning mentioned to him that they were going to the theatre. Sarah Bernhardt[23] was visiting the town, and they had a box, which he had insisted on their taking. By now he had forgotten about it, and her smart attire was an offense to him. But he concealed this feeling when he recollected that he had himself insisted on their taking a box and going, because it was an aesthetic pleasure, beneficial and instructive for the children.

Praskovya Fyodorovna came in satisfied with herself, but yet with something of a guilty air. She sat down, asked how he was, as he saw, simply for the sake of asking, and not for the sake of learning anything, knowing indeed that there was nothing to learn, and began telling him how absolutely necessary it was; how she would not have gone for anything, but the box had been taken, and Liza, their daughter, and Petrishtchev (the examining lawyer, the daughter's suitor) were going, and that it was out of the question to let them go alone. But that she would have liked much better to stay with him. If only he would be sure to follow the doctor's prescription while she was away.

"Oh, and Fyodor Dmitryevitch" (the suitor) "would like to come in. May he? And Liza?"

"Yes, let them come in."

The daughter came in, in evening clothes, her fresh young body showing, while his body made him suffer so. But she made a show of it; she was strong, healthy, obviously in love, and impatient of the illness, suffering, and death that hindered her happiness.

Fyodor Dmitryevitch came in too in evening dress, his hair curled *à la*

[22] Evening affair.

[23] Immensely popular French actress (1844–1923), who toured widely in Europe, the United States, and Russia.

Capoul,[24] with his long sinewy neck tightly fenced round by a white collar, with his vast expanse of white chest and strong thighs displayed in narrow black trousers, with one white glove in his hand and a crush opera hat.

Behind him crept in unnoticed the little high school boy in his new uniform, poor fellow, in gloves, and with those awful blue rings under his eyes that Ivan Ilyitch knew the meaning of.

He always felt sorry for his son. And pitiable indeed was his scared face of sympathetic suffering. Except Gerasim, Ivan Ilyitch fancied that Volodya was the only one that understood and was sorry.

They all sat down; again they asked how he was. A silence followed. Liza asked her mother about the opera-glass. An altercation ensued between the mother and daughter as to who had taken it, and where it had been put. It turned into an unpleasant squabble.

Fyodor Dmitryevitch asked Ivan Ilyitch whether he had seen Sarah Bernhardt? Ivan Ilyitch could not at first catch the question that was asked him, but then he said, "No, have you seen her before?"

"Yes, in *Adrienne Lecouvreur.*"[25]

Praskovya Fyodorovna observed that she was particularly good in that part. The daughter made some reply. A conversation sprang up about the art and naturalness of her acting, that conversation that is continually repeated and always the same.

In the middle of the conversation Fyodor Dmitryevitch glanced at Ivan Ilyitch and relapsed into silence. The others looked at him and became mute, too. Ivan Ilyitch was staring with glittering eyes straight before him, obviously furious with them. This had to be set right, but it could not anyhow be set right. This silence had somehow to be broken. No one would venture on breaking it, and all began to feel alarmed that the decorous deception was somehow breaking down, and the facts would be exposed to all. Liza was the first to pluck up courage. She broke the silence. She tried to cover up what they were all feeling, but inadvertently she gave it utterance.

"*If we are going,* though, it's time to start," she said, glancing at her watch, a gift from her father; and with a scarcely perceptible meaning smile to the young man, referring to something only known to themselves, she got up with a rustle of her skirts.

They all got up, said good-bye, and went away. When they were gone, Ivan Ilyitch fancied he was easier; there was no falsity—that had gone away with them, but the pain remained. That continual pain, that continual terror, made nothing harder, nothing easier. It was always worse.

Again came minute after minute, hour after hour, still the same and still no end, and ever more terrible the inevitable end.

"Yes, send Gerasim," he said in answer to Pyotr's question.

[24] In the fashionable Capoul style (French).

[25] A light, commercial play by the immensely prolific French playwright Eugène Scribe. Tolstoy disliked his work.

IX

Late at night his wife came back. She came in on tiptoe, but he heard her, opened his eyes, and made haste to close them again. She wanted to send away Gerasim and sit up with him herself instead. He opened his eyes and said, "No, go away."

"Are you in great pain?"

"Always the same."

"Take some opium."

He agreed, and drank it. She went away.

Till three o'clock he slept a miserable sleep. It seemed to him that he and his pain were being thrust somewhere into a narrow, deep, black sack, and they kept pushing him further and further in, and still could not thrust him to the bottom. And this operation was awful to him, and was accompanied with agony. And he was afraid, and yet wanted to fall into it, and struggled and yet tried to get into it. And all of a sudden he slipped and fell and woke up. Gerasim, still the same, is sitting at the foot of the bed half-dozing peacefully, patient. And he is lying with his wasted legs clad in stockings, raised on Gerasim's shoulders, the same candle burning in the alcove, and the same interminable pain.

"Go away, Gerasim," he whispered.

"It's all right, sir. I'll stay a bit longer."

"No, go away."

He took his legs down, lay sideways on his arm, and he felt very sorry for himself. He only waited till Gerasim had gone away into the next room; he could restrain himself no longer, and cried like a child. He cried at his own helplessness, at his awful loneliness, at the cruelty of people, at the cruelty of God, at the absence of God.

"Why hast Thou done all this? What brought me to this? Why, why torture me so horribly?"

He did not expect an answer, and wept indeed that there was and could be no answer. The pain grew more acute again, but he did not stir, did not call.

He said to himself, "Come, more then; come, strike me! But what for? What have I done to Thee? what for?"

Then he was still, ceased weeping, held his breath, and was all attention; he listened, as it were, not to a voice uttering sounds, but to the voice of his soul, to the current of thoughts that rose up within him.

"What is it you want?" was the first clear idea capable of putting into words that he grasped.

"What? Not to suffer, to live," he answered.

And again he was utterly plunged into attention so intense that even the pain did not distract him.

"To live? Live how?" the voice of his soul was asking.

"Why, live as I used to live before—happily and pleasantly."

"As you used to live before—happily and pleasantly?" queried the voice. And he began going over in his imagination the best moments of his pleasant life. But strange to say, all these best moments of his pleasant life seemed now not at all what they had seemed then. All—except the first memories of childhood—there, in his childhood there had been something really pleasant in which one could have lived if it had come back. But the creature who had this pleasant experience was no more; it was like a memory of some one else.

As soon as he reached the beginning of what had resulted in him as he was now, Ivan Ilyitch, all that had seemed joys to him then now melted away before his eyes and were transformed into something trivial, and often disgusting.

And the further he went from childhood, the nearer to the actual present, the more worthless and uncertain were the joys. It began with life at the school of jurisprudence. Then there had still been something genuinely good; then there had been gaiety; then there had been friendship; then there had been hopes. But in the higher classes these good moments were already becoming rarer. Later on, during the first period of his official life, at the governor's, good moments appeared; but it was all mixed, and less and less of it was good. And further on even less was good, and the further he went the less good there was.

His marriage . . . as gratuitous as the disillusion of it and the smell of his wife's breath and the sensuality, the hypocrisy! And that deadly official life, and anxiety about money, and so for one year, and two, and ten, and twenty, and always the same thing. And the further he went, the more deadly it became. "As though I had been going steadily downhill, imagining that I was going uphill. So it was in fact. In public opinion I was going uphill, and steadily as I got up it, life was ebbing away from me. . . . And now the work's done, there's nothing left but to die.

"But what is this? What for? It cannot be! It cannot be that life has been so senseless, so loathsome? And if it really was so loathsome and senseless, then why die, and die in agony? There's something wrong.

"Can it be I have not lived as one ought?" suddenly came into his head. "But how not so, when I've done everything as it should be done?" he said, and at once dismissed this only solution of all the enigma of life and death as something utterly out of the question.

"What do you want now? To live? Live how? Live as you live at the courts when the usher booms out: 'The Judge is coming!' . . . The judge is coming, the judge is coming," he repeated to himself. "Here he is, the judge! But I'm not to blame!" he shrieked in fury. "What's it for?" And he left off crying, and turning with his face to the wall, fell to pondering always on the same question, "What for, why all this horror?"

But however much he pondered, he could not find an answer. And whenever the idea struck him, as it often did, that it all came of his never having lived as he ought, he thought of all the correctness of his life and dismissed the strange idea.

X

Another fortnight had passed. Ivan Ilyitch could not now get up from the sofa. He did not like lying in bed, and lay on the sofa. And lying almost all the time facing the wall, in loneliness he suffered all the inexplicable agonies, and in loneliness pondered always that inexplicable question, "What is it? Can it be true that it's death?" And an inner voice answered, "Yes, it is true." "Why these agonies?" and a voice answered, "For no reason." Beyond and besides this there was nothing.

From the very beginning of his illness, ever since Ivan Ilyitch first went to the doctor's, his life had been split up into two contradictory moods, which were continually alternating—one was despair and the anticipation of an uncomprehended and awful death; the other was hope and an absorbed watching over the actual condition of his body. First there was nothing confronting him but a kidney or intestine which had temporarily declined to perform its duties, then there was nothing but unknown awful death, which there was no escaping.

These two moods had alternated from the very beginning of the illness; but the further the illness progressed, the more doubtful and fantastic became the conception of the kidney, and the more real the sense of approaching death.

He had but to reflect on what he had been three months before and what he was now, to reflect how steadily he had been going downhill, for every possibility of hope to be shattered.

Of late, in the loneliness in which he found himself, lying with his face to the back of the sofa, a loneliness in the middle of a populous town and of his numerous acquaintances and his family, a loneliness than which none more complete could be found anywhere—not at the bottom of the sea, not deep down in the earth;—of late in this fearful loneliness Ivan Ilyitch had lived only in imagination in the past. One by one the pictures of his past rose up before him. It always began from what was nearest in time and went back to the most remote, to childhood, and rested there. If Ivan Ilyitch thought of the stewed prunes that had been offered him for dinner that day, his mind went back to the damp, wrinkled French plum of his childhood, of its peculiar taste and the flow of saliva when the stone was sucked; and along with this memory of a taste there rose up a whole series of memories of that period—his nurse, his brother, his playthings. "I mustn't . . . it's too painful," Ivan Ilyitch said to himself, and he brought himself back to the present. The button on the back of the sofa and the creases in the morocco.[26] "Morocco's dear, and doesn't wear well; there was a quarrel over it. But the morocco was different, and different too the quarrel when we tore father's portfolio and were punished, and mamma bought us the tarts." And again his mind rested on his childhood, and again it was painful, and he tried to drive it away and think of something else.

And again at that point, together with that chain of associations, quite another chain of memories came into his heart, of how his illness had grown up and become more acute. It was the same there, the further back the more life there had been. There had been both more that was good in life and more of life itself. And the two began to melt into one. "Just as the pain goes on getting worse and worse, so has my whole life gone on getting

[26] A fine leather made from goatskin, often used as a furniture-covering in the nineteenth century.

worse and worse," he thought. One light spot was there at the back, at the beginning of life, and then it kept getting blacker and blacker, and going faster and faster. "In inverse ratio to the square of the distance from death," thought Ivan Ilyitch. And the image of a stone falling downwards with increasing velocity sank into his soul. Life, a series of increasing sufferings, falls more and more swiftly to the end, the most fearful sufferings. "I am falling." He shuddered, shifted himself, would have resisted, but he knew beforehand that he could not resist; and again, with eyes weary with gazing at it, but unable not to gaze at what was before him, he stared at the back of the sofa and waited, waited expecting that fearful fall and shock and dissolution. "Resistance is impossible," he said to himself. "But if one could at least comprehend what it's for? Even that's impossible. It could be explained if one were to say that I hadn't lived as I ought. But that can't be alleged," he said to himself, thinking of all the regularity, correctness, and propriety of his life. "That really can't be admitted," he said to himself, his lips smiling ironically as though some one could see his smile and be deceived by it. "No explanation! Agony, death. . . . What for?"

XI

So passed a fortnight. During that fortnight an event occurred that had been desired by Ivan Ilyitch and his wife. Petrishtchev made a formal proposal. This took place in the evening. Next day Praskovya Fyodorovna went in to her husband, resolving in her mind how to inform him of Fyodor Dmitryevitch's proposal, but that night there had been a change for the worse in Ivan Ilyitch. Praskovya Fyodorovna found him on the same sofa, but in a different position. He was lying on his face, groaning, and staring straight before him with a fixed gaze.

She began talking of remedies. He turned his stare on her. She did not finish what she had begun saying; such hatred of her in particular was expressed in that stare.

"For Christ's sake, let me die in peace," he said.

She would have gone away, but at that moment the daughter came in and went up to say good morning to him. He looked at his daughter just as at his wife, and to her inquiries how he was, he told her drily that they would soon all be rid of him. Both were silent, sat a little while, and went out.

"How are we to blame?" said Liza to her mother. "As though we had done it! I'm sorry for papa, but why punish us?"

At the usual hour the doctor came. Ivan Ilyitch answered, "Yes, no," never taking his exasperated stare from him, and towards the end he said, "Why, you know that you can do nothing, so let me be."

"We can relieve your suffering," said the doctor.

"Even that you can't do; let me be."

The doctor went into the drawing-room and told Praskovya Fyodorovna that it was very serious, and that the only resource left them was opium to relieve his sufferings, which must be terrible. The doctor said his physical sufferings were terrible, and that was true; but even more terrible than his physical sufferings were his mental sufferings, and in that lay his chief misery.

His moral sufferings were due to the fact that during that night, as he looked at the sleepy, good-natured, broad-cheeked face of Gerasim, the thought had suddenly come into his head, "What if in reality all my life, my conscious life, has been not the right thing?" The thought struck him that what he had regarded before as an utter impossibility, that he had spent his life not as he ought, might be the truth. It struck him that those scarcely detected impulses of struggle within him against what was considered good by persons of higher position, scarcely detected impulses which he had dismissed, that they might be the real thing, and everything else might be not the right thing. And his official work, and his ordering of his daily life and of his family, and these social and official interests,—all that might be not the right thing. He tried to defend it all to himself. And suddenly he felt all the weakness of what he was defending. And it was useless to defend it.

"But if it's so," he said to himself, "and I am leaving life with the consciousness that I have lost all that was given me, and there's no correcting it, then what?" He lay on his back and began going over his whole life entirely anew. When he saw the footman in the morning, then his wife, then his daughter, then the doctor, every movement they made, every word they uttered, confirmed for him the terrible truth that had been revealed to him in the night. In them he saw himself, saw all in which he had lived, and saw distinctly that it was all not the right thing; it was a horrible, vast deception that concealed both life and death. This consciousness intensified his physical agonies, multiplied them tenfold. He groaned and tossed from side to side and pulled at the covering over him. It seemed to him that it was stifling him and weighing him down. And for that he hated them.

They gave him a big dose of opium; he sank into unconsciousness; but at dinner-time the same thing began again. He drove them all away, and tossed from side to side.

His wife came to him and said, "Jean, darling, do this for my sake" (for my sake?). "It can't do harm, and it often does good. Why, it's nothing. And often in health people——"

He opened his eyes wide.

"What? Take the sacrament? What for? No. Besides . . ."

She began to cry.

"Yes, my dear. I'll send for our priest, he's so nice."

"All right, very well," he said.

When the priest came and confessed him he was softened, felt as it were a relief from his doubts, and consequently from his sufferings, and there came a moment of hope. He began once more thinking of the intestinal appendix and the possibility of curing it. He took the sacrament with tears in his eyes.

When they laid him down again after the sacrament for a minute, he felt comfortable, and again the hope of life sprang up. He began to think about the operation which had been suggested to him. "To live, I want to live," he said to himself. His wife came in to congratulate him; she uttered the customary words and added—

"It's quite true, isn't it, that you're better?"

Without looking at her, he said, "Yes."

Her dress, her figure, the expression of her face, the tone of her voice,—all told him the same: "Not the right thing. All that in which you lived and are living is lying, deceit, hiding life and death away from you." And as soon as he had formed that thought, hatred sprang up in him, and with that hatred agonizing physical sufferings, and with these sufferings the sense of inevitable, approaching ruin. Something new was happening; there were screwing and shooting pains, and a tightness in his breathing.

The expression of his face as he uttered that "Yes" was terrible. After uttering that "Yes," looking her straight in the face, he turned on to his face, with a rapidity extraordinary in his weakness, and shrieked—

"Go away, go away, let me be!"

XII

From that moment there began the scream that never ceased for three days, and was so awful that through two closed doors one could not hear it without horror. At the moment when he answered his wife he grasped that he had fallen, that there was no return, that the end had come, quite the end, while doubt was still as unsolved, still remained doubt.

"Oo! Oo—o! Oo!" he screamed in varying intonations. He had begun screaming, "I don't want to!" and so had gone on screaming on the same vowel sound—oo!

All those three days, during which time did not exist for him, he was struggling in that black sack into which he was being thrust by an unseen resistless force. He struggled as the man condemned to death struggles in the hands of the executioner, knowing that he cannot save himself. And every moment he felt that in spite of all his efforts to struggle against it, he was getting nearer and nearer to what terrified him. He felt that his agony was due both to his being thrust into this black hole and still more to his not being able to get right into it. What hindered him from getting into it was the claim that his life had been good. That justification of his life held him fast and would not let him get forward, and it caused him more agony than all.

All at once some force struck him in the chest, in the side, and stifled his breathing more than ever; he rolled forward into the hole, and there at the end there was some sort of light. It had happened with him, as it had sometimes happened to him in a railway carriage, when he had thought he was going forward while he was going back, and all of a sudden recognized his real direction.

"Yes, it has all been not the right thing," he said to himself, "but that's no matter." He could, he could do the right thing. "What is the right thing?" he asked himself, and suddenly he became quiet.

This was at the end of the third day, two hours before his death. At that very moment the schoolboy had stealthily crept into his father's room and gone up to his bedside. The dying man was screaming and waving his arms. His hand fell on the schoolboy's head. The boy snatched it, pressed it to his lips, and burst into tears.

At that very moment Ivan Ilyitch had rolled into the hole, and caught sight of the light, and it was revealed to him that his life had not been what it ought to have been, but that that could still be set right. He asked himself, "What is the right thing?"—and became quiet, listening. Then he felt some one was kissing his hand. He opened his eyes and glanced at his son. He felt sorry for him. His wife went up to him. He glanced at her. She was gazing at him with open mouth, the tears unwiped streaming over her nose and cheeks, a look of despair on her face. He felt sorry for her.

"Yes, I'm making them miserable," he thought. "They're sorry, but it will be better for them when I die." He would have said this, but had not the strength to utter it. "Besides, why speak, I must act," he thought. With a glance to his wife he pointed to his son and said—

"Take away . . . sorry for him. . . . And you too . . ." He tried to say "forgive," but said "forgo" . . . and too weak to correct himself, shook his hand, knowing that He would understand Whose understanding mattered.

And all at once it became clear to him that what had tortured him and would not leave him was suddenly dropping away all at once on both sides and on ten sides and on all sides. He was sorry for them, must act so that they might not suffer. Set them free and be free himself of those agonies. "How right and how simple!" he thought. "And the pain?" he asked himself. "Where's it gone? Eh, where are you, pain?"

He began to watch for it.

"Yes, here it is. Well, what of it, let the pain be.

"And death. Where is it?"

He looked for his old accustomed terror of death, and did not find it. "Where is it? What death?" There was no terror, because death was not either.

In the place of death there was light.

"So this is it!" he suddenly exclaimed aloud.

"What joy!"

To him all this passed in a single instant, and the meaning of that instant suffered no change after. For those present his agony lasted another two hours. There was a rattle in his throat, a twitching in his wasted body. Then the rattle and the gasping came at longer and longer intervals.

"It is over!" some one said over him.

He caught those words and repeated them in his soul.

"Death is over," he said to himself. "It's no more."

He drew in a breath, stopped midway in the breath, stretched and died.

Henrik Ibsen

(1828–1906)

Henrik Ibsen, the schoolbook cliché has it, is the Father of Modern Drama. The label is an oversimplification; modern drama had a number of fathers (an artistic, if not a biological, possibility). And Father Ibsen has had more than his share of trouble with his children, whose attitudes have ranged from dutiful imitation to outright rebellion. But the label does suggest Ibsen's achievement, not only a dozen or so luminous, timeless plays, but the articulation of a viable "idea of a theater" for the modern age. In the longest view, the idea of a theater has appeared only three times in Western literature—in Periclean Athens in the fifth century B.C., *in Renaissance Europe between about 1580 and 1700, and in the modern period since about 1880. At each of these points, playwrights have achieved the supremely difficult task of creating a theater and a dramatic form capable of expressing their ages' views of human life richly and complexly. Ibsen took the debased and mechanical theater in which he served a long, wearying apprenticeship and forged from its elements a dramatic form rooted deeply enough in the popular theater to be stageworthy and accessible and at the same time rich and subtle enough to express a comprehensive view of modern life and to probe multiple levels of existence. His themes are not only the ills of society but also the most private problems of the inner life of the individual, problems of what Ibsen called "spiritual emancipation and purification." His artistic children, even the most rebellious, have not outgrown his influence.*

The modern theater may be said to date from December 4, 1879, the publication date of A Doll House. *It took Ibsen fifty-one years of grueling apprenticeship to reach that date. He was born in 1828 in Skien, Norway, a tiny logging town about a hundred miles southwest of what is now Oslo (then called Christiania). His childhood was lonely and poverty-stricken, especially after the bankruptcy of his businessman father when Ibsen was eight. When he was fifteen, he was sent as an apothecary's apprentice to Grimstad, another tiny town farther down the Oslo Fjord, where he remained for six years, feeling, as he recalled later, "on a war footing with the little community where I felt I was being suppressed by my situation and by circumstances in general." He fathered an illegitimate child upon a housemaid ten years his senior and contributed to the child's support for fifteen years—a "buried secret" like those which appear so frequently in his mature plays—and he wrote his first play,* Catiline *(1849).* Catiline *was a stiff, amateurish play which turned the first-century* B.C. *Roman revolutionary into a haunted, brooding, Byronic figure; it nevertheless announced, as Ibsen himself observed twenty-five years later, some of his major themes, including "the conflict between one's aims and one's abilities, between what man proposes and what is actually possible."*

Ibsen left Grimstad when he was twenty-one, determined to be a writer rather than a druggist. Despite a rigorous program of self-education, he failed a portion of his entrance examinations for the University of Christiania and instead used Catiline, *which had been privately printed in a tiny edition, as his entrée into the Norwegian theater, such as it was. In 1851, he was engaged as a resident playwright in Bergen. He worked in the theater for the next thirteen years, first in Bergen for six and then in Christiania for seven more. He did everything from sweeping the stage to stage-managing, and he wrote eight plays, mostly in verse and mostly on Norwegian legendary and historical subjects, which were produced, in several instances with modest success. Ibsen came to despise the workaday theater—he called it "a daily abortion"—but his consummate sense of the stage can be traced to this prolonged experience in actual production.*

In 1864, Ibsen, depressed, defeated, and deeply in debt, obtained a small government travel grant and went to Italy, where he was soon joined by his wife Suzannah, whom he had married in 1858, and their young son Sigurd. They were not to return to Norway, except for short visits, for twenty-seven years. Ibsen felt, he later wrote, that he had "escaped from the darkness into the light, from the mists through a tunnel out into the sunlight," and in a sudden burst of joyful energy, he wrote the work that catapulted him into fame, Brand *(1866). This was a "dramatic poem" not intended for the stage about a Norwegian priest whose defiant creed of "All or Nothing" plunges him into a tragic inner conflict between love and will. The play was an enormous success, going through fourteen editions in two years, and was followed quickly by* Peer Gynt *(1867), a complementary "dramatic poem" about a folklore hero who becomes the prototype of what Ibsen saw as contemporary spiritual vacillation and compromise. Following the publication of* Peer Gynt, *the Ibsens moved to Germany; they were to divide their residence between Germany and Italy for the next twenty-three years. Several years were consumed in work on what Ibsen thought would be his masterpiece,* Emperor and Galilean *(1873), a mammoth "world-historical" closet drama about the Roman Emperor who attempted to restore paganism after the triumph of Christianity.* Emperor and Galilean *was followed by a transitional work,* Pillars of Society *(1877), in which Ibsen experimented with ways of constructing a prose play of modern life.* Pillars of Society *inaugurated the series of twelve plays to which Ibsen was to devote the rest of his life and which constitute his chief contribution to the modern theater.*

In these plays, Ibsen renounced the romantic expansiveness of his earlier plays and adopted a radically different technique. All are set in contemporary Norway within middle-class homes, all are in prose, and all are thoroughly realistic, intended to make the spectator feel, as Ibsen said, "as if he were actually sitting, listening, and looking at events happening in real life." Style, in this case, is a direct expression of a philosophy of art. In these plays, Ibsen decisively renounced the idealist theory of art, in which its function is to inspire and uplift by presenting images of life as it should be, and adopted instead a realistic theory, in which art presents an interpretation of life as it is, thereby opening the way toward reform and improvement.

Ibsen's twelve realistic plays, which he suggested on at least one occasion formed an interrelated cycle, fall into four rather unequal groups. Pillars of Society *presents a narrow, hypocritical village society in which the revelation of a guilty secret from the past becomes the instrument of purgation for the main character.* A Doll House *(1879) and* Ghosts *(1881) further explore this metaphor within the context of marriage.* A Doll House *provoked a major scandal, intensified by* Ghosts, *in which Ibsen advanced even more forcefully the theme of the individual's responsibility to himself as supreme over even the most hallowed of social institutions. The response to these plays perhaps contributed to the themes of a second group—*An Enemy of the People *(1886),* The Wild Duck *(1884), and* Rosmersholm *(1886)—in which Ibsen explored the ambiguities of truth-telling and its consequences. Already in* Rosmersholm *social criticism began to be subordinated to the exploration of individual personalities, especially extreme, neurotic ones, and realistic technique began to be modified by an extensive use of symbolism. These tendencies continued in* The Lady from the Sea *(1888) and* Hedda Gabler *(1890), both complex studies in the psychological consequences of female subordination. Ibsen himself explicitly linked his last four plays as an interrelated subgroup:* The Master Builder *(1892),* Little Eyolf *(1894),* John Gabriel Borkman *(1896), and* When We Dead Awaken *(1899). These plays have a rich, autumnal quality in their explorations of regret over failures and missed opportunities in the lives of strong-willed, titanic men; the style is symbolist rather than realistic, as the literal narratives are invaded by dream- and fantasy-material.*

The last few years of Ibsen's life were marked by a series of ambiguous but apparently platonic love affairs with much younger women: Helene Raff and Emilie

Bardach ("the May sun in a September life") and a young pianist named Hildur Andersen. These relationships left their mark on the final plays, especially in the ambiguous figure of Hilde Wangel in The Master Builder.

Ibsen and his wife took up permanent residence back in Norway in 1891. He suffered a severe stroke in 1900, followed by a second the following year, which left him unable to write. He remained an invalid for five more years, dying in 1906. His last word was "Tvertimod!" *("On the contrary!").*

Intellectually, Ibsen was a romantic liberal. Despite his reputation as a social critic, he never dealt in his plays with specific topical events. Even the more general targets of his criticism were matters hardly reformable by legislative measures: the pettiness and narrowness of small-town life, the excessive influence of the clergy, the power of commercial interests. Rather, he insisted throughout his life that reform must begin in the self-liberation of the individual.

*Ibsen's craftsmanship has been much praised but frequently for the wrong reasons. His dramaturgy in the narrowest sense is very much of the nineteenth century, and modern audiences must adopt a historical perspective if they are to accept comfortably his use of coincidence, his sometimes melodramatic, "cliff-hanger" act curtains, his characters' powers of total recall, and the almost frightening explicitness with which characters announce the themes of the plays they are in ("The spirit of truth and the spirit of freedom—*those *are the pillars of society," "I've been your doll-wife here, just as at home I was Papa's doll-child," etc.). Ibsen's formal mastery is not in his manipulation of such dated conventions but in the larger matter of shaping an entire story dramatically. At the center of each Ibsen play is an individual human life, glimpsed at a climactic moment of decision but gradually unfolded in its entirety in the course of the play. The contours of the lives of all these protagonists have certain similarities: a critical, self-limiting choice of a "mission" early in life, the gradual unfolding of the consequences of that choice, and an ecstatic moment of self-understanding leading sometimes to liberation, sometimes to death. It is this recurring myth of the self and its resonating implications through the levels of the family, the society, and the cosmos that link Ibsen's plays and give the reader the sense of titanic conflicts being worked out below the sometimes trivial events of the plays, the sense that the young James Joyce perhaps had in mind when he found the power of Ibsen's plays in "the naked drama—either the perception of a great truth, or the opening up of a great question, or a great conflict which is almost independent of the conflicting actors."*

All these generalizations apply to A Doll House. *(The play is usually known in English as* A Doll's House, *but the present translator, Rolf Fjelde, sensibly uses the English idiom that corresponds to the Norwegian title,* Et dukkehjem.*) The action of the play covers only a little over a day, but in its course Nora's entire life unfolds before us; her childhood as a "doll-child," her transition into a "doll-wife," her adoption of the misguided "mission" to win Helmer's lasting love through her great "secret," the collapse of this project, and the resurgence of her long-suppressed individuality. Past and present are thus constantly juxtaposed in the tight, "revelatory" structure, in which the revelation of past events becomes a major part of present action.*

A Doll House *aroused a storm of controversy when it was first published. Conservative readers and audiences indignantly rejected the depiction of what was after all a fairly conventional marriage as the systematic enslavement of the wife. But what they found most outrageous was the proposition that a woman's "most sacred duties" were not to her husband and children but to herself. The actress who first played Nora in Germany flatly refused to play the final scene as written, exclaiming, "I would never leave* my *children," and she presented Nora as viewing her sleeping children and sinking to the floor, unable to leave them. That final scene (in its authentic version) still retains its power, even in an age when the "angel of the house" has been partially demythologized.*

A Doll House *is a strong, polemical plea for women's liberation, but this particular kind of liberation is placed in a more general context of human liberation. Nora's father and husband and her society have enslaved her, but more basically, she has enslaved herself years ago by choosing, however unconsciously, something less than full selfhood. And now her greatest challenge is not to free herself from Helmer but to overcome her own instincts toward self-enslavement. The play is thus not only an exposure of marital enslavement but also a searching study of the psychology of the enslaved. Nineteen years after he wrote* A Doll House, *Ibsen was honored by the leading Norwegian feminist society for his services to women's rights. In responding to their tribute, he said, "I thank you for the toast, but must disclaim the honor of having consciously worked for the women's rights movement. I am not even quite clear as to just what this women's rights movement really is. To me it has seemed a problem of mankind in general." Ibsen was undoubtedly indulging his love of placing himself "on the contrary" here, but his words suggest a profound truth about* A Doll House. *Nora is correct when she tells Helmer, "It's a great sin what you and Papa did to me. You're to blame that nothing's become of me." But she moves beyond this view of herself as passive victim, which merely perpetuates her status as object, and accepts her own responsibility to bring about "the greatest miracle" of self-transformation. And for Ibsen, this is the greatest liberation of all.*

FURTHER READING *(prepared by J. H.):* Michael Meyer's massive *Ibsen: A Biography,* 1971, is the standard life, detailed and readable and with a great deal of information about the real-life sources of Ibsen's plays. Of historical interest but transcending that level are George Brandes, *Henrik Ibsen: A Critical Study,* 1898 (translated by Jessie Muir, 1964), by the Danish critic who was one of Ibsen's closest friends; and Bernard Shaw's *The Quintessence of Ibsenism,* 1891, by Ibsen's most famous disciple in England. More recent critical overviews are provided by Maurice Valency, *The Flower and the Castle,* 1963; and G. Wilson Knight, *Ibsen,* 1962. M. C. Bradbrook's *Ibsen the Norwegian: A Revaluation,* 1966; Brian W. Downs' *Ibsen: The Intellectual Background,* 1948, and *A Study of Six Plays by Ibsen,* 1950; and P. F. D. Tennant's *Ibsen's Dramatic Technique,* 1948, well represent Ibsen studies in England. James Hurt's *Catiline's Dream: An Essay on Ibsen's Plays,* 1972; and Charles R. Lyons' *Henrik Ibsen: The Divided Consciousness,* 1972, both attempt to relate the form of Ibsen's drama to his vision of life. Good collections of essays on Ibsen, with introductory bibliographies, are *Ibsen: A Collection of Critical Essays,* ed. Rolf Fjelde, 1965; and *Henrik Ibsen: A Critical Anthology,* ed. James McFarlane, 1970. The important subject of Ibsen's women characters is well treated in Elizabeth Hardwick, "Ibsen's Women," in *Seduction and Betrayal,* 1974.

A DOLL HOUSE

Translated by Rolf Fjelde

THE CHARACTERS

TORVALD HELMER, *a lawyer*
NORA, *his wife*
DR. RANK
MRS. LINDE
NILS KROGSTAD, *a bank clerk*
THE HELMERS' THREE SMALL CHILDREN
ANNE-MARIE, *their nurse*
HELENE, *a maid*
A DELIVERY BOY

The action takes place in HELMER*'s residence.*

ACT ONE

A comfortable room, tastefully but not expensively furnished. A door to the right in the back wall leads to the entryway; another to the left leads to HELMER*'s study. Between these doors, a piano. Midway in the left-hand wall a door, and further back a window. Near the window a round table with an armchair and a small sofa. In the right-hand wall, toward the rear, a door, and nearer the foreground a porcelain stove with two armchairs and a rocking chair beside it. Between the stove and the side door, a small table. Engravings on the walls. An* etagère[1] *with china figures and other small art objects; a small bookcase with richly bound books; the floor carpeted; a fire burning in the stove. It is a winter day.*

[*A bell rings in the entryway; shortly after we hear the door being unlocked.* NORA *comes into the room, humming happily to herself; she is wearing street clothes and carries an armload of packages, which she puts down on the table to the right. She has left the hall door open; and through it a* DELIVERY BOY *is seen, holding a Christmas tree and a basket, which he gives to the* MAID *who let them in.*]

NORA. Hide the tree well, Helene. The children mustn't get a glimpse of it till this evening, after it's trimmed. [*To the* DELIVERY BOY, *taking out her purse.*] How much?

DELIVERY BOY. Fifty, ma'am.

NORA. There's a crown. No, keep the change. [*The* BOY *thanks her and leaves.* NORA *shuts the door. She laughs softly to herself while taking off her street things. Drawing a bag of macaroons from her pocket, she eats a couple, then steals over and listens at her husband's study door.*] Yes, he's home. [*Hums again as she moves to the table right.*]

HELMER [*from the study*]. Is that my little lark twittering out there?

NORA [*busy opening some packages*]. Yes, it is.

HELMER. Is that my squirrel rummaging around?

[1] A piece of furniture with open shelves; a bookcase.

NORA. Yes!

HELMER. When did my squirrel get in?

NORA. Just now. [*Putting the macaroon bag in her pocket and wiping her mouth.*] Do come in, Torvald, and see what I've bought.

HELMER. Can't be disturbed. [*After a moment he opens the door and peers in, pen in hand.*] Bought, you say? All that there? Has the little spendthrift been out throwing money around again?

NORA. Oh, but Torvald, this year we really should let ourselves go a bit. It's the first Christmas we haven't had to economize.

HELMER. But you know we can't go squandering.

NORA. Oh yes, Torvald, we can squander a little now. Can't we? Just a tiny, wee bit. Now that you've got a big salary and are going to make piles and piles of money.

HELMER. Yes—starting New Year's. But then it's a full three months till the raise comes through.

NORA. Pooh! We can borrow that long.

HELMER. Nora! [*Goes over and playfully takes her by the ear.*] Are your scatterbrains off again? What if today I borrowed a thousand crowns, and you squandered them over Christmas week, and then on New Year's Eve a roof tile fell on my head, and I lay there—

NORA [*putting her hand on his mouth*]. Oh! Don't say such things!

HELMER. Yes, but what if it happened—then what?

NORA. If anything so awful happened, then it just wouldn't matter if I had debts or not.

HELMER. Well, but the people I'd borrowed from?

NORA. Them? Who cares about them! They're strangers.

HELMER. Nora, Nora, how like a woman! No, but seriously, Nora, you know what I think about that. No debts! Never borrow! Something of freedom's lost—and something of beauty, too—from a home that's founded on borrowing and debt. We've made a brave stand up to now, the two of us; and we'll go right on like that the little while we have to.

NORA [*going toward the stove*]. Yes, whatever you say, Torvald.

HELMER [*following her*]. Now, now, the little lark's wings mustn't droop. Come on, don't be a sulky squirrel. [*Taking out his wallet.*] Nora, guess what I have here.

NORA [*turning quickly*]. Money!

HELMER. There, see. [*Hands her some notes.*] Good grief, I know how costs go up in a house at Christmastime.

NORA. Ten—twenty—thirty—forty. Oh, thank you, Torvald; I can manage no end on this.

HELMER. You really will have to.

NORA. Oh yes, I promise I will! But come here so I can show you everything I bought. And so cheap! Look, new clothes for Ivar here—and a sword. Here a horse and a trumpet for Bob. And a doll and a doll's bed here for Emmy; they're nothing much, but she'll tear them to bits in no time anyway. And here I have dress material and handkerchiefs for the maids. Old Anne-Marie really deserves something more.

HELMER. And what's in that package there?

NORA [*with a cry*]. Torvald, no! You can't see that till tonight!

HELMER. I see. But tell me now, you little prodigal, what have you thought of for yourself?

NORA. For myself? Oh, I don't want anything at all.

HELMER. Of course you do. Tell me just what—within reason—you'd most like to have.

NORA. I honestly don't know. Oh, listen, Torvald—

HELMER. Well?

NORA [*fumbling at his coat buttons, without looking at him*]. If you want to give me something, then maybe you could—you could—

HELMER. Come on, out with it.

NORA [*hurriedly*]. You could give me money, Torvald. No more than you think you can spare; then one of these days I'll buy something with it.

HELMER. But Nora—

NORA. Oh, please, Torvald darling, do that! I beg you, please. Then I could hang the bills in pretty gilt paper on the Christmas tree. Wouldn't that be fun?

HELMER. What are those little birds called that always fly through their fortunes?

NORA. Oh yes, spendthrifts; I know all that. But let's do as I say, Torvald; then I'll have time to decide what I really need most. That's very sensible, isn't it?

HELMER [*smiling*]. Yes, very—that is, if you actually hung onto the money I give you, and you actually used it to buy yourself something. But it goes for the house and for all sorts of foolish things, and then I only have to lay out some more.

NORA. Oh, but Torvald—

HELMER. Don't deny it, my dear little Nora. [*Putting his arm around her waist.*] Spendthrifts are sweet, but they use up a frightful amount of money. It's incredible what it costs a man to feed such birds.

NORA. Oh, how can you say that! Really, I save everything I can.

HELMER [*laughing*]. Yes, that's the truth. Everything you can. But that's nothing at all.

NORA [*humming, with a smile of quiet satisfaction*]. Hm, if you only knew what expenses we larks and squirrels have, Torvald.

HELMER. You're an odd little one. Exactly the way your father was. You're never at a loss for scaring up money; but the moment you have it, it runs right out through your fingers; you never know what you've done with it. Well, one takes you as you are. It's deep in your blood. Yes, these things are hereditary, Nora.

NORA. Ah, I could wish I'd inherited many of Papa's qualities.

HELMER. And I couldn't wish you anything but just what you are, my sweet little lark. But wait; it seems to me you have a very—what should I call it?—a very suspicious look today—

NORA. I do?

HELMER. You certainly do. Look me straight in the eye.

NORA [*looking at him*]. Well?

HELMER [*shaking an admonitory finger*]. Surely my sweet tooth hasn't been running riot in town today, has she?

NORA. No. Why do you imagine that?

HELMER. My sweet tooth really didn't make a little detour through the confectioner's?

NORA. No, I assure you, Torvald—

HELMER. Hasn't nibbled some pastry?

NORA. No, not at all.

HELMER. Not even munched a macaroon or two?

NORA. No, Torvald, I assure you, really—

HELMER. There, there now. Of course I'm only joking.

NORA [*going to the table, right*]. You know I could never think of going against you.

HELMER. No, I understand that; and you *have* given me your word. [*Going over to her.*] Well, you keep your little Christmas secrets to yourself, Nora darling. I expect they'll come to light this evening, when the tree is lit.

NORA. Did you remember to ask Dr. Rank?

HELMER. No. But there's no need for that; it's assumed he'll be dining with us. All the same, I'll ask him when he stops by here this morning. I've ordered some fine wine. Nora, you can't imagine how I'm looking forward to this evening.

NORA. So am I. And what fun for the children, Torvald!

HELMER. Ah, it's so gratifying to know that one's gotten a safe, secure job, and with a comfortable salary. It's a great satisfaction, isn't it?

NORA. Oh, it's wonderful!

HELMER. Remember last Christmas? Three whole weeks before, you shut yourself in every evening till long after midnight, making flowers for the Christmas tree, and all the other decorations to surprise us. Ugh, that was the dullest time I've ever lived through.

NORA. It wasn't at all dull for me.

HELMER [*smiling*]. But the outcome *was* pretty sorry, Nora.

NORA. Oh, don't tease me with that again. How could I help it that the cat came in and tore everything to shreds.

HELMER. No, poor thing, you certainly couldn't. You wanted so much to please us all, and that's what counts. But it's just as well that the hard times are past.

NORA. Yes, it's really wonderful.

HELMER. Now I don't have to sit here alone, boring myself, and you don't have to tire your precious eyes and your fair little delicate hands—

NORA [*clapping her hands*]. No, is it really true, Torvald, I don't have to? Oh, how wonderfully lovely to hear! [*Taking his arm.*] Now I'll tell you just how I've thought we should plan things. Right after Christmas— [*The doorbell rings.*] Oh, the bell. [*Straightening the room up a bit.*] Somebody would have to come. What a bore!

HELMER. I'm not at home to visitors, don't forget.

MAID [*from the hall doorway*]. Ma'am, a lady to see you—

NORA. All right, let her come in.

MAID [*to* HELMER]. And the doctor's just come too.

HELMER. Did he go right to my study?

MAID. Yes, he did.

[HELMER *goes into his room. The* MAID *shows in* MRS. LINDE, *dressed in traveling clothes, and shuts the door after her.*]

MRS. LINDE [*in a dispirited and somewhat hesitant voice*]. Hello, Nora.

NORA [*uncertain*]. Hello—

MRS. LINDE. You don't recognize me.

NORA. No, I don't know—but wait, I think—[*Exclaiming.*] What! Kristine! Is it really you?

MRS. LINDE. Yes, it's me.

NORA. Kristine! To think I didn't recognize you. But then, how could I? [*More quietly.*] How you've changed, Kristine!

MRS. LINDE. Yes, no doubt I have. In nine—ten long years.

NORA. Is it so long since we met! Yes, it's all of that. Oh, these last eight years have been a happy time, believe me. And so now you've come in to town, too. Made the long trip in the winter. That took courage.

MRS. LINDE. I just got here by ship this morning.

NORA. To enjoy yourself over Christmas, of course. Oh, how lovely! Yes, enjoy ourselves, we'll do that. But take your coat off. You're not still cold? [*Helping her.*] There now, let's get cozy here by the stove. No, the easy chair there! I'll take the rocker here. [*Seizing her hands.*] Yes, now you have your old look again; it was only in that first moment. You're a bit more pale, Kristine—and maybe a bit thinner.

MRS. LINDE. And much, much older, Nora.

NORA. Yes, perhaps a bit older; a tiny, tiny bit; not much at all. [*Stopping short; suddenly serious.*] Oh, but thoughtless me, to sit here, chattering away. Sweet, good Kristine, can you forgive me?

MRS. LINDE. What do you mean, Nora?

NORA [*softly*]. Poor Kristine, you've become a widow.

MRS. LINDE. Yes, three years ago.

NORA. Oh, I knew it, of course; I read it in the papers. Oh, Kristine, you must believe me; I often thought of writing you then, but I kept postponing it, and something always interfered.

MRS. LINDE. Nora dear, I understand completely.

NORA. No, it was awful of me, Kristine. You poor thing, how much you must have gone through. And he left you nothing?

MRS. LINDE. No.

NORA. And no children?

MRS. LINDE. No.

NORA. Nothing at all, then?

MRS. LINDE. Not even a sense of loss to feed on.

NORA [*looking incredulously at her*]. But Kristine, how could that be?

MRS. LINDE [*smiling wearily and smoothing her hair*]. Oh, sometimes it happens, Nora.

NORA. So completely alone. How terribly hard that must be for you. I have three lovely children. You can't see them now; they're out with the maid. But now you must tell me everything—

MRS. LINDE. No, no, no, tell me about yourself.

NORA. No, you begin. Today I don't want to be selfish. I want to think only of you today. But there *is* something I must tell you. Did you hear of the wonderful luck we had recently?

MRS. LINDE. No, what's that?

NORA. My husband's been made manager in the bank, just think!

MRS. LINDE. Your husband? How marvelous!

NORA. Isn't it? Being a lawyer is such an uncertain living, you know, especially if one won't touch any cases that aren't clean and decent. And of course Torvald would never do that, and I'm with him completely there. Oh, we're simply delighted, believe me! He'll join the bank right after New Year's and start getting a huge salary and lots of commissions. From now on we can live quite differently—just as we want. Oh, Kristine, I feel so light and happy! Won't it be lovely to have stacks of money and not a care in the world?

MRS. LINDE. Well, anyway, it would be lovely to have enough for necessities.

NORA. No, not just for necessities, but stacks and stacks of money!

MRS. LINDE [*smiling*]. Nora, Nora, aren't you sensible yet? Back in school you were such a free spender.

NORA [*with a quiet laugh*]. Yes, that's what Torvald still says. [*Shaking her finger.*] But "Nora, Nora" isn't as silly as you all think. Really, we've been in no position for me to go squandering. We've had to work, both of us.

MRS. LINDE. You too?

NORA. Yes, at odd jobs—needlework, crocheting, embroidery, and such—[*Casually.*] and other things too. You remember that Torvald left the department when we were married? There was no chance of promotion in his office, and of course he needed to earn more money. But that first year he drove himself terribly. He took on all kinds of extra work that kept him going morning and night. It wore him down, and then he fell deathly ill. The doctors said it was essential for him to travel south.

MRS. LINDE. Yes, didn't you spend a whole year in Italy?

NORA. That's right. It wasn't easy to get away, you know. Ivar had just been born. But of course we had to go. Oh, that was a beautiful trip, and it saved Torvald's life. But it cost a frightful sum, Kristine.

MRS. LINDE. I can well imagine.

NORA. Four thousand, eight hundred crowns it cost. That's really a lot of money.

MRS. LINDE. But it's lucky you had it when you needed it.

NORA. Well, as it was, we got it from Papa.

MRS. LINDE. I see. It was just about the time your father died.

NORA. Yes, just about then. And, you know, I couldn't make that trip out to nurse him. I had to stay here, expecting Ivar any moment, and with my poor sick Torvald to care for. Dearest Papa, I never saw him again, Kristine. Oh, that was the worst time I've known in all my marriage.

MRS. LINDE. I know how you loved him. And then you went off to Italy?

NORA. Yes. We had the means now, and the doctors urged us. So we left a month after.

MRS. LINDE. And your husband came back completely cured?

NORA. Sound as a drum!

MRS. LINDE. But—the doctor?

NORA. Who?

MRS. LINDE. I thought the maid said he was a doctor, the man who came in with me.

NORA. Yes, that was Dr. Rank—but he's not making a sick call. He's our closest friend, and he stops by at least once a day. No, Torvald hasn't had a sick moment since, and the children are fit and strong, and I am, too. [*Jumping up and clapping her hands.*] Oh, dear God, Kristine, what a lovely thing to live and be happy! But how disgusting of me—I'm talking of nothing but my own affairs. [*Sits on a stool close by* KRISTINE, *arms resting across her knees.*] Oh, don't be angry with me! Tell me, is it really true that you weren't in love with your husband? Why did you marry him, then?

MRS. LINDE. My mother was still alive, but bedridden and helpless—and I had my two younger brothers to look after. In all conscience, I didn't think I could turn him down.

NORA. No, you were right there. But was he rich at the time?

MRS. LINDE. He was very well off, I'd say. But the business was shaky, Nora. When he died, it all fell apart, and nothing was left.

NORA. And then—?

MRS. LINDE. Yes, so I had to scrape up a living with a little shop and a little teaching and whatever else I could find. The last three years have been like one endless workday without a rest for me. Now it's over, Nora. My poor mother doesn't need me, for she's passed on. Nor the boys either; they're working now and can take care of themselves.

NORA. How free you must feel—

MRS. LINDE. No—only unspeakably empty. Nothing to live for now. [*Standing up anxiously.*] That's why I couldn't take it any longer out in that desolate hole. Maybe here it'll be easier to find something to do and keep my mind occupied. If I could only be lucky enough to get a steady job, some office work—

NORA. Oh, but Kristine, that's so dreadfully tiring, and you already look so tired. It would be much better for you if you could go off to a bathing resort.

MRS. LINDE [*going toward the window*]. I have no father to give me travel money, Nora.

NORA [*rising*]. Oh, don't be angry with me.

MRS. LINDE [*going to her*]. Nora dear, don't you be angry with me. The worst of my kind of situation is all the bitterness that's stored away. No one to work for, and yet you're always having to snap up your opportunities. You have to live; and so you grow selfish. When you told me the happy change in your lot, do you know I was delighted less for your sakes than for mine?

NORA. How so? Oh, I see. You think maybe Torvald could do something for you.

MRS. LINDE. Yes, that's what I thought.

NORA. And he will, Kristine! Just leave it to me; I'll bring it up so delicately—find something attractive to humor him with. Oh, I'm so eager to help you.

MRS. LINDE. How very kind of you, Nora, to be so concerned over me—doubly kind, considering you really know so little of life's burdens yourself.

NORA. I—? I know so little—?

MRS. LINDE [*smiling*]. Well, my heavens—a little needlework and such—Nora, you're just a child.

NORA [*tossing her head and pacing the floor*]. You don't have to act so superior.

MRS. LINDE. Oh?

NORA. You're just like the others. You all think I'm incapable of anything serious—

MRS. LINDE. Come now—

NORA. That I've never had to face the raw world.

MRS. LINDE. Nora dear, you've just been telling me all your troubles.

NORA. Hm! Trivia! [*Quietly.*] I haven't told you the big thing.

MRS. LINDE. Big thing? What do you mean?

NORA. You look down on me so, Kristine, but you shouldn't. You're proud that you worked so long and hard for your mother.

MRS. LINDE. I don't look down on a soul. But it *is* true: I'm proud—and happy, too—to think it was given to me to make my mother's last days almost free of care.

NORA. And you're also proud thinking of what you've done for your brothers.

MRS. LINDE. I feel I've a right to be.

NORA. I agree. But listen to this, Kristine—I've also got something to be proud and happy for.

MRS. LINDE. I don't doubt it. But whatever do you mean?

NORA. Not so loud. What if Torvald heard! He mustn't, not for anything in the world. Nobody must know, Kristine. No one but you.

MRS. LINDE. But what is it, then?

NORA. Come here. [*Drawing her down beside her on the sofa.*] It's true—I've also got something to be proud and happy for. I'm the one who saved Torvald's life.

MRS. LINDE. Saved—? Saved how?

NORA. I told you about the trip to Italy. Torvald never would have lived if he hadn't gone south—

MRS. LINDE. Of course; your father gave you the means—

NORA [*smiling*]. That's what Torvald and all the rest think, but—

MRS. LINDE. But—?

NORA. Papa didn't give us a pin. I was the one who raised the money.

MRS. LINDE. You? That whole amount?

NORA. Four thousand, eight hundred crowns. What do you say to that?

MRS. LINDE. But Nora, how was it possible? Did you win the lottery?

NORA [*disdainfully*]. The lottery? Pooh! No art to that.

MRS. LINDE. But where did you get it from then?

NORA [*humming, with a mysterious smile*]. Hmm, tra-la-la-la.

MRS. LINDE. Because you couldn't have borrowed it.

NORA. No? Why not?

MRS. LINDE. A wife can't borrow without her husband's consent.

NORA [*tossing her head*]. Oh, but a wife with a little business sense, a wife who knows how to manage—

MRS. LINDE. Nora, I simply don't understand—

NORA. You don't have to. Whoever said I *borrowed* the money? I could have gotten it other ways. [*Throwing herself back on the sofa.*] I could have gotten it from some admirer or other. After all, a girl with my ravishing appeal—

MRS. LINDE. You lunatic.

NORA. I'll bet you're eaten up with curiosity, Kristine.

MRS. LINDE. Now listen here, Nora—you haven't done something indiscreet?

NORA [*sitting up again*]. Is it indiscreet to save your husband's life?

MRS. LINDE. I think it's indiscreet that without his knowledge you—

NORA. But that's the point: he mustn't know! My Lord, can't you understand? He mustn't ever know the close call he had. It was to *me* the doctors came to say his life was in danger—that nothing could save him but a stay in the south. Didn't I try strategy then! I began talking about how lovely it would be for me to travel abroad like other young wives; I begged and I cried; I told him please to remember my condition, to be kind and indulge me; and then I dropped a hint that he could easily take out a loan. But at that, Kristine, he nearly exploded. He said I was frivolous, and it was his duty as man of the house not to indulge me in whims and fancies—as I think he called them. Aha, I thought, now you'll just have to be saved—and that's when I saw my chance.

MRS. LINDE. And your father never told Torvald the money wasn't from him?

NORA. No, never. Papa died right about then. I'd considered bringing him into my secret and begging him never to tell. But he was too sick at the time—and then, sadly, it didn't matter.

MRS. LINDE. And you've never confided in your husband since?

NORA. For heaven's sake, no! Are you serious? He's so strict on that subject. Besides—Torvald, with all his masculine pride—how painfully humiliating for him if he ever found out he was in debt to me. That would just ruin our relationship. Our beautiful, happy home would never be the same.

MRS. LINDE. Won't you ever tell him?

NORA [*thoughtfully, half smiling*]. Yes—maybe sometime, years from now, when I'm no longer so attractive. Don't laugh! I only mean when Torvald loves me less than now, when he stops enjoying my dancing and dressing up and reciting for him. Then it might be wise to have something in reserve—[*Breaking off.*] How ridiculous! That'll never happen— Well, Kristine, what do you think of my big secret? I'm capable of something too, hm? You can imagine, of course, how this thing hangs over me. It really hasn't been easy meeting the payments on time. In the business world there's what they call quarterly interest and what they call amortization, and these are always so terribly hard to manage. I've had to skimp a little here and there, wherever I could, you know. I could hardly spare anything from my house allowance, because Torvald has to live well. I couldn't let the children go poorly dressed; whatever I got for them, I felt I had to use up completely—the darlings!

MRS. LINDE. Poor Nora, so it had to come out of your own budget, then?

NORA. Yes, of course. But I was the one most responsible, too. Every time Torvald gave me money for new clothes and such, I never used more than half; always bought the simplest, cheapest outfits. It was a godsend that everything looks so well on me that Torvald never noticed. But it did weigh me down at times, Kristine. It *is* such a joy to wear fine things. You understand.

MRS. LINDE. Oh, of course.

NORA. And then I found other ways of making money. Last winter I was lucky enough to get a lot of copying to do. I locked myself in and sat writing every evening till late in the night. Ah, I was tired so often, dead tired. But still it was wonderful fun, sitting and working like that, earning money. It was almost like being a man.

MRS. LINDE. But how much have you paid off this way so far?

NORA. That's hard to say, exactly. These accounts, you know, aren't easy to figure. I only know that I've paid out all I could scrape together. Time and again I haven't known where to turn. [*Smiling.*] Then I'd sit here dreaming of a rich old gentleman who had fallen in love with me—

MRS. LINDE. What! Who is he?

NORA. Oh, really! And that he'd died, and when his will was opened, there in big letters it said, "All my fortune shall be paid over in cash, immediately, to that enchanting Mrs. Nora Helmer."

MRS. LINDE. But Nora dear—who *was* this gentleman?

NORA. Good grief, can't you understand? The old man never existed; that was only something I'd dream up time and again whenever I was at my wits' end for money. But it makes no difference now; the old fossil can go where he pleases for all I care; I don't need him or his will—because now I'm free. [*Jumping up.*] Oh, how lovely to think of that, Kristine! Carefree! To know you're carefree, utterly carefree; to be able to romp and play with the children, and to keep up a beautiful, charming home—everything just the way Torvald likes it! And think, spring is coming, with big blue skies. Maybe we can travel a little then. Maybe I'll see the ocean again. Oh yes, it *is* so marvelous to live and be happy!

[*The front doorbell rings.*]

MRS. LINDE [*rising*]. There's the bell. It's probably best that I go.

NORA. No, stay. No one's expected. It must be for Torvald.

MAID [*from the hall doorway*]. Excuse me, ma'am—there's a gentleman here to see Mr. Helmer, but I didn't know—since the doctor's with him—

NORA. Who is the gentleman?

KROGSTAD [*from the doorway*]. It's me, Mrs. Helmer.

[MRS. LINDE *starts and turns away toward the window.*]

NORA [*stepping toward him, tense, her voice a whisper*]. You? What is it? Why do you want to speak to my husband?

KROGSTAD. Bank business—after a fashion. I have a small job in the investment bank, and I hear now your husband is going to be our chief—

NORA. In other words, it's—

KROGSTAD. Just dry business, Mrs. Helmer. Nothing but that.

NORA. Yes, then please be good enough to step into the study. [*She nods indifferently as she sees him out by the hall door, then returns and begins stirring up the stove.*]

MRS. LINDE. Nora—who was that man?

NORA. That was a Mr. Krogstad—a lawyer.

MRS. LINDE. Then it really was him.

NORA. Do you know that person?

MRS. LINDE. I did once—many years ago. For a time he was a law clerk in our town.

NORA. Yes, he's been that.

MRS. LINDE. How he's changed.

NORA. I understand he had a very unhappy marriage.

MRS. LINDE. He's a widower now.

NORA. With a number of children. There now, it's burning. [*She closes the stove door and moves the rocker a bit to one side.*]

MRS. LINDE. They say he has a hand in all kinds of business.

NORA. Oh? That may be true; I wouldn't know. But let's not think about business. It's so dull.

[DR. RANK *enters from* HELMER'*s study.*]

RANK [*still in the doorway*]. No, no, really—I don't want to intrude, I'd just as soon talk a little while with your wife. [*Shuts the door, then notices* MRS. LINDE.] Oh, beg pardon. I'm intruding here too.

NORA. No, not at all. [*Introducing him.*] Dr. Rank, Mrs. Linde.

RANK. Well now, that's a name much heard in this house. I believe I passed the lady on the stairs as I came.

MRS. LINDE. Yes, I take the stairs very slowly. They're rather hard on me.

RANK. Uh-hm, some touch of internal weakness?

MRS. LINDE. More overexertion, I'd say.

RANK. Nothing else? Then you're probably here in town to rest up in a round of parties?

MRS. LINDE. I'm here to look for work.

RANK. Is that the best cure for overexertion?

MRS. LINDE. One has to live, Doctor.

RANK. Yes, there's a common prejudice to that effect.

NORA. Oh, come on, Dr. Rank—you really do want to live yourself.

RANK. Yes, I really do. Wretched as I am, I'll gladly prolong my torment indefinitely. All my patients feel like that. And it's quite the same, too, with the morally sick. Right at this moment there's one of those moral invalids in there with Helmer—

MRS. LINDE [*softly*]. Ah!

NORA. Who do you mean?

RANK. Oh, it's a lawyer, Krogstad, a type you wouldn't know. His character is rotten to the root—but even he began chattering all-importantly about how he had to *live.*

NORA. Oh? What did he want to talk to Torvald about?

RANK. I really don't know. I only heard something about the bank.

NORA. I didn't know that Krog—that this man Krogstad had anything to do with the bank.

RANK. Yes, he's gotten some kind of berth down there. [*To* MRS. LINDE.] I don't know if you also have, in your neck of the woods, a type of person who scuttles about breathlessly, sniffing out hints of moral corruption, and then maneuvers his victim into some sort of key position where he can keep an eye on him. It's the healthy these days that are out in the cold.

MRS. LINDE. All the same, it's the sick who most need to be taken in.

RANK [*with a shrug*]. Yes, there we have it. That's the concept that's turning society into a sanatorium.

[NORA, *lost in her thoughts, breaks out into quiet laughter and claps her hands.*]

RANK. Why do you laugh at that? Do you have any real idea of what society is?

NORA. What do I care about dreary old society? I was laughing at something quite different—something terribly funny. Tell me, Doctor—is everyone who works in the bank dependent now on Torvald?

RANK. Is that what you find so terribly funny?

NORA [*smiling and humming*]. Never mind, never mind! [*Pacing the floor.*] Yes, that's really immensely amusing: that we—that Torvald has so much power now over all those people. [*Taking the bag out of her pocket.*] Dr. Rank, a little macaroon on that?

RANK. See here, macaroons! I thought they were contraband here.

NORA. Yes, but these are some that Kristine gave me.

MRS. LINDE. What? I—?

NORA. Now, now, don't be afraid. You couldn't possibly know that Torvald had forbidden them. You see, he's worried they'll ruin my teeth. But hmp! Just this once! Isn't that so, Dr. Rank? Help yourself! [*Puts a macaroon in his mouth.*] And you too, Kristine. And I'll also have one, only a little one—or two, at the most. [*Walking about again.*] Now I'm really tremendously happy. Now there's just one last thing in the world that I have an enormous desire to do.

RANK. Well! And what's that?

NORA. It's something I have such a consuming desire to say so Torvald could hear.

RANK. And why can't you say it?

NORA. I don't dare. It's quite shocking.

MRS. LINDE. Shocking?

RANK. Well, then it isn't advisable. But in front of us you certainly can. What do you have such a desire to say so Torvald could hear?

NORA. I have such a huge desire to say—to hell and be damned!

RANK. Are you crazy?

MRS. LINDE. My goodness, Nora!

RANK. Go on, say it. Here he is.

NORA [*hiding the macaroon bag*]. Shh, shh, shh!

[HELMER *comes in from his study, hat in hand, overcoat over his arm.*]

NORA [*going toward him*]. Well, Torvald dear, are you through with him?

HELMER. Yes, he just left.

NORA. Let me introduce you—this is Kristine, who's arrived here in town.

HELMER. Kristine—? I'm sorry, but I don't know—

NORA. Mrs. Linde, Torvald dear. Mrs. Kristine Linde.

HELMER. Of course. A childhood friend of my wife's, no doubt?

MRS. LINDE. Yes, we knew each other in those days.

NORA. And just think, she made the long trip down here in order to talk with you.

HELMER. What's this?

MRS. LINDE. Well, not exactly—

NORA. You see, Kristine is remarkably clever in office work, and so she's terribly eager to come under a capable man's supervision and add more to what she already knows—

HELMER. Very wise, Mrs. Linde.

NORA. And then when she heard that you'd become a bank manager—the story was wired out to the papers—then she came in as fast as she could and—Really, Torvald, for my sake you can do a little something for Kristine, can't you?

HELMER. Yes, it's not at all impossible. Mrs. Linde, I suppose you're a widow?

MRS. LINDE. Yes.

HELMER. Any experience in office work?

MRS. LINDE. Yes, a good deal.

HELMER. Well, it's quite likely that I can make an opening for you—

NORA [*clapping her hands*]. You see, you see!

HELMER. You've come at a lucky moment, Mrs. Linde.

MRS. LINDE. Oh, how can I thank you?

HELMER. Not necessary. [*Putting his overcoat on.*] But today you'll have to excuse me—

RANK. Wait, I'll go with you. [*He fetches his coat from the hall and warms it at the stove.*]

NORA. Don't stay out long, dear.

HELMER. An hour; no more.

NORA. Are you going too, Kristine?

MRS. LINDE [*putting on her winter garments*]. Yes, I have to see about a room now.

HELMER. Then perhaps we can all walk together.

NORA [*helping her*]. What a shame we're so cramped here, but it's quite impossible for us to—

MRS. LINDE. Oh, don't even think of it! Good-bye, Nora dear, and thanks for everything.

NORA. Good-bye for now. Of course you'll be back this evening. And you too, Dr. Rank. What? If you're well enough? Oh, you've got to be! Wrap up tight now.

[*In a ripple of small talk the company moves out into the hall; children's voices are heard outside on the steps.*]

NORA. There they are! There they are! [*She runs to open the door. The children come in with their nurse,* ANNE-MARIE.] Come in, come in! [*Bends down and kisses them.*] Oh, you darlings—! Look at them, Kristine. Aren't they lovely!

RANK. No loitering in the draft here.

HELMER. Come, Mrs. Linde—this place is unbearable now for anyone but mothers.

[DR. RANK, HELMER, *and* MRS. LINDE *go down the stairs.* ANNE-MARIE *goes into the living room with the children.* NORA *follows, after closing the hall door.*]

NORA. How fresh and strong you look. Oh, such red cheeks you have! Like apples and roses. [*The children interrupt her throughout the following.*] And it was so much fun? That's wonderful. Really? You pulled both Emmy and Bob on the sled? Imagine, all together! Yes, you're a clever boy, Ivar. Oh, let me hold her a bit, Anne-Marie. My sweet little doll baby! [*Takes the smallest from the nurse and dances with her.*] Yes, yes, Mama will dance with Bob as well. What? Did you throw snowballs? Oh, if I'd only been there! No, don't bother, Anne-Marie—I'll undress them myself. Oh yes, let me. It's such fun. Go in and rest; you look half frozen. There's hot coffee waiting for you on the stove. [*The nurse goes into the room to the left.* NORA *takes the children's winter things off, throwing them about, while the children talk to her all at once.*] Is that so? A big dog chased you? But it didn't bite? No, dogs never bite little, lovely doll babies. Don't peek in the packages, Ivar! What is it? Yes, wouldn't you like to know. No, no, it's an ugly something. Well? Shall we play? What shall we play? Hide-and-seek? Yes, let's play hide-and-seek. Bob must hide first. I must? Yes, let me hide first. [*Laughing and shouting, she and the children play in and out of the living room and the adjoining room to the right. At last* NORA *hides under the table. The children come storming in, search, but cannot find her, then hear her muffled laughter, dash over to the table, lift the cloth up and find her. Wild shouting. She creeps forward as if to scare them. More shouts. Meanwhile, a knock at the hall door; no one has noticed it. Now the door half opens, and* KROGSTAD *appears. He waits a moment; the game goes on.*]

KROGSTAD. Beg pardon. Mrs. Helmer—

NORA [*with a strangled cry, turning and scrambling to her knees*]. Oh! What do you want?

KROGSTAD. Excuse me. The outer door was ajar; it must be someone forgot to shut it—

NORA [*rising*]. My husband isn't home, Mr. Krogstad.

KROGSTAD. I know that.

NORA. Yes—then what do you want here?

KROGSTAD. A word with you.

NORA. With—? [*To the children, quietly.*] Go in to Anne-Marie. What? No, the strange man won't hurt Mama. When he's gone, we'll play some more. [*She leads the children into the room to the left and shuts the door after them. Then, tense and nervous:*] You want to speak to me?

KROGSTAD. Yes, I want to.

NORA. Today? But it's not yet the first of the month—

KROGSTAD. No, it's Christmas Eve. It's going to be up to you how merry a Christmas you have.

NORA. What is it you want? Today I absolutely can't—

KROGSTAD. We won't talk about that till later. This is something else. You do have a moment to spare, I suppose?

NORA. Oh yes, of course—I do, except—

KROGSTAD. Good. I was sitting over at Olsen's Restaurant when I saw your husband go down the street—

NORA. Yes?

KROGSTAD. With a lady.

NORA. Yes. So?

KROGSTAD. If you'll pardon my asking: wasn't that lady a Mrs. Linde?

NORA. Yes.

KROGSTAD. Just now come into town?

NORA. Yes, today.

KROGSTAD. She's a good friend of yours?

NORA. Yes, she is. But I don't see—

KROGSTAD. I also knew her once.

NORA. I'm aware of that.

KROGSTAD. Oh? You know all about it. I thought so. Well, then let me ask you short and sweet: is Mrs. Linde getting a job in the bank?

NORA. What makes you think you can cross-examine me, Mr. Krogstad—you, one of my husband's employees? But since you ask, you might as well know—yes, Mrs. Linde's going to be taken on at the bank. And I'm the one who spoke for her, Mr. Krogstad. Now you know.

KROGSTAD. So I guessed right.

NORA [*pacing up and down*]. Oh, one does have a tiny bit of influence, I should hope. Just because I am a woman, don't think it means that—When one has a subordinate position, Mr. Krogstad, one really ought to be careful about pushing somebody who—hm—

KROGSTAD. Who has influence?

NORA. That's right.

KROGSTAD [*in a different tone*]. Mrs. Helmer, would you be good enough to use your influence on my behalf?

NORA. What? What do you mean?

KROGSTAD. Would you please make sure that I keep my subordinate position in the bank?

NORA. What does that mean? Who's thinking of taking away your position?

KROGSTAD. Oh, don't play the innocent with me. I'm quite aware that your friend would hardly relish the chance of running into me again; and I'm also aware now whom I can thank for being turned out.

NORA. But I promise you—

KROGSTAD. Yes, yes, yes, to the point: there's still time, and I'm advising you to use your influence to prevent it.

NORA. But Mr. Krogstad, I have absolutely no influence.

KROGSTAD. You haven't? I thought you were just saying—

NORA. You shouldn't take me so literally. I! How can you believe that I have any such influence over my husband?

KROGSTAD. Oh, I've known your husband from our student days. I don't think the great bank manager's more steadfast than any other married man.

NORA. You speak insolently about my husband, and I'll show you the door.

KROGSTAD. The lady has spirit.

NORA. I'm not afraid of you any longer. After New Year's, I'll soon be done with the whole business.

KROGSTAD [*restraining himself*]. Now listen to me, Mrs. Helmer. If necessary, I'll fight for my little job in the bank as if it were life itself.

NORA. Yes, so it seems.

KROGSTAD. It's not just a matter of income; that's the least of it. It's something else— All right, out with it! Look, this is the thing. You know, just like all the others, of course, that once, a good many years ago, I did something rather rash.

NORA. I've heard rumors to that effect.

KROGSTAD. The case never got into court; but all the same, every door was closed in my face from then on. So I took up those various activities you know about. I had to grab hold somewhere; and I dare say I haven't been among the worst. But now I want to drop all that. My boys are growing up. For their sakes, I'll have to win back as much respect as possible here in town. That job in the bank was like the first rung in my ladder. And now your husband wants to kick me right back down in the mud again.

NORA. But for heaven's sake, Mr. Krogstad, it's simply not in my power to help you.

KROGSTAD. That's because you haven't the will to—but I have the means to make you.

NORA. You certainly won't tell my husband that I owe you money?

KROGSTAD. Hm—what if I told him that?

NORA. That would be shameful of you. [*Nearly in tears.*] This secret—my joy and my pride—that he should learn it in such a crude and disgusting way—learn it from you. You'd expose me to the most horrible unpleasantness—

KROGSTAD. Only unpleasantness?

NORA [*vehemently*]. But go on and try. It'll turn out the worse for you, because then my husband will really see what a crook you are, and then you'll *never* be able to hold your job.

KROGSTAD. I asked if it was just domestic unpleasantness you were afraid of?

NORA. If my husband finds out, then of course he'll pay what I owe at once, and then we'd be through with you for good.

KROGSTAD [*a step closer*]. Listen, Mrs. Helmer—you've either got a very bad memory, or else no head at all for business. I'd better put you a little more in touch with the facts.

NORA. What do you mean?

KROGSTAD. When your husband was sick, you came to me for a loan of four thousand, eight hundred crowns.

NORA. Where else could I go?

KROGSTAD. I promised to get you that sum—

NORA. And you got it.

KROGSTAD. I promised to get you that sum, on certain conditions. You were so involved in your husband's illness, and so eager to finance your trip, that I guess you didn't think out all the details. It might just be a good idea to remind you. I promised you the money on the strength of a note I drew up.

NORA. Yes, and that I signed.

KROGSTAD. Right. But at the bottom I added some lines for your father to guarantee the loan. He was supposed to sign down there.

NORA. Supposed to? He did sign.

KROGSTAD. I left the date blank. In other words, your father would have dated his signature himself. Do you remember that?

NORA. Yes, I think—

KROGSTAD. Then I gave you the note for you to mail to your father. Isn't that so?

NORA. Yes.

KROGSTAD. And naturally you sent it at once—because only some five, six days later you brought me the note, properly signed. And with that, the money was yours.

NORA. Well, then; I've made my payments regularly, haven't I?

KROGSTAD. More or less. But—getting back to the point—those were hard times for you then, Mrs. Helmer.

NORA. Yes, they were.

KROGSTAD. Your father was very ill, I believe.

NORA. He was near the end.

KROGSTAD. He died soon after?

NORA. Yes.

KROGSTAD. Tell me, Mrs. Helmer, do you happen to recall the date of your father's death? The day of the month, I mean.

NORA. Papa died the twenty-ninth of September.

KROGSTAD. That's quite correct; I've already looked into that. And now we come to a curious thing—[*Taking out a paper.*] which I simply cannot comprehend.

NORA. Curious thing? I don't know—

KROGSTAD. This is the curious thing; that your father co-signed the note for your loan three days after his death.

NORA. How—? I don't understand.

KROGSTAD. Your father died the twenty-ninth of September. But look. Here your father dated his signature October second. Isn't that curious, Mrs. Helmer? [NORA *is silent.*] Can you explain it to me? [NORA *remains silent.*] It's also remarkable that the words "October second" and the year aren't written in your father's hand, but rather in one that I think I know. Well, it's easy to understand. Your father forgot perhaps to date his signature, and then someone or other added it, a bit sloppily, before anyone knew of his death. There's nothing wrong in that. It all comes down to the signature. And there's no question about *that,* Mrs. Helmer. It really *was* your father who signed his own name here, wasn't it?

NORA [*after a short silence, throwing her head back and looking squarely at him*]. No, it wasn't. *I* signed Papa's name.

KROGSTAD. Wait, now—are you fully aware that this is a dangerous confession?

NORA. Why? You'll soon get your money.

KROGSTAD. Let me ask you a question—why didn't you send the paper to your father?

NORA. That was impossible. Papa was so sick. If I'd asked him for his signature, I also would have had to tell him what the money was for. But I couldn't tell him, sick as he was, that my husband's life was in danger. That was just impossible.

KROGSTAD. Then it would have been better if you'd given up the trip abroad.

NORA. I couldn't possibly. The trip was to save my husband's life. I couldn't give that up.

KROGSTAD. But didn't you ever consider that this was a fraud against me?

NORA. I couldn't let myself be bothered by that. You weren't any concern of mine. I couldn't stand you, with all those cold complications you made, even though you knew how badly off my husband was.

KROGSTAD. Mrs. Helmer, obviously you haven't the vaguest idea of what you've involved yourself in. But I can tell you this: it was nothing more and nothing worse that I once did—and it wrecked my whole reputation.

NORA. You? Do you expect me to believe that you ever acted bravely to save your wife's life?

KROGSTAD. Laws don't inquire into motives.

NORA. Then they must be very poor laws.

KROGSTAD. Poor or not—if I introduce this paper in court, you'll be judged according to law.

NORA. This I refuse to believe. A daughter hasn't a right to protect her dying father from anxiety and care? A wife hasn't a right to save her husband's life? I don't know much about laws, but I'm sure that somewhere in the books these things are allowed. And you don't know anything about it—you who practice the law? You must be an awful lawyer, Mr. Krogstad.

KROGSTAD. Could be. But business—the kind of business we two are mixed up in—don't you think I know about that? All right. Do what you want now. But I'm telling you *this:* if I get shoved down a second time, you're going to keep me company. [*He bows and goes out through the hall.*]

NORA [*pensive for a moment, then tossing her head*]. Oh, really! Trying to frighten me! I'm not so silly as all that. [*Begins gathering up the children's clothes, but soon stops.*] But—? No, but that's impossible! I did it out of love.

THE CHILDREN [*in the doorway, left*]. Mama, that strange man's gone out the door.

NORA. Yes, yes, I know it. But don't tell anyone about the strange man. Do you hear? Not even Papa!

THE CHILDREN. No, Mama. But now will you play again?

NORA. No, not now.

THE CHILDREN. Oh, but Mama, you promised.

NORA. Yes, but I can't now. Go inside; I have too much to do. Go in, go in, my sweet darlings. [*She herds them gently back in the room and shuts the door after them. Settling on the sofa, she takes up a piece of embroidery and makes some stitches, but soon stops abruptly.*] No! [*Throws the work aside, rises, goes to the hall door and calls out.*] Helene! Let me have the tree in here. [*Goes to the table, left, opens the table drawer, and stops again.*] No, but that's utterly impossible!

MAID [*with the Christmas tree*]. Where should I put it, ma'am?

NORA. There. The middle of the floor.

MAID. Should I bring anything else?

NORA. No, thanks. I have what I need.

[*The* MAID, *who has set the tree down, goes out.*]

NORA [*absorbed in trimming the tree*]. Candles here—and flowers here. That terrible creature! Talk, talk, talk! There's nothing to it at all. The tree's going to be lovely. I'll do anything to please you, Torvald. I'll sing for you, dance for you—

[HELMER *comes in from the hall, with a sheaf of papers under his arm.*]

NORA. Oh! You're back so soon?

HELMER. Yes. Has anyone been here?
NORA. Here? No.
HELMER. That's odd. I saw Krogstad leaving the front door.
NORA. So? Oh yes, that's true. Krogstad was here a moment.
HELMER. Nora, I can see by your face that he's been here, begging you to put in a good word for him.
NORA. Yes.
HELMER. And it was supposed to seem like your own idea? You were to hide it from me that he'd been here. He asked you that, too, didn't he?
NORA. Yes, Torvald, but—
HELMER. Nora, Nora, and you could fall for that? Talk with that sort of person and promise him anything? And then in the bargain, tell me an untruth.
NORA. An untruth—?
HELMER. Didn't you say that no one had been here? [*Wagging his finger.*] My little songbird must never do that again. A songbird needs a clean beak to warble with. No false notes. [*Putting his arm about her waist.*] That's the way it should be, isn't it? Yes, I'm sure of it. [*Releasing her.*] And so, enough of that. [*Sitting by the stove.*] Ah, how snug and cozy it is here. [*Leafing among his papers.*]
NORA [*busy with the tree, after a short pause*]. Torvald!
HELMER. Yes.
NORA. I'm so much looking forward to the Stenborgs' costume party, day after tomorrow.
HELMER. And I can't wait to see what you'll surprise me with.
NORA. Oh, that stupid business!
HELMER. What?
NORA. I can't find anything that's right. Everything seems so ridiculous, so inane.
HELMER. So my little Nora's come to *that* recognition?
NORA [*going behind his chair, her arms resting on its back*]. Are you very busy, Torvald?
HELMER. Oh—
NORA. What papers are those?
HELMER. Bank matters.
NORA. Already?
HELMER. I've gotten full authority from the retiring management to make all necessary changes in personnel and procedure. I'll need Christmas week for that. I want to have everything in order by New Year's.
NORA. So that was the reason this poor Krogstad—
HELMER. Hm.
NORA [*still leaning on the chair and slowly stroking the nape of his neck*]. If you weren't so very busy, I would have asked you an enormous favor, Torvald.
HELMER. Let's hear. What is it?
NORA. You know, there isn't anyone who has your good taste—and I want so much to look well at the costume party. Torvald, couldn't you take over and decide what I should be and plan my costume?
HELMER. Ah, is my stubborn little creature calling for a lifeguard?
NORA. Yes, Torvald, I can't get anywhere without your help.

HELMER. All right—I'll think it over. We'll hit on something.

NORA. Oh, how sweet of you. [*Goes to the tree again. Pause.*] Aren't the red flowers pretty—? But tell me, was it really such a crime that this Krogstad committed?

HELMER. Forgery. Do you have any idea what that means?

NORA. Couldn't he have done it out of need?

HELMER. Yes, or thoughtlessness, like so many others. I'm not so heartless that I'd condemn a man categorically for just one mistake.

NORA. No, of course not, Torvald!

HELMER. Plenty of men have redeemed themselves by openly confessing their crimes and taking their punishment.

NORA. Punishment—?

HELMER. But now Krogstad didn't go that way. He got himself out by sharp practices, and that's the real cause of his moral breakdown.

NORA. Do you really think that would—?

HELMER. Just imagine how a man with that sort of guilt in him has to lie and cheat and deceive on all sides, has to wear a mask even with the nearest and dearest he has, even with his own wife and children. And with the children, Nora—that's where it's most horrible.

NORA. Why?

HELMER. Because that kind of atmosphere of lies infects the whole life of a home. Every breath the children take in is filled with the germs of something degenerate.

NORA [*coming closer behind him*]. Are you sure of that?

HELMER. Oh, I've seen it often enough as a lawyer. Almost everyone who goes bad early in life has a mother who's a chronic liar.

NORA. Why just—the mother?

HELMER. It's usually the mother's influence that's dominant, but the father's works in the same way, of course. Every lawyer is quite familiar with it. And still this Krogstad's been going home year in, year out, poisoning his own children with lies and pretense; that's why I call him morally lost. [*Reaching his hands out toward her.*] So my sweet little Nora must promise me never to plead his cause. Your hand on it. Come, come, what's this? Give me your hand. There, now. All settled. I can tell you it'd be impossible for me to work alongside of him. I literally feel physically revolted when I'm anywhere near such a person.

NORA [*withdraws her hand and goes to the other side of the Christmas tree*]. How hot it is here! And I've got so much to do.

HELMER [*getting up and gathering his papers*]. Yes, and I have to think about getting some of these read through before dinner. I'll think about your costume, too. And something to hang on the tree in gilt paper, I may even see about that. [*Putting his hand on her head.*] Oh you, my darling little songbird. [*He goes into his study and closes the door after him.*]

NORA [*softly, after a silence*]. Oh, really! it isn't so. It's impossible. It must be impossible.

ANNE-MARIE [*in the doorway, left*]. The children are begging so hard to come in to Mama.

NORA. No, no, no, don't let them in to me! You stay with them, Anne-Marie.

ANNE-MARIE. Of course, ma'am. [*Closes the door.*]

NORA [*pale with terror*]. Hurt my children—! Poison my home? [*A moment's pause; then she tosses her head.*] That's not true. Never. Never in all the world.

ACT TWO

Same room. Beside the piano the Christmas tree now stands stripped of ornament, burned-down candle stubs on its ragged branches. NORA'S *street clothes lie on the sofa.* NORA, *alone in the room, moves restlessly about; at last she stops at the sofa and picks up her coat.*

NORA [*dropping the coat again*]. Someone's coming! [*Goes toward the door, listens.*] No—there's no one. Of course—nobody's coming today, Christmas Day—or tomorrow, either. But maybe—[*Opens the door and looks out.*] No, nothing in the mailbox. Quite empty. [*Coming forward.*] What nonsense! He won't do anything serious. Nothing terrible could happen. It's impossible. Why, I have three small children.

[ANNE-MARIE, *with a large carton, comes in from the room to the left.*]

ANNE-MARIE. Well, at last I found the box with the masquerade clothes.

NORA. Thanks. Put it on the table.

ANNE-MARIE [*does so*]. But they're all pretty much of a mess.

NORA. Ahh! I'd love to rip them in a million pieces!

ANNE-MARIE. Oh, mercy, they can be fixed right up. Just a little patience.

NORA. Yes, I'll go get Mrs. Linde to help me.

ANNE-MARIE. Out again now? In this nasty weather? Miss Nora will catch cold—get sick.

NORA. Oh, worse things could happen— How are the children?

ANNE-MARIE. The poor mites are playing with their Christmas presents, but—

NORA. Do they ask for me much?

ANNE-MARIE. They're so used to having Mama around, you know.

NORA. Yes, but Anne-Marie, I *can't* be together with them as much as I was.

ANNE-MARIE. Well, small children get used to anything.

NORA. You think so? Do you think they'd forget their mother if she was gone for good?

ANNE-MARIE. Oh, mercy—gone for good!

NORA. Wait, tell me, Anne-Marie—I've wondered so often—how could you ever have the heart to give your child over to strangers?

ANNE-MARIE. But I had to, you know, to become little Nora's nurse.

NORA. Yes, but how could you *do* it?

ANNE-MARIE. When I could get such a good place? A girl who's poor and who's gotten in trouble is glad enough for that. Because that slippery fish, he didn't do a thing for me, you know.

NORA. But your daughter's surely forgotten you.

ANNE-MARIE. Oh, she certainly has not. She's written to me, both when she was confirmed and when she was married.

NORA [*clasping her about the neck*]. You old Anne-Marie, you were a good mother for me when I was little.

ANNE-MARIE. Poor little Nora, with no other mother but me.

NORA. And if the babies didn't have one, then I know that you'd— What silly talk! [*Opening the carton.*] Go in to them. Now I'll have to— Tomorrow you can see how lovely I'll look.

ANNE-MARIE. Oh, there won't be anyone at the party as lovely as Miss Nora. [*She goes off into the room, left.*]

NORA [*begins unpacking the box, but soon throws it aside*]. Oh, if I dared to go out. If only nobody would come. If only nothing would happen here while I'm out. What craziness—nobody's coming. Just don't think. This muff—needs a brushing. Beautiful gloves, beautiful gloves. Let it go. Let it go! One, two, three, four, five, six— [*With a cry.*] Oh, there they are! [*Poises to move toward the door, but remains irresolutely standing.* MRS. LINDE *enters from the hall, where she has removed her street clothes.*]

NORA. Oh, it's you, Kristine. There's no one else out there? How good that you've come.

MRS. LINDE. I hear you were up asking for me.

NORA. Yes, I just stopped by. There's something you really can help me with. Let's get settled on the sofa. Look, there's going to be a costume party tomorrow evening at the Stenborgs' right above us, and now Torvald wants me to go as a Neapolitan peasant girl and dance the tarantella[2] that I learned in Capri.

MRS. LINDE. Really, are you giving a whole performance?

NORA. Torvald says yes, I should. See, here's the dress. Torvald had it made for me down there; but now it's all so tattered that I just don't know—

MRS. LINDE. Oh, we'll fix that up in no time. It's nothing more than the trimmings—they're a bit loose here and there. Needle and thread? Good, now we have what we need.

NORA. Oh, how sweet of you!

MRS. LINDE [*sewing*]. So you'll be in disguise tomorrow, Nora. You know what? I'll stop by then for a moment and have a look at you all dressed up. But listen, I've absolutely forgotten to thank you for that pleasant evening yesterday.

NORA [*getting up and walking about*]. I don't think it was as pleasant as usual yesterday. You should have come to town a bit sooner, Kristine—Yes, Torvald really knows how to give a home elegance and charm.

MRS. LINDE. And you do, too, if you ask me. You're not your father's daughter for nothing. But tell me, is Dr. Rank always so down in the mouth as yesterday?

NORA. No, that was quite an exception. But he goes around critically ill all the time—tuberculosis of the spine, poor man. You know, his father was a disgusting thing who kept mistresses and so on—and that's why the son's been sickly from birth.

MRS. LINDE [*lets her sewing fall to her lap*]. But my dearest Nora, how do you know about such things?

NORA [*walking more jauntily*]. Hmp! When you've had three children, then

[2] A rapid, whirling southern Italian dance. Its name comes from the fact that it is popularly supposed to represent the death throes of someone bitten by a tarantula.

you've had a few visits from—from women who know something of medicine, and they tell you this and that.

MRS. LINDE [*resumes sewing; a short pause*]. Does Dr. Rank come here every day?

NORA. Every blessed day. He's Torvald's best friend from childhood, and *my* good friend, too. Dr. Rank almost belongs to this house.

MRS. LINDE. But tell me—is he quite sincere? I mean, doesn't he rather enjoy flattering people?

NORA. Just the opposite. Why do you think that?

MRS. LINDE. When you introduced us yesterday, he was proclaiming that he'd often heard my name in this house; but later I noticed that your husband hadn't the slightest idea who I really was. So how could Dr. Rank—?

NORA. But it's all true, Kristine. You see, Torvald loves me beyond words, and, as he puts it, he'd like to keep me all to himself. For a long time he'd almost be jealous if I even mentioned any of my old friends back home. So of course I dropped that. But with Dr. Rank I talk a lot about such things, because he likes hearing about them.

MRS. LINDE. Now listen, Nora; in many ways you're still like a child. I'm a good deal older than you, with a little more experience. I'll tell you something: you ought to put an end to all this with Dr. Rank.

NORA. What should I put an end to?

MRS. LINDE. Both parts of it, I think. Yesterday you said something about a rich admirer who'd provide you with money—

NORA. Yes, one who doesn't exist—worse luck. So?

MRS. LINDE. Is Dr. Rank well off?

NORA. Yes, he is.

MRS. LINDE. With no dependents?

NORA. No, no one. But—

MRS. LINDE. And he's over here every day?

NORA. Yes, I told you that.

MRS. LINDE. How can a man of such refinement be so grasping?

NORA. I don't follow you at all.

MRS. LINDE. Now don't try to hide it, Nora. You think I can't guess who loaned you the forty-eight hundred crowns?

NORA. Are you out of your mind? How could you think such a thing! A friend of ours, who comes here every single day. What an intolerable situation that would have been!

MRS. LINDE. Then it really wasn't him.

NORA. No, absolutely not. It never even crossed my mind for a moment— And he had nothing to lend in those days; his inheritance came later.

MRS. LINDE. Well, I think that was a stroke of luck for you, Nora dear.

NORA. No, it never would have occurred to me to ask Dr. Rank— Still, I'm quite sure that if I had asked him—

MRS. LINDE. Which you won't, of course.

NORA. No, of course not. I can't see that I'd ever need to. But I'm quite positive that if I talked to Dr. Rank—

MRS. LINDE. Behind your husband's back?

NORA. I've got to clear up this other thing; *that's* also behind his back. I've *got* to clear it all up.

MRS. LINDE. Yes, I was saying that yesterday, but—

NORA [*pacing up and down*]. A man handles these problems so much better than a woman—

MRS. LINDE. One's husband does, yes.

NORA. Nonsense. [*Stopping.*] When you pay everything you owe, then you get your note back, right?

MRS. LINDE. Yes, naturally.

NORA. And can rip it into a million pieces and burn it up—that filthy scrap of paper!

MRS. LINDE [*looking hard at her, laying her sewing aside, and rising slowly*]. Nora, you're hiding something from me.

NORA. You can see it in my face?

MRS. LINDE. Something's happened to you since yesterday morning. Nora, what is it?

NORA [*hurrying toward her*]. Kristine! [*Listening.*] Shh! Torvald's home. Look, go in with the children a while. Torvald can't bear all this snipping and stitching. Let Anne-Marie help you.

MRS. LINDE [*gathering up some of the things*]. All right, but I'm not leaving here until we've talked this out. [*She disappears into the room, left, as* TORVALD *enters from the hall.*]

NORA. Oh, how I've been waiting for you, Torvald dear.

HELMER. Was that the dressmaker?

NORA. No, that was Kristine. She's helping me fix up my costume. You know, it's going to be quite attractive.

HELMER. Yes, wasn't that a bright idea I had?

NORA. Brilliant! But then wasn't I good as well to give in to you?

HELMER. Good—because you give in to your husband's judgment? All right, you little goose, I know you didn't mean it like that. But I won't disturb you. You'll want to have a fitting, I suppose.

NORA. And you'll be working?

HELMER. Yes. [*Indicating a bundle of papers.*] See. I've been down to the bank. [*Starts toward his study.*]

NORA. Torvald.

HELMER [*stops*]. Yes.

NORA. If your little squirrel begged you, with all her heart and soul, for something—?

HELMER. What's that?

NORA. Then would you do it?

HELMER. First, naturally, I'd have to know what it was.

NORA. Your squirrel would scamper about and do tricks, if you'd only be sweet and give in.

HELMER. Out with it.

NORA. Your lark would be singing high and low in every room—

HELMER. Come on, she does that anyway.

NORA. I'd be a wood nymph and dance for you in the moonlight.

HELMER. Nora—don't tell me it's that same business from this morning?

NORA [*coming closer*]. Yes, Torvald, I beg you, please!

HELMER. And you actually have the nerve to drag that up again?

NORA. Yes, yes, you've got to give in to me; you *have* to let Krogstad keep his job in the bank.

HELMER. My dear Nora, I've slated his job for Mrs. Linde.

NORA. That's awfully kind of you. But you could just fire another clerk instead of Krogstad.

HELMER. This is the most incredible stubbornness! Because you go and give an impulsive promise to speak up for him, I'm expected to—

NORA. That's not the reason, Torvald. It's for your own sake. That man does writing for the worst papers; you said it yourself. He could do you any amount of harm. I'm scared to death of him—

HELMER. Ah, I understand. It's the old memories haunting you.

NORA. What do you mean by that?

HELMER. Of course, you're thinking about your father.

NORA. Yes, all right. Just remember how those nasty gossips wrote in the papers about Papa and slandered him so cruelly. I think they'd have had him dismissed if the department hadn't sent you up to investigate, and if you hadn't been so kind and open-minded toward him.

HELMER. My dear Nora, there's a notable difference between your father and me. Your father's official career was hardly above reproach. But mine is; and I hope it'll stay that way as long as I hold my position.

NORA. Oh, who can ever tell what vicious minds can invent? We could be so snug and happy now in our quiet, carefree home—you and I and the children, Torvald! That's why I'm pleading with you so—

HELMER. And just by pleading for him you make it impossible for me to keep him on. It's already known at the bank that I'm firing Krogstad. What if it's rumored around now that the new bank manager was vetoed by his wife—

NORA. Yes, what then—?

HELMER. Oh yes—as long as our little bundle of stubbornness gets her way—! I should go and make myself ridiculous in front of the whole office—give people the idea I can be swayed by all kinds of outside pressure. Oh, you can bet I'd feel the effects of that soon enough! Besides—there's something that rules Krogstad right out at the bank as long as I'm the manager.

NORA. What's that?

HELMER. His moral failings I could maybe overlook if I had to—

NORA. Yes, Torvald, why not?

HELMER. And I hear he's quite efficient on the job. But he was a crony of mine back in my teens—one of those rash friendships that crop up again and again to embarrass you later in life. Well, I might as well say it straight out: we're on a first-name basis. And that tactless fool makes no effort at all to hide it in front of others. Quite the contrary—he thinks that entitles him to take a familiar air around me, and so every other second he comes booming out with his "Yes, Torvald!" and "Sure thing, Torvald!" I tell you, it's been excruciating for me. He's out to make my place in the bank unbearable.

NORA. Torvald, you can't be serious about all this.

HELMER. Oh no? Why not?

NORA. Because these are such petty considerations.

HELMER. What are you saying? Petty? You think I'm petty!

NORA. No, just the opposite, Torvald dear. That's exactly why—

HELMER. Never mind. You call my motives petty; then I might as well be just that. Petty! All right! We'll put a stop to this for good. [*Goes to the hall door and calls.*] Helene!

NORA. What do you want?

HELMER [*searching among his papers*]. A decision. [*The* MAID *comes in.*] Look here; take this letter; go out with it at once. Get hold of a messenger and have him deliver it. Quick now. It's already addressed. Wait, here's some money.

MAID. Yes, sir. [*She leaves with the letter.*]

HELMER [*straightening his papers*]. There, now, little Miss Willful.

NORA [*breathlessly*]. Torvald, what was that letter?

HELMER. Krogstad's notice.

NORA. Call it back, Torvald! There's still time. Oh, Torvald, call it back! Do it for my sake—for your sake, for the children's sake! Do you hear, Torvald; do it? You don't know how this can harm us.

HELMER. Too late.

NORA. Yes, too late.

HELMER. Nora dear, I can forgive you this panic, even though basically you're insulting me. Yes, you are! Or isn't it an insult to think that *I* should be afraid of a courtroom hack's revenge? But I forgive you anyway, because this shows so beautifully how much you love me. [*Takes her in his arms.*] This is the way it should be, my darling Nora. Whatever comes, you'll see: when it really counts, I have strength and courage enough as a man to take on the whole weight myself.

NORA [*terrified*]. What do you mean by that?

HELMER. The whole weight, I said.

NORA [*resolutely*]. No, never in all the world.

HELMER. Good. So we'll share it, Nora, as man and wife. That's as it should be. [*Fondling her.*] Are you happy now? There, there, there—not these frightened dove's eyes. It's nothing at all but empty fantasies— Now you should run through your tarantella and practice your tambourine. I'll go to the inner office and shut both doors, so I won't hear a thing; you can make all the noise you like. [*Turning in the doorway.*] And when Rank comes, just tell him where he can find me. [*He nods to her and goes with his papers into the study, closing the door.*]

NORA [*standing as though rooted, dazed with fright, in a whisper*]. He really could do it. He will do it. He'll do it in spite of everything. No, not that, never, never! Anything but that! Escape! A way out— [*The doorbell rings.*] Dr. Rank! Anything but that! *Anything,* whatever it is! [*Her hands pass over her face, smoothing it; she pulls herself together, goes over and opens the hall door.* DR. RANK *stands outside, hanging his fur coat up. During the following scene, it begins getting dark.*]

NORA. Hello, Dr. Rank. I recognized your ring. But you mustn't go in to Torvald yet; I believe he's working.

RANK. And you?

NORA. For you, I always have an hour to spare—you know that. [*He has entered, and she shuts the door after him.*]

RANK. Many thanks. I'll make use of these hours while I can.

NORA. What do you mean by that? While you can?

RANK. Does that disturb you?

NORA. Well, it's such an odd phrase. Is anything going to happen?

RANK. What's going to happen is what I've been expecting so long—but I honestly didn't think it would come so soon.

NORA [*gripping his arm*]. What is it you've found out? Dr. Rank, you have to tell me!

RANK [*sitting by the stove*]. It's all over with me. There's nothing to be done about it.

NORA [*breathing easier*]. Is it you—then—?

RANK. Who else? There's no point in lying to one's self. I'm the most miserable of all my patients, Mrs. Helmer. These past few days I've been auditing my internal accounts. Bankrupt! Within a month I'll probably be laid out and rotting in the churchyard.

NORA. Oh, what a horrible thing to say.

RANK. The thing itself is horrible. But the worst of it is all the other horror before it's over. There's only one final examination left; when I'm finished with that, I'll know about when my disintegration will begin. There's something I want to say. Helmer with his sensitivity has such a sharp distaste for anything ugly. I don't want him near my sickroom.

NORA. Oh, but Dr. Rank—

RANK. I won't have him in there. Under no condition. I'll lock my door to him—As soon as I'm completely sure of the worst, I'll send you my calling card marked with a black cross, and you'll know then the wreck has started to come apart.

NORA. No, today you're completely unreasonable. And I wanted you so much to be in a really good humor.

RANK. With death up my sleeve? And then to suffer this way for somebody else's sins. Is there any justice in that? And in every single family, in some way or another, this inevitable retribution of nature goes on—

NORA [*her hands pressed over her ears*]. Oh, stuff! Cheer up! Please—be gay!

RANK. Yes, I'd just as soon laugh at it all. My poor, innocent spine, serving time for my father's gay army days.

NORA [*by the table, left*]. He was so infatuated with asparagus tips and *pâté de foie gras,* wasn't that it?

RANK. Yes—and with truffles.

NORA. Truffles, yes. And then with oysters, I suppose?

RANK. Yes, tons of oysters, naturally.

NORA. And then the port and champagne to go with it. It's so sad that all these delectable things have to strike at our bones.

RANK. Especially when they strike at the unhappy bones that never shared in the fun.

NORA. Ah, that's the saddest of all.

RANK [*looks searchingly at her*]. Hm.

NORA [*after a moment*]. Why did you smile?

RANK. No, it was you who laughed.

NORA. No, it was you who smiled, Dr. Rank!

RANK [*getting up*]. You're even a bigger tease than I'd thought.

NORA. I'm full of wild ideas today.

RANK. That's obvious.

NORA [*putting both hands on his shoulders*]. Dear, dear Dr. Rank, you'll never die for Torvald and me.

RANK. Oh, that loss you'll easily get over. Those who go away are soon forgotten.

NORA [*looks fearfully at him*]. You believe that?

RANK. One makes new connections, and then—

NORA. Who makes new connections?

RANK. Both you and Torvald will when I'm gone. I'd say you're well under way already. What was that Mrs. Linde doing here last evening?

NORA. Oh, come—you can't be jealous of poor Kristine?

RANK. O yes, I am. She'll be my successor here in the house. When I'm down under, that woman will probably—

NORA. Shh! Not so loud. She's right in there.

RANK. Today as well. So you see.

NORA. Only to sew on my dress. Good gracious, how unreasonable you are. [*Sitting on the sofa.*] Be nice now, Dr. Rank. Tomorrow you'll see how beautifully I'll dance; and you can imagine then that I'm dancing only for you—yes, and of course for Torvald, too—that's understood. [*Takes various items out of the carton.*] Dr. Rank, sit over here and I'll show you something.

RANK [*sitting*]. What's that?

NORA. Look here. Look.

RANK. Silk stockings.

NORA. Flesh-colored. Aren't they lovely? Now it's so dark here, but tomorrow— No, no, no, just look at the feet. Oh well, you might as well look at the rest.

RANK. Hm—

NORA. Why do you look so critical? Don't you believe they'll fit?

RANK. I've never had any chance to form an opinion on that.

NORA [*glancing at him a moment*]. Shame on you. [*Hits him lightly on the ear with the stockings.*] That's for you. [*Puts them away again.*]

RANK. And what other splendors am I going to see now?

NORA. Not the least bit more, because you've been naughty. [*She hums a little and rummages among her things.*]

RANK [*after a short silence*]. When I sit here together with you like this, completely easy and open, then I don't know—I simply can't imagine—whatever would have become of me if I'd never come into this house.

NORA [*smiling*]. Yes, I really think you feel completely at ease with us.

RANK [*more quietly, staring straight ahead*]. And then to have to go away from it all—

NORA. Nonsense, you're not going away.

RANK [*his voice unchanged*]. —and not even be able to leave some poor show of gratitude behind, scarcely a fleeting regret—no more than a vacant place that anyone can fill.

NORA. And if I asked you now for—? No—

RANK. For what?

NORA. For a great proof of your friendship—

RANK. Yes, yes?

NORA. No, I mean—for an exceptionally big favor—

RANK. Would you really, for once, make me so happy?

NORA. Oh, you haven't the vaguest idea what it is.

RANK. All right, then tell me.

NORA. No, but I can't, Dr. Rank—it's all out of reason. It's advice and help, too—and a favor—

RANK. So much the better. I can't fathom what you're hinting at. Just speak out. Don't you trust me?

NORA. Of course. More than anyone else. You're my best and truest friend, I'm sure. That's why I want to talk to you. All right, then, Dr. Rank: there's something you can help me prevent. You know how deeply, how inexpressibly dearly Torvald loves me; he'd never hesitate a second to give up his life for me.

RANK [*leaning close to her*]. Nora—do you think he's the only one—

NORA [*with a slight start*]. Who—?

RANK. Who'd gladly give up his life for you.

NORA [*heavily*]. I see.

RANK. I swore to myself you should know this before I'm gone. I'll never find a better chance. Yes, Nora, now you know. And also you know now that you can trust me beyond anyone else.

NORA [*rising, natural and calm*]. Let me by.

RANK [*making room for her, but still sitting*]. Nora—

NORA [*in the hall doorway*]. Helene, bring the lamp in. [*Goes over to the stove.*] Ah, dear Dr. Rank, that was really mean of you.

RANK [*getting up*]. That I've loved you just as deeply as somebody else? Was *that* mean?

NORA. No, but that you came out and told me. That was quite unnecessary—

RANK. What do you mean? Have you known—?

[*The* MAID *comes in with the lamp, sets it on the table, and goes out again.*]

RANK. Nora—Mrs. Helmer—I'm asking you: have you known about it?

NORA. Oh, how can I tell what I know or don't know? Really, I don't know what to say— Why did you have to be so clumsy, Dr. Rank! Everything was so good.

RANK. Well, in any case, you now have the knowledge that my body and soul are at your command. So won't you speak out?

NORA [*looking at him*]. After that?

RANK. Please, just let me know what it is.

NORA. You can't know anything now.

RANK. I have to. You mustn't punish me like this. Give me the chance to do whatever is humanly possible for you.

NORA. Now there's nothing you can do for me. Besides, actually, I don't need any help. You'll see—it's only my fantasies. That's what it is. Of course! [*Sits in the rocker, looks at him, and smiles.*] What a nice one you are, Dr. Rank. Aren't you a little bit ashamed, now that the lamp is here?

RANK. No, not exactly. But perhaps I'd better go—for good?

NORA. No, you certainly can't do that. You must come here just as you always have. You know Torvald can't do without you.

RANK. Yes, but *you*?

NORA. You know how much I enjoy it when you're here.

RANK. That's precisely what threw me off. You're a mystery to me. So many times I've felt you'd almost rather be with me than with Helmer.

NORA. Yes—you see, there are some people that one loves most and other people that one would almost prefer being with.

RANK. Yes, there's something to that.

NORA. When I was back home, of course I loved Papa most. But I always thought it was so much fun when I could sneak down to the maids' quarters, because they never tried to improve me, and it was always so amusing, the way they talked to each other.

RANK. Aha, so it's *their* place that I've filled.

NORA [*jumping up and going to him*]. Oh, dear, sweet Dr. Rank, that's not what I meant at all. But you can understand that with Torvald it's just the same as with Papa—

[*The* MAID *enters from the hall.*]

MAID. Ma'am—please! [*She whispers to* NORA *and hands her a calling card.*]

NORA [*glancing at the card*]. Ah! [*Slips it into her pocket.*]

RANK. Anything wrong?

NORA. No, no, not at all. It's only some—it's my new dress—

RANK. Really? But—there's your dress.

NORA. Oh, that. But this is another one—I ordered it—Torvald mustn't know—

RANK. Ah, now we have the big secret.

NORA. That's right. Just go in with him—he's back in the inner study. Keep him there as long as—

RANK. Don't worry. He won't get away. [*Goes into the study.*]

NORA [*to the* MAID]. And he's standing waiting in the kitchen?

MAID. Yes, he came up by the back stairs.

NORA. But didn't you tell him somebody was here?

MAID. Yes, but that didn't do any good.

NORA. He won't leave?

MAID. No, he won't go till he's talked with you, ma'am.

NORA. Let him come in, then—but quietly. Helene, don't breathe a word about this. It's a surprise for my husband.

MAID. Yes, yes, I understand—[*Goes out.*]

NORA. This horror—it's going to happen. No, no, no, it can't happen, it mustn't. [*She goes and bolts* HELMER's *door. The* MAID *opens the hall door for* KROGSTAD *and shuts it behind him. He is dressed for travel in a fur coat, boots, and a fur cap.*]

NORA [*going toward him*]. Talk softly. My husband's home.

KROGSTAD. Well, good for him.

NORA. What do you want?

KROGSTAD. Some information.

NORA. Hurry up, then. What is it?

KROGSTAD. You know, of course, that I got my notice.

NORA. I couldn't prevent it, Mr. Krogstad. I fought for you to the bitter end, but nothing worked.

KROGSTAD. Does your husband's love for you run so thin? He knows everything I can expose you to, and all the same he dares to—

NORA. How can you imagine he knows anything about this?

KROGSTAD. Ah, no—I can't imagine it either, now. It's not at all like my fine Torvald Helmer to have so much guts—

NORA. Mr. Krogstad, I demand respect for my husband!

KROGSTAD. Why, of course—all due respect. But since the lady's keeping it so carefully hidden, may I presume to ask if you're also a bit better informed than yesterday about what you've actually done?

NORA. More than you ever could teach me.

KROGSTAD. Yes, I *am* such an awful lawyer.

NORA. What is it you want from me?

KROGSTAD. Just a glimpse of how you are, Mrs. Helmer. I've been thinking about you all day long. A cashier, a night-court scribbler, a—well, a type like me also has a little of what they call a heart, you know.

NORA. Then show it. Think of my children.

KROGSTAD. Did you or your husband ever think of mine? But never mind. I simply wanted to tell you that you don't need to take this thing too seriously. For the present, I'm not proceeding with any action.

NORA. Oh no, really! Well—I knew that.

KROGSTAD. Everything can be settled in a friendly spirit. It doesn't have to get around town at all; it can stay just among us three.

NORA. My husband must never know anything of this.

KROGSTAD. How can you manage that? Perhaps you can pay me the balance?

NORA. No, not right now.

KROGSTAD. Or you know some way of raising the money in a day or two?

NORA. No way that I'm willing to use.

KROGSTAD. Well, it wouldn't have done you any good, anyway. If you stood in front of me with a fistful of bills, you still couldn't buy your signature back.

NORA. Then tell me what you're going to do with it.

KROGSTAD. I'll just hold onto it—keep it on file. There's no outsider who'll even get wind of it. So if you've been thinking of taking some desperate step—

NORA. I have.

KROGSTAD. Been thinking of running away from home—

NORA. I have!

KROGSTAD. Or even of something worse—

NORA. How could you guess that?

KROGSTAD. You can drop those thoughts.

NORA. How could you guess I was thinking of *that?*

KROGSTAD. Most of us think about *that* at first. I thought about it too, but I discovered I hadn't the courage—

NORA [*lifelessly*]. I don't either.

KROGSTAD [*relieved*]. That's true, you haven't the courage? You too?

NORA. I don't have it—I don't have it.

KROGSTAD. It would be terribly stupid, anyway. After that first storm at home blows out, why, then— I have here in my pocket a letter for your husband—

NORA. Telling everything?

KROGSTAD. As charitably as possible.

NORA [*quickly*]. He mustn't ever get that letter. Tear it up. I'll find some way to get money.

KROGSTAD. Beg pardon, Mrs. Helmer, but I think I just told you—

NORA. Oh, I don't mean the money I owe you. Let me know how much you want from my husband, and I'll manage it.

KROGSTAD. I don't want any money from your husband.

NORA. What do you want, then?

KROGSTAD. I'll tell you what. I want to recoup, Mrs. Helmer; I want to get on in the world—and there's where your husband can help me. For a year and a half I've kept myself clean of anything disreputable—all that time struggling with the worst conditions; but I was satisfied, working my way up step by step. Now I've been written right off, and I'm just not in the mood to come crawling back. I tell you, I want to move on. I want to get back in the bank—in a better position. Your husband can set up a job for me—

NORA. He'll never do that!

KROGSTAD. He'll do it. I know him. He won't dare breathe a word of protest. And once I'm in there together with him, you just wait and see! Inside of a year, I'll be the manager's right-hand man. It'll be Nils Krogstad, not Torvald Helmer, who runs the bank.

NORA. You'll never see the day!

KROGSTAD. Maybe you think you can—

NORA. I have the courage now—for *that.*

KROGSTAD. Oh, you don't scare me. A smart, spoiled lady like you—

NORA. You'll see; you'll see!

KROGSTAD. Under the ice, maybe? Down in the freezing, coal-black water? There, till you float up in the spring, ugly, unrecognizable, with your hair falling out—

NORA. You don't frighten me.

KROGSTAD. Nor do you frighten me. One doesn't do these things, Mrs. Helmer. Besides, what good would it be? I'd still have him safe in my pocket.

NORA. Afterwards? When I'm no longer—?

KROGSTAD. Are you forgetting that *I'll* be in control then over your final reputation? [NORA *stands speechless, staring at him.*] Good; now I've warned you. Don't do anything stupid. When Helmer's read my letter, I'll be waiting for his reply. And bear in mind that it's your husband himself who's forced me back to my old ways. I'll never forgive him for that. Good-bye, Mrs. Helmer. [*He goes out through the hall.*]

NORA [*goes to the hall door, opens it a crack, and listens*]. He's gone. Didn't leave the letter. Oh no, no, that's impossible too! [*Opening the door more and more.*] What's that? He's standing outside—not going downstairs. He's thinking it over? Maybe he'll—? [*A letter falls in the mailbox; then* KROGSTAD*'s footsteps are heard, dying away down a flight of stairs.* NORA *gives a muffled cry and runs over toward the sofa table. A short pause.*] In the mailbox. [*Slips warily over to the hall door.*] It's lying there. Torvald, Torvald—now we're lost!

MRS. LINDE [*entering with the costume from the room, left*]. There now, I can't see anything else to mend. Perhaps you'd like to try—

NORA [*in a hoarse whisper*]. Kristine, come here.

MRS. LINDE [*tossing the dress on the sofa*]. What's wrong? You look upset.

NORA. Come here. See that letter? *There!* Look—through the glass in the mailbox.

MRS. LINDE. Yes, yes, I see it.

NORA. That letter's from Krogstad—

MRS. LINDE. Nora—it's Krogstad who loaned you the money!

NORA. Yes, and now Torvald will find out everything.

MRS. LINDE. Believe me, Nora, it's best for both of you.

NORA. There's more you don't know. I forged a name.

MRS. LINDE. But for heaven's sake—?

NORA. I only want to tell you that, Kristine, so that you can be my witness.

MRS. LINDE. Witness? Why should I—?

NORA. If I should go out of my mind—it could easily happen—

MRS. LINDE. Nora!

NORA. Or anything else occurred—so I couldn't be present here—

MRS. LINDE. Nora, Nora, you aren't yourself at all!

NORA. And someone should try to take on the whole weight, all of the guilt, you follow me—

MRS. LINDE. Yes, of course, but why do you think—?

NORA. Then you're the witness that it isn't true, Kristine. I'm very much myself; my mind right now is perfectly clear; and I'm telling you: nobody else has known about this; I alone did everything. Remember that.

MRS. LINDE. I will. But I don't understand all this.

NORA. Oh, how could you ever understand it? It's the miracle now that's going to take place.

MRS. LINDE. The miracle?

NORA. Yes, the miracle. But it's so awful, Kristine. It mustn't take place, not for anything in the world.

MRS. LINDE. I'm going right over and talk with Krogstad.

NORA. Don't go near him; he'll do you some terrible harm!

MRS. LINDE. There was a time once when he'd gladly have done anything for me.

NORA. He?

MRS. LINDE. Where does he live?

NORA. Oh, how do I know? Yes. [*Searches in her pocket.*] Here's his card. But the letter, the letter—!

HELMER [*from the study, knocking on the door*]. Nora!

NORA [*with a cry of fear*]. Oh! What is it? What do you want?

HELMER. Now, now, don't be so frightened. We're not coming in. You locked the door—are you trying on the dress?

NORA. Yes, I'm trying it. I'll look just beautiful, Torvald.

MRS. LINDE [*who has read the card*]. He's living right around the corner.

NORA. Yes, but what's the use? We're lost. The letter's in the box.

MRS. LINDE. And your husband has the key?

NORA. Yes, always.

MRS. LINDE. Krogstad can ask for his letter back unread; he can find some excuse—

NORA. But it's just this time that Torvald usually—

MRS. LINDE. Stall him. Keep him in there. I'll be back as quick as I can. [*She hurries out through the hall entrance.*]

NORA [*goes to* HELMER'*s door, opens it, and peers in*]. Torvald!

HELMER [*from the inner study*]. Well—does one dare set foot in one's own living room at last? Come on, Rank, now we'll get a look— [*In the doorway.*] But what's this?

NORA. What, Torvald dear?

HELMER. Rank had me expecting some grand masquerade.

RANK [*in the doorway*]. That was my impression, but I must have been wrong.

NORA. No one can admire me in my splendor—not till tomorrow.

HELMER. But Nora dear, you look so exhausted. Have you practiced too hard?

NORA. No, I haven't practiced at all yet.

HELMER. You know, it's necessary—

NORA. Oh, it's absolutely necessary, Torvald. But I can't get anywhere without your help. I've forgotten the whole thing completely.

HELMER. Ah, we'll soon take care of that.

NORA. Yes, take care of me, Torvald, please! Promise me that? Oh, I'm so nervous. That big party— You must give up everything this evening for me. No business—don't even touch your pen. Yes? Dear Torvald, promise?

HELMER. It's a promise. Tonight I'm totally at your service—you little helpless thing. Hm—but first there's one thing I want to— [*Goes toward the hall door.*]

NORA. What are you looking for?

HELMER. Just to see if there's any mail.

NORA. No, no, don't do that, Torvald!

HELMER. Now what?

NORA. Torvald, please. There isn't any.

HELMER. Let me look, though. [*Starts out.* NORA, *at the piano, strikes the first notes of the tarantella.* HELMER, *at the door, stops.*] Aha!

NORA. I can't dance tomorrow if I don't practice with you.

HELMER [*going over to her*]. Nora dear, are you really so frightened?

NORA. Yes, so terribly frightened. Let me practice right now; there's still time before dinner. Oh, sit down and play for me, Torvald. Direct me. Teach me, the way you always have.

HELMER. Gladly, if it's what you want. [*Sits at the piano.*]

NORA [*snatches the tambourine up from the box, then a long varicolored shawl, which she throws around herself, whereupon she springs forward and cries out:*] Play for me now! Now I'll dance!

[HELMER *plays and* NORA *dances.* RANK *stands behind* HELMER *at the piano and looks on.*]

HELMER [*as he plays*]. Slower. Slow down.

NORA. Can't change it.

HELMER. Not so violent, Nora!

NORA. Has to be just like this.

HELMER [*stopping*]. No, no, that won't do at all.

NORA [*laughing and swinging her tambourine*]. Isn't that what I told you?

RANK. Let me play for her.

HELMER [*getting up*]. Yes, go on. I can teach her more easily then.

[RANK *sits at the piano and plays;* NORA *dances more and more wildly.* HELMER *has stationed himself by the stove and repeatedly gives her directions; she seems not to hear them; her hair loosens and falls over her shoulders; she does not notice, but goes on dancing.* MRS. LINDE *enters.*]

MRS. LINDE [*standing dumbfounded at the door*]. Ah—!

NORA [*still dancing*]. See what fun, Kristine!

HELMER. But Nora darling, you dance as if your life were at stake.

NORA. And it is.

HELMER. Rank, stop! This is pure madness. Stop it, I say!

[RANK *breaks off playing, and* NORA *halts abruptly.*]

HELMER [*going over to her*]. I never would have believed it. You've forgotten everything I taught you.

NORA [*throwing away the tambourine*]. You see for yourself.

HELMER. Well, there's certainly room for instruction here.

NORA. Yes, you see how important it is. You've got to teach me to the very last minute. Promise me that, Torvald?

HELMER. You can bet on it.

NORA. You mustn't, either today or tomorrow, think about anything else but me; you mustn't open any letters—or the mailbox—

HELMER. Ah, it's still the fear of that man—

NORA. Oh yes, yes, that too.

HELMER. Nora, it's written all over you—there's already a letter from him out there.

NORA. I don't know. I guess so. But you mustn't read such things now; there mustn't be anything ugly between us before it's all over.

RANK [*quietly to* HELMER]. You shouldn't deny her.

HELMER [*putting his arm around her*]. The child can have her way. But tomorrow night, after you've danced—

NORA. Then you'll be free.

MAID [*in the doorway, right*]. Ma'am, dinner is served.

NORA. We'll be wanting champagne, Helene.

MAID. Very good, ma'am. [*Goes out.*]

HELMER. So—a regular banquet, hm?

NORA. Yes, a banquet—champagne till daybreak! [*Calling out.*] And some macaroons, Helene. Heaps of them—just this once.

HELMER [*taking her hands*]. Now, now, now—no hysterics. Be my own little lark again.

NORA. Oh, I will soon enough. But go on in—and you, Dr. Rank. Kristine, help me put up my hair.

RANK [*whispering, as they go*]. There's nothing wrong—really wrong, is there?

HELMER. Oh, of course not. It's nothing more than this childish anxiety I was telling you about. [*They go out, right.*]

NORA. Well?

MRS. LINDE. Left town.

NORA. I could see by your face.

MRS. LINDE. He'll be home tomorrow evening. I wrote him a note.

NORA. You shouldn't have. Don't try to stop anything now. After all, it's a wonderful joy, this waiting here for the miracle.

MRS. LINDE. What is it you're waiting for?

NORA. Oh, you can't understand that. Go in to them; I'll be along in a moment.

[MRS. LINDE *goes into the dining room.* NORA *stands a short while as if composing herself; then she looks at her watch.*]

NORA. Five. Seven hours to midnight. Twenty-four hours to the midnight after, and then the tarantella's done. Seven and twenty-four? Thirty-one hours to live.

HELMER [*in the doorway, right*]. What's become of the little lark?

NORA [*going toward him with open arms*]. Here's your lark!

ACT THREE

Same scene. The table, with chairs around it, has been moved to the center of the room. A lamp on the table is lit. The hall door stands open. Dance music drifts down from the floor above. MRS. LINDE *sits at the table, absently paging through a book, trying to read, but apparently unable to focus her thoughts. Once or twice she pauses, tensely listening for a sound at the outer entrance.*

MRS. LINDE [*glancing at her watch*]. Not yet—and there's hardly any time left. If only he's not—[*Listening again.*] Ah, there he is. [*She goes out in the hall and cautiously opens the outer door. Quiet footsteps are heard on the stairs. She whispers:*] Come in. Nobody's here.

KROGSTAD [*in the doorway*]. I found a note from you at home. What's back of all this?

MRS. LINDE. I just *had* to talk to you.

KROGSTAD. Oh? And it just *had* to be here in this house?

MRS. LINDE. At my place it was impossible; my room hasn't a private entrance. Come in; we're all alone. The maid's asleep, and the Helmers are at the dance upstairs.

KROGSTAD [*entering the room*]. Well, well, the Helmers are dancing tonight? Really?

MRS. LINDE. Yes, why not?

KROGSTAD. How true—why not?

MRS. LINDE. All right, Krogstad, let's talk.

KROGSTAD. Do we two have anything more to talk about?

MRS. LINDE. We have a great deal to talk about.

KROGSTAD. I wouldn't have thought so.

MRS. LINDE. No, because you've never understood me, really.

KROGSTAD. Was there anything more to understand—except what's all too common in life? A calculating woman throws over a man the moment a better catch comes by.

MRS. LINDE. You think I'm so thoroughly calculating? You think I broke it off lightly?

KROGSTAD. Didn't you?

MRS. LINDE. Nils—is that what you really thought?

KROGSTAD. If you cared, then why did you write me the way you did?

MRS. LINDE. What else could I do? If I had to break off with you, then it was my job as well to root out everything you felt for me.

KROGSTAD [*wringing his hands*]. So that was it. And this—all this, simply for money!

MRS. LINDE. Don't forget I had a helpless mother and two small brothers. We couldn't wait for you, Nils; you had such a long road ahead of you then.

KROGSTAD. That may be; but you still hadn't the right to abandon me for somebody else's sake.

MRS. LINDE. Yes—I don't know. So many, many times I've asked myself if I did have that right.

KROGSTAD [*more softly*]. When I lost you, it was as if all the solid ground dissolved from under my feet. Look at me; I'm a half-drowned man now, hanging onto a wreck.

MRS. LINDE. Help may be near.

KROGSTAD. It was near—but then you came and blocked it off.

MRS. LINDE. Without my knowing it, Nils. Today for the first time I learned that it's you I'm replacing at the bank.

KROGSTAD. All right—I believe you. But now that you know, will you step aside?

MRS. LINDE. No, because that wouldn't benefit you in the slightest.

KROGSTAD. Not "benefit" me, hm! I'd step aside anyway.

MRS. LINDE. I've learned to be realistic. Life and hard, bitter necessity have taught me that.

KROGSTAD. And life's taught me never to trust fine phrases.

MRS. LINDE. Then life's taught you a very sound thing. But you do have to trust in actions, don't you?

KROGSTAD. What does that mean?

MRS. LINDE. You said you were hanging on like a half-drowned man to a wreck.

KROGSTAD. I've good reason to say that.

MRS. LINDE. I'm also like a half-drowned woman on a wreck. No one to suffer with; no one to care for.

KROGSTAD. You made your choice.

MRS. LINDE. There wasn't any choice then.

KROGSTAD. So—what of it?

MRS. LINDE. Nils, if only we two shipwrecked people could reach across to each other.

KROGSTAD. What are you saying?

MRS. LINDE. Two on one wreck are at least better off than each on his own.

KROGSTAD. Kristine!

MRS. LINDE. Why do you think I came into town?

KROGSTAD. Did you really have some thought of me?

MRS. LINDE. I have to work to go on living. All my born days, as long as I can remember, I've worked, and it's been my best and my only joy. But now I'm completely alone in the world; it frightens me to be so empty and lost. To work for yourself—there's no joy in that. Nils, give me something—someone to work for.

KROGSTAD. I don't believe all this. It's just some hysterical feminine urge to go out and make a noble sacrifice.

MRS. LINDE. Have you ever found me to be hysterical?

KROGSTAD. Can you honestly mean this? Tell me—do you know everything about my past?

MRS. LINDE. Yes.

KROGSTAD. And you know what they think I'm worth around here.

MRS. LINDE. From what you were saying before, it would seem that with me you could have been another person.

KROGSTAD. I'm positive of that.

MRS. LINDE. Couldn't it happen still?

KROGSTAD. Kristine—you're saying this in all seriousness? Yes, you are! I can see it in you. And do you really have the courage, then—?

MRS. LINDE. I need to have someone to care for; and your children need a mother. We both need each other. Nils, I have faith that you're good at heart—I'll risk everything together with you.

KROGSTAD [*gripping her hands*]. Kristine, thank you, thank you— Now I know I can win back a place in their eyes. Yes—but I forgot—

MRS. LINDE [*listening*]. Shh! The tarantella. Go now! Go on!

KROGSTAD. Why? What is it?

MRS. LINDE. Hear the dance up there? When that's over, they'll be coming down.

KROGSTAD. Oh, then I'll go. But—it's all pointless. Of course, you don't know the move I made against the Helmers.

MRS. LINDE. Yes, Nils, I know.

KROGSTAD. And all the same, you have the courage to—?

MRS. LINDE. I know how far despair can drive a man like you.

KROGSTAD. Oh, if I only could take it all back.

MRS. LINDE. You easily could—your letter's still lying in the mailbox.

KROGSTAD. Are you sure of that?

MRS. LINDE. Positive. But—

KROGSTAD [*looks at her searchingly*]. Is that the meaning of it, then? You'll save your friend at any price. Tell me straight out. Is that it?

MRS. LINDE. Nils—anyone who's sold herself for somebody else once isn't going to do it again.

KROGSTAD. I'll demand my letter back.

MRS. LINDE. No, no.

KROGSTAD. Yes, of course. I'll stay here till Helmer comes down; I'll tell him to give me my letter again—that it only involves my dismissal—that he shouldn't read it—

MRS. LINDE. No, Nils, don't call the letter back.

KROGSTAD. But wasn't that exactly why you wrote me to come here?

MRS. LINDE. Yes, in that first panic. But it's been a whole day and night since then, and in that time I've seen such incredible things in this house. Helmer's got to learn everything; this dreadful secret has to be aired; those two have to come to a full understanding; all these lies and evasions can't go on.

KROGSTAD. Well, then, if you want to chance it. But at least there's one thing I can do, and do right away—

MRS. LINDE [*listening*]. Go now, go quick! The dance is over. We're not safe another second.

KROGSTAD. I'll wait for you downstairs.

MRS. LINDE. Yes, please do; take me home.

KROGSTAD. I can't believe it; I've never been so happy. [*He leaves by way of the outer door; the door between the room and the hall stays open.*]

MRS. LINDE [*straightening up a bit and getting together her street clothes*]. How different now! How different! Someone to work for, to live for—a home to build. Well, it is worth the try! Oh, if they'd only come! [*Listening.*] Ah, there they are. Bundle up. [*She picks up her hat and coat.* NORA*'s and* HELMER*'s voices can be heard outside; a key turns in the lock, and* HELMER *brings* NORA *into the hall almost by force. She is wearing the Italian costume with a large black shawl about her; he has on evening dress, with a black domino*[3] *open over it.*]

NORA [*struggling in the doorway*]. No, no, no, not inside! I'm going up again. I don't want to leave so soon.

HELMER. But Nora dear—

NORA. Oh, I beg you, please, Torvald. From the bottom of my heart, *please*—only an hour more!

HELMER. Not a single minute, Nora darling. You know our agreement. Come on, in we go; you'll catch cold out here. [*In spite of her resistance, he gently draws her into the room.*]

MRS. LINDE. Good evening.

NORA. Kristine!

HELMER. Why, Mrs. Linde—are you here so late?

MRS. LINDE. Yes, I'm sorry, but I did want to see Nora in costume.

NORA. Have you been sitting here, waiting for me?

MRS. LINDE. Yes. I didn't come early enough; you were all upstairs; and then I thought I really couldn't leave without seeing you.

HELMER [*removing* NORA*'s shawl*]. Yes, take a good look. She's worth looking at, I can tell you that, Mrs. Linde. Isn't she lovely?

MRS. LINDE. Yes, I should say—

HELMER. A dream of loveliness, isn't she? That's what everyone thought at the party, too. But she's horribly stubborn—this sweet little thing. What's to be done with her? Can you imagine, I almost had to use force to pry her away.

NORA. Oh, Torvald, you're going to regret you didn't indulge me, even for just a half hour more.

HELMER. There, you see. She danced her tarantella and got a tumultuous hand—which was well earned, although the performance may have been a bit too naturalistic—I mean it rather overstepped the proprieties of art. But never mind—what's important is, she made a success, an overwhelming success. You think I could let her stay on after that and spoil the effect? Oh no; I took my lovely little Capri girl—my capricious little Capri girl, I should say—took her under my arm; one quick tour of the ballroom, a curtsy to every side, and then—as they say in nov-

[3] A large, loose, hooded cloak, designed to be worn with a mask for masquerades.

els—the beautiful vision disappeared. An exit should always be effective, Mrs. Linde, but that's what I can't get Nora to grasp. Phew, it's hot in here. [*Flings the domino on a chair and opens the door to his room.*] Why's it dark in here? Oh yes, of course. Excuse me. [*He goes in and lights a couple of candles.*]

NORA [*in a sharp, breathless whisper*]. So?

MRS. LINDE [*quietly*]. I talked with him.

NORA. And—?

MRS. LINDE. Nora—you must tell your husband everything.

NORA [*dully*]. I knew it.

MRS. LINDE. You've got nothing to fear from Krogstad, but you have to speak out.

NORA. I won't tell.

MRS. LINDE. Then the letter will.

NORA. Thanks, Kristine. I know now what's to be done. Shh!

HELMER [*reentering*]. Well, then, Mrs. Linde—have you admired her?

MRS. LINDE. Yes, and now I'll say good night.

HELMER. Oh, come, so soon? Is this yours, this knitting?

MRS. LINDE. Yes, thanks. I nearly forgot it.

HELMER. Do you knit, then?

MRS. LINDE. Oh yes.

HELMER. You know what? You should embroider instead.

MRS. LINDE. Really? Why?

HELMER. Yes, because it's a lot prettier. See here, one holds the embroidery so, in the left hand, and then one guides the needle with the right—so—in an easy, sweeping curve—right?

MRS. LINDE. Yes, I guess that's—

HELMER. But, on the other hand, knitting—it can never be anything but ugly. Look, see here, the arms tucked in, the knitting needles going up and down—there's something Chinese about it. Ah, that was really a glorious champagne they served.

MRS. LINDE. Yes, good night, Nora, and don't be stubborn anymore.

HELMER. Well put, Mrs. Linde!

MRS. LINDE. Good night, Mr. Helmer.

HELMER [*accompanying her to the door*]. Good night, good night. I hope you get home all right. I'd be very happy to—but you don't have far to go. Good night, good night. [*She leaves. He shuts the door after her and returns.*] There, now, at last we got her out the door. She's a deadly bore, that creature.

NORA. Aren't you pretty tired, Torvald?

HELMER. No, not a bit.

NORA. You're not sleepy?

HELMER. Not at all. On the contrary, I'm feeling quite exhilarated. But you? Yes, you really look tired and sleepy.

NORA. Yes, I'm very tired. Soon now I'll sleep.

HELMER. See! You see! I was right all along that we shouldn't stay longer.

NORA. Whatever you do is always right.

HELMER [*kissing her brow*]. Now my little lark talks sense. Say, did you notice what a time Rank was having tonight?

NORA. Oh, was he? I didn't get to speak with him.

HELMER. I scarcely did either, but it's a long time since I've seen him in such high spirits. [*Gazes at her a moment, then comes nearer her.*] Hm—it's marvelous, though, to be back home again—to be completely alone with you. Oh, you bewitchingly lovely young woman!

NORA. Torvald, don't look at me like that!

HELMER. Can't I look at my richest treasure? At all that beauty that's mine, mine alone—completely and utterly.

NORA [*moving around to the other side of the table*]. You mustn't talk to me that way tonight.

HELMER [*following her*]. The tarantella is still in your blood, I can see—and it makes you even more enticing. Listen. The guests are beginning to go. [*Dropping his voice.*] Nora—it'll soon be quiet through this whole house.

NORA. Yes, I hope so.

HELMER. You do, don't you, my love? Do you realize—when I'm out at a party like this with you—do you know why I talk to you so little, and keep such a distance away; just send you a stolen look now and then—you know why I do it? It's because I'm imagining then that you're my secret darling, my secret young bride-to-be, and that no one suspects there's anything between us.

NORA. Yes, yes; oh, yes, I know you're always thinking of me.

HELMER. And then when we leave and I place the shawl over those fine young rounded shoulders—over that wonderful curving neck—then I pretend that you're my young bride, that we're just coming from the wedding, that for the first time I'm bringing you into my house—that for the first time I'm alone with you—completely alone with you, your trembling young beauty! All this evening I've longed for nothing but you. When I saw you turn and sway in the tarantella—my blood was pounding till I couldn't stand it—that's why I brought you down here so early—

NORA. Go away, Torvald! Leave me alone. I don't want all this.

HELMER. What do you mean? Nora, you're teasing me. You will, won't you? Aren't I your husband—?

[*A knock at the outside door.*]

NORA [*startled*]. What's that?

HELMER [*going toward the hall*]. Who is it?

RANK [*outside*]. It's me. May I come in a moment?

HELMER [*with quiet irritation*]. Oh, what does he want now? [*Aloud.*] Hold on. [*Goes and opens the door.*] Oh, how nice that you didn't just pass us by!

RANK. I thought I heard your voice, and then I wanted so badly to have a look in. [*Lightly glancing about.*] Ah, me, these old familiar haunts. You have it snug and cozy in here, you two.

HELMER. You seemed to be having it pretty cozy upstairs, too.

RANK. Absolutely. Why shouldn't I? Why not take in everything in life? As much as you can, anyway, and as long as you can. The wine was superb—

HELMER. The champagne especially.

RANK. You noticed that too? It's amazing how much I could guzzle down.

NORA. Torvald also drank a lot of champagne this evening.

RANK. Oh?

NORA. Yes, and that always makes him so entertaining.

RANK. Well, why shouldn't one have a pleasant evening after a well-spent day?

HELMER. Well spent? I'm afraid I can't claim that.

RANK [*slapping him on the back*]. But I can, you see!

NORA. Dr. Rank, you must have done some scientific research today.

RANK. Quite so.

HELMER. Come now—little Nora talking about scientific research!

NORA. And can I congratulate you on the results?

RANK. Indeed you may.

NORA. Then they were good?

RANK. The best possible for both doctor and patient—certainty.

NORA [*quickly and searchingly*]. Certainty?

RANK. Complete certainty. So don't I owe myself a gay evening afterwards?

NORA. Yes, you're right, Dr. Rank.

HELMER. I'm with you—just so long as you don't have to suffer for it in the morning.

RANK. Well, one never gets something for nothing in life.

NORA. Dr. Rank—are you very fond of masquerade parties?

RANK. Yes, if there's a good array of odd disguises—

NORA. Tell me, what should we two go as at the next masquerade?

HELMER. You little featherhead—already thinking of the next!

RANK. We two? I'll tell you what: you must go as Charmed Life—

HELMER. Yes, but find a costume for *that!*

RANK. Your wife can appear just as she looks every day.

HELMER. That was nicely put. But don't you know what you're going to be?

RANK. Yes, Helmer, I've made up my mind.

HELMER. Well?

RANK. At the next masquerade I'm going to be invisible.

HELMER. That's a funny idea.

RANK. They say there's a hat—black, huge—have you never heard of the hat that makes you invisible? You put it on, and then no one on earth can see you.

HELMER [*suppressing a smile*]. Ah, of course.

RANK. But I'm quite forgetting what I came for. Helmer, give me a cigar, one of the dark Havanas.

HELMER. With the greatest pleasure. [*Holds out his case.*]

RANK. Thanks. [*Takes one and cuts off the tip.*]

NORA [*striking a match*]. Let me give you a light.

RANK. Thank you. [*She holds the match for him; he lights the cigar.*] And now good-bye.

HELMER. Good-bye, good-bye, old friend.

NORA. Sleep well, Doctor.

RANK. Thanks for that wish.

NORA. Wish me the same.

RANK. You? All right, if you like— Sleep well. And thanks for the light. [*He nods to them both and leaves.*]

HELMER [*his voice subdued*]. He's been drinking heavily.

NORA [*absently*]. Could be. [HELMER *takes his keys from his pocket and goes out in the hall.*] Torvald—what are you after?

HELMER. Got to empty the mailbox; it's nearly full. There won't be room for the morning papers.

NORA. Are you working tonight?

HELMER. You know I'm not. Why—what's this? Someone's been at the lock.

NORA. At the lock—?

HELMER. Yes, I'm positive. What do you suppose—? I can't imagine one of the maids—? Here's a broken hairpin. Nora, it's yours—

NORA [*quickly*]. Then it must be the children—

HELMER. You'd better break them of that. Hm, hm—well, opened it after all. [*Takes the contents out and calls into the kitchen.*] Helene! Helene, would you put out the lamp in the hall. [*He returns to the room, shutting the hall door, then displays the handful of mail.*] Look how it's piled up. [*Sorting through them.*] Now what's this?

NORA [*at the window*]. The letter! Oh, Torvald, no!

HELMER. Two calling cards—from Rank.

NORA. From Dr. Rank?

HELMER [*examining them*]. "Dr. Rank, Consulting Physician." They were on top. He must have dropped them in as he left.

NORA. Is there anything on them?

HELMER. There's a black cross over the name. See? That's a gruesome notion. He could almost be announcing his own death.

NORA. That's just what he's doing.

HELMER. What! You've heard something? Something he's told you?

NORA. Yes. That when those cards came, he'd be taking his leave of us. He'll shut himself in now and die.

HELMER. Ah, my poor friend! Of course I knew he wouldn't be here much longer. But so soon— And then to hide himself away like a wounded animal.

NORA. If it has to happen, then it's best it happens in silence—don't you think so, Torvald?

HELMER [*pacing up and down*]. He'd grown right into our lives. I simply can't imagine him gone. He with his suffering and loneliness—like a dark cloud setting off our sunlit happiness. Well, maybe it's best this way. For him, at least. [*Standing still.*] And maybe for us too, Nora. Now we're thrown back on each other, completely. [*Embracing her.*] Oh you, my darling wife, how can I hold you close enough? You know what, Nora—time and again I've wished you were in some terrible danger, just so I could stake my life and soul and everything, for your sake.

NORA [*tearing herself away, her voice firm and decisive*]. Now you must read your mail, Torvald.

HELMER. No, no, not tonight. I want to stay with you, dearest.

NORA. With a dying friend on your mind?

HELMER. You're right. We've both had a shock. There's ugliness between us—these thoughts of death and corruption. We'll have to get free of them first. Until then—we'll stay apart.

NORA [*clinging about his neck*]. Torvald—good night! Good night!

HELMER [*kissing her on the cheek*]. Good night, little songbird. Sleep well, Nora. I'll be reading my mail now. [*He takes the letters into his room and shuts the door after him.*]

NORA [*with bewildered glances, groping about, seizing* HELMER*'s domino, throwing it around her, and speaking in short, hoarse, broken whispers*]. Never see him again. Never, never. [*Putting her shawl over her head.*] Never see the children either—them, too. Never, never. Oh, the freezing black water! The depths—down— Oh, I wish it were over— He has it now; he's reading it—now. Oh no, no, not yet. Torvald, good-bye, you and the children— [*She starts for the hall; as she does,* HELMER *throws open his door and stands with an open letter in his hand.*]

HELMER. Nora!

NORA [*screams*]. Oh—!

HELMER. What is this? You know what's in this letter?

NORA. Yes, I know. Let me go! Let me out!

HELMER [*holding her back*]. Where are you going?

NORA [*struggling to break loose*]. You can't save me, Torvald!

HELMER [*slumping back*]. True! Then it's true what he writes? How horrible! No, no, it's impossible—it can't be true.

NORA. It *is* true. I've loved you more than all this world.

HELMER. Ah, none of your slippery tricks.

NORA [*taking one step toward him*]. Torvald—!

HELMER. What *is* this you've blundered into!

NORA. Just let me loose. You're not going to suffer for my sake. You're not going to take on my guilt.

HELMER. No more playacting. [*Locks the hall door.*] You stay right here and give me a reckoning. You understand what you've done? Answer! You understand?

NORA [*looking squarely at him, her face hardening*]. Yes. I'm beginning to understand everything now.

HELMER [*striding about*]. Oh, what an awful awakening! In all these eight years—she who was my pride and joy—a hypocrite, a liar—worse, worse—a criminal! How infinitely disgusting it all is! The shame! [NORA *says nothing and goes on looking straight at him. He stops in front of her.*] I should have suspected something of the kind. I should have known. All your father's flimsy values— Be still! All your father's flimsy values have come out in you. No religion, no morals, no sense of duty— Oh, how I'm punished for letting him off! I did it for your sake, and you repay me like this.

NORA. Yes, like this.

HELMER. Now you've wrecked all my happiness—ruined my whole future. Oh, it's awful to think of. I'm in a cheap little grafter's hands; he can do anything he wants with me, ask for anything, play with me like a puppet—and I can't breathe a word. I'll be swept down miserably into the depths on account of a featherbrained woman.

NORA. When I'm gone from this world, you'll be free.

HELMER. Oh, quit posing. Your father had a mess of those speeches too. What good would that ever do me if you were gone from this world, as you say? Not the slightest. He can still make the whole thing known; and if he does, I could be falsely suspected as your accomplice. They might even think that I was behind it—that I put you up to it. And all that I can thank you for—you that I've coddled the whole of our marriage. Can you see now what you've done to me?

NORA [*icily calm*]. Yes.

HELMER. It's so incredible, I just can't grasp it. But we'll have to patch up whatever we can. Take off the shawl. I said, take it off! I've got to appease him somehow or other. The thing has to be hushed up at any cost. And as for you and me, it's got to seem like everything between us is just as it was—to the outside world, that is. You'll go right on living in this house, of course. But you can't be allowed to bring up the children; I don't dare trust you with them—Oh, to have to say this to someone I've loved so much! Well, that's done with. From now on happiness doesn't matter; all that matters is saving the bits and pieces, the appearance—[*The doorbell rings.* HELMER *starts.*] What's that? And so late. Maybe the worst—? You think he'd—? Hide, Nora! Say you're sick. [NORA *remains standing motionless.* HELMER *goes and opens the door.*]

MAID [*half dressed, in the hall*]. A letter for Mrs. Helmer.

HELMER. I'll take it. [*Snatches the letter and shuts the door.*] Yes, it's from him. You don't get it; I'm reading it myself.

NORA. Then read it.

HELMER [*by the lamp*]. I hardly dare. We may be ruined, you and I. But—I've got to know. [*Rips open the letter, skims through a few lines, glances at an enclosure, then cries out joyfully.*] Nora! [NORA *looks inquiringly at him.*] Nora! Wait—better check it again— Yes, yes, it's true. I'm saved. Nora, I'm saved!

NORA. And I?

HELMER. You too, of course. We're both saved, both of us. Look. He's sent back your note. He says he's sorry and ashamed—that a happy development in his life—oh, who cares what he says! Nora, we're saved! No one can hurt you. Oh, Nora, Nora—but first, this ugliness all has to go. Let me see— [*Takes a look at the note.*] No, I don't want to see it; I want the whole thing to fade like a dream. [*Tears the note and both letters to pieces, throws them into the stove and watches them burn.*] There—now there's nothing left— He wrote that since Christmas Eve you—Oh, they must have been three terrible days for you, Nora.

NORA. I fought a hard fight.

HELMER. And suffered pain and saw no escape but—No, we're not going to dwell on anything unpleasant. We'll just be grateful and keep on repeating: it's over now, it's over! You hear me, Nora? You don't seem to realize—it's over. What's it mean—that frozen look? Oh, poor little Nora, I understand. You can't believe I've forgiven you. But I have, Nora; I swear I have. I know that what you did, you did out of love for me.

NORA. That's true.

HELMER. You loved me the way a wife ought to love her husband. It's simply the means that you couldn't judge. But you think I love you any the less for not knowing how to handle your affairs? No, no—just lean on me; I'll guide you and teach you. I wouldn't be a man if this feminine helplessness didn't make you twice as attractive to me. You mustn't mind those sharp words I said—that was all in the first confusion of thinking my world had collapsed. I've forgiven you, Nora; I swear I've forgiven you.

NORA. My thanks for your forgiveness. [*She goes out through the door, right.*]

HELMER. No, wait— [*Peers in.*] What are you doing in there?

NORA [*inside*]. Getting out of my costume.

HELMER [*by the open door*]. Yes, do that. Try to calm yourself and collect your thoughts again, my frightened little songbird. You can rest easy now; I've got wide wings to shelter you with. [*Walking about close by the door.*] How snug and nice our home is, Nora. You're safe here; I'll keep you like a hunted dove I've rescued out of a hawk's claws. I'll bring peace to your poor, shuddering heart. Gradually it'll happen, Nora; you'll see. Tomorrow all this will look different to you; then everything will be as it was. I won't have to go on repeating I forgive you; you'll feel it for yourself. How can you imagine I'd ever conceivably want to disown you—or even blame you in any way? Ah, you don't know a man's heart, Nora. For a man there's something indescribably sweet and satisfying in knowing he's forgiven his wife—and forgiven her out of a full and open heart. It's as if she belongs to him in two ways now: in a sense he's given her fresh into the world again, and she's become his wife and his child as well. From now on that's what you'll be to me—you little, bewildered, helpless thing. Don't be afraid of anything, Nora; just open your heart to me, and I'll be conscience and will to you both— [NORA *enters in her regular clothes.*] What's this? Not in bed? You've changed your dress?

NORA. Yes, Torvald, I've changed my dress.

HELMER. But why now, so late?

NORA. Tonight I'm not sleeping.

HELMER. But Nora dear—

NORA [*looking at her watch*]. It's still not so very late. Sit down, Torvald; we have a lot to talk over. [*She sits at one side of the table.*]

HELMER. Nora—what is this? That hard expression—

NORA. Sit down, This'll take some time. I have a lot to say.

HELMER [*sitting at the table directly opposite her*]. You worry me, Nora. And I don't understand you.

NORA. No, that's exactly it. You don't understand me. And I've never understood you either—until tonight. No, don't interrupt. You can just listen to what I say. We're closing out accounts, Torvald.

HELMER. How do you mean that?

NORA [*after a short pause*]. Doesn't anything strike you about our sitting here like this?

HELMER. What's that?

NORA. We've been married now eight years. Doesn't it occur to you that this is the first time we two, you and I, man and wife, have ever talked seriously together?

HELMER. What do you mean—seriously?

NORA. In eight whole years—longer even—right from our first acquaintance, we've never exchanged a serious word on any serious thing.

HELMER. You mean I should constantly go and involve you in problems you couldn't possibly help me with?

NORA. I'm not talking of problems. I'm saying that we've never sat down seriously together and tried to get to the bottom of anything.

HELMER. But dearest, what good would that ever do you?

NORA. That's the point right there: you've never understood me. I've been wronged greatly, Torvald—first by Papa, and then by you.

HELMER. What! By us—the two people who've loved you more than anyone else?

NORA [*shaking her head*]. You never loved me. You've thought it fun to be in love with me, that's all.

HELMER. Nora, what a thing to say!

NORA. Yes, it's true now, Torvald. When I lived at home with Papa, he told me all his opinions, so I had the same ones too; or if they were different I hid them, since he wouldn't have cared for that. He used to call me his doll-child, and he played with me the way I played with my dolls. Then I came into your house—

HELMER. How can you speak of our marriage like that?

NORA [*unperturbed*]. I mean, then I went from Papa's hands into yours. You arranged everything to your own taste, and so I got the same taste as you—or I pretended to; I can't remember. I guess a little of both, first one, then the other. Now when I look back, it seems as if I'd lived here like a beggar—just from hand to mouth. I've lived by doing tricks for you, Torvald. But that's the way you wanted it. It's a great sin what you and Papa did to me. You're to blame that nothing's become of me.

HELMER. Nora, how unfair and ungrateful you are! Haven't you been happy here?

NORA. No, never. I thought so—but I never have.

HELMER. Not—not happy!

NORA. No, only lighthearted. And you've always been so kind to me. But our home's been nothing but a playpen. I've been your doll-wife here, just as at home I was Papa's doll-child. And in turn the children have been my dolls. I thought it was fun when you played with me, just as they thought it fun when I played with them. That's been our marriage, Torvald.

HELMER. There's some truth in what you're saying—under all the raving exaggeration. But it'll all be different after this. Playtime's over; now for the schooling.

NORA. Whose schooling—mine or the children's?

HELMER. Both yours and the children's, dearest.

NORA. Oh, Torvald, you're not the man to teach me to be a good wife to you.

HELMER. And you can say that?

NORA. And I—how am I equipped to bring up children?

HELMER. Nora!

NORA. Didn't you say a moment ago that that was no job to trust me with?

HELMER. In a flare of temper! Why fasten on that?

NORA. Yes, but you were so very right. I'm not up to the job. There's another job I have to do first. I have to try to educate myself. You can't help me with that. I've got to do it alone. And that's why I'm leaving you now.

HELMER [*jumping up*]. What's that?

NORA. I have to stand completely alone, if I'm ever going to discover myself and the world out there. So I can't go on living with you.

HELMER. Nora, Nora!

NORA. I want to leave right away. Kristine should put me up for the night—

HELMER. You're insane! You've no right! I forbid you!

NORA. From here on, there's no use forbidding me anything. I'll take with me whatever is mine. I don't want a thing from you, either now or later.

HELMER. What kind of madness is this!

NORA. Tomorrow I'm going home—I mean, home where I came from. It'll be easier up there to find something to do.

HELMER. Oh, you blind, incompetent child!

NORA. I must learn to be competent, Torvald.

HELMER. Abandon your home, your husband, your children! And you're not even thinking what people will say.

NORA. I can't be concerned about that. I only know how essential this is.

HELMER. Oh, it's outrageous. So you'll run out like this on your most sacred vows.

NORA. What do you think are my most sacred vows?

HELMER. And I have to tell you that! Aren't they your duties to your husband and children?

NORA. I have other duties equally sacred.

HELMER. That isn't true. What duties are they?

NORA. Duties to myself.

HELMER. Before all else, you're a wife and a mother.

NORA. I don't believe in that anymore. I believe that, before all else, I'm a human being, no less than you—or anyway, I ought to try to become one. I know the majority thinks you're right, Torvald, and plenty of books agree with you, too. But I can't go on believing what the majority says, or what's written in books. I have to think over these things myself and try to understand them.

HELMER. Why can't you understand your place in your own home? On a point like that, isn't there one everlasting guide you can turn to? Where's your religion?

NORA. Oh, Torvald, I'm really not sure what religion is.

HELMER. What—?

NORA. I only know what the minister said when I was confirmed. He told me religion was this thing and that. When I get clear and away by myself, I'll go into that problem too. I'll see if what the minister said was right, or, in any case, if it's right for me.

HELMER. A young woman your age shouldn't talk like that. If religion can't move you, I can try to rouse your conscience. You do have some moral feeling? Or, tell me—has that gone too?

NORA. It's not easy to answer that, Torvald. I simply don't know. I'm all confused about these things. I just know I see them so differently from you. I find out, for one thing, that the law's not at all what I'd thought—but I can't get it through my head that the law is fair. A woman hasn't a right to protect her dying father or save her husband's life! I can't believe that.

HELMER. You talk like a child. You don't know anything of the world you live in.

NORA. No, I don't. But now I'll begin to learn for myself. I'll try to discover who's right, the world or I.

HELMER. Nora, you're sick; you've got a fever. I almost think you're out of your head.

NORA. I've never felt more clearheaded and sure in my life.

HELMER. And—clearheaded and sure—you're leaving your husband and children?

NORA. Yes.

HELMER. Then there's only one possible reason.

NORA. What?

HELMER. You no longer love me.

NORA. No. That's exactly it.

HELMER. Nora! You can't be serious!

NORA. Oh, this is so hard, Torvald—you've been so kind to me always. But I can't help it. I don't love you anymore.

HELMER [*struggling for composure*]. Are you also clearheaded and sure about that?

NORA. Yes, completely. That's why I can't go on staying here.

HELMER. Can you tell me what I did to lose your love?

NORA. Yes, I can tell you. It was this evening when the miraculous thing didn't come—then I knew you weren't the man I'd imagined.

HELMER. Be more explicit; I don't follow you.

NORA. I've waited now so patiently eight long years—for, my Lord, I know miracles don't come every day. Then this crisis broke over me, and such a certainty filled me: *now* the miraculous event would occur. While Krogstad's letter was lying out there, I never for an instant dreamed that you could give in to his terms. I was so utterly sure you'd say to him: go on, tell your tale to the whole wide world. And when he'd done that—

HELMER. Yes, what then? When I'd delivered my own wife into shame and disgrace—!

NORA. When he'd done that, I was so utterly sure that you'd step forward, take the blame on yourself and say: I am the guilty one.

HELMER. Nora—!

NORA. You're thinking I'd never accept such a sacrifice from you? No, of course not. But what good would my protests be against you? That was the miracle I was waiting for, in terror and hope. And to stave that off, I would have taken my life.

HELMER. I'd gladly work for you day and night, Nora—and take on pain and deprivation. But there's no one who gives up honor for love.

NORA. Millions of women have done just that.

HELMER. Oh, you think and talk like a silly child.

NORA. Perhaps. But you neither think nor talk like the man I could join myself to. When your big fright was over—and it wasn't from any threat against me, only for what might damage you—when all the danger was past, for you it was just as if nothing had happened. I was exactly the same, your little lark, your doll, that you'd have to handle with double care now that I'd turned out so brittle and frail. [*Gets up.*] Torvald—in that instant it dawned on me that for eight years I've been living here with a stranger, and that I'd even conceived three children—oh, I can't stand the thought of it! I could tear myself to bits.

HELMER [*heavily*]. I see. There's a gulf that's opened between us—that's clear. Oh, but Nora, can't we bridge it somehow?

NORA. The way I am now, I'm no wife for you.

HELMER. I have the strength to make myself over.

NORA. Maybe—if your doll gets taken away.

HELMER. But to part! To part from you! No, Nora, no—I can't imagine it.

NORA [*going out, right*]. All the more reason why it has to be. [*She re-enters with her coat and a small overnight bag, which she puts on a chair by the table.*]

HELMER. Nora, Nora, not now! Wait till tomorrow.

NORA. I can't spend the night in a strange man's room.

HELMER. But couldn't we live here like brother and sister—

NORA. You know very well how long that would last. [*Throws her shawl about her.*] Good-bye, Torvald. I won't look in on the children. I know they're in better hands than mine. The way I am now, I'm no use to them.

HELMER. But someday, Nora—someday—?

NORA. How can I tell? I haven't the least idea what'll become of me.

HELMER. But you're my wife, now and wherever you go.

NORA. Listen, Torvald—I've heard that when a wife deserts her husband's house just as I'm doing, then the law frees him from all responsibility. In any case, I'm freeing you from being responsible. Don't feel yourself bound, any more than I will. There has to be absolute freedom for us both. Here, take your ring back. Give me mine.

HELMER. That too?

NORA. That too.

HELMER. There it is.

NORA. Good. Well, now it's all over. I'm putting the keys here. The maids know all about keeping up the house—better than I do. Tomorrow, after I've left town, Kristine will stop by to pack up everything that's mine from home. I'd like those things shipped up to me.

HELMER. Over! All over! Nora, won't you ever think about me?

NORA. I'm sure I'll think of you often, and about the children and the house here.

HELMER. May I write you?

NORA. No—never. You're not to do that.

HELMER. Oh, but let me send you—

NORA. Nothing. Nothing.

HELMER. Or help you if you need it.

NORA. No. I accept nothing from strangers.

HELMER. Nora—can I never be more than a stranger to you?

NORA [*picking up the overnight bag*]. Ah, Torvald—it would take the greatest miracle of all—

HELMER. Tell me the greatest miracle!

NORA. You and I both would have to transform ourselves to the point that—Oh, Torvald, I've stopped believing in miracles.

HELMER. But I'll believe. Tell me! Transform ourselves to the point that—?

NORA. That our living together could be a true marriage. [*She goes out down the hall.*]

HELMER [*sinks down on a chair by the door, face buried in his hands*]. Nora! Nora! [*Looking about and rising.*] Empty. She's gone. [*A sudden hope leaps in him.*] The greatest miracle—?

[*From below, the sound of a door slamming shut.*]

Émile Zola

(1840–1902)

The name of the French novelist Émile Zola has come to be almost synonymous with that of the movement he founded, Naturalism. For many readers, especially English-language readers, he is known only as the writer who professed to operate as coldly and dispassionately as a laboratory scientist, trotting his guinea-pig characters through "experiments" designed to prove the hopeless and inexorable workings of "scientific determinism." The reader who gets past handbook definitions of "Naturalism" to turn to Zola's novels is likely to be struck by the disparity between principle and practice. L'Assommoir, Germinal, *and* Nana *are anything but sterile "experiments" in an outdated science. Instead, they are powerful, poetic novels, rich in myth and symbolism, teeming with vivid characters, and full of a romantic "excessiveness," to use one of Zola's own favorite words to describe his work. Zola the artist needs to be separated from his theories and placed in the company of the other great nineteenth-century "excessive" novelists: Balzac, Dickens, Tolstoy, and Dostoevsky.*

Zola was born in Paris in 1840, but was soon taken to Aix-en-Provence, where his father, an Italian engineer, was working on a canal project. The father died when Zola was seven, leaving the family in straitened circumstances. They remained for several years in Aix-en-Provence, where Zola received his early schooling. Baptistin Baille, who later pursued an academic career, and Paul Cézanne, destined for fame as a painter, were his closest friends. The family was forced to move back to Paris in 1857 to seek financial help from friends.

Zola, after completing his education, spent two years in grinding poverty, trying to find a job; the experience provided him with first-hand knowledge of the lives of the poor upon which he was to draw later. He worked for a time as a clerk in a shipping firm, a job he hated, but when he was twenty-two, he finally succeeded in getting a satisfactory job in the sales department of a large Paris publishing company. Stories for Ninon, *a collection of short stories, appeared in 1864, and his first novel,* Claude's Confessions, *followed the next year. Threatened with prosecution for obscenity, Zola resigned the publishing job and made his living by free-lance journalism. In* Thérèse Raquin *(1867) and* Madeleine Férat *(1868), Zola demonstrated his growing commitment to Naturalism and the "scientific" novel; in the preface to* Thérèse Raquin, *he wrote, "I chose persons dominated by their nerves and their blood, deprived of free will, led into every act of their lives by the fatalities of their flesh." Critics met both books with shock and rejection.*

In 1868–69, Zola conceived the mammoth project which was to make him famous. It was the Rougon-Macquart *cycle, a series of novels to be subtitled "The*

Natural and Social History of a Family under the Second Empire." (The Second Empire was the reign of Napoleon III, who seized power in a coup d'état *in 1851; it was to collapse, while Zola's cycle was in progress, in the Franco-Prussian War of 1870.) The cycle was intended to consist of ten novels (it eventually grew to twenty), and Zola expressed his intentions for it in the preface to the first novel of the series:*

> *I wish to show how a family, a small group of human beings, conducts itself in the society in which it is placed, flowering and giving birth to ten, twenty individuals who appear at first glance to be very dissimilar but who, upon examination, are seen to be intimately bound one to the other. Heredity has its laws, like gravity. By taking into account the twin question of temperaments and environments, I shall attempt to find and trace the thread which leads mathematically from one individual to the other. And when I have all the threads, I shall show this group in action in a single period of history.*

The fictional Rougon-Macquart family was to derive from Adélaïde Fouque, an unstable, hysterical woman born in 1768 and married at the age of eighteen to a stolid but ambitious farmer named Rougon, by whom she has one son. When Rougon dies two years later, Adélaïde takes as a lover a violent, alcoholic smuggler named Macquart, by whom she has a son and a daughter. The legitimate branch of the family is ambitious and law-abiding, while the illegitimate Macquart branch is unstable and violent. The unifying characteristic that the family derives from Adélaïde, Zola said, is "its overflow of appetites, the revolutionizing feature of our age, which encourages excessive self-indulgence." Zola based his ideas about heredity on the work of a Dr. Prosper Lucas, who in 1850 had developed a theory of "organic lesions," by which physiological damage to the brain or nervous system could be transmitted to future generations. Zola explained that the appetities of the Rougon-Macquarts were the result of "accidents to the nervous system and blood" of Adélaïde, her husband, and her lover. The Rougon-Macquart *novels were to trace the virtues and vices of the members of the family as they interacted with their physical and social environment.*

The first six novels of the Rougon-Macquart *series attracted some attention, but were only modest successes:* The Fortune of the Rougons *(1871),* The Kill *(1872),* The Belly of Paris *(1873),* The Conquest of Plassans *(1874),* The Abbe Mouret's Sin *(1875), and* His Excellency *(1876). In 1877, however,* L'Assommoir *became an enormous success, made Zola the best known writer in France, and insured the success of the rest of the series.* L'Assommoir *(the title is a piece of untranslatable French slang for a sleazy bar) is the story of Gervaise Macquart, first the mistress of a brutal hatmaker named Auguste Lantier and then the wife of a roofer named Coupeau, who slowly drinks himself to death. Readers were fascinated by Zola's meticulous detailing of slum life and moved by the warmth and compassion with which he drew his heroine, though many critics attacked the book for its sordidness and its "libel" of the working class. But readers bought the book, and within four years it had gone through ninety-one printings.*

A Love Episode *(1878) was followed by* Nana *(1880), the story of a prostitute and an even more spectacular success than* L'Assommoir. *Successive novels—* Piping Hot! *(1882),* The Ladies' Paradise *(1883), and* Joy of Life *(1884)— culminated in what is often regarded as Zola's finest novel:* Germinal *(1885), the epic story of an 1866 miners' strike. (The title, the name of one of the spring months in the French Revolutionary calendar, suggests the myth of death and renewal which runs not only through this novel but through the entire cycle.) The series was completed with* The Masterpiece *(1886),* Earth *(1887),* The Dream *(1888),* The Beast in Man *(1890),* Money *(1891),* The Debacle *(1892), and* Doctor Pascal *(1893). When the cycle was completed, Zola had devoted twenty-one years of his life to it, and it had made him one of the most famous writers in Europe.*

The year after the publication of the last volume in Rougon-Macquart, *Captain Alfred Dreyfus, a Jewish officer in the French army, was court-martialled for selling military secrets to Germany, found guilty, and sentenced to Devil's Island, the French penal colony off the coast of Guiana. Zola and a number of other supporters of Dreyfus believed him to be the innocent victim of anti-semitism and an attempt to conceal the real culprit, a Major Walsin-Esterhazy. After several years of controversy, Esterhazy was brought to trial in 1898 and, against the evidence, was acquitted. Zola immediately wrote a strong open letter to the President of France, entitled "I Accuse," and published it in a friendly newspaper. He openly accused officers of the Dreyfus court-martial and other high officers in the war office of lying and framing Dreyfus in order to hide Esterhazy's guilt. Zola's strategy was to provoke a libel suit in which the facts of the case could come out. He had his way: a fifteen-day trial, conducted unfairly by a hostile judge, ended in Zola's conviction and sentencing to a year in prison, with a large fine. On appeal, a new trial was granted, but Zola fled to England before the trial, hoping the passage of time would swing events in Dreyfus's favor. He was right; during his exile, a leading officer responsible for Dreyfus's conviction committed suicide, Esterhazy himself fled and confessed, and a new trial was ordered. The second court-martial brought in the absurd verdict of "guilty with extenuating circumstances"; Dreyfus was "pardoned" in 1899 and completely exonerated in 1906.*

Zola immediately returned to France when he received news that Dreyfus had been granted a new trial. In the midst of the Dreyfus controversy, he had completed a new, three-novel cycle called The Three Cities *(*Lourdes, *1894;* Rome, *1896; and* Paris, *1898), and now he vigorously continued work on a four-novel cycle called* The Four Gospels. Fruitfulness *was published in 1899,* Labor *in 1901, and* Truth *posthumously in 1903. A fourth novel,* Justice, *was never written, for on September 28, 1902, Zola was asphyxiated by carbon monoxide from a blocked chimney in his Paris home; his wife was also overcome but was saved. There is some inconclusive evidence that the chimney had been sabotaged by Dreyfus's enemies.*

Zola's great strengths as a writer—his meticulous descriptions of ordinary activities, his epic handling of crowd scenes, his power to raise realistic action to the level of myth, and his flowing, eloquent style—can be fully represented only by one of his major novels. But he also wrote a number of powerful short stories, often tossed off for magazines in the midst of his intensive work on his novels. "The Inundation" appeared in magazine form in 1875 and was reprinted in 1883 as part of the short-story collection Captain Burle. *The line between fact and fiction is characteristically thin in this story; it deals with a sensational news item, a flood which had ravaged the Garonne river valley in the Toulouse area two months before. The family in the story is fictional, but Zola presents the incident as typical of the suffering which the flood had caused. Zola's celebrated "research" in this case consisted only of memories of a railway journey through the area five years before and his reading of newspaper accounts of the disaster. (It has been pointed out that people drowned in the village of Saint-Jory could not be washed up at Toulouse, as happens at the end of the story.)*

But literal accuracy is subordinate to the imagination in this spare, tragic tale. Zola shapes his journalistic material to make it a Naturalistic Book of Job. This is an initiation story, in which Louis Roubieu looks back upon the ordeal which turned him from a prosperous, complacent bourgeois *into a shattered, haunted survivor crying out, "O God, why wilt Thou have me stay?" The use of Louis Roubieu as narrator gives the simple narrative two levels, one the brutal story of the flood itself, the other the story of Roubieu's compressed and long-delayed initiation into the blind, inhuman cruelty of the universe. Nature turns, for Roubieu, from the friendly partner of the beginning of the story into a terrifyingly indifferent killer, and he cries out, at the crucial moment of realization, "I recalled our afternoon walk, the meadows, the wheat fields, the vineyards, all so promising! They had all lied! Happiness had lied!" This brief, horrifying story captures something not only of Zola's fierce, uncompromising vision but also of his deep compassion for suffering humanity.*

FURTHER READING *(prepared by N. K. B.):* Joanna Richardson's illustrated *Zola,* 1978, is a balanced biography, particularly thorough on Zola's involvement with the Dreyfus case. Frederick William Hemmings, *Émile Zola,* 1953, rev. 1966, is an essential critical work on Zola, and his later study, *Life and Times of Émile Zola,* 1977, is equally illuminating. Jean-Albert Bédé, *Émile Zola,* 1974, is a brief reference guide, highlighting the key biographical events and literary works. E. M. Grant, *Émile Zola,* 1966, describes the biographical background and surveys chronologically Zola's works, themes, and techniques. Graham King, *Garden of Zola: Émile Zola and His Novels for English Readers,* 1978, explicates the fiction in detail and has an interesting chapter on translations of Zola, "The Perils of an English Reader." Winston R. Hewitt, *Through Those Living Pillars: Man and Nature in the Works of Émile Zola,* 1974, explores the importance of nature and natural imagery in Zola's works. Both Harry Levin, *The Gates of Horn: A Study of Five French Realists,* 1963, rev. 1966, and Martin Turnell, *The Art of French Fiction,* 1959, contain chapters on Zola's themes and techniques, placing him in the context of nineteenth-century French literature. Angus Wilson's study, *Émile Zola: An Introductory Study of His Novels,* 1952, is a provocative Freudian analysis.

THE INUNDATION[1]

Translated by Edward Vizetelly

I

My name is Louis Roubieu. I am seventy years of age and was born in the village of Saint-Jory, at a few leagues from Toulouse, on the banks of the Garonne. During fourteen years I battled with the soil in order to obtain from it enough bread to feed me. Affluence came at last, and only a month ago I was the richest farmer of the whole countryside.

Our home was blessed. Happiness had its abode under our roof. The sun was our ally, and I do not remember a bad harvest. We were nearly a dozen at the farm, all sharing the same happiness: myself, still hale and

[1] *L'Inondation* (English, "the inundation") is the French term used both for an ordinary flood and for the biblical Flood.

hearty, teaching the young ones how to work; my younger brother Pierre, a bachelor and formerly a sergeant in the army; my sister Agathe, a shrewd housewife, extremely stout and gay, who had come to live with us after her husband's death and whose laughter rang out from one end of the village to the other. Next came the whole brood: my son Jacques and Rose, his wife, with their three daughters, Aimée, Véronique and Marie. The first was married to Cyprien Bouisson, a strapping young fellow, to whom she had given two babies, one two years old and the other ten months old; Véronique, on her side, had just become engaged to Gaspard Rabuteau, while Marie, blond and very fair, looked more like a town-born lady than a farmer's daughter. This made up ten; I was both a grandfather and a great-grandfather.

When we assembled round the supper table I used to place my sister Agathe on my right, my brother Pierre on my left, and the children completed the circle, seated by order of seniority, down to the mite but ten months old. The whole lot ate heartily, and how gay they all were between each mouthful! I felt both pride and pleasure glowing in my veins when the little ones, stretching out their hands to me, shouted:

"Grandfather, give us some more bread. A big piece, Grandfather, please!"

Those were glorious days. The busy house sang through all its windows; in the evenings Pierre invented new games or told old stories of his regiment; on Sundays Aunt Agathe baked cakes for the girls, and Marie knew some beautiful hymns which she sang with the voice of a young chorister, looking like a saint, too, with her fair hair falling low on her neck and her hands folded in her lap. At the time of Aimée's marriage with Cyprien I had added a story to the house, and I used to say jokingly that when Véronique married Gaspard I should have to add another, and that if I did so at each successive wedding the house would end by reaching the sky. None of us wanted to leave it; we would rather have erected a town in the enclosure behind the farm. When the members of a large family agree, it is good to live and die on the spot where one was born.

This last spring the month of May was superb; the crops had not looked so promising for years. That day I went the round of the land with my son Jacques. We started at about three o'clock. Our meadows, still of a tender green, stretched alongside the Garonne; the grass had nearly reached its full height, and in a willow copse planted only last year there were shoots a yard long. We passed on, examining our cornfields and vineyards, the land bought bit by bit as our means increased. The wheat was growing apace; the vines were in full bloom, heralding a rich vintage. Jacques laughed his hearty laugh and, slapping me on the shoulder, said: "Well, Father, we shan't lack bread or wine. You must be in the good graces of God Almighty, as He lets money rain upon your land like this."

Jacques was right. I had no doubt gained the good graces of some saint in heaven, for all the good luck of the district appeared to fall on us. During a storm the hail would stop at the edge of our fields; if our neighbors' vines were ailing a protecting wall seemed to rise around ours, and gradually I had come to deem this just. Harming no one, I believed happiness to be my due.

On our way home we crossed some land belonging to us on the opposite side of the village. A plantation of mulberry trees was coming on splendidly, and the almond trees in a grove were bearing all they could. We chatted gaily and made plans for the future. As soon as we had saved the necessary capital, we would purchase certain patches of ground lying between our various lots and thus become the owners of an entire corner of the parish. If the crops turned out as well as they promised, our dream could be realized in the autumn.

As we drew near the farm we saw Rose gesticulating and shouting: "Come on, hurry up!"

One of our cows had just calved, and the whole household was astir. Aunt Agathe went rolling about, while the girls watched the little calf, whose advent seemed like an additional benison. Quite recently we had been compelled to enlarge our sheds, which contained nearly a hundred head of cattle without reckoning the horses.

"Another lucky day," I said. "We must have a bottle of good wine tonight."

Just then Rose took us aside to inform us that as Gaspard, Véronique's lover, had come to fix the wedding day, she had kept him to dinner. Gaspard, the eldest son of a farmer of Moranges, was a young man of twenty, known all through our part for his prodigious strength. At a public fete at Toulouse he had wrestled with and defeated Martial, the Lion of the South. Withal he was extremely good-natured and tenderhearted and so shy, indeed, that he blushed whenever Véronique's calm eyes met his own.

I told Rose to call him. He had stayed in the yard, helping the maids to hang out the linen of a three months' washing. When he entered the parlor, where we were all assembled, Jacques turned to me, saying, "It's for you to speak, Father."

"Well, my boy, you have come to settle the day," I said.

"Yes, that's why I came," he answered with a deep color on his cheeks.

"Don't blush, my lad," I resumed. "Shall we say the tenth of July, the day of Sainte Félicité? Today's the twenty-eighth of June, so you won't have long to wait. My poor dead wife's name was Félicité—it will be a good omen. Well, is it a settled thing?"

"Yes, all right; the day of Sainte Félicité will do," replied Gaspard.

Then, as he came up to Jacques and me, his hand fell on our outstretched palms with a might sufficient to fell an ox. Next he kissed Rose, calling her "mother." This stalwart young fellow with such redoubtable fists was losing sleep and flesh for love of Véronique; he told us that he should have fallen ill if we had not consented to let him have her.

"Now," I resumed, "let us go to our meal. All of you to your places. Thunder and lightning! I am as hungry as a wolf!"

That evening we sat down eleven. We had placed Gaspard and Véronique side by side, and he kept gazing at her, forgetting his supper and so disturbed by the thought that she was his that big tears moistened his eyelashes. Cyprien and Aimée, who had been married three years, smiled as they watched them; Jacques and Rose, with their twenty-five years of wedlock, were graver, still they stealthily exchanged moist glances, born of long-abiding tenderness. As for myself, I felt as if I were growing young again and living anew in those lovers, whose happiness seemed to bring a nook of paradise to our board. How excellent the soup tasted that evening! Aunt Agathe, who was always one for laughing, ventured to make a few jocose remarks, whereupon Pierre insisted upon relating his love passages with a lady of Lyons. Fortunately we had got to the dessert and were all talking at the same time. I had brought two bottles of sweet wine from the cellar, and we drank to Gaspard and Véronique's good luck, as the fashion is with us. Luck is never to quarrel, to have heaps of children and put by bags of money. Later on we had some singing; Gaspard knew some love ballads in our dialect, and by way of conclusion we asked Marie for a hymn. She stood up and began at once, her flutelike and delicate voice falling like a caress on the ear.

I had moved toward the window, and as Gaspard joined me I said, "There is nothing new over your way, is there?"

"No," he answered; "they talk a good deal about the heavy rains of the last few days; some say they might turn out badly."

It had, indeed, recently been raining during sixty consecutive hours, and since the previous day the Garonne had been greatly swollen; still we trusted her, and as long as she did not overflow we could not think of her as a dangerous neighbor. She was so useful; her expanse of water was so broad and gentle, and, moreover, peasants do not readily quit their homes even if the roof be about to fall.

"Nonsense," I said; "nothing will happen; it's the same every year. The river puts up its back as if it were in a rage, then it quiets down in a single night and subsides as gently as a lamb. Take my word, lad, it's only a joke. Just look out of the window and see what splendid weather we are having!"

Then with my hand I pointed to the sky.

It was seven o'clock; the sun was setting. All was blue; the sky showed like an immense expanse of azure, through which the sunset swam like golden dust. From above there slowly descended a delight, reaching to the verge of the distant horizon. I had never seen the village in such tender restfulness. A pink glow was fading under the eaves. I could hear a neighbor laughing and children chattering at the bend of the road opposite our house, while from farther off the lowing of herds returning to their sheds reached us, softened by the distance.

Meanwhile the deep roar of the Garonne sounded incessantly, but I was so used to the voice of the river that it seemed to be merely the voice of silence. By degrees the sky whitened and the village seemed falling into a serener sleep. It was the end of a beautiful day, and I fancied that all our happiness, our rich harvests, Véronique's engagement, came to us wafted from above, in the purity of the dying light. A benediction spread over us with the farewell of day.

I had returned to the center of the room where the girls were chatting merrily, and we were listening to them with smiling lips when suddenly, through the great peace of the twilight, an appalling shriek rang out—a shriek of terror and of death:

"The Garonne! The Garonne!"

II

We ran to the yard.

Saint-Jory lies at the very bottom of a dip in the land, lower than the river and some five hundred yards away from it. A screen of poplars dividing some meadows shuts out all view of the water.

We could see nothing, but the shriek still resounded: "The Garonne! The Garonne!"

Then coming from the road in front of us, two men and three women abruptly appeared, one of the latter holding a child in her arms. They were shouting, frenzied with terror, and running as fast as they could over the hard ground. Every now and then they looked back with scared faces, as if they were being pursued by a pack of wolves.

"What has happened?" cried Cyprien. "Can you make out anything, Grandfather?"

"No," I answered; "the leaves are not even stirring."

The low line of the horizon lay still and peaceful, but before I had done speaking a sharp exclamation broke from the others. Behind the fugitives, between the trunks of the poplars, over the tall grass, we caught sight of something resembling a pack of gray, yellowish spotted animals racing onward. They appeared on all sides—waves hurrying upon waves, an invasion of masses of water crested with foam, shaking white saliva, and making the ground quiver with the heavy gallop of their serried[2] ranks.

Then we also echoed the despairing cry, "The Garonne! The Garonne!"

The two men and the three women were still flying along the road, and they could hear the hideous gallop gaining upon them. Presently the waves formed in a single line, rolling and crashing with the thunder of charging battalions. Under their first onset three poplars snapped; their tall foliage tottered and disappeared. Then a shed was swollen up; a wall burst; unharnessed carts were carried away like wisps of straw. But the water seemed specially to pursue the fugitives. At a bend of the road, which is very steep at that particular spot, the flood suddenly fell in immense volume, cutting off their retreat. We saw them still attempting to run, splashing in the water, but silent now and maddened with fear. The waves rose to their knees; at last a huge billow dashed upon the woman who was carrying the child. Then all were submerged.

"Quick, quick!" I cried, "Come in! The house is strong. We have nothing to fear."

However, out of prudence we at once ascended to the second floor, making the girls pass before us; I was determined to be the last. Our house was built on a bank above the road, and the water was now slowly invading the yard with a soft little ripple. We were not much alarmed.

"Never mind," said Jacques reassuringly; "there is no danger. Do you remember, Father, how in '55 the water came into the yard just as it does now? It rose to a foot and then receded."

"It's a pity for the crops, anyhow," muttered Cyprien, half aloud.

"No, no; it won't be much," I said, noting the dilated, questioning eyes of the women. Aimée had laid her children on her bed and sat close to

[2] In dense rows.

them with Véronique and Marie. Aunt Agathe talked of warming some wine which she had brought with her in order to cheer us. Jacques and Rose looked out of the window, and I stood at the other with my brother, Cyprien and Gaspard.

"Come up, can't you?" I called to the two maids who were paddling about in the yard. "Don't stop there and get your legs wet."

"But the poor beasts," they answered; "they are frightened and will get killed in the sheds."

"Never mind! Come up. We will look after the cattle presently."

If the water continued to rise it would be impossible to save the cattle, but I thought it best not to alarm the servants. I tried to appear quite at ease and, leaning over the window sill, I gave an account of the progress of the flood. After rushing to the assault of the village the river had taken possession of even its narrowest lanes. The race of the charging waves had ceased; there was now a stealthy, invincible invasion. The hollow in which Saint-Jory lies was being transformed into a lake. In our yard the water had risen to a height of three feet already: I watched its ascent, but I affirmed that it remained stationary, and once I even hinted that it was subsiding.

"You will have to sleep here tonight, my boy," I said, turning to Gaspard; "that is, unless the roads get clear in a few hours, which might easily be the case."

He looked at me; his face was very pale, and I saw his eyes turn to Véronique, gleaming the while with intolerable anguish.

It was half-past eight. Out of doors it was still light—a white glimmer, unspeakably mournful, dropping from the pale sky. Before the maids joined us they had thought of bringing two lamps. I had them lit, hoping that they would brighten the darkening room in which we had taken refuge. Aunt Agathe now pushed a table forward and suggested a game of cards. The excellent woman, whose eyes sought mine anxiously every now and then, was especially desirous of diverting the children: her cheerfulness was grandly brave, and she laughed to conjure away the terror which she felt was creeping over all the others. The game was arranged; Aunt Agathe forced Aimée, Véronique and Marie into their chairs, placed the cards in their resistless fingers and began shuffling, dealing and cutting with such a flow of words that she almost stifled the sound of the rising flood. But our daughters could not fix their minds on the game; they remained pale, with feverish hands, bending their heads to listen. Every now and then one or another of them would turn uneasily and whisper:

"Grandfather, is it still rising?"

It *was* rising with fearful rapidity, but I answered carelessly, "No, no; go on playing—there is no danger."

Never before had I felt my heart wrung by such cruel dread. All the men had grouped themselves in front of the windows to shut out the appalling scene; we tried to look unconcerned when our faces were turned to the room, facing the lamps whose circular light fell on the table as amid the gentle peace of homely vigils. I remembered winter evenings when we had sat thus at the table. It was the same quiet picture, full of the soft warmth of affection. But while perfect peace dwelt within, I could hear behind my back the bellowing of the overflowing river, which was ever rising and rushing onward.

"Louis," whispered my brother Pierre, "the water is only three feet from the window; something must be done."

I pressed his arm to silence him, but it was too late to conceal our peril. The cattle had become frantic in the outhouses: we plainly heard the bleating and lowing of the maddened animals and particularly the wild shrieks of the horses who felt themselves in danger.

"Oh my God! My God!" murmured Aimée, who stood up, convulsed by a long shudder and with her closed fists pressed to her temples.

The women had all risen, and we were powerless to keep them from the windows; they stood there erect and mute, their hair lifted by a wind of terror. The twilight had come; a treacherous gleam hovered above the watery sheet; the pale sky looked like a white pall thrown over the earth; afar off some smoke was trailing; then everything became blurred: it was the close of a day of horror, sinking into a night of death. And not a human sound—only the dull roar of the infinitely widening expanse of water and the lowing and neighing of the frenzied animals!

"Oh God! Oh God!" repeated the women under their breath, as if afraid to speak aloud.

A loud crash silenced them. The infuriated cattle had broken through the stable doors; they passed by in the yellow flood, rolling as they were carried away by the current; the sheep were hurled along in droves like dead leaves whirling in pools; the cows and the horses struggled, trying to feel the ground but losing their footing; our big gray horse refused to die: he reared, stretched out his long neck and panted like the bellows of a forge till the eager waters dashed on his hindquarters, and then we saw him yield himself up and disappear.

Then for the first time we screamed; our cries seemed to come unconsciously, propelled by some alien will. With hands outstretched toward all those dear animals hurried away forever, we moaned and wept, sobbing aloud, giving vent to the tears and lamentations we had restrained. It was indeed our ruin! The crops lost, the cattle drowned, our fortune gone in a few brief hours! Oh, God was not just! We had not offended Him, and yet He had taken back all He had given! I shook my fist at heaven! I recalled our afternoon walk, the meadows, the wheat fields, the vineyards, all so promising! They had all lied! Happiness had lied! The very sun, when he had set so gently and calmly in the deep serenity of evening, had lied.

The flood was still rising, and all at once my brother Pierre, who had been watching it, exclaimed sharply: "Louis, look out! The water has reached the windows. We can't stay here."

These words broke upon our despair. I pulled myself together and, shrugging my shoulders, said, "After all, money is nothing. As long as we are all together and safe there is nothing to regret. We must begin work afresh; that is all."

"Yes, yes—you are right, Father," returned Jacques feverishly, "and we *are* safe—the walls are solid. Let us get upon the roof."

It was our only refuge. The water, after mounting the staircase step by step with a persevering gurgle, was entering at the door. We repaired to the loft, keeping close together, with the vague instinct which makes people in peril anxious to remain side by side. Cyprien alone had vanished. I called to him, and he came out of an adjoining room with a white, scared face. Then as I suddenly became aware of the absence of the two maids and stopped to wait for them, he looked at me strangely and whispered:

"Dead—the outbuilding where their room was has just given way."

The poor creatures must have gone to get their savings out of their boxes. Cyprien, in the same tone, told me that they had managed to throw a ladder across to the building where they slept and had used it as a bridge. I warned him to say nothing, but I felt a great chill at the back of my neck. It was the breath of death entering our house.

We did not even think of turning out the lamps when we went up to the roof in our turn; the cards remained spread out on the table; there was a foot of water in the room.

III

Fortunately the roof was broad and the incline a gentle one. It was reached by a skylight opening on to a little platform, upon which our party took refuge. The women sat down, and presently the men stepped out on the tiles to reconnoiter, going as far as the two tall chimney stacks at either end of the roof. I remained leaning against the aperture of the skylight, looking toward the four points of the horizon.

"Help cannot fail to come soon," I said with forced hopefulness. "The folks of Saintin have some boats, and they will pass this way. See over there, isn't that a lantern on the water?"

I received no answer. Pierre had mechanically lighted his pipe and was smoking so furiously that with every puff he spat out bits of the stem which he had broken between his teeth. Jacques and Cyprien stared into the distance with mournful faces, while Gaspard, with clenched fists, went on pacing the roof as if seeking for some outlet. The women, crouching and shuddering at our feet, covered their eyes to avoid the terrible sight. Presently, however, Rose, raising her head, looked round her.

"Where are the servants?" she asked. "Why don't they come up?"

I pretended not to hear, but she turned to me and fixed her eyes on mine.

"Where are the girls?" she repeated.

I turned away. I could not lie to her, and I felt that the deadly chill which had already touched me was passing over our wives and daughters. They had understood. Marie rose to her full height; a deep sigh parted her lips, and then, sinking down, she burst into a passion of tears. Aimée kept the heads of her two children in her lap, covering them up with her skirts as if to shield them. Véronique, who had her face in her hands, remained motionless. Aunt Agathe, growing paler, was repeatedly making the sign of the cross and muttering Paters and Aves.

All around us the scene was one of supreme grandeur. The night, which had now completely fallen, had the clear limpidity of summer darkness. There was no moon as yet, but the sky was studded with countless stars, and it was of so pure a blue that all the surrounding space was filled with an azure light. The horizon was so clearly defined that it seemed to harbor the twilight, and meanwhile the immense sheet of water, spreading out under the soft skies, became quite white, luminous as with a glow of its own, a phosphorescence which tipped the crest of every wave with tiny flamelets. Land was nowhere visible; the whole plain must have been submerged. One evening on the coast near Marseilles I had seen the sea looking like this and had remained gazing at it, transfixed with admiration.

"The water rises; the water rises," repeated my brother Pierre, still biting the stem of his pipe, which he had allowed to go out.

Indeed, the water was now only a yard from the edge of the roof. It was losing its tranquillity, its lakelike quietude, and currents were forming. When it reached a certain height we were no longer sheltered by the rising ground before the village, and as soon as this was covered, in less than an hour's time, the flood became threatening, lashing the houses with all the wreckage, staved-in barrels, timbers and trusses of hay, which it carried on its bosom. In the distance we heard the deafening shocks of the onsets against the walls. Poplars snapped and fell with a sinister splash, and houses crashed down like cartfuls of stones turned over on the roadside.

Jacques, unnerved by the women's sobs, kept on repeating: "We cannot stop here. Something must be done. Father, I implore you, let us try something."

Hesitating and stammering, I repeated after him: "Yes, yes, let us try something."

And none of us knew what to try. Gaspard proposed that he should take Véronique on his back and swim away with her. Pierre suggested a raft. They were both crazy. At last, however, Cyprien said: "If we could only reach the church."

And, indeed, high above the flood the church still rose up intact with its little square tower. We were separated from it by seven dwellings. Our house, the first of the village, adjoined a taller building, which in its turn leaned against its neighbor. It might be feasible to reach the presbytery by the roofs, and thence it would be easy to get into the church. Many of the villagers had already sought that refuge probably, for the neighboring roofs were deserted, and we heard a murmur of voices which certainly came from the belfry. But at best it was a perilous and uncertain undertaking.

"It is impossible," said Pierre. "Rambeau's house is too lofty; we should need some ladders."

"At any rate, I'll go and see," said Cyprien. "If we cannot get across I'll return; if we can we must all go, the men carrying the women."

I let him start. He was right: situated as we were, everything must be attempted. With the help of an iron clamp fixed to a chimney stack he had just succeeded in climbing onto the next house when his wife Aimée raised her eyes and saw that he was gone.

"Where is he?" she said. "I will not let him leave me. We are one—we must die together."

Then as she caught sight of him on the other roof she darted across the tiles, still carrying her children.

"Wait for me, Cyprien," she panted; "I am coming with you. I will die with you."

She would not be denied. Her husband, leaning over, implored her to remain with us, promising to return and assuring her that he was only acting for our common rescue. But shaking her head and with a wild look in her eyes, she still repeated excitedly: "I am coming with you. I will die with you."

He yielded; first he took the children, and then he helped his wife to climb up to him. We could see them walking slowly on the apex of the roof. Aimée had again taken her weeping children in her arms, and at every step Cyprien turned and supported her.

"As soon as she is in safety," I shouted, "come back to us."

I saw him wave his hand, but the roar of the water did not allow me to hear his answer. They were soon out of sight; they had descended onto the house beyond, the roof of which was lower. Five minutes later they again appeared on the third roof, which must have been very steep, for we could see that they were crawling up it on their knees. A sudden dread possessed me and, raising my hands to my mouth, I shouted out with all my strength: "Come back, come back!"

All of us, Pierre, Jacques and Gaspard, called to them to return; our voices seemed to stay them for a moment, but they soon moved on. They had reached the corner where the street turned in front of Rambeau's house, a tall building rising nearly nine feet above all the neighboring roofs. For a moment they wavered, and then Cyprien began to climb up a chimney with catlike agility. Aimée, who had evidently consented to wait for him, remained erect amid the tiles. We could plainly distinguish her clasping her babies to her bosom, standing out black against the clear sky and looking much taller than she really was. It was then that the awful catastrophe began.

Rambeau's house, originally intended for some business purposes, was very flimsily built, and, moreover, its frontage received the full shock of the current in the street. I fancied I could see it tremble under the onset of flood, and with bated breath I watched Cyprien's progress along the roof. Suddenly we heard a deep growl. The round moon had risen, freely pacing the sky, her yellow disk lighting up the immense lake with the clear brightness of a lamp. Not a single detail was lost to us. That growl was the noise of Rambeau's house falling in. A scream of terror escaped us as we saw Cyprien sink down. In that tempestuous crash we could only see the splashing of the waves under the remnants of the roof. Then all was calm again; the lake became level once more, with the black carcass of the submerged house bristling above the water with its snapped floors—a confused mass of tangled timbers, looking like the framework of some half-destroyed cathedral. Between those timbers I thought I could see a body moving, a living form wrestling with superhuman efforts.

"He lives!" I cried. "Ah, blessed be God, he lives! There, above that white sheet of water lit up by the moon!"

We shook with hysterical laughter and clapped our hands for joy, as if all danger had passed away.

"He will get up again," said Pierre.

"Yes, yes," explained Gaspard. "See? He is trying to catch hold of the beam on his left."

But our laughter was suddenly hushed. We remained dumb, silenced by anxiety. We had just realized in what an awful position Cyprien had now found himself. In the fall of the house his feet had been caught between two beams, and he was hanging head downward at a few inches above the water and quite unable to free himself. His agony was horrible. On the roof of the other house stood Aimée with her two children, shaken by convulsive shudders. There she remained, a witness of her husband's death struggle, never once taking her eyes off him. From her rigid lips there came a continuous lugubrious sound, like the howl of a dog frenzied by terror.

"We cannot let him die like that," said Jacques in distraction. "We must go to him."

"One might crawl down the beams, perhaps," muttered Pierre, "and disengage him."

They were already moving toward the nearest roof when the house it covered suddenly shook and crumbled in its turn. The way was cut off. Our blood froze in our veins. We seized each other's hands and pressed them nervously, unable to turn our eyes away from the ghastly sight.

Cyprien had at first attempted to stiffen himself, and with extraordinary muscular strength he had finally succeeded in getting farther away from the water and maintaining a sidelong position. But fatigue was mastering him; he tried to resist, to lay hold of the beams, beating the air with his arms in the hope of finding something to which he might cling; then, accepting death, he fell back and again hung down quite motionless. Death was slow to come; his hair barely touched the water, which was patiently rising—he must have felt its coolness on his head. A first wave wet his brow; another closed his eyes—slowly his head vanished from our view.

The women, huddled at our feet, hid their faces with their clasped hands. We fell on our knees with outstretched arms, stammering supplications and crying bitterly. On the other roof Aimée, still erect, with her children close pressed to her bosom, shrieked still louder and louder amid the night.

IV

I cannot tell how long the stupor of that crisis lasted. When I recovered my senses the water was higher still; it now reached the tiles, and our roof was only a narrow island, barely emerging from the immense watery expanse. On the right and left the houses had fallen. The sea was widening on all sides.

"We are moving," whispered Rose as she clutched at the tiles.

And, indeed, we all felt a pitching motion, as if the roof had changed into a floating raft; the heavy swell seemed to carry us along. It was only by turning to the motionless church tower that we got rid of this delusion and realized that we were on the same spot amid the angry surf.

It was then that the siege began in earnest. The current so far had followed the street, but the increasing wreckage that barred the way now caused it to flow back. A furious onset commenced. As soon as a plank or beam passed within the current's grasp it was seized, swung round and hurled like a ram against our house; the water never loosened its grasp; the current sucked the wreckage back merely to launch it again at our walls, which it assailed with regular repeated blows. Sometimes ten or twelve large pieces of wood would attack us at once on all sides. The water hissed; foamy splashes wet our feet. We heard the dull moan of the sonorous house filling with water and the creaking of the broken partitions, and whenever a more savage assault made the whole building quiver, we fancied that it was all over—that the walls were opening and giving us up to the river through their yawning breaches.

Gaspard, who had ventured to the very edge of the roof, succeeded in catching a passing beam, which he dragged out of the water with his powerful athletic arms.

"We must defend ourselves," he shouted.

Then Jacques, with the assistance of Pierre, endeavored to stop a long pole. I cursed my old age, which left me useless and as weak as a child. However, the defense was being organized; it was the fight of three men against the flood. Gaspard, armed with his beam, waited for the passing timbers, which the current turned into battering-rams, and kept them off at some little distance from the walls. The shock at times was so great that he fell down. Meantime Pierre and Jacques were maneuvering with their long pole, shoving away the nearer wreckage.

This fierce and senseless battle lasted during nearly an hour. As the time passed the combatants grew wildly excited; they beat the water, insulted it and swore at it. Gaspard hacked at it as if in a bodily struggle, lunged out with his beam as if he were trying to pierce a human breast. And all this time the water remained quietly obstinate, without a wound—invincible. Jacques and Pierre at last sank down on the roof, exhausted, and Gaspard, while making a final effort, saw the current wrest his beam from his grasp and hurl it against us. The struggle had become impossible.

Marie and Véronique, clasped in each other's arms, were repeating the same words in broken tones—words of terror, the echo of which still sounds incessantly in my ears: "I will not die! I will not die!"

Rose embraced them both, trying to reassure and comfort them, but at last she herself, trembling and shivering, lifted her white face and unconsciously cried aloud, "I will not die!"

Aunt Agathe alone remained quite silent. She had ceased praying and crossing herself. In a sort of dumb stupor she now let her eyes wander over the scene, and whenever they chanced to meet mine she still attempted a smile.

The water was lapping the tiles. No help could reach us now. We still heard the sound of voices issuing from the church; two lanterns had gleamed for an instant in the distance, then again the silence deepened amid the desolate immensity of the yellow expanse. In all probability the people of Saintin who owned some boats had been surprised by the flood before us.

Gaspard was still wandering about the roof, and suddenly he called to us, saying: "Look out! Help me—hold me tight!"

He had again snatched hold of a passing timber and was lying in wait for a huge black mass which was slowly swimming toward us. It was the broad, solid plank roof of a shed, wrenched away entire and floating like a raft. When it came within reach Gaspard arrested it, and, feeling that he was being dragged off, he called to us to help him. We seized him round the waist and clasped him tight. As soon as the wreck entered the current it advanced of its own accord against our roof, coming forward with so much violence that for a moment we feared we should see it fly asunder.

However, Gaspard boldly jumped upon this raft thus sent to us by Providence; he walked all over it to make sure of its strength, while Jacques and Pierre maintained it in position at the edge of our roof. Then he began to laugh and said exultingly, "You see, Grandfather, we are saved. Come, you women, leave off crying! It is as good as a real boat. Look here, my feet are dry. It can carry us all too. It feels like home already."

However, he thought it better to strengthen it and, securing some more beams, he bound them with some ropes which Pierre had happened to bring up with him on the chance of their being wanted. While thus engaged Gaspard once fell overboard, but he soon came up again and answered our cry of alarm with renewed hilarity.

"The Garonne knows me," he laughed; "I have often swum it for a league at a time." Then when he had got on the roof again he shook himself and exclaimed, "Come aboard—there's no time to lose!"

The women had fallen on their knees, and Gaspard had to carry Véronique and Marie to the middle of the raft, where he made them sit down. Rose and Agathe slipped off the tiles unaided and joined the girls. At that moment I again glanced toward the church. Aimée was still on the same roof, only she was now leaning against a chimney stack, holding her children aloft with rigidly uplifted arms. The water had risen to her waist.

"Do not worry, Grandfather," said Gaspard. "I promise you that we'll pick her up as we pass by."

Pierre and Jacques were already on the raft. I jumped after them. It tilted over a little on one side but seemed strong enough to carry us all. Gaspard was the last to leave the roof and gave each of us one of the poles which he had in readiness to be used as oars, he himself keeping a very long one, which he handled with great dexterity. He had taken command, and by his instructions we all pressed against the tiles with our poles, trying to shove off. But our efforts were fruitless; the raft seemed to adhere to the roof; at every fresh attempt we made the current hurled us back against the house. We were incurring great danger, for every fresh shock threatened to shatter the boards on which we stood.

Once more we became conscious of our impotency. We had thought ourselves saved, but we still belonged to the greedy river. I even began to regret that the women had left the roof, for I expected every minute to see them hurled into the furious water and carried away. But when I suggested that we should return to the house they one and all rebelled.

"No, no, let us try again," they pleaded, "or die here."

Gaspard was not laughing now. We multiplied our efforts, weighing on the poles with feverish strength, but all in vain. At last Pierre had an idea. He climbed onto the roof again and with a long rope managed to pull the raft to the left and get it out of the current. Then after he had jumped onto the raft again a few strokes of our poles enabled us to get into the open.

But Gaspard remembered his promise to rescue my poor Aimée, whose plaintive wail had not once ceased. To effect the rescue it was necessary to cross the street where raged that terrible current against which we had fought so desperately. He cast a questioning look at me. I was overcome. Never had I been placed in so cruel an alternative. Eight lives must be endangered, and yet if for their sakes I hesitated just one moment, I lacked the strength to resist the mother's lugubrious call.

"Yes, yes," I said to Gaspard. "We cannot go without her."

He bent his head in silence and began to ply his pole, taking advantage of such walls as were still standing. We slowly skirted the adjoining house, passing over our own cowsheds, but as soon as we turned the bend of the street we shrieked aloud. The current had captured us again and was carrying us off, forcing us back to our roof.

It lasted only a few seconds. We were indeed whirled away so suddenly that the screams we immediately raised expired amid the deafening crash of the raft against the tiles. It was rent asunder; the shivered boards were scattered, and we were hurled into the foaming whirlpool. I do not know what followed. I only remember that as I fell I saw Aunt Agathe lying at full length on the water, buoyed up by her skirts. Then without a struggle she slowly sank, her head thrown backward.

A sharp pain made me open my eyes. Pierre was dragging me by the hair along the tiles. I remained lying there, stupefied, with open eyes. Pierre had left me to dive again, and in the confusion of my mind I thought it strange when I espied Gaspard on the spot just vacated by my brother. The young man had Véronique in his arms. He laid her near me, plunged in again and brought up Marie, who was so white, rigid and motionless that I thought her dead. Then for the third time he threw himself into the water, but now he sought in vain and returned empty handed. Pierre had joined him; they were talking low, and I could not hear what they said. As they were coming, seemingly quite exhausted, up the incline of the roof I moaned out: "And Aunt Agathe and Jacques and Rose?"

They shook their heads; big tears were welling in their eyes. From the brief, husky words they spoke I gathered that Jacques's brains had been dashed out by a passing beam. Rose had clung to her husband's corpse and been dragged away with it. As for Aunt Agathe, she had not reappeared; we presumed that her body, driven forward by the current, had entered the house beneath us through one of the open windows.

Raising myself, I turned toward the chimney stack which Aimée had been clutching hold of a few moments previously. The flood had risen higher still; Aimée was no longer wailing; I only saw her two stiffened arms holding the children above the water. Then all collapsed: the sheet of water closed over her arms and her babes amid the sleepy glimmer of the full moon.

V

There were now only five of us on the roof. The water had left us but a narrow dry strip on the crest of the tiles. One of the chimney stacks had been swept away. We had to raise Véronique and Marie, who had fainted, and keep them erect to prevent the surf from wetting their legs. At last they regained consciousness, and our anguish increased as we saw them shivering in their soaked garments and heard them wailing that they would not die. We comforted them as one quiets children, assuring them that they were not going to die, that we would prevent death from taking them. But they no longer believed us; they realized that their life was nearly spent.

Each time that the word "die" fell like a knell from their lips their teeth chattered, and mutual dread threw them into each other's arms.

It was the end. A few ruined walls marked here and there the spot where the submerged village had stood. The church, alone intact, raised its belfry on high, and a sound of voices still proceeded from it, telling of people who were safely sheltered. In the distance the vast overflow of the raging waters roared continuously. We no longer heard the crash of crumbling houses, resembling the rough unloading of gravel on a road. The wreck was forsaken as if it were in mid-ocean, a thousand miles from land.

Once we fancied that we detected a splash of oars on our left: it was like a rhythmical, gentle beat growing clearer and nearer. Ah, what a hopeful music it seemed! We craned our necks forward to question space. We held our breath. But we saw nothing. The yellow expanse stretched out, spotted with black, shadowy things, but none of those things, crests of trees, fragments of shattered walls, were stirring. Tufts of herbage, empty barrels, planks, brought us delusive joys. We waved our handkerchiefs till, recognizing our error, we again became the prey of anxiety, wondering whence came the sound that ever fell upon our ears.

"Ah, I see it!" suddenly cried Gaspard. "A large boat—look, over there!"

And with his outstretched arm he pointed to a distant spot. Neither Pierre nor I could distinguish anything, but Gaspard obstinately insisted that it was a boat. The strokes of the oars became more distinct, and finally we all saw it. It was moving slowly, and it seemed to be circling round us without drawing any nearer. I remember that we then became almost mad, waving our arms, raving, shouting, insanely apostrophizing[3] the boat, insulting it and calling it a coward. The craft, still silent and dark, appeared to turn more slowly. Was it really a boat? I cannot tell; I only know that when we realized that it was gone we felt that it had carried our last hope away.

After that we expected every second to be engulfed in the fall of the house. By this time it must be undermined and was probably only held up by some stouter wall, which would drag down the whole building when it gave way. What especially terrified me was to feel the roof sinking under our weight; the house might possibly have resisted all night, but the tiles were loosened and broken by the attacking beams. We took refuge on the left, where the rafters seemed to be less impaired, but even there they soon seemed to weaken and would infallibly yield if the five of us remained together on so narrow a space.

For the last few moments my brother Pierre had mechanically placed his pipe between his lips again. He was twisting his thick, military-looking mustache and muttering confusedly, with his dark brows knit. The increasing peril which surrounded us on all sides and against which there was no possible fighting made him more and more irritated. He had two or three times spat into the water with angry contempt; then as we were sinking more and more, he made up his mind and walked down the slope of the roof.

[3] Speaking to a person who is not present.

"Pierre! Pierre!" I cried, afraid to understand.

He turned and answered quietly, "Good-by, Louis; this lasts too long to suit me, and my going will give you more room."

Then having thrown his pipe into the water, he resolutely flung himself after it, adding: "Good night; I've had enough of it!"

He did not rise again; he was but an indifferent swimmer, and no doubt he surrendered himself to the flood, brokenhearted by our ruin, the loss of those he loved, and feeling unwilling to survive them.

Two o'clock struck at the church tower. The night was almost over, that horrible night, so full of agony and tears. The dry strip under our feet was gradually becoming smaller. There was a soft gurgle of running water, with little caressing wavelets playing and tossing. Then again the current changed; the wreckage was carried to the right of the village, floating lazily along, as if the flood, now seemingly about to reach its greatest height, were resting, weary and satisfied.

All at once Gaspard removed his shoes and coat. During the last moment or two I had watched him wringing his hands and crushing his fingers. In answer to my question he said: "Listen, Grandfather. It kills me to wait here. I cannot stop any longer. Let me act—I can save her!"

He was alluding to Véronique. I attempted to reason with him, saying that he would never be strong enough to swim with the girl as far as the church. But he obstinately insisted, repeating: "I love her—I shall save her!"

I remained silent, simply drawing Marie to my breast. He thought, no doubt, that I was reproaching him with his loverlike selfishness.

"I will come back for Marie," he stammered; "I swear it. I will find a boat somehow and manage to get help. Trust me, Grandfather!"

He stripped, merely retaining his trousers, and then in a low and hurried voice he gave some urgent advice to Véronique, telling her not to struggle but to yield herself to him and, above all, not to get alarmed. The girl stared at him and huskily answered "Yes" to each sentence he spoke.

At last, having made the sign of the cross, although he was not habitually devout, he let himself slide down the roof, holding Véronique by a rope which he had passed under her arms. She gave a loud scream, beat the water with her limbs and fainted away.

"It is best so!" shouted Gaspard. "Now I can answer for her."

With unspeakable anguish I watched their progress. On the white water I easily discerned Gaspard's slightest movements; he supported the girl by means of the rope which he had also twined around himself, and he had thrown her partially across his right shoulder. Her dead weight occasionally made him sink, but he rallied, swimming on with supernatural energy.

I was getting hopeful, for he had already covered one third of the distance, when he struck against some obstacle—some wall hidden below the water's surface. The shock was appalling; they both disappeared. Then I saw Gaspard rise alone; the rope had broken. He plunged twice, and finally he reappeared, again carrying Véronique. He slung her upon his back, but as the supporting rope was gone, she weighed him down more heavily than before. In spite of this he was still advancing. A moment later, as they neared the church, I began to tremble violently; then suddenly I attempted to call out, for I had caught sight of some floating timber coming upon them sideways. My mouth remained wide open; a second concussion parted them; then the waters met again, but they were gone.

From that moment I remained stupefied, retaining merely the animal instinct of self-preservation and shrinking back whenever the water gained on me. Amid this stupor I continued hearing a sound of laughter without understanding whence it came. The day was rising in a great white dawn; the air was pleasant, very fresh and very calm, as it is beside a mere before the sunrise. But laughter still rang out, and on turning round I saw Marie standing near me in her dripping garments. It was she who was laughing!

How sweet and gentle she looked, poor darling, amid the advent of the morning! I saw her stoop, take a little water in the hollow of her palm and bathe her face. Then she twisted her rich golden hair and bound it round her head. She was dressing; she fancied herself back in her little room preparing for church on a Sunday morning while the bells were ringing merrily, and still she laughed her childish laughter, with a happy face and serene, clear eyes.

Her madness was contagious, for I began to laugh with her; terror had demented her, and it was a mercy vouchsafed by heaven, for she seemed conscious only of the enchanting beauty of the springtide dawn.

I watched her quietly, nodding gently and without comprehending. She went on with her toilet till she considered herself ready to start, and then, raising her pure crystalline voice, she began to sing one of her favorite hymns. Presently, however, she stopped, and, as if answering a call which she alone could hear, she cried: "I am coming! I am coming!"

Then resuming her chant, she descended the incline of the roof and stepped into the water, which softly, tenderly, closed over her without shock or struggle. For myself, I continued to smile, looking with a happy, contented face on the spot where she had disappeared.

After that I do not remember. I was quite alone on the roof, the water touching me. A single chimney stack remained standing, and I think I must have clung to it with all my strength, like an animal who refuses to perish. Beyond that I know nothing—nothing—all is black and vacant in my mind.

VI

Why am I here? I have been told that the people of Saintin arrived at about six o'clock with their boats and found me in a dead faint, hanging onto the chimney. The water had been so cruel as not to take me away with those I loved while I remained unconscious of my bereavement.

I—the old one—have obstinately lived on. All the others are gone, the children in swaddling clothes, the girls and their lovers, the young and the old married couples. And yet I remain living like a coarse, dry weed rooted to the stones. If I had the courage I would do what Pierre did. Like him, I would say, "Good night; I have had enough of this," and then I would fling myself into the Garonne, following the course that all the others have taken. I have not one child left me; my house is a ruin; my fields lie waste. Oh, for the nights when we all sat at the table, the elders in the center, the young ones in a row, when their merriment warmed my blood! Oh, for the grand days of harvest and vintage, when we all toiled together and came home in the gloaming, exultant in the pride of our wealth! Oh, for the handsome children and the fair vines, the lovely girls and the golden corn, the joy of my old age, the living reward of my whole life! Now that all this is dead and gone, tell me, O God, why wilt Thou have me stay?

I cannot be comforted. I want no help. I shall give my land to those of the village folk who possess children, for they will have the heart to clear it and till it afresh. Those who have no children need but a corner wherein to die.

I have had one wish, a last desire—I wanted to find the corpses of my dear ones and to bury them in our churchyard under a stone which would someday cover me also. I heard that a great many bodies which had been washed away by the river had been recovered at Toulouse, so I started to go and see them.

Was there ever so ghastly a scene? Nearly two thousand houses destroyed, seven hundred victims, all the bridges swept away, a whole district of the city razed, drowned in the mud; poignant tragedies, twenty thousand wretches half naked and dying of starvation, the town poisoned by the stench of unburied corpses and terrified by the fear of typhus. And mourning everywhere, funerals in all the streets, distress such as no alms could allay. But I walked on among the ruins of others, regardless of aught save my own—my own dear dead, the thought of whom weighed me down.

People told me that many bodies had been found and that they had already been buried in long rows in the cemetery. However, the precaution had been taken to photograph the unrecognized ones. It was among the piteous portraits shown me that I came across those of Gaspard and Véronique. The lovers were still clasped in a passionate embrace; they had given and received their nuptial kiss in death. They clung to each other so closely, mouth pressed to mouth and arms entwined, that it would have been impossible to part them without breaking their limbs. So they had been photographed together, and they slept united beneath the sod.

And that is all I have left, that horrible picture of those two fair children, disfigured and swollen by the water, but still bearing on their livid faces the imprint of their heroic love. I gaze upon them and I weep.

August Strindberg

(1849–1912)

The Swedish playwright August Strindberg, along with the Norwegian Henrik Ibsen, created the modern theater in the last years of the nineteenth century. Strindberg's contribution is much more problematic and difficult to define than Ibsen's. He wrote historical plays, brutal naturalistic dramas, and strange, visionary, symbolist plays (as well as novels, short stories, and a great mass of journalism—his collected works run to fifty-five volumes). No one play emerges as clearly his best or his most characteristic, and no one play has held the stage as firmly as, say, A Doll House *or* Ghosts. *Strindberg's impact has been a more general one; his dramatic kingdom is the exploration of the irrational and the unconscious, and he marked dramatic paths into these areas of experience later followed by the Expressionistic, Surrealistic, and Absurdist playwrights of the twentieth century. This influence began early and touched even his* bête noire *Ibsen, who bought a large portrait of Strindberg in 1895 and hung it in his study. It helped him to write, he said, to have "that madman staring down" at him, and Ibsen's late psychological dramas seem to have owed something to Strindberg's example.*

Strindberg was born in Stockholm in 1849, the son of an impoverished aristocratic father and an illiterate servant girl, a parentage he brooded over all his life and described in Son of a Servant *(1886), one volume of his voluminous, self-lacerating autobiography. His mother died when he was thirteen, and his father quickly married their housekeeper. Strindberg hated her and left home when he was eighteen. He entered the University of Uppsala, intending to study medicine, but failed his entrance examination in chemistry and dropped out. For several years, he supported himself by free-lance journalism and a string of odd jobs in Stockholm, meanwhile working on his first major play,* Master Olaf, *published in 1872 but not produced until 1881. This play, which came to be recognized as the first modern Swedish play, was the first in a series in which Strindberg attempted to use Swedish history as Shakespeare had used English history to create a national drama.*

In 1874, Strindberg met Siri von Essen, unhappily married to a guards officer, whom she left to become Strindberg's mistress. They were married in 1877, after she became pregnant with the first of their four children. Strindberg finally achieved literary success in 1879 with a satirical novel about Stockholm society named The Red Room. *Publication of the first volume of* Getting Married *(1884), a collection of stories about marital conflict, provoked a scandal and brought on him an indictment for blasphemy. He was acquitted, but became obsessed with the belief that the trial had been arranged by a conspiracy of feminists, of which Siri was a part. The second volume of* Getting Married *(1885) reflected this growing misogyny. Strindberg, during his marriage to Siri, also continued to write plays:* Lucky Peter's Travels *(1881),* The Father *(1887),* Comrades *(1888),* Miss Julie *(1888), and* Creditors *(1890). He was divorced from his wife in 1891.*

In 1892, Strindberg moved to Berlin, where he met a young journalist named Frida Uhl; they were married in 1893, but separated in 1894 and divorced in 1897. Strindberg's mental state had been deteriorating for some time, and about the time of his separation from Frida, he lapsed into a prolonged psychotic episode, the most severe of half a dozen in his life and one which he described in the autobiographical Inferno *(1897). During this period, much of it spent in Paris, he abandoned writing and engaged in various pseudo-scientific experiments, meanwhile tormented by paranoid fantasies of persecution by demons who hurled electrical shocks at him. The writing of* Inferno *apparently had a therapeutic effect on Strindberg, and he emerged from his madness in 1898. He also seems to have gained strength from adopting a mystical religious faith, strongly colored by theosophy. He returned to writing and over the next ten years wrote over thirty plays, including some of his most famous:* To Damascus *(1898 and 1904),* Gustav Vasa *and* Erik XIV *(both 1899),* The Dance of Death *(1901), and* A Dream Play *(1902). In addition, a flood of nondramatic writing poured from his pen: a third volume of his autobiography,* Alone *(1903), collections of short stories in 1902 and 1903, a satirical novel named* Black Banners *(1907), and voluminous polemical essays and articles.*

A third marriage took place in 1901, to a young Norwegian actress named Harriet Bosse; one child was born but the couple parted and were divorced in 1904.

Between 1907 and 1910, Strindberg was involved, with a young producer named August Falck, in the management of a small theater in Stockholm named The Intimate Theater and devoted to the production of his plays. For this theater, he wrote a set of "chamber plays," small-scale dramas modeled on chamber music, including Stormy Weather, The House That Burned, The Ghost Sonata, *and* The Pelican *(all 1907) and* The Black Glove *(1909). He died of stomach cancer in 1912.*

Strindberg's career inevitably raises difficult questions about the relationship between madness and art. It has been argued that Strindberg's art was the "sane" part of his life, an instrument of psychic distancing and self-mastery. But this is only partially true. Much of Strindberg's writing is quite literally mad, a flood of painful fantasy with little artistic shaping or control. And even at his best—in Miss Julie, The Father, *or* The Ghost Sonata*—the material is painfully warped and distorted by Strindberg's obsessive fantasies. What one critic has said of* The Father *might be applied to much of Strindberg's other work: "It is impossible to decide whether this is a sane play about a mad man or a mad play about a sane man." The reader or theatergoer who demands of art that it be completely objectified,* à la *Flaubert, with the artist invisible behind his work, coolly paring his fingernails, will not like Strindberg. But others with a more pluralistic view will find a raw, disturbing power in his work, a sense that they are in the presence of someone painfully reporting a journey into frightening and unfamiliar areas of experience.*

Miss Julie *was written in 1888 when Strindberg was a disciple of the French Naturalists, especially Émile Zola and the Goncourt brothers, Edmond and Jules, who added to a meticulous realism of detail a belief in scientific determinism. Man, for the Naturalists, was basically an animal in the natural world, and his behavior was a response to outer and inner forces—social and economic conditions as well as his heredity and biological needs—which he was unlikely to understand or control to any significant degree. The decisive influence upon the Naturalists was Charles Darwin's* Origin of Species *(1859), whose description of the battleground of nature where the "survival of the fittest" took place they applied quite directly to the interpretation of contemporary life.*

Strindberg's major plays of this period, including Miss Julie, *are all evolutionary battlefields in which highly developed, intelligent people fight for survival against more primitively organized types. The higher forms of life are likely to lose out to the lower in these encounters. Their characters, for one thing, are likely to be "characterless," that is, fluid, protean, and capable of change and development—possessing an advantage intellectually but a fatal weakness in the struggle for survival. Furthermore, the more primitive character is likely to be a "vampire," who can through sheer animal magnetism suck his opponent's strength and exercise a controlling power of suggestion over him. (Strindberg developed his theory of "vampirism" or "psychic assimilation" through the study of certain pseudo-scientific, occult accounts of "nerve* fluidum*" through which "spiritual emanations" traveled.) Thus, Strindberg developed a paradoxical theory of "the stronger": the cruder and more animal-like is likely to win out over the more intelligent, adaptable, and highly developed.*

All of these "ideas" appear in the Preface to Miss Julie, *a characteristic combination of the cranky and the brilliant. Strindberg explains his evolutionary drama with an irritating and foolish pose of Nietzschean brutality. "Perhaps," he writes, "there will come a time when we will be so enlightened that we will view with indifference the brutal, cynical, and heartless spectacle that life has to offer—perhaps when we have done with our imperfect, unreliable thought mechanisms which we call feelings, and which may be superfluous when our reflective organs have developed."*

More interesting than this Naturalist preaching are Strindberg's remarks on dramatic technique, the sections that have made this Preface one of the major documents in the early modern theater. Some of these remarks have to do with realistic innovations in staging: an angled setting with solid walls, real properties rather than painted ones, side-lighting rather than footlights, minimal makeup, and a completely darkened auditorium. Even more revolutionary are his comments on dramatic characterization and dialogue. Characters, he says, should be "characterless," that is, not dominated by one "character" or "humor" but complex, inconsistent, and multiply motivated. Dialogue should not be logically organized, like a catechism, but should be rambling and associational, reflecting the thought patterns of real life.

The play itself achieves these technical goals, while rising in content considerably above the brutality and misogyny of the Preface. Both Julie and Jean, though extreme, are credible characters, each radically divided, Julie split between an instinct for life and a powerful pull toward death, Jean torn between a sadistic desire to dominate and a masochistic tendency toward groveling submission. Miss Julie *is the starkest and most powerful of Strindberg's many treatments of the "Sex War," that inevitable and eternal struggle upon which Strindberg piled all his many tormented perceptions of human division. And perhaps part of the power of this complex play comes from our sense that the Sex War is not between the sexes at all but within Strindberg, between the Jean and the Julie in himself, the aristocrat and the "son of a servant."*

FURTHER READING *(prepared by W. J. R.):* The standard biography of Strindberg is Martin Lamm's massive *August Strindberg,* trans. by Harry G. Carlson, 1971, which includes critical interpretations of the major plays as well. Brita M. E. Mortensen and Brian W. Downs, *Strindberg: An Introduction to His Life and Work,* 1949, includes excellent discussions of the novels and short stories as well as the dramas. Gunnar Ollén's *August Strindberg,* trans. by Peter Tirner, 1972, contains brief descriptions of all the plays and also notes on some significant productions. Major works are also surveyed, in greater detail, in Walter Johnson's *August Strindberg,* 1972. Birgitta Steene's *The Greatest Fire: A Study of August Strindberg,* 1973, is an extensive critical analysis that attempts to correct earlier misconceptions of the author's vision and method. Evert Sprinchorn's *Strindberg as Dramatist,* 1982, traces the development of Strindberg's art through the four most significant groups of plays—ranging from his naturalist works to his "dream cycle." Strindberg's extensive use of mythic imagery in *Miss Julie* and several other plays is the subject of Harry G. Carlson's *Strindberg and the Poetry of Myth,* 1982. For shorter critical overviews of Strindberg's work, see the chapters on Strindberg in Eric Bentley, *The Playwright as Thinker,* 1945; Robert Brustein, *The Theater of Revolt,* 1962; Maurice Valency, *The Flower and the Castle,* 1963; and Richard Gilman, *The Making of Modern Drama,* 1974. *Strindberg: A Collection of Critical Essays,* ed. by Otto Reinert, 1971, contains studies of Strindberg's artistic temperament, his original contributions to theater, and several major plays.

MISS JULIE

A NATURALISTIC TRAGEDY IN ONE ACT

Translated by Arvid Paulson

THE AUTHOR'S PREFACE

In common with art generally, the theater has long seemed to me to be a *biblia pauperum,* i.e., a bible in pictures for those who cannot read the written or printed word. Similarly, the playwright has the semblance of being a lay preacher presenting the views and sentiments of his time in popular form—and in a form sufficiently popular so that the middle classes, from which theater audiences are chiefly drawn, can understand what it is all about without racking their brains.

Thus the theater has long been a public school for the young, for people not too well educated, and for women who still possess that primitive faculty of deceiving themselves and letting themselves be deceived; or, in brief, who are impressionable to illusion and susceptible to the suggestions of the author. For the self-same reason it has seemed to me as if, in our time—when the rudimentary, immature way of thinking (which is a process of the imagination) appears to be developing into reflection, inquiry and analysis—the theater, like religion, is in the throes of being abandoned as a moribund form of art for which we lack the conditions requisite to enjoyment. The profound crisis now sweeping through the whole of Europe gives credence to this assumption, and not least the fact that in those countries of culture which have given us the greatest thinkers of the age, namely England and Germany, the drama, in common with most of the other fine arts, is dead.

In other countries, however, efforts have been made to create a new form of drama by employing elements reflecting the ideas of modern times within the framework of the old forms. But on the one hand, there has not been sufficient time for these new ideas to have been so generally accepted that the audiences can fathom their purport and implication; on the other hand, some of the audiences have been so impassioned by partisan polemics and propaganda that it has been impossible to enjoy the play in a purely objective manner while one's innermost feelings and convictions are being assailed, and when an applauding or hissing majority displays a tyranny so openly as only a theater affords an opportunity for. And, furthermore, the new content has as yet been given no fresh form; as a result, the new wine has burst the old bottles.

In the present drama I have not attempted to create anything new (for that is an impossibility) but merely to modernize the form to meet the demands which, it occurs to me, people of our time are likely to make upon this art. To this end I have chosen (or rather, been captured by) a theme which may be said to lie outside the partisan and controversial issues of the day. The problem of social rise or downfall, of who is higher or lower, or who is better or worse, whether man or woman, is, has been and shall be of enduring interest. When I chose this theme from real life—as I heard it related a number of years ago, at which time I was greatly moved by the story—I saw in it the ingredients of a tragic drama. To see an individual on whom fortune has heaped an abundance of gifts go to her ruin and destruction, leaves us with a tragic feeling; to see a whole line die out is still more tragic. But perhaps there will come a time when we will be so enlightened that we will view with indifference the brutal, cynical and heartless spectacle that life has to offer—perhaps when we have done with our imperfect, unreliable thought mechanisms which we call feelings, and which may be superfluous when our reflective organs have developed.

The fact that the heroine in this play arouses our pity and compassion is due solely to our weakness and inability to resist such a feeling for fear that we ourselves may meet with the self-same fate. And the over-sensitive spectator may still not be content with feeling pity and compassion; the man with faith in the future may demand some sort of positive action or suggestion for doing away with the evil—in short, some stroke of policy. But, first of all, there is nothing absolutely evil; for the extinction of one family is nothing short of luck for another family that gets a chance to rise in the world. And the succession of rise and fall is one of life's greatest fascinations as luck is only relative. And to the man with a program who desires to rectify the unfortunate fact that the bird of prey devours the dove and that the lice eat the bird of prey, I wish to put this question: "Why should it be rectified?" Life is not so mathematically idiotic that it allows only the big to eat the small, for it happens just as often that the bee kills the lion or at least drives it mad.

That my tragedy has a depressing effect upon the many is the fault of these many. When we have grown as hardened as the first French revolutionaries were, then it will without question produce only a happy and wholesome impression to see the crown parks weeded out and ridded of rotting, super-annuated trees that too long have stood in the way of others, equally entitled to their day of vegetation—the kind of impression one experiences when one sees somebody with an incurable disease taken by death.

Not long ago I was upbraided by someone who thought my tragedy *The Father* was too sad. As if a tragedy were meant to be amusing! People are constantly clamoring pretentiously for the *joy of life*,[1] and play producers keep demanding farces—as if the joy of life consisted in being ludicrous and in depicting all human beings as if they were suffering from St. Vitus' dance, or idiocy. For my part, I find the joy of life in the hard and cruel battles of life; and to be able to add to my store of knowledge, to learn something, is enjoyment to me. It is for that reason I have chosen an unusual situation—yet one that teaches a moral; an exception, in brief,—but a rare exception that proves the rule and that no doubt will make all those who love the commonplace, feel offended. The next thing that will offend the simple-minded is the fact that my motivation for the action is not a

[1] Strindberg is alluding sardonically to Ibsen's *Ghosts* (1881), in which "the joy of life" (*livsglaede*) is a key phrase.

simple one and that the *raison d'être* is not a single one. A happening in life—and this is a fairly recent discovery!—is generally brought about by a whole series of more or less deep-lying motives; but as a rule the spectator selects the one which in his opinion seems the easiest to understand or that is most flattering to his own best judgment. A suicide takes place. "Bad business!" says the burgher. "Unrequited love!" say the women. "Physical illness!" says the invalid. "Crushed hopes!" says the human derelict. But now it is possible that the motive may be all or none of these things, and that the deceased may have concealed the actual motive by letting another be known that would cast a more favorable light over his memory!

The sad fate of Miss Julie I have motivated by a host of circumstances: the mother's fundamental instincts, the father's wrong upbringing of the girl, her own strange nature, and the suggestive influence of her fiancé upon an insipid, vapid and degenerated mind. In addition, and more directly, the festal mood of Midsummer Eve, the absence of her father, her monthly period, her preoccupancy with animals, the excitement of the dance, the long twilight of the night, the strongly aphrodisiac influence of the flowers, and lastly, the chance bringing together of the two alone in a secluded room—not to mention the aroused passion of a bold and aggressive man. Consequently my mode of procedure has been neither one-sidedly physiological nor psychological: I have neither placed the blame exclusively on traits inherited from the mother nor have I cast the blame on the girl's physical indisposition. By the same token, I have not put the blame solely on "immorality," and I have not merely preached a moral. For want of a priest, I have left this task to the cook.

I commend myself for the introduction of this multiplicity of motives; they are in keeping with the times. And if others have done the same thing before me, I will acknowledge with pride that I was not alone in my paradoxes—as all discoveries are called.

With regard to the delineation of the characters, I have made them somewhat lacking in character for the following reasons:

In the course of time the word *character* has been given many meanings. Originally it no doubt denoted the dominant trait in the soul-complex and was confused with temperament. With time it became the middle-class term for an automaton, an individual who had become so fixed in his nature—or who had adapted himself to a particular role in life and who, in a word, had ceased to grow—that people called him *a character.* On the other hand, a man who continued to develop, an able navigator on the river of life, who sailed not with sheets set fast but who veered down the wind to steer closer to the wind again—this man was called lacking in character. And this, of course, in a derogatory sense—because he was so hard to capture, to categorize, to keep an eye on.

This bourgeois notion of the fixed state of the soul was transmitted to the stage, where the middle-class element has always been in dominance. There a character became synonymous with a man permanently settled and finished, one who at all times appeared as a drunkard, a jolly jester, or as a deplorable, miserable figure. And for the purpose of characterization nothing more was needed than some physical defect such as a clubfoot, a wooden leg, a red nose—or that the actor in the role be given some repetitious phrase such as "That's splendid!" or "Barkis will be glad to do it!",[2] and so forth.

This one-sided manner of looking at human beings still survives in the great Molière. Harpagon[3] is a miser and nothing else, although he could have been both a miser and an excellent financier, a fine father, a good man in his community. And what is worse, his infirmity is precisely of utmost advantage to his son-in-law and daughter who are his heirs. For that reason they ought not to take him to task, even if they have to wait a little before they take to their nuptial bed. I do not believe, therefore, in simplified characters for the stage. An author's summary judgment upon men (this man is a fool; that one brutal; this one is jealous; that one stingy, etc.) ought to be challenged and rejected by the Naturalists who are aware of the richness of the human soul and who know that vice has another side to it that is very like virtue.

I have depicted my characters as modern characters, living in an age of transition at least more breathlessly hysterical than the period immediately preceding it. Thus I have made them more vacillating, disjointed: a blending of the old and the new. And it seems not improbable to me that modern ideas, absorbed through conversations and newspapers, could have filtered down to the domain of the domestics.

My souls (characters) are conglomerates of a past stage of civilization and our present one, scraps from books and newspapers, pieces of humanity, torn-off tatters of holiday clothes that have disintegrated and become rags—exactly as the soul is patched together. I have, besides, contributed a small fragment of evolutionary history by having the weaker character parrot words purloined from the stronger one, and by having the souls (the characters) borrow "ideas" (or suggestions, as they are called) from one another.

Miss Julie is a modern character. Not that the half-woman, the man-hater, has not existed since time immemorial but because she has now been discovered, has trod into the open and begun to create a stir. The half-woman of today is a type who pushes herself forward; today she is selling herself for power, decorations, aggrandizement, diplomas, as she did formerly for money; and the type is indicative of degeneration. It is not a wholesome type and it is not enduring, but unfortunately it can reproduce and transplant its misery in another generation. And degenerate men seem instinctively to choose their mates from among such women; and so they multiply and bring into the world progeny of indeterminate sex, to whom life becomes a torture. Fortunately, however, they come to an end, either from being unable to face and withstand life, or from the irresistible rebellion of their suppressed desires, or because their hope of coming up to men has been thwarted. It is a tragic type, revealing the spectacle of a desperate struggle against nature; tragic also as a Romantic inheritance now being put to flight by Naturalism, whose aim is only for happiness; for in order to achieve happiness, strong, virile and wholesome types are required.

[2] Strindberg is thinking of "character tags" like Tesman's in Ibsen's *Hedda Gabler* or Barkis's in Dickens's *David Copperfield.* (Actually, the line is "Barkis is willin'.")

[3] The title character in Molière's *The Miser* (1668).

But Miss Julie is also a remnant of the old war nobility, which is now giving way to the new aristocracy of the mind with its nervous driving force. She is a victim of the discord which a mother's "crime" produces in a family; a victim also of the delusions and deceptions of her time, of circumstances, of her own defective constitution—all of which adds up to the "fate" or "universal law" of days now past. The Naturalist has done away with the idea of guilt, as well as God; but the consequences of the act: punishment, imprisonment (or the fear of it)—*that* he cannot do away with for the simple reason that they are bound to remain. They will remain whether he (the Naturalist) lets the protagonists go free or not; for the injured parties are never so good-natured as outsiders (who have not been wronged) can be—at a price.

Even if the father for compelling reasons should take no vengeance, the daughter would avenge herself—as she does here—from that innate or acquired sense of honor which the upper classes have as their inheritance. From where? From the barbarian ages, from the original homeland of the Aryans, or from the chivalry of the Middle Ages? It is a beautiful thing, but these days it has become somewhat of a disadvantage to the preservation of the race. It is the nobleman's hara-kiri—which is the law of the Japanese, of his innermost conscience, that bids him cut open his own abdomen after receiving an insult from another man. The custom survives, in modified form, in the duel, also a privilege of the upper classes. And that is why Jean, the valet, remains alive; but Miss Julie cannot go on living once she has lost her honor. This is the advantage the serf has over the earl: that he is without this deadly superstition about honor. In all of us Aryans there is something of the nobleman, or Don Quixote, which makes us sympathize with the man who takes his own life after he has committed a dishonorable deed and so lost his honor. And we are noblemen enough to suffer when we see a person once considered great, suddenly topple and then be looked upon as dead and a nuisance. Yes—even if he should raise himself up again and make up for the past by performing an act of nobility. Jean, the valet, is a procreator, and he has acquired a distinct and separate character. He was born the son of a farmhand and has gradually taken on the characteristics of a gentleman. He finds it easy to learn, his senses are well developed (smell, taste, vision), and he has a feeling for beauty. He has already come up in the world; and he is hard and unscrupulous enough not to allow sensitiveness to interfere when it comes to using others for his purposes. He is already a stranger to those around him (the servants and farmhands) whom he looks down upon, as he does upon the life he has turned his back on. He avoids the menials and fears them because they know his secrets, pry into his scheming, watch with envy as he betters himself, and anticipate his downfall with glee. This accounts for the duality of his indeterminate character, which vacillates between love of power and glory and hatred against those who have it. He thinks of himself as an aristocrat. He has learned the secrets of good society. He is polished on the surface, but the inside is uncouth and vulgar. He has learned to wear formal clothes with taste, but one cannot be so certain that his body is clean.

He has respect for Miss Julie but is timid and apprehensive about Kristin (the cook), for she knows his precarious secrets. He is also sufficiently callous not to let the night's happenings interfere with his plans for the future. With the brutality of the serf and the lack of squeamishness of the ruler he can see blood without losing consciousness, and he can throw off any hardship or adversity. Consequently he emerges from the battlefield unscarred, and no doubt he will end up as a hotelkeeper; and if he fails to become a Roumanian count, his son will probably attend a university and may end up as a petty official.

For the rest, Jean gives a rather enlightening insight into the lower classes' conception of life—of life as they see it—when he speaks the truth, which he infrequently does; for rather than adhere to the truth he asks what will do him most good. When Miss Julie suggests that the lower classes must feel oppressed by those above them, Jean naturally agrees with her because his aim is to gain sympathy. But when he realizes that it is to his advantage to place himself apart from the common herd, he quickly takes back his words.

Aside from the fact that Jean is well on his way up in the world, he possesses an advantage over Miss Julie because of being a man. Sexually he is the aristocrat because of his male strength, his more acutely developed senses, and his capacity for taking the initiative.

His feeling of inferiority can principally be ascribed to the temporary social environment in which he lives, and he can probably rid himself of it when he sheds his servant's livery.

The mental attitude of the slave manifests itself in his inordinate respect for the count (as exemplified in the scene with the boots), and in his religious superstition. But his respectfulness is chiefly inspired by the fact that the count occupies a position of rank which he himself would like to attain. And this deference remains with him after he has won the affections of the count's daughter and seen the emptiness within the shell.

I find it hard to believe that a relationship of love in a higher sense could exist between two souls so different in nature. For this reason I have made Miss Julie imagine that she is in love—to justify her behavior, to blot out her transgression; and I let Jean think that if social conditions were different, he might be able to love her. I imagine love is much like the hyacinth: it has to strike roots in darkness *before* it can produce a healthy, hardy flower. In this instance, it shoots up instantaneously—and therefore the plant withers and dies so soon.

Finally there is Kristin. She is a female slave, obsequious and dull (from standing at the hot stove) and laden with morality and religion that serve as a cloak for her own immorality, and as a scapegoat. Her church-going is a means of lightheartedly and glibly unloading on Jesus her household thieveries and taking on a new lease of guiltlessness. Otherwise she is a subordinate figure, and therefore intentionally sketched much in the manner of the Pastor and the Doctor in *The Father*—the reason for this being that I wanted to have precisely this type of ordinary human being (such as country clergymen and country doctors usually are). If these subordinate figures of mine have appeared as abstractions to some, it is because everyday people go about their work in a somewhat detached manner. By that I mean that they are impersonal and that they show only *one* side of their personality. And as long as the spectator feels no need of seeing the other sides of their personality, my abstract characterization of them is quite correct.

As far as the dialogue is concerned, I have, to a certain degree, broken with tradition by not making catechists out of my characters; that is, they do not keep asking silly questions merely for the sake of bringing forth a clever or jocular retort. I have avoided the symmetrical, mathematical construction commonly used by the French in their dialogue. Instead I have had my characters use their brains only intermittently as people do in real life where, during a conversation, one cog in a person's brain may find itself, more or less by chance, geared into another cog; and where no topic is completely exhausted. That is the very reason that the dialogue rambles. In the early scenes it piles up material which is later worked up, gone over, repeated, expanded, rearranged and developed much like the theme in a musical composition.

The plot is tolerable enough, and as it is really concerned with only two persons, I have concentrated my attention on them. I have added only one other character, a minor one: Kristin (the cook), and have kept the spirit of the unfortunate father hovering over and in the background of the entire action. I have done this because I seem to have observed that the psychological course of events is what interests the people of our time most. I have also noticed that our souls, so hungry for knowledge, find no satisfaction in merely seeing something done; we want to know *how* and *why* it is done! What we want to see are the wires—the machinery! We want to examine the box with the false bottom, take hold of and feel the magic ring in an attempt to find where it is joined together; we want to scrutinize the cards and try to discover how they are marked.

In this attempt of mine I have had in mind the brothers de Goncourt's monographic novels[4] which, among all literature of modern times, have appealed to me most.

As far as the technical side is concerned, I have, as an experiment, done away with the division into acts. This I have done because I seem to have found that our decreasing capacity for illusion might be disturbed by intermissions, during which the theatergoer would have time to engage in reflection and thereby escape the author-mesmerizer's suggestive influence. The performance of *Miss Julie* will probably last one hour and a half. As people can listen to a lecture, a sermon, or a parliamentary proceeding lasting that length of time or longer, it has struck me that a theatrical piece ought not to fatigue an audience in a similar space of time. Already in 1872, in one of my earlier playwriting experiments, *The Outlaw,* I tried using this concentrated form, although without much success. The play was originally written in five acts, and when it was completed, I was cognizant of the chaotic and alarming effect it had upon me. I burned the manuscript and from out of the ashes rose a single, well-constructed act, fifty printed pages in length, that took one hour to perform. While the form of *Miss Julie* is not absolutely original, it nevertheless seems to be my own innovation; and as public taste appears to be changing, there may be prospects for its being accepted in our time.

My hope is that we may some day have audiences so educated that they will sit through a whole evening's performance of a play consisting only in one act. But to attain this, tests would have to be made.

4 Goncourt brothers, Edmond (1822–96) and Jules (1830–70), wrote a number of reali novels of Parisian life.

In order, however, to provide momentary interludes (or rest stops) for the audience and the actors without allowing the spectators to lose the illusion that the play has created, I have included three art forms, all integral parts of the drama, namely: the monologue, the pantomime, and the ballet. Originally they were part of the tragedies of antiquity, the monologue having been derived from the monody[5] and the ballet from the chorus.

The monologue has now been condemned by our realists as not being true to life; but if its motivation is sound, it can be made believable, and consequently it can be used to good advantage. It is, for instance, quite natural that an orator should walk up and down in his home practicing aloud his speech by himself; not at all improbable that an actor should rehearse the lines of his role in a stage voice; that a servant girl should babble to her cat; that a mother should prattle to her little child; that an old spinster should chatter with her parrot; that anyone might talk in his sleep. And in order that the actor, for once, may have an opportunity to do some independent work, free from any interference, suggestions or directions from the author, it may be preferable that the monologue scenes not be written out (in so many words) but merely indicated. For it is of small importance what is being said by a person in his sleep, or to a parrot, or a cat—it has no influence on the action in the play. A gifted actor may, however, improvise such a scene better than the author can, because the actor has become part and parcel of the situation and is imbued with the mood of it. In short, the author has no way of determining in advance how much small talk may be used and how long it should last without having the audience awakened from the spell it is under.

It is general knowledge that certain theaters in Italy have gone back to the art of improvising—and as a result have produced some creative artists. They follow, however, the author's general outline and suggestions; and this may well prove to be a step forward, not to say a new art form which may truly be said to be *creative*.

Wherever the monologue, on the other hand, has made for improbability, I have resorted to the pantomime; and there I have given the actors still wider scope for creating imagery—and to win individual acclaim. To prevent the audience from being strained to the utmost, I have designated that the music—for which there is ample justification owing to the fact that it is Midsummer Eve, with its traditional dancing—exert its seductive influence while the pantomime is going on. And I address a plea to the musical director that he consider carefully his choice of music selections, lest he conjure forth an atmosphere foreign to the play and lest he induce remembrances of strains from current operettas, or reminders of popular dance music, or of primitive folk airs which are too pronouncedly ethnographic.

The ballet which I have introduced could not have been replaced by a so-called mob (or ensemble) scene. Such scenes are generally badly acted and afford a lot of grinning fools, bent on attracting attention to themselves, an opportunity to shatter the illusion. As rustics usually do not im-

[5] A *monody* in Greek tragedy was an ode sung by a single voice, such as that of the chorus leader. A *chorus* was an ode sung by the full ensemble. Contrary to what Strindberg says, monologues and ballet-sequences in modern drama did not derive directly from these elements in classical tragedy.

provise into ditties their derision and jeers, but make use of already existing material (which frequently carries a double meaning) I have not composed their scurrilous innuendo but have chosen a little-known dance game, which I came across in the vicinity of Stockholm and wrote down. The words fit the actual happenings only to a degree and not entirely; but that is exactly my intention—for the wiliness and insidiousness in the slave makes him shrink from attacking in the open. Thus there must be no cackling buffoons in a serious drama such as this, no exhibition of coarse grinning in a situation which forever places the lid on the coffin of a family lineage.

With regard to the scenery, I have borrowed from impressionistic painting its asymmetry, its terse and pregnant concision, and in this way I think I have increased the possibilities for creating illusion. The very fact that the room is not seen in its entirety (nor all of its furnishings), gives us the incentive to conjecture. In brief, our imagination is set to work and fills in what is lacking before our eyes. I have also gained something by getting rid of the tiresome exits through doors, primarily because the doors in a stage set are made of canvas and move at the slightest touch. They can not even give expression to an angry father's temper when he, after an execrable dinner, gets up and leaves, slamming the door after him "so that the whole house shakes." On the stage "the whole house" (of canvas!) moves unsteadily from one side to the other. Similarly, I have used only one single setting, and this for two purposes: to blend the figures into the environment, and to break with the habit of using extravagant scenery. And with only one setting, one can expect it to be realistic in appearance. Yet there is nothing so hard to find on the stage as an interior set that comes close to looking as a room *should* look, no matter how convincingly the scenic artist otherwise can produce a volcano in eruption, or a waterfall. We may have to tolerate walls made of canvas, but it is about time that we stopped having shelves and kitchen utensils painted on it. There are so many other conventions on the stage that strain our imagination; certainly we might be freed from overexerting ourselves in an effort to believe that pots and pans painted on the scenery are real.

I have placed the rear wall and the table obliquely across the stage for the purpose of showing the actors full face and in half-profile while they face each other across the table. I once saw a setting in the opera *Aïda* that had a slanting backdrop, and it opened up to the eye unknown perspectives; and this arrangement did not have the look of having been made in a spirit of rebellion against the trying straight line.

Another innovation that is much needed is the removal of the footlights. The lighting is designed to make the actors appear plumper of face. But now let me ask: Why must all actors have plump faces? Does not the light from below tend to erase many of the sensitive, subtle character traits of the lower part of the face, and especially round the mouth? And does it not change the shape of the nose and cast a shadow effect above the eyes? Even if this were not so, there is one thing that is certain: that the eyes of the actors are suffering under a strain, making it difficult for them fully and effectively to project the varying expressions of the eyes across the footlights. For the light strikes the retina in places that under ordinary circumstances are protected (except in the case of sailors: they get the glare of the sun from the water), and consequently one seldom witnesses anything but a glare, a stare, or a crude rolling of the eyes—in the direction of the wings or upward toward the balconies—so that the whites of the eyes show. Very likely this also accounts for the tiresome habit of blinking with the eyelashes, especially by actresses. And whenever anyone on the stage has to speak with his eyes, there is only one way in which he can do it (and that a bad one): to gaze straight out into the audience, and so come in close contact with it from the stage apron outside the curtain line. Rightly or wrongly, this nuisance has been referred to as: "Greeting one's acquaintances!"

Would not sufficiently powerful lighting from the sides (with parabolas[6] or similar devices, for instance) be of help to the actor and enable him to project more completely the sensibility of expression and mobility of the eyes, which are the most important means of facial expression?

I have no illusions about being able to persuade the actors to play *for* the audience and not *to* it, although this would be highly desirable. Nor do I look forward with much hope to the day when I shall see an actor turn his back completely to the audience throughout an important scene; but I do wish that crucial scenes would not be given close to the prompter's box (in the center of the stage) as though the actors were performing a duet and expected it to be received by applause. I would like to have each scene played at the very place where the situation demands it to be played.

And so there must be no revolutionary changes, only minor modifications. To transform the stage into a room with the fourth wall removed, and to carry out the effect of realism by placing some pieces of furniture with their backs to the audience would, for the present, provoke an outcry.

And I would also like to say a word about the make-up, although I dare not hope that the actresses will pay much attention to me. They much prefer to look beautiful rather than look their part in the play. But it might be well to give a thought to whether it is expedient and becoming for the actor to smear his face with make-up until it becomes an abstraction and its character is obliterated by a mask. Let us imagine an actor who—in order to achieve an irascible, choleric look—applies a couple of bold, black lines between the eyes and that he, still looking wrathful with his ineradicable expression, has to smile in response to somebody's remark! What a horrible grimace it will result in! And again, how can the old man possibly wrinkle the false forehead of his wig (which is smooth as a billiard ball!) when he flies into a rage?

Presented on a small stage, a modern psychological drama, in which the most subtle reactions of the soul must be reflected by facial expression rather than by gesture, shouting and meaningless sound, would be a most practicable testing ground for the use of powerful lighting from the sides, with the participating actors using no make-up, or at least very little.

If, in addition, the visible orchestra with the disturbing glare from the lamps (on the music stands), and with the faces of orchestra members turned toward the audience, could be made invisible; and if the parquet ("orchestra") could be elevated so that the eyes of the spectators focused on a level higher than the actors' knees; if the stage boxes, with their giggling, snickering late dinner and supper party arrivals, could be got rid of; and if,

[6]Stage lights with curved reflectors.

in addition, we could have absolute darkness in the auditorium while the play is in progress; and if we, first and foremost, could have an intimate stage and an intimate theater—then we may see the inception of a new drama, and the theater could again become an institution for the entertainment of the cultured.

While waiting for this kind of theater to come into being, we may as well continue our writing and file it away in preparation for the repertory that is to come.

I have made an attempt! If I have not succeeded, there is time enough to make another!

CHARACTERS

MISS JULIE, *25 years old*
JEAN, *butler and valet, 30 years old*
KRISTIN, *cook, 35 years old*

The action takes place in the Count's kitchen on Midsummer Night's Eve.

A large kitchen the ceiling and side walls of which are masked by borders and draperies. The rear wall runs diagonally across the stage, from the right of the stage to the left, at a slight angle. On the wall, to the right, are two shelves with utensils of copper, iron, tin and other metals. The shelves are trimmed with fancy paper. Further over, on the left, can be seen three-quarters of a great arched doorway, which has two glass doors; through these doors are seen a fountain with a figure of Cupid, lilac shrubs in bloom and the tops of some Lombardy poplars. On the right, the corner of a large stove, faced with glazed bricks; a part of its hood is also seen. On the left, one end of the servants' dining table of white pine; around it are a few chairs. The stove is decorated with branches of birch, and twigs of juniper are strewn on the floor. On the table stands a large Japanese spice jar, filled with lilac blossoms. An ice-box, a kitchen table, and a sink. Above the door, a big, old-fashioned bell; to the right of the door, a speaking tube. Downstage, left, there is a triangular opening in the wall, inside which are doors upstage and downstage leading to JEAN'S *and* KRISTIN'S *rooms. Only the door leading to* JEAN'S *room (upstage) is visible.* KRISTIN *is standing at the stove. She is busy frying something. She wears a light-colored cotton dress and a kitchen apron.* JEAN *enters. He is wearing livery and carries a pair of large riding-boots with spurs which he puts down on the floor so that they are in full view of the audience.*

JEAN. Now Miss Julie's mad again—absolutely mad!

KRISTIN. So—you are back again, are you?

JEAN. I took the Count to the station, and when I came back and went by the barn, I stepped inside and had a dance. And there I saw Miss Julie leading the dance with the gamekeeper. But the instant she set eyes on me, she dashed straight over to me and asked me to dance the next waltz with her; and from that moment on she has been waltzing with me—and never in my life have I known anything like it! She is stark mad!

KRISTIN. She's always been crazy—but after the engagement was broken off two weeks ago, she is worse than ever.

JEAN. Just what was the trouble, I wonder? I thought he was a fine young man, even if he didn't have any money to speak of. . . . Oh, but they all have so many queer notions! [*He seats himself at one end of the table.*] Anyhow, don't you think it's strange that a lady like her—h'm—should want to stay at home with the help instead of going away with her father to visit some of their relatives?

KRISTIN. I suppose she is sort of embarrassed after the break-up with her fiancé—

JEAN. I shouldn't be surprised! But I must say, he was the sort who could stand up for himself. Did you hear, Kristin, how the whole thing happened? I watched it from beginning to end—although I never let on that I did.

KRISTIN. You don't mean it? You saw it—did you?

JEAN. I certainly did! They were together out in the stable-yard one evening—and Miss Julie was trying to "train" him, as she called it. What do you think she did? She had him jump over her riding crop—the way you train a dog to jump! And each time she gave him a whack with her riding crop. But the third time he snatched the whip from her hand and broke it into bits! And then he left.

KRISTIN. So that's what happened! Well, I never—

JEAN. Yes, that's the way it happened. . . . But now—what have you that's good to eat, Kristin?

KRISTIN [*dishes out from the pan and places a plate before* JEAN]. Oh, it's only a piece of kidney that I cut from the veal steak.

JEAN [*smells the food*]. Splendid! That's my special *délice.*[7] . . . [*He feels the plate.*] But you didn't heat the plate!

KRISTIN. I must say—you are more of a fuss-box than the Count himself when he wants to be particular. [*She runs her hand through his hair caressingly.*]

JEAN [*crossly*]. Stop that—stop pulling my hair! You know how sensitive I am about that!

KRISTIN. Why, why—you know I only do it because I love you—don't you know that!

JEAN [*eats.* KRISTIN *uncorks a bottle of ale*]. Beer on Midsummer Eve! No, thanks! I have something better than that. [*He pulls out a table drawer and produces a bottle of red wine with yellow seal.*] You see the yellow seal, don't you? Now bring me a glass! A glass with stem—*always*—when you drink it undiluted.

KRISTIN [*goes over to the stove and puts a small pan on the fire. Then she brings him a wine glass.*] God help the woman who gets you for a husband! I never knew anyone to fuss like you!

JEAN. Don't talk nonsense! You ought to be glad to get a fellow as fine as I! And I don't think it's hurt you any to have them call me your sweetheart! [*He tastes the wine.*] Good! Very good! Could be just a trifle warmer. [*He warms the glass with his hands.*] We bought this in Dijon. Four francs a liter from the cask—not counting the duty. What are you cooking over there that smells so horrible?

KRISTIN. Oh, it's some devilish mess that Miss Julie has me cook for Diana.

[7] "Delight" (French).

JEAN. You might be a little more careful with your expressions, Kristin!—But I don't see why you should stand and cook for that damned cur on Midsummer Eve! Is anything the matter with the bitch?

KRISTIN. Yes, she is sick. She has been sneaking out with the gatekeeper's pugdog, and now she's in trouble—and that's just what Miss Julie doesn't want, don't you see?

JEAN. The young lady is too haughty in some respects, and in others she has no pride at all—exactly like her mother, the countess, when she was alive. She was especially at home in the kitchen and in the stables, but she would never drive behind one horse only—she had to have at least two. She went around with dirty cuffs, but she had to have a crest on each button. And speaking of Miss Julie, she shows a lack of self-respect. She has no regard for her position. I could almost say she lacks refinement. Why, just now when she was dancing out there in the barn, she pulled the gamekeeper away from Anna and started to dance with him, without any ado. Would we do anything like that? We would not!—But that's what happens when aristocrats try to act like the common people—they become common! But she is splendid to look at! Gorgeous! Ah, what shoulders! And what—etcetera—

KRISTIN. Oh, stop your ranting! Haven't I heard what Clara says about her?—and she dresses her.

JEAN. Oh! Clara! You women are always jealous of one another! But don't *I* go out riding with her? . . . And can she dance!

KRISTIN. Listen, Jean—how about a dance with me when I get through with my work here?

JEAN. Why, certainly—why not?

KRISTIN. Is that a promise?

JEAN. Do I have to take an oath? When I say I'll do a thing, I do it!—Well, thanks for the snack, anyhow . . . it tasted good! [*He corks the wine bottle with gusto.*]

MISS JULIE [*appears suddenly in the doorway. She speaks to someone outside*]. I'll be back immediately—you just wait there . . .

[JEAN *quickly slips the bottle into the table drawer; then he rises respectfully.* MISS JULIE *enters and goes over to* KRISTIN *by the mirror.*]

MISS JULIE. Well, Kristin, is it ready?

[KRISTIN *indicates* JEAN*'s presence.*]

JEAN [*with gallantry*]. Do you ladies have secrets between you?

MISS JULIE [*with a flip of her handkerchief in his face*]. No inquisitiveness!

JEAN. Ah—what lovely fragrance—the smell of violets—

MISS JULIE [*coquettishly*]. So—you are impertinent, are you? Are you a connoisseur of scents, too? You are an expert at dancing. Now, now—no peeking! Go away!

JEAN [*impudently, yet with a semblance of politeness*]. Is it some sort of witches' brew for Midsummer Night that you two ladies are concocting? Something to help you look into the future and see what your lucky star has in store for you—and get a glimpse of your intended?

MISS JULIE [*tartly*]. You have to have good eyes for that! [*To* KRISTIN.] Pour it into a small bottle and put the cork in tight.—Now come and dance a schottische[8] with me, Jean.

JEAN [*hesitantly*]. I don't mean to be disrespectful, but I promised Kristin this dance . . .

MISS JULIE. Oh, she can dance the next one with you instead. How about it, Kristin? You'll loan me Jean, won't you?

KRISTIN. That's not for me to say. [*To* JEAN.] If Miss Julie condescends, it's not for you to say no. Go on, Jean, and be thankful to Miss Julie for the honor!

JEAN. If you will permit me to speak frankly, Miss Julie—and I hope you won't be offended—I wonder whether it's wise of you to dance more than one dance with the same partner . . . especially as people here are only too prone to misinterpret, to imagine things . . .

MISS JULIE [*flares up*]. What do you mean? What kind of interpretations? Just what is it you mean?

JEAN [*servilely*]. Since you refuse to understand, Miss Julie, I'll have to speak more plainly. It doesn't look good to single out one of your domestics in preference to some of the others, who would like to have the same honor paid to them . . .

MISS JULIE. Single out? Preference? What an idea! I am astonished! I—the mistress of the house—honor the people by attending their dance . . . and when I feel like dancing, I want to dance with someone who knows how to lead! I don't want to dance with someone who makes me look ridiculous!

JEAN. Just as you say, Miss Julie! I am at your service!

MISS JULIE [*in an appeasing tone of voice*]. Don't take it as an order now! Tonight we are celebrating! We all want to enjoy the holiday. We are all happy—and all just plain human beings . . . and rank doesn't count! Come now, give me your arm! You don't have to worry, Kristin—I am not going to take your sweetheart away from you!

[JEAN *offers her his arm: she takes it, and they go out.*]

The following scene is entirely in pantomime. It is to be played as if the actress were alone on the stage. Whenever necessary, she should turn her back to the audience and she should not look in the direction of the audience. She must be in no hurry, as though afraid that the audience might become impatient. KRISTIN *is alone. The faint sound of violin music in the distance, played in schottische tempo, is heard. She hums the tune while clearing* JEAN*'s place at the table, washes the dishes and utensils in the sink, dries them and puts them away in the cupboard. Then she removes her apron, takes out a small mirror from a drawer and places it on the table, supporting the mirror against the jar of lilacs. She lights a candle and heats a hairpin, with which she curls her forelock. This done, she goes to the door and stands there listening. Then she goes back to the table and discovers* MISS JULIE*'s forgotten handkerchief. She sniffs of it; then she distractedly smoothes it out and folds it carefully.*

[8] A kind of folk dance in two-four time, rather like a slow polka.

JEAN [*enters alone*]. She is mad, really! Dancing the way she does! The people are standing behind the doors, grinning at her. . . . What do you think has got into her, Kristin?

KRISTIN. Oh, she's having her period—and then she is always so peculiar.—Well, do you want to dance with me now?

JEAN. I hope you are not cross with me because I let you down a moment ago, are you?

KRISTIN. Certainly not! Not for a little thing like that—you ought to know that! And I know my place . . .

JEAN [*puts his arm round her waist*]. You show good sense, Kristin. You'll make a good wife. . . .

MISS JULIE [*enters. She is unpleasantly surprised. She speaks with forced good humor*]. Well—you are a fine young swain—running away from your partner!

JEAN. On the contrary, Miss Julie, I just hastened back to the one I deserted . . .

MISS JULIE [*changing tactics*]. Do you know—you dance as nobody else! But why do you wear your livery on a holiday like this? Take it off—this minute!

JEAN. Well—then I must ask you, Miss Julie, to step outside for a moment. . . . My black coat is hanging over there. . . .

[*He points toward it and goes over to the left.*]

MISS JULIE. You are not embarrassed because of me, are you? Just to change your coat?—Go into your room, then, and come back when you have changed. . . . Or you can stay here, and I'll turn my back.

JEAN. If you'll excuse me, then, Miss Julie. [*He goes to his room, on the left. One sees the movement of his arm while he is changing coats.*]

MISS JULIE [*to* KRISTIN]. Tell me, Kristin, is Jean your fiancé, is he? You seem to be so intimate.

KRISTIN. Fiancé? Well—yes, if you like! We call it being engaged.

MISS JULIE. Oh, you do?

KRISTIN. Well, you have been engaged yourself, Miss Julie, and . . .

MISS JULIE. Yes, but *we* were *properly* engaged.

KRISTIN. Just the same, nothing came of it.

[JEAN *re-enters, now dressed in a black cutaway and carrying a black bowler.*]

MISS JULIE [*regards him admiringly*]. *Très gentil, Monsieur Jean. Très gentil.*

JEAN. *Vous voulez plaisanter, madame!*

MISS JULIE. *Et vous voulez parlez français?*[9] Where have you learned that?

JEAN. In Switzerland—when I was steward in one of the largest hotels in Lucerne.

MISS JULIE. Why, you look a real gentleman in that cutaway! *Charmant!*[10] [*She seats herself at the table.*]

JEAN. Oh, you flatter me!

MISS JULIE [*offended*]. Flatter you?

[9] "Very elegant, Monsieur Jean! Very elegant!" "You wish to joke, madame." "And you wish to speak French?" (French.)

[10] "Charming!" (French).

JEAN. My natural modesty forbids me to believe that you could honestly pay compliments to anyone like me and that is why I had the audacity to assume that you were merely exaggerating—or, as it is called, engaging in flattery.

MISS JULIE. Where did you learn to phrase your words so nimbly? You must have visited the theaters a good deal?

JEAN. I've done that, too! Yes, I have been to many places.

MISS JULIE. But you were born here in the neighborhood, weren't you?

JEAN. My father was a farmhand on the county prosecutor's estate nearby. I remember seeing you when you were a child. But you never took any notice of me.

MISS JULIE. Oh, you do, really?

JEAN. Yes, and I especially remember one time . . . oh, but I can't tell you about that.

MISS JULIE. Oh, yes, do—go on—why not? This is just the time . . .

JEAN. No, really—I can't . . . not now! Some other time, perhaps . . .

MISS JULIE. Another time may be never. Is it anything so shocking?

JEAN. No, it isn't anything shocking at all—just the same I feel a little squeamish about it. Look at her there. [*He points to* KRISTIN *who has gone to sleep in a chair by the stove.*]

MISS JULIE. She'll make a delightful wife, won't she? Perhaps she snores, too?

JEAN. No—but she talks in her sleep.

MISS JULIE [*with sarcasm*]. How do you know?

JEAN [*with bravado*]. I have heard her. [*There is a silence. They eye each other.*]

MISS JULIE. Why don't you sit down?

JEAN. I couldn't—not in your presence!

MISS JULIE. And if I order you to?

JEAN. I would obey.

MISS JULIE. Sit down, then!—Oh, wait! Would you get me something to drink first . . .

JEAN. I don't know what there is in the ice-box here. I think there is only some beer.

MISS JULIE. That's not to be despised—and my tastes are so simple that I prefer it to wine.

JEAN [*takes out a bottle of ale from the ice-box, and opens it. Then he goes to the cupboard and brings out a glass and a plate, and serves her*]. If you please!

MISS JULIE. Thank you! Wouldn't you like some yourself?

JEAN. I am not particularly fond of beer—but since you insist . . .

MISS JULIE. Insist? I should think ordinary good manners would prompt you to keep me company . . .

JEAN. You are quite right, Miss Julie! [*He uncorks a bottle of ale and brings out another glass from the cupboard; then pours himself a glass of ale.*]

MISS JULIE. Now drink a toast to me! [JEAN *hesitates.*] Old as you are, I believe you are bashful.

JEAN [*kneeling, he raises his glass and jestingly parodies*]. To my sovereign and mistress!

MISS JULIE. Bravo! Now you must kiss my foot—as a crowning touch!

[JEAN *hesitates, and then he boldly takes her foot and gives it a light kiss.*]

MISS JULIE. Superb! You should have been an actor!

JEAN [*rises*]. We must not go on like this, Miss Julie . . . someone might come in and catch us—

MISS JULIE. Why should that matter?

JEAN. Because people would start to gossip, that's the reason! You should have heard their tongues wagging out there just now . . .

MISS JULIE. What did they say? Go on, tell me! Sit down . . .

JEAN [*sits down*]. I don't wish to hurt your feelings, Miss Julie—but they used expressions . . . that . . . well, they blurted out suspicions of a kind that . . . well, you can well imagine what kind— You are not a child, Miss Julie, and if you see a lady drinking alone with a man—and especially a servant—and at night—why—

MISS JULIE. What then? And besides, we are not alone. . . . Kristin is here, isn't she?

JEAN. Yes—asleep!

MISS JULIE. I'll wake her up! [*She rises.*] Kristin, are you asleep?

KRISTIN [*in her sleep*]. Bla-bla-bla-bla . . .

MISS JULIE. Kristin!—She is sound asleep!

KRISTIN [*still in her sleep*]. The Count's boots are polished—put on the coffee—I'll do it this minute—this very minute—phew—pish—ho— [*She snores.*]

MISS JULIE [*twists her nose*]. Wake up, will you?

JEAN [*sternly*]. One should never disturb people when they are asleep!

MISS JULIE [*in a sharp tone of voice*]. What's that?

JEAN. Anyone who stands at the stove all day long has a right to be tired at the end of the day. And sleep should be respected.

MISS JULIE [*in a different tone*]. It's considerate of you to think like that—it does you credit! Thank you! [*She extends her hand to him.*] Come outside with me and pick a few lilacs . . .

[KRISTIN *wakes, rises and goes sleepily to her bedroom, on the left.*]

JEAN. With you, Miss Julie?

MISS JULIE. Yes, with me!

JEAN. It would never do! Absolutely not!

MISS JULIE. I don't understand what you mean. . . . You couldn't possibly be imagining things, could you?

JEAN. No—not I . . . but the people.

MISS JULIE. What? That I am in love with a domestic?

JEAN. I am not conceited—but such things *have* happened. . . . And nothing is sacred to anybody.

MISS JULIE [*tartly*]. You talk like an aristocrat!

JEAN. Yes—and I *am!*

MISS JULIE. And *I*—am I lowering myself?

JEAN. Take my advice, Miss Julie, do not lower yourself! No one will believe you did it innocently. People will always say that you fell!

MISS JULIE. I have a higher opinion of people than you have. Come and let us see if I am right—Come on! [*She gives him a challenging glance.*]

JEAN. You know, Miss Julie, you are a very strange young lady!

MISS JULIE. Perhaps I am—but so are you strange! For that matter, everything is strange! Life, human beings—everything is scum and slime that floats and drifts on the surface until it sinks—sinks to the bottom! It makes me think of a dream that comes back to me ever so often: I am perched on top of a tall column and can see no way of getting down. When I gaze below, I feel dizzy. Yet I must get down; but I haven't the courage to jump. There is nothing to hold on to, and I hope that I may fall—but I don't. . . . Nevertheless I feel I cannot be at peace until I am down, down on the ground. . . . And if I should once reach the ground, I would want to be buried in the earth. Have you ever had such a feeling?

JEAN. No! *I* usually dream that I am lying underneath a tall tree in a dark forest. I have a desire to get up high, to the very top of the tree and look out over the bright landscape where the sun is shining—and to rob the bird's nest up there of its golden eggs. And I climb and climb; but the tree's trunk is so thick and so slippery, and the lowest branches are so high up. But I know that if I can only reach the first branch, I'll get to the top as easily as on a ladder. So far I have never reached it, but I am going to—even if it's only in my dreams.

MISS JULIE. Here I stand talking about dreams with you. . . . Come now! Only into the garden! [*She offers him her arm and they go out.*]

JEAN. We must sleep on nine midsummer blossoms tonight, Miss Julie; then our dreams will come true.

[MISS JULIE *and* JEAN *turn at the door.* JEAN *suddenly covers one eye with his hand.*]

MISS JULIE. Let me see what you have in your eye.

JEAN. Oh, its nothing . . . just a speck of dust. It'll disappear in a minute.

MISS JULIE. It was from my sleeve—it brushed against your eye. Sit down and let me help you! [*She takes him by the arm and leads him to a chair, takes hold of his head and bends it backward, then tries to remove the speck from his eye with the tip of her handkerchief.*] Sit still now, very still! [*She slaps him on the hand.*] Will you do as I tell you!—I believe the great, big, strong fellow is trembling! [*She feels his biceps.*] With arms like yours!

JEAN [*tries to dissuade her*]. Miss Julie!

MISS JULIE. Yes, Monsieur Jean!

JEAN. *Attention! Je ne suis qu'un homme!*[11]

MISS JULIE. Will you sit still!—There now! I got it out! Kiss my hand now and say "thank you"!

JEAN [*gets up from the chair*]. Miss Julie, will you please listen to me!—Kristin has gone to bed now.—Will you listen to me!

MISS JULIE. Kiss my hand first!

JEAN. Very well—but the blame will be yours!

MISS JULIE. Blame for what?

JEAN. For what? You are twenty-five years old, aren't you, and not a child? Don't you know it's dangerous to play with fire?

MISS JULIE. Not for me. I'm insured.

JEAN [*boldly*]. No, you are not! And if you are, you are not far from danger—you may trigger a combustion!

MISS JULIE. I presume you mean yourself!

JEAN. Yes. Not because it is I, but because I am a man, and young!

[11]"Careful! I'm only a man!" (French.)

MISS JULIE. Of prepossessing appearance. . . . What incredible conceit! Another Don Juan, perhaps! Or a Joseph![12] Upon my soul, I believe you are another Joseph!

JEAN. You do, do you?

MISS JULIE. Yes, I almost think so . . .

[JEAN *boldly goes up to her and tries to embrace and kiss her.*]

MISS JULIE [*boxes his ears*]. That'll teach you manners!

JEAN. Were you serious or were you jesting?

MISS JULIE. Serious.

JEAN. In that case, you were serious a moment ago also? You play much too seriously—and there is where the danger lies! Now I am tired of playing and beg to be excused so that I can go back to my work. The Count has to have his boots ready when he returns, and it's long past midnight.

[*He picks up a pair of boots.*]

MISS JULIE. Put down those boots!

JEAN. No. This is my work which I am hired to do—but I was never hired to be your playmate, and that's something I can never be. . . . I consider myself above that!

MISS JULIE. You are proud.

JEAN. In certain ways, yes—not in others.

MISS JULIE. Have you ever been in love?

JEAN. We don't use that word; but I have been fond of many girls—and once I felt sick because I couldn't have the one I wanted: sick, you know, like the princes in *A Thousand and One Nights*[13]—who could neither eat nor drink merely for love!

MISS JULIE. Who was the girl? [JEAN *does not answer.*] Who was she?

JEAN. That's something you couldn't force out of me.

MISS JULIE. If I ask you as an equal, ask you as a—friend. . . . Who was she?

JEAN. It was you!

MISS JULIE [*seats herself*]. How priceless!

JEAN. Yes, you may call it that! It was preposterous!—You see—it was that incident I was loath to tell you about, a moment ago—but now I shall. . . . Do you know how your world looks from below? No, you don't. Like hawks and falcons—whose backs we rarely see because they are always soaring high up in the sky. . . . I lived in my father's little shack with seven brothers and sisters and one pig out in the gray, barren fields where not even a tree grew. But from the windows I could see the wall enclosing the Count's park, with the apple trees rising above it. That was to me the Garden of Eden; and it was protected by a multitude of fierce angels with flaming swords. In spite of their presence, I and some other boys found our way to the tree of life. . . . Now you despise me, don't you?

[12] Don Juan is the legendary seducer of "a thousand and one women." Joseph is the Hebrew patriarch, who in his youth as a servant in Egypt tried to escape the unwelcome attentions of the wife of Potiphar, his master. See Genesis 39.

[13] *The Arabian Nights,* a collection of stories derived from India and Persia. Written in Arabic, the stories were first translated into a European language in a French translation of 1704–17.

MISS JULIE. Heavens, no—all boys steal apples!

JEAN. You say so now, but you have contempt for me just the same. . . . Well—one time I went into the Garden of Paradise with my mother, to weed the onion beds. Near the vegetable garden there was a Turkish pavilion standing in the shade of jasmine, and overgrown with honeysuckle. I had no idea what it could be used for; but I had never seen such a beautiful building.[14] . . . People went inside, then came out again; and one day the door was left open. I sneaked in and saw the walls were covered with pictures of emperors and kings; and hanging at the windows were red curtains with tassels. Now you understand where I was . . . I . . . [*He breaks off a spray of lilac and holds it close to her nostrils.*] I had never been inside the castle, and had never seen any place as grand as the church, but this was if anything more beautiful. . . . And no matter which way my thoughts went, they always returned to—to that backhouse. . . . And gradually it developed into a yearning to experience some day all of its splendor and charm.—*Enfin,*[15] I stole inside, gazed and admired, but just then I heard someone coming! There was only one exit for cultivated people—but for me there was another; and I had no choice but to take it . . .[16]

[MISS JULIE, *who meanwhile has accepted the lilac spray from* JEAN, *lets it drop on the table.*]

JEAN. . . . and then I took to my heels, plunged through a raspberry hedge, dashed across the strawberry patches and found myself on the rose terrace. There I gazed at a figure in pink dress and white stockings—it was you. I hid underneath a heap of weeds and lay there—lay there, imagine, with thistles pricking me and under dank, stinking earth. And as I watched you among the roses, I thought to myself: If it is true that a thief can get to heaven and be with the angels, why should it be impossible for a poor peasant child here on God's earth to get into the castle park and play with the Count's daughter . . .

MISS JULIE [*with an expression of pain*]. Do you think all poor children have the same thoughts that you had?

JEAN [*at first hesitantly, then with conviction*]. That all poor children . . . Yes—of course—of course . . .

MISS JULIE. It must be terrible to be poor!

JEAN. Oh, Miss Julie—oh! A dog may lie on the Countess's sofa—a horse have his nose stroked by a young lady—but a lackey . . . [*In a changed tone.*] Oh, of course, there are some who have the right stuff in them and who swing themselves up in the world—but that doesn't happen every day. Anyhow, do you know what I did? I ran down to the millpond and jumped in, with my clothes on. I was dragged out and given a thrashing. But the following Sunday when my father and the rest of the family had gone to visit my grandmother, I schemed to stay at home. I then washed myself with soap and warm water, put on my best clothes and went to church—where I knew I would see you! I saw you and went back home, determined to die. . . . But I wanted to die

[14] The "Turkish pavilion" is a privy. [15] "In short" (French).
[16] *another.* Through the pit for excrement.

beautifully and comfortably, without pain. I suddenly remembered that it was dangerous to sleep beneath an alder bush. We had a large one that was just blooming. I stripped it of its flowers; then made a bed of them in the oats-bin. Did you ever notice how smooth and silken oats are? Soft to the touch as the human skin. Well, I closed the lid, shut my eyes, and fell asleep. And when I woke up, I was very, very sick! . . . But as you see, I didn't die. What was in my mind, I really don't know! . . . I had no hope of ever winning you, of course—but you represented to me the hopelessness of ever rising above the social level to which I was born.

MISS JULIE. You know, you express yourself charmingly! Did you ever go to school?

JEAN. Briefly. But I have read a great many novels. And I have gone to the theater. Also I have listened to cultured people talking, and I've learned most from that.

MISS JULIE. You stand and listen to what we say?

JEAN. Certainly! And I have heard much—much—when I've been sitting on the carriage-box and when I've been at the oars in the rowboat. I once heard you, Miss Julie, and a girl friend of yours . . .

MISS JULIE. Oh!—What did you hear?

JEAN. Well, I don't know that I can tell you. . . . But I must say I was rather surprised; and I couldn't imagine where you had learned words like that. After all, perhaps there isn't such a great difference between people as one thinks—

MISS JULIE. Shame on you! We don't behave like you do when we are engaged!

JEAN [*with a penetrating look*]. Are you so sure? There is no use making yourself out so innocent, Miss Julie . . .

MISS JULIE. The man I gave my love to turned out to be a blackguard![17]

JEAN. That's what you always say—when it's over.

MISS JULIE. Always?

JEAN. Yes, always—at least that's what I think, having heard the same expression before—under such circumstances.

MISS JULIE. What sort of circumstances?

JEAN. Such as this one! The last time—

MISS JULIE. Stop! I don't want to hear any more!

JEAN. Strange to say, that's exactly what *she* said!—Well, now I must ask you to let me go to bed . . .

MISS JULIE [*softly*]. Go to bed at this hour—on Midsummer Eve?[18]

JEAN. Yes—I don't care the least bit about dancing with that riff-raff out there . . .

MISS JULIE. Go and get the key to the boathouse and take me for a row on the lake! I want to see the sunrise!

JEAN. Would that be a wise thing to do?

MISS JULIE. It sounds as if you were afraid of your reputation!

[17] Rascal.

[18] A folk festival celebrated especially in the Scandinavian countries. It originated as a pagan fertility festival and still carries overtones of sexual license.

JEAN. And why shouldn't I be? I don't want to be made to look ridiculous and I have no desire to be discharged without a reference just when I am hoping to start on my own. And besides, I feel I am under some obligation to Kristin . . .

MISS JULIE. Oh, so it's Kristin again?

JEAN. Yes—but it's you, too. Take my advice: go to bed!

MISS JULIE. Should I take orders from you?

JEAN. Yes, for once—I beg of you—for your own sake! It's long past midnight. Lack of sleep brings on feverish excitement; it intoxicates and makes one reckless. Go to bed! And besides, if I am not mistaken, I hear the people coming this way, and they will be looking for me. . . . If they find us here, you'll be under a cloud!

[*The crowd, approaching, is heard to sing.*]

There came two wedded maids from the wood—
Tridiridi-ralla tridiridi-ra.
The one had wet her little foot
Tridiridi-ralla-la.

They kept talking of nothing but money—
Tridiridi-ralla tridiridi-ra.
Yet they scarcely owned a farthing
Tridiridi-ralla-la.

Your ring I now give back to you
Tridiridi-ralla tridiridi-ra.
For I've another man in view
Tridiridi-ralla-la.

MISS JULIE. I know the people here, and I love them as they love me. Let them come and you'll see.

JEAN. No, Miss Julie, they don't love you. They accept your food, but spit at you behind your back! Believe me! Listen to them! Just listen to what they are singing. . . . No—don't listen!

MISS JULIE [*stands listening*]. What is it they are singing?

JEAN. It's an indecent parody! About you and me!

MISS JULIE. It's disgraceful! Shameless! What deceit!

JEAN. People like them are always cowardly! All you can do when you fight with rabble is to flee!

MISS JULIE. Flee? But where? We can't get out, and we can't go into Kristin's room . . .

JEAN. Well—into mine, then? We have to—there is no other way—and you can trust me. I am your friend, truly and respectfully . . .

MISS JULIE. But suppose—suppose they should look for you in your room?

JEAN. I'll bolt the door—and if they try to break in, I'll shoot! Come! [*He pleads with her, on his knees.*] Come, please!

MISS JULIE [*significantly*]. Will you promise me . . .
JEAN. I swear!

[MISS JULIE *goes quickly into his room, left.* JEAN *follows her excitedly.*]

Dressed in their holiday best and with flowers in their hats and caps, the farm people enter. Leading them is a fiddler. They place a keg of small beer and a firkin[19] *of corn brandy, both decorated with garlands of fresh green leaves, on the table; then they bring out glasses and start drinking, form a ring and begin to dance, singing to the tune of "There came two wedded maids from the wood." When they have finished the dance, they leave, singing.*

MISS JULIE *comes from* JEAN'*s room, alone. She sees the kitchen in a deplorable mess, and claps her hands together in dejection. Then she takes out her powder-puff and powders her face.*

JEAN [*enters with bravado*]. Don't you see! Did you hear them? Do you think you can stay here after this?
MISS JULIE. No! I don't think I can! But what are we going to do?
JEAN. Get away from here—travel—go far away from here . . .
MISS JULIE. Go away—travel. Yes, but where?
JEAN. To Switzerland—to the Italian lakes. . . . You have never been there, have you?
MISS JULIE. No—is it beautiful there?
JEAN. Ah! Eternal summer—orange groves—laurel trees. . . . Ah!
MISS JULIE. And when we are there—what shall we do?
JEAN. I'll start a hotel business—everything first class, and for exclusive guests . . .
MISS JULIE. A hotel?
JEAN. That's a lively business, believe me! All the time new faces, new languages, you never have time to worry or to be bored. . . . You nerve yourself against anything—you never have to look for something to do, for there is never any let-up. Bells ring day and night—you hear the train whistles—buses and carriages come and go—and all the time the money keeps rolling in. That's the life, I tell you!
MISS JULIE. Yes—that's living. . . . And what about me?
JEAN. You'll be the mistress of the house—its chief attraction and ornament! With your looks, and your style and manner, why, our success is assured from the start! It'll be colossal! You'll be sitting like a queen in the office and you'll keep the slaves moving by pressing an electric button—the guests file past your throne and place their tribute timidly before you—you have no idea how nervous it makes people to have their bills presented to them. I'll salt the bills, and you'll sugar them with your sweetest smile. . . . Ah, please—let us get away from here! [*He takes out a timetable from his pocket.*] Without delay—by the next train! We'll be in Malmö at six-thirty—in Hamburg at eight-forty in the morn-

[19] A small wooden cask.

ing—in Frankfort and Basel within a day—and we'll get to Como,[20] by way of St. Gothard, in—let me see—in three days. Three days!

MISS JULIE. That's all very well—but, Jean—you must give me courage. Tell me that you love me! Come and take me in your arms!

JEAN [*hesitates*]. I want to—but I lack the courage . . . ever to do it in this house again. I love you—you know that—you can't doubt that, can you, Miss Julie?

MISS JULIE [*shyly, with true womanly feeling*]. Miss Julie? Call me Julie! Between us there can no longer be any barriers! Call me Julie!

JEAN [*pathetically*]. I can't! As long as we are in this house, there are barriers between us. There is tradition—and there is the Count. Never in my life have I met *anyone* who strikes such awe into me! I have only to see his gloves lying on a chair, and I feel servile. . . . I have only to hear him ring upstairs, and I cringe like a shying horse—and even now when I look at his boots standing there so stiff and cocky, I feel a chill down my spine. [*He kicks at the boots.*] Superstition, prejudice, convention—knocked into us from childhood—but that can easily be got rid of. . . . All you have to do is to go to another country, to a republic, and there you will see how they prostrate themselves before my porter's uniform. . . . Yes, they'll bow and scrape—but here is one who won't! I wasn't born to crawl before others—I have the right stuff in me—I have character . . . and if I only get to the first branch, you watch me climb to the top! Today I am a lackey—next year I'll be in business for myself—ten years from now I'll be rich and retire—and then I'll move to Roumania and get myself a decoration—and I may, mark my words, I may end up a count!

MISS JULIE. Very nice, very nice!

JEAN. Yes—for in Roumania you can buy yourself a title—and so you may, after all, be a countess, Miss Julie. . . . *My* countess!

MISS JULIE. All that doesn't interest me at all—I'm leaving all that behind me! Tell me only that you love me . . . for if you don't . . . well—then what would I be?

JEAN. I'll tell you—I'll tell you a thousand times—later on! But not now—not here! And above all, let's not be sentimental, or everything will go wrong! We must look at this matter calmly, soberly, like sensible people. [*Takes out a cigar, bites off the butt end and lights it.*] Now you sit down there, and I'll sit here; then we'll talk it over as if nothing had happened.

MISS JULIE [*desperately*]. My God—haven't you any feelings?

JEAN. *If* I have feelings! There isn't a man with more feeling than I! But I know how to control myself!

MISS JULIE. A moment ago you kissed my slipper—and now . . .

JEAN [*brutally*]. That was then—now we have other things to think of!

MISS JULIE. Don't speak to me so cruelly!

JEAN. I am speaking sensibly, that's all! One folly has been committed—don't commit any more! The Count may be here any moment now; and before he comes, we must settle our future. Now—what do you think of my plans, Miss Julie? Do you approve of them?

[20] Town on Lake Como, in northern Italy, a famous resort.

MISS JULIE. They seem likely enough—but let me ask one question: Have you sufficient capital to start such a large undertaking?

JEAN [*chewing his cigar*]. Have I? Of course I have! I have my training in the business, my vast experience, my linguistic ability! That's a capital to be reckoned with, don't you think?

MISS JULIE. But you couldn't buy a railroad ticket with it, could you?

JEAN [*keeps chewing the cigar*]. That's quite true—and that is why I am looking for a partner who can advance the necessary funds.

MISS JULIE. Where do you expect to find such a person in a hurry?

JEAN. That is where *you* come in—if you want to be my partner—

MISS JULIE. I couldn't . . . and I haven't any money of my own. [*There is a silence.*]

JEAN. Then we'll have to drop the whole thing . . .

MISS JULIE. And so . . .

JEAN. And so . . . things remain as they are . . .

MISS JULIE. Do you think I'll remain under this roof as your mistress? Do you think I will allow the people here to point a finger at me? Do you think I could face my father after this? Never! Take me away from here—from this humiliation and disgrace! Oh, my God, what have I done? My God! . . . [*She breaks into tears.*]

JEAN. So, that's the tune you are singing *now?* What you have done?—What many others have done before you . . .

MISS JULIE [*screaming hysterically*]. And now you despise me! I'm falling—falling—

JEAN. Fall low enough—fall down to my level—then I'll raise you up again!

MISS JULIE. What dreadful power could have drawn me to you? The attraction of the weak to the strong, the ones on the decline to the ones rising? Or could it have been love? Is this what you call love? Do you know what love is?

JEAN. Do I? You may be sure I do! Do you think I never had an affair before?

MISS JULIE. What a way to speak! And such thoughts!

JEAN. That's the way I was brought up, and that's the way I am! Now don't get excited, and stop acting so prim and prudish! For now you are not a bit better than I am. . . . Come here, my little girl, let me treat you to a glass of something very special! [*He opens the table drawer and brings out the wine bottle; then he fills the two glasses which were used previously.*]

MISS JULIE. Where did you get this wine?

JEAN. From the wine cellar.

MISS JULIE. My father's burgundy!

JEAN. Isn't it good enough for his son-in-law?

MISS JULIE. And I drink beer!

JEAN. That only shows your taste is not as good as mine!

MISS JULIE. Thief!

JEAN. You are not going to give me away, are you?

MISS JULIE. Oh, God! To be the accomplice of a thief—and in my own home! Have I been under the influence of some intoxication? Have I been dreaming this Midsummer Night?—This festival of frolic and innocent merriment?

JEAN [*sarcastically*]. Innocent, h'm!

MISS JULIE [*paces back and forth*]. Could there be anyone in this world more miserable than I am?

JEAN. Why be miserable—after a conquest like yours? Think of Kristin in there—don't you think that she, too, has feelings . . .

MISS JULIE. I used to think so, but I no longer do! No—once a servant, always a servant!

JEAN. And once a whore—always a whore!

MISS JULIE [*on her knees, her hands clasped*]. Oh, God in heaven—put an end to my miserable life! Take me away from this filth—I am sinking down in it! Help me! Save me!

JEAN. I can't help feeling sorry for you. . . . When I lay in the onion bed and watched you in the rose garden, I—yes, I can tell you now—I had the same nasty thoughts that all boys have.

MISS JULIE. And you—you wanted to die for me!

JEAN. You mean in the oats-bin? I just made that up!

MISS JULIE. Just a lie, then!

JEAN. [*He is beginning to be sleepy.*] Not exactly! I think I once read somewhere in a newspaper about a chimney-sweep who went to sleep in a chest used for firewood. He had filled it with lilacs—because he was sued for non-support of his child . . .

MISS JULIE. So that's the kind of person you are . . .

JEAN. I had to make up something. Glitter and tinsel are what dazzle the women—and catch them.

MISS JULIE. Cad!

JEAN. Garbage!

MISS JULIE. And now you have seen the hawk's back!

JEAN. Not exactly its *back* . . .

MISS JULIE. And I was to be the first branch . . .

JEAN. But the branch was rotten . . .

MISS JULIE. I was to be the hotel sign . . .

JEAN. And I the hotel . . .

MISS JULIE. . . . Sitting behind the desk to attract and lure customers, falsify the bills and overcharge them . . .

JEAN. That would have been *my* business . . .

MISS JULIE. To think that the human soul can be so low, so rotten—

JEAN. Wash it clean, why don't you?

MISS JULIE. You lackey! You menial! Stand up when I speak to you!

JEAN. You—a menial's strumpet—whore to a lackey—keep your mouth shut and get out of here! Is it for you to rake me over the coals for being coarse and uncouth? Never have I seen any of our kind behave so vulgarly as you behaved tonight! Do you think a servant girl would accost a man the way you did? Did you ever see a girl of my class throw herself at a man as you did? That's something I have only seen done by animals and prostitutes!

MISS JULIE [*crushed*]. That's right! Stone me—trample on me—I deserve it—all of it! I am a wretched woman! But help me—help me out of this—if there *is* a way out of it!

JEAN [*now in a milder tone of voice*]. I would belittle myself if I denied having a share in the honor of seducing you; but do you really think that anyone of my class would have dared to cast a glance at you, if you yourself had not sent out the invitation? I still can't get over it—

MISS JULIE. And you take pride in it!

JEAN. Why not?—Although I must confess the victory was much too easy to give me any real intoxication!

MISS JULIE. Keep on being brutal!

JEAN [*rises*]. No—on the contrary, I ask you to forgive me for the things I just said! I never strike a defenseless person—least of all a woman. I won't deny that it gives me a certain satisfaction to discover that what dazzled us down below was nothing but cheap tinsel; that the hawk's back was only gray, like the rest of his fine feathers; that the delicate complexion was mere powder; that the polished nails had dirty edges; that the handkerchief could be soiled, despite its perfumed scent. . . . But on the other hand, it hurts me to realize that what I was striving to reach was so unsubstantial and artificial . . . it pains me to see that you have sunk so low that you are far beneath your own cook . . . it saddens me as when I see the autumn leaves torn into tatters by the rain and turned into mud.

MISS JULIE. You talk as if you already feel yourself above me?

JEAN. Of course I am! You see, I might be able to make you a countess—but you could never make me a count.

MISS JULIE. But you are a thief, and I am not!

JEAN. There are worse things than being a thief! Much worse! Besides, when I am employed in a household, I consider myself, in a way, a member of the family, related to it, so to speak; and to pick a berry or two when the bushes are full is not stealing. . . . [*His passion comes to life again.*] Miss Julie—you are a glorious woman—far too good for one like me! You are under the spell of some sort of intoxication, and now you want to cover up your mistake by deluding yourself that you love me! But you don't! You may be attracted to me physically—and in that case your love is no better than mine! But I am not content with being just an animal, to you; and I can never kindle any love in you for me—

MISS JULIE. Are you so sure of that?

JEAN. Do you mean to say that I could?—I could love you, yes—no doubt of that! You are beautiful, you are refined—[*He comes close to her and takes hold of her hand.*] . . . cultivated, and charming—when you feel like it; and I don't think that any man who has once fallen for you will ever stop loving you. [*He puts his arm round her waist.*] You are like mulled wine, strongly spiced—and a kiss from you. . . . [*He tries to lead her out of the kitchen. She gently frees herself from him.*]

MISS JULIE. Let me go! You will never win me that way . . .

JEAN. Then *how?* Not *that* way, you say. Not by caresses and pretty words—not by thoughtfulness about the future—trying to save you from disgrace! How then?

MISS JULIE. How? You ask how? I don't know . . . haven't a thought! I loathe you as I loathe a rat—but I can't escape you!

JEAN. Escape *with* me, then!

MISS JULIE [*straightens up*]. Escape? Yes, we must get away from here! But I am so tired!—Pour me a glass of wine!

[JEAN *serves her a glass.*]

MISS JULIE [*looking at her watch*]. But first we must have a talk—we still have a little time left. [*She empties her glass and holds it out for another drink.*]

JEAN. You must drink moderately, or it'll go to your head.

MISS JULIE. What does it matter?

JEAN. What does it matter? To be intoxicated is a sign of vulgarity. . . . What was it you wanted to tell me?

MISS JULIE. We have to get away from here! But first we must have a talk—that is, I must do the talking—for so far it is you who have done it all. You have told me about your life; now I shall tell you about mine—then we shall really know each other, before we begin our journey together.

JEAN. Wait a second! If you'll pardon my suggestion—don't you think you may regret it afterwards, if you bare your life's secrets?

MISS JULIE. Are you not my friend?

JEAN. Yes—in a way. . . . But don't put too much confidence in me.

MISS JULIE. You don't mean what you say—and besides: everybody knows my secrets. You see, my mother was not an aristocrat by birth. She came of quite simple stock. She was brought up in conformity with the ideas of her generation: equality of the sexes—the emancipation of women—and all that sort of thing. She looked upon marriage with downright aversion. Therefore, when my father proposed marriage to her, she replied that she would never be his wife—but—she married him just the same. I came into the world—against my mother's wishes, as I have learned; and now I was to be reared by my mother as a child of nature and in addition was to be taught all the things a boy has to learn, all in order to prove that a woman is quite as good as any man. I had to wear boy's clothes, had to learn how to handle horses, but I was never allowed in the cattle barn. I had to groom, harness and saddle my horse and had to go hunting—yes, I even had to try my hand at farming! And the farmhands were given women's chores to do, and the women did the men's work—and the upshot of it was that the estate almost went to rack and ruin, and we became the laughingstock of the whole countryside. . . . At last my father seems to have come out of his inertia, for he rebelled; and after that all went according to his will. My mother took sick—what the sickness was I never learned—but she frequently had spasms, shut herself up in the attic, or secluded herself in the garden—and sometimes she stayed out all night. Then came the great fire which you have heard about. The house, the stables, and the cattle barns burned down, and under suspicious circumstances that pointed to arson. The disaster happened, namely, the day after the quarterly insurance period had expired; and the insurance premium, that my father had forwarded by a messenger, had arrived too late because of the messenger's negligence or indifference. [*She fills up her glass, and drinks.*]

JEAN. You mustn't drink any more!

MISS JULIE. Ah, what do I care!—We were left with nothing, we had no place to sleep, except in the carriages. My father was desperate; he didn't know where to get money to build again. Then my mother suggested to him that he borrow from an old friend of hers—someone she had known in her youth, a brick manufacturer not far from here. Father got the loan, and without having to pay any interest—and this was a surprise to him. And the estate was rebuilt! [*She drinks again.*] Do you know who set the place on fire?

JEAN. The Countess, your mother . . .

MISS JULIE. Do you know who the brick manufacturer was?

JEAN. Your mother's lover?

MISS JULIE. Do you know whose money it was?

JEAN. Wait a second!—No—I don't—

MISS JULIE. It was my mother's.

JEAN. In other words, your father's—the Count's—unless they had made a marriage settlement.

MISS JULIE. No, there was none. My mother had a little money of her own. She didn't want my father to have charge of it, so she—entrusted it to her friend!

JEAN. And he helped himself to it!

MISS JULIE. Precisely! He appropriated the money. All this my father came to know. He couldn't bring action against him, couldn't repay his wife's lover, couldn't prove that the money was his wife's!—That was the revenge my mother took on him because he had made himself the master in his own house. He was on the verge of committing suicide when all this happened; as a matter of fact, there was a rumor that he tried to and didn't succeed. . . . However, he took a new lease of life, and my mother had to pay the penalty for her behavior! You can imagine what the next five years did to me! I felt sorry for my father, yet I took my mother's part because I didn't know the true circumstances. She had taught me to mistrust and hate men, for she herself hated men, as I told you before—and she made me swear never to become the slave of any man . . .

JEAN. And then you became engaged to the county prosecutor!

MISS JULIE. Yes—in order to make him my slave.

JEAN. And he refused?

MISS JULIE. He would have liked it, don't worry; but I didn't give him the chance. I became bored with him . . .

JEAN. I saw that you did—out in the stableyard.

MISS JULIE. What did you see?

JEAN. Exactly what happened—how he broke off the engagement.

MISS JULIE. That's a lie! It was I who broke the engagement!—Did he tell you he did? The scoundrel!

JEAN. I wouldn't call him a scoundrel. . . . You just hate men, Miss Julie.

MISS JULIE. Yes, I do! Most men! But occasionally—when my weakness comes over me—oh, the shame of it!

JEAN. You hate me, too, don't you?

MISS JULIE. I hate you no end! I should like to have you slaughtered like an animal!

JEAN. As one shoots a mad dog, eh?

MISS JULIE. Precisely!

JEAN. But as there is nothing here to shoot with, and no dog—what are we to do?

MISS JULIE. Get away from here!

JEAN. And then torture each other to death?

MISS JULIE. No—live life for a few brief days, for a week—for as long as we can—and then—die . . .

JEAN. Die? What nonsense! No—I think it would be far better to go into the hotel business.

MISS JULIE [*who, absorbed with her thoughts, has not heard what he said*]. . . . by Lake Como, where the sun is always shining—where the laurel tree is still greening at Christmas—and the oranges are golden red—

JEAN. Lake Como is a hole where it rains all the time, and I never saw any oranges there except in the grocery shops. But it's a good place for foreigners—and there are plenty of villas to be rented to lovers—and that is a business that pays! And do you know why? I'll tell you why—because they have to sign a six months' lease, and they never stay longer than three weeks!

MISS JULIE [*naïvely*]. Why only three weeks?

JEAN. Because they quarrel, of course. But the rent has to be paid in full just the same. And then the house is rented out again; and that's the way it goes—on and on—for people will always be in love, although their love doesn't last very long . . .

MISS JULIE. Then you don't care to die with me, do you?

JEAN. I don't care to die at all! Not only because I like to live, but because I consider suicide a sin against God, who gave us life.

MISS JULIE. You believe in God—*you?*

JEAN. Of course I do! I go to church every other Sunday. But now—quite frankly—now I am getting tired of all this talk, and I am going to bed.

MISS JULIE. Oh, you are, are you? And you think that will be a satisfactory ending? Do you know what a man owes to a woman he has taken advantage of?

JEAN [*takes out his purse and throws a coin on the table*]. There you are! Now I owe you nothing!

MISS JULIE [*pretends to ignore the insult*]. Are you aware of the legal consequences?

JEAN. It's too bad that the law provides no punishment for the woman who seduces a man!

MISS JULIE. Can you think of any way out of this other than going abroad, getting married, and being divorced?

JEAN. Suppose I refuse to enter into such a degrading marriage?

MISS JULIE. Degrading?

JEAN. Yes—for me! For, mind you, my lineage is cleaner and more respectable than yours—I have no pyromaniac in my family—

MISS JULIE. How can you be so sure of that?

JEAN. And how can you prove the opposite? We have no register of our ancestors—except in the police records! But I have seen your genealogical chart in the book on your drawing-room table. Do you know who your first ancestor was? A miller who let his wife sleep with the king one night during the Danish War!—I haven't any ancestors like that! I have no ancestry of any kind—but I can start a family tree of my own!

MISS JULIE. This is what I get for opening my heart to one like you, to an inferior . . . for betraying the honor of my family . . .

JEAN. You mean *dishonor!* . . . Well, I warned you—and now you see—People shouldn't drink, for then they start talking—and people should never be garrulous.

MISS JULIE. Oh, how I regret what I have done! How I regret it! Oh, if—at least—you had loved me!

JEAN. For the last time—what is it you want me to do? Do you want me to burst into tears? Do you want me to jump over your riding whip? Do you want me to kiss you?—to elope with you to Lake Como for three weeks?—and then. . . . What do you want me to do? What is it you want? This is getting to be intolerable! But that's what one gets for sticking one's nose into a female's business! Miss Julie—I know you must be suffering—but I can't understand you. . . . We have no such strange notions as you have—we don't hate as you do! To us love is nothing but playfulness—we play when our work is done. We haven't the whole day and the whole night for it like you! I think you must be sick. . . . Yes, I am sure you are!

MISS JULIE. You must treat me with kindness—you must speak to me like a human being . . .

JEAN. Yes, if you'll behave like one! You spit on me—but when I spit back, you object!

MISS JULIE. Oh, help me—help me! Tell me what to do—and where to go!

JEAN. In the name of Christ, I wish I knew myself!

MISS JULIE. I have behaved like a madwoman . . . but is there no way out of this?

JEAN. Stay here—and stop worrying! Nobody knows a thing.

MISS JULIE. I can't! They all know—and Kristin knows. . . .

JEAN. They know nothing—and they wouldn't believe such a thing!

MISS JULIE [*after a moment's hesitation*]. But—it might happen again!

JEAN. Yes—it might.

MISS JULIE. And have consequences? . . .

JEAN. Consequences? . . . What have I been thinking about? That never occurred to me!—Then there is only one thing to do. You must leave—and immediately! If I come with you, it would look suspicious—therefore you must go alone—go away—it doesn't matter where.

MISS JULIE. I—alone—but where? I couldn't do it!

JEAN. You must—and before the Count gets back! If you remain here, we both know what will happen. Having committed one mistake, it's easy to make another because the damage has already been done. . . . With time one gets more and more reckless—until finally one is caught! That's why I urge you to leave! Later on you can write to the Count and tell him everything—except that it was I!—He would never suspect, of course—and I don't think he would be eager to know!

MISS JULIE. I'll go, if you'll come with me . . .

JEAN. Are you stark staring mad, woman? Miss Julie eloping with her lackey! It would be in the newspapers before another day had passed. The Count would never get over it!

MISS JULIE. I can't go—and I can't stay here! Can't you help me! I am so tired, so dreadfully tired!—Order me to go! Make me move! I am no longer able to think—I can't bring myself to do anything!

JEAN. Now you see what sort of miserable creature you are, don't you? Why is your sort always so overbearing? Why do you strut with your noses in the air as if you were the lords of Creation?—Very well, then—I shall order you about! Go upstairs and get dressed, take enough money with you for traveling and then come down!

MISS JULIE [*almost in a whisper*]. Come upstairs with me—

JEAN. To your room?—Now you are mad again! [*He hesitates a moment.*] No! Go immediately! [*He takes her by the hand and escorts her to the door.*]

MISS JULIE [*walking toward the door*]. Why don't you speak gently to me, Jean?

JEAN. An order always sounds harsh.—Now you are beginning to find out how it feels . . .

[JULIE *leaves.* JEAN *is now alone. He gives a sigh of relief, seats himself at the table, takes out a pencil and a notebook, writes down some figures; now and then he counts aloud, all in pantomime, until* KRISTIN *enters. She is dressed for church-going; carries a white tie and a false shirt front with collar, for* JEAN.]

KRISTIN. In heaven's name—look at my kitchen! What's been going on here?

JEAN. Oh—it's Miss Julie—she brought them all inside. . . . Don't tell me you've been sleeping so soundly you didn't hear them?

KRISTIN. Yes, I slept like a log!

JEAN. And you are already dressed for church?

KRISTIN. Sure! You promised to come to communion with me today, didn't you?

JEAN. Why, of course—so I did, didn't I?—And I see you have my outfit there—let's get ready, then!

[JEAN *seats himself, and* KRISTIN *starts to put the dickey, collar and tie on him. There is a silence.*]

JEAN [*sleepily*]. What is the text for today?

KRISTIN. Oh—I think it's about the beheading of John the Baptist.[21]

JEAN. Then I imagine it's going to be a terribly long service!—Ouch, you are choking me!—Oh, I am so sleepy, so sleepy!

KRISTIN. Well, what have you been doing the whole night—you are all green in the face?

JEAN. I've been sitting here talking to Miss Julie. . . .

KRISTIN. She just has no decency, that one!

[*Silence.*]

JEAN. Tell me, Kristin, don't you think—

KRISTIN. What?

[21] Beheaded at the instigation of Herodias and Salome. See Matthew 14:1–12 and Mark 6:14–29.

JEAN. Isn't it strange, after all, when you think about it—that she—
KRISTIN. What is it that's so strange?
JEAN. Everything!

[*There is a pause.*]

KRISTIN [*with a glance at the wine glasses that stand on the table, half-filled*]. You haven't been drinking together, have you?
JEAN. Yes!
KRISTIN. You ought to be ashamed of yourself! Look me straight in the eye! [JEAN *affirms her suspicions.*] Can it be possible? Can it really be possible?
JEAN [*deliberates for a moment, then answers her*]. Yes—that's what happened.
KRISTIN. Why! I would never have believed it! Never! Shame on you! Shame on you!
JEAN. You are not jealous of her, are you?
KRISTIN. No, not of her! If it had been Clara or Sophie—I would have scratched your eyes out! Yes—yes, that's the way I feel—and I can't tell you just why I feel that way! Oh, but this is disgusting—disgusting!
JEAN. Do you hate her for it?
KRISTIN. No—I am furious with you! It was a shameless thing to do—shameless! I pity the girl!—To tell the truth, I don't care to stay in this house any longer—I want to feel some respect for the people I work for. . .
JEAN. Why do we have to have respect for them?
KRISTIN. Well, you tell me—you who know everything! You don't want to work for people who don't behave decently, do you? Do you? . . . I think it's degrading, that's what I think . . . .
JEAN. Yes—but it makes you feel good to know that they are not a bit better than we are!
KRISTIN. No—I don't look at it that way at all. If they are no better than we are—what's the use of trying to be like them—of becoming any better than we are? And think of the Count—think of him—who has had so much grief in his day! No—I won't stay here in this house any longer! . . . And with such as you!—Now—if it had been the county prosecutor—or someone who was a little bit better than you—
JEAN. What's that?
KRISTIN. That's just what I said! You may be good enough in your own way, but just the same there is a difference between high and low. . . . No—I'll never be able to get over this!—Miss Julie who was so proud—who acted so superior toward men. . . . You would never have thought that she would have let any man become intimate with her—and, least of all, a fellow like you! She—who was about to have her poor little Diana shot just because she was running after the gatekeeper's pugdog. . . . Can you imagine it! But I won't stay here any longer—the twenty-fourth of October I quit!
JEAN. And then?
KRISTIN. Well—since you bring the matter up—it's about time you looked around for something to do, for we are going to get married just the same.
JEAN. Yes—but what kind of place am I to look for? If I marry, I couldn't get a place like this.

KRISTIN. No, I know that. But you can get a job as a janitor or porter—or try to get a position in some government bureau. The government doesn't pay much, but it's security—and, besides, the wife and children get a pension.

JEAN [*with a grimace*]. That's all very good, but it doesn't exactly fit in with my plans just now to be thinking about dying for the benefit of wife and children. I must confess that my aspirations are aimed at something a little bit higher.

KRISTIN. You and your ideas, yes! But you have responsibilities, too! Try to think of them!

JEAN. Don't make me lose my temper by talking about responsibilities! I know what I have to do! [*He suddenly listens to some sound from outside.*] Anyhow, we have plenty of time to decide just what to do. Go and get ready now so we can go to church.

KRISTIN. Who can that be I hear walking upstairs?

JEAN. I've no idea—unless it's Clara.

KRISTIN [*as she is leaving*]. I don't suppose it could be the Count, could it? Could he have come home without anybody hearing him?

JEAN [*panic-stricken*]. The Count? Why, no—I would never think so. . . . If he had, he would have rung . . .

KRISTIN. Well, God help us. . . . I've never heard of anything like this! [*She goes out.*]

[*The sun has now risen and casts its rays on the treetops in the park. The light beams keep moving until they fall obliquely through the windows.* JEAN *goes over to the door and gives a sign to* JULIE *outside.*]

MISS JULIE [*comes inside. She is dressed for travel and carries a small birdcage, covered with a towel. She places the cage on a chair*]. I am ready now.

JEAN. Ssh! Kristin is awake!

MISS JULIE [*from this moment on, she shows signs of extreme nervousness*]. Does she suspect anything?

JEAN. Not a thing! She knows nothing!—Lord in heaven—how you look!

MISS JULIE. Look? Why—what's the matter?

JEAN. Your face is livid! You look like a corpse . . . and if you'll pardon me, your face is not clean!

MISS JULIE. Then I must wash my face! [*She goes over to the sink and washes her face and hands.*] Would you give me a towel?—Oh . . . I see the sun is rising . . .

JEAN. . . . and now the spell will be broken!

MISS JULIE. Yes, the trolls have been out this night!—But now, Jean,—you can come with me, do you hear, for I have all the money we need.

JEAN [*with disbelief and hesitation*]. You have enough?

MISS JULIE. Enough to start with. . . . Please come with me! I can't travel alone now. . . . Imagine my sitting alone on a stuffy train, squeezed in among crowds of passengers gaping at me . . . and with long stops at the stations, when I would like to fly away on wings. . . . No—I can't do it—I just can't do it! And then I'll be thinking of the past—memories of the midsummer days of my childhood—the church, covered with wreaths and garlands, with leaves of birch and with lilac—the festive dinner table—relatives and friends—and the afternoon in the park, with music and dancing, games and flowers. . . . Oh—no matter how one tries to get away from the past, the memories are there, packed into one's baggage. . . . They pursue one, hitched onto the tail of the train . . . and then comes remorse—and the pangs of conscience—

JEAN. I'll come with you, but let's hurry—before it's too late! We haven't a second to lose!

MISS JULIE. Hurry up and dress! [*She picks up the birdcage.*]

JEAN. But no baggage! Then we would be found out immediately!

MISS JULIE. No, nothing . . . only what we can take with us in our compartment.

JEAN [*who has just reached for his hat, stares at the birdcage*]. What's that you have there? What is it?

MISS JULIE. It's only my green siskin[22] . . . I couldn't go without her!

JEAN. Well, of all the—Are we going to take a birdcage with us now? You must be completely out of your mind! [*He tries to take the cage from her.*] Let go of the cage!

MISS JULIE. It's the one thing I am taking with me from my home—the only living thing that loves me since Diana was faithless to me. . . . Don't be cruel! Please let me take her with me!

JEAN. Put that cage down, I tell you—and don't talk so loud! Kristin can hear us!

MISS JULIE. No—I won't part with her to anyone else! I'd rather you killed her . . .

JEAN. Give me the little beast then—I'll chop its head off!

MISS JULIE. Oh—but—don't hurt her, please!—No—I can't let you . . .

JEAN. But I can—and I know how. . . . Give it to me!

MISS JULIE [*takes the bird out of the cage. She kisses it*]. Oh, my poor little Sérine, must your mother lose you—must you die?

JEAN. Let's have no scenes—it's now a question of life and death—of your own future. . . . Quick, now! [*He snatches the bird from her, goes over to the chopping block, and picks up the ax lying on it.* MISS JULIE *turns away her face.*] You should have learned how to kill chickens instead of how to shoot . . . [*He lets the hatchet fall on the bird's neck.*] . . . then the sight of a little blood wouldn't make you faint!

MISS JULIE [*screams*]. Let me die too! Kill me! You—who can take the life of an innocent little creature without even a tremble of the hand! Oh—how I hate you—how I loathe you! Now there is blood between us! I curse the day I was born, the day I was conceived!

JEAN. Stop cursing—it does you no good! Let's be off!

MISS JULIE [*approaches the chopping block, as if drawn to it against her will*]. No—I am not ready to go yet—I can't go—I must first see . . . [*She suddenly stops. She stands listening; all the while her eyes are riveted on the chopping block and the ax.*] You think I can't stand the sight of blood! You think I am such a weakling, do you?—Oh, I should like to see *your* blood—*your* brain—on the chopping block. . . . I should like to see your whole sex bathing in its own blood, like my little bird! I even

[22] A small European songbird, often kept as a pet.

think I could drink out of your skull—I would revel in bathing my feet in your caved-in chest—and I could devour your heart roasted! You think I am a weakling—you think that I am in love with you because my womb felt a craving for your seed—you think that I yearn to carry your offspring under my heart, to nourish it with my blood—to bear your child and your name? Come to think of it, what is your name? I have never heard your last name—I guess you haven't any. . . . I was to be Mrs. Gatekeeper—or Mme. Refuse-heap. . . . You dog who wear my collar—you lackey with my family crest on your buttons! I was to share you with my cook—a rival of my own servant! Oh, oh, oh!—You think I am a coward and that I am eager to flee! No—this time I am not leaving—come what may! When father returns he will find his chiffonier[23] ransacked and the money gone! Immediately he will ring that bell—his usual two rings for you, Jean,—and he will send for the sheriff . . . and then—then I shall tell the whole story! The whole story! Oh, what a relief it will be to get it over with. . . . If only that moment were here! And father will have a stroke and die! . . . And that will be the end of our family. And then, at last, we shall be at rest—find peace—eternal peace! . . . And the family coat of arms will be broken against the coffin—the noble line will be extinct—but the lackey's line will go on in an orphanage—reaping laurels in the gutter, and ending in prison . . .

JEAN. There's your royal blood talking! Bravo, Miss Julie! And don't forget to stuff the miller's skeleton in your family closet!

[KRISTIN *enters. She is dressed for church and carries a prayer book.*]

MISS JULIE [*rushes toward her and flings herself into her arms, as if to plead for protection*]. Help me, Kristin! Save me from this man!

KRISTIN [*stands cold and unmoved*]. What kind of spectacle is this on the sabbath morning? [*She notices the dead bird and the blood on the chopping block.*] And what's this piggish mess you have made here?—What's the meaning of all this? And why are you screaming and making so much noise?

MISS JULIE. Kristin—you are a woman—and you are my friend! Look out for this man—he is a villain!

JEAN [*somewhat abashed and timid*]. While you ladies are conversing, I am going in to shave. [*He goes into his room, left.*]

MISS JULIE. I want you to understand me—I want you to listen to me—

KRISTIN. No—I must say I can't understand all these goings-on! Where are you planning to go—you are dressed for traveling—and Jean had his hat on. . . . Why?—What's going on?

MISS JULIE. Listen to me, Kristin! You must listen to me—and then I'll tell you everything . . .

KRISTIN. I don't care to—I don't want to know . . .

MISS JULIE. You must—you must hear . . .

KRISTIN. Just what is it—what's it all about? Is it about this foolishness with Jean, is it?—Well, I don't let that bother me a bit—it's none of my

[23] Narrow chest of drawers.

concern. . . . But if you are thinking of tricking him into running away with you—then I'll soon put a stop to that!

MISS JULIE [*with extreme nervousness*]. Try to be calm, Kristin, and please listen to me! I can't stay here—and Jean can't stay here—and that is why we must leave . . .

KRISTIN. H'm, h'm!

MISS JULIE [*brightening*]. Oh, I know—I have an idea! Suppose the three of us—if we should go abroad—we three together—to Switzerland—and start a hotel business—I have the money, you see. . . . [*She dangles the handbag before* KRISTIN.] . . . and Jean and I would run the business—and I thought you could take charge of the kitchen. Don't you think that would be perfect?—Say that you will? Do come with us—then everything will be settled! Will you? Say yes! [*She puts her arms round* KRISTIN *and gives her a pat on the back.*]

KRISTIN [*coldly reflective*]. H'm, h'm!

MISS JULIE [*presto tempo*[24]]. You have never been out in the world, Kristin,—you must travel and see things. You have no idea what fun it is to travel by train! Always new people, new countries! And in Hamburg we stop over and look at the Zoological Garden—you will like that . . . and when we arrive in Munich, we have the museums there—and there you'll see Rubens and Raphael and other great masters, you know. . . . You have heard of Munich, haven't you?—There is where King Ludwig lived—the king, you know, who lost his mind.[25] . . . And then we'll visit his castles—his castles still are there; and they are beautiful like the castles in the fairy tales—and from there, you see, it is only a short distance to Switzerland—and the Alps! Think of it, they are covered with snow in the middle of the summer—and oranges grow there—and laurels that stay green the year round!

[JEAN *appears from the left. While he is sharpening his razor on a strop that he holds between his teeth and his left hand, he is listening with evident satisfaction to their conversation. Now and then he nods approvingly.*]

MISS JULIE [*tempo prestissimo*[26]]. And in Switzerland we'll buy a hotel—and I'll take care of the accounts while Jean looks after the guests—does the marketing—attends to the correspondence. . . . It'll be a hustle and bustle, believe me. . . . You hear the whistle of the train—the omnibus arrives—the bells ring, from the hotel rooms and the dining-room.—I make out the bills—and I know how to salt them, too. . . . You can't imagine how diffident tourists are when their bills are presented to them!—And you—you will preside in the kitchen! You won't have to stand at the stove yourself, of course,—and you will have to be dressed neatly and nicely so that you can show yourself among people . . . and with your looks—yes, I am not trying to flatter you—with your looks,

[24] Fast (musical term).

[25] King Ludwig II of Bavaria (1845–86) was incurably insane and had to be confined to his fantastic chateau on Lake Starnberg. He eventually drowned himself, forcing his doctor to share his death.

[26] Very fast (musical term).

you might very well get yourself a husband one fine day!—Some rich Englishman—why not? They are so easy to [*in a slackened pace*] . . . to capture . . . and then we'll build ourselves a villa at the edge of Lake Como. . . . Of course, it rains there a little occasionally, but . . . [*Her voice fades a little.*] . . . the sun must be shining there some time—even though the gloom seems to persist—and—so—well, we can always return home—and then go back again . . . [*There is a pause.*] . . . here—or somewhere else. . .

KRISTIN. Miss Julie, do you really believe all this yourself?

MISS JULIE [*crushed*]. . . . If I believe it—myself?

KRISTIN. Just that!

MISS JULIE. I don't know . . . I don't believe in anything anymore! [*She sinks down on the bench, puts her head between her hands and drops her head on the table.*] Not in anything! Not in anything!

KRISTIN [*turning toward the left where* JEAN *is standing*]. So-o, you were going to run away, were you?

JEAN [*crestfallen and looking foolish, he lays the razor on the table*]. Run away? Well—that's a strong word to use! Miss Julie told you about her project, didn't she? Well—she is tired now after being up all night . . . but her plan can very well be carried to success!

KRISTIN. Now you listen to me! Was it your intention that I was to be cook for that one—

JEAN [*sharply*]. You will be good enough to speak of your mistress in a proper manner! You understand me, don't you?

KRISTIN. Mistress, yes!

JEAN. Yes, mistress!

KRISTIN. Ha, listen—listen to him!

JEAN. Yes, that's just what you *should* do—listen—and talk a little less! Miss Julie *is* your mistress—and the very same thing that you now look down upon her for should make you feel contempt for yourself!

KRISTIN. I always had so much respect for myself that . . .

JEAN. . . . that you felt you could show disrespect for others!

KRISTIN. . . . that I could never let myself sink beneath my level! Nobody can say that the Count's cook has had any goings-on with the stablehand, or the fellow who looks after the pigs! No—nobody can say that!

JEAN. Yes—you are lucky to have been able to catch a fine fellow like me, that's all I can say!

KRISTIN. A fine fellow, indeed,—selling the oats from the Count's stable. . .

JEAN. You should talk about that—you, who take a rake-off from the grocer and let the butcher bribe you!

KRISTIN. I don't know what you mean . . .

JEAN. And you—you can't have any respect for the family you are working for! You—you—you!

KRISTIN. Are you coming with me to church now? You could stand a good sermon after your great triumph!

JEAN. No, I am not going to church today. . . . You have to go alone and confess your *own* exploits!

KRISTIN. Yes—that's what I intend to do, and I'll come back with enough forgiveness for us both! The Saviour suffered and died on the Cross for all our sins; and if we come to Him with faith and repentance in our hearts He will take all our trespasses upon Himself.

JEAN. Including petty grocery frauds?

MISS JULIE [*who suddenly lifts her head*]. Do you believe that, Kristin?

KRISTIN. That is my living faith, as sure as I stand here. It is the faith that was born in me as a child and that I have kept ever since, Miss Julie. . . . And where sin abounds, grace abounds much more . . .

MISS JULIE. Oh—if I only had your trusting faith! Oh, if I . . .

KRISTIN. Yes, but you see you can't have faith without God's special grace—and it is not given to all to receive that.

MISS JULIE. To whom is it given then?

KRISTIN. That, Miss Julie, is the great secret of the gift of grace . . . and God is no respecter of persons: in His Kingdom the last shall be first . . .

MISS JULIE. Well—but in that case He shows preference for the last, doesn't He?

KRISTIN [*continues*]. . . . and it's easier for a camel to go through the eye of a needle than for a rich man to enter the Kingdom of Heaven. You see, Miss Julie, that is the way it is!—But now I am going—alone—and on my way I'll stop and tell the stableman not to let out any of the horses to anybody . . . just in case anybody'd like to get away before the Count returns!—Goodbye! [*She goes out.*]

JEAN. What a bitch!—And all this just because of a green siskin!

MISS JULIE [*apathetically*]. Never mind the siskin!—Can you see any way out of this? Any way to end it?

JEAN [*thinking hard*]. No—I can't.

MISS JULIE. If you were in my place—what would you do?

JEAN. In your place? Let me think!—As a woman—of noble birth—who has fallen . . . I don't know. . . . Yes—now I think I know— [*His glance falls upon the razor.*]

MISS JULIE [*picks up the razor and makes a telling gesture*]. This, you mean?

JEAN. Yes . . . but *I* would never do it! Not I—for there is a difference between us two!

MISS JULIE. You mean—because you are a man and I a woman? What, then, is the difference?

JEAN. The same difference—as—between man and woman—

MISS JULIE [*with the razor in her hand*]. I want to do it . . . but I can't!—My father couldn't either—that time when he ought to have done it . . .

JEAN. No—he ought not to have done it! He had to take his revenge first!

MISS JULIE. And now my mother gets her revenge once more—through me!

JEAN. Did you ever love your father, Miss Julie? Did you?

MISS JULIE. Yes, I did—immensely—but, at the same time, I think I must have hated him. . . . I must have done so without being conscious of it! It was he who brought me up to look with contempt upon my own sex—to be part woman and part man! Who is to be blamed for the consequences? My father, my mother, or myself? Myself? Am I then really myself? There is nothing I can call my own; I haven't a thought that wasn't instilled in me by my father—not a passion that I didn't inherit from my mother . . . and that last notion of mine—the idea that all people are equal—that came from him, my fiancé . . . and that is why I call him a mischief-maker, a scoundrel! How can *I* possibly be to blame? To put the burden of blame on Jesus Christ as Kristin did just now—for that I have too much pride and too much sense, thanks to what my father taught me. . . . And as for the idea that a rich man may not enter Heaven—that's a lie; and Kristin, who has put her savings in the bank, won't get there either, for that matter! Now—who is to blame?—What does it matter who is to blame? After all, it is I who have to bear the burden of guilt and suffer the consequences. . . .

JEAN. Yes—but . . . [*Two abrupt rings interrupt him.* MISS JULIE *jumps to her feet;* JEAN *quickly changes his coat.*] The Count is back! What if Kristin . . . [*He goes over to the speaking tube and listens.*]

MISS JULIE. Could he have been to the chiffonier already?

JEAN. Yes, sir—this is Jean. [*He listens. The Count's voice is not heard by the audience.*] Yes, sir. —Yes, sir. Immediately!—At once, sir!—Yes, sir. In half an hour!

MISS JULIE [*in extreme agitation*]. What did he say? For God's sake—what did he say?

JEAN. He asked for his boots and his coffee in half an hour.

MISS JULIE. Half an hour, then! . . . Oh, I am so tired—I have no strength to do anything—not even to feel repentant—or to get away from here—or to stay here—to live—or to die! . . . Help me, please! Order me to do something—and I'll obey like a dog. . . . Do me this last service! Save my honor—save his good name! You know what I would like to have the will to do—yet don't like to do. . . . Use your willpower on me—and *make* me do it!

JEAN. I don't know why—but now *I* haven't any willpower either. I can't understand it. . . . It's just as if wearing this coat made it impossible for me to—to give orders to you; and now, after the Count spoke to me, I—well, I—I just can't explain it—but—oh, it's the damned menial in me . . . and if the Count should come in here this very minute, and he should order me to cut my throat, I believe I'd do it without the slightest hesitation!

MISS JULIE. Can't you make believe that you are he, and that I am you! You did a good piece of acting just now when you were on your knees—then you acted the nobleman—or, perhaps, you have seen a hypnotist when you've been to the theater? [JEAN *gives an affirmative nod.*] He tells his subject: "Pick up that broom!"—and he picks it up; he tells him to sweep—and he starts to sweep . . .

JEAN. But he must put his subject to sleep first . . .

MISS JULIE [*ecstatically*]. I am already asleep—the whole room is like a cloud of dust and smoke before me—and you look like a tall stove—and the stove looks like a man in black with a top hat—your eyes glow like embers in a fireplace—and your face is merely a patch of white ash . . . [*The sun's rays are now falling across the room and shine on* JEAN.] . . . It's so pleasantly warm . . . [*She rubs her hands together as if she were warming them by the fire.*] And how bright it is—and so peaceful!

JEAN [*takes the razor and places it in her hand*]. Here is the broom! Walk outside now while it's still light—out into the barn—and . . . [*He whispers in her ear.*]

MISS JULIE [*awake*]. Thank you! I'm going—to find rest. . . . But before I go, tell me—that even those who are among the first can receive the gift of grace. Please tell me that—even if you do not believe it!

JEAN. Among the first? No—that's something I cannot do. . . . But wait, Miss Julie. . . . Now I know the answer! Since you no longer are one of the first—you must be—among the last!

MISS JULIE. You are right!—I am among the—very last—I am the last! Oh!—But something holds me back again. . . . Tell me once again to go!

JEAN. No—I can't tell you again—I can't—

MISS JULIE. And the first shall be the last . . .

JEAN. Stop thinking—stop thinking! You are robbing me of all my strength—you are making me a coward. . . . What's that? I thought I heard the bell! No—but let's stuff it with paper. . . . Imagine, to be so afraid of a bell! Yes—but it isn't merely a bell—there is someone behind it—a hand that sets it in motion—and something else sets the hand in motion—but you can stop your ears—stop your ears—and then—yes, but then it keeps ringing louder than ever—keeps ringing until you answer—and then—it's too late! And then the sheriff appears on the scene—and then . . .

[*Two peremptory rings from the bell.*]

JEAN [*quails; then he straightens himself*]. It's horrible! But it's the only way to end it!—Go!

[MISS JULIE, *with the razor in her hand, walks firmly out through the door.*]

CURTAIN

Kate Chopin
(*1851–1904*)

One of the most striking events in the study of American literature in the last few decades has been the rediscovery of the late nineteenth-century novelist and short-story writer Kate Chopin. Beginning in the mid-1950s, a few scholars and critics began calling attention to Chopin's work, which had been out of print for over fifty years and which was remembered, if at all, only as minor local-color fiction. Within a dozen years, her complete works were republished and her masterpiece, The Awakening, *established itself as one of the classic American novels. The story is paralleled in American literary history only by Herman Melville's forty-year critical eclipse after his death and by William Faulkner's long neglect during his own lifetime until he was rediscovered by Malcolm Cowley in 1946. Chopin, like Melville and Faulkner, was ahead of her time; it was not until the resurgence of American feminism that the quality of her work could be adequately recognized by an appreciable number of readers.*

Kate Chopin was born Katherine O'Flaherty in St. Louis in 1851; her mother was a cultured French Creole and her father an Irish immigrant and a well-to-do merchant who died when Chopin was four years old. She attended private Catholic schools and was a fashionable nineteen-year-old debutante when she met and married Oscar Chopin, a twenty-five-year-old cotton merchant of French ancestry from New Orleans. The couple settled there and moved in the social circles of the Creole aristocracy for nine years, until Oscar Chopin's business failed and they moved with their children to Natchitoches Parish in rural Louisiana, where he managed part of the family plantation.

Oscar Chopin died suddenly in 1883, and the young widow, still only thirty-two years old, moved with her six children to her mother's home in St. Louis. Her mother died in 1885, however, and left Chopin without any close family. The following five years were a period of intellectual growth and transformation for Chopin. Her closest friend was her family doctor, Frederick Kolbenheyer (partial model for Dr. Mandelet in The Awakening*), a cultivated, well-read man who discussed books with her and encouraged her to try writing herself. She later said that she had "made her own acquaintance" during this period.*

Chopin's first published work, two short stories, appeared in periodicals in 1889; a novel, At Fault, *published in St. Louis at her own expense, followed in 1890.* At Fault *is a weak, didactic, anti-reform novel about a woman who makes the man she loves remarry the wife he divorced because of alcoholism; the woman continues drinking and all three lives are ruined. A second novel was written almost immediately, but Chopin was unable to find a publisher for it. She eventually destroyed the manuscript. Meanwhile, she was having increasing success in publishing her stories and sketches in national magazines, and she achieved national recognition with* Bayou Folk *(1894), a selection of her Louisiana "local color" stories.*

The critical success of Bayou Folk *seems to have given Chopin more confidence in her own powers and perceptions and set her on a course that was eventually to alienate her from her popular audience. She began increasingly to write about passionate, freedom-loving women in stories which were increasingly rejected by editors on moral grounds. Her second collection of stories,* A Night in Acadie, *appeared in 1897; genteel reviewers were less affirmative than they had been with* Bayou Folk, *finding an unpleasant note of "sensuality" in the stories.*

When A Night in Acadie *appeared, Chopin was already completing* The Awakening. *It was accepted by a publisher and appeared in 1899, arousing a storm of shocked protest. A St. Louis reviewer pronounced it "not a healthy book," a Chicago one placed it in "the overworked field of sex fiction," while one in Los Angeles found it "unhealthily introspective and morbid." One of the most interesting reviews was by twenty-six-year-old Willa Cather, who disliked the book but shrewdly compared Edna Pontellier to Flaubert's Madame Bovary and interpreted the book as an examination of the kind of woman who with an "unbalanced idealism" expects "the passion of love to fill and gratify every need of life." "Next time," Cather concluded, "I hope that Miss Chopin will devote that flexible iridescent style of hers to a better cause."*

There was to be no next time. Chopin's third collection of short stories was rejected a few months after the scandal of The Awakening. *Depressed and discouraged, she gave up writing altogether. She died five years later, at the age of fifty-three.*

In the context of the social and literary history of her time, Chopin was only mildly liberal. She lived in the South through the racial conflict of Reconstruction and the ruthless expansionism of the Gilded Age, but issues of race or class appear obliquely if at all in her work. In her period of self-examination following the deaths of her husband and mother, she stopped being a practicing Catholic. She read Darwin and was profoundly influenced by him, insisting thereafter that no serious writer could ignore his account of human nature. She disliked reform and was basically pessimistic about the ability of men and women to escape their "biological fates."

At the same time, she was not a Naturalist. She disliked Zola's novels, finding them too grim, and had the same objection to Hardy. She seems either not to have known or to have been indifferent to the work of the American Naturalists who were writing at the same time: Dreiser, Norris, Crane, and Garland, though she rejected with some impatience Garland's "sociological" subjects. The major influences upon her seem to have been French: Flaubert and, especially, Guy de Maupassant, whose mild realism she greatly admired. She belongs among the realists who dealt, as William Dean Howells recommended, with "the smiling aspects" of life; she was a lover, she wrote, of "brightness and gaiety and life and sunshine."

Chopin's recurring subject, in her mature short stories, is a woman's "awakening" to her true nature, the theme she develops at length in her final novel. Edna Pontellier's awakening is primarily into sensuality, but this awakening comes to involve, for her, large existential issues. She begins to "realize her position in the universe as a human being, and to recognize her relations as an individual to the world within and about her." Sexual freedom becomes the chief expression of a sense of an independent self: "I give myself where I choose," she tells Robert, when he inquires whether Pontellier would free her.

Edna's growth into sensuality and selfhood would be a simpler and a less interesting action if it were not accompanied by a contrary movement in the novel—a "going to sleep" in tension with the "awakening." She has been "self-contained" as a child and has spent most of her girlhood lost in daydreams and fantasies. She drops off to sleep at crucial points throughout the novel, sleeping through most of the day she first openly spends with Robert and experiencing "the old ennui" at the dinner party at which she celebrates her break with her husband. The ending of the novel is anticipated by a number of escapes into unconsciousness throughout and by the ambiguous symbolism of the sea, promising both sensuality and danger.

Despite these foreshadowings, the logic of the ending is elusive. Edna's explicit motivations for her final decision are revulsion at promiscuity—"Today it is Arobin; tomorrow it will be some one else"—and fear for her children—"but Raoul and Etienne!" But her children have not figured in her motivations before—through most of the novel they are visiting their grandmother—and we may wonder why a succession of lovers would be unwelcome, or at any rate worse than what she chooses. Perhaps more crucial than conscious motivation is Chopin's Darwinian pessimism about the possibility of changing one's nature. The ending also raises the general problem of the limits of Romantic individualism. Swimming "far out, where no woman had swum before," carries with it, for man or woman, the danger of not being able to swim back.

FURTHER READING *(prepared by N. K. B.):* For other fiction by Chopin, see *The Complete Works of Kate Chopin,* 2 vols., 1969, ed. by Per Seyersted. Seyersted has also written the most extensive biography, *Kate Chopin: A Critical Biography,* 1969, which includes a thorough examination of her stylistic methods and critical reception.

Daniel Rankin's early biography, *Kate Chopin and Her Creole Stories,* 1932, is valuable for the personal reminiscences included, and his antagonistic reaction to *The Awakening* is an interesting contrast to later studies. Nina Baym's introductory essay to *The Awakening and Selected Stories,* 1981, provides an illuminating survey of Chopin's life and writing career, viewed in the context of nineteenth-century fiction and women's writings. Margaret Culley, ed., *The Awakening: An Authoritative Text, Contexts, Criticism,* 1977, offers a shorter introduction; this edition also includes a wide sampling of contemporary reviews. Warner Berthoff, *The Ferment of Realism: American Literature 1894–1919,* 1965, acclaims Chopin for her rebellion against nineteenth-century social conventions. In "Local Color in *The Awakening,*" *Southern Review,* 6 (1970), 1031–1040, John R. May discusses the importance of setting in the novel. Donald A. Ringe, "Romantic Imagery in Kate Chopin's *The Awakening,*" *American Literature,* 43 (1972), 580–588, articulates the Romantic themes of the novel. In a detailed and provocative analysis, "Thanatos and Eros: Kate Chopin's *The Awakening,*" *American Quarterly,* 25 (1973), 449–471, Cynthia Griffin Wolff uses a psychoanalytic model to explain Edna's character and action.

THE AWAKENING

I

A green and yellow parrot, which hung in a cage outside the door, kept repeating over and over:

"*Allez vous-en! Allez vous-en! Sapristi!*[1] That's all right!"

He could speak a little Spanish, and also a language which nobody understood, unless it was the mocking-bird that hung on the other side of the door, whistling his fluty notes out upon the breeze with maddening persistence.

Mr. Pontellier, unable to read his newspaper with any degree of comfort, arose with an expression and an exclamation of disgust. He walked down the gallery and across the narrow "bridges" which connected the Lebrun cottages one with the other. He had been seated before the door of the main house. The parrot and the mocking-bird were the property of Madame Lebrun, and they had the right to make all the noise they wished. Mr. Pontellier had the privilege of quitting their society when they ceased to be entertaining.

He stopped before the door of his own cottage, which was the fourth one from the main building and next to the last. Seating himself in a wicker rocker which was there, he once more applied himself to the task of reading the newspaper. The day was Sunday; the paper was a day old. The Sunday papers had not yet reached Grand Isle.[2] He was already acquainted with the market reports, and he glanced restlessly over the editorials and bits of news which he had not had time to read before quitting New Orleans the day before.

Mr. Pontellier wore eye-glasses. He was a man of forty, of medium

[1] "Go away! Go away! Good lord!"

[2] An island fifty miles south of New Orleans in the Gulf of Mexico, popular as a summer resort among New Orleans Creoles.

height and rather slender build; he stooped a little. His hair was brown and straight, parted on one side. His beard was neatly and closely trimmed.

Once in a while he withdrew his glance from the newspaper and looked about him. There was more noise than ever over at the house. The main building was called "the house," to distinguish it from the cottages. The chattering and whistling birds were still at it. Two young girls, the Farival twins, were playing a duet from "Zampa"[3] upon the piano. Madame Lebrun was bustling in and out, giving orders in a high key to a yard-boy whenever she got inside the house, and directions in an equally high voice to a dining-room servant whenever she got outside. She was a fresh, pretty woman, clad always in white with elbow sleeves. Her starched skirts crinkled as she came and went. Farther down, before one of the cottages, a lady in black was walking demurely up and down, telling her beads. A good many persons of the *pension* had gone over to the *Chênière Caminada*[4] in Beaudelet's lugger[5] to hear mass. Some young people were out under the water-oaks playing croquet. Mr. Pontellier's two children were there—sturdy little fellows of four and five. A quadroon[6] nurse followed them about with a far-away, meditative air.

Mr. Pontellier finally lit a cigar and began to smoke, letting the paper drag idly from his hand. He fixed his gaze upon a white sunshade that was advancing at snail's pace from the beach. He could see it plainly between the gaunt trunks of the water-oaks and across the stretch of yellow camomile. The gulf looked far away, melting hazily into the blue of the horizon. The sunshade continued to approach slowly. Beneath its pink-lined shelter were his wife, Mrs. Pontellier, and young Robert Lebrun. When they reached the cottage, the two seated themselves with some appearance of fatigue upon the upper step of the porch, facing each other, each leaning against a supporting post.

"What folly! to bathe at such an hour in such heat!" exclaimed Mr. Pontellier. He himself had taken a plunge at daylight. That was why the morning seemed long to him.

"You are burnt beyond recognition," he added, looking at his wife as one looks at a valuable piece of personal property which has suffered some damage. She held up her hands, strong, shapely hands, and surveyed them critically, drawing up her lawn sleeves above the wrists. Looking at them reminded her of her rings, which she had given to her husband before leaving for the beach. She silently reached out to him, and he, understanding, took the rings from his vest pocket and dropped them into her open palm. She slipped them upon her fingers; then clasping her knees, she looked across at Robert and began to laugh. The rings sparkled upon her fingers. He sent back an answering smile.

"What is it?" asked Pontellier, looking lazily and amused from one to the other. It was some utter nonsense; some adventure out there in the water, and they both tried to relate it at once. It did not seem half so

[3] A once-popular opera by Louis Hérold. [4] Another island near Grand Isle.
[5] A small boat with "lugsails" (square sails on a slanting yard).
[6] A person who is one-fourth Negro.

amusing when told. They realized this, and so did Mr. Pontellier. He yawned and stretched himself. Then he got up, saying he had half a mind to go over to Klein's hotel and play a game of billiards.

"Come go along, Lebrun," he proposed to Robert. But Robert admitted quite frankly that he preferred to stay where he was and talk to Mrs. Pontellier.

"Well, send him about his business when he bores you, Edna," instructed her husband as he prepared to leave.

"Here, take the umbrella," she exclaimed, holding it out to him. He accepted the sunshade, and lifting it over his head descended the steps and walked away.

"Coming back to dinner?" his wife called after him. He halted a moment and shrugged his shoulders. He felt in his vest pocket; there was a ten-dollar bill there. He did not know; perhaps he would return for the early dinner and perhaps he would not. It all depended upon the company which he found over at Klein's and the size of "the game." He did not say this, but she understood it, and laughed, nodding good-by to him.

Both children wanted to follow their father when they saw him starting out. He kissed them and promised to bring them back bonbons and peanuts.

II

Mrs. Pontellier's eyes were quick and bright; they were a yellowish brown, about the color of her hair. She had a way of turning them swiftly upon an object and holding them there as if lost in some inward maze of contemplation or thought.

Her eyebrows were a shade darker than her hair. They were thick and almost horizontal, emphasizing the depth of her eyes. She was rather handsome than beautiful. Her face was captivating by reason of a certain frankness of expression and a contradictory subtle play of features. Her manner was engaging.

Robert rolled a cigarette. He smoked cigarettes because he could not afford cigars, he said. He had a cigar in his pocket which Mr. Pontellier had presented him with, and he was saving it for his after-dinner smoke.

This seemed quite proper and natural on his part. In coloring he was not unlike his companion. A clean-shaved face made the resemblance more pronounced than it would otherwise have been. There rested no shadow of care upon his open countenance. His eyes gathered in and reflected the light and languor of the summer day.

Mrs. Pontellier reached over for a palm-leaf fan that lay on the porch and began to fan herself, while Robert sent between his lips light puffs from his cigarette. They chatted incessantly: about the things around them; their amusing adventure out in the water—it had again assumed its entertaining aspect; about the wind, the trees, the people who had gone to the *Chênière;* about the children playing croquet under the oaks, and the

Farival twins, who were now performing the overture to "The Poet and the Peasant."[7]

Robert talked a good deal about himself. He was very young, and did not know any better. Mrs. Pontellier talked a little about herself for the same reason. Each was interested in what the other said. Robert spoke of his intention to go to Mexico in the autumn, where fortune awaited him. He was always intending to go to Mexico, but some way never got there. Meanwhile he held on to his modest position in a mercantile house in New Orleans, where an equal familiarity with English, French and Spanish gave him no small value as a clerk and correspondent.

He was spending his summer vacation, as he always did, with his mother at Grand Isle. In former times, before Robert could remember, "the house" had been a summer luxury of the Lebruns. Now, flanked by its dozen or more cottages, which were always filled with exclusive visitors from the *"Quartier Français,"*[8] it enabled Madame Lebrun to maintain the easy and comfortable existence which appeared to be her birthright.

Mrs. Pontellier talked about her father's Mississippi plantation and her girlhood home in the old Kentucky blue-grass country. She was an American woman, with a small infusion of French which seemed to have been lost in dilution. She read a letter from her sister, who was away in the East, and who had engaged herself to be married. Robert was interested, and wanted to know what manner of girls the sisters were, what the father was like, and how long the mother had been dead.

When Mrs. Pontellier folded the letter it was time for her to dress for the early dinner.

"I see Léonce isn't coming back," she said, with a glance in the direction whence her husband had disappeared. Robert supposed he was not, as there were a good many New Orleans club men over at Klein's.

When Mrs. Pontellier left him to enter her room, the young man descended the steps and strolled over toward the croquet players, where, during the half-hour before dinner, he amused himself with the little Pontellier children, who were very fond of him.

III

It was eleven o'clock that night when Mr. Pontellier returned from Klein's hotel. He was in an excellent humor, in high spirits, and very talkative. His entrance awoke his wife, who was in bed and fast asleep when he came in. He talked to her while he undressed, telling her anecdotes and bits of news and gossip that he had gathered during the day. From his trousers pockets he took a fistful of crumpled bank notes and a good deal of silver coin, which he piled on the bureau indiscriminately with keys, knife, handkerchief, and whatever else happened to be in his pockets. She was overcome with sleep, and answered him with little half utterances.

He thought it very discouraging that his wife, who was the sole object of

[7] This overture was another hackneyed parlor piece. *Poet and Peasant* is a light opera by Franz von Suppé.

[8] The French Quarter of New Orleans, home of the bulk of the Creole population.

his existence, evinced so little interest in things which concerned him, and valued so little his conversation.

Mr. Pontellier had forgotten the bonbons and peanuts for the boys. Notwithstanding he loved them very much, and went into the adjoining room where they slept to take a look at them and make sure that they were resting comfortably. The result of his investigation was far from satisfactory. He turned and shifted the youngsters about in bed. One of them began to kick and talk about a basket full of crabs.

Mr. Pontellier returned to his wife with the information that Raoul had a high fever and needed looking after. Then he lit a cigar and went and sat near the open door to smoke it.

Mrs. Pontellier was quite sure Raoul had no fever. He had gone to bed perfectly well, she said, and nothing had ailed him all day. Mr. Pontellier was too well acquainted with fever symptoms to be mistaken. He assured her the child was consuming at that moment in the next room.

He reproached his wife with her inattention, her habitual neglect of the children. If it was not a mother's place to look after children, whose on earth was it? He himself had his hands full with his brokerage business. He could not be in two places at once; making a living for his family on the street, and staying at home to see that no harm befell them. He talked in a monotonous, insistent way.

Mrs. Pontellier sprang out of bed and went into the next room. She soon came back and sat on the edge of the bed, leaning her head down on the pillow. She said nothing, and refused to answer her husband when he questioned her. When his cigar was smoked out he went to bed, and in half a minute he was fast asleep.

Mrs. Pontellier was by that time thoroughly awake. She began to cry a little, and wiped her eyes on the sleeve of her *peignoir*. Blowing out the candle, which her husband had left burning, she slipped her bare feet into a pair of satin *mules* at the foot of the bed and went out on the porch, where she sat down in the wicker chair and began to rock gently to and fro.

It was then past midnight. The cottages were all dark. A single faint light gleamed out from the hallway of the house. There was no sound abroad except the hooting of an old owl in the top of a water-oak, and the everlasting voice of the sea, that was not uplifted at that soft hour. It broke like a mournful lullaby upon the night.

The tears came so fast to Mrs. Pontellier's eyes that the damp sleeve of her *peignoir* no longer served to dry them. She was holding the back of her chair with one hand; her loose sleeve had slipped almost to the shoulder of her uplifted arm. Turning, she thrust her face, steaming and wet, into the bend of her arm, and she went on crying there, not caring any longer to dry her face, her eyes, her arms. She could not have told why she was crying. Such experiences as the foregoing were not uncommon in her married life. They seemed never before to have weighed much against the abundance of her husband's kindness and a uniform devotion which had come to be tacit and self-understood.

An indescribable oppression, which seemed to generate in some unfamiliar part of her consciousness, filled her whole being with a vague anguish. It was like a shadow, like a mist passing across her soul's summer day. It was strange and unfamiliar; it was a mood. She did not sit there inwardly upbraiding her husband, lamenting at Fate, which had directed her footsteps to the path which they had taken. She was just having a good cry all to herself. The mosquitoes made merry over her, biting her firm, round arms and nipping at her bare insteps.

The little stinging, buzzing imps succeeded in dispelling a mood which might have held her there in the darkness half a night longer.

The following morning Mr. Pontellier was up in good time to take the rockaway[9] which was to convey him to the steamer at the wharf. He was returning to the city to his business, and they would not see him again at the Island till the coming Saturday. He had regained his composure, which seemed to have been somewhat impaired the night before. He was eager to be gone, as he looked forward to a lively week in Carondelet Street.[10]

Mr. Pontellier gave his wife half of the money which he had brought away from Klein's hotel the evening before. She liked money as well as most women, and accepted it with no little satisfaction.

"It will buy a handsome wedding present for Sister Janet!" she exclaimed, smoothing out the bills as she counted them one by one.

"Oh! we'll treat Sister Janet better than that, my dear," he laughed, as he prepared to kiss her good-by.

The boys were tumbling about, clinging to his legs, imploring that numerous things be brought back to them. Mr. Pontellier was a great favorite, and ladies, men, children, even nurses, were always on hand to say good-by to him. His wife stood smiling and waving, the boys shouting, as he disappeared in the old rockaway down the sandy road.

A few days later a box arrived for Mrs. Pontellier from New Orleans. It was from her husband. It was filled with *friandises,* with luscious and toothsome bits—the finest of fruits, *patés,* a rare bottle or two, delicious syrups, and bonbons in abundance.

Mrs. Pontellier was always very generous with the contents of such a box; she was quite used to receiving them when away from home. The *patés* and fruit were brought to the dining-room; the bonbons were passed around. And the ladies, selecting with dainty and discriminating fingers and a little greedily, all declared that Mr. Pontellier was the best husband in the world. Mrs. Pontellier was forced to admit that she knew of none better.

IV

It would have been a difficult matter for Mr. Pontellier to define to his own satisfaction or any one else's wherein his wife failed in her duty toward their children. It was something which he felt rather than perceived, and he never voiced the feeling without subsequent regret and ample atonement.

If one of the little Pontellier boys took a tumble whilst at play, he was not apt to rush crying to his mother's arms for comfort; he would more likely pick himself up, wipe the water out of his eyes and the sand out of his

[9] A light four-wheeled carriage (named after Rockaway, New Jersey, where it was manufactured).

[10] Chief financial street in New Orleans and location of the Cotton Exchange.

mouth, and go on playing. Tots as they were, they pulled together and stood their ground in childish battles with doubled fists and uplifted voices, which usually prevailed against the other mother-tots. The quadroon nurse was looked upon as a huge encumbrance, only good to button up waists and panties and to brush and part hair; since it seemed to be a law of society that hair must be parted and brushed.

In short, Mrs. Pontellier was not a mother-woman. The mother-women seemed to prevail that summer at Grand Isle. It was easy to know them, fluttering about with extended, protecting wings when any harm, real or imaginary, threatened their precious brood. They were women who idolized their children, worshiped their husbands, and esteemed it a holy privilege to efface themselves as individuals and grow wings as ministering angels.

Many of them were delicious in the rôle; one of them was the embodiment of every womanly grace and charm. If her husband did not adore her, he was a brute, deserving of death by slow torture. Her name was Adèle Ratignolle. There are no words to describe her save the old ones that have served so often to picture the bygone heroine of romance and the fair lady of our dreams. There was nothing subtle or hidden about her charms; her beauty was all there, flaming and apparent: the spun-gold hair that comb nor confining pin could restrain; the blue eyes that were like nothing but sapphires; two lips that pouted, that were so red one could only think of cherries or some other delicious crimson fruit in looking at them. She was growing a little stout, but it did not seem to detract an iota from the grace of every step, pose, gesture. One would not have wanted her white neck a mite less full or her beautiful arms more slender. Never were hands more exquisite than hers, and it was a joy to look at them when she threaded her needle or adjusted her gold thimble to her taper middle finger as she sewed away on the little night-drawers or fashioned a bodice or a bib.

Madame Ratignolle was very fond of Mrs. Pontellier, and often she took her sewing and went over to sit with her in the afternoons. She was sitting there the afternoon of the day the box arrived from New Orleans. She had possession of the rocker, and she was busily engaged in sewing upon a diminutive pair of night-drawers.

She had brought the pattern of the drawers for Mrs. Pontellier to cut out—a marvel of construction, fashioned to enclose a baby's body so effectually that only two small eyes might look out from the garment, like an Eskimo's. They were designed for winter wear, when treacherous drafts came down chimneys and insidious currents of deadly cold found their way through key-holes.

Mrs. Pontellier's mind was quite at rest concerning the present material needs of her children, and she could not see the use of anticipating and making winter night garments the subject of her summer meditations. But she did not want to appear unamiable and uninterested, so she had brought forth newspapers, which she spread upon the floor of the gallery, and under Madame Ratignolle's directions she had cut a pattern of the impervious garment.

Robert was there, seated as he had been the Sunday before, and Mrs. Pontellier also occupied her former position on the upper step, leaning listlessly against the post. Beside her was a box of bonbons, which she held out at intervals to Madame Ratignolle.

That lady seemed at a loss to make a selection, but finally settled upon a stick of nougat, wondering if it were not too rich; whether it could possibly hurt her. Madame Ratignolle had been married seven years. About every two years she had a baby. At that time she had three babies, and was beginning to think of a fourth one. She was always talking about her "condition." Her "condition" was in no way apparent, and no one would have known a thing about it but for her persistence in making it the subject of conversation.

Robert started to reassure her, asserting that he had known a lady who had subsisted upon nougat during the entire—but seeing the color mount into Mrs. Pontellier's face he checked himself and changed the subject.

Mrs. Pontellier, though she had married a Creole,[11] was not thoroughly at home in the society of Creoles; never before had she been thrown so intimately among them. There were only Creoles that summer at Lebrun's. They all knew each other, and felt like one large family, among whom existed the most amicable relations. A characteristic which distinguished them and which impressed Mrs. Pontellier most forcibly was their entire absence of prudery. Their freedom of expression was at first incomprehensible to her, though she had no difficulty in reconciling it with a lofty chastity which in the Creole woman seems to be inborn and unmistakable.

Never would Edna Pontellier forget the shock with which she heard Madame Ratignolle relating to old Monsieur Farival the harrowing story of one of her *accouchements,*[12] withholding no intimate detail. She was growing accustomed to like shocks, but she could not keep the mounting color back from her cheeks. Oftener than once her coming had interrupted the droll story with which Robert was entertaining some amused group of married women.

A book had gone the rounds of the *pension.* When it came her turn to read it, she did so with profound astonishment. She felt moved to read the book in secret and solitude, though none of the others had done so—to hide it from view at the sound of approaching footsteps. It was openly criticized and freely discussed at table. Mrs. Pontellier gave over being astonished, and concluded that wonders would never cease.

V

They formed a congenial group sitting there that summer afternoon—Madame Ratignolle sewing away, often stopping to relate a story or incident with much expressive gesture of her perfect hands; Robert and Mrs. Pontellier sitting idle, exchanging occasional words, glances or smiles which indicated a certain advanced stage of intimacy and *camaraderie.*

He had lived in her shadow during the past month. No one thought anything of it. Many had predicted that Robert would devote himself to

[11] A Louisianan of French ancestry. Specifically, here, a member of the small circle of wealthy Creole "old families."

[12] Periods of confinement in childbirth.

Mrs. Pontellier when he arrived. Since the age of fifteen, which was eleven years before, Robert each summer at Grand Isle had constituted himself the devoted attendant of some fair dame or damsel. Sometimes it was a young girl, again a widow; but as often as not it was some interesting married woman.

For two consecutive seasons he lived in the sunlight of Mademoiselle Duvigné's presence. But she died between summers; then Robert posed as an inconsolable, prostrating himself at the feet of Madame Ratignolle for whatever crumbs of sympathy and comfort she might be pleased to vouchsafe.

Mrs. Pontellier liked to sit and gaze at her fair companion as she might look upon a faultless Madonna.

"Could any one fathom the cruelty beneath that fair exterior?" murmured Robert. "She knew that I adored her once, and she let me adore her. It was 'Robert, come; go; stand up; sit down; do this; do that; see if the baby sleeps; my thimble, please, that I left God knows where. Come and read Daudet[13] to me while I sew.' "

"*Par example!*[14] I never had to ask. You were always there under my feet, like a troublesome cat."

"You mean like an adoring dog. And just as soon as Ratignolle appeared on the scene, then it *was* like a dog. '*Passez! Adieu! Allez vous-en!*' "[15]

"Perhaps I feared to make Alphonse jealous," she interjoined, with excessive naïveté. That made them all laugh. The right hand jealous of the left! The heart jealous of the soul! But for that matter, the Creole husband is never jealous; with him the gangrene passion is one which has become dwarfed by disuse.

Meanwhile Robert, addressing Mrs. Pontellier, continued to tell of his one time hopeless passion for Madame Ratignolle; of sleepless nights, of consuming flames till the very sea sizzled when he took his daily plunge. While the lady at the needle kept up a little running, contemptuous comment:

"*Blagueur—farceur—gros bête, va!*"[16]

He never assumed this serio-comic tone when alone with Mrs. Pontellier. She never knew precisely what to make of it; at that moment it was impossible for her to guess how much of it was jest and what proportion was earnest. It was understood that he had often spoken words of love to Madame Ratignolle, without any thought of being taken seriously. Mrs. Pontellier was glad he had not assumed a similar rôle toward herself. It would have been unacceptable and annoying.

Mrs. Pontellier had brought her sketching materials, which she sometimes dabbled with in an unprofessional way. She liked the dabbling. She felt in it satisfaction of a kind which no other employment afforded her.

She had long wished to try herself on Madame Ratignolle. Never had that lady seemed a more tempting subject than at that moment, seated there like some sensuous Madonna, with the gleam of the fading day enriching her splendid color.

[13] Alphonse Daudet (1840–97) wrote lightly satirical, "local color" books about his native Provence.

[14] "For goodness sake!" [15] "Go on! Good bye! Go away!"

[16] "Humbug—joker—big blockhead, go on!"

Robert crossed over and seated himself upon the step below Mrs. Pontellier, that he might watch her work. She handled her brushes with a certain ease and freedom which came, not from long and close acquaintance with them, but from a natural aptitude. Robert followed her work with close attention, giving forth little ejaculatory expressions of appreciation in French, which he addressed to Madame Ratignolle.

"Mais ce n'est pas mal! Elle s'y connait, elle a de la force, oui."[17]

During his oblivious attention he once quietly rested his head against Mrs. Pontellier's arm. As gently she repulsed him. Once again he repeated the offense. She could not but believe it to be thoughtlessness on his part; yet that was no reason she should submit to it. She did not remonstrate, except again to repulse him quietly but firmly. He offered no apology.

The picture completed bore no resemblance to Madame Ratignolle. She was greatly disappointed to find that it did not look like her. But it was a fair enough piece of work, and in many respects satisfying.

Mrs. Pontellier evidently did not think so. After surveying the sketch critically she drew a broad smudge of paint across its surface, and crumpled the paper between her hands.

The youngsters came tumbling up the steps, the quadroon following at the respectful distance which they required her to observe. Mrs. Pontellier made them carry her paints and things into the house. She sought to detain them for a little talk and some pleasantry. But they were greatly in earnest. They had only come to investigate the contents of the bonbon box. They accepted without murmuring what she chose to give them, each holding out two chubby hands scoop-like, in the vain hope that they might be filled; and then away they went.

The sun was low in the west, and the breeze soft and languorous that came up from the south, charged with the seductive odor of the sea. Children, freshly befurbelowed,[18] were gathering for their games under the oaks. Their voices were high and penetrating.

Madame Ratignolle folded her sewing, placing thimble, scissors and thread all neatly together in the roll, which she pinned securely. She complained of faintness. Mrs. Pontellier flew for the cologne water and a fan. She bathed Madame Ratignolle's face with cologne, while Robert plied the fan with unnecessary vigor.

The spell was soon over, and Mrs. Pontellier could not help wondering if there were not a little imagination responsible for its origin, for the rose tint had never faded from her friend's face.

She stood watching the fair woman walk down the long line of galleries with the grace and majesty which queens are sometimes supposed to possess. Her little ones ran to meet her. Two of them clung about her white skirts, the third she took from its nurse and with a thousand endearments bore it along in her own fond, encircling arms. Though, as everybody well knew, the doctor had forbidden her to lift so much as a pin!

"Are you going bathing?" asked Robert of Mrs. Pontellier. It was not so much a question as a reminder.

"Oh, no," she answered, with a tone of indecision. "I'm tired; I think

[17] "That's not bad! She knows what she's doing, she has talent!"

[18] Dressed up with ruffles and flounces.

not." Her glance wandered from his face away toward the Gulf, whose sonorous murmur reached her like a loving but imperative entreaty.

"Oh, come!" he insisted. "You mustn't miss your bath. Come on. The water must be delicious; it will not hurt you. Come."

He reached up for her big, rough straw hat that hung on a peg outside the door, and put it on her head. They descended the steps, and walked away together toward the beach. The sun was low in the west and the breeze was soft and warm.

VI

Edna Pontellier could not have told why, wishing to go to the beach with Robert, she should in the first place have declined, and in the second place have followed in obedience to one of the two contradictory impulses which impelled her.

A certain light was beginning to dawn dimly within her,—the light which, showing the way, forbids it.

At that early period it served but to bewilder her. It moved her to dreams, to thoughtfulness, to the shadowy anguish which had overcome her the midnight when she had abandoned herself to tears.

In short, Mrs. Pontellier was beginning to realize her position in the universe as a human being, and to recognize her relations as an individual to the world within and about her. This may seem like a ponderous weight of wisdom to descend upon the soul of a young woman of twenty-eight—perhaps more wisdom than the Holy Ghost is usually pleased to vouchsafe to any woman.

But the beginning of things, of a world especially, is necessarily vague, tangled, chaotic, and exceedingly disturbing. How few of us ever emerge from such beginning! How many souls perish in its tumult!

The voice of the sea is seductive; never ceasing, whispering, clamoring, murmuring, inviting the soul to wander for a spell in abysses of solitude; to lose itself in mazes of inward contemplation.

The voice of the sea speaks to the soul. The touch of the sea is sensuous, enfolding the body in its soft, close embrace.

VII

Mrs. Pontellier was not a woman given to confidences, a characteristic hitherto contrary to her nature. Even as a child she had lived her own small life all within herself. At a very early period she had apprehended instinctively the dual life—that outward existence which conforms, the inward life which questions.

That summer at Grand Isle she began to loosen a little the mantle of reserve that had always enveloped her. There may have been—there must have been—influences, both subtle and apparent, working in their several ways to induce her to do this; but the most obvious was the influence of Adèle Ratignolle. The excessive physical charm of the Creole had first attracted her, for Edna had a sensuous susceptibility to beauty. Then the candor of the woman's whole existence, which every one might read, and which formed so striking a contrast to her own habitual reserve—this might have furnished a link. Who can tell what metals the gods use in forging the subtle bond which we call sympathy, which we might as well call love.

The two women went away one morning to the beach together, arm in arm, under the huge white sunshade. Edna had prevailed upon Madame Ratignolle to leave the children behind, though she could not induce her to relinquish a diminutive roll of needlework, which Adèle begged to be allowed to slip into the depths of her pocket. In some unaccountable way they had escaped from Robert.

The walk to the beach was no inconsiderable one, consisting as it did of a long, sandy path, upon which a sporadic and tangled growth that bordered it on either side made frequent and unexpected inroads. There were acres of yellow camomile reaching out on either hand. Further away still, vegetable gardens abounded, with frequent small plantations of orange or lemon trees intervening. The dark green clusters glistened from afar in the sun.

The women were both of goodly height, Madame Ratignolle possessing the more feminine and matronly figure. The charm of Edna Pontellier's physique stole insensibly upon you. The lines of her body were long, clean and symmetrical; it was a body which occasionally fell into splendid poses; there was no suggestion of the trim, stereotyped fashion-plate about it. A casual and indiscriminating observer, in passing, might not cast a second glance upon the figure. But with more feeling and discernment he would have recognized the noble beauty of its modeling, and the graceful severity of poise and movement, which made Edna Pontellier different from the crowd.

She wore a cool muslin that morning—white, with a waving vertical line of brown running through it; also a white linen collar and the big straw hat which she had taken from the peg outside the door. The hat rested any way on her yellow-brown hair, that waved a little, was heavy, and clung close to her head.

Madame Ratignolle, more careful of her complexion, had twined a gauze veil about her head. She wore dogskin gloves, with gauntlets that protected her wrists. She was dressed in pure white, with a fluffiness of ruffles that became her. The draperies and fluttering things which she wore suited her rich, luxuriant beauty as a greater severity of line could not have done.

There were a number of bath-houses along the beach, of rough but solid construction, built with small, protecting galleries facing the water. Each house consisted of two compartments, and each family at Lebrun's possessed a compartment for itself, fitted out with all the essential paraphernalia of the bath and whatever other conveniences the owners might desire. The two women had no intention of bathing; they had just strolled down to the beach for a walk and to be alone and near the water. The Pontellier and Ratignolle compartments adjoined one another under the same roof.

Mrs. Pontellier had brought down her key through force of habit. Unlocking the door of her bath-room she went inside, and soon emerged, bringing a rug, which she spread upon the floor of the gallery, and two huge hair pillows covered with crash,[19] which she placed against the front of the building.

The two seated themselves there in the shade of the porch, side by side, with their backs against the pillows and their feet extended. Madame Ratignolle removed her veil, wiped her face with a rather delicate handkerchief, and fanned herself with the fan which she always carried suspended somewhere about her person by a long, narrow ribbon. Edna removed her collar and opened her dress at the throat. She took the fan from Madame Ratignolle and began to fan both herself and her companion. It was very warm, and for a while they did nothing but exchange remarks about the heat, the sun, the glare. But there was a breeze blowing, a choppy, stiff wind that whipped the water into froth. It fluttered the skirts of the two women and kept them for a while engaged in adjusting, readjusting, tucking in, securing hair-pins and hat-pins. A few persons were sporting some distance away in the water. The beach was very still of human sound at that hour. The lady in black was reading her morning devotions on the porch of a neighboring bath-house. Two young lovers were exchanging their hearts' yearnings beneath the children's tent, which they had found unoccupied.

Edna Pontellier, casting her eyes about, had finally kept them at rest upon the sea. The day was clear and carried the gaze out as far as the blue sky went; there were a few white clouds suspended idly over the horizon. A lateen sail[20] was visible in the direction of Cat Island, and others to the south seemed almost motionless in the far distance.

"Of whom—of what are you thinking?" asked Adèle of her companion, whose countenance she had been watching with a little amused attention, arrested by the absorbed expression which seemed to have seized and fixed every feature into a statuesque repose.

"Nothing," returned Mrs. Pontellier, with a start, adding at once: "How stupid! But it seems to me it is the reply we make instinctively to such a question. Let me see," she went on, throwing back her head and narrowing her fine eyes till they shone like two vivid points of light. "Let me see. I was really not conscious of thinking of anything; but perhaps I can retrace my thoughts."

"Oh! never mind!" laughed Madame Ratignolle. "I am not quite so exacting. I will let you off this time. It is really too hot to think, especially to think about thinking."

"But for the fun of it," persisted Edna. "First of all, the sight of the water stretching so far away, those motionless sails against the blue sky, made a delicious picture that I just wanted to sit and look at. The hot wind beating in my face made me think—without any connection that I can trace—of a summer day in Kentucky, of a meadow that seemed as big as the ocean to the very little girl walking through the grass, which was higher

[19] A heavy cotton or linen fabric, with a rough, nubby surface.
[20] A long triangular sail.

than her waist. She threw out her arms as if swimming when she walked, beating the tall grass as one strikes out in the water. Oh, I see the connection now!"

"Where were you going that day in Kentucky, walking through the grass?"

"I don't remember now. I was just walking diagonally across a big field. My sun-bonnet obstructed the view. I could see only the stretch of green before me, and I felt as if I must walk on forever, without coming to the end of it. I don't remember whether I was frightened or pleased. I must have been entertained.

"Likely as not it was Sunday," she laughed; "and I was running away from prayers, from the Presbyterian service, read in a spirit of gloom by my father that chills me yet to think of."

"And have you been running away from prayers ever since, *ma chère?*"[21] asked Madame Ratignolle, amused.

"No! oh, no!" Edna hastened to say. "I was a little unthinking child in those days, just following a misleading impulse without question. On the contrary, during one period of my life religion took a firm hold upon me; after I was twelve and until—until—why, I suppose until now, though I never thought much about it—just driven along by habit. But do you know," she broke off, turning her quick eyes upon Madame Ratignolle and leaning forward a little so as to bring her face quite close to that of her companion, "sometimes I feel this summer as if I were walking through the green meadow again; idly, aimlessly, unthinking and unguided."

Madame Ratignolle laid her hand over that of Mrs. Pontellier, which was near her. Seeing that the hand was not withdrawn, she clasped it firmly and warmly. She even stroked it a little, fondly, with the other hand, murmuring in an undertone, *"Pauvre chérie."*[22]

The action was at first a little confusing to Edna, but she soon lent herself readily to the Creole's gentle caress. She was not accustomed to an outward and spoken expression of affection, either in herself or in others. She and her younger sister, Janet, had quarreled a good deal through force of unfortunate habit. Her older sister, Margaret, was matronly and dignified, probably from having assumed matronly and housewifely responsibilities too early in life, their mother having died when they were quite young. Margaret was not effusive; she was practical. Edna had had an occasional girl friend, but whether accidentally or not, they seemed to have been all of one type—the self-contained. She never realized that the reserve of her own character had much, perhaps everything, to do with this. Her most intimate friend at school had been one of rather exceptional intellectual gifts, who wrote fine-sounding essays, which Edna admired and strove to imitate; and with her she talked and glowed over the English classics, and sometimes held religious and political controversies.

Edna often wondered at one propensity which sometimes had inwardly disturbed her without causing any outward show or manifestation on her part. At a very early age—perhaps it was when she traversed the ocean of waving grass—she remembered that she had been passionately enamored of a dignified and sad-eyed cavalry officer who visited her father in Ken-

[21] "My dear." [22] "Poor dear."

tucky. She could not leave his presence when he was there, nor remove her eyes from his face, which was something like Napoleon's, with a lock of black hair falling across the forehead. But the cavalry officer melted imperceptibly out of her existence.

At another time her affections were deeply engaged by a young gentleman who visited a lady on a neighboring plantation. It was after they went to Mississippi to live. The young man was engaged to be married to the young lady, and they sometimes called upon Margaret, driving over of afternoons in a buggy. Edna was a little miss, just merging into her teens; and the realization that she herself was nothing, nothing, nothing to the engaged young man was a bitter affliction to her. But he, too, went the way of dreams.

She was a grown young woman when she was overtaken by what she supposed to be the climax of her fate. It was when the face and figure of a great tragedian[23] began to haunt her imagination and stir her senses. The persistence of the infatuation lent it an aspect of genuineness. The hopelessness of it colored it with the lofty tones of a great passion.

The picture of the tragedian stood enframed upon her desk. Any one may possess the portrait of a tragedian without exciting suspicion or comment. (This was a sinister reflection which she cherished.) In the presence of others she expressed admiration for his exalted gifts, as she handed the photograph around and dwelt upon the fidelity of the likeness. When alone she sometimes picked it up and kissed the cold glass passionately.

Her marriage to Léonce Pontellier was purely an accident, in this respect resembling many other marriages which masquerade as the decrees of Fate. It was in the midst of her secret great passion that she met him. He fell in love, as men are in the habit of doing, and pressed his suit with an earnestness and an ardor which left nothing to be desired. He pleased her; his absolute devotion flattered her. She fancied there was a sympathy of thought and taste between them, in which fancy she was mistaken. Add to this the violent opposition of her father and her sister Margaret to her marriage with a Catholic, and we need seek no further for the motives which led her to accept Monsieur Pontellier for her husband.

The acme of bliss, which would have been a marriage with the tragedian, was not for her in this world. As the devoted wife of a man who worshiped her, she felt she would take her place with a certain dignity in the world of reality, closing the portals forever behind her upon the realm of romance and dreams.

But it was not long before the tragedian had gone to join the cavalry officer and the engaged young man and a few others; and Edna found herself face to face with the realities. She grew fond of her husband, realizing with some unaccountable satisfaction that no trace of passion or excessive and fictitious warmth colored her affection, thereby threatening its dissolution.

She was fond of her children in an uneven, impulsive way. She would sometimes gather them passionately to her heart; she would sometimes forget them. The year before they had spent part of the summer with their

[23] Chopin probably had in mind the famous American Shakespearian actor Edwin Booth (1833–93).

grandmother Pontellier in Iberville. Feeling secure regarding their happiness and welfare, she did not miss them except with an occasional intense longing. Their absence was a sort of relief, though she did not admit this, even to herself. It seemed to free her of a responsibility which she had blindly assumed and for which Fate had not fitted her.

Edna did not reveal so much as all this to Madame Ratignolle that summer day when they sat with faces turned to the sea. But a good part of it escaped her. She had put her head down on Madame Ratignolle's shoulder. She was flushed and felt intoxicated with the sound of her own voice and the unaccustomed taste of candor. It muddled her like wine, or like a first breath of freedom.

There was the sound of approaching voices. It was Robert, surrounded by a troop of children, searching for them. The two little Pontelliers were with him, and he carried Madame Ratignolle's little girl in his arms. There were other children beside, and two nurse-maids followed, looking disagreeable and resigned.

The women at once rose and began to shake out their draperies and relax their muscles. Mrs. Pontellier threw the cushions and rug into the bath-house. The children all scampered off to the awning, and they stood there in a line, gazing upon the intruding lovers, still exchanging their vows and sighs. The lovers got up, with only a silent protest, and walked slowly away somewhere else.

The children possessed themselves of the tent, and Mrs. Pontellier went over to join them.

Madame Ratignolle begged Robert to accompany her to the house; she complained of cramp in her limbs and stiffness of the joints. She leaned draggingly upon his arm as they walked.

VIII

"Do me a favor, Robert," spoke the pretty woman at his side, almost as soon as she and Robert had started on their slow, homeward way. She looked up in his face, leaning on his arm beneath the encircling shadow of the umbrella which he had lifted.

"Granted; as many as you like," he returned, glancing down into her eyes that were full of thoughtfulness and some speculation.

"I only ask for one; let Mrs. Pontellier alone."

"Tiens!" he exclaimed, with a sudden, boyish laugh. *"Voilà que Madame Ratignolle est jalouse!"*[24]

"Nonsense! I'm in earnest; I mean what I say. Let Mrs. Pontellier alone."

"Why?" he asked; himself growing serious at his companion's solicitation.

"She is not one of us; she is not like us. She might make the unfortunate blunder of taking you seriously."

His face flushed with annoyance, and taking off his soft hat he began to beat it impatiently against his leg as he walked. "Why shouldn't she take me

[24]"So! Madame Ratignolle is jealous!"

seriously?" he demanded sharply. "Am I a comedian, a clown, a jack-in-the box? Why shouldn't she? You Creoles! I have no patience with you! Am I always to be regarded as a feature of an amusing programme? I hope Mrs. Pontellier does take me seriously. I hope she has discernment enough to find in me something besides the *blagueur*.[25] If I thought there was any doubt—"

"Oh, enough, Robert!" she broke into his heated outburst. "You are not thinking of what you are saying. You speak with about as little reflection as we might expect from one of those children down there playing in the sand. If your attentions to any married women here were ever offered with any intention of being convincing, you would not be the gentleman we all know you to be, and you would be unfit to associate with the wives and daughters of the people who trust you."

Madame Ratignolle had spoken what she believed to be the law and the gospel. The young man shrugged his shoulders impatiently.

"Oh! well! That isn't it," slamming his hat down vehemently upon his head. "You ought to feel that such things are not flattering to say to a fellow."

"Should our whole intercourse consist of an exchange of compliments? *Ma foi!*"[26]

"It isn't pleasant to have a woman tell you—" he went on, unheedingly, but breaking off suddenly: "Now if I were like Arobin—you remember Alcée Arobin and that story of the consul's wife at Biloxi?" And he related the story of Alcée Arobin and the consul's wife; and another about the tenor of the French Opera,[27] who received letters which should never have been written; and still other stories, grave and gay, till Mrs. Pontellier and her possible propensity for taking young men seriously was apparently forgotten.

Madame Ratignolle, when they had regained her cottage, went in to take the hour's rest which she considered helpful. Before leaving her, Robert begged her pardon for the impatience—he called it rudeness—with which he had received her well-meant caution.

"You made one mistake, Adèle," he said, with a light smile; "there is no earthly possibility of Mrs. Pontellier ever taking me seriously. You should have warned me against taking myself seriously. Your advice might then have carried some weight and given me subject for some reflection. *Au revoir*. But you look tired," he added, solicitously. "Would you like a cup of bouillon? Shall I stir you a toddy? Let me mix you a toddy with a drop of Angostura."

She acceded to the suggestion of bouillon, which was grateful and acceptable. He went himself to the kitchen, which was a building apart from the cottages and lying to the rear of the house. And he himself brought her the golden-brown bouillon, in a dainty Sèvres cup, with a flaky cracker or two on the saucer.

She thrust a bare, white arm from the curtain which shielded her open door, and received the cup from his hands. She told him he was a *bon*

[25] Humbug, fool. [26] "My word!" (literally, "My faith!").
[27] The New Orleans French Opera was one of the finest early opera companies in America.

garçon,[28] and she meant it. Robert thanked her and turned away toward "the house."

The lovers were just entering the grounds of the *pension.* They were leaning toward each other as the water-oaks bent from the sea. There was not a particle of earth beneath their feet. Their heads might have been turned upside-down, so absolutely did they tread upon blue ether. The lady in black, creeping behind them, looked a trifle paler and more jaded than usual. There was no sign of Mrs. Pontellier and the children. Robert scanned the distance for any such apparition. They would doubtless remain away till the dinner hour. The young man ascended to his mother's room. It was situated at the top of the house, made up of odd angles and a queer, sloping ceiling. Two broad dormer windows looked out toward the Gulf, and as far across it as a man's eye might reach. The furnishings of the room were light, cool, and practical.

Madame Lebrun was busily engaged at the sewing-machine. A little black girl sat on the floor, and with her hands worked the treadle of the machine. The Creole woman does not take any chances which may be avoided of imperiling her health.

Robert went over and seated himself on the broad sill of one of the dormer windows. He took a book from his pocket and began energetically to read it, judging by the precision and frequency with which he turned the leaves. The sewing-machine made a resounding clatter in the room; it was of a ponderous, by-gone make. In the lulls, Robert and his mother exchanged bits of desultory conversation.

"Where is Mrs. Pontellier?"

"Down at the beach with the children."

"I promised to lend her the Goncourt.[29] Don't forget to take it down when you go; it's there on the bookshelf over the small table." Clatter, clatter, clatter, bang! for the next five or eight minutes.

"Where is Victor going with the rockaway?"

"The rockaway? Victor?"

"Yes; down there in front. He seems to be getting ready to drive away somewhere."

"Call him." Clatter, clatter!

Robert uttered a shrill, piercing whistle which might have been heard back at the wharf.

"He won't look up."

Madame Lebrun flew to the window. She called "Victor!" She waved a handkerchief and called again. The young fellow below got into the vehicle and started the horse off at a gallop.

Madame Lebrun went back to the machine, crimson with annoyance. Victor was the younger son and brother—a *tête montée,*[30] with a temper which invited violence and a will which no ax could break.

"Whenever you say the word I'm ready to thrash any amount of reason into him that he's able to hold."

[28] "Good waiter" or "good boy."

[29] The Goncourt brothers, Edmond (1822–96) and Jules (1830–70), were famous for their realistic novels of Parisian life.

[30] Hothead.

"If your father had only lived!" Clatter, clatter, clatter, clatter, bang! It was a fixed belief with Madame Lebrun that the conduct of the universe and all things pertaining thereto would have been manifestly of a more intelligent and higher order had not Monsieur Lebrun been removed to other spheres during the early years of their married life.

"What do you hear from Montel?" Montel was a middle-aged gentleman whose vain ambition and desire for the past twenty years had been to fill the void which Monsieur Lebrun's taking off had left in the Lebrun household. Clatter, clatter, bang, clatter!

"I have a letter somewhere," looking in the machine drawer and finding the letter in the bottom of the work-basket. "He says to tell you he will be in Vera Cruz the beginning of next month"—clatter, clatter!—"and if you still have the intention of joining him"—bang! clatter, clatter, bang!

"Why didn't you tell me so before, mother? You know I wanted—" Clatter, clatter, clatter!

"Do you see Mrs. Pontellier starting back with the children? She will be in late to luncheon again. She never starts to get ready for luncheon till the last minute." Clatter, clatter! "Where are you going?"

"Where did you say the Goncourt was?"

IX

Every light in the hall was ablaze; every lamp turned as high as it could be without smoking the chimney or threatening explosion. The lamps were fixed at intervals against the wall, encircling the whole room. Some one had gathered orange and lemon branches, and with these fashioned graceful festoons between. The dark green of the branches stood out and glistened against the white muslin curtains which draped the windows, and which puffed, floated, and flapped at the capricious will of a stiff breeze that swept up from the Gulf.

It was Saturday night a few weeks after the intimate conversation held between Robert and Madame Ratignolle on their way from the beach. An unusual number of husbands, fathers, and friends had come down to stay over Sunday; and they were being suitably entertained by their families, with the material help of Madame Lebrun. The dining tables had all been removed to one end of the hall, and the chairs ranged about in rows and in clusters. Each little family group had had its say and exchanged its domestic gossip earlier in the evening. There was now an apparent disposition to relax; to widen the circle of confidences and give a more general tone to the conversation.

Many of the children had been permitted to sit up beyond their usual bedtime. A small band of them were lying on their stomachs on the floor looking at the colored sheets of the comic papers which Mr. Pontellier had brought down. The little Pontellier boys were permitting them to do so, and making their authority felt.

Music, dancing, and a recitation or two were the entertainments furnished, or rather, offered. But there was nothing systematic about the programme, no appearance of prearrangement nor even premeditation.

At an early hour in the evening the Farival twins were prevailed upon to play the piano. They were girls of fourteen, always clad in the Virgin's colors, blue and white, having been dedicated to the Blessed Virgin at their baptism. They played a duet from "Zampa," and at the earnest solicitation of every one present followed it with the overture to "The Poet and the Peasant."

"*Allez vous-en! Sapristi!*" shrieked the parrot outside the door. He was the only being present who possessed sufficient candor to admit that he was not listening to these gracious performances for the first time that summer. Old Monsieur Farival, grandfather of the twins, grew indignant over the interruption, and insisted upon having the bird removed and consigned to regions of darkness. Victor Lebrun objected; and his decrees were as immutable as those of Fate. The parrot fortunately offered no further interruption to the entertainment, the whole venom of his nature apparently having been cherished up and hurled against the twins in that one impetuous outburst.

Later a young brother and sister gave recitations, which every one present had heard many times at winter evening entertainments in the city.

A little girl performed a skirt dance in the center of the floor. The mother played her accompaniments and at the same time watched her daughter with greedy admiration and nervous apprehension. She need have had no apprehension. The child was mistress of the situation. She had been properly dressed for the occasion in black tulle and black silk tights. Her little neck and arms were bare, and her hair, artificially crimped, stood out like fluffy black plumes over her head. Her poses were full of grace, and her little black-shod toes twinkled as they shot out and upward with a rapidity and suddenness which were bewildering.

But there was no reason why every one should not dance. Madame Ratignolle could not, so it was she who gaily consented to play for the others. She played very well, keeping excellent waltz time and infusing an expression into the strains which was indeed inspiring. She was keeping up her music on account of the children, she said; because she and her husband both considered it a means of brightening the home and making it attractive.

Almost every one danced but the twins, who could not be induced to separate during the brief period when one or the other should be whirling around the room in the arms of a man. They might have danced together, but they did not think of it.

The children were sent to bed. Some went submissively; others with shrieks and protests as they were dragged away. They had been permitted to sit up till after the ice-cream, which naturally marked the limit of human indulgence.

The ice-cream was passed around with cake—gold and silver cake arranged on platters in alternate slices; it had been made and frozen during the afternoon back of the kitchen by two black women, under the supervision of Victor. It was pronounced a great success—excellent if it had only contained a little less vanilla or a little more sugar, if it had been frozen a degree harder, and if the salt might have been kept out of portions of it. Victor was proud of his achievement, and went about recommending it and urging every one to partake of it to excess.

After Mrs. Pontellier had danced twice with her husband, once with

Robert, and once with Monsieur Ratignolle, who was thin and tall and swayed like a reed in the wind when he danced, she went out on the gallery and seated herself on the low window-sill, where she commanded a view of all that went on in the hall and could look out toward the Gulf. There was a soft effulgence in the east. The moon was coming up, and its mystic shimmer was casting a million lights across the distant, restless water.

"Would you like to hear Mademoiselle Reisz play?" asked Robert, coming out on the porch where she was. Of course Edna would like to hear Mademoiselle Reisz play; but she feared it would be useless to entreat her.

"I'll ask her," he said. "I'll tell her that you want to hear her. She likes you. She will come." He turned and hurried away to one of the far cottages, where Mademoiselle Reisz was shuffling away. She was dragging a chair in and out of her room, and at intervals objecting to the crying of a baby, which a nurse in the adjoining cottage was endeavoring to put to sleep. She was a disagreeable little woman, no longer young, who had quarreled with almost every one, owing to a temper which was self-assertive and a disposition to trample upon the rights of others. Robert prevailed upon her without any too great difficulty.

She entered the hall with him during a lull in the dance. She made an awkward, imperious little bow as she went in. She was a homely woman, with a small weazened face and body and eyes that glowed. She had absolutely no taste in dress, and wore a batch of rusty black lace with a bunch of artificial violets pinned to the side of her hair.

"Ask Mrs. Pontellier what she would like to hear me play," she requested of Robert. She sat perfectly still before the piano, not touching the keys, while Robert carried her message to Edna at the window. A general air of surprise and genuine satisfaction fell upon every one as they saw the pianist enter. There was a settling down, and a prevailing air of expectancy everywhere. Edna was a trifle embarrassed at being thus signaled out for the imperious little woman's favor. She would not dare to choose, and begged that Mademoiselle Reisz would please herself in her selections.

Edna was what she herself called very fond of music. Musical strains, well rendered, had a way of evoking pictures in her mind. She sometimes liked to sit in the room of mornings when Madame Ratignolle played or practiced. One piece which that lady played Edna had entitled "Solitude." It was a short, plaintive, minor strain. The name of the piece was something else, but she called it "Solitude." When she heard it there came before her imagination the figure of a man standing beside a desolate rock on the seashore. He was naked. His attitude was one of hopeless resignation as he looked toward a distant bird winging its flight away from him.

Another piece called to her mind a dainty young woman clad in an Empire gown, taking mincing dancing steps as she came down a long avenue between tall hedges. Again, another reminded her of children at play, and still another of nothing on earth but a demure lady stroking a cat.

The very first chords which Mademoiselle Reisz struck upon the piano sent a keen tremor down Mrs. Pontellier's spinal column. It was not the first time she had heard an artist at the piano. Perhaps it was the first time she was ready, perhaps the first time her being was tempered to take an impress of the abiding truth.

She waited for the material pictures which she thought would gather and blaze before her imagination. She waited in vain. She saw no pictures of solitude, of hope, of longing, or of despair. But the very passions themselves were aroused within her soul, swaying it, lashing it, as the waves daily beat upon her splendid body. She trembled, she was choking, and the tears blinded her.

Mademoiselle had finished. She arose, and bowing her stiff, lofty bow, she went away, stopping for neither thanks nor applause. As she passed along the gallery she patted Edna upon the shoulder.

"Well, how did you like my music?" she asked. The young woman was unable to answer; she pressed the hand of the pianist convulsively. Mademoiselle Reisz perceived her agitation and even her tears. She patted her again upon the shoulder as she said:

"You are the only one worth playing for. Those others? Bah!" and she went shuffling and sidling on down the gallery toward her room.

But she was mistaken about "those others." Her playing had aroused a fever of enthusiasm. "What passion!" "What an artist!" "I have always said no one could play Chopin like Mademoiselle Reisz!" "That last prelude! *Bon Dieu!* It shakes a man!"

It was growing late, and there was a general disposition to disband. But some one, perhaps it was Robert, thought of a bath at that mystic hour and under that mystic moon.

X

At all events Robert proposed it, and there was not a dissenting voice. There was not one but was ready to follow when he led the way. He did not lead the way, however, he directed the way; and he himself loitered behind with the lovers, who had betrayed a disposition to linger and hold themselves apart. He walked between them, whether with malicious or mischievous intent was not wholly clear, even to himself.

The Pontelliers and Ratignolles walked ahead; the women leaning upon the arms of their husbands. Edna could hear Robert's voice behind them, and could sometimes hear what he said. She wondered why he did not join them. It was unlike him not to. Of late he had sometimes held away from her for an entire day, redoubling his devotion upon the next and the next, as though to make up for hours that had been lost. She missed him the days when some pretext served to take him away from her, just as one misses the sun on a cloudy day without having thought much about the sun when it was shining.

The people walked in little groups toward the beach. They talked and laughed; some of them sang. There was a band playing down at Klein's hotel, and the strains reached them faintly, tempered by the distance. There were strange, rare odors abroad—a tangle of the sea smell and of weeds and damp, new-plowed earth, mingled with the heavy perfume of a field of white blossoms somewhere near. But the night sat lightly upon the sea and the land. There was no weight of darkness; there were no shadows. The white light of the moon had fallen upon the world like the mystery and the softness of sleep.

Most of them walked into the water as though into a native element.

The sea was quiet now, and swelled lazily in broad billows that melted into one another and did not break except upon the beach in little foamy crests that coiled back like slow, white serpents.

Edna had attempted all summer to learn to swim. She had received instructions from both the men and women; in some instances from the children. Robert had pursued a system of lessons almost daily; and he was nearly at the point of discouragement in realizing the futility of his efforts. A certain ungovernable dread hung about her when in the water, unless there was a hand near by that might reach out and reassure her.

But that night she was like the little tottering, stumbling, clutching child, who of a sudden realizes its powers, and walks for the first time alone, boldly and with over-confidence. She could have shouted for joy. She did shout for joy, as with a sweeping stroke or two she lifted her body to the surface of the water.

A feeling of exultation overtook her, as if some power of significant import had been given her to control the working of her body and her soul. She grew daring and reckless, overestimating her strength. She wanted to swim far out, where no woman had swum before.

Her unlooked-for achievement was the subject of wonder, applause, and admiration. Each one congratulated himself that his special teachings had accomplished this desired end.

"How easy it is!" she thought. "It is nothing," she said aloud; "why did I not discover before that it was nothing. Think of the time I have lost splashing about like a baby!" She would not join the groups in their sports and bouts, but intoxicated with her newly conquered power, she swam out alone.

She turned her face seaward to gather in an impression of space and solitude, which the vast expanse of water, meeting and melting with the moonlit sky, conveyed to her excited fancy. As she swam she seemed to be reaching out for the unlimited in which to lose herself.

Once she turned and looked toward the shore, toward the people she had left there. She had not gone any great distance—that is, what would have been a great distance for an experienced swimmer. But to her unaccustomed vision the stretch of water behind her assumed the aspect of a barrier which her unaided strength would never be able to overcome.

A quick vision of death smote her soul, and for a second of time appalled and enfeebled her senses. But by an effort she rallied her staggering faculties and managed to regain the land.

She made no mention of her encounter with death and her flash of terror, except to say to her husband, "I thought I should have perished out there alone."

"You were not so very far, my dear; I was watching you," he told her.

Edna went at once to the bath-house, and she had put on her dry clothes and was ready to return home before the others had left the water. She started to walk away alone. They all called to her and shouted to her. She waved a dissenting hand, and went on, paying no further heed to their renewed cries which sought to detain her.

"Sometimes I am tempted to think that Mrs. Pontellier is capricious," said Madame Lebrun, who was amusing herself immensely and feared that Edna's abrupt departure might put an end to the pleasure.

"I know she is," assented Mr. Pontellier; "sometimes, not often."

Edna had not traversed a quarter of the distance on her way home before she was overtaken by Robert.

"Did you think I was afraid?" she asked him, without a shade of annoyance.

"No; I knew you weren't afraid."

"Then why did you come? Why didn't you stay out there with the others?"

"I never thought of it."

"Thought of what?"

"Of anything. What difference does it make?"

"I'm very tired," she uttered, complainingly.

"I know you are."

"You don't know anything about it. Why should you know? I never was so exhausted in my life. But it isn't unpleasant. A thousand emotions have swept through me tonight. I don't comprehend half of them. Don't mind what I'm saying; I am just thinking aloud. I wonder if I shall ever be stirred again as Mademoiselle Reisz's playing moved me tonight. I wonder if any night on earth will ever again be like this one. It is like a night in a dream. The people about me are like some uncanny, half-human beings. There must be spirits abroad tonight."

"There are," whispered Robert. "Didn't you know this was the twenty-eighth of August?"

"The twenty-eighth of August?"

"Yes. On the twenty-eighth of August, at the hour of midnight, and if the moon is shining—the moon must be shining—a spirit that has haunted these shores for ages rises up from the Gulf. With its own penetrating vision the spirit seeks some one mortal worthy to hold him company, worthy of being exalted for a few hours into realms of the semi-celestials. His search has always hitherto been fruitless, and he has sunk back, disheartened, into the sea. But tonight he found Mrs. Pontellier. Perhaps he will never wholly release her from the spell. Perhaps she will never again suffer a poor, unworthy earthling to walk in the shadow of her divine presence."

"Don't banter me," she said, wounded at what appeared to be his flippancy. He did not mind the entreaty, but the tone with its delicate note of pathos was like a reproach. He could not explain; he could not tell her that he had penetrated her mood and understood. He said nothing except to offer her his arm, for, by her own admission, she was exhausted. She had been walking alone with her arms hanging limp, letting her white skirts trail along the dewy path. She took his arm, but she did not lean upon it. She let her hand lie listlessly, as though her thoughts were elsewhere—somewhere in advance of her body, and she was striving to overtake them.

Robert assisted her into the hammock which swung from the post before her door out to the trunk of a tree.

"Will you stay out here and wait for Mr. Pontellier?" he asked.

"I'll stay out here. Good-night."

"Shall I get you a pillow?"

"There's one here," she said, feeling about, for they were in the shadow.

"It must be soiled; the children have been tumbling it about."

"No matter." And having discovered the pillow, she adjusted it beneath her head. She extended herself in the hammock with a deep breath of relief. She was not a supercilious or an over-dainty woman. She was not much given to reclining in the hammock, and when she did so it was with no cat-like suggestion of voluptuous ease, but with a beneficent repose which seemed to invade her whole body.

"Shall I stay with you till Mr. Pontellier comes?" asked Robert, seating himself on the outer edge of one of the steps and taking hold of the hammock rope which was fastened to the post.

"If you wish. Don't swing the hammock. Will you get my white shawl which I left on the window-sill over at the house?"

"Are you chilly?"

"No; but I shall be presently."

"Presently?" he laughed. "Do you know what time it is? How long are you going to stay out here?"

"I don't know. Will you get the shawl?"

"Of course I will," he said, rising. He went over to the house, walking along the grass. She watched his figure pass in and out of the strips of moonlight. It was past midnight. It was very quiet.

When he returned with the shawl she took it and kept it in her hand. She did not put it around her.

"Did you say I should stay till Mr. Pontellier came back?"

"I said you might if you wished to."

He seated himself again and rolled a cigarette, which he smoked in silence. Neither did Mrs. Pontellier speak. No multitude of words could have been more significant than those moments of silence, or more pregnant with the first-felt throbbings of desire.

When the voices of the bathers were heard approaching, Robert said good-night. She did not answer him. He thought she was asleep. Again she watched his figure pass in and out of the strips of moonlight as he walked away.

XI

"What are you doing out here, Edna? I thought I should find you in bed," said her husband, when he discovered her lying there. He had walked up with Madame Lebrun and left her at the house. His wife did not reply.

"Are you asleep?" he asked, bending down close to look at her.

"No." Her eyes gleamed bright and intense, with no sleepy shadows, as they looked into his.

"Do you know it is past one o'clock? Come on," and he mounted the steps and went into their room.

"Edna!" called Mr. Pontellier from within, after a few moments had gone by.

"Don't wait for me," she answered. He thrust his head through the door.

"You will take cold out there," he said, irritably. "What folly is this? Why don't you come in?"

"It isn't cold; I have my shawl."

"The mosquitoes will devour you."

"There are no mosquitoes."

She heard him moving about the room; every sound indicating impatience and irritation. Another time she would have gone in at his request. She would, through habit, have yielded to his desire; not with any sense of submission or obedience to his compelling wishes, but unthinkingly, as we walk, move, sit, stand, go through the daily treadmill of the life which has been portioned out to us.

"Edna, dear, are you not coming in soon?" he asked again, this time fondly, with a note of entreaty.

"No; I am going to stay out here."

"This is more than folly," he blurted out. "I can't permit you to stay out there all night. You must come in the house instantly."

With a writhing motion she settled herself more securely in the hammock. She perceived that her will had blazed up, stubborn and resistant. She could not at that moment have done other than denied and resisted. She wondered if her husband had ever spoken to her like that before, and if she had submitted to his command. Of course she had; she remembered that she had. But she could not realize why or how she should have yielded, feeling as she then did.

"Léonce, go to bed," she said. "I mean to stay out here. I don't wish to go in, and I don't intend to. Don't speak to me like that again; I shall not answer you."

Mr. Pontellier had prepared for bed, but he slipped on an extra garment. He opened a bottle of wine, of which he kept a small and select supply in a buffet of his own. He drank a glass of the wine and went out on the gallery and offered a glass to his wife. She did not wish any. He drew up the rocker, hoisted his slippered feet on the rail, and proceeded to smoke a cigar. He smoked two cigars; then he went inside and drank another glass of wine. Mrs. Pontellier again declined to accept a glass when it was offered to her. Mr. Pontellier once more seated himself with elevated feet, and after a reasonable interval of time smoked some more cigars.

Edna began to feel like one who awakens gradually out of a dream, a delicious, grotesque, impossible dream, to feel again the realities pressing into her soul. The physical need for sleep began to overtake her; the exuberance which had sustained and exalted her spirit left her helpless and yielding to the conditions which crowded her in.

The stillest hour of the night had come, the hour before dawn, when the world seems to hold its breath. The moon hung low, and had turned from silver to copper in the sleeping sky. The old owl no longer hooted, and the water-oaks had ceased to moan as they bent their heads.

Edna arose, cramped from lying so long and still in the hammock. She tottered up the steps, clutching feebly at the post before passing into the house.

"Are you coming in, Léonce?" she asked, turning her face toward her husband.

"Yes, dear," he answered, with a glance following a misty puff of smoke. "Just as soon as I have finished my cigar."

XII

She slept but a few hours. They were troubled and feverish hours, disturbed with dreams that were intangible, that eluded her, leaving only an impression upon her half-awakened senses of something unattainable. She was up and dressed in the cool of the early morning. The air was invigorating and steadied somewhat her faculties. However, she was not seeking refreshment or help from any source, either external or from within. She was blindly following whatever impulse moved her, as if she had placed herself in alien hands for direction, and freed her soul of responsibility.

Most of the people at that early hour were still in bed and asleep. A few, who intended to go over to the *Chênière* for mass, were moving about. The lovers, who had laid their plans the night before, were already strolling toward the wharf. The lady in black, with her Sunday prayer-book, velvet and gold-clasped, and her Sunday silver beads, was following them at no great distance. Old Monsieur Farival was up, and was more than half inclined to do anything that suggested itself. He put on his big straw hat, and taking his umbrella from the stand in the hall, followed the lady in black, never overtaking her.

The little negro girl who worked Madame Lebrun's sewing-machine was sweeping the galleries with long, absent-minded strokes of the broom. Edna sent her up into the house to awaken Robert.

"Tell him I am going to the *Chênière.* The boat is ready; tell him to hurry."

He had soon joined her. She had never sent for him before. She had never asked for him. She had never seemed to want him before. She did not appear conscious that she had done anything unusual in commanding his presence. He was apparently equally unconscious of anything extraordinary in the situation. But his face was suffused with a quiet glow when he met her.

They went together back to the kitchen to drink coffee. There was no time to wait for any nicety of service. They stood outside the window and the cook passed them their coffee and a roll, which they drank and ate from the window-sill. Edna said it tasted good. She had not thought of coffee nor of anything. He told her he had often noticed that she lacked forethought.

"Wasn't it enough to think of going to the *Chênière* and waking you up?" she laughed. "Do I have to think of everything?—as Léonce says when he's in a bad humor. I don't blame him; he'd never be in a bad humor if it weren't for me."

They took a short cut across the sands. At a distance they could see the curious procession moving toward the wharf—the lovers, shoulder to shoulder, creeping; the lady in black, gaining steadily upon them; old Monsieur Farival, losing ground inch by inch, and a young barefooted Spanish girl, with a red kerchief on her head and a basket on her arm, bringing up the rear.

Robert knew the girl, and he talked to her a little in the boat. No one present understood what they said. Her name was Mariequita. She had a round, sly, piquant face and pretty black eyes. Her hands were small, and she kept them folded over the handle of her basket. Her feet were broad and coarse. She did not strive to hide them. Edna looked at her feet, and noticed the sand and slime between her brown toes.

Beaudelet grumbled because Mariequita was there, taking up so much room. In reality he was annoyed at having old Monsieur Farival, who considered himself the better sailor of the two. But he would not quarrel with so old a man as Monsieur Farival, so he quarreled with Mariequita. The girl was deprecatory at one moment, appealing to Robert. She was saucy the next, moving her head up and down, making "eyes" at Robert and making "mouths" at Beaudelet.

The lovers were all alone. They saw nothing, they heard nothing. The lady in black was counting her beads for the third time. Old Monsieur Farival talked incessantly of what he knew about handling a boat, and of what Beaudelet did not know on the same subject.

Edna liked it all. She looked Mariequita up and down, from her ugly brown toes to her pretty black eyes, and back again.

"Why does she look at me like that?" inquired the girl of Robert.

"Maybe she thinks you are pretty. Shall I ask her?"

"No. Is she your sweetheart?"

"She's a married lady, and has two children."

"Oh! well! Francisco ran away with Sylvano's wife, who had four children. They took all his money and one of the children and stole his boat."

"Shut up!"

"Does she understand?"

"Oh, hush!"

"Are those two married over there—leaning on each other?"

"Of course not," laughed Robert.

"Of course not," echoed Mariequita, with a serious, confirmatory bob of the head.

The sun was high up and beginning to bite. The swift breeze seemed to Edna to bury the sting of it into the pores of her face and hands. Robert held his umbrella over her.

As they went cutting sidewise through the water, the sails bellied taut, with the wind filling and overflowing them. Old Monsieur Farival laughed sardonically at something as he looked at the sails, and Beaudelet swore at the old man under his breath.

Sailing across the bay to the *Chênière Caminada,* Edna felt as if she were being borne away from some anchorage which had held her fast, whose chains had been loosening—had snapped the night before when the mystic spirit was abroad, leaving her free to drift whithersoever she chose to set her sails. Robert spoke to her incessantly; he no longer noticed Mariequita. The girl had shrimps in her bamboo basket. They were covered with Spanish moss. She beat the moss down impatiently, and muttered to herself sullenly.

"Let us go to Grande Terre[31] tomorrow?" said Robert in a low voice.

"What shall we do there?"

"Climb up the hill to the old fort and look at the little wriggling gold snakes, and watch the lizards sun themselves."

[31] An island near Grand Isle.

She gazed away toward Grande Terre and thought she would like to be alone there with Robert, in the sun, listening to the ocean's roar and watching the slimy lizards writhe in and out among the ruins of the old fort.

"And the next day or the next we can sail to the Bayou Brulow,"[32] he went on.

"What shall we do there?"

"Anything—cast bait for fish."

"No; we'll go back to Grande Terre. Let the fish alone."

"We'll go wherever you like," he said. "I'll have Tonie come over and help me patch and trim my boat. We shall not need Beaudelet nor any one. Are you afraid of the pirogue?"[33]

"Oh, no."

"Then I'll take you some night in the pirogue when the moon shines. Maybe your Gulf spirit will whisper to you in which of these islands the treasures are hidden—direct you to the very spot, perhaps."

"And in a day we should be rich!" she laughed. "I'd give it all to you, the pirate gold and every bit of treasure we could dig up. I think you would know how to spend it. Pirate gold isn't a thing to be hoarded or utilized. It is something to squander and throw to the four winds, for the fun of seeing the golden specks fly."

"We'd share it, and scatter it together," he said. His face flushed.

They all went together up to the quaint little Gothic church of Our Lady of Lourdes, gleaming all brown and yellow with paint in the sun's glare.

Only Beaudelet remained behind, tinkering at his boat, and Mariequita walked away with her basket of shrimps, casting a look of childish ill-humor and reproach at Robert from the corner of her eye.

XIII

A feeling of oppression and drowsiness overcame Edna during the service. Her head began to ache, and the lights on the altar swayed before her eyes. Another time she might have made an effort to regain her composure; but her one thought was to quit the stifling atmosphere of the church and reach the open air. She arose, climbing over Robert's feet with a muttered apology. Old Monsieur Farival, flurried, curious, stood up, but upon seeing that Robert had followed Mrs. Pontellier, he sank back into his seat. He whispered an anxious inquiry of the lady in black, who did not notice him or reply, but kept her eyes fastened upon the pages of her velvet prayer-book.

"I felt giddy and almost overcome," Edna said, lifting her hands instinctively to her head and pushing her straw hat up from her forehead. "I couldn't have stayed through the service." They were outside in the shadow of the church. Robert was full of solicitude.

"It was folly to have thought of going in the first place, let alone staying. Come over to Madame Antoine's; you can rest there." He took her arm and led her away, looking anxiously and continuously down into her face.

How still it was, with only the voice of the sea whispering through the

[32] A village on the mainland near Grand Isle. [33] Canoe.

reeds that grew in the salt-water pools! The long line of little gray, weather-beaten houses nestled peacefully among the orange trees. It must always have been God's day on that low, drowsy island, Edna thought. They stopped, leaning over a jagged fence made of sea-drift, to ask for water. A youth, a mild-faced Acadian,[34] was drawing water from the cistern, which was nothing more than a rusty buoy, with an opening on one side, sunk in the ground. The water which the youth handed to them in a tin pail was not cold to taste, but it was cool to her heated face, and it greatly revived and refreshed her.

Madame Antoine's cot[35] was at the far end of the village. She welcomed them with all the native hospitality, as she would have opened her door to let the sunlight in. She was fat, and walked heavily and clumsily across the floor. She could speak no English, but when Robert made her understand that the lady who accompanied him was ill and desired to rest, she was all eagerness to make Edna feel at home and to dispose of her comfortably.

The whole place was immaculately clean, and the big, four-posted bed, snow-white, invited one to repose. It stood in a small side room which looked out across a narrow grass plot toward the shed, where there was a disabled boat lying keel upward.

Madame Antoine had not gone to mass. Her son Tonie had, but she supposed he would soon be back, and she invited Robert to be seated and wait for him. But he went and sat outside the door and smoked. Madame Antoine busied herself in the large front room preparing dinner. She was boiling mullets over a few red coals in the huge fireplace.

Edna, left alone in the little side room, loosened her clothes, removing the greater part of them. She bathed her face, her neck and arms in the basin that stood between the windows. She took off her shoes and stockings and stretched herself in the very center of the high, white bed. How luxurious it felt to rest thus in a strange, quaint bed, with its sweet country odor of laurel lingering about the sheets and mattress! She stretched her strong limbs that ached a little. She ran her fingers through her loosened hair for a while. She looked at her round arms as she held them straight up and rubbed them one after the other, observing closely, as if it were something she saw for the first time, the fine, firm quality and texture of her flesh. She clasped her hands easily above her head, and it was thus she fell asleep.

She slept lightly at first, half awake and drowsily attentive to the things about her. She could hear Madame Antoine's heavy, scraping tread as she walked back and forth on the sanded floor. Some chickens were clucking outside the windows, scratching for bits of gravel in the grass. Later she half heard the voices of Robert and Tonie talking under the shed. She did not stir. Even her eyelids rested numb and heavily over her sleepy eyes. The voices went on—Tonie's slow, Acadian drawl, Robert's quick, soft, smooth French. She understood French imperfectly unless directly addressed, and the voices were only part of the other drowsy, muffled sounds lulling her senses.

[34] Descendant of the French Canadians expelled from Acadia (Nova Scotia) in the eighteenth century who settled in Louisiana. "Cajun" is a corruption of "Acadian."

[35] Cottage.

When Edna awoke it was with the conviction that she had slept long and soundly. The voices were hushed under the shed. Madame Antoine's step was no longer to be heard in the adjoining room. Even the chickens had gone elsewhere to scratch and cluck. The mosquito bar was drawn over her; the old woman had come in while she slept and let down the bar. Edna arose quietly from the bed, and looking between the curtains of the window, she saw by the slanting rays of the sun that the afternoon was far advanced. Robert was out there under the shed, reclining in the shade against the sloping keel of the overturned boat. He was reading from a book. Tonie was no longer with him. She wondered what had become of the rest of the party. She peeped out at him two or three times as she stood washing herself in the little basin between the windows.

Madame Antoine had laid some coarse, clean towels upon a chair, and had placed a box of *poudre de riz*[36] within easy reach. Edna dabbed the powder upon her nose and cheeks as she looked at herself closely in the little distorted mirror which hung on the wall above the basin. Her eyes were bright and wide awake and her face glowed.

When she had completed her toilet she walked into the adjoining room. She was very hungry. No one was there. But there was a cloth spread upon the table that stood against the wall, and a cover was laid for one, with a crusty brown loaf and a bottle of wine beside the plate. Edna bit a piece from the brown loaf, tearing it with her strong, white teeth. She poured some of the wine into the glass and drank it down. Then she went softly out of doors, and plucking an orange from the low-hanging bough of a tree, threw it at Robert, who did not know she was awake and up.

An illumination broke over his whole face when he saw her and joined her under the orange tree.

"How many years have I slept?" she inquired. "The whole island seems changed. A new race of beings must have sprung up, leaving only you and me as past relics. How many ages ago did Madame Antoine and Tonie die? and when did our people from Grand Isle disappear from the earth?"

He familiarly adjusted a ruffle upon her shoulder.

"You have slept precisely one hundred years. I was left here to guard your slumbers; and for one hundred years I have been out under the shed reading a book. The only evil I couldn't prevent was to keep a broiled fowl from drying up."

"If it has turned to stone, still will I eat it," said Edna, moving with him into the house. "But really, what has become of Monsieur Farival and the others?"

"Gone hours ago. When they found that you were sleeping they thought it best not to awake you. Any way, I wouldn't have let them. What was I here for?"

"I wonder if Léonce will be uneasy!" she speculated, as she seated herself at table.

"Of course not; he knows you are with me," Robert replied, as he busied himself among sundry pans and covered dishes which had been left standing on the hearth.

[36] "Rice powder."

"Where are Madame Antoine and her son?" asked Edna.

"Gone to Vespers,[37] and to visit some friends, I believe. I am to take you back in Tonie's boat whenever you are ready to go."

He stirred the smoldering ashes till the broiled fowl began to sizzle afresh. He served her with no mean repast, dripping the coffee anew and sharing it with her. Madame Antoine had cooked little else than the mullets, but while Edna slept Robert had foraged the island. He was childishly gratified to discover her appetite, and to see the relish with which she ate the food which he had procured for her.

"Shall we go right away?" she asked, after draining her glass and brushing together the crumbs of the crusty loaf.

"The sun isn't as low as it will be in two hours," he answered.

"The sun will be gone in two hours."

"Well, let it go; who cares!"

They waited a good while under the orange trees, till Madame Antoine came back, panting, waddling, with a thousand apologies to explain her absence. Tonie did not dare to return. He was shy, and would not willingly face any woman except his mother.

It was very pleasant to stay there under the orange trees, while the sun dipped lower and lower, turning the western sky to flaming copper and gold. The shadows lengthened and crept out like stealthy, grotesque monsters across the grass.

Edna and Robert both sat upon the ground—that is, he lay upon the ground beside her, occasionally picking at the hem of her muslin gown.

Madame Antoine seated her fat body, broad and squat, upon a bench beside the door. She had been talking all the afternoon, and had wound herself up to the story-telling pitch.

And what stories she told them! But twice in her life she had left the *Chênière Caminada,* and then for the briefest span. All her years she had squatted and waddled there upon the island, gathering legends of the Baratarians[38] and the sea. The night came on, with the moon to lighten it. Edna could hear the whispering voices of dead men and the click of muffled gold.

When she and Robert stepped into Tonie's boat, with the red lateen sail, misty spirit forms were prowling in the shadows and among the reeds, and upon the water were phantom ships, speeding to cover.

XIV

The youngest boy, Etienne, had been very naughty, Madame Ratignolle said, as she delivered him into the hands of his mother. He had been unwilling to go to bed and had made a scene; whereupon she had taken charge of him and pacified him as well as she could. Raoul had been in bed and asleep for two hours.

The youngster was in his long white nightgown, that kept tripping him up as Madame Ratignolle led him along by the hand. With the other

[37] An evening church service.

[38] Pirates who operated in the area of Barataria Bay. The most famous was Jean Lafitte.

chubby fist he rubbed his eyes, which were heavy with sleep and ill humor. Edna took him in her arms, and seating herself in the rocker, began to coddle and caress him, calling him all manner of tender names, soothing him to sleep.

It was not more than nine o'clock. No one had yet gone to bed but the children.

Léonce had been very uneasy at first, Madame Ratignolle said, and had wanted to start at once for the *Chênière*. But Monsieur Farival had assured him that his wife was only overcome with sleep and fatigue, that Tonie would bring her safely back later in the day; and he had thus been dissuaded from crossing the bay. He had gone over to Klein's, looking up some cotton broker whom he wished to see in regard to securities, exchanges, stocks, bonds, or something of the sort, Madame Ratignolle did not remember what. He said he would not remain away late. She herself was suffering from heat and oppression, she said. She carried a bottle of salts and a large fan. She would not consent to remain with Edna, for Monsieur Ratignolle was alone, and he detested above all things to be left alone.

When Etienne had fallen asleep Edna bore him into the back room, and Robert went and lifted the mosquito bar that she might lay the child comfortably in his bed. The quadroon had vanished. When they emerged from the cottage Robert bade Edna good-night.

"Do you know we have been together the whole livelong day, Robert—since early this morning?" she said at parting.

"All but the hundred years when you were sleeping. Good-night."

He pressed her hand and went away in the direction of the beach. He did not join any of the others, but walked alone toward the Gulf.

Edna stayed outside, awaiting her husband's return. She had no desire to sleep or to retire; nor did she feel like going over to sit with the Ratignolles, or to join Madame Lebrun and a group whose animated voices reached her as they sat in conversation before the house. She let her mind wander back over her stay at Grand Isle; and she tried to discover wherein this summer had been different from any and every other summer of her life. She could only realize that she herself—her present self—was in some way different from the other self. That she was seeing with different eyes and making the acquaintance of new conditions in herself that colored and changed her environment, she did not yet suspect.

She wondered why Robert had gone away and left her. It did not occur to her to think he might have grown tired of being with her the livelong day. She was not tired, and she felt that he was not. She regretted that he had gone. It was so much more natural to have him stay when he was not absolutely required to leave her.

As Edna waited for her husband she sang low a little song that Robert had sung as they crossed the bay. It began with "Ah! *Si tu savais,*" and every verse ended with "*si tu savais.*"[39]

Robert's voice was not pretentious. It was musical and true. The voice, the notes, the whole refrain haunted her memory.

[39] "If you could know." Margaret Culley has identified this important song as a ballad, "Si Tu Savais," by Michael Balfe (1808–70), composer of *The Bohemian Girl.*

XV

When Edna entered the dining-room one evening a little late, as was her habit, an unusually animated conversation seemed to be going on. Several persons were talking at once, and Victor's voice was predominating, even over that of his mother. Edna had returned late from her bath, had dressed in some haste, and her face was flushed. Her head, set off by her dainty white gown, suggested a rich, rare blossom. She took her seat at table between old Monsieur Farival and Madame Ratignolle.

As she seated herself and was about to begin to eat her soup, which had been served when she entered the room, several persons informed her simultaneously that Robert was going to Mexico. She laid her spoon down and looked about her bewildered. He had been with her, reading to her all the morning, and had never even mentioned such a place as Mexico. She had not seen him during the afternoon; she had heard some one say he was at the house, upstairs with his mother. This she had thought nothing of, though she was surprised when he did not join her later in the afternoon, when she went down to the beach.

She looked across at him, where he sat beside Madame Lebrun, who presided. Edna's face was a blank picture of bewilderment, which she never thought of disguising. He lifted his eyebrows with the pretext of a smile as he returned her glance. He looked embarrassed and uneasy.

"When is he going?" she asked of everybody in general, as if Robert were not there to answer for himself.

"Tonight!" "This very evening!" "Did you ever!" "What possesses him!" were some of the replies she gathered, uttered simultaneously in French and English.

"Impossible!" she exclaimed. "How can a person start off from Grand Isle to Mexico at a moment's notice, as if he were going over to Klein's or to the wharf or down to the beach?"

"I said all along I was going to Mexico; I've been saying so for years!" cried Robert, in an excited and irritable tone, with the air of a man defending himself against a swarm of stinging insects.

Madame Lebrun knocked on the table with her knife handle.

"Please let Robert explain why he is going, and why he is going tonight," she called out. "Really, this table is getting to be more and more like Bedlam every day, with everybody talking at once. Sometimes—I hope God will forgive me—but positively, sometimes I wish Victor would lose the power of speech."

Victor laughed sardonically as he thanked his mother for her holy wish, of which he failed to see the benefit to anybody, except that it might afford her a more ample opportunity and license to talk herself.

Monsieur Farival thought that Victor should have been taken out in mid-ocean in his earliest youth and drowned. Victor thought there would be more logic in thus disposing of old people with an established claim for making themselves universally obnoxious. Madame Lebrun grew a trifle hysterical; Robert called his brother some sharp, hard names.

"There's nothing much to explain, mother," he said; though he explained, nevertheless—looking chiefly at Edna—that he could only meet the gentleman whom he intended to join at Vera Cruz by taking such and such a steamer, which left New Orleans on such a day; that Beaudelet was going out with his lugger-load of vegetables that night, which gave him an opportunity of reaching the city and making his vessel in time.

"But when did you make up your mind to all this?" demanded Monsieur Farival.

"This afternoon," returned Robert, with a shade of annoyance.

"At what time this afternoon?" persisted the old gentleman, with nagging determination, as if he were cross-questioning a criminal in a court of justice.

"At four o'clock this afternoon, Monsieur Farival," Robert replied, in a high voice and with a lofty air, which reminded Edna of some gentleman on the stage.

She had forced herself to eat most of her soup, and now she was picking the flaky bits of a *court bouillon*[40] with her fork.

The lovers were profiting by the general conversation on Mexico to speak in whispers of matters which they rightly considered were interesting to no one but themselves. The lady in black had once received a pair of prayer-beads of curious workmanship from Mexico, with very special indulgence attached to them, but she had never been able to ascertain whether the indulgence extended outside the Mexican border. Father Fochel of the Cathedral had attempted to explain it; but he had not done so to her satisfaction. And she begged that Robert would interest himself, and discover, if possible, whether she was entitled to the indulgence accompanying the remarkably curious Mexican prayer-beads.

Madame Ratignolle hoped that Robert would exercise extreme caution in dealing with the Mexicans, who, she considered, were a treacherous people, unscrupulous and revengeful. She trusted she did them no injustice in thus condemning them as a race. She had known personally but one Mexican, who made and sold excellent tamales, and whom she would have trusted implicitly, so soft-spoken was he. One day he was arrested for stabbing his wife. She never knew whether he had been hanged or not.

Victor had grown hilarious, and was attempting to tell an anecdote about a Mexican girl who served chocolate one winter in a restaurant in Dauphine Street.[41] No one would listen to him but old Monsieur Farival, who went into convulsions over the droll story.

Edna wondered if they had all gone mad, to be talking and clamoring at that rate. She herself could think of nothing to say about Mexico or the Mexicans.

"At what time do you leave?" she asked Robert.

"At ten," he told her. "Beaudelet wants to wait for the moon."

"Are you all ready to go?"

"Quite ready. I shall only take a hand-bag, and shall pack my trunk in the city."

He turned to answer some question put to him by his mother, and Edna, having finished her black coffee, left the table.

She went directly to her room. The little cottage was close and stuffy after leaving the outer air. But she did not mind; there appeared to be a hundred different things demanding her attention indoors. She began to

[40]Fish in wine sauce. [41]A street in the French Quarter.

set the toilet-stand to rights, grumbling at the negligence of the quadroon, who was in the adjoining room putting the children to bed. She gathered together stray garments that were hanging on the backs of chairs, and put each where it belonged in closet or bureau drawer. She changed her gown for a more comfortable and commodious wrapper. She rearranged her hair, combing and brushing it with unusual energy. Then she went in and assisted the quadroon in getting the boys to bed.

They were very playful and inclined to talk—to do anything but lie quiet and go to sleep. Edna sent the quadroon away to her supper and told her she need not return. Then she sat and told the children a story. Instead of soothing it excited them, and added to their wakefulness. She left them in heated argument, speculating about the conclusion of the tale which their mother promised to finish the following night.

The little black girl came in to say that Madame Lebrun would like to have Mrs. Pontellier go and sit with them over at the house till Mr. Robert went away. Edna returned answer that she had already undressed, that she did not feel quite well, but perhaps she would go over to the house later. She started to dress again, and got as far advanced as to remove her *peignoir*. But changing her mind once more she resumed the *peignoir,* and went outside and sat down before her door. She was overheated and irritable, and fanned herself energetically for a while. Madame Ratignolle came down to discover what was the matter.

"All that noise and confusion at the table must have upset me," replied Edna, "and moreover, I hate shocks and surprises. The idea of Robert starting off in such a ridiculously sudden and dramatic way! As if it were a matter of life and death! Never saying a word about it all morning when he was with me."

"Yes," agreed Madame Ratignolle. "I think it was showing us all—you especially—very little consideration. It wouldn't have surprised me in any of the others; those Lebruns are all given to heroics. But I must say I should never have expected such a thing from Robert. Are you not coming down? Come on, dear; it doesn't look friendly."

"No," said Edna, a little sullenly. "I can't go to the trouble of dressing again; I don't feel like it."

"You needn't dress; you look all right; fasten a belt around your waist. Just look at me!"

"No," persisted Edna; "but you go on. Madame Lebrun might be offended if we both stayed away."

Madame Ratignolle kissed Edna good-night, and went away, being in truth rather desirous of joining in the general and animated conversation which was still in progress concerning Mexico and the Mexicans.

Somewhat later Robert came up, carrying his hand-bag.

"Aren't you feeling well?" he asked.

"Oh, well enough. Are you going right away?"

He lit a match and looked at his watch. "In twenty minutes," he said. The sudden and brief flare of the match emphasized the darkness for a while. He sat down upon a stool which the children had left out on the porch.

"Get a chair," said Edna.

"This will do," he replied. He put on his soft hat and nervously took it off again, and wiping his face with his handkerchief, complained of the heat.

"Take the fan," said Edna, offering it to him.

"Oh, no! Thank you. It does no good; you have to stop fanning some time, and feel all the more uncomfortable afterward."

"That's one of the ridiculous things which men always say. I have never known one to speak otherwise of fanning. How long will you be gone?"

"Forever, perhaps. I don't know. It depends upon a good many things."

"Well, in case it shouldn't be forever, how long will it be?"

"I don't know."

"This seems to me perfectly preposterous and uncalled for. I don't like it. I don't understand your motive for silence and mystery, never saying a word to me about it this morning." He remained silent, not offering to defend himself. He only said, after a moment:

"Don't part from me in an ill-humor. I never knew you to be out of patience with me before."

"I don't want to part in any ill-humor," she said. "But can't you understand? I've grown used to seeing you, to having you with me all the time, and your action seems unfriendly, even unkind. You don't even offer an excuse for it. Why, I was planning to be together, thinking of how pleasant it would be to see you in the city next winter."

"So was I," he blurted. "Perhaps that's the—" He stood up suddenly and held out his hand. "Good-by, my dear Mrs. Pontellier; good-by. You won't—I hope you won't completely forget me." She clung to his hand, striving to detain him.

"Write to me when you get there, won't you, Robert?" she entreated.

"I will, thank you. Good-by."

How unlike Robert! The merest acquaintance would have said something more emphatic than "I will, thank you; good-by," to such a request.

He had evidently already taken leave of the people over at the house, for he descended the steps and went to join Beaudelet, who was out there with an oar across his shoulder waiting for Robert. They walked away in the darkness. She could only hear Beaudelet's voice; Robert had apparently not even spoken a word of greeting to his companion.

Edna bit her handkerchief convulsively, striving to hold back and to hide, even from herself as she would have hidden from another, the emotion which was troubling—tearing—her. Her eyes were brimming with tears.

For the first time she recognized anew the symptoms of infatuation which she had felt incipiently as a child, as a girl in her earliest teens, and later as a young woman. The recognition did not lessen the reality, the poignancy of the revelation by any suggestion or promise of instability. The past was nothing to her; offered no lesson which she was willing to heed. The future was a mystery which she never attempted to penetrate. The present alone was significant; was hers, to torture her as it was doing then with the biting conviction that she had lost that which she had held, that she had been denied that which her impassioned, newly awakened being demanded.

XVI

"Do you miss your friend greatly?" asked Mademoiselle Reisz one morning as she came creeping up behind Edna, who had just left her cottage on her way to the beach. She spent much of her time in the water since she had acquired finally the art of swimming. As their stay at Grand Isle drew near its close, she felt that she could not give too much time to a diversion which afforded her the only real pleasurable moments that she knew. When Mademoiselle Reisz came and touched her upon the shoulder and spoke to her, the woman seemed to echo the thought which was ever in Edna's mind; or, better, the feeling which constantly possessed her.

Robert's going had some way taken the brightness, the color, the meaning out of everything. The conditions of her life were in no way changed, but her whole existence was dulled, like a faded garment which seems to be no longer worth wearing. She sought him everywhere—in others whom she induced to talk about him. She went up in the mornings to Madame Lebrun's room, braving the clatter of the old sewing-machine. She sat there and chatted at intervals as Robert had done. She gazed around the room at the pictures and photographs hanging upon the wall, and discovered in some corner an old family album, which she examined with the keenest interest, appealing to Madame Lebrun for enlightenment concerning the many figures and faces which she discovered between its pages.

There was a picture of Madame Lebrun with Robert as a baby, seated in her lap, a round-faced infant with a fist in his mouth. The eyes alone in the baby suggested the man. And that was he also in kilts, at the age of five, wearing long curls and holding a whip in his hand. It made Edna laugh, and she laughed, too, at the portrait in his first long trousers; while another interested her, taken when he left for college, looking thin, long-faced, with eyes full of fire, ambition and great intentions. But there was no recent picture, none which suggested the Robert who had gone away five days ago, leaving a void and wilderness behind him.

"Oh, Robert stopped having his pictures taken when he had to pay for them himself! He found wiser use for his money, he says," explained Madame Lebrun. She had a letter from him, written before he left New Orleans. Edna wished to see the letter, and Madame Lebrun told her to look for it either on the table or the dresser, or perhaps it was on the mantelpiece.

The letter was on the bookshelf. It possessed the greatest interest and attraction for Edna; the envelope, its size and shape, the post-mark, the handwriting. She examined every detail of the outside before opening it. There were only a few lines, setting forth that he would leave the city that afternoon, that he had packed his trunk in good shape, that he was well, and sent her his love and begged to be affectionately remembered to all. There was no special message to Edna except a postscript saying that if Mrs. Pontellier desired to finish the book which he had been reading to her, his mother would find it in his room, among other books there on the table. Edna experienced a pang of jealousy because he had written to his mother rather than to her.

Every one seemed to take for granted that she missed him. Even her husband, when he came down the Saturday following Robert's departure, expressed regret that he had gone.

"How do you get on without him, Edna?" he asked.

"It's very dull without him," she admitted. Mr. Pontellier had seen Robert in the city, and Edna asked him a dozen questions or more. Where had they met? On Carondelet Street, in the morning. They had gone "in" and had a drink and cigar together. What had they talked about? Chiefly about his prospects in Mexico, which Mr. Pontellier thought were promising. How did he look? How did he seem—grave, or gay, or how? Quite cheerful, and wholly taken up with the idea of his trip, which Mr. Pontellier found altogether natural in a young fellow about to seek fortune and adventure in a strange, queer country.

Edna tapped her foot impatiently, and wondered why the children persisted in playing in the sun when they might be under the trees. She went down and led them out of the sun, scolding the quadroon for not being more attentive.

It did not strike her as in the least grotesque that she should be making of Robert the object of conversation and leading her husband to speak of him. The sentiment which she entertained for Robert in no way resembled that which she felt for her husband, or had ever felt, or ever expected to feel. She had all her life long been accustomed to harbor thoughts and emotions which never voiced themselves. They had never taken the form of struggles. They belonged to her and were her own, and she entertained the conviction that she had a right to them and that they concerned no one but herself. Edna had once told Madame Ratignolle that she would never sacrifice herself for her children, or for any one. Then had followed a rather heated argument; the two women did not appear to understand each other or to be talking the same language. Edna tried to appease her friend, to explain.

"I would give up the unessential; I would give my money, I would give my life for my children; but I wouldn't give myself. I can't make it more clear; it's only something which I am beginning to comprehend, which is revealing itself to me."

"I don't know what you would call the essential, or what you mean by the unessential," said Madame Ratignolle, cheerfully; "but a woman who would give her life for her children could do no more than that—your Bible tells you so. I'm sure I couldn't do more than that."

"Oh, yes you could!" laughed Edna.

She was not surprised at Mademoiselle Reisz's question the morning that lady, following her to the beach, tapped her on the shoulder and asked if she did not greatly miss her young friend.

"Oh, good morning, Mademoiselle; is it you? Why, of course I miss Robert. Are you going down to bathe?"

"Why should I go down to bathe at the very end of the season when I haven't been in the surf all summer," replied the woman, disagreeably.

"I beg your pardon," offered Edna, in some embarrassment, for she should have remembered that Mademoiselle Reisz's avoidance of the water had furnished a theme for much pleasantry. Some among them thought it was on account of her false hair, or the dread of getting the violets wet, while others attributed it to the natural aversion for water sometimes believed to accompany the artistic temperament. Mademoiselle offered Edna some chocolates in a paper bag, which she took from her pocket, by way of showing that she bore no ill feeling. She habitually ate chocolates for their sustaining quality; they contained much nutriment in small compass, she said. They saved her from starvation, as Madame Lebrun's table was utterly impossible; and no one save so impertinent a woman as Madame Lebrun could think of offering such food to people and requiring them to pay for it.

"She must feel very lonely without her son," said Edna, desiring to change the subject. "Her favorite son, too. It must have been quite hard to let him go."

Mademoiselle laughed maliciously.

"Her favorite son! Oh, dear! Who could have been imposing such a tale upon you? Aline Lebrun lives for Victor, and for Victor alone. She has spoiled him into the worthless creature he is. She worships him and the ground he walks on. Robert is very well in a way, to give up all the money he can earn to the family, and keep the barest pittance for himself. Favorite son, indeed! I miss the poor fellow myself, my dear. I liked to see him and to hear him about the place—the only Lebrun who is worth a pinch of salt. He comes to see me often in the city. I like to play to him. That Victor! hanging would be too good for him. It's a wonder Robert hasn't beaten him to death long ago."

"I thought he had great patience with his brother," offered Edna, glad to be talking about Robert, no matter what was said.

"Oh! he thrashed him well enough a year or two ago," said Mademoiselle. "It was about a Spanish girl, whom Victor considered that he had some sort of claim upon. He met Robert one day talking to the girl, or walking with her, or bathing with her, or carrying her basket—I don't remember what;—and he became so insulting and abusive that Robert gave him a thrashing on the spot that has kept him comparatively in order for a good while. It's about time he was getting another."

"Was her name Mariequita?" asked Edna.

"Mariequita—yes, that was it; Mariequita. I had forgotten. Oh, she's a sly one, and a bad one, that Mariequita!"

Edna looked down at Mademoiselle Reisz and wondered how she could have listened to her venom so long. For some reason she felt depressed, almost unhappy. She had not intended to go into the water; but she donned her bathing suit, and left Mademoiselle alone, seated under the shade of the children's tent. The water was growing cooler as the season advanced. Edna plunged and swam about with an abandon that thrilled and invigorated her. She remained a long time in the water, half hoping that Mademoiselle Reisz would not wait for her.

But Mademoiselle waited. She was very amiable during the walk back, and raved much over Edna's appearance in her bathing suit. She talked about music. She hoped that Edna would go to see her in the city, and wrote her address with the stub of a pencil on a piece of card which she found in her pocket.

"When do you leave?" asked Edna.

"Next Monday; and you?"

"The following week," answered Edna, adding, "It has been a pleasant summer, hasn't it, Mademoiselle?"

"Well," agreed Mademoiselle Reisz, with a shrug, "rather pleasant, if it hadn't been for the mosquitoes and the Farival twins."

XVII

The Pontelliers possessed a very charming home on Esplanade Street[42] in New Orleans. It was a large, double cottage, with a broad front veranda, whose round, fluted columns supported the sloping roof. The house was painted a dazzling white; the outside shutters, or jalousies, were green. In the yard, which was kept scrupulously neat, were flowers and plants of every description which flourishes in South Louisiana. Within doors the appointments were perfect after the conventional type. The softest carpets and rugs covered the floors; rich and tasteful draperies hung at doors and windows. There were paintings, selected with judgment and discrimination, upon the walls. The cut glass, the silver, the heavy damask which daily appeared upon the table were the envy of many women whose husbands were less generous than Mr. Pontellier.

Mr. Pontellier was very fond of walking about his house examining its various appointments and details, to see that nothing was amiss. He greatly valued his possessions, chiefly because they were his, and derived genuine pleasure from contemplating a painting, a statuette, a rare lace curtain—no matter what—after he had bought it and placed it among his household gods.

On Tuesday afternoons—Tuesday being Mrs. Pontellier's reception day[43]—there was a constant stream of callers—women who came in carriages or in the street cars, or walked when the air was soft and distance permitted. A light-colored mulatto boy, in dress coat and bearing a diminutive silver tray for the reception of cards, admitted them. A maid, in white fluted cap, offered the callers liqueur, coffee, or chocolate, as they might desire. Mrs. Pontellier, attired in a handsome reception gown, remained in the drawing-room the entire afternoon receiving her visitors. Men sometimes called in the evening with their wives.

This had been the programme which Mrs. Pontellier had religiously followed since her marriage, six years before. Certain evenings during the week she and her husband attended the opera or sometimes the play.

Mr. Pontellier left his home in the mornings between nine and ten o'clock, and rarely returned before half-past six or seven in the evening—dinner being served at half-past seven.

He and his wife seated themselves at table one Tuesday evening, a few weeks after their return from Grand Isle. They were alone together. The boys were being put to bed; the patter of their bare, escaping feet could be heard occasionally, as well as the pursuing voice of the quadroon, lifted in mild protest and entreaty. Mrs. Pontellier did not wear her usual Tuesday reception gown; she was in ordinary house dress. Mr. Pontellier, who was

[42] One of the wealthiest and most fashionable streets in the French Quarter.
[43] The day set aside each week to receive callers.

observant about such things, noticed it, as he served the soup and handed it to the boy in waiting.

"Tired out, Edna? Whom did you have? Many callers?" he asked. He tasted his soup and began to season it with pepper, salt, vinegar, mustard—everything within reach.

"There were a good many," replied Edna, who was eating her soup with evident satisfaction. "I found their cards when I got home; I was out."

"Out!" exclaimed her husband, with something like genuine consternation in his voice as he laid down the vinegar cruet and looked at her through his glasses. "Why, what could have taken you out on Tuesday? What did you have to do?"

"Nothing. I simply felt like going out, and I went out."

"Well, I hope you left some suitable excuse," said her husband, somewhat appeased, as he added a dash of cayenne pepper to the soup.

"No, I left no excuse. I told Joe to say I was out, that was all."

"Why, my dear, I should think you'd understand by this time that people don't do such things; we've got to observe *les convenances*[44] if we ever expect to get on and keep up with the procession. If you felt that you had to leave home this afternoon, you should have left some suitable explanation for your absence.

"This soup is really impossible; it's strange that woman hasn't learned yet to make a decent soup. Any free-lunch stand in town serves a better one. Was Mrs. Belthrop here?"

"Bring the tray with the cards, Joe. I don't remember who was here."

The boy retired and returned after a moment, bringing the tiny silver tray, which was covered with ladies' visiting cards. He handed it to Mrs. Pontellier.

"Give it to Mr. Pontellier," she said.

Joe offered the tray to Mr. Pontellier, and removed the soup.

Mr. Pontellier scanned the names of his wife's callers, reading some of them aloud, with comments as he read.

"'The Misses Delasidas.' I worked a big deal in futures for their father this morning; nice girls; it's time they were getting married. 'Mrs. Belthrop.' I tell you what it is, Edna; you can't afford to snub Mrs. Belthrop. Why, Belthrop could buy and sell us ten times over. His business is worth a good, round sum to me. You'd better write her a note. 'Mrs. James Highcamp.' Hugh! the less you have to do with Mrs. Highcamp, the better. 'Madame Laforcé.' Came all the way from Carrolton, too, poor old soul. 'Miss Wiggs,' 'Mrs. Eleanor Boltons.'" He pushed the cards aside.

"Mercy!" exclaimed Edna, who had been fuming. "Why are you taking the thing so seriously and making such a fuss over it?"

"I'm not making any fuss over it. But it's just such seeming trifles that we've got to take seriously; such things count."

The fish was scorched. Mr. Pontellier would not touch it. Edna said she did not mind a little scorched taste. The roast was in some way not to his fancy, and he did not like the manner in which the vegetables were served.

[44] The conventions or proprieties.

"It seems to me," he said, "we spend money enough in this house to procure at least one meal a day which a man could eat and retain his self-respect."

"You used to think the cook was a treasure," returned Edna, indifferently.

"Perhaps she was when she first came; but cooks are only human. They need looking after, like any other class of persons that you employ. Suppose I didn't look after the clerks in my office, just let them run things their own way; they'd soon make a nice mess of me and my business."

"Where are you going?" asked Edna, seeing that her husband arose from table without having eaten a morsel except a taste of the highly-seasoned soup.

"I'm going to get my dinner at the club. Good night." He went into the hall, took his hat and stick from the stand, and left the house.

She was somewhat familiar with such scenes. They had often made her very unhappy. On a few previous occcasions she had been completely deprived of any desire to finish her dinner. Sometimes she had gone into the kitchen to administer a tardy rebuke to the cook. Once she went to her room and studied the cookbook during an entire evening, finally writing out a menu for the week, which left her harassed with a feeling that, after all, she had accomplished no good that was worth the name.

But that evening Edna finished her dinner alone, with forced deliberation. Her face was flushed and her eyes flamed with some inward fire that lighted them. After finishing her dinner she went to her room, having instructed the boy to tell any other callers that she was indisposed.

It was a large, beautiful room, rich and picturesque in the soft, dim light which the maid had turned low. She went and stood at an open window and looked out upon the deep tangle of the garden below. All the mystery and witchery of the night seemed to have gathered there amid the perfumes and the dusky and tortuous outlines of flowers and foliage. She was seeking herself and finding herself in just such sweet, half-darkness which met her moods. But the voices were not soothing that came to her from the darkness and the sky above and the stars. They jeered and sounded mournful notes without promise, devoid even of hope. She turned back into the room and began to walk to and fro down its whole length, without stopping, without resting. She carried in her hands a thin handkerchief, which she tore into ribbons, rolled into a ball, and flung from her. Once she stopped, and taking off her wedding ring, flung it upon the carpet. When she saw it lying there, she stamped her heel upon it, striving to crush it. But her small boot heel did not make an indenture, not a mark upon the little glittering circlet.

In a sweeping passion she seized a glass vase from the table and flung it upon the tiles of the hearth. She wanted to destroy something. The crash and clatter were what she wanted to hear.

A maid, alarmed at the din of breaking glass, entered the room to discover what was the matter.

"A vase fell upon the hearth," said Edna. "Never mind; leave it till morning."

"Oh! you might get some of the glass in your feet, ma'am," insisted the young woman, picking up bits of the broken vase that were scattered upon the carpet. "And here's your ring, ma'am, under the chair."

Edna held out her hand, and taking the ring, slipped it upon her finger.

XVIII

The following morning Mr. Pontellier, upon leaving for his office, asked Edna if she would not meet him in town in order to look at some new fixtures for the library.

"I hardly think we need new fixtures, Léonce. Don't let us get anything new; you are too extravagant. I don't believe you ever think of saving or putting by."

"The way to become rich is to make money, my dear Edna, not to save it," he said. He regretted that she did not feel inclined to go with him and select new fixtures. He kissed her good-by, and told her she was not looking well and must take care of herself. She was unusually pale and very quiet.

She stood on the front veranda as he quitted the house, and absently picked a few sprays of jessamine that grew upon a trellis near by. She inhaled the odor of the blossoms and thrust them into the bosom of her white morning gown. The boys were dragging along the banquette[45] a small "express wagon," which they had filled with blocks and sticks. The quadroon was following them with little quick steps, having assumed a fictitious animation and alacrity for the occasion. A fruit vender was crying his wares in the street.

Edna looked straight before her with a self-absorbed expression upon her face. She felt no interest in anything about her. The street, the children, the fruit vender, the flowers growing there under her eyes, were all part and parcel of an alien world which had suddenly become antagonistic.

She went back into the house. She had thought of speaking to the cook concerning her blunders of the previous night; but Mr. Pontellier had saved her that disagreeable mission, for which she was so poorly fitted. Mr. Pontellier's arguments were usually convincing with those whom he employed. He left home feeling quite sure that he and Edna would sit down that evening, and possibly a few subsequent evenings, to a dinner deserving of the name.

Edna spent an hour or two in looking over some of her old sketches. She could see their shortcomings and defects, which were glaring in her eyes. She tried to work a little, but found she was not in the humor. Finally she gathered together a few of the sketches—those which she considered the least discreditable; and she carried them with her when, a little later, she dressed and left the house. She looked handsome and distinguished in her street gown. The tan of the seashore had left her face, and her forehead was smooth, white, and polished beneath her heavy yellow-brown

[45] Sidewalk.

hair. There were a few freckles on her face, and a small, dark mole near the under lip and one on the temple, half-hidden in her hair.

As Edna walked along the street she was thinking of Robert. She was still under the spell of her infatuation. She had tried to forget him, realizing the inutility of remembering. But the thought of him was like an obsession, ever pressing itself upon her. It was not that she dwelt upon details of their acquaintance, or recalled in any special or peculiar way his personality; it was his being, his existence, which dominated her thought, fading sometimes as if it would melt into the mist of the forgotten, reviving again with an intensity which filled her with an incomprehensible longing.

Edna was on her way to Madame Ratignolle's. Their intimacy, begun at Grand Isle, had not declined, and they had seen each other with some frequency since their return to the city. The Ratignolles lived at no great distance from Edna's home, on the corner of a side street, where Monsieur Ratignolle owned and conducted a drug store which enjoyed a steady and prosperous trade. His father had been in the business before him, and Monsieur Ratignolle stood well in the community and bore an enviable reputation for integrity and clear-headedness. His family lived in commodious apartments over the store, having an entrance on the side within the *porte cochère.*[46] There was something which Edna thought very French, very foreign, about their whole manner of living. In the large and pleasant salon which extended across the width of the house, the Ratignolles entertained their friends once a fortnight with a *soirée musicale,* sometimes diversified by card-playing. There was a friend who played upon the 'cello. One brought his flute and another his violin, while there were some who sang and a number who performed upon the piano with various degrees of taste and agility. The Ratignolles' *soirées musicales* were widely known, and it was considered a privilege to be invited to them.

Edna found her friend engaged in assorting the clothes which had returned that morning from the laundry. She at once abandoned her occupation upon seeing Edna, who had been ushered without ceremony into her presence.

"'Cité can do it as well as I; it is really her business," she explained to Edna, who apologized for interrupting her. And she summoned a young black woman, whom she instructed, in French, to be very careful in checking off the list which she handed her. She told her to notice particularly if a fine linen handkerchief of Monsieur Ratignolle's, which was missing last week, had been returned; and to be sure to set to one side such pieces as required mending and darning.

Then placing an arm around Edna's waist, she led her to the front of the house, to the salon, where it was cool and sweet with the odor of great roses that stood upon the hearth in jars.

Madame Ratignolle looked more beautiful than ever there at home, in a negligé which left her arms almost wholly bare and exposed the rich, melting curves of her white throat.

"Perhaps I shall be able to paint your picture some day," said Edna with a smile when they were seated. She produced the roll of sketches and

[46] A porch at the door of a building for sheltering persons entering or leaving carriages.

started to unfold them. "I believe I ought to work again. I feel as if I wanted to be doing something. What do you think of them? Do you think it worth while to take it up again and study some more? I might study for a while with Laidpore."

She knew that Madame Ratignolle's opinion in such a matter would be next to valueless, that she herself had not alone decided, but determined; but she sought the words of praise and encouragement that would help her to put heart into her venture.

"Your talent is immense, dear!"

"Nonsense!" protested Edna, well pleased.

"Immense, I tell you," persisted Madame Ratignolle, surveying the sketches one by one, at close range, then holding them at arm's length, narrowing her eyes, and dropping her head on one side. "Surely, this Bavarian peasant is worthy of framing; and this basket of apples! never have I seen anything more lifelike. One might almost be tempted to reach out a hand and take one."

Edna could not control a feeling which bordered upon complacency at her friend's praise, even realizing, as she did, its true worth. She retained a few of the sketches, and gave all the rest to Madame Ratignolle, who appreciated the gift far beyond its value and proudly exhibited the pictures to her husband when he came up from the store a little later for his midday dinner.

Mr. Ratignolle was one of those men who are called the salt of the earth. His cheerfulness was unbounded, and it was matched by his goodness of heart, his broad charity, and common sense. He and his wife spoke English with an accent which was only discernible through its un-English emphasis and a certain carefulness and deliberation. Edna's husband spoke English with no accent whatever. The Ratignolles understood each other perfectly. If ever the fusion of two human beings into one has been accomplished on this sphere it was surely in their union.

As Edna seated herself at table with them she thought, "Better a dinner of herbs," though it did not take her long to discover that it was no dinner of herbs, but a delicious repast, simple, choice, and in every way satisfying.

Monsieur Ratignolle was delighted to see her, though he found her looking not so well as at Grand Isle, and he advised a tonic. He talked a good deal on various topics, a little politics, some city news and neighborhood gossip. He spoke with an animation and earnestness that gave an exaggerated importance to every syllable he uttered. His wife was keenly interested in everything he said, laying down her fork the better to listen, chiming in, taking the words out of his mouth.

Edna felt depressed rather than soothed after leaving them. The little glimpse of domestic harmony which had been offered her gave her no regret, no longing. It was not a condition of life which fitted her, and she could see in it but an appalling and hopeless ennui. She was moved by a kind of commiseration for Madame Ratignolle,—a pity for that colorless existence which never uplifted its possessor beyond the region of blind contentment, in which no moment of anguish ever visited her soul, in which she would never have the taste of life's delirium. Edna vaguely wondered what she meant by "life's delirium." It had crossed her thought like some unsought, extraneous impression.

XIX

Edna could not help but think that it was very foolish, very childish, to have stamped upon her wedding ring and smashed the crystal vase upon the tiles. She was visited by no more outbursts, moving her to such futile expedients. She began to do as she liked and to feel as she liked. She completely abandoned her Tuesdays at home, and did not return the visits of those who had called upon her. She made no ineffectual efforts to conduct her household *en bonne ménagère,*[47] going and coming as it suited her fancy, and, so far as she was able, lending herself to any passing caprice.

Mr. Pontellier had been a rather courteous husband so long as he met a certain tacit submissiveness in his wife. But her new and unexpected line of conduct completely bewildered him. It shocked him. Then her absolute disregard for her duties as a wife angered him. When Mr. Pontellier became rude, Edna grew insolent. She had resolved never to take another step backward.

"It seems to me the utmost folly for a woman at the head of a household, and the mother of children, to spend in an atelier[48] days which would be better employed contriving for the comfort of her family."

"I feel like painting," answered Edna. "Perhaps I shan't always feel like it."

"Then in God's name paint! but don't let the family go to the devil. There's Madame Ratignolle; because she keeps up her music, she doesn't let everything else go to chaos. And she's more of a musician than you are a painter."

"She isn't a musician, and I'm not a painter. It isn't on account of painting that I let things go."

"On account of what, then?"

"Oh! I don't know. Let me alone; you bother me."

It sometimes entered Mr. Pontellier's mind to wonder if his wife were not growing a little unbalanced mentally. He could see plainly that she was not herself. That is, he could not see that she was becoming herself and daily casting aside that fictitious self which we assume like a garment with which to appear before the world.

Her husband let her alone as she requested, and went away to his office. Edna went up to her atelier—a bright room in the top of the house. She was working with great energy and interest, without accomplishing anything, however, which satisfied her even in the smallest degree. For a time she had the whole household enrolled in the service of art. The boys posed for her. They thought it amusing at first, but the occupation soon lost its attractiveness when they discovered that it was not a game arranged especially for their entertainment. The quadroon sat for hours before Edna's palette, patient as a savage, while the house-maid took charge of the children, and the drawing-room went undusted. But the house-maid, too, served her term as model when Edna perceived that the young woman's back and shoulders were molded on classic lines, and that her hair, loosened from its confining cap, became an inspiration. While Edna worked she sometimes sang low the little air, *"Ah! si tu savais!"*

[47] "As a good housekeeper." [48] Studio.

It moved her with recollections. She could hear again the ripple of the water, the flapping sail. She could see the glint of the moon upon the bay, and could feel the soft, gusty beating of the hot south wind. A subtle current of desire passed through her body, weakening her hold upon the brushes and making her eyes burn.

There were days when she was very happy without knowing why. She was happy to be alive and breathing, when her whole being seemed to be one with the sunlight, the color, the odors, the luxuriant warmth of some perfect Southern day. She liked then to wander alone into strange and unfamiliar places. She discovered many a sunny, sleepy corner, fashioned to dream in. And she found it good to dream and to be alone and unmolested.

There were days when she was unhappy, she did not know why,—when it did not seem worth while to be glad or sorry, to be alive or dead; when life appeared to her like a grotesque pandemonium and humanity like worms struggling blindly toward inevitable annihilation. She could not work on such a day, nor weave fancies to stir her pulses and warm her blood.

XX

It was during such a mood that Edna hunted up Mademoiselle Reisz. She had not forgotten the rather disagreeable impression left upon her by their last interview; but she nevertheless felt a desire to see her—above all, to listen while she played upon the piano. Quite early in the afternoon she started upon her quest for the pianist. Unfortunately she had mislaid or lost Mademoiselle Reisz's card, and looking up her address in the city directory, she found that the woman lived on Bienville Street, some distance away. The directory which fell into her hands was a year or more old, however, and upon reaching the number indicated, Edna discovered that the house was occupied by a respectable family of mulattoes who had *chambres garnies*[49] to let. They had been living there for six months, and knew absolutely nothing of a Mademoiselle Reisz. In fact, they knew nothing of any of their neighbors; their lodgers were all people of the highest distinction, they assured Edna. She did not linger to discuss class distinctions with Madame Pouponne, but hastened to a neighboring grocery store, feeling sure that Mademoiselle would have left her address with the proprietor.

He knew Mademoiselle Reisz a good deal better than he wanted to know her, he informed his questioner. In truth, he did not want to know her at all, or anything concerning her—the most disagreeable and unpopular woman who ever lived in Bienville Street. He thanked heaven she had left the neighborhood, and was equally thankful that he did not know where she had gone.

Edna's desire to see Mademoiselle Reisz had increased tenfold since these unlooked-for obstacles had arisen to thwart it. She was wondering who could give her the information she sought, when it suddenly occurred

[49] Furnished rooms.

to her that Madame Lebrun would be the one most likely to do so. She knew it was useless to ask Madame Ratignolle, who was on the most distant terms with the musician, and preferred to know nothing concerning her. She had once been almost as emphatic in expressing herself upon the subject as the corner grocer.

Edna knew that Madame Lebrun had returned to the city, for it was the middle of November. And she also knew where the Lebruns lived, on Chartres Street.

Their home from the outside looked like a prison, with iron bars before the door and lower windows. The iron bars were a relic of the old *régime,*[50] and no one had ever thought of dislodging them. At the side was a high fence enclosing the garden. A gate or door opening upon the street was locked. Edna rang the bell at this side garden gate, and stood upon the banquette, waiting to be admitted.

It was Victor who opened the gate for her. A black woman, wiping her hands upon her apron, was close at his heels. Before she saw them Edna could hear them in altercation, the woman—plainly an anomaly—claiming the right to be allowed to perform her duties, one of which was to answer the bell.

Victor was surprised and delighted to see Mrs. Pontellier, and he made no attempt to conceal either his astonishment or his delight. He was a dark-browed, good-looking youngster of nineteen, greatly resembling his mother, but with ten times her impetuosity. He instructed the black woman to go at once and inform Madame Lebrun that Mrs. Pontellier desired to see her. The woman grumbled a refusal to do part of her duty when she had not been permitted to do it all, and started back to her interrupted task of weeding the garden. Whereupon Victor administered a rebuke in the form of a volley of abuse, which, owing to its rapidity and incoherence, was all but incomprehensible to Edna. Whatever it was, the rebuke was convincing, for the woman dropped her hoe and went mumbling into the house.

Edna did not wish to enter. It was very pleasant there on the side porch, where there were chairs, a wicker lounge, and a small table. She seated herself, for she was tired from her long tramp; and she began to rock gently and smooth out the folds of her silk parasol. Victor drew up his chair beside her. He at once explained that the black woman's offensive conduct was all due to imperfect training, as he was not there to take her in hand. He had only come up from the island the morning before, and expected to return next day. He stayed all winter at the island; he lived there, and kept the place in order and got things ready for the summer visitors.

But a man needed occasional relaxation, he informed Mrs. Pontellier, and every now and again he drummed up a pretext to bring him to the city. My! but he had had a time of it the evening before! He wouldn't want his mother to know, and he began to talk in a whisper. He was scintillant with recollections. Of course, he couldn't think of telling Mrs. Pontellier all about it, she being a woman and not comprehending such things. But it all began with a girl peeping and smiling at him through the shutters as he passed by. Oh! but she was a beauty! Certainly he smiled back, and went up and talked to her. Mrs. Pontellier did not know him if she supposed he was

[50] That is, the period of Spanish rule (1762–1800).

one to let an opportunity like that escape him. Despite herself, the youngster amused her. She must have betrayed in her look some degree of interest or entertainment. The boy grew more daring, and Mrs. Pontellier might have found herself, in a little while, listening to a highly colored story but for the timely appearance of Madame Lebrun.

That lady was still clad in white, according to her custom of the summer. Her eyes beamed an effusive welcome. Would not Mrs. Pontellier go inside? Would she partake of some refreshment? Why had she not been there before? How was that dear Mr. Pontellier and how were those sweet children? Had Mrs. Pontellier ever known such a warm November?

Victor went and reclined on the wicker lounge behind his mother's chair, where he commanded a view of Edna's face. He had taken her parasol from her hands while he spoke to her, and he now lifted it and twirled it above him as he lay on his back. When Madame Lebrun complained that it was *so* dull coming back to the city; that she saw *so* few people now; that even Victor, when he came up from the island for a day or two, had *so* much to occupy him and engage his time; then it was that the youth went into contortions on the lounge and winked mischievously at Edna. She somehow felt like a confederate in crime, and tried to look severe and disapproving.

There had been but two letters from Robert, with little in them, they told her. Victor said it was really not worth while to go inside for the letters, when his mother entreated him to go in search of them. He remembered the contents, which in truth he rattled off very glibly when put to the test.

One letter was written from Vera Cruz and the other from the City of Mexico. He had met Montel, who was doing everything toward his advancement. So far, the financial situation was no improvement over the one he had left in New Orleans, but of course the prospects were vastly better. He wrote of the City of Mexico, the buildings, the people and their habits, the conditions of life which he found there. He sent his love to the family. He inclosed a check to his mother, and hoped she would affectionately remember him to all his friends. That was about the substance of the two letters. Edna felt that if there had been a message for her, she would have received it. The despondent frame of mind in which she had left home began again to overtake her, and she remembered that she wished to find Mademoiselle Reisz.

Madame Lebrun knew where Mademoiselle Reisz lived. She gave Edna the address, regretting that she would not consent to stay and spend the remainder of the afternoon, and pay a visit to Mademoiselle Reisz some other day. The afternoon was already well advanced.

Victor escorted her out upon the banquette, lifted her parasol, and held it over her while he walked to the car with her. He entreated her to bear in mind that the disclosures of the afternoon were strictly confidential. She laughed and bantered him a little, remembering too late that she should have been dignified and reserved.

"How handsome Mrs. Pontellier looked!" said Madame Lebrun to her son.

"Ravishing!" he admitted. "The city atmosphere has improved her. Some way she doesn't seem like the same woman."

XXI

Some people contended that the reason Mademoiselle Reisz always chose apartments up under the roof was to discourage the approach of beggars, peddlars and callers. There were plenty of windows in her little front room. They were for the most part dingy, but as they were nearly always open it did not make so much difference. They often admitted into the room a good deal of smoke and soot; but at the same time all the light and air that there was came through them. From her windows could be seen the crescent of the river, the masts of ships and the big chimneys of the Mississippi steamers. A magnificent piano crowded the apartment. In the next room she slept, and in the third and last she harbored a gasoline stove on which she cooked her meals when disinclined to descend to the neighboring restaurant. It was there also that she ate, keeping her belongings in a rare old buffet, dingy and battered from a hundred years of use.

When Edna knocked at Mademoiselle Reisz's front room door and entered, she discovered that person standing beside the window, engaged in mending or patching an old prunella gaiter.[51] The little musician laughed all over when she saw Edna. Her laugh consisted of a contortion of the face and all the muscles of the body. She seemed strikingly homely, standing there in the afternoon light. She still wore the shabby lace and the artificial bunch of violets on the side of her head.

"So you remembered me at last," said Mademoiselle. "I had said to myself, 'Ah, bah! she will never come.' "

"Did you want me to come?" asked Edna with a smile.

"I had not thought much about it," answered Mademoiselle. The two had seated themselves on a little bumpy sofa which stood against the wall. "I am glad, however, that you came. I have the water boiling back there, and was just about to make some coffee. You will drink a cup with me. And how is *la belle dame?*[52] Always handsome! always healthy! always contented!" She took Edna's hand between her strong wiry fingers, holding it loosely without warmth, and executing a sort of double theme upon the back and palm.

"Yes," she went on; "I sometimes thought: 'She will never come. She promised as those women in society always do, without meaning it. She will not come.' For I really don't believe you like me, Mrs. Pontellier."

"I don't know whether I like you or not," replied Edna, gazing down at the little woman with a quizzical look.

The candor of Mrs. Pontellier's admission greatly pleased Mademoiselle Reisz. She expressed her gratification by repairing forthwith to the region of the gasoline stove and rewarding her guest with the promised cup of coffee. The coffee and the biscuit accompanying it proved very acceptable to Edna, who had declined refreshment at Madame Lebrun's and was now beginning to feel hungry. Mademoiselle set the tray which she brought in upon a small table near at hand, and seated herself once again on the lumpy sofa.

"I have had a letter from your friend," she remarked, as she poured a little cream into Edna's cup and handed it to her.

[51] A kind of shoe with a cloth upper. [52] "The beautiful lady."

"My friend?"

"Yes, your friend Robert. He wrote to me from the City of Mexico."

"Wrote to *you*?" repeated Edna in amazement, stirring her coffee absently.

"Yes, to me. Why not? Don't stir all the warmth out of your coffee; drink it. Though the letter might as well have been sent to you; it was nothing but Mrs. Pontellier from beginning to end."

"Let me see it," requested the young woman, entreatingly.

"No; a letter concerns no one but the person who writes it and the one to whom it is written."

"Haven't you just said it concerned me from beginning to end?"

"It was written about you, not to you. 'Have you seen Mrs. Pontellier? How is she looking?' he asks. 'As Mrs. Pontellier says,' or 'as Mrs. Pontellier once said.' 'If Mrs. Pontellier should call upon you, play for her that Impromptu of Chopin's, my favorite. I heard it here a day or two ago, but not as you play it. I should like to know how it affects her,' and so on, as if he supposed we were constantly in each other's society."

"Let me see the letter."

"Oh, no."

"Have you answered it?"

"No."

"Let me see the letter."

"No, and again, no."

"Then play the Impromptu for me."

"It is growing late; what time do you have to be home?"

"Time doesn't concern me. Your question seems a little rude. Play the Impromptu."

"But you have told me nothing of yourself. What are you doing?"

"Painting!" laughed Edna. "I am becoming an artist. Think of it!"

"Ah! an artist! You have pretensions, Madame."

"Why pretensions? Do you think I could not become an artist?"

"I do not know you well enough to say. I do not know your talent or your temperament. To be an artist includes much; one must possess many gifts—absolute gifts—which have not been acquired by one's own effort. And, moreover, to succeed, the artist must possess the courageous soul."

"What do you mean by the courageous soul?"

"Courageous, *ma foi!* The brave soul. The soul that dares and defies."

"Show me the letter and play for me the Impromptu. You see that I have persistence. Does that quality count for anything in art?"

"It counts with a foolish old woman whom you have captivated," replied Mademoiselle, with her wriggling laugh.

The letter was right there at hand in the drawer of the little table upon which Edna had just placed her coffee cup. Mademoiselle opened the drawer and drew forth the letter, the topmost one. She placed it in Edna's hands, and without further comment arose and went to the piano.

Mademoiselle played a soft interlude. It was an improvisation. She sat low at the instrument, and the lines of her body settled into ungraceful curves and angles that gave it an appearance of deformity. Gradually and imperceptibly the interlude melted into the soft opening minor chords of the Chopin Impromptu.

Edna did not know when the Impromptu began or ended. She sat in the sofa corner reading Robert's letter by the fading light. Mademoiselle had glided from the Chopin into the quivering love-notes of Isolde's song,[53] and back again to the Impromptu with its soulful and poignant longing.

The shadows deepened in the little room. The music grew strange and fantastic—turbulent, insistent, plaintive and soft with entreaty. The shadows grew deeper. The music filled the room. It floated out upon the night, over the housetops, the crescent of the river, losing itself in the silence of the upper air.

Edna was sobbing, just as she had wept one midnight at Grand Isle when strange, new voices awoke in her. She arose in some agitation to take her departure. "May I come again, Mademoiselle?" she asked at the threshold.

"Come whenever you feel like it. Be careful; the stairs and landings are dark; don't stumble."

Mademoiselle reentered and lit a candle. Robert's letter was on the floor. She stooped and picked it up. It was crumpled and damp with tears. Mademoiselle smoothed the letter out, restored it to the envelope, and replaced it in the table drawer.

XXII

One morning on his way into town Mr. Pontellier stopped at the house of his old friend and family physician, Doctor Mandelet. The Doctor was a semi-retired physician, resting, as the saying is, upon his laurels. He bore a reputation for wisdom rather than skill—leaving the active practice of medicine to his assistants and younger contemporaries—and was much sought for in matters of consultation. A few families, united to him by bonds of friendship, he still attended when they required the services of a physician. The Pontelliers were among these.

Mr. Pontellier found the Doctor reading at the open window of his study. His house stood rather far back from the street, in the center of a delightful garden, so that it was quiet and peaceful at the old gentleman's study window. He was a great reader. He stared up disapprovingly over his eye-glasses as Mr. Pontellier entered, wondering who had the temerity to disturb him at that hour of the morning.

"Ah, Pontellier! Not sick, I hope. Come and have a seat. What news do you bring this morning?" He was quite portly, with a profusion of gray hair, and small blue eyes which age had robbed of much of their brightness but none of their penetration.

"Oh! I'm never sick, Doctor. You know that I come of tough fiber—of that old Creole race of Pontelliers that dry up and finally blow away. I came to consult—no, not precisely to consult—to talk to you about Edna. I don't know what ails her."

"Madame Pontellier not well?" marveled the Doctor. "Why, I saw

[53] The *Liebestod* ("Love-death" in German) from Richard Wagner's *Tristan and Isolde* (1857–59). In this passionate aria, Isolde bids the dead Tristan farewell and falls dead herself.

her—I think it was a week ago—walking along Canal Street, the picture of health, it seemed to me."

"Yes, yes; she seems quite well," said Mr. Pontellier, leaning forward and whirling his stick between his two hands; "but she doesn't act well. She's odd, she's not like herself. I can't make her out, and I thought perhaps you'd help me."

"How does she act?" inquired the doctor.

"Well, it isn't easy to explain," said Mr. Pontellier, throwing himself back in his chair. "She lets the housekeeping go to the dickens."

"Well, well; women are not all alike, my dear Pontellier. We've got to consider—"

"I know that; I told you I couldn't explain. Her whole attitude—toward me and everybody and everything—has changed. You know I have a quick temper, but I don't want to quarrel or be rude to a woman, especially my wife; yet I'm driven to it, and feel like ten thousand devils after I've made a fool of myself. She's making it devilishly uncomfortable for me," he went on nervously. "She's got some sort of notion in her head concerning the eternal rights of women; and—you understand—we meet in the morning at the breakfast table."

The old gentleman lifted his shaggy eyebrows, protruded his thick nether lip, and tapped the arms of his chair with his cushioned fingertips.

"What have you been doing to her, Pontellier?"

"Doing! *Parbleu!*"

"Has she," asked the Doctor, with a smile, "has she been associating of late with a circle of pseudo-intellectual women—super-spiritual superior beings? My wife has been telling me about them."

"That's the trouble," broke in Mr. Pontellier, "she hasn't been associating with any one. She has abandoned her Tuesdays at home, has thrown over all her acquaintances, and goes tramping about by herself, moping in the street-cars, getting in after dark. I tell you she's peculiar. I don't like it; I feel a little worried over it."

This was a new aspect for the Doctor. "Nothing hereditary?" he asked, seriously. "Nothing peculiar about her family antecedents, is there?"

"Oh, no, indeed! She comes of sound old Presbyterian Kentucky stock. The old gentleman, her father, I have heard, used to atone for his weekday sins with his Sunday devotions. I know for a fact, that his race horses literally ran away with the prettiest bit of Kentucky farming land I ever laid eyes upon. Margaret—you know Margaret—she has all the Presbyterianism undiluted. And the youngest is something of a vixen. By the way, she gets married in a couple of weeks from now."

"Send your wife up to the wedding," exclaimed the Doctor, foreseeing a happy solution. "Let her stay among her own people for a while; it will do her good."

"That's what I want her to do. She won't go to the marriage. She says a wedding is one of the most lamentable spectacles on earth. Nice thing for a woman to say to her husband!" exclaimed Mr. Pontellier, fuming anew at the recollection.

"Pontellier," said the Doctor, after a moment's reflection, "let your wife alone for a while. Don't bother her, and don't let her bother you. Woman, my dear friend, is a very peculiar and delicate organism—a sensitive and highly organized woman, such as I know Mrs. Pontellier to be, is especially peculiar. It would require an inspired psychologist to deal successfully with them. And when ordinary fellows like you and me attempt to cope with their idiosyncrasies the result is bungling. Most women are moody and whimsical. This is some passing whim of your wife, due to some cause or causes which you and I needn't try to fathom. But it will pass happily over, especially if you let her alone. Send her around to see me."

"Oh! I couldn't do that; there'd be no reason for it," objected Mr. Pontellier.

"Then I'll go around and see her," said the Doctor. "I'll drop in to dinner some evening *en bon ami.*"[54]

"Do! by all means," urged Mr. Pontellier. "What evening will you come? Say Thursday. Will you come Thursday?" he asked, rising to take his leave.

"Very well; Thursday. My wife may possibly have some engagement for me Thursday. In case she has, I shall let you know. Otherwise, you may expect me."

Mr. Pontellier turned before leaving to say:

"I am going to New York on business very soon. I have a big scheme on hand, and want to be on the field proper to pull the ropes and handle the ribbons. We'll let you in on the inside if you say so, Doctor," he laughed.

"No, I thank you, my dear sir," returned the Doctor. "I leave such ventures to you younger men with the fever of life still in your blood."

"What I wanted to say," continued Mr. Pontellier, with his hand on the knob; "I may have to be absent a good while. Would you advise me to take Edna along?"

"By all means, if she wishes to go. If not, leave her here. Don't contradict her. The mood will pass, I assure you. It may take a month, two, three months—possibly longer, but it will pass; have patience."

"Well, good-by, *à jeudi,*"[55] said Mr. Pontellier, as he let himself out.

The Doctor would have liked during the course of conversation to ask, "Is there any man in the case?" but he knew his Creole too well to make such a blunder as that.

He did not resume his book immediately, but sat for a while meditatively looking out into the garden.

XXIII

Edna's father was in the city, and had been with them several days. She was not very warmly or deeply attached to him, but they had certain tastes in common, and when together they were companionable. His coming was in the nature of a welcome disturbance; it seemed to furnish a new direction for her emotions.

He had come to purchase a wedding gift for his daughter, Janet, and an outfit for himself in which he might make a creditable appearance at her marriage. Mr. Pontellier had selected the bridal gift, as every one immediately connected with him always deferred to his taste in such matters. And his suggestions on the question of dress—which too often assumes the na-

[54] "As a good friend." [55] "Until Thursday."

ture of a problem—were of inestimable value to his father-in-law. But for the past few days the old gentleman had been upon Edna's hands, and in his society she was becoming acquainted with a new set of sensations. He had been a colonel in the Confederate army, and still maintained, with the title, the military bearing which had always accompanied it. His hair and mustache were white and silky, emphasizing the rugged bronze of his face. He was tall and thin, and wore his coats padded, which gave a fictitious breadth and depth to his shoulders and chest. Edna and her father looked very distinguished together, and excited a good deal of notice during their perambulations. Upon his arrival she began by introducing him to her atelier and making a sketch of him. He took the whole matter very seriously. If her talent had been ten-fold greater than it was, it would not have surprised him, convinced as he was that he had bequeathed to all of his daughters the germs of a masterful capability, which only depended upon their own efforts to be directed toward successful achievement.

Before her pencil he sat rigid and unflinching, as he had faced the cannon's mouth in days gone by. He resented the intrusion of the children, who gaped with wondering eyes at him, sitting so stiff up there in their mother's bright atelier. When they drew near he motioned them away with an expressive action of the foot, loath to disturb the fixed lines of his countenance, his arms, or his rigid shoulders.

Edna, anxious to entertain him, invited Mademoiselle Reisz to meet him, having promised him a treat in her piano playing; but Mademoiselle declined the invitation. So together they attended a *soirée musicale* at the Ratignolles'. Monsieur and Madame Ratignolle made much of the Colonel, installing him as the guest of honor and engaging him at once to dine with them the following Sunday, or any day which he might select. Madame coquetted with him in the most captivating and naïve manner, with eyes, gestures, and a profusion of compliments, till the Colonel's old head felt thirty years younger on his padded shoulders. Edna marveled, not comprehending. She herself was almost devoid of coquetry.

There were one or two men whom she observed at the *soirée musicale;* but she would never have felt moved to any kittenish display to attract their notice—to any feline or feminine wiles to express herself toward them. Their personality attracted her in an agreeable way. Her fancy selected them, and she was glad when a lull in the music gave them an opportunity to meet her and talk with her. Often on the street the glance of strange eyes had lingered in her memory, and sometimes had disturbed her.

Mr. Pontellier did not attend these *soirées musicales.* He considered them *bourgeois,* and found more diversion at the club. To Madame Ratignolle he said the music dispensed at her *soirées* was too "heavy," too far beyond his untrained comprehension. His excuse flattered her. But she disapproved of Mr. Pontellier's club, and she was frank enough to tell Edna so.

"It's a pity Mr. Pontellier doesn't stay home more in the evenings. I think you would be more—well, if you don't mind my saying it—more united, if he did."

"Oh! dear no!" said Edna, with a blank look in her eyes. "What should I do if he stayed home? We wouldn't have anything to say to each other."

She had not much of anything to say to her father, for that matter; but he did not antagonize her. She discovered that he interested her, though she realized that he might not interest her long; and for the first time in her life she felt as if she were thoroughly acquainted with him. He kept her busy serving him and ministering to his wants. It amused her to do so. She would not permit a servant or one of the children to do anything for him which she might do herself. Her husband noticed, and thought it was the expression of a deep filial attachment which he had never suspected.

The Colonel drank numerous "toddies" during the course of the day, which left him, however, imperturbed. He was an expert at concocting strong drinks. He had even invented some, to which he had given fantastic names, and for whose manufacture he required diverse ingredients that it devolved upon Edna to procure for him.

When Doctor Mandelet dined with the Pontelliers on Thursday he could discern in Mrs. Pontellier no trace of that morbid condition which her husband had reported to him. She was excited and in a manner radiant. She and her father had been to the race course, and their thoughts when they seated themselves at table were still occupied with the events of the afternoon, and their talk was still of the track. The Doctor had not kept pace with turf affairs. He had certain recollections of racing in what he called "the good old times" when the Lecompte stables flourished,[56] and he drew upon this fund of memories so that he might not be left out and seem wholly devoid of the modern spirit. But he failed to impose upon the Colonel, and was even far from impressing him with this trumped-up knowledge of bygone days. Edna had staked her father on his last venture, with the most gratifying results to both of them. Besides, they had met some very charming people, according to the Colonel's impressions. Mrs. Mortimer Merriman and Mrs. James Highcamp, who were there with Alcée Arobin, had joined them and had enlivened the hours in a fashion that warmed him to think of.

Mr. Pontellier himself had no particular leaning toward horse-racing, and was even rather inclined to discourage it as a pastime, especially when he considered the fate of that blue-grass farm in Kentucky. He endeavored, in a general way, to express a particular disapproval, and only succeeded in arousing the ire and opposition of his father-in-law. A pretty dispute followed, in which Edna warmly espoused her father's cause and the Doctor remained neutral.

He observed his hostess attentively from under his shaggy brows, and noted a subtle change which had transformed her from the listless woman he had known into a being who, for the moment, seemed palpitant with the forces of life. Her speech was warm and energetic. There was no repression in her glance or gesture. She reminded him of some beautiful, sleek animal waking up in the sun.

The dinner was excellent. The claret was warm and the champagne was cold, and under their beneficent influence the threatened unpleasantness melted and vanished with the fumes of the wine.

Mr. Pontellier warmed up and grew reminiscent. He told some amusing plantation experiences, recollections of old Iberville and his youth, when

[56] Like most of Chopin's references to places in New Orleans, this is an actual institution.

he hunted 'possum in company with some friendly darky; thrashed the pecan trees, shot the grosbec,[57] and roamed the woods and fields in mischievous idleness.

The Colonel, with little sense of humor and of the fitness of things, related a somber episode of those dark and bitter days, in which he had acted a conspicuous part and always formed a central figure. Nor was the Doctor happier in his selection, when he told the old, ever new and curious story of the waning of a woman's love, seeking strange, new channels, only to return to its legitimate source after days of fierce unrest. It was one of the many little human documents which had been unfolded to him during his long career as a physician. The story did not seem especially to impress Edna. She had one of her own to tell, of a woman who paddled away with her lover one night in a pirogue and never came back. They were lost amid the Baratarian Islands, and no one ever heard of them or found trace of them from that day to this. It was a pure invention. She said that Madame Antoine had related it to her. That, also, was an invention. Perhaps it was a dream she had had. But every glowing word seemed real to those who listened. They could feel the hot breath of the Southern night; they could hear the long sweep of the pirogue through the glistening moonlit water, the beating of birds' wings, rising startled from among the reeds in the salt-water pools; they could see the faces of the lovers, pale, close together, rapt in oblivious forgetfulness, drifting into the unknown.

The champagne was cold, and its subtle fumes played fantastic tricks with Edna's memory that night.

Outside, away from the glow of the fire and the soft lamplight, the night was chill and murky. The Doctor doubled his old-fashioned cloak across his breast as he strode home through the darkness. He knew his fellow-creatures better than most men; knew that inner life which so seldom unfolds itself to unanointed eyes. He was sorry he had accepted Pontellier's invitation. He was growing old, and beginning to need rest and an imperturbed spirit. He did not want the secrets of other lives thrust upon him.

"I hope it isn't Arobin," he muttered to himself as he walked. "I hope to heaven it isn't Alcée Arobin."

XXIV

Edna and her father had a warm, and almost violent dispute upon the subject of her refusal to attend her sister's wedding. Mr. Pontellier declined to interfere, to interpose either his influence or his authority. He was following Doctor Mandelet's advice, and letting her do as she liked. The Colonel reproached his daughter for her lack of filial kindness and respect, her want of sisterly affection and womanly consideration. His arguments were labored and unconvincing. He doubted if Janet would accept any excuse—forgetting that Edna had offered none. He doubted if Janet would ever speak to her again, and he was sure Margaret would not.

Edna was glad to be rid of her father when he finally took himself off

[57] A kind of finch, hunted as a gamebird in the South.

with his wedding garments and his bridal gifts, with his padded shoulders, his Bible reading, his "toddies" and ponderous oaths.

Mr. Pontellier followed him closely. He meant to stop at the wedding on his way to New York and endeavor by every means which money and love could devise to atone somewhat for Edna's incomprehensible action.

"You are too lenient, too lenient by far, Léonce," asserted the Colonel. "Authority, coercion are what is needed. Put your foot down good and hard; the only way to manage a wife. Take my word for it."

The Colonel was perhaps unaware that he had coerced his own wife into her grave. Mr. Pontellier had a vague suspicion of it which he thought it needless to mention at that late day.

Edna was not so consciously gratified at her husband's leaving home as she had been over the departure of her father. As the day approached when he was to leave her for a comparatively long stay, she grew melting and affectionate, remembering his many acts of consideration and his repeated expressions of an ardent attachment. She was solicitous about his health and his welfare. She bustled around, looking after his clothing, thinking about heavy underwear, quite as Madame Ratignolle would have done under similar circumstances. She cried when he went away, calling him her dear, good friend, and she was quite certain she would grow lonely before very long and go to join him in New York.

But after all, a radiant peace settled upon her when she at last found herself alone. Even the children were gone. Old Madame Pontellier had come herself and carried them off to Iberville with their quadroon. The old madame did not venture to say she was afraid they would be neglected during Léonce's absence; she hardly ventured to think so. She was hungry for them—even a little fierce in her attachment. She did not want them to be wholly "children of the pavement," she always said when begging to have them for a space. She wished them to know the country, with its streams, its fields, its woods, its freedom, so delicious to the young. She wished them to taste something of the life their father had lived and known and loved when he, too, was a little child.

When Edna was at last alone, she breathed a big, genuine sigh of relief. A feeling that was unfamiliar but very delicious came over her. She walked all through the house, from one room to another, as if inspecting it for the first time. She tried the various chairs and lounges, as if she had never sat and reclined upon them before. And she perambulated around the outside of the house, investigating, looking to see if windows and shutters were secure and in order. The flowers were like new acquaintances; she approached them in a familiar spirit, and made herself at home among them. The garden walks were damp, and Edna called to the maid to bring out her rubber sandals. And there she stayed, and stooped, digging around the plants, trimming, picking dead, dry leaves. The children's little dog came out, interfering, getting in her way. She scolded him, laughed at him, played with him. The garden smelled so good and looked so pretty in the afternoon sunlight. Edna plucked all the bright flowers she could find, and went into the house with them, she and the little dog.

Even the kitchen assumed a sudden interesting character which she had never before perceived. She went in to give directions to the cook, to say that the butcher would have to bring much less meat, that they would require only half their usual quantity of bread, of milk and groceries. She told the cook that she herself would be greatly occupied during Mr. Pontellier's absence, and she begged her to take all thought and responsibility of the larder upon her own shoulders.

That night Edna dined alone. The candelabra, with a few candles in the center of the table, gave all the light she needed. Outside the circle of light in which she sat, the large dining-room looked solemn and shadowy. The cook, placed upon her mettle, served a delicious repast—a luscious tenderloin broiled *à point.* The wine tasted good; the *marron glacé*[58] seemed to be just what she wanted. It was so pleasant, too, to dine in a comfortable *peignoir.*

She thought a little sentimentally about Léonce and the children, and wondered what they were doing. As she gave a dainty scrap or two to the doggie, she talked intimately to him about Etienne and Raoul. He was beside himself with astonishment and delight over these companionable advances, and showed his appreciation by his little quick, snappy barks and a lively agitation.

Then Edna sat in the library after dinner and read Emerson until she grew sleepy. She realized that she had neglected her reading, and determined to start anew upon a course of improving studies, now that her time was completely her own to do with as she liked.

After a refreshing bath, Edna went to bed. And as she snuggled comfortably beneath the eiderdown a sense of restfulness invaded her, such as she had not known before.

XXV

When the weather was dark and cloudy Edna could not work. She needed the sun to mellow and temper her mood to the sticking point. She had reached a stage when she seemed to be no longer feeling her way, working, when in the humor, with sureness and ease. And being devoid of ambition, and striving not toward accomplishment, she drew satisfaction from the work in itself.

On rainy or melancholy days Edna went out and sought the society of the friends she had made at Grand Isle. Or else she stayed indoors and nursed a mood with which she was becoming too familiar for her own comfort and peace of mind. It was not despair; but it seemed to her as if life were passing by, leaving its promise broken and unfulfilled. Yet there were other days when she listened, was led on and deceived by fresh promises which her youth held out to her.

She went again to the races, and again. Alcée Arobin and Mrs. Highcamp called for her one bright afternoon in Arobin's drag.[59] Mrs. Highcamp was a worldly but unaffected, intelligent, slim, tall blonde woman in the forties, with an indifferent manner and blue eyes that stared. She had a daughter who served her as a pretext for cultivating the society of young men of fashion. Alcée Arobin was one of them. He was a familiar

[58] *à point.* "Perfectly." *marron glacé.* Candied chestnut.

[59] A large four-horse coach.

figure at the race course, the opera, the fashionable clubs. There was a perpetual smile in his eyes, which seldom failed to awaken a corresponding cheerfulness in any one who looked into them and listened to his good-humored voice. His manner was quiet, and at times a little insolent. He possessed a good figure, a pleasing face, not overburdened with depth of thought or feeling; and his dress was that of the conventional man of fashion.

He admired Edna extravagantly, after meeting her at the races with her father. He had met her before on other occasions, but she had seemed to him unapproachable until that day. It was at his instigation that Mrs. Highcamp called to ask her to go with them to the Jockey Club to witness the turf event of the season.

There were possibly a few track men out there who knew the race horse as well as Edna, but there was certainly none who knew it better. She sat between her two companions as one having authority to speak. She laughed at Arobin's pretensions, and deplored Mrs. Highcamp's ignorance. The race horse was a friend and intimate associate of her childhood. The atmosphere of the stables and the breath of the blue grass paddock revived in her memory and lingered in her nostrils. She did not perceive that she was talking like her father as the sleek geldings ambled in review before them. She played for very high stakes, and fortune favored her. The fever of the game flamed in her cheeks and eyes, and it got into her blood and into her brain like an intoxicant. People turned their heads to look at her, and more than one lent an attentive ear to her utterances, hoping thereby to secure the elusive but ever-desired "tip." Arobin caught the contagion of excitement which drew him to Edna like a magnet. Mrs. Highcamp remained, as usual, unmoved, with her indifferent stare and uplifted eyebrows.

Edna stayed and dined with Mrs. Highcamp upon being urged to do so. Arobin also remained and sent away his drag.

The dinner was quiet and uninteresting, save for the cheerful efforts of Arobin to enliven things. Mrs. Highcamp deplored the absence of her daughter from the races, and tried to convey to her what she had missed by going to the "Dante reading" instead of joining them. The girl held a geranium leaf up to her nose and said nothing, but looked knowing and noncommittal. Mr. Highcamp was a plain, bald-headed man, who only talked under compulsion. He was unresponsive. Mrs. Highcamp was full of delicate courtesy and consideration toward her husband. She addressed most of her conversation to him at table. They sat in the library after dinner and read the evening papers together under the droplight;[60] while the younger people went into the drawing-room near by and talked. Miss Highcamp played some selections from Grieg upon the piano. She seemed to have apprehended all of the composer's coldness and none of his poetry. While Edna listened she could not help wondering if she had lost her taste for music.

When the time came for her to go home, Mr. Highcamp grunted a lame offer to escort her, looking down at his slippered feet with tactless concern. It was Arobin who took her home. The car ride was long, and it was late

[60] Suspended gas lamp.

when they reached Esplanade Street. Arobin asked permission to enter for a second to light his cigarette—his match safe[61] was empty. He filled his match safe, but did not light his cigarette until he left her, after she had expressed her willingness to go to the races with him again.

Edna was neither tired nor sleepy. She was hungry again, for the Highcamp dinner, though of excellent quality, had lacked abundance. She rummaged in the larder and brought forth a slice of Gruyère and some crackers. She opened a bottle of beer which she found in the icebox. Edna felt extremely restless and excited. She vacantly hummed a fantastic tune as she poked at the wood embers on the hearth and munched a cracker.

She wanted something to happen—something, anything; she did not know what. She regretted that she had not made Arobin stay a half hour to talk over the horses with her. She counted the money she had won. But there was nothing else to do, so she went to bed, and tossed there for hours in a sort of monotonous agitation.

In the middle of the night she remembered that she had forgotten to write her regular letter to her husband; and she decided to do so next day and tell him about her afternoon at the Jockey Club. She lay wide awake composing a letter which was nothing like the one which she wrote next day. When the maid awoke her in the morning Edna was dreaming of Mr. Highcamp playing the piano at the entrance of a music store on Canal Street, while his wife was saying to Alcée Arobin, as they boarded an Esplanade Street car:

"What a pity that so much talent has been neglected! but I must go."

When, a few days later, Alcée Arobin again called for Edna in his drag, Mrs. Highcamp was not with him. He said they would pick her up. But as that lady had not been apprised of his intention of picking her up, she was not at home. The daughter was just leaving the house to attend the meeting of a branch Folk Lore Society, and regretted that she could not accompany them. Arobin appeared nonplused, and asked Edna if there were any one else she cared to ask.

She did not deem it worth while to go in search of any of the fashionable acquaintances from whom she had withdrawn herself. She thought of Madame Ratignolle, but knew that her fair friend did not leave the house, except to take a languid walk around the block with her husband after nightfall. Mademoiselle Reisz would have laughed at such a request from Edna. Madame Lebrun might have enjoyed the outing, but for some reason Edna did not want her. So they went alone, she and Arobin.

The afternoon was intensely interesting to her. The excitement came back upon her like a remittent fever. Her talk grew familiar and confidential. It was no labor to become intimate with Arobin. His manner invited easy confidence. The preliminary stage of becoming acquainted was one which he always endeavored to ignore when a pretty and engaging woman was concerned.

He stayed and dined with Edna. He stayed and sat beside the wood fire. They laughed and talked; and before it was time to go he was telling her how different life might have been if he had known her years before. With ingenuous frankness he spoke of what a wicked, ill-disciplined boy he had

[61] Noncombustible container for matches.

been, and impulsively drew up his cuff to exhibit upon his wrist the scar from a saber cut which he had received in a duel outside of Paris when he was nineteen. She touched his hand as she scanned the red cicatrice[62] on the inside of his white wrist. A quick impulse that was somewhat spasmodic impelled her fingers to close in a sort of clutch upon his hand. He felt the pressure of her pointed nails in the flesh of his palm.

She arose hastily and walked toward the mantel.

"The sight of a wound or scar always agitates and sickens me," she said. "I shouldn't have looked at it."

"I beg your pardon," he entreated, following her; "it never occurred to me that it might be repulsive."

He stood close to her, and the effrontery in his eyes repelled the old, vanishing self in her, yet drew all her awakening sensuousness. He saw enough in her face to impel him to take her hand and hold it while he said his lingering good night.

"Will you go to the races again?" he asked.

"No," she said. "I've had enough of the races. I don't want to lose all the money I've won, and I've got to work when the weather is bright, instead of—"

"Yes; work; to be sure. You promised to show me your work. What morning may I come up to your atelier? Tomorrow?"

"No!"

"Day after?"

"No, no."

"Oh, please don't refuse me! I know something of such things. I might help you with a stray suggestion or two."

"No. Good night. Why don't you go after you have said good night? I don't like you," she went on in a high, excited pitch, attempting to draw away her hand. She felt that her words lacked dignity and sincerity, and she knew that he felt it.

"I'm sorry you don't like me. I'm sorry I offended you. How have I offended you? What have I done? Can't you forgive me?" And he bent and pressed his lips upon her hand as if he wished never more to withdraw them.

"Mr. Arobin," she complained, "I'm greatly upset by the excitement of the afternoon; I'm not myself. My manner must have misled you in some way. I wish you to go, please." She spoke in a monotonous, dull tone. He took his hat from the table, and stood with eyes turned from her, looking into the dying fire. For a moment or two he kept an impressive silence.

"Your manner has not misled me, Mrs. Pontellier," he said finally. "My own emotions have done that. I couldn't help it. When I'm near you, how could I help it? Don't think anything of it, don't bother, please. You see, I go when you command me. If you wish me to stay away, I shall do so. If you let me come back, I—oh! you will let me come back?"

He cast one appealing glance at her, to which she made no response. Alcée Arobin's manner was so genuine that it often deceived even himself.

Edna did not care or think whether it were genuine or not. When she was alone she looked mechanically at the back of her hand which he had

[62] Scar.

kissed so warmly. Then she leaned her head down on the mantelpiece. She felt somewhat like a woman who in a moment of passion is betrayed into an act of infidelity, and realizes the significance of the act without being wholly awakened from its glamour. The thought was passing vaguely through her mind, "What would he think?"

She did not mean her husband; she was thinking of Robert Lebrun. Her husband seemed to her now like a person whom she had married without love as an excuse.

She lit a candle and went up to her room. Alcée Arobin was absolutely nothing to her. Yet his presence, his manners, the warmth of his glances, and above all the touch of his lips upon her hand had acted like a narcotic upon her.

She slept a languorous sleep, interwoven with vanishing dreams.

XXVI

Alcée Arobin wrote Edna an elaborate note of apology, palpitant with sincerity. It embarrassed her; for in a cooler, quieter moment it appeared to her absurd that she should have taken his action so seriously, so dramatically. She felt sure that the significance of the whole occurrence had lain in her own self-consciousness. If she ignored his note it would give undue importance to a trivial affair. If she replied to it in a serious spirit it would still leave in his mind the impression that she had in a susceptible moment yielded to his influence. After all, it was no great matter to have one's hand kissed. She was provoked at his having written the apology. She answered in as light and bantering a spirit as she fancied it deserved, and said she would be glad to have him look in upon her at work whenever he felt the inclination and his business gave him the opportunity.

He responded at once by presenting himself at her home with all his disarming naïveté. And then there was scarcely a day which followed that she did not see him or was not reminded of him. He was prolific in pretexts. His attitude became one of good-humored subservience and tacit adoration. He was ready at all times to submit to her moods, which were as often kind as they were cold. She grew accustomed to him. They became intimate and friendly by imperceptible degrees, and then by leaps. He sometimes talked in a way that astonished her at first and brought the crimson into her face; in a way that pleased her at last, appealing to the animalism that stirred impatiently within her.

There was nothing which so quieted the turmoil of Edna's senses as a visit to Mademoiselle Reisz. It was then, in the presence of that personality which was offensive to her, that the woman, by her divine art, seemed to reach Edna's spirit and set it free.

It was misty, with heavy, lowering atmosphere, one afternoon, when Edna climbed the stairs to the pianist's apartments under the roof. Her clothes were dripping with moisture. She felt chilled and pinched as she entered the room. Mademoiselle was poking at a rusty stove that smoked a little and warmed the room indifferently. She was endeavoring to heat a pot of chocolate on the stove. The room looked cheerless and dingy to

Edna as she entered. A bust of Beethoven, covered with a hood of dust, scowled at her from the mantelpiece.

"Ah! here comes the sunlight!" exclaimed Mademoiselle, rising from her knees before the stove. "Now it will be warm and bright enough; I can let the fire alone."

She closed the stove door with a bang, and approaching, assisted in removing Edna's dripping mackintosh.

"You are cold; you look miserable. The chocolate will soon be hot. But would you rather have a taste of brandy? I have scarcely touched the bottle which you brought me for my cold." A piece of red flannel was wrapped around Mademoiselle's throat; a stiff neck compelled her to hold her head on one side.

"I will take some brandy," said Edna, shivering as she removed her gloves and overshoes. She drank the liquor from the glass as a man would have done. Then flinging herself upon the uncomfortable sofa she said, "Mademoiselle, I am going to move away from my house on Esplanade Street."

"Ah!" ejaculated the musician, neither surprised nor especially interested. Nothing ever seemed to astonish her very much. She was endeavoring to adjust the bunch of violets which had become loose from its fastening in her hair. Edna drew her down upon the sofa, and taking a pin from her own hair, secured the shabby artificial flowers in their accustomed place.

"Aren't you astonished?"

"Passably. Where are you going? to New York? to Iberville? to your father in Mississippi? where?"

"Just two steps away," laughed Edna, "in a little four-room house around the corner. It looks so cozy, so inviting and restful, whenever I pass by; and it's for rent. I'm tired looking after that big house. It never seemed like mine, anyway—like home. It's too much trouble. I have to keep too many servants. I am tired bothering with them."

"That is not your true reason, *ma belle*. There is no use in telling me lies. I don't know your reason, but you have not told me the truth." Edna did not protest or endeavor to justify herself.

"The house, the money that provides for it, are not mine. Isn't that enough reason?"

"They are your husband's," returned Mademoiselle, with a shrug and a malicious elevation of the eyebrows.

"Oh! I see there is no deceiving you. Then let me tell you: It is a caprice. I have a little money of my own from my mother's estate, which my father sends me by driblets. I won a large sum this winter on the races, and I am beginning to sell my sketches. Laidpore is more and more pleased with my work; he says it grows in force and individuality. I cannot judge of that myself, but I feel that I have gained in ease and confidence. However, as I said, I have sold a good many through Laidpore. I can live in the tiny house for little or nothing, with one servant. Old Celestine, who works occasionally for me, says she will come stay with me and do my work. I know I shall like it, like the feeling of freedom and independence."

"What does your husband say?"

"I have not told him yet. I only thought of it this morning. He will think I am demented, no doubt. Perhaps you think so."

Mademoiselle shook her head slowly. "Your reason is not yet clear to me," she said.

Neither was it quite clear to Edna herself; but it unfolded itself as she sat for a while in silence. Instinct had prompted her to put away her husband's bounty in casting off her allegiance. She did not know how it would be when he returned. There would have to be an understanding, an explanation. Conditions would some way adjust themselves, she felt; but whatever came, she had resolved never again to belong to another than herself.

"I shall give a grand dinner before I leave the old house!" Edna exclaimed. "You will have to come to it, Mademoiselle. I will give you everything that you like to eat and to drink. We shall sing and laugh and be merry for once." And she uttered a sigh that came from the very depths of her being.

If Mademoiselle happened to have received a letter from Robert during the interval of Edna's visits, she would give her the letter unsolicited. And she would seat herself at the piano and play as her humor prompted her while the young woman read the letter.

The little stove was roaring; it was red-hot, and the chocolate in the tin sizzled and sputtered. Edna went forward and opened the stove door, and Mademoiselle rising, took a letter from under the bust of Beethoven and handed it to Edna.

"Another! so soon!" she exclaimed, her eyes filled with delight. "Tell me, Mademoiselle, does he know that I see his letters?"

"Never in the world! He would be angry and would never write to me again if he thought so. Does he write to you? Never a line. Does he send you a message? Never a word. It is because he loves you, poor fool, and is trying to forget you, since you are not free to listen to him or to belong to him."

"Why do you show me his letters, then?"

"Haven't you begged for them? Can I refuse you anything? Oh! you cannot deceive me," and Mademoiselle approached her beloved instrument and began to play. Edna did not at once read the letter. She sat holding it in her hand, while the music penetrated her whole being like an effulgence, warming and brightening the dark places of her soul. It prepared her for joy and exultation.

"Oh!" she exclaimed, letting the letter fall to the floor. "Why did you not tell me?" She went and grasped Mademoiselle's hands up from the keys. "Oh! unkind! malicious! Why did you not tell me?"

"That he was coming back? No great news, *ma foi.* I wonder he did not come long ago."

"But when, when?" cried Edna, impatiently. "He does not say when."

"He says 'very soon.' You know as much about it as I do; it is all in the letter."

"But why? Why is he coming? Oh, if I thought—" and she snatched the letter from the floor and turned the pages this way and that way, looking for the reason, which was left untold.

"If I were young and in love with a man," said Mademoiselle, turning on the stool and pressing her wiry hands between her knees as she looked down at Edna, who sat on the floor holding the letter, "it seems to me he would have to be some *grand esprit;*[63] a man with lofty aims and ability to reach them; one who stood high enough to attract the notice of his fellow-men. It seems to me if I were young and in love I should never deem a man of ordinary caliber worthy of my devotion."

"Now it is you who are telling lies and seeking to deceive me, Mademoiselle; or else you have never been in love, and know nothing about it. Why," went on Edna, clasping her knees and looking up into Mademoiselle's twisted face, "do you suppose a woman knows why she loves? Does she select? Does she say to herself: 'Go to! Here is a distinguished statesman with presidential possibilities; I shall proceed to fall in love with him.' Or, 'I shall set my heart upon this musician, whose fame is on every tongue?' Or, 'This financier, who controls the world's money markets?'"

"You are purposely misunderstanding me, *ma reine.*[64] Are you in love with Robert?"

"Yes," said Edna. It was the first time she had admitted it, and a glow overspread her face, blotching it with red spots.

"Why?" asked her companion. "Why do you love him when you ought not to?"

Edna, with a motion or two, dragged herself on her knees before Mademoiselle Reisz, who took the glowing face between her two hands.

"Why? Because his hair is brown and grows away from his temples; because he opens and shuts his eyes, and his nose is a little out of drawing; because he has two lips and a square chin, and a little finger which he can't straighten from having played baseball too energetically in his youth. Because—"

"Because you do, in short," laughed Mademoiselle. "What will you do when he comes back?" she asked.

"Do? Nothing, except feel glad and happy to be alive."

She was already glad and happy to be alive at the mere thought of his return. The murky, lowering sky, which had depressed her a few hours before, seemed bracing and invigorating as she splashed through the streets on her way home.

She stopped at a confectioner's and ordered a huge box of bonbons for the children in Iberville. She slipped a card in the box, on which she scribbled a tender message and sent an abundance of kisses.

Before dinner in the evening Edna wrote a charming letter to her husband, telling him of her intention to move for a while into the little house around the block, and to give a farewell dinner before leaving, regretting that he was not there to share it, to help her out with the menu and assist her in entertaining the guests. Her letter was brilliant and brimming with cheerfulness.

XXVII

"What is the matter with you?" asked Arobin that evening. "I never found you in such a happy mood." Edna was tired by that time, and was reclining on the lounge before the fire.

[63] Great-spirited person. [64] "My dear" (literally, "my queen").

"Don't you know the weather prophet has told us we shall see the sun pretty soon?"

"Well, that ought to be reason enough," he acquiesced. "You wouldn't give me another if I sat here all night imploring you." He sat close to her on a low tabouret[65] and as he spoke his fingers lightly touched the hair that fell a little over her forehead. She liked the touch of his fingers through her hair, and closed her eyes sensitively.

"One of these days," she said, "I'm going to pull myself together for a while and think—try to determine what character of a woman I am; for, candidly, I don't know. By all the codes which I am acquainted with, I am a devilishly wicked specimen of the sex. But some way I can't convince myself that I am. I must think about it."

"Don't. What's the use? Why should you bother thinking about it when I can tell you what manner of woman you are." His fingers strayed occasionally down to her warm, smooth cheeks and firm chin, which was growing a little full and double.

"Oh, yes! You will tell me that I am adorable; everything that is captivating. Spare yourself the effort."

"No; I shan't tell you anything of the sort, though I shouldn't be lying if I did."

"Do you know Mademoiselle Reisz?" she asked irrelevantly.

"The pianist? I know her by sight. I've heard her play."

"She says queer things sometimes in a bantering way that you don't notice at the time and you find yourself thinking about afterward."

"For instance?"

"Well, for instance, when I left her today, she put her arms around me and felt my shoulder blades, to see if my wings were strong, she said. 'The bird that would soar above the level plain of tradition and prejudice must have strong wings. It is a sad spectacle to see the weaklings bruised, exhausted, fluttering back to earth.'"

"Whither would you soar?"

"I'm not thinking of any extraordinary flights. I only half comprehend her."

"I've heard she's partially demented," said Arobin.

"She seems to me wonderfully sane," Edna replied.

"I'm told she's extremely disagreeable and unpleasant. Why have you introduced her at a moment when I desired to talk of you?"

"Oh! talk of me if you like," cried Edna, clasping her hands beneath her head; "but let me think of something else while you do."

"I'm jealous of your thoughts tonight. They're making you a little kinder than usual; but some way I feel as if they were wandering, as if they were not here with me." She only looked at him and smiled. His eyes were very near. He leaned upon the lounge with an arm extended across her, while the other hand still rested upon her hair. They continued silently to look into each other's eyes. When he leaned forward and kissed her, she clasped his head, holding his lips to hers.

It was the first kiss of her life to which her nature had really responded. It was a flaming torch that kindled desire.

[65] A padded stool.

XXVIII

Edna cried a little that night after Arobin left her. It was only one phase of the multitudinous emotions which had assailed her. There was with her an overwhelming feeling of irresponsibility. There was the shock of the unexpected and the unaccustomed. There was her husband's reproach looking at her from the external things around her which he had provided for her external existence. There was Robert's reproach making itself felt by a quicker, fiercer, more overpowering love, which had awakened within her toward him. Above all, there was understanding. She felt as if a mist had been lifted from her eyes, enabling her to look upon and comprehend the significance of life, that monster made up of beauty and brutality. But among the conflicting sensations which assailed her, there was neither shame nor remorse. There was a dull pang of regret because it was not the kiss of love which had inflamed her, because it was not love which had held this cup of life to her lips.

XXIX

Without even waiting for an answer from her husband regarding his opinion or wishes in the matter, Edna hastened her preparations for quitting her home on Esplanade Street and moving into the little house around the block. A feverish anxiety attended her every action in that direction. There was no moment of deliberation, no interval of repose between the thought and its fulfillment. Early upon the morning following those hours passed in Arobin's society, Edna set about securing her new abode and hurrying her arrangements for occupying it. Within the precincts of her home she felt like one who has entered and lingered within the portals of some forbidden temple in which a thousand muffled voices bade her begone.

Whatever was her own in the house, everything which she had acquired aside from her husband's bounty, she caused to be transported to the other house, supplying simple and meager deficiencies from her own resources.

Arobin found her with rolled sleeves, working in company with the house-maid, when he looked in during the afternoon. She was splendid and robust, and had never appeared handsomer than in the old blue gown, with a red silk handkerchief knotted at random around her head to protect her hair from the dust. She was mounted upon a high step-ladder, unhooking a picture from the wall when he entered. He had found the front door open, and had followed his ring by walking in unceremoniously.

"Come down!" he said. "Do you want to kill yourself?" She greeted him with affected carelessness, and appeared absorbed in her occupation.

If he had expected to find her languishing, reproachful, or indulging in sentimental tears, he must have been greatly surprised.

He was no doubt prepared for any emergency, ready for any one of the foregoing attitudes, just as he bent himself easily and naturally to the situation which confronted him.

"Please come down," he insisted, holding the ladder and looking up at her.

"No," she answered; "Ellen is afraid to mount the ladder. Joe is working over at the 'pigeon house'—that's the name Ellen gives it, because it's so small and looks like a pigeon house—and some one has to do this."

Arobin pulled off his coat, and expressed himself ready and willing to tempt fate in her place. Ellen brought him one of her dust-caps, and went into contortions of mirth, which she found it impossible to control, when she saw him put it on before the mirror as grotesquely as he could. Edna herself could not refrain from smiling when she fastened it at his request. So it was he who in turn mounted the ladder, unhooking pictures and curtains, and dislodging ornaments as Edna directed. When he had finished he took off his dust-cap and went out to wash his hands.

Edna was sitting on the tabouret, idly brushing the tips of a feather duster along the carpet when he came in again.

"Is there anything more you will let me do?" he asked.

"That is all," she answered. "Ellen can manage the rest." She kept the young woman occupied in the drawing-room, unwilling to be left alone with Arobin.

"What about the dinner?" he asked; "the grand event, the *coup d'état?*"[66]

"It will be day after tomorrow. Why do you call it the '*coup d'état*'? Oh! it will be very fine; all my best of everything—crystal, silver and gold, Sèvres, flowers, music, and champagne to swim in. I'll let Léonce pay the bills. I wonder what he'll say when he sees the bills."

"And you ask me why I call it a *coup d'état*?" Arobin had put on his coat, and he stood before her and asked if his cravat was plumb. She told him it was, looking no higher than the tip of his collar.

"When do you go to the 'pigeon house?'—with all due acknowledgement to Ellen."

"Day after tomorrow, after the dinner. I shall sleep there."

"Ellen, will you very kindly get me a glass of water?" asked Arobin. "The dust in the curtains, if you will pardon me for hinting such a thing, has parched my throat to a crisp."

"While Ellen gets the water," said Edna, rising, "I will say good-by and let you go. I must get rid of this grime, and I have a million things to do and think of."

"When shall I see you?" asked Arobin, seeking to detain her, the maid having left the room.

"At the dinner, of course. You are invited."

"Not before?—not tonight or tomorrow morning or tomorrow noon or night? or the day after morning or noon? Can't you see yourself, without my telling you, what an eternity it is?"

He had followed her into the hall and to the foot of the stairway, looking up at her as she mounted with her face half turned to him.

"Not an instant sooner," she said. But she laughed and looked at him with eyes that at once gave him courage to wait and made it torture to wait.

[66] A sudden seizure of political power (literally, "stroke of state"). Arobin, in applying the term facetiously to the dinner party, is implying that Edna is deposing Pontellier.

XXX

Though Edna had spoken of the dinner as a very grand affair, it was in truth a very small affair and very select, in so much as the guests invited were few and were selected with discrimination. She had counted upon an even dozen seating themselves at her round mahogany board, forgetting for the moment that Madame Ratignolle was to the last degree *souffrante*[67] and unpresentable, and not foreseeing that Madame Lebrun would send a thousand regrets at the last moment. So there were only ten, after all, which made a cozy, comfortable number.

There were Mr. and Mrs. Merriman, a pretty, vivacious little woman in the thirties; her husband, a jovial fellow, something of a shallow-pate, who laughed a good deal at other people's witticisms, and had thereby made himself extremely popular. Mrs. Highcamp had accompanied them. Of course, there was Alcée Arobin; and Mademoiselle Reisz had consented to come. Edna had sent her a fresh bunch of violets with black lace trimmings for her hair. Monsieur Ratignolle brought himself and his wife's excuses. Victor Lebrun, who happened to be in the city, bent upon relaxation, had accepted with alacrity. There was a Miss Mayblunt, no longer in her teens, who looked at the world through lorgnettes and with the keenest interest. It was thought and said that she was intellectual; it was suspected of her that she wrote under a *nom de guerre*.[68] She had come with a gentleman by the name of Gouvernail, connected with one of the daily papers, of whom nothing special could be said, except that he was observant and seemed quiet and inoffensive. Edna herself made the tenth, and at half-past eight they seated themselves at table, Arobin and Monsieur Ratignolle on either side of their hostess.

Mrs. Highcamp sat between Arobin and Victor Lebrun. Then came Mrs. Merriman, Mr. Gouvernail, Miss Mayblunt, Mr. Merriman, and Mademoiselle Reisz next to Monsieur Ratignolle.

There was something extremely gorgeous about the appearance of the table, an effect of splendor conveyed by a cover of pale yellow satin under strips of lace-work. There were wax candles in massive brass candelabra, burning softly under yellow silk shades; full, fragrant roses, yellow and red, abounded. There were silver and gold, as she had said there would be, and crystal which glittered like the gems which the women wore.

The ordinary stiff dining chairs had been discarded for the occasion and replaced by the most commodious and luxurious which could be collected throughout the house. Mademoiselle Reisz, being exceedingly diminutive, was elevated upon cushions, as small children are sometimes hoisted at table upon bulky volumes.

"Something new, Edna?" exclaimed Miss Mayblunt, with lorgnette directed toward a magnificent cluster of diamonds that sparkled, that almost sputtered, in Edna's hair, just over the center of her forehead.

"Quite new; 'brand' new, in fact; a present from my husband. It arrived this morning from New York. I may as well admit that this is my birthday, and that I am twenty-nine. In good time I expect you to drink my health. Meanwhile, I shall ask you to begin with this cocktail, composed—would

[67] Suffering; ill. [68] Pseudonym.

you say 'composed?'" with an appeal to Miss Mayblunt—"composed by my father in honor of Sister Janet's wedding."

Before each guest stood a tiny glass that looked and sparkled like a garnet gem.

"Then, all things considered," spoke Arobin, "it might not be amiss to start out by drinking the Colonel's health in the cocktail which he composed, on the birthday of the most charming of women—the daughter whom he invented."

Mr. Merriman's laugh at this sally was such a genuine outburst and so contagious that it started the dinner with an agreeable swing that never slackened.

Miss Mayblunt begged to be allowed to keep her cocktail untouched before her, just to look at. The color was marvelous! She could compare it to nothing she had ever seen, and the garnet lights which it emitted were unspeakably rare. She pronounced the Colonel an artist, and stuck to it.

Monsieur Ratignolle was prepared to take things seriously: the *mets,* the *entre-mets,*[69] the service, the decorations, even the people. He looked up from his pompano[70] and inquired of Arobin if he were related to the gentleman of that name who formed one of the firm of Laitner and Arobin, lawyers. The young man admitted that Laitner was a warm personal friend, who permitted Arobin's name to decorate the firm's letterheads and to appear upon a shingle that graced Perdido Street.

"There are so many inquisitive people and institutions abounding," said Arobin, "that one is really forced as a matter of convenience these days to assume the virtue of an occupation if he has it not."[71]

Monsieur Ratignolle stared a little, and turned to ask Mademoiselle Reisz if she considered the symphony concerts up to the standard which had been set the previous winter. Mademoiselle Reisz answered Monsieur Ratignolle in French, which Edna thought a little rude, under the circumstances, but characteristic. Mademoiselle had only disagreeable things to say of the symphony concerts, and insulting remarks to make of all the musicians of New Orleans, singly and collectively. All her interest seemed to be centered upon the delicacies placed before her.

Mr. Merriman said that Mr. Arobin's remark about inquisitive people reminded him of a man from Waco the other day at the St. Charles Hotel—but as Mr. Merriman's stories were always lame and lacking point, his wife seldom permitted him to complete them. She interrupted him to ask if he remembered the name of the author whose book she had bought the week before to send to a friend in Geneva. She was talking "books" with Mr. Gouvernail and trying to draw from him his opinion upon current literary topics. Her husband told the story of the Waco man privately to Miss Mayblunt, who pretended to be greatly amused and to think it extremely clever.

Mrs. Highcamp hung with languid but unaffected interest upon the warm and impetuous volubility of her left-hand neighbor, Victor Lebrun. Her attention was never for a moment withdrawn from him after seating

[69] The main courses and the side dishes. [70] A fish, prized as a delicacy.

[71] Hamlet asks his mother Gertrude to "assume a virtue, if you have it not" (*Hamlet* III.iv.161).

herself at table; and when he turned to Mrs. Merriman, who was prettier and more vivacious than Mrs. Highcamp, she waited with easy indifference for an opportunity to reclaim his attention. There was the occasional sound of music, of mandolins, sufficiently removed to be an agreeable accompaniment rather than an interruption to the conversation. Outside the soft, monotonous splash of a fountain could be heard; the sound penetrated into the room with the heavy odor of jessamine that came through the open windows.

The golden shimmer of Edna's satin gown spread in rich folds on either side of her. There was a soft fall of lace encircling her shoulders. It was the color of her skin, without the glow, the myriad living tints that one may sometimes discover in vibrant flesh. There was something in her attitude, in her whole appearance when she leaned her head against the high-backed chair and spread her arms, which suggested the regal woman, the one who rules, who looks on, who stands alone.

But as she sat there amid her guests, she felt the old ennui overtaking her; the hopelessness which so often assailed her, which came upon her like an obsession, like something extraneous, independent of volition. It was something which announced itself; a chill breath that seemed to issue from some vast cavern wherein discords wailed. There came over her the acute longing which always summoned into her spiritual vision the presence of the beloved one, overpowering her at once with a sense of the unattainable.

The moments glided on, while a feeling of good fellowship passed around the circle like a mystic cord, holding and binding these people together with jest and laughter. Monsieur Ratignolle was the first to break the pleasant charm. At ten o'clock he excused himself. Madame Ratignolle was waiting for him at home. She was *bien souffrante,*[72] and she was filled with vague dread, which only her husband's presence could allay.

Mademoiselle Reisz arose with Monsieur Ratignolle, who offered to escort her to the car. She had eaten well; she had tasted the good, rich wines, and they must have turned her head, for she bowed pleasantly to all as she withdrew from table. She kissed Edna upon the shoulder, and whispered: *"Bonne nuit, ma reine; soyez sage."*[73] She had been a little bewildered upon rising, or rather, descending from her cushions, and Monsieur Ratignolle gallantly took her arm and led her away.

Mrs. Highcamp was weaving a garland of roses, yellow and red. When she had finished the garland, she laid it lightly upon Victor's black curls. He was reclining far back in the luxurious chair, holding a glass of champagne to the light.

As if a magician's wand had touched him, the garland of roses transformed him into a vision of Oriental beauty. His cheeks were the color of crushed grapes, and his dusky eyes glowed with a languishing fire.

"Sapristi!" exclaimed Arobin.

But Mrs. Highcamp had one more touch to add to the picture. She took from the back of her chair a white silken scarf, with which she had covered her shoulders in the early part of the evening. She draped it across the boy in graceful folds, and in a way to conceal his black, conventional evening dress. He did not seem to mind what she did to him, only smiled, showing a

[72]"Very ill." [73]"Good night, my dear; be good."

faint gleam of white teeth, while he continued to gaze with narrowing eyes at the light through his glass of champagne.

"Oh! to be able to paint in color rather than in words!" exclaimed Miss Mayblunt, losing herself in a rhapsodic dream as she looked at him.

"'There was a graven image of Desire
Painted with red blood on a ground of gold.'"[74]

murmured Gouvernail, under his breath.

The effect of the wine upon Victor was to change his accustomed volubility into silence. He seemed to have abandoned himself to a reverie, and to be seeing pleasing visions in the amber bead.

"Sing," entreated Mrs. Highcamp. "Won't you sing to us?"

"Let him alone," said Arobin.

"He's posing," offered Mr. Merriman; "let him have it out."

"I believe he's paralyzed," laughed Mrs. Merriman. And leaning over the youth's chair, she took the glass from his hand and held it to his lips. He sipped the wine slowly, and when he had drained the glass she laid it upon the table and wiped his lips with her little filmy handkerchief.

"Yes, I'll sing for you," he said, turning in his chair toward Mrs. Highcamp. He clasped his hands behind his head, and looking up at the ceiling began to hum a little, trying his voice like a musician tuning an instrument. Then, looking at Edna, he began to sing:

"Ah! si tu savais!"

"Stop!" she cried, "don't sing that. I don't want you to sing it," and she laid her glass so impetuously and blindly upon the table as to shatter it against a caraffe. The wine spilled over Arobin's legs and some of it trickled down upon Mrs. Highcamp's black gauze gown. Victor had lost all idea of courtesy, or else he thought his hostess was not in earnest, for he laughed and went on:

"Ah! si tu savais
Ce que tes yeux me disent"—[75]

"Oh! you mustn't! you mustn't," exclaimed Edna, and pushing back her chair she got up, and going behind him placed her hand over his mouth. He kissed the soft palm that pressed upon his lips.

"No, no, I won't, Mrs. Pontellier. I didn't know you meant it," looking up at her with caressing eyes. The touch of his lips was like a pleasing sting to her hand. She lifted the garland of roses from his head and flung it across the room.

"Come, Victor; you've posed long enough. Give Mrs. Highcamp her scarf."

[74] From "A Cameo," by A. C. Swinburne (1837–1909).

[75] "Ah! couldst thou but know what thine eyes tell me," from the Balfe song Robert sang earlier.

Mrs. Highcamp undraped the scarf from about him with her own hands. Miss Mayblunt and Mr. Gouvernail suddenly conceived the notion that it was time to say good night. And Mr. and Mrs. Merriman wondered how it could be so late.

Before parting from Victor, Mrs. Highcamp invited him to call upon her daughter, who she knew would be charmed to meet him and talk French and sing French songs with him. Victor expressed his desire and intention to call upon Miss Highcamp at the first opportunity which presented itself. He asked if Arobin were going his way. Arobin was not.

The mandolin players had long since stolen away. A profound stillness had fallen upon the broad, beautiful street. The voices of Edna's disbanding guests jarred like a discordant note upon the quiet harmony of the night.

XXXI

"Well?" questioned Arobin, who had remained with Edna after the others had departed.

"Well," she reiterated, and stood up, stretching her arms, and feeling the need to relax her muscles after having been so long seated.

"What next?" he asked.

"The servants are all gone. They left when the musicians did. I have dismissed them. The house has to be closed and locked, and I shall trot around to the pigeon house, and shall send Celestine over in the morning to straighten things up."

He looked around, and began to turn out some of the lights.

"What about upstairs?" he inquired.

"I think it is all right; but there may be a window or two unlatched. We had better look; you might take a candle and see. And bring me my wrap and hat on the foot of the bed in the middle room."

He went up with the light, and Edna began closing doors and windows. She hated to shut in the smoke and the fumes of the wine. Arobin found her cape and hat, which he brought down and helped her to put on.

When everything was secured and the lights put out, they left through the front door, Arobin locking it and taking the key, which he carried for Edna. He helped her down the steps.

"Will you have a spray of jessamine?" he asked, breaking off a few blossoms as he passed.

"No; I don't want anything."

She seemed disheartened, and had nothing to say. She took his arm, which he offered her, holding up the weight of her satin train with the other hand. She looked down, noticing the black line of his leg moving in and out so close to her against the yellow shimmer of her gown. There was the whistle of a railway train somewhere in the distance, and the midnight bells were ringing. They met no one in their short walk.

The "pigeon-house" stood behind a locked gate, and a shallow *parterre*[76]

[76] Garden with flower beds.

that had been somewhat neglected. There was a small front porch, upon which a long window and the front door opened. The door opened directly into the parlor; there was no side entry. Back in the yard was a room for servants, in which old Celestine had been ensconced.

Edna had left a lamp burning low upon the table. She had succeeded in making the room look habitable and homelike. There were some books on the table and a lounge near at hand. On the floor was a fresh matting, covered with a rug or two; and on the walls hung a few tasteful pictures. But the room was filled with flowers. These were a surprise to her. Arobin had sent them, and had had Celestine distribute them during Edna's absence. Her bedroom was adjoining, and across a small passage were the dining-room and kitchen.

Edna seated herself with every appearance of discomfort.

"Are you tired?" he asked.

"Yes, and chilled, and miserable. I feel as if I had been wound up to a certain pitch—too tight—and something inside of me had snapped." She rested her head against the table upon her bare arm.

"You want to rest," he said, "and to be quiet. I'll go; I'll leave you and let you rest."

"Yes," she replied.

He stood up beside her and smoothed her hair with his soft, magnetic hand. His touch conveyed to her a certain physical comfort. She could have fallen quietly asleep there if he had continued to pass his hand over her hair. He brushed the hair upward from the nape of her neck.

"I hope you will feel better and happier in the morning," he said. "You have tried to do too much in the past few days. The dinner was the last straw; you might have dispensed with it."

"Yes," she admitted; "it was stupid."

"No, it was delightful; but it has worn you out." His hand had strayed to her beautiful shoulders, and he could feel the response of her flesh to his touch. He seated himself beside her and kissed her lightly upon the shoulder.

"I thought you were going away," she said, in an uneven voice.

"I am, after I have said good night."

"Good night," she murmured.

He did not answer, except to continue to caress her. He did not say good night until she had become supple to his gentle, seductive entreaties.

XXXII

When Mr. Pontellier learned of his wife's intention to abandon her home and take up her residence elsewhere, he immediately wrote her a letter of unqualified disapproval and remonstrance. She had given reasons which he was unwilling to acknowledge as adequate. He hoped she had not acted upon her rash impulse; and begged her to consider first, foremost, and above all else, what people would say. He was not dreaming of scandal when he uttered this warning; that was a thing which would never have entered into his mind to consider in connection with his wife's name or his own. He was simply thinking of his financial integrity. It might get noised about that the Pontelliers had met with reverses, and were forced to conduct their *ménage*[77] on a humbler scale than heretofore. It might do incalculable mischief to his business prospects.

But remembering Edna's whimsical turn of mind of late, and foreseeing that she had immediately acted upon her impetuous determination, he grasped the situation with his usual promptness and handled it with his well-known business tact and cleverness.

The same mail which brought to Edna his letter of disapproval carried instructions—the most minute instructions—to a well-known architect concerning the remodeling of his home, changes which he had long contemplated, and which he desired carried forward during his temporary absence.

Expert and reliable packers and movers were engaged to convey the furniture, carpets, pictures—everything movable, in short—to places of security. And in an incredibly short time the Pontellier house was turned over to the artisans. There was to be an addition—a small snuggery;[78] there was to be frescoing, and hardwood flooring was to be put into such rooms as had not yet been subjected to this improvement.

Furthermore, in one of the daily papers appeared a brief notice to the effect that Mr. and Mrs. Pontellier were contemplating a summer sojourn abroad, and that their handsome residence on Esplanade Street was undergoing sumptuous alterations, and would not be ready for occupancy until their return. Mr. Pontellier had saved appearances!

Edna admired the skill of his maneuver, and avoided any occasion to balk his intentions. When the situation as set forth by Mr. Pontellier was accepted and taken for granted, she was apparently satisfied that it should be so.

The pigeon-house pleased her. It at once assumed the intimate character of a home, while she herself invested it with a charm which it reflected like a warm glow. There was with her a feeling of having descended in the social scale, with a corresponding sense of having risen in the spiritual. Every step which she took toward relieving herself from obligations added to her strength and expansion as an individual. She began to look with her own eyes; to see and to apprehend the deeper undercurrents of life. No longer was she content to "feed upon opinion" when her own soul had invited her.

After a little while, a few days, in fact, Edna went up and spent a week with her children in Iberville. They were delicious February days, with all the summer's promise hovering in the air.

How glad she was to see the children! She wept for very pleasure when she felt their little arms clasping her; their hard, ruddy cheeks pressed against her own glowing cheeks. She looked into their faces with hungry eyes that could not be satisfied with looking. And what stories they had to tell their mother! About the pigs, the cows, the mules! About riding to the mill behind Gluglu; fishing back in the lake with their Uncle Jasper; picking pecans with Lidie's little black brood, and hauling chips in their express wagon. It was a thousand times more fun to haul real chips for old lame

[77] Household. [78] A cozy room; a "den."

Susie's real fire than to drag painted blocks along the banquette on Esplanade Street!

She went with them herself to see the pigs and the cows, to look at the darkies laying the cane, to thrash the pecan trees, and catch fish in the back lake. She lived with them a whole week long, giving them all of herself, and gathering and filling herself with their young existence. They listened, breathless, when she told them the house in Esplanade Street was crowded with workmen, hammering, nailing, sawing, and filling the place with clatter. They wanted to know where their bed was; what had been done with their rocking-horse; and where did Joe sleep, and where had Ellen gone, and the cook? But, above all, they were fired with a desire to see the little house around the block. Was there any place to play? Were there any boys next door? Raoul, with pessimistic foreboding, was convinced that there were only girls next door. Where would they sleep, and where would papa sleep? She told them the fairies would fix it all right.

The old Madame was charmed with Edna's visit, and showered all manner of delicate attentions upon her. She was delighted to know that the Esplanade Street house was in a dismantled condition. It gave her the promise and pretext to keep the children indefinitely.

It was with a wrench and a pang that Edna left her children. She carried away with her the sound of their voices and the touch of their cheeks. All along the journey homeward their presence lingered with her like the memory of a delicious song. But by the time she had regained the city the song no longer echoed in her soul. She was again alone.

XXXIII

It happened sometimes when Edna went to see Mademoiselle Reisz that the little musician was absent, giving a lesson or making some small necessary household purchase. The key was always left in a secret hiding-place in the entry, which Edna knew. If Mademoiselle happened to be away, Edna would usually enter and wait for her return.

When she knocked at Mademoiselle Reisz's door one afternoon there was no response; so unlocking the door, as usual, she entered and found the apartment deserted, as she had expected. Her day had been quite filled up, and it was for a rest, for a refuge, and to talk about Robert, that she sought out her friend.

She had worked at her canvas—a young Italian character study—all the morning, completing the work without the model; but there had been many interruptions, some incident to her modest housekeeping, and others of a social nature.

Madame Ratignolle had dragged herself over, avoiding the too public thoroughfares, she said. She complained that Edna had neglected her much of late. Besides, she was consumed with curiosity to see the little house and the manner in which it was conducted. She wanted to hear all about the dinner party; Monsieur Ratignolle had left *so* early. What had happened after he left? The champagne and grapes which Edna sent over were *too* delicious. She had so little appetite; they had refreshed and toned her stomach. Where on earth was she going to put Mr. Pontellier in that little house, and the boys? And then she made Edna promise to go to her when her hour of trial overtook her.

"At any time—any time of the day or night, dear," Edna assured her.

Before leaving Madame Ratignolle said:

"In some way you seem to me like a child, Edna. You seem to act without a certain amount of reflection which is necessary in this life. That is the reason I want to say you mustn't mind if I advise you to be a little careful while you are living here alone. Why don't you have some one come and stay with you? Wouldn't Mademoiselle Reisz come?"

"No; she wouldn't wish to come, and I shouldn't want her always with me."

"Well, the reason—you know how evil-minded the world is—some one was talking of Alcée Arobin visiting you. Of course, it wouldn't matter if Mr. Arobin had not such a dreadful reputation. Monsieur Ratignolle was telling me that his attentions alone are considered enough to ruin a woman's name."

"Does he boast of his successes?" asked Edna, indifferently, squinting at her picture.

"No, I think not. I believe he is a decent fellow as far as that goes. But his character is so well known among the men. I shan't be able to come back and see you; it was very, very imprudent today."

"Mind the step!" cried Edna.

"Don't neglect me," entreated Madame Ratignolle; "and don't mind what I said about Arobin, or having some one to stay with you."

"Of course not," Edna laughed. "You may say anything you like to me." They kissed good-by. Madame Ratignolle had not far to go, and Edna stood on the porch a while watching her walk down the street.

Then in the afternoon Mrs. Merriman and Mrs. Highcamp had made their "party call." Edna felt that they might have dispensed with the formality. They had also come to invite her to play *vingt-et-un*[79] one evening at Mrs. Merriman's. She was asked to go early, to dinner, and Mr. Merriman or Mr. Arobin would take her home. Edna accepted in a half-hearted way. She sometimes felt very tired of Mrs. Highcamp and Mrs. Merriman.

Late in the afternoon she sought refuge with Mademoiselle Reisz, and stayed there alone, waiting for her, feeling a kind of repose invade her with the very atmosphere of the shabby, unpretentious little room.

Edna sat at the window, which looked out over the house-tops and across the river. The window frame was filled with pots of flowers, and she sat and picked the dry leaves from a rose geranium. The day was warm, and the breeze which blew from the river was very pleasant. She removed her hat and laid it on the piano. She went on picking the leaves and digging around the plants with her hat pin. Once she thought she heard Mademoiselle Reisz approaching. But it was a young black girl, who came in, bringing a small bundle of laundry, which she deposited in the adjoining room, and went away.

Edna seated herself at the piano, and softly picked out with one hand the bars of a piece of music which lay open before her. A half-hour went by. There was the occasional sound of people going and coming in the

[79]Twenty-one, a card game.

lower hall. She was growing interested in her occupation of picking out the aria, when there was a second rap at the door. She vaguely wondered what these people did when they found Mademoiselle's door locked.

"Come in," she called, turning her face toward the door. And this time it was Robert Lebrun who presented himself. She attempted to rise; she could not have done so without betraying the agitation which mastered her at sight of him, so she fell back upon the stool, only exclaiming, "Why, Robert!"

He came and clasped her hand, seemingly without knowing what he was saying or doing.

"Mrs. Pontellier! How do you happen—oh! how well you look! Is Mademoiselle Reisz not here? I never expected to see you."

"When did you come back?" asked Edna in an unsteady voice, wiping her face with her handkerchief. She seemed ill at ease on the piano stool, and he begged her to take the chair by the window. She did so, mechanically, while he seated himself on the stool.

"I returned day before yesterday," he answered, while he leaned his arm on the keys, bringing forth a crash of discordant sound.

"Day before yesterday!" she repeated, aloud; and went on thinking to herself, "day before yesterday," in a sort of an uncomprehending way. She had pictured him seeking her at the very first hour, and he had lived under the same sky since day before yesterday; while only by accident had he stumbled upon her. Mademoiselle must have lied when she said, "Poor fool, he loves you."

"Day before yesterday," she repeated, breaking off a spray of Mademoiselle's geranium; "then if you had not met me here today you wouldn't—when—that is, didn't you mean to come and see me?"

"Of course, I should have gone to see you. There have been so many things—" he turned the leaves of Mademoiselle's music nervously. "I started in at once yesterday with the old firm. After all there is as much chance for me here as there was there—that is, I might find it profitable some day. The Mexicans were not very congenial."

So he had come back because the Mexicans were not congenial; because business was as profitable here as there; because of any reason, and not because he cared to be near her. She remembered the day she sat on the floor, turning the pages of his letter, seeking the reason which was left untold.

She had not noticed how he looked—only feeling his presence; but she turned deliberately and observed him. After all, he had been absent but a few months, and was not changed. His hair—the color of hers—waved back from his temples in the same way as before. His skin was not more burned than it had been at Grand Isle. She found in his eyes, when he looked at her for one silent moment, the same tender caress, with an added warmth and entreaty which had not been there before—the same glance which had penetrated to the sleeping places of her soul and awakened them.

A hundred times Edna had pictured Robert's return, and imagined their first meeting. It was usually at her home, whither he had sought her out at once. She always fancied him expressing or betraying in some way his love for her. And here, the reality was that they sat ten feet apart, she at the window, crushing geranium leaves in her hand and smelling them, he twirling around on the piano stool, saying:

"I was very much surprised to hear of Mr. Pontellier's absence; it's a wonder Mademoiselle Reisz did not tell me; and your moving—mother told me yesterday. I should think you would have gone to New York with him, or to Iberville with the children, rather than be bothered here with housekeeping. And you are going abroad, too, I hear. We shan't have you at Grand Isle next summer; it won't seem—do you see much of Mademoiselle Reisz? She often spoke of you in the few letters she wrote."

"Do you remember that you promised to write to me when you went away?" A flush overspread his whole face.

"I couldn't believe that my letters would be of any interest to you."

"That is an excuse; it isn't the truth." Edna reached for her hat on the piano. She adjusted it, sticking the hat pin through the heavy coil of hair with some deliberation.

"Are you not going to wait for Mademoiselle Reisz?" asked Robert.

"No; I have found when she is absent this long, she is liable not to come back till late." She drew on her gloves, and Robert picked up his hat.

"Won't you wait for her?" asked Edna.

"Not if you think she will not be back till late," adding, as if suddenly aware of some discourtesy in his speech, "and I should miss the pleasure of walking home with you." Edna locked the door and put the key back in its hiding-place.

They went together, picking their way across muddy streets and sidewalks encumbered with the cheap display of small tradesmen. Part of the distance they rode in the car, and after disembarking, passed the Pontellier mansion, which looked broken and half torn asunder. Robert had never known the house, and looked at it with interest.

"I never knew you in your home," he remarked.

"I am glad you did not."

"Why?" She did not answer. They went on around the corner, and it seemed as if her dreams were coming true after all, when he followed her into the little house.

"You must stay and dine with me, Robert. You see I am all alone, and it is so long since I have seen you. There is so much I want to ask you."

She took off her hat and gloves. He stood irresolute, making some excuse about his mother who expected him; he even muttered something about an engagement. She struck a match and lit the lamp on the table; it was growing dusk. When he saw her face in the lamp-light, looking pained, with all the soft lines gone out of it, he threw his hat aside and seated himself.

"Oh! you know I want to stay if you will let me!" he exclaimed. All the softness came back. She laughed, and went and put her hand on his shoulder.

"This is the first moment you have seemed like the old Robert. I'll go tell Celestine." She hurried away to tell Celestine to set an extra place. She even sent her off in search of some added delicacy which she had not thought of for herself. And she recommended great care in dripping the coffee and having the omelet done to a proper turn.

When she reëntered, Robert was turning over magazines, sketches, and things that lay upon the table in great disorder. He picked up a photograph, and exclaimed:

"Alcée Arobin! What on earth is his picture doing here?"

"I tried to make a sketch of his head one day," answered Edna, "and he thought the photograph might help me. It was at the other house. I thought it had been left there. I must have packed it up with my drawing materials."

"I should think you would give it back to him if you have finished with it."

"Oh! I have a great many such photographs. I never think of returning them. They don't amount to anything." Robert kept on looking at the picture.

"It seems to me—do you think his head worth drawing? Is he a friend of Mr. Pontellier's? You never said you knew him."

"He isn't a friend of Mr. Pontellier's; he's a friend of mine. I always knew him—that is, it is only of late that I know him pretty well. But I'd rather talk about you, and know what you have been seeing and doing and feeling out there in Mexico." Robert threw aside the picture.

"I've been seeing the waves and the white beach of Grand Isle; the quiet, grassy street of the *Chênière;* the old fort at Grande Terre. I've been working like a machine, and feeling like a lost soul. There was nothing interesting."

She leaned her head upon her hand to shade her eyes from the light.

"And what have you been seeing and doing and feeling all these days?" he asked.

"I've been seeing the waves and the white beach of Grand Isle; the quiet, grassy street of the *Chênière Caminada;* the old sunny fort at Grande Terre. I've been working with a little more comprehension than a machine, and still feeling like a lost soul. There was nothing interesting."

"Mrs. Pontellier, you are cruel," he said, with feeling, closing his eyes and resting his head back in his chair. They remained in silence till old Celestine announced dinner.

XXXIV

The dining-room was very small. Edna's round mahogany would have almost filled it. As it was there was but a step or two from the little table to the kitchen, to the mantel, the small buffet, and the side door that opened out on the narrow brick-paved yard.

A certain degree of ceremony settled upon them with the announcement of dinner. There was no return to personalities. Robert related incidents of his sojourn in Mexico, and Edna talked of events likely to interest him, which had occurred during his absence. The dinner was of ordinary quality, except for the few delicacies which she had sent out to purchase. Old Celestine, with a bandana *tignon*[80] twisted about her head, hobbled in and out, taking a personal interest in everything; and she lingered occasionally to talk *patois*[81] with Robert, whom she had known as a boy.

[80] "Chignon," head scarf.

[81] Cajun speech, a dialect of French with many borrowings from English, Spanish, and American Indian languages.

He went out to a neighboring cigar stand to purchase cigarette papers, and when he came back he found that Celestine had served the black coffee in the parlor.

"Perhaps I shouldn't have come back," he said. "When you are tired of me, tell me to go."

"You never tire me. You must have forgotten the hours and hours at Grand Isle in which we grew accustomed to each other and used to being together."

"I have forgotten nothing at Grand Isle," he said, not looking at her, but rolling a cigarette. His tobacco pouch, which he laid upon the table, was a fantastic embroidered silk affair, evidently the handiwork of a woman.

"You used to carry your tobacco in a rubber pouch," said Edna, picking up the pouch and examining the needlework.

"Yes; it was lost."

"Where did you buy this one? In Mexico?"

"It was given to me by a Vera Cruz girl; they are very generous," he replied, striking a match and lighting his cigarette.

"They are very handsome, I suppose, those Mexican women; very picturesque, with their black eyes and their lace scarfs."

"Some are; others are hideous. Just as you find women everywhere."

"What was she like—the one who gave you the pouch? You must have known her very well."

"She was very ordinary. She wasn't of the slightest importance. I knew her well enough."

"Did you visit at her house? Was it interesting? I should like to know and hear about the people you met, and the impressions they made on you."

"There are some people who leave impressions not so lasting as the imprint of an oar upon the water."

"Was she such a one?"

"It would be ungenerous for me to admit that she was of that order and kind." He thrust the pouch back in his pocket, as if to put away the subject with the trifle which had brought it up.

Arobin dropped in with a message from Mrs. Merriman, to say that the card party was postponed on account of the illness of one of her children.

"How do you do, Arobin?" said Robert, rising from the obscurity.

"Oh! Lebrun. To be sure! I heard yesterday you were back. How did they treat you down in Mexique?"

"Fairly well."

"But not well enough to keep you there. Stunning girls, though, in Mexico. I thought I should never get away from Vera Cruz when I was down there a couple of years ago."

"Did they embroider slippers and tobacco pouches and hat-bands and things for you?" asked Edna.

"Oh! my! no! I didn't get so deep in their regard. I fear they made more impression on me than I made on them."

"You were less fortunate than Robert, then."

"I am always less fortunate than Robert. Has he been imparting tender confidences?"

"I've been imposing myself long enough," said Robert, rising, and shaking hands with Edna. "Please convey my regards to Mr. Pontellier when you write."

He shook hands with Arobin and went away.

"Fine fellow, that Lebrun," said Arobin when Robert had gone. "I never heard you speak of him."

"I knew him last summer at Grand Isle," she replied. "Here is that photograph of yours. Don't you want it?"

"What do I want with it? Throw it away." She threw it back on the table.

"I'm not going to Mrs. Merriman's," she said. "If you see her, tell her so. But perhaps I had better write. I think I shall write now, and say that I am sorry her child is sick, and tell her not to count on me."

"It would be a good scheme," acquiesced Arobin. "I don't blame you; stupid lot!"

Edna opened the blotter, and having procured paper and pen, began to write the note. Arobin lit a cigar and read the evening paper, which he had in his pocket.

"What is the date?" she asked. He told her.

"Will you mail this for me when you go out?"

"Certainly." He read to her little bits out of the newspaper, while she straightened things on the table.

"What do you want to do?" he asked, throwing aside the paper. "Do you want to go out for a walk or a drive or anything? It would be a fine night to drive."

"No; I don't want to do anything but just be quiet. You go away and amuse yourself. Don't stay."

"I'll go away if I must; but I shan't amuse myself. You know that I only live when I am near you."

He stood up to bid her good night.

"Is that one of the things you always say to women?"

"I have said it before, but I don't think I ever came so near meaning it," he answered with a smile. There were no warm lights in her eyes; only a dreamy, absent look.

"Good night. I adore you. Sleep well," he said, and he kissed her hand and went away.

She stayed alone in a kind of reverie—a sort of stupor. Step by step she lived over every instant of the time she had been with Robert after he had entered Mademoiselle Reisz's door. She recalled his words, his looks. How few and meager they had been for her hungry heart! A vision—a transcendently seductive vision of a Mexican girl arose before her. She writhed with a jealous pang. She wondered when he would come back. He had not said he would come back. She had been with him, had heard his voice and touched his hand. But some way he had seemed nearer to her off there in Mexico.

XXXV

The morning was full of sunlight and hope. Edna could see before her no denial—only the promise of excessive joy. She lay in bed awake, with bright eyes full of speculation. "He loves you, poor fool." If she could but get that conviction firmly fixed in her mind, what mattered about the rest? She felt she had been childish and unwise the night before in giving herself over to despondency. She recapitulated the motives which no doubt explained Robert's reserve. They were not insurmountable; they would not hold if he really loved her; they could not hold against her own passion, which he must come to realize in time. She pictured him going to his business that morning. She even saw how he was dressed; how he walked down one street, and turned the corner of another; saw him bending over his desk, talking to people who entered the office, going to his lunch, and perhaps watching for her on the street. He would come to her in the afternoon or evening, sit and roll his cigarette, talk a little, and go away as he had done the night before. But how delicious it would be to have him there with her! She would have no regrets, nor seek to penetrate his reserve if he still chose to wear it.

Edna ate her breakfast only half dressed. The maid brought her a delicious printed scrawl from Raoul, expressing his love, asking her to send him some bonbons, and telling her they had found that morning ten tiny white pigs all lying in a row beside Lidie's big white pig.

A letter also came from her husband, saying he hoped to be back early in March, and then they would get ready for that journey abroad which he had promised her so long, which he felt now fully able to afford; he felt able to travel as people should, without any thought of small economies—thanks to his recent speculations in Wall Street.

Much to her surprise she received a note from Arobin, written at midnight from the club. It was to say good morning to her, to hope she had slept well, to assure her of his devotion, which he trusted she in some faintest manner returned.

All these letters were pleasing to her. She answered the children in a cheerful frame of mind, promising them bonbons, and congratulating them upon their happy find of the little pigs.

She answered her husband with friendly evasiveness,—not with any fixed design to mislead him, only because all sense of reality had gone out of her life; she had abandoned herself to Fate, and awaited the consequences with indifference.

To Arobin's note she made no reply. She put it under Celestine's stove-lid.

Edna worked several hours with much spirit. She saw no one but a picture dealer, who asked her if it were true that she was going abroad to study in Paris.

She said possibly she might, and he negotiated with her for some Parisian studies to reach him in time for the holiday trade in December.

Robert did not come that day. She was keenly disappointed. He did not come the following day, nor the next. Each morning she awoke with hope, and each night she was a prey to despondency. She was tempted to seek him out. But far from yielding to the impulse, she avoided any occasion which might throw her in his way. She did not go to Mademoiselle Reisz's nor pass by Madame Lebrun's, as she might have done if he had still been in Mexico.

When Arobin, one night, urged her to drive with him, she went—out to the lake, on the Shell Road.[82] His horses were full of mettle, and even a little unmanageable. She liked the rapid gait at which they spun along, and

[82] A wide, well-paved road around Lake Pontchartrain, popular for carriage rides.

the quick, sharp sound of the horses' hoofs on the hard road. They did not stop anywhere to eat or to drink. Arobin was not needlessly imprudent. But they ate and they drank when they regained Edna's little dining-room—which was comparatively early in the evening.

It was late when he left her. It was getting to be more than a passing whim with Arobin to see her and be with her. He had detected the latent sensuality, which unfolded under his delicate sense of her nature's requirements like a torpid, torrid, sensitive blossom.

There was no despondency when she fell asleep that night; nor was there hope when she awoke in the morning.

XXXVI

There was a garden out in the suburbs; a small, leafy corner, with a few green tables under the orange trees. An old cat slept all day on the stone step in the sun, and an old *mulatresse*[83] slept her idle hours away in her chair at the open window, till some one happened to knock on one of the green tables. She had milk and cream cheese to sell, and bread and butter. There was no one who could make such excellent coffee or fry a chicken so golden brown as she.

The place was too modest to attract the attention of people of fashion, and so quiet as to have escaped the notice of those in search of pleasure and dissipation. Edna had discovered it accidentally one day when the high-board gate stood ajar. She caught sight of a little green table, blotched with the checkered sunlight that filtered through the quivering leaves overhead. Within she had found the slumbering *mulatresse,* the drowsy cat, and a glass of milk which reminded her of the milk she had tasted in Iberville.

She often stopped there during her perambulations; sometimes taking a book with her, and sitting an hour or two under the trees when she found the place deserted. Once or twice she took a quiet dinner there alone, having instructed Celestine beforehand to prepare no dinner at home. It was the last place in the city where she would have expected to meet any one she knew.

Still she was not astonished when, as she was partaking of a modest dinner late in the afternoon, looking into an open book, stroking the cat, which had made friends with her—she was not greatly astonished to see Robert come in at the tall garden gate.

"I am destined to see you only by accident," she said, shoving the cat off the chair beside her. He was surprised, ill at ease, almost embarrassed at meeting her thus so unexpectedly.

"Do you come here often?" he asked.

"I almost live here," she said.

"I used to drop in very often for a cup of Catiche's good coffee. This is the first time since I came back."

"She'll bring you a plate, and you will share my dinner. There's always enough for two—even three." Edna had intended to be indifferent and as reserved as he when she met him; she had reached the determination by a

[83] Mulatto woman, of mixed white and Negro descent.

laborious train of reasoning, incident to one of her despondent moods. But her resolve melted when she saw him before her, seated there beside her in the little garden, as if a designing Providence had led him into her path.

"Why have you kept away from me, Robert?" she asked, closing the book that lay open upon the table.

"Why are you so personal, Mrs. Pontellier? Why do you force me to idiotic subterfuges?" he exclaimed with sudden warmth. "I suppose there's no use telling you I've been very busy, or that I've been sick, or that I've been to see you and not found you at home. Please let me off with any one of these excuses."

"You are the embodiment of selfishness," she said. "You save yourself something—I don't know what—but there is some selfish motive, and in sparing yourself you never consider for a moment what I think, or how I feel your neglect and indifference. I suppose this is what you would call unwomanly; but I have got into a habit of expressing myself. It doesn't matter to me, and you may think me unwomanly if you like."

"No; I only think you cruel, as I said the other day. Maybe not intentionally cruel; but you seem to be forcing me into disclosures which can result in nothing; as if you would have me bare a wound for the pleasure of looking at it, without the intention or power of healing it."

"I'm spoiling your dinner, Robert; never mind what I say. You haven't eaten a morsel."

"I only came in for a cup of coffee." His sensitive face was all disfigured with excitement.

"Isn't this a delightful place?" she remarked. "I am so glad it has never actually been discovered. It is so quiet, so sweet, here. Do you notice there is scarcely a sound to be heard? It's so out of the way; and a good walk from the car. However, I don't mind walking. I always feel so sorry for women who don't like to walk; they miss so much—so many rare little glimpses of life; and we women learn so little of life on the whole.

"Catiche's coffee is always hot. I don't know how she manages it, here in the open air. Celestine's coffee gets cold bringing it from the kitchen to the dining-room. Three lumps! How can you drink it so sweet? Take some of the cress with your chop; it's so biting and crisp. Then there's the advantage of being able to smoke with your coffee out here. Now, in the city—aren't you going to smoke?"

"After a while," he said, laying a cigar on the table.

"Who gave it to you?" she laughed.

"I bought it. I suppose I'm getting reckless; I bought a whole box." She was determined not to be personal again and make him uncomfortable.

The cat made friends with him, and climbed into his lap when he smoked his cigar. He stroked her silky fur, and talked a little about her. He looked at Edna's book, which he had read; and he told her the end, to save her the trouble of wading through it, he said.

Again he accompanied her back to her home; and it was after dusk when they reached the little "pigeon-house." She did not ask him to remain, which he was grateful for, as it permitted him to stay without the discomfort of blundering through an excuse which he had no intention of considering. He helped her to light the lamp; then she went into her room to take off her hat and to bathe her face and hands.

When she came back Robert was not examining the pictures and magazines as before; he sat off in the shadow, leaning his head back on the chair as if in a reverie. Edna lingered a moment beside the table, arranging the books there. Then she went across the room to where he sat. She bent over the arm of his chair and called his name.

"Robert," she said, "are you asleep?"

"No," he answered, looking up at her.

She leaned over and kissed him—a soft, cool, delicate kiss, whose voluptuous sting penetrated his whole being—then she moved away from him. He followed, and took her in his arms, just holding her close to him. She put her hand up to his face and pressed his cheek against her own. The action was full of love and tenderness. He sought her lips again. Then he drew her down upon the sofa beside him and held her hand in both of his.

"Now you know," he said, "now you know what I have been fighting against since last summer at Grand Isle; what drove me away and drove me back again."

"Why have you been fighting against it?" she asked. Her face glowed with soft lights.

"Why? Because you were not free; you were Léonce Pontellier's wife. I couldn't help loving you if you were ten times his wife; but so long as I went away from you and kept away I could help telling you so." She put her free hand up to his shoulder, and then against his cheek, rubbing it softly. He kissed her again. His face was warm and flushed.

"There in Mexico I was thinking of you all the time, and longing for you."

"But not writing to me," she interrupted.

"Something put into my head that you cared for me; and I lost my senses. I forgot everything but a wild dream of your some way becoming my wife."

"Your wife!"

"Religion, loyalty, everything would give way if only you cared."

"Then you must have forgotten that I was Léonce Pontellier's wife."

"Oh! I was demented, dreaming of wild, impossible things, recalling men who had set their wives free, we have heard of such things."

"Yes, we have heard of such things."

"I came back full of vague, mad intentions. And when I got here—"

"When you got here you never came near me!" She was still caressing his cheek.

"I realized what a cur I was to dream of such a thing, even if you had been willing."

She took his face between her hands and looked into it as if she would never withdraw her eyes more. She kissed him on the forehead, the eyes, the cheeks, and the lips.

"You have been a very, very foolish boy, wasting your time dreaming of impossible things when you speak of Mr. Pontellier setting me free! I am no longer one of Mr. Pontellier's possessions to dispose of or not. I give myself where I choose. If he were to say, 'Here, Robert, take her and be happy; she is yours,' I should laugh at you both."

His face grew a little white. "What do you mean?" he asked.

There was a knock at the door. Old Celestine came in to say that Madame Ratignolle's servant had come around the back way with a message that Madame had been taken sick and begged Mrs. Pontellier to go to her immediately.

"Yes, yes," said Edna, rising; "I promised. Tell her yes—to wait for me. I'll go back with her."

"Let me walk over with you," offered Robert.

"No," she said; "I will go with the servant." She went into her room to put on her hat, and when she came in again she sat once more upon the sofa beside him. He had not stirred. She put her arms about his neck.

"Good-by, my sweet Robert. Tell me good-by." He kissed her with a degree of passion which had not before entered into his caress, and strained her to him.

"I love you," she whispered, "only you; no one but you. It was you who awoke me last summer out of a life-long, stupid dream. Oh! you have made me so unhappy with your indifference. Oh! I have suffered, suffered! Now you are here we shall love each other, my Robert. We shall be everything to each other. Nothing else in the world is of any consequence. I must go to my friend; but you will wait for me? No matter how late; you will wait for me, Robert?"

"Don't go; don't go! Oh! Edna, stay with me," he pleaded. "Why should you go? Stay with me, stay with me."

"I shall come back as soon as I can; I shall find you here." She buried her face in his neck, and said good-by again. Her seductive voice, together with his great love for her, had enthralled his senses, had deprived him of every impulse but the longing to hold her and keep her.

XXXVII

Edna looked in at the drug store. Monsieur Ratignolle was putting up a mixture himself, very carefully, dropping a red liquid into a tiny glass. He was grateful to Edna for having come; her presence would be a comfort to his wife. Madame Ratignolle's sister, who had always been with her at such trying times, had not been able to come up from the plantation, and Adèle had been inconsolable until Mrs. Pontellier so kindly promised to come to her. The nurse had been with them at night for the past week, as she lived a great distance away. And Dr. Mandelet had been coming and going all the afternoon. They were then looking for him any moment.

Edna hastened upstairs by a private stairway that led from the rear of the store to the apartments above. The children were all sleeping in a back room. Madame Ratignolle was in the salon, whither she had strayed in her suffering impatience. She sat on the sofa, clad in an ample white *peignoir,* holding a handkerchief tight in her hand with a nervous clutch. Her face was drawn and pinched, her sweet blue eyes haggard and unnatural. All her beautiful hair had been drawn back and plaited. It lay in a long braid on the sofa pillow, coiled like a golden serpent. The nurse, a comfortable looking *Griffe* woman[84] in white apron and cap, was urging her to return to her bedroom.

[84] A mulatto.

"There is no use, there is no use," she said at once to Edna. "We must get rid of Mandelet; he is getting too old and careless. He said he would be here at half-past seven; now it must be eight. See what time it is, Joséphine."

The woman was possessed of a cheerful nature, and refused to take any situation too seriously, especially a situation with which she was so familiar. She urged Madame to have courage and patience. But Madame only set her teeth hard into her under lip, and Edna saw the sweat gather in beads on her white forehead. After a moment or two she uttered a profound sigh and wiped her face with the handkerchief rolled in a ball. She appeared exhausted. The nurse gave her a fresh handkerchief, sprinkled with cologne water.

"This is too much!" she cried. "Mandelet ought to be killed! Where is Alphonse? Is it possible I am to be abandoned like this—neglected by every one?"

"Neglected, indeed!" exclaimed the nurse. Wasn't she there? And here was Mrs. Pontellier leaving, no doubt, a pleasant evening at home to devote to her? And wasn't Monsieur Ratignolle coming that very instant through the hall? And Joséphine was quite sure she had heard Doctor Mandelet's *coupé*.[85] Yes, there it was, down at the door.

Adèle consented to go back to her room. She sat on the edge of a little low couch next to her bed.

Doctor Mandelet paid no attention to Madame Ratignolle's upbraidings. He was accustomed to them at such times, and was too well convinced of her loyalty to doubt it.

He was glad to see Edna, and wanted her to go with him into the salon and entertain him. But Madame Ratignolle would not consent that Edna should leave her for an instant. Between agonizing moments, she chatted a little, and said it took her mind off her sufferings.

Edna began to feel uneasy. She was seized with a vague dread. Her own like experiences seemed far away, unreal, and only half remembered. She recalled faintly an ecstasy of pain, the heavy odor of chloroform, a stupor which had deadened sensation, and an awakening to find a little new life to which she had given being, added to the great unnumbered multitude of souls that come and go.

She began to wish she had not come; her presence was not necessary. She might have invented a pretext for staying away; she might even invent a pretext now for going. But Edna did not go. With an inward agony, with a flaming, outspoken revolt against the ways of Nature, she witnessed the scene of torture.

She was still stunned and speechless with emotion when later she leaned over her friend to kiss her and softly say good-by. Adèle, pressing her cheek, whispered in an exhausted voice: "Think of the children, Edna. Oh think of the children! Remember them!"

[85] A short carriage for two people.

XXXVIII

Edna still felt dazed when she got outside in the open air. The Doctor's *coupé* had returned for him and stood before the *porte cochère.* She did not wish to enter the *coupé,* and told Doctor Mandelet she would walk; she was not afraid, and would go alone. He directed his carriage to meet him at Mrs. Pontellier's, and he started to walk home with her.

Up—away up, over the narrow street between the tall houses, the stars were blazing. The air was mild and caressing, but cool with the breath of spring and the night. They walked slowly, the Doctor with a heavy, measured tread and his hands behind him; Edna, in an absent-minded way, as she had walked one night at Grand Isle, as if her thoughts had gone ahead of her and she was striving to overtake them.

"You shouldn't have been there, Mrs. Pontellier," he said. "That was no place for you. Adèle is full of whims at such times. There were a dozen women she might have had with her, unimpressionable women. I felt that it was cruel, cruel. You shouldn't have gone."

"Oh, well!" she answered, indifferently. "I don't know that it matters after all. One has to think of the children some time or other; the sooner the better."

"When is Léonce coming back?"

"Quite soon. Some time in March."

"And you are going abroad?"

"Perhaps—no, I am not going. I'm not going to be forced into doing things. I don't want to go abroad. I want to be let alone. Nobody has any right—except children, perhaps—and even then, it seems to me—or it did seem—" She felt that her speech was voicing the incoherency of her thoughts, and stopped abruptly.

"The trouble is," sighed the Doctor, grasping her meaning intuitively, "that youth is given up to illusions. It seems to be a provision of Nature; a decoy to secure mothers for the race. And Nature takes no account of moral consequences, of arbitrary conditions which we create, and which we feel obliged to maintain at any cost."

"Yes," she said. "The years that are gone seem like dreams—if one might go on sleeping and dreaming—but to wake up and find—oh! well! perhaps it is better to wake up after all, even to suffer, rather than to remain a dupe to illusions all one's life."

"It seems to me, my dear child," said the Doctor at parting, holding her hand, "you seem to me to be in trouble. I am not going to ask for your confidence. I will only say that if ever you feel moved to give it to me, perhaps I might help you. I know I would understand, and I tell you there are not many who would—not many, my dear."

"Some way I don't feel moved to speak of things that trouble me. Don't think I am ungrateful or that I don't appreciate your sympathy. There are periods of despondency and suffering which take possession of me. But I don't want anything but my own way. That is wanting a good deal, of course, when you have to trample upon the lives, the hearts, the prejudices of others—but no matter—still, I shouldn't want to trample upon the little lives. Oh! I don't know what I'm saying, Doctor. Good night. Don't blame me for anything."

"Yes, I will blame you if you don't come and see me soon. We will talk of things you never have dreamt of talking about before. It will do us both good. I don't want you to blame yourself, whatever comes. Good night, my child."

She let herself in at the gate, but instead of entering she sat upon the step of the porch. The night was quiet and soothing. All the tearing emotion of the last few hours seemed to fall away from her like a somber, uncomfortable garment, which she had but to loosen to be rid of. She went back to that hour before Adèle had sent for her; and her senses kindled afresh in thinking of Robert's words, the pressure of his arms, and the feeling of his lips upon her own. She could picture at that moment no greater bliss on earth than possession of the beloved one. His expression of love had already given him to her in part. When she thought that he was there at hand, waiting for her, she grew numb with the intoxication of expectancy. It was so late; he would be asleep perhaps. She would awaken him with a kiss. She hoped he would be asleep that she might arouse him with her caresses.

Still, she remembered Adèle's voice whispering, "Think of the children; think of them." She meant to think of them; that determination had driven into her soul like a death wound—but not tonight. Tomorrow would be time to think of everything.

Robert was not waiting for her in the little parlor. He was nowhere at hand. The house was empty. But he had scrawled on a piece of paper that lay in the lamplight:

"I love you. Good-by—because I love you."

Edna grew faint when she read the words. She went and sat on the sofa. Then she stretched herself out there, never uttering a sound. She did not sleep. She did not go to bed. The lamp sputtered and went out. She was still awake in the morning, when Celestine unlocked the kitchen door and came in to light the fire.

XXXIX

Victor, with hammer and nails and scraps of scantling,[86] was patching a corner of one of the galleries. Mariequita sat near by, dangling her legs, watching him work, and handing him nails from the tool-box. The sun was beating down upon them. The girl had covered her head with her apron folded into a square pad. They had been talking for an hour or more. She was never tired of hearing Victor describe the dinner at Mrs. Pontellier's. He exaggerated every detail, making it appear a veritable Lucullean[87] feast. The flowers were in tubs, he said. The champagne was quaffed from huge golden goblets. Venus rising from the foam[88] could have presented no more entrancing a spectacle than Mrs. Pontellier, blazing with beauty

[86] Small boards.

[87] Extravagant. Lucullus was a first-century B.C. Roman consul famous for his wealth and luxury.

[88] Venus, the Roman goddess of love, was born from the ocean foam.

and diamonds at the head of the board, while the other women were all of them youthful houris,[89] possessed of incomparable charms.

She got it into her head that Victor was in love with Mrs. Pontellier, and he gave her evasive answers, framed so as to confirm her belief. She grew sullen and cried a little, threatening to go off and leave him to his fine ladies. There were a dozen men crazy about her at the *Chénière;* and since it was the fashion to be in love with married people, why, she could run away any time she liked to New Orleans with Célina's husband.

Célina's husband was a fool, a coward, and a pig, and to prove it to her, Victor intended to hammer his head into a jelly the next time he encountered him. This assurance was very consoling to Mariequita. She dried her eyes, and grew cheerful at the prospect.

They were still talking of the dinner and the allurements of city life when Mrs. Pontellier herself slipped around the corner of the house. The two youngsters stayed dumb with amazement before what they considered to be an apparition. But it was really she in flesh and blood, looking tired and a little travel-stained.

"I walked up from the wharf," she said, "and heard the hammering. I supposed it was you, mending the porch. It's a good thing. I was always tripping over those loose planks last summer. How dreary and deserted everything looks!"

It took Victor some little time to comprehend that she had come in Beaudelet's lugger, that she had come alone, and for no purpose but to rest.

"There's nothing fixed up yet, you see. I'll give you my room; it's the only place."

"Any corner will do," she assured him.

"And if you can stand Philomel's cooking," he went on, "though I might try to get her mother while you are here. Do you think she would come?" turning to Mariequita.

Mariequita thought that perhaps Philomel's mother might come for a few days, and money enough.

Beholding Mrs. Pontellier make her appearance, the girl had at once suspected a lovers' rendezvous. But Victor's astonishment was so genuine, and Mrs. Pontellier's indifference so apparent, that the disturbing notion did not lodge long in her brain. She contemplated with the greatest interest this woman who gave the most sumptuous dinners in America, and who had all the men in New Orleans at her feet.

"What time will you have dinner?" asked Edna. "I'm very hungry; but don't get anything extra."

"I'll have it ready in little or no time," he said, bustling and packing away his tools. "You may go to my room to brush up and rest yourself. Mariequita will show you."

"Thank you," said Edna. "But, do you know, I have a notion to go down to the beach and take a good wash and even a little swim, before dinner?"

"The water is too cold!" they both exclaimed. "Don't think of it."

"Well, I might go down and try—dip my toes in. Why, it seems to me

[89]Nymphs; the beautiful virgins provided in Paradise to faithful Moslems.

the sun is hot enough to have warmed the very depths of the ocean. Could you get me a couple of towels? I'd better go right away, so as to be back in time. It would be a little too chilly if I waited till this afternoon."

Mariequita ran over to Victor's room, and returned with some towels, which she gave to Edna.

"I hope you have fish for dinner," said Edna, as she started to walk away; "but don't do anything extra if you haven't."

"Run and find Philomel's mother," Victor instructed the girl. "I'll go to the kitchen and see what I can do. By Gimminy! Women have no consideration! She might have sent me word."

Edna walked on down to the beach rather mechanically, not noticing anything special except that the sun was hot. She was not dwelling upon any particular train of thought. She had done all the thinking which was necessary after Robert went away, when she lay awake upon the sofa till morning.

She had said over and over to herself: "Today it is Arobin; tomorrow it will be some one else. It makes no difference to me, it doesn't matter about Léonce Pontellier—but Raoul and Etienne!" She understood now clearly what she had meant long ago when she said to Adèle Ratignolle that she would give up the unessential, but she would never sacrifice herself for her children.

Despondency had come upon her there in the wakeful night, and had never lifted. There was no one thing in the world that she desired. There was no human being whom she wanted near her except Robert; and she even realized that the day would come when he, too, and the thought of him would melt out of her existence, leaving her alone. The children appeared before her like antagonists who had overcome her; who had overpowered her and sought to drag her into the soul's slavery for the rest of her days. But she knew a way to elude them. She was not thinking of these things when she walked down to the beach.

The water of the Gulf stretched out before her, gleaming with the million lights of the sun. The voice of the sea is seductive, never ceasing, whispering, clamoring, murmuring, inviting the soul to wander in abysses of solitude. All along the white beach, up and down, there was no living thing in sight. A bird with a broken wing was beating the air above, reeling, fluttering, circling disabled down, down to the water.

Edna had found her old bathing suit still hanging, faded, upon its accustomed peg.

She put it on, leaving her clothing in the bath-house. But when she was there beside the sea, absolutely alone, she cast the unpleasant, pricking garments from her, and for the first time in her life she stood naked in the open air, at the mercy of the sun, the breeze that beat upon her, and the waves that invited her.

How strange and awful it seemed to stand naked under the sky! how delicious! She felt like some new-born creature, opening its eyes in a familiar world that it had never known.

The foamy wavelets curled up to her white feet, and coiled like serpents about her ankles. She walked out. The water was chill, but she walked on. The water was deep, but she lifted her white body and reached out with a long, sweeping stroke. The touch of the sea is sensuous, enfolding the body in its soft, close embrace.

She went on and on. She remembered the night she swam far out, and recalled the terror that seized her at the fear of being unable to regain the shore. She did not look back now, but went on and on, thinking of the blue-grass meadow that she had traversed when a little child, believing that it had no beginning and no end.

Her arms and legs were growing tired.

She thought of Léonce and the children. They were a part of her life. But they need not have thought that they could possess her, body and soul. How Mademoiselle Reisz would have laughed, perhaps sneered, if she knew! "And you call yourself an artist! What pretensions, Madame! The artist must possess the courageous soul that dares and defies."

Exhaustion was pressing upon and overpowering her.

"Good-by—because I love you." He did not know; he did not understand. He would never understand. Perhaps Doctor Mandelet would have understood if she had seen him—but it was too late; the shore was far behind her, and her strength was gone.

She looked into the distance, and the old terror flamed up for an instant, then sank again. Edna heard her father's voice and her sister Margaret's. She heard the barking of an old dog that was chained to the sycamore tree. The spurs of the cavalry officer clanged as he walked across the porch. There was the hum of bees, and the musky odor of pinks filled the air.

Anton Chekhov

(1860–1904)

Several streams flowed into the river that became the modern theater—the biting social realism of Ibsen, the hallucinatory dream visions of Strindberg, the defiant absurdism of Alfred Jarry—but none more important than that of the four major plays of the Russian dramatist Anton Chekhov. Uncle Vanya, The Seagull, The Three Sisters, *and* The Cherry Orchard *are plays that altered dramatic form to make it expressive of a distinctly "modern" view of human personality—multilayered, governed at least as much by unconscious forces as by conscious ones, full of tensions and contradictions between desire and action, expressed in language which, oftener than not, is designed to conceal or relieve half-understood feelings rather than to communicate. The dramatist Chekhov, inimitable, has nevertheless been imitated in some ways by most of the major dramatists of the twentieth century. His impact has been just as great upon the modern short story, which he created in the same sense that he created modern drama, altering the traditional form of short fiction to express the same sort of modern perception of human reality that his dramas express.*

Chekhov was born in 1860 in the southern Russian seaport town of Taganrog, where his father, a former serf and a rigid taskmaster to his family, ran a gradually failing grocery. Chekhov helped in the family business and attended the local schools, entering when he was nine the local gymnasium *or high school, where he remained for ten years. When he was sixteen, his father went bankrupt and escaped creditors by moving the family to Moscow. Chekhov remained behind, supporting himself for the last three years of his schooling by tutoring younger students. When he graduated at the age of nineteen, he followed the family to Moscow, where his father was slipping into bankruptcy again. Chekhov took over financial support of the family as well as entering the five-year medical program at Moscow University; he paid his own expenses and those of his family by free-lance writing of comic sketches for humorous magazines. He continued writing even after he became a doctor in 1884; the humorous, popular writing of the years between 1879 and 1888 forms an enormous body of work largely unknown today but crucial in the forming of his technical skill.*

The publication of a long story named "The Steppe" in a leading Russian literary journal in 1888 marked the beginning of a new phase in Chekhov's career. Already he had begun to experiment with stories and sketches in a more serious vein, and "The Steppe," an account of a journey through the Ukraine as seen through the eyes of a child, established the mode of his fiction for the last sixteen years of his life. A few of his earlier stories have been resurrected from the ephemeral journals in which they were published, but for the most part Chekhov's reputation in fiction rests upon about fifty stories written after 1888.

At the same time that Chekhov was moving in the direction of greater seriousness and complexity in his stories, he was experimenting with deepening and enriching his dramatic work. His Ivanov *(1887), a comparatively traditional work, had been successful both in Moscow and Petersburg, and he had written skillful short popular farces, or "vaudevilles"—"The Bear," "The Marriage Proposal," "The Wedding"—which are still frequently produced. But in 1888–89, he also wrote a long, rather verbose play named* The Wood Demon, *which, despite its failure in a Moscow production, represented a new experimental direction in Chekhov's playwriting. "The play is awfully strange," he confided to a friend, "and I wonder that such strange things should come from my pen."* The Wood Demon *was later to be transformed into* Uncle Vanya *(1897).*

Between 1890 and 1892, Chekhov was also deeply involved in medical and scientific work. In 1890, he made an extended trip to a Russian penal settlement on the remote island of Sakhalin, off the east coast of Siberia; he published the results of his investigation in The Island of Sakhalin *(1893–94). He also worked diligently in relief programs during the disastrous peasant famines of 1891 and 1892.*

From 1892 until 1898, Chekhov lived on a small estate he bought in the village of Melikhova, about fifty miles south of Moscow. He moved his elderly parents to the estate and cared for them, with the help of his unmarried sister Mariya, who became the housekeeper. The Melikhova years were among the most productive of Chekhov's life; he wrote many of his greatest short stories here, as well as a second full-length play, The Seagull, *disastrously produced in St. Petersburg in 1896 in one of the most humiliating experiences of Chekhov's life.*

During the later Melikhova years, Chekhov began to develop troubling symptoms of tuberculosis, the disease which had killed his irresponsible but lovable brother Nikolay in 1889. In 1897, he experienced a serious lung hemorrhage and was forced to sell the Melikhova estate and move to a villa in the more temperate climate of Yalta, a resort on the Crimean coast. The remaining seven years of his life were largely devoted to drama, although several of his greatest short stories, including "The Lady with a Dog," date from the Yalta years. In 1898, the failed Seagull *was revived as one of the first productions of the newly established Moscow Art Theater, under the direction of Konstantine Stanislavsky. It was an enormous success; the emblem of the Moscow Art Theater, one of the great theaters of the world, is still a stylized seagull. Chekhov, to provide Stanislavsky with a new play, offered* Uncle Vanya, *already radically revised from* The Wood Demon *and successfully produced in the provinces. It was produced at the Moscow Art Theater in 1899 and was also a success, though a more modest one than* The Seagull, *baffling many members of the audience.*

Chekhov's physical condition was worsening rapidly and he was unable to attend the Moscow performances of either The Seagull *or* Uncle Vanya. *He had, however, been able to attend one of the rehearsals of* The Seagull *and had fallen in love with Olga Knipper, the actress who played Nina; they were married in 1901, and the marriage was a very happy one, though Chekhov was confined to Yalta by his illness and Knipper, deeply committed to her work, remained in Moscow for the theater season each year. The Art Theater had toured the Crimea in 1900 and had performed both* The Seagull *and* Uncle Vanya *for Chekhov at Sevastapol and Yalta. His third play,* The Three Sisters, *was modestly successful in its first performance at the Moscow Art Theater in January, 1901; Chekhov, defying the advice of his doctors, had gone to Moscow and taken an active part in rehearsals.*

Chekhov began his masterpiece, The Cherry Orchard, *about the time of his marriage. The culmination of his rich, ironic technique, it took shape over a period of three years, reaching production on January 17, 1904, Chekhov's birthday and the occasion of an elaborate and moving series of tributes to him by his theatrical colleagues. He lived only six months more, dying in the German resort town of Badenweiler on July 14, 1904.*

Sigmund Freud once replied, when asked for a definition of a healthy life, that it consisted of being able to love and being able to work. He might have been describing Chekhov's view of life. Chekhov's world is an uncertain, indeterminate one which seems to be slowly falling apart. Social change, economic pressure, and philosophical doubt have left his characters uncertain of who they are and what goals they should adopt. All his plays and most of his stories take place not in the great centers of social and intellectual life but in the country in little provincial towns, and the sense of being out of touch with things, of being somehow in the backwaters, becomes symbolic of his characters' psychological positions as well. Chekhov's stories and plays meticulously etch the discouragement and disillusionment Russian intellectuals felt in the years following the failed reforms of Czar Alexander II in the 1860s and '70s and, at the same time, anticipate the modern Wasteland.

But Chekhov's work is never depressing or despairing. His characters may be confused or defeated, but their successes and failures are consistently placed against a background of a deep faith in the redemptive power of love and work, love even when it is refused or unreciprocated, work even when its long-range effects cannot be seen. In every Chekhov play and in many of the stories, someone eventually expresses Chekhov's faith in work, as Trofimov does, for example, in The Cherry Orchard: *"It is clear that to begin to live in the present we must first expiate our past, we must break with it; and we can expiate it only by suffering, by extraordinary unceasing labor." (The fact that, of all the characters in* The Cherry Orchard, *Trofimov is one of those least capable of either love or work is a Chekhovian irony that does not invalidate his point.)*

Chekhov never developed his simple faith into a systematic philosophy, and he seems to have been completely indifferent to the many pre-Revolutionary political movements fermenting in Russia during his lifetime. On one issue, however, he seems to have taken something of a stand, though a characteristically mild and indirect one. In the late 1880's, he had been much influenced by Tolstoy's doctrines of the holiness of the simple life and of nonresistance to violence and evil. Tolstoy's passivity and quietism were fundamentally alien to Chekhov's character, however, and in a number of stories of the nineties and in at least one play, The Three Sisters, he deals tellingly with the necessity to resist evil actively and with the illusions involved in fantasies of simple, earthy life. In the great story "Ward Number Six" (1892), for example, he tells the story of a doctor who does nothing to improve conditions in the wretched mental ward in his charge and ends up committed there himself. In The Three Sisters, the voracious Natalya gradually takes over the entire house of her sisters-in-law, who are unwilling ever to take a firm stand against her. And in the trio of 1898 stories, "The Man in a Shell," "Gooseberries," and "About Love," Chekhov deals with various sorts of self-deluded retreats from life and reality.

"Gooseberries" is one of Chekhov's greatest and most characteristic stories. On the surface, it seems curiously actionless and unresolved, a comic but shallow anecdote about a petty civil servant who acts out a sort of pop-cult Tolstoyan fantasy. But on second reading, the foolish Nikolay recedes in importance; we realize that the protagonist of the story is the frame-narrator Ivan Ivanovitch and that the climax of the story is his own spiritual crisis which his visit to his brother has triggered, his own vision of "general hypnotism." It seems a valid and moving vision, but we wonder. It has brought Ivan Ivanovitch to the point that "there is no spectacle more painful" than the sight of "a happy family sitting around the table drinking tea." Perhaps it is true that "the fact that lovely Pelagea was moving noiselessly about was better than any story."

Chekhov usually expressed his aims in drama in terms of a quiet, literal realism: "A play should be written in which people arrive, go away, have dinner, talk about the weather, and play cards. Life must be exactly as it is, and people as they are—not on stilts. . . . Let everything on the stage be just as complicated, and at the same time just as simple as it is in life." This will do as a loose description of The Cherry Orchard, but it does not suggest the play's meticulous artistry, in which each detail is as carefully controlled as in a lyric poem. Chekhov's plays are sometimes said to be "plotless," perhaps because people have trouble recognizing familiar plot elements when they are presented in unfamiliar ways. The Cherry Orchard has buried in it the rigid structure of a nineteenth-century "dispossession" melodrama, complete with foreclosing villain, grieving old mother, and paired young lovers. But Chekhov shifts the emphasis from melodramatic action to human reaction; the climactic auction, like most of the rest of the story, takes place offstage. And the stock characters are humanized and given contradictory motives. Lopahin loves the Ranevskys and is desperate to help them save their estate (though the ex-serf in him is also capable of gloating, understandably, over owning it himself). Lyubov, passionate, sentimental, charming, and self-destructive, is poles away from the white-haired old mother of theatrical cliché. And Trofimov and Anya are a most unexpected set of young lovers, being "above love" (at least according to Trofimov).

For the mechanical tricks of melodramatic plotting, Chekhov substitutes a simple pattern of arrival and departure ("people arrive and go away"); for stock theatrical characters, he substitutes real people, lovingly and meticulously observed ("not on stilts"); and for theatrical rhetoric, he substitutes the shifting, treacherous currents of *real speech, full of abrupt changes, apparent irrelevancies, and unconscious revelations of an emotional "subtext" under the "text" of rational intention. The result is one of the greatest of modern plays: a study of the decline and fall of a charming but doomed culture, a guarded but optimistic expression of hope for the future, and a timeless exploration of confused and groping but infinitely precious humanity.*

FURTHER READING *(prepared by W. J. R.):* Ronald Hingley's *A New Life of Anton Chekhov,* 1976, is a thorough biography based on much new Chekhov material. Other substantial biographies are David Magarshack's *Chekhov: A Life,* 1953, and Ernest J. Simmons's *Chekhov, A Biography,* 1962. *Anton Chekhov's Life and Thought: Selected Letters and Commentary,* ed. by Simon Karlinsky and trans. by Michael-Henry Heim and Simon Karlinsky, 1976, supplements a generous selection of Chekhov's letters with such extensive commentary that it amounts to a Chekhovian autobiography. Irina Kirk's *Anton Chekhov,* 1981, an introductory study, discusses Chekhov's artistic development, the short stories, and (more briefly) the major plays. David Magarshack's *Chekhov the Dramatist,* 1950, examines Chekhov's development as a playwright in terms of a distinction between plays of direct and of indirect action. Major plays are also discussed in Maurice Valency's *The Breaking String,* 1966, and J. L. Styan's *Chekhov in Performance,* 1971. Chekhov's artistry, his theater, and his personality are examined in *Chekhov: A Collection of Critical Essays,* ed. by Robert Louis Jackson, 1967. *Chekhov's Great Plays: A Critical Anthology,* ed. by Jean-Pierre Barricelli, 1981, is limited to drama and includes excellent essays by most of the leading recent Chekhov critics.

GOOSEBERRIES

Translated by Constance Garnett

The whole sky had been overcast with rain-clouds from early morning; it was a still day, not hot, but heavy, as it is in gray dull weather when the clouds have been hanging over the country for a long while, when one expects rain and it does not come. Ivan Ivanovitch, the veterinary surgeon, and Burkin, the high-school teacher, were already tired from walking, and the fields seemed to them endless. Far ahead of them they could just see the windmills of the village of Mironositskoe; on the right stretched a row of hillocks which disappeared in the distance behind the village, and they both knew that this was the bank of the river, that there were meadows, green willows, homesteads there, and that if one stood on one of the hillocks one could see from it the same vast plain, telegraph-wires, and a train which in the distance looked like a crawling caterpillar, and that in clear weather one could even see the town. Now, in still weather, when all nature seemed mild and dreamy, Ivan Ivanovitch and Burkin were filled with love of that countryside, and both thought how great, how beautiful a land it was.

"Last time we were in Prokofy's barn," said Burkin, "you were about to tell me a story."

"Yes; I meant to tell you about my brother."

Ivan Ivanovitch heaved a deep sigh and lighted a pipe to begin to tell his story, but just at that moment the rain began. And five minutes later heavy rain came down, covering the sky, and it was hard to tell when it would be over. Ivan Ivanovitch and Burkin stopped in hesitation; the dogs, already drenched, stood with their tails between their legs gazing at them feelingly.

"We must take shelter somewhere," said Burkin. "Let us go to Alehin's; it's close by."

"Come along."

They turned aside and walked through mown fields, sometimes going straight forward, sometimes turning to the right, till they came out on the road. Soon they saw poplars, a garden, then the red roofs of barns; there was a gleam of the river, and the view opened on to a broad expanse of water with a windmill and a white bath-house: this was Sofino, where Alehin lived.

The watermill was at work, drowning the sound of the rain; the dam was shaking. Here wet horses with drooping heads were standing near their carts, and men were walking about covered with sacks. It was damp, muddy, and desolate; the water looked cold and malignant. Ivan Ivanovitch and Burkin were already conscious of a feeling of wetness, messiness, and discomfort all over; their feet were heavy with mud, and when, crossing the dam, they went up to the barns, they were silent, as though they were angry with one another.

In one of the barns there was the sound of a winnowing machine,[1] the door was open, and clouds of dust were coming from it. In the doorway was standing Alehin himself, a man of forty, tall and stout, with long hair, more like a professor or an artist than a landowner. He had on a white shirt that badly needed washing, a rope for a belt, drawers instead of trousers, and his boots, too, were plastered up with mud and straw. His eyes and nose were black with dust. He recognized Ivan Ivanovitch and Burkin, and was apparently much delighted to see them.

"Go into the house, gentlemen," he said, smiling; "I'll come directly, this minute."

It was a big two-storied house. Alehin lived in the lower story, with arched ceilings and little windows, where the bailiffs had once lived; here everything was plain, and there was a smell of rye bread, cheap vodka, and harness. He went upstairs into the best rooms only on rare occasions, when visitors came. Ivan Ivanovitch and Burkin were met in the house by a maid-servant, a young woman so beautiful that they both stood still and looked at one another.

"You can't imagine how delighted I am to see you, my friends," said Alehin, going into the hall with them. "It is a surprise! Pelagea," he said, addressing the girl, "give our visitors something to change into. Only I must first go and wash, for I almost think I have not washed since spring. Wouldn't you like to come into the bath-house? and meanwhile they will get things ready here."

Beautiful Pelagea, looking so refined and soft, brought them towels and soap, and Alehin went to the bath-house with his guests.

"It's a long time since I had a wash," he said, undressing. "I have got a nice bath-house, as you see—my father built it—but I somehow never have time to wash."

[1] Threshing machine, to separate grain from chaff.

He sat down on the steps and soaped his long hair and his neck, and the water round him turned brown.

"Yes, I must say," said Ivan Ivanovitch meaningly, looking at his head.

"It's a long time since I washed . . ." said Alehin with embarrassment, giving himself a second soaping, and the water near him turned dark blue, like ink.

Ivan Ivanovitch went outside, plunged into the water with a loud splash, and swam in the rain, flinging his arms out wide. He stirred the water into waves which set the white lilies bobbing up and down; he swam to the very middle of the millpond and dived, and came up a minute later in another place, and swam on, and kept on diving, trying to touch the bottom.

"Oh, my goodness!" he repeated continually, enjoying himself thoroughly. "Oh, my goodness!" He swam to the mill, talked to the peasants there, then returned and lay on his back in the middle of the pond, turning his face to the rain. Burkin and Alehin were dressed and ready to go, but he still went on swimming and diving. "Oh, my goodness! . . ." he said. "Oh, Lord, have mercy on me! . . ."

"That's enough!" Burkin shouted to him.

They went back to the house. And only when the lamp was lighted in the big drawing-room upstairs, and Burkin and Ivan Ivanovitch, attired in silk dressing-gowns and warm slippers, were sitting in arm-chairs; and Alehin, washed and combed, in a new coat, was walking about the drawing-room, evidently enjoying the feeling of warmth, cleanliness, dry clothes, and light shoes; and when lovely Pelagea, stepping noiselessly on the carpet and smiling softly, handed tea and jam on a tray—only then Ivan Ivanovitch began on his story, and it seemed as though not only Burkin and Alehin were listening, but also the ladies, young and old, and the officers who looked down upon them sternly and calmly from their gold frames.

"There are two of us brothers," he began—"I, Ivan Ivanovitch, and my brother, Nikolay Ivanovitch, two years younger. I went in for a learned profession and became a veterinary surgeon, while Nikolay sat in a government office from the time he was nineteen. Our father, Tchimsha-Himalaisky, was a kantonist;[2] but he rose to be an officer and left us a little estate and the rank of nobility. After his death the little estate went in debts and legal expenses; but, anyway, we had spent our childhood running wild in the country. Like peasant children, we passed our days and nights in the fields and the woods, looked after horses, stripped the bark off the trees, fished, and so on. . . . And, you know, whoever has once in his life caught perch or has seen the migrating of the thrushes in autumn, watched how they float in flocks over the village on bright, cool days, he will never be a real townsman, and will have a yearning for freedom to the day of his death. My brother was miserable in the government office. Years passed by, and he went on sitting in the same place, went on writing the same papers and thinking of one and the same thing—how to get into the country. And this yearning by degrees passed into a definite desire, into a dream of buying himself a little farm somewhere on the banks of a river or a lake.

[2] Son of a common soldier, registered at birth in the army.

"He was a gentle, good-natured fellow, and I was fond of him, but I never sympathized with this desire to shut himself up for the rest of his life in a little farm of his own. It's the correct thing to say that a man needs no more than six feet of earth. But six feet is what a corpse needs, not a man. And they say, too, now, that if our intellectual classes are attracted to the land and yearn for a farm, it's a good thing. But these farms are just the same as six feet of earth. To retreat from town, from the struggle, from the bustle of life, to retreat and bury oneself in one's farm—it's not life, it's egoism, laziness, it's monasticism of a sort, but monasticism without good works. A man does not need six feet of earth or a farm, but the whole globe, all nature, where he can have room to display all the qualities and peculiarities of his free spirit.

"My brother Nikolay, sitting in his government office, dreamed of how he would eat his own cabbages, which would fill the whole yard with such a savory smell, take his meals on the green grass, sleep in the sun, sit for whole hours on the seat by the gate gazing at the fields and the forest. Gardening books and the agricultural hints in calendars were his delight, his favorite spiritual sustenance; he enjoyed reading newspapers, too, but the only thing he read in them were the advertisements of so many acres of arable land and a grass meadow with farm-houses and buildings, a river, a garden, a mill and millponds, for sale. And his imagination pictured the garden-paths, flowers and fruit, starling cotes, the carp in the pond, and all that sort of thing, you know. These imaginary pictures were of different kinds according to the advertisements which he came across, but for some reason in every one of them he had always to have gooseberries. He could not imagine a homestead, he could not picture an idyllic nook, without gooseberries.

"'Country life has its conveniences,' he would sometimes say. 'You sit on the verandah and you drink tea, while your ducks swim on the pond, there is a delicious smell everywhere, and . . . and the gooseberries are growing.'

"He used to draw a map of his property, and in every map there were the same things—(*a*) house for the family, (*b*) servants' quarters, (*c*) kitchen garden, (*d*) gooseberry-bushes. He lived parsimoniously, was frugal in food and drink, his clothes were beyond description; he looked like a beggar, but kept on saving and putting money in the bank. He grew fearfully avaricious. I did not like to look at him, and I used to give him something and send him presents for Christmas and Easter, but he used to save that too. Once a man is absorbed by an idea there is no doing anything with him.

"Years passed: he was transferred to another province. He was over forty, and he was still reading the advertisements in the papers and saving up. Then I heard he was married. Still with the same object of buying a farm and having gooseberries, he married an elderly and ugly widow without a trace of feeling for her, simply because she had filthy lucre. He went on living frugally after marrying her, and kept her short of food, while he put her money in the bank in his name.

"Her first husband had been a postmaster, and with him she was accustomed to pies and home-made wines, while with her second husband she did not get enough black bread; she began to pine away with this sort of life, and three years later she gave up her soul to God. And I need hardly say that my brother never for one moment imagined that he was responsible for her death. Money, like vodka, makes a man queer. In our town there was a merchant who, before he died, ordered a plateful of honey and ate up all his money and lottery tickets with the honey, so that no one might get the benefit of it. While I was inspecting cattle at a railway-station, a cattle-dealer fell under an engine and had his leg cut off. We carried him into the waiting-room, the blood was flowing—it was a horrible thing—and he kept asking them to look for his leg and was very much worried about it; there were twenty roubles in the boot on the leg that had been cut off, and he was afraid they would be lost."

"That's a story from a different opera," said Burkin.

"After his wife's death," Ivan Ivanovitch went on, after thinking for half a minute, "my brother began looking out for an estate for himself. Of course, you may look about for five years and yet end by making a mistake, and buying something quite different from what you have dreamed of. My brother Nikolay bought through an agent a mortgaged estate of three hundred and thirty acres, with a house for the family, with servants' quarters, with a park, but with no orchard, no gooseberry-bushes, and no duck-pond; there was a river, but the water in it was the color of coffee, because on one side of the estate there was a brickyard and on the other a factory for burning bones. But Nikolay Ivanovitch did not grieve much, he ordered twenty gooseberry-bushes, planted them, and began living as a country gentleman.

"Last year I went to pay him a visit. I thought I would go and see what it was like. In his letters my brother called his estate 'Tchumbaroklov Waste, alias Himalaiskoe.' I reached 'alias Himalaiskoe' in the afternoon. It was hot. Everywhere there were ditches, fences, hedges, fir-trees planted in rows, and there was no knowing how to get to the yard, where to put one's horse. I went up to the house, and was met by a fat red dog that looked like a pig. It wanted to bark, but it was too lazy. The cook, a fat, barefooted woman, came out of the kitchen, and she, too, looked like a pig, and said that her master was resting after dinner. I went in to see my brother. He was sitting up in bed with a quilt over his legs; he had grown older, fatter, wrinkled; his cheeks, his nose, and his mouth all stuck out—he looked as though he might begin grunting into the quilt at any moment.

"We embraced each other, and shed tears of joy and of sadness at the thought that we had once been young and now were both gray-headed and near the grave. He dressed, and led me out to show me the estate.

"'Well, how are you getting on here?' I asked.

"'Oh, all right, thank God; I am getting on very well.'

"He was no more a poor timid clerk, but a real landowner, a gentleman. He was already accustomed to it, had grown used to it, and liked it. He ate a great deal, went to the bath-house, was growing stout, was already at law with the village commune and both factories, and was very much offended when the peasants did not call him 'Your Honor.' And he concerned himself with the salvation of his soul in a substantial, gentlemanly manner, and performed deeds of charity, not simply, but with an air of consequence. And what deeds of charity! He treated the peasants for every sort of disease with soda and castor oil, and on his name-day had a thanksgiving service in the middle of the village, and then treated the peasants to a gallon of vodka—he thought that was the thing to do. Oh, those horrible gallons of vodka! One day the fat landowner hauls the peasants up before the district captain for trespass, and next day, in honor of a holiday, treats them to a gallon of vodka, and they drink and shout 'Hurrah!' and when they are drunk bow down to his feet. A change of life for the better, and being well-fed and idle develop in a Russian the most insolent self-conceit. Nikolay Ivanovitch, who at one time in the government office was afraid to have any views of his own, now could say nothing that was not gospel truth, and uttered such truths in the tone of a prime minister. 'Education is essential, but for the peasants it is premature.' 'Corporal punishment is harmful as a rule, but in some cases it is necessary and there is nothing to take its place.'

"'I know the peasants and understand how to treat them,' he would say. 'The peasants like me. I need only to hold up my little finger and the peasants will do anything I like.'

"And all this, observe, was uttered with a wise, benevolent smile. He repeated twenty times over 'We noblemen,' 'I as a noble'; obviously he did not remember that our grandfather was a peasant, and our father a soldier. Even our surname Tchimsha-Himalaisky, in reality so incongruous, seemed to him now melodious, distinguished, and very agreeable.

"But the point just now is not he, but myself. I want to tell you about the change that took place in me during the brief hours I spent at his country place. In the evening, when we were drinking tea, the cook put on the table a plateful of gooseberries. They were not bought, but his own gooseberries, gathered for the first time since the bushes were planted. Nikolay Ivanovitch laughed and looked for a minute in silence at the gooseberries, with tears in his eyes; he could not speak for excitement. Then he put one gooseberry in his mouth, looked at me with the triumph of a child who has at last received his favorite toy, and said:

"'How delicious!'

"And he ate them greedily, continually repeating, 'Ah, how delicious! Do taste them!'

"They were sour and unripe, but, as Pushkin says:

> "'Dearer to us the falsehood that exalts
> Than hosts of baser truths.'

"I saw a happy man whose cherished dream was so obviously fulfilled, who had attained his object in life, who had gained what he wanted, who was satisfied with his fate and himself. There is always, for some reason, an element of sadness mingled with my thoughts of human happiness, and, on this occasion, at the sight of a happy man I was overcome by an oppressive feeling that was close upon despair. It was particularly oppressive at night. A bed was made up for me in the room next to my brother's bedroom, and I could hear that he was awake, and that he kept getting up and going to the plate of gooseberries and taking one. I reflected how many satisfied, happy people there really are! What a suffocating force it is! You look at life: the insolence and idleness of the strong, the ignorance and brutishness of the weak, incredible poverty all about us, overcrowding, degeneration, drunkenness, hypocrisy, lying. . . . Yet all is calm and stillness in the houses and in the streets; of the fifty thousand living in a town, there is not one who would cry out, who would give vent to his indignation aloud. We see the people going to market for provisions, eating by day, sleeping by night, talking their silly nonsense, getting married, growing old, serenely escorting their dead to the cemetery; but we do not see and we do not hear those who suffer, and what is terrible in life goes on somewhere behind the scenes. . . . Everything is quiet and peaceful, and nothing protests but mute statistics: so many people gone out of their minds, so many gallons of vodka drunk, so many children dead from malnutrition. . . . And this order of things is evidently necessary; evidently the happy man only feels at ease because the unhappy bear their burdens in silence, and without that silence happiness would be impossible. It's a case of general hypnotism. There ought to be behind the door of every happy, contented man some one standing with a hammer continually reminding him with a tap that there are unhappy people; that however happy he may be, life will show him her laws sooner or later, trouble will come for him—disease, poverty, losses—and no one will see or hear, just as now he neither sees nor hears others. But there is no man with a hammer; the happy man lives at his ease, and trivial daily cares faintly agitate him like the wind in the aspen-tree—and all goes well.

"That night I realized that I, too, was happy and contented," Ivan Ivanovitch went on, getting up. "I, too, at dinner and at the hunt liked to lay down the law on life and religion, and the way to manage the peasantry. I, too, used to say that science was light, that culture was essential, but for the simple people reading and writing was enough for the time. Freedom is a blessing, I used to say; we can no more do without it than without air, but we must wait a little. Yes, I used to talk like that, and now I ask, 'For what reason are we to wait?'" asked Ivan Ivanovitch, looking angrily at Burkin. "Why wait, I ask you? What grounds have we for waiting? I shall be told, it can't be done all at once; every idea takes shape in life gradually, in its due time. But who is it says that? Where is the proof that it's right? You will fall back upon the natural order of things, the uniformity of phenomena; but is there order and uniformity in the fact that I, a living, thinking man, stand over a chasm and wait for it to close of itself, or to fill up with mud at the very time when perhaps I might leap over it or build a bridge across it? And again, wait for the sake of what? Wait till there's no strength to live? And meanwhile one must live, and one wants to live!

"I went away from my brother's early in the morning, and ever since then it has been unbearable for me to be in town. I am oppressed by its peace and quiet; I am afraid to look at the windows, for there is no spectacle more painful to me now than the sight of a happy family sitting around the table drinking tea. I am old and am not fit for the struggle; I am not even capable of hatred; I can only grieve inwardly, feel irritated and vexed; but at night my head is hot from the rush of ideas, and I cannot sleep. . . . Ah, if I were young!"

Ivan Ivanovitch walked backwards and forwards in excitement, and repeated: "If I were young!"

He suddenly went up to Alchin and began pressing first one of his hands and then the other.

"Pavel Konstantinovitch," he said in an imploring voice, "don't be calm and contented, don't let yourself be put to sleep! While you are young, strong, confident, be not weary in well-doing! There is no happiness, and there ought not to be; but if there is a meaning and an object in life, that meaning and object is not our happiness, but something greater and more rational. Do good!"

And all this Ivan Ivanovitch said with a pitiful, imploring smile, as though he were asking him a personal favor.

Then all three sat in arm-chairs at different ends of the drawing-room and were silent. Ivan Ivanovitch's story had not satisfied either Burkin or Alehin. When the generals and ladies gazed down from their gilt frames, looking in the dusk as though they were alive, it was dreary to listen to the story of the poor clerk who ate gooseberries. They felt inclined, for some reason, to talk about elegant people, about women. And their sitting in the drawing-room where everything—the chandeliers in their covers, the arm-chairs, and the carpet under their feet—reminded them that those very people who were now looking down from their frames had once moved about, sat, drunk tea in this room, and the fact that lovely Pelagea was moving noiselessly about was better than any story.

Alehin was fearfully sleepy; he had got up early, before three o'clock in the morning, to look after his work, and now his eyes were closing; but he was afraid his visitors might tell some interesting story after he had gone, and he lingered on. He did not go into the question whether what Ivan Ivanovitch had just said was right and true. His visitors did not talk of groats, nor of hay, nor of tar, but of something that had no direct bearing on his life, and he was glad and wanted them to go on.

"It's bed-time, though," said Burkin, getting up. "Allow me to wish you good-night."

Alehin said good-night and went downstairs to his own domain, while the visitors remained upstairs. They were both taken for the night to a big room where there stood two old wooden beds decorated with carvings, and in the corner was an ivory crucifix. The big cool beds, which had been made by the lovely Pelagea, smelt agreeably of clean linen.

Ivan Ivanovitch undressed in silence and got into bed.

"Lord forgive us sinners!" he said, and put his head under the quilt.

His pipe lying on the table smelt strongly of stale tobacco, and Burkin could not sleep for a long while, and kept wondering where the oppressive smell came from.

The rain was pattering on the window-panes all night.

THE CHERRY ORCHARD

Translated by Constance Garnett

CHARACTERS[1]

MADAME RANEVSKY (LYUBOV ANDREYEVNA), *the owner of the cherry orchard*
ANYA, *her daughter, aged seventeen*
VARYA, *her adopted daughter, aged twenty-four*
GAEV, LEONID ANDREYEVITCH, *brother of Madame Ranevsky*
LOPAHIN, YERMOLAY ALEXEYEVITCH, *a merchant*
TROFIMOV, PYOTR SERGEYEVITCH, *a student*
SEMYONOV-PISHTCHIK, *a landowner*
CHARLOTTA IVANOVNA, *a governess*
EPIHODOV, SEMYON PANTALEYEVITCH, *a clerk*
DUNYASHA, *a maid*
FIRS, *an old valet, aged eighty-seven*
YASHA, *a young valet*
A VAGRANT
THE STATIONMASTER
A POST-OFFICE CLERK
VISITORS
SERVANTS

The action takes place on the estate of MADAME RANEVSKY

ACT ONE

SCENE

A room, which has always been called the nursery. One of the doors leads into ANYA*'s room. Dawn, sun rises during the scene. May, the cherry trees in flower, but it is cold in the garden with the frost of early morning. Windows closed.*

[*Enter* DUNYASHA *with a candle and* LOPAHIN *with a book in his hand.*]

LOPAHIN. The train's in, thank God. What time is it?

DUNYASHA. Nearly two o'clock. [*Puts out the candle.*] It's daylight already.

LOPAHIN. The train's late! Two hours, at least. [*Yawns and stretches.*] I'm a pretty one; what a fool I've been. Came here on purpose to meet them at the station and dropped asleep. . . . Dozed off as I sat in the chair. It's annoying. . . . You might have waked me.

DUNYASHA. I thought you had gone. [*Listens.*] There, I do believe they're coming!

[1] The variety of names for the same person in nineteenth-century Russian literature is sometimes a source of confusion. Russians have three names: a given name (Lyubov or Leonid), a patronymic (Andreyevna, or "daughter of Andrey"; Andreyevitch, or "son of Andrey"), and a surname. A person may be addressed in a number of ways: by title and surname, as in "Madame Ranevsky" (formal), by given name and patronymic, as in "Lyubov Andreyevna" (respectful, but less formal), by given name alone, as in "Lyubov" or "Pyotr" (familiar), or by a diminutive of the given name: "Lyuba" or "Petya" (intimate or affectionate).

LOPAHIN. [*Listens.*] No, what with the luggage and one thing and another. [*A pause.*] Lyubov Andreyevna has been abroad five years; I don't know what she is like now. . . . She's a splendid woman. A good-natured, kind-hearted woman. I remember when I was a lad of fifteen, my poor father—he used to keep a little shop here in the village in those days—gave me a punch in the face with his fist and made my nose bleed. We were in the yard here, I forget what we'd come about—he had had a drop. Lyubov Andreyevna—I can see her now—she was a slim young girl then—took me to wash my face, and then brought me into this very room, into the nursery. "Don't cry, little peasant," says she, "it will be well in time for your wedding day." . . . [*A pause.*] Little peasant. . . . My father was a peasant, it's true, but here am I in a white waistcoat and brown shoes, like a pig in a bun shop. Yes, I'm a rich man, but for all my money, come to think, a peasant I was, and a peasant I am. [*Turns over the pages of the book.*] I've been reading this book and I can't make head or tail of it. I fell asleep over it. [*A pause.*]

DUNYASHA. The dogs have been awake all night, they feel that the mistress is coming.

LOPAHIN. Why, what's the matter with you, Dunyasha?

DUNYASHA. My hands are all of a tremble. I feel as though I should faint.

LOPAHIN. You're a spoilt soft creature, Dunyasha. And dressed like a lady too, and your hair done up. That's not the thing. One must know one's place.

[*Enter* EPIHODOV *with a nosegay; he wears a pea jacket and highly polished creaking topboots; he drops the nosegay as he comes in.*]

EPIHODOV [*picking up the nosegay*]. Here! the gardener's sent this, says you're to put it in the dining room. [*Gives* DUNYASHA *the nosegay.*]

LOPAHIN. And bring me some kvass.[2]

DUNYASHA. I will. [*Goes out.*]

EPIHODOV. It's chilly this morning, three degrees of frost, though the cherries are all in flower. I can't say much for our climate. [*Sighs.*] I can't. Our climate is not often propitious to the occasion. Yermolay Alexeyevitch, permit me to call your attention to the fact that I purchased myself a pair of boots the day before yesterday, and they creak, I venture to assure you, so that there's no tolerating them. What ought I to grease them with?

LOPAHIN. Oh, shut up! Don't bother me.

EPIHODOV. Every day some misfortune befalls me. I don't complain. I'm used to it, and I wear a smiling face. [DUNYASHA *comes in, hands* LOPAHIN *the kvass.*] I am going. [*Stumbles against a chair, which falls over.*] There! [*As though triumphant*] There you see now, excuse the expression, an accident like that among others. . . . It's positively remarkable. [*Goes out.*]

DUNYASHA. Do you know, Yermolay Alexeyevitch, I must confess, Epihodov has made me a proposal.

LOPAHIN. Ah!

[2] Russian beer made from barley, malt, and rye.

DUNYASHA. I'm sure I don't know. . . . He's a harmless fellow, but sometimes when he begins talking, there's no making anything of it. It's all very fine and expressive, only there's no understanding it. I've a sort of liking for him too. He loves me to distraction. He's an unfortunate man; every day there's something. They tease him about it—two and twenty misfortunes they call him.

LOPAHIN [*listening*]. There! I do believe they're coming.

DUNYASHA. They are coming! What's the matter with me? . . . I'm cold all over.

LOPAHIN. They really are coming. Let's go and meet them. Will she know me? It's five years since I saw her.

DUNYASHA [*in a flutter*]. I shall drop this very minute. . . . Ah, I shall drop.

[*There is a sound of two carriages driving up to the house.* LOPAHIN *and* DUNYASHA *go out quickly. The stage is left empty. A noise is heard in the adjoining rooms.* FIRS, *who has driven to meet* MADAME RANEVSKY, *crosses the stage hurriedly leaning on a stick. He is wearing old-fashioned livery and a high hat. He says something to himself, but not a word can be distinguished. The noise behind the scenes goes on increasing. A voice: "Come, let's go in here." Enter* LYUBOV ANDREYEVNA, ANYA, *and* CHARLOTTA IVANOVNA *with a pet dog on a chain, all in travelling dresses.* VARYA *in an outdoor coat with a kerchief over her head,* GAEV, SEMYONOV-PISHTCHIK, LOPAHIN, DUNYASHA *with bag and parasol, servants with other articles. All walk across the room.*]

ANYA. Let's come in here. Do you remember what room this is, mamma?

LYUBOV [*joyfully, through her tears*]. The nursery!

VARYA. How cold it is, my hands are numb. [*To* LYUBOV ANDREYEVNA] Your rooms, the white room and the lavender one, are just the same as ever, mamma.

LYUBOV. My nursery, dear delightful room. . . . I used to sleep here when I was little. . . . [*Cries.*] And here I am, like a little child. . . . [*Kisses her brother and* VARYA, *and then her brother again.*] Varya's just the same as ever, like a nun. And I knew Dunyasha. [*Kisses* DUNYASHA.]

GAEV. The train was two hours late. What do you think of that? Is that the way to do things?

CHARLOTTA [*to* PISHTCHIK]. My dog eats nuts, too.

PISHTCHIK [*wonderingly*]. Fancy that!

[*They all go out except* ANYA *and* DUNYASHA.]

DUNYASHA. We've been expecting you so long. [*Takes* ANYA'S *hat and coat.*]

ANYA. I haven't slept for four nights on the journey. I feel dreadfully cold.

DUNYASHA. You set out in Lent, there was snow and frost, and now? My darling! [*Laughs and kisses her.*] I *have* missed you, my precious, my joy. I must tell you . . . I can't put it off a minute. . . .

ANYA [*wearily*]. What now?

DUNYASHA. Epihodov, the clerk, made me a proposal just after Easter.

ANYA. It's always the same thing with you. . . . [*Straightening her hair*] I've lost all my hairpins. . . . [*She is staggering from exhaustion.*]

DUNYASHA. I don't know what to think, really. He does love me, he does love me so!

ANYA [*looking towards her door, tenderly*]. My own room, my windows just as though I had never gone away. I'm home! Tomorrow morning I shall get up and run into the garden. . . . Oh, if I could get to sleep! I haven't slept all the journey, I was so anxious and worried.

DUNYASHA. Pyotr Sergeyevitch came the day before yesterday.

ANYA [*joyfully*]. Petya!

DUNYASHA. He's asleep in the bathhouse, he has settled in there. I'm afraid of being in their way, says he. [*Glancing at her watch*] I was to have waked him, but Varvara Mihalovna told me not to. Don't you wake him, says she.

[*Enter* VARYA *with a bunch of keys at her waist.*]

VARYA. Dunyasha, coffee and make haste. . . . Mamma's asking for coffee.

DUNYASHA. This very minute. [*Goes out.*]

VARYA. Well, thank God, you've come. You're home again [*petting her*]. My little darling has come back! My precious beauty has come back again!

ANYA. I have had a time of it!

VARYA. I can fancy.

ANYA. We set off in Holy Week—it was so cold then, and all the way Charlotta would talk and show off her tricks. What did you want to burden me with Charlotta for?

VARYA. You couldn't have travelled all alone, darling. At seventeen!

ANYA. We got to Paris at last, it was cold there—snow. I speak French shockingly. Mamma lives on the fifth floor, I went up to her and there were a lot of French people, ladies, an old priest with a book. The place smelt of tobacco and so comfortless. I felt sorry, oh! so sorry for mamma all at once, I put my arms round her neck, and hugged her and wouldn't let her go. Mamma was as kind as she could be, and she cried. . . .

VARYA [*through her tears*]. Don't speak of it, don't speak of it!

ANYA. She had sold her villa at Mentone, she had nothing left, nothing. I hadn't a farthing left either, we only just had enough to get here. And mamma doesn't understand! When we had dinner at the stations, she always ordered the most expensive things and gave the waiters a whole rouble. Charlotta's just the same. Yasha too must have the same as we do; it's simply awful. You know Yasha is mamma's valet now, we brought him here with us.

VARYA. Yes, I've seen the young rascal.

ANYA. Well, tell me—have you paid the arrears on the mortgage?

VARYA. How could we get the money?

ANYA. Oh, dear! Oh, dear!

VARYA. In August the place will be sold.

ANYA. My goodness!

LOPAHIN. [*Peeps in at the door and moos like a cow.*] Moo! [*Disappears.*]

VARYA [*weeping*]. There, that's what I could do to him [*shakes her fist*].

ANYA [*embracing* VARYA, *softly*]. Varya, has he made you an offer? [VARYA *shakes her head.*] Why, but he loves you. Why is it you don't come to an understanding? What are you waiting for?

VARYA. I believe that there never will be anything between us. He has a lot to do, he has no time for me . . . and takes no notice of me. Bless the man, it makes me miserable to see him. . . . Everyone's talking of our being married, everyone's congratulating me, and all the while there's really nothing in it; it's all like a dream. [*In another tone*] You have a new brooch like a bee.

ANYA [*mournfully*]. Mamma bought it. [*Goes into her own room and in a light-hearted childish tone*] And you know, in Paris I went up in a balloon!

VARYA. My darling's home again! My pretty is home again!

[DUNYASHA *returns with the coffee pot and is making the coffee.*]

VARYA [*standing at the door*]. All day long, darling, as I go about looking after the house, I keep dreaming all the time. If only we could marry you to a rich man, then I should feel more at rest. Then I would go off by myself on a pilgrimage to Kiev, to Moscow . . . and so I would spend my life going from one holy place to another. . . . I would go on and on. . . . What bliss!

ANYA. The birds are singing in the garden. What time is it?

VARYA. It must be nearly three. It's time you were asleep, darling. [*Going into* ANYA's *room*] What bliss!

[YASHA *enters with a rug and a travelling bag.*]

YASHA. [*Crosses the stage, mincingly.*] May one come in here, pray?

DUNYASHA. I shouldn't have known you, Yasha. How you have changed abroad.

YASHA. H'm! . . . And who are you?

DUNYASHA. When you went away, I was that high. [*Shows distance from floor.*] Dunyasha, Fyodor's daughter. . . . You don't remember me!

YASHA. H'm! . . . You're a peach! [*Looks round and embraces her: she shrieks and drops a saucer.* YASHA *goes out hastily.*]

VARYA [*in the doorway, in a tone of vexation*]. What now?

DUNYASHA [*through her tears*]. I have broken a saucer.

VARYA. Well, that brings good luck.

ANYA [*coming out of her room*]. We ought to prepare mamma: Petya is here.

VARYA. I told them not to wake him.

ANYA [*dreamily*]. It's six years since father died. Then only a month later little brother Grisha was drowned in the river, such a pretty boy he was, only seven. It was more than mamma could bear, so she went away, went away without looking back [*shuddering*]. . . . How well I understand her, if only she knew! [*A pause.*] And Petya Trofimov was Grisha's tutor, he may remind her.

[*Enter* FIRS: *he is wearing a pea jacket and a white waistcoat.*]

FIRS. [*Goes up to the coffee pot, anxiously.*] The mistress will be served here. [*Puts on white gloves.*] Is the coffee ready? [*Sternly to* DUNYASHA] Girl! Where's the cream?

DUNYASHA. Ah, mercy on us! [*Goes out quickly.*]

FIRS [*fussing round the coffee pot*]. Ech! you good-for-nothing! [*Muttering to himself*] Come back from Paris. And the old master used to go to Paris too . . . horses all the way. [*Laughs.*]

VARYA. What is it, Firs?

FIRS. What is your pleasure? [*Gleefully*] My lady has come home! I have lived to see her again! Now I can die. [*Weeps with joy.*]

[*Enter* LYUBOV ANDREYEVNA, GAEV *and* SEMYONOV-PISHTCHIK; *the latter is in a short-waisted full coat of fine cloth, and full trousers.* GAEV, *as he comes in, makes a gesture with his arms and his whole body, as though he were playing billiards.*]

LYUBOV. How does it go? Let me remember. Cannon off the red!

GAEV. That's it—in off the white! Why, once, sister, we used to sleep together in this very room, and now I'm fifty-one, strange as it seems.

LOPAHIN. Yes, time flies.

GAEV. What do you say?

LOPAHIN. Time, I say, flies.

GAEV. What a smell of patchouli![3]

ANYA. I'm going to bed. Good night, mamma. [*Kisses her mother.*]

LYUBOV. My precious darling. [*Kisses her hands.*] Are you glad to be home? I can't believe it.

ANYA. Good night, uncle.

GAEV [*kissing her face and hands*]. God bless you! How like you are to your mother! [*To his sister*] At her age you were just the same, Lyuba.

[ANYA *shakes hands with* LOPAHIN *and* PISHTCHIK, *then goes out, shutting the door after her.*]

LYUBOV. She's quite worn out.

PISHTCHIK. Aye, it's a long journey, to be sure.

VARYA [*to* LOPAHIN *and* PISHTCHIK]. Well, gentlemen? It's three o'clock and time to say good-by.

LYUBOV. [*Laughs.*] You're just the same as ever, Varya. [*Draws her to her and kisses her.*] I'll just drink my coffee and then we will all go and rest. [FIRS *puts a cushion under her feet.*] Thanks, friend. I am so fond of coffee, I drink it day and night. Thanks, dear old man. [*Kisses* FIRS.]

VARYA. I'll just see whether all the things have been brought in. [*Goes out.*]

LYUBOV. Can it really be me sitting here? [*Laughs.*] I want to dance about and clap my hands. [*Covers her face with her hands.*] And I could drop asleep in a moment! God knows I love my country, I love it tenderly; I couldn't look out of the window in the train, I kept crying so. [*Through her tears*] But I must drink my coffee, though. Thank you, Firs, thanks, dear old man. I'm so glad to find you still alive.

[3] A penetrating East Indian perfume.

FIRS. The day before yesterday.

GAEV. He's rather deaf.

LOPAHIN. I have to set off for Harkov directly, at five o'clock. . . . It is annoying! I wanted to have a look at you, and a little talk. . . . You are just as splendid as ever.

PISHTCHIK [*breathing heavily*]. Handsomer, indeed. . . . Dressed in Parisian style . . . completely bowled me over.

LOPAHIN. Your brother, Leonid Andreyevitch here, is always saying that I'm a low-born knave, that I'm a money grubber, but I don't care one straw for that. Let him talk. Only I do want you to believe in me as you used to. I do want your wonderful tender eyes to look at me as they used to in the old days. Merciful God! My father was a serf of your father and of your grandfather, but you—you—did so much for me once, that I've forgotten all that; I love you as though you were my kin . . . more than my kin.

LYUBOV. I can't sit still, I simply can't. . . . [*Jumps up and walks about in violent agitation.*] This happiness is too much for me. . . . You may laugh at me, I know I'm silly. . . . My own bookcase. [*Kisses the bookcase.*] My little table.

GAEV. Nurse died while you were away.

LYUBOV. [*Sits down and drinks coffee.*] Yes, the Kingdom of Heaven be hers! You wrote me of her death.

GAEV. And Anastasy is dead. Squinting Petruchka has left me and is in service now with the police captain in the town. [*Takes a box of caramels out of his pocket and sucks one.*]

PISHTCHIK. My daughter, Dashenka, wishes to be remembered to you.

LOPAHIN. I want to tell you something very pleasant and cheering [*glancing at his watch*]. I'm going directly . . . there's no time to say much . . . well, I can say it in a couple of words. I needn't tell you your cherry orchard is to be sold to pay your debts; the 22nd of August is the date fixed for the sale; but don't you worry, dearest lady, you may sleep in peace, there is a way of saving it. . . . This is what I propose. I beg your attention! Your estate is not twenty miles from the town, the railway runs close by it, and if the cherry orchard and the land along the river bank were cut up into building plots and then let on lease for summer villas, you would make an income of at least 25,000 roubles a year out of it.

GAEV. That's all rot, if you'll excuse me.

LYUBOV. I don't quite understand you, Yermolay Alexeyevitch.

LOPAHIN. You will get a rent of at least 25 roubles a year for a three-acre plot from summer visitors, and if you say the word now, I'll bet you what you like there won't be one square foot of ground vacant by the autumn, all the plots will be taken up. I congratulate you; in fact, you are saved. It's a perfect situation with that deep river. Only, of course, it must be cleared—all the old buildings, for example, must be removed, this house too, which is really good for nothing and the old cherry orchard must be cut down.

LYUBOV. Cut down? My dear fellow, forgive me, but you don't know what you are talking about. If there is one thing interesting—remarkable indeed—in the whole province, it's just our cherry orchard.

LOPAHIN. The only thing remarkable about the orchard is that it's a very large one. There's a crop of cherries every alternate year, and then there's nothing to be done with them, no one buys them.

GAEV. This orchard is mentioned in the "Encyclopaedia."

LOPAHIN [*glancing at his watch*]. If we don't decide on something and don't take some steps, on the 22nd of August the cherry orchard and the whole estate too will be sold by auction. Make up your minds! There is no other way of saving it, I'll take my oath on that. No, no!

FIRS. In old days, forty or fifty years ago, they used to dry the cherries, soak them, pickle them, make jam too, and they used——

GAEV. Be quiet, Firs.

FIRS. And they used to send the preserved cherries to Moscow and to Harkov by the wagon-load. That brought the money in! And the preserved cherries in those days were soft and juicy, sweet and fragrant. . . . They knew the way to do them then. . . .

LYUBOV. And where is the recipe now?

FIRS. It's forgotten. Nobody remembers it.

PISHTCHIK [*to* LYUBOV ANDREYEVNA]. What's it like in Paris? Did you eat frogs there?

LYUBOV. Oh, I ate crocodiles.

PISHTCHIK. Fancy that now!

LOPAHIN. There used to be only the gentlefolks and the peasants in the country, but now there are these summer visitors. All the towns, even the small ones, are surrounded nowadays by these summer villas. And one may say for sure, that in another twenty years there'll be many more of these people and that they'll be everywhere. At present the summer visitor only drinks tea in his verandah, but maybe he'll take to working his bit of land too, and then your cherry orchard would become happy, rich and prosperous. . . .

GAEV [*indignant*]. What rot!

[*Enter* VARYA AND YASHA.]

VARYA. There are two telegrams for you, mamma. [*Takes out keys and opens an old-fashioned bookcase with a loud crack.*] Here they are.

LYUBOV. From Paris. [*Tears the telegrams, without reading them.*] I have done with Paris.

GAEV. Do you know, Lyuba, how old that bookcase is? Last week I pulled out the bottom drawer and there I found the date branded on it. The bookcase was made just a hundred years ago. What do you say to that? We might have celebrated its jubilee. Though it's an inanimate object, still it is a *book* case.

PISHTCHIK [*amazed*]. A hundred years! Fancy that now.

GAEV. Yes. . . . It is a thing . . . [*feeling the bookcase*]. Dear, honored, bookcase! Hail to thee who for more than a hundred years hast served the pure ideals of good and justice; thy silent call to fruitful labor has never flagged in those hundred years, maintaining [*in tears*] in the generations of man, courage and faith in a brighter future and fostering in us ideals of good and social consciousness. [*A pause.*]

LOPAHIN. Yes. . . .

LYUBOV. You are just the same as ever, Leonid.

GAEV [*a little embarrassed*]. Cannon off the right into the pocket!

LOPAHIN [*looking at his watch*]. Well, it's time I was off.

YASHA [*handing* LYUBOV ANDREYEVNA *medicine*]. Perhaps you will take your pills now.

PISHTCHIK. You shouldn't take medicines, my dear madam . . . they do no harm and no good. Give them here . . . honored lady. [*Takes the pillbox, pours the pills into the hollow of his hand, blows on them, puts them in his mouth and drinks off some kvass.*] There!

LYUBOV [*in alarm*]. Why, you must be out of your mind!

PISHTCHIK. I have taken all the pills.

LOPAHIN. What a glutton! [*All laugh.*]

FIRS. His honor stayed with us in Easter week, ate a gallon and a half of cucumbers. . . . [*Mutters.*]

LYUBOV. What is he saying?

VARYA. He has taken to muttering like that for the last three years. We are used to it.

YASHA. His declining years!

[CHARLOTTA IVANOVNA, *a very thin, lanky figure in a white dress with a lorgnette in her belt, walks across the stage.*]

LOPAHIN. I beg your pardon, Charlotta Ivanovna, I have not had time to greet you. [*Tries to kiss her hand.*]

CHARLOTTA [*pulling away her hand*]. If I let you kiss my hand, you'll be wanting to kiss my elbow, and then my shoulder.

LOPAHIN. I've no luck today! [*All laugh.*] Charlotta Ivanovna, show us some tricks!

LYUBOV. Charlotta, do show us some tricks!

CHARLOTTA. I don't want to. I'm sleepy. [*Goes out.*]

LOPAHIN. In three weeks' time we shall meet again. [*Kisses* LYUBOV ANDREYEVNA'S *hand.*] Good-by till then—I must go. [*To* GAEV] Good-by. [*Kisses* PISHTCHIK.] Good-by. [*Gives his hand to* VARYA, *then to* FIRS *and* YASHA.] I don't want to go. [*To* LYUBOV ANDREYEVNA] If you think over my plan for the villas and make up your mind, then let me know; I will lend you 50,000 roubles. Think of it seriously.

VARYA [*angrily*]. Well, do go, for goodness sake.

LOPAHIN. I'm going, I'm going. [*Goes out.*]

GAEV. Low-born knave! I beg pardon, though . . . Varya is going to marry him, he's Varya's fiancé.

VARYA. Don't talk nonsense, uncle.

LYUBOV. Well, Varya, I shall be delighted. He's a good man.

PISHTCHIK. He is, one must acknowledge, a most worthy man. And my Dashenka . . . says too that . . . she says . . . various things. [*Snores, but at once wakes up.*] But all the same, honored lady, could you oblige me . . . with a loan of 240 roubles . . . to pay the interest on my mortgage tomorrow?

VARYA [*dismayed*]. No, no.

LYUBOV. I really haven't any money.

PISHTCHIK. It will turn up. [*Laughs.*] I never lose hope. I thought everything was over, I was a ruined man, and lo and behold—the railway passed through my land and . . . they paid me for it. And something else will turn up again, if not today, then tomorrow . . . Dashenka'll win two hundred thousand . . . she's got a lottery ticket.

LYUBOV. Well, we've finished our coffee, we can go to bed.

FIRS. [*Brushes* GAEV, *reprovingly.*] You have got on the wrong trousers again! What am I to do with you?

VARYA [*softly*]. Anya's asleep. [*Softly opens the window.*] Now the sun's risen, it's not a bit cold. Look, mamma, what exquisite trees! My goodness! And the air! The starlings are singing!

GAEV. [*Opens another window.*] The orchard is all white. You've not forgotten it, Lyuba? That long avenue that runs straight, straight as an arrow, how it shines on a moonlight night. You remember? You've not forgotten?

LYUBOV [*looking out of the window into the garden*]. Oh, my childhood, my innocence! It was in this nursery I used to sleep, from here I looked out into the orchard, happiness waked with me every morning and in those days the orchard was just the same, nothing has changed. [*Laughs with delight.*] All, all white! Oh, my orchard! After the dark gloomy autumn, and the cold winter; you are young again, and full of happiness, the heavenly angels have never left you. . . . If I could cast off the burden that weighs on my heart, if I could forget the past!

GAEV. H'm! and the orchard will be sold to pay our debts; it seems strange. . . .

LYUBOV. See, our mother walking . . . all in white, down the avenue! [*Laughs with delight.*] It is she!

GAEV. Where?

VARYA. Oh, don't, mamma!

LYUBOV. There is no one. It was my fancy. On the right there, by the path to the arbor, there is a white tree bending like a woman. . . .

[*Enter* TROFIMOV *wearing a shabby student's uniform and spectacles.*]

LYUBOV. What a ravishing orchard! White masses of blossom, blue sky. . . .

TROFIMOV. Lyubov Andreyevna! [*She looks round at him.*] I will just pay my respects to you and then leave you at once. [*Kisses her hand warmly.*] I was told to wait until morning, but I hadn't the patience to wait any longer. . . .

[LYUBOV ANDREYEVNA *looks at him in perplexity.*]

VARYA [*through her tears*]. This is Petya Trofimov.

TROFIMOV. Petya Trofimov, who was your Grisha's tutor. . . . Can I have changed so much?

[LYUBOV ANDREYEVNA *embraces him and weeps quietly.*]

GAEV [*in confusion*]. There, there, Lyuba.

VARYA [*crying*]. I told you, Petya, to wait till tomorrow.

LYUBOV. My Grisha . . . my boy . . . Grisha . . . my son!

VARYA. We can't help it, mamma, it is God's will.

TROFIMOV [*softly through his tears*]. There . . . there.

LYUBOV [*weeping quietly*]. My boy was lost . . . drowned. Why? Oh, why, dear Petya? [*More quietly*] Anya is asleep in there, and I'm talking loudly . . . making this noise. . . . But, Petya? Why have you grown so ugly? Why do you look so old?

TROFIMOV. A peasant woman in the train called me a mangy-looking gentleman.

LYUBOV. You were quite a boy then, a pretty little student, and now your hair's thin—and spectacles. Are you really a student still? [*Goes towards the door.*]

TROFIMOV. I seem likely to be a perpetual student.

LYUBOV. [*Kisses her brother, then* VARYA.] Well, go to bed. . . . You are older too, Leonid.

PISHTCHIK. [*Follows her.*] I suppose it's time we were asleep. . . . Ugh! my gout. I'm staying the night! Lyubov Andreyevna, my dear soul, if you could . . . tomorrow morning . . . 240 roubles.

GAEV. That's always his story.

PISHTCHIK. 240 roubles . . . to pay the interest on my mortgage.

LYUBOV. My dear man, I have no money.

PISHTCHIK. I'll pay it back, my dear . . . a trifling sum.

LYUBOV. Oh, well. Leonid will give it you. . . You give him the money, Leonid.

GAEV. Me give it him! Let him wait till he gets it!

LYUBOV. It can't be helped, give it him. He needs it. He'll pay it back. [LYUBOV ANDREYEVNA, TROFIMOV, PISHTCHIK *and* FIRS *go out.* GAEV, VARYA *and* YASHA *remain.*]

GAEV. Sister hasn't got out of the habit of flinging away her money. [*To* YASHA] Get away, my good fellow, you smell of the hen house.

YASHA [*with a grin*]. And you, Leonid Andreyevitch, are just the same as ever.

GAEV. What's that? [*To* VARYA] What did he say?

VARYA [*to* YASHA]. Your mother has come from the village; she has been sitting in the servants' room since yesterday, waiting to see you.

YASHA. Oh, bother her!

VARYA. For shame!

YASHA. What's the hurry? She might just as well have come tomorrow. [*Goes out.*]

VARYA. Mamma's just the same as ever, she hasn't changed a bit. If she had her own way, she'd give away everything.

GAEV. Yes. [*A pause.*] If a great many remedies are suggested for some disease, it means that the disease is incurable. I keep thinking and racking my brains; I have many schemes, a great many, and that really means none. If we could only come in for a legacy from somebody, or marry our Anya to a very rich man, or we might go to Yaroslavl and try our luck with our old aunt, the Countess. She's very, very rich, you know.

VARYA. [*Weeps.*] If God would help us.

GAEV. Don't blubber. Aunt's very rich, but she doesn't like us. First, sister married a lawyer instead of a nobleman. . . . [ANYA *appears in the doorway.*] And then her conduct, one can't call it virtuous. She is good, and kind, and nice, and I love her, but, however one allows for extenuating circumstances, there's no denying that she's an immoral woman. One feels it in her slightest gesture.

VARYA [*in a whisper*]. Anya's in the doorway.

GAEV. What do you say? [*A pause.*] It's queer, there seems to be something wrong with my right eye. I don't see as well as I did. And on Thursday when I was in the district Court . . .

[*Enter* ANYA.]

VARYA. Why aren't you asleep, Anya?

ANYA. I can't get to sleep.

GAEV. My pet. [*Kisses* ANYA'S *face and hands.*] My child. [*Weeps.*] You are not my niece, you are my angel, you are everything to me. Believe me, believe . . .

ANYA. I believe you, uncle. Everyone loves you and respects you . . . but, uncle dear, you must be silent . . . simply be silent. What were you saying just now about my mother, about your own sister? What made you say that?

GAEV. Yes, yes . . . [*Puts his hand over his face.*] Really, that was awful! My God, save me! And today I made a speech to the bookcase . . . so stupid! And only when I had finished, I saw how stupid it was.

VARYA. It's true, uncle, you ought to keep quiet. Don't talk, that's all.

ANYA. If you could keep from talking, it would make things easier for you, too.

GAEV. I won't speak. [*Kisses* ANYA *and* VARYA'S *hands.*] I'll be silent. Only this is about business. On Thursday I was in the district Court; well, there was a large party of us there and we began talking of one thing and another, and this and that, and do you know, I believe that it will be possible to raise a loan on an I.O.U. to pay the arrears on the mortgage.

VARYA. If the Lord would help us!

GAEV. I'm going on Tuesday; I'll talk of it again. [*To* VARYA] Don't blubber. [*To* ANYA] Your mamma will talk to Lopahin; of course, he won't refuse her. And as soon as you're rested you shall go to Yaroslavl to the Countess, your great-aunt. So we shall all set to work in three directions at once, and the business is done. We shall pay off arrears, I'm convinced of it. [*Puts a caramel in his mouth.*] I swear on my honor, I swear by anything you like, the estate shan't be sold [*excitedly*]. By my own happiness, I swear it! Here's my hand on it, call me the basest, vilest of men, if I let it come to an auction! Upon my soul I swear it!

ANYA. [*Her equanimity has returned, she is quite happy.*] How good you are, uncle, and how clever! [*Embraces her uncle.*] I'm at peace now! Quite at peace! I'm happy!

[*Enter* FIRS.]

FIRS [*reproachfully*]. Leonid Andreyevitch, have you no fear of God? when are you going to bed?

GAEV. Directly, directly. You can go, Firs. I'll . . . yes, I will undress myself. Come, children, by-by. We'll go into details tomorrow, but now go to bed. [*Kisses* ANYA *and* VARYA] I'm a man of the eighties.[4] They run down that period, but still I can say I have had to suffer not a little for my convictions in my life. It's not for nothing that the peasant loves me. One must know the peasant! One must know how . . .

[4] The 1880's (twenty years before the time of the play) were a period of repressive reaction in Russia. Gaev idealizes the political attitudes of his class.

ANYA. At it again, uncle!

VARYA. Uncle dear, you'd better be quiet!

FIRS [*angrily*]. Leonid Andreyevitch!

GAEV. I'm coming. I'm coming. Go to bed. Potted the shot—there's a shot for you! A beauty! [*Goes out,* FIRS *hobbling after him.*]

ANYA. My mind's at rest now. I don't want to go to Yaroslavl, I don't like my great-aunt, but still my mind's at rest. Thanks to uncle. [*Sits down.*]

VARYA. We must go to bed. I'm going. Something unpleasant happened while you were away. In the old servants' quarters there are only the old servants, as you know—Efimyushka, Polya and Yevstigney—and Karp too. They began letting stray people in to spend the night—I said nothing. But all at once I heard they had been spreading a report that I gave them nothing but pease pudding to eat. Out of stinginess, you know. . . . And it was all Yevstigney's doing. . . . Very well, I said to myself. . . . If that's how it is, I thought, wait a bit. I sent for Yevstigney. . . . [*Yawns.*] He comes. . . . "How's this, Yevstigney," I said, "you could be such a fool as to? . . ." [*Looking at* ANYA] Anitchka! [*A pause.*] She's asleep. [*Puts her arm round* ANYA.] Come to bed . . . come along! [*Leads her.*] My darling has fallen asleep! Come . . . [*They go.*]

[*Far away beyond the orchard a shepherd plays on a pipe.* TROFIMOV *crosses the stage and, seeing* VARYA *and* ANYA, *stands still.*]

VARYA. 'Sh! asleep, asleep. Come, my own.

ANYA [*softly, half asleep*]. I'm so tired. Still those bells. Uncle . . . dear . . . mamma and uncle. . . .

VARYA. Come, my own, come along.

[*They go into* ANYA'S *room.*]

TROFIMOV [*tenderly*]. My sunshine! My spring.

ACT TWO

SCENE

The open country. An old shrine, long abandoned and fallen out of the perpendicular; near it a well, large stones that have apparently once been tombstones, and an old garden seat. The road to GAEV'S *house is seen. On one side rise dark poplars; and there the cherry orchard begins. In the distance a row of telegraph poles and far, far away on the horizon there is faintly outlined a great town, only visible in very fine clear weather. It is near sunset.* CHARLOTTA, YASHA *and* DUNYASHA *are sitting on the seat.* EPIHODOV *is standing near, playing something mournful on a guitar. All sit plunged in thought.* CHARLOTTA *wears an old forage cap; she has taken a gun from her shoulder and is tightening the buckle on the strap.*

CHARLOTTA [*musingly*]. I haven't a real passport of my own, and I don't know how old I am, and I always feel that I'm a young thing. When I was a little girl, my father and mother used to travel about to fairs and give performances—very good ones. And I used to dance *salto-mortale*[5]

[5] The "leap of death" (Italian), a standing somersault.

and all sorts of things. And when papa and mamma died, a German lady took me and had me educated. And so I grew up and became a governess. But where I came from, and who I am, I don't know. . . . Who my parents were, very likely they weren't married . . . I don't know. [*Takes a cucumber out of her pocket and eats.*] I know nothing at all. [*A pause.*] One wants to talk and has no one to talk to . . . I have nobody.

EPIHODOV. [*Plays on the guitar and sings.*] "What care I for the noisy world! What care I for friends or foes!" How agreeable it is to play on the mandolin!

DUNYASHA. That's a guitar, not a mandolin. [*Looks in a hand mirror and powders herself.*]

EPIHODOV. To a man mad with love, it's a mandolin. [*Sings.*] "Were her heart but aglow with love's mutual flame." [YASHA *joins in.*]

CHARLOTTA. How shockingly these people sing! Foo! Like jackals!

DUNYASHA [*to* YASHA]. What happiness, though, to visit foreign lands.

YASHA. Ah, yes! I rather agree with you there. [*Yawns, then lights a cigar.*]

EPIHODOV. That's comprehensible. In foreign lands everything has long since reached full complexion.

YASHA. That's so, of course.

EPIHODOV. I'm a cultivated man, I read remarkable books of all sorts, but I can never make out the tendency I am myself precisely inclined for, whether to live or to shoot myself, speaking precisely, but nevertheless I always carry a revolver. Here it is . . . [*Shows revolver.*]

CHARLOTTA. I've had enough, and now I'm going. [*Puts on the gun.*] Epihodov, you're a very clever fellow, and a very terrible one too, all the women must be wild about you. Br-r-r! [*Goes.*] These clever fellows are all so stupid; there's not a creature for me to speak to. . . . Always alone, alone, nobody belonging to me . . . and who I am, and why I'm on earth, I don't know. [*Walks away slowly.*]

EPIHODOV. Speaking precisely, not touching upon other subjects, I'm bound to admit about myself, that destiny behaves mercilessly to me, as a storm to a little boat. If, let us suppose, I am mistaken, then why did I wake up this morning, to quote an example, and look round, and there on my chest was a spider of fearful magnitude . . . like this. [*Shows with both hands.*] And then I take up a jug of kvass, to quench my thirst, and in it there is something in the highest degree unseemly of the nature of a cockroach. [*A pause.*] Have you read Buckle?[6] [*A pause.*] I am desirous of troubling you, Dunyasha, with a couple of words.

DUNYASHA. Well, speak.

EPIHODOV. I should be desirous to speak with you alone. [*Sighs.*]

DUNYASHA [*embarrassed*]. Well—only bring me my mantle first. It's by the cupboard. It's rather damp here.

EPIHODOV. Certainly. I will fetch it. Now I know what I must do with my revolver. [*Takes the guitar and goes off playing on it.*]

YASHA. Two and twenty misfortunes! Between ourselves, he's a fool. [*Yawns.*]

[6] Henry Thomas Buckle's *History of Civilization in England* (1857–61), popular in Russia for its presumably enlightened, rationalistic view of history. Epihodov's "ideas" are a jumble of half-understood "advanced thought."

DUNYASHA. God grant he doesn't shoot himself! [*A pause.*] I am so nervous, I'm always in a flutter. I was a little girl when I was taken into our lady's house, and now I have quite grown out of peasant ways, and my hands are white, as white as a lady's. I'm such a delicate, sensitive creature, I'm afraid of everything. I'm so frightened. And if you deceive me, Yasha, I don't know what will become of my nerves.

YASHA. [*Kisses her.*] You're a peach! Of course a girl must never forget herself; what I dislike more than anything is a girl being flighty in her behavior.

DUNYASHA. I'm passionately in love with you, Yasha; you are a man of culture—you can give your opinion about anything. [*A pause.*]

YASHA. [*Yawns.*] Yes, that's so. My opinion is this: if a girl loves anyone, that means that she has no principles. [*A pause.*] It's pleasant smoking a cigar in the open air. [*Listens.*] Someone's coming this way . . . it's the gentlefolk [DUNYASHA *embraces him impulsively.*] Go home, as though you had been to the river to bathe; go by that path, or else they'll meet you and suppose I have made an appointment with you here. That I can't endure.

DUNYASHA [*coughing softly*]. The cigar has made my head ache. . . .

[*Goes off.* YASHA *remains sitting near the shrine. Enter* LYUBOV ANDREYEVNA, GAEV *and* LOPAHIN.]

LOPAHIN. You must make up your mind once for all—there's no time to lose. It's quite a simple question, you know. Will you consent to letting the land for building or not? One word in answer: Yes or no? Only one word!

LYUBOV. Who is smoking such horrible cigars here? [*Sits down.*]

GAEV. Now the railway line has been brought near, it's made things very convenient. [*Sits down.*] Here we have been over and lunched in town. Cannon off the white! I should like to go home and have a game.

LYUBOV. You have plenty of time.

LOPAHIN. Only one word! [*Beseechingly*] Give me an answer!

GAEV [*yawning*]. What do you say?

LYUBOV. [*Looks in her purse.*] I had quite a lot of money here yesterday, and there's scarcely any left today. My poor Varya feeds us all on milk soup for the sake of economy; the old folks in the kitchen get nothing but pease pudding, while I waste my money in a senseless way. [*Drops purse, scattering gold pieces.*] There, they have all fallen out [*annoyed*]!

YASHA. Allow me, I'll soon pick them up. [*Collects the coins.*]

LYUBOV. Pray do, Yasha. And what did I go off to the town to lunch for? Your restaurant's a wretched place with its music and the tablecloth smelling of soap. . . . Why drink so much, Leonid? And eat so much? And talk so much? Today you talked a great deal again in the restaurant, and all so inappropriately. About the era of the 'seventies, about the decadents. And to whom? Talking to waiters about decadents![7]

LOPAHIN. Yes.

GAEV [*waving his hand*]. I'm incorrigible; that's evident. [*Irritably to* YASHA] Why is it you keep fidgeting about in front of us!

[7] Members of an anti-bourgeois movement in the arts in the 1890s.

YASHA. [*Laughs.*] I can't help laughing when I hear your voice.

GAEV [*to his sister*]. Either I or he . . .

LYUBOV. Get along! Go away, Yasha.

YASHA. [*Gives* LYUBOV ANDREYEVNA *her purse.*] Directly [*hardly able to suppress his laughter*]. This minute. . . . [*Goes off.*]

LOPAHIN. Deriganov, the millionaire, means to buy your estate. They say he is coming to the sale himself.

LYUBOV. Where did you hear that?

LOPAHIN. That's what they say in town.

GAEV. Our aunt in Yaroslavl has promised to send help; but when, and how much she will send, we don't know.

LOPAHIN. How much will she send? A hundred thousand? Two hundred?

LYUBOV. Oh, well! . . . Ten or fifteen thousand, and we must be thankful to get that.

LOPAHIN. Forgive me, but such reckless people as you are—such queer, unbusinesslike people—I never met in my life. One tells you in plain Russian your estate is going to be sold, and you seem not to understand it.

LYUBOV. What are we to do? Tell us what to do.

LOPAHIN. I do tell you every day. Every day I say the same thing. You absolutely must let the cherry orchard and the land on building leases; and do it at once, as quick as may be—the auction's close upon us! Do understand! Once make up your mind to build villas, and you can raise as much money as you like, and then you are saved.

LYUBOV. Villas and summer visitors—forgive me saying so—it's so vulgar.

GAEV. There I perfectly agree with you.

LOPAHIN. I shall sob, or scream, or fall into a fit. I can't stand it! You drive me mad! [*To* GAEV] You're an old woman!

GAEV. What do you say?

LOPAHIN. An old woman! [*Gets up to go.*]

LYUBOV [*in dismay*]. No, don't go! Do stay, my dear friend! Perhaps we shall think of something.

LOPAHIN. What is there to think of?

LYUBOV. Don't go, I entreat you! With you here it's more cheerful, anyway. [*A pause.*] I keep expecting something, as though the house were going to fall about our ears.

GAEV [*in profound dejection*]. Potted the white! It fails—a kiss.

LYUBOV. We have been great sinners. . . .

LOPAHIN. You have no sins to repent of.

GAEV. [*Puts a caramel in his mouth.*] They say I've eaten up my property in caramels. [*Laughs.*]

LYUBOV. Oh, my sins! I've always thrown my money away recklessly like a lunatic. I married a man who made nothing but debts. My husband died of champagne—he drank dreadfully. To my misery I loved another man, and immediately—it was my first punishment—the blow fell upon me, here, in the river . . . my boy was drowned and I went abroad—went away for ever, never to return, not to see that river again . . . I shut my eyes, and fled, distracted, and *he* after me . . . pitilessly, brutally. I bought a villa at Mentone,[8] for *he* fell ill there, and for three

[8] A resort on the Riviera.

years I had no rest day or night. His illness wore me out, my soul was dried up. And last year, when my villa was sold to pay my debts, I went to Paris and there he robbed me of everything and abandoned me for another woman; and I tried to poison myself. . . . So stupid, so shameful! . . . And suddenly I felt a yearning for Russia, for my country, for my little girl. . . . [*Dries her tears.*] Lord, Lord, be merciful! Forgive my sins! Do not chastise me more! [*Takes a telegram out of her pocket.*] I got this today from Paris. He implores forgiveness, entreats me to return. [*Tears up the telegram.*] I fancy there is music somewhere. [*Listens.*]

GAEV. That's our famous Jewish orchestra. You remember, four violins, a flute and a double bass.

LYUBOV. That still in existence? We ought to send for them one evening, and give a dance.

LOPAHIN. [*Listens.*] I can't hear. . . . [*Hums softly.*] "For money the Germans will turn a Russian into a Frenchman." [*Laughs.*] I did see such a piece at the theater yesterday! It was funny!

LYUBOV. And most likely there was nothing funny in it. You shouldn't look at plays, you should look at yourself a little oftener. How gray your lives are! How much nonsense you talk.

LOPAHIN. That's true. One may say honestly, we live a fool's life. [*Pause.*] My father was a peasant, an idiot; he knew nothing and taught me nothing, only beat me when he was drunk, and always with his stick. In reality I am just such another blockhead and idiot. I've learnt nothing properly. I write a wretched hand. I write so that I feel ashamed before folks, like a pig.

LYUBOV. You ought to get married, my dear fellow.

LOPAHIN. Yes . . . that's true.

LYUBOV. You should marry our Varya, she's a good girl.

LOPAHIN. Yes.

LYUBOV. She's a good-natured girl, she's busy all day long, and what's more, she loves you. And you have liked her for ever so long.

LOPAHIN. Well? I'm not against it. . . . She's a good girl. [*Pause.*]

GAEV. I've been offered a place in the bank: 6,000 roubles a year. Did you know?

LYUBOV. You would never do for that! You must stay as you are.

[*Enter* FIRS *with overcoat.*]

FIRS. Put it on, sir, it's damp.

GAEV [*putting it on*]. You bother me, old fellow.

FIRS. You can't go on like this. You went away in the morning without leaving word. [*Looks him over.*]

LYUBOV. You look older, Firs!

FIRS. What is your pleasure?

LOPAHIN. You look older, she said.

FIRS. I've had a long life. They were arranging my wedding before your papa was born. . . . [*Laughs.*] I was the head footman before the emancipation came.[9] I wouldn't consent to be set free then; I stayed on with the old master. . . . [*A pause.*] I remember what rejoicings they made and didn't know themselves what they were rejoicing over.

[9] The serfs were emancipated in Russia in 1861.

LOPAHIN. Those were fine old times. There was flogging anyway.

FIRS [*not hearing*]. To be sure! The peasants knew their place, and the masters knew theirs; but now they're all at sixes and sevens, there's no making it out.

GAEV. Hold your tongue, Firs. I must go to town tomorrow. I have been promised an introduction to a general, who might let us have a loan.

LOPAHIN. You won't bring that off. And you won't pay your arrears, you may rest assured of that.

LYUBOV. That's all his nonsense. There is no such general.

[*Enter* TROFIMOV, ANYA, *and* VARYA.]

GAEV. Here come our girls.

ANYA. There's mamma on the seat.

LYUBOV [*tenderly*]. Come here, come along. My darlings! [*Embraces* ANYA *and* VARYA.] If you only knew how I love you both. Sit beside me, there, like that.

[*All sit down.*]

LOPAHIN. Our perpetual student is always with the young ladies.

TROFIMOV. That's not your business.

LOPAHIN. He'll soon be fifty, and he's still a student.

TROFIMOV. Drop your idiotic jokes.

LOPAHIN. Why are you so cross, you queer fish?

TROFIMOV. Oh, don't persist!

LOPAHIN. [*Laughs.*] Allow me to ask you what's your idea of me?

TROFIMOV. I'll tell you my idea of you, Yermolay Alexeyevitch: you are a rich man, you'll soon be a millionaire. Well, just as in the economy of nature a wild beast is of use, who devours everything that comes in his way, so you too have your use.

[*All laugh.*]

VARYA. Better tell us something about the planets, Petya.

LYUBOV. No, let us go on with the conversation we had yesterday.

TROFIMOV. What was it about?

GAEV. About pride.

TROFIMOV. We had a long conversation yesterday, but we came to no conclusion. In pride, in your sense of it, there is something mystical. Perhaps you are right from your point of view; but if one looks at it simply, without subtlety, what sort of pride can there be, what sense is there in it, if a man in his physiological formation is very imperfect, if in the immense majority of cases he is coarse, dull-witted, profoundly unhappy? One must give up glorification of self. One should work, and nothing else.

GAEV. One must die in any case.

TROFIMOV. Who knows? And what does it mean—dying? Perhaps man has a hundred senses, and only the five we know are lost at death, while the other ninety-five remain alive.

LYUBOV. How clever you are, Petya!

LOPAHIN [*ironically*]. Fearfully clever!

TROFIMOV. Humanity progresses, perfecting its powers. Everything that is beyond its ken now will one day become familiar and comprehensible; only we must work, we must with all our powers aid the seeker after truth. Here among us in Russia the workers are few in number as yet.

The vast majority of the intellectual people I know, seek nothing, do nothing, are not fit as yet for work of any kind. They call themselves intellectual, but they treat their servants as inferiors, behave to the peasants as though they were animals, learn little, read nothing seriously, do practically nothing, only talk about science and know very little about art. They are all serious people, they all have severe faces, they all talk of weighty matters and air their theories, and yet the vast majority of us—ninety-nine per cent.—live like savages, at the least thing fly to blows and abuse, eat piggishly, sleep in filth and stuffiness, bugs everywhere, stench and damp and moral impurity. And it's clear all our fine talk is only to divert our attention and other people's. Show me where to find the crèches[10] there's so much talk about, and the reading rooms? They only exist in novels: in real life there are none of them. There is nothing but filth and vulgarity and Asiatic apathy. I fear and dislike very serious faces. I'm afraid of serious conversations. We should do better to be silent.

LOPAHIN. You know, I get up at five o'clock in the morning, and I work from morning to night; and I've money, my own and other people's, always passing through my hands, and I see what people are made of all round me. One has only to begin to do anything to see how few honest, decent people there are. Sometimes when I lie awake at night, I think: "Oh! Lord, thou hast given us immense forests, boundless plains, the widest horizons, and living here we ourselves ought really to be giants."

LYUBOV. You ask for giants! They are no good except in storybooks; in real life they frighten us.

[EPIHODOV *advances in the background, playing on the guitar.*]

LYUBOV [*dreamily*]. There goes Epihodov.

ANYA [*dreamily*]. There goes Epihodov.

GAEV. The sun has set, my friends.

TROFIMOV. Yes.

GAEV [*not loudly, but, as it were, declaiming*]. O nature, divine nature, thou art bright with eternal luster, beautiful and indifferent! Thou, whom we call mother, thou dost unite within thee life and death! Thou dost give life and dost destroy!

VARYA [*in a tone of supplication*]. Uncle!

ANYA. Uncle, you are at it again!

TROFIMOV. You'd much better be cannoning off the red!

GAEV. I'll hold my tongue, I will.

[*All sit plunged in thought. Perfect stillness. The only thing audible is the muttering of* FIRS. *Suddenly there is a sound in the distance, as it were from the sky—the sound of a breaking harp string, mournfully dying away.*]

LYUBOV. What is that?

LOPAHIN. I don't know. Somewhere far away a bucket fallen and broken in the pits. But somewhere very far away.

[10] Day nurseries or child-care centers.

GAEV. It might be a bird of some sort—such as a heron.

TROFIMOV. Or an owl.

LYUBOV. [*Shudders.*] I don't know why, but it's horrid. [*A pause.*]

FIRS. It was the same before the calamity—the owl hooted and the samovar hissed all the time.

GAEV. Before what calamity?

FIRS. Before the emancipation. [*A pause.*]

LYUBOV. Come, my friends, let us be going; evening is falling. [*To* ANYA] There are tears in your eyes. What is it, darling? [*Embraces her.*]

ANYA. Nothing, mamma; it's nothing.

TROFIMOV. There is somebody coming.

[*The* WAYFARER *appears in a shabby white forage cap and an overcoat; he is slightly drunk.*]

WAYFARER. Allow me to inquire, can I get to the station this way?

GAEV. Yes. Go along that road.

WAYFARER. I thank you most feelingly [*coughing*]. The weather is superb. [*Declaims*] My brother, my suffering brother! . . . Come out to the Volga! Whose groan do you hear? . . . [*To* VARYA] Mademoiselle, vouchsafe a hungry Russian thirty kopeks.

[VARYA *utters a shriek of alarm.*]

LOPAHIN [*angrily*]. There's a right and a wrong way of doing everything!

LYUBOV [*hurriedly*]. Here, take this. [*Looks in her purse.*] I've no silver. No matter—here's gold for you.

WAYFARER. I thank you most feelingly! [*Goes off.*]

[*Laughter.*]

VARYA [*frightened*]. I'm going home—I'm going . . . Oh, mamma, the servants have nothing to eat, and you gave him gold!

LYUBOV. There's no doing anything with me. I'm so silly! When we get home, I'll give you all I possess. Yermolay Alexeyevitch, you will lend me some more . . . !

LOPAHIN. I will.

LYUBOV. Come, friends, it's time to be going. And Varya, we have made a match of it for you. I congratulate you.

VARYA [*through her tears*]. Mamma, that's not a joking matter.

LOPAHIN. "Ophelia, get thee to a nunnery!"[11]

GAEV. My hands are trembling; it's a long while since I had a game of billiards.

LOPAHIN. "Ophelia! Nymph, in thy orisons be all my sins remember'd."

LYUBOV. Come, it will soon be suppertime.

VARYA. How he frightened me! My heart's simply throbbing.

LOPAHIN. Let me remind you, ladies and gentlemen: on the 22nd of August the cherry orchard will be sold. Think about that! Think about it!

[*All go off, except* TROFIMOV *and* ANYA.]

ANYA [*laughing*]. I'm grateful to the wayfarer! He frightened Varya and we are left alone.

[11] Lopahin is quoting in a garbled version *Hamlet* III.i.139–42, from a scene in which Hamlet alternately woos and abuses Ophelia. Lopahin seems merely to be trying to be "elegant," and fails to realize the horrible inappropriateness of the line.

TROFIMOV. Varya's afraid we shall fall in love with each other, and for days together she won't leave us. With her narrow brain she can't grasp that we are above love. To eliminate the petty and transitory which hinders us from being free and happy—that is the aim and meaning of our life. Forward! We go forward irresistibly towards the bright star that shines yonder in the distance. Forward! Do not lag behind, friends.

ANYA. [*Claps her hands.*] How well you speak! [*A pause.*] It is divine here today.

TROFIMOV. Yes, it's glorious weather.

ANYA. Somehow, Petya, you've made me so that I don't love the cherry orchard as I used to. I used to love it so dearly. I used to think that there was no spot on earth like our garden.

TROFIMOV. All Russia is our garden. The earth is great and beautiful—there are many beautiful places in it. [*A pause.*] Think only, Anya, your grandfather, and great-grandfather, and all your ancestors were slave owners—the owners of living souls—and from every cherry in the orchard, from every leaf, from every trunk there are human creatures looking at you. Cannot you hear their voices? Oh, it is awful! Your orchard is a fearful thing, and when in the evening or at night one walks about the orchard, the old bark on the trees glimmers dimly in the dusk, and the old cherry trees seem to be dreaming of centuries gone by and tortured by fearful visions. Yes! We are at least two hundred years behind, we have really gained nothing yet, we have no definite attitude to the past, we do nothing but theorize or complain of depression or drink vodka. It is clear that to begin to live in the present we must first expiate our past, we must break with it; and we can expiate it only by suffering, by extraordinary unceasing labor. Understand that, Anya.

ANYA. The house we live in has long ceased to be our own, and I shall leave it, I give you my word.

TROFIMOV. If you have the house keys, fling them into the well and go away. Be free as the wind.

ANYA [*in ecstasy*]. How beautifully you said that!

TROFIMOV. Believe me, Anya, believe me! I am not thirty yet, I am young, I am still a student, but I have gone through so much already! As soon as winter comes I am hungry, sick, careworn, poor as a beggar, and what ups and downs of fortune have I not known! And my soul was always, every minute, day and night, full of inexplicable forebodings. I have a foreboding of happiness, Anya. I see glimpses of it already.

ANYA [*pensively*]. The moon is rising.

[EPIHODOV *is heard playing still the same mournful song on the guitar. The moon rises. Somewhere near the poplars* VARYA *is looking for* ANYA *and calling "Anya! where are you?"*]

TROFIMOV. Yes, the moon is rising. [*A pause.*] Here is happiness—here it comes! It is coming nearer and nearer; already I can hear its footsteps. And if we never see it—if we may never know it—what does it matter? Others will see it after us.

VARYA'S VOICE. Anya! Where are you?

TROFIMOV. That Varya again! [*Angrily*] It's revolting!

ANYA. Well, let's go down to the river. It's lovely there.
TROFIMOV. Yes, let's go.

[*They go.*]

VARYA'S VOICE. Anya! Anya!

ACT THREE

SCENE

A drawing room divided by an arch from a larger drawing room. A chandelier burning. The Jewish orchestra, the same that was mentioned in Act II, is heard playing in the anteroom. It is evening. In the larger drawing room they are dancing the grand chain.[12] *The voice of* SEMYONOV-PISHTCHIK: "Promenade à une paire!" *Then enter the drawing room in couples first* PISHTCHIK *and* CHARLOTTA IVANOVNA, *then* TROFIMOV *and* LYUBOV ANDREYEVNA, *thirdly* ANYA *with the* POST OFFICE CLERK, *fourthly* VARYA *with the* STATION MASTER, *and other guests.* VARYA *is quietly weeping and wiping away her tears as she dances. In the last couple is* DUNYASHA. *They move across the drawing room.* PISHTCHIK *shouts:* "Grand rond, balancez!" *and* "Les Cavaliers à genou et remerciez vos dames."

[FIRS *in a swallow-tail coat brings in seltzer water on a tray.* PISHTCHIK *and* TROFIMOV *enter the drawing room.*]

PISHTCHIK. I am a full-blooded man; I have already had two strokes. Dancing's hard work for me, but as they say, if you're in the pack, you must bark with the rest. I'm as strong, I may say, as a horse. My parent, who would have his joke—may the Kingdom of Heaven be his!—used to say about our origin that the ancient stock of the Semyonov-Pishtchiks was derived from the very horse that Caligula made a member of the senate. [*Sits down.*] But I've no money, that's where the mischief is. A hungry dog believes in nothing but meat. . . . [*Snores, but at once wakes up.*] That's like me . . . I can think of nothing but money.

TROFIMOV. There really is something horsy about your appearance.

PISHTCHIK. Well . . . a horse is a fine beast . . . a horse can be sold.

[*There is the sound of billiards being played in an adjoining room.* VARYA *appears in the arch leading to the larger drawing room.*]

TROFIMOV [*teasing*]. Madame Lopahin! Madame Lopahin!

VARYA [*angrily*]. Mangy-looking gentleman!

TROFIMOV. Yes, I am a mangy-looking gentleman, and I'm proud of it!

VARYA [*pondering bitterly*]. Here we have hired musicians and nothing to pay them! [*Goes out.*]

TROFIMOV [*to* PISHTCHIK]. If the energy you have wasted during your life-

[12] A popular ballroom dance. In the following lines, *"Promenade à une paire"* (Promenade by couples), *"Grand rond, balancez"* (Grand round and swing), and *"Les Cavaliers à genou et remerciez vos dames"* (Gentlemen, kneel and thank your partners) are calls in the dance. Even in their reduced circumstances, the Ranevskys dance fashionable French dances rather than Russian ones.

time in trying to find the money to pay your interest, had gone to something else, you might in the end have turned the world upside down.

PISHTCHIK. Nietzsche, the philosopher, a very great and celebrated man . . . of enormous intellect . . . says in his works, that one can make forged bank notes.[13]

TROFIMOV. Why, have you read Nietzsche?

PISHTCHIK. What next . . . Dashenka told me. . . . And now I am in such a position, I might just as well forge bank notes. The day after tomorrow I must pay 310 roubles—130 I have procured. [*Feels in his pockets, in alarm.*] The money's gone! I have lost my money! [*Through his tears*] Where's the money? [*Gleefully*] Why, here it is behind the lining. . . . It has made me hot all over.

[*Enter* LYUBOV ANDREYEVNA *and* CHARLOTTA IVANOVNA.]

LYUBOV. [*Hums the Lezginka.*] Why is Leonid so long? What can he be doing in town? [*To* DUNYASHA] Offer the musicians some tea.

TROFIMOV. The sale hasn't taken place, most likely.

LYUBOV. It's the wrong time to have the orchestra, and the wrong time to give a dance. Well, never mind. [*Sits down and hums softly.*]

CHARLOTTA. [*Gives* PISHTCHIK *a pack of cards.*] Here's a pack of cards. Think of any card you like.

PISHTCHIK. I've thought of one.

CHARLOTTA. Shuffle the pack now. That's right. Give it here, my dear Mr. Pishtchik. *Ein, zwei, drei*[14]—now look, it's in your breast pocket.

PISHTCHIK [*taking a card out of his breast pocket*]. The eight of spades! Perfectly right! [*Wonderingly*] Fancy that now!

CHARLOTTA [*holding pack of cards in her hands, to* TROFIMOV]. Tell me quickly which is the top card.

TROFIMOV. Well, the queen of spades.

CHARLOTTA. It is! [*To* PISHTCHIK] Well, which card is uppermost?

PISHTCHIK. The ace of hearts.

CHARLOTTA. It is! [*Claps her hands, pack of cards disappears.*] Ah! what lovely weather it is today!

[*A mysterious feminine voice which seems coming out of the floor answers her.* "Oh, yes, it's magnificent weather, madam."]

CHARLOTTA. You are my perfect ideal.

VOICE. And I greatly admire you too, madam.

STATION MASTER [*applauding*]. The lady ventriloquist—bravo!

PISHTCHIK [*wonderingly*]. Fancy that now! Most enchanting Charlotta Ivanovna. I'm simply in love with you.

CHARLOTTA. In love? [*Shrugging shoulders*] What do you know of love, *guter Mensch, aber schlechter Musikant.*[15]

TROFIMOV. [*Pats* PISHTCHIK *on the shoulder.*] You dear old horse. . . .

[13] As usual, Pishtchik has everything garbled. The German philosopher Friedrich Nietzsche (1844–1900) argued that the Superman (the natural aristocrat) was "beyond good and evil," but Nietzsche did not issue a general warrant for forgery.

[14] "One, two, three" (German). [15] "A good man but a bad musician" (German).

CHARLOTTA. Attention, please! Another trick! [*Takes a travelling rug from a chair.*] Here's a very good rug; I want to sell it [*shaking it out*]. Doesn't anyone want to buy it?

PISHTCHIK [*wonderingly*]. Fancy that!

CHARLOTTA. *Ein, zwei, drei!* [*Quickly picks up rug she has dropped; behind the rug stands* ANYA; *she makes a curtsey, runs to her mother, embraces her and runs back into the larger drawing room amidst general enthusiasm.*]

LYUBOV. [*Applauds.*] Bravo! Bravo!

CHARLOTTA. Now again! *Ein, zwei, drei!* [*Lifts up the rug; behind the rug stands* VARYA, *bowing.*]

PISHTCHIK [*wonderingly*]. Fancy that now!

CHARLOTTA. That's the end. [*Throws the rug at* PISHTCHIK, *makes a curtsey, runs into the larger drawing room.*]

PISHTCHIK. [*Hurries after her.*] Mischievous creature! Fancy! [*Goes out.*]

LYUBOV. And still Leonid doesn't come. I can't understand what he's doing in the town so long! Why, everything must be over by now. The estate is sold, or the sale has not taken place. Why keep us so long in suspense?

VARYA [*trying to console her*]. Uncle's bought it. I feel sure of that.

TROFIMOV [*ironically*]. Oh, yes!

VARYA. Great-aunt sent him an authorization to buy it in her name, and transfer the debt. She's doing it for Anya's sake, and I'm sure God will be merciful. Uncle will buy it.

LYUBOV. My aunt in Yaroslavl sent fifteen thousand to buy the estate in her name, she doesn't trust us—but that's not enough even to pay the arrears. [*Hides her face in her hands.*] My fate is being sealed today, my fate . . .

TROFIMOV [*teasing* VARYA]. Madame Lopahin.

VARYA [*angrily*]. Perpetual student! Twice already you've been sent down from the University.

LYUBOV. Why are you angry, Varya? He's teasing you about Lopahin. Well, what of that? Marry Lopahin if you like, he's a good man, and interesting; if you don't want to, don't! Nobody compels you, darling.

VARYA. I must tell you plainly, mamma, I look at the matter seriously; he's a good man, I like him.

LYUBOV. Well, marry him. I can't see what you're waiting for.

VARYA. Mamma. I can't make him an offer myself. For the last two years, everyone's been talking to me about him. Everyone talks; but he says nothing or else makes a joke. I see what it means. He's growing rich, he's absorbed in business, he has no thoughts for me. If I had money, were it ever so little, if I had only a hundred roubles, I'd throw everything up and go far away. I would go into a nunnery.

TROFIMOV. What bliss!

VARYA [*to* TROFIMOV]. A student ought to have sense! [*In a soft tone with tears*] How ugly you've grown, Petya! How old you look! [*To* LYUBOV ANDREYEVNA, *no longer crying*] But I can't do without work, mamma; I must have something to do every minute.

[*Enter* YASHA.]

YASHA [*hardly restraining his laughter*]. Epihodov has broken a billiard cue! [*Goes out.*]

VARYA. What is Epihodov doing here? Who gave him leave to play billiards? I can't make these people out. [*Goes out.*]

LYUBOV. Don't tease her, Petya. You see she has grief enough without that.

TROFIMOV. She is so very officious, meddling in what's not her business. All the summer she's given Anya and me no peace. She's afraid of a love affair between us. What's it to do with her? Besides, I have given no grounds for it. Such triviality is not in my line. We are above love!

LYUBOV. And I suppose I am beneath love. [*Very uneasily*] Why is it Leonid's not here? If only I could know whether the estate is sold or not! It seems such an incredible calamity that I really don't know what to think. I am distracted . . . I shall scream in a minute . . . I shall do something stupid. Save me, Petya, tell me something, talk to me!

TROFIMOV. What does it matter whether the estate is sold today or not? That's all done with long ago. There's no turning back, the path is overgrown. Don't worry yourself, dear Lyubov Andreyevna. You mustn't deceive yourself; for once in your life you must face the truth!

LYUBOV. What truth? You see where the truth lies, but I seem to have lost my sight, I see nothing. You settle every great problem so boldly, but tell me, my dear boy, isn't it because you're young—because you haven't yet understood one of your problems through suffering? You look forward boldly, and isn't it that you don't see and don't expect anything dreadful because life is still hidden from your young eyes? You're bolder, more honest, deeper than we are, but think, be just a little magnanimous, have pity on me. I was born here, you know, my father and mother lived here, my grandfather lived here, I love this house. I can't conceive of life without the cherry orchard, and if it really must be sold, then sell me with the orchard. [*Embraces* TROFIMOV, *kisses him on the forehead.*] My boy was drowned here. [*Weeps.*] Pity me, my dear kind fellow.

TROFIMOV. You know I feel for you with all my heart.

LYUBOV. But that should have been said differently, so differently. [*Takes out her handkerchief, telegram falls on the floor.*] My heart is so heavy today. It's so noisy here my soul is quivering at every sound, I'm shuddering all over, but I can't go away; I'm afraid to be quiet and alone. Don't be hard on me, Petya . . . I love you as though you were one of ourselves. I would gladly let you marry Anya—I swear I would—only, my dear boy, you must take your degree, you do nothing—you're simply tossed by fate from place to place. That's so strange. It is, isn't it? And you must do something with your beard to make it grow somehow. [*Laughs.*] You look so funny!

TROFIMOV. [*Picks up the telegram.*] I've no wish to be a beauty.

LYUBOV. That's a telegram from Paris. I get one every day. One yesterday and one today. That savage creature is ill again, he's in trouble again. He begs forgiveness, beseeches me to go, and really I ought to go to Paris to see him. You look shocked, Petya. What am I to do, my dear boy, what am I to do? He is ill, he is alone and unhappy, and who'll look after him, who'll keep him from doing the wrong thing, who'll give him his medicine at the right time? And why hide it or be silent? I love him, that's clear. I love him! I love him! He's a millstone about my neck, I'm going to the bottom with him, but I love that stone and can't live without it. [*Presses* TROFIMOV's *hand.*] Don't think ill of me, Petya, don't tell me anything, don't tell me . . .

TROFIMOV [*through his tears*]. For God's sake forgive my frankness: why, he robbed you!

LYUBOV. No! No! No! You mustn't speak like that. [*Covers her ears.*]

TROFIMOV. He is a wretch! You're the only person that doesn't know it! He's a worthless creature! A despicable wretch!

LYUBOV [*getting angry, but speaking with restraint*]. You're twenty-six or twenty-seven years old, but you're still a schoolboy.

TROFIMOV. Possibly.

LYUBOV. You should be a man at your age! You should understand what love means! And you ought to be in love yourself. You ought to fall in love! [*Angrily*] Yes, yes, and it's not purity in you, you're simply a prude, a comic fool, a freak.

TROFIMOV [*in horror*]. The things she's saying!

LYUBOV. I am above love! You're not above love, but simply as our Firs here says, "You are a good-for-nothing." At your age not to have a mistress!

TROFIMOV [*in horror*]. This is awful! The things she is saying! [*Goes rapidly into the larger drawing room clutching his head.*] This is awful! I can't stand it! I'm going. [*Goes off, but at once returns.*] All is over between us! [*Goes off into the anteroom.*]

LYUBOV. [*Shouts after him.*] Petya! Wait a minute! You funny creature! I was joking! Petya!

[*There is a sound of somebody running quickly downstairs and suddenly falling with a crash.* ANYA *and* VARYA *scream, but there is a sound of laughter at once.*]

LYUBOV. What has happened?

[ANYA *runs in.*]

ANYA [*laughing*]. Petya's fallen downstairs! [*Runs out.*]

LYUBOV. What a queer fellow that Petya is!

[*The* STATION MASTER *stands in the middle of the larger room and reads "The Magdalene," by Alexey Tolstoy.*[16] *They listen to him, but before he has recited many lines strains of a waltz are heard from the anteroom and the reading is broken off. All dance.* TROFIMOV, ANYA, VARYA *and* LYUBOV ANDREYEVNA *come in from the anteroom.*]

LYUBOV. Come, Petya—come, pure heart! I beg your pardon. Let's have a dance! [*Dances with* PETYA.]

[ANYA *and* VARYA *dance.* FIRS *comes in, puts his stick down near the side door.* YASHA *also comes into the drawing room and looks on at the dancing.*]

YASHA. What is it, old man?

[16] A sentimental "parlor piece" in which Christ appears at a fashionable banquet.

FIRS. I don't feel well. In the old days we used to have generals, barons and admirals dancing at our balls, and now we send for the post office clerk and the station master and even they're not overanxious to come. I am getting feeble. The old master, the grandfather, used to give sealing wax for all complaints. I have been taking sealing wax for twenty years or more. Perhaps that's what's kept me alive.

YASHA. You bore me, old man! [*Yawns.*] It's time you were done with.

FIRS. Ach, you're a good-for-nothing! [*Mutters.*]

[TROFIMOV *and* LYUBOV ANDREYEVNA *dance in the larger room and then on to the stage.*]

LYUBOV. *Merci.* I'll sit down a little. [*Sits down.*] I'm tired.

[*Enter* ANYA.]

ANYA [*excitedly*]. There's a man in the kitchen has been saying that the cherry orchard's been sold today.

LYUBOV. Sold to whom?

ANYA. He didn't say to whom. He's gone away.

[*She dances with* TROFIMOV, *and they go off into the larger room.*]

YASHA. There was an old man gossiping there, a stranger.

FIRS. Leonid Andreyevitch isn't here yet, he hasn't come back. He has his light overcoat on, *demi-saison,*[17] he'll catch cold for sure. Ach! Foolish young things!

LYUBOV. I feel as though I should die. Go, Yasha, find out to whom it has been sold.

YASHA. But he went away long ago, the old chap. [*Laughs.*]

LYUBOV [*with slight vexation*]. What are you laughing at? What are you pleased at?

YASHA. Epihodov is so funny. He's a silly fellow, two and twenty misfortunes.

LYUBOV. Firs, if the estate is sold, where will you go?

FIRS. Where you bid me, there I'll go.

LYUBOV. Why do you look like that? Are you ill? You ought to be in bed.

FIRS. Yes [*ironically*]. Me go to bed and who's to wait here? Who's to see to things without me? I'm the only one in all the house.

YASHA [*to* LYUBOV ANDREYEVNA]. Lyubov Andreyevna, permit me to make a request of you; if you go back to Paris again, be so kind as to take me with you. It's positively impossible for me to stay here [*looking about him; in an undertone*]. There's no need to say it, you see for yourself—an uncivilized country, the people have no morals, and then the dullness! The food in the kitchen's abominable, and then Firs runs after one muttering all sorts of unsuitable words. Take me with you, please do!

[*Enter* PISHTCHIK.]

PISHTCHIK. Allow me to ask you for a waltz, my dear lady. [LYUBOV ANDREYEVNA *goes with him.*] Enchanting lady, I really must borrow of you just 180 roubles [*dances*], only 180 roubles. [*They pass into the larger room.*]

YASHA. [*Hums softly.*] "Knowest thou my soul's emotion."

[17] "Between seasons"; light, "all-weather" clothing (French).

[*In the larger drawing room, a figure in a gray top hat and in check trousers is gesticulating and jumping about. Shouts of* "Bravo, Charlotta Ivanovna."]

DUNYASHA. [*She has stopped to powder herself.*] My young lady tells me to dance. There are plenty of gentlemen, and too few ladies, but dancing makes me giddy and makes my heart beat. Firs, the post office clerk said something to me just now that quite took my breath away.

[*Music becomes more subdued.*]

FIRS. What did he say to you?

DUNYASHA. He said I was like a flower.

YASHA. [*Yawns.*] What ignorance! [*Goes out.*]

DUNYASHA. Like a flower. I am a girl of such delicate feelings, I am awfully fond of soft speeches.

FIRS. Your head's being turned.

[*Enter* EPIHODOV.]

EPIHODOV. You have no desire to see me, Dunyasha. I might be an insect. [*Sighs.*] Ah! life!

DUNYASHA. What is it you want?

EPIHODOV. Undoubtedly you may be right. [*Sighs.*] But of course, if one looks at it from that point of view, if I may so express myself, you have, excuse my plain speaking, reduced me to a complete state of mind. I know my destiny. Every day some misfortune befalls me and I have long ago grown accustomed to it, so that I look upon my fate with a smile. You gave me your word, and though I——

DUNYASHA. Let us have a talk later, I entreat you, but now leave me in peace, for I am lost in reverie. [*Plays with her fan.*]

EPIHODOV. I have a misfortune every day, and if I may venture to express myself, I merely smile at it, I even laugh.

[VARYA *enters from the larger drawing room.*]

VARYA. You still have not gone, Epihodov. What a disrespectful creature you are, really! [*To* DUNYASHA] Go along, Dunyasha! [*To* EPIHODOV] First you play billiards and break the cue, then you go wandering about the drawing room like a visitor!

EPIHODOV. You really cannot, if I may so express myself, call me to account like this.

VARYA. I'm not calling you to account, I'm speaking to you. You do nothing but wander from place to place and don't do your work. We keep you as a counting-house clerk, but what use you are I can't say.

EPIHODOV [*offended*]. Whether I work or whether I walk, whether I eat or whether I play billiards, is a matter to be judged by persons of understanding and my elders.

VARYA. You dare to tell me that! [*Firing up*] You dare! You mean to say I've no understanding. Begone from here! This minute!

EPIHODOV [*intimidated*]. I beg you to express yourself with delicacy.

VARYA [*beside herself with anger*]. This moment! get out! away! [*He goes towards the door, she following him.*] Two and twenty misfortunes! Take yourself off! Don't let me set eyes on you! [EPIHODOV *has gone out, behind the door his voice,* "I shall lodge a complaint against you."] What! You're coming back? [*Snatches up the stick* FIRS *has put down near the door.*] Come! Come! Come! I'll show you! What! You're coming? Then take that! [*She swings the stick, at the very moment that* LOPAHIN *comes in.*]

LOPAHIN. Very much obliged to you!

VARYA [*angrily and ironically*]. I beg your pardon!

LOPAHIN. Not at all! I humbly thank you for your kind reception!

VARYA. No need of thanks for it. [*Moves away, then looks round and asks softly*] I haven't hurt you?

LOPAHIN. Oh, no! Not at all! There's an immense bump coming up, though!

VOICES FROM LARGER ROOM. Lopahin has come! Yermolay Alexeyevitch!

PISHTCHIK. What do I see and hear? [*Kisses* LOPAHIN.] There's a whiff of cognac about you, my dear soul, and we're making merry here too!

[*Enter* LYUBOV ANDREYEVNA.]

LYUBOV. Is it you, Yermolay Alexeyevitch? Why have you been so long? Where's Leonid?

LOPAHIN. Leonid Andreyevitch arrived with me. He is coming.

LYUBOV [*in agitation*]. Well! Well! Was there a sale? Speak!

LOPAHIN [*embarrassed, afraid of betraying his joy*]. The sale was over at four o'clock. We missed our train—had to wait till half-past nine. [*Sighing heavily*] Ugh! I feel a little giddy.

[*Enter* GAEV. *In his right hand he has purchases, with his left hand is wiping away his tears.*]

LYUBOV. Well, Leonid? What news? [*Impatiently, with tears*] Make haste, for God's sake!

GAEV. [*Makes her no answer, simply waves his hand. To* FIRS, *weeping*] Here, take them; there's anchovies, Kertch herrings. I have eaten nothing all day. What I have been through! [*Door into the billiard room is open. There is heard a knocking of balls and the voice of* YASHA *saying "Eighty-seven."* GAEV'S *expression changes, he leaves off weeping.*] I am fearfully tired. Firs, come and help me change my things. [*Goes to his own room across the larger drawing room.*]

PISHTCHIK. How about the sale? Tell us, do!

LYUBOV. Is the cherry orchard sold?

LOPAHIN. It is sold.

LYUBOV. Who has bought it?

LOPAHIN. I have bought it.

[*A pause.* LYUBOV *is crushed; she would fall down if she were not standing near a chair and table.* VARYA *takes keys from her waistband, flings them on the floor in middle of drawing room and goes out.*]

LOPAHIN. I have bought it! Wait a bit, ladies and gentlemen, pray. My head's a bit muddled, I can't speak. [*Laughs.*] We came to the auction. Deriganov was there already. Leonid Andreyevitch only had 15,000 and Deriganov bid 30,000, besides the arrears, straight off. I saw how the land lay. I bid against him. I bid 40,000, he bid 45,000, I said 55, and so he went on, adding 5 thousands and I adding 10. Well . . . So it ended. I bid 90, and it was knocked down to me. Now the cherry orchard's mine! Mine! [*Chuckles.*] My God, the cherry orchard's mine! Tell me that I'm drunk, that I'm out of my mind, that it's all a dream. [*Stamps with his feet.*] Don't laugh at me! If my father and my grandfather could rise from their graves and see all that has happened! How their Yermolay, ignorant, beaten Yermolay, who used to run about barefoot in winter, how that very Yermolay has bought the finest estate in the world! I have bought the estate where my father and grandfather were slaves, where they weren't even admitted into the kitchen. I am asleep, I am dreaming! It is all fancy, it is the work of your imagination plunged in the darkness of ignorance. [*Picks up keys, smiling fondly.*] She threw away the keys; she means to show she's not the housewife now. [*Jingles the keys.*] Well, no matter. [*The orchestra is heard tuning up.*] Hey, musicians! Play! I want to hear you. Come, all of you, and look how Yermolay Lopahin will take the axe to the cherry orchard, how the trees will fall to the ground! We will build houses on it and our grandsons and great-grandsons will see a new life springing up there. Music! Play up!

[*Music begins to play.* LYUBOV ANDREYEVNA *has sunk into a chair and is weeping bitterly.*]

LOPAHIN [*reproachfully*]. Why, why didn't you listen to me? My poor friend! Dear lady, there's no turning back now. [*With tears*] Oh, if all this could be over, oh, if our miserable disjointed life could somehow soon be changed!

PISHTCHIK. [*Takes him by the arm, in an undertone.*] She's weeping, let us go and leave her alone. Come. [*Takes him by the arm and leads him into the larger drawing room.*]

LOPAHIN. What's that? Musicians, play up! All must be as I wish it. [*With irony*] Here comes the new master, the owner of the cherry orchard! [*Accidentally tips over a little table, almost upsetting the candelabra.*] I can pay for everything!

[*Goes out with* PISHTCHIK. *No one remains on the stage or in the larger drawing room except* LYUBOV, *who sits huddled up, weeping bitterly. The music plays softly.* ANYA *and* TROFIMOV *come in quickly.* ANYA *goes up to her mother and falls on her knees before her.* TROFIMOV *stands at the entrance to the larger drawing room.*]

ANYA. Mamma! Mamma, you're crying, dear, kind, good mamma! My precious! I love you! I bless you! The cherry orchard is sold, it is gone, that's true, that's true! But don't weep, mamma! Life is still before you, you have still your good, pure heart! Let us go, let us go, darling, away from here! We will make a new garden, more splendid than this one; you will see it, you will understand. And joy, quiet, deep joy, will sink into your soul like the sun at evening! And you will smile, mamma! Come, darling, let us go!

ACT FOUR

SCENE

Same as in First Act. There are neither curtains on the windows nor pictures on the walls: only a little furniture remains piled up in a corner as if for sale. There is a sense of desolation; near the outer door and in the background of the scene are packed trunks, travelling bags, etc. On the left the door is open, and from here the voices of VARYA *and* ANYA *are audible.* LOPAHIN *is standing waiting.* YASHA *is holding a tray with glasses full of champagne. In front of the stage* EPIHODOV *is tying up a box. In the background behind the scene a hum of talk from the peasants who have come to say good-by. The voice of* GAEV: "Thanks, brothers, thanks!"

YASHA. The peasants have come to say good-by. In my opinion, Yermolay Alexeyevitch, the peasants are good-natured, but they don't know much about things.

[*The hum of talk dies away. Enter across front of stage* LYUBOV ANDREYEVNA *and* GAEV. *She is not weeping, but is pale; her face is quivering—she cannot speak.*]

GAEV. You gave them your purse, Lyuba. That won't do—that won't do!

LYUBOV. I couldn't help it! I couldn't help it!

[*Both go out.*]

LOPAHIN [*in the doorway, calls after them*]. You will take a glass at parting? Please do. I didn't think to bring any from the town, and at the station I could only get one bottle. Please take a glass. [*A pause.*] What? You don't care for any? [*Comes away from the door.*] If I'd known, I wouldn't have bought it. Well, and I'm not going to drink it. [YASHA *carefully sets the tray down on a chair.*] You have a glass, Yasha, anyway.

YASHA. Good luck to the travellers, and luck to those that stay behind! [*Drinks.*] This champagne isn't the real thing, I can assure you.

LOPAHIN. It cost eight roubles the bottle. [*A pause.*] It's devilish cold here.

YASHA. They haven't heated the stove today—it's all the same since we're going. [*Laughs.*]

LOPAHIN. What are you laughing for?

YASHA. For pleasure.

LOPAHIN. Though it's October, it's as still and sunny as though it were summer. It's just right for building! [*Looks at his watch; says in doorway*] Take note, ladies and gentlemen, the train goes in forty-seven minutes; so you ought to start for the station in twenty minutes. You must hurry up!

[TROFIMOV *comes in from out of doors wearing a greatcoat.*]

TROFIMOV. I think it must be time to start, the horses are ready. The devil only knows what's become of my galoshes; they're lost. [*In the doorway.*] Anya! My galoshes aren't here. I can't find them.

LOPAHIN. And I'm getting off to Harkov. I am going in the same train with you. I'm spending all the winter at Harkov. I've been wasting all my time gossiping with you and fretting with no work to do. I can't get on without work. I don't know what to do with my hands, they flap about so queerly, as if they didn't belong to me.

TROFIMOV. Well, we're just going away, and you will take up your profitable labors again.

LOPAHIN. Do take a glass.

TROFIMOV. No, thanks.

LOPAHIN. Then you're going to Moscow now?

TROFIMOV. Yes. I shall see them as far as the town, and tomorrow I shall go on to Moscow.

LOPAHIN. Yes, I daresay, the professors aren't giving any lectures, they're waiting for your arrival.

TROFIMOV. That's not your business.

LOPAHIN. How many years have you been at the University?

TROFIMOV. Do think of something newer than that—that's stale and flat. [*Hunts for galoshes.*] You know we shall most likely never see each other again, so let me give you one piece of advice at parting: don't wave your arms about—get out of the habit. And another thing, building villas, reckoning up that the summer visitors will in time become independent farmers—reckoning like that, that's not the thing to do either. After all, I am fond of you: you have fine delicate fingers like an artist, you've a fine delicate soul.

LOPAHIN. [*Embraces him.*] Good-by, my dear fellow. Thanks for everything. Let me give you money for the journey, if you need it.

TROFIMOV. What for? I don't need it.

LOPAHIN. Why, you haven't got a halfpenny.

TROFIMOV. Yes, I have, thank you. I got some money for a translation. Here it is in my pocket, [*anxiously*] but where can my galoshes be!

VARYA [*from the next room*]. Take the nasty things! [*Flings a pair of galoshes onto the stage.*]

TROFIMOV. Why are you so cross, Varya? h'm! . . . but those aren't my galoshes.

LOPAHIN. I sowed three thousand acres with poppies in the spring, and now I have cleared forty thousand profit. And when my poppies were in flower, wasn't it a picture! So here, as I say, I made forty thousand, and I'm offering you a loan because I can afford to. Why turn up your nose? I am a peasant—I speak bluntly.

TROFIMOV. Your father was a peasant, mine was a chemist—and that proves absolutely nothing whatever. [LOPAHIN *takes out his pocketbook.*] Stop that—stop that. If you were to offer me two hundred thousand I wouldn't take it. I am an independent man, and everything that all of you, rich and poor alike, prize so highly and hold so dear, hasn't the slightest power over me—it's like so much fluff fluttering in the air. I can get on without you. I can pass by you. I am strong and proud. Humanity is advancing towards the highest truth, the highest happiness, which is possible on earth, and I am in the front ranks.

LOPAHIN. Will you get there?

TROFIMOV. I shall get there. [*A pause.*] I shall get there, or I shall show others the way to get there.

[*In the distance is heard the stroke of an axe on a tree.*]

LOPAHIN. Good-by, my dear fellow; it's time to be off. We turn up our noses at one another, but life is passing all the while. When I am working hard without resting, then my mind is more at ease, and it seems to me as though I too know what I exist for; but how many people there are in Russia, my dear boy, who exist, one doesn't know what for. Well, it doesn't matter. That's not what keeps things spinning. They tell me Leonid Andreyevitch has taken a situation. He is going to be a clerk at the bank—6,000 roubles a year. Only, of course, he won't stick to it—he's too lazy.

ANYA [*in the doorway*]. Mamma begs you not to let them chop down the orchard until she's gone.

TROFIMOV. Yes, really, you might have the tact. [*Walks out across the front of the stage.*]

LOPAHIN. I'll see to it! I'll see to it! Stupid fellows! [*Goes out after him.*]

ANYA. Has Firs been taken to the hospital?

YASHA. I told them this morning. No doubt they have taken him.

ANYA [*to* EPIHODOV, *who passes across the drawing room*]. Semyon Pantaleyevitch, inquire, please, if Firs has been taken to the hospital.

YASHA [*in a tone of offense*]. I told Yegor this morning—why ask a dozen times?

EPIHODOV. Firs is advanced in years. It's my conclusive opinion no treatment would do him good; it's time he was gathered to his fathers. And I can only envy him. [*Puts a trunk down on a cardboard hatbox and crushes it.*] There, now, of course—I knew it would be so.

YASHA [*jeeringly*]. Two and twenty misfortunes!

VARYA [*through the door*]. Has Firs been taken to the hospital?

ANYA. Yes.

VARYA. Why wasn't the note for the doctor taken too?

ANYA [*from the adjoining room*]. Where's Yasha? Tell him his mother's come to say good-by to him.

YASHA. [*Waves his hand.*] They put me out of all patience! [DUNYASHA *has all this time been busy about the luggage. Now, when* YASHA *is left alone, she goes up to him.*]

DUNYASHA. You might just give me one look, Yasha. You're going away. You're leaving me. [*Weeps and throws herself on his neck.*]

YASHA. What are you crying for? [*Drinks the champagne.*] In six days I shall be in Paris again. Tomorrow we shall get into the express train and roll away in a flash. I can scarcely believe it! *Vive la France!* It doesn't suit me here—it's not the life for me; there's no doing anything. I have seen enough of the ignorance here. I have had enough of it. [*Drinks champagne.*] What are you crying for? Behave yourself properly, and then you won't cry.

DUNYASHA. [*Powders her face, looking in a pocket mirror.*] Do send me a letter from Paris. You know how I loved you, Yasha—how I loved you! I am a tender creature, Yasha.

YASHA. Here they are coming!

[*Busies himself about the trunks, humming softly. Enter* LYUBOV ANDREYEVNA, GAEV, ANYA *and* CHARLOTTA IVANOVNA.]

GAEV. We ought to be off. There's not much time now [*looking at* YASHA]. What a smell of herrings!

LYUBOV. In ten minutes we must get into the carriage. [*Casts a look about the room.*] Farewell, dear house, dear old home of our fathers! Winter will pass and spring will come, and then you will be no more; they will tear you down! How much those walls have seen! [*Kisses her daughter passionately.*] My treasure, how bright you look! Your eyes are sparkling like diamonds! Are you glad? Very glad?

ANYA. Very glad! A new life is beginning, mamma.

GAEV. Yes, really, everything is all right now. Before the cherry orchard was sold, we were all worried and wretched, but afterwards, when once the question was settled conclusively, irrevocably, we all felt calm and even cheerful. I am a bank clerk now—I am a financier—cannon off the red. And you, Lyuba, after all, you are looking better; there's no question of that.

LYUBOV. Yes. My nerves are better, that's true. [*Her hat and coat are handed to her.*] I'm sleeping well. Carry out my things, Yasha. It's time. [*To* ANYA] My darling, we shall soon see each other again. I am going to Paris. I can live there on the money your Yaroslavl auntie sent us to buy the estate with—hurrah for auntie!—but that money won't last long.

ANYA. You'll come back soon, mamma, won't you? I'll be working up for my examination in the high school, and when I have passed that, I shall set to work and be a help to you. We will read all sorts of things together, mamma, won't we? [*Kisses her mother's hands.*] We will read in the autumn evenings. We'll read lots of books, and a new wonderful world will open out before us [*dreamily*]. Mamma, come soon.

LYUBOV. I shall come, my precious treasure. [*Embraces her.*]

[*Enter* LOPAHIN. CHARLOTTA *softly hums a song.*]

GAEV. Charlotta's happy; she's singing!

CHARLOTTA. [*Picks up a bundle like a swaddled baby.*] By, by, my baby. [*A baby is heard crying: "Ooah! ooah!"]* Hush, hush, my pretty boy! [*Ooah! ooah!*] Poor little thing! [*Throws the bundle back.*] You must please find me a situation. I can't go on like this.

LOPAHIN. We'll find you one, Charlotta Ivanovna. Don't you worry yourself.

GAEV. Everyone's leaving us. Varya's going away. We have become of no use all at once.

CHARLOTTA. There's nowhere for me to be in the town. I must go away. [*Hums.*] What care I . . .

[*Enter* PISHTCHIK.]

LOPAHIN. The freak of nature!

PISHTCHIK [*gasping*]. Oh! . . . let me get my breath. . . . I'm worn out . . . my most honored . . . Give me some water.

GAEV. Want some money, I suppose? Your humble servant! I'll go out of the way of temptation. [*Goes out.*]

PISHTCHIK. It's a long while since I have been to see you . . . dearest lady. [*To* LOPAHIN] You are here . . . glad to see you . . . a man of immense intellect . . . take . . . here [*gives* LOPAHIN] . . . 400 roubles. That leaves me owing 840.

LOPAHIN [*shrugging his shoulders in amazement*]. It's like a dream. Where did you get it?

PISHTCHIK. Wait a bit . . . I'm hot . . . a most extraordinary occurrence! Some Englishmen came along and found in my land some sort of white clay. [*To* LYUBOV ANDREYEVNA] And 400 for you . . . most lovely . . . wonderful. [*Gives money.*] The rest later. [*Sips water.*] A young man in the train was telling me just now that a great philosopher advises jumping off a housetop. "Jump!" says he; "the whole gist of the problem lies in that." [*Wonderingly*] Fancy that, now! Water, please!

LOPAHIN. What Englishmen?

PISHTCHIK. I have made over to them the rights to dig the clay for twenty-four years . . . and now, excuse me . . . I can't stay . . . I must be trotting on. I'm going to Znoikovo . . . to Kardamanovo. . . . I'm in debt all round. [*Sips.*] . . . To your very good health! . . . I'll come in on Thursday.

LYUBOV. We are just off to the town, and tomorrow I start for abroad.

PISHTCHIK. What! [*In agitation*] Why to the town? Oh, I see the furniture . . . the boxes. No matter . . . [*through his tears*] . . . no matter . . . men of enormous intellect . . . these Englishmen. . . . Never mind . . . be happy. God will succor you . . . no matter . . . everything in this world must have an end. [*Kisses* LYUBOV ANDREYEVNA'S *hand.*] If the rumor reaches you that my end has come, think of this . . . old horse, and say: "There once was such a man in the world . . . Semyonov Pishtchik . . . the Kingdom of Heaven be his!" . . . most extraordinary weather . . . yes. [*Goes out in violent agitation, but at once returns and says in the doorway*] Dashenka wishes to be remembered to you. [*Goes out.*]

LYUBOV. Now we can start. I leave with two cares in my heart. The first is leaving Firs ill. [*Looking at her watch*] We have still five minutes.

ANYA. Mamma, Firs has been taken to the hospital. Yasha sent him off this morning.

LYUBOV. My other anxiety is Varya. She is used to getting up early and working; and now, without work, she's like a fish out of water. She is thin and pale, and she's crying, poor dear! [*A pause.*] You are well aware, Yermolay Alexeyevitch, I dream of marrying her to you, and everything seemed to show that you would get married. [*Whispers to* ANYA *and motions to* CHARLOTTA *and both go out.*] She loves you—she suits you. And I don't know—I don't know why it is you seem, as it were, to avoid each other. I can't understand it!

LOPAHIN. I don't understand it myself, I confess. It's queer somehow, altogether. If there's still time, I'm ready now at once. Let's settle it straight off, and go ahead; but without you, I feel I shan't make her an offer.

LYUBOV. That's excellent. Why, a single moment's all that's necessary. I'll call her at once.

LOPAHIN. And there's champagne all ready too [*looking into the glasses*]. Empty! Someone's emptied them already. [YASHA *coughs.*] I call that greedy.

LYUBOV [*eagerly*]. Capital! We will go out. Yasha, *allez!*[18] I'll call her in. [*At the door*] Varya, leave all that; come here. Come along! [*Goes out with* YASHA.]

LOPAHIN [*looking at his watch*]. Yes.

[18] "Go!"

[*A pause. Behind the door, smothered laughter and whispering, and, at last, enter* VARYA.]

VARYA [*looking a long while over the things*]. It is strange, I can't find it anywhere.

LOPAHIN. What are you looking for?

VARYA. I packed it myself, and I can't remember. [*A pause.*]

LOPAHIN. Where are you going now, Varvara Mihailova?

VARYA. I? To the Ragulins. I have arranged to go to them to look after the house—as a housekeeper.

LOPAHIN. That's in Yashnovo? It'll be seventy miles away. [*A pause.*] So this is the end of life in this house!

VARYA [*looking among the things*]. Where is it? Perhaps I put it in the trunk. Yes, life in this house is over—there will be no more of it.

LOPAHIN. And I'm just off to Harkov—by this next train. I've a lot of business there. I'm leaving Epihodov here, and I've taken him on.

VARYA. Really!

LOPAHIN. This time last year we had snow already, if you remember; but now it's so fine and sunny. Though it's cold, to be sure—three degrees of frost.

VARYA. I haven't looked. [*A pause.*] And besides, our thermometer's broken.

[*A pause. Voice at the door from the yard:* "Yermolay Alexeyevitch!"]

LOPAHIN [*as though he had long been expecting this summons*]. This minute!

[LOPAHIN *goes out quickly.* VARYA *sitting on the floor and laying her head on a bag full of clothes, sobs quietly. The door opens.* LYUBOV ANDREYEVNA *comes in cautiously.*]

LYUBOV. Well? [*A pause.*] We must be going.

VARYA. [*Has wiped her eyes and is no longer crying.*] Yes, mamma, it's time to start. I shall have time to get to the Ragulins today, if only you're not late for the train.

LYUBOV [*in the doorway*]. Anya, put your things on.

[*Enter* ANYA, *then* GAEV *and* CHARLOTTA IVANOVNA. GAEV *has on a warm coat with a hood. Servants and cabmen come in.* EPIHODOV *bustles about the luggage.*]

LYUBOV. Now we can start on our travels.

ANYA [*joyfully*]. On our travels!

GAEV. My friends—my dear, my precious friends! Leaving this house forever, can I be silent? Can I refrain from giving utterance at leave-taking to those emotions which now flood all my being?

ANYA [*supplicatingly*]. Uncle!

VARYA. Uncle, you mustn't!

GAEV [*dejectedly*]. Cannon and into the pocket . . . I'll be quiet. . . .

[*Enter* TROFIMOV *and afterwards* LOPAHIN.]

TROFIMOV. Well, ladies and gentlemen, we must start.

LOPAHIN. Epihodov, my coat!

LYUBOV. I'll stay just one minute. It seems as though I have never seen before what the walls, what the ceilings in this house were like, and now I look at them with greediness, with such tender love.

GAEV. I remember when I was six years old sitting in that window on Trinity Day watching my father going to church.

LYUBOV. Have all the things been taken?

LOPAHIN. I think all. [*Putting on overcoat, to* EPIHODOV] You, Epihodov, mind you see everything is right.

EPIHODOV [*in a husky voice*]. Don't you trouble, Yermolay Alexeyevitch.

LOPAHIN. Why, what's wrong with your voice?

EPIHODOV. I've just had a drink of water, and I choked over something.

YASHA [*contemptuously*]. The ignorance!

LYUBOV. We are going—and not a soul will be left here.

LOPAHIN. Not till the spring.

VARYA. [*Pulls a parasol out of a bundle, as though about to hit someone with it.* LOPAHIN *makes a gesture as though alarmed.*] What is it? I didn't mean anything.

TROFIMOV. Ladies and gentlemen, let us get into the carriage. It's time. The train will be in directly.

VARYA. Petya, here they are, your galoshes, by that box. [*With tears*] And what dirty old things they are!

TROFIMOV [*putting on his galoshes*]. Let us go, friends!

GAEV [*greatly agitated, afraid of weeping*]. The train—the station! Double balk, ah!

LYUBOV. Let us go!

LOPAHIN. Are we all here? [*Locks the side door on left.*] The things are all here. We must lock up. Let us go!

ANYA. Good-by, home! Good-by to the old life!

TROFIMOV. Welcome to the new life!

[TROFIMOV *goes out with* ANYA. VARYA *looks round the room and goes out slowly.* YASHA *and* CHARLOTTA IVANOVNA, *with her dog, go out.*]

LOPAHIN. Till the spring, then! Come, friends, till we meet!

[*Goes out.* LYUBOV ANDREYEVNA *and* GAEV *remain alone. As though they had been waiting for this, they throw themselves on each other's necks, and break into subdued smothered sobbing, afraid of being overheard.*]

GAEV [*in despair*]. Sister, my sister!

LYUBOV. Oh, my orchard!—my sweet, beautiful orchard! My life, my youth, my happiness, good-by! good-by!

VOICE OF ANYA [*calling gaily*]. Mamma!

VOICE OF TROFIMOV [*gaily, excitedly*]. Aa—oo!

LYUBOV. One last look at the walls, at the windows. My dear mother loved to walk about this room.

GAEV. Sister, sister!

VOICE OF ANYA. Mamma!
VOICE OF TROFIMOV. Aa—oo!
LYUBOV. We are coming.

[*They go out. The stage is empty. There is the sound of the doors being locked up, then of the carriages driving away. There is silence. In the stillness there is the dull stroke of an axe on a tree, clanging with a mournful lonely sound. Footsteps are heard.* FIRS *appears in the doorway on the right. He is dressed as always—in a pea jacket and white waistcoat with slippers on his feet. He is ill.*]

FIRS. [*Goes up to the doors, and tries the handles.*] Locked! They have gone. . . . [*Sits down on sofa.*] They have forgotten me. . . . Never mind . . . I'll sit here a bit. . . . I'll be bound Leonid Andreyevitch hasn't put his fur coat on and has gone off in his thin overcoat. [*Sighs anxiously.*] I didn't see after him. . . . These young people . . . [*Mutters something that can't be distinguished.*] Life has slipped by as though I hadn't lived. [*Lies down.*] I'll lie down a bit. . . . There's no strength in you, nothing left you—all gone! Ech! I'm good for nothing.

[*Lies motionless. A sound is heard that seems to come from the sky, like a breaking harp string, dying away mournfully. All is still again, and there is heard nothing but the strokes of the axe far away in the orchard.*]

The Modern Period

JUST as it is difficult for a swimming man to see the ocean, so it is difficult for us to bring a clear perspective to the study of the literature of the present and of the recent past. Our own literary history is still writing itself. Like Menelaus seizing Proteus, we can take a grip on it for a moment, but the minute we let go, it changes shape again. And we must add to the dynamic, protean quality of an ongoing literature the additional complication of our own personal involvement in it. The American critic Lionel Trilling has identified the urgent, personal quality as the major "modern element in modern literature." "No literature," he writes, "has ever been so shockingly personal as ours—it asks every question that is forbidden in polite society. It asks us if we are content with our marriages, with our family lives, with our professional lives, with our friends." To a degree, understanding modern literature inevitably implies the formidable problem of understanding ourselves.

What is the *modern?* From one point of view, the word says very little. In ordinary language, it merely means "up-to-date" or "pertaining to the present time" and therefore can have no fixed meaning. Sophocles was modern in 450 B.C., Dante in 1300 A.D., but their modernity has nothing to do with T. S. Eliot's in 1922 or Thomas Pynchon's in 1973. *Modern* would thus seem to be the most neutral and noncommittal of terms, less fixed even than *eighteenth-century* or *nineteenth-century,* not to mention such interpretative labels as *neoclassic* or *romantic.* In practice, though, *modernism* has come to mean something very specific in literary history, not just whatever is current but a time-bound movement, roughly coinciding with the twentieth century and developing certain artistic principles as specific as those of neoclassicism or romanticism. It is significant that twentieth-century artists should have settled upon such a slippery, ever-changing word as *modern* to describe their work, which has itself demonstrated a pattern of rapid and accelerating change. But change itself can be a principle of continuity; there can be, paradoxically, a "tradition of the new," as the art critic Harold Rosenberg has pointed out. We may not be able to freeze the stream of that tradition, as it surges around us, but we can chart a few currents in it.

One such current is the persistent conviction throughout twentieth-century literature that our age is unique, that modern experience is qualitatively different from that of any time in the past. Some critics, taking a very long view, have seen modern culture, with its pervasive secularism, its dominance by scientific technology, and its overwhelmingly individualist coloring, as the logical culmination of forces set in motion during the Renaissance; modernism is, for them, an extension of Renaissance individualism. Others have identified modernism as a late phase of romanticism, a continuing response to the collapse of traditional values and authority signaled by the French Revolution, or as a development of the demystifying impulses of late nineteenth-century realism. But most critics, while acknowledging the survivals of the past into modern culture, have sensed something fundamentally new in that culture. And modern artists have, for the most part, held the same view. "On or about December 1910 human nature changed," Virginia Woolf wrote in 1924. D. H. Lawrence had the same feeling, though he dated the change five years later: "It was in 1915 the old world ended," he wrote in *Kangaroo* (1923).

One is tempted to ask the exact time of day and if Woolf and Lawrence were sure that their watches were accurate. But of course their comparative precision is a rhetorical flourish as well as an allusion to certain symbolic events: the death of England's King Edward VII and the opening of the first Post-Impressionist exhibition in London (both 1910) and the first full year of World War I (1915). More important than getting an exact fix on precise dates is understanding what this presumed "change in human nature" amounted to. At its most fundamental level, the change was a massive disillusionment, an erosion of faith not only in religion but in a number of secular principles as well, principles which at least seemed to have formed the basis of all of Western civilization. The disillusionment was to some degree intellectual, the result of a wide range of late nineteenth-century theories and discoveries that collectively implied a radical revision of traditional Western ideas. Karl Marx's *Capital* (1867–94) shook the imperialist ideology of Western Europe by finding in history not the pattern of progress toward domination of the world by the "enlightened" bourgeoisie of Europe but an inevitable movement, to be hurried along by revolution, toward a struggle between the capitalist middle class and the nonpropertied proletariat that would end in the triumph of the workers. Charles Darwin's *Origin of Species* (1859) and *The Descent of Man* (1871) similarly seemed to remove mind from human history, on an even broader scale, by placing man in the animal world in the grip of determinative forces not of reason but of brute survival. Sir James G. Frazer, in *The Golden Bough* (1890) struck another blow against the popular theory of progress by showing the continuities and similarities between "primitive" and "civilized" cultures. The German philosopher Friedrich Nietzsche's *Birth of Tragedy* (1872), which glorified the Dionysian forces in life, had an enormous impact on late nineteenth-century Europe; in Nietzsche's reconsideration of Greek history, Apollo and Socrates became the villains rather than the heroic light-bringers they seemed to the nineteenth-century imagination. Faith in ordinary, cause-and-effect reasoning was further eroded from a very different source by Max Planck's proposal in 1900 of the quantum theory of atomic and subatomic particles; its model of discrete bits (*quanta*) of energy behaving in apparently discontinuous and unpredictable ways seized the imaginations of people who took the theory far beyond the limits of physics. And Sigmund Freud's *Interpretation of Dreams* (1899) created a new model of human personality itself as complex, multilayered, and governed, in large part, by irrational and unconscious survivals of childhood fantasy.

This compressed collage of names and ideas can only suggest the nature of the disillusionment out of which modernism rose. In a sense it contains nothing new; class struggle, the animal side of man, primitivism, the power of Dionysus, irrationality, and the unconscious had been central to much nineteenth-century thought. But these ideas never succeeded, in the nineteenth century, in destroying the generally prevalent faith in religion, progress, and materialism. That faith weakened in the face of contrary evidence late in the century and died in the apocalyptic experience of the First World War.

Modern artists just after World War I (and some in the years just before it) found themselves in a world deprived of a number of traditional ways of ordering experience. They could no longer accept the premises of the existence of a God, of man's right to a certain dignity by virtue of his special place in creation, of the supremacy of reason in human affairs, or even of life as being self-evidently worth living. The heavens were, for the first time in history, empty. Of course, not all people rejected these premises any more than all people reject them now. (A perennial piece of graffiti reads: "God is dead—Nietzsche." "Nietzsche is dead—God.") But the main tendency of modern Western culture has been to deny or question them.

Much of modern literature was born from this new spiritual confrontation with emptiness. But the exploration of the void has not been predominantly despairing or nihilistic. Just as frequently, it has been joyful and affirmative. The search for new ways of ordering experience meaningfully has ended as often in hope as in despair, whether the ground for affirmation be personal relationships, social idealism, rediscovery of man's roots in nature, or a kind of indefinable animal vitality. As often as not, "gaiety," in W. B. Yeats's words, "transfigures all that dread."

Disillusioned and contemplating a cosmos and a society either without order or so complexly ordered as to defy understanding, most modern writers have looked within themselves for a principle of order. The most striking feature of modern literature has therefore been its overwhelming preoccupation with the self, the nature of consciousness, and the processes of perception. In its subjectivity, modern literature has paralleled the development of other arts, such as painting, which moved in the late nineteenth century from the Impressionistic concern with the viewer's coloring of the external world in the act of perception, through a gradual withdrawal from the outside world into the viewer's consciousness, to the complete immersion in the mind typical of modern abstract painting.

Crucial to early modern literary explorations of individual perception were the theory and practice of the French Symbolist poets. Charles Baudelaire (1821–67), Arthur Rimbaud (1854–91), Paul Verlaine (1844–96), and Stéphane Mallarmé (1842–98) reacted against both the materialism of their society and the crudity of naturalism by withdrawing into an ideal world of art. The Symbolists aimed to capture the most evanescent of personal experiences in shimmering, open-ended, essentially private symbols. Their quixotic goal was to express the inexpressible, or rather to evoke it subtly. "Poetry," Mallarmé wrote, "should not inform but suggest and evoke, not name things but create their atmosphere." Echoes of Symbolist doctrines linger not only in the pervasive symbolic method of the early modern novelists, poets, and dramatists but also in a number of explicit statements about narrative form and meaning, such as Conrad's description of Marlow's narrative method in *Heart of Darkness*: "To him the meaning of an episode was not inside like a kernel but outside, enveloping the tale which brought it out only as a glow brings out a haze, in the likeness of one of those misty halos that sometimes are made visible by the spectral illumination of moonshine." They linger also in Virginia Woolf's description of life as the novelist should seek to represent it—"not a series of gig lamps symmetrically arranged; but a luminous halo, a semi-transparent envelope surrounding us from the beginning of consciousness to the end"—and in the young James Joyce's quest for epiphanic moments of enlightenment through bits of concrete experience.

The Symbolists' concentration upon single moments of individual perception anticipated the modernists' pervasive concern with fragmentation. As general laws and large systems lost their persuasiveness, they left behind small fragments of irreducible experience to be manipulated and reordered in new ways. As the Cubist painters shattered the features of a human face and reassembled them, perhaps with both eyes on one side of a profile, so modernist writers shattered and reassembled the elements of their art. Conrad's literary impressionism approaches a kind of literary cubism in a novel such as *Lord Jim,* a series of nonchronological fragments glimpsed, to use Marlow's own metaphor, through brief rifts in an enveloping fog. Character, too, is disassembled into its fragmentary components, not held together by an overarching theory of human types or any other simple psychology. Strindberg's "characterless" dramatic characters are of this complex sort. "I have depicted my characters as modern characters," he pointed out in his preface to *Miss Julie* (1888), "vacillating, disjointed: a blending of the old and the new . . . . My characters are conglomerates of a past stage of civilization and our present one, scraps from books and newspapers, pieces of humanity, torn-off tatters of holiday clothes that have disintegrated and become rags—exactly as the soul is patched together." The "heap of broken images" that is T. S. Eliot's *The Waste Land,* the disjointed fragments of a story the six characters bring to the theater in Luigi Pirandello's *Six Characters in Search of an Author,* and the brief, snapshot scenes of Bertolt Brecht's Epic Theater are all expressions of the modern writer's sense that fragments are all that one can honestly treat. Fragments alone are freed from suspect traditional systems of order.

The disintegration of experience into fragments suggests the negative side of modernism; the Symbolists' attempt to divine the significance of each luminous bit and the search for new forms of organizing the fragments suggest the positive side. The simplest organizational method was juxtaposition, as in collage. Early modern painters experimented with this method, and Ezra Pound used it when he edited the first version of Eliot's *Waste Land* to remove the transitions between the separate sections. Even more far-reaching was stream-of-consciousness, a technique associated ordinarily with fiction but implicit also in poetry or even drama which takes its form from the fluid, associational, often illogical, moment-to-moment sequence of ideas, feelings, and impressions of a single mind. Inevitably, traditional literary forms melt before such subjectivity and are replaced by unique, make-it-up-as-you-go-along ones in which each work seems tailored to its own content. Genres overlap and merge, so that poetry can incorporate sections of flat prose and novels can employ the lyricism, the rhythmic qualities, and the symbolism traditionally associated with poetry. The forms of the past are shamelessly raided and employed, but mainly for ironic effect, as when *The Waste Land* briefly shapes itself into a series of sonnets, *Heart of Darkness* reminds us for a moment of a boys' adventure story, or the Producer in *Six Characters* tries to force the characters' inchoate tale into the iron form of melodrama.

An equally important shaping principle in modern literature has been what might be called the "stream-of-*un*consciousness," the use of the irrational logic of dreams and fantasies. The modernists' search for an alternative logic to what they perceived as a sterile, exhausted rationality led them repeatedly to the shadowy structures of the dream. Strindberg, in his preface to *A Dream Play* (1902), described his idea of these structures: "The author has sought to reproduce the disconnected, yet apparently logical, form of the dream. Anything is possible and plausible. Time and space do not exist; the imagination, grounding itself only slightly in reality, spins and weaves new patterns, mixing memory, experience, free invention, absurdity, and improvisation. Characters divide, double, redouble, evaporate, condense, float out of each other, converge. But there is a consciousness transcending all—the consciousness of the dreamer." Like Strindberg, the French Surrealists of the 1920's sought to capture the dream for literature, through hypnosis, drugs, revery, and automatic writing; for them, the "surreality" of dreams held a truth more profound than the logic of waking reality. But even for other writers who did not attempt to recreate dreams directly, the workings of the unconscious held a fascination so great that Freud's explanations in *The Interpretation of Dreams* of the principles of dream-logic—its symbolizings, compressions and divisions of characters and ideas, and its mysterious redistributions of emotional associations—are almost as useful for interpreting modern literature as they are for interpreting dreams.

Myth, as a sort of collective dream, has been mined also for its power to give shape to experience, but myth in modernism has been stripped, for the most part, of its religious and magical associations. When James Joyce built *Ulysses,* the story of a day in Dublin, June 16, 1904, on the foundation of the sequence of episodes in the *Odyssey,* T. S. Eliot found the idea promising for modern literature: "In using the myth, in manipulating the continuous parallel between contemporaneity and antiquity, Mr. Joyce is pursuing a method which others must pursue after him . . . . It is simply a way of controlling, of ordering, of giving a shape and a significance to the immense panorama of futility and anarchy which is contemporary history . . . . It is, I seriously believe, a step toward making the modern world possible for art." Eliot himself employed the "mythic method" in 1922, the same year *Ulysses* was published, when he built *The Waste Land* upon the structure of the ancient fertility myth of the dying and reviving king. Eliot was right in predicting that many later writers would find in allusion and myth a way of structuring modern experience: Yeats with the story of Leda and the swan and a great many other myths, both pagan and Christian; Mann with the Faust-legend and the story of Joseph and his brothers; Porter and many others with the mythic descent to the underworld; Faulkner with the myth of Eden; and dozens of other modern writers with dozens of other myths.

The modern writer's quest for order created by individual consciousness has led inevitably to a preoccupation with the artist himself and with the artistic process. The twentieth century has been the great age of the *Bildungsroman* (the growing-up story) and the *Künstlerroman* (the artist-story), along with their equivalents in poetry and drama. One of the great modern masterpieces, Marcel Proust's *Remembrance of Things Past* (1913–27), is a seven-volume narrative about the writer himself and his quest for an artistic subject. D. H. Lawrence's *Sons and Lovers* (1913), Thomas Mann's *Death in Venice* (1913) and *Doctor Faustus* (1947), James Joyce's *A Portrait of the Artist as a Young Man* (1916), Virginia Woolf's *To the Lighthouse* (1927), and a host of other works explore either the writer's own development as an artist or that of a thinly veiled surrogate. The themes of these works are seldom narrowly aesthetic; art becomes an exemplary activity, representing the pattern-making which the openness and indeterminancy of modern life forces all of us to engage in. Thus the artist becomes the modern hero, the prototype of the modern person thinking and feeling.

The same pattern-making impulse may account for the formalism and the reflexivity of much modern art. It is as if the artist were saying, "If I cannot see an order in the world around me, I can at least explore the order within the microcosm of my work. And perhaps that order will help me perceive order in the larger world as well." Modern literature is full of metafiction, metapoetry, and metatheater, self-reflexive literature about literature, in which literary forms come to stand for the forms of life. Much modern drama carries to its logical conclusion Jaques' observation in *As You Like It* that "all the world's a stage, and all the men and women merely players." In Luigi Pirandello's *Six Characters in Search of an Author* (1921), the six characters invade a play rehearsal and launch an attack upon the actors' definitions of "theater" and "life," leaving them at least half-convinced that life consists only in wearing a series of "naked masks." Or perhaps all the world's a novel, as it seems to be in the work of writers from Joseph Conrad through Samuel Beckett and Jorge Luis Borges to Peter Handke. Or perhaps it's a poem, as it is in *The Waste Land,* in W. B. Yeats's "Sailing to Byzantium," in W. H. Auden's "In Memory of W. B. Yeats," and in many other modern poems. Art folds back upon itself in "the act of finding," as Wallace Stevens wrote, "what will suffice."

Not all modern literature has the sort of problematical, existential, self-conscious quality we have been describing. The Soviet Union and the other socialist countries of eastern Europe have rejected modern Western literature as a product of decadent bourgeois individualism. Writers in these countries have cultivated a style that appears to Western eyes naively realistic. And even in the West, many major writers have run counter to the prevailingly existential current by adhering to traditional or dogmatic systems, as the older Eliot did with Anglo-Catholicism and as Bertolt Brecht did with Marxism.

Perhaps a century from now the landscape of twentieth-century literature will look very different. There may be a reordering of "major" and "minor" writers, and what we think of as "modernism" may then appear to be, on the one hand, only part of a much larger movement we today have not seen the end of, or on the other, a series of smaller, distinct movements. Already, many critics see modernism as having been superseded, perhaps in 1930 or 1945 or even in 1970, by a "post-modernist" movement. (The term has a nicely paradoxical quality about it.) Post-modernism, it seems, has moved in two almost opposite directions simultaneously: conservatively, toward a comparatively simple and direct realism, and, futuristically, toward a conception of literature as abstract game. However this may be, modern literature (and perhaps post-modern literature as well) has been an extraordinarily rich and vital response to the pressures of our difficult and exhilarating century.

FURTHER READING *(prepared by J. H.):* A good starting point for the study of modern literature is *Modernism,* ed. Malcolm Bradbury and James McFarlane, 1974, in the Pelican Guides to European Literature series. This volume includes thirty-four essays by a number of critics on important topics in modernism, including its history in different countries and its expression in various genres. *The Modern Tradition: Backgrounds of Modern Literature,* ed. Richard Ellmann and Charles Feidelson, Jr., 1965, constitutes a small library in itself of key documents in the intellectual history of modernism. Of the many collections of essays on modernism, one of the best is *Literary Modernism,* ed. Irving Howe, 1967, which includes previously published essays, including Lionel Trilling's brilliant "On the Modern Element in Modern Literature," Stephen Spender's "The Modern as Vision of the Whole," and José Ortega y Gasset's "The Dehumanization of Art." Howe's introduction, "The Idea of the Modern," is one of the best short treatments of the subject. A classic essay not included in the Howe collection is Harry Levin's "What Was Modernism?" in *Refractions,* 1966. Maurice Beebe's "What Modernism Was," his introduction to a special issue on modernism of the *Journal of Modern Literature,* 3 (1973–74), 1065–1084, is also excellent; he includes a bibliography of the subject.

On the relationship of modernism to Symbolism, see Edmund Wilson's *Axel's Castle: A Study in the Imaginative Literature of 1870–1930,* 1945. On the relation of modernism to romanticism, see Jacques Barzun, *Classic, Romantic, and Modern,* 1962; Gabriel Josipovici, "Modernism and Romanticism," in *The World and the Book: A Study of Modern Fiction,* 1971; and Robert Langbaum, *The Modern Spirit: Essays on the Continuity of Nineteenth- and Twentieth-Century Literature,* 1970.

On "post-modernism," see John Barth's "The Literature of Exhaustion," originally published in the *Atlantic Monthly* of August, 1967, and often reprinted; *Innovations: Essays on Art and Ideas,* ed. Bernard Bergonzi, 1968; and Ihab Hassan's "POSTmodernISM," *New Literary History,* 3 (1971), 5–30.

Sigmund Freud

(1856–1939)

The question of whether the work of Sigmund Freud is science or art has never been settled, least of all by Freud himself, who recognized and delighted in the ambiguity. Through his early work, especially, he held himself to the precision of a scientific method and vocabulary, while at the same time drawing freely for examples and language upon a wide range of literature and art; his pages are studded with references to his favorite literary works: Greek tragedy, Shakespeare's plays, Milton's Paradise Lost, *and the works of German Romanticism. He insisted throughout his life that not he but the poets had discovered the unconscious and that his contribution had consisted of systematizing their insights through "a few psychological formulas." He was a magnificent writer himself;* The Interpretation of Dreams *and the great case studies are monuments of Austrian literature. It is not a denigration of psychoanalysis to say it is a great imaginative creation, the flowering of the literary tradition which was rooted in Rousseau and which flourished throughout the nineteenth century in the Romantics' abiding interest in the individual self and how it emerges from childhood experience. It is no wonder that a recent student of psychoanalysis has concluded that it is faltering as a science and that "Freud's future place will be in the realm of art, not science."*

Freud was born in 1856 in Freiberg, Moravia (now Příbor, Czechoslovakia), the son of a prosperous Jewish wool merchant. The family moved to Vienna when Freud was four and he was educated there at the excellent Sperl Gymnasium and the University of Vienna, where he received his medical degree in 1881. Plans for a research career were changed in 1882, when he met and fell in love with Martha Bernays and decided that, if he was to support a wife, he would have to go into private practice. Over the four years of their engagement, he was on the staff first of the Vienna General Hospital and then of a private psychiatric clinic. He treated patients, continued research on the physiology of the brain which he had begun as a medical student, became a lecturer in neuropathology at the University, and attended a crucial four-month series of lectures in Paris by the famous neurologist Jean Charcot, who had begun to experiment with the treatment of hysteria by hypnotism. In 1886, Freud married Martha Bernays and set up a private psychiatric practice in Vienna, which was to continue for the next fifty-one years.

The story of the rest of Freud's life is essentially the story of the development of psychoanalysis, a rigorous and deeply personal exploration against heavy odds into unknown territories of the human mind. The beginnings of psychoanalysis were in a series of hysteric patients Freud treated, along with another Viennese physician, Josef Breuer, beginning in 1882. ("Hysteria" is a neurotic condition characterized by violent emotional outbursts, depression, and various impairments of sensory and motor functions.) Breuer, like Charcot, was experimenting with hypnosis in the treatment of these patients and had discovered that if a patient could be induced to remember and describe the circumstances of the onset of his illness, the symptoms tended to disappear, at least temporarily. The most famous of these patients was "Anna O.," a twenty-one-year-old girl who had suffered a partial paralysis and impairments of speech and sight after the death of her father; Breuer broke off her treatment abruptly when he discovered that she was sexually attracted to him. The success of "the talking cure" suggested a psychological rather than a physiological basis for hysteria, and this insight became the subject of Studies in Hysteria *(1895), upon which Breuer and Freud collaborated. By the time the book was published, Breuer and Freud had already gone their separate ways, because of Breuer's inability to accept Freud's growing conviction that sexual experiences were invariably at the basis of hysterical conditions. Between 1892 and 1897, Freud gradually abandoned hypnosis in favor of "free association," a process of encouraging the patient to talk freely about his or her memories, withholding and censoring nothing, while the therapist quietly listened. He also developed his theory of "childhood seduction"; on the evidence of a detailed study of thirteen cases, he concluded that "the cause of hysteria is a passive sexual experience before puberty:* i.e., *a traumatic seduction."*

Perhaps the most important creative period in Freud's life was the three years between 1897 and 1900. His father, Jakob Freud, died in 1896, triggering powerful conflicts in Freud which amounted to a serious psychoneurosis. He embarked upon a rigorous, systematic psychoanalysis (he began to use the word first in 1896) of himself, to which he devoted an hour at the end of each working day and which he reported, sometimes cryptically, in letters to his intimate friend Wilhelm Fliess. The product of this self-analysis was the abandonment of the seduction theory, the formulation of the theory of the Oedipus complex, and the writing of The Interpretation of Dreams. *Freud abandoned the seduction theory when he realized that sexual molestation of children, though doubtless more common than generally acknowledged, could not be as universal as it appeared to be among his patients (and at the same time discovered that his own father was not free from "incestuous incrimination"). He concluded that effects like those of actual molestation could be produced by fantasies representing the wishes of children to sleep with parents of the opposite sex, the basis of the theory of the Oedipus complex. The extent to which* The Interpretation of Dreams *grew out of his own self-analysis Freud himself acknowledged in his preface to the second edition in 1908: "For this book has a further subjective significance for me personally—a significance which I only grasped after I had completed it. It was, I found, a portion of my own self-analysis, my reaction to my father's death—that is to say, to the most important event, the most poignant loss, of a man's life." On the foundation of his own self-examination, Freud established the main outlines of psychoanalysis in* The Interpretation of Dreams: *the theory of the unconscious, the ways in which dreams represent reality, and the development of infantile sexuality, including the Oedipus complex.*

For the rest of his life Freud elaborated and modified the model of psychoanalysis presented in The Interpretation of Dreams. The Psychopathology of Everyday Life *(1901) and* Jokes and their Relation to the Unconscious *(1905) explained how everyday "slips" and jokes, respectively, reveal the workings of unconscious wishes. Also appearing in 1905 were the important* Three Essays on the Theory of Sexuality *("The Sexual Aberrations," "Infantile Sexuality," and "The Transformations of Puberty") and the first of the great case studies: "Dora." "Little Hans" and "The Rat Man" appeared in 1909, "Dr. Schreber" and "The Wolf Man" in 1911 and 1918.* Beyond the Pleasure Principle *(1920) introduced, in connection with a study of the "repetition compulsion" (the drive to repeat patterns of behavior), the important, and controversial, theory of a "death instinct."* The Ego and the Id *(1923) elaborated Freud's spatial metaphor of the mind as divided into ego, superego, and id.* The Future of an Illusion *(1927),* Civilization and its Discontents *(1930), and* Moses and Monotheism *(1939) turned from individual psychology to apply psychoanalytical insights to broad questions of human culture.*

Much of Freud's energy during the latter part of his life was also devoted to defending and disseminating the principles of psychoanalysis personally. A small group of interested friends which met on Wednesday evenings at Freud's house beginning in 1902 grew into the Vienna Psychoanalytical Society in 1908 and the International Psychoanalytical Association in 1910. Freud's relationships with his disciples and associates were often difficult; one after another broke away, often with much bitterness: first Alfred Adler, then Wilhelm Stekel, and finally Carl Jung.

In 1917, Freud, a heavy cigar-smoker, first noticed a painful swelling in the roof of his mouth, eventually diagnosed as cancer in 1923. Over the next sixteen years, he underwent thirty-three painful operations; in his last years, he had to wear a bulky prosthetic device to separate his mouth from his nasal cavity. Also, in 1938, the Nazis marched into Vienna, with Freud and his "Jewish" psychology high on their blacklists; his books had been publicly burned in Berlin in 1933. The Nazis, under international pressure, agreed to allow him to leave Austria, and Freud reluctantly yielded to his friends' urgings and left Vienna for London. He died there in 1939.

Freud himself noted that his case studies read like carefully constructed fiction; "It strikes me myself as strange that the case histories I write should read like short stories and that, as one might say, they lack the serious stamp of science." "The Case of Miss Lucy R." is one of the 1895 Studies in Hysteria, *and thus stands only on the threshold of psychoanalysis. Freud is already committed to the concept of the unconscious and to the proposition that neurosis can reflect painful events that have been repressed. He also recognizes the sexual basis of neurosis; he is not satisfied with the initial explanation of the trauma and delves deeper until he uncovers an episode with a sexual content that underlies the ones divulged earlier. But he lacks, thus far, an awareness of infantile sexuality; Miss Lucy R.'s trauma was an embarrassing episode of adult sexual feeling, barely below the surface of consciousness. It is interesting to speculate what Freud might have made of this delicate English governess tormented by the smell of burning pastry if he had encountered her a few years later. Perhaps he might have been more attentive to Miss Lucy R.'s association of the smell of her employer's cigar with the fact that "they constantly smoke at home" and looked more closely into the nature of her attraction to this odd employer who can become so angry if anyone kisses his motherless children on the lips.*

But the literary interest of "The Case of Miss Lucy R." does not rest primarily in its content but in its structure. As early as 1913, a reader compared Freud's manner in his case studies to that of Sherlock Holmes, who relentlessly brushed aside superficial explanations to ferret out the hidden truth. Sometimes Freud even sounds like Holmes: "As plausible as this sounded, it did not satisfy me," he tells the reader before returning to Miss Lucy for more memories and associations. The world of Freud's case studies is the world of modern fiction, in which narrative is not the presentation of finished conclusions about reality but a series of probing, often inconclusive investigations into a problematical world inhabited by complex, multilayered human beings who do not yield up their secrets easily. Conrad did not have to read Freud before he created his Marlow, brooding out the secrets of a Lord Jim or a Kurtz, nor did Joyce have to read him before he stripped away Gabriel Conroy's layers of defenses to bring him to self-confrontation. But both they and the other great fictionalists of the twentieth century reflect the view of human beings in the world that Freud first mapped.

FURTHER READING *(prepared by J. H.):* The standard life of Freud is still Ernest Jones, *The Life and Work of Sigmund Freud,* 3 vols., 1953–57. A briefer account, with a short but reliable summary of the development of Freud's ideas, is Richard Wollheim's *Sigmund Freud,* 1971. A fuller study of Freud's thought is Philip Rieff's *Freud: The Mind of the Moralist,* 3rd ed., 1979. The best study of Freud as a writer is perhaps Stanley Edgar Hyman's *The Tangled Bank,* 1962, which also includes studies of Darwin, Marx, and Frazer as literary figures. *Freud: A Collection of Critical Essays,* ed. Perry Meisel, 1981, in the Twentieth Century Views series, has a long, excellent introduction by the editor on "Freud as Literature" and assembles a number of major essays on Freud's significance to literature. On the related topic of the psychoanalytic interpretation of literature, the novice might well start with Norman Holland's *The Dynamics of Literary Response,* 1968; Holland's later turn toward "identity theory" as a tool of literary analysis is well represented in *Poems in Persons,* 1973. Ernst Kris's *Psychoanalytic Explorations in Art,* 1952, and Simon O. Lesser's *Fiction and the Unconscious,* 1957, can also be recommended. There are a number of useful collections of psychoanalytical essays on literature; among them are *Psychoanalysis and Literature,* ed. Hendrik M. Ruitenbeek, 1964, and *The Practice of Psychoanalytic Criticism,* ed. Leonard Tennenhouse, 1976.

THE CASE OF MISS LUCY R.

Translated by A. A. Brill

Towards the end of 1892 a friendly colleague recommended to me a young lady whom he had been treating for chronic recurrent purulent rhinitis[1]. . . . She finally complained of new symptoms which this experienced physician could no longer refer to local affections. She had lost all perception of smell and was almost constantly bothered by one or two subjective sensations of smell. This she found very irksome. In addition to this she was depressed in spirits, weak, and complained of a heavy head, loss of appetite, and an incapacity for work.

This young lady visited me from time to time during my office hours—she was a governess in the family of a factory superintendent living in the suburbs of Vienna. She was an English lady of rather delicate constitution, anemic, and with the exception of her nasal trouble was in good health. Her first statements concurred with those of her physician. She suffered from depression and lassitude, and was tormented by subjective sensations of smell. Of hysterical signs, she showed a quite distinct general analgesia without tactile impairment, the fields of vision showed no narrowing on coarse testing with the hand, the nasal mucous membrane was totally analgesic and reflexless, tactile sensation was absent, and the perception of this organ was abolished for specific as well as for other stimuli, such as ammonia or acetic acid.[2] The purulent nasal catarrh was then in a state of improvement.

On first attempting to understand this case the subjective sensations of smell had to be taken as recurrent hallucinations interpreting persistent

[1]Nasal inflammation.

[2]Freud examines Miss R. for the sorts of disorders of sensory and motor functions associated with a hysteria neurosis. She has no pain but retains feeling except in the nasal membrane, has experienced no narrowing of her field of vision, but cannot smell even strong odors.

hysterical symptoms. The depression was perhaps the affect[3] belonging to the trauma[4] and there must have been an episode during which the present subjective sensations were objective. This episode must have been the trauma, the symbols of which recurred in memory as sensations of smell. Perhaps it would be more correct to consider the recurring hallucinations of smell with the accompanying depression as equivalents of hysterical attacks. The nature of recurrent hallucinations really makes them unfit to take the part of continuous symptoms, and this really did not occur in this rudimentarily developed case. On the other hand it was absolutely to be expected that the subjective sensations of smell would show such a specialization as to be able to correspond in its origin to a very definite and real object.

This expectation was soon fulfilled, for on being asked what odor troubled her most she stated that it was an odor of burned pastry. I could then assume that the odor of burned pastry really occurred in the traumatic event. It is quite unusual to select sensations of smell as memory symbols of traumas, but it is quite obvious why these were here selected. She was afflicted with purulent rhinitis, hence the nose and its perceptions were in the foreground of her attention. All I knew about the life of the patient was that she took care of two children whose mother died a few years ago from a grave and acute disease.

As a starting point of the analysis I decided to use the "odor of burned pastry." I will now relate the history of this analysis. It could have occurred under more favorable conditions, but as a matter of fact what should have taken place in one session was extended over a number of them. She could only visit me during my office hours, during which I could devote to her but little of my time. One single conversation had to be extended for over a week as her duties did not permit her to come to me often from such a distance, so that the conversation was frequently broken off and resumed at the next session.

On attempting to hypnotize Miss Lucy R. she did not merge into the somnambulic[5] state. I therefore was obliged to forego somnambulism and the analysis was made while she was in a state not perhaps differing much from the normal . . . .

Miss Lucy R. . . . lay calmly in a degree of mild suggestibility, her eyes constantly closed, the features immobile, the limbs without motion. I asked her whether she remembered on what occasion the smell perception of burned pastry originated.—"Oh, yes, I know it well. It was about two months ago, two days before my birthday. I was with the children (two girls) in the school room playing and teaching them to cook, when a letter just left by the letter carrier was brought in. From its postmark and handwriting I recognized it as one sent to me by my mother from Glasgow and I wished to open it and read it. The children then came running over, pulled the letter out of my hand and exclaimed, 'No, you must not read it now, it is probably a congratulatory letter for your birthday and we will keep it for you until then.' While the children were thus playing there was a sudden

[3]Feeling or emotion. [4]Shock; painful emotional experience with lasting effects.
[5]Hypnotic.

diffusion of an intense odor. The children forgot the pastry which they were cooking and it became burned. Since then I have been troubled by this odor, it is really always present but is more marked during excitement."

"Do you see this scene distinctly before you?"—"As clearly as I experienced it."—"What was there in it that so excited you?"—"I was touched by the affection which the children displayed towards me."—"But weren't they always so affectionate?"—"Yes, but I just got the letter from my mother."—"I can't understand in what way the affection of the little ones and the letter from the mother contrasted, a thing which you appear to intimate."—"I had the intention of going to my mother and my heart became heavy at the thought of leaving those dear children."—"What is the matter with your mother? Was she so lonesome that she wanted you, or was she sick just then and you expected some news?"—"No, she is delicate but not really sick, and has a companion with her."—"Why then were you obliged to leave the children?"—"This house had become unbearable to me. The housekeeper, the cook, and the French maid seemed to be under the impression that I was too proud for my position. They united in intriguing against me and told the grandfather of the children all sorts of things about me, and when I complained to both gentlemen I did not receive the support which I expected. I then tendered my resignation to the master (father of the children) but he was very friendly, asking me to reconsider it for two weeks before taking any definite steps. It was while I was in that state of indecision that the incident occurred. I thought that I would leave the house but have remained."—"Aside from the attachment of the children is there anything particular which attracts you to them?"—"Yes, my mother is distantly related to their mother and when the latter was on her death bed I promised her to do my utmost in caring for the children, that I would not forsake them, and be a mother to them, and this promise I broke when offering my resignation."

The analysis of the subjective sensation of smell seemed completed. It was once objective and intimately connected with an experience, a small scene, in which contrary affects conflicted, sorrow at forsaking the children, and the mortification which despite all urged her to this decision. Her mother's letter naturally recalled the motives of this decision because she thought of returning to her mother. The conflict of the affects raised this moment to a trauma and the sensation of smell which was connected with it remained as its symbol. The only thing to be explained was the fact that out of all the sensory perceptions of that scene, the perception of smell was selected as the symbol, but I was already prepared to use the chronic nasal affliction as an explanation. On being directly questioned she stated that just at that time she suffered from a severe coryza[6] and could scarcely smell anything, but in her excitement she perceived the odor of burned pastry; it penetrated the organically motived anosmia.[7]

As plausible as this sounded it did not satisfy me; there seemed to be something lacking. There was no acceptable reason wherefore this series of excitements and this conflict of affects should have led to hysteria. Why did

[6]Head-cold, stuffed nose. [7]Loss of sense of smell.

it not all remain on a normal psychological basis? In other words, what justified the conversion[8] under discussion? Why did she not recall the scenes themselves instead of the sensations connected with them which she preferred as symbols for her recollection? Such questions might seem superfluous and impertinent when dealing with old hysterias in which the mechanism of conversion was habitual, but this girl first acquired hysteria through this trauma, or at least through this slight distress.

From the analysis of similar cases I already knew that where hysteria is to be newly acquired one psychic determinant is indispensible; namely, that some presentation must intentionally be repressed from consciousness and excluded from associative elaboration.[9]

In this intentional repression I also find the reason for the conversion of the sum of excitement, be it partial or total. The sum of excitement which is not to enter into psychic association more readily finds the wrong road to bodily innervation.[10] The reason for the repression itself could only be a disagreeable feeling, the incompatibility of one of the repressible ideas with the ruling presentation-mass of the ego.[11] The repressed presentation then avenges itself by becoming pathogenic.[12]

From this I concluded that Miss Lucy R. merged into that moment of hysterical conversion, which must have been under the determinations of that trauma which she intentionally left in the darkness and which she took pains to forget. On considering her attachment for the children and her sensitiveness towards the other persons of the household, there remained but one interpretation, which I was bold enough to impart to her. I told her that I did not believe that all these things were simply due to her affection for the children, but that I thought that she was rather in love with her master, perhaps unwittingly, that she really nurtured the hope of taking the place of the mother, and it was for that reason that she became so sensitive towards the servants with whom she had lived peacefully for years. She feared lest they would notice something of her hope and scoff at her.

She answered in her laconic manner: "Yes, I believe it is so."—"But if you knew that you were in love with the master, why did you not tell me so?"—"But I did not know it, or rather, I did not wish to know it. I wished to crowd it out of my mind, never to think of it, and of late I have been successful."

"Why did you not wish to admit it to yourself? Were you ashamed because you loved a man?"—"O, no, I am not unreasonably prudish; one is certainly not responsible for one's own feelings. I only felt chagrined because it was my employer in whose service I was and in whose house I lived, and toward whom I could not feel as independent as towards another. What is more, I am a poor girl and he is a rich man of a prominent family, and if anybody should have had any inkling about my feelings they would have ridiculed me."

After this I encountered no resistances in elucidating the origin of this

[8]The representation of a repressed memory or emotion by a physical symptom.
[9]Integration with other thoughts and experiences.
[10]Stimulation, excitation.
[11]With the dominant self-conception, one's ideas of oneself. [12]Disease-producing.

affection. She told me that the first years of her life in that house were passed uneventfully. She fulfilled her duties without thinking about unrealizable wishes. One day, however, the serious, and very busy and hitherto very reserved master engaged her in conversation about the exigencies of rearing the children. He became milder and more cordial than usual, he told her how much he counted on her in the bringing up of his orphaned children, and looked at her rather peculiarly. It was in this moment that she began to love him, and gladly occupied herself with the pleasing hopes which she conceived during that conversation. However, as this was not followed by anything else, and despite her waiting and persevering no other confidential heart-to-heart talk followed, she decided to crowd it out of her mind. She quite agreed with me that the look in connection with the conversation was probably intended for the memory of his deceased wife. She was also perfectly convinced that her love was hopeless.

After this conversation I expected a decided change in her condition but for a time it did not take place. She continued depressed and moody—a course of hydrotherapy[13] which I ordered for her at the same time refreshed her somewhat mornings. The odor of burned pastry did not entirely disappear, though it became rarer and feebler. It appeared only, as she said, when she was very much excited.

The continuation of this memory symbol led me to believe that besides the principal scene it represented many smaller side traumas and I therefore investigated everything that might have been in any way connected with the scene of the burned pastry. We thus passed through the theme of family friction, the behavior of the grandfather and others, and with that the sensation of burned odor gradually disappeared. Just then there was a lengthy interruption occasioned by a new nasal affliction . . . .

On her return she informed me that she received many Christmas presents from both gentlemen as well as from the household servants, as if they were trying to appease her and wipe away the recollection of the conflicts of the last months. These frank advances made no impression on her.

On questioning her on another occasion about the odor of burned pastry she stated that it had entirely disappeared, but instead she was now bothered by another and similar odor like the smoke of a cigar. This odor really existed before; it was only concealed by the odor of the pastry but now appeared by itself.

I was not very much pleased with the success of my treatment. What occurred here is what a mere symptomatic treatment is generally blamed for, namely, that it removes one symptom only to make room for another. Nevertheless, I immediately set forth to remove this new memory symbol by analysis.

This time I did not know whence this subjective sensation of smell originated, nor on what important occasion it was objective. On being questioned she said, "They constantly smoke at home, I really don't know whether the smell which I feel has any particular significance." I then proposed that she should try to recall things under the pressure of my hands.[14]

[13]Water-treatments, therapeutic baths.

[14]Freud helped patients who could not be hypnotized to remember things by telling them that they would remember when he placed his hands on their heads.

I have already mentioned that her recollections were plastically vivid, that she was a "visual." Indeed under the pressure of my hands a picture came into her mind—at first only slowly and fragmentarily. It was the dining room of the house in which she waited with the children for the arrival of the gentlemen from the factory for dinner.—"Now we are all at the table, the gentlemen, the French maid, the housekeeper, the children and I. It is the same as usual."—"Just keep on looking at that picture. It will soon become developed and specialized."—"Yes, there is a guest, the chief accountant, an old gentleman who loves the children like his own grandchildren, but he dines with us so frequently that it is nothing unusual."—"Just have patience, keep on looking at the picture, something will certainly happen."—"Nothing happens. We leave the table, the children take leave and go with us up to the second floor as usual."—"Well?"—"It really is something unusual, I now recognize the scene. As the children take leave the chief accountant attempts to kiss them, but my master jumps up and shouts at him, 'Don't kiss the children!' I then experienced a stitch in the heart, and as the gentlemen were smoking, this odor remained in my memory."

This, therefore, was the second, deeper seated scene causing the trauma and leaving the memory symbol. But why was this scene so effective? I then asked her which scene happened first, this one or the one with the burned pastry?—"The last scene happened first by almost two months."—"Why did you feel the stitch at the father's interference? The reproof was not meant for you."—"It was really not right to rebuke an old gentleman in such manner who was a dear friend and a guest, it could have been said quietly."—"Then you were really affected by your master's impetuosity? Were you perhaps ashamed of him, or have you thought, 'If he could become so impetuous to an old friend guest over such a trifle, how would he act towards me if I were his wife?'"—"No, that is not it."—"But still it was about his impetuosity?"—"Yes, about the kissing of the children, he never liked that." Under the pressure of my hands there emerged a still older scene which was the real effective trauma and which bestowed on the scene with the chief accountant the traumatic effectivity.

A few months before a lady friend visited the house and on leaving kissed both children on the lips. The father, who was present, controlled himself and said nothing to the lady, but when she left he was very angry at the unfortunate governess. He said that he held her responsible for this kissing; that it was her duty not to tolerate it; that she was neglecting her duties in allowing such things, and that if it ever happened again he would entrust the education of his children to some one else. This occurred while she believed herself loved and waited for a repetition of that serious and friendly talk. This episode shattered all her hopes. She thought: "If he can upbraid and threaten me on account of such a trifle, of which I am entirely innocent, I must have been mistaken, he never entertained any tenderer feelings towards me, else he would have been considerate."—It was evidently this painful scene that came to her as the father reprimanded the chief accountant for attempting to kiss the children.

On being visited by Miss Lucy R. two days after the last analysis I had to ask her what pleasant things happened to her. She looked as though transformed, she smiled and held her head aloft. For a moment I thought that after all I probably mistook the conditions and that the governess of the children had now become the bride of the master. But she soon dissipated all my suppositions, saying, "Nothing new happened. You really do not know me. You have always seen me while I was sick and depressed. I am otherwise always cheerful. On awaking yesterday morning my burden was gone and since then I feel well."—"What do you think of your chances in the house?"—"I am perfectly clear about that. I know that I have none, and I am not going to be unhappy about it."—"Will you now be able to get along with the others in the house?"—"I believe so, because most of the trouble was due to my sensitiveness."—"Do you still love the master?"—"Certainly I love him, but that does not bother me much. One can think and feel as one wishes."

I now examined her nose and found that the pain and the reflex sensations had almost completely reappeared. She could distinguish odors, but she was uncertain when they were very intense. What part the nasal trouble played in the anosmia I must leave undecided.

The whole treatment extended over a period of nine weeks. Four months later I accidentally met the patient at one of our summer resorts—she was cheerful and stated that her health continued to be good . . . .

Joseph Conrad
(1857–1924)

To take up a new language at the age of twenty, as Joseph Conrad did, is to accept a challenge. To make a career as a professional, indeed a creative, writer in the new language is an act of hardihood, and Conrad did that too. More *(as William Faulkner would say): he became one of the masters of English prose style, in a highly adjectival vein disastrous to imitate (unless one is Faulkner, who did so) but eminently right for Conrad himself in his heavily atmospheric tales. Even this linguistic miracle, however, is only the beginning of Conrad's achievement. Author of some of the best adventure fiction in any language, he also—and more fundamentally—explored troubled minds and souls. Starting from the realist tradition of the nineteenth-century novels, and retaining much of their rich texture and verisimilitude, he went on to pioneer modernist methods, especially in the handling of narrative time and multiple or less-than-reliable points of view. He was one of the great symbolists. In short, he was close to being the complete literary artist. And even if, some centuries hence, the world should lose all interest in art, Conrad will remain indispensable to cultural history, for his vivid anatomies of colonialism, imperialism, the Third World as it appears to the Westerner, and—still more broadly—his critique of the Western* mythos *of Enlightened Progress. Indeed, those two words come startlingly alive in* Heart of Darkness, *with its complex symbolic title and its ironically labeled "pilgrims" whose heavenly city is made not of ethereal alabaster but of material ivory.*

Conrad's life divides into two halves: an adventurous far-flung career as a seaman and a second career as a writer, spent almost entirely in a small corner of England. He was born in 1857, as Józef Teodor Konrad Nalecz Korzeniowski, in

Berdyczew, a Polish town that had been absorbed into Russia (and today again is part of the Soviet Union). His parents, Apollo and Evelina Korzeniowski, were descended from landed gentry. When his son was four, Apollo—poet, translator, and fervent Polish nationalist—was consigned for political reasons to exile in northern Russia; mother and son joined him there. Climatic hardships took their toll, Evelina dying when the boy was seven. The despondent Apollo died four years later, in Krakow. (Conrad's fiction is haunted by the image of a selfless yet egotistic believer willing to risk disaster for his ideals.) The orphan Józef came under the care of his benevolent uncle Tadeusz Bobrowski, who saw to his ward's schooling in that city. The restless and romantic teenager, like the Marlow he created in his later fiction, aspired to explore the great world, and, after having eroded his uncle's opposition, he took a social step down by entering the French merchant marine at the age of sixteen as an apprentice seaman. For four years he sailed in French ships (steamers he despised as "locomotives"), to the West Indies and South America. During this period Conrad seems to have had some covert escapades, in Latin America and in Spain, where he smuggled guns in the service of Don Carlos, the claimant of the Spanish throne. In Marseilles he also incurred a mysterious chest-wound, possibly from a duel over a woman (as he wanted people to believe), possibly from an attempted suicide (which would be consistent with his chronic tendency to depression).

When he was twenty, Conrad took a decisive step by shifting from the French to the English merchant service, partly in order to evade the Russian draft, from which British ships claimed exemption for their men. In the next sixteen years, under the British flag, Conrad continued to see the world—chiefly in voyages to Australia, India, and the Indonesian islands—while also getting to know England and, more important, English. He worked and studied his way up, qualifying as mate, then captain, and becoming a British citizen along the way. In 1890, between sea assignments, he commanded a river boat on the Congo. The million square miles of the Belgian Congo region, only recently opened up by the famous explorer Henry Morton Stanley, were at the time the personal property of King Leopold II, a rapacious man whose philanthropic rhetoric was a screen for one of the most infamous chapters in the history of European imperialism. Conrad, whose moral sensibilities had not been nurtured in a hothouse, later called the episode "the vilest scramble for loot that ever disfigured the history of human conscience and geographical exploration." Some of the atrocities committed in the Congo are evoked by Marlow's account in Heart of Darkness, *which in other ways too follows closely the author's real-life experiences. Conrad's health was permanently impaired, and the inner man was likewise transformed, according to his own testimony. Before that time, he said, he had been "a mere animal"—a curious and intriguing metaphor in view of the discoveries Marlow makes about human nature in the story.*

By 1894, when Conrad's seagoing career ended, he had been writing for several years, and in 1895, under his simplified and Englished name, he launched his prolific career as an author of fiction with Almayer's Folly, *which like many of Conrad's novels still to come drew on his experiences and observations in places remote from Europe. In the following year he married Jessie George, an Englishwoman, and settled down in the county of Kent, in southeast England, his home for the rest of his life. Over the next seventeen years he produced in steady succession sixteen books, some of them ranking with the best fiction in English, including such masterpieces as* Heart of Darkness *(1899, included in* Youth, *1902),* Lord Jim *(1900),* Nostromo *(1904),* The Secret Agent *(1907), and* Under Western Eyes *(1911). His friends and admirers were a kind of turn-of-the-century pantheon, including Stephen Crane, Henry James, H. G. Wells, Rudyard Kipling, W. H. Hudson, John Galsworthy, Arnold Bennett, Ford Madox Ford (who co-authored three books with Conrad), and several other eminent people. Yet despite this kind of backing, for novels of the highest excellence with the inherent popular appeal of exotic places and adventurous action, Conrad's works did not sell widely, and his life was a grinding struggle with low spirits, poor health, and poverty. Not until* Chance *(1912-14) and* Victory *(1915) were published did he score popular and financial success. Thereafter he was a celebrity, idolized during an American visit in 1923 and offered British knighthood (which he declined) in 1924. He died of a heart attack that same year and was buried in the Roman Catholic churchyard in Canterbury, the city at the spiritual center of his adopted country.*

Although it lacks the epic scale of, say, Nostromo, Heart of Darkness *is Conrad at his best and near his most characteristic. The presence of Conrad's alter ego Marlow (who appears in several other works); the skillful dislocations of narrative sequence, which moves psychologically toward climactic insight rather than chronologically; the appropriately tropical luxuriance of the heightened language; the gropings toward understanding, by Marlow, implicitly by his shipboard listeners, and by the reader; the portentous mood infused into words, events, objects, and setting; perhaps above all the nearly unparalleled density of the relentless but somehow unobtrusive symbolic imagery—all these working together make up a novel that, for power disciplined by art, has few equals in fiction. At no point in* Heart of Darkness *can one sink a drill without discovering several of its many strata. It synthesizes historical epochs—from the Roman to the Elizabethan to the modern English and European. It penetrates anthropological time and space as well, tracing a deceptively long path from "civilization" to the "primitive" that, we come to see, is at most a single step. It makes a timely statement about Belgium and other colonial powers, its theme transcending the 1890s without blurring the journalistic details. It relates a particular man's growth—or attempt to grow—into knowledge of the world and of himself. It explores not only for the truth but for the meaning and usefulness of the very notion of truth. Its images are unforgettable, especially in their eerie juxtapositions and superimpositions: grass growing through the pavements of a white city, and, far away, through the rib cage of a human skeleton; a woman's arms extended in grief on a jungle riverbank and in a European drawing room; the popping of a gunboat's shells into an impassive continent and a fusillade directed as idly into riverside foliage; the "scientific" measurement of heads by a European doctor and the impaled heads around a jungle station; an accountant's immaculate starched collar and an adventurer's clownlike patchwork apparel; the preternatural stillness of the jungle and the voice of a fallen missionary, at once the symbol of his power and of his ineffectuality.*

Heart of Darkness *is an endlessly discussed, endlessly discussable work. Does Marlow find and face truth, or does he finally take refuge in still another saving form of illusion? If the "civilized" pilgrim-profiteers and the deluded emissaries of spiritual light are more contemptible than the "savages," why is "restraint," normally considered a civilized trait, so imperative when the wild is calling? What, exactly, does Marlow mean by the "inborn strength" and "deliberate belief" that he contrasts with mere "principles" as the only safeguard against the darkness without and within the human heart? And how is that bulwark related to the saving power of practical work? In what sense are Kurtz's appalling last words an "affirmation, a moral victory"? Why does Marlow lie to Kurtz's "Intended"? Does he, in fact, lie to her or does he ironically equivocate? In the dense thematic interweaving of* Heart of Darkness, *each of these and of many similar questions is the end of a string that, unlike Ariadne's in the ancient myth, leads into a labyrinth without guaranteeing that it has an exit. It is an interesting fact, and symptomatic of Conrad's power and insight, that readers continue to debate such issues even while wondering whether they are resolvable, either as critical problems within the novel itself or outside it, as questions about the real-life darkness of the human heart.*

FURTHER READING (*prepared by W. J. R.):* The three finest biographies in order of usefulness for the student of Conrad's art are Jocelyn Baines's *Joseph Conrad: A Critical Biography,* 1960; Frederick R. Karl's *Joseph Conrad: The Three Lives,* 1979; and Bernard C. Meyer's *Joseph Conrad: A Psychoanalytic Biography,* 1967. For important studies of the real-life sources of Conrad's stories, see J. D. Gordan's *Joseph Conrad: The Making of a Novelist,* 1940, and Norman Sherry's *Conrad's Eastern World,* 1966, and *Conrad's Western World,* 1971. The ideology and politics of Conrad's fiction have been studied by Eloise Knapp Hsay, *The Political Novels of Joseph Conrad,* 1963; Avrom Fleishman, *Conrad's Politics: Community and Anarchy in the Fiction of Joseph Conrad,* 1967; and R. F. Lee, *Conrad's Colonialism,* 1969. Ian Watt's *Conrad in the Nineteenth Century,* 1979, is probably the most significant study of the novelist since Albert Guerard's *Conrad the Novelist,* 1958. Guerard's opening essay, "The Journey Within," has been frequently reprinted in collections of critical essays on Conrad. Other valuable studies of his fiction may be found in Thomas Moser's *Joseph Conrad: Achievement and Decline,* 1957; Leo Gurko's *Joseph Conrad: Giant in Exile,* 1962; Adam Gillon's *The Eternal Solitary,* 1960; Frederick R. Karl's *A Reader's Guide to Joseph Conrad,* 1960; and Jacques Berthoud's *Joseph Conrad: The Major Phase,* 1978. The Norton Critical Edition of *Heart of Darkness,* ed. Robert Kimbrough, 1971, includes illuminating selections from both primary and secondary sources. *Joseph Conrad: A Collection of Criticism,* ed. Frederick R. Karl, 1975, and *Conrad: A Collection of Critical Essays,* ed. Marvin Mudrick, 1966, are also useful.

HEART OF DARKNESS

I

The Nellie, a cruising yawl, swung to her anchor without a flutter of the sails, and was at rest. The flood had made, the wind was nearly calm, and being bound down the river, the only thing for it was to come to[1] and wait for the turn of the tide.

The sea-reach of the Thames stretched before us like the beginning of an interminable waterway. In the offing[2] the sea and the sky were welded together without a joint, and in the luminous space the tanned sails of the barges drifting up with the tide seemed to stand still in red clusters of canvas sharply peaked, with gleams of varnished sprits. A haze rested on the low shores that ran out to sea in vanishing flatness. The air was dark above Gravesend,[3] and farther back still seemed condensed into a mournful gloom, brooding motionless over the biggest, and the greatest, town on earth.

[1] Anchor. [2] Horizon.

[3] A town twenty-five miles east of London, where the Thames begins to widen toward the sea.

The Director of Companies was our captain and our host. We four affectionately watched his back as he stood in the bows looking to seaward. On the whole river there was nothing that looked half so nautical. He resembled a pilot, which to a seaman is trustworthiness personified. It was difficult to realize his work was not out there in the luminous estuary, but behind him, within the brooding gloom.

Between us there was, as I have already said somewhere, the bond of the sea. Besides holding our hearts together through long periods of separation, it had the effect of making us tolerant of each other's yarns—and even convictions. The Lawyer—the best of old fellows—had, because of his many years and many virtues, the only cushion on deck, and was lying on the only rug. The Accountant had brought out already a box of dominoes, and was toying architecturally with the bones. Marlow sat cross-legged right aft, leaning against the mizzen-mast. He had sunken cheeks, a yellow complexion, a straight back, an ascetic aspect, and, with his arms dropped, the palms of hands outwards, resembled an idol. The director, satisfied the anchor had good hold, made his way aft and sat down amongst us. We exchanged a few words lazily. Afterwards there was silence on board the yacht. For some reason or other we did not begin that game of dominoes. We felt meditative, and fit for nothing but placid staring. The day was ending in a serenity of still and exquisite brilliance. The water shone pacifically; the sky, without a speck, was a benign immensity of unstained light; the very mist on the Essex marshes was like a gauzy and radiant fabric, hung from the wooded rises inland, and draping the low shores in diaphanous folds. Only the gloom to the west, brooding over the upper reaches, became more sombre every minute, as if angered by the approach of the sun.

And at last, in its curved and imperceptible fall, the sun sank low, and from glowing white changed to a dull red without rays and without heat, as if about to go out suddenly, stricken to death by the touch of that gloom brooding over a crowd of men.

Forthwith a change came over the waters, and the serenity became less brilliant but more profound. The old river in its broad reach rested unruffled at the decline of day, after ages of good service done to the race that peopled its banks, spread out in the tranquil dignity of a waterway leading to the uttermost ends of the earth. We looked at the venerable stream not in the vivid flush of a short day that comes and departs for ever, but in the august light of abiding memories. And indeed nothing is easier for a man who has, as the phrase goes, "followed the sea" with reverence and affection, than to evoke the great spirit of the past upon the lower reaches of the Thames. The tidal current runs to and fro in its unceasing service, crowded with memories of men and ships it has borne to the rest of home or to the battles of the sea. It had known and served all the men of whom the nation is proud, from Sir Francis Drake to Sir John Franklin,[4] knights all, titled and untitled—the great knights-errant of the sea. It had borne all the ships whose names are like jewels flashing in the night of time, from the *Golden*

[4] Drake was the Elizabethan admiral who sailed around the globe in the *Golden Hind* (Deer) in 1577–1580. Franklin was a seeker of the Northwest Passage, in the ships *Erebus* and *Terror*, in 1845–1847.

Hind returning with her round flanks full of treasure, to be visited by the Queen's Highness and thus pass out of the gigantic tale, to the *Erebus* and *Terror,* bound on other conquests—and that never returned. It had known the ships and the men. They had sailed from Deptford, from Greenwich, from Erith[5]—the adventurers and the settlers; kings' ships and the ships of men on 'Change;[6] captains, admirals, the dark "interlopers" of the Eastern trade, and the commissioned "generals" of East India[7] fleets. Hunters for gold or pursuers of fame, they all had gone out on that stream, bearing the sword, and often the torch, messengers of the might within the land, bearers of a spark from the sacred fire. What greatness had not floated on the ebb of that river into the mystery of an unknown earth! . . . The dreams of men, the seed of commonwealths, the germs of empires.

The sun set; the dusk fell on the stream, and lights began to appear along the shore. The Chapman lighthouse, a three-legged thing erect on a mud-flat, shone strongly. Lights of ships moved in the fairway[8]—a great stir of lights going up and going down. And farther west on the upper reaches the place of the monstrous town was still marked ominously on the sky, a brooding gloom in sunshine, a lurid glare under the stars.

"And this also," said Marlow suddenly, "has been one of the dark places of the earth."

He was the only man of us who still "followed the sea." The worst that could be said of him was that he did not represent his class. He was a seaman, but he was a wanderer, too, while most seamen lead, if one may so express it, a sedentary life. Their minds are of the stay-at-home order, and their home is always with them—the ship; and so is their country—the sea. One ship is very much like another, and the sea is always the same. In the immutability of their surroundings the foreign shores, the foreign faces, the changing immensity of life, glide past, veiled not by a sense of mystery but by a slightly disdainful ignorance; for there is nothing mysterious to a seaman unless it be the sea itself, which is the mistress of his existence and as inscrutable as Destiny. For the rest, after his hours of work, a casual stroll or a casual spree on shore suffices to unfold for him the secret of a whole continent, and generally he finds the secret not worth knowing. The yarns of seamen have a direct simplicity, the whole meaning of which lies within the shell of a cracked nut. But Marlow was not typical (if his propensity to spin yarns be excepted), and to him the meaning of an episode was not inside like a kernel but outside, enveloping the tale which brought it out only as a glow brings out a haze, in the likeness of one of those misty halos that sometimes are made visible by the spectral illumination of moonshine.

His remark did not seem at all surprising. It was just like Marlow. It was accepted in silence. No one took the trouble to grunt even; and presently he said, very slow—

"I was thinking of very old times, when the Romans[9] first came here, nineteen hundred years ago—the other day. . . . Light came out of this

[5] *Deptford . . . Erith.* Ports downstream from London. [6] The financial market.

[7] The East India Company was officially chartered; "interlopers" were unauthorized traders.

[8] Main channel.

[9] Beginning with Julius Caesar, the Romans conquered and then occupied much of Britain between 54 B.C. and 442 A.D.

river since—you say Knights? Yes; but it is like a running blaze on a plain, like a flash of lightning in the clouds. We live in the flicker—may it last as long as the old earth keeps rolling! But darkness was here yesterday. Imagine the feelings of a commander of a fine—what d'ye call 'em?—trireme[10] in the Mediterranean, ordered suddenly to the north; run overland across the Gauls[11] in a hurry; put in charge of one of these craft the legionaries—a wonderful lot of handy men they must have been, too—used to build, apparently by the hundred, in a month or two, if we may believe what we read. Imagine him here—the very end of the world, a sea the colour of lead, a sky the colour of smoke, a kind of ship about as rigid as a concertina—and going up this river with stores, or orders, or what you like. Sand-banks, marshes, forests, savages,—precious little to eat fit for a civilized man, nothing but Thames water to drink. No Falernian[12] wine here, no going ashore. Here and there a military camp lost in a wilderness, like a needle in a bundle of hay—cold, fog, tempests, disease, exile, and death,—death skulking in the air, in the water, in the bush. They must have been dying like flies here. Oh, yes—he did it. Did it very well, too, no doubt, and without thinking much about it either, except afterwards to brag of what he had gone through in his time, perhaps. They were men enough to face the darkness. And perhaps he was cheered by keeping his eye on a chance of promotion to the fleet at Ravenna[13] by and by, if he had good friends in Rome and survived the awful climate. Or think of a decent young citizen in a toga—perhaps too much dice, you know—coming out here in the train of some prefect,[14] or tax-gatherer, or trader even, to mend his fortunes. Land in a swamp, march through the woods, and in some inland post feel the savagery, the utter savagery, had closed round him,—all that mysterious life of the wilderness that stirs in the forest, in the jungles, in the hearts of wild men. There's no initiation either into such mysteries. He has to live in the midst of the incomprehensible, which is also detestable. And it has a fascination, too, that goes to work upon him. The fascination of the abomination—you know, imagine the growing regrets, the longing to escape, the powerless disgust, the surrender, the hate."

He paused.

"Mind," he began again, lifting one arm from the elbow, the palm of the hand outwards, so that, with his legs folded before him, he had the pose of a Buddha[15] preaching in European clothes and without a lotus-flower—"Mind, none of us would feel exactly like this. What saves us is efficiency—the devotion to efficiency. But these chaps were not much account, really. They were no colonists; their administration was merely a squeeze, and nothing more, I suspect. They were conquerors, and for that you want only brute force—nothing to boast of, when you have it, since your strength is just an accident arising from the weakness of others. They grabbed what they could get for the sake of what was to be got. It was just robbery with violence, aggravated murder on a great scale, and men going at it blind—as is very proper for those who tackle a darkness. The conquest of the earth,

[10] Galley with three levels of oars. [11] Inhabitants of what is now France and Belgium.
[12] A gourmet wine. [13] An important base of the Roman fleet, on the Adriatic Sea.
[14] High Roman administrator.
[15] Statue of the Indian founder of Buddhism, often represented atop a lotus flower; also, a Buddhist wise man.

which mostly means the taking it away from those who have a different complexion or slightly flatter noses than ourselves, is not a pretty thing when you look into it too much. What redeems it is the idea only. An idea at the back of it; not a sentimental pretence but an idea; and an unselfish belief in the idea—something you can set up, and bow down before, and offer a sacrifice to. . . ."

He broke off. Flames glided in the river, small green flames, red flames, white flames, pursuing, overtaking, joining, crossing each other—then separating slowly or hastily. The traffic of the great city went on in the deepening night upon the sleepless river. We looked on, waiting patiently—there was nothing else to do till the end of the flood; but it was only after a long silence, when he said, in a hesitating voice, "I suppose you fellows remember I did once turn fresh-water sailor for a bit," that we knew we were fated, before the ebb began to run, to hear about one of Marlow's inconclusive experiences.

"I don't want to bother you much with what happened to me personally," he began, showing in this remark the weakness of many tellers of tales who seem so often unaware of what their audience would best like to hear; "yet to understand the effect of it on me you ought to know how I got out there, what I saw, how I went up that river to the place were I first met the poor chap. It was the farthest point of navigation and the culminating point of my experience. It seemed somehow to throw a kind of light on everything about me—and into my thoughts. It was sombre enough, too—and pitiful—not extraordinary in any way–not very clear either. No, not very clear. And yet it seemed to throw a kind of light.

"I had then, as you remember, just returned to London after a lot of Indian Ocean, Pacific, China Seas—a regular dose of the East—six years or so, and I was loafing about, hindering you fellows in your work and invading your homes, just as though I had got a heavenly mission to civilize you. It was very fine for a time, but after a bit I did get tired of resting. Then I began to look for a ship—I should think the hardest work on earth. But the ships wouldn't even look at me. And I got tired of that game, too.

"Now when I was a little chap I had a passion for maps. I would look for hours at South America, or Africa, or Australia, and lose myself in all the glories of exploration. At that time there were many blank spaces on the earth, and when I saw one that looked particularly inviting on a map (but they all look that) I would put my finger on it and say, When I grow up I will go there. The North Pole was one of these places, I remember. Well, I haven't been there yet, and shall not try now. The glamour's off. Other places were scattered about the Equator, and in every sort of latitude all over the two hemispheres. I have been in some of them, and . . . well, we won't talk about that. But there was one yet—the biggest, the most blank, so to speak—that I had a hankering after.

"True, by this time it was not a blank space any more. It had got filled since my boyhood with rivers and lakes and names. It had ceased to be a blank space of delightful mystery—a white patch for a boy to dream gloriously over. It had become a place of darkness. But there was in it one river[16] especially, a mighty big river, that you could see on the map, resem-

[16] The Congo, flowing through central Africa into the South Atlantic.

bling an immense snake uncoiled, with its head in the sea, its body at rest curving afar over a vast country, and its tail lost in the depths of the land. And as I looked at the map of it in a shop-window, it fascinated me as a snake would a bird—a silly little bird. Then I remembered there was a big concern, a Company for trade on that river. Dash it all! I thought to myself, they can't trade without using some kind of craft on that lot of fresh water—steamboats! Why shouldn't I try to get charge of one? I went on along Fleet Street,[17] but could not shake off the idea. The snake had charmed me.

"You understand it was a Continental concern, that Trading society; but I have a lot of relations living on the Continent, because it's cheap and not so nasty as it looks, they say.

"I am sorry to own I began to worry them. This was already a fresh departure for me. I was not used to get things that way, you know. I always went my own road and on my own legs where I had a mind to go. I wouldn't have believed it of myself; but, then—you see—I felt somehow I must get there by hook or by crook. So I worried them. The men said 'My dear fellow,' and did nothing. Then—would you believe it?—I tried the women. I, Charlie Marlow, set the women to work—to get a job. Heavens! Well, you see, the notion drove me. I had an aunt, a dear enthusiastic soul. She wrote: 'It will be delightful. I am ready to do anything, anything for you. It is a glorious idea. I know the wife of a very high personage in the Administration, and also a man who has lots of influence with,' etc., etc. She was determined to make no end of fuss to get me appointed skipper of a river steamboat, if such was my fancy.

"I got my appointment—of course; and I got it very quick. It appears the Company had received news that one of their captains had been killed in a scuffle with the natives. This was my chance, and it made me the more anxious to go. It was only months and months afterwards, when I made the attempt to recover what was left of the body, that I heard the original quarrel arose from a misunderstanding about some hens. Yes, two black hens. Fresleven—that was the fellow's name, a Dane—thought himself wronged somehow in the bargain, so he went ashore and started to hammer the chief of the village with a stick. Oh, it didn't surprise me in the least to hear this, and at the same time to be told that Fresleven was the gentlest, quietest creature that ever walked on two legs. No doubt he was; but he had been a couple of years already out there engaged in the noble cause, you know, and he probably felt the need at last of asserting his self-respect in some way. Therefore he whacked the old nigger mercilessly, while a big crowd of his people watched him, thunderstruck, till some man—I was told the chief's son—in desperation at hearing the old chap yell, made a tentative jab with a spear at the white man—and of course it went quite easy between the shoulder-blades. Then the whole population cleared into the forest, expecting all kinds of calamities to happen, while, on the other hand, the steamer Fresleven commanded left also in a bad panic, in charge of the engineer, I believe. Afterwards nobody seemed to trouble much about Fresleven's remains, till I got out and stepped into his shoes. I couldn't let it rest, though; but when an opportunity offered at last to meet

[17] Busy commercial street in London.

my predecessor, the grass growing through his ribs was tall enough to hide his bones. They were all there. The supernatural being had not been touched after he fell. And the village was deserted, the huts gaped black, rotting, all askew within the fallen enclosures. A calamity had come to it, sure enough. The people had vanished. Mad terror had scattered them, men, women, and children, through the bush, and they had never returned. What became of the hens I don't know either. I should think the cause of progress got them, anyhow. However, through this glorious affair I got my appointment, before I had fairly begun to hope for it.

"I flew around like mad to get ready, and before forty-eight hours I was crossing the Channel to show myself to my employers, and sign the contract. In a very few hours I arrived in a city[18] that always makes me think of a whited sepulchre.[19] Prejudice no doubt. I had no difficulty in finding the Company's offices. It was the biggest thing in the town, and everybody I met was full of it. They were going to run an over-sea empire, and make no end of coin by trade.

"A narrow and deserted street in deep shadow, high houses, innumerable windows with venetian blinds, a dead silence, grass sprouting between the stones, imposing carriage archways right and left, immense double doors standing ponderously ajar. I slipped through one of these cracks, went up a swept and ungarnished staircase, as arid as a desert, and opened the first door I came to. Two women, one fat and the other slim, sat on straw-bottomed chairs, knitting black wool. The slim one got up and walked straight at me—still knitting with down-cast eyes—and only just as I began to think of getting out of her way, as you would for a somnambulist,[20] stood still, and looked up. Her dress was as plain as an umbrella-cover, and she turned round without a word and preceded me into a waiting-room. I gave my name, and looked about. Deal[21] table in the middle, plain chairs all round the walls, on one end a large shining map, marked with all the colours of a rainbow. There was a vast amount of red—good to see at any time, because one knows that some real work is done in there, a deuce of a lot of blue, a little green, smears of orange, and, on the East Coast, a purple patch, to show where the jolly pioneers of progress drink the jolly lager-beer. However, I wasn't going into any of these. I was going into the yellow.[22] Dead in the centre. And the river was there—fascinating—deadly—like a snake. Ough! A door opened, a whitehaired secretarial head, but wearing a compassionate expression, appeared, and a skinny forefinger beckoned me into the sanctuary. Its light was dim, and a heavy writing-desk squatted in the middle. From behind that structure came out an impression of pale plumpness in a frock-coat. The great man himself. He was five feet six, I should judge, and had his grip on the handle-end of ever so many millions. He shook hands, I fancy, murmured vaguely, was satisfied with my French. *Bon voyage.*

[18] Brussels, capital of Belgium, whose king, Leopold II, owned the vast Congo region in 1890, the approximate time of this story.

[19] Jesus, in accusing the Pharisees of hypocrisy, likened them to whited sepulchers (tombs), gleaming without but corrupt within. See Matthew 23:27.

[20] Sleepwalker. [21] Plain fir or pine.

[22] The colors distinguish lands controlled by the various European colonial powers; for example, red is British, purple German or perhaps Dutch, yellow the Belgian Congo.

"In about forty-five seconds I found myself again in the waiting-room with the compassionate secretary, who, full of desolation and sympathy, made me sign some document. I believe I undertook amongst other things not to disclose any trade secrets. Well, I am not going to.

"I began to feel slightly uneasy. You know I am not used to such ceremonies, and there was something ominous in the atmosphere. It was just as though I had been let into some conspiracy—I don't know—something not quite right; and I was glad to get out. In the outer room the two women knitted black wool feverishly. People were arriving, and the younger one was walking back and forth introducing them. The old one sat on her chair. Her flat cloth slippers were propped up on a foot-warmer, and a cat reposed on her lap. She wore a starched white affair on her head, had a wart on one cheek, and silver-rimmed spectacles hung on the tip of her nose. She glanced at me above the glasses. The swift and indifferent placidity of that look troubled me. Two youths with foolish and cheery countenances were being piloted over, and she threw at them the same quick glance of unconcerned wisdom. She seemed to know all about them and about me, too. An eerie feeling came over me. She seemed uncanny and fateful. Often far away there I thought of these two, guarding the door of Darkness, knitting black wool as for a warm pall,[23] one introducing, introducing continuously to the unknown, the other scrutinizing the cheery and foolish faces with unconcerned old eyes. *Ave!* Old knitter of black wool. *Morituri te salutant.*[24] Not many of those she looked at ever saw her again—not half, by a long way.

"There was yet a visit to the doctor. 'A simple formality,' assured me the secretary, with an air of taking an immense part in all my sorrows. Accordingly a young chap wearing his hat over the left eyebrow, some clerk I suppose,—there must have been clerks in the business, though the house was as still as a house in a city of the dead—came from somewhere upstairs, and led me forth. He was shabby and careless, with inkstains on the sleeves of his jacket, and his cravat was large and billowy, under a chin shaped like the toe of an old boot. It was a little too early for the doctor, so I proposed a drink, and thereupon he developed a vein of joviality. As we sat over our vermouths he glorified the Company's business, and by and by I expressed casually my surprise at him not going out there. He became very cool and collected all at once. 'I am not such a fool as I look, quoth Plato to his disciples,' he said sententiously, emptied his glass with great resolution, and we rose.

"The old doctor felt my pulse, evidently thinking of something else the while. 'Good, good for there,' he mumbled, and then with a certain eagerness asked me whether I would let him measure my head. Rather surprised, I said Yes, when he produced a thing like calipers and got the dimensions back and front and every way, taking notes carefully. He was an unshaven little man in a threadbare coat like a gaberdine, with his feet in slippers, and I thought him a harmless fool. 'I always ask leave, in the interests of science, to measure the crania of those going out there,' he said.

[23] Cloth spread over a coffin.

[24] *Ave . . . salutant.* The salute to the Emperor by the Roman gladiators in the arena: "Hail! Those who are about to die salute you."

'And when they come back, too?' I asked. 'Oh, I never see them,' he remarked; 'and, moreover, the changes take place inside, you know.' He smiled, as if at some quiet joke. 'So you are going out there. Famous.[25] Interesting, too.' He gave me a searching glance, and made another note. 'Ever any madness in your family?' he asked, in a matter-of-fact tone. I felt very annoyed. 'Is that question in the interests of science, too?' 'It would be,' he said, without taking notice of my irritation, 'interesting for science to watch the mental changes of individuals, on the spot, but . . .' 'Are you an alienist?'[26] I interrupted. 'Every doctor should be— a little,' answered that original, imperturbably. 'I have a little theory which you Messieurs who go out there must help me to prove. This is my share in the advantages my country shall reap from the possession of such a magnificent dependency. The mere wealth I leave to others. Pardon my questions, but you are the first Englishman coming under my observation . . .' I hastened to assure him I was not in the least typical. 'If I were,' said I, 'I wouldn't be talking like this with you.' 'What you say is rather profound, and probably erroneous,' he said, with a laugh. 'Avoid irritation more than exposure to the sun. Adieu. How do you English say, eh? Good-bye. Ah! Good-bye. Adieu. In the tropics one must before everything keep calm.' . . . He lifted a warning forefinger. . . . *'Du calme, du calme. Adieu.'*

"One thing more remained to do—say good-bye to my excellent aunt. I found her triumphant. I had a cup of tea—the last decent cup of tea for many days—and in a room that most soothingly looked just as you would expect a lady's drawing-room to look, we had a long quiet chat by the fireside. In the course of these confidences it became quite plain to me I had been represented to the wife of the high dignitary, and goodness knows to how many more people besides, as an exceptional and gifted creature—a piece of good fortune for the Company—a man you don't get hold of every day. Good heavens! and I was going to take charge of a two-penny-half-penny river-steamboat with a penny whistle[27] attached! It appeared, however, I was also one of the Workers, with a capital—you know. Something like an emissary of light, something like a lower sort of apostle. There had been a lot of such rot let loose in print and talk just about that time, and the excellent woman, living right in the rush of all that humbug, got carried off her feet. She talked about 'weaning those ignorant millions from their horrid ways,' till, upon my word, she made me quite uncomfortable. I ventured to hint that the Company was run for profit.

" 'You forget, dear Charlie, that the labourer is worthy of his hire,'[28] she said, brightly. It's queer how out of touch with truth women are. They live in a world of their own, and there has never been anything like it, and never can be. It is too beautiful altogether, and if they were to set it up it would go to pieces before the first sunset. Some confounded fact we men have been living contentedly with ever since the day of creation would start up and knock the whole thing over.

"After this I got embraced, told to wear flannel, be sure to write often, and so on—and I left. In the street—I don't known why—a queer feeling

[25] Splendid. [26] Psychiatrist. [27] A small, inexpensive musical pipe.

[28] *labourer . . . hire.* Jesus' words to his disciples in sending them forth as missionaries; Luke 10:7.

came to me that I was an impostor. Odd thing that I, who used to clear out for any part of the world at twenty-four hours' notice, with less thought than most men give to the crossing of a street, had a moment—I won't say of hesitation, but of startled pause, before this commonplace affair. The best way I can explain it to you is by saying that, for a second or two, I felt as though, instead of going to the centre of a continent, I were about to set off for the centre of the earth.

"I left in a French steamer, and she called in every blamed port they have out there, for, as far as I could see, the sole purpose of landing soldiers and custom-house officers. I watched the coast. Watching a coast as it slips by the ship is like thinking about an enigma. There it is before you—smiling, frowning, inviting, grand, mean, insipid, or savage, and always mute with an air of whispering, Come and find out. This one was almost featureless, as if still in the making, with an aspect of monotonous grimness. The edge of a colossal jungle, so dark-green as to be almost black, fringed with white surf, ran straight, like a ruled line, far, far away along a blue sea whose glitter was blurred by a creeping mist. The sun was fierce, the land seemed to glisten and drip with steam. Here and there grayish-whitish specks showed up clustered inside the white surf, with a flag flying above them perhaps. Settlements some centuries old, and still no bigger than pinheads on the untouched expanse of their background. We pounded along, stopped, landed soldiers; went on, landed custom-house clerks to levy toll in what looked like a God-forsaken wilderness, with a tin shed and a flagpole lost in it; landed more soldiers—to take care of the custom-house clerks, presumably. Some, I heard, got drowned in the surf; but whether they did or not, nobody seemed particularly to care. They were just flung out there, and on we went. Every day the coast looked the same, as though we had not moved; but we passed various places—trading places—with names like Gran' Bassam, Little Popo; names that seemed to belong to some sordid farce acted in front of a sinister back-cloth. The idleness of a passenger, my isolation amongst all these men with whom I had no point of contact, the oily and languid sea, the uniform sombreness of the coast, seemed to keep me away from the truth of things, within the toil[29] of a mournful and senseless delusion. The voice of the surf heard now and then was a positive pleasure, like the speech of a brother. It was something natural, that had its reason, that had a meaning. Now and then a boat from the shore gave one a momentary contact with reality. It was paddled by black fellows. You could see from afar the white of their eyeballs glistening. They shouted, sang; their bodies streamed with perspiration; they had faces like grotesque masks—these chaps; but they had bone, muscle, a wild vitality, an intense energy of movement, that was as natural and true as the surf along their coast. They wanted no excuse for being there. They were a great comfort to look at. For a time I would feel I belonged still to a world of straightforward facts; but the feeling would not last long. Something would turn up to scare it away. Once, I remember, we came upon a man-of-war anchored off the coast. There wasn't even a shed there, and she was shelling the bush. It appears the French had one of their wars going on thereabouts. Her ensign[30] dropped limp like a rag; the

[29] Net; trap. [30] Flag.

muzzles of the long six-inch guns stuck out all over the low hull; the greasy, slimy swell swung her up lazily and let her down, swaying her thin masts. In the empty immensity of earth, sky, and water, there she was, incomprehensible, firing into a continent. Pop, would go one of the six-inch guns; a small flame would dart and vanish, a little white smoke would disappear, a tiny projectile would give a feeble screech—and nothing happened. Nothing could happen. There was a touch of insanity in the proceeding, a sense of lugubrious drollery in the sight; and it was not dissipated by somebody on board assuring me earnestly there was a camp of natives—he called them enemies!—hidden out of sight somewhere.

"We gave her her letters (I heard the men in that lonely ship were dying of fever at the rate of three a day) and went on. We called at some more places with farcical names, where the merry dance of death and trade goes on in a still and earthy atmosphere as of an overheated catacomb;[31] all along the formless coast bordered by dangerous surf, as if Nature herself had tried to ward off intruders; in and out of rivers, streams of death in life, whose banks were rotting into mud, whose waters, thickened into slime, invaded the contorted mangroves,[32] that seemed to writhe at us in the extremity of an impotent despair. Nowhere did we stop long enough to get a particularized impression, but the general sense of vague and oppressive wonder grew upon me. It was like a weary pilgrimage amongst hints for nightmares.

"It was upward of thirty days before I saw the mouth of the big river. We anchored off the seat of the government. But my work would not begin till some two hundred miles farther on. So as soon as I could I made a start for a place thirty miles higher up.

"I had my passage on a little sea-going steamer. Her captain was a Swede, and knowing me for a seaman, invited me on the bridge. He was a young man, lean, fair, and morose, with lanky hair and a shuffling gait. As we left the miserable little wharf, he tossed his head contemptuously at the shore. 'Been living there?' he asked. I said, 'Yes.' 'Fine lot these government chaps—are they not?' he went on, speaking English with great precision and considerable bitterness. 'It is funny what some people will do for a few francs a month. I wonder what becomes of that kind when it goes up country?' I said to him I expected to see that soon. 'So-o-o!' he exclaimed. He shuffled athwart,[33] keeping one eye ahead vigilantly. 'Don't be too sure,' he continued. 'The other day I took up a man who hanged himself on the road. He was a Swede, too.' 'Hanged himself! Why, in God's name?' I cried. He kept on looking out watchfully. 'Who knows? The sun too much for him, or the country perhaps.'

"At last we opened a reach.[34] A rocky cliff appeared, mounds of turned-up earth by the shore, houses on a hill, others with iron roofs, amongst a waste of excavations, or hanging to the declivity. A continuous noise of the rapids above hovered over this scene of inhabited devastation. A lot of people, mostly black and naked, moved about like ants. A jetty projected into the river. A blinding sunlight drowned all this at times in a sudden recrudescence of glare. 'There's your Company's station,' said the

[31] Underground tunnel containing graves. [32] Tropical evergreens.
[33] Sideways. [34] Straight stretch between curves of the river.

Swede, pointing to three wooden barrack-like structures on the rocky slope. 'I will send your things up. Four boxes did you say? So. Farewell.'

"I came upon a boiler wallowing in the grass, then found a path leading up the hill. It turned aside for the boulders, and also for an undersized railway-truck lying there on its back with its wheels in the air. One was off. The thing looked as dead as the carcass of some animal. I came upon more pieces of decaying machinery, a stack of rusty rails. To the left a clump of trees made a shady spot, where dark things seemed to stir feebly. I blinked, the path was steep. A horn tooted to the right, and I saw the black people run. A heavy and dull detonation shook the ground, a puff of smoke came out of the cliff, and that was all. No change appeared on the face of the rock. They were building a railway. The cliff was not in the way or anything; but this objectless blasting was all the work going on.

"A slight clinking behind me made me turn my head. Six black men advanced in a file, toiling up the path. They walked erect and slow, balancing small baskets full of earth on their heads, and the clink kept time with their footsteps. Black rags were wound round their loins, and the short ends behind waggled to and fro like tails. I could see every rib, the joints of their limbs were like knots in a rope; each had an iron collar on his neck, and all were connected together with a chain whose bights[35] swung between them, rhythmically clinking. Another report from the cliff made me think suddenly of that ship of war I had seen firing into a continent. It was the same kind of ominous voice; but these men could by no stretch of imagination be called enemies. They were called criminals, and the outraged law, like the bursting shells, had come to them, an insoluble mystery from the sea. All their meagre breasts panted together, the violently dilated nostrils quivered, the eyes stared stonily up-hill. They passed me within six inches, without a glance, with that complete, deathlike indifference of unhappy savages. Behind this raw matter one of the reclaimed, the product of the new forces at work, strolled despondently, carrying a rifle by its middle. He had a uniform jacket with one button off, and seeing a white man on the path, hoisted his weapon to his shoulder with alacrity. This was simple prudence, white men being so much alike at a distance that he could not tell who I might be. He was speedily reassured, and with a large, white, rascally grin, and a glance at his charge,[36] seemed to take me into partnership in his exalted trust. After all, I also was a part of the great cause of these high and just proceedings.

"Instead of going up, I turned and descended to the left. My idea was to let that chain-gang get out of sight before I climbed the hill. You know I am not particularly tender; I've had to strike and to fend off. I've had to resist and to attack sometimes—that's only one way of resisting—without counting the exact cost, according to the demands of such sort of life as I had blundered into. I've seen the devil of violence, and the devil of greed, and the devil of hot desire; but, by all the stars! these were strong, lusty, red-eyed devils, that swayed and drove men—men, I tell you. But as I stood on this hillside, I foresaw that in the blinding sunshine of that land I would become acquainted with a flabby, pretending, weak-eyed devil of a rapacious and pitiless folly. How insidious he could be, too, I was only to find

[35] Slack lengths. [36] Those in his custody.

out several months later and a thousand miles farther. For a moment I stood appalled, as though by a warning. Finally I descended the hill, obliquely, towards the trees I had seen.

"I avoided a vast artificial hole somebody had been digging on the slope, the purpose of which I found it impossible to divine. It wasn't a quarry or a sandpit, anyhow. It was just a hole. It might have been connected with the philanthropic desire of giving the criminals something to do. I don't know. Then I nearly fell into a very narrow ravine, almost no more than a scar in the hillside. I discovered that a lot of imported drainage-pipes for the settlement had been tumbled in there. There wasn't one that was not broken. It was a wanton smash-up. At last I got under the trees. My purpose was to stroll into the shade for a moment; but no sooner within than it seemed to me I had stepped into the gloomy circle of some Inferno. The rapids were near, and an uninterrupted, uniform, headlong, rushing noise filled the mournful stillness of the grove, where not a breath stirred, not a leaf moved, with a mysterious sound—as though the tearing pace of the launched earth had suddenly become audible.

"Black shapes crouched, lay, sat between the trees leaning against the trunks, clinging to the earth, half coming out, half effaced within the dim light, in all the attitudes of pain, abandonment, and despair. Another mine[37] on the cliff went off, followed by a slight shudder of the soil under my feet. The work was going on. The work! And this was the place where some of the helpers had withdrawn to die.

"They were dying slowly—it was very clear. They were not enemies, they were not criminals, they were nothing earthly now,—nothing but black shadows of disease and starvation, lying confusedly in the greenish gloom. Brought from all the recesses of the coast in all the legality of time contracts, lost in uncongenial surroundings, fed on unfamiliar food, they sickened, became inefficient, and were then allowed to crawl away and rest. These moribund shapes were free as air—and nearly as thin. I began to distinguish the gleam of the eyes under the trees. Then, glancing down, I saw a face near my hand. The black bones reclined at full length with one shoulder against the tree, and slowly the eyelids rose and the sunken eyes looked up at me, enormous and vacant, a kind of blind, white flicker in the depths of the orbs, which died out slowly. The man seemed young—almost a boy—but you know with them it's hard to tell. I found nothing else to do but to offer him one of my good Swede's ship's biscuits I had in my pocket. The fingers closed slowly on it and held—there was no other movement and no other glance. He had tied a bit of white worsted round his neck—Why? Where did he get it? Was it a badge—an ornament—a charm—a propitiatory act? Was there any idea at all connected with it? It looked startling round his black neck, this bit of white thread from beyond the seas.

"Near the same tree two more bundles of acute angles sat with their legs drawn up. One, with his chin propped on his knees, stared at nothing, in an intolerable and appalling manner: his brother phantom rested its forehead, as if overcome with a great weariness; and all about others were scattered in every pose of contorted collapse, as in some picture of a mas-

[37] Explosive device.

sacre or a pestilence. While I stood horror-struck, one of these creatures rose to his hands and knees, and went off on all-fours towards the river to drink. He lapped out of his hand, then sat up in the sunlight, crossing his shins in front of him, and after a time let his woolly head fall on his breastbone.

"I didn't want any more loitering in the shade, and I made haste towards the station. When near the buildings I met a white man, in such an unexpected elegance of get-up that in the first moment I took him for a sort of vision. I saw a high starched collar, white cuffs, a light alpaca jacket, snowy trousers, a clean necktie, and varnished boots. No hat. Hair parted, brushed, oiled, under a green-lined parasol held in a big white hand. He was amazing, and had a pen-holder behind his ear.

"I shook hands with this miracle, and I learned he was the Company's chief accountant, and that all the book-keeping was done at this station. He had come out for a moment, he said, 'to get a breath of fresh air.' The expression sounded wonderfully odd, with its suggestion of sedentary desk-life. I wouldn't have mentioned the fellow to you at all, only it was from his lips that I first heard the name of the man who is so indissolubly connected with the memories of that time. Moreover, I respected the fellow. Yes; I respected his collars, his vast cuffs, his brushed hair. His appearance was certainly that of a hairdresser's dummy; but in the great demoralization of the land he kept up his appearance. That's backbone. His starched collars and got-up shirt-fronts were achievements of character. He had been out nearly three years; and, later, I could not help asking him how he managed to sport such linen. He had just the faintest blush, and said modestly, 'I've been teaching one of the native women about the station. It was difficult. She had a distaste for the work.' Thus this man had verily accomplished something. And he was devoted to his books, which were in apple-pie order.

"Everything else in the station was in a muddle,—heads, things, buildings. Strings of dusty niggers with splay feet arrived and departed; a stream of manufactured goods, rubbishy cottons, beads, and brass-wire sent into the depths of darkness, and in return came a precious trickle of ivory.

"I had to wait in the station for ten days—an eternity. I lived in a hut in the yard, but to be out of the chaos I would sometimes get into the accountant's office. It was built of horizontal planks, and so badly put together that, as he bent over his high desk, he was barred from neck to heels with narrow strips of sunlight. There was no need to open the big shutter to see. It was hot there, too; big flies buzzed fiendishly, and did not sting, but stabbed. I sat generally on the floor, while, of faultless appearance (and even slightly scented), perching on a high stool, he wrote, he wrote. Sometimes he stood up for exercise. When a truckle-bed with a sick man (some invalid agent from up-country) was put in there, he exhibited a gentle annoyance. 'The groans of this sick person,' he said, 'distract my attention. And without that it is extremely difficult to guard against clerical errors in this climate.'

"One day he remarked, without lifting his head, 'In the interior you will no doubt meet Mr. Kurtz.' On my asking who Mr. Kurtz was, he said he was a first-class agent; and seeing my disappointment at this information, he added slowly, laying down his pen, 'He is a very remarkable person.'

Further questions elicited from him that Mr. Kurtz was at present in charge of a trading post, a very important one, in the true ivory-country, at 'the very bottom of there. Sends in as much ivory as all the others put together. . . .' He began to write again. The sick man was too ill to groan. The flies buzzed in a great peace.

"Suddenly there was a growing murmur of voices and a great tramping of feet. A caravan had come in. A violent babble of uncouth sounds burst out on the other side of the planks. All the carriers were speaking together, and in the midst of the uproar the lamentable voice of the chief agent was heard 'giving it up' tearfully for the twentieth time that day. . . . He rose slowly. 'What a frightful row,' he said. He crossed the room gently to look at the sick man, and returning, said to me, 'He does not hear.' 'What! Dead?' I asked, startled. 'No, not yet,' he answered, with great composure. Then, alluding with a toss of the head to the tumult in the station-yard, 'When one has got to make correct entries, one comes to hate those savages—hate them to the death.' He remained thoughtful for a moment. 'When you see Mr. Kurtz,' he went on, 'tell him from me that everything here'—he glanced at the desk—'is very satisfactory. I don't like to write to him—with those messengers of ours you never know who may get hold of your letter—at that Central Station.' He stared at me for a moment with his mild, bulging eyes. 'Oh, he will go far, very far,' he began again. 'He will be a somebody in the Administration before long. They, above—the Council in Europe, you know—mean him to be.'

"He turned to his work. The noise outside had ceased, and presently in going out I stopped at the door. In the steady buzz of flies the homeward-bound agent was lying flushed and insensible; the other, bent over his books, was making correct entries of perfectly correct transactions; and fifty feet below the doorstep I could see the still treetops of the grove of death.

"Next day I left that station at last, with a caravan of sixty men, for a two-hundred-mile tramp.

"No use telling you much about that. Paths, paths, everywhere; a stamped-in network of paths spreading over the empty land, through long grass, through burnt grass, through thickets, down and up chilly ravines, up and down stony hills ablaze with heat; and a solitude, a solitude, nobody, not a hut. The population had cleared out a long time ago. Well, if a lot of mysterious niggers armed with all kinds of fearful weapons suddenly took to traveling on the road between Deal[38] and Gravesend, catching the yokels right and left to carry heavy loads for them, I fancy every farm and cottage thereabouts would get empty very soon. Only here the dwellings were gone, too. Still I passed through several abandoned villages. There's something pathetically childish in the ruins of grass walls. Day after day, with the stamp and shuffle of sixty pair of bare feet behind me, each pair under a 60-lb. load. Camp, cook, sleep, strike camp, march. Now and then a carrier dead in harness, at rest in the long grass near the path, with an empty water-gourd and his long staff lying by his side. A great silence around and above. Perhaps on some quiet night the tremor of far-off drums, sinking, swelling, a tremor vast, faint; a sound weird, appealing,

[38] A port on the English Channel.

suggestive, and wild—and perhaps with as profound a meaning as the sound of bells in a Christian country. Once a white man in an unbuttoned uniform, camping on the path with an armed escort of lank Zanzibaris,[39] very hospitable and festive—not to say drunk. Was looking after the upkeep of the road, he declared. Can't say I saw any road or any upkeep, unless the body of a middle-aged negro, with a bullet-hole in the forehead, upon which I absolutely stumbled three miles farther on, may be considered as a permanent improvement. I had a white companion, too, not a bad chap, but rather too fleshy and with the exasperating habit of fainting on the hot hillsides, miles away from the least bit of shade and water. Annoying, you know, to hold your own coat like a parasol over a man's head while he is coming-to. I couldn't help asking him once what he meant by coming there at all. 'To make money, of course. What do you think?' he said, scornfully. Then he got fever, and had to be carried in a hammock slung under a pole. As he weighed sixteen stone[40] I had no end of rows with the carriers. They jibbed,[41] ran away, sneaked off with their loads in the night—quite a mutiny. So, one evening, I made a speech in English with gestures, not one of which was lost to the sixty pairs of eyes before me, and the next morning I started the hammock off in front all right. An hour afterwards I came upon the whole concern wrecked in a bush—man, hammock, groans, blankets, horrors. The heavy pole had skinned his poor nose. He was very anxious for me to kill somebody, but there wasn't the shadow of a carrier near. I remembered the old doctor—'It would be interesting for science to watch the mental changes of individuals, on the spot.' I felt I was becoming scientifically interesting. However, all that is to no purpose. On the fifteenth day I came in sight of the big river again, and hobbled into the Central Station. It was on a back water surrounded by scrub and forest, with a pretty border of smelly mud on one side, and on the three others enclosed by a crazy fence of rushes. A neglected gap was all the gate it had, and the first glance at the place was enough to let you see the flabby devil was running that show. White men with long staves in their hands appeared languidly from amongst the buildings, strolling up to take a look at me, and then retired out of sight somewhere. One of them, a stout, excitable chap with black moustaches, informed me with great volubility and many digressions, as soon as I told him who I was, that my steamer was at the bottom of the river. I was thunderstruck. What, how, why? Oh, it was 'all right.' The 'manager himself' was there. All quite correct. 'Everybody had behaved splendidly! splendidly!'—'you must,' he said in agitation, 'go and see the general manager at once. He is waiting!'

"I did not see the real significance of that wreck at once. I fancy I see it now, but I am not sure—not at all. Certainly the affair was too stupid—when I think of it—to be altogether natural. Still . . . But at the moment it presented itself simply as a confounded nuisance. The steamer was sunk. They had started two days before in a sudden hurry up the river with the manager on board, in charge of some volunteer skipper, and before they had been out three hours they tore the bottom out of her on stones, and she sank near the south bank. I asked myself what I was to do there, now

[39] Hired men from Zanzibar, a large island off the east coast of Africa.
[40] Fourteen-pound British unit of weight; thus, 224 pounds. [41] Balked.

my boat was lost. As a matter of fact, I had plenty to do in fishing my command out of the river. I had to set about it the very next day. That, and the repairs when I brought the pieces to the station, took some months.

"My first interview with the manager was curious. He did not ask me to sit down after my twenty-mile walk that morning. He was commonplace in complexion, in feature, in manners, and in voice. He was of middle size and of ordinary build. His eyes, of the usual blue, were perhaps remarkably cold, and he certainly could make his glance fall on one as trenchant and heavy as an axe. But even at these times the rest of his person seemed to disclaim the intention. Otherwise there was only an indefinable, faint expression of his lips, something stealthy—a smile—not a smile—I remember it, but I can't explain. It was unconscious, this smile was, though just after he had said something it got intensified for an instant. It came at the end of his speeches like a seal applied on the words to make the meaning of the commonest phrase appear absolutely inscrutable. He was a common trader, from his youth up employed in these parts—nothing more. He was obeyed, yet he inspired neither love nor fear, nor even respect. He inspired uneasiness. That was it! Uneasiness. Not a definite mistrust—just uneasiness—nothing more. You have no idea how effective such a . . . a . . . faculty can be. He had no genius for organizing, for initiative, or for order even. That was evident in such things as the deplorable state of the station. He had no learning, and no intelligence. His position had come to him—why? Perhaps because he was never ill . . . He had served three terms of three years out there . . . Because triumphant health in the general rout of constitutions is a kind of power in itself. When he went home on leave he rioted on a large scale—pompously. Jack[42] ashore—with a difference—in externals only. This one could gather from his casual talk. He originated nothing, he could keep the routine going—that's all. But he was great. He was great by this little thing that it was impossible to tell what could control such a man. He never gave that secret away. Perhaps there was nothing within him. Such a suspicion made one pause—for out there there were no external checks. Once when various tropical diseases had laid low almost every 'agent' in the station, he was heard to say, 'Men who come out here should have no entrails.' He sealed the utterance with that smile of his, as though it had been a door opening into a darkness he had in his keeping. You fancied you had seen things—but the seal was on. When annoyed at mealtimes by the constant quarrels of the white men about precedence, he ordered an immense round table to be made, for which a special house had to be built. This was the station's mess-room. Where he sat was the first place—the rest were nowhere. One felt this to be his unalterable conviction. He was neither civil nor uncivil. He was quiet. He allowed his 'boy'—an overfed young negro from the coast—to treat the white men, under his very eyes, with provoking insolence.

"He began to speak as soon as he saw me. I had been very long on the road. He could not wait. Had to start without me. The up-river stations had to be relieved. There had been so many delays already that he did not know who was dead and who was alive, and how they got on—and so on, and so on. He paid no attention to my explanations, and, playing with a stick of

[42] Jack-tar; sailor.

sealing-wax, repeated several times that the situation was 'very grave, very grave.' There were rumours that a very important station was in jeopardy, and its chief, Mr. Kurtz, was ill. Hoped it was not true. Mr. Kurtz was . . . I felt weary and irritable. Hang Kurtz, I thought. I interrupted him by saying I had heard of Mr. Kurtz on the coast. 'Ah! So they talk of him down there,' he murmured to himself. Then he began again, assuring me Mr. Kurtz was the best agent he had, an exceptional man, of the greatest importance to the Company; therefore I could understand his anxiety. He was, he said, 'very, very uneasy.' Certainly he fidgeted on his chair a good deal, exclaimed, 'Ah, Mr. Kurtz!' broke the stick of sealing-wax and seemed dumfounded by the accident. Next thing he wanted to know 'how long it would take to' . . . I interrupted him again. Being hungry, you know, and kept on my feet too, I was getting savage. 'How can I tell?' I said. 'I haven't even seen the wreck yet—some months, no doubt.' All this talk seemed to me so futile. 'Some months,' he said. 'Well, let us say three months before we can make a start. Yes. That ought to do the affair.' I flung out of his hut (he lived all alone in a clay hut with a sort of verandah) muttering to myself my opinion of him. He was a chattering idiot. Afterwards I took it back when it was borne in upon me startlingly with what extreme nicety he had estimated the time requisite for the 'affair.'

"I went to work the next day, turning, so to speak, my back on that station. In that way only it seemed to me I could keep my hold on the redeeming facts of life. Still, one must look about sometimes; and then I saw this station, these men strolling aimlessly about in the sunshine of the yard. I asked myself sometimes what it all meant. They wandered here and there with their absurd long staves in their hands, like a lot of faithless pilgrims bewitched inside a rotten fence. The word 'ivory' rang in the air, was whispered, was sighed. You would think they were praying to it. A taint of imbecile rapacity blew through it all, like a whiff from some corpse. By Jove! I've never seen anything so unreal in my life. And outside, the silent wilderness surrounding this cleared speck on the earth struck me as something great and invincible, like evil or truth, waiting patiently for the passing away of this fantastic invasion.

"Oh, those months! Well, never mind. Various things happened. One evening a grass shed full of calico, cotton prints, beads, and I don't know what else, burst into a blaze so suddenly that you would have thought the earth had opened to let an avenging fire consume all that trash. I was smoking my pipe quietly by my dismantled steamer, and saw them all cutting capers in the light, with their arms lifted high, when the stout man with moustaches came tearing down to the river, a tin pail in his hand, assured me that everybody was 'behaving splendidly, splendidly,' dipped about a quart of water and tore back again. I noticed there was a hole in the bottom of his pail.

"I strolled up. There was no hurry. You see the thing had gone off like a box of matches. It had been hopeless from the very first. The flame had leaped high, driven everybody back, lighted up everything—and collapsed. The shed was already a heap of embers glowing fiercely. A nigger was being beaten near by. They said he had caused the fire in some way; be that as it may, he was screeching most horribly. I saw him, later, for several days, sitting in a bit of shade looking very sick and trying to recover himself: afterwards he arose and went out—and the wilderness without a sound took him into its bosom again. As I approached the glow from the dark I found myself at the back of two men, talking. I heard the name of Kurtz pronounced, then the words, 'take advantage of this unfortunate accident.' One of the men was the manager. I wished him a good evening. 'Did you ever see anything like it—eh? it is incredible,' he said, and walked off. The other man remained. He was a first-class agent, young, gentlemanly, a bit reserved, with a forked little beard and a hooked nose. He was stand-offish with the other agents, and they on their side said he was the manager's spy upon them. As to me, I had hardly ever spoken to him before. We got into talk, and by and by we strolled away from the hissing ruins. Then he asked me to his room, which was in the main building of the station. He struck a match, and I perceived that this young aristocrat had not only a silver-mounted dressing-case but also a whole candle all to himself. Just at that time the manager was the only man supposed to have any right to candles. Native mats covered the clay walls; a collection of spears, assegais,[43] shields, knives was hung up in trophies. The business intrusted to this fellow was the making of bricks—so I had been informed; but there wasn't a fragment of a brick anywhere in the station, and he had been there more than a year—waiting. It seems he could not make bricks without something, I don't know what—straw[44] maybe. Anyways, it could not be found there, and as it was not likely to be sent from Europe, it did not appear clear to me what he was waiting for. An act of special creation[45] perhaps. However, they were all waiting—all the sixteen or twenty pilgrims of them—for something; and upon my word it did not seem an uncongenial occupation, from the way they took it, though the only thing that ever came to them was disease—as far as I could see. They beguiled the time by backbiting and intriguing against each other in a foolish kind of way. There was an air of plotting about that station, but nothing came of it, of course. It was as unreal as everything else—as the philanthropic pretence of the whole concern, as their talk, as their government, as their show of work. The only real feeling was a desire to get appointed to a trading-post where ivory was to be had, so that they could earn percentages. They intrigued and slandered and hated each other only on that account,—but as to effectually lifting a little finger—oh, no. By heavens! there is something after all in the world allowing one man to steal a horse while another must not look at a halter. Steal a horse straight out. Very well. He has done it. Perhaps he can ride. But there is a way of looking at a halter that would provoke the most charitable of saints into a kick.

"I had no idea why he wanted to be sociable, but as we chatted in there it suddenly occurred to me the fellow was trying to get at something—in fact, pumping me. He alluded constantly to Europe, to the people I was supposed to know there—putting leading questions as to my acquaintances in the sepulchral city, and so on. His little eyes glittered like mica discs—with curiosity—though he tried to keep up a bit of superciliousness. At first I

[43] Javelins used by south-African tribes.

[44] The ancient Hebrews, enslaved in Egypt, were required to deliver their usual quota of bricks though deprived of the straw needed to make them, an instance of senseless tyranny. See Exodus 5.

[45] The belief, rejected by evolutionists, that God created each species separately.

was astonished, but very soon I became awfully curious to see what he would find out from me. I couldn't possibly imagine what I had in me to make it worth his while. It was very pretty to see how he baffled himself, for in truth my body was full only of chills, and my head had nothing in it but that wretched steamboat business. It was evident he took me for a perfectly shameless prevaricator. At last he got angry, and, to conceal a movement of furious annoyance, he yawned. I rose. Then I noticed a small sketch in oils, on a panel, representing a woman, draped and blindfolded, carrying a lighted torch. The background was sombre—almost black. The movement of the woman was stately, and the effect of the torch-light on the face was sinister.

"It arrested me, and he stood by civilly, holding an empty half-pint champagne bottle (medical comforts) with the candle stuck in it. To my question he said Mr. Kurtz had painted this—in this very station more than a year ago—while waiting for means to go to his trading-post. "Tell me, pray,' said I, 'who is this Mr. Kurtz?'

"'The chief of the Inner Station,' he answered in a short tone, looking away. 'Much obliged,' I said, laughing. 'And you are the brickmaker of the Central Station. Everyone knows that.' He was silent for a while. 'He is a prodigy,' he said at last. 'He is an emissary of pity, and science, and progress, and devil knows what else. We want,' he began to declaim suddenly, 'for the guidance of the cause intrusted to us by Europe, so to speak, higher intelligence, wide sympathies, a singleness of purpose.' 'Who says that?' I asked. 'Lots of them,' he replied. 'Some even write that; and so *he* comes here, a special being, as you ought to know.' 'Why ought I to know?' I interrupted, really surprised. He paid no attention. 'Yes. To-day he is chief of the best station, next year he will be assistant-manager, two years more and . . . but I daresay you know what he will be in two years' time. You are of the new gang—the gang of virtue. The same people who sent him specially also recommended you. Oh, don't say no. I've my own eyes to trust.' Light dawned upon me. My dear aunt's influential acquaintances were producing an unexpected effect upon that young man. I nearly burst into a laugh. 'Do you read the Company's confidential correspondence?' I asked. He hadn't a word to say. It was great fun. 'When Mr. Kurtz,' I continued, severely, 'is General Manager, you won't have the opportunity.'

"He blew the candle out suddenly, and we went outside. The moon had risen. Black figures strolled about listlessly, pouring water on the glow, whence proceeded a sound of hissing; steam ascended in the moonlight, the beaten nigger groaned somewhere. 'What a row the brute makes!' said the indefatigable man with the moustaches, appearing near us. 'Serve him right. Transgression—punishment—bang! Pitiless, pitiless. That's the only way. This will prevent all conflagrations for the future. I was just telling the manager . . .' He noticed my companion, and became crestfallen all at once. 'Not in bed yet,' he said, with a kind of servile heartiness; 'it's so natural. Ha! Danger—agitation.' He vanished. I went on to the river-side, and the other followed me. I heard a scathing murmur at my ear. 'Heap of muffs—go to.' The pilgrims could be seen in knots gesticulating, discussing. Several had still their staves in their hands. I verily believe they took these sticks to bed with them. Beyond the fence the forest stood up spectrally in the moonlight, and through the dim stir, through the faint sounds of that lamentable courtyard, the silence of the land went home to one's very heart—its mystery, its greatness, the amazing reality of its concealed life. The hurt nigger moaned feebly somewhere near by, and then fetched a deep sigh that made me mend my pace away from there. I felt a hand introducing itself under my arm. 'My dear sir,' said the fellow, 'I don't want to be misunderstood, and especially by you, who will see Mr. Kurtz long before I can have that pleasure. I wouldn't like him to get a false idea of my disposition. . . .'

"I let him run on, this papier-maché Mephistopheles,[46] and it seemed to me that if I tried I could poke my forefinger through him, and would find nothing inside but a little loose dirt, maybe. He, don't you see, had been planning to be assistant-manager by and by under the present man, and I could see that the coming of that Kurtz had upset them both not a little. He talked precipitately, and I did not try to stop him. I had my shoulders against the wreck of my steamer, hauled up on the slope like a carcass of some big river animal. The smell of mud, of primeval mud, by Jove! was in my nostrils, the high stillness of primeval forest was before my eyes; there were shiny patches on the black creek. The moon had spread over everything a thin layer of silver—over the rank grass, over the mud, upon the wall of matted vegetation standing higher than the wall of a temple, over the great river I could see through a sombre gap glittering, glittering, as it flowed broadly by without a murmur. All this was great, expectant, mute, while the man jabbered about himself. I wondered whether the stillness on the face of the immensity looking at us two were meant as an appeal or as a menace. What were we who had strayed in here? Could we handle that dumb thing, or would it handle us? I felt how big, how confoundedly big, was that thing that couldn't talk, and perhaps was deaf as well. What was in there? I could see a little ivory coming out from there, and I had heard Mr. Kurtz was in there. I had heard enough about it, too—God knows! Yet somehow it didn't bring any image with it—no more than if I had been told an angel or a fiend was in there. I believed it in the same way one of you might believe there are inhabitants in the planet Mars. I knew once a Scotch sailmaker who was certain, dead sure, there were people in Mars. If you asked him for some idea how they looked and behaved, he would get shy and mutter something about 'walking on all-fours.' If you as much as smiled, he would—though a man of sixty—offer to fight you. I would not have gone so far as to fight for Kurtz, but I went for him near enough to a lie. You know I hate, detest, and can't bear a lie, not because I am straighter than the rest of us, but simply because it appalls me. There is a taint of death, a flavour of mortality in lies—which is exactly what I hate and detest in the world—what I want to forget. It makes me miserable and sick, like biting something rotten would do. Temperament, I suppose. Well, I went near enough to it by letting the young fool there believe anything he liked to imagine as to my influence in Europe. I became in an instant as much of a pretence as the rest of the bewitched pilgrims. This simply because I had a notion it somehow would be of help to that Kurtz whom at the time I did not see—you understand. He was just a word for me. I did not see the man in the name any more than you do. Do you see him? Do you see the story?

[46] The devil who bargains for the legendary Faust's soul.

Do you see anything? It seems to me I am trying to tell you a dream—making a vain attempt, because no relation of a dream can convey the dream-sensation, that commingling of absurdity, surprise, and bewilderment in a tremor of struggling revolt, that notion of being captured by the incredible which is of the very essence of dreams . . ."

He was silent for a while.

". . . No, it is impossible; it is impossible to convey the life-sensation of any given epoch of one's existence—that which makes its truth, its meaning—its subtle and penetrating essence. It is impossible. We live, as we dream—alone. . . ."

He paused again as if reflecting, then added—

"Of course in this you fellows see more than I could then. You see me, whom you know. . . ."

It had become so pitch dark that we listeners could hardly see one another. For a long time already he, sitting apart, had been no more to us than a voice. There was not a word from anybody. The others might have been asleep, but I was awake. I listened, I listened on the watch for the sentence, for the word, that would give me the clue to the faint uneasiness inspired by this narrative that seemed to shape itself without human lips in the heavy night-air of the river.

". . . Yes—I let him run on," Marlow began again, "and think what he pleased about the powers that were behind me. I did! And there was nothing behind me! There was nothing but that wretched, old, mangled steamboat I was leaning against, while he talked fluently about 'the necessity for every man to get on.' 'And when one comes out here, you conceive, it is not to gaze at the moon.' Mr. Kurtz was a 'universal genius,' but even a genius would find it easier to work with 'adequate tools—intelligent men.' He did not make bricks—why, there was a physical impossibility in the way—as I was well aware; and if he did secretarial work for the manager, it was because 'no sensible man rejects wantonly the confidence of his superiors.' Did I see it? I saw it. What more did I want? What I really wanted was rivets, by heaven! Rivets. To get on with the work—to stop the hole. Rivets I wanted. There were cases of them down at the coast—cases—piled up—burst—split! You kicked a loose rivet at every second step in that station yard on the hillside. Rivets had rolled into the grove of death. You could fill your pockets with rivets for the trouble of stooping down—and there wasn't one rivet to be found where it was wanted. We had plates that would do, but nothing to fasten them with. And every week the messenger, a lone negro, letter-bag on shoulder and staff in hand, left our station for the coast. And several times a week a coast caravan came in with trade goods—ghastly glazed calico that made you shudder only to look at it, glass beads value about a penny a quart, confounded spotted cotton handkerchiefs. And no rivets. Three carriers could have brought all that was wanted to set that steamboat afloat.

"He was becoming confidential now, but I fancy my unresponsive attitude must have exasperated him at last, for he judged it necessary to inform me he feared neither God nor devil, let alone any mere man. I said I could see that very well, but what I wanted was a certain quantity of rivets—and rivets were what really Mr. Kurtz wanted, if he had only known it. Now letters went to the coast every week. . . . 'My dear sir,' he cried, 'I write from dictation.' I demanded rivets. There was a way—for an intelligent man. He changed his manner; became very cold, and suddenly began to talk about a hippopotamus; wondered whether sleeping on board the steamer (I stuck to my salvage night and day) I wasn't disturbed. There was an old hippo that had the bad habit of getting out on the bank and roaming at night over the station grounds. The pilgrims used to turn out in a body and empty every rifle they could lay hands on at him. Some even had sat up o' nights for him. All this energy was wasted, though. 'That animal has a charmed life,' he said; 'but you can say this only of brutes in this country. No man—you apprehend me?—no man here bears a charmed life.' He stood there for a moment in the moonlight with his delicate hooked nose set a little askew, and his mica eyes glittering without a wink, then, with a curt Good-night, he strode off. I could see he was disturbed and considerably puzzled, which made me feel more hopeful than I had been for days. It was a great comfort to turn from that chap to my influential friend, the battered, twisted, ruined, tin-pot steamboat. I clambered on board. She rang under my feet like an empty Huntley & Palmer biscuit-tin kicked along a gutter; she was nothing so solid in make, and rather less pretty in shape, but I had expended enough hard work on her to make me love her. No influential friend would have served me better. She had given me a chance to come out a bit—to find out what I could do. No, I don't like work. I had rather laze about and think of all the fine things that can be done. I don't like work—no man does—but I like what is in the work,—the chance to find yourself. Your own reality—for yourself, not for others—what no other man can ever know. They can only see the mere show, and never can tell what it really means.

"I was not surprised to see somebody sitting aft, on the deck, with his legs dangling over the mud. You see I rather chummed with the few mechanics there were in that station, whom the other pilgrims naturally despised—on account of their imperfect manners, I suppose. This was the foreman—a boiler-maker by trade—a good worker. He was a lank, bony, yellow-faced man, with big intense eyes. His aspect was worried, and his head was as bald as the palm of my hand; but his hair in falling seemed to have stuck to his chin, and had prospered in the new locality, for his beard hung down to his waist. He was a widower with six young children (he had left them in charge of a sister of his to come out there), and the passion of his life was pigeon-flying. He was an enthusiast and a connoisseur. He would rave about pigeons. After work hours he used sometimes to come over from his hut for a talk about his children and his pigeons; at work, when he had to crawl in the mud under the bottom of the steamboat, he would tie up that beard of his in a kind of white serviette[47] he brought for the purpose. It had loops to go over his ears. In the evening he could be seen squatted on the bank rinsing that wrapper in the creek with great care, then spreading it solemnly on a bush to dry.

"I slapped him on the back and shouted, 'We shall have rivets!' He scrambled to his feet exclaiming, 'No! Rivets!' as though he couldn't believe his ears. Then in a low voice, 'You . . . eh?' I don't know why we behaved like lunatics. I put my finger to the side of my nose and nodded mysteri-

[47] Napkin.

ously. 'Good for you!' he cried, snapped his fingers above his head, lifting one foot. I tried a jig. We capered on the iron deck. A frightful clatter came out of that hulk, and the virgin forest on the other bank of the creek sent it back in a thundering roll upon the sleeping station. It must have made some of the pilgrims sit up in their hovels. A dark figure obscured the lighted doorway of the manager's hut, vanished, then, a second or so after, the doorway itself vanished, too. We stopped, and the silence driven away by the stamping of our feet flowed back again from the recesses of the land. The great wall of vegetation, an exuberant and entangled mass of trunks, branches, leaves, boughs, festoons, motionless in the moonlight, was like a rioting invasion of soundless life, a rolling wave of plants, piled up, crested, ready to topple over the creek, to sweep every little man of us out of his little existence. And it moved not. A deadened burst of mighty splashes and snorts reached us from afar, as though an ichthyosaurus[48] had been taking a bath of glitter in the great river. 'After all,' said the boiler-maker in a reasonable tone, 'why shouldn't we get the rivets?' Why not, indeed! I did not know of any reason why we shouldn't. 'They'll come in three weeks,' I said, confidently.

"But they didn't. Instead of rivets there came an invasion, an infliction, a visitation. It came in sections during the next three weeks, each section headed by a donkey carrying a white man in new clothes and tan shoes, bowing from that elevation right and left to the impressed pilgrims. A quarrelsome band of footsore sulky niggers trod on the heels of the donkey; a lot of tents, camp-stools, tin boxes, white cases, brown bales would be shot down in the courtyard, and the air of mystery would deepen a little over the muddle of the station. Five such instalments came, with their absurd air of disorderly flight with the loot of innumerable outfit shops and provision stores, that, one would think, they were lugging, after a raid, into the wilderness for equitable division. It was an inextricable mess of things decent in themselves but that human folly made look like the spoils of thieving.

"This devoted band called itself the Eldorado[49] Exploring Expedition, and I believe they were sworn to secrecy. Their talk, however, was the talk of sordid buccaneers: it was reckless without hardihood, greedy without audacity, and cruel without courage; there was not an atom of foresight or of serious intention in the whole batch of them, and they did not seem aware these things are wanted for the work of the world. To tear treasure out of the bowels of the land was their desire, with no more moral purpose at the back of it than there is in burglars breaking into a safe. Who paid the expenses of the noble enterprise I don't know; but the uncle of our manager was leader of that lot.

"In exterior he resembled a butcher in a poor neighbourhood, and his eyes had a look of sleepy cunning. He carried his fat paunch with ostentation on his short legs, and during the time his gang infested the station spoke to no one but his nephew. You could see these two roaming about all day long with their heads close together in an everlasting confab.[50]

[48] Primeval marine reptile.
[49] The name of a legendary Latin American kingdom supposed to be rich in gold and gems.
[50] Talk.

"I had given up worrying myself about the rivets. One's capacity for that kind of folly is more limited than you would suppose. I said Hang!—and let things slide. I had plenty of time for meditation, and now and then I would give some thought to Kurtz. I wasn't very interested in him. No. Still, I was curious to see whether this man, who had come out equipped with moral ideas of some sort, would climb to the top after all and how he would set about his work when there."

II

"One evening as I was lying flat on the deck of my steamboat, I heard voices approaching—and there were the nephew and the uncle strolling along the bank. I laid my head on my arm again, and had nearly lost myself in a doze, when somebody said in my ear, as it were: 'I am as harmless as a little child, but I don't like to be dictated to. Am I the manager—or am I not? I was ordered to send him there. It's incredible.' . . . I became aware that the two were standing on the shore alongside the forepart of the steamboat, just below my head. I did not move; it did not occur to me to move: I was sleepy. 'It *is* unpleasant,' grunted the uncle. 'He has asked the Administration to be sent there,' said the other, 'with the idea of showing what he could do; and I was instructed accordingly. Look at the influence that man must have. Is it not frightful?' They both agreed it was frightful, then made several bizarre remarks: 'Make rain and fine weather—one man—the Council—by the nose'—bits of absurd sentences that got the better of my drowsiness, so that I had pretty near the whole of my wits about me when the uncle said, 'The climate may do away with this difficulty for you. Is he alone there?' 'Yes,' answered the manager; 'he sent his assistant down the river with a note to me in these terms: "Clear this poor devil out of the country, and don't bother sending more of that sort. I had rather be alone than have the kind of men you can dispose of with me." It was more than a year ago. Can you imagine such impudence!' 'Anything since then?' asked the other, hoarsely. 'Ivory,' jerked the nephew; 'lots of it—prime sort—lots—most annoying, from him.' 'And with that?' questioned the heavy rumble. 'Invoice,' was the reply fired out, so to speak. Then silence. They had been talking about Kurtz.

"I was broad awake by this time, but, lying perfectly at ease, remained still, having no inducement to change my position. 'How did that ivory come all this way?' growled the elder man, who seemed very vexed. The other explained that it had come with a fleet of canoes in charge of an English half-caste clerk Kurtz had with him; that Kurtz had apparently intended to return himself, the station being by that time bare of goods and stores, but after coming three hundred miles, had suddenly decided to go back, which he started to do alone in a small dugout with four paddlers, leaving the half-caste to continue down the river with the ivory. The two fellows there seemed astounded at anybody attempting such a thing. They were at a loss for an adequate motive. As to me, I seemed to see Kurtz for the first time. It was a distinct glimpse: the dugout, four paddling savages, and the lone white man turning his back suddenly on the headquarters, on relief, on thoughts of home—perhaps; setting his face towards the depths of the wilderness, towards his empty and desolate station. I did not know the motive. Perhaps he was just simply a fine fellow who stuck to his work for its own sake. His name, you understand, had not been pronounced once. He was 'that man.' The half-caste, who, as far as I could see, had conducted a difficult trip with great prudence and pluck, was invariably alluded to as 'that scoundrel.' The 'scoundrel' had reported that the 'man' had been very ill—had recovered imperfectly. . . . The two below me moved away then a few paces, and strolled back and forth at some little distance. I heard: 'Military post—doctor—two hundred miles—quite alone now—unavoidable delays—nine months—no news—strange rumours.' They approached again, just as the manager was saying, 'No one, as far as I know, unless a species of wandering trader—a pestilential fellow, snapping ivory from the natives.' Who was it they were talking about now? I gathered in snatches that this was some man supposed to be in Kurtz's district, and of whom the manager did not approve. 'We will not be free from unfair competition till one of these fellows is hanged for an example,' he said. 'Certainly,' grunted the other; 'get him hanged! Why not? Anything—anything can be done in this country. That's what I say; nobody here, you understand, *here,* can endanger your position. And why? You stand the climate—you outlast them all. The danger is in Europe; but there before I left I took care to——' They moved off and whispered, then their voices rose again. 'The extraordinary series of delays is not my fault. I did my best.' The fat man sighed. 'Very sad.' 'And the pestiferous absurdity of his talk,' continued the other; 'he bothered me enough when he was here. "Each station should be like a beacon on the road towards better things, a centre for trade of course, but also for humanizing, improving, instructing." Conceive you—that ass! And he wants to be manager! No, it's——' Here he got choked by excessive indignation, and I lifted my head the least bit. I was surprised to see how near they were—right under me. I could have spat upon their hats. They were looking on the ground, absorbed in thought. The manager was switching his leg with a slender twig: his sagacious relative lifted his head. 'You have been well since you came out this time?' he asked. The other gave a start. 'Who? I? Oh! Like a charm—like a charm. But the rest—oh, my goodness! All sick. They die so quick, too, that I haven't the time to send them out of the country—it's incredible!' 'H'm. Just so,' grunted the uncle. 'Ah! my boy, trust to this—I say, trust to this.' I saw him extend his short flipper of an arm for a gesture that took in the forest, the creek, the mud, the river,—seemed to beckon with a dishonouring flourish before the sunlit face of the land a treacherous appeal to the lurking death, to the hidden evil, to the profound darkness of its heart. It was so startling that I leaped to my feet and looked back at the edge of the forest, as though I had expected an answer of some sort to that black display of confidence. You know the foolish notions that come to one sometimes. The high stillness confronted these two figures with its ominous patience, waiting for the passing away of a fantastic invasion.

"They swore aloud together—out of sheer fright, I believe—then pretending not to know anything of my existence, turned back to the station. The sun was low; and leaning forward side by side, they seemed to be tugging painfully uphill their two ridiculous shadows of unequal length, that trailed behind them slowly over the tall grass without bending a single blade.

"In a few days the Eldorado Expedition went into the patient wilderness, that closed upon it as the sea closes over a diver. Long afterwards the news came that all the donkeys were dead. I know nothing as to the fate of the less valuable animals. They, no doubt, like the rest of us, found what they deserved. I did not inquire. I was then rather excited at the prospect of meeting Kurtz very soon. When I say very soon I mean it comparatively. It was just two months from the day we left the creek when we came to the bank below Kurtz's station.

"Going up that river was like travelling back to the earliest beginnings of the world, when vegetation rioted on the earth and the big trees were kings. An empty stream, a great silence, an impenetrable forest. The air was warm, thick, heavy, sluggish. There was no joy in the brilliance of sunshine. The long stretches of the waterway ran on, deserted, into the gloom of overshadowed distances. On silvery sandbanks hippos and alligators sunned themselves side by side. The broadening waters flowed through a mob of wooded islands; you lost your way on that river as you would in a desert, and butted all day long against shoals, trying to find the channel, till you thought yourself bewitched and cut off for ever from everything you had known once—somewhere—far away—in another existence perhaps. There were moments when one's past came back to one, as it will sometimes when you have not a moment to spare to yourself; but it came in the shape of an unrestful and noisy dream, remembered with wonder amongst the overwhelming realities of this strange world of plants, and water, and silence. And this stillness of life did not in the least resemble a peace. It was the stillness of an implacable force brooding over an inscrutable intention. It looked at you with a vengeful aspect. I got used to it afterwards; I did not see it any more; I had no time. I had to keep guessing at the channel; I had to discern, mostly by inspiration, the signs of hidden banks; I watched for sunken stones; I was learning to clap my teeth smartly before my heart flew out, when I shaved by a fluke some infernal sly old snag that would have ripped the life out of the tin-pot steamboat and drowned all the pilgrims; I had to keep a look-out for the signs of dead wood we could cut up in the night for next day's steaming. When you have to attend to things of that sort, to the mere incidents of the surface, the reality—the reality, I tell you—fades. The inner truth is hidden—luckily, luckily. But I felt it all the same; I felt often its mysterious stillness watching me at my monkey tricks, just as it watches you fellows performing on your respective tight-ropes for—what is it? half-a-crown a tumble——"

"Try to be civil, Marlow," growled a voice, and I knew there was at least one listener awake besides myself.

"I beg your pardon. I forgot the heartache which makes up the rest of the price. And indeed what does the price matter, if the trick be well done? You do your tricks very well. And I didn't do badly either, since I managed not to sink that steamboat on my first trip. It's a wonder to me yet. Imagine a blindfolded man set to drive a van over a bad road. I sweated and shivered over that business considerably, I can tell you. After all, for a seaman, to scrape the bottom of the thing that's supposed to float all the time under his care is the unpardonable sin. No one may know of it, but you never forget the thump—eh? A blow on the very heart. You remember it, you dream of it, you wake up at night and think of it—years after—and go hot and cold all over. I don't pretend to say that steamboat floated all the time. More than once she had to wade for a bit, with twenty cannibals splashing around and pushing. We had enlisted some of these chaps on the way for a crew. Fine fellows—cannibals—in their place. They were men one could work with, and I am grateful to them. And, after all, they did not eat each other before my face: they had brought along a provision of hippo-meat which went rotten, and made the mystery of the wilderness stink in my nostrils. Phoo! I can sniff it now. I had the manager on board and three or four pilgrims with their staves—all complete. Sometimes we came upon a station close by the bank, clinging to the skirts of the unknown, and the white men rushing out of a tumble-down hovel, with great gestures of joy and surprise and welcome, seemed very strange—had the appearance of being held there captive by a spell. The word ivory would ring in the air for a while—and on we went again into the silence, along empty reaches, round the still bends, between the high walls of our winding way, reverberating in hollow claps the ponderous beat of the stern-wheel. Trees, trees, millions of trees, massive, immense, running up high; and at their foot, hugging the bank against the stream, crept the little begrimed steamboat, like a sluggish beetle crawling on the floor of a lofty portico.[51] It made you feel very small, very lost, and yet it was not altogether depressing, that feeling. After all, if you were small, the grimy beetle crawled on—which was just what you wanted it to do. Where the pilgrims imagined it crawled to I don't know. To some place where they expected to get something. I bet! For me it crawled towards Kurtz—exclusively; but when the steam-pipes started leaking we crawled very slow. The reaches opened before us and closed behind, as if the forest had stepped leisurely across the water to bar the way for our return. We penetrated deeper and deeper into the heart of darkness. It was very quiet there. At night sometimes the roll of drums behind the curtain of trees would run up the river and remain sustained faintly, as if hovering in the air high over our heads, till the first break of day. Whether it meant war, peace, or prayer we could not tell. The dawns were heralded by the descent of a chill stillness; the wood-cutters slept, their fires burned low; the snapping of a twig would make you start. We were wanderers on a prehistoric earth, on an earth that wore the aspect of an unknown planet. We could have fancied ourselves the first of men taking possession of an accursed inheritance, to be subdued at the cost of profound anguish and of excessive toil. But suddenly, as we struggled round a bend, there would be a glimpse of rush walls, of peaked grass-roofs, a burst of yells, a whirl of black limbs, a mass of hands clapping, of feet stamping, of bodies swaying, of eyes rolling, under the droop of heavy and motionless foliage. The steamer toiled along slowly on the edge of a black and incomprehensible frenzy. The prehistoric man was cursing us, praying to us, welcoming us—who could tell? We were cut off from the comprehension of our surroundings; we glided past like phantoms, wondering and secretly appalled, as sane men would be before an enthusiastic

[51] Porch with tall columns.

outbreak in a madhouse. We could not understand because we were too far and could not remember, because we were travelling in the night of first ages, of those ages that are gone, leaving hardly a sign—and no memories.

"The earth seemed unearthly. We are accustomed to look upon the shackled form of a conquered monster, but there—there you could look at a thing monstrous and free. It was unearthly, and the men were—— No, they were not inhuman. Well, you know, that was the worst of it—this suspicion of their not being inhuman. It would come slowly to one. They howled and leaped, and spun, and made horrid faces; but what thrilled you was just the thought of their humanity—like yours—the thought of your remote kinship with this wild and passionate uproar. Ugly. Yes, it was ugly enough; but if you were man enough you would admit to yourself that there was in you just the faintest trace of a response to the terrible frankness of that noise, a dim suspicion of there being a meaning in it which you—you so remote from the night of first ages—could comprehend. And why not? The mind of man is capable of anything—because everything is in it, all the past as well as all the future. What was there after all? Joy, fear, sorrow, devotion, valour, rage—who can tell?—but truth—truth stripped of its cloak of time. Let the fool gape and shudder—the man knows, and can look on without a wink. But he must at least be as much of a man as these on the shore. He must meet that truth with his own true stuff—with his own inborn strength. Principles won't do. Acquisitions, clothes, pretty rags—rags that would fly off at the first good shake. No; you want a deliberate belief. An appeal to me in this fiendish row—is there? Very well; I hear; I admit, but I have a voice, too, and for good or evil mine is the speech that cannot be silenced. Of course, a fool, what with sheer fright and fine sentiments, is always safe. Who's that grunting? You wonder I didn't go ashore for a howl and a dance? Well, no—I didn't. Fine sentiments, you say? Fine sentiments, be hanged! I had no time. I had to mess about with white-lead and strips of woollen blanket helping to put bandages on those leaky steampipes—I tell you. I had to watch the steering, and circumvent those snags, and get the tin-pot along by hook or by crook. There was surface-truth enough in these things to save a wiser man. And between whiles I had to look after the savage who was fireman. He was an improved specimen; he could fire up a vertical boiler. He was there below me, and, upon my word, to look at him was as edifying as seeing a dog in a parody of breeches and a feather hat, walking on his hind-legs. A few months of training had done for that really fine chap. He squinted at the steam-gauge and at the water-gauge with an evident effort of intrepidity—and he had filed teeth, too, the poor devil, and the wool of his pate shaved into queer patterns, and three ornamental scars on each of his cheeks. He ought to have been clapping his hands and stamping his feet on the bank, instead of which he was hard at work, a thrall to strange witchcraft, full of improving knowledge. He was useful because he had been instructed; and what he knew was this—that should the water in that transparent thing disappear, the evil spirit inside the boiler would get angry through the greatness of his thirst, and take a terrible vengeance. So he sweated and fired up and watched the glass fearfully (with an impromptu charm, made of rags, tied to his arm, and a piece of polished bone, as big as a watch, stuck flatways through his lower lip), while the wooded banks slipped past us slowly, the short noise was left behind, the interminable miles of silence—and we crept on, towards Kurtz. But the snags were thick, the water was treacherous and shallow, the boiler seemed indeed to have a sulky devil in it, and thus neither that fireman nor I had any time to peer into our creepy thoughts.

"Some fifty miles below the Inner Station we came upon a hut of reeds, an inclined and melancholy pole, with the unrecognizable tatters of what had been a flag of some sort flying from it, and a neatly stacked wood-pile. This was unexpected. We came to the bank, and on the stack of firewood found a flat piece of board with some faded pencil-writing on it. When deciphered it said: 'Wood for you. Hurry up. Approach cautiously.' There was a signature, but it was illegible—not Kurtz— a much longer word. 'Hurry up.' Where? Up the river? 'Approach cautiously.' We had not done so. But the warning could not have been meant for the place where it could be only found after approach. Something was wrong above. But what—and how much? That was the question. We commented adversely upon the imbecility of that telegraphic style. The bush around said nothing, and would not let us look very far, either. A torn curtain of red twill hung in the doorway of the hut, and flapped sadly in our faces. The dwelling was dismantled; but we could see a white man had lived there not very long ago. There remained a rude table—a plank on two posts; a heap of rubbish reposed in a dark corner, and by the door I picked up a book. It had lost its covers, and the pages had been thumbed into a state of extremely dirty softness; but the back had been lovingly stitched afresh with white cotton thread, which looked clean yet. It was an extraordinary find. Its title was, *An Inquiry into some Points of Seamanship,* by a man Towser, Towson—some such name—Master in his Majesty's Navy. The matter looked dreary reading enough, with illustrative diagrams and repulsive tables of figures, and the copy was sixty years old. I handled this amazing antiquity with the greatest possible tenderness, lest it should dissolve in my hands. Within, Towson or Towser was inquiring earnestly into the breaking strain of ships' chains and tackle, and other such matters. Not a very enthralling book; but at the first glance you could see there a singleness of intention, an honest concern for the right way of going to work, which made these humble pages, thought out so many years ago, luminous with another than a professional light. The simple old sailor, with his talk of chains and purchases,[52] made me forget the jungle and the pilgrims in a delicious sensation of having come upon something unmistakably real. Such a book being there was wonderful enough; but still more astounding were the notes penciled in the margin, and plainly referring to the text. I couldn't believe my eyes! They were in cipher! Yes, it looked like cipher. Fancy a man lugging with him a book of that description into this nowhere and studying it—and making notes—in cipher at that! It was an extravagant mystery.

"I had been dimly aware for some time of a worrying noise, and when I lifted my eyes I saw the wood-pile was gone, and the manager, aided by all the pilgrims, was shouting at me from the river-side. I slipped the book into my pocket. I assure you to leave off reading was like tearing myself away from the shelter of an old and solid friendship.

[52] Instruments such as blocks-and-tackle used to move objects.

"I started the lame engine ahead. 'It must be this miserable trader—this intruder,' exclaimed the manager, looking back malevolently at the place we had left. 'He must be English,' I said. 'It will not save him from getting into trouble if he is not careful,' muttered the manager darkly. I observed with assumed innocence that no man was safe from trouble in this world.

"The current was more rapid now, the steamer seemed at her last gasp, the stern-wheel flopped languidly, and I caught myself listening on tiptoe for the next beat of the boat, for in sober truth I expected the wretched thing to give up every moment. It was like watching the last flickers of a life. But still we crawled. Sometimes I would pick out a tree a little way ahead to measure our progress towards Kurtz by, but I lost it invariably before we got abreast. To keep the eyes so long on one thing was too much for human patience. The manager displayed a beautiful resignation. I fretted and fumed and took to arguing with myself whether or no I would talk openly with Kurtz; but before I could come to any conclusion it occurred to me that my speech or my silence, indeed any action of mine, would be a mere futility. What did it matter what any one knew or ignored? What did it matter who was manager? One gets sometimes such a flash of insight. The essentials of this affair lay deep under the surface, beyond my reach, and beyond my power of meddling.

"Towards the evening of the second day we judged ourselves about eight miles from Kurtz's station. I wanted to push on; but the manager looked grave, and told me the navigation up there was so dangerous that it would be advisable, the sun being very low already, to wait where we were till next morning. Moreover, he pointed out that if the warning to approach cautiously were to be followed, we must approach in daylight—not at dusk, or in the dark. This was sensible enough. Eight miles meant nearly three hours' steaming for us, and I could also see suspicious ripples at the upper end of the reach. Nevertheless, I was annoyed beyond expression at the delay, and most unreasonably, too, since one night more could not matter much after so many months. As we had plenty of wood, and caution was the word, I brought up in the middle of the stream. The reach was narrow, straight, with high sides like a railway cutting. The dusk came gliding into it long before the sun had set. The current ran smooth and swift, but a dumb immobility sat on the banks. The living trees, lashed together by the creepers and every living bush of the undergrowth, might have been changed into stone, even to the slenderest twig, to the lightest leaf. It was not sleep—it seemed unnatural, like a state of trance. Not the faintest sound of any kind could be heard. You looked on amazed, and began to suspect yourself of being deaf—then the night came suddenly, and struck you blind as well. About three in the morning some large fish leaped, and the loud splash made me jump as though a gun had been fired. When the sun rose there was a white fog, very warm and clammy, and more blinding than the night. It did not shift or drive; it was just there, standing all round you like something solid. At eight or nine, perhaps, it lifted as a shutter lifts. We had a glimpse of the towering multitude of trees, of the immense matted jungle, with the blazing little ball of the sun hanging over it—all perfectly still—and then the white shutter came down again, smoothly, as if sliding in greased grooves. I ordered the chain, which we had begun to heave in, to be paid out again. Before it stopped running with a muffled rattle, a cry, a very loud cry as of infinite desolation soared slowly in the opaque air. It ceased. A complaining clamour, modulated in savage discords, filled our ears. The sheer unexpectedness of it made my hair stir under my cap. I don't know how it struck the others: to me it seemed as though the mist itself had screamed, so suddenly, and apparently from all sides at once, did this tumultuous and mournful uproar arise. It culminated in a hurried outbreak of almost intolerably excessive shrieking, which stopped short, leaving us stiffened in a variety of silly attitudes, and obstinately listening to the nearly as appalling and excessive silence. 'Good God! What is the meaning——' stammered at my elbow one of the pilgrims, a little fat man, with sandy hair and red whiskers, who wore side-spring boots, and pink pyjamas tucked into his socks. Two others remained open-mouthed a whole minute, then dashed into the little cabin, to rush out incontinently and stand darting scared glances, with Winchesters[53] at 'ready' in their hands. What we could see was just the steamer we were on, her outlines blurred as though she had been on the point of dissolving, and a misty strip of water, perhaps two feet broad, around her—and that was all. The rest of the world was nowhere, as far as our eyes and ears were concerned. Just nowhere. Gone, disappeared; swept off without leaving a whisper or a shadow behind.

"I went forward, and ordered the chain to be hauled in short, so as to be ready to trip the anchor and move the steamboat at once if necessary. 'Will they attack?' whispered an awed voice. 'We will be all butchered in this fog,' murmured another. The faces twitched with the strain, the hands trembled slightly, the eyes forgot to wink. It was very curious to see the contrast of expressions of the white men and of the black fellows of our crew, who were as much strangers to that part of the river as we, though their homes were only eight hundred miles away. The whites, of course greatly discomposed, had besides a curious look of being painfully shocked by such an outrageous row. The others had an alert, naturally interested expression; but their faces were essentially quiet, even those of the one or two who grinned as they hauled at the chain. Several exchanged short, grunting phrases, which seemed to settle the matter to their satisfaction. Their headman, a young, broad-chested black, severely draped in dark-blue fringed cloths, with fierce nostrils and his hair all done up artfully in oily ringlets, stood near me. 'Aha!' I said, just for good fellowship's sake. 'Catch 'im,' he snapped, with a bloodshot widening of his eyes and a flash of sharp teeth—'catch 'im. Give 'im to us.' 'To you, eh?' I asked; 'what would you do with them?' 'Eat 'im!' he said, curtly, and, leaning his elbow on the rail, looked out into the fog in a dignified and profoundly pensive attitude. I would no doubt have been properly horrified, had it not occurred to me that he and his chaps must be very hungry; that they must have been growing increasingly hungry for at least this month past. They had been engaged for six months (I don't think a single one of them had any clear idea of time, as we at the end of countless ages have. They still belonged to the beginnings of time—had no inherited experience to teach them as it were), and of course, as long as there was a piece of paper written over in accordance with some farcical law or other made down the river, it didn't

[53] A brand of repeater rifle.

enter anybody's head to trouble how they would live. Certainly they had brought with them some rotten hippo-meat, which couldn't have lasted very long, anyway, even if the pilgrims hadn't, in the midst of a shocking hullabaloo, thrown a considerable quantity of it overboard. It looked like a high-handed proceeding; but it was really a case of legitimate self-defense. You can't breathe dead hippo waking, sleeping, and eating, and at the same time keep your precarious grip on existence. Besides that, they had given them every week three pieces of brass wire, each about nine inches long; and the theory was they were to buy their provisions with that currency in river-side villages. You can see how *that* worked. There were either no villages, or the people were hostile, or the director, who like the rest of us fed out of tins, with an occasional old he-goat thrown in, didn't want to stop the steamer for some more or less recondite reason. So, unless they swallowed the wire itself, or made loops of it to snare the fishes with, I don't see what good their extravagant salary could be to them. I must say it was paid with a regularity worthy of a large and honourable trading company. For the rest, the only thing to eat—though it didn't look eatable in the least—I saw in their possession was a few lumps of some stuff like half-cooked dough, of a dirty lavender colour, they kept wrapped in leaves, and now and then swallowed a piece of, but so small that it seemed done more for the looks of the thing than for any serious purpose of sustenance. Why in the name of all the gnawing devils of hunger they didn't go for us—they were thirty to five—and have a good tuck-in[54] for once, amazes me now when I think of it. They were big powerful men, with not much capacity to weigh the consequences, with courage, with strength, even yet, though their skins were no longer glossy and their muscles no longer hard. And I saw that something restraining, one of those human secrets that baffle probability, had come into play there. I looked at them with a swift quickening of interest—not because it occurred to me I might be eaten by them before very long, though I own to you that just then I perceived—in a new light, as it were—how unwholesome the pilgrims looked, and I hoped, yes I positively hoped, that my aspect was not so—what shall I say?—so—unappetizing: a touch of fantastic vanity which fitted well with the dream-sensation that pervaded all my days at that time. Perhaps I had a little fever, too. One can't live with one's finger everlastingly on one's pulse. I had often 'a little fever,' or a little touch of other things—the playful paw-strokes of the wilderness, the preliminary trifling before the more serious onslaught which came in due course. Yes; I looked at them as you would on any human being, with a curiosity of their impulses, motives, capacities, weaknesses, when brought to the test of an inexorable physical necessity. Restraint! What possible restraint? Was it superstition, disgust, patience, fear—or some kind of primitive honour? No fear can stand up to hunger, no patience can wear it out, disgust simply does not exist where hunger is; and as to superstition, beliefs, and what you may call principles, they are less than chaff in a breeze. Don't you know the devilry of lingering starvation, its exasperating torment, its black thoughts, its sombre and brooding ferocity? Well, I do. It takes a man all his inborn strength to fight hunger properly. It's really easier to face bereavement, dishonour, and the perdi-

[54] Dinner.

tion of one's soul—than this kind of prolonged hunger. Sad, but true. And these chaps, too, had no earthly reason for any kind of scruple. Restraint! I would just as soon have expected restraint from a hyena prowling amongst the corpses of a battlefield. But there was the fact facing me—the fact dazzling, to be seen, like the foam on the depths of the sea, like a ripple on an unfathomable enigma, a mystery greater—when I thought of it—than the curious, inexplicable note of desperate grief in this savage clamour that had swept by us on the river-bank, behind the blind whiteness of the fog.

"Two pilgrims were quarrelling in hurried whispers as to which bank. 'Left.' 'No, no; how can you? Right, right, of course.' 'It is very serious,' said the manager's voice behind me; 'I would be desolated if anything should happen to Mr. Kurtz before we came up.' I looked at him, and had not the slightest doubt he was sincere. He was just the kind of man who would wish to preserve appearances. That was his restraint. But when he muttered something about going on at once, I did not even take the trouble to answer him. I knew, and he knew, that it was impossible. Were we to let go our hold of the bottom, we would be absolutely in the air—in space. We wouldn't be able to tell where we were going to—whether up or down stream, or across—till we fetched against one bank or the other,—and then we wouldn't know at first which it was. Of course I made no move. I had no mind for a smash-up. You couldn't imagine a more deadly place for a shipwreck. Whether drowned at once or not, we were sure to perish speedily in one way or another. 'I authorize you to take all the risks,' he said, after a short silence. 'I refuse to take any,' I said, shortly; which was just the answer he expected, though its tone might have surprised him. 'Well, I must defer to your judgment. You are captain,' he said, with marked civility. I turned my shoulder to him in sign of my appreciation, and looked into the fog. How long would it last? It was the most hopeless look-out. The approach to this Kurtz grubbing for ivory in the wretched bush was beset by as many dangers as though he had been an enchanted princess sleeping in a fabulous castle. 'Will they attack, do you think?' asked the manager, in a confidential tone.

"I did not think they would attack, for several obvious reasons. The thick fog was one. If they left the bank in their canoes they would get lost in it, as we would be if we attempted to move. Still, I had also judged the jungle of both banks quite impenetrable—and yet eyes were in it, eyes that had seen us. The river-side bushes were certainly very thick; but the undergrowth behind was evidently penetrable. However, during the short lift I had seen no canoes anywhere in the reach—certainly not abreast of the steamer. But what made the idea of attack inconceivable to me was the nature of the noise—of the cries we had heard. They had not the fierce character boding immediate hostile intention. Unexpected, wild, and violent as they had been, they had given me an irresistible impression of sorrow. The glimpse of the steamboat had for some reason filled those savages with unrestrained grief. The danger, if any, I expounded, was from our proximity to a great human passion let loose. Even extreme grief may ultimately vent itself in violence—but more generally takes the form of apathy. . . .

"You should have seen the pilgrims stare! They had no heart to grin, or even to revile me: but I believe they thought me gone mad—with fright, maybe. I delivered a regular lecture. My dear boys, it was no good bothering. Keep a lookout? Well, you may guess I watched the fog for the signs of lifting as a cat watches a mouse; but for anything else our eyes were of no more use to us than if we had been buried miles deep in a heap of cotton-wool. It felt like it, too—choking, warm, stifling. Besides, all I said, though it sounded extravagant, was absolutely true to fact. What we afterwards alluded to as an attack was really an attempt at repulse. The action was very far from being aggressive—it was not even defensive, in the usual sense: it was undertaken under the stress of desperation, and in its essence was purely protective.

"It developed itself, I should say, two hours after the fog lifted, and its commencement was at a spot, roughly speaking, about a mile and a half below Kurtz's station. We had just floundered and flopped round a bend, when I saw an islet, a mere grassy hummock of bright green, in the middle of the stream. It was the only thing of the kind; but as we opened the reach more, I perceived it was the head of a long sandbank, or rather of a chain of shallow patches stretching down the middle of the river. They were discoloured, just awash, and the whole lot was seen just under the water, exactly as a man's backbone is seen running down the middle of his back under the skin. Now, as far as I did see, I could go to the right or to the left of this. I didn't know either channel, of course. The banks looked pretty well alike, the depth appeared the same; but as I had been informed the station was on the west side, I naturally headed for the western passage.

"No sooner had we fairly entered it than I became aware it was much narrower than I had supposed. To the left of us there was the long uninterrupted shoal, and to the right a high, steep bank heavily overgrown with bushes. Above the bush the trees stood in serried[55] ranks. The twigs overhung the current thickly, and from distance to distance a large limb of some tree projected rigidly over the stream. It was then well on in the afternoon, the face of the forest was gloomy, and a broad strip of shadow had already fallen on the water. In this shadow we steamed up—very slowly, as you may imagine. I sheered her well inshore—the water being deepest near the bank, as the sounding-pole informed me.

"One of my hungry and forbearing friends was sounding in the bows just below me. This steamboat was exactly like a decked scow.[56] On the deck, there were two little teak-wood houses, with doors and windows. The boiler was in the fore-end, and the machinery right astern. Over the whole there was a light roof, supported on stanchions. The funnel projected through that roof, and in front of the funnel a small cabin built of light planks served for a pilot-house. It contained a couch, two camp-stools, a loaded Martini-Henry[57] leaning in one corner, a tiny table, and the steering-wheel. It had a wide door in front and a broad shutter at each side. All these were always thrown open, of course. I spent my days perched up there on the extreme fore-end of that roof, before the door. At night I slept, or tried to, on the couch. An athletic black belonging to some coast tribe, and educated by my poor predecessor, was the helmsman. He sported a pair of brass earrings, wore a blue cloth wrapper from the waist to the ankles, and thought all the world of himself. He was the most unsta-

[55] In dense rows. [56] Flat-bottomed rectangular-shaped boat. [57] A powerful rifle.

ble kind of fool I had ever seen. He steered with no end of a swagger while you were by; but if he lost sight of you, he became instantly the prey of an abject funk,[58] and would let that cripple of a steamboat get the upper hand of him in a minute.

"I was looking down at the sounding-pole, and feeling much annoyed to see at each try a little more of it stick out of that river, when I saw my poleman give up the business suddenly, and stretch himself flat on the deck, without even taking the trouble to haul his pole in. He kept hold on it though, and it trailed in the water. At the same time the fireman, whom I could also see below me, sat down abruptly before his furnace and ducked his head. I was amazed. Then I had to look at the river mighty quick, because there was a snag in the fairway. Sticks, little sticks, were flying about—thick: they were whizzing before my nose, dropping below me, striking behind me against my pilot-house. All this time the river, the shore, the woods, were very quiet—perfectly quiet. I could only hear the heavy splashing thump of the stern-wheel and the patter of these things. We cleared the snag clumsily. Arrows, by Jove! We were being shot at! I stepped in quickly to close the shutter on the land-side. That fool-helmsman, his hands on the spokes, was lifting his knees high, stamping his feet, champing his mouth, like a reined-in horse. Confound him! And we were staggering within ten feet of the bank. I had to lean right out to swing the heavy shutter, and I saw a face amongst the leaves on the level with my own, looking at me very fierce and steady; and then suddenly, as though a veil had been removed from my eyes, I made out, deep in the tangled gloom, naked breasts, arms, legs, glaring eyes,—the bush was swarming with human limbs in movement, glistening, of bronze colour. The twigs shook, swayed, and rustled, the arrows flew out of them, and then the shutter came to. 'Steer her straight,' I said to the helmsman. He held his head rigid, face forward; but his eyes rolled, he kept on lifting and setting down his feet gently, his mouth foamed a little. 'Keep quiet!' I said in a fury. I might just as well have ordered a tree not to sway in the wind. I darted out. Below me there was a great scuffle of feet on the iron deck; confused exclamations; a voice screamed, 'Can you turn back?' I caught sight of a V-shaped ripple on the water ahead. What? Another snag! A fusillade burst out under my feet. The pilgrims had opened with their Winchesters, and were simply squirting lead into that bush. A deuce of a lot of smoke came up and drove slowly forward. I swore at it. Now I couldn't see the ripple of the snag either. I stood in the doorway, peering, and the arrows came in swarms. They might have been poisoned, but they looked as though they wouldn't kill a cat. The bush began to howl. Our woodcutters raised a warlike whoop; the report of a rifle just at my back deafened me. I glanced over my shoulder, and the pilot-house was yet full of noise and smoke when I made a dash at the wheel. The fool-nigger had dropped everything, to throw the shutter open and let off that Martini-Henry. He stood before the wide opening, glaring, and I yelled at him to come back, while I straightened the sudden twist out of that steamboat. There was no room to turn even if I had wanted to, the snag was somewhere very near ahead in that confounded smoke, there was no time to

[58] Panic or depression.

lose, so I just crowded her into the bank—right into the bank, where I knew the water was deep.

"We tore slowly along the overhanging bushes in a whirl of broken twigs and flying leaves. The fusillade below stopped short, as I had foreseen it would when the squirts got empty. I threw my head back to a glinting whizz that traversed the pilot-house, in at one shutter hole and out at the other. Looking past that mad helmsman, who was shaking the empty rifle and yelling at the shore, I saw vague forms of men running bent double, leaping, gliding, distinct, incomplete, evanescent. Something big appeared in the air before the shutter, the rifle went overboard, and the man stepped back swiftly, looked at me over his shoulder in an extraordinary, profound, familiar manner, and fell upon my feet. The side of his head hit the wheel twice, and the end of what appeared a long cane clattered round and knocked over a little camp-stool. It looked as though after wrenching that thing from somebody ashore he had lost his balance in the effort. The thin smoke had blown away, we were clear of the snag, and looking ahead I could see that in another hundred yards or so I would be free to sheer off, away from the bank; but my feet felt so very warm and wet that I had to look down. The man had rolled on his back and stared straight up at me; both his hands clutched that cane. It was the shaft of a spear that, either thrown or lunged through the opening, had caught him in the side just below the ribs; the blade had gone in out of sight, after making a frightful gash; my shoes were full; a pool of blood lay very still, gleaming dark-red under the wheel; his eyes shone with an amazing lustre. The fusillade burst out again. He looked at me anxiously, gripping the spear like something precious, with an air of being afraid I would try to take it away from him. I had to make an effort to free my eyes from his gaze and attend to the steering. With one hand I felt above my head for the line of the steam whistle, and jerked out screech after screech hurriedly. The tumult of angry and warlike yells was checked instantly, and then from the depths of the woods went out such a tremulous and prolonged wail of mournful fear and utter despair as may be imagined to follow the flight of the last hope from the earth. There was a great commotion in the bush; the shower of arrows stopped, a few dropping shots rang out sharply—then silence, in which the languid beat of the stern-wheel came plainly to my ears. I put the helm hard a-starboard at the moment when the pilgrim in pink pyjamas, very hot and agitated, appeared in the doorway. 'The manager sends me ——' he began in an official tone, and stopped short. 'Good God!' he said, glaring at the wounded man.

"We two whites stood over him, and his lustrous and inquiring glance enveloped us both. I declare it looked as though he would presently put to us some question in an understandable language; but he died without uttering a sound, without moving a limb, without twitching a muscle. Only in the very last moment, as though in response to some sign we could not see, to some whisper we could not hear, he frowned heavily, and that frown gave to his black death-mask an inconceivably sombre, brooding, and menacing expression. The lustre of inquiring glance faded swiftly into vacant glassiness. 'Can you steer?' I asked the agent eagerly. He looked very dubious; but I made a grab at his arm, and he understood at once I meant him to steer whether or no. To tell you the truth, I was morbidly anxious to change my shoes and socks. 'He is dead,' murmured the fellow, immensely impressed. 'No doubt about it,' said I, tugging like mad at the shoe-laces. 'And by the way, I suppose Mr. Kurtz is dead as well by this time.'

"For the moment that was the dominant thought. There was a sense of extreme disappointment, as though I had found out I had been striving after something altogether without a substance. I couldn't have been more disgusted if I had travelled all this way for the sole purpose of talking with Mr. Kurtz. Talking with . . . I flung one shoe overboard, and became aware that that was exactly what I had been looking forward to—a talk with Kurtz. I made the strange discovery that I had never imagined him as doing, you know, but as discoursing. I didn't say to myself, 'Now I will never see him,' or 'Now I will never shake him by the hand,' but, 'now I will never hear him.' The man presented himself as a voice. Not of course that I did not connect him with some sort of action. Hadn't I been told in all the tones of jealousy and admiration that he had collected, bartered, swindled, or stolen more ivory than all the other agents together? That was not the point. The point was in his being a gifted creature, and that of all his gifts the one that stood out preëminently, that carried with it a sense of real presence, was his ability to talk, his words—the gift of expression, the bewildering, the illuminating, the most exalted and the most contemptible, the pulsating stream of light, or the deceitful flow from the heart of an impenetrable darkness.

"The other shoe went flying unto the devil-god of that river. I thought, By Jove! it's all over. We are too late; he has vanished—the gift has vanished, by means of some spear, arrow, or club. I will never hear that chap speak after all,—and my sorrow had a startling extravagance of emotion, even such as I had noticed in the howling sorrow of these savages in the bush. I couldn't have felt more of lonely desolation somehow, had I been robbed of a belief or had missed my destiny in life. . . . Why do you sigh in this beastly way, somebody? Absurd? Well, absurd. Good Lord! mustn't a man ever—— Here, give me some tobacco." . . .

There was a pause of profound stillness, then a match flared, and Marlow's lean face appeared, worn, hollow, with downward folds and dropped eyelids, with an aspect of concentrated attention; and as he took vigorous draws at his pipe, it seemed to retreat and advance out of the night in the regular flicker of the tiny flame. The match went out.

"Absurd!" he cried. "This is the worst of trying to tell. . . . Here you all are, each moored with two good addresses, like a hulk with two anchors, a butcher round one corner, a policeman round another, excellent appetites, and temperature normal—you hear—normal from year's end to year's end. And you say, Absurd! Absurd be—exploded! Absurd! My dear boys, what can you expect from a man who out of sheer nervousness had just flung overboard a pair of new shoes! Now I think of it, it is amazing I did not shed tears. I am, upon the whole, proud of my fortitude. I was cut to the quick at the idea of having lost the inestimable privilege of listening to the gifted Kurtz. Of course I was wrong. The privilege was waiting for me. Oh, yes, I heard more than enough. And I was right, too. A voice. He was very little more than a voice. And I heard—him—it—this voice—other voices—all of them were so little more than voices—and the memory of that time itself lingers around me, impalpable, like a dying vibration of one immense jabber, silly, atrocious, sordid, savage, or simply mean, without any kind of sense. Voices, voices—even the girl herself—now—"

He was silent for a long time.

"I laid[59] the ghost of his gifts at last with a lie," he began, suddenly. "Girl! What? Did I mention a girl? Oh, she is out of it—completely. They—the women I mean—are out of it—should be out of it. We must help them to stay in that beautiful world of their own, lest ours gets worse. Oh, she had to be out of it. You should have heard the disinterred body of Mr. Kurtz saying, 'My Intended.' You would have perceived directly then how completely she was out of it. And the lofty frontal bone of Mr. Kurtz! They say the hair goes on growing sometimes, but this—ah—specimen, was impressively bald. The wilderness had patted him on the head, and, behold, it was like a ball—an ivory ball; it had caressed him, and—lo!—he had withered; it had taken him, loved him, embraced him, got into his veins, consumed his flesh, and sealed his soul to its own by the inconceivable ceremonies of some devilish initiation. He was its spoiled and pampered favourite. Ivory? I should think so. Heaps of it, stacks of it. The old mud shanty was bursting with it. You would think there was not a single tusk left either above or below the ground in the whole country. 'Mostly fossil,' the manager had remarked, disparagingly. It was no more fossil than I am; but they call it fossil when it is dug up. It appears these niggers do bury the tusks sometimes—but evidently they couldn't bury this parcel deep enough to save the gifted Mr. Kurtz from his fate. We filled the steamboat with it, and had to pile a lot on the deck. Thus he could see and enjoy as long as he could see, because the appreciation of this favour had remained with him to the last. You should have heard him say, 'My ivory.' Oh yes, I heard him. 'My Intended, my ivory, my station, my river, my——' everything belonged to him. It made me hold my breath in expectation of hearing the wilderness burst into a prodigious peal of laughter that would shake the fixed stars in their places. Everything belonged to him—but that was a trifle. The thing was to know what he belonged to, how many powers of darkness claimed him for their own. That was the reflection that made you creepy all over. It was impossible—it was not good for one either—trying to imagine. He had taken a high seat amongst the devils of the land—I mean literally. You can't understand. How could you?—with solid pavement under your feet, surrounded by kind neighbours ready to cheer you or to fall on you, stepping delicately between the butcher and the policeman, in the holy terror of scandal and gallows and lunatic asylums—how can you imagine what particular region of the first ages a man's untrammelled feet may take him into by the way of solitude—utter solitude without a policeman—by the way of silence—utter silence, where no warning voice of a kind neighbour can be heard whispering of public opinion? These little things make all the great difference. When they are gone you must fall back upon your own innate strength, upon your own capacity for faithfulness. Of course you may be too much of a fool to go wrong—too dull even to know you are being assaulted by the powers of darkness. I take it, no fool ever made a bargain for his soul with the devil: the fool is too

[59] Put to rest.

much of a fool, or the devil too much of a devil—I don't know which. Or you may be such a thunderingly exalted creature as to be altogether deaf and blind to anything but heavenly sights and sounds. Then the earth for you is only a standing place—and whether to be like this is your loss or your gain I won't pretend to say. But most of us are neither one nor the other. The earth for us is a place to live in, where we must put up with sights, with sounds, with smells, too, by Jove!—breathe dead hippo, so to speak, and not be contaminated. And there, don't you see? your strength comes in, the faith in your ability for the digging of unostentatious holes to bury the stuff in—your power of devotion, not to yourself, but to an obscure, back-breaking business. And that's difficult enough. Mind, I am not trying to excuse or even explain—I am trying to account to myself for—for—Mr. Kurtz—for the shade of Mr. Kurtz. This initiated wraith from the back of Nowhere honoured me with its amazing confidence before it vanished altogether. This was because it could speak English to me. The orginal Kurtz had been educated partly in England, and—as he was good enough to say himself—his sympathies were in the right place. His mother was half-English, his father was half-French. All Europe contributed to the making of Kurtz; and by and by I learned that, most appropriately, the International Society for the Suppression of Savage Customs had intrusted him with the making of a report, for its future guidance. And he had written it, too. I've seen it. I've read it. It was eloquent, vibrating with eloquence, but too high-strung, I think. Seventeen pages of close writing he had found time for! But this must have been before his—let us say—nerves, went wrong, and caused him to preside at certain midnight dances ending with unspeakable rites, which—as far as I reluctantly gathered from what I heard at various times—were offered up to him—do you understand?—to Mr. Kurtz himself. But it was a beautiful piece of writing. The opening paragraph, however, in the light of later information, strikes me now as ominous. He began with the argument that we whites, from the point of development we had arrived at, 'must necessarily appear to them [savages] in the nature of supernatural beings—we approach them with the might as of a deity,' and so on, and so on. 'By the simple exercise of our will we can exert a power for good practically unbounded,' etc., etc. From that point he soared and took me with him. The peroration was magnificent, though difficult to remember, you know. It gave me the notion of an exotic Immensity ruled by an august Benevolence. It made me tingle with enthusiasm. This was the unbounded power of eloquence—of words—of burning noble words. There were no practical hints to interrupt the magic current of phrases, unless a kind of note at the foot of the last page, scrawled evidently much later, in an unsteady hand, may be regarded as the exposition of a method. It was very simple, and at the end of that moving appeal to every altruistic sentiment it blazed at you, luminous and terrifying, like a flash of lightning in a serene sky: 'Exterminate all the brutes!' The curious part was that he had apparently forgotten all about that valuable postscriptum, because, later on, when he in a sense came to himself, he repeatedly entreated me to take good care of 'my pamphlet' (he called it), as it was sure to have in the future a good influence upon his career. I had full information about all these things, and, besides, as it turned out, I was to have the care of his memory.

I've done enough for it to give me the indisputable right to lay it, if I choose, for an everlasting rest in the dust-bin[60] of progress amongst all the sweepings and, figuratively speaking, all the dead cats of civilization. But then, you see, I can't choose. He won't be forgotten. Whatever he was, he was not common. He had the power to charm or frighten rudimentary souls into an aggravated witch-dance in his honour; he could also fill the small souls of the pilgrims with bitter misgivings: he had one devoted friend at least, and he had conquered one soul in the world that was neither rudimentary nor tainted with self-seeking. No; I can't forget him, though I am not prepared to affirm the fellow was exactly worth the life we lost in getting to him. I missed my late helmsman awfully,—I missed him even while his body was still lying in the pilot-house. Perhaps you will think it passing strange this regret for a savage who was no more account than a grain of sand in a black Sahara. Well, don't you see, he had done something, he had steered; for months I had him at my back—a help—an instrument. It was a kind of partnership. He steered for me—I had to look after him, I worried about his deficiencies, and thus a subtle bond had been created, of which I only became aware when it was suddenly broken. And the intimate profundity of that look he gave me when he received his hurt remains to this day in my memory—like a claim of distant kinship affirmed in a supreme moment.

"Poor fool! If he had only left that shutter alone. He had no restraint, no restraint—just like Kurtz—a tree swayed by the wind. As soon as I had put on a dry pair of slippers, I dragged him out after first jerking the spear out of his side, which operation I confess I performed with my eyes shut tight. His heels leaped together over the little door-step; his shoulders were pressed to my breast; I hugged him from behind desperately. Oh! he was heavy, heavy; heavier than any man on earth, I should imagine. Then without more ado I tipped him overboard. The current snatched him as though he had been a wisp of grass, and I saw the body roll over twice before I lost sight of it for ever. All the pilgrims and the manager were then congregated on the awning-deck about the pilot-house, chattering at each other like a flock of excited magpies, and there was a scandalized murmur at my heartless promptitude. What they wanted to keep that body hanging about for I can't guess. Embalm it, maybe. But I had also heard another, and a very ominous, murmur on the deck below. My friends the woodcutters were likewise scandalized, and with a better show of reason—though I admit that the reason itself was quite inadmissible. Oh, quite! I had made up my mind that if my late helmsman was to be eaten, the fishes alone should have him. He had been a very second-rate helmsman while alive, but now he was dead he might have become a first-class temptation, and possibly cause some startling trouble. Besides, I was anxious to take the wheel, the man in pink pyjamas showing himself a hopeless duffer at the business.

"This I did directly the simple funeral was over. We were going half-speed, keeping right in the middle of the stream, and I listened to the talk about me. They had given up Kurtz, they had given up the station; Kurtz was dead, and the station had been burnt—and so on—and so on. The

[60] British term for garbage can.

red-haired pilgrim was beside himself with the thought that at least this poor Kurtz had been properly avenged. 'Say! We must have made a glorious slaughter of them in the bush. Eh? What do you think? Say?' He positively danced, the bloodthirsty little gingery[61] beggar. And he had nearly fainted when he saw the wounded man! I could not help saying, 'You made a glorious lot of smoke, anyhow.' I had seen, from the way the tops of the bushes rustled and flew, that almost all the shots had gone too high. You can't hit anything unless you take aim and fire from the shoulder; but these chaps fired from the hip with their eyes shut. The retreat, I maintained—and I was right—was caused by the screeching of the steam-whistle. Upon this they forgot Kurtz, and began to howl at me with indignant protests.

"The manager stood by the wheel murmuring confidentially about the necessity of getting well away down the river before dark at all events, when I saw in the distance a clearing on the river-side and the outlines of some sort of building. 'What's this?' I asked. He clapped his hands in wonder. 'The station!' he cried. I edged in at once, still going half-speed.

"Through my glasses I saw the slope of a hill interspersed with rare trees and perfectly free from undergrowth. A long decaying building on the summit was half buried in the high grass; the large holes in the peaked roof gaped black from afar; the jungle and the woods made a background. There was no enclosure or fence of any kind; but there had been one apparently, for near the house half-a-dozen slim posts remained in a row, roughly trimmed, and with their upper ends ornamented with round carved balls. The rails, or whatever there had been between, had disappeared. Of course the forest surrounded all that. The river-bank was clear, and on the water-side I saw a white man under a hat like a cart-wheel beckoning persistently with his whole arm. Examining the edge of the forest above and below, I was almost certain I could see movements—human forms gliding here and there. I steamed past prudently, then stopped the engines and let her drift down. The man on the shore began to shout, urging us to land. 'We have been attacked,' screamed the manager. 'I know—I know. It's all right,' yelled back the other, as cheerful as you please. 'Come along. It's all right. I am glad.'

"His aspect reminded me of something I had seen—something funny I had seen somewhere. As I manoeuvred to get alongside, I was asking myself, 'What does this fellow look like?' Suddenly I got it. He looked like a harlequin.[62] His clothes had been made of some stuff that was brown holland[63] probably, but it was covered with patches all over, with bright patches, blue, red, and yellow,—patches on the back, patches on the front, patches on elbows, on knees; coloured binding around his jacket, scarlet edging at the bottom of his trousers; and the sunshine made him look extremely gay and wonderfully neat withal, because you could see how beautifully all this patching had been done. A beardless, boyish face, very fair, no features to speak of, nose peeling, little blue eyes, smiles and frowns chasing each other over that open countenance like sunshine and shadow on a wind-swept plain. 'Look out, captain!' he cried; 'there's a snag

[61] Red-headed.

[62] The gaudily dressed clown in the style of Italian improvised comedy called *commedia dell'arte*.

[63] Unbleached, often glazed, cotton or linen.

lodged in here last night.' What! Another snag? I confess I swore shamefully. I had nearly holed my cripple, to finish off that charming trip. The harlequin on the bank turned his little pug-nose up to me. 'You English?' he asked, all smiles. 'Are you?' I shouted from the wheel. The smiles vanished, and he shook his head as if sorry for my disappointment. Then he brightened up. 'Never mind!' he cried, encouragingly. 'Are we in time?' I asked. 'He is up there,' he replied, with a toss of the head up the hill, and becoming gloomy all of a sudden. His face was like the autumn sky, overcast one moment and bright the next.

"When the manager, escorted by the pilgrims, all of them armed to the teeth, had gone to the house this chap came on board. 'I say, I don't like this. These natives are in the bush,' I said. He assured me earnestly it was all right. 'They are simple people,' he added; 'well, I am glad you came. It took me all my time to keep them off.' 'But you said it was all right,' I cried. 'Oh, they meant no harm,' he said; and as I stared he corrected himself, 'Not exactly.' Then vivaciously, 'My faith, your pilot-house wants a clean-up!' In the next breath he advised me to keep enough steam on the boiler to blow the whistle in case of any trouble. 'One good screech will do more for you than all your rifles. They are simple people,' he repeated. He rattled away at such a rate he quite overwhelmed me. He seemed to be trying to make up for lots of silence, and actually hinted, laughing, that such was the case. 'Don't you talk with Mr. Kurtz?' I said. 'You don't talk with that man—you listen to him,' he exclaimed with severe exaltation. 'But now ——' He waved his arm, and in the twinkling of an eye was in the uttermost depths of despondency. In a moment he came up again with a jump, possessed himself of both my hands, shook them continuously, while he gabbled: 'Brother sailor . . . honour . . . pleasure . . . delight . . . introduce myself . . . Russian . . . son of an arch-priest . . . Government of Tambov[64] . . . What? Tobacco! English tobacco; the excellent English tobacco! Now, that's brotherly. Smoke? Where's a sailor that does not smoke?'

"The pipe soothed him, and gradually I made out he had run away from school, had gone to sea in a Russian ship; ran away again; served some time in English ships; was now reconciled with the arch-priest. He made a point of that. 'But when one is young one must see things, gather experience, ideas; enlarge the mind.' 'Here!' I interrupted. 'You can never tell! Here I met Mr. Kurtz,' he said, youthfully solemn and reproachful. I held my tongue after that. It appears he had persuaded a Dutch trading-house on the coast to fit him out with stores and goods, and had started for the interior with a light heart, and no more idea of what would happen to him than a baby. He had been wandering about that river for nearly two years alone, cut off from everybody and everything. 'I am not so young as I look. I am twenty-five,' he said. 'At first old Van Shuyten would tell me to go to the devil,' he narrated with keen enjoyment; 'but I stuck to him, and talked and talked, till at last he got afraid I would talk the hind-leg off his favourite dog, so he gave me some cheap things and a few guns, and told me he hoped he would never see my face again. Good old Dutchman, Van Shuyten. I've sent him one small lot of ivory a year ago, so that he can't call me a little thief when I get back. I hope he got it. And for the rest I don't

[64] Region in central Russia.

care. I had some wood stacked for you. That was my old house. Did you see?'

"I gave him Towson's book. He made as though he would kiss me, but restrained himself. 'The only book I had left, and I thought I had lost it,' he said, looking at it ecstatically. 'So many accidents happen to a man going about alone, you know. Canoes get upset sometimes—and sometimes you've got to clear out so quick when the people get angry.' He thumbed the pages. 'You made notes in Russian?' I asked. He nodded. 'I thought they were written in cipher,' I said. He laughed, then became serious. 'I had lots of trouble to keep these people off,' he said. 'Did they want to kill you?' I asked. 'Oh, no!' he cried, and checked himself. 'Why did they attack us?' I pursued. He hesitated, then said shamefacedly, 'They don't want him to go.' 'Don't they?' I said, curiously. He nodded a nod full of mystery and wisdom. 'I tell you,' he cried, 'this man has enlarged my mind.' He opened his arms wide, staring at me with his little blue eyes that were perfectly round."

III

"I looked at him, lost in astonishment. There he was before me, in motley,[65] as though he had absconded from a troupe of mimes, enthusiastic, fabulous.[66] His very existence was improbable, inexplicable, and altogether bewildering. He was an insoluble problem. It was inconceivable how he had existed, how he had succeeded in getting so far, how he had managed to remain—why he did not instantly disappear. 'I went a little farther,' he said, 'then still a little farther—till I had gone so far that I don't know how I'll ever get back. Never mind. Plenty time. I can manage. You take Kurtz away quick—quick—I tell you.' The glamour of youth enveloped his particoloured rags, his destitution, his loneliness, the essential desolation of his futile wanderings. For months—for years—his life hadn't been worth a day's purchase; and there he was gallantly, thoughtlessly alive, to all appearance indestructible solely by the virtue of his few years and of his unreflecting audacity. I was seduced into something like admiration—like envy. Glamour urged him on, glamour kept him unscathed. He surely wanted nothing from the wilderness but space to breathe in and to push on through. His need was to exist, and to move onwards at the greatest possible risk, and with a maximum of privation. If the absolutely pure, uncalculating, unpractical spirit of adventure had ever ruled a human being, it ruled this be-patched youth. I almost envied him the possession of this modest and clear flame. It seemed to have consumed all thought of self so completely, that even while he was talking to you, you forgot that it was he—the man before your eyes—who had gone through these things. I did not envy him his devotion to Kurtz, though. He had not meditated over it. It came to him, and he accepted it with a sort of eager fatalism. I must say that to me it appeared about the most dangerous thing in every way he had come upon so far.

"They had come together unavoidably, like two ships becalmed near

[65] Clown's many-colored apparel. [66] Like a creature of fable.

each other, and lay rubbing sides at last. I suppose Kurtz wanted an audience, because on a certain occasion, when encamped in the forest, they had talked all night, or more probably Kurtz had talked. 'We talked of everything,' he said, quite transported at the recollection. 'I forgot there was such a thing as sleep. The night did not seem to last an hour. Everything! Everything! . . . Of love, too.' 'Ah, he talked to you of love!' I said, much amused. 'It isn't what you think,' he cried, almost passionately. 'It was in general. He made me see things—things.'

"He threw his arms up. We were on deck at the time, and the headman of my wood-cutters, lounging near by, turned upon him his heavy and glittering eyes. I looked around, and I don't know why, but I assure you that never, never before, did this land, this river, this jungle, the very arch of this blazing sky, appear to me so hopeless and so dark, so impenetrable to human thought, so pitiless to human weakness. 'And, ever since, you have been with him, of course?' I said.

"On the contrary. It appears their intercourse had been very much broken by various causes. He had, as he informed me proudly, managed to nurse Kurtz through two illnesses (he alluded to it as you would to some risky feat), but as a rule Kurtz wandered alone, far in the depths of the forest. 'Very often coming to this station, I had to wait days and days before he would turn up,' he said. 'Ah, it was worth waiting for!—sometimes.' 'What was he doing? exploring or what?' I asked. 'Oh, yes, of course'; he had discovered lots of villages, a lake, too—he did not know exactly in what direction; it was dangerous to inquire too much—but mostly his expeditions had been for ivory. 'But he had no goods to trade with by that time,' I objected. 'There's a good lot of cartridges left even yet,' he answered, looking away. 'To speak plainly, he raided the country,' I said. He nodded. 'Not alone, surely!' He muttered something about the villages round that lake. 'Kurtz got the tribe to follow him, did he?' I suggested. He fidgeted a little. 'They adored him,' he said. The tone of these words was so extraordinary that I looked at him searchingly. It was curious to see his mingled eagerness and reluctance to speak of Kurtz. The man filled his life, occupied his thoughts, swayed his emotions. 'What can you expect?' he burst out; 'he came to them with thunder and lightning, you know—and they had never seen anything like it—and very terrible. He could be very terrible. You can't judge Mr. Kurtz as you would an ordinary man. No, no, no! Now—just to give you an idea—I don't mind telling you, he wanted to shoot me, too, one day—but I don't judge him.' 'Shoot you!' I cried. 'What for?' 'Well, I had a small lot of ivory the chief of that village near my house gave me. You see I used to shoot game for them. Well, he wanted it, and wouldn't hear reason. He declared he would shoot me unless I gave him the ivory and then cleared out of the country, because he could do so, and had a fancy for it, and there was nothing on earth to prevent him killing whom he jolly well pleased. And it was true, too. I gave him the ivory. What did I care! But I didn't clear out. No, no. I couldn't leave him. I had to be careful, of course, till we got friendly again for a time. He had his second illness then. Afterwards I had to keep out of the way; but I didn't mind. He was living for the most part in those villages on the lake. When he came down to the river, sometimes he would talk to me, and sometimes it was better for me to be careful. This man suffered too much. He hated all this, and somehow he couldn't get away. When I had a chance I begged him to try and leave while there was time; I offered to go back with him. And he would say yes, and then he would remain; go off on another ivory hunt; disappear for weeks; forget himself amongst these people—forget himself—you know.' 'Why! he's mad,' I said. He protested indignantly. Mr. Kurtz couldn't be mad. If I had heard him talk, only two days ago, I wouldn't dare hint at such a thing. . . . I had taken up my binoculars while we talked, and was looking at the shore, sweeping the limit of the forest at each side and at the back of the house. The consciousness of there being people in that bush, so silent, so quiet—as silent and quiet as the ruined house on the hill—made me uneasy. There was no sign on the face of nature of this amazing tale that was not so much told as suggested to me in desolate exclamations, completed by shrugs, in interrupted phrases, in hints ending in deep sighs. The woods were unmoved, like a mask—heavy, like the closed door of a prison—they looked with their air of hidden knowledge, of patient expectation, of unapproachable silence. The Russian was explaining to me that it was only lately that Mr. Kurtz had come down to the river, bringing along with him all the fighting men of that lake tribe. He had been absent for several months—getting himself adored, I suppose—and had come down unexpectedly, with the intention to all appearance of making a raid either across the river or down stream. Evidently the appetite for more ivory had got the better of the—what shall I say?—less material aspirations. However he had got much worse suddenly. 'I heard he was lying helpless, and so I came up—took my chance,' said the Russian. 'Oh, he is bad, very bad.' I directed my glass to the house. There were no signs of life, but there was the ruined roof, the long mud wall peeping above the grass, with three little square window-holes, no two of the same size; all this brought within reach of my hand, as it were. And then I made a brusque movement, and one of the remaining posts of that vanished fence leaped up in the field of my glass. You remember I told you I had been struck at the distance by certain attempts at ornamentation, rather remarkable in the ruinous aspect of the place. Now I had suddenly a nearer view, and its first result was to make me throw my head back as if before a blow. Then I went carefully from post to post with my glass, and I saw my mistake. These round knobs were not ornamental but symbolic; they were expressive and puzzling, striking and disturbing—food for thought and also for vultures if there had been any looking down from the sky; but at all events for such ants as were industrious enough to ascend the pole. They would have been even more impressive, those heads on the stakes, if their faces had not been turned to the house. Only one, the first I had made out, was facing my way. I was not so shocked as you may think. The start back I had given was really nothing but a movement of surprise. I had expected to see a knob of wood there, you know. I returned deliberately to the first I had seen—and there it was, black, dried, sunken, with closed eyelids,—a head that seemed to sleep at the top of that pole, and, with the shrunken dry lips showing a narrow white line of the teeth, was smiling, too, smiling continuously at some endless and jocose dream of that eternal slumber.

"I am not disclosing any trade secrets. In fact, the manager said afterwards that Mr. Kurtz's methods had ruined the district. I have no opinion on that point, but I want you clearly to understand that there was nothing exactly profitable in these heads being there. They only showed that Mr. Kurtz lacked restraint in the gratification of his various lusts, that there was something wanting in him—some small matter which, when the pressing need arose, could not be found under his magnificent eloquence. Whether he knew of this deficiency himself I can't say. I think the knowledge came to him at last—only at the very last. But the wilderness had found him out early, and had taken on him a terrible vengeance for the fantastic invasion. I think it had whispered to him things about himself which he did not know, things of which he had no conception till he took counsel with this great solitude—and the whisper had proved irresistibly fascinating. It echoed loudly within him because he was hollow at the core. . . . I put down the glass, and the head that had appeared near enough to be spoken to seemed at once to have leaped away from me into inaccessible distance.

"The admirer of Mr. Kurtz was a bit crestfallen. In a hurried, indistinct voice he began to assure me he had not dared to take these—say, symbols—down. He was not afraid of the natives; they would not stir till Mr. Kurtz gave the word. His ascendancy was extraordinary. The camps of these people surrounded the place, and the chiefs came every day to see him. They would crawl. . . . 'I don't want to know anything of the ceremonies used when approaching Mr. Kurtz,' I shouted. Curious, this feeling that came over me that such details would be more intolerable than those heads drying on the stakes under Mr. Kurtz's windows. After all, that was only a savage sight, while I seemed at one bound to have been transported into some lightless region of subtle horrors, where pure, uncomplicated savagery was a positive relief, being something that had a right to exist—obviously—in the sunshine. The young man looked at me with surprise. I suppose it did not occur to him that Mr. Kurtz was no idol of mine. He forgot I hadn't heard any of these splendid monologues on, what was it? on love, justice, conduct of life—or what not. If it had come to crawling before Mr. Kurtz, he crawled as much as the veriest savage of them all. I had no idea of the conditions, he said: these heads were the heads of rebels. I shocked him excessively by laughing. Rebels! What would be the next definition I was to hear? There had been enemies, criminals, workers—and these were rebels. Those rebellious heads looked very subdued to me on their sticks. 'You don't know how such a life tries a man like Kurtz,' cried Kurtz's last disciple. 'Well, and you?' I said. 'I! I! I am a simple man. I have no great thoughts. I want nothing from anybody. How can you compare me to . . . ?' His feelings were too much for speech, and suddenly he broke down. 'I don't understand,' he groaned. 'I've been doing my best to keep him alive, and that's enough. I had no hand in all this. I have no abilities. There hasn't been a drop of medicine or a mouthful of invalid food for months here. He was shamefully abandoned. A man like this, with such ideas. Shamefully! Shamefully! I—I—haven't slept for the last ten nights. . .'

"His voice lost itself in the calm of the evening. The long shadows of the forest had slipped down hill while we talked, had gone far beyond the ruined hovel, beyond the symbolic row of stakes. All this was in the gloom, while we down there were yet in the sunshine, and the stretch of the river abreast of the clearing glittered in a still and dazzling splendour, with a murky and overshadowed bend above and below. Not a living soul was seen on the shore. The bushes did not rustle.

"Suddenly round the corner of the house a group of men appeared, as though they had come up from the ground. They waded waist-deep in the grass, in a compact body, bearing an improvised stretcher in their midst. Instantly, in the emptiness of the landscape, a cry arose whose shrillness pierced the still air like a sharp arrow flying straight to the very heart of the land; and, as if by enchantment, streams of human beings—of naked human beings—with spears in their hands, with bows, with shields, with wild glances and savage movements, were poured into the clearing by the dark-faced and pensive forest. The bushes shook, the grass swayed for a time, and then everything stood still in attentive immobility.

"'Now, if he does not say the right thing to them we are all done for,' said the Russian at my elbow. The knot of men with the stretcher had stopped, too, half-way to the steamer, as if petrified. I saw the man on the stretcher sit up, lank and with an uplifted arm, above the shoulders of the bearers. 'Let us hope that the man who can talk so well of love in general will find some particular reason to spare us this time,' I said. I resented bitterly the absurd danger of our situation, as if to be at the mercy of that atrocious phantom had been a dishonouring necessity. I could not hear a sound, but through my glasses I saw the thin arm extended commandingly, the lower jaw moving, the eyes of that apparition shining darkly far in its bony head that nodded with grotesque jerks. Kurtz—Kurtz—that means short in German—don't it? Well, the name was as true as everything else in his life—and death. He looked at least seven feet long. His covering had fallen off, and his body emerged from it pitiful and appalling as from a winding-sheet.[67] I could see the cage of his ribs all astir, the bones of his arm waving. It was as though an animated image of death carved out of old ivory had been shaking its hand with menaces at a motionless crowd of men made of dark and glittering bronze. I saw him open his mouth wide—it gave him a weirdly voracious aspect, as though he had wanted to swallow all the air, all the earth, all the men before him. A deep voice reached me faintly. He must have been shouting. He fell back suddenly. The stretcher shook as the bearers staggered forward again, and almost at the same time I noticed that the crowd of savages was vanishing without any perceptible movement of retreat, as if the forest that had ejected these beings so suddenly had drawn them in again as the breath is drawn in a long aspiration.

"Some of the pilgrims behind the stretcher carried his arms—two shot-guns, a heavy rifle, and a light revolver-carbine—the thunderbolts of that pitiful Jupiter.[68] The manager bent over him murmuring as he walked beside his head. They laid him down in one of the little cabins—just a room for a bedplace and a camp-stool or two, you know. We had brought his belated correspondence, and a lot of torn envelopes and open letters littered his bed. His hand roamed feebly amongst these pages. I was struck by the fire of his eyes and the composed languor of his expression. It was not so much the exhaustion of disease. He did not seem in pain. This shadow looked satiated and calm, as though for the moment it had had its fill of all the emotions.

[67] Wrapping for a corpse. [68] Ruler of the classical gods.

"He rustled one of the letters, and looking straight in my face said, 'I am glad.' Somebody had been writing to him about me. These special recommendations were turning up again. The volume of tone he emitted without effort, almost without the trouble of moving his lips, amazed me. A voice! a voice! It was grave, profound, vibrating, while the man did not seem capable of a whisper. However, he had enough strength in him—factitious no doubt—to very nearly make an end of us, as you shall hear directly.

"The manager appeared silently in the doorway; I stepped out at once and he drew the curtain after me. The Russian, eyed curiously by the pilgrims, was staring at the shore. I followed the direction of his glance.

"Dark human shapes could be made out in the distance, flitting indistinctly against the gloomy border of the forest, and near the river two bronze figures, leaning on tall spears, stood in the sunlight under fantastic head-dresses of spotted skins, warlike and still in statuesque repose. And from right to left along the lighted shore moved a wild and gorgeous apparition of a woman.

"She walked with measured steps, draped in striped and fringed cloths, treading the earth proudly, with a slight jingle and flash of barbarous ornaments. She carried her head high; her hair was done in the shape of a helmet; she had brass leggings to the knee, brass wire gauntlets to the elbow, a crimson spot on her tawny cheek, innumerable necklaces of glass beads on her neck; bizarre things, charms, gifts of witch-men, that hung about her, glittered and trembled at every step. She must have had the value of several elephant tusks upon her. She was savage and superb, wild-eyed and magnificent; there was something ominous and stately in her deliberate progress. And in the hush that had fallen suddenly upon the whole sorrowful land, the immense wilderness, the colossal body of the fecund and mysterious life seemed to look at her, pensive, as though it had been looking at the image of its own tenebrous[69] and passionate soul.

"She came abreast of the steamer, stood still, and faced us. Her long shadow fell to the water's edge. Her face had a tragic and fierce aspect of wild sorrow and of dumb pain mingled with the fear of some struggling, half-shaped resolve. She stood looking at us without a stir, and like the wilderness itself, with an air of brooding over an inscrutable purpose. A whole minute passed, and then she made a step forward. There was a low jingle, a glint of yellow metal, a sway of fringed draperies, and she stopped as if her heart had failed her. The young fellow by my side growled. The pilgrims murmured at my back. She looked at us all as if her life had depended upon the unswerving steadiness of her glance. Suddenly she opened her bared arms and threw them up rigid above her head, as though in an uncontrollable desire to touch the sky, and at the same time the swift shadows darted out on the earth, swept around on the river, gathering the steamer into a shadowy embrace. A formidable silence hung over the scene.

"She turned away slowly, walked on, following the bank, and passed into the bushes to the left. Once only her eyes gleamed back at us in the dusk of the thickets before she disappeared.

"'If she had offered to come aboard I really think I would have tried to

[69] Dark.

shoot her,' said the man of patches, nervously. 'I have been risking my life every day for the last fortnight to keep her out of the house. She got in one day and kicked up a row about those miserable rags I picked up in the storeroom to mend my clothes with. I wasn't decent. At least it must have been that, for she talked like a fury to Kurtz for an hour, pointing at me now and then. I don't understand the dialect of this tribe. Luckily for me, I fancy Kurtz felt too ill that day to care, or there would have been mischief. I don't understand. . . . No—it's too much for me. Ah, well, it's all over now.'

"At this moment I heard Kurtz's deep voice behind the curtain: 'Save me!—save the ivory, you mean. Don't tell me. Save *me!* Why, I've had to save you. You are interrupting my plans now. Sick! Sick! Not so sick as you would like to believe. Never mind. I'll carry my ideas out yet—I will return. I'll show you what can be done. You with your little peddling notions—you are interfering with me. I will return. I. . . .'

"The manager came out. He did me the honour to take me under the arm and lead me aside. 'He is very low, very low,' he said. He considered it necessary to sigh, but neglected to be consistently sorrowful. 'We have done all we could for him—haven't we? But there is no disguising the fact, Mr. Kurtz has done more harm than good to the Company. He did not see the time was not ripe for vigorous action. Cautiously, cautiously—that's my principle. We must be cautious yet. The district is closed to us for a time. Deplorable! Upon the whole, the trade will suffer. I don't deny there is a remarkable quantity of ivory—mostly fossil. We must save it, at all events—but look how precarious the position is—and why? Because the method is unsound.' 'Do you,' said I, looking at the shore, 'call it "unsound method?"' 'Without doubt,' he exclaimed, hotly. 'Don't you?' . . . 'No method at all,' I murmured after a while. 'Exactly,' he exulted. 'I anticipated this. Shows a complete want of judgment. It is my duty to point it out in the proper quarter.' 'Oh,' said I, 'that fellow—what's his name?—the brickmaker, will make a readable report for you.' He appeared confounded for a moment. It seemed to me I had never breathed an atmosphere so vile, and I turned mentally to Kurtz for relief—positively for relief. 'Nevertheless I think Mr. Kurtz is a remarkable man,' I said with emphasis. He started, dropped on me a cold heavy glance, said very quietly, 'he *was,*' and turned his back on me. My hour of favour was over; I found myself lumped along with Kurtz as a partisan of methods for which the time was not ripe: I was unsound! Ah! but it was something to have at least a choice of nightmares.

"I had turned to the wilderness really, not to Mr. Kurtz, who, I was ready to admit, was as good as buried. And for a moment it seemed to me as if I also were buried in a vast grave full of unspeakable secrets. I felt an intolerable weight oppressing my breast, the smell of the damp earth, the unseen presence of victorious corruption, the darkness of an impenetrable night. . . . The Russian tapped me on the shoulder. I heard him mumbling and stammering something about 'brother seaman—couldn't conceal—knowledge of matters that would affect Mr. Kurtz's reputation.' I waited. For him evidently Mr. Kurtz was not in his grave; I suspect that for him Mr. Kurtz was one of the immortals. 'Well!' said I at last, 'speak out. As it happens, I am Mr. Kurtz's friend—in a way.'

"He stated with a good deal of formality that had we not been 'of the same profession,' he would have kept the matter to himself without regard to consequences. 'He suspected there was an active ill will towards him on the part of these white men that——' 'You are right,' I said, remembering a certain conversation I had overheard. 'The manager thinks you ought to be hanged.' He showed a concern at this intelligence which amused me at first. 'I had better get out of the way quietly,' he said, earnestly. 'I can do no more for Kurtz now, and they would soon find some excuse. What's to stop them? There's a military post three hundred miles from here.' 'Well, upon my word,' said I, 'perhaps you had better go if you have any friends amongst the savages near by.' 'Plenty,' he said, 'They are simple people—and I want nothing, you know.' He stood biting his lip, then: 'I don't want any harm to happen to these whites here, but of course I was thinking of Mr. Kurtz's reputation—but you are a brother seaman and——' 'All right,' said I, after a time. 'Mr. Kurtz's reputation is safe with me.' I did not know how truly I spoke.

"He informed me, lowering his voice, that it was Kurtz who had ordered the attack to be made on the steamer. 'He hated sometimes the idea of being taken away—and then again. . . . But I don't understand these matters. I am a simple man. He thought it would scare you away—that you would give it up, thinking him dead. I could not stop him. Oh, I had an awful time of it this last month.' 'Very well,' I said. 'He is all right now.' 'Ye-e-es,' he muttered, not very convinced apparently. 'Thanks,' said I; 'I shall keep my eyes open.' 'But quiet—eh?' he urged, anxiously. 'It would be awful for his reputation if anybody here——' I promised a complete discretion with great gravity. 'I have a canoe and three black fellows waiting not very far. I am off. Could you give me a few Martini-Henry cartridges?' I could, and did, with proper secrecy. He helped himself, with a wink at me, to a handful of my tobacco. 'Between sailors—you know—good English tobacco.' At the door of the pilot-house he turned round—'I say, haven't you a pair of shoes you could spare?' He raised one leg. 'Look.' The soles were tied with knotted strings sandal-wise under his bare feet. I rooted out an old pair, at which he looked with admiration before tucking it under his left arm. One of his pockets (bright red) was bulging with cartridges, from the other (dark blue) peeped 'Towson's Inquiry,' etc., etc. He seemed to think himself excellently well equipped for a renewed encounter with the wilderness. 'Ah! I'll never, never meet such a man again. You ought to have heard him recite poetry—his own, too, it was, he told me. Poetry!' He rolled his eyes at the recollection of these delights. 'Oh, he enlarged my mind!' 'Good-bye,' said I. He shook hands and vanished in the night. Sometimes I ask myself whether I had ever really seen him—whether it was possible to meet such a phenomenon! . . .

"When I woke up shortly after midnight his warning came to my mind with its hint of danger that seemed, in the starred darkness, real enough to make me get up for the purpose of having a look round. On the hill a big fire burned, illuminating fitfully a crooked corner of the station-house. One of the agents with a picket[70] of a few of our blacks, armed for the purpose, was keeping guard over the ivory; but deep within the forest, red gleams that wavered, that seemed to sink and rise from the ground

[70] Band of sentries.

amongst confused columnar shapes of intense blackness, showed the exact position of the camp where Mr. Kurtz's adorers were keeping their uneasy vigil. The monotonous beating of a big drum filled the air with muffled shocks and a lingering vibration. A steady droning sound of many men chanting each to himself some weird incantation came out from the black, flat wall of the woods as the humming of bees comes out of a hive, and had a strange narcotic effect upon my half-awake senses. I believe I dozed off leaning over the rail, till an abrupt burst of yells, an overwhelming outbreak of a pent-up and mysterious frenzy, woke me up in a bewildered wonder. It was cut short all at once, and the low droning went on with an effect of audible and soothing silence. I glanced casually into the little cabin. A light was burning within, but Mr. Kurtz was not there.

"I think I would have raised an outcry if I had believed my eyes. But I didn't believe them at first—the thing seemed so impossible. The fact is I was completely unnerved by a sheer blank fright, pure abstract terror, unconnected with any distinct shape of physical danger. What made this emotion so overpowering was—how shall I define it?—the moral shock I received, as if something altogether monstrous, intolerable to thought and odious to the soul, had been thrust upon me unexpectedly. This lasted of course the merest fraction of a second, and then the usual sense of commonplace, deadly danger, the possibility of a sudden onslaught and massacre, or something of the kind, which I saw impending, was positively welcome and composing. It pacified me, in fact, so much, that I did not raise an alarm.

"There was an agent buttoned up inside an ulster[71] and sleeping on a chair on deck within three feet of me. The yells had not awakened him; he snored very slightly; I left him to his slumbers and leaped ashore. I did not betray Mr. Kurtz—it was ordered I should never betray him—it was written I should be loyal to the nightmare of my choice. I was anxious to deal with this shadow by myself alone,—and to this day I don't know why I was so jealous of sharing with any one the peculiar blackness of that experience.

"As soon as I got on the bank I saw a trail—a broad trail through the grass. I remember the exultation with which I said to myself, 'He can't walk—he is crawling on all-fours—I've got him.' The grass was wet with dew. I strode rapidly with clenched fists. I fancy I had some vague notion of falling upon him and giving him a drubbing. I don't know. I had some imbecile thoughts. The knitting old woman with the cat obtruded herself upon my memory as a most improper person to be sitting at the other end of such an affair. I saw a row of pilgrims squirting lead in the air out of Winchesters held to the hip. I thought I would never get back to the steamer, and imagined myself living alone and unarmed in the woods to an advanced age. Such silly things—you know. And I remember I confounded the beat of the drum with the beating of my heart, and was pleased at its calm regularity.

"I kept to the track though—then stopped to listen. The night was very clear; a dark blue space, sparkling with dew and starlight, in which black things stood very still. I thought I could see a kind of motion ahead of me. I was strangely cocksure of everything that night. I actually left the track and

[71]Long, heavy overcoat.

ran in a wide semicircle (I verily believe chuckling to myself) so as to get in front of that stir, of that motion I had seen—if indeed I had seen anything. I was circumventing Kurtz as though it had been a boyish game.

"I came upon him, and, if he had not heard me coming, I would have fallen over him, too, but he got up in time. He rose, unsteady, long, pale, indistinct, like a vapour exhaled by the earth, and swayed slightly, misty and silent before me; while at my back the fires loomed between the trees, and the murmur of many voices issued from the forest. I had cut him off cleverly; but when actually confronting him I seemed to come to my senses, I saw the danger in its right proportion. It was by no means over yet. Suppose he began to shout? Though he could hardly stand, there was still plenty of vigour in his voice. 'Go away—hide yourself,' he said, in that profound tone. It was very awful. I glanced back. We were within thirty yards from the nearest fire. A black figure stood up, strode on long black legs, waving long black arms, across the glow. It had horns—antelope horns, I think—on its head. Some sorcerer, some witch-man, no doubt: it looked fiend-like enough. 'Do you know what you are doing?' I whispered. 'Perfectly,' he answered, raising his voice for that single word: it sounded to me far off and yet loud, like a hail through a speaking-trumpet. If he makes a row we are lost, I thought to myself. This clearly was not a case for fisticuffs, even apart from the very natural aversion I had to beat that Shadow—this wandering and tormented thing. 'You will be lost,' I said—'utterly lost.' One gets sometimes such a flash of inspiration, you know. I did say the right thing, though indeed he could not have been more irretrievably lost than he was at this very moment, when the foundations of our intimacy were being laid—to endure—to endure—even to the end—even beyond.

"'I had immense plans,' he muttered irresolutely. 'Yes,' said I; 'but if you try to shout I'll smash your head with——' There was not a stick or a stone near. 'I will throttle you for good,' I corrected myself. 'I was on the threshold of great things,' he pleaded, in a voice of longing, with a wistfulness of tone that made my blood run cold. 'And now for this stupid scoundrel——' 'Your success in Europe is assured in any case,' I affirmed, steadily. I did not want to have the throttling of him, you understand—and indeed it would have been very little use for any practical purpose. I tried to break the spell—the heavy, mute spell of the wilderness—that seemed to draw him to its pitiless breast by the awakening of forgotten and brutal instincts, by the memory of gratified and monstrous passions. This alone, I was convinced, had driven him out to the edge of the forest, to the bush, towards the gleam of fires, the throb of drums, the drone of weird incantations; this alone had beguiled his unlawful soul beyond the bounds of permitted aspirations. And, don't you see, the terror of the position was not in being knocked on the head—though I had a very lively sense of that danger, too—but in this, that I had to deal with a being to whom I could not appeal in the name of anything high or low. I had, even like the niggers, to invoke him—himself—his own exalted and incredible degradation. There was nothing either above or below him, and I knew it. He had kicked himself loose of the earth. Confound the man! he had kicked the very earth to pieces. He was alone, and I before him did not know whether I stood on the ground or floated in the air. I've been telling you what we said—

repeating the phrases we pronounced—but what's the good? They were common everyday words—the familiar, vague sounds exchanged on every waking day of life. But what of that? They had behind them, to my mind, the terrific suggestiveness of words heard in dreams, of phrases spoken in nightmares. Soul! If anybody had ever struggled with a soul, I am the man. And I wasn't arguing with a lunatic either. Believe me or not, his intelligence was perfectly clear—concentrated, it is true, upon himself with horrible intensity, yet clear; and therein was my only chance—barring, of course, the killing him there and then, which wasn't so good, on account of unavoidable noise. But his soul was mad. Being alone in the wilderness, it had looked within itself, and, by heavens! I tell you, it had gone mad. I had—for my sins, I suppose—to go through the ordeal of looking into it myself. No eloquence could have been so withering to one's belief in mankind as his final burst of sincerity. He struggled with himself, too. I saw it,—I heard it. I saw the inconceivable mystery of a soul that knew no restraint, no faith, and no fear, yet struggling blindly with itself. I kept my head pretty well; but when I had him at last stretched on the couch, I wiped my forehead, while my legs shook under me as though I had carried half a ton on my back down that hill. And yet I had only supported him, his bony arm clasped round my neck—and he was not much heavier than a child.

"When next day we left at noon, the crowd, of whose presence behind the curtain of trees I had been acutely conscious all the time, flowed out of the woods again, filled the clearing, covered the slope with a mass of naked, breathing, quivering, bronze bodies. I steamed up a bit, then swung downstream, and two thousand eyes followed the evolutions of the splashing, thumping, fierce river-demon beating the water with its terrible tail and breathing black smoke into the air. In front of the first rank, along the river, three men, plastered with bright red earth from head to foot, strutted to and fro restlessly. When we came abreast again, they faced the river, stamped their feet, nodded their horned heads, swayed their scarlet bodies; they shook towards the fierce river-demon a bunch of black feathers, a mangy skin with a pendent tail—something that looked like a dried gourd; they shouted periodically together strings of amazing words that resembled no sounds of human language; and the deep murmurs of the crowd, interrupted suddenly, were like the responses of some satanic litany.

"We had carried Kurtz into the pilot-house: there was more air there. Lying on the couch, he stared through the open shutter. There was an eddy in the mass of human bodies, and the woman with helmeted head and tawny cheeks rushed out to the very brink of the stream. She put out her hands, shouted something, and all that wild mob took up the shout in a roaring chorus of articulated, rapid, breathless utterance.

"'Do you understand this?' I asked.

"He kept on looking out past me with fiery, longing eyes, with a mingled expression of wistfulness and hate. He made no answer, but I saw a smile, a smile of indefinable meaning, appear on his colourless lips that a moment after twitched convulsively. 'Do I not?' he said slowly, gasping, as if the words had been torn out of him by a supernatural power.

"I pulled the string of the whistle, and I did this because I saw the pilgrims on deck getting out their rifles with an air of anticipating a jolly lark. At the sudden screech there was a movement of abject terror through that wedged mass of bodies. 'Don't! don't you frighten them away,' cried someone on deck disconsolately. I pulled the string time after time. They broke and ran, they leaped, they crouched, they swerved, they dodged the flying terror of the sound. The three red chaps had fallen flat, face down on the shore, as though they had been shot dead. Only the barbarous and superb woman did not so much as flinch, and stretched tragically her bare arms after us over the sombre and glittering river.

"And then that imbecile crowd down on the deck started their little fun, and I could see nothing more for smoke.

"The brown current ran swiftly out of the heart of darkness, bearing us down towards the sea with twice the speed of our upward progress; and Kurtz's life was running swiftly, too, ebbing, ebbing out of his heart into the sea of inexorable time. The manager was very placid, he had no vital anxieties now, he took us both in with a comprehensive and satisfied glance: the 'affair' had come off as well as could be wished. I saw the time approaching when I would be left alone of the party of 'unsound method.' The pilgrims looked upon me with disfavour. I was, so to speak, numbered with the dead. It is strange how I accepted this unforeseen partnership, this choice of nightmares forced upon me in the tenebrous land invaded by these mean and greedy phantoms.

"Kurtz discoursed. A voice! a voice! It rang deep to the very last. It survived his strength to hide in the magnificent folds of eloquence the barren darkness of his heart. Oh, he struggled! he struggled! The wastes of his weary brain were haunted by shadowy images now—images of wealth and fame revolving obsequiously round his unextinguishable gift of noble and lofty expression. My Intended, my station, my career, my ideas—these were the subjects for the occasional utterances of elevated sentiments. The shade of the original Kurtz frequented the bedside of the hollow sham, whose fate it was to be buried presently in the mould of primeval earth. But both the diabolic love and the unearthly hate of the mysteries it had penetrated fought for the possession of that soul satiated with primitive emotions, avid of lying fame, of sham distinction, of all the appearances of success and power.

"Sometimes he was contemptibly childish. He desired to have kings meet him at railway-stations on his return from some ghastly Nowhere, where he intended to accomplish great things. 'You show them you have in you something that is really profitable, and then there will be no limits to the recognition of your ability,' he would say. 'Of course you must take care of the motives—right motives—always.' The long reaches that were like one and the same reach, monotonous bends that were exactly alike, slipped past the steamer with their multitude of secular[72] trees looking patiently after this grimy fragment of another world, the forerunner of change, of conquest, of trade, of massacres, of blessings. I looked ahead—piloting. 'Close the shutter,' said Kurtz suddenly one day; 'I can't bear to look at this.' I did so. There was a silence. 'Oh, but I will wring your heart yet!' he cried at the invisible wilderness.

"We broke down—as I had expected—and had to lie up for repairs at

[72] Enduring for ages.

the head of an island. This delay was the first thing that shook Kurtz's confidence. One morning he gave me a packet of papers and a photograph—the lot tied together with a shoe-string. 'Keep this for me,' he said. 'This noxious fool' (meaning the manager) 'is capable of prying into my boxes when I am not looking.' In the afternoon I saw him. He was lying on his back with closed eyes, and I withdrew quietly, but I heard him mutter, 'Live rightly, die, die . . .' I listened. There was nothing more. Was he rehearsing some speech in his sleep, or was it a fragment of a phrase from some newspaper article? He had been writing for the papers and meant to do so again, 'for the furthering of my ideas. It's a duty.'

"His was an impenetrable darkness. I looked at him as you peer down at a man who is lying at the bottom of a precipice where the sun never shines. But I had not much time to give him, because I was helping the engine-driver to take to pieces the leaky cylinders, to straighten a bent connecting-rod, and in other such matters. I lived in an infernal mess of rust, filings, nuts, bolts, spanners, hammers, ratchet-drills—things I abominate, because I don't get on with them. I tended the little forge we fortunately had aboard; I toiled wearily in a wretched scrap-heap—unless I had the shakes too bad to stand.

"One evening coming in with a candle I was startled to hear him say a little tremulously, 'I am lying here in the dark waiting for death.' The light was within a foot of his eyes. I forced myself to murmur, 'Oh, nonsense!' and stood over him as if transfixed.

"Anything approaching the change that came over his features I have never seen before, and hope never to see again. Oh, I wasn't touched. I was fascinated. It was as though a veil had been rent. I saw on that ivory face the expression of sombre pride, of ruthless power, of craven terror—of an intense and hopeless despair. Did he live his life again in every detail of desire, temptation, and surrender during that supreme moment of complete knowledge? He cried in a whisper at some image, at some vision—he cried out twice, a cry that was no more than a breath—

"'The horror! The horror!'

"I blew the candle out and left the cabin. The pilgrims were dining in the mess-room, and I took my place opposite the manager, who lifted his eyes to give me a questioning glance, which I successfully ignored. He leaned back, serene, with that peculiar smile of his sealing the unexpressed depths of his meanness. A continuous shower of small flies streamed upon the lamp, upon the cloth, upon our hands and faces. Suddenly the manager's boy put his insolent black head in the doorway, and said in a tone of scathing contempt—

"'Mistah Kurtz—he dead.'

"All the pilgrims rushed out to see. I remained, and went on with my dinner. I believe I was considered brutally callous. However, I did not eat much. There was a lamp in there—light, don't you know—and outside it was so beastly, beastly dark. I went no more near the remarkable man who had pronounced a judgment upon the adventures of his soul on this earth. The voice was gone. What else had been there? But I am of course aware that next day the pilgrims buried something in a muddy hole.

"And then they very nearly buried me.

"However, as you see, I did not go to join Kurtz there and then. I did not. I remained to dream the nightmare out to the end, and to show my loyalty to Kurtz once more. Destiny. My destiny! Droll thing life is—that mysterious arrangement of merciless logic for a futile purpose. The most you can hope from it is some knowledge of yourself—that comes too late—a crop of unextinguishable regrets. I have wrestled with death. It is the most unexciting contest you can imagine. It takes place in an impalpable grayness, with nothing under foot, with nothing around, without spectators, without clamour, without glory, without the great desire of victory, without the great fear of defeat, in a sickly atmosphere of tepid scepticism, without much belief in your own right, and still less in that of your adversary. If such is the form of ultimate wisdom, then life is a greater riddle than some of us think it to be. I was within a hair's breadth of the last opportunity for pronouncement, and I found with humiliation that probably I would have nothing to say. This is the reason why I affirm that Kurtz was a remarkable man. He had something to say. He said it. Since I had peeped over the edge myself, I understand better the meaning of his stare, that could not see the flame of the candle, but was wide enough to embrace the whole universe, piercing enough to penetrate all the hearts that beat in the darkness. He had summed up—he had judged. 'The horror!' He was a remarkable man. After all, this was the expression of some sort of belief; it had candour, it had conviction, it had a vibrating note of revolt in its whisper, it had the appalling face of a glimpsed truth—the strange commingling of desire and hate. And it is not my own extremity I remember best—a vision of grayness without form filled with physical pain, and a careless contempt for the evanescence of all things—even of this pain itself. No! It is his extremity that I seem to have lived through. True, he had made that last stride, he had stepped over the edge, while I had been permitted to draw back my hesitating foot. And perhaps in this is the whole difference; perhaps all the wisdom, and all truth, and all sincerity, are just compressed into that inappreciable moment of time in which we step over the threshold of the invisible. Perhaps! I like to think my summing-up would not have been a word of careless contempt. Better his cry—much better. It was an affirmation, a moral victory paid for by innumerable defeats, by abominable terrors, by abominable satisfactions. But it was a victory! That is why I have remained loyal to Kurtz to the last, and even beyond, when a long time after I heard once more, not his own voice, but the echo of his magnificent eloquence thrown to me from a soul as translucently pure as a cliff of crystal.

"No, they did not bury me, though there is a period of time which I remember mistily, with a shuddering wonder, like a passage through some inconceivable world that had no hope in it and no desire. I found myself back in the sepulchral city resenting the sight of people hurrying through the streets to filch a little money from each other, to devour their infamous cookery, to gulp their unwholesome beer, to dream their insignificant and silly dreams. They trespassed upon my thoughts. They were intruders whose knowledge of life was to me an irritating pretence, because I felt so sure they could not possibly know the things I knew. Their bearing, which was simply the bearing of commonplace individuals going about their business in the assurance of perfect safety, was offensive to me like the outrageous flauntings of folly in the face of a danger it is unable to comprehend.

I had no particular desire to enlighten them, but I had some difficulty in restraining myself from laughing in their faces, so full of stupid importance. I daresay I was not very well at that time. I tottered about the streets—there were various affairs to settle—grinning bitterly at perfectly respectable persons. I admit my behaviour was inexcusable, but then my temperature was seldom normal in these days. My dear aunt's endeavours to 'nurse up my strength' seemed altogether beside the mark. It was not my strength that wanted nursing, it was my imagination that wanted soothing. I kept the bundle of papers given me by Kurtz, not knowing exactly what to do with it. His mother had died lately, watched over, as I was told, by his Intended. A clean-shaved man, with an official manner and wearing gold-rimmed spectacles, called on me one day and made inquiries, at first circuitous, afterwards suavely pressing, about what he was pleased to denominate certain 'documents.' I was not surprised, because I had had two rows with the manager on the subject out there. I had refused to give up the smallest scrap out of that package, and I took the same attitude with the spectacled man. He became darkly menacing at last, and with much heat argued that the Company had the right to every bit of information about its 'territories.' And, said he, 'Mr. Kurtz's knowledge of unexplored regions must have been necessarily extensive and peculiar—owing to his great abilities and to the deplorable circumstances in which he had been placed: therefore——' I assured him Mr. Kurtz's knowledge, however extensive, did not bear upon the problems of commerce or administration. He invoked then the name of science. 'It would be an incalculable loss if,' etc., etc. I offered him the report on the 'Suppression of Savage Customs,' with the postscriptum torn off. He took it eagerly, but ended by sniffing at it with an air of contempt. 'This is not what we had a right to expect,' he remarked. 'Expect nothing else,' I said. 'There are only private letters.' He withdrew upon some threat of legal proceedings, and I saw him no more; but another fellow, calling himself Kurtz's cousin, appeared two days later, and was anxious to hear all the details about his dear relative's last moments. Incidentally he gave me to understand that Kurtz had been essentially a great musician. 'There was the making of an immense success,' said the man, who was an organist, I believe, with lank gray hair flowing over a greasy coat-collar. I had no reason to doubt his statement; and to this day I am unable to say what was Kurtz's profession, whether he ever had any—which was the greatest of his talents. I had taken him for a painter who wrote for the papers, or else for a journalist who could paint—but even the cousin (who took snuff during the interview) could not tell me what he had been—exactly. He was a universal genius—on that point I agreed with the old chap, who thereupon blew his nose noisily into a large cotton handkerchief and withdrew in senile agitation, bearing off some family letters and memoranda without importance. Ultimately a journalist anxious to know something of the fate of his 'dear colleague' turned up. This visitor informed me Kurtz's proper sphere ought to have been politics 'on the popular side.' He had furry straight eyebrows, bristly hair cropped short, an eye-glass on a broad ribbon, and becoming expansive, confessed his opinion that Kurtz really couldn't write a bit—'but heavens! how that man could talk. He electrified large meetings. He had faith—don't you see?—he had the faith. He could get himself to believe anything—anything. He would have been a splendid leader of an extreme party.' 'What party?' I asked. 'Any party,' answered the other. 'He was an—an—extremist.' Did I not think so? I assented. Did I know, he asked, with a sudden flash of curiosity, 'what it was that had induced him to go out there?' 'Yes,' said I, and forthwith handed him the famous Report for publication, if he thought fit. He glanced through it hurriedly, mumbling all the time, judged 'it would do,' and took himself off with this plunder.

"Thus I was left at last with a slim packet of letters and the girl's portrait. She struck me as beautiful—I mean she had a beautiful expression. I know that the sunlight can be made to lie, too, yet one felt that no manipulation of light and pose could have conveyed the delicate shade of truthfulness upon those features. She seemed ready to listen without mental reservation, without suspicion, without a thought for herself. I concluded I would go and give her back her portrait and those letters myself. Curiosity? Yes; and also some other feeling perhaps. All that had been Kurtz's had passed out of my hands: his soul, his body, his station, his plans, his ivory, his career. There remained only his memory and his Intended—and I wanted to give that up, too, to the past, in a way—to surrender personally all that remained of him with me to that oblivion which is the last word of our common fate. I don't defend myself. I had no clear perception of what it was I really wanted. Perhaps it was an impulse of unconscious loyalty, or the fulfilment of one of those ironic necessities that lurk in the facts of human existence. I don't know. I can't tell. But I went.

"I thought his memory was like the other memories of the dead that accumulate in every man's life—a vague impress on the brain of shadows that had fallen on it in their swift and final passage; but before the high and ponderous door, between the tall houses of a street as still and decorous as a well-kept alley in a cemetery, I had a vision of him on the stretcher, opening his mouth voraciously, as if to devour all the earth with all its mankind. He lived then before me; he lived as much as he had ever lived—a shadow insatiable of splendid appearances, of frightful realities; a shadow darker than the shadow of the night, and draped nobly in the folds of a gorgeous eloquence. The vision seemed to enter the house with me—the stretcher, the phantom-bearers, the wild crowd of obedient worshippers, the gloom of the forests, the glitter of the reach between the murky bends, the beat of the drum, regular and muffled like the beating of a heart—the heart of a conquering darkness. It was a moment of triumph for the wilderness, an invading and vengeful rush which, it seemed to me, I would have to keep back alone for the salvation of another soul. And the memory of what I had heard him say afar there, with the horned shapes stirring at my back, in the glow of fires, within the patient woods, those broken phrases came back to me, were heard again in their ominous and terrifying simplicity. I remembered his abject pleading, his abject threats, the colossal scale of his vile desires, the meanness, the torment, the tempestuous anguish of his soul. And later on I seemed to see his collected languid manner, when he said one day, 'This lot of ivory now is really mine. The Company did not pay for it. I collected it myself at a very great personal risk. I am afraid they will try to claim it as theirs though. H'm. It is a difficult case. What do you think I ought to do—resist? Eh? I want no more than justice.' . . . He wanted no more than justice—no more than justice. I rang the bell before a mahogany door on the first floor,[73] and while I waited he seemed to stare at me out of the glassy panel—stare with that wide and immense stare embracing, condemning, loathing all the universe. I seemed to hear the whispered cry, 'The horror! The horror!'

"The dusk was falling. I had to wait in a lofty drawing-room with three long windows from floor to ceiling that were like three luminous and bedraped columns. The bent gilt legs and backs of the furniture shone in indistinct curves. The tall marble fireplace had a cold and monumental whiteness. A grand piano stood massively in a corner; with dark gleams on the flat surfaces like a sombre and polished sarcophagus.[74] A high door opened—closed. I rose.

"She came forward, all in black, with a pale head, floating towards me in the dusk. She was in mourning. It was more than a year since his death, more than a year since the news came; she seemed as though she would remember and mourn forever. She took both my hands in hers and murmured, 'I had heard you were coming.' I noticed she was not very young—I mean not girlish. She had a mature capacity for fidelity, for belief, for suffering. The room seemed to have grown darker, as if all the sad light of the cloudy evening had taken refuge on her forehead. This fair hair, this pale visage, this pure brow, seemed surrounded by an ashy halo from which the dark eyes looked out at me. Their glance was guileless, profound, confident, and trustful. She carried her sorrowful head as though she were proud of that sorrow, as though she would say, I—I alone know how to mourn for him as he deserves. But while we were still shaking hands, such a look of awful desolation came upon her face that I perceived she was one of those creatures that are not the playthings of Time. For her he had died only yesterday. And, by Jove! the impression was so powerful that for me, too, he seemed to have died only yesterday—nay, this very minute. I saw her and him in the same instant of time—his death and her sorrow—I saw her sorrow in the very moment of his death. Do you understand? I saw them together—I heard them together. She had said, with a deep catch of the breath, 'I have survived'; while my strained ears seemed to hear distinctly, mingled with her tone of despairing regret, the summing-up whisper of his eternal condemnation. I asked myself what I was doing there, with a sensation of panic in my heart as though I had blundered into a place of cruel and absurd mysteries not fit for a human being to behold. She motioned me to a chair. We sat down. I laid the packet gently on the little table, and she put her hand over it. . . . 'You knew him well,' she murmured, after a moment of mourning silence.

"'Intimacy grows quickly out there,' I said. 'I knew him as well as it is possible for one man to know another.'

"'And you admired him,' she said. 'It was impossible to know him and not to admire him. Was it?'

"'He was a remarkable man,' I said, unsteadily. Then before the appealing fixity of her gaze, that seemed to watch for more words on my lips, I went on, 'It was impossible not to——'

[73] What Americans call the second floor. [74] Stately stone coffin.

"'Love him,' she finished eagerly, silencing me into an appalled dumbness. 'How true! how true! But when you think that no one knew him so well as I! I had all his noble confidence. I knew him best.'

"'You knew him best,' I repeated. And perhaps she did. But with every word spoken the room was growing darker, and only her forehead, smooth and white, remained illumined by the unextinguishable light of belief and love.

"'You were his friend,' she went on. 'His friend,' she repeated, a little louder. 'You must have been, if he had given you this, and sent you to me. I feel I can speak to you—and oh! I must speak. I want you—you who have heard his last words—to know I have been worthy of him. . . . It is not pride. . . . Yes! I am proud to know I understood him better than any one on earth—he told me so himself. And since his mother died I have had no one—no one—to—to——'

"I listened. The darkness deepened. I was not even sure whether he had given me the right bundle. I rather suspect he wanted me to take care of another batch of his papers which, after his death, I saw the manager examining under the lamp. And the girl talked, easing her pain in the certitude of my sympathy; she talked as thirsty men drink. I had heard that her engagement with Kurtz had been disapproved by her people. He wasn't rich enough or something. And indeed I don't know whether he had not been a pauper all his life. He had given me some reason to infer that it was his impatience of comparative poverty that drove him out there.

"'. . . Who was not his friend who had heard him speak once?' she was saying. 'He drew men towards him by what was best in them.' She looked at me with intensity. 'It is the gift of the great,' she went on, and the sound of her low voice seemed to have the accompaniment of all the other sounds, full of mystery, desolation, and sorrow, I had ever heard—the ripple of the river, the soughing of the trees swayed by the wind, the murmurs of the crowds, the faint ring of incomprehensible words cried from afar, the whisper of a voice speaking from beyond the threshold of an eternal darkness. 'But you have heard him! You know!' she cried.

"'Yes, I know,' I said with something like despair in my heart, but bowing my head before the faith that was in her, before that great and saving illusion that shone with an unearthly glow in the darkness, in the triumphant darkness from which I could not have defended her—from which I could not even defend myself.

"'What a loss to me—to us!'—she corrected herself with beautiful generosity; then added in a murmur, 'To the world.' By the last gleams of twilight I could see the glitter of her eyes, full of tears—of tears that would not fall.

"'I have been very happy—very fortunate—very proud,' she went on. 'Too fortunate. Too happy for a little while. And now I am unhappy for—for life.'

"She stood up; her fair hair seemed to catch all the remaining light in a glimmer of gold. I rose, too.

"'And of all this,' she went on, mournfully, 'of all his promise, and of all his greatness, of his generous mind, of his noble heart, nothing remains—nothing but a memory. You and I——'

"'We shall always remember him,' I said, hastily.

"'No!' she cried. 'It is impossible that all this should be lost—that such a life should be sacrificed to leave nothing—but sorrow. You know what vast plans he had. I knew of them, too—I could not perhaps understand—but others knew of them. Something must remain. His words, at least, have not died.'

"'His words will remain,' I said.

"'And his example,' she whispered to herself. 'Men looked up to him—his goodness shone in every act. His example——'

"'True,' I said; 'his example, too. Yes, his example. I forgot that.'

"'But I do not. I cannot—I cannot believe—not yet. I cannot believe that I shall never see him again, that nobody will see him again, never, never, never.'

"She put out her arms as if after a retreating figure, stretching them back and with clasped pale hands across the fading and narrow sheen of the window. Never see him! I saw him clearly enough then. I shall see this eloquent phantom as long as I live, and I shall see her, too, a tragic and familiar Shade, resembling in this gesture another one, tragic also, and bedecked with powerless charms, stretching bare brown arms over the glitter of the infernal stream, the stream of darkness. She said suddenly very low, 'He died as he lived.'

"'His end,' said I, with dull anger stirring in me, 'was in every way worthy of his life.'

"'And I was not with him,' she murmured. My anger subsided before a feeling of infinite pity.

"'Everything that could be done——' I mumbled.

"'Ah, but I believed in him more than any one on earth—more than his own mother, more than—himself. He needed me! Me! I would have treasured every sigh, every word, every sign, every glance.'

"I felt like a chill grip on my chest. 'Don't,' I said, in a muffled voice.

"'Forgive me. I—I—have mourned so long in silence—in silence. . . . You were with him—to the last? I think of his loneliness. Nobody near to understand him as I would have understood. Perhaps no one to hear. . . .'

"'To the very end,' I said, shakily. 'I heard his very last words. . . .' I stopped in a fright.

"'Repeat them,' she murmured in a heart-broken tone. 'I want—I want—something—something—to—live with.'

"I was on the point of crying at her, 'Don't you hear them?' The dusk was repeating them in a persistent whisper all around us, in a whisper that seemed to swell menacingly like the first whisper of a rising wind. 'The horror! the horror!'

"'His last word—to live with,' she insisted. 'Don't you understand I loved him—I loved him—I loved him!'

"I pulled myself together and spoke slowly.

"'The last word he pronounced was—your name.'

"I heard a light sigh and then my heart stood still, stopped dead short by an exulting and terrible cry, by the cry of inconceivable triumph and of unspeakable pain. 'I knew it—I was sure!' . . . She knew. She was sure. I heard her weeping; she had hidden her face in her hands. It seemed to me that the house would collapse before I could escape, that the heavens would fall upon my head. But nothing happened. The heavens do not fall for such a trifle. Would they have fallen, I wonder, if I had rendered Kurtz that justice which was his due? Hadn't he said he wanted only justice? But I couldn't. I could not tell her. It would have been too dark—too dark altogether. . . ."

Marlow ceased, and sat apart, indistinct and silent, in the pose of a meditating Buddha. Nobody moved for a time. "We have lost the first of the ebb," said the Director, suddenly. I raised my head. The offing was barred by a black bank of clouds, and the tranquil waterway leading to the uttermost ends of the earth flowed sombre under an overcast sky—seemed to lead into the heart of an immense darkness.

William Butler Yeats

(1865–1939)

"The greatest poet of our time—certainly the greatest in this language, and so far as I am able to judge, in any language"—this was T. S. Eliot's judgment of William Butler Yeats soon after his death in 1939. Another fellow poet, W. H. Auden, paid, in verse, an equally strong, if more ambiguous, tribute: "You were silly like us: your gift survived it all; / The parish of rich women, physical decay, / Yourself; mad Ireland hurt you into poetry." The silliness is certainly there in Yeats; the greatness is in his power to pass his experiences through the Byzantine fire of his imagination and turn them into great poetry.

Yeats's life and personality were battlefields of ambivalence and contradiction. A shy, retiring man, he nevertheless was a vigorous crusader for Irish national literature, an efficient manager of the Abbey Theatre, and eventually an Irish senator ("a smiling public man"). One of the most local of poets, combing Irish folklore and history for his subjects and his imagery, he was at the same time profoundly modern in his intellectual cosmopolitanism, not only drawing upon the classics of Western literature and thought but also, often for the first time in the West, tapping the riches of Japan, China, and India. Rejecting the often acrimonious division between Catholic and Protestant in his native land, he nevertheless immersed himself in a sort of composite religious mysticism drawn from a wide range of world religions and partially devised by himself. It is no wonder that Yeats constructed an elaborate mythological system based upon "masks" and "anti-selves" and that his poems are full of rich, unresolved tensions between recurring opposites.

Yeats's life and career do not present an orderly progression through certain "periods," but rather a restless oscillation among his central preoccupations: a fierce devotion to "pure" art, an equally fierce commitment to an Irish national art, withdrawal into ecstatic mysticism, and involvement in the affairs of the world. Born in Dublin in 1865, Yeats was the first of four children of John Butler Yeats, who had thrown over the practice of the law to become a portrait painter, and Susan Pollexfen Yeats, the quiet and devout daughter of a prominent family in County Sligo, in northwestern Ireland. Yeats's childhood and youth were divided among Dublin; London, where his father was studying art and seeking commissions; and Sligo, with his *mother's family. After a brief flirtation with art school in Dublin, Yeats settled for a time in London, where his first book—*The Wanderings of Oisin*—appeared in 1889. Despite its Irish proper names, the book was a lengthy, ethereal, Shelleyan allegory.*

The 1890's were a period of rapid development for Yeats. He had already become interested in the patriot John O'Leary's calls for an Irish national literature, and he was further galvanized by his first meeting, in 1889, with Maud Gonne, a famous Dublin beauty and a fervent nationalist, for whom he cherished a hopeless love the rest of his life. Yeats wrote a play, The Countess Cathleen *(1892), for Maud Gonne, and in* The Celtic Twilight, *a collection of essays published in 1893, he renewed O'Leary's call for Irish art to express Irish nationalism. His meeting in 1896 with Lady Augusta Gregory, a wealthy Irish widow with an interest in writing, led to the founding of the Irish Literary Theatre in 1899 and of the Abbey Theatre in 1904. The Abbey became one of the greatest of twentieth-century theater companies, nurturing the dramatic talents not only of Yeats and Lady Gregory, who became a skilled writer of folk comedies, but also of John Millington Synge and, later, Sean O'Casey.*

The other major thread of Yeats's development during the '90s was his evolving of an elaborate body of symbolism. His study of Shelley, Blake (whose works he edited during this decade), and the French Symbolists led him to a conviction that most major poets had drawn upon a fully developed system of complementary symbols, and he consciously set out to elaborate such a system for himself. He drew not only upon the symbols of Shelley and Blake but also upon the mystical systems of the Theosophists, the Rosicrucians, and the spiritualists. He had always been attracted to magic and in London had been a member of the Theosophical Society, a late-nineteenth-century cult which, under its charismatic leader Madame Helena Petrovna Blavatsky, sought to unite mankind by reviving ancient occult knowledge; he also belonged to the Order of the Golden Dawn, led by MacGregor Mathers, which shared many of the Theosophists' concerns but was more willing to attempt "phenomena," or feats of magic. From both literary and occult sources, Yeats built up a body of recurring symbols—the rose, the lily, the swan, the cross—and he added to them symbols of his own devising, many from Irish legend.

This body of symbolism first appeared fully in The Wind Among the Reeds *(1899), a book whose impact upon the modern movement the Yeats critic Richard Ellmann has compared to that of Wordsworth's* Lyrical Ballads *(1798) upon the Romantic movement. Almost precisely a century before, Wordsworth had called for man to return to the "mighty presence" of nature for strength and renewal; Yeats called for man to turn back into himself to discover a second nature, a nature not "half created, half perceived" as for Wordsworth, but almost wholly created by the human mind, for whom seas, stars, and roses were merely emblems of inner reality.*

After the achievement of The Wind Among the Reeds, *and under the influence of his practical, public work with the Abbey Theatre and his study of translations of Irish poetry, Yeats characteristically swung back from the symbolic pole of his work toward the realistic one. The poems in* In the Seven Woods *(1903),* The Green Helmet *(1910), and* Responsibilities *(1914), though they retained some Yeatsian symbolism, for the most part used more themes from ordinary life, a more concrete imagery, and a more direct, colloquial diction. This spirit is expressed in a short poem in* Responsibilities, *"A Coat," in which the poet rejects his coat "covered with embroideries / Out of old mythologies" and asserts that "there's more enterprise / In walking naked."*

Ezra Pound, American expatriate and fervent crusader for the "modern," whom Yeats first met in 1909, helped interest Yeats, who was already disillusioned by the coarse literal-mindedness of Abbey audiences, in the Noh plays of Japan, and Yeats wrote the first of his many small chamber plays for dancers in 1916: At the Hawk's Well. *In the same year, the Easter Rising, which was planned as a general rebellion against English rule but diminished to a gallant defense of the Dublin General Post Office, held by nationalists who proclaimed an Irish republic, was swiftly and brutally put down by the English. With a Yeatsian doubleness of vision, the arcane withdrawal of* At the Hawk's Well *was balanced by the guarded but genuine celebration, in a series of poems, of the "terrible beauty" of the Rising.*

In 1917, Yeats proposed marriage to Iseult Gonne, daughter of the Maud Gonne who had refused his repeated proposals. Iseult, too, refused, and a few weeks later, Yeats proposed to Georgie Hyde-Lees and was accepted. On his honeymoon, Yeats suggested that his bride try automatic writing, by which the subject lets the hand move, ouija-board style, without conscious control. Yeats was delighted with the results, concluded that Mrs. Yeats had strong psychic powers, and used the texts produced as the basis of A Vision *(1925), the exposition of his comprehensive mythology. The Yeatses paid £35 for a ruined Norman tower at Ballylee, in Galway, near Coole Park, Lady Gregory's home, where Yeats had spent many summers, and had it remodeled into a home. They divided their time between the tower and a house in Dublin. A daughter was born in 1919 and a son in 1921. In 1922 Yeats became a senator of the new Irish Free State, and in 1923 he received the Nobel Prize.*

Whether because of his marriage, the satisfaction of recognition both in Ireland and internationally, or the achievement of a creatively balanced tension among the potentially conflicting elements of his art, Yeats's poetry of the 1920s represents his finest achievement. The volumes The Tower *(1928) and* The Winding Stair *(1933), which contain such masterpieces as the two Byzantium poems, "Leda and the Swan," and "Among School Children," combine a direct, concrete diction and a rich and suggestive, though unobtrusive, symbolism to speak powerfully of many of Yeats's central concerns.*

The last decade of Yeats's life was dominated by yet another conflict, that between mortality and the urge to live, and this conflict found its way into a surprising group of poems of his old age. In 1927, Yeats contracted a serious lung ailment from which he was never to recover fully. He had to give up residence in the Ballylee tower after 1929 and spent much of his time during these later years in Italy and the south of France. In 1934, he underwent a "Steinach operation," a procedure to retard aging by regulating the production of hormones; Yeats regarded it as a success. Much of his writing during the '30s was devoted to drama and to rewriting A Vision, *a revised version of which appeared in 1937. But he also continued to write poetry voluminously, much of which was published posthumously, in* Last Poems and Plays *(1940). In many of these last poems, Yeats adopted the mask of a "wild old wicked man" raging against the dying of the light and returning, his "ladder" of speculation and mythologizing gone, to the "foul rag-and-bone shop of the heart." He died in southern France in 1939. His heirs had to wait until 1948, after World War II, to bring his body back to Sligo and reinter it in the churchyard at Drumcliffe, under the epitaph stipulated in "Under Ben Bulben": "Cast a cold eye on life, on death. Horseman, pass by!"*

The serious reader of Yeats must sooner or later come to terms with the symbolism of the system outlined in A Vision, *either reading all the poems after 1922 as fully understandable only in the light of the system, ignoring it completely and attending only to the poems' intrinsic meanings, or (most sensibly) consulting the system when it is needed and ignoring it otherwise.* A Vision *is very complex, but the elements of it needed for reading all but a few of the poems are fairly simple. Its basis is a cyclic system which, in good occult fashion, can show the "correspondences" among world history, national history, and the individual life. The cycle is the "Great Wheel," a circle divided into twenty-eight segments derived from the phases of the moon. Each of the twenty eight phases is identified with certain characteristics and values; phases opposite each other on the circle are opposite in qualities as well. The Great Wheel thus yields twenty-eight phases through which world history and national histories pass, as well as twenty-eight personality types, each with its implicit opposite or "mask."*

The other basic conceptual representation in A Vision *consists of two "gyres." These gyres, or whirling cones, are represented as pointed in opposite directions and interpenetrating each other. Like the lunar phases of the Great Wheel, the gyres represent a balancing of opposites, one gyre representing external fate, the other standing for internal destiny (as well as a number of other opposites). A cross section of these two whirling, interlocked cones will produce a representation of the mingled qualities of an individual personality, with complex balancings of fate and free will, the physical and the spiritual, space and time, the moral and the aesthetic, the "objective" and the "subjective," and other oppositions. The gyres, like the wheel, have historical and cosmic meanings as well as personal ones.*

A Vision *is also of interest in its own right, not just as a guide to the poems based on it. It can be read as an intensely subjective veiled self-analysis in which Yeats tries to come to terms with the divisions he feels in his own personality. But from another point of view, it is an essentially objective attempt to escape the divisions of a single self and attain a "unity" (a favorite Yeats word) in which all possible individual conflicts and antitheses can be contained. It is, in other words, Yeats's most elaborate poetic metaphor, if not his richest.*

Yeats's attitude toward his system was ambiguous. At times, he seemed to imply a literal belief in it; at other times, he seemed to regard it merely as scaffolding to be kicked away after it had been used, mere "stylistic arrangements of experience." The ordinary reader of Yeats will be more likely to adopt the latter attitude and be moved not by the system but by the poetry.

In imagining vividly the rape of Leda by the swan Zeus, Yeats wonders, "Did she put on his knowledge with his power / Before the indifferent beak could let her drop?" "Knowledge" and "power"—these are favorite words of Yeats's throughout his career. They suggest the choice (seldom clear-cut) the individual must make between cultivation of the self and involvement in the external world, with the danger that knowledge will make one "lack all conviction," while power will fill one with a misguided "passionate intensity." A few of Yeats's poems may be identified as "knowledge" poems or "power" poems, but in most of them knowledge and power are held in a dynamic balance, along with the other resonant oppositions that radiate out from this central one. It is this complex, essentially dramatic sense of the world, along with Yeats's miraculous mastery of language, that has made him the most memorable poet of the twentieth century.

FURTHER READING *(prepared by N. K. B.):* The standard edition of Yeats's poetry is *The Variorum Edition of the Poems of W. B. Yeats*, ed. by Peter Allt and Russell K. Alspach, 1957. General readers can consult M. L. Rosenthal's *Selected Poems and Two Plays of William Butler Yeats*, 1962, for a good selection, introductory essay, and glossary of explanatory notes. The first authorized biography, Joseph Hone's *W. B. Yeats, 1865–1939,* 1942, rev. 1962, is based on personal acquaintance with the poet and was written with full access to unpublished materials. As a detailed, factual account, Hone's book is standard reading, but it should be supplemented with A. Norman Jeffares, *W. B. Yeats: Man and Poet,* 1949, rev. 1962, and Richard Ellmann's *Yeats: The Man and the Masks,* 1948. Ellmann's critical biography was the first to describe and evaluate Yeats's debt to the occult. Ellmann's later work, *The Identity of Yeats,* 1954, rev. 1964, is a brilliant study demonstrating the coherence of Yeats's thought and technique throughout his changing poetic styles. Balachandra Rajan, *W. B. Yeats: A Critical Introduction,* 1965, is a compact, readable summary of the poetic and dramatic works. John Unterecker, *A Reader's Guide to W. B. Yeats,* 1959, rev. 1971, is particularly perceptive on Yeats's imagery. A. Norman Jeffares's two introductory studies, *The Poetry of W. B. Yeats,* 1961, and *W. B. Yeats,* 1971, contain brief but helpful biographical comments and explications. In *The Poetry of W. B. Yeats,* 1941, Louis MacNeice argues for the unity of Yeats's canon, emphasizing the later poems, and demonstrates the importance of studying his revisions. Thomas Parkinson, *W. B. Yeats, Self-Critic: A Study of His Early Verse,* 1951, thoroughly examines the poetic apprenticeship; Parkinson's later work, *W. B. Yeats: The Later Poetry,* 1964, is a major contribution to the study of Yeats's compositional methods, as reflected in textual revisions and variants. For more extensive commentary on revisions of selected poems, see Jon Stallworthy, *Between the Lines: Yeats's Poetry in the Making,* 1963, and *Vision and Revision in Yeats's Last Poems,* 1969. *The Permanence of Yeats,* ed. by James Hall and Martin Steinmann, 1950, is a gathering of the finest early criticism, but readers should also consult *Yeats: A Collection of Critical Essays,* ed. by John Unterecker, 1963, which includes excerpts from seven major studies, including Hugh Kenner's important article on the ordering of Yeats's published poems, "The Sacred Book of the Arts," and part of Frank Kermode's *Romantic Image,* 1957. *W. B. Yeats: The Critical Heritage,* ed. by A. Norman Jeffares, 1977, provides an elaborate survey and sample of critical responses to Yeats's poetry, drama, and prose.

THE LAKE ISLE OF INNISFREE[1]

I will arise and go now, and go to Innisfree,
And a small cabin build there, of clay and wattles[2] made:
Nine bean-rows will I have there, a hive for the honeybee,
And live alone in the bee-loud glade.

And I shall have some peace there, for peace comes dropping slow,
Dropping from the veils of the morning to where the cricket sings;
There midnight's all a glimmer, and noon a purple glow,
And evening full of the linnet's wings.

I will arise and go now, for always night and day
I hear lake water lapping with low sounds by the shore;
While I stand on the roadway, or on the pavements grey,
I hear it in the deep heart's core.

[1] An island in Lough Gill in County Sligo. This poem was suggested by Henry David Thoreau's *Walden* (1854).

[2] Interwoven poles and branches.

TO IRELAND IN THE COMING TIMES

Know, that I would accounted be
True brother of a company
That sang, to sweeten Ireland's wrong,
Ballad and story, rann[1] and song;
Nor be I any less of them,
Because the red-rose-bordered hem
Of her[2], whose history began
Before God made the angelic clan,
Trails all about the written page.
When Time began to rant and rage
The measure of her flying feet
Made Ireland's heart begin to beat;
And Time bade all his candles flare
To light a measure here and there;
And may the thoughts of Ireland brood
Upon a measured quietude.

Nor may I less be counted one
With Davis, Mangan, Ferguson,[3]
Because, to him who ponders well,
My rhymes more than their rhyming tell
Of things discovered in the deep,
Where only body's laid asleep.
For the elemental creatures[4] go
About my table to and fro,
That hurry from unmeasured mind
To rant and rage in flood and wind;
Yet he who treads in measured ways
May surely barter gaze for gaze.
Man ever journeys on with them
After the red-rose-bordered hem.
Ah, faeries, dancing under the moon,
A Druid[5] land, a Druid tune!

While still I may, I write for you
The love I lived, the dream I knew.
From our birthday, until we die,
Is but the winking of an eye;
And we, our singing and our love,
What measurer Time has lit above,

[1] Verse or stanza (an Irish term).
[2] The rose. Yeats identified this as "the Eternal Rose of Beauty and of Peace," but it has many more complex meanings for him, including mystic rapture and divinity.
[3] Irish poets: Thomas Osborne Davis (1814–45), James Clarence Mangan (1803–49), and Samuel Ferguson (1810–86).
[4] Spirits associated with the four elements (earth, air, fire, and water).
[5] Having to do with an ancient Celtic priesthood.

And all benighted things that go
About my table to and fro,
Are passing on to where may be,
In truth's consuming ecstasy,
No place for love and dream at all;
For God goes by with white footfall.
I cast my heart into my rhymes,
That you, in the dim coming times,
May know how my heart went with them
After the red-rose-bordered hem.

HE REMEMBERS FORGOTTEN BEAUTY

When my arms wrap you round I press
My heart upon the loveliness
That has long faded from the world;
The jewelled crowns that kings have hurled
In shadowy pools, when armies fled;
The love-tales wrought with silken thread
By dreaming ladies upon cloth
That has made fat the murderous moth;
The roses that of old time were
Woven by ladies in their hair,
The dew-cold lilies ladies bore
Through many a sacred corridor
Where such grey clouds of incense rose
That only God's eyes did not close:
For that pale breast and lingering hand
Come from a more dream-heavy land,
A more dream-heavy hour than this;
And when you sigh from kiss to kiss
I hear white Beauty sighing, too,
For hours when all must fade like dew,
But flame on flame, and deep on deep,
Throne over throne where in half sleep,
Their swords upon their iron knees,
Brood her high lonely mysteries.

A COAT

I made my song a coat
Covered with embroideries
Out of old mythologies
From heel to throat;
But the fools caught it,
Wore it in the world's eyes

As though they'd wrought it.
Song, let them take it,
For there's more enterprise
In walking naked.

EASTER 1916[1]

I have met them at close of day
Coming with vivid faces
From counter or desk among grey
Eighteenth-century houses.
I have passed with a nod of the head
Or polite meaningless words,
Or have lingered awhile and said
Polite meaningless words,
And thought before I had done
Of a mocking tale or a gibe
To please a companion
Around the fire at the club,
Being certain that they and I
But lived where motley is worn:
All changed, changed utterly:
A terrible beauty is born.

That woman's[2] days were spent
In ignorant good-will,
Her nights in argument
Until her voice grew shrill.
What voice more sweet than hers
When, young and beautiful,
She rode to harriers?[3]
This man[4] had kept a school
And rode our wingèd horse;[5]
This other[6] his helper and friend
Was coming into his force;

[1] A general rebellion against British rule in Ireland was planned for Easter Sunday, 1916. When a German ship bringing arms was intercepted by the British, attempts were made to postpone the Rising, but they failed and the rebellion began on the Monday after Easter. The nationalists seized the Dublin General Post Office and proclaimed an Irish Republic. The British regained the Post Office, however, and executed sixteen of the nationalist leaders and imprisoned about two thousand of the participants. As Yeats indicates, he was personally acquainted with many of the leaders.

[2] Constance Gore-Booth, a fervent nationalist from the Sligo aristocracy. She was imprisoned for her role in the Rising.

[3] Hunting dogs that resemble small foxhounds.

[4] Padraic Pearse, headmaster of St. Enda's school and a poet. He was one of the seven signers of the proclamation of independence and was executed by the British.

[5] Pegasus, horse of the Muses (since Pearse was a poet).

[6] Thomas MacDonagh, executed for his part in the Rising, was a poet and playwright.

He might have won fame in the end,
So sensitive his nature seemed,
So daring and sweet his thought.
This other man[7] I had dreamed
A drunken, vainglorious lout.
He had done most bitter wrong
To some who are near my heart,
Yet I number him in the song;
He, too, has resigned his part
In the casual comedy;
He, too, has been changed in his turn,
Transformed utterly:
A terrible beauty is born.

Hearts with one purpose alone
Through summer and winter seem
Enchanted to a stone
To trouble the living stream.
The horse that comes from the road,
The rider, the birds that range
From cloud to tumbling cloud,
Minute by minute they change;
A shadow of cloud on the stream
Changes minute by minute;
A horse-hoof slides on the brim,
And a horse plashes within it;
The long-legged moor-hens dive,
And hens to moor-cocks call;
Minute by minute they live:
The stone's in the midst of all.

Too long a sacrifice
Can make a stone of the heart.
O when may it suffice?
That is Heaven's part, our part
To murmur name upon name,
As a mother names her child
When sleep at last has come
On limbs that had run wild.
What is it but nightfall?
No, no, not night but death;
Was it needless death after all?
For England may keep faith
For all that is done and said.[8]
We know their dream; enough
To know they dreamed and are dead;

[7] Major John MacBride, who had married Maud Gonne, whom Yeats loved. They separated after two years.

[8] The English Parliament had voted Home Rule for Ireland, but it had not yet been implemented.

And what if excess of love
Bewildered them till they died?
I write it out in a verse—
MacDonagh and MacBride
And Connolly[9] and Pearse
Now and in time to be,
Wherever green is worn,
Are changed, changed utterly:
A terrible beauty is born.

THE SECOND COMING[1]

Turning and turning in the widening gyre[2]
The falcon cannot hear the falconer;
Things fall apart; the centre cannot hold;
Mere anarchy is loosed upon the world,
The blood-dimmed tide is loosed, and everywhere
The ceremony of innocence is drowned;
The best lack all conviction, while the worst
Are full of passionate intensity.[3]

Surely some revelation is at hand;
Surely the Second Coming is at hand.
The Second Coming! Hardly are those words out
When a vast image out of *Spiritus Mundi*[4]
Troubles my sight: somewhere in sands of the desert
A shape with lion body and the head of a man,
A gaze blank and pitiless as the sun,
Is moving its slow thighs, while all about it
Reel shadows of the indignant desert birds.
The darkness drops again; but now I know
That twenty centuries of stony sleep
Were vexed to nightmare by a rocking cradle,[5]
And what rough beast, its hour come round at last,
Slouches towards Bethlehem to be born?

[9] James Connolly was commander in chief of the Easter Rising and was among those executed.

[1] An ironic allusion to Christ's promised return. Yeats saw history, as he explained in *A Vision* (1925, 1937), as a series of cycles ("gyres"). This poem suggests that the end of the Christian "gyre" is at hand and that it will be succeeded by an irrational, authoritarian cycle.

[2] A cone-shaped spiral. The reference here is to the falcon's literal flight, but the gyre-shape had a mystical meaning for Yeats and formed the basis of his diagram of history in *A Vision*.

[3] *The blood-dimmed tide . . . passionate intensity.* A reference to the Russian Revolution (1917).

[4] Latin for "Spirit of the World," a collective unconscious which Yeats held to be the storehouse of archetypal images such as that of the Sphinx.

[5] The cradle of Christ.

SAILING TO BYZANTIUM[1]

I

That is no country for old men. The young
In one another's arms, birds in the trees
—Those dying generations—at their song,
The salmon-falls, the mackerel-crowded seas,
Fish, flesh, or fowl, commend all summer long
Whatever is begotten, born, and dies.
Caught in that sensual music all neglect
Monuments of unageing intellect.

II

An aged man is but a paltry thing,
A tattered coat upon a stick, unless
Soul clap its hands and sing, and louder sing
For every tatter in its mortal dress,
Nor is there singing school but studying
Monuments of its own magnificence;
And therefore I have sailed the seas and come
To the holy city of Byzantium.

III

O sages standing in God's holy fire
As in the gold mosaic of a wall,[2]
Come from the holy fire, perne in a gyre,[3]
And be the singing-masters of my soul.
Consume my heart away; sick with desire
And fastened to a dying animal
It knows not what it is; and gather me
Into the artifice of eternity.

IV

Once out of nature I shall never take
My bodily form from any natural thing,
But such a form as Grecian goldsmiths make
Of hammered gold and gold enamelling
To keep a drowsy Emperor awake;[4]
Or set upon a golden bough to sing

[1] Byzantium (modern Istanbul) was the capital of the Byzantine Empire in the fifth and sixth centuries. Yeats makes it a symbol of the timeless world of art, but he was interested in the historical city as well, writing in *A Vision* of the integration of matter and spirit in Byzantine art. He regarded the highly stylized Byzantine art as "impersonal" and expressive of "the vision of a whole people."

[2] Yeats is referring to Byzantine mosaics like those on the walls of the famous Church of Hagia Sophia in Byzantium.

[3] Whirl in a spiral, a mystical movement for Yeats.

[4] *But such a form. . .Emperor awake.* Yeats said he had read of such singing artificial birds in the Byzantine Emperor's palace.

To lords and ladies of Byzantium
Of what is past, or passing, or to come.

TWO SONGS FROM A PLAY[1]

I

I saw a staring virgin[2] stand
Where holy Dionysus died,
And tear the heart out of his side,
And lay the heart upon her hand
And bear that beating heart away;
And then did all the Muses[3] sing
Of Magnus Annus[4] at the spring,
As though God's death were but a play.

Another Troy must rise and set,
Another lineage feed the crow,[5]
Another Argo's painted prow
Drive to a flashier bauble yet.
The Roman Empire stood appalled:
It dropped the reigns of peace and war
When that fierce virgin and her Star[6]
Out of the fabulous darkness called.

II

In pity for man's darkening thought
He walked that room and issued thence
In Galilean turbulence;
The Babylonian starlight brought
A fabulous, formless darkness in;
Odour of blood when Christ was slain

[1] The play was *The Resurrection* (1927). These two closely related songs refer to Yeats's cyclic theory of history. In the first, the death and rebirth of Dionysus are paralleled with those of Christ in the succeeding cycle. The second song develops the contrast between "Babylonian starlight" and Christ's "Galilean turbulence," but internalizes the contrast to man's own imagination ("resinous heart").

[2] Athene. Dionysus' heart was removed and swallowed by Zeus so that Dionysus might be reborn.

[3] The nine sister goddesses in Greek mythology who presided over the arts.

[4] Latin for the "Great Year," the 26,000 years in which a complete cycle of the precession of the equinoxes takes place. In Yeats's system, it represents one turning of the "Great Wheel" and is made up of twelve cycles of approximately two thousand years each.

[5] That is, the equivalent of the Trojan War must take place in another cycle. The crow is thought of as the scavenger of battlefields. Argo was the name of the ship in which Jason sailed to seek the Golden Fleece.

[6] Mary and Christ, paralleled with Athene and Dionysus.

Made all Platonic tolerance vain
And vain all Doric discipline.[7]

Everything that man esteems
Endures a moment or a day.
Love's pleasure drives his love away,
The painter's brush consumes his dreams;
The herald's cry, the soldier's tread
Exhaust his glory and his might:
Whatever flames upon the night
Man's own resinous heart has fed.

LEDA AND THE SWAN[1]

A sudden blow: the great wings beating still
Above the staggering girl, her thighs caressed
By the dark webs, her nape caught in his bill,
He holds her helpless breast upon his breast.

How can those terrified vague fingers push
The feathered glory from her loosening thighs?
And how can body, laid in that white rush,
But feel the strange heart beating where it lies?

A shudder in the loins engenders there
The broken wall, the burning roof and tower
And Agamemnon dead.
Being so caught up,
So mastered by the brute blood of the air,
Did she put on his knowledge with his power
Before the indifferent beak could let her drop?

AMONG SCHOOL CHILDREN

I

I walk through the long schoolroom questioning;
A kind old nun in a white hood replies;
The children learn to cipher and to sing,
To study reading-books and history,
To cut and sew, be neat in everything

[7] *Platonic tolerance. . .Doric discipline.* The teachings of Plato and other Greek philosophers.

[1] In Greek mythology, Zeus took the form of a swan to rape the mortal Leda. From the union, in Yeats's version of the myth, were born the twin sisters Clytemnestra (wife and slayer of Agamemnon) and Helen, cause of the Trojan War ("the burning roof and tower"). Yeats thinks of Zeus's act as an "annunciation" inaugurating Greek civilization.

In the best modern way—the children's eyes
In momentary wonder stare upon
A sixty-year-old smiling public man.[1]

II

I dream of a Ledaean body,[2] bent
Above a sinking fire, a tale that she
Told of a harsh reproof, or trivial event
That changed some childish day to tragedy—
Told, and it seemed that our two natures blent
Into a sphere from youthful sympathy,
Or else, to alter Plato's parable,[3]
Into the yolk and white of the one shell.

III

And thinking of that fit of grief or rage
I look upon one child or t'other there
And wonder if she stood so at that age—
For even daughters of the swan can share
Something of every paddler's heritage—
And had that colour upon cheek or hair,
And thereupon my heart is driven wild:
She stands before me as a living child.

IV

Her present image floats into the mind—
Did Quattrocento finger[4] fashion it
Hollow of cheek as though it drank the wind
And took a mess of shadows for its meat?
And I though never of Ledaean kind
Had pretty plumage once—enough of that,
Better to smile on all that smile, and show
There is a comfortable kind of old scarecrow.

V

What youthful mother, a shape upon her lap
Honey of generation had betrayed,
And that must sleep, shriek, struggle to escape
As recollection or the drug decide,
Would think her son, did she but see that shape
With sixty or more winters on its head,
A compensation for the pang of his birth,
Or the uncertainty of his setting forth?

[1] Yeats was not only a famous poet, but after 1922 an Irish Senator.
[2] A body like Leda's. (See "Leda and the Swan.") Yeats is referring to Maud Gonne.
[3] Aristophanes, in Plato's *Symposium*, says that the two sexes were originally one but were divided like an egg cut in two.
[4] The hand of a fifteenth-century Italian artist, such as Leonardo da Vinci.

VI

Plato thought nature but a spume that plays
Upon a ghostly paradigm of things;[5]
Solider Aristotle played the taws
Upon the bottom of a king of kings;[6]
World-famous golden-thighed Pythagoras
Fingered upon a fiddle-stick or strings
What a star sang and careless Muses heard:[7]
Old clothes upon old sticks to scare a bird.

VII

Both nuns and mothers worship images,
But those the candles light are not as those
That animate a mother's reveries,
But keep a marble or a bronze repose.
And yet they too break hearts—O Presences
That passion, piety or affection knows,
And that all heavenly glory symbolise—
O self-born mockers of man's enterprise;

VIII

Labour is blossoming or dancing where
The body is not bruised to pleasure soul,
Nor beauty born out of its own despair,
Nor blear-eyed wisdom out of midnight oil.
O chestnut-tree, great-rooted blossomer,
Are you the leaf, the blossom or the bole?[8]
O body swayed to music, O brightening glance,
How can we know the dancer from the dance?

CRAZY JANE TALKS WITH THE BISHOP[1]

I met the Bishop on the road
And much said he and I.
'Those breasts are flat and fallen now,
Those veins must soon be dry;
Live in a heavenly mansion,
Not in some foul sty.'

[5] *Plato thought. . .of things.* An allusion to Plato's theory of forms, in which the visible world merely reflects ideal forms, which are the true reality.

[6] *Solider Aristotle. . .king of kings.* Aristotle was tutor to the young Alexander the Great, whom he presumably whipped ("played the taws"). Aristotle was "solider" than Plato because he emphasized the close study of the visible world.

[7] The sixth-century B.C. Greek philosopher Pythagoras developed the theory of musical harmony. According to legend, he had a thighbone of gold.

[8] Trunk.

[1] This is one of a series of seven "Crazy Jane" poems, in which old, half-mad Jane speaks wisdom as King Lear's Fool does.

'Fair and foul are near of kin,
And fair needs foul,' I cried.
'My friends are gone, but that's a truth
Nor grave nor bed denied,
Learned in bodily lowliness
And in the heart's pride.

'A woman can be proud and stiff
When on love intent;
But Love has pitched his mansion in
The place of excrement;
For nothing can be sole or whole
That has not been rent.'

LAPIS LAZULI[1]

(FOR HARRY CLIFTON)

I have heard that hysterical women say
They are sick of the palette and fiddle-bow,
Of poets that are always gay,
For everybody knows or else should know
That if nothing drastic is done
Aeroplane and Zeppelin[2] will come out,
Pitch like King Billy[3] bomb-balls in
Until the town lie beaten flat.

All perform their tragic play,
There struts Hamlet, there is Lear,
That's Ophelia, that Cordelia;
Yet they, should the last scene be there,
The great stage curtain about to drop,
If worthy their prominent part in the play,
Do not break up their lines to weep.
They know that Hamlet and Lear are gay;
Gaiety transfiguring all that dread.
All men have aimed at, found and lost;
Black out; Heaven blazing into the head:
Tragedy wrought to its uttermost.
Though Hamlet rambles and Lear rages,
And all the drop-scenes drop at once
Upon a hundred thousand stages,
It cannot grow by an inch or an ounce.

[1] A deep-blue, semiprecious stone. Yeats actually had a piece carved in the manner he describes.
[2] A lighter-than-air dirigible used for military purposes by the Germans in World War I.
[3] King William III, who defeated the army of the deposed King James II at the Battle of the Boyne in 1690.

On their own feet they came, or on shipboard,
Camel-back, horse-back, ass-back, mule-back,
Old civilisations put to the sword.
Then they and their wisdom went to rack:
No handiwork of Callimachus,[4]
Who handled marble as if it were bronze,
Made draperies that seemed to rise
When sea-wind swept the corner, stands;
His long lamp-chimney shaped like the stem
Of a slender palm, stood but a day;
All things fall and are built again,
And those that build them again are gay.

Two Chinamen, behind them a third,
Are carved in lapis lazuli,
Over them flies a long-legged bird,
A symbol of longevity;
The third, doubtless a serving-man,
Carries a musical instrument.

Every discoloration of the stone,
Every accidental crack or dent,
Seems a water-course or an avalanche,
Or lofty slope where it still snows
Though doubtless plum or cherry-branch
Sweetens the little half-way house
Those Chinamen climb towards, and I
Delight to imagine them seated there;
There, on the mountain and the sky,
On all the tragic scene they stare.
One asks for mournful melodies;
Accomplished fingers begin to play.
Their eyes mid many wrinkles, their eyes,
Their ancient, glittering eyes, are gay.

THE CIRCUS ANIMALS' DESERTION

I

I sought a theme and sought for it in vain,
I sought it daily for six weeks or so.
Maybe at last, being but a broken man,
I must be satisfied with my heart, although
Winter and summer till old age began
My circus animals were all on show,

[4] Fifth-century B.C. Greek sculptor, famous for his carved draperies, produced with a running drill.

Those stilted boys, that burnished chariot,
Lion and woman and the Lord knows what.[1]

II

What can I but enumerate old themes?
First that sea-rider Oisin[2] led by the nose
Through three enchanted islands, allegorical dreams,
Vain gaiety, vain battle, vain repose,
Themes of the embittered heart, or so it seems,
That might adorn old songs or courtly shows;
But what cared I that set him on to ride,
I, starved for the bosom of his faery bride?

And then a counter-truth filled out its play,
The Countess Cathleen was the name I gave it;
She, pity-crazed, had given her soul away,
But masterful Heaven had intervened to save it.[3]
I thought my dear must her own soul destroy,
So did fanaticism and hate enslave it,[4]
And this brought forth a dream and soon enough
This dream itself had all my thought and love.

And when the Fool and Blind Man stole the bread
Cuchulain fought the ungovernable sea;[5]
Heart-mysteries there, and yet when all is said
It was the dream itself enchanted me:
Character isolated by a deed
To engross the present and dominate memory.
Players and painted stage took all my love,
And not those things that they were emblems of.

III

Those masterful images because complete
Grew in pure mind, but out of what began?
A mound of refuse or the sweepings of a street,
Old kettles, old bottles, and a broken can,
Old iron, old bones, old rags, that raving slut
Who keeps the till. Now that my ladder's gone,
I must lie down where all the ladders start,
In the foul rag-and-bone shop of the heart.

[1] *Those stilted boys. . .the Lord knows what.* The "stilted boys" are the tragic characters (wearing *cotherni,* or Greek thick-soled shoes) in Yeats's plays. The "burnished chariot" is Fergus's in such poems by Yeats as "Who Goes with Fergus?" The "lion and woman" are the sphinx in both "The Double Vision of Michael Robartes" and "The Second Coming."

[2] *that sea-rider Oisin.* In Yeats's 1889 poem *The Wanderings of Oisin* (pronounced "ush-een").

[3] *The Countess Cathleen. . .to save it. The Countess Cathleen* (1892) deals with an Irish countess who sells her soul to the devil to get food for her starving people, but whom God saves anyway, valuing the spirit above the deed.

[4] Maud Gonne, whose nationalist fervor Yeats disapproved of.

[5] *And when the Fool. . .ungovernable sea.* In the play *On Baile's Strand* (1904).

UNDER BEN BULBEN[1]

I

Swear by what the sages spoke
Round the Mareotic Lake
That the Witch of Atlas knew,
Spoke and set the cocks a-crow.[2]

Swear by those horsemen, by those women[3]
Complexion and form prove superhuman,
That pale, long-visaged company
That air in immortality
Completeness of their passions won;
Now they ride the wintry dawn
Where Ben Bulben sets the scene.

Here's the gist of what they mean.

II

Many times man lives and dies
Between his two eternities,
That of race and that of soul,
And ancient Ireland knew it all.
Whether man die in his bed
Or the rifle knocks him dead,
A brief parting from those dear
Is the worst man has to fear.
Though grave-diggers' toil is long,
Sharp their spades, their muscles strong,
They but thrust their buried men
Back in the human mind again.

III

You that Mitchel's prayer have heard,
'Send war in our time, O Lord!'[4]
Know that when all words are said
And a man is fighting mad,
Something drops from eyes long blind,

[1] One of Yeats's last poems, written September 4, 1938. Ben Bulben is a mountain in County Sligo, overlooking the village of Drumcliff, where Yeats left directions that he be buried.

[2] *Round the Mareotic Lake. . .cocks a-crow.* The Mareotic Lake is Lake Mareotis, near Alexandria, where both the Neo-Pythagorean philosophers (first century A.D.) and the Christian Neo-Platonists (third century A.D.) flourished. *The Witch of Atlas* is a poem by Percy Bysshe Shelley which mentions Lake Mareotis. Presumably what both the "sages" and the Witch of Atlas knew was the secret of timeless beauty.

[3] *those horsemen. . .those women.* The *sidhe* or Irish fairies who ride through the countryside around Ben Bulben.

[4] *'Send war. . .O Lord.'* John Mitchel (1815-75?), founder of the United Irishmen, wrote in his journal from prison, "Give us war in our time, O Lord!"

He completes his partial mind,
For an instant stands at ease,
Laughs aloud, his heart at peace.
Even the wisest man grows tense
With some sort of violence
Before he can accomplish fate,
Know his work or choose his mate.

IV

Poet and sculptor, do the work,
Nor let the modish painter shirk
What his great forefathers did,
Bring the soul of man to God.
Make him fill the cradles right.

Measurement began our might:[5]
Forms a stark Egyptian thought,
Forms that gentler Phidias wrought.
Michael Angelo left a proof
On the Sistine Chapel roof,
Where but half-awakened Adam
Can disturb globe-trotting Madam
Till her bowels are in heat,
Proof that there's a purpose set
Before the secret working mind:
Profane perfection of mankind.

Quattrocento[6] put in paint
On backgrounds for a God or Saint
Gardens where a soul's at ease;
Where everything that meets the eye,
Flowers and grass and cloudless sky,
Resemble forms that are or seem
When sleepers wake and yet still dream,
And when it's vanished still declare,
With only bed and bedstead there,
That heavens had opened.
                                        Gyres run on;
When that greater dream had gone
Calvert and Wilson, Blake and Claude,[7]
Prepared a rest for the people of God,

[5] Yeats is reviewing the development of art and thought according to his view of history. "Measurement" is Babylonian mathematics; Phidias was a fifth-century B.C. Greek sculptor; Michael Angelo (or Michelangelo) was the sixteenth-century Italian painter and sculptor who designed and painted the Sistine Chapel.

[6] The art of fifteenth-century Italy.

[7] *Calvert. . .Claude.* Edward Calvert, nineteenth-century wood-engraver; Richard Wilson, eighteenth-century landscape painter; William Blake, nineteenth-century poet and engraver; Claude Lorrain, seventeenth-century landscape painter. All these provided images for Yeats's poetry, as did Samuel Palmer (line 66), nineteenth-century landscape painter and etcher.

Palmer's phrase, but after that
Confusion fell upon our thought.

V

Irish poets, learn your trade,
Sing whatever is well made,
Scorn the sort now growing up
All out of shape from toe to top,
Their unremembering hearts and heads
Base-born products of base beds.
Sing the peasantry, and then
Hard-riding country gentlemen,
The holiness of monks, and after
Porter-drinkers' randy laughter;
Sing the lords and ladies gay
That were beaten into the clay
Through seven heroic centuries;
Cast your mind on other days
That we in coming days may be
Still the indomitable Irishry.

VI

Under bare Ben Bulben's head
In Drumcliff churchyard Yeats is laid.
An ancestor was rector there
Long years ago, a church stands near,
By the road an ancient cross.
No marble, no conventional phrase;
On limestone quarried near the spot
By his command these words are cut:
Cast a cold eye
On life, on death.
Horseman, pass by![8]

[8] *Cast a cold eye. . .pass by!* The inscription on Yeats's tombstone.

Luigi Pirandello

(1867–1936)

"Life," Luigi Pirandello wrote, "is a continuous flow which we continually try to stop, to fix in concepts and ideals. But inside ourselves, in what we call our soul, the flow continues indistinctly, under the wire, past the limits that we set when we formed consciousness and built a personality. During certain stormy moments, inundated by the flow, all our fictitious forms collapse ignominiously."

Pirandello's perception of the tension between man's fragile, partial, provisional conscious mind and the surging, vital, unknowable forces of "life" is a distinctly and painfully modern one. (His "flood within ourselves" is very close to Freud's Unconscious.) It was Pirandello's achievement as a dramatist to find a dramatic form that not only expressed this perception but actually embodied it. The stage itself, in Pirandello's hands, becomes a metaphor for a view of human personality as dizzyingly multiple and of reality as essentially unknowable. *Six Characters in Search of an Author*, as his English translator Frederick May rightly suggests, is to the theater what Eliot's *Waste Land* is to poetry: a work which redefines the medium itself to express a radically modern sense of the world.

Pirandello was born in Sicily in 1867, the son of a prosperous family of sulfur-merchants. He resisted his father's desire for him to enter the family business and attended first the University of Rome and then the University of Bonn, where he received a doctorate in philology in 1891; his thesis was on the dialect of his hometown in Sicily. Three years later he entered into an arranged marriage with Antonietta Portulano, the daughter of another family of wealthy sulfur-dealers. The marriage gave Pirandello an independent income and allowed the couple to settle in Rome, where he led the life of a leisured man of letters, publishing an occasional volume of poetry and contributing short stories to literary magazines. The marriage produced three children.

In 1903, a catastrophic landslide destroyed the sulfur mines of both the Pirandellos and the Portulanos, plunging both families into poverty. Pirandello had to seek employment teaching Italian in a girls' school in Rome. His wife, already weakened by a difficult childbirth, reacted to the disaster first with a six-month hysterical paralysis and then with a progressive psychosis. Pirandello cared for her at home for sixteen years, the victim of her paranoia and irrational jealousy, until her increasing violence forced him to commit her to an institution in 1919. (Amazingly, she remained there for forty years, dying in 1959.) It is hard not to see in this tragedy the roots of Pirandello's later themes. The essential unknowability of other people, the fragility of surface forms and ideals, and the multiple selves within each personality were not merely theoretical issues for Pirandello.

Now driven by financial need, Pirandello began to write voluminously. His early career was devoted mainly to fiction; solid success came in 1904 with *The Late Mattia Pascal*, a novel which anticipated the conflict between being and seeming which dominated his later writing. Other successes followed: several collections of earthy, realistic short stories and several novels, including *The Old and Young* (1913), *The Notebooks of Serafino Gubbio, Cinematograph Operator* (1916), and *One, None, and a Hundred Thousand* (1925–26).

Pirandello wrote his first play, *The Vise*, in 1898, but discouraged by difficulties in getting it produced, he did not return to the theater until 1915. *Right You Are (If You Think So)* (1917), an ironic study of the relativity of truth, was a modest success and ignited an enormous burst of dramatic creativity that was to continue through the '20s. His first major theatrical success was *As Before, Better than Before* (1920); immediately after its production, he wrote, within a five-week period, both *Six Characters in Search of an Author* and *Henry IV*, his masterpieces. (Pirandello was always an extraordinarily fast writer; he wrote *Right You Are* in six days, *Six Characters* in three weeks, and *Henry IV* in two weeks.) The productions in Rome of *Six Characters* in 1921 and *Henry IV* in 1922 brought Pirandello international fame. Productions of the two plays followed in Paris, London, Berlin, and New York, and Pirandello's subsequent plays were eagerly competed *for:* To Clothe the Naked *(1923),* The Life I Gave You *(1924),* Each in His Own Way *(1924),* Diana and Tuda *(1927),* The New Colony *(1928),* Lazarus *(1929),* Tonight We Improvise *(1930),* As You Desire Me *(1930), and* When Somebody is Somebody *(1933). He received the Nobel Prize in 1934.*

World fame achieved, Pirandello in 1925 founded the Art Theater, an Italian national theater based in Rome but committed to touring the world with his plays; the company appeared all over Europe and even toured South America. Financial losses forced the theater to close, however, in 1928. When Mussolini assumed dictatorial powers in the same year, Pirandello committed himself enthusiastically to the new regime, accepting subsidies and honors from the Fascists and publicly supporting their policies, even contributing his Nobel medal to be melted down to support the Italian invasion of Abyssinia. Many attempts have been made to reconcile Pirandello's Fascism with the ironic skepticism toward all systems that characterizes his creative work. It is unnecessary to conclude that he was merely cynically opportunistic; if all systems are equally suspect, there is a temptation to accept one that at least promises order. The plays of the Fascist period—especially The New Colony, Lazarus, *and* The Mountain Giants *(1936, unfinished)—have been read as withdrawals into myth in reaction to the rigors of the Fascist state. These later years were also marked by a deep, continuing love for the Italian actress Marta Abba. Pirandello died in 1936, leaving instructions for the most private and spartan of funerals: "Dead, let me not be clothed. Let me be placed, naked, in a sheet. No flowers on the bed, no lighted candle. . . . The cart, the horse, the driver,* e basta!"

Italian critics have held that Pirandello's achievement is greater in fiction than in drama, but there is no doubt that his world stature rests primarily upon his plays, especially Henry IV *and the plays that he called his trilogy of "the theater in the theater":* Six Characters in Search of An Author, Each in His Own Way, *and* Tonight We Improvise. *"Pirandellism," as it has influenced modern drama, is the self-conscious exposure of the theater itself as a metaphor for human life. This "metatheater" (to use the American critic Lionel Abel's term), the exploration of the proposition that "all the world's a stage," is perhaps as old as the theater itself, but it was Pirandello who revived it in peculiarly modern terms and placed it at the center of his art.*

The basic premise of Six Characters in Search of an Author*—six (ultimately seven) "characters" invade the rehearsal of a play—sets up a situation which generates a series of dazzling paradoxes about the relation of art to life and initiates a dramatic action designed to lead the commonsensical Producer and his actors to that vertiginous, Pirandellian moment when the "fictitious forms" of consciousness collapse under the surging "flood" of life, a moment reached at the very end of the play.*

The spine of the play is the ongoing debate between the Father and the Producer over the comparative "reality" of ordinary human beings and "characters." Insofar as anyone wins the debate, it is probably the Father, who superficially seems to be Pirandello's spokesman. (In some productions, the Father has even been made up to look like Pirandello, pointed beard and all.) But it is a serious misreading of the play to miss the dramatic irony in the presentation of the Father. His arguments that the characters of art are more "real" than ordinary people because they are exempt from temporal change and because they can be seen from only one point of view are absurd (in several senses); his defense of the fixed and the unchanging sounds suspiciously like not a defense of life but a wish for death. The unthinking animal vitality of the actors is much more attractive than the Father's tortured self-consciousness.

The crucial character in this play is perhaps not the Father but one who never appears, that mysteriously absent Author. Why did he abandon his characters and their shadowy, half-finished plot? The critic Eric Bentley has pointed out that the three incidents in the fragmentary "characters" plot are close to primitive fantasy: a father seducing his daughter, a son seeing his parents making love, and a child murdering a sibling. Perhaps our absent Author has abandoned his characters because they have led him onto psychologically dangerous ground. But behind even the Author, in a Pirandellian layering of reality, is Pirandello himself, who dramatizes, in the finished play, not merely the Father's specious philosophizing but all the paradoxes and conflicts of the parallel projects of playwriting and encountering the mysterious flood of life.

NOTE ON THE TEXT

The text of Six Characters in Search of an Author *reprinted here differs considerably from the version generally known in America. Previous English translations of the play have been based upon Pirandello's original 1921 version. Frederick May's translation is the first English version based on Pirandello's final, definitive version of the play.*

FURTHER READING *(prepared by N. K. B.): Naked Masks,* ed. Eric Bentley, 1952, contains other plays by Pirandello, an excellent introduction, a biographical note, and Pirandello's Preface to *Six Characters in Search of an Author.* Gaspare Giudice, *Pirandello,* 1975, trans. by Alastair Hamilton, provides the fullest account of the writer's absorbing life; Renate Matthaei, *Luigi Pirandello,* 1973, also contains much biographical detail, in addition to analyzing the major plays. Walter Starkie's *Luigi Pirandello,* 1926, rev. 1937, 1965, has the enthusiasm of an early study and remains one of the most readable introductions to the playwright and his plays. In *The Drama of Luigi Pirandello,* 1935, rev. 1957, Domenico Vittorini examines those plays written between 1918 and 1935 and places Pirandello's work in the context of Italian literary traditions. Anne Paolucci's *Pirandello's Theater,* 1974, focuses on the experimental quality of the later plays but argues for the unity of his entire work. Olga Ragusa, *Luigi Pirandello,* 1981, provides explications of selected plays in order to demonstrate Pirandello's early interest in psychology and the occult. Glauco Cambon, ed., *Pirandello: A Collection of Critical Essays,* 1967, is a valuable compendium of critical views, including Francis Fergusson's essay on theatricality in *Six Characters.* Oscar Büdel, *Pirandello,* 1966, rev. 1969, establishes the importance of Relativism in Pirandello's technique. Roger W. Oliver, *Dreams of Passion: The Theater of Luigi Pirandello,* 1979, interprets the drama according to the theory of perception articulated in Pirandello's essay "On Humor," with a lengthy analysis of *Six Characters.* A well-documented, thorough study, A. Richard Sogliuzzo's *Luigi Pirandello, Director: The Playwright in the Theatre,* 1982, demonstrates the role of Pirandello's theories in his own productions.

SIX CHARACTERS IN SEARCH OF AN AUTHOR

A PLAY IN THE MAKING

Translated by Frederick May

THE CHARACTERS OF THE PLAY IN THE MAKING

THE FATHER
THE MOTHER
THE STEPDAUGHTER
THE SON
THE BOY *(non-speaking)*
THE LITTLE GIRL *(non-speaking)*
MADAME PACE[1] *(who is called into being)*

THE ACTORS IN THE COMPANY

THE PRODUCER[2]
THE LEADING LADY
THE LEADING MAN
THE SECOND FEMALE LEAD[3]
THE INGENUE
THE JUVENILE LEAD
OTHER ACTORS AND ACTRESSES
THE STAGE MANAGER
THE PROMPTER
THE PROPERTY MAN
THE FOREMAN OF THE STAGE CREW
THE PRODUCER'S SECRETARY
THE COMMISSIONAIRE[4]
STAGE HANDS AND OTHER THEATER PERSONNEL

DAYTIME: THE STAGE OF A THEATER

N.B.—*The play has neither acts nor scenes. Its performance will be interrupted twice: once—though the curtain will not be lowered—when the* PRODUCER *and the principal* CHARACTERS *go away to write the script and the* ACTORS *leave the stage, and a second time when the Man on the Curtain lets it fall by mistake.*

When the audience enters the auditorium the curtain is up and the stage is just as it would be during the daytime. There is no set and there are no wings; it is empty and in almost total darkness. This is in order that right from the very beginning the audience shall receive the impression of being present, not at a performance of a carefully rehearsed play, but at a performance of a play that suddenly happens.

Two small flights of steps, one right and one left, give access to the stage from the auditorium.

On the stage itself, the prompter's dome has been removed, and is standing just to one side of the prompt box.[5]

[1] Pronounced "pah-chay" ("peace" in Italian).
[2] "Director" in American theater-terminology.
[3] Referred to as "The Second Actress" in the text. [4] Doorman, caretaker.
[5] Older theaters and opera houses had a pit in the stage down center for a prompter or chorus conductor. His head was concealed by a shield called the "prompter's dome."

Downstage, on the other side, a small table and an armchair with its back turned to the audience have been set for the PRODUCER.

Two more small tables, one rather larger than the other, together with several chairs, have been set downstage so that they are ready if needed for the rehearsal. There are other chairs scattered about to the left and to the right for the actors, and, in the background, to one side and almost hidden, there is a piano.

When the house lights go down the FOREMAN *comes on to the stage through the door back. He is dressed in blue dungarees and carries his tools in a bag slung at his belt. From a corner at the back of the stage he takes one or two slats of wood, brings them down front, kneels down and starts nailing them together. At the sound of his hammer the* STAGE-MANAGER *rushes in from the direction of the dressing rooms.*

STAGE-MANAGER. Hey! What are you doing?

FOREMAN. What am I doing? Hammering . . . nails.

STAGE-MANAGER. At this time of day? [*He looks at his watch.*] It's gone half-past ten! The Producer'll be here any minute now and he'll want to get on with his rehearsal.

FOREMAN. And let me tell *you* something . . . I've got to have time to do *my* work, too.

STAGE-MANAGER. You'll get it, you'll get it. . . . But you can't do that *now.*

FOREMAN. When can I do it then?

STAGE-MANAGER. After the rehearsal. Now, come on. . . . Clear up all this mess, and let me get on with setting the second act of *The Game As He Played It.*[6]

[*The* FOREMAN *gathers his pieces of wood together, muttering and grumbling all the while, and goes off. Meanwhile, the* ACTORS OF THE COMPANY *have begun to come on to the stage through the door back. First one comes in, then another, then two together . . . just as they please. There are nine or ten of them in all—as many as you would suppose you would need for the rehearsal of Pirandello's play,* The Game As He Played It, *which has been called for today. As they come in they greet one another and the* STAGE-MANAGER *with a cheery "Good morning." Some of them go off to their dressing-rooms; others, and among them the* PROMPTER, *who is carrying the prompt copy rolled up under his arm, remain on the stage, waiting for the* PRODUCER *to come and start the rehearsal. While they are waiting—some of them standing, some seated about in small groups—they exchange a few words*

[6] A (nonexistent) play by Pirandello.

among themselves. One lights a cigarette, another complains about the part that he's been given and a third reads out an item of news from a theatrical journal for the benefit of the other actors. It would be best if all the ACTORS AND ACTRESSES *could be dressed in rather bright and gay clothes. This first improvised scene should be played very naturally and with great vivacity. After a while, one of the comedy men can sit down at the piano and start playing a dance-tune. The younger* ACTORS AND ACTRESSES *start dancing.*]

STAGE-MANAGER [*clapping his hands to restore order*]. Come on, now, come on! That's enough of that! Here's the producer!

[*The music and dancing come to a sudden stop. The* ACTORS *turn and look out into the auditorium and see the* PRODUCER, *who is coming in through the door. He comes up the gangway between the stalls, bowler hat on head, stick under arm, and a large cigar in his mouth, to the accompaniment of a chorus of "Good-mornings" from the* ACTORS *and climbs up one of the flights of steps on to the stage. His* SECRETARY *offers him his post—a newspaper or so, a script.*]

PRODUCER. Any letters?

SECRETARY. None at all. This is all the post there is.

PRODUCER [*handing him back the script*]. Put it in my office. [*Then, looking around and turning to the* STAGE-MANAGER.] Oh, you can't see a thing here! Ask them to give us a spot of light, please.

STAGE-MANAGER. Right you are!

[*He goes off to give the order and a short while after the whole of the right side of the stage, where the* ACTORS *are standing, is lit up by a bright white light. In the meantime the* PROMPTER *has taken his place in his box, switched on his light and spread his script out in front of him.*]

PRODUCER [*clapping his hands*]. Come on, let's get started! [*To the* STAGE-MANAGER.] Anyone missing?

STAGE-MANAGER. The Leading Lady.

PRODUCER. As usual! [*Looks at his watch.*] We're ten minutes late already. Make a note, will you, please, to remind me to give her a good talking-to about being so late? It might teach her to get to rehearsals on time in the future.

[*He has scarcely finished his rebuke when the voice of the* LEADING LADY *is heard at the back of the auditorium.*]

LEADING LADY. No, please don't! Here I am! Here I am!

[*She is dressed completely in white, with a large and rather dashing and provocative hat, and is carrying a dainty little lap-dog. She runs down the aisle and hastily climbs up the steps on to the stage.*]

PRODUCER. You've set your heart on always keeping us waiting, haven't you?

LEADING LADY. Forgive me! I hunted everywhere for a taxi so that I should get here on time! But you haven't started yet, anyway. And I don't come on immediately. [*Then, calling the* STAGE-MANAGER *by name, she gives him the lap-dog.*] Please put him in my dressing-room . . . and mind you shut the door!

PRODUCER [*grumblingly*]. And she has to bring a dog along too! As if there weren't enough dogs around here! [*He claps his hands again and turns to the* PROMPTER.] Come on now, let's get on with Act II of *The Game As He Played It*. [*He sits down in the armchair.*] Now, ladies and gentlemen, who's on?

[*The* ACTORS AND ACTRESSES *clear away from the front of the stage and go and sit to one side, except for the three who start the scene, and the* LEADING LADY. *She had paid no attention to the* PRODUCER'S *question and has seated herself at one of the little tables.*]

PRODUCER [*to the* LEADING LADY]. Ah! So you're in this scene, are you?

LEADING LADY. Me? Oh, no!

PRODUCER [*annoyed*]. Then for God's sake get off!

[*And the* LEADING LADY *gets up and goes and sits with the others.*]

PRODUCER [*to the* PROMPTER]. Now, let's get started!

PROMPTER [*reading from his script*]. "The house of Leone Gala. A strange room, half dining-room, half study."

PRODUCER [*turning to the* STAGE-MANAGER]. We'll use the red set.

STAGE-MANAGER [*making a note on a sheet of paper*]. The red set. Right!

PROMPTER [*continuing to read from his script*]. "A table laid for a meal and a desk with books and papers. Bookshelves with books on them. Glass-fronted cupboards containing valuable china. A door back leading into Leone's bedroom. A side door left, leading into the kitchen. The main entrance is right."

PRODUCER [*getting up and pointing*]. Right! Now listen carefully—over there, the main entrance. And over here, the kitchen. [*Turning to the actor who is to play the part of Socrates.*] You'll make your entrances and exits this side. [*To the* STAGE-MANAGER.] We'll have that green-baize door at the back there . . . and some curtains. [*He goes and sits down again.*]

STAGE-MANAGER [*making a note*]. Right you are!

PROMPTER [*reading*]. "Scene I. Leone Gala, Guido Venanzi, Filippo, who is called Socrates." [*To the* PRODUCER.] Do I have to read the stage directions as well?

PRODUCER. Yes, yes, of course! I've told you that a hundred times!

PROMPTER [*reading*]. "When the curtain rises, Leone Gala, wearing a cook's hat and apron, is busy beating an egg in a basin with a wooden spoon. Filippo, also dressed as a cook, is beating another egg. Guido Venanzi is sitting listening to them."

LEADING MAN [*to the* PRODUCER]. Excuse me, but do I really have to wear a cook's hat?

PRODUCER [*irritated by this observation*]. So it seems! That's certainly what's written there! [*He points to the script.*]

LEADING MAN. Forgive me for saying so, but it's ridiculous.

PRODUCER [*bounding to his feet in fury*]. Ridiculous! Ridiculous! What do you expect me to do if the French haven't got any more good comedies to send us, and we're reduced to putting on plays by Pirandello? And if you can understand *his* plays . . . you're a better man than I am! He deliberately goes out of his way to annoy people, so that by the time the play's through everybody's fed up . . . actors, critics, audience, everybody!

[*The* ACTORS *laugh. Then getting up and going over to the* LEADING MAN, *the* PRODUCER *cries*]:

Yes, my dear fellow, a cook's hat! And you beat eggs! And do you think that, having these eggs to beat, you then have nothing more on your hands? Oh, no, not a bit of it. . . . You have to represent the shell of the eggs that you're beating!

[*The* ACTORS *start laughing again and begin to make ironical comments among themselves.*]

Shut up! And listen when I'm explaining things! [*Turning again to the* LEADING MAN.] Yes, my dear fellow, the shell . . . or, as you might say, the empty form of reason, without that content of instinct which is blind! You are reason and your wife is instinct, in a game where you play the parts which have been given you. And all the time you're playing your part, you are the self-willed puppet of yourself. Understand?

LEADING MAN [*spreading out his hands*]. Me? No!

PRODUCER [*returning to his seat*]. Neither do I! However, let's get on with it! It's going to be a wonderful flop, anyway! [*In a confidential tone.*] I suggest you turn to the audience a bit more . . . about three-quarters face. Otherwise, what with the abstruseness of the dialogue, and the audience's not being able to hear you, the whole thing'll go to hell. [*Clapping his hands again.*] Now, come along! *Come along!* Let's get started!

PROMPTER. Excuse me, sir, do you mind if I put the top back on my box? There's a bit of a draft.

PRODUCER. Of course! Go ahead! Go ahead!

[*Meanwhile the* COMMISSIONAIRE *has entered the auditorium. He is wearing a braided cap and having covered the length of the aisle, he comes up to the edge of the stage to announce the arrival of the* SIX CHARACTERS *to the* PRODUCER. *They have followed the* COMMISSIONAIRE *into the auditorium and have walked behind him as he has come up to the stage. They look about them, a little perplexed and a little dismayed.*

In any production of this play it is imperative that the producer should use every means possible to avoid any confusion between the SIX CHARACTERS *and the* ACTORS. *The placings of the two groups, as they will be indicated in the stage-directions once the* CHARACTERS *are on the stage, will no doubt help. So, too, will their being lit in different colors. But the most effective and most suitable method of distinguishing them that suggests itself, is the use of special masks for the* CHARACTERS, *masks specially made from some material which will not grow limp with perspiration and will at the same time be light enough to be worn by the actors playing these parts. They should be cut so as to leave the eyes, the nose and the mouth free. In this way the deep significance of the play can be brought out. The* CHARACTERS *should not, in fact, appear as phantasms, but as created realities, unchangeable creations of the imagination and, therefore, more real and more consistent than the ever-changing naturalness of the* ACTORS. *The masks will assist in giving the impression of figures constructed by art, each one fixed immutably in the expression of that sentiment which is fundamental to it. That is to say in* REMORSE *for the* FATHER, REVENGE *for the* STEPDAUGHTER, CONTEMPT *for the* SON *and* SORROW *for the* MOTHER. *Her mask should have wax tears fixed in the corners of the eyes and coursing down the cheeks, just like those which are carved and painted in the representations of the Mater Dolorosa*[7] *that are to be seen in churches. Her dress, too, should be of a special material and cut. It should be severely plain, its folds stiff, giving in fact the appearance of having been carved, and not of being made of any material that*

[7] Mary, mother of Christ, sorrowing for her son, a favorite subject of ecclesiastical art.

you can just go out and buy or have cut out and made up into a dress by any ordinary dressmaker.

The FATHER *is a man of about fifty. He is not bald but his reddish hair is thin at the temples. His moustache is thick and coils over his still rather youthful-looking mouth, which all too often falls open in a purposeless, uncertain smile. His complexion is pale and this is especially noticeable when one has occasion to look at his forehead, which is particularly broad. His blue, oval-shaped eyes are very clear and piercing. He is wearing a dark jacket and light-colored trousers. At times his manner is all sweetness and light, at others it is hard and harsh.*

The MOTHER *appears as a woman crushed and terrified by an intolerable weight of shame and abasement. She is dressed in a modest black and wears a thick crêpe widow's veil. When she lifts her veil she reveals a wax-like face; it is not, however, at all sickly-looking. She keeps her eyes downcast all the time. The* STEPDAUGHTER, *who is eighteen, is defiant, bold, arrogant—almost shamelessly so. She is very beautiful. She, too, is dressed in mourning but carries it with a decided air of showy elegance. She shows contempt for the very timid, dejected, half-frightened manner of her younger brother, a rather grubby and unprepossessing* BOY *of fourteen, who is also dressed in black. On the other hand she displays a very lively tenderness for her small sister, a* LITTLE GIRL *of about four, who is wearing a white frock with a black silk sash round her waist.*

The SON *is a tall young man of twenty-two. He is wearing a mauve colored overcoat and has a long green scarf twisted round his neck. He appears as if he has stiffened into an attitude of contempt for the* FATHER *and of supercilious indifference towards the* MOTHER.]

COMMISSIONAIRE [*cap in hand*]. Excuse me, sir.
PRODUCER [*snapping at him rudely*]. Now what's the matter?
COMMISSIONAIRE. There are some people here, sir, asking for you.

[*The* PRODUCER *and the* ACTORS *turn in astonishment and look out into the auditorium.*]

PRODUCER [*furiously*]. But I've got a rehearsal on at the moment! And you know quite well that no one's allowed in here while a rehearsal's going on. [*Then addressing the* CHARACTERS.] Who are you? What do you want?

FATHER [*he steps forward, followed by the others, and comes to the foot of one of the flights of steps*]. We are here in search of an author.

PRODUCER [*caught between anger and utter astonishment*]. In search of an author? Which author?

FATHER. Any author, sir.

PRODUCER. But there's no author here. . . . We're not rehearsing a new play.

STEPDAUGHTER [*vivaciously, as she rushes up the steps*]. So much the better! Then so much the better, sir! *We* can be your new play.

ONE OF THE ACTORS [*amidst the lively comments and laughter of the others*]. Oh, just listen to her! *Listen* to her!

FATHER [*following the* STEPDAUGHTER *on to the stage*]. Yes, but if there isn't any author. . . . [*To the* PRODUCER.] Unless *you'd* like to be the author. . . .

[*Holding the* LITTLE GIRL *by the hand, the* MOTHER, *followed by the* BOY, *climbs up the first few steps leading to the stage and stands there expectantly. The* SON *remains morosely below.*]

PRODUCER. Are you people trying to be funny?

FATHER. No. . . . How can you suggest such a thing? On the contrary, we are bringing you a terrible and grievous drama.

STEPDAUGHTER. And we might make your fortune for you.

PRODUCER. Perhaps you'll do me the kindness of getting out of this theater! We've got no time to waste on lunatics!

FATHER [*he is wounded by this, but replies in a gentle tone*]. Oh. . . . But you know very well, don't you, that life is full of things that are infinitely absurd, things that, for all their impudent absurdity, have no need to masquerade as truth, because they are true.

PRODUCER. What the devil are you talking about?

FATHER. What I'm saying is that reversing the usual order of things, forcing oneself to a contrary way of action, may well be construed as madness. As, for instance, when we create things which have all the appearance of reality in order that they shall look like the realities themselves. But allow me to observe that if this indeed be madness, it is, nonetheless, the sole *raison d'être* of your profession.

[*The* ACTORS *stir indignantly at this.*]

PRODUCER [*getting up and looking him up and down*]. Oh, yes? So you think ours is a profession of lunatics, do you?

FATHER. Yes, making what isn't true *seem* true . . . without having to . . . for fun. . . . Isn't it your function to give life on the stage to imaginary characters?

PRODUCER [*immediately, making himself spokesman for the growing anger of his actors*]. I should like you to know, my dear sir, that the actor's profession is a most noble one. And although nowadays, with things in the state they are, our playwrights give us stupid comedies to act, and puppets to represent instead of men, I'd have you know that it is our boast that we have given life, here on these very boards, to immortal works!

[*The* ACTORS *satisfiedly murmur their approval and applaud the* PRODUCER.]

FATHER [*breaking in and following hard on his argument*]. There you are! Oh, that's it exactly! To living beings . . . to beings who are more alive than those who breathe and wear clothes! Less real, perhaps, but truer! We're in complete agreement!

[*The* ACTORS *look at each other in utter astonishment.*]

PRODUCER. But . . . What on earth! . . . But you said just now . . .

FATHER. No, I said that because of your . . . because you shouted at us that you had no time to waste on lunatics . . . while nobody can know better than you that nature makes use of the instrument of human fantasy to pursue her work of creation on a higher level.

PRODUCER. True enough! True enough! But where does all this get us?

FATHER. Nowhere. I only wish to show you that one is born into life in so many ways, in so many forms. . . . As a tree, or as a stone; as water or as a butterfly. . . . Or as a woman. And that one can be born a character.

PRODUCER [*ironically, feigning amazement*]. And you, together with these other people, were born a character?

FATHER. Exactly. And alive, as you see. [*The* PRODUCER *and the* ACTORS *burst out laughing as if at some huge joke.*] [*Hurt.*] I'm sorry that you laugh like that because, I repeat, we carry within ourselves a terrible and grievous drama, as you can deduce for yourselves from this woman veiled in black.

[*And so saying, he holds out his hand to the* MOTHER *and helps her up the last few steps and, continuing to hold her hand, leads her with a certain tragic solemnity to the other side of the stage, which immediately lights up with a fantastic kind of light. The* LITTLE GIRL *and the* BOY *follow their* MOTHER. *Next the* SON *comes up and goes and stands to one side, in the background. Then the* STEPDAUGHTER *follows him on to the stage; she stands downstage, leaning against the proscenium arch. The* ACTORS *are at first completely taken aback and then, caught in admiration at this development, they burst into applause—just as if they had had a show put on for their benefit.*]

PRODUCER [*at first utterly astonished and then indignant*]. Shut up! What the . . .! [*Then turning to the* CHARACTERS.] And you get out of here! Clear out of here! [*To the* STAGE-MANAGER.] For God's sake, clear them out!

STAGE-MANAGER [*coming forward, but then stopping as if held back by some strange dismay*]. Go away! Go away!

FATHER [*to the* PRODUCER]. No, no! Listen. . . . We. . . .

PRODUCER [*shouting*]. I tell you, we've got work to do!

LEADING MAN. You can't go about playing practical jokes like this. . . .

FATHER [*resolutely coming forward*]. I wonder at your incredulity. Is it perhaps that you're not accustomed to seeing the characters created by an author leaping to life up here on the stage, when they come face to face with each other? Or is it, perhaps, that there's no script there [*he points to the prompt box*] that contains us?

STEPDAUGHTER [*smiling, she steps towards the* PRODUCER; *then, in a wheedling voice*]. Believe me, sir, we really are six characters . . . and very, very interesting! But we've been cut adrift.

FATHER [*brushing her aside*]. Yes, that's it, we've been cut adrift. [*And then immediately to the* PRODUCER.] In the sense, you understand, that the author who created us as living beings, either couldn't or wouldn't put us materially into the world of art. And it was truly a crime . . . because he who has the good fortune to be born a living character may snap his fingers at Death even. He will never die! Man . . . The writer . . . The instrument of creation . . . Will die. . . . But what is created by him will never die. And in order to live eternally he has not the slightest need of extraordinary gifts or of accomplishing prodigies. Who was Sancho Panza? Who was Don Abbondio?[8] And yet they live eternally because—living seeds—they had the good fortune to find a fruitful womb—a fantasy which knew how to raise and nourish them, and to make them live through all eternity.

PRODUCER. All this is very, very fine indeed. . . . But what do you want here?

FATHER. We wish to live, sir!

PRODUCER [*ironically*]. Through all eternity?

FATHER. No, sir; just for a moment . . . in you.

AN ACTOR. Listen to him! . . . listen to him!

LEADING LADY. They want to live in us!

JUVENILE LEAD [*pointing to the* STEPDAUGHTER]. I've no objection . . . so long as I get her.

FATHER. Listen! Listen! The play is in the making. [*To the* PRODUCER.] But if you and your actors are willing, we can settle it all between us without further delay.

PRODUCER [*annoyed*]. But what do you want to settle? We don't go in for that sort of concoction here! We put on comedies and dramas here.

FATHER. Exactly! That's the very reason why we came to you.

PRODUCER. And where's the script?

FATHER. It is in us, sir. [*The* ACTORS *laugh.*] The drama is in us. *We* are the drama and we are impatient to act it—so fiercely does our inner passion urge us on.

[8] *Sancho Panza . . . Don Abbondio.* Sancho Panza is the groom in Miguel de Cervantes' *Don Quixote* (1605, 1616). Don Abbondio is the parish priest in Alessandro Manzoni's romantic novel *I Promessi Sposi (The Betrothed,* 1825–26).

STEPDAUGHTER [*scornful, treacherous, alluring, with deliberate shamelessness*]. My passion. . . . If you only knew! My passion . . . for him!

[*She points to the* FATHER *and makes as if to embrace him, but then bursts into strident laughter.*]

FATHER [*at once, angrily*]. You keep out of this for the moment! And please don't laugh like that!

STEPDAUGHTER. Oh . . . mayn't I? Then perhaps *you'll* allow me, ladies and gentlemen. . . . Although it's scarcely two months since my father died . . . just you watch how I can dance and sing!

[*Mischievously she starts to sing Dave Stamper's "Prends garde à Tchou-Tchin-Tchou" in the fox-trot or slow one-step version by François Salabert. She sings the first verse, accompanying it with a dance.*]

Les chinois sont un peuple malin,
De Shangaï à Pékin,
Ils ont mis des écriteaux partout:
Prenez garde à Tchou-Tchin-Tchou![9]

[*While she is singing and dancing, the* ACTORS, *and especially the younger ones, as if attracted by some strange fascination, move towards her and half raise their hands as though to catch hold of her. She runs away, and when the* ACTORS *burst into applause, and the* PRODUCER *rebukes her, she stands where she is, quietly, abstractedly, and as if her thoughts were far away.*]

ACTORS AND ACTRESSES [*laughing and clapping*]. Well done! Jolly good!

PRODUCER [*irately*]. Shut up! What do you think this is . . . a cabaret? [*Then taking the* FATHER *a little to one side, he says with a certain amount of consternation.*] Tell me something. . . . Is she mad?

FATHER. What do you mean, mad? It's worse than that!

STEPDAUGHTER [*immediately rushing up to the* PRODUCER]. Worse! Worse! Oh it's something very much worse than that! Listen! Let's put this drama on at once. . . . Please! Then you'll see that at a certain moment I . . . when this little darling here. . . . [*Takes the* LITTLE GIRL *by the hand and brings her over to the* PRODUCER.] . . . Isn't she a dear? [*Takes her in her arms and kisses her.*] You little darling! . . . You dear little darling! [*Puts her down again, adding in a moved tone, almost without wishing to.*] Well, when God suddenly takes this child away from her poor mother, and that little imbecile there [*roughly grabbing hold of the* BOY *by the sleeve and*

[9] *Prends garde à Tchou-Tchin-Tchou.* French version of "Beware of Chu-Chin-Chow," a popular song of 1917. *Chou Chin Chow* was an enormously popular New York musical revue by Frederic Norton and Oscar Asche, and this song, from the *Ziegfeld Follies of 1917,* alludes to its success: "The Chinese are a cunning folk / From Shanghai to Peking, / They've put up posters everywhere: / Beware of *Chu Chin Chow!*"

thrusting him forward] does the stupidest of all stupid things, like the idiot he is [*pushing him back towards the* MOTHER] . . . Then you will see me run away. Yes, I shall run away! And, oh, how I'm longing for that moment to come! Because after all the very intimate things that have happened between him and me [*with a horrible wink in the direction of the* FATHER] I can't remain any longer with these people . . . having to witness my mother's anguish because of that queer fish there [*pointing to the* SON]. Look at him! Look at him! See how indifferent, how frigid he is . . . because he's the legitimate son . . . *he* is! He despises me, he despises him [*pointing to the* BOY], he despises that dear little creature. . . . Because we're bastards! Do you understand? . . . Because we're *bastards!* [*She goes up to the* MOTHER *and embraces her.*] And he doesn't want to recognize this poor woman as his mother. . . . This poor woman . . . who is the mother of us all! He looks down on her as if she were only the mother of us three bastards! The wretch! [*She says all this very quickly and very excitedly. She raises her voice at the word 'bastards' and the final 'wretch' is delivered in a low voice and almost spat out.*]

MOTHER [*to the* PRODUCER, *an infinity of anguish in her voice*]. Please, in the name of these two little children . . . I beg you. . . . [*She grows faint and sways on her feet.*] Oh, my God! [*Consternation and bewilderment among the* ACTORS.]

FATHER [*rushing over to support her, accompanied by most of the* ACTORS]. Quick . . . a chair. . . . A chair for this poor widow!

ACTORS [*rushing over*]. Has she fainted? Has she fainted?

PRODUCER. Quick, get a chair . . . get a chair!

[*One of the* ACTORS *brings a chair, the others stand around, anxious to help in any way they can. The* MOTHER *sits on the chair; she attempts to prevent the* FATHER *from lifting the veil which hides her face.*]

FATHER. Look at her. . . . Look at her. . . .

MOTHER. No, No! My God! Stop it, please!

FATHER. Let them see you. [*He lifts her veil.*]

MOTHER [*rising and covering her face with her hands in desperation*]. I beg you, sir, . . . Don't let this man carry out his plan! You must prevent him. . . . It's horrible!

PRODUCER [*utterly dumbfounded*]. I don't get this at all. . . . I haven't got the slightest idea what you're talking about. [*To the* FATHER.] Is this lady your wife?

FATHER [*immediately*]. Yes, sir, my wife.

PRODUCER. Then how does it come about that she's a widow if you're still alive?

[*The* ACTORS *find relief for their bewilderment and astonishment in a noisy burst of laughter.*]

FATHER [*wounded, speaking with sharp resentment*]. Don't laugh! Don't laugh like that, for pity's sake! It is in this fact that her drama lies. She had another man. Another man who ought to be here.

MOTHER [*with a cry*]. No! No!

STEPDAUGHTER. He's got the good luck to be dead. . . . He died two months ago, as I just told you. We're still wearing mourning for him, as you can see.

FATHER. But it's not because he's dead that he's not here. No, he's not here because . . . Look at her! Look at her, please, and you'll understand immediately! Her drama does not lie in the love of two men for whom she, being incapable of love, could feel nothing. . . . Unless, perhaps, it be a little gratitude . . . to him, not to me. She is not a woman. . . . She is a mother. And her drama. . . . And how powerful it is! How powerful it is! . . . Her drama lies entirely, in fact, in these four children. . . . The children of the two men that she had.

MOTHER. Did you say that I had them? Do you dare to say that I *had* these two men . . . to suggest that I wanted them? [*To the* PRODUCER.] It was his doing. He gave him to me! He forced him on me! He forced me. . . . He forced me to go away with that other man!

STEPDAUGHTER [*at once, indignantly*]. It's not true!

MOTHER [*startled*]. Not true?

STEPDAUGHTER. It's not true! It's not true, I say.

MOTHER. And what can you possibly know about it?

STEPDAUGHTER. It's not true! [*To the* PRODUCER.] Don't believe her! Do you know why she said that? Because of him. [*Pointing to the* SON.] That's why she said it! Because she tortures herself, wears herself out with anguish, because of the indifference of that son of hers. She wants him to believe that if she abandoned him when he was two years old it was because he [*pointing to the* FATHER] forced her to do it.

MOTHER [*forcefully*]. He forced me to do it! He forced me, as God is my witness! [*To the* PRODUCER.] Ask him [*pointing to her* HUSBAND] if it's not true! Make him tell my son! She [*pointing to her* DAUGHTER] knows nothing at all about the matter.

STEPDAUGHTER. I know that while my father lived you were always happy. . . . You had a peaceful and contented life together. Deny it if you can!

MOTHER. I don't deny it! No. . . .

STEPDAUGHTER. He was always most loving, always kindness itself towards you. [*To the* BOY, *angrily*.] Isn't it true? Go on. . . . Say it's true! Why don't you speak, you stupid little idiot?

MOTHER. Leave the poor boy alone! Why do you want to make me appear an ungrateful woman? I don't want to say anything against your father. . . . I only said that it wasn't my fault, and that it wasn't just to satisfy my own desires that I left his house and abandoned my son.

FATHER. What she says is true. It was my doing.

[*There is a pause.*]

LEADING MAN [*to the other* ACTORS]. My God! What a show!

LEADING LADY. And we're the audience this time!

JUVENILE LEAD. For once in a while.

PRODUCER [*who is beginning to show a lively interest*]. Let's listen to this! Let's hear what they've got to say!

[*And saying this he goes down the steps into the auditorium and stands in front of the stage, as if to get an impression of the scene from the audience's point of view.*]

SON [*without moving from where he is, speaking coldly, softly, ironically*]. Yes! Listen to the chunk of philosophy you're going to get now! He will tell you all about the Daemon of Experiment.

FATHER. You're a cynical idiot, as I've told you a hundred times. [*Down to the* PRODUCER.] He mocks me because of this expression that I've discovered in my own defense.

SON [*contemptuously*]. Words! Words!

FATHER. Yes! Words! Words! They can always bring consolation to us. . . . To everyone of us. . . . When we're confronted by something for which there's no explanation. . . . When we're face to face with an evil that consumes us. . . . The consolation of finding a word that tells us nothing, but that brings us peace.

STEPDAUGHTER. And dulls our sense of remorse, too. Yes! That above all!

FATHER. Dulls our sense of remorse? No, that's not true. It wasn't with words alone that I quietened remorse within me.

STEPDAUGHTER. No, you did it with a little money as well. Yes! Oh, yes! with a little money as well! With the hundred lire that he was going to offer me . . . as payment, ladies and gentlemen!

[*A movement of horror on the part of the* ACTORS.]

SON [*contemptuously to his* STEPSISTER]. That was vile!

STEPDAUGHTER. Vile? There they were, in a pale blue envelope, on the little mahogany table in the room behind Madame Pace's shop. Madame Pace. . . . One of those *Madames* who pretend to sell *Robes et Manteaux*[10] so that they can attract us poor girls from decent families into their workrooms.

SON. And she's bought the right to tyrannize over the whole lot of us with those hundred lire that he was going to pay her. . . . But by good fortune. . . . And let me emphasize this. . . . He had no reason to pay her anything.

STEPDAUGHTER. Yes, but it was a very near thing! Oh, yes, it was, you know! [*She bursts out laughing.*]

MOTHER [*rising to protest*]. For shame! For shame!

STEPDAUGHTER [*immediately*]. Shame? No! This is my revenge! I'm trembling with desire. . . . Simply trembling with desire to live that scene! That room. . . . Over here is the shop-window with all the coats in it. . . . And over there the divan, the long mirror and a screen. . . . And in front of the window that little mahogany table. . . . And the pale blue envelope with the hundred lire inside. Yes, I can see it quite clearly! I'd only have to stretch out my hand and I could pick it up! But you gentlemen really ought to turn your backs now, because I'm almost naked. I no longer blush, because he's the one who does the blushing now [*pointing to the* FATHER]. But, let me tell you, he was very pale then. . . . Very pale indeed! [*To the* PRODUCER.] You can believe *me*!

PRODUCER. I haven't the vaguest idea what you're talking about!

[10] Dresses and cloaks (French).

FATHER. I can well believe it! When you get things hurled at you like that. Put your foot down. . . . And let me speak before you believe all these horrible slanders she's so viciously heaping upon me. . . . Without letting me get a word of explanation in.

STEPDAUGHTER. Ah, but this isn't the place for your long-winded fairy-stories, you know!

FATHER. But I'm not going to. . . . I want to explain things to him!

STEPDAUGHTER. Oh yes . . . I bet you do! You'll explain everything so that it suits you, won't you?

[*At this point the* PRODUCER *comes back on stage to restore order.*]

FATHER. But can't you see that here we have the cause of all the trouble! In the use of words! Each one of us has a whole world of things inside him. . . . And each one of us has his own particular world. How can we understand each other if into the words which I speak I put the sense and the value of things as I understand them within myself. . . . While at the same time whoever is listening to them inevitably assumes them to have the sense and value that they have for him. . . . The sense and value that they have in the world that he has within him? We think we understand one another. . . . But we never really do understand! Look at this situation, for example! All my pity, all the pity that I feel for this woman [*pointing to the* MOTHER] *she* sees as the most ferocious cruelty.

MOTHER. But you turned me out of the house!

FATHER. There! Do you hear? I turned her out! She really believed that I was turning her out!

MOTHER. You know how to talk . . . I don't. . . . But believe me [*turning to the* PRODUCER] after he had married me. . . . Goodness knows why! For I was a poor, humble woman. . . .

FATHER. But it was just because of that. . . . It was your humility that I loved in you. I married you for your humility, believing . . . [*He breaks off, for she is making gestures of contradiction. Then, seeing how utterly impossible it is to make her understand him, he opens his arms wide in a gesture of despair and turns to the* PRODUCER.] No! . . . You see? She says no! It's terrifying, believe me! It's really terrifying, this deafness [*he taps his forehead*]. . . . This mental deafness of hers! Affection. . . . Yes! . . . For her children! But deaf. . . . Mentally deaf. . . . Deaf to the point of desperation.

STEPDAUGHTER. True enough! But now you make him tell us what good all his cleverness has ever done us.

FATHER. If we could only foresee all the ill that can result from the good that we believe we are doing.

[*Meanwhile the* LEADING LADY, *with ever-increasing fury, has been watching the* LEADING MAN, *who is busy carrying on a flirtation with the* STEPDAUGHTER. *Unable to stand it any longer she now steps forward and says to the* PRODUCER.]

LEADING LADY. Excuse me, but are you going on with the rehearsal?

PRODUCER. Why, of course! Of course! But just at the moment I want to hear what these people have to say!

JUVENILE LEAD. This is really something quite new!

INGENUE. It's most interesting!

LEADING LADY. For those that are interested! [*And she looks meaningly in the direction of the* LEADING MAN.]

PRODUCER [*to the* FATHER]. But you'll have to explain everything clearly. [*He goes and sits down.*]

FATHER. Yes. . . . Well. . . . You see . . . I had a poor man working under me. . . . He was my secretary, and devoted to me. . . . Who understood *her* in every way. . . . In everything [*pointing to the* MOTHER]. Oh, there wasn't the slightest suspicion of anything wrong. He was a good man. A humble man. . . . Just like her. . . . They were incapable . . . both of them . . . not only of doing evil . . . but even of thinking it!

STEPDAUGHTER. So, instead, he thought about it for them! And then got on with it.

FATHER. It's not true! I thought that what I should be doing would be for their good. . . . And for mine, too. . . . I confess it! Yes, things had come to such a pass that I couldn't say a single word to either of them without their immediately exchanging an understanding look. . . . Without the one's immediately trying to catch the other's eye. . . . For advice as to how to take what I had said. . . . So that I shouldn't get into a bad temper. As you'll readily appreciate it was enough to keep me in a state of continual fury. . . . Of intolerable exasperation!

PRODUCER. But. . . . Forgive my asking. . . . Why didn't you give this secretary of yours the sack?

FATHER. That's exactly what I did do, as a matter of fact. But then I had to watch that poor woman wandering forlornly about the house like some poor lost creature. . . . Like one of those stray animals you take in out of charity.

MOTHER. But . . .

FATHER [*immediately turning on her, as if to forestall what she is about to say*]. Your son! You were going to tell him about your son, weren't you?

MOTHER. But first of all he tore my son away from me!

FATHER. Not out of any desire to be cruel though! I took him away so that, by living in the country, in contact with Nature, he might grow up strong and healthy.

STEPDAUGHTER [*pointing to him, ironically*]. And just look at him!

FATHER [*immediately*]. And is it my fault, too, that he's grown up the way he has? I sent him to a wet-nurse in the country . . . a peasant's wife . . . because my wife didn't seem strong enough to me. . . . Although she came of a humble family, and it was for that reason that I'd married her! Just a whim maybe. . . . But then . . . what was I to do? I've always had this cursed longing for a certain solid moral healthiness.

[*At this the* STEPDAUGHTER *breaks out afresh into noisy laughter.*]

Make her stop that noise! I can't stand it!

PRODUCER. Be quiet! Let me hear what he has to say, for God's sake!

[*At the* PRODUCER'S *rebuke she immediately returns to her former attitude. . . . Absorbed and distant, a half-smile on her lips. The* PRODUCER *comes down off the stage again to see how it looks from the auditorium.*]

FATHER. I could no longer stand the sight of that woman near me [*pointing to the* MOTHER]. Not so much because of the irritation she caused me . . . the nausea . . . the very real nausea with which she inspired me. . . . But rather because of the pain . . . the pain and the anguish that I was suffering on her account.

MOTHER. And he sent me away!

FATHER. Well provided with everything. . . . To that other man. . . . So that she might be free of me.

MOTHER. And so that he might be free as well!

FATHER. Yes, I admit it. And a great deal of harm came as a result of it. . . . But I meant well. . . . And I did it more for her sake than for my own. I swear it! [*He folds his arms. Then immediately turning to the* MOTHER.] Did I ever lose sight of you? Tell me, did I ever lose sight of you until that fellow took you away suddenly to some other town . . . all unknown to me. . . . Just because he'd got some queer notion into his head about the interest I was showing in you. . . . An interest which was pure, I assure you, sir. . . . Without the slightest suspicion of any ulterior motive about it! I watched the new little family that grew up around her with incredible tenderness. She can testify to that [*he points to the* STEPDAUGHTER].

STEPDAUGHTER. Oh, I most certainly can! I was such a sweet little girl. . . . Such a sweet little girl, you see. . . . With plaits down to my shoulders . . . and my knickers a little bit longer than my frock. I used to see him standing there by the door of the school as I came out. He came to see how I was growing up. . . .

FATHER. Oh, this is vile! Treacherous! Infamous!

STEPDAUGHTER. Oh, no! What makes you say it's infamous?

FATHER. It's infamous! Infamous! [*Then turning excitedly to the* PRODUCER *he goes on in an explanatory tone.*] After she'd gone away [*pointing to the* MOTHER], my house suddenly seemed empty. She had been a burden on my spirit, but she had filled my house with her presence! Left alone I wandered through the rooms like some lost soul. This boy here [*pointing to the* SON], having been brought up away from home . . . I don't know . . . But . . . But when he returned home he no longer seemed to be my son. With no mother to link him to me, he grew up entirely on his own. . . . A creature apart . . . absorbed in himself . . . with no tie of intellect or affection to bind him to me. And then. . . . And, strange as it may seem, it's the simple truth . . . I became curious about her little family. . . . Gradually I was attracted to this family which had come into being as a result of what I had done. And the thought of it began to fill the emptiness that I felt all around me. I felt a real need . . . a very real need . . . to believe that she was happy, at peace, absorbed in the simple everyday duties of life. I wanted to look on her as being fortunate because she was far removed from the complicated torments of my spirit. And so, to have some proof of this, I used to go and watch that little girl come out of school.

STEPDAUGHTER. I should just say he did! He used to follow me along the street. He would smile at me and when I reached home he'd wave to me

. . . like this. I would look at him rather provocatively, opening my eyes wide. I didn't know who he might be. I told my mother about him and she knew at once who it must be. [*The* MOTHER *nods agreement.*] At first she didn't want to let me go to school again. . . . And she kept me away for several days. And when I did go back, I saw him waiting for me at the door again . . . looking so ridiculous . . . with a brown paper bag in his hand. He came up to me and patted me. . . . And then he took a lovely large straw hat out of the bag . . . with lots of lovely little roses on it. . . . And all for me.

PRODUCER. This is a bit off the point, you know.

SON [*contemptuously*]. Yes. . . . Literature! Literature!

FATHER. Literature indeed! This is life! Passion!

PRODUCER. It may be. But you certainly can't act this sort of stuff!

FATHER. I agree with you. Because all this is only leading up to the main action. I'm not suggesting that this part should be acted. And as a matter of fact, as you can quite well see, she [*pointing to the* STEPDAUGHTER] is no longer that little girl with plaits down to her shoulders. . . .

STEPDAUGHTER. . . . and her knickers a little bit longer than her frock!

FATHER. It is now that the drama comes! Something new, something complex. . . .

STEPDAUGHTER [*coming forward, her voice gloomy, fierce*]. As soon as my father died. . . .

FATHER [*at once, not giving her a chance to continue*]. . . . they fell into the most wretched poverty! They came back here. . . . And because of her stupidity [*pointing to the* MOTHER] I didn't know a thing about it. It's true enough that she can hardly write her own name. . . . But she might have got her daughter or that boy to write and tell me that they were in need!

MOTHER. Now tell me, sir, how was I to know that this was how he'd feel?

FATHER. That's exactly where you went wrong, in never having got to know how I felt about anything.

MOTHER. After so many years away from him. . . . And after all that had happened. . . .

FATHER. And is it my fault that that fellow took you away from here as he did? [*Turning to the* PRODUCER.] I tell you, they disappeared overnight. . . . He'd found some sort of a job away from here . . . I couldn't trace them at all. . . . So, of necessity, my interest in them dwindled. And this was how it was for quite a number of years. The drama broke out, unforeseen and violent in its intensity, when they returned. . . . When I was impelled by the demands of my miserable flesh, which is still alive with desire. . . . Oh, the wretchedness, the unutterable wretchedness of the man who's alone and who detests the vileness of casual affairs! When he's not old enough to do without a woman, and not really young enough to be able to go and look for one without feeling a sense of shame. Wretchedness, did I say? It's horrible! It's horrible! Because no woman is any longer capable of giving him love. And when he realizes this, he ought to do without. . . . Yes, yes, I know! . . . Each one of us, when he appears before his fellow men, is clothed with a certain dignity. But deep down inside himself he knows what unconfessable things go on in the secrecy of his own heart. We give way

. . . we give way to temptation. . . . Only to rise up again immediately, filled with a great eagerness to re-establish our dignity in all its solid entirety. . . . Just as if it were a tombstone on some grave in which we had buried, in which we had hidden from our eyes, every sign, and the very memory itself of our shame. And everyone is just like that! Only there are some of us who lack the courage to talk about certain things.

STEPDAUGHTER. They've got the courage to do them, though. . . . All of them!

FATHER. Yes, all of them! But only in secret! And that's why it needs so much more courage to talk about them! A man's only got to mention these things, and the words have hardly left his lips before he's been labelled a cynic. And all the time it's not true. He's just like everybody else. . . . In fact he's better than they are, because he's not afraid to reveal with the light of his intelligence that red blush of shame which is inherent in human bestiality. . . . That shame to which bestial man closes his eyes, in order not to see it. And woman. . . . Yes, woman. . . . What kind of a being is she? She looks at you, tantalizingly, invitingly. You take her in your arms! And no sooner is she clasped firmly in your arms than she shuts her eyes. It is the sign of her mission, the sign by which she says to man, "Blind yourself, for I am blind."

STEPDAUGHTER. And what about when she no longer shuts her eyes? When she no longer feels the need to hide her blushing shame from herself by closing her eyes? When she sees instead . . . dry-eyed and dispassionate . . . the blushing shame of man, who has blinded himself without love? Oh, what disgust, what unutterable disgust, does she feel then for all these intellectual complications, for all this philosophy which reveals the beast in man and then tries to save him, tries to excuse him . . . I just can't stand here and listen to him! Because when a man is obliged to "simplify" life bestially like that—when he throws overboard every vestige of "humanity," every chaste desire, every pure feeling. . . . All sense of idealism, of duty, of modesty and of shame. . . . Then nothing is more contemptible, infuriating and revoltingly nauseating than their maudlin remorse. . . . Those crocodile tears!

PRODUCER. Now let's get back to the point! Let's get to the point! This is just a lot of beating about the bush!

FATHER. Very well. But a fact is like a sack. . . . When it's empty it won't stand up. And in order to make it stand up you must first of all pour into it all the reasons and all the feelings which have caused it to exist. I couldn't possibly be expected to know that when that man died and they returned here in such utter poverty, she [*pointing to the* MOTHER] would go out to work as a dress-maker in order to support the children. . . . Nor that, of all people, she'd gone to work for that . . . for Madame Pace.

STEPDAUGHTER. Who's a high-class dress-maker, if you ladies and gentlemen would really like to know. On the surface she does work for only the best sort of people. But she arranges things so that these fine ladies act as a screen . . . without prejudice to the others . . . who are only so-so.

MOTHER. Believe me, it never entered my head for one moment that that old hag gave me work because she had her eye on my daughter. . . .

STEPDAUGHTER. Poor Mummy! Do you know what that woman used to do when I took her back the work that my mother had done? She would point out to me how the material had been ruined by giving it to my mother to sew. . . . Oh, she'd grumble about this! And she'd grumble about that! And so, you understand, I had to pay for it. . . . And all the time this poor creature thought she was sacrificing herself for me and for those two children, as she sat up all night sewing away at work for Madame Pace. [*Gestures and exclamations of indignation from the* ACTORS.]

PRODUCER [*immediately*]. And it was there, one day, that you met . . .

STEPDAUGHTER [*pointing to the* FATHER]. . . . him! Yes, him! An old client! Now there's a scene for you to put on! Absolutely superb!

FATHER. With her . . . the Mother . . . arriving. . . .

STEPDAUGHTER [*immediately, treacherously*]. . . . almost in time!

FATHER [*a cry*]. No! In time! In time! Fortunately I recognized her in time! And I took them all back home with me! Now you can imagine what the situation is like for both of us. She, just as you see her. . . . And I, no longer able to look her in the face.

STEPDAUGHTER. It's utterly ridiculous! How can I possibly be expected, after all that, to be a modest young miss . . . well-bred and virtuous . . . in accordance with his confounded aspirations for a "solid moral healthiness"?

FATHER. My drama lies entirely in this one thing. . . . In my being conscious that each one of us believes himself to be a single person. But it's not true. . . . Each one of us is many persons. . . . Many persons . . . according to all the possibilities of being that there are within us. . . . With some people we are one person. . . . With others we are somebody quite different. . . . And all the time we are under the illusion of always being one and the same person for everybody. . . . We believe that we are always this one person in whatever it is we may be doing. But it's not true! It's not true! And we see this very clearly when by some tragic chance we are, as it were, caught up whilst in the middle of doing something and find ourselves suspended in mid-air. And then we perceive that all of us was not in what we were doing, and that it would, therefore, be an atrocious injustice to us to judge us by that action alone. . . . To keep us suspended like that. . . . To keep us in a pillory . . . throughout all existence . . . as if our whole life were completely summed up in that one deed. Now do you understand the treachery of this girl? She surprised me somewhere where I shouldn't have been . . . and doing something that I shouldn't have been doing with her. . . . She surprised an aspect of me that should never have existed for her. And now she is trying to attach to me a reality such as I could never have expected I should have to assume for her. . . . The reality that lies in one fleeting, shameful moment of my life. And this, this above all, is what I feel most strongly about. And as you can see, the drama acquires a tremendous value from this concept. Then there's the position of the others. . . . His . . . [*pointing to the* SON].

SON [*shrugging his shoulders scornfully*]. Leave me alone! I've got nothing to do with all this!

FATHER. What do you mean . . . you've got nothing to do with all this?

SON. I've got nothing to do with it. . . . And I don't want to have anything to do with it, because, as you quite well know, I wasn't meant to be mixed up in all this with the rest of you!

STEPDAUGHTER. Common, that's what we are! And he's a fine gentleman! But, as you may have noticed, every now and again I fix him with a contemptuous look, and he lowers his eyes. . . . Because he knows the harm he's done me!

SON [*scarcely looking at her*]. I?

STEPDAUGHTER. Yes, you! You! It's all your fault that I became a prostitute! [*A movement of horror from the* ACTORS.] Did you or did you not deny us, by the attitude you adopted—I won't say the intimacy of your home—but even that mere hospitality which makes guests feel at their ease? We were invaders who had come to disturb the kingdom of your legitimacy. I should just like you [*this to the* PRODUCER] to be present at certain little scenes that took place between him and me. He says that I tyrannized over everybody. . . . But it was just because of the way that he behaved that I took advantage of the thing that he calls "vile". . . . Why I exploited the reason for my coming into his house with my mother. . . . Who is his mother as well! And I went into that house as mistress of it!

SON [*slowly coming forward*]. It's all very easy for them. . . . It's fine sport. . . . All of them ganging-up against me. But just imagine the position of a son whose fate it is one fine day, while he's sitting quietly at home, to see arriving an impudent and brazen young woman who asks for his father—and heaven knows what her business is with him! Later he sees her come back, as brazen as ever, bringing that little girl with her. And finally he sees her treating his father—without knowing in the least why—in a very equivocal and very much to-the-point manner . . . asking him for money, in a tone of voice which leads you to suppose that he must give it to her. . . . Must give it to her, because he has every obligation to do so. . . .

FATHER. As indeed I have! It's an obligation I owe your mother!

SON. How should I know that? When had I ever seen or even heard of her? Then one day I see her arrive with *her* [*pointing to the* STEPDAUGHTER] together with that boy and the little girl. And they say to me, "This is *your* mother, too, you know." Little by little I begin to understand. . . . Largely as a result of the way she goes on [*pointing to the* STEPDAUGHTER *again*]. . . . Why it is that they've come to live with us. . . . So suddenly. . . . So unexpectedly. . . . What I feel, what I experience, I neither wish, nor am able, to express. I wouldn't even wish to confess it to myself. No action, therefore, can be hoped for from me in this affair. Believe me, I am a dramatically unrealized character . . . and I do not feel the least bit at ease in their company. So please leave me out of it!

FATHER. What! But it's just because you're like that. . . .

SON [*in violent exasperation*]. And what do you know about it? How do you know what I'm like? When have you ever bothered yourself about me?

FATHER. I admit it! I admit it! But isn't that a dramatic situation in itself? This aloofness of yours, which is so cruel to me and to your mother. . . . Your mother who returns home and sees you almost for the first time. . . . You're so grown up that she doesn't recognize you, but she knows that you're her son. [*Pointing to the* MOTHER *and addressing the* PRODUCER.] There, look! She's crying!

STEPDAUGHTER [*angrily, stamping her foot*]. Like the fool she is!

FATHER [*pointing to the* STEPDAUGHTER]. She can't stand him! [*Then returning to the subject of the* SON.] He says he's got nothing to do with all this, when, as a matter of fact, almost the whole action hinges on him. Look at that little boy. . . . See how he clings to his mother all the time, frightened and humiliated. . . . And it's *his* fault that he's like that! Perhaps his position is the most painful of all. . . . More than any of them he feels himself to be an outsider. And so the poor little chap feels mortified, humiliated at being taken into my home . . . out of charity, as it were. [*Confidentially.*] He's just like his father. Humble. . . . Doesn't say a word. . . .

PRODUCER. I don't think it's a good idea to have him in. You've no idea what a nuisance boys are on the stage.

FATHER. Oh, . . . but he won't be a nuisance for long. . . . He disappears almost immediately. And the little girl, too. . . . In fact, she's the first to go.

PRODUCER. This is excellent! I assure you I find this all very interesting. . . . Very interesting indeed! I can see we've got the makings of a pretty good play here.

STEPDAUGHTER [*trying to butt in*]. When you've got a character like me!

FATHER [*pushing her to one side in his anxiety to hear what decision the* PRODUCER *has come to*]. You be quiet!

PRODUCER [*continuing, heedless of the interruption*]. And it's certainly something new. . . . Ye-es! . . .

FATHER. Absolutely brand new!

PRODUCER. You had a nerve, though, I must say. . . . Coming here and chucking the idea at me like that. . . .

FATHER. Well, you understand, born as we are for the stage. . . .

PRODUCER. Are you amateur actors?

FATHER. No . . . I say that we're born for the stage because . . .

PRODUCER. Oh, don't try and come that one with me! You're an old hand at this game.

FATHER. No. I only act as much as anyone acts the part that he sets himself to perform, or the part that he is given in life. And in me it is passion itself, as you can see, that always becomes a little theatrical of its own accord . . . as it does in everyone . . . once it becomes exalted.

PRODUCER. Oh well, that as may be! That as may be! . . . But you do understand, without an author . . . I could give you the address of somebody who'd . . .

FATHER. No! . . . Look here. . . . You be the author!

PRODUCER. Me? What the devil are you talking about?

FATHER. Yes, you! You! Why not?

PRODUCER. Because I've never written anything in my life! That's why not!

FATHER. Then why not try your hand at it now? There's nothing to it. Everybody's doing it! And your job's made all the easier for you because we are here, all of us, alive before you. . . .

PRODUCER. That's not enough!

FATHER. Not enough? When you see us live our drama. . . .

PRODUCER. Yes! Yes! But we'll still need somebody to write the play.

FATHER. No. . . . Someone to take it down possibly, while we act it out, scene by scene. It'll be quite sufficient if we make a rough sketch of it first and then have a run through.

PRODUCER [*climbing back on to the stage, tempted by this*]. H'm! . . . You almost succeed in tempting me. . . . H'm! It would be rather fun! We could certainly have a shot at it.

FATHER. Of course! Oh, you'll see what wonderful scenes 'll emerge! I can tell you what they are here and now.

PRODUCER. You tempt me. . . . You tempt me. . . . Let's have a go at it! . . . Come with me into my office. [*Turning to the* ACTORS.] You can have a few minutes' break. . . . But don't go too far away. I want you all back again in about a quarter of an hour or twenty minutes. [*To the* FATHER.] Well, let's see what we can make of it! We might get something really extraordinary out of it. . . .

FATHER. There's no *might* about it! They'd better come along too, don't you think? [*Pointing to the other* CHARACTERS.]

PRODUCER. Yes, bring 'em along! Bring 'em along! [*Starts going off and then turns back to the* ACTORS.] Now remember, don't be late back! You've got a quarter of an hour!

[*The* PRODUCER *and the* SIX CHARACTERS *cross the stage and disappear. The* ACTORS *remain looking at one another in astonishment.*]

LEADING MAN. Is he serious? What's he going to do?

JUVENILE LEAD. This is utter madness!

A THIRD ACTOR. Does he expect us to knock up a play in five minutes?

JUVENILE LEAD. Yes . . . like the actors in the old Commedia dell' Arte.[11]

LEADING LADY. Well, if he thinks that I'm going to have anything to do with fun and games of that sort. . . .

INGENUE. And you certainly don't catch me joining in!

A FOURTH ACTOR. I should like to know who those people are. [*He is alluding to the* CHARACTERS.]

THIRD ACTOR. Who do you think they're likely to be? They're probably escaped lunatics. . . . Or crooks!

JUVENILE LEAD. And does he really take what they say seriously?

INGENUE. Vanity! That's what it is. . . . The vanity of appearing as an author!

LEADING MAN. It's absolutely unheard of! If the stage has come to this. . . .

A FIFTH ACTOR. I'm rather enjoying it!

THIRD ACTOR. Oh, well! After all, we shall have the pleasure of seeing what comes of it all!

And talking among themselves in this way the ACTORS *leave the stage. Some go out through the door back, some go in the direction of the dressing-rooms. The curtain remains up.*

The performance is suspended for twenty minutes.

[11]Form of comic theater in sixteenth- to eighteenth-century Italy. It used improvised dialogue and masked, stock characters such as Harlequin, Columbine, and Scaramouche.

The call-bells ring, warning the audience that the performance is about to be resumed.

The ACTORS, *the* STAGE-MANAGER, *the* FOREMAN *of the stage crew, the* PROMPTER *and the* PROPERTY MAN *reassemble on stage. Some come from the dressing-rooms, some through the door back, some even from the auditorium. The* PRODUCER *enters from his office accompanied by the* SIX CHARACTERS.

The houselights are extinguished and the stage lighting is as before.

PRODUCER. Now come on, ladies and gentlemen! Are we all here? Let me have your attention please! Now let's make a start! [*Then calls the* FOREMAN.]

FOREMAN. Yes, sir?

PRODUCER. Set the stage for the parlor scene. A couple of flats and a door will do. As quickly as you can!

[*The* FOREMAN *runs off at once to carry out this order and is setting the stage as directed whilst the* PRODUCER *is making his arrangements with the* STAGE-MANAGER, *the* PROPERTY MAN, *the* PROMPTER *and the* ACTORS. *The flats he has set up are painted in pink and gold stripes.*]

PRODUCER [*to* PROPERTY MAN]. Just have a look, please, and see if we've got some sort of sofa or divan in the props room.

PROPERTY MAN. There's the green one, sir.

STEPDAUGHTER. No, no, green won't do! It was yellow . . . yellow flowered plush. . . . A huge thing . . . and most comfortable.

PROPERTY MAN. Well, we haven't got anything like that.

PRODUCER. It doesn't matter! Give me what there is!

STEPDAUGHTER. What do you mean, it doesn't matter? Madame Pace's famous sofa!

PRODUCER. We only want it for this run-through. Please don't interfere. [*To the* STAGE-MANAGER.] Oh, and see if we've got a shop-window . . . something rather long and narrowish is what we want.

STEPDAUGHTER. And a little table . . . the little mahogany table for the pale blue envelope!

STAGE-MANAGER [*to* PRODUCER]. There's that little one. . . . You know, the gold-painted one.

PRODUCER. That'll do fine! Shove it on!

FATHER. You need a long mirror.

STEPDAUGHTER. And the screen! I must have a screen, please. . . . Else how can I manage?

STAGE-MANAGER. Don't you worry, Miss! We've got masses of them!

PRODUCER [*to the* STEPDAUGHTER]. And some clothes-hangers and so on, h'm?

STEPDAUGHTER. Oh, yes, lots!

PRODUCER [*to the* STAGE-MANAGER]. See how many we've got and get somebody to bring them up.

STAGE-MANAGER. Right you are, sir, I'll see to it!

[*The* STAGE-MANAGER *goes off about his business and while the* PRODUCER *is talking to the* PROMPTER *and later to the* CHARACTERS *and* ACTORS, *he gets the stage hands to bring up the furniture and properties and proceeds to arrange them in what he thinks is the best sort of order.*]

PRODUCER [*to the* PROMPTER]. Now if you'll get into position while they're setting the stage. . . . Look, here's an outline of the thing. . . . Act I . . . Act II . . . [*he holds out some sheets of paper to him*]. But you'll really have to excel yourself this time.

PROMPTER. You mean, take it down in shorthand?

PRODUCER [*pleasantly surprised*]. Oh, good man! Can you do shorthand?

PROMPTER. I mayn't know much about prompting, but shorthand. . . .

PRODUCER. Better and better. [*Turning to a* STAGE-HAND.] Go and get some paper out of my room. . . . A large stack. . . . As much as you can find!

[*The* STAGE-HAND *hurries off and returns shortly with a thick stack of paper which he gives to the* PROMPTER.]

PRODUCER [*to the* PROMPTER]. Follow the scenes closely as we play them and try and fix the lines . . . or at least the most important ones. [*Then, turning to the* ACTORS.] Right, ladies and gentlemen, clear the stage, please! No, come over this side [*he waves them over to his left*] . . . and pay careful attention to what goes on.

LEADING LADY. Excuse me, but we . . .

PRODUCER [*forestalling what she is going to say*]. There won't be any improvising to do, don't you worry!

LEADING MAN. What *do* we have to do, then?

PRODUCER. Nothing. For the moment all you've got to do is to stay over there and watch what happens. You'll get your parts later. Just now we're going to have a rehearsal . . . or as much of one as we can in the circumstances! And *they'll* be doing the rehearsing [*he points to the* CHARACTERS].

FATHER [*in consternation, as if he had tumbled from the clouds into the midst of all the confusion on stage*]. We are? But, excuse me, in what way will it be a rehearsal?

PRODUCER. Well . . . a rehearsal . . . a rehearsal for *their* benefit. [*He points to the* ACTORS.]

FATHER. But if we're the characters . . .

PRODUCER. Just so, "the characters." But it's not characters that act here. It's actors who do the acting here. The characters remain there, in the script [*he points to the prompt box*]. . . . When there is a script!

FATHER. Precisely! And since there is no script and you have the good fortune to have the characters here alive before your very eyes. . . .

PRODUCER. Oh, this is wonderful! Do you want to do everything on your own? Act . . . present yourselves to the public?

FATHER. Yes, just as we are.

PRODUCER. And let me tell you you'd make a wonderful sight!

LEADING MAN. And what use should we be then?

PRODUCER. You're not going to pretend that you can act, are you? Why, it's enough to make a cat laugh. . . . [*And as a matter of fact, the* ACTORS *burst out laughing.*] There you are, you see, they're laughing at the idea! [*Then, remembering.*] But, to the point! I must tell you what your parts are. That's not so very difficult. They pretty well cast themselves. [*To the* SECOND ACTRESS.] You, the Mother. [*To the* FATHER.] We'll have to find a name for her.

FATHER. Amalia.

PRODUCER. But that's your wife's name. We can hardly call her by her real name.

FATHER. And why not, when that's her name? But, perhaps, if it has to be that lady . . . [*a slight gesture to indicate the* SECOND ACTRESS] I see *her* [*pointing to the* MOTHER] as Amalia. But do as you like. . . . [*His confusion grows.*] I don't know what to say to you. . . . I'm already beginning. . . . I don't know how to express it . . . to hear my own words ringing false . . . as if they had another sound from the one I had meant to give them. . . .

PRODUCER. Now don't you worry about that! Don't you worry about it at all! We'll think about how to get the right tone of voice. And as for the name. . . . If you want it to be Amalia, Amalia it shall be. Or we'll find some other name. Just for the present we'll refer to the characters in this way. [*To the* JUVENILE LEAD.] You, the Son. . . [*To the* LEADING LADY.] And you'll play the Stepdaughter, of course. . . .

STEPDAUGHTER [*excitedly*]. What! What did you say? That woman there. . . . Me! [*She bursts out laughing.*]

PRODUCER [*angrily*]. And what's making you laugh?

LEADING LADY [*indignantly*]. Nobody has ever dared to laugh at me before! Either you treat me with respect or I'm walking out!

STEPDAUGHTER. Oh, no, forgive me! I wasn't laughing at you.

PRODUCER [*to* STEPDAUGHTER]. You should feel yourself honored to be played by . . .

LEADING LADY [*immediately, disdainfully*]. . . . "that woman there."

STEPDAUGHTER. But my remark wasn't meant as a criticism of you . . . I was thinking about myself. . . . Because I can't see myself in you at all. I don't know how to . . . you're not a bit like me!

FATHER. Yes, that's the point I wanted to make! Look . . . all that we express. . . .

PRODUCER. What do you mean . . . *all that you express?* Do you think that this whatever-it-is that you express is something you've got inside you? Not a bit of it.

FATHER. Why . . . aren't even the things we express our own?

PRODUCER. Of course they aren't! The things that you express become material here for the actors, who give it body and form, voice and gesture. And, let me tell you, my actors have given expression to much loftier material than this. This stuff of yours is so trivial that, believe me, if it comes off on the stage, the credit will all be due to my actors.

FATHER. I don't dare to contradict you! But please believe me when I tell you that we . . . who have these bodies . . . these features. . . . Who are as you see us now. . . . We are suffering horribly. . . .

PRODUCER [*cutting in impatiently*]. . . . But the make-up will remedy all that. . . . At least as far as your faces are concerned!

FATHER. Perhaps. . . . But what about our voices? . . . What about our gestures? . . .

PRODUCER. Now, look here! You, as yourself, just cannot exist here! Here there's an actor who'll play you. And let that be an end to all this argument!

FATHER. I understand. . . . And now I think I see why our author didn't wish to put us on the stage after all. . . . He saw us as we are. . . . Alive. . . . He saw us as living beings. . . . I don't want to offend your actors. . . . Heaven forbid that I should! . . . But I think that seeing myself acted now . . . by I don't know whom . . .

LEADING MAN [*rising with some dignity and coming over, followed by a laughing group of young actresses*]. By me, if you have no objection.

FATHER [*humbly, mellifluously*]. I am deeply honored, sir. [*He bows.*] But. . . . Well. . . . I think that however much of his art this gentleman puts into absorbing me into himself. . . . However much he wills it. . . . [*He becomes confused.*]

LEADING MAN. Go on! Go on! [*The* ACTRESSES *laugh.*]

FATHER. Well, I should say that the performance he'll give. . . . Even if he makes himself up to look as much like me as he can. . . .I should say that with his figure . . . [*All the* ACTORS *laugh*] . . . it will be difficult for it to be a performance of me . . . of me as I really am. It will rather be . . . leaving aside the question of his appearance. . . . It will be how he interprets what I am . . . how he sees me. . . . If he sees me as anything at all. . . . And not as I, deep down within myself, feel myself to be. And it certainly seems to me that whoever is called upon to criticize us will have to take this into account.

PRODUCER. So you're already thinking about what the critics will say, are you? And here am I, still trying to get the play straight! The critics can say what they like. We'd be much better occupied in thinking about getting the play on. . . . If we can. [*Stepping out of the group and looking around him.*] Now, come on, let's make a start! Is everything ready? [*To the* ACTORS *and* CHARACTERS.] Come on, don't clutter up the place! Let me see how it looks! [*He comes down from the stage.*] And now, don't let's lose any more time! [*To the* STEPDAUGHTER.] Do you think the set looks all right?

STEPDAUGHTER. To be perfectly honest, I just don't recognize it at all!

PRODUCER. Good Lord, you surely didn't hope that we were going to reconstruct that room behind Madame Pace's shop here on the stage, did you? [*To the* FATHER.] You did tell me it had flowered wallpaper, didn't you?

FATHER. Yes, white.

PRODUCER. Well, it's not white—and it's got stripes on it—but it'll have to do! As for the furniture, I think we've more or less got everything we need. Bring that little table down here a bit! [*The* STAGE HANDS *do so. Then he says to the* PROPERTY MAN.] Now, will you go and get an envelope. . . . A pale blue one if you can. . . . And give it to that gentleman. [*He points to the* FATHER.]

PROPERTY MAN. The kind you put letters in?

PRODUCER and FATHER. Yes, the kind you put letters in!

PROPERTY MAN. Yes, sir! At once, sir! [*Exit.*]

PRODUCER. Now, come on! First scene—the young lady. [*The* LEADING LADY *comes forward.*] No! No! Wait a moment! I said the young lady! [*Pointing to the* STEPDAUGHTER.] You stay there and watch. . . .

STEPDAUGHTER [*immediately adding*]. . . . how I make it live!

LEADING LADY [*resentfully*]. I'll know how to make it live, don't you worry, once I get started!

PRODUCER [*with his hands to his head*]. Ladies and gentlemen, don't let's have any arguing! Please! Right! Now . . . The first scene is between the young lady and Madame Pace. Oh! [*He looks around rather helplessly and then comes back on stage.*] What about this Madame Pace?

FATHER. She's not with us, sir.

PRODUCER. And what do we do about her?

FATHER. But she's alive! She's alive too!

PRODUCER. Yes, yes! But where is she?

FATHER. If you'll just allow me to have a word with your people. . . . [*Turning to the* ACTRESSES.] I wonder if you ladies would do me the kindness of lending me your hats for a moment.

THE ACTRESSES [*a chorus . . . half-laughing, half-surprised*]. What?
Our hats?
What did he say?
Why?
Listen to the man!

PRODUCER. What are you going to do with the women's hats?

[*The* ACTORS *laugh.*]

FATHER. Oh, nothing . . . I just want to put them on these pegs for a moment. And perhaps one of you ladies would be so kind as to take off your coat, too.

THE ACTORS [*laughter and surprise in their voices*]. Their coats as well?
And after that?
The man must be mad!

ONE OR TWO OF THE ACTRESSES [*surprise and laughter in their voices*]. But why?
Only our coats?

FATHER. So that I can hang them here. . . . Just for a moment or so. . . . Please do me this favor. Will you?

THE ACTRESSES [*they take off their hats. One or two take off their coats as well, all laughing the while. They go over and hang the coats here and there on the pegs and hangers*].
And why not?
Here you are!
This really is funny!
Do we have to put them on show?

FATHER. Precisely. . . . You have to put them on show. . . . Like this!

PRODUCER. Is one allowed to know what you're up to?

FATHER. Why, yes. If we set the stage better, who knows whether she may not be attracted by the objects of her trade and perhaps appear among us. . . . [*He invites them to look towards the door at the back of the stage.*] Look! Look!

[*The door opens and* MADAME PACE *comes in and takes a few steps forward.*

She is an enormously fat old harridan of a woman, wearing a pompous carrot-colored tow wig with a red rose stuck into one side of it, in the Spanish manner. She is heavily made up and dressed with clumsy elegance in a stylish red silk dress. In one hand she carries an ostrich feather fan; the other hand is raised and a lighted cigarette is poised between two fingers. Immediately they see this apparition, the ACTORS *and the* PRODUCER *bound off the stage with howls of fear, hurling themselves down the steps into the auditorium and making as if to dash up the aisle. The* STEPDAUGHTER, *however, rushes humbly up to* MADAME PACE, *as if greeting her mistress.*]

STEPDAUGHTER [*rushing up to her*]. Here she is! Here she is!

FATHER [*beaming*]. It's Madame Pace! What did I tell you? Here she is!

PRODUCER [*his first surprise overcome, he is now indignant*]. What sort of a game do you call this?

LEADING MAN. JUVENILE LEAD. INGENUE. LEADING LADY.	*Almost at the same moment and all speaking at once.*	Hang it all, what's going on? Where did *she* spring from? They were keeping her in reserve! So it's back to the music hall and conjuring tricks, is it?

FATHER [*dominating the protesting voices*]. One moment, please! Why should you wish to destroy this prodigy of reality, which was born, which was evoked, attracted and formed by this scene itself? . . . A reality which has more right to live here than you have. . . . Because it is so very much more alive than you are. . . . Why do you want to spoil it all, just because of some niggling, vulgar convention of truth? . . . Which of you actresses will be playing the part of Madame Pace? Well, *that* woman *is* Madame Pace! Grant me at least that the actress who plays her will be less true than she is. . . . For *she* is Madame Pace in person! Look! My daughter recognized her and went up to her at once. Now, watch this scene! Just watch it! [*Hesitantly the* PRODUCER *and the* ACTORS *climb back on to the stage. But while the* ACTORS *have been protesting and the* FATHER *has been replying to them, the scene between the* STEPDAUGHTER *and* MADAME PACE *has begun. It is carried on in an undertone, very quietly—naturally in fact—in a manner that would be quite impossible on the stage. When the* ACTORS *obey the* FATHER'S *demand that they shall watch what is happening, they see that* MADAME PACE *has already put her hand under the* STEPDAUGHTER'S *chin to raise her head and is talking to her. Hearing her speak in a completely unintelligible manner they are held for a moment. But almost immediately their attention flags.*]

PRODUCER. Well?

LEADING MAN. But what's she saying?

LEADING LADY. We can't hear a thing!

JUVENILE LEAD. Speak up! Louder!

STEPDAUGHTER [*she leaves* MADAME PACE *and comes down to the group of* ACTORS. MADAME PACE *smiles—a priceless smile*]. Did you say, "Louder?" What do you mean, "Louder?" What we're talking about is scarcely the sort of thing to be shouted from the roof-tops. I was able to yell it out just now so that I could shame *him* [*pointing to the* FATHER]. . . . So that I could have my revenge! But it's quite another matter for Madame Pace. . . . It would mean prison for her.

PRODUCER. Indeed? So that's how it is, is it? But let me tell you something, my dear young lady. . . . Here in the theater you've got to make yourself heard! The way you're doing this bit at the moment even those of us who're on stage can't hear you! Just imagine what it'll be like with an audience out front. This scene's got to be got over. And anyway there's nothing to prevent you from speaking up when you're on together. . . . We shan't be here to listen to you. . . . We're only here now because it's a rehearsal. Pretend you're alone in the room behind the shop, where nobody can hear you.

[*The* STEPDAUGHTER *elegantly, charmingly—and with a mischievous smile—wags her finger two or three times in disagreement.*]

PRODUCER. What do you mean, "No?"

STEPDAUGHTER [*in a mysterious whisper*]. There's someone who'll hear us if *she* [*pointing to* MADAME PACE] speaks up.

PRODUCER [*in utter consternation*]. Do you mean to say that there's somebody else who's going to burst in on us? [*The* ACTORS *make as if to dive off the stage again.*]

FATHER. No! No! They're alluding to me. I have to be there, waiting behind the door. . . . And Madame Pace knows it. So, if you'll excuse me, I'll go. . . . So that I'm all ready to make my entrance. [*He starts off towards the back of the stage.*]

PRODUCER [*stopping him*]. No! No! Wait a moment! When you're here you have to respect the conventions of the theater! Before you get ready to go on to that bit. . . .

STEPDAUGHTER. No! Let's get on with it at once! At once! I'm dying with desire, I tell you . . . to live this scene. . . . To live it! If he wants to get on with it right away, I'm more than ready!

PRODUCER [*shouting*]. But first of all, the scene between you and her [*pointing to* MADAME PACE] has got to be got over! Do you understand?

STEPDAUGHTER. Oh, my God! She's just been telling me what *you* already know. . . . That once again my mother's work has been badly done. . . . That the dress is spoiled. . . . And that I must be patient if she is to go on helping us in our misfortune.

MADAME PACE [*stepping forward, a grand air of importance about her*]. But, yes, *señor, porque* I not want to make profit . . . to take advantàge. . . .

PRODUCER [*more than a touch of terror in his voice*]. What? Does she speak like that?

[*The* ACTORS *burst into noisy laughter.*]

STEPDAUGHTER [*laughing too*]. Yes, she speaks like that, half in English, half in Spanish. . . . It's most comical.

MADAME PACE. Ah, no, it does not to me seem good manners that you laugh of me when I . . . force myself to . . . *hablar,* as I can, English, *señor!*

PRODUCER. Indeed, no! It's very wrong of us! You speak like that! Yes, speak like that, Madame! It'll bring the house down! We couldn't ask for anything better. It'll bring a little comic relief into the crudity of the situation. Yes, you talk like that! It's absolutely wonderful!

STEPDAUGHTER. Wonderful! And why not? When you hear a certain sort of suggestion made to you in a lingo like that. . . . There's not much doubt about what your answer's going to be. . . . Because it almost seems like a joke. You feel inclined to laugh when you hear there's an "old *señor*" who wants to "amuse himself with me." An "old *señor*," eh, Madame?

MADAME PACE. Not so very old. . . . Not quite so young, yes? And if he does not please to you. . . . Well, he has . . . *prudencia.*

MOTHER [*absorbed as they are in the scene the* ACTORS *have been paying no attention to her. Now, to their amazement and consternation, she leaps up and attacks* MADAME PACE. *At her cry they jump, then hasten smilingly to restrain her, for she, meanwhile, has snatched off* MADAME PACE'S *wig and has thrown it to the ground*]. You old devil! You old witch! You murderess! Oh, my daughter!

STEPDAUGHTER [*rushing over to restrain her* MOTHER]. No, Mummy, no! Please!

FATHER [*rushing over at the same time*]. Calm yourself, my dear! Just be calm! Now . . . come and sit down again!

MOTHER. Take that woman out of my sight, then!

[*In the general excitement the* PRODUCER, *too, has rushed over and the* STEPDAUGHTER *now turns to him.*]

STEPDAUGHTER. It's impossible for my mother to remain here!

FATHER [*to the* PRODUCER]. They can't be here together. That's why, when we first came, that woman wasn't with us. If they're on at the same time the whole thing is inevitably given away in advance.

PRODUCER. It doesn't matter! It doesn't matter a bit! This is only a first run-through. . . . Just to give us a rough idea how it goes. Everything'll come in useful . . . I can sort out the bits and pieces later. . . . I'll make something out of it, even if it is all jumbled up. [*Turning to the* MOTHER *and leading her back to her chair.*] Now, please be calm, and sit down here, nice and quietly.

[*Meanwhile the* STEPDAUGHTER *has gone down center stage again. She turns to* MADAME PACE.]

STEPDAUGHTER. Go on, Madame, go on!

MADAME PACE [*offended*]. Ah, no thank you! Here I do not do nothing more with your mother present!

STEPDAUGHTER. Now, come on! Show in the "old *señor*" who wants to "amuse himself with me." [*Turning imperiously on the rest.*] Yes, this scene has got to be played. So let's get on with it! [*To* MADAME PACE.] You can go!

MADAME PACE. Ah, I am going . . . I am going. . . . Most assuredly I am going! [*Exit furiously, ramming her wig back on and glowering at the* ACTORS, *who mockingly applaud her.*]

STEPDAUGHTER [*to the* FATHER]. And now you make your entrance! There's no need for you to go out and come in again! Come over here! Pretend that you've already entered! Now, I'm standing here modestly, my eyes on the ground. Come on! Speak up! Say, "Good afternoon, Miss," in that special tone of voice . . . you know. . . . Like somebody who's just come in from the street.

PRODUCER [*by this time he is down off the stage*]. Listen to her! Are you running this rehearsal, or am I? [*To the* FATHER, *who is looking perplexed and undecided.*] Go on, do as she tells you! Go to the back of the stage. . . . Don't exit! . . . And then come forward again.

[*The* FATHER *does as he is told. He is troubled and very pale. But as he approaches from the back of the stage he smiles, already absorbed in the reality of his created life. He smiles as if the drama which is about to break upon him is as yet unknown to him. The* ACTORS *become intent on the scene which is beginning.*]

PRODUCER [*whispering quickly to the* PROMPTER, *who has taken up his position*]. Get ready to write now!

THE SCENE

FATHER [*coming forward, a new note in his voice*]. Good afternoon, Miss.

STEPDAUGHTER [*her head bowed, speaking with restrained disgust*]. Good afternoon!

FATHER [*studying her a little, looking up into her face from under the brim of her hat (which almost hides it), and perceiving that she is very young, exclaims, almost to himself, a little out of complacency, a little, too, from the fear of compromising himself in a risky adventure*]. H'm! But. . . . M'm. . . . This won't be the first time, will it? The first time that you've been here?

STEPDAUGHTER [*as before*]. No, sir.

FATHER. You've been here before? [*And since the* STEPDAUGHTER *nods in affirmation*] More than once? [*He waits a little while for her reply, resumes his study of her, again looking up into her face from under the brim of her hat, smiles and then says.*] Then . . . well . . . it shouldn't any longer be so. . . . May I take off your hat?

STEPDAUGHTER [*immediately forestalling him, unable to restrain her disgust*]. No, sir, I'll take it off myself! [*Convulsed, she hurriedly takes it off.*]

[*The* MOTHER *is on tenterhooks throughout. The* TWO CHILDREN *cling to their* MOTHER *and they, she and the* SON *form a group on the side opposite the* ACTORS, *watching the scene. The* MOTHER *follows the words and the actions of the* STEPDAUGHTER *and the* FATHER *with varying expressions of sorrow, of indignation, of anxiety and of horror; from time to time she hides her face in her hands and sobs.*]

MOTHER. Oh, my God! My God!

FATHER [*he remains for a moment as if turned to stone by this sob. Then he resumes in the same tone of voice as before*]. Here, let me take it. I'll hang it up for you. [*He takes the hat from her hands.*] But such a charming, such a dear little head really ought to have a much smarter hat than this! Would you like to come and help me choose one from among these hats of Madame's? Will you?

INGENUE [*breaking in*]. Oh, I say! Those are *our* hats!

PRODUCER [*at once, furiously*]. For God's sake, shut up! Don't try to be funny! We're doing our best to rehearse this scene, in case you weren't aware of the fact! [*Turning to* STEPDAUGHTER.] Go on from where you left off, please.

STEPDAUGHTER [*continuing*]. No thank you, sir.

FATHER. Come now, don't say no. Do say you'll accept it. . . . Just to please me. I shall be most upset if you won't. . . . Look, here are some rather nice ones. And then it would please Madame. She puts them out on show on purpose, you know.

STEPDAUGHTER. No . . . listen! I couldn't wear it.

FATHER. You're thinking perhaps about what they'll say when you come home wearing a new hat? Well now, shall I tell you what to do? Shall I tell you what to say when you get home?

STEPDAUGHTER [*quickly—she is at the end of her tether*]. No, it's not that! I couldn't wear it because I'm . . . As you see. . . . You should have noticed already . . . [*indicating her black dress*].

FATHER. That you're in mourning! Of course. . . . Oh, forgive me! Of course! Oh, I beg your pardon! Believe me. . . . I'm most profoundly sorry. . . .

STEPDAUGHTER [*summoning all her strength and forcing herself to conquer her contempt, her indignation and her nausea*]. Stop! Please don't say any more! I really ought to be thanking you. There's no need for you to feel so very sorry or upset! Please don't give another thought to what I said! I, too, you understand. . . . [*Tries hard to smile and adds.*] I really must forget that I'm dressed like this!

PRODUCER [*interrupting them; he climbs back on to the stage and turns to the* PROMPTER]. Hold it! Stop a minute! Don't write that down. Leave out that last bit. [*Turning to the* FATHER *and the* STEPDAUGHTER.] It's going very well! Very well indeed! [*Then to the* FATHER.] And then you go on as we arranged. [*To the* ACTORS.] Rather delightful, that bit where he offers her the hat, don't you think?

STEPDAUGHTER. Ah, but the best bit's coming now! Why aren't we going on?

PRODUCER. Now be patient, please! Just for a little while! [*Turning to the* ACTORS.] Of course it'll have to be treated rather lightly. . . .

LEADING MAN. . . . M'm . . . and put over slickly. . . .

LEADING LADY. Of course! There's nothing difficult about it at all. [*To the* LEADING MAN.] Shall we try it now?

LEADING MAN. As far as I'm . . . I'll go and get ready for my entrance. [*Exit to take up his position outside the door back.*]

PRODUCER [*to the* LEADING LADY]. Now, look. . . . The scene between you and Madame Pace is finished. I'll get down to writing it up properly afterwards. You're standing. . . . Where are you going?

LEADING LADY. Just a moment! I want to put my hat back on. . . . [*Goes over, takes her hat down and puts it on.*]

PRODUCER. Good! Now you stand here. With your head bowed down a bit.

STEPDAUGHTER [*amused*]. But she's not dressed in black!

LEADING LADY. I *shall* be dressed in black. . . . And much more becomingly than you are!

PRODUCER [*to the* STEPDAUGHTER]. Shut up . . . please! And watch! You'll learn something. [*Claps his hands.*] Now come on! Let's get going! Entrance! [*He goes down from the stage again to see how it looks from out front. The door back opens and the* LEADING MAN *steps forward. He has the lively, raffish, self-possessed air of an elderly gallant. The playing of this scene by the* ACTORS *will appear from the very first words as something completely different from what was played before, without its having, even in the slightest degree, the air of a parody. It should appear rather as if the scene has been touched up. Quite naturally the* FATHER *and the* STEPDAUGHTER, *not being able to recognize themselves at all in the* LEADING LADY *and* LEADING MAN, *yet hearing them deliver the very words they used, react in a variety of ways, now with a gesture, now with a smile, with open protest even, to the impression they receive. They are surprised, lost in wonder, in suffering . . . as we shall see. The* PROMPTER'S *voice is clearly heard throughout the scene.*]

LEADING MAN. Good afternoon, Miss!

FATHER [*immediately, unable to restrain himself*]. No! No! [*And the* STEPDAUGHTER, *seeing the* LEADING MAN *enter in this way, bursts out laughing.*]

PRODUCER [*infuriated*]. Shut up! And once and for all . . . Stop that laughing! We shan't get anywhere if we go on like this!

STEPDAUGHTER [*moving away from the proscenium*]. Forgive me . . . but I couldn't help laughing! This lady [*pointing to the* LEADING LADY] stands just where you put her, without budging an inch . . . But if she's meant to be me. . . . I can assure you that if I heard anybody saying "Good afternoon" to me in that way and in that tone of voice I'd burst out laughing. . . . So I had to, you see.

FATHER [*coming forward a little, too*]. Yes, that's it exactly. . . . His manner. . . . The tone of voice. . . .

PRODUCER. To hell with your manner and your tone of voice! Just stand to one side, if you don't mind, and let me get a look at this rehearsal.

LEADING MAN [*coming forward*]. Now if I've got to play an old fellow who's coming into a house of rather doubtful character. . . .

PRODUCER. Oh, don't take any notice of him! Now, *please!* Start again, please! It was going very nicely. [*There is a pause—he is clearly waiting for the* LEADING MAN *to begin again.*] Well?

LEADING MAN. Good afternoon, Miss.

LEADING LADY. Good afternoon!

LEADING MAN [*repeating the* FATHER'S *move—that is, looking up into the* LEADING LADY'S *face from under the brim of her hat; but then expressing very clearly first his satisfaction and then his fear*]. M'm . . . this won't be the first time, I hope. . . .

FATHER [*unable to resist the temptation to correct him*]. Not "hope"—"will it?", "will it?"

PRODUCER. You say "will it?" . . . It's a question.

LEADING MAN [*pointing to the* PROMPTER]. I'm sure he said "hope."

PRODUCER. Well, it's all one! "Hope" or whatever it was! Go on, please! Go on. . . . Oh, there was one thing . . . I think perhaps it ought not to be quite so heavy. . . . Hold on, I'll show you what I mean. Watch me. . . . [*Comes back on to the stage. Then, making his entrance, he proceeds to play the part.*] Good afternoon, Miss.

LEADING LADY. Good afternoon. . . .

PRODUCER. M'm. . . . [*Turning to the* LEADING MAN *to impress on him the way he has looked up at the* LEADING LADY *from under the brim of her hat.*] Surprise, fear and satisfaction. [*Then turning back to the* LEADING LADY.] It won't be the first time, will it, that you've been here? [*Turning again to the* LEADING MAN *inquiringly.*] Is that clear? [*To the* LEADING LADY.] And then you say, "No, sir." [*To the* LEADING MAN.] There you are. . . . It wants to be a little more . . . what shall I say? . . . A little more *flexible*. A little more *souple!* [*He goes down from the stage again.*]

LEADING LADY. No, sir. . . .

LEADING MAN. You've been here before? More than once?

PRODUCER. Wait a minute! You must let her [*pointing to the* LEADING LADY] get her nod in first. You've been here before? [*The* LEADING LADY *lifts her head a little, closing her eyes painfully as if in disgust and then when the* PRODUCER *says* Down, *nods twice.*]

STEPDAUGHTER [*unable to restrain herself*]. Oh, my God! [*And immediately she puts her hand over her mouth to stifle her laughter.*]

PRODUCER [*turning*]. What's the matter?

STEPDAUGHTER [*immediately*]. Nothing! Nothing!

PRODUCER [*to the* LEADING MAN]. It's your cue. . . . Carry straight on.

LEADING MAN. More than once? Well then . . . Come along. . . . May I take off your hat?

[*The* LEADING MAN *says this last line in such a tone of voice and accompanies it with such a gesture that the* STEPDAUGHTER, *who has remained with her hands over her mouth, can no longer restrain herself. She tries desperately to prevent herself from laughing but a noisy burst of laughter comes irresistibly through her fingers.*]

LEADING LADY [*turning indignantly*]. I'm not going to stand here and be made a fool of by that woman!

LEADING MAN. And neither am I. Let's pack the whole thing in.

PRODUCER [*shouting at the* STEPDAUGHTER]. Once and for all, will you shut up!

STEPDAUGHTER. Yes. . . . Forgive me, please! . . . Forgive me!

PRODUCER. The trouble with you is that you've got no manners! You go too far!

FATHER [*trying to intervene*]. Yes, sir, you're quite right! Quite right! But you must forgive her. . . .

PRODUCER [*climbing back on to the stage*]. What do you want me to forgive? It's absolutely disgusting the way she's behaving!

FATHER. Yes. . . . But . . . Oh, believe me . . . Believe me, it has such a strange effect. . . .

PRODUCER. Strange! How do you mean, "Strange"? What's so strange about it?

FATHER. You see, sir, I admire . . . I admire your actors. . . . That gentleman there [*pointing to the* LEADING MAN] and that lady [*pointing to the* LEADING LADY] . . . But . . . Well . . . The truth is . . . They're certainly not us!

PRODUCER. I should hope not! How do you expect them to be *you* if they're actors?

FATHER. Just so, actors. And they play our parts well, both of them. But when they act . . . To us they seem to be doing something quite different. They want to be the same . . . And all the time they just aren't.

PRODUCER. But how aren't they the same? What are they then?

FATHER. Something that becomes theirs . . . And no longer ours.

PRODUCER. But that's inevitable! I've told you that already.

FATHER. Yes, I understand . . . I understand that. . . .

PRODUCER. Well then, let's hear no more on the subject! [*Turning to the* ACTORS.] We'll run through it later by ourselves in the usual way. I've always had a strong aversion to holding rehearsals with the author present. He's never satisfied! [*Turning to the* FATHER *and the* STEPDAUGHTER.] Now, come on, let's get on with it! And let's see if we can have no more laughing! [*To the* STEPDAUGHTER.]

STEPDAUGHTER. Oh, I shan't laugh any more! I promise you! My big bit's coming now. . . . Just you wait and see!

PRODUCER. Well, then. . . . When you say, "Please don't give another thought to what I said! I, too, you understand. . . ." [*Turning to the* FATHER.] You come in at once with, "I understand! I understand!" and immediately ask . . .

STEPDAUGHTER [*interrupting him*]. What? What does he ask?

PRODUCER. . . . why you're in mourning.

STEPDAUGHTER. Oh, no! That's not it at all! Listen! When I told him that I mustn't think about my being in mourning, do you know what his answer was? "Well, then, let's take this little frock off at once, shall we?"

PRODUCER. That would be wonderful! Wonderful! That *would* bring the house down!

STEPDAUGHTER. But it's the truth!

PRODUCER. But what's the truth got to do with it? Acting's what *we're* here for! Truth's all very fine . . . But only up to a point.

STEPDAUGHTER. And what do you want then?

PRODUCER. You'll see! You'll see. Leave everything to me.

STEPDAUGHTER. No, I won't! What you'd like to do, no doubt, is to concoct a romantic, sentimental little affair out of my disgust, out of all the reasons, each more cruel, each viler than the other, why I am this sort of woman, why I am what I am! An affair with him! He asks me why I'm in mourning and I reply with tears in my eyes that my father died only two months ago. No! No! He must say what he said then, "Well, then, let's take this little frock off at once, shall we?" And I . . . my heart still grieving for my father's death. . . . I went behind there . . . Do you understand? . . . There, behind that screen! And then, my fingers trembling with shame and disgust, I took off my frock, undid my brassière. . . .

PRODUCER [*running his hands through his hair*]. For God's sake! What on earth are you saying, girl?

STEPDAUGHTER [*crying out excitedly*]. The truth! The truth!

PRODUCER. Yes, it probably is the truth! I'm not denying it! And I understand . . . I fully appreciate all your horror. But you must realize that we simply can't put this kind of thing on the stage.

STEPDAUGHTER. Oh, you can't, can't you? If that's how things are, thanks very much! I'm going!

PRODUCER. No! No! Look here! . . .

STEPDAUGHTER. I'm going! I'm not stopping here! You worked it all out together, didn't you? . . . The pair of you. . . . You and him. . . . When you were in there. . . . You worked out what was going to be possible on the stage. Oh, thanks very much! I understand! He wants to jump to the bit where he presents his spiritual torments! [*This is said harshly.*] But I want to present my own drama! *Mine! Mine!*

PRODUCER [*his shoulders shaking with annoyance*]. Ah! There we have it! *Your* drama! Look here . . . you'll have to forgive me for telling you this . . . but there isn't only your part to be considered! Each of the others has his drama, too. [*He points to the* FATHER.] He has his and your Mother has hers. You can't have one character coming along like this, becoming too prominent, invading the stage in and out of season and overshadowing all the rest. All the characters must be contained within one harmonious picture, and presenting only what it is proper to present. I'm very well aware that everyone carries a complete life within himself and that he wants to put it before the whole world. But it's here that we run into difficulties: how are we to bring out only just so much as is absolutely necessary? . . . And at the same time, of course, to take into account all the other characters. . . . And yet in that small fragment we have to be able to hint at all the rest of the secret life of that character. Ah, it would be all very pleasant if each character could have a nice little monologue. . . . Or without making any bones about it, give a lecture, in which he could tell his audience what's bubbling and boiling away inside him. [*His tone is good-humored, conciliatory.*] You must restrain yourself. And believe me, it's in your own interest, too. Because all this fury . . . this exasperation and this disgust . . . They make a bad impression. Especially when . . . And pardon me for mentioning this. . . . You yourself have confessed that you'd had other men there at Madame Pace's before him. . . . And more than once!

STEPDAUGHTER [*bowing her head. She pauses a moment in recollection and then, a deeper note in her voice*]. That is true! But you must remember that those other men mean *him* for me, just as much as he himself does!

PRODUCER [*uncomprehending*]. What? The other men mean *him?* What do you mean?

STEPDAUGHTER. Isn't it true that in the case of someone who's gone wrong, the person who was responsible for the first fault is responsible for all the faults which follow? And in my case, he is responsible. . . . Has been ever since before I was born. Look at him, and see if it isn't true!

PRODUCER. Very well, then! And does this terrible weight of remorse that is resting on his spirit seem so slight a thing to you? Give him the chance of acting it!

STEPDAUGHTER. How? How can he act all his "noble" remorse, all his "moral" torments, if you want to spare him all the horror of one day finding in his arms. . . . After he had asked her to take off her frock . . . her grief still undulled by time. . . . The horror of finding in his arms that child. . . . A woman now, and a fallen woman already. . . . That child whom he used to go and watch as she came out of school? [*She says these last words in a voice trembling with emotion. The* MOTHER, *hearing her talk like this, is overcome by distress which expresses itself at first in stifled sobs. Finally she breaks out into a fit of bitter crying. Everyone is deeply moved. There is a long pause.*]

STEPDAUGHTER [*gravely and resolutely, as soon as the* MOTHER *shows signs of becoming a little quieter*]. At the moment we are here, unknown as yet by the public. Tomorrow you will present us as you wish. . . . Making up your play in your own way. But would you really like to see our drama? To see it flash into life as it did in reality?

PRODUCER. Why, of course! I couldn't ask for anything better, so that from now on I can use as much as possible of it.

STEPDAUGHTER. Well, then, ask my Mother to leave us.

MOTHER [*rising, her quiet weeping changed to a sharp cry*]. No! No! Don't you allow them to do it! Don't allow them to do it!

PRODUCER. But it's only so that I can see how it goes.

MOTHER. I can't bear it! I can't bear it!

PRODUCER. But since it's already happened, I don't understand!

MOTHER. No, it's happening now! It happens all the time! My torment is no pretense, sir. I am alive and I am present always. . . . At every moment of my torment. . . . A torment which is for ever renewing itself. Always alive and always present. But those two children there. . . . Have you heard them say a single word? They can no longer speak! They cling to me still. . . . In order to keep my torment living and present! But for themselves they no longer exist! They no longer exist! And she [*pointing to the* STEPDAUGHTER] . . . She has run away. . . . Run away from me and is lost. . . . Lost! . . . And if I see her here before me it is for this reason and for this reason alone. . . . To renew at all times. . . . Forever. . . . To bring before me again, present and living, the anguish that I have suffered on her account too.

FATHER [*solemnly*]. The eternal moment, as I told you, sir. She [*he points to the* STEPDAUGHTER] . . . She is here in order to fix me. . . . To hold me suspended throughout all eternity. . . . In the pillory of that one fleeting shameful moment in my life. She cannot renounce her rôle. . . . And you, sir, cannot really spare me my agony.

PRODUCER. Quite so, but I didn't say that I wouldn't present it. As a matter of fact it'll form the basis of the first act. . . . Up to the point where she surprises you [*pointing to the* MOTHER].

FATHER. That is right. Because it is my sentence. All our passion. . . . All our suffering. . . . Which must culminate in *her* cry [*pointing to the* MOTHER].

STEPDAUGHTER. I can still hear it ringing in my ears! That cry sent me mad! You can play me just as you like. . . . It doesn't matter. Dressed, if you like, provided that I can have my arms bare at least. . . . Just my arms bare. . . . Because, you see, standing there . . . [*She goes up to the* FATHER *and rests her head on his chest.*] With my head resting on his chest like this . . . and with my arms round his neck . . . I could see a vein throbbing away in my arm. And then . . . Just as if that pulsing vein alone gave me a sense of horror . . . I shut my eyes tight and buried my head in his chest. [*Turning towards the* MOTHER.] Scream, Mummy! Scream! [*She buries her head in the* FATHER'S *chest and, raising her shoulders as if in order not to hear the cry, adds in a voice stifled with torment.*] Scream, as you screamed then!

MOTHER [*rushing upon them to separate them*]. No! No! She's my daughter! [*And having torn her daughter away.*] You brute! You brute! She's my daughter! Can't you see that she's my daughter?

PRODUCER [*retreating at the cry right up to the footlights, amid the general dismay of the* ACTORS]. Excellent! Excellent! And then . . . Curtain! Curtain!

FATHER [*rushing over to him convulsively*]. Yes, because that's how it really happened!

PRODUCER [*quite convinced, admiration in his voice*]. Oh, yes, we must have the curtain there. . . . That cry and then . . . Curtain! Curtain!

[*At the repeated shouts of the* PRODUCER *the* STAGE-HAND *on the curtain lets it down, leaving the* PRODUCER *and the* FATHER *between it and the footlights.*]

PRODUCER [*looking up, his arms raised*]. Oh, the damned fool! I say, "Curtain" . . . Meaning that I want the act to end there. . . . And he really does go and bring the curtain down. [*To the* FATHER, *lifting up a corner of the curtain.*] Oh, yes! That's absolutely wonderful! Very good indeed! That'll get them! There's no *if or but* about it. . . . That line and then . . . *Curtain!* We've got something in that first act . . . or I'm a Dutchman! [*Disappears through the curtain with the* FATHER.]

When the curtain goes up again the audience sees that the STAGE-HANDS *have dismantled the previous set and put on in its place a small garden fountain. On one side of the stage the* ACTORS *are sitting in a row, and on the other side, the* CHARACTERS. *The* PRODUCER *is standing in a meditative attitude in the middle of the stage with his hand clenched over his mouth. There is a brief pause; then:*

PRODUCER [*with a shrug of his shoulders*]. Oh, well! . . . Let's get on with Act II! Now if you'll only leave it all to me, as we agreed, everything'll sort itself out.

STEPDAUGHTER. This is where we make our entry into his house . . . [*Pointing to the* FATHER.] In spite of him! [*Pointing to the* SON.]

PRODUCER [*out of patience*]. Yes, yes! But leave it to me, I tell you!

STEPDAUGHTER. Well. . . . So long as it's made quite clear that it was against his wishes.

MOTHER [*from the corner, shaking her head*]. For all the good that's come of it. . . .

STEPDAUGHTER [*turning to her quickly*]. That doesn't matter! The more harm that it's done us, the more remorse for him!

PRODUCER [*impatiently*]. I understand all that! I'll take it all into account! Don't you worry about it!

MOTHER [*a supplicant note in her voice*]. But I do beg you, sir . . . To set my conscience at rest. . . . To make it quite plain that I tried in every way I could to . . .

STEPDAUGHTER [*interrupting contemptuously and continuing her* MOTHER'S *speech*]. . . . to pacify me, to persuade me not to get my own back. . . . [*To the* PRODUCER.] Go on . . . do what she asks you! Give her that satisfaction. . . . Because she's quite right, you know! I'm enjoying myself no end, because . . . Well, just look. . . . The meeker she is, the more she tries to wriggle her way into his heart, the more he holds himself aloof, the more distant he becomes. I can't think why she bothers!

PRODUCER. Are we going to get started on the second act or are we not?

STEPDAUGHTER. I won't say another word! But, you know, it won't be possible to play it all in the garden, as you suggested.

PRODUCER. Why not?

STEPDAUGHTER. Because he [*pointing to the* SON *again*] shuts himself up in his room all the time. . . . Holding himself aloof. . . . And, what's more, there's all the boy's part. . . . Poor bewildered little devil. . . . As I told you, all that takes place indoors.

PRODUCER. I know all about that! On the other hand you do understand that we can hardly stick up notices telling the audience what the scene is. . . . *Or* change the set three or four times in one act.

LEADING MAN. They used to in the good old days.

PRODUCER. Oh, yes. . . . When the intelligence of the audience was about up to the level of that little girl's there. . . .

LEADING LADY. And it does make it easier to get the sense of illusion.

FATHER [*immediately, rising*]. Illusion, did you say? For Heaven's sake, please don't use the word illusion! Please don't use that word. . . . It's a particularly cruel one for us!

PRODUCER [*astounded*]. And why's that?

FATHER. It's cruel! Cruel! You should have known that!

PRODUCER. What ought we to say then? We were referring to the illusion that we have to create on this stage . . . for the audience. . . .

LEADING MAN. . . . with our acting. . . .

PRODUCER. . . . the illusion of a reality!

FATHER. I understand, sir. But you . . . Perhaps you can't understand us. Forgive me! Because . . . you see . . . for you and for your actors, all this is only . . . and quite rightly so. . . . All this is only a game.

LEADING LADY [*indignantly interrupting him*]. What do you mean, a game? We're not children! We're serious actors!

FATHER. I don't deny it! And in fact, in using the term, I was referring to your art which must, as this gentleman has said, create a perfect illusion of reality.

PRODUCER. Precisely!

FATHER. Now just consider the fact that we [*pointing quickly to himself and to the other* FIVE CHARACTERS] as ourselves, have no other reality outside this illusion!

PRODUCER [*in utter astonishment, looking round at his actors who show the same bewildered amazement*]. And what does all that mean?

FATHER [*the ghost of a smile on his face. There is a brief pause while he looks at them all*]. As I said. . . . What other reality should we have? What for you is an illusion that you have to create, for us, on the other hand, is our sole reality. The only reality we know. [*There is a short pause. Then he takes a step or two towards the* PRODUCER *and adds.*] But it's not only true in our case, you know. Just think it over. [*He looks into his eyes.*] Can you tell me who you are? [*And he stands there pointing his index finger at him.*]

PRODUCER [*disturbed, a half-smile on his lips*]. What? Who am I? I'm myself!

FATHER. And suppose I were to tell you that that wasn't true? Suppose I told you that you were me? . . .

PRODUCER. I should say that you were mad! [*The* ACTORS *laugh.*]

FATHER. You're quite right to laugh, because here everything's a game. [*To the* PRODUCER.] And you can object, therefore, that it's only in fun that that gentleman [*pointing to the* LEADING MAN] who is *himself* must be *me* who, on the contrary, am myself. . . . That is, *the person you see here.* There, you see. I've caught you in a trap! [*The* ACTORS *laugh again.*]

PRODUCER [*annoyed*]. But you said all this not ten minutes ago! Do we have to go over all that again?

FATHER. No. As a matter of fact that wasn't what I intended. I should like to invite you to abandon this game. . . . [*Looking at the* LEADING LADY *as if to forestall what she will say.*] Your art! Your art! . . . The game that it is customary for you and your actors to play here in this theater. And once again I ask you in all seriousness. . . . Who are you?

PRODUCER [*turning to the* ACTORS *in utter amazement, an amazement not unmixed with irritation*]. What a cheek the fellow has! A man who calls himself a character comes here and asks me who I am!

FATHER [*with dignity, but in no way haughtily*]. A character, sir, may always ask a man who he is. Because a character has a life which is truly his, marked with his own special characteristics. . . . And as a result he is always somebody! Whilst a man. . . . And I'm not speaking of you personally at the moment. . . . Man in general . . . Can quite well be nobody.

PRODUCER. That as may be! But you're asking *me* these questions. Me, do you understand? The Producer! The boss!

FATHER [*softly, with gentle humility*]. But only in order to know if you, you as you really are now, are seeing yourself as, for instance, after all the time that has gone by, you see yourself as you were at some point in the past. . . . With all the illusions that you had then . . . with everything . . . all the things you had deep down inside you . . . everything that made up your external world . . . everything as it appeared to you then . . . and as it *was*, as it was in reality for you then! Well . . . thinking back on those illusions which you no longer have . . . on all those things that no longer *seem* to be what they *were* once upon a time . . . don't you feel that . . . I won't say these boards. . . . No! . . . That the very earth itself is slipping away from under your feet, when you reflect that in the same way this *you* that you now feel yourself to be . . . all your reality as it is today . . . is destined to seem an illusion tomorrow?

PRODUCER [*not having understood much of all this, and somewhat taken aback by this specious argument*]. Well? And where does all this get us, anyway?

FATHER. Nowhere. I only wanted to make you see that if we [*again pointing to himself and to the other* CHARACTERS] have no reality outside the world of illusion, it would be as well if you mistrusted your own reality. . . . The reality that you breathe and touch today. . . . Because like the reality of yesterday, it is fated to reveal itself as a mere illusion tomorrow.

PRODUCER [*deciding to make fun of him*]. Oh, excellent! And so you'd say that you and this play of yours that you've been putting on for my benefit are more real than I am?

FATHER [*with the utmost seriousness*]. Oh, without a doubt.

PRODUCER. Really?

FATHER. I thought that you'd understood that right from the very beginning.

PRODUCER. More real than I am?

FATHER. If your reality can change from one day to the next. . . .

PRODUCER. But everybody knows that it can change like that! It's always changing. . . . Just like everybody else's!

FATHER [*with a cry*]. No, ours doesn't change! You see. . . . That's the difference between us! Our reality doesn't change. . . . It can't change. . . . It can never be in any way different from what it is. . . . Because it is already fixed. . . . Just as it is. . . . For ever! For ever it is *this* reality. . . . It's terrible! . . . This immutable reality. . . . It should make you shudder to come near us!

PRODUCER [*quickly, suddenly struck by an idea. He moves over and stands squarely in front of him*]. I should like to know, however, when anyone ever saw a character step out of his part and begin a long dissertation on it like the one you've just been making. . . . Expounding it. . . . Explaining it. . . . Can you tell me? . . . I've never seen it happen before!

FATHER. You have never seen it happen before because authors usually hide the details of their work of creation. Once the characters are alive. . . . Once they are standing truly alive before their author. . . . He does nothing but follow the words and gestures that they suggest to him. . . . And he must want them to be what they themselves want to be. For woe betide him if he doesn't do what they wish him to do! When a character is born he immediately acquires such an independence. . . . Even of his own author. . . . That everyone can imagine him in a whole host of situations in which his author never thought of placing him. . . . They can even imagine his acquiring, sometimes, a significance that the author never dreamed of giving him.

PRODUCER. Yes. . . . I know all that!

FATHER. Well, then, why are you so astonished at seeing us? Just imagine what a misfortune it is for a character to be born alive. . . . Created by the imagination of an author who afterwards sought to deny him life. . . . Now tell me whether a character who has been left unrealized in this way. . . . Living, yet without a life. . . . Whether this character hasn't the right to do what we are doing now. . . . Here and now. . . . For your benefit? . . . After we had spent . . . Oh, such ages, believe me! . . . Doing it for his benefit . . . Trying to persuade him, trying to urge him to realize us. . . . First of all I would present myself to him. . . . Then she would . . . [*pointing to the* STEPDAUGHTER]. . . . And then her poor Mother. . . .

STEPDAUGHTER [*coming forward as if in a trance*]. Yes, what he says is true. . . . I would go and tempt him. . . . There, in his gloomy study. . . . Just at twilight. . . . He would be sitting there, sunk in an armchair. . . . Not bothering to stir himself and switch on the light. . . . Content to let the room get darker and darker. . . . Until the whole room was filled with a darkness that was alive with our presence. . . . We were there to tempt him. . . . [*And then, as if she saw herself as still in that study and irritated by the presence of all those actors.*] Oh, go away. . . . All of you! Leave us alone! Mummy . . . and her son. . . . I and the little girl. . . . The boy by himself. . . . Always by himself. . . . Then he and I together [*a faint gesture in the direction of the* FATHER]. And then. . . . By myself. . . . By myself . . . alone in that darkness [*a sudden turn round as if she wished to seize and fix the vision that she has of herself, the living vision of herself that she sees shining in the darkness*]. Yes, my life! Ah, what scenes, what wonderful scenes we suggested to him! And I . . . I tempted him more than any of them. . . .

FATHER. Indeed you did! And it may well be that it's all your fault that he wouldn't give us the life we asked for. . . . You were too persistent. . . . Too impudent. . . . You exaggerated too much. . . .

STEPDAUGHTER. What? When it was he who wanted me to be what I am? [*She goes up to the* PRODUCER *and says confidentially.*] I think it's much more likely that he refused because he felt depressed . . . or because of his contempt for the theater. . . . Or at least, for the present-day theater with all its pandering to the box-office. . . .

PRODUCER. Let's get on! Let's get on, for God's sake! Let's have some action!

STEPDAUGHTER. It looks to me as if we've got too much action for you already. . . . Just staging our entry into his house [*pointing to the* FATHER]. You yourself said that you couldn't stick up notices or be changing the set every five minutes.

PRODUCER. And neither can we! Of course we can't! What we've got to do is to combine and group all the action into one continuous well-knit scene. . . . Not the sort of thing that you want. . . . With, first of all, your younger brother coming home from school and wandering about the house like some lost soul. . . . Hiding behind doors and brooding on a plan that . . . What did you say it does to him?

STEPDAUGHTER. Dries him up. . . . Shrivels him up completely.

PRODUCER. M'm! Well, as you said. . . . And all the time you can see it more and more clearly in his eyes. . . . Wasn't that what you said?

STEPDAUGHTER. Yes. . . . Just look at him! [*Pointing to where he is standing by his* MOTHER.]

PRODUCER. And then, at the same time, you want the child to be playing in the garden, blissfully unaware of everything. The boy in the house, the little girl in the garden. . . . I ask you!

STEPDAUGHTER. Yes . . . happily playing in the sun! That is the only pleasure that I have. . . . Her happiness. . . . All the joy that she gets from playing in the garden. . . . After the wretchedness and the squalor of that horrible room where we all four slept together. . . . And she had to sleep with me. . . . Just think of it. . . . My vile contaminated body next to hers! . . . With her holding me tight in her loving, innocent, little arms! She only had to get a glimpse of me in the garden and she'd run up to me and take me by the hand. She wasn't interested in the big flowers . . . she'd run about looking for the . . . "weeny" ones. . . . So that she could point them out to me. . . . And she'd be so happy. . . . So excited. . . .

[*As she says this she is torn by the memory of it all and gives a long, despairing cry, dropping her head on to her hands which are lying loosely on the little table in front of her. At the sight of her emotion everyone is deeply moved. The* PRODUCER *goes up to her almost paternally and says comfortingly.*]

PRODUCER. We'll have the garden in. . . . Don't you worry. . . . We'll have the garden scene in. . . . Just you wait and see. . . . You'll be quite satisfied with how I arrange it. . . . We'll play everything in the garden. [*Calling a* STAGE-HAND.] Hey [*his name*]! Let me have something in the shape of a tree or two. . . . A couple of not-too-large cypresses in front of this fountain! [*Two small cypress trees descend from the flies. The* FOREMAN *dashes up and fixes them with struts and nails.*]

PRODUCER [*to the* STEPDAUGHTER]. That'll do. . . . For the moment anyway. . . . It'll give us a rough idea. [*Calls to the* STAGE-HAND *again.*] Oh [*his name*], let me have something for a sky, will you?

STAGE-HAND [*up aloft*]. Eh?

PRODUCER. Something for a sky! A backcloth to go behind the fountain! [*And a white backcloth descends from the flies.*]

PRODUCER. Not white! I said I wanted a sky! Oh, well, it doesn't matter. . . . Leave it! Leave it! . . . I'll fix it myself. . . . [*Calls.*] Hey! . . . You there on the lights! . . . Everything off. . . . And let me have the moonlight blues on! . . . Blues in the batten! . . . A couple of blue spots on the backcloth! . . . Yes, that's it! That's just right!

[*There is now a mysterious moonlit effect about the scene, and the* ACTORS *are prompted to move about and to speak as they would if they were indeed walking in a moonlit garden.*]

PRODUCER [*to the* STEPDAUGHTER]. There, do you see? Now the Boy, instead of hiding behind doors inside the house, can move about the garden and hide behind these trees. But, you know, it'll be rather difficult to find a little girl to play that scene with you. . . . The one where she shows you the flowers. [*Turning to the* BOY.] Now come down here a bit!

Let's see how it works out! [*Then, since the* BOY *doesn't move.*] Come on! Come on! [*He drags him forward and tries to make him hold his head up. But after every attempt down it falls again.*] Good God, here's a fine how d'ye do. . . . There's something queer about this boy. . . . What's the matter with him? . . . My God, he'll have to say *something*. . . . [*He goes up to him, puts a hand on his shoulder and places him behind one of the trees.*] Now. . . . Forward a little! . . . Let me see you! . . . M'm! . . . Now hide yourself. . . . That's it! Now try popping your head out a bit . . . Take a look round. . . . [*He goes to one side to study the effect and the* BOY *does what he has been told to do. The* ACTORS *look on, deeply affected and quite dismayed.*] That's excellent! . . . Yes, excellent! [*Turning again to the* STEPDAUGHTER.] Suppose the little girl were to catch sight of him there as he was looking out, and run over to him. . . . Wouldn't that drag a word or two out of him?

STEPDAUGHTER [*rising*]. It's no use your hoping that he'll speak. . . . At least not so long as *he's* here [*pointing to the* SON]. If you want him to speak, you'll have to send *him* away first.

SON [*going resolutely towards the steps down into the auditorium*]. Willingly! I'm only too happy to oblige! Nothing could possibly suit me better!

PRODUCER [*immediately catching hold of him*]. Hey! Oh no you don't! Where are you going? You hang on a minute!

[*The* MOTHER *rises in dismay, filled with anguish at the thought that he really is going away. She instinctively raises her arms to prevent him from going, without, however, moving from where she is standing.*]

SON [*he has reached the footlights*]. I tell you . . . There's absolutely nothing for me to do here! Let me go, please! Let me go! [*This to the* PRODUCER.]

PRODUCER. What do you mean . . . There's nothing for you to do?

STEPDAUGHTER [*placidly, ironically*]. Don't bother to hold him back! He won't go away!

FATHER. He has to play that terrible scene with his Mother in the garden.

SON [*immediately, fiercely, resolutely*]. I'm not playing anything! I've said that all along! [*To the* PRODUCER.] Let me go!

STEPDAUGHTER [*running over, then addressing the* PRODUCER]. Do you mind? [*She gets him to lower the hand with which he has been restraining the* SON.] Let him go! [*Then turning to the* SON, *as soon as the* PRODUCER *has dropped his arm.*] Well, go on. . . . Leave us!

[*The* SON *stands where he is, still straining in the direction of the steps, but, as if held back by some mysterious force, he cannot go down them. Then, amidst the utter dismay and anxious bewilderment of the* ACTORS, *he wanders slowly along the length of the footlights in the direction of the other flight of steps. Once there, he again finds himself unable to descend, much as he would wish to. The* STEPDAUGHTER *has watched his progress in-*

tently, her eyes challenging, defiant. Now she bursts out laughing.]

STEPDAUGHTER. He can't, you see! He can't leave us! He must remain here. . . . He has no choice but to remain with us! He's chained to us. . . . Irrevocably! But if I . . . Who really do run away when what is inevitable happens. . . . And I run away because of my hatred for him. . . . I run away just because I can no longer bear the sight of him. . . . Well, if I can still stay here. . . . If I can still put up with his company and with having to have him here before my eyes. . . . Do you think it's likely that he can run away? Why, he has to stay here with that precious father of his. . . . With his mother. . . . Because now she has no other children but him. . . . [*Turning to her* MOTHER.] Come on, Mummy! Come on. . . . [*Turning to the* PRODUCER *and pointing to the* MOTHER.] There. . . . You see. . . . She'd got up to prevent him from going. . . . [*To her* MOTHER, *as if willing her actions by some magic power.*] Come on! Come on! [*Then to the* PRODUCER.] You can imagine just how reluctant she is to give this proof of her affection in front of your actors. But so great is her desire to be with him that . . . There! . . . You see? . . . She's willing to live out again her scene with him! [*And as a matter of fact the* MOTHER *has gone up to her* SON, *and scarcely has the* STEPDAUGHTER *finished speaking before she makes a gesture to indicate her agreement.*]

SON [*immediately*]. No! No! You're not going to drag me into this! If I can't get away, I shall stay here! But I repeat that I'm not going to do any acting at all!

FATHER [*trembling with excitement, to the* PRODUCER]. You can force him to act!

SON. Nobody can force me!

FATHER. I can and I will!

STEPDAUGHTER. Wait! Wait! First of all the little girl has to go to the fountain. . . . [*Goes over to the* LITTLE GIRL. *She drops on to her knees in front of her and takes her face in her hands.*] Poor little darling. . . . You're looking so bewildered. . . . With those beautiful big eyes. . . . You must be wondering just where you are. We're on a stage, dear! What's a stage? Well . . . It's a place where you play at being serious. They put on plays here. And now *we're* putting a play on. Really and truly! Even you. . . . [*Embracing her, clasping her to her breast and rocking her for a moment or so.*] Oh, you little darling. . . . My dear little darling, what a terrible play for you. . . . What a horrible end they've thought out for you! The garden, the fountain. . . . Yes, it's a make-believe fountain. . . . The pity is, darling, that everything's make-believe here. . . . But perhaps you like a make-believe fountain better than a real one. . . . So that you can play in it. . . . M'm? No. . . . It'll be a game for the others. . . . Not for you unfortunately . . . Because you're real. . . . And you really play by a real fountain. . . . A lovely big green one, with masses of bamboo palms casting shadows. . . . Looking at your reflection in the water. . . . And lots and lots of little baby ducklings swimming about in it, breaking the shadow into a thousand little ripples. You try to take hold of one of the ducklings. . . . [*With a shriek which fills everybody with dismay.*] No, Rosetta, no! Your Mummy's not looking after you. . . . And all because of that swine there. . . . Her son! I feel as if all the devils in hell were loose inside me. . . . And he . . . [*Leaves the* LITTLE GIRL *and turns with her usual scorn to the* BOY.] What are you doing . . . drooping there like that? . . . Always the little beggar-boy! It'll be your fault too if that baby drowns. . . . Because of the way you go on. . . . As if I didn't pay for everybody when I got you into his house. [*Seizing his arm to make him take his hand out of his pocket.*] What have you got there? What are you trying to hide? Out with it! Take that hand out of your pocket! [*She snatches his hand out of his pocket and to everybody's horror reveals that it is clenched round a revolver. She looks at him for a little while, as if satisfied. Then she says somberly.*] M'm! Where did you get that gun from? . . . And how did you manage to lay your hands on it? [*And since the* BOY, *in his utter dismay—his eyes are staring and vacant—does not reply.*] You idiot! If I'd been you I shouldn't have killed myself. . . . I'd have killed one of *them*. . . . Or the pair of them! Father and son together!

[*She hides him behind the cypress tree where he was lurking before. Then she takes the* LITTLE GIRL *by the hand and leads her towards the fountain. She puts her into the basin of the fountain, and makes her lie down so that she is completely hidden. Finally she goes down on her knees and buries her head in her hands on the rim of the basin of the fountain.*]

PRODUCER. That's it! Good! [*Turning to the* SON.] And at the same time. . . .

SON [*angrily*]. What do you mean . . . "And at the same time"? Oh, no! . . . Nothing of the sort! There never was any scene between her and me! [*Pointing to the* MOTHER.] You make her tell you what really happened! [*Meanwhile the* SECOND ACTRESS *and the* JUVENILE LEAD *have detached themselves from the group of* ACTORS *and are standing gazing intently at the* MOTHER *and the* SON *so that later they can act these parts.*]

MOTHER. Yes, it's true, sir! I'd gone to his room at the time.

SON. There! Did you hear? To my room! Not into the garden!

PRODUCER. That doesn't matter at all! As I said we'll have to run all the action together into one composite scene!

SON [*becoming aware that the* JUVENILE LEAD *is studying him*]. What do *you* want?

JUVENILE LEAD. Nothing! I was just looking at you.

SON [*turning to the* SECOND ACTRESS]. Oh! . . . And *you're* here too, are you? All ready to play *her* part, I suppose? [*Pointing to the* MOTHER.]

PRODUCER. That's the idea! And if you want my opinion you ought to be damned grateful for all the attention they're paying you.

SON. Indeed? Thank you! But hasn't it dawned on you yet that you aren't going to be able to stage this play? Not even the tiniest vestige of us is to be found in you. . . . And all the time your actors are studying us from the outside. Do you think it's possible for us to live confronted by a mirror which, not merely content with freezing us in that particular picture which is the fixing of our expression, has to throw an image back at us which we can no longer recognize? . . . Our own features, yes. . . . But twisted into a horrible grimace.

FATHER. He's quite right! He's quite right, you know!

PRODUCER [*to the* JUVENILE LEAD *and* SECOND ACTRESS]. Right you are! Get back with the others!

SON. It's no use your bothering! I'm not having anything to do with this!

PRODUCER. You be quiet for the moment, and let me listen to what your mother has to say! [*To the* MOTHER.] You were saying? . . . You'd gone to his room? . . .

MOTHER. Yes, I'd gone to his room. . . . I couldn't bear the strain any longer! I wanted to pour out my heart to him. . . . I wanted to tell him of all the anguish that was tormenting me. . . . But as soon as he saw me come in . .

SON. There was no scene between us! I rushed out of the room. . . . I didn't want to get involved in any scenes! Because I never have been involved in any! Do you understand?

MOTHER. Yes! That *is* what happened! That is what happened.

PRODUCER. But for the purposes of this play we've simply *got* to have a scene between you and him! Why . . . it's absolutely *essential*!

MOTHER. I'm quite ready to take part in one! Oh, if you could only find some way to give me an opportunity of speaking to him . . . if only for a moment. . . . So that I can pour out my heart to him!

FATHER [*going up to the* SON, *in a great rage*]. You'll do what she asks, do you understand? You'll do what your Mother asks!

SON [*more stubbornly than ever*]. I'm doing nothing!

FATHER [*taking hold of him by the lapels of his coat and shaking him*]. My God, you'll do what I tell you! Or else . . . Can't you hear how she's pleading with you? Haven't you a spark of feeling in you for your Mother?

SON [*grappling with the* FATHER]. No, I haven't! For God's sake let's have done with all this. . . . Once and for all, let's have done with it!

[*General agitation. The* MOTHER *is terrified and tries to get between them in order to separate them.*]

MOTHER. Please! *Please!*

FATHER [*without relinquishing his hold*]. You must obey me! You *must!*

SON [*struggling with him and finally hurling him to the ground. He falls near the steps amidst general horror*]. What's come over you? Why are you in this terrible state of frenzy? Haven't you any sense of decency? . . . Going about parading your shame. . . . And ours, too. I'm having nothing to do with this affair! Nothing, do you hear? And by making this stand I am interpreting the wishes of our author, who didn't wish to put us on the stage!

PRODUCER. Oh, God! You come along here and . . .

SON [*pointing to the* FATHER]. *He* did! I didn't!

PRODUCER. Aren't you here now?

SON. It was he who wanted to come. . . . And he dragged us all along with him. Then the pair of them went in there with you and agreed on what was to go into the play. But he didn't only stick to what really did occur. . . . No, as if that wasn't enough for any man, he had to put in things that never even happened.

PRODUCER. Well, then, you tell me what really happened! You can at least do that! You rushed out of your room without saying a word?

SON [*he hesitates for a moment*]. Without saying a word! I didn't want to get involved in a scene!

PRODUCER [*pressing him*]. And then? What did you do then?

SON [*everybody's attention is on him; amidst the anguished silence he takes a step or two across the front of the stage*]. Nothing. . . . As I was crossing the garden . . . [*he breaks off and becomes gloomy and absorbed*].

PRODUCER [*urging him to speak, very much moved by this extraordinary reserve*]. Well? As you were crossing the garden?

SON [*in exasperation, shielding his face with his arm*]. Why do you want to force me to tell you? It's horrible!

[*The* MOTHER *is trembling all over and stifled sobs come from her as she looks towards the fountain.*]

PRODUCER [*slowly, quietly . . . he has seen where the* MOTHER *is looking and he now turns to the* SON *with growing apprehension*]. The little girl?

SON [*staring straight in front of him, out into the auditorium*]. There . . . In the fountain. . . .

FATHER [*from where he is on the floor, pointing with tender pity to the* MOTHER]. She was following him. . . .

PRODUCER [*anxiously to the* SON]. And what did you do?

SON [*slowly, continuing to stare in front of him*]. I rushed up to the fountain. . . . I was about to dive in and fish her out. . . . Then all of a sudden I pulled up short. . . . Behind that tree I saw something that made my blood run cold. . . . The boy. . . . The boy was standing there. . . . Stock still. . . . With madness in his eyes. . . . Staring like some insane creature at his little sister, who was lying drowned in the fountain! [*The* STEPDAUGHTER, *who has all this while been bent over the fountain in order to hide the* LITTLE GIRL, *is sobbing desperately—her sobs coming like an echo from the background. There is a pause.*] I moved towards him. . . . And then . . . [*And from behind the trees where the* BOY *is hidden a revolver shot rings out.*]

MOTHER [*with a heartrending cry she rushes behind the trees accompanied by the* SON *and all the* ACTORS. *There is general confusion*]. Oh, my son! My son! [*And then amidst the general hubbub and shouting.*] Help! Oh, help!

PRODUCER [*amidst all the shouting, he tries to clear a space while the* BOY *is carried off behind the skycloth*]. Is he wounded? Is he badly hurt?

[*By now everybody, except for the* PRODUCER *and the* FATHER, *who is still on the ground by the steps, has disappeared behind the skycloth. They can be heard muttering and exclaiming in great consternation. Then first from one side, then from the other, the* ACTORS *re-enter.*]

LEADING LADY [*re-entering right, very much moved*]. He's dead, poor boy! He's dead! Oh what a terrible thing to happen!

LEADING MAN [*re-entering left, laughing*]. What do you mean, dead? It's all make-believe! It's all just a pretense! Don't get taken in by it!

OTHER ACTORS [*entering from the right*]. Make-believe? Pretense? Reality! Reality! He's dead!

OTHERS [*from the left*]. No! Make-believe! It's all a pretense!

FATHER [*rising and crying out to them*]. What do you mean, pretense? Reality, ladies and gentlemen, reality! Reality! [*And desperation in his face, he too disappears behind the backcloth*].

PRODUCER [*at the end of his tether*]. Pretense! Reality! Go to hell, the whole lot of you! Lights! Lights! Lights!

[*The stage and the auditorium are suddenly flooded with very bright light. The* PRODUCER *breathes again as if freed from a tremendous burden. They all stand there looking into one another's eyes, in an agony of suspense and dismay.*]

PRODUCER. My God! Nothing like this has ever happened to me before! I've lost a whole day on their account! [*He looks at his watch.*] You can go home now. . . . All of you! There's nothing we can do now! It's too late to start rehearsing again! I'll see you all this evening. [*And as soon as the* ACTORS *have said "Goodbye!" and gone he calls out to the* ELECTRICIAN.] Hey [*his name*]! Everything off! [*He has hardly got the words out before the theater is plunged for a moment into utter darkness.*] Hell! You might at least leave me one light on, so that I can see where I'm going!

And immediately behind the backcloth, a green flood lights up. It projects the silhouettes of the CHARACTERS *(minus the* BOY *and the* LITTLE GIRL*), clear-cut and huge, on to the backcloth. The* PRODUCER *is terrified and leaps off the stage. As he does so the green flood is switched off—rather as if its having come on in the first instance had been due to the* ELECTRICIAN'S *having pulled the wrong switch—and the stage is again lit in blue. Slowly the* CHARACTERS *come in and advance to the front of the stage. The* SON *comes in first, from the right, followed by the* MOTHER, *who has her arms outstretched towards him. Then the* FATHER *comes in from the left. They stop half-way down the stage and stand there like people in a trance. Last of all the* STEPDAUGHTER *comes in from the left and runs towards the steps which lead down into the auditorium. With her foot on the top step she stops for a moment to look at the other three and bursts into strident laughter. Then she hurls herself down the steps and runs up the aisle. She stops at the back of the auditorium and turns to look at the three figures standing on the stage. She bursts out laughing again. And when she has disappeared from the auditorium you can still hear her terrible laughter coming from the foyer beyond. A short pause and then,*

CURTAIN

Thomas Mann

(1875–1955)

To be a German citizen in the first half of the twentieth century, to be deeply committed to German culture and to feel that one is in the tradition of Goethe, Schiller, and Wagner, and at the same time be forced to witness and participate in the debacle that is modern German history is a fearful challenge for an artist. Yet this was the position of Thomas Mann, the greatest German novelist of his time, and the dilemma provided the underlying subject, at least indirectly, of much of his voluminous work. A profoundly philosophical novelist, Mann concerned himself even in his early stories with the contrary forces that lead to social growth or decay. Mann was forced to revise many of his views, but he remained throughout his career an eloquent spokesman for traditional, humane values and an acute analyst of the forces in modern life that threaten those values.

Mann was born in 1875 in the Baltic seaport town of Lübeck, in west Germany, into a family that had been prosperous merchants in the region since medieval times. After his father's death when Mann was sixteen, he moved with his family to Munich, where he attended the university (without, however, taking a degree), worked briefly in an insurance office, and wrote for a satirical magazine. In his early twenties, he decided to devote himself to writing, as his older brother Heinrich had already done. (Heinrich had a successful career as a novelist; he is now best remembered for the novel dramatized in Josef von Sternberg's 1930 film The Blue Angel.*) Mann's early stories, of which a collection appeared in 1898, dealt recurringly with the ambiguities of the artist's role, as both interpreter and falsifier of life. They also showed the influence of the romantic irrationalism of Schopenhauer and Nietzsche and the composer Wagner.*

Mann's first novel, Buddenbrooks *(1900), was a massive family novel which continued the exploration of the tension between art and ordinary, middle-class life by showing, over three generations, how a preoccupation with art saps the vitality of the younger heirs of a vigorous family of businessmen. A nostalgia for the virtues of bourgeois culture also pervaded the novellas* Tonio Kröger *and* Tristan *(both 1903), and the great novella* Death in Venice *(1912) further explored the threat of decadence inherent in the artist's role.*

The outbreak of World War I led Mann first to a polemical articulation of his social views and ultimately to a rethinking and modification of them. Reacting to his brother Heinrich's open criticism of the conservatism and nationalism of German culture, Mann in 1918 published a polemical treatise, Reflections of an Unpolitical Man, *in which he hotly defended "creative" irrationalism, conservatism, and authoritarianism against the claims of rationalistic democracy. Germany's defeat in the war and the chaos and extremism of German life under the short-lived Weimar Republic of the 1920s led him gradually to revise his views, and in a series of essays, he began to espouse democratic principles. This intellectual development is reflected in* The Magic Mountain *(1924), in which a mountaintop tuberculosis sanitarium comes to serve as a model of the spiritual state of Europe. Much of this long novel of ideas is devoted to debates between the humanistic and democratic Settembrini and the cynical, totalitarian Naphta. At the end, the protagonist, Hans Castorp, who has come to spend three weeks but spends seven years in the death-haunted enchantment of the sanitarium, sides, somewhat skeptically but decisively, with Settembrini and leaves for a life of action and service to others. Some of the same tensions between traditional values and newer ones appear in* Disorder and Early Sorrow *(1926).*

As the shadow of the coming of Nazism began to fall across Germany, Mann became even more outspoken in his defense of humane values. In Mario and the Magician *(1930), he caricatured the Nazis in the figure of a shabby, cynical illusionist; in the same year, he delivered a courageous address in Berlin, "An Appeal to*

Reason," calling for the middle and working classes to join together to oppose the rising barbarity of the Nazis. When Hitler took power in 1933, Mann and his wife were on vacation in Switzerland. Warned by friends, they did not return to Germany, but spent the following five years near Zurich. They came to America in 1938, settling first in Princeton, New Jersey, and then in southern California. The Nazis had stripped him of German citizenship in 1936; he became a U.S. citizen in 1944.

Mann spent much of the 1930s and 1940s working on his cycle of novels Joseph and His Brothers, *in which he reinterpreted the biblical story as a fable of the issues of his own day. Israel, in his treatment, is the home of the mythic, the tribal, and the collective. Joseph is forced out of this traditional environment into Egypt, the home of change, history, and individualism, thus paralleling Mann's own spiritual history and that of his time, as he saw it. Some of these same themes appear in the witty, ironic* Lotte in Weimar *(1939), known in America as* The Beloved Returns; *here Lotte Kestner, the heroine of Goethe's semi-autobiographical* Werther, *comes as an old woman to renew her relationship with her old lover, now a world-famous writer. But Goethe refuses to return to the past and teaches Lotte that one must accept time and change. The novels of the war years also include* Doctor Faustus *(1947), begun in 1943; it traces, through the music of the German composer Adrian Leverkühn, the movement of Germany from humanism to Nazi primitivism. The novel has been called the greatest literary treatment of music as well as the most profound artistic treatment of Nazism.*

Mann refused to live again in Germany after the war, although he visited both East and West Germany several times. He left the United States in 1952 to settle once more in Switzerland, where he died in 1955.

"Felix Krull" was written and published as a short story fairly early in Mann's career, but he regarded it as a fragment and for years intended to return to it and develop it into a novel. He finally did so at the end of his career, with The Confessions of Felix Krull, Confidence Man *(1955). Even as a novel, it remained a fragment; Mann intended to continue the story with a sequel but died before doing so. The novel lacks the wit and charm of the short story, one of Mann's deftest characterizations of a favorite type, the artist as shape-changer, actor, and con man.*

The conflict of citizen and artist is a basic theme in Mann's work (as it is in that of his great contemporary Joyce, who dramatized the conflict in the figures of Leopold Bloom and Stephen Dedalus in Ulysses*). Professor Cornelius is one of Mann's most moving portraits of the bourgeois citizen. His story is consummately crafted; Mann, despite his skill in the large-scale novel, is perhaps at his best in his tightly constructed novellas.* Disorder and Early Sorrow *seems at first to be a fragile, almost eventless story of domestic life. But as it develops, the story becomes a complex layering of social values and generational conflict. The professor's traditional world is crumbling under the pressures of post-war economic and social disorder. He is far from unsympathetic with the values of the "big folks," his children, but he finds them disturbing and hard to understand, and he sits in his study upstairs, surrounded by his books and listening to the tumult of the party downstairs, in a rich image of social disjunction. The story moves from "disorder" to "early sorrow" in the culminating episode of Ellie's bedtime suffering. Her painful fall from innocence into experience is paralleled by her father's reaction. The small, domestic action of the story opens up into large perspectives as Cornelius meditates upon his own love of history, his "timeless" love for his daughter, and his own fear of falling from the deathlike, artlike stasis of finished history into the experience of the frightening but living present.*

FURTHER READING (*prepared by N. K. B.*): Although not strictly a biography, *Thomas Mann: A Chronicle of His Life,* by Hans Burgin and Hans-Otto Mayer, 1969, trans. by Eugene Dobson, contains a detailed list of key events in Mann's life and career, with valuable cross-references to the notebooks, letters, and publication history of major works. Thomas Mann's *A Sketch of My Life,* trans. by H. T. Lowe-Porter, 1960, is an informal account. Nigel Hamilton, *The Brothers Mann: The Lives of Heinrich and Thomas Mann, 1871–1950 and 1875–1955,* 1979, is a major study of the background and biographies of the two figures. For concise introductions to Mann's life and writing, see Joseph R. Stern, *Thomas Mann,* 1967; R. J. Hollingdale, *Thomas Mann: A Critical Study,* 1971; and Martin Swales, *Thomas Mann: A Study,* 1980. Henry Hatfield, *Thomas Mann,* 1951, rev. 1962, contains a biographical sketch and surveys Mann's artistic development, including an analysis of "Felix Krull." Ignace Feuerlicht, *Thomas Mann,* 1968, discusses both "Felix Krull" and *Disorder and Early Sorrow* in his introductory study, which stresses the autobiographical features of Mann's work. In *Thomas Mann: The Uses of Tradition,* 1974, T. J. Reed views Mann in the context of German and European literary traditions. Erich Heller's provocative study *Thomas Mann: The Ironic German,* 1958, rev. 1961, also examines Mann's debt to the cultural milieu. T. E. Apter's *Thomas Mann: The Devil's Advocate,* 1979, demonstrates the strong influence of German Romanticism on Mann's career. Fritz Kaufmann, *Thomas Mann: The World as Will and Representation,* 1957, investigates the philosophical foundations underlying Mann's fiction and themes. For an analysis of Mann's early work, see Joseph Brennan, *Thomas Mann's World,* 1942. In *From the Magic Mountain: Mann's Later Masterpieces,* 1979, Henry Hatfield demonstrates the importance of Mann's later phase and documents his political positions. J. M. Lindsay, *Thomas Mann,* 1954, also stresses the later work but argues for the overall unity of Mann's creative output. Henry Hatfield, ed., *Thomas Mann: A Collection of Critical Essays,* 1964, provides twelve essays by German, British, and American scholars, including Robert Heilman's study of "Felix Krull." *The Stature of Thomas Mann,* ed. Charles Neider, 1947, is the most comprehensive gathering of Mann scholarship from the first half of the twentieth century.

FELIX KRULL

Translated by H. T. Lowe–Porter

As I take my pen in hand, in ample leisure and complete retirement—in sound health too, though tired, so very tired that I shall hardly be able to proceed save in small stages and with frequent pauses for rest—as I take up my pen, then, to commit my confessions to the long-suffering paper, in the neat and pleasing calligraphy of which I am master, I own to a fleeting misgiving on the score of my own fitness for the task in hand. Am I, I ask myself, equipped by previous training for this intellectual enterprise? However, since every word that I have to say concerns solely my own personal and peculiar experiences, errors, and passions and hence should be entirely within my compass; so the only doubt which can arise is whether I command the necessary tact and gifts of expression, and in my view these are less the fruit of a regular course of study than of natural parts and a favorable atmosphere in youth. For the latter I have not lacked; I come of an upper-class if somewhat loose-living home, and my sister Olympia and I had the benefit for some months of the ministrations of a Fräulein from

Vevey[1]—though it is true that she had to leave, in consequence of a rivalry between her and my mother, of which my father was the object. My godfather Maggotson, with whom I was in daily and intimate contact, was an artist of considerable merit; everybody in the little town called him professor, though that enviable title was his more by courtesy than by right. My father, his size and obesity notwithstanding, had great personal charm, and he always laid stress upon lucid and well-chosen language. There was French blood in the family from the grandmother's side and he himself had spent some of his young years in France—he used to say that he knew Paris like his waistcoat pocket. His French pronunciation was excellent and he was fond of introducing into his conversation little expressions like *"C'est ça," "épatant," "parfaitement," "à mon gout,"*[2] and so on. Up till the end of his life he was a great favorite with the female sex. I have said all this of course by way of preface and somewhat out of the due order of my tale. As for myself I have a natural instinct for good form, upon which throughout my career of fraud I have always been able to rely, as my story will only too abundantly show. I think therefore that I may commit it to writing without further misgivings on this score. I am resolved to practice the utmost candor, regardless whether I incur the reproach of vanity or shamelessness—for what moral value or significance can confessions like mine possess if they have not the value of perfect sincerity?

The Rhine valley brought me forth—that region favored of heaven, mild and without ruggedness either in its climate or in the nature of its soil, abounding in cities and villages peopled by a blithe and laughter-loving folk—truly of all the regions of the earth it must be one of the sweetest. Here on these slopes exposed to the southern sun and sheltered from rude winds by the hills of the Rhine valley lie those flourishing resorts the very sound of whose names makes the heart of the toper to laugh: Rüdesheim, Johannisberg, Rauenthal[3]—and here too that most estimable little town where forty years ago I saw the light. It lies slightly westward of the bend made by the river at Mainz. Containing some four thousand souls, it is famous for its wine-cellars and is one of the chief landing-places for the steamers which ply up and down the Rhine. Thus the gay city of Mainz was very near, the Taunus baths patronized by high society, Homburg, Langenschwalbach, and Schlangenbad. This last we could reach by a half-hour's journey on a narrow-gauge road; and how often in the pleasant time of year did we make excursions thither, my parents, my sister Olympia, and I, by train, by carriage, or by boat! Many other excursions we made too, in all directions, for everywhere nature smiled and the hand of man and his fertile brain had spread out pleasures for our delectation. I can still see my father, clad in his comfortable summer suit with a pattern of small checks, as he used to sit with us in the arbor of some inn garden, rather far off the table, for his paunch prevented him from drawing up close, rapt in enjoyment of a dish of prawns washed down with golden wine. Often my god-

[1] A *Fräulein* (literally, "young woman") is a nursemaid. Vevey is in western Switzerland.
[2] "That's right," "Wonderful!" "Exactly," "To my taste."
[3] Places where famous Rhine wines are made.

father Maggotson was with us, looking at the scene through his big round glasses and absorbing great and small into his artist soul.

My poor father was the proprietor of the firm of Engelbert Krull, makers of the now extinct brand of sparkling wine called Lorley Extra Cuvée. The cellars of the firm lay on the Rhine not far from the landing-stage, and often as a lad I used to play in the cool vaults or follow the stone-paved lanes that led in all directions among the high-tiered shelves, meditating upon the army of bottles that lay in slanting rows upon their sides. "There you lie," I would apostrophize them—though of course at that time I had no power to put my thoughts into apposite words—"there you lie in this subterranean twilight and within you there is clearing and mellowing that bubbling golden sap which shall make so many pairs of eyes to sparkle and so many hearts to throb with heightened zest. You are not much to look at now; but one day you will mount up to the light and be arrayed in festal splendor and there will be parties and weddings and little celebrations in private rooms and your corks will pop up to the ceiling and kindle mirth and levity and desire in the hearts of men."—Some such ideas as these the boy strove to express; and so much at least was true, that the firm of Engelbert Krull laid great stress upon the exterior of their wares, those last touches which in the trade are known as the coiffure. The compressed corks were fastened with silver wire and gold cords sealed with purple wax, yes, actually a stately round seal such as one sees on documents. The necks were wrapped in a fullness of silver foil and on the swelling body was a flaring label with gilt flourishes round the edge. This label had been concocted by my godfather Maggotson. It bore several coats of arms and stars, my father's monogram, and the name of the brand: Lorley Extra Cuvée, all in gilt letters, and a female figure arrayed in a few spangles and a necklace, sitting on the top of a rock with her legs crossed, combing her flowing hair. But unfortunately it appears that the quality of the wine did not correspond to the splendor of its setting-out. "Krull," I have heard my godfather say, "I have the greatest respect for you personally; but really the police ought to condemn your wine. A week ago I was foolish enough to drink half a bottle and my constitution has not yet recovered from the shock. What sort of stuff do you dose it with—petroleum, fusel oil? Anyhow, it's poison. You ought to be afraid to sell it." My poor father's was a soft nature, he could not bear hard words and was always thrown into a distress. "It's all right for you to joke, Maggotson," he would answer, gently caressing his belly with his finger-tips, as was his habit, "but there is such a prejudice against the domestic product, I have to keep down the price and make the public believe it is getting something for its money. Anyhow, the competition is so fierce that I shall not be able to go on for long." Thus my poor father.

Our villa was a charming little property seated on a slope commanding a view of the Rhine. The front garden ran downhill and rejoiced in many crockeryware adornments: dwarfs, toadstools, and animals in lifelike poses; there was a looking-glass ball on a stand, which grotesquely distorted the faces of the passers-by; an aeolian harp,[4] several grottoes, and a foun-

[4] A wind-harp; box-shaped instrument with strings that produce sounds when the wind blows over them.

tain whose spray made an ingenious design in the air while silver-fish swam in the basin. As for our domestic interior, it was after my father's heart, who above all things liked comfort and good cheer. Cosy nooks invited one to sit down; there was a real spinning-wheel in one corner, and endless trifles and knick-knacks. Mussel-shells, glass boxes, bottles of smelling-salts stood about on étagères[5] and velvet-topped tables. A multiplicity of down cushions in silk-embroidered covers were distributed on sofas and day-beds, for my father loved to lie soft. The curtain-rods were halberds,[6] and the portières very jolly, made of colored beads and rushes, which look quite like a solid door, but you can pass through without lifting your hand, when they fall behind you with a whispering sound. Above the wind-screen was an ingenious device which played the first bar of "Wine, Women, and Song" in a pleasing little tinkle whenever the door opened or shut.

Such was the home upon which, on a mild rainy Sunday in May, I first opened my eyes. From now on I mean to follow the order of events and not run ahead of my story. If report tells true, the birth was slow and difficult and did not come to pass without help from the family doctor, whose name was Mecum. It appears that I—if I may use the first person to refer to that far-away and foreign little being—was extremely inactive and made no attempt to second my mother's efforts, showing no zeal to enter a world which I was yet to love with such an ardent love. However, I was a healthy and well-formed infant and throve at the breast of my excellent wet-nurse in a way to encourage the liveliest hopes for my future. Yet the most mature reflection inclines me to associate this reluctance to exchange the darkness of the womb for the light of day with the extraordinary gift and passion for sleep which has been mine all my life. They tell me that I was a quiet child, that I did not cry and break the peace, but was given to sleep and napping, to a degree most comfortable to my nurses. And however great my subsequent love of the world, which caused me to mingle in it in all sorts of guises and to attach it to myself by all possible means, yet I feel that in night and slumber always my true home was to be found. Even without physical fatigue I have always fallen asleep with the greatest ease and enjoyment, lost myself in far and dreamless forgetfulness, and waked after ten or twelve or even fourteen hours' oblivion more refreshed and gratified than even by all the satisfactions and successes of my waking hours. Is there a contradiction here between this love of sleep and my great urge towards life and love of which it will be in place to speak hereafter? I have said that I have concentrated much thought upon this matter and several times I have had the clearest perception that there is no contradiction but rather a hidden connection and correspondence. And it is the fact that now, when I have aged and grown weary so that I feel none of my old irresistible compulsion towards the society of men, but live in complete retirement, only now is my power of sleep impaired, so that I am in a sense a stranger to it, my slumbers being short and light and fleeting; whereas even in the prison—where there was much opportunity—I slept better than in the soft beds of the most luxurious hotels. But I am fallen into my old error of getting ahead of my story.

Often enough I heard from my parents' lips that I was a Sunday child;

[5]Open-shelved cabinets. [6]Medieval weapons, combining spear and battle-ax.

and though I was brought up to despise all forms of superstition I have always thought there was some significance in the fact, taken in connection with my Christian name of Felix (for so I was christened, after my godfather Maggotson) and my physical fineness and sense of well-being. Yes, I have always believed that I was *felix*,[7] a favored child of the gods; and I may say that, on the whole, events do not show me to have been mistaken in this lively conviction. Indeed, it is peculiarly characteristic of my career that whatever misfortune and suffering it may have held always seemed like a divergence from the natural order, a cloud, as it were, through which my native sunniness continued to shine.—After which digression into the abstract I will once more return to depict in its broad outlines the scene of my early youth.

A child full of fantasy, I afforded the family much amusement by my imaginative flights. I have often been told, and seem still to remember, how when I was still in dresses it pleased me to pretend that I was the Kaiser. In this game I would persist for hours at a time. Sitting in my little go-cart, which my nurse would push about the garden or the lower floors of the house, I would draw down my mouth as far as I could, so that my upper lip was lengthened out of all proportion, and blink my eyes slowly until what with the strain and the strength of my feelings they would presently grow red and fill with tears. Quite overcome with the burden of my age and dignity I would sit silent in my go-cart, my nurse having been instructed to tell all the passers-by how things stood, for I should have taken it hard had they failed to fall in with my whim. "This is the Kaiser I am pushing about here," she would say, carrying her hand to her temple in an awkward salute; and everybody would pay me homage. My godfather Maggotson, who loved his joke, would play up to me in every way. "Look, there he goes, the hoary old hero!" he would say, with an exaggeratedly deep obeisance. Then he would pretend to be the populace and stand beside my path tossing his hat in the air, his stick, even his glasses, shouting: "Hurrah, hurrah!" and laughing fit to kill himself when out of the excess of my emotions the tears would roll down my long-drawn face.

I used to play the same sort of game when I was much older and could no longer expect my elders to fall in with them. I did not miss their cooperation, glorying as I did in my free and incommunicable flights of imagination. I awoke one morning, for instance, filled with the idea that I was a prince, a prince eighteen years old, named Karl; and prince I remained all day long, for the inestimable advantage of this kind of game was that it never needed to be interrupted, not even during the almost insupportable hours which I spent at school. I moved about clothed in a sort of amiable aloofness, holding lively imaginary converse with my governor or adjutant; and the secret of my own superiority which I hugged to my breast filled me with a perfectly indescribable pride and joy. What a glorious gift is the fancy, what subtle satisfactions it affords! The boys I knew, being ignorant of this priceless advantage which I possessed, seemed to me dull and limited louts indeed, unable to enter the kingdom where I was at home at no cost to myself and simply by an act of the will. They were all very simple fellows, with coarse hair and red hands. They would have had a hard time

[7] "Happy" (Latin).

indeed convincing themselves that they were princes—and very foolish they would have looked. Whereas my hair was as silken-soft as one seldom sees it in boys, and light in color; together with my blue-gray eyes it formed a fascinating contrast to the golden brownness of my skin, so that I hovered on the border-line between blond and brunet and might have been considered either. I had good hands and early began to care for them: well-shaped without being too narrow, never clammy, but dry and just warm enough to be pleasant. The finger-nails too were the kind that it is a pleasure to look at. And my voice, even before it changed, had an ingratiating note and could fall so flatteringly upon the ear that I liked above all things to listen to it myself when I was alone and could blissfully engage in long, plausible, but quite meaningless colloquies with my aide-de-camp, accompanying them with extravagant gestures and attitudes. Such, then, were the physical advantages which I possessed; but these things are mostly very intangible, well-nigh impossible to put into words even for one equipped with a high degree of literary skill, and only recognizable in their effects. However that may be, I could not for long have disguised from myself that I was made of finer stuff than my schoolmates, and take no shame to myself for frankly admitting that such was the case. It is nothing to me to be accused of conceit; I should need to be either a fool or a hypocrite to write myself down an average person when I am but honoring the truth in repeating that I am made of finer stuff.

I grew up very much by myself, for my sister Olympia was several years older than I; and indulged as pastime in various mental quiddities,[8] of which I will cite one or two. I had taken it into my head to study that mysterious force the human will and to practice in myself how far it was capable of extension into regions considered beyond human powers. It is a well-known fact that the muscles controlling the pupils of our eyes react involuntarily in accordance with the strength of the light upon them. I decided to test whether this reaction could be brought under control of the will. I would stand before my mirror and concentrate all my powers upon the effort to expand or contract my pupils. And I protest that these obstinate efforts were actually crowned with success. At first, while I stood bathed in perspiration, my color coming and going, there would be an irregular flicker and fluctuation. But by practice I actually succeeded in narrowing the pupils to the merest points and then expanding them to great round pools of blackness. The fearful joy I felt at this result was actually accompanied by a physical shuddering before the mysteries of our human nature.

It was at this time, too, I often amused myself by a sort of introspection which even today has not lost all charm for me. I would inquire of myself: which is better, to see the world small or to see it large? The significance of the question was this: great men, I thought, field-marshals, statesmen, conquerors, and leading spirits generally that rise above the mass of mankind must be so constituted as to see the world small, like a chess-board, else they would never command the necessary ruthlessness to regulate the common weal and woe according to their own will. Yet it was quite possible, on the other hand, that such a diminishing point of view, as it were, might lead to

[8] Eccentricities.

one doing nothing at all. For if you saw the world and human beings in it as small and insignificant and were early persuaded that nothing was worth while, you could easily sink into indifference and indolence and contemptuously prefer your own peace of mind to any influence you might exert upon the spirits of men. And added to that your own supine detachment from mankind would certainly give offense and cut you off still further from any success you might have had in despite of yourself. Then is it better, I would next inquire, to think of the world and human nature as great, glorious, and important, worthy the expenditure of every effort to the end of achieving some meed of esteem and good report? Yet again, how easily can such a point of view lead to self-detraction and loss of confidence, so that the fickle world passes you by with a smile as a simpleton, in favor of more self-confident lovers! Though on the other hand such genuine credulity and artlessness has its good side too, since men cannot but be flattered by the way you look up to them; and if you devote yourself to making this impression, it will give weight and seriousness to your life, lend it meaning in your own eyes, and lead to your advancement. In this wise would I speculate and weigh the pros and cons; but always it has lain in my nature to take up the second position, seeing the world and mankind as great and glorious phenomena, capable of affording such priceless satisfactions that no effort on my part could seem disproportionate to the rewards I might reap.

Ideas of this kind were certainly calculated to isolate me from my schoolmates and companions, who of course spent their time in more commonplace and traditional occupations. But it is also a fact that these boys, most of whose fathers were either civil servants or the owners of vineyards, were instructed to avoid my society. I early discovered this, for on inviting one of them to our home he made no bones of telling me that he had been forbidden to associate with me because my family was not respectable. The experience not only wounded my pride but made me covet an intercourse which otherwise I could not have craved. But there is no doubt that the current opinion about our household and the goings-on there was in large measure justified.

I have referred above to the disturbance in our family circle due to the presence of our Fräulein from Vevey. My poor father was infatuated with this girl and ran after her until he succeeded in gaining his ends, or so it seemed, for dissensions arose between him and my mother and he departed for Mainz, where he remained for several weeks restoring his equilibrium with the joys of a bachelor life. My mother took entirely the wrong course, I am convinced, in treating my poor father with such a lack of consideration. She was a woman of insignificant mental parts; but what was more to the point, her human weaknesses were no less apparent than his own. My sister Olympia, a fat and fleshly-minded creature who later went on the stage and had some small success there, took after her in this respect—the difference between them and my poor father being that theirs was a heavy and sensual greed of pleasure, whereas his follies were never without a certain ease and grace. Mother and daughter lived in unusual intimacy—I recall once seeing my mother measure Olympia's thigh with a tape-measure, which gave me to think for several hours. Another time, when I was old enough to have some intuitive understanding of such matters though no words to express them in, I watched unseen and saw my mother and sister flirting with a young painter who was doing some work about the house. He was a dark-eyed lad in a white smock and they painted upon him a green moustache with his own paint. In the end they roused him to such a pitch that they fled giggling up the attic stair and he pursued them thither. My parents bored each other to tears and got relief by filling the house with guests from Mainz and Wiesbaden so that our house was the scene of a continual round of gaieties. It was a promiscuous crew who frequented these gatherings: actors and actresses, young business men, the sickly young infantry lieutenant who later proposed to my sister; a Jewish banker with a wife whose charms gushed appallingly out of her jet-spangled frock; a journalist in a velvet waistcoat with a lock of hair falling over his brow, who every time brought along a new wife. They would arrive for seven o'clock dinner, and the feasting, the dancing and piano-playing, the skylarking and shrieks of laughter would go on all night. Particularly at carnival-time and the vintage season the waves of pleasure rose very high. My father, who was very clever in such things, would set off the most splendid fireworks in the garden; all the company would be masked and unearthly light would play upon the crockery dwarfs. All restraint was abandoned. At that time it was my sorry lot to attend the high school of our little town; and often I would go down to the dining-room at seven o'clock or half past with face new-washed, to eat my breakfast and find the guests still at their after-dinner coffee, rumpled, sallow, and hollow-eyed, blinking at the daylight; they would receive me into their midst with shoutings.

When still quite young I was allowed with my sister Olympia to take part in the festivities. Even when alone we always set a good table, and my father drank champagne mixed with sodawater. But at these parties there were endless courses prepared by a chef from Wiesbaden with the assistance of our own cook: the most tempting succession of sweets, savories, and ices. Lorley Extra Cuvée flowed in streams, but many good wines were served as well. I was particularly fond of the bouquet of Berncasteler Doctor. Later in life I made acquaintance with many of the noblest wines and could order Grand Vin Château Margaux or Grand Cru Mouton-Rothschild, two very fine wines, as to the manner born.

I love to call up the picture of my father as he presided at the head of the table, with his white imperial, and his belly confined in a white silk waistcoat. His voice was weak and sometimes he would be seized by self-consciousness and look down at his plate. Yet his enjoyment was to be read in his eyes and in his shining red face. *"C'est épatant,"* he would say. *"Parfaitement"*—and with his fingers, which curved backwards at the tips, he would give delicate touches to the table-service. My mother and sister meanwhile were abandoned to a gross and soulless gluttony, between courses flirting with their table-mates behind their fans.

After dinner, when the gas-chandeliers began to be wreathed in smoke, came dancing and forfeit-playing.[9] When the evening was advanced I used to be sent to bed; but as sleep, in that din, was out of the question, I would wrap myself in my red woollen coverlet and in this becoming disguise return to the feast, where I was received with cries of joy from all the females.

[9] Playing games that involve playful penalties.

Refreshments such as wine jellies, lemonade, punch, herring salad, were served in relays until the morning coffee. The dance was free and untrammelled, the games of forfeits were pretext for much kissing and caressing; the ladies bent over the backs of their chairs to give the gentlemen stimulating glimpses into the bosoms of their frocks; and the climax of the evening arrived when some humorist turned out the gas and there was a general scramble in the dark.

These parties were undoubtedly the cause of the unfavorable criticism which spread about the town; but according to the reports which came to my ears it was their economic aspect that was the target for gossip. For it was only too well known that my father's business was at a desperate pass and that the dining and wining and fireworks must give it the *coup de grâce.*[10] I was sensitive enough to feel the hostile atmosphere when I was still very young; it united, as I have said, with certain peculiarities of my own character to give me on the whole a great deal of pain. The more cordially, then, did I appreciate an incident which took place at about this time; I set it down here with peculiar pleasure.

I was eight years old when my family and I spent some weeks one summer at the famous and neighboring resort of Langenschwalbach. My father took mud baths for his gout, and my mother and sister made themselves talked about for the size and shape of their hats. Of the society we frequented there is little good to be said. The residential class, as usual, avoided us. The better-class guests kept themselves to themselves as they usually do; and such society as we could get had not much to recommend it. Yet I liked Langenschwalbach and later on often made such resorts the scene of my operations. The tranquil, well-regulated existence and the sight of aristocratic and well-groomed people in the gardens and on the tennis courts satisfied an inward craving of my soul. But the strongest attraction of all was the daily concert given by a well-trained orchestra to the guests of the cure. Though I have never attained to skill in any branch of the art I was a fanatical lover of music; even as a child I could not tear myself away from the pretty little pavilion where a becomingly uniformed band played selections and potpourris under the direction of their gypsy leader. Hours on end I would crouch on the steps of that little temple of art, enchanted to my very marrow by the ordered succession of sweet sounds and watching with rapture every motion of the musicians as they attacked their instruments. In particular I was thrilled by the gestures of the violinists and when I went home I delighted my parents with an imitation performed on two sticks, one long and one short. The swinging movement of the left arm in producing a soulful tone, the soft gliding motion from one position to the next, the dexterity of the fingering in virtuoso passages and cadenzas, the fine and supple bowing of the right wrist, the cheek cuddled in such utter abandonment to the violin—all this I succeeded in reproducing so faithfully that the family, especially my father, burst into enthusiastic applause. And being in good spirits due to the beneficial effect of the baths, he conceived the following little joke, with the connivance of the long-haired and almost speechless little bandmaster. They bought a small cheap violin and plentifully smeared the bow with

[10] Death-blow (French).

vaseline. As a rule not much attention was paid to my appearance; but now I was arrayed in a pretty sailor suit with gilt buttons and lanyard all complete, also silk stockings and shiny patent-leather shoes. And one Sunday I took my place at the side of the little conductor during the afternoon promenade concert and assisted in the performance of a Hungarian dance, doing with my violin and my vaselined bow what I had done with my two sticks. My success was tremendous. The public, gentle and simple, streamed up from all sides and assembled before the pavilion to look at the infant prodigy. My pale face, my utter absorption in my task, the lock of hair falling over my brow, my childish hands and wrists in the full, tapering sleeves of the pretty blue sailor suit—in short, my whole touching and astonishing little figure captured all hearts. When I finished with a full sweep of the bow across all the fiddle-strings, the garden resounded with applause and delighted cries from male and female throats. The bandmaster stowed my bow and fiddle safely away and I was set down on the ground, where I was overwhelmed with praises and caresses. The most aristocratic ladies and gentlemen stroked my hair, patted my cheeks and hands, called me an angel child and an amazing little devil. An old Russian princess in violet silk and white side-curls took my head between her beringed hands and kissed my brow, all beaded as it was with perspiration. Then in a pitch of enthusiasm she snatched a lyre-shaped diamond brooch from her throat and with a perfect torrent of ecstatic French pinned it on the front of my blouse. My family approached and my father made excuses for the defects of my playing on the score of my tender years. I was escorted to the confectioner's, where at three different tables I was regaled with chocolate and cream cakes. The scions of the noble family of Siebenklingen, whom I had admired from afar while they regarded me with cold disdain, came up and asked me to play croquet, and while our parents drank coffee together I went off with the children in the seventh heaven of delight, my diamond brooch upon my blouse. That was one of the happiest days of my life, perhaps quite the happiest. The cry was set up that I should play again; actually the management of the Casino approached my father and asked for an encore; but he refused, saying that he had only permitted me to play by way of exception and that repeated public appearances were not consistent with my social position. And besides our stay in Bad Langenschwalbach was drawing to a close.

I wish now to speak of my godfather Maggotson, by no means an ordinary man. He was short and thickset in build, with thin and prematurely gray hair, which he wore parted over one ear and brushed across his crown. He was clean-shaven, with a hooked nose and thin, compressed lips, and wore large round glasses with celluloid rims. His face was further remarkable for the fact that it was bald above the eyes, having no brows to speak of; also for the somewhat acidulous disposition it betrayed—to which, indeed, he was wont to give expression in words, as for instance in his cynical explanation of the name he bore. "Nature," he would say, "is full of corruption and blow-flies, and I am her offspring. Therefore am I called Maggotson. But as for why I am called Felix, that God alone knows." He came from Cologne, where he had once moved in the best social circles and often acted as carnival steward. But for reasons which remained obscure he had been obliged to leave Cologne; he had gone into retirement in our little town, where he very soon—a considerable time before my birth—became an intimate of our household. At all our evening companies he was a regular and indispensable guest and in high favor with young and old. He would purse his lips and fix the ladies through his round glasses, with appraising eyes, until they would screech for mercy, putting their hands before their faces and begging him to turn away his gaze. Apparently they feared the penetrating artist eye; but he, it would seem, did not share in their awe of his calling, and not infrequently made ironic allusions to the nature of artists. "Phidias,"[11] he would say, "also called Pheidias, was a man of more than average gifts—as might perhaps be gathered from the fact that he was convicted for theft and put in jail at Athens for having appropriated to his own use the gold and ivory entrusted to him for his statue of Athena. But Pericles,[12] who had discovered him, had him set free, thereby proving himself to be a connoisseur not only of art but of artists as well; and Phidias—or Pheidias—went to Olympia, where he was commissioned to make the great chryselephantine[13] statue of the Olympian Zeus. But what did he do? He stole the gold and ivory again—and there in the prison at Olympia he died. An extraordinary combination, my friends. But that is the way people are. They want people to be talented—which is already something out of the ordinary. But when it comes to the other qualities which go with the talents—and perhaps are essential to them—oh, no, they don't care for these at all, they refuse to have any understanding of them." Thus my godfather. I have set down his remarks verbatim because he repeated them so often that I know them by heart.

I have said that we lived on terms of mutual regard: yes, I believe that I enjoyed his especial favor, and often as I grew older it was my especial delight to serve as his model, dressing up in all sorts of costumes, of which he possessed a large and varied collection. His studio was a sort of lumber-room[14] with a large window under the roof of a little house standing by itself down on the Rhine. He rented this house and lived in it with an old serving-woman, and there I would pose for him hours at a time, perched on a rude model-throne while he brushed and scraped and painted away. Several times I sat for him in the nude for a large picture with a Greek mythological subject, destined to adorn the dining-room of a wine-dealer in Mainz. When I did this my godfather was not chary of his praise; and indeed I was a little like a young god, slender, graceful, yet powerful in build, with a golden skin and proportions that lacked little of perfection. If there was a fault it lay in that my legs were a little too short; but my godfather consoled me for this defect by saying that Goethe, that prince of the intellect, had been short-legged too and certainly had never been hampered thereby. The hours devoted to these sittings form an especial chapter in my memory. Yet I enjoyed even more, I think, the "dressing up" itself; and that took place not only in the studio but at our house as well. Often when my godfather was to sup with us he would send up a large bundle of costumes, wigs, and accessories and try them all on me after the meal, sketching any particularly good effect on the lid of a pasteboard box.

[11] Greek sculptor (fifth century B.C.). He is said to have supervised the sculpture for the great works on the Acropolis.

[12] Athenian statesman (fifth century B.C.).

[13] Overlaid with gold and ivory.

[14] Storeroom.

"He has a head for costumes," he would say, meaning that everything became me, and that in each disguise which I assumed I looked better and more natural than in the last. I might appear as a Roman flute-player in a short smock, a wreath of roses twined in my black locks; as an English page in snug-fitting satin with lace collar and plumed hat; as a Spanish bullfighter in spangled jacket and large round sombrero; as a youthful abbé of the Watteau period,[15] with cap and bands, mantle and buckled shoes; as an Austrian officer in white military tunic with sash and dagger; or as a German mountaineer in leather shorts and hobnailed boots, with the bock's-beard[16] stuck in his green felt hat—whatever the costume, the mirror assured me that I was born to wear it, and my audience declared that I looked to the life exactly the person whom I aimed to represent. My godfather even asserted that with the aid of costume and wig I seemed able to put on not only whatever social rank or national characteristics I chose, but that I could actually adapt myself to any given period or century. For each age, my godfather would say, imparts to its children its own physiognomical stamp; whereas I, in the costume of a Florentine dandy of the end of the Middle Ages, could look as though I had stepped from a contemporary portrait, and yet be no less convincing in the full-bottomed wig which was the fashionable ideal of a later century.—Ah, those were glorious hours! But when they were over and I resumed my dull and ordinary dress, how stale, flat, and unprofitable seemed all the world by contrast,[17] in what deep dejection did I spend the rest of the evening!

Of my godfather I shall say no more in this place. Later on, at the end of my strenuous career, this extraordinary man intervened decisively in my destiny and saved me from despair.

I search my mind for further impressions of my youth, and am reminded at once of the day when I first attended the theater, at Wiesbaden, with my parents. I should interpolate here that in what I have so far set down I have not too anxiously adhered to the chronological order but have treated my younger days as a whole and moved freely within them from episode to episode. When I posed to my godfather as a Greek god I was sixteen or seventeen years old and thus no longer a child, though very backward at school. But my first visit to the theater fell in my fourteenth year—though even so my physical and mental maturity, as will presently be seen, was well advanced and my sensitiveness to certain classes of impressions much keener than is ordinarily the case. What I saw that evening made the strongest impression on me and gave me food for perennial reflection.

We had first visited a Viennese café, where I drank sweet punch and my father imbibed absinthe through a straw—and this already was calculated to stir me to my depths. But how put into words the fever which possessed me when we drove in a droshky[18] to the theater and entered the lighted auditorium with its tiers of boxes? The women fanning their bosoms in the

[15] That is, of the seventeenth and eighteenth centuries. Antoine Watteau was a French painter (1684–1721).

[16] Decorative tuft of hair, like a goat's beard.

[17] "How weary, stale, flat, and unprofitable / Seem to me all the uses of this world!" (*Hamlet,* I.ii.133–134.)

[18] A kind of Russian carriage.

balcony, the men leaning over their chairs to chat; the hum and buzz of conversation in the stalls where we presently took our seats; the odors which streamed from hair and clothing to mingle with that of the illuminating gas; the confusion of sounds as the orchestra tuned up; the voluptuous frescoes displaying whole cascades of rosy foreshortenings—certainly all this could not but spur my youthful senses and prepare my mind for all the extraordinary scenes to follow. I had never before save in church seen so many people gathered together; and this playhouse, with its impressively complex seating-arrangements and its elevated stage where the elect, in brilliant costumes and to musical accompaniment, performed their dialogues and dances and developed the activities required by the plot—certainly all that was in my eyes a church where pleasure was the god; where men in need of edification gathered in the darkness to gaze upwards open-mouthed at a sphere of bright perfection where each saw embodied the desire of his heart.

The piece was an unpretentious offering to the comic muse—I have even forgotten its name. Its scene was laid in Paris, which delighted my poor father's heart, and it centered round the figure of an idle young attaché, the traditional fascinator and lady-killer, played by the highly popular leading man, whose name was Müller-Rosé. I heard his real name from my father, who rejoiced in his personal acquaintance, and the picture of this man will remain forever in my memory. He is probably old and worn-out by now, like me, but at that time his power to dazzle all the world, myself included, made upon me so strong an impression that it belongs to the decisive experiences of my life. I say to dazzle, and it will be seen hereafter how much meaning I would convey by that word. But first I will essay to set down from my still very lively recollections the impression which Müller-Rosé made upon me. On his first entrance he was dressed all in black—yet he radiated brilliance. He was supposed to come from some resort of the gay world and to be slightly intoxicated—a state which he knew how to counterfeit to perfection, yet without any suggestion of grossness. He wore a black cloak with a satin lining, patent-leather shoes, evening dress, white kid gloves, and a top hat which sat far back on his glistening locks, arranged in the then fashionable military parting, which ran all the way to the back of the neck. And every article of all this was so irreproachable, so well-pressed, and sat with a flawless perfection such as in real life could not endure above a quarter of an hour and made him seem like a being from another world. In particular the top hat, light-heartedly askew on his head, was the very pattern and mirror of what a top hat should be, without one grain of dust and with the most beautiful reflections, exactly as though they had been painted on. And this superb figure had a face to match, of a rosy fineness like wax, with almond-shaped, black-rimmed eyes, a small, short, straight nose and an extremely clear-cut, coral-red mouth and a little black moustache, even as though it were drawn with a paint-brush, following the outline of his arched upper lip. Reeling with a supple poise such as drunken men in everyday life do not possess, he gave his hat and stick to an attendant, slipped out of his cloak, and stood there in full evening fig, with diamond studs in his pleated shirt-front. As he drew off his gloves, laughing and rattling on in a silvery voice, you could see that his hands were white as milk outside and adorned with diamond rings, but inside pink like his face. He stood before the footlights at one side of the stage and trilled the first verse of a song all about what a wonderful life it was to be an attaché and a favorite with the ladies. Then he spread out his arms and snapped his fingers and waltzed apparently delirious with bliss over to the other side of the stage, where he sang the second verse and made his exit. Being recalled by loud applause, he sang the third and last verse in front of the prompter's box. And then with easy grace he began unfolding his rôle as called for by the plot. He was supposed to be very rich, which in itself lent his figure an almost magical charm. He appeared in a succession of "changes": immaculate white sports clothes with a red belt; a full-dress, slightly outré uniform—yes, in one delicate and hair-raising situation, pale-blue silk underdrawers. The complications of the plot were audacious, adventurous, and risqué by turns. One saw him at the feet of a countess, at a champagne supper with two predatory daughters of joy, and standing with raised pistol confronting his fatuous rival in a duel. And not one of these elegant but strenuous occupations had power to derange one fold of his shirt-front, extinguish any of the brilliance of his top hat, or deepen the delicate tint of his complexion. He moved so easily within the frame of the musical and dramatic conventions that they seemed, so far from restricting him, to release him from the limitations of everyday life. He seemed pervaded to the finger-tips by a magic which we know how to express only by the vague and inadequate word "talent"—the exercise of which obviously gave him as much pleasure as it did us. He would fit his fingers round the silver crook of his cane, would let his hands glide into his trouser pockets, and these actions, even his getting out of a chair, his very exits and entrances, had a quality of conscious gratification which filled the heart of the beholder with joy. Yes, that was it: Müller-Rosé heightened our joy of life—if the phrase is adequate to express that feeling, mingled of pain and pleasure, envy, yearning, hope, and irresistible love which the sight of the consummately charming can kindle in the human soul.

The public in the stalls was composed of middle-class citizens and their wives, clerks, one-year service men, and little girls in blouses; and despite the rapture of my own sensations I was able and eager to look about me and interpret the feelings of the audience. On all these faces sat a look of almost silly bliss. They were rapt in self-forgetful absorption, a smile played about their lips, sweeter and more lively in the little shop-girls, more brooding and dreamy in the grown-up women, while on the faces of the men it expressed the benevolent admiration which simple fathers feel in the presence of sons who have passed beyond their own sphere and realized the dreams of their youth. As for the clerks and the young soldiers, everything stood wide open in their upturned faces—eyes, mouths, nostrils, everything. And their smiles seemed to be saying: "Suppose it was us, standing up there in our underdrawers—how should we be making out? And look how he knows how to behave with those shameless hussies, just as though he were no better than they!"—When Müller-Rosé left the stage a power seemed to have gone out of the audience, all their shoulders sagged. When he stormed triumphantly from the back-stage to the footlights, holding a note with arms outspread, every bosom seemed to heave in his direction and the ladies' satin bodices creaked at the seams. Yes, as we sat there in the darkness we were like a swarm of night-flying insects rushing blind, dumb, and drunken into the flame.

My father was royally entertained. He had followed the French custom and carried hat and stick into the theater with him. When the curtain fell he put on the one and with the other banged on the floor loud and long. *"C'est épatant,"* said he several times, quite weak with enthusiasm. At last it was all over and we were outside in the lobby, among a crowd of clerks who were quite uplifted and trying to walk, talk, and hold their canes like the hero of the evening. My father said to me: "Come along, let's go and shake hands with him. Good Lord, weren't we on pretty good terms once, Müller and I? He will be delighted to see me again." So we instructed our ladies to wait for us in the vestibule and went off to pay our respects. We passed through the director's box, next the stage and already dark, then through a little door and behind the scenes. Stagehands were clearing away in the eerie darkness. A little creature in red livery, who had been a lift-boy in the play, stood leaning against the wall sunk in reverie. My poor father pinched her playfully where her figure was amplest and asked her the way to the dressing-rooms, which she pointed out with rather an ill grace. We went through a whitewashed corridor, where uncovered gas-jets flared in the confined air. From behind several doors issued loud laughter or angry voices, and my father gestured with his thumb to call my attention to them as we went on. At the end of the narrow passage he knocked on the last door, laying his ear to his knuckle. From within came a gruff shout: "Who's there?" or "What the devil do you want?" or words to that effect. "May I come in?" asked my father in reply, whereupon the voice instructed him to do something else with which I would not sully the pages of my narrative. My father smiled his deprecating little smile and called through the door: "Müller, it's Krull, Engelbert Krull. I suppose I may shake you by the hand, after all these years?" There was a laugh from inside and the voice said: "Oh, so it's you, old horse! Always on the hunt for some sport, eh?" And as we opened the door it went on: "I suppose you won't take any harm from my nakedness!" We went in. I shall never forget the disgusting sight that offered itself to my boyish eyes.

Müller-Rosé was seated at a grubby dressing-table in front of a dusty and speckled mirror with side wings. He had nothing on but a pair of grey tricot drawers, and a man in shirt-sleeves was massaging his back, the sweat running down his own face. The actor's visage glistened with salve and he was busy wiping if off with a towel already stiff with rouge and grease paint. Half of his countenance still had the rosy coating which had made him radiant on the stage but now looked merely pink and silly beside the cheesy pallor of the man's natural complexion. He had taken off the chestnut-brown wig and I saw that he was red-haired. One of his eyes still had deep black shadows beneath it and metallic dust clung to the lashes; the other was inflamed and watery and leered up at us with an indescribably *gamin* expression. All this I might have borne. But not the pimples with which Müller-Rosé's back, chest, shoulders, and upper arms were thickly strewn. They were horrible pimples, red-rimmed, suppurating, some of them even bleeding; even today I cannot repress a shudder at the thought of them. I find that our capacity for disgust is in direct proportion to our capacity for enjoyment, to our eagerness for the pleasures which this world can give. A cool and indifferent nature could never be so shaken by disgust as I was at that moment. Worst of all was the air of the room, compounded of sweat and exhalations from the pots and jars and sticks of grease paint which strewed the table. At first I thought I could not stand it above a minute without being sick.

However, I stood and looked—but I can add nothing to this description of Müller-Rosé's dressing-room. Perhaps I should reproach myself for having so little that is objective to report of my first visit to a theater—if I were not writing primarily for my own amusement and only secondarily for any public I may have. I am not bent on sustaining any dramatic suspense, leaving such effects to the writers of imaginative tales, who must contrive to give their inventions the beautiful and symmetrical proportions of a work of art—whereas my material is derived from my own experiences alone and I feel I may dispose it as seems to me good. Thus I shall linger upon such events as were of especial value or significance to me, neglecting no necessary detail to bring them out; passing over more lightly those of less personal moment. I have well-nigh forgotten what passed between my father and Müller-Rosé on that occasion—probably because other matters took my attention. For it is undoubtedly true that we receive stronger impressions through the senses than through the mind. I recall that the singer—though surely the applause which had greeted him that evening must have left him in no great doubt as to his triumph—kept asking my father whether it had "gone over" or how well it had "gone over." I perfectly understood how he felt. I have even a vague memory of some rather ordinary turns of phrase which he wove into the conversation, as for instance, in reply to some insinuation of my father's: "Shut your jaw—" then adding in the same breath: "over a quid of tobacco, there's some on the stand." But, as I said, I lent but half an ear to this or other specimens of his mental quality, being altogether taken up by my own sense impressions.

"So this, then"—ran my thoughts—"this pimpled and smeary individual is the charmer at whom the indistinguished masses were just now gazing up blissful-eyed! This repulsive worm is the reality of the glorious butterfly in whom all those deluded onlookers thought to see realized all their own secret dreams of beauty, grace and perfection! He is just like one of those disgusting little creatures which have the power of being phosphorescent in the evening." But the grown-up people in the audience, who on the whole must know about life and who yet were so frightfully eager to be deceived, must they not have been aware of the deception? Or did they just privately not consider it one? And that is quite possible. For when you come to think about it, which is the "real" shape of the glow-worm: the insignificant little creature crawling about on the flat of your hand, or the poetic spark that swims through the summer night? Who would presume to say? Rather call up the picture you saw before: the swarm of moths and gnats, rushing blindly and irresistibly into the flame. With what unanimity in the work of self-delusion! What can it be, then, but that such an instinctive need as this is implanted by God Himself in the heart of man, to satisfy which the Müller-Rosés are created? Here beyond a doubt is operative in life a wise and indispensable economy, in the service of which such men are kept and rewarded. How much admiration is his due for the success which he achieved tonight and achieves every night! Let us then smother what disgust we feel, in the realization that he knows all about his frightful pimples and yet—with the help of grease paint, lighting, music, and distance—can move before his audience with such complete assurance as to make them see in him their heart's ideal and thereby endlessly to enliven and edify them. And more: let us ask ourselves what it was that urged this miserable mountebank to learn the art of transfiguring himself nightly. What are the secret sources of the charm which possessed him and radiated from his finger-tips? The question needs but to be asked to be answered: who does not know the magic, the ineffable sweetness—for which any words we have are all too pale—of the power which teaches the glow-worm to light the night? This man could not hear too often nor too emphatically that his performance gave pleasure, pleasure beyond the ordinary. It was the yearning of all his being towards that host of yearning souls, it was that inspired and winged his art. He gave us joy of life, we in our turn sated his craving for applause; and was this not a mutual satisfaction, a true marriage of desires?

The above lines indicate the main current of the thoughts which surged through my eager and overheated brain as I sat there in Müller-Rosé's dressing-room, yes, and for days and weeks afterwards possessed my musings and my dreams. And always they were accompanied by emotions so profound and shattering, such a drunkenness of yearning, hope, and joy, that even today, despite my great fatigue, the memory of them makes my heart beat faster. In those days my feelings were of such violence that they threatened to burst my frame; often they made me somewhat ailing and thus served me as a pretext for stopping away from school.

It would be superfluous to dwell upon the reasons for my growing aversion to this odious institution. I am only able to live when my mind and my fancy are completely free; and thus it is that the memory of my years in prison is actually less hateful to me than those of the ostensibly more honorable bond of slavery and fear which chafed my sensitive boyish soul when I was forced to attend at the ugly little white box of a school-building down in the town. Add to these feelings the isolation from which I suffered, the grounds of which I have set forth above, and it will surprise nobody that I early had the idea of taking more holidays than the law allowed.

And in carrying out my idea another game I had long practiced was of signal service to me: that of imitating my father's handwriting. A father is the natural and nearest model for the growing boy striving to adapt himself to the adult world. Physical structure as well as the more mysterious bond between them incline the boy to admire all that in the parent of which he is still incapable himself and to strive to imitate it—or rather it is perhaps his very admiration which unconsciously leads him to develop along the lines which the laws of inheritance have laid down. At the time when I was still digging great pothooks in my slate I already dreamed of guiding a steel pen with my father's swiftness and skill; and how many scraps of paper I covered later on with efforts to copy his hand from memory, my fingers arranged round the pen in the same delicate fashion as his. His writing was not in fact very hard to imitate, for my poor father wrote a childish hand, like a copybook, quite undeveloped, its only peculiarity being that the letters were very tiny and prolonged immoderately by hairlines in a way I have never seen anywhere else. This mannerism I soon mastered to the life. In contrast to the angular Gothic character of the script the signature, *E. Krull,* had a Latin *ductus.*[19] It was surrounded by a perfect cloud of flourishes, which at first sight looked difficult to copy, but were in reality so simple in conception that I succeeded almost better with the signature than with anything else. The lower half of the *E* made a bold curve to the right, in whose open lap, as it were, the remaining syllable was neatly nestled. A second flourish rose from the *u,* embracing everything before it, cutting the curve of the *E* in two places and ending in an *s*-shaped down-stroke flanked like the curve of the *E* with rows of dots. The whole signature was higher than it was long, it was both naïve and bizarre; thus it lent itself so well to my purpose that in the end the inventor of it could not himself have distinguished between my products and his own.

Of course I very soon made practical use of a gift which had been acquired solely for my amusement. I employed it to gain my mental freedom—as follows: "My son Felix," I wrote, "had severe cramps on the 7th of this month and had to stop away from school. Regretfully yours, E. Krull." Or: "An infected sore on the gum as well as a sprained right arm obliged my son Felix to keep his bed from the 10th to the 14th. Regret his not having been able to attend school. Faithfully yours, E. Krull." My efforts being crowned with success, nothing hindered me from spending the school hours of one day or even of several roaming about outside the town, lying stretched in the leafy, whispering shade of some green pasture, dreaming the dreams peculiar to my youth and state. Sometimes I hid in the ruins of the old episcopal seat on the Rhine; sometimes, even, in winter and rough weather in the hospitable studio of my godfather, who indeed chid[20] me for my conduct, but in tones which showed that he had a certain sympathy with the motives which led to it.

But now and again it came about that I lay in bed at home–and not always, as I have explained above, without any justification. It is a favorite theory of mine that every deception which has not a higher truth at its root but is simply a barefaced lie is by the very fact so gross and palpable that nobody can fail to see through it. Only one kind of lie has a chance of being effective: that which is quite undeserving of the name of deceit, being but the product of a lively imagination which has not yet entered wholly into the realm of the actual and acquired those tangible signs by which alone it can be estimated at its proper worth. True, I was a sturdy boy, who never aside from the usual childish ails had anything the matter with him. Yet when one morning I decided to avoid trouble and suffering by stopping in bed I was by no means practicing a gross perversion of the actual situation. For why should I have gone to meet trouble, when I possessed the means of rendering powerless at will the arm of my oppressors? The higher truth actually was that the tension and depression due to my imaginative flights was not seldom so overpowering that they became actual suffering; together with my fear of what the day might bring forth they were enough to produce a basis of solid fact for my pretenses to rest upon. I needed to put no strain upon myself to command the sympathy and concern of my people and the family doctor.

On a certain day, when the need for freedom and the possession of my

[19] Flowing quality. [20] Chided; scolded.

own soul had become overpowering, I began with producing my symptoms with myself as sole audience. The extreme limit of the hour for rising was overpassed in dreams; breakfast had been brought in and was cooling on the table downstairs; all the stupid louts in town were on their dull schoolward way; daily life had begun, and I was irretrievably committed to a course of rebellion against my taskmasters. The audacity of my conduct was enough to make my heart flutter and my cheek turn pale. I noted that my finger-nails had taken on a bluish tint. The morning was cold and I needed to throw off the covers for only a few moments and to lie relaxed—when I had brought on a most convincing attack of shivers and teeth-chattering. All that I am saying is of course highly indicative of my character and temperament. I have always been very sensitive, susceptible, and in need of cherishing; and everything I have accomplished in life has been the result of self-conquest—yes, to be regarded as a moral achievement of a high order. If it were otherwise I should never, either then or later, have succeeded by mere voluntary relaxation of mind and body in producing the appearance of physical suffering and thus inclining those about me to tenderness and concern. To counterfeit illness effectively could never be within the powers of the coarse-grained man. But anybody who is made of finer stuff—if I may be pardoned for repeating the phrase—is always, though he may never be ill in the rude sense of the word, on familiar terms with suffering and can control its symptoms by intuition.

I closed my eyes and then opened them to their widest extent, making them look appealing and plaintive. I knew without the aid of a glass that my hair was rumpled from sleep and fell in damp strands on my brow. My face being already pale, I made it look sunken by a device of my own, drawing in the cheeks and holding them imperceptibly with the teeth from inside. This made my chin look longer too and gave me the appearance of having got thin overnight. A dilating of the nostrils and almost painful twitching of the muscles at the corners of the eyes contributed to the effect. I put my basin on a chair by my bed, folded my blue-nailed fingers across my breast, chattered my teeth from time to time, and thus awaited the moment when somebody should come to look me up.

That would not be too early; my parents loved to lie abed and it might be two or three school hours had passed before it became known that I was still in the house. Then my mother came upstairs and into the room and asked if I were ill. I looked at her large-eyed, as though in my dazed condition it was hard for me to tell who she was. Then I said yes, I thought I must be ill. What was the matter? Oh, my head, and the ache in my bones—"and why am I so cold?" I went on, in a monotonous voice, articulating with difficulty and tossing myself from side to side of the bed. My mother looked sympathetic. I do not believe that she took my sufferings very seriously, but as her sensibilities were very much in excess of her reason she could not bring herself to spoil the game but instead joined in and began to support me in my performance. "Poor child," she said, laying her forefinger on my cheek and shaking her head in pity, "don't you want something to eat?" I declined with a shudder, pressing my chin on my chest. The iron consistency of my performance sobered her somewhat; she was startled out of her enjoyment of the game, for that anybody should on such grounds refrain from food and drink was quite beyond her. She looked at me with a growing sense of reality. When she had got so far I assisted her to a decision by a display of art as arduous as it was effective. Starting up in bed with fitful and shuddering motions I drew my basin towards me and bent over it with frightful twitchings and contortions of my whole body, such as could not be witnessed without sympathetic convulsions by anyone not possessed of a heart of stone. "Nothing in me," I gasped between my writhings, lifting my wry and wasted face from the basin. "Gave it all up in the night"; and then I nerved myself to a protracted climax of such gaspings and chokings that it seemed I should never again get my breath. My mother held my head and repeatedly called me by my name in anxious and urgent tones, to bring me to myself. When my limbs began at length to relax, "I will send for Dusing!" she cried, and ran out of the room. Exhausted but with an indescribable and joyful sense of satisfaction, I fell back upon my pillows.

How often had I imagined to myself such a scene, how often passed through all its stages in my mind before I ventured to put it into operation! I hope that I may be understood when I say that I felt as though I were in a joyful dream when for the first time I put it into practice and achieved a complete success. It is not everybody can do such a thing. One may dream of it—but one does not do it. Suppose, a man thinks, that something awful were to happen to me: if I were to fall in a faint or blood were to burst out of my nose, or if I were to have some kind of seizure—then how suddenly the world's harsh unconcern would turn into attention, sympathy, and tardy remorse! But the flesh is obtusely strong and enduring, it holds out long after the mind has felt the need of sympathy and care; it will not manifest the alarming tangible symptoms which would make everybody imagine himself in a like state of suffering and speak with admonishing voice to the conscience of the world. But I—I had produced these symptoms, as effectively as though I had had nothing to do with their appearance. I had improved upon nature, realized a dream; and he alone who has tried to create a compelling and effective reality out of nothing, out of sheer inward knowledge and contemplation—in short, out of a combination of nothing but fantasy and his own personality—he alone can understand the strange and dreamlike satisfaction with which I rested from my creative task.

An hour later came Medical Inspector Dusing. He had been our family physician ever since the death of old Dr. Mecum, the practitioner who had ushered me into the world. Dr. Dusing was tall and stooped, with an awkward carriage and bristling mouse-colored hair. He was constantly either caressing his long nose with thumb and forefinger or else rubbing his large bony hands. This man might have been dangerous to my enterprise. Not, I think, through his professional ability, which I believe to have been meager—though indeed a genuine scholar serving science with single mind and heart for its own sake would have been easiest of all to deceive. No, but Dr. Dusing might have seen through me by virtue of a certain crude knowledge of human frailty which he possessed and which is often the whole stock-in-trade of inferior natures. This unworthy follower of Esculapius[21]

[21] Roman god of medicine.

was both stupid and striving and had been appointed to office through personal influence, adroit exploitation of wine-house acquaintances, and the receipt of patronage; he was always driving to Wiesbaden to further his interests in the exercise of his office. It was very telling that he did not keep to the rule of first come, first served in his waiting-room, but took the more influential patients first, leaving the simpler ones to sit. His manner towards the former class was obsequious, towards the latter harsh and cynical, often betraying that he did not believe in their complaints. I am convinced that he would not have stopped at any lie, corruption, or bribery which would ingratiate him with his superiors or recommend him as a zealous party man with the ruling powers; such behavior was consistent with the shrewd practical sense which in default of higher qualifications he relied upon to see him to his goal. My poor father's position was already very dubious; yet as a taxpayer and a business man he belonged to the influential classes of the town, and Dr. Dusing naturally wished to stand well with such a client. It is even possible that the wretched man enjoyed corruption for corruption's sake and found that a sufficient reason for conniving at my fraud. In any case, he would come in and sit down at my bedside with the usual phrases, saying: "Well, well, what's all this?" or "What have we here?" and the moment would come when a wink, a smile, or a significant little pause would indicate to me that we were partners in deception at the little game of shamming sick—"school-sick," as he was pleased to call it. Never did I make the smallest return to his advances. Not out of caution, for he would probably not have betrayed me, but out of pride and the genuine contempt I felt for him. I only looked more dismal and helpless, my cheeks grew hollower, my breathing shorter and more difficult, my mouth more lax, at each attempt he made to seduce me. I was quite prepared to go through another attack of vomiting if needs must; and so persistently did I fail to understand his worldly wisdom that in the end he had to abandon that line of attack in favor of a more strictly professional one.

That presented some difficulty. First because he was actually stupid; and second because the clinical picture I presented was very general and indefinite in its character. He thumped my chest and listened to me all over, peered into my throat by means of the handle of a tablespoon, gave me great discomfort by taking my temperature, and finally for better or worse was driven to pass judgment. "Just the megrims,"[22] said he. "Nothing to worry about. The usual attack. And our young friend's tummy always acts in sympathy. He must be quiet, see no visitors, he must not talk, better lie in a darkened room. I'll write a prescription—a little caffeine and citric acid will do no harm, it's always the best thing." If there were any cases of flu in the town, he would say: "Flu, my dear lady, with a gastric complication. That is what our young friend has caught. Not much inflammation of the passages as yet; still there is some. Do you notice any, my child? Do you feel like coughing? There is a little fever too; it will probably increase in the course of the day. The pulse is rapid and irregular." And he could think of nothing more, save to prescribe a certain bittersweet tonic

[22] Low spirits, the "blues."

wine from the chemist's. I was nothing loth; I found it most soothing and comforting, now that the battle had been won.

Indeed, the doctor's calling is not different from any other: its practitioners are for the most part ordinary empty-headed folk, ready to see what is not there and to deny the obvious. Any untrained person, if he loves and has knowledge of the flesh, is their superior and in the mysteries of the art can lead them by the nose. The inflammation of the air passages was something I had not thought of, so I had not included it in my performance. But once I had forced the doctor to drop the theory of "school-sickness," he had to fall back on flu, and to that end had to assume that my throat was irritated and my tonsils swollen, which was just as little the case as the other. He was quite right about the fever—though the fact entirely disproved his first diagnosis by presenting a genuine clinical phenomenon. Medical science teaches that fever can only be caused by the infection of the blood through some agency or other and that fever on other than physical grounds does not exist. That is absurd. My readers will be as convinced as I am myself that I was not ill in the ordinary sense when Inspector Dusing examined me. But I was highly excited; I had concentrated my whole being upon an act of the will; I was drunk with the intensity of my performance in the rôle of parodying nature—a performance which had to be masterly lest it become ridiculous; I was delirious with the alternate tension and relaxation necessary to give actuality in my own eyes and others' to a condition which did not exist; and all this so heightened and enhanced my organic processes that the doctor could actually read the result off the thermometer. The same explanation applies to the pulse. When the Inspector's head lay on my chest and I inhaled the animal odor of his dry grey hair, I had it in my power to feel a violent reaction that made my heart beat fast and unevenly. And as for my stomach, Dr. Dusing always said that it was affected, whatever other diagnosis he produced; and it was true enough that the organ was uncommonly sensitive, pulsing and contracting with every stir of feeling, so that where others under stress of circumstances speak of a throbbing heart, I might always speak of a throbbing stomach. Of this phenomenon the doctor was aware and he was not a little impressed by it.

So he prescribed his acid drops or his tonic wine and stopped awhile gossiping with my mother; I lay meantime breathing short-windedly through my flaccid lips and looking vacantly at the ceiling. My father would probably come in, too, and look at me with an embarrassed self-conscious air, avoiding my eye. He would take occasion to consult the doctor about his gout. Then I was left alone, to spend the day—perhaps two or three days—on short commons[23] (which I did not mind, because they made the food taste better) and in peace and freedom, given over to dreams of the brilliant future. When my youthful appetite rebelled at the diet of rusks[24] and gruel, I would slip out of my bed, open my writing-desk, and resort to the store of chocolate which nearly always lay there.

Where did I get my chocolate? It came into my possession in a strange, almost fantastic way. On a corner of the busiest street in our little city there

[23] Rations. [24] Dry toast, zwieback.

was an excellent delicatessen shop, a branch, if I mistake not, of a Wiesbaden firm. It supplied the wants of the best society and was most attractive. My way to school led me past this shop and many times I had entered it with a small coin in my hand to buy cheap sweets, such as fruit drops or barley sugar. But one day on going in I found it empty, not only of purchasers but also of attendants. There was a little bell on a spring over the door, and this had rung as I entered; but either the inner room was empty or the occupants did not hear the bell—I was and remained alone. And at first the emptiness surprised and startled me, it even gave me an uncanny feeling; but presently I began to look about me, for never before had I been able to contemplate undisturbed the delights of such a spot. It was a narrow room, with a rather high ceiling, and crammed from top to bottom with goodies. There were rows and rows of hams, sausages of all shapes and colors—white, yellow, red, and black; fat and lean and round and long—lines of tins and conserves, cocoas and teas, bright translucent glasses of honey, marmalade, and jam; bottles plump and bottles slender, filled with liqueurs and punch—all these things crowded the shelves from floor to ceiling. Then there were glass showcases where smoked mackerel, lampreys, flounders, and eels were displayed on platters to tempt the appetite. There were dishes of Italian salad, lobsters spreading their claws on blocks of ice, sprats pressed flat and gleaming goldenly from opened boxes; choice fruits—garden strawberries and grapes beautiful as though they came from the Promised Land; tiers of sardine tins and those fascinating little white earthenware jars of caviar and *foie gras*. Plump chickens dangled their necks from the top shelf, and there were trays of cooked meats, ham, tongue, beef, and veal, smoked salmon and breast of goose, with the slender slicing-knife lying ready to hand. There were all sorts of cheeses under glass bells, brick-red, milk-white, and marbled, also the creamy ones that ooze in a golden wave out of their silver foil. Artichokes, bundles of asparagus, truffles, little liver sausages in silver paper—all these things lay heaped in rich abundance; while on other tables stood open tin boxes full of fine biscuits, spice cakes piled in criss-cross layers, and glass urns full of dessert bonbons and crystallized fruits.

I stood transfixed. Holding my breath and cocking my ears I drank in the enchanting atmosphere of the place and the medley of odors from chocolate and smoked fish and earthy truffles. My fancy ran riot with memories of fairy stories of the paradise of children, of underground treasure-chambers where children born on Sunday might enter and fill their pockets with precious stones. It seemed like a dream; everyday laws and dull regulations were all suspended, one might give free rein to one's desires and let fancy rove in blissful unrestraint. I was seized with such a fever of desire on beholding this paradise of plenty entirely given over to my single person that I felt my very limbs to twitch. It took great self-control not to burst out in a paean of jubilation at so much richness and so much freedom. I spoke into the silence, saying: "Good day" in quite a loud voice; I can still remember how the strained tones of my voice died away into the stillness. No one answered. And the water ran into my mouth in streams at that very moment. One quick and noiseless step and I stood beside one of the laden tables. I made one rapturous grab into the nearest glass urn, slipped my fistful of pralines into my coat pocket, gained the door, and by another second was round the corner of the street.

No doubt I shall be accused of common theft. I will not deny the accusation, I will simply retreat and not confront anyone who chooses to take the paltry word into his mouth. But the word—the poor, cheap, worn-out word, which does violence to all the finer meanings of life—is one thing, and quite another the living, primeval, and absolute deed, forever shining with newness and originality. It is only out of habit and sheer mental indolence that we come to regard them as the same thing. And the truth is that the word, as used to describe or characterize a deed, is no better than one of these wire fly-killers that always miss the fly. Moreover, whenever it is a question of an act, it is not the what nor the why that matters (although the second is the more important), but simply and solely the who. Whatever I have done and committed, it has always been first of all *my* deed, not Tom's, Dick's, or Harry's: and though I have had to swallow, especially at the hands of the law, having the same name applied to me as to ten thousand others, I have always rebelled against such an unnatural comparison, in the unshakable conviction that I am a favorite of the powers that be and actually compact of different flesh and blood. The reader will forgive me this excursion into the abstract, and it may be that it ill becomes me, for I have no training or warrant for that kind of metaphysical thought. But I consider it my duty either to reconcile him so far as possible with the idiosyncrasies of my existence or else to prevent him from reading further.

When I got home I went up to my room, still in my overcoat, spread my treasure-trove out on my table, and examined it. I almost disbelieved that it was still there—for how often do not priceless things come to us in our dreams, yet when we wake our hands are empty? Imagine my lively joy—like that of a man waking from such a dream to find his treasure materialized on his bed-quilt—in examining my bonbons! They were of the best quality, wrapped in silver paper, filled with sweet liqueur and flavored creams; but it was not alone their quality that enraptured me; even more it was the winning over of my dream treasure into my waking hand that made up the sum of my delight—a delight too great for me not to think of repeating it as occasion offered. Whatever the explanation—I did not cudgel my brains to find one—the shop proved to be often open and unwatched at the noon hour, as I could tell by strolling slowly past the door with my school-satchel on my back. I would return and go in, having learned to open the door so softly that the little bell did not jingle. By way of precaution I would say: "Good day"—and then take what was nearest, never too much, always with wise moderation, a handful of bonbons, a tablet of chocolate, a slice of cake—very probably nothing was ever missed. But these dreamlike occasions on which I clutched with open hand the sweets of life were accompanied by such an expansion of my whole personality that they gave me anew the sensations with which certain trains of thought and introspection had already made me familiar.

At this point—though not without having laid aside the flowing pen to pause and collect my thoughts—I wish to enter at more length with my unknown reader upon a theme already glanced at earlier in these confessions. Let me say at once that such a reader will be disappointed if he expects from me any lightness of tone or lewdness of expression. No, for the dictates of morality and good form demand that discretion and sobriety be united with the candor which I promised at the outset of my enterprise. Pleasure in the salacious for its own sake, though an almost universal fault, has always been incomprehensible to me, and verbal excesses of this kind I have always found the most repulsive of all, since they are the cheapest and have not the excuse of passion. People laugh and joke about these matters precisely as though they were dealing with the simplest and most amusing subject in the world, whereas the exact opposite is the truth; and to talk of them in that loose and airy way is to surrender to the whinnyings of the mob the most important and mysterious concern of nature and of life. But to my confession.

First of all I must make it clear that the above-mentioned concern began very early to play a rôle with me, to occupy my thoughts, shape my fancies, and form the content of my childish enterprises—long, that is, before I had any words for it or could possibly form any general ideas of its nature or bearing. For a considerable time, that is, I regarded my tendency to such thoughts and the lively pleasure I had in them to be private and personal to myself. Nobody else, I thought, would understand them, and it was in fact advisable not to talk of them at all. Lacking any other means of description, I grouped all my emotions and fancies together under the heading of "the great joy" or "the best of all" and guarded them as a priceless secret. And thanks to this jealous reserve, thanks also to my isolation, and to a third cause to which I shall presently come, I long remained in this state of intellectual ignorance which so little corresponded to the liveliness of my senses. For as far back as I can remember, this "great joy" took up a commanding position in my inner life—indeed it probably began to do so farther back than my conscious memory extends. For small children are to that extent "innocent" in that they are unconscious; but that they are so in the sense of angelic purity is without doubt a sentimental superstition which would not stand the test of an objective examination. For myself, at least, I have it from an unexceptionable source, that even at my nurse's breast I displayed the clearest evidence of certain feelings—and this tradition has always seemed highly credible to me, as indicative of the eagerness of my nature.

In fact my penchant for the pleasures of love bordered on the extraordinary; even today it is my conviction that it far exceeded the usual measure. That this was so I had early grounds for suspecting; but my suspicions were converted to certainty on the evidence of that person who told me of my susceptible behavior while still at the breast. With this person I sustained for several years a secret relationship. I refer to our housemaid Genoveva, who had been with us from a child and was in the beginning of her thirties when I reached sixteen. She was the daughter of a sergeant-major and had for a long time been engaged to the station-master at a little station between Frankfurt and Nieder-Lahnstein. She had a good deal of feeling for the refinements of life, and although she performed all the hard work of the house her position was as much housekeeper as servant. The marriage was—for lack of money—only a distant prospect; and the long waiting must have been a genuine hardship to the poor girl. In person she was a well-developed blonde with a lively green eye and mincing ways.

But despite the prospect of spending her best years in renunciation she never listened to proposals from a lower sphere of society—advances from soldiers, working-men, or such people—for she did not reckon herself with common folk, feeling disgust for their speech and the way they smelled. The case was different with the son of the house, who aroused her approbation as he developed, and might give her the feeling that in satisfying him she both as it were performed a domestic duty and also improved her own station in society. Thus it happened that my desires did not encounter any serious resistance. I need not go into great detail—the episode had the usual features, too well known to be of interest to a cultured audience.

One evening my godfather Maggotson had supped with us, and we had spent the evening trying on costumes. When I went up to bed it happened—very likely so contrived by her—that I met Genoveva at the door of my attic room. We stopped to talk, by degrees moved over into the room itself, and ended by occupying it together for the night. I well remember my mood: it was one of gloom, disillusion, and boredom such as often seized upon me at the end of an evening devoted to the exercise of my "head for costumes"—only this time even more severe than usual. I had resumed my ordinary garb with loathing, I had the impulse to tear it off—but not the desire to forget my misery in slumber. For it seemed to me that the only possible consolation was to be found in Genoveva's arms—yes, to tell the whole truth, I felt that in complete intimacy with her I should find the continuation and consummation of my brilliant evening and the proper goal of my ramblings through my godfather's wardrobe of costumes. However that may be, at least the soul-satisfying, unimaginable delight I discovered on Genoveva's white, well-nourished breast defies all description. I cried out for very bliss, I felt myself mounting heavenwards. And it was not of a selfish nature, my desire: for so I was constructed that it was kindled only by the mutual joy of Genoveva.

Of course every possibility of comparison is out of the question; I can neither demonstrate nor disprove, but I was then and am now convinced that with me the satisfaction of love is twicc as sweet and twice as poignant as with the average man. But it would be doing me an injustice to conclude that on the score of my unusual endowment I became a libertine and lady-killer. My difficult and dangerous life made great demands on my powers of concentration—I had to take care not to exhaust myself. I have observed that with some the act of love is a trifle which they perfunctorily discharge and go their way as though nothing had happened. As for me, the tribute which I paid was so great as to leave me for the time quite vacant and empty of the power to act. True, I have often exceeded, for the flesh is weak and I found my amorous requirements only too easily met. But in the end and on the whole I was of a temper too manly and too serious not to be called back from sensual relaxation to a necessary and healthful austerity. Moreover, the purely physical satisfaction is surely the grosser part of that which I had as a child instinctively called "the great joy." It enervates by satisfying us all too completely; it makes us bad lovers of the world, because on the one hand it robs life of its bloom and enchantment and on the other it impoverishes our own power to charm, since only he who desires is amiable, not he who is sated. For my part, I know many kinds of satisfaction finer and more subtle than the crude act which after all is but a limited and illusory satisfaction of appetite; and I am convinced that he has but a crude notion of enjoyment whose activities are directed only and immediately to the definite goal. My desires were always upon a broader, larger, and more general scale; they found the sweetest feeding where others might not seek; they were never precisely defined or specialized—and for this reason among others it was that despite my special aptitude I remained so long innocent and unconscious, yes, actually my whole life long a child and dreamer.

And herewith I leave a subject in dealing with which I believe I have not for a moment transgressed the canons of propriety and good taste, and hasten forwards to the tragic moment which terminated my sojourn under my parents' roof, and formed the turning-point of my career. I begin by mentioning the betrothal of my sister Olympia to Second Lieutenant Deibel of the second Nassau regiment No. 88, stationed in Mainz. The betrothal was attended by celebrations on a grand scale but led up to no other consequences. For the stress of circumstances proved too much for it; it was broken off and my sister—after the collapse of our family life—went on the stage. Deibel was a sickly young man, very ignorant of life. He was a constant guest at our parties, where, heated by dancing, forfeit-playing, and Berncasteler Doctor and fired by the judicious glimpses of their charms vouchsafed by the ladies of our household, he fell wildly in love with Olympia. With the concupiscence of weak-chested persons the world over, and probably overestimating our position and consequence, he actually one evening went on his knees and, almost shedding tears in his ardor, implored her to be his. To this day I do not understand how Olympia had the face to accept him, for certainly she did not respond to the feelings he professed and was doubtless informed by my mother of the true state of our affairs. But she probably thought it was high time to be sure of some refuge, no matter how frail, from the oncoming storm; she may even have thought that her engagement to an officer in the army, however poor his prospects, might delay the catastrophe. My poor father was appealed to for his consent and gave it with an embarrassed air and not much to say; whereupon the family event was communicated to the assembled guests, who received the news with loud acclaim and baptized it, so to say, with streams of Lorley Extra Cuvée. After that, Lieutenant Deibel came almost daily to our house from Mainz, and did no little damage to his health by constant attendance upon the object of his sickly desire. I once entered the room where the betrothed pair had been for some little time alone and found him looking so distracted and moribund that I am convinced the turn which affairs presently took was for him a piece of unmixed good fortune.

As for me, my mind was occupied in these weeks almost wholly with the fascinating subject of the change of name which my sister's marriage would entail upon her. I remember that I envied her almost to bitterness. She who for so long had been called Olympia Krull would sign herself in future Olympia Deibel—and that fact alone possessed all the charm of novelty. How tiresome it is to sign all one's life long the same name to letters and papers! The hand grows paralyzed with irritation and disgust—what a pleasurable refreshment and stimulation then of the whole being comes of being able to give oneself a new name and to hear oneself addressed by it! It seemed to me a positive advantage which the female sex has over the male that at least once in life the opportunity is afforded of this tonic and restorative—whereas to the male any change is as good as forbidden by law. I, personally, not having been born to lead the flabby and protected existence of the great bourgeois class, have often overstepped a prohibition which ran counter both to my safety and my dislike of the humdrum and everyday. I displayed in the process, if I may say so, a very pretty gift of invention; and there was a peculiar easy grace in the act whereby I, for the first time in my life, laid aside like a soiled and worn-out garment the name to which I was born, to assume another which for elegance and euphony far surpassed that of Lieutenant Deibel.

But in the midst of the betrothal episode events had taken their course, and ruin—to express myself poetically—knocked with harsh knuckles upon the door of our home. Those malicious rumors about my poor father's business, the studied avoidance we suffered from all and sundry, the gossip about our domestic affairs—all these were most cruelly confirmed by the event, to the unlovely satisfaction of the croakers. The consuming public had more and more refrained from buying our brand of wine. Lowering the price of course did not improve the product, nor did the alluring design produced against his better judgment by my good-natured godfather have any effect in staying the disaster. Ruin fell upon my poor father in the spring of my eighteenth year.

I was of course at that time entirely lacking in business sense—nor am I now any better off in that respect, since my own career, based on imagination and self-discipline, gave me no commercial training. Accordingly I refrain from trying my pen on a subject of which I have no knowledge and from burdening the reader with an account of the misfortunes of the Lorley wine company. But I feel impelled to give expression to the great sympathy which in these last months I felt for my father. He sank more and more into a speechless melancholy and would sit somewhere about the house with his head bent and the fingers of his right hand gently stroking his rounded belly, ceaselessly and rapidly blinking his eyes. He made frequent pathetic trips to Mainz, probably to try to get hold of some money; he would return from these excursions greatly dejected, wiping his face and eyes with a little batiste handkerchief. It was only at the evening parties, which we still held in our villa, when he sat at table with his napkin tied round his neck, his guest about him, and his glass in his hand, presiding over the feast, that anything like comfort revisited him. Yet in the course of one such evening there occurred a most unpleasant quarrel between my poor father and the Jewish banker, husband of the jet-laden female. He, as I then learned, was one of the most hardened cut-throats who ever lured harried and unwary business folk into their nets. Very soon thereafter came that serious and ominous day—yet for me refreshing in its novel excitement—when the factory and business premises of my father did not open and a group of cold-eyed, tight-lipped gentlemen appeared at our villa to attach our possessions. My poor father, in the choicest of phrases, had declared his bankruptcy before the courts and appended to his declaration that naïve and flourishing signature of his which I so well knew how to imitate; and with due solemnity proceedings in bankruptcy were instituted.

On that day our disgrace gave me occasion to stop away from school—

and I may say here that it was never granted me to finish my course. This was firstly due to my never having troubled to conceal my aversion to the despotism and dullness which characterized that institution, and secondly because our domestic circumstances and ultimate disruption filled the masters with venom and contempt. At the Easter holidays after my poor father's failure they refused to give me my leaving-certificate, thus offering me the alternative of putting up with an inferior position unsuited to my age or of leaving the school and losing the advantages of a certificate. In the joyful consciousness that my native parts were adequate to make up for the loss of such extremely limited advantages, I chose the latter course.

Our financial collapse was complete; it became clear that my poor father had put it off so long and involved himself so deeply in the toils of the usurers only because he was aware that when the crash came it would reduce him to beggary. Everything came under the hammer: the warehouses (but who wanted to buy so notoriously bad a product as my father's wine?), the real estate—that is, the cellars and our villa, laden as those were with mortgages to two-thirds of their value, the interest on which had not been paid for years; the dwarfs, the toadstools and crockery animals in the garden—yes, the glass ball and the aeolian harp went the same sad way. The inside of the house was stripped of every charm: the spinning-wheel, the down cushions, the glass boxes and smelling-bottles all went at public auction, not even the halberds over the windows and the glass bead curtains were spared, and if the little device over the ventilator that played "Wine, Women, and Song" when the door was opened, still jingled unmindful of the desolation, it was only because it had not been noticed by its legal owners.

One could scarcely say at first that my father looked like a broken man. His face even expressed a certain satisfaction that his affairs, having passed beyond his own competence, now found themselves in such good hands; and since the bank which had purchased our property let us for very pity remain for the present within its bare walls, we still had a roof over our heads. Temperamentally easy-going and good-natured, he could not credit his fellow human beings with being so puritanically cruel as to reject him utterly; he was simple enough to try to form a local company with himself as director. His proposals were brusquely repulsed, as also other efforts he made to re-establish himself in life—though if he had been successful he would doubtless have proceeded upon his old courses of feastings and fireworks. But when everything failed he at last recognized the fact; and probably considering that he was in the way of us others, who might make better headway without him, he resolved to make an end of himself.

Five months had passed since the beginning of the bankruptcy proceedings; it was early autumn. Since Easter I had not gone back to school and was enjoying my temporary freedom and lack of prospects. We had gathered in our bare dining-room, my mother, my sister Olympia, and I, to eat our meager meal, and were waiting for the head of the family. But when we had finished our soup and he did not appear, we sent Olympia, who had always been his favorite, to summon him. She had been gone scarcely three minutes when we heard her give a prolonged scream and then run still screaming upstairs and down and then distractedly up again. Frightened to my very marrow and ready for the worst, I went to my father's room. There he lay, upon the floor, with his clothing opened; his hand was resting upon the roundness of his belly, and beside him lay the fatal shining thing with which he had shot himself in his gentle heart. Our maid Genoveva and I lifted him to the sofa, and while she ran for the doctor, my sister Olympia still rushed screaming through the house, and my mother out of very fear would not venture out of the dining-room, I stood beside the earthly husk of my progenitor, now growing cold, with my hand over my eyes, and paid him the abundant tribute of my tears.

DISORDER AND EARLY SORROW

Translated by H. T. Lowe-Porter

The principal dish at dinner had been croquettes made of turnip greens. So there follows a trifle,[1] concocted out of those dessert powders we use nowadays,[2] that taste like almond soap. Xaver, the youthful manservant, in his outgrown striped jacket, white woolen gloves, and yellow sandals, hands it round, and the "big folk" take this opportunity to remind their father, tactfully, that company is coming today.

The "big folk" are two, Ingrid and Bert. Ingrid is brown-eyed, eighteen, and perfectly delightful. She is on the eve of her exams, and will probably pass them, if only because she knows how to wind masters, and even headmasters, round her finger. She does not, however, mean to use her certificate once she gets it; having leanings towards the stage, on the ground of her ingratiating smile, her equally ingratiating voice, and a marked and irresistible talent for burlesque. Bert is blond and seventeen. He intends to get done with school somehow, anyhow, and fling himself into the arms of life. He will be a dancer, or a cabaret actor, possibly even a waiter—but not a waiter anywhere else save at Cairo, the night-club, whither he has once already taken flight, at five in the morning, and been brought back crestfallen. Bert bears a strong resemblance to the youthful manservant, Xaver Kleinsgutl, of about the same age as himself; not because he looks common—in features he is strikingly like his father, Professor Cornelius—but by reason of an approximation of types, due in its turn to far-reaching compromises in matters of dress and bearing generally. Both lads wear their heavy hair very long on top, with a cursory parting in the middle, and give their heads the same characteristic toss to throw it off the forehead. When one of them leaves the house, by the garden gate, bareheaded in all weathers, in a blouse rakishly girded with a leather strap, and sheers off bent well over with his head on one side; or else mounts his push-bike—Xaver makes free with his employers', of both sexes, or even, in acutely irresponsible mood, with the Professor's own—Dr. Cornelius from his bedroom window cannot, for the life of him, tell whether he is

[1] A dessert made of sponge cake spread with a jam or other filling and covered with custard.

[2] That is, during the difficult inflationary period that followed World War I. *Disorder and Early Sorrow* was written in 1925.

looking at his son or his servant. Both, he thinks, look like young moujiks.[3] And both are impassioned cigarette-smokers, though Bert has not the means to compete with Xaver, who smokes as many as thirty a day, of a brand named after a popular cinema star. The big folk call their father and mother the "old folk"—not behind their backs, but as a form of address and in all affection: "Hullo, old folks," they will say; though Cornelius is only forty-seven years old and his wife eight years younger. And the Professor's parents, who lead in his household the humble and hesitant life of the really old, are on the big folk's lips the "ancients." As for the "little folk," Ellie and Snapper, who take their meals upstairs with blue-faced Ann—so-called because of her prevailing facial hue—Ellie and Snapper follow their mother's example and address their father by his first name, Abel. Unutterably comic it sounds, in its pert, confiding familiarity; particularly on the lips, in the sweet accents, of five-year-old Eleanor, who is the image of Frau Cornelius's baby pictures and whom the Professor loves above everything else in the world.

"Darling old thing," says Ingrid affably, laying her large but shapely hand on his, as he presides in proper middle-class style over the family table, with her on his left and the mother opposite: "Parent mine, may I ever so gently jog your memory, for you have probably forgotten: this is the afternoon we were to have our little jollification, our turkey-trot with eats to match. You haven't a thing to do but just bear up and not funk it; everything will be over by nine o'clock."

"Oh—ah!" says Cornelius, his face falling. "Good!" he goes on, and nods his head to show himself in harmony with the inevitable. "I only meant—is this really the day? Thursday, yes. How time flies! Well, what time are they coming?"

"Half past four they'll be dropping in, I should say," answers Ingrid, to whom her brother leaves the major rôle in all dealings with the father. Upstairs, while he is resting, he will hear scarcely anything, and from seven to eight he takes his walk. He can slip out by the terrace if he likes.

"Tut!" says Cornelius deprecatingly, as who should say: "You exaggerate." But Bert puts in: "It's the one evening in the week Wanja doesn't have to play. Any other night he'd have to leave by half past six, which would be painful for all concerned."

Wanja is Ivan Herzl, the celebrated young leading man at the Stadttheater.[4] Bert and Ingrid are on intimate terms with him, they often visit him in his dressing-room and have tea. He is an artist of the modern school, who stands on the stage in strange and, to the Professor's mind, utterly affected dancing attitudes, and shrieks lamentably. To a professor of history, all highly repugnant; but Bert has entirely succumbed to Herzl's influence, blackens the lower rim of his eyelids—despite painful but fruitless scenes with the father—and with youthful carelessness of the ancestral anguish declares that not only will he take Herzl for his model if he becomes a dancer, but in case he turns out to be a waiter at the Cairo he means to walk precisely thus.

Cornelius slightly raises his brows and makes his son a little bow—indicative of the unassumingness and self-abnegation that befits his age.

[3] Russian peasants. [4] Municipal theater.

You could not call it a mocking bow or suggestive in any special sense. Bert may refer it to himself or equally to his so talented friend.

"Who else is coming?" next inquires the master of the house. They mention various people, names all more or less familiar, from the city, from the suburban colony, from Ingrid's school. They still have some telephoning to do, they say. They have to phone Max. This is Max Hergesell, an engineering student; Ingrid utters his name in the nasal drawl which according to her is the traditional intonation of all the Hergesells. She goes on to parody it in the most abandonedly funny and lifelike way, and the parents laugh until they nearly choke over the wretched trifle. For even in these times when something funny happens people have to laugh.

From time to time the telephone bell rings in the Professor's study, and the big folk run across, knowing it is their affair. Many people had to give up their telephones the last time the price rose, but so far the Corneliuses have been able to keep theirs, just as they have kept their villa, which was built before the war, by dint of the salary Cornelius draws as professor of history—a million marks,[5] and more or less adequate to the chances and changes of postwar life. The house is comfortable, even elegant, though sadly in need of repairs that cannot be made for lack of materials, and at present disfigured by iron stoves with long pipes. Even so, it is still the proper setting of the upper middle class, though they themselves look odd enough in it, with their worn and turned clothing and altered way of life. The children, of course, know nothing else; to them it is normal and regular, they belong by birth to the "villa proletariat." The problem of clothing troubles them not at all. They and their like have evolved a costume to fit the time, by poverty out of taste for innovation: in summer it consists of scarcely more than a belted linen smock and sandals. The middle-class parents find things rather more difficult.

The big folk's table napkins hang over their chair-backs, they talk with their friends over the telephone. These friends are the invited guests who have rung up to accept or decline or arrange; and the conversation is carried on in the jargon of the clan, full of slang and high spirits, of which the old folk understand hardly a word. These consult together meantime about the hospitality to be offered to the impending guests. The Professor displays a middle-class ambitiousness: he wants to serve a sweet—or something that looks like a sweet—after the Italian salad and brownbread sandwiches. But Frau Cornelius says that would be going too far. The guests would not expect it, she is sure—and the big folk, returning once more to their trifle, agree with her.

The mother of the family is of the same general type as Ingrid, though not so tall. She is languid; the fantastic difficulties of the housekeeping have broken and worn her. She really ought to go and take a cure,[6] but feels incapable; the floor is always swaying under her feet, and everything seems upside down. She speaks of what is uppermost in her mind: the eggs, they simply must be bought today. Six thousand marks apiece they are, and just so many are to be had on this one day of the week at one single shop fifteen minutes' journey away. Whatever else they do, the big folk must go

[5] This high monthly salary reflects the runaway inflation in postwar Germany.
[6] Rest cure, at a spa.

and fetch them immediately after luncheon, with Danny, their neighbor's son, who will soon be calling for them; and Xaver Kleinsgutl will don civilian garb and attend his young master and mistress. For no single household is allowed more than five eggs a week; therefore the young people will enter the shop singly, one after another, under assumed names, and thus wring twenty eggs from the shopkeeper for the Cornelius family. This enterprise is the sporting event of the week for all participants, not excepting the moujik Kleinsgutl, and most of all for Ingrid and Bert, who delight in misleading and mystifying their fellowmen and would revel in the performance even if it did not achieve one single egg. They adore impersonating fictitious characters; they love to sit in a bus and carry on long lifelike conversations in a dialect which they otherwise never speak, the most commonplace dialogue about politics and people and the price of food, while the whole bus listens open-mouthed to this incredibly ordinary prattle, though with a dark suspicion all the while that something is wrong somewhere. The conversation waxes ever more shameless, it enters into revolting detail about these people who do not exist. Ingrid can make her voice sound ever so common and twittering and shrill as she impersonates a shopgirl with an illegitimate child, said child being a son with sadistic tendencies, who lately out in the country treated a cow with such unnatural cruelty that no Christian could have borne to see it. Bert nearly explodes at her twittering, but restrains himself and displays a grisly sympathy; he and the unhappy shopgirl entering into a long, stupid, depraved, and shuddery conversation over the particular morbid cruelty involved; until an old gentleman opposite, sitting with his ticket folded between his index finger and his seal ring, can bear it no more and makes public protest against the nature of the themes these young folk are discussing with such particularity. He uses the Greek plural: "themata." Whereat Ingrid pretends to be dissolving in tears, and Bert behaves as though his wrath against the old gentleman was with difficulty being held in check and would probably burst out before long. He clenches his fists, he gnashes his teeth, he shakes from head to foot; and the unhappy old gentleman, whose intentions had been of the best, hastily leaves the bus at the next stop.

Such are the diversions of the big folk. The telephone plays a prominent part in them: they ring up any and everybody—members of government, opera singers, dignitaries of the Church—in the character of shop assistants, or perhaps as Lord or Lady Doolittle. They are only with difficulty persuaded that they have the wrong number. Once they emptied their parents' card-tray[7] and distributed its contents among the neighbors' letter-boxes, wantonly, yet not without enough impish sense of the fitness of things to make it highly upsetting, God only knowing why certain people should have called where they did.

Xaver comes in to clear away, tossing the hair out of his eyes. Now that he has taken off his gloves you can see the yellow chain-ring[8] on his left hand. And as the Professor finishes his watery eight-thousand-mark beer and lights a cigarette, the little folk can be heard scrambling down the stair, coming, by established custom, for their after-dinner call on Father and

[7] Tray where visitors left their calling-cards.
[8] Wrist chain affected by young bohemians of the time.

Mother. They storm the dining-room, after a struggle with the latch, clutched by both pairs of little hands at once; their clumsy small feet twinkle over the carpet, in red felt slippers with the socks falling down on them. With prattle and shoutings each makes for his own place: Snapper to Mother, to climb on her lap, boast of all he has eaten, and thump his fat little tum; Ellie to her Abel, so much hers because she is so very much his; because she consciously luxuriates in the deep tenderness—like all deep feeling, concealing a melancholy strain—with which he holds her small form embraced; in the love in his eyes as he kisses her little fairy hand or the sweet brow with its delicate tracery of tiny blue veins.

The little folk look like each other, with the strong undefined likeness of brother and sister. In clothing and haircut they are twins. Yet they are sharply distinguished after all, and quite on sex lines. It is a little Adam and a little Eve. Not only is Snapper the sturdier and more compact, he appears consciously to emphasize his four-year-old masculinity in speech, manner, and carriage, lifting his shoulders and letting the little arms hang down quite like a young American athlete, drawing down his mouth when he talks and seeking to give his voice a gruff and forthright ring. But all this masculinity is the result of effort rather than natively his. Born and brought up in these desolate, distracted times, he has been endowed by them with an unstable and hypersensitive nervous system and suffers greatly under life's disharmonies. He is prone to sudden anger and outbursts of bitter tears, stamping his feet at every trifle; for this reason he is his mother's special nursling and care. His round, round eyes are chestnut brown and already inclined to squint, so that he will need glasses in the near future. His little nose is long, the mouth small—the father's nose and mouth they are, more plainly than ever since the Professor shaved his pointed beard and goes smooth-faced. The pointed beard had become impossible—even professors must make some concession to the changing times.

But the little daughter sits on her father's knee, his Eleonorchen,[9] his little Eve, so much more gracious a little being, so much sweeter-faced than her brother—and he holds his cigarette away from her while she fingers his glasses with her dainty wee hands. The lenses are divided for reading and distance, and each day they tease her curiosity afresh.

At bottom he suspects that his wife's partiality may have a firmer basis than his own: that Snapper's refractory masculinity perhaps is solider stuff than his own little girl's more explicit charm and grace. But the heart will not be commanded, that he knows; and once and for all his heart belongs to the little one, as it has since the day she came, since the first time he saw her. Almost always when he holds her in his arms he remembers that first time: remembers the sunny room in the Women's Hospital, where Ellie first saw the light, twelve years after Bert was born. He remembers how he drew near, the mother smiling the while, and cautiously put aside the canopy of the diminutive bed that stood beside the large one. There lay the little miracle among the pillows: so well formed, so encompassed, as it were, with the harmony of sweet proportions, with little hands that even then, though so much tinier, were beautiful as now; with wide-open eyes blue as

[9] "Little Eleanor," an affectionate diminutive form of "Eleanor."

the sky and brighter than the sunshine—and almost in that very second he felt himself captured and held fast. This was love at first sight, love everlasting: a feeling unknown, unhoped for, unexpected—in so far as it could be a matter of conscious awareness; it took entire possession of him, and he understood, with joyous amazement, that this was for life.

But he understood more. He knows, does Dr. Cornelius, that there is something not quite right about this feeling, so unaware, so undreamed of, so involuntary. He has a shrewd suspicion that it is not by accident it has so utterly mastered him and bound itself up with his existence; that he had—even subconsciously—been preparing for it, or, more precisely, been prepared for it. There is, in short, something in him which at a given moment was ready to issue in such a feeling; and this something, highly extraordinary to relate, is his essence and quality as a professor of history. Dr. Cornelius, however, does not actually say this, even to himself; he merely realizes it, at odd times, and smiles a private smile. He knows that history professors do not love history because it is something that comes to pass, but only because it is something that *has* come to pass; that they hate a revolution like the present one[10] because they feel it is lawless, incoherent, irrelevant—in a word, unhistoric; that their hearts belong to the coherent, disciplined, historic past. For the temper of timelessness, the temper of eternity—thus the scholar communes with himself when he takes his walk by the river before supper—that temper broods over the past; and it is a temper much better suited to the nervous system of a history professor than are the excesses of the present. The past is immortalized; that is to say, it is dead; and death is the root of all godliness and all abiding significance. Dr. Cornelius, walking alone in the dark, has a profound insight into this truth. It is this conservative instinct of his, his sense of the eternal, that has found in his love for his little daughter a way to save itself from the wounding inflicted by the times. For father love, and a little child on its mother's breast—are not these timeless, and thus very, very holy and beautiful? Yet Cornelius, pondering there in the dark, descries something not perfectly right and good in his love. Theoretically, in the interests of science, he admits it to himself. There is something ulterior about it, in the nature of it; that something is hostility, hostility against the history of today, which is still in the making and thus not history at all, in behalf of the genuine history that has already happened—that is to say, death. Yes, passing strange though all this is, yet it is true; true in a sense, that is. His devotion to this priceless little morsel of life and new growth has something to do with death, it clings to death as against life; and that is neither right nor beautiful—in a sense. Though only the most fanatical asceticism could be capable, on no other ground than such casual scientific perception, of tearing this purest and most precious of feelings out of his heart.

He holds his darling on his lap and her slim rosy legs hang down. He raises his brows as he talks to her, tenderly, with a half-teasing note of respect, and listens enchanted to her high, sweet little voice calling him Abel. He exchanges a look with the mother, who is caressing her Snapper and reading him a gentle lecture. He must be more reasonable, he must learn self-control; today again, under the manifold exasperations of life, he

[10] That is, the revolution in society after the war.

has given way to rage and behaved like a howling dervish. Cornelius casts a mistrustful glance at the big folk now and then, too; he thinks it not unlikely they are not unaware of those scientific preoccupations of his evening walks. If such be the case they do not show it. They stand there leaning their arms on their chair-backs and with a benevolence not untinctured with irony look on at the parental happiness.

The children's frocks are of a heavy, brick-red stuff, embroidered in modern "arty" style. They once belonged to Ingrid and Bert and are precisely alike, save that little knickers come out beneath Snapper's smock. And both have their hair bobbed. Snapper's is a streaky blond, inclined to turn dark. It is bristly and sticky and looks for all the world like a droll, badly fitting wig. But Ellie's is chestnut brown, glossy and fine as silk, as pleasing as her whole little personality. It covers her ears—and these ears are not a pair, one of them being the right size, the other distinctly too large. Her father will sometimes uncover this little abnormality and exclaim over it as though he had never noticed it before, which both makes Ellie giggle and covers her with shame. Her eyes are now golden brown, set far apart and with sweet gleams in them—such a clear and lovely look! The brows above are blond; the nose still unformed, with thick nostrils and almost circular holes; the mouth large and expressive, with a beautifully arching and mobile upper lip. When she laughs, dimples come in her cheeks and she shows her teeth like loosely strung pearls. So far she has lost but one tooth, which her father gently twisted out with his handkerchief after it had grown very wobbling. During this small operation she had paled and trembled very much. Her cheeks have the softness proper to her years, but they are not chubby; indeed, they are rather concave, due to her facial structure, with its somewhat prominent jaw. On one, close to the soft fall of her hair, is a downy freckle.

Ellie is not too well pleased with her looks—a sign that already she troubles about such things. Sadly she thinks it is best to admit it once for all, her face is "homely"; though the rest of her, "on the other hand," is not bad at all. She loves expressions like "on the other hand"; they sound choice and grown-up to her, and she likes to string them together, one after the other: "very likely," "probably," "after all." Snapper is self-critical too, though more in the moral sphere: he suffers from remorse for his attacks of rage and considers himself a tremendous sinner. He is quite certain that heaven is not for such as he; he is sure to go to "the bad place" when he dies, and no persuasions will convince him to the contrary—as that God sees the heart and gladly makes allowances. Obstinately he shakes his head, with the comic, crooked little peruke,[11] and vows there is no place for him in heaven. When he has a cold he is immediately quite choked with mucus; rattles and rumbles from top to toe if you even look at him; his temperature flies up at once and he simply puffs. Nursy is pessimistic on the score of his constitution: such fat-blooded children as he might get a stroke any minute. Once she even thought she saw the moment at hand: Snapper had been in one of his berserker rages, and in the ensuing fit of penitence stood himself in the corner with his back to the room. Suddenly Nursy noticed that his face had gone all blue, far bluer, even, than her own. She raised the

[11] Wig. (Snapper's hair looks like a wig.)

alarm, crying out that the child's all too rich blood had at length brought him to his final hour; and Snapper, to his vast astonishment, found himself, so far from being rebuked for evil-doing, encompassed in tenderness and anxiety—until it turned out that his color was not caused by apoplexy but by the distempering[12] on the nursery wall, which had come off on his tear-wet face.

Nursy has come downstairs too, and stands by the door, sleek-haired, owl-eyed, with her hands folded over her white apron, and a severely dignified manner born of her limited intelligence. She is very proud of the care and training she gives her nurslings and declares that they are "enveloping wonderfully." She has had seventeen suppurated teeth lately removed from her jaws and been measured for a set of symmetrical yellow ones in dark rubber gums; these now embellish her peasant face. She is obsessed with the strange conviction that these teeth of hers are the subject of general conversation, that, as it were, the sparrows on the housetops chatter of them. "Everybody knows I've had a false set put in," she will say; "there has been a great deal of foolish talk about them." She is much given to dark hints and veiled innuendo: speaks, for instance, of a certain Dr. Bleifuss,[13] whom every child knows, and "there are even some in the house who pretend to be him." All one can do with talk like this is charitably to pass it over in silence. But she teaches the children nursery rhymes: gems like:

"Puff, puff, here comes the train!
Puff, puff, toot, toot,
Away it goes again,"

Or that gastronomical jingle, so suited, in its sparseness, to the times, and yet seemingly with a blitheness of its own:

"Monday we begin the week,
Tuesday there's a bone to pick.
Wednesday we're half way through,
Thursday what a great to-do!
Friday we eat what fish we're able,
Saturday we dance round the table.
Sunday brings us pork and greens—
Here's a feast for kings and queens!"

Also a certain four-line stanza with a romantic appeal, unutterable and unuttered:

"Open the gate, open the gate
And let the carriage drive in.
Who is it in the carriage sits?
A lordly sir with golden hair."

Or, finally that ballad about golden-haired Marianne who sat on a, sat on a, sat on a stone, and combed out her, combed out her, combed out her

[12] Water-soluble paint. [13] "Dr. Leadfoot."

hair; and about bloodthirsty Rudolph, who pulled out a, pulled out a, pulled out a knife—and his ensuing direful end. Ellie enunciates all these ballads charmingly, with her mobile little lips, and sings them in her sweet little voice—much better than Snapper. She does everything better than he does, and he pays her honest admiration and homage and obeys her in all things except when visited by one of his attacks. Sometimes she teaches him, instructs him upon the birds in the picture book and tells him their proper names: "This is a chaffinch, Buddy, this is a bullfinch, this is a cowfinch." He has to repeat them after her. She gives him medical instruction too, teaches him the names of diseases, such as infammation of the lungs, infammation of the blood, infammation of the air. If he does not pay attention and cannot say the words after her, she stands him in the corner. Once she even boxed his ears, but was so ashamed that she stood herself in the corner for a long time. Yes, they are fast friends, two souls with but a single thought, and have all their adventures in common. They come home from a walk and relate as with one voice that they have seen two moolies and a teenty-weenty baby calf. They are on familiar terms with the kitchen, which consists of Xaver and the ladies Hinterhofer, two sisters once of the lower middle class who, in these evil days, are reduced to living *"au pair"*[14] as the phrase goes and officiating as cook and housemaid for their board and keep. The little ones have a feeling that Xaver and the Hinterhofers are on much the same footing with their father and mother as they are themselves. At least sometimes, when they have been scolded, they go downstairs and announce that the master and mistress are cross. But playing with the servants lacks charm compared with the joys of playing upstairs. The kitchen could never rise to the height of the games their father can invent. For instance, there is "four gentlemen taking a walk." When they play it Abel will crook his knees until he is the same height with themselves and go walking with them, hand in hand. They never get enough of this sport; they could walk round and round the dining-room a whole day on end, five gentlemen in all, counting the diminished Abel.

Then there is the thrilling cushion game. One of the children, usually Ellie, seats herself, unbeknownst to Abel, in his seat at table. Still as a mouse she awaits his coming. He draws near with his head in the air, descanting in loud, clear tones upon the surpassing comfort of his chair; and sits down on top of Ellie. "What's this, what's this?" says he. And bounces about, deaf to the smothered giggles exploding behind him. "Why have they put a cushion in my chair? And what a queer, hard, awkward-shaped cushion it is!" he goes on. "Frightfully uncomfortable to sit on!" And keeps pushing and bouncing about more and more on the astonishing cushion and clutching behind him into the rapturous giggling and squeaking, until at last he turns round, and the game ends with a magnificent climax of discovery and recognition. They might go through all this a hundred times without diminishing by an iota its power to thrill.

Today is no time for such joys. The imminent festivity disturbs the atmosphere, and besides there is work to be done, and, above all, the eggs to be got. Ellie has just time to recite "Puff, puff," and Cornelius to discover that her ears are not mates, when they are interrupted by the arrival of

[14] As unpaid servants who work for their room and board.

Danny, come to fetch Bert and Ingrid. Xaver, meantime, has exchanged his striped livery for an ordinary coat, in which he looks rather rough-and-ready, though as brisk and attractive as ever. So then Nursy and the children ascend to the upper regions, the Professor withdraws to his study to read, as always after dinner, and his wife bends her energies upon the sandwiches and salad that must be prepared. And she has another errand as well. Before the young people arrive she has to take her shopping basket and dash into town on her bicycle, to turn into provisions a sum of money she has in hand, which she dares not keep lest it lose all value.

Cornelius reads, leaning back in his chair, with his cigar between his middle and index fingers. First he reads Macaulay[15] on the origin of the English public debt at the end of the seventeenth century; then an article in a French periodical on the rapid increase in the Spanish debt towards the end of the sixteenth. Both these for his lecture on the morrow. He intends to compare the astonishing prosperity which accompanied the phenomenon in England with its fatal effects a hundred years earlier in Spain, and to analyze the ethical and psychological grounds of the difference in results. For that will give him a chance to refer back from the England of William III, which is the actual subject in hand, to the time of Philip II and the Counter-Reformation, which is his own special field. He has already written a valuable work on this period; it is much cited and got him his professorship. While his cigar burns down and gets strong, he excogitates a few pensive sentences in a key of gentle melancholy, to be delivered before his class next day: about the practically hopeless struggle carried on by the belated Philip against the whole trend of history: against the new, the kingdom-disrupting power of the Germanic ideal of freedom and individual liberty. And about the persistent, futile struggle of the aristocracy, condemned by God and rejected of man, against the forces of progress and change. He savors his sentences; keeps on polishing them while he puts back the books he has been using; then goes upstairs for the usual pause in his day's work, the hour with drawn blinds and closed eyes, which he so imperatively needs. But today, he recalls, he will rest under disturbed conditions, amid the bustle of preparations for the feast. He smiles to find his heart giving a mild flutter at the thought. Disjointed phrases on the theme of black-clad Philip and his times mingle with a confused consciousness that they will soon be dancing down below. For five minutes or so he falls asleep.

As he lies and rests he can hear the sound of the garden gate and the repeated ringing at the bell. Each time a little pang goes through him, of excitement and suspense, at the thought that the young people have begun to fill the floor below. And each time he smiles at himself again—though even his smile is slightly nervous, is tinged with the pleasurable anticipations people always feel before a party. At half past four—it is already

[15]Thomas Babington Macaulay, English historian (1800–1859). The lecture Cornelius is planning relates economic conditions to ethical and religious matters by comparing conditions in seventeenth-century England, the time of William III, to those in sixteenth-century Spain, the time of Philip II and the Counter-Reformation (a reform movement within the Roman Catholic Church in response to the sixteenth-century Reformation, led by Martin Luther). The topic obviously concerns him because of the implicit parallel with the Germany of his own day.

dark—he gets up and washes at the wash-stand. The basin has been out of repair for two years. It is supposed to tip, but has broken away from its socket on one side and cannot be mended because there is nobody to mend it; neither replaced because no shop can supply another. So it has to be hung up above the vent and emptied by lifting in both hands and pouring out the water. Cornelius shakes his head over this basin, as he does several times a day—whenever, in fact, he has occasion to use it. He finishes his toilet with care, standing under the ceiling light to polish his glasses till they shine. Then he goes downstairs.

On his way to the dining-room he hears the gramophone already going, and the sound of voices. He puts on a polite, society air; at his tongue's end is the phrase he means to utter: "Pray don't let me disturb you," as he passes directly into the dining-room for his tea. "Pray don't let me disturb you"—it seems to him precisely the *mot juste;*[16] towards the guests cordial and considerate, for himself a very bulwark.

The lower floor is lighted up, all the bulbs in the chandelier are burning save one that has burned out. Cornelius pauses on a lower step and surveys the entrance hall. It looks pleasant and cozy in the bright light, with its copy of Marées[17] over the brick chimney-piece, its wainscoted walls—wainscoted in soft wood—and red-carpeted floor, where the guests stand in groups, chatting, each with his tea-cup and slice of bread-and-butter spread with anchovy paste. There is a festal haze, faint scents of hair and clothing and human breath come to him across the room, it is all characteristic and familiar and highly evocative. The door into the dressing-room is open, guests are still arriving.

A large group of people is rather bewildering at first sight. The Professor takes in only the general scene. He does not see Ingrid, who is standing just at the foot of the steps, in a dark silk frock with a pleated collar falling softly over the shoulders, and bare arms. She smiles up at him, nodding and showing her lovely teeth.

"Rested?" she asks, for his private ear. With a quite unwarranted start he recognizes her, and she presents some of her friends.

"May I introduce Herr Zuber?" she says. "And this is Fräulein Plaichinger."

Herr Zuber is insignificant. But Fräulein Plaichinger is a perfect Germania,[18] blond and voluptuous, arrayed in floating draperies. She has a snub nose, and answers the Professor's salutation in the high, shrill pipe so many stout women have.

"Delighted to meet you," he says. "How nice of you to come! A classmate of Ingrid's, I suppose?"

And Herr Zuber is a golfing partner of Ingrid's. He is in business; he works in his uncle's brewery. Cornelius makes a few jokes about the thinness of the beer and professes to believe that Herr Zuber could easily do something about the quality if he would. "But pray don't let me disturb you," he goes on, and turns towards the dining-room.

"There comes Max," says Ingrid. "Max, you sweep, what do you mean

[16] The exact word (French).

[17] The works of the German painter Hans von Marées (1837–1887) had been rediscovered and become popular in the 1890s.

[18] Female figure embodying Germany.

by rolling up at this time of day?" For such is the way they talk to each other, offensively to an older ear; of social forms, of hospitable warmth, there is no faintest trace. They all call each other by their first names.

A young man comes up to them out of the dressing-room and makes his bow; he has an expanse of white shirt-front and a little black string tie. He is as pretty as a picture, dark, with rosy cheeks, clean-shaven of course, but with just a sketch of side-whisker. Not a ridiculous or flashy beauty, not like a gypsy fiddler, but just charming to look at, in a winning, well-bred way, with kind dark eyes. He even wears his dinner-jacket a little awkwardly.

"Please don't scold me, Cornelia," he says; "it's the idiotic lectures." And Ingrid presents him to her father as Herr Hergesell.

Well, and so this is Herr Hergesell. He knows his manners, does Herr Hergesell, and thanks the master of the house quite ingratiatingly for his invitation as they shake hands. "I certainly seem to have missed the bus," says he jocosely. "Of course I have lectures today up to four o'clock; I would have; and after that I had to go home to change." Then he talks about his pumps, with which he has just been struggling in the dressing-room.

"I brought them with me in a bag," he goes on. "Mustn't tramp all over the carpet in our brogues—it's not done. Well, I was ass enough not to fetch along a shoe-horn, and I find I simply can't get in! What a sell! They are the tightest I've ever had, the numbers don't tell you a thing, and all the leather today is just cast iron. It's not leather at all. My poor finger"—he confidingly displays a reddened digit and once more characterizes the whole thing as a "sell," and a putrid sell into the bargain. He really does talk just as Ingrid said he did, with a peculiar nasal drawl, not affectedly in the least, but merely because that is the way of all the Hergesells.

Dr. Cornelius says it is very careless of them not to keep a shoe-horn in the cloak-room and displays proper sympathy with the mangled finger. "But now you *really* must not let me disturb you any longer," he goes on. "*Auf wiedersehen!*"[19] And he crosses the hall into the dining-room.

There are guests there too, drinking tea; the family table is pulled out. But the Professor goes at once to his own little upholstered corner with the electric light bulb above it—the nook where he usually drinks his tea. His wife is sitting there talking with Bert and two other young men, one of them Herzl, whom Cornelius knows and greets; the other a typical "Wandervogel"[20] named Möller, a youth who obviously neither owns nor cares to own the correct evening dress of the middle classes (in fact, there is no such thing any more), nor to ape the manners of a gentleman (and, in fact, there is no such thing any more either). He has a wilderness of hair, horn spectacles, and a long neck, and wears golf stockings and a belted blouse. His regular occupation, the Professor learns, is banking, but he is by way of being an amateur folklorist and collects folksongs from all localities and in all languages. He sings them, too, and at Ingrid's command has brought his guitar; it is hanging in the dressing-room in an oilcloth case. Herzl, the actor, is small and slight, but he has a strong growth of black beard, as you can tell by the thick coat of powder on his cheeks. His

[19] "Until we meet again!"; Goodbye.

[20] A "bird of passage," a wanderer belonging to a German youth movement.

eyes are larger than life, with a deep and melancholy glow. He has put on rouge besides the powder—those dull carmine high-lights on the cheeks can be nothing but a cosmetic. "Queer," thinks the Professor. "You would think a man would be one thing or the other—not melancholic and use face paint at the same time. It's a psychological contradiction. How can a melancholy man rouge? But here we have a perfect illustration of the abnormality of the artist soul-form. It can make possible a contradiction like this—perhaps it even consists in the contradiction. All very interesting—and no reason whatever for not being polite to him. Politeness is a primitive convention—and legitimate. . . . Do take some lemon, Herr Hofschauspieler!"[21]

Court actors and court theaters—there are no such things any more, really. But Herzl relishes the sound of the title, notwithstanding he is a revolutionary artist. This must be another contradiction inherent in his soul-form; so, at least, the Professor assumes, and he is probably right. The flattery he is guilty of is a sort of atonement for his previous hard thoughts about the rouge.

"Thank you so much—it's really too good of you, sir," says Herzl, quite embarrassed. He is so overcome that he almost stammers; only his perfect enunciation saves him. His whole bearing towards his hostess and the master of the house is exaggeratedly polite. It is almost as though he had a bad conscience in respect of his rouge; as though an inward compulsion had driven him to put it on, but now, seeing it through the Professor's eyes, he disapproves of it himself, and thinks, by an air of humility towards the whole of unrouged society, to mitigate its effect.

They drink their tea and chat: about Möller's folksongs, about Basque folksongs and Spanish folksongs; from which they pass to the new production of *Don Carlos*[22] at the Stadttheater, in which Herzl plays the title-rôle. He talks about his own rendering of the part and says he hopes his conception of the character has unity. They go on to criticize the rest of the cast, the setting, and the production as a whole; and Cornelius is struck, rather painfully, to find the conversation trending towards his own special province, back to Spain and the Counter-Reformation. He has done nothing at all to give it this turn, he is perfectly innocent, and hopes it does not look as though he had sought an occasion to play the professor. He wonders, and falls silent, feeling relieved when the little folk come up to the table. Ellie and Snapper have on their blue velvet Sunday frocks; they are permitted to partake in the festivities up to bed-time. They look shy and large-eyed as they say how-do-you-do to the strangers and, under pressure, repeat their names and ages. Herr Möller does nothing but gaze at them solemnly, but Herzl is simply ravished. He rolls his eyes up to heaven and puts his hands over his mouth; he positively blesses them. It all, no doubt, comes from his heart, but he is so addicted to theatrical methods of making an impression and getting an effect that both words and behavior ring frightfully false. And even his enthusiasm for the little folk looks too much like part of his general craving to make up for the rouge on his cheeks.

[21] "Mr. Court-Theater Actor!"
[22] A play by the German Romantic playwright Friedrich Schiller (1759–1805).

The tea-table has meanwhile emptied of guests, and dancing is going on in the hall. The children run off, the Professor prepares to retire. "Go and enjoy yourselves," he says to Möller and Herzl, who have sprung from their chairs as he rises from his. They shake hands and he withdraws into his study, his peaceful kingdom, where he lets down the blinds, turns on the desk lamp, and sits down to his work.

It is work which can be done, if necessary, under disturbed conditions: nothing but a few letters and a few notes. Of course, Cornelius's mind wanders. Vague impressions float through it: Herr Hergesell's refractory pumps, the high pipe in that plump body of the Plaichinger female. As he writes, or leans back in his chair and stares into space, his thoughts go back to Herr Möller's collection of Basque folksongs, to Herzl's posings and humility, to "his" Carlos and the court of Philip II. There is something strange, he thinks, about conversations. They are so ductile, they will flow of their own accord in the direction of one's dominating interest. Often and often he has seen this happen. And while he is thinking, he is listening to the sounds next door—rather subdued, he finds them. He hears only voices, no sound of footsteps. The dancers do not glide or circle round the room; they merely walk about over the carpet, which does not hamper their movements in the least. Their way of holding each other is quite different and strange, and they move to the strains of the gramophone, to the weird music of the new world. He concentrates on the music and makes out that it is a jazz-band record, with various percussion instruments and the clack and clatter of castanets, which, however, are not even faintly suggestive of Spain, but merely jazz like the rest. No, not Spain. . . . His thoughts are back at their old round.

Half an hour goes by. It occurs to him it would be no more than friendly to go and contribute a box of cigarettes to the festivities next door. Too bad to ask the young people to smoke their own—though they have probably never thought of it. He goes into the empty dining-room and takes a box from his supply in the cupboard: not the best ones, nor yet the brand he himself prefers, but a certain long, thin kind he is not averse to getting rid of—after all, they are nothing but youngsters. He takes the box into the hall, holds it up with a smile, and deposits it on the mantel-shelf. After which he gives a look round and returns to his own room.

There comes a lull in dance and music. The guests stand about the room in groups or round the table at the window or are seated in a circle by the fireplace. Even the built-in stairs, with their worn velvet carpet, are crowded with young folk as in an amphitheater: Max Hergesell is there, leaning back with one elbow on the step above and gesticulating with his free hand as he talks to the shrill, voluptuous Plaichinger. The floor of the hall is nearly empty, save just in the center: there, directly beneath the chandelier, the two little ones in their blue velvet frocks clutch each other in an awkward embrace and twirl silently round and round, oblivious of all else. Cornelius, as he passes, strokes their hair, with a friendly word; it does not distract them from their small solemn preoccupation. But at his own door he turns to glance round and sees young Hergesell push himself off the stair by his elbow—probably because he noticed the Professor. He comes down into the arena, takes Ellie out of her brother's arms, and dances with her himself. It looks very comic, without the music, and he crouches down just as Cornelius does when he goes walking with the four gentlemen, holding the fluttered Ellie as though she were grown up and taking little "shimmying" steps. Everybody watches with huge enjoyment, the gramophone is put on again, dancing becomes general. The Professor stands and looks, with his hand on the door-knob. He nods and laughs; when he finally shuts himself into his study the mechanical smile still lingers on his lips.

Again he turns over pages by his desk lamp, takes notes, attends to a few simple matters. After a while he notices that the guests have forsaken the entrance hall for his wife's drawing-room, into which there is a door from his own study as well. He hears their voices and the sounds of a guitar being tuned. Herr Möller, it seems, is to sing—and does so. He twangs the strings of his instrument and sings in a powerful bass a ballad in a strange tongue, possibly Swedish. The Professor does not succeed in identifying it, though he listens attentively to the end, after which there is great applause. The sound is deadened by the portière that hangs over the dividing door. The young bank-clerk begins another song. Cornelius goes softly in.

It is half-dark in the drawing-room; the only light is from the shaded standard lamp, beneath which Möller sits, on the divan, with his legs crossed, picking his strings. His audience is grouped easily about; as there are not enough seats, some stand, and more, among them many young ladies, are simply sitting on the floor with their hands clasped round their knees or even with their legs stretched out before them. Hergesell sits thus, in his dinner-jacket, next the piano, with Fräulein Plaichinger beside him. Frau Cornelius is holding both children on her lap as she sits in her easy-chair opposite the singer. Snapper, the Boeotian,[23] begins to talk loud and clear in the middle of the song and has to be intimidated with hushings and finger-shakings. Never, never would Ellie allow herself to be guilty of such conduct. She sits there daintily erect and still on her mother's knee. The Professor tries to catch her eye and exchange a private signal with his little girl; but she does not see him. Neither does she seem to be looking at the singer. Her gaze is directed lower down.

Möller sings the "joli tambour":[24]

> "Sire, mon roi, donnez-moi votre fille—"[25]

They are all enchanted. "How good!" Hergesell is heard to say, in the odd, nasally condescending Hergesell tone. The next one is a beggar ballad, to a tune composed by young Möller himself; it elicits a storm of applause:

> "Gypsy lassie a-goin' to the fair,
> Huzza!
> Gypsy laddie a-goin' to be there—
> Huzza, diddlety umpty dido!"

[23] A barbarian. (The ancient Athenians joked about the provinciality of the residents of Boeotia, a remote area of Greece.)

[24] The "pretty drum" (French), a kind of folksong.

[25] "Lord, my king, give me your daughter."

Laughter and high spirits, sheer reckless hilarity, reigns after this jovial ballad. "Frightfully good!" Hergesell comments again, as before. Follows another popular song, this time a Hungarian one; Möller sings it in its own outlandish tongue, and most effectively. The Professor applauds with ostentation. It warms his heart and does him good, this outcropping of artistic, historic, and cultural elements all amongst the shimmying. He goes up to young Möller and congratulates him, talks about the songs and their sources, and Möller promises to lend him a certain annotated book of folksongs. Cornelius is the more cordial because all the time, as fathers do, he has been comparing the parts and achievements of this young stranger with those of his own son, and being gnawed by envy and chagrin. This young Möller, he is thinking, is a capable bank clerk (though about Möller's capacity he knows nothing whatever) and has this special gift besides, which must have taken talent and energy to cultivate. "And here is my poor Bert, who knows nothing and can do nothing and thinks of nothing except playing the clown, without even talent for that!" He tries to be just; he tells himself that, after all, Bert has innate refinement; that probably there is a good deal more to him than there is to the successful Möller; that perhaps he has even something of the poet in him, and his dancing and table-waiting are due to mere boyish folly and the distraught times. But paternal envy and pessimism win the upper hand; when Möller begins another song, Dr. Cornelius goes back to his room.

He works as before, with divided attention, at this and that, while it gets on for seven o'clock. Then he remembers a letter he may just as well write, a short letter and not very important, but letter-writing is wonderful for the way it takes up the time, and it is almost half past when he has finished. At half past eight the Italian salad will be served; so now is the prescribed moment for the Professor to go out into the wintry darkness to post his letters and take his daily quantum of fresh air and exercise. They are dancing again, and he will have to pass through the hall to get his hat and coat; but they are used to him now, he need not stop and beg them not to be disturbed. He lays away his papers, takes up the letters he has written, and goes out. But he sees his wife sitting near the door of his room and pauses a little by her easy-chair.

She is watching the dancing. Now and then the big folk or some of their guests stop to speak to her; the party is at its height, and there are more onlookers than these two: blue-faced Ann is standing at the bottom of the stairs, in all the dignity of her limitations. She is waiting for the children, who simply cannot get their fill of these unwonted festivities, and watching over Snapper, lest his all too rich blood be churned to the danger-point by too much twirling round. And not only the nursery but the kitchen takes an interest: Xaver and the two ladies Hinterhofer are standing by the pantry door looking on with relish. Fräulein Walburga, the elder of the two sunken sisters (the culinary section—she objects to being called a cook), is a whimsical, good-natured sort, brown-eyed, wearing glasses with thick circular lenses; the nose-piece is wound with a bit of rag to keep it from pressing on her nose. Fräulein Cecilia is younger, though not so precisely young either. Her bearing is as self-assertive as usual, this being her way of sustaining her dignity as a former member of the middle class. For Fräulein Cecilia feels acutely her descent into the ranks of domestic service. She positively declines to wear a cap or other badge of servitude, and her hardest trial is on the Wednesday evening when she has to serve the dinner while Xaver has his afternoon out. She hands the dishes with averted face and elevated nose—a fallen queen; and so distressing is it to behold her degradation that one evening when the little folk happened to be at table and saw her they both with one accord burst into tears. Such anguish is unknown to young Xaver. He enjoys serving and does it with an ease born of practice as well as talent, for he was once a "piccolo."[26] But otherwise he is a thorough-paced good-for-nothing and windbag—with quite distinct traits of character of his own, as his long-suffering employers are always ready to concede, but perfectly impossible and a bag of wind for all that. One must just take him as he is, they think, and not expect figs from thistles. He is the child and product of the disrupted times, a perfect specimen of his generation, follower of the revolution, Bolshevist sympathizer. The Professor's name for him is the "minute-man," because he is always to be counted on in any sudden crisis, if only it address his sense of humor or love of novelty, and will display therein amazing readiness and resource. But he utterly lacks a sense of duty and can as little be trained to the performance of the daily round and common task as some kinds of dog can be taught to jump over a stick. It goes so plainly against the grain that criticism is disarmed. One becomes resigned. On grounds that appealed to him as unusual and amusing he would be ready to turn out of his bed at any hour of the night. But he simply cannot get up before eight in the morning, he cannot do it, he will not jump over the stick. Yet all day long the evidence of this free and untrammelled existence, the sound of his mouth organ, his joyous whistle, or his raucous but expressive voice lifted in song, rises to the hearing of the world abovestairs; and the smoke of his cigarettes fills the pantry. While the Hinterhofer ladies work he stands and looks on. Of a morning while the Professor is breakfasting, he tears the leaf off the study calendar—but does not lift a finger to dust the room. Dr. Cornelius has often told him to leave the calendar alone, for he tends to tear off two leaves at a time and thus to add to the general confusion. But young Xaver appears to find joy in this activity, and will not be deprived of it.

Again, he is fond of children, a winning trait. He will throw himself into games with the little folk in the garden, make and mend their toys with great ingenuity, even read aloud from their books—and very droll it sounds in his thick-lipped pronunciation. With his whole soul he loves the cinema; after an evening spent there he inclines to melancholy and yearning and talking to himself. Vague hopes stir in him that some day he may make his fortune in that gay world and belong to it by rights—hopes based on his shock of hair and his physical agility and daring. He likes to climb the ash tree in the front garden, mounting branch by branch to the very top and frightening everybody to death who sees him. Once there he lights a cigarette and smokes it as he sways to and fro, keeping a lookout for a cinema director who might chance to come along and engage him.

If he changed his striped jacket for mufti,[27] he might easily dance with the others and no one would notice the difference. For the big folk's friends

[26] Apprentice waiter. [27] Ordinary street clothing.

are rather anomalous in their clothing: evening dress is worn by a few, but it is by no means the rule. There is quite a sprinkling of guests, both male and female, in the same general style as Möller the ballad-singer. The Professor is familiar with the circumstances of most of this young generation he is watching as he stands beside his wife's chair; he has heard them spoken of by name. They are students at the high school or at the School of Applied Art; they lead, at least the masculine portion, that precarious and scrambling existence which is purely the product of the time. There is a tall, pale, spindling youth, the son of a dentist, who lives by speculation. From all the Professor hears, he is a perfect Aladdin.[28] He keeps a car, treats his friends to champagne suppers, and showers presents upon them on every occasion, costly little trifles in mother-of-pearl and gold. So today he has brought gifts to the young givers of the feast: for Bert a gold lead-pencil, and for Ingrid a pair of earrings of barbaric size, great gold circlets that fortunately do not have to go through the little ear lobe, but are fastened over it by means of a clip. The big folk come laughing to their parents to display these trophies; and the parents shake their heads even while they admire—Aladdin bowing over and over from afar.

The young people appear to be absorbed in their dancing—if the performance they are carrying out with so much still concentration can be called dancing. They stride across the carpet, slowly, according to some unfathomable prescript, strangely embraced; in the newest attitude, tummy advanced and shoulders high, waggling the hips. They do not get tired, because nobody could. There is no such thing as heightened color or heaving bosoms. Two girls may dance together or two young men—it is all the same. They move to the exotic strains of the gramophone, played with the loudest needles to procure the maximum of sound: shimmies, foxtrots, one-steps, double foxes, African shimmies, Java dances, and Creole polkas, the wild musky melodies follow one another, now furious, now languishing, a monotonous Negro program in unfamiliar rhythm, to a clacking, clashing, and strumming orchestral accompaniment.

"What is that record?" Cornelius inquires of Ingrid, as she passes him by in the arms of the pale young speculator, with reference to the piece then playing, whose alternate languors and furies he finds comparatively pleasing and showing a certain resourcefulness in detail.

"*Prince of Pappenheim:* 'Console thee, dearest child,' " she answers, and smiles pleasantly back at him with her white teeth.

The cigarette smoke wreathes beneath the chandelier. The air is blue with a festal haze compact of sweet and thrilling ingredients that stir the blood with memories of green-sick pains and are particularly poignant to those whose youth—like the Professor's own—has been oversensitive. . . . The little folk are still on the floor. They are allowed to stay up until eight, so great is their delight in the party. The guests have got used to their presence; in their own way, they have their place in the doings of the evening. They have separated, anyhow: Snapper revolves all alone in the middle of the carpet, in his little blue velvet smock, while Ellie is running

[28] Fabulously rich person (from a story in the *Arabian Nights:* "Aladdin and His Wonderful Lamp").

after one of the dancing couples, trying to hold the man fast by his coat. It is Max Hergesell and Fräulein Plaichinger. They dance well, it is a pleasure to watch them. One has to admit that these mad modern dances, when the right people dance them, are not so bad after all—they have something quite taking. Young Hergesell is a capital leader, dances according to rule, yet with individuality. So it looks. With what aplomb can he walk backwards—when space permits! And he knows how to be graceful standing still in a crowd. And his partner supports him well, being unsuspectedly lithe and buoyant, as fat people often are. They look at each other, they are talking, paying no heed to Ellie, though others are smiling to see the child's persistence. Dr. Cornelius tries to catch up his little sweetheart as she passes and draw her to him. But Ellie eludes him, almost peevishly; her dear Abel is nothing to her now. She braces her little arms against his chest and turns her face away with a persecuted look. Then escapes to follow her fancy once more.

The Professor feels an involuntary twinge. Uppermost in his heart is hatred for this party, with its power to intoxicate and estrange his darling child. His love for her—that not quite disinterested, not quite unexceptionable love of his—is easily wounded. He wears a mechanical smile, but his eyes have clouded, and he stares fixedly at a point in the carpet, between the dancers' feet.

"The children ought to go to bed," he tells his wife. But she pleads for another quarter of an hour; she has promised already, and they do love it so! He smiles again and shakes his head, stands so a moment and then goes across to the cloakroom, which is full of coats and hats and scarves and overshoes. He has trouble in rummaging out his own coat, and Max Hergesell comes out of the hall, wiping his brow.

"Going out, sir?" he asks, in Hergesellian accents, dutifully helping the older man on with his coat. "Silly business this, with my pumps," he says. "They pinch like hell. The brutes are simply too tight for me, quite apart from the bad leather. They press just here on the ball of my great toe"—he stands on one foot and holds the other in his hand—"it's simply unbearable. There's nothing for it but to take them off; my brogues will have to do the business. . . . Oh, let me help you, sir."

"Thanks," says Cornelius. "Don't trouble. Get rid of your own tormentors. . . . Oh, thanks very much!" For Hergesell has gone on one knee to snap the fasteners of his snowboots.

Once more the Professor expresses his gratitude; he is pleased and touched by so much sincere respect and youthful readiness to serve. "Go and enjoy yourself," he counsels. "Change your shoes and make up for what you have been suffering. Nobody can dance in shoes that pinch. Good-bye, I must be off to get a breath of fresh air."

"I'm going to dance with Ellie now," calls Hergesell after him. "She'll be a first-rate dancer when she grows up, and that I'll swear to.'

"Think so?" Cornelius answers, already half out. "Well, you are a connoisseur, I'm sure. Don't get curvature of the spine with stooping."

He nods again and goes. 'Fine lad," he thinks as he shuts the door. "Student of engineering. Knows what he's bound for, got a good clear head, and so well set up and pleasant too." And again paternal envy rises as he compares his poor Bert's status with this young man's, which he puts in the rosiest light that his son's may look the darker. Thus he sets out on his evening walk.

He goes up the avenue, crosses the bridge, and walks along the bank on the other side as far as the next bridge but one. The air is wet and cold, with a little snow now and then. He turns up his coat collar and slips the crook of his cane over the arm behind his back. Now and then he ventilates his lungs with a long deep breath of the night air. As usual when he walks, his mind reverts to his professional preoccupations, he thinks about his lectures and the things he means to say tomorrow about Philip's struggle against the Germanic revolution, things steeped in melancholy and penetratingly just. Above all just, he thinks. For in one's dealings with the young it behoves one to display the scientific spirit, to exhibit the principles of enlightenment—not only for purposes of mental discipline, but on the human and individual side, in order not to wound them or indirectly offend their political sensibilities; particularly in these days, when there is so much tinder in the air, opinions are so frightfully split up and chaotic, and you may so easily incur attacks from one party or the other, or even give rise to scandal, by taking sides on a point of history. "And taking sides is unhistoric anyhow," so he muses. "Only justice, only impartiality is historic." And could not, properly considered, be otherwise. . . . For justice can have nothing of youthful fire and blithe, fresh, loyal conviction. It is by nature melancholy. And, being so, has secret affinity with the lost cause and the forlorn hope rather than with the fresh and blithe and loyal—perhaps this affinity is its very essence and without it it would not exist at all! . . . "And is there then no such thing as justice?" the Professor asks himself, and ponders the question so deeply that he absently posts his letters in the next box and turns round to go home. This thought of his is unsettling and disturbing to the scientific mind—but is it not after all itself scientific, psychological, conscientious, and therefore to be accepted without prejudice, no matter how upsetting? In the midst of which musings Dr. Cornelius finds himself back at his own door.

On the outer threshold stands Xaver, and seems to be looking for him.

"Herr Professor," says Xaver, tossing back his hair, "go upstairs to Ellie straight off. She's in a bad way."

"What's the matter?" asks Cornelius in alarm. "Is she ill?"

"No-o, not to say ill," answers Xaver. "She's just in a bad way and crying fit to bust her little heart. It's along o' that chap with the shirtfront that danced with her—Herr Hergesell. She couldn't be got to go upstairs peaceably, not at no price at all, and she's b'en crying bucketfuls."

"Nonsense," says the Professor, who has entered and is tossing off his things in the cloakroom. He says no more; opens the glass door and without a glance at the guests turns swiftly to the stairs. Takes them two at a time, crosses the upper hall and the small room leading into the nursery. Xaver follows at his heels, but stops at the nursery door.

A bright light still burns within, showing the gay frieze that runs all round the room, the large row of shelves heaped with a confusion of toys, the rocking-horse on his swaying platform, with red-varnished nostrils and raised hoofs. On the linoleum lie other toys—building blocks, railway trains, a little trumpet. The two white cribs stand not far apart, Ellie's in the window corner, Snapper's out in the room.

Snapper is asleep. He has said his prayers in loud, ringing tones, prompted by Nurse, and gone off at once into vehement, profound, and rosy slumber—from which a cannonball fired at close range could not rouse him. He lies with both fists flung back on the pillows on either side of the tousled head with its funny crooked little slumber-tossed wig.

A circle of females surrounds Ellie's bed: not only blue-faced Ann is there, but the Hinterhofer ladies too, talking to each other and to her. They make way as the Professor comes up and reveal the child sitting all pale among her pillows, sobbing and weeping more bitterly than he has ever seen her sob and weep in her life. Her lovely little hands lie on the coverlet in front of her, the nightgown with its narrow lace border has slipped down from her shoulder—such a thin, birdlike little shoulder—and the sweet head Cornelius loves so well, set on the neck like a flower on its stalk, her head is on one side, with the eyes rolled up to the corner between wall and ceiling above her head. For there she seems to envisage the anguish of her heart and even to nod to it—either on purpose or because her head wobbles as her body is shaken with the violence of her sobs. Her eyes rain down tears. The bow-shaped lips are parted, like a little *mater dolorosa's,*[29] and from them issue long, low wails that in nothing resemble the unnecessary and exasperating shrieks of a naughty child, but rise from the deep extremity of her heart and wake in the Professor's own a sympathy that is well-nigh intolerable. He has never seen his darling so before. His feelings find immediate vent in an attack on the ladies Hinterhofer.

"What about the supper?" he asks sharply. "There must be a great deal to do. Is my wife being left to do it alone?"

For the acute sensibilities of the former middle class this is quite enough. The ladies withdraw in righteous indignation, and Xaver Kleingutl jeers at them as they pass out. Having been born to low life instead of achieving it, he never loses a chance to mock at their fallen state.

"Childie, childie," murmurs Cornelius, and sitting down by the crib enfolds the anguished Ellie in his arms. "What is the trouble with my darling?"

She bedews his face with her tears.

"Abel . . . Abel . . ." she stammers between sobs. "Why—isn't Max—my brother? Max ought to be—my brother!"

Alas, alas! What mischance is this? Is this what the party has wrought, with its fatal atmosphere? Cornelius glances helplessly up at blue-faced Ann standing there in all the dignity of her limitations with her hands before her on her apron. She purses up her mouth and makes a long face. "It's pretty young," she says, "for the female instincts to be showing up."

"Hold your tongue," snaps Cornelius, in his agony. He has this much to be thankful for, that Ellie does not turn from him now; she does not push him away as she did downstairs, but clings to him in her need, while she reiterates her absurd, bewildered prayer that Max might be her brother, or

[29] A *mater dolorosa* is the conventional figure in art of Mary grieving for Christ.

with a fresh burst of desire demands to be taken downstairs so that he can dance with her again. But Max, of course, is dancing with Fräulein Plaichinger, that behemoth who is his rightful partner and has every claim upon him; whereas Ellie—never, thinks the Professor, his heart torn with the violence of his pity, never has she looked so tiny and birdlike as now, when she nestles to him shaken with sobs and all unaware of what is happening in her little soul. No, she does not know. She does not comprehend that her suffering is on account of Fraülein Plaichinger, fat, overgrown, and utterly within her rights in dancing with Max Hergesell, whereas Ellie may only do it once, by way of a joke, although she is incomparably the more charming of the two. Yet it would be quite mad to reproach young Hergesell with the state of affairs or to make fantastic demands upon him. No, Ellie's suffering is without help or healing and must be covered up. Yet just as it is without understanding, so it is also without restraint—and that is what makes it so horribly painful. Xaver and blue-faced Ann do not feel this pain, it does not affect them—either because of native callousness or because they accept it as the way of nature. But the Professor's fatherly heart is quite torn by it, and by a distressful horror of this passion, so hopeless and so absurd.

Of no avail to hold forth to poor Ellie on the subject of the perfectly good little brother she already has. She only casts a distraught and scornful glance over at the other crib, where Snapper lies vehemently slumbering, and with fresh tears calls again for Max. Of no avail either the promise of a long, long walk tomorrow, all five gentlemen, round and round the dining room table; or a dramatic description of the thrilling cushion games they will play. No, she will listen to none of all this, nor to lying down and going to sleep. She will not sleep, she will sit bolt upright and suffer. . . . But on a sudden they stop and listen, Abel and Ellie; listen to something miraculous that is coming to pass, that is approaching by strides, two strides, to the nursery door, that now overwhelmingly appears. . . .

It is Xaver's work, not a doubt of that. He has not remained by the door where he stood to gloat over the ejection of the Hinterhofers. No, he has bestirred himself, taken a notion; likewise steps to carry it out. Downstairs he has gone, twitched Herr Hergesell's sleeve, and made a thick-lipped request. So here they both are. Xaver, having done his part, remains by the door; but Max Hergesell comes up to Ellie's crib; in his dinner jacket, with his sketchy side-whiskers and charming black eyes; obviously quite pleased with his rôle of swan knight[30] and fairy prince, as one who should say: "See, here am I, now all losses are restored and sorrows end!"[31]

Cornelius is almost as much overcome as Ellie herself.

"Just look," he says feebly, "look who's here. This is uncommonly good of you, Herr Hergesell."

"Not a bit of it," says Hergesell. "Why shouldn't I come to say good-night to my fair partner?"

And he approaches the bars of the crib, behind which Ellie sits struck mute. She smiles blissfully through her tears. A funny, high little note that

[30]Lohengrin, in Wagner's opera (1847) of that name, enters in one scene in a boat drawn by swans.

[31]Shakespeare's Sonnet 30: "But if the while I think on thee, dear friend, / All losses are restor'd and sorrows end."

is half a sigh of relief comes from her lips, then she looks dumbly up at her swan knight with her golden-brown eyes—tear-swollen though they are, so much more beautiful than the fat Plaichinger's. She does not put up her arms. Her joy, like her grief, is without understanding; but she does not do that. The lovely little hands lie quiet on the coverlet, and Max Hergesell stands with his arms leaning over the rail as on a balcony.

"And now," he says smartly, "she need not 'sit the livelong night and weep upon her bed'!"[32] He looks at the Professor to make sure he is receiving due credit for the quotation. "Ha ha!" he laughs, "she's beginning young. 'Console thee, dearest child!' Never mind, you're all right! Just as you are you'll be wonderful! You've only got to grow up. . . . And you'll lie down and go to sleep like a good girl, now I've come to say good-night? And not cry any more, little Lorelei?"[33]

Ellie looks up at him, transfigured. One birdlike shoulder is bare; the Professor draws the lace-trimmed nighty over it. There comes into his mind a sentimental story he once read about a dying child who longs to see a clown he had once, with unforgettable ecstasy, beheld in a circus. And they bring the clown to the bedside marvellously arrayed, embroidered before and behind with silver butterflies; and the child dies happy. Max Hergesell is not embroidered, and Ellie, thank God, is not going to die, she has only been "in a bad way." But, after all, the effect is the same. Young Hergesell leans over the bars of the crib and rattles on, more for the father's ear than the child's, but Ellie does not know that—and the father's feelings towards him are a most singular mixture of thankfulness, embarrassment, and hatred.

"Good night, little Lorelei," says Hergesell, and gives her his hand through the bars. Her pretty, soft, white little hand is swallowed up in the grasp of his big, strong, red one. "Sleep well," he says, "and sweet dreams! But don't dream about me—God forbid! Not at your age—ha ha!" And then the fairy clown's visit is at an end. Cornelius accompanies him to the door. "No, no, positively, no thanks called for, don't mention it," he largeheartedly protests; and Xaver goes downstairs with him, to help serve the Italian salad.

But Dr. Cornelius returns to Ellie, who is now lying down, with her cheek pressed into her flat little pillow.

"Well, wasn't that lovely?" he says as he smooths the covers. She nods, with one last little sob. For a quarter of an hour he sits beside her and watches while she falls asleep in her turn, beside the little brother who found the right way so much earlier than she. Her silky brown hair takes the enchanting fall it always does when she sleeps; deep, deep lie the lashes over the eyes that late so abundantly poured forth their sorrow; the angelic mouth with its bowed upper lip is peacefully relaxed and a little open. Only now and then comes a belated catch in her slow breathing.

And her small hands, like pink and white flowers, lie so quietly, one on the coverlet, the other on the pillow by her face—Dr. Cornelius, gazing, feels his heart melt with tenderness as with strong wine.

[32] From a lyric in Johann Wolfgang von Goethe's *Wilhelm Meister's Apprenticeship* (1796), Chapter 13.

[33] A siren who, in German legend, lured sailors onto rocks along the Rhine with her singing.

"How good," he thinks, "that she breathes in oblivion with every breath she draws! That in childhood each night is a deep wide gulf between one day and the next. Tomorrow, beyond all doubt, young Hergesell will be a pale shadow, powerless to darken her little heart. Tomorrow, forgetful of all but present joy, she will walk with Abel and Snapper, all five gentlemen, round and round the table, will play the ever-thrilling cushion game."

Heaven be praised for that!

James Joyce

(1882–1941)

It is extraordinary that the greatest poet of the twentieth century, William Butler Yeats, and the greatest novelist, James Joyce, were both from the tiny island of Ireland. And both were not only from Ireland but quintessentially of Ireland; Irish life provided the materials of their art, cosmopolitan as that art came to be. Both wrote primarily of themselves, transforming their self-perceptions, their experiences, and their friends into symbols. But Yeats's art was essentially compressive; remaining in Ireland, he distilled his observations into brief, luminous lyrics. Joyce's was expansive; through his prolonged, self-imposed exile from Ireland, he wove his memories of Irish life into a series of ever longer and more inclusive books, climaxing his career with an extraordinary Dublin epic grounded in the story of a Dublin publican's family but reaching out to include all of human history. Dubliners *(1914),* A Portrait of the Artist as a Young Man *(1916),* Ulysses *(1922), and* Finnegans Wake *(1939) remain stories of Dublin life at the turn of the century while at the same time they stand at the pinnacle of international modern fiction.*

Joyce was born in Dublin in 1882. The members of his family were to cast their shadows over his major fictional characters. The father was John Stanislaus Joyce, the mother was Mary Jane ("May") Murray Joyce, and there were nine brothers and sisters who survived infancy; the one closest to Joyce was Stanislaus, two years younger than he. Joyce described his father, under the guise of "Simon Dedalus" in A Portrait of the Artist as a Young Man, *as "a medical student, an oarsman, a tenor, an amateur actor, a shouting politician, a small landlord, a small investor, a drinker, a good fellow, a storyteller, somebody's secretary, something in a distillery, a tax-gatherer, a bankrupt and at present a praiser of his own past." May Joyce was a gentle, devout woman with a good training in music. "Stannie" was a quiet, studious boy who remained unflinchingly loyal to his older brother and whom Joyce came to regard, with considerable ambivalence, as a sort of shadow self.*

The story of Joyce's childhood and youth in Dublin is one of the gradual but steady decline of the family fortunes and of his own self-separation from them. John Joyce had begun his marriage with a good income from inherited property and from a political appointment as collector of taxes for the city of Dublin. When Joyce was six, he was sent to Clongowes Wood College, an expensive boarding school run by the Jesuits. John Joyce lost his job as tax collector, however, because of irregularities in his accounts, and drifted through a series of jobs toward bankruptcy. Joyce had to drop out of Clongowes Wood; after two years at home, he completed his elementary education at Belvedere College, where he and Stanislaus were admitted without fees. He remained there between the ages of eleven and sixteen, distinguishing himself academically, and then entered University College, Dublin, a Jesuit institution founded by Cardinal Newman as an alternative to the almost wholly Protestant Trinity College, Dublin. During his university years, Joyce read widely, often outside the curriculum, and began to write seriously, producing not only several published critical essays but also poems and notebooks of "epiphanies," the word Joyce borrowed from theology to refer to intense moments when the truth about a person or thing was revealed. He graduated in 1902, with a respectable second-class degree in Latin.

After graduating, Joyce considered studying medicine, attended a few lectures in Dublin, and then went to Paris, where he spent a few months, quickly giving up the idea of becoming a doctor. He returned to Dublin in April, 1903, after receiving the telegram, memorable from its use in Ulysses, *"MOTHER DYING COME HOME FATHER." His mother died in August, and Joyce remained in Dublin for a little over a year more, teaching for a short time, beginning an autobiographical novel named* Stephen Hero, *writing some short stories for a farmers' magazine,* The Irish Homestead, *and sharing, for ten days, a rented Martello tower with a medical-student friend named Oliver St. John Gogarty, later to become the "Buck Mulligan" of* Ulysses.

In June, 1904, Joyce met a girl from Galway named Nora Barnacle, then working as a chambermaid in Finn's Hotel in Dublin. Their first date was on June 16, 1904 (commemorated by Joyce's selection of that date for "Bloomsday," the day of the entire action of Ulysses*). The two fell in love; since Joyce was opposed to marriage as an institution and could not live unmarried with Nora in Dublin, he persuaded her to go abroad with him. They left Dublin in October, 1904, and went to Pola, a small Adriatic seaport then controlled by Austria, now part of Yugoslavia. After a few months they moved to Trieste, where they remained, with a brief interlude in Rome, until 1915, Joyce supporting them by teaching English in the local Berlitz school. Stanislaus joined them in Trieste in 1905; a son, Georgio, was born the same year, and a daughter, Lucia Anna, in 1907.*

In 1905, too, Joyce submitted the first version of Dubliners, *a collection of short stories, to a publisher; it was repeatedly rejected and even after acceptance was subjected to censorship by publishers and printers who objected to the stories' sexual frankness, their use of such obscenities as "bloody," and their use of real names of people and places. Joyce meanwhile had begun in 1907 to revise* Stephen Hero *into a tighter, more carefully controlled "work in five chapters." Both* Dubliners *and* A Portrait of the Artist as a Young Man *were published in 1914 (*A Portrait *in serial form in a literary review named* The Egoist, *with book publication following in 1916). Both works were favorably reviewed and began to bring Joyce a wide reputation.*

When World War I broke out in 1915, the Joyces were allowed to leave Trieste for neutral Zurich. They remained there until 1919, with Joyce giving private English lessons and working on the early chapters of Ulysses. *This book had started as another short story for* Dubliners *about a "Mr. Hunter" but quickly grew into a massive novel which recreates the action of the* Odyssey *in a single day in 1904 Dublin, with the Stephen Dedalus of* A Portrait *in the role of Telemachus and Leopold Bloom, an advertising solicitor, and his musical wife Molly as Odysseus and Penelope. After the war, the Joyces returned to Trieste briefly and then moved to Paris in 1920. By now Joyce had obtained some measure of relief from money worries, first through grants from the Royal Literary Society and Mrs. Edith Rockefeller McCormick and later through a continuing series of subsidies from Harriet Shaw Weaver, a well-to-do English feminist and patron of the arts. In 1917, however, he had begun to suffer from increasing difficulties with his eyesight; between that time and 1930, he underwent twenty-five painful operations for iritis, glaucoma, and cataracts which left his vision seriously impaired.*

When Ulysses *was published on Joyce's fortieth birthday, February 2, 1922, a storm of outrage broke around his head. Serial publication of the early chapters of the book in the American* Little Review *had already been banned in 1920, and now the postal authorities banned it in both England and America. For more than ten years, English and American readers could get the book only in smuggled, surreptitious copies from Paris. Finally in 1933, an American court ruled that it was not obscene. An American edition appeared the following year, and the English followed suit in 1936. (The book was never banned in Ireland, but it was not allowed for sale either until long after it was available elsewhere.)*

Even before the completion of Ulysses, *Joyce had been planning a "night" book to complement his "day" book,* Ulysses, *and he wrote the first pages of the new work in March, 1923. Its composition was to stretch out over sixteen years, with sections appearing periodically in magazines and in pamphlet form as parts of a "Work in Progress." Joyce's last years were saddened by the mental illness of his daughter; what began as mild eccentricity gradually became advanced schizophrenia, and it was necessary to place her in a mental hospital in 1932. "Work in Progress," completed and given the title* Finnegans Wake, *was published in 1939, its long-awaited appearance disappointingly neglected under the urgency of news of the impending war. When France fell to the Nazis in 1940, the Joyces fled again to Zurich, where Joyce died in January, 1941, of a perforated ulcer.*

In Joyce's own day, his work was greeted with incomprehension and hostility by the general public and by a sizable portion of the literary establishment. (And even by a number of his fellow modernist novelists: Virginia Woolf thought Ulysses *was the work of "a queasy undergraduate scratching his pimples," although she later relented, and D. H. Lawrence told his wife that Molly's monologue was "the dirtiest, most indecent, obscene thing ever written. Yes, it is, Frieda. . . . It is filthy.") His admirers generally praised his work for its technical experimentation and stylistic brilliance. T. S. Eliot praised Joyce for his use in* Ulysses *of the "mythical method" and recognized the parallel (not really a very close one) with his own treatment of the Fisher King myth in a modern setting in* The Waste Land, *published the same year as* Ulysses. *A great deal of attention has been paid to Joyce's "stream of consciousness" technique, by which the narrative follows the flow of consciousness of one or more characters, a technique Joyce experimented with in* Dubliners, *developed fully in* A Portrait *and* Ulysses, *and transcended in the flowing, multilayered dream language of* Finnegans Wake.

Joyce was a daring experimentalist, and the difficulty of his books can still intimidate. A Portrait *is by no means easy reading; it takes a number of deep breaths to get through* Ulysses *the first time; and* Finnegans Wake *remains literally a closed book to all except a growing but still comparatively small number of enthusiasts who have accepted the challenge, if not of spending their entire lives on it, as Joyce suggested (only half facetiously), of spending enough time on it to open up its flood of comic invention and warm humanity.*

It is the comedy and the humanity that are likely to strike contemporary readers more than the obscenity and the obscurity, accustomed as we are to sexual frankness greater than Molly's and puzzles more difficult than Ulysses. *Joyce is above all a great comic writer, not only in the Irish blarneying that fills his pages but in his vision of life. Joyce's world, like that of the other great modernists, was fragmented, the fragmentation defined for him, as the critic Charles Peake has pointed out, as the split between the extraordinariness of the romantic, self-absorbed Artist (Stephen Dedalus) and the ordinariness of the earthy, life-accepting Citizen (Leopold Bloom). This split, which Joyce found within himself as well as in his family and in the modern world, he was able to resolve through the reconciling power of the comic imagination, which can soar into the ethereal while carrying the ordinary with it all the way.*

Dubliners *is a collection of fifteen stories of Dublin life. On the first page of the first story, "The Sisters," the nameless young narrator whispers the word "paralysis" to himself and says that he "longed to be nearer to it and to look upon its deadly work." In a sense, all the stories in the collection explore paralysis in Irish life, through successive sequences devoted to childhood, adolescence, mature life, and public life (Joyce's own categories). "Araby," the third story in the childhood group, illustrates Joyce's short-story technique vividly. There is a Chekhovian plotlessness about the structure; the story is held together by symbols and images rather than by external action. (Notice, for example, the way the word* blind *and related images of seeing and blindness wind their way through the story.) And it culminates in the sort of moment not of overt action but of self-revelation that Joyce called an "epiphany."*

Joyce wrote "The Dead," the last and greatest story in Dubliners, *in 1907, two years after he had submitted the first version of* Dubliners *to a publisher. Part of the impulse for the story came from Joyce's feeling that he had not been quite fair to Dublin in the other stories of* Dubliners; *he had left out, he told his brother Stanislaus, "its ingenuous insularity and its hospitality." He also drew upon an experience of his wife Nora; in Galway in 1903, Michael ("Sonny") Bodkin had courted her and had died after standing in the rain under her window and singing to her. The model for Gabriel was partially Joyce himself; other partial models were his father and a friend named Constantine Curran. One critic has aptly suggested that Gabriel may be Joyce's portrait of himself if he had remained in the paralysis of Dublin.*

The finished story, however, transforms whatever is autobiographical in the material into a polished and complex work of art. Every detail from the opening line ("Lily, the caretaker's daughter, was literally run off her feet") contributes to the title metaphor and leads Gabriel inexorably to his moving and epiphanic moment of self-realization in the last lines.

FURTHER READING (*prepared by J. H.*): One of the finest literary biographies ever written is Richard Ellmann's *James Joyce,* 2nd ed., 1982. There are a great many introductory books which briefly survey all the major works. Among those that can be recommended are Anthony Burgess's popularly written *Re Joyce,* 1965; A. Walton Litz's *James Joyce,* 1972; William York Tindall's *A Reader's Guide to James Joyce,* 1959; John Gross's *Joyce,* 1971; Matthew Hodgart's *James Joyce: A Student's Guide,* 1978; and Sydney Bolt's *A Preface to James Joyce,* 1981. In the same category but more ambitious and correspondingly more lastingly useful are Hugh Kenner's *Dublin's Joyce,* 1955, and Charles H. Peake's *James Joyce: The Citizen and the Artist,* 1977. A number of important critical essays are collected in the Twentieth Century Views volume *Joyce: A Collection of Critical Essays,* ed. William M. Chace, 1974. The study of *Ulysses* and *Finnegans Wake* requires special tools which need not be listed here. On the short stories in *Dubliners, James Joyce's "Dubliners": Critical Essays,* ed.

Clive Hart, 1969, can be especially recommended; it includes a comprehensive essay on each story, written by a major Joyce critic. Other good collections of essays on *Dubliners* include *"Dubliners": A Collection of Critical Essays,* ed. Peter Garrett, 1968; and the Viking Critical Edition of *Dubliners,* ed. Robert Scholes and A. Walton Litz, 1969. Detailed, page-by-page glosses on the stories are provided in Don Gifford, *Joyce Annotated: Dubliners and A Portrait of the Artist as a Young Man,* 2nd ed., 1982.

ARABY

North Richmond Street, being blind,[1] was a quiet street except at the hour when the Christian Brothers' School[2] set the boys free. An uninhabited house of two storeys stood at the blind end, detached from its neighbours in a square ground. The other houses of the street, conscious of decent lives within them, gazed at one another with brown imperturbable faces.

The former tenant of our house, a priest, had died in the back drawing-room. Air, musty from having been long enclosed, hung in all the rooms, and the waste room behind the kitchen was littered with old useless papers. Among these I found a few paper-covered books, the pages of which were curled and damp: *The Abbot,* by Walter Scott, *The Devout Communicant* and *The Memoirs of Vidocq.*[3] I liked the last best because its leaves were yellow. The wild garden behind the house contained a central apple-tree and a few straggling bushes under one of which I found the late tenant's rusty bicycle-pump. He had been a very charitable priest; in his will he had left all his money to institutions and the furniture of his house to his sister.

When the short days of winter came dusk fell before we had well eaten our dinners. When we met in the street the houses had grown sombre. The space of sky above us was the colour of ever-changing violet and towards it the lamps of the street lifted their feeble lanterns. The cold air stung us and we played till our bodies glowed. Our shouts echoed in the silent street. The career of our play brought us through the dark muddy lanes behind the houses where we ran the gantlet of the rough tribes from the cottages,[4] to the back doors of the dark dripping gardens where odours arose from the ashpits, to the dark odorous stables where a coachman smoothed and combed the horse or shook music from the buckled harness. When we returned to the street light from the kitchen windows had filled the areas. If my uncle was seen turning the corner we hid in the shadow until we had seen him safely housed. Or if Mangan's sister came out on the doorstep to

[1] Dead-end.

[2] The Irish Christian Brothers were a lay order which boasted of its conservatism. Their schools were thought of as educationally and socially inferior to those of the Jesuits.

[3] Sir Walter Scott's *The Abbot* (1820) is a romantic historical novel about Mary Queen of Scots. Bernard Benstock has pointed out that there were two books called *The Devout Communicant,* one a Catholic manual by a Franciscan friar named Pacificus Baker and the other an anti-Catholic tract by Abednego Seller; Joyce doubtless intended the ambiguity. *The Memoirs of Vidocq* were the sensational, spurious memoirs of François Eugène Vidocq (1775–1857), an ex-criminal who became chief of detectives in the Paris police.

[4] Children from the poorer houses.

call her brother in to his tea we watched her from our shadow peer up and down the street. We waited to see whether she would remain or go in and, if she remained, we left our shadow and walked up to Mangan's steps resignedly. She was waiting for us, her figure defined by the light from the half-opened door. Her brother always teased her before he obeyed and I stood by the railings looking at her. Her dress swung as she moved her body and the soft rope of her hair tossed from side to side.

Every morning I lay on the floor in the front parlour watching her door. The blind was pulled down to within an inch of the sash so that I could not be seen. When she came out on the doorstep my heart leaped. I ran to the hall, seized my books and followed her. I kept her brown figure always in my eye and, when we came near the point at which our ways diverged, I quickened my pace and passed her. This happened morning after morning. I had never spoken to her, except for a few casual words, and yet her name was like a summons to all my foolish blood.

Her image accompanied me even in places the most hostile to romance. On Saturday evenings when my aunt went marketing I had to go to carry some of the parcels. We walked through the flaring streets, jostled by drunken men and bargaining women, amid the curses of labourers, the shrill litanies of shop-boys who stood on guard by the barrels of pigs' cheeks, the nasal chanting of street-singers, who sang a *come-all-you* about O'Donovan Rossa,[5] or a ballad about the troubles in our native land. These noises converged in a single sensation of life for me: I imagined that I bore my chalice[6] safely through a throng of foes. Her name sprang to my lips at moments in strange prayers and praises which I myself did not understand. My eyes were often full of tears (I could not tell why) and at times a flood from my heart seemed to pour itself out into my bosom. I thought little of the future. I did not know whether I would ever speak to her or not or, if I spoke to her, how I could tell her of my confused adoration. But my body was like a harp and her words and gestures were like fingers running upon the wires.

One evening I went into the back drawing-room in which the priest had died. It was a dark rainy evening and there was no sound in the house. Through one of the broken panes I heard the rain impinge upon the earth, the fine incessant needles of water playing in the sodden beds. Some distant lamp or lighted window gleamed below me. I was thankful that I could see so little. All my senses seemed to desire to veil themselves and, feeling that I was about to slip from them, I pressed the palms of my hands together until they trembled, murmuring: "*O love! O love!*" many times.

At last she spoke to me. When she addressed the first words to me I was so confused that I did not know what to answer. She asked me was I going to *Araby*.[7] I forgot whether I answered yes or no. It would be a splendid bazaar, she said; she would love to go.

[5] A "come-all-you" is any narrative ballad, for which "Come all you noble Irishmen . . ." (or "lads and lassies," or whatever) is a stock opening. O'Donovan Rossa, or "Dynamite Rossa," was Jeremiah O'Donovan (1831–1915), a legendary Irish revolutionary imprisoned in 1865.

[6] The cup used for the wine in the celebration of the Eucharist.

[7] An "Araby" bazaar was held in Dublin on May 14–19, 1894. Joyce probably also had in mind, for its exotic and Eastern associations, a lush popular song named "I'll Sing Thee Songs of Araby," with words by W. G. Wills and music by Frederick Clay.

—And why can't you? I asked.

While she spoke she turned a silver bracelet round and round her wrist. She could not go, she said, because there would be a retreat[8] that week in her convent. Her brother and two other boys were fighting for their caps and I was alone at the railings. She held one of the spikes, bowing her head towards me. The light from the lamp opposite our door caught the white curve of her neck, lit up her hair that rested there and, falling, lit up the hand upon the railing. It fell over one side of her dress and caught the white border of a petticoat, just visible as she stood at ease.

—It's well for you, she said.

—If I go, I said, I will bring you something.

What innumerable follies laid waste my waking and sleeping thoughts after that evening! I wished to annihilate the tedious intervening days. I chafed against the work of school. At night in my bedroom and by day in the classroom her image came between me and the page I strove to read. The syllables of the word *Araby* were called to me through the silence in which my soul luxuriated and cast an Eastern enchantment over me. I asked for leave to go to the bazaar on Saturday night. My aunt was surprised and hoped it was not some Freemason affair.[9] I answered few questions in class. I watched my master's face pass from amiability to sternness; he hoped I was not beginning to idle. I could not call my wandering thoughts together. I had hardly any patience with the serious work of life which, now that it stood between me and my desire, seemed to me child's play, ugly monotonous child's play.

On Saturday morning I reminded my uncle that I wished to go to the bazaar in the evening. He was fussing at the hallstand, looking for the hat-brush, and answered me curtly:

—Yes, boy, I know.

As he was in the hall I could not go into the front parlour and lie at the window. I left the house in bad humour and walked slowly towards the school. The air was pitilessly raw and already my heart misgave me.

When I came home to dinner my uncle had not yet been home. Still it was early. I sat staring at the clock for some time and, when its ticking began to irritate me, I left the room. I mounted the staircase and gained the upper part of the house. The high cold empty gloomy rooms liberated me and I went from room to room singing. From the front window I saw my companions playing below in the street. Their cries reached me weakened and indistinct and, leaning my forehead against the cool glass, I looked over at the dark house where she lived. I may have stood there for an hour, seeing nothing but the brown-clad figure cast by my imagination, touched discreetly by the lamplight at the curved neck, at the hand upon the railings and at the border below the dress.

When I came downstairs again I found Mrs Mercer sitting at the fire. She was an old garrulous woman, a pawnbroker's widow, who collected used stamps for some pious purpose. I had to endure the gossip of the tea-table. The meal was prolonged beyond an hour and still my uncle did

[8] Period of withdrawal from the world for religious exercises and meditation.

[9] The Masons were thought to be anti-Catholic. The name "Araby" apparently makes the aunt think of the oriental trappings of the Masonic order.

not come. Mrs Mercer stood up to go: she was sorry she couldn't wait any longer, but it was after eight o'clock and she did not like to be out late, as the night air was bad for her. When she had gone I began to walk up and down the room, clenching my fists. My aunt said:

—I'm afraid you may put off your bazaar for this night of Our Lord.

At nine o'clock I heard my uncle's latchkey in the halldoor. I heard him talking to himself and heard the hallstand rocking when it had received the weight of his overcoat. I could interpret these signs. When he was midway through his dinner I asked him to give me the money to go to the bazaar. He had forgotten.

—The people are in bed and after their first sleep now, he said.

I did not smile. My aunt said to him energetically:

—Can't you give him the money and let him go? You've kept him late enough as it is.

My uncle said he was very sorry he had forgotten. He said he believed in the old saying: *All work and no play makes Jack a dull boy.* He asked me where I was going and, when I had told him a second time he asked me did I know *The Arab's Farewell to his Steed.*[10] When I left the kitchen he was about to recite the opening lines of the piece to my aunt.

I held a florin[11] tightly in my hand as I strode down Buckingham Street towards the station. The sight of the streets thronged with buyers and glaring with gas recalled to me the purpose of my journey. I took my seat in a third-class carriage of a deserted train. After an intolerable delay the train moved out of the station slowly. It crept onward among ruinous houses and over the twinkling river. At Westland Row Station a crowd of people pressed to the carriage doors; but the porters moved them back, saying that it was a special train for the bazaar. I remained alone in the bare carriage. In a few minutes the train drew up beside an improvised wooden platform. I passed out on to the road and saw by the lighted dial of a clock that it was ten minutes to ten. In front of me was a large building which displayed the magical name.

I could not find any sixpenny entrance and, fearing that the bazaar would be closed, I passed in quickly through a turnstile, handing a shilling to a weary-looking man. I found myself in a big hall girdled at half its height by a gallery. Nearly all the stalls were closed and the greater part of the hall was in darkness. I recognised a silence like that which pervades a church after a service. I walked into the centre of the bazaar timidly. A few people were gathered about the stalls which were still open. Before a curtain, over which the words *Café Chantant*[12] were written in coloured lamps, two men were counting money on a salver. I listened to the fall of the coins.

Remembering with difficulty why I had come I went over to one of the stalls and examined porcelain vases and flowered tea-sets. At the door of the stall a young lady was talking and laughing with two young gentlemen. I remarked their English accents and listened vaguely to their conversation.

[10] A piece of sentimental "parlor poetry" by Lady Caroline Norton (1808–1877). The poem has some points of similarity with "Araby" in that the speaker, after lamenting the sale of his horse, awakens from "the fevered dream," flings "them back their gold," and rides off into the desert.

[11] A coin worth two shillings.

[12] "Singing cafe," a "French" cafe with musical entertainment.

—O, I never said such a thing!
—O, but you did!
—O, but I didn't!
—Didn't she say that?
—Yes. I heard her.
—O, there's a . . . fib!

Observing me the young lady came over and asked me did I wish to buy anything. The tone of her voice was not encouraging; she seemed to have spoken to me out of a sense of duty. I looked humbly at the great jars that stood like eastern guards at either side of the dark entrance to the stall and murmured:

—No, thank you.

The young lady changed the position of one of the vases and went back to the two young men. They began to talk of the same subject. Once or twice the young lady glanced at me over her shoulder.

I lingered before her stall, though I knew my stay was useless, to make my interest in her wares seem the more real. Then I turned away slowly and walked down the middle of the bazaar. I allowed the two pennies to fall against the sixpence in my pocket. I heard a voice call from one end of the gallery that the light was out. The upper part of the hall was now completely dark.

Gazing up into the darkness I saw myself as a creature driven and derided by vanity; and my eyes burned with anguish and anger.

THE DEAD

Lily, the caretaker's daughter, was literally run off her feet. Hardly had she brought one gentleman into the little pantry behind the office on the ground floor and helped him off with his overcoat than the wheezy hall-door bell clanged again and she had to scamper along the bare hallway to let in another guest. It was well for her she had not to attend to the ladies also. But Miss Kate and Miss Julia had thought of that and had converted the bathroom upstairs into a ladies' dressing-room. Miss Kate and Miss Julia were there, gossiping and laughing and fussing, walking after each other to the head of the stairs, peering down over the banisters and calling down to Lily to ask her who had come.

It was always a great affair, the Misses Morkan's annual dance. Everybody who knew them came to it, members of the family, old friends of the family, the members of Julia's choir, any of Kate's pupils that were grown up enough, and even some of Mary Jane's pupils too. Never once had it fallen flat. For years and years it had gone off in splendid style as long as anyone could remember; ever since Kate and Julia, after the death of their brother Pat, had left the house in Stoney Batter and taken Mary Jane, their only niece, to live with them in the dark gaunt house on Usher's Island, the upper part of which they had rented from Mr Fulham, the corn-factor[1] on the ground floor. That was a good thirty years ago if it was a day. Mary

[1] Grain merchant.

Jane, who was then a little girl in short clothes, was now the main prop of the household, for she had the organ in Haddington Road.[2] She had been through the Academy and gave a pupils' concert every year in the upper room of the Antient Concert Rooms.[3] Many of her pupils belonged to the better-class families on the Kingstown and Dalkey line. Old as they were, her aunts also did their share. Julia, though she was quite grey, was still the leading soprano in Adam and Eve's,[4] and Kate, being too feeble to go about much, gave music lessons to beginners on the old square piano in the back room. Lily, the caretaker's daughter, did housemaid's work for them. Though their life was modest, they believed in eating well; the best of everything: diamond-bone sirloins, three-shilling tea and the best bottled stout. But Lily seldom made a mistake in the orders so that she got on well with her three mistresses. They were fussy, that was all. But the only thing they would not stand was back answers.

Of course they had good reason to be fussy on such a night. And then it was long after ten o'clock and yet there was no sign of Gabriel and his wife. Besides they were dreadfully afraid that Freddy Malins might turn up screwed.[5] They would not wish for worlds that any of Mary Jane's pupils should see him under the influence; and when he was like that it was sometimes very hard to manage him. Freddy Malins always came late but they wondered what could be keeping Gabriel: and that was what brought them every two minutes to the banisters to ask Lily had Gabriel or Freddy come.

—O, Mr Conroy, said Lily to Gabriel when she opened the door for him, Miss Kate and Miss Julia thought you were never coming. Goodnight, Mrs Conroy.

—I'll engage they did, said Gabriel, but they forget that my wife here takes three mortal hours to dress herself.

He stood on the mat, scraping the snow from his goloshes, while Lily led his wife to the foot of the stairs and called out:

—Miss Kate, here's Mrs Conroy.

Kate and Julia came toddling down the dark stairs at once. Both of them kissed Gabriel's wife, said she must be perished alive and asked was Gabriel with her.

—Here I am as right as the mail, Aunt Kate! Go on up. I'll follow, called out Gabriel from the dark.

He continued scraping his feet vigorously while the three women went upstairs, laughing, to the ladies' dressing-room. A light fringe of snow lay like a cape on the shoulders of his overcoat and like toecaps on the toes of his goloshes; and, as the buttons of his overcoat slipped with a squeaking noise through the snow-stiffened frieze,[6] a cold fragrant air from out-of-doors escaped from crevices and folds.

—Is it snowing again, Mr Conroy? asked Lily.

She had preceded him into the pantry to help him off with his overcoat. Gabriel smiled at the three syllables she had given his surname and glanced at her. She was a slim, growing girl pale in complexion and with hay-coloured hair. The gas in the pantry made her look still paler. Gabriel had

[2] That is, had the organist's job in a church in Haddington Road.
[3] A Dublin concert hall. Joyce competed in a singing contest there in 1904.
[4] A large church on Merchant's Quay in central Dublin.
[5] Drunk. [6] A heavy, woolen cloth.

known her when she was a child and used to sit on the lowest step nursing a rag doll.

—Yes, Lily, he answered, and I think we're in for a night of it.

He looked up at the pantry ceiling, which was shaking with the stamping and shuffling of feet on the floor above, listened for a moment to the piano and then glanced at the girl, who was folding his overcoat carefully at the end of a shelf.

—Tell me, Lily, he said in a friendly tone, do you still go to school?

—O no, sir, she answered. I'm done schooling this year and more.

—O, then, said Gabriel gaily, I suppose we'll be going to your wedding one of these fine days with your young man, eh?

The girl glanced back at him over her shoulder and said with great bitterness:

—The men that is now is only all palaver and what they can get out of you.

Gabriel coloured as if he felt he had made a mistake and, without looking at her, kicked off his goloshes and flicked actively with his muffler at his patent-leather shoes.

He was a stout tallish young man. The high colour of his cheeks pushed upwards even to his forehead where it scattered itself in a few formless patches of pale red; and on his hairless face there scintillated restlessly the polished lenses and the bright gilt rims of the glasses which screened his delicate and restless eyes. His glossy black hair was parted in the middle and brushed in a long curve behind his ears where it curled slightly beneath the groove left by his hat.

When he had flicked lustre into his shoes he stood up and pulled his waistcoat down more tightly on his plump body. Then he took a coin rapidly from his pocket.

—O Lily, he said, thrusting it into her hands, it's Christmas-time, isn't it? Just . . . here's a little. . . .

He walked rapidly towards the door.

—O no, sir! cried the girl, following him. Really, sir, I wouldn't take it.

—Christmas-time! Christmas-time! said Gabriel, almost trotting to the stairs and waving his hand to her in deprecation.

The girl, seeing that he had gained the stairs, called out after him:

—Well, thank you, sir.

He waited outside the drawing-room door until the waltz should finish, listening to the skirts that swept against it and to the shuffling of feet. He was still discomposed by the girl's bitter and sudden retort. It had cast a gloom over him which he tried to dispel by arranging his cuffs and the bows of his tie. He then took from his waistcoat pocket a little paper and glanced at the headings he had made for his speech. He was undecided about the lines from Robert Browning for he feared they would be above the heads of his hearers. Some quotation that they would recognise from Shakespeare or from the Melodies[7] would be better. The indelicate clacking of the men's heels and the shuffling of their soles reminded him that their grade of culture differed from his. He would only make himself

[7] Thomas Moore's *Irish Melodies* (1807–34), a popular collection in which Moore wrote new words to traditional Irish melodies.

ridiculous by quoting poetry to them which they could not understand. They would think that he was airing his superior education. He would fail with them just as he had failed with the girl in the pantry. He had taken up a wrong tone. His whole speech was a mistake from first to last, an utter failure.

Just then his aunts and his wife came out of the ladies' dressing-room. His aunts were two small plainly dressed old women. Aunt Julia was an inch or so the taller. Her hair, drawn low over the tops of her ears, was grey; and grey also, with darker shadows, was her large flaccid face. Though she was stout in build and stood erect her slow eyes and parted lips gave her the appearance of a woman who did not know where she was or where she was going. Aunt Kate was more vivacious. Her face, healthier than her sister's, was all puckers and creases, like a shrivelled red apple, and her hair, braided in the same old-fashioned way, had not lost its ripe nut colour.

They both kissed Gabriel frankly. He was their favourite nephew, the son of their dead elder sister, Ellen, who had married T. J. Conroy of the Port and Docks.[8]

—Gretta tells me you're not going to take a cab back to Monkstown to-night, Gabriel, said Aunt Kate.

—No, said Gabriel, turning to his wife, we had quite enough of that last year, hadn't we? Don't you remember, Aunt Kate, what a cold Gretta got out of it? Cab windows rattling all the way, and the east wind blowing in after we passed Merrion. Very jolly it was. Gretta caught a dreadful cold.

Aunt Kate frowned severely and nodded her head at every word.

—Quite right, Gabriel, quite right, she said. You can't be too careful.

—But as for Gretta there, said Gabriel, she'd walk home in the snow if she were let.

Mrs Conroy laughed.

—Don't mind him, Aunt Kate, she said. He's really an awful bother, what with green shades for Tom's eyes at night and making him do the dumb-bells, and forcing Eva to eat the stirabout.[9] The poor child! And she simply hates the sight of it! . . . O, but you'll never guess what he makes me wear now!

She broke out into a peal of laughter and glanced at her husband, whose admiring and happy eyes had been wandering from her dress to her face and hair. The two aunts laughed heartily too, for Gabriel's solicitude was a standing joke with them.

—Goloshes! said Mrs Conroy. That's the latest. Whenever it's wet underfoot I must put on my goloshes. To-night even he wanted me to put them on, but I wouldn't. The next thing he'll buy me will be a diving suit.

Gabriel laughed nervously and patted his tie reassuringly while Aunt Kate nearly doubled herself, so heartily did she enjoy the joke. The smile soon faded from Aunt Julia's face and her mirthless eyes were directed towards her nephew's face. After a pause she asked:

—And what are goloshes, Gabriel?

—Goloshes, Julia! exclaimed her sister. Goodness me, don't you know what goloshes are? You wear them over your . . . over your boots, Gretta, isn't it?

[8] That is, of the government office regulating the harbor. [9] Porridge, oatmeal.

—Yes, said Mrs Conroy. Guttapercha[10] things. We both have a pair now. Gabriel says everyone wears them on the continent.

—O, on the continent, murmured Aunt Julia, nodding her head slowly.

Gabriel knitted his brows and said, as if he were slightly angered:

—It's nothing very wonderful but Gretta thinks it very funny because she says the word reminds her of Christy Minstrels.[11]

—But tell me, Gabriel, said Aunt Kate, with brisk tact. Of course, you've seen about the room. Gretta was saying . . .

—O, the room is all right, replied Gabriel. I've taken one in the Gresham.[12]

—To be sure, said Aunt Kate, by far the best thing to do. And the children, Gretta, you're not anxious about them?

—O, for one night, said Mrs Conroy. Besides, Bessie will look after them.

—To be sure, said Aunt Kate again. What a comfort it is to have a girl like that, one you can depend on! There's that Lily, I'm sure I don't know what has come over her lately. She's not the girl she was at all.

Gabriel was about to ask his aunt some questions on this point but she broke off suddenly to gaze after her sister who had wandered down the stairs and was craning her neck over the banisters.

—Now, I ask you, she said, almost testily, where is Julia going? Julia! Julia! Where are you going?

Julia, who had gone halfway down one flight, came back and announced blandly:

—Here's Freddy.

At the same moment a clapping of hands and a final flourish of the pianist told that the waltz had ended. The drawing-room door was opened from within and some couples came out. Aunt Kate drew Gabriel aside hurriedly and whispered into his ear:

—Slip down, Gabriel, like a good fellow and see if he's all right, and don't let him up if he's screwed. I'm sure he's screwed. I'm sure he is.

Gabriel went to the stairs and listened over the banisters. He could hear two persons talking in the pantry. Then he recognised Freddy Malins' laugh. He went down the stairs noisily.

—It's such a relief, said Aunt Kate to Mrs Conroy, that Gabriel is here. I always feel easier in my mind when he's here. . . . Julia, there's Miss Daly and Miss Power will take some refreshment. Thanks for your beautiful waltz, Miss Daly. It made lovely time.

A tall wizen-faced man, with a stiff grizzled moustache and swarthy skin, who was passing out with his partner, said:

—And may we have some refreshment, too, Miss Morkan?

—Julia, said Aunt Kate summarily, and here's Mr Browne and Miss Furlong. Take them in, Julia, with Miss Daly and Miss Power.

—I'm the man for the ladies, said Mr Browne, pursing his lips until his moustache bristled and smiling in all his wrinkles. You know, Miss Morkan, the reason they are so fond of me is—

He did not finish his sentence, but, seeing that Aunt Kate was out of

[10] A tough plastic substance resembling rubber.

[11] Famous minstrel company organized by E. P. Christy. American blackface minstrels were popular in nineteenth-century Dublin.

[12] A fashionable Dublin hotel.

earshot, at once led the three young ladies into the back room. The middle of the room was occupied by two square tables placed end to end, and on these Aunt Julia and the caretaker were straightening and smoothing a large cloth. On the sideboard were arrayed dishes and plates, and glasses and bundles of knives and forks and spoons. The top of the closed square piano served also as a sideboard for viands and sweets. At a smaller sideboard in one corner two young men were standing, drinking hop-bitters.[13]

Mr Browne led his charges thither and invited them all, in jest, to some ladies' punch, hot, strong and sweet. As they said they never took anything strong he opened three bottles of lemonade for them. Then he asked one of the young men to move aside, and, taking hold of the decanter, filled out for himself a goodly measure of whisky. The young men eyed him respectfully while he took a trial sip.

—God help me, he said, smiling, it's the doctor's orders.

His wizened face broke into a broader smile, and the three young ladies laughed in musical echo to his pleasantry, swaying their bodies to and fro, with nervous jerks of their shoulders. The boldest said:

—O, now, Mr Browne, I'm sure the doctor never ordered anything of the kind.

Mr Browne took another sip of his whisky and said, with sidling mimicry:

—Well, you see, I'm like the famous Mrs Cassidy, who is reported to have said: *Now, Mary Grimes, if I don't take it, make me take it, for I feel I want it.*

His hot face had leaned forward a little too confidentially and he had assumed a very low Dublin accent so that the young ladies, with one instinct, received his speech in silence. Miss Furlong, who was one of Mary Jane's pupils, asked Miss Daly what was the name of the pretty waltz she had played; and Mr Browne, seeing that he was ignored, turned promptly to the two young men who were more appreciative.

A red-faced young woman, dressed in pansy,[14] came into the room, excitedly clapping her hands and crying:

—Quadrilles! Quadrilles![15]

Close on her heels came Aunt Kate, crying:

—Two gentlemen and three ladies, Mary Jane!

—O, here's Mr Bergin and Mr Kerrigan, said Mary Jane. Mr Kerrigan, will you take Miss Power? Miss Furlong, may I get you a partner, Mr Bergin. O, that'll just do now.

—Three ladies, Mary Jane, said Aunt Kate.

The two young gentlemen asked the ladies if they might have the pleasure, and Mary Jane turned to Miss Daly.

—O, Miss Daly, you're really awfully good, after playing for the last two dances, but really we're so short of ladies to-night.

—I don't mind in the least, Miss Morkan.

—But I've a nice partner for you, Mr Bartell D'Arcy, the tenor. I'll get him to sing later on. All Dublin is raving about him.

—Lovely voice, lovely voice! said Aunt Kate.

As the piano had twice begun the prelude to the first figure Mary Jane led her recruits quickly from the room. They had hardly gone when Aunt Julia wandered slowly into the room, looking behind her at something.

[13] A kind of malt liquor. [14] Violet. [15] A ballroom dance for four-couple "sets."

—What is the matter, Julia? asked Aunt Kate anxiously. Who is it?

Julia, who was carrying in a column of table-napkins, turned to her sister and said, as if the question had surprised her:

—It's only Freddy, Kate, and Gabriel with him.

In fact right behind her Gabriel could be seen piloting Freddy Malins across the landing. The latter, a young man of about forty, was of Gabriel's size and build, with very round shoulders. His face was fleshy and pallid, touched with colour only at the thick hanging lobes of his ears and at the wide wings of his nose. He had coarse features, a blunt nose, a convex and receding brow, tumid and protruded lips. His heavy-lidded eyes and the disorder of his scanty hair made him look sleepy. He was laughing heartily in a high key at a story which he had been telling Gabriel on the stairs and at the same time rubbing the knuckles of his left fist backwards and forwards into his left eye.

—Good-evening, Freddy, said Aunt Julia.

Freddy Malins bade the Misses Morkan good-evening in what seemed an offhand fashion by reason of the habitual catch in his voice and then, seeing that Mr Browne was grinning at him from the sideboard, crossed the room on rather shaky legs and began to repeat in an undertone the story he had just told to Gabriel.

—He's not so bad, is he? said Aunt Kate to Gabriel.

Gabriel's brows were dark but he raised them quickly and answered:

—O, no, hardly noticeable.

—Now, isn't he a terrible fellow! she said. And his poor mother made him take the pledge on New Year's Eve. But come on, Gabriel, into the drawing-room.

Before leaving the room with Gabriel she signalled to Mr Browne by frowning and shaking her forefinger in warning to and fro. Mr Browne nodded in answer and, when she had gone, said to Freddy Malins:

—Now, then, Teddy, I'm going to fill you out a good glass of lemonade just to buck you up.

Freddy Malins, who was nearing the climax of his story, waved the offer aside impatiently but Mr Browne, having first called Freddy Malins' attention to a disarray in his dress, filled out and handed him a full glass of lemonade. Freddy Malins' left hand accepted the glass mechanically, his right hand being engaged in the mechanical readjustment of his dress. Mr Browne, whose face was once more wrinkling with mirth, poured out for himself a glass of whisky while Freddy Malins exploded, before he had well reached the climax of his story, in a kink of high-pitched bronchitic laughter and, setting down his untasted and overflowing glass, began to rub the knuckles of his left fist backwards and forwards into his left eye, repeating words of his last phrase as well as his fit of laughter would allow him.

. . . .

Gabriel could not listen while Mary Jane was playing her Academy piece,[16] full of runs and difficult passages, to the hushed drawing-room.

[16] Demonstration piece prepared as part of her study at the Dublin Royal Academy of Music.

He liked music but the piece she was playing had no melody for him and he doubted whether it had any melody for the other listeners, though they had begged Mary Jane to play something. Four young men, who had come from the refreshment-room to stand in the doorway at the sound of the piano, had gone away quietly in couples after a few minutes. The only persons who seemed to follow the music were Mary Jane herself, her hands racing along the key-board or lifted from it at the pauses like those of a priestess in momentary imprecation, and Aunt Kate standing at her elbow to turn the page.

Gabriel's eyes, irritated by the floor, which glittered with beeswax under the heavy chandelier, wandered to the wall above the piano. A picture of the balcony scene in *Romeo and Juliet* hung there and beside it was a picture of the two murdered princes in the Tower[17] which Aunt Julia had worked in red, blue and brown wools when she was a girl. Probably in the school they had gone to as girls that kind of work had been taught, for one year his mother had worked for him as a birthday present a waistcoat of purple tabinet, with little foxes' heads upon it, lined with brown satin and having round mulberry buttons. It was strange that his mother had had no musical talent though Aunt Kate used to call her the brains carrier of the Morkan family. Both she and Julia had always seemed a little proud of their serious and matronly sister. Her photograph stood before the pierglass.[18] She held an open book on her knees and was pointing out something in it to Constantine who, dressed in a man-o'-war suit, lay at her feet. It was she who had chosen the names of her sons for she was very sensible of the dignity of family life. Thanks to her, Constantine was now senior curate in Balbriggan and, thanks to her, Gabriel himself had taken his degree in the Royal University. A shadow passed over his face as he remembered her sullen opposition to his marriage. Some slighting phrases she had used still rankled in his memory; she had once spoken of Gretta as being country cute and that was not true of Gretta at all. It was Gretta who had nursed her during all her last long illness in their house at Monkstown.

He knew that Mary Jane must be near the end of her piece for she was playing again the opening melody with runs of scales after every bar and while he waited for the end the resentment died down in his heart. The piece ended with a trill of octaves in the treble and a final deep octave in the bass. Great applause greeted Mary Jane as, blushing and rolling up her music nervously, she escaped from the room. The most vigorous clapping came from the four young men in the doorway who had gone away to the refreshment-room at the beginning of the piece but had come back when the piano had stopped.

Lancers[19] were arranged. Gabriel found himself partnered with Miss Ivors. She was a frank-mannered talkative young lady, with a freckled face and prominent brown eyes. She did not wear a low-cut bodice and the large brooch which was fixed in the front of her collar bore on it an Irish device.

When they had taken their places she said abruptly:

—I have a crow to pluck with you.

[17] Richard III was said to have ordered the murders of his two nephews, sons of Edward IV, in the Tower of London, 1483.

[18] A large mirror filling the space between two windows. [19] A kind of quadrille.

—With me? said Gabriel.

She nodded her head gravely.

—What is it? asked Gabriel, smiling at her solemn manner.

—Who is G. C.? answered Miss Ivors, turning her eyes upon him.

Gabriel coloured and was about to knit his brows, as if he did not understand, when she said bluntly:

—O, innocent Amy! I have found out that you write for *The Daily Express*. Now, aren't you ashamed of yourself?

—Why should I be ashamed of myself? asked Gabriel, blinking his eyes and trying to smile.

—Well, I'm ashamed of you, said Miss Ivors frankly. To say you'd write for a rag like that. I didn't think you were a West Briton.[20]

A look of perplexity appeared on Gabriel's face. It was true that he wrote a literary column every Wednesday in *The Daily Express*, for which he was paid fifteen shillings. But that did not make him a West Briton surely. The books he received for review were almost more welcome than the paltry cheque. He loved to feel the covers and turn over the pages of newly printed books. Nearly every day when his teaching in the college was ended he used to wander down the quays to the second-hand booksellers, to Hickey's on Bachelor's Walk, to Web's or Massey's on Aston's Quay, or to O'Clohissey's in the by-street. He did not know how to meet her charge. He wanted to say that literature was above politics. But they were friends of many years' standing and their careers had been parallel, first at the University and then as teachers: he could not risk a grandiose phrase with her. He continued blinking his eyes and trying to smile and murmured lamely that he saw nothing political in writing reviews of books.

When their turn to cross[21] had come he was still perplexed and inattentive. Miss Ivors promptly took his hand in a warm grasp and said in a soft friendly tone:

—Of course, I was only joking. Come, we cross now.

When they were together again she spoke of the University question[22] and Gabriel felt more at ease. A friend of hers had shown her his review of Browning's poems. That was how she had found out the secret: but she liked the review immensely. Then she said suddenly:

—O, Mr Conroy, will you come for an excursion to the Aran Isles[23] this summer? We're going to stay there a whole month. It will be splendid out in the Atlantic. You ought to come. Mr Clancy is coming, and Mr Kilkelly and Kathleen Kearney. It would be splendid for Gretta too if she'd come. She's from Connacht,[24] isn't she?

—Her people are, said Gabriel shortly.

—But you will come, won't you? said Miss Ivors, laying her warm hand eagerly on his arm.

—That fact is, said Gabriel, I have already arranged to go—

[20] Pejorative term for an English-oriented Irishman.

[21] A step in the Lancers quadrille.

[22] The question of how to provide educational opportunities for Roman Catholics other than the heavily Protestant Trinity College, Dublin.

[23] Islands off the west coast of Ireland, valued by nationalists as a place where the Irish language and customs had been preserved.

[24] An area in western Ireland.

—Go where? asked Miss Ivors.

—Well, you know, every year I go for a cycling tour with some fellows and so—

—But where? asked Miss Ivors.

—Well, we usually go to France or Belgium or perhaps Germany, said Gabriel awkwardly.

—And why do you go to France and Belgium, said Miss Ivors, instead of visiting your own land?

—Well, said Gabriel, it's partly to keep in touch with the languages and partly for a change.

—And haven't you your own language to keep in touch with—Irish? asked Miss Ivors.

—Well, said Gabriel, if it comes to that, you know, Irish is not my language.

Their neighbours had turned to listen to the cross-examination. Gabriel glanced right and left nervously and tried to keep his good humour under the ordeal which was making a blush invade his forehead.

—And haven't you your own land to visit, continued Miss Ivors, that you know nothing of, your own people, and your own country?

—O, to tell you the truth, retorted Gabriel suddenly, I'm sick of my own country, sick of it!

—Why? asked Miss Ivors.

Gabriel did not answer for his retort had heated him.

—Why? repeated Miss Ivors.

They had to go visiting together[25] and, as he had not answered her, Miss Ivors said warmly:

—Of course, you've no answer.

Gabriel tried to cover his agitation by taking part in the dance with great energy. He avoided her eyes for he had seen a sour expression on her face. But when they met in the long chain he was surprised to feel his hand firmly pressed. She looked at him from under her brows for a moment quizzically until he smiled. Then, just as the chain was about to start again, she stood on tiptoe and whispered into his ear:

—West Briton!

When the lancers were over Gabriel went away to a remote corner of the room where Freddy Malins' mother was sitting. She was a stout feeble old woman with white hair. Her voice had a catch in it like her son's and she stuttered slightly. She had been told that Freddy had come and that he was nearly all right. Gabriel asked her whether she had had a good crossing. She lived with her married daughter in Glasgow and came to Dublin on a visit once a year. She answered placidly that she had had a beautiful crossing and that the captain had been most attentive to her. She spoke also of the beautiful house her daughter kept in Glasgow, and of all the friends they had there. While her tongue rambled on Gabriel tried to banish from his mind all memory of the unpleasant incident with Miss Ivors. Of course the girl or woman, or whatever she was, was an enthusiast but there was a time for all things. Perhaps he ought not to have answered her like that. But she had no right to call him a West Briton before people, even in joke.

[25] Another step in the Lancers quadrille.

She had tried to make him ridiculous before people, heckling him and staring at him with her rabbit's eyes.

He saw his wife making her way towards him through the waltzing couples. When she reached him she said into his ear:

—Gabriel, Aunt Kate wants to know won't you carve the goose as usual. Miss Daly will carve the ham and I'll do the pudding.

—All right, said Gabriel.

—She's sending in the younger ones first as soon as this waltz is over so that we'll have the table to ourselves.

—Were you dancing? asked Gabriel.

—Of course I was. Didn't you see me? What row had you with Molly Ivors?

—No row. Why? Did she say so?

—Something like that. I'm trying to get that Mr D'Arcy to sing. He's full of conceit, I think.

—There were no words, said Gabriel moodily, only she wanted me to go for a trip to the west of Ireland and I said I wouldn't.

His wife clasped her hands excitedly and gave a little jump.

—O, do go, Gabriel, she cried. I'd love to see Galway again.

—You can go if you like, said Gabriel coldly.

She looked at him for a moment, then turned to Mrs Malins and said:

—There's a nice husband for you, Mrs Malins.

While she was threading her way back across the room Mrs Malins, without adverting to the interruption, went on to tell Gabriel what beautiful places there were in Scotland and beautiful scenery. Her son-in-law brought them every year to the lakes and they used to go fishing. Her son-in-law was a splendid fisher. One day he caught a fish, a beautiful big fish, and the man in the hotel boiled it for their dinner.

Gabriel hardly heard what she said. Now that supper was coming near he began to think again about his speech and about the quotation. When he saw Freddy Malins coming across the room to visit his mother Gabriel left the chair free for him and retired into the embrasure of the window. The room had already cleared and from the back room came the clatter of plates and knives. Those who still remained in the drawing-room seemed tired of dancing and were conversing quietly in little groups. Gabriel's warm trembling fingers tapped the cold pane of the window. How cool it must be outside! How pleasant it would be to walk out alone, first along by the river and then through the park![26] The snow would be lying on the branches of the trees and forming a bright cap on the top of the Wellington Monument.[27] How much more pleasant it would be there than at the supper-table!

He ran over the headings of his speech: Irish hospitality, sad memories, the Three Graces, Paris, the quotation from Browning. He repeated to himself a phrase he had written in his review: *One feels that one is listening to a thought-tormented music.* Miss Ivors had praised the review. Was she sincere? Had she really any life of her own behind all her propagandism? There had never been any ill-feeling between them until that night. It

[26] Phoenix Park, on the west side of Dublin.
[27] A large monument to the Duke of Wellington at the east end of Phoenix Park.

unnerved him to think that she would be at the supper-table, looking up at him while he spoke with her critical quizzing eyes. Perhaps she would not be sorry to see him fail in his speech. An idea came into his mind and gave him courage. He would say, alluding to Aunt Kate and Aunt Julia: *Ladies and Gentlemen, the generation which is now on the wane among us may have had its faults but for my part I think it had certain qualities of hospitality, of humour, of humanity, which the new and very serious and hypereducated generation that is growing up around us seems to me to lack.* Very good: that was one for Miss Ivors. What did he care that his aunts were only two ignorant old women?

A murmur in the room attracted his attention. Mr Browne was advancing from the door, gallantly escorting Aunt Julia, who leaned upon his arm, smiling and hanging her head. An irregular musketry of applause escorted her also as far as the piano and then, as Mary Jane seated herself on the stool, and Aunt Julia, no longer smiling, half turned so as to pitch her voice fairly into the room, gradually ceased. Gabriel recognised the prelude. It was that of an old song of Aunt Julia's—*Arrayed for the Bridal.*[28] Her voice, strong and clear in tone, attacked with great spirit the runs which embellish the air and though she sang very rapidly she did not miss even the smallest of the grace notes. To follow the voice, without looking at the singer's face, was to feel and share the excitement of swift and secure flight. Gabriel applauded loudly with all the others at the close of the song and loud applause was borne in from the invisible supper-table. It sounded so genuine that a little colour struggled into Aunt Julia's face as she bent to replace in the music-stand the old leather-bound song-book that had her initials on the cover. Freddy Malins, who had listened with his head perched sideways to hear her better, was still applauding when everyone else had ceased and talking animatedly to his mother who nodded her head gravely and slowly in acquiescence. At last, when he could clap no more, he stood up suddenly and hurried across the room to Aunt Julia whose hand he seized and held in both his hands, shaking it when words failed him or the catch in his voice proved too much for him.

—I was just telling my mother, he said, I never heard you sing so well, never. No, I never heard your voice so good as it is to-night. Now! Would you believe that now? That's the truth. Upon my word and honour that's the truth. I never heard your voice sound so fresh and so . . . so clear and fresh, never.

Aunt Julia smiled broadly and murmured something about compliments as she released her hand from his grasp. Mr Browne extended his open hand towards her and said to those who were near him in the manner of a showman introducing a prodigy to an audience:

—Miss Julia Morkan, my latest discovery!

He was laughing very heartily at this himself when Freddy Malins turned to him and said:

—Well, Browne, if you're serious you might make a worse discovery. All I can say is I never heard her sing half so well as long as I am coming here. And that's the honest truth.

[28] A "parlor" arrangement by George Linley of the aria "*Son vergin vezzosa*" from Bellini's opera *I Puritani.* The song, an ecstatic description of a girl on her wedding day, contrasts sharply with Aunt Julia's aged appearance.

—Neither did I, said Mr Browne. I think her voice has greatly improved.

Aunt Julia shrugged her shoulders and said with meek pride:

—Thirty years ago I hadn't a bad voice as voices go.

—I often told Julia, said Aunt Kate emphatically, that she was simply thrown away in that choir. But she never would be said by me.

She turned as if to appeal to the good sense of the others against a refractory child while Aunt Julia gazed in front of her, a vague smile of reminiscence playing on her face.

—No, continued Aunt Kate, she wouldn't be said or led by anyone, slaving there in that choir night and day, night and day. Six o'clock on Christmas morning! And all for what?

—Well, isn't it for the honour of God, Aunt Kate? asked Mary Jane, twisting round on the piano-stool and smiling.

Aunt Kate turned fiercely on her niece and said:

—I know all about the honour of God, Mary Jane, but I think it's not at all honourable for the pope to turn out the women out of the choirs that have slaved there all their lives and put little whipper-snappers of boys over their heads.[29] I suppose it is for the good of the Church if the pope does it. But it's not just, Mary Jane, and it's not right.

She had worked herself into a passion and would have continued in defence of her sister for it was a sore subject with her but Mary Jane, seeing that all the dancers had come back, intervened pacifically:

—Now, Aunt Kate, you're giving scandal to Mr Browne who is of the other persuasion.[30]

Aunt Kate turned to Mr Browne, who was grinning at this allusion to his religion, and said hastily:

—O, I don't question the pope's being right. I'm only a stupid old woman and I wouldn't presume to do such a thing. But there's such a thing as common everyday politeness and gratitude. And if I were in Julia's place I'd tell that Father Healey straight up to his face . . .

—And besides, Aunt Kate, said Mary Jane, we really are all hungry and when we are hungry we are all very quarrelsome.

—And when we are thirsty we are also quarrelsome, added Mr Browne.

—So that we had better go to supper, said Mary Jane, and finish the discussion afterwards.

On the landing outside the drawing-room Gabriel found his wife and Mary Jane trying to persuade Miss Ivors to stay for supper. But Miss Ivors, who had put on her hat and was buttoning her cloak, would not stay. She did not feel in the least hungry and she had already overstayed her time.

—But only for ten minutes, Molly, said Mrs Conroy. That won't delay you.

—To take a pick itself, said Mary Jane, after all your dancing.

—I really couldn't, said Miss Ivors.

—I am afraid you didn't enjoy yourself at all, said Mary Jane hopelessly.

—Ever so much, I assure you, said Miss Ivors, but you really must let me run off now.

[29] Pope Pius X, in 1903, forbade women to sing in choirs and ordered the use of boys' choirs instead.

[30] Protestant.

—But how can you get home? asked Mrs Conroy.

—O, it's only two steps up the quay.[31]

Gabriel hesitated a moment and said:

—If you will allow me, Miss Ivors, I'll see you home if you really are obliged to go.

But Miss Ivors broke away from them.

—I won't hear of it, she cried. For goodness sake go in to your suppers and don't mind me. I'm quite well able to take care of myself.

—Well, you're the comical girl, Molly, said Mrs Conroy frankly.

—*Beannacht libh,*[32] cried Miss Ivors, with a laugh, as she ran down the staircase.

Mary Jane gazed after her, a moody puzzled expression on her face, while Mrs Conroy leaned over the banisters to listen for the hall-door. Gabriel asked himself was he the cause of her abrupt departure. But she did not seem to be in ill humour: she had gone away laughing. He stared blankly down the staircase.

At that moment Aunt Kate came toddling out of the supper-room, almost wringing her hands in despair.

—Where is Gabriel? she cried. Where on earth is Gabriel? There's everyone waiting in there, stage to let,[33] and nobody to carve the goose!

—Here I am, Aunt Kate! cried Gabriel, with sudden animation, ready to carve a flock of geese, if necessary.

A fat brown goose lay at one end of the table and at the other end, on a bed of creased paper strewn with sprigs of parsley, lay a great ham, stripped of its outer skin and peppered over with crust crumbs, a neat paper frill round its shin and beside this was a round of spiced beef. Between these rival ends ran parallel lines of side-dishes: two little minsters of jelly, red and yellow; a shallow dish full of blocks of blancmange and red jam, a large green leaf-shaped dish with a stalk-shaped handle, on which lay bunches of purple raisins and peeled almonds, a companion dish on which lay a solid rectangle of Smyrna figs, a dish of custard topped with grated nutmeg, a small bowl full of chocolates and sweets wrapped in gold and silver papers and a glass vase in which stood some tall celery stalks. In the centre of the table there stood, as sentries to a fruit-stand which upheld a pyramid of oranges and American apples, two squat old-fashioned decanters of cut glass, one containing port and the other dark sherry. On the closed square piano a pudding in a huge yellow dish lay in waiting and behind it were three squads of bottles of stout and ale and minerals, drawn up according to the colours of their uniforms, the first two black, with brown and red labels, the third and smallest squad white, with transverse green sashes.

Gabriel took his seat boldly at the head of the table and, having looked to the edge of the carver, plunged his fork firmly into the goose. He felt quite at ease now for he was an expert carver and liked nothing better than to find himself at the head of a well-laden table.

—Miss Furlong, what shall I send you? he asked. A wing or a slice of the breast?

[31] One of the docks along the Liffey River in Dublin. [32] "Farewell" (Gaelic).

[33] *stage to let.* An expression meaning things are delayed.

—Just a small slice of the breast.

—Miss Higgins, what for you?

—O, anything at all, Mr Conroy.

While Gabriel and Miss Daly exchanged plates of goose and plates of ham and spiced beef Lily went from guest to guest with a dish of hot floury potatoes wrapped in a white napkin. This was Mary Jane's idea and she had also suggested apple sauce for the goose but Aunt Kate had said that plain roast goose without any apple sauce had always been good enough for her and she hoped she might never eat worse. Mary Jane waited on her pupils and saw that they got the best slices and Aunt Kate and Aunt Julia opened and carried across from the piano bottles of stout and ale for the gentlemen and bottles of minerals for the ladies. There was a great deal of confusion and laughter and noise, the noise of orders and counter-orders, of knives and forks, of corks and glass-stoppers. Gabriel began to carve second helpings as soon as he had finished the first round without serving himself. Everyone protested loudly so that he compromised by taking a long draught of stout for he had found the carving hot work. Mary Jane settled down quietly to her supper but Aunt Kate and Aunt Julia were still toddling round the table, walking on each other's heels, getting in each other's way and giving each other unheeded orders. Mr Browne begged of them to sit down and eat their suppers and so did Gabriel but they said there was time enough, so that, at last, Freddy Malins stood up and, capturing Aunt Kate, plumped her down on her chair amid general laughter.

When everyone had been well served Gabriel said, smiling:

—Now, if anyone wants a little more of what vulgar people call stuffing let him or her speak.

A chorus of voices invited him to begin his own supper and Lily came forward with three potatoes which she had reserved for him.

—Very well, said Gabriel amiably, as he took another preparatory draught, kindly forget my existence, ladies and gentlemen, for a few minutes.

He set to his supper and took no part in the conversation with which the table covered Lily's removal of the plates. The subject of talk was the opera company which was then at the Theatre Royal. Mr Bartell D'Arcy, the tenor, a dark-complexioned young man with a smart moustache, praised very highly the leading contralto of the company but Miss Furlong thought she had a rather vulgar style of production. Freddy Malins said there was a negro chieftain singing in the second part of the Gaiety pantomime who had one of the finest tenor voices he had ever heard.

—Have you heard him? he asked Mr Bartell D'Arcy across the table.

—No, answered Mr Bartell D'Arcy carelessly.

—Because, Freddy Malins explained, now I'd be curious to hear your opinion of him. I think he has a grand voice.

—It takes Teddy to find out the really good things, said Mr Browne familiarly to the table.

—And why couldn't he have a voice too? asked Freddy Malins sharply. Is it because he's only a black?

Nobody answered this question and Mary Jane led the table back to the legitimate opera. One of her pupils had given her a pass for *Mignon*.[34] Of course it was very fine, she said, but it made her think of poor Georgina Burns. Mr Browne could go back farther still, to the old Italian companies that used to come to Dublin—Tietjens, Ilma de Murzka, Campanini, the great Trebelli, Giuglini, Ravelli, Aramburo.[35] Those were the days, he said, when there was something like singing to be heard in Dublin. He told too of how the top gallery of the old Royal[36] used to be packed night after night, of how one night an Italian tenor had sung five encores to *Let Me Like a Soldier Fall*,[37] introducing a high C every time, and of how the gallery boys would sometimes in their enthusiasm unyoke the horses from the carriage of some great *prima donna* and pull her themselves through the streets to her hotel. Why did they never play the grand old operas now, he asked, *Dinorah, Lucrezia Borgia?*[38] Because they could not get the voices to sing them: that was why.

—Oh, well, said Mr Bartell D'Arcy, I presume there are as good singers to-day as there were then.

—Where are they? asked Mr Browne defiantly.

—In London, Paris, Milan, said Mr Bartell D'Arcy warmly. I suppose Caruso,[39] for example, is quite as good, if not better than any of the men you have mentioned.

—Maybe so, said Mr Browne. But I may tell you I doubt it strongly.

—O, I'd give anything to hear Caruso sing, said Mary Jane.

—For me, said Aunt Kate, who had been picking a bone, there was only one tenor. To please me, I mean. But I suppose none of you ever heard of him.

—Who was he, Miss Morkan? asked Mr Bartell D'Arcy politely.

—His name, said Aunt Kate, was Parkinson. I heard him when he was in his prime and I think he had then the purest tenor voice that was ever put into a man's throat.

—Strange, said Mr Bartell D'Arcy. I never even heard of him.

—Yes, yes, Miss Morkan is right, said Mr Browne. I remember hearing of old Parkinson but he's too far back for me.

—A beautiful pure sweet mellow English tenor, said Aunt Kate with enthusiasm.

Gabriel having finished, the huge pudding was transferred to the table. The clatter of forks and spoons began again. Gabriel's wife served out spoonfuls of the pudding and passed the plates down the table. Midway down they were held up by Mary Jane, who replenished them with raspberry or orange jelly or with blancmange and jam. The pudding was of Aunt Julia's making and she received praises for it from all quarters. She herself said that it was not quite brown enough.

[34] Opera by Ambroise Thomas (1866).

[35] These are all names of famous opera singers of the nineteenth century.

[36] A Dublin theater that burned down in 1880.

[37] A melodramatic tenor aria from the opera *Maritana* (1845), by William Vincent Wallace, words by Edward Fitzball.

[38] *Dinorah* (1859) is an opera by Giacomo Meyerbeer; *Lucrezia Borgia* (1833) is by Gaetano Donizetti.

[39] The great tenor Enrico Caruso (1874–1921) was at the height of his career in 1904, the time of the story.

—Well, I hope, Miss Morkan, said Mr Browne, that I'm brown enough for you because, you know, I'm all brown.

All the gentlemen, except Gabriel, ate some of the pudding out of compliment to Aunt Julia. As Gabriel never ate sweets the celery had been left for him. Freddy Malins also took a stalk of celery and ate it with his pudding. He had been told that celery was a capital thing for the blood and he was just then under doctor's care. Mrs Malins, who had been silent all through the supper, said that her son was going down to Mount Melleray[40] in a week or so. The table then spoke of Mount Melleray, how bracing the air was down there, how hospitable the monks were and how they never asked for a penny-piece from their guests.

—And do you mean to say, asked Mr Browne incredulously, that a chap can go down there and put up there as if it were a hotel and live on the fat of the land and then come away without paying a farthing?

—O, most people give some donation to the monastery when they leave, said Mary Jane.

—I wish we had an institution like that in our Church, said Mr Browne candidly.

He was astonished to hear that the monks never spoke, got up at two in the morning and slept in their coffins. He asked what they did it for.

—That's the rule of the order, said Aunt Kate firmly.[41]

—Yes, but why? asked Mr Browne.

Aunt Kate repeated that it was the rule, that was all. Mr Browne still seemed not to understand. Freddy Malins explained to him, as best he could, that the monks were trying to make up for the sins committed by all the sinners in the outside world. The explanation was not very clear for Mr Browne grinned and said:

—I like that idea very much but wouldn't a comfortable spring bed do them as well as a coffin?

—The coffin, said Mary Jane, is to remind them of their last end.

As the subject had grown lugubrious it was buried in a silence of the table during which Mrs Malins could be heard saying to her neighbour in an indistinct undertone:

—They are very good men, the monks, very pious men.

The raisins and almonds and figs and apples and oranges and chocolates and sweets were now passed about the table and Aunt Julia invited all the guests to have either port or sherry. At first Mr Bartell D'Arcy refused to take either but one of his neighbours nudged him and whispered something to him upon which he allowed his glass to be filled. Gradually as the last glasses were being filled the conversation ceased. A pause followed, broken only by the noise of the wine and by unsettlings of chairs. The Misses Morkan, all three, looked down at the tablecloth. Someone coughed once or twice and then a few gentlemen patted the table gently as a signal for silence. The silence came and Gabriel pushed back his chair and stood up.

The patting at once grew louder in encouragement and then ceased altogether. Gabriel leaned his ten trembling fingers on the tablecloth and

[40] Trappist monastery in southern Ireland.
[41] Aunt Kate is misinformed; the Trappists have no such rule.

smiled nervously at the company. Meeting a row of upturned faces he raised his eyes to the chandelier. The piano was playing a waltz tune and he could hear the skirts sweeping against the drawing-room door. People, perhaps, were standing in the snow on the quay outside, gazing up at the lighted windows and listening to the waltz music. The air was pure there. In the distance lay the park where the trees were weighted with snow. The Wellington Monument wore a gleaming cap of snow that flashed westward over the white field of Fifteen Acres.[42]

He began:

—Ladies and Gentlemen.

—It has fallen to my lot this evening, as in years past, to perform a very pleasing task but a task for which I am afraid my poor powers as a speaker are all too inadequate.

—No, no! said Mr Browne.

—But, however that may be, I can only ask you to-night to take the will for the deed and to lend me your attention for a few moments while I endeavour to express to you in words what my feelings are on this occasion.

—Ladies and Gentlemen. It is not the first time that we have gathered together under this hospitable roof, around this hospitable board. It is not the first time that we have been the recipients—or perhaps, I had better say, the victims—of the hospitality of certain good ladies.

He made a circle in the air with his arm and paused. Everyone laughed or smiled at Aunt Kate and Aunt Julia and Mary Jane who all turned crimson with pleasure. Gabriel went on more boldly:

—I feel more strongly with every recurring year that our country has no tradition which does it so much honour and which it should guard so jealously as that of its hospitality. It is a tradition that is unique as far as my experience goes (and I have visited not a few places abroad) among the modern nations. Some would say, perhaps, that with us it is rather a failing than anything to be boasted of. But granted even that, it is, to my mind, a princely failing, and one that I trust will long be cultivated among us. Of one thing, at least, I am sure. As long as this one roof shelters the good ladies aforesaid—and I wish from my heart it may do so for many and many a long year to come—the tradition of genuine warm-hearted courteous Irish hospitality, which our forefathers have handed down to us and which we in turn must hand down to our descendants, is still alive among us.

A hearty murmur of assent ran round the table. It shot through Gabriel's mind that Miss Ivors was not there and that she had gone away discourteously: and he said with confidence in himself:

—Ladies and Gentlemen.

—A new generation is growing up in our midst, a generation actuated by new ideas and new principles. It is serious and enthusiastic for these new ideas and its enthusiasm, even when it is misdirected, is, I believe, in the main sincere. But we are living in a sceptical and, if I may use the phrase, a thought-tormented age: and sometimes I fear that this new generation, educated or hypereducated as it is, will lack those qualities of humanity, of hospitality, of kindly humour which belonged to an older day. Listening

[42] Part of Phoenix Park.

to-night to the names of all those great singers of the past it seemed to me, I must confess, that we were living in a less spacious age. Those days might, without exaggeration, be called spacious days: and if they are gone beyond recall let us hope, at least, that in gatherings such as this we shall still speak of them with pride and affection, still cherish in our hearts the memory of those dead and gone great ones whose fame the world will not willingly let die.[43]

—Hear, hear! said Mr Browne loudly.

—But yet, continued Gabriel, his voice falling into a softer inflection, there are always in gatherings such as this sadder thoughts that will recur to our minds: thoughts of the past, of youth, of changes, of absent faces that we miss here to-night. Our path through life is strewn with many such sad memories: and were we to brood upon them always we could not find the heart to go on bravely with our work among the living. We have all of us living duties and living affections which claim, and rightly claim, our strenuous endeavours.

—Therefore, I will not linger on the past. I will not let any gloomy moralising intrude upon us here to-night. Here we are gathered together for a brief moment from the bustle and rush of our everyday routine. We are met here as friends, in the spirit of good-fellowship, as colleagues, also to a certain extent, in the true spirit of *camaraderie,* and as the guests of—what shall I call them?—the Three Graces[44] of the Dublin musical world.

The table burst into applause and laughter at this sally. Aunt Julia vainly asked each of her neighbours in turn to tell her what Gabriel had said.

—He says we are the Three Graces, Aunt Julia, said Mary Jane.

Aunt Julia did not understand but she looked up, smiling, at Gabriel, who continued in the same vein:

—Ladies and Gentlemen.

—I will not attempt to play to-night the part that Paris played on another occasion.[45] I will not attempt to choose between them. The task would be an invidious one and one beyond my poor powers. For when I view them in turn, whether it be our chief hostess herself, whose good heart, whose too good heart, has become a byword with all who know her, or her sister, who seems to be gifted with perennial youth and whose singing must have been a surprise and a revelation to us all to-night, or, last but not least, when I consider our youngest hostess, talented, cheerful, hardworking and the best of nieces, I confess, Ladies and Gentlemen, that I do not know to which of them I should award the prize.

Gabriel glanced down at his aunts and, seeing the large smile on Aunt Julia's face and the tears which had risen to Aunt Kate's eyes, hastened to his close. He raised his glass of port gallantly, while every member of the company fingered a glass expectantly, and said loudly:

—Let us toast them all three together. Let us drink to their health,

[43] *the world . . . die.* Gabriel is echoing a phrase of Milton's here, about his hopes as a poet (*The Reason of Church Government,* Preface to Book II).

[44] In classical mythology, the three Graces, daughters of Zeus, were Aglaia (brilliance), Euphrosyne (joy), and Thalia (bloom). They presided over all beauty and charm.

[45] The shepherd Paris had to judge the beauty of Hera, Athena, and Aphrodite. His choice of Aphrodite began the Trojan War.

wealth, long life, happiness and prosperity and may they long continue to hold the proud and self-won position which they hold in their profession and the position of honour and affection which they hold in our hearts.

All the guests stood up, glass in hand, and turning towards the three seated ladies, sang in unison, with Mr Browne as leader:

For they are jolly gay fellows,
For they are jolly gay fellows,
For they are jolly gay fellows,
Which nobody can deny.

Aunt Kate was making frank use of her handkerchief and even Aunt Julia seemed moved. Freddy Malins beat time with his pudding-fork and the singers turned towards one another, as if in melodious conference, while they sang with emphasis:

Unless he tells a lie,
Unless he tells a lie,

Then, turning once more towards their hostesses, they sang:

For they are jolly gay fellows,
For they are jolly gay fellows,
For they are jolly gay fellows,
Which nobody can deny.

The acclamation which followed was taken up beyond the door of the supper-room by many of the other guests and renewed time after time, Freddy Malins acting as officer with his fork on high.

. . . .

The piercing morning air came into the hall where they were standing so that Aunt Kate said:

—Close the door, somebody. Mrs Malins will get her death of cold.

—Browne is out there, Aunt Kate, said Mary Jane.

—Browne is everywhere, said Aunt Kate, lowering her voice.

Mary Jane laughed at her tone.

—Really, she said archly, he is very attentive.

—He has been laid on[46] here like the gas, said Aunt Kate in the same tone, all during the Christmas.

She laughed herself this time good-humouredly and then added quickly:

—But tell him to come in, Mary Jane, and close the door. I hope to goodness he didn't hear me.

At that moment the hall-door was opened and Mr Browne came in from the doorstep, laughing as if his heart would break. He was dressed in a long green overcoat with mock astrakhan cuffs and collar and wore on his head an oval fur cap. He pointed down the snow-covered quay from where the sound of shrill prolonged whistling was borne in.

[46] Provided like one of the utilities.

—Teddy will have all the cabs in Dublin out, he said.

Gabriel advanced from the little pantry behind the office, struggling into his overcoat and, looking round the hall, said:

—Gretta not down yet?

—She's getting on her things, Gabriel, said Aunt Kate.

—Who's playing up there? asked Gabriel.

—Nobody. They're all gone.

—O no, Aunt Kate, said Mary Jane. Bartell D'Arcy and Miss O'Callaghan aren't gone yet.

—Someone is strumming at the piano, anyhow, said Gabriel.

Mary Jane glanced at Gabriel and Mr Browne and said with a shiver:

—It makes me feel cold to look at you two gentlemen muffled up like that. I wouldn't like to face your journey home at this hour.

—I'd like nothing better this minute, said Mr Browne stoutly, than a rattling fine walk in the country or a fast drive with a good spanking goer between the shafts.

—We used to have a very good horse and trap at home, said Aunt Julia sadly.

—The never-to-be-forgotten Johnny, said Mary Jane, laughing.

Aunt Kate and Gabriel laughed too.

—Why, what was wonderful about Johnny? asked Mr Browne.

—The late lamented Patrick Morkan, our grandfather, that is, explained Gabriel, commonly known in his later years as the old gentleman, was a glue-boiler.

—O, now, Gabriel, said Aunt Kate, laughing, he had a starch mill.

—Well, glue or starch, said Gabriel, the old gentleman had a horse by the name of Johnny. And Johnny used to work in the old gentleman's mill, walking round and round in order to drive the mill. That was all very well; but now comes the tragic part about Johnny. One fine day the old gentleman thought he'd like to drive out with the quality to a military review in the park.

—The Lord have mercy on his soul, said Aunt Kate compassionately.

—Amen, said Gabriel. So the old gentleman, as I said, harnessed Johnny and put on his very best tall hat and his very best stock collar and drove out in grand style from his ancestral mansion somewhere near Back Lane, I think.

Everyone laughed, even Mrs Malins, at Gabriel's manner and Aunt Kate said:

—O now, Gabriel, he didn't live in Back Lane, really. Only the mill was there.

—Out from the mansion of his forefathers, continued Gabriel, he drove with Johnny. And everything went on beautifully until Johnny came in sight of King Billy's statue:[47] and whether he fell in love with the horse King Billy sits on or whether he thought he was back again in the mill, anyhow he began to walk round the statue.

Gabriel paced in a circle round the hall in his goloshes amid the laughter of the others.

[47] Statue of King William III, who defeated the army of the deposed King James II, defender of Irish Catholicism, at the Battle of the Boyne in 1690.

—Round and round he went, said Gabriel, and the old gentleman, who was a very pompous old gentleman, was highly indignant. *Go on, sir! What do you mean, sir? Johnny! Johnny! Most extraordinary conduct! Can't understand the horse!*

The peal of laughter which followed Gabriel's imitation of the incident was interrupted by a resounding knock at the hall-door. Mary Jane ran to open it and let in Freddy Malins. Freddy Malins, with his hat well back on his head and his shoulders humped with cold, was puffing and steaming after his exertions.

—I could only get one cab, he said.

—O, we'll find another along the quay, said Gabriel.

—Yes, said Aunt Kate. Better not keep Mrs Malins standing in the draught.

Mrs Malins was helped down the front steps by her son and Mr Browne and, after many manoeuvres, hoisted into the cab. Freddy Malins clambered in after her and spent a long time settling her on the seat, Mr Browne helping him with advice. At last she was settled comfortably and Freddy Malins invited Mr Browne into the cab. There was a good deal of confused talk, and then Mr Browne got into the cab. The cabman settled his rug over his knees, and bent down for the address. The confusion grew greater and the cabman was directed differently by Freddy Malins and Mr Browne, each of whom had his head out through a window of the cab. The difficulty was to know where to drop Mr Browne along the route and Aunt Kate, Aunt Julia and Mary Jane helped the discussion from the doorstep with cross-directions and contradictions and abundance of laughter. As for Freddy Malins he was speechless with laughter. He popped his head in and out of the window every moment, to the great danger of his hat, and told his mother how the discussion was progressing till at last Mr Browne shouted to the bewildered cabman above the din of everybody's laughter:

—Do you know Trinity College?

—Yes, sir, said the cabman.

—Well, drive bang up against Trinity College gates, said Mr Browne, and then we'll tell you where to go. You understand now?

—Yes, sir, said the cabman.

—Make like a bird for Trinity College.

—Right, sir, cried the cabman.

The horse was whipped up and the cab rattled off along the quay amid a chorus of laughter and adieus.

Gabriel had not gone to the door with the others. He was in a dark part of the hall gazing up the staircase. A woman was standing near the top of the first flight, in the shadow also. He could not see her face but he could see the terracotta and salmonpink panels of her skirt which the shadow made appear black and white. It was his wife. She was leaning on the banisters, listening to something. Gabriel was surprised at her stillness and strained his ear to listen also. But he could hear little save the noise of laughter and dispute on the front steps, a few chords struck on the piano and a few notes of a man's voice singing.

He stood still in the gloom of the hall, trying to catch the air that the voice was singing and gazing up at his wife. There was grace and mystery in her attitude as if she were a symbol of something. He asked himself what is a woman standing on the stairs in the shadow, listening to distant music, a symbol of. If he were a painter he would paint her in that attitude. Her blue felt hat would show off the bronze of her hair against the darkness and the dark panels of her skirt would show off the light ones. *Distant Music* he would call the picture if he were a painter.

The hall-door was closed; and Aunt Kate, Aunt Julia and Mary Jane came down the hall, still laughing.

—Well, isn't Freddy terrible? said Mary Jane. He's really terrible.

Gabriel said nothing but pointed up the stairs towards where his wife was standing. Now that the hall-door was closed the voice and the piano could be heard more clearly. Gabriel held up his hand for them to be silent. The song seemed to be in the old Irish tonality and the singer seemed uncertain both of his words and of his voice. The voice, made plaintive by distance and by the singer's hoarseness, faintly illuminated the cadence of the air with words expressing grief:

O, the rain falls on my heavy locks
And the dew wets my skin,
My babe lies cold . . .[48]

—O, exclaimed Mary Jane. It's Bartell D'Arcy singing and he wouldn't sing all the night. O, I'll get him to sing a song before he goes.

—O, do, Mary Jane, said Aunt Kate.

Mary Jane brushed past the others and ran to the staircase but before she reached it the singing stopped and the piano was closed abruptly.

—O, what a pity! she cried. Is he coming down, Gretta?

Gabriel heard his wife answer yes and saw her come down towards them. A few steps behind her were Mr Bartell D'Arcy and Miss O'Callaghan.

—O, Mr D'Arcy, cried Mary Jane, it's downright mean of you to break off like that when we were all in raptures listening to you.

—I have been at him all the evening, said Miss O'Callaghan, and Mrs Conroy too and he told us he had a dreadful cold and couldn't sing.

—O, Mr D'Arcy, said Aunt Kate, now that was a great fib to tell.

—Can't you see that I'm as hoarse as a crow? said Mr D'Arcy roughly.

He went into the pantry hastily and put on his overcoat. The others, taken aback by his rude speech, could find nothing to say. Aunt Kate wrinkled her brows and made signs to the others to drop the subject. Mr D'Arcy stood swathing his neck carefully and frowning.

—It's the weather, said Aunt Julia, after a pause.

—Yes, everybody has colds, said Aunt Kate readily, everybody.

—They say, said Mary Jane, we haven't had snow like it for thirty years; and I read this morning in the newspapers that the snow is general all over Ireland.

—I love the look of snow, said Aunt Julia sadly.

—So do I, said Miss O'Callaghan. I think Christmas is never really Christmas unless we have the snow on the ground.

[48] The song is "The Lass of Aughrim," a version of a song also known as "Lord Gregory" (Child ballad number 76). The lass stands in the rain outside the castle of Lord Gregory, her child's father, begging to be taken in. Joyce learned this song from his Galway wife Nora.

—But poor Mr D'Arcy doesn't like the snow, said Aunt Kate, smiling.

Mr D'Arcy came from the pantry, fully swathed and buttoned, and in a repentant tone told them the history of his cold. Everyone gave him advice and said it was a great pity and urged him to be very careful of his throat in the night air. Gabriel watched his wife who did not join in the conversation. She was standing right under the dusty fanlight and the flame of the gas lit up the rich bronze of her hair which he had seen her drying at the fire a few days before. She was in the same attitude and seemed unaware of the talk about her. At last she turned towards them and Gabriel saw that there was colour on her cheeks and that her eyes were shining. A sudden tide of joy went leaping out of his heart.

—Mr D'Arcy, she said, what is the name of that song you were singing?

—It's called *The Lass of Aughrim,* said Mr D'Arcy, but I couldn't remember it properly. Why? Do you know it?

—*The Lass of Aughrim,* she repeated. I couldn't think of the name.

—It's a very nice air, said Mary Jane. I'm sorry you were not in voice tonight.

—Now, Mary Jane, said Aunt Kate, don't annoy Mr D'Arcy. I won't have him annoyed.

Seeing that all were ready to start she shepherded them to the door where good night was said:

—Well, good-night, Aunt Kate, and thanks for the pleasant evening.

—Good-night, Gabriel. Good-night, Gretta!

—Good-night, Aunt Kate, and thanks ever so much. Good-night Aunt Julia.

—O, good-night, Gretta, I didn't see you.

—Good-night, Mr D'Arcy. Good-night, Miss O'Callaghan.

—Good-night, Miss Morkan.

—Good-night, again.

—Good-night, all. Safe home.

—Good-night. Good night.

The morning was still dark. A dull yellow light brooded over the houses and the river; and the sky seemed to be descending. It was slushy underfoot; and only streaks and patches of snow lay on the roofs, on the parapets of the quay and on the area railings. The lamps were still burning redly in the murky air and, across the river, the palace of the Four Courts[49] stood out menacingly against the heavy sky.

She was walking on before him with Mr Bartell D'Arcy, her shoes in a brown parcel tucked under one arm and her hands holding her skirt up from the slush. She had no longer any grace of attitude but Gabriel's eyes were still bright with happiness. The blood went bounding along his veins; and the thoughts went rioting through his brain, proud, joyful, tender, valorous.

She was walking on before him so lightly and so erect that he longed to run after her noiselessly, catch her by the shoulders and say something foolish and affectionate into her ear. She seemed to him so frail that he longed to defend her against something and then to be alone with her. Moments of their secret life together burst like stars upon his memory. A

[49] The Irish law courts.

heliotrope envelope was lying beside his breakfast-cup and he was caressing it with his hand. Birds were twittering in the ivy and the sunny web of the curtain was shimmering along the floor: he could not eat for happiness. They were standing on the crowded platform and he was placing a ticket inside the warm palm of her glove. He was standing with her in the cold, looking in through a grated window at a man making bottles in a roaring furnace. It was very cold. Her face, fragrant in the cold air, was quite close to his; and suddenly he called out to the man at the furnace:

—Is the fire hot, sir?

But the man could not hear with the noise of the furnace. It was just as well. He might have answered rudely.

A wave of yet more tender joy escaped from his heart and went coursing in warm flood along his arteries. Like the tender fire of stars moments of their life together, that no one knew of or would ever know of, broke upon and illumined his memory. He longed to recall to her those moments, to make her forget the years of their dull existence together and remember only their moments of ecstasy. For the years, he felt, had not quenched his soul or hers. Their children, his writing, her household cares had not quenched all their souls' tender fire. In one letter that he had written to her then he had said: *Why is it that words like these seem to me so dull and cold? Is it because there is no word tender enough to be your name?*

Like distant music these words that he had written years before were borne towards him from the past. He longed to be alone with her. When the others had gone away, when he and she were in their room in the hotel, then they would be alone together. He would call her softly:

—Gretta!

Perhaps she would not hear at once: she would be undressing. Then something in his voice would strike her. She would turn and look at him. . . .

At the corner of Winetavern Street they met a cab. He was glad of its rattling noise as it saved him from conversation. She was looking out of the window and seemed tired. The others spoke only a few words, pointing out some building or street. The horse galloped along wearily under the murky morning sky, dragging his old rattling box after his heels, and Gabriel was again in a cab with her, galloping to catch the boat, galloping to their honeymoon.

As the cab drove across O'Connell Bridge Miss O'Callaghan said:

—They say you never cross O'Connell Bridge without seeing a white horse.

—I see a white man this time, said Gabriel.

—Where? asked Mr Bartell D'Arcy.

Gabriel pointed to the statue, on which lay patches of snow.[50] Then he nodded familiarly to it and waved his hand.

—Good-night, Dan, he said gaily.

When the cab drew up before the hotel Gabriel jumped out and, in spite of Mr Bartell D'Arcy's protest, paid the driver. He gave the man a shilling over his fare. The man saluted and said:

[50] The statue is of Daniel O'Connell (1775–1847), the Irish nationalist after whom the bridge is named.

—A prosperous New Year to you, sir.

—The same to you, said Gabriel cordially.

She leaned for a moment on his arm in getting out of the cab and while standing at the curbstone, bidding the others good-night. She leaned lightly on his arm, as lightly as when she had danced with him a few hours before. He had felt proud and happy then, happy that she was his, proud of her grace and wifely carriage. But now, after the kindling again of so many memories, the first touch of her body, musical and strange and perfumed, sent through him a keen pang of lust. Under cover of her silence he pressed her arm closely to his side; and, as they stood at the hotel door, he felt that they had escaped from their lives and duties, escaped from home and friends and run away together with wild and radiant hearts to a new adventure.

An old man was dozing in a great hooded chair in the hall. He lit a candle in the office and went before them to the stairs. They followed him in silence, their feet falling in soft thuds on the thickly carpeted stairs. She mounted the stairs behind the porter, her head bowed in the ascent, her frail shoulders curved as with a burden, her skirt girt tightly about her. He could have flung his arms about her hips and held her still for his arms were trembling with desire to seize her and only the stress of his nails against the palms of his hands held the wild impulse of his body in check. The porter halted on the stairs to settle his guttering candle. They halted too on the steps below him. In the silence Gabriel could hear the falling of the molten wax into the tray and the thumping of his own heart against his ribs.

The porter led them along a corridor and opened a door. Then he set his unstable candle down on a toilet-table and asked at what hour they were to be called in the morning.

—Eight, said Gabriel.

The porter pointed to the tap of the electric-light and began a muttered apology but Gabriel cut him short.

—We don't want any light. We have light enough from the street. And I say, he added, pointing to the candle, you might remove that handsome article, like a good man.

The porter took up his candle again, but slowly for he was surprised by such a novel idea. Then he mumbled good-night and went out. Gabriel shot the lock to.

A ghostly light from the street lamp lay in a long shaft from one window to the door. Gabriel threw his overcoat and hat on a couch and crossed the room towards the window. He looked down into the street in order that his emotion might calm a little. Then he turned and leaned against a chest of drawers with his back to the light. She had taken off her hat and cloak and was standing before a large swinging mirror, unhooking her waist. Gabriel paused for a few moments, watching her, and then said:

—Gretta!

She turned away from the mirror slowly and walked along the shaft of light towards him. Her face looked so serious and weary that the words would not pass Gabriel's lips. No, it was not the moment yet.

—You looked tired, he said.

—I am a little, she answered.

—You don't feel ill or weak?

—No, tired: that's all.

She went on to the window and stood there, looking out. Gabriel waited again and then, fearing that diffidence was about to conquer him, he said abruptly:

—By the way, Gretta!

—What is it?

—You know that poor fellow Malins? he said quickly.

—Yes. What about him?

—Well, poor fellow, he's a decent sort of chap, after all, continued Gabriel in a false voice. He gave me back that sovereign I lent him and I didn't expect it really. It's a pity he wouldn't keep away from that Browne, because he's not a bad fellow at heart.

He was trembling now with annoyance. Why did she seem so abstracted? He did not know how he could begin. Was she annoyed, too, about something? If she would only turn to him or come to him of her own accord! To take her as she was would be brutal. No, he must see some ardour in her eyes first. He longed to be master of her strange mood.

—When did you lend him the pound? she asked, after a pause.

Gabriel strove to restrain himself from breaking out in brutal language about the sottish Malins and his pound. He longed to cry to her from his soul, to crush her body against his, to overmaster her. But he said:

—O, at Christmas, when he opened that little Christmas-card shop in Henry Street.

He was in such a fever of rage and desire that he did not hear her come from the window. She stood before him for an instant, looking at him strangely. Then, suddenly raising herself on tiptoe and resting her hands lightly on his shoulders, she kissed him.

—You are a very generous person, Gabriel, she said.

Gabriel, trembling with delight at her sudden kiss and at the quaintness of her phrase, put his hands on her hair and began smoothing it back, scarcely touching it with his fingers. The washing had made it fine and brilliant. His heart was brimming over with happiness. Just when he was wishing for it she had come to him of her own accord. Perhaps her thoughts had been running with his. Perhaps she had felt the impetuous desire that was in him, and then the yielding mood had come upon her. Now that she had fallen to him so easily he wondered why he had been so diffident.

He stood, holding her head between his hands. Then, slipping one arm swiftly about her body and drawing her towards him, he said softly:

—Gretta dear, what are you thinking about?

She did not answer nor yield wholly to his arm. He said again, softly:

—Tell me what it is, Gretta. I think I know what is the matter. Do I know?

She did not answer at once. Then she said in an outburst of tears:

—O, I am thinking about that song, *The Lass of Aughrim.*

She broke loose from him and ran to the bed and, throwing her arms across the bed-rail, hid her face. Gabriel stood stock-still for a moment in astonishment and then followed her. As he passed in the way of the cheval-glass[51] he caught sight of himself in full length, his broad, well-filled shirt-front, the face whose expression always puzzled him when he saw it in a mirror and his glimmering gilt-rimmed eyeglasses. He halted a few paces from her and said:

—What about the song? Why does that make you cry?

She raised her head from her arms and dried her eyes with the back of her hand like a child. A kinder note than he had intended went into his voice.

—Why, Gretta? he asked.

—I am thinking about a person long ago who used to sing that song.

—And who was the person long ago? asked Gabriel, smiling.

—It was a person I used to know in Galway when I was living with my grandmother, she said.

The smile passed away from Gabriel's face. A dull anger began to gather again at the back of his mind and the dull fires of his lust began to glow angrily in his veins.

—Someone you were in love with? he asked ironically.

—It was a young boy I used to know, she answered, named Michael Furey. He used to sing that song, *The Lass of Aughrim.* He was very delicate.

Gabriel was silent. He did not wish her to think that he was interested in this delicate boy.

—I can see him so plainly, she said, after a moment. Such eyes as he had: big dark eyes! And such an expression in them—an expression!

—O then, you were in love with him? said Gabriel.

—I used to go out walking with him, she said, when I was in Galway.

A thought flew across Gabriel's mind.

—Perhaps that was why you wanted to go to Galway with that Ivors girl? he said coldly.

She looked at him and asked in surprise:

—What for?

Her eyes made Gabriel feel awkward. He shrugged his shoulders and said:

—How do I know? To see him perhaps.

She looked away from him along the shaft of light towards the window in silence.

—He is dead, she said at length. He died when he was only seventeen. Isn't it a terrible thing to die so young as that?

—What was he? asked Gabriel, still ironically.

—He was in the gasworks, she said.

Gabriel felt humiliated by the failure of his irony and by the evocation of this figure from the dead, a boy in the gasworks. While he had been full of memories of their secret life together, full of tenderness and joy and desire, she had been comparing him in her mind with another. A shameful consciousness of his own person assailed him. He saw himself as a ludicrous figure, acting as a pennyboy[52] for his aunts, a nervous well-meaning sentimentalist, orating to vulgarians and idealising his own clownish lusts, the pitiable fatuous fellow he had caught a glimpse of in the mirror. Instinc-

[51] A long mirror mounted to swing in a frame. [52] Errand boy.

tively he turned his back more to the light lest she might see the shame that burned upon his forehead.

He tried to keep up his tone of cold interrogation but his voice when he spoke was humble and indifferent.

—I suppose you were in love with this Michael Furey, Gretta, he said.

—I was great with him at that time, she said.

Her voice was veiled and sad. Gabriel, feeling now how vain it would be to try to lead her whither he had purposed, caressed one of her hands and said, also sadly:

—And what did he die of so young, Gretta? Consumption, was it?

—I think he died for me, she answered.

A vague terror seized Gabriel at this answer as if, at that hour when he had hoped to triumph, some impalpable and vindictive being was coming against him, gathering forces against him in its vague world. But he shook himself free of it with an effort of reason and continued to caress her hand. He did not question her again for he felt that she would tell him of herself. Her hand was warm and moist: it did not respond to his touch but he continued to caress it just as he had caressed her first letter to him that spring morning.

—It was in the winter, she said, about the beginning of the winter when I was going to leave my grandmother's and come up here to the convent. And he was ill at the time in his lodgings in Galway and wouldn't be let out and his people in Oughterard[53] were written to. He was in decline, they said, or something like that. I never knew rightly.

She paused for a moment and sighed.

—Poor fellow, she said. He was very fond of me and he was such a gentle boy. We used to go out together, walking, you know, Gabriel, like the way they do in the country. He was going to study singing only for his health. He had a very good voice, poor Michael Furey.

—Well; and then? asked Gabriel.

—And then when it came to the time for me to leave Galway and come up to the convent he was much worse and I wouldn't be let see him so I wrote a letter saying I was going up to Dublin and would be back in the summer and hoping he would be better then.

She paused for a moment to get her voice under control and then went on;

—Then the night before I left I was in my grandmother's house in Nuns' Island, packing up, and I heard gravel thrown up against the window. The window was so wet I couldn't see so I ran downstairs as I was and slipped out the back into the garden and there was the poor fellow at the end of the garden, shivering.

—And did you not tell him to go back? asked Gabriel.

—I implored of him to go home at once and told him he would get his death in the rain. But he said he did not want to live. I can see his eyes as well as well! He was standing at the end of the wall where there was a tree.

—And did he go home? asked Gabriel.

—Yes, he went home. And when I was only a week in the convent he

[53] A village near Galway, in western Ireland.

died and he was buried in Oughterard where his people came from. O, the day I heard that, that he was dead!

She stopped, choking with sobs, and, overcome by emotion flung herself downward on the bed, sobbing in the quilt. Gabriel held her hand for a moment longer, irresolutely, and then, shy of intruding on her grief, let it fall gently and walked quietly to the window.

She was fast asleep.

Gabriel, leaning on his elbow, looked for a few moments unresentfully on her tangled hair and half-open mouth, listening to her deep-drawn breath. So she had had that romance in her life: a man had died for her sake. It hardly pained him now to think how poor a part he, her husband, had played in her life. He watched her while she slept as though he and she had never lived together as man and wife. His curious eyes rested long upon her face and on her hair: and, as he thought of what she must have been then, in that time of her first girlish beauty, a strange, friendly pity for her entered his soul. He did not like to say even to himself that her face was no longer beautiful but he knew that it was no longer the face for which Michael Furey had braved death.

Perhaps she had not told him all the story. His eyes moved to the chair over which she had thrown some of her clothes. A petticoat string dangled to the floor. One boot stood upright, its limp upper fallen down: the fellow of it lay upon its side. He wondered at his riot of emotions of an hour before. From what had it proceeded? From his aunt's supper, from his own foolish speech, from the wine and dancing, the merry-making when saying good-night in the hall, the pleasure of the walk along the river in the snow. Poor Aunt Julia! She, too, would soon be a shade with the shade of Patrick Morkan and his horse. He had caught that haggard look upon her face for a moment when she was singing *Arrayed for the Bridal.* Soon, perhaps, he would be sitting in that same drawing-room, dressed in black, his silk hat on his knees. The blinds would be drawn down and Aunt Kate would be sitting beside him, crying and blowing her nose and telling him how Julia had died. He would cast about in his mind for some words that might console her, and would find only lame and useless ones. Yes, yes: that would happen very soon.

The air of the room chilled his shoulders. He stretched himself cautiously along under the sheets and lay down beside his wife. One by one they were all becoming shades. Better pass boldly into that other world, in the full glory of some passion, than fade and wither dismally with age. He thought of how she who lay beside him had locked in her heart for so many years that image of her lover's eyes when he had told her that he did not wish to live.

Generous tears filled Gabriel's eyes. He had never felt like that himself towards any woman but he knew that such a feeling must be love. The tears gathered more thickly in his eyes and in the partial darkness he imagined he saw the form of a young man standing under a dripping tree. Other forms were near. His soul had approached that region where dwell the vast hosts of the dead. He was conscious of, but could not apprehend, their wayward and flickering existence. His own identity was fading out into a grey impalpable world: the solid world itself which these dead had one time reared and lived in was dissolving and dwindling.

A few light taps upon the pane made him turn to the window. It had begun to snow again. He watched sleepily the flakes, silver and dark, falling obliquely against the lamplight. The time had come for him to set out on his journey westward. Yes, the newspapers were right: snow was general all over Ireland. It was falling on every part of the dark central plain, on the treeless hills, falling softly upon the Bog of Allen[54] and, farther westward, softly falling into the dark mutinous Shannon waves.[55] It was falling, too, upon every part of the lonely churchyard on the hill where Michael Furey lay buried. It lay thickly drifted on the crooked crosses and headstones, on the spears of the little gate, on the barren thorns. His soul swooned slowly as he heard the snow falling faintly through the universe and faintly falling, like the descent of their last end, upon all the living and the dead.

[54] The Bog of Allen is just southwest of Dublin.
[55] Waves on the Shannon river, near Limerick, in southwest Ireland.

Virginia Woolf

(1882–1941)

"Examine for a moment," Virginia Woolf wrote, "an ordinary mind on an ordinary day. The mind receives a myriad impressions—trivial, fantastic, evanescent, or engraved with the sharpness of steel. . . . Life is not a series of gig lamps symmetrically arranged; but a luminous halo, a semi-transparent envelope surrounding us from the beginning of consciousness to the end. Is it not the task of the novelist to convey this varying, this unknown and uncircumscribed spirit, whatever aberration or complexity it may display, with as little mixture of the alien and external as possible?" Woolf's project of placing an individual consciousness at the center of fiction, as opposed to the "alien and external," is one she shares with many other major modern novelists. Her "luminous halo" reminds us of the famous description of Marlow's symbolist narrative style in Conrad's Heart of Darkness: *"To him the meaning of an episode was not inside like a kernel but outside, enveloping the tale which brought it out only as a glow brings out a haze, in the likeness of one of these misty halos that sometimes are made visible by the spectral illumination of moonshine." And the project of exploring "an ordinary mind on an ordinary day" has been undertaken repeatedly by modern novelists from Conrad through Joyce, Proust, and Faulkner up to current writers. But the statement is also a very precise description of Woolf's own fluid and subtle fiction and its exploration of the flow of consciousness, "whatever aberration or complexity it may display."*

Woolf was born in London in 1882. Her father was Sir Leslie Stephen, one of the leading men of letters of Victorian England, author of a History of English Thought in the Eighteenth Century *and editor of the* Dictionary of National Biography; *her mother was Julia Pattle Stephen, a famous beauty and equally famous hostess to the literary figures who gathered at the Stephen home: George*

Meredith, Henry James, J. A. Symonds, and most of the other prominent writers of the day. Her father's learning and industry and her mother's social and domestic mastery were models Woolf struggled with all her life, until she exorcised them in her greatest novel, To the Lighthouse (1927).

Julia Stephen died when Woolf was thirteen. Leslie Stephen reacted by plunging into an exaggerated and melodramatic mourning that was to continue for the rest of his life, while Woolf had the first of a series of mental breakdowns that were to recur periodically the rest of her life. A second breakdown, including a suicide attempt, followed the death of her father in 1904, when she was twenty-two. When she recovered, she moved, with her sister Vanessa and her brothers Thoby and Adrian, from the family home in Kensington, London, to 46 Gordon Square in the less fashionable and more bohemian area of Bloomsbury. The Stephen sisters and brothers, in their new Bloomsbury home, formed the initial nucleus of what within a few years would be famous as the "Bloomsbury group," a circle of artists and intellectuals who would have a major impact upon the culture of England between the wars. The circle, many of whom knew the Stephen sons at Cambridge, eventually included the biographer Lytton Strachey, the economist J. M. Keynes, the art critic Roger Fry, the novelist E. M. Forster, and a number of lesser names.

Virginia Stephen married Leonard Woolf, a journalist and political writer, in 1912; the following year, her first novel, which she had worked on for six years, appeared: The Voyage Out. Publication of the book was followed by a third breakdown, which lasted, with brief respites, for four years.

In 1917, the Woolfs bought a hand press and founded the Hogarth Press in their home, partly as a therapeutic diversion for Virginia. It had a long and distinguished history, publishing not only some of Woolf's books but such other important works as T. S. Eliot's Poems (1919). A second novel, Night and Day, appeared in 1919 as well, followed by Monday or Tuesday, a collection of stories, in 1920. Both The Voyage Out and Night and Day had been comparatively traditional in form, but in the stories of Monday or Tuesday, Woolf began to experiment with a more fluid, subjective style that deemphasized external action, capturing instead the moment-to-moment flow of consciousness of her characters. She pursued this style in her next novel, Jacob's Room (1922), and in Mrs. Dalloway (1925). Her finest novel, To the Lighthouse, appeared in 1927. Woolf used the language of psychoanalysis to describe the personal meaning of this novel, which explored through the character of Lily Briscoe her struggles to come to terms with the images of her parents, depicted in Mr. and Mrs. Ramsey. "I suppose that I did for myself what psychoanalysts do for their patients. I expressed some very long felt and deeply felt emotion. And in expressing it I explained it and then laid it to rest." The three-part structure of To the Lighthouse—a long, stream-of-consciousness account of a day in the life of the Ramseys and their guests, a shorter poetic account of the passing of ten years, and then another stream-of-consciousness description of another day—perfectly achieves the organic relation between fluid consciousness and form Woolf aspired to.

A love affair with Vita Sackville-West inspired the amusing but uncharacteristic Orlando (1928), a mock-biography that pursues a single character from Elizabethan times to the present, the protagonist changing sexes to fit each age. In The Waves (1931), Woolf returned to her more characteristic kind of experimentation, following the streams of consciousness of six characters at selected moments throughout their lives and juxtaposing them with a fragmented account of a single day on the seashore. The concern with the contrast between personal time and larger, more impersonal temporal units continued in The Years (1937), which traces, in a more *traditional form than her immediately preceding novels, the history of the Pargiter family from 1880 to 1936, and in* Between the Acts *(1941), a short novel that balances a single day in the lives of a group of villagers against a village pageant embodying the whole range of English history.*

Woolf's voluminous writing of the 1930s also included several volumes of her collected literary criticism, which had made her one of the most admired critics of her age; Flush *(1933), a fanciful biography of the Brownings presented as the biography of Mrs. Browning's dog; and a long biography of her friend the art critic Roger Fry (1940). In* A Room of One's Own *(1929) and* Three Guineas *(1938), as well as many of her critical essays, she championed the cause of women writers and the more general emancipation of women.*

In 1941, sensing the coming of another mental breakdown, Virginia Woolf, then living with her husband in a rural cottage near Rodmell, drowned herself in the nearby river Ouse.

To Woolf, her life as a writer was inseparable from her life as a woman. "A woman's writing is always feminine; it cannot help being feminine; at its best it is most feminine," she wrote (though characteristically complicating her position by adding, "the only difficulty lies in defining what we mean by feminine"). Feminine experience, she believed, had not received adequate expression in literature because of conventions that denied women education equal to men's and burdened them with social and domestic duties that stood in the way of writing. "Five hundred pounds and a room of one's own" was the famous formula she proposed as the prerequisite for success as a writer. But Woolf's feminism was not confined to external social conditions; she explored feminine psychology in her greatest characters—Clarissa Dalloway, Mrs. Ramsey, Lily Briscoe—despite her awareness of the difficulty in "defining what we mean by feminine."

Some of the finest and most characteristic passages in Woolf's fiction are party scenes: the last episode in Mrs. Dalloway, *for example, Mrs. Ramsey's dinner party in* To the Lighthouse, *and another of Mrs. Dalloway's parties in "The New Dress." Parties have an almost ceremonial meaning to Woolf; Mrs. Ramsey and Mrs. Dalloway are both "artists of life" whose parties serve some of the functions of art in providing structures for organizing experience and orchestrating the subtleties of human relationships. But balancing such female artists of life are such equally characteristic female figures as Lily Briscoe and Mabel Waring, insecure outsiders, excluded from life's feasts and doubting their adequacy as women. "The New Dress," published in 1927, the same year as* To the Lighthouse, *presents a view of one of these parties through the mind of an "outsider." Woolf's representation of Mabel Waring's flow of consciousness as she desperately sneaks looks into mirrors, masochistically imagines herself as a dressmaker's dummy stuck full of pins, and defensively wishes she had married a rich, adventurous man or found "some wonderful, helpful, astonishing book" to transform her life is a tiny masterpiece of Woolf's narrow but powerful art.*

FURTHER READING *(prepared by N. K. B.):* The standard biography is Quentin Bell's *Virginia Woolf,* 2 vols., 1972, a balanced, detailed account. Phyllis Rose's *Woman of Letters: A Life of Virginia Woolf,* 1978, is a feminist reading of Woolf's life, stressing her role as a professional writer and social critic. The best supplements to these biographies are *The Diary of Virginia Woolf,* 5 vols., ed. Anne Oliver Bell, 1977 ff., and *The Letters of Virginia Woolf,* 6 vols., ed. Nigel Nicolson and Joanne Trautmann, 1975 ff. Susan Gorsky's *Virginia Woolf,* 1978, summarizes key biographical events and surveys the major themes and techniques in both the fiction and the essays. Joan Bennett's *Virginia Woolf,* 1945, is a penetrating study of Woolf's narrative style. Jean Guiguet's *Virginia Woolf and Her Works,* trans. by Jean Stewart, 1965, claims that Woolf's main preoccupation lies in her "quest for reality," and analyzes provocatively the relationship between her life and art. In *Virginia Woolf: The Inward Voyage,* 1970, Harvena Richter examines subjective viewpoints in Woolf's fiction. Mitchell Leaska's *The Novels of Virginia Woolf From Beginning to End,* 1977, emphasizes the multiple perspectives of the personae in Woolf's fiction. Herbert Marder's *Feminism and Art,* 1968, examines the social criticism in both fiction and nonfiction. For collections of essays in Woolf criticism, see Claire Sprague, ed., *Virginia Woolf: A Collection of Critical Essays,* 1971, and Jane Marcus, ed., *New Feminist Essays on Virginia Woolf,* 1981, a provocative and illuminating sample of criticism and research. *Virginia Woolf: The Critical Heritage,* ed. by Robin Majumdar and Allen McLaurin, 1975, offers the widest collection of contemporary British and American reviews between 1915 and 1941.

THE NEW DRESS

Mabel had her first serious suspicion that something was wrong as she took her cloak off and Mrs. Barnet, while handing her the mirror and touching the brushes and thus drawing her attention, perhaps rather markedly, to all the appliances for tidying and improving hair, complexion, clothes, which existed on the dressing table, confirmed the suspicion—that it was not right, not quite right, which growing stronger as she went upstairs and springing at her, with conviction as she greeted Clarissa Dalloway, she went straight to the far end of the room, to a shaded corner where a looking-glass hung and looked. No! It was not *right.* And at once the misery which she always tried to hide, the profound dissatisfaction—the sense she had had, ever since she was a child, of being inferior to other people—set upon her, relentlessly, remorselessly, with an intensity which she could not beat off, as she would when she woke at night at home, by reading Borrow or Scott;[1] for oh these men, oh these women, all were thinking—"What's Mabel wearing? What a fright she looks! What a hideous new dress!"—their eyelids flickering as they came up and then their lids shutting rather tight. It was her own appalling inadequacy; her cowardice; her mean, water-sprinkled blood that depressed her. And at once the whole of the room where, for ever so many hours, she had planned with the little dressmaker how it was to go, seemed sordid, repulsive; and her own drawing-room so shabby, and herself, going out, puffed up with vanity as she touched the letters on the hall table and said: "How dull!" to show off—all this now seemed unutterably silly, paltry, and provincial. All this had been absolutely destroyed, shown up, exploded, the moment she came into Mrs. Dalloway's drawing-room.

What she had thought that evening when, sitting over the teacups, Mrs. Dalloway's invitation came, was that, of course, she could not be fashionable. It was absurd to pretend it even—fashion meant cut, meant style, meant thirty guineas at least—but why not be original? Why not be herself,

[1] George Borrow (1803–81) wrote travel books, especially about life among the gypsies. Sir Walter Scott (1771–1832) was famous for his historical romances.

anyhow? And, getting up, she had taken that old fashion book of her mother's, a Paris fashion book of the time of the Empire,[2] and had thought how much prettier, more dignified, and more womanly they were then, and so set herself—oh, it was foolish—trying to be like them, pluming herself in fact, upon being modest and old-fashioned and very charming, giving herself up, no doubt about it, to an orgy of self-love, which deserved to be chastised, and so rigged herself out like this.

But she dared not look in the glass. She could not face the whole horror—the pale yellow, idiotically old-fashioned silk dress with its long skirt and its high sleeves and its waist and all the things that looked so charming in the fashion book, but not on her, not among all these ordinary people. She felt like a dressmaker's dummy standing there, for young people to stick pins into.

"But, my dear, it's perfectly charming!" Rose Shaw said, looking her up and down with that little satirical pucker of the lips which she expected—Rose herself being dressed in the height of the fashion, precisely like everybody else, always.

"We are all like flies trying to crawl over the edge of the saucer," Mabel thought, and repeated the phrase as if she were crossing herself, as if she were trying to find some spell to annul this pain, to make this agony endurable. Tags of Shakespeare, lines from books she had read ages ago, suddenly came to her when she was in agony, and she repeated them over and over again. "Flies trying to crawl," she repeated. If she could say that over often enough and make herself see the flies, she would become numb, chill, frozen, dumb. Now she could see flies crawling slowly out of a saucer of milk with their wings stuck together; and she strained and strained (standing in front of the looking-glass, listening to Rose Shaw) to make herself see Rose Shaw and all the other people there as flies, trying to hoist themselves out of something, or into something, meagre, insignificant, toiling flies. But she could not see them like that, not other people. She saw herself like that—she was a fly, but the others were dragonflies, butterflies, beautiful insects, dancing, fluttering, skimming, while she alone dragged herself up out of the saucer. (Envy and spite, the most detestable of the vices, were her chief faults.)

"I feel like some dowdy, decrepit, horribly dingy old fly," she said, making Robert Haydon stop just to hear her say that, just to reassure herself by furbishing up a poor weak-kneed phrase and so showing how detached she was, how witty, that she did not feel in the least out of anything. And, of course, Robert Haydon answered something quite polite, quite insincere, which she saw through instantly, and said to herself, directly he went (again from some book), "Lies, lies, lies!" For a party makes things either much more real, or much less real, she thought; she saw in a flash to the bottom of Robert Haydon's heart; she saw through everything. She saw the truth. *This* was true, this drawing-room, this self, and the other false. Miss Milan's little work-room was really terribly hot, stuffy, sordid. It smelt of clothes and cabbage cooking; and yet, when Miss Milan put the glass in her hand, and she looked at herself with the dress on, finished, an extraordinary bliss

[2]The time of the first French Empire, 1804–15. Women's fashions in the Empire were characterized by high waistlines and free-hanging, undraped skirts.

shot through her heart. Suffused with light, she sprang into existence. Rid of cares and wrinkles, what she had dreamed of herself was there—a beautiful woman. Just for a second (she had not dared look longer, Miss Milan wanted to know about the length of the skirt), there looked at her, framed in the scrolloping[3] mahogany, a grey-white, mysteriously smiling, charming girl, the core of herself, the soul of herself; and it was not vanity only, not only self-love that made her think it good, tender, and true. Miss Milan said that the skirt could not well be longer; if anything the skirt, said Miss Milan, puckering her forehead, considering with all her wits about her, must be shorter; and she felt, suddenly, honestly, full of love for Miss Milan, much, much fonder of Miss Milan than of anyone in the whole world, and could have cried for pity that she should be crawling on the floor with her mouth full of pins, and her face red and her eyes bulging—that one human being should be doing this for another, and she saw them all as human beings merely, and herself going off to her party, and Miss Milan pulling the cover over the canary's cage, or letting him pick a hempseed from between her lips, and the thought of it, of this side of human nature and its patience and its endurance and its being content with such miserable, scanty, sordid, little pleasures filled her eyes with tears.

And now the whole thing had vanished. The dress, the room, the love, the pity, the scrolloping looking-glass, and the canary's cage—all had vanished, and here she was in a corner of Mrs. Dalloway's drawing-room, suffering tortures, woken wide awake to reality.

But it was all so paltry, weak-blooded, and petty-minded to care so much at her age with two children, to be still so utterly dependent on people's opinions and not have principles or convictions, not to be able to say as other people did, "There's Shakespeare! There's death! We're all weevils in a captain's biscuit"—or whatever it was that people did say.

She faced herself straight in the glass; she pecked at her left shoulder; she issued out into the room, as if spears were thrown at her yellow dress from all sides. But instead of looking fierce or tragic, as Rose Shaw would have done—Rose would have looked like Boadicea[4]—she looked foolish and self-conscious, and simpered like a schoolgirl and slouched across the room, positively slinking, as if she were a beaten mongrel, and looked at a picture, an engraving. As if one went to a party to look at a picture! Everybody knew why she did it—it was from shame, from humiliation.

"Now the fly's in the saucer," she said to herself, "right in the middle, and can't get out, and the milk," she thought, rigidly staring at the picture, "is sticking its wings together."

"It's so old-fashioned," she said to Charles Burt, making him stop (which by itself he hated) on his way to talk to someone else.

She meant, or she tried to make herself think that she meant, that it was the picture and not her dress, that was old-fashioned. And one word of praise, one word of affection from Charles would have made all the difference to her at the moment. If he had only said, "Mabel, you're looking charming tonight!" it would have changed her life. But then she ought to

[3] Apparently an invented word, combining "scrolled" and "scalloped."

[4] Stately and regal, like the first-century A.D. British queen who led an unsuccessful revolt against the Romans.

have been truthful and direct. Charles said nothing of the kind, of course. He was malice itself. He always saw through one, especially if one were feeling particularly mean, paltry, or feeble-minded.

"Mabel's got a new dress!" he said, and the poor fly was absolutely shoved into the middle of the saucer. Really, he would like her to drown, she believed. He had no heart, no fundamental kindness, only a veneer of friendliness. Miss Milan was much more real, much kinder. If only one could feel that and stick to it, always. "Why," she asked herself—replying to Charles much too pertly, letting him see that she was out of temper, or "ruffled" as he called it ("Rather ruffled?" he said and went on to laugh at her with some woman over there)—"Why," she asked herself, "can't I feel one thing always, feel quite sure that Miss Milan is right, and Charles wrong and stick to it, feel sure about the canary and pity and love and not be whipped all round in a second by coming into a room full of people?" It was her odious, weak, vacillating character again, always giving at the critical moment and not being seriously interested in conchology, etymology, botany, archeology, cutting up potatoes and watching them fructify like Mary Dennis, like Violet Searle.

Then Mrs. Holman, seeing her standing there, bore down upon her. Of course a thing like a dress was beneath Mrs. Holman's notice, with her family always tumbling downstairs or having the scarlet fever. Could Mabel tell her if Elmthorpe was ever let for August and September? Oh, it was a conversation that bored her unutterably!—it made her furious to be treated like a house agent or a messenger boy, to be made use of. Not to have value, that was it, she thought, trying to grasp something hard, something real, while she tried to answer sensibly about the bathroom and the south aspect and the hot water to the top of the house; and all the time she could see little bits of her yellow dress in the round looking-glass which made them all the size of boot-buttons or tadpoles; and it was amazing to think how much humiliation and agony and self-loathing and effort and passionate ups and downs of feeling were contained in a thing the size of a threepenny bit. And what was still odder, this thing, this Mabel Waring, was separate, quite disconnected; and though Mrs. Holman (the black button) was leaning forward and telling her how her eldest boy had strained his heart running, she could see her, too, quite detached in the looking-glass, and it was impossible that the black dot, leaning forward, gesticulating, should make the yellow dot, sitting solitary, self-centred, feel what the black dot was feeling, yet they pretended.

"So impossible to keep boys quiet"—that was the kind of thing one said.

And Mrs. Holman, who could never get enough sympathy and snatched what little there was greedily, as if it were her right (but she deserved much more for there was her little girl who had come down this morning with a swollen knee-joint), took this miserable offering and looked at it suspiciously, grudgingly, as if it were a halfpenny when it ought to have been a pound and put it away in her purse, must put up with it, mean and miserly though it was, times being hard, so very hard; and on she went, creaking, injured Mrs. Holman, about the girl with the swollen joints. Ah, it was tragic, this greed, this clamour of human beings, like a row of cormorants, barking and flapping their wings for sympathy—it was tragic, could one have felt it and not merely pretended to feel it!

But in her yellow dress tonight she could not wring out one drop more; she wanted it all, all for herself. She knew (she kept on looking into the glass, dipping into that dreadfully showing-up blue pool) that she was condemned, despised, left like this in a backwater, because of her being like this a feeble, vacillating creature; and it seemed to her that the yellow dress was a penance which she had deserved, and if she had been dressed like Rose Shaw, in lovely, clinging green with a ruffle of swansdown, she would have deserved that; and she thought that there was no escape for her—none whatever. But it was not her fault altogether, after all. It was being one of a family of ten; never having money enough, always skimping and paring; and her mother carrying great cans, and the linoleum worn on the stair edges, and one sordid little domestic tragedy after another—nothing catastrophic, the sheep farm failing, but not utterly; her eldest brother marrying beneath him but not very much—there was no romance, nothing extreme about them all. They petered out respectably in seaside resorts; every watering-place had one of her aunts even now asleep in some lodging with the front windows not quite facing the sea. That was so like them—they had to squint at things always. And she had done the same—she was just like her aunts. For all her dreams of living in India, married to some hero like Sir Henry Lawrence, some empire builder (still the sight of a native in a turban filled her with romance), she had failed utterly. She had married Hubert, with his safe, permanent underling's job in the Law Courts, and they managed tolerably in a smallish house, without proper maids, and hash when she was alone or just bread and butter, but now and then—Mrs. Holman was off, thinking her the most dried-up, unsympathetic twig she had ever met, absurdly dressed, too, and would tell everyone about Mabel's fantastic appearance—now and then, thought Mabel Waring, left alone on the blue sofa, punching the cushion in order to look occupied, for she would not join Charles Burt and Rose Shaw, chattering like magpies and perhaps laughing at her by the fireplace—now and then, there did come to her delicious moments, reading the other night in bed, for instance, or down by the sea on the sand in the sun, at Easter—let her recall it—a great tuft of pale sand-grass standing all twisted like a shock of spears against the sky, which was blue like a smooth china egg, so firm, so hard, and then the melody of the waves—"Hush, hush," they said, and the children's shouts paddling—yes, it was a divine moment, and there she lay, she felt, in the hand of the Goddess who was the world; rather a hard-hearted, but very beautiful Goddess, a little lamb laid on the altar (one did think these silly things, and it didn't matter so long as one never said them). And also with Hubert sometimes she had quite unexpectedly—carving the mutton for Sunday lunch, for no reason, opening a letter, coming into a room—divine moments, when she said to herself (for she would never say this to anybody else), "This is it. This has happened. This is it!" And the other way about it was equally surprising—that is, when everything was arranged—music, weather, holidays, every reason for happiness was there—then nothing happened at all. One wasn't happy, It was flat, just flat, that was all.

Her wretched self again, no doubt! She had always been a fretful, weak, unsatisfactory mother, a wobbly wife, lolling about in a kind of twilight existence with nothing very clear or very bold, or more one thing than another, like all her brothers and sisters, except perhaps Herbert—they were all the same poor water-veined creatures who did nothing. Then in the midst of this creeping, crawling life, suddenly she was on the crest of a wave. That wretched fly—where had she read the story that kept coming into her mind about the fly and the saucer?—struggled out. Yes, she had those moments. But now that she was forty, they might come more and more seldom. By degrees she would cease to struggle any more. But that was deplorable! That was not to be endured! That made her feel ashamed of herself!

She would go to the London Library tomorrow. She would find some wonderful, helpful, astonishing book, quite by chance, a book by a clergyman, by an American no one had ever heard of; or she would walk down the Strand and drop, accidentally, into a hall where a miner was telling about the life in the pit, and suddenly she would become a new person. She would be absolutely transformed. She would wear a uniform; she would be called Sister Somebody; she would never give a thought to clothes again. And forever after she would be perfectly clear about Charles Burt and Miss Milan and this room and that room; and it would be always, day after day, as if she were lying in the sun or carving the mutton. It would be it!

So she got up from the blue sofa, and the yellow button in the looking-glass got up too, and she waved her hand to Charles and Rose to show them she did not depend on them one scrap, and the yellow button moved out of the looking-glass, and all the spears were gathered into her breast as she walked towards Mrs. Dalloway and said, "Good night."

"But it's too early to go," said Mrs. Dalloway, who was always so charming.

"I'm afraid I must," said Mabel Waring. "But," she added in her weak, wobbly voice which only sounded ridiculous when she tried to strengthen it, "I have enjoyed myself enormously."

"I have enjoyed myself," she said to Mr. Dalloway, whom she met on the stairs.

"Lies, lies, lies!" she said to herself, going downstairs, and "Right in the saucer!" she said to herself as she thanked Mrs. Barnet for helping her and wrapped herself, round and round and round, in the Chinese cloak she had worn these twenty years.

Franz Kafka

(1883–1924)

Dreams and nightmares have had an important place in literature since its beginning, from Cassandra's visionary hallucinations in Agamemnon *through Dante's great dream-vision of the afterlife in* The Divine Comedy *to Joyce's "funferall" dream-novel,* Finnegans Wake. *Some of the most powerful and characteristic modern literary dreams were those of a tall, lanky, melancholy Jewish lawyer from*

Prague, who spent his days in a bureaucratic insurance office listening to workers' insurance claims and his nights in writing stories that read like a series of nightmares. Dreams, as Freud pointed out, are among the most personal and idiosyncratic of phenomena, but paradoxically, Kafka's dream-stories, while profoundly rooted in his own lonely, neurotic personality, have struck deep chords in a wide range of readers. It is almost as if Kafka's nightmares of faceless, anonymous authority and of the individual's loneliness, alienation, and despair were collective dreams of the twentieth century.

Franz Kafka was born in 1883, in Prague, Czechoslovakia, a city whose twentieth-century history strangely echoes Kafka's fables of mindless tyranny and oppression. He was the oldest surviving child of six children; his father was a wealthy, self-made Jewish merchant whose struggles to succeed had made him an outspoken and domineering defender of traditional authority, while his mother was a simple, submissive woman with little sympathy for Kafka's artistic interests. He distinguished himself at a fine high school in Prague and then studied law at the University of Prague, receiving his doctorate when he was twenty-three. After a year of legal apprenticeship, he took a job with the accident claims division of the Workers' Accident Insurance Institute for the Kingdom of Bohemia. He stuck to that job steadily for nine years and then, after he developed tuberculosis, intermittently for another five, resigning only two years before his early death. Listening to stories of accidents and hardships and of dealing with governmental and business bureaucracy, tasks to which he devoted each day from eight to two, undoubtedly contributed to the themes of the stories he began writing after working hours.

Kafka's first published work appeared in a Prague magazine in 1909; he was to publish very little during his lifetime, most of his work appearing posthumously. He moved, however, in the circles of Prague Jewish intellectuals and artists, including the theologian Martin Buber, the novelist Franz Werfel, and especially Max Brod, his closest friend and, later, his editor and biographer. By 1913, Kafka had written enough short pieces to publish a collection, Meditation; *the same year, he wrote "The Judgment," a story about his father, which he felt represented a great personal and artistic breakthrough, as well as "The Metamorphosis" and the first sections of the novel published after his death as* Amerika *(1927).*

Also in 1913, Kafka met and fell in love with a German girl named Felice Bauer. Their odd courtship continued for five years, Kafka vacillating between the desire to marry and the desire to devote all his time to his art. During these years, he wrote the famous short story "The Penal Colony" and the novel The Trial *(posthumously published in 1925). When World War I broke out, Kafka, as a civil servant, was exempt from military service, but the war's senselessness and brutality confirmed his own vision of the nightmarishness of history.*

In 1917, Kafka discovered that he had tuberculosis. He took a medical leave from his job and began a series of treatments that were to continue the rest of his life. In 1920, he was in a sanitarium in the Tatra Mountains on the Polish border in northern Czechoslovakia. About this time he had an intense, tortured love affair with his Czech translator, Milena Jesenska, which again he broke off, ostensibly to devote all his time to writing. He was also working on his famous novel The Castle *(1926), about a land surveyor named K. and his attempts to enter the castle to which he has been summoned.*

During the final years of his life, Kafka's health deteriorated rapidly. In 1923, he fell in love with Dora Dymant and settled with her in Berlin; he asked Dora's father for permission to marry her but was refused. In the winter of 1923–24 he moved into a series of clinics and sanitariums. He died, Dora at his side, on June 3, 1924, at a sanitarium in Kierling, near Vienna. His surviving family, including his sisters, all perished several years later in Nazi concentration camps.

Kafka left instructions that all his manuscripts were to be destroyed and that work already published was not to be republished. His friend Max Brod took the responsibility of disregarding these instructions, however, and published, over a period of several years, the bulk of Kafka's work. By the 1930s Kafka was well-known in France, England, and the United States; his fame in Germany had to wait until the fall of the Hitler regime in 1945, but since then he has become one of the most famous and influential of German-language authors there as well.

The American critic Philip Rahv has pointed out a "nuclear fable" that underlies Kafka's most characteristic works. In each of them, a unique, intelligent, unpredictable individual is thrust into a baffling, automatic, depersonalized world where he must struggle to maintain his individuality against a system that tries to force him into a dazed, acquiescent behavior which fits the externally imposed expectations of the system. The result is a painful, disorienting conflict between one's inner sense of self and the pressures of the identity imposed from without. The personal roots of this recurring fable were undoubtedly Kafka's relations with his domineering, intimidating father. This relationship, as Kafka saw it, is recorded in the painful, self-lacerating "Letter to His Father" (1919), a letter which never reached Hermann Kafka:

> *Dear Father:*
>
> *You asked me recently why I maintain that I am afraid of you. As usual, I was unable to think of any answer to your question, partly for the very reason that I am afraid of you, and partly because an explanation of the grounds for this fear would mean going into far more details than I could even approximately keep in mind while talking.*

The letter does not ultimately answer the question of why Hermann Kafka, overpowering as he was, remained so potent a force in his son's life. But he did remain so, not only in the stories of explicit paternal tyranny but in others in which the father's power is projected upon a frightening, depersonalizing universe.

It would be a mistake, however, to regard Kafka's stories as merely transcriptions of his neurotic fantasies, ripped raw from his unconscious. Kafka is one of the most artful of writers, and his oneiric tales are the products of careful craftsmanship and laborious revision. He was a close student not only of the German Romantic writers, including Goethe, Kleist, Grillparzer, and Von Hofmannstal (a major influence), but also of Flaubert, Dostoevsky, Tolstoy, and Dickens, all of whom left some mark upon his work. He also took a lively interest in social and political affairs; from his adolescence he was a socialist, and in his later years he was a supporter of Zionism, under the influence of both Max Brod and Dora Dymant. Despite his atheism, he took an intense interest in Judaism and was especially influenced by the Jewish mystical movement known as Hasidism. Many of the most apparently private of Kafka's stories have social, philosophical, and religious dimensions that reflect these varied interests.

The first sentence of "The Metamorphosis"—"As Gregor Samsa awoke one morning from uneasy dreams he found himself transformed in his bed into a gigantic insect"—is one of the most famous in modern fiction, not only for its startling content but also for its calm, matter-of-fact style, which sets the tone for the rest of the story. The premise of the story is dreamlike; as Freud pointed out, one of the most important mechanisms of the "dream-work" is symbolization. Gregor Samsa feels himself to be an insect and has been treated like an insect; the story makes the dreamlike leap from "I feel like an insect" to "I am an insect." Gregor has been treated like an insect by his family and by his employer, and he is not blameless: he may feel an insectlike guilt over having displaced his father as breadwinner and head of the family. The causes are complex, but whatever they are, they have led Gregor to the ultimate alienation, loss of even his physical humanity. He is the ultimate "underground man," and his plight may even have been suggested by the incident in Dostoevsky's Notes from Underground *in which the officer on the Nevsky Prospect takes the narrator by the shoulders and moves him to the side, as if he were nothing more than "a curious insect."*

Once Gregor's metamorphosis has been accomplished, in that opening line, the story proceeds inexorably to his death, as it does for the protagonist in another story often linked to Kafka's: Tolstoy's The Death of Ivan Ilyitch, *in which Ivan, like Gregor, feels that he is being punished but has committed no crime. But Ivan's story ends in illumination and joy at the last moment: "'So this is it!' he suddenly exclaimed aloud, 'What joy!'" The only affirmative note in "The Metamorphosis" comes after Gregor's death, when his loved sister ambiguously and with an unconscious callousness reaffirms life by springing to her feet and stretching her young body.*

FURTHER READING *(prepared by N. K. B.)*: *The Complete Stories*, ed. Nahum N. Glatzer, 1946, includes all stories published during Kafka's life, as well as posthumous stories. Ronald Hayman's *Kafka: A Biography*, 1982, argues that the fiction mirrors Kafka's experience. Max Brod, Kafka's close friend and literary executor, has written a standard work, *Franz Kafka: A Biography*, trans. by G. Humphreyes Roberts and Richard Winston, 1947, rev. 1960. Richard and Clara Winston have edited and translated Kafka's *Letters to Friends, Family, and Editors*, 1977. Meno Spann's *Franz Kafka*, 1976, includes an informative introduction to Kafka's life and writings, with important commentary on individual works. Walter Sokel's *Franz Kafka*, 1966, is a brief study that emphasizes the autobiographical elements in Kafka's writings. Erich Heller's *The Disinherited Mind*, 1952, and his *Franz Kafka*, 1975, are major contributions to Kafka scholarship. Ronald Gray's *Franz Kafka*, 1973, surveys the writing career and suggests the philosophical and religious themes pervading individual works. Mark Spilka's comparative study *Dickens and Kafka*, 1963, illuminates Kafka's style. Heinz Politzer's *Franz Kafka: Parable and Paradox*, 1962, examines his narrative technique. *The Commentators' Despair: The Interpretations of Kafka's Metamorphosis*, ed. Stanley Corngold, 1973, includes a wide variety of critical readings. Ronald Gray, ed., *Kafka: A Collection of Critical Essays*, 1962, includes essays on Kafka's life, themes, and techniques, including a reading of "The Metamorphosis" by Johannes Pfeiffer. Angel Flores has edited several compendiums of Kafka scholarship, including *The Kafka Problem*, 1946, a milestone in Kafka criticism in English; *Franz Kafka Today*, ed. Flores and Homer Swander, 1958; and *The Kafka Debate: New Perspectives for Our Time*, 1977, which contains thirty-three essays. J. P. Stern, ed., *The World of Franz Kafka*, 1980, contains essays on Kafka's life and background. Kenneth Hughes, ed., *Franz Kafka: An Anthology of Marxist Criticism*, 1981, surveys and reprints important Marxist interpretations, including an essay by Hannah Arendt and Howard Fast's "The Metamorphosis" from his *Literature and Reality*, 1950.

THE METAMORPHOSIS

Translated by Willa and Edwin Muir

I

As Gregor Samsa awoke one morning from uneasy dreams he found himself transformed in his bed into a gigantic insect. He was lying on his hard, as it were armor-plated, back and when he lifted his head a little he could see his dome-like brown belly divided into stiff arched segments on top of which the bed quilt could hardly keep in position and was about to slide off completely. His numerous legs, which were pitifully thin compared to the rest of his bulk, waved helplessly before his eyes.

What has happened to me? he thought. It was no dream. His room, a regular human bedroom, only rather too small, lay quiet between the four familiar walls. Above the table on which a collection of cloth samples was unpacked and spread out—Samsa was a commercial traveler—hung the picture which he had recently cut out of an illustrated magazine and put into a pretty gilt frame. It showed a lady, with a fur cap on and a fur stole, sitting upright and holding out to the spectator a huge fur muff into which the whole of her forearm had vanished!

Gregor's eyes turned next to the window, and the overcast sky—one could hear rain drops beating on the window gutter—made him quite melancholy. What about sleeping a little longer and forgetting all this nonsense, he thought, but it could not be done, for he was accustomed to sleep on his right side and in his present condition he could not turn himself over. However violently he forced himself towards his right side he always rolled on to his back again. He tried it at least a hundred times, shutting his eyes to keep from seeing his struggling legs, and only desisted when he began to feel in his side a faint dull ache he had never experienced before.

Oh God, he thought, what an exhausting job I've picked on! Traveling about day in, day out. It's much more irritating work than doing the actual business in the office, and on top of that there's the trouble of constant traveling, of worrying about train connections, the bed and irregular meals, casual acquaintances that are always new and never become intimate friends. The devil take it all! He felt a slight itching up on his belly; slowly pushed himself on his back nearer to the top of the bed so that he could lift his head more easily; identified the itching place which was surrounded by many small white spots the nature of which he could not understand and made to touch it with a leg, but drew the leg back immediately, for the contact made a cold shiver run through him.

He slid down again into his former position. This getting up early, he thought, makes one quite stupid. A man needs his sleep. Other commercials live like harem women. For instance, when I come back to the hotel of a morning to write up the orders I've got, these others are only sitting down to breakfast. Let me just try that with my chief; I'd be sacked on the spot. Anyhow, that might be quite a good thing for me, who can tell? If I didn't have to hold my hand because of my parents I'd have given notice long ago, I'd have gone to the chief and told him exactly what I think of him. That would knock him endways from his desk! It's a queer way of doing, too, this sitting on high at a desk and talking down to employees, especially when they have to come quite near because the chief is hard of hearing. Well, there's still hope; once I've saved enough money to pay back my parents' debts to him—that should take another five or six years—I'll do it without fail. I'll cut myself completely loose then. For the moment, though, I'd better get up, since my train goes at five.

He looked at the alarm clock ticking on the chest. Heavenly Father! he thought. It was half-past six o'clock and the hands were quietly moving on, it was even past the half-hour, it was getting on toward a quarter to seven. Had the alarm clock not gone off? From the bed one could see that it had been properly set for four o'clock; of course it must have gone off. Yes, but was it possible to sleep quietly through that ear-splitting noise? Well, he had not slept quietly, yet apparently all the more soundly for that. But what was he to do now? The next train went at seven o'clock; to catch that he would need to hurry like mad and his samples weren't even packed up, and he himself wasn't feeling particularly fresh and active. And even if he did catch the train he wouldn't avoid a row with the chief, since the firm's porter would have been waiting for the five o'clock train and would have long since reported his failure to turn up. The porter was a creature of the chief's, spineless and stupid. Well, supposing he were to say he was sick? But that would be most unpleasant and would look suspicious, since during his five years' employment he had not been ill once. The chief himself would be sure to come with the sick-insurance doctor, would reproach his parents with their son's laziness and would cut all excuses short by referring to the insurance doctor, who of course regarded all mankind as perfectly healthy malingerers. And would he be so far wrong on this occasion? Gregor really felt quite well, apart from a drowsiness that was utterly superfluous after such a long sleep, and he was even unusually hungry.

As all this was running through his mind at top speed without his being able to decide to leave his bed—the alarm clock had just struck a quarter to seven—there came a cautious tap at the door behind the head of his bed. "Gregor," said a voice—it was his mother's—"it's a quarter to seven. Hadn't you a train to catch?" That gentle voice! Gregor had a shock as he heard his own voice answering hers, unmistakably his own voice, it was true, but with a persistent horrible twittering squeak behind it like an undertone, that left the words in their clear shape only for the first moment and then rose up reverberating round them to destroy their sense, so that one could not be sure one had heard them rightly. Gregor wanted to answer at length and explain everything, but in the circumstances he confined himself to saying: "Yes, yes, thank you, Mother, I'm getting up now." The wooden door between them must have kept the change in his voice from being noticeable outside, for his mother contented herself with this statement and shuffled away. Yet this brief exchange of words had made the other members of the family aware that Gregor was still in the house, as they had not expected, and at one of the side doors his father was already knocking, gently, yet with his fist. "Gregor, Gregor," he called, "what's the matter with you?" And after a little while he called again in a deeper voice: "Gregor! Gregor!" At the other side door his sister was saying in a low, plaintive tone: "Gregor? Aren't you well? Are you needing anything?" He answered them both at once: "I'm just ready," and did his best to make his voice sound as normal as possible by enunciating the words very clearly and leaving long pauses between them. So his father went back to his breakfast, but his sister whispered: "Gregor, open the door, do." However, he was not thinking of opening the door, and felt thankful for the prudent habit he had acquired in traveling of locking all doors during the night, even at home.

His immediate intention was to get up quietly without being disturbed, to put on his clothes and above all eat his breakfast, and only then to consider what else was to be done, since in bed, he was well aware, his meditations would come to no sensible conclusion. He remembered that often enough in bed he had felt small aches and pains, probably caused by awkward postures, which had proved purely imaginary once he got up, and he looked forward eagerly to seeing this morning's delusions gradually fall away. That the change in his voice was nothing but the precursor of a severe chill, a standing ailment of commercial travelers, he had not the least possible doubt.

To get rid of the quilt was quite easy; he had only to inflate himself a little and it fell off by itself. But the next move was difficult, especially because he was so uncommonly broad. He would have needed arms and hands to hoist himself up; instead he had only the numerous little legs which never stopped waving in all directions and which he could not control in the least. When he tried to bend one of them it was the first to stretch itself straight; and did he succeed at last in making it do what he wanted, all the other legs meanwhile waved the more wildly in a high degree of unpleasant agitation. "But what's the use of lying idle in bed," said Gregor to himself.

He thought that he might get out of bed with the lower part of his body first, but this lower part, which he had not yet seen and of which he could form no clear conception, proved too difficult to move; it shifted so slowly; and when finally, almost wild with annoyance, he gathered his forces together and thrust out recklessly, he had miscalculated the direction and bumped heavily against the lower end of the bed, and the stinging pain he felt informed him that precisely this lower part of his body was at the moment probably the most sensitive.

So he tried to get the top part of himself out first, and cautiously moved his head towards the edge of the bed. That proved easy enough, and despite its breadth and mass the bulk of his body at last slowly followed the movement of his head. Still, when he finally got his head free over the edge of the bed he felt too scared to go on advancing, for after all if he let himself fall in this way it would take a miracle to keep his head from being injured. And at all costs he must not lose consciousness now, precisely now; he would rather stay in bed.

But when after a repetition of the same efforts he lay in his former position again, sighing, and watched his little legs struggling against each other more wildly than ever, if that were possible, and saw no way of bringing any order into this arbitrary confusion, he told himself again that it was impossible to stay in bed and that the most sensible course was to risk everything for the smallest hope of getting away from it. At the same time he did not forget meanwhile to remind himself that cool reflection, the coolest possible, was much better than desperate resolves. In such moments he focused his eyes as sharply as possible on the window, but, unfortunately, the prospect of the morning fog, which muffled even the other side of the narrow street, brought him little encouragement and comfort. "Seven o'clock already," he said to himself when the alarm clock chimed again, "seven o'clock already and still such a thick fog." And for a little while he lay quiet, breathing lightly, as if perhaps expecting such complete repose to restore all things to their real and normal condition.

But then he said to himself: "Before it strikes a quarter past seven I must be quite out of this bed, without fail. Anyhow, by that time someone will have come from the office to ask for me, since it opens before seven." And he set himself to rocking his whole body at once in a regular rhythm, with the idea of swinging it out of the bed. If he tipped himself out in that way he could keep his head from injury by lifting it at an acute angle when he fell. His back seemed to be hard and was not likely to suffer from a fall on the carpet. His biggest worry was the loud crash he would not be able to help making, which would probably cause anxiety, if not terror, behind all the doors. Still, he must take the risk.

When he was already half out of the bed—the new method was more a game than an effort, for he needed only to hitch himself across by rocking to and fro—it struck him how simple it would be if he could get help. Two strong people—he thought of his father and the servant girl—would be amply sufficient; they would only have to thrust their arms under his convex back, lever him out of the bed, bend down with their burden and then be patient enough to let him turn himself right over on to the floor, where it was to be hoped his legs would then find their proper function. Well, ignoring the fact that the doors were all locked, ought he really to call for help? In spite of his misery he could not suppress a smile at the very idea of it.

He had got so far that he could barely keep his equilibrium when he rocked himself strongly, and he would have to nerve himself very soon for the final decision since in five minutes' time it would be a quarter past seven—when the front doorbell rang. "That's someone from the office," he said to himself, and grew almost rigid, while his little legs only jigged about all the faster. For a moment everything stayed quiet. "They're not going to open the door," said Gregor to himself, catching at some kind of irrational hope. But then of course the servant girl went as usual to the door with her heavy tread and opened it. Gregor needed only to hear the first good morning of the visitor to know immediately who it was—the chief clerk himself. What a fate, to be condemned to work for a firm where the smallest omission at once gave rise to the gravest suspicion! Were all employees in a body nothing but scoundrels, was there not among them one single loyal devoted man who, had he wasted only an hour or so of the firm's time in a morning, was so tormented by conscience as to be driven out of his mind and actually incapable of leaving his bed? Wouldn't it really have been sufficient to send an apprentice to inquire—if any inquiry were necessary at all—did the chief clerk himself have to come and thus indicate to the entire family, an innocent family, that this suspicious circumstance could be investigated by no one less versed in affairs than himself? And more through the agitation caused by these reflections than through any act of will Gregor swung himself out of bed with all his strength. There was a loud thump, but it was not really a crash. His fall was broken to some extent by the carpet, his back, too, was less stiff than he thought, and so there was merely a dull thud, not so very startling. Only he had not lifted his head carefully enough and had hit it; he turned it and rubbed it on the carpet in pain and irritation.

"That was something falling down in there," said the chief clerk in the next room to the left. Gregor tried to suppose to himself that something like what had happened to him today might some day happen to the chief clerk; one really could not deny that it was possible. But as if in brusque reply to this supposition the chief clerk took a couple of firm steps in the next-door room and his patent-leather boots creaked. From the right-hand room his sister was whispering to inform him of the situation: "Gregor, the chief clerk's here." "I know," muttered Gregor to himself; but he didn't dare to make his voice loud enough for his sister to hear it.

"Gregor," said his father now from the left-hand room, "the chief clerk has come and wants to know why you didn't catch the early train. We don't know what to say to him. Besides, he wants to talk to you in person. So open the door, please. He will be good enough to excuse the untidiness of your room." "Good morning, Mr. Samsa," the chief clerk was calling amiably meanwhile. "He's not well," said his mother to the visitor, while his father was still speaking through the door, "he's not well, sir, believe me. What else would make him miss a train! The boy thinks about nothing but his work. It makes me almost cross the way he never goes out in the evenings; he's been here the last eight days and has stayed at home every single evening. He just sits there quietly at the table reading a newspaper or looking through railway timetables. The only amusement he gets is doing fretwork. For instance, he spent two or three evenings cutting out a little picture frame; you would be surprised to see how pretty it is; it's hanging in his room; you'll see it in a minute when Gregor opens the door. I must say I'm glad you've come, sir; we should never have got him to unlock the door by ourselves; he's so obstinate; and I'm sure he's unwell, though he wouldn't have it to be so this morning." "I'm just coming," said Gregor slowly and carefully, not moving an inch for fear of losing one word of the conversation. "I can't think of any other explanation, madam," said the chief clerk. "I hope it's nothing serious. Although on the other hand I must say that we men of business—fortunately or unfortunately—very often simply have to ignore any slight indisposition, since business must be attended to." "Well, can the chief clerk come in now?" asked Gregor's father impatiently, again knocking on the door. "No," said Gregor. In the left-hand room a painful silence followed this refusal; in the right-hand room his sister began to sob.

Why didn't his sister join the others? She was probably newly out of bed and hadn't even begun to put on her clothes yet. Well, why was she crying? Because he wouldn't get up and let the chief clerk in, because he was in danger of losing his job, and because the chief would begin dunning his parents again for the old debts? Surely these were things one didn't need to worry about for the present. Gregor was still at home and not in the least thinking of deserting the family. At the moment, true, he was lying on the carpet and no one who knew the condition he was in could seriously expect him to admit the chief clerk. But for such a small discourtesy, which could plausibly be explained away somehow later on, Gregor could hardly be dismissed on the spot. And it seemed to Gregor that it would be much more sensible to leave him in peace for the present than to trouble him with tears and entreaties. Still, of course, their uncertainty bewildered them all and excused their behavior.

"Mr. Samsa," the chief clerk called now in a louder voice, "what's the matter with you? Here you are, barricading yourself in your room, giving only 'yes' and 'no' for answers, causing your parents a lot of unnecessary trouble and neglecting—I mention this only in passing—neglecting your business duties in an incredible fashion. I am speaking here in the name of your parents and of your chief, and I beg you quite seriously to give me an immediate and precise explanation. You amaze me, you amaze me. I thought you were a quiet, dependable person, and now all at once you seem bent on making a disgraceful exhibition of yourself. The chief did hint to me early this morning a possible explanation for your disappearance—with reference to the cash payments that were entrusted to you recently—but I almost pledged my solemn word of honor that this could not be so. But now that I see how incredibly obstinate you are, I no longer have the slightest desire to take your part at all. And your position in the firm is not so unassailable. I came with the intention of telling you all this in private, but since you are wasting my time so needlessly I don't see why your parents shouldn't hear it too. For some time past your work has been most unsatisfactory; this is not the season of the year for a business boom, of course, we admit that, but a season of the year for doing no business at all, that does not exist, Mr. Samsa, must not exist."

"But, sir," cried Gregor, beside himself and in his agitation forgetting everything else, "I'm just going to open the door this very minute. A slight illness, an attack of giddiness, has kept me from getting up. I'm still lying in bed. But I feel all right again. I'm getting out of bed now. Just give me a moment or two longer! I'm not quite so well as I thought. But I'm all right, really. How a thing like that can suddenly strike one down! Only last night I was quite well, my parents can tell you, or rather I did have a slight presentiment. I must have showed some sign of it. Why didn't I report it at the office! But one always thinks that an indisposition can be got over without staying in the house. Oh, sir, do spare my parents! All that you're reproaching me with now has no foundation; no one has ever said a word to me about it. Perhaps you haven't looked at the last orders I sent in. Anyhow, I can still catch the eight-o'clock train, I'm much the better for my few hours' rest. Don't let me detain you here, sir; I'll be attending to business very soon, and do be good enough to tell the chief so and to make my excuses to him!"

And while all this was tumbling out pell-mell and Gregor hardly knew what he was saying, he had reached the chest quite easily, perhaps because of the practice he had had in bed, and was now trying to lever himself upright by means of it. He meant actually to open the door, actually to show himself and speak to the chief clerk; he was eager to find out what the others, after all their insistence, would say at the sight of him. If they were horrified then the responsibility was no longer his and he could stay quiet. But if they took it calmly, then he had no reason either to be upset, and could really get to the station for the eight-o'clock train if he hurried. At first he slipped down a few times from the polished surface of the chest, but at length with a last heave he stood upright; he paid no more attention to the pains in the lower part of his body, however they smarted. Then he let himself fall against the back of a near-by chair, and clung with his little legs to the edges of it. That brought him into control of himself again and he stopped speaking, for now he could listen to what the chief clerk was saying.

"Did you understand a word of it?" the chief clerk was asking; "surely he can't be trying to make fools of us?" "Oh dear," cried his mother, in tears, "perhaps he's terribly ill and we're tormenting him. Grete! Grete!" she called out then. "Yes, Mother?" called his sister from the other side. They were calling to each other across Gregor's room. "You must go this minute for the doctor. Gregor is ill. Go for the doctor, quick. Did you hear how he was speaking?" "That was no human voice," said the chief clerk in a voice noticeably low beside the shrillness of the mother's. "Anna! Anna!" his father was calling through the hall to the kitchen, clapping his hands, "get a locksmith at once!" And the two girls were already running through the hall with a swish of skirts—how could his sister have got dressed so quickly?—and were tearing the front door open. There was no sound of its closing again; they had evidently left it open, as one does in houses where some great misfortune has happened.

But Gregor was now much calmer. The words he uttered were no longer understandable, apparently, although they seemed clear enough to him, even clearer than before, perhaps because his ear had grown accustomed to the sound of them. Yet at any rate people now believed that something was wrong with him, and were ready to help him. The positive certainty with which these first measures had been taken comforted him. He felt himself drawn once more into the human circle and hoped for great and remarkable results from both the doctor and the locksmith, without really distinguishing precisely between them. To make his voice as clear as possible for the decisive conversation that was now imminent he coughed a little, as quietly as he could, of course, since this noise too might not sound like a human cough for all he was able to judge. In the next room meanwhile there was complete silence. Perhaps his parents were sitting at the table with the chief clerk, whispering, perhaps they were all leaning against the door and listening.

Slowly Gregor pushed the chair towards the door, then let go of it, caught hold of the door for support—the soles at the end of his little legs were somewhat sticky—and rested against it for a moment after his efforts. Then he set himself to turning the key in the lock with his mouth. It seemed, unhappily, that he hadn't really any teeth—what could he grip the key with?—but on the other hand his jaws were certainly very strong; with their help he did manage to set the key in motion, heedless of the fact that he was undoubtedly damaging them somewhere, since a brown fluid issued from his mouth, flowed over the key and dripped on the floor. "Just listen to that," said the chief clerk next door; "he's turning the key." That was a great encouragement to Gregor; but they should all have shouted encouragement to him, his father and mother too: "Go on, Gregor," they should have called out, "keep going, hold on to that key!" And in the belief that they were all following his efforts intently, he clenched his jaws recklessly on the key with all the force at his command. As the turning of the key progressed he circled round the lock, holding on now only with his mouth, pushing on the key, as required, or pulling it down again with all the weight of his body. The louder click of the finally yielding lock literally quickened Gregor. With a deep breath of relief he said to himself: "So I didn't need the locksmith," and laid his head on the handle to open the door wide.

Since he had to pull the door towards him, he was still invisible when it was really wide open. He had to edge himself slowly round the near half of the double door, and to do it very carefully if he was not to fall plump upon his back just on the threshold. He was still carrying out this difficult manoeuvre, with no time to observe anything else, when he heard the chief clerk utter a loud "Oh!"—it sounded like a gust of wind—and now he could see the man, standing as he was nearest to the door, clapping one hand before his open mouth and slowly backing away as if driven by some invisible steady pressure. His mother—in spite of the chief clerk's being there her hair was still undone and sticking up in all directions—first clasped her hands and looked at his father, then took two steps towards Gregor and fell on the floor among her outspread skirts, her face quite hidden on her breast. His father knotted his fist with a fierce expression on his face as if he meant to knock Gregor back into his room, then looked uncertainly round the living room, covered his eyes with his hands and wept till his great chest heaved.

Gregor did not go now into the living room, but leaned against the inside of the firmly shut wing of the door, so that only half his body was visible and his head above it bending sideways to look at the others. The light had meanwhile strengthened; on the other side of the street one could see clearly a section of the endlessly long, dark-gray building opposite—it was a hospital—abruptly punctuated by its row of regular windows; the rain was still falling, but only in large singly discernible and literally singly splashing drops. The breakfast dishes were set out on the table lavishly, for breakfast was the most important meal of the day to Gregor's father, who lingered it out for hours over various newspapers. Right opposite Gregor on the wall hung a photograph of himself on military service, as a lieutenant, hand on sword, a carefree smile on his face, inviting one to respect his uniform and military bearing. The door leading to the hall was open, and one could see that the front door stood open too, showing the landing beyond and the beginning of the stairs going down.

"Well," said Gregor, knowing perfectly that he was the only one who had retained any composure, "I'll put my clothes on at once, pack up my samples and start off. Will you only let me go? You see, sir, I'm not obstinate, and I'm willing to work; traveling is a hard life, but I couldn't live without it. Where are you going, sir? To the office? Yes? Will you give a true account of all this? One can be temporarily incapacitated, but that's just the moment for remembering former services and bearing in mind that later on, when the incapacity has been got over, one will certainly work with all the more industry and concentration. I'm loyally bound to serve the chief, you know that very well. Besides, I have to provide for my parents and my sister. I'm in great difficulties, but I'll get out of them again. Don't make things any worse for me than they are. Stand up for me in the firm. Travelers are not popular there, I know. People think they earn sacks of money and just have a good time. A prejudice there's no particular reason for revising. But you, sir, have a more comprehensive view of affairs than the rest of the staff, yes, let me tell you in confidence, a more comprehensive view than the chief himself, who, being the owner, lets his judgment easily be swayed against one of his employees. And you know very well that the traveler, who is never seen in the office almost the whole year round, can so easily fall a victim to gossip and ill luck and unfounded complaints, which he mostly knows nothing about, except when he comes back exhausted from his rounds, and only then suffers in person from their evil consequences, which he can no longer trace back to the original causes. Sir, sir, don't go away without a word to me to show that you think me in the right at least to some extent!"

But at Gregor's very first words the chief clerk had already backed away and only stared at him with parted lips over one twitching shoulder. And while Gregor was speaking he did not stand still one moment but stole away towards the door, without taking his eyes off Gregor, yet only an inch at a time, as if obeying some secret injunction to leave the room. He was already at the hall, and the suddenness with which he took his last step out of the living room would have made one believe he had burned the sole of his foot. Once in the hall he stretched his right arm before him towards the staircase, as if some supernatural power were waiting there to deliver him.

Gregor perceived that the chief clerk must on no account be allowed to go away in this frame of mind if his position in the firm were not to be endangered to the utmost. His parents did not understand this so well; they had convinced themselves in the course of years that Gregor was settled for life in this firm, and besides they were so preoccupied with their immediate troubles that all foresight had forsaken them. Yet Gregor had this foresight. The chief clerk must be detained, soothed, persuaded and finally won over; the whole future of Gregor and his family depended on it! If only his sister had been there! She was intelligent; she had begun to cry while Gregor was still lying quietly on his back. And no doubt the chief clerk, so partial to ladies, would have been guided by her; she would have shut the door of the flat and in the hall talked him out of his horror. But she was not there, and Gregor would have to handle the situation himself. And without remembering that he was still unaware what powers of movement he possessed, without even remembering that his words in all possibility, indeed in all likelihood, would again be unintelligible, he let go the wing of the door, pushed himself through the opening, started to walk towards the chief clerk, who was already ridiculously clinging with both hands to the railing on the landing; but immediately, as he was feeling for a support, he fell down with a little cry upon all his numerous legs. Hardly was he down when he experienced for the first time this morning a sense of physical comfort; his legs had firm ground under them; they were completely obedient, as he noted with joy; they even strove to carry him forward in whatever direction he chose; and he was inclined to believe that a final relief from all his sufferings was at hand. But in the same moment as he found himself on the floor, rocking with suppressed eagerness to move, not far from his mother, indeed just in front of her, she, who had seemed so completely crushed, sprang all at once to her feet, her arms and fingers outspread, cried: "Help, for God's sake, help!" bent her head down as if to see Gregor better, yet on the contrary kept backing senselessly away; had quite forgotten that the laden table stood behind her; sat upon it hastily, as if in absence of mind, when she bumped into it; and seemed altogether unaware that the big coffee pot beside her was upset and pouring coffee in a flood over the carpet.

"Mother, Mother," said Gregor in a low voice, and looked up at her. The chief clerk, for the moment, had quite slipped from his mind; instead, he could not resist snapping his jaws together at the sight of the streaming coffee. That made his mother scream again. She fled from the table and fell into the arms of his father, who hastened to catch her. But Gregor had now no time to spare for his parents; the chief clerk was already on the stairs; with his chin on the banister he was taking one last backward look. Gregor made a spring, to be as sure as possible of overtaking him; the chief clerk must have divined his intention, for he leaped down several steps and vanished; he was still yelling "Ugh!" and it echoed through the whole staircase.

Unfortunately, the flight of the chief clerk seemed completely to upset Gregor's father, who had remained relatively calm until now, for instead of running after the man himself, or at least not hindering Gregor in his pursuit, he seized in his right hand the walking stick which the chief clerk had left behind on a chair, together with a hat and greatcoat, snatched in his left hand a large newspaper from the table and began stamping his feet and flourishing the stick and the newspaper to drive Gregor back into his room. No entreaty of Gregor's availed, indeed no entreaty was even understood; however humbly he bent his head his father only stamped on the floor the more loudly. Behind his father his mother had torn open a window, despite the cold weather, and was leaning far out of it with her face in her hands. A strong draught set in from the street to the staircase, the window curtains blew in, the newspapers on the table fluttered, stray pages whisked over the floor. Pitilessly Gregor's father drove him back, hissing and crying "Shoo!" like a savage. But Gregor was quite unpracticed in walking backwards, it really was a slow business. If he only had a chance to turn round he could get back to his room at once, but he was afraid of exasperating his father by the slowness of such a rotation and at any moment the stick in his father's hand might hit him a fatal blow on the back or on the head. In the end, however, nothing else was left for him to do since to his horror he observed that in moving backwards he could not even control the direction he took; and so, keeping an anxious eye on his father all the time over his shoulder, he began to turn round as quickly as he could, which was in reality very slowly. Perhaps his father noted his good intentions, for he did not interfere except every now and then to help him in the manoeuvre from a distance with the point of the stick. If only he would have stopped making that unbearable hissing noise! It made Gregor quite lose his head. He had turned almost completely round when the hissing noise so distracted him that he even turned a little the wrong way again. But when at last his head was fortunately right in front of the doorway, it appeared that his body was too broad simply to get through the opening. His father, of course, in his present mood was far from thinking of such a thing as opening the other half of the door, to let Gregor have enough space. He had merely the fixed idea of driving Gregor back into his room as quickly as possible. He would never have suffered Gregor to make the circumstantial preparations for standing up on end and perhaps slipping his way through the door. Maybe he was now making more noise than ever to urge Gregor forward, as if no obstacle impeded him; to Gregor, anyhow, the noise in his rear sounded no longer like the voice of one single father; this was really no joke, and Gregor thrust himself—come what might—into the doorway. One side of his body rose up, he was tilted at an angle in the doorway, his flank was quite bruised, horrid blotches stained the white door, soon he was stuck fast and, left to himself, could not have moved at all, his legs on one side fluttered trembling in the air, those on the other were crushed painfully to the floor—when from behind his father gave him a strong push which was literally a deliverance and he flew far into the room, bleeding freely. The door was slammed behind with the stick, and then at last there was silence.

II

Not until it was twilight did Gregor awake out of a deep sleep, more like a swoon than a sleep. He would certainly have waked up of his own accord not much later, for he felt himself sufficiently rested and well-slept, but it seemed to him as if a fleeting step and a cautious shutting of the door leading into the hall had aroused him. The electric lights in the street cast a pale sheen here and there on the ceiling and the upper surfaces of the furniture, but down below, where he lay, it was dark. Slowly, awkwardly trying out his feelers, which he now first learned to appreciate, he pushed his way to the door to see what had been happening there. His left side felt like one single long, unpleasantly tense scar, and he had actually to limp on his two rows of legs. One little leg, moreover, had been severely damaged in the course of that morning's events—it was almost a miracle that only one had been damaged—and trailed uselessly behind him.

He had reached the door before he discovered what had really drawn him to it: the smell of food. For there stood a basin filled with fresh milk in which floated little sops of white bread. He could almost have laughed with joy, since he was now still hungrier than in the morning, and he dipped his head almost over the eyes straight into the milk. But soon in disappointment he withdrew it again; not only did he find it difficult to feed because of his tender left side—and he could only feed with the palpitating collaboration of his whole body—he did not like the milk either, although milk had been his favorite drink and that was certainly why his sister had set it there for him; indeed it was almost with repulsion that he turned away from the basin and crawled back to the middle of the room.

He could see through the crack of the door that the gas was turned on in the living room, but while usually at this time his father made a habit of reading the afternoon newspaper in a loud voice to his mother and occasionally to his sister as well, not a sound was now to be heard. Well, perhaps his father had recently given up this habit of reading aloud, which his sister had mentioned so often in conversation and in her letters. But there was the same silence all around, although the flat was certainly not empty of occupants. "What a quiet life our family has been leading," said Gregor to himself, and as he sat there motionless staring into the darkness he felt great pride in the fact that he had been able to provide such a life for his parents and sister in such a fine flat. But what if all the quiet, the comfort, the contentment were now to end in horror? To keep himself from being lost in such thoughts Gregor took refuge in movement and crawled up and down the room.

Once during the long evening one of the side doors was opened a little and quickly shut again, later the other side door too; someone had apparently wanted to come in and then thought better of it. Gregor now stationed himself immediately before the living-room door, determined to persuade any hesitating visitor to come in or at least to discover who it might be; but the door was not opened again and he waited in vain. In the early morning, when the doors were locked, they had all wanted to come in; now that he had opened one door and the other had apparently been opened during the day, no one came in and even the keys were on the other side of the doors.

It was late at night before the gas went out in the living room, and Gregor could easily tell that his parents and his sister had all stayed awake until then, for he could clearly hear the three of them stealing away on tiptoe. No one was likely to visit him, not until the morning, that was certain; so he had plenty of time to meditate at his leisure on how he was to arrange his life afresh. But the lofty, empty room in which he had to lie flat on the floor filled him with an apprehension he could not account for, since it had been his very own room for the past five years and with a half-unconscious action, not without a slight feeling of shame, he scuttled under the sofa, where he felt comfortable at once, although his back was a little cramped and he could not lift his head up, and his only regret was that his body was too broad to get the whole of it under the sofa.

He stayed there all night, spending the time partly in a light slumber, from which his hunger kept waking him up with a start, and partly in worrying and sketching vague hopes, which all led to the same conclusion, that he must lie low for the present and, by exercising patience and the utmost consideration, help the family to bear the inconvenience he was bound to cause them in his present condition.

Very early in the morning, it was still almost night, Gregor had the chance to test the strength of his new resolutions, for his sister, nearly fully dressed, opened the door from the hall and peered in. She did not see him at once, yet when she caught sight of him under the sofa—well, he had to be somewhere, he couldn't have flown away, could he?—she was so startled that without being able to help it she slammed the door shut again. But as if regretting her behavior she opened the door again immediately and came in on tiptoe, as if she were visiting an invalid or even a stranger. Gregor had pushed his head forward to the very edge of the sofa and watched her. Would she notice that he had left the milk standing, and not for lack of hunger, and would she bring in some other kind of food more to his taste? If she did not do it of her own accord, he would rather starve than draw her attention to the fact, although he felt a wild impulse to dart out from under the sofa, throw himself at her feet and beg her for something to eat. But his sister at once noticed, with surprise, that the basin was still full, except for a little milk that had been spilt all around it, she lifted it immediately, not with her bare hands, true, but with a cloth and carried it away. Gregor was wildly curious to know what she would bring instead, and made various speculations about it. Yet what she actually did next, in the goodness of her heart, he could never have guessed at. To find out what he liked she brought him a whole selection of food, all set out on an old newspaper. There were old, half-decayed vegetables, bones from last night's supper covered with a white sauce that had thickened; some raisins and almonds; a piece of cheese that Gregor would have called uneatable two days ago; a dry roll of bread, a buttered roll, and a roll both buttered and salted. Besides all that, she set down again the same basin, into which she had poured some water, and which was apparently to be reserved for his exclusive use. And with fine tact, knowing that Gregor would not eat in her presence, she withdrew quickly and even turned the key, to let him understand that he could take his ease as much as he liked. Gregor's legs all whizzed towards the food. His wounds must have healed completely, moreover, for he felt no disability, which amazed him and made him reflect how more than a month ago he had cut one finger a little with a knife and had still suffered pain from the wound only the day before yesterday. Am I less sensitive now? he thought, and sucked greedily at the cheese, which above all the other edibles attracted him at once and strongly. One after another and with tears of satisfaction in his eyes he quickly devoured the cheese, the vegetables and the sauce; the fresh food, on the other hand, had no charms for him, he could not even stand the smell of it and actually dragged away to some little distance the things he could eat. He had long finished his meal and was only lying lazily on the same spot when his sister turned the key slowly as a sign for him to retreat. That roused him at once, although he was nearly asleep, and he hurried under the sofa again. But it took considerable self-control for him to stay under the sofa, even for the short time his sister was in the room, since the large meal had swollen his body somewhat and he was so cramped he could hardly breathe. Slight attacks of breathlessness afflicted him and his eyes were starting a little out of his head as he watched his unsuspecting sister sweeping together with a broom not only the remains of what he had eaten but even the things he had not touched, as if these were now of no use to anyone, and hastily shoveling it all into a bucket, which she covered with a wooden lid and carried away. Hardly had she turned her back when Gregor came from under the sofa and stretched and puffed himself out.

In this manner Gregor was fed, once in the early morning while his parents and the servant girl were still asleep, and a second time after they had all had their midday dinner, for then his parents took a short nap and the servant girl could be sent out on some errand or other by his sister. Not that they would have wanted him to starve, of course, but perhaps they could not have borne to know more about his feeding than from hearsay, perhaps too his sister wanted to spare them such little anxieties wherever possible, since they had quite enough to bear as it was.

Under what pretext the doctor and the locksmith had been got rid of on that first morning Gregor could not discover, for since what he said was not understood by the others, it never struck any of them, not even his sister, that he could understand what they said, and so whenever his sister came into his room he had to content himself with hearing her utter only a sigh now and then and an occasional appeal to the saints. Later on, when she had got a little used to the situation—of course she could never get completely used to it—she sometimes threw out a remark which was kindly meant or could be so interpreted. "Well, he liked his dinner today," she would say when Gregor had made a good clearance of his food; and when he had not eaten, which gradually happened more and more often, she would say almost sadly: "Everything's been left standing again."

But although Gregor could get no news directly, he overheard a lot from the neighboring rooms, and as soon as voices were audible, he would run to the door of the room concerned and press his whole body against it. In the first few days especially there was no conversation that did not refer to him somehow, even if only indirectly. For two whole days there were family consultations at every mealtime about what should be done; but also between meals the same subject was discussed, for there were always at least two members of the family at home, since no one wanted to be alone in the flat and to leave it quite empty was unthinkable. And on the very first of these days the household cook—it was not quite clear what and how much she knew of the situation—went down on her knees to his mother and begged leave to go and when she departed, a quarter of an hour later, gave thanks for her dismissal with tears in her eyes as if for the greatest benefit that could have been conferred on her, and without any prompting swore a solemn oath that she would never say a single word to anyone about what had happened.

Now Gregor's sister had to cook too, helping her mother; true, the cooking did not amount to much, for they ate scarcely anything. Gregor was always hearing one of the family vainly urging another to eat and getting no answer but: "Thanks, I've had all I want," or something similar. Perhaps they drank nothing either. Time and again his sister kept asking his father if he wouldn't like some beer and offered kindly to go and fetch it herself, and when he made no answer suggested that she could ask the concierge to fetch it, so that he need feel no sense of obligation, but then a round "No" came from his father and no more was said about it.

In the course of that very first day Gregor's father explained the family's financial position and prospects to both his mother and his sister. Now and then he rose from the table to get some voucher or memorandum out of the small safe he had rescued from the collapse of his business five years earlier. One could hear him opening the complicated lock and rustling papers out and shutting it again. This statement made by his father was the first cheerful information Gregor had heard since his imprisonment. He had been of the opinion that nothing at all was left over from his father's business; at least his father had never said anything to the contrary, and of course he had not asked him directly. At that time Gregor's sole desire was to do his utmost to help the family to forget as soon as possible the catastrophe which had overwhelmed the business and thrown them all into a state of complete despair. And so he had set to work with unusual ardor and almost overnight had become a commercial traveler instead of a little clerk, with of course much greater chances of earning money, and his success was immediately translated into good round coin which he could lay on the table for his amazed and happy family. These had been fine times, and they had never recurred, at least not with the same sense of glory, although later on Gregor had earned so much money that he was able to meet the expenses of the whole household and did so. They had simply got used to it, both the family and Gregor; the money was gratefully accepted and gladly given, but there was no special uprush of warm feeling. With his sister alone had he remained intimate, and it was a secret plan of his that she, who loved music, unlike himself, and could play movingly on the violin, should be sent next year to study at the Conservatorium, despite the great expense that would entail, which must be made up in some other way. During his brief visits home the Conservatorium was often mentioned in the talks he had with his sister, but always merely as a beautiful dream which could never come true, and his parents discouraged even these innocent references to it; yet Gregor had made up his mind firmly about it and meant to announce the fact with due solemnity on Christmas Day.

Such were the thoughts, completely futile in his present condition, that went through his head as he stood clinging upright to the door and listening. Sometimes out of sheer weariness he had to give up listening and let his head fall negligently against the door, but he always had to pull himself together again at once, for even the slight sound his head made was audible next door and brought all conversation to a stop. "What can he be doing now?" his father would say after a while, obviously turning towards the door, and only then would the interrupted conversation gradually be set going again.

Gregor was now informed as amply as he could wish—for his father tended to repeat himself in his explanations, partly because it was a long time since he had handled such matters and partly because his mother could not always grasp things at once—that a certain amount of investments, a very small amount it was true, had survived the wreck of their fortunes and had even increased a little because the dividends had not been touched meanwhile. And besides that, the money Gregor brought home every month—he had kept only a few dollars for himself—had never been quite used up and now amounted to a small capital sum. Behind the door Gregor nodded his head eagerly, rejoiced at this evidence of unexpected thrift and foresight. True, he could really have paid off some more of his father's debts to the chief with this extra money, and so brought much nearer the day on which he could quit his job, but doubtless it was better the way his father had arranged it.

Yet this capital was by no means sufficient to let the family live on the interest of it; for one year, perhaps, or at the most two, they could live on the principal, that was all. It was simply a sum that ought not to be touched and should be kept for a rainy day; money for living expenses would have to be earned. Now his father was still hale enough but an old man, and he had done no work for the past five years and could not be expected to do much; during these five years, the first years of leisure in his laborious though unsuccessful life, he had grown rather fat and become sluggish. And Gregor's old mother, how was she to earn a living with her asthma, which troubled her even when she walked through the flat and kept her lying on a sofa every other day panting for breath beside an open window? And was his sister to earn her bread, she who was still a child of seventeen and whose life hitherto had been so pleasant, consisting as it did in dressing herself nicely, sleeping long, helping in the housekeeping, going out to a few modest entertainments and above all playing the violin? At first whenever the need for earning money was mentioned Gregor let go his hold on the door and threw himself down on the cool leather sofa beside it, he felt so hot with shame and grief.

Often he just lay there the long nights through without sleeping at all, scrabbling for hours on the leather. Or he nerved himself to the great effort of pushing an armchair to the window, then crawled up over the window sill and, braced against the chair, leaned against the windowpanes, obviously in some recollection of the sense of freedom that looking out of a window always used to give him. For in reality day by day things that were even a little way off were growing dimmer to his sight; the hospital across the street, which he used to execrate for being all too often before his eyes, was now quite beyond his range of vision, and if he had not known that he lived in Charlotte Street, a quiet street but still a city street, he might have believed that his window gave on a desert waste where gray sky and gray land blended indistinguishably into each other. His quick-witted sister only needed to observe twice that the armchair stood by the window; after that whenever she had tidied the room she always pushed the chair back to the same place at the window and even left the inner casements open.

If he could have spoken to her and thanked her for all she had to do for him, he could have borne her ministrations better; as it was, they oppressed him. She certainly tried to make as light as possible of whatever was disagreeable in her task, and as time went on she succeeded, of course, more and more, but time brought more enlightenment to Gregor too. The very way she came in distressed him. Hardly was she in the room when she rushed to the window, without even taking time to shut the door, careful as she was usually to shield the sight of Gregor's room from the others, and as if she were almost suffocating tore the casements open with hasty fingers, standing then in the open draught for a while even in the bitterest cold and drawing deep breaths. This noisy scurry of hers upset Gregor twice a day; he would crouch trembling under the sofa all the time, knowing quite well that she would certainly have spared him such a disturbance had she found it at all possible to stay in his presence without opening the window.

On one occasion, about a month after Gregor's metamorphosis, when there was surely no reason for her to be still startled at his appearance, she came a little earlier than usual and found him gazing out of the window, quite motionless, and thus well placed to look like a bogey. Gregor would not have been surprised had she not come in at all, for she could not immediately open the window while he was there, but not only did she retreat, she jumped back as if in alarm and banged the door shut; a stranger might well have thought that he had been lying in wait for her there meaning to bite her. Of course he hid himself under the sofa at once, but he had to wait until midday before she came again, and she seemed more ill at ease than usual. This made him realize how repulsive the sight of him still was to her, and that it was bound to go on being repulsive, and what an effort it must cost her not to run away even from the sight of the small portion of his body that stuck out from under the sofa. In order to spare her that, therefore, one day he carried a sheet on his back to the sofa—it cost him four hours' labor—and arranged it there in such a way as to hide him completely, so that even if she were to bend down she could not see him. Had she considered the sheet unnecessary, she would certainly have stripped it off the sofa again, for it was clear enough that this curtaining and confining of himself was not likely to conduce to Gregor's comfort, but she left it where it was, and Gregor even fancied that he caught a thankful glance from her eye when he lifted the sheet carefully a very little with his head to see how she was taking the new arrangement.

For the first fortnight his parents could not bring themselves to the point of entering his room, and he often heard them expressing their appreciation of his sister's activities, whereas formerly they had frequently scolded her for being as they thought a somewhat useless daughter. But now, both of them often waited outside the door, his father and his mother, while his sister tidied his room, and as soon as she came out she had to tell them exactly how things were in the room, what Gregor had eaten, how he had conducted himself this time and whether there was not perhaps some slight improvement in his condition. His mother, moreover, began relatively soon to want to visit him, but his father and sister dissuaded her at first with arguments which Gregor listened to very attentively and altogether approved. Later, however, she had to be held back by main force, and when she cried out: "Do let me in to Gregor, he is my unfortunate son! Can't you understand that I must go to him?" Gregor thought that it might be well to have her come in, not every day, of course, but perhaps once a week; she understood things, after all, much better than his sister, who was only a child despite the efforts she was making and had perhaps taken on so difficult a task merely out of childish thoughtlessness.

Gregor's desire to see his mother was soon fulfilled. During the daytime he did not want to show himself at the window, out of consideration for his parents, but he could not crawl very far around the few square yards of floor space he had, nor could he bear lying quietly at rest all during the night, while he was fast losing any interest he had ever taken in food, so that for mere recreation he had formed the habit of crawling crisscross over the walls and ceiling. He especially enjoyed hanging suspended from the ceiling; it was much better than lying on the floor; one could breathe more freely; one's body swung and rocked lightly; and in the almost blissful absorption induced by this suspension it could happen to his own surprise that he let go and fell plump on the floor. Yet he now had his body much better under control than formerly, and even such a big fall did him no harm. His sister at once remarked the new distraction Gregor had found for himself—he left traces behind him of the sticky stuff on his soles wherever he crawled—and she got the idea in her head of giving him as wide a field as possible to crawl in and of removing the pieces of furniture that hindered him, above all the chest of drawers and the writing desk. But that was more than she could manage all by herself; she did not dare ask her father to help her; and as for the servant girl, a young creature of sixteen who had had the courage to stay on after the cook's departure, she could not be asked to help, for she had begged as an especial favor that she might keep the kitchen door locked and open it only on a definite summons; so there was nothing left but to apply to her mother at an hour when her father was out. And the old lady did come, with exclamations of joyful eagerness, which, however, died away at the door of Gregor's room.

Gregor's sister, of course, went in first, to see that everything was in order before letting his mother enter. In great haste Gregor pulled the sheet lower and rucked it more in folds so that it really looked as if it had been thrown accidentally over the sofa. And this time he did not peer out from under it; he renounced the pleasure of seeing his mother on this occasion and was only glad that she had come at all. "Come in, he's out of sight," said his sister, obviously leading her mother in by the hand. Gregor could now hear the two women struggling to shift the heavy old chest from its place, and his sister claiming the greater part of the labor for herself, without listening to the admonitions of her mother who feared she might overstrain herself. It took a long time. After at least a quarter of an hour's tugging his mother objected that the chest had better be left where it was, for in the first place it was too heavy and could never be got out before his father came home; standing in the middle of the room like that it would only hamper Gregor's movements, while in the second place it was not at all certain that removing the furniture would be doing a service to Gregor. She was inclined to think to the contrary; the sight of the naked walls made her own heart heavy, and why shouldn't Gregor have the same feeling, considering that he had been used to his furniture for so long and might feel forlorn without it. "And doesn't it look," she concluded in a low voice—in fact she had been almost whispering all the time as if to avoid letting Gregor, whose exact whereabouts she did not know, hear even the tones of her voice, for she was convinced that he could not understand her words—"doesn't it look as if we were showing him, by taking away his furniture, that we have given up hope of his ever getting better and are just leaving him coldly to himself? I think it would be best to keep his room exactly as it has always been, so that when he comes back to us he will find everything unchanged and be able all the more easily to forget what has happened in between."

On hearing these words from his mother Gregor realized that the lack of all direct human speech for the past two months together with the monotony of family life must have confused his mind, otherwise he could not account for the fact that he had quite earnestly looked forward to having his room emptied of furnishing. Did he really want his warm room, so comfortably fitted with old family furniture, to be turned into a naked den in which he would certainly be able to crawl unhampered in all directions but at the price of shedding simultaneously all recollection of his human background? He had indeed been so near the brink of forgetfulness that only the voice of his mother, which he had not heard for so long, had drawn him back from it. Nothing should be taken out of his room; everything must stay as it was; he could not dispense with the good influence of the furniture on his state of mind; and even if the furniture did hamper him in his senseless crawling round and round, that was no drawback but a great advantage.

Unfortunately his sister was of the contrary opinion; she had grown accustomed, and not without reason, to consider herself an expert in Gregor's affairs as against her parents, and so her mother's advice was now enough to make her determined on the removal not only of the chest and the writing desk, which had been her first intention, but of all the furniture except the indispensable sofa. This determination was not, of course, merely the outcome of childish recalcitrance and of the self-confidence she had recently developed so unexpectedly and at such cost; she had in fact perceived that Gregor needed a lot of space to crawl about in, while on the other hand he never used the furniture at all, so far as could be seen. Another factor might have been also the enthusiastic temperament of an adolescent girl, which seeks to indulge itself on every opportunity and which now tempted Grete to exaggerate the horror of her brother's circumstances in order that she might do all the more for him. In a room where Gregor lorded it all alone over empty walls no one save herself was likely ever to set foot.

And so she was not to be moved from her resolve by her mother, who seemed moreover to be ill at ease in Gregor's room and therefore unsure of herself, was soon reduced to silence and helped her daughter as best she could to push the chest outside. Now, Gregor could do without the chest, if need be, but the writing desk he must retain. As soon as the two women had got the chest out of his room, groaning as they pushed it, Gregor stuck his head out from under the sofa to see how he might intervene as kindly and cautiously as possible. But as bad luck would have it, his mother was the first to return, leaving Grete clasping the chest in the room next door where she was trying to shift it all by herself, without of course moving it from the spot. His mother however was not accustomed to the sight of him; it might sicken her and so in alarm Gregor backed quickly to the other end of the sofa, yet could not prevent the sheet from swaying a little in front. That was enough to put her on the alert. She paused, stood still for a moment and then went back to Grete.

Although Gregor kept reassuring himself that nothing out of the way was happening, but only a few bits of furniture were being changed round, he soon had to admit that all this trotting to and fro of the two women, their little ejaculations and the scraping of furniture along the floor affected him like a vast disturbance coming from all sides at once, and however much he tucked in his head and legs and cowered to the very floor he was bound to confess that he would not be able to stand it for long. They were clearing his room out; taking away everything he loved; the chest in which he kept his fret saw and other tools was already dragged off; they were now loosening the writing desk which had almost sunk into the floor, the desk at which he had done all his homework when he was at the commercial academy, at the grammar school before that, and, yes, even at the primary school—he had no more time to waste in weighing the good intentions of the two women, whose existence he had by now almost forgotten, for they were so exhausted that they were laboring in silence and nothing could be heard but the heavy scuffling of their feet.

And so he rushed out—the women were just leaning against the writing desk in the next room to give themselves a breather—and four times changed his direction, since he really did not know what to rescue first; then on the wall opposite, which was already otherwise cleared, he was struck by the picture of the lady muffled in so much fur and quickly crawled up to it and pressed himself to the glass, which was a good surface to hold on to and comforted his hot belly. This picture at least, which was entirely hidden beneath him, was going to be removed by nobody. He turned his head towards the door of the living room so as to observe the women when they came back.

They had not allowed themselves much of a rest and were already coming; Grete had twined her arm round her mother and was almost supporting her. "Well, what shall we take now?" said Grete, looking round. Her eyes met Gregor's on the wall. She kept her composure, presumably because of her mother, bent her head down to her mother, to keep her from looking up, and said, although in a fluttering, unpremeditated voice: "Come, hadn't we better go back to the living room for a moment?" Her intentions were clear enough to Gregor; she wanted to bestow her mother in safety and then chase him down from the wall. Well, just let her try it! He clung to his picture and would not give it up. He would rather fly in Grete's face.

But Grete's words had succeeded in disquieting her mother, who took a step to one side, caught sight of the huge brown mass on the flowered wallpaper, and before she was really conscious that what she saw was Gregor screamed in a loud, hoarse voice: "Oh God, oh God!" fell with outspread arms over the sofa as if giving up and did not move. "Gregor!" cried his sister, shaking her fist and glaring at him. This was the first time she had directly addressed him since his metamorphosis. She ran into the next room for some aromatic essence with which to rouse her mother from her fainting fit. Gregor wanted to help too—there was still time to rescue the picture—but he was stuck fast to the glass and had to tear himself loose; he then ran after his sister into the next room as if he could advise her, as he used to do; but then had to stand helplessly behind her; she meanwhile searched among various small bottles and when she turned round started in alarm at the sight of him; one bottle fell on the floor and broke; a splinter of glass cut Gregor's face and some kind of corrosive medicine splashed him; without pausing a moment longer Grete gathered up all the bottles she could carry and ran to her mother with them; she banged the door shut with her foot. Gregor was now cut off from his mother, who was perhaps nearly dying because of him; he dared not open the door for fear of frightening away his sister, who had to stay with her mother; there was nothing he could do but wait; and harassed by self-reproach and worry he began now to crawl to and fro, over everything, walls, furniture and ceiling, and finally in his despair, when the whole room seemed to be reeling round him, fell down on to the middle of the big table.

A little while elapsed. Gregor was still lying there feebly and all around was quiet; perhaps that was a good omen. Then the doorbell rang. The servant girl was of course locked in her kitchen, and Grete would have to open the door. It was his father. "What's been happening?" were his first words; Grete's face must have told him everything. Grete answered in a muffled voice, apparently hiding her head on his breast: "Mother has been fainting, but she's better now. Gregor's broken loose." "Just what I expected," said his father, "just what I've been telling you, but you women would never listen." It was clear to Gregor that his father had taken the worst interpretation of Grete's all too brief statement and was assuming that Gregor had been guilty of some violent act. Therefore Gregor must now try to propitiate his father, since he had neither time nor means for an explanation. And so he fled to the door of his own room and crouched against it, to let his father see as soon as he came in from the hall that his son had the good intention of getting back into his room immediately and that it was not necessary to drive him there, but that if only the door were opened he would disappear at once.

Yet his father was not in the mood to perceive such fine distinctions. "Ah!" he cried as soon as he appeared, in a tone which sounded at once angry and exultant. Gregor drew his head back from the door and lifted it to look at his father. Truly, this was not the father he had imagined to himself; admittedly he had been too absorbed of late in his new recreation of crawling over the ceiling to take the same interest as before in what was happening elsewhere in the flat, and he ought really to be prepared for some changes. And yet, and yet, could that be his father? The man who used to lie wearily sunk in bed whenever Gregor set out on a business journey; who welcomed him back of an evening lying in a long chair in a dressing gown; who could not really rise to his feet but only lifted his arms in greeting, and on the rare occasions when he did go out with his family, on one or two Sundays a year and on high holidays, walked between Gregor and his mother, who were slow walkers anyhow, even more slowly than they did, muffled in his old greatcoat, shuffling laboriously forward with the help of his crook-handled stick which he set down most cautiously at every step and, whenever he wanted to say anything, nearly always came to a full stop and gathered his escort around him? Now he was standing there in fine shape; dressed in a smart blue uniform with gold buttons, such as bank messengers wear; his strong double chin bulged over the stiff high collar of his jacket; from under his bushy eyebrows his black eyes darted fresh and penetrating glances; his onetime tangled white hair had been combed flat on either side of a shining and carefully exact parting. He pitched his cap, which bore a gold monogram, probably the badge of some bank, in a wide sweep across the whole room on to a sofa and with the tail-ends of his jacket thrown back, his hands in his trouser pockets, advanced with a grim visage towards Gregor. Likely enough he did not himself know what he meant to do; at any rate he lifted his feet uncommonly high, and Gregor was dumbfounded at the enormous size of his shoe soles. But Gregor could not risk standing up to him, aware as he had been from the very first day of his new life that his father believed only the severest measures suitable for dealing with him. And so he ran before his father, stopping when he stopped and scuttling forward again when his father made any kind of move. In this way they circled the room several times without anything decisive happening; indeed the whole operation did not even look like a pursuit because it was carried out so slowly. And so Gregor did not leave the floor, for he feared that his father might take as a piece of peculiar wickedness any excursion of his over the walls or the ceiling. All the same, he could not stay this course much longer, for while his father took one step he had to carry out a whole series of movements. He was already beginning to feel breathless, just as in his former life his lungs had not been very dependable. As he was staggering along, trying to concentrate his energy on running, hardly keeping his eyes open; in his dazed state never even thinking of any other escape than simply going forward; and having almost forgotten that the walls were free to him, which in this room were well provided with finely carved pieces of furniture full of knobs and crevices—suddenly something lightly flung landed close behind him and rolled before him. It was an apple; a second apple followed immediately; Gregor came to a stop in alarm; there was no point in running on, for his father was determined to bombard him. He had filled his pockets with fruit from the dish on the sideboard and was now shying apple after apple, without taking particularly good aim for the moment. The small red apples rolled about the floor as if magnetized and cannoned into each other. An apple thrown without much force grazed Gregor's back and glanced off harmlessly. But another following immediately landed right on his back and sank in; Gregor wanted to drag himself forward, as if this startling, incredible pain could be left behind him; but he felt as if nailed to the spot and flattened himself out in a complete derangement of all his senses. With his last conscious look he saw the door of his room being torn open and his mother rushing out ahead of his screaming sister, in her underbodice, for her daughter had loosened her clothing to let her breathe more freely and recover from her swoon, he saw his mother rushing towards his father, leaving one after another behind her on the floor her loosened petticoats, stumbling over her petticoats straight to his father and embracing him, in complete union with him—but here Gregor's sight began to fail—with her hands clasped round his father's neck as she begged for her son's life.

III

The serious injury done to Gregor, which disabled him for more than a month—the apple went on sticking in his body as a visible reminder, since no one ventured to remove it—seemed to have made even his father recollect that Gregor was a member of the family, despite his present unfortunate and repulsive shape, and ought not to be treated as an enemy, that, on the contrary, family duty required the suppression of disgust and the exercise of patience, nothing but patience.

And although his injury had impaired, probably forever, his powers of movement, and for the time being it took him long, long minutes to creep across his room like an old invalid—there was no question now of crawling up the wall—yet in his own opinion he was sufficiently compensated for this worsening of his condition by the fact that towards evening the living-room door, which he used to watch intently for an hour or two beforehand, was always thrown open, so that lying in the darkness of his room, invisible to the family, he could see them all at the lamp-lit table and listen to their talk, by general consent as it were, very different from his earlier eavesdropping.

True, their intercourse lacked the lively character of former times, which he had always called to mind with a certain wistfulness in the small hotel bedrooms where he had been wont to throw himself down, tired out, on damp bedding. They were now mostly very silent. Soon after supper his father would fall asleep in his armchair; his mother and sister would admonish each other to be silent; his mother, bending low over the lamp, stitched at fine sewing for an underwear firm; his sister, who had taken a job as a salesgirl, was learning shorthand and French in the evenings on the chance of bettering herself. Sometimes his father woke up, and as if quite unaware that he had been sleeping said to his mother: "What a lot of sewing you're doing today!" and at once fell asleep again, while the two women exchanged a tired smile.

With a kind of mulishness his father persisted in keeping his uniform on even in the house; his dressing gown hung uselessly on its peg and he slept fully dressed where he sat, as if he were ready for service at any moment and even here only at the beck and call of his superior. As a result, his uniform, which was not brand-new to start with, began to look dirty, despite all the loving care of the mother and sister to keep it clean, and Gregor often spent whole evenings gazing at the many greasy spots on the garment, gleaming with gold buttons always in a high state of polish, in which the old man sat sleeping in extreme discomfort and yet quite peacefully.

As soon as the clock struck ten his mother tried to rouse his father with gentle words and to persuade him after that to get into bed, for sitting there he could not have a proper sleep and that was what he needed most, since he had to go on duty at six. But with the mulishness that had obsessed him since he became a bank messenger he always insisted on staying longer at the table, although he regularly fell asleep again and in the end only with the greatest trouble could be got out of his armchair and into his bed. However insistently Gregor's mother and sister kept urging him with gentle reminders, he would go on slowly shaking his head for a quarter of an hour, keeping his eyes shut, and refuse to get to his feet. The mother plucked at his sleeve, whispering endearments in his ear, the sister left her lessons to come to her mother's help, but Gregor's father was not to be caught. He would only sink down deeper in his chair. Not until the two women hoisted him up by the armpits did he open his eyes and look at them both, one after the other, usually with the remark: "This is a life. This is the peace and quiet of my old age." And leaning on the two of them he would heave himself up, with difficulty, as if he were a great burden to himself, suffer them to lead him as far as the door and then wave them off and go on alone, while the mother abandoned her needlework and the sister her pen in order to run after him and help him farther.

Who could find time, in this overworked and tired-out family, to bother about Gregor more than was absolutely needful? The household was reduced more and more; the servant girl was turned off; a gigantic bony charwoman with white hair flying round her head came in morning and evening to do the rough work; everything else was done by Gregor's mother, as well as great piles of sewing. Even various family ornaments, which his mother and sister used to wear with pride at parties and celebrations, had to be sold, as Gregor discovered of an evening from hearing them all discuss the prices obtained. But what they lamented most was the fact that they could not leave the flat which was much too big for their present circumstances, because they could not think of any way to shift Gregor. Yet Gregor saw well enough that consideration for him was not the main difficulty preventing the removal, for they could have easily shifted him in some suitable box with a few air holes in it; what really kept them from moving into another flat was rather their own complete hopelessness and the belief that they had been singled out for a misfortune such as had never happened to any of their relations or acquaintances. They fulfilled to the uttermost all that the world demands of poor people: the father fetched breakfast for the small clerks in the bank, the mother devoted her energy to making underwear for strangers, the sister trotted to and fro behind the counter at the behest of customers, but more than this they had not the strength to do. And the wound in Gregor's back began to nag at him afresh when his mother and sister, after getting his father into bed, came back again, left their work lying, drew close to each other and sat cheek by cheek; when his mother, pointing towards his room, said: "Shut that door now, Grete," and he was left again in darkness, while next door the women mingled their tears or perhaps sat dry-eyed staring at the table.

Gregor hardly slept at all by night or by day. He was often haunted by the idea that next time the door opened he would take the family's affairs in hand again just as he used to do; once more, after this long interval, there appeared in his thoughts the figures of the chief and the chief clerk, the commercial travelers and the apprentices, the porter who was so dull-witted, two or three friends in other firms, a chambermaid in one of the rural hotels, a sweet and fleeting memory, a cashier in a milliner's shop, whom he had wooed earnestly but too slowly—they all appeared, together with strangers or people he had quite forgotten, but instead of helping him and his family they were one and all unapproachable and he was glad when they vanished. At other times he would not be in the mood to bother about his family, he was only filled with rage at the way they were neglecting him, and although he had no clear idea of what he might care to eat he would make plans for getting into the larder to take the food that was after all his due, even if he were not hungry. His sister no longer took thought to bring him what might especially please him, but in the morning and at noon before she went to business hurriedly pushed into his room with her foot any food that was available, and in the evening cleared it out again with one sweep of the broom, heedless of whether it had been merely tasted, or—as most frequently happened—left untouched. The cleaning of his room, which she now did always in the evenings, could not have been more hastily done. Streaks of dirt stretched along the walls, here and there lay balls of dust and filth. At first Gregor used to station himself in some particularly filthy corner when his sister arrived, in order to reproach her with it, so to speak. But he could have sat there for weeks without getting her to make any improvement; she could see the dirt as well as he did, but she had simply made up her mind to leave it alone. And yet, with a touchiness that was new to her, which seemed anyhow to have infected the whole family, she jealously guarded her claim to be the sole caretaker of Gregor's room. His mother once subjected his room to a thorough cleaning, which was achieved only by means of several buckets of water—all this dampness of course upset Gregor too and he lay widespread, sulky and motionless on the sofa—but she was well punished for it. Hardly had his sister noticed the changed aspect of his room that evening than she rushed in high dudgeon into the living room and, despite the imploringly raised hands of her mother, burst into a storm of weeping, while her parents—her father had of course been startled out of his chair—looked on at first in helpless amazement; then they too began to go into action; the father reproached the mother on his right for not having left the cleaning of Gregor's room to his sister; shrieked at the sister on his left that never again was she to be allowed to clean Gregor's room; while the mother tried to pull the father into his bedroom, since he was beyond himself with agitation; the sister, shaken with sobs, then beat upon the table with her small fists; and Gregor hissed loudly with rage because not one of them thought of shutting the door to spare him such a spectacle and so much noise.

Still, even if the sister, exhausted by her daily work, had grown tired of looking after Gregor as she did formerly, there was no need for his mother's intervention or for Gregor's being neglected at all. The charwoman was there. This old widow, whose strong bony frame had enabled her to survive the worst a long life could offer, by no means recoiled from Gregor. Without being in the least curious she had once by chance opened the door of his room and at the sight of Gregor, who, taken by surprise, began to rush to and fro although no one was chasing him, merely stood there with her arms folded. From that time she never failed to open his door a little for a moment, morning and evening, to have a look at him. At first she even used to call him to her, with words which apparently she took to be friendly, such as: "Come along, then, you old dung beetle!" or "Look at the old dung beetle, then!" To such allocutions Gregor made no answer, but stayed motionless where he was, as if the door had never been opened. Instead of being allowed to disturb him so senselessly whenever the whim took her, she should rather have been ordered to clean out his room daily, that charwoman! Once, early in the morning—heavy rain was lashing on the windowpanes, perhaps a sign that spring was on the way—Gregor was so exasperated when she began addressing him again that he ran at her, as if to attack her, although slowly and feebly enough. But the charwoman instead of showing fright merely lifted high a chair that happened to be beside the door, and as she stood there with her mouth wide open it was clear that she meant to shut it only when she brought the chair down on Gregor's back. "So you're not coming any nearer?" she asked, as Gregor turned away again, and quietly put the chair back into the corner.

Gregor was now eating hardly anything. Only when he happened to pass the food laid out for him did he take a bit of something in his mouth as a pastime, kept it there for an hour at a time and usually spat it out again. At first he thought it was chagrin over the state of his room that prevented him from eating, yet he soon got used to the various changes in his room. It had become a habit in the family to push into his room things there was no room for elsewhere, and there were plenty of these now, since one of the rooms had been let to three lodgers. These serious gentlemen—all three of them with full beards, as Gregor once observed through a crack in the door—had a passion for order, not only in their own room but, since they were now members of the household, in all its arrangements, especially in the kitchen. Superfluous, not to say dirty, objects they could not bear. Besides, they had brought with them most of the furnishings they needed. For this reason many things could be dispensed with that it was no use trying to sell but that should not be thrown away either. All of them found their way into Gregor's room. The ash can likewise and the kitchen garbage can. Anything that was not needed for the moment was simply flung into

Gregor's room by the charwoman, who did everything in a hurry; fortunately Gregor usually saw only the object, whatever it was, and the hand that held it. Perhaps she intended to take the things away again as time and opportunity offered, or to collect them until she could throw them all out in a heap, but in fact they just lay wherever she happened to throw them, except when Gregor pushed his way through the junk heap and shifted it somewhat, at first out of necessity, because he had not room enough to crawl, but later with increasing enjoyment, although after such excursions, being sad and weary to death, he would lie motionless for hours. And since the lodgers often ate their supper at home in the common living room, the living-room door stayed shut many an evening, yet Gregor reconciled himself quite easily to the shutting of the door, for often enough on evenings when it was opened he had disregarded it entirely and lain in the darkest corner of his room, quite unnoticed by the family. But on one occasion the charwoman left the door open a little and it stayed ajar even when the lodgers came in for supper and the lamp was lit. They set themselves at the top end of the table where formerly Gregor and his father and mother had eaten their meals, unfolded their napkins and took knife and fork in hand. At once his mother appeared in the other doorway with a dish of meat and close behind her his sister with a dish of potatoes piled high. The food steamed with a thick vapor. The lodgers bent over the food set before them as if to scrutinize it before eating, in fact the man in the middle, who seemed to pass for an authority with the other two, cut a piece of meat as it lay on the dish, obviously to discover if it were tender or should be sent back to the kitchen. He showed satisfaction, and Gregor's mother and sister, who had been watching anxiously, breathed freely and began to smile.

The family itself took its meals in the kitchen. None the less, Gregor's father came into the living room before going into the kitchen and with one prolonged bow, cap in hand, made a round of the table. The lodgers all stood up and murmured something in their beards. When they were alone again they ate their food in almost complete silence. It seemed remarkable to Gregor that among the various noises coming from the table he could always distinguish the sound of their masticating teeth, as if this were a sign to Gregor that one needed teeth in order to eat, and that with toothless jaws even of the finest make one could do nothing. "I'm hungry enough," said Gregor sadly to himself, "but not for that kind of food. How these lodgers are stuffing themselves, and here am I dying of starvation!"

On that very evening—during the whole of his time there Gregor could not remember ever having heard the violin—the sound of violin-playing came from the kitchen. The lodgers had already finished their supper, the one in the middle had brought out a newspaper and given the other two a page apiece, and now they were leaning back at ease reading and smoking. When the violin began to play they pricked up their ears, got to their feet, and went on tiptoe to the hall door where they stood huddled together. Their movements must have been heard in the kitchen, for Gregor's father called out: "Is the violin-playing disturbing you, gentlemen? It can be stopped at once." "On the contrary," said the middle lodger, "could not Fräulein Samsa come and play in this room, beside us, where it is much more convenient and comfortable?" "Oh, certainly," cried Gregor's father, as if he were the violin-player. The lodgers came back into the living room and waited. Presently Gregor's father arrived with the music stand, his mother carrying the music and his sister with the violin. His sister quietly made everything ready to start playing; his parents, who had never let rooms before and so had an exaggerated idea of the courtesy due to lodgers, did not venture to sit down on their own chairs; his father leaned against the door, the right hand thrust between two buttons of his livery coat, which was formally buttoned up; but his mother was offered a chair by one of the lodgers and, since she left the chair just where he had happened to put it, sat down in a corner to one side.

Gregor's sister began to play; the father and mother, from either side, intently watched the movements of her hands. Gregor, attracted by the playing, ventured to move forward a little until his head was actually inside the living room. He felt hardly any surprise at his growing lack of consideration for the others; there had been a time when he prided himself on being considerate. And yet just on this occasion he had more reason than ever to hide himself, since owing to the amount of dust which lay thick in his room and rose into the air at the slightest movement, he too was covered with dust; fluff and hair and remnants of food trailed with him, caught on his back and along his sides; his indifference to everything was much too great for him to turn on his back and scrape himself clean on the carpet, as once he had done several times a day. And in spite of his condition, no shame deterred him from advancing a little over the spotless floor of the living room.

To be sure, no one was aware of him. The family was entirely absorbed in the violin-playing; the lodgers, however, who first of all had stationed themselves, hands in pockets, much too close behind the music stand so that they could all have read the music, which must have bothered his sister, had soon retreated to the window, half-whispering with downbent heads, and stayed there while his father turned an anxious eye on them. Indeed, they were making it more than obvious that they had been disappointed in their expectation of hearing good or enjoyable violin-playing, that they had had more than enough of the performance and only out of courtesy suffered a continued disturbance of their peace. From the way they all kept blowing the smoke of their cigars high in the air through nose and mouth one could divine their irritation. And yet Gregor's sister was playing so beautifully. Her face leaned sideways, intently and sadly her eyes followed the notes of music. Gregor crawled a little farther forward and lowered his head to the ground so that it might be possible for his eyes to meet hers. Was he an animal, that music had such an effect upon him? He felt as if the way were opening before him to the unknown nourishment he craved. He was determined to push forward till he reached his sister, to pull at her skirt and so let her know that she was to come into his room with her violin, for no one here appreciated her playing as he would appreciate it. He would never let her out of his room, at least, not so long as he lived; his frightful appearance would become, for the first time, useful to him; he would watch all the doors of his room at once and spit at intruders; but his sister should need no constraint, she should stay with him of her own free will; she should sit beside him on the sofa, bend down her ear to him and hear him confide that he had had the firm intention of sending her to the Conservatorium, and that, but for his mishap, last Christmas—surely

Christmas was long past?—he would have announced it to everybody without allowing a single objection. After this confession his sister would be so touched that she would burst into tears, and Gregor would then raise himself to her shoulder and kiss her on the neck, which, now that she went to business, she kept free of any ribbon or collar.

"Mr. Samsa!" cried the middle lodger, to Gregor's father, and pointed, without wasting any more words, at Gregor, now working himself slowly forwards. The violin fell silent, the middle lodger first smiled to his friends with a shake of the head and then looked at Gregor again. Instead of driving Gregor out, his father seemed to think it more needful to begin by soothing down the lodgers, although they were not at all agitated and apparently found Gregor more entertaining than the violin-playing. He hurried towards them and, spreading out his arms, tried to urge them back into their own room and at the same time to block their view of Gregor. They now began to be really a little angry, one could not tell whether because of the old man's behavior or because it had just dawned on them that all unwittingly they had such a neighbor as Gregor next door. They demanded explanations of his father, they waved their arms like him, tugged uneasily at their beards, and only with reluctance backed towards their room. Meanwhile Gregor's sister, who stood there as if lost when her playing was so abruptly broken off, came to life again, pulled herself together all at once after standing for a while holding violin and bow in nervelessly hanging hands and staring at her music, pushed her violin into the lap of her mother, who was still sitting in her chair fighting asthmatically for breath, and ran into the lodgers' room to which they were now being shepherded by her father rather more quickly than before. One could see the pillows and blankets on the beds flying under her accustomed fingers and being laid in order. Before the lodgers had actually reached their room she had finished making the beds and slipped out.

The old man seemed once more to be so possessed by his mulish self-assertiveness that he was forgetting all the respect he should show to his lodgers. He kept driving them on and driving them on until in the very door of the bedroom the middle lodger stamped his foot loudly on the floor and so brought him to a halt. "I beg to announce," said the lodger, lifting one hand and looking also at Gregor's mother and sister, "that because of the disgusting conditions prevailing in this household and family"—here he spat on the floor with emphatic brevity—"I give you notice on the spot. Naturally I won't pay you a penny for the days I have lived here; on the contrary I shall consider bringing an action for damages against you, based on claims—believe me—that will be easily susceptible of proof." He ceased and stared straight in front of him, as if he expected something. In fact his two friends at once rushed into the breach with these words: "And we too give notice on the spot." On that he seized the door-handle and shut the door with a slam.

Gregor's father, groping with his hands, staggered forward and fell into his chair; it looked as if he were stretching himself there for his ordinary evening nap, but the marked jerkings of his head, which was as if uncontrollable, showed that he was far from asleep. Gregor had simply stayed quietly all the time on the spot where the lodgers had espied him. Disappointment at the failure of his plan, perhaps also the weakness arising from extreme hunger, made it impossible for him to move. He feared, with a fair degree of certainty, that at any moment the general tension would discharge itself in a combined attack upon him, and he lay waiting. He did not react even to the noise made by the violin as it fell off his mother's lap from under her trembling fingers and gave out a resonant note.

"My dear parents," said his sister, slapping her hand on the table by way of introduction. "things can't go on like this. Perhaps you don't realize that, but I do. I won't utter my brother's name in the presence of this creature, and so all I say is: we must try to get rid of it. We've tried to look after it and to put up with it as far as is humanly possible, and I don't think anyone could reproach us in the slightest."

"She is more than right," said Gregor's father to himself. His mother, who was still choking for lack of breath, began to cough hollowly into her hand with a wild look in her eyes.

His sister rushed over to her and held her forehead. His father's thoughts seemed to have lost their vagueness at Grete's words; he sat more upright, fingering his service cap that lay among the plates still lying on the table from the lodgers' supper, and from time to time looked at the still form of Gregor.

"We must try to get rid of it," his sister now said explicitly to her father, since her mother was coughing too much to hear a word. "It will be the death of both of you, I can see that coming. When one has to work as hard as we do, all of us, one can't stand this continual torment at home on top of it. At least I can't stand it any longer." And she burst into such a passion of sobbing that her tears dropped on her mother's face, where she wiped them off mechanically.

"My dear," said the old man sympathetically, and with evident understanding, "but what can we do?"

Gregor's sister merely shrugged her shoulders to indicate the feeling of helplessness that had now overmastered her during her weeping fit, in contrast to her former confidence.

"If he could understand us," said her father, half questioningly; Grete, still sobbing, vehemently waved a hand to show how unthinkable that was.

"If he could understand us," repeated the old man, shutting his eyes to consider his daughter's conviction that understanding was impossible, "then perhaps we might come to some agreement with him. But as it is—"

"He must go," cried Gregor's sister, "that's the only solution, Father. You must just try to get rid of the idea that this is Gregor. The fact that we've believed it for so long is the root of all our trouble. But how can it be Gregor? If this were Gregor, he would have realized long ago that human beings can't live with such a creature, and he'd have gone away on his own accord. Then we wouldn't have any brother, but we'd be able to go on living and keep his memory in honor. As it is, this creature persecutes us, drives away our lodgers, obviously wants the whole apartment to himself and would have us all sleep in the gutter. Just look, Father," she shrieked all at once, "he's at it again!" And in an access of panic that was quite incomprehensible to Gregor she even quitted her mother, literally thrusting the chair from her as if she would rather sacrifice her mother than stay so near to Gregor, and rushed behind her father, who also rose up, being simply upset by her agitation, and half-spread his arms out as if to protect her.

Yet Gregor had not the slightest intention of frightening anyone, far less his sister. He had only begun to turn round in order to crawl back to his room, but it was certainly a startling operation to watch, since because of his disabled condition he could not execute the difficult turning movements except by lifting his head and then bracing it against the floor over and over again. He paused and looked round. His good intentions seemed to have been recognized; the alarm had only been momentary. Now they were all watching him in melancholy silence. His mother lay in her chair, her legs stiffly outstretched and pressed together, her eyes almost closing for sheer weariness; his father and his sister were sitting beside each other, his sister's arm around the old man's neck.

Perhaps I can go on turning round now, thought Gregor, and began his labors again. He could not stop himself from panting with the effort, and had to pause now and then to take breath. Nor did anyone harass him; he was left entirely to himself. When he had completed the turn-round he began at once to crawl straight back. He was amazed at the distance separating him from his room and could not understand how in his weak state he had managed to accomplish the same journey so recently, almost without remarking it. Intent on crawling as fast as possible, he barely noticed that not a single word, not an ejaculation from his family, interfered with his progress. Only when he was already in the doorway did he turn his head round, not completely, for his neck muscles were getting stiff, but enough to see that nothing had changed behind him except that his sister had risen to her feet. His last glance fell on his mother, who was not quite overcome by sleep.

Hardly was he well inside his room when the door was hastily pushed shut, bolted and locked. The sudden noise in his rear startled him so much that his little legs gave beneath him. It was his sister who had shown such haste. She had been standing ready waiting and had made a light spring forward. Gregor had not even heard her coming, and she cried "At last!" to her parents as she turned the key in the lock.

"And what now?" said Gregor to himself, looking round in the darkness. Soon he made the discovery that he was now unable to stir a limb. This did not surprise him, rather it seemed unnatural that he should ever actually have been able to move on these feeble little legs. Otherwise he felt relatively comfortable. True, his whole body was aching, but it seemed that the pain was gradually growing less and would finally pass away. The rotting apple in his back and the inflamed area around it, all covered with soft dust, already hardly troubled him. He thought of his family with tenderness and love. The decision that he must disappear was one that he held to even more strongly than his sister, if that were possible. In this state of vacant and peaceful meditation he remained until the tower clock struck three in the morning. The first broadening of light in the world outside the window entered his consciousness once more. Then his head sank to the floor of its own accord and from his nostrils came the last faint flicker of his breath.

When the charwoman arrived early in the morning—what between her strength and her impatience she slammed all the doors so loudly, never mind how often she had been begged not to do so, that no one in the whole apartment could enjoy any quiet sleep after her arrival—she noticed nothing unusual as she took her customary peep into Gregor's room. She thought he was lying motionless on purpose, pretending to be in the sulks; she credited him with every kind of intelligence. Since she happened to have the long-handled broom in her hand she tried to tickle him up with it from the doorway. When that too produced no reaction she felt provoked and poked at him a little harder, and only when she had pushed him along the floor without meeting any resistance was her attention aroused. It did not take her long to establish the truth of the matter, and her eyes widened, she let out a whistle, yet did not waste much time over it but tore open the door of the Samsas' bedroom and yelled into the darkness at the top of her voice: "Just look at this, it's dead; it's lying here dead and done for!"

Mr. and Mrs. Samsa started up in their double bed and before they realized the nature of the charwoman's announcement had some difficulty in overcoming the shock of it. But then they got out of bed quickly, one on either side, Mr. Samsa throwing a blanket over his shoulders, Mrs. Samsa in nothing but her nightgown; in this array they entered Gregor's room. Meanwhile the door of the living room opened, too, where Grete had been sleeping since the advent of the lodgers; she was completely dressed as if she had not been to bed, which seemed to be confirmed also by the paleness of her face. "Dead?" said Mrs. Samsa, looking questioningly at the charwoman, although she could have investigated for herself, and the fact was obvious enough without investigation. "I should say so," said the charwoman, proving her words by pushing Gregor's corpse a long way to one side with her broomstick. Mrs. Samsa made a movement as if to stop her, but checked it. "Well," said Mr. Samsa, "now thanks be to God." He crossed himself, and the three women followed his example. Grete, whose eyes never left the corpse, said: "Just see how thin he was. It's such a long time since he's eaten anything. The food came out again just as it went in." Indeed, Gregor's body was completely flat and dry, as could only now be seen when it was no longer supported by the legs and nothing prevented one from looking closely at it.

"Come in beside us, Grete, for a little while," said Mrs. Samsa with a tremulous smile, and Grete, not without looking back at the corpse, followed her parents into their bedroom. The charwoman shut the door and opened the window wide. Although it was so early in the morning a certain softness was perceptible in the fresh air. After all, it was already the end of March.

The three lodgers emerged from their room and were surprised to see no breakfast; they had been forgotten. "Where's our breakfast?" said the middle lodger peevishly to the charwoman. But she put her finger to her lips and hastily, without a word, indicated by gestures that they should go into Gregor's room. They did so and stood, their hands in the pockets of their somewhat shabby coats, around Gregor's corpse in the room where it was now fully light.

At that the door of the Samsas' bedroom opened and Mr. Samsa appeared in his uniform, his wife on one arm, his daughter on the other. They all looked a little as if they had been crying; from time to time Grete hid her face on her father's arm.

"Leave my house at once!" said Mr. Samsa, and pointed to the door without disengaging himself from the women. "What do you mean by that?" said the middle lodger, taken somewhat aback, with a feeble smile. The two others put their hands behind them and kept rubbing them together, as if in gleeful expectation of a fine set-to in which they were bound to come off the winners. "I mean just what I say," answered Mr. Samsa, and advanced in a straight line with his two companions towards the lodger. He stood his ground at first quietly, looking at the floor as if his thoughts were taking a new pattern in his head. "Then let us go, by all means," he said, and looked up at Mr. Samsa as if in a sudden access of humility he were expecting some renewed sanction for this decision. Mr. Samsa merely nodded briefly once or twice with meaningful eyes. Upon that the lodger really did go with long strides into the hall, his two friends had been listening and had quite stopped rubbing their hands for some moments and now went scuttling after him as if afraid that Mr. Samsa might get into the hall before them and cut them off from their leader. In the hall they all three took their hats from the rack, their sticks from the umbrella stand, bowed in silence and quitted the apartment. With a suspiciousness which proved quite unfounded Mr. Samsa and the two women followed them out to the landing; leaning over the banister they watched the three figures slowly but surely going down the long stairs, vanishing from sight at a certain turn of the staircase on every floor and coming into view again after a moment or so; the more they dwindled, the more the Samsa family's interest in them dwindled, and when a butcher's boy met them and passed them on the stairs coming up proudly with a tray on his head, Mr. Samsa and the two women soon left the landing and as if a burden had been lifted from them went back into their apartment.

They decided to spend this day in resting and going for a stroll; they had not only deserved such a respite from work, but absolutely needed it. And so they sat down at the table and wrote three notes of excuse, Mr. Samsa to his board of management, Mrs. Samsa to her employer and Grete to the head of her firm. While they were writing, the charwoman came in to say that she was going now, since her morning's work was finished. At first they only nodded without looking up, but as she kept hovering there they eyed her irritably. "Well?" said Mr. Samsa. The charwoman stood grinning in the doorway as if she had good news to impart to the family but meant not to say a word unless properly questioned. The small ostrich feather standing upright on her hat, which had annoyed Mr. Samsa ever since she was engaged, was waving gaily in all directions. "Well, what is it then?" asked Mrs. Samsa, who obtained more respect from the charwoman than the others. "Oh," said the charwoman, giggling so amiably that she could not at once continue, "just this, you don't need to bother about how to get rid of the thing next door. It's been seen to already." Mrs. Samsa and Grete bent over their letters again, as if preoccupied; Mr. Samsa, who perceived that she was eager to begin describing it all in detail, stopped her with a decisive hand. But since she was not allowed to tell her story, she remembered the great hurry she was in, being obviously deeply huffed: "Bye, everybody," she said, whirling off violently, and departed with a frightful slamming of doors.

"She'll be given notice tonight," said Mr. Samsa, but neither from his wife nor his daughter did he get any answer, for the charwoman seemed to have shattered again the composure they had barely achieved. They rose, went to the window and stayed there, clasping each other tight. Mr. Samsa turned in his chair to look at them and quietly observed them for a little. Then he called out: "Come along, now, do. Let bygones be bygones. And you might have some consideration for me." The two of them complied at once, hastened to him, caressed him and quickly finished their letters.

Then they all three left the apartment together, which was more than they had done for months, and went by tram into the open country outside the town. The tram, in which they were the only passengers, was filled with warm sunshine. Leaning comfortably back in their seats they canvassed their prospects for the future, and it appeared on closer inspection that these were not at all bad, for the jobs they had got, which so far they had never really discussed with each other, were all three admirable and likely to lead to better things later on. The greatest immediate improvement in their condition would of course arise from moving to another house; they wanted to take a smaller and cheaper but also better situated and more easily run apartment than the one they had, which Gregor had selected. While they were thus conversing, it struck both Mr. and Mrs. Samsa, almost at the same moment, as they became aware of their daughter's increasing vivacity, that in spite of all the sorrow of recent times, which had made her cheeks pale, she had bloomed into a pretty girl with a good figure. They grew quieter and half unconsciously exchanged glances of complete agreement, having come to the conclusion that it would soon be time to find a good husband for her. And it was like a confirmation of their new dreams and excellent intentions that at the end of their journey their daughter sprang to her feet first and stretched her young body.

D. H. Lawrence

(1885–1930)

D. H. Lawrence and James Joyce had a great deal in common: both spent most of their lives in exile from their native lands, England and Ireland, both labored to expand the boundaries of the novel, and both paid the price of having their major works banned because of their daring. But they greeted each other's work with hostility and incomprehension. Lawrence was repelled by Joyce's meticulous attention to detail: "'Did I feel a twinge in my little toe, or didn't I?' asks every character of Mr. Joyce," he wrote. Joyce, for his part, had this reaction to Lady Chatterley's Lover *(which he called* "Lady Chatterbox's Lover"*): "I read the first 2 pages of the usual sloppy English, and S. G. [Stuart Gilbert] read me a lyrical bit about nudism in the wood and the end which is a piece of propaganda in favor of something which, outside D. H. L.'s country at any rate, makes all the propaganda for itself." The incomprehension is understandable. Joyce, for all his daring, was fundamentally a classicist who packed as much of the Western literary tradition as he could into his books and then sought to retire behind them, "paring his fingernails." Lawrence was* *the quintessential romantic, renouncing tradition and placing himself squarely before the reader on every page of his books.*

D. H. Lawrence (the initials stand for David Herbert) was born in 1885 at Eastwood, Nottinghamshire, in the middle of the coal-mining area of England. His father was a miner, his mother a cultivated ex-schoolteacher who felt that she had married beneath her; their conflicts are recorded in Sons and Lovers, *Lawrence's first mature novel, and in many other works. Lawrence was able to attend Nottingham High School through a scholarship and, after a short period as a clerk and a pupil-teacher, went to University College, Nottingham. When he was twenty-three, he left college to become a teacher in Croydon and to write. His first novel,* The White Peacock, *appeared in 1911 and his second,* The Trespasser, *in 1912.*

In 1912, the crucial event in Lawrence's personal life occurred: he met Frieda von Richthofen Weekley, the aristocratic German wife of one of his professors at Nottingham. A month later, they eloped to the continent and began a lifetime of wandering and intense, strained involvement with each other that was to form a major subject of Lawrence's writing. After two years in Germany and Italy, Lawrence and Frieda returned to England and were married there in 1914. Sons and Lovers, *an autobiographical novel of his youth, was published in 1913; it was not a financial success but brought Lawrence's name to public attention. A collection of poems also appeared in 1913;* The Prussian Officer and Other Stories *appeared a year later.*

While Lawrence was abroad, he had been working on a long novel which became The Rainbow, *completed in 1915, and* Women in Love, *completed in 1916.* The Rainbow *was published in an expurgated edition in 1916 but was nevertheless officially condemned as obscene;* Women in Love *did not find a publisher for several years. Discouraged by this and other reverses, Lawrence spent the war years in restless movement. He became a friend of Lady Ottoline Morrell, a wealthy patroness of the arts, and hoped that she would help him set up a utopian community called "Rananim." Other friends included the critic John Middleton Murry, his writer-wife Katherine Mansfield, and the mathematician-philosopher Bertrand Russell, whom Lawrence met at Garsington Manor, Lady Ottoline's estate near Oxford. All of these friends appear in veiled form in* Women in Love. *In 1916, the Lawrences settled in a cottage in Cornwall, where they were persecuted by the police because of Lawrence's reputation as a critic of the war and because of Frieda's German background; they were finally forced to leave and settle in London for the duration of the war.*

After it ended, the Lawrences resumed their wanderings, living for short times in Germany, Italy, and Sicily. In 1920, a London publisher finally agreed to reissue The Rainbow *and to publish* Women in Love, *which appeared in 1921.* The Lost Girl *was published in 1920 and* Aaron's Rod *in 1922. The harsh attacks, especially upon* Women in Love, *in the English press hardened Lawrence's resolve to remain abroad; he and Frieda went to Ceylon in 1922 and then on to Australia, where he wrote* Kangaroo *(1923).*

Late in 1922, the Lawrences accepted an invitation from a wealthy American woman, Mabel Dodge Luhan, to join her in Taos, New Mexico; it was the beginning of an infatuation with the American Southwest and Mexico that was to profoundly affect Lawrence's thinking and his late works. In 1923, he left Taos for Mexico, where he studied Aztec civilization and began The Plumed Serpent *(1926). He returned to London late the same year and tried to persuade his friends to return with him to Mexico and establish his long-delayed utopian society. Only one agreed, and the project collapsed when Lawrence became seriously ill in Mexico in the winter of 1924–25 with what was initially diagnosed as malaria but eventually was discovered to be an advanced case of tuberculosis.*

Lawrence's last years were devoted to voluminous writing, carried out as he struggled against his illness. Settling in Florence, he wrote Etruscan Places *(1932), the last of a number of fine travel books, and his last novel,* Lady Chatterley's Lover, *a passionate love story in which Lawrence also summed up his appeal for a new relationship between men and women, which would, he believed, imply a regeneration of society. The novel was published in limited editions in Florence (1928) and Paris (1929) and in an expurgated edition in 1932; it was not to be published in an authentic version until 1959, when it provoked a famous obscenity trial. He also wrote the major stories "The Woman Who Rode Away" (1928) and "The Man Who Died" (1931), a great deal of poetry, and* Apocalypse *(1931), a commentary on the Book of Revelation. He died in 1930 in a tuberculosis sanitarium in the south of France, and his ashes were taken to New Mexico for burial. He was only forty-four.*

Lawrence was an intense, tormented man with a strong messianic streak. Underlying all his writing is a deep discontent with the modern world. He shared with many post-World War I writers the conviction that civilization was on the wrong track, that science, industrialization, and urbanization had produced a race of dehumanized robots, and that the solution lay in reawakening our irrational, emotional layers of being. "My great religion," he wrote, "is a belief in the blood, the flesh, as being wiser than the intellect." But more than most of his contemporaries, he was driven to translate his beliefs into ideologies and programs; a good part of his work is rather shrill polemic, calling for such projects as deindustrialization, the destruction of universal education, and compulsory training for boys in primitive combat.

At the heart of Lawrence's thinking, however, is his exploration of the marriage relationship. His thinking on this subject fluctuated considerably in the course of his career, but generally it tended toward an ambivalent emphasis both upon the violence and power struggles within the marriage bond and upon intimacy as a means of mystic knowledge. A key passage is Birkin's ideal of "star equilibrium" in Women in Love: *"not meeting and mingling, but an equilibrium, a pure balance of two single beings:—as the stars balance each other." Such an ideal combines ecstatic intimacy and an awareness of the essential otherness of the partner, precluding both sterile hostility and parasitic dependency.*

Lawrence was a fluent and prolific writer; he wrote more than sixty-five books, very uneven in quality. His finest achievements are his fourteen novels and his eight volumes of short stories. As a novelist, Lawrence did not share the "classical temper" of his contemporary Joyce; his novels are intense, lyrical, and visionary, with little attempt to create an objective world or autonomous characters. In his best novels— The Rainbow *and* Women in Love*—the reader is swept along by the intensity of their vision, the richness of their imagery, and the ecstatic rhythms of the prose. (Characteristically, Lawrence described even his prose style in sexual terms: the "continual, slightly modified repetition," he wrote, is a "pulsing, frictional to-and-fro which works up to culmination.")*

Many critics, however, have identified Lawrence's best work as his short stories, which combine the lyric qualities of the novels with a tighter discipline and sense of craftsmanship and, frequently, an earthy realism. Recurringly, the major conflict in Lawrence's stories is between the forces of repression and those of the vital unconscious. The protagonist has often stifled his own desires out of a middle-class genteelism, a fear of his own impulses, or too great a vulnerability to the needs of others. In the course of the action, he (or, often, she) must confront the "return of the repressed" and choose the forces of life or the forces of death. Sometimes it is too late, as it is for Elizabeth Bates, standing over the body of her dead husband, whom she realizes she has "known falsely." And sometimes it is not, as it is not for Mabel Pervin and Jack Fergusson, as they move out of the death-pond into each other's arms, "amazed, bewildered, and afraid."

FURTHER READING *(prepared by W. J. R.):* The most comprehensive biography is Edward Nehls's three-volume *D. H. Lawrence: A Composite Biography,* 1957–59, which uses letters, memoirs, and fictional writings to provide the most complex study of the phases of Lawrence's personal and intellectual life. Shorter, readable, and reliable biographies are Harry T. Moore's *The Life and Works of D. H. Lawrence,* 1951; and *The Intelligent Heart,* 1954, revised as *The Priest of Love,* 1974. More personal and less objective biographies include Frieda Lawrence's *Not I, But the Wind,* 1934, an intimate portrait of her husband; Jessie Chambers's *D. H. Lawrence: A Personal Record,* 1935, an account by the real-life Miriam of *Sons and Lovers;* and Richard Aldington's *Portrait of a Genius, But . . . ,* 1950. *A D. H. Lawrence Handbook,* edited by Keith Sagar, 1982, is a valuable general reference work on Lawrence. Major critical introductions to Lawrence's ideas and fiction include Mary Freeman's *D. H. Lawrence: A Basic Study of His Ideas,* 1955, an examination of Lawrence's humanistic rebellion against what he saw as a death-infested traditional culture; Mark Spilka's *The Love Ethic of D. H. Lawrence,* 1963; Julian Moynahan's *The Deed of Life: The Novels and Tales of D. H. Lawrence,* 1963; and H. M. Daleski's *The Forked Flame,* 1965. Less affirmative but equally significant studies of his work are Kingsley Widmer's *The Art of Perversity: D. H. Lawrence's Shorter Fiction,* 1962, which perceives Lawrence's rebellion as asocial, nihilistic, and demonic; Eliseo Vivas's *D. H. Lawrence: The Failure and Triumph of Art,* 1960, particularly valuable for its study of symbolic technique; and Graham Holderness's *D. H. Lawrence: History, Ideology, and Fiction,* 1981, a good study of the cultural, social, and ideological conflicts that underlie Lawrence's fiction. Carol Dix's *D. H. Lawrence and Women,* 1980, defends Lawrence against feminist objections to him. Among useful surveys are Philip Hobsbaum's *A Reader's Guide to D. H. Lawrence,* 1981; Keith Sagar's *The Art of D. H. Lawrence,* 1966; and Ronald Draper's *D. H. Lawrence,* 1964.

ODOUR OF CHRYSANTHEMUMS

I

The small locomotive engine, Number 4, came clanking, stumbling down from Selston with seven full wagons. It appeared round the corner with loud threats of speed, but the colt that it startled from among the gorse,[1] which still flickered indistinctly in the raw afternoon, outdistanced it at a canter. A woman, walking up the railway line to Underwood, drew back into the hedge, held her basket aside, and watched the footplate of the engine advancing. The trucks thumped heavily past, one by one, with slow inevitable movement, as she stood insignificantly trapped between the jolting black wagons and the hedge; then they curved away toward the

[1] A low, spiny shrub that grows on wastelands in Britain.

coppice[2] where the withered oak leaves dropped noiselessly, while the birds, pulling at the scarlet hips[3] beside the track, made off into the dusk that had already crept into the spinney.[4] In the open, the smoke from the engine sank and cleaved to the rough grass. The fields were dreary and forsaken, and in the marshy strip that led to the whimsey,[5] a reedy pit-pond, the fowls had already abandoned their run among the alders, to roost in the tarred fowl-house. The pit-bank[6] loomed up beyond the pond, flames like red sores licking its ashy sides, in the afternoon's stagnant light. Just beyond rose the tapering chimneys and the clumsy black headstocks[7] of Brinsley Colliery. The two wheels were spinning fast up against the sky, and the winding-engine[8] rapped out its little spasms. The miners were being turned up.

The engine whistled as it came into the wide bay of railway lines beside the colliery, where rows of trucks stood in harbour.

Miners, single, trailing and in groups, passed like shadows diverging home. At the edge of the ribbed level of sidings squat[9] a low cottage, three steps down from the cinder track. A large bony vine clutched at the house, as if to claw down the tiled roof. Round the bricked yard grew a few wintry primroses. Beyond, the long garden sloped down to a bush-covered brook course. There were some twiggy apple trees, winter-crack trees, and ragged cabbages. Beside the path hung dishevelled pink chrysanthemums, like pink cloths hung on bushes. A woman came stooping out of the felt-covered fowl-house, halfway down the garden. She closed and padlocked the door, then drew herself erect, having brushed some bits from her white apron.

She was a tall woman of imperious mien, handsome, with definite black eyebrows. Her smooth black hair was parted exactly. For a few moments she stood steadily watching the miners as they passed along the railway: then she turned toward the brook course. Her face was calm and set, her mouth was closed with disillusionment. After a moment she called:

"John!" There was no answer. She waited, and then said distinctly:

"Where are you?"

"Here!" replied a child's sulky voice from among the bushes. The woman looked piercingly through the dusk.

"Are you at that brook?" she asked sternly.

For answer the child showed himself before the raspberry-canes that rose like whips. He was a small, sturdy boy of five. He stood quite still, defiantly.

"Oh!" said the mother, conciliated. "I thought you were down at that wet brook—and you remember what I told you—"

The boy did not move or answer.

"Come, come on in," she said more gently, "it's getting dark. There's your grandfather's engine coming down the line!"

The lad advanced slowly, with resentful, taciturn movement. He was

[2] Thicket. [3] Seed pods of wild roses. [4] Grove of trees.
[5] A piece of mining equipment that raises water or ore out of the mine.
[6] Bank of slag or waste from the mine.
[7] Structure over a mine shaft that houses the surface part of the machinery. A colliery is a coal mine.
[8] Engine that raises and lowers men and materials in the mine. [9] Squatted.

dressed in trousers and waistcoat of cloth that was too thick and hard for the size of the garments. They were evidently cut down from a man's clothes.

As they went slowly toward the house he tore at the ragged wisps of chrysanthemums and dropped the petals in handfuls along the path.

"Don't do that—it does look nasty," said his mother. He refrained, and she, suddenly pitiful, broke off a twig with three or four wan flowers and held them against her face. When mother and son reached the yard her hand hesitated, and instead of laying the flower aside, she pushed it in her apron-band. The mother and son stood at the foot of the three steps looking across the bay of lines at the passing home of the miners. The trundle of the small train was imminent. Suddenly the engine loomed past the house and came to a stop opposite the gate.

The engine-driver, a short man with round grey beard, leaned out of the cab high above the woman.

"Have you got a cup of tea?" he said in a cheery, hearty fashion.

It was her father. She went in, saying she would mash.[10] Directly she returned.

"I didn't come to see you on Sunday," began the little grey-bearded man.

"I didn't expect you," said his daughter.

The engine-driver winced; then, reassuming his cheery, airy manner, he said:

"Oh, have you heard then? Well, and what do you think—?"

"I think it is soon enough," she replied.

At her brief censure the little man made an impatient gesture, and said coaxingly, yet with dangerous coldness:

"Well, what's a man to do? It's no sort of life for a man of my years, to sit at my own hearth like a stranger. And if I'm going to marry again it may as well be soon as late—what does it matter to anybody?"

The woman did not reply, but turned and went into the house. The man in the engine-cab stood assertive, till she returned with a cup of tea and a piece of bread and butter on a plate. She went up the steps and stood near the footplate of the hissing engine.

"You needn't 'a' brought me bread an' butter," said her father. "But a cup of tea"—he sipped appreciatively—"it's very nice." He sipped for a moment or two, then: "I hear as Walter's got another bout on," he said.

"When hasn't he?" said the woman bitterly.

"I heered tell of him in the 'Lord Nelson'[11] braggin' as he was going to spend that b— afore he went: half a sovereign that was."

"When?" asked the woman.

"A' Sat'day night—I know that's true."

"Very likely," she laughed bitterly. "He gives me twenty-three shillings."

"Aye, it's a nice thing, when a man can do nothing with his money but make a beast of himself!" said the grey-whiskered man. The woman turned her head away. Her father swallowed the last of his tea and handed her the cup.

"Aye," he sighed, wiping his mouth. "It's a settler,[12] it is—"

[10] Put the tea in to steep. [11] Name of a pub. [12] Final blow.

He put his hand on the lever. The little engine strained and groaned, and the train rumbled toward the crossing. The woman again looked across the metals. Darkness was settling over the spaces of the railway and trucks: the miners, in grey sombre groups, were still passing home. The winding-engine pulsed hurriedly, with brief pauses. Elizabeth Bates looked at the dreary flow of men, then she went indoors. Her husband did not come.

The kitchen was small and full of firelight; red coals piled glowing up the chimney mouth. All the life of the room seemed in the white, warm hearth and the steel fender reflecting the red fire. The cloth was laid for tea; cups glinted in the shadows. At the back, where the lowest stairs protruded into the room, the boy sat struggling with a knife and a piece of whitewood. He was almost hidden in the shadow. It was half-past four. They had but to await the father's coming to begin tea. As the mother watched her son's sullen little struggle with the wood, she saw herself in his silence and pertinacity; she saw the father in her child's indifference to all but himself. She seemed to be occupied by her husband. He had probably gone past his home, slunk past his own door, to drink before he came in, while his dinner spoiled and wasted in waiting. She glanced at the clock, then took the potatoes to strain them in the yard. The garden and fields beyond the brook were closed in uncertain darkness. When she rose with the saucepan, leaving the drain steaming into the night behind her, she saw the yellow lamps were lit along the high road that went up the hill away beyond the space of the railway lines and the field.

Then again she watched the men trooping home, fewer now and fewer.

Indoors the fire was sinking and the room was dark red. The woman put her saucepan on the hob,[13] and set a batter pudding near the mouth of the oven. Then she stood unmoving. Directly, gratefully, came quick young steps to the door. Someone hung on the latch a moment, then a little girl entered and began pulling off her outdoor things, dragging a mass of curls, just ripening from gold to brown, over her eyes with her hat.

Her mother chid[14] her for coming late from school, and said she would have to keep her at home the dark winter days.

"Why, mother, it's hardly a bit dark yet. The lamp's not lighted, and my father's not home."

"No, he isn't. But it's a quarter to five! Did you see anything of him?"

The child became serious. She looked at her mother with large, wistful blue eyes.

"No, mother, I've never seen him. Why? Has he come up an' gone past, to Old Brinsley? He hasn't, mother, 'cos I never saw him."

"He'd watch that," said the mother bitterly, "he'd take care as you didn't see him. But you may depend upon it, he's seated in the 'Prince o' Wales.'[15] He wouldn't be this late."

The girl looked at her mother piteously.

"Let's have our teas, mother, should we?" said she.

The mother called John to table. She opened the door once more and looked out across the darkness of the lines. All was deserted: she could not hear the winding-engines.

[13] Shelf on the side of a fireplace. [14] Chided; scolded. [15] Another pub.

"Perhaps," she said to herself, "he's stopped to get some ripping[16] done."

They sat down to tea. John, at the end of the table near the door, was almost lost in the darkness. Their faces were hidden from each other. The girl crouched against the fender slowly moving a thick piece of bread before the fire. The lad, his face a dusky mark on the shadow, sat watching her who was transfigured in the red glow.

"I do think it's beautiful to look in the fire," said the child.

"Do you?" said her mother. "Why?"

"It's so red, and full of little caves—and it feels so nice, and you can fair smell it."

"It'll want mending directly," replied the mother, "and then if your father comes he'll carry on and say there never is a fire when a man comes home sweating from the pit. A public-house is always warm enough."

There was silence till the boy said complainingly: "Make haste, our Annie."

"Well, I am doing! I can't make the fire do it no faster, can I?"

"She keeps wafflin'[17] it about so's to make 'er slow," grumbled the boy.

"Don't have such an evil imagination, child," replied the mother.

Soon the room was busy in the darkness with the crisp sound of crunching. The mother ate very little. She drank her tea determinedly, and sat thinking. When she rose her anger was evident in the stern unbending of her head. She looked at the pudding in the fender, and broke out:

"It is a scandalous thing as a man can't even come home to his dinner! If it's crozzled up[18] to a cinder I don't see why I should care. Past his very door he goes to get to a public-house, and here I sit with his dinner waiting for him—"

She went out. As she dropped piece after piece of coal on the red fire, the shadows fell on the walls, till the room was almost in total darkness.

"I canna see," grumbled the invisible John. In spite of herself, the mother laughed.

"You know the way to your mouth," she said. She set the dustpan outside the door. When she came again like a shadow on the hearth, the lad repeated, complaining sulkily:

"I canna see."

"Good gracious!" cried the mother irritably, "you're as bad as your father if it's a bit dusk!"

Nevertheless she took a paper spill[19] from a sheaf on the mantelpiece and proceeded to light the lamp that hung from the ceiling in the middle of the room. As she reached up, her figure displayed itself just rounding with maternity.

"Oh, mother—!" exclaimed the girl.

"What?" said the woman, suspended in the act of putting the lamp glass over the flame. The copper reflector shone handsomely on her, as she stood with uplifted arm, turning to face her daughter.

"You've got a flower in your apron!" said the child, in a little rapture at this unusual event.

[16] Cutting away coal. [17] Waving. [18] Shrivelled and burned.
[19] A long twist of paper.

"Goodness me!" exclaimed the woman, relieved. "One would think the house was afire." She replaced the glass and waited a moment before turning up the wick. A pale shadow was seen floating vaguely on the floor.

"Let me smell!" said the child, still rapturously, coming forward and putting her face to her mother's waist.

"Go along, silly!" said the mother, turning up the lamp. The light revealed their suspense so that the woman felt it almost unbearable. Annie was still bending at her waist. Irritably, the mother took the flowers out from her apron-band.

"Oh, mother—don't take them out!" Annie cried, catching her hand and trying to replace the sprig.

"Such nonsense!" said the mother, turning away. The child put the pale chrysanthemums to her lips, murmuring:

"Don't they smell beautiful!"

Her mother gave a short laugh.

"No," she said, "not to me. It was chrysanthemums when I married him, and chrysanthemums when you were born, and the first time they ever brought him home drunk, he'd got brown chrysanthemums in his button-hole."

She looked at the children. Their eyes and their parted lips were wondering. The mother sat rocking in silence for some time. Then she looked at the clock.

"Twenty minutes to six!" In a tone of fine bitter carelessness she continued: "Eh, he'll not come now till they bring him. There he'll stick! But he needn't come rolling in here in his pit-dirt, for *I* won't wash him. He can lie on the floor—Eh, what a fool I've been, what a fool! And this is what I came here for, to this dirty hole, rats and all, for him to slink past his very door. Twice last week—he's begun now—"

She silenced herself, and rose to clear the table.

While for an hour or more the children played, subduedly intent, fertile of imagination, united in fear of the mother's wrath, and in dread of their father's home-coming, Mrs. Bates sat in her rocking-chair making a "singlet" of thick cream-coloured flannel, which gave a dull wounded sound as she tore off the grey edge. She worked at her sewing with energy, listening to the children, and her anger wearied itself, lay down to rest, opening its eyes from time to time and steadily watching, its ears raised to listen. Sometimes even her anger quailed and shrank, and the mother suspended her sewing, tracing the footsteps that thudded along the sleepers[20] outside; she would lift her head sharply to bid the children "hush," but she recovered herself in time, and the footsteps went past the gate, and the children were not flung out of their play-world.

But at last Annie sighed, and gave in. She glanced at her wagon of slippers, and loathed the game. She turned plaintively to her mother.

"Mother!"—but she was inarticulate.

John crept out like a frog from under the sofa. His mother glanced up.

"Yes," she said, "just look at those shirt-sleeves!"

The boy held them out to survey them, saying nothing. Then somebody

[20] Cross ties of the railway track.

called in a hoarse voice away down the line, and suspense bristled in the room, till two people had gone by outside, talking.

"It is time for bed," said the mother.

"My father hasn't come," wailed Annie plaintively. But her mother was primed with courage.

"Never mind. They'll bring him when he does come—like a log." She meant there would be no scene. "And he may sleep on the floor till he wakes himself. I know he'll not go to work tomorrow after this!"

The children had their hands and faces wiped with a flannel. They were very quiet. When they had put on their nightdresses, they said their prayers, the boy mumbling. The mother looked down at them, at the brown silken bush of intertwining curls in the nape of the girl's neck, at the little black head of the lad, and her heart burst with anger at their father who caused all three such distress. The children hid their faces in her skirts for comfort.

When Mrs. Bates came down, the room was strangely empty, with a tension of expectancy. She took up her sewing and stitched for some time without raising her head. Meantime her anger was tinged with fear.

II

The clock struck eight and she rose suddenly, dropping her sewing on her chair. She went to the stairfoot door, opened it, listening. Then she went out, locking the door behind her.

Something scuffled in the yard, and she started, though she knew it was only the rats with which the place was overrun. The night was very dark. In the great bay of railway lines, bulked with trucks, there was no trace of light, only away back she could see a few yellow lamps at the pit-top, and the red smear of the burning pit-bank on the night. She hurried along the edge of the track, then, crossing the converging lines, came to the stile by the white gates, whence she emerged on the road. Then the fear which had led her shrank. People were walking up to New Brinsley; she saw the lights in the houses; twenty yards further on were the broad windows of the "Prince of Wales," very warm and bright, and the loud voices of men could be heard distinctly. What a fool she had been to imagine that anything had happened to him! He was merely drinking over there at the "Prince of Wales." She faltered. She had never yet been to fetch him, and she never would go. So she continued her walk toward the long straggling line of houses, standing blank on the highway. She entered a passage between the dwellings.

"Mr. Rigley?—Yes! Did you want him? No, he's not in at this minute."

The raw-boned woman leaned forward from her dark scullery and peered at the other, upon whom fell a dim light through the blind of the kitchen window.

"Is it Mrs. Bates?" she asked in a tone tinged with respect.

"Yes. I wondered if your Master was at home. Mine hasn't come yet."

"'Asn't 'e! Oh, Jack's been 'ome an' 'ad 'is dinner an' gone out. 'E's just gone for 'alf an hour afore bedtime. Did you call at the 'Prince of Wales'?"

"No—"

"No, you didn't like—! It's not very nice." The other woman was indulgent. There was an awkward pause. "Jack never said nothink about—about your Mester," she said.

"No!—I expect he's stuck in there!"

Elizabeth Bates said this bitterly, and with recklessness. She knew that the woman across the yard was standing at her door listening, but she did not care. As she turned:

"Stop a minute! I'll just go an' ask Jack if 'e knows anythink," said Mrs. Rigley.

"Oh, no—I wouldn't like to put—!"

"Yes, I will, if you'll just step inside an' see as th' childer doesn't come downstairs and set theirselves afire."

Elizabeth Bates, murmuring a remonstrance, stepped inside. The other woman apologized for the state of the room.

The kitchen needed apology. There were little frocks and trousers and childish undergarments on the squab[21] and on the floor, and a litter of playthings everywhere. On the black American cloth[22] of the table were pieces of bread and cake, crusts, slops, and a teapot with cold tea.

"Eh, ours is just as bad," said Elizabeth Bates, looking at the woman, not at the house. Mrs. Rigley put a shawl over her head and hurried out, saying:

"I shanna be a minute."

The other sat, noting with faint disapproval the general untidiness of the room. Then she fell to counting the shoes of various sizes scattered over the floor. There were twelve. She sighed and said to herself, "No wonder!"—glancing at the litter. There came the scratching of two pairs of feet on the yard, and the Rigleys entered. Elizabeth Bates rose. Rigley was a big man, with very large bones. His head looked particularly bony. Across his temple was a blue scar, caused by a wound got in the pit, a wound in which the coal-dust remained blue like tattooing.

"'Asna 'e come whoam yit?" asked the man, without any form of greeting, but with deference and sympathy. "I couldna say wheer 'e is—'e's non ower theer!"—he jerked his head to signify the "Prince of Wales."

"'E's 'appen gone up to th' 'Yew,'"[23] said Mrs. Rigley.

There was another pause. Rigley had evidently something to get off his mind:

"Ah left 'im finishin' a stint," he began. "Loose-all[24] 'ad bin gone about ten minutes when we com'n away, an' I shouted, 'Are ter comin', Walt?' an' 'e said, 'Go on, Ah shanna be but a'ef a minnit,' so we com'n ter th' bottom, me an' Bowers, thinkin' as 'e wor just behint, an' 'ud come up i' th' next bantle[25]—"

He stood perplexed, as if answering a charge of deserting his mate. Elizabeth Bates, now again certain of disaster, hastened to reassure him:

[21] Couch. [22] Oilcloth.

[23] "Maybe he's gone up to the 'Yew'" (another pub, the Yew Tree).

[24] The signal to stop work. [25] Group.

"I expect 'e's gone up to th' 'Yew Tree,' as you say. It's not the first time. I've fretted myself into a fever before now. He'll come home when they carry him."

"Ay, isn't it too bad!" deplored the other woman.

"I'll just step up to Dick's an' see if 'e *is* theer," offered the man, afraid of appearing alarmed, afraid of taking liberties.

"Oh, I wouldn't think of bothering you that far," said Elizabeth Bates, with emphasis, but he knew she was glad of his offer.

As they stumbled up the entry, Elizabeth Bates heard Rigley's wife run across the yard and open her neighbour's door. At this, suddenly all the blood in her body seemed to switch away from her heart.

"Mind!" warned Rigley. "Ah've said many a time as Ah'd fill up them ruts in this entry, sumb'dy 'll be breakin' their legs yit."

She recovered herself and walked quickly along with the miner.

"I don't like leaving the children in bed, and nobody in the house," she said.

"No, you dunna!" he replied courteously. They were soon at the gate of the cottage.

"Well, I shanna be many minnits. Dunna you be frettin' now, 'e'll be all right," said the butty.[26]

"Thank you very much, Mr. Rigley," she replied.

"You're welcome!" he stammered, moving away. "I shanna be many minnits."

The house was quiet. Elizabeth Bates took off her hat and shawl, and rolled back the rug. When she had finished, she sat down. It was a few minutes past nine. She was startled by the rapid chuff of the winding-engine at the pit, and the sharp whirr of the brakes on the rope as it descended. Again she felt the painful sweep of her blood, and she put her hand to her side, saying aloud, "Good gracious!—it's only the nine o'clock deputy[27] going down," rebuking herself.

She sat still, listening. Half an hour of this, and she was wearied out.

"What am I working myself up like this for?" she said pitiably to herself, "I s'll only be doing myself some damage."

She took out her sewing again.

At a quarter to ten there were footsteps. One person! She watched for the door to open. It was an elderly woman, in a black bonnet and a black woollen shawl—his mother. She was about sixty years old, pale, with blue eyes, and her face all wrinkled and lamentable. She shut the door and turned to her daughter-in-law peevishly.

"Eh, Lizzie, whatever shall we do, whatever shall we do!" she cried.

Elizabeth drew back a little, sharply.

"What is it, mother?" she said.

The elder woman seated herself on the sofa.

"I don't know, child, I can't tell you!"—she shook her head slowly. Elizabeth sat watching her, anxious and vexed.

[26] Buddy or workmate, sometimes with the special meaning of "foreman."
[27] Minor official in the mine; inspector.

"I don't know," replied the grandmother, sighing very deeply. "There's no end to my troubles, there isn't. The things I've gone through, I'm sure it's enough—" She wept without wiping her eyes, the tears running.

"But, mother," interrupted Elizabeth, "what do you mean? What is it?"

The grandmother slowly wiped her eyes. The fountains of her tears were stopped by Elizabeth's directness. She wiped her eyes slowly.

"Poor child! Eh, you poor thing!" she moaned. "I don't know what we're going to do, I don't—and you as you are—it's a thing, it is indeed!"

Elizabeth waited.

"Is he dead?" she asked, and at the words her heart swung violently, though she felt a slight flush of shame at the ultimate extravagance of the question. Her words sufficiently frightened the old lady, almost brought her to herself.

"Don't say so, Elizabeth! We'll hope it's not as bad as that; no, may the Lord spare us that, Elizabeth. Jack Rigley came just as I was sittin' down to a glass afore going to bed, an' 'e said, ''Appen[28] you'll go down th' line, Mrs. Bates. Walt's had an accident. 'Appen you'll go an' sit wi' 'er till we can get him home.' I hadn't time to ask him a word afore he was gone. An' I put my bonnet on an' come straight down, Lizzie. I thought to myself, 'Eh, that poor blessed child, if anybody should come an' tell her of a sudden, there's no knowin' what'll 'appen to 'er.' You mustn't let it upset you, Lizzie—or you know what to expect. How long is it, six months—or is it five, Lizzie? Ay!"—the old woman shook her head—"time slips on, it slips on! Ay!"

Elizabeth's thoughts were busy elsewhere. If he was killed—would she be able to manage on the little pension and what she could earn?—she counted up rapidly. If he was hurt—they wouldn't take him to the hospital—how tiresome he would be to nurse!—but perhaps she'd be able to get him away from the drink and his hateful ways. She would—while he was ill. The tears offered to come to her eyes at the picture. But what sentimental luxury was this she was beginning? She turned to consider the children. At any rate she was absolutely necessary for them. They were her business.

"Ay!" repeated the old woman, "it seems but a week or two since he brought me his first wages. Ay—he was a good lad, Elizabeth, he was, in his way. I don't know why he got to be such a trouble, I don't. He was a happy lad at home, only full of spirits. But there's no mistake he's been a handful of trouble, he has! I hope the Lord'll spare him to mend his ways. I hope so, I hope so. You've had a sight o' trouble with him, Elizabeth, you have indeed. But he was a jolly enough lad wi' me, he was, I can assure you. I don't know how it is. . . ."

The old woman continued to muse aloud, a monotonous irritating sound, while Elizabeth thought concentratedly, startled once, when she heard the winding-engine chuff quickly, and the brakes skirr with a shriek. Then she heard the engine more slowly, and the brakes made no sound. The old woman did not notice. Elizabeth waited in suspense. The mother-in-law talked, with lapses into silence.

"But he wasn't your son, Lizzie, an' it makes a difference. Whatever he was, I remember him when he was little, an' I learned to understand him and to make allowances. You've got to make allowances for them—"

[28] Maybe.

It was half-past ten, and the old woman was saying: "But it's trouble from beginning to end; you're never too old for trouble, never too old for that—" when the gate banged back, and there were heavy feet on the steps.

"I'll go, Lizzie, let me go," cried the old woman, rising. But Elizabeth was at the door. It was a man in pit-clothes.

"They're bringin' 'im, Missis," he said. Elizabeth's heart halted a moment. Then it surged on again, almost suffocating her.

"Is he—is it bad?" she asked.

The man turned away, looking at the darkness:

"The doctor says 'e'd been dead hours. 'E saw 'im i' th' lamp-cabin."

The old woman, who stood just behind Elizabeth, dropped into a chair, and folded her hands, crying: "Oh, my boy, my boy!"

"Hush!" said Elizabeth, with a sharp twitch of a frown. "Be still, mother, don't waken th' children: I wouldn't have them down for anything!"

The old woman moaned softly, rocking herself. The man was drawing away. Elizabeth took a step forward.

"How was it?" she asked.

"Well, I couldn't say for sure," the man replied, very ill at ease. "'E wor finishin' a stint an' th' butties 'ad gone, an' a lot o' stuff come down atop 'n 'im."

"And crushed him?" cried the widow, with a shudder.

"No," said the man, "it fell at th' back of 'im. 'E wor under th' face,[29] an' it niver touched 'im. It shut 'im in. It seems 'e wor smothered."

Elizabeth shrank back. She heard the old woman behind her cry:

"What?—what did 'e say it was?"

The man replied, more loudly: "'E wor smothered!"

Then the old woman wailed aloud, and this relieved Elizabeth.

"Oh, mother," she said, putting her hand on the old woman, "don't waken th' children, don't waken th' children."

She wept a little, unknowing, while the old mother rocked herself and moaned. Elizabeth remembered that they were bringing him home, and she must be ready. "They'll lay him in the parlour," she said to herself, standing a moment pale and perplexed.

Then she lighted a candle and went into the tiny room. The air was cold and damp, but she could not make a fire, there was no fireplace. She set down the candle and looked round. The candlelight glittered on the luster-glasses, on the two vases that held some of the pink chrysanthemums, and on the dark mahogany. There was a cold, deathly smell of chrysanthemums in the room. Elizabeth stood looking at the flowers. She turned away, and calculated whether there would be room to lay him on the floor, between the couch and the chiffonier. She pushed the chairs aside. There would be room to lay him down and to step round him. Then she fetched the old red tablecloth, and another old cloth, spreading them down to save her bit of carpet. She shivered on leaving the parlour; so, from the dresser-drawer she took a clean shirt and put it at the fire to air. All the time her mother-in-law was rocking herself in the chair and moaning.

"You'll have to move from there, mother," said Elizabeth. "They'll be bringing him in. Come in the rocker."

[29] The coal-face, exposed edge of the seam.

The old mother rose mechanically, and seated herself by the fire, continuing to lament. Elizabeth went into the pantry for another candle, and there, in the little penthouse under the naked tiles, she heard them coming. She stood still in the pantry doorway, listening. She heard them pass the end of the house, and come awkwardly down the three steps, a jumble of shuffling footsteps and muttering voices. The old woman was silent. The men were in the yard.

Then Elizabeth heard Matthews, the manager of the pit, say: "You go in first, Jim. Mind!"

The door came open, and the two women saw a collier backing into the room, holding one end of a stretcher, on which they could see the nailed pit-boots of the dead man. The two carriers halted, the man at the head stooping to the lintel of the door.

"Wheer will you have him?" asked the manager, a short, white-bearded man.

Elizabeth roused herself and came from the pantry carrying the unlighted candle.

"In the parlour," she said.

"In there, Jim!" pointed the manager, and the carriers backed round into the tiny room. The coat with which they had covered the body fell off as they awkwardly turned through the two doorways, and the women saw their man, naked to the waist, lying stripped for work. The old woman began to moan in a low voice of horror.

"Lay th' stretcher at th' side," snapped the manager, "an' put 'im on th' cloths. Mind now, mind! Look you now—!"

One of the men had knocked off a vase of chrysanthemums. He stared awkwardly, then they set down the stretcher. Elizabeth did not look at her husband. As soon as she could get in the room, she went and picked up the broken vase and the flowers.

"Wait a minute!" she said.

The three men waited in silence while she mopped up the water with a duster.

"Eh, what a job, what a job, to be sure!" the manager was saying, rubbing his brow with trouble and perplexity. "Never knew such a thing in my life, never! He'd no business to ha' been left. I never knew such a thing in my life! Fell over him clean as a whistle, an' shut him in. Not four foot of space, there wasn't—yet it scarce bruised him."

He looked down at the dead man, lying prone, half naked, all grimed with coal-dust.

"'Sphyxiated,' the doctor said. It *is* the most terrible job I've ever known. Seems as if it was done o' purpose. Clean over him, an' shut 'im in, like a mouse-trap"—he made a sharp, descending gesture with his hand.

The colliers standing by jerked aside their heads in hopeless comment.

The horror of the thing bristled upon them all.

Then they heard the girl's voice upstairs calling shrilly: "Mother, mother—who is it? Mother, who is it?"

Elizabeth hurried to the foot of the stairs and opened the door:

"Go to sleep!" she commanded sharply. "What are you shouting about? Go to sleep at once—there's nothing—"

Then she began to mount the stairs. They could hear her on the boards, and on the plaster floor of the little bedroom. They could hear her distinctly:

"What's the matter now?—what's the matter with you, silly thing?"—her voice was much agitated, with an unreal gentleness.

"I thought it was some men come," said the plaintive voice of the child. "Has he come?"

"Yes, they've brought him. There's nothing to make a fuss about. Go to sleep now, like a good child."

They could hear her voice in the bedroom, they waited whilst she covered the children under the bedclothes.

"Is he drunk?" asked the girl, timidly, faintly.

"No! No—he's not! He—he's asleep."

"Is he asleep downstairs?"

"Yes—and don't make a noise."

There was silence for a moment, then the men heard the frightened child again:

"What's that noise?"

"It's nothing, I tell you, what are you bothering for?"

The noise was the grandmother moaning. She was oblivious of everything, sitting on her chair rocking and moaning. The manager put his hand on her arm and bade her "Sh—sh!!"

The old woman opened her eyes and looked at him. She was shocked by this interruption, and seemed to wonder.

"What time is it?"—the plaintive thin voice of the child, sinking back unhappily into sleep, asked this last question.

"Ten o'clock," answered the mother more softly. Then she must have bent down and kissed the children.

Matthews beckoned to the men to come away. They put on their caps and took up the stretcher. Stepping over the body, they tiptoed out of the house. None of them spoke till they were far from the wakeful children.

When Elizabeth came down she found his mother alone on the parlour floor, leaning over the dead man, the tears dropping on him.

"We must lay him out," the wife said. She put on the kettle, then returning knelt at the feet, and began to unfasten the knotted leather laces. The room was clammy and dim with only one candle, so that she had to bend her face almost to the floor. At last she got off the heavy boots and put them away.

"You must help me now," she whispered to the old woman. Together they stripped the man.

When they arose, saw him lying in the naïve dignity of death, the women stood arrested in fear and respect. For a few moments they remained still, looking down, the old mother whimpering. Elizabeth felt countermanded. She saw him, how utterly inviolable he lay in himself. She had nothing to do with him. She could not accept it. Stooping, she laid her hand on him, in claim. He was still warm, for the mine was hot where he had died. His mother had his face between her hands, and was murmuring incoherently. The old tears fell in succession as drops from wet leaves; the mother was not weeping, merely her tears flowed. Elizabeth embraced the body of her husband, with cheek and lips. She seemed to be listening, inquiring, trying to get some connection. But she could not. She was driven away. He was impregnable.

She rose, went into the kitchen, where she poured warm water into a bowl, brought soap and flannel and a soft towel.

"I must wash him," she said.

Then the old mother rose stiffly, and watched Elizabeth as she carefully washed his face, carefully brushing the big blond moustache from his mouth with the flannel. She was afraid with a bottomless fear, so she ministered to him. The old woman, jealous, said:

"Let me wipe him!"—and she kneeled on the other side drying slowly as Elizabeth washed, her big black bonnet sometimes brushing the dark head of her daughter-in-law. They worked thus in silence for a long time. They never forgot it was death, and the touch of the man's dead body gave them strange emotions, different in each of the women; a great dread possessed them both, the mother felt the lie was given to her womb, she was denied; the wife felt the utter isolation of the human soul, the child within her was a weight apart from her.

At last it was finished. He was a man of handsome body, and his face showed no traces of drink. He was blond, full-fleshed, with fine limbs. But he was dead.

"Bless him," whispered his mother, looking always at his face, and speaking out of sheer terror. "Dear lad—bless him!" She spoke in a faint, sibilant ecstasy of fear and mother love.

Elizabeth sank down again to the floor, and put her face against his neck, and trembled and shuddered. But she had to draw away again. He was dead, and her living flesh had no place against his. A great dread and weariness held her: she was so unavailing. Her life was gone like this.

"White as milk he is, clear as a twelve-month baby, bless him, the darling!" the old mother murmured to herself. "Not a mark on him, clear and clean and white, beautiful as ever a child was made," she murmured with pride. Elizabeth kept her face hidden.

"He went peaceful, Lizzie—peaceful as sleep. Isn't he beautiful, the lamb? Ay—he must ha' made his peace, Lizzie. 'Appen he made it all right, Lizzie, shut in there. He'd have time. He wouldn't look like this if he hadn't made his peace. The lamb, the dear lamb. Eh, but he had a hearty laugh. I loved to hear it. He had the heartiest laugh, Lizzie, as a lad—"

Elizabeth looked up. The man's mouth was fallen back, slightly open under the cover of the moustache. The eyes, half shut, did not show glazed in the obscurity. Life with its smoky burning gone from him, had left him apart and utterly alien to her. And she knew what a stranger he was to her. In her womb was ice of fear, because of this separate stranger with whom she had been living as one flesh. Was this what it all meant—utter, intact separateness, obscured by heat of living? In dread she turned her face away. The fact was too deadly. There had been nothing between them, and yet they had come together, exchanging their nakedness repeatedly. Each time he had taken her, they had been two isolated beings, far apart as now. He was no more responsible than she. The child was like ice in her womb. For as she looked at the dead man, her mind, cold and detached, said clearly: "Who am I? What have I been doing? I have been fighting a husband who did not exist. *He* existed all the time. What wrong have I done? What was that I have been living with? There lies the reality, this man." And her soul died in her for fear: she knew she had never seen him, he had never seen her, they had met in the dark and had fought in the dark, not knowing whom they met nor whom they fought. And now she saw, and turned silent in seeing. For she had been wrong. She had said he was something he was not; she had felt familiar with him. Whereas he was apart all the while, living as she never lived, feeling as she never felt.

In fear and shame she looked at his naked body, that she had known falsely. And he was the father of her children. Her soul was torn from her body and stood apart. She looked at his naked body and was ashamed, as if she had denied it. After all, it was itself. It seemed awful to her. She looked at his face, and she turned her own face to the wall. For his look was other than hers, his way was not her way. She had denied him what he was—she saw it now. She had refused him as himself. And this had been her life, and his life. She was grateful to death, which restored the truth. And she knew she was not dead.

And all the while her heart was bursting with grief and pity for him. What had he suffered? What stretch of horror for this helpless man! She was rigid with agony. She had not been able to help him. He had been cruelly injured, this naked man, this other being, and she could make no reparation. There were the children—but the children belonged to life. This dead man had nothing to do with them. He and she were only channels through which life had flowed to issue in the children. She was a mother—but how awful she knew it now to have been a wife. And he, dead now, how awful he must have felt it to be a husband. She felt that in the next world he would be a stranger to her. If they met there, in the beyond, they would only be ashamed of what had been before. The children had come, for some mysterious reason, out of both of them. But the children did not unite them. Now he was dead, she knew how eternally he was apart from her, how eternally he had nothing more to do with her. She saw this episode of her life closed. They had denied each other in life. Now he had withdrawn. An anguish came over her. It was finished then: it had become hopeless between them long before he died. Yet he had been her husband. But how little!

"Have you got his shirt, 'Lizabeth?"

Elizabeth turned without answering, though she strove to weep and behave as her mother-in-law expected. But she could not, she was silenced. She went into the kitchen and returned with the garment.

"It is aired," she said, grasping the cotton shirt here and there to try. She was almost ashamed to handle him; what right had she or any one to lay hands on him; but her touch was humble on his body. It was hard work to clothe him. He was so heavy and inert. A terrible dread gripped her all the while: that he could be so heavy and utterly inert, unresponsive, apart. The horror of the distance between them was almost too much for her—it was so infinite a gap she must look across.

At last it was finished. They covered him with a sheet and left him lying, with his face bound. And she fastened the door of the little parlour, lest the children should see what was lying there. Then, with peace sunk heavy on her heart, she went about making tidy the kitchen. She knew she submitted to life, which was her immediate master. But from death, her ultimate master, she winced with fear and shame.

THE HORSE DEALER'S DAUGHTER

"Well, Mabel, and what are you going to do with yourself?" asked Joe, with foolish flippancy. He felt quite safe himself. Without listening for an answer, he turned aside, worked a grain of tobacco to the tip of his tongue, and spat it out. He did not care about anything, since he felt safe himself.

The three brothers and the sister sat round the desolate breakfast table, attempting some sort of desultory consultation. The morning's post had given the final tap to the family fortune, and all was over. The dreary dining-room itself, with its heavy mahogany furniture, looked as if it were waiting to be done away with.

But the consultation amounted to nothing. There was a strange air of ineffectuality about the three men, as they sprawled at table, smoking and reflecting vaguely on their own condition. The girl was alone, a rather short, sullen-looking young woman of twenty-seven. She did not share the same life as her brothers. She would have been good-looking, save for the impassive fixity of her face, "bull-dog," as her brothers called it.

There was a confused tramping of horses' feet outside. The three men all sprawled round in their chairs to watch. Beyond the dark holly-bushes that separated the strip of lawn from the highroad, they could see a cavalcade of shire horses[1] swinging out of their own yard, being taken for exercise. This was the last time. These were the last horses that would go through their hands. The young men watched with critical, callous look. They were all frightened at the collapse of their lives, and the sense of disaster in which they were involved left them no inner freedom.

Yet they were three fine, well-set fellows enough. Joe, the eldest, was a man of thirty-three, broad and handsome in a hot, flushed way. His face was red, he twisted his black moustache over a thick finger, his eyes were shallow and restless. He had a sensual way of uncovering his teeth when he laughed, and his bearing was stupid. Now he watched the horses with a glazed look of helplessness in his eyes, a certain stupor of downfall.

The great draught-horses swung past. They were tied head to tail, four of them, and they heaved along to where a lane branched off from the highroad, planting their great hoofs floutingly in the fine black mud, swinging their great rounded haunches sumptuously, and trotting a few sudden steps as they were led into the lane, round the corner. Every movement showed a massive, slumbrous strength, and a stupidity which held them in subjection. The groom at the head looked back, jerking the leading rope. And the cavalcade moved out of sight up the lane, the tail of the last horse bobbed up tight and stiff, held out taut from the swinging great haunches as they rocked behind the hedges in a motion like sleep.

[1] A breed of draft horses, bred in the English Midlands.

Joe watched with glazed hopeless eyes. The horses were almost like his own body to him. He felt he was done for now. Luckily he was engaged to a woman as old as himself, and therefore her father, who was steward of a neighbouring estate, would provide him with a job. He would marry and go into harness. His life was over, he would be a subject animal now.

He turned uneasily aside, the retreating steps of the horses echoing in his ears. Then, with foolish restlessness, he reached for the scraps of bacon-rind from the plates, and making a faint whistling sound, flung them to the terrier that lay against the fender. He watched the dog swallow them, and waited till the creature looked into his eyes. Then a faint grin came on his face, and in a high, foolish voice he said:

"You won't get much more bacon, shall you, you little bitch?"

The dog faintly and dismally wagged its tail, then lowered its haunches, circled round, and lay down again.

There was another helpless silence at the table. Joe sprawled uneasily in his seat, not willing to go till the family conclave was dissolved. Fred Henry, the second brother, was erect, clean-limbed, alert. He had watched the passing of the horses with more sang-froid.[2] If he was an animal, like Joe, he was an animal which controls, not one which is controlled. He was master of any horse, and he carried himself with a well-tempered air of mastery. But he was not master of the situations of life. He pushed his coarse brown moustache upwards, off his lip, and glanced irritably at his sister, who sat impassive and inscrutable.

"You'll go and stop with Lucy for a bit, shan't you?" he asked. The girl did not answer.

"I don't see what else you can do," persisted Fred Henry.

"Go as a skivvy,"[3] Joe interpolated laconically.

The girl did not move a muscle.

"If I was her, I should go in for training for a nurse," said Malcolm, the youngest of them all. He was the baby of the family, a young man of twenty-two, with a fresh, jaunty *museau.*[4]

But Mabel did not take any notice of him. They had talked at her and round her for so many years, that she hardly heard them at all.

The marble clock on the mantelpiece softly chimed the half-hour, the dog rose uneasily from the hearthrug and looked at the party at the breakfast table. But still they sat on in ineffectual conclave.

"Oh, all right," said Joe suddenly, apropos of nothing. "I'll get a move on."

He pushed back his chair, straddled his knees with a downward jerk, to get them free, in horsey fashion, and went to the fire. Still he did not go out of the room; he was curious to know what the others would do or say. He began to charge his pipe, looking down at the dog and saying, in a high, affected voice:

"Going wi' me? Going wi' me are ter? Tha'rt goin' further than tha counts on just now, dost hear?"

The dog faintly wagged its tail, the man stuck out his jaw and covered his pipe with his hands, and puffed intently, losing himself in the tobacco,

[2] Coolness, composure. [3] Servant.
[4] Face (French slang; literally "muzzle" or "snout").

looking down all the while at the dog with an absent brown eye. The dog looked up at him in mournful distrust. Joe stood with his knees stuck out, in real horsey fashion.

"Have you had a letter from Lucy?" Fred Henry asked of his sister.

"Last week," came the neutral reply.

"And what does she say?"

There was no answer.

"Does she *ask* you to go and stop there?" persisted Fred Henry.

"She says I can if I like."

"Well, then, you'd better. Tell her you'll come on Monday."

This was received in silence.

"That's what you'll do then, is it?" said Fred Henry, in some exasperation.

But she made no answer. There was a silence of futility and irritation in the room. Malcolm grinned fatuously.

"You'll have to make up your mind between now and next Wednesday," said Joe loudly, "or else find yourself lodgings on the kerbstone."

The face of the young woman darkened, but she sat on immutable.

"Here's Jack Fergusson!" exclaimed Malcolm, who was looking aimlessly out of the window.

"Where?" exclaimed Joe, loudly.

"Just gone past."

"Coming in?"

Malcolm craned his neck to see the gate.

"Yes," he said.

There was a silence. Mabel sat on like one condemned, at the head of the table. Then a whistle was heard from the kitchen. The dog got up and barked sharply. Joe opened the door and shouted:

"Come on."

After a moment a young man entered. He was muffled up in overcoat and a purple woollen scarf, and his tweed cap, which he did not remove, was pulled down on his head. He was of medium height, his face was rather long and pale, his eyes looked tired.

"Hello, Jack, Well, Jack!" exclaimed Malcolm and Joe. Fred Henry merely said, "Jack."

"What's doing?" asked the newcomer, evidently addressing Fred Henry.

"Same. We've got to be out by Wednesday. Got a cold?"

"I have—got it bad, too."

"Why don't you stop in?"

"*Me* stop in? When I can't stand on my legs, perhaps I shall have a chance." The young man spoke huskily. He had a slight Scotch accent.

"It's a knock-out, isn't it," said Joe, boisterously, "if a doctor goes round croaking with a cold. Looks bad for the patients, doesn't it?"

The young doctor looked at him slowly.

"Anything the matter with *you*, then?" he asked sarcastically.

"Not as I know of. Damn your eyes, I hope not. Why?"

"I thought you were very concerned about the patients, wondered if you might be one yourself."

"Damn it, no, I've never been patient to no flaming doctor, and hope I never shall be," returned Joe.

At this point Mabel rose from the table, and they all seemed to become aware of her existence. She began putting the dishes together. The young doctor looked at her, but did not address her. He had not greeted her. She went out of the room with the tray, her face impassive and unchanged.

"When are you off then, all of you?" asked the doctor.

"I'm catching the eleven-forty," replied Malcolm. "Are you goin' down wi' th' trap, Joe?"

"Yes, I've told you I'm going down wi' th' trap, haven't I?"

"We'd better be getting her in then. So long, Jack, if I don't see you before I go," said Malcolm, shaking hands.

He went out, followed by Joe, who seemed to have his tail between his legs.

"Well, this is the devil's own," exclaimed the doctor, when he was left alone with Fred Henry. "Going before Wednesday, are you?"

"That's the orders," replied the other.

"Where, to Northampton?"

"That's it."

"The devil!" exclaimed Fergusson, with quiet chagrin.

And there was silence between the two.

"All settled up, are you?" asked Fergusson.

"About."

There was another pause.

"Well, I shall miss yer, Freddy, boy," said the young doctor.

"And I shall miss thee, Jack," returned the other.

"Miss you like hell," mused the doctor.

Fred Henry turned aside. There was nothing to say. Mabel came in again, to finish clearing the table.

"What are *you* going to do, then, Miss Pervin?" asked Fergusson. "Going to your sister's, are you?"

Mabel looked at him with her steady, dangerous eyes, that always made him uncomfortable, unsettling his superficial ease.

"No," she said.

"Well, what in the name of fortune *are* you going to do? Say what you mean to do," cried Fred Henry, with futile intensity.

But she only averted her head, and continued her work. She folded the white table-cloth, and put on the chenille cloth.

"The sulkiest bitch that ever trod!" muttered her brother.

But she finished her task with perfectly impassive face, the young doctor watching her interestedly all the while. Then she went out.

Fred Henry stared after her, clenching his lips, his blue eyes fixing in sharp antagonism, as he made a grimace of sour exasperation.

"You could bray[5] her into bits, and that's all you'd get out of her," he said in a small, narrowed tone.

The doctor smiled faintly.

"What's she *going* to do, then?" he asked.

[5] Break.

"Strike me if *I* know!" returned the other.

There was a pause. Then the doctor stirred.

"I'll be seeing you to-night, shall I?" he said to his friend.

"Ay—where's it to be? Are we going over to Jessdale?"

"I don't know. I've got such a cold on me. I'll come round to the Moon and Stars, anyway."

"Let Lizzie and May miss their night for once, eh?"

"That's it—if I feel as I do now."

"All's one—"

The two young men went through the passage and down to the back door together. The house was large, but it was servantless now, and desolate. At the back was a small bricked house-yard, and beyond that a big square, gravelled fine and red, and having stables on two sides. Sloping, dank, winter-dark fields stretched away on the open sides.

But the stables were empty. Joseph Pervin, the father of the family, had been a man of no education, who had become a fairly large horse dealer. The stables had been full of horses, there was a great turmoil and come-and-go of horses and of dealers and grooms. Then the kitchen was full of servants. But of late things had declined. The old man had married a second time, to retrieve his fortunes. Now he was dead and everything was gone to the dogs, there was nothing but debt and threatening.

For months, Mabel had been servantless in the big house, keeping the home together in penury for her ineffectual brothers. She had kept house for ten years. But previously it was with unstinted means. Then, however brutal and coarse everything was, the sense of money had kept her proud, confident. The men might be foul-mouthed, the women in the kitchen might have bad reputations, her brothers might have illegitimate children. But so long as there was money, the girl felt herself established, and brutally proud, reserved.

No company came to the house, save dealers and coarse men. Mabel had no associates of her own sex, after her sister went away. But she did not mind. She went regularly to church, she attended to her father. And she lived in the memory of her mother, who had died when she was fourteen, and whom she had loved. She had loved her father, too, in a different way, depending upon him, and feeling secure in him, until at the age of fifty-four he married again. And then she had set hard against him. Now he had died and left them all hopelessly in debt.

She had suffered badly during the period of poverty. Nothing, however, could shake the curious sullen, animal pride that dominated each member of the family. Now, for Mabel, the end had come. Still she would not cast about her. She would follow her own way just the same. She would always hold the keys of her own situation. Mindless and persistent, she endured from day to day. Why should she think? Why should she answer anybody? It was enough that this was the end, and there was no way out. She need not pass any more darkly along the main street of the small town, avoiding every eye. She need not demean herself any more, going into the shops and buying the cheapest food. This was at an end. She thought of nobody, not even of herself. Mindless and persistent, she seemed in a sort of ecstasy to be coming nearer to her fulfilment, her own glorification, approaching her dead mother, who was glorified.

In the afternoon she took a little bag, with shears and sponge and a small scrubbing brush, and went out. It was a grey, wintry day, with saddened, dark green fields and an atmosphere blackened by the smoke of foundries not far off. She went quickly, darkly along the causeway, heeding nobody, through the town to the churchyard.

There she always felt secure, as if no one could see her, although as a matter of fact she was exposed to the stare of every one who passed along under the churchyard wall. Nevertheless, once under the shadow of the great looming church, among the graves, she felt immune from the world, reserved within the thick churchyard wall as in another country.

Carefully she clipped the grass from the grave, and arranged the pinky white, small chrysanthemums in the tin cross. When this was done, she took an empty jar from a neighbouring grave, brought water, and carefully, most scrupulously sponged the marble head-stone and the coping-stone.

It gave her sincere satisfaction to do this. She felt in immediate contact with the world of her mother. She took minute pains, went through the park in a state bordering on pure happiness, as if in performing this task she came into a subtle, intimate connection with her mother. For the life she followed here in the world was far less real than the world of death she inherited from her mother.

The doctor's house was just by the church. Fergusson, being a mere hired assistant, was slave to the country-side. As he hurried now to attend to the outpatients in the surgery, glancing across the graveyard with his quick eye, he saw the girl at her task at the grave. She seemed so intent and remote, it was like looking into another world. Some mystical element was touched in him. He slowed down as he walked, watching her as if spell-bound.

She lifted her eyes, feeling him looking. Their eyes met. And each looked away again at once, each feeling, in some way, found out by the other. He lifted his cap and passed on down the road. There remained distinct in his consciousness, like a vision, the memory of her face, lifted from the tombstone in the churchyard, and looking at him with slow, large, portentous eyes. It *was* portentous, her face. It seemed to mesmerize him. There was a heavy power in her eyes which laid hold of his whole being, as if he had drunk some powerful drug. He had been feeling weak and done before. Now the life came back into him, he felt delivered from his own fretted, daily self.

He finished his duties at the surgery as quickly as might be, hastily filling up the bottle of the waiting people with cheap drugs. Then, in perpetual haste, he set off again to visit several cases in another part of his round, before teatime. At all times he preferred to walk if he could, but particularly when he was not well. He fancied the motion restored him.

The afternoon was falling. It was grey, deadened, and wintry, with a slow, moist, heavy coldness sinking in and deadening all the faculties. But why should he think or notice? He hastily climbed the hill and turned across the dark green fields, following the black cinder-track. In the distance, across a shallow dip in the country, the small town was clustered like smouldering ash, a tower, a spire, a heap of low, raw, extinct houses. And on the nearest fringe of the town, sloping into the dip, was Oldmeadow, the Pervins' house. He could see the stables and the outbuildings distinctly, as they lay towards him on the slope. Well, he would not go there many more times! Another resource would be lost to him, another place gone: the only company he cared for in the alien, ugly little town he was losing. Nothing but work, drudgery, constant hastening from dwelling to dwelling among the colliers and the ironworkers. It wore him out, but at the same time he had a craving for it. It was a stimulant to him to be in the homes of the working people, moving as it were through the innermost body of their life. His nerves were excited and gratified. He could come so near, into the very lives of the rough, inarticulate, powerfully emotional men and women. He grumbled, he said he hated the hellish hole. But as a matter of fact it excited him, the contact with the rough, strongly-feeling people was a stimulant applied direct to his nerves.

Below Oldmeadow, in the green, shallow, soddened hollow of fields, lay a square, deep pond. Roving across the landscape, the doctor's quick eye detected a figure in black passing through the gate of the field, down towards the pond. He looked again. It would be Mabel Pervin. His mind suddenly became alive and attentive.

Why was she going down there? He pulled up on the path on the slope above, and stood staring. He could just make sure of the small black figure moving in the hollow of the failing day. He seemed to see her in the midst of such obscurity, that he was like a clairvoyant, seeing rather with the mind's eye than with ordinary sight. Yet he could see her positively enough, whilst he kept his eye attentive. He felt, if he looked away from her, in the thick, ugly falling dusk, he would lose her altogether.

He followed her minutely as she moved, direct and intent, like something transmitted rather than stirring in voluntary activity, straight down the field towards the pond. There she stood on the bank for a moment. She never raised her head. Then she waded slowly into the water.

He stood motionless as the small black figure walked slowly and deliberately towards the centre of the pond, very slowly, gradually moving deeper into the motionless water, and still moving forward as the water got up to her breast. Then he could see her no more in the dusk of the dead afternoon.

"There!" he exclaimed. "Would you believe it?"

And he hastened straight down, running over the wet, soddened fields, pushing through the hedges, down into the depression of callous wintry obscurity. It took him several minutes to come to the pond. He stood on the bank, breathing heavily. He could see nothing. His eyes seemed to penetrate the dead water. Yes, perhaps that was the dark shadow of her black clothing beneath the surface of the water.

He slowly ventured into the pond. The bottom was deep, soft clay, he sank in, and the water clasped dead cold round his legs. As he stirred he could smell the cold, rotten clay that fouled up into the water. It was objectionable in his lungs. Still, repelled and yet not heeding, he moved deeper into the pond. The cold water rose over his thighs, over his loins, upon his abdomen. The lower part of his body was all sunk in the hideous cold element. And the bottom was so deeply soft and uncertain, he was afraid of pitching with his mouth underneath. He could not swim, and was afraid.

He crouched a little, spreading his hands under the water and moving them round, trying to feel for her. The dead cold pond swayed upon his chest. He moved again, a little deeper, and again, with his hands underneath, he felt all around under the water. And he touched her clothing. But it evaded his fingers. He made a desperate effort to grasp it.

And so doing he lost his balance and went under, horribly, suffocating in the foul earthy water, struggling madly for a few moments. At last, after what seemed an eternity, he got his footing, rose again into the air and looked around. He gasped, and knew he was in the world. Then he looked at the water. She had risen near him. He grasped her clothing, and drawing her nearer, turned to take his way to land again.

He went very slowly, carefully, absorbed in the slow progress. He rose higher, climbing out of the pond. The water was now only about his legs; he was thankful, full of relief to be out of the clutches of the pond. He lifted her and staggered on to the bank, out of the horror of wet, grey clay.

He laid her down on the bank. She was quite unconscious and running with water. He made the water come from her mouth, he worked to restore her. He did not have to work very long before he could feel the breathing begin again in her; she was breathing naturally. He worked a little longer. He could feel her live beneath his hands; she was coming back. He wiped her face, wrapped her in his overcoat, looked round into the dim, dark grey world, then lifted her and staggered down the bank and across the fields.

It seemed an unthinkably long way, and his burden so heavy he felt he would never get to the house. But at last he was in the stable-yard, and then in the house-yard. He opened the door and went into the house. In the kitchen he laid her down on the hearthrug, and called. The house was empty. But the fire was burning in the grate.

Then again he kneeled to attend to her. She was breathing regularly, her eyes were wide open and as if conscious, but there seemed something missing in her look. She was conscious in herself, but unconscious of her surroundings.

He ran upstairs, took blankets from a bed, and put them before the fire to warm. Then he removed her saturated, earthy-smelling clothing, rubbed her dry with a towel, and wrapped her naked in the blankets. Then he went into the dining-room, to look for spirits. There was a little whisky. He drank a gulp himself, and put some into her mouth.

The effect was instantaneous. She looked full into his face, as if she had been seeing him for some time, and yet had only just become conscious of him.

"Dr. Fergusson?" she said.

"What?" he answered.

He was divesting himself of his coat, intending to find some dry clothing upstairs. He could not bear the smell of the dead, clayey water, and he was mortally afraid for his own health.

"What did I do?" she asked.

"Walked into the pond," he replied. He had begun to shudder like one sick, and could hardly attend to her. Her eyes remained full on him, he seemed to be going dark in his mind, looking back at her helplessly. The shuddering became quieter in him, his life came back in him, dark and unknowing, but strong again.

"Was I out of my mind?" she asked, while her eyes were fixed on him all the time.

"Maybe, for the moment," he replied. He felt quiet, because his strength had come back. The strange fretful strain had left him.

"Am I out of my mind now?" she asked.

"Are you?" he reflected a moment. "No," he answered truthfully, "I don't see that you are." He turned his face aside. He was afraid now, because he felt dazed, and felt dimly that her power was stronger than his, in this issue. And she continued to look at him fixedly all the time. "Can you tell me where I shall find some dry things to put on?" he asked.

"Did you dive into the pond for me?" she asked.

"No," he answered. "I walked in. But I went in overhead as well."

There was silence for a moment. He hesitated. He very much wanted to go upstairs to get into dry clothing. But there was another desire in him. And she seemed to hold him. His will seemed to have gone to sleep, and left him, standing there slack before her. But he felt warm inside himself. He did not shudder at all, though his clothes were sodden on him.

"Why did you?" she asked.

"Because I didn't want you to do such a foolish thing," he said.

"It wasn't foolish," she said, still gazing at him as she lay on the floor, with a sofa cushion under her head. "It was the right thing to do. *I* knew best, then."

"I'll go and shift these wet things," he said. But still he had not the power to move out of her presence, until she sent him. It was as if she had the life of his body in her hands, and he could not extricate himself. Or perhaps he did not want to.

Suddenly she sat up. Then she became aware of her own immediate condition. She felt the blankets about her, she knew her own limbs. For a moment it seemed as if her reason were going. She looked round, with wild eye, as if seeking something. He stood still with fear. She saw her clothing lying scattered.

"Who undressed me?" she asked, her eyes resting full and inevitable on his face.

"I did," he replied, "to bring you round."

For some moments she sat and gazed at him awfully, her lips parted.

"Do you love me, then?" she asked.

He only stood and stared at her, fascinated. His soul seemed to melt.

She shuffled forward on her knees, and put her arms round him, round his legs, as he stood there, pressing her breasts against his knees and thighs, clutching him with strange, convulsive certainty, pressing his thighs against her, drawing him to her face, her throat, as she looked up at him with flaring, humble eyes of transfiguration, triumphant in first possession.

"You love me," she murmured, in strange transport, yearning and triumphant and confident. "You love me. I know you love me, I know."

And she was passionately kissing his knees, through the wet clothing, passionately and indiscriminately kissing his knees, his legs, as if unaware of everything.

He looked down at the tangled wet hair, the wild, bare, animal shoulders. He was amazed, bewildered, and afraid. He had never thought of loving her. He had never wanted to love her. When he rescued her and restored her, he was a doctor, and she was a patient. He had had no single personal thought of her. Nay, this introduction of the personal element was very distasteful to him, a violation of his professional honour. It was horrible to have her there embracing his knees. It was horrible. He revolted from it, violently. And yet—and yet—he had not the power to break away.

She looked at him again, with the same supplication of powerful love, and that same transcendent, frightening light of triumph. In view of the delicate flame which seemed to come from her face like a light, he was powerless. And yet he had never intended to love her. He had never intended. And something stubborn in him could not give way.

"You love me," she repeated, in a murmur of deep rhapsodic assurance. "You love me."

Her hands were drawing him, drawing him down to her. He was afraid, even a little horrified. For he had, really, no intention of loving her. Yet her hands were drawing him towards her. He put out his hand quickly to steady himself, and grasped her bare shoulder. A flame seemed to burn the hand that grasped her soft shoulder. He had no intention of loving her: his whole will was against his yielding. It was horrible. And yet wonderful was the touch of her shoulders, beautiful the shining of her face. Was she perhaps mad? He had a horror of yielding to her. Yet something in him ached also.

He had been staring away at the door, away from her. But his hand remained on her shoulder. She had gone suddenly very still. He looked down at her. Her eyes were now wide with fear, with doubt, the light was dying from her face, a shadow of terrible greyness was returning. He could not bear the touch of her eyes' question upon him, and the look of death behind the question.

With an inward groan he gave way, and let his heart yield towards her. A sudden gentle smile came on his face. And her eyes, which never left his face, slowly, slowly filled with tears. He watched the strange water rise in her eyes, like some slow fountain coming up. And his heart seemed to burn and melt away in his breast.

He could not bear to look at her any more. He dropped on his knees, caught her head with his arms and pressed her face against his throat. She was very still. His heart, which seemed to have broken, was burning with a kind of agony in his breast. And he felt her slow, hot tears wetting his throat. But he could not move.

He felt the hot tears wet his neck and the hollows of his neck, and he remained motionless, suspended through one of man's eternities. Only now it had become indispensable to him to have her face pressed close to him; he could never let her go again. He could never let her head go away from the close clutch of his arm. He wanted to remain like that for ever, with his heart hurting him in a pain that was also life to him. Without knowing, he was looking down on her damp, soft brown hair.

Then, as it were suddenly, he smelt the horrid stagnant smell of that water. And at the same moment she drew away from him and looked at him. Her eyes were wistful and unfathomable. He was afraid of them, and he fell to kissing her, not knowing what he was doing. He wanted her eyes not to have that terrible, wistful, unfathomable look.

When she turned her face to him again, a faint delicate flush was glowing, and there was again dawning that terrible shining of joy in her eyes, which really terrified him, and yet which he now wanted to see, because he feared the look of doubt still more.

"You love me?" she said, rather faltering.

"Yes." The word cost him a painful effort. Not because it wasn't true. But because it was too newly true, the *saying* seemed to tear open again his newly-torn heart. And he hardly wanted it to be true, even now.

She lifted her face to him, and he bent forward and kissed her on the mouth, gently, with the one kiss that is an eternal pledge. And as he kissed her his heart strained again in his breast. He never intended to love her. But now it was over. He had crossed over the gulf to her, and all that he had left behind had shrivelled and become void.

After the kiss, her eyes again slowly filled with tears. She sat still, away from him, with her face drooped aside, and her hands folded in her lap. The tears fell very slowly. There was complete silence. He too sat there motionless and silent on the hearthrug. The strange pain of his heart that was broken seemed to consume him. That he should love her? That this was love! That he should be ripped open in this way! Him, a doctor! How they would all jeer if they knew! It was agony to him to think they might know.

In the curious naked pain of the thought he looked again to her. She was sitting there drooped into a muse. He saw a tear fall, and his heart flared hot. He saw for the first time that one of her shoulders was quite uncovered, one arm bare, he could see one of her small breasts; dimly, because it had become almost dark in the room.

"Why are you crying?" he asked, in an altered voice.

She looked up at him, and behind her tears the consciousness of her situation for the first time brought a dark look of shame to her eyes.

"I'm not crying, really," she said, watching him half frightened.

He reached his hand, and softly closed it on her bare arm.

"I love you! I love you!" he said in a soft, low vibrating voice, unlike himself.

She shrank, and dropped her head. The soft, penetrating grip of his hand on her arm distressed her. She looked up at him.

"I want to go," she said. "I want to go and get you some dry things."

"Why?" he said. "I'm all right."

"But I want to go," she said. "And I want you to change your things."

He released her arm, and she wrapped herself in the blanket, looking at him rather frightened. And still she did not rise.

"Kiss me," she said wistfully.

He kissed her, but briefly, half in anger.

Then, after a second, she rose nervously, all mixed up in the blanket. He watched her in her confusion, as she tried to extricate herself and wrap herself up so that she could walk. He watched her relentlessly, as she knew. And as she went, the blanket trailing, and as he saw a glimpse of her feet and her white leg, he tried to remember her as she was when he had wrapped her in the blanket. But then he didn't want to remember, because she had been nothing to him then, and his nature revolted from remembering her as she was when she was nothing to him.

A tumbling, muffled noise from within the dark house startled him. Then he heard her voice:—"There are clothes." He rose and went to the foot of the stairs, and gathered up the garments she had thrown down. Then he came back to the fire, to rub himself down and dress. He grinned at his own appearance when he had finished.

The fire was sinking, so he put on coal. The house was now quite dark, save for the light of a street-lamp that shone in faintly from beyond the holly trees. He lit the gas with matches he found on the mantelpiece. Then he emptied the pockets of his own clothes, and threw all his wet things in a heap into the scullery. After which he gathered up her sodden clothes, gently, and put them in a separate heap on the copper-top in the scullery.

It was six o'clock on the clock. His own watch had stopped. He ought to go back to the surgery. He waited, and still she did not come down. So he went to the foot of the stairs and called:

"I shall have to go."

Almost immediately he heard her coming down. She had on her best dress of black voile, and her hair was tidy, but still damp. She looked at him—and in spite of herself, smiled.

"I don't like you in those clothes," she said.

"Do I look a sight?" he answered.

They were shy of one another.

"I'll make you some tea," she said.

"No, I must go."

"Must you?" And she looked at him again with the wide, strained, doubtful eyes. And again, from the pain of his breast, he knew how he loved her. He went and bent to kiss her, gently, passionately, with his heart's painful kiss.

"And my hair smells so horrible," she murmured in distraction. "And I'm so awful, I'm so awful! Oh, no, I'm too awful." And she broke into bitter, heartbroken sobbing. "You can't want to love me, I'm horrible."

"Don't be silly, don't be silly," he said, trying to comfort her, kissing her, holding her in his arms. "I want you, I want to marry you, we're going to be married, quickly, quickly—tomorrow if I can."

But she only sobbed terribly, and cried:

"I feel awful. I feel awful. I feel I'm horrible to you."

"No, I want you, I want you," was all he answered, blindly, with that terrible intonation which frightened her almost more than her horror lest he should *not* want her.

T. S. Eliot

(1888–1965)

"Our civilization comprehends great variety and complexity, and this variety and complexity, playing upon a refined sensibility, must produce various and complex results. The poet must become more and more comprehensive, more allusive, more indirect, in order to force, to dislocate if necessary, language into his meaning." These lines, from T. S. Eliot's 1921 essay on "The Metaphysical Poets," come as close to describing and justifying the sometimes frustrating difficulties of modern poetry as any short statement could. And the image of the modern poet that they present—a "refined sensibility" bombarded by "great variety and complexity" and shattering and distorting his language in order to express that complexity—is a precise description of the quintessential modern poet, Eliot himself. As poet, critic, editor, and playwright, Eliot exerted an enormous influence on literature between the two wars, not only in England but internationally; the critic Richard Ellmann has pointed out that "for a span of years the latest verses in Arabic, Swahili, or Japanese were far more likely to be written like Eliot than like earlier poets in those languages or like other poets in English." And if contemporary poets are not so directly overwhelmed by Eliot's magisterial presence, they still build upon the general foundations that he laid down early in the century.

Thomas Stearns Eliot was born in St. Louis, Missouri, in 1888, into a prosperous, prominent family that had moved to Missouri from Massachusetts two generations before. Eliot's grandfather, who had come to St. Louis just after graduation from Harvard Divinity School, founded the first Unitarian church in St. Louis and established Washington University there. His son, the poet's father, departed somewhat from family tradition by going into business; he became a prosperous brick manufacturer. Eliot's mother, Charlotte Champe Stearns, had literary interests; she wrote poetry, a biography of her father-in-law, and a verse drama about the fifteenth-century religious reformer Savonarola. Many of Eliot's mature beliefs—his respect for tradition, his religious leanings, his class biases—can be traced back to his displaced New England family.

Eliot was educated at private schools in St. Louis and Massachusetts and then at Harvard, where he enrolled in 1906 and received a degree in philosophy only three years later. Two of his Harvard teachers, George Santayana and Irving Babbitt, exercised a continuing influence upon him; from Babbitt, especially, he acquired a strong anti-Romantic attitude. The following five years were full of turbulence and indecision for Eliot. He enrolled in graduate school in philosophy at Harvard where he was a teaching assistant for a year and then went to Paris to attend lectures by the philosopher Henri Bergson. While in France he read widely in the French Symbolist poets. The Symbolist movement, which had as its goal the expression of unique, personal, emotional responses at given moments through symbols that were often indefinite, apparently illogical, and sometimes private in their meaning, was to be one of the major influences upon Eliot's poetry. Charles Baudelaire, Jules Laforgue, and Stéphane Mallarmé were especially impressive figures for him. After two years back at Harvard, during which he read widely in Sanskrit and Oriental philosophy, Eliot returned to Europe on a travel grant; when war broke out, he settled in London. By 1915, he had decided to give up philosophy to pursue a career as a writer, to remain in England permanently, and to marry. He supported himself first by teach-

ing French and Latin in a grammar school, and then, for eight years, by working as a clerk in Lloyd's Bank. He married Vivien Haigh-Wood in 1915. His wife was subject to bouts of mental illness and the marriage was desperately unhappy, although they remained together for seventeen years, before separating in 1932. Eliot completed his Ph.D. thesis on the philosophy of F. H. Bradley in 1916, but the war prevented his returning to Harvard for his final oral examination and he never received the degree. Bradley's philosophy, which emphasized the uniqueness of individual experience, was to have a continuing influence upon Eliot's thought and poetry.

Eliot had written "The Love Song of J. Alfred Prufrock" in 1910, but it was not published until 1915, after Eliot's friend Ezra Pound had sent it to Harriet Monroe, editor of the famous Poetry *magazine in Chicago, and persuaded her to publish it, despite her initial judgment that it was "not poetry." Its publication in* Poetry *and as part of the collection* Prufrock and Other Observations *(1917) has been compared to the publication of William Wordsworth's and Samuel Taylor Coleridge's* Lyrical Ballads *in 1798; both inaugurated new ages in English poetry. The timid, anti-Romantic protagonist of "Prufrock," its dry, ironic tone, and its startlingly fresh imagery presented a model for modernist poetry that was to influence several generations of poets throughout the world.*

The years from 1915 to 1921 were difficult for Eliot. Financial and marital problems and a punishing schedule of work at the bank, voluminous journalism, and intensive poetic composition led him to a severe mental breakdown in 1921. Friends were able to arrange a leave of absence from the bank and complete rest and psychiatric care in Switzerland. He took the manuscript of The Waste Land *with him and with the editorial assistance of Ezra Pound gave the poem its final form. Its publication in 1922, first in Eliot's own review, the* Criterion, *then in the American* Dial, *and finally in book form, is generally regarded as the single most important event in the history of modern poetry. The promise of "The Love Song of J. Alfred Prufrock" was amply fulfilled in this frightening collage of fragments of memories, overheard conversations, and quotations, welded together only by the implied presence of a "refined sensibility" upon whom all this "variety and complexity" are being heaped and who staggers under their burden. Not even Eliot, apparently, was prepared either for the violent opposition to the poem ("a piece of tripe," was Amy Lowell's judgment) or for the fervency with which its admirers regarded it as the definitive description of their age. He regarded the claim that the poem expressed "the disillusionment of a generation" as "nonsense"; "I may have expressed for them," he wrote, "their own illusion of being disillusioned, but that did not form part of my intention." Nevertheless, the phrase* waste land *entered the language, along with* jazz age *and* lost generation, *as a definitive term for post-World War I disillusionment.*

In 1925, Eliot was able to leave Lloyd's Bank and join the publishing firm of Faber and Faber as an editor, a position he retained for the rest of his life. His reputation as a critic had already begun to rival his stature as a poet, and in a series of volumes of essays, he developed a critical position second only to his own poetic practice in its influence upon modern poetry: The Sacred Wood *(1920),* Homage to John Dryden *(1924),* For Lancelot Andrewes *(1928), and* Selected Essays *(1932).*

Eliot's development after The Waste Land *was steadily in the direction of literary, political, and religious conservatism and orthodoxy. In 1927, he became both an Anglo-Catholic and a British subject and was able to describe himself, apparently with a minimum of irony, as "classicist in literature, royalist in politics, and anglo-catholic in religion." The first major poetic fruit of his conversion was "Ash Wednesday" (1930), a poem based on the Anglican service and the Christian ascetic disciplines. The* Four Quartets, *long, interrelated poems that explored mystical experience, each with a five-part "meditative" structure like that of* The Waste Land, *began to appear in 1936 and were completed in 1943. Some critics have regarded the* Four Quartets *as Eliot's masterpiece; others have found them garrulous, mannered, and lacking in the intensity of the earlier poetry.*

Much of Eliot's energy in his later years was devoted to an attempt to create a modern poetic drama. His first completed play, Murder in the Cathedral *(1935), revived the style of Greek tragedy to tell the story of Thomas à Becket's martyrdom. In his later plays—*The Family Reunion *(1939),* The Cocktail Party *(1950),* The Confidential Clerk *(1954), and* The Elder Statesman *(1959)—he turned instead to the form of modern high comedy, in the manner of Noel Coward, a form which coexisted rather uneasily with the plays' mythic and religious themes.*

Vivian Eliot died in 1947; the couple had lived apart for the last fifteen years of her life. In 1957, Eliot married Valerie Fletcher and seems to have experienced a long-delayed personal happiness and peace. He died in 1965, at the age of seventy-two.

Eliot's major poems are all essentially dramatic monologues of a startlingly innovative kind. Prufrock is a speaker so timid that, if we are to believe the epigraph, he can persuade himself to talk only on the assurance that what he says will never be heard. He seems to be speaking to himself. Eliot denied that the "you and I" of the first line are merely two sides of Prufrock and said that "you" was a male companion, but it hardly matters, since Prufrock's self-preoccupation is so complete that any second party functions only as a mirror for himself. His soliloquy is a "love song" only in the most ironic sense; the whole poem is an elaborate rationalization for not seeking love. Love remains, for Prufrock, beneath the layers of fear, self-consciousness, and self-hate, only as a hopeless, fantasized yearning for the vitality of "a pair of ragged claws" and of "the mermaids singing, each to each."

The Waste Land *is probably also best read as a dramatic monologue. Eliot's original title, as we now know from the publication of the original manuscript in 1971, was "He Do the Police in Different Voices." This line is from Dickens's* Our Mutual Friend, *from a scene in which a widow praises her adopted son, Sloppy: "I do love a newspaper," she says. "You mightn't think it, but Sloppy is a beautiful reader of a newspaper. He do the Police in different voices."* The Waste Land *retains something of this air of a bravura display of mimicry. But who is the mimic? Eliot muddied the issue in his notes by identifying Tiresias as "the most important personage in the poem, uniting all the rest." But Tiresias cannot literally be the central consciousness, except perhaps as the most comprehensive of the many avatars of the speaker in this poem in which all the men are one man, all the women are one woman, and "the two sexes meet in Tiresias." The speaker of* The Waste Land *is the "refined sensibility" of Eliot's essay on the Metaphysical poets, upon whom the variety and complexity of the modern world are impinging. His mind is packed with cultural tradition—an anthropological account of the Grail legend,* The Divine Comedy, *the operas of Wagner, the story of the Crucifixion, French Symbolist poetry, and Jacobean drama—as well as such scraps of popular culture as music hall songs, bits of slang, and contemporary fashions. These bits of "found material" are set into a matrix of the flowing stream of consciousness of a man at the end of his tether, desperately shoring fragments against his ruin. Paradoxically, this portrait of an age gains its power from being first a dramatic portrait of a single mind.*

"The Hollow Men" has been called "a kind of coda to The Waste Land," *and it may even have been constructed from passages originally intended for that poem. The speaker, despite the "we" of the first line, is again a single individual (the "I" of Part II), and again his stream of consciousness is full of scraps of his reading, here predominantly* The Divine Comedy *and Joseph Conrad's* Heart of Darkness. *(Eliot recognized in Conrad's analysis of the psychology of a civilization in decline something close to his own vision: the epigraph to* The Waste Land *was originally to be "The horror! The horror!", Kurtz's last line in* Heart of Darkness.*)*

Eliot's criticism, as he acknowledged, was "programmatic" criticism, intended to explain and justify his own poetic practice. The important early essay "Tradition and the Individual Talent" redefined the word tradition *from a distinctly Eliotic point of view, so that it no longer implied conservatism or imitation of the past but rather a poet's consciousness of his relation to the whole range of previous literature. This conception of tradition, by which a "really new" work of art requires that "the whole existing order [of earlier works] must be, if ever so slightly, altered," does much to explain the meaning of the juxtaposition of past and present in* The Waste Land. *The essay "Hamlet and His Problems," also from* The Sacred Wood *(1921), introduced another key Eliot critical concept, the "objective correlative," which he defined as "a set of objects, a situation, a chain of events" that could serve as "the formula" for a particular emotion.* Hamlet, *he startlingly asserted, is an "artistic failure" because it lacks such an objective correlative for Hamlet's state of mind. The concept of the objective correlative is highly dubious, applied to* Hamlet, *but is obviously crucial in understanding Eliot's rejection of the sometimes vague images and imageless rhetoric of late-nineteenth-century poetry and his use of precise, hard-edged, concrete images in his own work.*

FURTHER READING *(prepared by N. K. B.):* For T. S. Eliot's other work, see *The Complete Poems and Plays,* 1969, and Frank Kermode, ed., *Selected Prose of T. S. Eliot,* 1975. Valerie Eliot, ed., *The Waste Land: A Facsimile and Transcript of the Original Drafts Including the Annotations of Ezra Pound,* 1971, is an indispensable tool for understanding the poem and contains a concise biography of Eliot during the years he composed it. Although there is no authorized biography, Herbert Howarth, *Notes on Some Figures Behind T. S. Eliot,* 1964, provides a detailed survey of Eliot's life through World War II. A. D. Moody, *Thomas Stearns Eliot: Poet,* 1979, demonstrates, through an analysis of Eliot's experimentation with style and form, the growth of his poetic imagination; the book also includes an analysis of "The Hollow Men" and *The Waste Land* manuscripts. Lyndall Gordon's *Eliot's Early Years,* 1977, examines unpublished poems of Eliot's apprenticeship as reflections of his personal experiences. Philip R. Headings's *T. S. Eliot,* 1964, rev. 1982, cogently introduces Eliot's techniques and themes. Helen Gardner, *The Art of T. S. Eliot,* 1949, is a major study of the late poems with particular attention to Eliot's metrical style and form. Elizabeth Drew, *T. S. Eliot: the Design of His Poetry,* 1950, provides a Jungian analysis of Eliot's themes. Grover Smith, Jr., *T. S. Eliot's Poetry and Plays,* 1956, examines the sources and influences in Eliot's work, including *The Waste Land.* F. O. Matthiessen's *The Achievement of T. S. Eliot,* 1935, rev. 1947, 1958, is an appreciative study emphasizing Eliot's technique. Hugh Kenner, *The Invisible Poet,* 1959, rev. 1964, analyzes the major texts, including *The Waste Land* and "The Hollow Men." Northrop Frye's *T. S. Eliot,* 1963, examines Eliot's central images. For explications of individual works, see George Williamson, *A Reader's Guide to T. S. Eliot,* 1953. Hugh Kenner, ed., *T. S. Eliot: A Collection of Critical Essays,* 1962, includes a biographical portrait by Wyndham Lewis. A. Walton Litz, ed., *Eliot in His Time,* 1973, includes two major essays on *The Waste Land* by Richard Ellmann and Robert Langbaum. Jay Martin, ed., *A Collection of Critical Essays on "The Waste Land,"* 1968, contains seven explications of individual sections of the poem. *T. S. Eliot: The Critical Heritage,* 2 vols., ed. by Michael Grant, 1982, contains the most comprehensive collection of reviews of the poetry and drama.

THE LOVE SONG OF J. ALFRED PRUFROCK

S'io credesse che mia risposta fosse
A persona che mai tornasse al mondo,
Questa fiamma staria senza piu scosse.
Ma perciocche giammai di questo fondo
Non torno vivo alcun, s'i'odo il vero,
Senza tema d'infamia ti rispondo.[1]

Let us go then, you and I,
When the evening is spread out against the sky
Like a patient etherised upon a table;
Let us go, through certain half-deserted streets,
The muttering retreats
Of restless nights in one-night cheap hotels
And sawdust restaurants with oyster-shells:
Streets that follow like a tedious argument
Of insidious intent
To lead you to an overwhelming question. . .
Oh, do not ask, "What is it?"
Let us go and make our visit.

In the room the women come and go
Talking of Michelangelo.

The yellow fog that rubs its back upon the window-panes,
The yellow smoke that rubs its muzzle on the window-panes
Licked its tongue into the corners of the evening,
Lingered upon the pools that stand in drains,
Let fall upon its back the soot that falls from chimneys,
Slipped by the terrace, made a sudden leap,
And seeing that it was a soft October night,
Curled once about the house, and fell asleep.

[1] These words are spoken to Dante by the spirit of Guido da Montefeltro, speaking from a flickering flame in the eighth circle of Hell.

If I believed that my reply were to anyone
who would ever return to the world,
this flame would remain quiet,
but since no one from this ditch
has ever returned alive, if I hear the truth,
I will answer without fear of infamy.
—(DANTE, *Inferno* XXVII. 61–66)

And indeed there will be time
For the yellow smoke that slides along the street,
Rubbing its back upon the window-panes;
There will be time, there will be time
To prepare a face to meet the faces that you meet;
There will be time to murder and create,
And time for all the works and days[2] of hands
That lift and drop a question on your plate;
Time for you and time for me,
And time yet for a hundred indecisions,
And for a hundred visions and revisions,
Before the taking of a toast and tea.

In the room the women come and go
Talking of Michelangelo.

And indeed there will be time
To wonder, "Do I dare?" and, "Do I dare?"
Time to turn back and descend the stair,
With a bald spot in the middle of my hair—
[They will say: "How his hair is growing thin!"]
My morning coat, my collar mounting firmly to the chin,
My necktie rich and modest, but asserted by a simple pin—
[They will say: "But how his arms and legs are thin!"]
Do I dare
Disturb the universe?
In a minute there is time
For decisions and revisions which a minute will reverse.

For I have known them all already, known them all:—
Have known the evenings, mornings, afternoons,
I have measured out my life with coffee spoons;
I know the voices dying with a dying fall
Beneath the music from a farther room.
So how should I presume?

And I have known the eyes already, known them all—
The eyes that fix you in a formulated phrase,
And when I am formulated, sprawling on a pin,
When I am pinned and wriggling on the wall,
Then how should I begin
To spit out all the butt-ends of my days and ways?
And how should I presume?

And I have known the arms already, known them all—

[2] *works and days.* An allusion to the *Works and Days* of the eighth-century B.C. Greek poet Hesiod. The allusion is ironic, since the *Works and Days* deals with the real labors of peasants rather than the idle chatter of this scene.

Arms that are braceleted and white and bare
[But in the lamplight, downed with light brown hair!]
Is it perfume from a dress
That makes me so digress?
Arms that lie along a table, or wrap about a shawl.
  And should I then presume?
  And how should I begin?

. . . . .

Shall I say, I have gone at dusk through narrow streets
And watched the smoke that rises from the pipes
Of lonely men in shirt-sleeves, leaning out of windows? . . .

  I should have been a pair of ragged claws
Scuttling across the floors of silent seas.

. . . . .

And the afternoon, the evening, sleeps so peacefully!
Smoothed by long fingers,
Asleep . . . tired . . . or it malingers,
Stretched on the floor, here beside you and me.
Should I, after tea and cakes and ices,
Have the strength to force the moment to its crisis?
But though I have wept and fasted, wept and prayed,
Though I have seen my head [grown slightly bald] brought in upon
    a platter,[3]
I am no prophet—and here's no great matter;
I have seen the moment of my greatness flicker,
And I have seen the eternal Footman hold my coat, and snicker,
And in short, I was afraid.

  And would it have been worth it, after all,
After the cups, the marmalade, the tea,
Among the porcelain, among some talk of you and me,
Would it have been worth while,
To have bitten off the matter with a smile,
To have squeezed the universe into a ball
To roll it toward some overwhelming question,
To say: "I am Lazarus,[4] come from the dead,
Come back to tell you all, I shall tell you all"—
If one, settling a pillow by her head,
  Should say: "That is not what I meant at all.
  That is not it, at all."

  And would it have been worth it, after all,
Would it have been worth while,
After the sunsets and the dooryards and the sprinkled streets,

[3] John the Baptist was beheaded and his head brought in upon a platter at the request of Salome. See Matthew 14:1–12.

[4] Lazarus was raised from the dead by Jesus. See John 11:1–44.

After the novels, after the teacups, after the skirts that trail along the
floor—
And this, and so much more?—
It is impossible to say just what I mean!
But as if a magic lantern threw the nerves in patterns on a screen:
Would it have been worth while
If one, settling a pillow or throwing off a shawl,
And turning toward the window, should say:
"That is not it at all,
That is not what I meant, at all."

. . . . .

No! I am not Prince Hamlet, nor was meant to be;
Am an attendant lord, one that will do
To swell a progress,[5] start a scene or two,
Advise the prince; no doubt, an easy tool,
Deferential, glad to be of use,
Politic, cautious, and meticulous;
Full of high sentence,[6] but a bit obtuse;
At times, indeed, almost ridiculous—
Almost, at times, the Fool.

I grow old . . . I grow old. . .
I shall wear the bottoms of my trousers rolled.

Shall I part my hair behind? Do I dare to eat a peach?
I shall wear white flannel trousers, and walk upon the beach.
I have heard the mermaids singing, each to each.

I do not think that they will sing to me.

I have seen them riding seaward on the waves
Combing the white hair of the waves blown back
When the wind blows the water white and black.

We have lingered in the chambers of the sea
By sea-girls wreathed with seaweed red and brown
Till human voices wake us, and we drown.

[5] A ceremonial procession, often represented in Elizabethan plays.
[6] Sententiously expressed opinions.

THE WASTE LAND[1]

"Nam Sibyllam quidem Cumis ego ipse oculis meis vidi in ampulla pendere, et cum illi pueri dicerent: Σίβυλλα τί θέλεις; *respondebat illa:* ἀποθανεῖν θέλω."[2]

FOR EZRA POUND
il miglior fabbro.[3]

I. THE BURIAL OF THE DEAD[4]

April is the cruellest month, breeding
Lilacs out of the dead land, mixing
Memory and desire, stirring
Dull roots with spring rain.
Winter kept us warm, covering
Earth in forgetful snow, feeding
A little life with dried tubers.
Summer surprised us, coming over the Starnbergersee[5]
With a shower of rain; we stopped in the colonnade,
And went on in sunlight, into the Hofgarten,[6]
And drank coffee, and talked for an hour.
Bin gar keine Russin, stamm' aus Litauen, echt deutsch.[7]

[1] Eliot provided fifty-two notes for *The Waste Land* when it was first published in book form in 1922 ("in order," according to his later statement, "to provide a few more pages of printed matter"). The notes given here are by the editors, except for those identified as quoted or abbreviated from Eliot's. Eliot's general note for the entire poem is as follows: "Not only the title, but the plan and a good deal of the incidental symbolism of the poem were suggested by Miss Jessie L. Weston's book on the Grail legend: *From Ritual to Romance* (Cambridge). Indeed, so deeply am I indebted, Miss Weston's book will elucidate the difficulties of the poem much better than my notes can do; and I recommend it (apart from the great interest of the book itself) to any who think such elucidation of the poem worth the trouble. To another work of anthropology I am indebted in general, one which has influenced our generation profoundly; I mean *The Golden Bough;* I have used especially the two volumes *Adonis, Attis, Osiris.* Anyone who is acquainted with these works will immediately recognise in the poem certain references to vegetation ceremonies."

[2] "For I saw with my own eyes the Sibyl hanging in a jar at Cumae, and when the boys asked, 'Sibyl, what do you want?' she answered, 'I want to die.'" This is from the *Satyricon* of Petronius (first century A.D.). The Cumaean Sibyl was a famous prophetess whom Virgil has guide Aeneas through Hades in the *Aeneid.* She had been granted eternal life by Apollo but she forgot to ask for eternal youth and so shrivelled until she was so small that she was kept in a jar.

[3] "The better maker" (Italian). Pound edited the original manuscript of *The Waste Land.* The phrase is quoted from Dante's *Purgatory* XXVI.117, where Dante applies it to the Provençal poet Arnaut Daniel.

[4] The title is from the Anglican burial service.

[5] A lake near Munich. The following lines echo a passage in *My Past,* the memoirs of the Austrian countess Marie Larisch, but according to Eliot's widow, Eliot derived them not from the book but from personal conversation with the countess.

[6] A public park in Munich.

[7] "I am no Russian, I'm from Lithuania, a true German" (German).

And when we were children, staying at the archduke's,
My cousin's, he took me out on a sled,
And I was frightened. He said, Marie,
Marie, hold on tight. And down we went.
In the mountains, there you feel free.
I read, much of the night, and go south in the winter.

What are the roots that clutch, what branches grow
Out of this stony rubbish? Son of man,[8]
You cannot say, or guess, for you know only
A heap of broken images, where the sun beats,
And the dead tree gives no shelter, the cricket no relief,[9]
And the dry stone no sound of water. Only
There is shadow under this red rock,
(Come in under the shadow of this red rock),[10]
And I will show you something different from either
Your shadow at morning striding behind you
Or your shadow at evening rising to meet you;
I will show you fear in a handful of dust.
Frisch weht der Wind
Der Heimat zu
Mein Irisch Kind,
Wo weilest du?[11]
"You gave me hyacinths first a year ago;
"They called me the hyacinth girl."
—Yet when we came back, late, from the Hyacinth garden,
Your arms full, and your hair wet, I could not
Speak, and my eyes failed, I was neither
Living nor dead, and I knew nothing,
Looking into the heart of light, the silence.
Oed' und leer das Meer.[12]

Madame Sosostris,[13] famous clairvoyante,
Had a bad cold, nevertheless
Is known to be the wisest woman in Europe,

[8] Eliot cites Ezekiel 2:1 as the source of this passage. The Lord says to Ezekiel, "Son of man, stand upon thy feet, and I will speak unto thee."

[9] Eliot cites Ecclesiastes 12:5. The passage is describing the aged, who "are afraid also of what is high, and terrors are in the way; the almond tree blossoms, the grasshopper drags itself along and desire fails."

[10] Isaiah 32:2 describes a great king who will be "like the shade of a great rock in a weary land," thus, according to Christian interpretation, foreshadowing Christ.

[11] Eliot identifies this verse as the sailor's song in Richard Wagner's *Tristan and Isolde* (1857–59), Act I: "Fresh blows the wind to the homeland; my Irish child, where are you waiting?"

[12] Eliot identifies this line also as from *Tristan and Isolde,* Act III: "Waste and empty is the sea." This is the report of a shepherd watching for the sail of a ship bringing Isolde from Cornwall to the dying Tristan.

[13] Eliot apparently derived the fortune-teller's fake Egyptian name from Aldous Huxley's novel *Chrome Yellow* (1921), in which a character uses the name "Sesostris, the Sorceress of Ecbatana" while telling fortunes at a fair.

With a wicked pack of cards.[14] Here, said she,
Is your card, the drowned Phoenician Sailor,
(Those are pearls that were his eyes.[15] Look!)
Here is Belladonna,[16] the Lady of the Rocks,
The lady of situations.
Here is the man with three staves, and here the Wheel,[17]
And here is the one-eyed merchant, and this card,
Which is blank, is something he carries on his back,
Which I am forbidden to see. I do not find
The Hanged Man. Fear death by water.
I see crowds of people, walking round in a ring.
Thank you. If you see dear Mrs. Equitone,
Tell her I bring the horoscope myself:
One must be so careful these days.

Unreal City,[18]
Under the brown fog of a winter dawn,
A crowd flowed over London Bridge, so many,
I had not thought death had undone so many.[19]
Sighs, short and infrequent, were exhaled,[20]
And each man fixed his eyes before his feet.
Flowed up the hill and down King William Street,
To where Saint Mary Woolnoth kept the hours

[14] "I am not familiar with the exact constitution of the Tarot pack of cards, from which I have obviously departed to suit my own convenience. The Hanged Man, a member of the traditional pack, fits my purpose in two ways: because he is associated in my mind with the Hanged God of Frazer, and because I associate him with the hooded figure in the passage of the disciples to Emmaus in Part V. The Phoenician Sailor and the Merchant appear later; also the 'crowds of people,' and Death by Water is executed in part IV. The Man with Three Staves (an authentic member of the Tarot pack) I associate, quite arbitrarily, with the Fisher King himself" (Eliot). The Tarot deck of cards, used widely for fortune-telling, is very old and uses as the names of suits the cup, lance, sword, and dish of the Grail legend. Jessie Weston discusses it in *From Ritual to Romance.* The figures on the cards, as Eliot notes, are identified with various characters in the poem. The Phoenician Sailor is both Mr. Eugenides (Part III) and Phlebas the Phoenician (Part IV). The Hanged Man is the "hooded figure" (Christ) of Part V. As Eliot also notes, the correspondences are not exact, and not every character has a corresponding card.

[15] *Those . . . his eyes.* A line from "Full Fathom Five Thy Father Lies," Ariel's song in Act I of Shakespeare's *Tempest.* Ariel is alluding to the presumed drowning of Ferdinand's father King Alonso.

[16] Both "beautiful lady" (Italian) and the name of a poison, deadly nightshade. She anticipates the neurotic lady of Part II. She is the "Lady of the Rocks" in ironic reference to Leonardo da Vinci's "Lady of the Rocks," a painting of the Virgin Mary, and to sirens who lure sailors onto the rocks (a typically ambivalent pairing of opposites in the poem). She is a "lady of situations" because of her presumed gossiping and intrigues.

[17] The Wheel of Fortune in the Tarot deck.

[18] "Cf. Baudelaire: *'Fourmillante cité, cité pleine de rêves, / Ou le spectre en plein jour raccroche le passant'*" (Eliot). The poem Eliot refers to is "The Seven Old Men" in Charles Baudelaire's *The Flowers of Evil* (1857): "Swarming city, city fitted with dreams, / Where the spectre in broad daylight accosts the passerby."

[19] "Cf. *Inferno* III, 55–57" (Eliot). When Dante arrives in Hell, he sees a long train of people and exclaims, "I had not thought death had undone so many!"

[20] "Cf. *Inferno* IV, 25–27" (Eliot). Here Dante is describing the virtuous pagans in the first circle of Hell.

With a dead sound on the final stroke of nine.[21]
There I saw one I knew, and stopped him, crying: "Stetson!
"You who were with me in the ships at Mylae![22]
"That corpse you planted last year in your garden,
"Has it begun to sprout? Will it bloom this year?
"Or has the sudden frost disturbed its bed?
"Oh keep the Dog far hence, that's friend to men,
"Or with his nails he'll dig it up again![23]
"You! hypocrite lecteur!—mon semblable,—mon frère!"[24]

II. A GAME OF CHESS[25]

The Chair she sat in, like a burnished throne,[26]
Glowed on the marble, where the glass
Held up by standards wrought with fruited vines
From which a golden Cupidon peeped out
(Another hid his eyes behind his wing)
Doubled the flames of sevenbranched candelabra
Reflecting light upon the table as
The glitter of her jewels rose to meet it,
From satin cases poured in rich profusion;
In vials of ivory and coloured glass
Unstoppered, lurked her strange synthetic perfumes,
Unguent, powdered, or liquid—troubled, confused
And drowned the sense in odours; stirred by the air
That freshened from the window, these ascended
In fattening the prolonged candle-flames,
Flung their smoke into the laquearia,[27]
Stirring the pattern on the coffered ceiling.
Huge sea-wood fed with copper

[21] "A phenomenon which I have often noticed" (Eliot). Saint Mary Woolnoth is a church in the "City," the financial district of London. King William Street is in the same area. The crowd is flowing over London Bridge to go to work.

[22] Naval battle in the First Punic War (260 B.C.), in which Rome defeated Carthage. The speaker merges this ancient war with the First World War, in which he and "Stetson" (a generalized figure, not a specific person) have recently fought.

[23] "Cf. the Dirge in Webster's *White Devil*" (Eliot). The lines Eliot refers to, in John Webster's play *The White Devil* (1612), are "But keep the wolf far thence, that's foe to men, / For with his nails he'll dig them up again" (V.iv.97–98). The switch from wolf to dog and the cliché of "man's best friend" domesticate the line but at the same time grotesquely juxtapose ancient fertility rites and modern suburban life.

[24] "V. Baudelaire, Preface to *Fleurs du Mal*" (Eliot). The line means, "Hypocrite reader!—my likeness—my brother!"

[25] The title of this section alludes to a play, *A Game at Chess,* by the Jacobean dramatist Thomas Middleton (c. 1570–1627). Closer to the action, though, is another Middleton play, *Women Beware Women,* in which an on-stage chess game parallels a cynical seduction in the next room. See note 36.

[26] "Cf. [Shakespeare's] *Antony and Cleopatra,* II.ii.190" (Eliot). The line is part of Enobarbus's description of Cleopatra: "The barge she sat in, like a burnished throne, / Burn'd on the water."

[27] "V. *Aeneid,* I.726" (Eliot). A "laquearia" is a panelled ceiling; the passage in the *Aeneid* Eliot cites as his source for the word describes Dido's lavish banquet for her lover Aeneas.

Burned green and orange, framed by the coloured stone,
In which sad light a carvèd dolphin swam.
Above the antique mantel was displayed
As though a window gave upon the sylvan scene[28]
The change of Philomel,[29] by the barbarous king
So rudely forced;[30] yet there the nightingale
Filled all the desert with inviolable voice
And still she cried, and still the world pursues,
"Jug Jug"[31] to dirty ears.
And other withered stumps of time
Were told upon the walls; staring forms
Leaned out, leaning, hushing the room enclosed.
Footsteps shuffled on the stair.
Under the firelight, under the brush, her hair
Spread out in fiery points
Glowed into words, then would be savagely still.

"My nerves are bad to-night. Yes, bad. Stay with me.
"Speak to me. Why do you never speak. Speak.
"What are you thinking of? What thinking? What?
"I never know what you are thinking. Think."

I think we are in rats' alley[32]
Where the dead men lost their bones.

"What is that noise?"
The wind under the door.[33]
"What is that noise now? What is the wind doing?"
Nothing again nothing.
"Do
"You know nothing? Do you see nothing? Do you remember
"Nothing?"

I remember
Those are pearls that were his eyes.[34]

[28] *sylvan scene.* "V. Milton, *Paradise Lost,* IV. 140" (Eliot). The passage Eliot refers to is a description of Eden, as first seen by Satan.

[29] "V. Ovid, *Metamorphoses,* VI, Philomela" (Eliot). In the *Metamorphoses,* Philomela is raped by her brother-in-law King Tereus, who cuts her tongue out so that she cannot denounce him. She is turned into a nightingale.

[30] "Cf. Part III, l. 204" (Eliot). In the line Eliot refers to, he returns to Tereus and the nightingale's song. There may be an echo here, too, of Milton's lines in "Lycidas" (1637): "I come to pluck your berries harsh and crude, / And with forced fingers rude, / Shatter your leaves before the mellowing year" (ll. 3–5). An important sub-theme in both "Lycidas" and *The Waste Land* is the difficulty of writing the poems, Milton's because of his immaturity, Eliot's because of the fragmentation of his culture. ("Lycidas" also involves a "death by water.")

[31] A conventional representation of the nightingale's song in Elizabethan verse.

[32] "Cf. Part III, l. 195" (Eliot): "bones cast in a little low dry garret, / Rattled by the rat's foot only, year to year."

[33] "Cf. Webster: 'Is the wind in that door still?'" (Eliot). The line is in John Webster's play *The Devil's Law Case* (1623), III.ii.162, where it is a question about whether a dying man is still breathing.

[34] "Cf. Part I, ll. 37, 48" (Eliot). The reference is again to Ariel's song in *The Tempest.*

"Are you alive, or not? Is there nothing in your head?"
But
O O O O that Shakespeherian Rag—
It's so elegant
So intelligent
"What shall I do now? What shall I do?"[35]
"I shall rush out as I am, and walk the street
"With my hair down, so. What shall we do to-morrow?
"What shall we ever do?"
The hot water at ten.
And if it rains, a closed car at four.
And we shall play a game of chess,[36]
Pressing lidless eyes and waiting for a knock upon the door.

When Lil's husband got demobbed,[37] I said—
I didn't mince my words, I said to her myself,
HURRY UP PLEASE ITS TIME[38]
Now Albert's coming back, make yourself a bit smart.
He'll want to know what you done with that money he gave you
To get yourself some teeth. He did, I was there.
You have them all out, Lil, and get a nice set,
He said, I swear, I can't bear to look at you.
And no more can't I, I said, and think of poor Albert,
He's been in the army four years, he wants a good time,
And if you don't give it him, there's others will, I said.
Oh is there, she said. Something o' that, I said.
Then I'll know who to thank, she said, and give me a straight look.
HURRY UP PLEASE ITS TIME
If you don't like it you can get on with it, I said.
Others can pick and choose if you can't.
But if Albert makes off, it won't be for lack of telling.
You ought to be ashamed, I said, to look so antique.
(And her only thirty-one.)
I can't help it, she said, pulling a long face,
It's them pills I took, to bring it off, she said.
(She's had five already, and nearly died of young George.)
The chemist[39] said it would be all right, but I've never been the same.
You *are* a proper fool, I said.
Well, if Albert won't leave you alone, there it is, I said,
What you get married for if you don't want children?
HURRY UP PLEASE ITS TIME
Well, that Sunday Albert was home, they had a hot gammon,[40]
And they asked me in to dinner, to get the beauty of it hot—
HURRY UP PLEASE ITS TIME
HURRY UP PLEASE ITS TIME

[35] Lines 128–31 are quoted from a 1912 popular song, "That Shakespearian Rag."
[36] "Cf. the game of chess in Middleton's *Women Beware Women*" (Eliot). See note 25.
[37] British slang for *demobilized* or discharged from the army.
[38] Traditional bartender's call at closing time in an English pub. [39] Druggist.
[40] Ham.

Goonight Bill. Goonight Lou. Goonight May. Goonight.
Ta ta. Goonight. Goonight.
Good night, ladies, good night, sweet ladies, good night, good night.[41]

III. THE FIRE SERMON[42]

The river's tent is broken: the last fingers of leaf
Clutch and sink into the wet bank. The wind
Crosses the brown land, unheard. The nymphs are departed.
Sweet Thames, run softly, till I end my song.[43]
The river bears no empty bottles, sandwich papers,
Silk handkerchiefs, cardboard boxes, cigarette ends
Or other testimony of summer nights. The nymphs are departed.
And their friends, the loitering heirs of city directors;
Departed, have left no addresses.
By the waters of Leman I sat down and wept . . .[44]
Sweet Thames, run softly till I end my song,
Sweet Thames, run softly, for I speak not loud or long.
But at my back in a cold blast I hear[45]
The rattle of the bones, and chuckle spread from ear to ear.
A rat crept softly through the vegetation
Dragging its slimy belly on the bank
While I was fishing in the dull canal
On a winter evening round behind the gashouse
Musing upon the king my brother's wreck
And on the king my father's death before him.[46]
White bodies naked on the low damp ground
And bones cast in a little low dry garret,
Rattled by the rat's foot only, year to year.
But at my back from time to time I hear[47]
The sound of horns and motors,[48] which shall bring
Sweeney to Mrs. Porter in the spring.
O the moon shone bright on Mrs. Porter

[41] This line quotes Ophelia's last words in her mad scene before she drowns herself (*Hamlet,* IV.v. 72–73). The lines blend with their modern analogue, the drinking song "Good Night, Ladies."

[42] The title alludes to the "Fire Sermon" of Buddha, sixth-century B.C. founder of Buddhism. See note 74.

[43] "V. Spenser, *Prothalamion*" (Eliot). This line is the refrain of the *Prothalamion* (or "wedding song") by Edmund Spenser (c. 1552–1599), which also includes the river-nymphs, the "silver-streaming" Thames, and the description of London which this section parodies.

[44] See Psalm 137: "By the waters of Babylon, there we sat down and wept, when we remembered Zion." Eliot wrote *The Waste Land* in Switzerland, near Lake Leman (Lake Geneva). "Leman" is also the Middle English word for "mistress."

[45] "Cf. Marvell, *To His Coy Mistress*" (Eliot). Eliot is alluding to a line in the poem by Andrew Marvell (1627–78): "But at my back I always hear / Time's winged chariot hurrying near."

[46] "Cf. *The Tempest,* I,ii" (Eliot). The lines are Ferdinand's: "Sitting upon a bank, / Weeping again the King my father's wrack, / This music crept by me upon the waters."

[47] Another allusion to "To His Coy Mistress." See note 45.

And on her daughter
They wash their feet in soda water[49]
Et O ces voix d'enfants, chantant dans la coupole![50]

Twit twit twit
Jug jug jug jug jug jug
So rudely forc'd.
Tereu[51]

Unreal City[52]
Under the brown fog of a winter noon
Mr. Eugenides, the Smyrna merchant[53]
Unshaven, with a pocket full of currants
C.i.f. London: documents at sight,[54]
Asked me in demotic[55] French
To luncheon at the Cannon Street Hotel
Followed by a weekend at the Metropole.[56]

At the violet hour, when the eyes and back
Turn upward from the desk, when the human engine waits
Like a taxi throbbing waiting,

[48] "Cf. Day, *Parliament of Bees:*
'When of a sudden, listening, you shall hear,
'A noise of horns and hunting, which shall bring
'Actaeon to Diana in the spring,
'Where all shall see her naked skin . . .'" (Eliot).
John Day (1547–c. 1640) was a minor Elizabethan poet. Actaeon, while hunting, accidentally came upon the goddess Diana bathing naked; as punishment, he was changed to a stag and torn apart by his own hounds.

[49] "I do not know the origins of the ballad from which these lines are taken: it was reported to me from Sydney, Australia" (Eliot). The song is an obscene parody of "Red Wing," sung in World War I: "O the moon shone bright on Mrs. Porter / And on the daughter / of Mrs. Porter. / They wash their feet in soda water, / And so they oughter, / To keep them clean."

[50] "V. Verlaine, *Parsifal*" (Eliot). The line is from a sonnet by Paul Verlaine (1844–1896). It means, "And O those voices of children, singing in the cupola!" The children are the children's choir at the end of Wagner's opera *Parsifal* (1877–82), singing as Parsifal's feet are ceremonially washed in preparation for his worship of the Grail. Here the children's voices ironically accompany, instead, the washing of Mrs. Porter's and her daughter's feet in soda water.

[51] See notes 30 and 31. "Tereu" is King Tereus; the line also echoes John Lyly's line in *Alexander and Campaspe* (1581): "'Tis the ravished nightingale; / Jug, jug, jug, jug, tereu, she cries."

[52] See note 18.

[53] Mr. Eugenides' name, ironically, means "well-born" in Greek. Smyrna is a Turkish seaport.

[54] "The currants were quoted at a price 'carriage and insurance free to London'; and the Bill of Lading etc. were to be handed to the buyer upon payment of the sight draft" (Eliot).

[55] Colloquial, vulgar.

[56] The Cannon Street Hotel in London was a large hotel near the Cannon Street Station, where boat trains departed for and arrived from the Continent; it was thus frequented by foreign businessmen. The Metropole was a luxury resort hotel in Brighton. Both hotels were said to be favorite meeting places for homosexual and other irregular liaisons. Weston, in *From Ritual to Romance,* describes how the Grail cult was spread by Levantine merchants. This modern merchant spreads a somewhat different cult.

I Tiresias, though blind, throbbing between two lives,[57]
Old man with wrinkled female breasts, can see
At the violet hour, the evening hour that strives
Homeward, and brings the sailor home from the sea,[58]
The typist home at teatime, clears her breakfast, lights
Her stove, and lays out food in tins.
Out of the window perilously spread
Her drying combinations[59] touched by the sun's last rays,
On the divan are piled (at night her bed)
Stockings, slippers, camisoles, and stays.
I Tiresias, old man with wrinkled dugs
Perceived the scene, and foretold the rest—
I too awaited the expected guest.
He, the young man carbuncular,[60] arrives,
A small house agent's clerk, with one bold stare,
One of the low on whom assurance sits
As a silk hat on a Bradford millionaire.[61]
The time is now propitious, as he guesses,
The meal is ended, she is bored and tired,
Endeavours to engage her in caresses
Which still are unreproved, if undesired.
Flushed and decided, he assaults at once;
Exploring hands encounter no defence;
His vanity requires no response,
And makes a welcome of indifference.
(And I Tiresias have foresuffered all
Enacted on this same divan or bed;
I who have sat by Thebes below the wall
And walked among the lowest of the dead.)[62]
Bestows one final patronising kiss,
And gropes his way, finding the stairs unlit . . .

[57] "Tiresias, although a mere spectator and not indeed a 'character,' is yet the most important personage in the poem, uniting all the rest. Just as the one-eyed merchant, seller of currants, melts into the Phoenician Sailor, and the latter is not wholly distinct from Ferdinand Prince of Naples, so all the women are one woman, and the two sexes meet in Tiresias. What Tiresias *sees,* in fact, is the substance of the poem. The whole passage from Ovid is of great anthropological interest" (Eliot). Eliot then quotes a passage from Ovid's *Metamorphoses* (III.320–38) which tells how Tiresias spent seven years as a woman. Later, asked to settle a quarrel between Jove and Juno over whether men or women enjoyed sex more, Tiresias agreed with Jove that women did. Angered, Juno blinded him, but Jove compensated him by giving him prophetic powers.

[58] "This may not appear as exact as Sappho's lines, but I had in mind the 'longshore' or 'day' fisherman, who returns at nightfall" (Eliot). Eliot seems to have in mind Sappho's poem to Hesperus, the evening star, that brings home "all things bright morning scattered." The line also recalls Robert Louis Stevenson's line in "Requiem": "Home is the sailor, home from the sea."

[59] One-piece underwear. [60] With boils.

[61] From the industrial town of Bradford, which thrived on war contracts during World War I; hence, a *nouveau riche* and a war profiteer.

[62] Tiresias lived in Thebes, where he foresaw the fates of Oedipus and Creon. After his death, he continued to prophesy in Hades.

She turns and looks a moment in the glass,
Hardly aware of her departed lover;
Her brain allows one half-formed thought to pass:
"Well now that's done: and I'm glad it's over."
When lovely woman stoops to folly[63] and
Paces about her room again, alone,
She smoothes her hair with automatic hand,
And puts a record on the gramophone.

"This music crept by me upon the waters"[64]
And along the Strand, up Queen Victoria Street.
O City city, I can sometimes hear
Beside a public bar in Lower Thames Street,
The pleasant whining of a mandoline
And a clatter and a chatter from within
Where fishmen lounge at noon: where the walls
Of Magnus Martyr[65] hold
Inexplicable splendour of Ionian white and gold.

The river sweats[66]
Oil and tar
The barges drift
With the turning tide
Red sails
Wide
To leeward, swing on the heavy spar.
The barges wash
Drifting logs
Down Greenwich reach
Past the Isle of Dogs.[67]

[63]"V. Goldsmith, the song in *The Vicar of Wakefield*" (Eliot). The song, in Oliver Goldsmith's 1766 novel, runs:

When lovely woman stoops to folly,
And finds too late that men betray;
What charm can soothe her melancholy,
What art can wash her guilt away?

The only art her guilt to cover,
To hide her shame from every eye,
To give repentance to her lover
And wring his bosom—is to die.

[64]"V. *The Tempest,* as above" (Eliot). See note 46.

[65]"The interior of St. Magnus Martyr is to my mind one of the finest among Wren's interiors. See *The Proposed Demolition of Nineteen City Churches:* (P. S. King & Son, Ltd.)" (Eliot). The church of St. Magnus Martyr, designed by the seventeenth-century architect Christopher Wren, is located near London Bridge.

[66]"The Song of the (three) Thames-daughters begins here. From line 292 to 306 inclusive they speak in turn. V. *Gotterdämmerung,* III.i: the Rhine-daughters" (Eliot). Eliot is referring to the Rhine Maidens in Richard Wagner's opera *The Twilight of the Gods* (1874). The modern women whose statements begin with line 292 ironically echo not only Wagner's Rhine Maidens but also Spenser's river nymphs.

[67]Greenwich reach is the stretch of the Thames near Greenwich; the Isle of Dogs is a peninsula extending into the Thames.

Weialala leia
Wallala leialala[68]

Elizabeth and Leicester[69]
Beating oars
The stern was formed
A gilded shell
Red and gold
The brisk swell
Rippled both shores
Southwest wind
Carried down stream
The peal of bells
White towers
Weialala leia
Wallala leialala

"Trams and dusty trees.
Highbury bore me. Richmond and Kew
Undid me.[70] By Richmond I raised my knees
Supine on the floor of a narrow canoe."

"My feet are at Moorgate,[71] and my heart
Under my feet. After the event
He wept. He promised 'a new start.'
I made no comment. What should I resent?"

"On Margate Sands.[72]
I can connect
Nothing with nothing.
The broken fingernails of dirty hands.
My people humble people who expect
Nothing."
la la

To Carthage then I came[73]

[68] This refrain is from the song of the Rhine Maidens in *The Twilight of the Gods.*

[69] "V. Froude, *Elizabeth,* Vol. I, ch. iv, letter of De Quadra to Philip of Spain: 'In the afternoon we were in a barge, watching the games on the river. (The queen) was alone with Lord Robert and myself on the poop, when they began to talk nonsense, and went so far that Lord Robert at last said, as I was on the spot there was no reason why they should not be married if the queen pleased'" (Eliot). Eliot quotes from *The Reign of Elizabeth,* by J. A. Froude (1818–1894). De Quadra was Spanish Ambassador to Elizabeth's court; Sir Robert was Robert Dudley, Earl of Leicester, a favorite of Elizabeth. Their sexual play on the Thames parallels the modern vignettes which follow.

[70] "Cf. *Purgatorio,* V, 133" (Eliot). The lines Eliot cites are translated, "Siena bore me; Maremma undid me," and are spoken by a woman named La Pia, who died in Maremma. Highbury is a suburb of London; Richmond and Kew are resort gardens near London.

[71] A slum area of London. [72] Seaside resort on the Thames.

[73] "V. St. Augustine's *Confessions:* 'to Carthage then I came, where a cauldron of unholy loves sang all about mine ears" (Eliot). St. Augustine (354–430) is describing his youthful debauchery.

Burning burning burning burning[74]
O Lord Thou pluckest me out[75]
O Lord Thou pluckest

burning

IV. DEATH BY WATER[76]

Phlebas the Phoenician, a fortnight dead,
Forgot the cry of gulls, and the deep sea swell
And the profit and loss.
A current under sea
Picked his bones in whispers. As he rose and fell
He passed the stages of his age and youth
Entering the whirlpool.
Gentile or Jew
O you who turn the wheel and look to windward,
Consider Phlebas, who was once handsome and tall as you.

V. WHAT THE THUNDER SAID[77]

After the torchlight red on sweaty faces
After the frosty silence in the gardens[78]
After the agony in stony places
The shouting and the crying
Prison and palace and reverberation
Of thunder of spring over distant mountains
He who was living is now dead
We who were living are now dying
With a little patience

[74] "The complete text of the Buddha's Fire Sermon (which corresponds in importance to the Sermon on the Mount), from which these words are taken, will be found translated in the late Henry Clarke Warren's *Buddhism in Translation* (Harvard Oriental Series). Mr. Warren was one of the great pioneers of Buddhist studies in the Occident" (Eliot).

[75] "From St. Augustine's *Confessions* again. The collocation of these two representatives of eastern and western asceticism, as the culmination of this part of the poem, is not an accident" (Eliot).

[76] This section is translated and adapted by Eliot from his poem in French "Dans le Restaurant."

[77] "In the first part of Part V three themes are employed: the journey to Emmaus, the approach to the Chapel Perilous (see Miss Weston's book) and the present decay of eastern Europe" (Eliot). The "journey to Emmaus" is the journey upon which the resurrected Christ's disciples met him but did not recognize him. (See Luke 24:13–16.) The "approach to the Chapel Perilous" is the final stage of the Grail hero's quest. The "present decay of eastern Europe" alludes to the aftermath of World War I and the Russian Revolution.

[78] Gethsemane, where Christ prayed before his arrest, and Golgotha, where he was crucified. This section is from the point of view of Christ's disciples between his crucifixion and the resurrection.

Here is no water but only rock
Rock and no water and the sandy road
The road winding above among the mountains
Which are mountains of rock without water
If there were water we should stop and drink
Amongst the rock one cannot stop or think
Sweat is dry and feet are in the sand
If there were only water amongst the rock
Dead mountain mouth of carious[79] teeth that cannot spit
Here one can neither stand nor lie nor sit
There is not even silence in the mountains
But dry sterile thunder without rain
There is not even solitude in the mountains
But red sullen faces sneer and snarl
From doors of mudcracked houses
If there were water
And no rock
If there were rock
And also water
And water
A spring
A pool among the rock
If there were the sound of water only
Not the cidada
And dry grass singing
But sound of water over a rock
Where the hermit-thrush sings in the pine trees[80]
Drip drop drip drop drop drop drop
But there is no water

Who is the third who walks always beside you?[81]
When I count, there are only you and I together
But when I look ahead up the white road
There is always another one walking beside you
Gliding wrapt in a brown mantle, hooded
I do not know whether a man or a woman
—But who is that on the other side of you?

[79] Decayed.

[80] "This is *Turdus aonalaschkae pallasii,* the hermit-thrush which I have heard in Quebec Province. Chapman says (*Handbook of Birds of Eastern North America*) 'it is most at home in secluded woodland and thickety retreats. . . . Its notes are not remarkable for variety or volume, but in purity and sweetness of tone and exquisite modulation they are unequalled.' Its 'water-dripping song' is justly celebrated" (Eliot). (This faintly absurd Eliotic note may gently parody Eliot's own notes as well as those of literal-minded academic editors.)

[81] "The following lines were stimulated by the account of one of the Antarctic expeditions (I forget which, but I think one of Shackleton's): it was related that the party of explorers, at the extremity of their strength, had the constant delusion that there was *one more member* than could actually be counted" (Eliot). The "third" is, however, Christ on the road to Emmaus.

What is that sound high in the air
Murmur of maternal lamentation
Who are those hooded hordes swarming
Over endless plains, stumbling in cracked earth
Ringed by the flat horizon only
What is the city over the mountains
Cracks and reforms and bursts in the violet air
Falling towers
Jerusalem Athens Alexandria
Vienna London
Unreal[82]

A woman drew her long black hair out tight
And fiddled whisper music on those strings
And bats with baby faces in the violet light
Whistled, and beat their wings
And crawled head downward down a blackened wall
And upside down in air were towers
Tolling reminiscent bells, that kept the hours
And voices singing out of empty cisterns and exhausted wells.

In this decayed hole among the mountains
In the faint moonlight, the grass is singing
Over the tumbled graves, about the chapel
There is the empty chapel,[83] only the wind's home.
It has no windows, and the door swings,
Dry bones can harm no one.
Only a cock stood on the rooftree
Co co rico co co rico[84]
In a flash of lightning. Then a damp gust
Bringing rain

Ganga[85] was sunken, and the limp leaves
Waited for rain, while the black clouds
Gathered far distant, over Himavant.[86]
The jungle crouched, humped in silence.
Then spoke the thunder

[82] "Cf. Hermann Hesse, *Blick ins Chaos*" (Eliot). The lines Eliot quotes from Hesse's *A Glimpse into Chaos* (1920) may be translated: "Already half of Europe, already at least half of Eastern Europe, is on the way to chaos, going drunkenly, in spiritual madness, along the edge of the abyss, singing drunkenly and rhapsodically, as Dimitri Karamazov [in Dostoevsky's *The Brothers Karamazov*] sang. The shocked bourgeoisie laughs at these songs; the saint and the seer hear them with tears."

[83] The Chapel Perilous, where the Grail Knight prepares for the final quest.

[84] Cockadoodledoo. The cock's crow heralds rebirth, dispels evil spirits, and recalls Peter's denial of Christ (Matthew 26).

[85] The Ganges river. [86] The Himalaya mountains.

Da
Datta:[87] what have we given?
My friend, blood shaking my heart
The awful daring of a moment's surrender
Which an age of prudence can never retract
By this, and this only, we have existed
Which is not to be found in our obituaries
Or in memories draped by the beneficent spider[88]
Or under seals broken by the lean solicitor
In our empty rooms
Da
Dayadhvam: I have heard the key[89]
Turn in the door once and turn once only
We think of the key, each in his prison
Thinking of the key, each confirms a prison
Only at nightfall, aethereal rumours
Revive for a moment a broken Coriolanus[90]
Da
Damyata: The boat responded
Gaily, to the hand expert with sail and oar
The sea was calm, your heart would have responded
Gaily, when invited, beating obedient
To controlling hands

I sat upon the shore
Fishing,[91] with the arid plain behind me
Shall I at least set my lands in order?
London Bridge is falling down falling down falling down
Poi s'ascose nel foco che gli affina[92]

[87]"'Datta, dayadhvam, damyata' (Give, sympathise, control). The fable of the meaning of the Thunder is found in the *Brihadaranyaka—Upanishad*, 5, 1" (Eliot). The fable Eliot refers to in the sacred Hindu text, the Upanishads, tells of how gods, men, and demons ask the god Prajápati what their duty is. He responds, in thunder, to each with the single syllable "Da." The men interpret this as *datta* (give alms), the demons as *dayadhvam* (sympathize with others), and the gods as *damyata* (control, practice self-restraint). All are correct, and the voice of the thunder ("da, da, da") continues to remind us of "the three great disciplines."

[88]"Cf. Webster, *The White Devil,* V,vi:

'. . . they'll remarry
Ere the worm pierce your winding-sheet, ere the spider
Make a thick curtain for your epitaphs'" (Eliot).

[89]lines 412–415. Eliot gives as the source of this passage Dante's line (*Inferno* XXXIII.46): "and below I heard the door of the horrible tower nailed up." Count Ugolino is describing how he and his young sons were starved to death. Eliot also quotes from F. H. Bradley, the philosopher upon whose work he wrote his doctoral dissertation, on how each person is locked within his own self: "the whole world for each [soul] is peculiar and private to that soul."

[90]Title character in Shakespeare's play. Coriolanus's pride and scorn for the masses make him a good example of one who fails to "sympathize."

[91]"V. Weston: *From Ritual to Romance;* chapter on the Fisher King" (Eliot).

[92]"V. *Purgatorio,* XXVI, 148" (Eliot). In Dante's passage, the poet Arnaut Daniel describes how he is purging his earthly lusts in Purgatory. With additional lines which Eliot provides in the note, the passage reads, "'And so I pray you, by that Virtue which guides you to the top of the stair, be reminded in time of my pain.' Then he hid himself in the fire which purifies them." Line 428 is translated by the last sentence of this passage.

Quando fiam uti chelidon[93]—O swallow swallow
Le Prince d'Aquitaine á la tour abolie[94]
These fragments I have shored against my ruins
Why then Ile fit you. Hieronymo's mad againe.[95]
Datta. Dayadhvam. Damyata.
            Shantih   shantih   shantih[96]

THE HOLLOW MEN

Mistah Kurtz—he dead.[1]
A penny for the Old Guy.[2]

I

We are the hollow men
We are the stuffed men
Leaning together
Headpiece filled with straw. Alas!
Our dried voices, when
We whisper together
Are quiet and meaningless
As wind in dry grass

[93] "V. *Pervigilium Veneris.* Cf. Philomela in Parts II and III" (Eliot). The line means "When shall I become as the swallow?" The *Pervigilium Veneris* (or "Vigil of Venus") is an anonymous late Latin poem which celebrates spring and Venus. It contains a reference to the Philomela myth used earlier in *The Waste Land;* Philomela longs to "become as the swallow" so that she "may cease to be silent."

[94] "V. Gerard de Nerval, Sonnet *El Desdichado*" (Eliot). The line (French), from "The Disinherited," by de Nerval (1808–1855), means, "The Prince of Aquitaine at the ruined tower." The line is a romantically melancholy self-description of the poet. The "ruined tower," a symbol of impotence, suggests the fall of civilizations and the "Tower Struck by Lightning" of the Tarot deck.

[95] "V. Kyd's *Spanish Tragedy*" (Eliot). In Thomas Kyd's Elizabethan revenge tragedy (c. 1587), subtitled "Hieronymo Is Mad Again," the main character, whose son has been murdered, is asked to write a court masque. Seeing a chance to take revenge through the play, he replies, "Why then Ile fit [or accommodate] you." Eliot seems to imply a comparison with himself and with *The Waste Land* as a poem to "fit" his audience.

[96] *Shantih.* "Repeated as here, a formal ending to an Upanishad. 'The Peace which passeth understanding' is our equivalent to this word" (Eliot).

[1] *Mistah Kurtz—he dead.* These are the words with which the manager's boy announces the death of Kurtz in Joseph Conrad's *Heart of Darkness* (1899). A number of details in "The Hollow Men" echo this work, including the central image. The colonialists in the novella are described as "hollow men": Marlow thinks he could poke his finger through the Brickmaker and "would find nothing inside but a little loose dirt, maybe," while Kurtz himself is "hollow at the core." The other major source of the image of hollowness is the first circle of Dante's *Inferno,* where live those who deserve "neither praise nor blame," never having committed themselves at all. References to both *The Divine Comedy* and *Heart of Darkness* pervade "The Hollow Men."

[2] *A penny for the Old Guy.* November 5, the anniversary of Guy Fawkes's attempt to blow up the Parliament buildings in 1605, is a folk holiday in England. On "Guy Fawkes Day," children make straw effigies of Guy Fawkes—"Old Guys"—and beg for pennies for fireworks.

Or rats' feet over broken glass
In our dry cellar

Shape without form, shade without colour,
Paralysed force, gesture without motion;

Those who have crossed
With direct eyes, to death's other Kingdom[3]
Remember us—if at all—not as lost
Violent souls, but only
As the hollow men
The stuffed men.

II

Eyes I dare not meet in dreams
In death's dream kingdom
These do not appear:
There, the eyes are
Sunlight on a broken column
There, is a tree swinging
And voices are
In the wind's singing
More distant and more solemn
Than a fading star.

Let me be no nearer
In death's dream kingdom
Let me also wear
Such deliberate disguises
Rat's coat, crowskin, crossed staves
In a field[4]
Behaving as the wind behaves
No nearer—

Not that final meeting
In the twilight kingdom[5]

[3] The hollow men live in one "death's Kingdom"; the literally dead live in the other. They have crossed "with direct eyes" as a sign of spiritual confidence and in an allusion to Beatrice's direct gaze, which Dante cannot meet at the end of the *Purgatory* and in canto IV of the *Paradise* in *The Divine Comedy*.

[4] English scarecrows frequently have dead animals and birds attached to them as a warning.

[5] Possibly a reference to Dante's meeting with Beatrice before entering Paradise (*Purgatory* XXX).

III

This is the dead land
This is cactus land
Here the stone images
Are raised, here they receive
The supplication of a dead man's hand
Under the twinkle of a fading star.

Is it like this
In death's other kingdom
Waking alone
At the hour when we are
Trembling with tenderness
Lips that would kiss
Form prayers to broken stone.

IV

The eyes are not here
There are no eyes here
In this valley of dying stars
In this hollow valley
This broken jaw of our lost kingdoms

In this last of meeting places
We grope together
And avoid speech
Gathered on this beach of the tumid river[6]

Sightless, unless
The eyes reappear
As the perpetual star
Multifoliate rose[7]
Of death's twilight kingdom
The hope only
Of empty men.

V

Here we go round the prickly pear
Prickly pear prickly pear
Here we go round the prickly pear
At five o'clock in the morning.[8]

[6] Both the Acheron, the river that encircles Hell in *The Divine Comedy,* and the Congo, in *Heart of Darkness.*

[7] The image of the blessed in Paradise in *The Divine Comedy* (*Paradise* XXXII).

[8] Parody of children's song, "Here We Go Round the Mulberry Bush."

Between the idea
And the reality[9]
Between the motion
And the act
Falls the Shadow[10]
For Thine is the Kingdom

Between the conception
And the creation
Between the emotion
And the response
Falls the Shadow
Life is very long

Between the desire
And the spasm
Between the potency
And the existence
Between the essence
And the descent
Falls the Shadow
For Thine is the Kingdom

For Thine is
Life is
For Thine is the

This is the way the world ends
This is the way the world ends
This is the way the world ends
Not with a bang but a whimper.[11]

[9] The Platonic distinction between abstract forms and concrete phenomena, but also echoing Shakespeare's *Julius Caesar,* II.i.63–65:

Between the acting of a dreadful thing
And the first motion, all the interim is
Like a phantasma or a hideous dream.

[10] Eliot connected this line with Ernest Dowson's poem *Cynara* (1896): "Last night, ah, yesternight, betwixt her lips and mine / There fell thy shadow, Cynara!" The "Shadow" here, which divides the various versions of desire and action, is possibly the Holy Ghost, or more precisely, the memory of a lost faith in the Holy Ghost, which blocks present action as the shadow of Cynara blocks present love.

[11] The imagery of the last line, contrasting the "bang" of positive action, whether for good or evil (like Guy Fawkes's plot), with the "whimper" of the hollow men, goes back to the Guy Fawkes Day fireworks of the epigraph.

TRADITION AND THE INDIVIDUAL TALENT

I

In English writing we seldom speak of tradition, though we occasionally apply its name in deploring its absence. We cannot refer to "the tradition" or to "a tradition"; at most, we employ the adjective in saying that the poetry of So-and-so is "traditional" or even "too traditional." Seldom, perhaps, does the word appear except in a phrase of censure. If otherwise, it is vaguely approbative, with the implication, as to the work approved, of some pleasing archaeological reconstruction. You can hardly make the word agreeable to English ears without this comfortable reference to the reassuring science of archaeology.

Certainly the word is not likely to appear in our appreciations of living or dead writers. Every nation, every race, has not only its own creative, but its own critical turn of mind; and is even more oblivious of the shortcomings and limitations of its critical habits than of those of its creative genius. We know, or think we know, from the enormous mass of critical writing that has appeared in the French language the critical method or habit of the French; we only conclude (we are such unconscious people) that the French are "more critical" than we, and sometimes even plume ourselves a little with the fact, as if the French were the less spontaneous. Perhaps they are; but we might remind ourselves that criticism is as inevitable as breathing, and that we should be none the worse for articulating what passes in our minds when we read a book and feel an emotion about it, for criticizing our own minds in their work of criticism. One of the facts that might come to light in this process is our tendency to insist, when we praise a poet, upon those aspects of his work in which he least resembles any one else. In these aspects or parts of his work we pretend to find what is individual, what is the peculiar essence of the man. We dwell with satisfaction upon the poet's difference from his predecessors, especially his immediate predecessors; we endeavour to find something that can be isolated in order to be enjoyed. Whereas if we approach a poet without this prejudice we shall often find that not only the best, but the most individual parts of his work may be those in which the dead poets, his ancestors, assert their immortality most vigorously. And I do not mean the impressionable period of adolescence, but the period of full maturity.

Yet if the only form of tradition, of handing down, consisted in following the ways of the immediate generation before us in a blind or timid adherence to its successes, "tradition" should positively be discouraged. We have seen many such simple currents soon lost in the sand; and novelty is better than repetition. Tradition is a matter of much wider significance. It cannot be inherited, and if you want it you must obtain it by great labour. It involves, in the first place, the historical sense, which we may call nearly indispensable to any one who would continue to be a poet beyond his twenty-fifth year; and the historical sense involves a perception, not only of the pastness of the past, but of its presence; the historical sense compels a man to write not merely with his own generation in his bones, but with a feeling that the whole of the literature of Europe from Homer and within it the whole of the literature of his own country has a simultaneous existence and composes a simultaneous order. This historical sense, which is a sense of the timeless as well as of the temporal and of the timeless and of the temporal together, is what makes a writer traditional. And it is at the same time what makes a writer most acutely conscious of his place in time, of his own contemporaneity.

No poet, no artist of any art, has his complete meaning alone. His significance, his appreciation is the appreciation of his relation to the dead poets and artists. You cannot value him alone; you must set him, for contrast and comparison, among the dead. I mean this as a principle of aesthetic, not merely historical, criticism. The necessity that he shall conform, that he shall cohere, is not onesided; what happens when a new work of art is created is something that happens simultaneously to all the works of art which preceded it. The existing monuments form an ideal order among themselves, which is modified by the introduction of the new (the really new) work of art among them. The existing order is complete before the new work arrives; for order to persist after the supervention of novelty, the *whole* existing order must be, if ever so slightly, altered; and so the relations, proportions, values of each work of art toward the whole are readjusted; and this is conformity between the old and the new. Whoever has approved this idea of order, of the form of European, of English literature will not find it preposterous that the past should be altered by the present as much as the present is directed by the past. And the poet who is aware of this will be aware of great difficulties and responsibilities.

In a peculiar sense he will be aware also that he must inevitably be judged by the standards of the past. I say judged, not amputated, by them; not judged to be as good as, or worse or better than, the dead; and certainly not judged by the canons of dead critics. It is a judgment, a comparison, in which two things are measured by each other. To conform merely would be for the new work not really to conform at all; it would not be new, and would therefore not be a work of art. And we do not quite say that the new is more valuable because it fits in; but its fitting in is a test of its value—a test, it is true, which can only be slowly and cautiously applied, for we are none of us infallible judges of conformity. We say: it appears to conform, and is perhaps individual, or it appears individual, and may conform; but we are hardly likely to find that it is one and not the other.

To proceed to a more intelligible exposition of the relation of the poet to the past: he can neither take the past as a lump, an indiscriminate bolus,[1] nor can he form himself wholly on one or two private admirations, nor can he form himself wholly upon one preferred period. The first course is inadmissible, the second is an important experience of youth, and the third is a pleasant and highly desirable supplement. The poet must be very conscious of the main current, which does not at all flow invariably through the most distinguished reputations. He must be quite aware of the obvious fact that art never improves, but that the material of art is never quite the same. He must be aware that the mind of Europe—the mind of his own coun-

[1] A large pill.

try—a mind which he learns in time to be much more important than his own private mind—is a mind which changes, and that this change is a development which abandons nothing *en route,* which does not superannuate either Shakespeare, or Homer, or the rock drawing of the Magdalenian draughtsmen.[2] That this development, refinement perhaps, complication certainly, is not, from the point of view of the artist, any improvement. Perhaps not even an improvement from the point of view of the psychologist or not to the extent which we imagine; perhaps only in the end based upon a complication in economics and machinery. But the difference between the present and the past is that the conscious present is an awareness of the past in a way and to an extent which the past's awareness of itself cannot show.

Some one said: "The dead writers are remote from us because we *know* so much more than they did." Precisely, and they are that which we know.

I am alive to a usual objection to what is clearly part of my programme for the *métier*[3] of poetry. The objection is that the doctrine requires a ridiculous amount of erudition (pedantry), a claim which can be rejected by appeal to the lives of poets in any pantheon. It will even be affirmed that much learning deadens or perverts poetic sensibility. While, however, we persist in believing that a poet ought to know as much as will not encroach upon his necessary receptivity and necessary laziness, it is not desirable to confine knowledge to whatever can be put into a useful shape for examinations, drawing-rooms, or the still more pretentious modes of publicity. Some can absorb knowledge, the more tardy must sweat for it. Shakespeare acquired more essential history from Plutarch[4] than most men could from the whole British Museum. What is to be insisted upon is that the poet must develop or procure the consciousness of the past and that he should continue to develop this consciousness throughout his career.

What happens is a continual surrender of himself as he is at the moment to something which is more valuable. The progress of an artist is a continual self-sacrifice, a continual extinction of personality.

There remains to define this process of depersonalization and its relation to the sense of tradition. It is in this depersonalization that art may be said to approach the condition of science. I, therefore, invite you to consider, as a suggestive analogy, the action which takes place when a bit of finely filiated[5] platinum is introduced into a chamber containing oxygen and sulphur dioxide.

II

Honest criticism and sensitive appreciation are directed not upon the poet but upon the poetry. If we attend to the confused cries of the newspaper critics and the *susurrus*[6] of popular repetition that follows, we shall hear the

[2] The prehistoric creators of the much admired cave drawings at La Madeleine, France.
[3] Practice, craft.
[4] The *Parallel Lives* of Plutarch (A.D. 46?–c. 120) were the major source of Shakespeare's Roman plays.
[5] Drawn out into a fine wire. [6] Murmuring (Latin).

names of poets in great numbers; if we seek not Blue-book knowledge,[7] but the enjoyment of poetry, and ask for a poem, we shall seldom find it. I have tried to point out the importance of the relation of the poem to other poems by other authors, and suggested the conception of poetry as a living whole of all the poetry that has ever been written. The other aspect of this Impersonal theory of poetry is the relation of the poem to its author. And I hinted, by an analogy, that the mind of the mature poet differs from that of the immature one not precisely in any valuation of "personality," not being necessarily more interesting, or having "more to say," but rather by being a more finely perfected medium in which special, or very varied, feelings are at liberty to enter into new combinations.

The analogy was that of the catalyst. When the two gases previously mentioned are mixed in the presence of a filament of platinum, they form sulphurous acid. This combination takes place only if the platinum is present; nevertheless the newly formed acid contains no trace of platinum, and the platinum itself is apparently unaffected; has remained inert, neutral, and unchanged. The mind of the poet is the shred of platinum. It may partly or exclusively operate upon the experience of the man himself; but, the more perfect the artist, the more completely separate in him will be the man who suffers and the mind which creates; the more perfectly will the mind digest and transmute the passions which are its material.

The experience, you will notice, the elements which enter the presence of the transforming catalyst, are of two kinds: emotions and feelings. The effect of a work of art upon the person who enjoys it is an experience different in kind from any experience not of art. It may be formed out of one emotion, or may be a combination of several; and various feelings, inhering for the writer in particular words or phrases or images, may be added to compose the final result. Or great poetry may be made without the direct use of any emotion whatever: composed out of feelings solely. Canto XV of the *Inferno* (Brunetto Latini) is a working up of the emotion evident in the situation; but the effect, though single as that of any work of art, is obtained by considerable complexity of detail. The last quatrain gives an image, a feeling attaching to an image, which "came," which did not develop simply out of what precedes, but which was probably in suspension in the poet's mind until the proper combination arrived for it to add itself to. The poet's mind is in fact a receptacle for seizing and storing up numberless feelings, phrases, images, which remain there until all the particles which can unite to form a new compound are present together.

If you compare several representative passages of the greatest poetry you see how great is the variety of types of combination, and also how completely any semi-ethical criterion of "sublimity" misses the mark. For it is not the "greatness," the intensity, of the emotions, the components, but the intensity of the artistic process, the pressure, so to speak, under which the fusion takes place, that counts. The episode of Paolo and Francesca[8] employs a definite emotion, but the intensity of the poetry is something quite different from whatever intensity in the supposed experience it may

[7] Official, conventional knowledge, from the blue covers in which government publications were bound.

[8] The lovers in Dante's *Inferno* V, treated with sympathy and tenderness.

give the impression of. It is no more intense, furthermore, than Canto XXVI, the voyage of Ulysses, which has not the direct dependence upon an emotion. Great variety is possible in the process of transmutation of emotion: the murder of Agamemnon, or the agony of Othello, gives an artistic effect apparently closer to a possible original than the scenes from Dante. In the *Agamemnon,* the artistic emotion approximates to the emotion of an actual spectator; in *Othello* to the emotion of the protagonist himself. But the difference between art and the event is always absolute; the combination which is the murder of Agamemnon is probably as complex as that which is the voyage of Ulysses. In either case there has been a fusion of elements. The ode of Keats contains a number of feelings which have nothing particular to do with the nightingale, but which the nightingale, partly, perhaps, because of its attractive name, and partly because of its reputation, served to bring together.

The point of view which I am struggling to attack is perhaps related to the metaphysical theory of the substantial unity of the soul: for my meaning is, that the poet has, not a "personality" to express, but a particular medium, which is only a medium and not a personality, in which impressions and experiences combine in peculiar and unexpected ways. Impressions and experiences which are important for the man may take no place in the poetry, and those which become important in the poetry may play quite a negligible part in the man, the personality.

I will quote a passage which is unfamiliar enough to be regarded with fresh attention in the light—or darkness—of these observations:

And now methinks I could e'en chide myself
For doating on her beauty, though her death
Shall be revenged after no common action.
Does the silkworm expend her yellow labours
For thee? For thee does she undo herself?
Are lordships sold to maintain ladyships
For the poor benefit of a bewildering minute?
Why does yon fellow falsify highways,
And put his life between the judge's lips,
To refine such a thing—keeps horse and men
To beat their valours for her? . . .[9]

In this passage (as is evident if it is taken in its context) there is a combination of positive and negative emotions: an intensely strong attraction toward beauty and an equally intense fascination by the ugliness which is contrasted with it and which destroys it. This balance of contrasted emotion is in the dramatic situation to which the speech is pertinent, but that situation alone is inadequate to it. This is, so to speak, the structural emotion, provided by the drama. But the whole effect, the dominant tone, is due to the fact that a number of floating feelings, having an affinity to this emotion by no means superficially evident, have combined with it to give us a new art emotion.

It is not in his personal emotions, the emotions provoked by particular

[9] From Cyril Tourneur's *The Revenger's Tragedy* (1607), III.v.67–78.

events in his life, that the poet is in any way remarkable or interesting. His particular emotions may be simple, or crude, or flat. The emotion in his poetry will be a very complex thing, but not with the complexity of the emotions of people who have very complex or unusual emotions in life. One error, in fact, of eccentricity in poetry is to seek for new human emotions to express; and in this search for novelty in the wrong place it discovers the perverse. The business of the poet is not to find new emotions, but to use the ordinary ones and, in working them up into poetry, to express feelings which are not in actual emotions at all. And emotions which he has never experienced will serve his turn as well as those familiar to him. Consequently, we must believe that "emotion recollected in tranquillity"[10] is an inexact formula. For it is neither emotion, nor recollection, nor, without distortion of meaning, tranquillity. It is a concentration, and a new thing resulting from the concentration, of a very great number of experiences which to the practical and active person would not seem to be experiences at all; it is a concentration which does not happen consciously or of deliberation. These experiences are not "recollected," and they finally unite in an atmosphere which is "tranquil" only in that it is a passive attending upon the event. Of course this is not quite the whole story. There is a great deal, in the writing of poetry, which must be conscious and deliberate. In fact, the bad poet is usually unconscious where he ought to be conscious, and conscious where he ought to be unconscious. Both errors tend to make him "personal." Poetry is not a turning loose of emotion, but an escape from emotion; it is not the expression of personality, but an escape from personality. But, of course, only those who have personality and emotions know what it means to want to escape from these things.

III

ὁ δὲ νους ἴσως θειότερόν τι καὶ ἀπαθές ἐστιν.[11]

This essay proposes to halt at the frontier of metaphysics or mysticism, and confine itself to such practical conclusions as can be applied by the responsible person interested in poetry. To divert interest from the poet to the poetry is a laudable aim: for it would conduce to a juster estimation of actual poetry, good and bad. There are many people who appreciate the expression of sincere emotion in verse, and there is a smaller number of people who can appreciate technical excellence. But very few know when there is an expression of *significant* emotion, emotion which has its life in the poem and not in the history of the poet. The emotion of art is impersonal. And the poet cannot reach this impersonality without surrendering himself wholly to the work to be done. And he is not likely to know what is to be done unless he lives in what is not merely the present, but the present

[10] Wordsworth's famous description of poetry in the Preface to *Lyrical Ballads* (1800). Actually, Wordsworth did not say that poetry is "emotion recollected in tranquillity" but that it "takes its origin" in such emotion.

[11] A line from Aristotle's *De Anima* (On the Soul), I.4: "The mind is doubtless more divine and less subject to passion."

moment of the past, unless he is conscious, not of what is dead, but of what is already living.

from HAMLET AND HIS PROBLEMS

. . . . So far from being Shakespeare's masterpiece, the play is most certainly an artistic failure. In several ways the play is puzzling, and disquieting as is none of the others. Of all the plays it is the longest and is possibly the one on which Shakespeare spent most pains; and yet he has left in it superfluous and inconsistent scenes which even hasty revision should have noticed. The versification is variable. Lines like

Look, the morn, in russet mantle clad,
Walks o'er the dew of yon high eastern hill,

are of the Shakespeare of *Romeo and Juliet.* The lines in Act v, sc.ii,

Sir, in my heart there was a kind of fighting
That would not let me sleep . . .
Up from my cabin,
My sea-gown scarf'd about me, in the dark
Grop'd I to find out them: had my desire;
Finger'd their packet;

are of his quite mature. Both workmanship and thought are in an unstable position. We are surely justified in attributing the play, with that other profoundly interesting play of "intractable" material and astonishing versification, *Measure for Measure,* to a period of crisis, after which follow the tragic successes which culminate in *Coriolanus. Coriolanus* may be not as "interesting" as *Hamlet,* but it is, with *Antony and Cleopatra,* Shakespeare's most assured artistic success. And probably more people have thought *Hamlet* a work of art because they found it interesting, than have found it interesting because it is a work of art. It is the "Mona Lisa" of literature.

The grounds of *Hamlet's* failure are not immediately obvious. Mr. Robertson is undoubtedly correct in concluding that the essential emotion of the play is the feeling of a son towards a guilty mother:

"[Hamlet's] tone is that of one who has suffered tortures on the score of his mother's degradation. . . . The guilt of a mother is an almost intolerable motive for drama, but it had to be maintained and emphasized to supply a psychological solution, or rather a hint of one."[1]

This, however, is by no means the whole story. It is not merely the "guilt of a mother" that cannot be handled as Shakespeare handled the suspicion of Othello, the infatuation of Antony, or the pride of Coriolanus. The subject might conceivably have expanded into a tragedy like these, intelligible, self-complete, in the sunlight. *Hamlet,* like the sonnets, is full of some

[1] John M. Robertson, *The Problem of Hamlet* (London: G. Allen & Unwin, 1919), p. 73. This is one of two books of which this essay is a review.

stuff that the writer could not drag to light, contemplate, or manipulate into art. And when we search for this feeling, we find it, as in the sonnets, very difficult to localize. You cannot point to it in the speeches; indeed, if you examine the two famous soliloquies you see the versification of Shakespeare, but a content which might be claimed by another, perhaps by the author of the *Revenge of Bussy d'Ambois,* Act v, sc. i.[2] We find Shakespeare's Hamlet not in the action, not in any quotations that we might select, so much as in an unmistakable tone which is unmistakably not in the earlier play.

The only way of expressing emotion in the form of art is by finding an "objective correlative"; in other words, a set of objects, a situation, a chain of events which shall be the formula of that *particular* emotion; such that when the external facts, which must terminate in sensory experience, are given, the emotion is immediately evoked. If you examine any of Shakespeare's more successful tragedies, you will find this exact equivalence; you will find that the state of mind of Lady Macbeth walking in her sleep has been communicated to you by a skillful accumulation of imagined sensory impressions; the words of Macbeth on hearing of his wife's death strike us as if, given the sequence of events, these words were automatically released by the last event in the series. The artistic "inevitability" lies in this complete adequacy of the external to the emotion; and this is precisely what is deficient in *Hamlet.* Hamlet (the man) is dominated by an emotion which is inexpressible, because it is in *excess* of the facts as they appear. And the supposed identity of Hamlet with his author is genuine to this point: that Hamlet's bafflement at the absence of objective equivalent to his feelings is a prolongation of the bafflement of his creator in the face of his artistic problem. Hamlet is up against the difficulty that his disgust is occasioned by his mother, but that his mother is not an adequate equivalent for it; his disgust envelops and exceeds her. It is thus a feeling which he cannot understand; he cannot objectify it, and it therefore remains to poison life and obstruct action. None of the possible actions can satisfy it; and nothing that Shakespeare can do with the plot can express Hamlet for him. And it must be noticed that the very nature of the *donnèes*[3] of the problem precludes objective equivalence. To have heightened the criminality of Gertrude would have been to provide the formula for a totally different emotion in Hamlet; it is just *because* her character is so negative and insignificant that she arouses in Hamlet the feeling which she is incapable of representing.

The "madness" of Hamlet lay to Shakespeare's hand; in the earlier play a simple ruse, and to the end, we may presume, understood as a ruse by the audience. For Shakespeare it is less than madness and more than feigned. The levity of Hamlet, his repetition of phrase, his puns, are not part of a deliberate plan of dissimulation, but a form of emotional relief. In the character Hamlet it is the buffoonery of an emotion which can find no outlet in action; in the dramatist it is the buffoonery of an emotion which he cannot express in art. The intense feeling, ecstatic or terrible, without an object or exceeding its object, is something which every person of sensibility

[2] A play by the Elizabethan George Chapman (1559–1634).
[3] The "givens," the set of assumptions upon which a literary work is based.

has known; it is doubtless a subject of study for pathologists. It often occurs in adolescence: the ordinary person puts these feelings to sleep, or trims down his feelings to fit the business world; the artist keeps them alive by his ability to intensify the world to his emotions. The Hamlet of Laforgue[4] is an adolescent; the Hamlet of Shakespeare is not, he has not that explanation and excuse. We must simply admit that here Shakespeare tackled a problem which proved too much for him. Why he attempted it at all is an insoluble puzzle; under compulsion of what experience he attempted to express the inexpressibly horrible, we cannot ever know. We need a great many facts in his biography; and we should like to know whether, and when, and after or at the same time as what personal experience, he read Montaigne, II. xii, *Apologie de Raimond Sebond.*[5] We should have, finally, to know something which is by hypothesis unknowable, for we assume it to be an experience which, in the manner indicated, exceeded the facts. We should have to understand things which Shakespeare did not understand himself.

[4] Eliot is alluding to an ironic modernization of the Hamlet story by the French Symbolist poet Jules Laforgue (1860–87): "Hamlet, or The Results of Filial Piety" (1885–86).

[5] "Apology for Raymond Sebond," a famous essay by Michel de Montaigne (1533–92); the essay's skeptical, questioning spirit has often been compared to that of *Hamlet.*

Katherine Anne Porter
(1890–1980)

"All the conscious and recollected years of my life," Katherine Anne Porter wrote in 1940, "have been lived to this day under the heavy threat of world catastrophe, and most of the energies of my mind and spirit have been spent in the effort to grasp the meaning of those threats, to trace them to their sources and to understand the logic of this majestic and terrible failure of the life of man in the Western world." At the time, Porter's reputation rested primarily upon a handful of beautifully crafted but rather fragile short stories, mostly about a girl growing up in Texas; it must have been startling to read that her theme was "the life of man in the Western world." But the statement was precisely true. Porter had the great short-story writer's gift of making the part stand for the whole, and the power of her art lies in the way small actions, firmly planted in a specific time and place, open up into large questions of human life, especially the tormented life of her own time.

Porter was born in 1890 in Indian Creek, Texas. Bits of her family history appear, slightly disguised, in a number of her stories. Her father's family had moved, just after the Civil War, from Kentucky to Texas, where they preserved something of the culture of Kentucky plantation life; Porter remembered that even in their poorest days they maintained a library and there were books all over the house. Her mother died when Porter was two, and the father moved the children to Kyle, Texas, to be reared by his mother, a vigorous, strong-willed woman remembered in several of Porter's stories. She too died when Porter was eleven, and the family moved to San

Antonio, where she attended convent schools. She ran away at sixteen and married, divorcing three years later. On her own, she moved to Chicago, where she remained three years, working on a newspaper and as an extra in the then-thriving Chicago movie industry. After moving back to Texas, she supported herself for a time singing Scottish ballads. In 1918 she took a job as a reporter for the Denver Rocky Mountain News. *After almost dying of influenza in Denver, she moved on to New York, where she worked as a free-lance writer for the next ten years, with interludes back in Texas and in Mexico.*

Porter's first published short story, "María Concepción," appeared in 1922; this and a series of other stories first published in magazines in the 1920s were collected under the title Flowering Judas and Other Stories *in 1930. She received a Guggenheim grant in 1931, which enabled her to spend a year in Mexico and then, in 1932, to go to Germany, where she met (and was appalled by) Hitler and other leading Nazis. In 1933, she married Eugene Pressly, of the U.S. diplomatic service, and remained in Paris for several years. The marriage ended in divorce in 1938; in the same year, she married Albert Erskine, Jr., an English professor at Louisiana State University, and then lived in Baton Rouge for four years.* Pale Horse, Pale Rider: Three Short Novels *appeared in 1939; it contained, besides the title novella,* Noon Wine *and* Old Mortality. *Divorced from Erskine in 1944, Porter led a somewhat nomadic life for several years, spending time in Hollywood as a screenwriter, appearing as a lecturer or a writer-in-residence at a number of colleges and universities, and eventually making her home in a Maryland suburb of Washington.*

When The Leaning Tower and Other Stories *appeared in 1944, Porter found herself the subject of a rather extensive legend. Her three collections of stories had not been commercially successful, but they had received high critical praise and had made her something of a "writer's writer," especially admired by her fellow artists. Little was known about her personal life, and rumors circulated that she was very beautiful (as she was), that she had been a bathing beauty in silent movies, that she had had a love affair with a Mexican revolutionary, that she had a trunkful of unpublished fiction, and that she was working on a long novel as well as a biography of Cotton Mather.*

The myth of the long novel was based on truth. She had begun to plan Ship of Fools *in 1932, when she read a fifteenth-century allegory by that name and decided to use it as the framework for a novel about her recent voyage to Germany. The novel was originally to be short and was to be included in the volume that contained* Pale Horse, Pale Rider. *After a number of false starts, Porter began writing the novel in 1941; she continued to work on it for twenty years, finishing it in 1961. Publication of fragments of the novel in various magazines had fed its legend, and its long-awaited publication in 1962 brought Porter her first major commercial success. The critical reception of the book was mixed, but on the whole favorable; one prestigious critic called it "the* Middlemarch *of a later day" (in reference to the social panorama of George Eliot's famous novel of 1871–72). Later critics have on the whole treated* Ship of Fools *favorably but have found it below the level of her finest short stories, some commenting that its best passages read like short stories.*

Porter's Collected Stories *appeared in 1965, her* Collected Essays and Occasional Writings *in 1970. A final book,* The Never Ending Wrong *(1977), dealt with the Sacco and Vanzetti case, in which two political radicals were executed for murder in 1927 after an unjust trial; Porter had been among those who demonstrated against the execution. She died in Washington in 1980, at the age of ninety.*

Porter herself identified the writers who were most influential in the development of her art. She once commented that, like other writers of her generation, she was educated "not at schools at all but by five writers: Henry James, James Joyce, W. B. Yeats, T. S. Eliot, and Ezra Pound." (She later added Virginia Woolf to this list.) This rollcall of Modernists may seem surprising, because at first glance Porter's fiction seems comparatively traditional in form, with clear story lines, consistent points of view, and a conservative narrative style. Her modernity lies not in obvious experimental techniques but in the complex layering by which she places simple actions in rich contexts of history and myth. She tells of reading a copy of Joyce's Dubliners *in a little Texas town soon after it appeared and of the "deep world of the imagination" it opened up to her. Her stories are like Joyce's in the care and the thoroughness with which they draw out meanings from slight experiences.*

Like Joyce, too, Porter is a highly autobiographical writer. She wrote mainly, she said, "from memory," drawing upon incidents in her own life around which she allowed other memories and details to accumulate until they formed a pattern. "Miranda" was the name she used to represent herself in her stories; Miranda appears in eight of the most important ones and seems to provide the narrative point of view for several others in which she is not named.

Pale Horse, Pale Rider *is based closely upon Porter's near-fatal bout with influenza in Denver in 1918, but it transcends autobiography in its artistry. The influenza Miranda succumbs to was part of a major epidemic that swept the country in the last year of World War I, a fact hinted at early in the story, and, juxtaposed with the carnage of the war, it provides the major metaphor of the story. Adam's name sets up resonances of the Eden myth, and Miranda's descent into illness, from which she emerges with a hard-won knowledge, echoes the myth of the descent into the underworld. The folksong of the title and the pale horseman of the Apocalypse who was to destroy a fourth of the world add other layerings of allusion. A simple story of a wartime love affair becomes a powerful lament for the "world catastrophe" of World War I, a dark prophecy of another impending war, and a searching personal examination of the relation of the individual to those catastrophes.*

FURTHER READING *(prepared by W. J. R.):* Joan Givner's *Katherine Anne Porter,* 1982, is a full-length biography. A good biographical sketch can be found in George Hendrick's *Katherine Anne Porter,* 1965. This work is also particularly good on Porter's Mexican stories. Excellent, widely varied critical evaluations of Porter's work appear in *Katherine Anne Porter: A Critical Symposium,* ed. Lodwick Hartley and George Gore, 1969. Sarah Youngblood's "Structural Imagery in *Pale Horse, Pale Rider*" offers a balanced interpretation of the novella. Glenway Wescott's "Katherine Anne Porter Personally" and Barbara Thompson's "An Interview" offer interesting personal views of the writer. John Edward Hardy's monograph *Katherine Anne Porter,* 1973, classifies the stories by four themes and discusses *Ship of Fools* as successful allegory. William Nance's *Katherine Anne Porter and the Art of Rejection,* 1963, an influential—and controversial—treatment of Porter's view of the world, treats the Miranda stories at length and also *Ship of Fools.* M. M. Liberman's *Katherine Anne Porter's Fiction,* 1971, synthesizes earlier criticism and is particularly good on *Ship of Fools, Old Mortality,* and *Noon Wine. Katherine Anne Porter: A Collection of Critical Essays,* ed. Robert Penn Warren, 1979, includes, among other things, Cleanth Brooks's influential essay on "The Grave," an interview with Porter, and several essays on *Ship of Fools.* For a feminist approach to *Pale Horse, Pale Rider, Old Mortality,* and several stories, see Barbara Harrell Carson's "Winning: Katherine Anne Porter's Women," in *The Authority of Experience: Essays in Feminist Criticism,* ed. Arlyn Diamond and Lee R. Edwards, 1977.

PALE HORSE, PALE RIDER

In sleep she knew she was in her bed, but not the bed she had lain down in a few hours since, and the room was not the same but it was a room she had known somewhere. Her heart was a stone lying upon her breast outside of her; her pulses lagged and paused, and she knew that something strange was going to happen, even as the early morning winds were cool through the lattice, the streaks of light were dark blue and the whole house was snoring in its sleep.

Now I must get up and go while they are all quiet. Where are my things? Things have a will of their own in this place and hide where they like. Daylight will strike a sudden blow on the roof startling them all up to their feet; faces will beam asking, Where are you going, What are you doing, What are you thinking, How do you feel, Why do you say such things, What do you mean? No more sleep. Where are my boots and what horse shall I ride? Fiddler or Graylie or Miss Lucy with the long nose and the wicked eye? How I have loved this house in the morning before we are all awake and tangled together like badly cast fishing lines. Too many people have been born here, and have wept too much here, and have laughed too much, and have been too angry and outrageous with each other here. Too many have died in this bed already, there are far too many ancestral bones propped up on the mantelpieces, there have been too damned many antimacassars[1] in this house, she said loudly, and oh, what accumulation of storied dust never allowed to settle in peace for one moment.

And the stranger? Where is that lank greenish stranger I remember hanging about the place, welcomed by my grandfather, my great-aunt, my five times removed cousin, my decrepit hound and my silver kitten? Why did they take to him, I wonder? And where are they now? Yet I saw him pass the window in the evening. What else besides them did I have in the world? Nothing. Nothing is mine, I have only nothing but it is enough, it is beautiful and it is all mine. Do I even walk about in my own skin or is it something I have borrowed to spare my modesty? Now what horse shall I borrow for this journey I do not mean to take, Graylie or Miss Lucy or Fiddler who can jump ditches in the dark and knows how to get the bit between his teeth? Early morning is best for me because trees are trees in one stroke, stones are stones set in shades known to be grass, there are no false shapes or surmises, the road is still asleep with the crust of dew unbroken. I'll take Graylie because he is not afraid of bridges.[2]

Come now, Graylie, she said, taking his bridle, we must outrun Death and the Devil. You are no good for it, she told the other horses standing saddled before the stable gate, among them the horse of the stranger, gray also, with tarnished nose and ears. The stranger swung into his saddle beside her, leaned far towards her and regarded her without meaning, the blank still stare of mindless malice that makes no threats and can bide its time. She drew Graylie around sharply, urged him to run. He leaped the low rose hedge and the narrow ditch beyond, and the dust of the lane flew

[1] Covers to protect the backs and arms of furniture.
[2] That spirits cannot cross water is a folk belief.

heavily under his beating hoofs. The stranger rode beside her, easily, lightly, his reins loose in his half-closed hand, straight and elegant in dark shabby garments that flapped upon his bones; his pale face smiled in an evil trance, he did not glance at her. Ah, I have seen this fellow before, I know this man if I could place him. He is no stranger to me.

She pulled Graylie up, rose in her stirrups and shouted, I'm not going with you this time—ride on! Without pausing or turning his head the stranger rode on. Graylie's ribs heaved under her, her own ribs rose and fell, Oh, why am I so tired, I must wake up. "But let me get a fine yawn first," she said, opening her eyes and stretching, "a slap of cold water in my face, for I've been talking in my sleep again, I heard myself but what was I saying?"

Slowly, unwillingly, Miranda drew herself up inch by inch out of the pit of sleep, waited in a daze for life to begin again. A single word struck in her mind, a gong of warning, reminding her for the day long what she forgot happily in sleep, and only in sleep. The war,[3] said the gong, and she shook her head. Dangling her feet idly with their slippers hanging, she was reminded of the way all sorts of persons sat upon her desk at the newspaper office. Every day she found someone there, sitting upon her desk instead of the chair provided, dangling his legs, eyes roving, full of his important affairs, waiting to pounce about something or other. "*Why* won't they sit in the chair? Should I put a sign on it, saying, 'For God's sake, sit here'?"

Far from putting up a sign, she did not even frown at her visitors. Usually she did not notice them at all until their determination to be seen was greater than her determination not to see them. Saturday, she thought, lying comfortably in her tub of hot water, will be pay day, as always. Or I hope always. Her thoughts roved hazily in a continual effort to bring together and unite firmly the disturbing oppositions in her day-to-day existence, where survival, she could see clearly, had become a series of feats of sleight of hand. I owe—let me see, I wish I had pencil and paper—well, suppose I *did* pay five dollars now on a Liberty Bond,[4] I couldn't possibly keep it up. Or maybe. Eighteen dollars a week. So much for rent, so much for food, and I mean to have a few things besides. About five dollars' worth. Will leave me twenty-seven cents. I suppose I can make it. I suppose I should be worried. I am worried. Very well, now I am worried and what next? Twenty-seven cents. That's not so bad. Pure profit, really. Imagine if they should suddenly raise me to twenty I should then have two dollars and twenty-seven cents left over. But they aren't going to raise me to twenty. They are in fact going to throw me out if I don't buy a Liberty Bond. I hardly believe that. I'll ask Bill. (Bill was the city editor.) I wonder if a threat like that isn't a kind of blackmail. I don't believe even a Lusk Committeeman[5] can get away with that.

Yesterday there had been two pairs of legs dangling, on either side of her typewriter, both pairs stuffed thickly into funnels of dark expensive-looking material. She noticed at a distance that one of them was oldish and

[3] The First World War. [4] Government savings bond sold to support the war effort.

[5] Member of a committee of the New York state legislature to investigate "seditious" activities; it was chaired by a state senator named Clayton Lusk. (Actually, the Lusk committee was not formed until after the war had ended.)

one was youngish, and they both of them had a stale air of borrowed importance which apparently they had got from the same source. They were both much too well nourished and the younger one wore a square little mustache. Being what they were, no matter what their business was it would be something unpleasant. Miranda had nodded at them, pulled out her chair and without removing her cap or gloves had reached into a pile of letters and sheets from the copy desk as if she had not a moment to spare. They did not move, or take off their hats. At last she had said "Good morning" to them, and asked if they were, perhaps, waiting for her?

The two men slid off the desk, leaving some of her papers rumpled, and the oldish man had inquired why she had not bought a Liberty Bond. Miranda had looked at him then, and got a poor impression. He was a pursy-faced man, gross-mouthed, with little lightless eyes, and Miranda wondered why nearly all of those selected to do the war work at home were of his sort. He might be anything at all, she thought; advance agent for a road show, promoter of a wildcat oil company, a former saloon keeper announcing the opening of a new cabaret, an automobile salesman—any follower of any one of the crafty, haphazard callings. But he was now all Patriot, working for the government. "Look here," he asked her, "do you know there's a war, or don't you?"

Did he expect an answer to that? Be quiet, Miranda told herself, this was bound to happen. Sooner or later it happens. Keep your head. The man wagged his finger at her, "Do you?" he persisted, as if he were prompting an obstinate child.

"Oh, the war," Miranda had echoed on a rising note and she almost smiled at him. It was habitual, automatic, to give that solemn, mystically uplifted grin when you spoke the words or heard them spoken. *"C'est la guerre,"*[6] whether you could pronounce it or not, was even better, and always, always, you shrugged.

"Yeah," said the younger man in a nasty way, "the war." Miranda, startled by the tone, met his eye; his stare was really stony, really viciously cold, the kind of thing you might expect to meet behind a pistol on a deserted corner. This expression gave temporary meaning to a set of features otherwise nondescript, the face of those men who have no business of their own. "We're having a war, and some people are buying Liberty Bonds and others just don't seem to get around to it," he said. "That's what we mean."

Miranda frowned with nervousness, the sharp beginnings of fear. "Are you selling them?" she asked, taking the cover off her typewriter and putting it back again.

"No, we're not selling them," said the older man. "We're just asking you why you haven't bought one." The voice was persuasive and ominous.

Miranda began to explain that she had no money, and did not know where to find any, when the older man interrupted: "That's no excuse, no excuse at all, and you know it, with the Huns overrunning martyred Belgium."[7]

[6] "That's war" (French).

[7] "Huns" and "the Boche" were negative slang terms for the Germans. Atrocity stories, many fabricated, about the German invasion of Belgium in 1914 were used to whip up American support for the war.

"With our American boys fighting and dying in Belleau Wood,"[8] said the younger man, "anybody can raise fifty dollars to help beat the Boche."

Miranda said hastily, "I have eighteen dollars a week and not another cent in the world. I simply cannot buy anything."

"You can pay for it five dollars a week," said the older man (they had stood there cawing back and forth over her head), "like a lot of other people in this office, and a lot of other offices besides are doing."

Miranda, desperately silent, had thought, "Suppose I were not a coward, but said what I really thought? Suppose I said to hell with this filthy war? Suppose I asked that little thug, What's the matter with you, why aren't you rotting in Belleau Wood? I wish you were . . ."

She began to arrange her letters and notes, her fingers refusing to pick up things properly. The older man went on making his little set speech. It was hard, of course. Everybody was suffering, naturally. Everybody had to do his share. But as to that, a Liberty Bond was the safest investment you could make. It was just like having the money in the bank. Of course. The government was back of it and where better could you invest?

"I agree with you about that," said Miranda, "But I haven't any money to invest."

And of course, the man had gone on, it wasn't so much her fifty dollars that was going to make any difference. It was just a pledge of good faith on her part. A pledge of good faith that she was a loyal American doing her duty. And the thing was safe as a church. Why, if he had a million dollars he'd be glad to put every last cent of it in these Bonds. . . . "You can't lose by it," he said, almost benevolently, "and you can lose a lot if you don't. Think it over. You're the only one in this whole newspaper office that hasn't come in. And every firm in this city has come in one hundred per cent. Over at the *Daily Clarion* nobody had to be asked twice."

"They pay better over there," said Miranda. "But next week, if I can. Not now, next week."

"See that you do," said the younger man. "This ain't any laughing matter."

They lolled away, past the Society Editor's desk, past Bill the City Editor's desk, past the long copy desk where old man Gibbons sat all night shouting at intervals, "Jarge! Jarge!" and the copy boy would come flying. "Never say *people* when you mean *persons,*" old man Gibbons had instructed Miranda, "and never say *practically,* say *virtually,* and don't for God's sake ever so long as I am at this desk use the barbarism *inasmuch* under any circumstances whatsoever. Now you're educated, you may go." At the head of the stairs her inquisitors had stopped in their fussy pride and vainglory, lighting cigars and wedging their hats more firmly over their eyes.

Miranda turned over in the soothing water, and wished she might fall asleep there, to wake up only when it was time to sleep again. She had a burning slow headache, and noticed it now, remembering she had waked up with it and it had in fact begun the evening before. While she dressed she tried to trace the insidious career of her headache, and it seemed reasonable to suppose it had started with the war. "It's been a headache, all

[8] Scene of a bloody battle in northern France in June, 1918.

right, but not quite like this." After the Committeemen had left, yesterday, she had gone to the cloakroom and had found Mary Townsend, the Society Editor, quietly hysterical about something. She was perched on the edge of the shabby wicker couch with ridges down the center, knitting on something rose-colored. Now and then she would put down her knitting, seize her head with both hands and rock, saying, "My *God*," in a surprised, inquiring voice. Her column was called Ye Towne Gossyp, so of course everybody called her Towney. Miranda and Towney had a great deal in common, and liked each other. They had both been real reporters once, and had been sent together to "cover" a scandalous elopement, in which no marriage had taken place, after all, and the recaptured girl, her face swollen, had sat with her mother, who was moaning steadily under a mound of blankets. They had both wept painfully and implored the young reporters to suppress the worst of the story. They had suppressed it, and the rival newspaper printed it all the next day. Miranda and Towney had taken their punishment together, and had been degraded publicly to routine female jobs, one to the theaters, the other to society. They had this in common, that neither of them could see what else they could possibly have done, and they knew they were considered fools by the rest of the staff—nice girls, but fools. At sight of Miranda, Towney had broken out in a rage, "I can't do it, I'll never be able to raise the money, I told them, I can't, I can't, but they wouldn't listen."

Miranda said, "I knew I wasn't the only person in this office who couldn't raise five dollars. I told them I couldn't, too, and I can't."

"My *God*," said Towney, in the same voice, "they told me I'd lose my job—"

"I'm going to ask Bill," Miranda said; "I don't believe Bill would do that."

"It's not up to Bill," said Towney. "He'd have to if they got after him. Do you suppose they could put us in jail?"

"I don't know," said Miranda. "If they do, we won't be lonesome." She sat down beside Towney and held her own head. "What kind of soldier are you knitting that for? It's a sprightly color, it ought to cheer him up."

"Like hell," said Towney, her needles going again. "I'm making this for myself. That's that."

"Well," said Miranda, "we won't be lonesome and we'll catch up on our sleep." She washed her face and put on fresh make-up. Taking clean gray gloves out of her pocket she went out to join a group of young women fresh from the country club dances, the morning bridge, the charity bazaar, the Red Cross workrooms, who were wallowing in good works. They gave tea dances and raised money, and with the money they bought quantities of sweets, fruit, cigarettes, and magazines for the men in the cantonment hospitals.[9] With this loot they were now setting out, a gay procession of high-powered cars and brightly tinted faces to cheer the brave boys who already, you might very well say, had fallen in defense of their country. It must be frightfully hard on them, the dears, to be floored like this when they're all crazy to get overseas and into the trenches as quickly as possible. Yes, and some of them are the cutest things you ever saw, I didn't know

[9]Temporary military hospitals.

there were so many good-looking men in this country, good heavens, I said, where do they come from? Well, my dear, you may ask yourself that question, who knows where they did come from? You're quite right, the way I feel about it is this, we must do everything we can to make them contented, but I draw the line at talking to them. I told the chaperons at those dances for enlisted men, I'll dance with them, every dumbbell who asks me, but I will NOT talk to them, I said, even if there is a war. So I danced hundreds of miles without opening my mouth except to say, Please keep your knees to yourself. I'm glad we gave those dances up. Yes, and the men stopped coming, anyway. But listen, I've heard that a great many of the enlisted men come from very good families; I'm not good at catching names, and those I did catch I'd never heard before, so I don't know . . . but it seems to me if they were from good families, you'd know it, wouldn't you? I mean, if a man is well bred he doesn't step on your feet, does he? At least not that. I used to have a pair of sandals ruined at every one of those dances. Well, I think any kind of social life is in very poor taste just now, I think we should all put on our Red Cross head dresses and wear them for the duration of the war—

Miranda, carrying her basket and her flowers, moved in among the young women, who scattered out and rushed upon the ward uttering girlish laughter meant to be refreshingly gay, but there was a grim determined clang in it calculated to freeze the blood. Miserably embarrassed at the idiocy of her errand, she walked rapidly between the long rows of high beds, set foot to foot with a narrow aisle between. The men, a selected presentable lot, sheets drawn up to their chins, not seriously ill, were bored and restless, most of them willing to be amused at anything. They were for the most part picturesquely bandaged as to arm or head, and those who were not visibly wounded invariably replied "Rheumatism" if some tactless girl, who had been solemnly warned never to ask this question, still forgot and asked a man what his illness was. The good-natured, eager ones, laughing and calling out from their hard narrow beds, were soon surrounded. Miranda, with her wilting bouquet and her basket of sweets and cigarettes, looking about, caught the unfriendly bitter eye of a young fellow lying on his back, his right leg in a cast and pulley. She stopped at the foot of his bed and continued to look at him, and he looked back with an unchanged, hostile face. Not having any, thank you and be damned to the whole business, his eyes said plainly to her, and will you be so good as to take your trash off my bed? For Miranda had set it down, leaning over to place it where he might be able to reach it if he would. Having set it down, she was incapable of taking it up again, but hurried away, her face burning, down the long aisle and out into the cool October sunshine, where the dreary raw barracks swarmed and worked with an aimless life of scurrying, dun-colored insects; and going around to a window near where he lay, she looked in, spying upon her soldier. He was lying with his eyes closed, his eyebrows in a sad bitter frown. She could not place him at all, she could not imagine where he came from nor what sort of being he might have been "in life," she said to herself. His face was young and the features sharp and plain, the hands were not laborer's hands but not well-cared-for hands either. They were good useful properly shaped hands, lying there on the coverlet. It occurred to her that it would be her luck to find him, instead of a jolly hungry puppy glad of a bite to eat and a little chatter. It is like turning a corner absorbed in your painful thoughts and meeting your state of mind embodied, face to face, she said. "My own feelings about this whole thing, made flesh. Never again will I come here, this is no sort of thing to be doing. This is disgusting," she told herself plainly. "Of course I would pick him out," she thought, getting into the back seat of the car she came in, "serves me right, I know better."

Another girl came out looking very tired and climbed in beside her. After a short silence, the girl said in a puzzled way, "I don't know what good it does, really. Some of them wouldn't take anything at all. I don't like this, do you?"

"I hate it," said Miranda.

"I suppose it's all right, though," said the girl, cautiously.

"Perhaps," said Miranda, turning cautious also.

That was for yesterday. At this point Miranda decided there was no good in thinking of yesterday, except for the hour after midnight she had spent dancing with Adam. He was in her mind so much, she hardly knew when she was thinking about him directly. His image was simply always present in more or less degree, he was sometimes nearer the surface of her thoughts, the pleasantest, the only really pleasant thought she had. She examined her face in the mirror between the windows and decided that her uneasiness was not all imagination. For three days at least she had felt odd and her expression was unfamiliar. She would have to raise that fifty dollars somehow, she supposed, or who knows what can happen? She was hardened to stories of personal disaster, of outrageous accusations and extraordinarily bitter penalties that had grown monstrously out of incidents very little more important than her failure—her refusal—to buy a Bond. No, she did not find herself a pleasing sight, flushed and shiny, and even her hair felt as if it had decided to grow in the other direction. I must do something about this, I can't let Adam see me like this, she told herself, knowing that even now at that moment he was listening for the turn of her door knob, and he would be in the hallway, or on the porch when she came out, as if by sheerest coincidence. The noon sunlight cast cold slanting shadows in the room where, she said, I suppose I live, and this day is beginning badly, but they all do now, for one reason or another. In a drowse, she sprayed perfume on her hair, put on her moleskin cap and jacket, now in their second winter, but still good, still nice to wear, again being glad she had paid a frightening price for them. She had enjoyed them all this time, and in no case would she have had the money now. Maybe she could manage for that Bond. She could not find the lock without leaning to search for it, then stood undecided a moment possessed by the notion that she had forgotten something she would miss seriously later on.

Adam was in the hallway, a step outside his own door; he swung about as if quite startled to see her, and said, "Hello. I don't have to go back to camp today after all—isn't that luck?"

Miranda smiled at him gaily because she was always delighted at the sight of him. He was wearing his new uniform, and he was all olive and tan and tawny, hay colored and sand colored from hair to boots. She half noticed again that he always began by smiling at her; that his smile faded gradually; that his eyes became fixed and thoughtful as if he were reading in a poor light.

They walked out together into the fine fall day, scuffling bright ragged leaves under their feet, turning their faces up to a generous sky really blue and spotless. At the first corner they waited for a funeral to pass, the mourners seated straight and firm as if proud in their sorrow.

"I imagine I'm late," said Miranda, "as usual. What time is it?"

"Nearly half past one," he said, slipping back his sleeve with an exaggerated thrust of his arm upward. The young soldiers were still self-conscious about their wrist watches. Such of them as Miranda knew were boys from southern and southwestern towns, far off the Atlantic seaboard, and they had always believed that only sissies wore wrist watches. "I'll slap you on the wrist watch," one vaudeville comedian would simper to another, and it was always a good joke, never stale.

"I think it's a most sensible way to carry a watch," said Miranda. "You needn't blush."

"I'm nearly used to it," said Adam, who was from Texas. "We've been told time and again how all the he-manly regular army men wear them. It's the horrors of war," he said; "are we downhearted? I'll say we are."[10]

It was the kind of patter going the rounds. "You look it," said Miranda.

He was tall and heavily muscled in the shoulders, narrow in the waist and flanks, and he was infinitely buttoned, strapped, harnessed into a uniform as tough and unyielding in cut as a strait jacket, though the cloth was fine and supple. He had his uniforms made by the best tailor he could find, he confided to Miranda one day when she told him how squish[11] he was looking in his new soldier suit. "Hard enough to make anything of the outfit, anyhow," he told her. "It's the least I can do for my beloved country, not to go around looking like a tramp." He was twenty-four years old and a Second Lieutenant in an Engineers Corps, on leave because his outfit expected to be sent over shortly. "Came in to make my will," he told Miranda, "and get a supply of toothbrushes and razor blades. By what gorgeous luck do you suppose," he asked her, "I happened to pick on your rooming house? How did I know you were there?"

Strolling, keeping step, his stout polished well-made boots setting themselves down firmly beside her thin-soled black suède, they put off as long as they could the end of their moment together, and kept up as well as they could their small talk that flew back and forth over little grooves worn in the thin upper surface of the brain, things you could say and hear clink reassuringly at once without disturbing the radiance which played and darted about the simple and lovely miracle of being two persons named Adam and Miranda, twenty-four years old each, alive and on the earth at the same moment: "Are you in the mood for dancing, Miranda?" and "I'm always in the mood for dancing, Adam!" but there were things in the way, the day that ended with dancing was a long way to go.

He really did look, Miranda thought, like a fine healthy apple this morning. One time or another in their talking, he had boasted that he had

[10] "Are we downhearted?" (supposed to be answered by shouts of "No!") was a catch phrase used at patriotic rallies.

[11] Stylish.

never had a pain in his life that he could remember. Instead of being horrified at this monster, she approved his monstrous uniqueness. As for herself, she had had too many pains to mention, so she did not mention them. After working for three years on a morning newspaper she had an illusion of maturity and experience; but it was fatigue merely, she decided, from keeping what she had been brought up to believe were unnatural hours, eating casually at dirty little restaurants, drinking bad coffee all night, and smoking too much. When she said something of her way of living to Adam, he studied her face a few seconds as if he had never seen it before, and said in a forthright way, "Why, it hasn't hurt you a bit, I think you're beautiful," and left her dangling there, wondering if he had thought she wished to be praised. She did wish to be praised, but not at that moment. Adam kept unwholesome hours too, or had in the ten days they had known each other, staying awake until one o'clock to take her out for supper; he smoked also continually, though if she did not stop him he was apt to explain to her exactly what smoking did to the lungs. "But," he said, "does it matter so much if you're going to war, anyway?"

"No," said Miranda, "and it matters even less if you're staying at home knitting socks. Give me a cigarette, will you?" They paused at another corner, under a half-foliaged maple, and hardly glanced at a funeral procession approaching. His eyes were pale tan with orange flecks in them, and his hair was the color of a haystack when you turn the weathered top back to the clear straw beneath. He fished out his cigarette case and snapped his silver lighter at her, snapped it several times in his own face, and they moved on, smoking.

"I can see you knitting socks," he said. "That would be just your speed. You know perfectly well you can't knit."

"I do worse," she said, soberly; "I write pieces advising other young women to knit and roll bandages and do without sugar and help win the war."

"Oh, well," said Adam, with the easy masculine morals in such questions, "that's merely your job, that doesn't count."

"I wonder," said Miranda. "How did you manage to get an extension of leave?"

"They just gave it," said Adam, "for no reason. The men are dying like flies out there, anyway. This funny new disease. Simply knocks you into a cocked hat."

"It seems to be a plague," said Miranda, "something out of the Middle Ages. Did you ever see so many funerals, ever?"

"Never did. Well, let's be strong minded and not have any of it. I've got four days more straight from the blue and not a blade of grass must grow under our feet. What about tonight?"

"Same thing," she told him, "but make it about half past one. I've got a special job beside my usual run of the mill."

"What a job you've got," said Adam, "nothing to do but run from one dizzy amusement to another and then write a piece about it."

"Yes, it's too dizzy for words," said Miranda. They stood while a funeral passed, and this time they watched it in silence. Miranda pulled her cap to an angle and winked in the sunlight, her head swimming slowly "like goldfish," she told Adam, "my head swims. I'm only half awake, I must have some coffee."

They lounged on their elbows over the counter of a drug store. "No more cream for the stay-at-homes," she said, "and only one lump of sugar. I'll have two or none; that's the kind of martyr I'm being. I mean to live on boiled cabbage and wear shoddy[12] from now on and get in good shape for the next round. No war is going to sneak up on me again."

"Oh, there won't be any more wars, don't you read the newspapers?"[13] asked Adam. "We're going to mop 'em up this time, and they're going to stay mopped, and this is going to be all."

"So they told me," said Miranda, tasting her bitter lukewarm brew and making a rueful face. Their smiles approved of each other, they felt they had got the right tone, they were taking the war properly. Above all, thought Miranda, no tooth-gnashing, no hair-tearing, it's noisy and unbecoming and it doesn't get you anywhere.

"Swill," said Adam rudely, pushing back his cup. "Is that all you're having for breakfast?"

"It's more than I want," said Miranda.

"I had buckwheat cakes, with sausage and maple syrup, and two bananas, and two cups of coffee, at eight o'clock, and right now, again, I feel like a famished orphan left in the ashcan. I'm all set," said Adam, "for broiled steak and fried potatoes and—"

"Don't go on with it," said Miranda, "it sounds delirious to me. Do all that after I'm gone." She slipped from the high seat, leaned against it slightly, glanced at her face in her round mirror, rubbed rouge on her lips and decided that she was past praying for.

"There's something terribly wrong," she told Adam. "I feel too rotten. It can't just be the weather, and the war."

"The weather is perfect," said Adam, "and the war is simply too good to be true. But since when? You were all right yesterday."

"I don't know," she said slowly, her voice sounding small and thin. They stopped as always at the open door before the flight of littered steps leading up to the newspaper loft. Miranda listened for a moment to the rattle of typewriters above, the steady rumble of presses below. "I wish we were going to spend the whole afternoon on a park bench," she said, "or drive to the mountains."

"I do too," he said; "let's do that tomorrow."

"Yes, tomorrow, unless something else happens. I'd like to run away," she told him; "let's both."

"Me?" said Adam. "Where I'm going there's no running to speak of. You mostly crawl about on your stomach here and there among the debris. You know, barbed wire and such stuff. It's going to be the kind of thing that happens once in a lifetime." He reflected a moment, and went on, "I don't know a darned thing about it, really, but they make it sound awfully messy. I've heard so much about it I feel as if I had been there and back. It's going to be an anticlimax," he said, "like seeing the pictures of a place so

[12] A cheap material made of reclaimed wool.
[13] According to patriotic rhetoric, World War I was "a war to end wars."

often you can't see it at all when you actually get there. Seems to me I've been in the army all my life."

Six months, he meant. Eternity. He looked so clear and fresh, and he had never had a pain in his life. She had seen them when they had been there and back and they never looked like this again. "Already the returned hero," she said, "and don't I wish you were."

"When I learned the use of the bayonet in my first training camp," said Adam, "I gouged the vitals out of more sandbags and sacks of hay than I could keep track of. They kept bawling at us, 'Get him, get that Boche, stick him before he sticks you'—and we'd go for those sandbags like wildfire, and honestly, sometimes I felt a perfect fool for getting so worked up when I saw the sand trickling out. I used to wake up in the night sometimes feeling silly about it."

"I can imagine," said Miranda. "It's perfect nonsense." They lingered, unwilling to say good-by. After a little pause, Adam, as if keeping up the conversation, asked, "Do you know what the average life expectation of a sapping party[14] is after it hits the job?"

"Something speedy, I suppose."

"Just nine minutes," said Adam; "I read that in your own newspaper not a week ago."

"Make it ten and I'll come along," said Miranda.

"Not another second," said Adam, "exactly nine minutes, take it or leave it."

"Stop bragging," said Miranda. "Who figured that out?"

"A noncombatant," said Adam, "a fellow with rickets."

This seemed very comic, they laughed and leaned towards each other and Miranda heard herself being a little shrill. She wiped the tears from her eyes. "My, it's a funny war," she said; "isn't it? I laugh every time I think about it."

Adam took her hand in both of his and pulled a little at the tips of her gloves and sniffed them. "What nice perfume you have," he said, "and such a lot of it, too. I like a lot of perfume on gloves and hair," he said, sniffing again.

"I've got probably too much," she said. "I can't smell or see or hear today. I must have a fearful cold."

"Don't catch cold," said Adam; "my leave is nearly up and it will be the last, the very last." She moved her fingers in her gloves as he pulled at the fingers and turned her hands as if they were something new and curious and of great value, and she turned shy and quiet. She liked him, she liked him, and there was more than this but it was no good even imagining, because he was not for her nor for any woman, being beyond experience already, committed without any knowledge or act of his own to death. She took back her hands. "Goodbye," she said finally, "until tonight."

She ran upstairs and looked back from the top. He was still watching her, and raised his hand without smiling. Miranda hardly ever saw anyone look back after he had said good-by. She could not help turning sometimes for one glimpse more of the person she had been talking with, as if that would save too rude and too sudden a snapping of even the lightest bond.

[14] A military detachment sent out to plant explosives under enemy fortifications.

But people hurried away, their faces already changed, fixed, in their straining towards their next stopping place, already absorbed in planning their next act or encounter. Adam was waiting as if he expected her to turn, and under his brows fixed in a strained frown, his eyes were very black.

At her desk she sat without taking off her jacket or cap, slitting envelopes and pretending to read the letters. Only Chuck Rouncivale, the sports reporter, and Ye Towne Gossyp were sitting on her desk today, and them she liked having there. She sat on theirs when she pleased. Towney and Chuck were talking and they went on with it.

"They say," said Towney, "that it is really caused by germs brought by a German ship to Boston, a camouflaged ship, naturally, it didn't come in under its own colors. Isn't that ridiculous?"

"Maybe it was a submarine," said Chuck, "sneaking in from the bottom of the sea in the dead of night. Now that sounds better."

"Yes, it does," said Towney; "they always slip up somewhere in these details . . . and they think the germs were sprayed over the city—it started in Boston, you know—and somebody reported seeing a strange, thick, greasy-looking cloud float up out of Boston Harbor and spread slowly all over that end of town. I think it was an old woman who saw it."

"Should have been," said Chuck.

"I read it in a New York newspaper," said Towney; "so it's bound to be true."

Chuck and Miranda laughed so loudly at this that Bill stood up and glared at them. "Towney still reads the newspapers," explained Chuck.

"Well, what's funny about that?" asked Bill, sitting down again and frowning into the clutter before him.

"It was a noncombatant saw that cloud," said Miranda.

"Naturally," said Towney.

"Member of the Lusk Committee, maybe," said Miranda.

"The Angel of Mons,"[15] said Chuck, "or a dollar-a-year man."[16]

Miranda wished to stop hearing, and talking, she wished to think for just five minutes of her own about Adam, really to think about him, but there was no time. She had seen him first ten days ago, and since then they had been crossing streets together, darting between trucks and limousines and pushcarts and farm wagons; he had waited for her in doorways and in little restaurants that smelled of stale frying fat; they had eaten and danced to the urgent whine and bray of jazz orchestras, they had sat in dull theaters because Miranda was there to write a piece about the play. Once they had gone to the mountains and, leaving the car, had climbed a stony trail, and had come out on a ledge upon a flat stone, where they sat and watched the lights change on a valley landscape that was, no doubt, Miranda said, quite apocryphal—"We need not believe it, but it is fine poetry," she told him; they had leaned their shoulders together there, and had sat quite still, watching. On two Sundays they had gone to the geological museum, and

[15] The figure of an angel was said to have appeared over the Allied lines at the battle of Mons, Belgium, in 1918.

[16] A businessman contributing to the war effort by doing government work for a token salary of a dollar a year.

had pored in shared fascination over bits of meteors, rock formations, fossilized tusks and trees, Indian arrows, grottoes from the silver and gold lodes. "Think of those old miners washing out their fortunes in little pans beside the streams," said Adam, "and inside the earth there was this—" and he had told her he liked better those things that took long to make; he loved airplanes too, all sorts of machinery, things carved out of wood or stone. He knew nothing much about them, but he recognized them when he saw them. He had confessed that he simply could not get through a book, any kind of book except textbooks on engineering; reading bored him to crumbs; he regretted now he hadn't brought his roadster, but he hadn't thought he would need a car; he loved driving, he wouldn't expect her to believe how many hundreds of miles he could get over in a day . . . he had showed her snapshots of himself at the wheel of his roadster; of himself sailing a boat, looking very free and windblown, all angles, hauling on the ropes; he would have joined the air force, but his mother had hysterics every time he mentioned it. She didn't seem to realize that dog fighting in the air was a good deal safer than sapping parties on the ground at night. But he hadn't argued, because of course she did not realize about sapping parties. And here he was, stuck, on a plateau a mile high with no water for a boat and his car at home, otherwise they could really have had a good time. Miranda knew he was trying to tell her what kind of person he was when he had his machinery with him. She felt she knew pretty well what kind of person he was, and would have liked to tell him that if he thought he had left himself at home in a boat or an automobile, he was much mistaken. The telephones were ringing, Bill was shouting at somebody who kept saying, "Well, but listen, well, but listen—" but nobody was going to listen, of course, nobody. Old man Gibbons bellowed in despair, "Jarge, Jarge—"

"Just the same," Towney was saying in her most complacent patriotic voice, "Hut Service[17] is a fine idea, and we should all volunteer even if they don't want us." Towney does well at this, thought Miranda, look at her; remembering the rose-colored sweater and the tight rebellious face in the cloakroom. Towney was now all open-faced glory and goodness, willing to sacrifice herself for her country. "After all," said Towney, "I *can* sing and dance well enough for the Little Theater, and I could write their letters for them, and at a pinch I might drive an ambulance. I have driven a Ford for years."

Miranda joined in: "Well, I can sing and dance too, but who's going to do the bed-making and the scrubbing up? Those huts are hard to keep, and it would be a dirty job and we'd be perfectly miserable; and as I've got a hard dirty job and am perfectly miserable, I'm going to stay at home."

"I think the women should keep out of it," said Chuck Rouncivale. "They just add skirts to the horrors of war." Chuck had bad lungs and fretted a good deal about missing the show. "I could have been there and back with a leg off by now; it would have served the old man right. Then he'd either have to buy his own hooch or sober up."

Miranda had seen Chuck on pay day giving the old man money for

[17] Volunteer work in Red Cross canteens ("huts") in the war zones.

hooch. He was a good-humored ingratiating old scoundrel, too, that was the worst of him. He slapped his son on the back and beamed upon him with the bleared eye of paternal affection while he took his last nickel.

"It was Florence Nightingale[18] ruined wars," Chuck went on. "What's the idea of petting soldiers and binding up their wounds and soothing their fevered brows? That's not war. Let 'em perish where they fall. That's what they're there for."

"You can talk," said Towney, with a slantwise glint at him.

"What's the idea?" asked Chuck, flushing and hunching his shoulders. "You know I've got this lung, or maybe half of it anyway by now."

"You're much too sensitive," said Towney. "I didn't mean a thing."

Bill had been raging about, chewing his half-smoked cigar, his hair standing up in a brush, his eyes soft and lambent but wild, like a stag's. He would never, thought Miranda, be more than fourteen years old if he lived for a century, which he would not, at the rate he was going. He behaved exactly like city editors in the moving pictures, even to the chewed cigar. Had he formed his style on the films, or had scenario writers seized once for all on the type Bill in its inarguable purity? Bill was shouting to Chuck: "*And* if he comes back here take him up the alley and saw his head off *by hand!*"

Chuck said, "He'll be back, don't worry." Bill said mildly, already off on another track, "Well, saw him off." Towney went to her own desk, but Chuck sat waiting amiably to be taken to the new vaudeville show. Miranda, with two tickets, always invited one of the reporters to go with her on Monday. Chuck was lavishly hardboiled and professional in his sports writing, but he had told Miranda that he didn't give a damn about sports, really; the job kept him out in the open, and paid him enough to buy the old man's hooch. He preferred shows and didn't see why women always had the job.

"Who does Bill want sawed today?" asked Miranda.

"That hoofer[19] you panned in this morning's," said Chuck. "He was up here bright and early asking for the guy that writes up the show business. He said he was going to take the goof who wrote that piece up the alley and bop him in the nose. He said . . ."

"I hope he's gone," said Miranda; "I do hope he had to catch a train."

Chuck stood up and arranged his maroon-colored turtle-necked sweater, glanced down at the peasoup tweed plus fours[20] and the hob-nailed tan boots which he hoped would help to disguise the fact that he had a bad lung and didn't care for sports, and said, "He's long gone by now, don't worry. Let's get going; you're late as usual."

Miranda, facing about, almost stepped on the toes of a little drab man in a derby hat. He might have been a pretty fellow once, but now his mouth drooped where he had lost his side teeth, and his sad red-rimmed eyes had given up coquetry. A thin brown wave of hair was combed out with brilliantine[21] and curled against the rim of the derby. He didn't move his

[18] English nursing reformer (1820–1910) who organized field hospitals in the Crimean War.
[19] Dancer in vaudeville.
[20] Loose sports knickers, so called because they were gathered four inches below the knee.
[21] A preparation for making hair glossy.

feet, but stood planted with a kind of inert resistance, and asked Miranda: "Are you the so-called dramatic critic on this hick newspaper?"

"I'm afraid I am," said Miranda.

"Well," said the little man, "I'm just asking for one minute of your valuable time." His underlip shot out, he began with shaking hands to fish about in his waistcoat pocket. "I just hate to let you get away with it, that's all." He riffled through a collection of shabby newspaper clippings. "Just give these the once-over, will you? And then let me ask you if you think I'm gonna stand for being knocked by a tanktown[22] critic," he said, in a toneless voice; "look here, here's Buffalo, Chicago, Saint Looey, Philadelphia, Frisco, besides New York. Here's the best publications in the business, *Variety,* the *Billboard,* they all broke down and admitted that Danny Dickerson knows his stuff. So you don't think so, hey? That's all I wanta ask you."

"No, I don't," said Miranda, as bluntly as she could, "and I can't stop to talk about it."

The little man leaned nearer, his voice shook as if he had been nervous for a long time. "Look here, what was there you didn't like about me? Tell me that."

Miranda said, "You shouldn't pay any attention at all. What does it matter what I think?"

"I don't care what you think, it ain't that," said the little man, "but these things get round and booking agencies back East don't know how it is out here. We get panned in the sticks and they think it's the same as getting panned in Chicago, see? They don't know the difference. They don't know that the more high class an act is the more the hick critics pan it. But I've been called the best in the business by the best in the business and I wanta know what you think is wrong with me."

Chuck said, "Come on, Miranda, curtain's going up." Miranda handed the little man his clippings, they were mostly ten years old, and tried to edge past him. He stepped before her again and said without much conviction, "If you was a man I'd knock your block off." Chuck got up at that and lounged over, taking his hands out of his pockets, and said, "Now you've done your song and dance you'd better get out. Get the hell out now before I throw you downstairs."

The little man pulled at the top of his tie, a small blue tie with red polka dots, slightly frayed at the knot. He pulled it straight and repeated as if he had rehearsed it, "Come out in the alley." The tears filled his thickened red lids. Chuck said, "Ah, shut up," and followed Miranda, who was running towards the stairs. He overtook her on the sidewalk. "I left him sniveling and shuffling his publicity trying to find the joker," said Chuck, "the poor old heel."

Miranda said, "There's too much of everything in this world just now. I'd like to sit down here on the curb, Chuck, and die, and never again see—I wish I could lose my memory and forget my own name . . . I wish—"

Chuck said, "Toughen up, Miranda. This is no time to cave in. Forget that fellow. For every hundred people in show business, there are ninety-nine like him. But you don't manage right, anyway. You bring it on yourself. All you have to do is play up the headliners, and you needn't even

[22] Small town, so called to suggest that all they had was a tank for trains to take on water.

mention the also-rans. Try to keep in mind that Rypinsky has got show business cornered in this town; please Rypinsky and you'll please the advertising department, please them and you'll get a raise. Hand-in-glove, my poor dumb child, will you never learn?"

"I seem to keep learning all the wrong things," said Miranda, hopelessly.

"You do for a fact," Chuck told her cheerfully. "You are as good at it as I ever saw. Now do you feel better?"

"This is a rotten show you've invited me to," said Chuck. "Now what are you going to do about it? If I were writing it up, I'd—"

"Do write it up," said Miranda. "You write it up this time. I'm getting ready to leave, anyway, but don't tell anybody yet."

"You mean it? All my life," said Chuck, "I've yearned to be a so-called dramatic critic on a hick newspaper, and this is positively my first chance."

"Better take it," Miranda told him. "It may be your last." She thought, This is the beginning of the end of something. Something terrible is going to happen to me. I shan't need bread and butter where I'm going. I'll will it to Chuck, he has a venerable father to buy hooch for. I hope they let him have it. Oh, Adam, I hope I see you once more before I go under with whatever is the matter with me. "I wish the war were over," she said to Chuck, as if they had been talking about that. "I wish it were over and I wish it had never begun."

Chuck had got out his pad and pencil and was already writing his review. What she had said seemed safe enough but how would he take it? "I don't care how it started or when it ends," said Chuck, scribbling away, "I'm not going to be there."

All the rejected men talked like that, thought Miranda. War was the one thing they wanted, now they couldn't have it. Maybe they had wanted badly to go, some of them. All of them had a sidelong eye for the women they talked with about it, a guarded resentment which said, "Don't pin a white feather[23] on me, you bloodthirsty female. I've offered my meat to the crows and they won't have it." The worst thing about war for the stay-at-homes is there isn't anyone to talk to any more. The Lusk Committee will get you if you don't watch out. Bread will win the war. Work will win, sugar will win, peach pits will win the war. Nonsense. *Not* nonsense, I tell you, there's some kind of valuable high explosive to be got out of peach pits.[24] So all the happy housewives hurry during the canning season to lay their baskets of peach pits on the altar of their country. It keeps them busy and makes them feel useful, and all these women running wild with the men away are dangerous, if they aren't given something to keep their little minds out of mischief. So rows of young girls, the intact cradles of the future, with their pure serious faces framed becomingly in Red Cross wimples,[25] roll cock-eyed bandages that will never reach a base hospital, and knit sweaters that will never warm a manly chest, their minds dwelling

[23] In the war hysteria, groups of women were organized to pin white feathers on draft-age men on the street, as a badge of cowardice.

[24] Peach pits were collected for the war effort, although it was unclear whether they could be used to make explosives, as Miranda has heard, or to make linings for gas masks.

[25] Red Cross volunteers wore stiff, white head coverings like those of nuns.

lovingly on all the blood and mud and the next dance at the Acanthus Club for the officers of the flying corps. Keeping still and quiet will win the war.

"I'm simply not going to be there," said Chuck, absorbed in his review. No, Adam will be there, thought Miranda. She slipped down in the chair and leaned her head against the dusty plush, closed her eyes and faced for one instant that was a lifetime the certain, the overwhelming and awful knowledge that there was nothing at all ahead for Adam and for her. Nothing. She opened her eyes and held her hands together palms up, gazing at them and trying to understand oblivion.

"Now look at this," said Chuck, for the lights had come on and the audience was rustling and talking again. "I've got it all done, even before the headliner comes on. It's old Stella Mayhew, and she's always good, she's been good for forty years, and she's going to sing 'O the blues ain't nothin' but the easy-going heart disease.' That's all you need to know about her. Now just glance over this. Would you be willing to sign it?"

Miranda took the pages and stared at them conscientiously, turning them over, she hoped, at the right moment, and gave them back. "Yes, Chuck, yes, I'd sign that. But I won't. We must tell Bill you wrote it, because it's your start, maybe."

"You don't half appreciate it," said Chuck. "You read it too fast. Here, listen to this—" and he began to mutter excitedly. While he was reading she watched his face. It was a pleasant face with some kind of spark of life in it, and a good severity in the modeling of the brow above the nose. For the first time since she had known him she wondered what Chuck was thinking about. He looked preoccupied and unhappy, he wasn't so frivolous as he sounded. The people were crowding into the aisle, bringing out their cigarette cases ready to strike a match the instant they reached the lobby; women with waved hair clutched at their wraps, men stretched their chins to ease them of their stiff collars, and Chuck said, "We might as well go now." Miranda, buttoning her jacket, stepped into the moving crowd, thinking, What did I ever know about them? There must be a great many of them here who think as I do, and we dare not say a word to each other of our desperation, we are speechless animals letting ourselves be destroyed, and why? Does anybody here believe the things we say to each other?

Stretched in unease on the ridge of the wicker couch in the cloakroom, Miranda waited for time to pass and leave Adam with her. Time seemed to proceed with more than usual eccentricity, leaving twilight gaps in her mind for thirty minutes which seemed like a second, and then hard flashes of light that shone clearly on her watch proving that three minutes is an intolerable stretch of waiting, as if she were hanging by her thumbs. At last it was reasonable to imagine Adam stepping out of the house in the early darkness into the blue mist that might soon be rain, he would be on the way, and there was nothing to think about him, after all. There was only the wish to see him and the fear, the present threat, of not seeing him again; for every step they took towards each other seemed perilous, drawing them apart instead of together, as a swimmer in spite of his most determined strokes is yet drawn slowly backward by the tide. "I don't want to love," she would think in spite of herself, "not Adam, there is no time and we are not ready for it and yet this is all we have—"

And there he was on the sidewalk, with his foot on the first step, and Miranda almost ran down to meet him. Adam, holding her hands, asked, "Do you feel well now? Are you hungry? Are you tired? Will you feel like dancing after the show?"

"Yes to everything," said Miranda, "yes, yes. . . ." Her head was like a feather, and she steadied herself on his arm. The mist was still mist that might be rain later, and though the air was sharp and clean in her mouth, it did not, she decided, make breathing any easier. "I hope the show is good, or at least funny," she told him, "but I promise nothing."

It was a long, dreary play, but Adam and Miranda sat very quietly together waiting patiently for it to be over. Adam carefully and seriously pulled off her glove and held her hand as if he were accustomed to holding her hand in theaters. Once they turned and their eyes met, but only once, and the two pairs of eyes were equally steady and noncommittal. A deep tremor set up in Miranda, and she set about resisting herself methodically as if she were closing windows and doors and fastening down curtains against a rising storm. Adam sat watching the monotonous play with a strange shining excitement, his face quite fixed and still.

When the curtain rose for the third act, the third act did not take place at once. There was instead disclosed a backdrop almost covered with an American flag improperly and disrespectfully exposed, nailed at each upper corner, gathered in the middle and nailed again, sagging dustily. Before it posed a local dollar-a-year man, now doing his bit as a Liberty Bond salesman. He was an ordinary man past middle life, with a neat little melon buttoned into his trousers and waistcoat, an opinionated tight mouth, a face and figure in which nothing could be read save the inept sensual record of fifty years. But for once in his life he was an important fellow in an impressive situation, and he reveled, rolling his words in an actorish tone.

"Looks like a penguin," said Adam. They moved, smiled at each other, Miranda reclaimed her hand, Adam folded his together and they prepared to wear their way again through the same old moldy speech with the same old dusty backdrop. Miranda tried not to listen, but she heard. These vile Huns—glorious Belleau Wood—our keyword is Sacrifice—Martyred Belgium—give till it hurts—our noble boys Over There—Big Berthas[26]—the death of civilization—the Boche—

"My head aches," whispered Miranda. "Oh, why won't he hush?"

"He won't," whispered Adam. "I'll get you some aspirin."

"In Flanders Field the poppies grow, Between the crosses row on row"[27]—"He's getting into the home stretch," whispered Adam—atrocities, innocent babes hoisted on Boche bayonets—your child and my child—if our children are spared these things, then let us say with all reverence that these dead have not died in vain—the war, the *war*, the WAR to end WAR, war for Democracy, for humanity, a safe world forever and ever—and to prove our faith in Democracy to each other, and to the world, let everybody get together and buy Liberty Bonds and do without sugar

[26] Large, long-range German cannons.

[27] Lines from "In Flanders Field," written in 1915 by John McCrae. The poem commemorates the many soldiers who were killed in Flanders (a part of Belgium) in 1914.

and wool socks—was that it? Miranda asked herself, Say that over, I didn't catch the last line. Did you mention Adam? If you didn't I'm not interested. What about Adam, you little pig? And what are we going to sing this time, "Tipperary" or "There's a Long, Long Trail"?[28] Oh, please do let the show go on and get over with. I must write a piece about it before I can go dancing with Adam and we have no time. Coal, oil, iron, gold, international finance, why don't you tell us about them, you little liar?

The audience rose and sang, "There's a Long, Long Trail A-winding," their opened mouths black and faces pallid in the reflected footlights; some of the faces grimaced and wept and had shining streaks like snail's tracks on them. Adam and Miranda joined in at the tops of their voices, grinning shamefacedly at each other once or twice.

In the street, they lit their cigarettes and walked slowly as always. "Just another nasty old man who would like to see the young ones killed," said Miranda in a low voice; "the tomcats try to eat the little tomkittens, you know. They don't fool you really, do they, Adam?"

The young people were talking like that about the business by then. They felt they were seeing pretty clearly through that game. She went on, "I hate these potbellied baldheads, too fat, too old, too cowardly, to go to war themselves, they know they're safe; it's you they are sending instead—"

Adam turned eyes of genuine surprise upon her. "Oh, *that* one," he said. "Now what could the poor sap do if they did take him? It's not his fault," he explained, "he can't do anything but talk." His pride in his youth, his forbearance and tolerance and contempt for that unlucky being breathed out of his very pores as he strolled, straight and relaxed in his strength. "What *could* you expect of him, Miranda?"

She spoke his name often, and he spoke hers rarely. The little shock of pleasure the sound of her name in his mouth gave her stopped her answer. For a moment she hesitated, and began at another point of attack. "Adam," she said, "the worst of war is the fear and suspicion and the awful expression in all the eyes you meet . . . as if they had pulled down the shutters over their minds and their hearts and were peering out at you, ready to leap if you make one gesture or say one word they do not understand instantly. It frightens me; I live in fear too, and no one should have to live in fear. It's the skulking about, and the lying. It's what war does to the mind and the heart, Adam, and you can't separate these two—what it does to them is worse than what it can do to the body."

Adam said soberly, after a moment, "Oh, yes, but suppose one comes back whole? The mind and the heart sometimes get another chance, but if anything happens to the poor old human frame, why, it's just out of luck, that's all."

"Oh, yes," mimicked Miranda. "It's just out of luck, that's all."

"If I didn't go," said Adam, in a matter-of-fact voice, "I couldn't look myself in the face."

So that's all settled. With her fingers flattened on his arm, Miranda was silent, thinking about Adam. No, there was no resentment or revolt in him. Pure, she thought, all the way through, flawless, complete, as the sacrificial

[28]"It's a Long Way to Tipperary" and "There's a Long, Long Trail A-Winding" were popular sentimental World War I songs.

lamb must be. The sacrificial lamb strode along casually, accommodating his long pace to hers, keeping her on the inside of the walk in the good American style, helping her across street corners as if she were a cripple—"I hope we don't come to a mud puddle, he'll carry me over it"—giving off whiffs of tobacco smoke, a manly smell of scentless soap, freshly cleaned leather and freshly washed skin, breathing through his nose and carrying his chest easily. He threw back his head and smiled into the sky which still misted, promising rain. "Oh, boy," he said, "what a night. Can't you hurry that review of yours so we can get started?"

He waited for her before a cup of coffee in the restaurant next to the pressroom, nicknamed The Greasy Spoon. When she came down at last, freshly washed and combed and powdered, she saw Adam first, sitting near the dingy big window, face turned to the street, but looking down. It was an extraordinary face, smooth and fine and golden in the shabby light, but now set in a blind melancholy, a look of pained suspense and disillusion. For just one split second she got a glimpse of Adam when he would have been older, the face of the man he would not live to be. He saw her then, rose, and the bright glow was there.

Adam pulled their chairs together at their table; they drank hot tea and listened to the orchestra jazzing "Pack Up Your Troubles."[29]

"In an old kit bag, and smoil, smoil, smoil," shouted half a dozen boys under the draft age, gathered around a table near the orchestra. They yelled incoherently, laughed in great hysterical bursts of something that appeared to be merriment, and passed around under the tablecloth flat bottles containing a clear liquid—for in this western city founded and built by roaring drunken miners, no one was allowed to take his alcohol openly—splashed it into their tumblers of ginger ale, and went on singing, "It's a Long Way to Tipperary." When the tune changed to "Madelon,"[30] Adam said, "Let's dance." It was a tawdry little place, crowded and hot and full of smoke, but there was nothing better. The music was gay; and life is completely crazy anyway, thought Miranda, so what does it matter? This is what we have, Adam and I, this is all we're going to get, this is the way it is with us. She wanted to say, "Adam, come out of your dream and listen to me. I have pains in my chest and my head and my heart and they're real. I am in pain all over, and you are in such danger as I can't bear to think about, and why can we not save each other?" When her hand tightened on his shoulder his arm tightened about her waist instantly, and stayed there, holding firmly. They said nothing but smiled continually at each other, odd changing smiles as though they had found a new language. Miranda, her face near Adam's shoulder, noticed a dark young pair sitting at a corner table, each with an arm around the waist of the other, their heads together, their eyes staring at the same thing, whatever it was, that hovered in space before them. Her right hand lay on the table, his hand over it, and her face was a blur with weeping. Now and then he raised her hand and kissed it, and set it down and held it, and her eyes would fill again. They were not

[29] Another popular World War I song: "Pack up your troubles in your old kit bag, and smile, smile, smile."

[30] A French dance song that became popular in the United States during the war.

shameless, they had merely forgotten where they were, or they had no other place to go, perhaps. They said not a word, and the small pantomime repeated itself, like a melancholy short film running monotonously over and over again. Miranda envied them. She envied that girl. At least she can weep if that helps, and he does not even have to ask, What is the matter? Tell me. They had cups of coffee before them, and after a long while—Miranda and Adam had danced and sat down again twice—when the coffee was quite cold, they drank it suddenly, then embraced as before, without a word and scarcely a glance at each other. Something was done and settled between them, at least; it was enviable, enviable, that they could sit quietly together and have the same expression on their faces while they looked into the hell they shared, no matter what kind of hell, it was theirs, they were together.

At the table nearest Adam and Miranda a young woman was leaning on her elbow, telling her young man a story. "And I don't like him because he's too fresh. He kept on asking me to take a drink and I kept telling him, I don't drink and he said, Now look here, I want a drink the worst way and I think it's mean of you not to drink with me, I can't sit up here and drink by myself, he said. I told him, You're not by yourself in the first place; I like that, I said, and if you want a drink go ahead and have it, I told him, why drag *me* in? So he called the waiter and ordered ginger ale and two glasses and I drank straight ginger ale like I always do but he poured a shot of hooch in his. He was awfully proud of that hooch, said he made it himself out of potatoes. Nice homemade likker, warm from the pipe, he told me, three drops of this and your ginger ale will taste like Mumm's Extry.[31] But I said, No, and I mean no, can't you get that through your bean? He took another drink and said, Ah, come on, honey, don't be so stubborn, this'll make your shimmy[32] shake. So I just got tired of the argument, and I said, I don't need to drink, to shake my shimmy, I can strut my stuff on tea, I said. Well, why don't you then, he wanted to know, and I just told him—"

She knew she had been asleep for a long time when all at once without even a warning footstep or creak of the door hinge, Adam was in the room turning on the light, and she knew it was he, though at first she was blinded and turned her head away. He came over at once and sat on the side of the bed and began to talk as if he were going on with something they had been talking about before. He crumpled a square of paper and tossed it in the fireplace.

"You didn't get my note," he said. "I left it under the door. I was called back suddenly to camp for a lot of inoculations. They kept me longer than I expected, I was late. I called the office and they told me you were not coming in today. I called Miss Hobbe here and she said you were in bed and couldn't come to the telephone. Did she give you my message?"

"No," said Miranda drowsily, "but I think I have been asleep all day. Oh, I do remember. There was a doctor here. Bill sent him. I was at the telephone once, for Bill told me he would send an ambulance and have me

[31] Mumm's Extra Dry is an expensive French champagne.

[32] Chemise, or dress. The "shimmy" or "shimmy shake" was a popular World War I dance that involved shaking the body from the shoulders down.

taken to the hospital. The doctor tapped my chest and left a prescription and said he would be back, but he hasn't come."

"Where is it, the prescription?" asked Adam.

"I don't know. He left it, though, I saw him."

Adam moved about searching the tables and the mantelpiece. "Here it is," he said. "I'll be back in a few minutes. I must look for an all-night drug store. It's after one o'clock. Good-by."

Good-by, good-by. Miranda watched the door where he had disappeared for quite a while, then closed her eyes, and thought. When I am not here I cannot remember anything about this room where I have lived for nearly a year, except that the curtains are too thin and there was never any way of shutting out the morning light. Miss Hobbe had promised heavier curtains, but they had never appeared. When Miranda in her dressing gown had been at the telephone that morning, Miss Hobbe had passed through, carrying a tray. She was a little red-haired nervously friendly creature, and her manner said all too plainly that the place was not paying and she was on the ragged edge.

"My dear *child,*" she said sharply, with a glance at Miranda's attire, "what is the matter?"

Miranda, with the receiver to her ear, said, "Influenza, I think."

"*Horrors,*" said Miss Hobbe, in a whisper, and the tray wavered in her hands. "Go back to bed at once . . . go at *once!*"

"I must talk to Bill first," Miranda had told her, and Miss Hobbe had hurried on and had not returned. Bill had shouted directions at her, promising everything, doctor, nurse, ambulance, hospital, her check every week as usual, everything, but she was to get back to bed and stay there. She dropped into bed, thinking that Bill was the only person she had ever seen who actually tore his own hair when he was excited enough . . . I suppose I should ask to be sent home, she thought, it's a respectable old custom to inflict your death on the family if you can manage it. No, I'll stay here, this is my business, but not in this room, I hope . . . I wish I were in the cold mountains in the snow, that's what I should like best; and all about her rose the measured ranges of the Rockies wearing their perpetual snow, their majestic blue laurels of cloud, chilling her to the bone with their sharp breath. Oh, no, I must have warmth—and her memory turned and roved after another place she had known first and loved best, that now she could see only in drifting fragments of palm and cedar, dark shadows and a sky that warmed without dazzling, as this strange sky had dazzled without warming her; there was the long slow wavering of gray moss in the drowsy oak shade, the spacious hovering of buzzards overhead, the smell of crushed water herbs along a bank, and without warning a broad tranquil river into which flowed all the rivers she had known. The walls shelved away in one deliberate silent movement on either side, and a tall sailing ship was moored near by, with a gangplank weathered to blackness touching the foot of her bed. Back of the ship was jungle, and even as it appeared before her, she knew it was all she had ever read or had been told or felt or thought about jungles; a writhing terribly alive and secret place of death, creeping with tangles of spotted serpents, rainbow-colored birds with malign eyes, leopards with humanly wise faces and extravagantly crested lions; screaming long-armed monkeys tumbling among broad fleshy leaves that glowed with sulphur-colored light and exuded the ichor[33] of death, and rotting trunks of unfamiliar trees sprawled in crawling slime. Without surprise, watching from her pillow, she saw herself run swiftly down this gangplank to the slanting deck, and standing there, she leaned on the rail and waved gaily to herself in bed, and the slender ship spread its wings and sailed away into the jungle. The air trembled with the shattering scream and the hoarse bellow of voices all crying together, rolling and colliding above her like ragged stormclouds, and the words became two words only rising and falling and clamoring about her head. Danger, danger, danger, the voices said, and War, war, war. There was her door half open, Adam standing with his hand on the knob, and Miss Hobbe with her face all out of shape with terror was crying shrilly, "I tell you, they must come for her *now,* or I'll put her on the sidewalk . . . I tell you, this is a plague, a plague, my God, and I've got a houseful of people to think about!"

Adam said, "I know that. They'll come for her tomorrow morning."

"Tomorrow morning, my God, they'd better come now!"

"They can't get an ambulance," said Adam, "and there aren't any beds. And we can't find a doctor or a nurse. They're all busy. That's all there is to it. You stay out of the room, and I'll look after her."

"Yes, you'll look after her, I can see that," said Miss Hobbe, in a particularly unpleasant tone.

"Yes, that's what I said," answered Adam, drily, "and you keep out."

He closed the door carefully. He was carrying an assortment of misshapen packages, and his face was astonishingly impassive.

"Did you hear that?" he asked, leaning over and speaking very quietly.

"Most of it," said Miranda, "it's a nice prospect, isn't it?"

"I've got your medicine," said Adam, "and you're to begin with it this minute. She can't put you out."

"So it's really as bad as that," said Miranda.

"It's as bad as anything can be," said Adam, "all the theaters and nearly all the shops and restaurants are closed, and the streets have been full of funerals all day and ambulances all night—"

"But not one for me," said Miranda, feeling hilarious and lightheaded. She sat up and beat her pillow into shape and reached for her robe. "I'm glad you're here, I've been having a nightmare. Give me a cigarette, will you, and light one for yourself and open all the windows and sit near one of them. You're running a risk," she told him, "don't you know that? Why do you do it?"

"Never mind," said Adam, "take your medicine," and offered her two large cherry-colored pills. She swallowed them promptly and instantly vomited them up. "*Do* excuse me," she said, beginning to laugh. "I'm so sorry." Adam without a word and with a very concerned expression washed her face with a wet towel, gave her some cracked ice from one of the packages, and firmly offered her two more pills. "That's what they always did at home," she explained to him, "and it worked." Crushed with humiliation, she put her hands over her face and laughed again, painfully.

"There are two more kinds yet," said Adam, pulling her hands from her face and lifting her chin. "You've hardly begun. And I've got other things,

[33] Watery fluid.

like orange juice and ice cream—they told me to feed you ice cream—and coffee in a thermos bottle, and a thermometer. You have to work through the whole lot so you'd better take it easy."

"This time last night we were dancing," said Miranda, and drank something from a spoon. Her eyes followed him about the room, as he did things for her with an absent-minded face, like a man alone; now and again he would come back, and slipping his hand under her head, would hold a cup or a tumbler to her mouth, and she drank, and followed him with her eyes again, without a clear notion of what was happening.

"Adam," she said, "I've just thought of something. Maybe they forgot St. Luke's Hospital. Call the sisters there and ask them not to be so selfish with their silly old rooms. Tell them I only want a very small dark ugly one for three days, or less. Do try them, Adam."

He believed, apparently, that she was still more or less in her right mind, for she heard him at the telephone explaining in his deliberate voice. He was back again almost at once, saying, "This seems to be my day for getting mixed up with peevish old maids. The sister said that even if they had a room you couldn't have it without doctor's orders. But they didn't have one, anyway. She was pretty sour about it."

"Well," said Miranda in a thick voice, "I think that's abominably rude and mean, don't you?" She sat up with a wide gesture of both arms, and began to retch again, violently.

"Hold it, as you were," called Adam, fetching the basin. He held her head, washed her face and hands with ice water, put her head straight on the pillow, and went over and looked out of the window. "Well," he said at last, sitting beside her again, "they haven't got a room. They haven't got a bed. They haven't even got a baby crib, the way she talked. So I think that's straight enough, and we may as well dig in."

"Isn't the ambulance coming?"

"Tomorrow, maybe."

He took off his tunic and hung it on the back of a chair. Kneeling before the fireplace, he began carefully to set kindling sticks in the shape of an Indian tepee, with a little paper in the center for them to lean upon. He lighted this and placed other sticks upon them, and larger bits of wood. When they were going nicely he added still heavier wood, and coal a few lumps at a time, until there was a good blaze, and a fire that would not need rekindling. He rose and dusted his hands together, the fire illuminated him from the back and his hair shone.

"Adam," said Miranda, "I think you're very beautiful." He laughed out at this, and shook his head at her. "What a hell of a word," he said, "for me." "It was the first that occurred to me," she said, drawing up on her elbow to catch the warmth of the blaze. "That's a good job, that fire."

He sat on the bed again, dragging up a chair and putting his feet on the rungs. They smiled at each other for the first time since he had come in that night. "How do you feel now?" he asked.

"Better, much better," she told him. "Let's talk. Let's tell each other what we meant to do."

"You tell me first," said Adam. "I want to know about you."

"You'd get the notion I had a very sad life," she said, "and perhaps it was, but I'd be glad enough to have it now. If I could have it back, it would be easy to be happy about almost anything at all. That's not true, but that's the way I feel now." After a pause, she said, "There's nothing to tell, after all, if it ends now, for all this time I was getting ready for something that was going to happen later, when the time came. So now it's nothing much."

"But it must have been worth having until now, wasn't it?" he asked seriously as if it were something important to know.

"Not if this is all," she repeated obstinately.

"Weren't you ever—happy?" asked Adam, and he was plainly afraid of the word; he was shy of it as he was of the word *love,* he seemed never to have spoken it before, and was uncertain of its sound or meaning.

"I don't know," she said, "I just lived and never thought about it. I remember things I liked, though, and things I hoped for."

"I was going to be an electrical engineer," said Adam. He stopped short. "And I shall finish up when I get back," he added, after a moment.

"Don't you love being alive?" asked Miranda. "Don't you love weather and the colors at different times of the day, and all the sounds and noises like children screaming in the next lot, and automobile horns and little bands playing in the street and the smell of food cooking?"

"I love to swim, too," said Adam.

"So do I," said Miranda; "we never did swim together."

"Do you remember any prayers?" she asked him suddenly. "Did you ever learn anything at Sunday School?"

"Not much," confessed Adam without contrition. "Well, the Lord's Prayer."

"Yes, and there's Hail Mary," she said, "and the really useful one beginning, I confess to Almighty God and to blessed Mary ever virgin and to the holy Apostles Peter and Paul—"

"Catholic," he commented.

"Prayers just the same, you big Methodist. I'll bet you *are* a Methodist."

"No, Presbyterian."

"Well, what others do you remember?"

"Now I lay me down to sleep—" said Adam.

"Yes, that one, and Blessed Jesus meek and mild—you see that my religious education wasn't neglected either. I even know a prayer beginning O Apollo.[34] Want to hear it?"

"No," said Adam, "you're making fun."

"I'm not," said Miranda, "I'm trying to keep from going to sleep. I'm afraid to go to sleep, I may not wake up. Don't let me go to sleep, Adam. Do you know Matthew, Mark, Luke and John? Bless the bed I lie upon?"

"If I should die before I wake, I pray the Lord my soul to take. Is that it?" asked Adam. "It doesn't sound right, somehow."

"Light me a cigarette, please, and move over and sit near the window. We keep forgetting about fresh air. You must have it." He lighted the cigarette and held it to her lips. She took it between her fingers and dropped it under the edge of her pillow. He found it and crushed it out in the saucer under the water tumbler. Her head swam in darkness for an instant, cleared, and she sat up in panic, throwing off the covers and break-

[34] The Greek god Apollo was, among other things, the god of healing.

ing into a sweat. Adam leaped up with an alarmed face, and almost at once was holding a cup of hot coffee to her mouth.

"You must have some too," she told him, quiet again, and they sat huddled together on the edge of the bed, drinking coffee in silence.

Adam said, "You must lie down again. You're awake now."

"Let's sing," said Miranda. "I know an old spiritual, I can remember some of the words." She spoke in a natural voice. "I'm fine now." She began in a hoarse whisper, "'Pale horse, pale rider, done taken my lover away[35] . . .' Do you know that song?"

"Yes," said Adam, "I heard Negroes in Texas sing it, in an oil field."

"I heard them sing it in a cotton field," she said; "it's a good song."

They sang that line together. "But I can't remember what comes next," said Adam.

"'Pale horse, pale rider,'" said Miranda, "(We really need a good banjo) 'done taken my lover away—'" Her voice cleared and she said, "But we ought to get on with it. What's the next line?"

"There's a lot more to it than that," said Adam, "about forty verses, the rider done taken away mammy, pappy, brother, sister, the whole family besides the lover—"

"But not the singer, not yet," said Miranda. "Death always leaves one singer to mourn. 'Death,'" she sang, "'oh, leave one singer to mourn—'"

"'Pale horse, pale rider,'" chanted Adam, coming in on the beat, "'done taken my lover away!' (I think we're good, I think we ought to get up an act—)"

"Go in Hut Service," said Miranda, "entertain the poor defenseless heroes Over There."

"We'll play banjos," said Adam; "I always wanted to play the banjo."

Miranda sighed, and lay back on the pillow and thought, I must give up, I can't hold out any longer. There was only that pain, only that room, and only Adam. There were no longer any multiple planes of living, no tough filaments of memory and hope pulling taut backwards and forwards holding her upright between them. There was only this one moment and it was a dream of time, and Adam's face, very near hers, eyes still and intent, was a shadow, and there was to be nothing more. . . .

"Adam," she said out of the heavy soft darkness that drew her down, down, "I love you, and I was hoping you would say that to me, too."

He lay down beside her with his arm under her shoulder, and pressed his smooth face against hers, his mouth moved towards her mouth and stopped. "Can you hear what I am saying?. . . What do you think I have been trying to tell you all this time?"

She turned towards him, the cloud cleared and she saw his face for an instant. He pulled the covers about her and held her, and said, "Go to sleep, darling, darling, if you will go to sleep now for one hour I will wake you up and bring you hot coffee and tomorrow we will find somebody to help. I love you, go to sleep—"

[35] A Black folksong. The pale horse and pale rider are from the book of Revelation 6:8: "And I saw, and behold, a pale horse, and its rider's name was Death, and Hades followed him; and they were given power over a fourth of the earth, to kill with sword and with famine and with pestilence and by wild beasts of the earth."

Almost with no warning at all, she floated into the darkness, holding his hand, in sleep that was not sleep but clear evening light in a small green wood, an angry dangerous wood full of inhuman concealed voices singing sharply like the whine of arrows and she saw Adam transfixed by a flight of these singing arrows that struck him in the heart and passed shrilly cutting their path through the leaves. Adam fell straight back before her eyes, and rose again unwounded and alive; another flight of arrows loosed from the invisible bow struck him again and he fell, and yet he was there before her untouched in a perpetual death and resurrection. She threw herself before him, angrily and selfishly she interposed between him and the track of the arrow, crying, No, no, like a child cheated in a game, It's my turn now, why must you always be the one to die? and the arrows struck her cleanly through the heart and through his body and he lay dead, and she still lived, and the wood whistled and sang and shouted, every branch and leaf and blade of grass had its own terrible accusing voice. She ran then, and Adam caught her in the middle of the room, running, and said, "Darling, I must have been asleep too. What happened, you screamed terribly?"

After he had helped her to settle again, she sat with her knees drawn up under her chin, resting her head on her folded arms and began carefully searching for her words because it was important to explain clearly. "It was a very odd sort of dream, I don't know why it could have frightened me. There was something about an old-fashioned valentine. There were two hearts carved on a tree, pierced by the same arrow—you know, Adam—"

"Yes, I know, honey," he said in the gentlest sort of way, and sat kissing her on the cheek and forehead with a kind of accustomedness, as if he had been kissing her for years, "one of those lace paper things."

"Yes, and yet they were alive, and were us, you understand—this doesn't seem to be quite the way it was, but it was something like that. It was in a wood—"

"Yes," said Adam. He got up and put on his tunic and gathered up the thermos bottle. "I'm going back to that little stand and get us some ice cream and hot coffee," he told her, "and I'll be back in five minutes, and you keep quiet. Good-by for five minutes," he said, holding her chin in the palm of his hand and trying to catch her eye, "and you be very quiet."

"Good-by," she said. "I'm awake again." But she was not, and the two alert young internes from the County hospital who had arrived, after frantic urgings from the noisy city editor of the Blue Mountain *News,* to carry her away in a police ambulance, decided that they had better go down and get the stretcher. Their voices roused her, she sat up, got out of bed at once and stood glancing about brightly. "Why, you're all right," said the darker and stouter of the two young men, both extremely fit and competent-looking in their white clothes, each with a flower in his buttonhole. "I'll just carry you." He unfolded a white blanket and wrapped it around her. She gathered up the folds and asked, "But where is Adam?" taking hold of the doctor's arm. He laid a hand on her drenched forehead, shook his head, and gave her a shrewd look. "Adam?"

"Yes," Miranda told him, lowering her voice confidentially, "he was here and now he is gone."

"Oh, he'll be back," the interne told her easily, "he's just gone round the block to get cigarettes. Don't worry about Adam. He's the least of your troubles."

"Will he know where to find me?" she asked, still holding back.

"We'll leave him a note," said the interne. "Come now, it's time we got out of here."

He lifted and swung her up to his shoulder. "I feel very badly," she told him; "I don't know why."

"I'll bet you do," said he, stepping out carefully, the other doctor going before them, and feeling for the first step of the stairs. "Put your arms around my neck," he instructed her. "It won't do you any harm and it's a great help to me."

"What's your name?" Miranda asked as the other doctor opened the front door and they stepped out into the frosty sweet air.

"Hildesheim," he said, in the tone of one humoring a child.

"Well, Dr. Hildesheim, aren't we in a pretty mess?"

"We certainly are," said Dr. Hildesheim.

The second young interne, still quite fresh and dapper in his white coat, though his carnation was withering at the edges, was leaning over listening to her breathing through a stethoscope, whistling thinly, "There's a Long, Long Trail—" From time to time he tapped her ribs smartly with two fingers, whistling. Miranda observed him for a few moments until she fixed his bright busy hazel eye not four inches from hers. "I'm not unconscious," she explained, "I know what I want to say." Then to her horror she heard herself babbling nonsense, knowing it was nonsense though she could not hear what she was saying. The flicker of attention in the eye near her vanished, the second interne went on tapping and listening, hissing softly under his breath.

"I wish you'd stop whistling," she said clearly. The sound stopped. "It's a beastly tune," she added. Anything, anything at all to keep her small hold on the life of human beings, a clear line of communication, no matter what, between her and the receding world. "Please let me see Dr. Hildesheim," she said, "I have something important to say to him. I must say it now." The second interne vanished. He did not walk away, he fled into the air without a sound, and Dr. Hildesheim's face appeared in his stead.

"Dr. Hildesheim, I want to ask you about Adam."

"That young man? He's been here, and left you a note, and has gone again," said Dr. Hildesheim, "and he'll be back tomorrow and the day after." His tone was altogether too merry and flippant.

"I don't believe you," said Miranda, bitterly, closing her lips and eyes and hoping she might not weep.

"Miss Tanner," called the doctor, "have you got that note?"

Miss Tanner appeared beside her, handed her an unsealed envelope, took it back, unfolded the note and gave it to her.

"I can't see it," said Miranda, after a pained search of the page full of hasty scratches in black ink.

"Here, I'll read it," said Miss Tanner. "It says, 'They came and took you while I was away and now they will not let me see you. Maybe tomorrow they will, with my love, Adam,'" read Miss Tanner in a firm dry voice, pronouncing the words distinctly. "Now, do you see?" she asked soothingly.

Miranda, hearing the words one by one, forgot them one by one. "Oh, read it again, what does it say?" she called out over the silence that pressed upon her, reaching towards the dancing words that just escaped as she almost touched them. "That will do," said Dr. Hildesheim, calmly authoritarian. "Where is that bed?"

"There is no bed yet," said Miss Tanner, as if she said, We are short of oranges. Dr. Hildesheim said, "Well, we'll manage something," and Miss Tanner drew the narrow trestle with bright crossed metal supports and small rubbery wheels into a deep jut of the corridor, out of the way of the swift white figures darting about, whirling and skimming like water flies all in silence. The white walls rose sheer as cliffs, a dozen frosted moons followed each other in perfect self-possession down a white lane and dropped mutely one by one into a snowy abyss.

What is this whiteness and silence but the absence of pain? Miranda lay lifting the nap of her white blanket softly between eased fingers, watching a dance of tall deliberate shadows moving behind a wide screen of sheets spread upon a frame. It was there, near her, on her side of the wall where she could see it clearly and enjoy it, and it was so beautiful she had no curiosity as to its meaning. Two dark figures nodded, bent, curtsied to each other, retreated and bowed again, lifted long arms and spread great hands against the white shadow of the screen; then with a single round movement, the sheets were folded back, disclosing two speechless men in white, standing, and another speechless man in white, lying on the bare springs of a white iron bed. The man on the springs was swathed smoothly from head to foot in white, with folded bands across the face, and a large stiff bow like merry rabbit ears dangled at the crown of his head.

The two living men lifted a mattress standing hunched against the wall, spread it tenderly and exactly over the dead man. Wordless and white they vanished down the corridor, pushing the wheeled bed before them. It had been an entrancing and leisurely spectacle, but now it was over. A pallid white fog rose in their wake insinuatingly and floated before Miranda's eyes, a fog in which was concealed all terror and all weariness, all the wrung faces and twisted backs and broken feet of abused, outraged living things, all the shapes of their confused pain and their estranged hearts; the fog might part at any moment and loose the horde of human torments. She put up her hands and said, Not yet, not yet, but it was too late. The fog parted and two executioners, white clad, moved towards her pushing between them with marvelously deft and practiced hands the misshapen figure of an old man in filthy rags whose scanty beard waggled under his opened mouth as he bowed his back and braced his feet to resist and delay the fate they had prepared for him. In a high weeping voice he was trying to explain to them that the crime of which he was accused did not merit the punishment he was about to receive; and except for this whining cry there was silence as they advanced. The soiled cracked bowls of the old man's hands were held before him beseechingly as a beggar's as he said, "Before God I am not guilty," but they held his arms and drew him onward, passed, and were gone.

The road to death is a long march beset with all evils, and the heart fails little by little at each new terror, the bones rebel at each step, the mind sets up its own bitter resistance and to what end? The barriers sink one by one, and no covering of the eyes shuts out the landscape of disaster, nor the sight of crimes committed there. Across the field came Dr. Hildesheim, his face a skull beneath his German helmet, carrying a naked infant writhing on the point of his bayonet, and a huge stone pot marked Poison in Gothic letters. He stopped before the well that Miranda remembered in a pasture on her father's farm, a well once dry but now bubbling with living water, and into its pure depths he threw the child and the poison, and the violated water sank back soundlessly into the earth. Miranda, screaming, ran with her arms above her head; her voice echoed and came back to her like a wolf's howl, Hildesheim is a Boche, a spy, a Hun, kill him, kill him before he kills you. . . . She woke howling, she heard the foul words accusing Dr. Hildesheim tumbling from her mouth; opened her eyes and knew she was in a bed in a small white room, with Dr. Hildesheim sitting beside her, two firm fingers on her pulse. His hair was brushed sleekly and his buttonhole flower was fresh. Stars gleamed through the window, and Dr. Hildesheim seemed to be gazing at them with no particular expression, his stethoscope dangling around his neck. Miss Tanner stood at the foot of the bed writing something on a chart.

"Hello," said Dr. Hildesheim, "at least you take it out in shouting. You don't try to get out of bed and go running around." Miranda held her eyes open with a terrible effort, saw his rather heavy, patient face clearly even as her mind tottered and slithered again, broke from its foundation and spun like a cast wheel in a ditch. "I didn't mean it, I never believed it, Dr. Hildesheim, you musn't remember it—" and was gone again, not being able to wait for an answer.

The wrong she had done followed her and haunted her dream: this wrong took vague shapes of horror she could not recognize or name, though her heart cringed at sight of them. Her mind, split in two, acknowledged and denied what she saw in the one instant, for across an abyss of complaining darkness her reasoning coherent self watched the strange frenzy of the other coldly, reluctant to admit the truth of its visions, its tenacious remorses and despairs.

"I know those are your hands," she told Miss Tanner, "I know it, but to me they are white tarantulas, don't touch me."

"Shut your eyes," said Miss Tanner.

"Oh, no," said Miranda, "for then I see worse things," but her eyes closed in spite of her will, and the midnight of her internal torment closed about her.

Oblivion, thought Miranda, her mind feeling among her memories of words she had been taught to describe the unseen, the unknowable, is a whirlpool of gray water turning upon itself for all eternity . . . eternity is perhaps more than the distance to the farthest star. She lay on a narrow ledge over a pit that she knew to be bottomless, though she could not comprehend it; the ledge was her childhood dream of danger, and she strained back against a reassuring wall of granite at her shoulders, staring into the pit, thinking, There it is, there it is at last, it is very simple; and soft carefully shaped words like oblivion and eternity are curtains hung before nothing at all. I shall not know when it happens, I shall not feel or remember, why can't I consent now, I am lost, there is no hope for me. Look, she told herself, there it is, that is death and there is nothing to fear. But she could not consent, still shrinking stiffly against the granite wall that was her childhood dream of safety, breathing slowly for fear of squandering breath, saying desperately, Look, don't be afraid, it is nothing, it is only eternity.

Granite walls, whirlpools, stars are things. None of them is death, nor the image of it. Death is death, said Miranda, and for the dead it has no attributes. Silenced she sank easily through deeps under deeps of darkness until she lay like a stone at the farthest bottom of life, knowing herself to be blind, deaf, speechless, no longer aware of the members of her own body, entirely withdrawn from all human concerns, yet alive with a peculiar lucidity and coherence; all notions of the mind, the reasonable inquiries of doubt, all ties of blood and the desires of the heart, dissolved and fell away from her, and there remained of her only a minute fiercely burning particle of being that knew itself alone, that relied upon nothing beyond itself for its strength; not susceptible to any appeal or inducement, being itself composed entirely of one single motive, the stubborn will to live. This fiery motionless particle set itself unaided to resist destruction, to survive and to be in its own madness of being, motiveless and planless beyond that one essential end. Trust me, the hard unwinking angry point of light said. Trust me. I stay.

At once it grew, flattened, thinned to a fine radiance, spread like a great fan and curved out into a rainbow through which Miranda, enchanted, altogether believing, looked upon a deep clear landscape of sea and sand, of soft meadow and sky, freshly washed and glistening with transparencies of blue. Why, of course, of course, said Miranda, without surprise but with serene rapture as if some promise made to her had been kept long after she had ceased to hope for it. She rose from her narrow ledge and ran lightly through the tall portals of the great bow that arched in its splendor over the burning blue of the sea and the cool green of the meadow on either hand.

The small waves rolled in and over unhurriedly, lapped upon the sand in silence and retreated; the grasses flurried before a breeze that made no sound. Moving towards her leisurely as clouds through the shimmering air came a great company of human beings, and Miranda saw in an amazement of joy that they were all the living she had known. Their faces were transfigured, each in its own beauty, beyond what she remembered of them, their eyes were clear and untroubled as good weather, and they cast no shadows. They were pure identities and she knew them every one without calling their names or remembering what relation she bore to them. They surrounded her smoothly on silent feet, then turned their entranced faces again towards the sea, and she moved among them easily as a wave among waves. The drifting circle widened, separated, and each figure was alone but not solitary; Miranda, alone too, questioning nothing, desiring nothing, in the quietude of her ecstasy, stayed where she was, eyes fixed on the overwhelming deep sky where it was always morning.

Lying at ease, arms under her head, in the prodigal warmth which flowed evenly from sea and sky and meadow, within touch but not touching the serenely smiling familiar beings about her, Miranda felt without warning a vague tremor of apprehension, some small flick of distrust in her joy; a thin frost touched the edges of this confident tranquillity; something, somebody, was missing, she had lost something, she had left something valuable in another country, oh, what could it be? There are no trees, no trees here, she said in fright, I have left something unfinished. A thought struggled at the back of her mind, came clearly as a voice in her ear. Where are the dead? We have forgotten the dead, oh, the dead, where are they? At once as if a curtain had fallen, the bright landscape faded, she was alone in a strange stony place of bitter cold, picking her way along a steep path of slippery snow, calling out, Oh, I must go back! But in what direction? Pain returned, a terrible compelling pain running through her veins like heavy fire, the stench of corruption filled her nostrils, the sweetish sickening smell of rotting flesh and pus; she opened her eyes and saw pale light through a coarse white cloth over her face, knew that the smell of death was in her body, and struggled to lift her hand. The cloth was drawn away; she saw Miss Tanner filling a hypodermic needle in her methodical expert way, and heard Dr. Hildesheim saying, "I think that will do the trick. Try another." Miss Tanner plucked firmly at Miranda's arm near the shoulder, and the unbelievable current of agony ran burning through her veins again. She struggled to cry out, saying, Let me go, let me go; but heard only incoherent sounds of animal suffering. She saw doctor and nurse glance at each other with the glance of initiates at a mystery, nodding in silence, their eyes alive with knowledgeable pride. They looked briefly at their handiwork and hurried away.

Bells screamed all off key, wrangling together as they collided in mid air, horns and whistles mingled shrilly with cries of human distress; sulphur colored light exploded through the black window pane and flashed away in darkness. Miranda waking from a dreamless sleep asked without expecting an answer, "What is happening?" for there was a bustle of voices and footsteps in the corridor, and a sharpness in the air; the far clamor went on, a furious exasperated shrieking like a mob in revolt.

The light came on, and Miss Tanner said in a furry voice, "Hear that? They're celebrating. It's the Armistice.[36] The war is over, my dear." Her hands trembled. She rattled a spoon in a cup, stopped to listen, held the cup out to Miranda. From the ward for old bedridden women down the hall floated a ragged chorus of cracked voices singing, "My country, 'tis of thee. . ."

Sweet land . . . oh, terrible land of this bitter world where the sound of rejoicing was a clamor of pain, where ragged tuneless old women, sitting up waiting for their evening bowl of cocoa, were singing, "Sweet land of Liberty—"

"Oh, say, can you see?" their hopeless voices were asking next, the hammer strokes of metal tongues drowning them out. "The war is over," said

[36] The end of World War I, November 11, 1918.

Miss Tanner, her underlip held firmly, her eyes blurred. Miranda said, "Please open the window, please, I smell death in here."

Now if real daylight such as I remember having seen in this world would only come again, but it is always twilight or just before morning, a promise of day that is never kept. What has become of the sun? That was the longest and loneliest night and yet it will not end and let the day come. Shall I ever see light again?

Sitting in a long chair, near a window, it was in itself a melancholy wonder to see the colorless sunlight slanting on the snow, under a sky drained of its blue. "Can this be my face?" Miranda asked her mirror. "Are these my own hands?" she asked Miss Tanner, holding them up to show the yellow tint like melted wax glimmering between the closed fingers. The body is a curious monster, no place to live in, how could anyone feel at home there? Is it possible I can ever accustom myself to this place? she asked herself. The human faces around her seemed dulled and tired, with no radiance of skin and eyes as Miranda remembered radiance; the once white walls of her room were now a soiled gray. Breathing slowly, falling asleep and waking again, feeling the splash of water on her flesh, taking food, talking in bare phrases with Dr. Hildesheim and Miss Tanner, Miranda looked about her with the covertly hostile eyes of an alien who does not like the country in which he finds himself, does not understand the language nor wish to learn it, does not mean to live there and yet is helpless, unable to leave it at his will.

"It is morning," Miss Tanner would say, with a sigh, for she had grown old and weary once for all in the past month, "morning again, my dear," showing Miranda the same monotonous landscape of dulled evergreens and leaden snow. She would rustle about in her starched skirts, her face bravely powdered, her spirit unbreakable as good steel, saying, "Look, my dear, what a heavenly morning, like a crystal," for she had an affection for the salvaged creature before her, the silent ungrateful human being whom she, Cornelia Tanner, a nurse who knew her business, had snatched back from death with her own hands. "Nursing is nine-tenths, just the same," Miss Tanner would tell the other nurses; "keep that in mind." Even the sunshine was Miss Tanner's own prescription for the further recovery of Miranda, this patient the doctors had given up for lost, and who yet sat here, visible proof of Miss Tanner's theory. She said, "Look at the sunshine, now," as she might be saying, "I ordered this for you, my dear, do sit up and take it."

"It's beautiful," Miranda would answer, even turning her head to look, thanking Miss Tanner for her goodness, most of all her goodness about the weather, "beautiful, I always loved it." And I might love it again if I saw it, she thought, but truth was, she could not see it. There was no light, there might never be light again, compared as it must always be with the light she had seen beside the blue sea that lay so tranquilly along the shore of her paradise. That was a child's dream of the heavenly meadow, the vision of repose that comes to a tired body in sleep, she thought, but I have seen it when I did not know it was a dream. Closing her eyes she would rest for a moment remembering that bliss which had repaid all the pain of the journey to reach it; opening them again she saw with a new anguish the dull world to which she was condemned, where the light seemed filmed over with cobwebs, all the bright surfaces corroded, the sharp planes melted and formless, all objects and beings meaningless, ah, dead and withered things that believed themselves alive!

At night, after the long effort of lying in her chair, in her extremity of grief for what she had so briefly won, she folded her painful body together and wept silently, shamelessly, in pity for herself and her lost rapture. There was no escape. Dr. Hildesheim, Miss Tanner, the nurses in the diet kitchen, the chemist, the surgeon, the precise machine of the hospital, the whole humane conviction and custom of society, conspired to pull her inseparable rack of bones and wasted flesh to its feet, to put in order her disordered mind, and to set her once more safely in the road that would lead her again to death.

Chuck Rouncivale and Mary Townsend came to see her, bringing her a bundle of letters they had guarded for her. They brought a basket of delicate small hothouse flowers, lilies of the valley with sweet peas and feathery fern, and above these blooms their faces were merry and haggard.

Mary said, "You *have* had a tussle, haven't you?" and Chuck said, "Well, you made it back, didn't you?" Then after an uneasy pause, they told her that everybody was waiting to see her again at her desk. "They've put me back on sports already, Miranda," said Chuck. For ten minutes Miranda smiled and told them how gay and what a pleasant surprise it was to find herself alive. For it will not do to betray the conspiracy and tamper with the courage of the living; there is nothing better than to be alive, everyone has agreed on that; it is past argument, and who attempts to deny it is justly outlawed. "I'll be back in no time at all," she said; "this is almost over."

Her letters lay in a heap in her lap and beside her chair. Now and then she turned one over to read the inscription, recognized this handwriting or that, examined the blotted stamps and the postmarks, and let them drop again. For two or three days they lay upon the table beside her, and she continued to shrink from them. "They will all be telling me again how good it is to be alive, they will say again they love me, they are glad I am living too, and what can I answer to that?" and her hardened, indifferent heart shuddered in despair at itself, because before it had been tender and capable of love.

Dr. Hildesheim said, "What, all these letters not opened yet?" and Miss Tanner said, "Read your letters, my dear, I'll open them for you." Standing beside the bed, she slit them cleanly with a paper knife. Miranda, cornered, picked and chose until she found a thin one in an unfamiliar handwriting. "Oh, no, now," said Miss Tanner, "take them as they come. Here, I'll hand them to you." She sat down, prepared to be helpful to the end.

What a victory, what triumph, what happiness to be alive, sang the letters in a chorus. The names were signed with flourishes like the circles in air of bugle notes, and they were the names of those she had loved best; some of those she had known well and pleasantly; and a few who meant nothing to her, then or now. The thin letter in the unfamiliar handwriting was from a strange man at the camp where Adam had been, telling her that Adam had died of influenza in the camp hospital. Adam had asked him, in case anything happened, to be sure to let her know.

If anything happened. To be sure to let her know. If anything happened. "Your friend, Adam Barclay," wrote the strange man. It had happened—she looked at the date—more than a month ago.

"I've been here a long time, haven't I?" she asked Miss Tanner, who was folding letters and putting them back in their proper envelopes.

"Oh, quite a while," said Miss Tanner, "but you'll be ready to go soon now. But you must be careful of yourself and not overdo, and you should come back now and then and let us look at you, because sometimes the aftereffects are very—"

Miranda, sitting up before the mirror, wrote carefully: "One lipstick, medium, one ounce flask Bois d'Hiver perfume, one pair of gray suéde gauntlets[37] without straps, two pairs gray sheer stockings without clocks[38]—"

Towney, reading after her, said, "Everything without something so that it will be almost impossible to get?"

"Try it, though," said Miranda, "they're nicer without. One walking stick of silvery wood with a silver knob."

"That's going to be expensive," warned Towney. "Walking is hardly worth it."

"You're right," said Miranda, and wrote in the margin, "a nice one to match my other things. Ask Chuck to look for this, Mary. Good looking and not too heavy." Lazarus,[39] come forth. Not unless you bring me my top hat and stick. Stay where you are then, you snob. Not at all. I'm coming forth. "A jar of cold cream," wrote Miranda, "a box of apricot powder—and, Mary, I don't need eye shadow, do I?" She glanced at her face in the mirror and away again. "Still, no one need pity this corpse if we look properly to the art of the thing."

Mary Townsend said, "You won't recognize yourself in a week."

"Do you suppose, Mary," asked Miranda, "I could have my old room back again?"

"That should be easy," said Mary. "We stored away all your things there with Miss Hobbe." Miranda wondered again at the time and trouble the living took to be helpful to the dead. But not quite dead now, she reassured herself, one foot in either world now; soon I shall cross back and be at home again. The light will seem real and I shall be glad when I hear that someone I know has escaped from death. I shall visit the escaped ones and help them dress and tell them how lucky they are, and how lucky I am still to have them. Mary will be back soon with my gloves and my walking stick, I must go now, I must begin saying good-by to Miss Tanner and Dr. Hildesheim. Adam, she said, now you need not die again, but still I wish you were here; I wish you had come back, what do you think I came back for, Adam, to be deceived like this?

At once he was there beside her, invisible but urgently present, a ghost but more alive than she was, the last intolerable cheat of her heart; for knowing it was false she still clung to the lie, the unpardonable lie of her bitter desire. She said, "I love you," and stood up trembling, trying by the mere act of her will to bring him to sight before her. If I could call you up

[37] Gloves. [38] Ornamental figures on the ankles or sides of stockings.
[39] Jesus raised Lazarus from the dead (John 11).

from the grave I would, she said, if I could see your ghost I would say, I believe . . . "I believe," she said aloud. "Oh, let me see you once more." The room was silent, empty, the shade was gone from it, struck away by the sudden violence of her rising and speaking aloud. She came to herself as if out of sleep. Oh, no, that is not the way, I must never do that, she warned herself. Miss Tanner said, "Your taxicab is waiting, my dear," and there was Mary. Ready to go.

No more war, no more plague, only the dazed silence that follows the ceasing of the heavy guns; noiseless houses with the shades drawn, empty streets, the dead cold light of tomorrow. Now there would be time for everything.

William Faulkner

(1897–1962)

The South has been to modern American literature what Ireland has been to modern British literature—the source of a body of writing distinguished for its rich, poetic language and its power to evoke a particular culture, rooted in a specific time and place, and at the same time to escape parochialism and speak with a universality that can capture an international audience. There are many literary Souths—Thomas Wolfe's North Carolina, Katherine Anne Porter's Texas, Eudora Welty's Mississippi—but the most famous is an imaginary one, Yoknapatawpha County, "William Faulkner, sole owner and proprietor" (as Faulkner once wrote on a map of his fictional world). The history, geography, and demography of Yoknapatawpha County gradually evolved in a dozen novels and many more short stories over a period of thirty years. The course of its development was, to quote the title of one of the best books on Faulkner, "from Jefferson to the world." Rooted in the Southern yarning and tale-telling of his hometown of Jefferson, Mississippi, Faulkner's saga, as it unfolds, becomes a spiritual history of the South, a meditation on the course of American history, and ultimately a mythic chronicle of man's fall into experience.

Faulkner was born in 1897 in New Albany, Mississippi, but his parents moved while he was still young to Oxford, home of the University of Mississippi, where his father first ran a livery stable and a hardware store and then became business manager of the university. Faulkner grew up among family tales of the South and of the Civil War; many centered around his great-grandfather, Colonel William C. Falkner (Faulkner added the "u" to the family name), who had fought for the Confederacy and after the war had built a railroad from Ripley into Tennessee and had even written a popular romantic novel, The White Rose of Memphis.

Always more interested in reading than in schooling, Faulkner dropped out of high school after two years and took a job in a bank, hoping to marry his sweetheart, Estelle Oldham. In 1918, when Estelle married another man and went to live with him in China, Faulkner joined the Canadian Royal Air Force. The war ended before he had finished his basic training, and he returned to Oxford, where he held a string of miscellaneous jobs, including a three-year stint as postmaster of the university post office. Meanwhile, he was learning to write; The Marble Faun, *a collection of poems, appeared in 1924 in a private edition. Part of 1925 was spent in New Orleans, where he met a number of writers, including Sherwood Anderson, who helped him arrange for the publication of his first novel,* Soldiers' Pay *(1926). Back in Oxford, Faulkner continued to work at a series of odd jobs while he wrote in the evenings and on weekends.* Mosquitoes, *a novel about literary life in New Orleans, appeared in 1927, but his third novel,* Flags in the Dust, *was rejected. Faulkner immediately set to work revising* Flags in the Dust *and writing a new novel,* The Sound and the Fury. *The revised* Flags in the Dust *appeared early in 1929 as* Sartoris; The Sound and the Fury *appeared later the same year. These two novels marked the end of Faulkner's apprenticeship and inaugurated the Yoknapatawpha cycle.*

Estelle Oldham returned to Oxford when her marriage ended in divorce, and she and Faulkner were married in 1929. They bought a rundown antebellum house just outside Oxford; Faulkner worked on it for years with his own hands. During the following twelve years, from 1930 to 1942, Faulkner produced the main body of his Yoknapatawpha series: As I Lay Dying *(1930),* Sanctuary *(1931),* Light in August *(1932),* Absalom, Absalom! *(1936),* The Unvanquished *(1938),* The Wild Palms *(1939),* The Hamlet *(1940), and* Go Down, Moses *(1942). These books were highly admired by a small circle of his fellow writers and by foreign readers, especially in France, but popular success escaped him; the lurid* Sanctuary *was the only one of his novels of the 1930s to succeed commercially. By 1945, Faulkner's books were out of print, and he had largely given up fiction and was writing films in Hollywood.*

The turning point in Faulkner's reputation came in 1945 with the publication of a collection of excerpts from his work, The Portable Faulkner, *edited by the prominent critic Malcolm Cowley. Cowley, in his long introduction, made clear the essential unity of Faulkner's work and arranged the selections so as to demonstrate the interrelationships among the Yoknapatawpha books.* The Portable Faulkner *was widely and favorably reviewed, and Faulkner's publisher responded to public demand by putting his novels back in print. A new novel,* Intruder in the Dust, *was a popular success in 1948. The following year, Faulkner was awarded the Nobel Prize. His* Collected Stories *appeared in 1950,* A Fable *in 1954, and* The Town *and* The Mansion, *the concluding volumes of the Snopes trilogy which he had begun with* The Hamlet, *in 1957 and 1959. His last novel,* The Reivers, *was published only a month before his death in Oxford in 1962.*

Faulkner's technique, like his materials, was an unexpected combination of down-home earthiness and cosmopolitan sophistication. He had studied closely the great works of the early Modernists, the Symbolist poetry of Charles Baudelaire, Paul Verlaine, and Stéphane Mallarmé, the poetry of T. S. Eliot, and the fiction of James Joyce, and he learned much from their intense concentration upon the ebb and flow of a single consciousness and from their use of symbolism and stream-of-consciousness narrative styles. The Sound and the Fury *broke new ground by making one of the four points of view from which the story is told that of a mentally retarded man; it is literally "a tale told by an idiot." Other novels are Conradian in their use of a ruminating, Marlow-like narrator whose spiralling meditations on the meaning of the action become the chief center of interest.*

The imaginary Yoknapatawpha County was built up like a jigsaw puzzle, not in historic sequence but in bits and pieces. In its completed form, the history of the county spans more than a century, from the displacement of its Indian inhabitants by white settlers through the creation of a plantation society, the collapse of that society in the Civil War, and the aftermath, the coming of the Snopeses, a new breed of sterile, locust-like scramblers displacing the Sartorises and their ordered world. The meaning of the history of the county lies, above all, in the values its people live by. The Sartoris world is a genuine community, bound together by deep respect for the wilderness and the land and by living codes of honor and chivalry. It is doomed, though, by the tragic flaw of slavery, and the War opens the gates to new values from the North and from the embittered misfits within the South, codes based on sterility, voracious self-interest, and exploitation of the land and of other people. There is thus a Chekhovian quality in Faulkner's work, a plangent sense of a lost world which, however, never becomes sentimentally nostalgic; he defends not an idealized past but the enduring qualities which, as he asserted in his Nobel Prize address, will make man "prevail."

"An Odor of Verbena" was originally published as a short story and later became a section of The Unvanquished*; the full novel traces the career of Colonel John Sartoris as seen through the eyes of his son Bayard. (Even Bayard's name contributes to the story's examination of codes of honor; he is named after a famous fifteenth-century French chivalric hero.) When* The Unvanquished *first appeared, many readers regarded it as a conventional Civil War romance, complete with dashing cavalrymen charging with plumes flying, sentimentalized Blacks defending their masters against the Yankees, and an idealized code of honor. "An Odor of Verbena" alone, the concluding section of the novel, is enough to refute this interpretation. Bayard, in the course of the story, is forced to confront the meaning of his father's code, now embodied in its "Greek amphora priestess," Drusilla Hawk. His choice of action places him among Faulkner's heroes, heroes not of flying plumes but of the human heart.*

FURTHER READING *(prepared by W. J. R.):* Joseph Blotner's *Faulkner*, 1974, is the definitive biography. Of the several anecdotal accounts of Faulkner's life, *William Faulkner of Oxford*, ed. James W. Webb and A. Wigfall Green, 1965, is the most reliable, collecting many reminiscences by Faulkner's fellow townspeople. Olga W. Vickery's *The Novels of William Faulkner*, 1959, rev. 1964, was one of the first important critical evaluations. Cleanth Brooks's *William Faulkner: The Yoknapatawpha Country*, 1963, rpt. 1966, and *William Faulkner: Toward Yoknapatawpha and Beyond*, 1978, are both valuable. The first examines the fourteen Yoknapatawpha novels and the backgrounds of Faulkner's fiction; the second deals with Faulkner's non-fictional prose, verse, and non-county fiction. Hyatt Waggoner's *William Faulkner: From Jefferson to the World*, 1959, is excellent both on individual works and on their interrelationships. Other comprehensive treatments of Faulkner include Warren Beck's *Faulkner*, 1976; John Pikoulis' *The Art of William Faulkner*, 1982; *William Faulkner: Four Decades of Criticism*, ed. Linda Welshimer Wagner, 1973 (a superior collection divided into "Development," "Works as a Whole," and "Method and Language"); and *Faulkner: A Collection of Critical Essays*, ed. Robert Penn Warren, 1966, which contains Malcolm Cowley's influential introduction to *The Portable Faulkner* and helpful genealogical tables. Thomas E. Dasher's *William Faulkner's Characters: An Index to Published and Unpublished Fiction*, 1981, is a helpful index to Faulkner's characters.

AN ODOR OF VERBENA

1

It was just after supper. I had just opened my *Coke*[1] on the table beneath the lamp; I heard Professor Wilkins' feet in the hall and then the instant of silence as he put his hand to the door knob, and I should have known. People talk glibly of presentiment, but I had none. I heard his feet on the stairs and then in the hall approaching and there was nothing in the feet because although I had lived in this house for three college years now and although both he and Mrs. Wilkins called me Bayard in the house, he would no more have entered my room without knocking than I would have entered his—or hers. Then he flung the door violently inward against the doorstop with one of those gestures with or by which an almost painfully unflagging preceptory of youth ultimately aberrates,[2] and stood there saying, "Bayard. Bayard, my son, my dear son."

I should have known; I should have been prepared. Or maybe I was prepared because I remember how I closed the book carefully, even marking the place, before I rose. He (Professor Wilkins) was doing something, bustling at something; it was my hat and cloak which he handed me and which I took although I would not need the cloak, unless even then I was thinking (although it was October, the equinox had not occurred) that the rains and the cool weather would arrive before I should see this room again and so I would need the cloak anyway to return to it if I returned, thinking "God, if he had only done this last night, flung that door crashing and bouncing against the stop last night without knocking so I could have gotten there before it happened, been there when it did, beside him on whatever spot, wherever it was that he would have to fall and lie in the dust and dirt."

"Your boy is downstairs in the kitchen," he said. It was not until years later that he told me (someone did; it must have been Judge Wilkins) how Ringo had apparently flung the cook aside and come on into the house and into the library where he and Mrs. Wilkins were sitting and said without preamble and already turning to withdraw: "They shot Colonel Sartoris this morning. Tell him I be waiting in the kitchen" and was gone before either of them could move. "He has ridden forty miles yet he refuses to eat anything." We were moving toward the door now—the door on my side of which I had lived for three years now with what I knew, what I knew now I must have believed and expected, yet beyond which I had heard the approaching feet yet heard nothing in the feet. "If there was just anything I could do."

"Yes, sir," I said. "A fresh horse for my boy. He will want to go back with me."

"By all means take mine—Mrs. Wilkins'," he cried. His tone was no different yet he did cry it and I suppose that at the same moment we both

[1] A law book, *Coke on Littleton*, by Sir Edward Coke (1552–1634).

[2] *preceptory . . . aberrates.* A teacher of youth breaks his pattern.

realised that was funny—a short-legged deep-barreled mare who looked exactly like a spinster music teacher, which Mrs. Wilkins drove to a basket phaeton[3]—which was good for me, like being doused with a pail of cold water would have been good for me.

"Thank you, sir," I said. "We won't need it. I will get a fresh horse for him at the livery stable when I get my mare." Good for me, because even before I finished speaking I knew that would not be necessary either, that Ringo would have stopped at the livery stable before he came out to the college and attended to that and that the fresh horse for him and my mare both would be saddled and waiting now at the side fence and we would not have to go through Oxford at all. Loosh would not have thought of that if he had come for me, he would have come straight to the college, to Professor Wilkins', and told his news and then sat down and let me take charge from then on. But not Ringo.

He followed me from the room. From now until Ringo and I rode away into the hot thick dusty darkness quick and strained for the overdue equinox like a laboring delayed woman, he would be somewhere either just beside me or just behind me and I never to know exactly nor care which. He was trying to find the words with which to offer me his pistol too. I could almost hear him: "Ah, this unhappy land, not ten years recovered from the fever yet still men must kill one another, still we must pay Cain's price in his own coin."[4] But he did not actually say it. He just followed me, somewhere beside or behind me as we descended the stairs toward where Mrs. Wilkins waited in the hall beneath the chandelier—a thin gray woman who reminded me of Granny, not that she looked like Granny probably but because she had known Granny—a lifted anxious still face which was thinking *Who lives by the sword shall die by it*[5] just as Granny would have thought, toward which I walked, had to walk not because I was Granny's grandson and had lived in her house for three college years and was about the age of her son when he was killed in almost the last battle nine years ago, but because I was now The Sartoris. (The Sartoris: that had been one of the concomitant flashes, along with the *at last it has happened* when Professor Wilkins opened my door.) She didn't offer me a horse and pistol, not because she liked me any less than Professor Wilkins but because she was a woman and so wiser than any man, else the men would not have gone on with the War for two years after they knew they were whipped. She just put her hands (a small woman, no bigger than Granny had been) on my shoulders and said, "Give my love to Drusilla and your Aunt Jenny. And come back when you can."

"Only I don't know when that will be," I said. "I don't know how many things I will have to attend to." Yes, I lied even to her; it had not been but a minute yet since he had flung that door bouncing into the stop yet already I was beginning to realise, to become aware of that which I still had no yardstick to measure save that one consisting of what, despite myself, despite

[3] A light, four-wheeled carriage.
[4] That is, through violence, as Cain killed Abel (Genesis 4).
[5] Jesus' words to a companion who cuts off the ear of a servant of the high priest (Matthew 26:52).

my raising and background (or maybe because of them) I had for some time known I was becoming and had feared the test of it; I remember how I thought while her hands still rested on my shoulders: *At least this will be my chance to find out if I am what I think I am or if I just hope; if I am going to do what I have taught myself is right or if I am just going to wish I were.*

We went on to the kitchen, Professor Wilkins still somewhere beside or behind me and still offering me the pistol and horse in a dozen different ways. Ringo was waiting; I remember how I thought then that no matter what might happen to either of us, I would never be The Sartoris to him. He was twenty-four too, but in a way he had changed even less than I had since that day when we had nailed Grumby's body to the door of the old compress.[6] Maybe it was because he had outgrown me, had changed so much that summer while he and Granny traded mules with the Yankees that since then I had had to do most of the changing just to catch up with him. He was sitting quietly in a chair beside the cold stove, spent-looking too who had ridden forty miles (at one time, either in Jefferson or when he was alone at last on the road somewhere, he had cried; dust was now caked and dried in the tear-channels on his face) and would ride forty more yet would not eat, looking up at me a little red-eyed with weariness (or maybe it was more than just weariness and so I would never catch up with him) then rising without a word and going on toward the door and I following and Professor Wilkins still offering the horse and the pistol without speaking the words and still thinking (I could feel that too) *Dies by the sword. Dies by the sword.*

Ringo had the two horses saddled at the side gate, as I had known he would—the fresh one for himself and my mare father had given me three years ago, that could do a mile under two minutes any day and a mile every eight minutes all day long. He was already mounted when I realised that what Professor Wilkins wanted was to shake my hand. We shook hands; I know he believed he was touching flesh which might not be alive tomorrow night and I thought for a second how if I told him what I was going to do, since we had talked about it, about how if there was anything at all in the Book, anything of hope and peace for His blind and bewildered spawn which He had chosen above all others to offer immortality, *Thou shalt not kill*[7] must be it, since maybe he even believed that he had taught it to me except that he had not, nobody had, not even myself since it went further than just having been learned. But I did not tell him. He was too old to be forced so, to condone even in principle such a decision; he was too old to have to stick to principle in the face of blood and raising and background, to be faced without warning and made to deliver like by a highwayman out of the dark: only the young could do that—one still young enough to have his youth supplied him gratis as a reason (not an excuse) for cowardice.

So I said nothing. I just shook his hand and mounted too, and Ringo and I rode on. We would not have to pass through Oxford now and so soon

[6] A building where cotton is compressed into bales.
[7] The sixth of the Ten Commandments (Exodus 20:13).

(there was a thin sickle of moon like the heel print of a boot in wet sand) the road to Jefferson lay before us, the road which I had travelled for the first time three years ago with Father and travelled twice at Christmas time and then in June and September and twice at Christmas time again and then June and September again each college term since alone on the mare, not even knowing that this was peace; and now this time and maybe last time who would not die (I knew that) but who maybe forever after could never again hold up his head. The horses took the gait which they would hold for forty miles. My mare knew the long road ahead and Ringo had a good beast too, had talked Hilliard at the livery stable out of a good horse too. Maybe it was the tears, the channels of dried mud across which his strain-reddened eyes had looked at me, but I rather think it was that same quality which used to enable him to replenish his and Granny's supply of United States Army letterheads[8] during that time—some outrageous assurance gained from too long and too close association with white people: the one whom he called Granny, the other with whom he had slept from the time we were born until Father rebuilt the house. We spoke one time, then no more:

"We could bushwhack him," he said. "Like we done Grumby that day. But I reckon that wouldn't suit that white skin you walks around in."

"No," I said. We rode on; it was October; there was plenty of time still for verbena although I would have to reach home before I would realise there was a need for it; plenty of time for verbena yet from the garden where Aunt Jenny puttered beside old Joby, in a pair of Father's old cavalry gauntlets, among the coaxed and ordered beds, the quaint and odorous old names, for though it was October no rain had come yet and hence no frost to bring (or leave behind) the first half-warm half-chill nights of Indian Summer—the drowsing air cool and empty for geese yet languid still with the old hot dusty smell of fox grape and sassafras—the nights when before I became a man and went to college to learn law Ringo and I, with lantern and axe and crokersack[9] and six dogs (one to follow the trail and five more just for the tonguing, the music) would hunt possum in the pasture where, hidden, we had seen our first Yankee that afternoon on the bright horse, where for the last year now you could hear the whistling of the trains which had no longer belonged to Mr. Redmond for a long while now and which at some instant, some second during the morning Father too had relinquished along with the pipe which Ringo said he was smoking, which slipped from his hand as he fell. We rode on, toward the house where he would be lying in the parlor now, in his regimentals[10] (sabre too) and where Drusilla would be waiting for me beneath all the festive glitter of the chandeliers, in the yellow ball gown and the sprig of verbena in her hair, holding the two loaded pistols (I could see that too, who had had no presentiment; I could see her, in the formal brilliant room arranged formally for obsequy, not tall, not slender as a woman is but as a youth, a boy, is motionless, in yellow, the face calm, almost bemused, the head simple

[8]Official stationery. [9]Burlap bag. [10]Dress uniform.

and severe, the balancing sprig of verbena above each ear, the two arms bent at the elbows, the two hands shoulder high, the two identical duelling pistols lying upon, not clutched in, one to each: the Greek amphora priestess[11] of a succinct and formal violence).

2

Drusilla said that he had a dream. I was twenty then and she and I would walk in the garden in the summer twilight while we waited for Father to ride in from the railroad. I was just twenty then: that summer before I entered the University to take the law degree which Father decided I should have and four years after the one, the day, the evening when Father and Drusilla had kept old Cash Benbow from becoming United States Marshal and returned home still unmarried and Mrs. Habersham herded them into her carriage and drove them back to town and dug her husband out of his little dim hole in the new bank and made him sign Father's peace bond for killing the two carpet baggers,[12] and took Father and Drusilla to the minister herself and saw that they were married. And Father had rebuilt the house too, on the same blackened spot, over the same cellar, where the other had burned, only larger, much larger: Drusilla said that the house was the aura of Father's dream just as a bride's trousseau and veil is the aura of hers. And Aunt Jenny had come to live with us now so we had the garden (Drusilla would no more have bothered with flowers than Father himself would have, who even now, even four years after it was over, still seemed to exist, breathe, in that last year of it while she had ridden in man's clothes and with her hair cut short like any other member of Father's troop, across Georgia and both Carolinas in front of Sherman's army)[13] for her to gather sprigs of verbena from to wear in her hair because she said verbena was the only scent you could smell above the smell of the horses and courage and so it was the only one that was worth the wearing. The railroad was hardly begun then and Father and Mr. Redmond were not only still partners, they were still friends, which as George Wyatt said was easily a record for Father, and he would leave the house at daybreak on Jupiter, riding up and down the unfinished line with two saddlebags of gold coins borrowed on Friday to pay the men on Saturday, keeping just two cross-ties ahead of the sheriff as Aunt Jenny said. So we walked in the dusk, slowly between Aunt Jenny's flower beds while Drusilla (in a dress now, who still would have worn pants all the time if Father had let her) leaned lightly on my arm and I smelled the verbena in her hair as I had smelled the rain in it and in Father's beard that night four years ago when he and Drusilla and Uncle Buck McCaslin found Grumby and then came home and found Ringo and me more than just

[11] Painting of a priestess on a Greek amphora, or vase.

[12] Northerners who went to the South after the Civil War to profit personally by the Reconstruction laws; so called because they were said to carry all their belongings in "carpet bags."

[13] In one of the decisive campaigns of the Civil War, the Northern general William Tecumseh Sherman took Atlanta in 1864 and then marched east across the South, devastating the countryside as he went.

asleep: escaped into that oblivion which God or Nature or whoever it was had supplied us with for the time being, who had had to perform more than should be required of children because there should be some limit to the age, the youth at least below which one should not have to kill. This was just after the Saturday night when I returned and I watched him clean the derringer[14] and reload it and we learned that the dead man was almost a neighbor, a hill man who had been in the first infantry regiment when it voted Father out of command: and we never to know if the man actually intended to rob Father or not because Father had shot too quick, but only that he had a wife and several children in a dirt-floored cabin in the hills, to whom Father the next day sent some money and she (the wife) walked into the house two days later while we were sitting at the dinner table and flung the money at Father's face.

"But nobody could have more of a dream than Colonel Sutpen," I said. He had been Father's second-in-command in the first regiment and had been elected colonel when the regiment deposed Father after Second Manassas, and it was Sutpen and not the regiment whom Father never forgave. He was underbred, a cold ruthless man who had come into the country about thirty years before the War, nobody knew from where except Father said you could look at him and know he would not dare to tell. He had got some land and nobody knew how he did that either, and he got money from somewhere—Father said they all believed he robbed steamboats, either as a card sharper or as an out-and-out highwayman—and built a big house and married and set up as a gentleman. Then he lost everything in the War like everybody else, all hope of descendants too (his son killed his daughter's fiancé on the eve of the wedding and vanished) yet he came back home and set out singlehanded to rebuild his plantation. He had no friends to borrow from and he had nobody to leave it to and he was past sixty years old, yet he set out to rebuild his place like it used to be; they told how he was too busy to bother with politics or anything; how when Father and the other men organised the nightriders to keep the carpet baggers from organising the Negroes into an insurrection, he refused to have anything to do with it. Father stopped hating him long enough to ride out to see Sutpen himself and he (Sutpen) came to the door with a lamp and did not even invite them to come in and discuss it; Father said, "Are you with us or against us?" and he said, "I'm for my land. If every man of you would rehabilitate his own land, the country will take care of itself" and Father challenged him to bring the lamp out and set it on a stump where they could both see to shoot and Sutpen would not. "Nobody could have more of a dream than that."

"Yes. But his dream is just Sutpen. John's is not. He is thinking of this whole country which he is trying to raise by its bootstraps, so that all the people in it, not just his kind nor his old regiment, but all the people, black and white, the women and children back in the hills who don't even own shoes—Don't you see?"

"But how can they get any good from what he wants to do for them if they are—after he has—"

[14] A short-barreled pocket pistol.

"Killed some of them? I suppose you include those two carpet baggers he had to kill to hold that first election, don't you?"

"They were men. Human beings."

"They were Northerners, foreigners who had no business here. They were pirates." We walked on, her weight hardly discernible on my arm, her head just reaching my shoulder. I had always been a little taller than she, even on that night at Hawkhurst while we listened to the niggers passing in the road, and she had changed but little since—the same boy-hard body, the close implacable head with its savagely cropped hair which I had watched from the wagon above the tide of crazed singing niggers as we went down into the river—the body not slender as women are but as boys are slender. "A dream is not a very safe thing to be near, Bayard. I know; I had one once. It's like a loaded pistol with a hair trigger: if it stays alive long enough, somebody is going to be hurt. But if it's a good dream, it's worth it. There are not many dreams in the world, but there are a lot of human lives. And one human life or two dozen—"

"Are not worth anything?"

"No. Not anything.—Listen. I hear Jupiter. I'll beat you to the house." She was already running, the skirts she did not like to wear lifted almost to her knees, her legs beneath it running as boys run just as she rode like men ride.

I was twenty then. But the next time I was twenty-four; I had been three years at the University and in another two weeks I would ride back to Oxford for the final year and my degree. It was just last summer, last August, and Father had just beat Redmond for the State legislature. The railroad was finished now and the partnership between Father and Redmond had been dissolved so long ago that most people would have forgotten they were ever partners if it hadn't been for the enmity between them. There had been a third partner but nobody hardly remembered his name now; he and his name both had vanished in the fury of the conflict which set up between Father and Redmond almost before they began to lay the rails, between Father's violent and ruthless dictatorialness and will to dominate (the idea was his; he did think of the railroad first and then took Redmond in) and that quality in Redmond (as George Wyatt said, he was not a coward or Father would never have teamed with him) which permitted him to stand as much as he did from Father, to bear and bear and bear until something (not his will nor his courage) broke in him. During the War Redmond had not been a soldier, he had had something to do with cotton for the Government; he could have made money himself out of it but he had not and everybody knew he had not, Father knew it, yet Father would even taunt him with not having smelled powder. He was wrong; he knew he was when it was too late for him to stop just as a drunkard reaches a point where it is too late for him to stop, where he promises himself that he will and maybe believes he will or can but it is too late. Finally they reached the point (they had both put everything they could mortgage or borrow into it for Father to ride up and down the line, paying the workmen and the waybills[15] on the rails at the last possible instant) where even Father realised that one of them would have to get out. So (they were not speaking

[15] Invoices; statements of charges due.

then; it was arranged by Judge Benbow) they met and agreed to buy or sell, naming a price which, in reference to what they had put into it, was ridiculously low but which each believed the other could not raise—at least Father claimed that Redmond did not believe he could raise it. So Redmond accepted the price, and found out that Father had the money. And according to Father, that's what started it, although Uncle Buck McCaslin said Father could not have owned a half interest in even one hog, let alone a railroad, and not dissolve the business either sworn enemy or death-pledged friend to his recent partner. So they parted and Father finished the road. By that time, seeing that he was going to finish it, some Northern people sold him a locomotive on credit which he named for Aunt Jenny, with a silver oil can in the cab with her name engraved on it; and last summer the first train ran into Jefferson, the engine decorated with flowers and Father in the cab blowing blast after blast on the whistle when he passed Redmond's house; and there were speeches at the station, with more flowers and a Confederate flag and girls in white dresses and red sashes and a band, and Father stood on the pilot of the engine and made a direct and absolutely needless allusion to Mr. Redmond. That was it. He wouldn't let him alone. George Wyatt came to me right afterward and told me. "Right or wrong," he said, "us boys and most of the other folks in this country know John's right. But he ought to let Redmond alone. I know what's wrong: he's had to kill too many folks, and that's bad for a man. We all know Colonel's brave as a lion, but Redmond ain't no coward either and there ain't any use in making a brave man that made one mistake eat crow all the time. Can't you talk to him?"

"I don't know," I said. "I'll try." But I had no chance. That is, I could have talked to him and he would have listened, but he could not have heard me because he had stepped straight from the pilot of that engine into the race for the Legislature. Maybe he knew that Redmond would have to oppose him to save his face even though he (Redmond) must have known that, after that train ran into Jefferson, he had no chance against Father, or maybe Redmond had already announced his candidacy and Father entered the race just because of that, I don't remember. Anyway they ran, a bitter contest in which Father continued to badger Redmond without reason or need, since they both knew it would be a landslide for Father. And it was, and we thought he was satisfied. Maybe he thought so himself, as the drunkard believes that he is done with drink; and it was that afternoon and Drusilla and I walked in the garden in the twilight and I said something about what George Wyatt had told me and she released my arm and turned me to face her and said, "This from you? You? Have you forgotten Grumby?"

"No," I said. "I never will forget him."

"You never will. I wouldn't let you. There are worse things than killing men, Bayard. There are worse things than being killed. Sometimes I think the finest thing that can happen to a man is to love something, a woman preferably, well, hard hard hard, then to die young because he believed what he could not help but believe and was what he could not (could not? would not) help but be." Now she was looking at me in a way she never had before. I did not know what it meant then and was not to know until tonight since neither of us knew then that two months later Father would be dead. I just knew that she was looking at me as she never had before and that the scent of the verbena in her hair seemed to have increased a hundred times, to have got a hundred times stronger, to be everywhere in the dusk in which something was about to happen which I had never dreamed of. Then she spoke. "Kiss me, Bayard."

"No. You are Father's wife."

"And eight years older than you are. And your fourth cousin too. And I have black hair. Kiss me, Bayard."

"No."

"Kiss me, Bayard." So I leaned my face down to her. But she didn't move, standing so, bent lightly back from me from the waist, looking at me; now it was she who said, "No." So I put my arms around her. Then she came to me, melted as women will and can, the arms with the wrist- and elbow-power to control horses about my shoulders, using the wrists to hold my face to hers until there was no longer need for the wrists; I thought then of the woman of thirty, the symbol of the ancient and eternal Snake[16] and of the men who have written of her, and I realised then the immitigable chasm between all life and all print—that those who can, do, those who cannot and suffer enough because they can't, write about it. Then I was free, I could see her again, I saw her still watching me with that dark inscrutable look, looking up at me now across her down-slanted face; I watched her arms rise with almost the exact gesture with which she had put them around me as if she were repeating the empty and formal gesture of all promise so that I should never forget it, the elbows angling outward as she put her hands to the sprig of verbena in her hair, I standing straight and rigid facing the slightly bent head, the short jagged hair, the rigid curiously formal angle of the bare arms gleaming faintly in the last of light as she removed the verbena sprig and put it into my lapel, and I thought how the War had tried to stamp all the women of her generation and class in the South into a type and how it had failed—the suffering, the identical experience (hers and Aunt Jenny's had been almost the same except that Aunt Jenny had spent a few nights with her husband before they brought him back home in an ammunition wagon while Gavin Breckbridge was just Drusilla's fiancé) was there in the eyes, yet beyond that was the incorrigibly individual woman: not like so many men who return from wars to live on Government reservations like so many steers, emasculate and empty of all save an identical experience which they cannot forget and dare not, else they would cease to live at that moment, almost interchangeable save for the old habit of answering to a given name.

"Now I must tell Father," I said.

"Yes," she said. "You must tell him. Kiss me." So again it was like it had been before. No. Twice, a thousand times and never like—the eternal and symbolical thirty to a young man, a youth, each time both cumulative and retroactive, immitigably unrepetitive, each wherein remembering excludes experience, each wherein experience antedates remembering; the skill without weariness, the knowledge virginal to surfeit, the cunning secret muscles to guide and control just as within the wrists and elbows lay slumbering the mastery of horses: she stood back, already turning, not looking

[16] That is, the Serpent of the Garden of Eden (Genesis 3).

at me when she spoke, never having looked at me, already moving swiftly on in the dusk: "Tell John. Tell him tonight."

I intended to. I went to the house and into the office at once; I went to the center of the rug before the cold hearth, I don't know why, and stood there rigid like soldiers stand, looking at eye level straight across the room and above his head and said, "Father" and then stopped. Because he did not even hear me. He said, "Yes, Bayard?" but he did not hear me although he was sitting behind the desk doing nothing, immobile, as still as I was rigid, one hand on the desk with a dead cigar in it, a bottle of brandy and a filled and untasted glass beside his hand, clothed quiet and bemused in whatever triumph it was he felt since the last overwhelming return of votes had come in late in the afternoon. So I waited until after supper. We went to the dining room and stood side by side until Aunt Jenny entered and then Drusilla, in the yellow ball gown, who walked straight to me and gave me one fierce inscrutable look then went to her place and waited for me to draw her chair while Father drew Aunt Jenny's. He had roused by then, not to talk himself but rather to sit at the head of the table and reply to Drusilla as she talked with a sort of feverish and glittering volubility—to reply now and then to her with that courteous intolerant pride which had lately become a little forensic, as if merely being in a political contest filled with fierce and empty oratory had retroactively made a lawyer of him who was anything and everything except a lawyer. Then Drusilla and Aunt Jenny rose and left us and he said, "Wait" to me who had made no move to follow and directed Joby to bring one of the bottles of wine which he had fetched back from New Orleans when he went there last to borrow money to liquidate his first private railroad bonds. Then I stood again like soldiers stand, gazing at eye level above his head while he sat half-turned from the table, a little paunchy now though not much, a little grizzled too in the hair though his beard was as strong as ever, with that spurious forensic air of lawyers and the intolerant eyes which in the last two years had acquired that transparent film which the eyes of carnivorous animals have and from behind which they look at a world which no ruminant ever sees, perhaps dares to see, which I have seen before on the eyes of men who have killed too much, who have killed so much that never again as long as they live will they ever be alone. I said again, "Father," then I told him.

"Hah?" he said. "Sit down." I sat down, I looked at him, watched him fill both glasses and this time I knew it was worse with him than not hearing: it didn't even matter. "You are doing well in the law, Judge Wilkins tells me. I am pleased to hear that. I have not needed you in my affairs so far, but from now on I shall. I have now accomplished the active portion of my aims in which you could not have helped me; I acted as the land and the time demanded and you were too young for that, I wished to shield you. But now the land and the time too are changing; what will follow will be a matter of consolidation, of pettifogging and doubtless chicanery in which I would be a babe in arms but in which you, trained in the law, can hold your own—our own. Yes, I have accomplished my aim, and now I shall do a little moral house-cleaning. I am tired of killing men, no matter what the necessity nor the end. Tomorrow, when I go to town and meet Ben Redmond, I shall be unarmed."

3

We reached home just before midnight; we didn't have to pass through Jefferson either. Before we turned in the gates I could see the lights, the chandeliers—hall, parlor, and what Aunt Jenny (without any effort or perhaps even design on her part) had taught even Ringo to call the drawing room, the light falling outward across the portico, past the columns. Then I saw the horses, the faint shine of leather and buckle-glints on the black silhouettes and then the men too—Wyatt and others of Father's old troop—and I had forgot that they would be there. I had forgot that they would be there; I remember how I thought, since I was tired and spent with strain, *Now it will have to begin tonight. I won't even have until tomorrow in which to begin to resist.* They had a watchman, a picquet[17] out, I suppose, because they seemed to know at once that we were in the drive. Wyatt met me, I halted the mare, I could look down at him and at the others gathered a few yards behind him with that curious vulture-like formality which Southern men assume in such situations.

"Well, boy," George said.

"Was it—" I said. "Was he—"

"It was all right. It was in front. Redmond ain't no coward. John had the derringer inside his cuff like always, but he never touched it, never made a move toward it." I have seen him do it, he showed me once: the pistol (it was not four inches long) held flat inside his left wrist by a clip he made himself of wire and an old clock spring; he would raise both hands at the same time, cross them, fire the pistol from beneath his left hand almost as if he were hiding from his own vision what he was doing; when he killed one of the men he shot a hole through his own coat sleeve. "But you want to get on to the house," Wyatt said. He began to stand aside, then he spoke again: "We'll take this off your hands, any of us. Me." I hadn't moved the mare yet and I had made no move to speak, yet he continued quickly, as if he had already rehearsed all this, his speech and mine, and knew what I would say and only spoke himself as he would have removed his hat on entering a house or used "sir" in conversing with a stranger: "You're young, just a boy, you ain't had any experience in this kind of thing. Besides, you got them two ladies in the house to think about. He would understand, all right."

"I reckon I can attend to it," I said.

"Sure," he said; there was no surprise, nothing at all, in his voice because he had already rehearsed this: "I reckon we all knew that's what you would say." He stepped back then; almost it was as though he and not I bade the mare to move on. But they all followed, still with that unctuous and voracious formality. Then I saw Drusilla standing at the top of the front steps, in the light from the open door and the windows like a theatre scene, in the yellow ball gown and even from here I believed that I could smell the verbena in her hair, standing there motionless yet emanating something louder than the two shots must have been—something voracious too and passionate. Then, although I had dismounted and someone had taken the

[17] Guard.

mare, I seemed to be still in the saddle and to watch myself enter that scene which she had postulated like another actor while in the background for chorus Wyatt and the others stood with the unctuous formality which the Southern man shows in the presence of death—that Roman holiday engendered by mist-born Protestantism grafted onto this land of violent sun, of violent alteration from snow to heat-stroke which has produced a race impervious to both. I mounted the steps toward the figure straight and yellow and immobile as a candle which moved only to extend one hand; we stood together and looked down at them where they stood clumped, the horses too gathered in a tight group beyond them at the rim of light from the brilliant door and windows. One of them stamped and blew his breath and jangled his gear.

"Thank you, gentlemen," I said. "My aunt and my—Drusilla thank you. There's no need for you to stay. Goodnight." They murmured, turning. George Wyatt paused, looking back at me.

"Tomorrow?" he said.

"Tomorrow." Then they went on, carrying their hats and tiptoeing, even on the ground, the quiet and resilient earth, as though anyone in that house awake would try to sleep, anyone already asleep in it whom they could have wakened. Then they were gone and Drusilla and I turned and crossed the portico, her hand lying light on my wrist yet discharging into me with a shock like electricity that dark and passionate voracity, the face at my shoulder—the jagged hair with a verbena sprig above each ear, the eyes staring at me with that fierce exaltation. We entered the hall and crossed it, her hand guiding me without pressure, and entered the parlor. Then for the first time I realised it—the alteration which is death—not that he was now just clay but that he was lying down. But I didn't look at him yet because I knew that when I did I would begin to pant; I went to Aunt Jenny who had just risen from a chair behind which Louvinia stood. She was Father's sister, taller than Drusilla but no older, whose husband had been killed at the very beginning of the War, by a shell from a Federal frigate at Fort Moultrie, come to us from Carolina six years ago. Ringo and I went to Tennessee Junction in the wagon to meet her. It was January, cold and clear and with ice in the ruts; we returned just before dark with Aunt Jenny on the seat beside me holding a lace parasol and Ringo in the wagon bed nursing a hamper basket containing two bottles of old sherry and the two jasmine cuttings which were bushes in the garden now, and the panes of colored glass which she had salvaged from the Carolina house where she and Father and Uncle Bayard were born and which Father had set in a fanlight above one of the drawing room windows for her—who came up the drive and Father (home now from the railroad) went down the steps and lifted her from the wagon and said, "Well, Jenny," and she said, "Well, Johnny," and began to cry. She stood too, looking at me as I approached—the same hair, the same high nose, the same eyes as Father's except that they were intent and very wise instead of intolerant. She said nothing at all, she just kissed me, her hands light on my shoulders. Then Drusilla spoke, as if she had been waiting with a sort of dreadful patience for the empty ceremony to be done, in a voice like a bell: clear, unsentient, on a single pitch, silvery and triumphant: "Come, Bayard."

"Hadn't you better go to bed now?" Aunt Jenny said.

"Yes," Drusilla said in that silvery ecstatic voice, "Oh yes. There will be plenty of time for sleep." I followed her, her hand again guiding me without pressure; now I looked at him. It was just as I had imagined it—sabre, plumes, and all—but with that alteration, that irrevocable difference which I had known to expect yet had not realised, as you can put food into your stomach which for a while the stomach declines to assimilate—the illimitable grief and regret as I looked down at the face which I knew—the nose, the hair, the eyelids closed over the intolerance—the face which I realised I now saw in repose for the first time in my life; the empty hands still now beneath the invisible stain of what had been (once, surely) needless blood, the hands now appearing clumsy in their very inertness, too clumsy to have performed the fatal actions which forever afterward he must have waked and slept with and maybe was glad to lay down at last—those curious appendages clumsily conceived to begin with yet with which man has taught himself to do so much, so much more than they were intended to do or could be forgiven for doing, which had now surrendered that life to which his intolerant heart had fiercely held; and then I knew that in a minute I would begin to pant. So Drusilla must have spoken twice before I heard her and turned and saw in the instant Aunt Jenny and Louvinia watching us, hearing Drusilla now, the unsentient bell quality gone now, her voice whispering into that quiet death-filled room with a passionate and dying fall: "Bayard." She faced me, she was quite near; again the scent of the verbena in her hair seemed to have increased a hundred times as she stood holding out to me, one in either hand, the two duelling pistols. "Take them, Bayard," she said, in the same tone in which she had said "Kiss me" last summer, already pressing them into my hands, watching me with that passionate and voracious exaltation, speaking in a voice fainting and passionate with promise: "Take them. I have kept them for you. I give them to you. Oh you will thank me, you will remember me who put into your hands what they say is an attribute only of God's, who took what belongs to heaven and gave it to you. Do you feel them? the long true barrels true as justice, the triggers (you have fired them) quick as retribution, the two of them slender and invincible and fatal as the physical shape of love?" Again I watched her arms angle out and upward as she removed the two verbena sprigs from her hair in two motions faster than the eye could follow, already putting one of them into my lapel and crushing the other in her other hand while she still spoke in that rapid passionate voice not much louder than a whisper: "There. One I give to you to wear tomorrow (it will not fade), the other I cast away, like this—" dropping the crushed bloom at her feet. "I abjure it. I abjure verbena forever more; I have smelled it above the odor of courage; that was all I wanted. Now let me look at you." She stood back, staring at me—the face tearless and exalted, the feverish eyes brilliant and voracious. "How beautiful you are: do you know it? How beautiful: young, to be permitted to kill, to be permitted vengeance, to take into your bare hands the fire of heaven that cast down Lucifer.[18] No; I. I gave it to you; I put it into your hands; Oh you will thank me, you will remember me when I am dead and you are an old man saying to himself, 'I

[18] The rebel archangel whom God cast out of Heaven.

have tasted all things.'—It will be the right hand, won't it?" She moved; she had taken my right hand which still held one of the pistols before I knew what she was about to do; she had bent and kissed it before I comprehended why she took it. Then she stopped dead still, still stooping in that attitude of fierce exultant humility, her hot lips and her hot hands still touching my flesh, light on my flesh as dead leaves yet communicating to it that battery charge dark, passionate and damned forever of all peace. Because they are wise, women are—a touch, lips or fingers, and the knowledge, even clairvoyance, goes straight to the heart without bothering the laggard brain at all. She stood erect now, staring at me with intolerable and amazed incredulity which occupied her face alone for a whole minute while her eyes were completely empty; it seemed to me that I stood there for a full minute while Aunt Jenny and Louvinia watched us, waiting for her eyes to fill. There was no blood in her face at all, her mouth open a little and pale as one of those rubber rings women seal fruit jars with. Then her eyes filled with an expression of bitter and passionate betrayal. "Why, he's not—" she said. "He's not—And I kissed his hand," she said in an aghast whisper; "*I kissed his hand*!" beginning to laugh, the laughter, rising, becoming a scream yet still remaining laughter, screaming with laughter, trying herself to deaden the sound by putting her hand over her mouth, the laughter spilling between her fingers like vomit, the incredulous betrayed eyes still watching me across the hand.

"Louvinia!" Aunt Jenny said. They both came to her. Louvinia touched and held her and Drusilla turned her face to Louvinia.

"I kissed his hand, Louvinia!" she cried. "Did you see it? *I kissed his hand*!" the laughter rising again, becoming the scream again yet still remaining laughter, she still trying to hold it back with her hand like a small child who has filled its mouth too full.

"Take her upstairs," Aunt Jenny said. But they were already moving toward the door, Louvinia half-carrying Drusilla, the laughter diminishing as they neared the door as though it waited for the larger space of the empty and brilliant hall to rise again. Then it was gone; Aunt Jenny and I stood there and I knew soon that I would begin to pant. I could feel it beginning like you feel regurgitation beginning, as though there were not enough air in the room, the house, not enough air anywhere under the heavy hot low sky where the equinox couldn't seem to accomplish, nothing in the air for breathing, for the lungs. Now it was Aunt Jenny who said "Bayard" twice before I heard her. "You are not going to try to kill him. All right."

"All right?" I said.

"Yes. All right. Don't let it be Drusilla, a poor hysterical young woman. And don't let it be him, Bayard, because he's dead now. And don't let it be George Wyatt and those others who will be waiting for you tomorrow morning. I know you are not afraid."

"But what good will that do?" I said. "What good will that do?" It almost began then; I stopped it just in time. "I must live with myself, you see."

"Then it's not just Drusilla? Not just him? Not just George Wyatt and Jefferson?"

"No," I said.

"Will you promise to let me see you before you go to town tomorrow?" I looked at her; we looked at one another for a moment. Then she put her hands on my shoulders and kissed me and released me, all in one motion. "Goodnight, son," she said. Then she was gone too and now it could begin. I knew that in a minute I would look at him and it would begin and I did look at him, feeling the long-held breath, the hiatus before it started, thinking how maybe I should have said, "Goodbye, Father" but did not. Instead I crossed to the piano and laid the pistols carefully on it, still keeping the panting from getting too loud too soon. Then I was outside on the porch and (I don't know how long it had been) I looked in the window and saw Simon squatting on a stool beside him. Simon had been his body servant during the War and when they came home Simon had a uniform too—a Confederate private's coat with a Yankee brigadier's star on it and he had put it on now too, like they had dressed Father, squatting on the stool beside him, not crying, not weeping the facile tears which are the white man's futile trait and which Negroes know nothing about but just sitting there, motionless, his lower lip slacked down a little; he raised his hand and touched the coffin, the black hand rigid and fragile-looking as a clutch of dead twigs, then dropped the hand; once he turned his head and I saw his eyes roll red and unwinking in his skull like those of a cornered fox. It had begun by that time; I panted, standing there, and this was it—the regret and grief, the despair out of which the tragic mute insensitive bones stand up that can bear anything, anything.

4

After a while the whippoorwills stopped and I heard the first day bird, a mockingbird. It had sung all night too but now it was the day song, no longer the drowsy moony fluting. Then they all began—the sparrows from the stable, the thrush that lived in Aunt Jenny's garden, and I heard a quail too from the pasture and now there was light in the room. But I didn't move at once. I still lay on the bed (I hadn't undressed) with my hands under my head and the scent of Drusilla's verbena faint from where my coat lay on a chair, watching the light grow, watching it turn rosy with the sun. After a while I heard Louvinia come up across the back yard and go into the kitchen; I heard the door and then the long crash of her armful of stovewood into the box. Soon they would begin to arrive—the carriages and buggies in the drive—but not for a while yet because they too would wait first to see what I was going to do. So the house was quiet when I went down to the diningroom, no sound in it except Simon snoring in the parlor, probably still sitting on the stool though I didn't look in to see. Instead I stood at the diningroom window and drank the coffee which Louvinia brought me, then I went to the stable; I saw Joby watching me from the kitchen door as I crossed the yard and in the stable Loosh looked up at me across Betsy's head, a curry comb in his hand, though Ringo didn't look at me at all. We curried Jupiter then. I didn't know if we would be able to without trouble or not, since always Father would come in first and touch him and tell him to stand and he would stand like a marble horse (or pale bronze rather) while Loosh curried him. But he stood for me too, a little restive but he stood, then that was done and now it was almost nine o'clock and soon they would begin to arrive and I told Ringo to bring Betsy on to the house.

I went on to the house and into the hall. I had not had to pant in some time now but it was there, waiting, a part of the alteration, as though by being dead and no longer needing air he had taken all of it, all that he had compassed and claimed and postulated between the walls which he had built, along with him. Aunt Jenny must have been waiting; she came out of the diningroom at once, without a sound, dressed, the hair that was like Father's combed and smooth above the eyes that were different from Father's eyes because they were not intolerant but just intent and grave and (she was wise too) without pity. "Are you going now?" she said.

"Yes." I looked at her. Yes, thank God, without pity. "You see, I want to be thought well of."

"I do," she said. "Even if you spend the day hidden in the stable loft, I still do."

"Maybe if she knew that I was going. Was going to town anyway."

"No," she said. "No, Bayard." We looked at one another. Then she said quietly, "All right. She's awake." So I mounted the stairs. I mounted steadily, not fast because if I had gone fast the panting would have started again or I might have had to slow for a second at the turn or at the top and I would not have gone on. So I went slowly and steadily, across the hall to her door and knocked and opened it. She was sitting at the window, in something soft and loose for morning in her bedroom only she never did look like morning in a bedroom because here was no hair to fall about her shoulders. She looked up, she sat there looking at me with her feverish brilliant eyes and I remembered I still had the verbena sprig in my lapel and suddenly she began to laugh again. It seemed to come not from her mouth but to burst out all over her face like sweat does and with a dreadful and painful convulsion as when you have vomited until it hurts you yet still you must vomit again—burst out all over her face except her eyes, the brilliant incredulous eyes looking at me out of the laughter as if they belonged to somebody else, as if they were two inert fragments of tar or coal lying on the bottom of a receptacle filled with turmoil: "I kissed his hand! *I kissed his hand*!" Louvinia entered, Aunt Jenny must have sent her directly after me; again I walked slowly and steadily so it would not start yet, down the stairs where Aunt Jenny stood beneath the chandelier in the hall as Mrs. Wilkins had stood yesterday at the University. She had my hat in her hand. "Even if you hid all day in the stable, Bayard," she said. I took the hat; she said quietly, pleasantly, as if she were talking to a stranger, a guest: "I used to see a lot of blockade runners[19] in Charleston. They were heroes in a way, you see—not heroes because they were helping to prolong the Confederacy but heroes in the sense that David Crockett or John Sevier[20] would have been to small boys or fool young women. There was one of them, an Englishman. He had no business there; it was the money of course, as with all of them. But he was the Davy Crockett to us because by

[19]During the Civil War, the North blockaded Southern ports. Blockade runners were sailors who slipped through the blockade.

[20]Famous frontiersmen. Crockett (1786–1836) was U.S. Representative from Tennessee; he died at the Alamo. Sevier (1745–1815) became Governor of Tennessee.

that time we had all forgot what money was, what you could do with it. He must have been a gentleman once or associated with gentlemen before he changed his name, and he had a vocabulary of seven words, though I must admit he got along quite well with them. The first four were, 'I'll have rum, thanks,' and then, when he had the rum, he would use the other three—across the champagne, to whatever ruffled bosom or low gown: 'No bloody moon.' No bloody moon, Bayard."

Ringo was waiting with Betsy at the front steps. Again he did not look at me, his face sullen, downcast even while he handed me the reins. But he said nothing, nor did I look back. And sure enough I was just in time; I passed the Compson carriage at the gates, General Compson lifted his hat as I did mine as we passed. It was four miles to town but I had not gone two of them when I heard the horse coming up behind me and I did not look back because I knew it was Ringo. I did not look back; he came up on one of the carriage horses, he rode up beside me and looked me full in the face for one moment, the sullen determined face, the eyes rolling at me defiant and momentary and red; we rode on. Now we were in town—the long shady street leading to the square, the new courthouse at the end of it; it was eleven o'clock now: long past breakfast and not yet noon so there were only women on the street, not to recognise me perhaps or at least not the walking stopped sudden and dead in midwalking as if the legs contained the sudden eyes, the caught breath, that not to begin until we reached the square and I thinking *If I could only be invisible until I reach the stairs to his office and begin to mount.* But I could not, I was not; we rode up to the Holston House and I saw the row of feet along the gallery rail come suddenly and quietly down and I did not look at them, I stopped Betsy and waited until Ringo was down then I dismounted and gave him the reins. "Wait for me here," I said.

"I'm going with you," he said, not loud; we stood there under the still circumspect eyes and spoke quietly to one another like two conspirators. Then I saw the pistol, the outline of it inside his shirt, probably the one we had taken from Grumby that day we killed him.

"No you ain't," I said.

"Yes I am."

"No you ain't." So I walked on, along the street in the hot sun. It was almost noon now and I could smell nothing except the verbena in my coat, as if it had gathered all the sun, all the suspended fierce heat in which the equinox could not seem to occur and were distilling it so that I moved in a cloud of verbena as I might have moved in a cloud of smoke from a cigar. Then George Wyatt was beside me (I don't know where he came from) and five or six others of Father's old troop a few yards behind, George's hand on my arm, drawing me into a doorway out of the avid eyes like caught breaths.

"Have you got that derringer?" George said.

"No," I said.

"Good," George said. "They are tricky things to fool with. Couldn't nobody but Colonel ever handle one right; I never could. So you take this. I tried it this morning and I know it's right. Here." He was already fumbling the pistol into my pocket, then the same thing seemed to happen to him that happened to Drusilla last night when she kissed my hand—something communicated by touch straight to the simple code by which he lived, without going through the brain at all: so that he too stood suddenly back, the pistol in his hand, staring at me with his pale outraged eyes and speaking in a whisper thin with fury: "Who are you? Is your name Sartoris? By God, if you don't kill him, I'm going to." Now it was not panting, it was a terrible desire to laugh, to laugh as Drusilla had, and say, "That's what Drusilla said." But I didn't. I said,

"I'm tending to this. You stay out of it. I don't need any help." Then his fierce eyes faded gradually, exactly as you turn a lamp down.

"Well," he said, putting the pistol back into his pocket. "You'll have to excuse me, son. I should have knowed you wouldn't do anything that would keep John from laying quiet. We'll follow you and wait at the foot of the steps. And remember: he's a brave man, but he's been sitting in that office by himself since yesterday morning waiting for you and his nerves are on edge."

"I'll remember," I said. "I don't need any help." I had started on when suddenly I said it without having any warning that I was going to: "No bloody moon."

"What?" he said. I didn't answer. I went on across the square itself now, in the hot sun, they following though not close so that I never saw them again until afterward, surrounded by the remote still eyes not following me yet either, just stopped where they were before the stores and about the door to the courthouse, waiting. I walked steadily on enclosed in the now fierce odor of the verbena sprig. Then shadow fell upon me; I did not pause, I looked once at the small faded sign nailed to the brick *B. J. Redmond. Atty at Law* and began to mount the stairs, the wooden steps scuffed by the heavy bewildered boots of countrymen approaching litigation and stained by tobacco spit, on down the dim corridor to the door which bore the name again, *B. J. Redmond* and knocked once and opened it. He sat behind the desk, not much taller than Father but thicker as a man gets who spends most of his time sitting and listening to people, freshly shaven and with fresh linen; a lawyer yet it was not a lawyer's face—a face much thinner than the body would indicate, strained (and yes, tragic; I know that now) and exhausted beneath the neat recent steady strokes of the razor, holding a pistol flat on the desk before him, loose beneath his hand and aimed at nothing. There was no smell of drink, not even of tobacco in the neat clean dingy room although I knew he smoked. I didn't pause. I walked steadily toward him. It was not twenty feet from door to desk yet I seemed to walk in a dreamlike state in which there was neither time nor distance, as though the mere act of walking was no more intended to encompass space than was his sitting. We didn't speak. It was as if we both knew what the passage of words would be and the futility of it; how he might have said, "Go out, Bayard. Go away, boy" and then, "Draw then. I will allow you to draw" and it would have been the same as if he had never said it. So we did not speak; I just walked steadily toward him as the pistol rose from the desk. I watched it, I could see the foreshortened slant of the barrel and I knew it would miss me though his hand did not tremble. I walked toward him, toward the pistol in the rocklike hand, I heard no bullet. Maybe I didn't even hear the explosion though I remember the sudden orange bloom and smoke as they appeared against his white shirt as they had appeared against Grumby's greasy Confederate coat; I still watched that foreshortened slant of barrel which I knew was not aimed at me and saw the second orange flash and smoke and heard no bullet that time either. Then I stopped; it was done then. I watched the pistol descend to the desk in short jerks; I saw him release it and sit back, both hands on the desk, I looked at his face and I knew too what it was to want air when there was nothing in the circumambience for the lungs. He rose, shoved the chair back with a convulsive motion and rose, with a queer ducking motion of his head; with his head still ducked aside and one arm extended as though he couldn't see and the other hand resting on the desk as if he couldn't stand alone, he turned and crossed to the wall and took his hat from the rack and with his head still ducked aside and one hand extended he blundered along the wall and passed me and reached the door and went through it. He was brave; no one denied that. He walked down those stairs and out onto the street where George Wyatt and the other six of Father's old troop waited and where the other men had begun to run now; he walked through the middle of them with his hat on and his head up (they told me how someone shouted at him: "Have you killed that boy too?"), saying no word, staring straight ahead and with his back to them, on to the station where the south-bound train was just in and got on it with no baggage, nothing, and went away from Jefferson and from Mississippi and never came back.

I heard their feet on the stairs then in the corridor then in the room, but for a while yet (it wasn't that long, of course) I still sat behind the desk as he had sat, the flat of the pistol still warm under my hand, my hand growing slowly numb between the pistol and my forehead. Then I raised my head; the little room was full of men. "My God!" George Wyatt cried. "You took the pistol away from him and then missed him, missed him *twice*?" Then he answered himself—that same rapport for violence which Drusilla had and which in George's case was actual character judgment: "No; wait. You walked in here without even a pocket knife and let him miss you twice. My God in heaven." He turned, shouting: "Get to hell out of here! You, White, ride out to Sartoris and tell his folks it's all over and he's all right. Ride!" So they departed, went away; presently only George was left, watching me with that pale bleak stare which was speculative yet not at all ratiocinative. "Well by God," he said. "—Do you want a drink?"

"No," I said. "I'm hungry. I didn't eat any breakfast."

"I reckon not, if you got up this morning aiming to do what you did. Come on. We'll go to the Holston House."

"No," I said. "No. Not there."

"Why not? You ain't done anything to be ashamed of. I wouldn't have done it that way, myself. I'd a shot at him once, anyway. But that's your way or you wouldn't have done it."

"Yes," I said. "I would do it again."

"Be damned if I would.—You want to come home with me? We'll have time to eat and then ride out there in time for the——" But I couldn't do that either.

"No," I said. "I'm not hungry after all. I think I'll go home."

"Don't you want to wait and ride out with me?"

"No, I'll go on."

"You don't want to stay here, anyway." He looked around the room again, where the smell of powder smoke still lingered a little, still lay somewhere on the hot dead air though invisible now, blinking a little with his fierce pale unintroverted eyes. "Well by God," he said again. "Maybe you're right, maybe there has been enough killing in your family without—Come on." We left the office. I waited at the foot of the stairs and soon Ringo came up with the horses. We crossed the square again. There were no feet on the Holston House railing now (it was twelve o'clock) but a group of men stood before the door who raised their hats and I raised mine and Ringo and I rode on.

We did not go fast. Soon it was one, maybe after; the carriages and buggies would begin to leave the square soon, so I turned from the road at the end of the pasture and I sat the mare, trying to open the gate without dismounting, until Ringo dismounted and opened it. We crossed the pasture in the hard fierce sun; I could have seen the house now but I didn't look. Then we were in the shade, the close thick airless shade of the creek bottom; the old rails still lay in the undergrowth where we had built the pen to hide the Yankee mules. Presently I heard the water, then I could see the sunny glints. We dismounted. I lay on my back, I thought *Now it can begin again if it wants to.* But it did not. I went to sleep. I went to sleep almost before I had stopped thinking. I slept for almost five hours and I didn't dream anything at all yet I waked myself up crying, crying too hard to stop it. Ringo was squatting beside me and the sun was gone though there was a bird of some sort still singing somewhere and the whistle of the northbound evening train sounded and the short broken puffs of starting where it had evidently stopped at our flag station. After a while I began to stop and Ringo brought his hat full of water from the creek but instead I went down to the water myself and bathed my face.

There was still a good deal of light in the pasture, though the whippoorwills had begun, and when we reached the house there was a mockingbird singing in the magnolia, the night song now, the drowsy moony one, and again the moon like the rim print of a heel in wet sand. There was just one light in the hall now and so it was all over though I could still smell the flowers even above the verbena in my coat. I had not looked at him again. I had started to before I left the house but I did not, I did not see him again and all the pictures we had of him were bad ones because a picture could no more have held him dead than the house could have kept his body. But I didn't need to see him again because he was there, he would always be there; maybe what Drusilla meant by his dream was not something which he possessed but something which he had bequeathed us which we could never forget, which would even assume the corporeal shape of him whenever any of us, black or white, closed our eyes. I went into the house. There was no light in the drawing room except the last of the afterglow which came through the western window where Aunt Jenny's colored glass was; I was about to go on upstairs when I saw her sitting there beside the window. She didn't call me and I didn't speak Drusilla's name, I just went to the door and stood there. "She's gone," Aunt Jenny said. "She took the evening train. She has gone to Montgomery, to Dennison." Denny had been married about a year now; he was living in Montgomery, reading law.

"I see," I said. "Then she didn't——" But there wasn't any use in that either; Jed White must have got there before one o'clock and told them. And besides, Aunt Jenny didn't answer. She could have lied to me but she didn't, she said,

"Come here." I went to her chair. "Kneel down. I can't see you."

"Don't you want the lamp?"

"No. Kneel down." So I knelt beside the chair. "So you had a perfectly splendid Saturday afternoon, didn't you? Tell me about it." Then she put her hands on my shoulders. I watched them come up as though she were trying to stop them; I felt them on my shoulders as if they had a separate life of their own and were trying to do something which for my sake she was trying to restrain, prevent. Then she gave up or she was not strong enough because they came up and took my face between them, hard, and suddenly the tears sprang and streamed down her face like Drusilla's laughing had. "Oh, damn you Sartorises!" she said. "Damn you! Damn you!"

As I passed down the hall the light came up in the diningroom and I could hear Louvinia laying the table for supper. So the stairs were lighted quite well. But the upper hall was dark. I saw her open door (that unmistakable way in which an open door stands open when nobody lives in the room any more) and I realised I had not believed that she was really gone. So I didn't look into the room. I went on to mine and entered. And then for a long moment I thought it was the verbena in my lapel which I still smelled. I thought that until I had crossed the room and looked down at the pillow on which it lay—the single sprig of it (without looking she would pinch off a half dozen of them and they would be all of a size, almost all of a shape, as if a machine had stamped them out) filling the room, the dusk, the evening with that odor which she said you could smell alone above the smell of horses.

Bertolt Brecht

(1898–1956)

Marxism, like Darwinism and Freudianism, has resonated through the culture of the twentieth century. Money, as a subject of literature, has had almost as long a history as love, but only with the publication of the first volume of Karl Marx's Capital *in 1869 did anyone try to see all culture—art, philosophy, religion, human nature itself—as a logical extension of economic conditions, a "superstructure" that sublimates the fundamental relationships of individuals and classes to the means of production. Marxist ideas have been expressed in literature in the productions of Socialist Realism, the style dictated by the Soviet Union and other Communist countries; in the plays of Bernard Shaw and Sean O'Casey; in the "proletarian" literature that appeared in the wake of the Great Depression of the 1930s; and in the post-World War II fiction of France, Germany, and England. The preeminent Marxist writer of* the twentieth century, however, is the German dramatist Bertolt Brecht, who not only explored the implications of Marxist thought in a series of masterful plays and poems but also created a Marxist theory of drama that has had a wide influence upon the other arts as well.

Brecht was born in 1898 into a prosperous and pious middle-class family in Augsburg, Bavaria. His father, the manager of a paper mill, was a Roman Catholic, but Brecht was raised in his mother's Lutheran faith; Brecht later mentioned the vigorous earthiness of Luther's translation of the Bible as a major influence upon his own style.

When Brecht was nineteen, he enrolled as a medical student at the University of Munich. His studies were interrupted by a year of military service during which he was assigned to a military hospital in his hometown of Augsburg. After the war, he returned to Munich but gradually drifted away from his medical studies into Munich theatrical life. Brecht played the guitar and sang his own songs in cafes. He also began to experiment with playwriting; Baal (1918), a wildly romantic play about a violently self-destructive young poet, was heavily influenced by the French symbolist poets Paul Verlaine and Arthur Rimbaud and by the expressionist playwrights August Strindberg and Frank Wedekind. Drums in the Night (1918), an equally nihilistic and cynical play about a returned German soldier set against the background of the communist Spartakist uprising of 1918, was produced by the Munich Kammerspiele Theater, won the prestigious Kleist Prize, and brought Brecht immediate fame. In the Jungle of Cities (1923) and an adaptation of Christopher Marlowe's Life of Edward II (1924) were also produced successfully in Munich.

The first, Munich phase of Brecht's career ended in 1924 with a move to Berlin and a job as dramaturg (play reader and literary advisor) in the Deutsches Theater, run by the great director Max Reinhardt. The cynicism and anarchy of Brecht's early plays had struck a responsive chord in members of his generation, many of them embittered and disillusioned by the bourgeois culture that had produced, it seemed, the horrors of the First World War. Now he turned in reaction, as many of his young contemporaries did, to Marxism, which seemed to promise a positive alternative to capitalism. The first fruit of his intensive study of Marxism was A Man's a Man (1925), a sardonic comedy that examines, against a background of a Kiplingesque India, the power of external conditions over even such seemingly immutable facts as human identity. The Threepenny Opera, an updating of John Gay's eighteenth-century satire The Beggar's Opera, with music by Kurt Weill, gave Brecht his first major popular success in 1928. Also belonging to this period are a series of short didactic plays developing points of Marxist doctrine and intended to be produced by amateur groups: The Flight of the Lindberghs (1929), The Didactic Play of Baden: On Consent (1929), The Exception and the Rule (1930), The Measures Taken (1930), and several others.

Brecht's outspoken Communist stance made it impossible for him to remain in Germany when Hitler came to power, and in 1933 he began a period of exile that was to last for fourteen years. He settled first in Denmark, moved to Sweden in 1939 and to Finland in 1940, and finally fled to the United States in 1941, settling in Santa Monica, California. Surprisingly, Brecht wrote his greatest plays during this period of enforced exile when his native land was in the grip of the forces that Brecht hated most. During the Nazi regime, he wrote a series of rather ephemeral anti-Nazi propaganda plays, including Fears and Miseries of the Third Reich (1938) and The Resistible Rise of Arturo Ui (1941), which depicts Hitler as a Chicago gangster. But the major work of the war years was a series of powerful, *poetic plays that combined the vitality of the first, nihilist period with the discipline of the second, didactic period:* Mother Courage and Her Children *(1939),* Galileo *(1939),* The Good Woman of Setzuan *(1940), and* The Caucasian Chalk Circle *(1945). In 1947, Brecht was called to testify before the House Committee on Un-American Activities; the Committee was poorly prepared, questioned Brecht ineptly, and dismissed him with thanks for his cooperation. He moved to Europe permanently the following day.*

The nine years that remained to Brecht were devoted more to production of his plays and to creating the famous Berliner Ensemble than to writing new plays. Settling first in Switzerland, Brecht, in 1949, accepted an offer from the government of East Germany to direct his own company in East Berlin. The company, which eventually occupied the old Schiffbauerdamm theater, where The Threepenny Opera *had played in 1928, became one of the finest theater companies of the world, rivalling the Moscow Art Theater and Dublin's Abbey Theatre in its influence upon world drama. Here Brecht directed the first German productions of many of his greatest plays and wrote a series of adaptations to furnish a repertoire for the new company:* The Private Tutor *(1950), based on an eighteenth-century play by Jacob Lenz;* Don Juan *(1952), based on the play by Molière;* Coriolanus *(1953), based on Shakespeare's play; and* Trumpets and Drums *(1956), based on George Farquhar's Restoration comedy* The Recruiting Officer. *The relationship between Brecht and the East German government was not always smooth; Brecht's practice did not follow the official government line of Socialist Realism, and in 1951, the government banned the production of his* Trial of Lucullus *on the grounds that it was too pacifist. Brecht died in Berlin in 1956.*

Surprisingly, despite Brecht's vehement rejection of the German tradition of philosopher-artists from Goethe through Nietzsche and Wagner to Thomas Mann, he can best be seen as belonging in some ways to that tradition. He had a profoundly moral conception of his art, one that he elaborated into a theory of drama, most fully expressed in A Little Organum for the Theater *(1948). This theory has come under fire from both Communist critics, who regard it as elitist and over-intellectualized, and Western capitalist critics, especially in America, who, when they want to praise Brecht, often insist that he "transcended" his theory to produce fundamentally traditional, "universal" plays. Basically, Brecht's theory of the "epic" (narrative) theater is a theory of the psychology of audience response. Traditional theater (what he called "Aristotelian" theater) encourages the spectator to identify uncritically with the main character and thereby to accept without question the values of the play's dramatic world. The playwright seeks to create the illusion that the play is happening in the present and to encourage the audience in a "willing suspension of disbelief" (to use Coleridge's phrase). Epic theater, in contrast, encourages the audience to maintain a skeptical detachment toward the characters and events of the play, not identifying uncritically with them but seeing them as examples of the relationship between "human nature" and social conditions. The epic playwright therefore organizes the action of his play into short, discrete segments and employs a number of "distancing devices" (*Verfremdungs-Effekts*) to discourage identification and to remind the spectator that he is watching a play, not real life: visible stage machinery, shifts in mode such as the introduction of verses, songs, and direct addresses to the audience, and stage settings that place realistic elements against nonrealistic backgrounds.*

It is easy to disagree with the theory of the Epic Theater as a general theory of drama, but Brecht was obviously writing what Eliot called "programmatic criticism," intended to explain and justify his own practice. And Brecht's great plays, far from "transcending" his theories, brilliantly validate them.

The Good Woman of Setzuan, *like all of Brecht's major plays, is set in a distant, largely imaginary society. Brecht cared little for historical realism; his India of* A Man's a Man, *his Chicago of* In the Jungle of Cities *and* St. Joan of the Stockyards *(1930), and his Yukon of* Mahagonny *(1929) are ludicrously inaccurate, and the Setzuan of* The Good Woman of Setzuan *has little to do with the real China. (When someone pointed out to Brecht that Setzuan, or Szechwan, was a province rather than a city, he merely laughed and declined to change his description.) Setzuan, like Brecht's India, Chicago, and Yukon, is modern capitalist society; its dreamlike unreality is a distancing device to throw into relief not historical or geographic fact but the theme of how a society based on competition can determine human nature. The Good Woman's enforced splitting into Shen Te and Shui Ta is a theatrical metaphor for the self-division inherent in a society that makes goodness and survival incompatible. The Good Woman becomes two people, as Kafka's Gregor Samsa in "The Metamorphosis" becomes an insect and Eliot's protagonist in* The Waste Land *becomes a schizophrenic when they are faced with similar modern threats to identity. And if Brecht, unlike Kafka or Eliot, believes that there is a political answer to these modern ills of alienation and self-division, he wisely withholds that answer. Shen Te's final desperate questions—"Could one change people? Can the world be changed?"—can be answered only by the audience.*

FURTHER READING *(prepared by N. K. B.):* Eric Bentley's edition of *Seven Plays by Bertolt Brecht,* 1961, provides a good sampling of other plays, in addition to an excellent critical introduction. Klaus Völker, *Brecht: A Biography,* 1978, trans. by John Nowell, 1979, consolidates much source material available on Brecht to provide an illuminating account. Frederic Ewen, *Bertolt Brecht: His Life, His Art, and His Times,* 1967, is an illustrated volume intended for the general reader. Willy Haas, *Bert Brecht,* 1970, contains many personal reminiscences and memoirs. Peter Demetz, ed., *Brecht: A Collection of Critical Essays,* 1962, includes discussions of Brecht's dramatic theories and major plays. Martin Esslin's *Bertolt Brecht,* 1969, is a brief introduction to the life and plays, and should be supplemented with Esslin's readable study *Brecht: The Man and His Work,* 1959, rev. 1971. The latter examines Brecht's theory and practice of drama; Esslin explains the cultural and aesthetic context for the idea of "Epic Theater" and gives a balanced account of Brecht's controversial relationship to the Communist Party. Claude Hill, *Bertolt Brecht,* 1975, discusses both major and neglected dramatic works in a chronological survey, with additional chapters on Brecht's theories and politics. In *The Theatre of Bertolt Brecht,* 1959, rev. 1968, John Willett thoroughly documents Brecht's own productions, with a careful study of his dramatic language. Ronald Gray, *Brecht the Dramatist,* 1976, surveys the plays as a reflection of the change in Brecht's political ideas, with a detailed explication of *The Good Woman of Setzuan.* Michael Morley's *Brecht,* 1977, also surveys the major works and includes an analysis of the nondramatic poetry as well. John Fuegi, *The Essential Brecht,* 1972, uses eight plays to argue the divergence between Brecht's theories and practice. In *Bertolt Brecht's Great Plays,* 1978, Alfred D. White offers a scene-by-scene explication of four plays, including *Good Woman.* Charles R. Lyons, *Bertolt Brecht: The Despair and the Polemic,* 1968, demonstrates the overall unity of Brecht's work and describes the relationship between Brecht's themes and politics. Jan Needle and Peter Thomson, in *Brecht,* 1981, invite a critical re-evaluation of Brecht's political views, as reflected in his theories of dramaturgy.

Two studies that discuss the influence of American culture on Brecht and the response to his work in the United States are James Lyon, *Bertolt Brecht in America,* 1980, and Patty Lee Parmalee, *Brecht's America,* 1981. Excellent essays on the contexts of Brecht's work are collected in *Brecht in Perspective,* ed. by Graham Bartram and Anthony Waine, 1982.

THE GOOD WOMAN OF SETZUAN

Translated by Eric Bentley

CHARACTERS

WONG, *a water seller*
THREE GODS
SHEN TE, *a prostitute, later a shopkeeper*
MRS. SHIN, *former owner of Shen Te's shop*
A FAMILY OF EIGHT *(husband, wife, brother, sister-in-law, grandfather, nephew, niece, boy)*
AN UNEMPLOYED MAN
A CARPENTER
MRS. MI TZU, *Shen Te's landlady*
YANG SUN, *an unemployed pilot, later a factory manager*
AN OLD WHORE
A POLICEMAN
AN OLD MAN
AN OLD WOMAN, *his wife*
MR. SHU FU, *a barber*
MRS. YANG, *mother of Yang Sun*
GENTLEMEN, VOICES, CHILDREN (3), etc.

PROLOGUE

At the gates of the half-westernized city of Setzuan. Evening. WONG *the Water Seller introduces himself to the audience.*

WONG. I sell water here in the city of Setzuan. It isn't easy. When water is scarce, I have long distances to go in search of it, and when it is plentiful, I have no income. But in our part of the world there is nothing unusual about poverty. Many people think only the gods can save the situation. And I hear from a cattle merchant—who travels a lot—that some of the highest gods are on their way here at this very moment. Informed sources have it that heaven is quite disturbed at all the complaining. I've been coming out here to the city gates for three days now to bid these gods welcome. I want to be the first to greet them. What about those fellows over there? No, no, they *work.* And that one there has ink on his fingers, he's no god, he must be a clerk from the cement factory. *Those* two are another story. They look as though they'd like to beat you. But gods don't need to beat you, do they? [*Enter* THREE GODS.] What about those three? Old-fashioned clothes—dust on their feet—they *must* be gods! [*He throws himself at their feet.*] Do with me what you will, illustrious ones!

FIRST GOD [*with an ear trumpet*]. Ah! [*He is pleased.*] So we were expected?

WONG [*giving them water*]. Oh, yes. And I *knew* you'd come.
FIRST GOD. We need somewhere to stay the night. You know of a place?
WONG. The whole town is at your service, illustrious ones! What sort of a place would you like?

[*The* GODS *eye each other.*]

FIRST GOD. Just try the first house you come to, my son.
WONG. That would be Mr. Fo's place.
FIRST GOD. Mr. Fo.
WONG. One moment! [*He knocks at the first house.*]
VOICE FROM MR. FO'S. No!

[WONG *returns a little nervously.*]

WONG. It's too bad. Mr. Fo isn't in. And his servants don't dare do a thing without his consent. He'll have a fit when he finds out who they turned away, won't he?
FIRST GOD [*smiling*]. He will, won't he?
WONG. One moment! The next house is Mr. Cheng's. Won't he be thrilled?
FIRST GOD. Mr. Cheng.

[WONG *knocks.*]

VOICE FROM MR. CHENG'S. Keep your gods. We have our own troubles!
WONG [*back with the* GODS]. Mr. Cheng is very sorry, but he has a houseful of relations. I think some of them are a bad lot, and naturally, he wouldn't like you to see them.
THIRD GOD. Are we so terrible?
WONG. Well, only with bad people, of course. Everyone knows the province of Kwan is always having floods.
SECOND GOD. Really? How's *that*?
WONG. Why, because they're so irreligious.
SECOND GOD. Rubbish. It's because they neglected the dam.
FIRST GOD [*to* SECOND]. Sh! [*To* WONG.] You're still in hopes, aren't you, my son?
WONG. Certainly. All Setzuan is competing for the honor! What happened up to now is pure coincidence. I'll be back. [*He walks away, but then stands undecided.*]
SECOND GOD. What did I tell you?
THIRD GOD. It *could* be pure coincidence.
SECOND GOD. The same coincidence in Shun, Kwan, and Setzuan? People just aren't religious any more, let's face the fact. Our mission has failed!
FIRST GOD. Oh come, we might run into a good person any minute.
THIRD GOD. How did the resolution read? [*Unrolling a scroll and reading from it.*] "The world can stay as it is if enough people are found living lives worthy of human beings." Good people, that is. Well, what about this Water Seller himself? *He's* good, or I'm very much mistaken.
SECOND GOD. You're very much mistaken. When he gave us a drink, I had the impression there was something odd about the cup. Well, look! [*He shows the cup to the* FIRST GOD.]
FIRST GOD. A false bottom!
SECOND GOD. The man is a swindler.
FIRST GOD. Very well, count *him* out. That's one man among millions. And as a matter of fact, we only need one on *our* side. These atheists are

saying, "The world must be changed because no one can *be* good and *stay* good." No one, eh? I say: let us find one—just one—and we have those fellows where we want them!

THIRD GOD [*to* WONG]. Water Seller, is it so hard to find a place to stay?

WONG. Nothing could be easier. It's just me. I don't go about it right.

THIRD GOD. Really? [*He returns to the others. A* GENTLEMAN *passes by.*]

WONG. Oh dear, they're catching on. [*He accosts the* GENTLEMAN.] Excuse the intrusion, dear sir, but three gods have just turned up. Three of the very highest. They need a place for the night. Seize this rare opportunity—to have real gods as your guests!

GENTLEMAN [*laughing*]. A new way of finding free rooms for a gang of crooks.

[*Exit* GENTLEMAN.]

WONG [*shouting at him*]. Godless rascal! Have you no religion, gentlemen of Setzuan? [*Pause.*] Patience, illustrious ones! [*Pause.*] There's only one person left. Shen Te, the prostitute. She *can't* say no. [*Calls up to a window.*] Shen Te!

[SHEN TE *opens the shutters and looks out.*]

WONG. *They're* here, and nobody wants them. Will you take them?

SHEN TE. Oh, no, Wong, I'm expecting a gentleman.

WONG. Can't you forget about him for tonight?

SHEN TE. The rent has to be paid tomorrow or I'll be out on the street.

WONG. This is no time for calculation, Shen Te.

SHEN TE. Stomachs rumble even on the Emperor's birthday, Wong.

WONG. Setzuan is one big dung hill!

SHEN TE. Oh, very well! I'll hide till my gentleman has come and gone. Then I'll take them. [*She disappears.*]

WONG. They mustn't see her gentleman or they'll know what she is.

FIRST GOD [*who hasn't heard any of this*]. I think it's hopeless.

[*They approach* WONG.]

WONG [*jumping, as he finds them behind him*]. A room has been found, illustrious ones! [*He wipes sweat off his brow.*]

SECOND GOD. Oh, good.

THIRD GOD. Let's see it.

WONG [*nervously*]. Just a minute. It has to be tidied up a bit.

THIRD GOD. Then we'll sit down here and wait.

WONG [*still more nervous*]. No, no! [*Holding himself back.*] Too much traffic, you know.

THIRD GOD [*with a smile*]. Of course, if you *want* us to move.

[*They retire a little. They sit on a doorstep.* WONG *sits on the ground.*]

WONG [*after a deep breath*]. You'll be staying with a single girl—the finest human being in Setzuan!

THIRD GOD. That's nice.

WONG [*to the audience*]. They gave me such a look when I picked up my cup just now.

THIRD GOD. You're worn out, Wong.

WONG. A little, maybe.

FIRST GOD. Do people here have a hard time of it?

WONG. The good ones do.

FIRST GOD. What about yourself?

WONG. You mean I'm not good. That's true. And I don't have an easy time either!

[*During this dialogue, a* GENTLEMAN *has turned up in front of* SHEN TE'S *house, and has whistled several times. Each time* WONG *has given a start.*]

THIRD GOD [*to* WONG, *softly*]. Psst! I think he's gone now.

WONG [*confused and surprised*]. Ye-e-es.

[*The* GENTLEMAN *has left now, and* SHEN TE *has come down to the street.*]

SHEN TE [*softly*]. Wong!

[*Getting no answer, she goes off down the street.* WONG *arrives just too late, forgetting his carrying pole.*]

WONG [*softly*]. Shen Te! Shen Te! [*To himself.*] So she's gone off to earn the rent. Oh dear, I can't go to the gods *again* with no room to offer them. Having failed in the service of the gods, I shall run to my den in the sewer pipe down by the river and hide from their sight!

[*He rushes off.* SHEN TE *returns, looking for him, but finding the gods. She stops in confusion.*]

SHEN TE. You are the illustrious ones? My name is Shen Te. It would please me very much if my simple room could be of use to you.

THIRD GOD. Where is the Water Seller, Miss . . . Shen Te?

SHEN TE. I missed him, somehow.

FIRST GOD. Oh, he probably thought you weren't coming, and was afraid of telling us.

THIRD GOD [*picking up the carrying pole*]. We'll leave this with you. He'll be needing it.

[*Led by* SHEN TE, *they go into the house. It grows dark, then light. Dawn. Again escorted by* SHEN TE, *who leads them through the half-light with a little lamp, the* GODS *take their leave.*]

FIRST GOD. Thank you, thank you, dear Shen Te, for your elegant hospitality! We shall not forget! And give our thanks to the Water Seller—he showed us a good human being.

SHEN TE. Oh, *I'm* not good. Let me tell you something: when Wong asked me to put you up, I hesitated.

FIRST GOD. It's all right to hesitate if you then go ahead! And in giving us that room you did much more than you knew. You proved that good people still exist, a point that has been disputed of late—even in heaven. Farewell!

SECOND GOD. Farewell!

THIRD GOD. Farewell!

SHEN TE. Stop, illustrious ones! I'm not sure you're right. I'd like to be good, it's true, but there's the rent to pay. And that's not all: I sell myself for a living. Even so I can't make ends meet, there's too much competition. I'd like to honor my father and mother and speak nothing but the truth and not covet my neighbor's house. I should love to stay with one man. But how? How is it done? Even breaking only a *few* of your commandments, I can hardly manage.

FIRST GOD [*clearing his throat*]. These thoughts are but, um, the misgivings of an unusually good woman!

THIRD GOD. Goodbye, Shen Te! Give our regards to the Water Seller!

SECOND GOD. And above all: be good! Farewell!

FIRST GOD. Farewell!

THIRD GOD. Farewell!

[*They start to wave goodbye.*]

SHEN TE. But everything is so expensive, I don't feel sure I can do it!

SECOND GOD. That's not in our sphere. We never meddle with economics.

THIRD GOD. One moment.

[*They stop.*]

Isn't it true she might do better if she had more money?

SECOND GOD. Come, come! How could we ever account for it Up Above?

FIRST GOD. Oh, there are ways. [*They put their heads together and confer in dumb show. To* SHEN TE, *with embarrassment.*] As you say you can't pay your rent, well, um, we're not paupers, so of course we *insist* on paying for our room. [*Awkwardly thrusting money into her hands.*] There! [*Quickly.*] But don't tell anyone! The incident is open to misinterpretation.

SECOND GOD. It certainly is!

FIRST GOD [*defensively*]. But there's no law against it! It was never decreed that a god mustn't pay hotel bills!

[*The* GODS *leave.*]

SCENE I

A small tobacco shop. The shop is not as yet completely furnished and hasn't started doing business.

SHEN TE [*to the audience*]. It's three days since the gods left. When they said they wanted to pay for the room, I looked down at my hand, and there was more than a thousand silver dollars! I bought a tobacco shop with the money, and moved in yesterday. I don't own the building, of course, but I can pay the rent, and I hope to do a lot of good here. Beginning with Mrs. Shin, who's just coming across the square with her pot. She had the shop before me, and yesterday she dropped in to ask for rice for her children.

[*Enter* MRS. SHIN. *Both women bow.*]

How do you do, Mrs. Shin.

MRS. SHIN. How do you do, Miss Shen Te. You like your new home?

SHEN TE. Indeed, yes. Did your children have a good night?

MRS. SHIN. In that hovel? The youngest is coughing already.

SHEN TE. Oh, dear!

MRS. SHIN. You're going to learn a thing or two in these slums.

SHEN TE. Slums? That's not what you said when you sold me the shop!

MRS. SHIN. Now don't start nagging! Robbing me and my innocent children of their home and then calling it a slum! That's the limit! [*She weeps.*]

SHEN TE [*tactfully*]. I'll get your rice.

MRS. SHIN. And a little cash while you're at it.

SHEN TE. I'm afraid I haven't sold anything yet.

MRS. SHIN [*screeching*]. I've got to have it. Strip the clothes from my back and then cut my throat, will you? I know what I'll do: I'll leave my children on your doorstep! [*She snatches the pot out of* SHEN TE'S *hands.*]

SHEN TE. Please don't be angry. You'll spill the rice.

[*Enter an elderly* HUSBAND *and* WIFE *with their shabbily-dressed* NEPHEW.]

WIFE. Shen Te, dear! You've come into money, they tell me. And we haven't a roof over our heads! A tobacco shop. We had one too. But it's gone. Could we spend the night here, do you think?

NEPHEW [*appraising the shop*]. Not bad!

WIFE. He's our nephew. We're inseparable!

MRS. SHIN. And who are these . . . ladies and gentlemen?

SHEN TE. They put me up when I first came in from the country. [*To the audience.*] Of course, when my small purse was empty, they put me out on the street, and they may be afraid I'll do the same to them. [*To the newcomers, kindly.*] Come in, and welcome, though I've only one little room for you—it's behind the shop.

HUSBAND. That'll do. Don't worry.

WIFE [*bringing* SHEN TE *some tea*]. We'll stay over here, so we won't be in your way. Did you make it a tobacco shop in memory of your first real home? We can certainly give you a hint or two! That's one reason we came.

MRS. SHIN [*to* SHEN TE]. Very nice! As long as you have a few customers too!

HUSBAND. Sh! A customer!

[*Enter an* UNEMPLOYED MAN, *in rags.*]

UNEMPLOYED MAN. Excuse me. I'm unemployed.

[MRS. SHIN *laughs.*]

SHEN TE. Can I help you?

UNEMPLOYED MAN. Have you any damaged cigarettes? I thought there might be some damage when you're unpacking.

WIFE. What nerve, begging for tobacco! [*Rhetorically.*] Why don't they ask for bread?

UNEMPLOYED MAN. Bread is expensive. One cigarette butt and I'll be a new man.

SHEN TE [*giving him cigarettes*]. That's very important—to be a new man. You'll be my first customer and bring me luck.

[*The* UNEMPLOYED MAN *quickly lights a cigarette, inhales, and goes off, coughing.*]

WIFE. Was that right, Shen Te, dear?

MRS. SHIN. If this is the opening of a shop, you can hold the closing at the end of the week.

HUSBAND. I bet he had money on him.

SHEN TE. Oh, no, he said he hadn't!

NEPHEW. How d'you know he wasn't lying?

SHEN TE [*angrily*]. How do you know he was?

WIFE [*wagging her head*]. You're too good, Shen Te, dear. If you're going to keep this shop, you'll have to learn to say No.

HUSBAND. Tell them the place isn't yours to dispose of. Belongs to . . . some relative who insists on all accounts being strictly in order . . .

MRS. SHIN. That's right! What do you think you are—a philanthropist?

SHEN TE [*laughing*]. Very well, suppose I ask you for my rice back, Mrs. Shin?

WIFE [*combatively, at* MRS. SHIN]. So that's *her* rice?

[*Enter the* CARPENTER, *a small man.*]

MRS. SHIN [*who, at the sight of him, starts to hurry away*]. See you tomorrow, Miss Shen Te! [*Exit* MRS. SHIN.]

CARPENTER. Mrs. Shin, it's you I want!

WIFE [*to* SHEN TE]. Has she some claim on you?

SHEN TE. She's hungry. That's a claim.

CARPENTER. Are you the new tenant? And filling up the shelves already? Well, they're not yours till they're paid for, ma'am. I'm the carpenter, so I should know.

SHEN TE. I took the shop "furnishings included."

CARPENTER. You're in league with that Mrs. Shin, of course. All right: I demand my hundred silver dollars.

SHEN TE. I'm afraid I haven't got a hundred silver dollars.

CARPENTER. Then you'll find it. Or I'll have you arrested.

WIFE [*whispering to* SHEN TE]. That relative: make it a cousin.

SHEN TE. Can't it wait till next month?

CARPENTER. No!

SHEN TE. Be a little patient, Mr. Carpenter, I can't settle all claims at once.

CARPENTER. Who's patient with me? [*He grabs a shelf from the wall.*] Pay up—or I take the shelves back!

WIFE. Shen Te! Dear! Why don't you let your . . . cousin settle this affair? [*To* CARPENTER.] Put your claim in writing. Shen Te's cousin will see you get paid.

CARPENTER [*derisively*]. Cousin, eh?

HUSBAND. Cousin, yes.

CARPENTER. I know these cousins!

NEPHEW. Don't be silly. He's a personal friend of mine.

HUSBAND. What a man! Sharp as a razor!

CARPENTER. All right. I'll put my claim in writing. [*Puts shelf on floor, sits on it, writes out bill.*]

WIFE [*to* SHEN TE]. He'd tear the dress off your back to get his shelves. Never recognize a claim! That's my motto.

SHEN TE. He's done a job, and wants something in return. It's shameful that I can't give it to him. What will the gods say?

HUSBAND. You did your bit when you took *us* in.

[*Enter the* BROTHER, *limping, and the* SISTER-IN-LAW, *pregnant.*]

BROTHER [*to* HUSBAND *and* WIFE]. So this is where you're hiding out! There's family feeling for you! Leaving us on the corner!

WIFE [*embarrassed, to* SHEN TE]. It's my brother and his wife. [*To them.*] Now stop grumbling, and sit quietly in that corner. [*To* SHEN TE.] It can't be helped. She's in her fifth month.

SHEN TE. Oh yes. Welcome!

WIFE [*to the couple*]. Say thank you.

[*They mutter something.*]

The cups are here. [*To* SHEN TE.] Lucky you bought this shop when you did!

SHEN TE [*laughing and bringing tea*]. Lucky indeed!

[*Enter* MRS. MI TZU, *the landlady.*]

MRS. MI TZU. Miss Shen Te? I am Mrs. Mi Tzu, your landlady. I hope our relationship will be a happy one. I like to think I give my tenants modern, personalized service. Here is your lease. [*To the others, as* SHEN TE *reads the lease.*] There's nothing like the opening of a little shop, is there? A moment of true beauty! [*She is looking around.*] Not very much on the shelves, of course. But everything in the gods' good time! Where are your references, Miss Shen Te?

SHEN TE. Do I *have* to have references?

MRS. MI TZU. After all, I haven't a notion who you are!

HUSBAND. Oh, *we'd* be glad to vouch for Miss Shen Te! We'd go through fire for her!

MRS. MI TZU. And who may *you* be?

HUSBAND [*stammering*]. Ma Fu, tobacco dealer.

MRS. MI TZU. Where is your shop, Mr. . . . Ma Fu?

HUSBAND. Well, um, I haven't a shop—I've just sold it.

MRS. MI TZU. I see. [*To* SHEN TE.] Is there no one else that knows you?

WIFE [*whispering to* SHEN TE]. Your cousin! Your cousin!

MRS. MI TZU. This is a respectable house, Miss Shen Te. I never sign a lease without certain assurances.

SHEN TE [*slowly, her eyes downcast*]. I have . . . a cousin.

MRS. MI TZU. On the square? Let's go over and see him. What does he do?

SHEN TE [*as before*]. He lives . . . in another city.

WIFE [*prompting*]. Didn't you say he was in Shung?

SHEN TE. That's right. Shung.

HUSBAND [*prompting*]. I had his name on the tip of my tongue. Mr. . . .

SHEN TE [*with an effort*]. Mr. . . . Shui . . . Ta.

HUSBAND. That's it! Tall, skinny fellow!

SHEN TE. Shui Ta!

NEPHEW [*to* CARPENTER]. *You* were in touch with him, weren't you? About the shelves?

CARPENTER [*surlily*]. Give him this bill. [*He hands it over.*] I'll be back in the morning.

[*Exit* CARPENTER.]

NEPHEW [*calling after him, but with his eyes on* MRS. MI TZU]. Don't worry! Mr. Shui Ta pays on the nail!

MRS. MI TZU [*looking closely at* SHEN TE]. I'll be happy to make his acquaintance, Miss Shen Te. [*Exit* MRS. MI TZU.]

[*Pause.*]

WIFE. By tomorrow morning she'll know more about you than you do yourself.

SISTER-IN-LAW [*to* NEPHEW]. This thing isn't built to last.

[*Enter* GRANDFATHER.]

WIFE. It's Grandfather! [*To* SHEN TE.] Such a good old soul!

[*The* Boy *enters.*]

Boy [*over his shoulder*]. Here they are!

Wife. And the boy, how he's grown! But he always could eat enough for ten.

[*Enter the* Niece.]

Wife [*to* Shen Te]. Our little niece from the country. There are more of us now than in your time. The less we had, the more there were of us; the more there were of us, the less we had. Give me the key. We must protect ourselves from unwanted guests. [*She takes the key and locks the door.*] Just make yourself at home. I'll light the little lamp.

Nephew [*a big joke*]. I hope her cousin doesn't drop in tonight! The strict Mr. Shui Ta!

[Sister-in-Law *laughs.*]

Brother [*reaching for a cigarette*]. One cigarette more or less . . .

Husband. One cigarette more or less.

[*They pile into the cigarettes. The* Brother *hands a jug of wine round.*]

Nephew. Mr. Shui Ta'll pay for it!

Grandfather [*gravely, to* Shen Te]. How do you do?

[Shen Te, *a little taken aback by the belatedness of the greeting, bows. She has the* Carpenter's *bill in one hand, the landlady's lease in the other.*]

Wife. How about a bit of a song? To keep Shen Te's spirits up?

Nephew. Good idea. Grandfather: you start!

Song of the Smoke

Grandfather.

I used to think (before old age beset me)
    That brains could fill the pantry of the poor.
But where did all my cerebration get me?
    I'm just as hungry as I was before.
            So what's the use?
                See the smoke float free
            Into ever colder coldness!
                It's the same with me.

Husband.

The straight and narrow path leads to disaster
    And so the crooked path I tried to tread.
That got me to disaster even faster.
    (They say we shall be happy when we're dead.)
            So what's the use, etc.

Niece.

You older people, full of expectation,
    At any moment now you'll walk the plank!
The future's for the younger generation!
    Yes, even if that future is a blank.
            So what's the use, etc.

NEPHEW [*to the* BROTHER]. Where'd you get that wine?

SISTER-IN-LAW [*answering for the* BROTHER]. He pawned the sack of tobacco.

HUSBAND [*stepping in*]. What? That tobacco was all we had to fall back on! You pig!

BROTHER. *You'd* call a man a pig because your wife was frigid! Did you refuse to drink it?

[*They fight. The shelves fall over.*]

SHEN TE [*imploringly*]. Oh, don't! Don't break everything! Take it, take it all, but don't destroy a gift from the gods!

WIFE [*disparagingly*]. This shop isn't big enough. I should never have mentioned it to Uncle and the others. When *they* arrive, it's going to be disgustingly overcrowded.

SISTER-IN-LAW. And did you hear our gracious hostess? She cools off quick!

[*Voices outside. Knocking at the door.*]

UNCLE'S VOICE. Open the door!

WIFE. Uncle? Is that you, Uncle?

UNCLE'S VOICE. Certainly, it's me. Auntie says to tell you she'll have the children here in ten minutes.

WIFE [*to* SHEN TE]. I'll have to let him in.

SHEN TE [*who scarcely hears her*].

The little lifeboat is swiftly sent down
Too many men too greedily
Hold on to it as they drown.

SCENE IA

WONG'S *den in a sewer pipe.*

WONG [*crouching there*]. All quiet! It's four days now since I left the city. The gods passed this way on the second day. I heard their steps on the bridge over there. They must be a long way off by this time, so I'm safe.

[*Breathing a sigh of relief, he curls up and goes to sleep. In his dream the pipe becomes transparent, and the* GODS *appear.*]

[*Raising an arm, as if in self-defense.*] I know, I know, illustrious ones! I found no one to give you a room—not in all Setzuan! There, it's out. Please continue on your way!

FIRST GOD [*mildly*]. But you did find someone. Someone who took us in for the night, watched over us in our sleep, and in the early morning lighted us down to the street with a lamp.

WONG. It was . . . Shen Te, that took you in?

THIRD GOD. Who else?

WONG. And I ran away! "She isn't coming," I thought, "she just can't afford it."

GODS [*singing*].

O you feeble, well-intentioned, and yet feeble chap!
Where there's need the fellow thinks there is no goodness!
When there's danger he thinks courage starts to ebb away!
Some people only see the seamy side!
What hasty judgment! What premature desperation!

WONG. I'm *very* ashamed, illustrious ones.

FIRST GOD. Do us a favor, Water Seller. Go back to Setzuan. Find Shen Te, and give us a report on her. We hear that she's come into a little money. Show interest in her goodness—for no one can be good for long if goodness is not in demand. Meanwhile we shall continue the search, and find other good people. After which, the idle chatter about the impossibility of goodness will stop!

[*The* GODS *vanish.*]

SCENE II

[*A knocking.*]

WIFE. Shen Te! Someone at the door. Where is she anyway?

NEPHEW. She must be getting the breakfast. Mr. Shui Ta will pay for it.

[*The* WIFE *laughs and shuffles to the door. Enter* MR. SHUI TA *and the* CARPENTER.]

WIFE. Who is it?

SHUI TA. I am Miss Shen Te's cousin.

WIFE. What?

SHUI TA. My name is Shui Ta.

WIFE. Her cousin?

NEPHEW. Her cousin?

NIECE. But that was a joke. She hasn't got a cousin.

HUSBAND. So early in the morning?

BROTHER. What's all the noise?

SISTER-IN-LAW. This fellow says he's her cousin.

BROTHER. Tell him to prove it.

NEPHEW. Right. If you're Shen Te's cousin, prove it by getting the breakfast.

SHUI TA [*whose regime begins as he puts out the lamp to save oil. Loudly, to all present, asleep or awake*]. Would you all please get dressed! Customers will be coming! I wish to open my shop!

HUSBAND. *Your* shop? Doesn't it belong to our good friend Shen Te?

[SHUI TA *shakes his head.*]

SISTER-IN-LAW. So we've been cheated. Where *is* the little liar?

SHUI TA. Miss Shen Te has been delayed. She wishes me to tell you there will be nothing she can do—now I am here.

WIFE [*bowled over*]. I thought she was *good!*

NEPHEW. Do you have to believe *him?*

HUSBAND. *I* don't.

NEPHEW. Then do something.

HUSBAND. Certainly! I'll send out a search party at once. You, you, you, and you, go out and look for Shen Te.

[*As the* GRANDFATHER *rises and makes for the door.*]

Not you, Grandfather, you and I will hold the fort.

SHUI TA. You won't find Miss Shen Te. She has suspended her hospitable activity for an unlimited period. There are too many of you. She asked me to say: this is a tobacco shop, not a gold mine.

HUSBAND. Shen Te never said a thing like that. Boy, food! There's a bakery on the corner. Stuff your shirt full when they're not looking!

SISTER-IN-LAW. Don't overlook the raspberry tarts.

HUSBAND. And don't let the policeman see you.

[*The* BOY *leaves.*]

SHUI TA. Don't you depend on this shop now? Then why give it a bad name, by stealing from the bakery?

NEPHEW. Don't listen to him. Let's find Shen Te. She'll give him a piece of her mind.

SISTER-IN-LAW. Don't forget to leave us some breakfast.

[BROTHER, SISTER-IN-LAW, *and* NEPHEW *leave.*]

SHUI TA [*to the* CARPENTER]. You see, Mr. Carpenter, nothing has changed since the poet, eleven hundred years ago, penned these lines:

A governor was asked what was needed
To save the freezing people in the city.
He replied:
"A blanket ten thousand feet long
To cover the city and all its suburbs."

[*He starts to tidy up the shop.*]

CARPENTER. Your cousin owes me money. I've got witnesses. For the shelves.

SHUI TA. Yes, I have your bill. [*He takes it out of his pocket.*] Isn't a hundred silver dollars rather a lot?

CARPENTER. No deductions! I have a wife and children.

SHUI TA. How many children?

CARPENTER. Three.

SHUI TA. I'll make you an offer. Twenty silver dollars.

[*The* HUSBAND *laughs.*]

CARPENTER. You're crazy. Those shelves are real walnut.

SHUI TA. Very well. Take them away.

CARPENTER. What?

SHUI TA. They cost too much. Please take them away.

WIFE. Not bad! [*And she, too, is laughing.*]

CARPENTER [*a little bewildered*]. Call Shen Te, someone! [*To* SHUI TA.] She's good!

SHUI TA. Certainly. She's ruined.

CARPENTER [*provoked into taking some of the shelves*]. All right, you can keep your tobacco on the floor.

SHUI TA [*to the* HUSBAND]. Help him with the shelves.

HUSBAND [*grins and carries one shelf over to the door where the* CARPENTER *now is*]. Goodbye, shelves!

CARPENTER [*to the* HUSBAND]. You dog! You want my family to starve?

SHUI TA. I repeat my offer. I have no desire to keep my tobacco on the floor. Twenty silver dollars.

CARPENTER [*with desperate aggressiveness*]. One hundred!

[SHUI TA *shows indifference, looks through the window. The* HUSBAND *picks up several shelves.*]

[*To* HUSBAND.] You needn't smash them against the doorpost, you idiot!

[*To* SHUI TA.] These shelves were made to measure. They're no use anywhere else!

SHUI TA. Precisely.

[*The* WIFE *squeals with pleasure.*]

CARPENTER [*giving up, sullenly*]. Take the shelves. Pay what you want to pay.

SHUI TA [*smoothly*]. Twenty silver dollars.

[*He places two large coins on the table. The* CARPENTER *picks them up.*]

HUSBAND [*brings the shelves back in*]. And quite enough too!

CARPENTER [*slinking off*]. Quite enough to get drunk on.

HUSBAND [*happily*]. Well, we got rid of him!

WIFE [*weeping with fun, gives a rendition of the dialogue just spoken*]. "Real walnut," says he. "Very well, take them away," says his lordship. "I have children," says he. "Twenty silver dollars," says his lordship. "They're no use anywhere else," says he. "Precisely," said his lordship! [*She dissolves into shrieks of merriment.*]

SHUI TA. And now: go!

HUSBAND. What's that?

SHUI TA. You're thieves, parasites. I'm giving you this chance. Go!

HUSBAND [*summoning all his ancestral dignity*]. That sort deserves no answer. Besides, one should never shout on an empty stomach.

WIFE. Where's that boy?

SHUI TA. Exactly. The boy. I want no stolen goods in this shop. [*Very loudly.*] I strongly advise you to leave! [*But they remain seated, noses in the air. Quietly.*] As you wish.

[SHUI TA *goes to the door. A* POLICEMAN *appears.* SHUI TA *bows.*]

I am addressing the officer in charge of this precinct?

POLICEMAN. That's right, Mr., um . . . what was the name, sir?

SHUI TA. Mr. Shui Ta.

POLICEMAN. Yes, of course, sir.

[*They exchange a smile.*]

SHUI TA. Nice weather we're having.

POLICEMAN. A little on the warm side, sir.

SHUI TA. Oh, a little on the warm side.

HUSBAND [*whispering to the* WIFE]. If he keeps it up till the boy's back, we're done for. [*Tries to signal* SHUI TA.]

SHUI TA [*ignoring the signal*]. Weather, of course, is one thing indoors, another out on the dusty street!

POLICEMAN. Oh, quite another, sir!

WIFE [*to the* HUSBAND]. It's all right as long as he's standing in the doorway—the boy will see him.

SHUI TA. Step inside for a moment! It's quite cool indoors. My cousin and I have just opened the place. And we attach the greatest importance to being on good terms with the, um, authorities.

POLICEMAN [*entering*]. Thank you, Mr. Shui Ta. It *is* cool!

HUSBAND [*whispering to the* WIFE]. And now the boy *won't* see him.

SHUI TA [*showing* HUSBAND *and* WIFE *to the* POLICEMAN]. Visitors, I think my cousin knows them. They were just leaving.

HUSBAND [*defeated*]. Ye-e-es, we were . . . just leaving.
SHUI TA. I'll tell my cousin you couldn't wait.

[*Noise from the street. Shouts of "Stop, thief!"*]

POLICEMAN. What's that?

[*The* BOY *is in the doorway with cakes and buns and rolls spilling out of his shirt. The* WIFE *signals desperately to him to leave. He gets the idea.*]

No, you don't! [*He grabs the* BOY *by the collar.*] Where's all this from?
BOY [*vaguely pointing*]. Down the street.
POLICEMAN [*grimly*]. So that's it. [*Prepares to arrest the* BOY.]
WIFE [*stepping in*]. And *we* knew nothing about it. [*To the* BOY.] Nasty little thief!
POLICEMAN [*dryly*]. Can you clarify the situation, Mr. Shui Ta?

[SHUI TA *is silent.*]

POLICEMAN [*who understands silence*]. Aha. You're all coming with me—to the station.
SHUI TA. I can hardly say how sorry I am that *my* establishment . . .
WIFE. Oh, he saw the boy leave not ten minutes ago!
SHUI TA. And to conceal the theft asked a policeman in?
POLICEMAN. Don't listen to her, Mr. Shui Ta, I'll be happy to relieve you of their presence one and all! [*To all three.*] Out! [*He drives them before him.*]
GRANDFATHER [*leaving last. Gravely*]. Good morning!
POLICEMAN. Good morning!

[SHUI TA, *left alone, continues to tidy up.* MRS. MI TZU *breezes in.*]

MRS. MI TZU. *You're* her cousin, are you? Then have the goodness to explain what all this means—police dragging people from a respectable house! By what right does your Miss Shen Te turn my property into a house of assignation?—Well, as you see, I know all!
SHUI TA. Yes. My cousin has the worst possible reputation: that of being poor.
MRS. MI TZU. No sentimental rubbish, Mr. Shui Ta. Your cousin was a common . . .
SHUI TA. Pauper. Let's use the uglier word.
MRS. MI TZU. I'm speaking of her conduct, not her earnings. But there must have *been* earnings, or how did she buy all this? Several elderly gentlemen took care of it, I suppose. I repeat: this is a respectable house! I have tenants who prefer not to live under the same roof with such a person.
SHUI TA [*quietly*]. How much do you want?
MRS. MI TZU [*he is ahead of her now*]. I beg your pardon?
SHUI TA. To reassure yourself. To reassure your tenants. How much will it cost?
MRS. MI TZU. You're a cool customer.
SHUI TA [*picking up the lease*]. The rent is high. [*He reads on.*] I assume it's payable by the month?
MRS. MI TZU. Not in her case.

SHUI TA [*looking up*]. What?

MRS. MI TZU. Six months' rent payable in advance. Two hundred silver dollars.

SHUI TA. Six . . . ! Sheer usury! And where am I to find it?

MRS. MI TZU. You should have thought of that before.

SHUI TA. Have you no heart, Mrs. Mi Tzu? It's true Shen Te acted foolishly, being kind to all those people, but she'll improve with time. I'll see to it she does. She'll work her fingers to the bone to pay her rent, and all the time be as quiet as a mouse, as humble as a fly.

MRS. MI TZU. Her social background . . .

SHUI TA. Out of the depths! She came out of the depths! And before she'll go back there, she'll work, sacrifice, shrink from nothing. . . . Such a tenant is worth her weight in gold, Mrs. Mi Tzu.

MRS. MI TZU. It's silver we were talking about, Mr. Shui Ta. Two hundred silver dollars or . . .

[*Enter the* POLICEMAN.]

POLICEMAN. Am I intruding, Mr. Shui Ta?

MRS. MI TZU. This tobacco shop is well-known to the police, I see.

POLICEMAN. Mr. Shui Ta has done us a service, Mrs. Mi Tzu. I am here to present our official felicitations!

MRS. MI TZU. That means less than nothing to me, sir. Mr. Shui Ta, all I can say is: I hope your cousin will find my terms acceptable. Good day, gentlemen. [*Exit.*]

SHUI TA. Good day, ma'am.

[*Pause.*]

POLICEMAN. Mrs. Mi Tzu a bit of a stumbling block, sir?

SHUI TA. She wants six months' rent in advance.

POLICEMAN. And you haven't got it, eh?

[SHUI TA *is silent.*]

But surely you can get it, sir? A man like you?

SHUI TA. What about a woman like Shen Te?

POLICEMAN. You're not staying, sir?

SHUI TA. No, and I won't be back. Do you smoke?

POLICEMAN [*taking two cigars, and placing them both in his pocket*]. Thank you, sir—I see your point. Miss Shen Te—let's mince no words—Miss Shen Te lived by selling herself. "What else could she have done?" you ask. "How else was she to pay the rent?" True. But the fact remains, Mr. Shui Ta, it is not respectable. Why not? A very deep question. But, in the first place, love—love isn't bought and sold like cigars, Mr. Shui Ta. In the second place, it isn't respectable to go waltzing off with someone that's paying his way, so to speak—it must be for love! Thirdly and lastly, as the proverb has it: not for a handful of rice but for love! [*Pause. He is thinking hard.*] "Well," you may say, "and what good is all this wisdom if the milk's already spilt?" Miss Shen Te is what she is. Is *where* she is. We have to face the fact that if she doesn't get hold of six months' rent pronto, she'll be back on the streets. The question then as I see it—everything in this world is a matter of opinion—the question as I see it is: *how* is she to get hold of this rent? How? Mr. Shui Ta: I don't know. [*Pause.*] I take that back, sir. It's just come to me. A husband. We must find her a husband!

[*Enter a little* OLD WOMAN.]

OLD WOMAN. A good cheap cigar for my husband, we'll have been married forty years tomorrow and we're having a little celebration.

SHUI TA. Forty years? And you still want to celebrate?

OLD WOMAN. As much as we can afford to. We have the carpet shop across the square. We'll be good neighbors, I hope?

SHUI TA. I hope so too.

POLICEMAN [*who keeps making discoveries*]. Mr. Shui Ta, you know what we need? We need capital. And how do we acquire capital? We get married.

SHUI TA [*to* OLD WOMAN]. I'm afraid I've been pestering this gentleman with my personal worries.

POLICEMAN [*lyrically*]. We can't pay six months' rent, so what do we do? We marry money.

SHUI TA. That might not be easy.

POLICEMAN. Oh, I don't know. She's a good match. Has a nice, growing business. [*To the* OLD WOMAN.] What do you think?

OLD WOMAN [*undecided*]. Well—

POLICEMAN. Should she put an ad in the paper?

OLD WOMAN [*not eager to commit herself*]. Well, if *she* agrees—

POLICEMAN. I'll write it for her. *You* lend us a hand, and *we* write an ad for you! [*He chuckles away to himself, takes out his notebook, wets the stump of a pencil between his lips, and writes away.*]

SHUI TA [*slowly*]. Not a bad idea.

POLICEMAN. "What . . . *respectable* . . . man . . . with small capital . . . widower . . . not excluded . . . desires . . . marriage . . . into flourishing . . . tobacco shop?" And now let's add: "am . . . pretty . . ." No! . . . "Prepossessing appearance."

SHUI TA. If you don't think that's an exaggeration?

OLD WOMAN. Oh, not a bit. I've seen her.

[*The* POLICEMAN *tears the page out of his notebook, and hands it over to* SHUI TA.]

SHUI TA [*with horror in his voice*]. How much luck we need to keep our heads above water! How many ideas! How many friends! [*To the* POLICEMAN.] Thank you, sir. I think I see my way clear.

SCENE III

Evening in the municipal park. Noise of a plane overhead. YANG SUN, *a young man in rags, is following the plane with his eyes: one can tell that the machine is describing a curve above the park.* YANG SUN *then takes a rope out of his pocket, looking anxiously about him as he does so. He moves toward a large willow. Enter* TWO PROSTITUTES, *one old, the other the* NIECE *whom we have already met.*

NIECE. Hello. Coming with me?

YANG SUN [*taken aback*]. If you'd like to buy me a dinner.

OLD WHORE. Buy you a dinner! [*To the* NIECE.] Oh, we know him—it's the unemployed pilot. Waste no time on him!

NIECE. But he's the only man left in the park. And it's going to rain.

OLD WHORE. Oh, how do you know?

[*And they pass by.* YANG SUN *again looks*

about him, again takes his rope, and this time throws it round a branch of the willow tree. Again he is interrupted. It is the TWO PROSTITUTES *returning—and in such a hurry they don't notice him.*]

NIECE. It's going to pour!

[*Enter* SHEN TE.]

OLD WHORE. There's that *gorgon* Shen Te! That *drove* your family out into the cold!

NIECE. It wasn't her. It was that cousin of hers. She offered to *pay* for the cakes. I've nothing against her.

OLD WHORE. I have, though. [*So that* SHEN TE *can hear.*] Now where could the little lady be off to? She may be rich now but that won't stop her snatching our young men, will it?

SHEN TE. I'm going to the tearoom by the pond.

NIECE. Is it true what they say? You're marrying a widower—with three children?

SHEN TE. Yes. I'm just going to see him.

YANG SUN [*his patience at breaking point*]. Move on there! This is a park, not a whorehouse!

OLD WHORE. Shut your mouth!

[*But the* TWO PROSTITUTES *leave.*]

YANG SUN. Even in the farthest corner of the park, even when it's raining, you can't get rid of them! [*He spits.*]

SHEN TE [*overhearing this*]. And what right have you to scold them? [*But at this point she sees the rope.*] Oh!

YANG SUN. Well, what are you staring at?

SHEN TE. That rope. What is it for?

YANG SUN. Think! Think! I haven't a penny. Even if I had, I wouldn't spend it on you. I'd buy a drink of water.

[*The rain starts.*]

SHEN TE [*still looking at the rope*]. What is the rope for? You mustn't!

YANG SUN. What's it to you? Clear out!

SHEN TE [*irrelevantly*]. It's raining.

YANG SUN. Well, don't try to come under this tree.

SHEN TE. Oh, no. [*She stays in the rain.*]

YANG SUN. Now go away. [*Pause.*] For one thing, I don't like your looks, you're bowlegged.

SHEN TE [*indignantly*]. That's not true!

YANG SUN. Well, don't show 'em to me. Look, it's raining. You better come under this tree.

[*Slowly, she takes shelter under the tree.*]

SHEN TE. Why did you want to do it?

YANG SUN. You really want to know? [*Pause.*] To get rid of you! [*Pause.*] You know what a flyer is?

SHEN TE. Of yes, I've met a lot of pilots. At the tearoom.

YANG SUN. You call *them* flyers? Think they know what a machine *is*? Just 'cause they have leather helmets? They gave the airfield director a bribe, that's the way *those* fellows got up in the air! Try one of them out sometime. "Go up to two thousand feet," tell him, "then let it fall, then pick it up again with a flick of the wrist at the last moment." Know what he'll say to that? "It's not in my contract." Then again, there's the landing problem. It's like landing on your own backside. It's no different, planes are human. Those fools don't understand. [*Pause.*] And I'm the biggest fool for reading the book on flying in the Peking school and skipping the page where it says: "we've got enough flyers and we don't need you." I'm a mail pilot and no mail. You understand that?

SHEN TE [*shyly*]. Yes. I do.

YANG SUN. No, you don't. You'd never understand that.

SHEN TE. When we were little we had a crane with a broken wing. He made friends with us and was very good-natured about our jokes. He would strut along behind us and call out to stop us going too fast for him. But every spring and autumn when the cranes flew over the villages in great swarms, he got quite restless. [*Pause.*] I understood that. [*She bursts out crying.*]

YANG SUN. Don't!

SHEN TE [*quieting down*]. No.

YANG SUN. It's bad for the complexion.

SHEN TE [*sniffling*]. I've stopped.

[*She dries her tears on her big sleeve. Leaning against the tree, but not looking at her, he reaches for her face.*]

YANG SUN. You can't even wipe your own face. [*He is wiping it for her with his handkerchief. Pause.*]

SHEN TE [*still sobbing*]. I don't know *anything!*

YANG SUN. You interrupted me! What for?

SHEN TE. It's such a rainy day. You only wanted to do . . . *that* because it's such a rainy day.

[*To the audience.*]

In our country
The evenings should never be somber
High bridges over rivers
The gray hour between night and morning
And the long, long winter:
Such things are dangerous
For, with all the misery,
A very little is enough
And men throw away an unbearable life.

[*Pause.*]

YANG SUN. Talk about yourself for a change.

SHEN TE. What about me? I have a shop.

YANG SUN [*incredulous*]. You have a shop, do you? Never thought of walking the streets?

SHEN TE. I *did* walk the streets. Now I have a shop.

YANG SUN [*ironically*]. A gift of the gods, I suppose!

SHEN TE. How did you know?

YANG SUN [*even more ironical*]. One fine evening the gods turned up saying: here's some money!

SHEN TE [*quickly*]. One fine morning.

YANG SUN [*fed up*]. This isn't much of an entertainment.

[*Pause.*]

SHEN TE. I can play the zither a little. [*Pause.*] And I can mimic men. [*Pause.*] I got the shop, so the first thing I did was to give my zither away. I can be as stupid as a fish now, I said to myself, and it won't matter.

I'm rich now, I said
I walk alone, I sleep alone
For a whole year, I said
I'll have nothing to do with a man.

YANG SUN. And now you're marrying one! The one at the tearoom by the pond?

[SHEN TE *is silent.*]

YANG SUN. What do you know about love?

SHEN TE. Everything.

YANG SUN. Nothing. [*Pause.*] Or d'you just mean you enjoyed it?

SHEN TE. No.

YANG SUN [*again without turning to look at her, he strokes her cheek with his hand*]. You like that?

SHEN TE. Yes.

YANG SUN [*breaking off*]. You're easily satisfied, I must say. [*Pause.*] What a town!

SHEN TE. You have no friends?

YANG SUN [*defensively*]. Yes, I have! [*Change of tone.*] But they don't want to hear I'm still unemployed. "What?" they ask. "Is there still water in the sea?" You have friends?

SHEN TE [*hesitating*]. Just a . . . cousin.

YANG SUN. Watch him carefully.

SHEN TE. He only came once. Then he went away. He won't be back.

[YANG SUN *is looking away.*]

But to be without hope, they say, is to be without goodness!

[*Pause.*]

YANG SUN. Go on talking. A voice is a voice.

SHEN TE. Once, when I was a little girl, I fell, with a load of brushwood. An old man picked me up. He gave me a penny too. Isn't it funny how people who don't have very much like to give some of it away? They must like to show what they can do, and how could they show it better than by being kind? Being wicked is just like being clumsy. When we sing a song, or build a machine, or plant some rice, we're being kind. You're kind.

YANG SUN. You make it sound easy.

SHEN TE. Oh, no. [*Little pause.*] Oh! A drop of rain!

YANG SUN. Where'd you feel it?

SHEN TE. Between the eyes.

YANG SUN. Near the right eye? Or the left?

SHEN TE. Near the left eye.

YANG SUN. Oh, good. [*He is getting sleepy.*] So you're through with men, eh?

SHEN TE [*with a smile*]. But I'm not bowlegged.

YANG SUN. Perhaps not.
SHEN TE. Definitely not.

[*Pause.*]

YANG SUN [*leaning wearily against the willow*]. I haven't had a drop to drink all day, I haven't eaten anything for *two* days. I couldn't love you if I tried.

[*Pause.*]

SHEN TE. I like it in the rain.

[*Enter* WONG *the Water Seller, singing.*]

THE SONG OF THE WATER SELLER IN THE RAIN

"Buy my water," I am yelling
And my fury restraining
For no water I'm selling
'Cause it's raining, 'cause it's raining!
    I keep yelling: "Buy my water!"
    But no one's buying
    Athirst and dying
    And drinking and paying!
    Buy water!
    Buy water, you dogs!

Nice to dream of lovely weather!
Think of all the consternation
Were there no precipitation
Half a dozen years together!
Can't you hear them shrieking: "Water!"
Pretending they adore me!
They all would go down on their knees before me!
Down on your knees!
Go down on your knees, you dogs!

What are lawns and hedges thinking?
What are fields and forests saying?
"At the cloud's breast we are drinking!
And we've no idea who's paying!"
    I keep yelling: "Buy my water!"
    But no one's buying
    Athirst and dying
    And drinking and paying!
    Buy water!
    Buy water, you dogs!

[*The rain has stopped now.* SHEN TE *sees* WONG *and runs toward him.*]

SHEN TE. Wong! You're back! Your carrying pole's at the shop.
WONG. Oh, thank you, Shen Te. And how is life treating *you?*

SHEN TE. I've just met a brave and clever man. And I want to buy him a cup of your water.

WONG [*bitterly*]. Throw back your head and open your mouth and you'll have all the water you need—

SHEN TE [*tenderly*].

I want *your* water, Wong
The water that has tired you so
The water that you carried all this way
The water that is hard to sell because it's been raining
I need it for the young man over there—he's a flyer!
A flyer is a bold man:
Braving the storms
In company with the clouds
He crosses the heavens
And brings to friends in far-away lands
The friendly mail!

[*She pays* WONG, *and runs over to* YANG SUN *with the cup. But* YANG SUN *is fast asleep.*]

[*Calling to* WONG, *with a laugh.*] He's fallen asleep! Despair and rain and I have worn him out!

SCENE IIIA

WONG'S *den. The sewer pipe is transparent, and the* GODS *again appear to* WONG *in a dream.*

WONG [*radiant*]. I've seen her, illustrious ones! And she hasn't changed!

FIRST GOD. That's good to hear.

WONG. She loves someone.

FIRST GOD. Let's hope the experience gives her the strength to stay good!

WONG. It does. She's doing good deeds all the time.

FIRST GOD. Ah? What sort? What sort of good deeds, Wong?

WONG. Well, she has a kind word for everybody.

FIRST GOD [*eagerly*]. And then?

WONG. Hardly anyone leaves her shop without tobacco in his pocket—even if he can't pay for it.

FIRST GOD. Not bad at all. Next?

WONG. She's putting up a family of eight.

FIRST GOD [*gleefully, to the* SECOND GOD]. Eight! [*To* WONG.] And that's not all, of course!

WONG. She bought a cup of water from me even though it was raining.

FIRST GOD. Yes, yes, yes, all these smaller good deeds!

WONG. Even they run into money. A little tobacco shop doesn't make so much.

FIRST GOD [*sententiously*]. A prudent gardener works miracles on the smallest plot.

WONG. She hands out rice every morning. That eats up half her earnings.

FIRST GOD [*a little disappointed*]. Well, as a beginning . . .

WONG. They call her the Angel of the Slums—whatever the Carpenter may say!

FIRST GOD. What's this? A carpenter speaks ill of her?

WONG. Oh, he only says her shelves weren't paid for in full.

SECOND GOD [*who has a bad cold and can't pronounce his n's and m's*]. What's this? Not paying a carpenter? Why was that?

WONG. I suppose she didn't have the money.

SECOND GOD [*severely*]. One pays what one owes, that's in our book of rules! First the letter of the law, then the spirit!

WONG. But it wasn't Shen Te, illustrious ones, it was her cousin. She called *him* in to help.

SECOND GOD. Then her cousin must never darken her threshold again!

WONG. Very well, illustrious ones! But in fairness to Shen Te, let me say that her cousin is a businessman.

FIRST GOD. Perhaps we should inquire what is customary? I find business quite unintelligible. But everybody's doing it. Business! Did the Seven Good Kings do business? Did Kung the Just sell fish?

SECOND GOD. In any case, such a thing must not occur again!

[*The* GODS *start to leave.*]

THIRD GOD. Forgive us for taking this tone with you. Wong, we haven't been getting enough sleep. The rich recommended us to the poor, and the poor tell us they haven't enough room.

SECOND GOD. Feeble, feeble, the best of them!

FIRST GOD. No great deeds! No heroic daring!

THIRD GOD. On such a *small* scale!

SECOND GOD. Sincere, yes, but what is actually *achieved?*

[*One can no longer hear them.*]

WONG [*calling after them*]. I've thought of something, illustrious ones: Perhaps you shouldn't ask—too—much—all—at—once!

SCENE IV

The square in front of SHEN TE'S *tobacco shop. Beside* SHEN TE'S *place, two other shops are seen: the carpet shop and a barber's. Morning. Outside* SHEN TE'S *the* GRANDFATHER, *the* SISTER-IN-LAW, *the* UNEMPLOYED MAN, *and* MRS. SHIN *stand waiting.*

SISTER-IN-LAW. She's been out all night again.

MRS. SHIN. No sooner did we get rid of that crazy cousin of hers than Shen Te herself starts carrying on! Maybe she does give us an ounce of rice now and then, but can you depend on her? Can you depend on her?

[*Loud voices from the barber's.*]

VOICE OF SHU FU. What are you doing in my shop? Get out—at once!

VOICE OF WONG. But sir. They all let me sell . . .

[WONG *comes staggering out of the barber's shop pursued by* MR. SHU FU, *the barber, a fat man carrying a heavy curling iron.*]

SHU FU. Get out, I said! Pestering my customers with your slimy old water! Get out! Take your cup!

[*He holds out the cup.* WONG *reaches out for it.* MR. SHU FU *strikes his hand with the curling iron, which is hot.* WONG *howls.*]

You had it coming, my man!

[*Puffing, he returns to his shop. The* UNEMPLOYED MAN *picks up the cup and gives it to* WONG.]

UNEMPLOYED MAN. You can report that to the police.

WONG. My hand! It's smashed up!

UNEMPLOYED MAN. Any bones broken?

WONG. I can't move my fingers.

UNEMPLOYED MAN. Sit down. I'll put some water on it.

[WONG *sits.*]

MRS. SHIN. The water won't cost you anything.

SISTER-IN-LAW. You might have got a bandage from Miss Shen Te till she took to staying out all night. It's a scandal.

MRS. SHIN [*despondently*]. If you ask me, she's forgotten we ever existed!

[*Enter* SHEN TE *down the street, with a dish of rice.*]

SHEN TE [*to the audience*]. How wonderful to see Setzuan in the early morning! I always used to stay in bed with my dirty blanket over my head afraid to wake up. This morning I saw the newspapers being delivered by little boys, the streets being washed by strong men, and fresh vegetables coming in from the country on ox carts. It's a long walk from where Yang Sun lives, but I feel lighter at every step. They say you walk on air when you're in love, but it's even better walking on the rough earth, on the hard cement. In the early morning, the old city looks like a great rubbish heap. Nice, though—with all its little lights. And the sky, so pink, so transparent, before the dust comes and muddies it! What a lot you miss if you never see your city rising from its slumbers like an honest old craftsman pumping his lungs full of air and reaching for his tools, as the poet says! [*Cheerfully, to her waiting guests.*] Good morning, everyone, here's your rice! [*Distributing the rice, she comes upon* WONG.] Good morning, Wong, I'm quite lightheaded today. On my way over, I looked at myself in all the shop windows. I'd love to be beautiful.

[*She slips into the carpet shop.* MR. SHU FU *has just emerged from his shop.*]

SHU FU [*to the audience*]. It surprises me how beautiful Miss Shen Te is looking today! I never gave her a passing thought before. But now I've been gazing upon her comely form for exactly three minutes! I begin to suspect I am in love with her. She is overpoweringly attractive! [*Crossly, to* WONG.] Be off with you, rascal!

[*He returns to his shop.* SHEN TE *comes back out of the carpet shop with the* OLD MAN *its proprietor and his wife—whom we have already met—the* OLD WOMAN.

[SHEN TE *is wearing a shawl. The* OLD MAN *is holding up a looking glass for her.*]

OLD WOMAN. Isn't it lovely? We'll give you a reduction because there's a little hole in it.

SHEN TE [*looking at another shawl on the* OLD WOMAN*'s arm*]. The other one's nice too.

OLD WOMAN [*smiling*]. Too bad there's no hole in that!

SHEN TE. That's right. My shop doesn't make very much.

OLD WOMAN. And your good deeds eat it all up! Be more careful, my dear . . .

SHEN TE [*trying on the shawl with the hole*]. Just now, I'm light-headed! Does the color suit me?

OLD WOMAN. You'd better ask a man.

SHEN TE [*to the* OLD MAN]. Does the color suit me?

OLD MAN. You'd better ask your young friend.

SHEN TE. I'd like to have your opinion.

OLD MAN. It suits you, very well. But wear it this way: the dull side out.

[SHEN TE *pays up.*]

OLD WOMAN. If you decide you don't like it, you can exchange it. [*She pulls* SHEN TE *to one side.*] Has he got money?

SHEN TE [*with a laugh*]. Yang Sun? Oh, no.

OLD WOMAN. Then how're you going to pay your rent?

SHEN TE. I'd forgotten about that.

OLD WOMAN. And next Monday is the first of the month! Miss Shen Te, I've got something to say to you. After we [*indicating her husband*] got to know you, we had our doubts about that marriage ad. We thought it would be better if you'd let *us* help you. Out of our savings. We reckon we could lend you two hundred silver dollars. We don't need anything in writing—you could pledge us your tobacco stock.

SHEN TE. You're prepared to lend money to a person like me?

OLD WOMAN. It's folks like you that need it. We'd think twice about lending anything to your cousin.

OLD MAN [*coming up*]. All settled, my dear?

SHEN TE. I wish the gods could have heard what your wife was just saying, Mr. Ma. They're looking for good people who're happy—and helping me makes you happy because you know it was love that got me into difficulties!

[*The old couple smile knowingly at each other.*]

OLD MAN. And here's the money, Miss Shen Te.

[*He hands her an envelope.* SHEN TE *takes it. She bows. They bow back. They return to their shop.*]

SHEN TE [*holding up her envelope*]. Look, Wong, here's six month's rent! Don't you believe in miracles now? And how do you like my new shawl?

WONG. For the young fellow I saw you with in the park?

[SHEN TE *nods.*]

MRS. SHIN. Never mind all that. It's time you took a look at his hand!

SHEN TE. Have you hurt your hand?

MRS. SHIN. That barber smashed it with his hot curling iron. Right in front of our eyes.

SHEN TE [*shocked at herself*]. And I never noticed! We must get you to a doctor this minute or who knows what will happen?

UNEMPLOYED MAN. It's not a doctor he should see, it's a judge. He can ask for compensation. The barber's filthy rich.

WONG. You think I have a chance?

MRS. SHIN [*with relish*]. If it's really good and smashed. But is it?

WONG. I think so. It's very swollen. Could I get a pension?

MRS. SHIN. You'd need a witness.

WONG. Well, you all saw it. You could all testify.

[*He looks round. The* UNEMPLOYED MAN, *the* GRANDFATHER, *and the* SISTER-IN-LAW *are all sitting against the wall of the shop eating rice. Their concentration on eating is complete.*]

SHEN TE [*to* MRS. SHIN]. You saw it yourself.

MRS. SHIN. I want nothin' to do with the police. It's against my principles.

SHEN TE [*to* SISTER-IN-LAW]. What about you?

SISTER-IN-LAW. Me? I wasn't looking.

SHEN TE [*to the* GRANDFATHER, *coaxingly*]. Grandfather, *you'll* testify, won't you?

SISTER-IN-LAW. And a lot of good that will do. He's simple-minded.

SHEN TE [*to the* UNEMPLOYED MAN]. You seem to be the only witness left.

UNEMPLOYED MAN. My testimony would only hurt him. I've been picked up twice for begging.

SHEN TE. Your brother is assaulted, and you shut your eyes?

He is hit, cries out in pain, and you are silent?
The beast prowls, chooses and seizes his victim, and you say:
"Because we showed no displeasure, he has spared us."

If no one present will be a witness, I will. I'll say I saw it.

MRS. SHIN [*solemnly*]. The name for that is perjury.

WONG. I don't know if I can accept that. Though maybe I'll have to. [*Looking at his hand.*] Is it swollen enough, do you think? The swelling's not going down?

UNEMPLOYED MAN. No, no, the swelling's holding up well.

WONG. Yes. It's *more* swollen if anything. Maybe my wrist is broken after all. I'd better see a judge at once.

[*Holding his hand very carefully, and fixing his eyes on it, he runs off.* MRS. SHIN *goes quickly into the barber's shop.*]

UNEMPLOYED MAN [*seeing her*]. She is getting on the right side of Mr. Shu Fu.

SISTER-IN-LAW. You and I can't change the world, Shen Te.

SHEN TE. Go away! Go away all of you!

[*The* UNEMPLOYED MAN, *the* SISTER-IN-LAW, *and the* GRANDFATHER *stalk off, eating and sulking.*]

[*To the audience.*]

They've stopped answering

They stay put
They do as they're told
They don't care
Nothing can make them look up
But the smell of food.

[*Enter* MRS. YANG, YANG SUN'S *mother, out of breath.*]

MRS. YANG. Miss Shen Te. My son has told me everything. I am Mrs. Yang, Sun's mother. Just think. He's got an offer. Of a job as a pilot. A letter has just come. From the director of the airfield in Peking!

SHEN TE. So he can fly again? Isn't that wonderful!

MRS. YANG [*less breathlessly all the time*]. They won't give him the job for nothing. They want five hundred silver dollars.

SHEN TE. We can't let money stand in his way, Mrs. Yang!

MRS. YANG. If only you could help him out!

SHEN TE. I have the shop. I can try! [*She embraces* MRS. YANG.] I happen to have two hundred with me now. Take it. [*She gives her the old couple's money.*] It was a loan but they said I could repay it with my tobacco stock.

MRS. YANG. And they were calling Sun the Dead Pilot of Setzuan! A friend in need!

SHEN TE. We must find another three hundred.

MRS. YANG. How?

SHEN TE. Let me think. [*Slowly.*] I know someone who can help. I didn't want to call on his services again, he's hard and cunning. But a flyer must fly. And I'll make this the last time.

[*Distant sound of a plane.*]

MRS. YANG. If the man you mentioned can do it. . . . Oh, look, there's the morning mail plane, heading for Peking!

SHEN TE. The pilot can see us, let's wave!

[*They wave. The noise of the engine is louder.*]

MRS. YANG. You know that pilot up there?

SHEN TE. Wave, Mrs. Yang! I know the pilot who *will* be up there. He gave up hope. But he'll do it now. One man to raise himself above the misery, above us all.

[*To the audience.*]

Yang Sun, my lover:
Braving the storms
In company with the clouds
Crossing the heavens
And bringing to friends in far-away lands
The friendly mail!

SCENE IVA

In front of the inner curtain. Enter SHEN TE, *carrying* SHUI TA'S *mask. She sings.*

THE SONG OF DEFENSELESSNESS

In our country
A useful man needs luck

Only if he finds strong backers can he prove himself useful
The good can't defend themselves and
Even the gods are defenseless.

Oh, why don't the gods have their own ammunition
And launch against badness their own expedition
Enthroning the good and preventing sedition
And bringing the world to a peaceful condition?

Oh, why don't the gods do the buying and selling
Injustice forbidding, starvation dispelling
Give bread to each city and joy to each dwelling?
Oh, why don't the gods do the buying and selling?

[*She puts on* SHUI TA'S *mask and sings in his voice.*]

You can only help one of your luckless brothers
By trampling down a dozen others

Why is it the gods do not feel indignation
And come down in fury to end exploitation
Defeat all defeat and forbid desperation
Refusing to tolerate such toleration?

Why is it?

SCENE V

SHEN TE'S *tobacco shop. Behind the counter,* MR. SHUI TA, *reading the paper.* MRS. SHIN *is cleaning up. She talks and he takes no notice.*

MRS. SHIN. And when certain rumors get about, what *happens* to a little place like this? It goes to pot. *I* know. So, if you want my advice, Mr. Shui Ta, find out just what exactly has been going on between Miss Shen Te and that Yang Sun from Yellow Street. And remember: a certain interest in Miss Shen Te has been expressed by the barber next door, a man with twelve houses and only one wife, who, for that matter, is likely to drop off at any time. A certain interest has been expressed. [*She relishes the phrase.*] He was even inquiring about her means and, if *that* doesn't prove a man is getting serious, what would? [*Still getting no response, she leaves with her bucket.*]

YANG SUN'S VOICE. Is that Miss Shen Te's tobacco shop?

MRS. SHIN'S VOICE. Yes, it is, but it's Mr. Shui Ta who's here today.

[SHUI TA *runs to the looking glass with the short, light steps of* SHEN TE, *and is just about to start primping, when he realizes his mistake, and turns away, with a short laugh. Enter* YANG SUN. MRS. SHIN *enters behind him and slips into the back room to eavesdrop.*]

YANG SUN. I am Yang Sun.

[SHUI TA *bows*.]

Is Miss Shen Te in?

SHUI TA. No.

YANG SUN. I guess you know our relationship? [*He is inspecting the stock.*] Quite a place! And I thought she was just talking big. I'll be flying again, all right. [*He takes a cigar, solicits and receives a light from* SHUI TA.] You think we can squeeze the other three hundred out of the tobacco stock?

SHUI TA. May I ask if it is your intention to sell at once?

YANG SUN. It was decent of her to come out with the two hundred but they aren't much use with the other three hundred still missing.

SHUI TA. Shen Te was overhasty promising so much. She might have to sell the shop itself to raise it. Haste, they say, is the wind that blows the house down.

YANG SUN. Oh, she isn't a girl to keep a man waiting. For one thing or the other, if you take my meaning.

SHUI TA. I take your meaning.

YANG SUN [*leering*]. Uh, huh.

SHUI TA. Would you explain what the five hundred silver dollars are for?

YANG SUN. Trying to sound me out? Very well. The director of the Peking airfield is a friend of mine from flying school. I give him five hundred: he gets me the job.

SHUI TA. The price is high.

YANG SUN. Not as these things go. He'll have to fire one of the present pilots—for negligence. Only the man he has in mind isn't negligent. Not easy, you understand. You needn't mention that part of it to Shen Te.

SHUI TA [*looking intently at* YANG SUN]. Mr. Yang Sun, you are asking my cousin to give up her possessions, leave her friends, and place her entire fate in your hands. I presume you intend to marry her?

YANG SUN. I'd be prepared to.

[*Slight pause.*]

SHUI TA. Those two hundred silver dollars would pay the rent here for six months. If you were Shen Te wouldn't you be tempted to continue business?

YANG SUN. What? Can you imagine Yang Sun the Flyer behind a counter? [*In an oily voice.*] "A strong cigar or a mild one, worthy sir?" Not in this century!

SHUI TA. My cousin wishes to follow the promptings of her heart, and, from her own point of view, she may even have what is called the right to love. Accordingly, she has commissioned me to help you to this post. There is nothing here that I am not empowered to turn immediately into cash. Mrs. Mi Tzu, the landlady, will advise me about the sale.

[*Enter* MRS. MI TZU.]

MRS. MI TZU. Good morning, Mr. Shui Ta, you wish to see me about the rent? As you know it falls due the day after tomorrow.

SHUI TA. Circumstances have changed, Mrs. Mi Tzu: my cousin is getting married. Her future husband here, Mr. Yang Sun, will be taking her to Peking. I am interested in selling the tobacco stock.

MRS. MI TZU. How much are you asking, Mr. Shui Ta?

YANG SUN. Three hundred sil—

SHUI TA. Five hundred silver dollars.
MRS. MI TZU. How much did she pay for it, Mr. Shui Ta?
SHUI TA. A thousand. And very little has been sold.
MRS. MI TZU. She was robbed. But I'll make you a special offer if you'll promise to be out by the day after tomorrow. Three hundred silver dollars.
YANG SUN [*shrugging*]. Take it, man, take it.
SHUI TA. It is not enough.
YANG SUN. Why not? Why not? Certainly, it's enough.
SHUI TA [*to* MRS. MI TZU]. Excuse me. [*Takes* YANG SUN *on one side*.] The tobacco stock is pledged to the old couple who gave my cousin the two hundred.
YANG SUN. Is it in writing?
SHUI TA. No.
YANG SUN [*to* MRS. MI TZU]. Three hundred will do.
MRS. MI TZU. Of course, I need an assurance that Miss Shen Te is not in debt.
YANG SUN. Mr. Shui Ta?
SHUI TA. She is not in debt.
YANG SUN. When can you let us have the money?
MRS. MI TZU. The day after tomorrow. And remember: I'm doing this because I have a soft spot in my heart for young lovers! [*Exit*.]
YANG SUN [*calling after her*]. Boxes, jars and sacks—three hundred for the lot and the pain's over! [*To* SHUI TA.] Where else can we raise money by the day after tomorrow?
SHUI TA. Nowhere. Haven't you enough for the trip and the first few weeks?
YANG SUN. Oh, certainly.
SHUI TA. How much, exactly?
YANG SUN. Oh, I'll dig it up, if I have to steal it.
SHUI TA. I see.
YANG SUN. Well, don't fall off the roof. I'll get to Peking somehow.
SHUI TA. Two people can't travel for nothing.
YANG SUN [*not giving* SHUI TA *a chance to answer*]. I'm leaving *her* behind. No millstones around *my* neck!
SHUI TA. Oh.
YANG SUN. Don't look at me like that!
SHUI TA. How precisely is my cousin to live?
YANG SUN. Oh, you'll think of something.
SHUI TA. A small request, Mr. Yang Sun. Leave the two hundred silver dollars here until you can show me two tickets for Peking.
YANG SUN. You learn to mind your own business, Mr. Shui Ta.
SHUI TA. I'm afraid Miss Shen Te may not wish to sell the shop when she discovers that. . .
YANG SUN. You don't know women. She'll want to. Even then.
SHUI TA [*a slight outburst*]. She is a human being, sir! And not devoid of common sense!
YANG SUN. Shen Te is a woman: she *is* devoid of common sense. I only have to lay my hand on her shoulder, and church bells ring.

SHUI TA [*with difficulty*]. Mr. Yang Sun!

YANG SUN. Mr. Shui Whatever-it-is!

SHUI TA. My cousin is devoted to you . . . because. . .

YANG SUN. Because I have my hands on her breasts. Give me a cigar. [*He takes one for himself, stuffs a few more in his pocket, then changes his mind and takes the whole box.*] Tell her I'll marry her, then bring me the three hundred. Or let her bring it. One or the other. [*Exit.*]

MRS. SHIN [*sticking her head out of the back room*]. Well, he has your cousin under his thumb, and doesn't care if all Yellow Street knows it!

SHUI TA [*crying out*]. I've lost my shop! And he doesn't love me! [*He runs berserk through the room, repeating these lines incoherently. Then stops suddenly and addresses* MRS. SHIN.] Mrs. Shin, you grew up in the gutter, like me. Are we lacking in hardness? I doubt it. If you steal a penny from me, I'll take you by the throat till you spit it out! You'd do the same to me. The times are bad, this city is hell, but we're like ants, we keep coming, up and up the walls, however smooth! Till bad luck comes. Being in love, for instance. *One* weakness is enough, and love is the deadliest.

MRS. SHIN [*emerging from the back room*]. You should have a little talk with Mr. Shu Fu the Barber. He's a real gentleman and just the thing for your cousin. [*She runs off.*]

SHUI TA.

A caress becomes a stranglehold
A sigh of love turns to a cry of fear
Why are there vultures circling in the air?
A girl is going to meet her lover.

[SHUI TA *sits down and* MR. SHU FU *enters with* MRS. SHIN.]

Mr. Shu Fu?

SHU FU. Mr. Shui Ta.

[*They both bow.*]

SHUI TA. I am told that you have expressed a certain interest in my cousin Shen Te. Let me set aside all propriety and confess: she is at this moment in grave danger.

SHU FU. Oh, dear!

SHUI TA. She has lost her shop, Mr. Shu Fu.

SHU FU. The charm of Miss Shen Te, Mr. Shui Ta, derives from the goodness, not of her shop, but of her heart. Men call her the Angel of the Slums.

SHUI TA. Yet her goodness has cost her two hundred silver dollars in a single day: we must put a stop to it.

SHU FU. Permit me to differ, Mr. Shui Ta. Let us rather open wide the gates to such goodness! Every morning, with pleasure tinged by affection, I watch her charitable ministrations. For they are hungry, and she giveth them to eat! Four of them, to be precise. Why only four? I ask. Why not four hundred? I hear she has been seeking shelter for the homeless. What about my humble cabins behind the cattle run? They are at her disposal. And so forth. And so on. Mr. Shui Ta, do you think Miss Shen Te could be persuaded to listen to certain ideas of mine? Ideas like these?

SHUI TA. Mr. Shu Fu, she would be honored.

[*Enter* WONG *and the* POLICEMAN. MR. SHU FU *turns abruptly away and studies the shelves.*]

WONG. Is Miss Shen Te here?

SHUI TA. No.

WONG. I am Wong the Water Seller. You are Mr. Shui Ta?

SHUI TA. I am.

WONG. I am a friend of Shen Te's.

SHUI TA. An intimate friend, I hear.

WONG [*to the* POLICEMAN]. You see? [*To* SHUI TA.] It's because of my hand.

POLICEMAN. He hurt his hand, sir, that's a fact.

SHUI TA [*quickly*]. You need a sling, I see. [*He takes a shawl from the back room, and throws it to* WONG.]

WONG. But that's her new shawl!

SHUI TA. She has no more use for it.

WONG. But she bought it to please someone!

SHUI TA. It happens to be no longer necessary.

WONG [*making the sling*]. She is my only witness.

POLICEMAN. Mr. Shui Ta, your cousin is supposed to have seen the Barber hit the Water Seller with a curling iron.

SHUI TA. I'm afraid my cousin was not present at the time.

WONG. But she was, sir! Just ask her! Isn't she in?

SHUI TA [*gravely*]. Mr. Wong, my cousin has her own troubles. You wouldn't wish her to add to them by committing perjury?

WONG. But it was she that told me to go to the judge!

SHUI TA. Was the judge supposed to heal your hand?

[MR. SHU FU *turns quickly around.* SHUI TA *bows to* SHU FU, *and vice versa.*]

WONG [*taking the sling off, and putting it back*]. I see how it is.

POLICEMAN. Well, I'll be on my way. [*To* WONG.] And you be careful. If Mr. Shu Fu wasn't a man who tempers justice with mercy, as the saying is, you'd be in jail for libel. Be off with you!

[*Exit* WONG, *followed by* POLICEMAN.]

SHUI TA. Profound apologies, Mr. Shu Fu.

SHU FU. Not at all, Mr. Shui Ta. [*Pointing to the shawl.*] The episode is over?

SHUI TA. It may take her time to recover. There are some fresh wounds.

SHU FU. We shall be discreet. Delicate. A short vacation could be arranged. . .

SHUI TA. First, of course, you and she would have to talk things over.

SHU FU. At a small supper in a small, but high-class, restaurant.

SHUI TA. I'll go and find her. [*Exit into back room.*]

MRS. SHIN [*sticking her head in again*]. Time for congratulations, Mr. Shu Fu?

SHU FU. Ah, Mrs. Shin! Please inform Miss Shen Te's guests they may take shelter in the cabins behind the cattle run!

[MRS. SHIN *nods, grinning.*]

[*To the audience.*] Well? What do you think of me, ladies and gentlemen? What could a man do more? Could he be less selfish? More farsighted?

A small supper in a small but . . . Does that bring rather vulgar and clumsy thoughts into your mind? Ts, ts, ts. Nothing of the sort will occur. She won't even be touched. Not even accidentally while passing the salt. An exchange of ideas only. Over the flowers on the table—white chrysanthemums by the way [*he writes down a note of this*]—yes, over the white chrysanthemums, two young souls will . . . shall I say "find each other"? We shall NOT exploit the misfortune of others. Understanding? Yes. An offer of assistance? Certainly. But quietly. Almost inaudibly. Perhaps with a single glance. A glance that could also—mean more.

MRS. SHIN [*coming forward*]. Everything under control, Mr. Shu Fu?

SHU FU. Oh, Mrs. Shin, what do you know about this worthless rascal Yang Sun?

MRS. SHIN. Why, he's the most worthless rascal. . .

SHU FU. Is he really? You're sure? [*As she opens her mouth.*] From now on, he doesn't exist! Can't be found anywhere!

[*Enter* YANG SUN.]

YANG SUN. What's been going on here?

MRS. SHIN. Shall I call Mr. Shui Ta, Mr. Shu Fu? He wouldn't want strangers in here!

SHU FU. Mr. Shui Ta is in conference with Miss Shen Te. Not to be disturbed!

YANG SUN. Shen Te here? I didn't see her come in. What kind of conference?

SHU FU [*not letting him enter the back room*]. Patience, dear sir! And if by chance I have an inkling who you are, pray take note that Miss Shen Te and I are about to announce our engagement.

YANG SUN. What?

MRS. SHIN. You didn't expect that, did you?

[YANG SUN *is trying to push past the barber into the back room when* SHEN TE *comes out.*]

SHU FU. My dear Shen Te, ten thousand apologies! Perhaps you. . .

YANG SUN. What is it, Shen Te? Have you gone crazy?

SHEN TE [*breathless*]. My cousin and Mr. Shu Fu have come to an understanding. They wish me to hear Mr. Shu Fu's plans for helping the poor.

YANG SUN. Your cousin wants to part us.

SHEN TE. Yes.

YANG SUN. And you've agreed to it?

SHEN TE. Yes.

YANG SUN. They told you I was bad.

[SHEN TE *is silent.*]

And suppose I am. Does that make me need you less? I'm low. Shen Te, I have no money, I don't do the right thing but at least I put up a fight! [*He is near her now, and speaks in an undertone.*] Have you no eyes? Look at him. Have you forgotten already?

SHEN TE. No.

YANG SUN. How it was raining?

SHEN TE. No.

YANG SUN. How you cut me down from the willow tree? Bought me water? Promised me money to fly with?

SHEN TE [*shakily*]. Yang Sun, what do you want?

YANG SUN. I want you to come with me.

SHEN TE [*in a small voice*]. Forgive me, Mr. Shu Fu, I want to go with Mr. Yang Sun.

YANG SUN. We're lovers you know. Give me the key to the shop.

[SHEN TE *takes the key from around her neck.* YANG SUN *puts it on the counter. To* MRS. SHIN.]

Leave it under the mat when you're through. Let's go, Shen Te.

SHU FU. But this is rape! Mr. Shui Ta!!

YANG SUN [*to* SHEN TE]. Tell him not to shout.

SHEN TE. Please don't shout for my cousin, Mr. Shu Fu. He doesn't agree with me, I know, but he's wrong. [*To the audience.*]

I want to go with the man I love
I don't want to count the cost
I don't want to consider if it's wise
I don't want to know if he loves me
I want to go with the man I love.

YANG SUN. That's the spirit.

[*And the couple leave.*]

SCENE VA

In front of the inner curtain. SHEN TE *in her wedding clothes, on the way to her wedding.*

SHEN TE. Something terrible has happened. As I left the shop with Yang Sun, I found the old carpet dealer's wife waiting in the street, trembling all over. She told me her husband has taken to his bed—sick with all the worry and excitement over the two hundred silver dollars they lent me. She said it would be best if I gave it back now. Of course, I had to say I would. She said she couldn't quite trust my cousin Shui Ta or even my fiancé Yang Sun. There were tears in her eyes. With my emotions in an uproar, I threw myself into Yang Sun's arms, I couldn't resist him. The things he'd said to Shui Ta had taught Shen Te nothing. Sinking into his arms, I said to myself:

To let no one perish, not even oneself
To fill everyone with happiness, even oneself
Is so good

How could I have forgotten those two old people? Yang Sun swept me away like a small hurricane. But he's not a bad man, and he loves me. He'd rather work in the cement factory than owe his flying to a crime. Though, of course, flying *is* a great passion with Sun. Now, on the way to my wedding, I waver between fear and joy.

SCENE VI

The "private dining room" on the upper floor of a cheap restaurant in a poor section of town. With SHEN TE: *the* GRANDFATHER, *the* SISTER-IN-LAW, *the* NIECE, MRS. SHIN, *the* UNEMPLOYED MAN. *In a corner, alone, a* PRIEST. *A* WAITER *pouring wine. Downstage,* YANG SUN *talking to his mother. He wears a dinner jacket.*

YANG SUN. Bad news, Mamma. She came right out and told me she can't sell the shop for me. Some idiot is bringing a claim because he lent her the two hundred she gave you.

MRS. YANG. What did *you* say? Of course, you can't marry her now.

YANG SUN. It's no use saying anything to *her*. I've sent for her cousin, Mr. Shui Ta. He said there was nothing in writing.

MRS. YANG. Good idea. I'll go out and look for him. Keep an eye on things.

[*Exit* MRS. YANG. SHEN TE *has been pouring wine.*]

SHEN TE [*to the audience, pitcher in hand*]. I wasn't mistaken in him. He's bearing up well. Though it must have been an awful blow—giving up flying. I do love him so. [*Calling across the room to him.*] Sun, you haven't drunk a toast with the bride!

YANG SUN. What do we drink to?

SHEN TE. Why, to the future!

YANG SUN. When the bridegroom's dinner jacket won't be a hired one!

SHEN TE. But when the bride's dress will still get rained on sometimes!

YANG SUN. To everything we ever wished for!

SHEN TE. May all our dreams come true!

[*They drink.*]

YANG SUN [*with loud conviviality*]. And now, friends, before the wedding gets under way, I have to ask the bride a few questions. I've no idea what kind of a wife she'll make, and it worries me. [*Wheeling on* SHEN TE.] For example. Can you make five cups of tea with three tea leaves?

SHEN TE. No.

YANG SUN. So I won't be getting very much tea. Can you sleep on a straw mattress the size of that book? [*He points to the large volume the* PRIEST *is reading.*]

SHEN TE. The two of us?

YANG SUN. The one of you.

SHEN TE. In that case, no.

YANG SUN. What a wife! I'm shocked!

[*While the audience is laughing, his mother returns. With a shrug of her shoulders, she tells* YANG SUN *the expected guest hasn't arrived. The* PRIEST *shuts the book with a bang, and makes for the door.*]

MRS. YANG. Where are *you* off to? It's only a matter of minutes.

PRIEST [*watch in hand*]. Time goes on, Mrs. Yang, and I've another wedding to attend to. Also a funeral.

MRS. YANG [*irately*]. D'you think we planned it this way? I was hoping to manage with one pitcher of wine, and we've run through two already.

[*Points to empty pitcher. Loudly.*] My dear Shen Te, I don't know where your cousin can be keeping himself!

SHEN TE. My cousin?

MRS. YANG. Certainly. I'm old fashioned enough to think such a close relative should attend the wedding.

SHEN TE. Oh, Sun, is it the three hundred silver dollars?

YANG SUN [*not looking her in the eye*]. Are you deaf? Mother says she's old fashioned. And I say I'm considerate. We'll wait another fifteen minutes.

HUSBAND. Another fifteen minutes.

MRS. YANG [*addressing the company*]. Now you all know, don't you, that my son is getting a job as a mail pilot?

SISTER-IN-LAW. In Peking, too, isn't it?

MRS. YANG. In Peking, too! The two of us are moving to Peking!

SHEN TE. Sun, tell your mother Peking is out of the question now.

YANG SUN. Your cousin'll tell her. If he agrees. I don't agree.

SHEN TE [*amazed, and dismayed*]. Sun!

YANG SUN. I hate this godforsaken Setzuan. What people! Know what they look like when I half close my eyes? Horses! Whinnying, fretting, stamping, screwing their necks up! [*Loudly.*] And what is it the thunder says? They are su-per-flu-ous! [*He hammers out the syllables.*] They've run their last race! They can go trample themselves to death! [*Pause.*] I've got to get out of here.

SHEN TE. But I've promised the money to the old couple.

YANG SUN. And since you always do the wrong thing, it's lucky your cousin's coming. Have another drink.

SHEN TE [*quietly*]. My cousin can't be coming.

YANG SUN. How d'you mean?

SHEN TE. My cousin can't be where I am.

YANG SUN. Quite a conundrum!

SHEN TE [*desperately*]. Sun, I'm the one that loves you. Not my cousin. He was thinking of the job in Peking when he promised you the old couple's money—

YANG SUN. Right. And that's why he's bringing the three hundred silver dollars. Here—to my wedding.

SHEN TE. He is not bringing the three hundred silver dollars.

YANG SUN. Huh? What makes you think that?

SHEN TE [*looking into his eyes*]. He says you only bought one ticket to Peking.

[*Short pause.*]

YANG SUN. That was yesterday. [*He pulls two tickets part way out of his inside pocket, making her look under his coat.*] Two tickets. I don't want Mother to know. She'll get left behind. I sold her furniture to buy these tickets, so you see. . .

SHEN TE. But what's to become of the old couple?

YANG SUN. What's to become of me? Have another drink. Or do you believe in moderation? If I drink, I fly again. And if you drink, you may learn to understand me.

SHEN TE. You want to fly. But I can't help you.

YANG SUN. "Here's a plane, my darling—but it's only got one wing!"

[*The* WAITER *enters.*]

WAITER. Mrs. Yang! Mrs. Yang!

MRS. YANG. Yes?

WAITER. Another pitcher of wine, ma'am?

MRS. YANG. We have enough, thanks. Drinking makes me sweat.

WAITER. Would you mind paying, ma'am?

MRS. YANG [*to everyone*]. Just be patient a few moments longer, everyone, Mr. Shui Ta is on his way over! [*To the* WAITER.] Don't be a spoilsport.

WAITER. I can't let you leave till you've paid your bill, ma'am.

MRS. YANG. But they know me here.

WAITER. That's just it.

PRIEST [*ponderously getting up*]. I humbly take my leave. [*And he does.*]

MRS. YANG [*to the others, desperately*]. Stay where you are, everybody! The priest says he'll be back in two minutes!

YANG SUN. It's no good, Mamma. Ladies and gentlemen, Mr. Shui Ta still hasn't arrived and the priest has gone home. We won't detain you any longer.

[*They are leaving now.*]

GRANDFATHER [*in the doorway, having forgotten to put his glass down*]. To the bride! [*He drinks, puts down the glass, and follows the others.*]

[*Pause.*]

SHEN TE. Shall I go too?

YANG SUN. You? Aren't you the bride? Isn't this your wedding? [*He drags her across the room, tearing her wedding dress.*] If we can wait, you can wait. Mother calls me her falcon. She wants to see me in the clouds. But I think it may be St. Nevercome's Day before she'll go to the door and see my plane thunder by. [*Pause. He pretends the guests are still present.*] Why such a lull in the conversation, ladies and gentlemen? Don't you like it here? The ceremony is only slightly postponed—because an important guest is expected at any moment. Also because the bride doesn't know what love is. While we're waiting, the bridegroom will sing a little song. [*He does so.*]

THE SONG OF ST. NEVERCOME'S DAY

On a certain day, as is generally known,
    One and all will be shouting: Hooray, hooray!
For the beggar maid's son has a solid-gold throne
    And the day is St. Nevercome's Day
On St. Nevercome's, Nevercome's, Nevercome's Day
He'll sit on his solid-gold throne

Oh, hooray, hooray! That day goodness will pay!
    That day badness will cost you your head!
And merit and money will smile and be funny
    While exchanging salt and bread
On St. Nevercome's, Nevercome's, Nevercome's Day
    While exchanging salt and bread

And the grass, oh, the grass will look down at the sky
    And the pebbles will roll up the stream

And all men will be good without batting an eye
They will make of our earth a dream
On St. Nevercome's, Nevercome's, Nevercome's Day
They will make of our earth a dream

And as for me, that's the day I shall be
A flyer and one of the best
Unemployed man, you will have work to do
Washerwoman, you'll get your rest
On St. Nevercome's, Nevercome's, Nevercome's Day
Washerwoman, you'll get your rest

MRS. YANG. It looks like he's not coming.

[*The three of them sit looking at the door.*]

SCENE VIA

WONG'S *den. The sewer pipe is again transparent and again the* GODS *appear to* WONG *in a dream.*

WONG. I'm so glad you've come, illustrious ones. It's Shen Te. She's in great trouble from following the rule about loving thy neighbor. Perhaps she's *too* good for this world!

FIRST GOD. Nonsense! You are eaten up by lice and doubts!

WONG. Forgive me, illustrious one, I only meant you might deign to intervene.

FIRST GOD. Out of the question! My colleague here intervened in some squabble or other only yesterday. [*He points to the* THIRD GOD *who has a black eye.*] The results are before us!

WONG. She had to call on her cousin again. But not even he could help. I'm afraid the shop is done for.

THIRD GOD [*a little concerned*]. Perhaps we should help after all?

FIRST GOD. The gods help those that help themselves.

WONG. What if we *can't* help ourselves, illustrious ones?

[*Slight pause.*]

SECOND GOD. Try, anyway! Suffering ennobles!

FIRST GOD. Our faith in Shen Te is unshaken!

THIRD GOD. We certainly haven't found any *other* good people. You can see where we spend our nights from the straw on our clothes.

WONG. You might help her find her way by—

FIRST GOD. The good man finds his own way here below!

SECOND GOD. The good woman too.

FIRST GOD. The heavier the burden, the greater her strength!

THIRD GOD. We're only onlookers, you know.

FIRST GOD. And everything will be all right in the end, O ye of little faith!

[*They are gradually disappearing through these last lines.*]

SCENE VII

The yard behind SHEN TE'S *shop. A few articles of furniture on a car.* SHEN TE *and* MRS. SHIN *are taking the washing off the line.*

MRS. SHIN. If you ask me, you should fight tooth and nail to keep the shop.

SHEN TE. How can I? I have to sell the tobacco to pay back the two hundred silver dollars today.

MRS. SHIN. No husband, no tobacco, no house and home! What are you going to live on?

SHEN TE. I can work. I can sort tobacco.

MRS. SHIN. Hey, look, Mr. Shui Ta's trousers! He must have left here stark naked!

SHEN TE. Oh, he may have another pair, Mrs. Shin.

MRS. SHIN. But if he's gone for good as you say, why has he left his pants behind?

SHEN TE. Maybe he's thrown them away.

MRS. SHIN. Can I take them?

SHEN TE. Oh, no.

[*Enter* MR. SHU FU, *running.*]

SHU FU. Not a word! Total silence! I know all. You have sacrificed your own love and happiness so as not to hurt a dear old couple who had put their trust in you! Not in vain does this district—for all its malevolent tongues!—call you the Angel of the Slums! That young man couldn't rise to your level, so you left him. And now, when I see you closing up the little shop, that veritable haven of rest for the multitude, well, I cannot, I cannot let it pass. Morning after morning I have stood watching in the doorway not unmoved—while you graciously handed out rice to the wretched. Is that never to happen again? Is the good woman of Setzuan to disappear? If only you would allow *me* to assist you! Now don't say anything! No assurances, no exclamations of gratitude! [*He has taken out his check book.*] Here! A blank check. [*He places it on the cart.*] Just my signature. Fill it out as you wish. Any sum in the world. I herewith retire from the scene, quietly, unobtrusively, making no claims, on tiptoe, full of veneration, absolutely selflessly . . . [*He has gone.*]

MRS. SHIN. Well! You're saved. There's always some idiot of a man . . . Now hurry! Put down a thousand silver dollars and let me fly to the bank before he comes to his senses.

SHEN TE. I can pay you for the washing without any check.

MRS. SHIN. What? You're not going to cash it just because you might have to marry him? Are you crazy? Men like him *want* to be led by the nose! Are you still thinking of that flyer? All Yellow Street knows how he treated you!

SHEN TE.

When I heard his cunning laugh, I was afraid
But when I saw the holes in his shoes, I loved him dearly.

MRS. SHIN. Defending that good for nothing after all that's happened!

SHEN TE [*staggering as she holds some of the washing*]. Oh!

MRS. SHIN [*taking the washing from her, dryly*]. So you feel dizzy when you stretch and bend? There couldn't be a little visitor on the way? If that's it, you can forget Mr. Shu Fu's blank check: it wasn't meant for a christening present!

[*She goes to the back with a basket.* SHEN TE'S *eyes follow* MRS. SHIN *for a moment. Then she looks down at her own body, feels her stomach, and a great joy comes into her eyes.*]

SHEN TE. O joy! A new human being is on the way. The world awaits him. In the cities the people say: he's got to be reckoned with, this new human being! [*She imagines a little boy to be present, and introduces him to the audience.*]

This is my son, the well-known flyer!
Say: Welcome
To the conqueror of unknown mountains and unreachable regions
Who brings us our mail across the impassable deserts!

[*She leads him up and down by the hand.*]

Take a look at the world, my son. That's a tree. Tree, yes. Say: "Hello, tree!" And bow. Like this. [*She bows.*] Now you know each other. And, look, here comes the Water Seller. He's a friend, give him your hand. A cup of fresh water for my little son, please. Yes, it *is* a warm day. [*Handing the cup.*] Oh dear, a policeman, we'll have to make a circle round *him.* Perhaps we can pick a few cherries over there in the rich Mr. Pung's garden. But we mustn't be seen. You want cherries? Just like children with fathers. No, no, you can't go straight at them like that. Don't pull. We must learn to be reasonable. Well, have it your own way. [*She has let him make for the cherries.*] Can you reach? Where to put them? Your mouth is the best place. [*She tries one herself.*] Mmm, they're good. But the policeman, we must run! [*They run.*] Yes, back to the street. Calm now, so no one will notice us. [*Walking the street with her child, she sings.*]

Once a plum—'twas in Japan—
Made a conquest of a man
But the man's turn soon did come
For he gobbled up the plum

[*Enter* WONG, *with a* CHILD *by the hand. He coughs.*]

SHEN TE. Wong!

WONG. It's about the Carpenter, Shen Te. He's lost his shop, and he's been drinking. His children are on the streets. This is one. Can you help?

SHEN TE [*to the child*]. Come here, little man. [*Takes him down to the footlights. To the audience.*]

You there! A man is asking you for shelter!
A man of tomorrow says: what about today?
His friend the conqueror, whom you know,
Is his advocate!

[*To* WONG.] He can live in Mr. Shu Fu's cabin. I may have to go there myself. I'm going to have a baby. That's a secret—don't tell Yang Sun—we'd only be in his way. Can you find the Carpenter for me?

WONG. I knew you'd think of something. [*To the* CHILD.] Goodbye, son, I'm going for your father.

Shen Te. What about your hand, Wong? I wanted to help, but my cousin . . .

Wong. Oh, I can get along with one hand, don't worry. [*He shows how he can handle his pole with his left hand alone.*]

Shen Te. But your right hand! Look, take this cart, sell everything that's on it, and go to the doctor with the money . . .

Wong. She's still good. But first I'll bring the Carpenter. I'll pick up the cart when I get back. [*Exit* Wong.]

Shen Te [*to the* Child]. Sit down over here, son, till your father comes.

[*The* Child *sits crosslegged on the ground. Enter the* Husband *and* Wife, *each dragging a large, full sack.*]

Wife [*furtively*]. You're alone, Shen Te, dear?

[Shen Te *nods. The* Wife *beckons to the* Nephew *offstage. He comes on with another sack.*]

Your cousin's away?

[Shen Te *nods.*]

He's not coming back?

Shen Te. No. I'm giving up the shop.

Wife. That's why we're here. We want to know if we can leave these things in your new home. Will you do us this favor?

Shen Te. Why, yes, I'd be glad to.

Husband [*cryptically*]. And if anyone asks about them, say they're yours.

Shen Te. Would anyone ask?

Wife [*with a glance back at her* Husband]. Oh, someone might. The police, for instance. They don't seem to like us. Where can we put it?

Shen Te. Well, I'd rather not get in any more trouble . . .

Wife. Listen to her! The good woman of Setzuan!

[Shen Te *is silent.*]

Husband. There's enough tobacco in those sacks to give us a new start in life. We could have our own tobacco factory!

Shen Te [*slowly*]. You'll have to put them in the back room.

[*The sacks are taken offstage, while the* Child *is left alone. Shyly glancing about him, he goes to the garbage can, starts playing with the contents, and eating some of the scraps. The others return.*]

Wife. We're counting on you, Shen Te!

Shen Te. Yes. [*She sees the* Child *and is shocked.*]

Husband. We'll see you in Mr. Shu Fu's cabins.

Nephew. The day after tomorrow.

Shen Te. Yes. Now, go. Go! I'm not feeling well.

[*Exeunt all three, virtually pushed off.*]

He is eating the refuse in the garbage can!
Only look at his little gray mouth!

[*Pause. Music.*]

As this is the world *my* son will enter
I will study to defend him.
To be good to you, my son,

I shall be a tigress to all others
If I have to.
And I shall have to.
[*She starts to go.*] One more time, then. I hope really the last.

[*Exit* SHEN TE, *taking* SHUI TA'S *trousers.* MRS. SHIN *enters and watches her with marked interest. Enter the* SISTER-IN-LAW *and the* GRANDFATHER.]

SISTER-IN-LAW. So it's true, the shop has closed down. And the furniture's in the back yard. It's the end of the road!

MRS. SHIN [*pompously*]. The fruit of high living, selfishness, and sensuality! Down the primrose path to Mr. Shu Fu's cabins—with you!

SISTER-IN-LAW. Cabins? Rat holes! He gave them to us because his soap supplies only went mouldy there!

[*Enter the* UNEMPLOYED MAN.]

UNEMPLOYED MAN. Shen Te is moving?

SISTER-IN-LAW. Yes. She was sneaking away.

MRS. SHIN. She's ashamed of herself, and no wonder!

UNEMPLOYED MAN. Tell her to call Mr. Shui Ta or she's done for this time!

SISTER-IN-LAW. Tell her to call Mr. Shui Ta or *we're* done for this time.

[*Enter* WONG *and* CARPENTER, *the latter with a* CHILD *on each hand.*]

CARPENTER. So we'll have a roof over our heads for a change!

MRS. SHIN. Roof? Whose roof?

CARPENTER. Mr. Shu Fu's cabins. And we have little Feng to thank for it. [FENG, *we find, is the name of the child already there; his* FATHER *now takes him. To the other two.*] Bow to your little brother, you two! [*The* CARPENTER *and the two new arrivals bow to* FENG.]

[*Enter* SHUI TA.]

UNEMPLOYED MAN. Sst! Mr. Shui Ta!

[*Pause.*]

SHUI TA. And what is this crowd here for, may I ask?

WONG. How do you do, Mr. Shui Ta? This is the Carpenter. Miss Shen Te promised him space in Mr. Shu Fu's cabins.

SHUI TA. That will not be possible.

CARPENTER. We can't go there after all?

SHUI TA. All the space is needed for other purposes.

SISTER-IN-LAW. You mean we have to get out? But we've got nowhere to go.

SHUI TA. Miss Shen Te finds it possible to provide employment. If the proposition interests you, you may stay in the cabins.

SISTER-IN-LAW [*with distaste*]. You mean *work?* Work for Miss Shen Te?

SHUI TA. Making tobacco, yes. There are three bales here already. Would you like to get them?

SISTER-IN-LAW [*trying to bluster*]. We have our own tobacco! We were in the tobacco business before you were born!

SHUI TA [*to the* CARPENTER *and the* UNEMPLOYED MAN]. You *don't* have your own tobacco. What about you?

[*The* CARPENTER *and the* UNEMPLOYED

MAN *get the point, and go for the sacks. Enter* MRS. MI TZU.]

MRS. MI TZU. Mr. Shui Ta? I've brought you your three hundred silver dollars.

SHUI TA. I'll sign your lease instead. I've decided not to sell.

MRS. MI TZU. What? You don't need the money for that flyer?

SHUI TA. No.

MRS. MI TZU. And you can pay six months' rent?

SHUI TA [*takes the barber's blank check from the cart and fills it out*]. Here is a check for ten thousand silver dollars. On Mr. Shu Fu's account. Look! [*He shows her the signature on the check.*] Your six months' rent will be in your hands by seven this evening. And now, if you'll excuse me.

MRS. MI TZU. So it's Mr. Shu Fu now. The flyer has been given his walking papers. These modern girls! In my day they'd have said she was flighty. That poor, deserted Mr. Yang Sun!

[*Exit* MRS. MI TZU. *The* CARPENTER *and the* UNEMPLOYED MAN *drag the three sacks back on the stage.*]

CARPENTER [*to* SHUI TA]. I don't know why I'm doing this for you.

SHUI TA. Perhaps your children want to eat, Mr. Carpenter.

SISTER-IN-LAW [*catching sight of the sacks*]. Was my brother-in-law here?

MRS. SHIN. Yes, he was.

SISTER-IN-LAW. I thought as much. I know those sacks! That's our tobacco!

SHUI TA. Really? I thought it came from my back room! Shall we consult the police on the point?

SISTER-IN-LAW [*defeated*]. No.

SHUI TA. Perhaps you will show me the way to Mr. Shu Fu's cabins?

[SHUI TA *goes off, followed by the* CARPENTER *and his two older children, the* SISTER-IN-LAW, *the* GRANDFATHER, *and the* UNEMPLOYED MAN. *Each of the last three drags a sack. Enter* OLD MAN *and* OLD WOMAN.]

MRS. SHIN. A pair of pants—missing from the clothes line one minute—and next minute on the honorable backside of Mr. Shui Ta!

OLD WOMAN. We thought Miss Shen Te was here.

MRS. SHIN [*preoccupied*]. Well, she's not.

OLD MAN. There was something she was going to give us.

WONG. She was going to help me too. [*Looking at his hand.*] It'll be too late soon. But she'll be back. This cousin has never stayed long.

MRS. SHIN [*approaching a conclusion*]. No, he hasn't, has he?

SCENE VIIA

The sewer pipe. WONG *asleep. In his dream, he tells the* GODS *his fears. The* GODS *seem tired from all their travels. They stop for a moment and look over their shoulders at the Water Seller.*

WONG. Illustrious ones, I've been having a bad dream. Our beloved Shen Te was in great distress in the rushes down by the river—the spot where the bodies of suicides are washed up. She kept staggering and holding her head down as if she was carrying something and it was dragging her down into the mud. When I called out to her, she said she had to take your Book of Rules to the other side, and not get it wet, or the ink would all come off. You had talked to her about the virtues, you know, the time she gave you shelter in Setzuan.

THIRD GOD. Well, but what do you suggest, my dear Wong?

WONG. Maybe a little relaxation of the rules, Benevolent One, in view of the bad times.

THIRD GOD. As for instance?

WONG. Well, um, good-will, for instance, might do instead of love?

THIRD GOD. I'm afraid that would create new problems.

WONG. Or, instead of justice, good sportsmanship?

THIRD GOD. That would only mean more work.

WONG. Instead of honor, outward propriety?

THIRD GOD. Still more work! No, no! The rules will have to stand, my dear Wong!

[*Wearily shaking their heads, all three journey on.*]

SCENE VIII

SHUI TA's *tobacco factory in* SHU FU's *cabins. Huddled together behind bars, several families, mostly women and children. Among these people the* SISTER-IN-LAW, *the* GRANDFATHER, *the* CARPENTER, *and his three children. Enter* MRS. YANG *followed by* YANG SUN.

MRS. YANG [*to the audience*]. There's something I just *have* to tell you: strength and wisdom are wonderful things. The strong and wise Mr. Shui Ta has transformed my son from a dissipated good-for-nothing into a model citizen. As you may have heard, Mr. Shui Ta opened a small tobacco factory near the cattle runs. It flourished. Three months ago—I shall never forget it—I asked for an appointment, and Mr. Shui Ta agreed to see us—me and my son. I can see him now as he came through the door to meet us . . .

[*Enter* SHUI TA, *from a door.*]

SHUI TA. What can I do for you, Mrs. Yang?

MRS. YANG. This morning the police came to the house. We find you've brought an action for breach of promise of marriage. In the name of Shen Te. You also claim that Sun came by two hundred silver dollars by improper means.

SHUI TA. That is correct.

MRS. YANG. Mr. Shui Ta, the money's all gone. When the Peking job didn't materialize, he ran through it all in three days. I know he's a good-for-nothing. He sold my furniture. He was moving to Peking without me. Miss Shen Te thought highly of him at one time.

SHUI TA. What do *you* say, Mr. Yang Sun?

YANG SUN. The money's gone.

SHUI TA [*to* MRS. YANG]. Mrs. Yang, in consideration of my cousin's incomprehensible weakness for your son, I am prepared to give him another chance. He can have a job—here. The two hundred silver dollars will be taken out of his wages.

YANG SUN. So it's the factory or jail?

SHUI TA. Take your choice.

YANG SUN. May I speak with Shen Te?

SHUI TA. You may not.

[*Pause.*]

YANG SUN [*sullenly*]. Show me where to go.

MRS. YANG. Mr. Shui Ta, you are kindness itself: the gods will reward you! [*To* YANG SUN.] And honest work will make a man of you, my boy.

[YANG SUN *follows* SHUI TA *into the factory.* MRS. YANG *comes down again to the footlights.*]

Actually, honest work didn't agree with him—at first. And he got no opportunity to distinguish himself till—in the third week—when the wages were being paid. . . .

[SHUI TA *has a bag of money. Standing next to his foreman—the former* UNEMPLOYED MAN—*he counts out the wages. It is* YANG SUN'S *turn.*]

UNEMPLOYED MAN [*reading*]. Carpenter, six silver dollars. Yang Sun, six silver dollars.

YANG SUN [*quietly*]. Excuse me, sir. I don't think it can be more than five. May I see? [*He takes the foreman's list.*] It says six working days. But that's a mistake, sir. I took a day off for court business. And I won't take what I haven't earned, however miserable the pay is!

UNEMPLOYED MAN. Yang Sun. Five silver dollars. [*To* SHUI TA.] A rare case, Mr. Shui Ta!

SHUI TA. How is it the book says six when it should say five?

UNEMPLOYED MAN. I must've made a mistake, Mr. Shui Ta. [*With a look at* YANG SUN.] It won't happen again.

SHUI TA [*taking* YANG SUN *aside*]. You don't hold back, do you? You give your all to the firm. You're even honest. Do the foreman's mistakes always favor the workers?

YANG SUN. He does have . . . friends.

SHUI TA. Thank you. May I offer you any little recompense?

YANG SUN. Give me a trial period of one week, and I'll prove my intelligence is worth more to you than my strength.

MRS. YANG SUN [*still down at the footlights*]. Fighting words, fighting words! That evening, I said to Sun: "If you're a flyer, then fly, my falcon! Rise in the world!" And he got to be foreman. Yes, in Mr. Shui Ta's tobacco factory, he worked real miracles.

[*We see* YANG SUN *with his legs apart standing behind the workers who are handing along a basket of raw tobacco above their heads.*]

YANG SUN. Faster! Faster! You, there, d'you think you can just stand around now you're not foreman any more? It'll be your job to lead us in song. Sing!

[UNEMPLOYED MAN *starts singing. The others join in the refrain.*]

SONG OF THE EIGHTH ELEPHANT

Chang had seven elephants—all much the same—
But then there was Little Brother
The seven, they were wild, Little Brother, he was tame
And to guard them Chang chose Little Brother
Run faster!
Mr. Chang has a forest park
Which must be cleared before tonight
And already it's growing dark!

When the seven elephants cleared that forest park
Mr. Chang rode high on Little Brother
While the seven toiled and moiled till dark
On his big behind sat Little Brother
Dig faster!
Mr. Chang has a forest park
Which must be cleared before tonight
And already it's growing dark!

And the seven elephants worked many an hour
Till none of them could work another
Old Chang, he looked sour, on the seven, he did glower
But gave a pound of rice to Little Brother
What was that?
Mr. Chang has a forest park
Which must be cleared before tonight
And already it's growing dark!

And the seven elephants hadn't any tusks
The one that had the tusks was Little Brother!
Seven are no match for one, if the one has a gun!
How old Chang did laugh at Little Brother!
Keep on digging!
Mr. Chang has a forest park
Which must be cleared before tonight
And already it's growing dark!

[*Smoking a cigar,* SHUI TA *strolls by.* YANG SUN, *laughing, has joined in the refrain of the third stanza and speeded up the tempo of the last stanza by clapping his hands.*]

MRS. YANG. And that's why I say: strength and wisdom are wonderful things. It took the strong and wise Mr. Shui Ta to bring out the best in Yang Sun. A real superior man is like a bell. If you ring it, it rings, and if you don't, it don't, as the saying is.

SCENE IX

SHEN TE'S *shop, now an office with club chairs and fine carpets. It is raining.* SHUI TA, *now fat, is just dismissing the* OLD MAN *and* OLD WOMAN. MRS. SHIN, *in obviously new clothes, looks on, smirking.*

SHUI TA. No! I can NOT tell you when we expect her back.

OLD WOMAN. The two hundred silver dollars came today. In an envelope. There was no letter, but it must be from Shen Te. We want to write and thank her. May we have her address?

SHUI TA. I'm afraid I haven't got it.

OLD MAN [*pulling* OLD WOMAN'S *sleeve*]. Let's be going.

OLD WOMAN. She's got to come back some time! [*They move off, uncertainly, worried.* SHUI TA *bows.*]

MRS. SHIN. They lost the carpet shop because they couldn't pay their taxes. The money arrived too late.

SHUI TA. They could have come to me.

MRS. SHIN. People don't like coming to you.

SHUI TA [*sits suddenly, one hand to his head*]. I'm dizzy.

MRS. SHIN. After all, you *are* in your seventh month. But old Mrs. Shin will be there in your hour of trial! [*She cackles feebly.*]

SHUI TA [*in a satisfied voice*]. Can I count on that?

MRS. SHIN. We all have our price, and mine won't be too high for the great Mr. Shui Ta! [*She opens* SHUI TA'S *collar.*]

SHUI TA. It's for the child's sake. All of this.

MRS. SHIN. "All for the child," of course.

SHUI TA. I'm so fat. People must notice.

MRS. SHIN. Oh no, they think it's 'cause you're rich.

SHUI TA [*more feelingly*]. What will happen to the child?

MRS. SHIN. You ask that nine times a day. Why, it'll have the best that money can buy!

SHUI TA. He must never see Shui Ta.

MRS. SHIN. Oh, no. Always Shen Te.

SHUI TA. What about the neighbors? There are rumors, aren't there?

MRS. SHIN. As long as Mr. Shu Fu doesn't find out, there's nothing to worry about. Drink this.

[*Enter* YANG SUN *in a smart business suit, and carrying a businessman's brief case.* SHUI TA *is more or less in* MRS. SHIN'S *arms.*]

YANG SUN [*surprised*]. I seem to be in the way.

SHUI TA [*ignoring this, rises with an effort*]. Till tomorrow, Mrs. Shin.

[MRS. SHIN *leaves with a smile, putting her new gloves on.*]

YANG SUN. Gloves now! She couldn't be fleecing you? And since when did *you* have a private life? [*Taking a paper from the brief case.*] You haven't been at your best lately, and things are getting out of hand. The police want to close us down. They say that at the most they can only permit twice the lawful number of workers.

SHUI TA [*evasively*]. The cabins are quite good enough.

YANG SUN. For the workers maybe, not for the tobacco. They're too damp. We must take over some of Mrs. Mi Tzu's buildings.

SHUI TA. Her price is double what I can pay.

YANG SUN. Not unconditionally. If she has me to stroke her knees she'll come down.

SHUI TA. I'll never agree to that.

YANG SUN. What's wrong? Is it the rain? You get so irritable whenever it rains.

SHUI TA. Never! I will never . . .

YANG SUN. Mrs. Mi Tzu'll be here in five minutes. *You* fix it. And Shu Fu will be with her . . . . What's all that noise?

[*During the above dialogue,* WONG *is heard off stage calling:* "The good Shen Te, where is she? Which of you has seen Shen Te, good people? Where is Shen Te?" *A knock. Enter* WONG.]

WONG. Mr. Shui Ta, I've come to ask when Miss Shen Te will be back, it's six months now . . . There are rumors. People say something's happened to her.

SHUI TA. I'm busy. Come back next week.

WONG [*excited*]. In the morning there was always rice on her doorstep—for the needy. It's been there again lately!

SHUI TA. And what do people conclude from this?

WONG. That Shen Te is still in Setzuan! She's been . . . [*He breaks off.*]

SHUI TA. She's been what? Mr. Wong, if you're Shen Te's friend, talk a little less about her, that's my advice to you.

WONG. I don't want your advice! Before she disappeared, Miss Shen Te told me something very important—she's pregnant!

YANG SUN. What? What was that?

SHUI TA [*quickly*]. The man is lying.

WONG. A good woman isn't so easily forgotten, Mr. Shui Ta.

[*He leaves.* SHUI TA *goes quickly into the back room.*]

YANG SUN [*to the audience*]. Shen Te pregnant? So that's why. Her cousin sent her away, so I wouldn't get wind of it. I have a son, a Yang appears on the scene, and what happens? Mother and child vanish into thin air! That scoundrel, that unspeakable . . . [*The sound of sobbing is heard from the back room.*] What was that? Someone sobbing? Who was it? Mr. Shui Ta the Tobacco King doesn't weep his heart out. And where does the rice come from that's on the doorstep in the morning?

[SHUI TA *returns. He goes to the door and looks out into the rain.*]

Where is she?

SHUI TA. Sh! It's nine o'clock. But the rain's so heavy, you can't hear a thing.

YANG SUN. What do you want to hear?

SHUI TA. The mail plane.

YANG SUN. What?

SHUI TA. I've been told *you* wanted to fly at one time. Is that all forgotten?

YANG SUN. Flying mail is night work. I prefer the daytime. And the firm is very dear to me—after all it belongs to my ex-fiancée, even if she's not around. And she's not, is she?

SHUI TA. What do you mean by that?

YANG SUN. Oh, well, let's say I haven't altogether—lost interest.

SHUI TA. My cousin might like to know that.

YANG SUN. I might not be indifferent—if I found she was being kept under lock and key.

SHUI TA. By whom?

YANG SUN. By you.

SHUI TA. What could you do about it?

YANG SUN. I could submit for discussion—my position in the firm.

SHUI TA. You are now my Manager. In return for a more appropriate position, you might agree to drop the enquiry into your ex-fiancée's whereabouts?

YANG SUN. I might.

SHUI TA. What position *would* be more appropriate?

YANG SUN. The one at the top.

SHUI TA. My own? [*Silence.*] And if I preferred to throw you out on your neck?

YANG SUN. I'd come back on my feet. With suitable escort.

SHUI TA. The police?

YANG SUN. The police.

SHUI TA. And when the police found no one?

YANG SUN. I might ask them not to overlook the back room. [*Ending the pretense.*] In short, Mr. Shui Ta, my interest in this young woman has not been officially terminated. I should like to see more of her. [*Into* SHUI TA'S *face.*] Besides, she's pregnant and needs a friend. [*He moves to the door.*] I shall talk about it with the Water Seller. [*Exit.*]

[SHUI TA *is rigid for a moment, then he quickly goes into the back room. He returns with* SHEN TE'S *belongings: underwear, etc. He takes a long look at the shawl of the previous scene. He then wraps the things in a bundle which, upon hearing a noise, he hides under the table. Enter* MRS. MI TZU *and* MR. SHU FU. *They put away their umbrellas and galoshes.*]

MRS. MI TZU. I thought your manager was here, Mr. Shui Ta. He combines charm with business in a way that can only be to the advantage of all of us.

SHU FU. You sent for us, Mr. Shui Ta?

SHUI TA. The factory is in trouble.

SHU FU. It always is.

SHUI TA. The police are threatening to close us down unless I can show that the extension of our facilities is imminent.

SHU FU. Mr. Shui Ta, I'm sick and tired of your constantly expanding projects. I place cabins at your cousin's disposal; you make a factory of them. I hand your cousin a check; you present it. Your cousin disappears and you find the cabins too small and talk of yet more . . .

SHUI TA. Mr. Shu Fu, I'm authorized to inform you that Miss Shen Te's return is now imminent.

SHU FU. Imminent? It's becoming his favorite word.

MRS. MI TZU. Yes, what does it mean?

SHUI TA. Mrs. Mi Tzu, I can pay you exactly half what you asked for your buildings. Are you ready to inform the police that I am taking them over?

MRS. MI TZU. Certainly, if I can take over your manager.

SHU FU. What?

MRS. MI TZU. He's so efficient.

SHUI TA. I'm afraid I need Mr. Yang Sun.

MRS. MI TZU. So do I.

SHUI TA. He will call on you tomorrow.

SHU FU. So much the better. With Shen Te likely to turn up at any moment, the presence of that young man is hardly in good taste.

SHUI TA. So we have reached a settlement. In what was once the good Shen Te's little shop we are laying the foundations for the great Mr. Shui Ta's twelve magnificent super tobacco markets. You will bear in mind that though they call me the Tobacco King of Setzuan, it is my cousin's interests that have been served . . .

VOICES [*off*]. The police, the police! Going to the tobacco shop! Something must have happened! [*Etc.*]

[*Enter* YANG SUN, WONG, *and the* POLICEMAN.]

POLICEMAN. Quiet there, quiet, quiet! [*They quiet down.*] I'm sorry, Mr. Shui Ta, but there's a report that you've been depriving Miss Shen Te of her freedom. Not that I believe all I hear but the whole city's in an uproar.

SHUI TA. That's a lie.

POLICEMAN. Mr. Yang Sun has testified that he heard someone sobbing in the back room.

SHU FU. Mrs. Mi Tzu and myself will testify that no one here has been sobbing.

MRS. MI TZU. We have been quietly smoking our cigars.

POLICEMAN. Mr. Shui Ta, I'm afraid I shall have to take a look at that room. [*He does so. The room is empty.*] No one there, of course, sir.

YANG SUN. But I heard sobbing. What's that? [*He finds the clothes.*]

WONG. Those are Shen Te's things. [*To crowd.*] Shen Te's clothes are here!

VOICES [*off. In sequence*]. Shen Te's clothes! They've been found under the table! Body of murdered girl still missing! Tobacco King suspected!

POLICEMAN. Mr. Shui Ta, unless you can tell us where the girl is, I'll have to ask you to come along.

SHUI TA. I do not know.

POLICEMAN. I can't say how sorry I am, Mr. Shui Ta. [*He shows him the door.*]

SHUI TA. Everything will be cleared up in no time. There are still judges in Setzuan.
YANG SUN. I heard sobbing!

SCENE IXA

WONG'S *den. For the last time, the* GODS *appear to the Water Seller in his dream. They have changed and show signs of a long journey, extreme fatigue, and plenty of mishaps. The* FIRST *no longer has a hat; the* THIRD *has lost a leg; all* THREE *are barefoot.*

WONG. Illustrious ones, at last you're here. Shen Te's been gone for months and today her cousin's been arrested. They think he murdered her to get the shop. But I had a dream and in this dream Shen Te said her cousin was keeping her prisoner. You must find her for us, illustrious ones!
FIRST GOD. We've found very few good people anywhere, and even they didn't keep it up. Shen Te is still the only one that stayed good.
SECOND GOD. If she *has* stayed good.
WONG. Certainly she has. But she's vanished.
FIRST GOD. That's the last straw. All is lost!
SECOND GOD. A little moderation, dear colleague!
FIRST GOD [*plaintively*]. What's the good of moderation now? If she can't be found, we'll have to resign! The world is a terrible place! Nothing but misery, vulgarity, and waste! Even the countryside isn't what it used to be. The trees are getting their heads chopped off by telephone wires, and there's such a noise from all the gunfire, and I can't stand those heavy clouds of smoke, and—
THIRD GOD. The place is absolutely unlivable! Good intentions bring people to the brink of the abyss, and good deeds push them over the edge. I'm afraid our book of rules is destined for the scrap heap—
SECOND GOD. It's people! They're a worthless lot!
THIRD GOD. The world is too cold!
SECOND GOD. It's people! They are too weak!
FIRST GOD. Dignity, dear colleagues, dignity! Never despair! As for this world, didn't we agree that we only have to find one human being who can stand the place? Well, we found her. True, we lost her again. We must find her again, that's all! And at once!
[*They disappear.*]

SCENE X

Courtroom. Groups: SHU FU *and* MRS. MI TZU; YANG SUN *and* MRS. YANG; WONG, *the* CARPENTER, *the* GRANDFATHER, *the* NIECE, *the* OLD MAN, *the* OLD WOMAN; MRS. SHIN, *the* POLICEMAN; *the* UNEMPLOYED MAN, *the* SISTER-IN-LAW.

OLD MAN. So much power isn't good for one man.
UNEMPLOYED MAN. And he's going to open twelve super tobacco markets!

WIFE. One of the judges is a friend of Mr. Shu Fu's.

SISTER-IN-LAW. Another one accepted a present from Mr. Shui Ta only last night. A great fat goose.

OLD WOMAN [*to* WONG]. And Shen Te is nowhere to be found.

WONG. Only the gods will ever know the truth.

POLICEMAN. Order in the court! My lords the judges!

[*Enter the* THREE GODS *in judges' robes. We overhear their conversation as they pass along the footlights to their bench.*]

THIRD GOD. We'll never get away with it, our certificates were so badly forged.

SECOND GOD. My predecessor's "sudden indigestion" will certainly cause comment.

FIRST GOD. But he *had* just eaten a whole goose.

UNEMPLOYED MAN. Look at that! *New* judges!

WONG. New judges. And what good ones!

[*The* THIRD GOD *hears this, and turns to smile at* WONG. *The* GODS *sit. The* FIRST GOD *beats on the bench with his gavel. The* POLICEMAN *brings in* SHUI TA *who walks with lordly steps. He is whistled at.*]

POLICEMAN [*to* SHUI TA]. Be prepared for a surprise. The judges have been changed.

[SHUI TA *turns quickly round, looks at them, and staggers.*]

NIECE. What's the matter now?

WIFE. The great Tobacco King nearly fainted.

HUSBAND. Yes, as soon as he saw the new judges.

WONG. Does *he* know who they are?

[SHUI TA *picks himself up, and the proceedings open.*]

FIRST GOD. Defendant Shui Ta, you are accused of doing away with your cousin Shen Te in order to take possession of her business. Do you plead guilty or not guilty?

SHUI TA. Not guilty, my lord.

FIRST GOD [*thumbing through the documents of the case*]. The first witness is the Policeman. I shall ask him to tell us something of the respective reputations of Miss Shen Te and Mr. Shui Ta.

POLICEMAN. Miss Shen Te was a young lady who aimed to please, my lord. She liked to live and let live, as the saying goes. Mr. Shui Ta, on the other hand, is a man of principle. Though the generosity of Miss Shen Te forced him at times to abandon half measures, unlike the girl, he was always on the side of the law, my lord. One time, he even unmasked a gang of thieves to whom his too trustful cousin had given shelter. The evidence, in short, my lord, proves that Mr. Shui Ta was *incapable* of the crime of which he stands accused!

FIRST GOD. I see. And are there others who could testify along, shall we say, the same lines?

[SHU FU *rises.*]

POLICEMAN [*whispering to* GODS]. Mr. Shu Fu—a very important person.

FIRST GOD [*inviting him to speak*]. Mr. Shu Fu!

SHU FU. Mr. Shui Ta is a businessman, my lord. Need I say more?

FIRST GOD. Yes.

SHU FU. Very well, I will. He is Vice President of the Council of Commerce and is about to be elected a Justice of the Peace. [*He returns to his seat.*]

WONG. Elected! *He* gave him the job!

[*With a gesture the* FIRST GOD *asks who* MRS. MI TZU *is.*]

POLICEMAN. Another very important person. Mrs. Mi Tzu.

FIRST GOD [*inviting her to speak*]. Mrs. Mi Tzu!

MRS. MI TZU. My lord, as Chairman of the Committee on Social Work, I wish to call attention to just a couple of eloquent facts: Mr. Shui Ta not only has erected a model factory with model housing in our city, he is a regular contributor to our home for the disabled. [*She returns to her seat.*]

POLICEMAN [*whispering*]. And she's a great friend of the judge that ate the goose!

FIRST GOD [*to the* POLICEMAN]. Oh, thank you. What next? [*To the Court, genially.*] Oh, yes. We should find out if any of the evidence is less favorable to the Defendant.

[WONG, *the* CARPENTER, *the* OLD MAN, *the* OLD WOMAN, *the* UNEMPLOYED MAN, *the* SISTER-IN-LAW, *and the* NIECE *come forward.*]

POLICEMAN [*whispering*]. Just the riff raff, my lord.

FIRST GOD [*addressing the "riff raff"*]. Well, um, riff raff—do you know anything of the Defendant, Mr. Shui Ta?

WONG. Too much, my lord.

UNEMPLOYED MAN. What don't we know, my lord?

CARPENTER. He ruined us.

SISTER-IN-LAW. He's a cheat.

NIECE. Liar.

WIFE. Thief.

BOY. Blackmailer.

BROTHER. Murderer.

FIRST GOD. Thank you. We should now let the Defendant state his point of view.

SHUI TA. I only came on the scene when Shen Te was in danger of losing what I had understood was a gift from the gods. Because I did the filthy jobs which someone had to do, they hate me. My activities were held down to the minimum, my lord.

SISTER-IN-LAW. He had us arrested!

SHUI TA. Certainly. You stole from the bakery!

SISTER-IN-LAW. Such concern for the bakery! You didn't want the shop for yourself, I suppose!

SHUI TA. I didn't want the shop overrun with parasites.

SISTER-IN-LAW. We had nowhere else to go.

SHUI TA. There were too many of you.

WONG. What about this old couple. Were *they* parasites?

OLD MAN. We lost our shop because of you!

OLD WOMAN. And we gave your cousin money!

SHUI TA. My cousin's fiancé was a flyer. The money had to go to *him.*

WONG. Did you care whether he flew or not? Did you care whether she married him or not? You wanted her to marry someone else! [*He points at* SHU FU.]

SHUI TA. The flyer unexpectedly turned out to be a scoundrel.

YANG SUN [*jumping up*]. Which was the reason you made him your Manager?

SHUI TA. Later on he improved.

WONG. And when he improved, you sold him to her? [*He points out* MRS. MI TZU.]

SHUI TA. She wouldn't let me have her premises unless she had him to stroke her knees!

MRS. MI TZU. What? The man's a pathological liar. [*To him.*] Don't mention my property to me as long as you live! Murderer! [*She rustles off, in high dudgeon.*]

YANG SUN [*pushing in*]. My lord, I wish to speak for the Defendant.

SISTER-IN-LAW. Naturally. He's your employer.

UNEMPLOYED MAN. And the worst slave driver in the country.

MRS. YANG. That's a lie! My lord, Mr. Shui Ta is a great man. He . . .

YANG SUN. He's this and he's that, but he is not a murderer, my lord. Just fifteen minutes before his arrest I heard Shen Te's voice in his own back room.

FIRST GOD. Oh? Tell us more!

YANG SUN. I heard sobbing, my lord!

FIRST GOD. But lots of women sob, we've been finding.

YANG SUN. Could I fail to recognize her voice?

SHU FU. No, you made her sob so often yourself, young man!

YANG SUN. Yes. But I also made her happy. Till he [*pointing at* SHUI TA] decided to sell her to you!

SHUI TA. Because you didn't love her.

WONG. Oh, no: it was for the money, my lord!

SHUI TA. And what was the money for, my lord? For the poor! And for Shen Te so she could go on being good!

WONG. For the poor? That he sent to his sweatshops? And why didn't you let Shen Te be good when you signed the big check?

SHUI TA. For the child's sake, my lord.

CARPENTER. What about *my* children? What did he do about them?

[SHUI TA *is silent.*]

WONG. The shop was to be a fountain of goodness. That was the gods' idea. You came and spoiled it!

SHUI TA. If I hadn't, it would have run dry!

MRS. SHIN. There's a lot in that, my lord.

WONG. What have you done with the good Shen Te, bad man? She *was* good, my lords, she was, I swear it! [*He raises his hand in an oath.*]

THIRD GOD. What's happened to your hand, Water Seller?

WONG [*pointing to* SHUI TA]. It's all his fault, my lord, *she* was going to send me to a doctor— [*To* SHUI TA.] You were her worst enemy!

SHUI TA. I was her only friend!

WONG. Where is she then? Tell us where your good friend is!

[*The excitement of this exchange has run through the whole crowd.*]

ALL. Yes, where is she? Where is Shen Te? [*Etc.*]

SHUI TA. Shen Te had to go.

WONG. Where? Where to?

SHUI TA. I cannot tell you! I cannot tell you!

ALL. Why? Why did she have to go away? [*Etc.*]

WONG [*into the din with the first words, but talking on beyond the others*]. Why not, why not? Why did she have to go away?

SHUI TA [*shouting*]. Because you'd all have torn her to shreds, that's why! My lords, I have a request. Clear the court! When only the judges remain, I will make a confession.

ALL [*except* WONG, *who is silent, struck by the new turn of events*]. So he's guilty? He's confessing! [*Etc.*]

FIRST GOD [*using the gavel*]. Clear the court!

POLICEMAN. Clear the court!

WONG. Mr. Shui Ta has met his match this time.

MRS. SHIN [*with a gesture toward the judges*]. You're in for a little surprise.

[*The court is cleared. Silence.*]

SHUI TA. Illustrious ones!

[*The* GODS *look at each other, not quite believing their ears.*]

SHUI TA. Yes, I recognize you!

SECOND GOD [*taking matters in hand, sternly*]. What have you done with our good woman of Setzuan?

SHUI TA. I have a terrible confession to make: I am she! [*He takes off his mask, and tears away his clothes.* SHEN TE *stands there.*]

SECOND GOD. Shen Te!

SHEN TE. Shen Te, yes. Shui Ta *and* Shen Te. Both.

Your injunction
To be good and yet to live
Was a thunderbolt:
It has torn me in two
I can't tell how it was
But to be good to others
And myself at the same time
I could not do it
Your world is not an easy one, illustrious ones!
When we extend our hand to a beggar, he tears it off for us
When we help the lost, we are lost ourselves.
And so
Since not to eat is to die
Who can long refuse to be bad?
As I lay prostrate beneath the weight of good intentions
Ruin stared me in the face
It was when I was unjust that I ate good meat
And hobnobbed with the mighty
Why?
Why are bad deeds rewarded?

Good ones punished?
I enjoy giving
I truly wished to be the Angel of the Slums
But washed by a foster-mother in the water of the gutter
I developed a sharp eye
The time came when pity was a thorn in my side
And, later, when kind words turned to ashes in my mouth
And anger took over
I became a wolf
Find me guilty, then, illustrious ones,
But know:
All that I have done I did
To help my neighbor
To love my lover
And to keep my little one from want
For your great, godly deeds, I was too poor, too small.

[*Pause.*]

FIRST GOD [*shocked*]. Don't go on making yourself miserable, Shen Te! We're overjoyed to have found you!

SHEN TE. I'm telling you I'm the bad man who committed all those crimes!

FIRST GOD [*using—or failing to use—his ear trumpet*]. The good woman who did all those good deeds?

SHEN TE. Yes, but the bad man too!

FIRST GOD [*as if something had dawned*]. Unfortunate coincidences! Heartless neighbors!

THIRD GOD [*shouting in his ear*]. But how is she to continue?

FIRST GOD. Continue? Well, she's a strong, healthy girl . . .

SECOND GOD. You didn't hear what she said!

FIRST GOD. I heard every word! She is confused, that's all! [*He begins to bluster.*] And what about this book of rules—we can't renounce our rules, can we? [*More quietly.*] Should the world be changed? How? By whom? The world should *not* be changed! [*At a sign from him, the lights turn pink, and music plays.*]

And now the hour of parting is at hand.
Dost thou behold, Shen Te, yon fleecy cloud?
It is our chariot. At a sign from me
'Twill come and take us back to whence we came
Above the azure vault and silver stars . . .

SHEN TE. No! Don't go, illustrious ones!

FIRST GOD.

Our cloud has landed now in yonder field
From whence it will transport us back to heaven.
Farewell, Shen Te, let not thy courage fail thee . . .

[*Exeunt* GODS.]

SHEN TE. What about the old couple? They've lost their shop! What about the Water Seller and his hand? And I've got to defend myself against the barber, because I don't love him! And against Sun, because I do love him! How? How?

[Shen Te's *eyes follow the* GODS *as they are imagined to step into a cloud which rises and moves forward over the orchestra and up beyond the balcony.*]

FIRST GOD [*from on high*]. We have faith in you, Shen Te!

SHEN TE. There'll be a child. And he'll have to be fed. I can't stay here. Where shall I go?

FIRST GOD. Continue to be good, good woman of Setzuan!

SHEN TE. I need my bad cousin!

FIRST GOD. But not very often!

SHEN TE. Once a week at least!

FIRST GOD. Once a month will be quite enough!

SHEN TE [*shrieking*]. No, no! Help!

[*But the cloud continues to recede as the* GODS *sing.*]

VALEDICTORY HYMN

What rapture, oh, it is to know
    A good thing when you see it
And having seen a good thing, oh,
    What rapture 'tis to flee it

Be good, sweet maid of Setzuan
    Let Shui Ta be clever
Departing, we forget the man
    Remember your endeavor

Because through all the length of days
    Her goodness faileth never
Sing hallelujah! May Shen Te's
    Good name live on forever!

SHEN TE. Help!

EPILOGUE

You're thinking, aren't you, that this is no right
Conclusion to the play you've seen tonight?
After a tale, exotic, fabulous,
A nasty ending was slipped up on us.
We feel deflated too. We too are nettled
To see the curtain down and nothing settled.
How could a better ending be arranged?
Could one change people? Can the world be changed?
Would new gods do the trick? Will atheism?
Moral rearmament? Materialism?
It is for you to find a way, my friends,
To help good men arrive at happy ends.
You write the happy ending to the play!
There must, there must, there's got to be a way!

Federico García Lorca
(1898–1936)

The greatest twentieth-century Spanish writer, perhaps the greatest since Cervantes, is the poet and playwright Federico García Lorca. In the early 1930s, Lorca and the generation of Spanish artists of which he was a part opened briefly the doors of Spain to the Modernist movement that had swept Europe a dozen years before, while at the same time remaining profoundly Spanish in their spirit and materials. The doors slammed shut again with the triumph of Franco's Nationalists in the Spanish Civil War, fought between 1936 and 1939, but Lorca and his contemporaries left behind a legacy of work which in other circumstances might have ushered in a new Golden Age of Spanish literature.

Lorca was born in 1898 in a small town near Granada. His father was a prosperous landowner and farmer, his mother a schoolteacher who taught him to play the piano and encouraged him in his reading, writing, and painting. The family moved to Granada when Lorca was eleven, and he attended a Jesuit school there in preparation for entering the University of Granada to study law. He soon abandoned law, however, to study literature, painting, and music. His virtuosity at the piano made him a welcome member of Granada artistic circles; there he formed a lifelong friendship with the composer Manuel de Falla and became friends as well with the sculptor Juan Cristóbal, the literary critic José Fernández Montesinos, and the concert guitarists Ángel Barrios and Andrés Segovia. He surprised these friends, who knew him primarily as a musician, with the publication of his first book, Impressions and Landscapes *(1918), about a trip to Castile.*

In 1919, Lorca left Granada for Madrid, where he took up a ten-year residency at the residencia de estudiantes *(residence of scholars) at the University of Madrid. This period was decisive in his career, since it was there that he came to know the leading Spanish artists of his own generation, including the film maker Luis Buñuel, the painter Salvador Dalí, and the poet Rafael Alberti. The* residencia *was also a world cultural center, and Lorca met such international artistic figures as François Mauriac, H. G. Wells, G. K. Chesterton, and Igor Stravinsky and became acquainted with such current movements in art as Dadaism and Surrealism. Lorca became known in this circle as an accomplished poet who preferred to recite his verse like a medieval troubadour rather than publish it. Volumes of poems, however, were published in 1921* (Book of Poems), *1924* (Songs), *and 1928* (Gypsy Ballads). *His first play,* The Butterfly's Evil Spell, *a fable about a cockroach who becomes charmed by the world of butterflies, was produced in 1920, but it was a disastrous failure. Other plays followed, notably* Mariana Pineda *(1927), his first theatrical success, produced in Barcelona with scenery by Dalí.*

The success of Mariana Pineda *and of* Gypsy Ballads *brought Lorca fame, but he succumbed to an extended period of severe depression in 1929. In an attempt to gain relief, he went to New York, where he briefly studied at Columbia University, but he soon left to stay with friends in Vermont. Lorca was shocked and horrified by the brutality of New York life; the result was a long poem named* The Poet in New York *(published posthumously in 1940), full of violent surrealistic images of cruelty and suffering. In America, he also became acquainted with the poetry of Walt Whitman, which was to become a major influence upon his own later work.*

Lorca left the United States after a year and a half and, after a trip to Havana, which restored his spirits, returned to Spain. The fall of the dictatorship of Primo de Rivera in 1930 and the establishment of a republican government in 1931 created an environment in which art could flourish, and Lorca's final five years were his most vital and productive ones. In 1932, he became the director of La Barraca, a touring theater company subsidized by the Ministry of National Education. This company, using a portable theater (a barraca, or "hut") seating four hundred, toured Spain, presenting classics of the Spanish theater to working-class audiences. Lorca was founder, stage director, and musical director for this company, and during the three years he worked with it, he developed a swift, simple, modern style of performance that blended theater, dance, music, and scene design into a single, integrated experience; the style was to have a decisive effect upon his own last plays.

Lorca continued to write voluminously during these years. His most famous single poem, "Lament for Ignacio Mejías," an elegy for a bullfighter friend, appeared in 1934, and during these years he also wrote the Arabic-influenced poems that were to appear after his death as the Divan of Tamarit. (A "divan" is a collection of poems.) He also wrote a number of plays, chief among them his three "rural tragedies": Blood Wedding (1933), Yerma (1934), and The House of Bernarda Alba (1936). These plays, based on themes of rural Spanish life, all deal with intense passions bursting through the bonds of traditional codes of behavior; all three employ a "total theater" technique of blending prose, poetry, music, and scene design to create a unified, powerful effect.

The republican government became progressively weaker during these years, and in July, 1936, the fascist "Insurgent" forces under Francisco Franco revolted in Spanish Morocco and invaded the mainland to inaugurate the Spanish Civil War. Lorca was in Granada at the time, and he went into hiding at the house of a friend, aware that his reputation as a homosexual, his connections with the republican government through La Barraca, and his friendship with republican supporters made him a prime target for the purges Franco's troops were carrying out. He was arrested on August 16 and executed by a firing squad two days later; he was only thirty-eight years old.

Lorca's three rural tragedies are generally conceded to be his finest work, and The House of Bernarda Alba, which he read to a small group of friends only a few weeks before his death, is usually regarded as the best play of the three. It is based upon a childhood memory of a household made up of a harsh widow and her daughters in a small town near Granada, and it is, before all else, a tough, compassionate study of the suffering of women under a repressive, male-oriented code of sexual roles and behavior. The cruelty implicit in the conservative sexual code becomes horrifyingly explicit in the episode that ends Act II. But Lorca also places his social theme within a more general context. His concern throughout his life with the tragic conflict between primitive passions and rigid conventions that frustrate their expression achieves its fullest statement in this play. The title recalls the House of Atreus and the other tragic houses of Greek drama, and the tragedy of Bernarda Alba's daughters becomes a tragedy of human beings in general. The house, with its thick, whitewashed walls against which a stallion obsessively kicks (opening of Act III), is only one of a number of images of enclosure and imprisonment that dominate the play. Bernarda Alba and her daughters are imprisoned not only in their house but also in the past, in their culture, in their female bodies, and finally in the human condition, trapped between the soaring demands of the human spirit and the bonds of earth.

FURTHER READING *(prepared by N. K. B.):* Until Jean-Louis Schonberg's comprehensive biography, *Federico García Lorca: L'Homme—L'oeuvre*, 1956, is translated into English, readers can rely on Arturo Barea's *Lorca: The Poet and His People*, trans. by Ilsa Barea, 1949; J. B. Trend's *Lorca and the Spanish Poetic Tradition*, 1956; and Edwin Honig's *García Lorca*, 1944, rev. 1963, which interprets the poetry and drama in relation to key biographical events. All three books discuss his relationship to Spanish literary tradition. Carl W. Cobb, *Federico García Lorca*, 1967, summarizes Lorca's life and examines his writing in the context of modern European literature, briefly explicating *The House of Bernarda Alba*. Robert Lima, *The Theatre of García Lorca*, 1963, stresses the poetic qualities of Lorca's drama and his experimentation with theatrical language. In *Lorca: The Theatre Beneath the Sand*, 1980, Gwynne Edwards relates the plays to European cultural and aesthetic movements and analyzes *The House of Bernarda Alba* at length as a "rural tragedy." Manuel Duran, ed., *Lorca: A Collection of Critical Essays*, 1962, contains key essays and excerpts from major studies, including Dámaso Alonso's "Lorca and the Expression of the Spanish Essence," an examination of Lorca's impact on his contemporaries, and Angel del Rio's "Lorca's Theater," a survey of the playwright's thematic and technical development. On nature in Lorca's poems and plays, see Joseph W. Zdenek, ed., *The World of Nature in the Works of Federico García Lorca*, 1980, which, along with other essays, includes Barry Weingarten's "Bernarda Alba: Nature as Unnatural."

THE HOUSE OF BERNARDA ALBA

A DRAMA ABOUT WOMEN IN THE VILLAGES OF SPAIN

Translated by James Graham-Lujan
and Richard L. O'Connell

CHARACTERS

BERNARDA, *age* 60
MARIA JOSEFA, *Bernarda's mother, age* 80
ANGUSTIAS, *Bernarda's daughter, age* 39
MAGDALENA, *Bernarda's daughter, age* 30
AMELIA, *Bernarda's daughter, age* 27
MARTIRIO, *Bernarda's daughter, age* 24
ADELA, *Bernarda's daughter, age* 20
A MAID, *age* 50
LA PONCIA, *a maid, age* 60
PRUDENCIA, *age* 50
WOMEN IN MOURNING

The writer states that these Three Acts are intended as a photographic document.

ACT I

A very white room in BERNARDA ALBA'S *house. The walls are white. There are arched doorways with jute curtains tied back with tassels and ruffles. Wicker chairs.*

On the walls, pictures of unlikely landscapes full of nymphs or legendary kings.

It is summer. A great brooding silence fills the stage. It is empty when the curtain rises. Bells can be heard tolling outside.

FIRST SERVANT [*entering*]. The tolling of those bells hits me right between the eyes.

PONCIA [*she enters, eating bread and sausage*]. More than two hours of mumbo jumbo. Priests are here from all the towns. The church looks beautiful. At the first responsory for the dead, Magdalena fainted.

FIRST SERVANT. She's the one who's left most alone.

PONCIA. She's the only one who loved her father. Ay! Thank God we're alone for a little. I came over to eat.

FIRST SERVANT. If Bernarda sees you . . . !

PONCIA. She's not eating today so she'd just as soon we'd all die of hunger! Domineering old tyrant! But she'll be fooled! I opened the sausage crock.

FIRST SERVANT [*with an anxious sadness*]. Couldn't you give me some for my little girl, Poncia?

PONCIA. Go ahead! And take a fistful of peas too. She won't know the difference today.

VOICE [*within*]. Bernarda!

PONCIA. There's the grandmother! Isn't she locked up tight?

FIRST SERVANT. Two turns of the key.

PONCIA. You'd better put the cross-bar up too. She's got the fingers of a lock-picker!

VOICE [*within*]. Bernarda!

PONCIA [*shouting*]. She's coming! [*To* THE SERVANT.] Clean everything up good. If Bernarda doesn't find things shining, she'll pull out the few hairs I have left.

SERVANT. What a woman!

PONCIA. Tyrant over everyone around her. She's perfectly capable of sitting on your heart and watching you die for a whole year without turning off that cold little smile she wears on her wicked face. Scrub, scrub those dishes!

SERVANT. I've got blood on my hands from so much polishing of everything.

PONCIA. She's the cleanest, she's the decentest, she's the highest everything! A good rest her poor husband's earned!

[*The bells stop.*]

SERVANT. Did all the relatives come?

PONCIA. Just hers. His people hate her. They came to see him dead and make the sign of the cross over him; that's all.

SERVANT. Are there enough chairs?

PONCIA. More than enough. Let them sit on the floor. When Bernarda's father died people stopped coming under his roof. She doesn't want them to see her in her "domain." Curse her!

SERVANT. She's been good to you.

PONCIA. Thirty years washing her sheets. Thirty years eating her leftovers. Nights of watching when she had a cough. Whole days peeking through a crack in the shutters to spy on the neighbors and carry her the tale. Life without secrets one from the other. But in spite of that—curse her! May the "pain of the piercing nail"[1] strike her in the eyes.

SERVANT. Poncia!

PONCIA. But I'm a good watchdog! I bark when I'm told and bite beggars' heels when she sics me on 'em. My sons work in her fields—both of them already married, but one of these days I'll have enough.

SERVANT. And then . . . ?

PONCIA. Then I'll lock myself up in a room with her and spit in her face—a whole year. "Bernarda, here's for this, that and the other!" Till I leave her—just like a lizard the boys have squashed. For that's what she is—she and her whole family! Not that I envy her her life. Five girls are left her, five ugly daughters—not counting Angustias the eldest, by her first husband, who had money—the rest of them, plenty of eyelets to embroider, plenty of linen petticoats, but bread and grapes when it comes to inheritance.[2]

SERVANT. Well, *I'd* like to have what they've got!

PONCIA. All we have is our hands and a hole in God's earth.

SERVANT. And that's the only earth they'll ever leave to us—to us who have nothing!

PONCIA [*at the cupboard*]. This glass has some specks.

SERVANT. Neither soap nor rag will take them off.

[*The bells toll.*]

PONCIA. The last prayer! I'm going over and listen. I certainly like the way our priest sings. In the Pater Noster his voice went up, and up—like a pitcher filling with water little by little. Of course, at the end his voice cracked, but it's glorious to hear it. No, there never was anybody like the old Sacristan—Tronchapinos. At my mother's Mass, may she rest in peace, he sang. The walls shook—and when he said "Amen," it was as if a wolf had come into the church. [*Imitating him.*] A-a-a-men! [*She starts coughing.*]

SERVANT. Watch out—you'll strain your windpipe!

PONCIA. I'd rather strain something else! [*Goes out laughing.*]

[THE SERVANT *scrubs. The bells toll.*]

SERVANT [*imitating the bells*]. Dong, dong, dong. Dong, dong, dong, May God forgive him!

BEGGAR WOMAN [*at the door, with a little girl*]. Blesséd be God!

SERVANT. Dong, dong, dong. I hope he waits many years for us! Dong, dong, dong.

BEGGAR [*loudly, a little annoyed*]. Blesséd be God!

SERVANT [*annoyed*]. Forever and ever!

BEGGAR. I came for the scraps.

[*The bells stop tolling.*]

SERVANT. You can go right out the way you came in. Today's scraps are for me.

BEGGAR. But you have somebody to take care of you—and my little girl and I are all alone!

[1] The evil eye; a Spanish curse. [2] Angustias, the oldest, is the only one with a dowry.

SERVANT. Dogs are alone too, and they live.

BEGGAR. They always give them to me.

SERVANT. Get out of here! Who let you in anyway? You've already tracked up the place. [THE BEGGAR WOMAN *and* LITTLE GIRL *leave.* THE SERVANT *goes on scrubbing.*] Floors finished with oil, cupboards, pedestals, iron beds—but us servants, we can suffer in silence—and live in mud huts with a plate and a spoon. I hope someday not a one will be left to tell it. [*The bells sound again.*] Yes, yes—ring away. Let them put you in a coffin with gold inlay and brocade to carry it on—you're no less dead than I'll be, so take what's coming to you, Antonio María Benavides—stiff in your broadcloth suit and your high boots—take what's coming to you! You'll never again lift my skirts behind the corral door!

[*From the rear door, two by two, women in mourning with large shawls and black skirts and fans begin to enter. They come in slowly until the stage is full.*]

SERVANT [*breaking into a wail*]. Oh, Antonio María Benavides, now you'll never see these walls, nor break bread in this house again! I'm the one who loved you most of all your servants. [*Pulling her hair.*] *Must* I live on after you've gone? Must I go on living?

[*The women finish coming in, and* BERNARDA *and her five daughters enter.* BERNARDA *leans on a cane.*]

BERNARDA [*to* THE SERVANT]. Silence!

SERVANT [*weeping*]. Bernarda!

BERNARDA. Less shrieking and more work. You should have had all this cleaner for the wake. Get out. This isn't your place.

[THE SERVANT *goes off crying.*]

The poor are like animals—they seem to be made of different stuff.

FIRST WOMAN. The poor feel their sorrows too.

BERNARDA. But they forget them in front of a plateful of peas.

FIRST GIRL [*timidly*]. Eating is necessary for living.

BERNARDA. At your age one doesn't talk in front of older people.

WOMAN. Be quiet, child.

BERNARDA. I've never taken lessons from anyone. Sit down. Magdalena, don't cry. If you want to cry, get under your bed. Do you hear me?

SECOND WOMAN [*to* BERNARDA]. Have you started to work the fields?

BERNARDA. Yesterday.

THIRD WOMAN. The sun comes down like lead.

FIRST WOMAN. I haven't known heat like this for years.

[*Pause. They all fan themselves.*]

BERNARDA. Is the lemonade ready?

PONCIA. Yes, Bernarda.

[*She brings in a large tray full of little white jars which she distributes.*]

BERNARDA. Give the men some.

PONCIA. They're already drinking in the patio.

BERNARDA. Let them get out the way they came in. I don't want them walking through here.

A GIRL [*to* ANGUSTIAS]. Pepe el Romano was with the men during the service.

ANGUSTIAS. There he was.

BERNARDA. His mother was there. She saw his mother. Neither she nor I saw Pepe . . .

GIRL. I thought . . .

BERNARDA. The one who *was* there was Darajalí, the widower. Very close to your Aunt. We all of us saw him.

SECOND WOMAN [*aside, in a low voice*]. Wicked, worse than wicked woman!

THIRD WOMAN. A tongue like a knife!

BERNARDA. Women in church shouldn't look at any man but the priest—and him only because he wears skirts. To turn your head is to be looking for the warmth of corduroy.

FIRST WOMAN. Sanctimonious old snake!

PONCIA [*between her teeth*]. Itching for a man's warmth.

BERNARDA [*beating with her cane on the floor*]. Blessèd be God!

ALL [*crossing themselves*]. Forever blessèd and praised.

BERNARDA. Rest in peace with holy company at your head.

ALL. Rest in peace!

BERNARDA. With the Angel Saint Michael, and his sword of justice.

ALL. Rest in peace!

BERNARDA. With the key that opens, and the hand that locks.

ALL. Rest in peace!

BERNARDA. With the most blessèd, and the little lights of the field.

ALL. Rest in peace!

BERNARDA. With our holy charity, and all souls on land and sea.

ALL. Rest in peace!

BERNARDA. Grant rest to your servant, Antonio María Benavides, and give him the crown of your blessèd glory.

ALL. Amen.

BERNARDA. [*She rises and chants.*] Requiem aeternam donat eis domine.

ALL [*standing and chanting in the Gregorian fashion*]. Et lux perpetua luce ab eis.[3]

[*They cross themselves.*]

FIRST WOMAN. May you have health to pray for his soul.

[*They start filing out.*]

THIRD WOMAN. You won't lack loaves of hot bread.

SECOND WOMAN. Nor a roof for your daughters.

[*They are all filing in front of* BERNARDA *and going out.* ANGUSTIAS *leaves by the door to the patio.*]

FOURTH WOMAN. May you go on enjoying your wedding wheat.

PONCIA. [*She enters, carrying a money bag.*] From the men—this bag of money for Masses.

BERNARDA. Thank them—and let them have a glass of brandy.

GIRL [*to* MAGDALENA]. Magdalena . . .

[3] "Grant them eternal rest, O Lord. And let the everlasting light shine upon them." (The Latin, like the prayer that precedes it, is rather garbled.)

BERNARDA [*to* MAGDALENA, *who is starting to cry*]. Sh-h-h-h! [*She beats with her cane on the floor.*]

[*All the women have gone out.*]

BERNARDA [*to the women who have just left*]. Go back to your houses and criticize everything you've seen! I hope it'll be many years before you pass under the archway of my door again.

PONCIA. You've nothing to complain about. The whole town came.

BERNARDA. Yes, to fill my house with the sweat from their wraps and the poison of their tongues.

AMELIA. Mother, don't talk like that.

BERNARDA. What other way is there to talk about this cursèd village with no river—this village full of wells where you drink water always fearful it's been poisoned?

PONCIA. Look what they've done to the floor!

BERNARDA. As though a herd of goats had passed through. [PONCIA *cleans the floor.*] Adela, give me a fan.

ADELA. Take this one. [*She gives her a round fan with green and red flowers.*]

BERNARDA [*throwing the fan on the floor*]. Is that the fan to give to a widow? Give me a black one and learn to respect your father's memory.

MARTIRIO. Take mine.

BERNARDA. And you?

MARTIRIO. I'm not hot.

BERNARDA. Well, look for another, because you'll need it. For the eight years of mourning, not a breath of air will get in this house from the street. We'll act as if we'd sealed up doors and windows with bricks. That's what happened in my father's house—and in my grandfather's house. Meantime, you can all start embroidering your hope-chest linens. I have twenty bolts of linen in the chest from which to cut sheets and coverlets. Magdalena can embroider them.

MAGDALENA. It's all the same to me.

ADELA [*sourly*]. If you don't want to embroider them—they can go without. That way yours will look better.

MAGDALENA. Neither mine nor yours. I know I'm not going to marry. I'd rather carry sacks to the mill. Anything except sit here day after day in this dark room.

BERNARDA. That's what a woman is for.

MAGDALENA. Cursed be all women.

BERNARDA. In this house you'll do what I order. You can't run with the story to your father any more. Needle and thread for women. Whiplash and mules for men. That's the way it has to be for people who have certain obligations.

[ADELA *goes out.*]

VOICE. Bernarda! Let me out!

BERNARDA [*calling*]. Let her out now!

[THE FIRST SERVANT *enters.*]

FIRST SERVANT. I had a hard time holding her. In spite of her eighty years, your mother's strong as an oak.

BERNARDA. It runs in the family. My grandfather was the same way.

SERVANT. Several times during the wake I had to cover her mouth with an empty sack because she wanted to shout out to you to give her dishwater to drink at least, and some dogmeat, which is what she says you feed her.

MARTIRIO. She's mean!

BERNARDA [*to* SERVANT]. Let her get some fresh air in the patio.

SERVANT. She took her rings and the amethyst earrings out of the box, put them on, and told me she wants to get married.

[*The daughters laugh.*]

BERNARDA. Go with her and be careful she doesn't get near the well.

SERVANT. You don't need to be afraid she'll jump in.

BERNARDA. It's not that—but the neighbors can see her there from their windows.

[THE SERVANT *leaves.*]

MARTIRIO. We'll go change our clothes.

BERNARDA. Yes, but don't take the 'kerchiefs from your heads.

[ADELA *enters.*]

And Angustias?

ADELA [*meaningfully*]. I saw her looking out through the cracks of the back door. The men had just gone.

BERNARDA. And you, what were *you* doing at the door?

ADELA. I went there to see if the hens had laid.

BERNARDA. But the men had already gone!

ADELA [*meaningfully*]. A group of them were still standing outside.

BERNARDA [*furiously*]. Angustias! Angustias!

ANGUSTIAS [*entering*]. Did you want something?

BERNARDA. For what—and at whom—were you looking?

ANGUSTIAS. Nobody.

BERNARDA. Is it decent for a woman of your class to be running after a man the day of her father's funeral? Answer me! Whom were you looking at?

[*Pause.*]

ANGUSTIAS. I . . .

BERNARDA. Yes, you!

ANGUSTIAS. Nobody.

BERNARDA. Soft! Honeytongue! [*She strikes her.*]

PONCIA [*running to her*]. Bernarda, calm down! [*She holds her.* ANGUSTIAS *weeps.*]

BERNARDA. Get out of here, all of you!

[*They all go out.*]

PONCIA. She did it not realizing what she was doing—although it's bad, of course. It really disgusted me to see her sneak along to the patio. Then she stood at the window listening to the men's talk which, as usual, was not the sort one should listen to.

BERNARDA. That's what they come to funerals for. [*With curiosity.*] What were they talking about?

PONCIA. They were talking about Paca la Roseta. Last night they tied her husband up in a stall, stuck her on a horse behind the saddle, and carried her away to the depths of the olive grove.

BERNARDA. And what did she do?

PONCIA. She? She was just as happy—they say her breasts were exposed and Maximiliano held on to her as if he were playing a guitar. Terrible!

BERNARDA. And what happened?

PONCIA. What had to happen. They came back almost at daybreak. Paca la Roseta with her hair loose and a wreath of flowers on her head.

BERNARDA. She's the only bad woman we have in the village.

PONCIA. Because she's not from here. She's from far away. And those who went with her are the sons of outsiders too. The men from here aren't up to a thing like that.

BERNARDA. No, but they like to see it, and talk about it, and suck their fingers over it.

PONCIA. They were saying a lot more things.

BERNARDA [*looking from side to side with a certain fear*]. What things?

PONCIA. I'm ashamed to talk about them.

BERNARDA. And my daughter heard them?

PONCIA. Of course!

BERNARDA. That one takes after her aunts: white and mealy-mouthed and casting sheep's eyes at any little barber's compliment. Oh, what one has to go through and put up with so people will be decent and not too wild!

PONCIA. It's just that your daughters are of an age when they ought to have husbands. Mighty little trouble they give you. Angustias must be much more than thirty now.

BERNARDA. Exactly thirty-nine.

PONCIA. Imagine. And she's never had a beau . . .

BERNARDA [*furiously*]. None of them has ever had a beau and they've never needed one! They get along very well.

PONCIA. I didn't mean to offend you.

BERNARDA. For a hundred miles around there's no one good enough to come near them. The men in this town are not of their class. Do you want me to turn them over to the first shepherd?

PONCIA. You should have moved to another town.

BERNARDA. That's it. To sell them!

PONCIA. No, Bernarda, to change. . . . Of course, any place else, they'd be the poor ones.

BERNARDA. Hold your tormenting tongue!

PONCIA. One can't even talk to you. Do we, or do we not share secrets?

BERNARDA. We do not. You're a servant and I pay you. Nothing more.

PONCIA. But . . .

SERVANT [*entering*]. Don Arturo's here. He's come to see about dividing the inheritance.

BERNARDA. Let's go. [*To* THE SERVANT.] You start whitewashing the patio. [*To* LA PONCIA.] And you start putting all the dead man's clothes away in the chest.

PONCIA. We could give away some of the things.

BERNARDA. Nothing—not a button even! Not even the cloth we covered his face with.

[*She goes out slowly, leaning on her cane. At the door she turns to look at the two servants. They go out. She leaves.*]

[AMELIA *and* MARTIRIO *enter.*]

AMELIA. Did you take the medicine?

MARTIRIO. For all the good it'll do me.

AMELIA. But you took it?

MARTIRIO. I do things without any faith, but like clockwork.

AMELIA. Since the new doctor came you look livelier.

MARTIRIO. I feel the same.

AMELIA. Did you notice? Adelaida wasn't at the funeral.

MARTIRIO. I know. Her sweetheart doesn't let her go out even to the front doorstep. Before, she was gay. Now, not even powder on her face.

AMELIA. These days a girl doesn't know whether to have a beau or not.

MARTIRIO. It's all the same.

AMELIA. The whole trouble is all these wagging tongues that won't let us live. Adelaida has probably had a bad time.

MARTIRIO. She's afraid of our mother. Mother is the only one who knows the story of Adelaida's father and where he got his lands. Everytime she comes here, Mother twists the knife in the wound. Her father killed his first wife's husband in Cuba so he could marry her himself. Then he left her there and went off with another woman who already had one daughter, and then he took up with this other girl, Adelaida's mother, and married her after his second wife died insane.

AMELIA. But why isn't a man like that put in jail?

MARTIRIO. Because men help each other cover up things like that and no one's able to tell on them.

AMELIA. But Adelaida's not to blame for any of that.

MARTIRIO. No. But history repeats itself. I can see that everything is a terrible repetition. And she'll have the same fate as her mother and grandmother—both of them wife to the man who fathered her.

AMELIA. What an awful thing!

MARTIRIO. It's better never to look at a man. I've been afraid of them since I was a little girl. I'd see them in the yard, yoking the oxen and lifting grain sacks, shouting and stamping, and I was always afraid to grow up for fear one of them would suddenly take me in his arms. God has made me weak and ugly and has definitely put such things away from me.

AMELIA. Don't say that! Enrique Humanas was after you and he liked you.

MARTIRIO. That was just people's ideas! One time I stood in my nightgown at the window until daybreak because he let me know through his shepherd's little girl that he was going to come, and he didn't. It was all just talk. Then he married someone else who had more money than I.

AMELIA. And ugly as the devil.

MARTIRIO. What do men care about ugliness? All they care about is lands, yokes of oxen, and a submissive bitch who'll feed them.

AMELIA. Ay!

[MAGDALENA *enters.*]

MAGDALENA. What are you doing?

MARTIRIO. Just here.

AMELIA. And you?

MAGDALENA. I've been going through all the rooms. Just to walk a little, and look at Grandmother's needlepoint pictures—the little woolen dog, and the black man wrestling with the lion—which we liked so much when we were children. Those were happier times. A wedding lasted ten days and evil tongues weren't in style. Today people are more refined. Brides wear white veils, just as in the cities, and we drink bottled wine, but we rot inside because of what people might say.

MARTIRIO. Lord knows what went on then!

AMELIA [*to* MAGDALENA]. One of your shoelaces has come untied.

MAGDALENA. What of it?

AMELIA. You'll step on it and fall.

MAGDALENA. One less!

MARTIRIO. And Adela?

MAGDALENA. Ah! She put on the green dress she made to wear for her birthday, went out to the yard, and began shouting: "Chickens! Chickens, look at me!" I had to laugh.

AMELIA. If Mother had only seen her!

MAGDALENA. Poor little thing! She's the youngest one of us and still has her illusions. I'd give something to see her happy.

[*Pause.* ANGUSTIAS *crosses the stage, carrying some towels.*]

ANGUSTIAS. What time is it?

MAGDALENA. It must be twelve.

ANGUSTIAS. So late?

AMELIA. It's about to strike.

[ANGUSTIAS *goes out.*]

MAGDALENA [*meaningfully*]. Do you know what? [*Pointing after* ANGUSTIAS.]

AMELIA. No.

MAGDALENA. Come on!

MARTIRIO. I don't know what you're talking about!

MAGDALENA. Both of you know it better than I do, always with your heads together, like two little sheep, but not letting anybody else in on it. I mean about Pepe el Romano!

MARTIRIO. Ah!

MAGDALENA [*mocking her*]. Ah! The whole town's talking about it. Pepe el Romano is coming to marry Angustias. Last night he was walking around the house and I think he's going to send a declaration soon.

MARTIRIO. I'm glad. He's a good man.

AMELIA. Me too. Angustias is well off.

MAGDALENA. Neither one of you is glad.

MARTIRIO. Magdalena! What do you mean?

MAGDALENA. If he were coming because of Angustias' looks, for Angustias as a woman, I'd be glad too, but he's coming for her money. Even though Angustias is our sister, we're her family here and we know she's old and sickly, and always has been the least attractive one of us! Because if she looked like a dressed-up stick at twenty, what can she look like now, now that she's forty?

MARTIRIO. Don't talk like that. Luck comes to the one who least expects it.

AMELIA. But Magdalena's right after all! Angustias has all her father's money; she's the only rich one in the house and that's why, now that

Father's dead and the money will be divided, they're coming for her.

MAGDALENA. Pepe el Romano is twenty-five years old and the best looking man around here. The natural thing would be for him to be after you, Amelia, or our Adela, who's twenty—not looking for the least likely one in this house, a woman who, like her father, talks through her nose.

MARTIRIO. Maybe he likes that!

MAGDALENA. I've never been able to bear your hypocrisy.

MARTIRIO. Heavens!

[ADELA *enters.*]

MAGDALENA. Did the chickens see you?

ADELA. What did you want me to do?

AMELIA. If Mother sees you, she'll drag you by your hair!

ADELA. I had a lot of illusions about this dress. I'd planned to put it on the day we were going to eat watermelons at the well. There wouldn't have been another like it.

MARTIRIO. It's a lovely dress.

ADELA. And one that looks very good on me. It's the best thing Magdalena's ever cut.

MAGDALENA. And the chickens, what did they say to you?

ADELA. They presented me with a few fleas that riddled my legs.

[*They laugh.*]

MARTIRIO. What you can do is dye it black.

MAGDALENA. The best thing you can do is give it to Angustias for her wedding with Pepe el Romano.

ADELA [*with hidden emotion*]. But Pepe el Romano . . .

AMELIA. Haven't you heard about it?

ADELA. No.

MAGDALENA. Well, now you know!

ADELA. But it can't be!

MAGDALENA. Money can do anything.

ADELA. Is that why she went out after the funeral and stood looking through the door? [*Pause.*] And that man would . . .

MAGDALENA. Would do anything.

[*Pause.*]

MARTIRIO. What are you thinking, Adela?

ADELA. I'm thinking that this mourning has caught me at the worst moment of my life for me to bear it.

MAGDALENA. You'll get used to it.

ADELA [*bursting out, crying with rage*]. I will not get used to it! I can't be locked up. I don't want my skin to look like yours. I don't want my skin's whiteness lost in these rooms. Tomorrow I'm going to put on my green dress and go walking in the streets. I want to go out!

[THE FIRST SERVANT *enters.*]

MAGDALENA [*in a tone of authority*]. Adela!

SERVANT. The poor thing! How she misses her father . . .

[*She goes out.*]

MARTIRIO. Hush!

AMELIA. What happens to one will happen to all of us.

[ADELA *grows calm.*]

MAGDALENA. The servant almost heard you.

SERVANT [*entering*]. Pepe el Romano is coming along at the end of the street.

[AMELIA, MARTIRIO, *and* MAGDALENA *run hurriedly*.]

MAGDALENA. Let's go see him!

[*They leave rapidly*.]

SERVANT [*to* ADELA]. Aren't you going?

ADELA. It's nothing to me.

SERVANT. Since he has to turn the corner, you'll see him better from the window of your room.

[THE SERVANT *goes out*. ADELA *is left on the stage, standing doubtfully; after a moment, she also leaves rapidly, going toward her room*. BERNARDA *and* LA PONCIA *come in*.]

BERNARDA. Damned portions and shares.

PONCIA. What a lot of money is left to Angustias!

BERNARDA. Yes.

PONCIA. And for the others, considerably less.

BERNARDA. You've told me that three times now, when you know I don't want it mentioned! Considerably less; a lot less! Don't remind me any more.

[ANGUSTIAS *comes in, her face heavily made up*.]

Angustias!

ANGUSTIAS. Mother.

BERNARDA. Have you dared to powder your face? Have you dared to wash your face on the day of your father's death?

ANGUSTIAS. He wasn't my father. Mine died a long time ago. Have you forgotten that already?

BERNARDA. You owe more to this man, father of your sisters, than to your own. Thanks to him, your fortune is intact.

ANGUSTIAS. We'll have to see about that first!

BERNARDA. Even out of decency! Out of respect!

ANGUSTIAS. Let me go out, Mother!

BERNARDA. Let you go out? After I've taken that powder off your face, I will. Spineless! Painted hussy! Just like your aunts. [*She removes the powder violently with her handkerchief*.] Now get out!

PONCIA. Bernarda, don't be so hateful!

BERNARDA. Even though my mother is crazy, I still have my five senses and I know what I'm doing.

[*They all enter*.]

MAGDALENA. What's going on here?

BERNARDA. Nothing's "going on here"!

MAGDALENA [*to* ANGUSTIAS]. If you're fighting over the inheritance, you're the richest one and can hang on to it all.

ANGUSTIAS. Keep your tongue in your pocketbook!

BERNARDA [*beating on the floor*]. Don't fool yourselves into thinking you'll sway me. Until I go out of this house feet first I'll give the orders for myself and for you!

[*Voices are heard and* MARIA JOSEFA, BERNARDA'S *mother, enters. She is very old and has decked out her head and breast with flowers.*]

MARIA JOSEFA. Bernarda, where is my mantilla?[4] Nothing, nothing of what I own will be for any of you. Not my rings nor my black moiré[5] dress. Because not a one of you is going to marry—not a one. Bernarda, give me my necklace of pearls.

BERNARDA [*to* THE SERVANT]. Why did you let her get in here?

SERVANT [*trembling*]. She got away from me!

MARIA JOSEFA. I ran away because I want to marry—I want to get married to a beautiful manly man from the shore of the sea. Because here the men run from women.

BERNARDA. Hush, Hush, Mother!

MARIA JOSEFA. No, no—I won't hush. I don't want to see these single women, longing for marriage, turning their hearts to dust; and I want to go to my home town. Bernarda, I want a man to get married to and be happy with!

BERNARDA. Lock her up!

MARIA JOSEFA. Let me go out, Bernarda!

[THE SERVANT *seizes* MARIA JOSEFA.]

BERNARDA. Help her, all of you!

[*They all grab the old woman.*]

MARIA JOSEFA. I want to get away from here! Bernarda! To get married by the shore of sea—by the shore of the sea!

QUICK CURTAIN

ACT II

A white room in BERNARDA'S *house. The doors on the left lead to the bedrooms.* BERNARDA'S *daughters are seated on low chairs, sewing.* MAGDALENA *is embroidering.* LA PONCIA *is with them.*

ANGUSTIAS. I've cut the third sheet.

MARTIRIO. That one goes to Amelia.

MAGDALENA. Angustias, shall I put Pepe's initials here too?

ANGUSTIAS [*dryly*]. No.

MAGDALENA [*calling*]. Adela, aren't you coming?

AMELIA. She's probably stretched out on the bed.

PONCIA. Something's wrong with that one. I find her restless, trembling, frightened—as if a lizard were between her breasts.

MARTIRIO. There's nothing, more or less, wrong with her than there is with all of us.

MAGDALENA. All of us except Angustias.

ANGUSTIAS. I feel fine, and anybody who doesn't like it can pop.

[4] A light, ornamental scarf worn over the head and shoulders.
[5] A fine fabric with a wavy, watered finish.

MAGDALENA. We all have to admit the nicest things about you are your figure and your tact.

ANGUSTIAS. Fortunately, I'll soon be out of this hell.

MAGDALENA. Maybe you won't get out!

MARTIRIO. Stop this talk!

ANGUSTIAS. Besides, a good dowry is better than dark eyes in one's face!

MAGDALENA. All you say just goes in one ear and out the other.

AMELIA [*to* LA PONCIA]. Open the patio door and see if we can get a bit of a breeze.

[LA PONCIA *opens the door*.]

MARTIRIO. Last night I couldn't sleep because of the heat.

AMELIA. Neither could I.

MAGDALENA. I got up for a bit of air. There was a black storm cloud and a few drops even fell.

PONCIA. It was one in the morning and the earth seemed to give off fire. I got up too. Angustias was still at the window with Pepe.

MAGDALENA [*with irony*]. That late? What time did he leave?

ANGUSTIAS. Why do you ask, if you saw him?

AMELIA. He must have left about one-thirty.

ANGUSTIAS. Yes. How did you know?

AMELIA. I heard him cough and heard his mare's hoofbeats.

PONCIA. But I heard him leave around four.

ANGUSTIAS. It must have been someone else!

PONCIA. No, I'm sure of it!

AMELIA. That's what it seemed to me, too.

MAGDALENA. That's very strange!

[*Pause*.]

PONCIA. Listen, Angustias, what did he say to you the first time he came by your window?

ANGUSTIAS. Nothing. What should he say? Just talked.

MARTIRIO. It's certainly strange that two people who never knew each other should suddenly meet at a window and be engaged.

ANGUSTIAS. Well, I didn't mind.

AMELIA. I'd have felt very strange about it.

ANGUSTIAS. No, because when a man comes to a window he knows, from all the busybodies who come and go and fetch and carry, that he's going to be told "yes."

MARTIRIO. All right, but he'd have to ask you.

ANGUSTIAS. Of course!

AMELIA [*inquisitively*]. And how did he ask you?

ANGUSTIAS. Why, no way:—"You know I'm after you. I need a good, well brought up woman, and that's you— if it's agreeable."

AMELIA. These things embarrass me!

ANGUSTIAS. They embarrass me too, but one has to go through it!

PONCIA. And did he say anything more?

ANGUSTIAS. Yes, he did all the talking.

MARTIRIO. And you?

ANGUSTIAS. I couldn't have said a word. My heart was almost coming out of my mouth. It was the first time I'd ever been alone at night with a man.

MAGDALENA. And such a handsome man.
ANGUSTIAS. He's not bad looking.
PONCIA. Those things happen among people who have an idea how to do things, who talk and say and move their hand. The first time my husband, Evaristo the Short-tailed, came to my window . . . Ha! Ha! Ha!
AMELIA. What happened?
PONCIA. It was very dark. I saw him coming along and as he went by he said, "Good evening," "Good evening," I said. Then we were both silent for more than half an hour. The sweat poured down my body. Then Evaristo got nearer and nearer as if he wanted to squeeze in through the bars and said in a very low voice—"Come here and let me feel you!"

[*They all laugh.* AMELIA *gets up, runs, and looks through the door.*]

AMELIA. Ay, I thought Mother was coming!
MAGDALENA. What she'd have done to us!

[*They go on laughing.*]

AMELIA. Sh-h-h! She'll hear us.
PONCIA. Then he acted very decently. Instead of getting some other idea, he went to raising birds, until he died. You aren't married but it's good for you to know, anyway, that two weeks after the wedding a man gives up the bed for the table, then the table for the tavern, and the woman who doesn't like it can just rot, weeping in a corner.
AMELIA. You liked it.
PONCIA. I learned how to handle him!
MARTIRIO. Is it true that you sometimes hit him?
PONCIA. Yes, and once I almost poked out one of his eyes!
MAGDALENA. All women ought to be like that!
PONCIA. I'm one of your mother's school. One time I don't know what he said to me, and then I killed all his birds—with the pestle!

[*They laugh.*]

MAGDALENA. Adela, child! Don't miss this.
AMELIA. Adela!

[*Pause.*]

MAGDALENA. I'll go see!

[*She goes out.*]

PONCIA. That child is sick!
MARTIRIO. Of course. She hardly sleeps!
PONCIA. What *does* she do, then?
MARTIRIO. How do I know what she does?
PONCIA. You probably know better than we do, since you sleep with just a wall between you.
ANGUSTIAS. Envy gnaws on people.
AMELIA. Don't exaggerate.
ANGUSTIAS. I can tell it in her eyes. She's getting the look of a crazy woman.
MARTIRIO. Don't talk about crazy women. This is one place you're not allowed to say that word.

[MAGDALENA *and* ADELA *enter.*]

MAGDALENA. Didn't you say she was asleep?
ADELA. My body aches.

MARTIRIO [*with a hidden meaning*]. Didn't you sleep well last night?

ADELA. Yes.

MARTIRIO. Then?

ADELA [*loudly*]. Leave me alone. Awake or asleep, it's no affair of yours. I'll do whatever I want to with my body.

MARTIRIO. I was just concerned about you!

ADELA. Concerned?—curious! Weren't you sewing? Well, continue! I wish I were invisible so I could pass through a room without being asked where I was going!

SERVANT [*entering*]. Bernarda is calling you. The man with the laces is here.

[*All but* ADELA *and* LA PONCIA *go out, and as* MARTIRIO *leaves, she looks fixedly at* ADELA.]

ADELA. Don't look at me like that! If you want, I'll give you my eyes, for they're younger, and my back to improve that hump you have, but look the other way when I go by.

PONCIA. Adela, she's your sister, and the one who most loves you besides!

ADELA. She follows me everywhere. Sometimes she looks in my room to see if I'm sleeping. She won't let me breathe, and always, "Too bad about that face!" "Too bad about that body! It's going to waste!" But I won't let that happen. My body will be for whomever I choose.

PONCIA [*insinuatingly, in a low voice*]. For Pepe el Romano, no?

ADELA [*frightened*]. What do you mean?

PONCIA. What I said, Adela!

ADELA. Shut up!

PONCIA [*loudly*]. Don't you think I've noticed?

ADELA. Lower your voice!

PONCIA. Then forget what you're thinking about!

ADELA. What do you know?

PONCIA. We old ones can see through walls. Where do you go when you get up at night?

ADELA. I wish you were blind!

PONCIA. But my head and hands are full of eyes, where something like this is concerned. I couldn't possibly guess your intentions. Why did you sit almost naked at your window, and with the light on and the window open, when Pepe passed by the second night he came to talk with your sister?

ADELA. That's not true!

PONCIA. Don't be a child! Leave your sister alone. And if you like Pepe el Romano, keep it to yourself. [ADELA *weeps*.] Besides, who says you can't marry him? Your sister Angustias is sickly. She'll die with her first child. Narrow waisted, old—and out of my experience I can tell you she'll die. Then Pepe will do what all widowers do in these parts: he'll marry the youngest and most beautiful, and that's you. Live on that hope, forget him, anything; but don't go against God's law.

ADELA. Hush.

PONCIA. I won't hush!

ADELA. Mind your own business. Snooper, traitor!

PONCIA. I'm going to stick to you like a shadow!

ADELA. Instead of cleaning the house and then going to bed and praying for the dead, you root around like an old sow about goings on between men and women—so you can drool over them.

PONCIA. I keep watch; so people won't spit when they pass our door.

ADELA. What a tremendous affection you've suddenly conceived for my sister.

PONCIA. I don't have any affection for any of you. I want to live in a decent house. I don't want to be dirtied in my old age!

ADELA. Save your advice. It's already too late. For I'd leap not over you, just a servant, but over my mother to put out this fire I feel in my legs and my mouth. What can you possibly say about me? That I lock myself in my room and will not open the door? That I don't sleep? I'm smarter than you! See if you can catch the hare with your hands.

PONCIA. Don't defy me, Adela, don't defy me! Because I can shout, light lamps, and make bells ring.

ADELA. Bring four thousand yellow flares and set them about the walls of the yard. No one can stop what has to happen.

PONCIA. You like him that much?

ADELA. That much! Looking in his eyes I seem to drink his blood in slowly.

PONCIA. I won't listen to you.

ADELA. Well, you'll have to! I've been afraid of you. But now I'm stronger than you!

[ANGUSTIAS *enters.*]

ANGUSTIAS. Always arguing!

PONCIA. Certainly. She insists that in all this heat I have to go bring her I don't know what from the store.

ANGUSTIAS. Did you buy me the bottle of perfume?

PONCIA. The most expensive one. And the face powder. I put them on the table in your room.

[ANGUSTIAS *goes out.*]

ADELA. And be quiet!

PONCIA. We'll see!

[MARTIRIO *and* AMELIA *enter.*]

MARTIRIO [*to* ADELA]. Did you see the laces?

AMELIA. Angustias', for her wedding sheets, are beautiful.

ADELA [*to* MARTIRIO, *who is carrying some lace*]. And these?

MARTIRIO. They're for me. For a nightgown.

ADELA [*with sarcasm*]. One needs a sense of humor around here!

MARTIRIO [*meaningfully*]. But only for me to look at. I don't have to exhibit myself before anybody.

PONCIA. No one ever sees us in our nightgowns.

MARTIRIO [*meaningfully, looking at* ADELA]. Sometimes they don't! But I love nice underwear. If I were rich, I'd have it made of Holland Cloth.[6] It's one of the few tastes I've left.

PONCIA. These laces are beautiful for babies' caps and christening gowns. I could never afford them for my own. Now let's see if Angustias will use them for hers. Once she starts having children, they'll keep her running night and day.

MAGDALENA. I don't intend to sew a stitch on them.

[6] A fine grade of cotton fabric.

AMELIA. And much less bring up some stranger's children. Look how our neighbors across the road are—making sacrifices for four brats.

PONCIA. They're better off than you. There at least they laugh and you can hear them fight.

MARTIRIO. Well, you go work for them, then.

PONCIA. No, fate has sent me to this nunnery!

[*Tiny bells are heard distantly as though through several thicknesses of wall.*]

MAGDALENA. It's the men going back to work.

PONCIA. It was three o'clock a minute ago.

MARTIRIO. With this sun!

ADELA [*sitting down*]. Ay! If only we could go out in the fields too!

MAGDALENA [*sitting down*]. Each class does what it has to!

MARTIRIO [*sitting down*]. That's it!

AMELIA [*sitting down*]. Ay!

PONCIA. There's no happiness like that in the fields right at this time of year. Yesterday morning the reapers arrived. Forty or fifty handsome young men.

MAGDALENA. Where are they from this year?

PONCIA. From far, far away. They came from the mountains! Happy! Like weathered trees! Shouting and throwing stones! Last night a woman who dresses in sequins and dances, with an accordion, arrived, and fifteen of them made a deal with her to take her to the olive grove. I saw them from far away. The one who talked with her was a boy with green eyes—tight knit as a sheaf of wheat.

AMELIA. Really?

ADELA. Are you sure?

PONCIA. Years ago another one of those women came here, and I myself gave my eldest son some money so he could go. Men need things like that.

ADELA. Everything's forgiven *them.*

AMELIA. To be born a woman's the worst possible punishment.

MAGDALENA. Even our eyes aren't our own.

[*A distant song is heard, coming nearer.*]

PONCIA. There they are. They have a beautiful song.

AMELIA. They're going out to reap now.

CHORUS.

The reapers have set out
Looking for ripe wheat;
They'll carry off the hearts
Of any girls they meet.

[*Tambourines and carrañacas*[7] *are heard. Pause. They all listen in the silence cut by the sun.*]

AMELIA. And they don't mind the sun!

MARTIRIO. They reap through flames.

ADELA. How I'd like to be a reaper so I could come and go as I pleased. Then we could forget what's eating us all.

[7] Folk percussion instruments.

MARTIRIO. What do you have to forget?
ADELA. Each one of us has something.
MARTIRIO [*intensely*]. Each one!
PONCIA. Quiet! Quiet!
CHORUS [*very distantly*].

Throw wide your doors and windows,
You girls who live in the town.
The reaper asks you for roses
With which to deck his crown.

PONCIA. What a song!
MARTIRIO [*with nostalgia*].

Throw wide your doors and windows,
You girls who live in the town.

ADELA [*passionately*].

The reaper asks you for roses
With which to deck his crown.

[*The song grows more distant.*]

PONCIA. Now they're turning the corner.
ADELA. Let's watch them from the window of my room.
PONCIA. Be careful not to open the shutters too much because they're likely to give them a push to see who's looking.

[*The three leave.* MARTIRIO *is left sitting on the low chair with her head between her hands.*]

AMELIA [*drawing near her*]. What's wrong with you?
MARTIRIO. The heat makes me feel ill.
AMELIA. And it's no more than that?
MARTIRIO. I was wishing it were November, the rainy days, the frost—anything except this unending summertime.
AMELIA. It'll pass and come again.
MARTIRIO. Naturally. [*Pause.*] What time did you go to sleep last night?
AMELIA. I don't know. I sleep like a log. Why?
MARTIRIO. Nothing. Only I thought I heard someone in the yard.
AMELIA. Yes?
MARTIRIO. Very late.
AMELIA. And weren't you afraid?
MARTIRIO. No. I've heard it other nights.
AMELIA. We'd better watch out! Couldn't it have been the shepherds?
MARTIRIO. The shepherds come at six.
AMELIA. Maybe a young, unbroken mule?
MARTIRIO [*to herself, with double meaning*]. That's it! That's it! An unbroken little mule.
AMELIA. We'll have to set a watch.
MARTIRIO. No. No. Don't say anything. It may be I've just imagined it.
AMELIA. Maybe.

[*Pause.* AMELIA *starts to go.*]

MARTIRIO. Amelia!
AMELIA [*at the door*]. What?

[*Pause.*]

MARTIRIO. Nothing.

[*Pause.*]

AMELIA. Why did you call me?

[*Pause.*]

MARTIRIO. It just came out. I didn't mean to.

[*Pause.*]

AMELIA. Lie down for a little.

ANGUSTIAS. [*She bursts in furiously, in a manner that makes a great contrast with previous silence.*] Where's that picture of Pepe I had under my pillow? Which one of you has it?

MARTIRIO. No one.

AMELIA. You'd think he was a silver St. Bartholomew.[8]

ANGUSTIAS. Where's the picture?

[PONCIA, MAGDALENA, *and* ADELA *enter.*]

ADELA. What picture?

ANGUSTIAS. One of you has hidden it on me.

MAGDALENA. Do you have the effrontery to say that?

ANGUSTIAS. I had it in my room, and now it isn't there.

MARTIRIO. But couldn't it have jumped out into the yard at midnight? Pepe likes to walk around in the moonlight.

ANGUSTIAS. Don't joke with me! When he comes I'll tell him.

PONCIA. Don't do that! Because it'll turn up. [*Looking at* ADELA.]

ANGUSTIAS. I'd like to know which one of you has it.

ADELA [*looking at* MARTIRIO]. Somebody has it! But not me!

MARTIRIO [*with meaning*]. Of course not you!

BERNARDA [*entering, with her cane*]. What scandal is this in my house in the heat's heavy silence? The neighbors must have their ears glued to the walls.

ANGUSTIAS. They've stolen my sweetheart's picture!

BERNARDA [*fiercely*]. Who? Who?

ANGUSTIAS. They have!

BERNARDA. Which one of you? [*Silence.*] Answer me! [*Silence.*] [*To* LA PONCIA.] Search their rooms! Look in their beds.[9] This comes of not tying you up with shorter leashes. But I'll teach you now! [*To* ANGUSTIAS.] Are you sure?

ANGUSTIAS. Yes.

BERNARDA. Did you look everywhere?

ANGUSTIAS. Yes, Mother.

[*They all stand in an embarrassed silence.*]

BERNARDA. At the end of my life—to make me drink the bitterest poison a mother knows. [*To* PONCIA.] Did you find it?

PONCIA. Here it is.

BERNARDA. Where did you find it?

PONCIA. It was. . .

BERNARDA. Say it! Don't be afraid.

[8] One of the Twelve Apostles; legendary missionary to India and Armenia.

[9] Poncia exits here and re-enters just before Bernarda says, "Did you find it?"

PONCIA [*wonderingly*]. Between the sheets in Martirio's bed.

BERNARDA [*to* MARTIRIO]. Is that true?

MARTIRIO. It's true.

BERNARDA [*advancing on her, beating her with her cane*]. You'll come to a bad end yet, you hypocrite! Trouble maker!

MARTIRIO [*fiercely*]. Don't hit me, Mother!

BERNARDA. All I want to.

MARTIRIO. If I let you! You hear me? Get back.

PONCIA. Don't be disrespectful to your mother!

ANGUSTIAS [*holding* BERNARDA]. Let her go, please!

BERNARDA. Not even tears in your eyes.

MARTIRIO. I'm not going to cry just to please you.

BERNARDA. Why did you take the picture?

MARTIRIO. Can't I play a joke on my sister? What else would I want it for?

ADELA [*leaping forward, full of jealousy*]. It wasn't a joke! You never like to play jokes. It was something else bursting in her breast—trying to come out. Admit it openly now.

MARTIRIO. Hush, and don't make me speak; for if I should speak the walls would close together one against the other with shame.

ADELA. An evil tongue never stops inventing lies.

BERNARDA. Adela!

MAGDALENA. You're crazy.

AMELIA. And you stone us all with your evil suspicions.

MARTIRIO. But some others do things more wicked!

ADELA. Until all at once they stand forth stark naked and the river carries them along.

BERNARDA. Spiteful!

ANGUSTIAS. It's not my fault Pepe el Romano chose me!

ADELA. For your money.

ANGUSTIAS. Mother!

BERNARDA. Silence!

MARTIRIO. For your fields and your orchards.

MAGDALENA. That's only fair.

BERNARDA. Silence, I say! I saw the storm coming but I didn't think it'd burst so soon. Oh, what an avalanche of hate you've thrown on my heart! But I'm not old yet—I have five chains for you, and this house my father built, so not even the weeds will know of my desolation. Out of here!

[*They go out.* BERNARDA *sits down desolately.* LA PONCIA *is standing close to the wall.* BERNARDA *recovers herself, and beats on the floor.*]

I'll have to let them feel the weight of my hand! Bernarda, remember your duty!

PONCIA. May I speak?

BERNARDA. Speak. I'm sorry you heard. A stranger is always out of place in a family.

PONCIA. What I've seen, I've seen.

BERNARDA. Angustias must get married right away.

PONCIA. Certainly. We'll have to get her away from here.

BERNARDA. Not her, him!

PONCIA. Of course. He's the one to get away from here. You've thought it all out.

BERNARDA. I'm not thinking. There are things that shouldn't and can't be thought out. I give orders.

PONCIA. And you think he'll be satisfied to go away?

BERNARDA [*rising*]. What are you imagining now?

PONCIA. He will, of course, marry Angustias.

BERNARDA. Speak up! I know you well enough to see that your knife's out for me.

PONCIA. I never knew a warning could be called murder.

BERNARDA. Have you some "warning" for me?

PONCIA. I'm not making any accusations, Bernarda. I'm only telling you to open your eyes and you'll see.

BERNARDA. See what?

PONCIA. You've always been smart, Bernarda. You've seen other people's sins a hundred miles away. Many times I've thought you could read minds. But, your children are your children, and now you're blind.

BERNARDA. Are you talking about Martirio?

PONCIA. Well, yes—about Martirio . . . [*With curiosity.*] I wonder why she hid the picture?

BERNARDA [*shielding her daughter*]. After all, she says it was a joke. What else could it be?

PONCIA [*scornfully*]. Do you believe that?

BERNARDA [*sternly*]. I don't merely believe it. It's so!

PONCIA. Enough of this. We're talking about your family. But if we were talking about your neighbor across the way, what would it be?

BERNARDA. Now you're beginning to pull the point of the knife out.

PONCIA [*always cruelly*]. No, Bernarda. Something very grave is happening here. I don't want to put the blame on your shoulders, but you've never given your daughters any freedom. Martirio is lovesick, I don't care what you say. Why didn't you let her marry Enrique Humanas? Why, on the very day he was coming to her window, did you send him a message not to come?

BERNARDA [*loudly*]. I'd do it a thousand times over! My blood won't mingle with the Humanas' while I live! His father was a shepherd.

PONCIA. And you see now what's happening to you with these airs!

BERNARDA. I have them because I can afford to. And you don't have them because you know where you came from!

PONCIA [*with hate*]. Don't remind me! I'm old now. I've always been grateful for your protection.

BERNARDA [*emboldened*]. You don't seem so!

PONCIA [*with hate, behind softness*]. Martirio will forget this.

BERNARDA. And if she doesn't—the worse for her. I don't believe this is that "very grave thing" that's happening here. Nothing's happening here. It's just that you wish it would! And if it should happen one day, you can be sure it won't go beyond these walls.

PONCIA. I'm not so sure of that! There are people in town who can also read hidden thoughts, from afar.

BERNARDA. How you'd like to see me and my daughters on our way to a whorehouse!

PONCIA. No one knows her own destiny!

BERNARDA. I know my destiny! And my daughters! The whorehouse was for a certain woman, already dead. . .

PONCIA [*fiercely*]. Bernarda, respect the memory of my mother!

BERNARDA. Then don't plague me with your evil thoughts!

[*Pause.*]

PONCIA. I'd better stay out of everything.

BERNARDA. That's what you ought to do. Work and keep your mouth shut. The duty of all who work for a living.

PONCIA. But we can't do that. Don't you think it'd be better for Pepe to marry Martirio or . . . yes! . . . Adela?

BERNARDA. No, I don't think so.

PONCIA [*with meaning*]. Adela! She's Romano's real sweetheart!

BERNARDA. Things are never the way we want them!

PONCIA. But it's hard work to turn them from their destined course. For Pepe to be with Angustias seems wrong to me—and to other people—and even to the wind. Who knows if they'll get what they want?

BERNARDA. There you go again! Sneaking up on me—giving me bad dreams. But I won't listen to you, because if all you say should come to pass—I'd scratch your face.

PONCIA. Frighten someone else with that.

BERNARDA. Fortunately, my daughters respect me and have never gone against my will!

PONCIA. That's right! But, as soon as they break loose they'll fly to the rooftops!

BERNARDA. And I'll bring them down with stones!

PONCIA. Oh, yes! You were always the bravest one!

BERNARDA. I've always enjoyed a good fight!

PONCIA. But aren't people strange. You should see Angustias' enthusiasm for her lover, at her age! And he seems very smitten too. Yesterday my oldest son told me that when he passed by with the oxen at four-thirty in the morning they were still talking.

BERNARDA. At four-thirty?

ANGUSTIAS [*entering*]. That's a lie!

PONCIA. That's what he told me.

BERNARDA [*to* ANGUSTIAS]. Speak up!

ANGUSTIAS. For more than a week Pepe has been leaving at one. May God strike me dead if I'm lying.

MARTIRIO [*entering*]. I heard him leave at four too.

BERNARDA. But did you see him with your eyes?

MARTIRIO. I didn't want to look out. Don't you talk now through the side window?

ANGUSTIAS. We talk through my bedroom window.

[ADELA *appears at the door.*]

MARTIRIO. Then. . .

BERNARDA. What's going on here?

PONCIA. If you're not careful, you'll find out! At least Pepe was at *one* of your windows—and at four in the morning too!

BERNARDA. Are you sure of that?

PONCIA. You can't be sure of anything in this life!

ADELA. Mother, don't listen to someone who wants us to lose everything we have.

BERNARDA. I know how to take care of myself! If the townspeople want to come bearing false witness against me, they'll run into a stone wall! Don't any of you talk about this! Sometimes other people try to stir up a wave of filth to drown us.

MARTIRIO. I don't like to lie.

PONCIA. So there must be something.

BERNARDA. There won't be anything. I was born to have my eyes always open. Now I'll watch without closing them 'til I die.

ANGUSTIAS. I have the right to know.

BERNARDA. You don't have any right except to obey. No one's going to fetch and carry for me. [*To* LA PONCIA.] And don't meddle in our affairs. No one will take a step without my knowing it.

SERVANT [*entering*]. There's a big crowd at the top of the street, and all the neighbors are at their doors!

BERNARDA [*to* PONCIA]. Run see what's happening!

[*The girls are about to run out.*]

Where are you going? I always knew you for window-watching women and breakers of your mourning. All of you, to the patio!

[*They go out.* BERNARDA *leaves. Distant shouts are heard.* MARTIRIO *and* ADELA *enter and listen, not daring to step farther than the front door.*]

MARTIRIO. You can be thankful I didn't happen to open my mouth.

ADELA. I would have spoken too.

MARTIRIO. And what were you going to say? Wanting isn't doing!

ADELA. I do what I can and what happens to suit me. You've wanted to, but haven't been able.

MARTIRIO. You won't go on very long.

ADELA. I'll have everything!

MARTIRIO. I'll tear you out of his arms!

ADELA [*pleadingly*]. Martirio, let me be!

MARTIRIO. None of us will have him!

ADELA. He wants me for his house!

MARTIRIO. I saw how he embraced you!

ADELA. I didn't want him to. It's as if I were dragged by a rope.

MARTIRIO. I'll see you dead first!

[MAGDALENA *and* ANGUSTIAS *look in. The tumult is increasing.* THE SERVANT *enters with* BERNARDA. PONCIA *also enters from another door.*]

PONCIA. Bernarda!

BERNARDA. What's happening?

PONCIA. Librada's daughter, the unmarried one, had a child and no one knows whose it is!

ADELA. A child?

PONCIA. And to hide her shame she killed it and hid it under the rocks, but the dogs, with more heart than most Christians, dug it out and, as though directed by the hand of God, left it at her door. Now they want to kill her. They're dragging her through the streets—and down the paths and across the olive groves the men are coming, shouting so the fields shake.

BERNARDA. Yes, let them all come with olive whips and hoe handles—let them all come and kill her!

ADELA. No, not to kill her!

MARTIRIO. Yes—and let us go out too!

BERNARDA. And let whoever loses her decency pay for it!

[*Outside a woman's shriek and a great clamor is heard.*]

ADELA. Let her escape! Don't you go out!

MARTIRIO [*looking at* ADELA]. Let her pay what she owes!

BERNARDA [*at the archway*]. Finish her before the guards come! Hot coals in the place where she sinned!

ADELA [*holding her belly*]. No! No!

BERNARDA. Kill her! Kill her!

CURTAIN

ACT III

Four white walls, lightly washed in blue, of the interior patio of BERNARDA ALBA'*s house. The doorways, illumined by the lights inside the rooms, give a tenuous glow to the stage.*

At the center there is a table with a shaded oil lamp about which BERNARDA *and her daughters are eating.* LA PONCIA *serves them.* PRUDENCIA *sits apart. When the curtain rises, there is a great silence interrupted only by the noise of plates and silverware.*

PRUDENCIA. I'm going. I've made you a long visit. [*She rises.*]

BERNARDA. But wait, Prudencia. We never see one another.

PRUDENCIA. Have they sounded the last call to rosary?[10]

PONCIA. Not yet.

[PRUDENCIA *sits down again.*]

BERNARDA. And your husband, how's he getting on?

PRUDENCIA. The same.

BERNARDA. We never see him either.

PRUDENCIA. You know how he is. Since he quarrelled with his brothers over the inheritance, he hasn't used the front door. He takes a ladder and climbs over the back wall.

BERNARDA. He's a real man! And your daughter?

PRUDENCIA. He's never forgiven her.

BERNARDA. He's right.

PRUDENCIA. I don't know what he told you. I suffer because of it.

BERNARDA. A daughter who's disobedient stops being a daughter and becomes an enemy.

[10] A devotion consisting of meditation on five sacred mysteries while reciting five decades of Ave Marias.

PRUDENCIA. I let water run. The only consolation I've left is to take refuge in the church, but, since I'm losing my sight, I'll have to stop coming so the children won't make fun of me.

[*A heavy blow is heard against the walls.*]

What's that?

BERNARDA. The stallion. He's locked in the stall and he kicks against the wall of the house. [*Shouting.*] Tether him and take him out in the yard! [*In a lower voice.*] He must be too hot.

PRUDENCIA. Are you going to put the new mares to him?

BERNARDA. At daybreak.

PRUDENCIA. You've known how to increase your stock.

BERNARDA. By dint of money and struggling.

PONCIA [*interrupting*]. And she has the best herd in these parts. It's a shame that prices are low.

BERNARDA. Do you want a little cheese and honey?

PRUDENCIA. I have no appetite.

[*The blow is heard again.*]

PONCIA. My God!

PRUDENCIA. It quivered in my chest!

BERNARDA [*rising, furiously*]. Do I have to say things twice? Let him out to roll on the straw. [*Pause. Then, as though speaking to the stableman.*] Well, then lock the mares in the corral, but let him run free or he may kick down the walls. [*She returns to the table and sits again.*] Ay, what a life!

PRUDENCIA. You have to fight like a man.

BERNARDA. That's it.

[ADELA *gets up from the table.*]

Where are you going?

ADELA. For a drink of water.

BERNARDA [*raising her voice*]. Bring a pitcher of cool water. [*To* ADELA.] You can sit down.

[ADELA *sits down.*]

PRUDENCIA. And Angustias, when will she get married?

BERNARDA. They're coming to ask for her within three days.

PRUDENCIA. You must be happy.

ANGUSTIAS. Naturally!

AMELIA [*to* MAGDALENA]. You've spilled the salt!

MAGDALENA. You can't possibly have worse luck than you're having.

AMELIA. It always brings bad luck.

BERNARDA. That's enough!

PRUDENCIA [*to* ANGUSTIAS]. Has he given you the ring yet?

ANGUSTIAS. Look at it. [*She holds it out.*]

PRUDENCIA. It's beautiful. Three pearls. In my day, pearls signified tears.

ANGUSTIAS. But things have changed now.

ADELA. I don't think so. Things go on meaning the same. Engagement rings should be diamonds.

PONCIA. The most appropriate.

BERNARDA. With pearls or without them, things are as one proposes.

MARTIRIO. Or as God disposes.

PRUDENCIA. I've been told your furniture is beautiful.

BERNARDA. It cost sixteen thousand *reales.*

PONCIA [*interrupting*]. The best is the wardrobe with the mirror.
PRUDENCIA. I never saw a piece like that.
BERNARDA. We had chests.
PRUDENCIA. The important thing is that everything be for the best.
ADELA. And that you never know.
BERNARDA. There's no reason why it shouldn't be.

[*Bells are heard very distantly.*]

PRUDENCIA. The last call. [*To* ANGUSTIAS.] I'll be coming back to have you show me your clothes.
ANGUSTIAS. Whenever you like.
PRUDENCIA. Good evening—God bless you!
BERNARDA. Good-bye, Prudencia.
ALL FIVE DAUGHTERS [*at the same time*]. God go with you!

[*Pause.* PRUDENCIA *goes out.*]

BERNARDA. Well, we've eaten.

[*They rise.*]

ADELA. I'm going to walk as far as the gate to stretch my legs and get a bit of fresh air.

[MAGDALENA *sits down in a low chair and leans against the wall.*]

AMELIA. I'll go with you.
MARTIRIO. I too.
ADELA [*with contained hate*]. I'm not going to get lost!
AMELIA. One needs company at night.

[*They go out.* BERNARDA *sits down.* ANGUSTIAS *is clearing the table.*]

BERNARDA. I've told you once already! I want you to talk to your sister Martirio. What happened about the picture was a joke and you must forget it.
ANGUSTIAS. You know she doesn't like me.
BERNARDA. Each one knows what she thinks inside. I don't pry into anyone's heart, but I want to put up a good front and have family harmony. You understand?
ANGUSTIAS. Yes.
BERNARDA. Then that's settled.
MAGDALENA. [*She is almost asleep.*] Besides, you'll be gone in no time. [*She falls asleep.*]
ANGUSTIAS. Not soon enough for me.
BERNARDA. What time did you stop talking last night?
ANGUSTIAS. Twelve-thirty.
BERNARDA. What does Pepe talk about?
ANGUSTIAS. I find him absent-minded. He always talks to me as though he were thinking of something else. If I ask him what's the matter, he answers—"We men have our worries."
BERNARDA. You shouldn't ask him. And when you're married, even less. Speak if he speaks, and look at him when he looks at you. That way you'll get along.
ANGUSTIAS. But, Mother, I think he's hiding things from me.

BERNARDA. Don't try to find out. Don't ask him, and above all, never let him see you cry.

ANGUSTIAS. I should be happy, but I'm not.

BERNARDA. It's all the same.

ANGUSTIAS. Many nights I watch Pepe very closely through the window bars and he seems to fade away—as though he were hidden in a cloud of dust like those raised by the flocks.

BERNARDA. That's just because you're not strong.

ANGUSTIAS. I hope so!

BERNARDA. Is he coming tonight?

ANGUSTIAS. No, he went into town with his mother.

BERNARDA. Good, we'll get to bed early. Magdalena!

ANGUSTIAS. She's asleep.

[ADELA, MARTIRIO, *and* AMELIA *enter.*]

AMELIA. What a dark night!

ADELA. You can't see two steps in front of you.

MARTIRIO. A good night for robbers, for anyone who needs to hide.

ADELA. The stallion was in the middle of the corral. White. Twice as large. Filling all the darkness.

AMELIA. It's true. It was frightening. Like a ghost.

ADELA. The sky has stars as big as fists.

MARTIRIO. This one stared at them till she almost cracked her neck.

ADELA. Don't you like them up there?

MARTIRIO. What goes on over the roof doesn't mean a thing to me. I have my hands full with what happens under it.

ADELA. Well, that's the way it goes with you!

BERNARDA. And it goes the same for you as for her.

ANGUSTIAS. Good night.

ADELA. Are you going to bed now?

ANGUSTIAS. Yes, Pepe isn't coming tonight.

[*She goes out.*]

ADELA. Mother, why, when a star falls or lightning flashes, does one say:
Holy Barbara,[11] blessed on high
May your name be in the sky
With holy water written high?

BERNARDA. The old people know many things we've forgotten.

AMELIA. I close my eyes so I won't see them.

ADELA. Not I. I like to see what's quiet and been quiet for years on end, running with fire.

MARTIRIO. But all that has nothing to do with us.

BERNARDA. And it's better not to think about it.

ADELA. What a beautiful night! I'd like to stay up till very late and enjoy the breeze from the fields.

BERNARDA. But we have to go to bed. Magdalena!

AMELIA. She's just dropped off.

[11] A virgin martyr (third or fourth century), said to have been killed by her father for being a Christian.

BERNARDA. Magdalena!

MAGDALENA [*annoyed*]. Leave me alone!

BERNARDA. To bed!

MAGDALENA [*rising, in a bad humor*]. You don't give anyone a moment's peace!

[*She goes off grumbling.*]

AMELIA. Good night!

[*She goes out.*]

BERNARDA. You two get along, too.

MARTIRIO. How is it Angustias' sweetheart isn't coming tonight?

BERNARDA. He went on a trip.

MARTIRIO [*looking at* ADELA]. Ah!

ADELA. I'll see you in the morning!

[*She goes out.* MARTIRIO *drinks some water and goes out slowly, looking at the door to the yard.* LA PONCIA *enters.*]

PONCIA. Are you still here?

BERNARDA. Enjoying this quiet and not seeing anywhere the "very grave thing" that's happening here—according to you.

PONCIA. Bernarda, let's not go any further with this.

BERNARDA. In this house there's no question of a yes or a no. My watchfulness can take care of anything.

PONCIA. Nothing's happening outside. That's true, all right. Your daughters act and are as though stuck in a cupboard. But neither you nor anyone else can keep watch inside a person's heart.

BERNARDA. My daughters breathe calmly enough.

PONCIA. That's your business, since you're their mother. I have enough to do just with serving you.

BERNARDA. Yes, you've turned quiet now.

PONCIA. I keep my place—that's all.

BERNARDA. The trouble is you've nothing to talk about. If there were grass in this house, you'd make it your business to put the neighbors' sheep to pasture here.

PONCIA. I hide more than you think.

BERNARDA. Do your sons still see Pepe at four in the morning? Are they still repeating this house's evil litany?

PONCIA. They say nothing.

BERNARDA. Because they can't. Because there's nothing for them to sink their teeth in. And all because my eyes keep constant watch!

PONCIA. Bernarda! I don't want to talk about this because I'm afraid of what you'll do. But don't you feel so safe.

BERNARDA. Very safe!

PONCIA. Who knows, lightning might strike suddenly. Who knows but what all of a sudden, in a rush of blood, your heart might stop.

BERNARDA. Nothing will happen here. I'm on guard now against all your suspicions.

PONCIA. All the better for you.

BERNARDA. Certainly, all the better!

SERVANT [*entering*]. I've just finished with the dishes. Is there anything else, Bernarda?

BERNARDA [*rising*]. Nothing. I'm going to get some rest.

PONCIA. What time do you want me to call you?

BERNARDA. No time. Tonight I intend to sleep well.

[*She goes out.*]

PONCIA. When you're powerless against the sea, it's easier to turn your back on it and not look at it.

SERVANT. She's so proud! She herself pulls the blindfold over her eyes.

PONCIA. I can do nothing. I tried to head things off, but now they frighten me too much. You feel this silence?—in each room there's a thunderstorm—and the day it breaks, it'll sweep all of us along with it. But I've said what I had to say.

SERVANT. Bernarda thinks nothing can stand against her, yet she doesn't know the strength a man has among women alone.

PONCIA. It's not all the fault of Pepe el Romano. It's true last year he was running after Adela; and she was crazy about him—but she ought to keep her place and not lead him on. A man's a man.

SERVANT. And some there are who believe he didn't have to talk many times with Adela.

PONCIA. That's true. [*In a low voice.*] And some other things.

SERVANT. I don't know what's going to happen here.

PONCIA. How I'd like to sail across the sea and leave this house, this battleground, behind!

SERVANT. Bernarda's hurrying the wedding and it's possible nothing will happen.

PONCIA. Things have gone much too far already. Adela is set[12] no matter what comes, and the rest of them watch without rest.

SERVANT. Martirio too. . .?

PONCIA. That one's the worst. She's a pool of poison. She sees El Romano is not for her, and she'd sink the world if it were in her hand to do so.

SERVANT. How bad they all are!

PONCIA. They're women without men, that's all. And in such matters even blood is forgotten. Sh-h-h! [*She listens.*]

SERVANT. What's the matter?

PONCIA. [*She rises.*] The dogs are barking.

SERVANT. Someone must have passed by the back door.

[ADELA *enters wearing a white petticoat and corselet.*]

PONCIA. Aren't you in bed yet?

ADELA. I want a drink of water. [*She drinks from a glass on the table.*]

PONCIA. I imagined you were asleep.

ADELA. I got thirsty and woke up. Aren't you two going to get some rest?

SERVANT. Soon now.

[ADELA *goes out.*]

PONCIA. Let's go.

SERVANT. We've certainly earned some sleep. Bernarda doesn't let me rest the whole day.

PONCIA. Take the light.

SERVANT. The dogs are going mad.

[12] Determined.

PONCIA. They're not going to let us sleep.

[*They go out. The stage is left almost dark.* MARIA JOSEFA *enters with a lamb in her arms.*]

MARIA JOSEFA [*singing*].

Little lamb, child of mine,
Let's go to the shore of the sea,
The tiny ant will be at his doorway,
I'll nurse you and give you your bread.
Bernarda, old leopard-face,
And Magdalena, hyena-face,
Little lamb. . .
Rock, rock-a-bye,
Let's go to the palms at Bethlehem's gate.

[*She laughs.*]

Neither you nor I would want to sleep
The door will open by itself
And on the beach we'll go and hide
In a little coral cabin.
Bernarda, old leopard-face,
And Magdalena, hyena-face,
Little lamb. . .
Rock, rock-a-bye,
Let's go to the palms at Bethlehem's gate.

[*She goes off singing.*]

[ADELA *enters. She looks about cautiously and disappears out the door leading to the corral.* MARTIRIO *enters by another door and stands in anguished watchfulness near the center of the stage. She also is in petticoats. She covers herself with a small black scarf.* MARIA JOSEFA *crosses before her.*]

MARTIRIO. Grandmother, where are you going?

MARIA JOSEFA. You are going to open the door for me? Who are you?

MARTIRIO. How did you get out here?

MARIA JOSEFA. I escaped. You, who are you?

MARTIRIO. Go back to bed.

MARIA JOSEFA. You're Martirio. Now I see you. Martirio, face of a martyr. And when are you going to have a baby? I've had this one.

MARTIRIO. Where did you get that lamb?

MARIA JOSEFA. I know it's a lamb. But can't a lamb be a baby? It's better to have a lamb than not to have anything. Old Bernarda, leopard-face, and Magdalena, hyena-face!

MARTIRIO. Don't shout.

MARIA JOSEFA. It's true. Everything's very dark. Just because I have white hair you think I can't have babies, but I can—babies and babies and babies. This baby will have white hair, and I'd have *this* baby, and another, and this *one* other; and with all of us with snow white hair we'll be like the waves—one, then another, and another. Then we'll all sit down and all of us will have white heads, and we'll be seafoam. Why isn't there any seafoam here? Nothing but mourning shrouds here.

MARTIRIO. Hush, hush.

MARIA JOSEFA. When my neighbor had a baby, I'd carry her some chocolate and later she'd bring me some, and so on—always and always and always. You'll have white hair, but your neighbors won't come. Now I have to go away, but I'm afraid the dogs will bite me. Won't you come with me as far as the fields? I don't like fields. I like houses, but open houses, and the neighbor women asleep in their beds with their little tiny tots, and the men outside sitting in their chairs. Pepe el Romano is a giant. All of you love him. But he's going to devour you because you're grains of wheat. No, not grains of wheat. Frogs with no tongues!

MARTIRIO [*angrily*]. Come, off to bed with you. [*She pushes her.*]

MARIA JOSEFA. Yes, but then you'll open the door for me, won't you?

MARTIRIO. Of course.

MARIA JOSEFA [*weeping*].

Little lamb, child of mine,
Let's go to the shore of the sea,
The tiny ant will be at his doorway,
I'll nurse you and give you your bread.

[MARTIRIO *locks the door through which* MARIA JOSEFA *came out and goes to the yard door. There she hesitates, but goes two steps farther.*]

MARTIRIO [*in a low voice*]. Adela! [*Pause. She advances to the door. Then, calling.*] Adela!

[ADELA *enters. Her hair is disarranged.*]

ADELA. And what are you looking for me for?

MARTIRIO. Keep away from him.

ADELA. Who are you to tell me that?

MARTIRIO. That's no place for a decent woman.

ADELA. How you wish *you'd* been there!

MARTIRIO [*shouting*]. This is the moment for me to speak. This can't go on.

ADELA. This is just the beginning. I've had strength enough to push myself forward—the spirit and looks you lack. I've seen death under this roof, and gone out to look for what was mine, what belonged to me.

MARTIRIO. That soulless man came for another woman. You pushed yourself in front of him.

ADELA. He came for the money, but his eyes were always on me.

MARTIRIO. I won't allow you to snatch him away. He'll marry Angustias.

ADELA. You know better than I he doesn't love her.

MARTIRIO. I know.

ADELA. You know because you've seen—he loves me, me!

MARTIRIO [*desperately*]. Yes.

ADELA [*close before her*]. He loves me, *me*! He loves me, *me!*

MARTIRIO. Stick me with a knife if you like, but don't tell me that again.

ADELA. That's why you're trying to fix it so I won't go away with him. It makes no difference to you if he puts his arms around a woman he doesn't love. Nor does it to me. He could be a hundred years with

Angustias, but for him to have his arms around me seems terrible to you—because you too love him! You love him!

MARTIRIO [*dramatically*]. Yes! Let me say it without hiding my head. Yes! My breast's bitter, bursting like a pomegranate. I love him!

ADELA [*impulsively, hugging her*]. Martirio, Martirio, I'm not to blame!

MARTIRIO. Don't put your arms around me! Don't try to smooth it over. My blood's no longer yours, and even though I try to think of you as a sister, I see you as just another woman. [*She pushes her away.*]

ADELA. There's no way out here. Whoever has to drown—let her drown. Pepe is mine. He'll carry me to the rushes along the river bank. . .

MARTIRIO. He won't!

ADELA. I can't stand this horrible house after the taste of his mouth. I'll be what he wants me to be. Everybody in the village against me, burning me with their fiery fingers; pursued by those who claim they're decent, and I'll wear, before them all, the crown of thorns that belongs to the mistress of a married man.

MARTIRIO. Hush!

ADELA. Yes, yes. [*In a low voice.*] Let's go to bed. Let's let him marry Angustias. I don't care any more, but I'll go off alone to a little house where he'll come to see me whenever he wants, whenever he feels like it.

MARTIRIO. That'll never happen! Not while I have a drop of blood left in my body.

ADELA. Not just weak you, but a wild horse I could force to his knees with just the strength of my little finger.

MARTIRIO. Don't raise that voice of yours to me. It irritates me. I have a heart full of a force so evil that, without my wanting to be, I'm drowned by it.

ADELA. You show us the way to love our sisters. God must have meant to leave me alone in the midst of darkness, because I can see you as I've never seen you before.

[*A whistle is heard and* ADELA *runs toward the door, but* MARTIRIO *gets in front of her.*]

MARTIRIO. Where are you going?

ADELA. Get away from that door!

MARTIRIO. Get by me if you can!

ADELA. Get away!

[*They struggle.*]

MARTIRIO [*shouts*]. Mother! Mother!

ADELA. Let me go!

[BERNARDA *enters. She wears petticoats and a black shawl.*]

BERNARDA. Quiet! Quiet! How poor I am without even a man to help me!

MARTIRIO [*pointing to* ADELA]. She was with him. Look at those skirts covered with straw!

BERNARDA [*going furiously toward* ADELA]. That's the bed of a bad woman!

ADELA [*facing her*]. There'll be an end to prison voices here!

[ADELA *snatches away her mother's cane and breaks it in two.*]

This is what I do with the tyrant's cane. Not another step. No one but Pepe commands me!

[MAGDALENA *enters.*]

MAGDALENA. Adela!

[LA PONCIA *and* ANGUSTIAS *enter.*]

ADELA. I'm his. [*To* ANGUSTIAS.] Know that—and go out in the yard and tell him. He'll be master in this house.

ANGUSTIAS. My God!

BERNARDA. The gun! Where's the gun?

[*She rushes out,* MARTIRIO *following.* AMELIA *enters and looks on frightened, leaning her head against the wall.*]

ADELA. No one can hold me back! [*She tries to go out.*]

ANGUSTIAS [*holding her*]. You're not getting out of here with your body's triumph! Thief! Disgrace of this house!

MAGDALENA. Let her go where we'll never see her again!

[*A shot is heard.*]

BERNARDA [*entering*]. Just try looking for him now!

MARTIRIO [*entering*]. That does away with Pepe el Romano.

ADELA. Pepe! My God! Pepe!

[*She runs out.*]

PONCIA. Did you kill him?

MARTIRIO. No. He raced away on his mare!

BERNARDA. It was my fault. A woman can't aim.

MAGDALENA. Then, why did you say. . .?

MARTIRIO. For her! I'd like to pour a river of blood over her head!

PONCIA. Curse you.

MAGDALENA. Devil!

BERNARDA. Although it's better this way!

[*A thud is heard.*]

Adela! Adela!

PONCIA [*at her door*]. Open this door!

BERNARDA. Open! Don't think the walls will hide your shame!

SERVANT [*entering*]. All the neighbors are up!

BERNARDA [*in a low voice, but like a roar*]. Open! Or I'll knock the door down! [*Pause. Everything is silent.*] Adela! [*She walks away from the door.*] A hammer!

[LA PONCIA *throws herself against the door. It opens and she goes in. As she enters, she screams and backs out.*]

What is it?

PONCIA. [*She puts her hand to her throat.*] May we never die like that!

[THE SISTERS *fall back.* THE SERVANT *crosses herself.* BERNARDA *screams and goes forward.*]

Don't go in!

BERNARDA. No, not I! Pepe, you're running now, alive, in the darkness, under the trees, but another day you'll fall. Cut her down! My daughter died a virgin. Take her to another room and dress her as though she were a virgin. No one will say anything about this! She died a virgin. Tell them, so that at dawn, the bells will ring twice.

MARTIRIO. A thousand times happy she, who had him.

BERNARDA. And I want no weeping. Death must be looked at face to face. Silence! [*To one daughter.*] Be still, I said! [*To another daughter.*] Tears when you're alone! We'll drown ourselves in a sea of mourning. She, the youngest daughter of Bernarda Alba, died a virgin. Did you hear me? Silence, silence, I said. Silence!

CURTAIN

Jorge Luis Borges
(1899–)

A group of remarkable writers, including Gabriel Garcia Márquez, Jorge Amado, Julio Cortázar, and Mario Vargas Llosa, have transformed Latin American literature, in the last quarter of a century, from a placid backwater of world literature into an important current in the main stream. The most prominent of these writers is the Argentinian Jorge Luis Borges. Borges' reputation, although he has written voluminously in a number of forms, rests almost exclusively upon about forty short prose tales, not quite sketches, not quite short stories—"fictions," he prefers to call them—which he wrote between about 1937 and 1955. Some of these fictions are brief, dreamlike fantasies, and others read, initially at least, like short autobiographical sketches that gradually open upon vistas of alternative realities. The effect is often vertiginous, as if the reader had rounded a corner or reached the top of a hill and suddenly glimpsed new worlds of the imagination.

Borges was born in Buenos Aires in 1899 into a family that had included a number of famous Argentine patriots. His father, a lawyer, teacher, and man of letters, was half English, and Borges learned English before he learned Spanish. In his father's well-stocked library, he read, as a child, many of the classics of storytelling—the Arabian Nights, Don Quixote, *Greek mythology, and the novels of Charles Dickens, Mark Twain, and H. G. Wells—which were to leave their mark on his own later fiction-making. In 1914, the family was in Europe when World War I broke out. They spent the war in Switzerland, where Borges completed his education at the Collège de Genève, becoming proficient in Latin, French, and German. After the war, he lived for a year in Majorca and a year in Spain, where at the age of twenty-one he became friends with members of the avant-garde Ultraist movement, who, influenced by the French Symbolists, advocated free verse and the supremacy of metaphor over direct statement.*

Borges returned to Buenos Aires in 1921, and over the next sixteen years, he led the life of an independent young man of letters in the artistic circles of the capital. He founded three literary magazines, which he used to promote Ultraist ideas in Argentina, published several volumes of poetry and essays, and wrote reviews and translations. A Universal History of Infamy, *a collection of bizarre sketches of criminals, some imaginary, appeared in 1936, and* The History of Eternity, *a collection of essays on ideas of eternity throughout history, in 1937; both foreshadowed some of Borges' later preoccupations.*

The turning point in Borges' career came in 1937–38, when he took a job in the Buenos Aires library, his father died, and he suffered a serious accident that left him with a severe head wound, blood poisoning, and a prolonged period of high fever. While convalescing from this close encounter with death, he began to write the fictions that were to make him famous, initially, he said, to see if he could still develop a lucid argument. The first collection of these pieces, The Garden of Forking Paths, *appeared in 1941; an expanded version,* Fictions, *followed in 1944. The main body of Borges' most characteristic work was completed with* The Aleph *(1949).*

Although Borges defines politics as "one of the forms of tedium," he strongly opposed Hitler in pro-German Argentina, and he was equally outspoken in his opposition to the dictatorship of Juan Perón, who came to power in 1946. Perón's government dismissed Borges from his library job and offered him a position as chicken inspector in the Buenos Aires city market. He was able to find a teaching post instead, but he remained under surveillance and his mother and sister were arrested. When Perón was overthrown in 1955, Borges became director of the National Library of Argentina, a member of the National Academy, and, a year later, Professor of English and North American Literature at the University of Buenos Aires.

Borges' eyesight began to deteriorate rapidly in the 1950s, as the result of the same hereditary eye disease that had blinded his father, and he eventually went almost totally blind. After 1955, he turned his attention more to poetry than to prose; his poetry, rather formal and classical, is radically different from his fictions. He did, however, publish a collection of stories which he regarded as experiments in "straightforward storytelling," Doctor Brodie's Report, *in 1970. He has traveled widely in recent years, especially in the United States, where he has taught and delivered lectures on a number of university campuses.*

Borges' brief, unsettling fictions have often been compared to Kafka's dream stories. In certain obvious ways, the parallel is not very exact; Kafka writes of the unconscious and irrational, whereas the pleasures of Borges' stories seem to be those of the conscious, rational mind. He is one of the most bookish of writers, and his stories often seem like his own "Library of Babel," where the whole world is reduced to a collection of books that include "the faithful catalogue of the Library, thousands and thousands of false catalogues, a demonstration of the fallacy of the true catalogue," and "a version of each book in all languages, the interpolations of every book in all books." His stories are highly rational, artificial constructions, full of logical puzzles, perceptual tricks, and dazzling paradoxes. The title of Labyrinths, *a collection of his stories in English, might be taken as descriptive of all his work. "Tlön, Uqbar, Orbis Tertius," for example, is among other things a progress through a labyrinth in which the reader, with the narrator, is repeatedly offered a choice between two "turnings": the real* Encyclopaedia Britannica *and its double, the plagiarized* Anglo-American Cyclopaedia; *a copy of the* Anglo-American Cyclopaedia *that contains an article on Uqbar and one that does not; a faulty, half-remembered quotation from an Uqbar thinker and the true version; and a dozen other "forking paths."*

Beneath the witty artificiality of Borges' fictions, however, there is a core of mystery that makes the comparison with Kafka just, despite their superficial differences. Borges' stories all play with systems of order, ways man has tried to make sense of the world, whether they be obscure heresies, philosophical systems, or artistic forms. But ultimately, all systems become equally provisional, and we are left with a sense of life as irreducibly enigmatic, all attempts to order it being merely fragments shored against our ruins. "Through the years," Borges has written, "a man peoples a space with images of provinces, kingdoms, mountains, bays, ships, islands, fishes, rooms, tools, stars, horses, and people. Shortly before his death he discovers that the patient labyrinth of lines traces the image of his own face."

FURTHER READING *(prepared by N. K. B.):* For an extensive collection of Borges' fiction, essays, and poetry, see Emir Rodriquez Monegal and Alastair Reid, eds., *Borges: A Reader,* 1981, which includes both little-known selections and major works spanning his entire career. *Labyrinths,* 1962, ed. by Donald A. Yates and James E. Irby, is a collection of Borges' fiction and essays, with an introductory chapter on his life and writing. Emir Rodriquez Monegal's *Jorge Luis Borges,* 1978, gives a detailed account of Borges' life, integrating critical commentary on the poetry and prose. For good introductions to Borges' major themes and artistry, see Martin Stabb's *Jorge Luis Borges,* 1970, a study of form that includes chapters on the poetry, fiction, and critical essays, including an analysis of "The Circular Ruins," and J. M. Cohen's *Jorge Luis Borges,* 1972, which analyzes the Argentinian context for Borges' early work. George McMurray's *Jorge Luis Borges,* 1980, emphasizes the philosophical concerns in the fiction. Ana Maria Barrenechea's *Borges: The Labyrinth Maker* (trans. by Robert Lima), 1965, contains a helpful summary of the dominant symbols in Borges' writing. Lowell Dunham and Ivar Ivask have edited a wide-ranging collection of essays on Borges, *The Cardinal Points of Borges,* 1971, which includes articles on his narrative style and critical reception. John Updike's "Books: The Author as Librarian," in the *New Yorker,* October 31, 1965, discusses Borges' innovative narrative techniques.

TLÖN, UQBAR, ORBIS TERTIUS

Translated by James E. Irby

1

I owe the discovery of Uqbar to the conjunction of a mirror and an encyclopedia. The mirror troubled the depths of a corridor in a country house on Gaona Street in Ramos Mejía; the encyclopedia is fallaciously called *The Anglo-American Cyclopaedia* (New York, 1917) and is a literal but delinquent reprint of the *Encyclopaedia Britannica* of 1902. The event took place some five years ago. Bioy Casares[1] had had dinner with me that evening and we became lengthily engaged in a vast polemic concerning the composition of a novel in the first person, whose narrator would omit or disfigure the facts and indulge in various contradictions which would permit a few readers—very few readers—to perceive an atrocious or banal reality. From the remote depths of the corridor, the mirror spied upon us. We discovered (such a discovery is inevitable in the late hours of the night) that mirrors have something monstrous about them. Then Bioy Casares recalled that

[1] Adolfo Bioy Casares (b. 1914) is a well-known Argentine author and a friend and collaborator of Borges. Throughout the story, Borges mingles real and fictitious people.

one of the heresiarchs[2] of Uqbar had declared that mirrors and copulation are abominable, because they increase the number of men. I asked him the origin of this memorable observation and he answered that it was reproduced in *The Anglo-American Cyclopaedia,* in its article on Uqbar. The house (which we had rented furnished) had a set of this work. On the last pages of Volume XLVI we found an article on Upsala; on the first pages of Volume XLVII, one on Ural-Altaic Languages, but not a word about Uqbar. Bioy, a bit taken aback, consulted the volumes of the index. In vain he exhausted all of the imaginable spellings: Ukbar, Ucbar, Ooqbar, Ookbar, Oukbahr . . . Before leaving, he told me that it was a region of Iraq or of Asia Minor. I must confess that I agreed with some discomfort. I conjectured that this undocumented country and its anonymous heresiarch were a fiction devised by Bioy's modesty in order to justify a statement. The fruitless examination of one of Justus Perthes' atlases fortified my doubt.

The following day, Bioy called me from Buenos Aires. He told me he had before him the article on Uqbar, in Volume XLVI of the encyclopedia. The heresiarch's name was not forthcoming, but there was a note on his doctrine, formulated in words almost identical to those he had repeated, though perhaps literarily inferior. He had recalled: *Copulation and mirrors are abominable.* The text of the encyclopedia said: *For one of those gnostics, the visible universe was an illusion or (more precisely) a sophism. Mirrors and fatherhood are abominable because they multiply and disseminate that universe.* I told him, in all truthfulness, that I should like to see that article. A few days later he brought it. This surprised me, since the scrupulous cartographical indices of Ritter's *Erdkunde*[3] were plentifully ignorant of the name Uqbar.

The tome Bioy brought was, in fact, Volume XLVI of the *Anglo-American Cyclopaedia.* On the half-title page and the spine, the alphabetical marking (Tor-Ups) was that of our copy, but, instead of 917, it contained 921 pages. These four additional pages made up the article on Uqbar, which (as the reader will have noticed) was not indicated by the alphabetical marking. We later determined that there was no other difference between the volumes. Both of them (as I believe I have indicated) are reprints of the tenth *Encyclopaedia Britannica.* Bioy had acquired his copy at some sale or other.

We read the article with some care. The passage recalled by Bioy was perhaps the only surprising one. The rest of it seemed very plausible, quite in keeping with the general tone of the work and (as is natural) a bit boring. Reading it over again, we discovered beneath its rigorous prose a fundamental vagueness. Of the fourteen names which figured in the geographical part, we only recognized three—Khorasan, Armenia, Erzerum[4]—interpolated in the text in an ambiguous way. Of the historical names, only one: the impostor magician Smerdis,[5] invoked more as a metaphor. The note seemed to fix the boundaries of Uqbar, but its nebulous reference points were rivers and craters and mountain ranges of that same region. We read, for example, that the lowlands of Tsai Khaldun and the Axa Delta marked the southern frontier and that on the islands of the delta wild

[2] Those who advance heresies, or unorthodox opinions. [3] Geography.
[4] Actual places in the Middle East.
[5] A usurper who seized the throne of Persia in the sixth century B.C.

horses procreate. All this, on the first part of page 918. In the historical section (page 920) we learned that as a result of the religious persecutions of the thirteenth century, the orthodox believers sought refuge on these islands, where to this day their obelisks remain and where it is not uncommon to unearth their stone mirrors. The section on Language and Literature was brief. Only one trait is worthy of recollection: it noted that the literature of Uqbar was one of fantasy and that its epics and legends never referred to reality, but to the two imaginary regions of Mlejnas and Tlön . . . The bibliography enumerated four volumes which we have not yet found, though the third—Silas Haslam: *History of the Land Called Uqbar,* 1874—figures in the catalogues of Bernard Quaritch's book shop.[6] The first, *Lesbare und lesenswerthe Bemerkungen über das Land Ukkbar in Klein-Asien,* dates from 1641 and is the work of Johannes Valentinus Andreä.[7] This fact is significant; a few years later, I came upon that name in the unsuspected pages of De Quincey[8] (*Writings,* Volume XIII) and learned that it belonged to a German theologian who, in the early seventeenth century, described the imaginary community of Rosae Crucis[9]—a community that others founded later, in imitation of what he had prefigured.

That night we visited the National Library. In vain we exhausted atlases, catalogues, annuals of geographical societies, travelers' and historians' memoirs: no one had ever been in Uqbar. Neither did the general index of Bioy's encyclopedia register that name. The following day, Carlos Mastronardi (to whom I had related the matter) noticed the black and gold covers of the *Anglo-American Cyclopaedia* in a bookshop on Corrientes and Talcahuano . . . He entered and examined Volume XLVI. Of course, he did not find the slightest indication of Uqbar.

2

Some limited and waning memory of Herbert Ashe, an engineer of the southern railways, persists in the hotel at Adrogué, amongst the effusive honeysuckles and in the illusory depths of the mirrors. In his lifetime, he suffered from unreality, as do so many Englishmen; once dead, he is not even the ghost he was then. He was tall and listless and his tired rectangular beard had once been red. I understand he was a widower, without children. Every few years he would go to England, to visit (I judge from some photographs he showed us) a sundial and a few oaks. He and my father had entered into one of those close (the adjective is excessive) English friendships that begin by excluding confidences and very soon dispense with dialogue. They used to carry out an exchange of books and newspapers and engage in taciturn chess games . . . I remember him in the hotel corri-

[6] "Haslam has also published *A General History of Labyrinths*" (Borges' note). Bernard Quaritch ran a famous London bookshop in the nineteenth century.

[7] *Readable and Valuable Observations on the Land of Uqbar in Asia Minor.* Andreä (1586–1654) was an actual German theologian, although the book is fictitious.

[8] Thomas De Quincey (1785–1859), English essayist.

[9] The Brotherhood of the Rosy Cross, an occult group. The modern movement originated in the writings of Andreä, but it claims roots in ancient Egypt.

dor, with a mathematics book in his hand, sometimes looking at the irrecoverable colors of the sky. One afternoon, we spoke of the duodecimal system of numbering (in which twelve is written as 10). Ashe said that he was converting some kind of tables from the duodecimal to the sexagesimal system (in which sixty is written as 10). He added that the task had been entrusted to him by a Norwegian, in Rio Grande do Sul. We had known him for eight years and he had never mentioned his sojourn in that region . . . We talked of country life, of the *capangas,*[10] of the Brazilian etymology of the word *gaucho*[11] (which some old Uruguayans still pronounce *gaúcho*) and nothing more was said—may God forgive me—of duodecimal functions. In September of 1937 (we were not at the hotel), Herbert Ashe died of a ruptured aneurysm. A few days before, he had received a sealed and certified package from Brazil. It was a book in large octavo. Ashe left it at the bar, where—months later—I found it. I began to leaf through it and experienced an astonished and airy feeling of vertigo which I shall not describe, for this is not the story of my emotions but of Uqbar and Tlön and Orbis Tertius. On one of the nights of Islam called the Night of Nights, the secret doors of heaven open wide and the water in the jars becomes sweeter; if those doors opened, I would not feel what I felt that afternoon. The book was written in English and contained 1001 pages. On the yellow leather back I read these curious words which were repeated on the title page: *A First Encyclopaedia of Tlön, Vol. XI. Hlaer to Jangn.* There was no indication of date or place. On the first page and on a leaf of silk paper that covered one of the color plates there was stamped a blue oval with this inscription: *Orbis Tertius.* Two years before I had discovered, in a volume of a certain pirated encyclopedia, a superficial description of a nonexistent country; now chance afforded me something more precious and arduous. Now I held in my hands a vast methodical fragment of an unknown planet's entire history, with its architecture and its playing cards, with the dread of its mythologies and the murmur of its languages, with its emperors and its seas, with its minerals and its birds and its fish, with its algebra and its fire, with its theological and metaphysical controversy. And all of it articulated, coherent, with no visible doctrinal intent or tone of parody.

In the "Eleventh Volume" which I have mentioned, there are allusions to preceding and succeeding volumes. In an article in the *N. R. F.* which is now classic, Néstor Ibarra has denied the existence of those companion volumes; Ezequiel Martínez Estrada[12] and Drieu La Rochelle have refuted that doubt, perhaps victoriously. The fact is that up to now the most diligent inquiries have been fruitless. In vain we have upended the libraries of the two Americas and of Europe. Alfonso Reyes,[13] tired of these subordinate sleuthing procedures, proposes that we should all undertake the task of reconstructing the many and weighty tomes that are lacking: *ex ungue leonem.*[14] He calculates, half in earnest and half jokingly, that a generation of *tlönistas* should be sufficient. This venturesome computation brings us back to the fundamental problem: Who are the inventors of Tlön? The

[10] Thugs (Brazilian Portuguese). [11] Cowboy (Brazilian Portuguese).
[12] Actual Argentine essayist (1895–1964). [13] An actual Mexican writer (1889–1959).
[14] "By the claw of the lion" (Latin). The full saying is "By the claw of the lion we know him," that is, the part implies the whole.

plural is inevitable, because the hypothesis of a lone inventor—an infinite Leibniz[15] laboring away darkly and modestly—has been unanimously discounted. It is conjectured that this brave new world is the work of a secret society of astronomers, biologists, engineers, metaphysicians, poets, chemists, algebraists, moralists, painters, geometers . . . directed by an obscure man of genius. Individuals mastering these diverse disciplines are abundant, but not so those capable of inventiveness and less so those capable of subordinating that inventiveness to a rigorous and systematic plan. This plan is so vast that each writer's contribution is infinitesimal. At first it was believed that Tlön was a mere chaos, an irresponsible license of the imagination; now it is known that it is a cosmos and that the intimate laws which govern it have been formulated, at least provisionally. Let it suffice for me to recall that the apparent contradictions of the Eleventh Volume are the fundamental basis for the proof that the other volumes exist, so lucid and exact is the order observed in it. The popular magazines, with pardonable excess, have spread news of the zoology and topography of Tlön; I think its transparent tigers and towers of blood perhaps do not merit the continued attention of *all* men. I shall venture to request a few minutes to expound its concept of the universe.

Hume noted for all time that Berkeley's arguments did not admit the slightest refutation nor did they cause the slightest conviction.[16] This dictum is entirely correct in its application to the earth, but entirely false in Tlön. The nations of this planet are congenitally idealist. Their language and the derivations of their language—religion, letters, metaphysics—all presuppose idealism. The world for them is not a concourse of objects in space; it is a heterogeneous series of independent acts. It is successive and temporal, not spatial. There are no nouns in Tlön's conjectural *Ursprache,*[17] from which the "present" languages and the dialects are derived: there are impersonal verbs, modified by monosyllabic suffixes (or prefixes) with an adverbial value. For example: there is no word corresponding to the word "moon," but there is a verb which in English would be "to moon" or "to moonate." "The moon rose above the river" is *hlör u fang axaxaxas mlö,* or literally: "upward behind the on-streaming it mooned."

The preceding applies to the languages of the southern hemisphere. In those of the northern hemisphere (on whose *Ursprache* there is very little data in the Eleventh Volume) the prime unit is not the verb, but the monosyllabic adjective. The noun is formed by an accumulation of adjectives. They do not say "moon," but rather "round airy-light on dark" or "pale-orange-of-the-sky" or any other such combination. In the example selected the mass of adjectives refers to a real object, but this is purely fortuitous.

[15] Gottfried Wilhelm Leibniz, seventeenth-century German mathematician and philosopher, invented the infinitesimal calculus. The English mathematician Sir Isaac Newton invented it independently at about the same time.

[16] The British idealist philosopher Bishop George Berkeley (1685–1753) argued that matter does not exist apart from its being perceived and that objects have a continuing existence only because they are continually observed by God. His theories were attacked by the Scottish skeptical philosopher David Hume (1711–1776).

[17] Original language (German).

The literature of this hemisphere (like Meinong's[18] subsistent world) abounds in ideal objects, which are convoked and dissolved in a moment, according to poetic needs. At times they are determined by mere simultaneity. There are objects composed of two terms, one of visual and another of auditory character: the color of the rising sun and the faraway cry of a bird. There are objects of many terms: the sun and the water on a swimmer's chest, the vague tremulous rose color we see with our eyes closed, the sensation of being carried along by a river and also by sleep. These second-degree objects can be combined with others; through the use of certain abbreviations, the process is practically infinite. There are famous poems made up of one enormous word. This word forms a *poetic object* created by the author. The fact that no one believes in the reality of nouns paradoxically causes their number to be unending. The languages of Tlön's northern hemisphere contain all the nouns of the Indo-European languages—and many others as well.

It is no exaggeration to state that the classic culture of Tlön comprises only one discipline: psychology. All others are subordinated to it. I have said that the men of this planet conceive the universe as a series of mental processes which do not develop in space but successively in time. Spinoza[19] ascribes to his inexhaustible divinity the attributes of extension and thought; no one in Tlön would understand the juxtaposition of the first (which is typical only of certain states) and the second—which is a perfect synonym of the cosmos. In other words, they do not conceive that the spatial persists in time. The perception of a cloud of smoke on the horizon and then of the burning field and then of the half-extinguished cigarette that produced the blaze is considered an example of association of ideas.

This monism or complete idealism invalidates all science. If we explain (or judge) a fact, we connect it with another; such linking, in Tlön, is a later state of the subject which cannot affect or illuminate the previous state. Every mental state is irreducible: the mere fact of naming it—i.e., of classifying it—implies a falsification. From which it can be deduced that there are no sciences on Tlön, not even reasoning. The paradoxical truth is that they do exist, and in almost uncountable number. The same thing happens with philosophies as happens with nouns in the northern hemisphere. The fact that every philosophy is by definition a dialectical game, a *Philosophie des Als Ob*,[20] has caused them to multiply. There is an abundance of incredible systems of pleasing design or sensational type. The metaphysicians of Tlön do not seek for the truth or even for verisimilitude, but rather for the astounding. They judge that metaphysics is a branch of fantastic literature. They know that a system is nothing more than the subordination of all aspects of the universe to any one such aspect. Even the phrase "all aspects" is rejectable, for it supposes the impossible addition of the present and of all past moments. Neither is it licit to use the plural "past moments," since it

[18] Alexius Meinong (1853–1920), Austrian philosopher and psychologist.

[19] The Dutch Jewish philosopher Baruch Spinoza (1632–1677) argued that all existence is embraced in one substance—God.

[20] A "philosophy of 'as if' " (German).

supposes another impossible operation . . . One of the schools of Tlön goes so far as to negate time: it reasons that the present is indefinite, that the future has no reality other than as a present hope, that the past has no reality other than as a present memory.[21] Another school declares that *all time* has already transpired and that our life is only the crepuscular and no doubt falsified and mutilated memory or reflection of an irrecoverable process. Another, that the history of the universe—and in it our lives and the most tenuous detail of our lives—is the scripture produced by a subordinate god in order to communicate with a demon.[22] Another, that the universe is comparable to those cryptographs in which not all the symbols are valid and that only what happens every three hundred nights is true. Another, that while we sleep here, we are awake elsewhere and that in this way every man is two men.

Amongst the doctrines of Tlön, none has merited the scandalous reception accorded to materialism. Some thinkers have formulated it with less clarity than fervor, as one might put forth a paradox. In order to facilitate the comprehension of this inconceivable thesis, a heresiarch of the eleventh century[23] devised the sophism of the nine copper coins, whose scandalous renown is in Tlön equivalent to that of the Eleatic paradoxes.[24] There are many versions of this "specious reasoning," which vary the number of coins and the number of discoveries; the following is the most common:

On Tuesday, X crosses a deserted road and loses nine copper coins. On Thursday, Y finds in the road four coins, somewhat rusted by Wednesday's rain. On Friday, Z discovers three coins in the road. On Friday morning, X finds two coins in the corridor of his house. The heresiarch would deduce from this story the reality—i.e., the continuity—of the nine coins which were recovered. *It is absurd* (he affirmed) *to imagine that four of the coins have not existed between Tuesday and Thursday, three between Tuesday and Friday afternoon, two between Tuesday and Friday morning. It is logical to think that they have existed—at least in some secret way, hidden from the comprehension of men—at every moment of those three periods.*

The language of Tlön resists the formulation of this paradox; most people did not even understand it. The defenders of common sense at first did no more than negate the veracity of the anecdote. They repeated that it was a verbal fallacy, based on the rash application of two neologisms not authorized by usage and alien to all rigorous thought: the verbs "find" and "lose," which beg the question, because they presuppose the identity of the first and of the last nine coins. They recalled that all nouns (man, coin,

[21] "Russell (*The Analysis of Mind,* 1921, page 159) supposes that the planet has been created a few minutes ago, furnished with a humanity that 'remembers' an illusory past" (Borges' note). The book is by the English mathematician and philosopher Bertrand Russell (1872–1970).

[22] Borges is alluding to Gnosticism, a second-century A.D. religious movement that stressed knowledge rather than faith as the key to salvation and postulated a number of gods, some of them evil. The early Christians declared it a heresy. Borges has written extensively on Gnosticism, especially in his essay "A Vindication of the False Basílides" in *Other Inquisitions* (1952).

[23] "A century, according to the duodecimal system, signifies a period of a hundred and forty-four years" (Borges' note).

[24] A series of paradoxes proposed by the fifth-century B.C. Greek philosopher Zeno, of the Eleatic school.

Thursday, Wednesday, rain) have only a metaphorical value. They denounced the treacherous circumstance "somewhat rusted by Wednesday's rain," which presupposes what is trying to be demonstrated: the persistence of the four coins from Tuesday to Thursday. They explained that *equality* is one thing and *identity* another, and formulated a kind of *reductio ad absurdum:*[25] the hypothetical case of nine men who on nine successive nights suffer a severe pain. Would it not be ridiculous—they questioned—to pretend that this pain is one and the same?[26] They said that the heresiarch was prompted only by the blasphemous intention of attributing the divine category of *being* to some simple coins and that at times he negated plurality and at other times did not. They argued: if equality implies identity, one would also have to admit that the nine coins are one.

Unbelievably, these refutations were not definitive. A hundred years after the problem was stated, a thinker no less brilliant than the heresiarch but of orthodox tradition formulated a very daring hypothesis. This happy conjecture affirmed that there is only one subject, that this indivisible subject is every being in the universe and that these beings are the organs and masks of the divinity. X is Y and is Z. Z discovers three coins because he remembers that X lost them; X finds two in the corridor because he remembers that the others have been found . . . The Eleventh Volume suggests that three prime reasons determined the complete victory of this idealist pantheism. The first, its repudiation of solipsism;[27] the second, the possibility of preserving the psychological basis of the sciences; the third, the possibility of preserving the cult of the gods. Schopenhauer[28] (the passionate and lucid Schopenhauer) formulates a very similar doctrine in the first volume of *Parerga und Paralipomena.*

The geometry of Tlön comprises two somewhat different disciplines: the visual and the tactile. The latter corresponds to our own geometry and is subordinated to the first. The basis of visual geometry is the surface, not the point. This geometry disregards parallel lines and declares that man in his movement modifies the forms which surround him. The basis of its arithmetic is the notion of indefinite numbers. They emphasize the importance of the concepts of greater and lesser, which our mathematicians symbolize as < and >. They maintain that the operation of counting modifies quantities and converts them from indefinite into definite sums. The fact that several individuals who count the same quantity should obtain the same result is, for the psychologists, an example of association of ideas or of a good exercise of memory. We already know that in Tlön the subject of knowledge is one and eternal.

In literary practices the idea of a single subject is also all-powerful. It is uncommon for books to be signed. The concept of plagiarism does not

[25] "Reduction to absurdity" (Latin), a way of disproving a proposition by showing that an absurdity results if it is pushed to its logical conclusion.

[26] "Today, one of the churches of Tlön Platonically maintains that a certain pain, a certain greenish tint of yellow, a certain temperature, a certain sound, are the only reality. All men, in the vertiginous moment of coitus, are the same man. All men who repeat a line from Shakespeare *are* William Shakespeare" (Borges' note).

[27] The theory that the self is the only thing that exists and that it can know only itself.

[28] Arthur Schopenhauer (1788–1869), German philosopher. The work referred to is a collection of essays on various topics published in 1851.

exist: it has been established that all works are the creation of one author, who is atemporal and anonymous. The critics often invent authors: they select two dissimilar works—the *Tao Te Ching* and the *1001 Nights,* say—attribute them to the same writer and then determine most scrupulously the psychology of this interesting *homme de lettres* . . .[29]

Their books are also different. Works of fiction contain a single plot, with all its imaginable permutations. Those of a philosophical nature invariably include both the thesis and the antithesis, the rigorous pro and con of a doctrine. A book which does not contain its counterbook is considered incomplete.

Centuries and centuries of idealism have not failed to influence reality. In the most ancient regions of Tlön, the duplication of lost objects is not infrequent. Two persons look for a pencil; the first finds it and says nothing; the second finds a second pencil, no less real, but closer to his expectations. These secondary objects are called *hrönir* and are, though awkward in form, somewhat longer. Until recently, the *hrönir* were the accidental products of distraction and forgetfulness. It seems unbelievable that their methodical production dates back scarcely a hundred years, but this is what the Eleventh Volume tells us. The first efforts were unsuccessful. However, the *modus operandi*[30] merits description. The director of one of the state prisons told his inmates that there were certain tombs in an ancient river bed and promised freedom to whoever might make an important discovery. During the months preceding the excavation the inmates were shown photographs of what they were to find. This first effort proved that expectation and anxiety can be inhibitory; a week's work with pick and shovel did not manage to unearth anything in the way of a *hrön* except a rusty wheel of a period posterior to the experiment. But this was kept in secret and the process was repeated later in four schools. In three of them the failure was almost complete; in the fourth (whose director died accidentally during the first excavations) the students unearthed—or produced—a gold mask, an archaic sword, two or three clay urns and the moldy and mutilated torso of a king whose chest bore an inscription which it has not yet been possible to decipher. Thus was discovered the unreliability of witnesses who knew of the experimental nature of the search . . . Mass investigations produce contradictory objects; now individual and almost improvised jobs are preferred. The methodical fabrication of *hrönir* (says the Eleventh Volume) has performed prodigious services for archaeologists. It has made possible the interrogation and even the modification of the past, which is now no less plastic and docile than the future. Curiously, the *hrönir* of second and third degree—the *hrönir* derived from another *hrön,* those derived from the *hrön* of a *hrön*—exaggerate the aberrations of the initial one; those of fifth degree are almost uniform; those of ninth degree become confused with those of the second; in those of the eleventh there is a purity of line not found in the original. The process is cyclical: the *hrön* of twelfth degree begins to fall off in quality. Stranger and more pure than any *hrön* is, at times, the *ur:* the object produced through suggestion, educed by hope. The great golden mask I have mentioned is an illustrious example.

Things become duplicated in Tlön; they also tend to become effaced

[29] Man of letters (French). [30] "Mode of operating" (Latin); procedure.

and lose their details when they are forgotten. A classic example is the doorway which survived so long as it was visited by a beggar and disappeared at his death. At times some birds, a horse, have saved the ruins of an amphitheater.

Postscript (1947). I reproduce the preceding article just as it appeared in the *Anthology of Fantastic Literature* (1940), with no omission other than that of a few metaphors and a kind of sarcastic summary which now seems frivolous. So many things have happened since then . . . I shall do no more than recall them here.

In March of 1941 a letter written by Gunnar Erfjord was discovered in a book by Hinton which had belonged to Herbert Ashe. The envelope bore a cancellation from Ouro Preto; the letter completely elucidated the mystery of Tlön. Its text corroborated the hypotheses of Martínez Estrada. One night in Lucerne or in London, in the early seventeenth century, the splendid history has its beginning. A secret and benevolent society (amongst whose members were Dalgarno and later George Berkeley)[31] arose to invent a country. Its vague initial program included "hermetic studies," philanthropy and the cabala.[32] From this first period dates the curious book by Andreä. After a few years of secret conclaves and premature syntheses it was understood that one generation was not sufficient to give articulate form to a country. They resolved that each of the masters should elect a disciple who would continue his work. This hereditary arrangement prevailed; after an interval of two centuries the persecuted fraternity sprang up again in America. In 1824, in Memphis (Tennessee), one of its affiliates conferred with the ascetic millionaire Ezra Buckley. The latter, somewhat disdainfully, let him speak—and laughed at the plan's modest scope. He told the agent that in America it was absurd to invent a country and proposed the invention of a planet. To this gigantic idea he added another, a product of his nihilism:[33] that of keeping the enormous enterprise secret. At that time the twenty volumes of the *Encyclopaedia Britannica* were circulating in the United States; Buckley suggested that a methodical encyclopedia of the imaginary planet be written. He was to leave them his mountains of gold, his navigable rivers, his pasture lands roamed by cattle and buffalo, his Negroes, his brothels and his dollars, on one condition: "The work will make no pact with the impostor Jesus Christ." Buckley did not believe in God, but he wanted to demonstrate to this nonexistent God that mortal man was capable of conceiving a world. Buckley was poisoned in Baton Rouge in 1828; in 1914 the society delivered to its collaborators, some three hundred in number, the last volume of the First Encyclopedia of Tlön. The edition was a secret one; its forty volumes (the vastest undertaking ever carried out by man) would be the basis for another more detailed edition, written not in English but in one of the lan-

[31] George Dalgarno (1626?–1687) was a Scottish educator who developed a system of teaching the deaf and attempted to develop a universal writing system independent of particular languages. For Berkeley, see note 16.

[32] A Jewish mystical system that views creation as taking place through "emanation" or radiations from the Godhead and interprets the Scriptures through numerological ciphers.

[33] "Buckley was a freethinker, a fatalist and a defender of slavery" (Borges' note). Nihilism is a doctrine that denies any objective basis for truth.

guages of Tlön. This revision of an illusory world, was called, provisionally, *Orbis Tertius*[34] and one of its modest demiurgi[35] was Herbert Ashe, whether as an agent of Gunnar Erfjord or as an affiliate, I do not know. His having received a copy of the Eleventh Volume would seem to favor the latter assumption. But what about the others?

In 1942 events became more intense. I recall one of the first of these with particular clarity and it seems that I perceived then something of its premonitory character. It happened in an apartment on Laprida Street, facing a high and light balcony which looked out toward the sunset. Princess Faucigny Lucinge had received her silverware from Poitiers. From the vast depths of a box embellished with foreign stamps, delicate immobile objects emerged: silver from Utrecht and Paris covered with hard heraldic fauna, and a samovar. Amongst them—with the perceptible and tenuous tremor of a sleeping bird—a compass vibrated mysteriously. The Princess did not recognize it. Its blue needle longed for magnetic north; its metal case was concave in shape; the letters around its edge corresponded to one of the alphabets of Tlön. Such was the first intrusion of this fantastic world into the world of reality.

I am still troubled by a stroke of chance which made me the witness of the second intrusion as well. It happened some months later, at a country store owned by a Brazilian in Cuchilla Negra. Amorim[36] and I were returning from Sant' Anna. The River Tacuarembó had flooded and we were obliged to sample (and endure) the proprietor's rudimentary hospitality. He provided us with some creaking cots in a large room cluttered with barrels and hides. We went to bed, but were kept from sleeping until dawn by the drunken ravings of an unseen neighbor, who intermingled inexplicable insults with snatches of *milongas*[37]—or rather with snatches of the same *milonga*. As might be supposed, we attributed this insistent uproar to the store owner's fiery cane liquor. By daybreak, the man was dead in the hallway. The roughness of his voice had deceived us: he was only a youth. In his delirium a few coins had fallen from his belt, along with a cone of bright metal, the size of a die. In vain a boy tried to pick up this cone. A man was scarcely able to raise it from the ground. I held it in my hand for a few minutes; I remember that its weight was intolerable and that after it was removed, the feeling of oppressiveness remained. I also remember the exact circle it pressed into my palm. This sensation of a very small and at the same time extremely heavy object produced a disagreeable impression of repugnance and fear. One of the local men suggested we throw it into the swollen river; Amorim acquired it for a few pesos. No one knew anything about the dead man, except that "he came from the border." These small, very heavy cones (made from a metal which is not of this world) are images of the divinity in certain regions of Tlön.

Here I bring the personal part of my narrative to a close. The rest is in the memory (if not in the hopes or fears) of all my readers. Let it suffice for me to recall or mention the following facts, with a mere brevity of words which the reflective recollection of all will enrich or amplify. Around 1944,

[34] "Third World" (Latin).
[35] Minor gods who create the material world, in Gnostic thought.
[36] Enrique Amorim (1900–1960), Uruguayan novelist. [37] Dance tunes.

a person doing research for the newspaper *The American* (of Nashville, Tennessee) brought to light in a Memphis library the forty volumes of the First Encyclopedia of Tlön. Even today there is a controversy over whether this discovery was accidental or whether it was permitted by the directors of the still nebulous *Orbis Tertius*. The latter is most likely. Some of the incredible aspects of the Eleventh Volume (for example, the multiplication of the *hrönir*) have been eliminated or attenuated in the Memphis copies; it is reasonable to imagine that these omissions follow the plan of exhibiting a world which is not too incompatible with the real world. The dissemination of objects from Tlön over different countries would complement this plan[38]. . . The fact is that the international press infinitely proclaimed the "find." Manuals, anthologies, summaries, literal versions, authorized re-editions and pirated editions of the Greatest Work of Man flooded and still flood the earth. Almost immediately, reality yielded on more than one account. The truth is that it longed to yield. Ten years ago any symmetry with a semblance of order—dialectical materialism, anti-Semitism, Nazism—was sufficient to entrance the minds of men. How could one do other than submit to Tlön, to the minute and vast evidence of an orderly planet? It is useless to answer that reality is also orderly. Perhaps it is, but in accordance with divine laws—I translate: inhuman laws—which we never quite grasp. Tlön is surely a labyrinth, but it is a labyrinth devised by men, a labyrinth destined to be deciphered by men.

The contact and the habit of Tlön have disintegrated this world. Enchanted by its rigor, humanity forgets over and again that it is a rigor of chess masters, not of angels. Already the schools have been invaded by the (conjectural) "primitive language" of Tlön; already the teaching of its harmonious history (filled with moving episodes) has wiped out the one which governed in my childhood; already a fictitious past occupies in our memories the place of another, a past of which we know nothing with certainty—not even that it is false. Numismatology,[39] pharmacology and archaeology have been reformed. I understand that biology and mathematics also await their avatars[40] . . . A scattered dynasty of solitary men has changed the face of the world. Their task continues. If our forecasts are not in error, a hundred years from now someone will discover the hundred volumes of the Second Encyclopedia of Tlön.

Then English and French and mere Spanish will disappear from the globe. The world will be Tlön. I pay no attention to all this and go on revising, in the still days at the Adrogué hotel, an uncertain Quevedian translation (which I do not intend to publish) of Browne's *Urn Burial*.[41]

[38] "There remains, of course, the problem of the *material* of some objects" (Borges' note).
[39] The study of coins. [40] Variant versions.
[41] An eccentric meditative work by the English writer Sir Thomas Browne (1605–1682).

THE CIRCULAR RUINS

Translated by Norman Thomas di Giovanni
in collaboration with the author

And if he left off dreaming about you. . . .
—THROUGH THE LOOKING-GLASS, *IV*

Nobody saw him come ashore in the encompassing night, nobody saw the bamboo craft run aground in the sacred mud, but within a few days everyone knew that the quiet man had come from the south and that his home was among the numberless villages upstream on the steep slopes of the mountain, where the Zend[1] language is barely tainted by Greek and where lepers are rare. The fact is that the gray man pressed his lips to the mud, scrambled up the bank without parting (perhaps without feeling) the brushy thorns that tore his flesh, and dragged himself, faint and bleeding, to the circular opening watched over by a stone tiger, or horse, which once was the color of fire and is now the color of ash. This opening is a temple which was destroyed ages ago by flames, which the swampy wilderness later desecrated, and whose god no longer receives the reverence of men. The stranger laid himself down at the foot of the image.

Wakened by the sun high overhead, he noticed—somehow without amazement—that his wounds had healed. He shut his pale eyes and slept again, not because of weariness but because he willed it. He knew that this temple was the place he needed for his unswerving purpose; he knew that downstream the encroaching trees had also failed to choke the ruins of another auspicious temple with its own fire-ravaged, dead gods; he knew that his first duty was to sleep. Along about midnight, he was awakened by the forlorn call of a bird. Footprints, some figs, and a water jug told him that men who lived nearby had looked on his sleep with a kind of awe and either sought his protection or else were in dread of his witchcraft. He felt the chill of fear and searched the crumbling walls for a burial niche, where he covered himself over with leaves he had never seen before.

His guiding purpose, though it was supernatural, was not impossible. He wanted to dream a man; he wanted to dream him down to the last detail and project him into the world of reality. This mystical aim had taxed the whole range of his mind. Had anyone asked him his own name or anything about his life before then, he would not have known what to answer. This forsaken, broken temple suited him because it held few visible things, and also because the neighboring villagers would look after his frugal needs. The rice and fruit of their offerings were nourishment enough for his body, whose one task was to sleep and to dream.

At the outset, his dreams were chaotic; later on, they were of a dialectic nature. The stranger dreamed himself at the center of a circular amphitheater which in some way was also the burnt-out temple. Crowds of silent

[1] There is no such language, but the name suggests the *Zend Avesta,* the scripture of Zoroastrianism, a religion originating in Persia in the sixth century B.C. and predicating a dualistic world dominated by the struggle between gods of goodness and gods of evil.

disciples exhausted the tiers of seats; the faces of the farthest of them hung centuries away from him and at a height of the stars, but their features were clear and exact. The man lectured on anatomy, cosmography, and witchcraft. The faces listened, bright and eager, and did their best to answer sensibly, as if they felt the importance of his questions, which would raise one of them out of an existence as a shadow and place him in the real world. Whether asleep or awake, the man pondered the answers of his phantoms and, not letting himself be misled by impostors, divined in certain of their quandaries a growing intelligence. He was in search of a soul worthy of taking a place in the world.

After nine or ten nights he realized, feeling bitter over it, that nothing could be expected from those pupils who passively accepted his teaching but that he might, however, hold hopes for those who from time to time hazarded reasonable doubts about what he taught. The former, although they deserved love and affection, could never become real; the latter, in their dim way, were already real. One evening (now his evenings were also given over to sleeping, now he was only awake for an hour or two at dawn) he dismissed his vast dream-school forever and kept a single disciple. He was a quiet, sallow, and at times rebellious young man with sharp features akin to those of his dreamer. The sudden disappearance of his fellow pupils did not disturb him for very long, and his progress, at the end of a few private lessons, amazed his teacher. Nonetheless, a catastrophe intervened. One morning, the man emerged from his sleep as from a sticky wasteland, glanced up at the faint evening light, which at first he confused with the dawn, and realized that he had not been dreaming. All that night and the next day, the hideous lucidity of insomnia weighed down on him. To tire himself out he tried to explore the surrounding forest, but all he managed, there in a thicket of hemlocks, were some snatches of broken sleep, fleetingly tinged with visions of a crude and worthless nature. He tried to reassemble his school, and barely had he uttered a few brief words of counsel when the whole class went awry and vanished. In his almost endless wakefulness, tears of anger stung his old eyes.

He realized that, though he may penetrate all the riddles of the higher and lower orders, the task of shaping the senseless and dizzying stuff of dreams is the hardest that a man can attempt—much harder than weaving a rope of sand or of coining the faceless wind. He realized that an initial failure was to be expected. He then swore he would forget the populous vision which in the beginning had led him astray, and he sought another method. Before attempting it, he spent a month rebuilding the strength his fever had consumed. He gave up all thoughts of dreaming and almost at once managed to sleep a reasonable part of the day. The few times he dreamed during this period he did not dwell on his dreams. Before taking up his task again, he waited until the moon was a perfect circle. Then, in the evening, he cleansed himself in the waters of the river, worshiped the gods of the planets, uttered the prescribed syllables of an all-powerful name, and slept. Almost at once, he had a dream of a beating heart.

He dreamed it throbbing, warm, secret. It was the size of a closed fist, a darkish red in the dimness of a human body still without a face or sex. With anxious love he dreamed it for fourteen lucid nights. Each night he perceived it more clearly. He did not touch it, but limited himself to witnessing it, to observing it, to correcting it now and then with a look. He felt it, he lived it from different distances and from many angles. On the fourteenth night he touched the pulmonary artery with a finger and then the whole heart, inside and out. The examination satisfied him. For one night he deliberately did not dream; after that he went back to the heart again, invoked the name of a planet, and set out to envision another of the principal organs. Before a year was over he came to the skeleton, the eyelids. The countless strands of hair were perhaps the hardest task of all. He dreamed a whole man, a young man, but the young man could not stand up or speak, nor could he open his eyes. Night after night, the man dreamed him asleep.

In the cosmogonies of the Gnostics,[2] the demiurges mold a red Adam who is unable to stand on his feet; as clumsy and crude and elementary as that Adam of dust was the Adam of dreams wrought by the nights of the magician. One evening the man was at the point of destroying all his handiwork (it would have been better for him had he done so), but in the end he restrained himself. Having exhausted his prayers to the gods of the earth and river, he threw himself down at the feet of the stone image that may have been a tiger or a stallion, and asked for its blind aid. That same evening he dreamed of the image. He dreamed it alive, quivering; it was no unnatural cross between tiger and stallion but at one and the same time both these violent creatures and also a bull, a rose, a thunderstorm. This manifold god revealed to him that its earthly name was Fire, that there in the circular temple (and in others like it) sacrifices had once been made to it, that it had been worshiped, and that through its magic the phantom of the man's dreams would be wakened to life in such a way that—except for Fire itself and the dreamer—every being in the world would accept him as a man of flesh and blood. The god ordered that, once instructed in the rites, the disciple should be sent downstream to the other ruined temple, whose pyramids still survived, so that in that abandoned place some human voice might exalt him. In the dreamer's dream, the dreamed one awoke.

The magician carried out these orders. He devoted a period of time (which finally spanned two years) to initiating his disciple into the riddles of the universe and the worship of Fire. Deep inside, it pained him to say goodbye to his creature. Under the pretext of teaching him more fully, each day he drew out the hours set aside for sleep. Also, he reshaped the somewhat faulty right shoulder. From time to time, he was troubled by the feeling that all this had already happened, but for the most part his days were happy. On closing his eyes he would think, "Now I will be with my son." Or, less frequently, "The son I have begotten awaits me and he will not exist if I do not go to him."

Little by little, he was training the young man for reality. On one occasion he commanded him to set up a flag on a distant peak. The next day, there on the peak, a fiery pennant shone. He tried other, similar exercises, each bolder than the one before. He realized with a certain bitterness that

[2] According to the doctrines of the second-century A.D. Gnostics, there was a hierarchy of 365 worlds, each identical with the one above it and each ruled by a "demiurge." The lowest world is our own, and its demiurge, our God, created man and the rest of the material world. See also "Tlön, Uqbar, Orbis Tertius," note 22.

his son was ready—and perhaps impatient—to be born. That night he kissed him for the first time and sent him down the river to the other temple, whose whitened ruins were still to be glimpsed over miles and miles of impenetrable forest and swamp. At the very end (so that the boy would never know he was a phantom, so that he would think himself a man like all men), the magician imbued with total oblivion his disciple's long years of apprenticeship.

His triumph and his peace were blemished by a touch of weariness. In the morning and evening dusk, he prostrated himself before the stone idol, perhaps imagining that his unreal son was performing the same rites farther down the river in other circular ruins. At night he no longer dreamed, or else he dreamed the way all men dream. He now perceived with a certain vagueness the sounds and shapes of the world, for his absent son was taking nourishment from the magician's decreasing consciousness. His life's purpose was fulfilled; the man lived on in a kind of ecstasy. After a length of time that certain tellers of the story count in years and others in half-decades, he was awakened one midnight by two rowers. He could not see their faces, but they spoke to him about a magic man in a temple up north who walked on fire without being burned. The magician suddenly remembered the god's words. He remembered that of all the creatures in the world, Fire was the only one who knew his son was a phantom. This recollection, comforting at first, ended by tormenting him. He feared that his son might wonder at this strange privilege and in some way discover his condition as a mere appearance. Not to be a man but to be the projection of another man's dreams—what an unparalleled humiliation, how bewildering! Every father cares for the child he has begotten—he has allowed—in some moment of confusion or happiness. It is understandable, then, that the magician should fear for the future of a son thought out organ by organ and feature by feature over the course of a thousand and one secret nights.

The end of these anxieties came suddenly, but certain signs foretold it. First (after a long drought), a far-off cloud on a hilltop, as light as a bird; next, toward the south, the sky, which took on the rosy hue of a leopard's gums; then, the pillars of smoke that turned the metal of the nights to rust; finally, the headlong panic of the forest animals. For what had happened many centuries ago was happening again. The ruins of the fire god's shrine were destroyed by fire. In a birdless dawn the magician saw the circling sheets of flame closing in on him. For a moment, he thought of taking refuge in the river, but then he realized that death was coming to crown his years and to release him from his labors. He walked into the leaping pennants of flame. They did not bite into his flesh, but caressed him and flooded him without heat or burning. In relief, in humiliation, in terror, he understood that he, too, was an appearance, that someone else was dreaming him.

Jean-Paul Sartre

(1905–1980)

Jean-Paul Sartre came close to being for the mid-twentieth century what Voltaire was for the Enlightenment and Goethe was for the Romantic movement, an artist-philosopher who both shaped and reflected the spirit of his age and who expressed that spirit in a flood of writing in a variety of forms, theoretical and philosophical as well as imaginative. For many of his contemporaries, even those who knew his work only secondhand, existentialism was the only persuasive faith in a frightening age notably lacking in faith, and Sartre was existentialism's exemplary figure, both because of his writings and because of his active, "committed" life.

Sartre was born in 1905 in Paris. His father died when he was still a baby, and he was reared by his grandfather, an uncle of Albert Schweitzer, the famous philosopher, musician, and African missionary. In The Words *(1964), an account of his early years, Sartre described himself as an ugly, lonely child who retreated into fantasy, which formed the basis of his mature concerns, metaphysics and fiction. He studied at the École Normale Supérieure in Paris, graduating in philosophy in 1929, and did further academic work in Egypt, Italy, Greece, and Germany, where he studied German philosophy under the famous existential phenomenologists Edmund Husserl and Martin Heidegger. In 1931, Sartre accepted a post as professor of philosophy in Le Havre. His early philosophical works showed the influence of Husserl and Heidegger:* Imagination *(1936),* Sketch for a Theory of the Emotions *(1939), and* The Psychology of Imagination *(1940).*

When World War II broke out, Sartre joined the French army; he was captured and spent nine months as a prisoner of war (1940–41). When he returned to Paris, he became an active member of the French Resistance and wrote for the underground newspapers that the Resistance published in defiance of the Nazi occupation. He never returned to teaching and after 1944 devoted all his time to writing.

Sartre's major philosophical work, Being and Nothingness, *appeared in 1943. In this book, Sartre presented a full existentialist theory of Being. The starting point for this philosophy is that God is dead and that therefore any ethical system must be based upon atheism. In the absence of God or any universal moral law, man is free to construct his own ethical system and his own meaning for his life; indeed, "condemned to freedom," he is obliged to do so. The emphasis in Sartre's ethics is upon action; man is not what he* is *but rather what he* does, *the sum total of all his actions. He must therefore become "engaged" in active life and take sides upon the issues of his time.*

Being and Nothingness *brought Sartre world fame as a philosopher, but by the time it was published he was already well known as a writer of fiction. (Sartre always regarded his philosophy and his fiction as complementary; indeed, fiction could sometimes deal more sensitively with the problems of individual existence with which he was concerned than formal philosophy could.) His first novel,* Nausea, *and his first collection of short shories,* The Wall, *both appeared in 1938.* Nausea *is the diary of a writer named Antoine Roquentin who finds himself nauseated by the variety and chaos of the external world and yearns for an orderly, controllable one, which he eventually finds in art. Sartre's only other novel was a massive, four-part work he never completed. Collectively entitled* Paths of Freedom, *it included* The Age of

Reason *(1945)*, The Reprieve *(1945)*, Iron in the Soul *(1949), and an unfinished fourth part, two chapters of which were published in 1949 under the title "Strange Friendship."*

During the war years, Sartre turned more to drama than to fiction. No Exit *(1944) and* The Flies *(1946), a version of the Orestes legend, reveal indirectly a disillusionment with the saving power of art suggested by* Nausea. *Under the growing influence of Marxism, Sartre began to suggest in these plays an escape from "nausea" through action in the world. The title of his 1948 play* Dirty Hands *makes this theme explicit; a person must be willing to "dirty his hands" in the real world, a theme developed further in* The Devil and the Good Lord *(1951),* Nekrassov *(1956), and* The Condemned of Altona *(1960).*

In a series of philosophical works written after the war, Sartre continued to develop his ideas, moving away from the pessimism of Being and Nothingness *toward humanism. In* Existentialism and Humanism *(1946),* The Problem of Method *(1960), and* Critique of Dialectical Reasoning *(1960), he continued to emphasize human freedom, but argued that one's own freedom inevitably depends upon the freedom of others and that one must accept responsibility for all the values implied by one's own way of living.*

In the 1950s, Sartre moved steadily closer to Communism, although he never became a party member. He traveled in the Soviet Union and in Cuba, where he supported Fidel Castro's regime. In 1967, he served as chairman of the Stockholm Vietnam War Crimes Tribunal, organized by Bertrand Russell to protest United States policy in Vietnam, and he urged Soviet intervention on behalf of the North in Vietnam. In 1964, he was awarded the Nobel Prize in literature, which he refused, explaining, "A writer must not accept official awards, because he would be adding the influence of the institution that crowned his work to the power of his pen. That is not fair to the reader."

Never married and firmly opposed to bourgeois marriage, Sartre formed a union in his student days with Simone de Beauvoir, who became as famous a writer as he; it was a stable relationship throughout his life. He died in 1980 at the age of seventy-four.

For a writer whose ideas are so complex and radical, Sartre's fiction is, at least on the surface, surprisingly traditional. It was influenced as strongly by detective stories, which he loved, as by philosophy. "The Wall," which first won him fame as a writer, is a suspense story with a melodramatic, O. Henry-like twist at the end. Nevertheless, it contains a cluster of Sartrian ideas, realized in a concrete, personal situation. Like many of his stories, "The Wall" reveals Sartre's interest in what he called "extreme cases"; it is under the pressure of desperate situations, he believed, that a person gains most in self-knowledge. Pablo Ibbieta's condemnation forces him into the crucial existential experience of confronting the reality of his own "absurd" mortality. In the space of a night, he undergoes a spiritual development that might ordinarily consume years (or never take place at all). The ending, contrived as it may seem, is an ironic, existentialist meditation upon the relation between one's self and one's actions in the world.

FURTHER READING *(prepared by N. K. B.)*: Sartre's dual career is reflected in the scholarship on his work, which typically focuses on either the literary or the philosophical and political. Philip Thody's *Sartre: A Biographical Introduction*, 1971, covers Sartre's career in both fields, surveying the dominant themes in the literary, philosophical, and political texts. Thody's earlier work, *Jean-Paul Sartre: A Literary and Political Study*, 1969, demonstrates how the language and imagery of the fiction and drama reflect Sartre's philosophical views. Iris Murdoch, *Sartre: Romantic Rationalist*, 1953, emphasizes the rationalist and existentialist currents in his work. In *Sartre: The Origins of a Style*, 1961, Frederic Jameson focuses on stylistics. Maurice Cranston, *Sartre*, 1962, examines Sartre's critical writings in light of his political theories. Dorothy McCall's *The Theatre of Jean-Paul Sartre*, 1969, emphasizes the structure and language of the plays, but her thematic explications are relevant to the fiction as well. Edith Kern, ed., *Sartre: A Collection of Critical Essays*, 1962, gathers key essays on the novels and plays and also includes a concise biographical introduction. In *The Literature of Possibility: A Study of Humanistic Existentialism*, 1959, Hazel Barnes argues that the fiction of both Sartre and Camus reveals their philosophical positions and explicates "The Wall" in this context. A later study by Barnes, *Sartre*, 1973, surveys the development of the philosophical positions taken in the drama and critical essays. Paul Arthur Schilpp, ed., *The Philosophy of Jean-Paul Sartre*, 1981, is a comprehensive collection of essays on the development of Sartre's thought. For brief, valuable introductions to Sartre and existentialism, see Alisdair Macintyre's essay in *Sartre: A Collection of Critical Essays*, 1971, ed. Mary Warnock, and Gordon E. Bigelow's "A Primer of Existentialism" in *College English*, 23 (December 1961), 171–178.

THE WALL

Translated by Maria Jolas

They pushed us into a large white room and my eyes began to blink because the light hurt them. Then I saw a table and four fellows seated at the table, civilians, looking at some papers. The other prisoners were herded together at one end and we were obliged to cross the entire room to join them. There were several I knew, and others who must have been foreigners. The two in front of me were blond with round heads. They looked alike. I imagine they were French. The smaller one kept pulling at his trousers, out of nervousness.

This lasted about three hours. I was dog-tired and my head was empty. But the room was well-heated, which struck me as rather agreeable; we had not stopped shivering for twenty-four hours. The guards led the prisoners in one after another in front of the table. Then the four fellows asked them their names and what they did. Most of the time that was all—or perhaps from time to time they would ask such questions as: "Did you help sabotage the munitions?" or, "Where were you on the morning of the ninth and what were you doing?" They didn't even listen to the replies, or at least they didn't seem to. They just remained silent for a moment and looked straight ahead, then they began to write. They asked Tom if it was true he had served in the International Brigade.[1] Tom couldn't say he hadn't because of the papers they had found in his jacket. They didn't ask Juan anything, but after he told them his name, they wrote for a long while.

"It's my brother José who's the anarchist," Juan said. "You know per-

[1] Units of international volunteers fighting on the Republican side in the Spanish Civil War (1936–1939).

fectly well he's not here now. I don't belong to any party. I never did take part in politics." They didn't answer.

Then Juan said, "I didn't do anything. And I'm not going to pay for what the others did."

His lips were trembling. A guard told him to stop talking and led him away. It was my turn.

"Your name is Pablo Ibbieta?"

I said yes.

The fellow looked at his papers and said, "Where is Ramon Gris?"

"I don't know."

"You hid him in your house from the sixth to the nineteenth."

"I did not."

They continued to write for a moment and the guards led me away. In the hall, Tom and Juan were waiting between two guards. We started walking. Tom asked one of the guards, "What's the idea?" "How do you mean?" the guard asked. "Was that just the preliminary questioning, or was that the trial?" "That was the trial," the guard said. "So now what? What are they going to do with us?" The guard answered drily, "The verdict will be told you in your cell."

In reality, our cell was one of the cellars of the hospital. It was terribly cold there because it was very drafty. We had been shivering all night long and it had hardly been any better during the day. I had spent the preceding five days in a cellar in the archbishop's palace, a sort of dungeon that must have dated back to the Middle Ages. There were lots of prisoners and not much room, so they housed them just anywhere. But I was not homesick for my dungeon. I hadn't been cold there, but I had been alone, and that gets to be irritating. In the cellar I had company. Juan didn't say a word; he was afraid, and besides, he was too young to have anything to say. But Tom was a good talker and knew Spanish well.

In the cellar there were a bench and four straw mattresses. When they led us back we sat down and waited in silence. After a while Tom said, "Our goose is cooked."

"I think so too," I said. "But I don't believe they'll do anything to the kid."

Tom said, "They haven't got anything on him. He's the brother of a fellow who's fighting, and that's all."

I looked at Juan. He didn't seem to have heard.

Tom continued, "You know what they do in Saragossa?[2] They lay the guys across the road and then they drive over them with trucks. It was a Moroccan deserter who told us that. They say it's just to save ammunition."

I said, "Well, it doesn't save gasoline."

I was irritated with Tom; he shouldn't have said that.

He went on, "There are officers walking up and down the roads with their hands in their pockets, smoking, and they see that it's done right. Do you think they'd put 'em out of their misery? Like hell they do. They just let 'em holler. Sometimes as long as an hour. The Moroccan said the first time he almost puked."

[2] Province in northeast Spain.

"I don't believe they do that here," I said, "unless they really are short of ammunition."

The daylight came in through four air vents and a round opening that had been cut in the ceiling, to the left, and which opened directly onto the sky. It was through this hole, which was ordinarily closed by means of a trapdoor, that they unloaded coal into the cellar. Directly under the hole, there was a big pile of coal dust; it had been intended for heating the hospital, but at the beginning of the war they had evacuated the patients and the coal had stayed there unused; it even got rained on from time to time, when they forgot to close the trapdoor.

Tom started to shiver. "God damn it," he said, "I'm shivering. There, it is starting again."

He rose and began to do gymnastic exercises. At each movement, his shirt opened and showed his white, hairy chest. He lay down on his back, lifted his legs in the air and began to do the scissors movement. I watched his big buttocks tremble. Tom was tough, but he had too much fat on him. I kept thinking that soon bullets and bayonet points would sink into that mass of tender flesh as though it were a pat of butter.

I wasn't exactly cold, but I couldn't feel my shoulders or my arms. From time to time, I had the impression that something was missing and I began to look around for my jacket. Then I would suddenly remember they hadn't given me a jacket. It was rather awkward. They had taken our clothes to give them to their own soldiers and had left us only our shirts and these cotton trousers the hospital patients wore in mid-summer. After a moment, Tom got up and sat down beside me, breathless.

"Did you get warmed up?"

"Damn it, no. But I'm all out of breath."

Around eight o'clock in the evening, a Major came in with two falangists.[3]

"What are the names of those three over there?" he asked the guard.

"Steinbock, Ibbieta and Mirbal," said the guard.

The Major put on his glasses and examined his list.

"Steinbock—Steinbock . . . Here it is. You are condemned to death. You'll be shot tomorrow morning."

He looked at his list again.

"The other two, also," he said.

"That's not possible," said Juan. "Not me."

The Major looked at him with surprise. "What's your name?"

"Juan Mirbal."

"Well, your name is here," said the Major, "and you're condemned to death."

"I didn't do anything," said Juan.

The Major shrugged his shoulders and turned toward Tom and me. "You are both Basque?"

"No, nobody's Basque."

[3] Fascists fighting against the Republic. The *Falange*, founded by José Antonio Primo de Rivera, son of the dictator, was a nationalist anti-Marxist youth group formed to oppose Socialist youth groups.

He appeared exasperated.

"I was told there were three Basques. I'm not going to waste my time running after them. I suppose you don't want a priest?"

We didn't even answer.

Then he said, "A Belgian doctor will be around in a little while. He has permission to stay with you all night."

He gave a military salute and left.

"What did I tell you?" Tom said. "We're in for something swell."

"Yes," I said. "It's a damned shame for the kid."

I said that to be fair, but I really didn't like the kid. His face was too refined and it was disfigured by fear and suffering, which had twisted all his features. Three days ago, he was just a kid with a kind of affected manner some people like. But now he looked like an aging fairy, and I thought to myself he would never be young again, even if they let him go. It wouldn't have been a bad thing to show him a little pity, but pity makes me sick, and besides, I couldn't stand him. He hadn't said anything more, but he had turned gray. His face and hands were gray. He sat down again and stared, round-eyed, at the ground. Tom was goodhearted and tried to take him by the arm, but the kid drew himself away violently and made an ugly face. "Leave him alone," I said quietly. "Can't you see he's going to start to bawl?" Tom obeyed regretfully. He would have liked to console the kid; that would have kept him occupied and he wouldn't have been tempted to think about himself. But it got on my nerves. I had never thought about death, for the reason that the question had never come up. But now it had come up, and there was nothing else to do but think about it.

Tom started talking. "Say, did you ever bump anybody off?" he asked me. I didn't answer. He started to explain to me that he had bumped off six fellows since August. He hadn't yet realized what we were in for, and I saw clearly he didn't *want* to realize it. I myself hadn't quite taken it in. I wondered if it hurt very much. I thought about the bullets; I imagined their fiery hail going through my body. All that was beside the real question; but I was calm, we had all night in which to realize it. After a while Tom stopped talking and I looked at him out of the corner of my eye. I saw that he, too, had turned gray and that he looked pretty miserable. I said to myself, "It's starting." It was almost dark, a dull light filtered through the air vents across the coal pile and made a big spot under the sky. Through the hole in the ceiling I could already see a star. The night was going to be clear and cold.

The door opened and two guards entered. They were followed by a blond man in a tan uniform. He greeted us.

"I'm the doctor," he said. "I've been authorized to give you any assistance you may require in these painful circumstances."

He had an agreeable, cultivated voice.

I said to him, "What are you going to do here?"

"Whatever you want me to do. I shall do everything in my power to lighten these few hours."

"Why did you come to us? There are lots of others: the hospital's full of them."

"I was sent here," he answered vaguely. "You'd probably like to smoke, wouldn't you?" he added suddenly. "I've got some cigarettes and even some cigars."

He passed around some English cigarettes and some *puros*,[4] but we refused them. I looked him straight in the eye and he appeared uncomfortable.

"You didn't come here out of compassion," I said to him. "In fact, I know who you are. I saw you with some fascists in the barracks yard the day I was arrested."

I was about to continue, when all at once something happened to me which surprised me: the presence of this doctor had suddenly ceased to interest me. Usually, when I've got hold of a man I don't let go. But somehow the desire to speak had left me. I shrugged my shoulders and turned away. A little later, I looked up and saw he was watching me with an air of curiosity. The guards had sat down on one of the mattresses. Pedro, the tall thin one, was twiddling his thumbs, while the other one shook his head occasionally to keep from falling asleep.

"Do you want some light?" Pedro suddenly asked the doctor. The other fellow nodded, "Yes." I think he was not over-intelligent, but doubtless he was not malicious. As I looked at his big, cold, blue eyes, it seemed to me the worst thing about him was his lack of imagination. Pedro went out and came back with an oil lamp which he set on the corner of the bench. It gave a poor light, but it was better than nothing; the night before we had been left in the dark. For a long while I stared at the circle of light the lamp threw on the ceiling. I was fascinated. Then, suddenly, I came to, the light circle paled, and I felt as if I were being crushed under an enormous weight. It wasn't the thought of death, and it wasn't fear; it was something anonymous. My cheeks were burning hot and my head ached.

I roused myself and looked at my two companions. Tom had his head in his hands and only the fat, white nape of his neck was visible. Juan was by far the worst off; his mouth was wide open and his nostrils were trembling. The doctor came over to him and touched him on the shoulder, as though to comfort him; but his eyes remained cold. Then I saw the Belgian slide his hand furtively down Juan's arm to his wrist. Indifferent, Juan let himself be handled. Then, as though absent-mindedly, the Belgian laid three fingers over his wrist; at the same time, he drew away somewhat and managed to turn his back to me. But I leaned over backward and saw him take out his watch and look at it a moment before relinquishing the boy's wrist. After a moment, he let the inert hand fall and went and leaned against the wall. Then, as if he had suddenly remembered something very important that had to be noted down immediately, he took a notebook from his pocket and wrote a few lines in it. "The son-of-a-bitch," I thought angrily. "He better not come and feel my pulse; I'll give him a punch in his dirty jaw."

He didn't come near me, but I felt he was looking at me. I raised my head and looked back at him. In an impersonal voice, he said, "Don't you think it's frightfully cold here?"

He looked purple with cold.

[4] Small cigars.

"I'm not cold," I answered him.

He kept looking at me with a hard expression. Suddenly I understood, and I lifted my hands to my face. I was covered with sweat. Here, in this cellar, in mid-winter, right in a draft, I was sweating. I ran my fingers through my hair, which was stiff with sweat; at the same time, I realized my shirt was damp and sticking to my skin. I had been streaming with perspiration for an hour, at least, and had felt nothing. But this fact hadn't escaped that Belgian swine. He had seen the drops rolling down my face and had said to himself that it showed an almost pathological terror; and he himself had felt normal and proud of it because he was cold. I wanted to get up and go punch his face in, but I had hardly started to make a move before my shame and anger had disappeared. I dropped back onto the bench with indifference.

I was content to rub my neck with my handkerchief because now I felt the sweat dripping from my hair onto the nape of my neck and that was disagreeable. I soon gave up rubbing myself, however, for it didn't do any good; my handkerchief was already wringing wet and I was still sweating. My buttocks, too, were sweating, and my damp trousers stuck to the bench.

Suddenly, Juan said, "You're a doctor, aren't you?"

"Yes," said the Belgian.

"Do people suffer—very long?"

"Oh! When . . . ? No, no," said the Belgian, in a paternal voice, "it's quickly over."

His manner was as reassuring as if he had been answering a paying patient.

"But I . . . Somebody told me—they often have to fire two volleys."

"Sometimes," said the Belgian, raising his head, "it just happens that the first volley doesn't hit any of the vital organs."

"So then they have to reload their guns and aim all over again?" Juan thought for a moment, then added hoarsely, "But that takes time!"

He was terribly afraid of suffering. He couldn't think about anything else, but that went with his age. As for me, I hardly thought about it any more and it certainly was not fear of suffering that made me perspire.

I rose and walked toward the pile of coal dust. Tom gave a start and looked at me with a look of hate. I irritated him because my shoes squeaked. I wondered if my face was as putty-colored as his. Then I noticed that he, too, was sweating. The sky was magnificent; no light at all came into our dark corner and I had only to lift my head to see the Big Bear.[5] But it didn't look the way it had looked before. Two days ago, from my cell in the archbishop's palace, I could see a big patch of sky and each time of day brought back a different memory. In the morning, when the sky was a deep blue, and light, I thought of beaches along the Atlantic; at noon, I could see the sun, and I remembered a bar in Seville where I used to drink manzanilla[6] and eat anchovies and olives; in the afternoon, I was in the shade, and I thought of the deep shadow which covers half of the arena while the other half gleams in the sunlight: it really gave me a pang to see the whole earth reflected in the sky like that. Now, however, no matter how much I looked up in the air, the sky no longer recalled any-

[5] A constellation. [6] Apple brandy.

thing. I liked it better that way. I came back and sat down next to Tom. There was a long silence.

Then Tom began to talk in a low voice. He had to keep talking, otherwise he lost his way in his own thoughts. I believe he was talking to me, but he didn't look at me. No doubt he was afraid to look at me, because I was gray and sweating. We were both alike and worse than mirrors for each other. He looked at the Belgian, the only one who was alive.

"Say, do you understand? I don't."

Then I, too, began to talk in a low voice. I was watching the Belgian. "Understand what? What's the matter?"

"Something's going to happen to us that I don't understand."

There was a strange odor about Tom. It seemed to me that I was more sensitive to odors than ordinarily. With a sneer, I said, "You'll understand, later."

"That's not so sure," he said stubbornly. "I'm willing to be courageous, but at least I ought to know . . . Listen, they're going to take us out into the courtyard. All right. The fellows will be standing in line in front of us. How many of them will there be?"

"Oh, I don't know. Five, or eight. Not more."

"That's enough. Let's say there'll be eight of them. Somebody will shout 'Shoulder arms!' and I'll see all eight rifles aimed at me. I'm sure I'm going to feel like going through the wall. I'll push against the wall as hard as I can with my back, and the wall won't give in. The way it is in a nightmare. . . . I can imagine all that. Ah, if you only knew how well I can imagine it!"

"Skip it!" I said. "I can imagine it too."

"It must hurt like the devil. You know they aim at your eyes and mouth so as to disfigure you," he added maliciously. "I can feel the wounds already. For the last hour I've been having pains in my head and neck. Not real pains—it's worse still. They're the pains I'll feel tomorrow morning. And after that, then what?"

I understood perfectly well what he meant, but I didn't want to seem to understand. As for the pains, I, too, felt them all through my body, like a lot of little gashes. I couldn't get used to them, but I was like him, I didn't think they were very important.

"After that," I said roughly, "you'll be eating daisies."

He started talking to himself, not taking his eyes off the Belgian, who didn't seem to be listening to him. I knew what he had come for, and that what we were thinking didn't interest him. He had come to look at our bodies, our bodies which were dying alive.

"It's like in a nightmare," said Tom. "You want to think of something, you keep having the impression you've got it, that you're going to understand, and then it slips away from you, it eludes you and it's gone again. I say to myself, afterwards, there won't be anything. But I don't really understand what that means. There are moments when I almost do—and then it's gone again. I start to think of the pains, the bullets, the noise of the shooting. I am a materialist, I swear it; and I'm not going crazy, either. But there's something wrong. I see my own corpse. That's not hard, but it's *I* who see it, with *my* eyes. I'll have to get to the point where I think—where I think I won't see anything more. I won't hear anything more, and the world will go on for the others. We're not made to think that way, Pablo.

Believe me, I've already stayed awake all night waiting for something. But this is not the same thing. This will grab us from behind, Pablo, and we won't be ready for it."

"Shut up," I said. "Do you want me to call a father confessor?"

He didn't answer. I had already noticed that he had a tendency to prophesy and call me "Pablo" in a kind of pale voice. I didn't like that very much, but it seems all the Irish are like that. I had a vague impression that he smelled of urine. Actually, I didn't like Tom very much, and I didn't see why, just because we were going to die together, I should like him any better. There are certain fellows with whom it would be different—with Ramon Gris, for instance. But between Tom and Juan, I felt alone. In fact, I liked it better that way. With Ramon I might have grown soft. But I felt terribly hard at that moment, and I wanted to stay hard.

Tom kept on muttering, in a kind of absent-minded way. He was certainly talking to keep from thinking. Naturally, I agreed with him, and I could have said everything he was saying. It's not *natural* to die. And since I was going to die, nothing seemed natural any more: neither the coal pile, nor the bench, nor Pedro's dirty old face. Only it was disagreeable for me to think the same things Tom thought. And I knew perfectly well that all night long, within five minutes of each other, we would keep on thinking things at the same time, sweating or shivering at the same time. I looked at him sideways and, for the first time, he seemed strange to me. He had death written on his face. My pride was wounded. For twenty-four hours I had lived side by side with Tom, I had listened to him, I had talked to him, and I knew we had nothing in common. And now we were as alike as twin brothers, simply because we were going to die together. Tom took my hand without looking at me.

"Pablo, I wonder . . . I wonder if it's true that we just cease to exist."

I drew my hand away.

"Look between your feet, you dirty dog."

There was a puddle between his feet and water was dripping from his trousers.

"What's the matter?" he said, frightened.

"You're wetting your pants," I said to him.

"It's not true," he said furiously. "I can't be . . . I don't feel anything."

The Belgian had come closer to him. With an air of false concern, he asked, "Aren't you feeling well?"

Tom didn't answer. The Belgian looked at the puddle without comment.

"I don't know what that is," Tom said savagely, "but I'm not afraid. I swear to you, I'm not afraid."

The Belgian made no answer. Tom rose and went to the corner. He came back, buttoning his fly, and sat down, without a word. The Belgian was taking notes.

We were watching the doctor. Juan was watching him too. All three of us were watching him because he was alive. He had the gestures of a living person, the interests of a living person; he was shivering in this cellar the way living people shiver; he had an obedient, well-fed body. We, on the other hand, didn't feel our bodies any more—not the same way, in any case. I felt like touching my trousers, but I didn't dare to. I looked at the

Belgian, well-planted on his two legs, master of his muscles—and able to plan for tomorrow. We were like three shadows deprived of blood; we were watching him and sucking his life like vampires.

Finally he came over to Juan. Was he going to lay his hand on the nape of Juan's neck for some professional reason, or had he obeyed a charitable impulse? If he had acted out of charity, it was the one and only time during the whole night. He fondled Juan's head and the nape of his neck. The kid let him do it, without taking his eyes off him. Then, suddenly, he took hold of the doctor's hand and looked at it in a funny way. He held the Belgian's hand between his own two hands and there was nothing pleasing about them, those two gray paws squeezing that fat red hand. I sensed what was going to happen and Tom sensed it, too. But all the Belgian saw was emotion, and he smiled paternally. After a moment, the kid lifted the big red paw to his mouth and started to bite it. The Belgian drew back quickly and stumbled toward the wall. For a second, he looked at us with horror. He must have suddenly understood that we were not men like himself. I began to laugh, and one of the guards started up. The other had fallen asleep with his eyes wide open, showing only the whites.

I felt tired and over-excited at the same time. I didn't want to think any more about what was going to happen at dawn—about death. It didn't make sense, and I never got beyond just words, or emptiness. But whenever I tried to think about something else I saw the barrels of rifles aimed at me. I must have lived through my execution twenty times in succession; one time I thought it was the real thing; I must have dozed off for a moment. They were dragging me toward the wall and I was resisting; I was imploring their pardon. I woke with a start and looked at the Belgian. I was afraid I had cried out in my sleep. But he was smoothing his mustache; he hadn't noticed anything. If I had wanted to, I believe I could have slept for a while. I had been awake for the last forty-eight hours, and I was worn out. But I didn't want to lose two hours of life. They would have had to come and wake me at dawn. I would have followed them, drunk with sleep, and I would have gone off without so much as "Gosh!" I didn't want it that way, I didn't want to die like an animal. I wanted to understand. Besides, I was afraid of having nightmares. I got up and began to walk up and down and, so as to think about something else, I began to think about my past life. Memories crowded in on me, helter-skelter. Some were good and some were bad—at least that was how I had thought of them *before*. There were faces and happenings. I saw the face of a little *novilero*[7] who had gotten himself horned during the *Feria*, in Valencia. I saw the face of one of my uncles, of Ramon Gris. I remembered all kinds of things that had happened: how I had been on strike for three months in 1926, and had almost died of hunger. I recalled a night I had spent on a beach in Granada; I hadn't eaten for three days, I was nearly wild, I didn't want to give up the sponge. I had to smile. With what eagerness I had run after happiness, and women, and liberty! And to what end? I had wanted to liberate Spain, I admired Py Margall,[8] I had belonged to the anarchist movement, I had

[7] Boy assigned to tend cattle, in this case bulls for bullfights. The *Feria* is a bullfighting festival.

[8] Revolutionary leader.

spoken at public meetings. I took everything as seriously as if I had been immortal.

At that time I had the impression that I had my whole life before me, and I thought to myself, "It's all a god-damned lie." Now it wasn't worth anything because it was finished. I wondered how I had ever been able to go out and have a good time with girls. I wouldn't have lifted my little finger if I had ever imagined that I would die like this. I saw my life before me finished, closed, like a bag, and yet what was inside was not finished. For a moment I tried to appraise it. I would have liked to say to myself, "It's been a good life." But it couldn't be appraised, it was only an outline. I had spent my time writing checks on eternity, and had understood nothing. Now, I didn't miss anything. There were a lot of things I might have missed: the taste of manzanilla, for instance, or the swims I used to take in summer in a little creek near Cadiz. But death had taken the charm out of everything.

Suddenly the Belgian had a wonderful idea.

"My friends," he said to us, "if you want me to—and providing the military authorities give their consent—I could undertake to deliver a word or some token from you to your loved ones. . . . "

Tom growled, "I haven't got anybody."

I didn't answer. Tom waited for a moment, then he looked at me with curiosity. "Aren't you going to send any message to Concha?"

"No."

I hated that sort of sentimental conspiracy. Of course, it was my fault, since I had mentioned Concha the night before, and I should have kept my mouth shut. I had been with her for a year. Even as late as last night, I would have cut my arm off with a hatchet just to see her again for five minutes. That was why I had mentioned her. I couldn't help it. Now I didn't care any more about seeing her. I hadn't anything more to say to her. I didn't even want to hold her in my arms. I loathed my body because it had turned gray and was sweating—and I wasn't even sure that I didn't loathe hers too. Concha would cry when she heard about my death; for months she would have no more interest in life. But still it was I who was going to die. When she looked at me something went from her to me. But I thought to myself that it was all over; if she looked at me *now* her gaze would not leave her eyes, it would not reach out to me. I was alone.

Tom, too, was alone, but not the same way. He was seated astride his chair and had begun to look at the bench with a sort of smile, with surprise, even. He reached out his hand and touched the wood cautiously, as though he were afraid of breaking something, then he drew his hand back hurriedly, and shivered. I wouldn't have amused myself touching that bench, if I had been Tom, that was just some more Irish play-acting. But somehow it seemed to me too that the different objects had something funny about them. They seemed to have grown paler, less massive than before. I had only to look at the bench, the lamp or the pile of coal dust to feel I was going to die. Naturally, I couldn't think clearly about my death, but I saw it everywhere, even on the different objects, the way they had withdrawn and kept their distance, tactfully, like people talking at the bedside of a dying person. It was *his own death* Tom had just touched on the bench.

In the state I was in, if they had come and told me I could go home quietly, that my life would be saved, it would have left me cold. A few hours, or a few years of waiting are all the same, when you've lost the illusion of being eternal. Nothing mattered to me any more. In a way, I was calm. But it was a horrible kind of calm—because of my body. My body—I saw with its eyes and I heard with its ears, but it was no longer I. It sweat and trembled independently, and I didn't recognize it any longer. I was obliged to touch it and look at it to know what was happening to it, just as if it had been someone else's body. At times I still felt it, I felt a slipping, a sort of headlong plunging, as in a falling airplane, or else I heard my heart beating. But this didn't give me confidence. In fact, everything that came from my body had something damned dubious about it. Most of the time it was silent, it stayed put and I didn't feel anything other than a sort of heaviness, a loathsome presence against me. I had the impression of being bound to an enormous vermin.

The Belgian took out his watch and looked at it.

"It's half-past three," he said.

The son-of-a-bitch! He must have done it on purpose. Tom jumped up. We hadn't yet realized the time was passing. The night surrounded us like a formless, dark mass; I didn't even remember it had started.

Juan started to shout. Wringing his hands, he implored, "I don't want to die! I don't want to die!"

He ran the whole length of the cellar with his arms in the air, then he dropped down onto one of the mattresses, sobbing. Tom looked at him with dismal eyes and didn't even try to console him any more. The fact was, it was no use; the kid made more noise than we did, but he was less affected, really. He was like a sick person who defends himself against his malady with a high fever. When there's not even any fever left, it's much more serious.

He was crying. I could tell he felt sorry for himself; he was thinking about death. For one second, one single second, I too felt like crying, crying out of pity for myself. But just the contrary happened. I took one look at the kid, saw his thin, sobbing shoulders, and I felt I was inhuman. I couldn't feel pity either for these others or for myself. I said to myself, "I want to die decently."

Tom had gotten up and was standing just under the round opening looking out for the first signs of daylight. I was determined, I wanted to die decently, and I only thought about that. But underneath, ever since the doctor had told us the time, I felt time slipping, flowing by, one drop at a time.

It was still dark when I heard Tom's voice.

"Do you hear them?"

"Yes."

People were walking in the courtyard.

"What the hell are they doing? After all, they can't shoot in the dark."

After a moment, we didn't hear anything more. I said to Tom, "There's the daylight."

Pedro got up yawning, and came and blew out the lamp. He turned to the man beside him. "It's hellish cold."

The cellar had grown gray. We could hear shots at a distance.

"It's about to start," I said to Tom. "That must be in the back courtyard."

Tom asked the doctor to give him a cigarette. I didn't want any; I didn't want either cigarettes or alcohol. From that moment on, the shooting didn't stop.

"Can you take it in?" Tom said.

He started to add something, then he stopped and began to watch the door. The door opened and a lieutenant came in with four soldiers. Tom dropped his cigarette.

"Steinbock?"

Tom didn't answer. Pedro pointed him out.

"Juan Mirbal?"

"He's the one on the mattress."

"Stand up," said the Lieutenant.

Juan didn't move. Two soldiers took hold of him by the armpits and stood him up on his feet. But as soon as they let go of him he fell down.

The soldiers hesitated a moment.

"He's not the first one to get sick," said the Lieutenant. "You'll have to carry him, the two of you. We'll arrange things when we get there." He turned to Tom. "All right, come along."

Tom left between two soldiers. Two other soldiers followed, carrying the kid by his arms and legs. He was not unconscious; his eyes were wide open and tears were rolling down his cheeks. When I started to go out, the Lieutenant stopped me.

"Are you Ibbieta?"

"Yes."

"You wait here. They'll come and get you later on."

They left. The Belgian and the two jailers left too, and I was alone. I didn't understand what had happened to me, but I would have liked it better if they had ended it all right away. I heard the volleys at almost regular intervals; at each one, I shuddered. I felt like howling and tearing my hair. But instead, I gritted my teeth and pushed my hands deep into my pockets, because I wanted to stay decent.

An hour later, they came to fetch me and took me up to the first floor in a little room which smelt of cigar smoke and was so hot it seemed to me suffocating. Here there were two officers sitting in comfortable chairs, smoking, with papers spread out on their knees.

"Your name is Ibbieta?"

"Yes."

"Where is Ramon Gris?"

"I don't know."

The man who questioned me was small and stocky. He had hard eyes behind his glasses.

"Come nearer," he said to me.

I went nearer. He rose and took me by the arms, looking at me in a way calculated to make me go through the floor. At the same time he pinched my arms with all his might. He didn't mean to hurt me; it was quite a game; he wanted to dominate me. He also seemed to think it was necessary to blow his fetid breath right into my face. We stood like that for a moment, only I felt more like laughing than anything else. It takes a lot more than that to intimidate a man who's about to die: it didn't work. He pushed me away violently and sat down again.

"It's your life or his," he said. "You'll be allowed to go free if you tell us where he is."

After all, these two bedizened fellows with their riding crops and boots were just men who were going to die one day. A little later than I, perhaps, but not a great deal. And there they were, looking for names among their papers, running after other men in order to put them in prison or do away with them entirely. They had their opinions on the future of Spain and on other subjects. Their petty activities seemed to me to be offensive and ludicrous. I could no longer put myself in their place. I had the impression they were crazy.

The little fat fellow kept looking at me, tapping his boots with his riding crop. All his gestures were calculated to make him appear like a spirited, ferocious animal.

"Well? Do you understand?"

"I don't know where Gris is," I said. "I thought he was in Madrid."

The other officer lifted his pale hand indolently. This indolence was also calculated. I saw through all their little tricks, and I was dumbfounded that men should still exist who took pleasure in that kind of thing.

"You have fifteen minutes to think it over," he said slowly. "Take him to the linen-room, and bring him back here in fifteen minutes. If he continues to refuse, he'll be executed at once."

They knew what they were doing. I had spent the night waiting. After that, they had made me wait another hour in the cellar, while they shot Tom and Juan, and now they locked me in the linen-room. They must have arranged the whole thing the night before. They figured that sooner or later people's nerves wear out and they hoped to get me that way.

They made a big mistake. In the linen-room I sat down on a ladder because I felt very weak, and I began to think things over. Not their proposition, however. Naturally I knew where Gris was. He was hiding in his cousins' house, about two miles outside the city. I knew, too, that I would not reveal his hiding place, unless they tortured me (but they didn't seem to be considering that). All that was definitely settled and didn't interest me in the least. Only I would have liked to understand the reasons for my own conduct. I would rather die than betray Gris. Why? I no longer liked Ramon Gris. My friendship for him had died shortly before dawn along with my love for Concha, along with my own desire to live. Of course I still admired him—he was hard. But it was not for that reason that I was willing to die in his place; his life was no more valuable than mine. No life was of any value. A man was going to be stood up against a wall and fired at till he dropped dead. It didn't make any difference whether it was I or Gris or somebody else. I knew perfectly well he was more useful to the Spanish cause than I was, but I didn't give a god-damn about Spain or anarchy, either; nothing had any importance now. And yet, there I was. I could save my skin by betraying Gris and I refused to do it. It seemed more ludicrous to me than anything else; it was stubbornness.

I thought to myself, "Am I hard-headed!" And I was seized with a strange sort of cheerfulness.

They came to fetch me and took me back to the two officers. A rat darted out under our feet and that amused me. I turned to one of the falangists and said to him, "Did you see that rat?"

He made no reply. He was gloomy, and took himself very seriously. As for me, I felt like laughing, but I restrained myself because I was afraid that if I started, I wouldn't be able to stop. The falangist wore mustaches. I kept after him, "You ought to cut off those mustaches, you fool."

I was amused by the fact that he let hair grow all over his face while he was still alive. He gave me a kind of half-hearted kick, and I shut up.

"Well," said the fat officer, "have you thought things over?"

I looked at them with curiosity, like insects of a very rare species.

"I know where he is," I said. "He's hiding in the cemetery. Either in one of the vaults, or in the gravediggers' shack."

I said that just to make fools of them. I wanted to see them get up and fasten their belts and bustle about giving orders.

They jumped to their feet.

"Fine. Moles, go ask Lieutenant Lopez for fifteen men. And as for you," the little fat fellow said to me, "if you've told the truth, I don't go back on my word. But you'll pay for this, if you're pulling our leg."

They left noisily and I waited in peace, still guarded by the falangists. From time to time I smiled at the thought of the face they were going to make. I felt dull and malicious. I could see them lifting up the gravestones, or opening the doors of the vaults one by one. I saw the whole situation as though I were another person: the prisoner determined to play the hero, the solemn falangists with their mustaches and the men in uniform running around among the graves. It was irresistibly funny.

After half an hour, the little fat fellow came back alone. I thought he had come to give the order to execute me. The others must have stayed in the cemetery.

The officer looked at me. He didn't look at all foolish.

"Take him out in the big courtyard with the others," he said. "When military operations are over, a regular tribunal will decide his case."

I thought I must have misunderstood.

"So they're not—they're not going to shoot me?" I asked.

"Not now, in any case. Afterwards, that doesn't concern me."

I still didn't understand.

"But why?" I said to him.

He shrugged his shoulders without replying, and the soldiers led me away. In the big courtyard there were a hundred or so prisoners, women and children and a few old men. I started to walk around the grass plot in the middle. I felt absolutely idiotic. At noon we were fed in the dining hall. Two or three fellows spoke to me. I must have known them, but I didn't answer. I didn't even know where I was.

Toward evening about ten new prisoners were pushed into the courtyard. I recognized Garcia, the baker.

He said to me, "Lucky dog! I didn't expect to find you alive."

"They condemned me to death," I said, "and then they changed their minds. I don't know why."

"I was arrested at two o'clock," Garcia said.

"What for?"

Garcia took no part in politics.

"I don't know," he said. "They arrest everybody who doesn't think the way they do."

He lowered his voice.

"They got Gris."

I began to tremble.

"When?"

"This morning. He acted like a damned fool. He left his cousins' house Tuesday because of a disagreement. There were any number of fellows who would have hidden him, but he didn't want to be indebted to anybody any more. He said, 'I would have hidden at Ibbieta's, but since they've got him, I'll go hide in the cemetery.'"

"In the cemetery?"

"Yes. It was the god-damnedest thing. Naturally they passed by there this morning; that had to happen. They found him in the gravediggers' shack. They opened fire at him and they finished him off."

"In the cemetery!"

Everything went around in circles, and when I came to I was sitting on the ground. I laughed so hard the tears came to my eyes.

Samuel Beckett
(1906–   )

When the Nobel committee awarded its prize to Samuel Beckett in 1969, part of its citation read, "In the realm of annihilation, the writing of Samuel Beckett rises like a miserere from all mankind, its muffled minor key sounding liberation to the oppressed and comfort to those in need." "Liberation" and "comfort" are not words that occur to most first readers of Beckett's spare, bleak stories and plays, but the further one travels in Beckett's strange world, the more just the committee's emphasis seems. The liberation and comfort do not come easily for Beckett; much of his work is devoted to stripping away the superficial reassurances—material possessions, social status, ideologies—by which most of us arrive at a more or less uneasy accommodation with existence. But when, the stripping done, we arrive at Beckett's unblinking vision of the core human condition, there is comfort. Tragedy and comedy converge, as they do for Yeats, with "gaiety transfiguring all that dread."

Beckett was born in 1906 at Foxrock, just outside Dublin, of Protestant, Anglo-Irish parents. He attended a good private school, Portora Royal School, in what later became Northern Ireland and then earned a bachelor's degree in Romance languages at Trinity College, Dublin. Having settled, he thought, upon an academic career, he became a lecturer in English at the École Normale Supérieure in Paris when he was twenty-two. In Paris, he met a number of avant-garde artists, among them James Joyce, who became a close friend. After two years, he returned to Dublin and a post as lecturer in French at Trinity, but resigned after two more years and decided to become a writer. For the next five years, he traveled restlessly around

Europe, finally settling in 1937 in Paris. A volume of short stories, More Pricks than Kicks, *appeared in 1934 and his first novel,* Murphy, *in 1938.*

When war broke out, Beckett remained in Paris and joined the French Underground. In 1942, learning that members of his group, "Gloria S.M.H.," had been arrested by the Nazis, he fled Paris for the unoccupied zone of France. He spent the rest of the war working as a farm laborer near Roussillon, in southeast France, and completing a second novel, Watt, *not published until 1953.*

When Beckett returned to Paris after the war, he plunged into an extraordinarily intensive four-year period of writing, between 1946 and 1950, during which he produced most of his major works. These included, in addition to a number of short stories, the trilogy of unconventional novels Molloy, Malone Dies, *and* The Unnamable *and the play* Waiting for Godot. *All of these works were written in French, because, Beckett explained, "in French, it is easier to write without style"; he himself later translated them into English. None of them was published until Beckett's wife (a pianist and a member of his Resistance group) finally persuaded a publisher to issue* Molloy *and* Malone Dies *(both in 1951) and* The Unnamable *(1953). International fame, however, did not come until the famous production in 1953 of* Waiting for Godot *at the tiny Théâtre de Babylone in Paris. The play ran for more than a year, to baffled but intrigued audiences, and soon found producers in London and New York.*

Beckett has commented, "I wrote all my work very fast—between 1946 and 1950. Since then I haven't written anything. Or at least nothing that has seemed to me valid." This seems to be a bit of Beckettian ironic self-deprecation, for he has kept up a steady output of works which, whether "valid" or not in whatever sense he had in mind, represent a logical development of the implications of the great works of the 1940s. Some of the more recent pieces rework earlier ones, but many of them are fresh work that moves in the direction of greater and greater compression and economy, perhaps in the direction of the silence that seems to be Beckett's ultimate ideal. Post-1950 fiction includes Stories and Texts for Nothing *(1955), which contains stories written in the 1940s;* How It Is *(1960), regarded by some as Beckett's finest fictional work;* The Lost Ones *(1966), an evocation of a purgatory-like world reminiscent of both Dante and science fiction;* Lessness *(1969), a five-page lyrical monologue; and* Company *(1980), a short, lyrical prose piece. His plays since* Waiting for Godot *have followed a similar course of reduction and compression:* Endgame *(1956), perhaps Beckett's greatest play;* All That Fall *(1956), one of a number of plays Beckett has written for radio;* Krapp's Last Tape *(1958);* Happy Days *(1961);* Play *(1962);* Film *(1963), a one-character filmscript written for Buster Keaton;* Eh Joe *(1965), a play for television;* Not I *(1972) and* That Time *(1975), both brief plays for one actor; and* Rockaby *(1981).*

The paradox of Beckett's work is its uniting of great philosophical sophistication and immediate, visceral appeal. Beckett has dissociated himself from the post-war French existentialists, but his work deals with the same fundamental questions of individual Being, taken as antecedent to more elaborate systems of meaning. What does it mean to say "I"? When I attempt to define myself, how can I unite the "I" who defines with the "I" being defined? How can I live my life meaningfully in the face of the absurd fact of my mortality?

Such questions define the area Beckett seems to refer to when he says, "My little exploration is the whole zone of being that has always been set aside by artists as something unusable—as something by definition incompatible with art." He carries out his exploration with a full consciousness of the work of philosophers who have dealt with this "zone of being," preeminently the seventeenth-century French philosopher René Descartes and his little-known Dutch disciple Arnold Geulincx.

But Beckett is a writer rather than a philosopher, and a comic writer at that. His triumph is not his contributions to ontology but his resonant, heartbreaking metaphors for existence—an old man writing as he dies, two tramps waiting by the side of the road, a woman sinking slowly into the ground—and his mastery of dramatic monologue. The vision on the jetty that the thirty-nine-year-old, tape-recorded Krapp reports echoes a similar experience Beckett had at the same age on a pier in Dublin harbor when he realized that dramatic monologue was the natural form for his work to take. Beckett's greatest works, in both fiction and drama, are flowing, stream-of-consciousness monologues in which particular characters and events seem to swim up out of the stream briefly and then sink back in. Even Didi and Gogo in Waiting for Godot *or Hamm and Clov in* Endgame *seem to be splittings of a single mind talking to itself. And the great* Trilogy *consists of a receding series of talkers who drop away until we arrive at the last monologist, the Unnamable, the voice of existence itself condemned to go on talking forever.*

Krapp's Last Tape *is a small masterpiece of Beckett's complex art. Krapp, like most of Beckett's protagonists, is basically a clown, and his routines with his keys, his bananas, and his bottle are broad music-hall gags. But the play is a metaphysical clown show: "Pascal's* Pensées *as played by the Fratellini clowns," in the words of the playwright Jean Anouilh about* Waiting for Godot. *The tape-recorder is used for all the slapstick comedy Beckett can get out of it, but it also becomes, with Krapp's bank of autobiographical tapes, a plangent metaphor for the time-cursed pathos of human existence.*

FURTHER READING *(prepared by N. K. B.):* Although critics often summarize major incidents in Beckett's life, Deirdre Bair's *Samuel Beckett*, 1978, provides the first detailed biography. Hugh Kenner's *Samuel Beckett: A Critical Study*, 1962, rev. 1968, is a provocative analysis of Beckett's style and themes, demonstrating the importance of Cartesian philosophy in his works. For a more concrete explication of individual texts, see Kenner's *Reader's Guide to Samuel Beckett*, 1973, which also contains a discussion of *Krapp's Last Tape*. Ruby Cohn's invaluable introduction to Beckett's themes and formal structures, *Samuel Beckett: The Comic Gamut*, 1962, emphasizes the comic devices in the drama and fiction. David T. Hesla, in *The Shape of Chaos: An Interpretation of the Art of Samuel Beckett*, 1971, relates Beckett's art to Western philosophical and intellectual traditions. Nathan Scott's *Samuel Beckett*, 1965, discusses Beckett in the context of the French literary tradition. In *Samuel Beckett*, 1976, John Pilling details the cultural and intellectual backgrounds of Beckett's career. Helene L. Baldwin's *Samuel Beckett's Real Silence*, 1981, demonstrates his concern with metaphysical and mystical themes. Martin Esslin, ed., *Samuel Beckett: A Collection of Critical Essays*, 1965, is the most useful compendium of international criticism on Beckett, including a succinct introduction by Esslin on the major themes. For specific readings of and reactions to *Krapp's Last Tape*, see *Samuel Beckett: The Critical Heritage*, 1979, ed. by Lawrence Graver and Raymond Federman.

KRAPP'S LAST TAPE

A PLAY IN ONE ACT

A late evening in the future.

KRAPP'S *den.*

Front centre a small table, the two drawers of which open towards audience.

Sitting at the table, facing front, i.e. across from the drawers, a wearish[1] *old man:* KRAPP.

Rusty black narrow trousers too short for him. Rusty black sleeveless waistcoat, four capacious pockets. Heavy silver watch and chain. Grimy white shirt open at neck, no collar. Surprising pair of dirty white boots, size ten at least, very narrow and pointed.

White face. Purple nose. Disordered grey hair. Unshaven.

Very near-sighted (but unspectacled). Hard of hearing.

Cracked voice. Distinctive intonation.

Laborious walk.

On the table a tape-recorder with microphone and a number of cardboard boxes containing reels of recorded tapes.

Table and immediately adjacent area in strong white light. Rest of stage in darkness.

KRAPP *remains a moment motionless, heaves a great sigh, looks at his watch, fumbles in his pockets, takes out an envelope, puts it back, fumbles, takes out a small bunch of keys, raises it to his eyes, chooses a key, gets up and moves to front of table. He stoops, unlocks first drawer, peers into it, feels about inside it, takes out a reel of tape, peers at it, puts it back, locks drawer, unlocks second drawer, peers into it, feels about inside it, takes out a large banana, peers at it, locks drawer, puts keys back in his pocket. He turns, advances to edge of stage, halts, strokes banana, peels it, drops skin at his feet, puts end of banana in his mouth and remains motionless, staring vacuously before him. Finally he bites off the end, turns aside and begins pacing to and fro at edge of stage, in the light, i.e. not more than four or five paces either way, meditatively eating banana. He treads on skin, slips, nearly falls, recovers himself, stoops and peers at skin and finally pushes it, still stooping, with his foot over the edge of stage into pit. He resumes his pacing, finishes banana, returns to table, sits down, remains a moment motionless, heaves a great sigh, takes keys from his pockets, raises them to his eyes, chooses key, gets up and moves to front of table, unlocks second drawer, takes out a second large banana, peers at it, locks drawer, puts back keys in his pocket, turns, advances to edge of stage, halts, strokes banana, peels it, tosses skin into pit, puts end of banana in his mouth and remains motionless, staring vacuously before him. Finally he has an idea, puts banana in his waistcoat pocket, the end emerging, and goes with all the speed he can muster backstage into darkness. Ten seconds. Loud pop of cork. Fifteen seconds. He comes back into light carrying an old*

[1] Lean, wizened.

ledger and sits down at table. He lays ledger on table, wipes his mouth, wipes his hands on the front of his waistcoat, brings them smartly together and rubs them.

KRAPP [*briskly*]. Ah! [*He bends over ledger, turns the pages, finds the entry he wants, reads.*] Box . . . thrree . . . spool . . . five. [*He raises his head and stares front. With relish.*] Spool! [*Pause.*] Spooool! [*Happy smile. Pause. He bends over table, starts peering and poking at the boxes.*] Box . . . thrree . . . thrree . . . four . . . two . . . [*with surprise*] nine! good God! . . . seven . . . ah! the little rascal! [*He takes up box, peers at it.*] Box thrree. [*He lays it on table, opens it and peers at spools inside.*] Spool . . . [*he peers at ledger*] . . . five . . . [*he peers at spools*] . . . five . . . five . . . ah! the little scoundrel! [*He takes out a spool, peers at it.*] Spool five. [*He lays it on table, closes box three, puts it back with the others, takes up the spool.*] Box thrree, spool five. [*He bends over the machine, looks up. With relish.*] Spooool! [*Happy smile. He bends, loads spool on machine, rubs his hands.*] Ah! [*He peers at ledger, reads entry at foot of page.*] Mother at rest at last . . . Hm . . . The black ball . . . [*He raises his head, stares blankly front. Puzzled.*] Black ball? . . . [*He peers again at ledger, reads.*] The dark nurse . . . [*He raises his head, broods, peers again at ledger, reads.*] Slight improvement in bowel condition . . . Hm . . . Memorable . . . what? [*He peers closer.*] Equinox, memorable equinox. [*He raises his head, stares blankly front. Puzzled.*] Memorable equinox? . . . [*Pause. He shrugs his shoulders, peers again at ledger, reads.*] Farewell to—[*he turns the page*]—love.

He raises his head, broods, bends over machine, switches on and assumes listening posture, i.e. leaning forward, elbows on table, hand cupping ear towards machine, face front.

TAPE [*strong voice, rather pompous, clearly* KRAPP'*s at a much earlier time*]. Thirty-nine today, sound as a—[*Settling himself more comfortably he knocks one of the boxes off the table, curses, switches off, sweeps boxes and ledger violently to the ground, winds tape back to beginning, switches on, resumes posture.*] Thirty-nine today, sound as a bell, apart from my old weakness, and intellectually I have now every reason to suspect at the . . . [*hesitates*] . . . crest of the wave—or thereabouts. Celebrated the awful occasion, as in recent years, quietly at the Winehouse. Not a soul. Sat before the fire with closed eyes, separating the grain from the husks. Jotted down a few notes, on the back of an envelope. Good to be back in my den, in my old rags. Have just eaten I regret to say three bananas and only with difficulty refrained from a fourth. Fatal things for a man with my condition. [*Vehemently.*] Cut 'em out! [*Pause.*] The new light above my table is a great improvement. With all this darkness round me I feel less alone. [*Pause.*] In a way. [*Pause.*] I love to get up and move about in it, then back here to . . . [*hesitates*] . . . me. [*Pause.*] Krapp.

[*Pause.*]

The grain, now what I wonder do I mean by that, I mean . . . [*hesitates*] . . . I suppose I mean those things worth having when all the dust has—when all *my* dust has settled. I close my eyes and try and imagine them.

[*Pause.* KRAPP *closes his eyes briefly.*]

Extraordinary silence this evening, I strain my ears and do not hear a sound. Old Miss McGlome always sings at this hour. But not tonight. Songs of her girlhood, she says. Hard to think of her as a girl. Wonderful woman though. Connaught,[2] I fancy. [*Pause.*] Shall I sing when I am her age, if I ever am? No. [*Pause.*] Did I sing as a boy? No. [*Pause.*] Did I ever sing? No.

[*Pause.*]

Just been listening to an old year, passages at random. I did not check in the book, but it must be at least ten or twelve years ago. At that time I think I was still living on and off with Bianca in Kedar Street. Well out of that, Jesus yes! Hopeless business. [*Pause.*] Not much about her, apart from a tribute to her eyes. Very warm. I suddenly saw them again. [*Pause.*] Incomparable! [*Pause.*] Ah well . . . [*Pause.*] These old P.M.s[3] are gruesome, but I often find them—[KRAPP *switches off, broods, switches on*]—a help before embarking on a new . . . [*hesitates*] . . . retrospect. Hard to believe I was ever that young whelp. The voice! Jesus! And the aspirations! [*Brief laugh in which* KRAPP *joins.*] And the resolutions! [*Brief laugh in which* KRAPP *joins.*] To drink less, in particular. [*Brief laugh of* KRAPP *alone.*] Statistics. Seventeen hundred hours, out of the preceding eight thousand odd, consumed on licensed premises[4] alone. More than 20%, say 40% of his waking life. [*Pause.*] Plans for a less . . . [*hesitates*] . . . engrossing sexual life. Last illness of his father. Flagging pursuit of happiness.

Unattainable laxation.[5] Sneers at what he calls his youth and thanks to God that it's over. [*Pause.*] False ring there. [*Pause.*] Shadows of the opus . . . magnum.[6] Closing with a—[*brief laugh*]—yelp to Providence. [*Prolonged laugh in which* KRAPP *joins.*] What remains of all that misery? A girl in a shabby green coat, on a railway-station platform? No?

[*Pause.*]

When I look—

KRAPP *switches off, broods, looks at his watch, gets up, goes backstage into darkness. Ten seconds. Pop of cork. Ten seconds. Second cork. Ten seconds. Third cork. Ten seconds. Brief burst of quavering song.*

KRAPP [*sings*]. Now the day is over,
Night is drawing nigh-igh,
Shadows—

Fit of coughing. He comes back into light, sits down, wipes his mouth, switches on, resumes his listening posture.

TAPE. —back on the year that is gone, with what I hope is perhaps a glint of the old eye to come, there is of course the house on the canal where mother lay a-dying, in the late autumn, after her long viduity [KRAPP *gives a start*], and the—[KRAPP *switches off, winds back tape a little, bends his ear closer to machine, switches on*]—a-dying, after her long viduity, and the—

[2] Northwestern province of Ireland. [3] Post mortems.
[4] Shops licensed to sell liquor. [5] Unwinding, relaxation.
[6] Of the great work (especially of literature).

KRAPP *switches off, raises his head, stares blankly before him. His lips move in the syllables of "viduity." No sound. He gets up, goes backstage into darkness, comes back with an enormous dictionary, lays it on table, sits down and looks up the word.*

KRAPP [*reading from dictionary*]. State—or condition of being—or remaining—a widow—or widower. [*Looks up. Puzzled.*] Being—or remaining? . . . [*Pause. He peers again at dictionary. Reading.*] "Deep weeds of viduity" . . . Also of an animal, especially a bird . . . the vidua or weaver-bird . . . Black plumage of male . . . [*He looks up. With relish.*] The vidua-bird!

[*Pause. He closes dictionary, switches on, resumes listening posture.*]

TAPE.—bench by the weir[7] from where I could see her window. There I sat, in the biting wind, wishing she were gone. [*Pause.*] Hardly a soul, just a few regulars, nursemaids, infants, old men, dogs. I got to know them quite well—oh by appearance of course I mean! One dark young beauty I recollect particularly, all white and starch, incomparable bosom, with a big black hooded perambulator, most funereal thing. Whenever I looked in her direction she had her eyes on me. And yet when I was bold enough to speak to her—not having been introduced—she threatened to call a policeman. As if I had designs on her virtue! [*Laugh. Pause.*] The face she had! The eyes! Like . . . [*hesitates*] . . . chrysolite![8] [*Pause.*] Ah well . . . [*Pause.*] I was there when—[KRAPP *switches off, broods, switches on again*]—the blind went down, one of those dirty brown roller affairs, throwing a ball for a little white dog, as chance would have it. I happened to look up and there it was. All over and done with, at last. I sat on for a few moments with the ball in my hand and the dog yelping and pawing at me. [*Pause.*] Moments. Her moments, my moments. [*Pause.*] The dog's moments. [*Pause.*] In the end I held it out to him and he took it in his mouth, gently, gently. A small, old, black, hard, solid rubber ball. [*Pause.*] I shall feel it, in my hand, until my dying day. [*Pause.*] I might have kept it. [*Pause.*] But I gave it to the dog.

[*Pause.*]

Ah well. . .

[*Pause.*]

Spiritually a year of profound gloom and indigence until that memorable night in March, at the end of the jetty,[9] in the howling wind, never to be forgotten, when suddenly I saw the whole thing. The vision, at last. This I fancy is what I have chiefly to record this evening, against the day when my work will be done and perhaps no place left in my memory, warm or cold, for the miracle that . . . [*hesitates*] . . . for the fire that set it alight. What I suddenly saw then was this, that the belief I had been going on all my life, namely—[KRAPP *switches off impatiently, winds tape forward, switches on again*]—great granite rocks the foam flying up in the light of the lighthouse and the wind-gauge spinning like a propellor, clear to me at last that the dark I have always struggled to keep under is in reality my most—[KRAPP *curses, switches off, winds tape forward, switches*

[7] Millpond. [8] Olivine, a pale green precious stone. [9] Wharf or pier.

on again]—unshatterable association until my dissolution of storm and night with the light of the understanding and the fire—[KRAPP *curses louder, switches off, winds tape forward, switches on again*]—my face in her breasts and my hand on her. We lay there without moving. But under us all moved, and moved us, gently, up and down, and from side to side.

[*Pause.*]

Past midnight. Never knew such silence. The earth might be uninhabited.

[*Pause.*]

Here I end—

[KRAPP *switches off, winds tape back, switches on again.*]

—upper lake, with the punt, bathed off the bank, then pushed out into the stream and drifted. She lay stretched out on the floorboards with her hands under her head and her eyes closed. Sun blazing down, bit of a breeze, water nice and lively. I noticed a scratch on her thigh and asked her how she came by it. Picking gooseberries, she said. I said again I thought it was hopeless and no good going on, and she agreed, without opening her eyes. [*Pause.*] I asked her to look at me and after a few moments—[*pause*]—after a few moments she did, but the eyes just slits, because of the glare. I bent over her to get them in the shadow and they opened. [*Pause. Low.*] Let me in. [*Pause.*] We drifted in among the flags and stuck. The way they went down, sighing, before the stem! [*Pause.*] I lay down across her with my face in her breasts and my hand on her. We lay there without moving. But under us all moved, and moved us, gently, up and down, and from side to side.

[*Pause.*]

Past midnight. Never knew—

KRAPP *switches off, broods. Finally he fumbles in his pockets, encounters the banana, takes it out, peers at it, puts it back, fumbles, brings out the envelope, fumbles, puts back envelope, looks at his watch, gets up and goes backstage into darkness. Ten seconds. Sound of bottle against glass, then brief siphon. Ten seconds. Bottle against glass alone. Ten seconds. He comes back a little unsteadily into light, goes to front of table, takes out keys, raises them to his eyes, chooses key, unlocks first drawer, peers into it, feels about inside, takes out reel, peers at it, locks drawer, puts keys back in his pocket, goes and sits down, takes reel off machine, lays it on dictionary, loads virgin reel on machine, takes envelope from his pocket, consults back of it, lays it on table, switches on, clears his throat and begins to record.*

KRAPP. Just been listening to that stupid bastard I took myself for thirty years ago, hard to believe I was ever as bad as that. Thank God that's all done with anyway. [*Pause.*] The eyes she had! [*Broods, realizes he is recording silence, switches off, broods. Finally.*] Everything there, everything, all the—[*Realizes this is not being recorded, switches on.*] Everything there, everything on this old muckball, all the light and dark and famine and feasting of . . . [*hesitates*] . . . the ages! [*In a shout.*] Yes! [*Pause.*] Let that go! Jesus! Take his mind off his homework! Jesus! [*Pause. Weary.*] Ah well, maybe he was right. [*Pause.*] Maybe he was right. [*Broods. Realizes. Switches off. Consults envelope.*] Pah! [*Crumples it and throws it away. Broods.*

Switches on.] Nothing to say, not a squeak. What's a year now? The sour cud and the iron stool. [*Pause.*] Revelled in the word spool. [*With relish.*] Spooool! Happiest moment of the past half million. [*Pause.*] Seventeen copies sold, of which eleven at trade price to free circulating libraries beyond the seas. Getting known. [*Pause.*] One pound six and something, eight I have little doubt. [*Pause.*] Crawled out once or twice, before the summer was cold. Sat shivering in the park, drowned in dreams and burning to be gone. Not a soul. [*Pause.*] Last fancies. [*Vehemently.*] Keep 'em under! [*Pause.*] Scalded the eyes out of me reading *Effie*[10] again, a page a day, with tears again. Effie . . . [*Pause.*] Could have been happy with her, up there on the Baltic, and the pines, and the dunes. [*Pause.*] Could I? [*Pause.*] And she? [*Pause.*] Pah! [*Pause.*] Fanny came in a couple of times. Bony old ghost of a whore. Couldn't do much, but I suppose better than a kick in the crutch. The last time wasn't so bad. How do you manage it, she said, at your age? I told her I'd been saving up for her all my life. [*Pause.*] Went to Vespers once, like when I was in short trousers. [*Pause. Sings.*]

Now the day is over,
Night is drawing nigh-igh,
Shadows—[*coughing, then almost inaudible*]—of the evening
Steal across the sky.

[*Gasping.*] Went to sleep and fell off the pew. [*Pause.*] Sometimes wondered in the night if a last effort mightn't—[*Pause.*] Ah finish your booze now and get to your bed. Go on with this drivel in the morning. Or leave it at that. [*Pause.*] Leave it at that. [*Pause.*] Lie propped up in the dark—and wander. Be again in the dingle[11] on a Christmas Eve, gathering holly, the red-berried. [*Pause.*] Be again on Croghan on a Sunday morning, in the haze, with the bitch, stop and listen to the bells. [*Pause.*] And so on. [*Pause.*] Be again, be again. [*Pause.*] All that old misery. [*Pause.*] Once wasn't enough for you. [*Pause.*] Lie down across her.

Long pause. He suddenly bends over machine, switches off, wrenches off tape, throws it away, puts on the other, winds it forward to the passage he wants, switches on, listens staring front.

TAPE.—gooseberries, she said. I said again I thought it was hopeless and no good going on, and she agreed, without opening her eyes. [*Pause.*] I asked her to look at me and after a few moments—[*pause*]—after a few moments she did, but the eyes just slits, because of the glare. I bent over her to get them in the shadow and they opened. [*Pause. Low.*] Let me in. [*Pause.*] We drifted in among the flags and stuck. The way they went down, sighing, before the stem! [*Pause.*] I lay down across her with my face in her breasts and my hand on her. We lay there without moving. But under us all moved, and moved us, gently, up and down, and from side to side.

[*Pause.* KRAPP'S *lips move. No sound.*]

[10] *Effi Briest* (1895), by the German novelist Theodor Fontane. [11] Wooded hollow.

Past midnight. Never knew such silence. The earth might be uninhabited.

[*Pause.*]

Here I end this reel. Box—[*pause*]—three, spool—[*pause*]—five. [*Pause.*] Perhaps my best years are gone. When there was a chance of happiness. But I wouldn't want them back. Not with the fire in me now. No, I wouldn't want them back.

[KRAPP *motionless staring before him. The tape runs on in silence.*]

CURTAIN

Richard Wright

(1908–1960)

"The Negro is America's metaphor," Richard Wright once wrote, and elsewhere, "Negro life in the U.S. dramatically symbolizes the struggles of a people whose forefathers lived in a warm, simple culture and who are now trying to live the new way of life that dominates our time: machine-civilization and all the consequences flowing from it. It must be understood that when I talk of the American Negroes, I am talking about everybody." For Wright, universality, or "talking about everybody," was not a flight away from engagement with the very specific issue of American racism; Native Son *(1940) tore the veil from the rage and frustration of urban American blacks and permanently changed the way both blacks and whites saw racial relations. But it was Wright's ability to see the Negro as metaphor as well as suffering individual that gave his work its psychological complexity and philosophical depth and made him a writer of international significance.*

Wright was born in Natchez, Mississippi, in 1908, the son of a sharecropper father and a mother trained as a schoolteacher but employed as a domestic servant. The father deserted the family when Wright was five, and for several years the family led a wandering existence through Mississippi, Tennessee, and Arkansas as the mother searched for employment. After she was disabled by a stroke when Wright was seven, he and his five-year-old brother Leon were placed in an orphanage. Eventually the family was reunited in Mississippi in the home of Wright's maternal grandmother, a stern Seventh Day Adventist with whom Wright was in constant conflict. When he graduated from high school in Jackson, Mississippi, he left home and found a job in Memphis, Tennessee.

After two years, the nineteen-year-old Wright determined to leave the South and made his way to Chicago, where he worked at a string of miscellaneous manual jobs before landing a job as a postal clerk. He had already begun writing before he left Memphis, and in Chicago he continued to write and to read widely. He joined the leftist John Reed Club, a writers' group, in 1933 and shortly afterward joined the Communist Party. He moved to New York in 1937 to become an editor and writer for the Daily Worker. *The following year his first book appeared:* Uncle Tom's Children, *a group of brutally naturalistic novellas about Southern racism.*

The publication of Native Son *in 1940 propelled Wright into international fame and was a landmark in black writing in America. The novel is a grim story of a black man named Bigger Thomas, who, after he unintentionally kills a white girl, comes to find in the role of murderer an alternative identity preferable to that imposed upon him by white society as a projection of its own weakness and cruelty. Unlike much previous black writing, including Wright's own,* Native Son *does not portray passive victims; it forces its readers to confront their own creation, a desperate, enraged killer. The book is a psychologically keen analysis of the making of a "nigger" (a word with which Bigger's name is intended to chime).* Native Son *was a commercial as well as critical success, a best seller, a Book of the Month Club selection, and the basis of a successful play directed on Broadway by Orson Welles the following year.*

During the early 1940s, Wright became increasingly disillusioned with Communism, resenting the restrictions it placed upon his work and coming to believe that the issue of racism was of minor importance in its program; he left the Party in 1944. As his enthusiasm for Communism waned, he read more intensively in Dostoevsky, Nietzsche, and Freud and in such existentialist philosophers as Kierkegaard. The influence of existentialism can be seen already in Native Son, *and it becomes prominent in "The Man Who Lived Underground," two sections of which were published in the literary magazine* Accent *in 1942 and which appeared complete in 1944. Wright's autobiography,* Black Boy *(1945), gave him another best-selling commercial success.*

Gertrude Stein admired Wright's work, and in 1945 she used her influence to have the French government invite him to Paris. His cordial reception and the absence of race prejudice there encouraged him to settle permanently in France with his wife and daughter. He became friends with Jean-Paul Sartre and Albert Camus and, with a group of French writers, founded Présence Africaine, *a journal of African culture. The fiction of the Paris years is generally regarded as representing a decline from the novels written in America. It includes* The Outsider *(1953), a Nietzschean study in identity;* Savage Holiday *(1954), a rather mechanical Freudian novel; and* The Long Dream *(1958), a maturation novel about a young Southern black who flees to Paris.* Black Power *(1954),* The Color Curtain *(1956), and* White Man, Listen *(1957) were all polemical books dealing with problems of the emerging nations of Africa.*

Wright died unexpectedly in 1960 of amoebic dysentery, contracted during one of his African trips. Three more books were published posthumously: Eight Men *(1961), a collection of stories including "The Man Who Lived Underground";* Lawd Today *(1963), a novel written in the thirties but previously unpublished; and* American Hunger *(1977), an autobiographical continuation of* Black Boy.

Wright shared with Sartre and Camus the existentialist concern with "extreme cases," with explosions of violence that force people into corners where the superficial falls away and the true self emerges. The action of "The Man Who Lived Underground," as in several other of Wright's stories, is triggered by an act of violence (or, in this case, a false accusation of such an act) and an ensuing flight and pursuit. The idea for the story actually came from the pulp magazine True Confessions *and in its first version began with a realistic account of the events leading up to Fred Daniels's flight. In the finished story, however, with its abrupt opening image of an anonymous man creeping into a sewer, the emphasis shifts from the reasons for the flight to the flight itself. The title and imagery of the story recall Dostoevsky's* Notes from Underground; *more generally the story reenacts the myth of the descent to the underworld, in which the hero returns with a gift for mankind. Fred Daniels obtains such a gift—the slant vision of American life as seen from the underground—but the prophet is rejected when he returns like Lazarus from the dead. Both the brutally realistic treatment of Fred Daniels's journey and the metaphoric overtones of his story typify the power and subtlety of Wright's art.*

FURTHER READING *(prepared by W. J. R.):* On Wright's life, see Constance Webb's *Richard Wright*, 1968. Webb, a personal friend of Wright's, devotes separate chapters to the major novels and includes a bibliography of Wright's writings. Russell Carl Brignano's *Richard Wright: An Introduction to the Man and His Works*, 1970, divides Wright's "public concerns" into four broad areas and discusses each in turn. The categories include race relations and Marxism. An excellent overview of Wright's career begins *Richard Wright: The Critical Reception*, ed. with introduction by John M. Reilly, 1978. Included here are critical responses to all of Wright's novels (excluding *Savage Holiday*). Keneth Kinnamon's *The Emergence of Richard Wright*, 1972, maintains a dual perspective on the literary aesthetics of Wright's fiction and poetry and on the elements of racial protest. Expatriatism, an important aspect of Wright's artistry, is the subject of Paul C. Sherr's "Richard Wright: The Expatriate Pattern," in *Modern Black Literature*, ed. S. Okechukwu Mezu, 1971; Sherr discusses in particular depth Gertrude Stein's noted esteem for Wright. *Twentieth Century Interpretations of "Native Son,"* ed. Houston A. Baker, Jr., 1972, offers ten essays, including Wright's "How Bigger Was Born."

THE MAN WHO LIVED UNDERGROUND

I've got to hide, he told himself. His chest heaved as he waited, crouching in a dark corner of the vestibule. He was tired of running and dodging. Either he had to find a place to hide, or he had to surrender. A police car swished by through the rain, its siren rising sharply. They're looking for me all over . . .[1] He crept to the door and squinted through the fogged plate glass. He stiffened as the siren rose and died in the distance. Yes, he had to hide, but where? He gritted his teeth. Then a sudden movement in the street caught his attention. A throng of tiny columns of water snaked into the air from the perforations of a manhole cover. The columns stopped abruptly, as though the perforations had become clogged; a gray spout of sewer water jutted up from underground and lifted the circular metal cover, juggled it for a moment, then let it fall with a clang.

He hatched a tentative plan: he would wait until the siren sounded far off, then he would go out. He smoked and waited, tense. At last the siren gave him his signal; it wailed, dying, going away from him. He stepped to the sidewalk, then paused and looked curiously at the open manhole, half expecting the cover to leap up again. He went to the center of the street and stooped and peered into the hole, but could see nothing. Water rustled in the black depths.

He started with terror; the siren sounded so near that he had the idea that he had been dreaming and had awakened to find the car upon him.

[1] In this story, repeated periods do not indicate omissions but are part of Wright's original punctuation.

He dropped instinctively to his knees and his hands grasped the rim of the manhole. The siren seemed to hoot directly above him and with a wild gasp of exertion he snatched the cover far enough off to admit his body. He swung his legs over the opening and lowered himself into watery darkness. He hung for an eternal moment to the rim by his finger tips, then he felt rough metal prongs and at once he knew that sewer workmen used these ridges to lower themselves into manholes. Fist over fist, he let his body sink until he could feel no more prongs. He swayed in dank space; the siren seemed to howl at the very rim of the manhole. He dropped and was washed violently into an ocean of warm, leaping water. His head was battered against a wall and he wondered if this were death. Frenziedly his fingers clawed and sank into a crevice. He steadied himself and measured the strength of the current with his own muscular tension. He stood slowly in water that dashed past his knees with fearful velocity.

He heard a prolonged scream of brakes and the siren broke off. Oh, God! They had found him! Looming above his head in the rain a white face hovered over the hole. "How did this damn thing get off?" he heard a policeman ask. He saw the steel cover move slowly until the hole looked like a quarter moon turned black. "Give me a hand here," someone called. The cover clanged into place, muffling the sights and sounds of the upper world. Knee-deep in the pulsing current, he breathed with aching chest, filling his lungs with the hot stench of yeasty rot.

From the perforations of the manhole cover, delicate lances of hazy violet sifted down and wove a mottled pattern upon the surface of the streaking current. His lips parted as a car swept past along the wet pavement overhead, its heavy rumble soon dying out, like the hum of a plane speeding through a dense cloud. He had never thought that cars could sound like that; everything seemed strange and unreal under here. He stood in darkness for a long time, knee-deep in rustling water, musing.

The odor of rot had become so general that he no longer smelled it. He got his cigarettes, but discovered that his matches were wet. He searched and found a dry folder in the pocket of his shirt and managed to strike one; it flared weirdly in the wet gloom, glowing greenishly, turning red, orange, then yellow. He lit a crumpled cigarette; then, by the flickering light of the match, he looked for support so that he would not have to keep his muscles flexed against the pouring water. His pupils narrowed and he saw to either side of him two steaming walls that rose and curved inward some six feet above his head to form a dripping, mouse-colored dome. The bottom of the sewer was a sloping V-trough. To the left, the sewer vanished in ashen fog. To the right was a steep down-curve into which water plunged.

He saw now that had he not regained his feet in time, he would have been swept to death, or had he entered any other manhole he would have probably drowned. Above the rush of the current he heard sharper juttings of water; tiny streams were spewing into the sewer from smaller conduits. The match died; he struck another and saw a mass of debris sweep past him and clog the throat of the down-curve. At once the water began rising rapidly. Could he climb out before he drowned? A long hiss sounded and the debris was sucked from sight; the current lowered. He understood now what had made the water toss the manhole cover; the down-curve had become temporarily obstructed and the perforations had become clogged.

He was in danger; he might slide into a down-curve; he might wander with a lighted match into a pocket of gas and blow himself up; or he might contract some horrible disease . . . Though he wanted to leave, an irrational impulse held him rooted. To the left, the convex ceiling swooped to a height of less than five feet. With cigarette slanting from pursed lips, he waded with taut muscles, his feet sloshing over the slimy bottom, his shoes sinking into spongy slop, the slate-colored water cracking in creamy foam against his knees. Pressing his flat left palm against the lowered ceiling, he struck another match and saw a metal pole nestling in a niche of the wall. Yes, some sewer workman had left it. He reached for it, then jerked his head away as a whisper of scurrying life whisked past and was still. He held the match close and saw a huge rat, wet with slime, blinking beady eyes and baring tiny fangs. The light blinded the rat and the frizzled head moved aimlessly. He grabbed the pole and let it fly against the rat's soft body; there was shrill piping and the grizzly body splashed into the dun-colored water and was snatched out of sight, spinning in the scuttling stream.

He swallowed and pushed on, following the curve of the misty cavern, sounding the water with the pole. By the faint light of another manhole cover he saw, amid loose wet brick, a hole with walls of damp earth leading into blackness. Gingerly he poked the pole into it; it was hollow and went beyond the length of the pole. He shoved the pole before him, hoisted himself upward, got to his hands and knees, and crawled. After a few yards he paused, struck to wonderment by the silence; it seemed that he had traveled a million miles away from the world. As he inched forward again he could sense the bottom of the dirt tunnel becoming dry and lowering slightly. Slowly he rose and to his astonishment he stood erect. He could not hear the rustling of the water now and he felt confoundingly alone, yet lured by the darkness and silence.

He crept a long way, then stopped, curious, afraid. He put his right foot forward and it dangled in space; he drew back in fear. He thrust the pole outward and it swung in emptiness. He trembled, imagining the earth crumbling and burying him alive. He scratched a match and saw that the dirt floor sheered away steeply and widened into a sort of cave some five feet below him. An old sewer, he muttered. He cocked his head, hearing a feathery cadence which he could not identify. The match ceased to burn.

Using the pole as a kind of ladder, he slid down and stood in darkness. The air was a little fresher and he could still hear vague noises. Where was he? He felt suddenly that someone was standing near him and he turned sharply, but there was only darkness. He poked cautiously and felt a brick wall; he followed it and the strange sounds grew louder. He ought to get out of here. This was crazy. He could not remain here for any length of time; there was no food and no place to sleep. But the faint sounds tantalized him; they were strange but familiar. Was it a motor? A baby crying? Music? A siren? He groped on, and the sounds came so clearly that he could feel the pitch and timbre of human voices. Yes, singing! That was it! He listened with open mouth. It was a church service. Enchanted, he groped toward the waves of melody.

Jesus, take me to your home above
And fold me in the bosom of Thy love . . .

The singing was on the other side of a brick wall. Excited, he wanted to watch the service without being seen. Whose church was it? He knew most of the churches in this area above ground, but the singing sounded too strange and detached for him to guess. He looked to the left, to the right, down to the black dirt, then upward and was startled to see a bright sliver of light slicing the darkness like the blade of a razor. He struck one of his two remaining matches and saw rusty pipes running along an old concrete ceiling. Photographically he located the exact position of the pipes in his mind. The match flame sank and he sprang upward; his hands clutched a pipe. He swung his legs and tossed his body onto the bed of pipes and they creaked, swaying up and down; he thought that the tier was about to crash, but nothing happened. He edged to the crevice and saw a segment of black men and women, dressed in white robes, singing, holding tattered songbooks in their black palms. His first impulse was to laugh, but he checked himself.

What was he doing? He was crushed with a sense of guilt. Would God strike him dead for that? The singing swept on and he shook his head, disagreeing in spite of himself. They oughtn't to do that, he thought. But he could think of no reason *why* they should not do it. Just singing with the air of the sewer blowing in on them . . . He felt that he was gazing upon something abysmally obscene, yet he could not bring himself to leave.

After a long time he grew numb and dropped to the dirt. Pain throbbed in his legs and a deeper pain, induced by the sight of those black people groveling and begging for something they could never get, churned in him. A vague conviction made him feel that those people should stand unrepentant and yield no quarter in singing and praying, yet *he* had run away from the police, had pleaded with them to believe in *his* innocence. He shook his head, bewildered.

How long had he been down here? He did not know. This was a new kind of living for him; the intensity of feelings he had experienced when looking at the church people sing made him certain that he had been down here a long time, but his mind told him that the time must have been short. In this darkness the only notion he had of time was when a match flared and measured time by its fleeting light. He groped back through the hole toward the sewer and the waves of song subsided and finally he could not hear them at all. He came to where the earth hole ended and he heard the noise of the current and time lived again for him, measuring the moments by the wash of water.

The rain must have slackened, for the flow of water had lessened and came only to his ankles. Ought he to go up into the streets and take his chances on hiding somewhere else? But they would surely catch him. The mere thought of dodging and running again from the police made him tense. No, he would stay and plot how to elude them. But what could he do down here? He walked forward into the sewer and came to another manhole cover; he stood beneath it, debating. Fine pencils of gold spilled suddenly from the little circles in the manhole cover and trembled on the surface of the current. Yes, street lamps . . . It must be night . . .

He went forward for about a quarter of an hour, wading aimlessly, poking the pole carefully before him. Then he stopped, his eyes fixed and intent. What's that? A strangely familiar image attracted and repelled him. Lit by the yellow stems from another manhole cover was a tiny nude body of a baby snagged by debris and half-submerged in water. Thinking that the baby was alive, he moved impulsively to save it, but his roused feelings told him that it was dead, cold, nothing, the same nothingness he had felt while watching the men and women singing in the church. Water blossomed about the tiny legs, the tiny arms, the tiny head, and rushed onward. The eyes were closed, as though in sleep; the fists were clenched, as though in protest; and the mouth gaped black in a soundless cry.

He straightened and drew in his breath, feeling that he had been staring for all eternity at the ripples of veined water skimming impersonally over the shriveled limbs. He felt as condemned as when the policemen had accused him. Involuntarily he lifted his hand to brush the vision away, but his arm fell listlessly to his side. Then he acted; he closed his eyes and reached forward slowly with the soggy shoe of his right foot and shoved the dead baby from where it had been lodged. He kept his eyes closed, seeing the little body twisting in the current as it floated from sight. He opened his eyes, shivered, placed his knuckles in the sockets, hearing the water speed in the somber shadows.

He tramped on, sensing at times a sudden quickening in the current as he passed some conduit whose waters were swelling the stream that slid by his feet. A few minutes later he was standing under another manhole cover, listening to the faint rumble of noises above ground. Streetcars and trucks, he mused. He looked down and saw a stagnant pool of gray-green sludge; at intervals a balloon pocket rose from the scum, glistening a bluish-purple, and burst. Then another. He turned, shook his head, and tramped back to the dirt cave by the church, his lips quivering.

Back in the cave, he sat and leaned his back against a dirt wall. His body was trembling slightly. Finally his senses quieted and he slept. When he awakened he felt stiff and cold. He had to leave this foul place, but leaving meant facing those policemen who had wrongly accused him. No, he could not go back aboveground. He remembered the beating they had given him and how he had signed his name to a confession, a confession which he had not even read. He had been too tired when they had shouted at him, demanding that he sign his name; he had signed it to end his pain.

He stood and groped about in the darkness. The church singing had stopped. How long had he slept? He did not know. But he felt refreshed and hungry. He doubled his fist nervously, realizing that he could not make a decision. As he walked about he stumbled over an old rusty iron pipe. He picked it up and felt a jagged edge. Yes, there was a brick wall and he could dig into it. What would he find? Smiling, he groped to the brick wall, sat, and began digging idly into damp cement. I can't make any noise, he cautioned himself. As time passed he grew thirsty, but there was no water. He had to kill time or go aboveground. The cement came out of the wall easily; he extracted four bricks and felt a soft draft blowing into his face. He stopped, afraid. What was beyond? He waited a long time and nothing happened; then he began digging again, soundlessly, slowly; he enlarged the hole and crawled through into a dark room and collided with another wall. He felt his way to the right; the wall ended and his fingers toyed in space, like the antennae of an insect.

He fumbled on and his feet struck something hollow, like wood. What's this? He felt with his fingers. Steps . . . He stooped and pulled off his shoes and mounted the stairs and saw a yellow chink of light shining and heard a low voice speaking. He placed his eye to a keyhole and saw the nude waxen figure of a man stretched out upon a white table. The voice, low-pitched and vibrant, mumbled indistinguishable words, neither rising nor falling. He craned his neck and squinted to see the man who was talking, but he could not locate him. Above the naked figure was suspended a huge glass container filled with a blood-red liquid from which a white rubber tube dangled. He crouched closer to the door and saw the tip end of a black object lined with pink satin. A coffin, he breathed. This is an undertaker's establishment. . . . A fine-spun lace of ice covered his body and he shuddered. A throaty chuckle sounded in the depths of the yellow room.

He turned to leave. Three steps down it occurred to him that a light switch should be nearby; he felt along the wall, found an electric button, pressed it, and a blinding glare smote his pupils so hard that he was sightless, defenseless. His pupils contracted and he wrinkled his nostrils at a peculiar odor. At once he knew that he had been dimly aware of this odor in the darkness, but the light had brought it sharply to his attention. Some kind of stuff they used to embalm, he thought. He went down the steps and saw piles of lumber, coffins, and a long workbench. In one corner was a tool chest. Yes, he could use tools, could tunnel through walls with them. He lifted the lid of the chest and saw nails, a hammer, a crowbar, a screwdriver, a light bulb, and a long length of electric wire. Good! He would lug these back to his cave.

He was about to hoist the chest to his shoulders when he discovered a door behind the furnace. Where did it lead? He tried to open it and found it securely bolted. Using the crowbar so as to make no sound, he pried the door open; it swung on creaking hinges, outward. Fresh air came to his face and he caught the faint roar of faraway sound. Easy now, he told himself. He widened the door and a lump of coal rattled toward him. A coalbin . . . Evidently the door led into another basement. The roaring noise was louder now, but he could not identify it. Where was he? He groped slowly over the coal pile, then ranged in darkness over a gritty floor. The roaring noise seemed to come from above him, then below. His fingers followed a wall until he touched a wooden ridge. A door, he breathed.

The noise died to a low pitch; he felt his skin prickle. It seemed that he was playing a game with an unseen person whose intelligence outstripped his. He put his ear to the flat surface of the door. Yes, voices . . . Was this a prize fight stadium? The sound of the voices came near and sharp, but he could not tell if they were joyous or despairing. He twisted the knob until he heard a soft click and felt the springy weight of the door swinging toward him. He was afraid to open it, yet captured by curiosity and wonder. He jerked the door wide and saw on the far side of the basement a furnace glowing red. Ten feet away was still another door, half ajar. He crossed and peered through the door into an empty, high-ceilinged corridor that terminated in a dark complex of shadow. The belling voices rolled about him and his eagerness mounted. He stepped into the corridor and the voices swelled louder. He crept on and came to a narrow stairway leading circularly upward; there was no question but that he was going to ascend those stairs.

Mounting the spiraled staircase, he heard the voices roll in a steady wave, then leap to crescendo, only to die away, but always remaining audible. Ahead of him glowed red letters: E—X—I—T. At the top of the steps he paused in front of a black curtain that fluttered uncertainly. He parted the folds and looked into a convex depth that gleamed with clusters of shimmering lights. Sprawling below him was a stretch of human faces, tilted upward, chanting, whistling, screaming, laughing. Dangling before the faces, high upon a screen of silver, were jerking shadows. A movie, he said with slow laughter breaking from his lips.

He stood in a box in the reserved section of a movie house and the impulse he had had to tell the people in the church to stop their singing seized him. These people were laughing at their lives, he thought with amazement. They were shouting and yelling at the animated shadows of themselves. His compassion fired his imagination and he stepped out of the box, walked out upon thin air, walked on down to the audience; and, hovering in the air just above them, he stretched out his hand to touch them . . . His tension snapped and he found himself back in the box, looking down into the sea of faces. No; it could not be done; he could not awaken them. He sighed. Yes, these people were children, sleeping in their living, awake in their dying.

He turned away, parted the black curtain, and looked out. He saw no one. He started down the white stone steps and when he reached the bottom he saw a man in trim blue uniform coming toward him. So used had he become to being underground that he thought that he could walk past the man, as though he were a ghost. But the man stopped. And he stopped.

"Looking for the men's room, sir?" the man asked, and, without waiting for an answer, he turned and pointed. "This way, sir. The first door to your right."

He watched the man turn and walk up the steps and go out of sight. Then he laughed. What a funny fellow! He went back to the basement and stood in the red darkness, watching the glowing embers in the furnace. He went to the sink and turned the faucet and the water flowed in a smooth silent stream that looked like a spout of blood. He brushed the mad image from his mind and began to wash his hands leisurely, looking about for the usual bar of soap. He found one and rubbed it in his palms until a rich lather bloomed in his cupped fingers, like a scarlet sponge. He scrubbed and rinsed his hands meticulously, then hunted for a towel; there was none. He shut off the water, pulled off his shirt, dried his hands on it; when he put it on again he was grateful for the cool dampness that came to his skin.

Yes, he was thirsty; he turned on the faucet again, bowled his fingers and when the water bubbled over the brim of his cupped palms, he drank in long, slow swallows. His bladder grew tight; he shut off the water, faced the wall, bent his head, and watched a red stream strike the floor. His nostrils wrinkled against acrid wisps of vapor; though he had tramped in the waters of the sewer, he stepped back from the wall so that his shoes, wet with sewer slime, would not touch his urine.

He heard footsteps and crawled quickly into the coalbin. Lumps rattled noisily. The footsteps came into the basement and stopped. Who was it? Had someone heard him and come down to investigate? He waited, crouching, sweating. For a long time there was silence, then he heard the clang of metal and a brighter glow lit the room. Somebody's tending the furnace, he thought. Footsteps came closer and he stiffened. Looming before him was a white face lined with coal dust, the face of an old man with watery blue eyes. Highlights spotted his gaunt cheekbones, and he held a huge shovel. There was a screechy scrape of metal against stone, and the old man lifted a shovelful of coal and went from sight.

The room dimmed momentarily, then a yellow glare came as coal flared at the furnace door. Six times the old man came to the bin and went to the furnace with shovels of coal, but not once did he lift his eyes. Finally he dropped the shovel, mopped his face with a dirty handkerchief, and sighed: "Wheeew!" He turned slowly and trudged out of the basement, his footsteps dying away.

He stood, and lumps of coal clattered down the pile. He stepped from the bin and was startled to see the shadowy outline of an electric bulb hanging above his head. Why had not the old man turned it on? Oh, yes . . . He understood. The old man had worked here for so long that he had no need for light; he had learned a way of seeing in his dark world, like those sightless worms that inch along underground by a sense of touch.

His eyes fell upon a lunch pail and he was afraid to hope that it was full. He picked it up; it was heavy. He opened it. *Sandwiches!* He looked guiltily around; he was alone. He searched farther and found a folder of matches and a half-empty tin of tobacco; he put them eagerly into his pocket and clicked off the light. With the lunch pail under his arm, he went through the door, groped over the pile of coal, and stood again in the lighted basement of the undertaking establishment. I've got to get those tools, he told himself. And turn off that light. He tiptoed back up the steps and switched off the light; the invisible voice still droned on behind the door. He crept down and, seeing with his fingers, opened the lunch pail and tore off a piece of paper bag and brought out the tin and spilled grains of tobacco into the makeshift concave. He rolled it and wet it with spittle, then inserted one end into his mouth and lit it: he sucked smoke that bit his lungs. The nicotine reached his brain, went out along his arms to his finger tips, down to his stomach, and over all the tired nerves of his body.

He carted the tools to the hole he had made in the wall. Would the noise of the falling chest betray him? But he would have to take a chance; he had to have those tools. He lifted the chest and shoved it; it hit the dirt on the other side of the wall with a loud clatter. He waited, listening; nothing happened. Head first, he slithered through and stood in the cave. He grinned, filled with a cunning idea. Yes, he would now go back into the basement of the undertaking establishment and crouch behind the coal pile and dig another hole. Sure! Fumbling, he opened the tool chest and extracted a crowbar, a screwdriver, and a hammer; he fastened them securely about his person.

With another lumpish cigarette in his flexed lips, he crawled back through the hole and over the coal pile and sat, facing the brick wall. He jabbed with the crowbar and the cement sheered away; quicker than he thought, a brick came loose. He worked an hour; the other bricks did not come easily. He sighed, weak from effort. I ought to rest a little, he thought. I'm hungry. He felt his way back to the cave and stumbled along the wall till he came to the tool chest. He sat upon it, opened the lunch pail, and took out two thick sandwiches. He smelled them. Pork chops . . . His mouth watered. He closed his eyes and devoured a sandwich, savoring the smooth rye bread and juicy meat. He ate rapidly, gulping down lumpy mouthfuls that made him long for water. He ate the other sandwich and found an apple and gobbled that up too, sucking the core till the last trace of flavor was drained from it. Then, like a dog, he ground the meat bones with his teeth, enjoying the salty, tangy marrow. He finished and stretched out full length on the ground and went to sleep . . .

. . . His body was washed by cold water that gradually turned warm and he was buoyed upon a stream and swept out to sea where waves rolled gently and suddenly he found himself walking upon the water how strange and delightful to walk upon the water and he came upon a nude woman holding a nude baby in her arms and the woman was sinking into the water holding the baby above her head and screaming *help* and he ran over the water to the woman and he reached her just before she went down and he took the baby from her hands and stood watching the breaking bubbles where the woman sank and he called *lady* and still no answer yes dive down there and rescue that woman but he could not take this baby with him and he stooped and laid the baby tenderly upon the surface of the water expecting it to sink but it floated and he leaped into the water and held his breath and strained his eyes to see through the gloomy volume of water but there was no woman and he opened his mouth and called *lady* and the water bubbled and his chest ached and his arms were tired but he could not see the woman and he called again *lady lady* and his feet touched sand at the bottom of the sea and his chest felt as though it would burst and he bent his knees and propelled himself upward and water rushed past him and his head bobbed out and he breathed deeply and looked around where was the baby the baby was gone and he rushed over the water looking for the baby calling *where is it* and the empty sky and sea threw back his voice *where is it* and he began to doubt that he could stand upon the water and then he was sinking and as he struggled the water rushed him downward spinning dizzily and he opened his mouth to call for help and water surged into his lungs and he choked . . .

He groaned and leaped erect in the dark, his eyes wide. The images of terror that thronged his brain would not let him sleep. He rose, made sure that the tools were hitched to his belt, and groped his way to the coal pile and found the rectangular gap from which he had taken the bricks. He took out the crowbar and hacked. Then dread paralyzed him. How long had he slept? Was it day or night now? He had to be careful. Someone might hear him if it were day. He hewed softly for hours at the cement, working silently. Faintly quivering in the air above him was the dim sound of yelling voices. Crazy people, he muttered. They're still there in that movie . . .

Having rested, he found the digging much easier. He soon had a dozen bricks out. His spirits rose. He took out another brick and his fingers fluttered in space. Good! What lay ahead of him? Another basement? He made the hole larger, climbed through, walked over an uneven floor and felt a metal surface. He lighted a match and saw that he was standing behind a furnace in a basement; before him, on the far side of the room, was a door. He crossed and opened it; it was full of odds and ends. Daylight spilled from a window above his head.

Then he was aware of a soft, continuous tapping. What was it? A clock? No, it was louder than a clock and more irregular. He placed an old empty box beneath the window, stood upon it, and looked into an areaway. He eased the window up and crawled through; the sound of the tapping came clearly now. He glanced about; he was alone. Then he looked upward at a series of window ledges. The tapping identified itself. That's a typewriter, he said to himself. It seemed to be coming from just above. He grasped the ridges of a rain pipe and lifted himself upward; through a half-inch opening of window he saw a doorknob about three feet away. No, it was not a doorknob; it was a small circular disk made of stainless steel with many fine markings upon it. He held his breath; an eerie white hand, seemingly detached from its arm, touched the metal knob and whirled it, first to the left, then to the right. It's a safe! . . . Suddenly he could see the dial no more; a huge metal door swung slowly toward him and he was looking into a safe filled with green wads of paper money, rows of coins wrapped in brown paper, and glass jars and boxes of various sizes. His heart quickened. Good Lord! The white hand went in and out of the safe, taking wads of bills and cylinders of coins. The hand vanished and he heard the muffled click of the big door as it closed. Only the steel dial was visible now. The typewriter still tapped in his ears, but he could not see it. He blinked, wondering if what he had seen was real. There was more money in that safe than he had seen in all his life.

As he clung to the rain pipe, a daring idea came to him and he pulled the screwdriver from his belt. If the white hand twirled that dial again, he would be able to see how far to left and right it spun and he would have the combination! His blood tingled. I can scratch the numbers right here, he thought. Holding the pipe with one hand, he made the sharp edge of the screwdriver bite into the brick wall. Yes, he could do it. Now, he was set. Now, he had a reason for staying here in the underground. He waited for a long time, but the white hand did not return. Goddamn! Had he been more alert, he could have counted the twirls and he would have had the combination. He got down and stood in the areaway, sunk in reflection.

How could he get into that room? He climbed back into the basement and saw wooden steps leading upward. Was that the room where the safe stood? Fearing that the dial was now being twirled, he clambered through the window, hoisted himself up the rain pipe, and peered; he saw only the naked gleam of the steel dial. He got down and doubled his fists. Well, he would explore the basement. He returned to the basement room and mounted the steps to the door and squinted through the keyhole; all was dark, but the tapping was still somewhere near, still faint and directionless. He pushed the door in; along one wall of a room was a table piled with radios and electrical equipment. A radio shop, he muttered.

Well, he could rig up a radio in his cave. He found a sack, slid the radio into it, and slung it across his back. Closing the door, he went down the steps and stood again in the basement, disappointed. He had not solved the problem of the steel dial and he was irked. He set the radio on the floor and again hoisted himself through the window and up the rain pipe and squinted; the metal door was swinging shut. Goddamn! He's worked the combination again. If I had been patient, I'd have had it! How could he get into that room? He *had* to get into it. He could jimmy the window, but it would be much better if he could get in without any traces. To the right of him, he calculated, should be the basement of the building that held the safe; therefore, if he dug a hole right *here*, he ought to reach his goal.

He began a quiet scraping; it was hard work, for the bricks were not damp. He eventually got one out and lowered it softly to the floor. He had to be careful; perhaps people were beyond this wall. He extracted a second layer of brick and found still another. He gritted his teeth, ready to quit. I'll dig one more, he resolved. When the next brick came out he felt air blowing into his face. He waited to be challenged, but nothing happened.

He enlarged the hole and pulled himself through and stood in quiet darkness. He scratched a match to flame and saw steps; he mounted and peered through a keyhole: Darkness . . . He strained to hear the typewriter, but there was only silence. Maybe the office had closed? He twisted the knob and swung the door in; a frigid blast made him shiver. In the shadows before him were halves and quarters of hogs and lambs and steers hanging from metal hooks on the low ceiling, red meat encased in folds of cold white fat. Fronting him was frost-coated glass from behind which came indistinguishable sounds. The odor of fresh raw meat sickened him and he backed away. A meat market, he whispered.

He ducked his head, suddenly blinded by light. He narrowed his eyes; the red-white rows of meat were drenched in yellow glare. A man wearing a crimson-spotted jacket came in and took down a bloody meat cleaver. He eased the door to, holding it ajar just enough to watch the man, hoping that the darkness in which he stood would keep him from being seen. The man took down a hunk of steer and placed it upon a bloody wooden block and bent forward and whacked with the cleaver. The man's face was hard, square, grim; a jet of mustache smudged his upper lip and a glistening cowlick of hair fell over his left eye. Each time he lifted the cleaver and brought it down upon the meat, he let out a short, deep-chested grunt. After he had cut the meat, he wiped blood off the wooden block with a sticky wad of gunny sack and hung the cleaver upon a hook. His face was proud as he placed the chunk of meat in the crook of his elbow and left.

The door slammed and the light went off; once more he stood in shadow. His tension ebbed. From behind the frosted glass he heard the man's voice: "Forty-eight cents a pound, ma'am." He shuddered, feeling that there was something he had to do. But what? He stared fixedly at the cleaver, then he sneezed and was terrified for fear that the man had heard him. But the door did not open. He took down the cleaver and examined the sharp edge smeared with cold blood. Behind the ice-coated glass a cash register rang with a vibrating, musical tinkle.

Absent-mindedly holding the meat cleaver, he rubbed the glass with his thumb and cleared a spot that enabled him to see into the front of the store.

The shop was empty, save for the man who was now putting on his hat and coat. Beyond the front window a wan sun shone in the streets; people passed and now and then a fragment of laughter or the whir of a speeding auto came to him. He peered closer and saw on the right counter of the shop a mosquito netting covering pears, grapes, lemons, oranges, bananas, peaches, and plums. His stomach contracted.

The man clicked out the light and he gritted his teeth, muttering, Don't lock the icebox door . . . The man went through the door of the shop and locked it from the outside. Thank God! Now, he would eat some more! He waited, trembling. The sun died and its rays lingered on in the sky, turning the streets to dusk. He opened the door and stepped inside the shop. In reverse letters across the front window was: NICK'S FRUITS AND MEATS. He laughed, picked up a soft ripe yellow pear and bit into it; juice squirted; his mouth ached as his saliva glands reacted to the acid of the fruit. He ate three pears, gobbled six bananas, and made away with several oranges, taking a bite out of their tops and holding them to his lips and squeezing them as he hungrily sucked the juice.

He found a faucet, turned it on, laid the cleaver aside, pursed his lips under the stream until his stomach felt about to burst. He straightened and belched, feeling satisfied for the first time since he had been underground. He sat upon the floor, rolled and lit a cigarette, his bloodshot eyes squinting against the film of drifting smoke. He watched a patch of sky turn red, then purple; night fell and he lit another cigarette, brooding. Some part of him was trying to remember the world he had left, and another part of him did not want to remember it. Sprawling before him in his mind was his wife, Mrs. Wooten for whom he worked, the three policemen who had picked him up . . . He possessed them now more completely than he had ever possessed them when he had lived above ground. How this had come about he could not say, but he had no desire to go back to them. He laughed, crushed the cigarette, and stood up.

He went to the front door and gazed out. Emotionally he hovered between the world aboveground and the world underground. He longed to go out, but sober judgment urged him to remain here. Then impulsively he pried the lock loose with one swift twist of the crowbar; the door swung outward. Through the twilight he saw a white man and a white woman coming toward him. He held himself tense, waiting for them to pass; but they came directly to the door and confronted him.

"I want to buy a pound of grapes," the woman said.

Terrified, he stepped back into the store. The white man stood to one side and the woman entered.

"Give me a pound of dark ones," the woman said.

The white man came slowly forward, blinking his eyes.

"Where's Nick?" the man asked.

"Were you just closing?" the woman asked.

"Yes, ma'am," he mumbled. For a second he did not breathe, then he mumbled again: "Yes, ma'am."

"I'm sorry," the woman said.

The street lamps came on, lighting the store somewhat. Ought he run? But that would raise an alarm. He moved slowly, dreamily, to a counter and lifted up a bunch of grapes and showed them to the woman.

"Fine," the woman said. "But isn't that more than a pound?"

He did not answer. The man was staring at him intently.

"Put them in a bag for me," the woman said, fumbling with her purse.

"Yes, ma'am."

He saw a pile of paper bags under a narrow ledge; he opened one and put the grapes in.

"Thanks," the woman said, taking the bag and placing a dime in his dark palm.

"Where's Nick?" the man asked again. "At supper?"

"Sir? Yes, sir," he breathed.

They left the store and he stood trembling in the doorway. When they were out of sight, he burst out laughing and crying. A trolley car rolled noisily past and he controlled himself quickly. He flung the dime to the pavement with a gesture of contempt and stepped into the warm night air. A few shy stars trembled above him. The look of things was beautiful, yet he felt a lurking threat. He went to an unattended newsstand and looked at a stack of papers. He saw a headline: HUNT NEGRO FOR MURDER.

He felt that someone had slipped up on him from behind and was stripping off his clothes; he looked about wildly, went quickly back into the store, picked up the meat cleaver where he had left it near the sink, then made his way through the icebox to the basement. He stood for a long time, breathing heavily. They know I didn't do anything, he muttered. But how could he prove it? He had signed a confession. Though innocent, he felt guilty, condemned. He struck a match and held it near the steel blade, fascinated and repelled by the dried blotches of blood. Then his fingers gripped the handle of the cleaver with all the strength of his body, he wanted to fling the cleaver from him, but he could not. The match flame wavered and fled; he struggled through the hole and put the cleaver in the sack with the radio. He was determined to keep it, for what purpose he did not know.

He was about to leave when he remembered the safe. Where was it? He wanted to give up, but felt that he ought to make one more try. Opposite the last hole he had dug, he tunneled again, plying the crowbar. Once he was so exhausted that he lay on the concrete floor and panted. Finally he made another hole. He wriggled through and his nostrils filled with the fresh smell of coal. He struck a match; yes, the usual steps led upward. He tiptoed to a door and eased it open. A fair-haired white girl stood in front of a steel cabinet, her blue eyes wide upon him. She turned chalky and gave a high-pitched scream. He bounded down the steps and raced to his hole and clambered through, replacing the bricks with nervous haste. He paused, hearing loud voices.

"What's the matter, Alice?"

"A man . . ."

"What man? Where?"

"A man was at that door . . ."

"Oh, nonsense!"

"He was looking at me through the door!"

"Aw, you're dreaming."

"I *did* see a man!"

The girl was crying now.

"There's nobody here."

Another man's voice sounded.

"What is it, Bob?"

"Alice says she saw a man in here, in that door!"

"Let's take a look."

He waited, poised for flight. Footsteps descended the stairs.

"There's nobody down here."

"The window's locked."

"And there's no door."

"You ought to fire that dame."

"Oh, I don't know. Women are that way."

"She's too hysterical."

The men laughed. Footsteps sounded again on the stairs. A door slammed. He sighed, relieved that he had escaped. But he had not done what he had set out to do; his glimpse of the room had been too brief to determine if the safe was there. He had to know. Boldly he groped through the hole once more; he reached the steps and pulled off his shoes and tip-toed up and peered through the keyhole. His head accidentally touched the door and it swung silently in a fraction of an inch; he saw the girl bent over the cabinet, her back to him. Beyond her was the safe. He crept back down the steps, thinking exultingly: I found it!

Now he had to get the combination. Even if the window in the areaway was locked and bolted, he could gain entrance when the office closed. He scoured through the holes he had dug and stood again in the basement where he had left the radio and the cleaver. Again he crawled out of the window and lifted himself up the rain pipe and peered. The steel dial showed lonely and bright, reflecting the yellow glow of an unseen light. Resigned to a long wait, he sat and leaned against the wall. From far off came the faint sounds of life aboveground; once he looked with a baffled expression at the dark sky. Frequently he rose and climbed the pipe to see the white hand spin the dial, but nothing happened. He bit his lip with impatience. It was not the money that was luring him, but the mere fact that he could get it with impunity. Was the hand now twirling the dial? He rose and looked, but the white hand was not in sight.

Perhaps it would be better to watch continuously? Yes; he clung to the pipe and watched the dial until his eyes thickened with tears. Exhausted, he stood again in the areaway. He heard a door being shut and he clawed up the pipe and looked. He jerked tense as a vague figure passed in front of him. He stared unblinkingly, hugging the pipe with one hand and holding the screwdriver with the other, ready to etch the combination upon the wall. His ears caught: *Dong . . . Dong . . . Dong . . . Dong . . . Dong . . . Dong . . . Dong* . . . Seven o'clock, he whispered. Maybe they were closing now? What kind of a store would be open as late as this? he wondered. Did anyone live in the rear? Was there a night watchman? Perhaps the safe was *already* locked for the night! Goddamn! While he had been eating in that shop, they had locked up everything . . . Then, just as he was about to give up, the white hand touched the dial and turned it once to the right and stopped at six. With quivering fingers, he etched 1—R—6 upon the brick wall with the tip of the screwdriver. The hand twirled the dial twice to the left and stopped at two, and he engraved 2—L—2 upon the wall. The dial was spun four times to the right and stopped at six again; he wrote 4—R—6. The dial rotated three times to the left and was centered straight up and down; he wrote 3—L—0. The door swung open and again he saw the piles of green money and the rows of wrapped coins. I got it, he said grimly.

Then he was stone still, astonished. There were two hands now. A right hand lifted a wad of green bills and deftly slipped it up the sleeve of a left arm. The hands trembled; again the right hand slipped a packet of bills up the left sleeve. He's stealing, he said to himself. He grew indignant, as if the money belonged to him. Though *he* had planned to steal the money, he despised and pitied the man. He felt that his stealing the money and the man's stealing were two entirely different things. He wanted to steal the money merely for the sensation involved in getting it, and he had no intention whatever of spending a penny of it; but he knew that the man who was now stealing it was going to spend it, perhaps for pleasure. The huge steel door closed with a soft click.

Though angry, he was somewhat satisfied. The office would close soon. I'll clean the place out, he mused. He imagined the entire office staff cringing with fear; the police would question everyone for a crime they had not committed, just as they had questioned him. And they would have no idea of how the money had been stolen until they discovered the holes he had tunneled in the walls of the basements. He lowered himself and laughed mischievously, with the abandoned glee of an adolescent.

He flattened himself against the wall as the window above him closed with rasping sound. He looked; somebody was bolting the window securely with a metal screen. That won't help you, he snickered to himself. He clung to the rain pipe until the yellow light in the office went out. He went back into the basement, picked up the sack containing the radio and cleaver, and crawled through the two holes he had dug and groped his way into the basement of the building that held the safe. He moved in slow motion, breathing softly. Be careful now, he told himself. There might be a night watchman . . . In his memory was the combination written in bold white characters as upon a blackboard. Eel-like he squeezed through the last hole and crept up the steps and put his hand on the knob and pushed the door in about three inches. Then his courage ebbed; his imagination wove dangers for him.

Perhaps the night watchman was waiting in there, ready to shoot. He dangled his cap on a forefinger and poked it past the jamb of the door. If anyone fired, they would hit his cap; but nothing happened. He widened the door, holding the crowbar high above his head, ready to beat off an assailant. He stood like that for five minutes; the rumble of a streetcar brought him to himself. He entered the room. Moonlight floated in from a side window. He confronted the safe, then checked himself. Better take a look around first . . . He stepped about and found a closed door. Was the night watchman in there? He opened it and saw a washbowl, a faucet, and a commode. To the left was still another door that opened into a huge dark room that seemed empty; on the far side of that room he made out the shadow of still another door. Nobody's here, he told himself.

He turned back to the safe and fingered the dial; it spun with ease. He laughed and twirled it just for fun. Get to work, he told himself. He turned the dial to the figures he saw on the blackboard of his memory; it was so easy that he felt that the safe had not been locked at all. The heavy door eased loose and he caught hold of the handle and pulled hard, but the door swung open with a slow momentum of its own. Breathless, he gaped at wads of green bills, rows of wrapped coins, curious glass jars full of white pellets, and many oblong green metal boxes. He glanced guiltily over his shoulder; it seemed impossible that someone should not call to him to stop.

They'll be surprised in the morning, he thought. He opened the top of the sack and lifted a wad of compactly tied bills; the money was crisp and new. He admired the smooth, cleancut edges. The fellows in Washington sure know how to make this stuff, he mused. He rubbed the money with his fingers, as though expecting it to reveal hidden qualities. He lifted the wad to his nose and smelled the fresh odor of ink. Just like any other paper, he mumbled. He dropped the wad into the sack and picked up another. Holding the bag, he thought and laughed.

There was in him no sense of possessiveness; he was intrigued with the form and color of the money, with the manifold reactions which he knew that men above-ground held toward it. The sack was one-third full when it occurred to him to examine the denominations of the bills; without realizing it, he had put many wads of one-dollar bills into the sack. Aw, nuts, he said in disgust. Take the big ones . . . He dumped the one-dollar bills onto the floor and swept all the hundred-dollar bills he could find into the sack, then he raked in rolls of coins with crooked fingers.

He walked to a desk upon which sat a typewriter, the same machine which the blond girl had used. He was fascinated by it; never in his life had he used one of them. It was a queer instrument of business, something beyond the rim of his life. Whenever he had been in an office where a girl was typing, he had almost always spoken in whispers. Remembering vaguely what he had seen others do, he inserted a sheet of paper into the machine; it went in lopsided and he did not know how to straighten it. Spelling in a soft diffident voice, he pecked out his name on the keys: *freddaniels*. He looked at it and laughed. He would learn to type correctly one of these days.

Yes, he would take the typewriter too. He lifted the machine and placed it atop the bulk of money in the sack. He did not feel that he was stealing, for the cleaver, the radio, the money, and the typewriter were all on the same level of value, all meant the same thing to him. They were the serious toys of the men who lived in the dead world of sunshine and rain he had left, the world that had condemned him, branded him guilty.

But what kind of a place is this? he wondered. What was in that dark room to his rear? He felt for his matches and found that he had only one left. He leaned the sack against the safe and groped forward into the room, encountering smooth, metallic objects that felt like machines. Baffled, he touched a wall and tried vainly to locate an electric switch. Well, he *had* to strike his last match. He knelt and struck it, cupping the flame near the floor with his palms. The place seemed to be a factory, with benches and tables. There were bulbs with green shades spaced about the tables; he turned on a light and twisted it low so that the glare was limited. He saw a half-filled packet of cigarettes and appropriated it. There were stools at the benches and he concluded that men worked here at some trade. He wandered and found a few half-used folders of matches. If only he could find more cigarettes! But there were none.

But what kind of a place was this? On a bench he saw a pad of paper captioned: PEER'S—MANUFACTURING JEWELERS. His lips formed an "O," then he snapped off the light and ran back to the safe and lifted one of the glass jars and stared at the tiny white pellets. Gingerly he picked up one and found that it was wrapped in tissue paper. He peeled the paper and saw a glittering stone that looked like glass, glinting white and blue sparks. Diamonds, he breathed.

Roughly he tore the paper from the pellets and soon his palm quivered with precious fire. Trembling, he took all four glass jars from the safe and put them into the sack. He grabbed one of the metal boxes, shook it, and heard a tinny rattle. He pried off the lid with the screwdriver. Rings! Hundreds of them . . . Were they worth anything? He scooped up a handful and jets of fire shot fitfully from the stones. These are diamonds too, he said. He pried open another box. Watches! A chorus of soft, metallic ticking filled his ears. For a moment he could not move, then he dumped all the boxes into the sack.

He shut the safe door, then stood looking around, anxious not to overlook anything. Oh! He had seen a door in the room where the machines were. What was in there? More valuables? He re-entered the room, crossed the floor, and stood undecided before the door. He finally caught hold of the knob and pushed the door in; the room beyond was dark. He advanced cautiously inside and ran his fingers along the wall for the usual switch, then he was stark still. *Something had moved in the room*! What was it? Ought he to creep out, taking the rings and diamonds and money? Why risk what he already had? He waited and the ensuing silence gave him confidence to explore further. Dare he strike a match? Would not a match flame make him a good target? He tensed again as he heard a faint sigh; he was now convinced that there was something alive near him, something that lived and breathed. On tiptoe he felt slowly along the wall, hoping that he would not collide with anything. Luck was with him; he found the light switch.

No; don't turn the light on. . . Then suddenly he realized that he did not know in what direction the door was. Goddamn! He had to turn the light on or strike a match. He fingered the switch for a long time, then thought of an idea. He knelt upon the floor, reached his arm up to the switch and flicked the button, hoping that if anyone shot, the bullet would go above his head. The moment the light came on he narrowed his eyes to see quickly. He sucked in his breath and his body gave a violent twitch and was still. In front of him, so close that it made him want to bound up and scream, was a human face.

He was afraid to move lest he touch the man. If the man had opened his eyes at that moment, there was no telling what he might have done. The man—long and rawboned—was stretched out on his back upon a little cot, sleeping in his clothes, his head cushioned by a dirty pillow; his face, clouded by a dark stubble of beard, looked straight up to the ceiling. The man sighed, and he grew tense to defend himself; the man mumbled and turned his face away from the light. I've got to turn off that light, he thought. Just as he was about to rise, he saw a gun and cartridge belt on the floor at the man's side. Yes, he would take the gun and cartridge belt, not to use them, but just to keep them, as one takes a memento from a country fair. He picked them up and was about to click off the light when his eyes fell upon a photograph perched upon a chair near the man's head; it was the picture of a woman, smiling, shown against a background of open fields; at the woman's side were two young children, a boy and a girl. He smiled indulgently; he could send a bullet into that man's brain and time would be over for him . . .

He clicked off the light and crept silently back into the room where the safe stood; he fastened the cartridge belt about him and adjusted the holster at his right hip. He strutted about the room on tiptoe, lolling his head nonchalantly, then paused, abruptly pulled the gun, and pointed it with grim face toward an imaginary foe. "Boom!" he whispered fiercely. Then he bent forward with silent laughter. That's just like they do it in the movies, he said.

He contemplated his loot for a long time, then got a towel from the washroom and tied the sack securely. When he looked up he was momentarily frightened by his shadow looming on the wall before him. He lifted the sack, dragged it down the basement steps, lugged it across the basement, gasping for breath. After he had struggled through the hole, he clumsily replaced the bricks, then tussled with the sack until he got it to the cave. He stood in the dark, wet with sweat, brooding about the diamonds, the rings, the watches, the money; he remembered the singing in the church, the people yelling in the movie, the dead baby, the nude man stretched out upon the white table . . . He saw these items hovering before his eyes and felt that some dim meaning linked them together, that some magical relationship made them kin. He stared with vacant eyes, convinced that all of these images, with their tongueless reality, were striving to tell him something . . .

Later, seeing with his fingers, he untied the sack and set each item neatly upon the dirt floor. Exploring, he took the bulb, the socket, and the wire out of the tool chest; he was elated to find a double socket at one end of the wire. He crammed the stuff into his pockets and hoisted himself upon the rusty pipes and squinted into the church; it was dim and empty. Somewhere in this wall were live electric wires; but where? He lowered himself, groped and tapped the wall with the butt of the screwdriver, listening vainly for hollow sounds. I'll just take a chance and dig, he said.

For an hour he tried to dislodge a brick, and when he struck a match, he found that he had dug a depth of only an inch! No use in digging here, he sighed. By the flickering light of a match, he looked upward, then lowered his eyes, only to glance up again, startled. Directly above his head, beyond the pipes, was a wealth of electric wiring. I'll be damned, he snickered.

He got an old dull knife from the chest and, seeing again with his fingers, separated the two strands of wire and cut away the insulation. Twice he received a slight shock. He scraped the wiring clean and managed to join the two twin ends, then screwed in the bulb. The sudden illumination blinded him and he shut his lids to kill the pain in his eyeballs. I've got that much done, he thought jubilantly.

He placed the bulb on the dirt floor and the light cast a blatant glare on the bleak clay walls. Next he plugged one end of the wire that dangled from the radio into the light socket and bent down and switched on the button; almost at once there was the harsh sound of static, but no words or music. Why won't it work? he wondered. Had he damaged the mechanism in any way? Maybe it needed grounding? Yes . . . He rummaged in the tool chest and found another length of wire, fastened it to the ground of the radio, and then tied the opposite end to a pipe. Rising and growing distinct, a slow strain of music entranced him with its measured sound. He sat upon the chest, deliriously happy.

Later he searched again in the chest and found a half-gallon can of glue; he opened it and smelled a sharp odor. Then he recalled that he had not even looked at the money. He took a wad of green bills and weighed it in his palm, then broke the seal and held one of the bills up to the light and studied it closely. *The United States of America will pay to the bearer on demand one hundred dollars*, he read in slow speech; then: *This note is legal tender for all debts, public and private* . . . He broke into a musing laugh, feeling that he was reading of the doings of people who lived on some far-off planet. He turned the bill over and saw on the other side of it a delicately beautiful building gleaming with paint and set amidst green grass. He had no desire whatever to count the money; it was what it stood for—the various currents of life swirling aboveground—that captivated him. Next he opened the rolls of coins and let them slide from their paper wrappings to the ground; the bright, new gleaming pennies and nickels and dimes piled high at his feet, a glowing mound of shimmering copper and silver. He sifted them through his fingers, listening to their tinkle as they struck the conical heap.

Oh, yes! He had forgotten. He would now write his name on the typewriter. He inserted a piece of paper and poised his fingers to write. But what was his name? He stared, trying to remember. He stood and glared about the dirt cave, his name on the tip of his lips. But it would not come to him. Why was he here? Yes, he had been running away from the police. But why? His mind was blank. He bit his lips and sat again, feeling a vague terror. But why worry? He laughed, then pecked slowly: *itwasalonghotday*. He was determined to type the sentence without making any mistakes. How did one make capital letters? He experimented and luckily discovered how to lock the machine for capital letters and then shift it back to lower case. Next he discovered how to make spaces, then he wrote neatly and correctly: *It was a long hot day*. Just why he selected that sentence he did not know; it was merely the ritual of performing the thing that appealed to him. He took the sheet out of the machine and looked around with stiff neck and hard eyes and spoke to an imaginary person:

"Yes, I'll have the contracts ready tomorrow."

He laughed. That's just the way they talk, he said. He grew weary of the game and pushed the machine aside. His eyes fell upon the can of glue, and a mischievous idea bloomed in him, filling him with nervous eagerness. He leaped up and opened the can of glue, then broke the seals on all the wads of money. I'm going to have some wallpaper, he said with a luxurious, physical laugh that made him bend at the knees. He took the towel with which he had tied the sack and balled it into a swab and dipped it into the can of glue and dabbed glue onto the wall; then he pasted one green bill by the side of another. He stepped back and cocked his head. Jesus! That's funny . . . He slapped his thighs and guffawed. He had triumphed over the world aboveground! He was free! If only people could see this! He wanted to run from this cave and yell his discovery to the world.

He swabbed all the dirt walls of the cave and pasted them with green bills; when he had finished the walls blazed with a yellow-green fire. Yes, this room would be his hide-out; between him and the world that had branded him guilty would stand this mocking symbol. He had not stolen the money; he had simply picked it up, just as a man would pick up firewood in a forest. And that was how the world aboveground now seemed to him, a wild forest filled with death.

The walls of money finally palled on him and he looked about for new interests to feed his emotions. The cleaver! He drove a nail into the wall and hung the bloody cleaver upon it. Still another idea welled up. He pried open the metal boxes and lined them side by side on the dirt floor. He grinned at the gold and fire. From one box he lifted up a fistful of ticking gold watches and dangled them by their gleaming chains. He stared with an idle smile, then began to wind them up; he did not attempt to set them at any given hour, for there was no time for him now. He took a fistful of nails and drove them into the papered walls and hung the watches upon them, letting them swing down by their glittering chains, trembling and ticking busily against the backdrop of green with the lemon sheen of the electric light shining upon the metal watch casings, converting the golden disks into blobs of liquid yellow. Hardly had he hung up the last watch than the idea extended itself; he took more nails from the chest and drove them into the green paper and took the boxes of rings and went from nail to nail and hung up the golden bands. The blue and white sparks from the stones filled the cave with brittle laughter, as though enjoying his hilarious secret. People certainly can do some funny things, he said to himself.

He sat upon the tool chest, alternately laughing and shaking his head soberly. Hours later he became conscious of the gun sagging at his hip and he pulled it from the holster. He had seen men fire guns in movies, but somehow his life had never led him into contact with firearms. A desire to feel the sensation others felt in firing came over him. But someone might hear. . . Well, what if they did? They would not know where the shot had come from. Not in their wildest notions would they think that it had come from under the streets! He tightened his fingers on the trigger; there was a deafening report and it seemed that the entire underground had caved in upon his eardrums; and in the same instant there flashed an orange-blue spurt of flame that died quickly but lingered on as a vivid after-image. He smelled the acrid stench of burnt powder filling his lungs and he dropped the gun abruptly.

The intensity of his feelings died and he hung the gun and cartridge belt upon the wall. Next he lifted the jars of diamonds and turned them bottom upward, dumping the white pellets upon the ground. One by one he picked them up and peeled the tissue paper from them and piled them in a neat heap. He wiped his sweaty hands on his trousers, lit a cigarette, and commenced playing another game. He imagined that he was a rich man who lived aboveground in the obscene sunshine and he was strolling through a park of a summer morning, smiling, nodding to his neighbors, sucking an after-breakfast cigar. Many times he crossed the floor of the cave, avoiding the diamonds with his feet, yet subtly gauging his footsteps so that his shoes, wet with sewer slime, would strike the diamonds at some undetermined moment. After twenty minutes of sauntering, his right foot smashed into the heap and diamonds lay scattered in all directions, glinting with a million tiny chuckles of icy laughter. Oh, shucks, he mumbled in mock regret, intrigued by the damage he had wrought. He continued walking, ignoring the brittle fire. He felt that he had a glorious victory locked in his heart.

He stooped and flung the diamonds more evenly over the floor and they showered rich sparks, collaborating with him. He went over the floor and trampled the stones just deeply enough for them to be faintly visible, as though they were set deliberately in the prongs of a thousand rings. A ghostly light bathed the cave. He sat on the chest and frowned. Maybe *any*thing's right, he mumbled. Yes, if the world as men had made it was right, then anything else was right, any act a man took to satisfy himself, murder, theft, torture.

He straightened with a start. What was happening to him? He was drawn to these crazy thoughts, yet they made him feel vaguely guilty. He would stretch out upon the ground, then get up; he would want to crawl again through the holes he had dug, but would restrain himself; he would think of going again up into the streets, but fear would hold him still. He stood in the middle of the cave, surrounded by green walls and a laughing floor, trembling. He was going to do something, but what? Yes, he was afraid of himself, afraid of doing some nameless thing.

To control himself, he turned on the radio. A melancholy piece of music rose. Brooding over the diamonds on the floor was like looking up into a sky full of restless stars; then the illusion turned into its opposite: he was high up in the air looking down at the twinkling lights of a sprawling city. The music ended and a man recited news events. In the same attitude in which he had contemplated the city, so now, as he heard the cultivated tone, he looked down upon land and sea as men fought, as cities were razed, as planes scattered death upon open towns, as long lines of trenches wavered and broke. He heard the names of generals and the names of mountains and the names of countries and the names and numbers of divisions that were in action on different battle fronts. He saw black smoke billowing from the stacks of warships as they neared each other over wastes of water and he heard their huge guns thunder as red-hot shells screamed across the surface of night seas. He saw hundreds of planes wheeling and droning in the sky and heard the clatter of machine guns as they fought each other and he saw planes falling in plumes of smoke and blaze of fire. He saw steel tanks rumbling across fields of ripe wheat to meet other tanks and there was a loud clang of steel as numberless tanks collided. He saw troops with fixed bayonets charging in waves against other troops who held fixed bayonets and men groaned as steel ripped into their bodies and they went down to die . . . The voice of the radio faded and he was staring at the diamonds on the floor at his feet.

He shut off the radio, fighting an irrational compulsion to act. He walked aimlessly about the cave, touching the walls with his finger tips. Suddenly he stood still. *What was the matter with him?* Yes, he knew . . . It was these walls; these crazy walls were filling him with a wild urge to climb out into the dark sunshine aboveground. Quickly he doused the light to banish the shouting walls, then sat again upon the tool chest. Yes, he was trapped. His muscles were flexed taut and sweat ran down his face. He knew now that he could not stay here and he could not go out. He lit a cigarette with shaking fingers; the match flame revealed the green-papered walls with militant distinctness; the purple on the gun barrel glinted like a threat; the meat cleaver brooded with its eloquent splotches of blood; the mound of silver and copper smoldered angrily; the diamonds winked at him from the floor; and the gold watches ticked and trembled, crowning time the king of consciousness, defining the limits of living . . . The match blaze died and he bolted from where he stood and collided brutally with the nails upon the walls. The spell was broken. He shuddered, feeling that, in spite of his fear, sooner or later he would go up into that dead sunshine and somehow say something to somebody about all this.

He sat again upon the tool chest. Fatigue weighed upon his forehead and eyes. Minutes passed and he relaxed. He dozed, but his imagination was alert. He saw himself rising, wading again in the sweeping water of the sewer; he came to a manhole and climbed out and was amazed to discover that he had hoisted himself into a room filled with armed policemen who were watching him intently. He jumped awake in the dark; he had not moved. He sighed, closed his eyes, and slept again; this time his imagination designed a scheme of protection for him. His dreaming made him feel that he was standing in a room watching over his own nude body lying stiff and cold upon a white table. At the far end of the room he saw a crowd of people huddled in a corner, afraid of his body. Though lying dead upon the table, he was standing in some mysterious way at his side, warding off the people, guarding his body, and laughing to himself as he observed the situation. They're scared of me, he thought.

He awakened with a start, leaped to his feet, and stood in the center of the black cave. It was a full minute before he moved again. He hovered between sleeping and waking, unprotected, a prey of wild fears. He could neither see nor hear. One part of him was asleep; his blood coursed slowly and his flesh was numb. On the other hand he was roused to a strange, high pitch of tension. He lifted his fingers to his face, as though about to weep. Gradually his hands lowered and he struck a match, looking about, expecting to see a door through which he could walk to safety; but there was no door, only the green walls and the moving floor. The match flame died and it was dark again.

Five minutes later he was still standing when the thought came to him that he had been asleep. Yes . . . But he was not yet fully awake; he was still queerly blind and dead. How long had he slept? Where was he? Then suddenly he recalled the green-papered walls of the cave and in the same instant he heard loud singing coming from the church beyond the wall. Yes, they woke me up, he muttered. He hoisted himself and lay atop the bed of pipes and brought his face to the narrow slit. Men and women stood here and there between pews. A song ended and a young black girl tossed back her head and closed her eyes and broke plaintively into another hymn:

Glad, glad, glad, oh, so glad
I got Jesus in my soul . . .

Those few words were all she sang, but what her words did not say, her emotions said as she repeated the lines, varying the mood and tempo, making her tone express meanings which her conscious mind did not know. Another woman melted her voice with the girl's, and then an old man's voice merged with that of the two women. Soon the entire congregation was singing:

Glad, glad, glad, oh, so glad
I got Jesus in my soul . . .

They're wrong, he whispered in the lyric darkness. He felt that their search for a happiness they could never find made them feel that they had committed some dreadful offense which they could not remember or understand. He was now in possession of the feeling that had gripped him when he had first come into the underground. It came to him in a series of questions: Why was this sense of guilt so seemingly innate, so easy to come by, to think, to feel, so verily physical? It seemed that when one felt this guilt one was retracing in one's feelings a faint pattern designed long before; it seemed that one was always trying to remember a gigantic shock that had left a haunting impression upon one's body which one could not forget or shake off, but which had been forgotten by the conscious mind, creating in one's life a state of eternal anxiety.

He had to tear himself away from this; he got down from the pipes. His nerves were so taut that he semed to feel his brain pushing through his skull. He felt that he had to do something, but he could not figure out what it was. Yet he knew that if he stood here until he made up his mind, he would never move. He crawled through the hole he had made in the brick wall and the exertion afforded him respite from tension. When he entered the basement of the radio store, he stopped in fear, hearing loud voices.

"Come on, boy! Tell us what you did with the radio!"

"Mister, I didn't steal the radio! I swear!"

He heard a dull thumping sound and he imagined a boy being struck violently.

"Please, mister!"

"Did you take it to a pawn shop?"

"No, sir! I didn't steal the radio! I got a radio at home," the boy's voice pleaded hysterically. "Go to my home and look!"

There came to his ears the sound of another blow. It was so funny that he had to clap his hand over his mouth to keep from laughing out loud. They're beating some poor boy, he whispered to himself, shaking his head. He felt a sort of distant pity for the boy and wondered if he ought to bring back the radio and leave it in the basement. No. Perhaps it was a good thing that they were beating the boy; perhaps the beating would bring to the boy's attention, for the first time in his life, the secret of his existence, the guilt that he could never get rid of.

Smiling, he scampered over a coal pile and stood again in the basement of the building where he had stolen the money and jewelry. He lifted himself into the areaway, climbed the rain pipe, and squinted through a two-inch opening of window. The guilty familiarity of what he saw made his muscles tighten. Framed before him in a bright tableau of daylight was the night watchman sitting upon the edge of a chair, stripped to the waist, his head sagging forward, his eyes red and puffy. The watchman's face and shoulders were stippled with red and black welts. Back of the watchman stood the safe, the steel door wide open, showing the empty vault. Yes, they think he did it, he mused.

Footsteps sounded in the room and a man in a blue suit passed in front of him, then another, then still another. Policemen, he breathed. Yes, they were trying to make the watchman confess, just as they had once made him confess to a crime he had not done. He stared into the room, trying to recall something. Oh. . . Those were the same policemen who had beaten him, had made him sign that paper when he had been too tired and sick to care. Now, they were doing the same thing to the watchman. His heart pounded as he saw one of the policemen shake a finger into the watchman's face.

"Why don't you admit it's an inside job, Thompson?" the policeman said.

"I've told you all I know," the watchman mumbled through swollen lips.

"But nobody was here but you!" the policeman shouted.

"I was sleeping," the watchman said. "It was wrong, but I was sleeping all that night!"

"Stop telling us that lie!"

"It's the truth!"

"When did you get the combination?"

"I don't know how to open the safe," the watchman said.

He clung to the rain pipe, tense; he wanted to laugh, but he controlled himself. He felt a great sense of power; yes, he could go back to the cave, rip the money off the walls, pick up the diamonds and rings, and bring them here and write a note, telling them where to look for their foolish toys. No. . . What good would that do? It was not worth the effort. The watchman was guilty; although he was not guilty of the crime of which he had been accused, he was guilty, had always been guilty. The only thing that worried him was that the man who had been really stealing was not being accused. But he consoled himself: they'll catch him sometime during his life.

He saw one of the policemen slap the watchman across the mouth.

"Come clean, you bastard!"

"I've told you all I know," the watchman mumbled like a child.

One of the police went to the rear of the watchman's chair and jerked it from under him; the watchman pitched forward upon his face.

"Get up!" a policeman said.

Trembling, the watchman pulled himself up and sat limply again in the chair.

"Now, are you going to talk?"

"I've told you all I know," the watchman gasped.

"Where did you hide the stuff?"

"I didn't take it!"

"Thompson, your brains are in your feet," one of the policemen said. "We're going to string you up and get them back into your skull."

He watched the policemen clamp handcuffs on the watchman's wrists and ankles; then they lifted the watchman and swung him upside-down and hoisted his feet to the edge of a door. The watchman hung, head down, his eyes bulging. They're crazy, he whispered to himself as he clung to the ridges of the pipe.

"You going to talk?" a policeman shouted into the watchman's ear. He heard the watchman groan.

"We'll let you hang there till you talk, see?"

He saw the watchman close his eyes.

"Let's take 'im down. He passed out," a policeman said.

He grinned as he watched them take the body down and dump it carelessly upon the floor. The policeman took off the handcuffs.

"Let 'im come to. Let's get a smoke," a policeman said.

The three policemen left the scope of his vision. A door slammed. He had an impulse to yell to the watchman that he could escape through the hole in the basement and live with him in the cave. But he wouldn't understand, he told himself. After a moment he saw the watchman rise and stand, swaying from weakness. He stumbled across the room to a desk, opened a drawer, and took out a gun. He's going to kill himself, he thought, intent, eager, detached, yearning to see the end of the man's actions. As the watchman stared vaguely about he lifted the gun to his temple; he stood like that for some minutes, biting his lips until a line of blood etched its way down a corner of his chin. No, he oughtn't do that, he said to himself in a mood of pity.

"Don't!" he half whispered and half yelled.

The watchman looked wildly about; he had heard him. But it did not help; there was a loud report and the watchman's head jerked violently and he fell like a log and lay prone, the gun clattering over the floor.

The three policemen came running into the room with drawn guns. One of the policemen knelt and rolled the watchman's body over and stared at a ragged, scarlet hole in the temple.

"Our hunch was right," the kneeling policeman said. "He was guilty, all right."

"Well, this ends the case," another policeman said.

"He knew he was licked," the third one said with grim satisfaction.

He eased down the rain pipe, crawled back through the holes he had made, and went back into his cave. A fever burned in his bones. He had to act, yet he was afraid. His eyes stared in the darkness as though propped open by invisible hands, as though they had become lidless. His muscles were rigid and he stood for what seemed to him a thousand years.

When he moved again his actions were informed with precision, his muscular system reinforced from a reservoir of energy. He crawled through the hole of earth, dropped into the gray sewer current, and sloshed ahead. When his right foot went forward at a street intersection, he fell backward and shot down into water. In a spasm of terror his right hand grabbed the concrete ledge of a down-curve and he felt the streaking water tugging violently at his body. The current reached his neck and for a moment he was still. He knew that if he moved clumsily he would be sucked under. He held onto the ledge with both hands and slowly pulled himself up. He sighed, standing once more in the sweeping water, thankful that he had missed death.

He waded on through sludge, moving with care, until he came to a web of light sifting down from a manhole cover. He saw steel hooks running up the side of the sewer wall; he caught hold and lifted himself and put his shoulder to the cover and moved it an inch. A crash of sound came to him as he looked into a hot glare of sunshine through which blurred shapes moved. Fear scalded him and he dropped back into the pallid current and stood paralyzed in the shadows. A heavy car rumbled past overhead, jarring the pavement, warning him to stay in his world of dark light, knocking the cover back into place with an imperious clang.

He did not know how much fear he felt, for fear claimed him completely; yet it was not a fear of the police or of people, but a cold dread at the thought of the actions he knew he would perform if he went out into that cruel sunshine. His mind said no; his body said yes; and his mind could not understand his feelings. A low whine broke from him and he was in the act of uncoiling. He climbed upward and heard the faint honking of auto horns. Like a frantic cat clutching a rag, he clung to the steel prongs and heaved his shoulder against the cover and pushed it off halfway. For a split second his eyes were drowned in the terror of yellow light and he was in a deeper darkness than he had ever known in the underground.

Partly out of the hole, he blinked, regaining enough sight to make out meaningful forms. An odd thing was happening: No one was rushing forward to challenge him. He had imagined the moment of his emergence as a desperate tussle with men who wanted to cart him off to be killed; instead, life froze about him as the traffic stopped. He pushed the cover aside, stood, swaying in a world so fragile that he expected it to collapse and drop him into some deep void. But nobody seemed to pay him heed. The cars were now swerving to shun him and the gaping hole.

"Why in hell don't you put up a red light, dummy?" a raucous voice yelled.

He understood; they thought that he was a sewer workman. He walked toward the sidewalk, weaving unsteadily through the moving traffic.

"Look where you're going, nigger!"

"That's right! Stay there and get killed!"

"You blind, you bastard?"

"Go home and sleep your drunk off!"

A policeman stood at the curb, looking in the opposite direction. When he passed the policeman, he feared that he would be grabbed, but nothing happened. Where was he? Was this real? He wanted to look about to get his bearings, but felt that something awful would happen to him if he did. He wandered into a spacious doorway of a store that sold men's clothing and saw his reflection in a long mirror: his cheekbones protruded from a hairy black face; his greasy cap was perched askew upon his head and his eyes were red and glassy. His shirt and trousers were caked with mud and hung loosely. His hands were gummed with a black stickiness. He threw back his head and laughed so loudly that passers-by stopped and stared.

He ambled on down the sidewalk, not having the merest notion of where he was going. Yet sleeping within him was the drive to go somewhere and say something to somebody. Half an hour later his ears caught the sound of spirited singing.

The Lamb, the Lamb, the Lamb
I hear thy voice a-calling
The Lamb, the Lamb, the Lamb
I feel thy grace a-falling

A church! He exclaimed. He broke into a run and came to brick steps leading downward to a subbasement. This is it! The church into which he had peered. Yes, he was going in and tell them. What? He did not know; but, once face to face with them, he would think of what to say. Must be Sunday, he mused. He ran down the steps and jerked the door open; the church was crowded and a deluge of song swept over him.

The Lamb, the Lamb, the Lamb
Tell me again your story
The Lamb, the Lamb, the Lamb
Flood my soul with your glory

He stared at the singing faces with a trembling smile.

"Say!" he shouted.

Many turned to look at him, but the song rolled on. His arm was jerked violently.

"I'm sorry, Brother, but you can't do that in here," a man said.

"But, mister!"

"You can't act rowdy in God's house, " the man said.

"He's filthy," another man said.

"But I want to tell 'em," he said loudly.

"He stinks," someone muttered.

The song had stopped, but at once another one began.

Oh, wondrous sight upon the cross
Vision sweet and divine
Oh, wondrous sight upon the cross
Full of such love sublime

He attempted to twist away, but other hands grabbed him and rushed him into the doorway.

"Let me alone!" he screamed, struggling.

"Get out!"

"He's drunk," somebody said. "He ought to be ashamed!"

"He acts crazy!"

He felt that he was failing and he grew frantic.

"But, mister, let me tell—"

"Get away from this door, or I'll call the police!"

He stared, his trembling smile fading in a sense of wonderment.

"The police," he repeated vacantly.

"Now, get!"

He was pushed toward the brick steps and the door banged shut. The waves of song came.

Oh, wondrous sight, wondrous sight
Lift my heavy heart above
Oh, wondrous sight, wondrous sight
Fill my weary soul with love

He was smiling again now. Yes, the police . . . That was it! Why had he not thought of it before? The idea had been deep down in him, and only now did it assume supreme importance. He looked up and saw a street sign: COURT STREET—HARTSDALE AVENUE. He turned and walked northward, his mind filled with the image of the police station. Yes, that was where they had beaten him, accused him, and had made him sign a confession of his guilt. He would go there and clear up everything, make a statement. What statement? He did not know. He was the statement, and since it was all so clear to him, surely he would be able to make it clear to others.

He came to the corner of Hartsdale Avenue and turned westward. Yeah, there's the station . . . A policeman came down the steps and walked past him without a glance. He mounted the stone steps and went through the door, paused; he was in a hallway where several policemen were standing, talking, smoking. One turned to him.

"What do you want, boy?"

He looked at the policeman and laughed.

"What in hell are you laughing about?" the policeman asked.

He stopped laughing and stared. His whole being was full of what he wanted to say to them, but he could not say it.

"Are you looking for the Desk Sergeant?"

"Yes, sir," he said quickly; then: "Oh, no, sir."

"Well, make up your mind, now."

Four policemen grouped themselves around him.

"I'm looking for the men," he said.

"What men?"

Peculiarly, at that moment he could not remember the names of the policemen; he recalled their beating him, the confession he had signed, and how he had run away from them. He saw the cave next to the church, the money on the walls, the guns, the rings, the cleaver, the watches, and the diamonds on the floor.

"They brought me here," he began.

"When?"

His mind flew back over the blur of the time lived in the underground blackness. He had no idea of how much time had elapsed, but the intensity of what had happened to him told him that it could not have transpired in a short space of time, yet his mind told him that time must have been brief.

"It was a long time ago." He spoke like a child relating a dimly remembered dream. "It was a long time," he repeated, following the promptings of his emotions. "They beat me . . . I was scared . . . I ran away."

A policeman raised a finger to his temple and made a derisive circle.

"Nuts," the policeman said.

"Do you know what place this is, boy?"

"Yes, sir. The police station," he answered sturdily, almost proudly.

"Well, who do you want to see?"

"The men," he said again, feeling that surely they knew the men. "You know the men," he said in a hurt tone.

"What's your name?"

He opened his lips to answer and no words came. He had forgotten. But what did it matter if he had? It was not important.

"Where do you live?"

Where did he live? It had been so long ago since he had lived up here in this strange world that he felt it was foolish even to try to remember. Then for a moment the old mood that had dominated him in the underground surged back. He leaned forward and spoke eagerly.

"They said I killed the woman."

"What woman?" a policeman asked.

"And I signed a paper that said I was guilty," he went on, ignoring their questions. "Then I ran off . . ."

"Did you run off from an institution?"

"No, sir," he said, blinking and shaking his head. "I came from under the ground. I pushed off the manhole cover and climbed out . . ."

"All right, now," a policeman said, placing an arm about his shoulder. "We'll send you to the psycho and you'll be taken care of."

"Maybe he's a Fifth Columnist!" a policeman shouted.

There was laughter and, despite his anxiety, he joined in. But the laughter lasted so long that it irked him.

"I got to find those men," he protested mildly.

"Say, boy, what have you been drinking?"

"Water," he said. "I got some water in a basement."

"Were the men you ran away from dressed in white, boy?"

"No, sir," he said brightly. "They were men like you."

An elderly policeman caught hold of his arm.

"Try and think hard. Where did they pick you up?"

He knitted his brows in an effort to remember, but he was blank inside. The policeman stood before him demanding logical answers and he could no longer think with his mind; he thought with his feelings and no words came.

"I was guilty," he said. "Oh, no, sir. I wasn't then, I mean, mister!"

"Aw, talk sense. Now, where did they pick you up?"

He felt challenged and his mind began reconstructing events in reverse; his feelings ranged back over the long hours and he saw the cave, the sewer, the bloody room where it was said that a woman had been killed.

"Oh, yes, sir," he said, smiling. "I was coming from Mrs. Wooten's."

"Who is she?"

"I work for her."

"Where does she live?"

"Next door to Mrs. Peabody, the woman who was killed."

The policemen were very quiet now, looking at him intently.

"What do you know about Mrs. Peabody's death, boy?"

"Nothing, sir. But they said I killed her. But it doesn't make any difference. I'm guilty!"

"What are you talking about, boy?"

His smile faded and he was possessed with memories of the underground; he saw the cave next to the church and his lips moved to speak. But how could he say it? The distance between what he felt and what these men meant was vast. Something told him, as he stood there looking into their faces, that he would never be able to tell them, that they would never believe him even if he told them.

"All the people I saw was guilty," he began slowly.

"Aw, nuts," a policeman muttered.

"Say," another policeman said, "that Peabody woman was killed over on Winewood. That's Number Ten's beat."

"Where's Number Ten?" a policeman asked.

"Upstairs in the swing room," someone answered.

"Take this boy up, Sam," a policeman ordered.

"O.K. Come along, boy."

An elderly policeman caught hold of his arm and led him up a flight of wooden stairs, down a long hall, and to a door.

"Squad Ten!" the policeman called through the door.

"What?" a gruff voice answered.

"Someone to see you!"

"About what?"

The old policeman pushed the door in and then shoved him into the room.

He stared, his lips open, his heart barely beating. Before him were the three policemen who had picked him up and had beaten him to extract the confession. They were seated about a small table, playing cards. The air was blue with smoke and sunshine poured through a high window, lighting up fantastic smoke shapes. He saw one of the policemen look up; the policeman's face was tired and a cigarette drooped limply from one corner of his mouth and both of his fat, puffy eyes were squinting and his hands gripped his cards.

"Lawson!" the man exclaimed.

The moment the man's name sounded he remembered the names of all of them: Lawson, Murphy, and Johnson. How simple it was. He waited, smiling, wondering how they would react when they knew that he had come back.

"Looking for me?" the man who had been called Lawson mumbled, sorting his cards. "For what?"

So far only Murphy, the red-headed one, had recognized him.

"Don't you-all remember me?" he blurted, running to the table.

All three of the policemen were looking at him now. Lawson, who seemed the leader, jumped to his feet.

"Where in hell have you been?"

"Do you know 'im, Lawson?" the old policeman asked.

"Huh?" Lawson frowned. "Oh, yes. I'll handle 'im." The old policeman left the room and Lawson crossed to the door and turned the key in the lock. "Come here, boy," he ordered in a cold tone.

He did not move; he looked from face to face. Yes, he would tell them about his cave.

"He looks batty to me," Johnson said, the one who had not spoken before.

"Why in hell did you come back here?" Lawson said.

"I—I just didn't want to run away no more," he said. "I'm all right, now." He paused; the men's attitude puzzled him.

"You've been hiding, huh?" Lawson asked in a tone that denoted that he had not heard his previous words. "You told us you were sick, and when we left you in the room, you jumped out of the window and ran away."

Panic filled him. Yes, they were indifferent to what he would say! They were waiting for him to speak and they would laugh at him. He had to rescue himself from this bog; he had to force the reality of himself upon them.

"Mister, I took a sackful of money and pasted it on the walls . . ." he began.

"I'll be damned," Lawson said.

"Listen," said Murphy, "let me tell you something for your own good. We don't want you, see? You're free, free as air. Now go home and forget it. It was all a mistake. We caught the guy who did the Peabody job. He wasn't colored at all. He was an Eyetalian."

"Shut up!" Lawson yelled. "Have you no sense!"

"But I want to tell 'im," Murphy said.

"We can't let this crazy fool go," Lawson exploded. "He acts nuts, but this may be a stunt . . ."

"I was down in the basement," he began in a childlike tone, as though repeating a lesson learned by heart; "and I went into a movie . . ." His voice failed. He was getting ahead of his story. First, he ought to tell them about the singing in the church, but what words could he use? He looked at them appealingly. "I went into a shop and took a sackful of money and diamonds and watches and rings . . . I didn't steal 'em, I'll give 'em all back. I just took 'em to play with . . ." He paused, stunned by their disbelieving eyes.

Lawson lit a cigarette and looked at him coldly.

"What did you do with the money?" he asked in a quiet, waiting voice.

"I pasted the hundred-dollar bills on the walls."

"What walls?" Lawson asked.

"The walls of the dirt room," he said, smiling, "the room next to the church. I hung up the rings and the watches and I stamped the diamonds into the dirt . . ." He saw that they were not understanding what he was saying. He grew frantic to make them believe, his voice tumbled on eagerly. "I saw a dead baby and a dead man . . ."

"Aw, you're nuts," Lawson snarled, shoving him into a chair.

"But, mister . . ."

"Johnson, where's the paper he signed?" Lawson asked.

"What paper?"

"The confession, fool!"

Johnson pulled out his billfold and extracted a crumpled piece of paper.

"Yes, sir, mister," he said, stretching forth his hand. "That's the paper I signed . . ."

Lawson slapped him and he would have toppled had his chair not struck a wall behind him. Lawson scratched a match and held the paper over the flame; the confession burned down to Lawson's fingertips.

He stared, thunderstruck; the sun of the underground was fleeing and the terrible darkness of the day stood before him. They did not believe him, but he *had* to make them believe him!

"But, mister . . ."

"It's going to be all right, boy," Lawson said with a quiet, soothing laugh. "I've burned your confession, see? You didn't sign anything." Lawson came close to him with the black ashes cupped in his palm. "You don't remember a thing about this, do you?"

"Don't you-all be scared of me," he pleaded, sensing their uneasiness. "I'll sign another paper, if you want me to. I'll show you the cave."

"What's your game, boy?" Lawson asked suddenly.

"What are you trying to find out?" Johnson asked.

"Who sent you here?" Murphy demanded.

"Nobody sent me, mister," he said. "I just want to show you the room . . ."

"Aw, he's plumb bats," Murphy said. "Let's ship 'im to the psycho."

"No," Lawson said. "He's playing a game and I wish to God I knew what it was."

There flashed through his mind a definite way to make them believe him; he rose from the chair with nervous excitement.

"Mister, I saw the night watchman blow his brains out because you accused him of stealing," he told them. "But he didn't steal the money and diamonds. I took 'em."

Tigerishly Lawson grabbed his collar and lifted him bodily.

"Who told you about that?"

"Don't get excited, Lawson," Johnson said. "He read about it in the papers."

Lawson flung him away.

"He couldn't have," Lawson said, pulling papers from his pocket. "I haven't turned in the reports yet."

"Then how *did* he find out?" Murphy asked.

"Let's get out of here," Lawson said with quick resolution. "Listen, boy, we're going to take you to a nice, quiet place, see?"

"Yes, sir," he said. "And I'll show you the underground."

"Goddamn," Lawson muttered, fastening the gun at his hip. He narrowed his eyes at Johnson and Murphy. "Listen," he spoke just above a whisper, "say nothing about this, you hear?"

"O.K.," Johnson said.

"Sure," Murphy said.

Lawson unlocked the door and Johnson and Murphy led him down the stairs. The hallway was crowded with policemen.

"What have you got there, Lawson?"

"What did he do, Lawson?"

"He's psycho, ain't he, Lawson?"

Lawson did not answer; Johnson and Murphy led him to the car parked at the curb, pushed him into the back seat. Lawson got behind the steering wheel and the car rolled forward.

"What's up, Lawson?" Murphy asked.

"Listen," Lawson began slowly, "we tell the papers that he spilled about the Peabody job, then he escapes. The Wop is caught and we tell the papers that we steered them wrong to trap the real guy, see? Now this dope shows up and acts nuts. If we let him go, he'll squeal that we framed him, see?"

"I'm all right, mister," he said, feeling Murphy's and Johnson's arm locked rigidly into his. "I'm guilty . . . I'll show you everything in the underground. I laughed and laughed . . ."

"Shut that fool up!" Lawson ordered.

Johnson tapped him across the head with a blackjack and he fell back against the seat cushion, dazed.

"Yes, sir," he mumbled. "I'm all right."

The car sped along Hartsdale Avenue, then swung onto Pine Street and rolled to State Street, then turned south. It slowed to a stop, turned in the middle of a block, and headed north again.

"You're going around in circles, Lawson," Murphy said.

Lawson did not answer; he was hunched over the steering wheel. Finally he pulled the car to a stop at a curb.

"Say, boy, tell us the truth," Lawson asked quietly. "Where did you hide?"

"I didn't hide, mister."

The three policemen were staring at him now; he felt that for the first time they were willing to understand him.

"Then what happened?"

"Mister, when I looked through all of those holes and saw how people were living, I loved 'em . . ."

"Cut out that crazy talk!" Lawson snapped. "Who sent you back here?"

"Nobody, mister."

"Maybe he's talking straight," Johnson ventured.

"All right," Lawson said. "Nobody hid you. Now, tell us *where* you hid."

"I went underground . . ."

"What goddamn underground do you keep talking about?"

"I just went . . ." He paused and looked into the street, then pointed to a manhole cover. "I went down in there and stayed."

"In the *sewer?*"

"Yes, sir."

The policemen burst into a sudden laugh and ended quickly. Lawson swung the car around and drove to Woodside Avenue; he brought the car to a stop in front of a tall apartment building.

"What're we going to do, Lawson?" Murphy asked.

"I'm taking him up to my place," Lawson said. "We've got to wait until night. There's nothing we can do now."

They took him out of the car and led him into a vestibule.

"Take the steps," Lawson muttered.

They led him up four flights of stairs and into the living room of a small apartment. Johnson and Murphy let go of his arms and he stood uncertainly in the middle of the room.

"Now, listen, boy," Lawson began, "forget those wild lies you've been telling us. Where did you hide?"

"I just went underground, like I told you."

The room rocked with laughter. Lawson went to a cabinet and got a bottle of whiskey; he placed glasses for Johnson and Murphy. The three of them drank.

He felt that he could not explain himself to them. He tried to muster all the sprawling images that floated in him; the images stood out sharply in his mind, but he could not make them have the meaning for others that they had for him. He felt so helpless that he began to cry.

"He's nuts, all right," Johnson said. "All nuts cry like that."

Murphy crossed the room and slapped him.

"Stop that raving!"

A sense of excitement flooded him; he ran to Murphy and grabbed his arm.

"Let me show you the cave," he said. "Come on, and you'll see!"

Before he knew it a sharp blow had clipped him on the chin; darkness covered his eyes. He dimly felt himself being lifted and laid out on the sofa. He heard low voices and struggled to rise, but hard hands held him down. His brain was clearing now. He pulled to a sitting posture and stared with glazed eyes. It had grown dark. How long had he been out?

"Say, boy," Lawson said soothingly, "will you show us the underground?"

His eyes shone and his heart swelled with gratitude. Lawson believed him! He rose, glad; he grabbed Lawson's arm, making the policeman spill whiskey from the glass to his shirt.

"Take it easy, goddammit," Lawson said.

"Yes, sir."

"O.K. We'll take you down. But you'd better be telling us the truth, you hear?"

He clapped his hands in wild joy.

"I'll show you everything!"

He had triumphed at last! He would now do what he had felt was compelling him all along. At last he would be free of his burden.

"Take 'im down," Lawson ordered.

They led him down to the vestibule; when he reached the sidewalk he saw that it was night and a fine rain was falling.

"It's just like when I went down," he told them.

"What?" Lawson asked.

"The rain," he said, sweeping his arm in a wide arc. "It was raining when I went down. The rain made the water rise and lift the cover off."

"Cut it out," Lawson snapped.

They did not believe him now, but they would. A mood of high selflessness throbbed in him. He could barely contain his rising spirits. They would see what he had seen; they would feel what he had felt. He would lead them through all the holes he had dug and . . . He wanted to make a hymn, prance about in physical ecstasy, throw his arm about the policemen in fellowship.

"Get into the car," Lawson ordered.

He climbed in and Johnson and Murphy sat at either side of him; Lawson slid behind the steering wheel and started the motor.

"Now, tell us where to go," Lawson said.

"It's right around the corner from where the lady was killed," he said.

The car rolled slowly and he closed his eyes, remembering the song he had heard in the church, the song that had wrought him to such a high pitch of terror and pity. He sang softly, lolling his head:

Glad, glad, glad, oh, so glad
I got Jesus in my soul . . .

"Mister," he said, stopping his song, "you ought to see how funny the rings look on the wall." He giggled. "I fired a pistol, too. Just once, to see how it felt."

"What do you suppose he's suffering from?" Johnson asked.

"Delusions of grandeur, maybe," Murphy said.

"Maybe it's because he lives in a white man's world," Lawson said.

"Say, boy, what did you eat down there?" Murphy asked, prodding Johnson anticipatorily with his elbow.

"Pears, oranges, bananas, and pork chops," he said.

The car filled with laughter.

"You didn't eat any watermelon?" Lawson asked, smiling.

"No, sir," he answered calmly. "I didn't see any."

The three policemen roared harder and louder.

"Boy, you're sure some case," Murphy said, shaking his head in wonder.

The car pulled to a curb.

"All right, boy," Lawson said. "Tell us where to go."

He peered through the rain and saw where he had gone down. The streets, save for a few dim lamps glowing softly through the rain, were dark and empty.

"Right there, mister," he said, pointing.

"Come on; let's take a look," Lawson said.

"Well, suppose he did hide down there," Johnson said, "what is that supposed to prove?"

"I don't believe he hid down there," Murphy said.

"It won't hurt to look," Lawson said. "Leave things to me."

Lawson got out of the car and looked up and down the street.

He was eager to show them the cave now. If he could show them what he had seen, then they would feel what he had felt and they in turn would show it to others and those others would feel as they had felt, and soon everybody would be governed by the same impulse of pity.

"Take 'im out," Lawson ordered.

Johnson and Murphy opened the door and pushed him out; he stood trembling in the rain, smiling. Again Lawson looked up and down the street; no one was in sight. The rain came down hard, slanting like black wires across the wind-swept air.

"All right," Lawson said. "Show us."

He walked to the center of the street, stopped and inserted a finger in one of the tiny holes of the cover and tugged, but he was too weak to budge it.

"Did you really go down in there, boy?" Lawson asked; there was a doubt in his voice.

"Yes, sir. Just a minute. I'll show you."

"Help 'im get that damn thing off," Lawson said.

Johnson stepped forward and lifted the cover; it clanged against the wet pavement. The hole gaped round and black.

"I went down in there," he announced with pride.

Lawson gazed at him for a long time without speaking, then he reached his right hand to his holster and drew his gun.

"Mister, I got a gun just like that down there," he said, laughing and looking into Lawson's face, "I fired it once then hung it on the wall. I'll show you."

"Show us how you went down," Lawson said quietly.

"I'll go down first, mister, and then you-all can come after me, hear?" he spoke like a little boy playing a game.

"Sure, sure," Lawson said soothingly. "Go ahead. We'll come."

He looked brightly at the policemen; he was bursting with happiness. He bent down and placed his hands on the rim of the hole and sat on the edge, his feet dangling into watery darkness. He heard the familiar drone of the gray current. He lowered his body and hung for a moment by his fingers, then he went downward on the steel prongs, hand over hand, until he reached the last rung. He dropped and his feet hit the water and he felt the stiff current trying to suck him away. He balanced himself quickly and looked back upward at the policemen.

"Come on, you-all!" he yelled, casting his voice above the rustling at his feet.

The vague forms that towered above him in the rain did not move. He laughed, feeling that they doubted him. But, once they saw the things he had done, they would never doubt again.

"Come on! The cave isn't far!" he yelled. "But be careful when your feet hit the water, because the current's pretty rough down here!"

Lawson still held the gun. Murphy and Johnson looked at Lawson quizzically.

"What are we going to do, Lawson?" Murphy asked.

"We are not going to follow that crazy nigger down into that sewer, are we?" Johnson asked.

"Come on, you-all!" he begged in a shout.

He saw Lawson raise the gun and point it directly at him. Lawson's face twitched, as though he were hesitating.

Then there was a thunderous report and a streak of fire ripped through his chest. He was hurled into the water, flat on his back. He looked in amazement at the blurred white faces looming above him. They shot me, he said to himself. The water flowed past him, blossoming in foam about his arms, his legs, and his head. His jaw sagged and his mouth gaped soundless. A vast pain gripped his head and gradually squeezed out consciousness. As from a great distance he heard hollow voices.

"What did you shoot him for, Lawson?"

"I had to."

"Why?"

"You've got to shoot his kind. They'd wreck things."

As though in a deep dream, he heard a metallic clank; they had replaced the manhole cover, shutting out forever the sound of wind and rain. From overhead came the muffled roar of a powerful motor and the swish of a speeding car. He felt the strong tide pushing him slowly into the middle of the sewer, turning him about. For a split second there hovered before his eyes the glittering cave, the shouting walls, and the laughing floor . . . Then his mouth was full of thick, bitter water. The current spun him around. He sighed and closed his eyes, a whirling object rushing alone in the darkness, veering, tossing, lost in the heart of the earth.

Albert Camus

(1913–1960)

Albert Camus' last published work was a collection of short stories entitled Exile and the Kingdom, *a phrase that encapsulates the painful division in human life around which all his work spirals. "Exile" is the condition of modern man—stripped of God, alienated from nature, tyrannized by frightening political ideologies, isolated from his fellows, and divided even against himself. "The Kingdom" is a kingdom of humanity man dreams of, in which, acknowledging the emptiness of the heavens, he can nevertheless take joy in his own animal vitality and in that of nature, living justly and lovingly with his fellows and with himself. Although he was identified with the post-World War II existentialists in France, Camus was less a formal philosopher than a novelist and meditative essayist whose intensely personal explorations of the human condition led him from a bleak vision of the absurdity of life to the guarded but moving humanism of his later works. A worldwide audience still finds this humanism timely and meaningful.*

Camus was born in 1913 in the town of Mondovi in Algeria. His father died less than a year later, in the First Battle of the Marne in World War I; his mother, who worked as a cleaning woman, then moved with her two children, her mother, and a brother into a two-room apartment in the working-class section of Algiers. There Camus spent his childhood. After grade school, he won a scholarship to high school. At sixteen, he enrolled as a philosophy student at the University of Algiers, but his studies were interrupted when he suffered the first of the tuberculosis attacks that recurred all his life. He was forced to abandon his plans for a career in college teaching.

Through the 1930s, Camus supported himself with a series of miscellaneous jobs in Algiers. He also read widely in both classic and modern French authors and was active in the theater, founding a company, the Workers' Theater, dedicated to performing for working-class audiences. For several years he acted, directed, and wrote plays for this company. He joined the Algerian Communist Party in 1934 but resigned a year later, disillusioned with its program. His first articles had been published while he was still at the university, and in 1937 he became a reporter, reviewer, and editorial writer for the Alger-Républicain. *In the same year his first book was published:* Betwixt and Between, *a collection of childhood reminiscences and travel sketches. In these sketches and in* Nuptials, *published the following year, Camus dealt with a theme that was to recur throughout his work: the contrast between man's loneliness, suffering, and mortality and his joy in life, a joy represented especially by the sensuality of the North African landscape.*

Camus left Algeria in 1942 for Paris to work in the French Resistance and to edit the underground Resistance newspaper Combat. The Stranger *was published just before he left Algeria, and he took with him the completed manuscript of* The Myth of Sisyphus*; the two works were to bring him international fame. Both works explore Camus' conception of the "absurd," man's position confronted with a world without hope or meaning and faced with the painful contradiction between his longing for immortality and his knowledge of his inevitable death. Meursault, the protagonist of* The Stranger, *is condemned to death less for killing an Arab (actually an act of self-defense) than for being a "stranger" to society's rituals (he did not weep at his mother's funeral). As Sartre does in "The Wall," Camus explores the spiritual development of a person awaiting imminent death. In prison, Meursault, while still rejecting society's dead conventions, moves beyond his previous perception of life as merely a series of meaningless sensual experiences to a vision of life as infinitely precious, not in spite of its absurdity but because of it. Similarly, in the famous ending of* The Myth of Sisyphus, *the mythic hero, condemned forever to roll a boulder up a mountain in Hades, triumphs over his fate by accepting its inherent meaninglessness: "The struggle itself toward the heights is enough to fill a man's heart. One must imagine Sisyphus happy."*

In Paris, Camus continued to write for the theater. The Misunderstanding *was produced in Paris in 1944, and* Caligula *followed in 1945; both developed the absurdist themes of* The Stranger *and* The Myth of Sisyphus. *Camus' most disastrous theatrical failure,* The State of Siege *(1948), was followed by his most brilliant success,* The Just Assassins *(1950). These four plays constitute his major achievement in drama, although he also adapted the work of several other writers for the stage, including William Faulkner's* Requiem for a Nun *(1956) and Fyodor Dostoevsky's* The Possessed *(1959).*

The Plague *(1947), a novel (or "chronicle," as Camus called it) about an epidemic in Oran, signals a shift in his concerns from the plight of the individual absurdist hero to the problem of values available to social man in an absurd world. Camus finds the answer in the human dignity and cooperation with which the people of Oran confront the plague, an epidemic that symbolizes both the universal threat of an indifferent universe and specifically the political tyranny of Nazi-style totalitarianism. In* The Plague *and the works following it, Camus' emphasis shifts from absurdity to revolt, an option he explores fully and directly in the long philosophical essay* The Rebel *(1951). A person becomes a rebel at the point where he says no to the oppressive patterns of society and accepts the challenge of forging personal and social values that affirm life. Camus' criticisms of collective, political "revolution," as opposed to individual, metaphysical "rebellion," alienated many of his politically committed contemporaries and led to an open break with Sartre.*

The Fall *(1956), a brilliantly ironic dramatic monologue, reveals yet another facet of Camus' thought, a new awareness of human duality. Evil is partially something we impose upon ourselves rather than something inflicted by a hostile universe. The complexity of the individual human being remains a central theme in the six stories that make up his last work,* Exile and the Kingdom *(1957). In this same year, he was awarded the Nobel Prize at the unusually young age of forty-four. Less than three years later, in 1960, he was killed in an automobile accident.*

"The Renegade" is one of the most powerful, and certainly the most shocking, of the stories in Exile and the Kingdom. *Technically, as the monologue of a tongueless slave, it recalls Camus' experience with the compression and immediacy of*

the stage, as well as the stream-of-consciousness monologues of Joyce and Faulkner. The French subtitle of the story, Un Esprit Confus *("A Confused Spirit"), is a guide to its meaning. In a realistic world that is nevertheless so stark that it hovers on the edge of surrealistic nightmare, the slave believes that he has achieved a Sisyphean liberation by freely choosing his slavery: "if I too become vicious I cease to be a slave." But one does not become free by exchanging one form of slavery for another. The slave's life has been one long exile, a truth he glimpses in his dying moments, in the last lines of this strange and troubling story.*

FURTHER READING *(prepared by N. K. B.):* Patrick McCarthy's detailed critical biography, *Camus,* 1982, emphasizes Camus' work as a political journalist and novelist and provides excellent background on the French rule in Algeria. Camus' eventful life has also been detailed in Herbert R. Lottman's *Albert Camus: A Biography,* 1979, and Morvan Lebesque's *Portrait of Camus,* 1971; both works provide ample background on Camus' political and philosophical development. Germaine Brée's *Camus,* 1961, summarizes key biographical incidents in light of additional evidence from Camus' notebooks and cogently discusses the fiction, with a short analysis of "The Renegade." For a clearly written introduction to Camus' philosophy and artistry, see Phillip H. Rhein's *Albert Camus,* 1969. Philip Thody's *Albert Camus, 1913–1960,* 1961, traces the development of Camus' style and includes a summary of his critical reception. In *Albert Camus and the Literature of Revolt,* 1960, John Cruickshank discusses Camus' persistent concern with political and existential freedom, focusing on the fictional and dramatic heroes and anti-heroes. Thomas Hanna, *The Thought and Art of Albert Camus,* 1958, shows how Camus' philosophy influenced his literary style and themes. Emmett Parker's *Albert Camus: The Artist in the Arena,* 1966, contains an in-depth account of the political context for Camus' fiction and non-fiction. Donald Lazere's *The Unique Creation of Albert Camus,* 1973, interprets Camus' work from a variety of critical perspectives, including psychoanalytic and Marxist, with a penetrating discussion of "The Renegade." Germaine Brée, ed., *Camus: A Collection of Critical Essays,* 1962, represents the international critical response to Camus, emphasizing the philosophical questions raised by his work and reprinting Jean-Paul Sartre's famous essay on *The Stranger.*

THE RENEGADE

Translated by Justin O'Brien

"What a jumble! What a jumble! I must tidy up my mind. Since they cut out my tongue, another tongue, it seems, has been constantly wagging somewhere in my skull, something has been talking, or someone, that suddenly falls silent and then it all begins again—oh, I hear too many things I never utter, what a jumble, and if I open my mouth it's like pebbles rattling together. Order and method, the tongue says, and then goes on talking of other matters simultaneously—yes, I always longed for order. At least one thing is certain, I am waiting for the missionary who is to come and take my place. Here I am on the trail, an hour away from Taghâsa, hidden in a pile of rocks, sitting on my old rifle. Day is breaking over the desert, it's still very cold, soon it will be too hot, this country drives men mad and I've been here I don't know how many years. . . . No, just a little longer. The missionary is to come this morning, or this evening. I've heard he'll come with a guide, perhaps they'll have but one camel between them. I'll wait. I am waiting, it's only the cold making me shiver. Just be patient a little longer, lousy slave!

But I have been patient for so long. When I was home on that high plateau of the Massif Central,[1] my coarse father, my boorish mother, the wine, the pork soup every day, the wine above all, sour and cold, and the long winter, the frigid wind, the snowdrifts, the revolting bracken—oh, I wanted to get away, leave them all at once and begin to live at last, in the sunlight, with fresh water. I believed the priest, he spoke to me of the seminary, he tutored me daily, he had plenty of time in that Protestant region, where he used to hug the walls as he crossed the village. He told me of the future and of the sun, Catholicism is the sun, he used to say, and he would get me to read, he beat Latin into my hard head ('The kid's bright but he's pig-headed'), my head was so hard that, despite all my falls, it has never once bled in my life: 'Bull-headed,' my pig of a father used to say. At the seminary they were proud as punch, a recruit from the Protestant region was a victory, they greeted me like the sun at Austerlitz.[2] The sun was pale and feeble, to be sure, because of the alcohol, they have drunk sour wine and the children's teeth are set on edge,[3] *gra gra,* one really ought to kill one's father, but after all there's no danger that *he*'ll hurl himself into missionary work since he's now long dead, the tart wine eventually cut through his stomach, so there's nothing left but to kill the missionary.

I have something to settle with him and with his teachers, with my teachers who deceived me, with the whole of lousy Europe, everybody deceived me. Missionary work, that's all they could say, go out to the savages and tell them: 'Here is my Lord, just look at him, he never strikes or kills, he issues his orders in a low voice, he turns the other cheek, he's the greatest of masters, choose him, just see how much better he's made me, offend me and you will see.' Yes, I believed, *gra gra,* and I felt better, I had put on weight, I was almost handsome, I wanted to be offended. When we would walk out in tight black rows, in summer, under Grenoble's[4] hot sun and would meet girls in cotton dresses, *I* didn't look away, I despised them, I waited for them to offend me, and sometimes they would laugh. At such times I would think: 'Let them strike me and spit in my face,' but their laughter, to tell the truth, came to the same thing, bristling with teeth and quips that tore me to shreds, the offense and the suffering were sweet to me! My confessor couldn't understand when I used to heap accusations on myself: 'No, no, there's good in you!' Good! There was nothing but sour wine in me, and that was all for the best, how can a man become better if he's not bad, I had grasped that in everything they taught me. That's the only thing I did grasp, a single idea, and, pig-headed bright boy, I carried it to its logical conclusion, I went out of my way for punishments, I groused at the normal, in short I too wanted to be an example in order to be noticed

[1] Mountainous plateau covering most of central France.

[2] Czechoslovakian village where, in 1805, Napoleon won his most brilliant victory, over the Russians and the Austrians.

[3] "The fathers have eaten a sour grape, and the children's teeth are set on edge" (Jeremiah 31:30).

[4] Town in southeast France.

and so that after noticing me people would give credit to what had made me better, through me praise my Lord.

Fierce sun! It's rising, the desert is changing, it has lost its mountain-cyclamen color, O my mountain, and the snow, the soft enveloping snow, no, it's a rather grayish yellow, the ugly moment before the great resplendence. Nothing, still nothing from here to the horizon over yonder where the plateau disappears in a circle of still soft colors. Behind me, the trail climbs to the dune hiding Taghâsa, whose iron name has been beating in my head for so many years. The first to mention it to me was the half-blind old priest who had retired to our monastery, but why do I say the first, he was the only one, and it wasn't the city of salt, the white walls under the blinding sun, that struck me in his account but the cruelty of the savage inhabitants and the town closed to all outsiders, only one of those who had tried to get in, one alone, to his knowledge, had lived to relate what he had seen. They had whipped him and driven him out into the desert after having put salt on his wounds and in his mouth, he had met nomads who for once were compassionate, a stroke of luck, and since then I had been dreaming about his tale, about the fire of the salt and the sky, about the House of the Fetish and his slaves, could anything more barbarous, more exciting be imagined, yes, that was my mission and I had to go and reveal to them my Lord.

They all expatiated on the subject at the seminary to discourage me, pointing out the necessity of waiting, that it was not missionary country, that I wasn't ready yet, I had to prepare myself specially, know who I was, and even then I had to go through tests, then they would see! But go on waiting, ah, no!—yes, if they insisted, for the special preparation and the tryouts because they took place at Algiers and brought me closer, but for all the rest I shook my pig-head and repeated the same thing, to get among the most barbarous and live as they did, to show them at home, and even in the House of the Fetish, through example, that my Lord's truth would prevail. They would offend me, of course, but I was not afraid of offenses, they were essential to the demonstration, and as a result of the way I endured them I'd get the upper hand of those savages like a strong sun. Strong, yes, that was the word I constantly had on the tip of my tongue, I dreamed of absolute power, the kind that makes people kneel down, that forces the adversary to capitulate, converts him in short, and the blinder, the crueler he is, the more he's sure of himself, mired in his own conviction, the more his consent establishes the royalty of whoever brought about his collapse. Converting good folk who had strayed somewhat was the shabby ideal of our priests, I despised them for daring so little when they could do so much, they lacked faith and I had it, I wanted to be acknowledged by the torturers themselves, to fling them on their knees and make them say: 'O Lord, here is thy victory,' to rule in short by the sheer force of words over an army of the wicked. Oh, I was sure of reasoning logically on that subject, never quite sure of myself otherwise, but once I get an idea I don't let go of it, that's my strong point, yes the strong point of the fellow they all pitied!

The sun has risen higher, my forehead is beginning to burn. Around me the stones are beginning to crack open with a dull sound, the only cool thing is the rifle's barrel, cool as the fields, as the evening rain long ago when the soup was simmering, they would wait for me, my father and mother who would occasionally smile at me, perhaps I loved them. But that's all in the past, a film of heat is beginning to rise from the trail, come on, missionary, I'm waiting for you, now I know how to answer the message, my new masters taught me, and I know they are right, you have to settle accounts with that question of love. When I fled the seminary in Algiers I had a different idea of the savages and only one detail of my imaginings was true, they are cruel. I had robbed the treasurer's office, cast off my habit, crossed the Atlas,[5] the upper plateaus and the desert, the bus-driver of the Trans-Sahara line made fun of me: 'Don't go there,' he too, what had got into them all, and the gusts of sand for hundreds of wind-blown kilometers, progressing and backing in the face of the wind, then the mountains again made up of black peaks and ridges sharp as steel, and after them it took a guide to go out on the endless sea of brown pebbles, screaming with heat, burning with the fires of a thousand mirrors, to the spot on the confines of the white country and the land of the blacks where stands the city of salt. And the money the guide stole from me, ever naïve I had shown it to him, but he left me on the trail—just about here, it so happens—after having struck me: 'Dog, there's the way, the honor's all mine, go ahead, go on, they'll show you,' and they did show me, oh yes, they're like the sun that never stops, except at night, beating sharply and proudly, that is beating me hard at this moment, too hard, with a multitude of lances burst from the ground, oh shelter, yes shelter, under the big rock, before everything gets muddled.

The shade here is good. How can anyone live in the city of salt, in the hollow of that basin full of dazzling heat? On each of the sharp right-angle walls cut out with a pickax and coarsely planed, the gashes left by the pickax bristle with blinding scales, pale scattered sand yellows them somewhat except when the wind dusts the upright walls and terraces, then everything shines with dazzling whiteness under a sky likewise dusted even to its blue rind. I was going blind during those days when the stationary fire would crackle for hours on the surface of the white terraces that all seemed to meet as if, in the remote past, they had all together tackled a mountain of salt, flattened it first, and then had hollowed out streets, the insides of houses and windows directly in the mass, or as if—yes, this is more like it, they had cut out their white, burning hell with a powerful jet of boiling water just to show that they could live where no one ever could, thirty days' travel from any living thing, in this hollow in the middle of the desert where the heat of day prevents any contact among creatures, separates them by a portcullis[6] of invisible flames and of searing crystals, where without transition the cold of night congeals them individually in their rock-salt shells, nocturnal dwellers in a dried-up icefloe, black Eskimoes suddenly shivering in their cubical igloos. Black because they wear long black garments, and the salt that collects even under their nails, that they continue tasting bitterly and swallowing during the sleep of those polar nights, the salt they drink in the water from the only spring in the hollow of a dazzling groove, often spots their dark garments with something like the trail of snails after a rain.

[5] Mountain range in north Africa. [6] Iron grating in the door of a fort.

Rain, O Lord, just one real rain, long and hard, rain from your heaven! Then at last the hideous city, gradually eaten away, would slowly and irresistibly cave in and, utterly melted in a slimy torrent, would carry off its savage inhabitants toward the sands. Just one rain, Lord! But what do I mean, what Lord, they are the lords and masters! They rule over their sterile homes, over their black slaves that they work to death in the mines and each slab of salt that is cut out is worth a man in the region to the south, they pass by, silent, wearing their mourning veils in the mineral whiteness of the streets, and at night, when the whole town looks like a milky phantom, they stoop down and enter the shade of their homes, where the salt walls shine dimly. They sleep with a weightless sleep and, as soon as they wake, they give orders, they strike, they say they are a united people, that their god is the true god, and that one must obey. They are my masters, they are ignorant of pity and, like masters, they want to be alone, to progress alone, to rule alone, because they alone had the daring to build in the salt and the sands a cold torrid city. And I . . .

What a jumble when the heat rises, I'm sweating, they never do, now the shade itself is heating up, I feel the sun on the stone above me, it's striking, striking like a hammer on all the stones and it's the music, the vast music of noon, air and stones vibrating over hundreds of kilometers, *gra*, I hear the silence as I did once before. Yes, it was the same silence, years ago, that greeted me when the guards led me to them, in the sunlight, in the center of the square, whence the concentric terraces rose gradually toward the lid of hard blue sky sitting on the edge of the basin. There I was, thrown on my knees in the hollow of that white shield, my eyes corroded by the swords of salt and fire issuing from all the walls, pale with fatigue, my ear bleeding from the blow given by my guide, and they, tall and black, looked at me without saying a word. The day was at its midcourse. Under the blows of the iron sun the sky resounded at length, a sheet of white-hot tin, it was the same silence, and they stared at me, time passed, they kept on staring at me, and I couldn't face their stares, I panted more and more violently, eventually I wept, and suddenly they turned their backs on me in silence and all together went off in the same direction. On my knees, all I could see, in the red-and-black sandals, was their feet sparkling with salt as they raised the long black gowns, the tip rising somewhat, the heel striking the ground lightly, and when the square was empty I was dragged to the House of the Fetish.

Squatting, as I am today in the shelter of the rock and the fire above my head pierces the rock's thickness, I spent several days within the dark of the House of the Fetish, somewhat higher than the others, surrounded by a wall of salt, but without windows, full of a sparkling night. Several days, and I was given a basin of brackish water and some grain that was thrown before me the way chickens are fed, I picked it up. By day the door remained closed and yet the darkness became less oppressive, as if the irresistible sun managed to flow through the masses of salt. No lamp, but by feeling my way along the walls I touched garlands of dried palms decorating the walls and, at the end, a small door, coarsely fitted, of which I could make out the bolt with my fingertips. Several days, long after—I couldn't count the days or the hours, but my handful of grain had been thrown me some ten times and I had dug out a hole for my excrements that I covered up in vain, the stench of an animal den hung on anyway—long after, yes, the door opened wide and they came in.

One of them came toward me where I was squatting in a corner. I felt the burning salt against my cheek, I smelled the dusty scent of the palms, I watched him approach. He stopped a yard away from me, he stared at me in silence, a signal, and I stood up, he stared at me with his metallic eyes that shone without expression in his brown horse-face, then he raised his hand. Still impassive, he seized me by the lower lip, which he twisted slowly until he tore my flesh and, without letting go, made me turn around and back up to the center of the room, he pulled on my lip to make me fall on my knees there, mad with pain and my mouth bleeding, then he turned away to join the others standing against the walls. They watched me moaning in the unbearable heat of the unbroken daylight that came in the wide-open door, and in that light suddenly appeared the Sorcerer with his raffia hair, his chest covered with a breastplate of pearls, his legs bare under a straw skirt, wearing a mask of reeds and wire with two square openings for the eyes. He was followed by musicians and women wearing heavy motley gowns that revealed nothing of their bodies. They danced in front of the door at the end, but a coarse, scarcely rhythmical dance, they just barely moved, and finally the Sorcerer opened the little door behind me, the masters did not stir, they were watching me, I turned around and saw the Fetish, his double ax-head, his iron nose twisted like a snake.

I was carried before him, to the foot of the pedestal, I was made to drink a black, bitter, bitter water, and at once my head began to burn, I was laughing, that's the offense, I have been offended. They undressed me, shaved my head and body, washed me in oil, beat my face with cords dipped in water and salt, and I laughed and turned my head away, but each time two women would take me by the ears and offer my face to the Sorcerer's blows while I could see only his square eyes, I was still laughing, covered with blood. They stopped, no one spoke but me, the jumble was beginning in my head, then they lifted me up and forced me to raise my eyes toward the Fetish, I had ceased laughing. I knew that I was now consecrated to him to serve him, adore him, no, I was not laughing any more, fear and pain stifled me. And there, in that white house, between those walls that the sun was assiduously burning on the outside, my face taut, my memory exhausted, yes, I tried to pray to the Fetish, he was all there was and even his horrible face was less horrible than the rest of the world. Then it was that my ankles were tied with a cord that permitted just one step, they danced again, but this time in front of the Fetish, the masters went out one by one.

The door once closed behind them, the music again, and the Sorcerer lighted a bark fire around which he pranced, his long silhouette broke on the angles of the white walls, fluttered on the flat surfaces, filled the room with dancing shadows. He traced a rectangle in a corner to which the women dragged me, I felt their dry and gentle hands, they set before me a bowl of water and a little pile of grain and pointed to the Fetish, I grasped that I was to keep my eyes fixed on him. Then the Sorcerer called them one after the other over to the fire, he beat some of them who moaned and who then went and prostrated themselves before the Fetish my god, while the Sorcerer kept on dancing and he made them all leave the room until only one was left, quite young, squatting near the musicians and not yet beaten. He held her by a shock of hair which he kept twisting around his wrist, she dropped backward with eyes popping until she finally fell on her back. Dropping her, the Sorcerer screamed, the musicians turned to the wall, while behind the square-eyed mask the scream rose to an impossible pitch, and the woman rolled on the ground in a sort of fit and, at last on all fours, her head hidden in her locked arms, she too screamed, but with a hollow, muffled sound, and in this position, without ceasing to scream and to look at the Fetish, the Sorcerer took her nimbly and nastily, without the woman's face being visible, for it was covered with the heavy folds of her garment. And, wild as a result of the solitude, *I* screamed too, yes, howled with fright toward the Fetish until a kick hurled me against the wall, biting the salt as I am biting this rock today with my tongueless mouth, while waiting for the man I must kill.

Now the sun has gone a little beyond the middle of the sky. Through the breaks in the rock I can see the hole it makes in the white-hot metal of the sky, a mouth voluble as mine, constantly vomiting rivers of flame over the colorless desert. On the trail in front of me, nothing, no cloud of dust on the horizon, behind me they must be looking for me, no, not yet, it's only in the late afternoon that they opened the door and I could go out a little, after having spent the day cleaning the House of the Fetish, set out fresh offerings, and in the evening the ceremony would begin, in which I was sometimes beaten, at others not, but always I served the Fetish, the Fetish whose image is engraved in iron in my memory and now in my hope also. Never had a god so possessed or enslaved me, my whole life day and night was devoted to him, and pain and the absence of pain, wasn't that joy, were due him and even, yes, desire, as a result of being present, almost every day, at that impersonal and nasty act which I heard without seeing it inasmuch as I now had to face the wall or else be beaten. But, my face up against the salt, obsessed by the bestial shadows moving on the wall, I listened to the long scream, my throat was dry, a burning sexless desire squeezed my temples and my belly as in a vise. Thus the days followed one another, I barely distinguished them as if they had liquefied in the torrid heat and the treacherous reverberation from the walls of salt, time had become merely a vague lapping of waves in which there would burst out, at regular intervals, screams of pain or possession, a long ageless day in which the Fetish ruled as this fierce sun does over my house of rocks, and now, as I did then, I weep with unhappiness and longing, a wicked hope consumes me, I want to betray, I lick the barrel of my gun and its soul inside, its soul, only guns have souls—oh, yes! the day they cut out my tongue, I learned to adore the immortal soul of hatred!

What a jumble, what a rage, *gra gra,* drunk with heat and wrath, lying prostrate on my gun. Who's panting here? I can't endure this endless heat, this waiting, I must kill him. Not a bird, not a blade of grass, stone, an arid desire, their screams, this tongue within me talking, and since they mutilated me, the long, flat, deserted suffering deprived even of the water of night, the night of which I would dream, when locked in with the god, in my den of salt. Night alone with its cool stars and dark fountains could save me, carry me off at last from the wicked gods of mankind, but ever locked up I could not contemplate it. If the newcomer tarries more, I shall see it at least rise from the desert and sweep over the sky, a cold golden vine that will hang from the dark zenith and from which I can drink at length, moisten this black dried hole that no muscle of live flexible flesh revives now, forget at last that day when madness took away my tongue.

How hot it was, really hot, the salt was melting or so it seemed to me, the air was corroding my eyes, and the Sorcerer came in without his mask. Almost naked under grayish tatters, a new woman followed him and her face, covered with a tattoo reproducing the mask of the Fetish, expressed only an idol's ugly stupor. The only thing alive about her was her thin flat body that flopped at the foot of the god when the Sorcerer opened the door of the niche. Then he went out without looking at me, the heat rose, I didn't stir, the Fetish looked at me over that motionless body whose muscles stirred gently and the woman's idol-face didn't change when I approached. Only her eyes enlarged as she stared at me, my feet touched hers, the heat then began to shriek, and the idol, without a word, still staring at me with her dilated eyes, gradually slipped onto her back, slowly drew her legs up and raised them as she gently spread her knees. But, immediately afterward, *gra,* the Sorcerer was lying in wait for me, they all entered and tore me from the woman, beat me dreadfully on the sinful place, what sin, I'm laughing, where is it and where is virtue, they clapped me against a wall, a hand of steel gripped my jaws, another opened my mouth, pulled on my tongue until it bled, was it I screaming with that bestial scream, a cool cutting caress, yes cool at last, went over my tongue. When I came to, I was alone in the night, glued to the wall, covered with hardened blood, a gag of strange-smelling dry grasses filled my mouth, it had stopped bleeding, but it was vacant and in that absence the only living thing was a tormenting pain. I wanted to rise, I fell back, happy, desperately happy to die at last, death too is cool and its shadow hides no god.

I did not die, a new feeling of hatred stood up one day, at the same time I did, walked toward the door of the niche, opened it, closed it behind me, I hated my people, the Fetish was there and from the depth of the hole in which I was I did more than pray to him, I believed in him and denied all I had believed up to then. Hail! he was strength and power, he could be destroyed but not converted, he stared over my head with his empty, rusty eyes. Hail! he was the master, the only lord, whose indisputable attribute was malice, there are no good masters. For the first time, as a result of offenses, my whole body crying out a single pain, I surrendered to him and approved his maleficent order, I adored in him the evil principle of the world. A prisoner of his kingdom—the sterile city carved out of a mountain of salt, divorced from nature, deprived of those rare and fleeting flowerings of the desert, preserved from those strokes of chance or marks of affection such as an unexpected cloud or a brief violent downpour that are familiar even to the sun or the sands, the city of order in short, right angles, square rooms, rigid men—I freely became its tortured, hate-filled citizen, I repudiated the long history that had been taught me. I had been misled, solely the reign of malice was devoid of defects, I had been misled, truth is square, heavy, thick, it does not admit distinctions, good is an idle dream, an intention constantly postponed and pursued with exhausting effort, a limit never reached, its reign is impossible. Only evil can reach its limits and reign absolutely, it must be served to establish its visible kingdom, then we shall see, but what does 'then' mean, only evil is present, down with Europe, reason, honor, and the cross. Yes, I was to be converted to the religion of my masters, yes indeed, I was a slave, but if I too become vicious I cease to be a slave, despite my shackled feet and my mute mouth. Oh, this heat is driving me crazy, the desert cries out everywhere under the unbearable light, and he, the Lord of kindness, whose very name revolts me, I disown him, for I know him now. He dreamed and wanted to lie, his tongue was cut out so that his word would no longer be able to deceive the world, he was pierced with nails even in his head, his poor head, like mine now, what a jumble, how weak I am, and the earth didn't tremble, I am sure, it was not a righteous man they had killed, I refuse to believe it, there are no righteous men but only evil masters who bring about the reign of relentless truth. Yes, the Fetish alone has power, he is the sole god of this world, hatred is his commandment, the source of all life, the cool water, cool like mint that chills the mouth and burns the stomach.

Then it was that I changed, they realized it, I would kiss their hands when I met them, I was on their side, never wearying of admiring them, I trusted them, I hoped they would mutilate my people as they had mutilated me. And when I learned that the missionary was to come, I knew what I was to do. That day like all the others, the same blinding daylight that had been going on so long! Late in the afternoon a guard was suddenly seen running along the edge of the basin, and, a few minutes later, I was dragged to the House of the Fetish and the door closed. One of them held me on the ground in the dark, under threat of his cross-shaped sword, and the silence lasted for a long time until a strange sound filled the ordinarily peaceful town, voices that it took me some time to recognize because they were speaking my language, but as soon as they rang out the point of the sword was lowered toward my eyes, my guard stared at me in silence. Then two voices came closer and I can still hear them, one asking why that house was guarded and whether they should break in the door, Lieutenant, the other said: 'No' sharply, then added, after a moment, that an agreement had been reached, that the town accepted a garrison of twenty men on condition that they would camp outside the walls and respect the customs. The private laughed, 'They're knuckling under,' but the officer didn't know, for the first time in any case they were willing to receive someone to take care of the children and that would be the chaplain, later on they would see about the territory. The other said they would cut off the chaplain's you know what if the soldiers were not there. 'Oh, no!' the officer answered. 'In fact, Father Beffort will come before the garrison; he'll be here in two days.' That was all I heard, motionless, lying under the sword, I was in pain, a wheel of needles and knives was whirling in me. They were crazy, they were crazy, they were allowing a hand to be laid on the city, on their invincible power, on the true god, and the fellow who was to come would not have his tongue cut out, he would show off his insolent goodness without paying for it, without enduring any offense. The reign of evil would be postponed, there would be doubt again, again time would be wasted dreaming of the impossible good, wearing oneself out in fruitless efforts instead of hastening the realization of the only possible kingdom and I looked at the sword threatening me, O sole power to rule over the world! O power, and the city gradually emptied of its sounds, the door finally opened, I remained alone, burned and bitter, with the Fetish, and I swore to him to save my new faith, my true masters, my despotic God, to betray well, whatever it might cost me.

Gra, the heat is abating a little, the stone has ceased to vibrate, I can go out of my hole, watch the desert gradually take on yellow and ocher tints that will soon be mauve. Last night I waited until they were asleep, I had blocked the lock on the door, I went out with the same step as usual, measured by the cord, I knew the streets, I knew where to get the old rifle, what gate wasn't guarded, and I reached here just as the night was beginning to fade around a handful of stars while the desert was getting a little darker. And now it seems days and days that I have been crouching in these rocks. Soon, soon, I hope he comes soon! In a moment they'll begin to look for me, they'll speed over the trails in all directions, they won't know that I left for them and to serve them better, my legs are weak, drunk with hunger and hate. Oh! over there, *gra,* at the end of the trail, two camels are growing bigger, ambling along, already multiplied by short shadows, they are running with that lively and dreamy gait they always have. Here they are, here at last!

Quick, the rifle, and I load it quickly. O Fetish, my god over yonder, may your power be preserved, may the offense be multiplied, may hate rule pitilessly over a world of the damned, may the wicked forever be masters, may the kingdom come, where in a single city of salt and iron black tyrants will enslave and possess without pity! And now, *gra gra,* fire on pity, fire on impotence and its charity, fire on all that postpones the coming of evil, fire twice, and there they are toppling over, falling, and the camels flee toward the horizon, where a geyser of black birds has just risen in the unchanged sky. I laugh, I laugh, the fellow is writhing in his detested habit, he is raising his head a little, he sees me—me his all-powerful shackled master, why does he smile at me, I'll crush that smile! How pleasant is the sound of a rifle butt on the face of goodness, today, today at last, all is consummated and everywhere in the desert, even hours away from here, jackals sniff the nonexistent wind, then set out in a patient trot toward the feast of carrion awaiting them. Victory! I raise my arms to a heaven moved to pity, a lavender shadow is just barely suggested on the opposite side, O nights of Europe, home, childhood, why must I weep in the moment of triumph?

He stirred, no the sound comes from somewhere else, and from the other direction here they come rushing like a flight of dark birds, my masters, who fall upon me, seize me, ah yes! strike, they fear their city sacked and howling, they fear the avenging soldiers I called forth, and this is only right, upon the sacred city. Defend yourselves now, strike! strike me first, you possess the truth! O my masters, they will then conquer the soldiers, they'll conquer the word and love, they'll spread over the deserts, cross the seas, fill the light of Europe with their black veils—strike the belly, yes, strike the eyes—sow their salt on the continent, all vegetation, all youth will die out, and dumb crowds with shackled feet will plod beside me in the world-wide desert under the cruel sun of the true faith, I'll not be alone. Ah! the pain, the pain they cause me, their rage is good and on this cross-shaped war-saddle where they are now quartering me, pity! I'm laughing, I love the blow that nails me down crucified.

How silent the desert is! Already night and I am alone, I'm thirsty. Still waiting, where is the city, those sounds in the distance, and the soldiers perhaps the victors, no, it can't be, even if the soldiers are victorious, they're not wicked enough, they won't be able to rule, they'll still say one must become better, and still millions of men between evil and good, torn, bewildered, O Fetish, why hast thou forsaken me? All is over, I'm thirsty, my body is burning, a darker night fills my eyes.

This long, this long dream, I'm awaking, no, I'm going to die, dawn is breaking, the first light, daylight for the living, and for me the inexorable sun, the flies. Who is speaking, no one, the sky is not opening up, no, no, God doesn't speak in the desert, yet whence comes that voice saying: 'If you consent to die for hate and power, who will forgive us?' Is it another tongue in me or still that other fellow refusing to die, at my feet, and repeating: 'Courage! courage! courage!'? Ah! supposing I were wrong again! Once fraternal men, sole recourse, O solitude, forsake me not! Here, here who are you, torn, with bleeding mouth, is it you, Sorcerer, the soldiers defeated you, the salt is burning over there, it's you my beloved master! Cast off that hate-ridden face, be good now, we were mistaken, we'll begin all over again, we'll rebuild the city of mercy, I want to go back home. Yes, help me, that's right, give me your hand. . . ."

A handful of salt fills the mouth of the garrulous slave.

Ralph Ellison

(1914–   )

The reputation of Ralph Ellison rests upon a single novel, but that novel, Invisible Man, *has taken its place among the masterpieces of twentieth-century world fiction. A complex, ambiguous work,* Invisible Man *examines the problem of growing up black in America from the perspective of cosmopolitan literary modernism. Ellison dipped his bucket in two wells: black life and culture ("the literary extension of the blues," one critic called the novel) and modern European art (the crucial literary influence upon him, by his own testimony, is T. S. Eliot's* The Waste Land*). Such evenhandedness has not always won the book friends, and a younger generation of black writers have attacked it sharply as—in the words of one of them—the work of "an Establishment writer, an Uncle Tom, an attacker of the sociological formulations of the civil rights movement." These hostile critics accuse Ellison of subjecting the vitality of black life to the paralyzing irony and nihilism of a decadent white Western art. But for other readers, both black and white, American and international, for whom the house of literature, including black literature, has many rooms, the novel remains, in one critic's words, "one of the best guides we have to a uniquely American reality."*

Ellison's background, which brought him into contact with a number of crucial areas of American culture, both black and white, helps to explain his artistic position. Born in Oklahoma City in 1914 to parents recently moved there from South Carolina, he grew up in a racial atmosphere somewhat more open than either the Deep South or the large urban centers. His father died when Ellison was three, and he was reared by a strong, intelligent mother who supported the family by working as a domestic servant but also canvassed for the Socialist party and was jailed several times for challenging local racial restrictions on housing. His mother encouraged his reading—she had named him after Ralph Waldo Emerson, hoping he would become a writer—and he was a good student in the segregated schools he attended. Oklahoma City was a flourishing center for jazz when Ellison was growing up; he developed a deep love for music and became friends with Jimmy Rushing, Hot Lips Paige, and Lester Young and the Blue Devils Orchestra, the members of which later formed the nucleus of the Count Basie Orchestra. Ellison himself became a good trumpet player and, for a time, considered a jazz career. In 1933, he enrolled in Tuskegee Institute in Alabama. After studying music there for three years, he left, without a degree, to study sculpture in New York.

In New York, Ellison met some of the writers who had contributed to the Harlem Renaissance of the 1920s, notably Langston Hughes, who encouraged him to write. He also met Richard Wright, who had recently arrived from Chicago and who also encouraged Ellison, publishing his first work in Wright's own magazine New Challenge *in 1937. In the following years, Ellison published a number of short stories and non-fiction pieces in various journals, including* The New Masses *and the* Antioch Review; *he also edited the* Negro Quarterly *for a few months in 1942. In 1943, Ellison tried to enlist as a trumpet player in the U.S. Navy band but was rejected and joined the Merchant Marine instead. After the war, aided by a writer's fellowship, he settled down to work on the novel which became* Invisible Man, *published in 1952. The book was an extraordinary success, winning the National Book Award in 1953 and being named in a poll of critics, conducted by* Book Week *in 1965, as "the most distinguished novel" of the past twenty years.*

In the wake of the success of his first novel, Ellison accepted a series of awards and appointments. He made a lecture tour of Germany in 1954 and spent two years in Rome, from 1955 to 1957, as a fellow of the American Academy of Arts and Letters. He held a series of distinguished visiting appointments at the University of Chicago, Rutgers, and Yale and, in 1970, became Albert Schweitzer Professor in Humanities at New York University. Shadow and Act, *a collection of essays on literature, folklore, and jazz, was published in 1964. He began work on a second novel in 1956; it has not yet appeared, although a legend has grown up around it comparable to that which gathered around Katherine Anne Porter's* Ship of Fools. *Ellison has done a number of readings from the manuscript, and brief sections of it have been published from time to time. A recent interviewer reports that the manuscript is now several thousand pages long and may eventually be published as a sequence of three novels.*

"Battle Royal" was published as a short story in 1947, five years before Invisible Man, *of which it forms the first chapter. Complete in itself, it nevertheless gains in richness by being considered in the context of the whole novel.* Invisible Man *is a "frame narrative" in which the entire story is told by a nameless narrator holed up, as we are told in a short prologue, in a secret basement room in New York where he keeps 1,369 electric lights blazing night and day to remind himself that he is visible. The story is a maturation narrative which takes the protagonist from the "battle*

royal" experience through the process of growing up, at a southern Negro college and then in New York, where he becomes first a member of the Brotherhood (the Communist party) and then "Rinehart," a Harlem gambler who is finally hunted by both blacks and whites in a nightmarish race riot. The Conradian device of the frame throws the emphasis of the story upon memory and perception; the action is presented in the restless, twisting, and mercurial language of the narrator, and as he remembers his experiences the incidents sometimes take on a surrealist quality. The speaker's quest for his own identity has led him through a series of roles available to blacks in America, none of which proves to be adequate. In the short, framing epilogue, however, he prepares to leave his underground: "Even hibernations can be overdone, come to think of it. Perhaps that's my greatest social crime, I've overstayed my hibernation, since there's a possibility that even an invisible man has a socially responsible role to play."

"Battle Royal," like the rest of Invisible Man, *thus presents a double perception of its action, that of the naive boy and that of the disillusioned older man looking back upon himself when young. The action is rooted in reality, but as it is filtered through memory it also takes on a Kafkaesque quality of symbolic nightmare; the elements in the brutal, racist men's smoker—moving from sex to violence to money to education—become a compressed allegory of the strategies of white oppression. And the grandfather's dream message at the end not only provides an interpretation of the fight but anticipates the issues of the rest of the novel: "To Whom It May Concern. Keep This Nigger-Boy Running."*

FURTHER READING *(prepared by W. J. R.):* Robert G. O'Meally's *The Craft of Ralph Ellison,* 1980, provides biographical information, with two chapters discussing the author's life and career. O'Meally also discusses *Invisible Man* and its effective use of surrealism. Barbara Christian's "Ralph Ellison: A Critical Study," in *Black Expression,* ed. Addison Gayle, Jr., 1970, discusses myth-making in *Invisible Man* and carefully charts the protagonist's movement from a fragile sense of self to invisibility. Another fine essay is Robert Bone's "Ralph Ellison and the Uses of Imagination," in *Anger, and Beyond,* ed. Herbert Hill, 1966. Bone discusses such important elements in Wright's fiction as jazz and politics. Bone's essay is one of the ten collected in *Twentieth Century Interpretations of "Invisible Man",* ed. John M. Reilly, 1970. A chronology of Ellison's life and a bibliography of works by and about him are included here. Additional essays (with some overlap from *Twentieth Century Interpretations*) constitute *The Merrill Studies in "Invisible Man,"* compiled by Ronald Gottesman, 1971. Susan L. Blake's "Ritual and Ritualization: Black Folklore in the Works of Ralph Ellison," *PMLA,* 94 (1979), 121–136, explores folklore as a means of reconciling the unique and universal aspects of black culture and experience. Blake uses *Invisible Man* and short stories in making her convincing argument.

BATTLE ROYAL

It goes a long way back, some twenty years. All my life I had been looking for something, and everywhere I turned someone tried to tell me what it was. I accepted their answers too, though they were often in contradiction and even self-contradictory. I was naïve. I was looking for myself and asking everyone except myself questions which I, and only I, could answer. It took me a long time and much painful boomeranging of my expectations to achieve a realization everyone else appears to have been born with: That I am nobody but myself. But first I had to discover that I am an invisible man!

And yet I am no freak of nature, nor of history. I was in the cards, other things having been equal (or unequal) eighty-five years ago. I am not ashamed of my grandparents for having been slaves. I am only ashamed of myself for having at one time been ashamed. About eighty-five years ago they were told that they were free, united with others of our country in everything pertaining to the common good, and, in everything social, separate like the fingers of the hand.[1] And they believed it. They exulted in it. They stayed in their place, worked hard, and brought up my father to do the same. But my grandfather is the one. He was an odd old guy, my grandfather, and I am told I take after him. It was he who caused the trouble. On his deathbed he called my father to him and said, "Son, after I'm gone I want you to keep up the good fight. I never told you, but our life is a war and I have been a *traitor* all my born days, a *spy* in the enemy's country ever since I give up my gun back in the Reconstruction.[2] Live with your head in the lion's mouth. I want you to overcome 'em with yeses, undermine 'em with grins, agree 'em to death and destruction, let 'em swoller you till they vomit or bust wide open." They thought the old man had gone out of his mind. He had been the meekest of men. The younger children were rushed from the room, the shades drawn and the flame of the lamp turned so low that it sputtered on the wick like the old man's breathing. "Learn it to the younguns," he whispered fiercely; then he died.

But my folks were more alarmed over his last words than over his dying. It was as though he had not died at all, his words caused so much anxiety. I was warned emphatically to forget what he had said and, indeed, this is the first time it has been mentioned outside the family circle. It had a tremendous effect upon me, however. I could never be sure of what he meant. Grandfather had been a quiet old man who never made any trouble, yet on his deathbed he had called himself a traitor and a spy, and he had spoken of his meekness as a dangerous activity. It became a constant puzzle which lay unanswered in the back of my mind. And whenever things went well for me I remembered my grandfather and felt guilty and uncomfortable. It was as though I was carrying out his advice in spite of myself. And to make it worse, everyone loved me for it. I was praised by the most lily-white men of the town. I was considered an example of desirable conduct—just as my grandfather had been. And what puzzled me was that the old man had defined it as *treachery*. When I was praised for my conduct I felt that in some way I was doing something that was really against the wishes of the white folks, that if they had understood they would have desired me to act just the opposite, that I should have been sulky and mean, and that that

[1] Booker T. Washingon, in his Atlanta Exposition Address of 1895, said, "In all things that are purely social we can be as separate as the fingers, yet one as the hand in all things essential to mutual progress." Washington (1858–1915), a black educator and president of Tuskegee Institute, a black school and later college in Tuskegee, Alabama, counseled his race to accept segregation and manual jobs. His views have been sharply criticized by subsequent black leaders; W. E. B. Dubois called Washington's Atlanta speech, delivered before a white audience, "the Atlanta Compromise."

[2] Period of social chaos and martial law in the South following the Civil War.

really would have been what they wanted, even though they were fooled and thought they wanted me to act as I did. It made me afraid that some day they would look upon me as a traitor and I would be lost. Still I was more afraid to act any other way because they didn't like that at all. The old man's words were like a curse. On my graduation day I delivered an oration in which I showed that humility was the secret, indeed, the very essence of progress. (Not that I believed this—how could I, remembering my grandfather?—I only believed that it worked.) It was a great success. Everyone praised me and I was invited to give the speech at a gathering of the town's leading white citizens. It was a triumph for our whole community.

It was in the main ballroom of the leading hotel. When I got there I discovered that it was on the occasion of a smoker, and I was told that since I was to be there anyway I might as well take part in the battle royal to be fought by some of my schoolmates as part of the entertainment. The battle royal came first.

All of the town's big shots were there in their tuxedoes, wolfing down the buffet foods, drinking beer and whiskey and smoking black cigars. It was a large room with a high ceiling. Chairs were arranged in neat rows around three sides of a portable boxing ring. The fourth side was clear, revealing a gleaming space of polished floor. I had some misgivings over the battle royal, by the way. Not from a distaste for fighting, but because I didn't care too much for the other fellows who were to take part. They were tough guys who seemed to have no grandfather's curse worrying their minds. No one could mistake their toughness. And besides, I suspected that fighting a battle royal might detract from the dignity of my speech. In those pre-invisible days I visualized myself as a potential Booker T. Washington. But the other fellows didn't care too much for me either, and there were nine of them. I felt superior to them in my way, and I didn't like the manner in which we were all crowded together into the servants' elevator. Nor did they like my being there. In fact, as the warmly lighted floors flashed past the elevator we had words over the fact that I, by taking part in the fight, had knocked one of their friends out of a night's work.

We were led out of the elevator through a rococo hall into an anteroom and told to get into our fighting togs. Each of us was issued a pair of boxing gloves and ushered out into the big mirrored hall, which we entered looking cautiously about us and whispering, lest we might accidentally be heard above the noise of the room. It was foggy with cigar smoke. And already the whiskey was taking effect. I was shocked to see some of the most important men of the town quite tipsy. They were all there—bankers, lawyers, judges, doctors, fire chiefs, teachers, merchants. Even one of the more fashionable pastors. Something we could not see was going on up front. A clarinet was vibrating sensuously and the men were standing up and moving eagerly forward. We were a small tight group, clustered together, our bare upper bodies touching and shining with anticipatory sweat; while up front the big shots were becoming increasingly excited over something we still could not see. Suddenly I heard the school superintendent, who had told me to come, yell, "Bring up the shines, gentlemen! Bring up the little shines!"

We were rushed up to the front of the ballroom, where it smelled even more strongly of tobacco and whiskey. Then we were pushed into place. I almost wet my pants. A sea of faces, some hostile, some amused, ringed around us, and in the center, facing us, stood a magnificent blonde—stark naked. There was dead silence. I felt a blast of cold air chill me. I tried to back away, but they were behind me and around me. Some of the boys stood with lowered heads, trembling. I felt a wave of irrational guilt and fear. My teeth chattered, my skin turned to goose flesh, my knees knocked. Yet I was strongly attracted and looked in spite of myself. Had the price of looking been blindness, I would have looked. The hair was yellow like that of a circus kewpie doll, the face heavily powdered and rouged, as though to form an abstract mask, the eyes hollow and smeared a cool blue, the color of a baboon's butt. I felt a desire to spit upon her as my eyes brushed slowly over her body. Her breasts were firm and round as the domes of East Indian temples, and I stood so close as to see the fine skin texture and beads of pearly perspiration glistening like dew around the pink and erected buds of her nipples. I wanted at one and the same time to run from the room, to sink through the floor, or go to her and cover her from my eyes and the eyes of the others with my body; to feel the soft thighs, to caress her and destroy her, to love her and murder her, to hide from her, and yet to stroke where below the small American flag tattooed upon her belly her thighs formed a capital V. I had a notion that of all in the room she saw only me with her impersonal eyes.

And then she began to dance, a slow sensuous movement; the smoke of a hundred cigars clinging to her like the thinnest of veils. She seemed like a fair bird-girl girdled in veils calling to me from the angry surface of some gray and threatening sea. I was transported. Then I became aware of the clarinet playing and the big shots yelling at us. Some threatened us if we looked and others if we did not. On my right I saw one boy faint. And now a man grabbed a silver pitcher from a table and stepped close as he dashed ice water upon him and stood him up and forced two of us to support him as his head hung and moans issued from his thick bluish lips. Another boy began to plead to go home. He was the largest of the group, wearing dark red fighting trunks much too small to conceal the erection which projected from him as though in answer to the insinuating low-registered moaning of the clarinet. He tried to hide himself with his boxing gloves.

And all the while the blonde continued dancing, smiling faintly at the big shots who watched her with fascination, and faintly smiling at our fear. I noticed a certain merchant who followed her hungrily, his lips loose and drooling. He was a large man who wore diamond studs in a shirtfront which swelled with the ample paunch underneath, and each time the blonde swayed her undulating hips he ran his hand through the thin hair of his bald head and, with his arms upheld, his posture clumsy like that of an intoxicated panda, wound his belly in a slow and obscene grind. This creature was completely hypnotized. The music had quickened. As the dancer flung herself about with a detached expression on her face, the men began reaching out to touch her. I could see their beefy fingers sink into the soft flesh. Some of the others tried to stop them and she began to move around the floor in graceful circles, as they gave chase, slipping and sliding over the polished floor. It was mad. Chairs went crashing, drinks were spilt, as they ran laughing and howling after her. They caught her just as she reached a door, raised her from the floor, and tossed her as college boys are tossed at a hazing, and above her red, fixed-smiling lips I saw the terror and disgust in her eyes, almost like my own terror and that which I saw in some of the other boys. As I watched, they tossed her twice and her soft breasts seemed to flatten against the air and her legs flung wildly as she spun. Some of the more sober ones helped her to escape. And I started off the floor, heading for the anteroom with the rest of the boys.

Some were still crying and in hysteria. But as we tried to leave we were stopped and ordered to get into the ring. There was nothing to do but what we were told. All ten of us climbed under the ropes and allowed ourselves to be blindfolded with broad bands of white cloth. One of the men seemed to feel a bit sympathetic and tried to cheer us up as we stood with our backs against the ropes. Some of us tried to grin. "See that boy over there?" one of the men said. "I want you to run across at the bell and give it to him right in the belly. If you don't get him, I'm going to get you. I don't like his looks." Each of us was told the same. The blindfolds were put on. Yet even then I had been going over my speech. In my mind each word was as bright as flame. I felt the cloth pressed into place, and frowned so that it would be loosened when I relaxed.

But now I felt a sudden fit of blind terror. I was unused to darkness. It was as though I had suddenly found myself in a dark room filled with poisonous cottonmouths. I could hear the bleary voices yelling insistently for the battle royal to begin.

"Get going in there!"

"Let me at that big nigger!"

I strained to pick up the school superintendent's voice, as though to squeeze some security out of that slightly more familiar sound.

"Let me at those black sonsabitches!" someone yelled.

"No, Jackson, no!" another voice yelled. "Here, somebody, help me hold Jack."

"I want to get at that ginger-colored nigger. Tear him limb from limb," the first voice yelled.

I stood against the ropes trembling. For in those days I was what they called ginger-colored, and he sounded as though he might crunch me between his teeth like a crisp ginger cookie.

Quite a struggle was going on. Chairs were being kicked about and I could hear voices grunting as with a terrific effort. I wanted to see, to see more desperately than ever before. But the blindfold was tight as a thick skin-puckering scab and when I raised my gloved hands to push the layers of white aside a voice yelled, "Oh, no, you don't, black bastard! Leave that alone!"

"Ring the bell before Jackson kills him a coon!" someone boomed in the sudden silence. And I heard the bell clang and the sound of the feet scuffling forward.

A glove smacked against my head. I pivoted, striking out stiffly as someone went past, and felt the jar ripple along the length of my arm to my shoulder. Then it seemed as though all nine of the boys had turned upon me at once. Blows pounded me from all sides while I struck out as best I could. So many blows landed upon me that I wondered if I were not the only blindfolded fighter in the ring, or if the man called Jackson hadn't succeeded in getting me after all.

Blindfolded, I could no longer control my motions. I had no dignity. I stumbled about like a baby or a drunken man. The smoke had become thicker and with each new blow it seemed to sear and further restrict my lungs. My saliva became like hot bitter glue. A glove connected with my head, filling my mouth with warm blood. It was everywhere. I could not tell if the moisture I felt upon my body was sweat or blood. A blow landed hard against the nape of my neck. I felt myself going over, my head hitting the floor. Streaks of blue light filled the black world behind the blindfold. I lay prone, pretending that I was knocked out, but felt myself seized by hands and yanked to my feet. "Get going, black boy! Mix it up!" My arms were like lead, my head smarting from blows. I managed to feel my way to the ropes and held on, trying to catch my breath. A glove landed in my midsection and I went over again, feeling as though the smoke had become a knife jabbed into my guts. Pushed this way and that by the legs milling around me, I finally pulled erect and discovered that I could see the black, sweat-washed forms weaving in the smoky-blue atmosphere like drunken dancers weaving to the rapid drum-like thuds of blows.

Everyone fought hysterically. It was complete anarchy. Everybody fought everybody else. No group fought together for long. Two, three, four, fought one, then turned to fight each other, were themselves attacked. Blows landed below the belt and in the kidney, with the gloves open as well as closed, and with my eye partly opened now there was not so much terror. I moved carefully, avoiding blows, although not too many to attract attention, fighting from group to group. The boys groped about like blind, cautious crabs crouching to protect their mid-sections, their heads pulled in short against their shoulders, their arms stretched nervously before them, with their fists testing the smoke-filled air like the knobbed feelers of hypersensitive snails. In one corner I glimpsed a boy violently punching the air and heard him scream in pain as he smashed his hand against a ring post. For a second I saw him bent over holding his hand, then going down as a blow caught his unprotected head. I played one group against the other, slipping in and throwing a punch then stepping out of range while pushing the others into the melee to take the blows blindly aimed at me. The smoke was agonizing and there were no rounds, no bells at three minute intervals to relieve our exhaustion. The room spun round me, a swirl of lights, smoke, sweating bodies surrounded by tense white faces. I bled from both nose and mouth, the blood spattering upon my chest.

The men kept yelling, "Slug him, black boy! Knock his guts out!"

"Uppercut him! Kill him! Kill that big boy!"

Taking a fake fall, I saw a boy going down heavily beside me as though we were felled by a single blow, saw a sneaker-clad foot shoot into his groin as the two who had knocked him down stumbled upon him. I rolled out of range, feeling a twinge of nausea.

The harder we fought the more threatening the men became. And yet, I had begun to worry about my speech again. How would it go? Would they recognize my ability? What would they give me?

I was fighting automatically when suddenly I noticed that one after another of the boys was leaving the ring. I was surprised, filled with panic, as though I had been left alone with an unknown danger. Then I understood. The boys had arranged it among themselves. It was the custom for the two men left in the ring to slug it out for the winner's prize. I discovered this too late. When the bell sounded two men in tuxedoes leaped into the ring and removed the blindfold. I found myself facing Tatlock, the biggest of the gang. I felt sick at my stomach. Hardly had the bell stopped ringing in my ears than it clanged again and I saw him moving swiftly toward me. Thinking of nothing else to do I hit him smash on the nose. He kept coming, bringing the rank sharp violence of stale sweat. His face was a black blank of a face, only his eyes alive—with hate of me and aglow with a feverish terror from what had happened to us all. I became anxious. I wanted to deliver my speech and he came at me as though he meant to beat it out of me. I smashed him again and again, taking his blows as they came. Then on a sudden impulse I struck him lightly and as we clinched, I whispered, "Fake like I knocked you out, you can have the prize."

"I'll break your behind," he whispered hoarsely.

"For *them?*"

"For *me,* sonofabitch!"

They were yelling for us to break it up and Tatlock spun me half around with a blow, and as a joggled camera sweeps in a reeling scene, I saw the howling red faces crouching tense beneath the cloud of blue-gray smoke. For a moment the world wavered, unraveled, flowed, then my head cleared and Tatlock bounced before me. That fluttering shadow before my eyes was his jabbing left hand. Then falling forward, my head against his damp shoulder, I whispered,

"I'll make it five dollars more."

"Go to hell!"

But his muscles relaxed a trifle beneath my pressure and I breathed, "Seven?"

"Give it to your ma," he said, ripping me beneath the heart.

And while I still held him I butted him and moved away. I felt myself bombarded with punches. I fought back with hopeless desperation. I wanted to deliver my speech more than anything else in the world, because I felt that only these men could judge truly my ability, and now this stupid clown was ruining my chances. I began fighting carefully now, moving in to punch him and out again with my greater speed. A lucky blow to his chin and I had him going too—until I heard a loud voice yell, "I got my money on the big boy."

Hearing this, I almost dropped my guard. I was confused: Should I try to win against the voice out there? Would not this go against my speech, and was not this a moment for humility, for nonresistance? A blow to my head as I danced about sent my right eye popping like a jack-in-the-box and settled my dilemma. The room went red as I fell. It was a dream fall, my body languid and fastidious as to where to land, until the floor became impatient and smashed up to meet me. A moment later I came to. An hypnotic voice said FIVE emphatically. And I lay there, hazily watching a dark red spot of my own blood shaping itself into a butterfly, glistening and soaking into the soiled gray world of the canvas.

When the voice drawled TEN I was lifted up and dragged to a chair. I sat dazed. My eye pained and swelled with each throb of my pounding heart and I wondered if now I would be allowed to speak. I was wringing wet, my mouth still bleeding. We were grouped along the wall now. The other boys ignored me as they congratulated Tatlock and speculated as to how much they would be paid. One boy whimpered over his smashed hand. Looking up front, I saw attendants in white jackets rolling the portable ring away and placing a small square rug in the vacant space surrounded by chairs. Perhaps, I thought, I will stand on the rug to deliver my speech.

Then the M.C. called to us, "Come on up here boys and get your money."

We ran forward to where the men laughed and talked in their chairs, waiting. Everyone seemed friendly now.

"There it is on the rug," the man said. I saw the rug covered with coins of all dimensions and a few crumpled bills. But what excited me, scattered here and there, were the gold pieces.

"Boys, it's all yours," the man said. "You get all you grab."

"That's right, Sambo," a blond man said, winking at me confidentially.

I trembled with excitement, forgetting my pain. I would get the gold and the bills, I thought. I would use both hands. I would throw my body against the boys nearest me to block them from the gold.

"Get down around the rug now," the man commanded, "and don't anyone touch it until I give the signal."

"This ought to be good," I heard.

As told, we got around the square rug on our knees. Slowly the man raised his freckled hand as we followed it upward with our eyes.

I heard, "These niggers look like they're about to pray!"

Then, "Ready," the man said. "Go!"

I lunged for a yellow coin lying on the blue design of the carpet, touching it and sending a surprised shriek to join those rising around me. I tried frantically to remove my hand but could not let go. A hot, violent force tore through my body, shaking me like a wet rat. The rug was electrified. The hair bristled up on my head as I shook myself free. My muscles jumped, my nerves jangled, writhed. But I saw that this was not stopping the other boys. Laughing in fear and embarrassment, some were holding back and scooping up the coins knocked off by the painful contortions of the others. The men roared above us as we struggled.

"Pick it up, goddamnit, pick it up!" someone called like a bass-voiced parrot. "Go on, get it!"

I crawled rapidly around the floor, picking up the coins, trying to avoid the coppers and to get greenbacks and the gold. Ignoring the shock by laughing, as I brushed the coins off quickly, I discovered that I could contain the electricity—a contradiction, but it works. Then the men began to push us onto the rug. Laughing embarrassedly, we struggled out of their hands and kept after the coins. We were all wet and slippery and hard to hold. Suddenly I saw a boy lifted into the air, glistening with sweat like a circus seal, and dropped, his wet back landing flush upon the charged rug, heard him yell and saw him literally dance upon his back, his elbows beating a frenzied tattoo upon the floor, his muscles twitching like the flesh of a horse stung by many flies. When he finally rolled off, his face was gray and no one stopped him when he ran from the floor amid booming laughter.

"Get the money," the M.C. called. "That's good hard American cash!"

And we snatched and grabbed, snatched and grabbed. I was careful not to come too close to the rug now, and when I felt the hot whiskey breath descend upon me like a cloud of foul air I reached out and grabbed the leg of a chair. It was occupied and I held on desperately.

"Leggo, nigger! Leggo!"

The huge face wavered down to mine as he tried to push me free. But my body was slippery and he was too drunk. It was Mr. Colcord, who owned a chain of movie houses and "entertainment palaces." Each time he grabbed me I slipped out of his hands. It became a real struggle. I feared the rug more than I did the drunk, so I held on, surprising myself for a moment by trying to topple *him* upon the rug. It was such an enormous idea that I found myself actually carrying it out. I tried not to be obvious, yet when I grabbed his leg, trying to tumble him out of the chair, he raised up roaring with laughter, and looking at me with soberness dead in the eye, kicked me viciously in the chest. The chair leg flew out of my hand and I felt myself going and rolled. It was as though I had rolled through a bed of hot coals. It seemed a whole century would pass before I would roll free, a century in which I was seared through the deepest levels of my body to the fearful breath within me and the breath seared and heated to the point of explosion. It'll all be over in a flash, I thought as I rolled clear. It'll all be over in a flash.

But not yet, the men on the other side were waiting, red faces swollen as though from apoplexy as they bent forward in their chairs. Seeing their fingers coming toward me I rolled away as a fumbled football rolls off the receiver's fingertips, back into the coals. That time I luckily sent the rug sliding out of place and heard the coins ringing against the floor and the boys scuffling to pick them up and the M.C. calling, "All right, boys, that's all. Go get dressed and get your money."

I was limp as a dish rag. My back felt as though it had been beaten with wires.

When we had dressed the M.C. came in and gave us each five dollars, except Tatlock, who got ten for being last in the ring. Then he told us to leave. I was not to get a chance to deliver my speech, I thought. I was going out into the dim alley in despair when I was stopped and told to go back. I returned to the ballroom, where the men were pushing back their chairs and gathering in groups to talk.

The M.C. knocked on a table for quiet. "Gentlemen," he said, "we almost forgot an important part of the program. A most serious part, gentlemen. This boy was brought here to deliver a speech which he made at his graduation yesterday . . ."

"Bravo!"

"I'm told that he is the smartest boy we've got out there in Greenwood. I'm told that he knows more big words than a pocket-sized dictionary."

Much applause and laughter.

"So now, gentlemen, I want you to give him your attention."

There was still laughter as I faced them, my mouth dry, my eye throbbing. I began slowly, but evidently my throat was tense, because they began shouting, "Louder! Louder!"

"We of the younger generation extol the wisdom of that great leader and educator,"[3] I shouted, "who first spoke these flaming words of wisdom: 'A ship lost at sea for many days suddenly sighted a friendly vessel. From the mast of the unfortunate vessel was seen a signal: "Water, water; we die of thirst!" The answer from the friendly vessel came back: "Cast down your bucket where you are." The captain of the distressed vessel, at last heeding the injunction, cast down his bucket, and it came up full of fresh sparkling water from the mouth of the Amazon River.' And like him I say, and in his words, 'To those of my race who depend upon bettering their condition in a foreign land, or who underestimate the importance of cultivating friendly relations with the Southern white man, who is his next-door neighbor, I would say: "Cast down your bucket where you are"—cast it down in making friends in every manly way of the people of all races by whom we are surrounded . . .'"

I spoke automatically and with such fervor that I did not realize that the men were still talking and laughing until my dry mouth, filling up with blood from the cut, almost strangled me. I coughed, wanting to stop and go to one of the tall brass, sandfilled spittoons to relieve myself, but a few of the men, especially the superintendent, were listening and I was afraid. So I gulped it down, blood, saliva and all, and continued. (What powers of endurance I had during those days! What enthusiasm! What a belief in the rightness of things!) I spoke even louder in spite of the pain. But still they talked and still they laughed, as though deaf with cotton in dirty ears. So I spoke with greater emotional emphasis. I closed my ears and swallowed blood until I was nauseated. The speech seemed a hundred times as long as before, but I could not leave out a single word. All had to be said, each memorized nuance considered, rendered. Nor was that all. Whenever I uttered a word of three or more syllables a group of voices would yell for me to repeat it. I used the phrase "social responsibility" and they yelled:

"What's that word you say, boy?"

"Social responsibility," I said.

"What?"

"Social . . ."

"Louder."

". . . responsibility."

"More!"

"Respon—"

"Repeat!"

"—sibility."

The room filled with the uproar of laughter until, no doubt, distracted by having to gulp down my blood, I made a mistake and yelled a phrase I had often seen denounced in newspaper editorials, heard debated in private.

"Social . . ."

[3] Booker T. Washington. The quotations that follow are from the 1895 Atlanta Exposition Speech.

"What?" they yelled.

". . . equality—"

The laughter hung smokelike in the sudden stillness. I opened my eyes, puzzled. Sounds of displeasure filled the room. The M.C. rushed forward. They shouted hostile phrases at me. But I did not understand.

A small dry mustached man in the front row blared out, "Say that slowly, son!"

"What, sir?"

"What you just said!"

"Social responsibility, sir," I said.

"You weren't being smart, were you, boy?" he said, not unkindly.

"No, sir!"

"You sure that about 'equality' was a mistake?"

"Oh, yes, sir," I said. "I was swallowing blood."

"Well, you had better speak more slowly so we can understand. We mean to do right by you, but you've got to know your place at all times. All right, now, go on with your speech."

I was afraid. I wanted to leave but I wanted also to speak and I was afraid they'd snatch me down.

"Thank you, sir," I said, beginning where I had left off, and having them ignore me as before.

Yet when I finished there was a thunderous applause. I was surprised to see the superintendent come forth with a package wrapped in white tissue paper, and gesturing for quiet, address the men.

"Gentlemen, you see that I did not overpraise this boy. He makes a good speech and some day he'll lead his people in the proper paths. And I don't have to tell you that that is important in these days and times. This is a good, smart boy, and so to encourage him in the right direction, in the name of the Board of Education I wish to present him a prize in the form of this . . ."

He paused, removing the tissue paper and revealing a gleaming calfskin brief case.

". . . in the form of this first-class article from Shad Whitmore's shop."

"Boy," he said, addressing me, "take this prize and keep it well. Consider it a badge of office. Prize it. Keep developing as you are and some day it will be filled with important papers that will help shape the destiny of your people."

I was so moved that I could hardly express my thanks. A rope of bloody saliva forming a shape like an undiscovered continent drooled upon the leather and I wiped it quickly away. I felt an importance that I had never dreamed.

"Open it and see what's inside," I was told.

My fingers a-tremble, I complied, smelling the fresh leather and finding an official-looking document inside. It was a scholarship to the state college for Negroes. My eyes filled with tears and I ran awkwardly off the floor.

I was overjoyed; I did not even mind when I discovered that the gold pieces I had scrambled for were brass pocket tokens advertising a certain make of automobile.

When I reached home everyone was excited. Next day the neighbors came to congratulate me. I even felt safe from grandfather, whose deathbed curse usually spoiled my triumphs. I stood beneath his photograph with my brief case in hand and smiled triumphantly into his stolid black peasant's face. It was a face that fascinated me. The eyes seemed to follow everywhere I went.

That night I dreamed I was at a circus with him and that he refused to laugh at the clowns no matter what they did. Then later he told me to open my brief case and read what was inside and I did, finding an official envelope stamped with the state seal; and inside the envelope I found another and another, endlessly, and I thought I would fall of weariness. "Them's years," he said. "Now open that one." And I did and in it I found an engraved document containing a short message in letters of gold. "Read it," my grandfather said. "Out loud!"

"To Whom It May Concern," I intoned. "Keep This Nigger-Boy Running."

I awoke with the old man's laughter ringing in my ears.

(It was a dream I was to remember and dream again for many years after. But at that time I had no insight into its meaning. First I had to attend college.)

Saul Bellow
(1915–)

In Saul Bellow's novel The Victim *(1947), Schlossberg, an elderly theatrical journalist and one of the first in a long line of "bughouse philosophers" in Bellow's stories, discusses acting: "I'll tell you. It's bad to be less than human and it's bad to be more than human. . . . So here is the whole thing, then. Good acting is what is exactly human. And if you say I am a tough critic, you mean I have a high opinion of what is human. This is my whole idea." What is exactly human has been Bellow's whole idea, too, in a series of brilliantly comic and profoundly serious novels that have explored the bewildering variety of models for self-definition in the chaos of modern life and searched for a conception of the human that is neither too mean nor too grandiose. Almost thirty years after* The Victim, *when he accepted the 1976 Nobel Prize for literature, Bellow reiterated his conviction that art should deal with "the main human enterprise" and should provide "a broader, more flexible, fuller, more coherent, more comprehensive account of what we human beings are, who we are, and what this life is for."*

Bellow's slant perspective on contemporary mass culture perhaps owes something to his background as an immigrant to Chicago as well as his Jewish intellectual's grasp of the range of European art and thought. Bellow was born in 1915 in Lachine, Quebec, to parents who had immigrated from Russia two years before. The family lived in a Montreal slum until Bellow was nine, when they moved to Chicago. Here Bellow attended the University of Chicago and Northwestern University, graduating in 1937 with honors in sociology and anthropology (fields echoed in unex-

pected ways in his fiction). After a brief period of graduate work in anthropology at the University of Wisconsin, he spent eight years teaching at Pestalozzi-Froebel Teachers College (1938–1942) and working in the editorial department of the Great Books project of the Encyclopedia Brittanica *(1943–1946).*

Bellow's first published story, "Two Morning Monologues," appeared in the Partisan Review *in 1941, and for several years he was closely identified with the* Partisan Review *group of urbane, politically committed Jewish writers and intellectuals, who included Isaac Rosenfeld, Delmore Schwartz, and Lionel Trilling. His first two novels,* Dangling Man *(1944) and* The Victim, *reflected the existentialist mood of the war and post-war years.* Dangling Man *is a 1940s* Notes from Underground *in which Joseph ("dangling" because he has quit his job and is waiting to be inducted into the army) is forced to consider, "How should a good man live; what ought he to do?"* The Victim, *the story of a small-time commercial journalist named Leventhal haunted by his double Allbee, who claims to have been ruined by Leventhal, also has a Dostoevskian model,* The Eternal Husband, *although the lover-cuckold relationship of the Dostoevsky story is transmuted into a Jew-Gentile relationship in* The Victim.

The Adventures of Augie March *(1953) represented a major and unexpected shift in the direction of Bellow's work. Without abandoning the moral concerns of his first novels, Bellow turned his attention from the sorrowful plights of such victim protagonists as Joseph and Leventhal to the joy and vitality of the tough street kid Augie March, an urban, Jewish Huckleberry Finn. And he moved from the small-scale, meticulously crafted form of* Dangling Man *and* The Victim *to a loose, expansive, picaresque form that he described as "catch-as-catch-can."* Augie March *is not Bellow's finest novel, but it first established the form and manner in which he was to do his finest work: an expansive, inclusive structure and a witty, mercurial, colloquially poetic style, often embodied in a first-person monologue.*

Seize the Day *(1956), a novella that traces one day in the life of Tommy Wilhelm, a middle-aged failure, temporarily reversed this trend, but* Henderson the Rain King *(1959) triumphantly confirmed it, through Henderson's sprawling, exuberantly comic account of his trip to Africa in quest of inner freedom and the exactly human. In* Herzog *(1964), perhaps Bellow's finest novel, he combined the comic excess of* Augie March *and* Henderson *with the careful craftsmanship of the early novels and* Seize the Day, *a combination he has achieved repeatedly in his later novels.* Mr. Sammler's Planet *(1970) won Bellow his third National Book Award (the first two were for* Augie March *and* Herzog*). The novel, in which the courtly European intellectual Mr. Sammler, almost literally returned from the grave of Nazi persecution, sardonically views the excesses of 1960s radicalism, took on an occasionally shrill, polemical tone that marred its effectiveness.* Humboldt's Gift *(1975), based upon Bellow's 1940s friendship with the poet Delmore Schwartz, returns to the mode of* Herzog *in its combination of bizarre comic characters, exuberant style, and searching criticism of American culture. These hallmarks of Bellow's fiction appear again in* The Dean's December *(1982).*

Although the novel remains Bellow's most successful form of expression, he has written a number of essays and other non-fictional works, several plays, and a good many short stories. Jerusalem and Back, *an account of a trip to Israel, appeared in 1976. A full-length play,* The Last Analysis, *ran for a month on Broadway in 1964, and three one-act plays collectively entitled* Under the Weather *were produced in New York and London and at Italy's Spoleto Festival in 1965–66.* Mosby's Memoirs and Other Stories, *a collection of six stories written in the*

1950s and 1960s, appeared in 1968. Bellow lives in Evanston, Illinois, and holds a professorial post on the Committee on Social Thought at the University of Chicago.

"Looking for Mr. Green" (1951), despite its early date, between The Victim *and* Augie March, *deals with some of Bellow's continuing preoccupations. Like Joseph in* Dangling Man, *Grebe has been forcibly yanked out of a sheltered background of academic humanism and forced to confront the reality of the contemporary world, although here the Depression rather than the army is the precipitating force. His subsistence job leads him into the frightening, disorienting world of the poverty-stricken black ghetto. Can the individual self survive in such a world? Does the individual mean anything? His supervisor Raynor, another humanist, is inclined to think not; in this world of appearances in which "nothing looks to be real, and everything stands for something else, and that thing for another thing, and that thing for a still further one," the only reality is survival, the difference between twenty-five and thirty-seven dollars a week. The Italian shopkeeper puts it more brutally; to him the ghetto dwellers are dehumanized, a "huge, hugging, despairing knot, a human wheel of heads, legs, bellies, arms, rolling through his shop." But Grebe cannot accept this view of humanity; if Mr. Green does not exist as an individual, Grebe's own marginal existence is called into doubt. (The inner link between the two is suggested by the similarity of "Grebe" and "Green.") Grebe's quest is for himself and for a conception of man that is neither more than human (philosophy's) nor less than human (the shopkeeper's) but "exactly human," and his quest is successful: "For after all, he* could *be found!"*

FURTHER READING (*prepared by W. J. R.*): Earl Rovit's *Saul Bellow,* 1965 (*University of Minnesota Pamphlets on American Writers,* No. 65), is a general introductory essay on the writer that discusses such topics as religion, the family unit, structure, and the development of the Bellow hero. Malcolm Bradbury's *Saul Bellow,* 1982, combines a general overview with shrewd insights into individual novels. Robert R. Dutton's *Saul Bellow,* 1971, discusses Bellow's rejection of the naturalistic vision of man; Dutton examines in detail Bellow's concept of "subangelic" man as it is presented in seven of the novels. A good survey of Bellow's techniques and literary concerns can be found in Irving Malin's *Saul Bellow's Fiction,* 1969, which examines such topics as theme, characterization, and imagery in separate chapters. Keith Michael Opdahl's *The Novels of Saul Bellow,* 1967, is also a good introduction to Bellow's fiction, with discussions of influences on Bellow's work (such as the psychological novel), aesthetic values, and other topics. Eight major works, including *Herzog* and *Humboldt's Gift,* are extensively explored in Eusebio L. Rodrigues's *Quest for the Human: An Exploration of Saul Bellow's Fiction,* 1981. Rodrigues's work is particularly good for its consideration of Bellow's language. John Jacob Clayton's important *Saul Bellow: In Defense of Man,* 1968, 2nd ed. 1979, discusses Bellow's attitudes toward American culture and examines six novels individually. Earl Rovit has edited *Saul Bellow: A Collection of Critical Essays,* 1975, which includes twelve essays and an interview with Bellow by Gordon Lloyd Harper.

LOOKING FOR MR. GREEN

Whatsoever thy hand findeth to do, do it with thy might. . .[1]

Hard work? No, it wasn't really so hard. He wasn't used to walking and stair-climbing, but the physical difficulty of his new job was not what George Grebe felt most. He was delivering relief checks in the Negro district, and although he was a native Chicagoan, this was not a part of the city he knew much about—it needed a depression to introduce him to it. No, it wasn't literally hard work, not as reckoned in foot-pounds, but yet he was beginning to feel the strain of it, to grow aware of its peculiar difficulty. He could find the streets and numbers, but the clients were not where they were supposed to be, and he felt like a hunter inexperienced in the camouflage of his game. It was an unfavorable day, too—fall, and cold, dark weather, windy. But, anyway, instead of shells in his deep trenchcoat pocket he had the cardboard of checks, punctured for the spindles of the file, the holes reminding him of the holes in player-piano paper. And he didn't look much like a hunter, either; his was a city figure entirely, belted up in this Irish conspirator's coat. He was slender without being tall, stiff in the back, his legs looking shabby in a pair of old tweed pants gone through and fringy at the cuffs. With this stiffness, he kept his head forward, so that his face was red from the sharpness of the weather; and it was an indoors sort of face with gray eyes that persisted in some kind of thought and yet seemed to avoid definiteness of conclusion. He wore sideburns that surprised you somewhat by the tough curl of the blond hair and the effect of assertion in their length. He was not so mild as he looked, nor so youthful; and nevertheless there was no effort on his part to seem what he was not. He was an educated man; he was a bachelor; he was in some ways simple; without lushing, he liked a drink; his luck had not been good. Nothing was deliberately hidden.

He felt that his luck was better than usual today. When he had reported for work that morning, he had expected to be shut up in the relief office at a clerk's job, for he had been hired downtown as a clerk, and he was glad to have, instead, the freedom of the streets and welcomed, at least at first, the vigor of the cold and even the blowing of the hard wind. But, on the other hand, he was not getting on with the distribution of the checks. It was true that it was a city job; nobody expected you to push too hard at a city job. His supervisor, that young Mr. Raynor, had practically told him that. Still, he wanted to do well at it. For one thing, when he knew how quickly he could deliver a batch of checks, he would know also how much time he could expect to clip for himself. And then, too, the clients would be waiting for their money. That was not the most important consideration, though it certainly mattered to him. No, but he wanted to do well, simply for doing-well's sake, to acquit himself decently of a job because he so rarely had a job to do that required just this sort of energy. Of this peculiar energy he now had a superabundance; once it had started to flow, it flowed all too heavily.

[1] Ecclesiastes 9:10.

And, for the time being, anyway, he was balked. He could not find Mr. Green.

So he stood in his big-skirted trenchcoat with a large envelope in his hand and papers showing from his pocket, wondering why people should be so hard to locate who were too feeble or sick to come to the station to collect their own checks. But Raynor had told him that tracking them down was not easy at first and had offered him some advice on how to proceed. "If you can see the postman, he's your first man to ask, and your best bet. If you can't connect with him, try the stores and tradespeople around. Then the janitor and the neighbors. But you'll find the closer you come to your man, the less people will tell you. They don't want to tell you anything."

"Because I'm a stranger."

"Because you're white. We ought to have a Negro doing this, but we don't at the moment, and of course you've got to eat, too, and this is public employment. Jobs have to be made. Oh, that holds for me, too. Mind you, I'm not letting myself out. I've got three years of seniority on you, that's all. And a law degree. Otherwise, you might be back of the desk and I might be going out into the field this cold day. The same dough pays us both and for the same, exact, identical reason. What's my law degree got to do with it? But you have to pass out these checks, Mr. Grebe, and it'll help if you're stubborn, so I hope you are."

"Yes, I'm fairly stubborn."

Raynor sketched hard with an eraser in the old dirt of his desk, left-handed, and said, "Sure, what else can you answer to such a question. Anyhow, the trouble you're going to have is that they don't like to give information about anybody. They think you're a plainclothes dick or an installment collector, or summons-server or something like that. Till you've been seen around the neighborhood for a few months and people know you're only from the relief."

It was dark, ground-freezing, pre-Thanksgiving weather; the wind played hob with the smoke, rushing it down, and Grebe missed his gloves, which he had left in Raynor's office. And no one would admit knowing Green. It was past three o'clock and the postman had made his last delivery. The nearest grocer, himself a Negro, had never heard the name Tulliver Green, or said he hadn't. Grebe was inclined to think that it was true, that he had in the end convinced the man that he wanted only to deliver a check. But he wasn't sure. He needed experience in interpreting looks and signs and, even more, the will not to be put off or denied and even the force to bully if need be. If the grocer did know, he had got rid of him easily. But since most of his trade was with reliefers, why should he prevent the delivery of a check? Maybe Green, or Mrs. Green, if there was a Mrs. Green, patronized another grocer. And was there a Mrs. Green? It was one of Grebe's great handicaps that he hadn't looked at any of the case records. Raynor should have let him read files for a few hours. But he apparently saw no need for that, probably considering the job unimportant. Why prepare systematically to deliver a few checks?

But now it was time to look for the janitor. Grebe took in the building in the wind and gloom of the late November day—trampled, frost-hardened lots on one side; on the other, an automobile junk yard and then the infinite work of Elevated frames, weak-looking, gaping with rubbish fires; two sets of leaning brick porches three stories high and a flight of cement stairs to the cellar. Descending, he entered the underground passage, where he tried the doors until one opened and he found himself in the furnace room. There someone rose toward him and approached, scraping on the coal grit and bending under the canvas-jacketed pipes.

"Are you the janitor?"

"What do you want?"

"I'm looking for a man who's supposed to be living here. Green."

"What Green?"

"Oh, you maybe have more than one Green?" said Grebe with new, pleasant hope. "This is Tulliver Green."

"I don't think I c'n help you, mister. I don't know any."

"A crippled man."

The janitor stood bent before him. Could it be that he was crippled? Oh, God! what if he was. Grebe's gray eyes sought with excited difficulty to see. But no, he was only very short and stooped. A head awakened from meditation, a strong-haired beard, low, wide shoulders. A staleness of sweat and coal rose from his black shirt and the burlap sack he wore as an apron.

"Crippled how?"

Grebe thought and then answered with the light voice of unmixed candor, "I don't know. I've never seen him." This was damaging, but his only other choice was to make a lying guess, and he was not up to it. "I'm delivering checks for the relief to shut-in cases. If he weren't crippled, he'd come to collect himself. That's why I said crippled. Bedridden, chair-ridden—is there anybody like that?"

This sort of frankness was one of Grebe's oldest talents, going back to childhood. But it gained him nothing here.

"No, suh. I've got four buildin's same as this that I take care of. I don' know all the tenants, leave alone the tenants' tenants. The rooms turn over so fast, people movin' in and out every day. I can't tell you."

The janitor opened his grimy lips, but Grebe did not hear him in the piping of the valves and the consuming pull of air to flame in the body of the furnace. He knew, however, what he had said.

"Well, all the same, thanks. Sorry I bothered you. I'll prowl around upstairs again and see if I can turn up someone who knows him."

Once more in the cold air and early darkness he made the short circle from the cellarway to the entrance crowded between the brickwork pillars and began to climb to the third floor. Pieces of plaster ground under his feet; strips of brass tape from which the carpeting had been torn away marked old boundaries at the sides. In the passage, the cold reached him worse than in the street; it touched him to the bone. The hall toilets ran like springs. He thought grimly as he heard the wind burning around the building with a sound like that of the furnace, that this was a great piece of constructed shelter. Then he struck a match in the gloom and searched for names and numbers among the writings and scribbles on the walls. He saw WHOODY-DOODY GO TO JESUS, and zigzags, caricatures, sexual scrawls, and curses. So the sealed rooms of pyramids were also decorated, and the caves of human dawn.

The information on his card was, TULLIVER GREEN—APT 3D. There were no names, however, and no numbers. His shoulders drawn up, tears of cold in his eyes, breathing vapor, he went the length of the corridor and told himself that if he had been lucky enough to have the temperament for it, he would bang on one of the doors and bawl out "Tulliver Green!" until he got results. But it wasn't in him to make an uproar and he continued to burn matches, passing the light over the walls. At the rear, in a corner of the hall, he discovered a door he had not seen before and he thought it best to investigate. It sounded empty when he knocked, but a young Negress answered, hardly more than a girl. She opened only a bit, to guard the warmth of the room.

"Yes, suh?"

"I'm from the district relief station on Prairie Avenue. I'm looking for a man named Tulliver Green to give him his check. Do you know him?"

No, she didn't; but he thought she had not understood anything of what he had said. She had a dream-bound, dream-blind face, very soft and black, shut off. She wore a man's jacket and pulled the ends together at her throat. Her hair was parted in three directions, at the sides and transversely, standing up at the front in a dull puff.

"Is there somebody around here who might know?"

"I jus' taken this room las' week."

He observed that she shivered, but even her shiver was somnambulistic and there was no sharp consciousness of cold in the big smooth eyes of her handsome face.

"All right, miss, thank you. Thanks," he said, and went to try another place.

Here he was admitted. He was grateful, for the room was warm. It was full of people, and they were silent as he entered—ten people, or a dozen, perhaps more, sitting on benches like a parliament. There was no light, properly speaking, but a tempered darkness that the window gave, and everyone seemed to him enormous, the men padded out in heavy work clothes and winter coats, and the women huge, too, in their sweaters, hats, and old furs. And, besides, bed and bedding, a black cooking range, a piano piled towering to the ceiling with papers, a dining room table of the old style of prosperous Chicago. Among these people Grebe, with his cold-heightened fresh color and his smaller stature, entered like a schoolboy. Even though he was met with smiles and goodwill, he knew, before a single word was spoken, that all the currents ran against him and that he would make no headway. Nevertheless he began. "Does anybody here know how I can deliver a check to Mr. Tulliver Green?"

"Green?" It was the man that had let him in who answered. He was in short sleeves, in a checkered shirt, and had a queer, high head, profusely overgrown and long as a shako;[2] the veins entered it strongly from his forehead. "I never heard mention of him. Is this where he live?"

"This is the address they gave me at the station. He's a sick man, and he'll need his check. Can't anybody tell me where to find him?"

He stood his ground and waited for a reply, his crimson wool scarf wound about his neck and drooping outside his trenchcoat, pockets weighted with the block of checks and official forms. They must have real-

[2] A high-crowned military cap, often of fur.

ized that he was not a college boy employed afternoons by a bill collector, trying foxily to pass for a relief clerk, recognized that he was an older man who knew himself what need was, who had had more than an average seasoning in hardship. It was evident enough if you looked at the marks under his eyes and at the sides of his mouth.

"Anybody know this sick man?"

"No, suh." On all sides he saw heads shaken and smiles of denial. No one knew. And maybe it was true, he considered, standing silent in the earthen, musky human gloom of the place as the rumble continued. But he could never really be sure.

"What's the matter with this man?" said shako-head.

"I've never seen him. All I can tell you is that he can't come in person for his money. It's my first day in this district."

"Maybe they given you the wrong number?"

"I don't believe so. But where else can I ask about him?" He felt that this persistence amused them deeply, and in a way he shared their amusement that he should stand up so tenaciously to them. Though smaller, though slight, he was his own man, he retracted nothing about himself, and he looked back at them, gray-eyed, with amusement and also with a sort of courage. On the bench some man spoke in his throat, the words impossible to catch, and a woman answered with a wild, shrieking laugh, which was quickly cut off.

"Well, so nobody will tell me?"

"Ain't nobody who knows."

"At least, if he lives here, he pays rent to someone. Who manages the building?"

"Greatham Company. That's on Thirty-ninth Street."

Grebe wrote it in his pad. But, in the street again, a sheet of wind-driven paper clinging to his leg while he deliberated what direction to take next, it seemed a feeble lead to follow. Probably this Green didn't rent a flat, but a room. Sometimes there were as many as twenty people in an apartment; the real-estate agent would know only the lessee. And not even the agent could tell you who the renters were. In some places the beds were even used in shifts, watchmen or jitney drivers[3] or short-order cooks in night joints turning out after a day's sleep and surrendering their beds to a sister, a nephew, or perhaps a stranger, just off the bus. There were large numbers of newcomers in this terrific, blight-bitten portion of the city between Cottage Grove and Ashland, wandering from house to house and room to room. When you saw them, how could you know them? They didn't carry bundles on their backs or look picturesque. You only saw a man, a Negro, walking in the street or riding in the car, like everyone else, with his thumb closed on a transfer. And therefore how were you supposed to tell? Grebe thought the Greatham agent would only laugh at his question.

But how much it would have simplified the job to be able to say that Green was old, or blind, or consumptive. An hour in the files, taking a few notes, and he needn't have been at such a disadvantage. When Raynor gave him the block of checks, he asked, "How much should I know about these people?" Then Raynor had looked as though he were preparing to accuse

[3] Bus drivers (from "jitney," or nickel, the original fare).

him of trying to make the job more important that it was. He smiled, because by then they were on fine terms, but nevertheless he had been getting ready to say something like that when the confusion began in the station over Staika and her children.

Grebe had waited a long time for this job. It came to him through the pull of an old schoolmate in the Corporation Counsel's office, never a close friend, but suddenly sympathetic and interested—pleased to show, moreover, how well he had done, how strongly he was coming on even in these miserable times. Well, he was coming through strongly, along with the Democratic administration itself. Grebe had gone to see him in City Hall, and they had had a counter lunch or beers at least once a month for a year, and finally it had been possible to swing the job. He didn't mind being assigned the lowest clerical grade, nor even being a messenger, though Raynor thought he did.

This Raynor was an original sort of guy and Grebe had taken to him immediately. As was proper on the first day, Grebe had come early, but he waited long, for Raynor was late. At last he darted into his cubicle of an office as though he had just jumped from one of those hurtling huge red Indian Avenue cars. His thin, rough face was wind-stung and he was grinning and saying something breathlessly to himself. In his hat, a small fedora, and his coat, the velvet collar a neat fit about his neck, and his silk muffler that set off the nervous twist of his chin, he swayed and turned himself in his swivel chair, feet leaving the ground; so that he pranced a little as he sat. Meanwhile he took Grebe's measure out of his eyes, eyes of an unusual vertical length and slighty sardonic. So the two men sat for a while, saying nothing, while the supervisor raised his hat from his miscombed hair and put it in his lap. His cold-darkened hands were not clean. A steel beam passed through the little makeshift room, from which machine belts once had hung. The building was an old factory.

"I'm younger than you; I hope you won't find it hard taking orders from me," said Raynor. "But I don't make them up, either. You're how old, about?"

"Thirty-five."

"And you thought you'd be inside doing paper work. But it so happens I have to send you out."

"I don't mind."

"And it's mostly a Negro load we have in this district."

"So I thought it would be."

"Fine. You'll get along. *C'est un bon boulot.*[4] Do you know French?"

"Some."

"I thought you'd be a university man."

"Have you been in France?" said Grebe.

"No, that's the French of the Berlitz School. I've been at it for more than a year, just as I'm sure people have been, all over the world, office boys in China and braves in Tanganyika. In fact, I damn well know it. Such is the attractive power of civilization. It's overrated, but what do you want? *Que voulez-vous?*[5] I get *Le Rire*[6] and all the spicy papers, just like in Tanganyika. It must be mystifying, out there. But my reason is that I'm aiming at the

[4] "It's a good job." [5] "What do you want?" [6] *Laughter,* a French comic magazine.

diplomatic service. I have a cousin who's a courier, and the way he describes it is awfully attractive. He rides in the *wagon-lits*[7] and reads books. While we—What did you do before?"

"I sold."

"Where?"

"Canned meat at Stop and Shop. In the basement."

"And before that?"

"Window shades, at Goldblatt's."

"Steady work?"

"No, Thursdays and Saturdays. I also sold shoes."

"You've been a shoe-dog, too. Well. And prior to that? Here it is in your folder." He opened the record. "Saint Olaf's College, instructor in classical languages. Fellow, University of Chicago, 1926–27. I've had Latin, too. Let's trade quotations—*'Dum spiro spero.'* "

" *'Da dextram misero.'* "

" *'Alea jacta est.'* "

" *'Excelsior.'* "[8]

Raynor shouted with laughter, and other workers came to look at him over the partition. Grebe also laughed, feeling pleased and easy. The luxury of fun on a nervous morning.

When they were done and no one was watching or listening, Raynor said rather seriously, "What made you study Latin in the first place? Was it for the priesthood?"

"No."

"Just for the hell of it? For the culture? Oh, the things people think they can pull!" He made his cry hilarious and tragic. "I ran my pants off so I could study for the bar, and I've passed the bar, so I get twelve dollars a week more than you as a bonus for having seen life straight and whole.[9] I'll tell you, as a man of culture, that even though nothing looks to be real, and everything stands for something else, and that thing for another thing, and that thing for a still further one—there ain't any comparison between twenty-five and thirty-seven dollars a week, regardless of the last reality. Don't you think that was clear to your Greeks? They were a thoughtful people, but they didn't part with their slaves."

This was a great deal more than Grebe had looked for in his first interview with his supervisor. He was too shy to show all the astonishment he felt. He laughed a little, aroused, and brushed at the sunbeam that covered his head with its dust. "Do you think my mistake was so terrible?"

"Damn right it was terrible, and you know it now that you've had the whip of hard times laid on your back. You should have been preparing yourself for trouble. Your people must have been well off to send you to the university. Stop me, if I'm stepping on your toes. Did your mother pamper you? Did your father give in to you? Were you brought up tenderly, with permission to go and find out what were the last things that

[7] Sleeping cars.

[8] "While I breathe, I hope," "Give your right hand to the wretched," "The die is cast," and "Higher."

[9] Matthew Arnold (1822–1888), in his poem "To a Friend," said that Sophocles "saw life steadily, and saw it whole."

everything else stands for while everybody else labored in the fallen world of appearances?"[10]

"Well, no, it wasn't exactly like that." Grebe smiled. *The fallen world of appearances!* no less. But now it was his turn to deliver a surprise. "We weren't rich. My father was the last genuine English butler in Chicago—"

"Are you kidding?"

"Why should I be?"

"In a livery?"

"In livery. Up on the Gold Coast."[11]

"And he wanted you to be educated like a gentleman?"

"He did not. He sent me to Armour Institute to study chemical engineering. But when he died, I changed schools."

He stopped himself, and considered how quickly Raynor had reached him. In no time he had your valise on the table and all your stuff unpacked. And afterward, in the streets, he was still reviewing how far he might have gone, and how much he might have been led to tell if they had not been interrupted by Mrs. Staika's great noise.

But just then a young woman, one of Raynor's workers, ran into the cubicle exclaiming, "Haven't you heard all the fuss?"

"We haven't heard anything."

"It's Staika, giving out with all her might. The reporters are coming. She said she phoned the papers and you know she did."

"But what is she up to?" said Raynor.

"She brought her wash and she's ironing it here, with our current, because the relief won't pay her electric bill. She has her ironing board set up by the admitting desk, and her kids are with her, all six. They never are in school more than once a week. She's always dragging them around with her because of her reputation."

"I don't want to miss any of this," said Raynor, jumping up. Grebe, as he followed with the secretary, said, "Who is this Staika?"

"They call her the 'Blood Mother of Federal Street.' She's a professional donor at the hospitals. I think they pay ten dollars a pint. Of course it's no joke, but she makes a very big thing out of it and she and the kids are in the papers all the time."

A small crowd, staff and clients divided by a plywood barrier, stood in the narrow space of the entrance, and Staika was shouting in a gruff, mannish voice, plunging the iron on the board and slamming it on the metal rest.

"My father and mother came in a steerage, and I was born in our house, Robey by Huron. I'm no dirty immigrant. I'm a U.S. citizen. My husband is a gassed veteran from France with lungs weaker'n paper, that hardly can he go to the toilet by himself. These six children of mine, I have to buy the shoes for their feet with my own blood. Even a lousy little white Communion necktie, that's a couple of drops of blood; a little piece of mosquito veil for my Vadja so she won't be ashamed in church for the other girls, they take my blood for it by Goldblatt. That's how I keep goin'. A fine thing if

[10] Platonic philosophy held that reality resided in abstract "forms" and that the visible world was one of mere appearances.

[11] A wealthy residential area along the shore of Lake Michigan in north Chicago.

I had to depend on the relief. And there's plenty of people on the rolls—fakes! There's nothin' *they* can't get, that can go and wrap bacon at Swift and Armour anytime. They're lookin' for them by the Yards. They never have to be out of work. Only they rather lay in their lousy beds and eat the public's money." She was not afraid, in a predominantly Negro station, to shout this way about Negroes.

Grebe and Raynor worked themselves forward to get a closer view of the woman. She was flaming with anger and with pleasure at herself, broad and huge, a golden-headed woman who wore a cotton cap laced with pink ribbon. She was barelegged and had on black gym shoes, her Hoover apron was open and her great breasts, not much restrained by a man's undershirt, hampered her arms as she worked at the kid's dress on the ironing board. And the children, silent and white, with a kind of locked obstinacy, in sheepskins and lumberjackets, stood behind her. She had captured the station, and the pleasure this gave her was enormous. Yet her grievances were true grievances. She was telling the truth. But she behaved like a liar. The look of her small eyes was hidden, and while she raged she also seemed to be spinning and planning.

"They send me out college caseworkers in silk pants to talk me out of what I got comin'. Are they better'n me? Who told them? Fire them. Let 'em go and get married, and then you won't have to cut electric from people's budget."

The chief supervisor, Mr. Ewing, couldn't silence her and he stood with folded arms at the head of his staff, bald, bald-headed, saying to his subordinates like the ex-school principal he was, "Pretty soon she'll be tired and go."

"No, she won't," said Raynor to Grebe. "She'll get what she wants. She knows more about the relief even than Ewing. She's been on the rolls for years, and she always gets what she wants because she puts on a noisy show. Ewing knows it. He'll give in soon. He's only saving face. If he gets bad publicity, the Commissioner'll have him on the carpet, downtown. She's got him submerged; she'll submerge everybody in time, and that includes nations and governments."

Grebe replied with his characteristic smile, disagreeing completely. Who would take Staika's orders, and what changes could her yelling ever bring about?

No, what Grebe saw in her, the power that made people listen, was that her cry expressed the war of flesh and blood, perhaps turned a little crazy and certainly ugly, on this place and this condition. And at first, when he went out, the spirit of Staika somehow presided over the whole district for him, and it took color from her; he saw her color, in the spotty curb fires, and the fires under the El, the straight alley of flamy gloom. Later, too, when he went into a tavern for a shot of rye, the sweat of beer, association with West Side Polish streets, made him think of her again.

He wiped the corners of his mouth with his muffler, a handkerchief being inconvenient to reach for, and went out again to get on with the delivery of his checks. The air bit cold and hard and a few flakes of snow formed near him. A train struck by and left a quiver in the frames and a bristling icy hiss over the rails.

Crossing the street, he descended a flight of board steps into a basement grocery, setting off a little bell. It was a dark, long store and it caught you with its stinks of smoked meat, soap, dried peaches, and fish. There was a fire wrinkling and flapping in the little stove, and the proprietor was waiting, an Italian with a long, hollow face and stubborn bristles. He kept his hands warm under his apron.

No, he didn't know Green. You knew people but not names. The same man might not have the same name twice. The police didn't know, either, and mostly didn't care. When somebody was shot or knifed, they took the body away and didn't look for the murderer. In the first place, nobody would tell them anything. So they made up a name for the coroner and called it quits. And in the second place, they didn't give a goddamn anyhow. But they couldn't get to the bottom of a thing even if they wanted to. Nobody would get to know even a tenth of what went on among these people. They stabbed and stole, they did every crime and abomination you ever heard of, men and men, women and women, parents and children, worse than the animals. They carried on their own way, and the horrors passed off like a smoke. There was never anything like it in the history of the whole world.

It was a long speech, deepening with every word in its fantasy and passion and becoming increasingly senseless and terrible: a swarm amassed by suggestion and invention, a huge, hugging, despairing knot, a human wheel of heads, legs, bellies, arms, rolling through his shop.

Grebe felt that he must interrupt him. He said sharply, "What are you talking about! All I asked was whether you knew this man."

"That isn't even the half of it. I been here six years. You probably don't want to believe this. But suppose it's true?"

"All the same," said Grebe, "there must be a way to find a person."

The Italian's close-spaced eyes had been queerly concentrated, as were his muscles, while he leaned across the counter trying to convince Grebe. Now he gave up the effort and sat down on his stool. "Oh—I suppose. Once in a while. But I been telling you, even the cops don't get anywhere."

"They're always after somebody. It's not the same thing."

"Well, keep trying if you want. I can't help you."

But he didn't keep trying. He had no more time to spend on Green. He slipped Green's check to the back of the block. The next name on the list was FIELD, WINSTON.

He found the backyard bungalow without the least trouble; it shared a lot with another house, a few feet of yard between. Grebe knew these two-shack arrangements. They had been built in vast numbers in the days before the swamps were filled and the streets raised, and they were all the same—a boardwalk along the fence, well under street level, three or four ball-headed posts for clotheslines, greening wood, dead shingles, and a long, long flight of stairs to the rear door.

A twelve-year-old boy let him into the kitchen, and there the old man was, sitting by the table in a wheelchair.

"Oh, it's d' Government man," he said to the boy when Grebe drew out his checks. "Go bring me my box of papers." He cleared a space on the table.

"Oh, you don't have to go to all that trouble," said Grebe. But Field laid out his papers: Social Security card, relief certification, letters from the state hospital in Manteno, and a naval discharge dated San Diego, 1920.

"That's plenty," Grebe said. "Just sign."

"You got to know who I am," the old man said. "You're from the Government. It's not your check, it's a Government check and you got no business to hand it over till everything is proved."

He loved the ceremony of it, and Grebe made no more objections. Field emptied his box and finished out the circle of cards and letters.

"There's everything I done and been. Just the death certificate and they can close book on me." He said this with a certain happy pride and magnificence. Still he did not sign; he merely held the little pen upright on the golden-green corduroy of his thigh. Grebe did not hurry him. He felt the old man's hunger for conversation.

"I got to get better coal," he said. "I send my little gran'son to the yard with my order and they fill his wagon with screening. The stove ain't made for it. It fall through the grate. The order says Franklin County egg-size coal."

"I'll report it and see what can be done."

"Nothing can be done, I expect. You know and I know. There ain't no little ways to make things better, and the only big thing is money. That's the only sunbeams, money. Nothing is black where it shines, and the only place you see black is where it ain't shining. What we colored have to have is our own rich. There ain't no other way."

Grebe sat, his reddened forehead bridged levelly by his close-cut hair and his cheeks lowered in the wings of his collar—the caked fire shone hard within the isinglass-and-iron frames, but the room was not comfortable—sat and listened while the old man unfolded his scheme. This was to create one Negro millionaire a month by subscription. One clever, good-hearted young fellow elected every month would sign a contract to use the money to start a business employing Negroes. This would be advertised by chain letters and word of mouth, and every Negro wage earner would contribute a dollar a month. Within five years there would be sixty millionaires.

"That'll fetch respect," he said with a throat-stopped sound that came out like a foreign syllable. "You got to take and organize all the money that gets thrown away on the policy wheel and horse race. As long as they can take it away from you, they got no respect for you. Money, that's d' sun of human kind!" Field was a Negro of mixed blood, perhaps Cherokee, or Natchez; his skin was reddish. And he sounded, speaking about a golden sun in this dark room, and looked, shaggy and slab-headed, with the mingled blood of his face and broad lips, the little pen still upright in his hand, like one of the underground kings of mythology, old judge Minos himself.[12]

And now he accepted the check and signed. Not to soil the slip, he held

[12] In Greek mythology, king of Crete and builder of the Labyrinth. After his death he became one of the judges in Hades.

it down with his knuckles. The table budged and creaked, the center of the gloomy, heathen midden[13] of the kitchen covered with bread, meat, and cans, and the scramble of papers.

"Don't you think my scheme'd work?"

"It's worth thinking about. Something ought to be done, I agree."

"It'll work if people will do it. That's all. That's the only thing, anytime. When they understand it in the same way, all of them."

"That's true," said Grebe, rising. His glance met the old man's.

"I know you got to go," he said. "Well, God bless you, boy, you ain't been sly with me. I can tell it in a minute."

He went back through the buried yard. Someone nursed a candle in a shed, where a man unloaded kindling wood from a sprawl-wheeled baby buggy and two voices carried on a high conversation. As he came up the sheltered passage he heard the hard boost of the wind in the branches and against the house fronts, and then, reaching the sidewalk, he saw the needle-eye red of cable towers in the open icy height hundreds of feet above the river and the factories—those keen points. From here, his view was obstructed all the way to the South Branch and its timber banks, and the cranes beside the water. Rebuilt after the Great Fire,[14] this part of the city was, not fifty years later, in ruins again, factories boarded up, buildings deserted or fallen, gaps of prairie between. But it wasn't desolation that this made you feel, but rather a faltering of organization that set free a huge energy, an escaped, unattached, unregulated power from the giant raw place. Not only must people feel it but, it seemed to Grebe, they were compelled to match it. In their very bodies. He no less than others, he realized. Say that his parents had been servants in their time, whereas he was not supposed to be one. He thought that they had never done any service like this, which no one visible asked for, and probably flesh and blood could not even perform. Nor could anyone show why it should be performed; or see where the performance would lead. That did not mean that he wanted to be released from it, he realized with a grimly pensive face. On the contrary. He had something to do. To be compelled to feel this energy and yet have no task to do—that was horrible; that was suffering; he knew what that was. It was now quitting time. Six o'clock. He could go home if he liked, to his room, that is, to wash in hot water, to pour a drink, lie down on his quilt, read the paper, eat some liver paste on crackers before going out to dinner. But to think of this actually made him feel a little sick, as though he had swallowed hard air. He had six checks left, and he was determined to deliver at least one of these: Mr. Green's check.

So he started again. He had four or five dark blocks to go, past open lots, condemned houses, old foundations, closed schools, black churches, mounds, and he reflected that there must be many people alive who had once seen the neighborhood rebuilt and new. Now there was a second layer of ruins; centuries of history accomplished through human massing. Numbers had given the place forced growth; enormous numbers had also broken it down. Objects once so new, so concrete that it could have occurred to

[13] A refuse heap, especially one uncovered by archaeologists.
[14] Much of Chicago burned in the Great Fire of 1871.

anyone they stood for other things, had crumbled. Therefore, reflected Grebe, the secret of them was out. It was that they stood for themselves by agreement, and were natural and not unnatural by agreement, and when the things themselves collapsed the agreement became visible. What was it, otherwise, that kept cities from looking peculiar? Rome, that was almost permanent, did not give rise to thoughts like these. And was it abidingly real? But in Chicago, where the cycles were so fast and the familiar died out, and again rose changed, and died again in thirty years, you saw the common agreement or covenant, and you were forced to think about appearances and realities. (He remembered Raynor and he smiled. Raynor was a clever boy.) Once you had grasped this, a great many things became intelligible. For instance, why Mr. Field should conceive such a scheme. Of course, if people were to agree to create a millionaire, a real millionaire would come into existence. And if you wanted to know how Mr. Field was inspired to think of this, why, he had within sight of his kitchen window the chart, the very bones of a successful scheme—the El with its blue and green confetti of signals. People consented to pay dimes and ride the crash-box cars, and so it was a success. Yet how absurd it looked; how little reality there was to start with. And yet Yerkes,[15] the great financier who built it, had known that he could get people to agree to do it. Viewed as itself, what a scheme of a scheme it seemed, how close to an appearance. Then, why wonder at Mr. Field's idea? He had grasped a principle. And then Grebe remembered, too, that Mr. Yerkes had established the Yerkes Observatory and endowed it with millions. Now, how did the notion come to him in his New York museum of a palace or his Aegean-bound yacht to give money to astronomers? Was he awed by the success of his bizarre enterprise and therefore ready to spend money to find out where in the universe being and seeming were identical? Yes, he wanted to know what abides; and whether flesh is Bible grass;[16] and he offered money to be burned in the fire of suns. Okay, then, Grebe thought further, these things exist because people consent to exist with them—we have got so far—and also there is a reality which doesn't depend on consent but within which consent is a game. But what about need, the need that keeps so many vast thousands in position? You tell me that, you *private* little gentleman and *decent* soul—he used these words against himself scornfully. Why is the consent given to misery? And why so painfully ugly? Because there is *something* that is dismal and permanently ugly? Here he sighed and gave it up, and thought it was enough for the present moment that he had a real check in his pocket for a Mr. Green who must be real beyond question. If only his neighbors didn't think they had to conceal him.

This time he stopped at the second floor. He struck a match and found a door. Presently a man answered his knock and Grebe had the check ready and showed it even before he began. "Does Tulliver Green live here? I'm from the relief."

The man narrowed the opening and spoke to someone at his back.

[15] Charles T. Yerkes (1837–1905), builder of the Chicago streetcar system and later of the London underground.

[16] "All flesh is grass, and all the goodliness thereof is as the flower of the field" (Isaiah 40:6).

"Does he live here?"

"Uh-uh. No."

"Or anywhere in this building? He's a sick man and he can't come for his dough." He exhibited the check in the light, which was smoky—the air smelled of charred lard—and the man held off the brim of his cap to study it.

"Uh-uh. Never seen the name."

"There's nobody around here that uses crutches?"

He seemed to think, but it was Grebe's impression that he was simply waiting for a decent interval to pass.

"No, suh. Nobody I ever see."

"I've been looking for this man all afternoon"—Grebe spoke out with sudden force—"and I'm going to have to carry this check back to the station. It seems strange not to be able to find a person to *give* him something when you're looking for him for a good reason. I suppose if I had bad news for him, I'd find him quick enough."

There was a responsive motion in the other man's face. "That's right, I reckon."

"It almost doesn't do any good to have a name if you can't be found by it. It doesn't stand for anything. He might as well not have any," he went on, smiling. It was as much of a concession as he could make to his desire to laugh.

"Well, now, there's a little old knot-back man I see once in a while. He might be the one you lookin' for. Downstairs."

"Where? Right side or left? Which door?"

"I don't know which. Thin-face little knot-back with a stick."

But no one answered at any of the doors on the first floor. He went to the end of the corridor, searching by matchlight, and found only a stairless exit to the yard, a drop of about six feet. But there was a bungalow near the alley, an old house like Mr. Field's. To jump was unsafe. He ran from the front door, through the underground passage and into the yard. The place was occupied. There was a light through the curtains, upstairs. The name on the ticket under the broken, scoop-shaped mailbox was Green! He exultantly rang the bell and pressed against the locked door. Then the lock clicked faintly and a long staircase opened before him. Someone was slowly coming down—a woman. He had the impression in the weak light that she was shaping her hair as she came, making herself presentable, for he saw her arms raised. But it was for support that they were raised; she was feeling her way downward, down the wall, stumbling. Next he wondered about the pressure of her feet on the treads; she did not seem to be wearing shoes. And it was a freezing stairway. His ring had got her out of bed, perhaps, and she had forgotten to put them on. And then he saw that she was not only shoeless but naked; she was entirely naked, climbing down while she talked to herself, a heavy woman, naked and drunk. She blundered into him. The contact of her breasts, though they touched only his coat, made him go back against the door with a blind shock. See what he had tracked down, in his hunting game!

The woman was saying to herself, furious with insult, "So I cain't ———k, huh? I'll show that son-of-a-bitch kin I, cain't I."

What should he do now? Grebe asked himself. Why, he should go. He should turn away and go. He couldn't talk to this woman. He couldn't keep her standing naked in the cold. But when he tried, he found himself unable to turn away.

He said, "Is this where Mr. Green lives?"

But she was still talking to herself and did not hear him.

"Is this Mr. Green's house?"

At last she turned her furious drunken glance on him. "What do you want?"

Again her eyes wandered from him; there was a dot of blood in their enraged brilliance. He wondered why she didn't feel the cold.

"I'm from the relief."

"Awright, what?"

"I've got a check for Tulliver Green."

This time she heard him and put out her hand.

"No, no, for *Mr.* Green. He's got to sign," he said. How was he going to get Green's signature tonight!

"I'll take it. He cain't."

He desperately shook his head, thinking of Mr. Field's precautions about identification. "I can't let you have it. It's for him. Are you Mrs. Green?"

"Maybe I is, and maybe I ain't. Who want to know?"

"Is he upstairs?"

"Awright. Take it up yourself, you goddamn fool."

Sure, he was a goddamn fool. Of course he could not go up because Green would probably be drunk and naked, too. And perhaps he would appear on the landing soon. He looked eagerly upward. Under the light was a high narrow brown wall. Empty! It remained empty!

"Hell with you, then!" he heard her cry. To deliver a check for coal and clothes, he was keeping her in the cold. She did not feel it, but his face was burning with frost and self-ridicule. He backed away from her.

"I'll come tomorrow, tell him."

"Ah, hell with you. Don' never come. What you doin' here in the night-time? Don' come back." She yelled so that he saw the breadth of her tongue. She stood astride in the long cold box of the hall and held on to the banister and the wall. The bungalow itself was shaped something like a box, a clumsy, high box pointing into the freezing air with its sharp, wintry lights.

"If you are Mrs. Green, I'll give you the check," he said, changing his mind.

"Give here, then." She took it, took the pen offered with it in her left hand, and tried to sign the receipt on the wall. He looked around, almost as though to see whether his madness was being observed, and came near believing that someone was standing on a mountain of used tires in the auto-junking shop next door.

"But are you Mrs. Green?" he now thought to ask. But she was already climbing the stairs with the check, and it was too late, if he had made an error, if he was now in trouble, to undo the thing. But he wasn't going to worry about it. Though she might not be Mrs. Green, he was convinced that Mr. Green was upstairs. Whoever she was, the woman stood for Green, whom he was not to see this time. Well, you silly bastard, he said to himself, so you think you found him. So what? Maybe you really did find him—what of it? But it was important that there was a real Mr. Green whom they could not keep him from reaching because he seemed to come as an emissary from hostile appearances. And though the self-ridicule was slow to diminish, and his face still blazed with it, he had, nevertheless, a feeling of elation, too. "For after all," he said, "he *could* be found!"

James Baldwin

(*1924–*)

The urgency and violence of twentieth-century history have often forced writers into especially close relationships with current events. William Butler Yeats's poetry is colored by the "terrible beauty" of the 1916 Easter Rising in Ireland, much of Thomas Mann's fiction is a complex reaction to the German defeat in World War I, and the work of the French existentialists of the 1940s was shaped in major ways by the Nazi occupation of France. The American civil rights movement of the 1960s similarly found its major literary interpreter in James Baldwin, who explored its meaning in a series of powerfully written and widely read essays and, less directly, in a number of fine novels and short stories. The essays collected in Notes of a Native Son *(1955),* Nobody Knows My Name *(1961), and* The Fire Next Time *(1963) brought Baldwin worldwide attention as one of the most accomplished essayists in American literary history, but they also placed him at the eye of a storm of controversy over his readings of racial issues. As the high passions of the 1960s recede with time, Baldwin has come to be regarded less as the spokesman of a movement and more as an imaginative writer whose interpretations of racial issues are grounded in his own complex personality.*

Baldwin was born in Harlem in 1924 to Berdis Jones, a domestic servant who three years later married David Baldwin, a brutal, paranoid laborer and storefront preacher by whom she had eight children. David Baldwin resented his wife's illegitimate son and subjected him to constant ridicule and abuse, from which Baldwin withdrew into a close relationship with his mother and into reading and schoolwork. While he was in De Witt Clinton High School, he also became a successful child preacher at the Fireside Pentecostal Church in Harlem, drawing large crowds for three years before losing his faith when he was sixteen.

Baldwin had already begun to write seriously while he was in high school, where he edited the school magazine, and he continued to write after graduation, while working in a defense plant in New Jersey. In 1943, Baldwin left home and settled in Greenwich Village, determined to become a writer. For the next five years, he supported himself by menial jobs and wrote at night, managing to sell a few magazine articles and beginning a novel. Richard Wright, whom he met in 1944, befriended him and helped him get a fellowship in 1945. A second award, the Rosenwald Fellowship, in 1948 enabled him to leave New York for Europe, where he remained for the next ten years, living in Paris, Switzerland, and the south of France.

The novel Baldwin had begun in Greenwich Village, Go Tell It on the Mountain, was completed in Europe and published in 1953. In this powerful and beautifully written novel, Baldwin drew upon his own early experiences for the story of a young Harlem boy named John Grimes with a gentle mother and a tyrannical stepfather and of Grimes's emotional conversion to fundamentalist religion. The critical praise with which Go Tell It on the Mountain was received was repeated in 1955, when Notes of a Native Son appeared. This collection of ten deeply personal essays on race had previously appeared in various magazines. In 1956, Baldwin's play The Amen Corner was produced at Howard University in Washington, D.C., and his second novel, Giovanni's Room, appeared. The Amen Corner returned to Baldwin's early religious experiences, telling the story of a woman evangelist, who is modeled upon a preacher named Mother Horn he had known in Harlem; the play was subsequently produced on Broadway in 1965. Giovanni's Room, in which the characters are white, deals not with race but with Baldwin's other major subject, homosexuality, in a story of an American student in Paris torn between two loves, for an Italian bartender named Giovanni and for the student's American fiancée.

Baldwin's return to the United States in 1957 inaugurated a second major stage in his career, a period of intense involvement with the civil rights movement. He visited the South for the first time soon after his return, became a member of the national advisory board of the Congress on Racial Equality, for several years wrote voluminously on civil rights issues, and spoke frequently and eloquently for the cause in person and on television. The essays of this period were collected in Nobody Knows My Name and The Fire Next Time. Nobody Knows My Name reprinted fifteen magazine articles and lectures, including three essays sharply critical of Richard Wright. These essays brought down upon Baldwin's head the wrath of the black radical leader Eldridge Cleaver, who in Soul on Ice (1968) defended Wright for his "profound political, economic, and social reference" and found in Baldwin a hatred of blacks and "a racial death-wish." Most of The Fire Next Time consisted of a long essay, "Down at the Cross; Letter From a Region of My Mind," which had created a sensation when it was first published in The New Yorker in 1962; it is perhaps Baldwin's finest essay.

Baldwin's first novel after his return to the United States was Another Country (1962), an ambitious work in which Baldwin brought his themes of race and sexuality together in the story of the suicide of a gifted black jazz drummer named Rufus Scott and the quests for love of his survivors: his sister Ida, his white friend Vivaldo Moore, and his bisexual white Southern lover Eric. Critics found the novel flawed and uneven, but it is Baldwin's fullest development of his interpretation of racism as rooted in white sexual repression and projected self-hate. Blues for Mr. Charlie, a play loosely based upon the killing of Emmett Till, a young black man lynched in 1955, ran for four months on Broadway in 1964, and Going to Meet the Man, a collection of short stories, was published in 1965.

A third period in Baldwin's career began in 1965 when he left the United States again and settled in Paris and Istanbul. His publications since then have included the novels Tell Me How Long the Train's Been Gone (1968), If Beale Street Could Talk (1974), and Just Above My Head (1979); a novella, This Morning, This Evening, So Soon (1967); three collections of essays; and miscellaneous other works, including screenplays, tape-recorded interviews, and a children's book.

"Sonny's Blues," originally published in 1957 and reprinted in 1965 in Going to Meet the Man, is one of Baldwin's most beautifully crafted stories and one of his richest explorations of the relationship between black culture and black identity. The *story might equally well be called "Sonny's Brother's Blues," for as it unfolds, it becomes the story less of Sonny's life than of the narrator's rediscovery of his own family and racial ties, his "brotherhood," in more than one sense. Sonny's arrest (which his brother, significantly, has to learn about from the newspaper) triggers a process of initiation for the narrator in which memories of the past become mingled with present encounters with Sonny and his world. In the final, climactic scene in the jazz club, when Sonny plays his triumphant "Am I Blue," his brother can join him in "leaving the shoreline and striking out for the deep water."*

FURTHER READING (*prepared by W. J. R.):* The most valuable single source of biographical information on Baldwin is Fern Eckman's *The Furious Passage of James Baldwin,* 1966, which is based primarily upon taped interviews with the author. Carolyn Wedin Sylvander's *James Baldwin,* 1980, begins with a biographical sketch, goes on to excellent appraisals of all the novels, and concludes with a discussion of Baldwin criticism. Baldwin's place in the tradition of black American writers is examined in Stanley Macebuh's *James Baldwin: A Critical Study,* 1973. Macebuh concentrates on Baldwin's novels and provides a good survey of black American literature. Diverse approaches to Baldwin's fiction are represented in *James Baldwin: A Collection of Critical Essays,* ed. Keneth Kinnamon, 1974, which includes Eldridge Cleaver's famous attack on Baldwin from his 1968 *Soul on Ice.* Baldwin is considered as novelist, essayist, playwright, and in other roles in *James Baldwin: A Critical Evaluation,* ed. Therman B. O'Daniel, 1977, which includes a bibliography of Baldwin's varied writings.

SONNY'S BLUES

I read about it in the paper, in the subway, on my way to work. I read it, and I couldn't believe it, and I read it again. Then perhaps I just stared at it, at the newsprint spelling out his name, spelling out the story. I stared at it in the swinging lights of the subway car, and in the faces and bodies of the people, and in my own face, trapped in the darkness which roared outside.

It was not to be believed and I kept telling myself that, as I walked from the subway station to the high school. And at the same time I couldn't doubt it. I was scared, scared for Sonny. He became real to me again. A great block of ice got settled in my belly and kept melting there slowly all day long, while I taught my classes algebra. It was a special kind of ice. It kept melting, sending trickles of ice water all up and down my veins, but it never got less. Sometimes it hardened and seemed to expand until I felt my guts were going to come spilling out or that I was going to choke or scream. This would always be at a moment when I was remembering some specific thing Sonny had once said or done.

When he was about as old as the boys in my classes his face had been bright and open, there was a lot of copper in it; and he'd had wonderfully direct brown eyes, and great gentleness and privacy. I wondered what he looked like now. He had been picked up, the evening before, in a raid on an apartment downtown, for peddling and using heroin.

I couldn't believe it: but what I mean by that is that I couldn't find any room for it anywhere inside me. I had kept it outside me for a long time. I hadn't wanted to know. I had had suspicions, but I didn't name them, I kept putting them away. I told myself that Sonny was wild, but he wasn't crazy. And he'd always been a good boy, he hadn't ever turned hard or evil or disrespectful, the way kids can, so quick, so quick, especially in Harlem. I didn't want to believe that I'd ever see my brother going down, coming to nothing, all that light in his face gone out, in the condition I'd already seen so many others. Yet it had happened and here I was, talking about algebra to a lot of boys who might, every one of them for all I knew, be popping off needles every time they went to the head.[1] Maybe it did more for them than algebra could.

I was sure that the first time Sonny had ever had horse,[2] he couldn't have been much older than these boys were now. These boys, now, were living as we'd been living then, they were growing up with a rush and their heads bumped abruptly against the low ceiling of their actual possibilities. They were filled with rage. All they really knew were two darknesses, the darkness of their lives, which was now closing in on them, and the darkness of the movies, which had blinded them to that other darkness, and in which they now, vindictively, dreamed, at once more together than they were at any other time, and more alone.

When the last bell rang, the last class ended, I let out my breath. It seemed I'd been holding it for all that time. My clothes were wet—I may have looked as though I'd been sitting in a steam bath, all dressed up, all afternoon. I sat alone in the classroom a long time. I listened to the boys outside, downstairs, shouting and cursing and laughing. Their laughter struck me for perhaps the first time. It was not the joyous laughter which—God knows why—one associates with children. It was mocking and insular, its intent was to denigrate. It was disenchanted, and in this, also, lay the authority of their curses. Perhaps I was listening to them because I was thinking about my brother and in them I heard my brother. And myself.

One boy was whistling a tune, at once very complicated and very simple, it seemed to be pouring out of him as though he were a bird, and it sounded very cool and moving through all that harsh, bright air, only just holding its own through all those other sounds.

I stood up and walked over to the window and looked down into the courtyard. It was the beginning of the spring and the sap was rising in the boys. A teacher passed through them every now and again, quickly, as though he or she couldn't wait to get out of that courtyard, to get those boys out of their sight and off their minds. I started collecting my stuff. I thought I'd better get home and talk to Isabel.

The courtyard was almost deserted by the time I got downstairs. I saw this boy standing in the shadow of a doorway, looking just like Sonny. I almost called his name. Then I saw that it wasn't Sonny, but somebody we used to know, a boy from around our block. He'd been Sonny's friend. He'd never been mine, having been too young for me, and, anyway, I'd never liked him. And now, even though he was a grown-up man, he still hung around that block, still spent hours on the street corners, was always high and raggy. I used to run into him from time to time and he'd often work around to asking me for a quarter or fifty cents. He always had some real good excuse, too, and I always gave it to him. I don't know why.

[1] Toilet. [2] Heroin.

But now, abruptly, I hated him. I couldn't stand the way he looked at me, partly like a dog, partly like a cunning child. I wanted to ask him what the hell he was doing in the school courtyard.

He sort of shuffled over to me, and he said, "I see you got the papers. So you already know about it."

"You mean about Sonny? Yes, I already know about it. How come they didn't get you?"

He grinned. It made him repulsive and it also brought to mind what he'd looked like as a kid. "I wasn't there. I stay away from them people."

"Good for you." I offered him a cigarette and I watched him through the smoke. "You come all the way down here just to tell me about Sonny?"

"That's right." He was sort of shaking his head and his eyes looked strange, as though they were about to cross. The bright sun deadened his damp dark brown skin and it made his eyes look yellow and showed up the dirt in his kinked hair. He smelled funky. I moved a little away from him and I said, "Well, thanks. But I already know about it and I got to get home."

"I'll walk you a little ways," he said. We started walking. There were a couple of kids still loitering in the courtyard and one of them said goodnight to me and looked strangely at the boy beside me.

"What're you going to do?" he asked me. "I mean, about Sonny?"

"Look. I haven't seen Sonny for over a year, I'm not sure I'm going to do anything. Anyway, what the hell *can* I do?"

"That's right," he said quickly, "ain't nothing you can do. Can't much help old Sonny no more, I guess."

It was what I was thinking and so it seemed to me he had no right to say it.

"I'm surprised at Sonny, though," he went on—he had a funny way of talking, he looked straight ahead as though he were talking to himself—"I thought Sonny was a smart boy, I thought he was too smart to get hung."

"I guess he thought so too," I said sharply, "and that's how he got hung. And how about you? You're pretty goddamn smart, I bet."

Then he looked directly at me, just for a minute. "I ain't smart," he said. "If I was smart, I'd have reached for a pistol a long time ago."

"Look. Don't tell *me* your sad story, if it was up to me, I'd give you one." Then I felt guilty—guilty, probably, for never having supposed that the poor bastard *had* a story of his own, much less a sad one, and I asked, quickly, "What's going to happen to him now?"

He didn't answer this. He was off by himself some place.

"Funny thing," he said, and from his tone we might have been discussing the quickest way to get to Brooklyn, "when I saw the papers this morning, the first thing I asked myself was if I had anything to do with it. I felt sort of responsible."

I began to listen more carefully. The subway station was on the corner, just before us, and I stopped. He stopped, too. We were in front of a bar and he ducked slightly, peering in, but whoever he was looking for didn't seem to be there. The juke box was blasting away with something black and bouncy and I half watched the barmaid as she danced her way from the juke box to her place behind the bar. And I watched her face as she laughingly responded to something someone said to her, still keeping time to the music. When she smiled one saw the little girl, one sensed the doomed, still-struggling woman beneath the battered face of the semi-whore.

"I never *give* Sonny nothing," the boy said finally, "but a long time ago I come to school high and Sonny asked me how it felt." He paused, I couldn't bear to watch him, I watched the barmaid, and I listened to the music which seemed to be causing the pavement to shake. "I told him it felt great." The music stopped, the barmaid paused and watched the juke box until the music began again. "It did."

All this was carrying me some place I didn't want to go. I certainly didn't want to know how it felt. It filled everything, the people, the houses, the music, the dark, quicksilver barmaid, with menace; and this menace was their reality.

"What's going to happen to him now?" I asked again.

"They'll send him away some place and they'll try to cure him." He shook his head. "Maybe he'll even think he's kicked the habit. Then they'll let him loose"—he gestured, throwing his cigarette into the gutter. "That's all."

"What do you mean, that's *all*?"

But I knew what he meant.

"I *mean*, that's *all*." He turned his head and looked at me, pulling down the corners of his mouth. "Don't you know what I mean?" he asked, softly.

"How the hell *would* I know what you mean?" I almost whispered it, I don't know why.

"That's right," he said to the air, "how would *he* know what I mean?" He turned toward me again, patient and calm, and yet I somehow felt him shaking, shaking as though he were going to fall apart. I felt that ice in my guts again, the dread I'd felt all afternoon; and again I watched the barmaid, moving about the bar, washing glasses, and singing. "Listen. They'll let him out and then it'll just start all over again. That's what I mean."

"You mean—they'll let him out. And then he'll just start working his way back in again. You mean he'll never kick the habit. Is that what you mean?"

"That's right," he said, cheerfully. "*You* see what I mean."

"Tell me," I said at last, "why does he want to die? He must want to die, he's killing himself, why does he want to die?"

He looked at me in surprise. He licked his lips. "He don't want to die. He wants to live. Don't nobody want to die, ever."

Then I wanted to ask him—too many things. He could not have answered, or if he had, I could not have borne the answers. I started walking. "Well, I guess it's none of my business."

"It's going to be rough on old Sonny," he said. We reached the subway station. "This is your station?" he asked. I nodded. I took one step down. "Damn!" he said, suddenly. I looked up at him. He grinned again. "Damn it if I didn't leave all my money home. You ain't got a dollar on you, have you? Just for a couple of days, is all."

All at once something inside gave and threatened to come pouring out of me. I didn't hate him any more. I felt that in another moment I'd start crying like a child.

"Sure," I said. "Don't sweat." I looked in my wallet and didn't have a dollar, I only had a five. "Here," I said. "That hold you?"

He didn't look at it—he didn't want to look at it. A terrible, closed look came over his face, as though he were keeping the number on the bill a secret from him and me. "Thanks," he said, and now he was dying to see me go. "Don't worry about Sonny. Maybe I'll write him or something."

"Sure," I said. "You do that. So long."

"Be seeing you," he said. I went on down the steps.

And I didn't write Sonny or send him anything for a long time. When I finally did, it was just after my little girl died, and he wrote me back a letter which made me feel like a bastard.

Here's what he said:

Dear brother,

You don't know how much I needed to hear from you. I wanted to write you many a time but I dug how much I must have hurt you and so I didn't write. But now I feel like a man who's been trying to climb up out of some deep, real deep and funky hole and just saw the sun up there, outside. I got to get outside.

I can't tell you much about how I got here. I mean I don't know how to tell you. I guess I was afraid of something or I was trying to escape from something and you know I have never been very strong in the head (smile). I'm glad Mama and Daddy are dead and can't see what's happened to their son and I swear if I'd known what I was doing I would never have hurt you so, you and a lot of other fine people who were nice to me and who believed in me.

I don't want you to think it had anything to do with me being a musician. It's more than that. Or maybe less than that. I can't get anything straight in my head down here and I try not to think about what's going to happen to me when I get outside again. Sometime I think I'm going to flip and *never* get outside and sometime I think I'll come straight back. I tell you one thing, though, I'd rather blow my brains out than go through this again. But that's what they all say, so they tell me. If I tell you when I'm coming to New York and if you could meet me, I sure would appreciate it. Give my love to Isabel and the kids and I was sure sorry to hear about little Gracie. I wish I could be like Mama and say the Lord's will be done, but I don't know it seems to me that trouble is the one thing that never does get stopped and I don't know what good it does to blame it on the Lord. But maybe it does some good if you believe it.

Your brother,
Sonny

Then I kept in constant touch with him and I sent him whatever I could and I went to meet him when he came back to New York. When I saw him many things I thought I had forgotten came flooding back to me. This was because I had begun, finally, to wonder about Sonny, about the life that Sonny lived inside. This life, whatever it was, had made him older and thinner and it had deepened the distant stillness in which he had always moved. He looked very unlike my baby brother. Yet, when he smiled, when we shook hands, the baby brother I'd never known looked out from the depths of his private life, like an animal waiting to be coaxed into the light.

"How you been keeping?" he asked me.

"All right. And you?"

"Just fine." He was smiling all over his face. "It's good to see you again."

"It's good to see you."

The seven years' difference in our ages lay between us like a chasm: I wondered if these years would ever operate between us as a bridge. I was remembering, and it made it hard to catch my breath, that I had been there when he was born; and I had heard the first words he had ever spoken. When he started to walk, he walked from our mother straight to me. I caught him just before he fell when he took the first steps he ever took in this world.

"How's Isabel?"

"Just fine. She's dying to see you."

"And the boys?"

"They're fine, too. They're anxious to see their uncle."

"Oh, come on. You know they don't remember me."

"Are you kidding? Of course they remember you."

He grinned again. We got into a taxi. We had a lot to say to each other, far too much to know how to begin.

As the taxi began to move, I asked, "You still want to go to India?"

He laughed. "You still remember that. Hell, no. This place is Indian enough for me."

"It used to belong to them," I said.

And he laughed again. "They damn sure knew what they were doing when they got rid of it."

Years ago, when he was around fourteen, he'd been all hipped on the idea of going to India. He read books about people sitting on rocks, naked, in all kinds of weather, but mostly bad, naturally, and walking barefoot through hot coals and arriving at wisdom. I used to say that it sounded to me as though they were getting away from wisdom as fast as they could. I think he sort of looked down on me for that.

"Do you mind," he asked, "if we have the driver drive alongside the park?[3] On the west side—I haven't seen the city in so long."

"Of course not," I said. I was afraid that I might sound as though I were humoring him, but I hoped he wouldn't take it that way.

So we drove along, between the green of the park and the stony, lifeless elegance of hotels and apartment buildings, toward the vivid, killing streets of our childhood. These streets hadn't changed, though housing projects jutted up out of them now like rocks in the middle of a boiling sea. Most of the houses in which we had grown up had vanished, as had the stores from which we had stolen, the basements in which we had first tried sex, the rooftops from which we had hurled tin cans and bricks. But houses exactly like the houses of our past yet dominated the landscape, boys exactly like the boys we once had been found themselves smothering in these houses, came down into the streets for light and air and found themselves encircled

[3] Central Park in Manhattan.

by disaster. Some escaped the trap, most didn't. Those who got out always left something of themselves behind, as some animals amputate a leg and leave it in the trap. It might be said, perhaps, that I had escaped, after all, I was a school teacher; or that Sonny had, he hadn't lived in Harlem for years. Yet, as the cab moved uptown through streets which seemed, with a rush, to darken with dark people, and as I covertly studied Sonny's face, it came to me that what we both were seeking through our separate cab windows was that part of ourselves which had been left behind. It's always at the hour of trouble and confrontation that the missing member aches.

We hit 110th Street and started rolling up Lenox Avenue.[4] And I'd known this avenue all my life, but it seemed to me again, as it had seemed on the day I'd first heard about Sonny's trouble, filled with a hidden menace which was its very breath of life.

"We almost there," said Sonny.

"Almost." We were both too nervous to say anything more.

We live in a housing project. It hasn't been up long. A few days after it was up it seemed uninhabitably new, now, of course, it's already rundown. It looks like a parody of the good, clean, faceless life—God knows the people who live in it do their best to make it a parody. The beat-looking grass lying around isn't enough to make their lives green, the hedges will never hold out the streets, and they know it. The big windows fool no one, they aren't big enough to make space out of no space. They don't bother with the windows, they watch the TV screen instead. The playground is most popular with the children who don't play at jacks, or skip rope, or roller skate, or swing, and they can be found in it after dark. We moved in partly because it's not too far from where I teach, and partly for the kids; but it's really just like the houses in which Sonny and I grew up. The same things happen, they'll have the same things to remember. The moment Sonny and I started into the house I had the feeling that I was simply bringing him back into the danger he had almost died trying to escape.

Sonny has never been talkative. So I don't know why I was sure he'd be dying to talk to me when supper was over the first night. Everything went fine, the oldest boy remembered him, and the youngest boy liked him, and Sonny had remembered to bring something for each of them; and Isabel, who is really much nicer than I am, more open and giving, had gone to a lot of trouble about dinner and was genuinely glad to see him. And she's always been able to tease Sonny in a way that I haven't. It was nice to see her face so vivid again and to hear her laugh and watch her make Sonny laugh. She wasn't, or, anyway, she didn't seem to be, at all uneasy or embarrassed. She chatted as though there were no subject which had to be avoided and she got Sonny past his first, faint stiffness. And thank God she was there, for I was filled with that icy dread again. Everything I did seemed awkward to me, and everything I said sounded freighted with hidden meaning. I was trying to remember everything I'd heard about dope addiction and I couldn't help watching Sonny for signs. I wasn't doing it out of malice. I was trying to find out something about my brother. I was dying to hear him tell me he was safe.

[4]Major street in Harlem, in north Manhattan; 110th Street is usually regarded as the southern boundary of Harlem.

"Safe!" my father grunted, whenever Mama suggested trying to move to a neighborhood which might be safer for children. "Safe, hell! Ain't no place safe for kids, nor nobody."

He always went on like this, but he wasn't, ever, really as bad as he sounded, not even on weekends, when he got drunk. As a matter of fact, he was always on the lookout for "something a little better," but he died before he found it. He died suddenly, during a drunken weekend in the middle of the war, when Sonny was fifteen. He and Sonny hadn't ever got on too well. And this was partly because Sonny was the apple of his father's eye. It was because he loved Sonny so much and was frightened for him, that he was always fighting with him. It doesn't do any good to fight with Sonny. Sonny just moves back, inside himself, where he can't be reached. But the principal reason that they never hit it off is that they were so much alike. Daddy was big and rough and loud-talking, just the opposite of Sonny, but they both had—that same privacy.

Mama tried to tell me something about this, just after Daddy died. I was home on leave from the army.

This was the last time I ever saw my mother alive. Just the same, this picture gets all mixed up in my mind with pictures I had of her when she was younger. The way I always see her is the way she used to be on a Sunday afternoon, say, when the old folks were talking after the big Sunday dinner. I always see her wearing pale blue. She'd be sitting on the sofa. And my father would be sitting in the easy chair, not far from her. And the living room would be full of church folks and relatives. There they sit, in chairs all around the living room, and the night is creeping up outside, but nobody knows it yet. You can see the darkness growing against the windowpanes and you hear the street noises every now and again, or maybe the jangling beat of a tambourine from one of the churches close by, but it's real quiet in the room. For a moment nobody's talking, but every face looks darkening, like the sky outside. And my mother rocks a little from the waist, and my father's eyes are closed. Everyone is looking at something a child can't see. For a minute they've forgotten the children. Maybe a kid is lying on the rug, half asleep. Maybe somebody's got a kid in his lap and is absent-mindedly stroking the kid's head. Maybe there's a kid, quiet and big-eyed, curled up in a big chair in the corner. The silence, the darkness coming, and the darkness in the faces frighten the child obscurely. He hopes that the hand which strokes his forehead will never stop—will never die. He hopes that there will never come a time when the old folks won't be sitting around the living room, talking about where they've come from, and what they've seen, and what's happened to them and their kinfolk.

But something deep and watchful in the child knows that this is bound to end, is already ending. In a moment someone will get up and turn on the light. Then the old folks will remember the children and they won't talk any more that day. And when light fills the room, the child is filled with darkness. He knows that every time this happens he's moved just a little closer to that darkness outside. The darkness outside is what the old folks have been talking about. It's what they've come from. It's what they endure. The child knows that they won't talk any more because if he knows too much about what's happened to *them*, he'll know too much too soon, about what's going to happen to *him*.

The last time I talked to my mother, I remember I was restless. I wanted to get out and see Isabel. We weren't married then and we had a lot to straighten out between us.

There Mama sat, in black, by the window. She was humming an old church song, *Lord, you brought me from a long ways off*. Sonny was out somewhere. Mama kept watching the streets.

"I don't know," she said, "if I'll ever see you again, after you go off from here. But I hope you'll remember the things I tried to teach you."

"Don't talk like that," I said, and smiled. "You'll be here a long time yet."

She smiled, too, but she said nothing. She was quiet for a long time. And I said, "Mama, don't you worry about nothing. I'll be writing all the time, and you be getting the checks. . . ."

"I want to talk to you about your brother," she said, suddenly. "If anything happens to me he ain't going to have nobody to look out for him."

"Mama," I said, "ain't nothing going to happen to you *or* Sonny. Sonny's all right. He's a good boy and he's got good sense."

"It ain't a question of his being a good boy," Mama said, "nor of his having good sense. It ain't only the bad ones, nor yet the dumb ones that gets sucked under." She stopped, looking at me. "Your Daddy once had a brother," she said, and she smiled in a way that made me feel she was in pain. "You didn't never know that, did you?"

"No," I said, "I never knew that," and I watched her face.

"Oh, yes," she said, "your Daddy had a brother." She looked out of the window again. "I know you never saw your Daddy cry. But *I* did—many a time, through all these years."

I asked her, "What happened to his brother? How come nobody's ever talked about him?"

This was the first time I ever saw my mother look old.

"His brother got killed," she said, "when he was just a little younger than you are now. I knew him. He was a fine boy. He was maybe a little full of the devil, but he didn't mean nobody no harm."

Then she stopped and the room was silent, exactly as it had sometimes been on those Sunday afternoons. Mama kept looking out into the streets.

"He used to have a job in the mill," she said, "and, like all young folks, he just liked to perform on Saturday nights. Saturday nights, him and your father would drift around to different places, go to dances and things like that, or just sit around with people they knew, and your father's brother would sing, he had a fine voice, and play along with himself on his guitar. Well, this particular Saturday night, him and your father was coming home from some place, and they were both a little drunk and there was a moon that night, it was bright like day. Your father's brother was feeling kind of good, and he was whistling to himself, and he had his guitar slung over his shoulder. They was coming down a hill and beneath them was a road that turned off from the highway. Well, your father's brother, being always kind of frisky, decided to run down this hill, and he did, with that guitar banging and clanging behind him, and he ran across the road, and he was making water behind a tree. And your father was sort of amused at him and he was still coming down the hill, kind of slow. Then he heard a car motor and that same minute his brother stepped from behind the tree, into the road, in the moonlight. And he started to cross the road. And your father started to run down the hill, he says he don't know why. This car was full of white men. They was all drunk, and when they seen your father's brother they let out a great whoop and holler and they aimed the car straight at him. They was having fun, they just wanted to scare him, the way they do sometimes, you know. But they was drunk. And I guess the boy, being drunk, too, and scared, kind of lost his head. By the time he jumped it was too late. Your father says he heard his brother scream when the car rolled over him, and he heard the wood of that guitar when it give, and he heard them strings go flying, and he heard them white men shouting, and the car kept on a-going and it ain't stopped till this day. And, time your father got down the hill, his brother weren't nothing but blood and pulp."

Tears were gleaming on my mother's face. There wasn't anything I could say.

"He never mentioned it," she said, "because I never let him mention it before you children. Your Daddy was like a crazy man that night and for many a night thereafter. He says he never in his life seen anything as dark as that road after the lights of that car had gone away. Weren't nothing, weren't nobody on that road, just your Daddy and his brother and that busted guitar. Oh, yes. Your Daddy never did really get right again. Till the day he died he weren't sure but that every white man he saw was the man that killed his brother."

She stopped and took out her handkerchief and dried her eyes and looked at me.

"I ain't telling you all this," she said, "to make you scared or bitter or to make you hate nobody. I'm telling you this because you got a brother. And the world ain't changed."

I guess I didn't want to believe this. I guess she saw this in my face. She turned away from me, toward the window again, searching those streets.

"But I praise my Redeemer," she said at last, "that He called your Daddy home before me. I ain't saying it to throw no flowers at myself, but, I declare, it keeps me from feeling too cast down to know I helped your father get safely through this world. Your father always acted like he was the roughest, strongest man on earth. And everybody took him to be like that. But if he hadn't had me there—to see his tears!"

She was crying again. Still, I couldn't move. I said, "Lord, Lord, Mama, I didn't know it was like that."

"Oh, honey," she said, "there's a lot that you don't know. But you are going to find out." She stood up from the window and came over to me. "You got to hold on to your brother," she said, "and don't let him fall, no matter what it looks like is happening to him and no matter how evil you gets with him. You going to be evil with him many a time. But don't you forget what I told you, you hear?"

"I won't forget," I said. "Don't you worry, I won't forget. I won't let nothing happen to Sonny."

My mother smiled as though she were amused at something she saw in my face. Then, "You may not be able to stop nothing from happening. But you got to let him know you's *there*."

Two days later I was married, and then I was gone. And I had a lot of things on my mind and I pretty well forgot my promise to Mama until I got shipped home on a special furlough for her funeral.

And, after the funeral, with just Sonny and me alone in the empty kitchen, I tried to find out something about him.

"What do you want to do?" I asked him.

"I'm going to be a musician," he said.

For he had graduated, in the time I had been away, from dancing to the juke box to finding out who was playing what, and what they were doing with it, and he had bought himself a set of drums.

"You mean, you want to be a drummer?" I somehow had the feeling that being a drummer might be all right for other people but not for my brother Sonny.

"I don't think," he said, looking at me very gravely, "that I'll ever be a good drummer. But I think I can play a piano."

I frowned. I'd never played the role of the older brother quite so seriously before, had scarcely ever, in fact, *asked* Sonny a damn thing. I sensed myself in the presence of something I didn't really know how to handle, didn't understand. So I made my frown a little deeper as I asked: "What kind of musician do you want to be?"

He grinned. "How many kinds do you think there are?"

"Be *serious*," I said.

He laughed, throwing his head back, and then looked at me. "I *am* serious."

"Well, then, for Christ's sake, stop kidding around and answer a serious question. I mean, do you want to be a concert pianist, you want to play classical music and all that, or—or what?" Long before I finished he was laughing again. "For Christ's *sake*, Sonny!"

He sobered, but with difficulty. "I'm sorry. But you sound so—*scared*!" and he was off again.

"Well, you may think it's funny now, baby, but it's not going to be so funny when you have to make your living at it, let me tell you *that*." I was furious because I knew he was laughing at me and I didn't know why.

"No," he said, very sober now, and afraid, perhaps, that he'd hurt me, "I don't want to be a classical pianist. That isn't what interests me. I mean"—he paused, looking hard at me, as though his eyes would help me to understand, and then gestured helplessly, as though perhaps his hand would help—"I mean, I'll have a lot of studying to do, and I'll have to study *everything*, but, I mean, I want to play *with*—jazz musicians." He stopped. "I want to play jazz," he said.

Well, the word had never before sounded as heavy, as real, as it sounded that afternoon in Sonny's mouth. I just looked at him and I was probably frowning a real frown by this time. I simply couldn't see why on earth he'd want to spend his time hanging around nightclubs, clowning around on bandstands, while people pushed each other around a dance floor. It seemed—beneath him, somehow. I had never thought about it before, had never been forced to, but I suppose I had always put jazz musicians in a class with what Daddy called "good-time people."

"Are you *serious*?"

"Hell, *yes*, I'm serious."

He looked more helpless than ever, and annoyed, and deeply hurt.

I suggested, helpfully: "You mean—like Louis Armstrong?"[5]

His face closed as though I'd struck him. "No. I'm not talking about none of that old-time, down home crap."

"Well, look, Sonny, I'm sorry, don't get mad. I just don't altogether get it, that's all. Name somebody—you know, a jazz musician you admire."

"Bird."

"Who?"

"Bird! Charlie Parker![6] Don't they teach you nothing in the goddamn army?"

I lit a cigarette. I was surprised and then a little amused to discover that I was trembling. "I've been out of touch," I said. "You'll have to be patient with me. Now. Who's this Parker character?"

"He's just one of the greatest jazz musicians alive," said Sonny, sullenly, his hands in his pockets, his back to me. "Maybe *the* greatest," he added, bitterly, "that's probably why *you* never heard of him."

"All right," I said, "I'm ignorant. I'm sorry. I'll go out and buy all the cat's records right away, all right?"

"It don't," said Sonny, with dignity, "make any difference to me. I don't care what you listen to. Don't do me any favors."

I was beginning to realize that I'd never seen him so upset before. With another part of my mind I was thinking that this would probably turn out to be one of those things kids go through and that I shouldn't make it seem important by pushing it too hard. Still, I didn't think it would do any harm to ask: "Doesn't all this take a lot of time? Can you make a living at it?"

He turned back to me and half leaned, half sat, on the kitchen table. "Everything takes time," he said, "and—well, yes, sure, I can make a living at it. But what I don't seem to be able to make you understand is that it's the only thing I want to do."

"Well, Sonny," I said, gently, "you know people can't always do exactly what they *want* to do—"

"*No*, I don't know that," said Sonny, surprising me. "I think people *ought* to do what they want to do, what else are they alive for?"

"You getting to be a big boy," I said desperately, "it's time you started thinking about your future."

"I'm thinking about my future," said Sonny, grimly. "I think about it all the time."

I gave up. I decided, if he didn't change his mind, that we could always talk about it later. "In the meantime," I said, "you got to finish school." We had already decided that he'd have to move in with Isabel and her folks. I knew this wasn't the ideal arrangement because Isabel's folks are inclined to be dicty[7] and they hadn't especially wanted Isabel to marry me. But I didn't know what else to do. "And we have to get you fixed up at Isabel's."

[5] Louis Armstrong (1900–1971), perhaps the greatest trumpet player in jazz history. He remained rooted in the "down home" Dixieland style, while also popularizing jazz for a white, middle-class audience.

[6] Charlie "Bird" Parker (1920–1955), alto saxophonist and one of the finest improvisers in the history of jazz. The central figure in the "bop" movement of the 1940s, he was also addicted to heroin.

[7] Dictatorial, bossy.

There was a long silence. He moved from the kitchen table to the window. "That's a terrible idea. You know it yourself."

"Do you have a *better* idea?"

He just walked up and down the kitchen for a minute. He was as tall as I was. He had started to shave. I suddenly had the feeling that I didn't know him at all.

He stopped at the kitchen table and picked up my cigarettes. Looking at me with a kind of mocking, amused defiance, he put one between his lips. "You mind?"

"You smoking already?"

He lit the cigarette and nodded, watching me through the smoke. "I just wanted to see if I'd have the courage to smoke in front of you." He grinned and blew a great cloud of smoke to the ceiling. "It was easy." He looked at my face. "Come on, now. I bet you was smoking at my age, tell the truth."

I didn't say anything but the truth was on my face, and he laughed. But now there was something very strained in his laugh. "Sure. And I bet that ain't all you was doing."

He was frightening me a little. "Cut the crap," I said. "We already decided that you was going to go and live at Isabel's. Now what's got into you all of a sudden?"

"*You* decided it," he pointed out. "*I* didn't decide nothing." He stopped in front of me, leaning against the stove, arms loosely folded. "Look, brother. I don't want to stay in Harlem no more, I really don't." He was very earnest. He looked at me, then over toward the kitchen window. There was something in his eyes I'd never seen before, some thoughtfulness, some worry all his own. He rubbed the muscle of one arm. "It's time I was getting out of here."

"Where do you want to *go*, Sonny?"

"I want to join the army. Or the navy, I don't care. If I say I'm old enough, they'll believe me."

Then I got mad. It was because I was so scared. "You must be crazy. You goddamn fool, what the hell do you want to go and join the *army* for?"

"I just told you. To get out of Harlem."

"Sonny, you haven't even finished *school*. And if you really want to be a musician, how do you expect to study if you're in the *army*?"

He looked at me, trapped, and in anguish. "There's ways. I might be able to work out some kind of deal. Anyway, I'll have the G.I. Bill when I come out."

"*If* you come out." We stared at each other. "Sonny, please. Be reasonable. I know the setup is far from perfect. But we got to do the best we can."

"I ain't learning nothing in school," he said. "Even when I go." He turned away from me and opened the window and threw his cigarette out into the narrow alley. I watched his back. "At least, I ain't learning nothing you'd want me to learn." He slammed the window so hard I thought the glass would fly out, and turned back to me. "And I'm sick of the stink of these garbage cans!"

"Sonny," I said, "I know how you feel. But if you don't finish school now, you're going to be sorry later that you didn't." I grabbed him by the shoulders. "And you only got another year. It ain't so bad. And I'll come back and I swear I'll help you do *whatever* you want to do. Just try to put up with it till I come back. Will you please do that? For me?"

He didn't answer and he wouldn't look at me.

"Sonny. You hear me?"

He pulled away. "I hear you. But you never hear anything *I* say."

I didn't know what to say to that. He looked out of the window and then back at me. "OK," he said, and sighed. "I'll try."

Then I said, trying to cheer him up a little, "They got a piano at Isabel's. You can practice on it."

And as a matter of fact, it did cheer him up for a minute. "That's right," he said to himself. "I forgot that." His face relaxed a little. But the worry, the thoughtfulness, played on it still, the way shadows play on a face which is staring into the fire.

But I thought I'd never hear the end of that piano. At first, Isabel would write me, saying how nice it was that Sonny was so serious about his music and how, as soon as he came in from school, or wherever he had been when he was supposed to be at school, he went straight to that piano and stayed there until suppertime. And, after supper, he went back to that piano and stayed there until everybody went to bed. He was at the piano all day Saturday and all day Sunday. Then he bought a record player and started playing records. He'd play one record over and over again, all day long sometimes, and he'd improvise along with it on the piano. Or he'd play one section of the record, one chord, one change, one progression, then he'd do it on the piano. Then back to the record. Then back to the piano.

Well, I really don't know how they stood it. Isabel finally confessed that it wasn't like living with a person at all, it was like living with sound. And the sound didn't make any sense to her, didn't make any sense to any of them—naturally. They began, in a way, to be afflicted by this presence that was living in their home. It was as though Sonny were some sort of god, or monster. He moved in an atmosphere which wasn't like theirs at all. They fed him and he ate, he washed himself, he walked in and out of their door; he certainly wasn't nasty or unpleasant or rude, Sonny isn't any of those things; but it was as though he were all wrapped up in some cloud, some fire, some vision all his own; and there wasn't any way to reach him.

At the same time, he wasn't really a man yet, he was still a child, and they had to watch out for him in all kinds of ways. They certainly couldn't throw him out. Neither did they dare to make a great scene about that piano because even they dimly sensed, as I sensed, from so many thousands of miles away, that Sonny was at that piano playing for his life.

But he hadn't been going to school. One day a letter came from the school board and Isabel's mother got it—there had, apparently, been other letters but Sonny had torn them up. This day, when Sonny came in, Isabel's mother showed him the letter and asked where he'd been spending his time. And she finally got it out of him that he'd been down in Greenwich Village, with musicians and other characters, in a white girl's apartment.

And this scared her and she started to scream at him and what came up, once she began—though she denies it to this day—was what sacrifices they were making to give Sonny a decent home and how little he appreciated it.

Sonny didn't play the piano that day. By evening, Isabel's mother had calmed down but then there was the old man to deal with, and Isabel herself. Isabel says she did her best to be calm but she broke down and started crying. She says she just watched Sonny's face. She could tell, by watching him, what was happening with him. And what was happening was that they penetrated his cloud, they had reached him. Even if their fingers had been a thousand times more gentle than human fingers ever are, he could hardly help feeling that they had stripped him naked and were spitting on that nakedness. For he also had to see that his presence, that music, which was life or death to him, had been torture for them and that they had endured it, not at all for his sake, but only for mine. And Sonny couldn't take that. He can take it a little better today than he could then but he's still not very good at it and, frankly, I don't know anybody who is.

The silence of the next few days must have been louder than the sound of all the music ever played since time began. One morning, before she went to work, Isabel was in his room for something and she suddenly realized that all of his records were gone. And she knew for certain that he was gone. And he was. He went as far as the navy would carry him. He finally sent me a postcard from some place in Greece and that was the first I knew that Sonny was still alive. I didn't see him any more until we were both back in New York and the war had long been over.

He was a man by then, of course, but I wasn't willing to see it. He came by the house from time to time, but we fought almost every time we met. I didn't like the way he carried himself, loose and dreamlike all the time, and I didn't like his friends, and his music seemed to be merely an excuse for the life he led. It sounded just that weird and disordered.

Then we had a fight, a pretty awful fight, and I didn't see him for months. By and by I looked him up, where he was living, in a furnished room in the Village, and I tried to make it up. But there were lots of other people in the room and Sonny just lay on his bed, and he wouldn't come downstairs with me, and he treated these other people at though they were his family and I weren't. So I got mad and then he got mad, and then I told him that he might just as well be dead as live the way he was living. Then he stood up and he told me not to worry about him any more in life, that he *was* dead as far as I was concerned. Then he pushed me to the door and the other people looked on as though nothing were happening, and he slammed the door behind me. I stood in the hallway, staring at the door. I heard somebody laugh in the room and then the tears came to my eyes. I started down the steps, whistling to keep from crying, I kept whistling to myself, *You going to need me, baby, one of these cold, rainy days.*

I read about Sonny's trouble in the spring. Little Grace died in the fall. She was a beautiful little girl. But she only lived a little over two years. She died of polio and she suffered. She had a slight fever for a couple of days, but it didn't seem like anything and we just kept her in bed. And we would certainly have called the doctor, but the fever dropped, she seemed to be all right. So we thought it had just been a cold. Then, one day, she was up, playing, Isabel was in the kitchen fixing lunch for the two boys when they'd come in from school, and she heard Grace fall down in the living room. When you have a lot of children you don't always start running when one of them falls, unless they start screaming or something. And, this time, Gracie was quiet. Yet, Isabel says that when she heard that *thump* and then that silence, something happened to her to make her afraid. And she ran to the living room and there was little Grace on the floor, all twisted up, and the reason she hadn't screamed was that she couldn't get her breath. And when she did scream, it was the worst sound, Isabel says, that she'd ever heard in all her life, and she still hears it sometimes in her dreams. Isabel will sometimes wake me up with a low, moaning, strangling sound and I have to be quick to awaken her and hold her to me and where Isabel is weeping against me seems a mortal wound.

I think I may have written Sonny the very day that little Grace was buried. I was sitting in the living room in the dark, by myself, and I suddenly thought of Sonny. My trouble made his real.

One Saturday afternoon, when Sonny had been living with us, or anyway, been in our house, for nearly two weeks, I found myself wandering aimlessly about the living room, drinking from a can of beer, and trying to work up courage to search Sonny's room. He was out, he was usually out whenever I was home, and Isabel had taken the children to see their grandparents. Suddenly I was standing still in front of the living room window, watching Seventh Avenue. The idea of searching Sonny's room made me still. I scarcely dared to admit to myself what I'd be searching for. I didn't know what I'd do if I found it. Or if I didn't.

On the sidewalk across from me, near the entrance to a barbecue joint, some people were holding an old-fashioned revival meeting. The barbecue cook, wearing a dirty white apron, his conked[8] hair reddish and metallic in the pale sun, and a cigarette between his lips, stood in the doorway, watching them. Kids and older people paused in their errands and stood there, along with some older men and a couple of very tough-looking women who watched everything that happened on the avenue, as though they owned it, or were maybe owned by it. Well, they were watching this, too. The revival was being carried on by three sisters in black, and a brother. All they had were their voices and their Bibles and a tambourine. The brother was testifying[9] and while he testified two of the sisters stood together, seeming to say, amen, and the third sister walked around with the tambourine outstretched and a couple of people dropped coins into it. Then the brother's testimony ended and the sister who had been taking up the collection dumped the coins into her palm and transferred them to the pocket of her long black robe. Then she raised both hands, striking the tambourine against the air, and then against one hand, and she started to sing. And the two other sisters and the brother joined in.

It was strange, suddenly, to watch, though I had been seeing these meetings all my life. So, of course, had everybody else down there. Yet, they paused and watched and listened and I stood still at the window. "*'Tis the old ship of Zion*," they sang, and the sister with the tambourine kept a steady, jangling beat, "*it has rescued many a thousand!*" Not a soul under the

[8] Chemically straightened.

[9] Making emotional declarations of religious beliefs and experiences.

sound of their voices was hearing this song for the first time, not one of them had been rescued. Nor had they seen much in the way of rescue work being done around them. Neither did they especially believe in the holiness of the three sisters and the brother, they knew too much about them, knew where they lived, and how. The woman with the tambourine, whose voice dominated the air, whose face was bright with joy, was divided by very little from the woman who stood watching her, a cigarette between her heavy, chapped lips, her hair a cuckoo's nest, her face scarred and swollen from many beatings, and her black eyes glittering like coal. Perhaps they both knew this, which was why, when, as rarely, they addressed each other, they addressed each other as Sister. As the singing filled the air the watching, listening faces underwent a change, the eyes focusing on something within; the music seemed to soothe a poison out of them; and time seemed, nearly, to fall away from the sullen, belligerent, battered faces, as though they were fleeing back to their first condition, while dreaming of their last. The barbecue cook half shook his head and smiled, and dropped his cigarette and disappeared into his joint. A man fumbled in his pockets for change and stood holding it in his hand impatiently, as though he had just remembered a pressing appointment further up the avenue. He looked furious. Then I saw Sonny, standing on the edge of the crowd. He was carrying a wide, flat notebook with a green cover, and it made him look, from where I was standing, almost like a schoolboy. The coppery sun brought out the copper in his skin, he was very faintly smiling, standing very still. Then the singing stopped, the tambourine turned into a collection plate again. The furious man dropped in his coins and vanished, so did a couple of the women, and Sonny dropped some change in the plate, looking directly at the woman with a little smile. He started across the avenue, toward the house. He has a slow, loping walk, something like the way Harlem hipsters walk, only he's imposed on this his own half-beat. I had never really noticed it before.

I stayed at the window, both relieved and apprehensive. As Sonny disappeared from my sight, they began singing again. And they were still singing when his key turned in the lock.

"Hey," he said.

"Hey, yourself. You want some beer?"

"No. Well, maybe." But he came up to the window and stood beside me, looking out. "What a warm voice," he said.

They were singing *If I could only hear my mother pray again*!

"Yes," I said, "and she can sure beat that tambourine."

"But what a terrible song," he said, and laughed. He dropped his notebook on the sofa and disappeared into the kitchen. "Where's Isabel and the kids?"

"I think they went to see their grandparents. You hungry?"

"No." He came back into the living room with his can of beer. "You want to come some place with me tonight?"

I sensed, I don't know how, that I couldn't possibly say no. "Sure. Where?"

He sat down on the sofa and picked up his notebook and started leafing through it. "I'm going to sit in with some fellows in a joint in the Village."

"You mean, you're going to play, tonight?"

"That's right." He took a swallow of his beer and moved back to the window. He gave me a sidelong look. "If you can stand it."

"I'll try," I said.

He smiled to himself and we both watched as the meeting across the way broke up. The three sisters and the brother, heads bowed, were singing *God be with you till we meet again*. The faces around them were very quiet. Then the song ended. The small crowd dispersed. We watched the three women and the lone man walk slowly up the avenue.

"When she was singing before," said Sonny, abruptly, "her voice reminded me for a minute of what heroin feels like sometimes—when it's in your veins. It makes you feel sort of warm and cool at the same time. And distant. And—and sure." He sipped his beer, very deliberately not looking at me. I watched his face. "It makes you feel—in control. Sometimes you've got to have that feeling."

"Do you?" I sat down slowly in the easy chair.

"Sometimes." He went to the sofa and picked up his notebook again. "Some people do."

"In order," I asked, "to play?" And my voice was very ugly, full of contempt and anger.

"Well"—he looked at me with great, troubled eyes, as though, in fact, he hoped his eyes would tell me things he could never otherwise say—"they *think* so. And *if* they think so—!"

"And what do *you* think?" I asked.

He sat on the sofa and put his can of beer on the floor. "I don't know," he said, and I couldn't be sure if he were answering my question or pursuing his thoughts. His face didn't tell me. "It's not so much to *play*. It's to *stand* it, to be able to make it at all. On any level." He frowned and smiled: "In order to keep from shaking to pieces."

"But these friends of yours," I said, "they seem to shake themselves to pieces pretty goddamn fast."

"Maybe." He played with the notebook. And something told me that I should curb my tongue, that Sonny was doing his best to talk, that I should listen. "But of course you only know the ones that've gone to pieces. Some don't—or at least they haven't *yet* and that's just about all *any* of us can say." He paused. "And then there are some who just live, really, in hell, and they know it and they see what's happening and they go right on. I don't know." He sighed, dropped the notebook, folded his arms. "Some guys, you can tell from the way they play, they on something *all* the time. And you can see that, well, it makes something real for them. But of course," he picked up his beer from the floor and sipped it and put the can down again, "they *want* to, too, you've got to see that. Even some of them that say they don't—*some*, not all."

"And what about you?" I asked—I couldn't help it. "What about you? Do *you* want to?"

He stood up and walked to the window and I remained silent for a long time. Then he sighed. "Me," he said. Then: "While I was downstairs before, on my way here, listening to that woman sing, it struck me all of a sudden how much suffering she must have had to go through—to sing like that. It's *repulsive* to think you have to suffer that much."

I said: "But there's no way not to suffer—is there, Sonny?"

"I believe not," he said and smiled, "but that's never stopped anyone from trying." He looked at me. "Has it?" I realized, with this mocking look, that there stood between us, forever, beyond the power of time or forgiveness, the fact that I had held silence—so long!—when he had needed human speech to help him. He turned back to the window. "No, there's no way not to suffer. But you try all kinds of ways to keep from drowning in it, to keep on top of it, and to make it seem—well, like *you*. Like you did something, all right, and now you're suffering for it. You know?" I said nothing. "Well you know," he said, impatiently, "why *do* people suffer? Maybe it's better to do something to give it a reason, *any* reason."

"But we just agreed," I said, "that there's no way not to suffer. Isn't it better, then, just to—take it?"

"But nobody just takes it," Sonny cried, "that's what I'm telling you! *Everybody* tries not to. You're just hung up on the *way* some people try—it's not *your* way!"

The hair on my face began to itch, my face felt wet. "That's not true," I said, "that's not true. I don't give a damn what other people do, I don't even care how they suffer. I just care how *you* suffer." And he looked at me. "Please believe me," I said, "I don't want to see you—die—trying not to suffer."

"I won't," he said flatly, "die trying not to suffer. At least, not any faster than anybody else."

"But there's no need," I said, trying to laugh, "is there? in killing yourself."

I wanted to say more, but I couldn't. I wanted to talk about will power and how life could be—well, beautiful. I wanted to say that it was all within; but was it? or, rather, wasn't that exactly the trouble? And I wanted to promise that I would never fail him again. But it would all have sounded—empty words and lies.

So I made the promise to myself and prayed that I would keep it.

"It's terrible sometimes, inside," he said, "that's what's the trouble. You walk these streets, black and funky and cold, and there's not really a living ass to talk to, and there's nothing shaking, and there's no way of getting it out—that storm inside. You can't talk it and you can't make love with it, and when you finally try to get with it and play it, you realize *nobody's* listening. So *you've* got to listen. You got to find a way to listen."

And then he walked away from the window and sat on the sofa again, as though all the wind had suddenly been knocked out of him. "Sometimes you'll do *anything* to play, even cut your mother's throat." He laughed and looked at me. "Or your brother's." Then he sobered. "Or your own." Then: "Don't worry. I'm all right now and I think I'll *be* all right. But I can't forget—where I've been. I don't mean just the physical place I've been, I mean where I've *been*. And *what* I've been."

"What have you been, Sonny?" I asked.

He smiled—but sat sideways on the sofa, his elbow resting on the back, his fingers playing with his mouth and chin, not looking at me. "I've been something I didn't recognize, didn't know I could be. Didn't know anybody could be." He stopped, looking inward, looking helplessly young, looking old. "I'm not talking about it now because I feel *guilty* or anything like that—maybe it would be better if I did, I don't know. Anyway, I can't really talk about it. Not to you, not to anybody," and now he turned and faced me. "Sometimes, you know, and it was actually when I was most *out* of the world, I felt that I was in it, that I was *with* it, really, and I could play or I didn't really have to *play*, it just came out of me, it was there. And I don't know how I played, thinking about it now, but I know I did awful things, those times, sometimes, to people. Or it wasn't that I *did* anything to them—it was that they weren't real." He picked up the beer can; it was empty; he rolled it between his palms: "And other times—well, I needed a fix, I needed to find a place to lean, I needed to clear a space to *listen*—and I couldn't find it, and I—went crazy, I did terrible things to *me*, I was terrible *for* me." He began pressing the beer can between his hands, I watched the metal begin to give. It glittered, as he played with it like a knife, and I was afraid he would cut himself, but I said nothing. "Oh well. I can never tell you. I was all by myself at the bottom of something, stinking and sweating and crying and shaking, and I smelled it, you know? *my* stink, and I thought I'd die if I couldn't get away from it and yet, all the same, I knew that everything I was doing was just locking me in with it. And I didn't know," he paused, still flattening the beer can, "I didn't know, I still *don't* know, something kept telling me that maybe it was good to smell your own stink, but I didn't think that *that* was what I'd been trying to do—and—who can stand it?" and he abruptly dropped the ruined beer can, looking at me with a small, still smile, and then rose, walking to the window as though it were the lodestone rock. I watched his face, he watched the avenue. "I couldn't tell you when Mama died—but the reason I wanted to leave Harlem so bad was to get away from drugs. And then, when I ran away, that's what I was running from—really. When I came back, nothing had changed, *I* hadn't changed, I was just—older." And he stopped, drumming with his fingers on the windowpane. The sun had vanished, soon darkness would fall. I watched his face. "It can come again," he said, almost as though speaking to himself. Then he turned to me. "It can come again," he repeated. "I just want you to know that."

"All right," I said, at last. "So it can come again. All right."

He smiled, but the smile was sorrowful. "I had to try to tell you," he said.

"Yes," I said. "I understand that."

"You're my brother," he said, looking straight at me, and not smiling at all.

"Yes," I repeated, "yes. I understand that."

He turned back to the window, looking out. "All that hatred down there," he said, "all that hatred and misery and love. It's a wonder it doesn't blow the avenue apart."

We went to the only nightclub on a short, dark street, downtown. We squeezed through the narrow, chattering, jampacked bar to the entrance of the big room, where the bandstand was. And we stood there for a moment, for the lights were very dim in this room and we couldn't see. Then, "Hello, boy," said the voice and an enormous black man, much older than Sonny or myself, erupted out of all that atmospheric lighting and put an arm around Sonny's shoulder. "I been sitting right here," he said, "waiting for you."

He had a big voice, too, and heads in the darkness turned toward us.

Sonny grinned and pulled a little away, and said, "Creole, this is my brother. I told you about him."

Creole shook my hand. "I'm glad to meet you, son," he said, and it was clear that he was glad to meet me *there*, for Sonny's sake. And he smiled, "You got a real musician in *your* family," and he took his arm from Sonny's shoulder and slapped him, lightly, affectionately, with the back of his hand.

"Well. Now I've heard it all," said a voice behind us. This was another musician, and a friend of Sonny's, a coal-black, cheerful-looking man, built close to the ground. He immediately began confiding to me, at the top of his lungs, the most terrible things about Sonny, his teeth gleaming like a lighthouse and his laugh coming up out of him like the beginning of an earthquake. And it turned out that everyone at the bar knew Sonny, or almost everyone; some were musicians, working there, or nearby, or not working, some were simply hangers-on, and some were there to hear Sonny play. I was introduced to all of them and they were all very polite to me. Yet, it was clear that, for them, I was only Sonny's brother. Here, I was in Sonny's world. Or, rather: his kingdom. Here, it was not even a question that his veins bore royal blood.

They were going to play soon and Creole installed me, by myself, at a table in a dark corner. Then I watched them, Creole, and the little black man, and Sonny, and the others, while they horsed around, standing just below the bandstand. The light from the bandstand spilled just a little short of them and, watching them laughing and gesturing and moving about, I had the feeling that they, nevertheless, were being most careful not to step into that circle of light too suddenly: that if they moved into the light too suddenly, without thinking, they would perish in flame. Then, while I watched, one of them, the small black man, moved into the light and crossed the bandstand and started fooling around with his drums. Then—being funny and being, also, extremely ceremonious—Creole took Sonny by the arm and led him to the piano. A woman's voice called Sonny's name and a few hands started clapping. And Sonny, also being funny and being ceremonious, and so touched, I think, that he could have cried, but neither hiding it nor showing it, riding it like a man, grinned, and put both hands to his heart and bowed from the waist.

Creole then went to the bass fiddle and a lean, very bright-skinned brown man jumped up on the bandstand and picked up his horn. So there they were, and the atmosphere on the bandstand and in the room began to change and tighten. Someone stepped up to the microphone and announced them. Then there were all kinds of murmurs. Some people at the bar shushed others. The waitress ran around, frantically getting in the last orders, guys and chicks got closer to each other, and the lights on the bandstand, on the quartet, turned to a kind of indigo. Then they all looked different there. Creole looked about him for the last time, as though he were making certain that all his chickens were in the coop, and then he—jumped and struck the fiddle. And there they were.

All I know about music is that not many people ever really hear it. And even then, on the rare occasions when something opens within, and the music enters, what we mainly hear, or hear corroborated, are personal, private, vanishing evocations. But the man who creates the music is hearing something else, is dealing with the roar rising from the void and imposing order on it as it hits the air. What is evoked in him, then, is of another order, more terrible because it has no words, and triumphant, too, for that same reason. And his triumph, when he triumphs, is ours. I just watched Sonny's face. His face was troubled, he was working hard, but he wasn't with it. And I had the feeling that, in a way, everyone on the bandstand was waiting for him, both waiting for him and pushing him along. But as I began to watch Creole, I realized that it was Creole who held them all back. He had them on a short rein. Up there, keeping the beat with his whole body, wailing on the fiddle, with his eyes half closed, he was listening to everything, but he was listening to Sonny. He was having a dialogue with Sonny. He wanted Sonny to leave the shoreline and strike out for the deep water. He was Sonny's witness that deep water and drowning were not the same thing—he had been there, and he knew. And he wanted Sonny to know. He was waiting for Sonny to do the things on the keys which would let Creole know that Sonny was in the water.

And, while Creole listened, Sonny moved, deep within, exactly like someone in torment. I had never before thought of how awful the relationship must be between the musician and his instrument. He has to fill it, this instrument, with the breath of life, his own. He has to make it do what he wants it to do. And a piano is just a piano. It's made out of so much wood and wires and little hammers and big ones, and ivory. While there's only so much you can do with it, the only way to find this out is to try; to try and make it do everything.

And Sonny hadn't been near a piano for over a year. And he wasn't on much better terms with his life, not the life that stretched before him now. He and the piano stammered, started one way, got scared, stopped; started another way, panicked, marked time, started again; then seemed to have found a direction, panicked again, got stuck. And the face I saw on Sonny I'd never seen before. Everything had been burned out of it, and, at the same time, things usually hidden were being burned in, by the fire and fury of the battle which was occurring in him up there.

Yet, watching Creole's face as they neared the end of the first set, I had the feeling that something had happened, something I hadn't heard. Then they finished, there was scattered applause, and then, without an instant's warning, Creole started into something else, it was almost sardonic, it was *Am I Blue*. And, as though he commanded, Sonny began to play. Something began to happen. And Creole let out the reins. The dry, low, black man said something awful on the drums, Creole answered, and the drums talked back. Then the horn insisted, sweet and high, slightly detached perhaps, and Creole listened, commenting now and then, dry, and driving, beautiful and calm and old. Then they all came together again, and Sonny was part of the family again. I could tell this from his face. He seemed to have found, right there beneath his fingers, a damn brand-new piano. It seemed that he couldn't get over it. Then, for a while, just being happy with Sonny, they seemed to be agreeing with him that brand-new pianos certainly were a gas.

Then Creole stepped forward to remind them that what they were playing was the blues. He hit something in all of them, he hit something in me, myself, and the music tightened and deepened, apprehension began to beat the air. Creole began to tell us what the blues were all about. They were not about anything very new. He and his boys up there were keeping it new, at the risk of ruin, destruction, madness, and death, in order to find new ways to make us listen. For, while the tale of how we suffer, and how we are delighted, and how we may triumph is never new, it always must be heard. There isn't any other tale to tell, it's the only light we've got in all this darkness.

And this tale, according to that face, that body, those strong hands on those strings, has another aspect in every country, and a new depth in every generation. Listen, Creole seemed to be saying, listen. Now these are Sonny's blues. He made the little black man on the drums know it, and the bright, brown man on the horn. Creole wasn't trying any longer to get Sonny in the water. He was wishing him Godspeed. Then he stepped back, very slowly, filling the air with the immense suggestion that Sonny speak for himself.

Then they all gathered around Sonny and Sonny played. Every now and again one of them seemed to say, amen. Sonny's fingers filled the air with life, his life. But that life contained so many others. And Sonny went all the way back, he really began with the spare, flat statement of the opening phrase of the song. Then he began to make it his. It was very beautiful because it wasn't hurried and it was no longer a lament. I seemed to hear with what burning he had made it his, with what burning we had yet to make it ours, how we could cease lamenting. Freedom lurked around us and I understood, at last, that he could help us to be free if we would listen, that he would never be free until we did. Yet, there was no battle in his face now, I heard what he had gone through, and would continue to go through until he came to rest in earth. He had made it his: that long line, of which we knew only Mama and Daddy. And he was giving it back, as everything must be given back, so that, passing through death, it can live forever. I saw my mother's face again, and felt, for the first time, how the stones of the road she had walked on must have bruised her feet. I saw the moonlit road where my father's brother died. And it brought something else back to me, and carried me past it, I saw my little girl again and felt Isabel's tears again, and I felt my own tears begin to rise. And I was yet aware that this was only a moment, that the world waited outside, as hungry as a tiger, and that trouble stretched above us, longer than the sky.

Then it was over. Creole and Sonny let out their breath, both soaking wet, and grinning. There was a lot of applause and some of it was real. In the dark, the girl came by and I asked her to take drinks to the bandstand. There was a long pause, while they talked up there in the indigo light and after awhile I saw the girl put a Scotch and milk on top of the piano for Sonny. He didn't seem to notice it, but just before they started playing again, he sipped from it and looked toward me, and nodded. Then he put it back on top of the piano. For me, then, as they began to play again, it glowed and shook above my brother's head like the very cup of trembling.[10]

[10] "Behold, I have taken out of thine hand the cup of trembling, even the dregs of the cup of my fury; thou shalt no more drink it again" (Isaiah 51:22).

Flannery O'Connor

(1925–1964)

The American novelist and short story writer Flannery O'Connor found herself, as a writer, a woman, and, especially, a Roman Catholic, very much in the alienated, odd-man-out position of many modern writers, whatever their faith. "I have found," she said, "from reading my own writing, that my subject in fiction is the action of grace in territory held largely by the devil. I have also found that what I write is read by an audience which puts little stock either in grace or the devil." The result is a shocking, grotesque fiction of extremes: "It's not necessary to point out that the look of this fiction is going to be wild, that it is almost of necessity going to be violent and comic, because of the discrepancies that it seeks to combine." The "wild" fiction O'Connor produced in her tragically short life has placed her in the distinguished company of other Southern American writers who have won a worldwide audience.

Mary Flannery O'Connor was born in Savannah, Georgia, in 1925, the only child of Edward and Regina Cline O'Connor, both devout Roman Catholics. When she was thirteen, her father discovered that he suffered from disseminated lupus, an incurable disease in which the body attacks its own tissues, and the family moved to the mother's old home in Milledgeville, Georgia. Edward O'Connor died of his ailment in 1941, a year before his daughter graduated from high school. After graduation, O'Connor attended the Georgia State College for Women in Milledgeville, majoring in English and social studies and writing for the college newspaper and literary magazine. The stories written during her college years won her a scholarship to the Writers' Workshop at the University of Iowa; she spent three years there and another at the writers' colony at Yaddo, in New York State. Her first story appeared in 1946 in the literary magazine Accent; *others followed quickly in a variety of periodicals.*

O'Connor moved to New York in 1948, taking with her the partially completed manuscript of her first novel, Wise Blood, *four chapters of which were published in magazines in 1948 and 1949. In 1950, she became very ill with what was diagnosed as disseminated lupus, although her doctors managed to save her life with blood transfusions and were able to arrest the disease with injections of a new cortisone derivative. When she was released from the hospital, she moved back to Georgia; too weak to climb stairs, she moved with her mother to a dairy farm the family owned outside Milledgeville where she could have a bedroom and study on the ground floor. There she lived and worked for the rest of her life.*

Wise Blood, published in 1952, is a grotesque tragicomedy about a young man named Hazel Motes who leaves his home in Tennessee to go to a city named Taulkinham (obviously Atlanta) to preach his own religion, the "church of truth without Jesus Christ Crucified." (His puzzled landlady asks him, "Protestant? Or something foreign?" "He said no mam, it was Protestant.") Hazel murders a man hired by a fake evangelist named Onnie Jay Holy to impersonate Hazel, takes a fifteen-year-old mistress named Sabbath Lily, buys an old Essex car which becomes the symbol of his calling ("Nobody with a good car needs to be justified," he says), blinds himself with lime, and eventually is martyred by the police. Reviewers were puzzled by the book's strange mingling of religious symbols, grotesque violence, and broad backwoods comedy. O'Connor's intentions were somewhat clarified in a note she wrote for the 1962 second edition of the novel, in which she described it as "a comic novel about a Christian *malgré lui*, and as such, very serious." Hazel is a modern prophet of negativism who rejects the sacrificial blood of Christ in favor of the "wise blood" of his own natural body but whose own crazed passion leads him, mysteriously, to become a true prophet of Christ's blood.

Wise Blood was followed in 1955 by *A Good Man Is Hard to Find*. This collection of ten short stories included, in addition to the famous title story about an escaped convict who murders an entire family, several other of O'Connor's most important stories, notably "The Artificial Nigger," "Good Country People," "The Displaced Person," and "The River." A second novel, *The Violent Bear It Away*, was published in 1960; it too is about a reluctant young prophet. Francis Marion Tarwater, the great-nephew of a drunken prophet, moonshiner, and chicken-fighter and the nephew of an equally crazed apostle of rationality, begins his ministry by drowning his uncle's idiot son in the process of baptizing him. Satan, who has directed the drowning of the boy, returns to drug and rape Tarwater at the end of the novel. But Tarwater sets fire to the woods, burns away his sins, becomes a true prophet, and finally trudges off into the distance "in the bleeding stinking mad shadow of Jesus."

In 1964, an abdominal operation reactivated O'Connor's lupus, and her health began to deteriorate rapidly. Writing against time, she completed the stories for another collection before she died in August of that year. Her last stories appeared in 1965 as *Everything That Rises Must Converge*. This book contains some of O'Connor's best work, including the title story, "Parker's Back," "The Lame Shall Enter First," and "The Enduring Chill."

O'Connor's work has often been compared to Faulkner's as an example of "Southern Grotesque," but the parallel is not really very close. For all its extravagance and eccentricity, Faulkner's world remains rooted in the realities of Southern life; O'Connor's, despite her keen eye for detail, her ear for the turns of Southern speech, and her richly Southern comic sense, has much more the quality of an allegorical dream landscape. Her South is a version of the modern Wasteland, inhabited by lost, confused souls whose obscure passions for the divine, in the absence of any coherent faith, explode in twisted, grotesque, and darkly comic ways. Her vision of life is not just Catholic, but Catholic in the mystic and ascetic tradition of St. John of the Cross, as the critic Stanley Edgar Hyman has pointed out. Her Southern folk humor expresses a radically dualistic vision of the world and a sense of the immediate presence of both Christ and the Devil ("the dragon by the roadside"); her work resembles *Huckleberry Finn* as imagined by Fyodor Dostoevsky.

When the Reverend Bevel Summers, standing in the water, shouts, "Believe Jesus or the devil!" he defines, despite the absurd figure he presents, the basic opposi-

tion in "The River." Harry is a child pilgrim bound away from his shallow, secular family toward salvation. Along the way, he encounters true malevolence in the children who trick him into letting the hog out and in the demonic figure of Mr. Paradise, who comes to jeer at the preacher and to discount his claims by exhibiting his unhealed cancer. When Mr. Paradise pursues Harry to attack him sexually, his giant candy cane becomes a grotesque parody of the shepherd's crook of Christian symbolism. As he stands in the water like "a giant pig," he is linked to the real pig as an image of human debasement, and he finally degenerates even further to "some ancient water monster," an image of primal evil. The muddy river really does become "the rich red river of Jesus' Blood"; according to O'Connor, Harry "has been baptized and so he goes to his Maker; this is a good end"—a stern judgment but one typical of O'Connor's strange and radical art.

FURTHER READING (*prepared by W. J. R.):* Dorothy Walters's *Flannery O'Connor,* 1973, a good introduction, includes biographical information and chapters on *Wise Blood* and *The Violent Bear It Away.* Dorothy Tuck McFarland's *Flannery O'Connor,* 1976, contains synopses of the short stories and introduces the main critical issues. James A. Grimshaw, Jr.'s *The Flannery O'Connor Companion,* 1981, also is a good introduction, with summaries of all the stories, a chapter on O'Connor's nonfiction, and a guide to her characters. Ten excellent essays on O'Connor's religious views are collected in *The Added Dimension: The Art and Mind of Flannery O'Connor,* ed. Melvin J. Friedman and Lewis A. Lawson, 1966, 2nd ed. 1977, which also contains some of the author's correspondence. Martha Stephens's *The Question of Flannery O'Connor,* 1973, appraises the fiction as an expression of "joyless faith" and discusses the tension between this element and O'Connor's "high comedy." Miles Orvell's *The Invisible Parade: The Fiction of Flannery O'Connor,* 1972, traces the influence of American Romanticism and humor on O'Connor's work. Orvell's discussion of O'Connor's often harsh rejections of secular humanism is particularly good. Stuart L. Burns's "O'Connor and the Critics: An Overview," *Mississippi Quarterly,* 27 (1974), 483–95, is a useful guide to books on O'Connor, pointing out the many redundant (and sometimes untenable) interpretations of her work.

THE RIVER

The child stood glum and limp in the middle of the dark living room while his father pulled him into a plaid coat. His right arm was hung in the sleeve but the father buttoned the coat anyway and pushed him forward toward a pale spotted hand that stuck through the half-open door.

"He ain't fixed right," a loud voice said from the hall.

"Well then for Christ's sake fix him," the father muttered. "It's six o'clock in the morning." He was in his bathrobe and barefooted. When he got the child to the door and tried to shut it, he found her looming in it, a speckled skeleton in a long pea-green coat and felt helmet.

"And his and my carfare," she said. "It'll be twict we have to ride the car."

He went in the bedroom again to get the money and when he came back, she and the boy were both standing in the middle of the room. She was taking stock. "I couldn't smell those dead cigarette butts long if I was ever to come sit with you," she said, shaking him down in his coat.

"Here's the change," the father said. He went to the door and opened it wide and waited.

After she had counted the money she slipped it somewhere inside her coat and walked over to a watercolor hanging near the phonograph. "I know what time it is," she said, peering closely at the black lines crossing into broken planes of violent color. "I ought to. My shift goes on at 10 P.M. and don't get off till 5 and it takes me one hour to ride the Vine Street car."

"Oh, I see," he said; "well, we'll expect him back tonight, about eight or nine?"

"Maybe later," she said. "We're going to the river to a healing. This particular preacher don't get around this way often. I wouldn't have paid for that," she said, nodding at the painting, "I would have drew it myself."

"All right, Mrs. Connin, we'll see you then," he said, drumming on the door.

A toneless voice called from the bedroom, "Bring me an icepack."

"Too bad his mamma's sick," Mrs. Connin said. "What's her trouble?"

"We don't know," he muttered.

"We'll ask the preacher to pray for her. He's healed a lot of folks. The Reverend Bevel Summers. Maybe she ought to see him sometime."

"Maybe so," he said. "We'll see you tonight," and he disappeared into the bedroom and left them to go.

The little boy stared at her silently, his nose and eyes running. He was four or five. He had a long face and bulging chin and half-shut eyes set far apart. He seemed mute and patient, like an old sheep waiting to be let out.

"You'll like this preacher," she said. "The Reverend Bevel Summers. You ought to hear him sing."

The bedroom door opened suddenly and the father stuck his head out and said, "Good-by, old man. Have a good time."

"Good-by," the little boy said and jumped as if he had been shot.

Mrs. Connin gave the watercolor another look. Then they went out into the hall and rang for the elevator. "I wouldn't have drew it," she said.

Outside the gray morning was blocked off on either side by the unlit empty buildings. "It's going to fair up later," she said, "but this is the last time we'll be able to have any preaching at the river this year. Wipe your nose, Sugar Boy."

He began rubbing his sleeve across it but she stopped him. "That ain't nice," she said. "Where's your handkerchief?"

He put his hands in his pockets and pretended to look for it while she waited. "Some people don't care how they send one off," she murmured to her reflection in the coffee shop window. "You pervide." She took a red and blue flowered handkerchief out of her pocket and stooped down and began to work on his nose. "Now blow," she said and he blew. "You can borry it. Put it in your pocket."

He folded it up and put it in his pocket carefully and they walked on to the corner and leaned against the side of a closed drugstore to wait for the car. Mrs. Connin turned up her coat collar so that it met her hat in the back. Her eyelids began to droop and she looked as if she might go to sleep against the wall. The little boy put a slight pressure on her hand.

"What's your name?" she asked in a drowsy voice. "I don't know but only your last name. I should have found out your first name."

His name was Harry Ashfield and he had never thought at any time before of changing it. "Bevel," he said.

Mrs. Connin raised herself from the wall. "Why ain't that a coincident!" she said. "I told you that's the name of this preacher!"

"Bevel," he repeated.

She stood looking down at him as if he had become a marvel to her. "I'll have to see you meet him today," she said. "He's no ordinary preacher. He's a healer. He couldn't do nothing for Mr. Connin though. Mr. Connin didn't have the faith but he said he would try anything once. He had this griping in his gut."

The trolley appeared as a yellow spot at the end of the deserted street.

"He's gone to the government hospital now," she said, "and they taken one-third of his stomach. I tell him he better thank Jesus for what he's got left but he says he ain't thanking nobody. Well I declare," she murmured, "Bevel!"

They walked out to the tracks to wait. "Will he heal me?" Bevel asked.

"What you got?"

"I'm hungry," he decided finally.

"Didn't you have your breakfast?"

"I didn't have time to be hungry yet then," he said.

"Well when we get home we'll both have us something," she said. "I'm ready myself."

They got on the car and sat down a few seats behind the driver and Mrs. Connin took Bevel on her knees. "Now you be a good boy," she said, "and let me get some sleep. Just don't get off my lap." She lay her head back and as he watched, gradually her eyes closed and her mouth fell open to show a few long scattered teeth, some gold and some darker than her face; she began to whistle and blow like a musical skeleton. There was no one in the car but themselves and the driver and when he saw she was asleep, he took out the flowered handkerchief and unfolded it and examined it carefully. Then he folded it up again and unzipped a place in the innerlining of his coat and hid it in there and shortly he went to sleep himself.

Her house was a half-mile from the end of the car line, set back a little from the road. It was tan paper brick with a porch across the front of it and a tin top. On the porch there were three little boys of different sizes with identical speckled faces and one tall girl who had her hair up in so many aluminum curlers that it glared like the roof. The three boys followed them inside and closed in on Bevel. They looked at him silently, not smiling.

"That's Bevel," Mrs. Connin said, taking off her coat. "It's a coincident he's named the same as the preacher. These boys are J. C., Spivey, and Sinclair, and that's Sarah Mildred on the porch. Take off that coat and hang it on the bed post, Bevel."

The three boys watched him while he unbuttoned the coat and took it off. Then they watched him hang it on the bed post and then they stood, watching the coat. They turned abruptly and went out the door and had a conference on the porch.

Bevel stood looking around him at the room. It was part kitchen and part bedroom. The entire house was two rooms and two porches. Close to his foot the tail of a light-colored dog moved up and down between two floor boards as he scratched his back on the underside of the house. Bevel jumped on it but the hound was experienced and had already withdrawn when his feet hit the spot.

The walls were filled with pictures and calendars. There were two round photographs of an old man and woman with collapsed mouths and another picture of a man whose eyebrows dashed out of two bushes of hair and clashed in a heap on the bridge of his nose; the rest of his face stuck out like a bare cliff to fall from. "That's Mr. Connin," Mrs. Connin said, standing back from the stove for a second to admire the face with him, "but it don't favor him any more." Bevel turned from Mr. Connin to a colored picture over the bed of a man wearing a white sheet. He had long hair and a gold circle around his head and he was sawing on a board while some children stood watching him. He was going to ask who that was when the three boys came in again and motioned for him to follow them. He thought of crawling under the bed and hanging onto one of the legs but the three boys only stood there, speckled and silent, waiting, and after a second he followed them at a little distance out on the porch and around the corner of the house. They started off through a field of rough yellow weeds to the hog pen, a five-foot boarded square full of shoats, which they intended to ease him over into. When they reached it, they turned and waited silently, leaning against the side.

He was coming very slowly, deliberately bumping his feet together as if he had trouble walking. Once he had been beaten up in the park by some strange boys when his sitter forgot him, but he hadn't known anything was going to happen that time until it was over. He began to smell a strong odor of garbage and to hear the noises of a wild animal. He stopped a few feet from the pen and waited, pale but dogged.

The three boys didn't move. Something seemed to have happened to them. They stared over his head as if they saw something coming behind him but he was afraid to turn his own head and look. Their speckles were pale and their eyes were still and gray as glass. Only their ears twitched slightly. Nothing happened. Finally, the one in the middle said, "She'd kill us," and turned, dejected and hacked, and climbed up on the pen and hung over, staring in.

Bevel sat down on the ground, dazed with relief, and grinned up at them.

The one sitting on the pen glanced at him severely. "Hey you," he said after a second, "if you can't climb up and see these pigs you can lift that bottom board off and look in thataway." He appeared to offer this as a kindness.

Bevel had never seen a real pig but he had seen a pig in a book and knew they were small fat pink animals with curly tails and round grinning faces and bow ties. He leaned forward and pulled eagerly at the board.

"Pull harder," the littlest boy said. "It's nice and rotten. Just lift out thet nail."

He eased a long reddish nail out of the soft wood.

"Now you can lift up the board and put your face to the . . ." a quiet voice began.

He had already done it and another face, gray, wet and sour, was pushing into his, knocking him down and back as it scraped out under the plank. Something snorted over him and charged back again, rolling him over and pushing him up from behind and then sending him forward, screaming through the yellow field, while it bounded behind.

The three Connins watched from where they were. The one sitting on the pen held the loose board back with his dangling foot. Their stern faces didn't brighten any but they seemed to become less taut, as if some great need had been partly satisfied. "Maw ain't going to like him lettin out thet hawg," the smallest one said.

Mrs. Connin was on the back porch and caught Bevel up as he reached the steps. The hog ran under the house and subsided, panting, but the child screamed for five minutes. When she had finally calmed him down, she gave him his breakfast and let him sit on her lap while he ate it. The shoat climbed the two steps onto the back porch and stood outside the screen door, looking in with his head lowered sullenly. He was long-legged and hump-backed and part of one of his ears had been bitten off.

"Git away!" Mrs. Connin shouted. "That one yonder favors Mr. Paradise that has the gas station," she said. "You'll see him today at the healing. He's got the cancer over his ear. He always comes to show he ain't been healed."

The shoat stood squinting a few seconds longer and then moved off slowly. "I don't want to see him," Bevel said.

They walked to the river, Mrs. Connin in front with him and the three boys strung out behind and Sarah Mildred, the tall girl, at the end to holler if one of them ran out on the road. They looked like the skeleton of an old boat with two pointed ends, sailing slowly on the edge of the highway. The white Sunday sun followed at a little distance, climbing fast through a scum of gray cloud as if it meant to overtake them. Bevel walked on the outside edge, holding Mrs. Connin's hand and looking down into the orange and purple gulley that dropped off from the concrete.

It occurred to him that he was lucky this time that they had found Mrs. Connin who would take you away for the day instead of an ordinary sitter who only sat where you lived or went to the park. You found out more when you left where you lived. He had found out already this morning that he had been made by a carpenter named Jesus Christ. Before he had thought it had been a doctor named Sladewall, a fat man with a yellow mustache who gave him shots and thought his name was Herbert, but this must have been a joke. They joked a lot where he lived. If he had thought about it before, he would have thought Jesus Christ was a word like "oh" or "damn" or "God," or maybe somebody who had cheated them out of something sometime. When he had asked Mrs. Connin who the man in the sheet in the picture over her bed was, she had looked at him a while with her mouth open. Then she had said, "That's Jesus," and she had kept on looking at him.

In a few minutes she had got up and got a book out of the other room. "See here," she said, turning over the cover, "this belonged to my great grandmamma. I wouldn't part with it for nothing on earth." She ran her finger under some brown writing on a spotted page. "Emma Stevens Oakley, 1832," she said. "Ain't that something to have? And every word of it the gospel truth." She turned the next page and read him the name: "The Life of Jesus Christ for Readers Under Twelve." Then she read him the book.

It was a small book, pale brown on the outside with gold edges and a smell like old putty. It was full of pictures, one of the carpenter driving a crowd of pigs out of a man. They were real pigs, gray and sour-looking, and Mrs. Connin said Jesus had driven them all out of this one man. When she finished reading, she let him sit on the floor and look at the pictures again.

Just before they left for the healing, he had managed to get the book inside his innerlining without her seeing him. Now it made his coat hang down a little farther on one side than the other. His mind was dreamy and serene as they walked along and when they turned off the highway onto a long red clay road winding between banks of honeysuckle, he began to make wild leaps and pull forward on her hand as if he wanted to dash off and snatch the sun which was rolling away ahead of them now.

They walked on the dirt road for a while and then they crossed a field stippled with purple weeds and entered the shadows of a wood where the ground was covered with thick pine needles. He had never been in woods before and he walked carefully, looking from side to side as if he were entering a strange country. They moved along a bridle path that twisted downhill through crackling red leaves, and once, catching at a branch to keep himself from slipping, he looked into two frozen green-gold eyes enclosed in the darkness of a tree hole. At the bottom of the hill, the woods opened suddenly onto a pasture dotted here and there with black and white cows and sloping down, tier after tier, to a broad orange stream where the reflection of the sun was set like a diamond.

There were people standing on the near bank in a group, singing. Long tables were set up behind them and a few cars and trucks were parked in a road that came up by the river. They crossed the pasture, hurrying, because Mrs. Connin, using her hand for a shed over her eyes, saw the preacher already standing out in the water. She dropped her basket on one of the tables and pushed the three boys in front of her into the knot of people so that they wouldn't linger by the food. She kept Bevel by the hand and eased her way up to the front.

The preacher was standing about ten feet out in the stream where the water came up to his knees. He was a tall youth in khaki trousers that he had rolled up higher than the water. He had on a blue shirt and a red scarf around his neck but no hat and his light-colored hair was cut in sideburns that curved into the hollows of his cheeks. His face was all bone and red light reflected from the river. He looked as if he might have been nineteen years old. He was singing in a high twangy voice, above the singing on the bank, and he kept his hands behind him and his head tilted back.

He ended the hymn on a high note and stood silent, looking down at the water and shifting his feet in it. Then he looked up at the people on the bank. They stood close together, waiting; their faces were solemn but expectant and every eye was on him. He shifted his feet again.

"Maybe I know why you come," he said in the twangy voice, "maybe I don't.

"If you ain't come for Jesus, you ain't come for me. If you just come to see can you leave your pain in the river, you ain't come for Jesus. You can't leave your pain in the river," he said. "I never told nobody that." He stopped and looked down at his knees.

"I seen you cure a woman oncet!" a sudden high voice shouted from the hump of people. "Seen that woman git up and walk out straight where she had limped in!"

The preacher lifted one foot and then the other. He seemed almost but not quite to smile. "You might as well go home if that's what you come for," he said.

Then he lifted his head and arms and shouted, "Listen to what I got to say, you people! There ain't but one river and that's the River of Life, made out of Jesus' Blood. That's the river you have to lay your pain in, in the River of Faith, in the River of Life, in the River of Love, in the rich red river of Jesus' Blood, you people!"

His voice grew soft and musical. "All the rivers come from that one River and go back to it like it was the ocean sea and if you believe, you can lay your pain in that River and get rid of it because that's the River that was made to carry sin. It's a River full of pain itself, pain itself, moving toward the Kingdom of Christ, to be washed away, slow, you people, slow as this here old red water river round my feet.

"Listen," he sang, "I read in Mark about an unclean man, I read in Luke about a blind man, I read in John about a dead man! Oh you people hear! The same blood that makes this River red, made that leper clean, made that blind man stare, made that dead man leap! You people with trouble," he cried, "lay it in that River of Blood, lay it in that River of Pain, and watch it move away toward the Kingdom of Christ."

While he preached, Bevel's eyes followed drowsily the slow circles of two silent birds revolving high in the air. Across the river there was a low red and gold grove of sassafras with hills of dark blue trees behind it and an occasional pine jutting over the skyline. Behind, in the distance, the city rose like a cluster of warts on the side of the mountain. The birds revolved downward and dropped lightly in the top of the highest pine and sat hunch-shouldered as if they were supporting the sky.

"If it's this River of Life you want to lay your pain in, then come up," the preacher said, "and lay your sorrow here. But don't be thinking this is the last of it because this old red river don't end here. This old red suffering stream goes on, you people, slow to the Kingdom of Christ. This old red river is good to Baptize in, good to lay your faith in, good to lay your pain in, but it ain't this muddy water here that saves you. I been all up and down this river this week," he said. "Tuesday I was in Fortune Lake, next day in Ideal, Friday me and my wife drove to Lulawillow to see a sick man there. Them people didn't see no healing," he said and his face burned redder for a second. "I never said they would."

While he was talking a fluttering figure had begun to move forward with a kind of butterfly movement—an old woman with flapping arms whose head wobbled as if it might fall off any second. She managed to lower herself at the edge of the bank and let her arms churn in the water. Then she bent farther and pushed her face down in it and raised herself up finally, streaming wet; and still flapping, she turned a time or two in a blind circle until someone reached out and pulled her back into the group.

"She's been that way for thirteen years," a rough voice shouted. "Pass the hat and give this kid his money. That's what he's here for." The shout, directed out to the boy in the river, came from a huge old man who sat like a humped stone on the bumper of a long ancient gray automobile. He had on a gray hat that was turned down over one ear and up over the other to expose a purple bulge on his left temple. He sat bent forward with his hands hanging between his knees and his small eyes half closed.

Bevel stared at him once and then moved into the folds of Mrs. Connin's coat and hid himself.

The boy in the river glanced at the old man quickly and raised his fist. "Believe Jesus or the devil!" he cried. "Testify to one or the other!"

"I know from my own self-experience," a woman's mysterious voice called from the knot of people, "I know from it that this preacher can heal. My eyes have been opened! I testify to Jesus!"

The preacher lifted his arms quickly and began to repeat all that he had said before about the River and the Kingdom of Christ and the old man sat on the bumper, fixing him with a narrow squint. From time to time Bevel stared at him again from around Mrs. Connin.

A man in overalls and a brown coat leaned forward and dipped his hand in the water quickly and shook it and leaned back, and a woman held a baby over the edge of the bank and splashed its feet with water. One man moved a little distance away and sat down on the bank and took off his shoes and waded out into the stream; he stood there for a few minutes with his face tilted as far back as it would go, then he waded back and put on his shoes. All this time, the preacher sang and did not appear to watch what went on.

As soon as he stopped singing, Mrs. Connin lifted Bevel up and said, "Listen here, preacher, I got a boy from town today that I'm keeping. His mamma's sick and he wants you to pray for her. And this is a coincident—his name is Bevel! Bevel," she said, turning to look at the people behind her, "same as his. Ain't that a coincident, though?"

There were some murmurs and Bevel turned and grinned over her shoulder at the faces looking at him. "Bevel," he said in a loud jaunty voice.

"Listen," Mrs. Connin said, "have you ever been Baptized, Bevel?"

He only grinned.

"I suspect he ain't ever been Baptized," Mrs. Connin said, raising her eyebrows at the preacher.

"Swang him over here," the preacher said and took a stride forward and caught him.

He held him in the crook of his arm and looked at the grinning face. Bevel rolled his eyes in a comical way and thrust his face forward, close to the preacher's. "My name is Bevvvuuuuul," he said in a loud deep voice and let the tip of his tongue slide across his mouth.

The preacher didn't smile. His bony face was rigid and his narrow gray eyes reflected the almost colorless sky. There was a loud laugh from the old man sitting on the car bumper and Bevel grasped the back of the preacher's collar and held it tightly. The grin had already disappeared from his face. He had the sudden feeling that this was not a joke. Where he lived everything was a joke. From the preacher's face, he knew immediately that nothing the preacher said or did was a joke. "My mother named me that," he said quickly.

"Have you ever been Baptized?" the preacher asked.

"What's that?" he murmured.

"If I Baptize you," the preacher said, "you'll be able to go to the Kingdom of Christ. You'll be washed in the river of suffering, son, and you'll go by the deep river of life. Do you want that?"

"Yes," the child said, and thought, I won't go back to the apartment then, I'll go under the river.

"You won't be the same again," the preacher said. "You'll count." Then he turned his face to the people and began to preach and Bevel looked over his shoulder at the pieces of the white sun scattered in the river. Suddenly the preacher said, "All right, I'm going to Baptize you now," and without more warning, he tightened his hold and swung him upside down and plunged his head into the water. He held him under while he said the words of Baptism and then he jerked him up again and looked sternly at the gasping child. Bevel's eyes were dark and dilated. "You count now," the preacher said. "You didn't even count before."

The little boy was too shocked to cry. He spit out the muddy water and rubbed his wet sleeve into his eyes and over his face.

"Don't forget his mamma," Mrs. Connin called. "He wants you to pray for his mamma. She's sick."

"Lord," the preacher said, "we pray for somebody in affliction who isn't here to testify. Is your mother sick in the hospital?" he asked. "Is she in pain?"

The child stared at him. "She hasn't got up yet," he said in a high dazed voice. "She has a hangover." The air was so quiet he could hear the broken pieces of the sun knocking in the water.

The preacher looked angry and startled. The red drained out of his face and the sky appeared to darken in his eyes. There was a loud guffaw from the bank and Mr. Paradise shouted, "Haw! Cure the afflicted woman with the hangover!" and began to beat his knee with his fist.

"He's had a long day," Mrs. Connin said, standing with him in the door of the apartment and looking sharply into the room where the party was going on. "I reckon it's past his regular bedtime." One of Bevel's eyes was closed and the other half closed; his nose was running and he kept his mouth open and breathed through it. The damp plaid coat dragged down on one side.

That would be her, Mrs. Connin decided, in the black britches—long black satin britches and barefoot sandals and red toenails. She was lying on half the sofa, with her knees crossed in the air and her head propped on the arm. She didn't get up.

"Hello Harry," she said. "Did you have a big day?" She had a long pale face, smooth and blank, and straight sweet-potato-colored hair, pulled back.

The father went off to get the money. There were two other couples. One of the men, blond with little violet-blue eyes, leaned out of his chair and said, "Well Harry, old man, have a big day?"

"His name ain't Harry. It's Bevel," Mrs. Connin said.

"His name is Harry," *she* said from the sofa. "Whoever heard of anybody named Bevel?"

The little boy had seemed to be going to sleep on his feet, his head drooping farther and farther forward; he pulled it back suddenly and opened one eye; the other was stuck.

"He told me this morning his name was Bevel," Mrs. Connin said in a shocked voice. "The same as our preacher. We been all day at a preaching and healing at the river. He said his name was Bevel, the same as the preacher's. That's what he told me."

"Bevel!" his mother said. "My God! what a name."

"This preacher is name Bevel and there's no better preacher around," Mrs. Connin said. "And furthermore," she added in a defiant tone, "he Baptized this child this morning!"

His mother sat straight up. "Well the nerve!" she muttered.

"Furthermore," Mrs. Connin said, "he's a healer and he prayed for you to be healed."

"Healed!" she almost shouted. "Healed of what for Christ's sake?"

"Of your affliction," Mrs. Connin said icily.

The father had returned with the money and was standing near Mrs. Connin waiting to give it to her. His eyes were lined with red threads. "Go on, go on," he said, "I want to hear more about her affliction. The exact nature of it has escaped . . ." He waved the bill and his voice trailed off. "Healing by prayer is mighty inexpensive," he murmured.

Mrs. Connin stood a second, staring into the room, with a skeleton's appearance of seeing everything. Then, without taking the money, she turned and shut the door behind her. The father swung around, smiling vaguely, and shrugged. The rest of them were looking at Harry. The little boy began to shamble toward the bedroom.

"Come here, Harry," his mother said. He automatically shifted his direction toward her without opening his eye any farther. "Tell me what happened today," she said when he reached her. She began to pull off his coat.

"I don't know," he muttered.

"Yes you do know," she said, feeling the coat heavier on one side. She unzipped the innerlining and caught the book and a dirty handkerchief as they fell out. "Where did you get these?"

"I don't know," he said and grabbed for them. "They're mine. She gave them to me."

She threw the handkerchief down and held the book too high for him to reach and began to read it, her face after a second assuming an exaggerated comical expression. The others moved around and looked at it over her shoulder. "My God," somebody said.

One of the men peered at it sharply from behind a thick pair of glasses. "That's valuable," he said. "That's a collector's item," and he took it away from the rest of them and retired to another chair.

"Don't let George go off with that," his girl said.

"I tell you it's valuable," George said. "1832."

Bevel shifted his direction again toward the room where he slept. He shut the door behind him and moved slowly in the darkness to the bed and sat down and took off his shoes and got under the cover. After a minute a shaft of light let in the tall silhouette of his mother. She tiptoed lightly across the room and sat down on the edge of his bed. "What did that dolt of a preacher say about me?" she whispered. "What lies have you been telling today, honey?"

He shut his eye and heard her voice from a long way away, as if he were under the river and she on top of it. She shook his shoulder. "Harry," she said, leaning down and putting her mouth to his ear, "tell me what he said." She pulled him into a sitting position and he felt as if he had been drawn up from under the river. "Tell me," she whispered and her bitter breath covered his face.

He saw the pale oval close to him in the dark. "He said I'm not the same now," he muttered. "I count."

After a second, she lowered him by his shirt front onto the pillow. She hung over him an instant and brushed her lips against his forehead. Then she got up and moved away, swaying her hips lightly through the shaft of light.

He didn't wake up early but the apartment was still dark and close when he did. For a while he lay there, picking his nose and eyes. Then he sat up in bed and looked out the window. The sun came in palely, stained gray by the glass. Across the street at the Empire Hotel, a colored cleaning woman was looking down from an upper window, resting her face on her folded arms. He got up and put on his shoes and went to the bathroom and then into the front room. He ate two crackers spread with anchovy paste, that he found on the coffee table, and drank some ginger ale left in a bottle and looked around for his book but it was not there.

The apartment was silent except for the faint humming of the refrigerator. He went into the kitchen and found some raisin bread heels and spread a half jar of peanut butter between them and climbed up on the tall kitchen stool and sat chewing the sandwich slowly, wiping his nose every now and then on his shoulder. When he finished he found some chocolate milk and drank that. He would rather have had the ginger ale he saw but they left the bottle openers where he couldn't reach them. He studied what was left in the refrigerator for a while—some shriveled vegetables that she had forgot were there and a lot of brown oranges that she bought and didn't squeeze; there were three or four kinds of cheese and something fishy in a paper bag; the rest was a pork bone. He left the refrigerator door open and wandered back into the dark living room and sat down on the sofa.

He decided they would be out cold until one o'clock and that they would all have to go to a restaurant for lunch. He wasn't high enough for the table yet and the waiter would bring a highchair and he was too big for a highchair. He sat in the middle of the sofa, kicking it with his heels. Then he got up and wandered around the room, looking into the ashtrays at the butts as if this might be a habit. In his own room he had picture books and blocks but they were for the most part torn up; he found the way to get new ones was to tear up the ones he had. There was very little to do at any time but eat; however, he was not a fat boy.

He decided he would empty a few of the ashtrays on the floor. If he only emptied a few, she would think they had fallen. He emptied two, rubbing the ashes carefully into the rug with his finger. Then he lay on the floor for a while, studying his feet which he held up in the air. His shoes were still damp and he began to think about the river.

Very slowly, his expression changed as if he were gradually seeing appear what he didn't know he'd been looking for. Then all of a sudden he knew what he wanted to do.

He got up and tiptoed into their bedroom and stood in the dim light there, looking for her pocketbook. His glance passed her long pale arm hanging off the edge of the bed down to the floor, and across the white mound his father made, and past the crowded bureau, until it rested on the pocketbook hung on the back of a chair. He took a car-token out of it and half a package of Life Savers. Then he left the apartment and caught the car at the corner. He hadn't taken a suitcase because there was nothing from there he wanted to keep.

He got off the car at the end of the line and started down the road he and Mrs. Connin had taken the day before. He knew there wouldn't be anybody at her house because the three boys and the girl went to school and Mrs. Connin had told him she went out to clean. He passed her yard and walked on the way they had gone to the river. The paper brick houses were far apart and after a while the dirt place to walk on ended and he had to walk on the edge of the highway. The sun was pale yellow and high and hot.

He passed a shack with an orange gas pump in front of it but he didn't see the old man looking out at nothing in particular from the doorway. Mr. Paradise was having an orange drink. He finished it slowly, squinting over the bottle at the small plaid-coated figure disappearing down the road. Then he set the empty bottle on a bench and, still squinting, wiped his sleeve over his mouth. He went in the shack and picked out a peppermint stick, a foot long and two inches thick, from the candy shelf, and stuck it in his hip pocket. Then he got in his car and drove slowly down the highway after the boy.

By the time Bevel came to the field speckled with purple weeds, he was dusty and sweating and he crossed it at a trot to get into the woods as fast as he could. Once inside, he wandered from tree to tree, trying to find the path they had taken yesterday. Finally he found a line worn in the pine needles and followed it until he saw the steep trail twisting down through the trees.

Mr. Paradise had left his automobile back some way on the road and had walked to the place where he was accustomed to sit almost every day, holding an unbaited fishline in the water while he stared at the river passing in front of him. Anyone looking at him from a distance would have seen an old boulder half hidden in the bushes.

Bevel didn't see him at all. He only saw the river, shimmering reddish yellow, and bounded into it with his shoes and his coat on and took a gulp. He swallowed some and spit the rest out and then he stood there in water up to his chest and looked around him. The sky was a clear pale blue, all in one piece—except for the hole the sun made—and fringed around the bottom with treetops. His coat floated to the surface and surrounded him like a strange gay lily pad and he stood grinning in the sun. He intended not to fool with preachers any more but to Baptize himself and to keep on going this time until he found the Kingdom of Christ in the river. He didn't mean to waste any more time. He put his head under the water at once and pushed forward.

In a second he began to gasp and sputter and his head reappeared on the surface; he started under again and the same thing happened. The river wouldn't have him. He tried again and came up, choking. This was the way it had been when the preacher held him under—he had had to fight with something that pushed him back in the face. He stopped and thought suddenly: it's another joke, it's just another joke! He thought how far he had come for nothing and he began to hit and splash and kick the filthy river. His feet were already treading on nothing. He gave one low cry of pain and indignation. Then he heard a shout and turned his head and saw something like a giant pig bounding after him, shaking a red and white club and shouting. He plunged under once and this time, the waiting current caught him like a long gentle hand and pulled him swiftly forward and down. For an instant he was overcome with surprise; then since he was moving quickly and knew that he was getting somewhere, all his fury and his fear left him.

Mr. Paradise's head appeared from time to time on the surface of the water. Finally, far downstream, the old man rose like some ancient water monster and stood empty-handed, staring with his dull eyes as far down the river line as he could see.

Peter Handke

(1942–)

"Philosophy," the modern linguistic philosopher Ludwig Wittgenstein wrote, "is a fight against the fascination which forms of expression exert upon us." So is literature, the young Austrian novelist and playwright Peter Handke would add. "The progress of literature," he has declared, "consists of the gradual removal of unnecessary fictions." Handke's spare, ascetic dramas and fictions are "meta-literature," to use a word which has been employed to describe writing that takes as a part of its subject the nature of writing itself. Such a concern is as old as the episode in the Phaiákian court in Homer's Odyssey, *in which a blind harper, Homer, sings a song about a blind harper, Demódokos, singing a song about a hero, Odysseus, who tells stories. It is also as modern as logical positivism, existentialism, and contemporary French structuralism, all of which have explored how the self is shaped by the nature of language and which have all left their mark upon Handke. But Handke is not primarily a philosopher any more than Homer was; his achievement is not to have demonstrated philosophical positions but to have created from his meta-literary structures brilliant new literary forms to explore fresh and deeply affecting areas of experience.*

Handke was born in 1942 in the small town of Griffen, in the Austrian province of Carinthia, near the Yugoslavian border, and spent his childhood there, except for the four years between 1944 and 1948, when the family lived in Berlin during the collapse of Hitler's Reich and its aftermath. He was educated at a Jesuit seminary and, in law, at the University of Graz; both the Jesuit legalist tradition and Handke's study of the law appear to have left their mark upon his precise, sometimes dry style.

Handke became almost immediately famous in German literary circles in 1966, when he was twenty-four years old and had just completed his course at Graz. In Princeton, New Jersey, on the last day of the annual meeting of Group 47, the German writers' organization founded in 1947 to plan the course of post-Nazi German writing, Handke suddenly rose from the audience and delivered a scathing attack upon the established writers present, their "trifling and idiotic" emphasis upon "descriptive" (rather than analytical) writing, and the "superannuated" criticism that supported it. Handke's brash and well-calculated performance drew cheers and applause even from the writers he was attacking. His first novel, The Hornets, *had just been published, and within weeks of the conference, his first play,* Offending the Audience, *was a major success in a production in Frankfurt.*

Through the 1960s, Handke was known primarily as a dramatist. Offending the Audience, *an attempt to do "something onstage against the stage," consists of four actors who enter, announce that no play will take place, and, in a rhythmic, precise series of statements, analyze the nature of the theater and then the audience, including their intelligence, their appearance, and their smell. Handke refused to call this piece a "play," instead coining the term* Sprechstücke *("speaking piece"); he followed it with several other similar speaking pieces, including* Prophecy *and* Self-Accusation *(both 1966) and* Calling for Help *(1967). Handke's first full-length play,* Kaspar, *was produced in 1968. Based remotely upon the story of Kaspar Hauser, a boy discovered in Nuremburg in 1828 who had been kept in a closet for sixteen years and had never learned to talk, the play presents a clownlike figure bombarded by invisible "prompter" voices who first teach him to speak and then to adopt the values of orderly society. Learning his lesson too well, Kaspar deteriorates in the second half into a haunted, self-conscious modern man finally stripped even of the language he has learned. Critics in several countries found the play the most important since Samuel Beckett's* Waiting for Godot. My Foot My Tutor, *a mime play, followed in 1969.* The Ride Across Lake Constance, *which appeared in 1970, is an eerie, dreamlike play in which a group of characters in a hotel lobby express themselves solely in a series of disjointed, self-conscious theatrical clichés. Other plays for radio, television, and the stage have also been produced, most notably* They Are Dying Out *(1975), but none has matched the success of* Kaspar.

Meanwhile, Handke's work as a writer of fiction gradually came to the fore. The Hornets *was followed by another novel,* The Peddler *(1967), but his first major success in fiction came in 1970 with* The Goalie's Anxiety at the Penalty Kick. *Like much of Handke's fiction, this novel deals with a mental breakdown, in this case that of Bloch, a construction worker and ex-soccer player who finds himself gradually losing his sense of the rules by which we perceive reality and communicate our sense of it. In the course of his collapse, he murders a girl he has picked up, flees, and then waits for the police to arrest him.* Short Letter, Long Farewell *(1972) is a powerful short novel about a German writer's travels across America after he receives a disturbing message from his estranged wife: "I am in New York. Please do not look for me, it would not be nice for you to find me." The novel explores various American myths and roles and culminates in a meeting with the American film director John Ford. (Handke makes pervasive use of popular culture in his fiction, including movies, television, and popular music.)* A Moment of True Feeling *(1975) again deals with an extreme mental state, through the story of an Austrian diplomat in Paris who dreams he has committed a murder and undergoes a progressive "fracture of the mind."* The Left-Handed Woman *(1976) explores not the alienated sensibility of the earlier novels but its converse, a "paradisiac state" of joyful acceptance of the external world; Handke made it into a film.*

Handke's best works to date are probably Kaspar *and* A Sorrow Beyond Dreams *(1972), his account of his mother's life and her suicide. In dealing with this most emotional of subjects, Handke is especially eager not to fall into the cotton-wool language and attitudes by which we distance ourselves from grief or even into the easy generalizations by which we come to "know" someone. The biography thus has two complementary subjects: the mother's struggle to be a person and Handke's struggle to describe her as she was. The mother (we never learn her name) contends with the constrictions of Austrian farm life, the pressures of Nazism, the restraints upon women, and her own inner confusion in her struggle for identity, a partially successful effort despite her ultimate voluntary withdrawal from life. Handke's struggle to speak the truth is equally fierce, almost as if the challenge of writing about this subject were a test of his whole vocation as a writer. The German title,* Wunschloses Unglück, *contains a bitter irony not suggested by the graceful but rather loose English translation; it means, approximately, "A Satisfying Misery," with the bitter suggestion that for a writer a mother's death is a challenging and satisfying "subject" as well as a source of grief. The subtitle, "A Life Story," has its irony, too, because the story is about a death. But the biography is both a life and a story, and Handke sees living and writing as parallel projects. His mother fights her way toward an identity past all the cultural assumptions embodied in language, assumptions Handke makes us conscious of by capitalizing emotionally loaded words: "ADMIRERS," "BACK IN PEACETIME," "GENTLEMEN." Handke fights his way toward the truth past similar veils of conventionalized feeling. But his almost pedantic precision never softens the visceral pain of his loss in this story of death that is also a hymn to life.*

FURTHER READING (*prepared by J. H.*): June Schlueter's *The Plays and Novels of Peter Handke,* 1981, is the fullest treatment in English of Handke's work. Nicholas Hern's *Peter Handke: Theatre and Anti-Theatre,* 1971, includes a brief biographical sketch, short interpretations of the early plays, and some translated extracts. An important essay by Handke himself on his work is "Brecht, Play, Theatre, Agitation," in *Theatre Quarterly* 1 (1971). An illuminating interview with him by Artur Joseph appeared in *Tulane Drama Review* 15 (1971), 57–58. J. L. Styan includes a brief survey of Handke's theater work in *Modern Drama in Theory and Practice,* Vol. 3, 1981, pp. 173–76. Richard Gilman includes a chapter on Handke in *The Making of Modern Drama,* 1974; and Ronald Hayman has a good essay, "Peter Handke and The Sentence," in *Theatre and Anti-Theatre,* 1979. Many of the observations these critics make about Handke's plays can be extended also to his fiction, on which good criticism in English is even more sparse. Frank Kermode's "The Model of a Modern Modernist," *New York Review of Books,* May 1, 1975, introduces American readers to Handke, whom Kermode calls "the most interesting young writer in German today." Another good English-language critic of Handke is Stanley Kauffmann, whose reviews in the *New Republic* are worth looking up; see especially his review of *Short Letter, Long Farewell* in the issue of Sept. 28, 1974.

A SORROW BEYOND DREAMS

A LIFE STORY

Translated by Ralph Manheim

He not busy being born is busy dying.
—Bob Dylan[1]

Dusk was falling quickly. It was just after 7 p.m., and the month was October.
—Patricia Highsmith, *A Dog's Ransom*[2]

The Sunday edition of the *Kärntner Volkszeitung* carried the following item under "Local News": "In the village of A. (G. township), a housewife, aged 51, committed suicide on Friday night by taking an overdose of sleeping pills."

My mother has been dead for almost seven weeks; I had better get to work before the need to write about her, which I felt so strongly at her funeral, dies away and I fall back into the dull speechlessness with which I reacted to the news of her suicide. Yes, get to work: for, intensely as I sometimes feel the need to write about my mother, this need is so vague that if I didn't work at it I would, in my present state of mind, just sit at my typewriter pounding out the same letters over and over again. This sort of kinetic therapy alone would do me no good; it would only make me passive and apathetic. I might just as well take a trip—if I were traveling, my mindless dozing and lounging around wouldn't get on my nerves so much.

During the last few weeks I have been more irritable than usual; disorder, cold, and silence drive me to distraction; I can't see a bread crumb or a bit of fluff on the floor without bending down to pick it up. Thinking about this suicide, I become so insensible that I am sometimes startled to find that an object I have been holding hasn't fallen out of my hand. Yet I long for such moments, because they shake me out of my apathy and clear my head. My sense of horror makes me feel better: at last my boredom is gone; an unresisting body, no more exhausting distances, a painless passage of time.

The worst thing right now would be sympathy, expressed in a word or even a glance. I would turn away or cut the sympathizer short, because I need the feeling that what I am going through is incomprehensible and incommunicable; only then does the horror seem meaningful and real. If anyone talks to me about it, the boredom comes back, and everything is unreal again. Nevertheless, for no reason at all, I sometimes tell people about my mother's suicide, but if they dare to mention it I am furious.

[1] From "It's Alright, Ma (I'm Only Bleeding)," on the album *Bringing It All Back Home* (1965).

[2] An American suspense novel, published in 1972.

What I really want them to do is change the subject and tease me about something.

In his latest movie someone asks James Bond whether his enemy, whom he has just thrown over a stair rail, is *dead*. His answer—"Let's hope so!"—made me laugh with relief. Jokes about dying and being dead don't bother me at all; on the contrary, they make me feel good.

Actually, my moments of horror are brief, and what I feel is not so much horror as unreality; seconds later, the world closes in again, and if someone is with me I try to be especially attentive, as though I had just been rude.

Now that I've begun to write, these states seem to have dwindled and passed, probably because I try to describe them as accurately as possible. In describing them, I begin to remember them as belonging to a concluded period of my life, and the effort of remembering and formulating keeps me so busy that the short daydreams of the last few weeks have stopped. I look back on them as intermittent "states": suddenly my day-to-day world—which, after all, consists only of images repeated ad nauseam over a period of years and decades since they were new—fell apart, and my mind became so empty that it ached.

That is over now; I no longer fall into these states. When I write, I necessarily write about the past, about something which, at least while I am writing, is behind me. As usual when engaged in literary work, I am alienated from myself and transformed into an object, a remembering and formulating machine. I am writing the story of my mother, first of all because I think I know more about her and how she came to her death than any outside investigator who might, with the help of a religious, psychological, or sociological guide to the interpretation of dreams, arrive at a facile explanation of this interesting case of suicide; but second in my own interest, because having something to do brings me back to life; and lastly because, like an outside investigator, though in a different way, I would like to represent this VOLUNTARY DEATH as an exemplary case.

Of course, all these justifications are arbitrary and could just as well be replaced by others that would be equally arbitrary. In any case, I experienced moments of extreme speechlessness and needed to formulate them—the motive that has led men to write from time immemorial.

In my mother's pocketbook, when I arrived for the funeral, I found a post-office receipt for a registered letter bearing the number 432. On Friday afternoon, before going home and taking the sleeping pills, she had mailed a registered letter containing a copy of her will to my address in Frankfurt. (But why also SPECIAL DELIVERY?) On Monday I went to the same post office to telephone. That was two and a half days after her death. On the desk in front of the post-office clerk, I saw the yellow roll of registration stickers; nine more registered letters had been mailed over the weekend; the next number was 442, and this image was so similar to the number I had in my head that at first glance I became confused and thought for a moment nothing had happened. The desire to tell someone about it cheered me up. It was such a bright day; the snow; we were eating soup with liver dumplings; "it began with . . ."; if I started like this, it would all seem to be made up, I would not be extorting personal sympathy from my listener or reader, I would merely be telling him a rather fantastic story.[3]

* * *

Well then, it began with my mother being born more than fifty years ago in the same village where she died. At that time all the land that was good for anything in the region belonged either to the church or to noble landowners; part of it was leased to the population, which consisted mostly of artisans and small peasants. The general indigence was such that few peasants owned their land. For practical purposes, the conditions were the same as before 1848; serfdom had been abolished in a merely formal sense.[4] My grandfather—he is still living, aged eighty-six—was a carpenter; in addition, he and his wife worked a few acres of rented farm and pasture land. He was of Slovenian descent and illegitimate. Most of the children born to small peasants in those days were illegitimate, because, years after attaining sexual maturity, few small peasants were in possession of living quarters or the means to support a household. His mother was the daughter of a rather well-do-do peasant, who, however, never regarded his hired man, my grandfather's father, as anything more than the "baby-maker." Nevertheless, my grandfather's mother inherited money enough to buy a small farm.

And so it came about that my grandfather was the first of his line—generations of hired men with blanks in their baptismal certificates, who had been born and who died in other people's houses and left little or no inheritance because their one and only possession, their Sunday suit, had been lowered into the grave with them—to grow up in surroundings where he could really feel at home and who was not merely tolerated in return for his daily toil.

Recently the financial section of one of our newspapers carried an apologia for the economic principles of the Western world. Property, it said, was MATERIALIZED FREEDOM. This may in his time have been true of my grandfather, the first in a long line of peasants fettered by poverty to own anything at all, let alone a house and a piece of land. The consciousness of owning something had so liberating an effect that after generations of will-lessness a will could now make its appearance: the will to become still freer. And that meant only one thing—justifiably so for my grandfather in his situation—to enlarge his property, for the farm he started out with was so small that nearly all his labors went into holding on to it. The ambitious smallholder's only hope lay in saving.

So my grandfather saved, until the inflation of the twenties ate up all his savings. Then he began to save again, not only by setting aside unneeded money but also and above all by compressing his own needs and demanding the same frugality of his children as well; his wife, being a woman, had never so much as dreamed that any other way of life was possible.

He continued to save toward the day when his children would need

[3] Asterisks here and later in *A Sorrow Beyond Dreams* indicate divisions of the narrative, not omissions of part of the text.

[4] Slovenia, now a part of Yugoslavia, was controlled by Germany until 1918. Serfdom was abolished there in the aftermath of the Revolutions of 1848.

SETTLEMENTS for marriage or to set themselves up in a trade. The idea that any of his savings might be spent before then on their EDUCATION couldn't possibly have entered his head, especially where his daughters were concerned. And even in his sons the centuries-old dread of becoming a homeless pauper was so deeply ingrained that one of them, who more by accident than by design had obtained a scholarship to the Gymnasium,[5] found those unfamiliar surroundings unbearable after only a few days. He walked the thirty miles from the provincial capital at night, arriving home on a Saturday, which was housecleaning day; without a word he started sweeping the yard: the noise he made with his broom in the early dawn told the whole story. He became a proficient and contented carpenter.

He and his older brother were killed early in the Second World War. In the meantime, my grandfather had gone on saving and once again lost his savings in the Depression of the thirties. His saving meant that he neither drank nor smoked, and played cards only on Sunday; but even the money he won in his Sunday card games—and he played so carefully that he almost always won—went into savings; at the most, he would slip his children a bit of small change. After the war, he started saving again; today he receives a government pension and is still at it.

The surviving son, a master carpenter with twenty workers in his employ, has no need to save. He invests, which means that he *can* drink and gamble; in fact, it's expected of him. Unlike his father, who all his life has been speechless and in every way self-denying, he has at least developed speech of a kind, though he uses it only in the town council, where he represents a small and obscure political party with visions of a grandiose future rooted in a grandiose past.

For a woman to be born into such surroundings was in itself deadly. But perhaps there was one comfort: no need to worry about the future. The fortune-tellers at our church fairs took a serious interest only in the palms of the young men; a girl's future was a joke.

No possibilities, it was all settled in advance: a bit of flirtation, a few giggles, brief bewilderment, then the alien, resigned look of a woman starting to keep house again, the first children, a bit of togetherness after the kitchen work, from the start not listened to, and in turn listening less and less, inner monologues, trouble with her legs, varicose veins, mute except for mumbling in her sleep, cancer of the womb, and finally, with death, destiny fulfilled. The girls in our town used to play a game based on the stations in a woman's life: Tired/Exhausted/Sick/Dying/Dead.

My mother was the next to last of five children. She was a good pupil; her teachers gave her the best possible marks and especially praised her neat handwriting. And then her school years were over. Learning had been a mere child's game; once your compulsory education was completed and you began to grow up, there was no need of it. After that a girl stayed home, getting used to the staying at home that would be her future.

No fears, except for an animal fear in the dark and in storms; no changes, except for the change between heat and cold, wet and dry, comfort and discomfort.

The passage of time was marked by church festivals, slaps in the face for

[5] Secondary school to prepare students for the university.

secret visits to the dance hall, fits of envy directed against her brothers, and the pleasure of singing in the choir. Everything else that happened in the world was a mystery; no newspapers were read except the Sunday bulletin of the diocese, and then only the serial.

Sundays: boiled beef with horseradish sauce, the card game, the women humbly sitting there, a family photograph showing the first radio.

My mother was high-spirited; in the photographs she propped her hands on her hips or put her arm over her younger brother's shoulder. She was always laughing and seemed incapable of doing anything else.

Rain—sun; outside—inside: feminine feelings were very much dependent on the weather, because "outside" was seldom allowed to mean anything but the yard and "inside" was invariably the house, without a room of one's own.

The climate in that region is extremely variable: cold winters and sultry summers, but at sunset or even in the shade of a tree you shivered. Rain and more rain; from early September on, whole days of damp fog outside the tiny windows (they are hardly any larger today); drops of water on the clotheslines; toads jumping across your path in the dark; gnats, bugs, and moths even in the daytime; worms and wood lice under every log in the woodshed. You couldn't help becoming dependent on those things; there was nothing else. Seldom: desireless and somehow happy; usually: desireless and a little unhappy.

No possibility of comparison with a different way of life: richer? less hemmed in?

It began with my mother suddenly wanting something. She wanted to learn, because in learning her lessons as a child she had felt something of herself. Just as when we say, "I feel like myself." For the first time, a desire, and she didn't keep it to herself; she spoke of it time and time again, and in the end it became an obsession with her. My mother told me she had "begged" my grandfather to let her learn something. But it was out of the question, disposed of with a wave of the hand, unthinkable.

Still, our people had a traditional respect for accomplished facts: a pregnancy, a war, the state, ritual, and death. When at the age of fifteen or sixteen my mother ran away from home to learn cooking at some Hôtel du Lac,[6] my grandfather let her have her own way, *because she was already gone;* and besides, there wasn't much to be learned about cooking.

No other course was open to her; scullery maid, chambermaid, assistant cook, head cook. "People will always eat." In the photographs, a flushed face, glowing cheeks, arm in arm with bashful, serious-looking girl friends; she was the life of the party; self-assured gaiety ("Nothing can happen to me"); exuberant, sociable, nothing to hide.

City life: short skirts ("knee huggers"), high-heeled shoes, permanent wave, earrings, unclouded joy of life. Even a stay abroad! Chambermaid in the Black Forest, flocks of ADMIRERS, kept at a DISTANCE! Dates, dancing, entertainment, fun; hidden fear of sex ("They weren't my type"). Work, pleasure; heavyhearted, lighthearted; Hitler had a nice voice on the radio. The homesickness of those who can't afford anything; back at the Hôtel du Lac ("I'm doing the bookkeeping now"); glowing references ("Fräulein . . .

[6] Resort hotel.

has shown aptitude and willingness to learn. So conscientious, frank, and cheerful that we find it hard . . . She is leaving our establishment of her own free will"). Boat rides, all-night dances, never tired.

On April 10, 1938, the Yes to Germany![7] "The Führer[8] arrived at 4:15 p.m., after a triumphal passage through the streets of Klagenfurt to the strains of the Badenweiler March. The rejoicing of the masses seemed to know no bounds. The thousands of swastika flags in the spas and summer resorts were reflected in the already ice-free waters of the Wörthersee. The airplanes of the old Reich and our native planes vied with one another in the clouds overhead."

The newspapers advertised plebiscite badges and silk or paper flags. After football games the teams marched off with a regulation *"Sieg Heil!"*[9] The letter A was replaced by the letter D on the bumpers of motor vehicles.[10] On the radio: 6:15, call to arms; 6:35, motto of the day; 6:40, gymnastics; 8–12 p.m., Radio Königsberg: Richard Wagner concert followed by entertainment and dance music.

"How to mark your ballot on April 10: make a *bold* cross in the *larger* circle under the word YES."

Thieves just out of jail were locked up again when they claimed that the objects found in their possession had been bought in department stores that MEANWHILE HAD GONE OUT OF EXISTENCE because they had belonged to Jews.

Demonstrations, torchlight parades, mass meetings. Buildings decorated with the new national emblem SALUTED; forests and mountains peaks DECKED THEMSELVES OUT; the historic events were represented to the rural population as a drama of nature.

"We were kind of excited," my mother told me. For the first time, people did things together. Even the daily grind took on a festive mood, "until late into the night." For once, everything that was strange and incomprehensible in the world took on meaning and became part of a larger context; even disagreeable, mechanical work was festive and meaningful. Your automatic movements took on an athletic quality, because you saw innumerable others making the same movements. A new life, in which you felt protected, yet free.

The rhythm became an existential ritual. "Public need before private greed, the community comes first." You were at home wherever you went; no more homesickness. Addresses on the back of photographs; you bought your first date book (or was it a present?)—all at once you had so many friends and there was so much going on that it became possible to FORGET something. She had always wanted to be proud of something, and now, because what she was doing was somehow important, she actually was proud, not of anything in particular, but in general—a state of mind, a newly attained awareness of being alive—and she was determined never to give up that vague pride.

She still had no interest in politics: what was happening before her eyes

[7] After Nazi troops entered Austria on March 12, 1938, a plebiscite held throughout that country on April 10 recorded a vote of more than ninety-nine percent in favor of Germany's absorbing of Austria.

[8] Hitler. [9] "Hail victory!" (a Nazi salute).

[10] That is, "D" for "Deutschland" (Germany) rather than "A" for "Austria."

was something entirely different from politics—a masquerade, a newsreel festival, a secular church fair. "Politics" was something colorless and abstract, not a carnival, not a dance, not a band in local costume, in short, nothing VISIBLE. Pomp and ceremony on all sides. And what was "politics"? A meaningless word, because, from your schoolbooks on, everything connected with politics had been dished out in catchwords unrelated to any tangible reality and even such images as were used were devoid of human content: oppression as chains or boot heel, freedom as mountaintop, the economic system as a reassuringly smoking factory chimney or as a pipe enjoyed after the day's work, the social system as a descending ladder: "Emperor—King—Nobleman—Burgher—Peasant—Weaver/Carpenter—Beggar—Gravedigger"; a game, incidentally, that could be played properly only in the prolific families of peasants, carpenters, and weavers.

* * *

That period helped my mother to come out of her shell and become independent. She acquired a presence and lost her last fear of human contact: her hat awry, because a young fellow was pressing his head against hers, while she merely laughed into the camera with an expression of self-satisfaction. (The fiction that photographs can "tell us" anything—but isn't all formulation, even of things that have really happened, more or less a fiction? *Less,* if we content ourselves with a mere record of events; *more,* if we try to formulate in depth? And the more fiction we put into a narrative, the more likely it is to interest others, because people identify more readily with formulations than with recorded facts. Does this explain the need for poetry? "Breathless on the riverbank" is one of Thomas Bernhard's formulations.[11])

* * *

The war—victory communiqués introduced by portentous music, pouring from the "people's radio sets," which gleamed mysteriously in dimly lit "holy corners"—further enhanced people's sense of self, because it "increased the uncertainty of all circumstances" (Clausewitz)[12] and made the day-to-day happenings that had formerly been taken for granted seem excitingly fortuitous. For my mother the war was not a childhood nightmare that would color her whole emotional development as it did mine; more than anything else, it was contact with a fabulous world, hitherto known to her only from travel folders. A new feeling for distances, for how things had been BACK IN PEACETIME, and most of all for other individuals, who up until then had been confined to the shadowy roles of casual friends, dance partners, and fellow workers. And also for the first time, a family feeling: "Dear Brother . . . I am looking at the map to see where you might be now . . . Your sister . . ."

And in the same light of her first love: a German party member, in civilian life a savings-bank clerk, now an army paymaster, which gave him a rather special standing. She was soon in a family way. He was married,

[11] Contemporary German poet and novelist (born 1931).

[12] Karl von Clausewitz (1780–1831), a Prussian general whose *On War* is the definitive textbook of traditional military strategy.

and she loved him dearly; anything he said was all right with her. She introduced him to her parents, went hiking with him, kept him company in his soldier's loneliness.

"He was so attentive to me, and I wasn't afraid of him the way I had been with other men."

He did the deciding and she trailed along. Once he gave her a present—perfume. He also lent her a radio for her room and later took it away again. "At that time" he still read books, and together they read one entitled *By the Fireside*. On the way down from a mountain pasture on one of their hikes, they had started to run. My mother broke wind and my father reproved her; a little later he too let a fart escape him and followed it with a slight cough, hem-hem. In telling me of this incident years later, she bent double and giggled maliciously, though at the same time her conscience troubled her because she was belittling her only love. She herself thought it comical that she had once loved someone, especially a man like him. He was smaller than she, many years older, and almost bald; she walked beside him in low-heeled shoes, always at pains to adapt her step to his, her hand repeatedly slipping off his inhospitable arm; an ill-matched, ludicrous couple. And yet, twenty years later, she still longed to feel for someone what she had then felt for that savings-bank wraith. But there never was ANOTHER: everything in her life had conspired to inculcate a kind of love that remains fixated on a particular irreplaceable object.

It was after graduating from the Gymnasium that I first saw my father: on his way to the rendezvous, he chanced to come toward me in the street; he was wearing sandals, a piece of paper was folded over his sunburned nose, and he was leading a collie on a leash. Then, in a small café in her home village, he met his former love; my mother was excited, my father embarrassed; standing by the jukebox at the other end of the café, I picked out Elvis Presley's "Devil in Disguise." My mother's husband had got wind of all this, but he had merely sent his youngest son to the café as an indication that he was in the know. After buying himself an ice-cream cone, the child stood next to his mother and the stranger, asking her from time to time, always in the same words, if she was going home soon. My father put sunglasses over his regular glasses, said something now and then to the dog, and finally announced that he "might as well" pay up. "No, no, it's on me," he said, when my mother also took her purse out of her handbag. On the trip we took together, the two of us wrote her a postcard. In every hotel we went to, he let it be known that I was his son, for fear we'd be taken for homosexuals (Article 175).[13] Life had disappointed him, he had become more and more lonely. "Now that I know people, I've come to appreciate animals," he said, not quite in earnest of course.

* * *

Shortly before I was born, my mother married a German army sergeant, who had been COURTING her for some time and didn't mind her having a child by someone else. "It's this one or none!" he had decided the first time he laid eyes on her, and bet his buddies that he would get her or, conversely, that she would take him. She found him repulsive, but everyone

[13] Homosexuality was a crime under the Nazi criminal code.

harped on her duty (to give the child a father); for the first time in her life she let herself be intimidated and laughed rather less. Besides, it impressed her that someone should have taken a shine to her.

"Anyway, I figured he'd be killed in the war," she told me. "But then all of a sudden I started worrying about him."

In any case, she was now entitled to a family allotment. With the child she went to Berlin to stay with her husband's parents. They tolerated her. When the first bombs fell, she went back home—the old story. She began to laugh again, sometimes so loudly that everyone cringed.

She forgot her husband, squeezed her child so hard that it cried, and kept to herself in this house where, after the death of her brothers, those who remained looked uncomprehendingly through one another. Was there, then, nothing more? Had that been all? Masses for the dead, childhood diseases, drawn curtains, correspondence with old acquaintances of carefree days, making herself useful in the kitchen and in the fields, running out now and then to move the child into the shade; then, even here in the country, air-raid sirens, the population scrambling into the cave shelters, the first bomb crater, later used for children's games and as a garbage dump.

The days were haunted, and once again the outside world, which years of daily contact had wrested from the nightmares of childhood and made familiar, became an impalpable ghost.

My mother looked on in wide-eyed astonishment. Fear didn't get the better of her; but sometimes, infected by the general fright, she would burst into a sudden laugh, partly because she was ashamed that her body had suddenly made itself so churlishly independent. In her childhood and even more so in her young girlhood, "Aren't you ashamed?" or "You ought to be ashamed!" had run in her ears like a litany. In this rural, Catholic environment, any suggestion that a woman might have a life of her own was an impertinence: disapproving looks, until shame, at first acted out in fun, became real and frightened away the most elementary feelings. Even in joy, a "woman's blush," because joy was something to be ashamed of; in sadness, she turned red rather than pale and instead of bursting into tears broke out in sweat.

In the city my mother had thought she had found a way of life that more or less suited her, that at least made her feel good. Now she came to realize that by excluding every other alternative, other people's way of life had set itself up as the one and only *hope of salvation*. When, in speaking of herself, she went beyond a statement of fact, she was silenced by a glance.

A bit of gaiety, a dance step while working, the humming of a song hit, were foolishness, and soon she herself thought so, because no one reacted and she was left alone with her gaiety. In part, the others lived their own lives as an example; they ate so little as an example, were silent in each other's presence as an example, and went to confession only to remind the stay-at-homes of their sins.

And so she was starved. Her little attempts to explain herself were futile mutterings. She felt free—but there was nothing she could do about it. The others, to be sure, were children; but it was oppressive to be looked at so reproachfully, especially by children.

When the war was over, my mother remembered her husband and, though no one had asked for her, went to Berlin. Her husband, who had also forgotten that he had once courted her on a bet, was living with a girl friend in Berlin; after all, there had been a war on.

But she had her child with her, and without enthusiasm they both took the path of duty.

They lived in a sublet room in Berlin-Pankow. The husband worked as a streetcar motorman and drank, worked as a streetcar conductor and drank, worked as a baker and drank. Taking with her her second child, who had been born in the meantime, his wife went to see his employer and begged him to give her husband one more chance, the old story.

In this life of misery, my mother lost her country-round cheeks and achieved a certain chic. She carried her head high and acquired a graceful walk. Whatever she put on was becoming to her. She had no need of fox furs. When her husband sobered up and clung to her and told her he loved her, she gave him a merciful, pitying smile. By then, she had no illusions about anything.

They went out a good deal, an attractive couple. When he was drunk, he got FRESH and she had to be SEVERE with him. Then he would beat her because she had nothing to say to him, when it was he who brought home the bacon.

Without his knowledge, she gave herself an abortion with a knitting needle.

For a time he lived with his parents; then they sent him back to her. Childhood memories: the fresh bread that he sometimes brought home; the black, fatty loaves of pumpernickel around which the dismal room blossomed into life; my mother's words of praise.

In general, these memories are inhabited more by things than by people: a dancing top in a deserted street amid ruins, oat flakes in a sugar spoon, gray mucus in a tin spittoon with a Russian trademark; of people, only separated parts: hair, cheeks, knotted scars on fingers; from her childhood days my mother had a swollen scar on her index finger; I held on to it when I walked beside her.

* * *

And so she was nothing and never would be anything; it was so obvious that there was no need of a forecast. She already said "in my day," though she was not yet thirty. Until then, she hadn't resigned herself, but now life became so hard that for the first time she had to listen to reason. She listened to reason, but understood nothing.

She had already begun to work something out and even, as far as possible, to live accordingly. She said to herself: "Be sensible"—the reason reflex—and "All right, I'll behave."

And so she budgeted herself and also learned to budget people and objects, though on that score there was little to be learned: the people in her life—her husband, whom she couldn't talk to, and her children, whom she couldn't yet talk to—hardly counted, and objects were available only in minimal quantities. Consequently, she became petty and niggardly: Sunday shoes were not to be worn on weekdays, street clothes were to be hung up as soon as you got home, her shopping bag wasn't a toy, the warm bread was for the next day. (Later on, my confirmation watch was locked up right after my confirmation.)

Because she was helpless, she disciplined herself, which went against her grain and made her touchy. She hid her touchiness behind an anxious, exaggerated dignity, but at the slightest provocation a defenseless, panic-stricken look shone through. She was easily humiliated.

Like her father, she thought the time had come to deny herself everything, but then with a shamefaced laugh she would ask the children to let her lick their candy.

The neighbors liked her and admired her for her Austrian sociability and gaiety; they thought her FRANK and SIMPLE, not coquettish and affected like city people; there was no fault to be found with her.

She also got on well with the Russians, because she could make herself understood in Slovenian. With them she talked and talked, saying everything she was able to say in the words common to both languages; that unburdened her.

But she never had any desire for an affair. Her heart had grown heavy too soon: the shame that had always been preached at her had finally become a part of her. An affair, to her mind, could only mean someone "wanting something" of her, and that put her off; she, after all, didn't want anything of anybody. The men she later liked to be with were GENTLEMEN: their company gave her a pleasant feeling that took the place of affection. As long as there was someone to talk with, she felt relaxed and almost happy. She let no one come too close; she could have been approached only with the delicacy which in former days had enabled her to feel that she belonged to herself—but that was long ago; she remembered it only in her dreams.

She became sexless; everything went into the trivia of daily life.

She wasn't lonely; at most, she sensed that she was only a half. But there was no one to supply the other half. "We rounded each other out so well," she said, thinking back on her days with the savings-bank clerk; that was her ideal of eternal love.

* * *

The postwar period; the big city—in this city, city life was no longer possible. You took shortcuts, up hill and down dale through the rubble, to get there sooner, but even so you found yourself at the end of a long line, jostled by fellow citizens who had ceased to be anything more than elbows and eyes looking into space. A short, unhappy laugh; like the rest of them, you looked away from yourself, into space; like the rest of them, you gave yourself away, showed that you needed something; still, you tried to assert yourself; pathetic, because that made you just like the people around you: something pushing and pushed, shoving and shoved, cursing and cursed at. In her new situation, her mouth, which up until then had been open at least occasionally—in youthful amazement (or in feminine acting-as-if), in rural fright, at the end of a daydream that lightened her heavy heart—was kept closed with exaggerated firmness, as a sign of adaptation to a universal determination which, because there was so little to be *personally* determined about, could never be more than a pretense.

A masklike face—not rigid as a mask but with a masklike immobility—a disguised voice, which for fear of attracting attention not only spoke the foreign dialect but mimicked the foreign turns of phrase—"Mud in your eye!"—"Keep your paws off that!"—"You're sure shoveling it in today!"—a copied posture, with a bend at the hips and one foot thrust forward . . . all this in order to become, not a different person, but a TYPE: to change from a prewar type to a postwar type, from a country bumpkin to a city person, adequately described in the words: TALL, SLIM, DARK-HAIRED.

In thus becoming a type, she felt freed from her own history, because now she saw herself through the eyes of a stranger making an erotic appraisal.

And so an emotional life that never had a chance of achieving bourgeois composure acquired a superficial stability by clumsily imitating the bourgeois system of emotional relations, prevalent especially among women, the system in which "So-and-so is my type but I'm not his," or "I'm his but he's not mine," or in which "We're made for each other" or "can't stand the sight of each other"—in which clichés are taken as binding rules and any *individual* reaction, which takes some account of an actual person, becomes a deviation. For instance, my mother would say of my father, "Actually, he wasn't my type." And so this typology became a guide to life; it gave you a pleasantly objective feeling about yourself; you stopped worrying about your origins, your possibly dandruff-ridden, sweaty-footed individuality, or the daily renewed problem of how to go on living; being a type relieved the human molecule of his humiliating loneliness and isolation; he lost himself, yet now and then he was somebody, if only briefly.

Once you became a type, you floated through the streets, buoyed up by all the things you could pass with indifference, repelled by everything which, in forcing you to stop, brought you back bothersomely to yourself: the lines outside the shops, a high bridge across the Spee,[14] a shop window with baby carriages in it. (She had given herself another secret abortion.) Always on the move to get away from yourself and keep your peace of mind. Motto: "Today I won't think of anything; today I'll enjoy myself."

At times it worked and everything personal was swallowed up by the typical. Then even sadness was only a passing phase, a suspension of good cheer: "Forsaken, forsaken, / Like a pebble in the street, That's how forsaken I am"; with the foolproof melancholy of this phony folk song, she contributed her share to the general merriment; the next item on the program might, for instance, be the ribald tone of a male voice getting ready to tell a joke. And then, with a sense of release, you could join in the laughter.

At home, of course, she was alone with the FOUR WALLS; some of the bounce was still there, a hummed tune, a dance step while taking off her shoes, a brief desire to jump out of her skin. And then she was dragging herself around the room again, from husband to child, from child to husband, from one thing to another.

Her calculations always went wrong; the little bourgeois recipes for salvation had stopped working, because in actual fact her living conditions—the one-room apartment, the constant worry about where the next meal was coming from, the fact that communication with her LIFE COMPANION

[14] The Spee River, which flows through Berlin before joining the Havel River at Spandau.

was confined almost exclusively to gestures, involuntary mimicry, and embarrassed sexual intercourse—were actually prebourgeois. It was only by leaving the house that she could get anything at all out of life. Outside: the victor type; inside: the weaker half, the eternal loser! What a life!

Whenever she told me about it later on—and *telling* about it was a need with her—she would shake with disgust and misery, but too feebly to shake them *off*; her shudders only revived her horror.

From my childhood: ridiculous sobs in the toilet, nose blowing, inflamed eyes. She was; she became; she became nothing.

* * *

(Of course what is written here about a particular person is rather general; but only such generalizations, in explicit disregard of my mother as a possibly unique protagonist in a possibly unique story, can be of interest to anyone but myself. Merely to relate the vicissitudes of a life that came to a sudden end would be pure presumption.

(The dangers of all these abstractions and formulations is of course that they tend to become independent. When that happens, the individual that gave rise to them is forgotten—like images in a dream, phrases and sentences enter into a chain reaction, and the result is a literary ritual in which an individual life ceases to be anything more than a pretext.

(These two dangers—the danger of merely telling what happened and the danger of a human individual becoming painlessly submerged in poetic sentences—have slowed down my writing, because in every sentence I am afraid of losing my balance. This is true of every literary effort, but especially in this case, where the facts are so overwhelming that there is hardly anything to think out.

(Consequently, I first took the facts as my starting point and looked for ways of formulating them. But I soon noticed that in looking for formulations I was moving away from the facts. I then adopted a new approach—starting not with the facts but with the already available formulations, the linguistic deposit of man's social experience. From my mother's life, I sifted out the elements that were already foreseen in these formulas, for only with the help of a ready-made public language was it possible to single out from among all the irrelevant facts of this life the few that cried out to be made public.

(Accordingly, I compare, sentence by sentence, the stock of formulas applicable to the biography of a woman with my mother's particular life; the actual work of writing follows from the agreements and contradictions between them. The essential is to avoid mere quotations; even when sentences look quoted, they must never allow one to forget that they deal with someone who to my mind at least is distinct. Only then, only if a sentence is firmly and circumspectly centered on my personal or, if you will, private subject, do I feel that I can use it.

(Another specific feature of this story is that I do not, as is usually the case, let every sentence carry me further away from the inner life of my characters, so as finally, in a liberated and serene holiday mood, to look at them from outside as isolated insects. Rather, I try with unbending earnestness to penetrate my character. And because I cannot fully capture her in any sentence, I keep having to start from scratch and never arrive at the usual sharp and clear bird's-eye view.

(Ordinarily, I start with myself and my own headaches; in the course of my writing, I detach myself from them more and more, and then in the end I ship myself and my headaches off to market as a commodity—but in this case, since I am only a *writer* and can't take the role of the *person written about*, such detachment is impossible. I can only move myself into the distance; my mother can never become for me, as I can for myself, a wingèd art object flying serenely through the air. She refuses to be isolated and remains unfathomable; my sentences crash in the darkness and lie scattered on the paper.

(In stories we often read that something or other is "unnamable" or "indescribable"; ordinarily this strikes me as a cheap excuse. This story, however, is really about the nameless, about speechless moments of terror. It is about moments when the mind boggles with horror, states of fear so brief that speech always comes too late; about dream happenings so gruesome that the mind perceives them physically as worms. The blood curdles, the breath catches, "a cold chill crept up my back, my hair stood on end"—states experienced while listening to a ghost story, while turning on a water faucet that you can quickly turn off again, on the street in the evening with a beer bottle in one hand; in short, it is a record of states, not a well-rounded story with an anticipated, hence comforting, end.

(At best, I am able to capture my mother's story for brief moments in dreams, because then her feelings become so palpable that I experience them as doubles and am identical with them; but these are precisely the moments I have already mentioned, in which extreme need to communicate coincides with extreme speechlessness. That is why I affect the usual biographical pattern and write: "At that time . . . later," "Because . . . although," "was . . . became . . . became nothing," hoping in this way to dominate the horror. That, perhaps, is the comical part of my story.)

* * *

In the early summer of 1948, my mother left the eastern sector of Germany with her husband and two children, carrying the little girl, who was just a year old, in a shopping bag. They had no papers. They crossed two borders illegally, both in the gray of dawn; once a Russian border guard shouted "Halt," and my mother's answer in Slovenian served as a password; those days became fixed in the boy's mind as a triad of gray dawn, whispers, and danger. Happy excitement on the train ride through Austria, and then she was back in the house where she was born, where two small rooms were turned over to her and her family. Her husband was employed as foreman by her carpenter brother; she herself was reincorporated into the household.

In the city she had not been proud of having children; here she was, and often showed herself with them. She no longer took any nonsense from anyone. In the old days her only reaction had been a bit of back talk; now she laughed. She could laugh anyone to silence. Her husband, in particular, got laughed at so vigorously whenever he started discussing his numerous projects that he soon faltered and looked vacantly out the window. True, he would start in again the next day. (That period lives for me in the sound of my mother laughing at people!) She also interrupted the children with her laughter when they wanted something; it was ridiculous to express desires in earnest. In the meantime, she brought her third child into the world.

She took to the native dialect again, though of course only in fun: she was a woman who had been ABROAD. Almost all her old girl friends had by then returned to their native village; they had made only brief excursions to the city or across the borders.

In this life, confined almost entirely to housekeeping and making ends meet, you didn't confide in your friends; at the most, friendship meant familiarity. It was plain from the start that all had the same troubles—the only difference was that some took them more lightly than others, a matter of temperament.

In this section of the population, people without troubles were an oddity—freaks. Drunks didn't get talkative, only more taciturn; they might bellow or brawl for a while, but then they sank back into themselves, until at closing time they would start sobbing for no known reason and hug or thrash whoever was nearest to them.

No one had anything to say about himself, even in church, at Easter confession, when at least once a year there was an opportunity to reveal something of oneself, there was only a mumbling of catchwords out of the catechism, and the word "I" seemed stranger to the speaker himself than a chunk out of the moon. If in talking about himself anyone went beyond relating some droll incident, he was said to be "peculiar." Personal life, if it had ever developed a character of its own, was depersonalized except for dream tatters swallowed up by the rites of religion, custom, and good manners; little remained of the human individual, and indeed, the word "individual" was known only in pejorative combinations.

The sorrowful Rosary; the glorious Rosary; the harvest festival; the plebiscite celebration; ladies' choice; the drinking of brotherhood; April Fools' pranks; wakes; kisses on New Year's Eve: in these rituals all private sorrow, ambition, hunger for communication, sense of the unique, wanderlust, sexual drive, and in general all reactions to a lopsided world in which the roles were reversed, were projected outward, so that no one was a problem to himself.

All spontaneity—taking a walk on a weekday, falling in love a second time, or, if you were a woman, going to the tavern by yourself for a schnapps—was frowned upon; in a pinch you could ask someone to dance or join in a song "spontaneously," but that was all. Cheated out of your own biography and feelings, you became "skittish"; you shied away from people, stopped talking, or, more seriously touched, went from house to house screaming.

The above-mentioned rites then functioned as a consolation. This consolation didn't address itself to you as a person; it simply swallowed you up, so that in the end you as an individual were content to be nothing, or at least nothing much.

You lost interest in personal matters and stopped inquiring about them.

All questions became empty phrases, and the answers were so stereotyped that there was no need to involve *people* in them; *objects* sufficed; the cool grave, the sweet heart of Jesus, the sweet Lady of Sorrows, became fetishes for the death wish that sweetened your daily afflictions; in the midst of these consoling fetishes, you ceased to exist. And because your days were spent in unchanging association with the same things, they became sacred to you; not leisure but work was sweet. Besides, there was nothing else.

You no longer had eyes for anything. "Curiosity" ceased to be a human characteristic and became a womanish vice.

But my mother was curious by nature and had no consoling fetishes. Instead of losing herself in her work, she took it in her stride; consequently she was discontented. The *Weltschmerz*[15] of the Catholic religion was alien to her; she believed only in happiness in this world, and that was a matter of luck; she herself had had bad luck.

She'd show them, though.

But how?

How she would have loved to be really frivolous! And then she actually did something frivolous: "I've been frivolous today, I've bought myself a blouse." All the same—and that was a good deal in those surroundings—she took to smoking and even smoked in public.

Many of the local women were secret drinkers; their thick, twisted lips repelled her: that wasn't the way to show them. At the most she would get tipsy, and then she would drink to lifelong friendship with everyone in sight, and soon she was on friendly terms with all the younger notables. Even in this little village there was a kind of "society," consisting of the few who were somewhat better off than the rest, and she was welcome in their gatherings. Once, disguised as a Roman matron, she won first prize at a masked ball. At least in its merrymaking, country society thought of itself as classless—as long as you were NEAT, CLEAN, and JOLLY.

* * *

At home she was "Mother"; even her husband addressed her as "Mother" more often than by her first name. That was all right with her; for one thing, it corresponded to her feeling about her husband: she had never regarded him as anything resembling a sweetheart.

Now it was she who saved. Her saving, to be sure, could not, like her father's, mean setting money aside. It was pure *scrimping*; you curtailed your needs to the point where they became vices, and then you curtailed them some more.

But even in this wretchedly narrow sphere, she comforted herself with the thought that she was at least imitating the *pattern* of middle-class life: ludicrous as it might seem, it was still possible to classify purchases as necessary, merely useful, and luxurious.

Only food was necessary; winter fuel was useful; everything else was a luxury.

[15] "World pain" (German), sadness over the disparity between the world as it is and an ideal of how it should be.

If only once a week, she derived a pleasurable feeling of pride from the fact that a little something was left over for luxury. "We're still better off than the rest of them."

She indulged in the following luxuries: a seat in the ninth row at the movies, followed by a glass of wine and soda water; a one- or two-schilling bar of Bensdorp chocolate to give the children the next morning; once a year, a bottle of homemade eggnog; on occasional winter Sundays she would whip up the cream she had saved during the week by keeping the milk pot between the two panes of the double windows overnight. "What a feast!" I would write if it were my own story; but it was only the slavish aping of an unattainable life style, a child's game of earthly paradise.

Christmas: necessities were packaged as presents. We surprised each other with such necessities as underwear, stockings, and handkerchiefs, and the beneficiary said he had WISHED for just that! We pretended that just about everything that was given to us, except food, was a present; I was sincerely grateful for the most indispensable school materials and spread them out beside my bed like presents.

* * *

A budgeted life, determined by the hourly wages she totted up for her husband, always hoping to discover a forgotten half hour; dread of rainy spells, when the wages were next to nothing, which he passed in their little room talking to her or looking resentfully out the window.

In the winter, when there was no building, her husband spent his unemployment benefits on drink. She went from tavern to tavern looking for him; with gleeful malice, he would show her what was left. She ducked to avoid his blows. She stopped talking to him. The children, repelled and frightened by her silence, clung to their contrite father. Witch! The children looked at her with hostility; she was so stern and unbending. They slept with pounding hearts when their parents were out and pulled the blanket over their heads when toward morning the husband pushed the wife into the room. At every step she stopped until he pushed her. Both were obstinately mute. Then finally she opened her mouth and said what he had been waiting to hear: "You beast! You beast!" whereupon he was able to beat her in earnest. To every blow she responded with a short, crushing laugh.

They seldom looked at each other except in these moments of open hatred; then they looked deep and unflinchingly into each other's eyes, he from below, she from above. The children under the blanket heard only the shoving and breathing, and occasionally the rattling of dishes in the cupboard. Next morning they made their own breakfast while husband and wife lay in bed, he dead to the world, she with her eyes closed, pretending to be asleep. (Undoubtedly, this kind of account seems copied, borrowed from accounts of other incidents; an old story interchangeable with other old stories; unrelated to the time when it took place; in short, it smacks of the nineteenth century. But just that seems necessary, for, at least in that part of the world and under the given economic conditions, such anachronistic, interchangeable nineteenth-century happenings were still the rule. And even today the Town Hall bulletin board is taken up almost entirely by notices to the effect that So-and-so and So-and-so are forbidden to enter the taverns.)

* * *

She never ran away. She had learned her place. "I'm only waiting for the children to grow up." A third abortion, this time followed by a severe hemorrhage. Shortly before she was forty, she became pregnant again. An abortion was no longer possible; the child was born.

The word "poverty" was a fine, somehow noble word. It evoked an image out of old schoolbooks: poor but clean. Cleanliness made the poor socially acceptable. Social progress meant teaching people to be clean; once the indigent had been cleaned up, "poverty" became a title of honor. Even in the eyes of the poor, the squalor of destitution applied only to the filthy riffraff of foreign countries.

"The tenant's visiting card is his windowpane."

And so the have-nots obediently bought soap with the money provided for that purpose by the progressive authorities. As paupers, they had shocked the official mind with repulsive, but for that very reason palpable, images; now, as a reclaimed and cleansed "poorer class," their life became so unimaginably abstract that they could be forgotten. Squalid misery can be described in concrete terms; poverty can only be intimated in symbols.

Moreover, the graphic accounts of squalor were concerned only with its physically disgusting aspect; they *produced* disgust by the relish they took in it, so that disgust, instead of being translated into action, merely became a reminder of the anal, shit-eating phase.

In certain households, for instance, there was only one bowl; at night it was used as a chamberpot and by day for kneading bread dough. Undoubtedly the bowl was washed out with boiling water in between, so there was little harm done; the dual use of the bowl became disgusting only when it was *described*: "They relieve themselves in the same bowl they eat out of."—"Ugh!" Words convey this sort of passive, complacent disgust much better than the sight of the phenomena they refer to. (A memory of my own: shuddering while describing spots of egg yolk on a dressing gown.) Hence my distaste for descriptions of misery; for in hygienic, but equally miserable, poverty, there is nothing to describe.

Accordingly, when the word "poverty" comes up, I always think: "once upon a time"; and, for the most part, one hears it in the mouth of persons who have gone through it in the past, a word connected with childhood; not "I was poor" but "I was the child of poor parents" (Maurice Chevalier):[16] a quaint note to season memoirs with. But at the thought of my mother's living conditions, I am unable to embroider on my memory. From the first, she was under pressure to keep up the forms: in country schools, the subject most stressed for girls was called "the outward form and appearance of written work"; in later life, this found its continuation in a woman's obliga-

[16] French actor and singer (1888–1972).

tion to keep up the appearancc of a united family; not cheerful poverty but formally perfect squalor; and gradually, in its daily effort to keep up appearances, her face lost its soul.

Maybe we would have felt better in formless squalor; we might have achieved a degree of proletarian class-consciousness. But in that part of the world there was no proletariat, at most, beggars and tramps; no one fought or even talked back; the totally destitute were merely embarrassed; poverty was indeed a disgrace.

* * *

Nevertheless, my mother, who had not learned to take all this for granted, was humiliated by the eternal stringency. In symbolic terms: she was no longer a NATIVE WHO HAD NEVER SEEN A WHITE MAN; she was capable of imagining a life that was something more than lifelong housework. If someone had given her the slightest hint, she would have got the right idea.

If, would have.

What actually happened: a nature play with a human prop that was systematically dehumanized. Pleading with her brother not to dismiss her husband for drunkenness; pleading with the local radio spotter not to report her unregistered radio; pleading with the bank for a building loan, protesting that she was a good citizen and would prove worthy of it; from office to office for a certificate of indigence, which had to be renewed each year if her son, who was now at the university, was to obtain a scholarship; applications for sick relief, family allowances, reduction of church taxes—most of which depended on the benevolent judgment of the authorities, but even if you had a legal right to something, you had to prove it over and over again in such detail that when the "Approved" stamp finally came, you received it with gratitude, as a favor.

* * *

No machines in the house; everything was still done by hand. Objects out of a past century, now generally transfigured with nostalgia: not only the coffee mill, which you had actually come to love as a toy—also the GOOD OLD ironing board, the COZY hearth, the often-mended cooking pots, the DANGEROUS poker, the STURDY wheelbarrow, the ENTERPRISING weed cutter, the SHINING BRIGHT KNIVES, which over the years had been ground to a vanishing narrowness by BURLY scissors grinders, the FIENDISH thimble, the STUPID darning egg, the CLUMSY OLD flatiron, which provided variety by having to be put back on the stove every so often, and finally the PRIZE PIECE, the foot-and hand-operated Singer sewing machine. But the golden haze is all in the manner of listing.

Another way of listing would be equally idyllic; your aching back; your hands scalded in the wash boiler, then frozen red while hanging up the clothes (how the frozen washing crackled as you folded it up!); an occasional nosebleed when you straightened up after hours of bending over; being in such a hurry to get through with the day's work that you went marketing with the telltale blood spot on the back of your skirt; the eternal moaning about little aches and pains, because after all you were only a woman. Women among themselves: not "How are you feeling?" but "Are you feeling better?"

All that is known. It proves nothing; its demonstrative value is destroyed by the habit of thinking in terms of advantages and disadvantages, the most evil of all ways of looking at life. "Everything has its advantages and disadvantages." Once that is said, the unbearable becomes bearable—a mere disadvantage, and what after all is a disadvantage but a necessary adjunct of every advantage?

An advantage, as a rule, was merely the absence of a disadvantage: *no* noise, *no* responsibility, *not* working for strangers, *not* having to leave your home and children every day. The disadvantages that were absent made up for those that were present.

So it wasn't really so bad; you could do it with one hand tied behind your back. Except that no end was in sight.

Today was yesterday, yesterday was always. Another day behind you, another week gone, and Happy New Year. What will we have to eat tomorrow? Has the mailman come? What have you been doing around the house all day?

Setting the table, clearing the table: "Has everybody been served?" Open the curtains, draw the curtains; turn the light on, turn the light out; "Why do you always leave the light on in the bathroom?"; folding, unfolding; emptying, filling; plugging in, unplugging. "Well, that does it for today."

The first electrical appliance: an iron, a marvel she had "always longed for." Embarrassment, as though she had been unworthy of it: "What have I done to deserve it? From now on I'll always look forward to ironing! Maybe I'll have a little more time for myself."

The mixer, the electric stove, the refrigerator, the washing machine: more and more time for herself. But she only stood there stiff with terror, dizzy after her long years as the good household fairy. But she had also had to husband her feelings so much that she expressed them only in slips of the tongue, and then did her best to gloss them over. The animal spirits that had once filled her whole body now showed themselves only seldom; one finger of her heavy, listless hand would quiver, and instantly this hand would be covered by the other.

* * *

But my mother had not been crushed for good. She began to assert herself. No longer obliged to work her fingers to the bone, she gradually became herself again. She got over her skittishness. She showed people the face with which she felt more or less at ease.

She read newspapers, but preferred books with stories she could compare with her own life. She read the books I was reading, first Fallada, Knut Hamsun, Dostoevsky, Maxim Gorky, then Thomas Wolfe and William Faulkner.[17] What she said about books could not have been put into print; she merely told me what had particularly caught her attention. "I'm not like that," she sometimes said, as though the author had written about

[17] Hans Fallada was the pseudonym of the German novelist Rudolf Ditzen (1893–1947). Knut Hamsun (1859–1952) was a Norwegian novelist and poet. Fyodor Dostoevsky (1821–1881) and Maxim Gorky (1868–1936) were both Russian writers. Thomas Wolfe (1900–1938) and William Faulkner (1897–1962) were American writers.

her. To her, every book was an account of her own life, and in reading she came to life; for the first time, she came out of her shell; she learned to talk about *herself*; and with each book she had more ideas on the subject. Little by little, I learned something about her.

* * *

Up until then she had got on her own nerves, her own presence had made her uncomfortable; now she lost herself in reading and conversation, and emerged with a new feeling about herself. "It's making me young again."

True, books to her were only stories out of the past, never dreams of the future; in them she found everything she had missed and would never make good. Early in life she had dismissed all thought of a future. Thus, her second spring was merely a transfiguration of her past experience.

Literature didn't teach her to start thinking of herself but showed her it was too late for that. She COULD HAVE made something of herself. Now, at the most, she gave SOME thought to herself, and now and then after shopping she would treat herself to a cup of coffee at the tavern and worry a LITTLE LESS about what people might think.

She became indulgent toward her husband; when he started talking, she let him finish; she no longer stopped him after the first sentence with a nod so violent that it made him swallow his words. She felt sorry for him; often her pity left her defenseless when he wasn't suffering at all and she merely thought of him in connection with some object which to her mind stood for her own past despair: a washbasin with cracked enamel, a tiny electric hot plate, blackened by boiled-over milk.

When a member of the family was absent, she surrounded him with images of loneliness; if he wasn't at home with her, he was sure to be alone. Cold, hunger, unfriendly people: and it was all her fault. She included her despised husband in these guilt feelings and worried about him when he had to manage without her; even during her frequent stays at the hospital, once on suspicion of cancer, her conscience tormented her: her poor husband at home wasn't getting anything hot to eat.

Her sympathy for him when he was absent prevented her from ever feeling lonely; only a brief moment of forsakenness when she had him on her hands again; the irrepressible distaste inspired by his wobbly knees and the drooping seat of his trousers. "If only I had a man I could look up to"; it was no good having to despise someone all the time.

This visible disgust in her very first gesture, attenuated over the years into a patient, polite looking-up from whatever she happened to be doing, only crushed him the more. She had always thought him WEAK-KNEED. He often made the mistake of asking her why she couldn't bear him. Invariably she answered: "What makes you think that?" He persisted: was he really so repulsive? She comforted him, and all the while her loathing grew. They were growing old together; the thought didn't move her, but on the surface it made life easier, because he got out of the habit of beating her and bullying her.

Exhausted by the daily labors that got him nowhere, he became sickly and gentle. He woke from his maunderings into a real loneliness, to which she could respond only in his absence.

They hadn't grown apart; they had never been really together. A sentence from a letter: "My husband has calmed down." And she lived more calmly beside him, drawing satisfaction from the thought that she had always been and always would be a mystery to him.

* * *

She began to take an interest in politics; she no longer voted like her husband, for his employer's and her brother's party. Now she voted Socialist; and after a while her husband, who felt an increasing need to lean on her, did so too. But she never believed that politics could be of any help to her personally. She cast her ballot as a gift, never expecting anything in return. "The Socialists do more for the workers"—but she didn't feel herself to be a worker.

The preoccupations that meant more and more to her, as housekeeping took up less of her time, had no place in what she knew of the Socialist system. She remained alone with her sexual disgust, repressed till it found an outlet only in dreams, with the fog-dampened bedclothes and the low ceiling over her head. The things that really mattered to her were not political. Of course there was a flaw in her reasoning—but what was it? And what politician could explain it to her? And in what words?

Politicians lived in another world. When you asked them a question, they didn't answer; they merely stated their positions. "You can't talk about most things anyway." Politics was concerned only with the things that could be talked about; you had to handle the rest for yourself, or leave it to God. And besides, if a politician were to take an interest in you personally, you'd bolt. That would be getting too intimate.

* * *

She was gradually becoming an individual.

* * *

Away from the house, she took on an air of dignity; sitting beside me as I drove the secondhand car I had bought her, she looked unsmilingly straight ahead. At home she no longer bellowed when she sneezed, and she didn't laugh as loudly as before.

(At her funeral, her youngest son was to remember how on his way home in those days he had heard her, while still a long way off, screaming with laughter.)

When shopping, she dispensed token greetings to the right and left; she went to the hairdresser's more often and had her nails manicured. This was no longer the assumed dignity with which she had run the gauntlet in the days of postwar misery—today no one could destroy her composure with a glance.

But sometimes at home, while her husband, his back turned to her, his shirttails hanging out, his hands thrust deep into his pockets, silent except for an occasional suppressed cough, gazed down into the valley and her youngest son sat snotnosed on the kitchen sofa reading a Mickey Mouse comic book, she would sit at the table in her new, erect posture, angrily rapping her knuckles on the table edge, and then suddenly raise her hand to her cheek. At this her husband, as often as not, would leave the house, stand outside the door for a while clearing his throat, and come in again.

She sat there with her hand on her cheek until her son asked for a slice of bread with something on it. To stand up she had to prop herself on both hands.

Another son wrecked the car and was thrown in jail for driving without a license. Like his father, he drank, and again she went from tavern to tavern. What a brood! He paid no attention to her reproofs, she always said the same thing, she lacked the vocabulary that might have had some effect on him. "Aren't you ashamed?"—"I know," he said.—"You could at least get yourself a room somewhere else."—"I know." He went on living at home, duplicated her husband, and even damaged the next car. She packed his bag and put it outside the house; he left the country. She dreamed the worst about him, wrote him a letter signed "Your unhappy mother," and he came right back. And so on. She felt that she was to blame. She took it hard.

And then the always identical objects all about her, in always the same places! She tried to be untidy, but her daily puttings-away had become too automatic. If only she could die! But she was afraid of death. Besides, she was too curious. "I've always had to be strong; I'd much rather have been weak."

She had no hobbies; she didn't collect anything or swap anything. She had stopped doing crossword puzzles. She had given up pasting photographs in albums; she just put them away somewhere.

She took no part in public life; once a year she gave blood and wore the blood donor's badge on her coat. One day she was introduced on the radio as the hundred thousandth donor of the year and rewarded with a gift basket.

Now and then she went bowling at the new automatic bowling alley. She giggled with her mouth closed when the tenpins all toppled over and the bell rang.

Once, on the Heart's Desire radio program, relatives in East Berlin sent the whole family greetings, followed by Handel's Hallelujah Chorus.

She dreaded the winter, when they all spent their days in one room; no one came to see her; when she heard a sound and looked up, it was always her husband again: "Oh, it's you."

She began having bad headaches. She couldn't keep pills down; at first suppositories helped, but not for long. Her head throbbed so that she could only touch it, ever so gently, with her fingertips. Each week the doctor gave her an injection that eased the pain for a while. But soon the injections became ineffectual. The doctor told her to keep her head warm, and she went about with a scarf on her head. She took sleeping pills but usually woke up soon after midnight; then she would cover her face with her pillow. She lay awake trembling until it was light, and the trembling lasted all day. The pain made her see ghosts.

In the meantime her husband had been sent to a sanatorium with tuberculosis; he wrote affectionate letters, he begged her to let him lie beside her again. Her answers were friendly.

The doctor didn't know what was wrong with her; the usual female trouble? change of life?

She was so weak that often when she reached out for something, she missed her aim; her hands hung down limp at her sides. After washing the lunch dishes, she lay down awhile on the kitchen sofa; it was too cold in the bedroom. Sometimes her headache was so bad that she didn't recognize anyone. Nothing interested her. When her head was throbbing, we had to raise our voices to talk to her. She lost all sense of balance and orientation, bumped into the corners of things, and fell down stairs. It hurt her to laugh, she only grimaced now and then. The doctor said it was probably a strangulated nerve. She hardly spoke above a whisper, she was even too miserable to complain. She let her head droop, first on one side, then on the other, but the pain followed her.

"I'm not human anymore."

* * *

Once, when staying with her summer before last, I found her lying on her bed with so wretched a look on her face that I didn't dare go near her. A picture of animal misery, as in a zoo. It was a torment to see how shamelessly she had turned herself inside out; everything about her was dislocated, split, open, inflamed, a tangle of entrails. And she looked at me from far away as if I were her BROKEN HEART, as Karl Rossmann was for the humiliated stoker in Kafka's novel.[18] BROKEN HEART. Frightened and exasperated, I left the room.

Only since then have I been fully aware of my mother. Before that, I kept forgetting her, at the most feeling an occasional pang when I thought about the idiocy of her life. Now she imposed herself on me, took on body and reality, and her condition was so palpable that at some moments it became a part of me.

The people in the neighborhood also began to see her with other eyes; as though she had been chosen to bring their own lives home to them. They still asked why and wherefore, but only on the surface; they understood her without asking.

* * *

She became insensible, she couldn't remember anything or recognize even the most familiar objects. More and more often, when her youngest son came home from school, he found a note on the table saying she had gone out, he should make himself some sandwiches or go next door to eat. These notes, torn from an account book, piled up in the drawer.

She was no longer able to play the housewife. Her whole body was sore when she woke up in the morning. She dropped everything she picked up, and would gladly have followed it in its fall.

Doors got in her way; the mold seemed to rain from the walls as she passed.

She watched television but couldn't follow. She moved her hands this way and that to keep from falling asleep.

Sometimes in her walks she forgot herself. She sat at the edge of the woods, as far as possible from the houses, or beside the brook below an abandoned sawmill. Looking at the grain fields or the water didn't take away her pain but deadened it intermittently. Her feelings dovetailed with the things she looked at; every sight was a torment; she would turn to

[18] The novel is Franz Kafka's *Amerika* (1927).

another, and that too would torment her. But in between there were dead points, when the whirligig world left her a moment's peace. At such moments, she was merely tired; thoughtlessly immersed in the water, she rested from the turmoil.

Then again everything in her clashed with the world around her; panic-stricken, she struggled to keep her balance, but the feeling was too strong and her peace was gone. She had to stand up and move on.

She had to walk very slowly because, as she told me, the horror strangled her.

She walked and walked until she was so tired she had to sit down again. But soon she had to stand up and go on.

So the time passed, and often she failed to notice that it was getting dark. She was night-blind and had difficulty in finding her way home. Outside the house, she stopped and sat down on a bench, afraid to go in.

Then, after a long while, the door opened very slowly and my mother stood there with vacant eyes, like a ghost.

But in the house as well she wandered about, mistaking doors and directions. Often she had no idea how she had come to be where she was or how the time had passed. She had lost all sense of time and place.

She lost all desire to see anyone; at the most she would sit in the tavern, among the people from the tourist buses, who were in too much of a hurry to look her in the face. She couldn't dissemble any more; she had put all that behind her. One look at her and anyone was bound to see what was wrong.

She was afraid of losing her mind. Quickly, for fear it would be too late, she wrote a few letters of farewell.

Her letters were full of urgency, as if she had tried to etch herself into the paper. In that period of her life, writing had ceased to be an extraneous effort, as it is for most people in her circumstances; it had become a reflex, independent of her will. Yet there was hardly anything one could talk to her about; every word reminded her of some horror and threw her off balance. "I can't talk. Don't torture me." She turned away, turned again, turned further away. Then she had to close her eyes, and silent tears ran uselessly down her averted face.

* * *

She went to see a neurologist in the provincial capital. With him she could talk; a doctor was someone she could confide in. She herself was surprised at how much she told him. It was only in speaking that she began really to remember. The doctor nodded at everything she said, recognized every particular as a symptom, and by subsuming them under a name—"nervous breakdown"—organized them into a system. That comforted her. He knew what was wrong with her; at least he had a name for her condition. And she wasn't the only one; there were others in the waiting room.

On her next visit, it amused her to observe these people. The doctor advised her to take walks in the open air. He prescribed a medicine that somewhat relieved the pressure on her head. A trip would help, she needed a change. On each visit she paid cash, because the Workers Health Insurance didn't provide for treatment of this kind. And then she was depressed again, because of the expense.

Sometimes she searched desperately for a word for something. Usually she knew it, she merely wanted others to share in her thought. She looked back with nostalgia at the brief period when she had recognized no one and understood nothing.

As it wore off, her illness became an affectation; now she only played at being sick. She pretended that her head was in a muddle as a defense against her thoughts, which had become clear again; for, once her head was perfectly clear, she could only regard herself as an individual case and the consolation of belonging to a group was no longer available to her. She exaggerated her forgetfulness and absent-mindedness in order to be encouraged, when she finally did remember or show that she had understood everything perfectly, with a "You see! You're much better now!"—as though all the horror had consisted in losing her memory and being unable to join in the conversation.

* * *

You couldn't joke with her. Teasing about her condition didn't help her. SHE TOOK EVERYTHING LITERALLY. If anyone started clowning to cheer her up, she burst into tears.

* * *

In midsummer she went to Yugoslavia for four weeks. At first she only sat in her darkened hotel room, touching and feeling her head. She couldn't read, her thoughts got in the way. Every few minutes she went to the bathroom and washed her hands and face.

Then she ventured out and dabbled in the water. This was her first vacation away from home and her first visit to the seashore. She liked the sea; at night there was often a storm, and then she didn't mind lying awake. She bought a straw hat to shield her from the sun and sold it back the day she left. Every afternoon she went to a café and ordered an espresso. She wrote cards and letters to all her friends in which she spoke only incidentally of herself.

She recovered her sense of time and awareness of her surroundings. She listened curiously to the conversations at the other tables and tried to figure out the relationships between the people.

Toward evening when the heat had let up she took walks; she went to villages nearby and looked into the doorless houses. Her amazement was real; she had never seen such dire poverty. Her headaches stopped and so did her thoughts. For a time she was outside the world. She felt pleasantly bored.

Back home, she was her old talkative self. She had plenty to talk about. She let me go with her on her walks. Now and then we went to the tavern for dinner and she got into the habit of drinking a Campari before her meal. She still clutched at her head, but by then it was little more than a tic. She remembered that a year ago a man had actually spoken to her in a café. "But he was very polite!" Next summer she thought she would go to some northern country where it wasn't so hot.

She took it easy, sat in the garden with her friends, smoking and fanning the wasps out of her coffee.

The weather was sunny and mild. The fir trees on the hills round about were veiled in mist all day, and for a time they were not as dark as usual. She put up fruit and vegetables for the winter, and thought of adopting a child.

* * *

I was already too busy with my own life. In the middle of August, I went back to Germany and left her to her own resources. During the following months I was working on a book. I heard from her occasionally.

"My head spins a little. Some days are hard to bear." "It's cold and cheerless, the fog doesn't lift until mid-morning. I sleep late, and when I finally crawl out of bed, I have no desire to do anything. And adopting a child is out of the question right now. They won't give me one because my husband has tuberculosis."

"Whenever a pleasant thought crops up, a door closes and I'm alone again with my nightmares. I'd be so glad to write something more cheerful, but there isn't anything. When I start a conversation, he doesn't know what I'm talking about, so I prefer to say nothing. Somehow I was looking forward to seeing him again, but when he's here I can't bear the sight of him. I know I ought to find some way of making life bearable, I keep thinking about it, but nothing occurs to me. Just read this and forget it as fast as you can, that's my advice."

"I can't stand it in the house anymore, so I'm always gadding about somewhere. I've been getting up a little earlier, that's the hardest time for me; I have to force myself to do something, or I'd just go back to bed. There's a terrible loneliness inside me, I don't feel like talking to anyone. I'd often like to drink a little something in the evening, but I mustn't, because if I did my medicine wouldn't take effect. Yesterday I went to Klagenfurt, I roamed around all day and caught the last local home."

In October she didn't write. During the fine autumn days someone would meet her walking slowly down the street and prod her to walk a little faster. She was always asking her friends to join her in a cup of coffee at the tavern. People invited her out on Sunday excursions and she was glad to go. She went with friends to the last church fairs of the year. Sometimes she even went to a football game. She would look on indulgently as her friends cheered and whistled, and hardly open her mouth. But when in the course of his re-election campaign the Chancellor stopped in the village and handed out carnations, she pushed boldly through the crowd and asked for one: "Haven't you got one for me?" "I beg your pardon, ma'am."

* * *

Early in November she wrote: "I'm not logical enough to think things through to the end, and my head aches. Sometimes it buzzes and whistles so that I can't bear any outside noise.

"I talk to myself, because I can't say anything to other people anymore. Sometimes I feel like a machine. I'd like to go away somewhere, but when it gets dark I'm afraid of not finding the way home again. In the morning there's a dense fog and then everything is so quiet. Every day I do the same work, and every morning the place is a mess again. There's never any end to it. I really wish I were dead. When I'm out in the street and I see a car coming, I want to fall in front of it. But how can I be sure it would work?

"Yesterday I saw Dostoevsky's 'The Gentle Spirit'[19] on TV; all night long I saw the most gruesome things, I wasn't dreaming, I really saw them, some men were going around naked and instead of genitals they had intestines hanging out. My husband is coming home on December 1. I keep feeling more and more uneasy. I can't see how it will be possible to live with him. We each look in a different direction and the loneliness only gets worse. I'm cold now, I think I'll take a walk."

* * *

She often shut herself up in the house. When people started telling her their troubles, she stopped them short. She treated them all very harshly, silenced them with a wave of her hand or with her sudden laugh. Other people were irritating children; at best she felt slightly sorry for them.

She was often cross. There was something about her way of finding fault that often made people feel like hypocrites.

When her picture was taken, she was no longer able to compose her face. She puckered her forehead and raised her cheeks in a smile, but there was an incurable sadness in her eyes; her pupils were out of kilter, displaced from the center of her irises.

Mere existence had become a torture to her.

But at the same time she had a horror of death.

"Take walks in the woods!" (The neurologist.)

"But it's dark in the woods!" the local veterinarian, her occasional confidant, said contemptuously after her death.

* * *

Day and night the fog hung on. At noon she tried putting the light out and immediately turned it on again. What should she look at? Cross her arms and put her hands on her shoulders. From time to time, an invisible buzz saw, a rooster who thought all day that the day was just dawning and crowed until late afternoon; and then at closing time the factory whistles.

At night the fog pressed against the windowpanes. At irregular intervals she could hear a drop of water running down the glass outside. She kept the heating pad on all night in her bed. Every morning the fire was out in the kitchen stove. "I don't want to pull myself together any more." She was no longer able to close her eyes. There had been a GREAT FALL (Franz Grillparzer)[20] in her consciousness.

* * *

(From this point on, I shall have to be careful to keep my story from telling itself.)

* * *

She wrote letters of farewell to everyone in her family. She not only knew what she was doing, she also knew why she could no longer do anything else. "You won't understand," she wrote to her husband. "But it's unthinka-

[19] An 1876 story by Fyodor Dostoevsky in which a grieving husband tries to understand why his wife committed suicide.

[20] Austrian playwright (1791–1872), famous for his tragedies.

ble that I should go on living." To me she wrote a registered special-delivery letter, enclosing a copy of her will. "I have begun to write several times, but it's no comfort, no help to me." All her letters were headed not only with the date as usual but also with the day of the week: "Thursday, November 18, 1971."

The next day she took the local to the district capital and had the prescription our family doctor had given her refilled: a hundred sleeping pills. Though it was not raining, she also bought a red umbrella with a handsome, slightly curved, wooden handle.

Late that afternoon she took the local back. As a rule this train is almost empty. She was seen by one or two people. She went home and ate dinner at the house next door, where her daughter was living. Everything as usual: "We even told jokes."

Then, in her own house, she watched television with her youngest son. A movie from the "Father and Son" series was being shown.

She sent the child to bed; the television was still playing. She had been to the hairdresser's the day before and had had her nails done. She turned off the television, went to her bedroom, and hung up her brown two-piece dress in the wardrobe. She took all the sleeping pills and all her anti-depression pills. She put on menstrual pants, stuffed diapers inside, put on two more pairs of pants and an ankle-length nightgown, tied a scarf under her chin, and lay down in the bed. She did not turn on the heating pad. She stretched out and laid one hand on the other. At the end of her letter to me, which otherwise contained only instructions for her funeral, she wrote that she was perfectly calm, glad at last to be falling asleep in peace. But I'm sure that wasn't true.

* * *

The following afternoon, on receiving the news of her death, I flew to Austria. The plane was half empty; it was a steady, quiet flight, the air clear and cloudless, the lights of changing cities far below. Reading the paper, drinking beer, looking out the window, I gradually sank into a tired, impersonal sense of well-being. Yes, I thought over and over again, carefully enunciating my thoughts to myself: THAT DOES IT. THAT DOES IT. THAT DOES IT. GOOD. GOOD. GOOD. And throughout the flight I was beside myself with pride that she had committed suicide. Then the plane prepared to land and the lights grew larger and larger. Dissolved in a boneless euphoria against which I was powerless, I moved through the almost deserted airport building. In the train the next morning, I listened to a woman who was one of the Vienna Choirboys' singing teachers. Even when they grew up, she was telling her companion, the Choirboys were unable to stand on their own feet. She had a son who was one of them. On a tour in South America, he was the only one who had managed on his pocket money. He had even brought some of it back. She had reason to hope that he, at least, would have some sense when he grew up. I couldn't stop listening.

I was met at the station and driven home in the car. Snow had fallen during the night; now it was cloudless, the sun was shining, it was cold, the air sparkled with frost. What a contradiction to be driving through a serenely civilized countryside—in weather that made this countryside so much a part of the unchanging deep-blue space above it that no further change seemed thinkable—to a house of mourning and a corpse that might already have begun to rot! During the drive I was unable to get my bearings or form a picture of what was to come, and the dead body in the cold bedroom found me utterly unprepared.

Chairs had been set up in a row and women sat drinking the wine that had been served them. I sensed that little by little, as they looked at the dead woman, they began to think of themselves.

The morning before the funeral I was alone in the room with the body for a long while. At first my feelings were at one with the custom of the deathwatch. Even her dead body seemed cruelly forsaken and in need of love. Then I began to be bored and looked at the clock. I had decided to spend at least an hour with her. The skin under her eyes was shriveled, and here and there on her face there were still drops of holy water. Her belly was somewhat bloated from the effect of the pills. I compared the hands on her bosom with a fixed point at the end of the room to make sure she was not breathing after all. The furrow between her nose and upper lip was gone. Sometimes, after looking at her for a while, I didn't know what to think. At such moments my boredom was at its height and I could only stand distraught beside the corpse. When the hour was over, I didn't want to leave; I stayed in the room beyond the time I had set myself.

Then she was photographed. From which side did she look best? "The sugar-side of the dead."

The burial ritual depersonalized her once and for all, and relieved everyone. It was snowing hard as we followed her mortal remains. Only her name had to be inserted in the religious formulas. "Our beloved sister . . ." On our coats candle wax, which was later ironed out.

It was snowing so hard that you couldn't get used to it; you kept looking at the sky to see if it was letting up. One by one, the candles went out and were not lighted again. How often, it passed through the mind, I had read of someone catching a fatal illness while attending a funeral.

The woods began right outside the graveyard wall. Fir woods on a rather steep hill. The trees were so close together that you could see only the tops of even the second row, and from then on treetops after treetops. The people left the grave quickly. Standing beside it, I looked up at the motionless trees; for the first time it seemed to me that nature was really merciless. So these were the facts! The forest spoke for itself. Apart from these countless treetops nothing counted; in the foreground, an episodic jumble of shapes, which gradually receded from the picture. I felt mocked and helpless. All at once, in my impotent rage, I felt the need of writing something about my mother.

In the house that evening I climbed the stairs. Suddenly I took several steps at one bound, giggling in an unfamiliar voice, as if I had become a ventriloquist. I ran up the last few steps. Once upstairs I thumped my chest lustily and hugged myself. Then slowly, with a sense of self-importance, as though I were the holder of a unique secret, I went back down the stairs.

It is not true that writing has helped me. In my weeks of preoccupation with the story, the story has not ceased to preoccupy me. Writing has not, as I at first supposed, been a remembering of a concluded period in my life, but merely a constant pretense at remembering, in the form of sentences that only lay claim to detachment. Even now I sometimes wake up with a start, as though in response to some inward prodding, and, breathless with horror, feel that I am literally rotting away from second to second. The air in the darkness is so still that, losing their balance, torn from their moorings, the things of my world fly soundlessly about: in another minute they will come crashing down from all directions and smother me. In these tempests of dread, I become magnetic like a decaying animal and, quite otherwise than in undirected pleasure, where all my feelings play together freely, I am attacked by an undirected, objective horror.

Obviously narration is only an act of memory; on the other hand, it holds nothing in reserve for future use; it merely derives a little pleasure from states of dread by trying to formulate them as aptly as possible; from enjoyment of horror it produces enjoyment of memory.

Often during the day I have a sense of being watched. I open doors and look out. Every sound seems to be an attempt on my life.

Sometimes, of course, as I worked on my story, my frankness and honesty weighed on me and I longed to write something that would allow me to lie and dissemble a bit, a play, for instance.

Once, when I was slicing bread, my knife slipped; instantly, I remembered how in the morning she used to cut thin slices of bread and pour warm milk on them for the children.

Often, as she passed by, she would quickly wipe out the children's ears and nostrils with her saliva. I always shrank back from the saliva smell.

Once, while mountain climbing with a group of friends, she started off to one side to relieve herself. I was ashamed of her and started to bawl, so she held it in.

In the hospital she was always in a big ward with a lot of other people. Yes, those things still exist! Once in such a hospital ward she pressed my hand for a long while.

When everyone had been served and had finished eating, she would daintily pop the remaining scraps into her mouth.

(These, of course, are anecdotes. But in this context scientific inferences would be just as anecdotal. All words and phrases are too mild.)

The eggnog bottle in the sideboard!

My painful memory of her daily motions, especially in the kitchen.

When she was angry, she didn't beat the children; at the most, she would wipe their noses violently.

Fear of death when I wake up at night and the light is on in the hallway.

Some years ago I had the idea of making an adventure movie with all the members of my family; it would have had nothing to do with me personally.

As a child, she was moonstruck.

She died on a Friday, and during the first few weeks it was on Fridays that her death agony was most present to me. Every Friday the dawn was painful and dark. The yellow streetlights in the night mist; dirty snow and sewer smell; folded arms in the television chair; the last toilet flushing, twice.

Often while at work on my story I felt that writing music would be more in keeping with its incidents. Sweet New England . . .

"Perhaps there are new, unsuspected kinds of despair that are unknown to us," said a village schoolmaster in a crime-thriller series. *The Commissar.*

All the jukeboxes in the region had a record titled WORLD-WEARY POLKA.

The first signs of spring—mud, puddles, warm wind, and snowless trees. Far away, far beyond my typewriter.

"She took her secret with her to the grave."

In one dream she had a second face, but it too was rather worn.

She was kindly.

Then again, something cheerful: in a dream I saw all sorts of things that were intolerably painful to look at. Suddenly someone came along and in a twinkling took the painful quality out of all these things. LIKE TAKING DOWN AN OUT-OF-DATE POSTER. The metaphor was part of my dream.

One summer day I was in my grandfather's room, looking out the window. There wasn't much to be seen: a street led uphill through the village to a building that was painted dark ("Schönbrunn") yellow, an old-time inn; there it turned off to one side. It was a SUNDAY AFTERNOON, the street was DESERTED. All at once, I had a bitter-tasting feeling for the man who lived in that room; I felt that he would soon die. But this feeling was softened by the knowledge that his death would be a natural one.

Horror is something perfectly natural; the mind's horror vacui.[21] A thought is taking shape, then suddenly it notices that there is nothing more to think. Whereupon it crashes to the ground like a figure in a comic strip who suddenly realizes that he has been walking on air.

Someday I shall write about all this in greater detail.

Written January—February 1972

[21] "Horror of the vacuum," or of emptiness.

Chronology

NEOCLASSICISM THROUGH ROMANTICISM

Political and Social Events	*Intellectual and Cultural Events*
1620 Pilgrims land at Plymouth Rock	
	1624 Franz Hals, *The Laughing Cavalier*
	1628 William Harvey, *Essay on the Motion of the Heart and Blood*
	1636 Harvard College founded
	1637 René Descartes, *Discourse on Method*
1642–1660 English Civil War, Commonwealth, and Protectorate	1642 Rembrandt, *The Night Watch*
1643 Louis XIV crowned King of France	
	1653 Jean-Baptiste Lully becomes court composer at Paris
1669 Peter the Great begins reform and modernization of Russia	1669 Blaise Pascal, *Pensées*
	1690 John Locke, *An Essay Concerning Human Understanding*
1692 Witchcraft trials at Salem, Massachusetts	
1701–14 War of the Spanish Succession: a general European war over succession to the Spanish empire but more generally over the balance of power in Europe. It resulted in France's loss of much of its empire and the ascendancy of England	1704 Johann Sebastian Bach's first cantatas composed
	1709 First piano built
	1710 George Berkeley, *Treatise Concerning the Principles of Human Knowledge*
1714 George I of the German House of Hanover crowned King of England	
1715 Louis XV crowned King of France. His rule, which extended to 1774, was corrupt and extravagant; it prepared the way for the French Revolution	1717 Jean Watteau, *Embarkation of Cythera*
	1729 Johann Sebastian Bach, *St. Matthew Passion*
1740 Maria Theresa Empress of Hapsburg lands; her succession precipitated the general European War of the Austrian Succession (1740–48)	1738 Methodist Church founded by John Wesley and George Whitefield
	1739 David Hume, *A Treatise of Human Nature*
Frederick II crowned King of Prussia (ruled until 1786)	1742 George Frederick Handel, *Messiah*

Molière (1622–1673)

Jean Racine (1639–1699)

Jonathan Swift (1667–1745)

Alexander Pope (1688–1744)

Voltaire (1694–1778)

Jean-Jacques Rousseau (1712–1778)

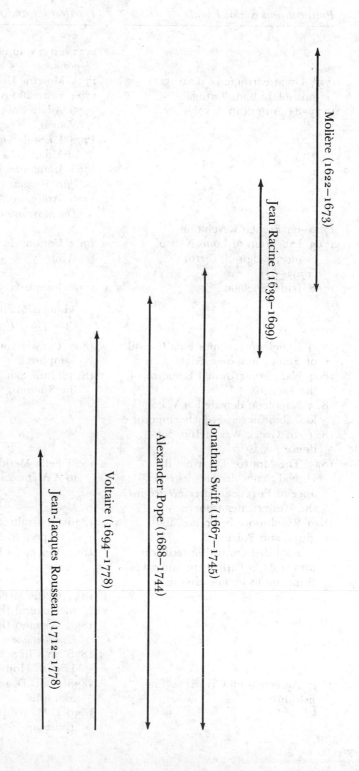

Political and Social Events	*Intellectual and Cultural Events*
	1751 First volumes of French *Encyclopédie*
1755 Great earthquake destroys most of Lisbon, Portugal	1755 Moscow University founded
	1763 Excavations begun at Pompeii
1775–83 American Revolution	1776 Adam Smith, *The Wealth of Nations*
	1778 La Scala Opera House opens in Milan
	1781 Immanuel Kant, *Critique of Pure Reason*
	1786 Wolfgang Amadeus Mozart, *The Marriage of Figaro*
1789–99 French Revolution	
1793 Execution of Louis XVI of France; Reign of Terror (1793–94)	1793 Cotton gin invented by Eli Whitney
1798 Irish rebellion	1798 Joseph Haydn, *The Creation*
	Thomas Malthus, *Essay on the Principle of Population*
1799 Napoleon becomes First Consul of France in a *coup d'état*	1807 Ludwig von Beethoven, Fifth Symphony
1804 Napoleon crowned Emperor of the French	1814 Franz Schubert, "Gretchen at the Spinning Wheel"
1815 Napoleon defeated at Waterloo, abdicates as French Emperor	
1821–29 Greek War of Independence	
1823 The Monroe Doctrine: the United States declares its resistance to European interference in the Western hemisphere	1826 Felix Mendelssohn, Overture to *A Midsummer Night's Dream*
1830 Revolutions in France, Belgium, and Poland	1830 First railroad in England, from Liverpool to Manchester
1832 English Reform Bill redistributes seats in Parliament and gives franchise to middle-class men	1831 Vincenzio Bellini, *Norma*
	1834 Cyrus McCormick patents a mechanical reaper
	1835 Gaetano Donizetti, *Lucia di Lammermoor*
	1836 Sir Charles Barry designs the English Houses of Parliament
1837 Accession of Victoria to English throne	1838 Louis Daguerre takes first photographs
	1839 J. M. W. Turner, *The Fighting Téméraire*

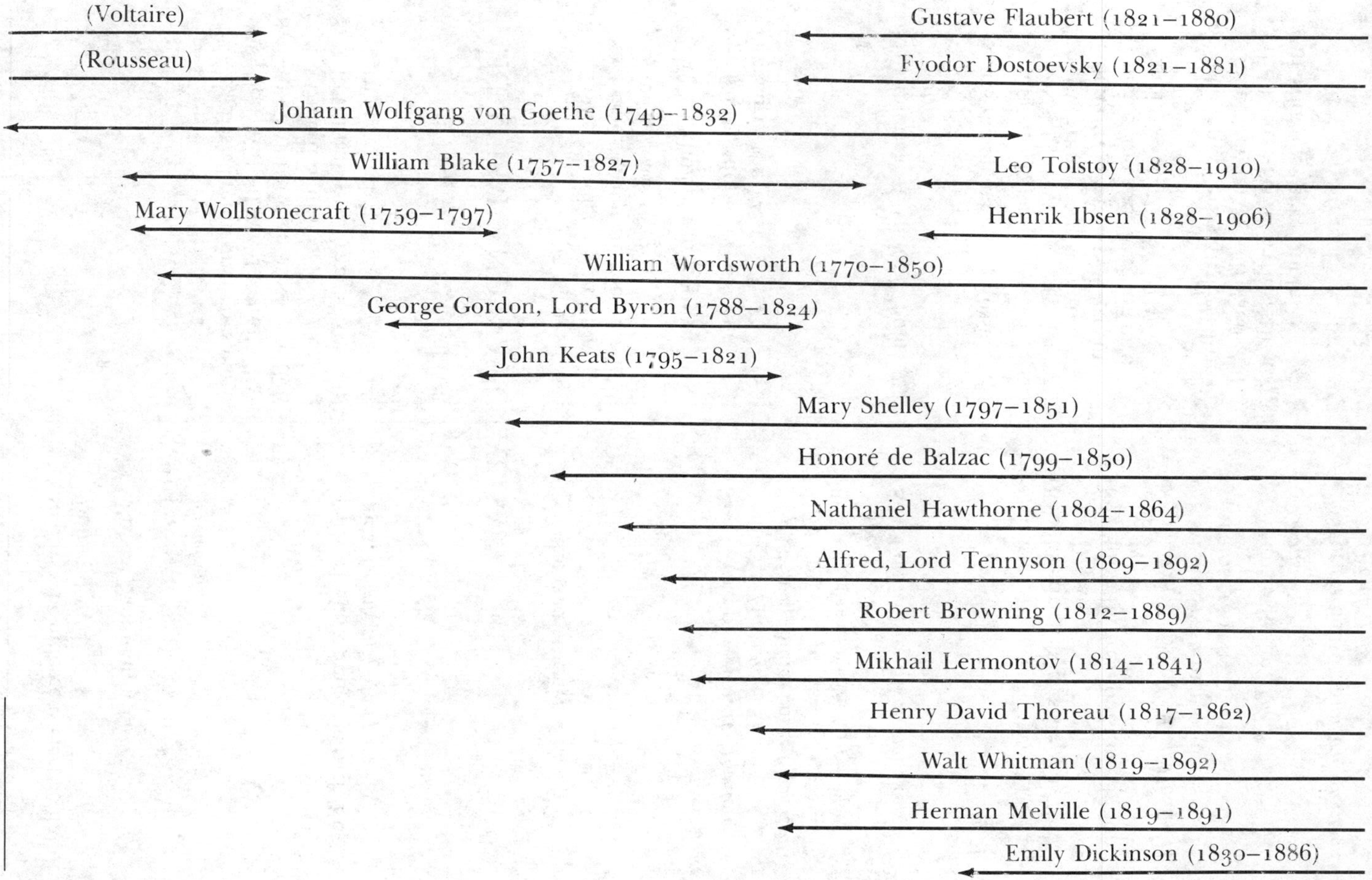
(Voltaire)
Gustave Flaubert (1821–1880)
(Rousseau)
Fyodor Dostoevsky (1821–1881)
Johann Wolfgang von Goethe (1749–1832)
William Blake (1757–1827)
Leo Tolstoy (1828–1910)
Mary Wollstonecraft (1759–1797)
Henrik Ibsen (1828–1906)
William Wordsworth (1770–1850)
George Gordon, Lord Byron (1788–1824)
John Keats (1795–1821)
Mary Shelley (1797–1851)
Honoré de Balzac (1799–1850)
Nathaniel Hawthorne (1804–1864)
Alfred, Lord Tennyson (1809–1892)
Robert Browning (1812–1889)
Mikhail Lermontov (1814–1841)
Henry David Thoreau (1817–1862)
Walt Whitman (1819–1892)
Herman Melville (1819–1891)
Emily Dickinson (1830–1886)

Political and Social Events	*Intellectual and Cultural Events*
	1840 First incandescent electric light bulb
	Robert Schumann, *Lieder*
	1843 Sören Kierkegaard, *Fear and Trembling*
1845–47 Irish famine increases emigration to the United States	
1846–48 War between Mexico and the United States	
1848 Revolutions in France, Austria, Germany, and Italy	1848 Karl Marx and Friedrich Engels, *Communist Manifesto*

REALISM AND NATURALISM

	1850 Richard Wagner, *Lohengrin*
1851 Louis Napoleon seizes power in France to initiate the Second Empire (until 1870)	
Great Exhibition in London	
1853 Commodore Perry opens Japan to the West	1853 Giuseppi Verdi, *Il Trovatore* and *La Traviata*
	1857 Charles Baudelaire, *Flowers of Evil*
	1859 Charles Darwin, *Origin of Species*
1861 American Civil War (until 1865)	1864 Leo Tolstoy, *War and Peace*
Serfs emancipated in Russia	
Unification of Italy	
1870–71 Franco-Prussian War, resulting in creation of German Empire and the French Third Empire	1872 Friedrich Nietzsche, *The Birth of Tragedy*
	1874 First Impressionist exhibition in Paris
	1879 Henrik Ibsen, *A Doll House*
1882 Phoenix Park murders: British Chief Secretary for Ireland and the Under-Secretary assassinated in Phoenix Park, Dublin	1884 Louis Pasteur inoculates against rabies
	Auguste Rodin, *The Burghers of Calais*
	Georges Seurat, *Sunday Afternoon on Grande Jatte*

Lives of Authors

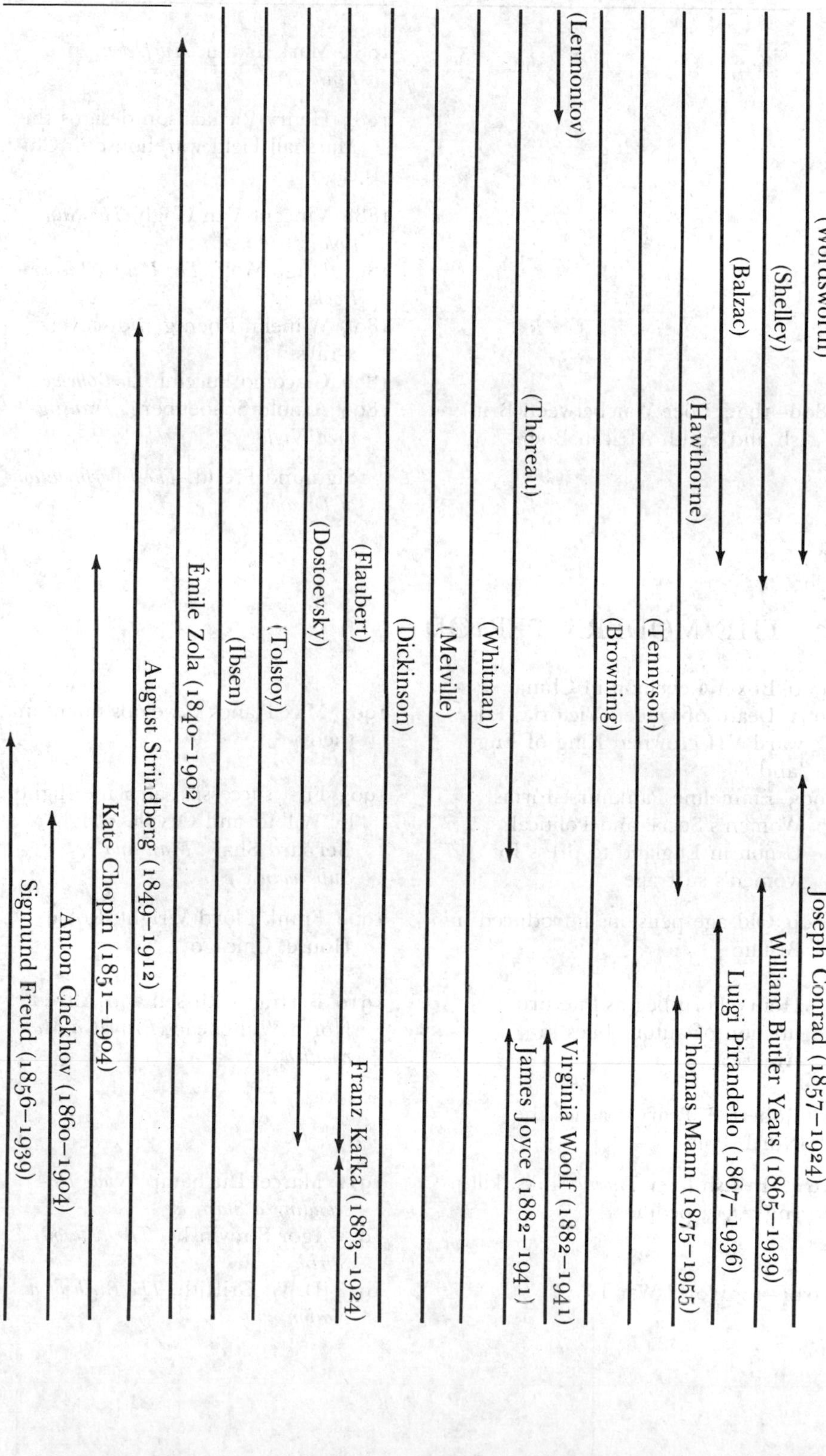
(Wordsworth)
Joseph Conrad (1857–1924)
(Shelley)
William Butler Yeats (1865–1939)
(Balzac)
Luigi Pirandello (1867–1936)
(Hawthorne)
Thomas Mann (1875–1955)
(Tennyson)
(Browning)
Virginia Woolf (1882–1941)
(Lermontov)
(Thoreau)
James Joyce (1882–1941)
(Whitman)
(Melville)
(Dickinson)
(Flaubert)
Franz Kafka (1883–1924)
(Dostoevsky)
(Tolstoy)
(Ibsen)
Émile Zola (1840–1902)
August Strindberg (1849–1912)
Kate Chopin (1851–1904)
Anton Chekhov (1860–1904)
Sigmund Freud (1856–1939)

Political and Social Events	*Intellectual and Cultural Events*
	1884 Mark Twain, *Huckleberry Finn*
	1885 Henry Richardson designs the Marshall Field warehouse in Chicago
	1888 Vincent Van Gogh, *The Sunflowers*
	1891 Hugo Wolf, *The Italian Lieder Book*
	1895 Wilhelm Roentgen discovers x-rays
	1896 Giacomo Puccini, *La Bohème*
1899–1902 Boer War between British and South African Boers	1899 Arnold Schoenberg, *Transfigured Night*
	Sigmund Freud, *The Interpretation of Dreams*

THE MODERN PERIOD

1900 Boxer Rebellion in China	
1901 Death of Queen Victoria; Edward VII crowned King of England	1901 Max Planck develops quantum theory
1903 Emmeline Pankhurst forms Women's Social and Political Union in England to press for women's suffrage	1903 First successful airplane flight by Wilbur and Orville Wright Bernard Shaw, *Man and Superman*
1909 Old age pensions introduced in Britain	1909 Frank Lloyd Wright, Robie House, Chicago
Henry Ford begins line production of automobiles in America	1910 Bertrand Russell and Alfred North Whitehead, *Principia Mathematica*
Robert E. Peary reaches the North Pole	
1912 British liner *Titanic* sinks, killing 1,513 people	1912 Marcel Duchamp, *Nude Descending a Staircase*
	1913 Igor Stravinsky, *The Rite of Spring*
1914–18 World War I	1914 D. W. Griffith, *The Birth of a Nation*

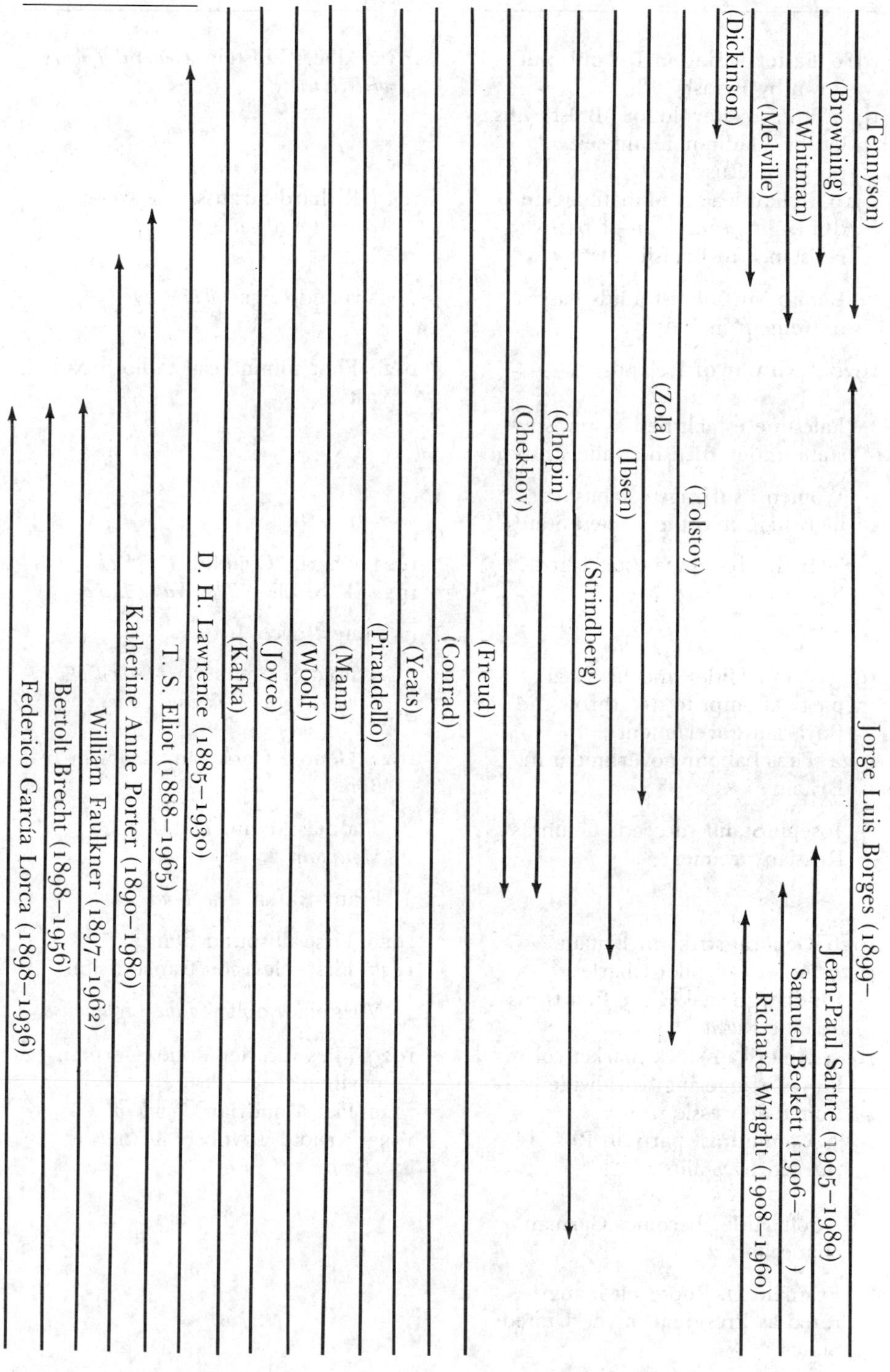

(Tennyson)
(Browning)
(Whitman)
(Melville)
(Dickinson)
Jorge Luis Borges (1899–)
Jean-Paul Sartre (1905–1980)
Samuel Beckett (1906–)
Richard Wright (1908–1960)
(Tolstoy)
(Zola)
(Ibsen)
(Strindberg)
(Chopin)
(Chekhov)
(Freud)
(Conrad)
(Yeats)
(Pirandello)
(Mann)
(Woolf)
(Joyce)
(Kafka)
D. H. Lawrence (1885–1930)
T. S. Eliot (1888–1965)
Katherine Anne Porter (1890–1980)
William Faulkner (1897–1962)
Bertolt Brecht (1898–1956)
Federico García Lorca (1898–1936)

Political and Social Events	*Intellectual and Cultural Events*
1916 Easter Rising in Ireland, put down by British	1915 Albert Einstein, *General Theory of Relativity*
1917 Russian Revolution: Bolsheviks led by Vladimir Lenin seize power in Russia	
1919 Indian leader Mahatma Gandhi begins campaign of passive resistance to British rule	1919 Richard Strauss, *The Woman Without a Shadow*
Benito Mussolini founds Fascist movement in Italy	Fernand Léger, *The City*
1920 Civil war in Ireland	1920 First commercial radio broadcast
Palestine established as Jewish state under British administration	
Women's suffrage established in Britain and the United States	
1921 Irish Free State established	1921 Charlie Chaplin, *The Kid*
	1922 T. S. Eliot, *The Waste Land*
	James Joyce, *Ulysses*
1923 Adolf Hitler and his Nazi party attempt to overthrow the Bavarian government	Arnold Schoenberg, *Method of Composing with Twelve Tones*
1924 First Labour government in Britain	1924 George Gershwin, *Rhapsody in Blue*
Joseph Stalin succeeds Lenin as Russian premier	Thomas Mann, *The Magic Mountain*
	Franz Kafka, *The Trial*
1926 General strike in Britain	1926 First all-sound films
1927 American pilot Charles Lindbergh makes the first transatlantic flight	1927 First television transmission
	Virginia Woolf, *To the Lighthouse*
1929 American stock market collapses, triggering worldwide economic depression	1929 Mies van der Rohe, German pavilion
	1930 Piet Mondrian, *Fox Trot*
1933 Communist party in Russia purged by Stalin	1933 Arnold Toynbee, *A Study of History*
Adolf Hitler becomes German chancellor	
Franklin D. Roosevelt inaugurated as President of the United States	

Lives of Authors

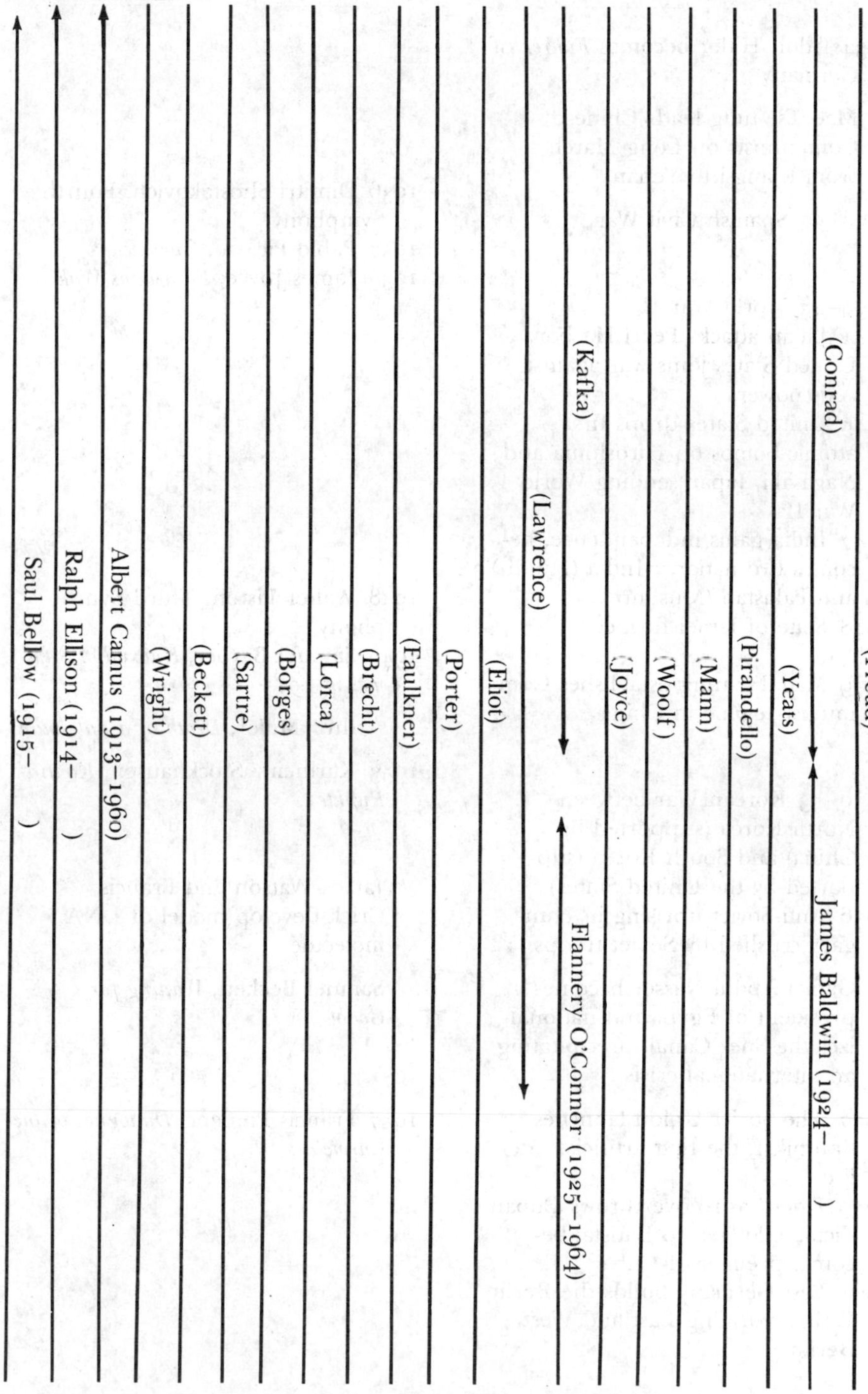
(Freud)
(Conrad)
(Yeats)
James Baldwin (1924–)
(Pirandello)
(Mann)
(Woolf)
(Joyce)
(Kafka)
Flannery O'Connor (1925–1964)
(Lawrence)
(Eliot)
(Porter)
(Faulkner)
(Brecht)
(Lorca)
(Borges)
(Sartre)
(Beckett)
(Wright)
Albert Camus (1913–1960)
Ralph Ellison (1914–)
Saul Bellow (1915–)

Political and Social Events

1934 Adolf Hitler becomes *Führer* of Germany

Mao Tse-tung leads Chinese Communists on Long March from Kiangsi to Yenan

1936–39 Spanish Civil War

1939–45 World War II

1941 Japan attacks Pearl Harbor; United States joins war against Axis powers

1945 United States drops first atomic bombs on Hiroshima and Nagasaki, Japan, ending World War II

1947 India gains independence, becomes two nations: India (Hindu) and Pakistan (Muslim)

1948 State of Israel formed

1949 Mao Tse-tung establishes Communist regime in China

1950–53 Korean War between North Korea (supported by China) and South Korea (supported by the United States)

1956 Anti-Soviet uprising in Hungary crushed by Soviet troops

Gamal Abdul Nasser becomes president of Egypt and nationalizes the Suez Canal, precipitating an international crisis

1957 The Soviet Union launches Sputnik I, the first artificial satellite

1959 Fidel Castro overthrows Cuban dictator Fulgencio Batista, becomes premier of Cuba

1961 East Germany builds the Berlin Wall, separating East and West Berlin

Intellectual and Cultural Events

1936 Dimitri Shostakovich, Fourth Symphony

1937 Pablo Picasso, *Guernica*

1939 James Joyce, *Finnegans Wake*

1948 Walter Piston, Third Symphony

1949 Samuel Barber, *Knoxville: Summer of 1915*

Arthur Miller, *Death of a Salesman*

1953 Karlheinz Stockhausen, *Kontra-Punkte*

James Watson and Francis Crick develop model of DNA molecule

Samuel Beckett, *Waiting for Godot*

1957 Francis Poulenc, *Dialogues of the Carmelites*

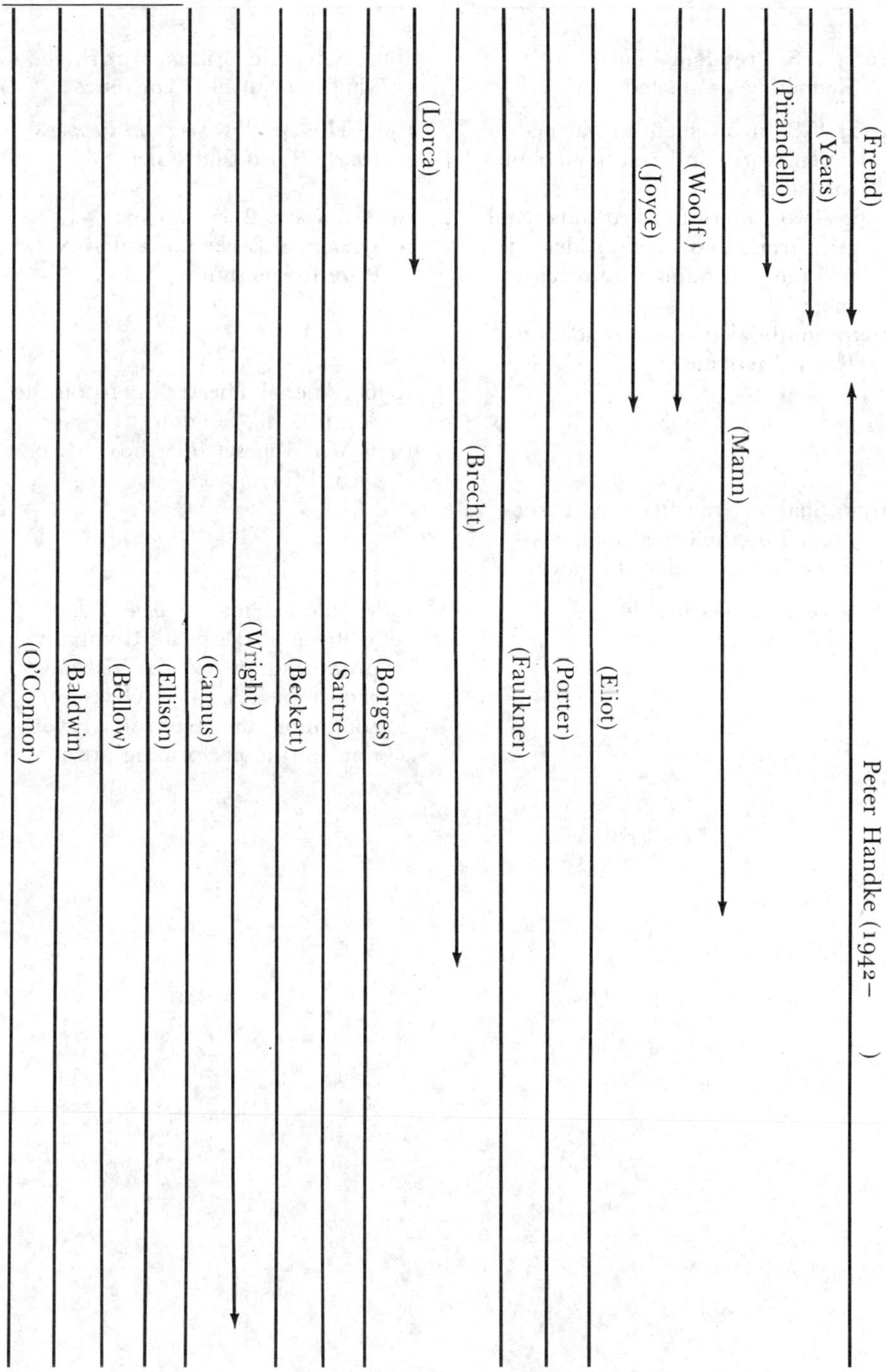
Peter Handke (1942–)
(Freud)
(Yeats)
(Pirandello)
(Mann)
(Woolf)
(Joyce)
(Eliot)
(Porter)
(Faulkner)
(Brecht)
(Lorca)
(Borges)
(Sartre)
(Beckett)
(Wright)
(Camus)
(Ellison)
(Bellow)
(Baldwin)
(O'Connor)

Political and Social Events	*Intellectual and Cultural Events*
1963 U.S. President John F. Kennedy assassinated	1962 Benjamin Britten, *War Requiem* Vatican Council II convenes
1964 U.S. involvement in war between North and South Vietnam increases	1967 The Beatles, *Sergeant Pepper's Lonely Hearts Club Band*
1969 Two American astronauts, Neil Armstrong and Edwin Aldrin, Jr., become first humans to reach the moon	1968 Luciano Berio, *Sinfonia* 1969 Samuel Beckett awarded Nobel Prize for literature
1975 South Vietnam surrenders to North Vietnam	
	1976 National Theatre opens on the South Bank, London 1977 *Star Wars* sets new box office record for movies
1979 Shah of Iran flees and is succeeded by the exiled religious leader the Ayatollah Khomeini	
Russian forces invade Afghanistan	1981 Harold Pinter, *Family Voices* 1983 Royal Shakespeare Company production of *Nicholas Nickleby* shown on U.S. cable television, continuing the "electronic revolution" in the performing arts

Lives of Authors

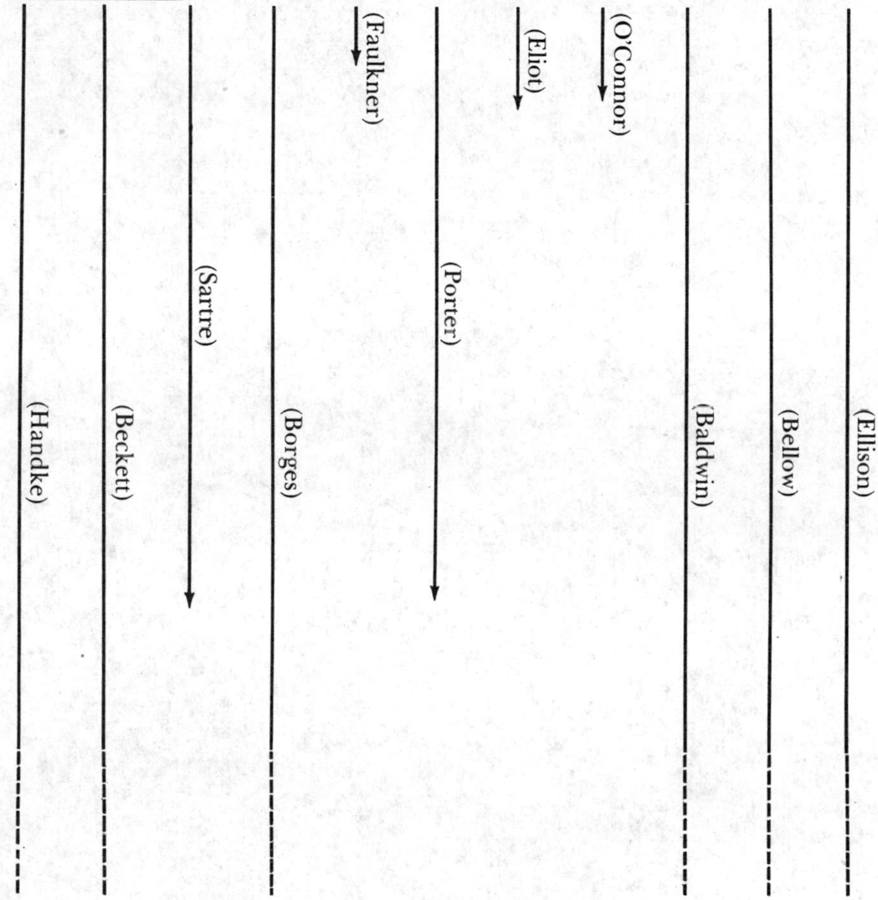

Index

Note: First lines of short and middle-length poems are in roman type. Titles of long works are in italics. Titles of short works are in italics in the general alphabetical listing but in roman type when listed as sub-entries under their authors' names.